THE UNIVERSITY ATLAS

Twenty-first Edition

GEORGE PHILIP

LONDON · MELBOURNE · MILWAUKEE

Edited by
Harold Fullard, M.Sc., Consultant Cartographer,
H. C. Darby, C.B.E., Litt.D., F.B.A., Emeritus Professor of
Geography, University of Cambridge and
B. M. Willett, B.A., Cartographic Editor,
D. Gaylard, Assistant Cartographic Editor

Maps prepared by the cartographic staff of George
Philip under the direction of A. G. Poynter, M.A.,
Director of Cartography.

First Edition February 1937
Twenty-first Edition Spring 1981

British Library Cataloguing in Publication Data
The university atlas. – 21st ed
  1. Atlases, British
  I. Fullard, Harold
  II. Darby, Henry Clifford
  912   G1019

ISBN 0 540 05378 3

Preface

During the course of over forty years since its original publication the University Atlas has been through twenty editions, each of which has in its turn been revised and improved.

For the eighth edition in 1958, the atlas was completely redesigned because it was considered that only an entirely new version would meet the needs of the post-war years. In that edition we made two significant changes: a substantial increase in the scale of the sectional maps, and a re-arrangement of the atlas into an easily portable size, convenient for frequent use and able to stand on a bookshelf.

For the twelfth edition in 1967, the style of colouring of the maps was completely changed to provide lighter and clearer layer colours. This in turn made possible the inclusion of hill-shading to complement the layer colouring and bring out clearly relief features without impairing the detail of names, settlements and communications.

For the nineteenth edition in 1978 the content of the atlas was completely re-examined, and the lay-out of a large number of maps was redesigned – in particular those covering Asia, Australasia and Latin America. This enabled larger scales to be provided for (a) China, south-east Asia, Japan, the Tashkent area and the southern Urals; (b) south-east Australia and New Guinea; and (c) Mexico, the West Indies and eastern Brazil. Other new maps covered the Indian Ocean, the North Sea, the French departments, the Benelux countries, Switzerland, Alaska and California. The design of yet other maps was altered to secure a more effective presentation, e.g., the world maps of climate.

As in previous editions, international boundaries have been drawn to show the *de facto* situation where there are rival claims to territory. The preliminary matter includes a summary of the projections used, and also climatic graphs for over 200 stations.

Spellings of names are in the forms given in the latest official lists, and generally agree with the rules of the Permanent Committee on Geographical Names and the United States Board on Geographic Names. A list of changed place names and names for which alternatives are often used appears with the index which contains over 50,000 entries.

We gratefully acknowledge the help of many official organisations and individuals, and especially thank the Meteorological Office for extracting data for the climate graphs.

H. FULLARD
H.C. DARBY

Contents

World

Europe & The British Isles

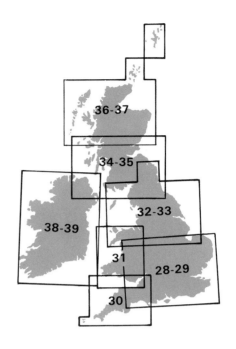

Europe

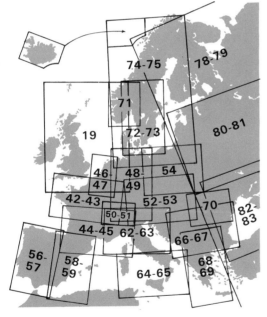

Asia

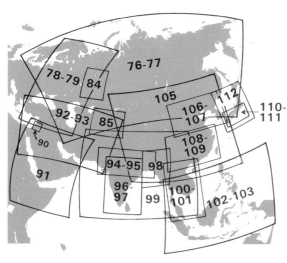

Africa

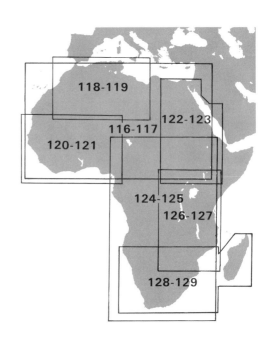

Australasia

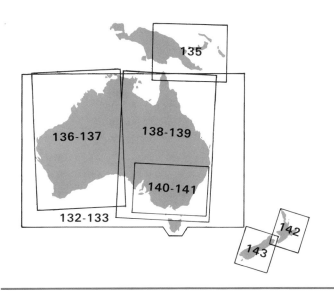

The Americas

Index

Principal Countries of the World

Country	Area in thousands of square km	Population in thousands	Density of population per sq. km	Capital Population in thousands
Afghanistan	647	15 108	23	Kabul (588)
Albania	29	2 608	90	Tiranë (192)
Algeria	2 382	18 515	8	Algiers (1 503)
Angola	1 247	6 732	5	Luanda (475)
Argentina	2 767	26 393	10	Buenos Aires (8 436)
Australia	7 687	14 249	2	Canberra (215)
Austria	84	7 508	89	Vienna (1 590)
Bangladesh	144	84 655	588	Dacca (1 730)
Belgium	31	9 840	317	Brussels (1 042)
Belize	23	153	7	Belmopan (4)
Benin	113	3 377	30	Porto-Novo (104)
Bhutan	47	1 240	26	Thimphu (60)
Bolivia	1 099	5 137	5	Sucre (63) / La Paz (655)
Botswana	600	726	1	Gaborone (37)
Brazil	8 512	115 397	14	Brasilia (763)
Brunei	6	201	35	Bandar Seri Begawan (37)
Bulgaria	111	8 814	79	Sofia (1 032)
Burma	677	32 205	48	Rangoon (2 276)
Burundi	28	4 256	152	Bujumbura (157)
Cambodia	181	8 574	47	Phnom Penh (2 000)
Cameroon	475	8 058	17	Yaoundé (314)
Canada	9 976	23 499	2	Ottawa (693)
Central African Rep.	623	2 370	4	Bangui (187)
Chad	1 284	4 309	3	Ndjamena (179)
Chile	757	10 857	14	Santiago (3 692)
China	9 597	975 230	102	Peking (7 570)
Colombia	1 139	25 645	23	Bogota (2 855)
Congo	342	1 459	4	Brazzaville (290)
Costa Rica	51	2 111	41	San José (395)
Cuba	115	9 728	85	Havana (1 861)
Cyprus	9	616	66	Nicosia (147)
Czechoslovakia	128	15 138	118	Prague (1 176)
Denmark	43	5 104	119	Copenhagen (1 251)
Djibouti	22	113	5	Djibouti (62)
Dominican Republic	49	5 124	104	Santo Domingo (818)
Ecuador	284	7 814	28	Quito (743)
Egypt	1 001	41 000	41	Cairo (5 084)
El Salvador	21	4 365	208	San Salvador (366)
Equatorial Guinea	28	346	12	Rey Malabo (37)
Ethiopia	1 222	29 705	24	Addis Abeba (1 196)
Fiji	18	607	34	Suva (118)
Finland	337	4 752	14	Helsinki (825)
France	547	53 278	97	Paris (9 863)
French Guiana	91	60	1	Cayenne (25)
Gabon	268	538	2	Libréville (186)
Gambia	11	569	52	Banjul (48)
Germany, East	108	16 756	155	East Berlin (1 111)
Germany, West	249	61 310	246	Bonn (284)
Ghana	239	10 969	46	Accra (738)
Greece	132	9 360	71	Athens (2 101)
Greenland	2 176	51	0.02	Godthåb (9)
Guatemala	109	6 621	61	Guatemala (717)
Guinea	246	4 763	19	Conakry (526)
Guinea-Bissau	36	777	22	Bissau (109)
Guyana	215	820	4	Georgetown (187)
Haiti	28	4 833	173	Port-au-Prince (746)
Honduras	112	3 439	31	Tegucigalpa (274)
Hong Kong	1	4 606	4 386	Victoria (849)
Hungary	93	10 699	115	Budapest (2 082)
Iceland	103	224	2	Reykjavik (83)
India	3 288	638 388	194	Delhi (3 647)
Indonesia	2 027	145 100	72	Jakarta (4 576)
Iran	1 648	35 213	21	Tehran (4 496)
Iraq	435	12 327	28	Baghdad (2 969)
Irish Republic	70	3 365	48	Dublin (545)
Israel	21	3 689	177	Jerusalem (376)
Italy	301	56 697	188	Rome (2 898)
Ivory Coast	322	7 613	24	Abidjan (850)
Jamaica	11	2 133	194	Kingston (573)
Japan	372	114 898	309	Tokyo (11 695)
Jordan	98	2 984	30	Amman (712)
Kenya	583	14 856	26	Nairobi (835)
Korea, North	121	17 072	141	Pyongyang (1 500)
Korea, South	98	37 019	378	Seoul (6 879)
Kuwait	18	1 199	67	Kuwait (775)
Laos	237	3 546	15	Vientiane (177)
Lebanon	10	3 012	301	Beirut (702)
Lesotho	30	1 214	40	Maseru (29)
Liberia	111	1 742	16	Monrovia (172)
Libya	1 760	2 748	2	Tripoli (551)
Luxembourg	3	356	137	Luxembourg (78)
Madagascar	587	8 289	14	Antananarivo (378)
Malawi	118	5 669	48	Lilongwe (103)
Malaysia	330	12 960	39	Kuala Lumpur (452)
Mali	1 240	6 290	5	Bamako (404)
Malta	0.3	340	1 062	Valletta (14)
Mauritania	1 031	1 544	2	Nouakchott (135)
Mauritius	2	924	462	Port Louis (141)
Mexico	1 973	66 944	34	Mexico (13 994)
Mongolia	1 565	1 576	1	Ulan Bator (400)
Morocco	447	18 906	42	Rabat (596)
Mozambique	783	11 756	15	Maputo (384)
Namibia	824	852	1	Windhoek (61)
Nepal	141	13 421	95	Katmandu (210)
Netherlands	41	13 986	341	Amsterdam (965)
New Zealand	269	3 107	12	Wellington (328)
Nicaragua	130	2 395	18	Managua (500)
Niger	1 267	4 994	4	Niamey (130)
Nigeria	924	77 217	78	Lagos (1 477)
Norway	324	4 059	13	Oslo (645)
Oman	212	839	4	Muscat (25)
Pakistan	804	76 770	95	Islamabad (77)
Panama	76	1 826	24	Panama (440)
Papua New Guinea	462	3 000	6	Port Moresby (113)
Paraguay	407	2 888	7	Asunción (565)
Peru	1 285	16 819	13	Lima (3 303)
Philippines	300	46 351	154	Manila (1 438)
Poland	313	35 010	112	Warsaw (1474)
Portugal	92	9 798	107	Lisbon (1 612)
Puerto Rico	9	3 317	372	San Juan (515)
Romania	238	21 855	92	Bucharest (1 934)
Rwanda	26	4 508	173	Kigali (90)
Saudi Arabia	2 150	7 866	4	Riyadh (667)
Senegal	196	5 381	27	Dakar (799)
Sierra Leone	72	3 292	45	Freetown (214)
Singapore	0.6	2 334	4 024	Singapore (2 308)
Somali Republic	638	3 443	5	Mogadishu (230)
South Africa	1 221	27 700	23	Pretoria (562) / Cape Town (1 097)
Spain	505	37 109	74	Madrid (3 520)
Sri Lanka	66	14 346	217	Colombo (607)
Sudan	2 506	17 376	7	Khartoum (334)
Surinam	163	374	2	Paramaribo (151)
Swaziland	17	544	32	Mbabane (24)
Sweden	450	8 278	18	Stockholm (1 375)
Switzerland	41	6 337	155	Berne (284)
Syria	185	8 088	44	Damascus (1 142)
Taiwan	36	15 500	431	Taipei (3 050)
Tanzania	945	16 553	18	Dar-es-Salaam (757)
Thailand	514	45 100	88	Bangkok (4 702)
Togo	56	2 409	43	Lomé (135)
Trinidad and Tobago	5	1 133	222	Port of Spain (63)
Tunisia	164	6 077	37	Tunis (944)
Turkey	781	43 210	54	Ankara (1 701)
Uganda	236	12 780	54	Kampala (331)
United Arab Emirates	84	711	9	Abu Dhabi (236)
U.S.S.R.	22 402	263 400	12	Moscow (8 011)
United Kingdom	245	55 836	228	London (6 877)
United States	9 363	218 059	23	Washington (3 021)
Upper Volta	274	6 554	24	Ouagadougou (169)
Uruguay	178	2 864	16	Montevideo (1 230)
Venezuela	912	13 122	14	Caracas (2 576)
Vietnam	330	49 890	151	Hanoi (2 571)
Western Samoa	3	151	53	Apia (32)
Yemen (Sana)	195	5 642	29	Sana (448)
Yemen (South)	288	1 853	6	Aden (285)
Yugoslavia	256	21 914	86	Belgrade (775)
Zaïre	2 345	27 745	12	Kinshasa (2 008)
Zambia	753	5 649	8	Lusaka (559)
Zimbabwe	391	6 930	18	Salisbury (616)

Climate Graphs

The climate graphs should be used in conjunction with the maps illustrating the climate of the World, and also the more detailed maps of the climates of the Continents and the British Isles. For each of the Continents and the British Isles about thirty different stations have been selected so that practically every type of climate throughout the world is covered by the graphs. Complete temperature, pressure and rainfall statistics have been obtained for all except a few stations where pressure statistics were not available. Wherever possible the graphs show average observations based upon long period means, and in all other cases over as long a period as possible. The latest available statistics have been consulted throughout.

Small maps are given on each sheet of graphs showing the location of every station. The figure after the name of the station gives the height in metres of the station above sea-level, so that comparisons between stations can be made after allowing for elevation. For temperature, measurements are given in degrees Centigrade; for pressure, millibars; and for rainfall, in millimetres. The temperature graphs show the monthly means of daily maximum and minimum actual temperatures: from these the mean monthly actual temperatures can easily be determined. The mean annual range of temperature is given above the temperature graphs.
The pressure graphs show the mean monthly pressure at sea-level, except in cases of high-level stations, where the height to which the pressure has been reduced is noted.

The rainfall graphs show the average monthly rainfall, and above them is given the average total annual rainfall. These graphs have been drawn to show the rainfall on the same scale for all stations to facilitate true comparisons between them. Where the rainfall graph extends over to the temperature graph the rainfall scale has been continued at the side of the graph.

On the temperature maps the actual temperatures and sea-level isotherms for the two extreme months of the year, January and July, are given. This information is supplemented by the graphs so that a far more complete picture of temperature changes can now be visualized. A comparison of stations in high latitudes with those in low latitudes renders apparent the importance of the seasonal changes due to insolation. In high latitudes the annual range of temperature is considerable. It decreases gradually as the equator is approached where there is scarcely any variation throughout the year. Another important factor in determining the range is the position of a station in relation to the sea, which exercises a strong moderating influence. The graphs for Africa illustrate the differences in seasons in the northern and southern hemispheres. The influence of the sea also shows itself in the small differences between the mean daily maxima and minima of seaside stations as compared with inland stations. Those most remote from the sea experience a large diurnal range.

The graphs reveal very clearly the intimate connection existing between temperature and pressure. This is perhaps nowhere more clearly indicated than in Asia, where the intense winter cold of the interior coincides with a high pressure system, and the warmth of summer with a low pressure system. As the graphs deal only with land stations all the great pressure systems of the world cannot be demonstrated. Their influence is discernible however in the pressure graphs for many of the stations, e.g., the permanent low pressure system centred on Iceland and the permanent high pressure system based on the Azores, seen in the graphs for Reykjavík and Lisboa respectively, and the permanent equatorial low pressures. One further factor having an important bearing on local climate in high mountain regions deserves mention, namely, the influence of height in reducing pressure. Reduced to sea-level, the pressures for Quito and Guayaquil would appear to be the same, but the graphs reveal the differences which actually exist.

The rainfall maps in the atlas show broadly seasonal rainfall for summer and winter. These are now supplemented by the rainfall graphs, a study of which enables greater distinctions to be drawn between the various rainfall regions, by showing both the amount of precipitation and the months in which it occurs—factors of prime significance for vegetation. In classifying the different rainfall regimes attention should be paid to the factor of relief and the connection noted between the low pressures and convectional rains of equatorial regions.

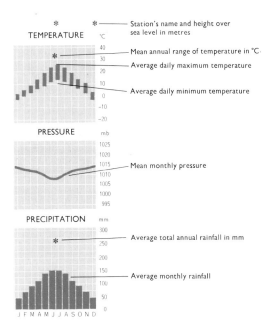

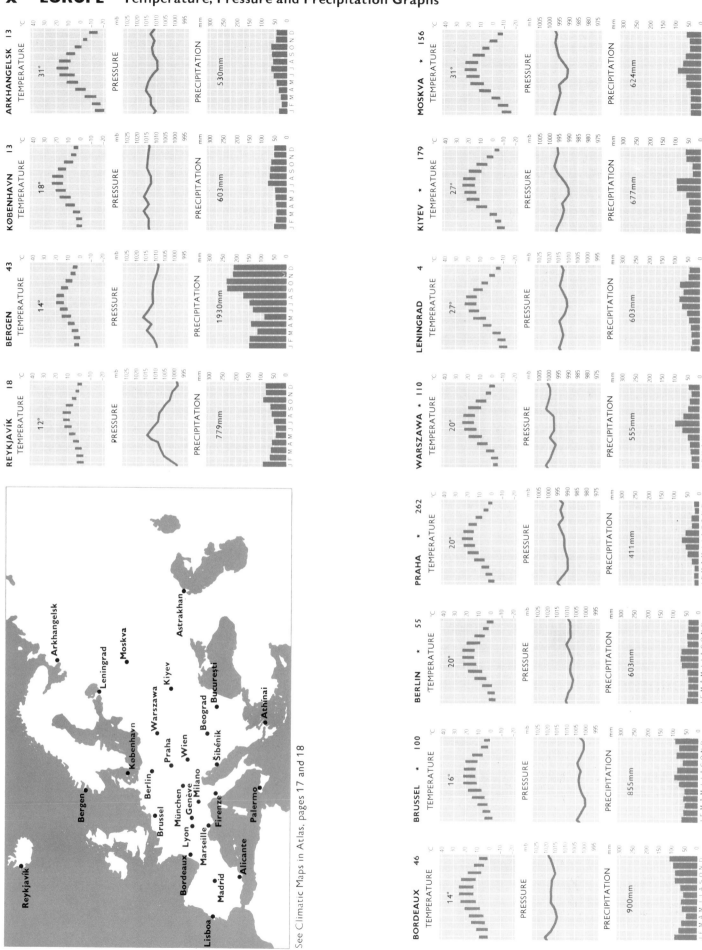

See Climatic Maps in Atlas, pages 17 and 18

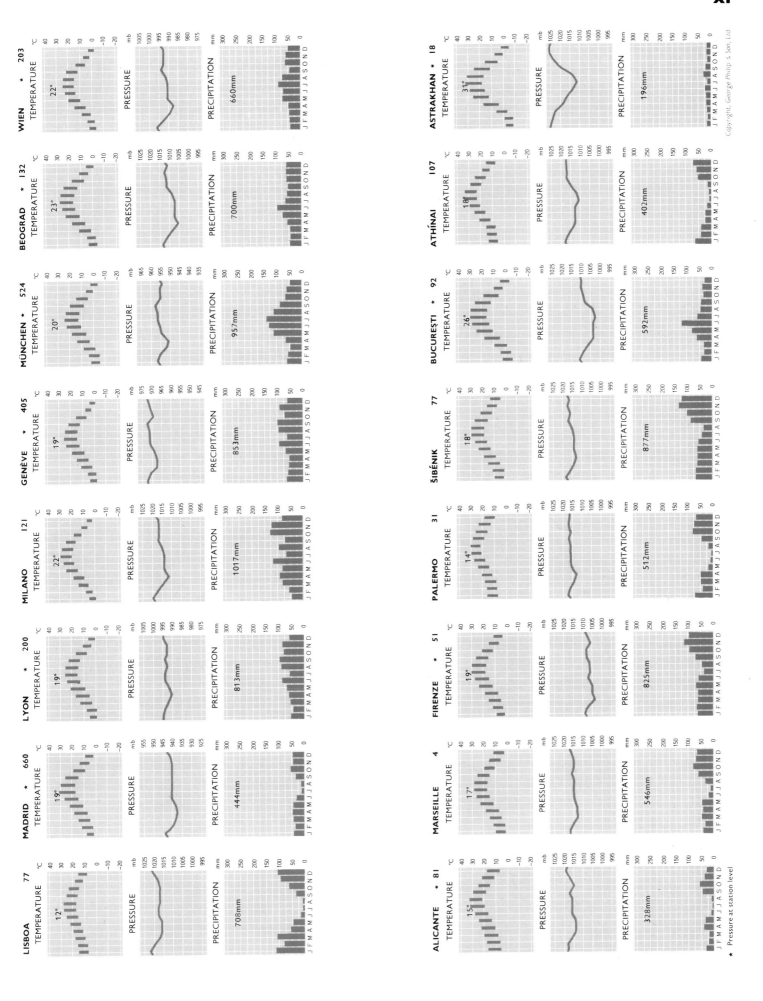

LISBOA 77
TEMPERATURE
12°
PRESSURE
PRECIPITATION
708mm

MADRID ★ 660
TEMPERATURE
19°
PRESSURE
PRECIPITATION
444mm

LYON ★ 200
TEMPERATURE
19°
PRESSURE
PRECIPITATION
813mm

MILANO 121
TEMPERATURE
22°
PRESSURE
PRECIPITATION
1017mm

GENÈVE ★ 405
TEMPERATURE
19°
PRESSURE
PRECIPITATION
853mm

MÜNCHEN ★ 524
TEMPERATURE
20°
PRESSURE
PRECIPITATION
957mm

BEOGRAD ★ 132
TEMPERATURE
23°
PRESSURE
PRECIPITATION
700mm

WIEN ★ 203
TEMPERATURE
22°
PRESSURE
PRECIPITATION
660mm

ALICANTE ★ 81
TEMPERATURE
15°
PRESSURE
PRECIPITATION
328mm

MARSEILLE 4
TEMPERATURE
17°
PRESSURE
PRECIPITATION
546mm

FIRENZE ★ 51
TEMPERATURE
19°
PRESSURE
PRECIPITATION
825mm

PALERMO 31
TEMPERATURE
14°
PRESSURE
PRECIPITATION
512mm

ŠIBÉNIK 77
TEMPERATURE
18°
PRESSURE
PRECIPITATION
877mm

BUCUREŞTI ★ 92
TEMPERATURE
26°
PRESSURE
PRECIPITATION
592mm

ATHÍNAI 107
TEMPERATURE
18°
PRESSURE
PRECIPITATION
402mm

ASTRAKHAN ★ 18
TEMPERATURE
31°
PRESSURE
PRECIPITATION
196mm

★ Pressure at station level

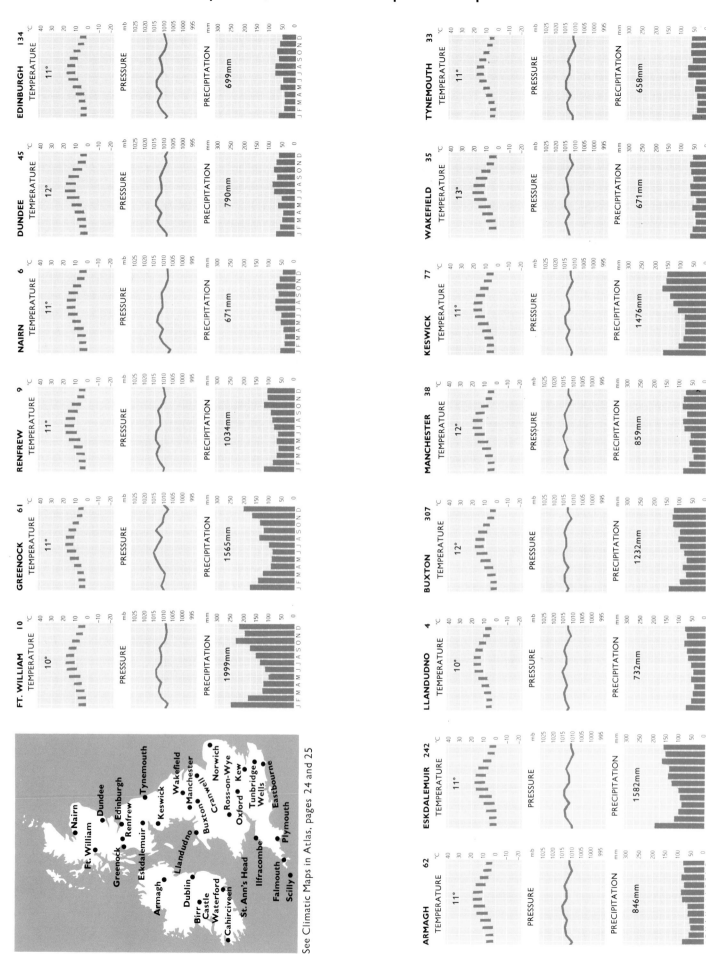

See Climatic Maps in Atlas, pages 24 and 25

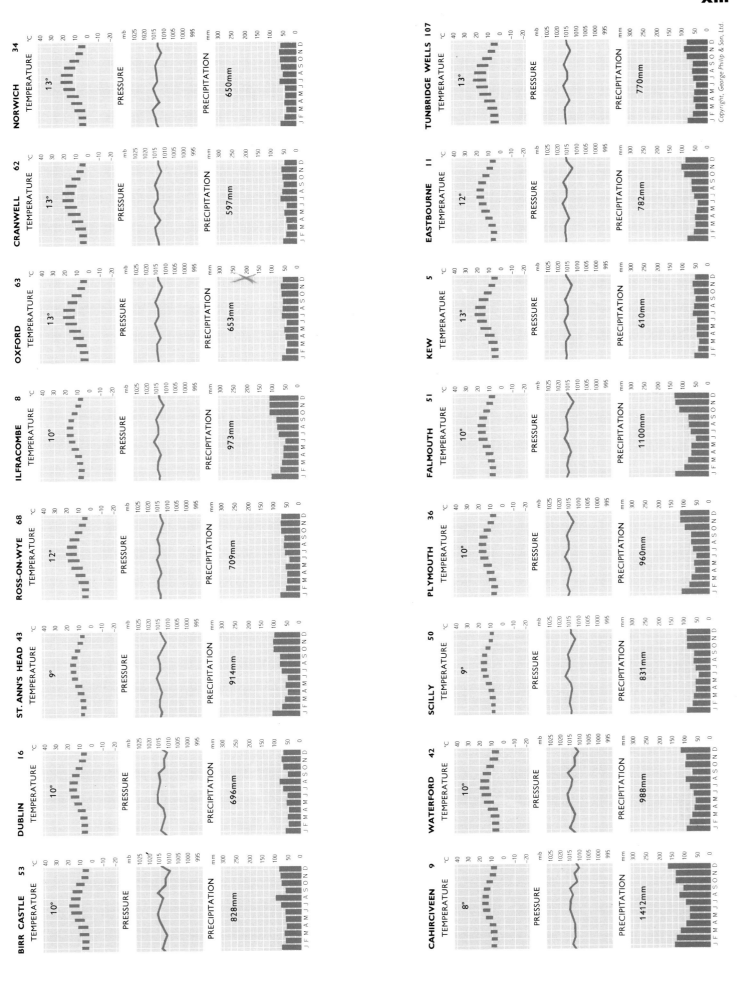

NORWICH 34
TEMPERATURE
°C
40 30 20 10 0 -10 -20
13°
PRESSURE
mb
1025 1020 1015 1010 1005 1000 995
PRECIPITATION
mm
300 250 200 150 100 50 0
650mm
J F M A M J J A S O N D

CRANWELL 62
TEMPERATURE
°C
40 30 20 10 0 -10 -20
13°
PRESSURE
mb
1025 1020 1015 1010 1005 1000 995
PRECIPITATION
mm
300 250 200 150 100 50 0
597mm
J F M A M J J A S O N D

OXFORD 63
TEMPERATURE
°C
40 30 20 10 0 -10 -20
13°
PRESSURE
mb
1025 1020 1015 1010 1005 1000 995
PRECIPITATION
mm
300 250 200 150 100 50 0
653mm
J F M A M J J A S O N D

ILFRACOMBE 8
TEMPERATURE
°C
40 30 20 10 0 -10 -20
10°
PRESSURE
mb
1025 1020 1015 1010 1005 1000 995
PRECIPITATION
mm
300 250 200 150 100 50 0
973mm
J F M A M J J A S O N D

ROSS-ON-WYE 68
TEMPERATURE
°C
40 30 20 10 0 -10 -20
12°
PRESSURE
mb
1025 1020 1015 1010 1005 1000 995
PRECIPITATION
mm
300 250 200 150 100 50 0
709mm
J F M A M J J A S O N D

ST. ANN'S HEAD 43
TEMPERATURE
°C
40 30 20 10 0 -10 -20
9°
PRESSURE
mb
1025 1020 1015 1010 1005 1000 995
PRECIPITATION
mm
300 250 200 150 100 50 0
914mm
J F M A M J J A S O N D

DUBLIN 16
TEMPERATURE
°C
40 30 20 10 0 -10 -20
10°
PRESSURE
mb
1025 1020 1015 1010 1005 1000 995
PRECIPITATION
mm
300 250 200 150 100 50 0
696mm
J F M A M J J A S O N D

BIRR CASTLE 53
TEMPERATURE
°C
40 30 20 10 0 -10 -20
10°
PRESSURE
mb
1025 1020 1015 1010 1005 1000 995
PRECIPITATION
mm
300 250 200 150 100 50 0
828mm
J F M A M J J A S O N D

TUNBRIDGE WELLS 107
TEMPERATURE
°C
40 30 20 10 0 -10 -20
13°
PRESSURE
mb
1025 1020 1015 1010 1005 1000 995
PRECIPITATION
mm
300 250 200 150 100 50 0
770mm
J F M A M J J A S O N D

EASTBOURNE 11
TEMPERATURE
°C
40 30 20 10 0 -10 -20
12°
PRESSURE
mb
1025 1020 1015 1010 1005 1000 995
PRECIPITATION
mm
300 250 200 150 100 50 0
782mm
J F M A M J J A S O N D

KEW 5
TEMPERATURE
°C
40 30 20 10 0 -10 -20
13°
PRESSURE
mb
1025 1020 1015 1010 1005 1000 995
PRECIPITATION
mm
300 250 200 150 100 50 0
610mm
J F M A M J J A S O N D

FALMOUTH 51
TEMPERATURE
°C
40 30 20 10 0 -10 -20
10°
PRESSURE
mb
1025 1020 1015 1010 1005 1000 995
PRECIPITATION
mm
300 250 200 150 100 50 0
1100mm
J F M A M J J A S O N D

PLYMOUTH 36
TEMPERATURE
°C
40 30 20 10 0 -10 -20
10°
PRESSURE
mb
1025 1020 1015 1010 1005 1000 995
PRECIPITATION
mm
300 250 200 150 100 50 0
960mm
J F M A M J J A S O N D

SCILLY 50
TEMPERATURE
°C
40 30 20 10 0 -10 -20
9°
PRESSURE
mb
1025 1020 1015 1010 1005 1000 995
PRECIPITATION
mm
300 250 200 150 100 50 0
831mm
J F M A M J J A S O N D

WATERFORD 42
TEMPERATURE
°C
40 30 20 10 0 -10 -20
10°
PRESSURE
mb
1025 1020 1015 1010 1005 1000 995
PRECIPITATION
mm
300 250 200 150 100 50 0
988mm
J F M A M J J A S O N D

CAHIRCIVEEN 9
TEMPERATURE
°C
40 30 20 10 0 -10 -20
8°
PRESSURE
mb
1025 1020 1015 1010 1005 1000 995
PRECIPITATION
mm
300 250 200 150 100 50 0
1412mm
J F M A M J J A S O N D

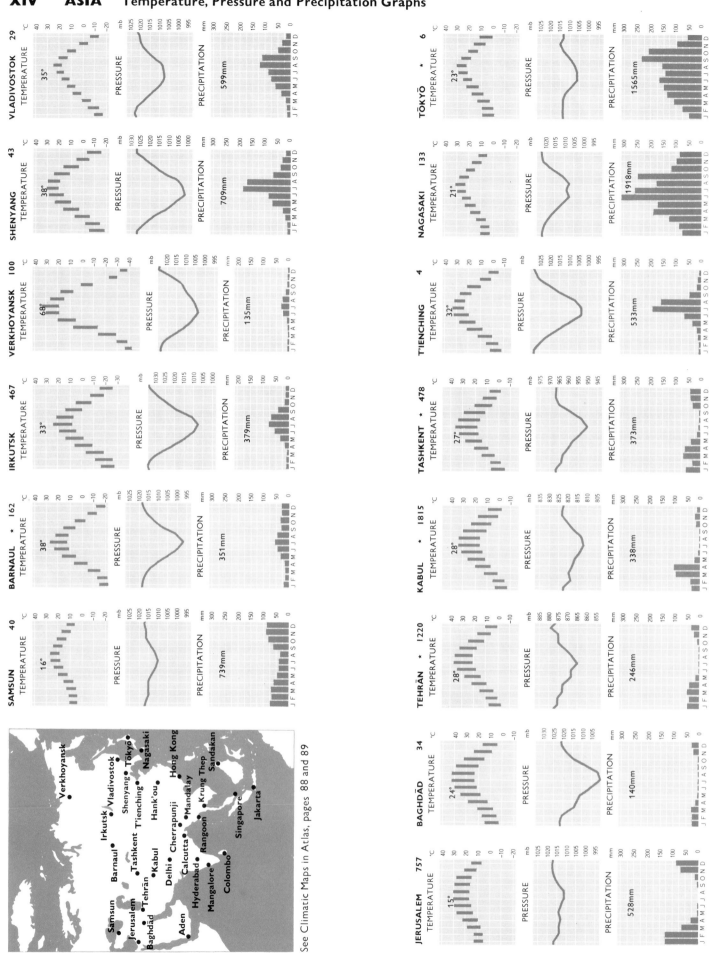

See Climatic Maps in Atlas, pages 88 and 89

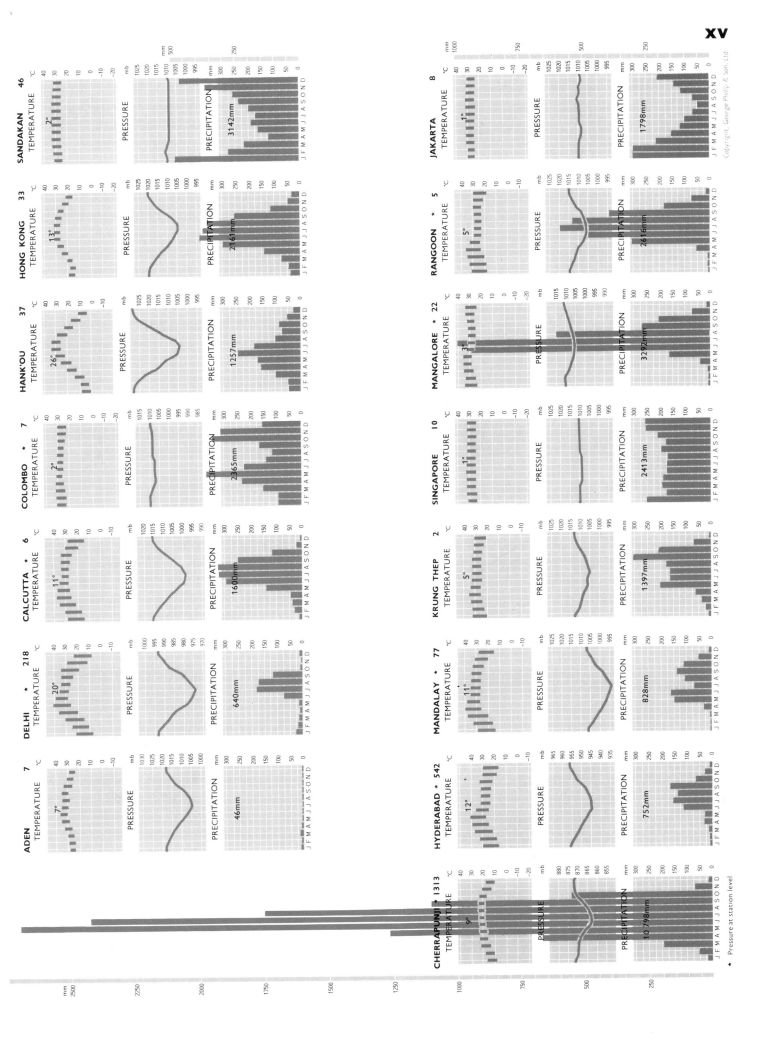

SANDAKAN 46
TEMPERATURE °C
2°
PRESSURE mb
PRECIPITATION mm
3142mm

HONG KONG 33
TEMPERATURE °C
13°
PRESSURE mb
PRECIPITATION mm
2161mm

HANK'OU 37
TEMPERATURE °C
26°
PRESSURE mb
PRECIPITATION mm
1257mm

COLOMBO ★ 7
TEMPERATURE °C
2°
PRESSURE mb
PRECIPITATION mm
2365mm

CALCUTTA ★ 6
TEMPERATURE °C
11°
PRESSURE mb
PRECIPITATION mm
1600mm

DELHI ★ 218
TEMPERATURE °C
20°
PRESSURE mb
PRECIPITATION mm
640mm

ADEN 7
TEMPERATURE °C
7°
PRESSURE mb
PRECIPITATION mm
46mm

JAKARTA 8
TEMPERATURE °C
1°
PRESSURE mb
PRECIPITATION mm
1798mm

RANGOON ★ 5
TEMPERATURE °C
5°
PRESSURE mb
PRECIPITATION mm
2616mm

MANGALORE ★ 22
TEMPERATURE °C
3°
PRESSURE mb
PRECIPITATION mm
3292mm

SINGAPORE 10
TEMPERATURE °C
1°
PRESSURE mb
PRECIPITATION mm
2413mm

KRUNG THEP 2
TEMPERATURE °C
5°
PRESSURE mb
PRECIPITATION mm
1397mm

MANDALAY ★ 77
TEMPERATURE °C
11°
PRESSURE mb
PRECIPITATION mm
828mm

HYDERABAD ★ 542
TEMPERATURE °C
12°
PRESSURE mb
PRECIPITATION mm
752mm

CHERRAPUNJI ★ 1313
TEMPERATURE °C
9°
PRESSURE mb
PRECIPITATION mm
10 798mm

★ Pressure at station level

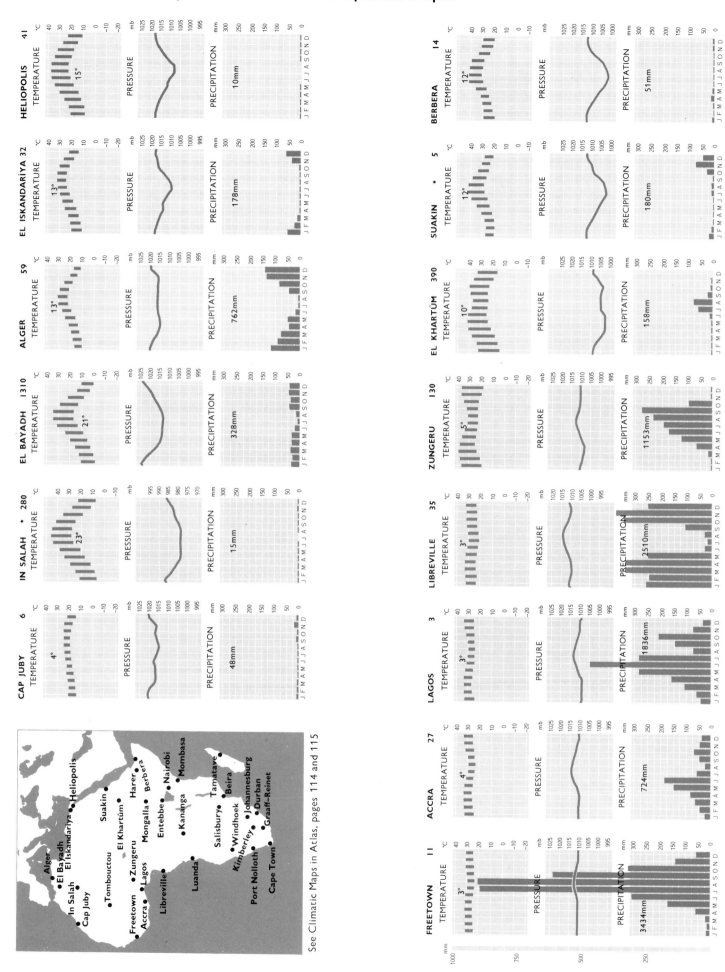

See Climatic Maps in Atlas, pages 114 and 115

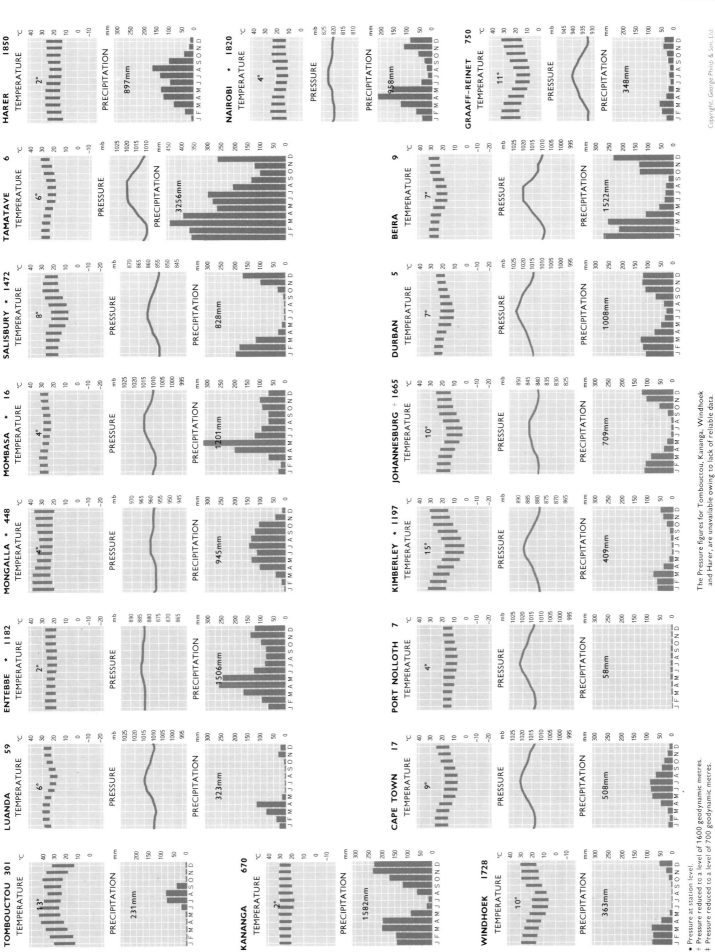

The Pressure figures for Tombouctou, Kananga, Windhoek and Harer, are unavailable owing to lack of reliable data.

★ Pressure at station level.
† Pressure reduced to a level of 1600 geodynamic metres.
‡ Pressure reduced to a level of 700 geodynamic metres.

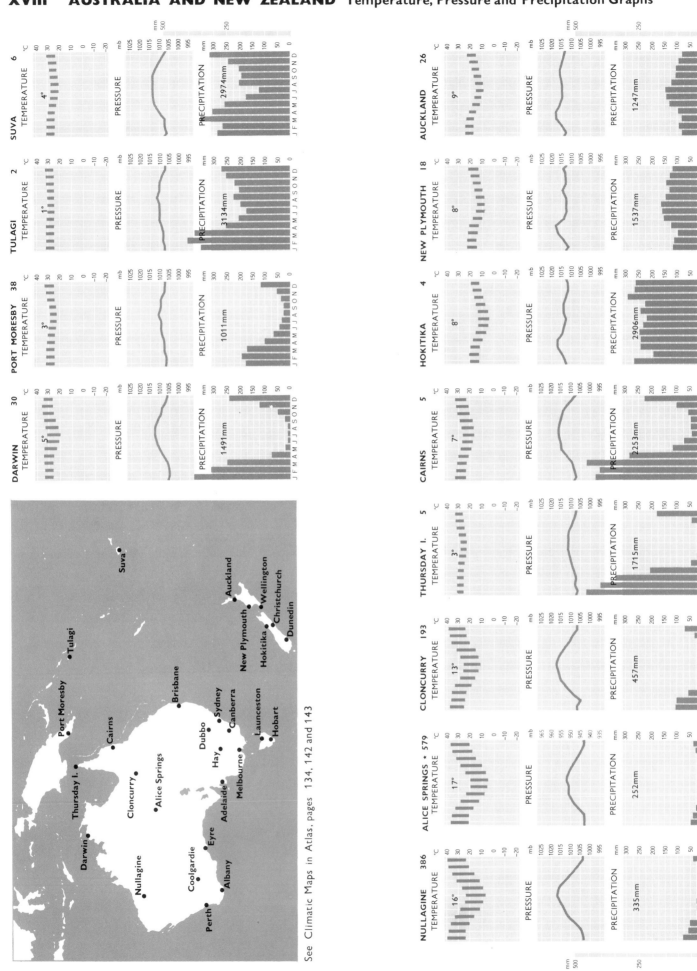

See Climatic Maps in Atlas, pages 134, 142 and 143

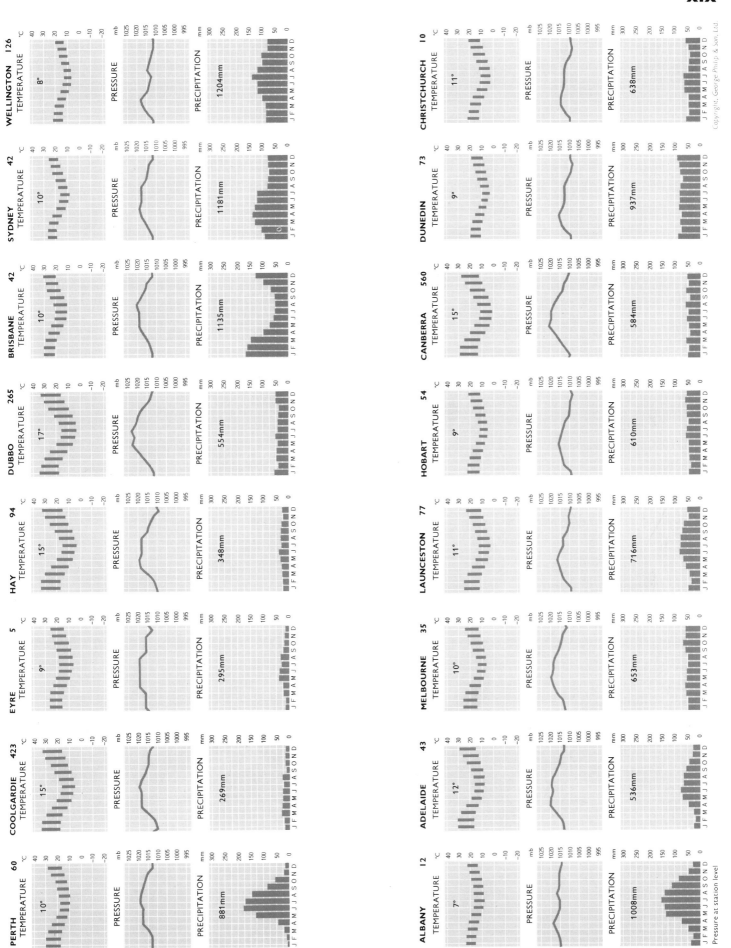

* Pressure at station level

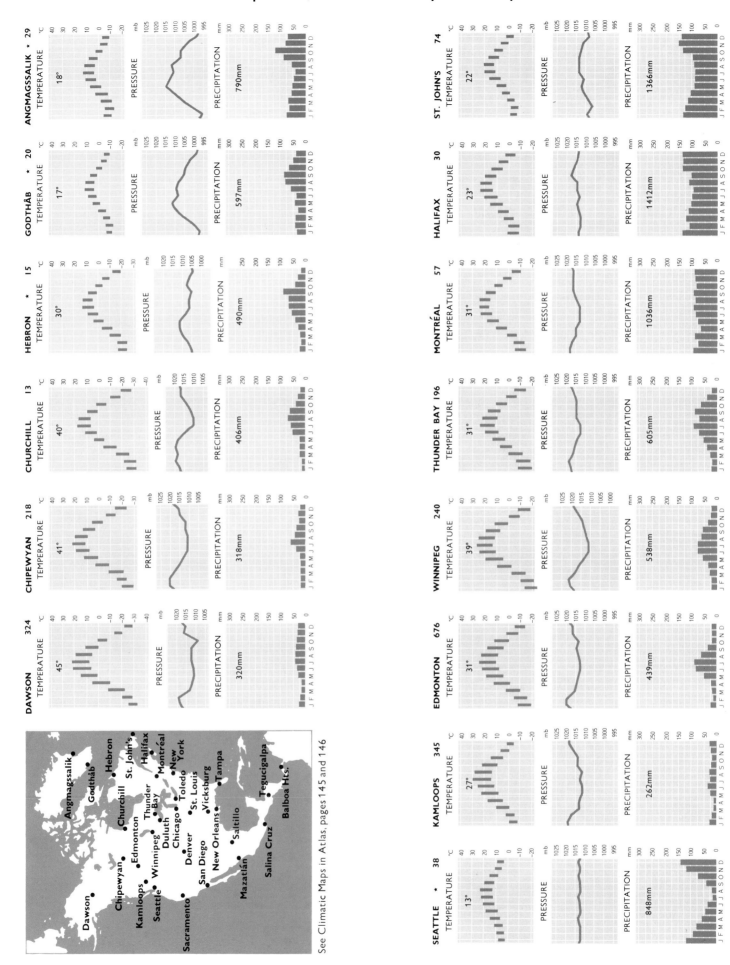

See Climatic Maps in Atlas, pages 145 and 146

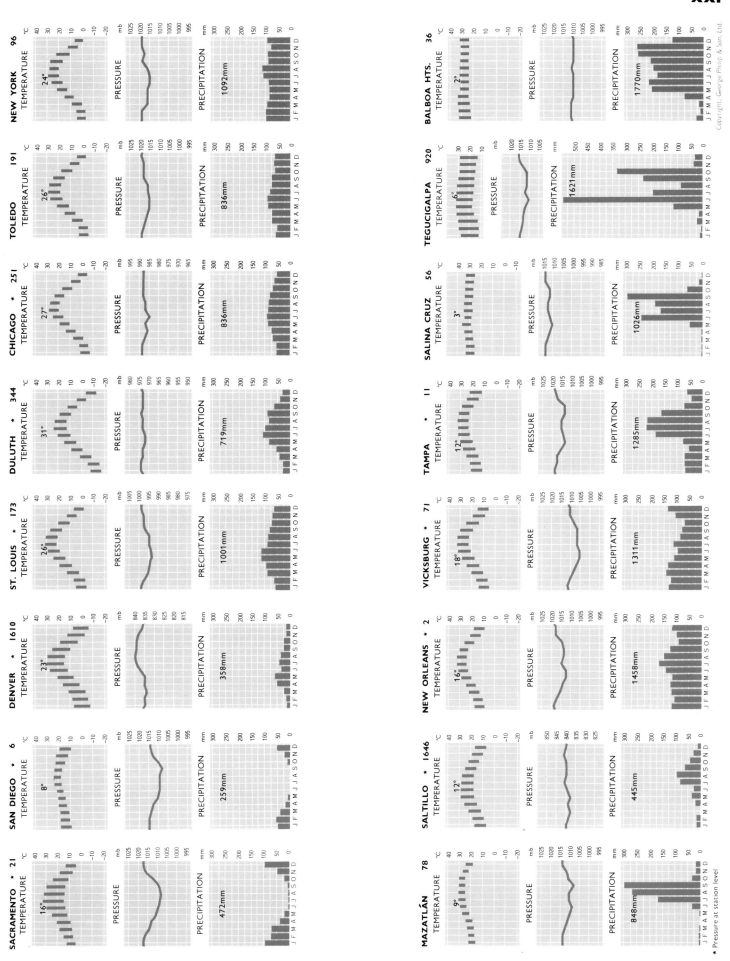

XXI

Copyright, George Philip & Son, Ltd.

* Pressure at station level

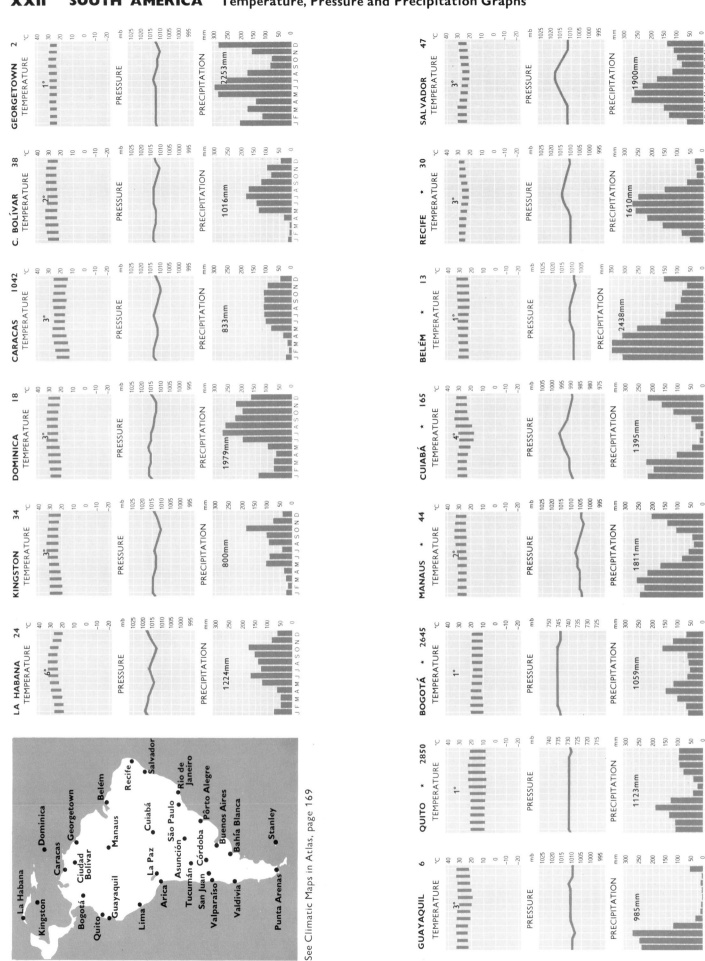

See Climatic Maps in Atlas, page 169

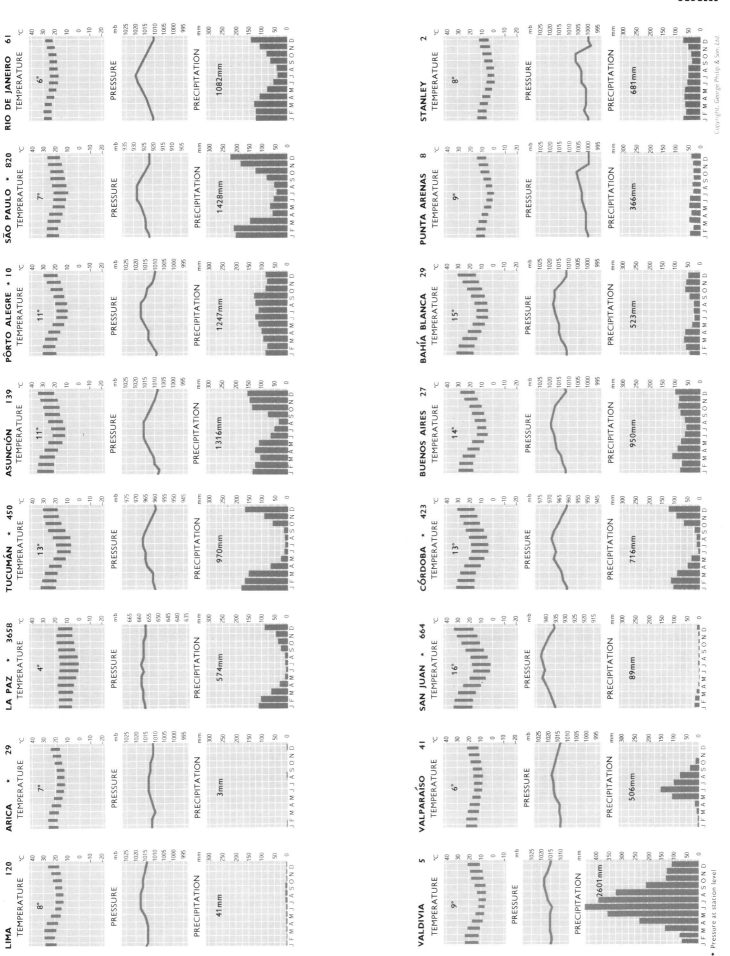

RIO DE JANEIRO 61
TEMPERATURE °C
6°
PRESSURE mb
PRECIPITATION mm
1082mm
J F M A M J J A S O N D

SÃO PAULO ★ 820
TEMPERATURE °C
7°
PRESSURE mb
PRECIPITATION mm
1428mm
J F M A M J J A S O N D

PÔRTO ALEGRE ★ 10
TEMPERATURE °C
11°
PRESSURE mb
PRECIPITATION mm
1247mm
J F M A M J J A S O N D

ASUNCIÓN 139
TEMPERATURE °C
11°
PRESSURE mb
PRECIPITATION mm
1316mm
J F M A M J J A S O N D

TUCUMÁN ★ 450
TEMPERATURE °C
13°
PRESSURE mb
PRECIPITATION mm
970mm
J F M A M J J A S O N D

LA PAZ ★ 3658
TEMPERATURE °C
4°
PRESSURE
PRECIPITATION mm
574mm
J F M A M J J A S O N D

ARICA ★ 29
TEMPERATURE °C
7°
PRESSURE mb
PRECIPITATION mm
3mm
J F M A M J J A S O N D

LIMA 120
TEMPERATURE °C
8°
PRESSURE mb
PRECIPITATION mm
41mm
J F M A M J J A S O N D

STANLEY 2
TEMPERATURE °C
8°
PRESSURE mb
PRECIPITATION mm
681mm
J F M A M J J A S O N D

PUNTA ARENAS 8
TEMPERATURE °C
9°
PRESSURE mb
PRECIPITATION mm
366mm
J F M A M J J A S O N D

BAHÍA BLANCA 29
TEMPERATURE °C
15°
PRESSURE mb
PRECIPITATION mm
523mm
J F M A M J J A S O N D

BUENOS AIRES 27
TEMPERATURE °C
14°
PRESSURE mb
PRECIPITATION mm
950mm
J F M A M J J A S O N D

CÓRDOBA ★ 423
TEMPERATURE °C
13°
PRESSURE mb
PRECIPITATION mm
716mm
J F M A M J J A S O N D

SAN JUAN ★ 664
TEMPERATURE °C
16°
PRESSURE mb
PRECIPITATION mm
89mm
J F M A M J J A S O N D

VALPARAÍSO 41
TEMPERATURE °C
6°
PRESSURE mb
PRECIPITATION mm
506mm
J F M A M J J A S O N D

VALDIVIA 5
TEMPERATURE °C
9°
PRESSURE mb
PRECIPITATION mm
2601mm
J F M A M J J A S O N D

★ Pressure at station level

Projections Used

GENERAL REFERENCE

Abbreviations of measures used — ft Feet; mm { Millimetres / Millimeters } cm { Centimetres / Centimeters } m { Metres / Meters } km { Kilometres / Kilometers } mb Millibars

———3386——— Principal Shipping Routes
(Distances in Nautical Miles)

City and Town symbols in order of size

⬡ ⬡ ◼ ◉ ● ◎ ○ ○ ○

∴ Sites of Archæological or Historical Importance

〰〰〰 International Boundaries

⎯ ⎯⎯ ⎯⎯ International Boundaries (Undemarcated or Undefined)

〰〰〰 Internal Boundaries

〰 Principal Roads

⎯⎯⎯ Tracks, Seasonal and other Roads

⊣--⊢ Road Tunnels

〰 Principal Railways

〰 Other Railways

⎯⎯⎯ Railways under construction

⊣--⊢ Railway Tunnels

⎯⎯⎯ Principal Canals

⎯⎯⎯ Principal Oil Pipelines

⎯⎯⎯ Principal Air Routes

✧ Principal Airports

〰 Perennial Streams

⎯⎯⎯ Seasonal Streams

Seasonal Lakes, Salt Flats

Swamps, Marshes

Wells in Desert

Permanent Ice

⊃⊂ Passes

▲ 8848 Height above sea-level
▼ 8050 Depth below sea-level } in metres
1134 Height of lake-level

CONVERSION SCALE

ft   m

30 000 — 9000
— 8000
24 000 — 7000
— 6000
18 000 — 5000
— 4000
12,000 — 3000
9000 — 2000
6000 — 1000
3000 — 500
Sea Level 0 — 0 Sea Level
— 500
— 1000
1000 — 2000
— 3000
2000 — 4000
— 5000
3000 — 6000
— 7000
4000 — 8000
— 9000
5000 — 10 000
— 11 000
6000 — 12 000
7000
fathoms   m

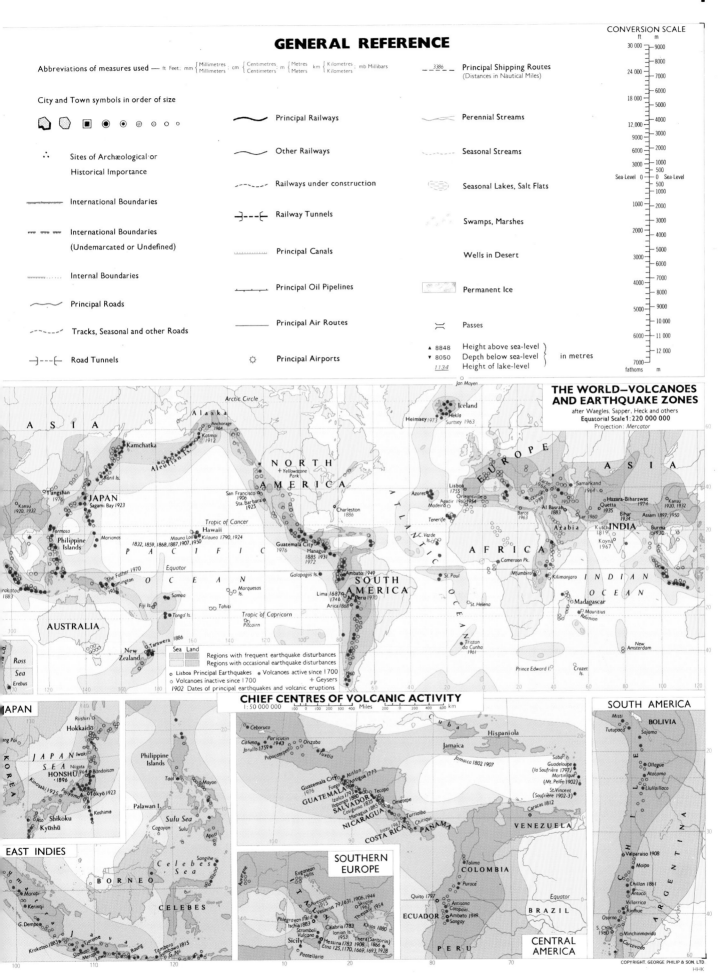

THE WORLD—VOLCANOES AND EARTHQUAKE ZONES
after Waegles, Sapper, Heck and others
Equatorial Scale 1:220 000 000
Projection: Mercator

Sea Land
Regions with frequent earthquake disturbances
Regions with occasional earthquake disturbances
○ Lisboa Principal Earthquakes   ● Volcanoes active since 1700
○ Volcanoes inactive since 1700   + Geysers
1902 Dates of principal earthquakes and volcanic eruptions

CHIEF CENTRES OF VOLCANIC ACTIVITY
1: 50 000 000
100 0 100 200 300 400 Miles   200 0 200 400 600 km

JAPAN

EAST INDIES

SOUTHERN EUROPE

SOUTH AMERICA

CENTRAL AMERICA

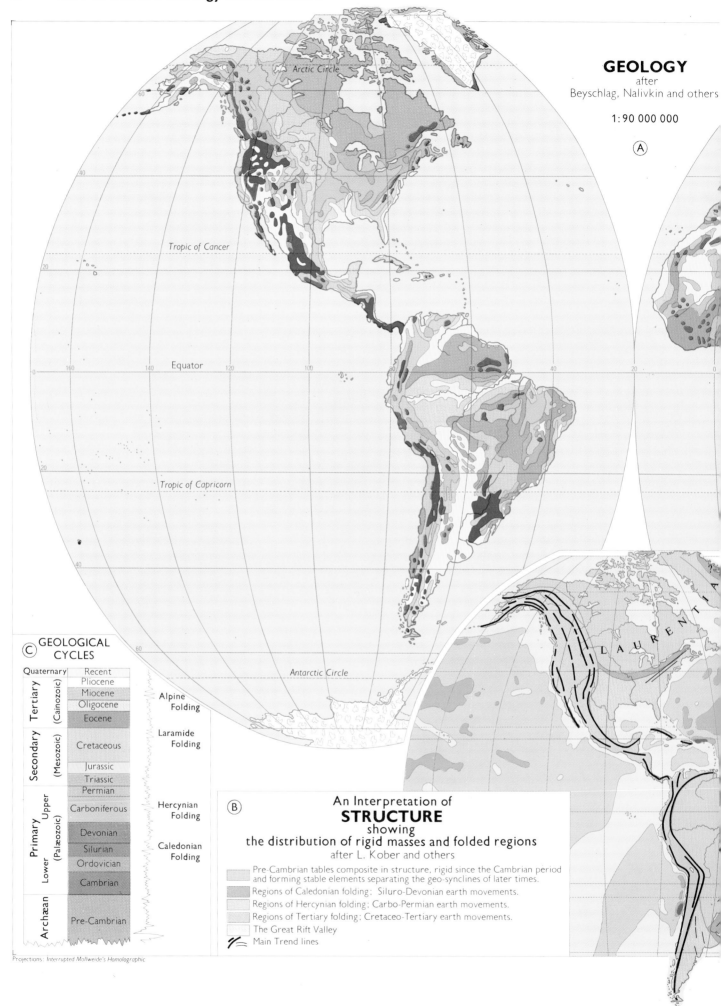

GEOLOGY
after
Beyschlag, Nalivkin and others

1:90 000 000

Ⓐ

Ⓒ **GEOLOGICAL
CYCLES**

Quaternary		Recent	
Tertiary (Cainozoic)	Secondary (Mesozoic)	Pliocene	
		Miocene	Alpine Folding
		Oligocene	
		Eocene	
		Cretaceous	Laramide Folding
		Jurassic	
		Triassic	
Primary (Palæozoic)	Upper	Permian	
		Carboniferous	Hercynian Folding
	Lower	Devonian	
		Silurian	Caledonian Folding
		Ordovician	
		Cambrian	
Archæan		Pre-Cambrian	

Ⓑ   An Interpretation of
STRUCTURE
showing
the distribution of rigid masses and folded regions
after L. Kober and others

Pre-Cambrian tables composite in structure, rigid since the Cambrian period
and forming stable elements separating the geo-synclines of later times.

Regions of Caledonian folding; Siluro-Devonian earth movements.

Regions of Hercynian folding; Carbo-Permian earth movements.

Regions of Tertiary folding; Cretaceo-Tertiary earth movements.

The Great Rift Valley

Main Trend lines

Projections: *Interrupted Mollweide's Homolographic*

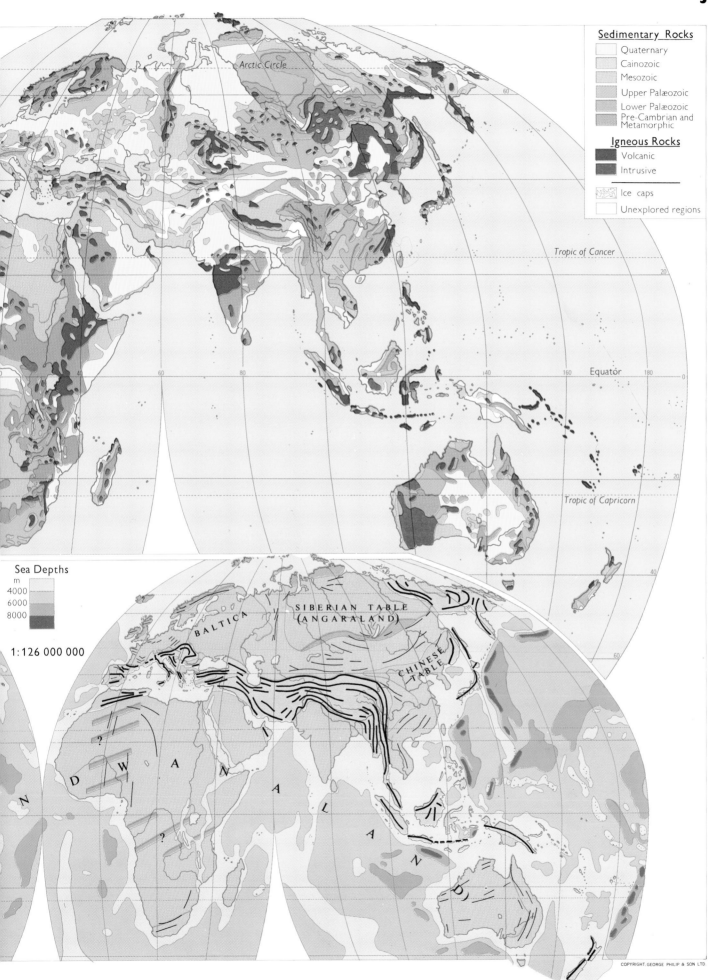

3

Sedimentary Rocks
- Quaternary
- Cainozoic
- Mesozoic
- Upper Palæozoic
- Lower Palæozoic
- Pre-Cambrian and Metamorphic

Igneous Rocks
- Volcanic
- Intrusive

Ice caps

Unexplored regions

Arctic Circle

Tropic of Cancer

Equator

Tropic of Capricorn

Sea Depths
m
4000
6000
8000

1:126 000 000

BALTICA

SIBERIAN TABLE
(ANGARALAND)

CHINESE
TABLE

N D W A N A L A N

?
?

Köppen's classification recognises five major climatic regions corresponding broadly to the five principal vegetation types and these are designated by the letters A, B, C, D and E. Each one of these is subdivided on the basis of temperature and rainfall.

CLIMATIC REGIONS   after Köppen

TROPICAL RAINY CLIMATES A

Af	Rain Forest Climate
Am	Monsoon Climate
Aw	Savanna Climate

All mean monthly temperatures above 18°C and an annual variation in temperature of less than 6°C.

All monthly temperatures above 18°C but with an annual variation in temperature of less than 12°C.

The division of the three major A groups as far as rainfall is concerned is illustrated by the graph below:-

DRY CLIMATES B

| BS | Steppe Climate |
| BW | Desert Climate |

The principal difference between this grouping and groups A, C, D and E is the combination of a wide range of temperatures with low rainfall.

The differing criteria for separating the Steppe and Desert climates are shown by the graph below:-

- - - - summer rainfall
——— winter rainfall
—·—· rainfall evenly distributed

WARM TEMPERATE RA
CLIMATES C

This climatic group is separ of the coldest month below the warmest month is over

Cw	Dry Winter C
Cs	Dry Summer (Mediterra
Cf	Climate with Dry Season

COPYRIGHT. GEORGE. PHILIP & SON. LTD.

COLD TEMPERATE RAINY CLIMATES D

Dw	Dry Winter Climate	The mean temperature of the coldest month is below −3°C but the mean temperature of the warmest month is still over 10°C.
Df	Dry Summer Climate	

POLAR CLIMATES E

ET	Tundra Climate	The mean temperature of the warmest month is below 10°C giving permanently frozen subsoil.
EF	Polar Climate	The mean temperature of the warmest month is below 0°C giving permanent ice and snow.

The classification is in some cases subdivided by the addition of the following letters after the major types:-

Used with groups C and D	a	Hot summer—mean temperature of the hottest month above 22°C and with more than four months of over 10°C.
	b	Warm summer—mean temperature of the hottest month below 22°C but still with more than four months of over 10°C.
	c	Cool short summer—mean temperature of the hottest month below 22°C but with less than four months of over 10°C.
Used with group D	d	Cool short summer and cold winter—mean temperature of the hottest month below 22°C, and of the coldest month below −38°C.
Used with group B	h	Hot dry climate—mean annual temperature above 18°C.
	k	Cool dry climate—mean annual temperature below 18°C.
Used with group E	H	Polar climate due to elevation being over 1500m

having the mean temperature
. The mean temperature of

t month of summer has at least
s much rain as the driest
nth.

t month of winter has at least
s as much rain as the driest
ummer. The driest summer
lf has less than 30mm rainfall.

ll throughout the year.

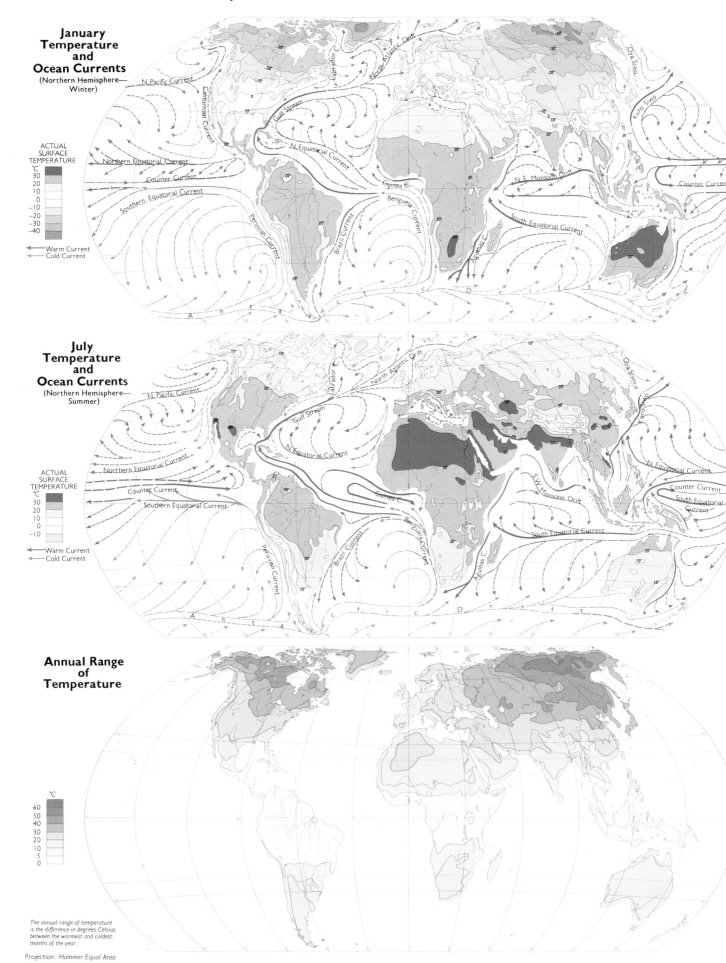

January Temperature and Ocean Currents
(Northern Hemisphere— Winter)

ACTUAL
SURFACE
TEMPERATURE
°C
30
20
10
0
-10
-20
-30
-40

← Warm Current
← Cold Current

N. Pacific Current
Californian Current
Labrador C.
North Atlantic Drift
Oya Siwo
Kuro Siwo
Gulf Stream
N. Equatorial Current
Northern Equatorial Current
Counter Current
Guinea C.
N. E. Monsoon Drift
Counter Current
Southern Equatorial Current
South Equatorial Current
Benguela Current
Peruvian Current
Brazil Current
Agulhas C.
A n t a r c t i c   D r i f t

July Temperature and Ocean Currents
(Northern Hemisphere— Summer)

ACTUAL
SURFACE
TEMPERATURE
°C
30
20
10
0
-10

← Warm Current
← Cold Current

N. Pacific Current
Labrador C.
North Atlantic Drift
Oya Siwo
Kuro Siwo
Gulf Stream
N. Equatorial Current
Northern Equatorial Current
Counter Current
Counter Current
Guinea C.
S.W. Monsoon Drift
Southern Equatorial Current
South Equatorial Current
South Equatorial Current
Benguela Current
Peruvian Current
Brazil Current
Agulhas C.
A n t a r c t i c   D r i f t

Annual Range of Temperature

°C
60
50
40
30
20
10
5
0

The annual range of temperature is the difference in degrees Celsius between the warmest and coldest months of the year.

Projection: *Hammer Equal Area*

1:190 000 000

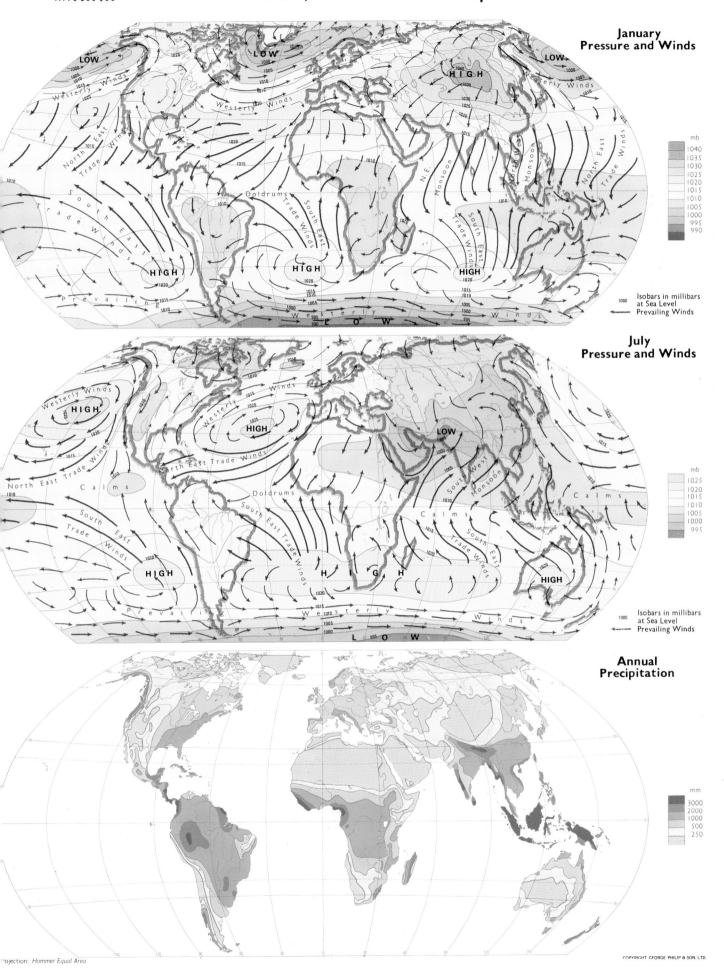

January
Pressure and Winds

mb
1040
1035
1030
1025
1020
1015
1010
1005
1000
995
990

1000   Isobars in millibars
at Sea Level
Prevailing Winds

July
Pressure and Winds

mb
1025
1020
1015
1010
1005
1000
995

1000   Isobars in millibars
at Sea Level
Prevailing Winds

Annual
Precipitation

mm
3000
2000
1000
500
250

Projection: *Hammer Equal Area*

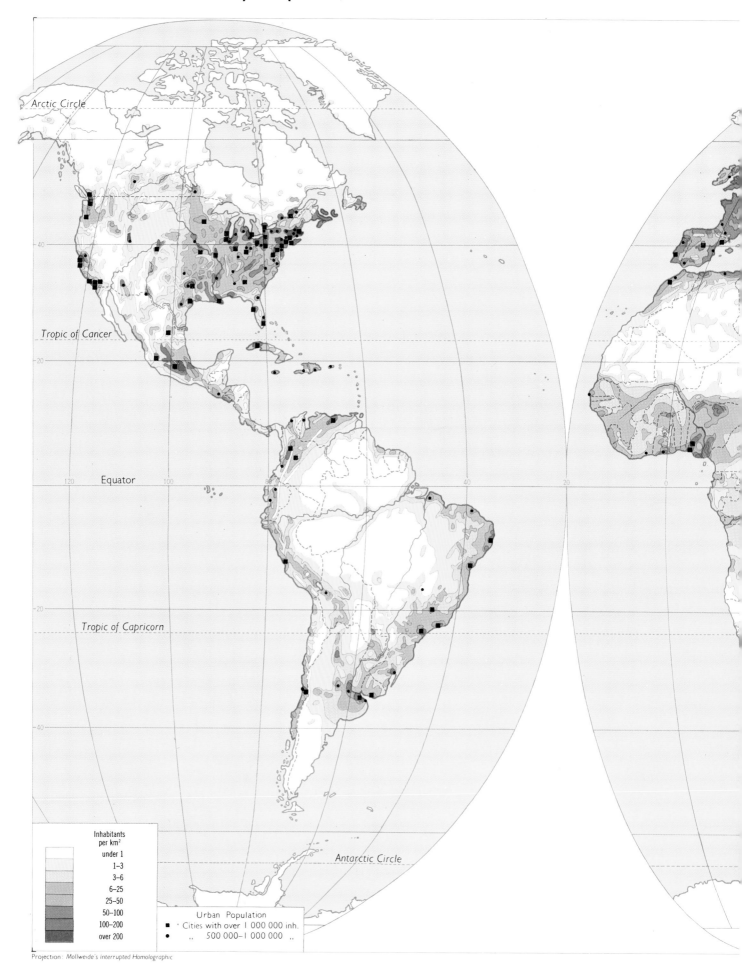

Arctic Circle

Tropic of Cancer

Equator

Tropic of Capricorn

Antarctic Circle

Inhabitants per km²	
under 1	
1–3	
3–6	
6–25	
25–50	
50–100	
100–200	
over 200	

Urban Population
■ Cities with over 1 000 000 inh.
● ,,   500 000–1 000 000 ,,

Projection: Mollweide's interrupted Homolographic

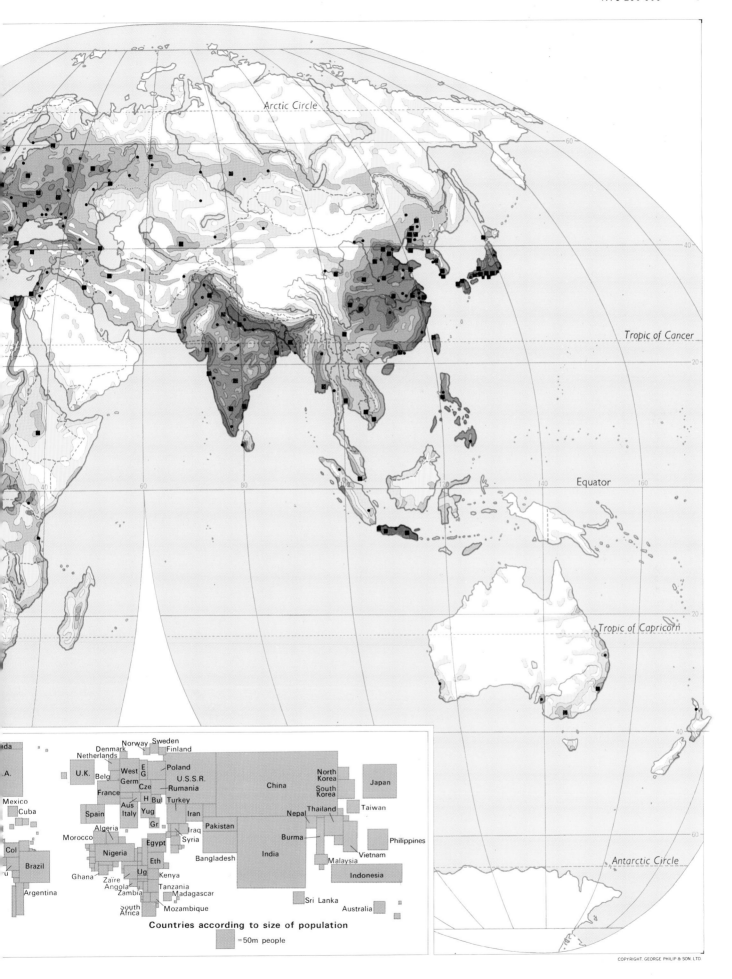

Arctic Circle

60

40

Tropic of Cancer

20

Equator

Tropic of Capricorn

40

60

Antarctic Circle

40   60   80   100   120   140   160

Countries according to size of population

=50m people

Norway Sweden
Denmark
Netherlands Finland
U.K. West E Poland
Belg Germ G North
.A. Cze U.S.S.R. Korea Japan
France Rumania China South
Mexico Aus H Bul Turkey Korea Taiwan
Cuba Spain Italy Yug Iran Nepal Thailand
Algeria Gr Iraq Pakistan Philippines
Col Morocco Egypt Syria Burma Vietnam
Brazil Nigeria Eth Bangladesh India Malaysia
Ghana Ug Kenya Indonesia
Zaïre Tanzania
Angola Madagascar Sri Lanka
Zambia Australia
Argentina South Mozambique
Africa

Projection: *Hammer Equal Area*

ARCTIC REGIONS

EUREKA
TEMPERATURE
Range 51.7°C
Eureka
80°00'N
85°56'W
PRESSURE
M.S.L.
ANNUAL
PRECIPITATION
Total 58.2mm.
J F M A M J J A S O N D

Arctic Explorers
Cook 1778
Franklin 1826–47
McClure 1850–53
Nordenskiöld ("Vega") 1878–79
De Long 1881
Nansen ("Fram") 1893–96
Abruzzi & Cagni 1899–1900
Sverdrup 1902
Peary 1892–1906
Amundsen 1903–6 & 1926
Peary 1908–9
Knud Rasmussen 1912
Koch 1913
Stefánsson 1914–15
Byrd 1926 (by air)
Wilkins 1928 (by air)
Lindsay 1934
Papanin (Drift of Soviet
Expedition) 1937–38
"Sedov" 1937–40
Knuth (Danish Pearyland
Expedition) 1948–49

Projection: Zenithal Equidistant

Progress of Exploration
Coasts explored before   1800
  "   "   between 1800 &
  "   "   between 1850 &
  "   "   since   1900
+ Byrd   Highest latitudes reached by explo
1926   wit

Seas open all
Extreme limi
drift-ice
Seas covered
pack-ice in S
Seas permane
covered by p
Ice-caps and
permanent ic

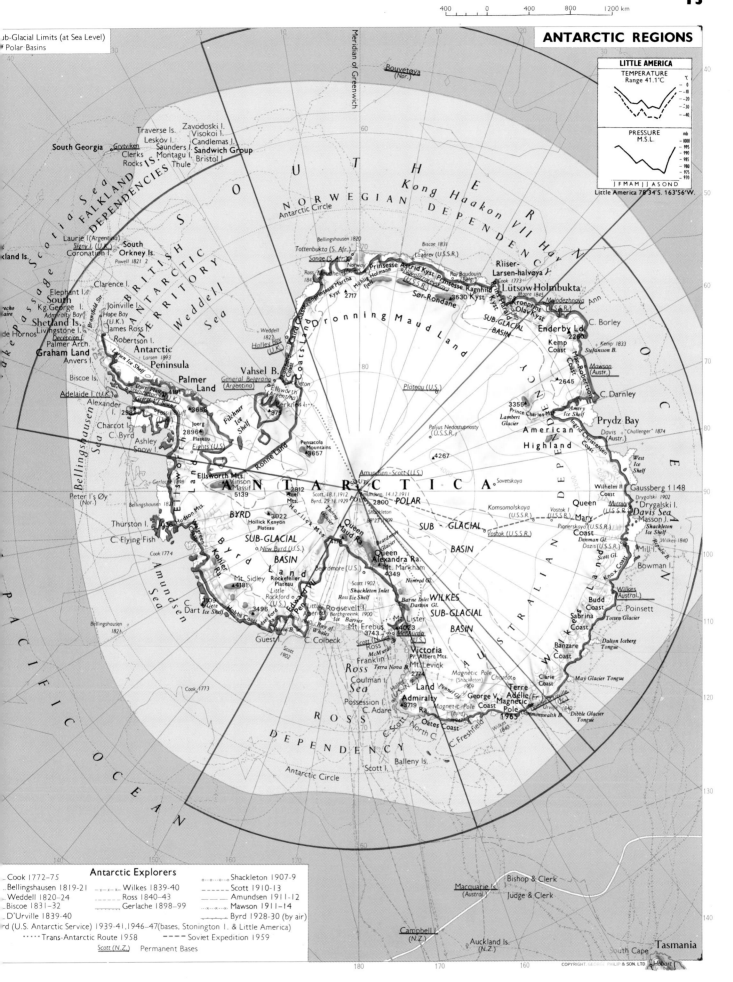

1 : 35 000 000

400 0 400 800 1200 km

13

ANTARCTIC REGIONS

LITTLE AMERICA
TEMPERATURE
Range 41.1°C

PRESSURE
M.S.L.

J F M A M J J A S O N D
Little America 78°34'S. 163°56'W.

Meridian of Greenwich

S O U T H E R N

Kong Haakon VII Hav

NORWEGIAN DEPENDENCY

Bouvetøya (Nor.)

Antarctic Circle

Traverse Is.
Zavodoski I.
Visokoi I.
Leskov I.
Candlemas I.
South Georgia Grytviken
Saunders I. Sandwich Group
Clerks Montagu I. Bristol I.
Rocks I.S. Thule

Scotia Sea FALKLAND DEPENDENCIES

kland Is.

Laurie I.(Argentina)
Signy I. (U.K.) South
Coronation I. Orkney Is.
Powell 1821 2

BRITISH ANTARCTIC TERRITORY

Weddell Sea

Clarence I.

Elephant I.
South
Kg.George I.
Admiralty Bay
Shetland Is. Livingstone I. Hope Bay (U.K.)
Deception I. James Ross I.
Robertson I.
Graham Land Antarctic
Anvers I. Peninsula
Larsen 1893
Biscoe Is.
Vahsel B.
Palmer General Belgrano (Argentina)
Land Berkner I.
Adelaide I. (U.K.)
Alexander I. Fossil Bluff (U.K.)
Charcot I.
Ashley Snow I. Joerg

Filchner Ice Shelf

Ronne Land

Pensacola Mountains

Coats Land

Dronning Maud Land

Prinsesse Astrid Kyst
Prinsesse Ragnhild Kyst
Sør-Rondane

Lützow Holmbukta
Kronprins Olav Kyst
Molodezhnaya (U.S.S.R.)

C. Ann

Enderby Ld.
Kemp Coast
Mawson (Austr.)

C. Borley

SUB-GLACIAL BASIN

C. Darnley

Prince Charles Mts.
Lambert Glacier
Amery Ice Shelf

Prydz Bay
Davis (Austr.)
"Challenger" 1874

American Highland

Plateau (U.S.)

Poljus Nedostupnosty (U.S.S.R.)

Amundsen-Scott (U.S.)

ANTARCTICA

Soovetskaya

West Ice Shelf

Ellsworth Mts.
Vinson Massif

POLAR

Queen Mary Coast

Wilhelm II Coast
Gaussberg 1148

Davis Sea
Drygalski 1902
Masson I.
Shackleton Ice Shelf
Wilkes 1840

BYRD

Hollick Kenyon Plateau
New Byrd (U.S.)

Byrd Land

SUB-GLACIAL BASIN

Komsomolskaya (U.S.S.R.)
Vostok I (U.S.S.R.)
Vostok (U.S.S.R.)

SUB - GLACIAL BASIN

Pionerskaya (U.S.S.R.)

Denman Gl.
Oazis (U.S.S.R.)

Bowman I.

Thurston I.
C. Flying Fish

Amundsen Sea

Mt. Sidley
Rockefeller Plateau
Little Rockford (U.S.)

Queen Maud Ra.

Queen Alexandra Ra.
Mt. Markham
4349

Nimrod Gl.

WILKES
SUB-GLACIAL BASIN

Budd Coast
Sabrina Coast
Banzare Coast

C. Poinsett
Totten Glacier
Dalton Iceberg Tongue

Shackleton Inlet
Ross Ice Shelf

Roosevelt I.
Borchgrevink 1900

Mt. Lister

Mt. Erebus
3743
Mt. Terror

Barne Inlet
Darwin Gl.

Clarie Coast

May Glacier Tongue

Victoria

Pr. Albert Mts.
Mt. Levick
2774

Magnetic Pole (Shackleton) 1909

Terre Adélie (Fr.)

George V Coast
Magnetic Pole 1965

Dibble Glacier Tongue

Ross Sea

Franklin I.
Terra Nova B.

Coulman I.

Possession I.
C. Adare

Admiralty Ra.
3719

Oates Coast

North C.
C. Freshfield

Commonwealth B.

ROSS DEPENDENCY

Balleny Is.

Antarctic Circle

Scott I.

PACIFIC OCEAN

Antarctic Explorers

Cook 1772–75
Bellingshausen 1819–21   Wilkes 1839–40
Weddell 1820–24   Ross 1840–43
Biscoe 1831–32   Gerlache 1898–99
D'Urville 1839–40
rd (U.S. Antarctic Service) 1939–41,1946–47(bases, Stonington I. & Little America)
Trans-Antarctic Route 1958   Soviet Expedition 1959
Scott (N.Z.)   Permanent Bases

Shackleton 1907-9
Scott 1910-13
Amundsen 1911-12
Mawson 1911–14
Byrd 1928-30 (by air)

Macquarie Is. (Austral.)

Bishop & Clerk
Judge & Clerk

Campbell I. (N.Z.)

Auckland Is. (N.Z.)

South Cape

Tasmania
Hobart

COPYRIGHT. GEORGE PHILIP & SON, LTD.

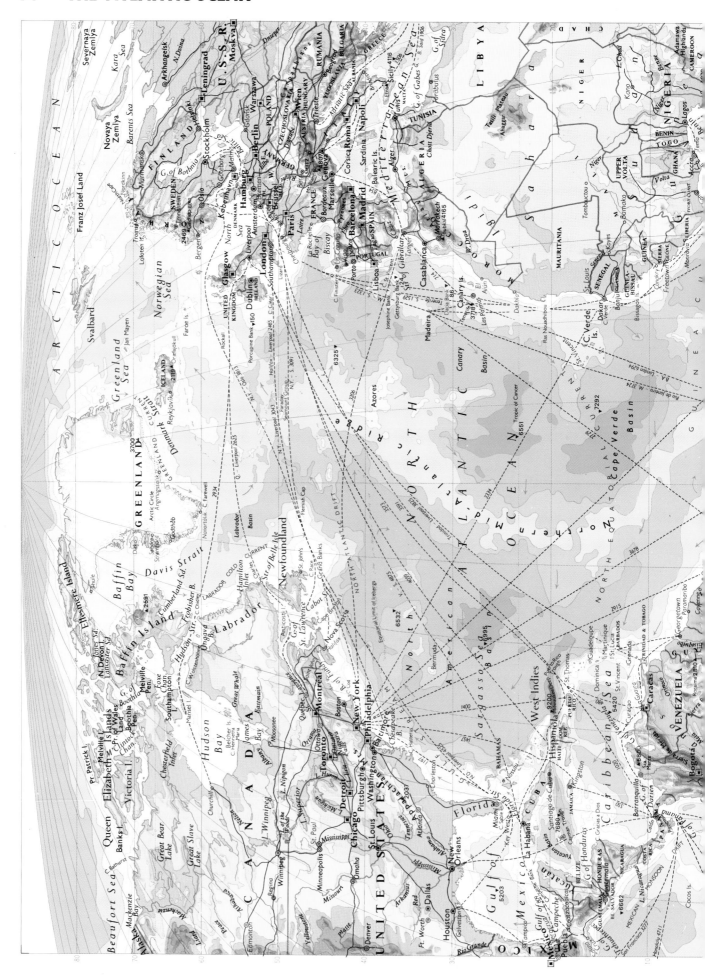

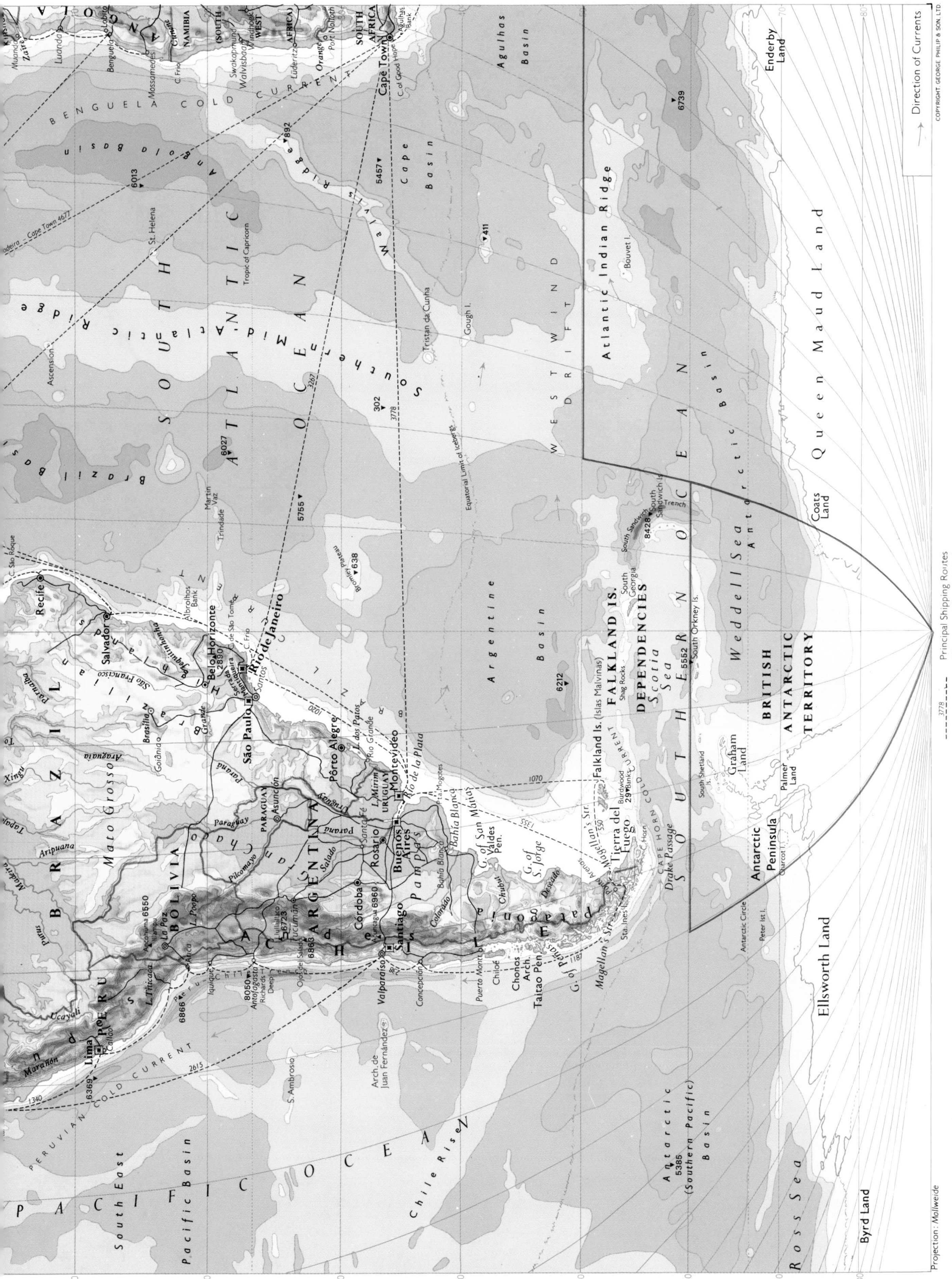
SOUTH ATLANTIC OCEAN
PACIFIC OCEAN
SOUTHERN OCEAN
BRAZIL
BOLIVIA
PERU
PARAGUAY
URUGUAY
ARGENTINA
CHILE
FALKLAND IS.
FALKLAND IS. DEPENDENCIES
BRITISH ANTARCTIC TERRITORY
SOUTH AFRICA
NAMIBIA
Recife
Salvador
Belo Horizonte
Rio de Janeiro
São Paulo
Brasília
Pôrto Alegre
Montevideo
Buenos Aires
Rosario
Córdoba
Santiago
Valparaiso
Asunción
La Paz
Lima
Callao
Cape Town
C. of Good Hope
Lüderitz
Walvis Bay
Swakopmund
Windhoek
Moçâmedes
Benguela
Luanda
St. Helena
Ascension
Tristan da Cunha
Gough I.
Bouvet I.
South Georgia
South Sandwich Is.
South Orkney Is.
South Shetland Is.
Falkland Is. (Islas Malvinas)
Tierra del Fuego
C. Horn
Drake Passage
Scotia Sea
Weddell Sea
Ross Sea
Graham Land
Palmer Land
Antarctic Peninsula
Ellsworth Land
Byrd Land
Coats Land
Queen Maud Land
Enderby Land
Brazil Basin
Angola Basin
Cape Basin
Agulhas Basin
Argentine Basin
South East Pacific Basin
Antarctic (Southern Pacific) Basin
Atlantic Indian Ridge
Mid Atlantic Ridge
Walvis Ridge
Chile Rise
BENGUELA COLD CURRENT
PERUVIAN COLD CURRENT
WEST WIND DRIFT
CAPE HORN COLD CURRENT
Equatorial Limit of Icebergs
Tropic of Capricorn
Antarctic Circle
Direction of Currents
Principal Shipping Routes (Distances in Nautical Miles)
Projection: Mollweide
m 6000 4000 3000 2000 1500 1000 400 200 0
0 200 2000 4000 5000 6000 8000 m

1:20 000 000

200 0 200 400 600 800 km

Ob

Mountains

Ural

Iz. 1617

Pechora

Tundra

Kanin
Peninsula

Mezen

N. Dvina

Kola
Peninsula

White
Sea

Onega

L.Onega

Ladoga

Chudskoye

Finland

Svir

Neva

L.Torne

Kebnekaise
▲2123

Lapland

L.Inari

Onega

Obshchiyv

Kama

Volga

Rybinsk
Res.

Oka

Volga

Don

Ural

Volga

Volga Uplands

Tsimlyansk
Res.

Don

Caspian

Volga

CASPIAN
SEA
-28

Caucasus

5633
▲

Elbrus 5633

Terek

Kuban

Kura

Aras

Armenia

Araks

L.Van

Kurdistan

Sivan

Euphrates

Anatolia

Taurus

3710
▲

BLACK SEA

2211
▲

Crimea

Sea of
Azov

Str. of Kerch

Bosporus

Central Russian Uplands

Ukraine

Dnepr
(Dnieper)

Bug

Danube

Pripyat
(Pripet)
Marshes

Dnestr (Dniester)

Danube

Carpathians

Transylvanian Alps

Wallachia

Balkans

Rhodope

Balkan Peninsula

Pindus

Aegean
Sea

Morea

Ionian Is.

Ionian
Sea

Str.of Otranto

ADRIATIC SEA

Dinaric Alps

Plain of
Hungary

Danube

Tisza

Mures

Morava

Sava

Sudetes

Moravian
Heights

Bohemian For.

Carpathians

2655
▲

Bakony For.

North

European

Plain

Nied. Silesia

Odra (Oder)

Wisła
(Vistula)

Niemen

G. of
Riga

Gotland

BALTIC SEA

G. of Bothnia

Vänern

Vättern

Mälaren

Indalsi

Ume

Lule

Skagerrak

Kattegat

Jutland

Elbe

Weser

Harz
1142

Erz Geb

Ez Geb

Bohemian For.

Danube

Black For.

Vosges

Jura

Alps

4807
▲

Mt. Blanc
4807

Apennines

Vesuvius
1277

Tiber

Tyrrhenian
Sea

Corsica

Sardinia

Str. of Bonifacio

Ligurian
Sea

Po

Rhône

Cévennes

Central
Massif

Mt. Dore
1886

Ardennes

Meuse

Eifel

Rhine

Netherlands

Heligoland

Weser
wald

Thuringer
wald

Main

Jura

Lindesnes

Vesterålen

Lofoten

Kjolen

Scandinavia

Galdhøpiggen
▲2469

3734

NORWEGIAN

SEA

North Cape

Nordkinn

North Cape

Mts.

Iceland

Hekla 1491
▲

Vatnajökull

Örœfa
2119

Arctic Circle

Faroe Is.

Shetland Is.

Orkney Is.

Hebrides

Fisher Bank

Dogger Bank

NORTH

SEA

Ben Nevis
1347
▲

British
Isles

Great Britain

Snowdon
1085

Thames

Ireland

Irish Sea

Rockall

ATLANTIC

OCEAN

Land's End

English Channel

Brittany

Bay of
Biscay

Loire

Seine

Garonne

Gironde

Valentia I.

C. Clear

C. Finisterre

Douro

Sa. da Estrela

Iberian

Peninsula

Old
Castile

New
Castile

Cantabrian Mts.

Pico de Aneto

Pyrenees

3404

Sa. de Guadarrama

Sierra Morena

Andalusia

Guadalquivir

Sa. Nevada

3478

Tagus

MEDITERRANEAN

Str. of Gibraltar

Rif

Maritime Atlas

Balearic Is.

C. St.
Vincent

C. Trafalgar

C. Spartel

C. St.
Roca (Tejo)

Ebro

Sicily
3263

Etna 3263

Str. of Messina

Calabria

C. Bon

C. Blanco

m 4000 2000 1000 400 200 0 200

4000 2000

1:40 000 000

400 0 400 800 1200 1600 km

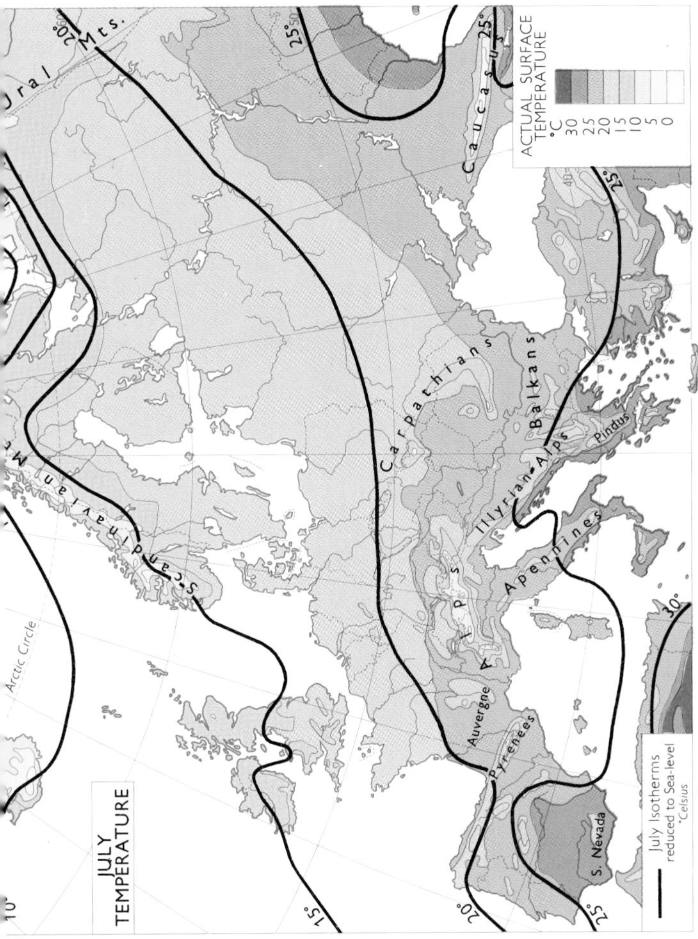

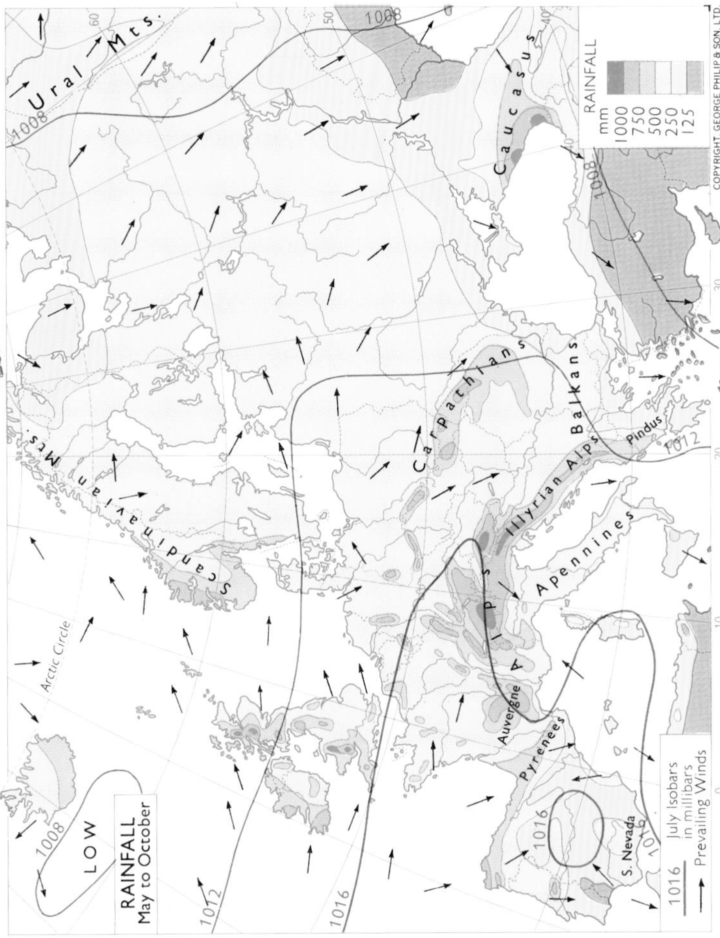

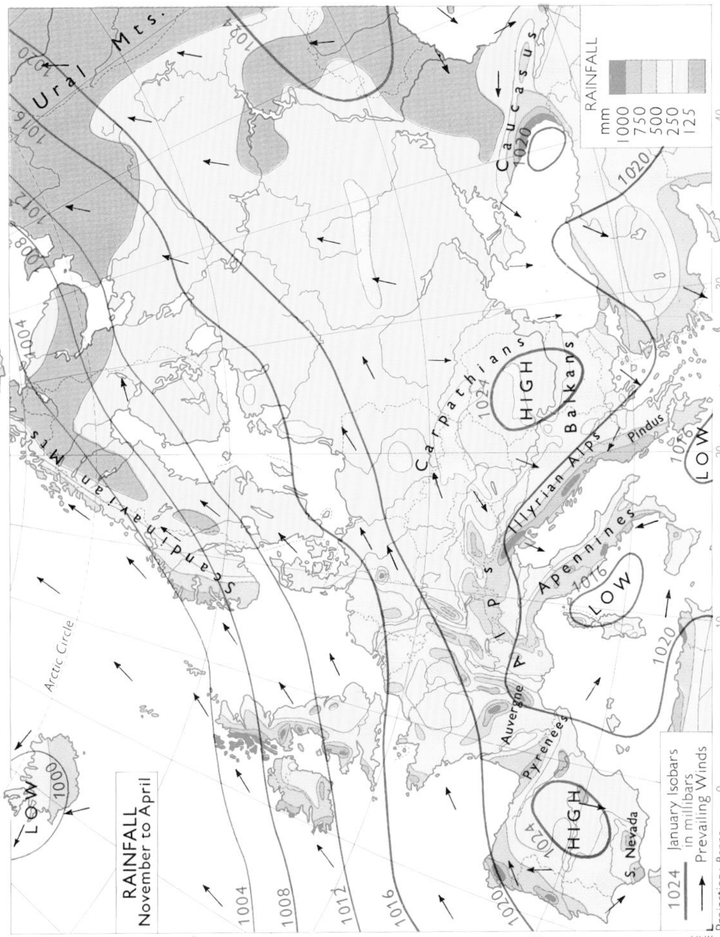

JULY TEMPERATURE

ACTUAL SURFACE TEMPERATURE
°C
30
25
20
15
10
5
0

Ural Mts.

Caucasus

Carpathians

Illyrian Alps

Balkans

Pindus

Alps

Apennines

Scandinavian Mts.

Auvergne

Pyrenees

S. Nevada

Arctic Circle

July Isotherms reduced to Sea-level
°Celsius

JANUARY TEMPERATURE

ACTUAL SURFACE TEMPERATURE
°C
10
5
0
-5
-10
-15
-20

Ural Mts.

Caucasus

Carpathians

Illyrian Alps

Balkans

Pindus

Alps

Apennines

Scandinavian Mts.

Auvergne

Pyrenees

S. Nevada

Arctic Circle

January Isotherms reduced to Sea-level
°Celsius

60

50

40

RAINFALL May to October

RAINFALL
mm
1000
750
500
250
125

Ural Mts.

Caucasus

Carpathians

Illyrian Alps

Balkans

Pindus

Alps

Apennines

Scandinavian Mts.

Auvergne

Pyrenees

S. Nevada

Arctic Circle

LOW

1008

1012

1016

July Isobars in millibars
Prevailing Winds

COPYRIGHT GEORGE PHILIP & SON LTD

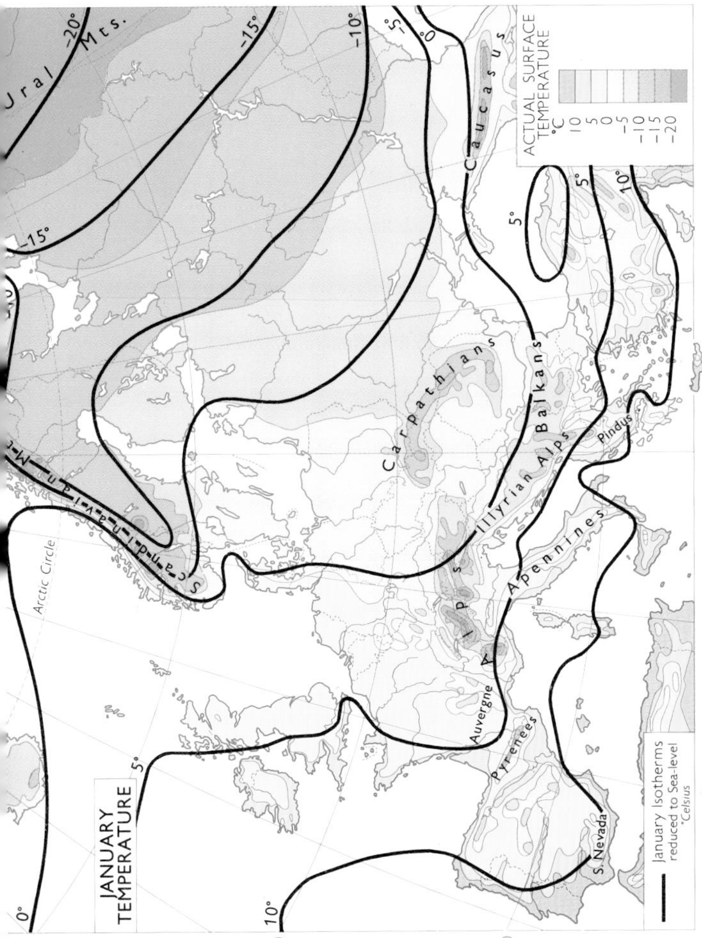

RAINFALL November to April

RAINFALL
mm
1000
750
500
250
125

Ural Mts.

Caucasus

Carpathians

Illyrian Alps

Balkans

Pindus

Alps

Apennines

Scandinavian Mts.

Auvergne

Pyrenees

S. Nevada

Arctic Circle

HIGH

LOW

LOW

LOW

HIGH

1000
1004
1008
1012
1016
1020
1024

January Isobars in millibars
Prevailing Winds

HHK Projection: Bonne

1:35 000 000

400   0   400   800   1200 km

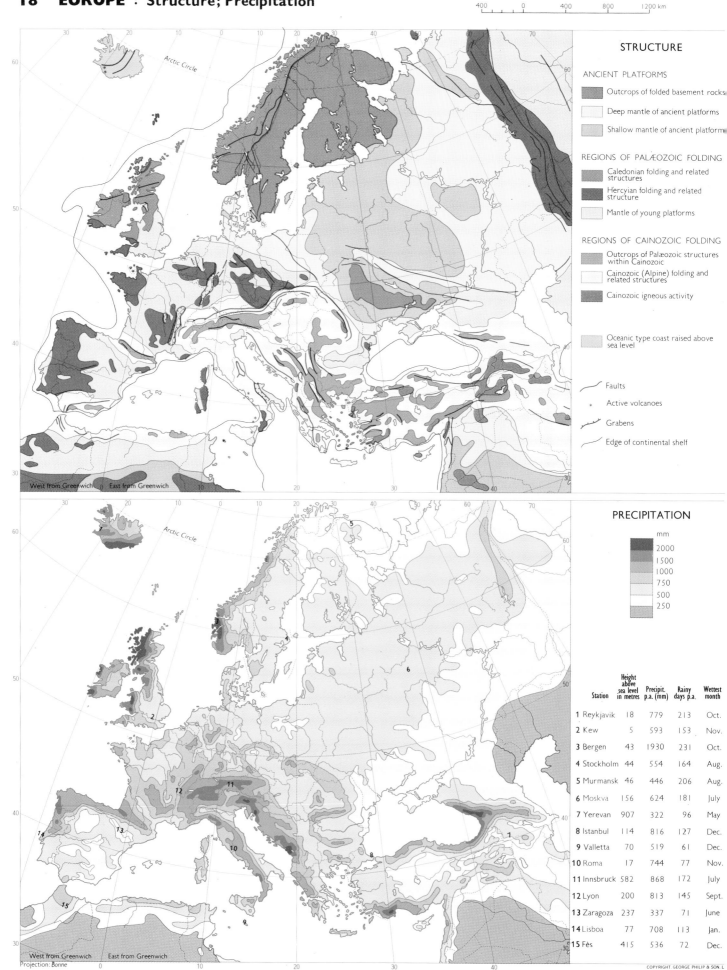

STRUCTURE

ANCIENT PLATFORMS

- Outcrops of folded basement rocks
- Deep mantle of ancient platforms
- Shallow mantle of ancient platform

REGIONS OF PALÆOZOIC FOLDING

- Caledonian folding and related structures
- Hercyian folding and related structure
- Mantle of young platforms

REGIONS OF CAINOZOIC FOLDING

- Outcrops of Palæozoic structures within Cainozoic
- Cainozoic (Alpine) folding and related structures
- Cainozoic igneous activity

- Oceanic type coast raised above sea level

- Faults
- Active volcanoes
- Grabens
- Edge of continental shelf

Arctic Circle

West from Greenwich   East from Greenwich

PRECIPITATION

mm
- 2000
- 1500
- 1000
- 750
- 500
- 250

Station	Height above sea level in metres	Precipit. p.a. (mm)	Rainy days p.a.	Wettest month
1 Reykjavik	18	779	213	Oct.
2 Kew	5	593	153	Nov.
3 Bergen	43	1930	231	Oct.
4 Stockholm	44	554	164	Aug.
5 Murmansk	46	446	206	Aug.
6 Moskva	156	624	181	July
7 Yerevan	907	322	96	May
8 Istanbul	114	816	127	Dec.
9 Valletta	70	519	61	Dec.
10 Roma	17	744	77	Nov.
11 Innsbruck	582	868	172	July
12 Lyon	200	813	145	Sept.
13 Zaragoza	237	337	71	June
14 Lisboa	77	708	113	Jan.
15 Fès	415	536	72	Dec.

Arctic Circle

West from Greenwich   East from Greenwich

Projection: Bonne

1:6 000 000

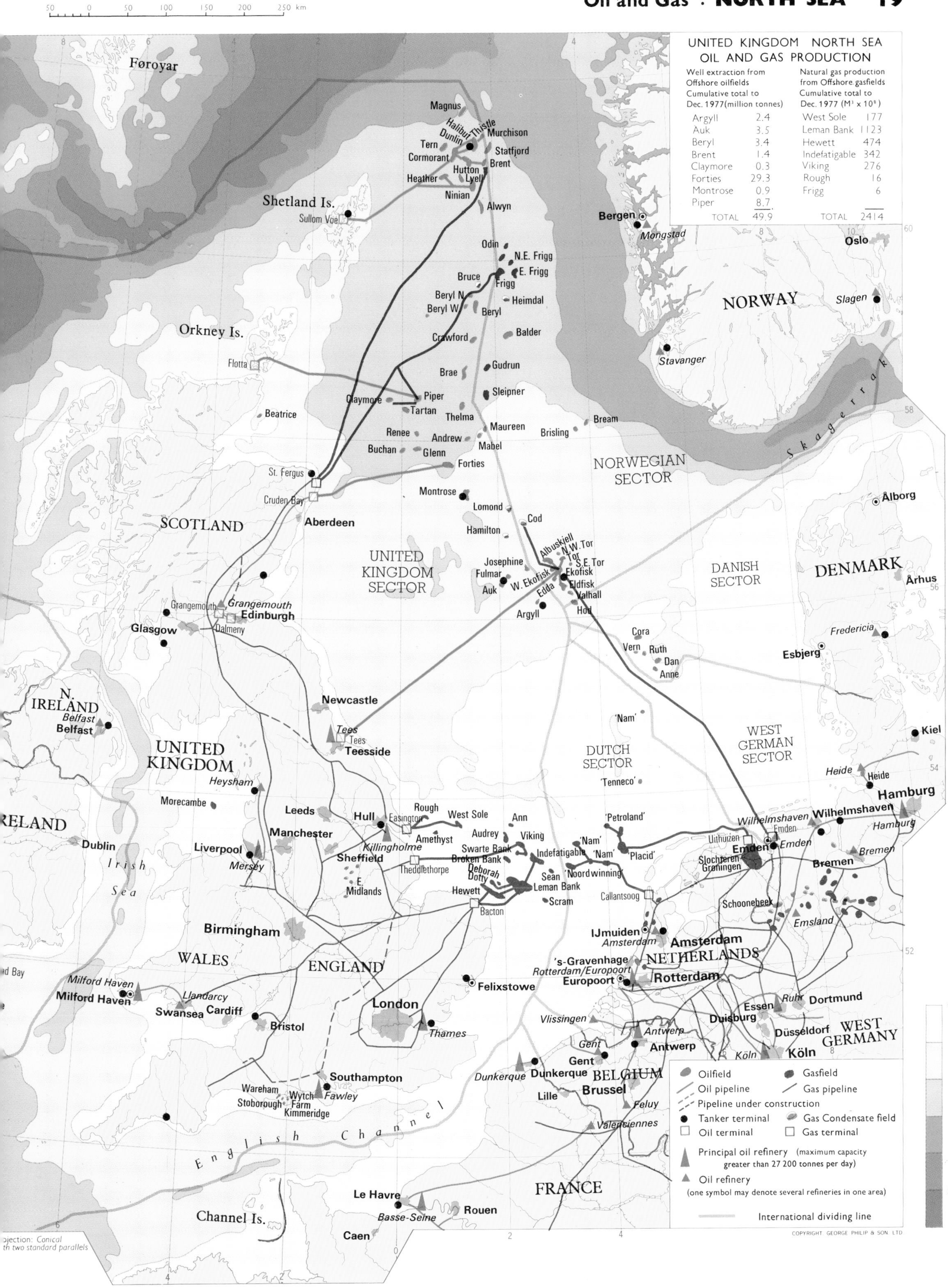

50 0 50 100 150 200 250 km

Føroyar

UNITED KINGDOM NORTH SEA OIL AND GAS PRODUCTION

Well extraction from Offshore oilfields Cumulative total to Dec. 1977 (million tonnes)		Natural gas production from Offshore gasfields Cumulative total to Dec. 1977 ($M^3 \times 10^8$)	
Argyll	2.4	West Sole	177
Auk	3.5	Leman Bank	1123
Beryl	3.4	Hewett	474
Brent	1.4	Indefatigable	342
Claymore	0.3	Viking	276
Forties	29.3	Rough	16
Montrose	0.9	Frigg	6
Piper	8.7		
TOTAL	49.9	TOTAL	2414

Magnus
Halibut Thistle
Dunlin Murchison
Tern
Cormorant Statfjord
Hutton Brent
Heather Lyell
Ninian
Alwyn

Shetland Is.
Sullom Voe

Bergen
Mongstad

Oslo

Odin
N.E. Frigg
E. Frigg
Bruce Frigg Heimdal
Beryl N Beryl
Beryl W
Crawford Balder

NORWAY

Slagen

Orkney Is.

Brae Gudrun
Sleipner

Flotta

Stavanger

Beatrice
Claymore Piper
Tartan
Thelma
Renee Maureen Brisling
Andrew Mabel Bream
Buchan Glenn
Forties

NORWEGIAN
SECTOR

Skagerrak

St. Fergus
Cruden Bay
Montrose
Lomond

SCOTLAND Aberdeen Hamilton Cod

Ålborg

UNITED
KINGDOM
SECTOR

Josephine Albuskjell
Fulmar N.W.Tor
Auk Tor
W. Ekofisk S.E. Tor
Edda Ekofisk
Eldfisk
Argyll Valhall
Hod

DANISH
SECTOR

DENMARK

Århus

Grangemouth Grangemouth
Edinburgh
Glasgow Dalmeny

Cora
Vern Ruth
Dan
Anne

Fredericia
Esbjerg

N. IRELAND
Belfast
Belfast

Newcastle
Tees
Tees
Teesside

'Nam'

WEST
GERMAN
SECTOR

Kiel

UNITED
KINGDOM

Heysham

Morecambe

DUTCH
SECTOR

'Tenneco'

Heide Heide

Hamburg
Hamburg

IRELAND

Dublin

Irish
Sea

Leeds
Hull Easington
Manchester Rough West Sole Ann
Amethyst Audrey Viking
Liverpool Killingholme Swarte Bank
Mersey Sheffield Broken Bank
Theddlethorpe Deborah Indefatigable
E. Dotty 'Nam'
Midlands Sean Leman Bank
Hewett Scram

'Petroland'

Uithuizen Emden Emden
Slochteren Emden
Groningen

'Nam' 'Placid'
Noordwinning

Wilhelmshaven Wilhelmshaven

Bremen Bremen

Birmingham
WALES ENGLAND

Milford Haven
Milford Haven
Llandarcy
Swansea Cardiff
Bristol

Bacton

Callantsoog

Schoonebeek

Emsland

IJmuiden
Amsterdam
Amsterdam

's-Gravenhage
Rotterdam/Europoort
Europoort Rotterdam

NETHERLANDS

Essen Ruhr Dortmund
Duisburg
Düsseldorf Köln

WEST
GERMANY

d Bay

London
Thames

Felixstowe

Vlissingen
Gent Antwerp
Gent Antwerp
BELGIUM

Köln Köln

m

50
100

Wareham
Stoborough Wytch Fawley
Kimmeridge Farm

Southampton

Dunkerque Dunkerque
Lille Brussel
Brussel

Feluy

Valenciennes

200

500

1000

English Channel

FRANCE

Oilfield		Gasfield
Oil pipeline		Gas pipeline
Pipeline under construction		
Tanker terminal		Gas Condensate field
Oil terminal		Gas terminal

Principal oil refinery (maximum capacity greater than 27 200 tonnes per day)

Oil refinery (one symbol may denote several refineries in one area)

International dividing line

Le Havre
Basse-Seine Rouen

Channel Is.

Caen

Projection: Conical
with two standard parallels

COPYRIGHT GEORGE PHILIP & SON LTD

1:20 000 000

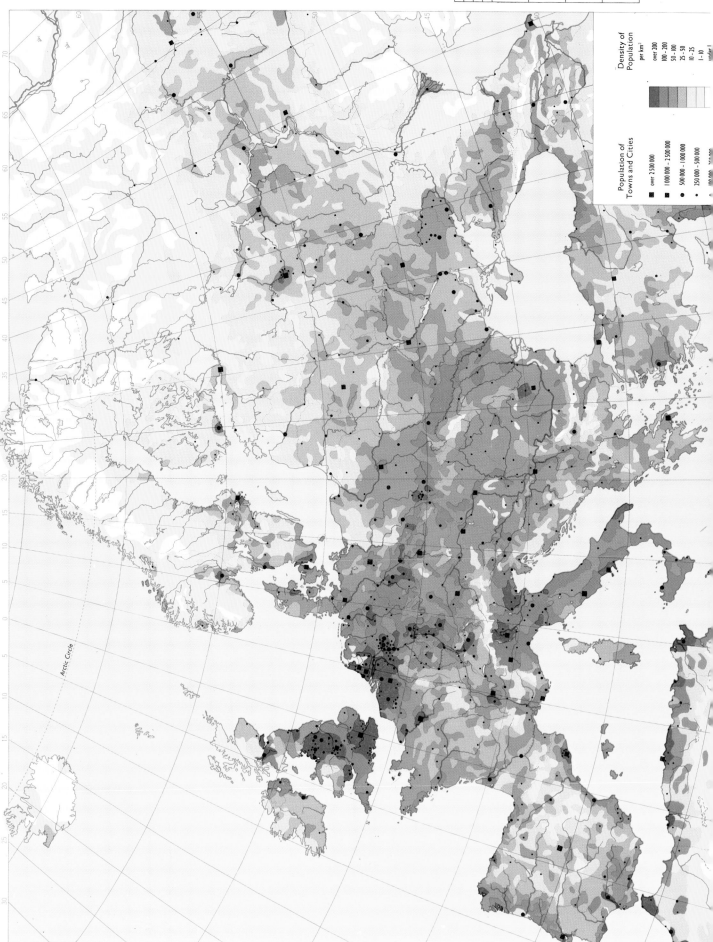

Density of
Population
per km²

over 200
100 - 200
50 - 100
25 - 50
10 - 25
1 - 10

Population of
Towns and Cities

over 2 500 000
1 000 000 - 2 500 000
500 000 - 1 000 000
250 000 - 500 000

Arctic Circle

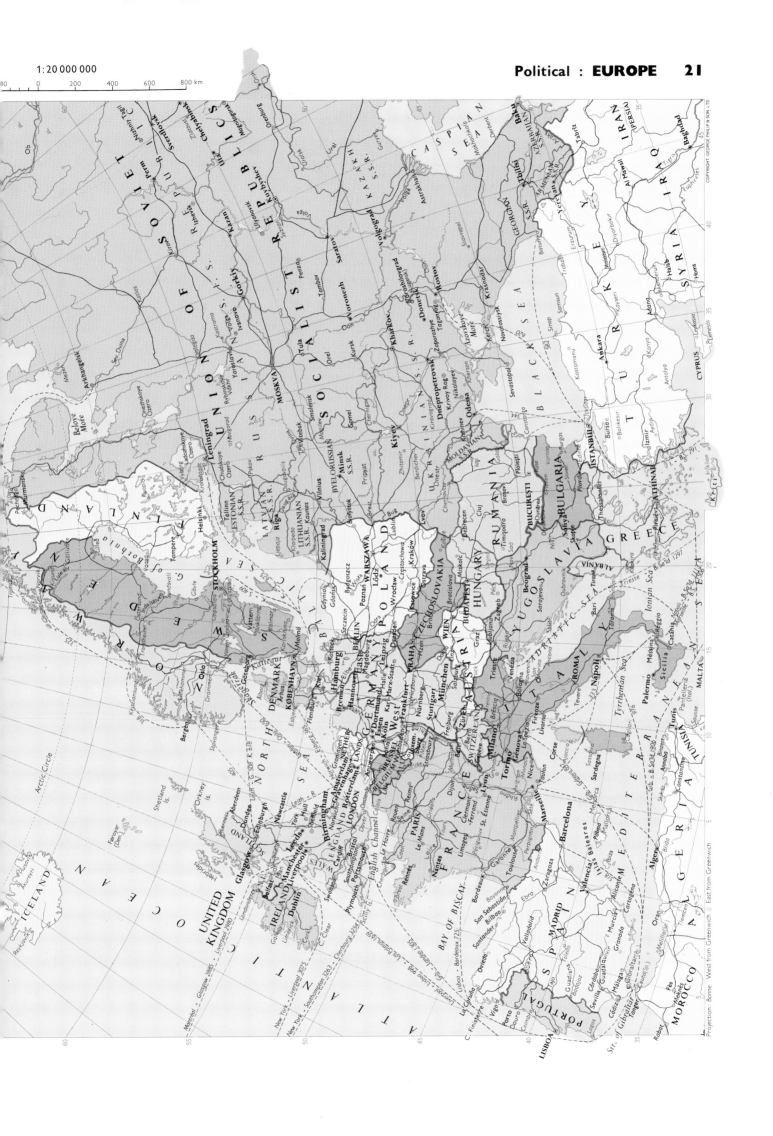

1 : 20 000 000

0   200   400   600   800 km

Projection: Bonne   West from Greenwich 0 East from Greenwich

1 : 4 000 000

50 0 50 100 150 km

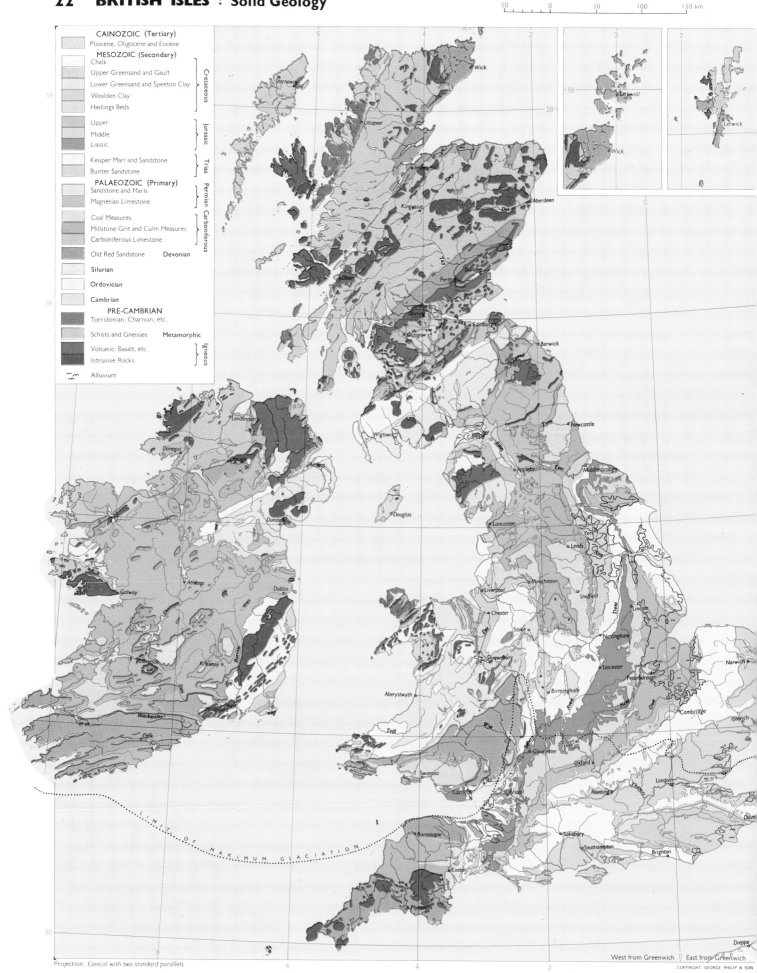

CAINOZOIC (Tertiary)
Pliocene, Oligocene and Eocene

MESOZOIC (Secondary)
Chalk
Upper Greensand and Gault
Lower Greensand and Speeton Clay
Wealden Clay
Hastings Beds

Upper
Middle
Liassic

Keuper Marl and Sandstone
Bunter Sandstone

PALAEOZOIC (Primary)
Sandstone and Marls
Magnesian Limestone

Coal Measures
Millstone Grit and Culm Measures
Carboniferous Limestone

Old Red Sandstone   Devonian

Silurian

Ordovician

Cambrian

PRE-CAMBRIAN
Torridonian, Charnian, etc.

Schists and Gneisses   Metamorphic

Volcanic: Basalt, etc.
Intrusive Rocks

Alluvium

Cretaceous
Jurassic
Trias
Permian
Carboniferous
Igneous

Projection: Conical with two standard parallels

West from Greenwich | East from Greenwich

COPYRIGHT. GEORGE PHILIP & SON.

1:4 000 000

50 0 50 100 150 km

ection: Conical with two standard parallels

West from Greenwich East from Greenwich

COPYRIGHT. GEORGE PHILIP & SON. LTD.

m
1000
400
200
100
0
0
50
100
200
m

1:4 000 000

ANNUAL PRECIPITATION
AND
ISOBARS

ANNUAL PRECIPITATION

mm
2500
2000
1500
1250
1000
750
625
500

ANNUAL ISOBARS

1011 mb   (in Millibars)

WIND ROSES

Frequency of wind
from each direction
is indicated by the
length of each arrow

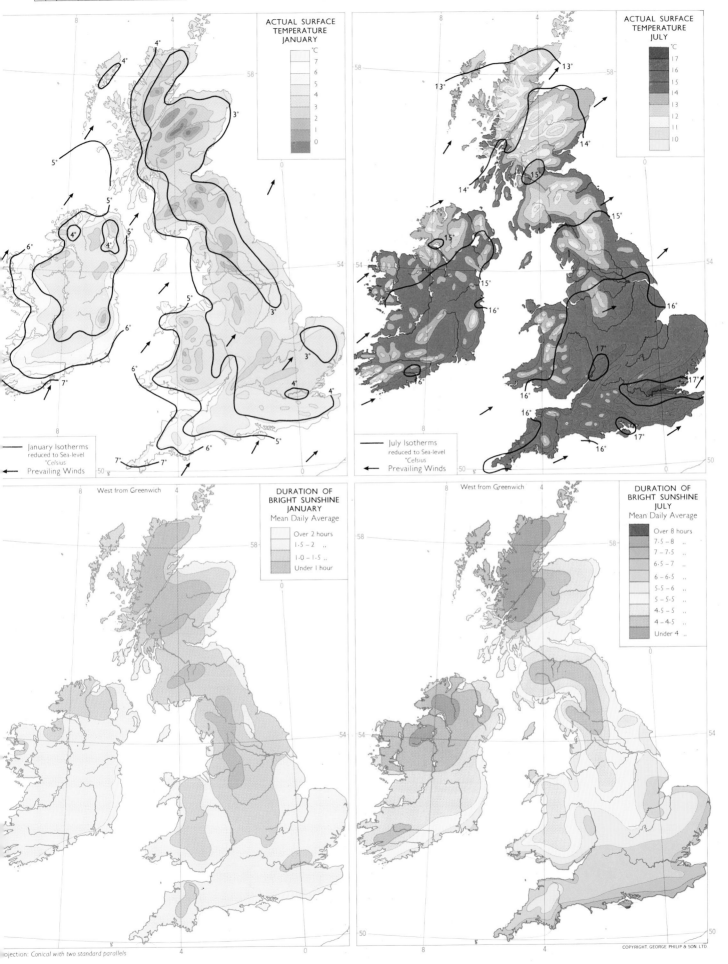

1 : 8 500 000

50 0 50 100 150 200 250 300 km

ACTUAL SURFACE TEMPERATURE JANUARY

°C
7
6
5
4
3
2
1
0

—— January Isotherms
reduced to Sea-level
Celsius
←— Prevailing Winds

ACTUAL SURFACE TEMPERATURE JULY

°C
17
16
15
14
13
12
11
10

—— July Isotherms
reduced to Sea-level
Celsius
←— Prevailing Winds

West from Greenwich

DURATION OF BRIGHT SUNSHINE JANUARY
Mean Daily Average

Over 2 hours
1·5 – 2 „
1·0 – 1·5 „
Under 1 hour

West from Greenwich

DURATION OF BRIGHT SUNSHINE JULY
Mean Daily Average

Over 8 hours
7·5 – 8 „
7 – 7·5 „
6·5 – 7 „
6 – 6·5 „
5·5 – 6 „
5 – 5·5 „
4·5 – 5 „
4 – 4·5 „
Under 4 „

Projection: Conical with two standard parallels

1 : 4 000 000

50   0   50   100   150 km

West from Greenwich   East from Greenwich

COPYRIGHT, GEORGE PHILIP & SON, L™

1 : 4 000 000

50   0   50   100   150 km

The DISTRICTS of Northern Ireland have been numbered and can be identified by reference to this table.

1	Londonderry	14	Craigavon
2	Limavady	15	Armagh
3	Coleraine	16	Newry & Mourne
4	Ballymoney	17	Banbridge
5	Moyle	18	Down
6	Larne	19	Lisburn
7	Ballymena	20	Antrim
8	Magherafelt	21	Newtownabbey
9	Cookstown	22	Carrickfergus
10	Strabane	23	North Down
11	Omagh	24	Ards
12	Fermanagh	25	Castlereagh
13	Dungannon	26	Belfast

1 Merseyside
2 Greater Manchester
3 West Yorkshire
4 South Yorkshire
5 West Glamorgan
6 Mid Glamorgan
7 South Glamorgan

Projection: Conical with two standard parallels

West from Greenwich   0   East from Greenwich

1:1 000 000

10   0   10   20   30   40 km

West from Greenwich   East from Greenwich

═══ Motorways
════ Motorways under construction

COPYRIGHT. GEORGE PHILIP & SON. LTD.

1:1 000 000

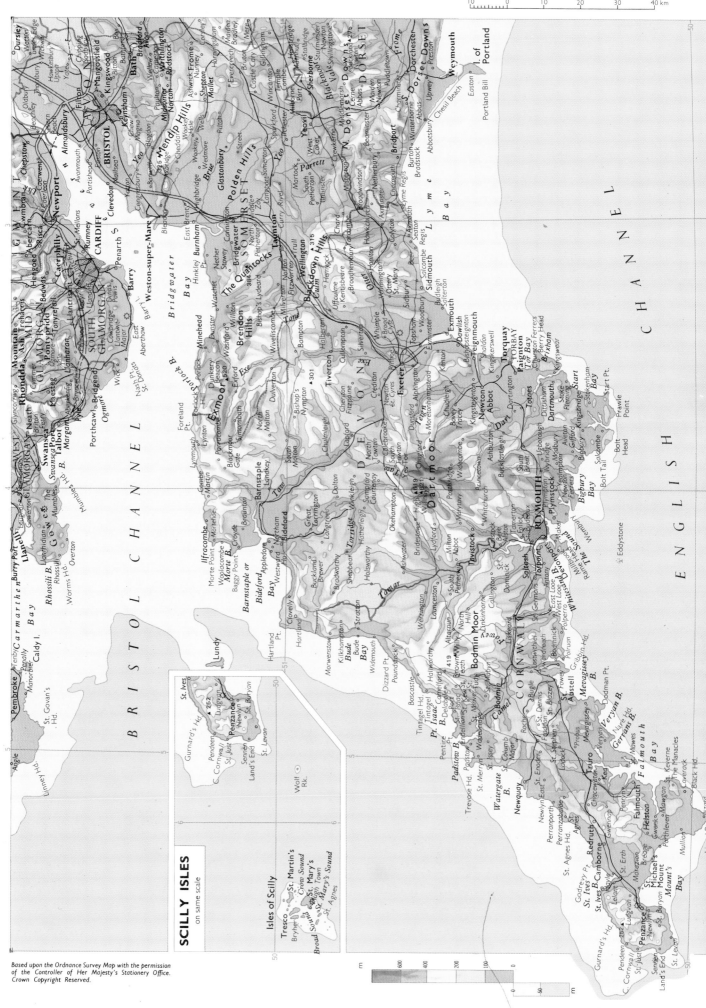

BRISTOL   CHANNEL

ENGLISH   CHANNEL

SCILLY ISLES
on same scale

Isles of Scilly

1:1 000 000

10   0   10   20   30   40 km

m
1000
800
600
400
200
100
0
50
100
m

on: Conical with two standard parallels

═══ Motorways
════ Motorways under construction

West from Greenwich

COPYRIGHT GEORGE PHILIP & SON LTD.

Based upon the Ordnance Survey Map with the permission of the Controller of Her Majesty's Stationery Office. Crown Copyright Reserved.

IRISH

SEA

Projection: Conical with two standard parallels

━━━ Motorways
═══ Motorways under construction

m
1000
800
600
400
200
100
0
0
50
m

1:1 000 000

10   0   10   20   30   40 km

Continuation
Northwards
on same scale

N O R T H

S E A

BORDERS

Berwick on
Tweed

Holy I.

Budle Bay

Farne Is.

CHEVIOT HILLS

The Cheviot
▲816

Breamish

Alnwick

NORTHUMBERLAND

Morpeth

Ashington
Newbiggin

HADRIAN'S WALL

Blyth

Whitley B.

NEWCASTLE
UPON TYNE

Tynemouth
South
Shields
Wallsend   Jarrow

Hexham

Gateshead   TYNE AND
WEAR

Sunderland

Consett
Stanley
Chester le
Street

Washington
Houghton
le Spring

Durham

Hartley
Seaton Delaval
Earsdon   Whitley Bay
Tynemouth
Wallsend
South Shields
Gateshead   Jarrow
TYNE AND WEAR
Sunderland
Washington
Houghton le Spring
Seaham
Murton
Easington Colliery
Horden
Peterlee
Wheatley
Hill   Castle Eden
Hartlepool

Billingham
Stockton
on Tees
Thornaby
on Tees   Middlesbrough
Redcar
Marske by the Sea
Saltburn by the Sea
Staithes
Kettle Ness
Hinderwell   Whitby
Robin Hood's Bay

CLEVELAND

Guisborough

Cleveland Hills
▲454
North York
Moors

Fylingdales
Moor

Scarborough

YORKSHIRE

Northallerton

Vale of Pickering

Filey
Filey Bay
Hunmanby

Flamborough
Flamborough
Head

Bridlington
Bridlington
Bay

Ripon

York

Driffield

Skipsea

Beeford

Hornsea

LEEDS

Beverley

Leven

HUMBERSIDE

Holderness

Aldbrough

HULL

Withernsea

Humber

Scunthorpe

Grimsby
Cleethorpes

Spurn Hd.

Mouth of the Humber

Doncaster

Donna Nook

LINCOLNSHIRE

Louth

Mablethorpe

Sutton-on-Sea

Rotherham

Gainsborough

Market Rasen

Alford

SHEFFIELD

Worksop

Lincoln

Skegness

Chesterfield

Mansfield

Newark
on-Trent

Sleaford

Boston

The Wash

NOTTINGHAM

Grantham

NORFOLK

Derby

DERBYSHIRE

West from Greenwich   East from Greenwich

COPYRIGHT GEORGE PHILIP & SON LTD.

Based upon the Ordnance Survey Map with the permission
of the Controller of Her Majesty's Stationery Office.
Crown Copyright Reserved.

West from Greenw

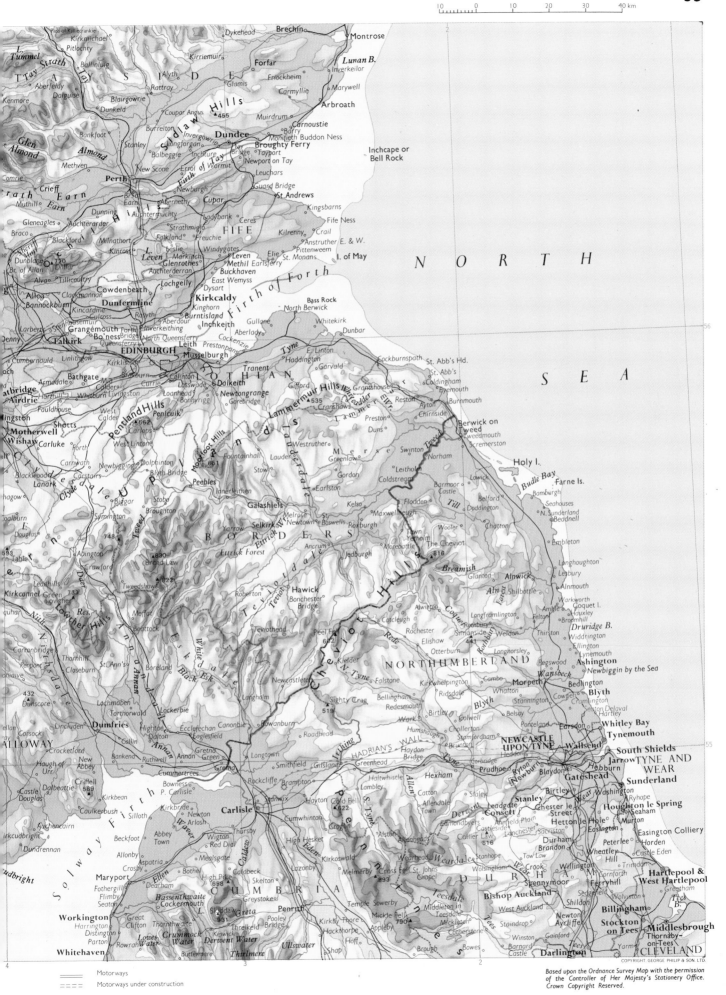

1 : 1 000 000

10   0   10   20   30   40 km

Motorways
Motorways under construction

SHETLAND ISLANDS
on same scale

Herma Ness
Haroldswick
Baltasound
Bluemull Sd.
Balta
Unst
Ramna Stacks
Cullivoe
Uyeasound
Mu Ness
Point of Fethaland
Whale Firth
Fetlar
The Faither
North Roe
Mid Yell Sd.
The Snap
Ronas Hill 450
Yell
Esha Ness
Hillswick
Burravoe
SHETLAND
Lunna Ness
St. Magnus Bay
Brae
Skaw Taing
Out Skerries
Muckle Roe
Voe
Whalsay
Papa Stour
S Nesting Bay
The Háa
Sd. of Papa
Sandness
Walls
Score Hd.
Vaila
Easter Skeld
Gruting Voe
Lerwick
I. of Noss
Scalloway
Bressay
Hamnavoe
293
Bard Hd.
West Burra
Bressay Sd.
Kettla Ness
Helli Ness
Hoswick
Mousa
St. Ninian's I.
Scousburgh
Boddam
Fitful Hd.
B. of Quendale
Sumburgh Hd.

Butt of Lewis
Port of Ness
South Dell
Ness
Borve
Cellar Hd.
Barvas
Tolsta Hd.
Carloway
North Tolsta
291
Newmarket
Broad Bay
Tiumpan Hd.
Shawbost
Back
Gallan Hd.
Great Bernera
Stornoway
Melbost
Eye Peninsula
Portaguiran
Uig
Callanish
Bayble
L. Roag
Lewis
Chicken Hd.
Aird Brenish
575
Gisla
Lochs
Crossbost
Loch Langavat
Balallan
L. Ersort
Cromore
Scarp
Kintravay
Park
Gravir
Kebock Hd.
Husinish
N. Harris
571
L. Shell
Husinish Pt.
Ardvourlie Castle
799
Beinn Mhor
W. L. Tarbert
Taransay
Ardhasig
Tarbert
Sd. of Shiant
Shiant Is.
Sd. of Taransay
L. Seaforth
WESTERN
Toe Hd.
Scalpay
E.L. Tarbert
Pabbay
S. Harris
Scarastavore
Sound of Harris
Leverburgh
Berneray
Rodel
Renish Pt.
Rubha Hunish
Haskeir Is.
Sd. of Pabbay
ISLES
Griminish Pt.
Kilmaluag
Soilas
Vaternish Pt.
North Uist
Lochmaddy
Loch Snizort
Paible
L. Maddy
Clachan
Uig
Trotternish
Sound of Monach
L. Eport
Waternish
The Storr
Monach Is.
Baleshare
Carinish
347 Eaval
Dunvegan Head
Stein
719
Milovaig
Rona
Grimsay
Ronay
Lephin
Gramisdale
Dunvegan
Roskhill
Benbecula
488
Portree
Ardivachar Pt.
Wiay
Bracadale
L. Bee
Bagh nam Faoileann
Coillore
L. Bracadale
Minginish
L. Harport
Howmore
Carbost
Drynoch
Scalpay
South Uist
605 Hecla
Fernilea
Sligachan
620 B. Mhor
Rubha Ardvule
Cuillin Hills
Bla Bheinn
L. Eynort
Glenbrittle
1009
928
Daliburgh
Lochboisdale
Rubh'an Dunain
L. Boisdale
Soay Sd.
Soay
L. Scavaig
Isle Ornsay
Teangue
Sound of Barra
Sd. of Eriskay
Canna
Eriskay
Cuillin Sound
Greian Hd.
Sanday
Kinloch
Barra
Sd. of Canna
Pt. of Sleat
Castlebay
384
Bruernish Pt.
Rhum
810
Vatersay
Sandray
Eigg
Pabbay
394
Mingulay
Sd. of Eigg
Berneray
Muck
Barra Head
241

L. Inche
L. Laxfor
Handa I.
Eddrachillis Bay
Pt. of Stoer
Drumbeg
Assyn
Stoer
Enard Bay
Rhu Coigach
Summer Isles
L. Lurgainn
L. Broom
Greenstone Pt.
Gruinard B.
Mellon Charles
An Teallach 1062
L. na Seala
Aultbea
Longa I.
Fionn Loch
L. Gairloch
Ewe
Gairloch
Melvaig
Poolewe
Henderson
Kerrysdale
Talladale 981 Sloch
L. Maree
W
Kinlochewe
1053
L. Torridon
1397
Torridon
Fasag
Achnas
Shieldaig
Coulags
Achnashellach
Applecross Forest
Carron
Applecross
Monar
1052 L. Mo
Kishorn
Lochcarron
Sgu
Toscaig
Stromemore
Carn Eig
Crowlin Is.
Carron
Stromeferry
1182
Kyle of Lochalsh
Plockton
Auchtertyre
Kyleakin
L. Alsh
Dornie
Glenelg
Invershi
L. Chr
11
The Saddle
1010
Glen Shiel
Broadford
L. Hourn
L. Quoich
Glen
Ladhar B. 1019
Knoydart
Tom
Armadale
Sound of Sleat
Inverie
1040
L. Nevis
Sgurr na Ciche
Ardvasar
Mallaig
L. Arkaig
Morar
983
Culvain
Loch Morar
Arisaig
Lechailort
Glenfinnan
Caledo
Kinlochell
Shona
882
Cur
Moidart
Corr
Kinlochmoidart
L. Eil
L. Moidart
S
Ardnamurchan
888
Ardgour
North
Pt. of Ardnamurchan
Salen
Sunart
Corran
Kilchoan
527
Strontian
Sorisdale
Mingary
L. Sunart
South
Coll
Clabhach
Morvern
Arinagour
Caliach Pt.
Tobermory
Drimnin
Calgary
Dervaig
Sd. of Mull
Lochaline
L. Frisa
Loch Linnhe
L. Etive
Tiree
Scarinish
Treshnish Isles
L. Tuath
Lismore I.
Hynish B.
Passage of Tiree
Salen
Hynish

m
1000
800
600
400
200
100
0
0
50
100
m

1:1 000 000

10   0   10   20   30   40 km

ORKNEY ISLANDS
on same scale

Pentland Firth

NORTH

SEA

West from Greenwich

1:1 250 000

10   0   10   20   30   40   50 km

Motorways

West from Greenwich

Projection: Conical with two standard parallels

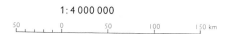

1 : 4 000 000

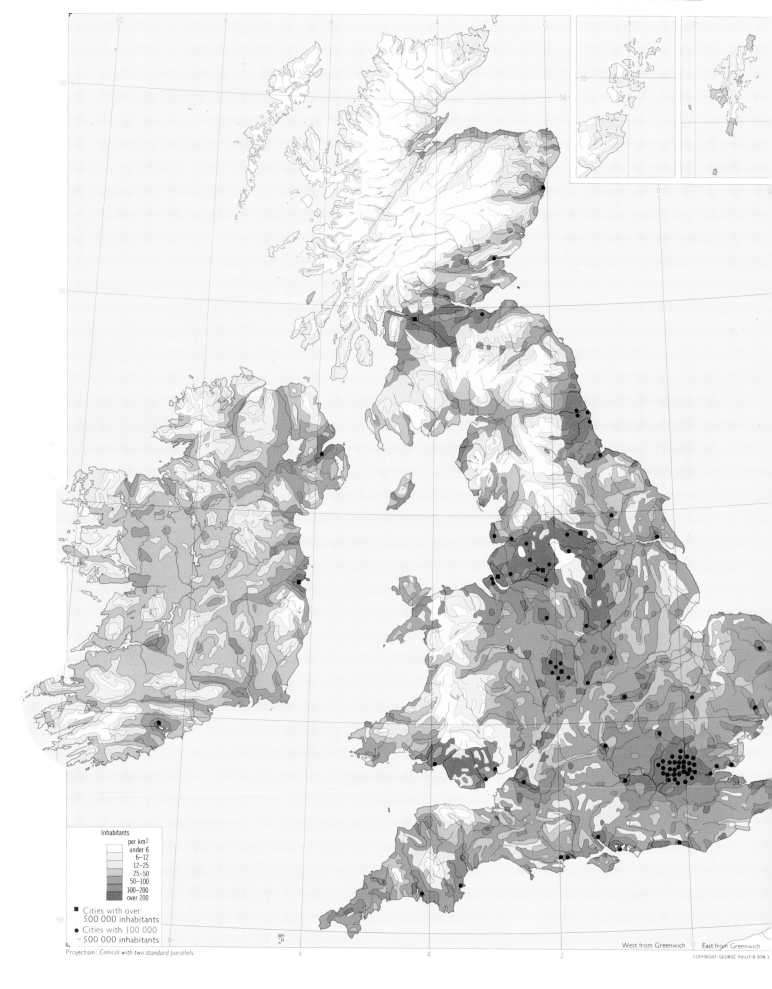

Inhabitants
per km²
under 6
6–12
12–25
25–50
50–100
100–200
over 200

■ Cities with over
500 000 inhabitants

● Cities with 100 000
– 500 000 inhabitants

Projection : Conical with two standard parallels

West from Greenwich   East from Greenwich

COPYRIGHT. GEORGE PHILIP & SON. L

1:5 000 000

50   0   50   100   150   200 km

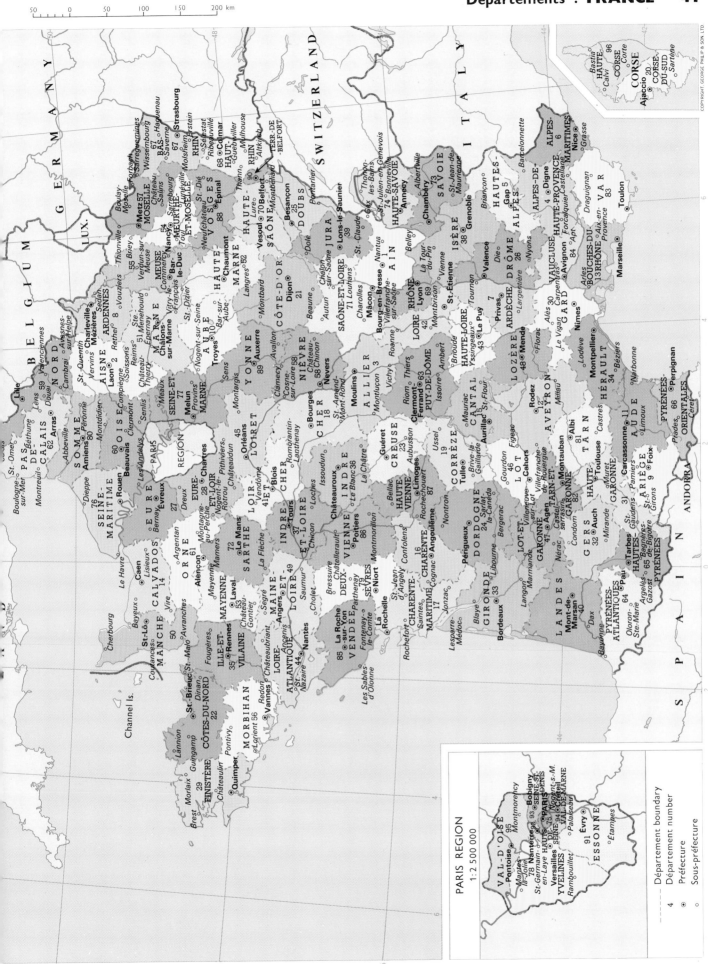

COPYRIGHT GEORGE PHILIP & SON LTD

CORSE 96
Bastia
HAUTE-
Calvi   CORSE
CORSE-
Ajaccio   DU-SUD
Sartène   20

PARIS REGION
1:2 500 000

VAL-D'OISE 95
Pontoise
Montmorency
Bobigny 93 SEINE-ST.-
78 Nanterre 92 PARIS DENIS
St-Germain- DE- 75
en-Laye HAUTS- Nogent-s.-M.
Versailles SEINE 94
YVELINES VAL DE MARNE
Créteil
Palaiseau
Rambouillet   91 Évry
ESSONNE
Étampes

----- Département boundary
4   Département number
◉   Préfecture
○   Sous-préfecture

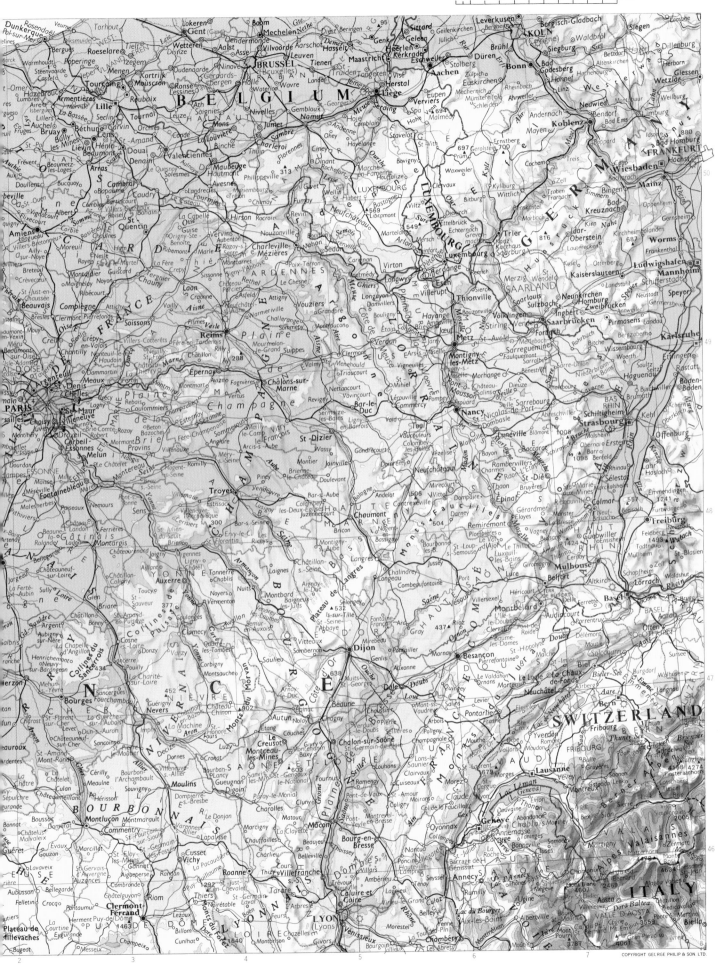

1 : 2 500 000

10 0 10 20 30 40 50 60 70 80 90 100 km

1 : 2 500 000

10 0 10 20 30 40 50 60 70 80 90 100 km

SWITZERLAND

FRANCE

ITALY

CORSICA

LIGURIAN SEA

Golfo di Génova

MEDITERRANEAN SEA

Lion

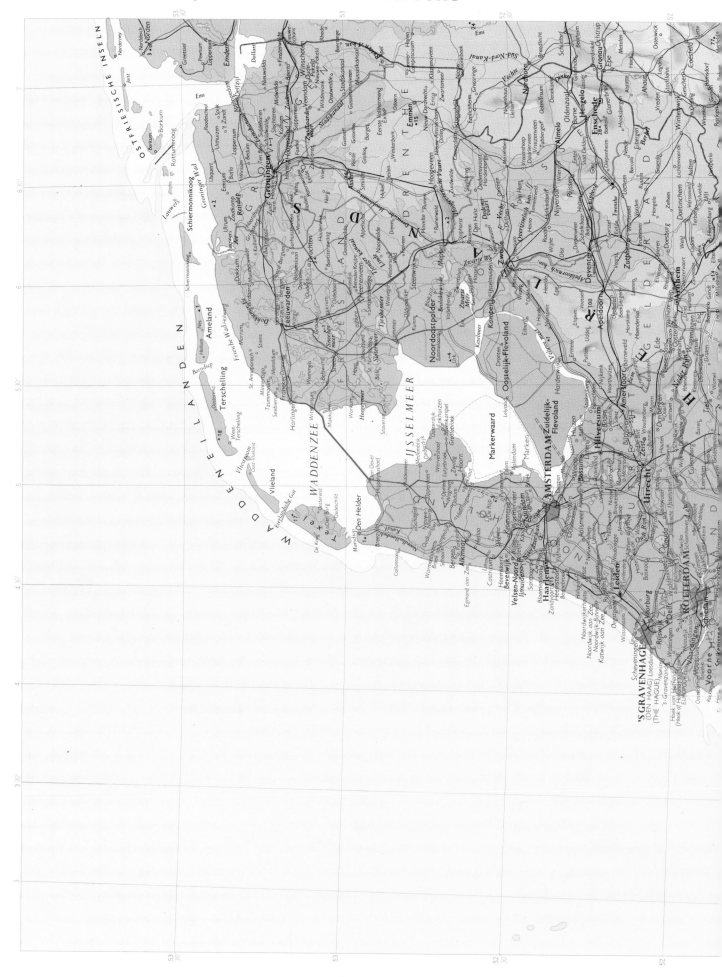

1:1 250 000

10 5 0 10 20 30 40 50 km

COPYRIGHT GEORGE PHILIP & SON LTD.

Projection: Conical with two standard parallels 3°30' and 5°30'

East from Greenwich

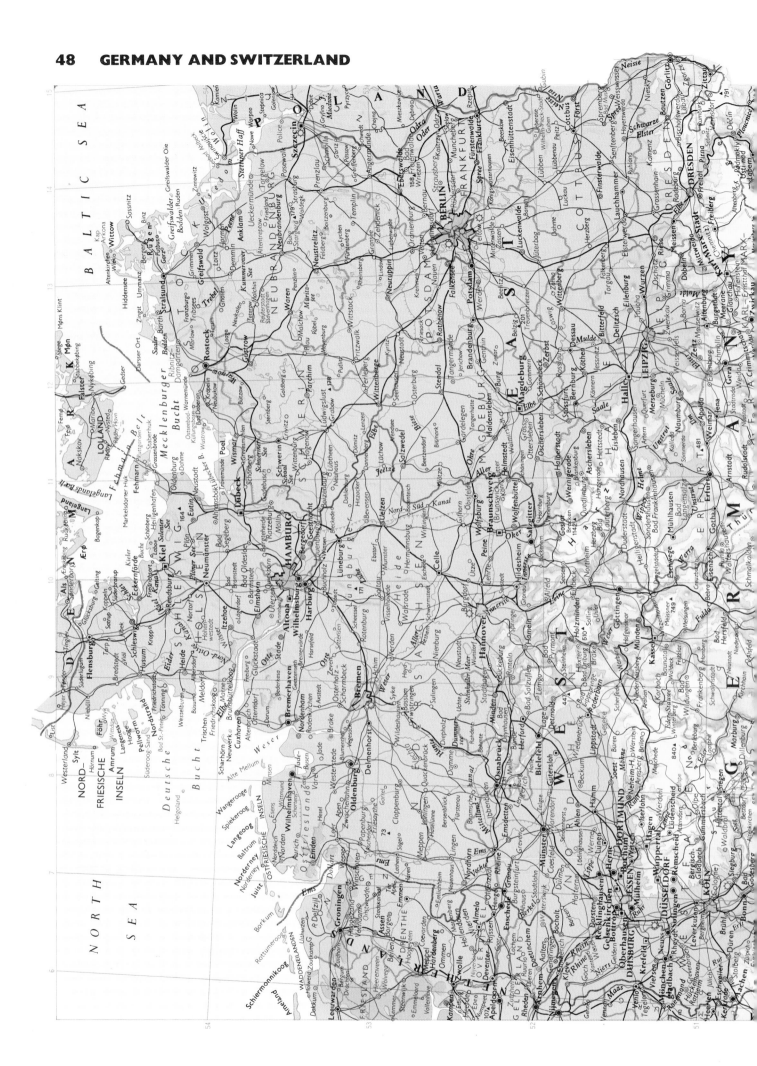

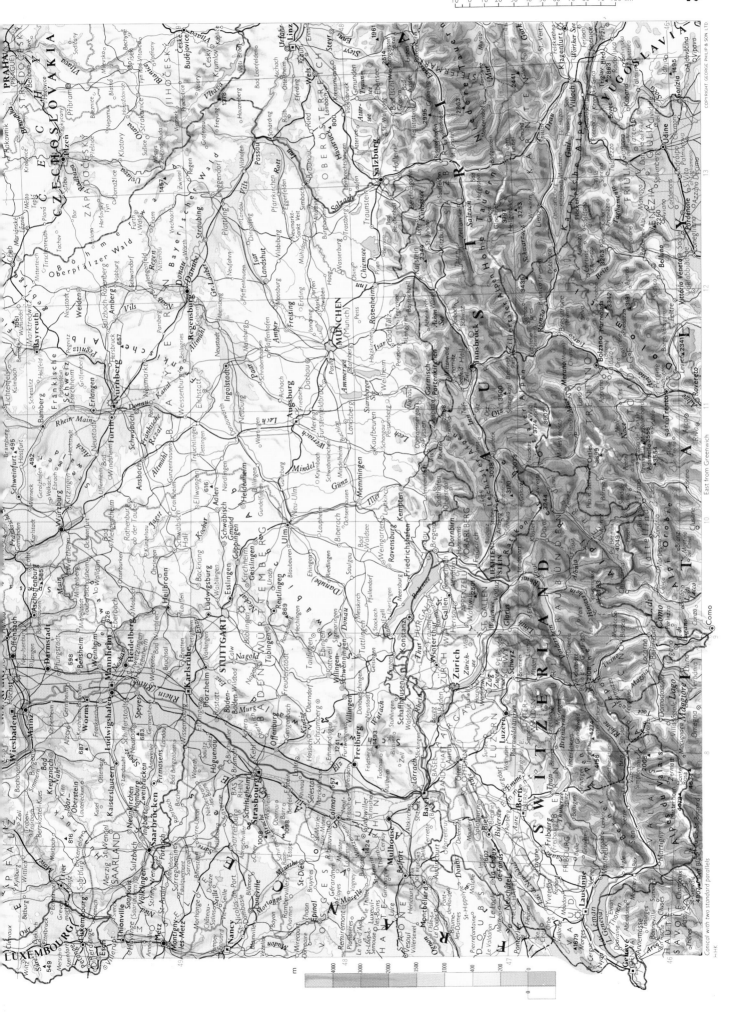

1 : 2 500 000

10 0 10 20 30 40 50 60 70 80 90 100 km

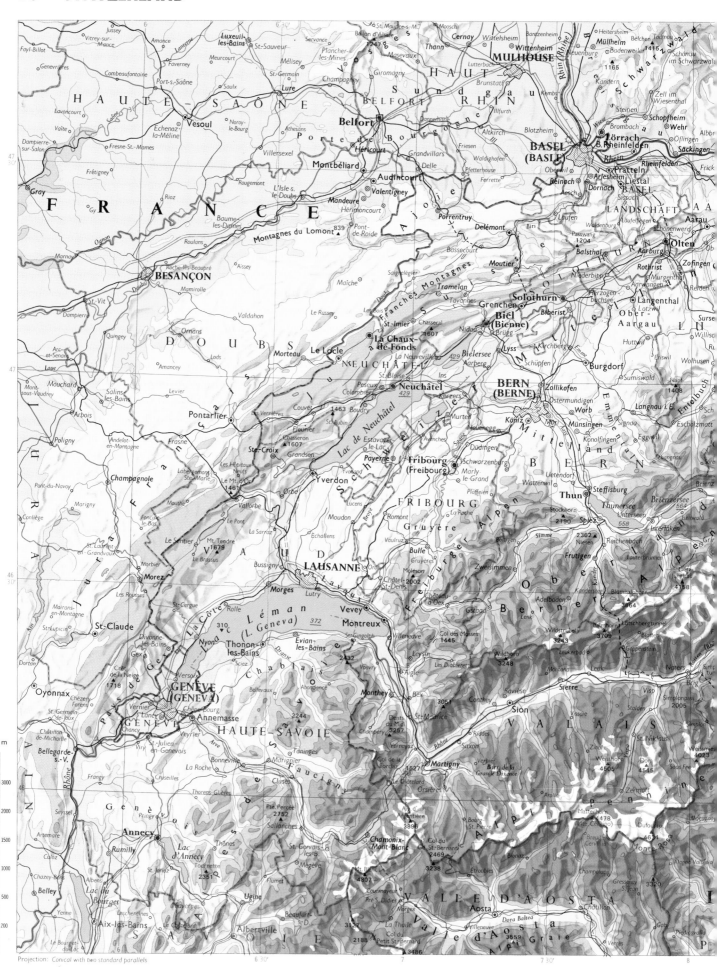

Projection: Conical with two standard parallels

1 : 1 000 000

10   5   0   10   20   30   40 km

W. GERMANY

BAYERN

AUSTRIA

TIROL

SWITZERLAND

THURGAU

VORARLBERG

SCHWYZ

GLARUS

GRAUBÜNDEN

TICINO

LOMBARDIA

ITALY

ZÜRICH

Konstanz

Friedrichshafen

Lindau

Bregenz

Dornbirn

St. Gallen

Winterthur

Feldkirch

Vaduz

Chur

Davos

St. Moritz

Bellinzona

Locarno

Lugano

Como

Lecco

BÉRGAMO

Lago di Como

Lago Maggiore

Lago di Lugano

East from Greenwich

COPYRIGHT. GEORGE PHILIP & SON. LTD.

Projection: Conical with two standard parallels

1:2 500 000

10 0 10 20 30 40 50 60 70 80 90 100 km

East from Greenwich

COPYRIGHT. GEORGE PHILIP & SON. LTD.

1:3 000 000

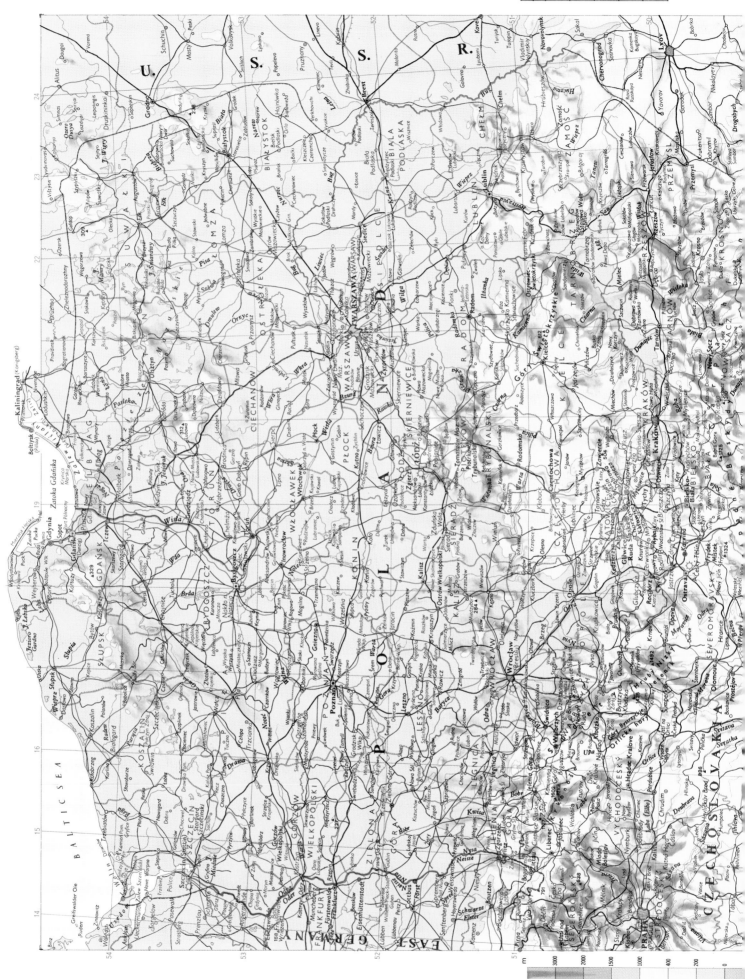

1:5 000 000

50   0   50   100   150   200 km

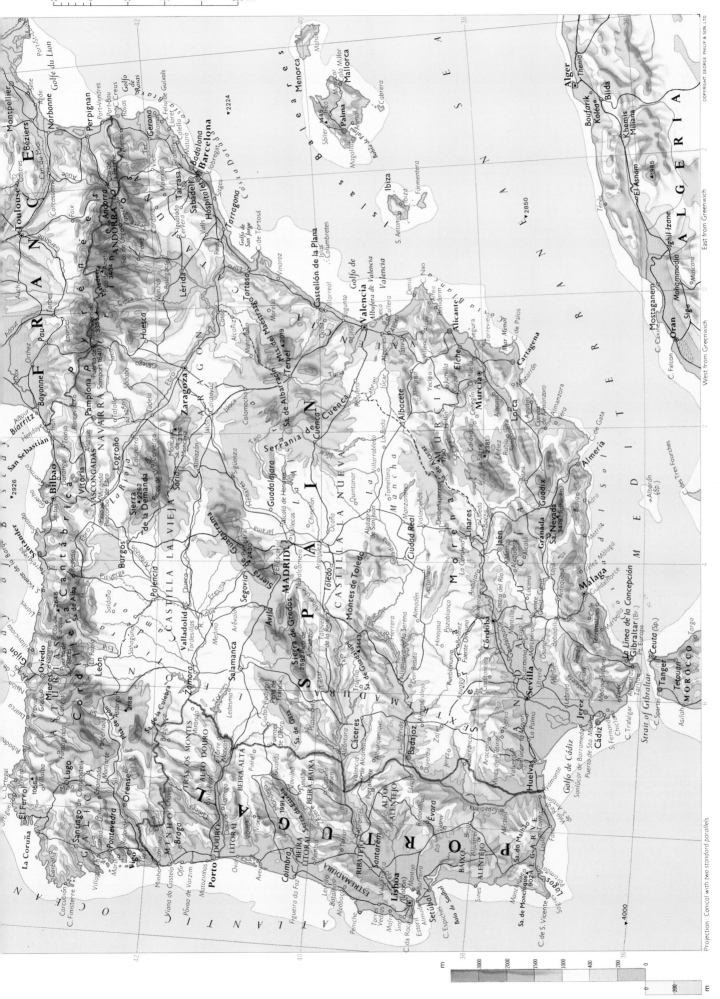

1 : 2 500 000

10 0 10 20 30 40 50 60 70 80 90 100 km

MEDITERRANEAN

SEA

Golfo de Almería

MOROCCO

Strait of Gibraltar

Golfo de Cádiz

Projection: Conical with two standard parallels

West from Greenwich

COPYRIGHT GEORGE PHILIP & SON LTD.

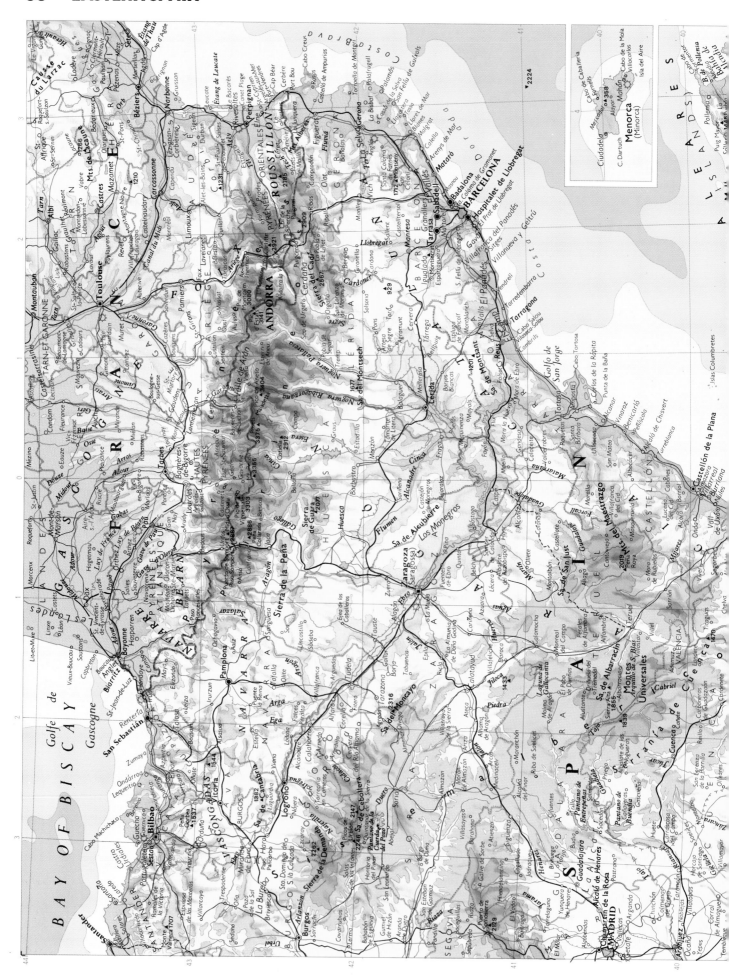

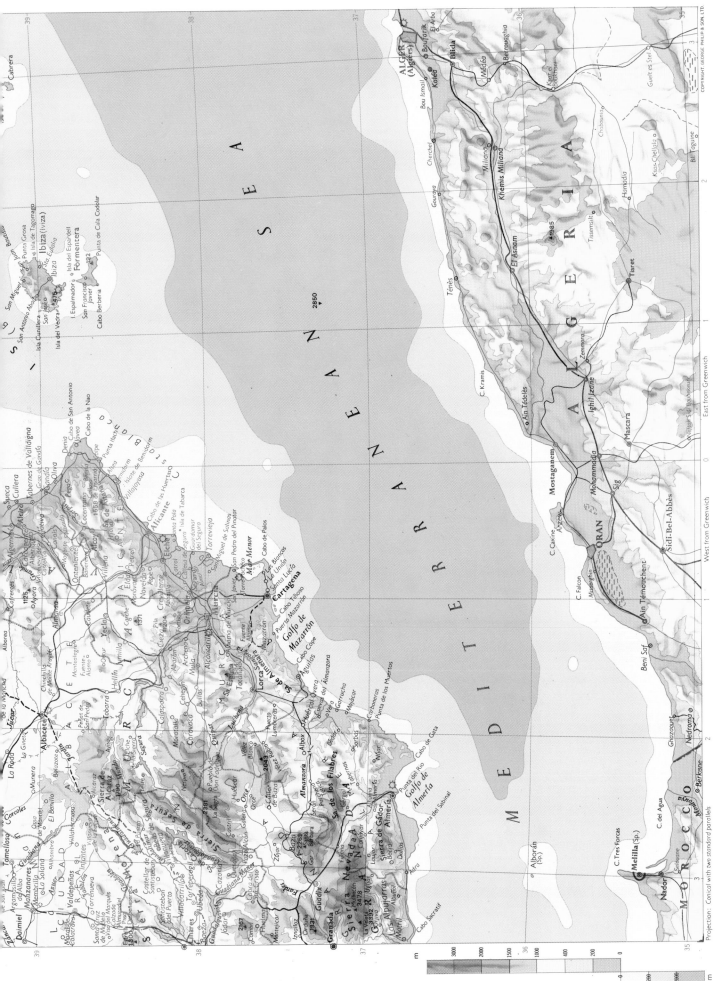

1 : 2 500 000

10 0 10 20 30 40 50 60 70 80 90 100 km

COPYRIGHT GEORGE PHILIP & SON LTD.

Projection: Conical with two standard parallels

East from Greenwich

West from Greenwich

M E D I T E R R A N E A N   S E A

A L G E R I A

M O R O C C O

ALGER (Algiers)

ORAN

Cartagena

Alicante

Albacete

Almería

Granada

Lorca

Murcia

Ibiza (Iviza)

Formentera

Mostaganem

Sidi-Bel-Abbès

Tiaret

Blida

Médéa

Mascara

Melilla (Sp.)

m

3000
2000
1500
1000
400
200
0
m

Projection: Conical with two
standard parallels.

West from Greenwich   East from Greenwich

1:10 000 000

100 0 100 200 300 400 km

BLACK SEA

AEGEAN SEA

Ionian Sea

POLAND

Warszawa · Brest · Łódź · Radom · Lublin · Kielce · Chorzów · Kraków · Wrocław · Przemyśl · Lvov · Poznań · Płock

UKRAINSKAYA S.S.R.

Kiyev · Zhitomir · Vinnitsa · Chernigov · Sumy · Kharkov · Poltava · Kremenchug · Kirovograd · Dnepropetrovsk · Krivoy Rog · Zaporozhye · Donetsk · Makeyevka · Gorlovka · Rostov · Novocherkassk · Taganrog · Zhdanov (Mariupol) · Nikolayev · Kherson · Odessa · Melitopol · Berdyansk

U. S. S. R.

Volgograd · Voroshilovgrad · Shakhty · Kamensk-Shakhtinskiy · Krasnodar · Stavropol · Armavir · Maykop · Novorossiysk · Tuapse · Sochi

MOLDAVIAN S.S.R.

Kishinev · Bendery · Tiraspol

RUMANIA

Bucureşti · Ploieşti · Braşov · Galaţi · Brăila · Constanţa · Craiova · Cluj · Arad · Timişoara · Sibiu · Oradea · Iaşi

HUNGARY

Budapest · Szeged · Debrecen · Pécs · Miskolc · Kecskemét · Hódmezővásárhely

BULGARIA

Sofiya · Plovdiv · Varna · Burgas · Edirne · Musala 2925

YUGOSLAVIA

Beograd · Novi Sad · Subotica · Sarajevo · Skopje · Niš · Kragujevac · Sava · Mostar · Dubrovnik (Ragusa)

ALBANIA

Tirana · Durrës · Bitola · Elbasan · Shkodër

GREECE

Athínai · Thessaloníki · Pátrai · Piraiévs · Lárisa · Vólos · Kérkira · Kefallinía · Pelopónnisos · Kikládhes · Náxos · Kríti · Iráklion · Khaniá · Ródhos · Límnos · Lésvos · Khíos · Évvoia

TURKEY

Istanbul · Ankara · Izmir · Bursa · Konya · Adana · Kayseri · Eskişehir · Afyon Karahisar · Antalya · Sivas · Trabzon · Samsun · Gaziantep · Üsküdar · İzmit · Balıkesir · Manisa · Denizli · Mersin · Tarsus · Iskenderun · Antakya

SYRIA

Halab · Hamā · Homs · Tarābulus · Al Ladhiqiyah · Baniyas

LEBANON

Bayrūt (Beirut) · Dimashq (Damascus) · Sayda

ISRAEL

Tel Aviv-Yafo · Haifa · Jerusalem · Gaza

JORDAN

Ammān · Ma'ān

CYPRUS

Levkosia (Nicosia) · Lemesós · Larnaca · Ammókhostos (Famagusta)

EGYPT

El Qâhira · El Iskandariya · Tanta · Bûr Saîd · El Suweis · El Faiyûm · Beni Suêf · El Mahalla el Kubra · Dumyât · El 'Arîsh

LIBYA

Banghāzī · Al Marj (Barce) · Cyrene · Derna · Tobruq

MEDITERRANEAN SEA

Sea of Azov · Kerch · Krymskaya (Crimea) · Simferopol · Sevastopol · Yalta · Feodosiya · Yevpatoriya

Danube · Dnepr · Don · Nile

Division between Greeks
and Turks in Cyprus;
Turks to the north.

Projection: Conical with two standard parallels

East from Greenwich

1:2 500 000

10 0 10 20 30 40 50 60 70 80 90 100 km

FOR CONTINUATION SEE PAGE 66

Iles Sanguinaires
G. d'Ajaccio
Tavaco
Pertelo
Inaudine
2136 Zonza
Favone
Solenzara
CORSE
CORSICA
C. di Muro
Propriano
Levie
G. de Valinco
Sartène
Porto-Vecchio
CORSE-DU-SUD
Iles Cerbicales
Bonifacio
I. de
Cavallo

Bouches de Bonifacio
Maddalena
Santa Teresa Gallura
La Maddalena
Caprera
Punta dello Scorno
Pto. Cervo
Costa
Asinara
Golfo dell'
Arzachena
Smeralda
41
Asinara
Coghinas
Aggius
Calangiánus
Golfo Aranci
G. di Olbia
Porto Tórres
Témpio Pausánia
Olbia
Tavolara
Sorso
1362
Olbia
Sénnori
M. Limbara
Sássari
Ósilo
C. dell'Argentiera
Úschiri
Posada
Fertília
Íttiri
L. al Coghinas
Ozieri
Tanaunella
Álghero
Pattada
Buddusò
Siniscola
C. Comino
Villanova
1259
Bonárva
1150
Bitti
Monteleone
Orune
Bosa
Macomer
Órune
Dorgali
Temo
Núoro
Golfo di
Ghilarza
Oliena
Orosei
C. Mannu
L. del Tirso
Fonni
Gavino
40
Tirso
Sorgono
Monti del
C. di Monte Santu
Cábras
1834
Gennargentu
Oristano
SARDEGNA
Baunei
M. Arci
Lacóni
Arbatax
Golfo di
812
Arborea
SARDEGNA
Lanusei
Oristano
Arborea
Tortolì
Terralba
Mannu
Ierzu
SARDINIA
Núrri
Mándas
Gúspini
Fluminendosa
Villaputzu
Arbus
San Gavino
Sanluri
Monreale
1236
Gonnosfanádiga
Senorbì
Muravera
Fluminimaggiore
M. Línas
Villacidro
S. Vito
C. Ferrato
Serramanna
Dolianova
Iglésias
Cíxerri
Assémini
Sestu
Sta. Serpedi
Portoscuso
Síliqua
Sinnai
1069
C. Spartivento
Carloforte
Maracalagonis
Selárgius
Carbónia
Quartu Sant'Elena
San Pietro
1116
Cagliari
Sant'Antioco
Santadi
Golfo di
Sant'
Porto Botte
Pula
Cágliari
Serpentara
Antíoco
Teulada
C. Carbonara
G. di Pálmas
C. Spartivento

T Y R R H E N I A N

3719

S E A

3589

1 : 2 500 000

10 0 10 20 30 40 50 60 70 80 90 100 km

ADRIATIC

SEA

A L B A N I A

Drini
Shëngjini Lezha Rrësheni
Rubiku
K. iMyzhllit
te Skenderbeut Laçi Burrela Mati
Bishti i Palles Ishmi TIRANA Kruja
Shijaku DURRES Kavaja
Durrës Tirana
(Durazzo) (Tiranë)
Kalaja e Turrës Pegini Rrogozhina
Shkumbini ELBASANI
Fieri Lushnja Samani o. Stalin
Vlora Levani Berati
Kep i Gjuhës Karaburuni VLORA Tepelena 2130
Dukati Gribës
Himara

Strait of Otranto

Laguna e Nartës l. Sazan

Gjiri i Vlorës

Otranto
C. d'Otranto

Othonoi
Erikoúsa
Samothráki Kérkira Kassiópi
Korakiána Liapádhes
Kérkira
(Corfu) Kérkira
Gastoúri
Áyios Matthaíos
Argyrádhes Levkími

A D R I A T I C

S E A

Monte Sant'Angelo
G. di Manfredónia

Manfredónia
Barletta
Trani
Bisceglie
Molfetta
Giovinazzo
Bari
Mola di Bari
Polignano a Mare
Monopoli
Fasano
Ostuni
Bríndisi
Francavilla Fontana Mesagne
Squinzano
Trepuzzi
Lecce
Copertino
Nardò Galatina
Máglie
Gallípoli
Racale Casarano Ugento Tricase
Presicce
C. Santa Maria di Leuca Gagliano del Capo

Golfo di
Táranto

TARANTO
Sinni

IONIAN

3065

S E A

IONIAN
S E A

CALABRIA

Isole Eólie o Lípari (Æolian Is.)

Strómboli 926

Panarea
Filicudi Salina
962
Alicudi 602 Lípari
499 Vulcano

Golfo di
Sant'Eufémia

Golfo di Squillace

Catanzaro

Capa Stilo

Messina
Réggio di Calábria
Str. di Messina

Catánia
Golfo di
Catánia
Siracusa

M E D I T E R R A N E A N   S E A

4116

COPYRIGHT, GEORGE PHILIP & SON, LTD.
HHK

Projection: Conical with two standard parallels

East from Greenwich

FOR CONTINUATION SEE PAGE 63

1:2 500 000

10 0 10 20 30 40 50 60 70 80 90 100 km

1:2 500 000

10 0 10 20 30 40 50 60 70 80 90 100 km

SEA OF CRETE

(Sea of Candia)

ARKHIPÉLAGOS

KIKLÁDHES
(CYCLADES)

ATTIKI KAI

PELOPONNISOS

DHODHEKANISOS
(DODECANESE)

Continuation Eastwards
on same scale

Projection: Conical with two standard parallels

East from Greenwich

COPYRIGHT GEORGE PHILIP & SON LTD.

m 3000 2000 1500 1000 400 200 0

m 0 200 2000

1:2 500 000

1:2 500 000

10 0 10 20 30 40 50 60 70 80 90 100 km

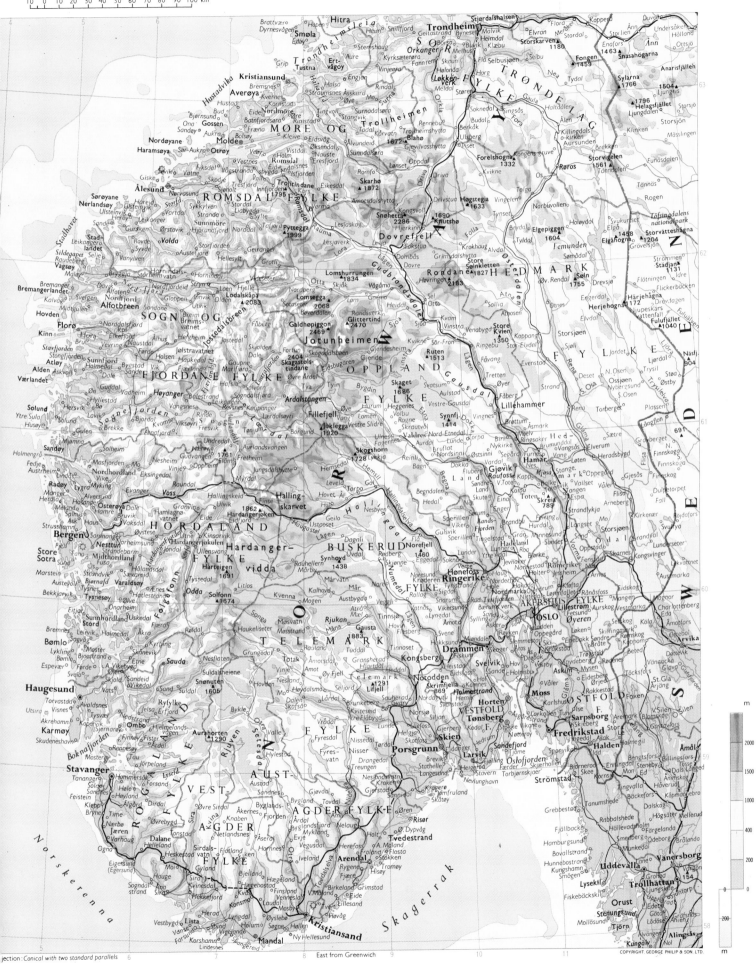

jection: Conical with two standard parallels

East from Greenwich

COPYRIGHT GEORGE PHILIP & SON LTD.

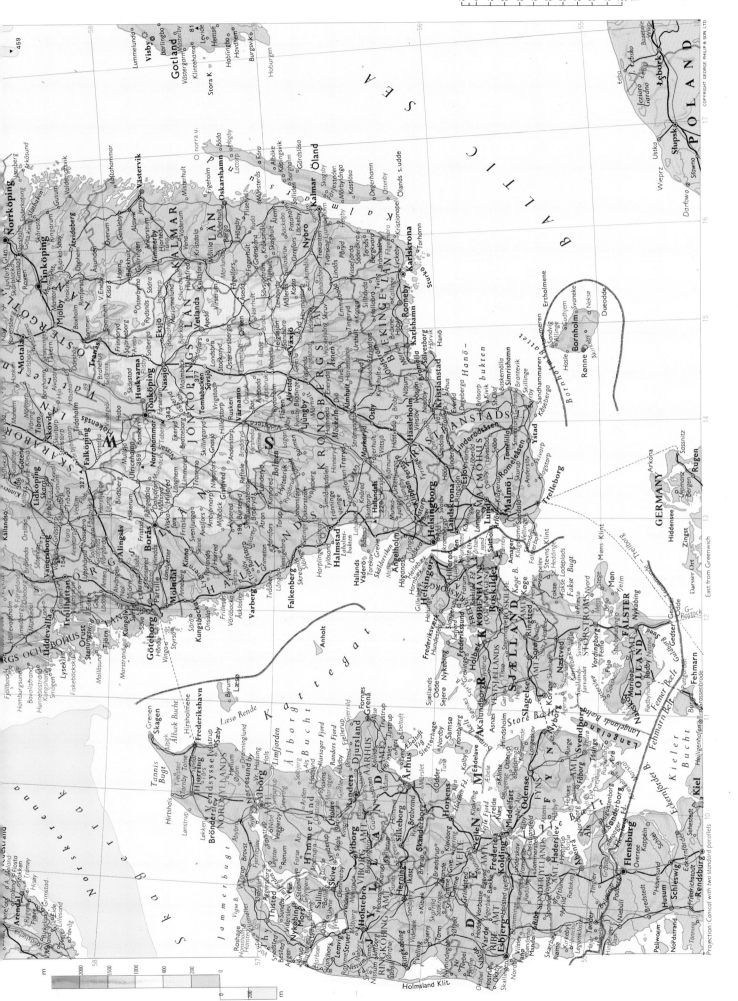

1:2 500 000

10 0 10 20 30 40 50 60 70 80 90 100 km

POLAND

BALTIC SEA

Gotland

Visby

Öland

Kalmar

KALMAR LÄN

Oskarshamn

Västervik

Norrköping

Linköping

ÖSTERGÖTLAND

Motala

Mjölby

Nässjö

Jönköping

JÖNKÖPINGS LÄN

Huskvarna

Tranås

Värnamo

KRONOBERGS LÄN

Växjö

Ljungby

Älmhult

Nybro

Karlskrona

BLEKINGE LÄN

Ronneby

Karlshamn

Bornholm

Rønne

SKARABORGS LÄN

Skövde

Falköping

Lidköping

Vänersborg

Trollhättan

Alingsås

Borås

Mölndal

Göteborg

Partille

Kungsbacka

Varberg

Falkenberg

Halmstad

HALLANDS LÄN

Helsingborg

Landskrona

Lund

MALMÖHUS LÄN

Malmö

Trelleborg

Ystad

KRISTIANSTADS LÄN

Kristianstad

Hässleholm

Kattegat

Anholt

Læsø

Frederikshavn

Skagen

Hjørring

Ålborg

NORDJYLLANDS AMT

VENDSYSSEL

Limfjorden

Thisted

Struer

Holstebro

RINGKØBING AMT

Viborg

VIBORG AMT

Skive

Randers

ÅRHUS AMT

Århus

Silkeborg

Herning

JYLLAND

Skanderborg

Horsens

VEJLE AMT

Vejle

Fredericia

Kolding

RIBE AMT

Esbjerg

Varde

Ringkøbing

Holmsland Klit

SØNDERJYLLANDS AMT

Haderslev

Åbenrå

Sønderborg

Als

Flensburg

Schleswig

Rendsburg

Kiel

GERMANY

Fehmarn

FYN

FYNS AMT

Odense

Middelfart

Svendborg

Ærø

Langeland

SJÆLLAND

København

Roskilde

ROSKILDE AMT

VESTSJÆLLANDS AMT

Slagelse

Kalundborg

Korsør

Næstved

STORSTRØMS AMT

Vordingborg

Nykøbing

FALSTER

LOLLAND

Maribo

Nakskov

Rødby

Gedser

Møn

Helsingør

FREDERIKSBORG AMT

Frederikssund

Frederiksværk

Hillerød

København

Køge

Projection: Conical with two standard parallels

East from Greenwich

COPYRIGHT GEORGE PHILIP & SON LTD.

DENMARK

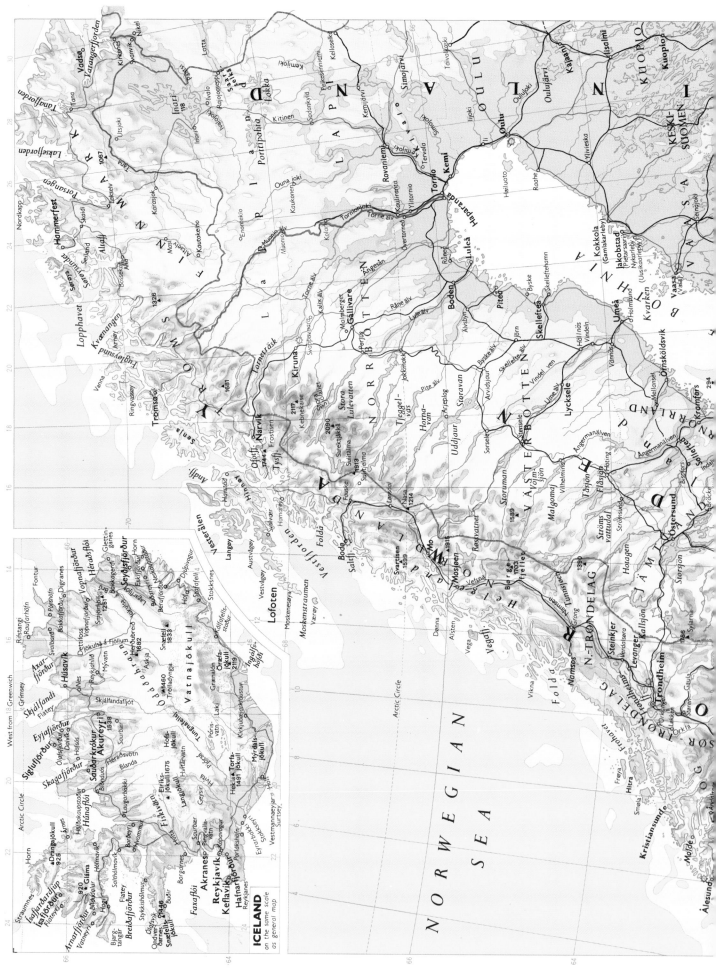

ICELAND
on the same scale
as general map

1:5 000 000

50   0   50   100   150   200 km

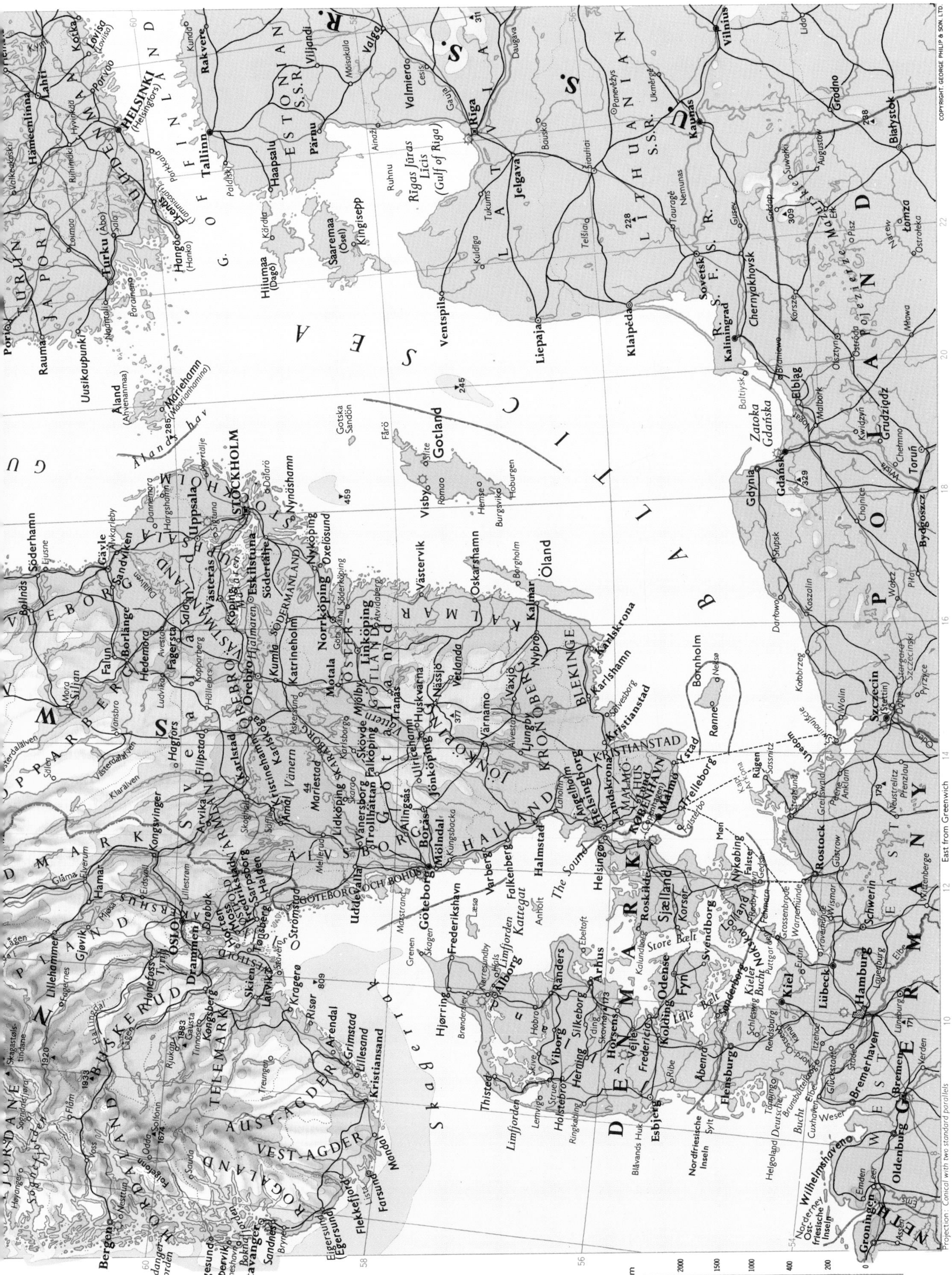

B A L T I C   S E A

S W E D E N

N O R W A Y

D E N M A R K

F I N L A N D

G E R M A N Y

P O L A N D

E S T O N I A N   S.S.R.

L A T V I A N   S.S.R.

L I T H U A N I A N   S.S.R.

R.S.F.S.R.

HELSINKI (Helsingfors)

Turku (Åbo)

Tallinn

Pärnu

Riga

Valmiera

Jelgava

Liepaja

Klaipėda

Kaliningrad

Chernyakhovsk

Kaunas

Vilnius

Grodno

Białystok

Łomża

Gdynia

Gdańsk

Elbląg

Grudziądz

Toruń

Bydgoszcz

Szczecin (Stettin)

Słupsk

Rostock

Lübeck

Hamburg

Bremen

Oldenburg

Wilhelmshaven

Bremerhaven

Kiel

Flensburg

Schwerin

STOCKHOLM

Uppsala

Gävle

Västerås

Örebro

Norrköping

Linköping

Jönköping

Göteborg

Malmö

KØBENHAVN

Helsingborg

Kristianstad

Karlskrona

Kalmar

Visby

Gotland

Öland

Bornholm

Rügen

Rigas Jūras Līcis (Gulf of Riga)

Ålands hav

G. O F   F I N L A N D

O S L O

Drammen

Kristiansand

Stavanger

Bergen

Skagerrak

Kattegat

Rīga

Ventspils

Saaremaa (Ösel)

Hiiumaa (Dagö)

East from Greenwich

Projection: Conical with two standard parallels

COPYRIGHT GEORGE PHILIP & SON LTD.

m 2000 1500 1000 400 200 0

R.S.F.S.R.
1. Daghestan A.S.S.R.
2. Kabardino–Balkar A.S.S.R.
3. Mari A.S.S.R.
4. Mordovian A.S.S.R.
5. North Ossetian A.S.S.R.
6. Tatar A.S.S.R.
7. Udmurt A.S.S.R.
8. Chuvash A.S.S.R.
9. Checheno–Ingush A.S.S.R.
AZERBAIJAN
10. Nakhichevan A.S.S.R.
GEORGIA
11. Abkhaz A.S.S.R.
12. Adzhar A.S.S.R.

Projection: Conical Orthomorphic with two standard parallels

East from Greenwich

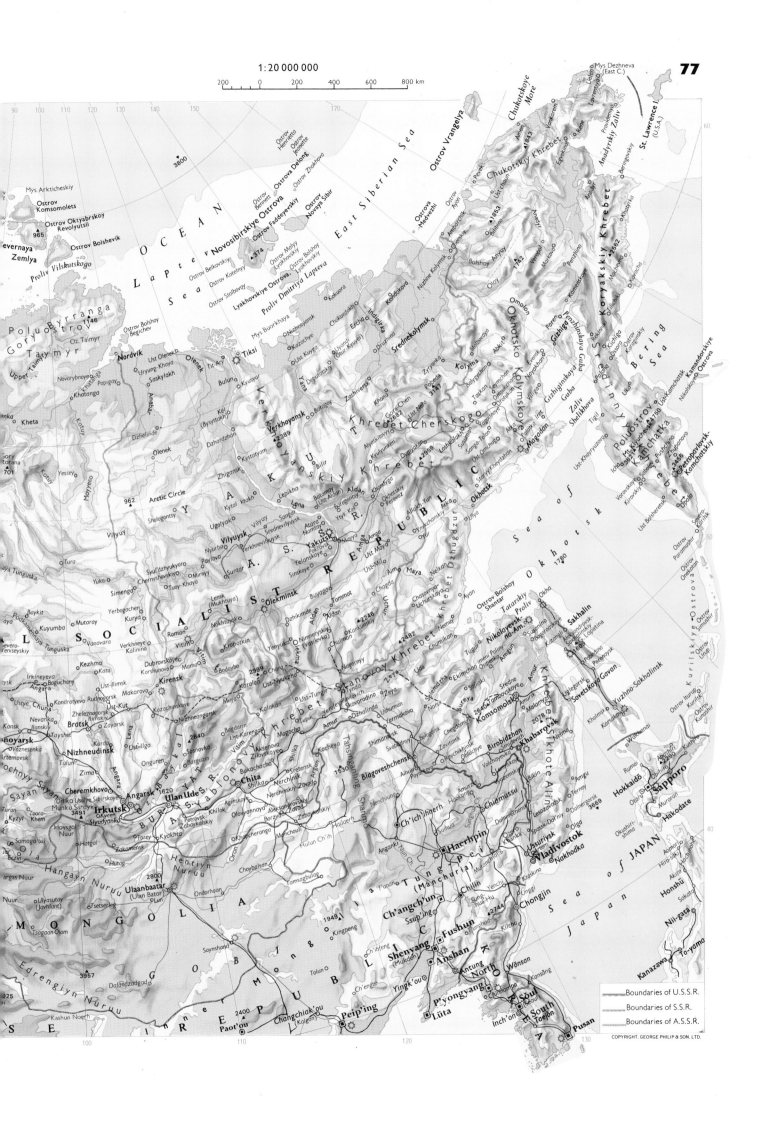

1:10 000 000

100   0   100   200   300   400 km

COPYRIGHT. GEORGE PHILIP & SON LTD.

Projection: Conical with two standard parallels

Division between Greeks and Turks
in Cyprus; Turks to the North.

East from Greenwich

1 Kabardino-Balkar A.S.S.R.
2 North Ossetian A.S.S.R.
3 Nakhichevan A.S.S.R. (Azer.)
4 Checheno-Ingush A.S.S.R.
  Karagiye Depression

S T E P P E   S. S. R.

K A Z A K H S K A Y A

Nizmennost

Kaspiyskaya

C A S P I A N   S E A

Kara
Bogaz
Gol.

Krasnovodsk

Nebit-
Dag

A L B O R Z

TEHRÁN

Demāvend 5604

Semnān

KALMYK A.S.S.R.

Volgograd
(Stalingrad)

Astrakhan

Ergeni Vozvyshennost

BAKU

A Z E R B A I J A N
S. S. R.

P E R S I A

DAGESTAN
A.S.S.R.

Makhachkala

Grozny

Ordzhonikidze

Elbrus 5633

K a v k a z

C a u c a s u s

GEORGIAN S.S.R.

Tbilisi

ARMENIAN
S.S.R.

Yerevan

Ararat
5165

Tabriz

Volgodonsk

Rostov

Taganrog

Azovskoye More
(Sea of Azov)

Krasnodar

Stavropol

Armavir

Maykop

Sochi

Sukhumi

Batumi

Trabzon

A B K H A Z S K

B L A C K   S E A

Novorossiysk

KHARKOV

U K R A I N I A N   S. S. R.

Donetsk

Zaporozhye

Krivoy
Rog

Dnepropetrovsk

Nikolayev

Kherson

Krymskiy P-ov.
(Crimea)

Simferopol

Sevastopol

Yalta

Feodosiya

Kerch

MOLDAVIAN
S.S.R.

Kishinev

Odessa

R U M A N I A

BUCUREŞTI
(Bucharest)

B U L G A R I A

Varna

Burgas

Constanţa

İSTANBUL

Bursa

İzmir
(Smyrna)

T U R K E Y

A n a t o l i a

Ankara

Konya

Adana

Kayseri

Sivas

Erzurum

Diyarbakır

Malatya

CYPRUS

M E D I T E R R A N E A N   S E A

L e v a n t

S Y R I A

Halab

Hama'

Homs

Dimashq
(Damascus)

Bayrūt
(Beirut)

I R A Q

Baghdad

Al Mawşil

Dijah (Tigris)

Nahr al Furāt

Bādiyat ash Shām

Kirkūk

Projection : Conical with two standard parallels

1 : 5 000 000

50   0   50   100   150   200 km

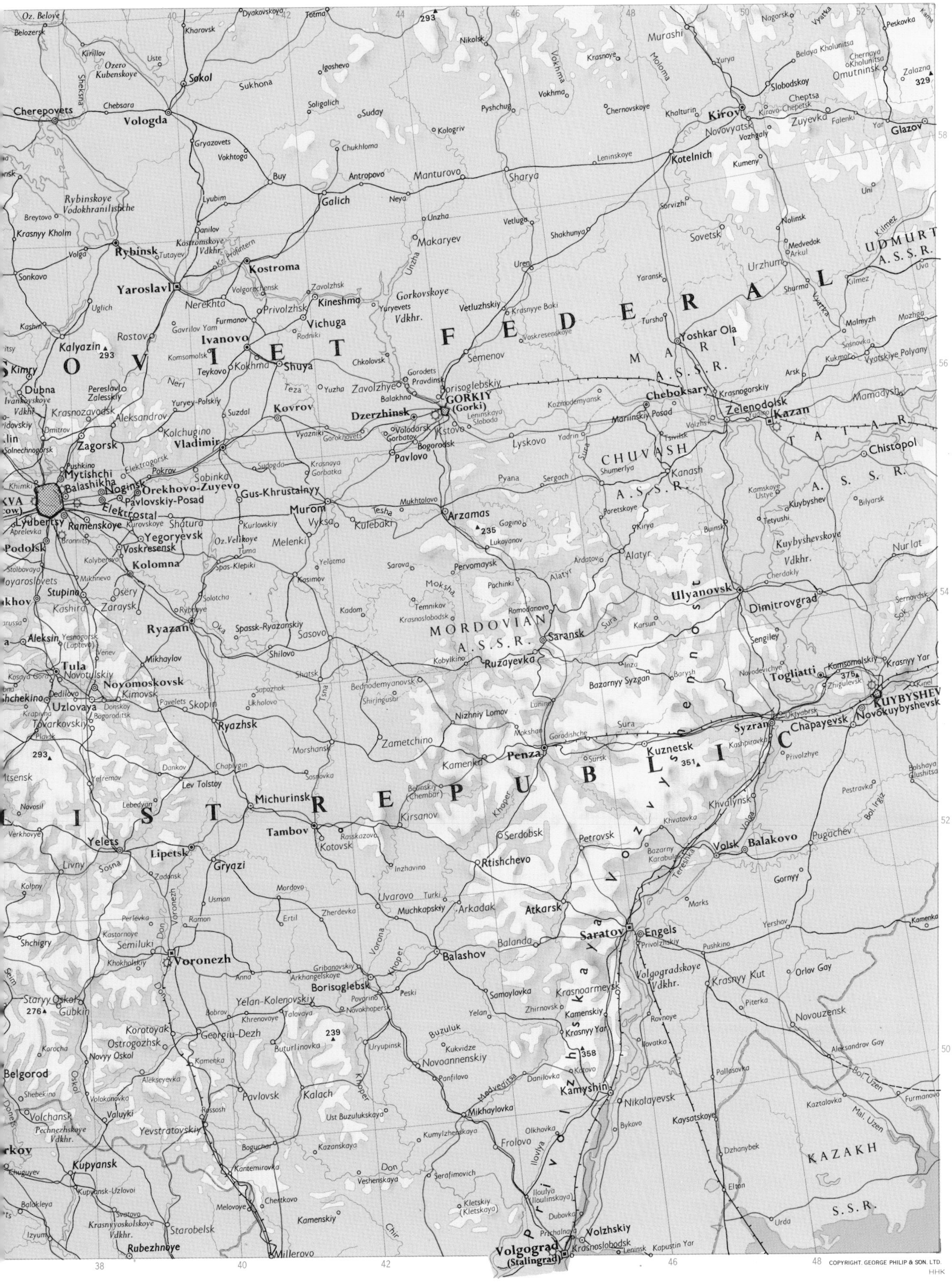

Oz. Beloye
Belozersk
Kirillov
Ozera Kubenskoye
Uste
Sheksna
Cherepovets
Vologda
Sokol
Chebsara
Gryazovets
Vokhtoga
Dyakovskoye
Totma
Sukhona
Suday
Soligalich
Kologriv
Igoshevo
Nikolsk
Vokhma
Vokhma
Pyshchug
Chernovskoye
Krasnoye
Moloma
Murashi
Nagorsk
Vyatka
Peskovka
Kama
Belaya Kholunitsa
Chernaya
Omutninsk
Kholunitsa
Zalazna
329
293

Breytovo
Krasnyy Kholm
Rybinskoye Vodokhranilishche
Danilov
Lyubim
Buy
Antropovo
Manturovo
Neya
Sharya
Vetluga
Shakhunya
Leninskoye
Kotelnich
Kumeny
Yurya
Slobodskoy
Kirovo-Chepetsk
Cheptsa
Kirov
Novovyatsk
Vozhgaly
Zuyevka
Falenki
Yar
Glazov
Uni
UDMURT
A.S.S.R.
Uva
58

Sonkovo
Volga
Rybinsk
Yaroslavl
Tutayev
Kostromskoye Vdkhr.
Kr. Profintern
Kostroma
Zavolzhsk
Kineshma
Makaryev
Unzha
Uren
Urzhum
Arkul
Medvedok
Nolinsk
Sovetsk
Sorvizhi
Yaransk
Shurma
Kilmez
Mozhga
Malmyzh
Kukmor
Vyatskiye Polyany
Mamadysh
56

Kashin
Kalyazin
293
Kimry
Uglich
Rostov
Nerekhta
Gavrilov Yam
Privolzhsk
Furmanov
Ivanovo
Vichuga
Rodniki
Yuryevets
Vetluzhskiy
Krasnyye Baki
Voskresenskoye
Tursha
Yoshkar Ola
M A R I   A.S.S.R.
Krasnogorskiy
Sovsnovka
Arsk
Kazan
TATAR
Chistopol

Dubna
Pereslavl Zalesskiy
Komsomolsk
Teykovo
Kokhma
Shuya
Chkalovsk
Semenov
Gorodets
Pravdinsk
Borisoglebskiy
Kozmodemyansk
Mariinskiy Posad
Cheboksary
Zelenodolsk
Volzhsk
Vasilsursk

Ivankovskoye Vdkhr.
Krasnozavodsk
Aleksandrov
Kolchugino
Yuryev-Polskiy
Suzdal
Kovrov
Vyazniki
Gorokhovets
Volodarsk
Leninskaya Sloboda
Balakhna
GORKIY (Gorki)
Kstovo
Lyskovo
Yadrin
CHUVASH A.S.S.R.
Shumerlya
Kanash
Tsivilsk
Buinsk
Tetyushi
Bilyarsk
Kuybyshev

Dmitrov
Zagorsk
Solnechnogorsk
Klin
Pushkino
Mytishchi
Balashikha
Elektrogorsk
Pokrov
Sobinka
Vladimir
Dzerzhinsk
Pavlovo
Bogorodsk
Krasnaya Gorbatka
Sudogda
Pyana
Sergach
Kamskoye Ustye
Nurlat

MKVA (Moscow)
Lyubertsy
Noginsk
Orekhovo-Zuyevo
Pavlovskiy-Posad
Elektrostal
Gus-Khrustalnyy
Murom
Tesha
Mukhtolovo
Arzamas
235
Gagino
Poretskoye
Alatyr
Kirya
Kuybyshevskoye Vdkhr.
Cherdakly
Ulyanovsk
Dimitrovgrad

Apreleyka
Podolsk
Ramenskoye
Yegoryevsk
Voskresensk
Kurovskoye
Shatura
Kurlovskiy
Vyksa
Kulebaki
Oz. Velikoye
Tuma
Melenki
Yelatma
Sarova
Pervomaysk
Lukoyanov
Ardatov
Alatyr
Sura
Karsun
Inza
Novodevichye
Sengiley
Togliatti
375
Komsomolskiy
Krasnyy Yar

Stolbovaya
Stupino
Kolomna
Mikhnevo
Kolyberovo
Spas-Klepiki
Kasimov
Kadom
Temnikov
Moksha
Pochinki
Romanovo
Saransk
Barysh
Zhigulevsk
Oktyabrsk
KUYBYSHEV
Novokuybyshevsk

Osery
Zaraysk
Rybnoye
Solotcha
Oka
Sasovo
MORDOVIAN A.S.S.R.
Krasnoslobodsk
Kobylkino
Ruzayevka
Sura
Bazarnyy Syzgan
Syzran
Kashpirovka
Privolzhye
Bolshaya Glushitsa

Kashira
Ryazan
Spassk-Ryazanskiy
Shilovo
Shatsk
Bednodemyanovsk
Shingursk
Lunino
Nizhniy Lomov
Mokshan
Gorodishche
Sura
Kuznetsk
351
Privolzhsk
Chapayevsk

Aleksin
Yesnogorsk (Laptevo)
Novomoskovsk
Kimovsk
Mikhaylov
Sapozhok
Skopin
Ryazhsk
Chaplygin
Morshansk
Zametchino
Mokshar
Penza
Syzran
Kamenka
Kuznetsk
Pestravka

Tula
Novotulskiy
Dedilovo
Kimovsk
Bogoroditsk
Uzlovaya
Pavelets
Dankov
Lev Tolstoy
Kirsanov
Khvalynsk
Khvatovka
Balashov
Volsk
Balakovo
Pugachev
Gornyy
Bol. Irgiz

Shchekino
Krapivna
Tovarkovskiy
Plavsk
293
Yefremov
Lebedyan
Michurinsk
Rasskazovo
Serdobsk
Petrovsk
Bazarny Karabulak
Marks
Pallasovka

Novosil
Lipetsk
Gryazi
Kotovsk
Tambov
Inzhavino
Rtishchevo
Atkarsk
Yershov

Mtsensk
Yelets
Livny
Sosna
Zadonsk
Mordovo
Usman
Uvarovo
Turki
Arkadak
Saratov
Engels
Privolzhskiy
Pushkino
Krasnyy Kut
Orlov Gay

Kolpny
Shchigry
Perlevka
Ramon
Don
Voronezh
Zherdevka
Ertil
Muchkapskiy
Balanda
Samoylovka
Krasnoarmeysk
Volgogradskoye Vdkhr.
Krasnyy Yar
Piterka
Novouzensk

Semiluki
Voronezh
Anna
Gribanovskiy
Arkhangelskoye
Borisoglebsk
Peski
Yelan
Zhirnovsk
Kamenskiy
Krasnyy Yar
Novatka
Aleksandrov Gay

Staryy Oskol
276
Gubkin
Khokhalskiy
Kastornoye
Davydovka
Georgiu-Dezh
239
Buturlinovka
Uryupinsk
Buzuluk
Kukvidze
Novoannenskiy
Panfilovo
358
Danilovka
Kotovo
Nikolayevsk
Kaztalovka
Furmanovo
Mal. Uzen
KAZAKH

Belgorod
Shebekino
Novyy Oskol
Alekseyevka
Kamenka
Ostrogozhsk
Korotoyak
Pavlovsk
Kalach
Kazanskaya
Mikhaylovka
Kamyshin
Bykovo
Kaysatskoye
S.S.R.

Volchansk
Pechenezhskoye Vdkhr.
Valuyki
Rossosh
Buturlinovka
Boguchar
Kantemirovka
Chir
Frolovo
Ilovlya
Olkhovka
Elton
Urda

Kharkov
Kupyansk
Yevstratovskiy
Kamenskiy
Veshenskaya
Serafimovich
Ilovlya
Iloulinskaya
Dubovka
Dzhanybek

Balakleya
Kupyansk-Uzlovoi
Svatova
Krasnyy Oskol Vdkhr.
Starobelsk
Melovoye
Chertkovo
Kamenskiy
Kletskiy (Kletskaya)
Prichalnaya
Volzhskiy
Kapustin Yar

Izyum
Rubezhnoye
Millerovo
Volgograd (Stalingrad)
Krasnoslobodsk
Lenin

SOVIET FEDERAL SOCIALIST REPUBLIC

COPYRIGHT. GEORGE PHILIP & SON. LTD.
HHK

Projection: Conical with two standard parallels

1:5 000 000

50   0   50   100   150   200 km

Yelan-Kolenovskiy   Povorino   Peski   Samoylovka   Krasnoarmeysk   Krasnyy Kut   Orlov Gay   Oz. Chalkar   Chalkar
Bobrov   Khrenovoye   Talovaya   Zhirnovsk   Rovnoye   Novouzensk   Dzhambeyty
Georgiu-Dezh   239   Buturlinovka   Uryupinsk   Novakhoperskiy   Yelan   Kamensk   Nikolayevsk   Vozyshennost   Volgogradskoye   Novouzensk   Mergenevskiy   Karsha
gozhsk   Kamenka   Pavlovsk   Kalach   Novoannenskiy   Buzuluk   Panfilovo   Medveditsa   Danilovka   Krasnyy   Vdkhr.   Aleksandrov Gay   Bol. Uzen   Furmanovo   Bazartobe
Rossosh   Boguchar   Kazanskaya   Serafimovich   Ilovlya   Krasny   358   Kaysatskoye   Mal. Uzen   Antonovo   Kalmykovo
Kantemirovka   Veshenskaya   Don   Frolovo   Mikhaylovka   Olkhovka   Bykovo   Dzhanybek   Elton   Urda   Makhambet   Topoli
Melovoye   Chertkovo   Kletskiy   Dubovka   Leninsk   Kapustin Yar   Vladimirovka   Verkhniy Baskunchak   (Yamankhalinka)   Inderborskiy
Millerovo   Kamenskiy   Surovikino   Volgograd   Krasnoslobodsk   Akhtubinsk   Shungay   Zelënyy   Novobogatinskoye
Voroshilovgrad   Kamensk-Shakhtinskiy   Morozovsk   Kolach na Donu   Krasnoarmeysk   Volzhskiy   (Petropavlovskiy)   Guryev
(Lugansk)   Belaya Kalitva   Tsimlyanskoye   Chernyshkovskiy   Volga   Kopanovka   Yenotayevka   -28
Gukovo   Krasnodonetskaya   Vdkhr.   Kotelnikovo   Obilnoye   Staryy Biryuzyak   Krasnyy Yar   Guryev
Shakhty   Tsimlyansk   Volgodonsk   Dubovskoye   Zavetnoye   Zimovniki   Kuberle   Astrakhan   Krasnoye   Kamyzyak
Novocherkassk   Bolshaya Martynovka   KALMYK   Krasnyy Yar   -28
Rostov   Bataysk   Veselovskoye   Manych   Proletarskaya   A.S.S.R.   Astrakhan   Kultay
Vdkhr.   Mechetinskaya   Remontnoye   Krasnoye   Kaspiyskiy   Mumra   Mangyshlakskiy
Zernograd   Oz. Manych-Gudilo   Elista   Liman   Zaliv
Kushchevskaya   Yegorlykskaya   Gigant   (Stepnoi)   Beloye Ozero   M. Tyub Karagan   P-ov Mangyshlak
Salsk   Leninsk   Priyutnoye   Kuma   Fort Shevchenko
Peschanokopskoye   Yegorlyk   Divnoye   Staryy Biryuzyak   Shevchenko
Pavlovskaya   Belaya Glina   Krasnogvardeyskoye   Ipatovo   Kalaus   Arzgir   Beloye Ozero   Tyuleniy   O. Kulaly
Tikhoretsk   Novoaleksandrovskaya   Svetlograd   Bryanskoye   O. Chechen
Korenovsk   Krapotkin   Izobil'nyy   (Petrovskoye)   Prikumsk   Vladimirovka   Kizlyar   Lopatin   Aleksandriyskaya
Ust-Labinsk   Kurgannaya   Blagodarnoye   Zelenokumsk   Staryy Biryuzyak   Tyuleniy
Armavir   Stavropol   831   (Kurgannaya)   Nevinnomyssk   (Vorontsovo-Aleksandrovskoye)   CASPIAN
Maykop   Labinsk   Kuban   Kursavka   Zelenokumsk   Terek   -28
Apsheronsk   Cherkessk   Mineralnyye Vody   Georgievsk   Prokhladnyy   Mozdok   CHECHENO-   Kizlyar
Neftegorsk   Dakhovskaya   Yessentuki   Pyatigorsk   Mayskiy   Malgobek   INGUSH   Gudermes   Makhachkala
Kislovodsk   Karachayevsk   Nalchik   Nartkala   Beslan   Groznyy   A.S.S.R.   Sulak   Kumtorkala   Kaspiysk
Sochi   Krasnaya Polyana   Teberda   KABARDINO-   Elkhotovo   Kizil Yurt   Buynaksk   SEA
Adler   Gagra   BALKAR A.S.S.R.   Elbrus   Ordzhonikidze   Sadon   Khasavyurt   Izberbash   Novokayakent   800
ABKHAZ   Kodori   5633   Nartkala   Sayasan   Khunzakh   Akusha   DAGESTANSKIY   Derbent
Gudauta   A.S.S.R.   5203   Balta   Kazbek   Tebulos   Agvali   Kakhib   Akusha   Dagestanskiye Ogni
Novy Afon   Sukhumi   Tkvarcheli   Dzhvari   5047   4492   Khunzakh   Kuli   Modzhalis   Kasumkent
Ochamchire   Gali   Zugdidi   Rioni   Oni   Tsageri   Mikha-Tskhakaya   Kutaisi   Tiyarata   Khachmas
GEORGIA   Sachkhere   Tskhinvali   Dusheti   Telavi   Kvareli   Samurs   Akhty   Mikhaylovka
Anaklia   Tkibuli   Chiatura   (Stalinir)   Gori   Mtskheta   Logodekhi   Zakataly   Kuba   Divichi
Poti   Khashuri   Kaspi   Kvareli   Gurdzhaani   Kutkashen   Siazan
Kobuleti   Makharadze   S.S.R.   Borzhomi   Tbilisi   Signakhi   Citeli   Sheki   Bazar Dyuzi   Baba-dag
Batumi   Khulo   Akhaltsikhe   Khrami   Rustavi   Ckaro   Alazan   (Nukha)   4466   3629   Sumgait
ADZHAR A.S.S.R.   Vale   Manueli   Iori   Mirzaani   Mingechaurskoye   Khachmas   Artem
Hopa   Borchka   Shaumyani   Akstafa   Alazan   Vdkhr.   Mashtaga
Pazar   Makharadze   Akhalkalaki   Kura   Zakataly   Agdash   Shemakha   BAKU
Rize   Artvin   Ardahan   Kirovakan   Dilizhan   Kirovabad   Chanlar   Yevlakh   Genkchay   Zyrya
Trabzon   Surmene   Çildir   Leninakan   Sevan   Mir-Bashir   Barda   Terter   Lyaki   Kazi Magomed
Çakirgol   3063   Kars   Aragats   Chardakhlu   Mingechaur   AZERBAIJAN   S.S.R.
3937   Kaçkar   Oltu   Sarikamis   4090   Ozero   Tauz   Agdzhabedi   Ali-Bayramly   Alyata
Bayburt   Norman   Digor   Echmiadzin   Sevan   Martuni   Imishly   M. Byandovan
Eğri   Tortum   Aras   Kagizman   Yerevan   Agdam   Sabirabad   Karachala
Egentani   ARMENIAN A.S.S.R.

1:5 000 000

50   0   50   100   150   200 km

K O M I
A.S.S.R.

Obyachevo
Kazhim
Veslyana
Vishera
Gora
Denezhkin
Kamen
▲1493
Massava
Pelym
Konda

Nagorsk
Lesnoy
Kay
Gayny
Bondyug
Cherdyn
Krasnovishersk
Pokrovsk-Uralskiy
Severouralsk
Sama
Lozva
Shaim

Vyatka
Rudnichnyy
Kosa
Kosa
Yuria
Borovsk
Solikamsk
Gora Konzhakovskiy
Kamen ▲1569
Karpinsk
Krasnoturinsk
Serov
Mezhdurechensk

Belaya
Kholunitsa
Chernaya
Kholunitsa
Kudymkar
Pozhva
Chermoz
Usolye
Berezniki
Kamskoye
Vdkhr.
Kizel
Gubakha
Malomalsk
Lobva
Lyalya
Novaya
Lyalya
Verkhoturye
Gari

Kirov
Slobodskoy
Omutninsk
Afanasyevo
Zalazna
Aleksandrovsk
Kytlym
Kachkanar
Krasnouralsk
Basyanovskiy
Bolotovskoye
Tabory

Novovyatsk
Cheptsa
Peskovka
Kama
Kama
Dobryanka
Pashiya
Usva
Nizh. Salda
Turinsk
Tavda

Zuyevka
Falenki
Glazov
Vereshchagino
Nytva
Ocher
Chusovoy
Lysva
Chusovaya
Kushva
Verkhnyaya Salda
Alapayevsk
Irbit
Nitsa
Tura

Kumeny
Yar
Kez
Debessy
Perm
Nizhniy Tagil
Verkhniy Tagil
Nevyansk
Rezh
Artemovskiy
Bulandsh
Troitskiy
Tyume

Nolinsk
Medvedok
Arkul
Igra
Zura
Kungur
Shalya
Kuzino
Pervouralsk
Revda
Asbest
Sukhoy Log
Talitsa
Pyshn

Urzhum
Kilmez
Yakshur
Bodya
Osa
Achit
Nizhniye Sergi
SVERDLOVSK
Beloyarskiy
Bogdanovich
Kamyshlov

Shurma
Kilmez
U D M U R T
A.S.S.R.
Votkinsk
Vorkinskoye
Vdkhr.
Krasnoufimsk
Ufa
Polevskoy
Sysert
Kamensk
Uralskiy
Dalmatovo

Malmyzh
Uva
Izhevsk
Chaykovskiy
Chernushka
Mikhaylovskiy
Verkhniy Ufaley
Iset
Shadrinsk

Mozhga
Agryz
Sarapul
Kambarka
Yangul
Askino
Nyazepetrovsk
Kasli
Uksyanskoye
Kargapolye
Kurg

Mamadysh
Yelabuga
Menzelinsk
Burayevo
Izh
Kama
Duvan
Verkhniye
Kigi
Kusa
Karabash
Brodokalmak
Techa
Miass

Kuybyshevskoye
Vdkhr.
Buklyan
Naberezhnyye
Chelny
Dyurtyuli
B A S H K I R
Krasnyy Klyuch
Kyshtym
Argayash
Mishkino

Chistopol
Zainsk
Birsk
Ay
Berdyaush
Zlatoust
Kusa
Chelyabinsk
Shumikha

T A T A R
A.S.S.R.
Bilyarsk
Aktash
Tumutuk
Almetyevsk
Blagoveshchensk
Kushnarenkovo
Asha
Minyar
Yuryuzan
Satka
Miass
Chebarkul
Kopeysk
Shchuchye

Leninogorsk
Bugulma
Tuymazy
Chishmy
Ufa
Chernikovsk
Iglino
Katav
Ivanovsk
Bakal
Korkino
Yemanzhelinsk
Kurtamysh

Nurlat
Oktyabrskiy
Davlekanovo
Inzer
Gora Iremel
▲1582
Yuzhno-Uralsk
Uvelskiy
Zverinogolovskoye

Sernovodsk
Isakly
Belebey
Rayevskiy
A.S.S.R.
Gora
Yamantau
▲1638
Tirlyanskiy
Uchaly
Plast
Ust Uyskoye

Bugulma
Krasnousolskiy
Zigazinskiy
Beloretsk
Verkhneuralsk
Troitsk
Uy
Vedenka

Abdulino
Sterlitamak
Petrovskoye
Gora
Bol. Shatan
▲1270
Magnitogorsk
Komsomolets
Borovskoye

Krasnyy Yar
Timashevo
Kinel
Bol. Kinel
Buguruslan
Salavat
Ishimbay
Verkhniy Avzyan
Agapovka
Varna
Fedorovka

KUYBYSHEV
Novokuybyshevsk
Koltubanovskiy
Tok
Ivanovka
Ponomarevka
Meleuz
Bakr Uzyak
Ural
Kartaly
Kustanay

Alekseyevka
Buzuluk
Samara
Grachevka
Sorochinsk
Mrakovo
Siboy
Kizilskoye
Aktobe
Rudnyy

Bolshaya
Glushitsa
Andreyevka
Bulanovo
Tyulgan
Kumertau
Yermolayevo
Baymak
Tobol
Kushmu

Novo-Sergiyevskiy
Sakmara
Sakmara
Buribay
Iriklinskoye
Vdkhr.
Dzhetygara
Ozero
Kushmuru
Kushm

Darinskoye
Ural
Ilek
Orenburg
Saraktash
Krasnoyarskiy
Shilda
Livanovka
Ozero
Sarymoin

Uralsk
Aksay
Ilek
Krasnyy Kholm
Ural
Kuvandyk
Gay
Iriklinskiy
Adamovka
Zhailma
Ozero
Aksuat

Chilik
Dubenskiy
Mednogorsk
Novoorsk
Kumak
Svetlyy
Oz.
Zhetykol
Oz. Ayke

Chapayevo
Utva
Sol Iletsk
Akbulak
Novotroitsk
Orsk
Grigoryevka
Dombarovskiy
Oz. Shalkar
Yega Kara
Ozero
Sarykopa

Mergeneva
Oz.
Chalkar
Chalkar
Dzhambeyty
Martuk
Batamshinskiy
Khromtau
Oz. Shalkar
Karashatau
Suykbulak

Karsha
Ural
Karatobe
Bol. Khoba
Aktyubinsk
Alga
Karabutak
Turgay
Zha

Novoalekseyevka
K A Z A K H   S.S.R.
Turgay

m
1500
1000
400
200
50
0

1:5 000 000

50   0   50   100   150   200 km

Projection: Conical with two standard parallels.

East from Greenwich

COPYRIGHT GEORGE PHILIP & SON LTD.

m 6000 4000 3000 2000 1500 1000 400 200 0

1:50 000 000

500   0   500   1000   1500   2000 km

PACIFIC OCEAN

Aleutians

Bering Str.

C. Dezhneva

Kamchatka Peninsula

Sea of Okhotsk

Kolyma Ra.

Gydan Ra. (Kolyma)

Wrangel I.

New Siberian Is.

Indigirka

Verkhoyansk Range

Lena

Aldan

Stanovoy Ra.

Yablonovy Ra.

Amur

Sikhote Alin Ra.

Sakhalin I.

Sea of Japan

Hokkaido

Kurile Is.

Honshu

Shikoku

Kyushu

Korea Str.

Korea

Yellow Sea

East China Sea

Ryukyu Is.

Formosa

Bonin Is.

Caroline Is.

Philippine Is.

Luzon

Mindanao

Palawan

Sulu Sea

Borneo

Celebes Sea

Celebes

Moluccas

Halmahera

New Guinea

Ceram

Banda Sea

Arafura Sea

Timor

Flores

Java Sea

East

Sunda

Sumatra

Str. of Malacca

Malay Peninsula

G. of Siam

Menam

Mekong

Irrawaddy

Salween

Bay of Bengal

Andaman Is.

Nicobar Is.

Ceylon

Palk Strait

Eastern Ghats

Western Ghats

Deccan

Godavari

Krishna

C. Comorin

Maldive Is.

Laccadive Is.

INDIAN OCEAN

Equator

Amirantes

Seychelles

Socotra (C. Guardafui)

G. of Aden

Somali Peninsula

Red Sea

Nile

Libyan Desert

Mediterranean Sea

Adriatic Sea

Rhône

British Isles

North Sea

Iceland

Greenland

Arctic Circle

Scandinavia

Finland

Baltic Sea

North European Plain

Vistula

Oder

Elbe

Danube

Carpathians

Bosporus

Black Sea

Anatolia

Cyprus

Taurus Mts.

Dead Sea

Syrian Desert

Suez Canal

Mesopotamia

Tigris

Euphrates

Arabia

Al Rub al Khali

Persian Gulf

G. of Oman

Arabian Sea

Ararat 5165

Caucasus

Elbruz 5633

Elburz Mts.

Caspian Sea

Plateau of Iran

Great Salt Desert

Zagros

Kola Pen.

White Sea

North Cape

Kolguyev

Novaya Zemlya

Barents Sea

Svalbard

Kara Sea

Severnaya Zemlya

Taimyr Peninsula

Cheyuskin

ARCTIC OCEAN

Yenisei

Central Siberian Plateau

Lower Tunguska

Ob

Angara

Yenisei

Lena

Baikal

Sayan Mts.

Selenga

Plateau of Mongolia

Great Khingan Mts.

Manchurian Plain

Sungari

Po Hai

Hwang

Great Plain of China

China

Hwang

Yellow Sea

Si-kiang

Hainan

Hong (Red)

Ton-kin

G. of Tongking

West Siberian Plain

Irtysh

Tobol

Irtysh

Narodnaya 1894

Ural Mountains

1640?

Steppes

Volga

Ural

Don

Dnieper

N. Dvina

Central Russian Uplands

L. Balkhash

Ili

Chu

Syr Darya

Aral Sea

Turanian Plain

Amu Darya

Kyzyl Kum

Altai

Tien Shan

Belukha 4506

Turfan Basin

Tarim

Lop Nor

Takla Makan

Tarim Basin

Kunlun Shan

Plateau of Tibet

Koko Nor

Tsangpo

Brahmaputra

Himalaya

Everest 8848

Pamirs

Communism Pk. 7495

Karakoram Ra. 8611

Hindu Kush 7690

Helmand

Hari-rud

Sulaiman Ra.

Thar

Indus

Ganga

Yamuna

Narmada

Tapti

m   6000   4000   2000   1000   400   200   10   0

0   -200   2000   4000   6000   8000

1:50 000 000

500   0   500   1000   1500   2000 km

Projection: Bonne

COPYRIGHT. GEORGE PHILIP & SON, LTD.

1:100 000 000

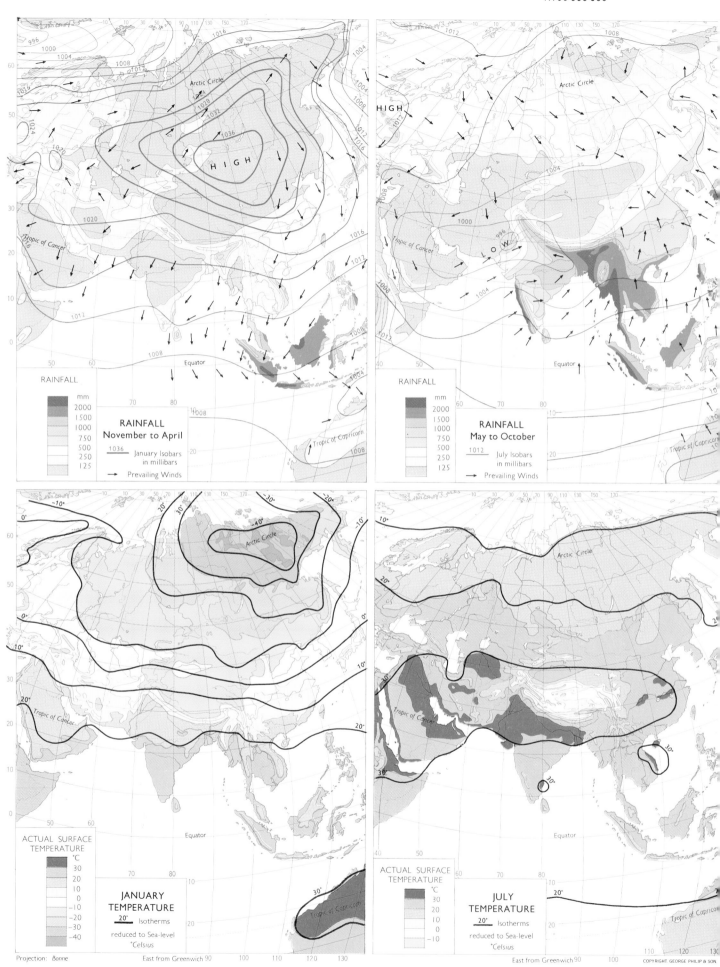

RAINFALL

mm
2000
1500
1000
750
500
250
125

RAINFALL
November to April

1036 ―― January Isobars
in millibars

→ Prevailing Winds

RAINFALL

mm
2000
1500
1000
750
500
250
125

RAINFALL
May to October

1012 ―― July Isobars
in millibars

→ Prevailing Winds

ACTUAL SURFACE
TEMPERATURE

°C
30
20
10
0
-10
-20
-30
-40

**JANUARY
TEMPERATURE**

20° ―― Isotherms

reduced to Sea-level
°Celsius

ACTUAL SURFACE
TEMPERATURE

°C
30
20
10
0
-10

**JULY
TEMPERATURE**

20° ―― Isotherms

reduced to Sea-level
°Celsius

Projection: *Bonne*   East from Greenwich 90

East from Greenwich 90

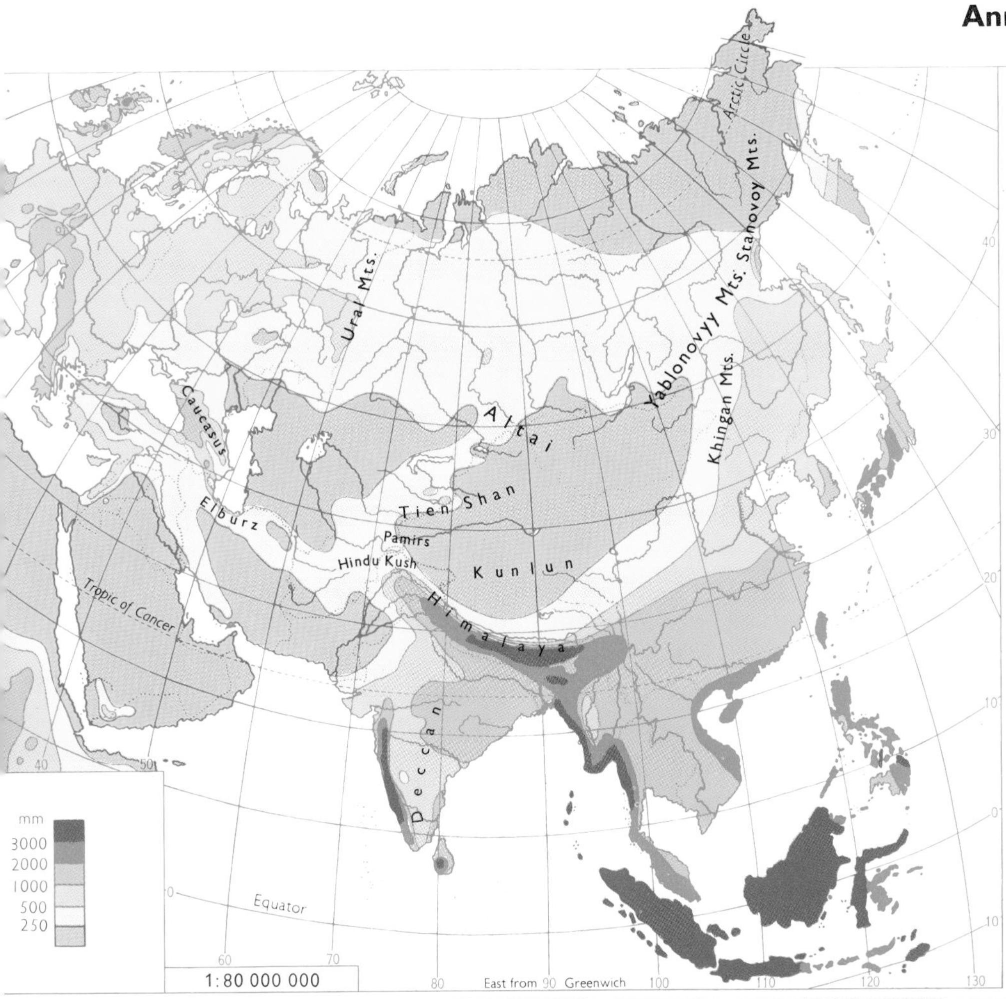

INDIA:
MONSOONS

THEIR EVOLUTION
IS SHOWN BY
MONTHLY
CLIMATE
MAPS

RAINFALL
mm per month

mm
25
50
100
200
400

—— ISOTHERMS
Temperature in degrees Celsius

—— ISOBARS
(Pressure in millibars)

⟵ WINDS

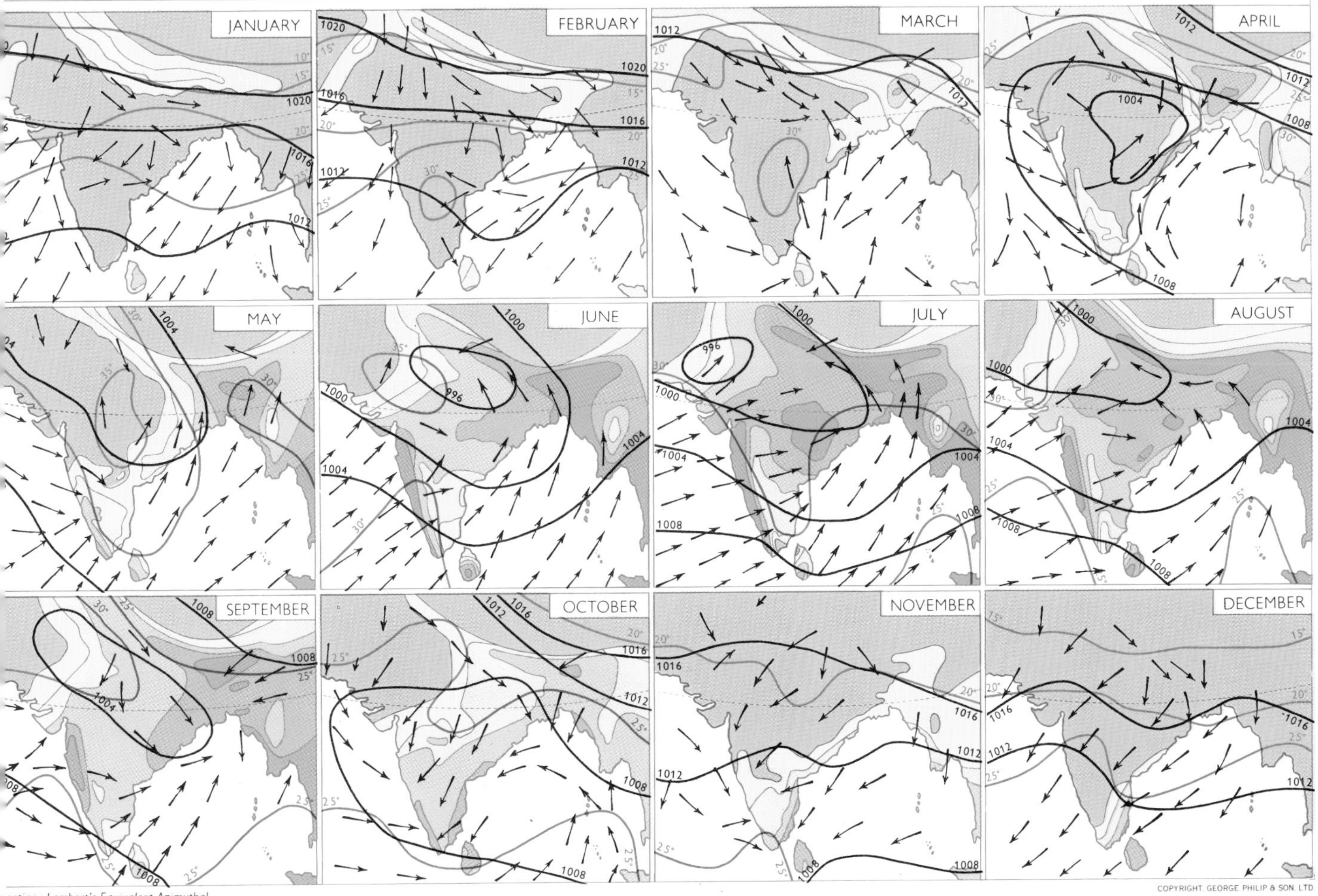

mm
3000
2000
1000
500
250

1:80 000 000

Equator

East from Greenwich

JANUARY FEBRUARY MARCH APRIL

MAY JUNE JULY AUGUST

SEPTEMBER OCTOBER NOVEMBER DECEMBER

ection: Lambert's Equivalent Azimuthal

COPYRIGHT GEORGE PHILIP & SON LTD

1:1 000 000

10   0   10   20   30   40 km

- - - - 1949-1967 Armistice lines between
· · · · · · · · Israel and the Arab States.

Projection: Conical with two standard parallels   East from Greenwich

Continuation
Southwards
1:2 500 000
0   10   20   30 k

1:15 000 000

100 0 100 200 300 400 500 600 km

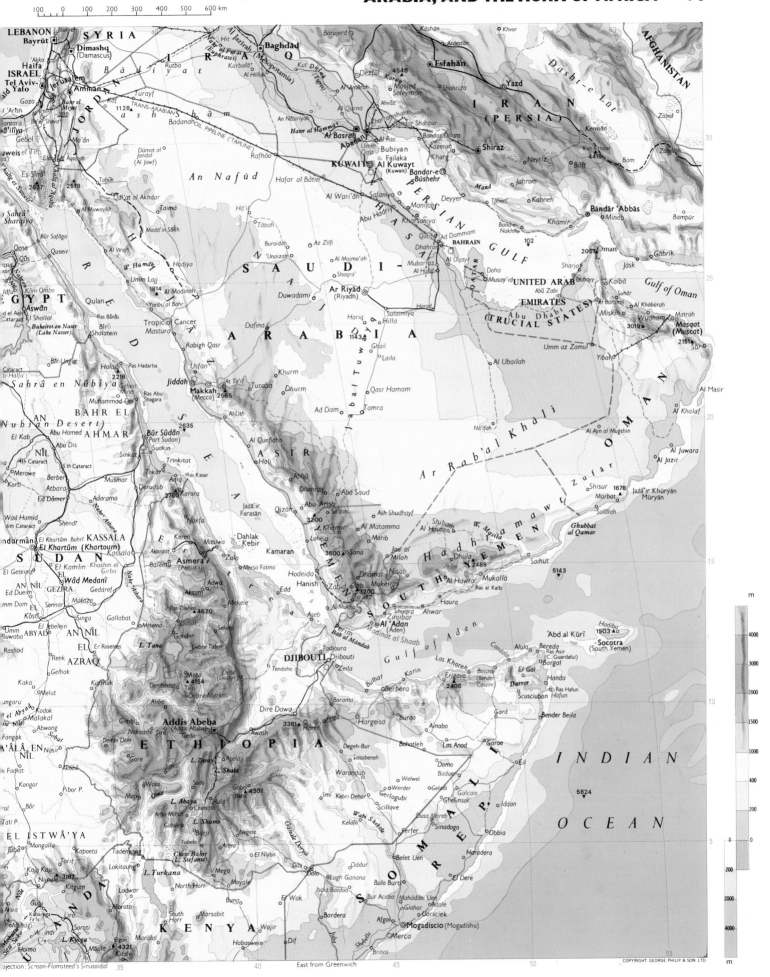

East from Greenwich

Projection: Senson-Flamsteed's Sinusoidal

COPYRIGHT GEORGE PHILIP & SON. LTD

m

4000
3000
2000
1500
1000
400
200
0
200
2000
4000

m

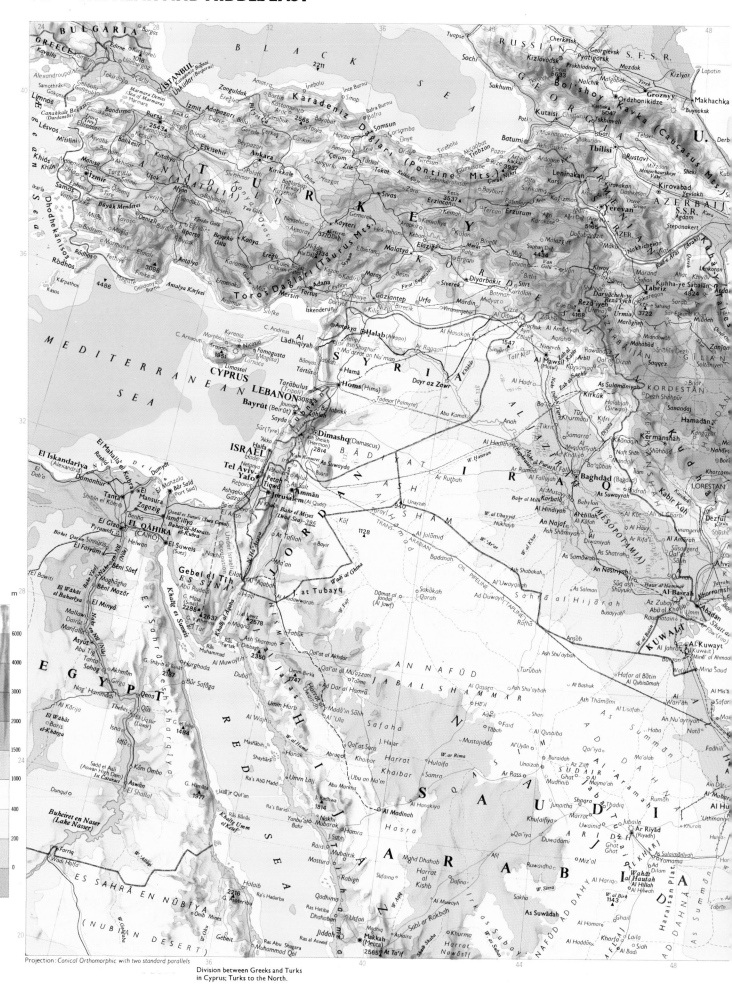

Division between Greeks and Turks
in Cyprus; Turks to the North.

KAZAKH S.S.R.

Aralskoye More

Muynak

KARA-KALPAKISCHE A.S.S.R.

PESKI KYZYLKUM

KAZAKH S.S.R.

Turkestan

Dzhambul

Gora Manas

Talass

Naryn

Chimkent

Arys

Lenger 4488

Kok-Yangak

Tösh-Kumyr

KAZAKH S.S.R.

Plato Ustyurt

U Z B E K   S.S.R.

Chimbai

Kungrod

Nukus

Chirchik

Tashkent

Angren

Namangan

Kokand

Andizhan

Leninsk

Margelan

Osh

Dzhalal-Abad

K I R G I Z   S.S.R.

Tien Shan

Kashgar (Shufu)

Yangi Hisar

CHINA

7579

Tashaus

Urgench

Turtkul

Khiva

Yangi Yul

Fergana

Kanibadam

Isfara

Uch Kurgan

Ulugh Chat

S.S.R.

Zaliv

Kara Bogaz Gol

Krasnovodski Poluostrov

Ozero Sarykamish

2169

Gizhduvan

Dzhizak

Ura Tyube

Sulyukta

Pik Lenina

7134

TADZHIK

Bukhara

Kagan

Samarkand

Dushanbe

Ordzhonikidzeabad

7495

Pik Kommunizma

Pamirs

4109

TURKMEN S.S.R.

Nebit Dag

Kizyl Arvat

KARA KUM

Chardzhou

Karshi

Guzar

Denau

Regar

Kurgan-Tyube

Kulyab

Khorog

Murgab

7789

Ashkhabad

K o p p e h   D a g

Kazandzhik

Mary (Mery)

Bairam Ali

Iolotan

Kerki

Karakumskiy Canal

Termez

Mazar-i-Sharif

BADAKHSHAN

PESHAWAR

Mashhad (Meshed)

Kuh-e Binalud

3314

Neyshabur

Kashaf

Salehabad

Band-i-Turkistan

3494

Qala Nau

H I N D U   K U S H

TAKHAR

Kabul

Jalalabad

NANGARHAR

Peshawar

RAWALPINDI

Rawalpindi

I R A N

DASHT-E KAVIR (Great Salt Desert)

KHORASAN

Herat

Safed Koh

3588

Ghazni

WARDAK

PAKTIA

3513

ISMAIL KHAN

A F G H A N I S T A N

4148

URUZGAN

GHAZNI

ZABUL

Kandahar

HELMAND

KANDAHAR

Registan

Quetta

3693

D E R A

B A L U C H I S T A N

P A K I S T A N

Dasht-i-Margo

CHAKHANSUR

Ghazai Hills

2462

MULTAN

Multan

BAHAWALPUR

Kerman

3992

4419

3962

Zahedan (Duzdab)

Dasht-i-Tahlab

Siahan Range

Central Makran Range

2480

Sukkur

Rohri

INDIA

GREAT INDIAN DESERT

F A R S

Shiraz

Persepolis

K E R M A N

SISTAN

Iranshahr

Makran Coast Range

KARACHI

Karachi

Hyderabad

KUTCH

Gulf of Kutch

Jamnagar

Bandar Abbas

Qeshm

Str. of Hormuz

Gwadar

Pasni

Ormara

Rann of Kutch

G U L F

Oman

Khasab

Ras al Khaima

Dubayy

Sharjah

Ajman

Fujaira

Gulf of Oman

Tropic of Cancer

A R A B I A N

EMIRATES

Al Wahat al Buraimi

ARAB Dhabi

Abu Zabi

Masqat (Muscat)

4122

UNITED

(TRUCIAL STATES)

O M A N

East from Greenwich

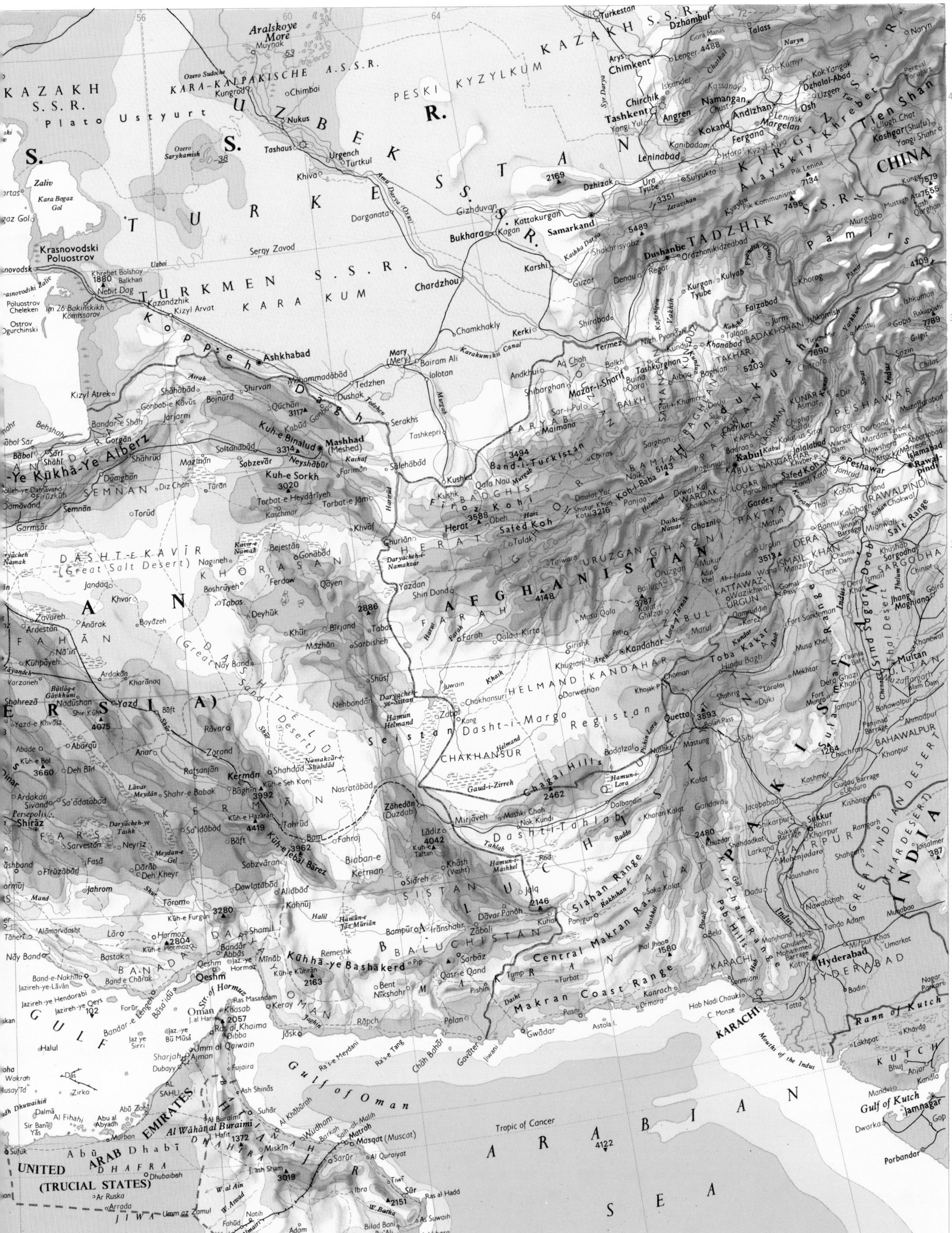

COPYRIGHT. GEORGE PHILIP & SON. LTD

S E A

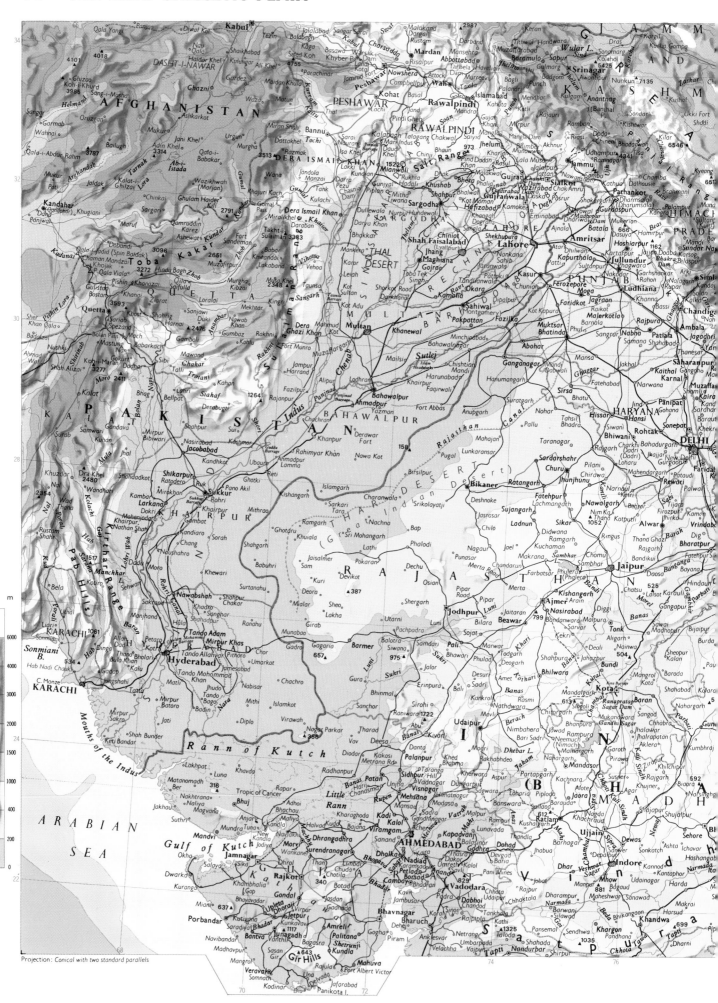

Projection: Conical with two standard parallels

1:6 000 000

50 0 50 100 150 200 250 km

JAMMU AND KASHMIR
On same scale as Main Map

East from Greenwich

COPYRIGHT. GEORGE PHILIP & SON. LTD.

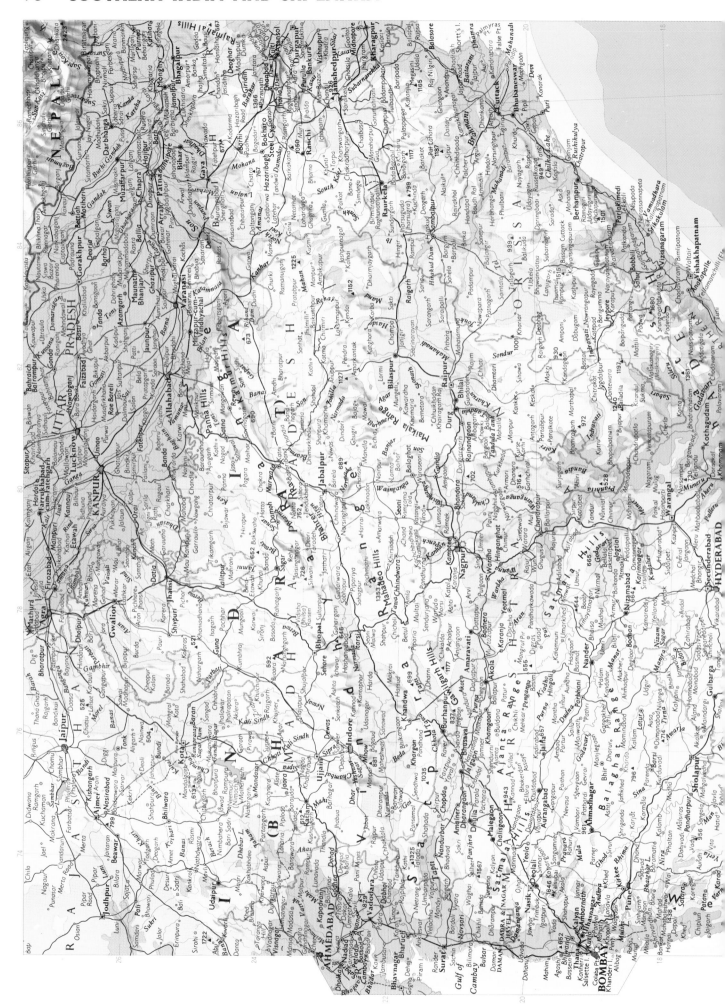

1 : 6 000 000

50   0   50   100   150   200   250 km

East from 80°Greenwich

Projection: Conical with two standard parallels
HHI

B A Y   O F   B E N G A L

Coromandel Coast

A R A B I A N   S E A

M   a   l   a   b   a   r   C   o   a   s   t

Eikalpeni Bank

St. Mary's Is.

Coondapur

Androth I.

Kalpeni I.

KARNATAKA

GOA

TAMIL NADU

MADRAS

BANGALORE

Mysore

Coimbatore

Calicut
(Kozhikode)

Cochin

Trivandrum

C. Comorin

Pondicherry
Cuddalore

Nellore

SRI LANKA
(CEYLON)

Colombo

Galle

Trincomalee

Jaffna

Palk Strait

Gulf   of   Mannar

G   u   l   f   o   f   M   a   n   n   a   r

(M a n n a r)

m
3000
2000
500
400
200
0

m
0
200
2000
4000

1:6 000 000

50 0 50 100 150 200 250 km

BAY

OF

BENGAL

Mouths of the Ganga

The Sandheads

TIBET

CHINESE   REPUBLIC

BHUTAN

INDIA

ARUNACHAL PRADESH

ASSAM

NAGALAND

MANIPUR

MEGHALAYA

BANGLADESH

DACCA

TRIPURA

MIZORAM

CALCUTTA

Sundarbans

KHULNA

Chittagong

CHIN

SAGAING

KACHIN

CHIN

BURMA

Mandalay

Rangoon

Bassein

PEGU

KAYAH

THAILAND

Tropic of Cancer

ARAKAN

MAGWE

TENASSERIM

G. of Martaban

Mouths of the Irrawaddy

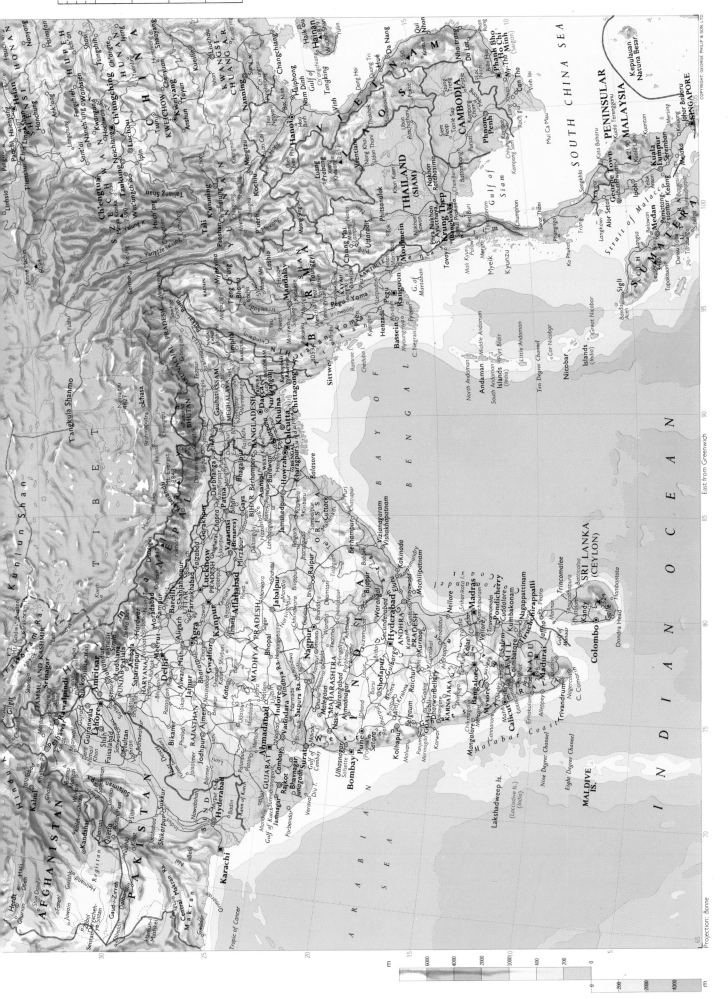

1:20 000 000

200   0   200   400   600   800 km

Projection: Bonne

East from Greenwich

COPYRIGHT GEORGE PHILIP & SON LTD

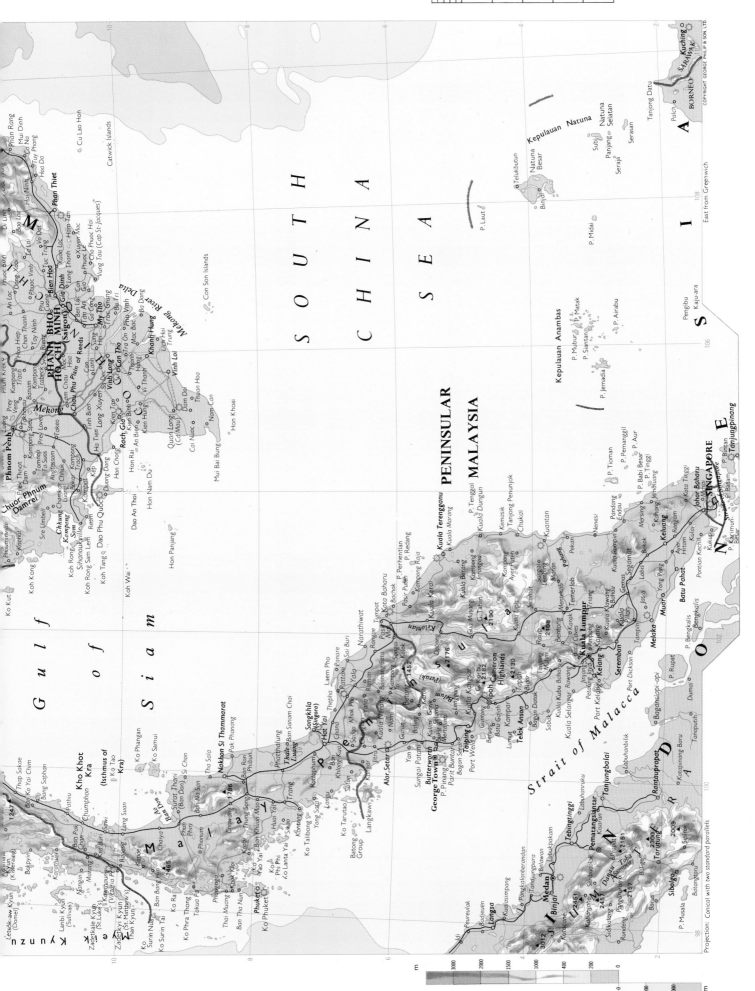

Projection: Mercator

East from Greenwich

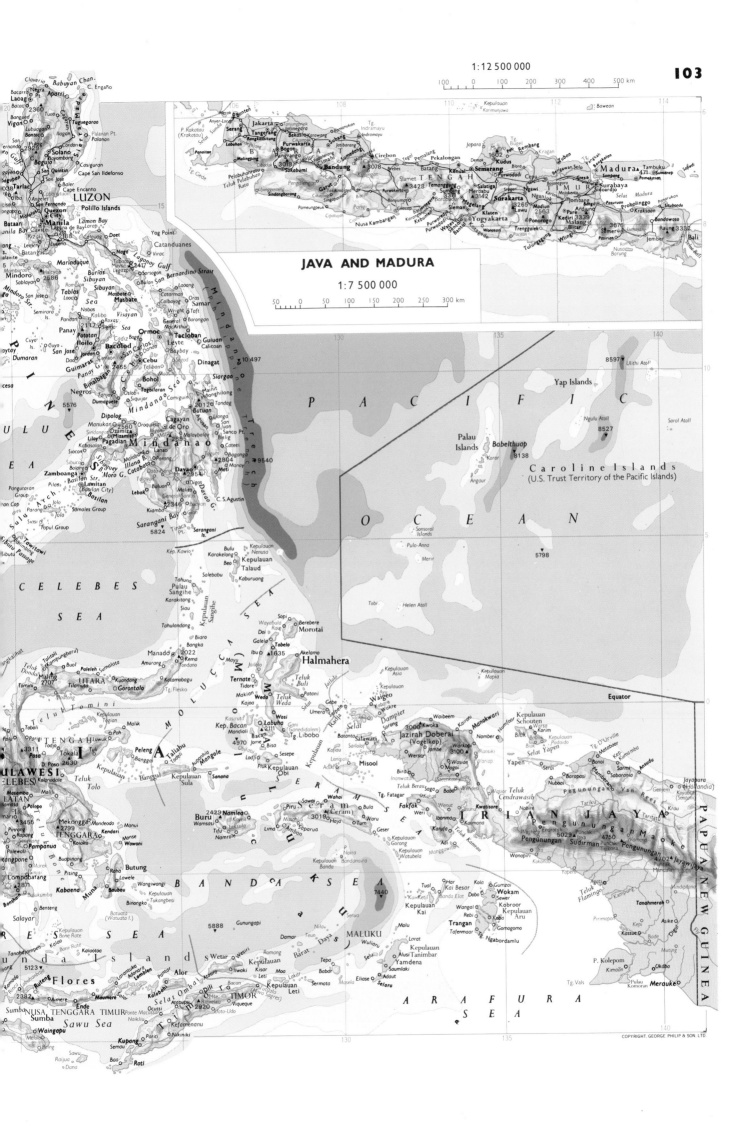

1:12 500 000

100   0   100   200   300   400   500 km

JAVA AND MADURA

1:7 500 000

50   0   50   100   150   200   250   300 km

LUZON

PACIFIC

OCEAN

CELEBES
SEA

Caroline Islands
(U.S. Trust Territory of the Pacific Islands)

Palau
Islands

Yap Islands

Equator

Halmahera

Mindanao

SULU
SEA

Zamboanga

Ternate
Tidore

Manado

UTARA

TENGAH

SULAWESI
(CELEBES)

TENGGARA

MOLUCCA SEA

SERAM SEA

CERAM SEA

Seram

Buru

MALUKU

BANDA SEA

FLORES SEA

Flores

TIMOR

NUSA TENGGARA TIMUR

Sumba

Sawu Sea

SUNDA Islands

ARAFURA
SEA

IRIAN JAYA

Pegunungan Maoke

PAPUA NEW GUINEA

COPYRIGHT GEORGE PHILIP & SON LTD.

1 : 30 000 000

200 0 200 400 600 800 1000 km

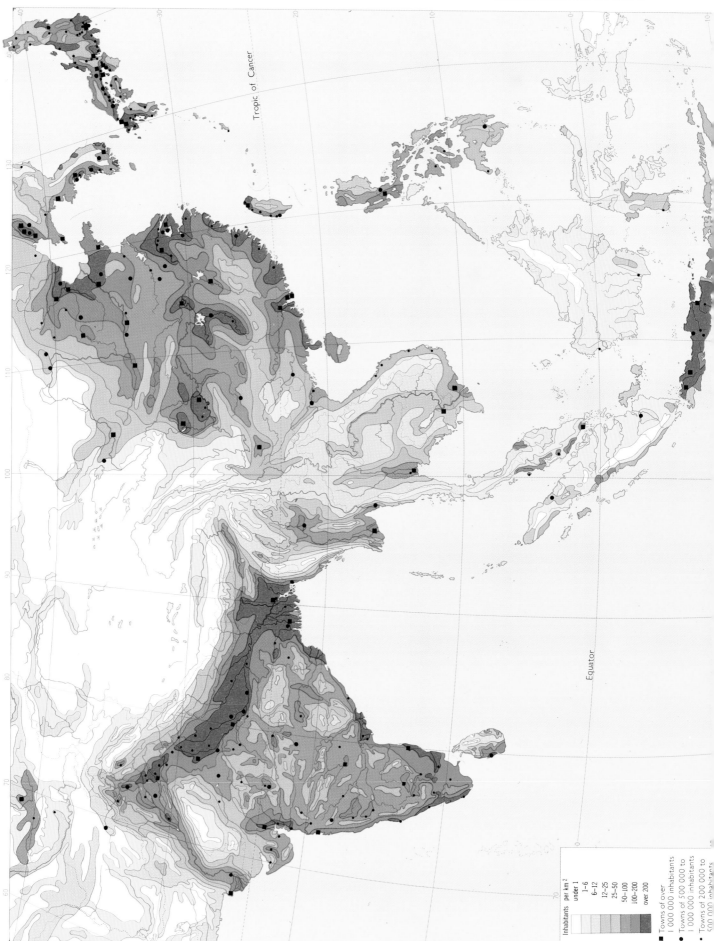

Tropic of Cancer

Equator

Inhabitants	per km²
	under 1
	1–6
	6–12
	12–25
	25–50
	50–100
	100–200
	over 200

■ Towns of over
   1 000 000 inhabitants

● Towns of 500 000 to
   1 000 000 inhabitants

● Towns of 200 000 to
   500 000 inhabitants

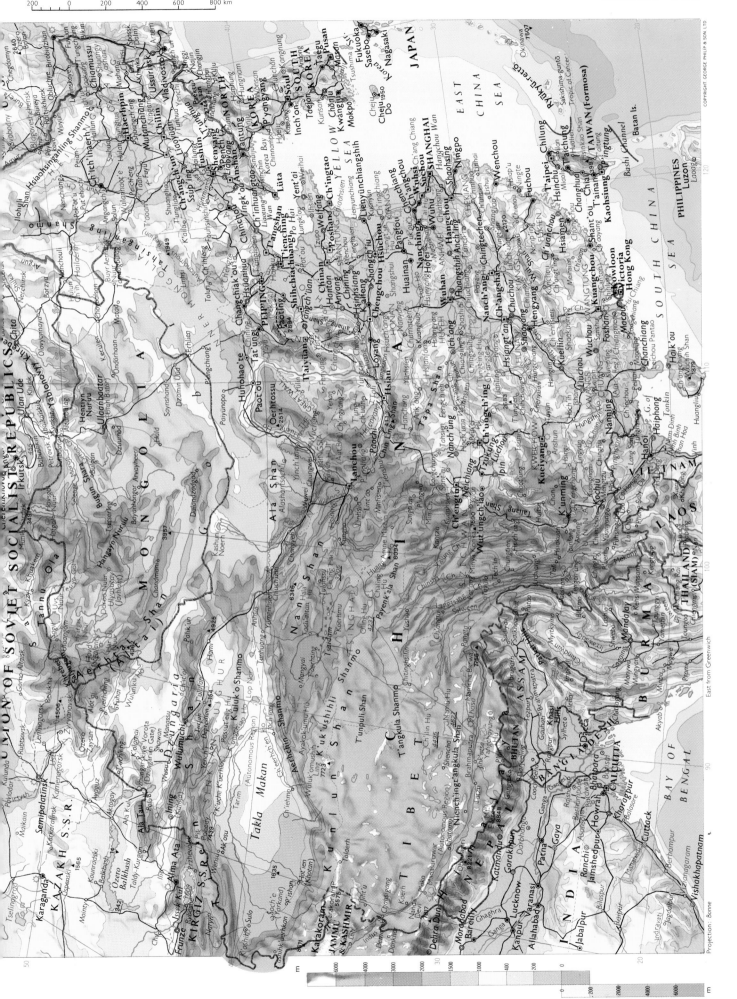

1:20 000 000

200   0   200   400   600   800 km

Projection: Bonne

East from Greenwich

COPYRIGHT GEORGE PHILIP & SON LTD

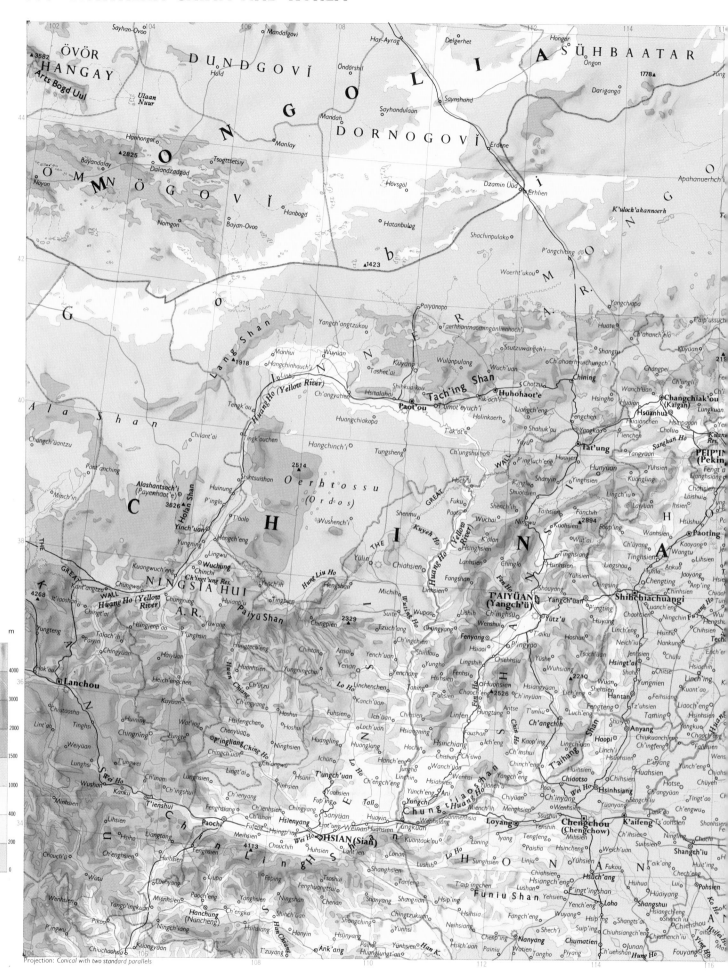

Projection: Conical with two standard parallels

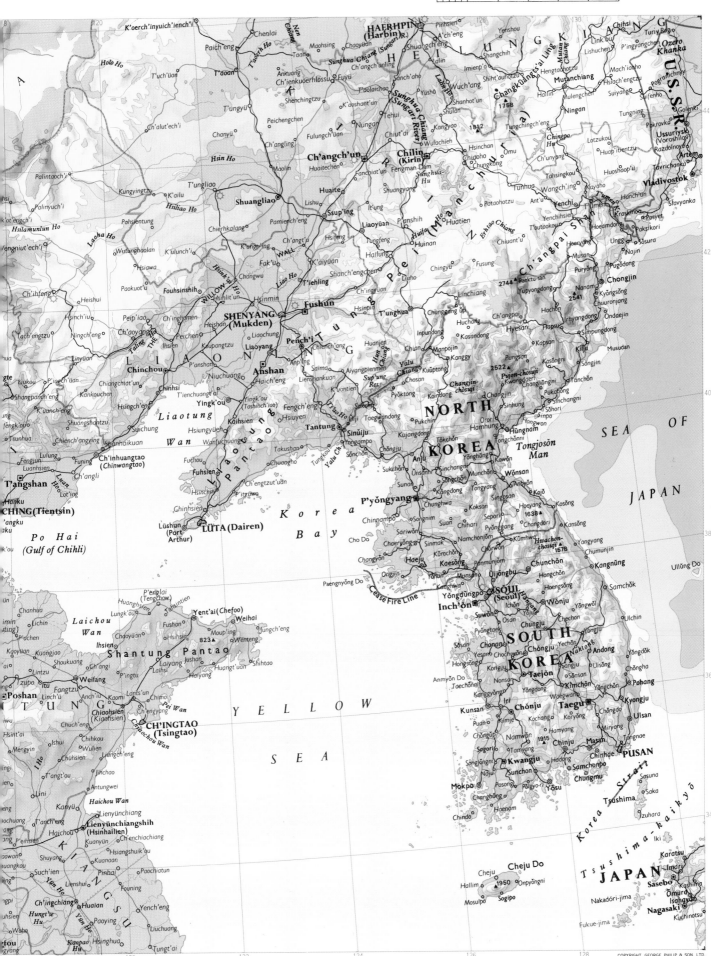

A

K'oerch'inyuich'iench'i

Chenlai

Pihsien

Holo Ho

Nen Chiang

HAERHPIN (Harbin) R.

Yenshou

A'ch'eng

Maohsing Chaoyang Shuangch'eng

Shangchih

CHISHIH

Turiy Reg

H E I L U N G K I A N G

Ozero Khanka

Paich'eng

Tuch'uan

T'aoan

Ankuang Ch'ienkuoerhlossu Fuyu

Sanch'aho Wuch'ang

Shiht'ouhotzu

Hengtaohotzu

Pokrovka

grafichnyi

pragnichnyi

T'ch'uan

Sunghua Chiang (Sungari)

Ch'angch'unling

Lalin

Imienp'o

Mutanchiang

Mulengcheng

Suiyang

Tungning

Turiy Reg

U.S.S.R.

T'ungyü Shenchingtzu Peichengchen

T'aolaichao Yushu Shanot'un

1758

Halfin

Ningan

Suifenho

Ussuriysk (Voroshilov)

Razdolnoye

Chanyü

Ch'angling

Nungan

Kangyao Shulan

1812

Tungchingch'eng

Lotzukou

Pokrovka

Artem

Hsin Ho

Maolin Huaitechen

Fanchiat'un Fengman Dam

Ch'unyang

Chingpo Hu

Huap'itientzu

Tahsingkou

Wang'ch'ing

Kayao

Vladivostok

Slavyanka

Kungyingtzu K'ailu

Huaite It'ung

Sunghua-Hu

Potaohotzu

Ant'u

Yenchi

Tumen

Hunch'un

Kraskino

Posyet

Ch'angch'un

Chilin (Kirin)

Shuangyang

Tunhua

T'outaoku

Yenchihsien

Hoemdong

Paksikori

Sōsura

Pahsientung Chierhkalang

Shuangliao Lishu Ssup'ing

Liaoyüan P'anshih

Huina Huatien

Ch'angpai Shan

Unggi

Najin

Laoha Ho K'angp'ing Hsifeng Tungfeng

Huinan

Fusung

Musan

Puryŏng

Pugŏdong

42

Hsiawa Changwu WALL Fak'u

K'aiyüan

Shanch'engchen Chingyü

Erhtao Chiang

2744 ▲ Paektu-san

Yupyŏngdong

Nanam

Chongjin

Kuanch'eng Hsinlit'un Liao Ho T'iehling

Hsinpin T'unghua

Chungang up

2541

Kyŏngsŏng

Chuuronjong

Ōndaejin

Paokuot'u Fouhsinshih Hsinmin

Fushun

Huanjen

Ch'angpai Hochon

Irhyangdong

Kasandong Hyesan Hapsu

Simpundong

Kiju

Musudan

SHENYANG (Mukden)

Pench'i

Chiench'ang

Hun Chiang Manpojin

Kanggye Kapsan

Kasŏng-ni Sŏngjin

Heishan Liaoyang

Anp'ing Huanjen Chian

Yalu Kanggy

2522▲

Pungsan Changhŭng-ni

Tanch'on

Chinchou Niuchuang **Anshan**

Haich'eng Saima Lienshankuan

Aiyangpienmen

Chosan Sup'ung Res.

Changjin-chosuji

Kwangdaeri Pukch'ŏng

Kuuptong Changjin

Sinch'angni

Kaihsien Yingk'ou (Tashihch'iao) Hsiuyen

Tsao Ho Uiji Taegwandong

Pyŏktong Kangdong Hongwon Sinpo

NORTH

T'ienchuang Hsingch'eng Yingk'ou

Wantienho Fengch'eng

K'uantien Ch'osan

Chian

Hamhung **KOREA**

Tōkchōn

Hŭngnam

Liaotung Pantao

Tantung **Sinŭiju**

Kujangdong

Pukchin

SEA OF

Chinhsi Shanhaikuan Wan Wanfuchuang Takushan Tungkou

Yongampo Sŏnch'ŏn

Anju Yŏnghŭng Tongjosŏn Man

T'angshan Luan Ho Fuchou

Chuangho

Yalu Ch' Sinanju Munch'on **Wŏnsan**

Fengjun Lulung Ch'inhuangtao (Chinwangtao)

Fuhsien P'itzuwa Ch'engtzut'uan

Sukch'ŏn Sinch'angni

Singosan Anbyŏn

JAPAN

Luanhsien Lot'ing Ch'angli

Kangdong Tongyang Munch'on

Kojō

Hanku CHING (Tientsin) Ghinhsien

Lüshun (Port Arthur)

Sunan Chunghwa Kangsŏng Kōsong

'angku **LÜTA (Dairen)**

P'yŏngyang

Koksan Sepor**i**

1638▲

aku

K o r e a B a y

Chinnampo Songnim Suan Chihari

Pyŏnggang Changdori Kansŏng

Po Hai (Gulf of Chihli)

Cho Do Sariwŏn Sinmak

Kŭmhwa Hwachon-chosuji

38

Changyŏn Sinmak Namch'onjŏm Ch'ŏrwŏn

1578

P'eriglai (Tengchow)

Haeju Kŭmch'ŏn Kaesŏng

Panmunjom Chunch'ŏn

Yangyang

Huanghsien Lungk'ou T'ahsintien

Changyŏng Ongjin Kŭmhwa

Hongch'ŏn Kangnŭng

Ullŭng Do

Laichou Wan Fushan Yent'ai (Chefoo)

Weihai

Paengnyŏng Do Cease Fire Line

SEOUL

Haengsŏng Samch'ŏk

Chaoyüan Hsihsia 823▲ Jungch'eng

Yŏngdŭngpo **Inch'ŏn**

Hongch'ŏn Wŏnju

Yŏngwŏl Ulchin

Ihsien Mouping Wenteng

Suwŏn Ich'ŏn

Osan Chungju Chechon

Shoukuang Ch'angi Laiyang Jushan Shihtao

Sŏsan P'yŏngt'aek Ch'ŏngju

SOUTH

Yŏngju

Yŏngdŏk

Weifang P'ingtu Haiyang

Anmyŏn Do Yesan Ch'ŏnan Chŏngju Naktong

Andong

Ch'ŏngha

Fangtzu Linch'u Kaomi Lants'un Chimo

Taech'ŏnni

Hongsŏng Kongju **KOREA**

Sangju Uisŏng

Poshan Chiaohsien (Kiaohsien)

Chimo

Taejŏn

Kimch'ŏn

Yŏngch'ŏn **Pohang**

Chiao-chou Wan

Anmyŏn Do Nonsan Yŏngdong Waegwan Kyŏngju

Mengyin Ishui Wulien

CH'INGTAO (Tsingtao)

Kunsan **Chŏnju** **Taegu**

Iho T'angt'ou

Puan Kŭmje Kochang Koryŏng Ch'ŏngdo Ulsan

Lini

Y E L L O W

S E A

Chŏngŭp Namwŏn Hamyang Miryang Tongnae

Chanhua Kanyü Lienyünchiang

Sagori Tamyang 1915 Chinju **Masan**

Chindo Haenam Chinhae **PUSAN**

Lienyünchiangshih (Hsinhailien) Kuanyün

Songjŏngni **Kwangju** Hadong Samch'ŏnpo Chungmu

Kiangnan Ho Kuantaokou Hsiangshuik'ou

Sunch'ŏn P'olgyo Yŏsu

Korea Strait

Tsushima

Saka

sasuna

Izuhara

Iki

Karatsu

Such'ien Pinhai Paochiatun

Mokp'o Changhŭng Posong

Kuchinotsu

J A P A N

Ch'ingchiang Huaian

Cheju **Cheju Do**

Nakadóri-jima Ōmura Isahaya

Hungtse Hu Yün Ho Yench'eng

Hallim 1950 Onpyŏngni

Sasebo Gōshima

Nagasaki

Mosulpo Sogipo

Fukue-jima

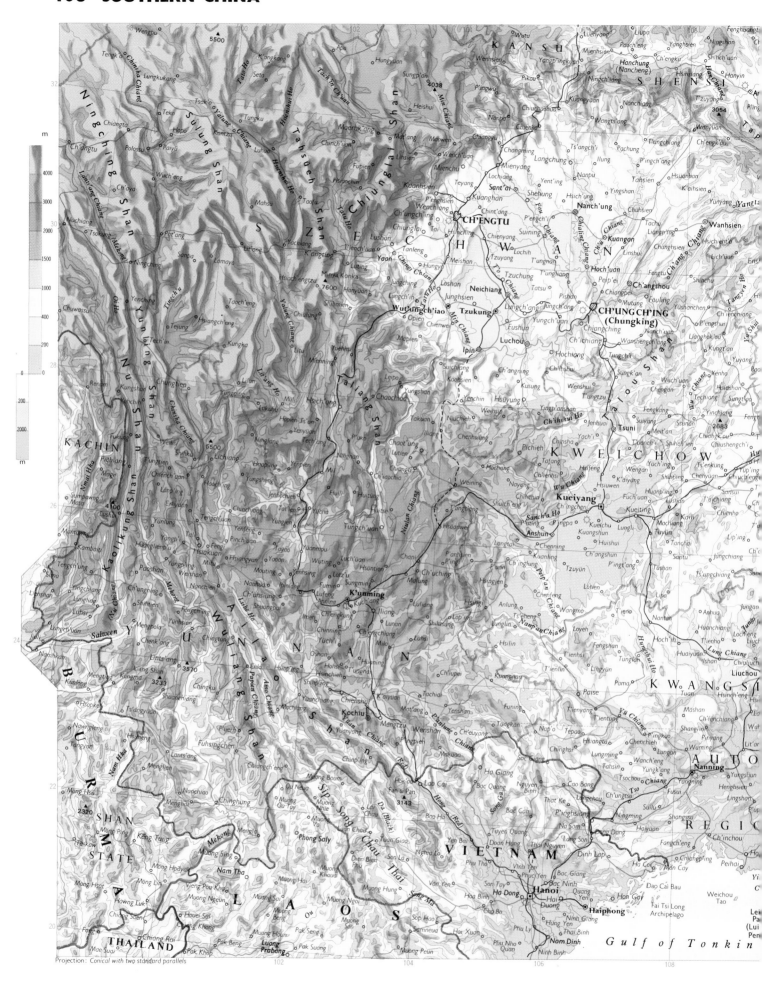

1:6 000 000

50 0 50 100 150 200 250 km

SEA OF JAPAN

SOUTH KOREA

CHŪGOKU-DISTRICT

HONSHŪ

KYŪSHŪ
KYŪSHŪ-DISTRICT

SHIKOKU
SHIKOKU-DISTRICT

Projection:
Lambert's Conformal
Conic

1:2 500 000

10 0 10 20 30 40 50 60 70 80 90 100 km

CHŪBU-DISTRICT

Kanazawa

Ū

ISHIKAWA

Komatsu

Kaga

Mikuni

Fukui

Echizen-Misaki

Sabae

FUKUI

Takefu

Ōno

Wakasa-Wan

Tsuruga

Hokuriku Tunnel

Obama

KYŌTO

Ōtsu

Kusatsu

Himi

Takaoka

Shinminato

Uozu

Namerikawa

Toyama

Heiya

TOYAMA

Tonami

Oyabe

Tsubata

Oyama

Johana

Kamioka

Takayama

Shirakawa

Furukawa

Hida-Sammyaku

Hotaka-Dake

Ōmachi

Nakano

Nagano

Suzaka

Nakanojō

Shiran-San 2578

Nikkō

Chuzenji-Ko

Imaichi

TOCHIGI

Utsunomiya

Kanuma

Karasuyama

Hitachi-ota

Hitachi

Kashima-

Nada

NAGOYA

Toyota

AICHI

Okazaki

Hekinan

Shinshiro

Toyokawa

Toyohashi

Hamamatsu

Enshū-Nada

KINKI-DISTRICT

Kumano-Nada

Kii-Hantō

NAKAYAMA

Tanabe

Shingū

Kushimoto

Shio-no-Misaki

PACIFIC OCEAN

East from Greenwich

COPYRIGHT. GEORGE PHILIP & SON. LTD.

Hachijō-Jima

Aoga-Shima

Mikura-Jima

Miyake-Jima

Kōzu-Shima

Nii-Jima

To-Shima

Shikine-Jima

Ō-Shima

Mihara-Yama
755

Sumisu-Jima

m

3000

2000

1500

1000

400

200

0

200

2000

4000

m

1 : 7 500 000

50   0   50   100   150   200   250   300 km

CHINA

U.S.S.R.

Sikhote Alin

KOREA

KOREA

Pusan

SEA   OF   JAPAN

Sea of Okhotsk

Wakkanai
Rebun-Tō
Rishiri-Tō
Teshio
Otoineppu
Monbetsu
HOKKAIDŌ
Rumoi
Shibatsu
Kitami
Abashiri
Asahigawa
Daisetsu-Zan 2290
Otaru
Bibai
Iwamisawa
Obihiro
Kushiro
Sapporo
Tomakomai
Poroshiri Dake 2052
Muroran
Okushiri-Tō
Esashi
Hakodate
Esan-Misaki
Matsumae
Tsugaru-Kaikyō
Aomori
Hirosaki
Hachinohe
Kuji
Akita
Morioka
Miyako
Honjō
Hanamaki
Kamaishi
Yokote
Ichinoseki
Sakata
Shinjō
Tsuruoka
Ishinomaki
Yamagata
Shiogama
Sendai
Sado
Shibata
Yonezawa
Fukushima
Niigata
Nagaoka
Kashiwazaki
Koriyama
Wajima
Nagano
Takada
Iwaki
Nanao
Nagano
Kanazawa
Toyama
Matsumoto
Utsunomiya
Hitachi
Takaoka
Takasaki
Mito
Fukui
Takayama
Chichibu
Tsuchiura
CHŪBU
Takefu
Tsuruga
Gifu
TŌKYŌ
Chōshi
Tottori
Maizuru
Hikone
Nagoya
Kōfu
Chiba
Matsue
Toyooka
Kyōto
Yokkaichi
Shimizu
Yokohama
Yonago
Ōsaka
Okazaki
Shizuoka
Yokosuka
CHŪGOKU
Himeji
Kōbe
Nara
Numazu
Atami
Tsu
Hamamatsu
Hiroshima
Kurashiki
Sakai
Toyohashi
Okayama
Wakayama
Kishiwada
Onomichi
Owase
KINKI
Kure
Takamatsu
Shimonoseki
Tokushima
KYŪSHŪ
Matsuyama
Shingū
SHIKOKU
Fukuoka
Kitakyūshū
Kōchi
Sasebo
Kurume
Ōita
Muroto-Misaki
Nagasaki
Kumamoto
Nakamura
Kagoshima
Miyazaki
KYŪSHŪ
Kanoya
Makurazaki
Ōsumi-Shotō
Tane-ga-Shima
Yaku-Jima

PACIFIC

OCEAN

PACIFIC

OCEAN

RYŪKYŪ ISLAND
Continuation southwards
in same scale

Ōsumi-Sh
Tokara-Kaik
Naze
Amami Ō Sh
Tokunoshima
Okinoerabu-Jima
Okinawa-Jima
Kerama-Shotō
Naha
Miyako-Jima
Hirara
Yaeyama-Shotō
Yonaguni-Jima
Ishigaki-Jima
Iriomote-Jima
Nansei-Shotō Trench
7507

Projection : Bonne   East from Greenwich   COPYRIGHT GEORGE PHILIP & SON

1:40 000 000

400 0 400 800 1200 1600 km

SPAIN

Madeira
(Port.)

Islas
Canarias

Tenerife

El Aaiun

Dakhla

Dērik

MAURITANIA
Nouakchott

SENEGAL
BISSAU
GUINEA
Bissau
Conakry
Freetown
SIERRA
LEONE
Monrovia
LIBERIA

Tanger Gibraltar (Br.)
Tetouan
Casablanca
Rabat Fès
MOROCCO
Marrakech
Essaouira
Ifni
Dra

Alger
Oran
Constantine
Annaba
Bizerte
Tunis
TUNISIA
Sfax
Djerid
Tripolitaine

ALGERIA

In Salah

Ghadames
Ghat

S a h a r a

MALI
Tombouctou
Kayes
Bamako
Kankan
UPPER
VOLTA
Ouagadougou
IVORY
COAST
Kumasi
Abidjan
GHANA
Accra
TOGO
BENIN
Lomé
Porto Novo
Sekondi-
Takoradi

Niamey
Sokoto
Kano
Kaduna
Maiduguri
N I G E R I A
Ibadan
Lagos
Enugu
Port Harcourt

Agades

N I G E R   C H A D

Lac
Tchad
Ndjamena
Abéché

Marzuq
Al Jawf

L I B Y A

MALTA
Sicilia
Tarābulus
Banghāzī

TURKEY
Athínai
Kriti
CYPRUS

Mediterranean Sea

Siwa
El Faiyûm
EGYPT
Asyût
Aswân

EL QAHIRA
El Suweis
Bûr Said

Halab
SYRIA
Tel Aviv-
Yafo
ISRAEL
JORDAN
Dimashq

Al Mawsil
Baghdad
IRAQ
Al Basrah
KUWAIT

Tehrān
Esfahān
IRAN

Persian Gulf
BAHRAIN
QATAR

Tropic of Cancer

SAUDI-
ARABIA
Al Madīnah
Makkah

Asir

Wadi-Halfa
Es Sahrâ
En Nûbiya
Bûr Sûdan

Dongola
Esh Shimâliya
Atbara
Omdurmân
El Khartûm
Kordofân
El Obeid
El Fâsher
Dârfûr

S U D A N

Kassala
Asmera
Mitsiwa

YEMEN
Madinat al Shaâb
SOUTH YEMEN
Al Adan (Aden)
Berbera
DJIBOUTI
Djibouti

G. of Aden
Socotra
(South Yemen)
Ras Asir

A'Âlâ
Bahr el
Ghazâl
Wâw
El Istwâ'ya
Malakâl
L. Tana
Addis Abeba
ETHIOPIA
Harer
Shebele

SOMALI REP.
Mogadishu

CENTRAL AFRICAN
REP.
Bangui
Oubangi

CAMEROON
Yaoundé
Rey Malabo
Macias Nguema Biyoga
(Fernando Póo)
EQUATORIAL
GUINEA
Mbini
Douala
Libreville
GABON
C. Lopez

SÃO TOMÉ AND
PRÍNCIPE
Pagalu
(Annobón)

Gulf of Guinea

CONGO
Brazzaville
Kinshasa
Pointe Noire
Cabinda
Boma
Luanda

Z A I R E
Mbandaka
Kisangani
L. Idi
Amin Dada
Kasai
Ilebo
Bukama
Shaba
Lubumbashi
Kananga

L. Mobutu
Sese Seko
UGANDA
Kampala
RWANDA
BURUNDI
Bujumbura
Kigoma
Tabora
Dodoma
T A N Z A N I A
Dar-es-Salaam
Zanzibar
Pemba

KENYA
L. Victoria
Kisumu
Nairobi
Mombasa
Equator
Kismayu

INDIAN
OCEAN

Aldabra Is.
Arch. des Comores
Cabo
Delgado
Ruvuma

ATLANTIC

OCEAN

Ascension
(Br.)

West from Greenwich East from Greenwich

A N G O L A
Huambo
Benguela
Lobito
Moçâmedes
Cunene
Cubango

Z A M B I A
Lusaka
Livingstone
MALAWI
Lilongwe
Zomba
Blantyre
Malawi
L. Mweru

MOZAMBIQUE
Moçambique
Quelimane
Chinde
Beira
Mozambique Channel
Majunga

Diego-
Suarez
Tamatave
MADAGASCAR
MAURITIUS
Réunion
(Fr.)
Tananarive
Fianarantsoa
Tuléar

ZIMBABWE
Salisbury
Bulawayo

NAMIBIA
(SOUTH WEST
AFRICA)
Windhoek
Swakopmund
Walvis-
baai
Lüderitz

BOTSWANA
Kalahari
Gaborone

Tropic of Capricorn

TRANSVAAL
Pretoria
Johannesburg
Vaal
O.V.
Bloemfontein
NATAL
Durban
SOUTH AFRICA
CAPE
PROVINCE
Kimberley
Oranje
Cape
Town
Kaap die Goeie Hoop
(Cape of Good Hope)
East
London
Port
Elizabeth
Maputo
SWAZ
LES

Pr. Edward Is.
(S.A.)

LES. Lesotho
O.F.S. Orange Free State
SWAZ. Swaziland

COPYRIGHT. GEORGE PHILIP & SON LTD
HHI

DENSITY OF POPULATION
1:80 000 000
Inhabitants
per km²   per km²
under 1   12- 25
1- 3   25- 50
3- 6   50-100
6-12   over 100
Towns of over 200 000 inhabitants
Section: Zenithal Equidistant

Tanger
Rabat
Casablanca
Safi
Marrakech
Melilla
Alger
Oran
Tunis
Sfax
Tarābulus
Banghāzī
Constantine
Annaba

El Iskandarîya
Bûr Said
El Suweis
El Qahira
Aswan

Tropic of Cancer
Omdurman
El Khartûm

Kano
Ilorin
Ogbomosho
Oshogbo
Ibadan
Kumasi
Lagos
Abidjan
Accra
Douala
Port Harcourt
Addis Abeba

Equator
Libreville
Brazzaville
Kinshasa
Luanda
Kananga
Kisangani
Nairobi
Mombasa
Dar es Salaam

Lubumbashi
Kitwe
Lusaka
Bulawayo
Salisbury
Tananarive
Tropic of Capricorn

Pretoria
Johannesburg
Maputo
Durban
Cape Town
Port Elizabeth

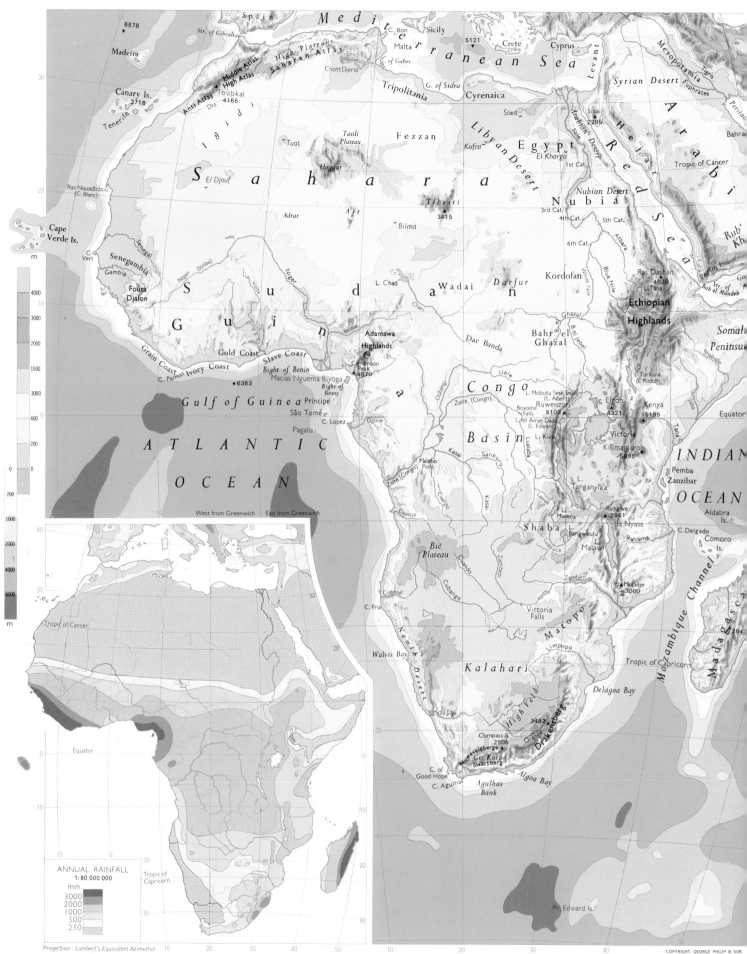

1:40 000 000

400   0   400   800   1200   1600 km

m

4000
3000
2000
1500
1000
400
200
0

0

200
1000
2000
4000
6000

m

ANNUAL RAINFALL
1:80 000 000

mm
3000
2000
1000
500
250

Projection: Lambert's Equivalent Azimuthal

1:80 000 000

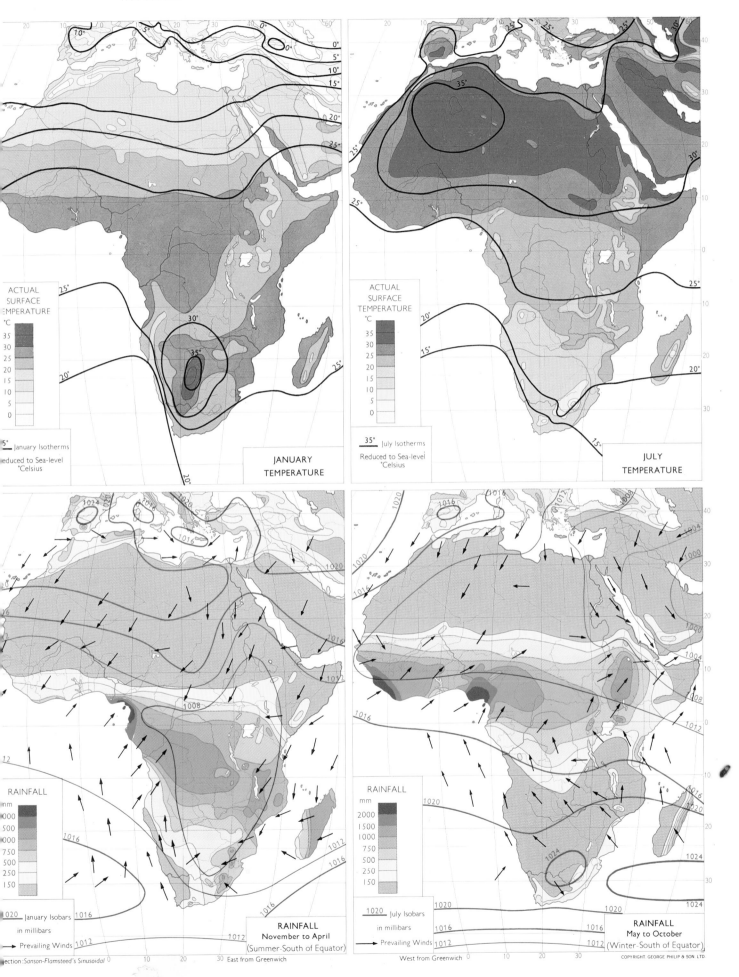

ACTUAL
SURFACE
TEMPERATURE
°C
35
30
25
20
15
10
5
0

5° January Isotherms
Reduced to Sea-level
°Celsius

JANUARY
TEMPERATURE

ACTUAL
SURFACE
TEMPERATURE
°C
35
30
25
20
15
10
5
0

35° July Isotherms
Reduced to Sea-level
°Celsius

JULY
TEMPERATURE

RAINFALL
mm
2000
1500
1000
750
500
250
150

1020 January Isobars
in millibars
Prevailing Winds

RAINFALL
November to April
(Summer-South of Equator)

RAINFALL
mm
2000
1500
1000
750
500
250
150

1020 July Isobars
in millibars
Prevailing Winds

RAINFALL
May to October
(Winter-South of Equator)

Projection: Sanson-Flamsteed's Sinusoidal 0

East from Greenwich

West from Greenwich 0

COPYRIGHT GEORGE PHILIP & SON LTD

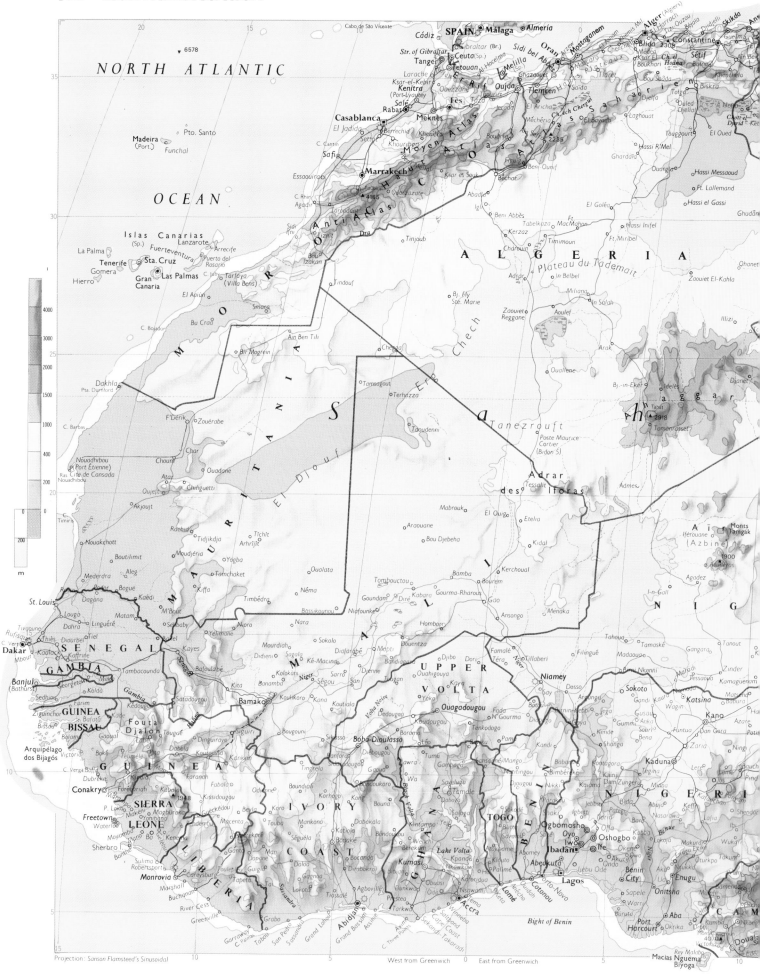

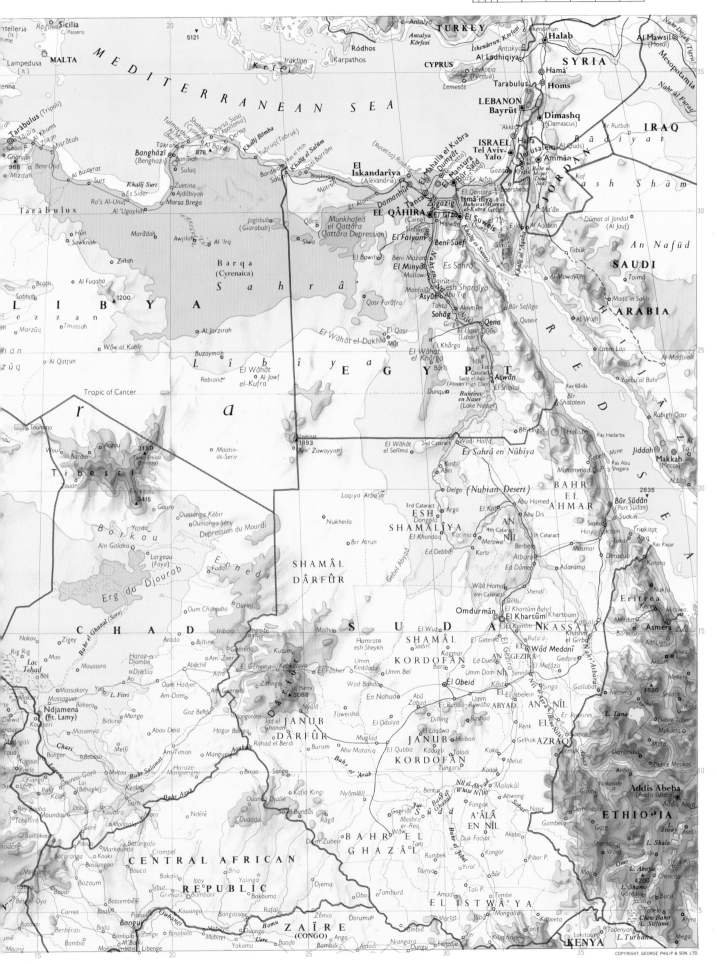

1:15 000 000

100   0   100   200   300   400   500   600 km

MEDITERRANEAN SEA

TURKEY

Antalya
Antalya Körfezi
İskenderun Körfezi
İskenderun
Al Mawsil
(Mosul)

CYPRUS
Lefkoşia
(Nicosia)
Lemesós

Al Ladhiqiya
Ḥamā
Homs
Tarabulus

SYRIA

Halab

Mesopotamia
Nahr Dijla (Tigris)

Ródhos
Kríti
Iraklion
Karpathos

Antiochia
Hama
Damascus

LEBANON
Bayrūt

Dimashq
(Damascus)

IRAQ

Ar Rutban

Bādiyat

Sicilia
C. Passero
Pantelleria
(It.)
Ragusa

MALTA

Lampedusa
(It.)

Tarabulus (Tripoli)
Tājūra
Al Khums
Zliţan
Misrātah

Ghuryān
Banghāzī
(Benghazi)

Al Bayḍā
Ra's Lānūf

'Akko
Haifa
Tel Aviv-
Yafo
Jerusalem
(Al Quds)

ISRAEL

JORDAN
Amman

Irbid
Beersheba

Ma'ān

An Nafūd

SAUDI

ARABIA

Madīnat

Al Madīnah

RED

SEA

Makkah
(Mecca)

Jiddah

Bûr Sûdân
(Port Sudan)

BAHR
EL
AHMAR

ETHIOPIA

Addis Abeba
(Addis Ababa)

KENYA

L. Turkana

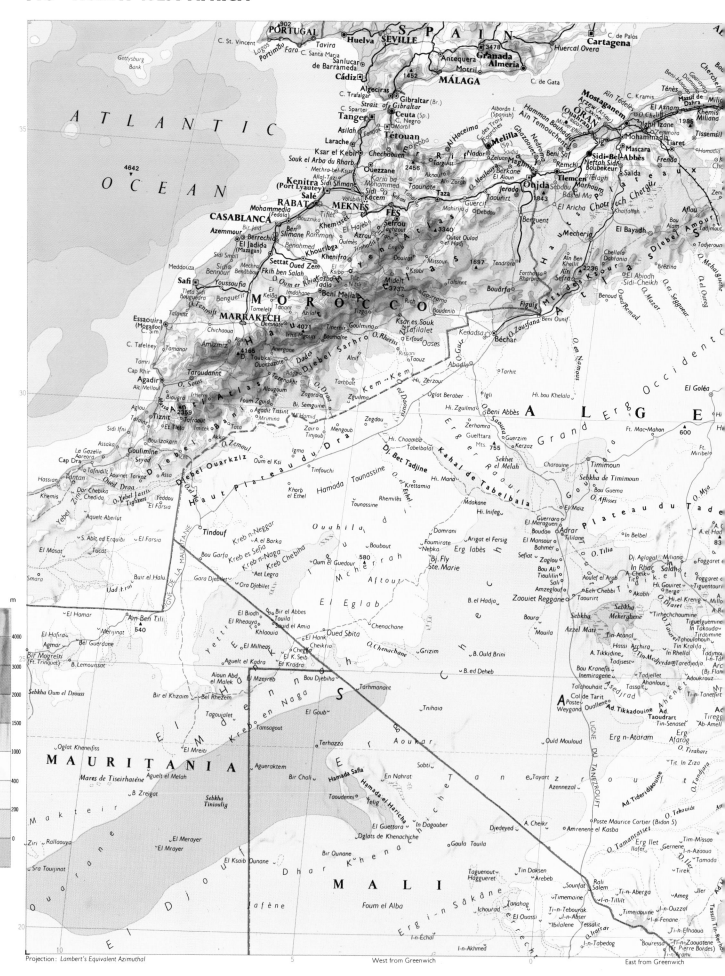

50 0 50 100 150 200 250 300 km

MEDITERRANEAN SEA

SICILY

C. Spartivento

Marsala

Etna 3340

CATANIA

Caltanissetta

Siracusa

Agrigento

Ragusa

C. Passero

Pantelleria
(Italian)

Gozo
Valletta
MALTA

Linosa I.
(Italian)

Lampione I.
Lampedusa
(Italian)

Bejaia

C. Bougaroun

Djidjelli

Skikda

Annaba

El Kala

Menzel
Bourguiba
Bizerte (Binzert)

Mateur
Ariana
Halq el Oued

TUNIS

Nabeul
Hammamet

Menzel-Temime

Kelibia

CONSTANTINE

Guelma

Béja

Zaghouan

Enfidha

Kalaa-Kebira

Sétil

El Eulma

Souk
Ahras

Sousse
Monastir

Moknine

Batna

Aïn Beïda

Kairouan

El Mahdia

Khenchela

Tébessa

Sbeitla

Msaken

Rass Kaboudia

Djebiniana

Biskra

Gafsa

Sfax

Iles Kerkenna

Chott
Melrhir

Maharès

G. de Gabès

Nefta

Chott el Fedjadj

Gabès

Djerba I.

Tozeur

Chott
Djerid

Kebili
Hamma

El Kantara

Zarzis

El Oued

Douz

Médenine

Bahiret el Bibane

Touggourt

Ksar Rhilane

Ben
Gardane

Tarābulus
(Tripoli)

Zuwārah

Al'Ulaylot

Al Wāṭiyah

Homs (Al Khums)

Leptis Magna (Labdah)

Tūkrah

Al Abyār

Banghāzī
(Benghazi)

Baninah

Suluq

Dehibat

Nālūt

Jabal Nafūsah

Gharyān

968 Wādī
Banī Walīd

Misurata

Khalij Surt
(Gulf of Sidra)

Kurkūrah

Antolāt

Wāzin

Jādū

Az Zintān

716

Mizdah

Al Jabal al Gharb

Surt

Zueitina

AL JABAL AL GHARB

Al Qaryah
ash Sharqīyah

MISRĀTAH

Ghudāmis

Al Hammādah al Hamrā'

SABHAH

Al Haruj al Aswad

LIBYA

NIGER

CHAD

COPYRIGHT. GEORGE PHILIP & SON. LTD.

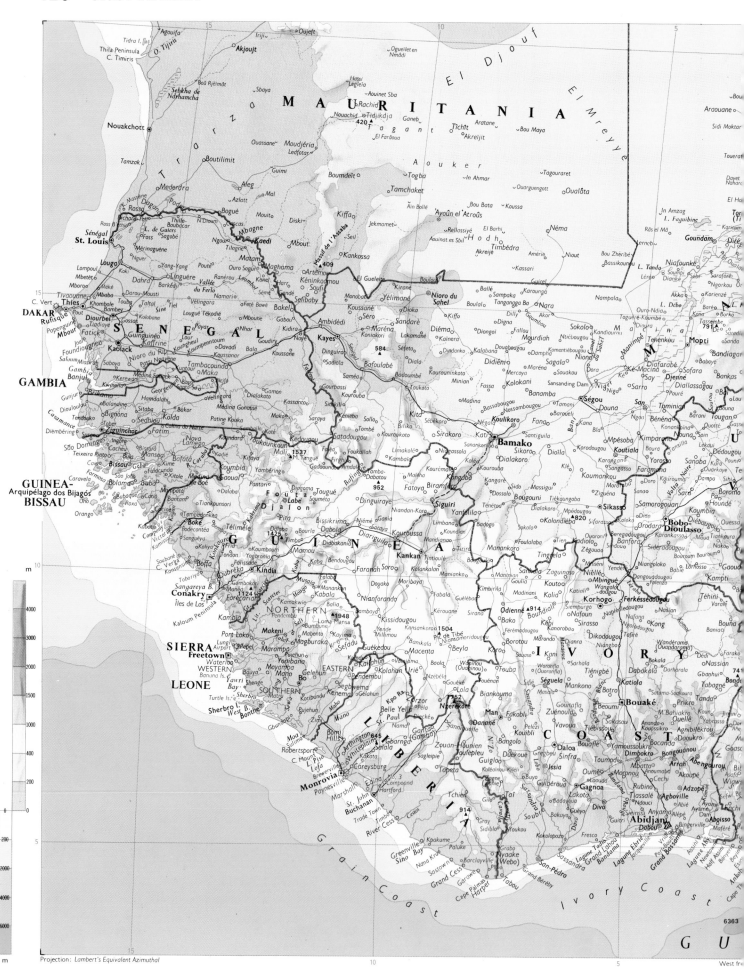

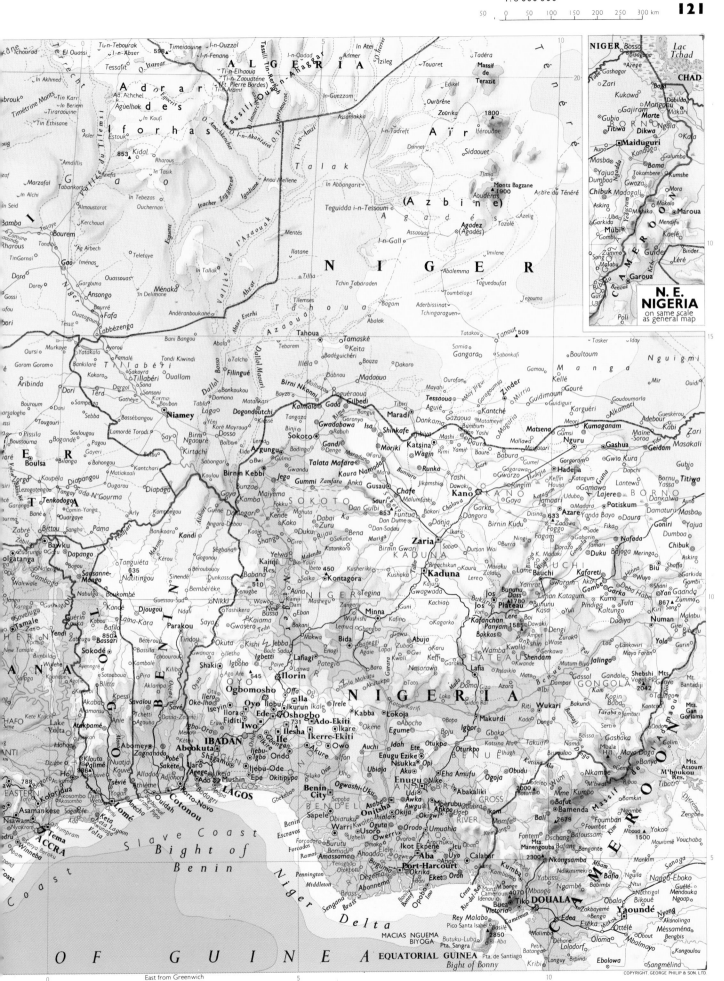

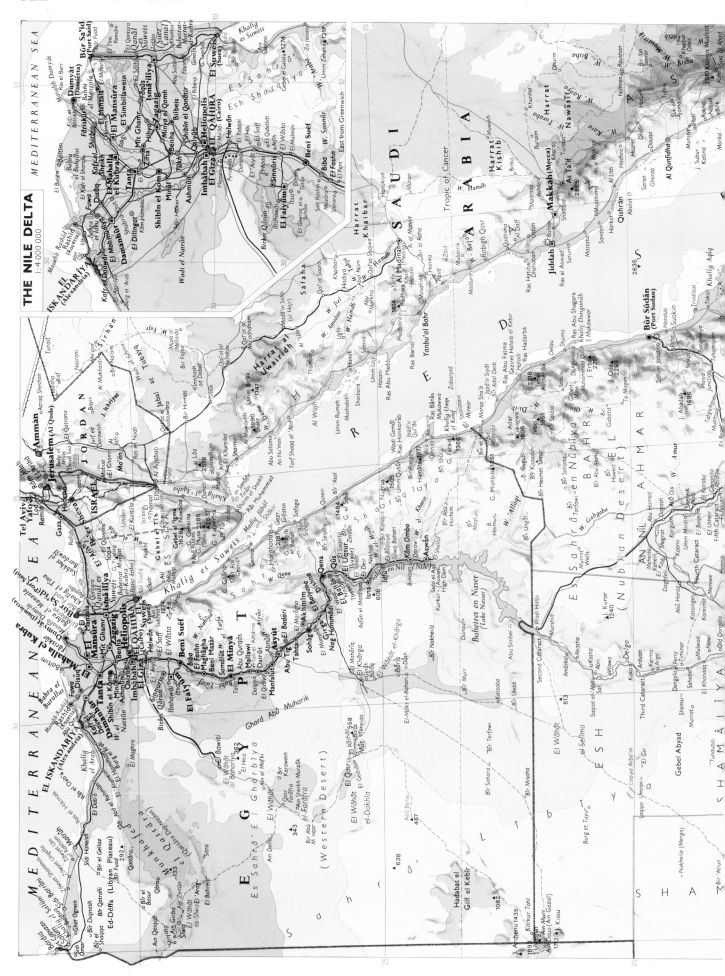

THE NILE DELTA
1:4 000 000

1:8 000 000

50 0 50 100 150 200 250 300 km

Projection: Lambert's Equivalent Azimuthal

East from Greenwich

COPYRIGHT GEORGE PHILIP & SON LTD

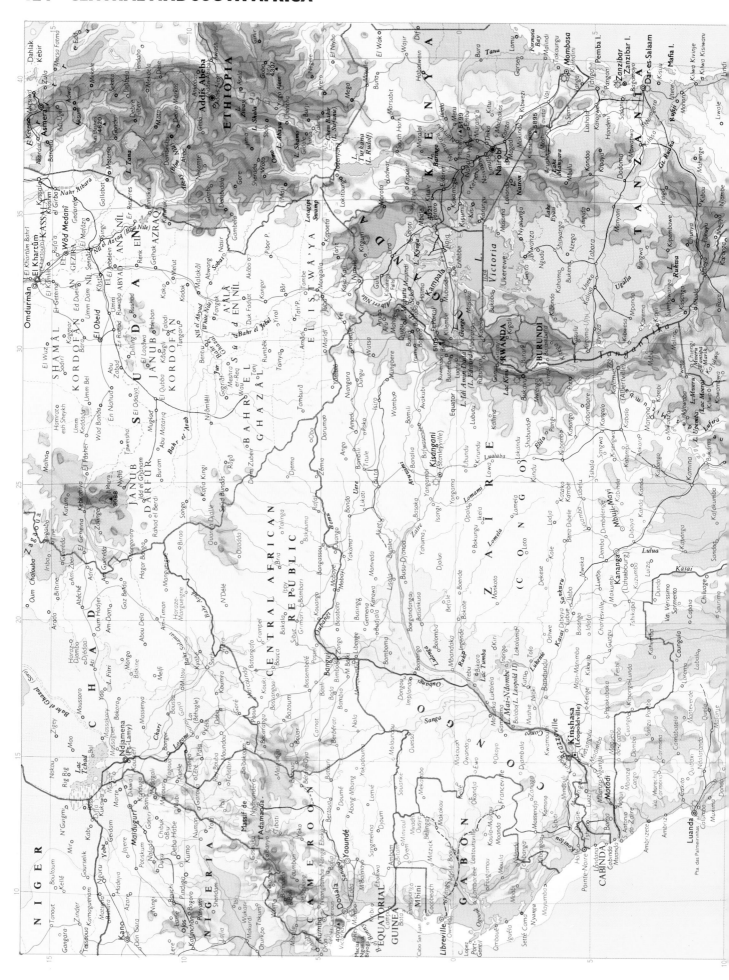

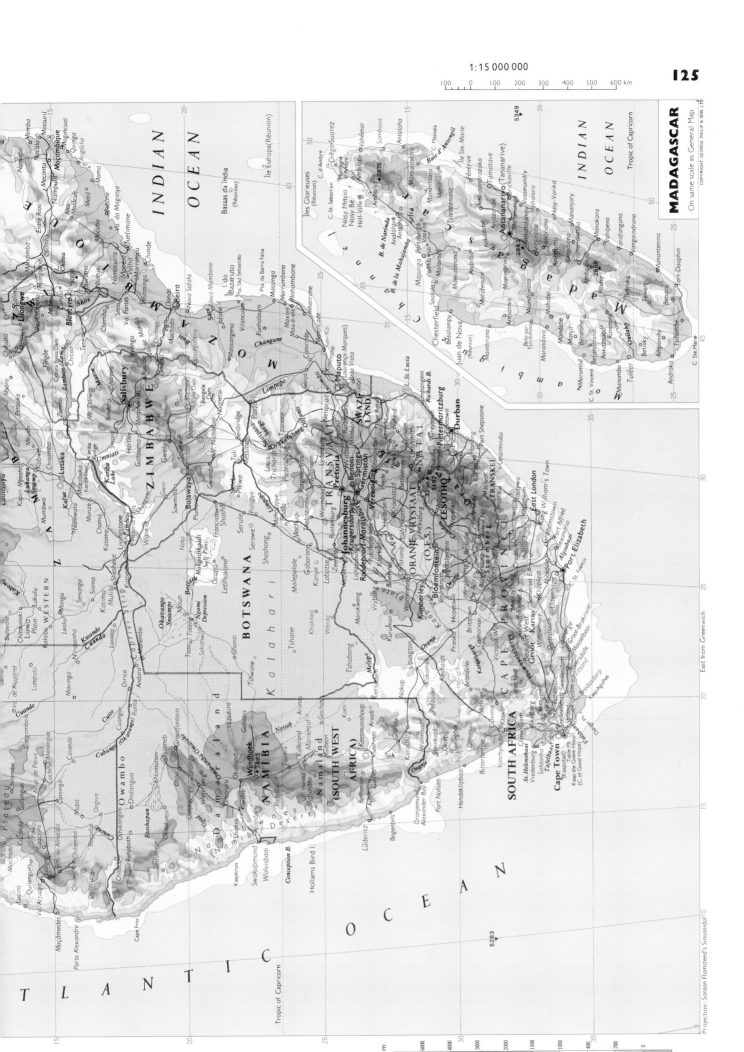

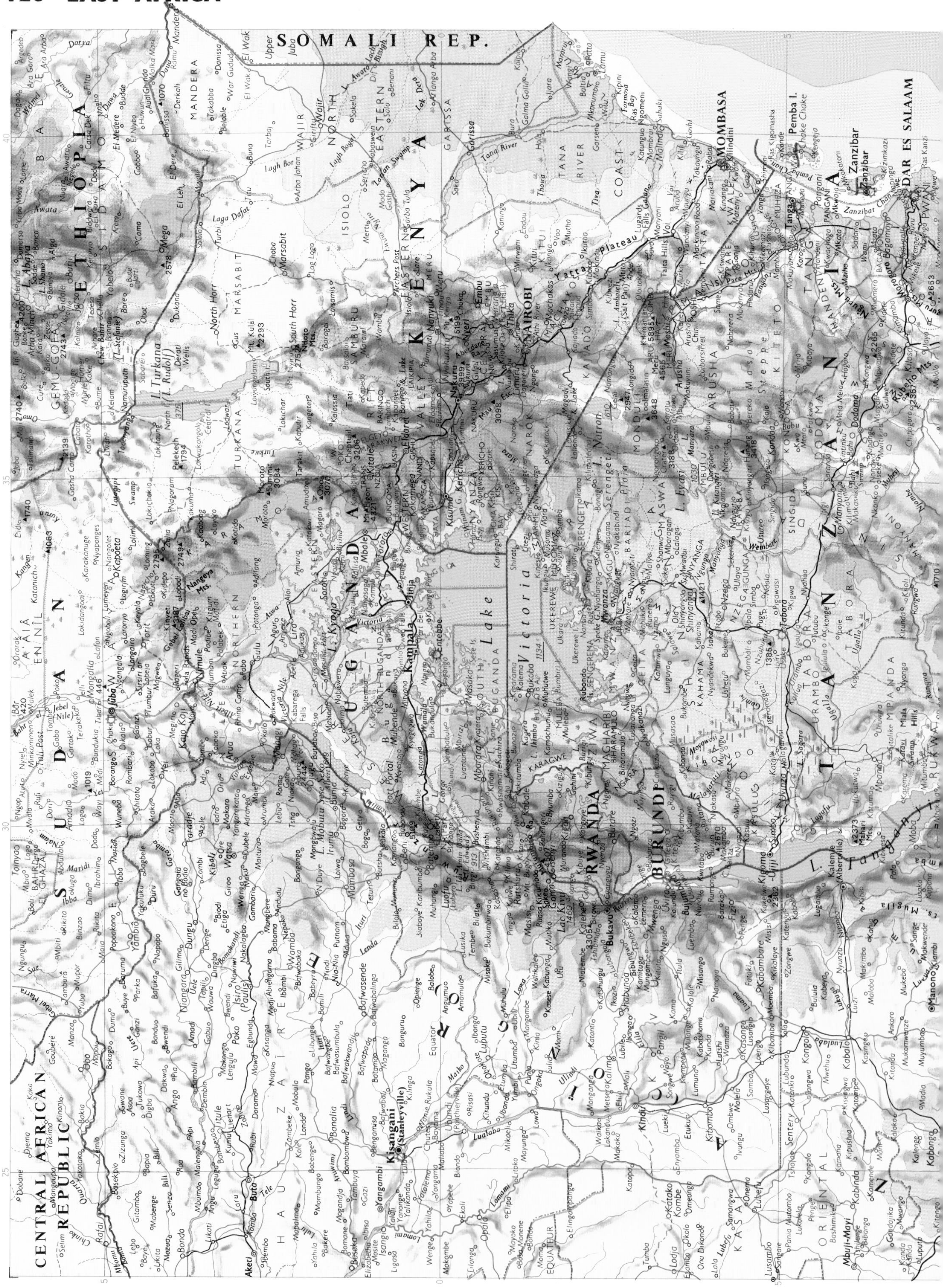

SOMALI REP.

ETHIOPIA

SUDAN

KENYA

UGANDA

TANZANIA

ZAIRE

RWANDA

BURUNDI

CENTRAL AFRICAN REPUBLIC

NAIROBI

MOMBASA

DAR ES SALAAM

Zanzibar

Pemba I.

L. Turkana (L. Rudolf)

Lake Victoria

L. Tanganyika

L. Kyoga

Kampala

Jinja

Entebbe

Kisangani (Stanleyville)

GEMU GOFA

SIDAMO

MARSABIT

ISIOLO

EASTERN

COAST

RIFT VALLEY

NORTHERN

ORIENTAL

KASAI

EQUATOR

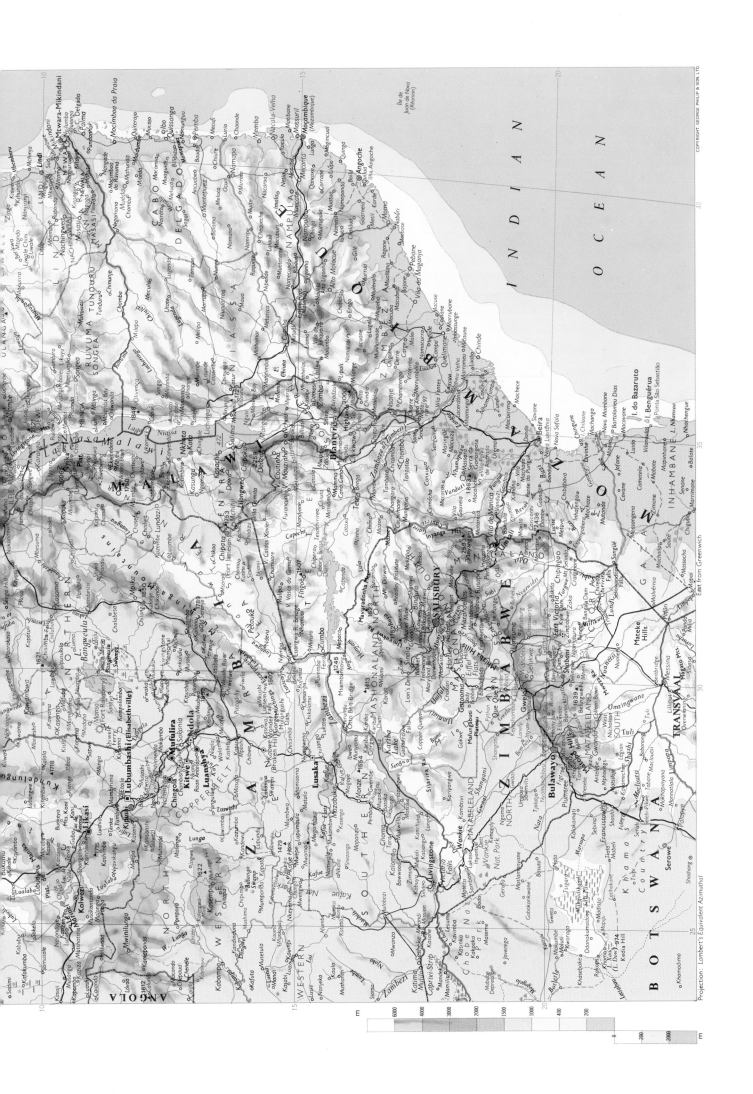

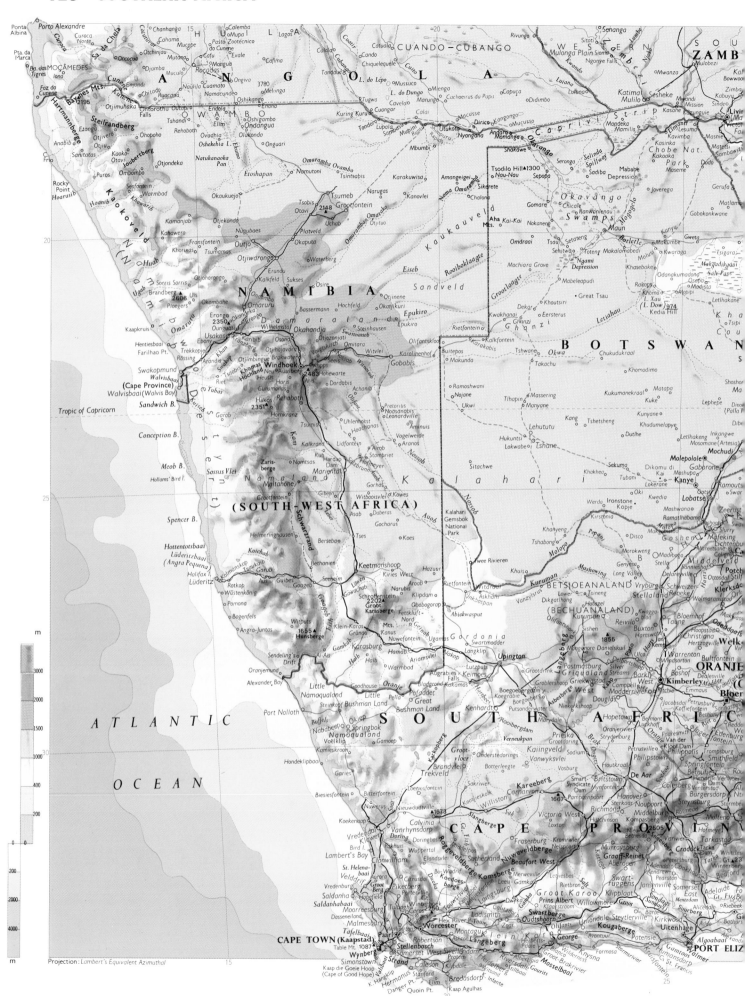

ATLANTIC

OCEAN

Projection: Lambert's Equivalent Azimuthal

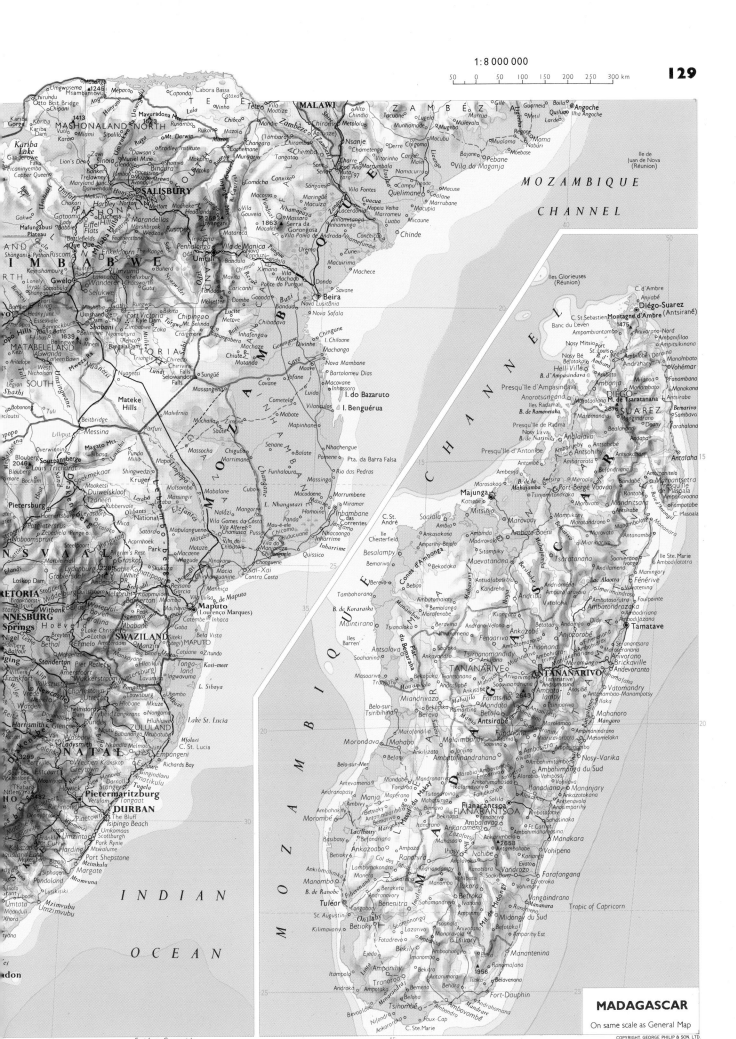

1:8 000 000

50 0 50 100 150 200 250 300 km

MOZAMBIQUE

CHANNEL

INDIAN

OCEAN

MADAGASCAR

On same scale as General Map

COPYRIGHT. GEORGE. PHILIP & SON. LTD.

East from Greenwich

Tropic of Capricorn

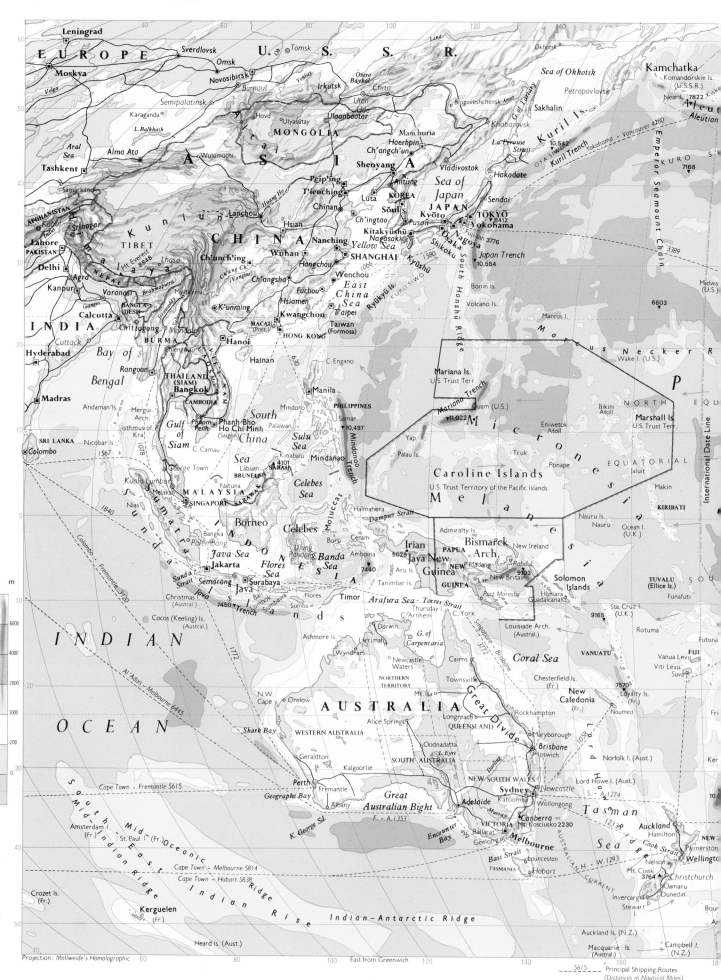

_ _ _ _ _ 5615 _ _ _ Principal Shipping Routes
(Distances in Nautical Miles)

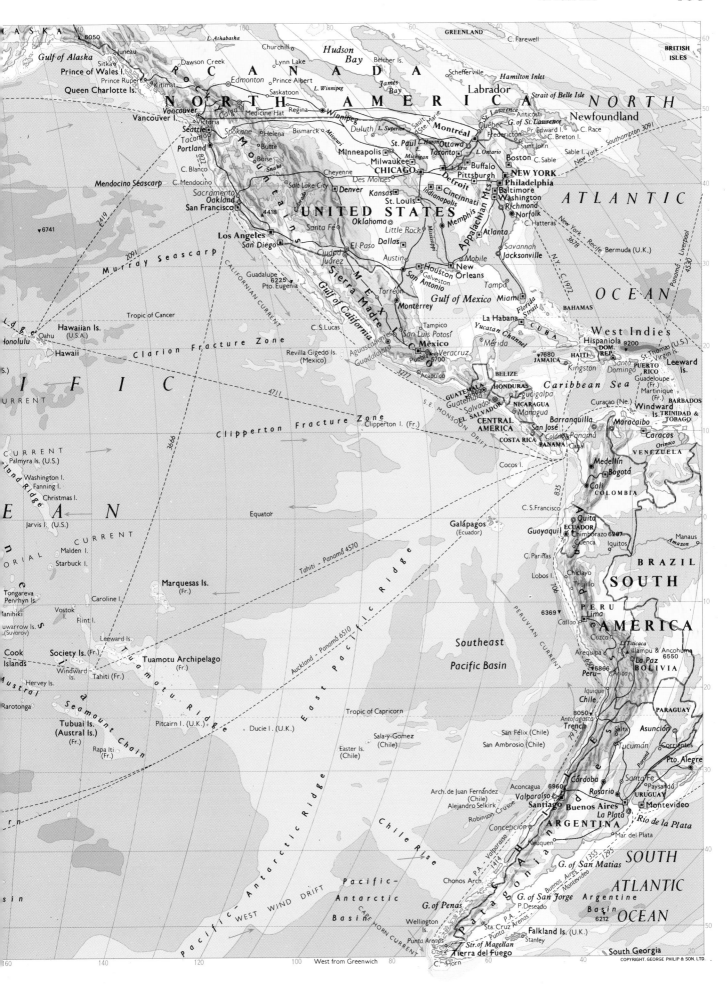

ALASKA   6050   L. Athabaska   Churchill   GREENLAND   C. Farewell   60   BRITISH ISLES

Gulf of Alaska   Juneau   Dawson Creek   Lynn Lake   Hudson Bay   Belcher Is.   C. Farewell   BRITISH ISLES

Prince of Wales I.   Sitka   C A N A D A   James Bay   Scheffervllle   Hamilton Inlet

Prince Rupert   Kitimat   Edmonton   Prince Albert   L. Winnipeg   Labrador   Strait of Belle Isle   NORTH

Queen Charlotte Is.   N O R T H   A M E R I C A   Newfoundland   50

Vancouver   Calgary   Medicine Hat   Regina   Saskatoon   Winnipeg   Duluth   St. Lawrence   Anticosti   Québec   G. of St. Lawrence   Pr. Edward I.   C. Race

Vancouver I.   Victoria   Spokane   Helena   Bismarck   Missouri   Sault Ste. Marie   Montréal   Fredericton   C. Breton I.   Sable I.   New York – Southampton 3091

Seattle   Butte   St. Paul   Ottawa   Toronto   Saint John   Sable I.

Tacoma   Portland   Boise   Snake   Minneapolis   Milwaukee   Michigan   Huron   Buffalo   Boston   C. Sable

Cheyenne   Des Moines   CHICAGO   Erie   Detroit   Pittsburgh   NEW YORK   40

Mendocino Seascarp   C. Blanco   C. Mendocino   Salt Lake City   Denver   Kansas   St. Louis   Cincinnati   Philadelphia   A T L A N T I C

Sacramento   4418   Colorado   Kansas   Indianapolis   Washington   Baltimore

Oakland   UNITED STATES   Santa Fé   Oklahoma   Memphis   Richmond   Norfolk

San Francisco   Little Rock   Atlanta   C. Hatteras   New York – Recife 3678   O C E A N

6741   Los Angeles   Santa Fé   Dallas   Mobile   Savannah   Jacksonville   Bermuda (U.K.)

San Diego   El Paso   Austin   Houston   New Orleans   Jacksonville

Murray Seascarp   2091   Ciudad Juárez   San Antonio   Galveston   Tampa   N.Y.- C. 1972

Guadalupe   6225   M E X I C O   Torreón   Gulf of Mexico   Miami   BAHAMAS

Tropic of Cancer   Pto. Eugenia   Sierra Madre   Monterrey   Florida Strait   CUBA   West Indies

Clarion Fracture Zone   C.S. Lucas   Tampico   La Habana   Yucatan Channel   Hispaniola   9200   St. Thomas (U.S.)

Honolulu   Hawaiian Is. (U.S.A.)   San Luis Potosí   Mérida   JAMAICA   7680   HAITI   DOM. REP.   Virgin Is.

Hawaii   Revilla Gigedo Is. (Mexico)   Aguascalientes   México   Veracruz   Kingston   Santo Domingo   PUERTO RICO   Leeward Is.

Guadalajara   Puebla   5700   Caribbean Sea   Guadeloupe (Fr.)   Martinique (Fr.)

3277   Acapulco   BELIZE   BARBADOS

Clipperton Fracture Zone   GUATEMALA   HONDURAS   S.E. MONSOON DRIFT   Windward Is.   TRINIDAD & TOBAGO

4711   Clipperton I. (Fr.)   Guatemala   Tegucigalpa   NICARAGUA   Curacao (Ne.)   Maracaibo   Caracas

Salvador   Managua   CENTRAL AMERICA   Barranquilla   Orinoco

Cocos I.   San José   Panamá   VENEZUELA

COSTA RICA   PANAMA   Canal   Colón   Medellín   Bogotá

Palmyra Is. (U.S.)   Cali   COLOMBIA

Washington I.   Fanning I.

Christmas I.   835   Quito

Equator   Galápagos (Ecuador)   ECUADOR   Chimborazo 6267   Manaus

Jarvis I. (U.S.)   Guayaquil   Cuenca   Iquitos   Amazon   0

Tahiti – Panamá 4570   C. Pariñas   BRAZIL

Malden I.   Starbuck I.   Chiclayo   SOUTH

Tongareva   Marquesas Is. (Fr.)   Lobos I.   Trujillo   70b

Penrhyn I.   706   PERU   10

Manihiki   Caroline I.   C.S. Francisco   6369   Lima   AMERICA

Suwarrow Is. (Suvorov)   Vostok   Flint I.   Callao   Cuzco

Cook Islands   Society Is. (Fr.)   Southeast   Arequipa   Illampu & Ancohuma 6550

Windward Is.   Tahiti (Fr.)   Pacific Basin   La Paz   6866   BOLIVIA

Hervey Is.   Tuamotu Archipelago (Fr.)   Peru-   Arica   20

Rarotonga   Austral   Iquique   Chile

Tubuai Is. (Austral Is.) (Fr.)   Pitcairn I. (U.K.)   Ducie I. (U.K.)   Tropic of Capricorn   8050   Antofagasta   PARAGUAY

Rapa Iti (Fr.)   Sala-y-Gomez (Chile)   Trench   Salta   Asunción

Seamount Chain   Easter I. (Chile)   San Félix (Chile)   Tucumán   Corrientes

San Ambrosio (Chile)   PA.   Pto. Alegre

Arch. de Juan Fernández (Chile)   Aconcagua 6960   Córdoba   Santa Fé   Paysandú   30

Valparaíso   Rosario   URUGUAY

Alejandro Selkirk   Santiago   Buenos Aires   La Plata   Montevideo

Robinson Crusoe   Concepción   ARGENTINA   Río de la Plata

Neuquen   Mar del Plata

Chonos Arch.   1355   1795   SOUTH

Chile Rise   Buenos Aires   Montevideo

G. of San Matias   ATLANTIC

Pacific-   G. of Penas   P. Deseado   G. of San Jorge   Argentine

Antarctic   Wellington   Basin   6212   OCEAN

Basin   Sta. Cruz Arenas   40

Pacific-Antarctic Ridge   WEST WIND DRIFT   CAPE HORN CURRENT   Str. of Magellan   Falkland Is. (U.K.)

Punta Arenas   Stanley   South Georgia   50

160   140   120   100   West from Greenwich   80   60   40   COPYRIGHT. GEORGE PHILIP & SON. LTD.

1:14 000 000

100 0 100 200 300 400 500 600 km

Wessel
ish Co. Is.
Wilberforce B.
Melville B.
C. Arnhem
P. Bradshaw
Caledon B.
C. Grey
ue Mud B.
Alyangula
Groote Eylandt
C. Beatrice

Gulf of

r Edward Pellew Group
Vanderlin I.

Carpentaria
Bight

rroloola
Mornington
I.
C. van
Diemen
Wellesley Is.
Bentinck I.

N

Y

BARKLY
stral Downs

Camooweal
Dobbyn

Burketown
Normanton
Croydon
Einasleigh
Forsyth

Thursday I.   Banks I.
Prince of Wales I. C. York
Newcastle B.
Endeavour Str.
P. Musgrave
Shelburne B.
Duifken Pt. Weipa C. Grenville
Albatross B. Temple B.
Archer C. Weymouth
Cape C. Direction
Holroyd

York
Peninsula
Coleman
Coen

Mitchell

Chillagoe Mareeba

CORAL

SEA

CORAL

SEA ISLANDS

TERRITORY

Misima I.
Louisiade
Archipelago
Rossel I.
Tagula I.

Rennell

San Cristóbal

10

Princess Charlotte B.
C. Melville Bathurst B.
Osprey Rf.
C. Flattery
C. Bedford Cooktown
C. Tribulation
Trinity Bay
Mossman
C. Grafton
Cairns
Atherton
Bartle Frere 1612
Innisfail

Great Barrier Reef

15

Gilbert
Normanton
Croydon
Dobbyn
Mount Isa
Kajabbi

Leichhardt
Norman
Gregory Ra.

Newcastle
Ra.

Einasleigh
Forsyth

Hinchinbrook I.
Ingham Palm Is.
Halifax B.

Lihou Rfs
& Cays.

Mary
Kathleen
Cloncurry
Duchess
Urandangi
Dajarra

Julia Cr.
Richmond

Flinders

Selwyn
Selwyn Range
LANDSBOROUGH

Pentland
Hughenden

Charters
Towers

FLINDERS

Townsville
C. Cleveland
C. Bowling Green
Ayr Home Hill

Proserpine Bowen
Collinsville Whitsunday I.
Netherdale Cumberland Is.
Mackay

Bird I.

20

QUEENSLAND

Winton
Boulia

Muttaburra

Great Dividing
Belyando

Peak Ra. Isaac Broad Sd.
1274
St. Lawrence
C. Palmerston
C. Townshend
Townshend I.

Swain
Rfs.

Saumarez Rf.

Chesterfield Is.

Bellona Rfs.

PACIFIC

Diamantina

Bedourie

Longreach
Ilfracombe Barcaldine Alpha
CAPRICORN

Aramac
Clermont
Emerald
Blackall Nogoa

Drummond Ra.

Springsure
1312
Expedition Ra.
Dawson

Mt. Morgan
Gladstone
Biloela
Monto

Rockhampton
Keppel B.
C. Capricorn
Curtis I.
P. Curtis
Bustard Head

Cato I.

Tropic of Capricorn

OCEAN

Thomson
Barcoo

Jundah
Yaraka

Warrego Ra.

Augathella

Theodore

Childers
Burnett

Bundaberg
Hervey
Sandy C.
Bay
Fraser I.

Windorah
Adavale

L. Yamma
Yamma

Quilpie
Charleville
Mitchell
Roma

Taroom Gayndah
Wandoan Maryborough
Murgon Pialba
WARREGO Miles Wondai
Condamine Dalby
Kingaroy
Nanango

Gympie

Bribie I.
Nambour

25

Cooper Creek
Streszlecki Cr.

Grey Range

Thargomindah

Wyandra
Cunnamulla

BALONNE
St. George

Moonie

Toowoomba

Ipswich
Brisbane

Moreton B.

Moreton I.
Southport
N. Stradbroke I.

r
rt

L. Eyre
(North)
on-52

L.
Gregory
L. Blanche

Tibooburra

Paroo

Paroo
Chan.

Dirranbandi

Mungindi

Goondiwindi

Warwick

Stanthorpe

Tenterfield
Casino
Lismore
C. Byron
Ballina

RALIA

L. Eyre (South)
L. Callabonna

Bourke

Barwon
Walgett

Gwydir

Mac Intyre

Moree
Warialda

Inverell Glen
Innes
The Round Mountain
Grafton
Clarence

30

Leigh Creek
omera
Pimba
Copley

Flinders

St. Mary's Pk.
1089
Hawker

L. Frome

NEW

SOUTH

Coonamble

Narrabri
Gilgandra

Liverpool
Plains

Liverpool Ra. 1585

Narrambri

Tamworth
Gunnedah

New England Ra.

Armidale

Kempsey
Macleay
Port Macquarie

Coffs
Harbour

Taree
Barrington Tops

WALES

Lord Howe I.

Torrens
es
Pt. Augusta

Mt. Brown
965
rendum
Hill

Main Barrier Ra.
BARRIER
Broken Hill
Menindee

Wilcannia

Cobar
Nyngan

Dubbo

Bogan

Castlereagh

Mudgee

Wellington

Singleton
Maitland
Cessnock

Muswellbrook
Sugarloaf Pt.
P. Stephens

Newcastle

Darling

Ivanhoe

Roto

Condobolin
Hillston Cargelligo

Parkes
Forbes

Orange
Bathurst

Lithgow
Katoomba
Penrith

Hawkesbury R.

anges
Quorn
hyalla

C. Northumberland
Port Fairy
Warrnambool

Discovery B.
C. Bridgewater

Colac

Port. Phillip
Phillip I.
Wonthaggi

Bass
King I.

Strait

Hunter I.
C. Grim
Sandy C.
Macquarie Harb.

Burnie
Zeehan Mt. Ossa 1617
Queenstown

TASMANIA

Low Rocky Pt.
P. Davey

Devonport

Ulverstone
Beaconsfield
Mt. Ossa 1621
Great L.
New
Norfolk
Hobart

Scottsdale
Launceston
Ben Lomond
St. Marys
Freycinet
Penin.

Tasman Penin.
C. Arthur
Storm B.
Bruny I.
S.E. Cape

Cape Barren I.
C. Portland Flinders I.
Furneaux
Group
Clarke I.

35

OCEAN

TASMAN

SEA

140
145
150
155
160

1:60 000 000

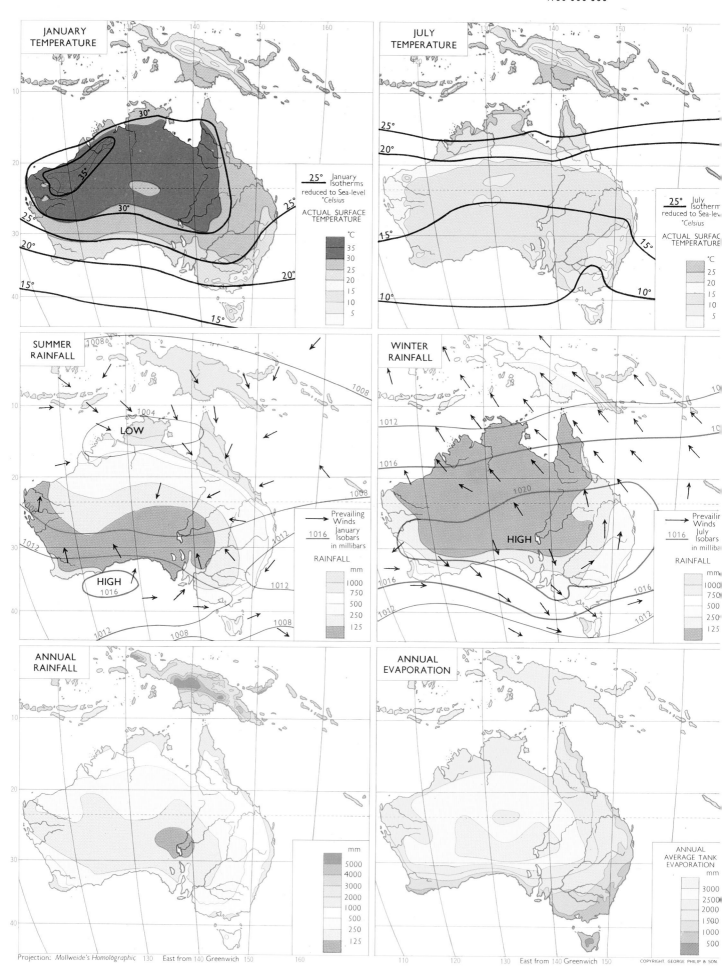

JANUARY
TEMPERATURE

25° January
Isotherms
reduced to Sea-level
°Celsius

ACTUAL SURFACE
TEMPERATURE

°C
35
30
25
20
15
10
5

JULY
TEMPERATURE

25° July
Isotherm
reduced to Sea-lev
°Celsius

ACTUAL SURFAC
TEMPERATURE

°C
25
20
15
10
5

SUMMER
RAINFALL

LOW

HIGH

→ Prevailing
Winds
January
1016 Isobars
in millibars

RAINFALL

mm
1000
750
500
250
125

WINTER
RAINFALL

HIGH

→ Prevaili
Winds
July
1016 Isobars
in milliba

RAINFALL

mm
1000
750
500
250
125

ANNUAL
RAINFALL

mm
5000
4000
3000
2000
1000
500
250
125

ANNUAL
EVAPORATION

ANNUAL
AVERAGE TANK
EVAPORATION
mm
3000
2500
2000
1500
1000
500

Projection: *Mollweide's Homolographic* 130 East from 140 Greenwich 150 160

110 120 130 East from 140 Greenwich 150

COPYRIGHT GEORGE PHILIP & SON

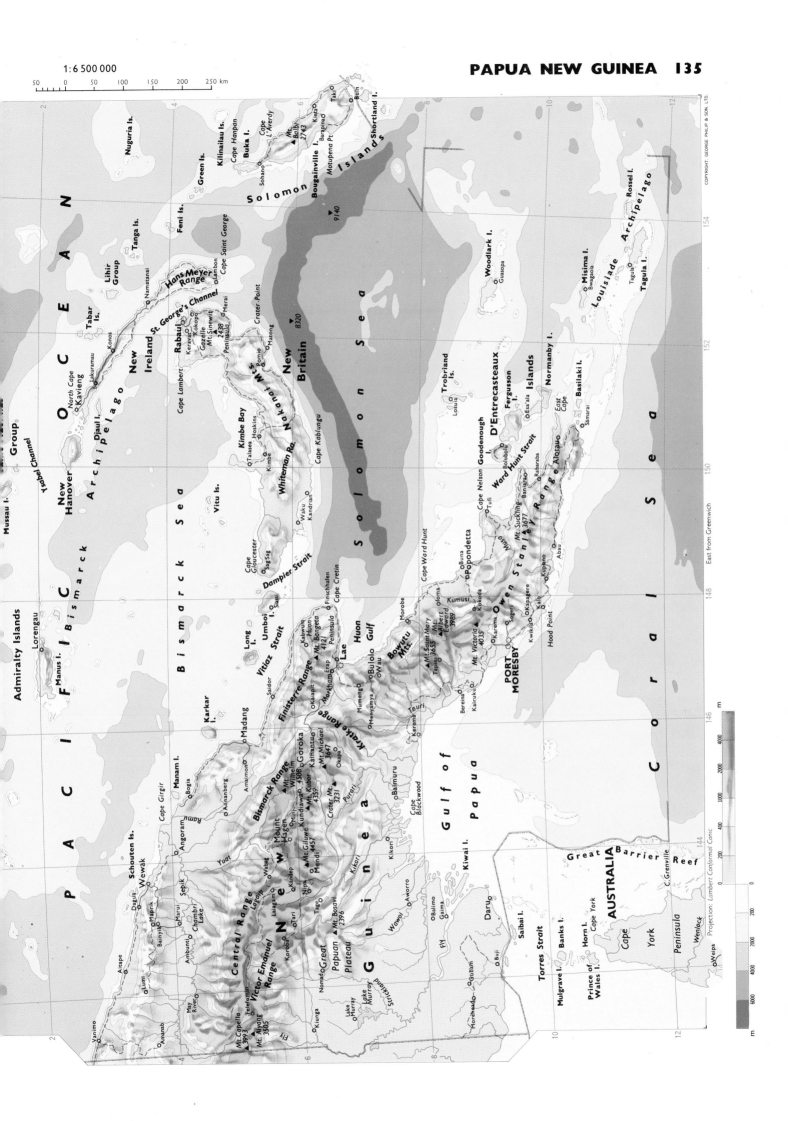

1:6 500 000

50 0 50 100 150 200 250 km

P A C I F I C   O C E A N

Nuguria Is.

Kilinailau Is.
Green Is.
Cape Hanpan
Buka I.
Cape L'Averdy
TakiO
BuinO
Mt. Balbi
2743
Sohano
KietaO
Barapinao
MotupenaPt
Bougainville I.
9140

S o l o m o n   I s l a n d s

Shortland I.

Feni Is.
Tanga Is.
Namatanai
Lambon
Merai
Crater Point

Lihir
Group
Tabar Is.
Hans Meyer
Range
St. George's Channel
Cape Saint George
Matong
Pomio

Mussau I.

Admiralty Islands

New Hanover
Ysabel Channel
North Cape
Kavieng
Archipelago
Lakuraman
Konos

New
Ireland
Djaul I.

Rabaul
Keravat
Kokopo
Gazelle
Peninsula
Mt. Sinewit
2438

New
Britain
8320

Nakanai Ra.
Whiteman Ra.
Kandrian
Waku

S o l o m o n   S e a

Woodlark I.
Guasopa

Misima I.
Bwagaoia

Rossel I.
Tagula
Louisiade Archipelago
Tagula I.

Lorengau
Manus I.
Schouten Is.

B i s m a r c k   S e a

Cape Lambert
Hoskins
Talasea
Kimbe
Kimbe Bay

Vitu Is.

Cape Gloucester
Sag Sag
Dampier Strait
Siassi
Cape Cretin
Finschhafen

Long I.
Umboi I.
Vitiaz Strait
Saidor
Kabwum
Huon
Peninsula
Mt. Bangeta
4121

Cape Kablungu

Trobriand
Is.
Losuia

Kitava
D'Entrecasteaux
Goodenough
Islands
Bolubolu
Fergusson
I.
Esa'ala
Normanby I.

East
Cape
Basilaki I.
Samarai

C o r a l   S e a

Karkar I.
Manam I.
Bogia
Cape Girgir
Madang

Bainyik
Maprik
Dagua
Wewak
Angoram
Ramu
Annanberg
Amaimon

Finisterre Range
Erap
Lae
Markham
OkaiainO
Mumeng
Bulolo
Wau
Menyamya

Huon
Gulf
Morobe

Kratke Range

Boyutu Mts.
Tauri
Keramo

Cape Ward Hunt
Buna
Popondetta
Kokoda
Kumusi
Kapapere
Sogeri

Mt. Suckling
3677
Banijao
Rabaraba
Ward Hunt Strait
Tufi
Cape Nelson

Owen Stanley Range
Abau
Alotau

Mt. Wilhelm
4508
Goroka
Kainantu
Mt. Michael
3647
Okapa

Bismarck Range
Mt. Hagen
Mt. Kubor
4359
Kundiawa
Crater Mt.
3231
Purari

Mt. Giluwe
4457
Mendi
Nipa
Kandep
Tago

N e w

G u i n e a

Central Range
Victor Emanuel Range
Mt. Capella
3993
Mt. Aiyang
3605
Telefomin
May
River
Yanimo
Aitape
Lumi
Amanab

Lake
Murray
Kiunga
Fly
Nomad
Great
Papuan
Plateau
Mt. Bosavi
2396

Kikori
Kikori
Baimuru
Cape
Blackwood
G u l f   o f   P a p u a

PORT
MORESBY
Mt. Victoria
4035
Mt. Albert
Edward
3989
Mt. Saint Mary
3655
Tapini
Bereina
Kairuku
Karema
Kwikila
Hood Point

Kiwai I.
Daru
Balimo
Gaima
Morehead
OBuji
Wowoi
Aworro

Torres Strait
Saibai I.
Mulgrave I.
Banks I.
Prince of
Wales I.
Horn I.
Cape York
Cape
York
Peninsula
C. Grenville

A U S T R A L I A
Great Barrier Reef
Weipa

East from Greenwich

Projection: Lambert Conformal Conic

m
4000
2000
1000
400
200
0
200
2000
4000
6000
m

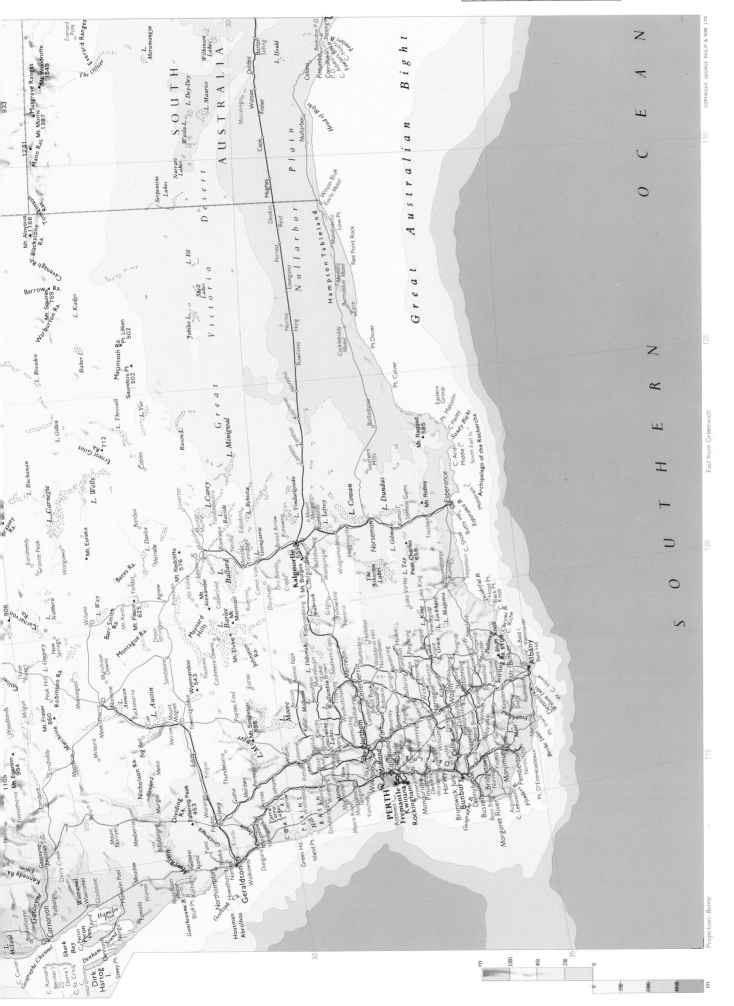

1:8 000 000

50 0 50 100 150 200 250 300 km

SOUTHERN OCEAN

S O U T H

A U S T R A L I A

Great Victoria Desert

Nullarbor Plain

Hampton Tableland

Great Australian Bight

PERTH
Fremantle
Kwinana
Rockingham

Kalgoorlie
Esperance

Geraldton

Albany

COPYRIGHT GEORGE PHILIP & SON, LTD.

East from Greenwich

Projection: Bonne

m
1000
400
200
0

m
0
200
2000
4000

Projection: *Alber's Equal area with two standard parallels*

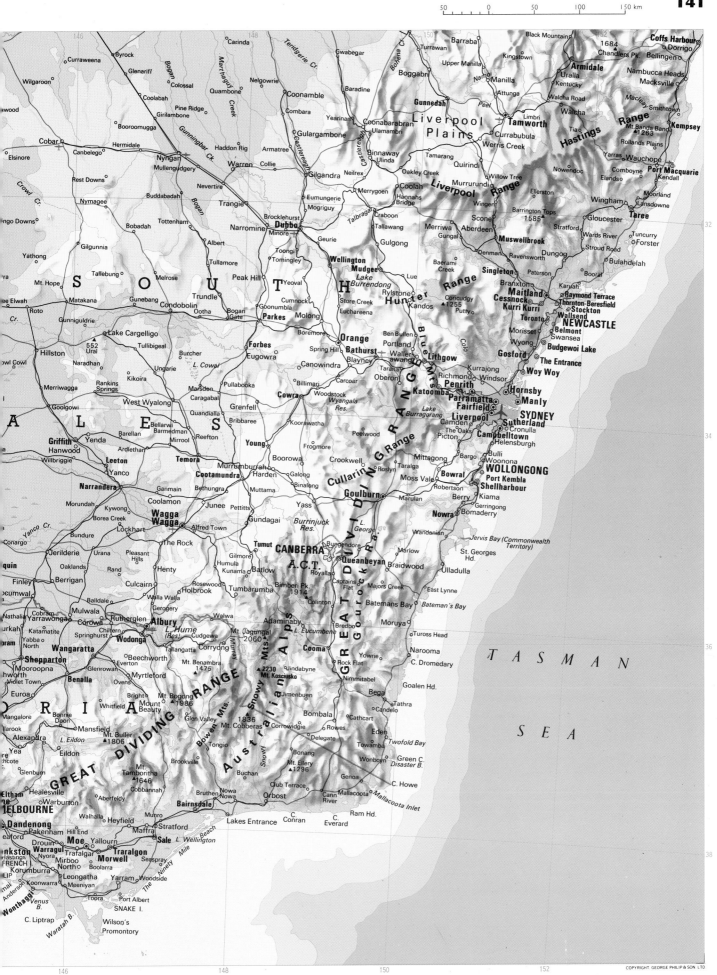

1 : 4 000 000

50   0   50   100   150 km

1:3 500 000

20 0 20 40 60 80 100 km

JANUARY
TEMPERATURE
1:25 000 000

ACTUAL SURFACE
TEMPERATURE
°C
20
15
10
5
0

20° Isotherms
reduced to Sea-level
°Celsius

JULY
TEMPERATURE
1:25 000 000

TASMAN

SEA

Ahipara B.
Hokianga Harb.

C. Maria
van Diemen
North C.
Parengarenga Harb.
C. Reinga
Ninety Mile Beach
Rangaunu B.
Doubless B.
Whangaroa Harb.
Bay of Islands
Cavalli I.
C. Brett
Poor Knights Island
Whangaruru Harb.
Whangarei
Whangarei Harb.
Bream Head
Bream Bay
Hen & Chickens Islands
Bream Tail
Dargaville
Needles Point
Port Fitzroy
Lit. Barrier I.
Great Barrier I.
C. Rodney
C. Barrier
Cuvier I.
Kawau I.
Mercury Is.
Mercury B.
Haurakai Gulf
Port Charles
C. Colville
Coromandel
Coromandel Peninsula
Birkenhead
Takapuna
Devonport
AUCKLAND
Mt. Roskill
Onehunga
Mt. Wellington
Manukau
Papakura
Pukekohe
Manukau Harb.
Whangamata
Mayor I.
Thames
Waihi
White I.
C. Runaway
Te Kaha
Hicks Bay
East C.
Hamilton
Cambridge
Tauranga
Mt. Maunganui
Bay of Plenty
Matata
Whakatane
Ohiwa Harbour
Opotiki
Raukumara Ra.
Te Araroa
Waipiro
Tokomaru Bay
Raglan Harb.
Frankton
Morrinsville
Matamata
Te Puke
Rotorua
Te Karaka
Tolaga Bay
Aotea Harb.
Te Awamutu
Putaruru
L. Tarawera
Mt. Tarawera 1111
Ormond
Gisborne
Poverty Bay
Kawhia Harb.
Tokoroa
KAINGAROA STATE FOREST
Murupara
Galatea
Tuaheni Pt.
Tirua Pt.
Te Kuiti
Rangitaiki
Waikare Iti
Waikaremoana
North Taranaki Bight
Taumarunui
Lake Taupo
Taupo
Frasertown
Mahia Peninsula
Portland I.
New Plymouth
Mt. Egmont
Stratford
C. Egmont
Ruapehu 2796
NAT. PARK
Ahimanawa Ra.
Kaweka Ra.
Hawke Bay
Napier
Taradale
Clive
C. Kidnappers
Hastings
Havelock North
Hawera
South Taranaki Bight
Waverley
Ruahine Ra.
Waipawa
Waipukurau
Wanganui
Marton
Feilding
Dannevirke
Woodville
Palmerston North
Manawatu
Foxton
Levin
Masterton
Carterton
Otaki
Kapiti I.
Paraparaumu
Paekakariki
Mauriceville
Castlepoint
Upr. Hutt
Lr. Hutt
WELLINGTON
Petone
Wainuiomata
Aorangi Mts. 983
Martinborough
Flat Pt.
C. Palliser
Palliser Bay

Golden Bay
C. Farewell
Farewell Spit
Separation Pt.
D'Urville Island
Stephens I.
French Pass
Tasman Bay
Nelson
Stoke
Picton
Cloudy B.
Blenheim
Richmond Ra.
MARLBOROUGH
Kaikoura Ra.
Seaward Kaikouras
C. Campbell

SUMMER AND
WINTER RAINFALL
mm
1000
750
500
250

1012 Isobars
in millibars
→ Prevailing Winds

SUMMER
RAINFALL
November to April
1:25 000 000

WINTER
RAINFALL
May to October
1:25 000 000

m
3000
2000
1000
400
200
0
200
2000
m

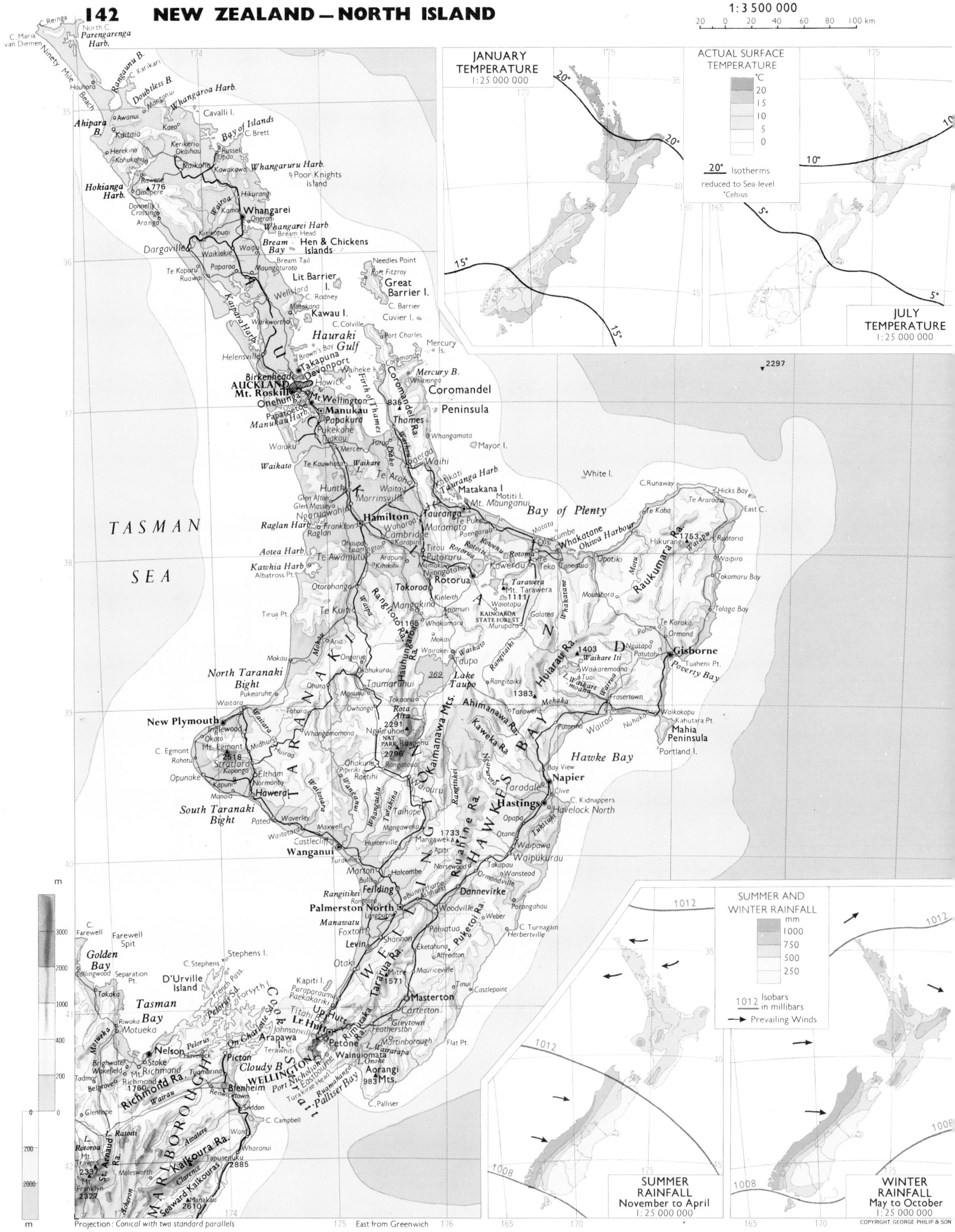

Projection: Conical with two standard parallels

East from Greenwich

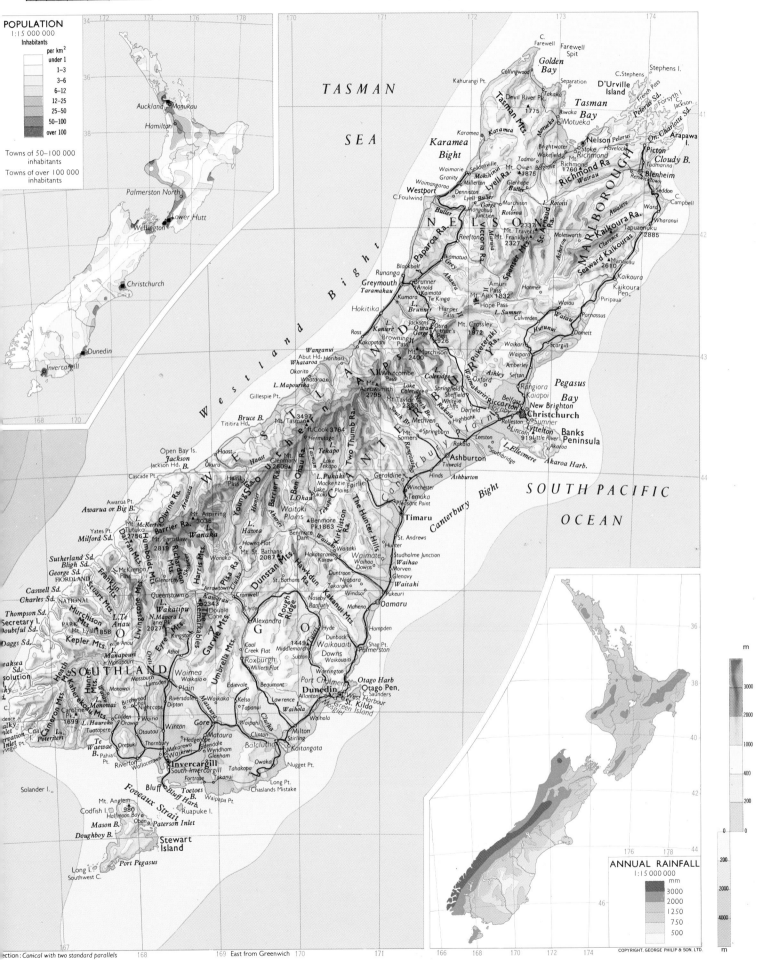

1 : 3 500 000

20 0 20 40 60 80 100 km

POPULATION

1 : 15 000 000

Inhabitants per km²

	under 1
	1–3
	3–6
	6–12
	12–25
	25–50
	50–100
	over 100

Towns of 50–100 000 inhabitants

Towns of over 100 000 inhabitants

ANNUAL RAINFALL

1 : 15 000 000

mm

	3000
	2000
	1250
	750
	500

Projection: Conical with two standard parallels

East from Greenwich

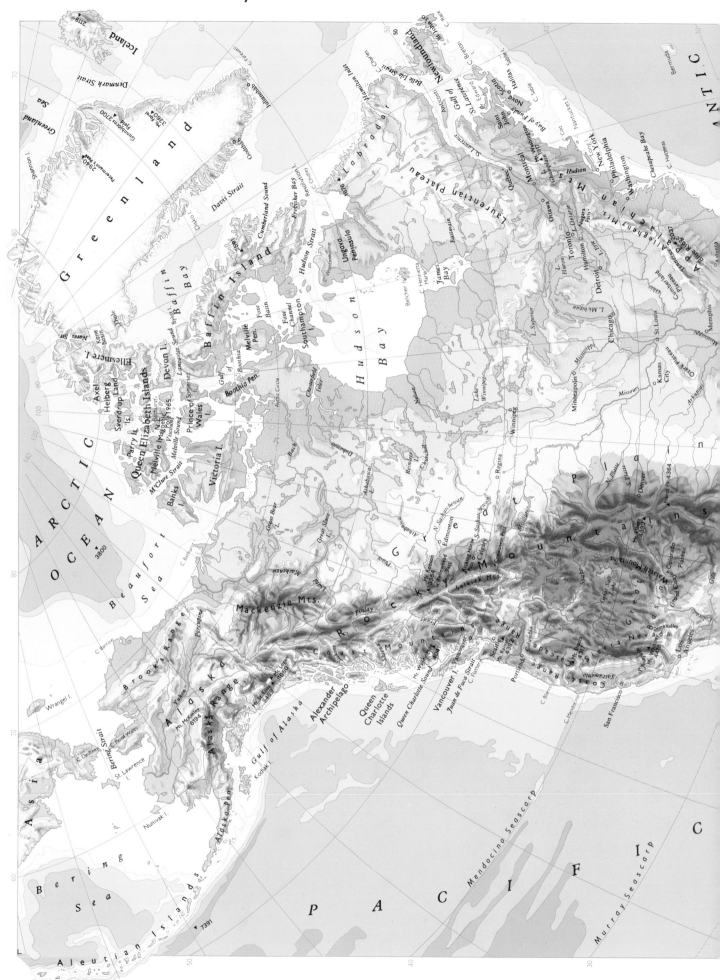

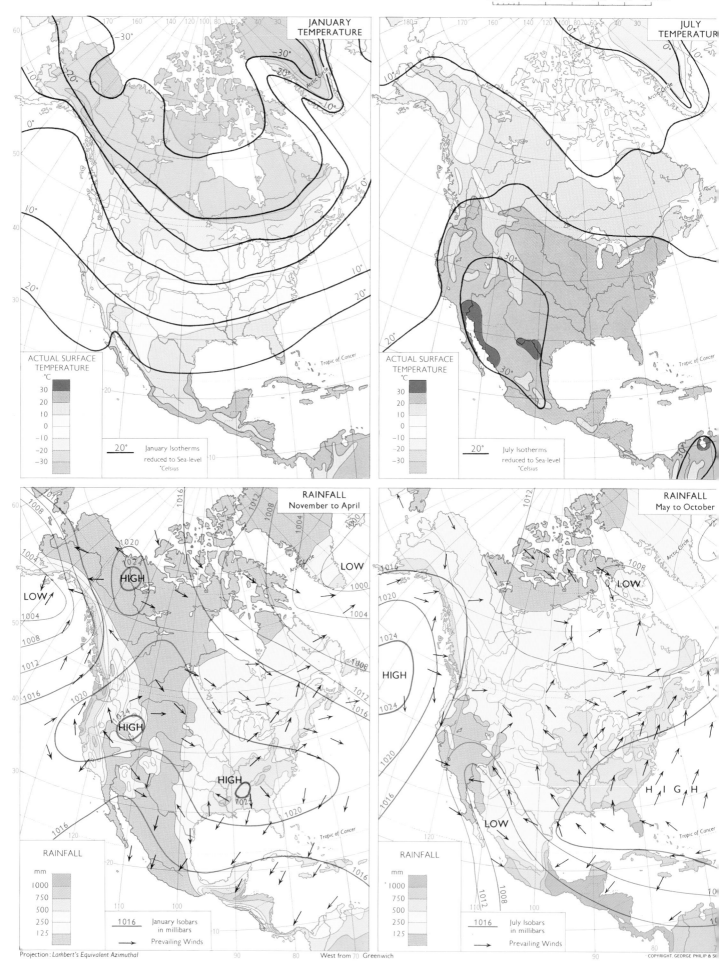

1:70 000 000

500   0   500   1000   1500   2000   2500 km

JANUARY
TEMPERATURE

JULY
TEMPERATURE

ACTUAL SURFACE
TEMPERATURE
°C
30
20
10
0
−10
−20
−30

—20°— January Isotherms
reduced to Sea-level
°Celsius

ACTUAL SURFACE
TEMPERATURE
°C
30
20
10
0
−10
−20
−30

—20°— July Isotherms
reduced to Sea-level
°Celsius

Tropic of Cancer

Arctic Circle

RAINFALL
November to April

RAINFALL
May to October

LOW

HIGH

LOW

HIGH

HIGH

LOW

HIGH

LOW

H I G H

RAINFALL

mm
1000
750
500
250
125

—1016— January Isobars
in millibars
→ Prevailing Winds

RAINFALL

mm
1000
750
500
250
125

—1016— July Isobars
in millibars
→ Prevailing Winds

Projection : Lambert's Equivalent Azimuthal

West from Greenwich

COPYRIGHT. GEORGE PHILIP & SON

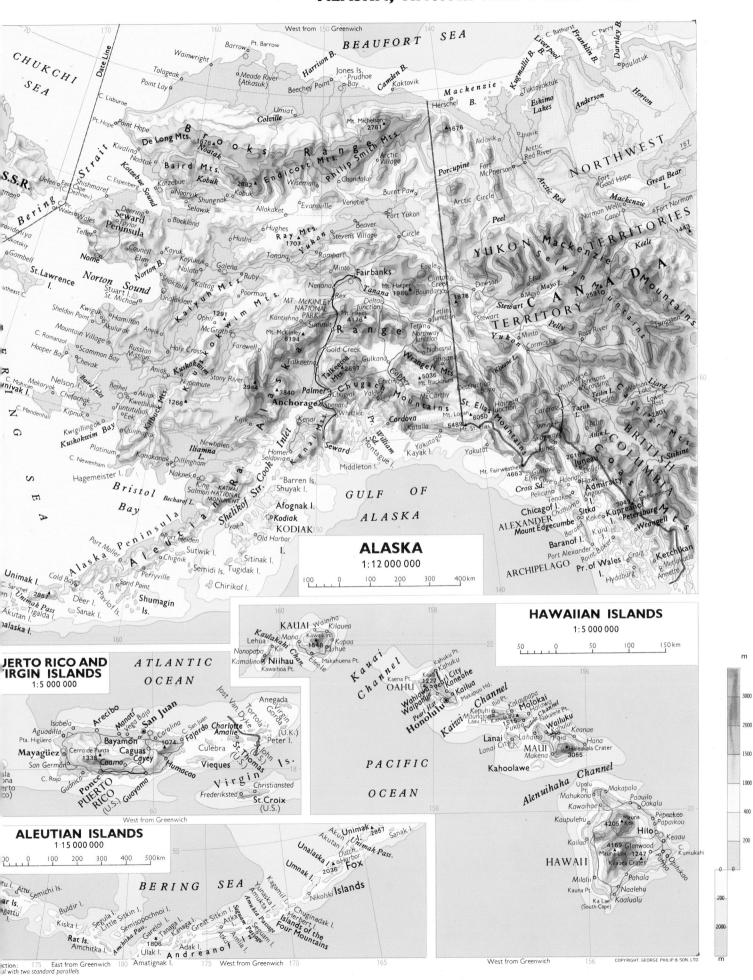

ALASKA

1:12 000 000

100   0   100   200   300   400km

HAWAIIAN ISLANDS

1:5 000 000

50   0   50   100   150km

PUERTO RICO AND VIRGIN ISLANDS

1:5 000 000

ALEUTIAN ISLANDS

1:15 000 000

0   100   200   300   400   500km

COPYRIGHT GEORGE PHILIP & SON LTD.

m
3000
2000
1500
1000
400
200
0
200
2000
m

ALASKA
1:30 000 000

Projection: Bonne

1:15 000 000

100   0   100   200   300   400   500   600 km

GREENLAND

ATLANTIC

BAFFIN BAY

Davis Strait

Cumberland Peninsula

Cumberland Sd.

Frobisher Bay

Hudson Strait

Ungava Bay

Ungava Peninsula

COAST OF LABRADOR

NEWFOUNDLAND

QUEBEC

James Bay

St. John's

Gulf of St. Lawrence

PR. EDWARD I.

NOVA SCOTIA

NEW BRUNSWICK

MAINE

Halifax

MONTRÉAL

Québec

OTTAWA

TORONTO

NEW HAMPSHIRE

Boston

NEW YORK

VERMONT

MASS.

CONN.

RHODE I.

NEW YORK

Buffalo

PENNSYLVANIA

NEW JERSEY

DETROIT

Cleveland

OHIO

INDIANA

OCEAN

West from Greenwich

COPYRIGHT. GEORGE PHILIP & SON. LTD.

N. W. T E R R I T O R I E S

M A N I T O B A

H U D S O N   B A Y

North Belcher Is.
Baker's Dozen Is.
Kugong I.
Belcher Islands
Flaherty
Tukarak I.
Innetalling I.
Nastapoka Is.
Nastapoka
L. Guillaume-Delisle
L. à l'Eau Claire
Petite Baleine
Lac Bier

Stupart
Knee L.
Gods
Niskibi
Black Duck
Fort Severn
Winisk
Wabuk Pt.
C. Lookout
C. Henrietta Maria
Long I.
Merry I.
Poste-de-la-Baleine
Grand Baleine

Edmund L.
Gods L.
Sharpe L.
Red Sucker L.
Sill L.
Sachigo
Beaverstone
Beaver
Severn
Winisk
Sutton
Kinushseo
Lakitusaki
Lake River
Pte. Louis-XIV
Burton
Roggan
Roggan River
Julian L.
Craven L.
Kanaaupscow

J A M E S   B A Y

Ponask L.
Sachigo Lake
Bearskin Lake
Severn L.
Severn
Fawn
Winisk
W i n i s k
Shamattawa
Attawapiskat
Attawapiskat
Ekwan Pt.
North Twin I.
South Twin I.
Akimiski I.
Weston I.
Fort George
Castor
Nouveau Comptoir
Yasinski
Sakami
L. Sakami
L. de Corve

Finger L.
Sandy Lake
Sandy L.
Favourable Lake
Big Trout Lake
Shibogama
Wunnummin L.
Chipai L.
Winisk
Ekwan
Missisa L.
Kapiskau
Tredely I.
Charlton
Duncan
Opinaca
L. Opinaca
Lac Rossignol

MacDowell L. 396
Pipestone
North Caribou L.
Mameigwess L.
Attawapiskat
Attawapiskat
Albany
Kinoje
Fort Albany
Rupert R.
Fort Rupert (Rupert House)
Rupert
Némiscau
Boyd L.
Low L.

O N T A R I O

Q

Casummit Lake
Birch L.
Trout L.
Bowman
Cat L.
Central Patricia
Pickle Lake
Otoskwin
Lansdowne House
Missisa
Atikameg
Moosonee
Moose Factory
Nouveau Comptoir
Némiscau
Eastmain
Eastmain
Rupert
Mesgouez
Némiscau
L. Evans
L. Troilus

Hudson
Mamitaki L.
Sturgeon L.
Sioux Lookout
Savant Lake
St. Joseph L.
Fort Hope
Eabamet
Ogoki
Kwataboahegan
Hannah B.
Moose River
Moose Factory
Broadback
Dana
L. Evans
Waswanipi
Opémisca
556
Chibou

L A K E   S U P E R I O R

Duluth
Superior
Ashland
Thunder Bay
Isle Royale
Michipicoten
Sault Ste. Marie
Sudbury
North Bay
Timmins
Kirkland Lake
Rouyn
Noranda
Val-d'Or

W I S C O N S I N

M I C H I G A N

Milwaukee
Green Bay
Madison
Chicago
Rockford
Grand Rapids
Flint
Detroit
Windsor
Toledo
Cleveland

Georgian Bay
Parry Sound
North Bay
Pembroke
Ottawa
Hull
Trois-Rivières
Joliette

L A K E   H U R O N

Lake Huron
Owen Sound
Barrie
Orillia
Peterborough
Kingston
Brockville
Cornwall

L A K E   O N T A R I O

Toronto
Hamilton
St. Catharines
Rochester
Buffalo
Syracuse
London
Niagara Falls

L A K E   E R I E

I N D I A N A

O H I O

P E N N S Y L V A N I A

I L L I N O I S

Lambert's Equivalent Azimuthal

m
1500
1000
400
200
0
200
2000
4000
m

1:7 000 000

50   0   50   100   150   200   250   300 km

COAST OF NEWFOUNDLAND

LABRADOR

QUEBEC

NEWFOUNDLAND

Long Range Mts.

Corner Brook

GULF OF ST. LAWRENCE

Î. d'Anticosti

Îs. de la Madeleine (Quebec)

PRINCE EDWARD ISLAND

Charlottetown

Cabot Strait

SAINT-PIERRE ET MIQUELON (Fr.)

St. John's

Avalon Peninsula

NEW BRUNSWICK

NOVA SCOTIA

Cape Breton Island

MAINE

Fredericton

Saint John

Bay of Fundy

Halifax

Dartmouth

Yarmouth

Sable I. (Nova Scotia)

ATLANTIC OCEAN

BOSTON

Portland

St. Lawrence

West from Greenwich

70   65   60

COPYRIGHT GEORGE PHILIP & SON LTD.

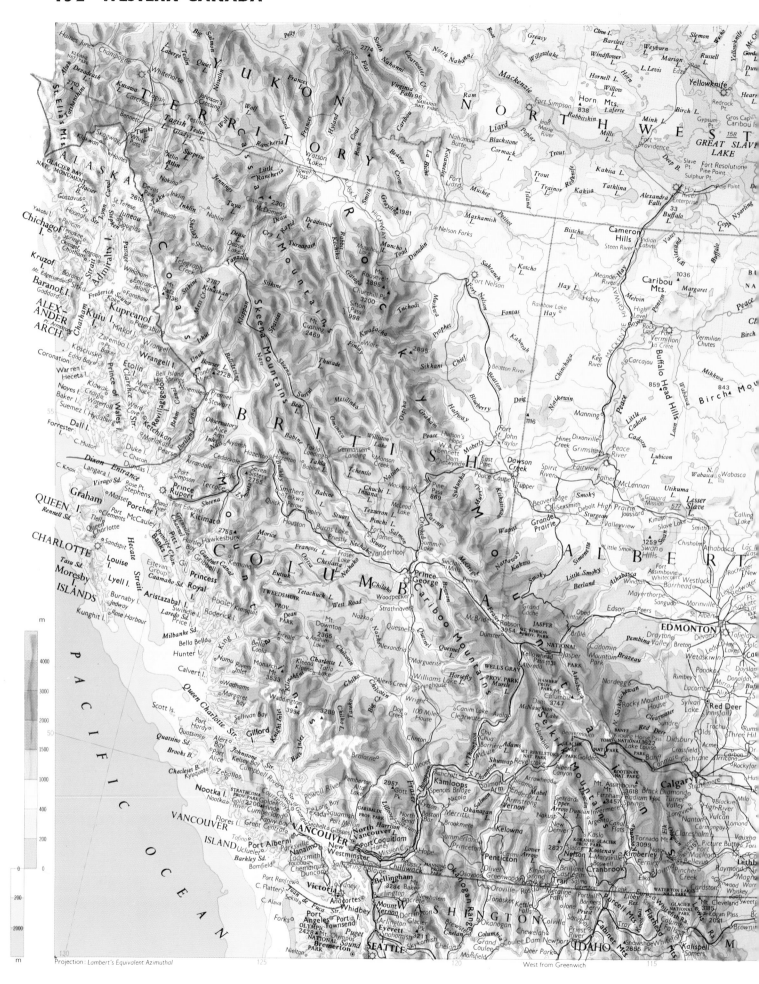

Projection: Lambert's Equivalent Azimuthal   West from Greenwich

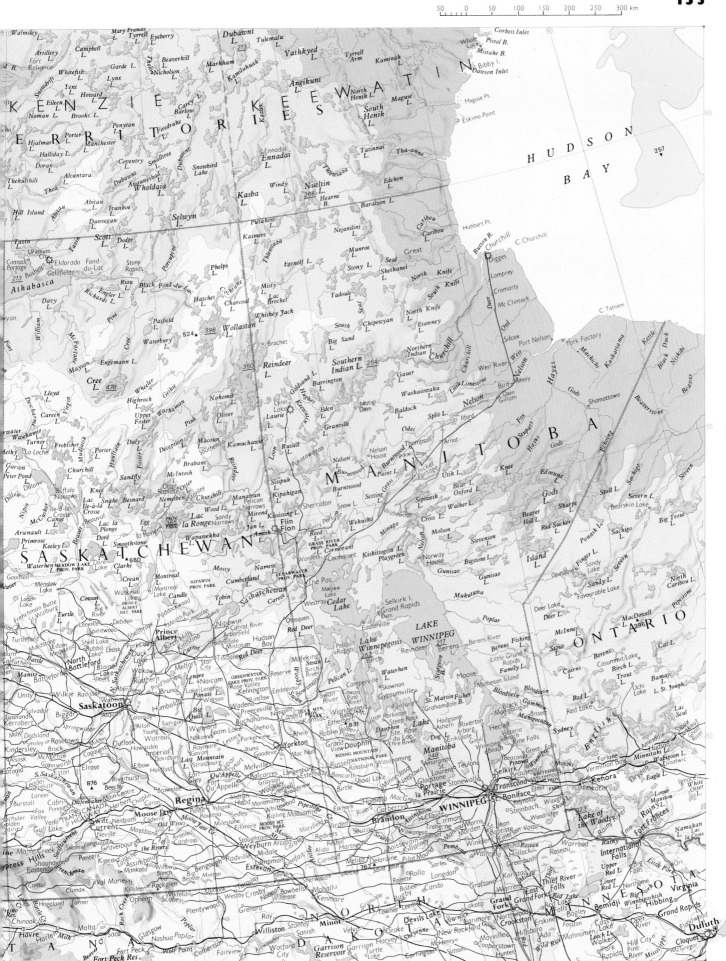

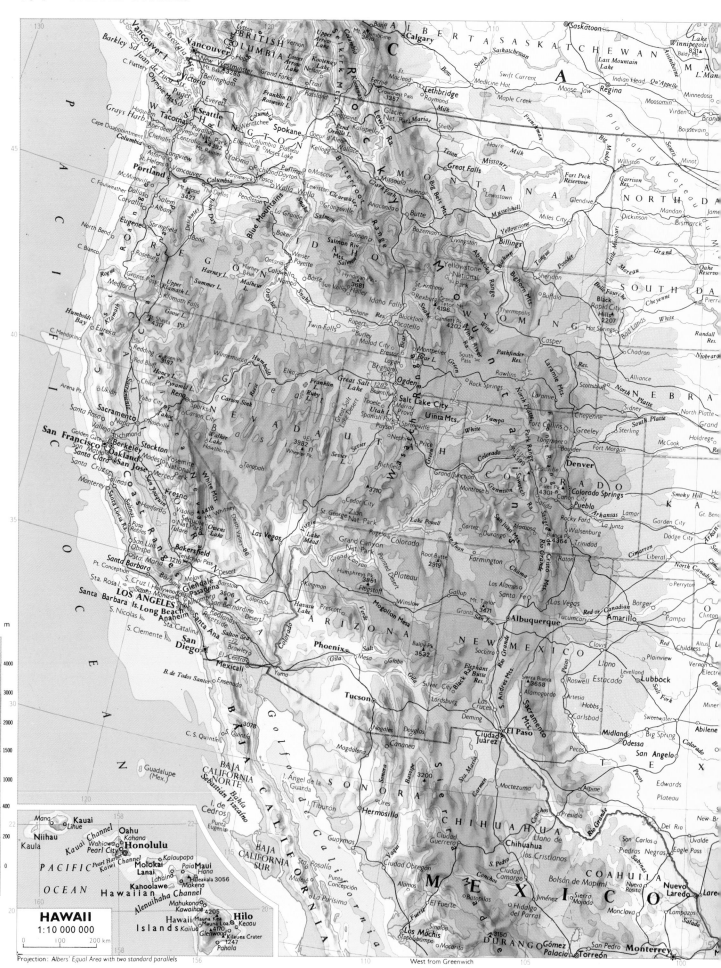

HAWAII
1:10 000 000

0   100   200 km

Projection: Albers' Equal Area with two standard parallels

West from Greenwich

1:12 000 000

100   0   100   200   300   400   500 km

G U L F   O F   M E X I C O

A T L A N T I C   O C E A N

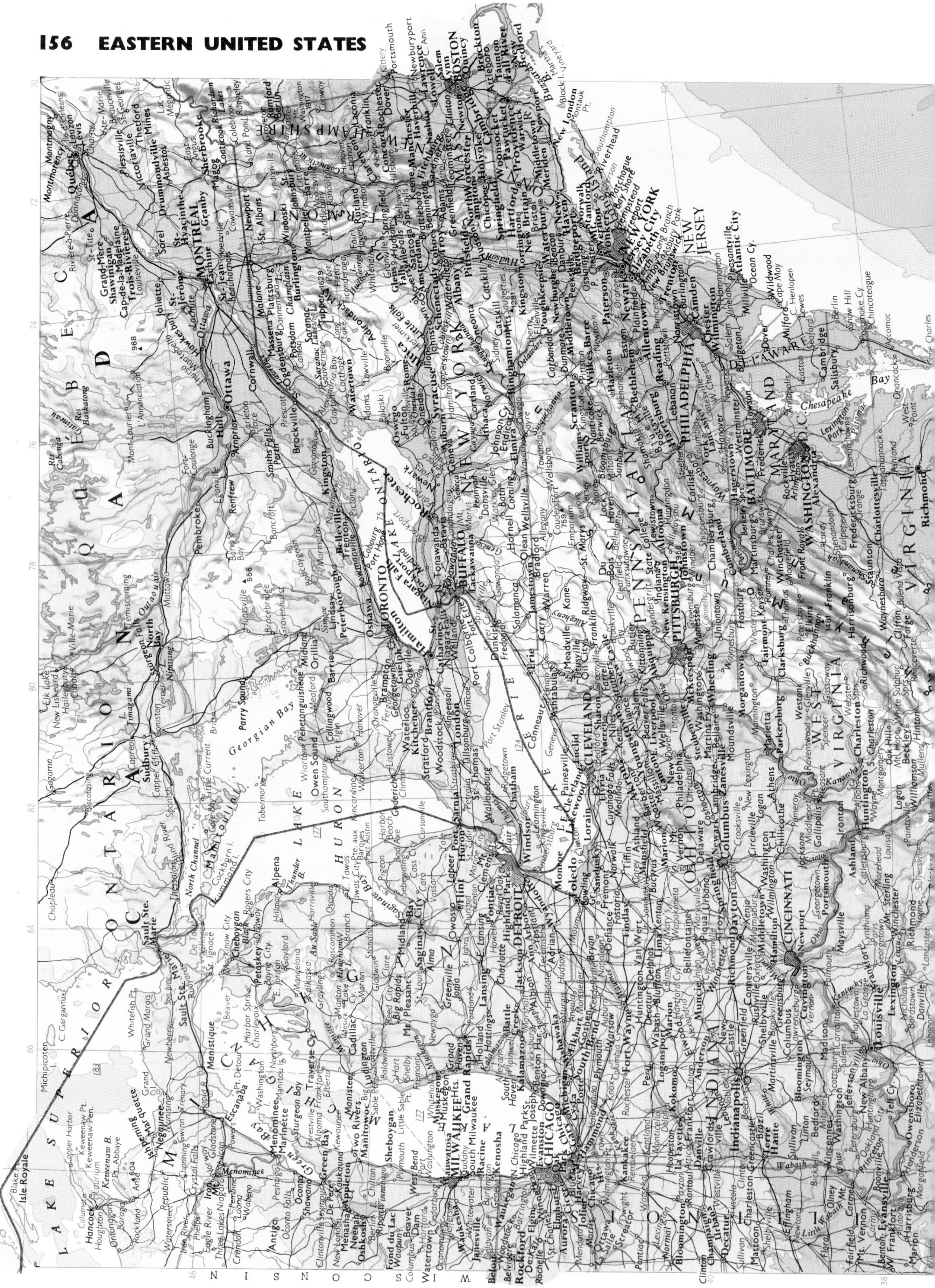

LAKE SUPERIOR
LAKE MICHIGAN
LAKE HURON
LAKE ERIE
LAKE ONTARIO
Georgian Bay
QUEBEC
ONTARIO
MICHIGAN
WISCONSIN
ILLINOIS
INDIANA
OHIO
PENNSYLVANIA
NEW YORK
NEW JERSEY
DELAWARE
MARYLAND
WEST VIRGINIA
VIRGINIA
MONTREAL
OTTAWA
TORONTO
CHICAGO
MILWAUKEE
DETROIT
CLEVELAND
BUFFALO
PITTSBURGH
CINCINNATI
PHILADELPHIA
BALTIMORE
WASHINGTON
BOSTON
NEW YORK CITY

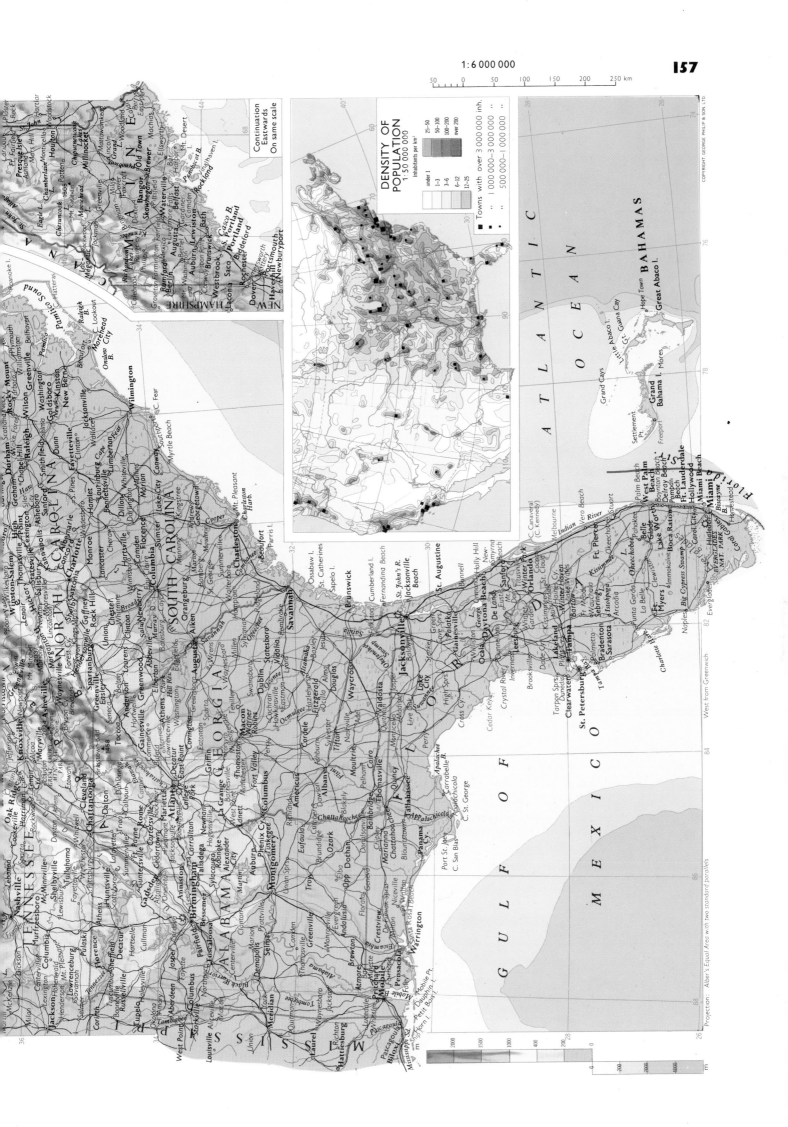

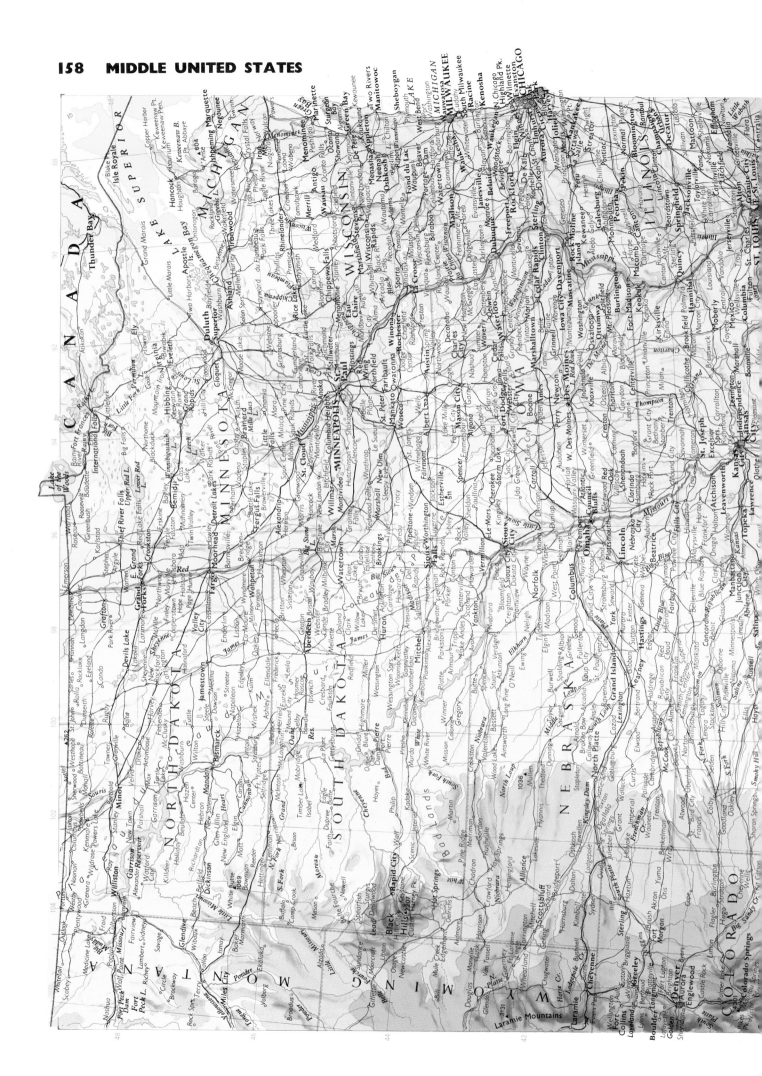

1:6 000 000

0   50   100   150   200   250 km

GULF OF MEXICO

West from Greenwich

Projection: Albers' Equal Area with two standard parallels

COPYRIGHT GEORGE PHILIP & SON LTD

Continuation Southwards on same scale

1:6 000 000

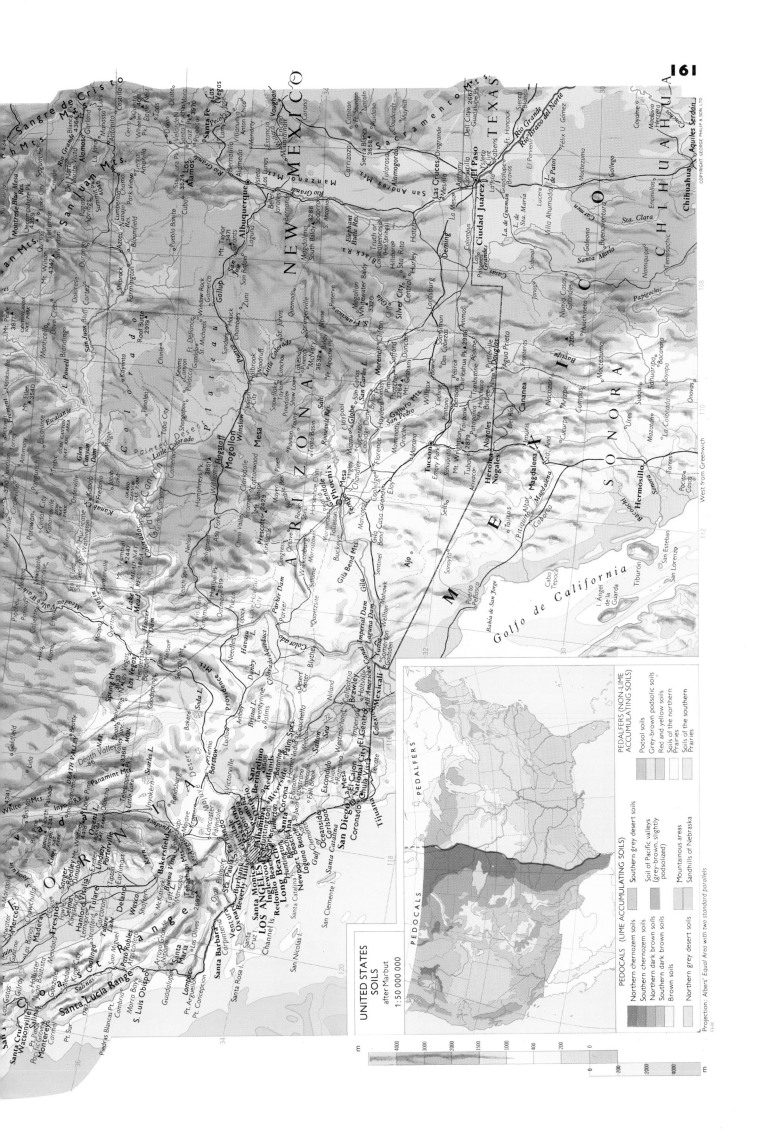

**UNITED STATES
SOILS**

after Marbut

1:50 000 000

PEDOCALS (LIME ACCUMULATING SOILS)

Northern chernozem soils
Southern chernozem soils
Northern dark brown soils
Southern dark brown soils
Brown soils
Northern grey desert soils
Southern grey desert soils
Soil of Pacific valleys
(grey-brown, slightly
podsolized)
Mountainous areas
Sandhills of Nebraska

**PEDALFERS (NON-LIME
ACCUMULATING SOILS)**

Podsol soils
Grey-brown podsolic soils
Red and yellow soils
Soils of the northern
Prairies
Soils of the southern
Prairies

Projection: Albers' Equal Area with two standard parallels

COPYRIGHT GEORGE PHILIP & SON LTD

West from Greenwich

1:3 000 000

20 0 20 40 60 80 100 120 km

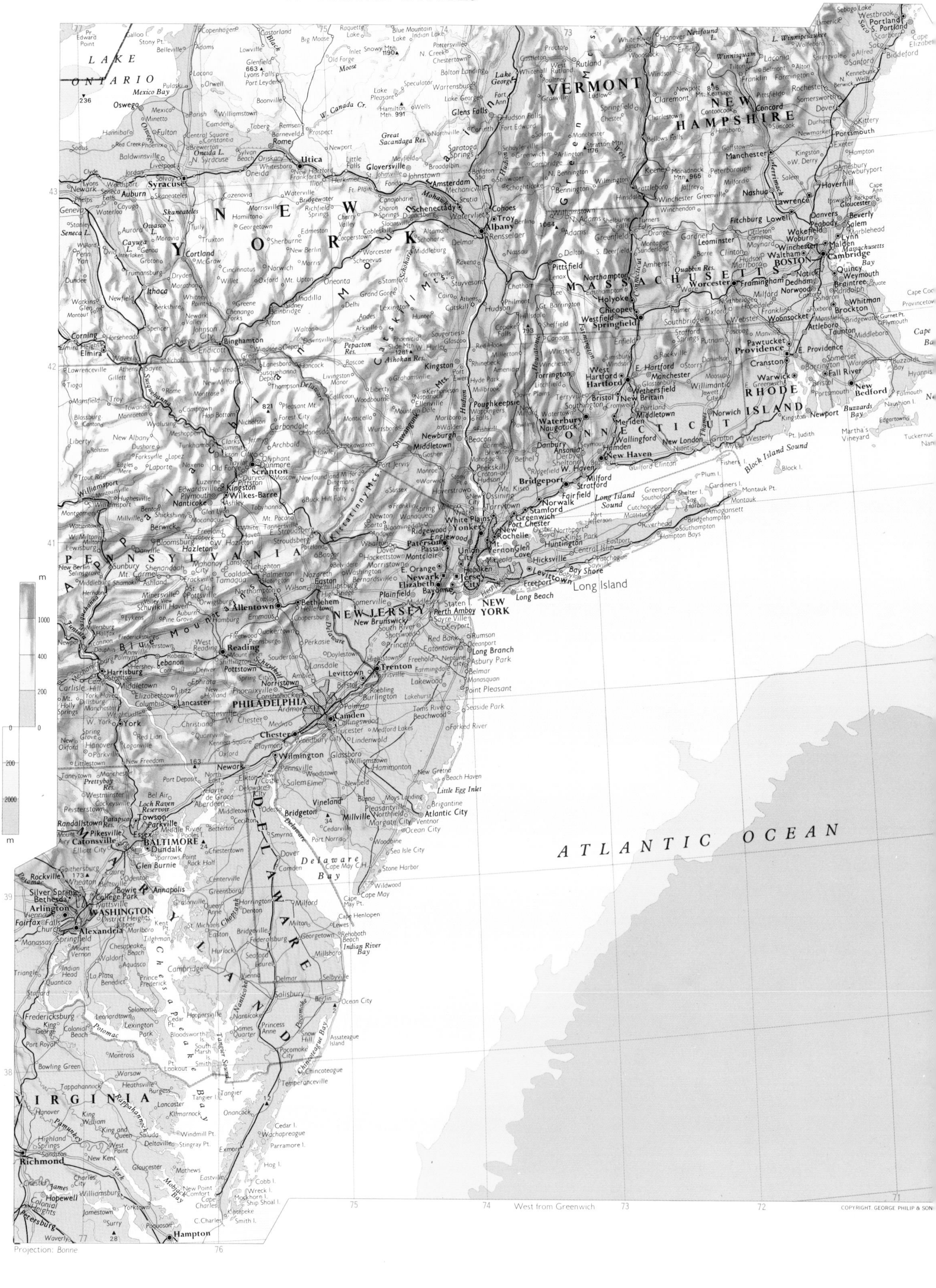

LAKE ONTARIO

NEW YORK

VERMONT

NEW HAMPSHIRE

MASSACHUSETTS

RHODE ISLAND

CONNECTICUT

PENNSYLVANIA

NEW JERSEY

NEW YORK

Long Island

MARYLAND

DELAWARE

VIRGINIA

ATLANTIC OCEAN

Boston
Providence
New York
Philadelphia
Baltimore
Washington
Richmond
Harrisburg
Albany
Scranton
Allentown
Reading
Trenton
Camden
Wilmington
Atlantic City

Delaware Bay

Chesapeake Bay

West from Greenwich

m
1000
400
200
0
200
2000
m

Projection: Bonne

COPYRIGHT. GEORGE PHILIP & SON

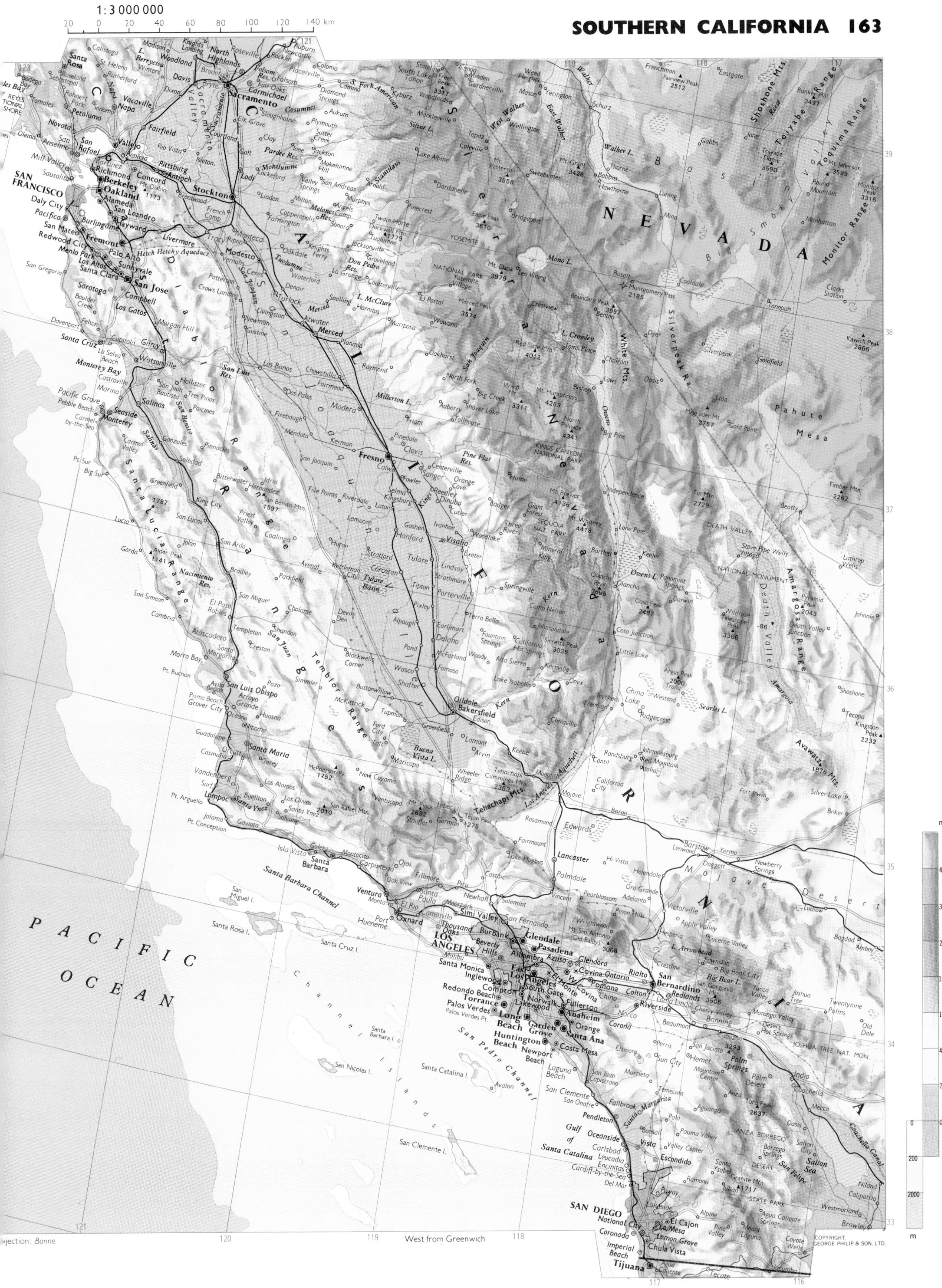

1:3 000 000

20 0 20 40 60 80 100 120 140 km

PACIFIC OCEAN

NEVADA

SAN FRANCISCO
Daly City
Pacifica
San Mateo
Redwood City
Menlo Park
Palo Alto
Sunnyvale
Santa Clara
San Jose
Saratoga
Los Gatos
Campbell
Fremont
Hayward
San Leandro
Alameda
Oakland
Berkeley
Richmond
San Rafael
Novato
Petaluma
Santa Rosa
Napa
Vallejo
Concord
Antioch
Pittsburg
Stockton
Livermore
Modesto
Tracy
Ripon
Turlock
Merced
Los Banos
Chowchilla
Madera
Fresno
Clovis
Sanger
Reedley
Dinuba
Visalia
Tulare
Hanford
Lemoore
Corcoran
Porterville
Delano
Wasco
Shafter
Bakersfield
Oildale
Santa Cruz
Watsonville
Salinas
Monterey
Seaside
Pacific Grove
Carmel-by-the-Sea
Hollister
King City
Paso Robles
San Luis Obispo
Arroyo Grande
Pismo Beach
Grover City
Santa Maria
Lompoc
Santa Barbara
Ventura
Oxnard
Port Hueneme
Thousand Oaks
Simi Valley
San Fernando
Glendale
Burbank
Pasadena
LOS ANGELES
Santa Monica
Beverly Hills
Inglewood
Compton
Torrance
Redondo Beach
Palos Verdes
Long Beach
Garden Grove
Huntington Beach
Newport Beach
Santa Ana
Anaheim
Orange
Costa Mesa
Fullerton
Pomona
Ontario
Riverside
San Bernardino
Redlands
Colton
Corona
Oceanside
Carlsbad
Escondido
Vista
SAN DIEGO
National City
Chula Vista
Imperial Beach
Coronado
Tijuana

YOSEMITE NATIONAL PARK
Mono L.
KINGS CANYON NATIONAL PARK
SEQUOIA NAT. PARK
Mt Whitney 4418
DEATH VALLEY NATIONAL MONUMENT
Mojave Desert
JOSHUA TREE NAT. MON.
ANZA BORREGO DESERT STATE PARK
Salton Sea
Coachella Canal

Sacramento Valley
San Joaquin Valley
Santa Lucia Range
Temblor Range
Tehachapi Mts.
Shoshone Mts.
Toiyabe Range
Monitor Range
White Mts.
Owens L.
Tulare Basin

Santa Barbara Channel
Channel Islands
San Miguel I.
Santa Rosa I.
Santa Cruz I.
Santa Catalina I.
San Clemente I.
San Nicolas I.
San Pedro Channel
Gulf of Santa Catalina

Projection: Bonne   West from Greenwich   COPYRIGHT GEORGE PHILIP & SON. LTD.

m
4000
3000
2000
1500
1000
400
200
0
200
2000
m

PACIFIC

OCEAN

m
4000
3000
2000
1500
1000
400
200
0
0
200
2000
4000

m

REFERENCE TO NUMBERS
1 Federal District   5 México
2 Aguascalientes   6 Morelos
3 Guanajuato   7 Querétaro
4 Hidalgo   8 Tlaxcala

Projection: Bi-polar oblique Conical Orthomorphic   110   West from Greenwich   105

1:8 000 000

50   0   50   100   150   200   250   300 km

GULF   OF

MEXICO

G U L F

UNITED **S T A T E S**

ARKANSAS

MISSISSIPPI

ALABAMA

GEORGIA

FLORIDA

LOUISIANA

TEXAS

Denison
Sherman   Paris   Hope   Camden   Greenville   Tuscaloosa   Opelika
Denton   Greenville   Texarkana   Texarkana   El Dorado   Greenville   Columbus
FORT WORTH   DALLAS   Marshall   Monroe   Vicksburg   Meridian   Selma   Americus   Cordele
Cleburne   Longview   Shreveport   Jackson   Montgomery   Phenix City   Albany   Waycross
Hillsboro   Tyler   Corsicana   Natchez   Laurel   Troy   Chattahoochee   Valdosta
Brownwood   Waco   Palestine   Nacogdoches   Alexandria   Hattiesburg   Dothan   Tallahassee
Temple   Lufkin   Mc Comb   Bogalusa   Mobile   Panama City   Pensacola   Lake City
Huntsville   Trinity   Baton Rouge   Biloxi   Apalachee Bay
Austin   Bryan   Beaumont   Lafayette   NEW ORLEANS   Gulfport   Suwannee
HOUSTON   Port Arthur   Atchafalaya Bay   Breton Sound   C. San Blas
SAN ANTONIO   Rosenberg   Galveston   Terrebonne B.   Mississippi Delta   Clearwater
Victoria

Corpus Christi

O   F

Alice
Kingsville
Laredo

Camargo   Laguna Madre
Mc Allen   Harlingen
Reynosa   Brownsville
M.R. Reynosa   Matamoros
Valle Hermoso   Santa Teresa
San Fernando   Laguna Madre

M E X I C O

CUBA
Guane
La Fé

TAMAULIPAS
Santander-Jiménez
La Pesca
Soto la Marina
Sierra de Tamaulipas
Aldama   Pta. Jerez
Ciudad Mante   La Esperanza
Ciudad Madero
Ciudad Victoria   Tampico
Ciudad Valles   Pánuco
Laguna de Tamiahua
Temapal   Ozuluama   C. Rojo
Tamazunchale   Tantoyuca
Chicontepec   Tuxpan
Chapopote   Poza Rica   Papantla
Rio   Nautla
Huauchinango   Misantla
Tulancingo   Furbero
Teziutlán
MEXICO   Jalapa   Zempoala
Tlaxcala   PUEBLA   Coatepec   Veracruz
Amecameca   Orizaba
Córdoba
Tehuacán   Cosamaloapan   Alvarado
San Andrés   Tlacotalpan
Tuxtla
Acatlán   Coatzacoalcos
Cárdenas   Frontera   Paraíso   Palizada
Minatitlán   Villahermosa
Acayucan   TABASCO
Jesús Carranza   Macuspana
Tlaxiaco   Ixtlán de Juárez   Presa Miguel Alemán
Oaxaca   Monte Albán   Matías Romero
Ocotlán   Tuxtla Gutiérrez   San Cristóbal de las Casas
Tlacolula   Ixtepec   Juchitán   CHIAPAS   Comitán
OAXACA   Tehuantepec   Tonalá   Chiapa
Salina Cruz   Arriaga
Golfo de Tehuantepec   Istmo de Tehuantepec
Huixtla
Tapachula   GUATEMALA

Golfo
de
Campeche

Isla Desterrada
Isla Pérez

Canal de Yucatán
C. San Antonio
Corrientes

Progreso   Pta. Yalkubul   Rio Lagartos   C. Catoche
Dzilam de Bravo   El Cuyo   Pto. Juárez
Dzibilchaltún   Motul   Temax   Tizimín   El Diaz
Mérida   Izamal   Espita   Puerto Morelos
YUCATÁN   Soluta   Chichén Itzá   Valladolid   Isla Cozumel
Maxcanú   Mayapán   Ticul   Cozumel
Calkini   Peto   Vigía Chico
Tenabo   Tekax   B. de la Ascensión
Bolonchenticul
Campeche   Hopelchén   B. del Espíritu Santo
Etznó   Felipe Carrillo Puerto   QUINTANA
San José Carpizo   Pedro Antonio Santos   ROO
Champotón   Juárez   Bacalar   Banco
Chenkán   Chetumal   B. de   Chinchorro
Ciudad del Carmen   Laguna de Términos   Corozal   Chetumal
CAMPECHE   Ambergris Cay
Concepción   Orange Walk
Uaxactún   Turneffe Is.
Benque Viejo   Belize City   BELIZE
Tikal   Belmopan   Stann Creek
L. Petén Itzá   Islas de la Bahía
Flores   Golfo de Honduras   Roatán   Puerto Castilla   Iriona
Maya Mts.   Monkey River   La Ceiba
San Luis   San Antonio   Puerto Barrios   Tela
Punta Gorda   Puerto Cortés   San Pedro Sula   HONDURAS
Livingston   El Progreso
GUATEMALA   Cobán   Zacapa   Santa Barbara
Cuchumatanes   Chiquimula   Juticalpa
Huehuetenango   Jalapa   Tegucigalpa
San Marcos   Totonicapán   Antigua   GUATEMALA

COPYRIGHT GEORGE PHILIP & SON LTD.

GULF OF MEXICO

Fort Myers
Fort Lauderdale
Boca Raton
West Palm Beach
West End
Freeport
Grand Bahama I.
Hope Town
Little Abaco I.
Naples
C. Romano
Everglades
Hialeah
MIAMI
Bimini Is.
Berry Is.
Nassau
New Provid. I.
Andros Town
Dry Tortugas
C. Sable
Florida Bay
Florida City
Key West
Adelaide
(Havana) LA HABANA
MARIANAO
San Antonio de los Baños
Guanabacoa
Santo Cruz del Norte
Matanzas
Canal Nicolas
Cay Sal Bank
Pinar del Río
Bahía Honda
Guanajay
Güines
Jovellanos
Cárdenas
Colón
Sagua la Grande
Santa Clara
Caibarién
Placetas
Morón
Cienfuegos
Trinidad
Sancti-Spíritus
Ciego de Avila
I. de Pinos
Nueva Gerona
Archipiélago de los Canarreos
Júcaro
Tunas de Zaza
Florida
Camagüey
Cayman Islands (Br.)
Georgetown
Grand Cayman
Cayman Brac
Little Cayman
Montego Bay
JAMAICA

GUATEMALA
Cobán
Huehuetenango
San Marcos
Totonicapán
Sololá
Antigua
GUATEMALA
Quezaltenango
Retalhuleu
Mazatenango
Escuintla
Coatepeque
Amatitlán
Jalapa
Zacapa
Chiquimula
HONDURAS
San Pedro Sula
El Progreso
La Ceiba
Tela
Puerto Cortés
Puerto Barrios
Santa Bárbara
Tegucigalpa
Comayagua
La Paz
EL SALVADOR
SAN SALVADOR
Santa Ana
Ahuachapán
Sonsonate
Suchitoto
Cojutepeque
Zacatecoluca
Usulután
San Miguel
Golfo de Fonseca
NICARAGUA
Chinandega
León
Estelí
Matagalpa
MANAGUA
Masaya
Granada
Diriamba
Boaco
Juigalpa
Bluefields
Lago de Nicaragua
Isla de Ometepe
Rivas
San Juan del Sur
COSTA RICA
Liberia
Puntarenas
Alajuela
SAN JOSÉ
Cartago
Limón
Pen. de Nicoya
David
Puerto Armuelles
PANAMÁ
Colón
Golfo de Panamá

CARIBBEAN

Swan Islands (U.S.A. & Honduras)
Islas de la Bahía
Laguna Caratasca
Mosquitia
C. Gracias á Dios
Cayos Miskitos (Nicaragua)
Puerto Cabezas
I. de Providencia (Colombia)
I. de San Andrés (Colombia)
Islas del Maíz (Nicaragua, U.S.A.)
Cayos de Albuquerque (Colombia)
Archipiélago de las Mulatas
Golfo del Darién

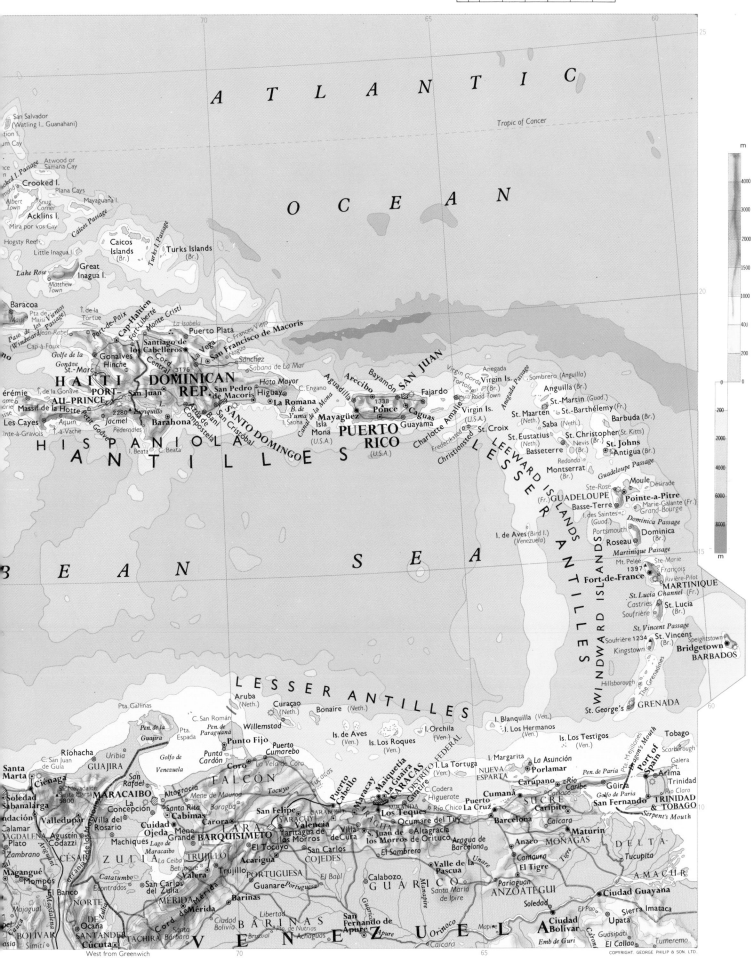

1 : 8 000 000

50   0   50   100   150   200   250   300 km

A T L A N T I C

Tropic of Cancer

O C E A N

m
4000
3000
2000
1500
1000
400
200
0
200
2000
4000
6000
8000
m

San Salvador
(Watling I., Guanahani)
tion I.
um Cay

Crooked I.
Plana Cays
Albert
Town
Snug
Corner
Mayaguana I.
Acklins I.
Mira por vos Cay

Hogsty Reef

Little Inagua I.
Lake Rose
Great
Inagua I.
Matthew
Town

Caicos
Islands
(Br.)
Turks Islands
(Br.)

Baracoa
Pta. de
Maisí Maisí
Paso de los
(Windward)Jean-Rebel
Cap-à-Foux
no

Î. de la
Tortue
Port-de-Paix
Cap-Haïtien
Fort-Liberté
Monte Cristi
La Isabela
Puerto Plata

San Francisco de Macorís
Vega
Santiago de
los Cabelleros
C. Frances Viejo

SAN JUAN
Bayamón
Virgin Gorda
Tortola
Virgin Is.
(Br.)
Anegada
Sombrero (Anguilla)
Anguilla (Br.)

Golfe de la
Gonâve
St.-Marc
Gonaïves
Hinche
Cord.
Central
3175
Sánchez
Sabana de la Mar
Hato Mayor
Arecibo
Road Town
St.-Martin (Guad.)
Anegada Passage
St.-Barthélemy (Fr.)

HAITI
érémie
amé
arie
sse
PORT-
AU-PRINCE
San Juan
DOMINICAN REP.
San Pedro
de Macorís
Higüey
C. Engano
Aguadilla
Mayagüez
Ponce
1338
Caguas
Fajardo
Virgin Is.
(U.S.A.)
St. Maarten
(Neth.)
Saba (Neth.)
St. Christopher (St. Kitts)
Nevis (Br.)
St. Johns
Barbuda (Br.)

Les Cayes
Aquin
Î.-à-Vache
Jacmel
2280
Enriquillo
Azua de
Compostela
San Cristóbal
Barahona
SANTO DOMINGO
B. de
Yuma
I. Saona
Canal de la Mona
Guayama
Charlotte Amalie
St. Croix
St. Eustatius
(Neth.)
Basseterre
(Br.)
St. Johns
Antigua (Br.)

Massif de la Hotte
HISPANIOLA
I. Beata
C. Beata
Isla
Mona
(U.S.A.)
PUERTO
RICO
(U.S.A.)
Fredericksted
Christiansted
Redonda
Montserrat
(Br.)
Guadeloupe Passage

A N T I L L E S
Ste-Rose
L E E W A R D   I S L A N D S
GUADELOUPE
(Fr.)
Basse-Terre
I. des Saintes
(Guad.)
Moule
Désirade
Pointe-à-Pitre
Marie-Galante (Fr.)
Grand-Bourg
Dominica Passage

I. de Aves (Bird I.)
(Venezuela)
Portsmouth
Roseau
Dominica
(Br.)

Martinique Passage

B E A N   S E A
L E S S E R
Mt. Pelée
1397
Ste-Marie
François
Rivière-Pilot
FORT-DE-FRANCE
MARTINIQUE
(Fr.)

W I N D W A R D   I S L A N D S
St. Lucia Channel (Fr.)
Castries
Soufrière
St. Lucia
(Br.)

A N T I L L E S
St. Vincent Passage
Soufrière 1234
Kingstown
St. Vincent
(Br.)
Speightstown
Bridgetown
BARBADOS

The Grenadines
Hillsborough
St. George's
GRENADA

L E S S E R   A N T I L L E S

Pta. Gallinas
Aruba
(Neth.)
Curaçao
(Neth.)
Bonaire (Neth.)
I. Blanquilla (Ven.)
I. Los Hermanos
(Ven.)
Is. Los Testigos
(Ven.)
Tobago
Scarborough

C. San Román
Pen. de
Paraguaná
Willemstad
Is. de Aves
(Ven.)
Is. Los Roques
(Ven.)
I. Orchila
(Ven.)
I. Margarita
La Asunción
NUEVA
ESPARTA
Porlamar
Galera
Pt.

Ríohacha
Uribia
Pen. de la
Guajira
Pta.
Espada
Golfo de
Venezuela
Punta
Cardón
Puerto
Fijo
Puerto
Cumarebo
I. La Tortuga
(Ven.)
Pen. de Paria
Carúpano
Río
Caribe
Güiria
Port of
Spain
Arima
Trinidad

Santa
Marta
C. San Juan
de Guía
GUAJIRA
Coro
La Vela de Coro
Tucacas
Maiquetía
La Guaira
DISTRITO
FEDERAL
Puerto
La Cruz
Cumaná
Caripe
Golfo de Paria
San Fernando
TRINIDAD
& TOBAGO
Soledad
Cienaga
Sierra Nevada de
Santa Marta
5800
MARACAIBO
Altagracia
Mene de Mauroa
FALCON
Puerto
Cabello
Maracay
CARACAS
Guaire
Higuerote
Río Chico
MIRANDA
Barcelona
SUCRE
Caripito
Serpent's Mouth
Sabanalarga
La Concepción
Santa Rita
Cabimas
Baragua
San Felipe
Tocuyo
Valencia
YARACUY
CARABOBO
Los Teques
Ocumare del Tuy
Maturín
MONAGAS
ndación
Valledupar
Villa del
Rosario
Cuidad
Ojeda
Mene
Grande
Carora
LARA
Yaritagua de
los Morros
Villa
de
Cura
S. Juan de
los Morros de Orituco
Altagracia
Aragua de
Barcelona
Anaco
Calamar
CESAR
Machiques
ZULIA
La Ceiba
Lago de
Maracaibo
TRUJILLO
Acarigua
El Tocuyo
COJEDES
San Carlos
El Sombrero
Cantaura
El Tigre
DELTA-
Tucupita
Magangué
Mompós
Banco
Catatumbo
San Carlos
del Zulia
Valera
TRUJILLO
PORTUGUESA
Guanare
El Baúl
Calabozo
Valle de la
Pascua
Pariaguan
ANZOATEGUI
Ciudad Guayana
AMACUR

MAGDALENA
Plato
Zambrano
Majagual
Magangué
NORTE
DE
SANTANDER
Ocaña
Cúcuta
TACHIRA
San Carlos de
Santa
Bárbara
MÉRIDA
Mérida
Cord. de Mérida
Barinas
BARINAS
Libertad
San
Fernando de
Apure
Ciudad
Bolivia
Pto. de Nutrias
Achaguas
Apure
Guárico
Manapire
Santa María
de Ipire
Soledad
Orinoco
Caicara
Ciudad
Bolívar
El Pao
Upata
Sierra Imataca
Guasipati
El Callao
Tumeremo
Emb de Guri
Caroni

BOLÍVAR
Simití
V E N E Z U E L A
Embalse de Guri

West from Greenwich

COPYRIGHT. GEORGE PHILIP & SON. LTD.

1 : 30 000 000

200   0   200   400   600   800   1000 km

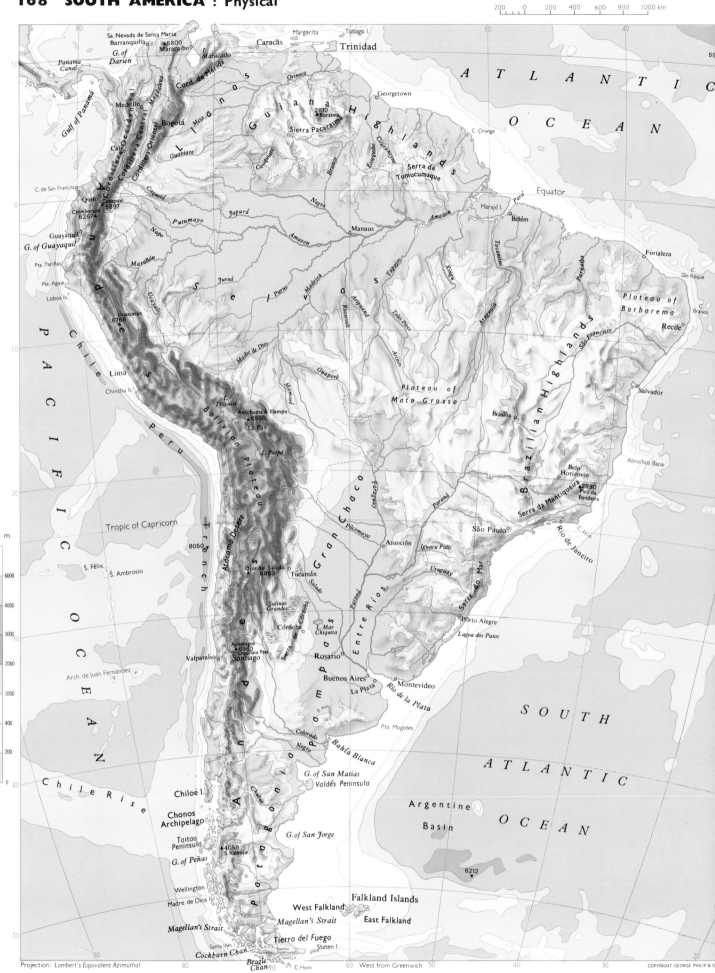

Sa. Nevada de Santa Marta
Barranquilla
Maracaibo
Margarita
Caracas
Tobago I.
Trinidad

Panama
Canal
G. of
Darien
▲5800
L. Maracaibo
Cord. de Mérida
Llanos
Orinoco
Guiana Highlands
Georgetown
C. Orange

ATLANTIC

OCEAN

Medellín
Bogotá
Cordillera Occidental
Cordillera Central
Cordillera Oriental
Magdalena
Cali
Guaviare
Meta
Sierra Pacaraima
▲2810 Roraima
Serra de Tumucumaque

C. de San Francisco
Quito Cotopaxi
▲5897
Caquetá
Putumayo
Napo
Japurá
Negro
Amazon
Equator

Chimborazo
6267
Guayaquil
G. of Guayaquil
Marañón
Ucayali
Juruá
Purus
Amazon
Madeira
Manaus
Marajó I.
Pará
Belém
Tocantins

Pta. Pariñas
Pta. Aguja
Lobos Is.
Huascarán
6768
Madre de Dios
Juruá
Selvas
Tapajos
Xingu
Araguaia
Parnaiba
Fortaleza
São Roque
Plateau of Borborema
Recife
C. Branco

Lima
Chincha Is.
L. Titicaca
Ancohuma & Illampu
▲6550
La Paz
Guaporé
Mamoré
Tietê Pires
Arinos
São Francisco
Salvador
Brazilian Highlands

Chile
Peru Trench
Bolivian Plateau
L. Poopó
Plateau of Mato Grosso
Brasília
Abrolhos Bank

Tropic of Capricorn
Atacama Desert
Gran Chaco
Paraguay
Paraná
Belo Horizonte
▲2890 Pico da Bandeira
Serra da Mantiqueira

8050
S. Félix
S. Ambrosio
Ojos del Salado
6863
Tucumán
Salado
Pilcomayo
Asunción
Iguaçu Falls
Uruguay
São Paulo
Serra do Mar
Rio de Janeiro
C. Frio

PACIFIC

OCEAN

Salinas Grandes
Córdoba
Sierra de Córdoba
L. Mar Chiquita
Entre Rios
Paraná
Pôrto Alegre
Lagoa dos Patos

Aconcagua
▲6960
Uspallata Pass
Valparaíso
Santiago
Arch. de Juan Fernández
Rosario
Pampas
Buenos Aires
La Plata
Montevideo
Río de la Plata
Pta. Mogotes

SOUTH

ATLANTIC

Colorado
Negro
Bahía Blanca

Chile Rise
G. of San Matias
Valdés Peninsula
Argentine
Basin

OCEAN

Chiloé I.
Chubut
Patagonia
Chonos Archipelago
Taitao Peninsula
▲4058 S. Valentin
G. of San Jorge
G. of Peñas

▲6212

Wellington
Madre de Dios I.
Magellan's Strait
West Falkland
Falkland Islands
East Falkland

Santa Inés I.
Cockburn Chan.
Beagle Chan.
Tierra del Fuego
Staten I.
C. Horn

m
6000
4000
3000
2000
1000
400
200
0
200
2000
4000
6000
8000
m

Projection: Lambert's Equivalent Azimuthal

West from Greenwich

COPYRIGHT. GEORGE PHILIP & S

1:80 000 000

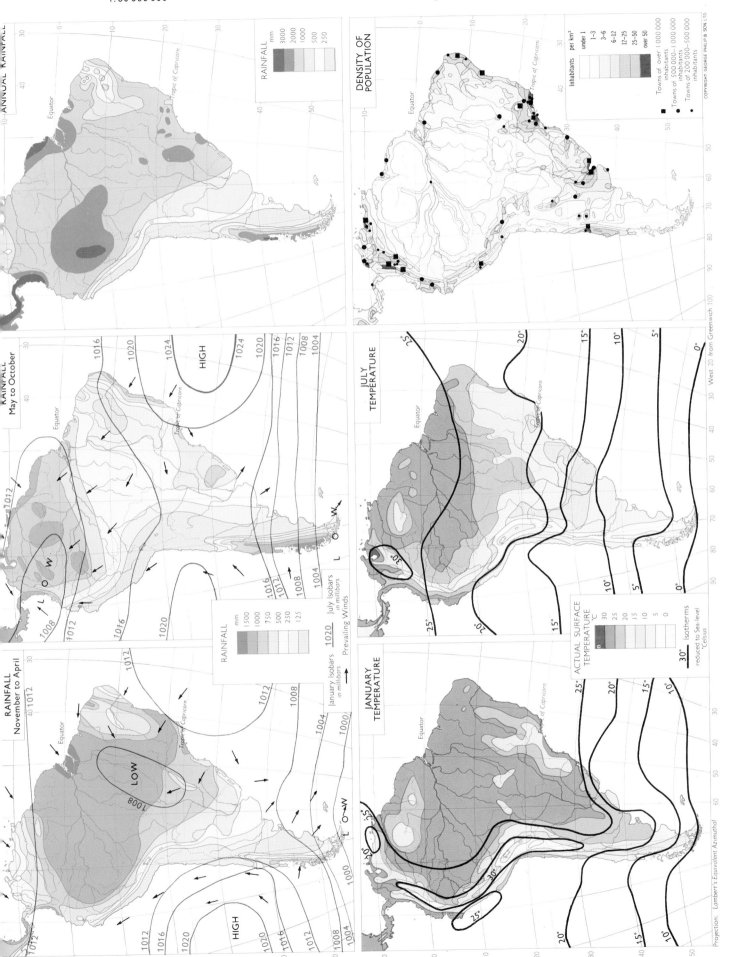

ANNUAL RAINFALL

RAINFALL
mm
3000
2000
1000
500
250

DENSITY OF POPULATION

per km²
under 1
1-3
3-6
6-12
12-25
25-50
over 50

Towns of over 1 000 000 inhabitants
Towns of 500 000–1 000 000 inhabitants
Towns of 200 000–500 000 inhabitants

COPYRIGHT GEORGE PHILIP & SON, LTD.

RAINFALL
May to October

HIGH
1016
1020
1024
1024
1020
1016
1012
1008
1004
1012
1008
LOW
1008
1012
1016
1020

RAINFALL
mm
1500
1000
750
500
250
125

1020 July Isobars in millibars
Prevailing Winds

JULY TEMPERATURE
25°
20°
15°
10°
5°
0°
30°
25°
30°

ACTUAL SURFACE TEMPERATURE
°C
30
25
20
15
10
5
0

30° Isotherms
reduced to Sea-level
°Celsius

RAINFALL
November to April

LOW
1008
1012
1016
1020
1012
1016
1020
HIGH
1020
1016
1012
1008
1004
1008
1004
1000
1000

1020 January Isobars in millibars
Prevailing Winds

JANUARY TEMPERATURE
25°
20°
15°
10°
35°
30°
25°
20°
30°
20°
15°
10°

Equator
Tropic of Capricorn

West 20 from Greenwich 100

Projection: Lambert's Equivalent Azimuthal

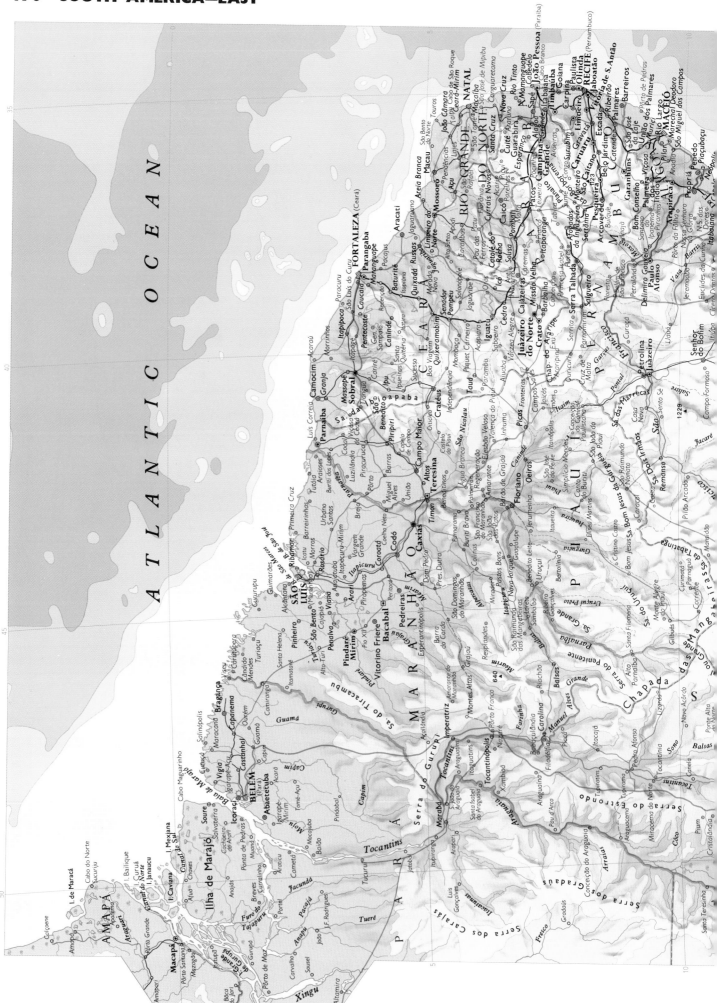

ATLANTIC OCEAN

1:8 000 000

50 0 50 100 150 200 250 300 km

ATLANTIC OCEAN

Tropic of Capricorn

West from Greenwich

COPYRIGHT GEORGE PHILIP & SON LTD

Projection: Lambert's Equivalent Azimuthal 50

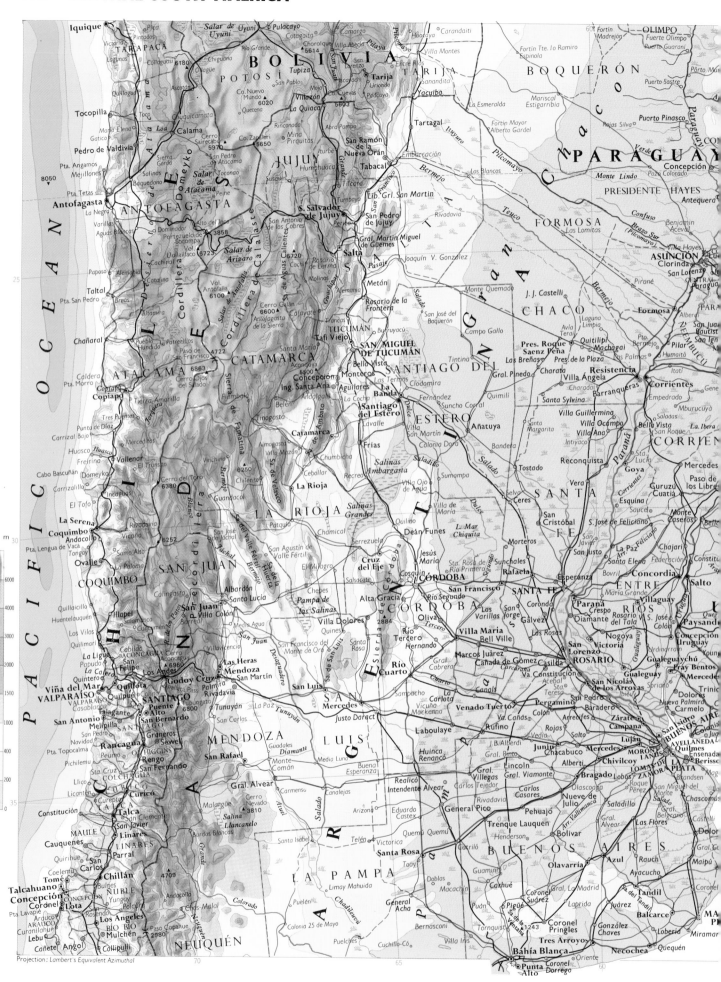

1 : 8 000 000

50 0 50 100 150 200 250 300 km

BELO
HORIZONTE

N. Lima
Itabirito

Congonhas

Vitória
Itaquari
Vila
Velha

Cons.
Lafaiete

Ouro
Prêto

Ponte Nova

Pico da
Bandeira
2890

Carangola

Guarapari

Castelo

Cachoeiro
de Itapemirim

Três Lagoas
Andradina
Mirassol
Olímpia
S. Seb.
do Paraíso
Passos
Oliveira
Campo Belo
Muriaé
Alegre
Itaperuna

Xavantina
Mirandópolis
S. José
do Rio Prêto
Bebedouro
Reprêsa de
Furnas
São João
del Rei
Ubá
Cambuci
Guarus

Araçatuba
Caranduva
Ribeirão
Prêto
Guaxupé
Três
Pontas
Barbacena
Cataguases
CAMPOS

Panorama
Adamantina
Penápolis
Taquaritinga
Jaboticabal
Novo
Horizonte
Mococa
Alfenas
Varginha
Lavras
Leopoldina
Itaperuna
Cabo de
São Tomé

Pres.
Epitácio
Birigui
Tupã
Lins
Araraquara
São
Carlos
Casa
Branca
Poços de
Caldas
Pouso
Três
Corações
Juiz de Fora
Três
Rios
Paraíba do Sul

Pôrto São José
Presidente
Prudente
Martinópolis
Marília
Garça
São João
da Boa Vista
Araras
Pinhal
Alegre
São
Lourenço
Itajubá
2787
Volta
Redonda
Barra do Piraí
Nova Friburgo
Macaé

Paranavaí
Rancharia
Paraguaçu
Paulista
Bariri
Jaú
Rio Claro
Limeira
Mogi-Mirim
Americana
Cruzeiro
Guaratinguetá
Barra
Mansa
Mar
Petrópolis

Nova
Esperança
Assis
Santa Cruz
do Rio Pardo
Piracicaba
Botucatu
Itu
Guararema
Paulista
Bragança
Nova Iguaçu
DUQUE DE CAXIAS
RIO DE JANEIRO

Maringá
Cianorte
Londrina
Cornélio
Procópio
Ourinhos
Avaré
Tatuí
CAMPINAS
Jundiaí
Taubaté
S. J. dos Campos
Angra dos Reis
NITERÓI
SÃO GONÇALO

Cruzeiro
do Oeste
Apucarana
Jacarèzinho
Itapetininga
SÃO PAULO
Jacareí
Ilha Grande
Baía da Ilha Grande
Cabo Frio
La. de Araruama

Guaíra
Mandaguari
Arapongas
Joaquim
Távora
Itaporanga
SANTO ANDRÉ
Mogi das Cruzes
Pta. de Juatinga
Tropic of Capricorn

PARANÁ
Itararé
Itapeva
Paranapiacaba
São Vicente
Santos
Ilha de São Sebastião
Pta. do Boi

Pitanga
Ibaití
Jaguariaíva
Apiaí
Juquiá
Guarujá
Itanhaém

Cascavel
Fóz do Iguaçu
Iguaçu Falls
Guarapuava
Sa. das Araras
Prudentópolis
Castro
Serra
Registro
Iguape

Iraí
Iguazú
Falls
Laranjeiras
do Sul
Palmeira
Ponta Grossa
Ilha Comprida

Bernardo
de Irigoyen
Iratí
Lapa
CURITIBA
Antonina
Ilha do Cardoso

Eldorado
San Pedro
União da
Vitória
Rio Negro
Paranaguá

MISIONES
Pto. União
Mafra
Guaratuba

Uruguaí
Cleveland
Palmas
Caçador
São Francisco do Sul

Obera
Chapecó
Joaçaba
Blumenau
Joinvile

N. Alem
Santa Cecília
Brusque
Itajaí

San
Javier
Erechim
Campos Novos
SANTA CATARINA
Rio do Sul
Ilha de Santa Catarina

Santa Rosa
Lajes
Florianópolis

Caràzinho
Passo Fundo
1808

São
Ângelo
Ijuí

São Luís
Gonzaga
Cruz Alta
Vacaria
Tubarão
Laguna

Guaporé
Araranguá
Cabo Santa Marta Grande

RIO GRANDE
Bento Gonçalves
Criciúma

Santa Maria
Santa Cruz
do Sul
Caxias do Sul

Montenegro
Nôvo Hamburgo
Taquara

Cachoeira do Sul
São
Leopoldo
Osorio

Rio Pardo
PORTO ALEGRE

DO SUL
Encantadas

São
Gabriel
Caçapava
do Sul
Camaquã

Dom Pedrito
Camaquã
Mostardas

Bagé
Canguçu
ATLANTIC

Pelotas
Lagoa dos Patos

Melo
Rio Grande

Jaguarão

OCEAN

Sta. Clara
de Olimar
Lagoa Mirim

del Yi
Treinta y Tres
Lagoa Mangueira

José Batlle
y Ordoñez
Santa Vitória do Palmar

Lascano

Aigua
Castillos

Minas
Rocha

San Carlos

Maldonado

IDEO

GROSSO

Maracaju

Rio Brilhante

Dourados
Pôrto São José

Juan Caballero

Anambaí

Paraná

MATO

ALTO PARANÁ

Misiones

Santa Rosa

BRAZIL

5304

West from Greenwich

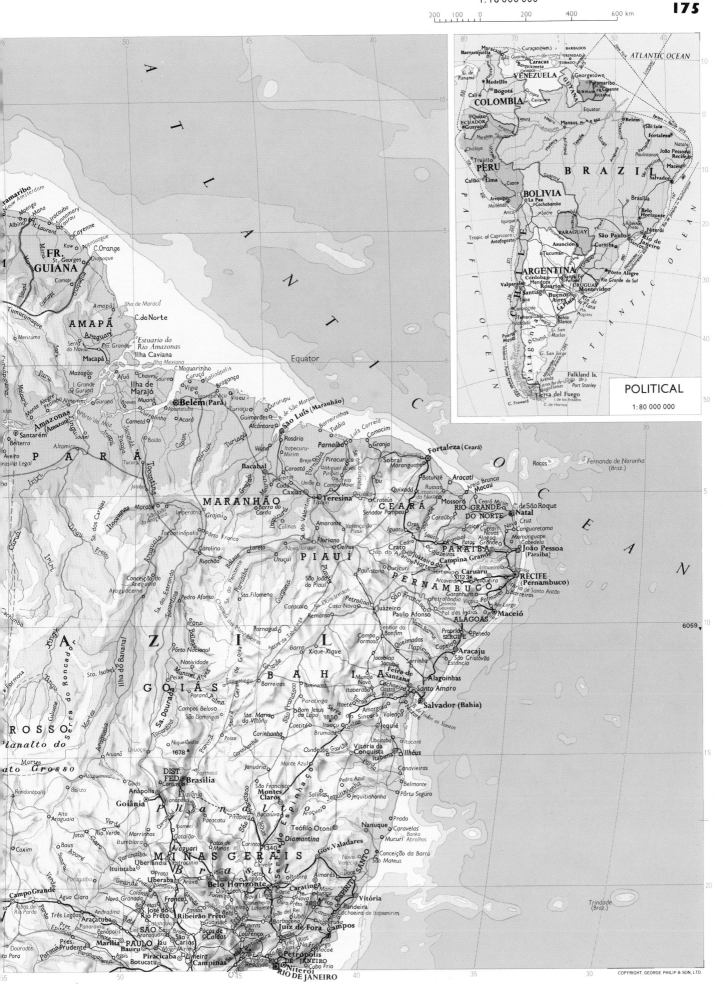

1 : 16 000 000

200 100 0   200   400   600 km

ATLANTIC OCEAN

BARBADOS

TRINIDAD

Curaçao (Neth.)

Barranquilla
La Guaira
Caracas
Maracaibo
Barquisimeto
G. de Panamá
VENEZUELA
GUYANA
Georgetown
Paramaribo
SURINAM
FR. GUIANA
Cayenne
Medellín
Cali
Bogotá
COLOMBIA
Equator
Belém
São Luís
Natal
Fortaleza
Quito
ECUADOR
Guayaquil
Manaus
Iquitos
Marañón
B R A Z I L
João Pessoa
Recife
Chiclayo
Trujillo
PERU
Lima
Callao
Cuzco
BOLIVIA
La Paz
Cochabamba
Sucre
Corumbá
Brasília
Salvador
Arequipa
Mollendo
Arica
Iquique
Tropic of Capricorn
Antofagasta
PARAGUAY
Asunción
Tucumán
São Paulo
Rio de Janeiro
Niterói
Curitiba
Belo Horizonte
Ribeirão Preto
Valparaíso
Santiago
Talca
ARGENTINA
Córdoba
Mendoza
Rosário
Santa Fé
Pôrto Alegre
Rio Grande do Sul
URUGUAY
Montevideo
Buenos Aires
La Plata
Rio de la Plata
Bahía Blanca
Concepción
Bogotás
Valdivia
Puerto Montt
G. San Matías
Patagonia
G. San Jorge
Falkland Is.
(Br.)
Port Stanley
Estrecho de Magallanes
Tierra del Fuego
C. Froward
C. de Hornos
C. de los Estados
ATLANTIC OCEAN
PACIFIC OCEAN

POLITICAL

1 : 80 000 000

A T L A N T I C

Paramaribo
Nieuw Amsterdam
Moengo
Mana
Iracoubo
Sinnamary
Kourou
Albina
St. Laurent
Cayenne
Kaw
C. Orange
Oyapock
Approuague
FR. GUIANA
Oiapoque
Camopi
Tumucumaque
Amapá
Serra do Navio
Pta. Grande
Ilha de Maracá
C. do Norte
Araguari
Macapá
Estuário do Rio Amazonas
Ilha Caviana
AMAPÁ
Afuá
Ilha Mexiana
C. Maguarinho
Chaves
Soure
Mazagão
I. Grande de Gurupá
Ilha de Marajó
Curuçá
Salinópolis
Bragança
Breves
Muaná
Vigia
Viseu
Belém (Pará)
Abaetetuba
Cametá
Acará
Santarém
Amazonas (Amazon)
Almeirim
Gurupá
Baião
Cachoeira
PARÁ
Aveiro
Altamira
Brasília Legal
Xingu
Iriri
Tocantins
Tocantins
Marabá
S. dos Carajás
Imperatriz
Grajaú
Tocantinópolis
Pôrto Franco
Carolina
MARANHÃO
Barra do Corda
Balsas
Riachão
Loreto
Conceição do Araguaia
Araguacema
Araguaia
Pedro Afonso
Pôrto Nacional
Natividade
Manuel Alves
Taguatinga
Sta. Maria da Vitória
Dianópolis
Campos Belos
GOIÁS
Niquelândia
Uruaçu
1678
Aruanã
Goiás
Ceres
Anápolis
Luziânia
Brasília
DIST. FED.
Corumbá
Goiânia
Vianópolis
Ipameri
Catalão
MATO GROSSO
Planalto do Mato Grosso
Rondonópolis
Baliza
Alto Araguaia
Jataí
Rio Verde
Itumbiara
Patos de Minas
Araguari
Uberlândia
Uberaba
Coxim
Aporé
Paranaíba
Campo Grande
Ribas do Rio Pardo
Três Lagoas
Paraná
Andradina
Araçatuba
Birigui
Pres. Epitácio
Pres. Prudente
Marília
Bauru
Dourados
Ponta Porã
Jaú
Botucatu
Assis
Itararé
MATO GROSSO DO SUL

B de São Marcos
São Luís (Maranhão)
Barreirinhas
Tutóia
Turiaçu
Cururupu
Guimarães
Alcântara
Rosário
Parnaíba
Luís Correia
Camocim
Granja
Itapecuru-Mirim
Brejo
Piracuruca
Sobral
Coroatá
Miguel Alves
Piripiri
Ibu
Maranguape
Fortaleza (Ceará)
Bacabal
Codó
União
Campo Maior
Baturité
Aracati
Caxias
Timon
Teresina
Oeiras
Quixadá
Quixeramobim
Macau
Colinas
Amarante
Valença do Piauí
Crateús
CEARÁ
Senador Pompeu
Mossoró
Areia Branca
PIAUÍ
Floriano
Iguatu
Oros
Icó
RIO GRANDE DO NORTE
Ceará Mirim
C. de São Roque
Natal
Nova Iorque
São João do Piauí
Caicó
Currais Novos
Canguaretama
Uruçuí
Sta. Filomena
Picos
Sousa
Catolé
Pombal
Patos
Alagoa Grande
Mamanguape
Cabedelo
Chap. do Araripe
Juàzeiro do Norte
Campina Grande
João Pessoa (Paraíba)
Caracol
Dois Irmãos
Crato
Cajazeiras
PARAÍBA
Caruaru
Remanso
Casa Nova
Petrolina
Juàzeiro
Ouricuri
Arcoverde
Limoeiro
Pesqueira
RECIFE (Pernambuco)
C. de Santo Antão
Pornagul
Paulistana
Sertânea
PERNAMBUCO
Garanhuns
Vitória
Palmares
Petrolândia
Pal dos Índios
Rio Largo
Campo Formoso
Senhor do Bonfim
Paulo Afonso
Gravatá
Maceió
ALAGOAS
Barra
Xique-Xique
Queimadas
Itapicuru
Própria
Penedo
Jacobina
Serrinha
Capela
SERGIPE
6059
São Cristóvão
Aracaju
BAHIA
Itaberaba
Mundo Novo
Feira de Santana
Estância
Barreiras
Irecê
Alagoinhas
Ibotirama
Castro Alves
Santo Amaro
Cachoeira
Paratinga
Itaetê
1850
Amargosa
Valença
Salvador (Bahia)
Bom Jesus da Lapa
Serra
Ituaçu
Itabuna
B. de Todos os Santos
Caetité
Brumado
Jequié
Carinhanha
Januária
Ubaitaba
Itacaré
Condeúba
Gavião
Vitória da Conquista
Ilhéus
Monte Azul
Canavieiras
Salinas
Pedra Azul
Belmonte
Francisco Sá
Jequitinhonha
Pôrto Seguro
Montes Claros
Araçuaí
Prado
Bocaiúva
Nanuque
Caravelas
Diamantina
Teófilo Otoni
Mucuri
Abrolhos
Pirapora
1340
Gov. Valadares
Conceição da Barra
Nova Venécia
São Mateus
Corinto
Patos de Minas
MINAS GERAIS
Carvelos
Manhuaçu
Aimorés
São Francisco
Sete Lagoas
Sabará
Colatina
Linhares
Belo Horizonte
Caratinga
Araxá
Bom Despacho
Itabira
2890
Vitória
Oliveira
Ouro Prêto
Bandeira
Cachoeiro de Itapemirim
Franca
Formiga
Conselheiro Lafaiete
Barbacena
Ubá
Itaperuna
Ribeirão Preto
Passos
Nova Lima
Barra
Leopoldina
Campos
Guaxupé
São Carlos
Mogi-Mirim
Juiz de Fora
Poços de Caldas
Araraquara
Lavras
Sta. Rita
Rios
Nova Friburgo
São Lourenço
Macaé
Piracicaba
Campinas
Limeira
Petrópolis
RIO DE JANEIRO
Niterói
Cabo Frio
Resende
Volta Redonda
RIO DE JANEIRO

B R A Z I L
P A R Á
A M A Z O N A S

O C E A N

Rocas
Fernando de Noronha (Braz.)

Trindade (Braz.)

Equator

COPYRIGHT. GEORGE PHILIP & SON, LTD.

1:16 000 000

200 100 0 200 400 600 km

PARAGUAY

BRAZIL

RIO GRANDE DO SUL

URUGUAY

BUENOS AIRES

MONTEVIDEO

Mar del Plata

SOUTH ATLANTIC OCEAN

Golfo San Matías

Península Valdés

Golfo San Jorge

Comodoro Rivadavia

Bahía Grande

FALKLAND ISLANDS
(ISLAS MALVINAS)
(Br.)
West Falkland   Stanley
East Falkland

South Georgia
(Br.)

Estrecho de Magallanes
(Magellan's Str.)

Punta Arenas

Tierra
del Fuego

Cabo de Hornos (C.Horn)

Projection: Sanson-Flamsteed's Sinusoidal   West from Greenwich   COPYRIGHT GEORGE PHILIP & SON

The number printed in bold type against each index entry indicates the map page where the feature will be found. The geographical coordinates which follow the name are sometimes only approximate but are close enough for the place name to be located.

An open square □ signifies that the name refers to an administrative subdivision of a country while a solid square ■ follows the name of a country. (□) follows the old county names of the U.K.

The alphabetical order of names composed of two or more words is governed primarily by the first word and then by the second. This rule applies even if the second word is a description or its abbreviation, R.,L.,I. for example. Names composed of a proper name (Gibraltar) and a description (Strait of) are positioned alphabetically by the proper name. If the same place name occurs twice or more times in the index and all are in the same country, each is followed by the name of the administrative subdivision in which it is located. The names are placed in the alphabetical order of the subdivisions. If the same place name occurs twice or more in the index and the places are in different countries they will be followed by their country names, the latter governing the alphabetical order. In a mixture of these situations the primary order is fixed by the alphabetical sequence of the countries and the secondary order by that of the country subdivisions.

Aabenraa-Sønderborg Amt □ Afognak I

A

Aabenraa-Sønderborg Amt □ 73 55 0N 9 30 E
Aachen 48 50 47N 6 4 E
Aadorf 15 47 30N 8 55 E
Aaiun 116 27 9N 13 12W
Aal 73 55 39N 8 18 E
Aâlâ en Nîl □ 123 8 50N 29 55 E
Aalen 49 48 49N 10 6 E
Aalma ech Chaab 90 33 7N 35 9 E
Aalsmeer 46 52 17N 4 43 E
Aalsö 73 56 23N 10 52 E
Aalst, Belg. 47 50 56N 4 2 E
Aalst, Neth. 152 50 57N 4 20 E
Aalten 46 51 56N 6 35 E
Aalter 47 51 5N 3 28 E
Aarau 50 47 23N 8 4 E
Aarburg 50 47 2N 7 16 E
Aardenburg 47 51 16N 3 28 E
Aare, R. 50 47 33N 8 14 E
Aareavaara 74 67 27N 23 29 E
Aargau □ 50 47 26N 8 10 E
Aarhus Amt □ 73 56 15N 10 15 E
Aarle 47 51 30N 5 38 E
Aarschot 47 50 59N 4 49 E
Aarsele 47 51 0N 3 26 E
Aartrijke 47 51 7N 3 6 E
Aarwangen 50 47 15N 7 46 E
Aasleagh 38 53 37N 9 40W
Aastrup 73 55 34N 8 49 E
Aba, Congo 126 3 58N 30 17 E
Aba, Nigeria 121 5 10N 7 19 E
Âbâ, Jazîrat 123 13 30N 32 31 E
Abadan 92 30 22N 48 20 E
Abade, Ethiopia 123 9 22N 38 3 E
Abade, Iran 93 31 8N 52 40 E
Abadin 56 43 21N 7 29W
Abadla 118 31 2N 2 45W
Abaeté 171 19 9 S 45 27W
Abaeté, R. 171 18 2 S 45 12W
Abaetetuba 170 1 40 S 48 50W
Abai 173 25 58 S 55 54W
Abak 121 4 58N 7 50 E
Abakaliki 121 6 22N 8 2 E
Abakan 77 53 40N 91 10 E
Abal Nam 122 25 20N 38 37 E
Abalemma 121 16 12N 7 50 E
Aballetuba 170 1 40 S 51 15W
Abanilla 59 38 12N 1 3W
Abano Terme 63 45 22N 11 46 E
Abarán 59 38 12N 1 23W
Abarqu 93 31 10N 53 20 E
Abasan 90 31 19N 34 21 E
Abasberes 123 11 33N 35 23 E
Abashiri 112 44 0N 144 15 E
Abashiri-Wan 112 44 0N 144 30 E
Abau 135 10 11 S 148 46 E
Abaújszántó 53 48 16N 21 12 E
Abaya L. 123 6 30N 37 50 E
Abbadia San Salvatore 63 42 53N 11 40 E
Abbay, R., (Nîl el Azraq) 123 10 17N 35 22 E
Abbaye, Pt. 156 46 58N 88 4W
Abbetorp 73 56 57N 16 8 E
Abbeville, France 43 50 6N 1 49 E
Abbeville, La., U.S.A. 159 30 0N 92 7W
Abbeville, S.C., U.S.A. 157 34 12N 82 21W
Abbey 39 53 7N 8 25W
Abbey Town 32 54 50N 3 18W
Abbeydorney 39 52 21N 9 40W
Abbeyfeale 39 52 23N 9 20W
Abbeyleix 39 52 55N 7 20W
Abbeyside 39 52 5N 7 36W
Abbiategrasso 62 45 23N 8 55 E
Abbieglassie 139 27 15 S 147 28 E
Abbotabad 94 34 10N 73 15 E
Abbots Bromley 28 52 50N 1 52W
Abbots Langley 29 51 43N 0 25W
Abbotsbury 28 50 40N 2 36W
Abbotsford, Can. 152 49 0N 122 10W
Abbotsford, U.S.A. 158 44 55N 90 20W
Abcoude 46 52 17N 4 59 E
'Abd al Kuri 91 12 5N 52 20 E
Abdulino 84 53 42N 53 40 E
Abe, L. 123 11 8N 41 47 E
Abéché 117 13 50N 20 35 E
Abejar 58 41 48N 2 47W
Abekr 123 12 45N 28 50 E
Abêlessa 118 22 58N 4 47 E
Abelti 123 8 10N 37 30 E
Abengourou 120 6 42N 3 27W
Åbenrå 73 55 3N 9 25 E
Abeokuta 121 7 3N 3 19 E
Aber 126 2 12N 32 25 E
Aber-soch 31 52 50N 4 31W
Aberaeron 31 52 15N 4 16W
Aberayron = Aberaeron 31 52 15N 4 16W
Abercarn 31 51 39N 3 9W
Aberchirder 37 57 34N 2 40W
Abercorn 139 25 12 S 151 5 E
Abercorn = Mbala 127 8 46 S 31 17 E
Abercrave 31 51 48N 3 42W
Aberdare 31 51 43N 3 27W
Aberdare Ra. 126 0 15 S 36 50 E
Aberdaron 31 52 48N 4 41W
Aberdeen, Austral. 141 32 9 S 150 56 E
Aberdeen, Can. 153 52 20N 106 8W
Aberdeen, S. Afr. 128 32 28 S 24 2 E
Aberdeen, U.K. 37 57 9N 2 6W
Aberdeen, Md., U.S.A. 162 39 30N 76 14W
Aberdeen, S.D., U.S.A. 158 45 30N 98 30W
Aberdeen, Wash., U.S.A. 160 47 0N 123 50W
Aberdeen (□) 26 57 18N 2 30W
Aberdour 35 56 2N 3 18W
Aberdovey 31 52 33N 4 3W
Aberdulais 31 51 41N 3 46W
Aberfeldy, Austral. 141 37 42 S 146 22 E
Aberfeldy, U.K. 37 56 37N 3 50W
Aberffraw 31 53 11N 4 28W
Aberfoyle 34 56 10N 4 23W
Abergaria-a-Velha 56 40 41N 8 32W
Abergavenny 31 51 49N 3 1W
Abergele 31 53 17N 3 35W
Abergwili 31 51 52N 4 18W
Abergynolwyn 31 52 39N 3 58W
Aberkenfig 31 51 33N 3 36W
Aberlady 35 56 0N 2 51W
Abernathy 159 33 49N 101 49W
Abernethy 35 56 19N 3 18W
Aberporth 31 52 8N 4 32W
Abersychan 31 51 44N 3 3W
Abertillery 31 51 44N 3 9W
Aberystwyth 31 52 25N 4 6W
Abha 122 18 0N 42 34 E
Abhayapuri 98 26 24N 90 38 E
Abidiya 122 18 18N 34 3 E
Abidjan 120 5 26N 3 58W
Abilene, Kans., U.S.A. 158 39 0N 97 16W
Abilene, Texas, U.S.A. 159 32 22N 99 40W
Abingdon, U.K. 28 51 40N 1 17W
Abingdon, Ill., U.S.A. 158 40 53N 90 23W
Abingdon, Va., U.S.A. 157 36 46N 81 56W
Abington 35 55 30N 3 42W
Abington Reef 138 18 0 S 149 35 E
Abitan L. 153 60 27N 107 15W
Abitan, R. 153 59 53N 109 3W
Abitibi L. 150 48 40N 79 40W
Abiy Adi 123 13 39N 39 3 E
Abkhaz A.S.S.R. □ 83 43 0N 41 0 E
Abkit 77 64 10N 157 10 E
Abnûb 122 27 18N 31 4 E
Åbo = Turku 75 60 27N 22 14 E
Abo, Massif d' 119 21 41N 16 8 E
Abocho 121 7 35N 6 56 E
Abohar 94 30 10N 74 10 E
Aboisso 120 5 30N 3 5W
Abomey 121 7 10N 2 5 E
Abondance 45 46 18N 6 42 E
Abong Mbang 124 4 0N 13 8 E
Abonnema 121 4 41N 6 49 E
Abony 53 47 12N 20 3 E
Aboso 120 5 23N 1 57W
Abou Deïa 117 11 20N 19 20 E
Aboyne 37 57 4N 2 48W
Abqaiq 92 26 0N 49 45 E
Abra Pampa 172 22 43 S 65 42W
Abrantes 57 39 24N 8 7W
Abraveses 56 40 41N 7 55 E
Abreojos, Pta. 164 26 50N 113 40W
Abreschviller 43 48 39N 7 6 E
Abrets, Les 45 45 32N 5 35 E
Abri, Esh Shimâliya, Sudan 123 20 50N 30 27 E
Abri, Kordofân, Sudan 123 11 40N 30 21 E
Abrolhos, Arquipélago dos 171 18 0 S 38 30W
Abrolhos, banka 171 18 0 S 38 0W
Abrud 70 46 19N 23 5 E
Abruzzi □ 63 42 15N 14 0 E
Absaroka Ra. 160 44 40N 110 0W
Abū al Khasib 92 30 25N 48 0 E
Abū 'Ali 92 27 20N 49 27 E
Abu Arish 91 16 53N 42 48 E
Abû Ballas 122 24 26N 27 36 E
Abu Deleiq 123 15 57N 33 48 E
Abū Dhabī 93 24 28N 54 36 E
Abû Dis 90 31 47N 35 16 E
Abu Dis 122 19 12N 33 38 E
Abu Dom 123 16 18N 32 25 E
Abû Gabra 123 11 2N 26 50 E
Abū Ghōsh 90 31 48N 35 6 E
Abû Gubeiha 123 11 30N 31 15 E
Abu Habl, W. 123 12 37N 31 0 E
Abu Hamed 122 19 32N 33 13 E
Abû Haraz, Esh Shimâliya, Sudan 122 19 8N 32 18 E
Abû Haraz, Nîl el Azraq, Sudan 123 14 35N 34 30 E
Abû Higar 123 12 50N 33 59 E
Abu Kamal 92 34 30N 41 0 E
Abu Markha 92 25 4N 38 22 E
Abu Qîr 122 31 18N 30 0 E
Abu Qireiya 122 24 5N 35 28 E
Abu Qurqâs 122 28 1N 30 44 E
Abu Salama 122 27 10N 35 51 E
Abû Simbel 122 22 18N 31 40 E
Abu Tig 122 27 4N 31 15 E
Abu Tiga 123 12 47N 34 12 E
Abû Zabad 123 12 25N 29 10 E
Abu Zenîma 122 29 0N 33 15 E
Abuja 121 9 16N 7 2 E
Abunã 174 9 40 S 65 20W
Abunã, R. 174 9 41 S 65 20W
Aburatsu 110 31 34N 131 24 E
Aburo, Mt. 126 2 4N 30 53 E
Abut Hd. 143 43 7 S 170 15 E
Abwong 123 9 2N 32 14 E
Åby 73 58 40N 16 10 E
Aby, Lagune 120 5 15N 3 14W
Acacías 174 3 59N 73 46W
Acajutla 166 13 36N 89 50W
Açallândia 170 5 0 S 47 50W
Acámbaro 164 20 0N 100 40W
Acaponeta 164 22 30N 105 20W
Acapulco de Juárez 165 16 51N 99 56W
Acarai, Serra 175 1 50N 57 50W
Acaraú 170 2 53 S 40 7W
Acari 170 6 31 S 36 38W
Acarigua 174 9 33N 69 12W
Acatlan 165 18 10N 98 3W
Acayucán 165 17 59N 94 58W
Accéglio 62 44 28N 6 59 E
Accomac 156 37 43N 75 40W
Accra 121 5 35N 0 6W
Accrington 32 53 46N 2 22W
Acebal 172 33 20 S 60 50W
Aceh □ 102 4 0N 97 30 E
Acerenza 65 40 50N 15 58 E
Acerra 65 40 57N 14 22 E
Aceuchal 57 38 39N 6 30W
Achaguas 174 7 46N 68 14W
Achak Gomba 99 33 30N 96 25 E
Achalpur 96 21 22N 77 32 E
Achavanich 37 58 22N 3 25W
Achel 47 51 15N 5 29 E
A'ch'eng 107 45 33N 127 0 E
Achenkirch 52 47 32N 11 45 E
Achensee 52 47 26N 11 45 E
Acher 94 23 10N 72 32 E
Achern 49 48 37N 8 5 E
Acheron, R. 143 42 16 S 173 4 E
Achill 38 53 56N 9 55W
Achill Hd. 38 53 59N 10 15W
Achill I. 38 53 58N 10 5W
Achill Sd. 38 53 53N 9 55W
Achillbeg I. 38 53 51N 9 58W
Achim 48 53 1N 9 2 E
Achimota 121 5 35N 0 15W
Achinsk 77 56 20N 90 20 E
Achisay 85 43 35N 68 53 E
Achit 84 56 48N 57 54 E
Achnasheen 36 57 35N 5 5W
Achnashellach 36 57 28N 5 20W
Achol 123 6 35N 31 32 E
A'Chralaig, Mt. 36 57 11N 5 10W
Acireale 65 37 37N 15 9 E
Ackerman 159 33 20N 89 8W
Acklin's I. 167 22 30N 74 0W
Acland, Mt. 133 24 50 S 148 20 E
Aclare 38 54 4N 8 54W
Acle 29 52 38N 1 32 E
Acme 152 51 33N 113 30W
Aconcagua 172 32 50 S 70 0W
Aconcagua □ 172 32 15 S 70 30W
Aconcagua, Cerro 172 32 39 S 70 0W
Aconquija, Mt. 172 27 0 S 66 0W
Acopiara 170 6 6 S 39 27W
Açores, Is. dos 14 38 44N 29 0W
Acquapendente 63 42 45N 11 50 E
Acquasanta 63 42 46N 13 24 E
Acquaviva delle Fonti 65 40 53N 16 50 E
Acqui 62 44 40N 8 28 E
Acre = 'Akko 90 32 35N 35 4 E
Acre □ 174 9 1 S 71 0W
Acre, R. 174 10 45 S 68 25W
Acri 65 39 29N 16 23 E
Acs 53 47 42N 18 0 E
Acton Burnell 28 52 37N 2 41W
Açu 170 5 34 S 36 54W
Ad Dam 91 20 33N 44 45 E
Ad Dammam 92 26 20N 50 5 E
Ad Dar al Hamra 92 27 20N 37 45 E
Ad Dawhah 93 25 15N 51 35 E
Ad Dilam 92 23 55N 47 10 E
Ada, Ethiopia 123 8 48N 38 51 E
Ada, Ghana 121 5 44N 0 40 E
Ada, Minn., U.S.A. 158 47 20N 96 30W
Ada, Okla., U.S.A. 159 34 50N 96 45W
Ada, Yugo. 66 45 49N 20 9 E
Adair C. 12 71 50N 71 0W
Adaja, R. 56 41 15N 4 50W
Adale 91 2 58N 46 27 E
Ådalslinden 72 63 27N 16 55 E
Adam 93 22 15N 57 28 E
Adamantina 171 21 42 S 51 4W
Adamaoua, Massif de l' 121 7 20N 12 20 E
Adamawa Highlands = Adamaoua 121 7 20N 12 20 E
Adamello, Mt. 62 46 10N 10 34 E
Adami Tulu 123 7 53N 38 41 E
Adaminaby 141 36 0 S 148 45 E
Adamovka 84 51 32N 59 56 E
Adams, Mass., U.S.A. 162 42 38N 73 8W
Adams, N.Y., U.S.A. 162 43 50N 76 3W
Adams, Wis., U.S.A. 158 43 59N 89 50W
Adam's Bridge 97 9 15N 79 40 E
Adams L. 152 51 10N 119 40W
Adams Mt. 160 46 10N 121 28W
Adam's Peak 97 6 55N 80 45 E
Adamuz 57 38 2N 4 32W
Adana 92 37 0N 35 16 E
Adanero 56 40 56N 4 36W
Adapazari 92 40 48N 30 25 E
Adarama 123 17 10N 34 52 E
Adare 39 52 34N 8 48W
Adare, C. 13 71 0 S 171 0 E
Adavale 139 25 52 S 144 32 E
Adayio 123 14 29N 40 50 E
Adda, R. 62 45 25N 9 30 E
Addis Ababa = Addis Abeba 123 9 2N 38 42 E
Addis Abeba 123 9 2N 38 42 E
Addis Alem 123 9 0N 38 17 E
Addlestone 29 51 22N 0 30W
Addo 29 33 32 S 25 44 E
Addu Atoll 87 0 30 S 73 0 E
Adebour 121 13 17N 11 50 E
Adel 157 31 10N 83 28W
Adelaide, Austral. 140 34 52 S 138 30 E
Adelaide, Bahamas 166 25 0N 77 31W
Adelaide I. 13 67 15 S 68 30W
Adelaide Pen. 148 68 15N 97 30W
Adelaide River 136 13 15 S 131 7 E
Adelanto 163 34 35N 117 22W
Adelboden 50 46 29N 7 33 E
Adele, I. 136 15 32 S 123 9 E
Adélie, Terre 13 67 0 S 140 0 E
Ademuz 58 40 5N 1 13W
Aden 91 12 50N 45 0 E
Aden, G. of 91 13 0N 50 0 E
Adendorp 128 33 25 S 24 30 E
Adhoi 94 23 26N 70 32 E
Adi 103 4 15 S 133 30 E
Adi Daro 123 14 20N 38 14 E
Adi Keyih 123 14 51N 39 22 E
Adi Kwala 123 14 38N 38 48 E
Adi Ugri 123 14 58N 38 48 E
Adieu, C. 137 32 0 S 132 10 E
Adieu Pt. 136 15 14 S 124 35 E
Adigala 123 10 24N 42 15 E
Adige, R. 63 45 9N 11 25 E
Adigrat 123 14 20N 39 26 E
Adilabad 96 19 33N 78 35 E
Adin 160 41 10N 121 0W
Adin Khel 93 32 45N 68 5 E
Adinkerke 47 51 5N 2 36 E
Adirampattinam 97 10 28N 79 20 E
Adirondack Mts. 156 44 0N 74 15W
Adis Dera 123 10 12N 38 46 E
Adjohon 121 6 41N 2 32 E
Adjud 70 46 7N 27 10 E
Adjumani 126 3 20N 31 50 E
Adlavik Is. 151 55 2N 58 45W
Adler 83 43 28N 39 52 E
Adliswil 51 47 19N 8 32 E
Admer 119 20 21N 5 27 E
Admer, Erg d' 119 24 0N 9 5 E
Admiralty B. 13 62 0 S 59 0W
Admiralty G. 136 14 20 S 125 55 E
Admiralty I. 147 57 40N 134 35W
Admiralty Inlet 160 48 0N 122 40W
Admiralty Is. 135 2 0 S 147 0 E
Admiralty Ra. 13 72 0 S 164 0 E
Ado 121 6 36N 2 56 E
Ado Ekiti 121 7 38N 5 12 E
Adok 123 8 10N 30 20 E
Adola 123 11 14N 41 44 E
Adonara 103 8 15 S 123 5 E
Adoni 97 15 33N 77 18W
Adony 53 47 6N 18 52 E
Adour, R. 44 43 32N 1 32W
Adra, India 95 23 30N 86 42 E
Adra, Spain 59 36 43N 3 3W
Adraj 91 20 1N 51 0 E
Adrano 65 37 40N 14 49 E
Adrar 118 27 51N 0 11W
Adrar des Iforhas 121 19 40N 1 40 E
Adrasman 85 40 38N 69 58 E
Adré 117 13 40N 22 20 E
Adri 119 27 32N 13 2 E
Adria 63 45 4N 12 3 E
Adrian, Mich., U.S.A. 156 41 55N 84 0W
Adrian, Tex., U.S.A. 159 35 19N 102 37W
Adriatic Sea 60 43 0N 16 0 E
Adrigole 39 51 44N 9 42W
Adua 103 1 45 S 129 50 E
Aduku 126 2 03N 32 45 E
Adula 51 46 30N 9 3 E
Adung Long 98 28 7N 97 42 E
Adur 97 9 8N 76 40 E
Adwa, Ethiopia 123 14 15N 38 52 E
Adwa, Si Arab. 92 27 15N 42 35 E
Adwick le Street 33 53 35N 1 12W
Adzhar A.S.S.R. □ 83 42 0N 42 0 E
Adzopé 120 6 7N 3 49W
Æbelø I. 73 55 39N 10 10 E
Æbeltoft 73 56 12N 10 41 E
Æbeltoft Vig. B. 73 56 9N 10 35 E
Ægean Is. 61 38 0N 25 0 E
Ægean Sea 61 37 0N 25 0 E
Aenemuiden 47 51 30N 3 40 E
Ænes 71 60 5N 6 8 E
Æolian Is. = Eólie, I. 65 38 40N 15 7 E
Aerhchin Shanmo 105 38 0N 88 0 E
Aerhshan 105 47 93N 119 59 E
Aerht'ai Shan 105 48 0N 90 0 E
Æro 73 54 53N 10 20 E
Ærø 73 54 52N 10 25 E
Ærøskøbing 73 54 53N 10 24 E
Aesch 50 47 28N 7 36 E
Aëtós 69 37 15N 21 50 E
Afafi, Massif d' 119 22 11N 14 48 E
Afanasyevo 84 58 52N 53 15 E
Afándou 69 36 18N 28 12 E
Afarag, Erg 118 23 50N 2 47 E
Afdera, Mt. 123 13 16N 41 5 E
Affreville = Khemis Miliania 118 36 11N 2 14 E
Affric, L. 36 57 15N 5 5W
Affric, R. 37 57 15N 4 50W
Afghanistan ■ 93 33 0N 65 0 E
Afgoi 91 2 7N 44 59 E
Afif 92 23 53N 42 56 E
Afikpo 121 5 53N 7 54 E
Aflisses, O. 118 28 30N 0 50 E
Aflou 118 34 7N 2 3 E
Afodo 123 10 18N 34 49 E
Afogados da Ingàzeira 170 7 45 S 37 39W
Afognak I. 147 58 10N 152 50W

Afragola Al Wakrah

Afragola 65 40 54N 14 15 E
Africa 114 10 0N 20 0 E
Afton 162 42 14N 75 31W
Aftout 118 26 50N 3 45W
Afuá 170 0 15 S 50 10W
Afula 90 32 37N 35 17 E
Afyon Karahisar 92 38 20N 30 15 E
Agadès 121 16 58N 7 59 E
Agadir 118 30 28N 9 35W
Agadir Tissint 118 29 57N 7 16W
Agano, R. 112 37 50N 139 30 E
Agapa 77 71 27N 89 15 E
Agapovka 84 53 18N 59 8 E
Agar 94 23 40N 76 2 E
Agaro 123 7 50N 36 38 E
Agartala 98 23 50N 91 23 E
Agassiz 152 49 14N 121 46W
Agat 123 15 38N 38 16 E
Agattu I. 147 52 25N 172 30 E
Agbelouvé 121 6 35N 1 14 E
Agboville 120 5 55N 4 15W
Agdam 83 40 0N 46 58 E
Agdash 83 40 44N 47 22 E
Agde 44 43 19N 3 28 E
Agde, C. d' 44 43 16N 3 28 E
Agdz 118 30 47N 6 30W
Agen 44 44 12N 0 38 E
Ageo 111 35 58N 139 36 E
Ager Tay 119 20 0N 17 41 E
Agersø 73 55 13N 11 12 E
Agger 73 56 47N 8 13 E
Aggersborg 73 57 0N 9 16 E
Aggius 64 40 56N 9 4 E
Aghalee 38 54 32N 6 17W
Aghavannagh 39 52 55N 6 25W
Aghern 39 52 5N 8 10W
Aghil Mts. 93 36 0N 77 0 E
Aghil Pass 93 36 15N 76 35 E
Aginskoye 77 51 6N 114 32 E
Agira 65 37 40N 14 30 E
Aglou 118 29 50N 9 50W
Agly, R. 44 42 46N 3 3 E
Agna Branca 170 7 57 S 47 19W
Agnes 137 28 0 S 120 30 E
Agnew 137 28 1 S 120 30 E
Agnews Hill 38 54 51N 5 55W
Agnibilékrou 120 7 10N 3 11W
Agnita 70 45 59N 24 40 E
Agnone 65 41 49N 14 20 E
Ago 111 33 36N 135 29 E
Agofie 121 8 27N 0 15 E
Agogna, R. 62 45 8N 8 42 E
Agogo, Ghana 121 6 50N 1 1W
Agogo, Sudan 123 7 50N 28 45 E
Agon 42 49 2N 1 34W
Agön 72 61 33N 17 25 E
Agon I. 72 61 34N 17 23 E
Ágordo 63 46 18N 12 2 E
Agout, R. 44 43 47N 1 41 E
Agra 94 27 17N 77 58 E
Agrado 174 2 15N 75 46W
Agramunt 58 41 48N 1 6 E
Agreda 58 41 51N 1 55W
Agri 73 56 14N 10 32 E
Ağri Daği 92 39 50N 44 15 E
Agri, R. 65 40 17N 16 15 E
Agrigento 64 37 19N 13 33 E
Agrinion 69 38 37N 21 27 E
Agrøpoli 65 40 23N 14 59 E
Agryz 84 56 33N 53 2 E
Agua Caliente, Mexico 164 26 30N 108 20W
Agua Caliente, U.S.A. 163 32 29N 116 59W
Agua Caliente Springs 163 32 56N 116 19W
Agua Clara 175 20 25 S 52 45W
Agua Prieta 164 31 20N 109 32W
Aguadas 174 5 40N 75 38W
Aguadilla 147 18 27N 67 10W
Aguadulce 166 8 15N 80 32W
Aguanaval, R. 164 23 45N 103 10W
Aguanga 163 33 27N 116 51W
Aguanus, R. 151 50 13N 62 5W
Aguapeí, R. 171 21 0 S 51 0W
Aguapey, R. 172 29 7 S 56 36W
Aguaray Guazú, R. 172 24 47 S 57 19W
Aguarico, R. 174 0 0 77 30W
Aguas Blancas 172 24 15 S 69 55W
Aguas Calientes, Sierra de 172 25 26 S 67 27W
Águas Formosas 171 17 5 S 40 57W
Aguas, R. 58 41 20N 0 30W
Aguascalientes 164 22 0N 102 12W
Aguascalientes □ 164 22 0N 102 20W
Agudo 57 38 59N 4 52W
Águeda 56 40 34N 8 27W
Agueda, R. 56 40 45N 6 37W
Aguelt el Kadra 118 25 3N 7 6W
Agueni N'Ikko 118 32 29N 5 47W
Aguié 121 13 31N 7 46 E
Aguilafuente 56 41 13N 4 7W
Aguilar 57 37 31N 4 40W
Aguilar de Campóo 56 42 47N 4 15W
Aguilares 172 27 26 S 65 35W
Aguilas 59 37 23N 1 35W
Aguja, C. de la 174 11 18N 74 12W
Aguja, Pta. 174 6 0 S 81 0W
Agulaa 123 13 40N 39 40 E
Agulhas, Kaap 128 34 52 S 20 0 E
Agung 102 8 20 S 115 28 E
Agur, Israel 90 31 42N 34 55 E
Agur, Uganda 126 2 28N 32 55 E
Agūš 70 46 28N 26 15 E
Agusan, R. 103 9 20N 125 50 E
Agvali 83 42 36N 46 8 E
Aha Mts. 128 19 45 S 21 0 E
Ahaggar 119 23 0N 6 30 E
Ahamansu 121 7 38N 0 35 E
Ahar 92 38 35N 47 0 E
Ahascragh 38 53 24N 8 20W
Ahaura 143 42 20 S 171 32 E
Ahaura, R. 143 42 21 S 171 34 E
Ahaus 48 52 4N 7 1 E
Ahelledjem 119 26 37N 6 58 E
Ahimanawa Ra. 130 39 5 S 176 30 E
Ahipara B. 142 35 5 S 173 5 E
Ahiri 96 19 30N 80 0 E
Ahlen 48 51 45N 7 52 E
Ahmad Wal 94 29 18N 65 58 E
Ahmadabad (Ahmedabad) 94 23 0N 72 40 E
Ahmadnagar (Ahmednagar) 96 19 7N 74 46 E
Ahmadpur 94 29 12N 71 10 E
Ahmar Mts. 123 9 20N 41 15 E
Ahoada 121 5 8N 6 36 E
Ahoghill 38 54 52N 6 23W
Ahome 164 25 55N 109 11W
Ahr, R. 48 50 25N 6 52 E
Ahrensbök 48 54 0N 10 34 E
Ahrweiler 48 50 31N 7 3 E
Ahsā, Wahatāal 92 25 50N 49 0 E
Ahuachapán 166 13 54N 89 52W
Ahuriri, R. 143 44 31 S 170 12 E
Åhus 73 55 56N 14 18 E
Ahvāz 92 31 20N 48 40 E
Ahvenanmaa 75 60 15N 20 0 E
Ahzar 121 15 30N 3 20 E
Aibaq 93 36 15N 68 5 E
Aichach 49 48 28N 11 9 E
Aichi-ken □ 111 35 0N 137 15 E
Aidone 65 37 26N 14 26 E
Aiello Cálabro 65 39 6N 16 12 E
Aigle 50 46 18N 6 58 E
Aignay-le-Duc 43 47 40N 4 43 E
Aigre 44 45 54N 0 1 E
Aigua 173 34 13 S 54 46W
Aigueperse 44 46 3N 3 13 E
Aigues-Mortes 45 43 35N 4 12 E
Aiguilles 45 44 47N 6 51 E
Aiguillon 44 44 18N 0 21 E
Aiguillon, L' 44 46 20N 1 16W
Aigurande 44 46 27N 1 49 E
Aihui 105 50 16N 127 28 E
Aija 174 9 50 S 77 45W
Aijal 98 23 40N 92 44 E
Aiken 157 33 34N 81 50W
Ailao Shan 108 24 0N 101 30 E
Aillant-sur-Tholon 43 47 52N 3 20 E
Aillik 151 55 11N 59 18W
Ailly-sur-Noye 43 49 45N 2 20 E
Ailsa Craig, I. 34 55 15N 5 7W
Aim 77 59 0N 133 55 E
Aimere 103 8 45 S 121 3 E
Aimogasta 172 28 33 S 66 50W
Aimorés 171 19 30 S 41 4W
Aimorés, Serra dos 171 17 50 S 40 30W
Ain □ 45 46 5N 5 20 E
Ain Banaiyah 93 23 0N 51 0 E
Aïn-Beïda 119 35 50N 7 35 E
Ain ben Khellil 118 33 15N 0 49W
Ain Ben Tili 118 25 59N 9 27W
Aïn Benian 118 36 48N 2 55 E
'Ain Dalla 122 27 20N 27 23 E
Ain Dar 92 25 55N 49 10 E
Ain el Mafki 122 27 30N 28 15 E
Ain Girba 122 29 20N 25 14 E
Aïn M'lila 119 36 2N 6 35 E
Ain Qeiqab 122 29 42N 24 55 E
Ain, R. 45 45 52N 5 11 E
Aïn Rich 118 34 38N 24 55 E
Aïn-Sefra 118 32 47N 0 37W
Ain Sheikh Murzûk 122 26 47N 27 45 E
Ain Sukhna 122 29 32N 32 20 E
Aïn Tédelès 118 36 0N 0 21 E
Aïn-Témouchent 118 35 16N 1 8W
Aïn Touta 119 35 26N 5 54 E
Ain Zeitûn 122 29 10N 25 48 E
Aïn Zorah 118 34 37N 3 32W
Ainabo 91 9 0N 46 25 E
Ainazi 80 57 50N 24 24 E
Aine Galakka 117 18 10N 18 30 E
Aínos Óros 69 38 10N 20 35 E
Ainsdale 32 53 37N 3 2W
Ainsworth 158 42 33N 99 52W
Aioi 110 34 48N 134 28 E
Aion 77 69 50N 169 0 E
Aipe 174 3 13N 75 15W
Aïr 121 18 30N 8 0 E
Airaines 43 49 58N 1 55 E
Aird Brenish, C. 36 58 8N 7 8W
Aird, The, dist. 37 57 26N 4 30W
Airdrie 35 55 53N 3 57W
Aire 43 50 37N 2 22 E
Aire, Isla del 58 39 48N 4 16 E
Aire, R. 43 49 18N 5 0 E
Aire-sur-l'Adour 44 43 42N 0 15W
Aireys Inlet 140 38 29 S 144 5 E
Airolo 51 46 32N 8 37 E
Airvault 42 46 50N 0 8W
Aisgill 32 54 23N 2 21W
Aishihik 147 61 40N 137 46W
Aisne □ 43 49 42N 3 40 E
Aisne, R. 43 49 26N 2 50 E
Aït Melloul 118 30 25N 9 29W
Aitana, Sierra de 59 38 35N 0 24W
Aitape 135 3 11 S 142 22 E
Aith 37 59 8N 2 38W
Aitkin 158 46 32N 93 43W
Aitolía Kai Akarnanía □ 69 38 45N 21 18 E
Aitolikón 69 38 26N 21 21 E
Aitoska Planina 67 42 45N 27 30 E
Aiuaba 170 6 38 S 40 7W
Aiud 70 46 19N 23 44 E
Aix-en-Provence 45 43 32N 5 27 E
Aix-la-Chapelle = Aachen 48 50 47N 6 4 E
Aix-les-Bains 45 45 41N 5 53 E
Aix-les-Thermes 44 42 43N 1 51 E
Aix-sur-Vienne 44 45 48N 1 8 E
Aiyang, Mt. 135 5 10 S 141 20 E
Aiyangpienmen 107 40 55N 124 30 E
Aiyansh 152 55 17N 129 2W
Aiyina 69 37 45N 23 26 E
Aiyínion 68 40 28N 22 28 E
Aiyion 69 38 15N 22 5 E
Aizenay 42 46 44N 1 38W
Aizpute 80 56 43N 21 40 E
Aizuwakamatsu 112 37 30N 139 56 E
Ajaccio 45 41 55N 8 40 E
Ajaccio, G. d' 45 41 52N 8 40 E
Ajalpán 165 18 22N 97 15W
Ajana 137 27 56 S 114 35 E
Ajanta Ra. 96 20 28N 75 50 E
Ajax, Mt. 143 42 35 S 172 5 E
Ajdabiyah 119 30 54N 20 4 E
Ajdīr, Raïs 119 33 4N 11 44 E
AjdovTUina 63 45 54N 13 54 E
Ajibar 123 10 35N 38 36 E
'Ajlun 90 32 18N 35 47 E
Ajman 93 25 25N 55 30 E
Ajmer 94 26 28N 74 37 E
Ajo 161 32 18N 112 54W
Ajoie 50 47 22N 7 0 E
Ajok 123 9 15N 28 28 E
Ajua 120 4 50N 1 55W
Ak Dağ 92 36 30N 30 0 E
Akaba 121 8 10N 1 2 E
Akabli 118 26 49N 1 31 E
Akaishi-Dake 111 35 27N 138 9 E
Akaishi-Sammyaku 111 35 25N 138 10 E
Akaki Beseka 123 8 55N 38 45 E
Akala 123 15 39N 36 13 E
Akaroa 143 43 49 S 172 59 E
Akaroa Harb. 131 43 54 S 172 59 E
Akasha 122 21 10N 30 32 E
Akashi 110 34 45N 135 0 E
Akbou 119 36 31N 4 31 E
Akbulak 84 51 1N 55 37 E
Akdala 85 45 2N 74 35 E
Akechi 111 35 18N 137 23 E
Akegbe 121 6 17N 7 28 E
Akelamo 103 1 35N 129 40 E
Akershus Fylke □ 71 60 10N 11 15 E
Akeru, R. 96 17 25N 80 0 E
Aketi 124 2 38N 23 47 E
Akhaïa □ 69 38 5N 21 45 E
Akhalkalaki 83 41 27N 43 25 E
Akhaltsikhe 83 41 40N 43 0 E
Akharnaí 69 38 5N 23 44 E
Akhelóös, R. 69 39 5N 21 25 E
Akhendriá 69 34 58N 25 16 E
Akhéron, R. 68 39 31N 20 29 E
Akhisar 92 38 56N 27 48 E
Akhladhókambos 69 37 31N 22 35 E
Akhmîm 122 26 31N 31 47 E
Akhnur 95 32 52N 74 45 E
Akhtopol 67 42 6N 27 56 E
Akhtubinsk (Petropavlovskiy) 83 48 27N 46 7 E
Akhty 83 41 30N 47 45 E
Akhtyrka 80 50 25N 35 0 E
Aki 110 33 30N 133 54 E
Aki-Nada 110 34 5N 132 40 E
Akiak 147 60 50N 161 12W
Akimiski I. 150 52 50N 81 30W
Akimovka 82 46 44N 35 0 E
Akincilar 69 37 57N 27 25 E
Akinum 138 6 15 S 149 30 E
Åkirkeby 73 55 4N 14 55 E
Akita 112 39 45N 140 0 E
Akita-ken □ 112 39 40N 140 30 E
Akjoujt 120 19 45N 14 15W
Akka 118 29 28N 8 9W
'Akko 90 32 35N 35 4 E
Akkol, Kazakh, U.S.S.R. 85 45 0N 75 39 E
Akkol, Kazakh, U.S.S.R. 85 43 36N 70 45 E
Akköy 69 37 30N 27 18 E
Akkrum 46 53 3N 5 50 E
Aklampa 121 8 15N 2 10 E
Aklavik, Can. 147 68 12N 135 0W
Aklavik, N.W.T., Can. 147 68 12N 135 0W
Akmuz 85 41 15N 76 10 E
Aknoul 118 34 40N 3 55W
Akō 110 34 45N 134 24 E
Ako 121 10 19N 10 48 E
Akobo, R. 123 7 10N 34 25 E
Akola 96 20 42N 77 2 E
Akonolinga 121 3 50N 12 18 E
Akordat 123 15 30N 37 40 E
Akosombo Dam 121 6 20N 0 5 E
Ak'osu 105 41 15N 80 14 E
Akot, India 96 21 10N 77 10 E
Akot, Sudan 123 6 31N 30 9 E
Akpatok I. 149 60 25N 68 8W
Akranes 74 64 19N 22 6W
Åkrehamn 71 59 15N 5 10 E
Akreïjit 120 18 19N 9 11W
Akrítas Venétiko, Ákra 69 36 43N 21 54 E
Akron, Colo., U.S.A. 158 40 13N 103 15W
Akron, Ohio, U.S.A. 156 41 7N 81 31W
Akrotíri, Ákra 68 40 26N 25 27W
Aksai Chih, L. 95 35 15N 79 55 E
Aksaray 92 38 25N 34 2 E
Aksarka 76 66 31N 67 50 E
Aksehir 92 38 18N 31 30 E
Aksenovo Zilovskoye 77 53 20N 117 40 E
Aksuat, Ozero 84 51 32N 64 34 E
Aksum 123 14 5N 38 40 E
Aktash, R.S.F.S.R., U.S.S.R. 84 52 2N 52 7 E
Aktash, Uzbek S.S.R., U.S.S.R. 85 39 55N 65 55 E
Aktobe 84 52 55N 62 22 E
Aktogay 85 44 25N 76 44 E
Aktyubinsk 79 50 17N 57 10 E
Aktyuz 85 42 54N 76 7 E
Aku 121 6 40N 7 18 E
Akulurak 147 62 40N 164 35W
Akun I. 147 54 15N 165 30W
Akune 110 32 1N 130 12 E
Akure 121 7 15N 5 5 E
Akureyri 74 65 40N 18 6W
Akusha 83 42 18N 47 30 E
Akutan I. 147 53 30N 166 0W
Akzhar 85 43 8N 71 37 E
Al Abyār 119 32 9N 20 29 E
Al Amadiyah 92 37 5N 43 30 E
Al Amārah 92 31 55N 47 15 E
Al Aqabah 92 29 37N 35 0 E
Al Ashkhara 93 21 50N 59 30 E
Al Ayn al Mugshin 91 19 35N 54 40 E
Al 'Azīzīyah 119 32 30N 13 1 E
Al Badi 92 22 0N 46 35 E
Al Barah 90 31 55N 35 12 E
Al Barkāt 119 24 56N 10 14 E
Al Basrah 92 30 30N 47 50 E
Al Baydā 117 32 30N 21 40 E
Al Bu'ayrāt 119 31 24N 15 44 E
Al Buqay'ah 90 32 15N 35 30 E
Al Dīwaniyah 92 32 0N 45 0 E
Al Fallujah 92 33 20N 43 55 E
Al Fāw 92 30 0N 48 30 E
Al Hadithan 92 34 0N 41 13 E
Al Hamad 92 31 30N 39 30 E
Al Hamar 92 22 23N 46 6 E
Al Hariq 92 23 29N 46 27 E
Al Hasakah 92 36 35N 40 45 E
Al Hauta 91 16 5N 48 20 E
Al Havy 92 32 5N 46 5 E
Al Hillah, Iraq 92 32 30N 44 25 E
Al Hillah, Si Arab. 92 23 35N 46 50 E
Al Hilwah 92 23 24N 46 48 E
Al Hindiya 92 32 30N 44 10 E
Al Hoceïma 118 35 8N 3 58W
Al Hufrah, Awbārī, Libya 119 25 32N 14 1 E
Al Hufrah, Misrātah, Libya 119 29 5N 18 3 E
Al Hufuf 92 25 25N 49 45 E
Al Husayyāt 119 30 24N 20 37 E
Al Husn 90 32 29N 35 52 E
Al Irq 117 29 5N 21 35 E
Al Ittihad = Madinat al Shaab 91 12 50N 45 0 E
Al Jahrah 92 29 25N 47 40 E
Al Jalāmid 92 31 20N 39 45 E
Al Jarzirah 117 26 10N 21 20 E
Al Jawf 117 24 10N 23 24 E
Al Jazir 91 18 30N 56 31 E
Al Jubail 92 27 0N 49 50 E
Al Juwara 91 19 0N 57 13 E
Al Khābūrah 93 23 57N 57 5 E
Al Khalih 90 31 32N 35 6 E
Al Khums (Homs) 119 32 40N 14 17 E
Al Kut 92 32 30N 46 0 E
Al Kuwayt 92 29 20N 48 0 E
Al Ladhiqiyah 92 35 30N 35 45 E
Al Līth 122 20 9N 40 15 E
Al Madīnah 92 24 35N 39 52 E
Al-Mafraq 90 32 17N 36 14 E
Al Majma'ah 92 25 57N 45 22 E
Al Manamah 93 26 10N 50 30 E
Al Marj 117 32 25N 20 30 E
Al Masīrah 91 20 25N 58 50 E
Al Mawsil 92 36 15N 43 5 E
Al Miqdadīyah 92 34 0N 45 0 E
Al Mubarraz 92 25 30N 49 40 E
Al Muharraq 93 26 15N 50 40 E
Al Mukha 91 13 18N 43 15 E
Al Musayyib 92 32 40N 44 25 E
Al Muwaylih 92 27 40N 35 30 E
Al Qaddāhīyah 119 31 15N 15 9 E
Al Qamishli 92 37 10N 41 10 E
Al Qaryah ash Sharqīyah 119 30 28N 13 40 E
Al Qaşabāt 119 32 39N 14 1 E
Al Qatif 92 26 35N 50 0 E
Al Qaţrun 119 24 56N 15 3 E
Al Quaisūmah 92 28 10N 46 20 E
Al Quds 90 31 47N 35 10 E
Al Qunfidha 122 19 3N 41 4 E
Al Quraiyat 93 23 17N 58 53 E
Al Qurnah 92 31 1N 47 25 E
Al 'Ula 92 26 35N 38 0 E
Al Uqaylah 119 30 12N 19 10 E
Al Uqayr 92 25 40N 50 15 E
Al' Uwayqilah 92 30 30N 42 10 E
Al 'Uyūn 92 26 30N 43 50 E
Al Wajh 122 26 10N 36 30 E
Al Wakrah 93 25 10N 51 40 E

Al Warīah Almaden

Al Warīah	92	27 50N	47 30 E
Al Wātīyah	119	32 28N	11 57 E
Ala, Italy	62	45 46N	11 0 E
Ala, Sweden	72	61 13N	17 9 E
Ala Shan	105	40 0N	104 0 E
Alabama □	157	31 0N	87 0W
Alabama, R.	157	31 30N	87 35W
Alaçati	69	38 16N	26 23 E
Alaejos	56	41 18N	5 13W
Alagna Valsésia	62	45 51N	7 56 E
Alagôa Grande	170	7 3 S	35 35W
Alagôas □	170	9 0 S	36 0W
Alagoinhas	171	12 0 S	38 20W
Alagón	58	41 46N	1 12W
Alagón, R.	56	39 50N	6 50W
Alajuela	166	10 2N	84 8W
Alakamisy	129	21 19 S	47 14 E
Alakurtti	78	67 0N	30 30 E
Alam Ajaib	122	25 55N	27 14 E
Alameda, Spain	57	37 12N	4 39W
Alameda, Calif., U.S.A.	163	37 46N	122 15W
Alameda, N. Mex., U.S.A.	161	35 10N	106 43W
Alameda, S.D., U.S.A.	160	43 2N	112 30W
Alamitos, Sierra de los	164	26 30N	102 20W
Alamo	161	37 21N	115 10W
Alamogordo	161	32 59N	106 0W
Alamos	164	27 0N	109 0W
Alamosa	161	37 30N	106 0W
Åland	75	60 15N	20 0 E
Aland	96	17 36N	76 35 E
Alandroal	57	38 41N	7 24W
Ålands hav	75	60 10N	19 30 E
Alange, Presa de	57	38 45N	6 18W
Alangouassou	120	7 30N	4 34W
Alanis	57	38 3N	5 43W
Alanya	92	36 38N	32 0 E
Alaotra, L.	129	17 30 S	48 30 E
Alapayevsk	84	57 52N	61 42 E
Alar del Rey	56	42 38N	4 20W
Alaraz	56	40 45N	5 17W
Alaşehir	79	38 23N	28 30 E
Alashantsoch'i	106	38 59N	105 45 E
Alaska □	147	65 0N	150 0W
Alaska, G. of	147	58 0N	145 0W
Alaska Highway	152	60 0N	130 0W
Alaska Pen.	147	56 0N	160 0W
Alaska Range	147	62 50N	151 0W
Alássio	62	44 1N	8 10 E
Alatri	64	41 44N	13 21 E
Alatyr	81	54 45N	46 35 E
Alatyr, R.	81	54 45N	45 30 E
Alausí	174	2 0 S	78 50W
Álava □	58	42 48N	2 28W
Alava, C.	160	48 10N	124 40W
Alaverdi	83	41 2N	44 37 E
Alawoona	140	34 45 S	140 30 E
Alaykel	85	40 15N	74 25 E
Alayor	58	39 57N	4 8 E
Alayskiy Khrebet	85	39 45N	72 0 E
Alazan, R.	83	41 25N	46 35 E
Alba	62	44 41N	8 1 E
Alba □	70	46 10N	23 30 E
Alba de Tormes	56	40 50N	5 30W
Alba-Iulia	70	46 8N	23 39 E
Albac	70	46 28N	23 1 E
Albacete	59	39 0N	1 50W
Albacete □	59	38 50N	2 0W
Albacutya, L.	140	35 45 S	141 58 E
Albæk	73	57 36N	10 25 E
Ålbæk Bugt	73	57 35N	10 40 E
Albaida	59	38 51N	0 31W
Albalate de las Nogueras	58	40 22N	2 18W
Albalate del Arzobispo	58	41 6N	0 31W
Albania ■	68	41 0N	20 0 E
Albano Laziale	64	41 44N	12 40 E
Albany, Austral.	137	35 1 S	117 58 E
Albany, Ga., U.S.A.	157	31 40N	84 10W
Albany, Minn., U.S.A.	158	45 37N	94 38W
Albany, N.Y., U.S.A.	162	42 29N	73 47W
Albany, Oreg., U.S.A.	160	44 41N	123 0W
Albany, Tex., U.S.A.	159	32 45N	99 20W
Albany, R.	150	52 17N	81 31W
Albardón	172	31 20 S	68 30W
Albarracín	58	40 25N	1 26W
Albarracín, Sierra de	58	40 30N	1 30W
Albatross B.	138	12 45 S	141 30 E
Albatross Pt.	142	38 7 S	174 44 E
Albegna, R.	63	42 40N	11 28 E
Albemarle	157	35 27N	80 15W
Albemarle Sd.	157	36 0N	76 30W
Albenga	62	44 3N	8 12 E
Alberche, R.	56	40 10N	4 30W
Alberdi	172	26 14 S	58 20W
Alberes, Mts.	58	42 28N	2 56W
Alberga	139	27 12 S	135 28 E
Alberga, R.	136	26 50 S	133 40 E
Alberique	59	39 7N	0 31W
Alberni	152	49 20N	124 50W
Albersdorf	48	54 8N	9 19 E
Albert, Austral.	141	32 22 S	147 30 E
Albert, Can.	151	45 51N	64 38W
Albert, France	43	50 0N	2 38 E
Albert Canyon	152	51 8N	117 41W
Albert Edward, Mt.	135	8 20 S	147 24 E
Albert Edward Ra.	136	18 17 S	127 57 E
Albert L., Austral.	140	35 30 S	139 10 E
Albert L., U.S.A.	160	42 40N	120 8W
Albert Lea	158	43 32N	93 20W
Albert, L. = Mobutu Sese Seko, L.	126	1 30N	31 0 E
Albert Nile, R.	126	3 16N	31 38 E
Albert Town	167	22 37N	74 33 E
Alberta □	152	54 40N	115 0W
Alberti	172	35 1 S	60 16W
Albertinia	128	34 11 S	21 34 E
Albertirsa	53	47 14N	19 37 E
Albertkanaal	47	51 14N	4 26 E
Alberton	151	46 50N	64 0W
Albertville	45	45 40N	6 22 E
Albertville = Kalemie	126	5 55 S	29 9 E
Albi	44	43 56N	2 9 E
Albia	158	41 0N	92 50W
Albina	175	5 37N	54 15W
Albina, Pta.	128	15 52 S	11 44 E
Albino	62	45 47N	9 48 E
Albion, Idaho, U.S.A.	160	42 21N	113 37W
Albion, Mich., U.S.A.	156	42 15N	84 45W
Albion, Nebr., U.S.A.	158	41 47N	98 0W
Alblasserdam	46	51 52N	4 40 E
Albocácer	58	40 21N	0 1 E
Alböke	73	56 57N	16 47 E
Alborán, I.	57	35 57N	3 0W
Alborea	59	39 17N	1 24W
Ålborg	73	57 2N	9 54 E
Ålborg Bugt	73	56 50N	10 35 E
Alborz, Reshteh-Ye Kūkhā-Ye	93	36 0N	52 0 E
Albox	59	37 23N	2 8W
Albreda	152	52 35N	119 10W
Albrighton	28	52 38N	2 17W
Albuera, La	57	38 45N	6 49W
Albufeira	57	37 5N	8 15W
Albula, R.	51	46 38N	9 30 E
Albuñol	59	36 48N	3 11W
Albuquerque	161	35 5N	106 47W
Albuquerque, Cayos de	166	12 10N	81 50W
Alburno, Mte.	65	40 32N	15 20 E
Alburquerque	57	39 15N	6 59W
Albury	141	36 3 S	146 56 E
Albuskjell, oilfield	19	56 40N	3 0 E
Alby	72	62 30N	15 28 E
Alcácer do Sal	57	38 22N	8 33W
Alcalá de Chisvert	58	40 19N	0 13 E
Alcalá de Guadaira	57	37 20N	5 50W
Alcalá de Henares	58	40 28N	3 22W
Alcalá de los Gazules	57	36 29N	5 43W
Alcalá la Real	57	37 27N	3 57W
Alcamo	64	37 59N	12 55 E
Alcanadre	58	42 24N	2 7W
Alcanadre, R.	58	41 43N	0 12W
Alcanar	58	40 33N	0 28 E
Alcanede	57	39 25N	8 49W
Alcanena	57	39 27N	8 40W
Alcañices	57	41 41N	6 21W
Alcaníz	58	41 2N	0 8W
Alcântara	170	2 20 S	44 30W
Alcántara	57	39 41N	6 57W
Alcantara L.	153	60 57N	108 9W
Alcantarilla	59	37 59N	1 12W
Alcaracejos	57	38 24N	4 58W
Alcaraz	59	38 40N	2 29W
Alcaraz, Sierra de	59	38 40N	2 20W
AlcáRovas	57	38 23N	8 9W
Alcarria, La	58	40 31N	2 45W
Alcaudete	57	37 35N	4 5W
Alcázar de San Juan	59	39 24N	3 12W
Alcester	28	52 13N	1 52W
Alcira	59	39 9N	0 30W
Alcoa	157	35 50N	84 0W
Alcobaça, Brazil	171	17 30 S	39 13W
Alcobaça, Port.	57	39 32N	9 0W
Alcobendas	58	40 32N	3 38W
Alcolea del Pinar	58	41 2N	2 28W
Alcora	58	40 5N	0 14W
Alcoutim	57	37 25N	7 28W
Alcova	160	42 37N	106 52W
Alcoy	59	38 43N	0 30W
Alcubierre, Sierra de	58	41 45N	0 22W
Alcublas	58	39 48N	0 43W
Alcudia	58	39 51N	3 9 E
Alcudia, Bahía de	58	39 45N	3 14 E
Alcudia, Sierra de la	57	38 34N	4 30W
Aldabra Is.	11	9 22 S	46 28 E
Aldama	165	22 25N	98 4W
Aldan	77	58 40N	125 30 E
Aldan, R.	77	62 30N	135 10 E
Aldborough	33	54 6N	1 21W
Aldbourne	28	51 28N	1 38W
Aldbrough	33	53 50N	0 7W
Aldeburgh	29	52 9N	1 35 E
Aldeia Nova	57	37 55N	7 24W
Alden I.	71	61 19N	4 45 E
Alder	160	45 27N	112 3W
Alder Pk.	163	35 53N	12 22W
Alderbury	28	51 4N	1 45W
Alderley Edge	32	53 18N	2 15W
Aldermaston	28	51 23N	1 9W
Alderney, I.	42	49 42N	2 12W
Aldershot	29	51 15N	0 43W
Aldersyde	152	50 40N	113 53W
Aldingham	32	54 8N	3 3W
Aledo	158	41 10N	90 50W
Alefa	123	11 55N	36 55 E
Aleg	120	17 3N	13 55W
Alegre	173	20 50 S	41 30W
Alegrete	173	29 40 S	56 0W
Aleisk	76	52 40N	83 0 E
Alejandro Selkirk, I.	131	33 50 S	80 15W
Aleksandriya, U.S.S.R.	79	50 45N	26 22 E
Aleksandriya, U.S.S.R.	82	48 42N	33 3 E
Aleksandriyskaya	83	43 59N	47 0 E
Aleksandrov	81	56 23N	38 44 E
Aleksandrov Gay.	81	50 15N	48 35 E
Aleksandrovac	66	44 28N	21 13 E
Aleksandrovka	82	48 55N	32 20 E
Aleksandrovo	67	43 14N	24 51 E
Aleksandrovsk	84	59 9N	57 33 E
Aleksandrovsk-Sakhaliniskiy	77	50 50N	142 20 E
Aleksandrovskiy Zavod	77	50 40N	117 50 E
Aleksandrovskoye	76	60 35N	77 50 E
Aleksandrów Kujawski	54	52 53N	18 43 E
Aleksandrów Łódzki	54	51 49N	19 17 E
Alekseyevka, R.S.F.S.R., U.S.S.R.	81	50 43N	38 40 E
Alekseyevka, R.S.F.S.R., U.S.S.R.	84	52 35N	51 17 E
Aleksin	81	54 31N	37 9 E
Aleksinac	66	43 31N	21 42 E
Além Paraíba	173	21 52 S	42 41W
Alemania, Argent.	172	25 40 S	65 30W
Alemania, Chile	172	25 10 S	69 55W
Ålen	71	62 51N	11 17 E
Alençon	42	48 27N	0 4 E
Alentejo, Alto-	55	39 0N	7 40W
Alentejo, Baixo-	55	38 0N	8 30W
Alenuihaha Chan.	147	20 25N	156 0W
Aleppo	92	36 10N	37 15 E
Aléria	45	42 5N	9 26 E
Alert B.	152	50 30N	127 35W
Alès	45	44 9N	4 5 E
Aleşd	70	47 3N	22 22 E
Alessándria	62	44 54N	8 37 E
Ålestrup	73	56 42N	9 29 E
Ålesund	71	62 28N	6 12 E
Alet	123	8 14N	29 2 E
Alet-les-Bains	44	43 0N	2 14 E
Aletschgletscher	50	46 28N	8 2 E
Aletschhorn	50	46 28N	8 0 E
Aleutian Is.	147	52 0N	175 0W
Aleutian Ra.	147	55 0N	155 0W
Alexander	158	47 51N	103 40W
Alexander Arch.	147	57 0N	135 0W
Alexander B.	128	28 36 S	16 33 E
Alexander City	157	32 58N	85 57W
Alexander I.	13	69 0 S	70 0W
Alexander, Mt.	137	28 58 S	120 16 E
Alexandra, Austral.	141	37 8 S	145 40 E
Alexandra, N.Z.	143	45 14 S	169 25 E
Alexandra Falls	152	60 29N	116 18W
Alexandria, Austral.	138	19 5 S	136 40 E
Alexandria, Brazil	171	6 25 S	38 1W
Alexandria, B.C., Can.	152	52 35N	122 27W
Alexandria, Ont., Can.	150	45 19N	74 38W
Alexandria, Rumania	70	43 57N	25 24 E
Alexandria, S. Afr.	128	33 38 S	26 28 E
Alexandria, U.K.	34	55 59N	4 40W
Alexandria, Ind., U.S.A.	156	40 18N	85 40W
Alexandria, La., U.S.A.	159	31 20N	92 30W
Alexandria, Minn., U.S.A.	158	45 50N	95 20W
Alexandria, S.D., U.S.A.	158	43 40N	97 45W
Alexandria, Va., U.S.A.	162	38 47N	77 1W
Alexandria = El Iskandarîya	122	31 0N	30 0 E
Alexandria Bay	156	44 20N	75 52W
Alexandrina, L.	140	35 25 S	139 10 E
Alexandroúpolis	68	40 50N	25 54 E
Alexis Creek	152	52 0N	123 20W
Alexis, R.	151	52 33N	56 8W
Alfambra	58	40 33N	1 5W
Alfândega da Fé	56	41 20N	6 59W
Alfaro	58	42 10N	1 50W
Alfatar	67	43 59N	27 13 E
Alfeld	48	52 0N	9 49 E
Alfenas	173	21 40 S	44 0W
Alfiós, R.	69	37 36N	21 54 E
Alfonsine	63	44 30N	12 1 E
Alford, Grampian, U.K.	37	57 13N	2 42W
Alford, Lincs., U.K.	33	53 16N	0 10 E
Alfred	162	43 28N	70 40W
Alfred Town	141	35 8 S	147 30 E
Alfredton	142	40 41 S	175 54 E
Alfreton	33	53 6N	1 22W
Alfriston	29	50 48N	0 10 E
Alfta	72	61 21N	16 4 E
Alftanes	74	64 29N	22 10W
Alga	84	49 53N	57 20 E
Algaba, La	57	37 27N	6 1W
Algar	57	36 40N	5 39W
Ålgård	71	58 46N	5 53 E
Ålgård	71	58 46N	5 53 E
Algarinejo	57	37 19N	4 9W
Algarve	57	37 15N	8 10W
Algeciras	57	36 9N	5 28W
Algemesí	59	39 11N	0 27W
Alger	118	36 42N	3 8 E
Algeria ■	118	35 10N	3 11 E
Alghero	64	40 34N	8 20 E
Algiers = Alger	118	36 42N	3 8 E
Algoabaai	128	33 50 S	25 45 E
Algodonales	57	36 54N	5 24W
Algodor, R.	56	39 51N	3 48W
Algoma, Mich., U.S.A.	156	44 35N	87 27W
Algoma, Oreg., U.S.A.	160	42 25N	121 54W
Algonquin Prov. Pk.	150	45 50N	78 30W
Alhama de Almería	59	36 57N	2 34W
Alhama de Aragón	58	41 18N	1 54W
Alhama de Granada	57	37 0N	3 59W
Alhama de Murcia	59	37 51N	1 25W
Alhambra, Spain	59	38 54N	3 4W
Alhambra, U.S.A.	163	34 8N	118 10W
Alhaurín el Grande	57	36 39N	4 41W
Alhucemas = Al-Hoceïma	118	35 8N	3 58W
Ali al Gharbi	92	32 30N	46 45 E
Ali Bayramly	83	39 43N	48 52 E
Ali Khel	94	33 56N	69 35 E
Ali Sabieh	123	11 10N	42 44 E
Àlia	64	37 47N	13 42 E
Aliabad	93	28 10N	57 35 E
Aliaga	58	40 40N	0 42W
Aliakmon, R.	68	40 10N	22 0 E
Alibag	96	18 38N	72 56 E
Alibo	123	9 52N	37 5 E
Alibunar	66	45 5N	20 57 E
Alicante	59	38 23N	0 30W
Alicante □	59	38 30N	0 37W
Alice, S. Afr.	128	32 48 S	26 55 E
Alice, U.S.A.	159	27 47N	98 1W
Alice Arm	152	55 29N	129 31W
Alice Downs	136	17 45 S	127 56 E
Alice, Punta dell'	65	39 23N	17 10 E
Alice, R., Queens., Austral.	138	15 35 S	142 20 E
Alice, R., Queens., Austral.	138	24 2 S	144 50 E
Alice Springs	138	23 40 S	135 50 E
Alicedale	128	33 15 S	26 4 E
Aliceville	157	33 9N	88 10W
Alick Cr.	138	20 35 S	142 10 E
Alicudi, I.	65	38 33N	14 20 E
Alida	153	49 25N	101 55W
Aligarh, India	93	27 55N	78 10 E
Aligarh, Raj., India	94	25 55N	76 15 E
Aligarh, Ut. P., India	94	27 55N	78 10 E
Aligudarz	92	33 25N	49 45 E
Alijó	56	41 16N	7 27W
Alimena	65	37 42N	14 4 E
Alimnía	69	36 16N	27 43 E
Aling Kangri	99	31 45N	84 45 E
Alingaabro	73	56 56N	10 32 E
Alingsås	73	57 56N	12 31 E
Alipore	95	22 32N	88 24 E
Alipur	94	29 25N	70 55 E
Alipur Duar	98	26 30N	89 35 E
Aliquippa	156	40 38N	80 18W
Aliste, R.	56	41 48N	6 14W
Alivérion	69	38 24N	24 2 E
Aliwal North	128	30 45 S	26 45 E
Alix	152	52 24N	113 11W
Aljezur	57	37 18N	8 49W
Aljustrel	57	37 55N	8 10W
Alkamari	121	13 27N	11 10 E
Alken	47	50 53N	5 18 E
Alkhalaf	91	20 30N	58 13 E
Alkmaar	46	52 37N	4 45 E
All American Canal	161	32 45N	115 0W
Allada	121	6 41N	2 9 E
Allah Dad	94	25 38N	67 34 E
Allahabad	95	25 25N	81 58 E
Allakaket	147	66 30N	152 45W
Allakh Yun	77	60 50N	137 5 E
Allal Razi	118	34 30N	6 39W
Allan	153	51 53N	106 4W
Allanche	44	45 14N	2 57 E
Allanmyo	98	19 16N	95 17 E
Allanridge	128	27 45 S	26 40 E
Allansford	140	38 26 S	142 39 E
Allanton	143	45 55 S	170 15 E
Allanwater	150	50 14N	90 10W
Allaqi, Wadi	122	22 15N	34 55 E
Allard Lake	151	50 40N	63 10W
Allariz	56	42 11N	7 50W
Allassac	44	45 15N	1 29 E
Alle	47	49 51N	4 58 E
Allegan	156	42 32N	85 52W
Allegheny Mts.	156	38 0N	80 0W
Allegheny, R.	156	41 14N	79 50W
Allègre	44	45 12N	3 41 E
Allen, Bog of	39	53 15N	7 0W
Allen, L.	38	54 30N	8 5W
Allen R.	35	54 53N	2 13W
Allenby (Hussein) Bridge	90	31 53N	35 33 E
Allendale	35	54 55N	2 15W
Allende	164	28 20N	100 50W
Allenheads	35	54 49N	2 12W
Allentown	162	40 36N	75 30W
Allentsteig	52	48 41N	15 20 E
Allenwood	39	53 16N	6 53W
Alleppey	97	9 30N	76 28 E
Allerőd	73	55 54N	12 19 E
Alleur	47	50 39N	5 31 E
Allevard	45	45 24N	6 5 E
Alliance, Nebr., U.S.A.	158	42 10N	102 50W
Alliance, Ohio, U.S.A.	156	40 53N	81 7W
Allier □	44	46 25N	3 0 E
Allier, R.	43	46 57N	3 4 E
Alligator Cr., Queens., Austral.	138	21 20 S	149 12 E
Alligator Cr., Queens., Austral.	138	19 23 S	146 58 E
Allihies	39	51 39N	10 4W
Allingåbrl	73	56 28N	10 20 E
Allingåbro	73	56 28N	10 20 E
Allinge	73	55 17N	14 50 E
Alliston	150	44 9N	79 52W
Alloa	35	56 7N	3 49W
Allonby	32	54 45N	3 27W
Allos	45	44 15N	6 38 E
Alma, Can.	151	48 35N	71 40W
Alma, Kans., U.S.A.	158	39 1N	96 22W
Alma, Mich., U.S.A.	156	43 25N	84 40W
Alma, Nebr., U.S.A.	158	40 10N	99 25W
Alma, Wis., U.S.A.	158	44 19N	91 54W
Alma Ata	85	43 15N	76 57 E
Almada	57	38 40N	9 9W
Almaden	138	17 22 S	144 40 E

Almadén

Amungen

Almadén	**57**	38 49N	4 52W
Almagro	**57**	38 50N	3 45W
Almalyk	**85**	40 50N	69 35E
Almanor, L.	**160**	40 15N	121 11W
Almansa	**59**	38 51N	1 5W
Almanza	**56**	42 39N	5 3W
Almanzor, Pico de	**56**	40 15N	5 18W
Almanzora, R.	**59**	37 22N	2 21W
Almarcha, La	**58**	39 41N	2 24W
Almas	**171**	11 33S	47 9W
Almaş, Mţii	**70**	44 49N	22 12E
Almazán	**58**	41 30N	2 30W
Almazora	**58**	39 57N	0 3W
Almeirim, Brazil	**175**	1 30S	52 0W
Almeirim, Port.	**57**	39 12N	8 37W
Almelo	**46**	52 22N	6 42E
Almenar	**58**	41 43N	2 12W
Almenara, Brazil	**171**	16 11S	40 42W
Almenara, Spain	**58**	39 46N	0 14W
Almenara, Sierra de	**59**	37 34N	1 32W
Almendralejo	**57**	38 41N	6 26W
Almería	**59**	36 52N	2 32W
Almería □	**59**	37 20N	2 20W
Almería, G. de	**59**	36 41N	2 28W
Almetyevsk	**84**	54 53N	52 20E
Almhult	**73**	56 32N	14 10E
Almirante	**166**	9 10N	82 30W
Almiropótamos	**69**	38 16N	24 11E
Almirós	**69**	39 11N	22 45E
Almodôvar	**57**	37 31N	8 2W
Almodóvar del Campo	**57**	38 43N	4 10W
Almogia	**57**	36 50N	4 32W
Almonaster la Real	**57**	37 52N	6 48W
Almond R.	**35**	56 27N	3 27W
Almondsbury	**28**	51 33N	2 34W
Almonte, R.	**57**	39 41N	6 12W
Almora	**95**	29 38N	79 4E
Almoradi	**59**	38 7N	0 46W
Almorox	**56**	40 14N	4 24W
Almoustarat	**121**	17 35N	0 8E
Älmult	**73**	56 33N	14 8E
Almuñécar	**57**	36 43N	3 41W
Almunia, La de Doña Godina	**58**	41 29N	1 23W
Almvik	**73**	57 49N	16 30E
Aln, R.	**35**	55 24N	1 35W
Alness	**37**	57 41N	4 15W
Alness R.	**37**	57 45N	4 20W
Alnif	**118**	31 10N	5 8W
Alnmouth	**35**	55 24N	1 37W
Alnön I.	**72**	62 26N	17 33E
Alnwick	**35**	55 25N	1 42W
Aloi	**126**	2 16N	33 10E
Alon	**98**	22 12N	95 5E
Alonsa	**153**	50 50N	99 0W
Alor, I.	**103**	8 15S	124 30E
Alor Setar	**101**	6 7N	100 22E
Alora	**57**	36 49N	4 46W
Alosno	**57**	37 33N	7 7W
Alot'ai	**105**	47 52N	88 7E
Alotau	**135**	10 16S	150 30E
Alougoum	**118**	30 17N	6 56W
Aloysius Mt.	**137**	26 0S	128 38E
Alpaugh	**163**	35 53N	119 29W
Alpedrinha	**56**	40 6N	7 27W
Alpena	**156**	45 6N	83 24W
Alpercatas, R.	**170**	6 2S	44 19W
Alpes-de-Haute-Provence □	**45**	44 8N	6 10E
Alpes-Maritimes □	**45**	43 55N	7 10E
Alpes Valaisannes	**50**	46 4N	7 30E
Alpha	**138**	23 39S	146 37E
Alphen	**47**	51 29N	4 58E
Alphen aan den Rijn	**46**	52 7N	4 40E
Alphington	**30**	50 41N	3 32W
Alpi Apuan	**62**	44 7N	10 14E
Alpi Craie	**43**	45 40N	7 0E
Alpi Lepontine	**51**	46 22N	8 27E
Alpi Orobie	**62**	46 7N	10 0E
Alpi Retiche	**51**	46 45N	10 0E
Alpiarça	**57**	39 15N	8 35W
Alpine, Ariz., U.S.A.	**161**	33 57N	109 4W
Alpine, Calif., U.S.A.	**163**	32 50N	116 46W
Alpine, Tex., U.S.A.	**159**	30 35N	103 35W
Alpnach	**51**	46 57N	8 17E
Alrewas	**28**	52 43N	1 44W
Alrø	**73**	55 52N	10 5E
Alroy Downs	**138**	19 20S	136 5E
Als	**73**	56 46N	10 18E
Alsace	**43**	48 15N	7 25E
Alsager	**32**	53 7N	2 20W
Alsask	**153**	51 21N	109 59W
Alsásua	**58**	42 54N	2 10W
Alseda	**73**	57 27N	15 20E
Alsen	**72**	63 23N	13 56E
Alsfeld	**48**	50 44N	9 19E
Alsh, L.	**36**	57 15N	5 39W
Alsónémedi	**53**	47 34N	19 15E
Alsten	**74**	65 58N	12 40E
Alston	**32**	54 48N	2 26W
Alta	**74**	69 57N	23 10E
Alta Gracia	**172**	31 40S	64 30W
Alta Lake	**152**	50 10N	123 0W
Alta, Sierra	**58**	40 31N	1 30W
Alta Sierra	**163**	35 42N	118 33W
Altaelva	**74**	69 46N	23 45E
Altafjorden	**74**	70 5N	23 5E
Altagracia	**174**	10 45N	71 30W
Altai = Aerht'ai Shan	**105**	48 0N	90 0E
Altamaha, R.	**157**	31 50N	82 0W
Altamira, Brazil	**175**	3 0S	52 10W
Altamira, Chile	**172**	25 47S	69 51W
Altamira, Colomb.	**174**	2 3N	75 47W
Altamira, Mexico	**165**	22 24N	97 55W
Altamira, Cuevas de	**56**	43 20N	4 5W
Altamont	**162**	42 43N	74 3W
Altamura	**65**	40 50N	16 33E
Altanbulag	**54**	50 19N	106 30E
Altar	**164**	30 40N	111 50W
Altarnun	**30**	50 35N	4 30W
Altata	**164**	24 30N	108 0W
Altavista	**156**	37 9N	79 22W
Altdorf	**51**	46 52N	8 36E
Altea	**59**	38 38N	0 2W
Altenberg	**48**	50 46N	13 47E
Altenbruch	**48**	53 48N	8 44E
Altenburg	**48**	50 59N	12 28E
Altenkirchen	**48**	50 41N	7 38E
Altenmarkt	**52**	47 43N	14 39E
Alter do Chão	**57**	39 12N	7 40W
Altkirch	**43**	47 37N	7 15E
Altnaharra	**37**	58 17N	4 27W
Alto Adige = Trentino-Alto Adige	**62**	46 5N	11 0E
Alto Araguaia	**175**	17 15S	53 20W
Alto Chindio	**127**	16 19S	35 25E
Alto Cuchumatanes	**164**	15 30N	91 10W
Alto del Inca	**172**	24 10S	68 10W
Alto Ligonha	**127**	15 30S	38 11E
Alto Molocue	**127**	15 50S	37 35E
Alto Paraná □	**173**	25 0S	54 50W
Alto Parnaíba	**170**	9 6S	45 57W
Alto Santo	**170**	5 31S	38 15W
Alto Turi	**170**	2 54S	45 38W
Alto Uruguay, R.	**173**	27 0S	53 30W
Alton, U.K.	**29**	51 8N	0 59W
Alton, Ill., U.S.A.	**158**	38 55N	90 5W
Alton, N.H., U.S.A.	**162**	43 27N	71 13W
Alton Downs	**139**	26 7S	138 57E
Altona	**48**	53 32N	9 56E
Altoona	**156**	40 32N	78 24W
Altopáscio	**62**	43 50N	10 40E
Altos	**170**	5 3S	42 28W
Altrincham	**32**	53 25N	2 21W
Altstätten	**51**	47 22N	9 33E
Alturas	**160**	41 36N	120 37W
Altus	**159**	34 30N	99 25W
Alucra	**83**	40 22N	38 47E
Aluksône	**80**	57 24N	27 3E
Alula	**91**	11 50N	50 45E
Alupka	**82**	44 23N	34 2E
Alushta	**82**	44 40N	34 25E
Alusi	**103**	7 35S	131 40E
Alustante	**58**	40 36N	1 40W
Alva, U.K.	**35**	56 9N	3 49W
Alva, U.S.A.	**159**	36 50N	98 50W
Alvaiázere	**56**	39 49N	8 23W
Ålvangen	**73**	58 0N	12 7E
Älvängen	**73**	57 58N	12 8E
Alvarado, Mexico	**165**	18 40N	95 50W
Alvarado, U.S.A.	**159**	32 25N	97 15W
Alvaro Obregón, Presa	**164**	27 55N	109 52W
Alvastra	**73**	58 20N	14 44E
Alvdal	**71**	62 6N	10 37E
Alvear	**172**	29 5S	56 30W
Alvechurch	**28**	52 22N	1 58W
Alverca	**57**	38 56N	9 1W
Alveringen	**47**	51 1N	2 43E
Alvesta	**73**	56 54N	14 35E
Älvho	**72**	61 30N	14 45E
Alvie, Austral.	**140**	38 14S	143 30E
Alvie, U.K.	**37**	57 10N	3 50W
Alvin	**159**	29 23N	95 12W
Alvito	**57**	38 15N	8 0W
Älvkarleby	**75**	60 32N	17 40E
Alvra, Pic d'	**51**	46 35N	9 50E
Älvros	**72**	62 3N	14 38E
Älvsborgs län □	**73**	58 30N	12 30E
Älvsby	**74**	65 42N	20 52E
Älvsbyn	**74**	65 40N	20 0E
Alvsered	**73**	57 14N	12 51E
Alwar	**94**	27 38N	76 34E
Alwaye	**97**	10 8N	76 24E
Alwinton	**35**	55 20N	2 7W
Alwyn, oilfield	**19**	60 30N	1 45E
Alyangula	**133**	13 55S	136 30E
Alyaskitovyy	**77**	64 45N	141 30E
Alyata	**83**	39 58N	49 25E
Alyth	**37**	56 38N	3 15W
Alzada	**158**	45 3N	104 22W
Alzano Lombardo	**62**	45 44N	9 43E
Alzette, R.	**47**	49 45N	6 6E
Alzey	**49**	49 48N	8 4E
Am-Dam	**117**	12 40N	20 35E
Am Djeress	**117**	16 15N	22 50E
Am Guereda	**117**	12 53N	21 14E
Am Timan	**117**	11 0N	20 10E
Am-Zoer	**124**	14 13N	21 23E
Amadeus, L.	**137**	24 54S	131 0E
Amadi, Congo	**126**	3 40N	26 40E
Amadi, Sudan	**123**	5 29N	30 25E
Amadi, Zaïre	**126**	3 40N	26 40E
Amadia	**92**	37 6N	43 30E
Amadjuak	**149**	64 0N	72 39W
Amadjuak L.	**149**	65 0N	71 8W
Amadora	**57**	38 45N	9 13W
Amaga	**174**	6 3N	75 42W
Amagansett	**162**	40 58N	72 8W
Amagasaki	**111**	34 42N	135 20E
Amager	**73**	55 37N	12 35E
Amagi	**110**	33 25N	130 39E
Amagunze	**121**	6 20N	7 40E
Amaimon	**135**	5 12S	145 30E
Amakusa-Nada	**110**	32 35N	130 5E
Amakusa-Shotō	**110**	32 15N	130 10E
Åmål	**72**	59 2N	12 40E
Åmål	**72**	59 3N	12 42E
Amalapuram	**96**	16 35N	81 55E
Amalfi, Colomb.	**174**	6 55N	75 4W
Amalfi, Italy	**65**	40 39N	14 34E
Amaliás	**69**	37 47N	21 22E
Amalner	**96**	21 5N	75 5E
Amambaí	**173**	23 5S	55 13W
Amambaí, R.	**173**	23 22S	53 56W
Amambay □	**173**	23 0S	56 0W
Amambay, Cordillera de	**173**	20 30S	56 0W
Amami-O-Shima	**112**	28 0N	129 0E
Amanab	**135**	3 40S	141 14E
Amandola	**63**	42 59N	13 21E
Amanfrom	**121**	7 20N	0 25E
Amangeldy	**76**	50 10N	65 10E
Amantea	**65**	39 8N	16 3E
Amapá	**170**	2 5N	50 50W
Amapá □	**170**	1 40N	52 0W
Amar Gedid	**123**	14 27N	25 13E
Amara, Iraq	**92**	31 57N	47 12E
Amara, Sudan	**123**	10 25N	34 10E
Amarante, Brazil	**170**	6 14S	42 50W
Amarante, Port.	**56**	41 16N	8 5W
Amarante do Maranhão	**170**	5 36S	46 45W
Amaranth	**153**	50 36N	98 43W
Amarapura	**98**	21 54N	96 3E
Amaravati, R.	**97**	10 50N	77 42E
Amaravati = Amraoti	**96**	20 55N	77 45E
Amareleja	**57**	38 12N	7 13W
Amargosa	**171**	13 2S	39 36W
Amargosa, R.	**163**	36 14N	116 51W
Amargosa Ra., mts	**163**	36 25N	116 40W
Amarillo	**159**	35 14N	101 46W
Amaro Leite	**171**	13 58S	49 9W
Amaro, Mt.	**63**	42 5N	14 6E
Amarpur, India	**99**	23 30N	91 45E
Amarpur, Bihar, India	**95**	25 5N	87 0E
Amarpur, Tripura, India	**99**	23 30N	91 45E
Amasra	**92**	41 45N	32 30E
Amassama	**121**	5 1N	6 2E
Amasya	**92**	40 40N	35 50E
Amatignak I.	**147**	51 19N	179 10W
Amatikulu	**129**	29 3S	31 33E
Amatitlán	**166**	14 29N	90 38W
Amatrice	**63**	42 38N	13 16E
Amay	**47**	50 33N	5 19E
Amazon, R.	**175**	2 0S	53 30W
Amazonas □, Brazil	**174**	4 20S	64 0W
Amazonas □, Colomb.	**174**	1 0S	72 0W
Amazonas □, Venez.	**174**	3 30N	66 0W
Amazonas, R.	**175**	2 0S	53 30W
Ambad	**96**	19 38N	75 50E
Ambahakily	**129**	21 36S	43 41E
Ambala	**94**	30 23N	76 56E
Ambalangoda	**97**	6 15N	80 5E
Ambalapuzha	**97**	9 25N	76 25E
Ambalavao	**129**	21 50S	46 56E
Ambalindum	**138**	23 23S	134 40E
Ambam	**124**	2 20N	11 15E
Ambanifilao	**129**	12 48S	49 47E
Ambanja	**129**	13 40S	48 27E
Ambararata	**129**	13 41S	48 27E
Ambarchik	**77**	69 40N	162 20E
Ambarijeby	**129**	14 56S	47 41E
Ambarnath	**96**	19 12N	73 22E
Ambaro, B. d'	**129**	13 23S	48 38E
Ambasamudram	**97**	8 43N	77 25E
Ambato	**174**	1 5S	78 42W
Ambato-Boéni	**129**	16 28S	46 43E
Ambato, Sierra de	**172**	28 25N	66 10W
Ambatolampy	**129**	19 20S	47 35E
Ambatondrazaka	**129**	17 55S	48 28E
Ambatosoratra	**129**	17 37S	48 31E
Ambenja	**129**	15 17S	46 58E
Ambeno	**103**	9 20S	124 30E
Amberg	**49**	49 25N	11 52E
Ambergris Cay	**165**	18 0N	88 0W
Ambérieu-en-Bugey	**45**	45 57N	5 20E
Amberley	**143**	43 9S	172 44E
Ambert	**44**	45 33N	3 44E
Ambevongo	**129**	15 25S	42 26E
Ambia	**129**	16 11S	45 33E
Ambidédi	**120**	14 35N	11 47W
Ambikapur	**95**	23 15N	83 15E
Ambikol	**122**	21 20N	30 50E
Ambilobé	**125**	13 10S	49 3E
Ambinanindrano	**129**	20 5S	48 23E
Ambjörnarp	**73**	57 25N	13 17E
Amble	**35**	55 20N	1 36W
Ambler	**162**	40 9N	75 13W
Ambleside	**32**	54 26N	2 58W
Amblève	**47**	50 21N	6 10E
Amblève, R.	**47**	50 25N	5 45E
Ambo, Begemdir & Simen, Ethiopia	**123**	12 20N	37 30E
Ambo, Shewa, Ethiopia	**123**	9 0N	37 48E
Ambo, Peru	**174**	10 5S	76 10W
Ambodifototra	**129**	16 59S	49 52E
Ambodilazana	**129**	18 6S	49 10E
Ambohimahasoa	**129**	21 7S	47 13E
Ambohimanga du Sud	**129**	20 52S	47 36E
Ambon	**103**	3 35S	128 20E
Ambongao, Cones d'	**129**	17 0S	45 0E
Amboseli L.	**126**	2 40S	37 10E
Ambositra	**129**	20 31S	47 25E
Amboy	**163**	34 33N	115 51W
Ambre, C. d'	**129**	12 40S	49 10E
Ambre, Mt. d'	**125**	12 30S	49 10E
Ambriz	**124**	7 48S	13 8E
Ambrizete	**124**	7 10S	12 52E
Ambunti	**135**	4 13S	142 52E
Ambut	**97**	12 48N	78 43E
Amby	**139**	26 30S	148 11E
Amchitka I.	**147**	51 30N	179 0W
Amchitka P.	**147**	51 30N	179 0W
Amderma	**76**	69 45N	61 30E
Ameca	**164**	20 30N	104 0W
Ameca, R.	**164**	20 40N	105 15W
Amecameca	**165**	19 10N	98 57W
Ameland	**46**	53 27N	5 45E
Amélia	**63**	42 34N	12 25E
Amèlie-les-Bains-Palalda	**44**	42 29N	2 41E
Amen	**77**	68 45N	180 0E
Amendolaro	**65**	39 58N	16 34E
Amenia	**162**	41 51N	73 33W
America	**47**	51 27N	5 59E
American Falls	**160**	42 46N	112 56W
American Falls Res.	**160**	43 0N	112 50W
American Highland	**13**	73 0S	75 0E
Americana	**173**	22 45S	47 20W
Americus	**157**	32 0N	84 10W
Amersfoort, Neth.	**46**	52 9N	5 23E
Amersfoort, S. Afr.	**129**	26 59S	29 53E
Amersham	**29**	51 40N	0 38W
Amery, Austral.	**137**	31 9S	117 5E
Amery, Can.	**153**	56 34N	94 3W
Ames	**158**	42 0N	93 40W
Amesbury, U.K.	**28**	51 10N	1 46W
Amesbury, U.S.A.	**162**	42 50N	70 52W
Amesdale	**153**	50 2N	92 55W
Ameson	**150**	49 50N	84 35W
Amethyst, gasfield	**19**	53 38N	0 40E
Amfiklia	**69**	38 38N	22 35E
Amfilokhia	**69**	38 52N	21 9E
Amfípolis	**68**	40 48N	23 52E
Ámfissa	**69**	38 32N	22 22E
Amga, R.	**77**	61 0N	132 0E
Amgu	**77**	45 45N	137 15E
Amherst, Burma	**99**	16 2N	97 20E
Amherst, Can.	**151**	45 48N	64 8W
Amherst, Mass., U.S.A.	**162**	42 21N	72 30W
Amherst, Tex., U.S.A.	**159**	34 0N	102 24W
Amherst, Mt.	**136**	18 11S	126 59E
Amherstburg	**150**	42 6N	83 6W
Amiata Mte.	**63**	42 54N	11 40E
Amiens	**43**	49 54N	2 16E
Amigdhalokefáli	**69**	35 23N	23 30E
Amili	**98**	28 25N	95 52E
Amindaion	**68**	40 42N	21 42E
Amirante Is.	**11**	6 0S	53 0E
Amisk L.	**153**	54 35N	102 15W
Amistati, Presa	**164**	29 24N	101 0W
Amite	**159**	30 47N	90 31W
Åmli	**71**	58 45N	8 32E
Amlia I.	**147**	52 5N	173 30W
Amlwch	**31**	53 24N	4 21W
Amm Adam	**123**	16 20N	36 1E
'Ammân	**90**	32 0N	35 52E
Ammanford	**31**	51 48N	4 0W
Ammerån	**72**	63 9N	16 13E
Ammerån	**72**	63 9N	16 13E
Ammersee	**49**	48 0N	11 7E
Ammerzoden	**46**	51 45N	5 13E
Ammi'ad	**90**	32 55N	35 32E
Amnat Charoen	**100**	15 51N	104 38E
Amne Machin	**105**	34 30N	100 0E
Amnéville	**43**	49 16N	6 9E
Amo Chiang, R.	**108**	22 56N	101 47E
Amorebieta	**58**	43 13N	2 44W
Amorgós	**69**	36 50N	25 57E
Amory	**57**	33 59N	88 30W
Amos	**150**	48 35N	78 5W
Åmot	**71**	59 54N	9 54E
Åmot	**71**	59 34N	8 0E
Åmotsdal	**71**	59 37N	8 26E
Amour, Djebel	**118**	33 42N	1 37E
Amoy = Hsiamen	**109**	24 25N	118 4E
Amozoc	**165**	19 2N	98 3W
Ampang	**101**	3 8N	101 45E
Ampanihy	**129**	24 40S	44 45E
Amparihy Est.	**129**	23 57S	47 20E
Ampasindava, B. d'	**129**	13 40S	48 15E
Ampasindava, Presqu'île d'	**129**	13 42S	47 55W
Amper	**121**	9 25N	9 40E
Ampère	**119**	35 44N	5 27E
Ampleforth	**33**	54 13N	1 8W
Ampombiantambo	**129**	12 42S	48 57E
Amposta	**58**	40 43N	0 34E
Ampotaka	**129**	25 3S	44 41E
Ampoza	**129**	22 20S	44 44E
Ampthill	**29**	52 3N	0 30W
Amqa	**90**	32 59N	35 10E
Amqui	**151**	48 28N	67 27W
Amraoti	**96**	20 55N	77 45E
Amreli	**94**	21 35N	71 17E
Amrenene el Kasba	**118**	22 10N	0 30E
Amriswil	**51**	47 33N	9 18E
Amritsar	**94**	31 35N	74 57E
Amroha	**95**	28 53N	78 30E
Amrum	**48**	54 37N	8 21E
Amsel	**119**	22 47N	5 29E
Amsterdam, Neth.	**46**	52 23N	4 54E
Amsterdam, U.S.A.	**162**	42 58N	74 10W
Amsterdam, I.	**11**	37 30S	77 30E
Amstetten	**52**	48 7N	14 51E
Amu Darya, R.	**76**	37 50N	65 0E
Amuay	**174**	11 50N	70 10W
Amukta I.	**147**	52 29N	171 20W
Amund Ringnes I.	**12**	78 20N	96 25W
Amundsen Gulf	**148**	71 0N	124 0W
Amundsen Sea	**13**	72 0S	115 0W
Amungen	**72**	61 10N	15 40E

Amuntai Anza

Amuntai 102 2 28S 115 25E
Amur, R. 77 53 30N 122 30E
Amurang 103 1 5N 124 40E
Amuri Pass 143 42 31S 172 11E
Amurrio 58 43 3N 3 0W
Amurzet 77 47 50N 131 5E
Amusco 56 42 10N 4 28W
Amvrakikós Kólpos 69 39 0N 20 55E
Amvrosiyvka 83 47 43N 38 30E
Amzeglouf 118 26 50N 0 1E
An 98 22 29N 96 54E
An Bien 101 9 45N 105 0E
An Geata Mór, (Binghamstown) 38 54 13N 10 0W
An Hoa 100 15 30N 108 20E
An Loc 101 11 40N 106 50E
An Nafud 92 28 15N 41 0E
An Najaf 92 32 3N 44 15E
An-Nāqūrah 90 33 7N 35 8E
An Nasiriyah 92 31 0N 46 15E
An Nawfaliyah 119 30 54N 17 58E
An Nhon (Binh Dinh) 100 13 55N 109 7E
An Nîl □ 123 17 30N 33 0E
An Nîl el Abyad □ 123 14 0N 32 15E
An Nu'ayriyah 92 27 30N 48 30E
An Teallach, Mt. 36 57 49N 5 18W
An Thoi, Dao 101 9 58N 104 0E
An Tuc 100 13 57N 108 39E
An Uaimh 38 53 39N 6 40W
Ana-Sira 71 58 17N 6 25E
Anabta 90 32 19N 35 7E
Anabuki 110 34 2N 134 11E
Anaco 174 9 27N 64 28W
Anaconda 160 46 7N 113 0W
Anacortes 160 48 30N 122 40W
Anadarko 159 35 4N 98 15W
Anadia, Brazil 170 9 42S 36 18W
Anadia, Port. 56 40 26N 8 27W
Anadolu 92 38 0N 29 0E
Anadyr 77 64 35N 177 20E
Anadyr, R. 77 66 50N 171 0E
Anadyrskiy Zaliv 77 64 0N 180 0E
Anáfi 69 36 22N 25 48E
Anafópoulo 69 36 17N 25 50E
Anagni 64 41 44N 13 8E
Anah 92 34 25N 42 0E
Anaheim 163 33 50N 118 0W
Anahim Lake 152 52 28N 125 18W
Anáhuac 164 27 14N 100 9W
Anai Mudi, Mt. 97 10 12N 77 20E
Anaimalai Hills 97 10 20N 76 40E
Anajás 170 0 59S 49 57W
Anajatuba 170 3 16S 44 37W
Anakapalle 96 17 42N 83 06E
Anakie 138 23 32S 147 45E
Anaklia 83 42 22N 41 35E
Analalava 129 14 35S 48 0E
Analapasy 129 25 11S 46 40E
Anam 121 6 19N 6 41E
Anambar, R. 94 30 10N 68 50E
Anambas, Kepulauan 102 3 20N 106 30E
Anamoose 158 47 55N 100 7W
Anamosa 158 42 7N 91 17W
Anamur 92 36 8N 32 58E
Anan 110 33 54N 134 40E
Anand 94 22 32N 72 59E
Anandpur 96 21 16N 86 13E
Anánes 69 36 33N 24 9E
Anantapur 97 14 39N 77 42E
Anantnag 95 33 45N 75 10E
Ananyev 82 47 44N 29 57E
Anapa 82 44 55N 37 25E
Anápolis 171 16 15S 48 50W
Anar 93 30 55N 55 13E
Anarak 93 33 25N 53 40E
Anatolia = Anadolu 92 38 0N 29 0E
Anatone 160 46 9N 117 4W
Añatuya 172 28 20S 62 50W
Anaunethad L. 153 60 55N 104 25W
Anaye 117 19 15N 12 50E
Anbyŏn 107 39 1N 127 35E
Ancaster 33 52 59N 0 32W
Ancenis 42 47 21N 1 10W
Anch'i 109 25 3N 118 13E
Anch'ing 109 30 37N 117 0E
Anch'iu 107 36 25N 119 10E
Ancholme, R. 33 53 42N 0 32W
Anchorage 147 61 10N 149 50W
Ancião 56 39 56N 8 27W
Ancohuma, Nevada 174 16 0S 68 50W
Ancon 164 8 57N 79 33W
Ancón 174 11 50S 77 10W
Ancona 63 43 37N 13 30E
Ancrum 35 55 31N 2 35W
Ancud 176 42 0S 73 50W
Ancud, G. de 176 42 0S 73 0W
Andacollo, Argent. 172 37 10S 70 42W
Andacollo, Chile 172 30 15S 71 10W
Andado 138 25 25S 135 15E
Andalgalá 172 27 40S 66 30W
Åndalsnes 71 62 35N 7 43E
Andalucía 57 37 35N 5 0W
Andalusia 157 31 51N 86 30W
Andalusia = Andalucía 57 37 35N 5 0W
Andaman Is. 101 12 30N 92 30E
Andaman Sea 101 13 0N 96 0E
Andaman Str. 101 12 15N 92 20E
Andara 128 18 2S 21 9E
Andaraí 171 12 48S 41 20W
Andeer 51 46 36N 9 26E
Andelfingen 51 47 36N 8 41E
Andelot 43 46 51N 5 56E
Andelys, Les 42 49 15N 1 25E
Andenne 47 50 30N 5 5E
Andéranboukane 121 15 26N 3 2E
Anderlecht 47 50 50N 4 19E
Anderlues 47 50 25N 4 16E
Andermatt 51 46 38N 8 35E
Andernach 48 50 24N 7 25E
Andernos 44 44 44N 1 6W
Anderslöv 73 55 26N 13 19E
Anderson, Austral. 141 38 32S 145 27E
Anderson, Calif., U.S.A. 160 40 30N 122 19W
Anderson, Ind., U.S.A. 156 40 5N 85 40W
Anderson, Mo., U.S.A. 159 36 43N 94 29W
Anderson, S.C., U.S.A. 157 34 32N 82 40W
Anderson, Mt. 129 25 5S 30 42E
Anderson, R. 147 69 42N 129 0W
Anderstorp 73 57 19N 13 39E
Andes 162 42 12N 74 47W
Andes, mts. 174 20 0S 68 0W
Andfjorden 74 69 10N 16 20E
Andhra, L. 96 18 30N 73 32E
Andhra Pradesh □ 97 15 0N 80 0E
Andikíthira 69 35 52N 23 15E
Andímilos 69 36 47N 24 12E
Andíparos 69 37 0N 25 3E
Andípaxoi 69 39 9N 20 13E
Andípsara 69 38 30N 25 29E
Andizhan 76 41 10N 72 0E
Andkhui 93 36 52N 65 8E
Andohararo 129 22 58S 43 45E
Andol 96 17 51N 78 4E
Andong 107 36 40N 128 43E
Andorra ■ 58 42 30N 1 30E
Andorra La Vella 58 42 31N 1 32E
Andover, U.K. 28 51 13N 1 29W
Andover, U.S.A. 162 40 59N 74 44W
Andradina 171 20 54S 51 23W
Andrahary, Mt. 129 13 37S 49 17E
Andraitx 58 39 35N 2 25E
Andramasina 129 19 11S 47 35E
Andrano-Velona 129 18 10S 46 52E
Andranopasy 129 21 17S 43 44E
Andreanof Is. 147 51 0N 178 0W
Andreapol 80 56 40N 32 17E
Andreas 32 54 23N 4 25W
Andrespol 54 51 45N 19 34E
Andrew, oilfield 19 58 4N 1 24E
Andrews, S.C., U.S.A. 157 33 29N 79 30W
Andrews, Tex., U.S.A. 159 32 18N 102 33W
Andreyevka 84 52 19N 51 55E
Ándria 65 41 13N 16 17E
Andrian 65 46 30N 11 13E
Andriba 129 17 30S 46 58E
Andrijevica 66 42 45N 19 48E
Andrítsaina 69 37 29N 21 52E
Androka 129 24 58S 44 2E
Ándros 69 37 50N 24 50E
Andros I. 166 24 30N 78 0W
Andros Town 166 24 43N 77 47W
Andrychów 54 49 51N 19 18E
Andújar 57 38 3N 4 5W
Aneby 73 57 48N 14 49E
Anécho 121 6 12N 1 34E
Anegada I. 147 18 45N 64 20W
Anergane 118 31 4N 7 14W
Aneto, Pico de 58 42 37N 0 40E
Anfeg 119 22 29N 5 58E
Anfu 109 27 23N 114 37E
Ang Thong 100 14 35N 100 31E
Anga 77 60 35N 132 0E
Angamos, Punta 172 23 1S 70 32W
Anganch'i 98 47 9N 123 48E
Angara, R. 77 58 30N 97 0E
Angarsk 77 52 30N 104 0E
Angas Downs 137 24 49S 132 14E
Angas Ra. 137 23 0S 127 50E
Angaston 140 34 30S 139 8E
Ånge 72 62 31N 15 35E
Ångebo 72 61 58N 16 22E
Angel de la Guarda, I. 164 29 30N 113 30W
Ängelholm 73 56 15N 12 58E
Angellala 139 26 24S 146 54E
Angels Camp 163 38 8N 120 30W
Ängelsberg 72 59 58N 16 0E
Angenong 99 31 57N 94 10E
Anger, R. 123 9 30N 36 35E
Angereb 123 13 11N 37 7E
Angereb, R. 123 14 0N 36 0E
Ångermanälven 72 62 40N 18 0E
Angermünde 48 53 1N 14 0E
Angers 42 47 30N 0 35W
Angerville 43 48 19N 2 0E
Ångesån 74 66 50N 22 15E
Anghiari 63 43 32N 12 3E
Angical 171 12 0S 44 42W
Angical do Piauí 171 6 5S 42 44W
Angikuni L. 153 62 0N 100 0W
Angkor 100 13 22N 103 50E
Angle 31 51 40N 5 3W
Anglem Mt. 143 46 45S 167 53E
Anglès 58 41 57N 2 38E
Anglesey (□) 26 53 17N 4 20W
Anglesey, I. 31 53 17N 4 20W
Anglet 44 43 29N 1 31W
Angleton 159 29 12N 95 23W
Angleur 47 50 36N 5 35E
Anglure 43 48 35N 3 50E
Angmagssalik 12 65 40N 37 20W
Angmering 29 50 48N 0 28W
Ango 126 4 10N 26 5E
Angoche 127 16 8S 40 0E
Angoche, I. 127 16 20S 39 50E
Angol 172 37 56S 72 45W
Angola 156 41 40N 85 0W
Angola ■ 125 12 0S 18 0E
Angoon 147 57 40N 134 40W
Angoram 135 4 4S 144 4E
Angoulême 44 45 39N 0 10E
Angoumois 44 45 30N 0 25E
Angra dos Reis 173 23 0S 44 10W
Angra-Juntas 128 27 39S 15 31E
Angran 76 80 59N 69 3E
Angren 85 41 1N 70 12E
Angtassom 101 11 1N 104 41E
Angu 126 3 25N 24 28E
Anguilla, I. 167 18 14N 63 5W
Angurugu 138 14 0S 136 25E
Angus (□) 26 56 45N 2 55W
Angus, Braes of 37 56 51N 3 0W
Anhanduí, R. 173 21 46S 52 9W
Anhée 47 50 18N 4 53E
Anholt 73 56 42N 11 33E
Anhsi 105 40 30N 96 0E
Anhsiang 109 29 24N 112 9E
Anhua, Hunan, China 109 28 22N 111 10E
Anhua, Kwangsi-Chuang, China 108 25 10N 108 21E
Anhwei □ 109 33 15N 116 50E
Ani, Kiangsi, China 109 28 50N 115 32E
Ani, Shansi, China 106 35 3N 111 2E
Aniak 147 61 58N 159 50W
Anicuns 171 16 28S 49 58W
Ánidhros 69 36 38N 25 43E
Anié 121 7 42N 1 8E
Animas 161 31 58N 108 58W
Ånimskog 73 58 53N 12 35E
Anin 101 15 36N 97 50E
Anivorano 129 18 44S 48 58E
Anjangaon 96 21 10N 77 20E
Anjar 94 23 6N 70 10E
Anjen 109 26 42N 113 19E
Anjiabé 129 12 7S 49 20E
Anjidiv I. 97 14 40N 74 10E
Anjō 111 34 57N 137 5E
Anjou 42 47 20N 0 15W
Anjozorobe 129 18 22S 47 52E
Anju 107 39 36N 125 40E
Anka 121 12 13N 5 58E
Ank'ang 108 32 38N 109 5E
Ankara 92 40 0N 32 54E
Ankaramena 129 21 57S 46 39E
Ankazoabo 129 22 18S 44 31E
Ankazobé 129 18 20S 47 10E
Ankazotokana 129 21 20S 48 9E
Ankisabé 129 19 17S 46 29E
Anklesvar 96 21 38N 73 3E
Ankober 123 9 35N 39 40E
Ankoro 126 6 45S 26 55E
Ankuang 107 45 19N 123 40E
Ankuo 106 38 25N 115 19E
Anlu 109 31 12N 113 38E
Anlung 108 25 6N 106 31E
Ånmyŏn Do 107 36 25N 126 25E
Ånn 72 63 19N 12 34E
Ann Arbor 156 42 17N 83 45W
Ann C., Antarct. 13 66 30S 50 30E
Ann C., U.S.A. 162 42 39N 70 37W
Ann, gasfield 19 53 40N 2 5E
Ånn L. 72 63 15N 12 35E
Anna, U.S.A. 159 37 28N 89 10W
Anna, U.S.S.R. 81 51 38N 40 23E
Anna Branch, R. 139 34 2S 141 50E
Anna Plains 136 19 17S 121 37E
Annaba 119 36 50N 7 46E
Annaberg-Buchholz 48 50 34N 12 58E
Annagassan 38 53 53N 6 20W
Annagh Hd. 38 54 15N 10 5W
Annaka 111 36 19N 138 54E
Annalee, R. 38 54 3N 7 15W
Annalong 38 54 7N 5 55W
Annam = Trung-Phan 101 16 30N 107 30E
Annamitique, Chaîne 100 17 0N 106 0E
Annan 35 55 0N 3 17W
Annan, R. 35 54 58N 3 18W
Annanberg 135 4 52S 144 42E
Annandale 35 55 10N 3 25W
Annapolis 162 39 0N 76 30W
Annapolis Royal 151 44 44N 65 32W
Annapurna 95 28 34N 83 50E
Annascaul 39 52 10N 10 3W
Anne, oilfield 19 55 24N 5 7E
Annean, L. 137 26 54S 118 14E
Anneberg 73 57 32N 12 6E
Annecy 45 45 55N 6 8E
Annecy, L. d' 45 45 52N 6 10E
Annemasse 45 46 12N 6 16E
Annestown 39 52 8N 7 18W
Annette 147 55 2N 131 35W
Annfield Plain 33 54 52N 1 45W
Annie Peak 137 33 53S 119 59E
Anning 108 24 58N 102 30E
Anningie 136 21 50S 133 7E
Anniston 157 33 45N 85 50W
Annobón = Pagalu 114 1 35S 3 35E
Annonay 45 45 15N 4 40E
Annonciation, L' 150 46 25N 74 55W
Annot 45 43 58N 6 38E
Annotto Bay 166 18 17N 77 3W
Annuello 140 34 53S 142 55E
Annville 162 40 18N 76 32W
Áno Arkhánai 69 35 16N 25 11E
Áno Porróia 68 41 17N 23 2E
Áno Viánnos 69 35 2N 25 21E
Anoka 158 45 10N 93 26W
Anorotsangana 129 13 56S 47 55E
Anp'ing, Hopei, China 106 38 13N 115 31E
Anp'ing, Liaoning, China 107 41 10N 123 30E
Ans 47 50 39N 5 32E
Ansai 106 36 54N 109 10E
Ansbach 49 49 17N 10 34E
Anse au Loup, L' 151 51 32N 56 50W
Anse, L' 150 46 47N 88 28W
Anseba, R. 123 16 15N 37 45E
Anserma 174 5 13N 75 48W
Anseroeul 47 50 43N 3 32E
Anshan 107 41 3N 122 58E
Anshun 105 26 2N 105 57E
Ansley 158 41 19N 99 24W
Ansó 58 42 51N 0 48W
Anson 159 32 46N 99 54W
Anson B. 136 13 20S 130 6E
Ansongo 121 15 25N 0 35E
Ansonia 162 41 21N 73 6W
Ansonville 150 48 46N 80 43W
Anstey 28 52 41N 1 14W
Anstey Hill 109 34 51S 138 44E
Anstruther 35 56 14N 2 40W
Ansudu 103 2 11S 139 22E
Antabamba 174 14 40S 73 0W
Antakya 92 36 14N 36 10E
Antalaha 129 14 57S 50 20E
Antalya 92 36 52N 30 45E
Antalya Körfezi 92 36 15N 31 30E
Antananarivo 125 18 55S 47 35E
Antanimbaribé 129 21 30S 44 48E
Antarctic Pen. 13 67 0S 60 0W
Antarctica 125 90 0S 0 0
Antela, Laguna 56 42 7N 7 40W
Antelope 127 21 2S 28 31E
Anten 73 58 5N 12 22E
Antenor Navarro 170 6 44S 38 27W
Antequera, Parag. 172 24 8S 57 7W
Antequera, Spain 57 37 5N 4 33W
Antero Mt. 161 38 45N 106 43W
Anthemoús 68 40 31N 23 15E
Anthony, Kans., U.S.A. 159 37 8N 98 2W
Anthony, N. Mex., U.S.A. 161 32 1N 106 37W
Anthony Lagoon 138 18 0S 135 30E
Anti Atlas, Mts. 118 30 30N 6 30W
Antibes 45 43 34N 7 6E
Antibes, C. d' 45 43 31N 7 7E
Anticosti, Î. de 151 49 30N 63 0W
Antifer, C. d' 42 49 41N 0 10E
Antigo 158 45 8N 89 5W
Antigonish 151 45 38N 61 58W
Antigua 166 14 34N 90 41W
Antigua Bahama, Canal de la 166 22 10N 77 30W
Antigua, I. 167 17 0N 61 50W
Antilla 166 20 40N 75 50W
Antimony 161 38 7N 112 0W
Antioch 163 38 7N 121 45W
Antioquia 174 6 40N 75 55W
Antioquia □ 174 7 0N 75 30W
Antipodes Is. 130 49 45S 178 40E
Antler 158 48 58N 101 18W
Antler, R. 153 49 8N 101 0W
Antlers 159 34 15N 95 35W
Antofagasta 172 23 50S 70 30W
Antofagasta □ 172 24 0S 69 0W
Antofagasta de la Sierra 172 26 5S 67 20W
Antofallá 172 25 30S 68 5W
Antofalla, Salar de 172 25 40S 67 45W
Antoing 47 50 34N 3 27E
Anton 159 33 49N 102 5W
Anton Chico 161 35 12N 105 5W
Antongil, B. d' 129 15 30S 49 50E
Antonibe 129 15 7S 47 24E
Antonibe, Presqu'île d' 129 15 30S 49 50E
Antonina 173 25 26S 48 42W
Antonito 161 37 4N 106 1W
Antonovo 83 49 25N 51 42E
Antony 30 50 22N 4 13W
Antrain 42 48 28N 1 30W
Antrim 38 54 43N 6 13W
Antrim □ 38 54 42N 6 20W
Antrim Co. 38 54 58N 6 20W
Antrim, Mts. of 38 54 57N 6 8W
Antrim Plateau 136 18 8S 128 20E
Antrodoco 63 42 25N 13 4E
Antropovo 81 58 26N 42 51E
Antsalova 129 18 40S 44 37E
Antse 106 35 5N 112 15E
Antsirabé 129 19 55S 47 2E
Antsohihy 129 14 50S 47 50E
Ant'u 107 43 6N 128 54E
Antung 107 40 10N 124 18E
Antungwei 107 35 10N 119 20E
Antwerp 140 36 17S 142 4E
Antwerp = Antwerpen 47 51 13N 4 25E
Antwerpen 47 51 13N 4 25E
Antwerpen □ 47 51 15N 4 40E
Antz'u 106 39 31N 116 41E
Anupgarh 94 29 10N 73 10E
Anuradhapura 97 8 22N 80 28E
Anvaing 47 50 41N 3 34E
Anvers = Antwerp(en) 47 51 13N 4 25E
Anvers I. 13 64 30S 63 40W
Anvik 147 62 37N 160 20W
Anxious B. 139 33 24S 134 45E
Anyama 120 5 30N 4 3W
Anyang 106 36 7N 114 26E
Anyer-Lor 103 6 6S 105 56E
Anyüan 109 25 9N 115 21E
Anza, Jordan 90 32 22N 35 12E
Anza, U.S.A. 163 33 35N 116 39W

Anza Borrego Desert State Park **Arizpe**

Anza Borrego Desert State Park	**163**	33 0N	116 26W
Anzhero-Sudzhensk	**76**	56 10N	83 40 E
Ánzio	**64**	41 28N	12 37 E
Aoga-Shima	**111**	32 28N	139 46 E
Aoiz	**58**	42 46N	1 22W
Aomori	**112**	40 45N	140 45 E
Aomori-ken □	**112**	40 45N	140 40 E
Aonla	**95**	28 16N	79 11 E
Aono-Yama	**110**	34 28N	131 48 E
Aorangi Mts.	**142**	41 49 S	175 22 E
Aoreora	**118**	28 51N	10 53W
Aosta	**62**	45 43N	7 20 E
Aoudéras	**121**	17 45N	8 20 E
Aouinet Torkoz	**118**	28 31N	9 46W
Aoukar □	**118**	23 50N	2 45W
Aouker	**120**	23 48N	4 0W
Aoulef el Arab	**118**	26 55N	1 2 E
Aoullouz	**118**	30 44N	8 1W
Apa	**108**	32 55N	101 40 E
Apa, R.	**172**	22 6 S	58 2W
Apache, Ariz., U.S.A.	**161**	31 46N	109 6W
Apache, Okla., U.S.A.	**159**	34 53N	98 22W
Apahanuerhch'i	**106**	43 58N	116 2 E
Apalachee B.	**157**	30 0N	84 0W
Apalachicola	**157**	29 40N	85 0W
Apalachicola, R.	**157**	30 0N	85 0W
Apapa	**121**	6 25N	3 25 E
Apaporis, R.	**174**	0 30 S	70 30W
Aparecida do Taboado	**171**	20 5 S	51 5W
Aparri	**103**	18 22N	121 38 E
Aparurén	**174**	5 6N	62 8W
Apateu	**70**	46 36N	21 47 E
Apatin	**66**	45 40N	19 0 E
Apatzingán	**164**	19 0N	102 20W
Apeldoorn	**46**	52 13N	5 57 E
Apeldoornsch Kanal	**46**	52 29N	6 5 E
Apen	**48**	53 12N	7 47 E
Apenam	**102**	8 35 S	116 13 E
Apennines	**16**	44 20N	10 20 E
Apía	**174**	5 5N	75 58W
Apiacás, Serra dos	**174**	9 50 S	57 0W
Apiaí	**174**	24 31 S	48 50W
Apinajé	**171**	11 31 S	48 18W
Apiti	**142**	39 58 S	175 54 E
Apizaco	**165**	19 26N	98 9W
Aplahové	**121**	6 56N	1 41 E
Aplao	**174**	16 0 S	72 40W
Apo, Mt.	**103**	6 53N	125 14 E
Apodi	**170**	5 39 S	37 48W
Apolda	**48**	51 1N	11 30 E
Apollo Bay	**140**	38 45 S	143 40 E
Apollonia, Greece	**69**	36 58N	24 43 E
Apollonia, Libya	**117**	32 52N	21 59 E
Apolo	**174**	14 30 S	68 30W
Aporé, R.	**171**	19 27 S	50 57W
Aporema	**170**	1 14N	50 49W
Apostle Is.	**158**	46 50N	90 30W
Apóstoles	**173**	28 0 S	56 0W
Apostolovo	**82**	47 39N	33 39 E
Apoteri	**174**	4 2N	58 32W
Appalachian Mts.	**156**	38 0N	80 0W
Appelscha	**46**	52 57N	6 21 E
Appeninni	**65**	41 0N	15 0 E
Appeninno Ligure	**62**	44 30N	9 0 E
Appenzell	**51**	47 20N	9 25 E
Appenzell-Ausser Rhoden □	**51**	47 23N	9 23 E
Appenzell-Inner Rhoden □	**51**	47 20N	9 25 E
Appiano	**63**	46 27N	11 17 E
Appingedam	**46**	53 19N	6 51 E
Apple Valley	**163**	34 30N	117 11W
Appleby	**32**	54 35N	2 29W
Applecross	**36**	57 26N	5 50W
Applecross For.	**36**	57 27N	5 40W
Appledore, Devon, U.K.	**30**	51 3N	4 12W
Appledore, Kent, U.K.	**29**	51 2N	0 47 E
Appleton	**156**	44 17N	88 25W
Approuague	**170**	4 20N	52 0W
Apreivka	**81**	55 33N	37 4 E
Apricena	**65**	41 47N	15 25 E
Aprigliano	**65**	39 17N	16 19 E
Aprília	**64**	41 38N	12 38 E
Apsheronsk	**83**	44 28N	39 42 E
Apsley Str.	**136**	11 35 S	130 28 E
Apt	**45**	43 53N	5 24 E
Apucarana	**173**	23 55 S	51 33W
Apulia = Puglia	**65**	41 0N	16 30 E
Apure □	**174**	7 10N	68 50W
Apure, R.	**174**	8 0N	69 20W
Apurímac, R.	**174**	12 10 S	73 30W
Apurito, R.	**174**	7 50N	67 0W
Apuseni, Munţii	**70**	46 30N	22 45 E
Aq Chah	**93**	37 0N	66 5 E
'Aqaba	**122**	29 31N	35 0 E
'Aqaba, Khalīj al	**92**	28 15N	33 20 E
Aqîq	**122**	18 14N	38 12 E
Aqîq, Khalîg	**122**	18 20N	38 10 E
'Aqraba	**90**	32 9N	35 20 E
'Aqrah	**92**	36 46N	43 45 E
Aquanish	**151**	50 14N	62 2W
Aquasco	**162**	38 35N	76 43W
Aquidaba	**171**	10 17 S	37 2W
Aquidauana	**175**	20 30 S	55 50W
Aquila, L'	**63**	42 21N	13 24 E
Aquiles Serdán	**164**	28 37N	105 54W
Aquin	**167**	18 16N	73 24W
Ar Ramadi	**92**	33 25N	43 20 E
Ar-Ramthā	**90**	32 34N	36 0 E
Ar Rass	**92**	25 50N	43 40 E
Ar Rifai	**92**	31 50N	46 10 E
Ar Riyād	**92**	24 41N	46 42 E
Ar Rub 'al Khālī	**91**	21 0N	51 0 E
Ar Rutbah	**92**	33 0N	40 15 E
Arab, Khalîg el	**122**	30 55N	29 0 E
Arab, Shott al	**92**	30 0N	48 31 E
Araba	**121**	13 7N	5 0 E
Arabatskaya Strelka	**82**	45 40N	35 0 E
Arabba	**63**	46 30N	11 51 E
Arabelo	**174**	4 55N	64 13W
Arabia	**86**	25 0N	45 0 E
Arabian Desert	**122**	28 0N	32 20 E
Arabian Sea	**86**	16 0N	65 0 E
Aracajú	**170**	10 55 S	37 4W
Aracataca	**174**	10 38N	74 9W
Aracati	**170**	4 30 S	37 44W
Araçatuba	**173**	21 10 S	50 30W
Aracena	**57**	37 53N	6 38W
Aracruz	**171**	19 49 S	40 16W
Araçuaí	**171**	16 52 S	42 4W
Araçuaí, R.	**171**	16 46 S	42 2W
Arad	**66**	46 10N	21 20 E
Arada	**117**	15 0N	20 20 E
Aradu Nou	**66**	46 8N	21 20 E
Arafura Sea	**103**	10 0 S	135 0 E
Aragats	**83**	40 30N	44 15 E
Aragón	**58**	41 25N	1 0W
Aragón, R.	**58**	42 35N	0 50W
Aragona	**64**	37 24N	13 36 E
Aragua □	**174**	10 0N	67 10W
Aragua de Barcelona	**174**	9 28N	64 49W
Araguacema	**170**	8 50 S	49 20W
Araguaçu	**171**	12 49 S	49 51W
Araguaia, R.	**170**	7 0 S	49 15W
Araguaína	**170**	7 12 S	48 12W
Araguari	**171**	18 38 S	48 11W
Araguari, R.	**170**	1 0N	51 40W
Araguatins	**170**	5 38 S	48 7W
Araioses	**170**	2 53 S	41 55W
Arak	**118**	25 20N	3 45 E
Arāk	**92**	34 0N	49 40 E
Arakan □	**98**	19 0N	94 15 E
Arakan Coast	**99**	19 0N	94 0 E
Arakan Yoma	**98**	20 0N	94 30 E
Arákhova	**69**	38 28N	22 35 E
Araks, R. = Aras, Rud-e	**92**	39 10N	47 10 E
Aral Sea = Aralskoye More	**76**	44 30N	60 0 E
Aralsk	**76**	46 50N	61 20 E
Aralskoye More	**76**	44 30N	60 0 E
Aramac	**138**	22 58 S	145 14 E
Arambagh	**95**	22 53N	87 48 E
Aramǔ, Mţii de	**70**	47 10N	22 30 E
Aran Fawddwy, Mt.	**31**	52 48N	3 40W
Aran, I.	**38**	55 0N	8 30W
Aran Is.	**39**	53 5N	9 42W
Aranci	**64**	41 5N	3 40W
Aranci, Golfo	**64**	41 0N	9 35 E
Aranda de Duero	**58**	41 39N	3 42W
Aranđelovac	**66**	44 18N	20 37 E
Aranga	**142**	35 44 S	173 40 E
Aranjuez	**56**	40 1N	3 40W
Aranos	**125**	24 9 S	19 7 E
Aransas Pass	**159**	28 0N	97 9W
Aranyaprathet	**101**	13 41N	102 30 E
Aranzazu	**174**	5 16N	75 30W
Arao	**110**	32 59N	130 25 E
Araouane	**120**	18 55N	3 30W
Arapahoe	**158**	40 22N	99 53W
Arapari	**170**	5 34 S	49 15W
Arapawa I.	**131**	41 13 S	174 20 E
Arapey Grande, R.	**172**	30 55 S	57 49W
Arapiraca	**170**	9 45 S	36 39W
Arapkir	**92**	39 5N	38 30 E
Arapongas	**173**	23 29 S	51 28W
Arapuni	**130**	38 3 S	175 37 E
Araranguá	**173**	29 0 S	49 30W
Araraquara	**171**	21 50 S	48 0W
Araras	**173**	5 15 S	60 35W
Ararás, Serra dos	**173**	25 0 S	53 10W
Ararat, Austral.	**140**	37 16 S	143 0 E
Ararat, Turkey	**92**	39 50N	44 15 E
Ararat, Mt. = Ağri Daği	**92**	39 50N	44 15 E
Arari	**170**	3 28 S	44 47W
Araria	**95**	26 9N	87 33 E
Araripe	**171**	7 12 S	40 8W
Araripe, Chapada do	**170**	7 20 S	40 0W
Araripina	**170**	7 33 S	40 34W
Araro	**123**	4 41N	38 50 E
Araruama, Lagoa de	**173**	22 53 S	42 12W
Araruna	**170**	6 52 S	35 44W
Åras	**71**	59 42N	10 31 E
Aras, Rud-e	**92**	39 10N	47 10 E
Araticu	**170**	1 58 S	49 51W
Arauca	**174**	7 0N	70 40W
Arauca □	**174**	6 40N	71 0W
Arauca, R.	**174**	7 30N	69 0W
Arauco	**172**	37 16 S	73 25W
Arauco □	**172**	37 40 S	73 25W
Araújos	**171**	19 56 S	45 14W
Arauquita	**174**	7 2N	71 25W
Araure	**174**	9 34N	69 13W
Arawa	**123**	9 57N	41 58 E
Arawhata	**143**	43 59 S	168 38 E
Arawhata, R.	**143**	44 0 S	168 40 E
Araxá	**171**	19 35 S	46 55W
Araya, Pen. de	**174**	10 40N	64 0W
Arba	**123**	9 0N	40 20 E
Arba Jahan	**126**	2 5N	39 2 E
Arba, L'	**118**	36 40N	3 9 E
'Arba Minch	**123**	6 0N	37 30 E
Arbah, Wadi al	**90**	30 30N	35 5 E
Arbatax	**64**	39 57N	9 42 E
Arbedo	**51**	46 12N	9 3 E
Arbeláez	**174**	4 17N	74 26W
Arbīl	**92**	36 15N	44 5 E
Arboga	**72**	59 24N	15 52 E
Arbois	**43**	46 55N	5 46 E
Arbon	**51**	47 31N	9 26 E
Arbore	**123**	5 3N	36 50 E
Arborea	**64**	39 46N	8 34 E
Arborfield	**153**	53 6N	103 39W
Arborg	**153**	50 54N	97 13W
Arbrå	**72**	61 28N	16 22 E
Arbresle, L'	**45**	45 50N	4 26 E
Arbroath	**37**	56 34N	2 35W
Arbuckle	**160**	39 3N	122 2W
Arbus	**64**	39 30N	8 33 E
Arbuzinka	**82**	47 52N	31 25 E
Arc	**43**	47 28N	5 34 E
Arcachon	**44**	44 40N	1 10W
Arcachon, Bassin d'	**44**	44 42N	1 10W
Arcadia, Fla., U.S.A.	**157**	27 20N	81 50W
Arcadia, La., U.S.A.	**159**	32 34N	92 53W
Arcadia, Nebr., U.S.A.	**158**	41 29N	99 4W
Arcadia, Wis., U.S.A.	**158**	44 13N	91 29W
Arcata	**160**	40 55N	124 4W
Arcévia	**63**	43 29N	12 58 E
Archangel = Arkhangelsk	**78**	64 40N	41 0 E
Archar	**66**	43 50N	22 54 E
Archbald	**162**	41 30N	75 31W
Archena	**59**	38 9N	1 16W
Archer B.	**138**	13 20 S	141 30 E
Archer, R.	**138**	13 25 S	142 50 E
Archers Post	**126**	0 35N	37 35 E
Archidona	**57**	37 6N	4 22W
Archiestown	**37**	57 28N	3 20W
Arci, Monte	**64**	39 47N	8 44 E
Arcidosso	**63**	42 51N	11 30 E
Arcila = Asilah	**118**	35 29N	6 0W
Arcis-sur-Aube	**43**	48 32N	4 10 E
Arckaringa	**139**	27 56 S	134 45 E
Arckaringa Cr.	**139**	28 10 S	135 22 E
Arco, Italy	**62**	45 55N	10 54 E
Arco, U.S.A.	**160**	43 45N	113 16W
Arcola	**153**	49 40N	102 30W
Arcoona	**140**	31 2 S	137 1 E
Arcos, Brazil	**171**	20 17 S	45 32W
Arcos, Spain	**58**	41 12N	2 16W
Arcos de los Frontera	**57**	36 45N	5 49W
Arcot	**97**	12 53N	79 20 E
Arcoverde	**170**	8 25 S	37 4W
Arctic Ocean	**12**	78 0N	160 0W
Arctic Red, R.	**147**	66 0N	132 0W
Arctic Red River	**147**	67 15N	134 0W
Arctic Village	**147**	68 5N	145 45W
Arda, R., Bulg.	**67**	41 40N	25 40 E
Arda, R., Italy	**62**	44 53N	9 52 E
Ardabil	**92**	38 15N	48 18 E
Ardagh	**39**	52 30N	9 5W
Ardakan	**93**	30 20N	52 5 E
Årdal	**71**	59 9N	6 13 E
Ardales	**57**	36 53N	4 51W
Årdalstangen	**71**	61 14N	7 43 E
Ardara	**38**	54 47N	8 25W
Ardatov	**81**	54 51N	46 15 E
Ardavasar	**36**	57 3N	5 54 E
Ardbeg	**34**	55 38N	6 6W
Ardcath	**38**	53 36N	6 21W
Ardcharnich	**36**	57 52N	5 5W
Ardchyle	**34**	56 26N	4 24W
Ardèche □	**45**	44 42N	4 16 E
Ardee	**38**	53 51N	6 32W
Arden Stby.	**73**	56 46N	9 52 E
Ardennes	**47**	49 30N	5 10 E
Ardennes □	**43**	49 35N	4 40 E
Ardentes	**43**	46 45N	1 50 E
Ardentinny	**34**	56 3N	4 56 E
Arderin, Mt.	**39**	53 3N	7 40W
Ardestan	**93**	33 20N	52 25 E
Ardfert	**39**	52 20N	9 49W
Ardfinnan	**39**	52 20N	7 53W
Ardglass	**38**	54 16N	5 38W
Ardgour	**36**	56 45N	5 25W
Ardgroom	**39**	51 44N	9 53W
Árdhas, R.	**68**	41 36N	26 25 E
Ardhasig	**36**	57 55N	6 51W
Ardhéa	**68**	40 58N	22 3 E
Ardila, R.	**57**	38 10N	7 20W
Ardingly	**29**	51 3N	0 3W
Ardino	**67**	41 34N	25 9 E
Ardivachar Pt.	**36**	57 23N	7 25W
Ardkearagh	**39**	51 48N	10 11W
Ardkeen	**38**	54 27N	5 31W
Ardlethan	**141**	34 22 S	146 53 E
Ardlui	**34**	56 19N	4 43W
Ardmore, Austral.	**138**	21 39 S	139 11 E
Ardmore, Okla., U.S.A.	**159**	34 10N	97 5W
Ardmore, Pa., U.S.A.	**162**	39 58N	75 18W
Ardmore, S.D., U.S.A.	**158**	43 0N	103 40W
Ardmore Hd.	**39**	51 58N	7 43W
Ardmore Pt.	**34**	55 40N	6 0W
Ardnacrusha	**39**	52 43N	8 38W
Ardnamurchan, Pen.	**36**	56 43N	6 0W
Ardnamurchan Pt.	**36**	56 44N	6 14W
Ardnaree	**38**	54 6N	9 8W
Ardnave Pt.	**34**	55 54N	6 20W
Ardooie	**47**	50 59N	3 13 E
Ardore Marina	**65**	38 11N	16 10 E
Ardrahan	**39**	53 10N	8 48W
Ardres	**43**	50 50N	2 0 E
Ardrishaig	**34**	56 0N	5 27W
Ardrossan, Austral.	**140**	34 26 S	137 53 E
Ardrossan, U.K.	**34**	55 39N	4 50W
Ards □	**38**	54 35N	5 30W
Ards Pen.	**38**	54 30N	5 25W
Ardud	**70**	47 37N	22 52 E
Ardunac	**83**	41 8N	42 5 E
Ardvoulie Castle	**36**	58 0N	6 45W
Ardwell	**37**	57 20N	3 5W
Åre	**72**	63 22N	13 15 E
Arecibo	**147**	18 29N	66 42W
Areia Branca	**170**	5 0 S	37 0W
Aremark	**71**	59 15N	11 42 E
Arena de la Ventana, Punta	**164**	24 4N	109 52W
Arenales, Cerro	**176**	47 5 S	73 40W
Arenas	**56**	43 17N	4 50W
Arenas de San Pedro	**56**	40 12N	5 5W
Arenas, Pta.	**174**	10 20N	62 39W
Arendal	**71**	58 28N	8 46 E
Arendonk	**47**	51 19N	5 5 E
Arendsee	**48**	52 52N	11 27 E
Arenig Fach, Mt.	**31**	52 55N	3 45 E
Arenig Fawr, Mt.	**31**	52 56N	3 45W
Arenys de Mar	**58**	41 35N	2 33 E
Arenzano	**62**	44 24N	8 40 E
Areópolis	**69**	36 40N	22 22 E
Arequipa	**174**	16 20 S	71 30W
Arero	**123**	4 41N	38 50 E
Arês	**171**	6 11 S	35 9W
Arès	**44**	44 47N	1 8W
Arévalo	**56**	41 3N	4 43W
Arezzo	**63**	43 28N	11 50 E
Arga, R.	**58**	42 30N	1 50W
Argalastí	**68**	39 13N	23 13 E
Argamasilla de Alba	**59**	39 8N	3 5W
Arganda	**58**	40 19N	3 26W
Arganil	**56**	40 13N	8 3W
Argayash	**84**	55 29N	60 52 E
Argelès-Gazost	**44**	43 0N	0 6W
Argelès-sur-Mer	**44**	42 34N	3 1 E
Argent-sur-Sauldre	**43**	47 33N	2 25 E
Argenta, Can.	**152**	50 20N	116 55W
Argenta, Italy	**63**	44 37N	11 50 E
Argentan	**42**	48 45N	0 1W
Argentário, Mte.	**63**	42 23N	11 11 E
Argentat	**44**	45 6N	1 56 E
Argentera	**62**	44 23N	6 58 E
Argenteuil	**43**	48 57N	2 14 E
Argentia	**151**	47 18N	53 58W
Argentiera, C. dell'	**64**	40 44N	8 8 E
Argentière, Aiguilles d'	**50**	45 58N	7 2 E
Argentina	**174**	0 34N	74 17W
Argentina ■	**176**	35 0 S	66 0W
Argentino, L.	**176**	50 10 S	73 0W
Argenton-sur-Creuse	**44**	46 36N	1 30 E
Argentré	**42**	48 5N	0 40W
Argeş □	**70**	45 0N	24 45 E
Argeş, R.	**70**	44 30N	25 50 E
Arghandab, R.	**94**	32 15N	66 23 E
Argo	**122**	19 28N	30 30 E
Argo, I.	**122**	19 28N	30 30 E
Argolikós Kólpos	**69**	37 20N	22 52 E
Argolís □	**69**	37 38N	22 50 E
Argonne	**43**	49 0N	5 20 E
Árgos	**69**	37 40N	22 43 E
Árgos Orestikón	**68**	40 27N	21 26 E
Argostólion	**69**	38 12N	20 33 E
Arguedas	**58**	42 11N	1 36W
Arguello, Pt.	**163**	34 34N	120 40W
Argun, R.	**77**	53 20N	121 28 E
Argungu	**121**	12 40N	4 31 E
Argus Pk.	**163**	35 52N	117 26W
Argyle	**158**	48 23N	96 49W
Argyle Downs	**136**	16 17 S	128 47 E
Argyle, L.	**136**	16 20 S	128 40 E
Argyll (□)	**26**	56 18N	5 15W
Argyll, Dist.	**34**	56 14N	5 10W
Argyll, oilfield	**19**	56 8N	3 5 E
Argyrádhes	**68**	39 27N	19 58 E
Århus	**73**	56 8N	10 11 E
Aria	**142**	38 33 S	175 0 E
Ariamsvlei	**128**	28 9 S	19 51 E
Ariana	**119**	36 52N	10 12 E
Ariano Irpino	**65**	41 10N	15 4 E
Ariano nel Polèsine	**63**	44 56N	12 5 E
Aribinda	**121**	14 17N	0 52W
Arica, Chile	**174**	18 32 S	70 20W
Arica, Colomb.	**174**	2 0 S	71 50W
Arica, Peru	**174**	1 30 S	75 30W
Arid, C.	**137**	34 1 S	123 10 E
Arida	**111**	33 29N	135 44 E
Ariège □	**44**	42 56N	1 30 E
Ariège, R.	**44**	42 56N	1 25 E
Arieş, R.	**70**	46 24N	23 20 E
Arilje	**66**	43 44N	20 7 E
Arima	**167**	10 38N	61 17W
Arinagour	**34**	56 38N	6 31W
Arinos, R.	**174**	11 15 S	57 0W
Ario de Rosales	**164**	19 12N	101 42W
Aripuanã	**174**	9 25 S	60 30W
Aripuanã, R.	**174**	7 30 S	60 25W
Ariquemes	**174**	9 55 S	63 6W
Arisaig	**36**	56 55N	5 50W
Arisaig, Sd. of	**36**	56 50N	5 50W
Arîsh, W. el	**122**	30 25N	34 52 E
Arismendi	**174**	8 29N	68 22W
Arissa	**123**	11 10N	41 35 E
Aristazabal, I.	**152**	52 40N	129 10W
Arita	**110**	33 11N	129 54 E
Arivaca	**161**	31 37N	111 25W
Arivonimamo	**129**	19 1 S	47 11 E
Ariyalur	**97**	11 8N	79 8 E
Ariza	**58**	41 19N	2 3W
Arizaro, Salar de	**172**	24 40 S	67 50W
Arizona	**172**	35 45 S	65 25W
Arizona □	**161**	34 20N	111 30W
Arizpe	**164**	30 20N	110 11W

Arjang Atalaia

Name	Map	Lat.	Long.
Arjang	72	59 24N	12 9 E
Årjäng	72	59 24N	12 8 E
Arjeplog	74	66 3N	18 2 E
Arjona, Colomb.	174	10 14N	75 22W
Arjona, Spain	57	37 56N	4 4W
Arjuno	103	7 49S	112 19 E
Arka	77	60 15N	142 0 E
Arkadak	81	51 58N	43 19 E
Arkadelphia	159	34 5N	93 0W
Arkadhia □	69	37 30N	22 20 E
Arkaig, L.	36	56 58N	5 10W
Arkansas □	159	35 0N	92 30W
Arkansas City	159	37 4N	97 3W
Arkansas, R.	159	35 20N	93 30W
Árkathos, R.	68	39 20N	21 4 E
Arkhángelos	69	36 13N	28 7 E
Arkhangelsk	78	64 40N	41 0 E
Arkhangelskoye	81	51 32N	40 58 E
Arkiko	123	15 33N	39 30 E
Arkle R.	32	54 25N	2 0W
Arklow	39	52 48N	6 10W
Arklow Hd.	39	52 46N	6 10W
Arkoi	69	37 24N	26 44 E
Arkona, Kap	48	54 41N	13 26 E
Arkonam	97	13 7N	79 43 E
Arkösund	73	58 29N	16 56 E
Arkoúdhi	69	38 33N	20 43 E
Arkticheskiy, Mys	77	81 10N	95 0 E
Arkul	84	57 17N	50 3 E
Arkville	162	42 9N	74 37W
Arlanc	44	45 25N	3 42 E
Arlanza, R.	56	42 6N	4 0W
Arlanzón, R.	56	42 12N	4 0W
Arlberg Pass	49	49 9N	10 12 E
Arlee	160	47 10N	114 4W
Arles	45	43 41N	4 40 E
Arlesheim	50	47 30N	7 37 E
Arless	39	52 53N	7 1W
Arlington, S. Afr.	129	28 1S	27 53 E
Arlington, Oreg., U.S.A.	160	45 48N	120 6W
Arlington, S.D., U.S.A.	158	44 25N	97 4W
Arlington, Va., U.S.A.	162	38 52N	77 5W
Arlington, Vt., U.S.A.	162	43 5N	73 9W
Arlington, Wash., U.S.A.	160	48 11N	122 4W
Arlon	47	49 42N	5 49 E
Arlöv	73	55 38N	13 5 E
Arly	121	11 35N	1 28 E
Armadale, Austral.	137	32 12S	116 0 E
Armadale, Lothian, U.K.	35	55 54N	3 42W
Armadale, Skye, U.K.	36	57 24N	5 54W
Armagh, Can.	137	46 41N	70 32W
Armagh, U.K.	38	54 22N	6 40W
Armagh □	38	54 18N	6 37W
Armagh Co.	38	54 16N	6 35W
Armagnac	44	43 44N	0 10 E
Armançon, R.	43	47 51N	4 7 E
Armavir	83	45 2N	41 7 E
Armenia	174	4 35N	75 45W
Armenian S.S.R. □	83	40 0N	41 0 E
Armeniş	70	45 13N	22 17 E
Armentières	43	50 40N	2 50 E
Armero	174	4 58N	74 54W
Armidale	141	30 30S	151 40 E
Armour	158	43 20N	98 25W
Armoy	38	55 8N	6 20W
Arms	150	49 34N	86 3W
Armstead	160	45 0N	112 56W
Armstrong, B.C., Can.	152	50 25N	119 10W
Armstrong, Ont., Can.	150	50 18N	89 4W
Armstrong, U.S.A.	159	26 59N	90 48W
Armstrong Cr.	136	16 35S	131 40 E
Armur	96	18 48N	78 16 E
Arnaia	68	40 30N	23 40 E
Arnarfjörður	74	65 48N	23 40W
Arnay-le-Duc	43	47 10N	4 27 E
Arnedillo	58	42 13N	2 14W
Arnedo	58	42 12N	2 5W
Árnes	74	66 1N	21 31W
Årnes	71	60 7N	11 28 E
Arnett	159	36 9N	99 44W
Arney	38	54 17N	7 41W
Arnhem	46	51 58N	5 55 E
Arnhem B.	138	12 20S	136 10 E
Arnhem, C.	138	12 20S	137 0 E
Arnhem Ld.	138	13 10S	135 0 E
Arni	97	12 43N	79 19 E
Árnissa	68	40 47N	21 49 E
Arno Bay	140	33 54S	136 34 E
Arno, R.	62	43 44N	10 20 E
Arnold, N.Z.	143	42 29S	171 25 E
Arnold, U.K.	33	53 0N	1 8W
Arnold, Calif., U.S.A.	163	38 15N	120 20W
Arnold, Nebr., U.S.A.	158	41 29N	100 10W
Arnoldstein	52	46 33N	13 43 E
Arnot	153	55 46N	96 41W
Arnøy	74	70 9N	20 40 E
Arnprior	150	45 26N	76 21W
Arnsberg	48	51 25N	8 10 E
Arnside	32	54 12N	2 49W
Arnstadt	48	50 50N	10 56 E
Aroa	174	10 26N	68 54W
Aroab	125	26 41S	19 39 E
Aroánia Óri	69	37 56N	22 12 E
Aroche	57	37 56N	6 57W
Aroeiras	170	7 31S	35 41W
Arolla	50	46 2N	7 29 E
Arolsen	48	51 23N	9 1 E
Arona	62	45 45N	8 32 E
Arosa	51	46 47N	9 41 E
Arosa, Ría de	56	42 28N	8 57W
Arpajon, Cantal, France	44	44 54N	2 28 E
Arpajon, Seine et Oise, France	43	48 37N	2 12 E
Arpino	64	41 40N	13 35 E
Arra Mts.	39	52 50N	8 22W
Arrabury	139	26 45S	141 0 E
Arrah	95	25 35N	84 32 E
Arraias	171	12 56S	46 57W
Arraias, R.	170	7 30S	49 20W
Arraiolos	57	38 44N	7 59W
Arran, I.	34	55 34N	5 12W
Arrandale	152	54 57N	130 0W
Arras	43	50 17N	2 46 E
Arreau	44	42 54N	0 22 E
Arrecife	116	28 59N	13 40W
Arrecifes	172	34 06S	60 9W
Arrée, Mts. d'	42	48 26N	3 55W
Arriaga, Chiapas, Mexico	165	16 15N	93 52W
Arriaga, San Luís de Potosi, Mexico	164	21 55N	101 23W
Arrild	73	55 8N	8 58 E
Arrililah P.O.	138	23 43S	143 54 E
Arrino	137	29 30S	115 40 E
Arrochar	34	56 12N	4 45W
Arrojado, R.	171	13 24S	44 20W
Arromanches-les-Bains	42	49 20N	0 38W
Arronches	57	39 8N	7 16W
Arrou	42	48 6N	1 8 E
Arrow L.	38	54 3N	8 20W
Arrow Rock Res.	160	43 45N	115 50W
Arrowhead	152	50 40N	117 55W
Arrowhead, L.	163	34 16N	117 10W
Arrowsmith, Mt.	143	30 7N	141 38 E
Arrowtown	143	44 57S	168 50 E
Arroyo de la Luz	57	39 30N	6 38W
Arroyo Grande	163	35 9N	120 32W
Ars	73	56 48N	9 30 E
Ars	44	46 13N	1 30W
Ars-sur-Moselle	43	49 5N	6 4 E
Arsenault L.	153	53 6N	108 32W
Arsiero	63	45 49N	11 22 E
Arsikere	97	13 15N	76 15 E
Arsk	81	56 10N	49 50 E
Årskogen	72	62 8N	17 20 E
Árta	69	39 8N	21 2 E
Artá	58	39 40N	3 20 E
Arta □	68	39 15N	26 0 E
Arteaga	164	18 50N	102 20W
Arteijo	56	43 19N	8 29W
Artem,Os.	83	40 28N	50 20 E
Artémou	120	15 38N	12 16W
Artemovsk	82	48 35N	37 55 E
Artemovski	83	54 45N	93 35 E
Artemovskiy	84	57 21N	61 54 E
Artenay	43	48 5N	1 50 E
Artern	48	51 22N	11 18 E
Artesa de Segre	58	41 54N	1 3 E
Artesia	159	32 55N	104 25W
Artesia Wells	159	28 17N	99 18W
Artesian	158	44 2N	97 54W
Arth	51	47 4N	8 31 E
Arthez-de-Béarn	44	43 29N	0 38W
Arthington	120	6 35N	10 45W
Arthur Cr.	138	22 30S	136 25 E
Arthur Pt.	138	22 7S	150 3 E
Arthur, R.	138	41 2S	144 40 E
Arthur's Pass	143	42 54S	171 35 E
Arthur's Town	167	24 38N	75 42W
Arthurstown	39	52 15N	6 58W
Artigas	172	30 20S	56 30W
Artigavan	38	54 51N	7 24W
Artik	83	40 38N	44 50 E
Artillery L.	153	63 9N	107 52W
Artois	43	50 20N	2 30 E
Artotína	69	38 42N	22 2 E
Artvin	92	41 14N	41 44 E
Aru, Kepulauan	103	6 0S	134 30 E
Arua	126	3 1N	30 58 E
Aruanã	171	15 0S	51 10W
Aruba I.	167	12 30N	70 0W
Arudy	44	43 7N	0 28W
Arumpo	140	33 48S	142 55 E
Arun, R.	95	27 30N	87 15 E
Arun R.	29	50 48N	0 33W
Arunachal Pradesh □	98	28 0N	95 0 E
Arundel	29	50 52N	0 32W
Aruppukottai	97	9 31N	78 8 E
Arusha	126	3 20S	36 40 E
Arusha □	126	4 0S	36 30 E
Arusha Chini	126	3 32S	37 20 E
Arusi □	123	7 45N	39 00 E
Aruvi,Aru	97	8 48N	79 53 E
Aruwimi, R.	126	1 30N	25 0 E
Arva	38	53 57N	7 35W
Arvada	160	44 43N	106 6W
Arvaklu	97	8 20N	79 58 E
Arvayheer	105	46 15N	102 48 E
Arve, R.	45	46 11N	6 8 E
Arvi	96	20 59N	78 16 E
Arvida	151	48 25N	71 14W
Arvidsjaur	74	65 35N	19 10 E
Arvika	72	59 40N	12 36 E
Arvin	163	35 12N	118 50W
Arys	85	42 26N	68 48 E
Arys, R.	85	42 45N	68 15 E
Arzachena	64	41 5N	9 27 E
Arzamas	81	55 27N	43 55 E
Arzew	118	35 50N	0 23W
Arzgir	83	45 18N	44 23 E
Arzignano	63	45 30N	11 20 E
As	47	51 1N	5 35 E
Aš	52	50 13N	12 12 E
As Salt	90	32 2N	35 43 E
As Samawah	92	31 15N	45 15 E
As-Samū	90	31 24N	35 4 E
As Sulaimānīyah	92	35 35N	45 29 E
As Sulṭbn	119	31 4N	17 8 E
As Suwaih	93	22 10N	59 33 E
As Suwayda	92	32 40N	36 30 E
As Suwayrah	92	32 55N	45 0 E
Asab	128	25 30S	18 0 E
Asaba	121	6 12N	6 38 E
Asadabad	92	34 50N	48 10 E
Asafo	120	6 20N	2 40W
Asahi	111	35 43N	140 39 E
Asahi-Gawa, R.	110	34 36N	133 58 E
Asahikawa	112	43 45N	142 30 E
Asale, L.	123	14 0N	40 20 E
Asama-Yama	111	36 24N	138 31 E
Asamankese	121	5 50N	0 40W
Asankrangwa	120	5 45N	2 30W
Asansol	95	23 40N	87 1 E
Asarna	72	62 40N	14 20 E
Åsarna	72	62 39N	14 22 E
Asbe Teferi	123	9 4N	40 49 E
Asbesberge	128	29 0S	23 0 E
Asbest	84	57 0N	61 30 E
Asbestos	151	45 47N	71 58W
Asbury Park	162	40 15N	74 1W
Ascensión	164	31 6N	107 59W
Ascensión, B. de la	165	19 50N	87 20W
Ascension, I.	15	8 0S	14 15W
Aschach	49	48 23N	14 0 E
Aschaffenburg	49	49 58N	9 8 E
Aschendorf	48	53 2N	7 22 E
Aschersleben	48	51 45N	11 28 E
Asciano	63	43 14N	11 32 E
Áscoli Piceno	63	42 51N	13 34 E
Áscoli Satriano	65	41 11N	15 32 E
Ascona	51	46 9N	8 46 E
Ascope	174	7 46S	79 8W
Ascot	29	51 24N	0 41W
Ascotán	172	21 45S	68 17W
Aseb	123	13 0N	42 40 E
Åseda	73	57 10N	15 20 E
Aseda	73	57 10N	15 20 E
Asedjrad	118	24 51N	1 29 E
Asela	123	8 0N	39 0 E
Asenovgrad	67	42 1N	24 51 E
Åseral	71	58 37N	7 25 E
Åseral	71	58 38N	7 26 E
Asfeld	43	49 27N	4 5 E
Asfordby	29	52 45N	0 57W
Asfûn el Matâ'na	122	25 26N	32 30 E
Åsgårdstrand	71	59 22N	10 27 E
Ash	29	51 17N	1 16 E
Ash Fork	161	35 14N	112 32W
Ash Grove	159	37 21N	93 36W
Ash Shām,Bādiyat	92	31 30N	40 0 E
Ash Shāmīyah	92	31 55N	44 35 E
Ash Shatrah	92	31 30N	46 10 E
Ash Shuna	90	32 32N	35 34 E
Asha	84	55 0N	57 16 E
Ashaira	122	21 40N	40 40 E
Ashanti	121	7 30N	2 0W
Ashau	100	16 6N	107 22 E
Ashbourne, Ireland	38	53 31N	6 24W
Ashbourne, U.K.	33	53 2N	1 44W
Ashburn	157	31 42N	83 40W
Ashburton, N.Z.	143	43 53S	171 48 E
Ashburton, U.K.	30	50 31N	3 45W
Ashburton Downs	136	23 25S	117 4 E
Ashburton, R., Austral.	136	21 40S	114 56 E
Ashburton, R., N.Z.	131	44 2S	171 50 E
Ashby-de-la-Zouch	28	52 45N	1 29W
Ashchurch	28	52 0N	2 7W
Ashcroft	152	50 40N	121 20W
Ashdod	90	31 49N	34 35 E
Ashdot Ya'aqov	90	32 39N	35 35 E
Ashdown Forest	29	51 4N	0 2 E
Asheboro	157	35 43N	79 46W
Asherton	159	28 25N	99 43W
Asheville	157	35 39N	82 30W
Asheweig, R.	150	54 17N	87 12W
Ashford, Austral.	139	29 15S	151 3 E
Ashford, Derby., U.K.	33	53 13N	1 43W
Ashford, Kent, U.K.	29	51 8N	0 53 E
Ashford, U.S.A.	160	46 45N	122 2W
Ashikaga	111	36 28N	139 29 E
Ashington	35	55 12N	1 35W
Ashio	111	36 38N	139 27 E
Ashizuri-Zaki	110	32 35N	132 50 E
Ashkarkot	94	33 3N	67 58 E
Ashkhabad	76	38 0N	57 50 E
Ashland, Kans., U.S.A.	159	37 13N	99 43W
Ashland, Ky., U.S.A.	156	38 25N	82 40W
Ashland, Me., U.S.A.	151	46 34N	68 26W
Ashland, Mont., U.S.A.	160	45 41N	106 12W
Ashland, Nebr., U.S.A.	158	41 5N	96 27W
Ashland, Ohio, U.S.A.	156	40 52N	82 20W
Ashland, Oreg., U.S.A.	160	42 10N	122 38W
Ashland, Pa., U.S.A.	162	40 45N	76 22W
Ashland, Va., U.S.A.	156	37 46N	77 30W
Ashland, Wis., U.S.A.	158	46 40N	90 52W
Ashley, N.D., U.S.A.	158	46 3N	99 23W
Ashley, Pa., U.S.A.	162	41 14N	75 53W
Ashmont	152	54 7N	111 29W
Ashmore Is.	136	12 14S	123 50 E
Ashmore Reef	136	12 14S	123 5 E
Ashmûn	122	30 18N	30 55 E
Ashokan Res.	162	41 56N	74 13W
Ashquelon	90	31 42N	34 55 E
Ashtabula	156	41 52N	80 50W
Ashti	96	18 50N	75 15 E
Ashton, S. Afr.	128	33 50S	20 5 E
Ashton, U.S.A.	160	44 6N	111 30W
Ashton-in-Makerfield	32	53 29N	2 39W
Ashton-u.-Lyne	32	53 30N	2 8 E
Ashuanipi, L.	151	52 45N	66 15W
Ashurst	142	40 16S	175 45 E
Ashurstwood	29	51 6N	0 2 E
Ashwater	30	50 43N	4 18W
Ashwick	28	51 13N	2 31W
Asia	86	45 0N	75 0 E
Asia, Kepulauan	103	1 0N	131 13 E
Asiago	63	45 52N	11 30 E
Asifabad	96	19 30N	79 24 E
Asilah	118	35 29N	6 0W
Asinara	64	41 5N	8 15 E
Asinara, G. dell'	64	41 0N	8 30 E
Asinara I.	64	41 5N	8 15 E
Asino	76	57 0N	86 0 E
Asir	91	18 40N	42 30 E
Asir, Ras	91	11 55N	51 10 E
Aska	96	19 37N	84 42 E
Askeaton	39	52 37N	8 58W
Asker	71	59 50N	10 26 E
Askersund	73	58 53N	14 55 E
Askim	71	59 35N	11 10 E
Askino	84	56 5N	56 34 E
Askja	74	65 3N	16 48W
Askloster	73	57 13N	12 11 E
Askrigg	32	54 19N	2 6W
Asl	122	29 33N	32 44 E
Aslackby	33	52 53N	0 23W
Asmar	93	35 10N	71 27 E
Asmera (Asmara)	123	15 19N	38 55 E
Asnæs	73	55 40N	11 0 E
Åsnen	73	56 35N	15 45 E
Åsnes	71	60 37N	11 59 E
Asni	118	31 17N	7 58W
Aso	110	33 0N	130 42 E
Aso-Zan	110	32 53N	131 6 E
Asoa	126	4 35N	25 48 E
Ásola	62	45 12N	10 25 E
Asotin	160	46 14N	117 2W
Aspatria	32	54 45N	3 20W
Aspe	59	38 20N	0 40W
Aspen	161	39 12N	106 56W
Aspermont	159	33 11N	100 15W
Aspiring, Mt.	143	44 23S	168 46 E
Aspres	45	44 32N	5 44 E
Aspur	94	23 58N	74 7 E
Asquith	153	52 8N	107 13W
Assa	118	28 35N	9 6W
Assaba, Massif de l'	120	16 10N	11 45W
Assam □	98	25 45N	92 30 E
Assamakka	121	19 21N	5 38 E
Assateague I.	162	38 5N	75 6W
Asse	47	50 54N	4 6 E
Assebroek	47	51 11N	3 17 E
Assekrem	119	23 16N	5 49 E
Assémini	64	39 18N	9 0 E
Assen	46	53 0N	6 35 E
Assendelft	46	52 29N	4 45 E
Assenede	47	51 14N	3 46 E
Assens, Odense, Denmark	73	56 41N	10 3 E
Assens, Randers, Denmark	73	55 16N	9 55 E
Assesse	47	50 22N	5 2 E
Assiniboia	153	49 40N	105 59W
Assiniboine, R.	153	49 53N	97 8W
Assinica L.	150	50 30N	75 20W
Assinie	120	5 9N	3 17W
Assis	173	22 40S	50 20W
Assisi	63	43 4N	12 36 E
Ássos	69	38 22N	20 33 E
Assynt	36	58 25N	5 10W
Assynt, L.	36	58 25N	5 15W
Astakidha	69	35 53N	26 50 E
Astalfort	44	44 4N	0 40 E
Astara	79	38 30N	48 50 E
Astee	39	52 33N	9 36W
Asten	47	51 24N	5 45 E
Asti	62	44 54N	8 11 E
Astillero	56	43 24N	3 49W
Astipálaia	69	36 32N	26 22 E
Aston, C.	149	70 10N	67 40W
Aston Clinton	29	51 48N	0 44W
Astorga	56	42 29N	6 8W
Astoria	160	46 16N	123 50W
Åstorp	73	56 6N	12 55 E
Astrakhan	83	46 25N	48 5 E
Astudillo	56	42 12N	4 22W
Asturias	56	43 15N	6 0W
Astwood Bank	28	52 15N	1 55W
Asunción	172	25 21S	57 30W
Asunción, La	174	11 2N	63 53W
Åsunden	73	57 47N	13 18 E
Asutri	123	15 25N	35 45 E
Aswa, R.	126	2 30N	33 5 E
Aswad,Rasal	122	21 20N	39 0 E
Aswân	122	24 4N	32 57 E
Aswân High Dam = Sadd el Aali	122	24 5N	32 54 E
Asyût	122	27 11N	31 4 E
Asyûti, Wadi	122	27 18N	31 20 E
Aszód	53	47 39N	19 28 E
At Tafilah	92	30 45N	35 30 E
At Ta'if	122	21 5N	40 27 E
Atacama	172	25 40S	67 40W
Atacama □	172	27 30S	70 0W
Atacama, Desierto de	176	24 0S	69 20W
Atacama, Salar de	172	24 0S	68 20W
Ataco	174	3 35N	75 23W
Atakor	119	23 27N	5 31 E
Atakpamé	121	7 31N	1 13 E
Atalaia	114	9 25S	36 0W

Atalándi Ayutla

Atalándi 69 38 39N 22 58 E
Atalaya 174 10 45 S 73 50W
Ataléia 171 18 3 S 41 6W
Atami 111 35 0N 139 55 E
Atankawng 98 25 50N 97 47 E
Atar 116 20 30N 13 5W
Atara 77 63 10N 129 10 E
Ataram, Erg d' 118 23 57N 2 0 E
Atarfe 57 37 13N 3 40W
Atascadero 163 35 32N 120 44W
Atasu 76 48 30N 71 0 E
Atauro 103 8 10 S 125 30 E
Atbara 122 17 42N 33 59 E
Atbara, R. 122 17 40N 33 56 E
Atbashi 85 41 10N 75 48 E
Atbashi, Khrebet 85 40 50N 75 30 E
Atchafalaya B. 159 29 30N 91 20W
Atchison 158 39 40N 95 0W
Atebubu 121 7 47N 1 0W
Ateca 58 41 20N 1 49W
Aterno, R. 63 42 18N 13 45 E
Atesine, Alpi 62 46 55N 11 30 E
Atessa 63 42 5N 14 27 E
Ath 47 50 38N 3 47 E
Ath Thamami 92 27 45N 35 30 E
Athabasca 152 54 45N 113 20W
Athabasca, L. 153 59 15N 109 15W
Athabasca, R. 153 58 40N 110 50W
Athboy 38 53 37N 6 55W
Athea 39 52 27N 9 18W
Athenry 39 53 18N 8 45W
Athens, Ala., U.S.A. 157 34 49N 86 58W
Athens, Ga., U.S.A. 157 33 56N 83 24W
Athens, N.Y., U.S.A. 162 42 15N 73 48W
Athens, Ohio, U.S.A. 156 39 52N 82 6W
Athens, Pa., U.S.A. 162 41 57N 76 36W
Athens, Tex., U.S.A. 159 32 11N 95 48W
Athens = Athínai 69 37 58N 23 46 E
Atherstone 28 52 35N 1 32W
Atherton, Austral. 138 17 17 S 145 30 E
Atherton, U.K. 32 53 32N 2 30W
Athiéme 121 6 37N 1 40 E
Athínai 69 37 58N 23 46 E
Athleague 38 53 34N 8 17W
Athlone 38 53 26N 7 57W
Athni 96 16 44N 75 6 E
Athol 143 45 30 S 168 35 E
Atholl, Forest of 37 56 51N 3 50W
Atholville 151 47 59N 66 43W
Áthos, Mt. 68 40 9N 24 22 E
Athus 47 49 34N 5 50 E
Athy 39 53 0N 7 0W
Ati 123 13 5N 29 2 E
Atiak 126 3 12N 32 2 E
Atiamuri 142 38 24 S 176 5 E
Atico 174 16 14 S 73 40W
Atienza 58 41 12N 2 52W
Atikokan 150 48 45N 91 37W
Atikonak L. 151 52 40N 64 32W
Atka, U.S.A. 147 52 5N 174 40W
Atka, U.S.S.R. 77 60 50N 151 48 E
Atkarsk 81 51 55N 45 2 E
Atkasuk (Meade River) 147 70 30N 157 20W
Atkinson 158 42 35N 98 59W
Atlanta, Ga., U.S.A. 157 33 50N 84 24W
Atlanta, Tex., U.S.A. 159 33 7N 94 8W
Atlantic 158 41 25N 95 0W
Atlantic City 162 39 25N 74 25W
Atlantic Ocean 14 0 0 20 0W
Atlántico □ 174 10 45N 75 0W
Atlas, Great, Mts. 114 33 0N 5 0W
Atlin 147 59 31N 133 41W
Atlin Lake 147 59 26N 133 45W
'Atlit 90 32 42N 34 56 E
Atløy 71 61 21N 4 58 E
Atmakur 97 14 37N 79 40 E
Atmore 157 31 2N 87 30W
Atnarko 152 52 25N 126 0W
Atō 110 34 25N 131 40 E
Atoka 159 34 22N 96 10W
Atokos 69 38 28N 20 49 E
Atolia 163 35 19N 117 37W
Atotonilco el Alto 164 20 20N 98 40W
Atouguia 57 39 20N 9 20W
Atoyac, R. 165 16 30N 97 31W
Atrafors 73 57 02N 12 40 E
Atrak, R. 93 37 50N 57 0 E
Ätran 73 57 7N 12 57 E
Atrato, R. 174 6 40N 77 0W
Atrauli 94 28 2N 78 20 E
Atri 63 42 35N 14 0 E
Atsbi 122 13 52N 39 50 E
Atsumi 111 34 35N 137 4 E
Atsumi-Wan 111 34 44N 137 13 E
Atsuta 112 43 24N 141 26 E
Attalla 157 34 2N 86 5W
Attawapiskat 150 52 56N 82 24W
Attawapiskat, L. 150 52 18N 87 54W
Attawapiskat, R. 150 52 57N 82 18W
Attendorn 48 51 8N 7 54 E
Attersee 52 47 55N 13 31 E
Attert 47 49 45N 5 47 E
Attica 156 40 20N 87 15W
Attichy 43 49 25N 3 3 E
Attigny 43 49 28N 4 35 E
Attikamagen L. 151 55 0N 66 30W
Attikí Kai Arkhipélagos □ 69 38 10N 23 40 E
Attil 90 32 23N 35 4 E
Attleboro 162 41 56N 71 18W
Attleborough 29 52 32N 1 1 E
Attock 94 33 52N 72 20 E
Attopeu 100 14 48N 106 50 E
Attu 147 52 55N 173 10W
Attunga 141 30 55 S 150 50 E
Attur 97 11 35N 78 30 E
Attymon 39 53 20N 8 37W
Atuel, R. 172 36 17 S 66 50W
Atvidaberg 73 58 12N 16 0 E
Atwater 163 37 21N 120 37W
Atwood 158 39 52N 101 3W
Au Sable Pt. 150 46 0N 86 0W
Au Sable, R. 156 44 25N 83 20W
Aubagne 45 43 17N 5 37 E
Aubange 47 49 34N 5 48 E
Aubarede Pt. 103 17 15N 122 20 E
Aube □ 43 48 15N 4 0 E
Aubel 47 50 42N 5 51 E
Aubenas 45 44 37N 4 24 E
Aubenton 43 49 50N 4 12 E
Auberry 163 37 7N 119 29W
Aubigny-sur-Nère 43 47 30N 2 24 E
Aubin 44 44 33N 2 15 E
Aubrac, Mts. d' 44 44 38N 2 58 E
Auburn, Ala., U.S.A. 157 32 37N 85 30W
Auburn, Calif., U.S.A. 160 38 50N 121 4W
Auburn, Ind., U.S.A. 156 41 20N 85 0W
Auburn, Nebr., U.S.A. 158 40 25N 95 50W
Auburn, N.Y., U.S.A. 162 42 57N 76 39W
Auburn, Penn., U.S.A. 162 40 36N 76 6W
Auburn Range 139 25 15 S 150 30 E
Auburndale 157 28 5N 81 45W
Aubusson 44 45 57N 2 11 E
Auch 44 43 39N 0 36 E
Auchel 43 50 30N 2 29 E
Auchenblae 37 56 54N 2 26W
Auchencairn 35 54 51N 3 52W
Auchi 121 7 6N 6 13 E
Auchinleck 34 55 28N 4 18W
Auchness 37 58 0N 4 36W
Auchterarder 35 56 18N 3 43W
Auchterderran 35 56 8N 3 16W
Auchtermuchty 35 56 18N 3 15W
Auchtertyre 36 57 17N 5 35W
Auckland 142 36 52 S 174 46 E
Auckland □ 142 38 35 S 177 0 E
Auckland Is. 142 51 0 S 166 0 E
Aude □ 44 43 8N 2 28 E
Aude, R. 44 44 13N 3 15 E
Auden 150 50 14N 87 53W
Auderghem 47 50 49N 4 26 E
Auderville 42 49 43N 1 57W
Audierne 42 48 1N 4 34W
Audincourt 43 47 30N 6 50 E
Audlem 32 52 59N 2 31W
Audo Ra. 123 6 20N 41 50 E
Audrey, gasfield 19 53 35N 2 0 E
Audubon 158 41 43N 94 56W
Aue 48 50 34N 12 43 E
Auerbach 48 50 30N 12 25 E
Auffay 42 49 43N 1 07 E
Augathella 139 25 48 S 146 35 E
Augher 38 54 25N 7 10W
Aughnacloy 38 54 25N 6 58W
Aughrim, Clare, Ireland 39 53 0N 8 57W
Aughrim, Galway, Ireland 39 53 18N 8 19W
Aughrim, Wicklow, Ireland 39 52 52N 6 20W
Aughrus More 38 53 34N 10 10W
Augrabies Falls 128 28 35 S 20 20 E
Augsburg 49 48 22N 10 54 E
Augusta, Italy 65 37 14N 15 12 E
Augusta, Ark., U.S.A. 159 35 17N 91 25W
Augusta, Ga., U.S.A. 157 33 29N 81 59W
Augusta, Kans., U.S.A. 159 37 40N 97 0W
Augusta, Me., U.S.A. 151 44 20N 69 46 E
Augusta, Mont., U.S.A. 160 47 30N 112 29W
Augusta, Wis., U.S.A. 158 44 41N 91 8W
Augustenborg 73 54 57N 9 53 E
Augustine 159 31 30N 94 37W
Augusto Cardosa 127 12 40 S 34 50 E
Augustów 54 53 51N 23 00 E
Augustus Downs 138 18 35 S 139 55 E
Augustus I. 136 15 20 S 124 30 E
Augustus, Mt. 137 24 20 S 116 50 E
Auk, oilfield 19 56 25N 2 15 E
Aukan 123 15 29N 40 50 E
Aukum 163 38 34N 120 43W
Auld, L. 136 22 32 S 123 44 E
Auldearn 37 57 34N 3 50W
Aulla 62 44 12N 9 57 E
Aulnay 44 46 2N 0 22W
Aulne, R. 42 48 17N 4 16W
Ault 158 40 40N 104 42W
Ault-Onival 42 50 5N 1 29 E
Aultbea 36 57 50N 5 36W
Aulus-les-Bains 44 42 49N 1 19 E
Aumale 43 49 46N 1 46 E
Aumont-Aubrac 44 44 43N 3 17 E
Auna 121 10 9N 4 42 E
Aundh 96 17 33N 74 23 E
Aunis 44 46 0N 0 50W
Auponhia 103 1 58 S 125 27 E
Aups 45 43 37N 6 15 E
Aur, P. 101 2 35N 104 10 E
Aura 98 26 59N 97 57 E
Aurahorten, Mt. 71 59 15N 6 53 E
Auraiya 95 26 28N 79 33 E
Aurangabad, Bihar, India 95 24 45N 84 18 E
Aurangabad, Maharashtra, India 96 19 50N 75 23 E
Auray 42 47 40N 3 0W
Aurès 119 35 8N 6 30 E
Aurich 48 53 28N 7 30 E
Aurilândia 171 16 44 S 50 28W
Aurillac 44 44 55N 2 26 E
Aurlandsvangen 71 60 55N 7 12 E
Auronza 63 46 33N 12 27 E
Aurora, Brazil 171 6 57 S 38 58W
Aurora, S. Afr. 128 32 40 S 18 29 E
Aurora, Colo., U.S.A. 158 39 44N 104 55W
Aurora, Ill., U.S.A. 156 41 42N 88 12W
Aurora, Mo., U.S.A. 159 36 58N 93 42W
Aurora, Nebr., U.S.A. 158 40 55N 98 0W
Aurora, N.Y., U.S.A. 162 42 45N 76 42W
Aurskog 71 59 55N 11 26 E
Aurukun Mission 138 13 20 S 141 45 E
Aus 128 26 35 S 16 12 E
Auskerry I. 37 59 2N 2 35W
Aust-Agder fylke □ 75 58 55N 7 40 E
Austad 71 58 58N 7 37 E
Austerlitz = Slavikov 53 49 10N 16 52 E
Austevoll 71 60 5N 5 13 E
Austin, Austral. 137 27 40 S 117 50 E
Austin, Minn., U.S.A. 158 43 37N 92 59W
Austin, Nev., U.S.A. 160 39 30N 117 1W
Austin, Tex., U.S.A. 159 30 20N 97 45W
Austin, L. 137 27 40 S 118 0 E
Austral Downs 138 20 30 S 137 45 E
Austral Is. = Tubuai, Îles 143 25 0 S 150 0 E
Australia ■ 133 23 0 S 135 0 E
Australian Alps 141 36 30 S 148 8 E
Australian Cap. Terr. 139 35 15 S 149 8 E
Australian Dependency 13 73 0 S 90 0 E
Austria ■ 52 47 0N 14 0 E
Austvågøy 74 68 20N 14 40 E
Autelbas 47 49 39N 5 52 E
Auterive 44 43 21N 1 29 E
Authie, R. 43 50 22N 1 38 E
Autlan 164 19 40N 104 30W
Autun 43 46 58N 4 17 E
Auvelais 47 50 27N 4 38 E
Auvergne, Austral. 136 15 39 S 130 1 E
Auvergne, France 44 45 20N 3 0 E
Auxerre 43 47 48N 3 32 E
Auxi-le-Château 43 50 15N 2 8 E
Auxonne 43 47 10N 5 20 E
Auzances 44 46 2N 2 30 E
Avaldsnes 71 59 21N 5 20 E
Avallon 43 47 30N 3 53 E
Avalon 163 33 21N 118 20W
Avalon Pen. 151 47 30N 53 20W
Avalon Res. 159 32 30N 104 30W
Avanigadda 97 16 0N 80 56 E
Avaré 173 23 4 S 48 58W
Ávas 68 40 57N 25 56 E
Avawatz Mts. 163 35 30N 116 20W
Avebury 28 51 25N 1 52W
Aveh 92 35 40N 49 15 E
Aveiro, Brazil 175 3 10 S 55 5W
Aveiro, Port. 56 40 37N 8 38W
Aveiro □ 56 40 40N 8 35W
Avelgem 47 50 47N 3 27 E
Avellaneda 172 34 50 S 58 10W
Avellino 65 40 54N 14 46 E
Avenal 163 36 0N 120 8W
Avenchen 50 46 53N 7 2 E
Averøya 71 63 0N 7 35 E
Aversa 65 40 58N 14 11 E
Avery 160 47 22N 115 56W
Aves, Islas de 174 12 0N 67 40W
Avesnes-sur-Helpe 43 50 8N 3 55 E
Avesta 72 60 9N 16 10 E
Aveton Gifford 30 50 17N 3 51W
Aveyron □ 44 44 22N 2 45 E
Avezzano 63 42 2N 13 24 E
Avgó 69 35 33N 25 37 E
Aviá Terai 172 26 45 S 60 50W
Aviano 63 46 3N 12 35 E
Avich, L. 34 56 17N 5 25W
Aviemore 37 57 11N 3 50W
Avigliana 62 45 7N 7 13 E
Avigliano 65 40 44N 15 41 E
Avignon 45 43 57N 4 50 E
Ávila 56 40 39N 4 43W
Ávila □ 56 40 30N 5 0W
Avila Beach 163 35 11N 120 44W
Ávila, Sierra de 56 40 40N 5 0W
Avilés 56 43 35N 5 57W
Avionárion 69 38 31N 24 8 E
Avisio, R. 63 46 14N 11 18 E
Aviz 57 39 4N 7 53W
Avize 43 48 59N 4 0 E
Avoca, Austral. 139 37 5 S 143 26 E
Avoca, Ireland 39 52 52N 6 13W
Avoca, R., Austral. 140 35 40 S 143 43 E
Avoca, R., Ireland 39 52 48N 6 10W
Avoch 37 57 34N 4 10W
Avola, Can. 152 51 45N 119 19W
Avola, Italy 65 36 56N 15 7 E
Avon 158 43 0N 98 3W
Avon □ 28 51 30N 2 40W
Avon Downs 133 19 58 S 137 25 E
Avon Is. 133 19 37 S 158 17 E
Avon, R., Austral. 137 31 40 S 116 7 E
Avon, R., Avon, U.K. 28 51 30N 2 43W
Avon, R., Grampian, U.K. 37 57 25N 3 25W
Avon, R., Hants., U.K. 28 50 44N 1 45W
Avon, R., Warwick, U.K. 28 52 0N 2 9W
Avondale, N.Z. 142 36 54 S 174 42 E
Avondale, Rhod. 127 17 43 S 30 58 E
Avonlea 153 50 0N 105 0W
Avonmouth 28 51 30N 2 42W
Avranches 42 48 40N 1 20W
Avrig 70 45 43N 24 21 E
Avrillé 44 46 28N 1 28W
Avtovac 66 43 9N 18 35 E
Avu Meru □ 126 3 20 S 36 50 E
Awag el Baqar 123 10 10N 33 10 E
Awaji 111 34 32N 135 1 E
Awaji-Shima 110 34 30N 134 50 E
Awali 93 26 0N 50 30 E
Awantipur 95 33 55N 75 3 E
Awanui 142 35 4 S 173 17 E
Awarja, R. 96 18 0N 76 15 E
Awarta 90 32 10N 35 17 E
Awarua Pt. 143 44 15 S 168 5 E
Awasa, L. 123 7 0N 38 30 E
Awash 123 9 1N 40 10 E
Awash, R. 123 11 30N 42 0 E
Awaso 120 6 15N 2 22W
Awatere, R. 143 41 37 S 174 10 E
Awbarī 119 26 46N 12 57 E
Awe, L. 34 56 15N 5 15W
Aweil 123 8 42N 27 20 E
Awgu 121 6 4N 7 24 E
Awjilah 117 29 8N 21 7 E
Aworro 135 7 43 S 143 11 E
Ax-les-Thermes 44 42 44N 1 50 E
Axarfjörður 74 66 15N 16 45W
Axbridge 28 51 17N 2 50W
Axe Edge 32 53 14N 2 2W
Axe R. 28 51 17N 2 52W
Axel 47 51 16N 3 55 E
Axel Heiberg I. 12 80 0N 90 0W
Axelfors 73 57 26N 13 7 E
Axholme, Isle of 33 53 30N 1 10 E
Axim 120 4 51N 2 15W
Axintele 70 44 37N 26 47 E
Axiós, R. 68 40 57N 22 35 E
Axmarsbruk 72 61 3N 17 10 E
Axminster 30 50 47N 3 1W
Axmouth 30 50 43N 3 2W
Axstedt 48 53 26N 8 43 E
Axvall 73 58 23N 13 34 E
Ay 43 49 3N 4 0 E
Ay, R. 84 56 8N 57 40 E
Ayabaca 174 4 40 S 79 53W
Ayabe 111 35 20N 135 20 E
Ayacucho, Argent. 172 37 5 S 58 20W
Ayacucho, Peru 174 13 0 S 74 0W
Ayaguz 76 48 10N 80 0 E
Ayakkuduk 85 41 12N 65 12 E
Ayakok'umu Hu 105 37 30N 89 20 E
Ayakudi 97 10 57N 77 6 E
Ayamonte 57 37 12N 7 24W
Ayan 77 56 30N 138 16 E
Ayancık 82 41 57N 34 18 E
Ayapel 174 8 19N 75 9W
Ayapel, Sa. de 174 7 45N 75 30W
Ayaş 82 40 10N 32 14 E
Ayaviri 174 14 50 S 70 35W
Aydın □ 92 37 40N 27 40 E
Aye 47 50 14N 5 18 E
Ayenngré 121 8 40N 1 1 E
Ayer Hitam 101 1 55N 103 11 E
Ayeritam 101 5 24N 100 15 E
Ayers Rock 136 25 23 S 131 5 E
Ayiá 68 39 43N 22 45 E
Ayia Anna 69 38 52N 23 24 E
Ayía Marína, Kásos, Greece 69 35 27N 26 53 E
Ayía Marína, Leros, Greece 69 37 11N 26 48 E
Ayía Paraskeví 68 39 14N 26 16 E
Ayía Rouméli 69 35 14N 23 58 E
Ayiássos 69 39 5N 26 23 E
Áyios Andréas 69 37 21N 22 45 E
Áyios Evstrátios 68 39 34N 24 58 E
Áyios Ioánnis, Ákra 69 35 20N 25 40 E
Áyios Kírikos 69 37 34N 26 17 E
Áyios Matthaíos 68 39 30N 19 47 E
Áyios Míron 69 35 15N 25 1 E
Áyios Nikólaos 69 35 11N 25 41 E
Áyios Pétros 69 38 38N 20 33 E
Áyios Yeóryios 69 37 28N 23 57 E
Aykathonísi 69 37 28N 27 0 E
Ayke, Ozero 84 51 57N 61 36 E
Aylesbury 29 51 48N 0 49W
Aylesford 29 51 18N 0 29 E
Aylmer L. 148 64 0N 108 30W
Aylsham 29 52 48N 1 16 E
Ayn Zālah 92 36 45N 42 35 E
'Ayn Zaqqūt 119 29 0N 19 30 E
Ayna 59 38 34N 2 3W
Aynho 28 51 59N 1 15W
Ayni 85 39 23N 68 32 E
Ayolas 172 27 10 S 56 59W
Ayom 123 7 49N 28 23 E
Ayon, Ostrov 77 69 50N 169 0 E
Ayora 59 39 3N 1 3W
Ayr, Austral. 138 19 35 S 147 25 E
Ayr, U.K. 34 55 28N 4 37W
Ayr (□) 26 55 25N 4 25W
Ayr, Heads of 34 55 25N 4 43W
Ayr, R. 34 55 29N 4 40W
Ayre, Pt. of 37 58 55N 2 43W
Ayre, Pt. of I.o.M. 32 54 27N 4 21W
Aysgarth 32 54 18N 2 0W
Aysha 123 10 50N 42 23 E
Ayton 138 15 45 S 145 25 E
Ayton, Borders, U.K. 35 55 51N 2 6W
Ayton, N. Yorks., U.K. 33 54 15N 0 29W
Aytos 67 42 47N 27 16 E
Aytoska Planina 67 42 45N 27 30 E
Ayu, Kepulauan 103 0 35N 131 5 E
Ayutla, Guat. 166 14 40N 92 10W

Ayutla **Balasore**

Ayutla, Mexico **165** 16 58N 99 17W
Ayutthaya = Phra Nakhon Si A. **101** 14 25N 100 30 E
Ayvalık **92** 39 20N 26 46 E
Aywaille **47** 50 28N 5 40 E
Az Zahiriya **90** 31 25N 34 58 E
Az Zahran **92** 26 10N 50 7 E
Az-Zarqā **90** 32 5N 36 4 E
Az Zāwiyah **119** 32 52N 12 56 E
Az-Zilfī **92** 26 12N 44 52 E
Az Zintān **119** 31 59N 12 9 E
Az Zubayr **92** 30 20N 47 50 E
Azambuja **57** 39 4N 8 51W
Azamgarh **95** 26 35N 83 13 E
Azaouak, Vallée de l' **121** 15 50N 3 20 E
Azärbāijān □ **92** 37 0N 44 30 E
Azare **121** 11 55N 10 10 E
Azay-le-Rideau **42** 47 16N 0 30 E
Azazga **119** 36 48N 4 22 E
Azbine = Aïr **121** 18 0N 8 0 E
Azeffoun **119** 36 51N 4 26 E
Azemmour **118** 33 14N 9 20W
Azerbaijan S.S.R. □ **83** 40 20N 48 0 E
Azezo **123** 12 28N 37 15 E
Azilal, Beni Mallal **118** 32 0N 6 30W
Azimganj **95** 24 14N 84 16 E
Aznalcóllar **57** 37 32N 6 17W
Azogues **174** 2 35 S 78 0W
Azor **90** 32 2N 34 48 E
Azores, Is. **14** 38 44N 29 0W
Azov **83** 47 3N 39 25 E
Azov Sea = Azovskoye More **82** 46 0N 36 30 E
Azovskoye More **82** 46 0N 36 30 E
Azovy **76** 64 55N 64 35 E
Azpeitia **58** 43 12N 2 19W
Azrou **118** 33 28N 5 19W
Aztec **161** 36 54N 108 0W
Azúa de Compostela **167** 18 25N 70 44W
Azuaga **57** 38 16N 5 39W
Azuara **58** 41 15N 0 53W
Azuara, R. **58** 41 12N 0 55W
Azúcar, Presa del **165** 26 0N 99 5W
Azuer, R. **57** 38 50N 3 15W
Azuero, Pen. de **166** 7 30N 80 30W
Azul **172** 36 42 S 59 43W
Azusa **163** 34 8N 117 52W
Azzaba **119** 36 48N 7 6 E
Azzano Décimo **63** 45 53N 12 46 E

B

B. Curri **68** 42 22N 20 5 E
Ba Don **100** 17 45N 106 26 E
Ba Dong **101** 9 40N 106 33 E
Ba Ngoi = Cam Lam **101** 11 50N 109 10 E
Ba, R. **56** 13 5N 109 0 E
Ba Tri **101** 10 2N 106 36 E
Baa **103** 10 50 S 123 0 E
Baamonde **56** 43 7N 7 44W
Baar **51** 47 12N 8 32 E
Baarle Nassau **47** 51 27N 4 56 E
Baarlo **47** 51 20N 6 6 E
Baarn **46** 52 12N 5 17 E
Bāb el Māndeb **91** 12 35N 43 25 E
Baba Burnu **68** 39 29N 26 2 E
Baba dag **83** 41 0N 48 55 E
Baba, Mt. **67** 42 44N 23 59 E
Babaçulândia **170** 7 13 S 47 46W
Babadag **70** 44 53N 28 44 E
Babaeski **67** 41 26N 27 6 E
Babahoyo **174** 1 40 S 79 30W
Babakin **137** 32 7 S 118 1 E
Babana **121** 10 31N 3 46 E
Babar, Alg. **119** 35 10N 7 6 E
Babar, Pak. **94** 31 7N 69 32 E
Babar, I. **103** 8 0 S 129 30 E
Babarkach **94** 29 45N 68 0 E
Babayevo **81** 59 24N 35 55 E
Babb **160** 48 56N 113 27W
Babbitt **163** 38 32N 118 39W
Babenhausen **49** 49 57N 8 56 E
Babi Besar, P. **101** 2 25N 103 59 E
Babia Gora **54** 49 38N 19 38 E
Babile **123** 9 16N 42 11 E
Babinda **138** 17 20 S 145 56 E
Babine **152** 55 20N 126 35W
Babine L. **152** 54 48N 126 0W
Babine, R. **152** 55 45N 127 44W
Babo **103** 2 30 S 133 30 E
Babócsa **53** 46 2N 17 21 E
Babol **93** 36 40N 52 50 E
Babol Sar **93** 36 45N 52 45 E
Baboma **126** 2 30N 28 10 E
Baborówo Kietrz **53** 50 7N 18 1 E
Baboua **124** 5 49N 14 58 E
Babuna, mts. **66** 41 30N 21 40 E
Babura **121** 12 51N 8 59 E
Babusar Pass **95** 35 12N 73 59 E
Babushkin **81** 55 45N 37 40 E
Babušnica **66** 43 7N 22 27 E
Babylon, Iraq **92** 32 40N 44 30 E
Babylon, U.S.A. **162** 40 42N 73 20W
Bač **66** 45 29N 19 17 E
Bac Can **100** 22 08N 105 49 E
Bac Giang **100** 21 16N 106 11 E
Bac Kan **101** 22 5N 105 50 E
Bac Lieu = Vinh Loi **101** 9 17N 105 43 E
Bac Ninh **100** 21 13N 106 4 E
Bac Phan **100** 22 0N 105 0 E
Bac Quang **100** 22 30N 104 48 E
Bacabal **170** 4 15N 44 45W
Bacalar **165** 18 12N 87 53W
Bacan, Pulau **103** 0 50 S 127 30 E
Bacarès, Le **44** 42 47N 3 3 E
Bacarra **103** 18 15N 120 37 E
Baccarat **43** 48 28N 6 42 E
Bacchus Marsh **140** 37 43 S 144 27 E
Bacerac **164** 30 18N 108 50W
Bach Long Vi, Dao **100** 20 10N 107 40 E
Bachaquero **174** 9 56N 71 8W
Bacharach **49** 50 3N 7 46 E
Bachclina **76** 57 45N 67 20 E
Bachok **101** 6 4N 102 25 E
Bachuma **123** 6 31N 36 1 E
Bačina **66** 43 42N 21 23 E
Back **36** 58 17N 6 20W
Back, R. **148** 65 10N 104 0W
Bačka Palanka **66** 45 17N 19 27 E
Bačka Topola **66** 45 49N 19 39 E
Bäckefors **73** 58 48N 12 9 E
Bački Petrovac **66** 45 29N 19 32 E
Backnang **49** 48 57N 9 26 E
Backstairs Passage **133** 35 40 S 138 5 E
Bacolod **103** 10 40N 122 57 E
Bacqueville **42** 49 47N 1 0 E
Bacs-Kiskun □ **53** 46 43N 19 30 E
Bácsalmás **53** 46 8N 19 17 E
Bacton **29** 52 50N 1 29 E
Bacuit **103** 11 20N 119 20 E
Bacup **32** 53 42N 2 12W
Bacǔu **70** 46 35N 26 55 E
Bacǔu □ **70** 46 30N 26 45 E
Bad Aussee **52** 47 43N 13 45 E
Bad Axe **150** 43 48N 82 59W
Bad Bergzabem **49** 49 6N 8 0 E
Bad Bramstedt **48** 53 56N 9 53 E
Bad Doberan **48** 54 6N 11 55 E
Bad Driburg **48** 51 44N 9 0 E
Bad Ems **49** 50 22N 7 44 E
Bad Frankenhausen **48** 51 21N 11 3 E
Bad Freienwalde **52** 52 46N 14 2 E
Bad Godesberg **48** 50 41N 7 4 E
Bad Hersfeld **48** 50 52N 9 42 E
Bad Hofgastein **52** 47 17N 13 6 E
Bad Homburg **49** 50 17N 8 33 E
Bad Honnef **48** 50 39N 7 13 E
Bad Ischl **52** 47 44N 13 38 E
Bad Kissingen **49** 50 11N 10 5 E
Bad Kreuznach **49** 49 47N 7 47 E
Bad Lands **158** 43 40N 102 10W
Bad Lauterberg **48** 51 38N 10 29 E
Bad Leonfelden **52** 48 31N 14 18 E
Bad Lippspringe **48** 51 47N 8 46 E
Bad Mergentheim **49** 49 29N 9 47 E
Bad Münstereifel **48** 50 33N 6 46 E
Bad Nauheim **49** 50 24N 8 45 E
Bad Oeynhausen **48** 52 16N 8 45 E
Bad Oldesloe **48** 53 56N 10 17 E
Bad Orb **49** 50 16N 9 21 E
Bad Pyrmont **48** 51 59N 9 5 E
Bad, R. **158** 44 10N 100 50W
Bad Ragaz **51** 47 0N 9 30 E
Bad St. Peter **48** 54 23N 8 32 E
Bad Salzuflen **48** 52 8N 8 44 E
Bad Segeberg **48** 53 58N 10 16 E
Bad Tölz **49** 47 43N 11 34 E
Bad Waldsee **49** 47 56N 9 46 E
Bad Wildungen **48** 51 7N 9 10 E
Bad Wimpfen **49** 49 12N 9 10 E
Bad Windsheim **49** 49 29N 10 25 E
Badagara **97** 11 35N 75 40 E
Badagri **121** 6 25N 2 55 E
Badajoz **57** 38 50N 6 59W
Badajoz □ **57** 38 40N 6 30W
Badakhshan □ **93** 36 30N 71 0 E
Badalona **58** 41 26N 2 15 E
Badalzai **94** 29 50N 65 35 E
Badampahar **96** 22 10N 86 10 E
Badanah **92** 30 58N 41 30 E
Badas **102** 4 33N 114 25 E
Badas, Kepulauan **102** 0 45N 107 5 E
Baddo, R. **93** 28 15N 65 0 E
Bade **103** 7 10 S 139 35 E
Baden, Austria **53** 48 1N 16 13 E
Baden, Switz. **51** 47 28N 8 18 E
Baden-Baden **49** 48 45N 8 15 E
Baden Park **140** 32 8 S 144 12 E
Baden-Württemberg □ **49** 48 40N 9 0 E
Badenoch **37** 58 16N 4 5W
Badenscoth **37** 57 27N 2 30W
Badeso **123** 9 58N 40 52 E
Badgastein **52** 47 7N 13 9 E
Badger, Can. **151** 49 0N 56 4W
Badger, U.S.A. **163** 36 38N 119 1W
Badghis □ **93** 35 0N 63 0 E
Badgom **95** 34 1N 74 45 E
Badhoevedorp **46** 52 20N 4 47 E
Badia Polesine **63** 45 6N 11 30 E
Badin **94** 24 38N 68 54 E
Badnera **96** 20 48N 77 44 E
Badogo **120** 11 2N 8 13W
Badrinath **95** 30 45N 79 30 E
Baduen **91** 7 15N 47 40 E
Badulla **97** 7 1N 81 7 E
Badupi **98** 21 36N 93 27 E
Bække **73** 55 35N 9 6 E
Baena **57** 37 37N 4 20W
Baerami Creek **141** 32 27 S 150 27 E
Baetas **174** 6 5 S 62 15W
Baexem **47** 51 13N 5 53 E
Baeza, Ecuador **174** 0 25 S 77 45W
Baeza, Spain **59** 37 57N 3 25W
Bafa **93** 31 40N 55 25 E
Bafa Gölü **69** 37 30N 27 29 E
Bafatá **120** 12 8N 15 20W
Baffin Bay **12** 72 0N 64 0W
Baffin I. **149** 68 0N 75 0W
Bafia **121** 4 40N 11 10 E
Bafilo **121** 9 22N 1 22 E
Bafing, R. **120** 11 40N 10 45W
Baflo **46** 53 22N 6 31 E
Bafoulabé **120** 13 50N 10 55W
Bafq **93** 31 40N 55 20 E
Bafra **82** 41 34N 35 54 E
Baft **93** 29 15N 56 38 E
Bafut **121** 6 6N 10 2 E
Bafwakwandji **126** 1 12N 26 52 E
Bafwasende **126** 1 3N 27 5 E
Bagalkot **96** 16 10N 75 40 E
Bagamoyo **126** 6 28 S 38 55 E
Bagamoyo □ **126** 6 20 S 38 30 E
Bagan Datok **101** 3 59N 100 47 E
Bagan Serai **101** 5 1N 100 32 E
Bagan Siapiapi **102** 2 12N 100 50 E
Baganga **103** 7 34N 126 33 E
Bagasra **94** 21 59N 71 77 E
Bagawi **123** 12 20N 34 18 E
Bagdad **163** 34 35N 115 53W
Bagdarin **77** 54 26N 113 36 E
Bagé **173** 31 20 S 54 15W
Bagenalstown = Muine Bheag **39** 52 42N 6 57W
Baggs **160** 41 8N 107 46W
Baggy Pt. **30** 51 11N 4 12W
Bagh **95** 33 59N 73 45 E
Bagh nam Faoileann, B. **36** 57 22N 7 13W
Baghdād **92** 33 20N 44 30 E
Bagherhat **98** 22 40N 89 47 E
Bagheria **64** 38 5N 13 30 E
Baghin **93** 30 12N 56 45 E
Baghlan **93** 36 12N 69 0 E
Baghlan □ **93** 36 0N 68 30 E
Baginbun Hd. **39** 52 10N 6 50W
Bagley **158** 47 30N 95 22W
Bagnacavallo **63** 44 25N 11 58 E
Bagnara Cálabra **65** 38 16N 15 49 E
Bagnères-de-Bigorre **44** 43 5N 0 9 E
Bagnères-de-Luchon **44** 42 47N 0 38 E
Bagni di Lucca **62** 44 1N 10 37 E
Bagno di Romagna **63** 43 50N 11 59 E
Bagnoles-de-l'Orne **42** 48 32N 0 25W
Bagnolo Mella **62** 45 27N 10 14 E
Bagnols-les-Bains **44** 44 30N 3 40 E
Bagnols-sur-Cèze **45** 44 10N 4 36 E
Bagnorégio **63** 42 38N 12 7 E
Bagolino **62** 45 49N 10 28 E
Bagotville **151** 48 22N 70 54W
Bagrdan **66** 44 5N 21 11 E
Bagshot **29** 51 22N 0 41W
Baguio **103** 16 26N 120 34 E
Bahabón de Esgueva **58** 41 52N 3 43W
Bahadurabad **98** 25 11N 89 44 E
Bahadurgarh **94** 28 40N 76 57 E
Bahama, Canal Viejo de **166** 22 10N 77 30W
Bahama Is. **167** 24 40N 74 0W
Bahamas ■ **167** 24 0N 74 0W
Baharîya, El Wâhât el **122** 28 0N 28 50 E
Bahau **101** 2 48N 102 26 E
Bahawalnagar **94** 30 0N 73 15 E
Bahawalpur **94** 29 37N 71 40 E
Bahawalpur □ **94** 29 5N 71 3 E
Baheri **95** 28 45N 79 34 E
Baheta **123** 13 27N 42 10 E
Bahi **126** 5 58 S 35 21 E
Bahi Swamp **126** 6 10 S 35 0 E
Bahía = Salvador **171** 13 0 S 38 30W
Bahía □ **171** 12 0N 42 0W
Bahía Blanca **172** 38 35 S 62 13W
Bahía de Caráquez **174** 0 40 S 80 27W
Bahía Honda **166** 22 54N 83 10W
Bahía, Islas de la **166** 16 45N 86 15W
Bahía Laura **176** 48 10 S 66 30W
Bahía Negra **174** 20 5 S 58 5W
Bahir Dar Giyorgis **123** 11 33N 37 25 E
Bahmer **118** 27 32N 0 10W
Bahönye **53** 46 25N 17 28 E
Bahr Aouk **124** 9 20N 20 40 E
Bahr Dar **123** 11 37N 37 10 E
Bahr el Abiad **123** 9 30N 31 40 E
Bahr el Ahmer □ **122** 20 0N 35 0 E
Bahr el Arab **123** 9 50N 27 10 E
Bahr el Azraq **123** 10 30N 35 0 E
Bahr el Ghazâl □ **123** 7 0N 28 0 E
Bahr el Ghazâl, R. **123** 9 0N 30 0 E
Bahr el Jebel **123** 7 30N 30 30 E
Bahr Salamat **124** 10 0N 19 0 E
Bahr Yûsef **122** 28 25N 30 35 E
Bahra **92** 21 25N 39 32 E
Bahra el Burullus **122** 31 28N 30 48 E
Bahra el Manzala **122** 31 28N 32 01 E
Bahraich **95** 27 38N 81 50 E
Bahrain ■ **93** 26 0N 50 35 E
Bahramabad **93** 30 28N 56 2 E
Bahu Kalat **93** 25 50N 61 20 E
Bai **120** 13 35N 3 28W
Bai Bung, Mui **101** 8 38N 104 44 E
Bai Duc **100** 18 3N 105 49 E
Bai Thuong **100** 19 54N 105 23 E
Baia-Mare **70** 47 40N 23 17 E
Baia-Sprie **70** 47 41N 23 43W
Baião **170** 2 40 S 49 40W
Baïbokoum **117** 7 40N 14 45 E
Baidoa **91** 3 8N 43 30 E
Baie Comeau **151** 49 12N 68 10W
Baie de l'Abri **151** 50 3N 67 0W
Baie Johan Beetz **151** 50 18N 62 50W
Baie St. Paul **151** 47 28N 70 32W
Baie Trinité **151** 49 25N 67 20W
Baie Verte **151** 49 55N 56 12W
Baignes **44** 45 28N 0 25W
Baigneux-les-Juifs **43** 47 31N 4 39 E
Ba'ījī **92** 35 0N 43 30 E
Baikal, L. **77** 53 0N 108 0 E
Bailadila, Mt. **96** 18 43N 81 15 E
Baildon **33** 53 52N 1 46W
Baile Atha Cliath = Dublin **39** 53 20N 6 18W
Bailei **123** 6 44N 40 18 E
Bailén **57** 38 8N 3 48W
Baileux **47** 50 2N 4 23 E
Bailhongal **97** 15 55N 74 53 E
Bailique, Ilha **170** 1 2N 49 58W
Bailleul **43** 50 44N 2 41 E
Baillieborough **38** 53 55N 7 0W
Baimuru **135** 7 35 S 144 51 E
Bain-de-Bretagne **42** 47 50N 1 40W
Bainbridge, U.K. **32** 54 18N 2 7W
Bainbridge, Ga., U.S.A. **157** 30 53N 84 34W
Bainbridge, N.Y., U.S.A. **162** 42 17N 75 29W
Baing **103** 10 14 S 120 34 E
Bainville **158** 48 8N 104 10W
Bainyik **135** 3 40 S 143 4 E
Baird **159** 32 25N 99 25W
Baird Inlet **147** 64 49N 164 18W
Baird Mts. **147** 67 10N 160 15W
Bairnsdale **141** 37 48 S 147 36 E
Baissa **121** 7 14N 10 38 E
Baitadi **95** 29 35N 80 25 E
Baixa Grande **171** 11 57 S 40 11W
Baiyuda **122** 17 35N 32 07 E
Baja **53** 46 12N 18 59 E
Baja California **164** 32 10N 115 12W
Baja, Pta. **164** 29 50N 116 0W
Bajah, Wadi **122** 23 14N 39 20 E
Bajana **94** 23 7N 71 49 E
Bajimba **139** 29 22 S 152 0 E
Bajimba, Mt. **139** 29 17 S 152 6 E
Bajina Bašta **66** 43 58N 19 35 E
Bajitpur **95** 24 13N 91 0 E
Bajmok **66** 45 57N 19 24 E
Bajo Boquete **167** 8 49N 82 27W
Bajoga **121** 10 57N 11 20 E
Bajool **138** 23 40 S 150 35 E
Bak **53** 46 43N 16 51 E
Bakal **84** 54 56N 58 48 E
Bakala **117** 6 15N 20 20 E
Bakanas **85** 44 50N 76 15 E
Bakar **63** 45 18N 14 32 E
Bakel, Neth. **47** 51 30N 5 45 E
Bakel, Senegal **120** 14 56N 12 20W
Baker, Calif., U.S.A. **163** 35 16N 116 8W
Baker, Mont., U.S.A. **158** 46 22N 104 12W
Baker, Nev., U.S.A. **160** 38 59N 114 7W
Baker, Oreg., U.S.A. **160** 44 50N 117 55W
Baker Is. **130** 0 10N 176 35 E
Baker, L., Austral. **137** 26 54 S 126 5 E
Baker, L., Can. **148** 64 0N 96 0W
Baker Lake **148** 64 20N 96 3W
Baker Mt. **160** 48 50N 121 49W
Baker's Dozen Is. **150** 56 45N 78 45W
Bakersfield **163** 35 25N 119 0W
Bakewell **33** 53 13N 1 40W
Bakhchisaray **82** 44 40N 33 45 E
Bakhmach **80** 51 10N 32 45 E
Bakhtiari □ **92** 32 0N 49 0 E
Bakia **123** 5 18N 25 45 E
Bakinskikh Komissarov **92** 39 20N 49 15 E
Bakırköy **67** 40 59N 28 53 E
Bakkafjörðr **74** 66 2N 14 48W
Bakkagerði **74** 65 31N 13 49W
Bakke **71** 58 25N 6 39 E
Bakony Forest = Bakony Hegység **53** 47 10N 17 30 E
Bakony Hegység **53** 47 10N 17 30 E
Bakony, R. **53** 47 35N 17 54 E
Bakori **121** 11 34N 7 25 E
Bakouma **117** 5 40N 22 56 E
Bakov **52** 50 27N 14 55 E
Bakpakty **85** 44 35N 76 40 E
Bakr Uzyak **84** 52 59N 58 38 E
Baku **83** 40 25N 49 45 E
Bakwanga = Mbuji Mayi **124** 6 9 S 23 40 E
Bal'a **90** 32 20N 35 6 E
Bala, L. = Tegid, L. **31** 52 53N 3 38W
Balabac I. **102** 8 0N 117 0 E
Balabac, Selat **102** 7 53N 117 5 E
Balabagh **94** 34 25N 70 12 E
Balabakk **92** 34 0N 36 10 E
Balabalagan, Kepulauan **102** 2 20 S 117 30 E
Balaghat **96** 21 49N 80 12 E
Balaghat Ra. **96** 18 50N 76 30 E
Balaguer **58** 41 50N 0 50 E
Balakhna **81** 56 35N 43 32 E
Balaklava, Austral. **140** 34 7 S 138 22 E
Balaklava, U.S.S.R. **82** 44 30N 33 30 E
Balakleya **82** 49 28N 36 55 E
Balakovo **81** 52 4N 47 55 E
Balallan **36** 58 5N 6 35W
Balancán **165** 17 48N 91 32W
Balanda **81** 51 30N 44 40 E
Balangir **96** 20 43N 83 35 E
Balapur **96** 21 22N 76 45 E
Balashikha **81** 55 45N 37 59 E
Balashov **81** 51 30N 43 10 E
Balasinor **94** 22 57N 73 23 E
Balasore **96** 21 35N 87 3 E

Balassagyarmat **Bangor**

Balassagyarmat	**53**	48 4N	19 15 E
Balât	**122**	25 36N	29 19 E
Balaton	**53**	46 50N	17 40 E
Balatonfüred	**53**	46 58N	17 54 E
Balatonszentgyörgy	**53**	46 41N	17 19 E
Balazote	**59**	38 54N	2 09W
Balbeggie	**35**	56 26N	3 19W
Balbi, Mt.	**135**	5 55 S	154 58 E
Balblair	**37**	57 39N	4 11W
Balboa	**166**	9 0N	79 30W
Balbriggan	**38**	53 35N	6 10W
Balcarce	**172**	38 0 S	58 10W
Balcarres	**153**	50 50N	103 35W
Balchik	**67**	43 28N	28 11 E
Balclutha	**143**	46 15 S	169 45 E
Bald Hd.	**137**	35 6 S	118 1 E
Bald Hill, W. Australia, Austral.	**137**	31 36 S	116 13 E
Bald Hill, W. Australia, Austral.	**137**	24 55 S	119 57 E
Bald I.	**137**	34 57 S	118 27 E
Bald Knob	**159**	35 20N	91 35W
Baldegger-See	**51**	47 12N	8 17 E
Balder, oilfield	**19**	59 10N	2 20 E
Balderton	**33**	53 3N	0 46W
Baldock	**29**	51 59N	0 11W
Baldock L.	**153**	56 33N	97 57W
Baldoyle	**38**	53 24N	6 10W
Baldwin, Fla., U.S.A.	**156**	30 15N	82 10W
Baldwin, Mich., U.S.A.	**156**	43 54N	85 53W
Baldwinsville	**162**	43 10N	76 19W
Bale	**63**	45 4N	13 46 E
Baleares □	**58**	39 30N	3 0 E
Baleares, Islas	**58**	39 30N	3 0 E
Balearic Is. = Baleares, Islas	**58**	39 30N	3 0 E
Baleia, Ponta da	**171**	17 40 S	39 7W
Balen	**47**	51 10N	5 10 E
Baler	**103**	15 46N	121 34 E
Balerna	**51**	45 52N	9 0 E
Baleshare I.	**36**	57 30N	7 21W
Balezino	**84**	58 2N	53 6 E
Balfate	**166**	15 48N	86 25W
Balfe's Creek	**138**	20 12 S	145 55 E
Balfour, S. Afr.	**129**	26 38 S	28 35 E
Balfour, U.K.	**37**	59 2N	2 54W
Balfour Downs	**137**	22 45 S	120 50 E
Balfouriyya	**90**	32 38N	35 18 E
Balfron	**34**	56 4N	4 20W
Bali	**121**	5 54N	10 0 E
Bali □	**102**	8 20 S	115 0 E
Bali, I.	**102**	8 20 S	115 0 E
Bali, Selat	**103**	8 30 S	114 35 E
Baligród	**54**	49 20N	22 17 E
Balikesir	**92**	39 35N	27 58 E
Balikpapan	**102**	1 10 S	116 55 E
Balimbing	**103**	5 10N	120 3 E
Balimo	**135**	8 6 S	142 57 E
Baling	**101**	5 41N	100 55 E
Balintore	**37**	57 45N	3 55W
Balipara	**99**	26 50N	92 45 E
Balit	**95**	36 15N	74 40 E
Baliza	**175**	16 0 S	52 20W
Balk	**46**	52 54N	5 35 E
Balkan Mts. = Stara Planina	**67**	43 15N	23 0 E
Balkan Pen.	**16**	42 0N	22 0 E
Balkh = Wazirabad	**93**	36 44N	66 47 E
Balkh □	**93**	36 30N	67 0 E
Balkhash	**76**	46 50N	74 50 E
Balkhash, Ozero	**76**	40 0N	74 50 E
Balla, Ireland	**38**	53 48N	9 7W
Balla, Pak.	**99**	24 10N	91 35 E
Ballachulish	**36**	56 40N	5 10W
Balladonia	**137**	32 27 S	123 51 E
Ballagan Pt.	**38**	54 0N	6 6W
Ballaghaderreen	**38**	53 55N	8 35W
Ballantrae	**34**	55 6N	5 0W
Ballara	**140**	32 19 S	140 45 E
Ballarat	**139**	37 33 S	143 50 E
Ballard, L.	**137**	29 20 S	120 10 E
Ballarpur	**96**	19 50N	79 23 E
Ballater	**37**	57 2N	3 2W
Ballaugh	**32**	54 20N	4 32W
Balldale	**141**	36 20N	146 33 E
Ballenas, Canal de las	**164**	29 10N	113 45W
Balleni	**70**	45 48N	27 51 E
Balleny Is.	**13**	66 30 S	163 0 E
Ballia	**95**	25 46N	84 12 E
Ballickmoyler	**39**	52 54N	7 2W
Ballidu	**137**	30 35 S	116 45 E
Ballina, Austral.	**139**	28 50 S	153 31 E
Ballina, Mayo, Ireland	**38**	54 7N	9 10W
Ballina, Tipp., Ireland	**39**	52 49N	8 27W
Ballinagar	**39**	53 15N	7 21W
Ballinagh = Bellananagh	**38**	53 55N	7 25W
Ballinalack	**38**	53 38N	7 28W
Ballinalea	**39**	53 0N	6 8W
Ballinalee	**38**	53 46N	7 40W
Ballinamallard	**38**	54 30N	7 36W
Ballinameen	**38**	53 54N	8 19W
Ballinamore	**38**	54 3N	7 48W
Ballinamore Bridge	**38**	53 30N	8 24W
Ballinascarty	**39**	51 40N	8 52W
Ballinasloe	**39**	53 20N	8 12W
Ballincollig	**39**	51 52N	8 35W
Ballindaggin	**39**	52 33N	6 43W
Ballinderry	**38**	53 2N	8 13W
Ballinderry R.	**38**	54 40N	6 32W
Ballindine	**38**	53 40N	8 57W
Ballineen	**39**	51 43N	8 57W
Balling	**73**	56 38N	8 51 E
Ballingarry, Lim., Ireland	**39**	53 1N	8 3W
Ballingarry, Tipp., Ireland	**39**	52 29N	8 50W
Ballingarry, Tipp., Ireland	**39**	52 35N	7 32W
Ballingeary	**39**	51 51N	9 13W
Ballinger	**159**	31 45N	99 58W
Ballinhassig	**39**	51 48N	8 33W
Ballinlough	**38**	53 45N	8 39W
Ballinluig	**37**	56 40N	3 40W
Ballinrobe	**38**	53 36N	9 13W
Ballinskelligs	**39**	51 50N	10 17W
Ballinskelligs B.	**39**	51 46N	10 11W
Ballintober	**38**	53 43N	8 25W
Ballintoy	**38**	55 13N	6 20W
Ballintra	**38**	54 35N	8 9W
Ballinunty	**39**	52 36N	7 40W
Ballinure	**39**	52 34N	7 46W
Ballivian	**172**	22 41 S	62 10W
Ballivor	**38**	53 32N	6 50W
Ballo Pt.	**79**	8 55N	13 18W
Balloch	**34**	56 0N	4 35W
Ballon	**39**	48 10N	0 16 E
Ballston Spa	**162**	43 0N	73 51W
Ballybay	**38**	54 8N	6 52W
Ballybofey	**38**	54 48N	7 47W
Ballyboghil	**38**	53 32N	6 16W
Ballybogy	**38**	55 8N	6 33W
Ballybunion	**39**	52 30N	9 40W
Ballycanew	**39**	52 37N	6 18W
Ballycarney	**39**	52 35N	6 44W
Ballycastle	**38**	55 12N	6 15W
Ballycastle B.	**38**	55 12N	6 15W
Ballyclare, Ireland	**38**	53 40N	8 0W
Ballyclare, U.K.	**38**	54 46N	6 0W
Ballyclerahan	**39**	52 25N	7 48W
Ballycolla	**39**	52 53N	7 27W
Ballyconneely	**38**	53 27N	10 5W
Ballyconneely B.	**38**	53 23N	10 8W
Ballyconnell	**38**	54 7N	7 35W
Ballycotton	**39**	51 50N	8 0W
Ballycroy	**38**	54 2N	9 49W
Ballydavid	**39**	53 12N	8 28W
Ballydavid Hd.	**39**	52 15N	10 20W
Ballydehob	**39**	51 34N	9 28W
Ballydonegan	**39**	51 37N	10 12W
Ballydonegan B.	**39**	51 38N	10 6W
Ballyduff, Kerry, Ireland	**39**	52 27N	9 40W
Ballyduff, Waterford, Ireland	**39**	52 9N	8 2W
Ballyforan	**38**	53 29N	8 18W
Ballygar	**38**	53 33N	8 20W
Ballygarrett	**39**	52 34N	6 15W
Ballygawley	**38**	54 27N	7 2W
Ballyglass	**38**	53 45N	9 9W
Ballygorman	**38**	55 23N	7 20W
Ballyhahill	**39**	52 33N	9 13W
Ballyhaise	**38**	54 3N	7 20W
Ballyhalbert	**38**	54 30N	5 28W
Ballyhaunis	**38**	53 47N	8 47W
Ballyheige I.	**39**	52 22N	9 51W
Ballyhoura Hills	**39**	52 18N	8 33W
Ballyjamesduff	**38**	53 52N	7 11W
Ballylanders	**39**	52 25N	8 21W
Ballylaneen	**39**	52 10N	7 25W
Ballylongford	**39**	52 34N	9 30W
Ballylooby	**39**	52 20N	7 59W
Ballylynan	**39**	52 57N	7 02W
Ballymacoda	**39**	51 53N	7 56W
Ballymagorry	**38**	54 52N	7 26W
Ballymahon	**39**	53 35N	7 45W
Ballymena	**38**	54 53N	6 18W
Ballymena □	**38**	54 53N	6 18W
Ballymoe	**38**	53 41N	8 28W
Ballymoney	**38**	55 5N	6 30W
Ballymoney □	**38**	55 5N	6 23W
Ballymore	**39**	53 30N	7 40W
Ballymore Eustace	**39**	53 8N	6 38W
Ballymote	**38**	54 5N	8 30W
Ballymurphy	**39**	52 33N	6 52W
Ballymurray	**38**	53 36N	8 8W
Ballynabola	**39**	52 21N	6 50W
Ballynacally	**39**	52 42N	9 7W
Ballynacargy	**38**	53 35N	7 32W
Ballynacorra	**39**	51 53N	8 10W
Ballynagore	**38**	53 24N	7 29W
Ballynahinch	**38**	54 24N	5 55W
Ballynahown	**38**	53 21N	7 52W
Ballynameen	**38**	54 58N	6 41W
Ballynamona	**39**	52 5N	8 39W
Ballynure	**38**	54 47N	5 59W
Ballyquintin, Pt.	**38**	54 20N	5 30W
Ballyragget	**39**	52 47N	7 20W
Ballyroan	**39**	52 57N	7 20W
Ballyronan	**38**	54 43N	6 32W
Ballyroney	**38**	54 17N	6 8W
Ballysadare	**38**	54 12N	8 30W
Ballyshannon	**38**	54 30N	8 10W
Ballyvaughan	**39**	53 7N	9 10W
Ballyvourney	**39**	51 57N	9 10W
Ballyvoy	**38**	55 11N	6 11W
Ballywalter	**38**	54 33N	5 30W
Ballywilliam	**39**	52 27N	6 52W
Balmaceda	**176**	46 0 S	71 50W
Balmaclellan	**35**	55 6N	4 5W
Balmazújváros	**53**	47 37N	21 21 E
Balmedie	**37**	57 14N	2 4W
Balmhorn	**50**	46 26N	7 42 E
Balmoral	**140**	37 15 S	141 48 E
Balmoral For.	**37**	57 0N	3 15W
Balmorhea	**159**	31 2N	103 41W
Balnapaling	**37**	57 42N	4 2W
Balonne, R.	**139**	28 47 S	147 56 E
Balovale	**125**	13 30 S	23 15 E
Balquhidder	**34**	56 22N	4 22W
Balrampur	**95**	27 30N	82 20 E
Balranald	**140**	34 38 S	143 33 E
Balş	**70**	44 22N	24 5 E
Balsas	**165**	18 0N	99 40W
Balsas, R., Goias, Brazil	**170**	9 0 S	48 0W
Balsas, R., Maranhão, Brazil	**170**	7 15 S	44 35W
Balsas, R., Mexico	**164**	18 30N	101 20W
Bålsta	**72**	59 35N	17 30 E
Balsthal	**50**	47 19N	7 41 E
Balta, Rumania	**70**	44 54N	22 38 E
Balta, U.S.A.	**158**	48 12N	100 7W
Balta, U.S.S.R.	**82**	48 2N	29 45 E
Balta, I.	**36**	60 44N	0 49W
Baltanás	**56**	41 56N	4 15W
Baltasound	**36**	60 47N	0 53W
Baltic Sea	**75**	56 0N	20 0 E
Baltiisk	**75**	54 38N	19 55 E
Baltim	**122**	31 35N	31 10 E
Baltimore, Ireland	**39**	51 29N	9 22W
Baltimore, U.S.A.	**162**	39 18N	76 37W
Baltinglass	**39**	52 57N	6 42W
Baltrum	**48**	53 43N	7 25 E
Baluchistan □	**93**	27 30N	65 0 E
Balurghat	**95**	25 15N	88 44 E
Balvicar	**34**	56 17N	5 38W
Balygychan	**77**	63 56N	154 12 E
Bam	**93**	29 7N	58 14 E
Bam La	**99**	29 25N	98 35 E
Bama	**121**	11 33N	13 33 E
Bamako	**120**	12 34N	7 55W
Bamba	**121**	17 5N	1 0W
Bambari	**117**	5 40N	20 35 E
Bambaroo	**107**	18 50 S	146 11 E
Bamberg, Ger.	**49**	49 54N	10 53 E
Bamberg, U.S.A.	**157**	33 19N	81 1W
Bambesi	**123**	9 45N	34 40 E
Bambey	**120**	14 42N	16 28W
Bambili	**126**	3 40N	26 0 E
Bamboo	**138**	14 34 S	143 20 E
Bambouti	**126**	5 25N	27 12 E
Bambuí	**171**	20 1 S	45 58W
Bamburgh	**35**	55 36N	1 42W
Bamenda	**121**	5 57N	10 11 E
Bamfield	**152**	48 45N	125 10W
Bamford	**33**	53 21N	1 41W
Bamian □	**93**	35 0N	67 0 E
Bamkin	**121**	6 3N	11 27 E
Bampton, Devon, U.K.	**30**	50 59N	3 29W
Bampton, Oxon., U.K.	**28**	51 44N	1 33W
Bampur	**93**	27 15N	60 21 E
Bampur, R.	**93**	27 20N	59 30 E
Ban Aranyaprathet	**100**	13 41N	102 30 E
Ban Ban	**100**	19 31N	103 15 E
Ban Bang Hin	**101**	9 32N	98 35 E
Ban Bua Chum	**101**	15 11N	101 12 E
Ban Bua Yai	**100**	15 33N	102 26 E
Ban Chiang Klang	**100**	19 15N	100 55 E
Ban Chik	**100**	17 15N	102 22 E
Ban Choho	**100**	15 2N	102 9 E
Ban Dan Lan Hoi	**100**	17 0N	99 35 E
Ban Don	**100**	12 53N	107 48 E
Ban Don = Surat Thani	**101**	9 8N	99 20 E
Ban Don, Go	**101**	9 20N	99 25 E
Ban Dong	**100**	19 14N	100 3 E
Ban Hong	**100**	18 18N	98 50 E
Ban Houei Sai	**101**	20 22N	100 32 E
Ban Kaeng	**100**	17 29N	100 7 E
Ban Kantang	**101**	7 25N	99 31 E
Ban Keun	**100**	18 22N	102 35 E
Ban Khai	**100**	12 46N	101 18 E
Ban Khe Bo	**101**	19 10N	104 39 E
Ban Kheun	**100**	20 13N	101 7 E
Ban Khlong Kua	**101**	6 57N	100 8 E
Ban Khuan Mao	**101**	7 50N	99 37 E
Ban Khun Yuam	**100**	18 49N	97 57 E
Ban Ko Yai Chim	**101**	11 17N	99 26 E
Ban Kok	**100**	16 40N	103 40 E
Ban Laem	**100**	13 13N	99 59 E
Ban Lao Ngam	**100**	15 28N	106 10 E
Ban Le Kathe	**100**	15 49N	98 53 E
Ban Mae Chedi	**100**	19 11N	99 31 E
Ban Mae Laeng	**100**	20 1N	99 17 E
Ban Mae Sariang	**100**	18 0N	97 56 E
Ban Me Thuot	**100**	12 40N	108 3 E
Ban Mi	**100**	15 3N	100 32 E
Ban Muong Mo	**100**	19 4N	103 58 E
Ban Na Mo	**100**	17 7N	105 40 E
Ban Na San	**101**	8 33N	99 52 E
Ban Na Tong	**100**	20 56N	101 47 E
Ban Nam Bac	**100**	20 38N	102 20 E
Ban Nam Ma	**100**	22 2N	101 37 E
Ban Ngang	**100**	15 59N	106 11 E
Ban Nong Bok	**100**	17 5N	104 48 E
Ban Nong Boua	**100**	15 40N	106 33 E
Ban Nong Pling	**100**	15 40N	100 10 E
Ban Pak Chan	**101**	10 32N	98 51 E
Ban Phai	**100**	16 4N	102 44 E
Ban Pong	**100**	13 50N	99 55 E
Ban Ron Phibun	**101**	8 9N	99 51 E
Ban Sanam Chai	**101**	7 33N	100 25 E
Ban Sangkha	**100**	14 37N	103 52 E
Ban Tak	**100**	17 2N	99 4 E
Ban Tako	**100**	14 5N	102 40 E
Ban Takua Pa	**101**	8 55N	98 25 E
Ban Tha Dua	**100**	17 59N	98 39 E
Ban Tha Li	**100**	17 37N	101 25 E
Ban Tha Nun	**101**	8 12N	98 18 E
Ban Thahine	**100**	14 12N	105 33 E
Ban Thateng	**101**	15 25N	106 27 E
Ban Xien Kok	**100**	20 54N	100 39 E
Ban Yen Nhan	**100**	20 57N	106 2 E
Baña, La, Punta de	**58**	40 33N	0 40 E
Banadar Daryay Oman □	**93**	25 30N	56 0 E
Banadia	**174**	6 54N	71 49W
Banagher	**39**	53 12N	8 0W
Banalia	**126**	1 32N	25 5 E
Banam	**101**	11 20N	105 17 E
Banamba	**120**	13 29N	7 22W
Banana	**138**	24 28 S	150 8 E
Bananal, I. do	**171**	11 30 S	50 30W
Banaras = Varanasi	**95**	25 22N	83 8 E
Banas, R., Gujarat, India	**94**	24 25N	72 30 E
Banas, R., Madhya Pradesh, India	**95**	24 15N	81 30 E
Bânâs, Ras.	**122**	23 57N	35 50 E
Banat □	**66**	45 45N	21 15 E
Banbridge	**38**	54 21N	6 17W
Banbridge □	**38**	54 21N	6 16W
Banbury	**28**	52 4N	1 21W
Banchory	**37**	57 3N	2 30W
Bancroft	**150**	45 3N	77 51W
Bancroft = Chililabombwe	**127**	12 18 S	27 43 E
Band	**67**	46 30N	24 25 E
Band-i-Turkistan, Ra.	**93**	35 2N	64 0 E
Banda	**95**	25 30N	80 26 E
Banda Aceh	**102**	5 35N	95 20 E
Banda Banda, Mt.	**141**	31 10 S	152 28 E
Banda Elat	**103**	5 40 S	133 5 E
Banda, Kepulauan	**103**	4 37 S	129 50 E
Banda, La	**172**	27 45 S	64 10W
Banda, Punta	**164**	31 47N	116 50W
Banda Sea	**103**	6 0 S	130 0 E
Bandama, R.	**120**	6 32N	5 30W
Bandanwara	**94**	26 9N	74 38 E
Bandar = Masulipatnam	**97**	16 12N	81 12 E
Bandar 'Abbās	**93**	27 15N	56 15 E
Bandar-e Būshehr	**93**	28 55N	50 55 E
Bandar-e Chārak	**93**	26 45N	54 20 E
Bandar-e Deylam	**92**	30 5N	50 10 E
Bandar-e Lengeh	**93**	26 35N	54 58 E
Bandar-e Ma'shur	**92**	30 35N	49 10 E
Bandar-e-Nakhīlu	**93**	26 58N	53 30 E
Bandar-e Rīg	**93**	29 30N	50 45 E
Bandar-e Shah	**93**	37 0N	54 10 E
Bandar-e-Shahpur	**92**	30 30N	49 5 E
Bandar-i-Pahlavi	**92**	37 30N	49 30 E
Bandar Maharani = Muar	**101**	2 3N	102 34 E
Bandar Penggaram = Batu Pahat	**101**	1 50N	102 56 E
Bandar Seri Begawan	**102**	4 52N	115 0 E
Bandawe	**127**	11 58 S	34 5 E
Bande, Belg.	**47**	50 10N	5 25 E
Bande, Spain	**56**	42 3N	7 58W
Bandeira, Pico da	**173**	20 26 S	41 47W
Bandeirante	**171**	13 41 S	50 48W
Bandera, Argent.	**172**	28 55 S	62 20W
Bandera, U.S.A.	**159**	29 45N	99 3W
Banderas, Bahía de	**164**	20 40N	105 30W
Bandi-San	**112**	37 36N	140 4 E
Bandia, R.	**96**	19 30N	80 25 E
Bandiagara	**120**	14 12N	3 29W
Bandirma	**92**	40 20N	28 0 E
Bandon	**39**	51 44N	8 45W
Bandon, R.	**39**	51 40N	8 11W
Bandula	**127**	19 0 S	33 7 E
Bandundu	**124**	3 15 S	17 22 E
Bandung	**103**	6 36 S	107 48 E
Bandya	**137**	27 40 S	122 5 E
Bañeres	**59**	38 44N	0 38W
Banes	**167**	21 0N	75 42W
Bañeza, La	**56**	42 17N	5 54W
Banff, Can.	**152**	51 10N	115 34W
Banff, U.K.	**37**	57 40N	2 32W
Banff Nat. Park	**152**	51 30N	116 15W
Banfora	**120**	10 40N	4 40W
Bang Fai, R.	**100**	16 57N	104 45 E
Bang Hieng, R.	**100**	16 24N	105 40 E
Bang Krathum	**100**	16 34N	100 18 E
Bang Lamung	**100**	13 3N	100 56 E
Bang Mun Nak	**100**	16 2N	100 23 E
Bang Pa In	**100**	14 14N	100 35 E
Bang Rakam	**100**	16 45N	100 7 E
Bang Saphan	**101**	11 14N	99 28 E
Bangala Dam	**127**	21 7 S	31 25 E
Bangalore	**97**	12 59N	77 40 E
Bangangte	**121**	5 8N	10 32 E
Bangaon	**95**	23 0N	88 47 E
Bangassou	**124**	4 55N	23 55 E
Bangeta, Mt.	**135**	6 21 S	147 3 E
Banggai	**103**	1 40 S	123 30 E
Banggi, P.	**102**	7 50N	117 0 E
Banghāzī	**119**	32 11N	20 3 E
Bangil	**103**	7 36 S	112 50 E
Bangjang	**123**	11 23N	32 41 E
Bangka, Pulau, Celebes, Indon.	**103**	1 50N	125 5 E
Bangka, Pulau, Sumatera, Indon.	**102**	2 0 S	105 50 E
Bangka, Selat	**102**	3 30 S	105 30 E
Bangkalan	**103**	7 2 S	112 46 E
Bangkinang	**102**	0 18N	100 5 E
Bangko	**102**	2 5 S	102 9 E
Bangkok = Krung Thep	**100**	13 45N	100 31 E
Bangladesh ■	**98**	24 0N	90 0 E
Bangolo	**120**	7 1N	7 29W
Bangor, Me., U.S.A.	**151**	44 48N	68 42W

Bangor Bassevelde

Bangor, Pa., U.S.A.	**162**	40 51N	75 13W
Bangor, N.I., U.K.	**38**	54 40N	5 40W
Bangor, Wales, U.K.	**31**	53 13N	4 9W
Bangued	**103**	17 40N	120 37 E
Bangui	**124**	4 23N	18 35 E
Banguru	**126**	0 30N	27 10 E
Bangweulu, L.	**127**	11 0 S	30 0 E
Bangweulu Swamp	**127**	11 20 S	30 15 E
Banham	**29**	52 27N	1 3 E
Bani	**167**	18 16N	70 22W
Bani Bangou	**121**	15 3N	2 42 E
Bani, Djebel	**118**	29 16N	8 0W
Bani Na'im	**90**	31 31N	35 10 E
Bani, R.	**120**	12 40N	6 30W
Bani Suhayla	**90**	31 21N	34 19 E
Bania	**120**	9 4N	3 6W
Baniara	**135**	9 44 S	149 54 E
Banihal Pass	**95**	33 30N	75 12 E
Banīnah	**119**	32 0N	20 12 E
Baniyas	**92**	35 10N	36 0 E
Banja Luka	**66**	44 49N	17 26 E
Banjak, Kepulauan	**102**	2 10N	97 10 E
Banjar	**103**	7 24 S	108 30 E
Banjarmasin	**102**	3 20 S	114 35 E
Banjarnegara	**103**	7 24 S	109 42 E
Banjul	**120**	13 28N	16 40W
Banka Banka	**138**	18 50 S	134 0 E
Bankend	**35**	55 2N	3 31W
Bankeryd	**73**	57 53N	14 6 E
Banket	**127**	17 27 S	30 19 E
Bankfoot	**35**	56 30N	3 31W
Bankhead	**37**	57 11N	2 10W
Bankilaré	**121**	14 35N	0 44 E
Bankipore	**95**	25 35N	85 10 E
Banks I., B.C., Can.	**152**	53 20N	130 0W
Banks I., N. W. Terr., Can.	**12**	73 15N	121 30W
Banks I., P.N.G.	**135**	10 10 S	142 15 E
Banks Peninsula	**143**	43 45 S	173 15 E
Banks Str.	**138**	40 40 S	148 10 E
Bankura	**95**	23 11N	87 18 E
Bankya	**66**	42 43N	23 8 E
Bann R., Down, U.K.	**38**	54 30N	6 31W
Bann R., Londonderry, U.K.	**38**	55 10N	6 34W
Bannalec	**42**	47 57N	3 42W
Bannang Sata	**101**	6 16N	101 16 E
Bannerton	**140**	34 42 S	142 47 E
Banning, Can.	**150**	48 44N	91 56W
Banning, U.S.A.	**163**	33 58N	116 58W
Banningville = Bandundu	**124**	3 15 S	17 22 E
Bannockburn, Rhod.	**127**	20 17 S	29 48 E
Bannockburn, U.K.	**35**	56 5N	3 55W
Bannow	**39**	52 12N	6 50W
Bannow B.	**39**	52 13N	6 48W
Bannu	**93**	33 0N	70 18 E
Bañolas	**58**	42 16N	2 44 E
Banon	**45**	44 2N	5 38 E
Baños de la Encina	**57**	38 10N	3 46W
Baños de Molgas	**56**	42 15N	7 40W
Bánovce	**53**	48 44N	18 16 E
Banská Bystrica	**53**	48 46N	19 14 E
Banská Stiavnica	**53**	48 25N	18 55 E
Banško	**67**	41 52N	23 28 E
Banswara	**94**	23 32N	74 24 E
Bantama	**121**	7 48N	0 42W
Bante	**121**	8 25N	1 53 E
Banteer	**39**	52 8N	8 53W
Banten	**103**	6 5 S	106 8 E
Bantry	**39**	51 40N	9 28W
Bantry, B.	**39**	51 35N	9 50W
Bantul	**103**	7 55 S	110 19 E
Bantva	**94**	21 29N	70 12 E
Bantval	**97**	12 55N	75 0 E
Banu	**93**	35 35N	69 5 E
Banwell	**28**	51 19N	2 51W
Banya	**67**	42 33N	24 50 E
Banyo	**121**	6 52N	11 45 E
Banyuls	**44**	42 29N	3 8 E
Banyumas	**103**	7 32 S	109 18 E
Banyuwangi	**103**	8 13 S	114 21 E
Banzare Coast	**13**	66 30 S	125 0 E
Banzyville = Mobayi	**124**	4 15N	21 8 E
Bao Ha	**100**	22 11N	104 21 E
Bao Lac	**100**	22 57N	105 40 E
Bao Loc	**101**	11 32N	107 48 E
Bap	**94**	27 23N	72 18 E
Bapatla	**97**	15 55N	80 30 E
Bapaume	**43**	50 7N	2 50 E
Bâqa el Gharbiya	**90**	32 25N	35 2 E
Baqūbah	**92**	33 45N	44 50 E
Baquedano	**172**	23 20 S	69 52W
Bar, U.S.S.R.	**82**	49 4N	27 40 E
Bar, Yugo.	**66**	42 8N	19 8 E
Bar Harbor	**151**	44 15N	68 20W
Bar-le-Duc	**43**	48 47N	5 10 E
Bar-sur-Aube	**43**	48 14N	4 40 E
Bar-sur-Seine	**43**	48 7N	4 20 E
Barabai	**102**	2 32 S	115 34 E
Barabinsk	**76**	55 20N	78 20 E
Baraboo	**158**	43 28N	89 46W
Baracoa	**167**	20 20N	74 30W
Baradero	**172**	33 52 S	59 29W
Baradine	**141**	30 56 S	149 4 E
Baraga	**158**	46 49N	88 29W
Barahona, Dom. Rep.	**167**	18 13N	71 7W
Barahona, Spain	**58**	41 17N	2 39W
Barail Range	**99**	25 15N	93 20 E
Barakhola	**99**	25 0N	92 45 E
Barakot	**95**	21 33N	84 59 E
Barakula	**139**	26 30 S	150 33 E
Baralaba	**138**	24 13 S	149 50 E
Baralzon L.	**153**	60 0N	98 3W
Baramati	**96**	18 11N	74 33 E
Baramba	**96**	20 25N	85 23 E
Barameiya	**122**	18 32N	36 38 E
Baramula	**95**	34 15N	74 20 E
Baran	**94**	25 9N	76 40 E
Baranoa	**174**	10 48N	74 55W
Baranof I.	**147**	57 0N	135 10W
Baranovichi	**80**	53 10N	26 0 E
Baranów Sandomierski	**54**	50 29N	21 30 E
Baranya □	**53**	46 0N	18 15 E
Barão de Cocais	**171**	19 56 S	43 28W
Barão de Grajaú	**170**	6 45 S	43 1W
Barão de Melgaço	**174**	11 50 S	60 45W
Baraolt	**70**	46 5N	25 34 E
Barapasi	**103**	2 15 S	137 5 E
Barapina	**135**	6 21 S	155 25 E
Barasat	**95**	22 46N	88 31 E
Barasoli	**123**	13 38N	42 0W
Barat Daya, Kepuluan	**103**	7 30 S	128 0 E
Barataria B.	**159**	29 15N	89 45W
Baraut	**94**	29 13N	77 7 E
Baraya	**174**	3 10N	75 4W
Barbacena	**173**	21 15 S	43 56W
Barbacoas, Colomb.	**174**	1 45N	78 0W
Barbacoas, Venez.	**174**	9 29N	66 58W
Barbados ■	**167**	13 0N	59 30W
Barbalha	**170**	7 19 S	39 17W
Barban	**63**	45 0N	14 4 E
Barbastro	**58**	42 2N	0 5 E
Barbate	**57**	36 13N	5 56W
Barberton, S. Afr.	**129**	25 42 S	31 2 E
Barberton, U.S.A.	**156**	41 0N	81 40W
Barbigha	**95**	25 21N	85 47 E
Barbourville	**157**	36 57N	83 52W
Barbuda I.	**167**	17 30N	61 40W
Barca d'Alva	**56**	41 0N	7 0W
Barca, La	**164**	20 20N	102 40W
Barcaldine	**138**	23 33 S	145 13 E
Barcarrota	**57**	38 31N	6 51W
Barce = Al Marj	**117**	32 25N	20 40 E
Barcellona Pozzo di Gotto	**65**	38 8N	15 15 E
Barcelona, Spain	**58**	41 21N	2 10 E
Barcelona, Venez.	**174**	10 10N	64 40W
Barcelona □	**58**	41 30N	2 0 E
Barcelonette	**45**	44 23N	6 40 E
Barcelos	**174**	1 0 S	63 0W
Barcin	**54**	52 52N	17 55 E
Barcoo, R.	**138**	28 29 S	137 46 E
Barcs	**53**	45 58N	17 28 E
Barczewo	**54**	53 50N	20 42 E
Bard, Hd.	**36**	60 6N	1 5W
Barda	**83**	40 25N	47 10 E
Bardai	**119**	21 25N	17 0 E
Bardas Blancas	**172**	35 49 S	69 45W
Bardejov	**53**	49 18N	21 15 E
Bardera	**91**	2 20N	42 27 E
Bardi	**62**	44 38N	9 43 E
Bardiyah	**117**	31 45N	25 0 E
Bardney	**33**	53 13N	0 19W
Bardo	**54**	50 31N	16 42 E
Bardoc	**137**	30 18 S	121 12 E
Bardoli	**96**	21 12N	73 5 E
Bardsey, I.	**31**	52 46N	4 47W
Bardsey Sound	**31**	52 47N	4 46W
Bardstown	**156**	37 50N	85 29W
Bareilly	**95**	28 22N	79 27 E
Barellan	**141**	34 16 S	146 24 E
Barengapara	**98**	25 14N	90 14 E
Barentin	**42**	49 33N	0 58 E
Barenton	**42**	48 38N	0 50W
Barents Sea	**12**	73 0N	39 0 E
Barentu	**123**	15 2N	37 35 E
Barfleur	**42**	49 40N	1 17W
Barford	**28**	52 15N	1 35W
Barga	**62**	44 5N	10 30 E
Bargal	**91**	11 25N	51 0 E
Bargara	**138**	24 50 S	152 25 E
Barge	**62**	44 43N	7 19 E
Barge, La	**160**	41 12N	110 4W
Bargnop	**123**	9 32N	28 25 E
Bargo	**141**	34 18 S	150 35 E
Bargoed	**31**	51 42N	3 22W
Bargteheide	**48**	53 42N	10 13 E
Barguzin	**77**	53 37N	109 37 E
Barh	**95**	25 29N	85 46 E
Barhaj	**95**	26 18N	83 44 E
Barham	**29**	51 12N	1 10 E
Barhi	**95**	24 15N	85 25 E
Bari, India	**94**	26 39N	77 39 E
Bari, Italy	**65**	41 6N	16 52 E
Bari Doab	**94**	30 20N	73 0 E
Baria = Phuoc Le	**101**	10 39N	107 19 E
Bariadi □	**126**	2 45 S	34 40 E
Barika	**118**	35 23N	5 22 E
Barinas	**174**	8 36N	70 15W
Barinas □	**174**	8 10N	69 50W
Baring C.	**148**	70 0N	117 30W
Baringo	**126**	0 47N	36 16 E
Baringo □	**126**	0 55N	36 0 E
Baringo, L.	**126**	0 47N	36 16 E
Barinitas	**174**	8 45N	70 25W
Baripada	**96**	21 57N	86 45 E
Bariri	**171**	22 4 S	48 44W
Bârîs	**122**	24 42N	30 31 E
Barisal	**98**	22 30N	90 20 E
Barisan, Bukit	**102**	3 30 S	102 15 E
Barito, R.	**102**	2 50 S	114 50 E
Barjac	**45**	44 20N	4 22 E
Barjols	**45**	43 34N	6 2 E
Barjūji, W.	**119**	25 26N	12 12 E
Bark L.	**150**	46 58N	82 25W
Barka	**122**	17 30N	37 34 E
Barkah	**93**	23 40N	58 0 E
Barker, Mt.	**139**	35 4 S	138 55 E
Barking	**29**	51 31N	0 10 E
Barkley Sound	**152**	48 50N	125 10W
Barkly Downs	**138**	20 30 S	138 30 E
Barkly East	**129**	30 58 S	27 33 E
Barkly Tableland	**138**	19 50 S	138 40 E
Barkly West	**128**	28 5 S	24 31 E
Barkol, Wadi	**122**	17 40N	32 0 E
Barksdale	**159**	29 47N	100 2W
Barlborough	**33**	53 17N	1 17W
Barlby	**33**	53 48N	1 3W
Barlee, L.	**137**	29 15 S	119 30 E
Barlee, Mt.	**137**	24 35 S	128 10 E
Barlee Ra.	**137**	23 30 S	116 0 E
Barlett	**163**	36 29N	118 2W
Barletta	**65**	41 20N	16 17 E
Barlinek	**54**	53 0N	15 15 E
Barlingbo	**73**	57 35N	18 27 E
Barlow L.	**153**	62 00N	103 0W
Barmby Moor	**33**	53 55N	0 47W
Barmedman	**141**	34 9 S	147 21 E
Barmer	**94**	25 45N	71 20 E
Barmera	**140**	34 15 S	140 28 E
Barmoor	**35**	55 38N	2 0W
Barmouth	**31**	52 44N	4 3W
Barmstedt	**48**	53 47N	9 46 E
Barna	**39**	53 14N	9 10W
Barnaderg	**38**	53 29N	8 43W
Barnagar	**94**	23 7N	75 19 E
Barnard Castle	**32**	54 33N	1 55W
Barnato	**141**	31 38 S	145 0 E
Barnaul	**76**	53 20N	83 40 E
Barnby Moor	**33**	53 21N	1 0W
Barne Inlet	**13**	80 15 S	160 0 E
Barnes	**141**	36 2 S	144 47 E
Barnesville	**157**	33 6N	84 9W
Barnet	**29**	51 37N	0 15W
Barnetby le Wold	**33**	53 34N	0 24W
Barneveld, Neth.	**96**	52 7N	5 36 E
Barneveld, U.S.A.	**162**	43 16N	75 14W
Barneville	**42**	49 23N	1 46W
Barney, Mt.	**133**	28 17 S	152 44 E
Barngo	**138**	25 3 S	147 20 E
Barnhart	**159**	31 10N	101 8W
Barnoldswick	**32**	53 55N	2 11W
Barnsley	**33**	53 33N	1 29W
Barnstaple	**30**	51 5N	4 3W
Barnstaple B.	**30**	51 5N	4 25W
Barnsville	**158**	46 43N	96 28W
Baro	**121**	8 35N	6 18 E
Baro, R.	**123**	8 25N	33 40 E
Baroda	**94**	25 29N	76 35 E
Baroda = Vadodara, India	**93**	22 20N	73 10 E
Baroda = Vadodara, Gujarat, India	**94**	22 20N	73 10 E
Baron Ra.	**136**	23 30 S	127 45 E
Barpali	**96**	21 11N	83 35 E
Barpathar	**98**	26 17N	93 53 E
Barpeta	**95**	26 20N	91 10 E
Barqa	**117**	27 0N	20 0 E
Barqin	**119**	27 33N	13 34 E
Barques, Pte. aux	**156**	44 5N	82 55W
Barquinha	**57**	39 28N	8 25W
Barquísimeto	**174**	9 58N	69 13W
Barr, France	**43**	48 25N	7 28 E
Barr, U.K.	**34**	55 13N	4 44W
Barr Smith Ra.	**137**	27 10 S	120 15 E
Barra, Brazil	**170**	11 5 S	43 10W
Barra, Gambia	**120**	13 21N	16 36W
Barra da Estiva	**171**	13 38 S	41 19W
Barra de Navidad	**164**	19 12N	104 41W
Barra do Corda	**170**	5 30 S	45 10W
Barra do Mendes	**171**	11 43 S	42 4W
Barra do Piraí	**173**	22 30 S	43 50W
Barra Falsa, Pta. da	**129**	22 58 S	35 37 E
Barra Hd.	**36**	56 47N	7 40W
Barra, I.	**36**	57 0N	7 30W
Barra Mansa	**173**	22 35 S	44 12W
Barra, Sd. of	**36**	57 4N	7 25W
Barraba	**141**	30 21 S	150 35 E
Barrackpur	**95**	22 44N	88 30 E
Barrafranca	**65**	37 22N	14 10 E
Barranca, Lima, Peru	**174**	10 45 S	77 50W
Barranca, Loreto, Peru	**174**	4 50 S	76 50W
Barrancabermeja	**174**	7 0N	73 50W
Barrancas, Colomb.	**174**	10 57N	72 50W
Barrancas, Venez.	**174**	8 55N	62 5W
Barrancos	**57**	38 10N	6 58W
Barranqueras	**172**	27 30 S	59 0W
Barranquilla, Atlántico, Colomb.	**174**	11 0N	74 50W
Barranquilla, Vaupés, Colomb.	**174**	1 39N	72 19W
Barras, Brazil	**170**	4 15 S	42 18W
Barras, Colomb.	**174**	1 45 S	73 13W
Barraute	**150**	48 26N	77 38W
Barre, U.S.A.	**156**	44 15N	72 30W
Barre, U.S.A.	**162**	42 26N	72 6W
Barreal	**172**	31 33 S	69 28W
Barreiras	**171**	12 8 S	45 0W
Barreirinhas	**170**	2 30 S	42 50W
Barreiro	**57**	38 40N	9 6W
Barreiros	**170**	8 49 S	35 12W
Barrême	**45**	43 57N	6 23 E
Barren I.	**101**	12 17N	95 50 E
Barren Is., Madag.	**129**	18 25 S	43 40 E
Barren Is., U.S.A.	**147**	58 45N	152 0W
Barren Junc.	**139**	30 5 S	149 0 E
Barretos	**171**	20 30 S	48 35W
Barrhead, Can.	**152**	54 10N	114 24W
Barrhead, U.K.	**34**	55 48N	4 23W
Barrhill	**34**	55 7N	4 46W
Barrie	**150**	44 24N	79 40W
Barrier, C.	**142**	36 25 S	175 32 E
Barrier Ra., Austral.	**140**	31 0 S	141 30 E
Barrier Ra., N.Z.	**143**	44 5 S	169 42 E
Barrier Rf., Gt.	**138**	19 0 S	149 0 E
Barrière	**152**	51 12N	120 7W
Barrington, Austral.	**133**	31 58 S	151 55 E
Barrington, Ill., U.S.A.	**156**	42 8N	88 5W
Barrington, R.I., U.S.A.	**162**	41 43N	71 20W
Barrington L.	**153**	56 55N	100 15W
Barrington Tops.	**141**	32 6 S	151 28 E
Barringun	**139**	29 1 S	145 41 E
Barrow	**147**	71 16N	156 50W
Barrow Creek T.O.	**138**	21 30 S	133 55 E
Barrow I.	**136**	20 45 S	115 20 E
Barrow-in-Furness	**32**	54 8N	3 15W
Barrow Pt.	**138**	14 20 S	144 40 E
Barrow, Pt.	**147**	71 22N	156 30W
Barrow, R.	**39**	52 10N	6 57W
Barrow Ra.	**137**	26 0 S	127 40 E
Barrow Strait	**12**	74 20N	95 0W
Barrow upon Humber	**33**	53 41N	0 22W
Barrowford	**32**	53 51N	2 14W
Barruecopardo	**56**	41 4N	6 40W
Barruelo	**56**	42 54N	4 17W
Barry, S. Glam., U.K.	**31**	51 23N	3 19W
Barry, Tayside, U.K.	**35**	56 29N	2 45W
Barry I.	**31**	51 23N	3 17W
Barry's Bay	**150**	45 29N	77 41W
Barry's Pt.	**39**	51 36N	8 40W
Barsalogho	**121**	13 25N	1 3W
Barsat	**95**	36 10N	72 45 E
Barsi	**96**	18 10N	75 50 E
Barsø	**73**	55 7N	9 33 E
Barsoi	**99**	25 48N	87 57 E
Barstow, Calif., U.S.A.	**163**	34 58N	117 2W
Barstow, Tex., U.S.A.	**170**	31 30N	103 25W
Barthélemy, Col	**100**	19 26N	104 6 E
Bartica	**174**	6 25N	58 40W
Bartle Frere, Mt.	**138**	17 27 S	145 50 E
Bartlesville	**159**	36 50N	95 58W
Bartlett	**159**	30 46N	97 30W
Bartlett, L.	**152**	63 5N	118 20W
Bartolomeu Dias	**127**	21 10 S	35 8 E
Barton	**33**	54 28N	1 38W
Barton Siding	**137**	30 31 S	132 39 E
Barton-upon-Humber	**33**	53 41N	0 27W
Bartoszyce	**54**	54 15N	20 55 E
Bartow	**157**	27 53N	81 49W
Barú, I. de	**174**	10 15N	75 35W
Baruth	**48**	52 3N	13 31 E
Barvas	**36**	58 21N	6 31W
Barvaux	**47**	50 21N	5 29 E
Barvenkovo	**82**	48 57N	37 0 E
Barwani	**94**	22 2N	74 57 E
Barwell	**28**	52 35N	1 22W
Barysh	**81**	49 2N	25 18 E
Bas-Rhin □	**43**	48 40N	7 30 E
Bašaid	**66**	45 38N	20 25 E
Basa'idu	**93**	26 35N	55 20 E
Basal	**94**	33 33N	72 13 E
Basalt	**163**	38 0N	118 15W
Basankusa	**124**	1 5N	19 50 E
Basawa	**94**	34 15N	70 50 E
Bascharage	**47**	49 34N	5 55 E
Bascuñán, Cabo	**172**	28 52 S	71 35W
Basècles	**47**	50 32N	3 39 E
Basel (Basle)	**50**	47 35N	7 35 E
Basel Landschaft □	**50**	47 26N	7 45 E
Basel-Stadt □	**50**	47 35N	7 35 E
Basento, R.	**65**	40 35N	16 10 E
Bashi Channel	**105**	21 15N	122 0 E
Bashkir A.S.S.R. □	**84**	54 0N	57 0 E
Basilaki, I.	**135**	10 35 S	151 0 E
Basilan, Selat	**103**	6 50N	122 0 E
Basilanl, I.	**103**	6 35N	122 0 E
Basildon	**29**	51 34N	0 29 E
Basilicata □	**65**	40 30N	16 0 E
Basim	**96**	20 3N	77 0 E
Basin	**160**	44 22N	108 2W
Basing	**28**	51 16N	1 3W
Basingstoke	**28**	51 15N	1 5W
Basirhat	**98**	22 40N	88 54 E
Baskatong Res.	**150**	46 46N	75 50W
Baskerville C.	**136**	17 10 S	122 15 E
Basle = Basel	**50**	47 35N	7 35 E
Basmat	**96**	19 15N	77 12 E
Basoda	**94**	23 52N	77 54 E
Basodino	**51**	46 25N	8 28 E
Basoka	**126**	1 16N	23 40 E
Basongo	**124**	4 15 S	20 20 E
Basque Provinces = Vascongadas	**58**	42 50N	2 45W
Basra = Al Basrah	**92**	30 30N	47 50 E
Bass Rock	**35**	56 5N	2 40W
Bass Strait	**138**	39 15 S	146 30 E
Bassano, del Grappa	**63**	45 45N	11 45 E
Bassari	**121**	9 19N	0 57 E
Bassas da India	**125**	22 0 S	39 0 E
Basse	**120**	13 13N	14 15W
Basse-Terre, I.	**167**	16 0N	61 40W
Bassecourt	**50**	47 20N	7 15 E
Bassée, La	**43**	50 31N	2 49 E
Bassein, Burma	**98**	16 30N	94 30 E
Bassein, India	**96**	19 26N	72 48 E
Bassein Myit	**99**	16 45N	94 30 E
Bassenthwaite, L.	**32**	54 40N	3 14W
Basseterre	**167**	17 17N	62 43W
Bassett, Nebr., U.S.A.	**158**	42 37N	99 30W
Bassett, Va., U.S.A.	**157**	36 48N	79 59W
Bassevelde	**47**	51 15N	3 41 E

Bassi **94** 30 44N 76 21 E
Bassigny **43** 48 0N 5 10 E
Bassikounou **120** 15 55N 6 1W
Bassilly **47** 50 40N 3 56 E
Bassum **48** 52 50N 8 42 E
Båstad **73** 56 25N 12 51 E
Båstad **73** 56 25N 12 51 E
Bastak **93** 27 15N 54 25 E
Bastar **96** 19 25N 81 40 E
Basti **95** 26 52N 82 55 E
Bastia **45** 42 40N 9 30 E
Bastia Umbra **63** 43 4N 12 34 E
Bastide, La **44** 44 35N 3 55 E
Bastogne **47** 50 1N 5 43 E
Baston **29** 52 43N 0 19W
Bastrop **159** 30 5N 97 22W
Basuto **128** 19 50 S 26 25 E
Basutoland = Lesotho **129** 29 0 S 28 0 E
Basyanovskiy **84** 58 19N 60 44 E
Bat Yam **90** 32 2N 34 44 E
Bata, Eq. Guin. **124** 1 57N 9 50 E
Bata, Rumania **70** 46 1N 22 4 E
Bataan **103** 14 40N 120 25 E
Bataan Pen. **103** 14 38N 120 30 E
Batabanó **166** 22 40N 82 20W
Batabanó, G. de **167** 22 30N 82 30W
Batac **103** 18 3N 120 34 E
Batagoy **77** 67 38N 134 38 E
Batak **67** 41 57N 24 12 E
Batalha **57** 39 40N 8 50W
Batama **126** 0 58N 26 33 E
Batamay **77** 63 30N 129 15 E
Batamshinskiy **84** 50 36N 58 16 E
Batang **103** 6 55 S 109 40 E
Batangafo **117** 7 25N 18 20 E
Batangas **103** 13 35N 121 10 E
Batanta, I. **103** 0 55N 130 40 E
Bataszék **66** 46 10N 18 44 E
Batatais **173** 20 54 S 47 37W
Batavia **156** 43 0N 78 10W
Bataysk **83** 47 3N 39 45 E
Batchelor **136** 13 4 S 131 1 E
Bateman's B. **141** 35 40 S 150 12 E
Batemans Bay **141** 35 44 S 150 11 E
Bates Ra. **137** 27 25 S 121 0 E
Batesburg **157** 33 54N 81 32W
Batesville, Ark., U.S.A. **159** 35 48N 91 40W
Batesville, Miss., U.S.A. **159** 34 17N 89 58W
Batesville, Tex., U.S.A. **159** 28 59N 99 38W
Batetski **80** 58 47N 30 16 E
Bath, U.K. **28** 51 22N 2 22W
Bath, Maine, U.S.A. **151** 43 50N 69 49W
Bath, N.Y., U.S.A. **156** 42 20N 77 17W
Batheay **101** 11 59N 104 57 E
Bathford **28** 51 23N 2 18W
Bathgate **35** 55 54N 3 38W
Bâthie, La **46** 45 37N 6 28 E
Bathmen **46** 52 15N 6 29 E
Bathurst, Austral. **141** 33 25 S 149 31 E
Bathurst, Can. **151** 47 37N 65 43W
Bathurst B. **138** 14 16 S 144 25 E
Bathurst C. **147** 70 30N 128 30W
Bathurst, C. **147** 70 34N 128 0W
Bathurst, Gambia = Banjul **120** 13 28N 16 40W
Bathurst Harb. **138** 43 15 S 146 10 E
Bathurst I., Austral. **136** 11 30 S 130 10 E
Bathurst I., Can. **12** 76 30N 130 10W
Bathurst Inlet **148** 66 50N 108 1W
Batie **120** 9 53N 2 53W
Batley **33** 53 43N 1 38W
Batlow **141** 35 31 S 148 9 E
Batman **92** 37 55N 41 5 E
Batna **119** 35 34N 6 15 E
Batoka **127** 16 45 S 27 15 E
Baton Rouge **159** 30 30N 91 5W
Batong, Ko **101** 6 32N 99 12 E
Batopilas **164** 27 45N 107 45W
Batouri **124** 4 30N 14 25 E
Battambang **100** 13 7N 103 12 E
Batticaloa **97** 7 43N 81 45 E
Battice **47** 50 39N 5 50 E
Battipáglia **65** 40 38N 15 0 E
Battir **90** 31 44N 35 8 E
Battle, Can. **153** 52 58N 110 52W
Battle, U.K. **29** 50 55N 0 30 E
Battle Camp **138** 15 20 S 144 40 E
Battle Creek **156** 42 20N 85 36W
Battle Harbour **151** 52 16N 55 35W
Battle Lake **158** 46 20N 95 43W
Battle Mountain **160** 40 45N 117 0W
Battle, R. **153** 52 43N 108 15W
Battlefields **127** 18 37 S 29 47 E
Battleford **153** 52 45N 108 15W
Battonya **53** 46 16N 21 3 E
Batu Caves **101** 3 15N 101 40 E
Batu Gajah **101** 4 28N 101 3 E
Batu, Kepulauan **102** 0 30 S 98 25 E
Batu, Mt. **123** 6 55N 39 45 E
Batu Pahat **101** 1 50N 102 56 E
Batuata, P. **103** 6 30 S 122 20 E
Batulaki **103** 5 40N 125 30 E
Batumi **83** 41 30N 41 30 E
Baturadja **102** 4 11 S 104 15 E
Baturité **170** 4 28 S 38 45W
Baturité, Serra de **170** 4 25 S 39 0W
Baubau **103** 5 25 S 123 50 E
Bauchi **121** 10 22N 9 48 E
Bauchi □ **121** 10 0N 10 0 E
Baud **42** 47 52N 3 1W
Baudette **158** 48 46N 94 35W
Baudouinville = Moba **126** 7 0 S 29 48 E
Baudour **47** 50 29N 3 50 E
Bauer, C. **139** 32 44 S 134 4 E
Baugé **42** 47 31N 0 8W
Bauhinia Downs **138** 24 35 S 149 18 E
Baule, La **42** 47 18N 2 23W
Bauma **51** 47 3N 8 53 E
Baume les Dames **43** 47 22N 6 22 E
Baunei **64** 40 2N 9 41 E
Bauru **173** 22 10 S 49 0W
Baús **175** 18 22 S 52 47W
Bauska **80** 56 25N 25 15 E
Bautzen **48** 51 11N 14 25 E
Baux, Les **45** 43 45N 4 51 E
BavaniŠte **66** 44 49N 20 53 E
Bavaria = Bayern **49** 49 7N 11 30 E
Båven **72** 59 35N 17 30 E
Bavispe, R. **164** 29 30N 109 11W
Bawdsey **29** 52 1N 1 27 E
Bawdwin **98** 23 5N 97 50 E
Bawean **102** 5 46 S 112 35 E
Bawku **121** 11 3N 0 19W
Bawlake **98** 19 11N 97 21 E
Bawnboy **38** 54 8N 7 40W
Bawtry **33** 53 25N 1 1W
Baxley **157** 31 43N 82 23W
Baxter Springs **159** 37 3N 94 45W
Bay Bulls **151** 47 19N 52 50W
Bay City, Mich., U.S.A. **156** 43 35N 83 51W
Bay City, Oreg., U.S.A. **160** 45 45N 123 58W
Bay City, Tex., U.S.A. **159** 28 59N 95 55W
Bay de Verde **151** 48 5N 52 54W
Bay, Laguna de **103** 14 20N 121 11 E
Bay of Islands **142** 35 15 S 174 6 E
Bay St. Louis **159** 30 18N 89 22W
Bay Shore **162** 40 44N 73 15W
Bay Springs **159** 31 58N 89 18W
Bay View **142** 39 25 S 176 50 E
Baya **127** 11 53 S 27 25 E
Bayamo **166** 20 20N 76 40W
Bayamón **147** 18 24N 66 10W
Bayan Kara Shan **99** 34 0N 98 0 E
Bayan-Ovoo **106** 47 47N 112 5 E
Bayana **94** 26 55N 77 18 E
Bayanaul **76** 50 45N 75 45 E
Bayandalay **106** 43 30N 103 29 E
Bayanga **124** 2 53N 16 19 E
Bayanhongor **105** 46 8N 100 43 E
Bayard **158** 41 48N 103 17W
Baybay **103** 10 40N 124 55 E
Bayble **36** 58 12N 6 13W
Bayburt **92** 40 15N 40 20 E
Bayerischer Wald **49** 49 0N 13 0 E
Bayern □ **49** 49 7N 11 30 E
Bayeux **42** 49 17N 0 42W
Bayfield **158** 46 50N 90 48W
Bayir **92** 30 45N 36 55 E
Baykadam **85** 43 48N 69 58 E
Baykal, Oz. **77** 53 0N 108 0 E
Baykit **77** 61 50N 95 50 E
Baykonur **76** 47 48N 65 50 E
Baymak **84** 52 36N 58 19 E
Baynes Mts. **128** 17 15 S 13 0 E
Bayombong **103** 16 30N 121 10 E
Bayon **43** 48 30N 6 20 E
Bayona **56** 42 6N 8 52W
Bayonne, France **44** 43 30N 1 28W
Bayonne, U.S.A. **162** 40 41N 74 7W
Bayovar **174** 5 50 S 81 0W
Baypore, R. **97** 11 10N 75 47 E
Bayram-Ali **76** 37 37N 62 10 E
Bayreuth **49** 49 56N 11 35 E
Bayrischzell **49** 47 39N 12 1 E
Bayrūt **92** 33 53N 35 31 E
Baysun **85** 38 12N 67 12 E
Bayt Aula **90** 31 37N 35 2 E
Bayt Fajjar **90** 31 38N 35 9 E
Bayt Fūrīk **90** 32 11N 35 20 E
Bayt Jala **90** 31 43N 35 11 E
Bayt Lahm **90** 31 43N 35 12 E
Bayt Rīma **90** 32 2N 35 6 E
Bayt Sāhūr **90** 31 42N 35 13 E
Bayt Ummar **90** 31 38N 35 7 E
Bayta at Tahtā **90** 32 9N 35 18 E
Baytin **90** 31 56N 35 14 E
Baytown **159** 29 42N 94 57W
Bayzhansay **85** 43 14N 69 54 E
Bayzo **121** 13 52N 4 35 E
Baza **59** 37 30N 2 47W
Bazar Dyuzi **83** 41 12N 48 10 E
Bazarny Karabulak **81** 52 30N 46 20 E
Bazarnyy Syzgan **81** 53 45N 46 40 E
Bazartobe **83** 49 26N 51 45 E
Bazaruto, I. do **129** 21 40 S 35 28 E
Bazas **44** 44 27N 0 13W
Bazuriye **90** 33 15N 35 16 E
Beabula **141** 34 26 S 145 9 E
Beach **158** 46 57N 104 0W
Beach Haven **162** 39 34N 74 14W
Beachley **28** 51 37N 2 39W
Beachport **140** 37 29 S 140 0 E
Beachwood **162** 39 55N 74 8W
Beachy Head **29** 50 44N 0 16 E
Beacon, Austral. **137** 30 26 S 117 52 E
Beacon, U.S.A. **162** 41 32N 73 58W
Beaconia **153** 50 25N 96 31W
Beaconsfield, Austral. **133** 41 11 S 146 48 E
Beaconsfield, U.K. **29** 51 36N 0 39W
Beadnell **35** 55 33N 1 38W
Beagle Bay **136** 16 32 S 122 54 E
Beagle, Canal **176** 55 0 S 68 30W
Bealanana **129** 14 33N 48 44 E
Bealey **143** 43 2 S 171 36 E
Beaminster **28** 50 48N 2 44W
Bear I. **39** 51 38N 9 50W
Bear I. (Nor.) **12** 74 30N 19 0 E
Bear L., B.C., Can. **152** 56 10N 126 52W
Bear L., Man., Can. **153** 55 8N 96 0W
Bear L., U.S.A. **160** 42 0N 111 20W
Bearcreek **160** 45 11N 109 6W
Beardmore **150** 49 36N 87 57W
Beardmore Glacier **13** 84 30 S 170 0 E
Beardstown **158** 40 0N 90 25W
Bearn **44** 43 28N 0 36W
Bearpaw Mt. **160** 48 15N 109 55W
Bearsden **34** 55 55N 4 21W
Bearskin Lake **150** 53 58N 91 2W
Bearsted **29** 51 15N 0 35 E
Beas de Segura **59** 38 15N 2 53W
Beasain **58** 43 3N 2 11W
Beata, C. **167** 17 40N 71 30W
Beata, I. **167** 17 34N 71 31W
Beatrice, Rhod. **127** 18 15 S 30 55 E
Beatrice, U.S.A. **158** 40 20N 96 40W
Beatrice, C. **138** 14 20 S 136 55 E
Beatrice, oilfield **19** 58 7N 3 6W
Beattock **35** 55 19N 3 27W
Beatton, R. **152** 56 15N 120 45W
Beatton River **152** 57 26N 121 20W
Beatty **163** 36 58N 116 46W
Beaucaire **45** 43 48N 4 39 E
Beauce, Plaines de **43** 48 10N 2 0 E
Beauceville **151** 46 13N 70 46W
Beaudesert **139** 27 59 S 153 0 E
Beaufort, Austral. **140** 37 25 S 143 25 E
Beaufort, Malay. **102** 5 30N 115 40 E
Beaufort, N.C., U.S.A. **157** 34 45N 76 40W
Beaufort, S.C., U.S.A. **157** 32 25N 80 40W
Beaufort Sea **12** 72 0N 140 0W
Beaufort-West **128** 32 18 S 22 36 E
Beaugency **43** 47 47N 1 38 E
Beauharnois **150** 45 20N 73 52W
Beaujeu **45** 46 10N 4 35 E
Beaujolais **45** 46 0N 4 25 E
Beaulieu, Loiret, France **44** 47 31N 2 49 E
Beaulieu, Vendée, France **45** 46 41N 1 37W
Beaulieu, U.K. **28** 50 49N 1 27W
Beaulieu, R. **152** 62 3N 113 11W
Beauly **37** 57 29N 4 27W
Beauly Firth **37** 57 30N 4 20W
Beauly, R. **37** 57 26N 4 28W
Beaumaris **31** 53 16N 4 7W
Beaumetz-les-Loges **43** 50 15N 2 40 E
Beaumont, Belg. **47** 50 15N 4 14 E
Beaumont, France **44** 44 45N 0 46 E
Beaumont, N.Z. **143** 45 50 S 169 33 E
Beaumont, Calif., U.S.A. **163** 33 56N 116 58W
Beaumont, Tex., U.S.A. **159** 30 5N 94 8W
Beaumont-le-Roger **42** 49 4N 0 47 E
Beaumont-sur-Oise **43** 49 9N 2 17 E
Beaune **43** 47 2N 4 50 E
Beaune-la-Rolande **43** 48 4N 2 25 E
Beauraing **47** 50 7N 4 57 E
Beausejour **153** 50 5N 96 35 E
Beausset, Le **45** 43 10N 5 46 E
Beauvais **43** 49 25N 2 8 E
Beauval **153** 55 9N 107 37W
Beauvoir, Deux Sèvres, France **44** 46 12N 0 30W
Beauvoir, Vendée, France **42** 46 55N 2 1W
Beaver, Alaska, U.S.A. **147** 66 20N 147 30W
Beaver, Okla., U.S.A. **159** 36 52N 100 31W
Beaver, Utah, U.S.A. **161** 38 20N 112 45W
Beaver City **158** 40 13N 99 50W
Beaver Dam **158** 43 28N 88 50W
Beaver Falls **156** 40 44N 80 20W
Beaver Hill L. **153** 54 16N 94 59W
Beaver I. **150** 45 40N 85 31W
Beaver, R. **152** 59 52N 124 20W
Beaver, R **150** 55 55N 87 48W
Beaver, R. **153** 55 26N 107 45W
Beaverhill L., Man., Can. **153** 54 5N 94 50W
Beaverhill L., N.W.T., Can. **153** 63 2N 111 22W
Beaverhill L., Alb., **152** 53 27N 112 32W
Beaverlodge **152** 55 11N 119 29W
Beavermouth **152** 51 32N 117 23W
Beaverstone, R. **150** 54 59N 89 25W
Beawar **94** 26 3N 74 18 E
Bebedouro **173** 21 0 S 48 25W
Bebington **32** 53 23N 3 1W
Beboa **129** 17 22 S 44 33 E
Bebra **48** 50 59N 9 48 E
Beccles **29** 52 27N 1 33 E
Bečej **66** 45 36N 20 3 E
Beceni **70** 45 23N 26 48 E
Becerreá **56** 42 51N 7 10W
Béchar **118** 31 38N 2 18 E
Becharof L. **147** 58 0N 156 30W
Bechuanaland = Botswana **125** 23 0 S 24 0 E
Bechyně **52** 49 17N 14 29 E
Beckermet **32** 54 26N 3 31W
Beckfoot **32** 54 50N 3 25W
Beckingham **33** 53 24N 0 49W
Beckley **156** 37 50N 81 8W
Bécon **42** 47 30N 0 50W
Bečva, R. **53** 49 31N 17 40 E
Bedale **33** 54 18N 1 35W
Bédar **59** 37 11N 1 59W
Bédarieux **44** 43 37N 3 10 E
Bédarrides **45** 44 2N 4 54 E
Beddone, Mt. **138** 25 50 S 134 20 E
Bedele **123** 8 31N 35 44 E
Bedel, Pereval **85** 41 26N 78 26 E
Bederkesa **48** 53 37N 8 50 E
Bedford, Can. **150** 45 7N 72 59W
Bedford, S. Afr. **128** 32 40 S 26 10 E
Bedford, U.K. **29** 52 8N 0 29W
Bedford, Ind., U.S.A. **156** 38 50N 86 30W
Bedford, Iowa, U.S.A. **158** 40 40N 94 41W
Bedford, Ohio, U.S.A. **156** 41 23N 81 32W
Bedford, Va., U.S.A. **156** 37 25N 79 30W
Bedford □ **29** 52 4N 0 28W
Bedford, C. **138** 15 14 S 145 21 E
Bedford Downs **136** 17 19 S 127 20 E
Bedford Level **29** 52 25N 0 5 E
Bedków **54** 51 36N 19 44 E
Bedlington **35** 55 8N 1 35W
Bednesti **152** 53 50N 123 10W
Bednja, R. **63** 46 12N 16 25 E
Bednodemyanovsk **81** 53 55N 43 15 E
Bedourie **138** 24 30 S 139 30 E
Bedretto **51** 46 31N 8 31 E
Bedum **47** 53 18N 6 36 E
Bedwas **31** 51 36N 3 10W
Bedworth **28** 52 28N 1 29W
Bedzin **54** 50 19N 19 7 E
Bee L. **36** 57 22N 7 21W
Beebyn **137** 27 0 S 117 48 E
Beech Grove **156** 39 40N 86 2W
Beechey Point **147** 70 27N 149 18W
Beechworth **141** 36 22 S 146 43 E
Beechy **153** 50 53N 107 24W
Beeford **33** 53 58N 0 18W
Beek, Gelderland, Neth. **46** 51 55N 6 11 E
Beek, Limburg, Neth. **47** 50 57N 5 48 E
Beek, Noord Brabant, Neth. **47** 51 32N 5 38 E
Beekbergen **46** 52 10N 5 58 E
Beelitz **48** 52 14N 12 58 E
Beemem **47** 51 9N 3 21 E
Beenleigh **139** 27 43 S 153 10 E
Beer **30** 50 41N 3 5W
Be'er Sheva' **90** 31 15N 34 48 E
Be'er Sheva', N. **90** 31 12N 34 40 E
Be'er Toviyyao **90** 31 44N 34 42 E
Be'eri **90** 31 25N 34 30 E
Be'erotayim **90** 32 19N 34 59 E
Beersheba = Be'er Sheva' **90** 31 15N 34 48 E
Beerta **46** 53 11N 7 6 E
Beerze, R. **46** 51 39N 5 20 E
Beesd **46** 51 53N 5 11 E
Beesel **47** 51 16N 6 2 E
Beeskow **48** 52 9N 14 14 E
Beeston **33** 52 55N 1 11W
Beetaloo **138** 17 15 S 133 50 E
Beetsterzwaag **46** 53 4N 6 5 E
Beetzendorf **48** 52 42N 11 6 E
Beeville **159** 28 27N 97 44W
Befale **124** 0 25N 20 45 E
Befandriana **125** 21 55 S 44 0 E
Befotaka, Diégo-Suarez, Madag. **129** 14 30 S 48 0 E
Befotaka, Fianarantsoa, Madag. **129** 23 49 S 47 0 E
Beg, L. **38** 54 48N 6 28W
Bega **141** 36 41 S 149 51 E
Bega, Canalul **66** 45 37N 20 46 E
Begelly **31** 51 45N 4 44W
Begemdir & Simen □ **123** 13 55N 37 30 E
Begna **71** 60 41N 9 42 E
Begonte **56** 43 10N 7 40W
Begu-Sarai **95** 25 24N 86 9 E
Beguildy **31** 52 25N 3 11W
Béhagle = Lai **117** 9 25N 16 30 E
Behara **125** 24 55 S 46 20 E
Behbehan **92** 30 30N 50 15 E
Behror **94** 27 51N 76 20 E
Behshahr **93** 36 45N 53 35 E
Beida (Al Bayda) **117** 32 30N 21 40 E
Beighton **33** 53 21N 1 21W
Beilen **46** 52 52N 6 27 E
Beilngries **49** 49 1N 11 27 E
Beilpajah **140** 32 54 S 143 52 E
Beilul **123** 13 2N 42 20 E
Beinn a' Ghlo, Mt. **37** 56 51N 3 42W
Beinn Mhor, Mt. **36** 57 59N 6 39W
Beira **127** 19 50 S 34 52 E
Beira-Alta **55** 40 35N 7 35W
Beira-Baixa **55** 40 2N 7 30W
Beira-Litoral **55** 40 5N 8 30W
Beirut = Bayrūt **92** 33 53N 35 31 E
Beit Bridge **127** 14 58 S 30 15 E
Beit Hanum **90** 31 32N 34 32 E
Beit Lahiya **90** 31 32N 34 30 E
Beit 'Ur et Tahta **90** 31 54N 35 5 E
Beit Yosef **90** 32 34N 35 33 E
Beitbridge **127** 22 12 S 30 0 E
Beith **34** 55 45N 4 38W
Beituniya **90** 31 54N 35 10 E
Beiuş **70** 46 40N 22 21 E
Beja **57** 38 2N 7 53W
Béja **119** 36 43N 9 12 E
Beja □ **57** 37 55N 7 55W
Béjaïa **119** 36 42N 5 2 E
Béjar **56** 40 23N 5 46W
Bejestan **93** 34 30N 58 5 E
Bekabad **85** 40 13N 69 14 E
Bekasi **103** 6 20 S 107 0 E
Békés **53** 46 47N 21 9 E
Békés □ **53** 46 45N 21 0 E
Békéscsaba **53** 46 40N 21 10 E
Bekily **129** 24 13 S 45 19 E
Bekkevoort **47** 50 57N 4 58 E
Bekkjarvik **71** 60 1N 5 13 E

Bekoji Berghem

Bekoji 123 7 40N 38 20 E
Bekok 101 2 20N 103 7 E
Bekopaka 129 19 9 S 44 45 E
Bekwai 121 6 30N 1 34W
Bel Air 162 39 32N 76 21W
Bela, India 95 25 50N 82 0 E
Bela, Pak. 94 26 12N 66 20 E
Bela Crkva 66 44 55N 21 27 E
Bela Palanka 66 43 13N 22 17 E
Bela Vista, Brazil 173 22 12 S 56 20W
Bela Vista, Mozam. 129 26 10 S 32 44 E
Bélâbre 44 46 34N 1 8 E
Belaia, Mt. 123 11 25N 36 8 E
Belalcázar 57 38 35N 5 10W
Belanovica 66 44 15N 20 23 E
Belavenona 129 24 50 S 47 4 E
Belawan 102 3 33N 98 32 E
Belaya Glina 83 46 5N 40 48 E
Belaya Kalitva 83 48 13N 40 50 E
Belaya Kholunitsa 84 58 41N 50 13 E
Belaya, R. 84 54 54N 53 33 E
Belaya Tserkov 80 49 45N 30 10 E
Belbroughton 28 52 23N 2 5W
Belceşti 70 47 19N 27 7 E
Bełchatów 54 51 21N 19 22 E
Belcher, C. 12 75 0N 160 0W
Belcher Is. 150 56 15N 78 45W
Belchite 58 41 18N 0 43W
Belclare 38 53 29N 8 55W
Belcoo 38 54 18N 7 52W
Belderg 38 54 18N 9 33W
Beldringe 73 55 28N 10 21 E
Belebey 84 54 7N 54 7 E
Belém de São Francisco 170 8 46 S 38 58W
Belém (Pará) 170 1 20 S 48 30W
Belén, Argent. 172 27 40 S 67 5W
Belén, Colomb. 174 1 26N 75 56W
Belén, Parag. 172 23 30 S 57 6W
Belen 161 34 40N 106 50W
Belene 67 43 39N 25 10 E
Bélesta 44 42 55N 1 56 E
Belet Uen 91 4 30N 45 5 E
Belev 81 53 50N 36 5 E
Belfast, N.Z. 143 43 27 S 172 39 E
Belfast, S. Afr. 129 25 42 S 30 2 E
Belfast, U.K. 38 54 35N 5 56W
Belfast, U.S.A. 151 44 30N 69 0W
Belfast □ 38 54 35N 5 56W
Belfast, L. 38 54 40N 5 50W
Belfeld 47 51 18N 6 6 E
Belfeoram 151 47 32N 55 30W
Belfield 158 46 54N 103 11W
Belford 35 55 36N 1 50W
Belfort 43 47 38N 6 50 E
Belfort □ 43 47 38N 6 52 E
Belfry 160 45 10N 109 2W
Belgaum 97 15 55N 74 35 E
Belgioioso 62 45 9N 9 21 E
Belgium ■ 47 51 30N 5 0 E
Belgooly 138 51 44N 8 30W
Belgorod 82 50 35N 36 35 E
Belgorod Dnestrovskiy 82 46 11N 30 23 E
Belgrade 160 45 50N 111 10W
Belgrade = Beograd 66 44 50N 20 37 E
Belgrove 143 41 27 S 172 59 E
Belhaven 157 35 34N 76 35W
Beli 121 7 52N 10 58 E
Beli Drim, R. 66 42 25N 20 34 E
Beli Manastir 66 45 45N 18 36 E
Beli Timok, R. 66 43 39N 22 14 E
Belice, R. 64 37 44N 12 58 E
Belinga 124 1 10N 13 2 E
Belingwe 127 20 29 S 29 57 E
Belingwe, N., mt. 127 20 37 S 29 55 E
Belinsky (Chembar) 81 53 0N 43 25 E
Belinţ 66 45 48N 21 54 E
Belinyu 102 1 35 S 105 50 E
Beliton, Is. 102 3 10 S 107 50 E
Belitung, I. 102 3 10 S 107 50 E
Beliu 70 46 30N 22 0 E
Belize ■ 165 17 0N 88 30W
Belize City 165 17 25N 88 0W
Beljanica 66 44 08N 21 43 E
Bell 151 53 50N 53 10 E
Bell Bay 138 41 6 S 146 53 E
Bell I. 151 50 46N 55 35W
Bell Irving, R. 152 56 12N 129 5W
Bell Peninsula 149 63 50N 82 0W
Bell, R. 150 49 48N 77 38W
Bell Rock = Inchcape Rock 35 56 26N 2 24W
Bell Ville 172 32 40 S 62 40W
Bella Bella 152 52 10N 128 10W
Bella Coola 152 52 25N 126 40W
Bella Unión 172 30 15 S 57 40W
Bella Vista, Corrientes, Argent. 172 28 33 S 59 0W
Bella Vista, Tucuman, Argent. 172 27 10 S 65 25W
Bella Yella 120 7 24N 10 9W
Bellacorick 38 54 8N 9 35W
Bellaghy 38 54 50N 6 31W
Bellágio 62 45 59N 9 15 E
Bellaire 156 40 1N 80 46W
Bellananagh 38 53 55N 7 25W
Bellarena 38 55 7N 6 57W
Bellarwi 141 34 6 S 147 13 E
Bellary 97 15 10N 76 56 E
Bellata 139 29 53 S 149 46 E
Bellavary 38 53 54N 9 9W
Belle Fourche 158 44 43N 103 52W
Belle Fourche, R. 158 44 25N 105 0W
Belle Glade 157 26 43N 80 38W
Belle Ile 42 47 20N 3 10W
Belle Isle 151 51 57N 55 25W
Belle-Isle-en-Terre 42 48 33N 3 23W
Belle Isle, Str. of 151 51 30N 56 30W
Belle, La 157 26 45N 81 22W
Belle Plaine, Iowa, U.S.A. 158 41 51N 92 18W
Belle Plaine, Minn., U.S.A. 158 44 35N 93 48W
Belledonne 45 45 11N 6 0 E
Belledune 151 47 55N 65 50W
Belleek 38 54 30N 8 6W
Bellefontaine 156 40 20N 83 45W
Bellefonte 156 40 56N 77 45W
Bellegarde, Ain, France 45 46 4N 5 49 E
Bellegarde, Creuse, France 43 45 59N 2 19 E
Bellegarde, Loiret, France 43 48 0N 2 26 E
Belleoram 151 47 31N 55 25W
Belleville, Can. 150 44 10N 77 23W
Belleville, Rhône, France 45 46 7N 4 45 E
Belleville, Vendée, France 42 46 48N 1 28W
Belleville, Ill., U.S.A. 158 38 30N 90 0W
Belleville, Kans., U.S.A. 158 39 51N 97 38W
Belleville, N.Y., U.S.A. 162 43 46N 76 10W
Bellevue, Can. 152 49 35N 114 22W
Bellevue, U.S.A. 160 43 25N 144 23W
Belley 45 45 46N 5 41 E
Bellin (Payne Bay) 149 60 0N 70 0W
Bellingen 141 30 25 S 152 50 E
Bellingham, U.K. 35 55 09N 2 16W
Bellingham, U.S.A. 160 48 45N 122 27W
Bellingshausen Sea 13 66 0 S 80 0W
Bellinzona 51 46 11N 9 1 E
Bello 174 6 20N 75 33W
Bellona Reefs 133 21 26 S 159 0 E
Bellows Falls 162 43 10N 72 30W
Bellpat 94 29 0N 68 5 E
Bellpuig 58 41 37N 1 1 E
Belluno 63 46 8N 12 6 E
Bellville 159 29 58N 96 18W
Belmar 162 40 10N 74 2W
Bélmez 57 38 17N 5 17W
Belmont, Austral. 141 33 4 S 151 42 E
Belmont, U.S.A. 162 43 27N 71 29W
Belmonte, Brazil 171 16 0 S 39 0W
Belmonte, Port. 56 40 21N 7 20W
Belmonte, Spain 58 39 34N 2 43W
Belmopan 165 17 18N 88 30W
Belmore 140 33 34 S 141 13 E
Belmullet 38 54 13N 9 58W
Belo Horizonte 171 19 55 S 43 56W
Belo Jardim 170 8 20 S 36 26W
Belo-sur-Mer 129 20 42 S 44 33 E
Belo-sur-Tsiribihana 129 19 40 S 43 30 E
Belogorsk, R.S.F.S.R., U.S.S.R. 77 51 0N 128 20 E
Belogorsk, Ukraine, U.S.S.R. 82 45 3N 34 35 E
Belogradchik 66 43 37N 22 40 E
Belogradets 67 43 22N 27 18 E
Beloha 129 25 10 S 45 3 E
Beloit, Kans., U.S.A. 158 39 32N 98 9W
Beloit, Wis., U.S.A. 158 42 35N 89 0W
Belokholunitskiy 81 58 55N 50 43 E
Belomorsk 78 64 35N 34 30 E
Belonia 98 23 15N 91 30 E
Belopolye 80 51 14N 34 20 E
Beloretsk 84 53 58N 58 24 E
Belovo 76 54 30N 86 0 E
Beloyarskiy 84 56 45N 61 24 E
Beloye More 78 66 0N 38 0 E
Beloye, Oz. 78 60 10N 37 35 E
Beloye Ozero 83 45 15N 46 50 E
Belozersk 81 60 0N 37 30 E
Belpasso 65 37 37N 15 0 E
Belper 33 53 2N 1 29W
Belsay 35 55 6N 1 53W
Belsele 47 51 9N 4 6 E
Belsito 64 37 50N 13 47 E
Beltana 140 30 48 S 138 25 E
Belterra 175 2 45 S 55 0W
Beltinci 63 46 37N 16 20 E
Belton, Humberside, U.K. 33 53 33N 0 49W
Belton, Norfolk, U.K. 29 52 35N 1 39 E
Belton, S.C., U.S.A. 157 34 31N 82 39W
Belton, Tex., U.S.A. 159 31 4N 97 30W
Beltra, Mayo, Ireland 38 53 57N 9 24W
Beltra, Sligo, Ireland 38 54 12N 8 36W
Beltra L. 38 53 56N 9 28W
Beltsy 82 47 48N 28 0 E
Belturbet 38 54 6N 7 28W
Belukha 76 49 50N 86 50 E
Beluran 102 5 48N 117 35 E
Beluša 53 49 5N 18 27 E
Belušić 66 43 50N 21 10 E
Belvedere Maríttimo 65 39 37N 15 52 E
Belvès 44 44 46N 1 0 E
Belvidere, Ill., U.S.A. 158 42 15N 88 55W
Belvidere, N.J., U.S.A. 162 40 48N 75 5W
Belville 38 54 40N 9 22W
Belvis de la Jara 57 39 45N 4 57W
Belyando, R. 138 21 38 S 146 50 E
Belyj Jar 76 58 26N 84 39 E
Belyy 80 55 48N 32 51 E
Belyy, Ostrov 76 73 30N 71 0 E
Belyye Vody 85 42 25N 69 50 E
Belz 80 50 23N 24 1 E
Belzig 48 52 8N 12 36 E
Belzoni 159 33 12N 90 30W
Bemaraha, Plat. du 129 18 40 S 44 45 E
Bemarivo, Majunga, Madag. 129 17 6 S 44 31 E
Bemarivo, Tuléar, Madag. 129 21 45 S 44 45 E
Bemarivo, R. 129 21 45 S 44 45 E
Bemavo 129 21 33 S 45 25 E
Bembéréke 121 10 11N 2 43 E
Bembesi 127 20 0 S 28 58 E
Bembesi, R. 127 20 0 S 28 58 E
Bembézar, R. 57 38 0N 5 20W
Bembridge 28 50 41N 1 4W
Bemidji 158 47 30N 94 50W
Bemmel 46 51 54N 5 54 E
Ben Alder 37 55 59N 4 30W
Ben Avon 37 57 6N 3 28W
Ben Bheigeir, Mt. 34 55 43N 6 6W
Ben Bullen 141 33 12 S 150 2 E
Ben Chonzine 35 56 27N 4 0W
Ben Cruachan, Mt. 34 56 26N 5 8W
Ben Dearg 37 57 47N 4 58W
Ben Dearg, mt. 37 56 54N 3 49W
Ben Dhorain 37 58 7N 3 50W
Ben Dorian 34 56 30N 4 42W
Ben Gardane 119 33 11N 11 11 E
Ben Hee 37 58 16N 4 43W
Ben Hope, mt. 37 58 24N 4 36W
Ben Klibreck 37 58 14N 4 25W
Ben Lawers, mt. 37 56 33N 4 13W
Ben Lomond, mt. 139 30 1 S 151 43 E
Ben Lomond mt. 138 41 38 S 147 42 E
Ben Lomond, mt. 34 56 12N 4 39W
Ben Loyal 37 58 25N 4 25W
Ben Luc 101 10 39N 106 29 E
Ben Lui, mt. 34 56 24N 4 50W
Ben Macdhui 37 57 4N 3 40W
Ben Mhor 36 57 16N 7 21W
Ben More, Mull, U.K. 34 56 26N 6 2W
Ben More, Perth, U.K. 34 56 23N 4 31W
Ben More Assynt 37 58 7N 4 51W
Ben Nevis, mt., N.Z. 143 45 15 S 169 0 E
Ben Nevis, mt., U.K. 36 56 48N 5 0W
Ben Ohau Ra. 143 44 1 S 170 4 E
Ben Quang 100 17 3N 106 55 E
Ben Stack 36 58 20N 4 58W
Ben Tharsiunn 37 57 47N 4 20W
Ben Venue 34 56 13N 4 28W
Ben Vorlich 34 56 22N 4 15W
Ben Wyvis, mt. 37 57 40N 4 35W
Bena 121 11 20N 5 50 E
Bena Dibele 124 4 4 S 22 50 E
Benagalbón 57 36 45N 4 15W
Benagerie 140 31 25 S 140 22 E
Benahmed 118 33 4N 7 9W
Benalla 141 36 30 S 146 0 E
Benambra, Mt. 141 36 31 S 147 34 E
Benamejí 57 37 16N 4 33W
Benanee 140 34 31 S 142 52 E
Benares = Varanasi 95 25 22N 83 8 E
Benavente, Port. 57 38 59N 8 49W
Benavente, Spain 56 42 2N 5 43W
Benavides, Spain 56 42 30N 5 54W
Benavides, U.S.A. 159 27 35N 98 28W
Benbane Hd. 38 55 15N 6 30W
Benbaun, Mt. 38 53 30N 9 50W
Benbecula, I. 36 57 26N 7 21W
Benbonyathe, Mt. 140 30 25 S 139 11 E
Benburb 38 54 25N 6 42W
Bencubbin 137 30 48 S 117 52 E
Bend 160 44 2N 121 15W
Bendel □ 121 6 0N 6 0 E
Bender Beila 91 9 30N 50 48 E
Bender Cassim 91 11 12N 49 18 E
Bendering 137 32 23 S 118 18 E
Bendery 82 46 50N 29 50 E
Bendigo 140 36 40 S 144 15 E
Beneden Knijpe 46 52 58N 5 59 E
Benedick 162 38 31N 76 41W
Beneditinos 170 5 27 S 42 22W
Benedito Leite 170 7 13 S 44 34W
Benei Beraq 129 32 5N 34 50 E
Bénéna 120 13 9N 4 17W
Beneraird, Mt. 34 55 4N 4 57W
Benešov 52 49 46N 14 41 E
Bénestroff 43 48 54N 6 45 E
Benet 44 46 22N 0 35W
Benevento 65 41 7N 14 45 E
Benfeld 43 48 22N 7 34 E
Beng Lovea 100 12 36N 105 34 E
Benga 127 16 11 S 33 40 E
Bengal, Bay of 65 15 0N 00 90 E
Bengawan Solo 103 7 5 S 112 25 E
Benghazi = Banghãzī 119 32 11N 20 3 E
Bengkalis 102 1 30N 102 10 E
Bengkulu 102 3 50 S 102 12 E
Bengkulu □ 102 3 48 S 102 16 E
Bengough 153 49 25N 105 10W
Benguela 125 12 37 S 13 25 E
Benguerir 118 32 16N 7 56W
Benguérua, Î. 129 21 58 S 35 28 E
Benha 122 30 26N 31 8 E
Beni 126 0 30N 29 27 E
Beni Abbès 118 30 5N 2 5W
Beni Haoua 118 36 30N 1 30 E
Benî Mazâr 122 28 32N 30 44 E
Beni Mellal 118 32 21N 6 21W
Beni Ounif 118 32 0N 1 10W
Beni, R. 174 10 30 S 66 0W
Beni Saf 118 35 17N 1 15W
Benî Suêf 122 29 5N 31 6 E
Beniah L. 152 63 23N 112 17W
Benicarló 58 40 23N 0 23 E
Benicia 163 38 3N 122 9W
Benidorm 59 38 33N 0 9W
Benidorm, Islote de 59 38 31N 0 9W
Benin ■ 121 10 0N 2 0 E
Benin, Bight of 121 5 0N 3 0 E
Benin City 121 6 20N 5 31 E
Benington 33 52 59N 0 5 E
Benisa 59 38 43N 0 03 E
Benjamin Aceval 172 24 58 S 57 34W
Benjamin Constant 174 4 40 S 70 15W
Benjamin Hill 164 30 10N 111 10W
Benkelman 158 40 7N 101 32W
Benlidi 138 24 35 S 144 50 E
Benmore Pk. 143 44 25 S 170 8 E
Bennane Hd. 34 55 9N 5 2W
Bennebroek 46 52 19N 4 36 E
Bennekom 46 52 0N 5 41 E
Bennett 147 59 56N 134 53W
Bennettsbridge 39 52 36N 7 12W
Bennettsville 157 34 38N 79 39W
Bennington 162 42 52N 73 12W
Benoa 102 8 50 S 115 20 E
Bénodet 42 47 53N 4 7W
Benoni 129 26 11 S 28 18 E
Benoud 118 32 20N 0 16 E
Benque Viejo 165 17 5N 89 8W
Bensheim 49 49 40N 8 38 E
Benson, U.K. 28 51 37N 1 6W
Benson, U.S.A. 161 31 59N 110 19W
Bent 93 26 20N 59 25 E
Benteng 103 6 10 S 120 30 E
Bentinck I. 138 17 3 S 139 35 E
Bentiu 123 9 10N 29 55 E
Bentley, Hants., U.K. 29 51 12N 0 52W
Bentley, S. Yorks, U.K. 33 53 33N 1 9W
Bento Gonçalves 173 29 10 S 51 31W
Benton, Ark., U.S.A. 159 34 30N 92 35W
Benton, Calif., U.S.A. 163 37 48N 118 32W
Benton, Ill., U.S.A. 158 38 0N 88 55W
Benton, Pa., U.S.A. 162 41 12N 76 23W
Benton Harbor 156 42 10N 86 28W
Bentong 101 3 31N 101 55 E
Bentu Liben 123 8 32N 38 21 E
Benue □ 121 7 30N 7 30 E
Benue Plateau □ 121 8 0N 8 30 E
Benue, R. 121 7 50N 6 30 E
Benwee Hd. 38 54 20N 9 50W
Beo 103 4 25N 126 50 E
Beograd 66 44 50N 20 37 E
Beowawe 160 40 45N 117 0W
Beppu 110 33 15N 131 30 E
Beppu-Wan 110 33 18N 131 34 E
Ber Dagan 90 32 1N 34 49 E
Bera 98 24 5N 89 37 E
Beragh 38 54 34N 7 10W
Berakit 123 14 38N 39 29 E
Berati 68 40 43N 19 59 E
Berber 122 18 0N 34 0 E
Berbéra 117 10 33N 16 35 E
Berbera 91 10 30N 45 2 E
Berbérati 124 4 15N 15 40 E
Berberia, Cabo 59 38 39N 1 24 E
Berbice, R. 174 5 20N 58 10W
Berceto 62 44 30N 10 0 E
Berchtesgaden 49 47 37N 13 1 E
Berck-sur-Mer 43 50 25N 1 36 E
Berdichev 82 49 57N 28 30 E
Berdsk 76 54 47N 83 2 E
Berdyansk 82 46 45N 36 50 E
Berdyaush 84 55 9N 59 9 E
Bere Alston 30 50 29N 4 11W
Bere Regis 28 50 45N 2 13W
Berea 156 37 35N 84 18W
Berebere 103 2 25N 128 45 E
Bereda 91 11 45N 51 0 E
Bereina 135 8 39 S 146 30 E
Berekum 120 7 29N 2 34W
Berenice 122 24 2N 35 25 E
Berens I. 153 52 18N 97 18W
Berens, R. 153 51 21N 97 0W
Berens River 153 52 25N 97 0W
Beresteckho 80 50 22N 25 5 E
Bereşti 70 46 6N 27 50 E
Berettyo, R. 53 47 32N 21 47 E
Berettyóújfalu 53 47 13N 21 33 E
Beretǔu, R. 70 47 30N 22 7 E
Berevo 129 19 44 S 44 58 E
Berevo-sur-Ranobe 129 17 14 S 44 17 E
Bereza 80 52 31N 24 51 E
Berezhany 80 49 26N 24 58 E
Berezina, R. 80 54 10N 28 10 E
Berezna 80 51 35N 30 46 E
Berezniki 84 59 24N 56 46 E
Berezovka 82 47 25N 30 55 E
Berezovo 76 64 0N 65 0 E
Berg 71 59 10N 11 18 E
Berga, Spain 58 42 6N 1 48 E
Berga, Kalmar, Sweden 73 57 14N 16 3 E
Berga, Kronoberg, Sweden 73 56 55N 14 0 E
Bergama 92 39 8N 27 15 E
Bergambacht 46 51 56N 4 48 E
Bérgamo 62 45 42N 9 40 E
Bergantiños 56 43 20N 8 40W
Bergedorf 48 53 28N 10 12 E
Bergeijk 47 51 19N 5 21 E
Bergen, Ger. 48 54 24N 13 26 E
Bergen, Norway 71 60 23N 5 20 E
Bergen-Binnen 46 52 40N 4 43 E
Bergen-op-Zoom 47 51 30N 4 18 E
Bergerac 44 44 51N 0 30 E
Bergheim 48 50 57N 6 38 E
Berghem 46 51 46N 5 33 E

Bergisch-Gladbach **Billesdon**

Bergisch-Gladbach	**48**	50 59N	7 9E
Bergkvara	**73**	56 23N	16 5E
Bergschenhoek	**46**	51 59N	4 30E
Bergsjö	**72**	61 59N	17 3E
Berguent	**118**	34 1N	2 0W
Bergues	**43**	50 58N	2 24E
Bergum	**46**	53 13N	5 59E
Bergvik	**72**	61 16N	16 50E
Berhala, Selat	**102**	1 0S	104 15E
Berhampore	**95**	24 2N	88 27E
Berhampur	**96**	19 15N	84 54E
Berheci, R.	**70**	46 7N	27 19E
Berhungra	**139**	34 46S	147 52E
Bering Sea	**130**	58 0N	167 0E
Bering Str.	**147**	66 0N	170 0W
Beringarra	**137**	26 0S	116 55E
Beringen, Belg.	**47**	51 3N	5 14E
Beringen, Switz.	**51**	47 38N	8 34E
Beringovskiy	**77**	63 3N	179 19E
Berislav	**82**	46 50N	33 30E
Berisso	**172**	34 40S	58 0W
Berja	**59**	36 50N	2 56W
Berkane	**118**	34 52N	2 20W
Berkel, R.	**46**	52 8N	6 12E
Berkeley	**163**	37 52N	122 20W
Berkeley Springs	**156**	39 38N	78 12W
Berkhamsted	**29**	51 45N	0 33W
Berkhout	**46**	52 38N	4 59E
Berkner I.	**13**	79 30S	50 0W
Berkovitsa	**67**	43 16N	23 8E
Berkshire	**162**	42 19N	76 11W
Berkshire □	**28**	51 30N	1 20W
Berkshire Downs	**28**	51 30N	1 30W
Berkyk	**71**	62 50N	9 59E
Berlaar	**47**	51 7N	4 39E
Berland, R.	**152**	54 0N	116 50W
Berlanga	**57**	38 17N	5 50W
Berlave	**47**	51 2N	4 0E
Berleburg	**48**	51 3N	8 22E
Berlenga, I.	**75**	39 25N	9 30W
Berlick	**47**	51 22N	6 9E
Berlin, Ger.	**48**	52 32N	13 24E
Berlin, Md., U.S.A.	**162**	38 19N	75 12W
Berlin, N.H., U.S.A.	**156**	44 29N	71 10W
Berlin, N.Y., U.S.A.	**162**	42 42N	73 23W
Berlin, E. □	**48**	52 30N	13 30E
Berlin, W. □	**48**	52 30N	13 20E
Bermeja, Sierra	**57**	36 45N	5 11W
Bermejo, R., Formosa, Argent.	**172**	26 30S	58 50W
Bermejo, R., San Juan, Argent.	**172**	30 0S	68 0W
Bermeo	**58**	43 25N	2 47W
Bermillo de Sayago	**56**	41 22N	6 8W
Bermuda, I.	**10**	32 45N	65 0W
Bern (Berne)	**50**	46 57N	7 28E
Bern (Berne) □	**50**	46 45N	7 40E
Bernalda	**65**	40 24N	16 44E
Bernalillo	**161**	35 17N	106 37W
Bernam, R.	**101**	3 45N	101 5E
Bernardo de Irigoyen	**173**	26 15S	53 40W
Bernardsville	**162**	40 43N	74 34W
Bernasconi	**172**	37 55S	63 44W
Bernau	**49**	47 53N	12 20E
Bernay	**42**	49 5N	0 35E
Berndorf	**52**	47 59N	16 1E
Berne = Bern	**50**	46 57N	7 28E
Berner Alpen	**50**	46 27N	7 35E
Berneray, I.	**36**	56 47N	7 38W
Bernese Oberland = Oberland	**50**	46 27N	7 35E
Bernier I.	**137**	24 50S	113 12E
Bernina Pass	**51**	46 22N	9 54E
Bernina, Piz	**51**	46 20N	9 54E
Bernissart	**47**	50 28N	3 39E
Beroroha	**125**	21 40S	45 10E
Béroubouey	**121**	10 34N	2 46E
Beroun	**52**	49 57N	14 5E
Berounka, R.	**52**	50 0N	13 47E
Berovo	**66**	41 42N	22 51E
Berrahal	**119**	36 54N	7 33E
Berre	**45**	43 28N	5 11E
Berre, Étang de	**45**	43 27N	5 5E
Berrechid	**118**	33 18N	7 36W
Berri	**140**	34 14S	140 35E
Berriedale	**37**	58 12N	3 30W
Berriew	**31**	52 36N	3 12W
Berrigan	**141**	35 38S	145 49E
Berrouaghia	**118**	36 10N	2 53E
Berrwillock	**140**	35 36S	142 59E
Berry, Austral.	**141**	34 46S	150 43E
Berry, France	**43**	47 0N	2 0E
Berry Hd.	**30**	50 24N	3 29W
Berry Is.	**166**	25 40N	77 50W
Berryville	**159**	36 23N	93 35W
Bersenbrück	**48**	52 33N	7 56E
Berst Ness	**37**	59 16N	3 0W
Berthaund	**158**	40 21N	105 5W
Berthier Is.	**136**	14 29S	124 59E
Berthold	**158**	48 19N	101 45W
Bertincourt	**43**	50 5N	2 58E
Bertoua	**124**	4 30N	13 45E
Bertraghboy, B.	**38**	53 22N	9 54W
Bertrand	**158**	40 35N	99 38W
Bertrange	**47**	49 37N	6 3E
Bertrix	**47**	49 51N	5 15E
Beruas	**101**	4 30N	100 47E
Berufjörður	**74**	64 48N	14 29W
Berur Hayil	**90**	31 34N	34 38E
Berwick	**162**	41 4N	76 17W
Berwick (□)	**26**	55 46N	2 30W
Berwick-upon-Tweed	**35**	55 47N	2 0W
Berwyn Mts.	**31**	52 54N	3 26W
Beryl N., oilfield	**19**	59 37N	1 30E
Beryl, oilfield	**19**	59 28N	1 30E
Beryl W., oilfield	**19**	59 32N	1 20E
Berzasca	**66**	44 39N	21 58E
Berzence	**53**	46 12N	17 11E
Besal	**95**	35 4N	73 56E
Besalampy	**129**	16 43S	44 29E
Besançon	**43**	47 9N	6 0E
Besar	**102**	2 40S	116 0E
Beserah	**101**	3 50N	103 21E
Beshenkovichi	**80**	55 2N	29 29E
Beška	**66**	45 8N	20 6E
Beskids, Mts.	**53**	49 35N	18 40E
Beslan	**83**	43 22N	44 28E
Besna Kobila	**66**	42 31N	22 10E
Besnard L.	**153**	55 25N	106 0W
Beşparmak Daği	**69**	37 32N	27 30E
Bessarabiya	**70**	46 20N	29 0E
Bessarabka	**82**	46 21N	28 51E
Bessbrook	**38**	54 12N	6 25W
Bessèges	**45**	44 18N	4 8E
Bessemer	**158**	46 27N	90 0W
Bessin	**42**	49 21N	1 0W
Bessines-sur-Gartempe	**42**	46 6N	1 22E
Best	**47**	51 31N	5 23E
Bet Alfa	**90**	32 31N	35 25E
Bet Guvrin	**90**	31 37N	34 54E
Bet Hashitta	**90**	32 31N	35 27E
Bet Ha'tmeq	**90**	32 58N	35 8E
Bet Qeshet	**90**	32 41N	35 21E
Bet She'an	**90**	32 30N	35 30E
Bet Tadjine, Djebel	**118**	29 0N	3 30W
Bet Yosef	**90**	32 34N	35 33E
Betafo	**129**	19 50S	46 51E
Betanzos	**56**	43 15N	8 12W
Bétaré-Oya	**124**	5 40N	14 5E
Betekom	**47**	50 59N	4 47E
Bétera	**58**	39 35N	0 28W
Bethal	**129**	26 27S	29 28E
Bethanien	**125**	26 31S	17 8E
Bethany, S. Afr.	**128**	29 34S	25 59E
Bethany, U.S.A.	**158**	40 18N	94 0W
Bethany = Eizariya	**90**	31 47N	35 15E
Bethel, U.S.A.	**147**	60 50N	161 50W
Bethel, Conn., U.S.A.	**162**	41 22N	73 25W
Bethesda, U.K.	**31**	53 11N	4 3W
Bethesda, U.S.A.	**162**	38 59N	77 6W
Bethlehem, S. Afr.	**129**	28 14S	28 18E
Bethlehem, U.S.A.	**162**	40 39N	75 24W
Bethlehem = Bayt Lahm	**90**	31 43N	35 12E
Bethulie	**128**	30 30S	25 59E
Béthune	**43**	50 30N	2 38E
Béthune, R.	**42**	49 56N	1 5E
Bethungra	**141**	34 45S	147 51E
Betijoque	**174**	9 23N	70 44W
Betim	**171**	19 58S	44 13W
Betioky	**129**	23 48S	44 20E
Beton Bazoches	**43**	48 42N	3 15E
Betong	**101**	5 45N	101 5E
Betoota	**138**	25 40S	140 42E
Betroka	**129**	23 16S	46 0E
Betsiamites	**151**	48 56N	68 40W
Betsiamites, R.	**151**	48 56N	68 40W
Betsiboka, R.	**129**	17 0S	47 0E
Betsjoeanaland	**128**	26 30S	22 30E
Bettembourg	**47**	49 31N	6 6E
Betterton	**162**	39 52N	76 4W
Betteshanger	**29**	51 14N	1 20E
Bettiah	**95**	26 48N	84 33E
Bettles	**147**	66 54N	150 50W
Bèttola	**62**	44 46N	9 35E
Bettws Bledrws	**31**	52 9N	4 2W
Bettyhill	**37**	58 31N	4 12W
Betul	**96**	21 48N	77 59E
Betung	**102**	2 0S	103 10E
Betws-y-Coed	**31**	53 4N	3 49W
Beuca	**70**	44 14N	24 56E
Beuil	**45**	44 6N	7 0E
Beulah, Can.	**153**	50 16N	101 02W
Beulah, U.S.A.	**158**	47 18N	101 47W
Beuvronne, La	**46**	48 59N	2 41E
Bevensen	**48**	53 5N	10 34E
Beveren	**47**	51 12N	4 16E
Beverley, Austral.	**137**	32 9S	116 56E
Beverley, U.K.	**33**	53 52N	0 26W
Beverlo	**47**	51 7N	5 13E
Beverly, Can.	**152**	53 36N	113 21W
Beverly, Mass., U.S.A.	**162**	42 32N	70 50W
Beverly, Wash., U.S.A.	**160**	46 55N	119 59W
Beverly Hills	**163**	34 4N	118 29W
Beverwijk	**46**	52 28N	4 38E
Bewdley	**28**	52 23N	2 19W
Bex	**50**	46 15N	7 0E
Bexhill	**29**	50 51N	0 29E
Bexley	**29**	51 26N	0 10E
Beyin	**120**	5 1N	2 41W
Beykoz	**67**	41 8N	29 7E
Beyla	**120**	8 30N	8 38W
Beynat	**44**	45 8N	1 44E
Beyneu	**76**	45 10N	55 3E
Beypazaı	**92**	40 10N	31 48E
Beyşehir Gölü	**92**	37 40N	31 45E
Bezdan	**66**	45 28N	18 57E
Bezerros	**171**	8 14S	35 45W
Bezet	**90**	33 4N	35 8E
Bezhitsa	**80**	53 19N	34 17E
Béziers	**44**	43 20N	3 12E
Bezwada = Vijayawada	**97**	16 31N	80 39E
Bhachau	**93**	23 20N	70 16E
Bhadarwah	**95**	32 58N	75 46E
Bhadra, R.	**97**	13 0N	76 0E
Bhadrakh	**96**	21 10N	86 30E
Bhadravati	**97**	13 49N	76 15E
Bhagalpur	**95**	25 10N	87 0E
Bhairab	**98**	22 51N	89 34E
Bhairab Bazar	**98**	24 4N	90 58E
Bhaisa	**96**	19 10N	77 58E
Bhakkar	**94**	31 40N	71 5E
Bhakra Dam	**95**	31 30N	76 45E
Bhamo	**98**	24 15N	97 15E
Bhamragarh	**96**	19 30N	80 40E
Bhandara	**96**	21 5N	79 42E
Bhanrer Ra.	**94**	23 40N	79 45E
Bharat = India	**93**	24 0N	78 0E
Bharatpur	**94**	27 15N	77 30E
Bharuch	**96**	21 47N	73 0E
Bhatghar L.	**96**	18 10N	73 48E
Bhatiapara Ghat	**98**	23 13N	89 42E
Bhatkal	**97**	13 58N	74 35E
Bhatpara	**95**	22 50N	88 25E
Bhattiprolu	**97**	16 7N	80 45E
Bhaun	**94**	32 55N	72 40E
Bhaunagar = Bhavnagar	**94**	21 45N	72 10E
Bhavani	**97**	11 27N	77 43E
Bhavani, R.	**97**	11 30N	77 15E
Bhavnagar	**94**	21 45N	72 10E
Bhawanipatna	**96**	19 55N	83 30E
Bhera	**94**	32 29N	72 57E
Bhilsa = Vidisha	**94**	23 28N	77 53E
Bhilwara	**94**	25 25N	74 38E
Bhima, R.	**96**	17 20N	76 30E
Bhimber	**95**	32 59N	74 3E
Bhimvaram	**96**	16 30N	81 30E
Bhind	**95**	26 30N	78 46E
Bhir	**96**	19 4N	75 58E
Bhiwandi	**96**	19 15N	73 0E
Bhiwani	**94**	28 50N	76 9E
Bhola	**98**	22 45N	90 35E
Bhongir	**96**	17 30N	78 56E
Bhopal	**94**	23 20N	77 53E
Bhor	**96**	18 12N	73 53E
Bhubaneswar	**96**	20 15N	85 50E
Bhuj	**94**	23 15N	69 49E
Bhumibol Dam	**100**	17 15N	98 58E
Bhusaval	**96**	21 15N	69 49E
Bhutan ■	**98**	27 25N	89 50E
Biafra, B. of = Bonny, Bight of	**121**	3 30N	9 20E
Biak	**103**	1 0S	136 0E
Biała	**54**	50 24N	17 40E
Biała Piska	**54**	53 37N	22 5E
Biała Podlaska	**54**	52 4N	23 6E
Biała Podlaska □	**54**	52 0N	23 0E
Biała, R.	**54**	49 46N	20 53E
Białogard	**54**	54 2N	15 58E
Biały Bór	**54**	53 53N	16 51E
Białystok	**54**	53 10N	23 10E
Białystok □	**54**	53 9N	23 10E
Biancavilla	**65**	37 39N	14 50E
Biano Plateau = Manika Plateau	**127**	9 55S	26 24E
Biaro	**103**	2 5N	125 26E
Biarritz	**44**	43 29N	1 33W
Biasca	**51**	46 22N	8 58E
Biba	**122**	28 55N	31 0E
Bibaï	**112**	43 19N	141 52E
Bibby I.	**153**	61 55N	93 0W
Biberach	**49**	48 5N	9 49E
Biberist	**50**	47 11N	7 34E
Bibey, R.	**56**	42 24N	7 13W
Bibiani	**120**	6 30N	2 8W
Bibile	**97**	7 10N	81 25E
Biboohra	**138**	16 56S	145 25E
Bibungwa	**126**	2 40S	28 15E
Bibury	**28**	51 46N	1 50W
Bic	**151**	48 20N	68 41W
Bicaj	**68**	42 0N	20 25E
Bicaz	**70**	46 53N	26 5E
Biccari	**65**	41 23N	15 12E
Bicester	**28**	51 53N	1 9W
Biche, La, R.	**152**	59 57N	123 50W
Bichena	**123**	10 28N	38 10E
Bickerton I.	**138**	13 45S	136 10E
Bicknell, Ind., U.S.A.	**156**	38 50N	87 20W
Bicknell, Utah, U.S.A.	**161**	38 16N	111 35W
Bicsad	**70**	47 56N	23 28E
Bicton	**28**	52 43N	2 47W
Bida	**121**	9 3N	5 58E
Bidar	**96**	17 55N	77 35E
Biddeford	**151**	43 30N	70 28W
Biddenden	**29**	51 7N	0 40E
Biddu	**90**	31 50N	35 8E
Biddulph	**32**	53 8N	2 11W
Biddwara	**123**	5 11N	38 34E
Biddya	**90**	32 7N	35 4E
Bideford	**30**	51 1N	4 13W
Bideford Bay	**30**	51 5N	4 20W
Bidford on Avon	**28**	52 9N	1 53W
Bidor	**101**	4 6N	101 15E
Bidura	**140**	34 10S	143 21E
Bié	**125**	12 22S	16 55E
Bié Plateau	**125**	12 0S	16 0E
Bieber	**160**	41 4N	121 6W
Biel (Bienne)	**50**	47 8N	7 14E
Bielawa	**54**	50 43N	16 37E
Bielé Karpaty	**53**	49 5N	18 0E
Bielefeld	**48**	52 2N	8 31E
Bielersee	**50**	47 6N	7 5E
Biella	**62**	45 33N	8 3E
Bielsk Podlaski	**54**	52 47N	23 12E
Bielsko-Biała	**54**	49 50N	19 8E
Bielsko-Biała □	**54**	49 45N	19 15E
Bien Hoa	**101**	10 57N	106 49E
Bienfait	**153**	49 10N	102 50W
Bienne = Biel	**50**	47 8N	7 14E
Bienvenida	**57**	38 18N	6 12W
Bienville, L.	**150**	55 5N	72 40W
Biescas	**58**	42 37N	0 20W
Biesiesfontein	**128**	30 57S	17 58E
Bietigheim	**49**	48 57N	9 8E
Bievre	**47**	49 57N	5 1E
Biferno, R.	**65**	41 40N	14 38E
Big B.	**151**	55 43N	60 35W
Big Bear City	**163**	34 16N	116 51W
Big Bear L.	**163**	34 15N	116 56W
Big Beaver	**153**	49 10N	105 10W
Big Beaver House	**150**	52 59N	89 50W
Big Bell	**137**	27 21S	117 40E
Big Belt Mts.	**160**	46 50N	111 30W
Big Bend	**129**	26 50S	32 2E
Big Bend Nat. Park	**159**	29 15N	103 15W
Big Black, R.	**159**	32 35N	90 30W
Big Blue, R.	**158**	40 20N	96 40W
Big Cr.	**152**	51 42N	122 41W
Big Creek	**163**	37 11N	119 14W
Big Cypress Swamp	**157**	26 12N	81 10W
Big Delta	**147**	64 15N	145 0W
Big Falls	**158**	48 11N	93 48W
Big Horn	**160**	46 11N	107 25W
Big Horn Mts. = Bighorn Mts.	**160**	44 30N	107 30W
Big Horn R.	**160**	45 30N	108 10W
Big Lake	**159**	31 12N	101 25W
Big Moose	**162**	43 49N	74 58W
Big Muddy, R.	**158**	48 25N	104 45W
Big Pine	**163**	37 12N	118 17W
Big Piney	**160**	42 32N	110 3W
Big Quill L.	**153**	51 55N	105 22W
Big, R.	**151**	54 50N	58 55W
Big Rapids	**156**	43 42N	85 27W
Big River	**153**	53 50N	107 0W
Big Sable Pt.	**156**	44 5N	86 30W
Big Salmon	**147**	61 50N	136 0W
Big Sand L.	**153**	57 45N	99 45W
Big Sandy	**160**	48 12N	110 9W
Big Sandy Cr.	**158**	38 52N	103 11W
Big Sioux, R.	**158**	44 20N	96 53W
Big Smoky Valley	**163**	38 30N	117 15W
Big Snowy Mt.	**160**	46 50N	109 15W
Big Spring	**159**	32 10N	101 25W
Big Springs	**158**	41 4N	102 3W
Big Stone City	**158**	45 20N	96 30W
Big Stone Gap	**157**	36 52N	82 45W
Big Stone L.	**158**	44 25N	96 35W
Big Sur	**163**	36 15N	121 48W
Big Trout L.	**150**	53 40N	90 0W
Biganos	**44**	44 39N	0 59W
Bigbury	**30**	50 17N	3 52W
Bigbury B.	**30**	50 18N	3 58W
Bigerymunal, Mt.	**137**	27 25S	120 40E
Bigfork	**160**	48 3N	114 2W
Biggar	**153**	52 4N	108 0W
Bigge I.	**136**	14 35S	125 10E
Biggenden	**139**	25 31S	152 4E
Biggleswade	**29**	52 6N	0 16W
Bighorn Mts.	**160**	44 30N	107 30W
Bignona	**120**	12 52N	16 23W
Bigorre	**44**	43 5N	0 2E
Bigstone L.	**153**	53 42N	95 44W
Bigtimber	**160**	45 53N	110 0W
Bigwa	**126**	7 10S	39 10E
Bihaó	**63**	44 49N	15 57E
Bihar	**95**	25 5N	85 40E
Bihar □	**95**	25 0N	86 0E
Biharamulo	**126**	2 25S	31 25E
Biharamulo □	**126**	2 30S	31 20E
Biharkeresztes	**53**	47 8N	21 44E
Bihé Plateau	**125**	12 0S	16 0E
Bihor □	**70**	47 0N	22 10E
Bihor, Munţii	**70**	46 29N	22 47E
Bijagós, Arquipélago dos	**120**	11 15N	16 10W
Bijaipur	**94**	26 2N	77 36E
Bijapur, Mad. P., India	**96**	18 50N	80 50E
Bijapur, Mysore, India	**96**	16 50N	75 55E
Bijar	**92**	35 52N	47 35E
Bijeljina	**66**	44 46N	19 17E
Bijni	**98**	26 30N	90 40E
Bijnor	**94**	29 27N	78 11E
Bikaner	**94**	28 2N	73 18E
Bikapur	**95**	26 30N	82 7E
Bikin	**77**	46 50N	134 20E
Bikini, atoll	**130**	12 0N	167 30E
Bikoro	**124**	0 48S	18 15E
Bikoué	**121**	5 55S	11 50E
Bilād Banī Bū 'Ali	**93**	22 0N	59 20E
Bilara	**94**	26 14N	73 53E
Bilaspara	**98**	26 13N	90 14E
Bilaspur, India	**99**	22 2N	82 15E
Bilaspur, Mad. P., India	**95**	22 2N	82 15E
Bilaspur, Punjab, India	**94**	31 19N	76 50E
Bilauk Taungdan	**100**	13 0N	99 0E
Bilbao	**58**	43 16N	2 56W
Bilbor	**70**	47 18N	25 30E
Bíldudalur	**74**	65 41N	23 36W
Bilecik	**92**	40 5N	30 5E
Bileóa	**66**	42 53N	18 27E
Bilibino	**77**	68 3N	166 20E
Bilibiza	**127**	12 30S	40 20E
Bilin	**98**	17 14N	97 15E
Bilir	**77**	65 40N	131 20E
Bilishti	**68**	40 37N	20 59E
Bill	**158**	43 18N	105 18W
Billa	**121**	8 55N	12 15E
Billabalong	**137**	27 25S	115 49E
Billericay	**29**	51 38N	0 25E
Billesdon	**29**	52 38N	0 56W

Billiluna Blenheim

Billiluna 136 19 37 S 127 41 E
Billimari 71 33 41 S 148 37 E
Billingham 33 54 36N 1 18W
Billinghay 33 53 5N 0 17W
Billings 160 45 43N 108 29W
Billingsfors 72 58 59N 12 15 E
Billingshurst 29 51 2N 0 28W
Billom 44 45 43N 3 20 E
Bilma 117 18 50N 13 30 E
Bilo Gora 66 45 53N 17 15 E
Biloela 138 24 24 S 150 31 E
Biloxi 159 30 30N 89 0W
Bilpa Morea Claypan 138 25 0 S 140 0 E
Bilston 28 52 34N 2 5W
Bilthoven 46 52 8N 5 12 E
Biltine 117 14 40N 20 50 E
Bilugyun 98 16 24N 97 32 E
Bilyana 138 18 5 S 145 50 E
Bilyarsk 84 54 58N 50 22 E
Bilzen 47 50 52N 5 31 E
Bima 103 8 22 S 118 49 E
Bimban 122 24 24N 32 54 E
Bimberi Peak, mt. 141 35 44 S 148 51 E
Bimbila 121 8 54N 0 5 E
Bimbo 124 4 15N 18 33 E
Bina-Etawah 94 24 13N 78 14 E
Binačka Morava, R. 66 42 30N 19 35 E
Binalbagan 103 10 12N 122 50 E
Binalong 141 34 40 S 148 39 E
Binatang 102 2 10N 111 40 E
Binbrook 33 53 26N 0 9W
Binche 47 50 26N 4 10 E
Binda 139 27 52 S 147 21 E
Bindi Bindi 137 30 37 S 116 22 E
Bindle 139 27 40 S 148 45 E
Bindura 127 17 18 S 31 18 E
Bingara, N.S.W., Austral. 139 29 52 S 150 36 E
Bingara, Queens., Austral. 139 28 10 S 144 37 E
Bingen 49 49 57N 7 53 E
Bingerville 120 5 18N 3 49W
Bingham, U.K. 33 52 57N 0 55W
Bingham, U.S.A. 151 45 5N 69 50W
Bingham Canyon 160 40 31N 112 10W
Binghamton 38 42 9N 75 54W
Bingley 32 53 51N 1 50W
Bingöl 92 39 20N 41 0 E
Binh Dinh = An Nhon 100 13 55N 109 7 E
Binh Khe 100 13 57N 108 51 E
Binh Son 100 15 20N 108 40 E
Binjai 102 3 50N 98 30 E
Binnaway 141 31 28 S 149 24 E
Binongko 103 5 55 S 123 55 E
Binscarth 153 50 37N 101 17W
Bint 93 26 22N 59 25 E
Bint Jaibail 90 33 8N 35 25 E
Bintan 102 1 0N 104 0 E
Bintulu 102 3 10N 113 0 E
Binyamina 90 32 32N 34 56 E
Binza 123 5 25N 28 40 E
Binzert = Bizerte 119 37 15N 9 50 E
Bio-Bío □ 172 37 35 S 72 0W
Bio Culma 123 7 20N 42 15 E
Biograd 63 43 56N 15 29 E
Biokovo 66 43 23N 17 0 E
Biougra 118 30 15N 9 14W
Biq'at Bet Netofa 90 32 49N 35 22 E
Bir 93 19 0N 75 54 E
Bîr Abû Hashim 122 23 42N 34 6 E
Bîr Abû M'nqar 122 26 33N 27 33 E
Bir Adal Deib 122 22 35N 36 10 E
Bir al Malfa 119 31 58N 15 18 E
Bir 'Asal 122 25 55N 34 20 E
Bir Autrun 117 18 15N 26 40 E
Bîr Dhu'fân 119 31 59N 14 32 E
Bîr Diqnash 122 31 3N 25 23 E
Bîr el Abbes 118 26 7N 6 9W
Bir-el-Ater 119 34 46N 8 3 E
Bîr el Basur 122 29 51N 25 49 E
Bîr el Gellaz 122 30 50N 26 40 E
Bîr el Shaqqa 122 30 54N 25 1 E
Bîr Fuad 122 30 35N 26 28 E
Bir Haimur 122 22 45N 33 40 E
Bîr Kanayis 122 24 59N 33 15 E
Bîr Kerawein 122 27 10N 28 25 E
Bîr Lemouissat 118 25 0N 10 32W
Bîr Maql 122 23 7N 33 40 E
Bîr Misaha 122 22 13N 27 59 E
Bir Mogreïn, (Fort Trinquet) 116 25 10N 11 25W
Bîr Murr 122 23 28N 30 10 E
Bir Nabala 90 31 52N 35 12 E
Bîr Nakheila 122 24 1N 30 50 E
Bîr Qâtrani 122 30 55N 26 10 E
Bîr Ranga 122 24 25N 35 15 E
Bîr Ras 123 12 0N 44 0 E
Bîr Sahara 122 22 54N 28 40 E
Bîr Seiyâla 122 25 10N 34 50 E
Bir Semguine 118 30 1N 5 39W
Bîr Shalatein 122 23 5N 35 25 E
Bîr Shebb 122 22 25N 29 40 E
Bîr Shût 122 23 50N 35 15 E
Bîr Terfawi 122 22 57N 28 55 E
Bîr Umm Qubûr 122 24 35N 34 2 E
Bîr Ungât 122 22 8N 33 48 E
Bîr Za'farâna 122 29 10N 32 40 E
Bîr Zāmus 119 24 16N 15 6 E
Bîr Zeidûn 122 25 45N 34 40 E
Bir Zeit 90 31 59N 35 11 E
Bira 103 2 3 S 132 2 E
Bîra 70 47 2N 27 3 E
Biramfero 120 11 40N 9 10W
Birao 117 10 20N 22 40 E
Birawa 126 2 20 S 28 48 E
Bîrca 70 43 59N 23 36 E
Birch 29 51 50N 0 54 E
Birch Hills 153 52 59N 105 25W
Birch I. 153 52 26N 99 54W
Birch L., N.W.T., Can. 152 62 4N 116 33W
Birch L., Ont., Can. 150 51 23N 92 18W
Birch L., U.S.A. 150 47 48N 91 43W
Birch Mts. 152 57 30N 113 10W
Birch River 153 52 24N 101 6W
Birchington 29 51 22N 1 18 E
Birchip 140 35 56 S 142 55 E
Birchiş 70 45 58N 22 0 E
Birchwood 143 45 55 S 167 53 E
Bird 153 56 30N 94 13W
Bird City 158 39 48N 101 33W
Bird I., Austral. 133 22 10 S 155 28 E
Bird I., S. Afr. 128 32 3 S 18 17 E
Birdaard 46 53 18N 5 53 E
Birdhip 139 35 52 S 142 50 E
Birdlip 28 51 50N 2 7W
Birdsville 138 25 51 S 139 20 E
Birdum 136 15 39 S 133 13 E
Birecik 92 37 0N 38 0 E
Bireuen 102 5 14N 96 39 E
Birhan 123 10 45N 37 55 E
Birifo 120 13 30N 14 0 E
Birigui 173 21 18 S 50 16W
Birimgan 138 22 41 S 147 25 E
Birjand 93 32 57N 59 10 E
Birk 122 18 8N 41 30 E
Birka 122 22 11N 40 38 E
Birkdale 32 53 38N 3 2W
Birkenhead, N.Z. 142 36 49 S 174 46 E
Birkenhead, U.K. 32 53 24N 3 1W
Birket Qârûn 122 29 30N 30 40 E
Birkfeld 52 47 21N 15 45 E
Birkhadem 118 36 43N 3 3 E
Bîrlad 70 46 15N 27 38 E
Birmingham, U.K. 28 52 30N 1 55W
Birmingham, U.S.A. 157 33 31N 86 50W
Birmitrapur 96 22 30N 84 10 E
Birni Ngaouré 121 13 5N 2 51 E
Birni Nkonni 121 13 55N 5 15 E
Birnin Gwari 121 11 0N 6 45 E
Birnin Kebbi 121 12 32N 4 12 E
Birnin Kudu 121 11 30N 9 29 E
Birobidzhan 77 48 50N 132 50 E
Birqin 90 32 23N 35 15 E
Birr 39 53 7N 7 55W
Birrie, R. 139 29 43 S 146 37 E
Birs, R. 50 47 24N 7 32 E
Birsilpur 94 28 11N 72 58 E
Birsk 84 55 25N 55 30 E
Birtin 70 46 59N 22 31 E
Birtle 153 50 30N 101 5W
Birtley, Northumberland, U.K. 35 55 5N 2 12W
Birtley, Tyne & Wear, U.K. 35 54 53N 1 34W
Birur 93 13 30N 75 55 E
Biryuchiy, Ostrov 82 46 10N 35 0 E
Birzai 80 56 11N 24 45 E
Bîrzava 70 46 7N 21 59 E
Bisa 103 1 10 S 127 40 E
Bisáccia 65 41 0N 15 20 E
Bisacquino 64 37 42N 13 13 E
Bisai 111 35 16N 136 44 E
Bisalpur 95 28 14N 79 48 E
Bisbal, La 58 41 58N 3 2 E
Bisbee 161 31 30N 110 0W
Biscay, B. of 14 45 0N 2 0W
Biscayne B. 157 25 40N 80 12W
Biscéglie 65 41 14N 16 30 E
Bischofshofen 52 47 26N 13 14 E
Bischofswerda 48 51 8N 14 11 E
Bischofszell 51 47 29N 9 15 E
Bischwiller 43 48 41N 7 50 E
Biscoe I. 13 66 0 S 67 0W
Biscostasing 150 47 18N 82 9W
Biscucuy 174 9 22N 69 59W
Biševo, I. 63 42 57N 16 3 E
Bisha 123 15 30N 37 31 E
Bisha, Wadi 122 20 30N 43 0 E
Bishop, Calif., U.S.A. 163 37 20N 118 26W
Bishop, Tex., U.S.A. 159 27 35N 97 49W
Bishop Auckland 33 54 40N 1 40W
Bishop's Castle 28 52 29N 3 0W
Bishop's Cleeve 28 51 56N 2 3W
Bishop's Falls 151 49 2N 55 30W
Bishop's Frome 28 52 8N 2 29W
Bishops Lydeard 28 51 4N 3 12W
Bishop's Nympton 30 50 58N 3 44W
Bishop's Stortford 29 51 52N 0 11 E
Bishop's Waltham 28 50 57N 1 13W
Bishopsteignton 30 50 32N 3 32W
Bishopstoke 28 50 58N 1 19W
Bisignano 65 30 30N 16 17 E
Bisina, L. 126 1 38N 33 56 E
Biskra 119 34 50N 5 44 E
Biskupiec 54 53 53N 20 58 E
Bislig 103 8 15N 126 27 E
Bismarck 158 46 49N 100 49W
Bismarck Arch. 135 2 30 S 150 0 E
Bismarck Ra. 135 5 35 S 145 0 E
Bismarck Sea 135 4 10 S 146 50 E
Bismark 48 52 39N 11 31 E
Biso 126 1 44N 31 26 E
Bison 158 45 34N 102 28W
Bispfors 74 63 1N 16 39 E
Bispgarden 72 63 2N 16 40 E
Bissagos = Bijagós 120 11 15N 16 10W
Bissau 120 11 45N 15 45W
Bissett 153 51 2N 95 41W
Bissikrima 120 10 50N 10 58W
Bistcho L. 152 59 45N 118 50W
Bistreţu 70 43 54N 23 23 E
Bistrica = Ilirska Bistrica 63 45 34N 14 14 E
Bistriţa 70 47 9N 24 35 E
Bistriţa Năsăud □ 70 47 15N 24 30 E
Bistriţa, R. 70 47 10N 24 30 E
Bistriţei, Munţii 70 47 15N 25 40 E
Biswan 95 27 29N 81 2 E
Bisztynek 54 54 8N 20 53 E
Bitam 124 2 5N 11 25 E
Bitche 43 48 58N 7 25 E
Bitkine 124 11 59N 18 13 E
Bitlis 92 38 20N 42 3 E
Bitola (Bitolj) 66 41 5N 21 21 E
Bitonto 65 41 7N 16 40 E
Bitter Creek 160 41 39N 108 36W
Bitter L., Gt. 122 30 15N 32 40 E
Bitter L. = Buheirat-Murrat el Kubra 122 30 15N 32 40 E
Bitterfeld 48 51 36N 12 20 E
Bitterfontein 128 31 0 S 18 32 E
Bitteroot, R. 160 46 30N 114 20W
Bitterroot Range 160 46 0N 114 20W
Bitterwater 163 36 23N 121 0W
Bitti 64 40 29N 9 20 E
Bitton 28 51 25N 2 27W
Bittou 121 11 17N 0 18W
Bitumount 152 57 26N 112 40W
Biu 121 10 40N 12 3 E
Bivolari 70 47 31N 27 27 E
Bivolu 70 47 16N 25 58 E
Biwa-Ko 111 35 15N 135 45 E
Biwabik 158 47 33N 92 19W
Biylikol, Ozero 85 43 5N 70 45 E
Biysk 76 52 40N 85 0 E
Bizana 129 30 50 S 29 52 E
Bizen 110 34 43N 134 8 E
Bizerte (Binzert) 119 37 15N 9 50 E
Bjandovan, Mys 83 39 45N 49 28 E
Bjargtangar 74 65 30N 24 30W
Bjärka-Säby 73 58 16N 15 44 E
Bjarnanes 74 64 20N 15 6W
Bjelasica 66 42 50N 19 40 E
Bjelo Polje 66 43 1N 19 45 E
Bjelovar 66 45 56N 16 49 E
Bjerringbro 73 56 23N 9 39 E
Björbo 72 60 27N 14 44 E
Björkhamre 72 61 24N 16 25 E
Björkhult 73 57 50N 15 40 E
Björneborg 72 59 14N 14 16 E
Bjuv 73 56 5N 12 55 E
Bla Bheinn 36 57 14N 6 7W
Blaby 28 52 34N 1 10W
Blace 66 43 18N 21 17 E
Blachownia 54 50 49N 18 56 E
Black Combe, mt. 32 54 16N 3 20W
Black Diamond 152 50 45N 114 14W
Black Esk R. 35 55 14N 3 13W
Black Forest = Schwarzwald 49 48 0N 8 0 E
Black Hd., Ireland 39 53 9N 9 18W
Black Hd., Antrim, U.K. 38 54 56N 5 42W
Black Hd., Cornwall, U.K. 30 50 1N 5 6W
Black Hills 158 44 0N 103 50W
Black I. 153 51 12N 96 30W
Black Island Sd. 162 41 10N 71 45W
Black Isle, Reg. 37 57 35N 4 15W
Black L., Can. 153 59 12N 105 15W
Black L., U.S.A. 156 45 28N 84 15W
Black Mesa, Mt. 159 36 57N 102 55W
Black Mt. = Mynydd Du 31 51 45N 3 45W
Black Mountain 141 30 18 S 151 39 E
Black Mts. 31 51 52N 3 5W
Black Pt. 137 34 30 S 119 25 E
Black R. 38 53 54N 7 42W
Black, R., Ark., U.S.A. 159 36 15N 90 45W
Black, R., N.Y., U.S.A. 162 43 59N 76 40W
Black, R., Wis., U.S.A. 158 44 18N 90 52W
Black, R., Vietnam = Da, R. 100 21 15N 105 20 E
Black Range, Mts. 161 33 30N 107 55W
Black River 166 18 0N 77 50W
Black Rock 140 32 50 S 138 44 E
Black Sea 21 43 30N 35 0 E
Black Volta, R. 120 9 0N 2 40W
Black Warrior, R. 157 33 0N 87 45W
Blackall 138 24 25 S 145 45 E
Blackball 143 42 22 S 171 26 E
Blackbull 138 17 55 S 141 45 E
Blackburn 32 53 44N 2 30W
Blackburn, Mt. 147 61 5N 142 3W
Blackbutt 139 26 51 S 152 6 E
Blackdown Hills 28 50 57N 3 15W
Blackduck 158 47 43N 94 32W
Blackfoot 160 43 13N 112 12W
Blackfoot, R. 160 47 0N 113 35W
Blackford 35 56 15N 3 48W
Blackie 152 50 36N 113 37W
Blackmoor Gate 30 51 9N 3 55W
Blackmoor Vale 28 50 54N 2 28W
Blackpool 32 53 48N 3 3W
Blackridge 138 22 35 S 147 35 E
Blackrock 39 53 18N 6 11W
Blacks Harbour 151 45 3N 66 49W
Blacksburg 156 37 17N 80 23W
Blacksod B. 38 54 6N 10 0W
Blacksod Pt. 38 54 7N 10 5W
Blackstairs Mt. 39 52 33N 6 50W
Blackstone 156 37 6N 78 0W
Blackstone, R. 152 61 5N 122 55W
Blackstone Ra. 137 26 00 S 129 00 E
Blackville 151 46 44N 65 50W
Blackwater, Austral. 138 23 35 S 148 53 E
Blackwater, Can. 152 53 20N 123 0W
Blackwater, Ireland 39 52 26N 6 20W
Blackwater Cr. 139 25 56 S 144 30 E
Blackwater, R., Limerick, Ireland 39 51 55N 7 50W
Blackwater, R., Meath, Ireland 38 53 40N 6 40W
Blackwater, R., Essex, U.K. 29 51 44N 0 53 E
Blackwater, R., Ulster, U.K. 38 54 31N 6 35W
Blackwater Res. 37 56 42N 4 45W
Blackwell 159 36 55N 97 20W
Blackwells Corner 163 35 37N 119 47W
Blackwood 35 55 40N 3 56W
Blackwood, C. 135 7 49 S 144 31 E
Bladel 47 51 22N 5 13 E
Bladinge 73 56 52N 14 29 E
Blädinge 73 56 52N 14 29 E
Blaenau Ffestiniog 31 53 0N 3 57W
Blaenavon 31 51 46N 3 5W
Blagaj 66 43 16N 17 55 E
Blagdon 28 51 19N 2 42W
Blagnac 44 43 38N 1 24 E
Blagodarnoye 83 45 7N 43 37 E
Blagoevgrad (Gorna Dzhumayo) 66 42 2N 23 5 E
Blagoveshchensk, Amur, U.S.S.R. 77 50 20N 127 30 E
Blagoveshchensk, Urals, U.S.S.R. 84 55 1N 55 59 E
Blagoveshchenskoye 85 43 18N 74 12 E
Blaina 31 51 46N 3 10W
Blaine 160 48 59N 122 43W
Blaine Lake 153 52 51N 106 52W
Blainville 43 48 33N 6 23 E
Blair 158 41 38N 96 10W
Blair Athol 138 22 42 S 147 31 E
Blair Atholl 37 56 46N 3 50W
Blairgowrie 37 56 36N 3 20W
Blairmore 152 49 40N 114 25W
Blaj 70 46 10N 23 57 E
Blake Pt. 158 48 12N 88 27W
Blakely 157 31 22N 85 0W
Blakeney, Glos., U.K. 28 51 45N 2 29W
Blakeney, Norfolk, U.K. 29 52 57N 1 1 E
Blâmont 43 48 35N 6 50 E
Blanc, C., Maurit. 116 20 50N 17 0W
Blanc, C., Tunisia 119 37 15N 9 56 E
Blanc, Le 44 46 37N 1 3 E
Blanc, Mont 45 45 48N 6 50 E
Blanc Sablon 151 51 24N 57 8W
Blanca, Bahía 176 39 10 S 61 30W
Blanca Peak 161 37 35N 105 29W
Blanchard 159 35 8N 97 40W
Blanche, C. 139 33 1 S 134 9 E
Blanche L., S. Austral., Austral. 139 29 15 S 139 40 E
Blanche L., W. Austral., Austral. 136 22 25 S 123 17 E
Blanco, S. Afr. 128 33 55 S 22 23 E
Blanco, U.S.A. 159 30 7N 98 30W
Blanco, C., C. Rica 166 9 34N 85 8W
Blanco, C., Peru 174 4 10 S 81 10W
Blanco, C., Spain 59 39 21N 2 51 E
Blanco, C., U.S.A. 160 42 50N 124 40W
Blanco, R. 172 31 54 S 69 42W
Blanda 74 65 20N 19 40W
Blandford Forum 28 50 52N 2 10W
Blanding 161 37 35N 109 30W
Blanes 58 41 40N 2 48 E
Blangy 43 49 14N 0 17 E
Blanice, R. 52 49 10N 14 5 E
Blankenberge 47 51 20N 3 9 E
Blankenburg 48 51 46N 10 56 E
Blanquefort 44 44 55N 0 38W
Blanquilla, La 174 11 51N 64 37W
Blanquillo 173 32 53 S 55 37W
Blansko 53 49 22N 16 40 E
Blantyre 127 15 45 S 35 0 E
Blaricum 46 52 16N 5 14 E
Blarney 39 51 57N 8 35W
Błaski 54 51 38N 18 30 E
Blatná 52 49 25N 13 52 E
Blatnitsa 67 43 41N 28 32 E
Blatten 50 46 16N 8 0 E
Blåvands Huk 75 55 33N 8 4 E
Blaydon 35 54 56N 1 47W
Blaye 44 45 8N 0 40W
Blaye-les-Mines 44 44 1N 2 8 E
Blayney 141 33 32 S 149 14 E
Blaze, Pt. 136 12 56 S 130 11 E
Błazowa 54 49 53N 22 7 E
Bleadon 28 51 18N 2 57W
Blean 29 51 18N 1 3 E
Bleasdale Moors 32 53 57N 2 40W
Bleckede 48 53 18N 10 43 E
Bled 63 46 27N 14 7 E
Blednaya, Gora 76 65 50N 65 30 E
Bléharis 47 50 31N 3 25 E
Bleiburg 52 46 35N 14 49 E
Blejeşti 70 44 19N 25 27 E
Blekinge län □ 73 56 20N 15 20 E
Blenheim 143 41 38 S 174 5 E

Bléone, R Booral

Bléone, R.	45	44 5N	6 0E
Bletchingdon	28	51 51N	1 16W
Bletchley	29	51 59N	0 44W
Bleymard, Le	44	44 30N	3 42E
Blidet Amor	119	32 59N	5 58E
Blidö	72	59 37N	18 53E
Blidsberg	73	57 56N	13 30E
Bligh Sound	143	44 47S	167 32E
Blind River	150	46 10N	82 58W
Blinishti	68	41 52N	19 58E
Blinnenhorn	51	46 26N	8 19E
Blisworth	29	52 11N	0 56W
Blitar	103	8 5S	112 11E
Blitta	121	8 23N	1 6E
Block I.	162	41 11N	71 35W
Blockley	28	52 1N	1 45W
Bloemendaal	46	52 24N	4 39E
Bloemfontein	128	29 6S	26 14E
Bloemhof	128	27 38S	25 32E
Blofield	29	52 38N	1 25E
Blois	42	47 35N	1 20E
Blokziji	46	52 43N	5 58E
Blomskog	72	59 16N	12 2E
Blonduós	74	65 40N	20 12W
Bloodsworth Is.	162	38 9N	76 3W
Bloodvein, R.	153	51 47N	96 43W
Bloody Foreland	38	55 10N	8 18W
Bloomer	158	45 8N	91 30W
Bloomfield, Iowa, U.S.A.	158	40 44N	92 26W
Bloomfield, N. Mexico, U.S.A.	161	36 46N	107 59W
Bloomfield, Nebr., U.S.A.	158	42 38N	97 15W
Bloomfield R.	138	15 56S	145 22E
Bloomingdale	162	41 33N	74 26W
Bloomington, Ill., U.S.A.	158	40 49N	89 0W
Bloomington, Ind., U.S.A.	156	39 10N	86 30W
Bloomsburg	162	41 0N	76 30W
Blora	103	6 57S	111 25E
Blossburg	162	41 40N	77 4W
Blouberg	129	23 8S	29 0E
Blountstown	157	30 28N	85 5W
Bloxham	28	52 1N	1 22W
Bludenz	52	47 10N	9 50E
Blue I.	156	41 40N	87 40W
Blue Lake	160	40 53N	124 0W
Blue Mesa Res.	161	38 30N	107 15W
Blue Mountain Lake	162	43 52N	74 30W
Blue Mountain Peak	167	18 0N	76 40W
Blue Mts., Austral.	133	33 40S	150 0E
Blue Mts., Jamaica	167	18 0N	76 40W
Blue Mts., Ore., U.S.A.	160	45 15N	119 0W
Blue Mts., Pa., U.S.A.	156	40 30N	76 0W
Blue Mud B.	138	13 30S	136 0E
Blue Nile = Nîl el Azraq	123	12 30N	34 30E
Blue Nile □ = An Nîl el Azraq □	123	12 30N	34 30E
Blue Nile, R. = Nîl el Azraq	123	10 30N	35 0E
Blue Ridge, Mts.	157	36 30N	80 15W
Blue Stack Mts.	38	54 46N	8 5W
Blueberry, R.	152	56 45N	120 49W
Bluefield	156	37 18N	81 14W
Bluefields	166	12 0N	83 50W
Bluemull Sd.	36	60 45N	1 0W
Blueskin B.	143	45 44S	170 38E
Bluff, Austral.	138	23 35S	149 4E
Bluff, N.Z.	143	46 37S	168 20E
Bluff, U.S.A.	147	64 50N	147 15W
Bluff Downs	138	19 37S	145 30E
Bluff Harbour	143	46 36S	168 21E
Bluff Knoll, Mt	137	34 24S	118 15E
Bluff Pt.	137	27 50S	114 5E
Bluffton	156	40 43N	85 9W
Blumenau	173	27 0S	49 0W
Blumenthal	48	53 5N	12 20E
Blümisalphorn	50	46 30N	7 47E
Blundeston	29	52 33N	1 42E
Blunt	158	44 32N	100 0W
Bly	160	42 23N	121 0W
Blyberg	72	61 9N	14 11E
Blyth, Austral.	140	33 49S	138 28E
Blyth, Northumberland, U.K.	35	55 8N	1 32W
Blyth, Notts., U.K.	33	53 22N	1 2W
Blyth Bridge	35	55 41N	3 22W
Blyth, R.	35	55 8N	1 30W
Blythburgh	29	52 19N	1 36E
Blythe	161	33 40N	114 33W
Blyton	33	53 25N	0 42W
Bo, Norway	71	59 25N	9 3E
Bo, S. Leone	120	7 55N	11 50W
Bo Duc	101	11 58N	106 50E
Bō-no-Misaki	110	31 15N	130 13E
Boa I.	38	54 30N	7 50W
Boa Nova	171	14 22S	40 10W
Boa Viagem	170	5 7S	39 44W
Boa Vista	174	2 48N	60 30W
Boaco	166	12 29N	85 35W
Boal	56	43 25N	6 49W
Boat of Garten	37	57 15N	3 45W
Boatman	139	27 16S	146 55E
Bobadah	141	32 19S	146 41E
Bobbili	96	18 35N	83 30E
Bóbbio	62	44 47N	9 22E
Bobcaygeon	150	44 33N	78 33W
Böblingen	57	48 41N	9 1E
Bobo-Dioulasso	120	11 8N	4 13W
Boboc	67	45 13N	26 59E
Bobolice	54	53 58N	16 37E
Boboshevo	66	42 9N	23 0E
Bobov Dol	66	42 20N	23 0E
Bóbr, R.	54	51 50N	15 15E
Bobrinets	82	48 4N	32 5E
Bobrov	81	51 5N	40 2E
Bobruysk	80	53 10N	29 15E
Bobures	174	9 15N	71 11W
Boca de Uracoa	174	9 8N	62 20W
Bôca do Acre	174	8 50S	67 27W
Bocage	41	49 0N	1 0W
Bocaiúva	171	17 7S	43 49W
Bocanda	120	7 5N	4 31W
Bocaranga	117	7 0N	15 35E
Bocas del Dragon	174	11 0N	61 50W
Bocas del Toro	166	9 15N	82 20W
Bocdam	36	59 55N	1 16W
Boceguillas	58	41 20N	3 39W
Bochnia	54	49 58N	20 27E
Bocholt, Belg.	47	51 10N	5 35E
Bocholt, Ger.	48	51 50N	6 35E
Bochov	52	50 9N	13 3E
Bochum	48	51 28N	7 12E
Bockenem	48	52 1N	10 8E
Bocoyna	164	27 52N	107 35W
Bocq, R.	47	50 20N	4 55E
Boçsa Montanŭ	66	45 21N	21 47E
Boda	124	4 19N	17 26E
Böda	73	57 15N	17 3E
Boda	74	57 15N	17 0E
Bodaybo	77	57 50N	114 0E
Boddam	37	57 28N	1 46W
Boddington	137	32 50S	116 30E
Bodedern	31	53 17N	4 29W
Bodegraven	46	52 5N	4 46E
Boden	74	65 50N	21 42E
Bodenham	28	52 9N	2 41W
Bodensee	51	47 35N	9 25E
Bodenteich	48	52 49N	10 41E
Boderg, L.	38	53 52N	8 0W
Bodhan	96	18 40N	77 55E
Bodiam	29	51 1N	0 33E
Bodinayakkanur	97	10 2N	77 10E
Bodinga	121	12 58N	5 10E
Bodinnick	30	50 20N	4 37W
Bodio	51	46 23N	8 55E
Bodmin	30	50 28N	4 44W
Bodmin Moor	30	50 33N	4 36W
Bodø	74	67 17N	14 24E
Bodrog, R.	53	48 15N	21 35E
Bodrum	92	37 5N	27 30E
Bódva, R.	53	48 19N	20 45E
Bodyke	39	52 53N	8 38W
Boechout	47	51 10N	4 30E
Boegoebergdam	128	29 7S	22 9E
Boekelo	46	52 12N	6 49E
Boelenslaan	46	53 10N	6 10E
Boën	45	45 44N	4 0E
Boende	124	0 24S	21 12E
Boerne	159	29 48N	98 41W
Boertange	46	53 1N	7 12E
Boezinge	47	50 54N	2 52E
Boffa	120	10 16N	14 3W
Bofin L.	38	53 51N	7 55W
Bofors	72	59 19N	14 34E
Bogale	98	21 16N	92 24E
Bogalusa	159	30 50N	89 55W
Bogan Gate	141	33 7S	147 49E
Bogan, R.	141	32 45S	148 8E
Bogantungan	138	23 41S	147 17E
Bogata	159	33 26N	95 10W
Bogatió	66	44 51N	19 30E
Bogdan, Mt.	67	42 37N	24 20E
Bogdanovitch	84	56 47N	62 1E
Bogenfels	125	27 25S	15 25E
Bogense	73	55 34N	10 5E
Boggabilla	139	28 36S	150 24E
Boggabri	141	30 45S	150 0E
Boggeragh Mts.	39	52 2N	8 55W
Boghari = Ksar el Boukhari	118	35 51N	2 52E
Bogia	135	4 9S	145 0E
Bognor Regis	29	50 47N	0 40W
Bogø	73	54 55N	12 2E
Bogo	103	11 3N	124 0E
Bogodukhov	80	50 9N	35 33E
Bogong, Mt.	141	36 47S	147 17E
Bogor	103	6 36S	106 48E
Bogoro	121	9 37N	9 29E
Bogoroditsk	81	53 47N	38 8E
Bogorodsk	81	56 4N	43 30E
Bogorodskoye	77	52 22N	140 30E
Bogoso	120	5 38N	2 3W
Bogotá	174	4 34N	74 0W
Bogotol	76	56 15N	89 50E
Bogra	98	24 51N	89 22E
Boguchany	77	58 40N	97 30E
Boguchar	83	49 55N	40 32E
Bogué	120	16 45N	14 10W
Boguslav	82	49 47N	30 53E
Boguszów Lubawka	54	50 43N	15 56E
Bohain	43	49 59N	3 28E
Bohemia	52	50 0N	14 0E
Bohemia Downs	136	18 53S	126 14E
Bohemian Forest = Böhmerwald	49	49 30N	12 40E
Bohena Cr.	139	30 17S	149 42E
Boheraphuca	39	53 1N	7 45W
Bohinjska Bistrica	63	46 17N	14 1E
Böhmerwald	49	49 30N	12 40E
Bohmte	48	52 24N	8 20E
Bohola	38	53 54N	9 4W
Boholl, I.	103	9 50N	124 10E
Bohotleh	91	8 20N	46 25E
Boi	121	9 35N	9 27E
Boi, Pta. de	173	23 55S	45 15W
Boiano	65	41 28N	14 29E
Boiestown	151	46 27N	66 26W
Boigu I.	138	9 15S	143 30E
Boileau, C.	136	17 40S	122 7E
Boipeba, I. de	171	13 39S	38 55W
Bois, Les	50	47 11N	6 50E
Bois, R.	171	18 35S	50 2W
Boischot	47	51 3N	4 47E
Boisdale L.	36	57 9N	7 19W
Boise	160	43 43N	116 9W
Boise City	159	36 45N	102 30W
Boissevain	153	49 15N	100 0W
Boite, R.	63	46 24N	12 13E
Boitzenburg	48	55 16N	13 36E
Boizenburg	48	53 22N	10 42E
Bojador C.	116	26 0N	14 30W
Bojanow	54	51 43N	16 42E
Bøjden	73	55 6N	10 7E
Bojnurd	93	37 30N	57 20E
Bojonegoro	103	7 11S	111 54E
Boju	121	7 22N	7 55E
Boka	66	45 22N	20 52E
Boka Kotorska	66	42 23N	18 32E
Bokala	120	8 31N	4 33W
Boké	120	10 56N	14 17W
Bokhara, R.	139	29 55S	146 42E
Bokkos	121	9 17N	9 1E
Boknafjorden	71	59 14N	5 40E
Bokombayevskoye	85	47 7N	77 0E
Bokoro	117	12 25N	17 14E
Bokote	124	0 12S	21 8E
Bokpyin	101	11 18N	98 42E
Boksitogorsk	80	59 32N	33 56E
Bokungu	124	0 35S	22 50E
Bol, Chad	124	13 30N	15 0E
Bol, Yugo.	63	43 18N	16 38E
Bolama	120	11 30N	15 30W
Bolan Pass	93	29 50N	67 20E
Bolangum	140	36 42S	142 54E
Bolaños, R.	164	22 0N	104 10W
Bolbec	42	49 30N	0 30E
Bolchereche	76	56 4N	74 45E
Boldeşti	70	45 3N	26 2E
Bole	123	6 36N	37 20E
Bolekhov	80	49 0N	24 0E
Bolesławiec	54	51 17N	15 37E
Bolgary	78	55 3N	48 50E
Bolgatanga	121	10 44N	0 53W
Bolgrad	82	45 40N	28 32E
Boli	123	6 2N	28 48E
Bolinao C.	103	16 30N	119 55E
Bolívar, Argent.	172	36 15S	60 53W
Bolívar, Antioquía, Colomb.	174	5 50N	76 1W
Bolívar, Cauca, Colomb.	174	2 0N	77 0W
Bolivar, Mo., U.S.A.	159	37 38N	93 22W
Bolivar, Tenn., U.S.A.	159	35 14N	89 0W
Bolívar □	174	9 0N	74 40W
Bolivia ■	174	17 6S	64 0W
Boljevac	66	43 51N	21 58E
Bolkhov	81	53 25N	36 0E
Bollène	45	44 18N	4 45E
Bollington	32	53 18N	2 8W
Bollnäs	72	61 21N	16 24E
Bollon	139	28 2S	147 29E
Bollstabruk	72	63 1N	17 40E
Bollullos	57	37 19N	6 32W
Bolmen	73	56 55N	13 40E
Bolney	29	50 59N	0 11W
Bolo Silase	123	8 51N	39 27E
Bolobo	124	2 6S	16 20E
Bologna	63	44 30N	11 20E
Bologne	43	48 10N	5 8E
Bologoye	80	57 55N	34 0E
Bolomba	124	0 35N	19 0E
Bolonchenticul	165	20 0N	89 49W
Bolong	103	6 6N	122 16E
Bolotovskoye	84	58 31N	62 28E
Boloven, Cao Nguyen	100	15 10N	106 30E
Bolpur	95	23 40N	87 45E
Bolsena	63	42 40N	11 58E
Bolsena, L. di	63	42 35N	11 55E
Bolshaya Glushitsa	81	52 24N	50 29E
Bolshaya Khobda, R.	84	50 50N	54 53E
Bolshaya Kinel, R.	84	53 14N	50 30E
Bolshaya Lepetrikha	82	47 11N	33 57E
Bolshaya Martynovka	83	47 12N	41 46E
Bolshaya Shatan, Gora	84	53 37N	58 3E
Bolshevik, Ostrov	77	78 30N	102 0E
Bolshezemelskaya Tundra	78	67 0N	56 0E
Bolshoi Kavkas	83	42 50N	44 0E
Bolshoi Tuters, O.	80	59 44N	26 57E
Bolshoy Atlym	76	62 25N	66 50E
Bolshoy Tokmak	82	47 16N	35 42E
Bol'soj T'uters, O.	80	59 44N	26 57E
Bolsover	33	53 14N	1 18W
Bolsward	46	53 3N	5 32E
Bolt Head	30	50 13N	3 48W
Bolt Tail	30	50 13N	3 55W
Boltaña	58	42 28N	0 4E
Boltigen	50	46 38N	7 24E
Bolton	32	53 35N	2 26W
Bolton Abbey	32	53 59N	1 53W
Bolton by Bowland	32	53 56N	2 21W
Bolton Landing	162	43 32N	73 35W
Bolton le Sands	32	54 7N	2 49W
Bolton-on-Dearne	33	53 31N	1 19W
Bolu	92	40 45N	31 35E
Bolubolu	135	9 21S	150 20E
Bolus Hd.	39	51 48N	10 20W
Bolvadin	92	38 45N	31 57E
Bolzano (Bozen)	63	46 30N	11 20E
Bom Conselho	170	9 42S	37 26W
Bom Despacho	171	19 43S	45 15W
Bom Jardim	171	7 47S	35 35W
Bom Jesus	170	9 4S	44 22W
Bom Jesus da Gurguéia, Serra	170	9 0S	43 0W
Bom Jesus da Lapa	171	13 15S	43 25W
Boma	124	5 50S	13 4E
Bomaderry	141	34 52S	150 37E
Bōmba, Khalīj	117	32 20N	23 15E
Bomba, La	164	31 53N	115 2W
Bombala	141	36 56S	149 15E
Bombarral	57	39 15N	9 9W
Bombay	96	18 55N	72 50E
Bomboma	124	2 25N	18 55E
Bombombwa	126	2 18N	19 3E
Bomi Hills	120	7 1N	10 38E
Bomili	126	1 45N	27 5E
Bomokandi, R.	126	3 10N	28 15E
Bomongo	124	1 27N	18 21E
Bomu, R.	124	4 40N	23 30E
Bon C.	119	37 1N	11 2E
Bon Sar Pa	100	12 24N	107 35E
Bonaduz	15	46 49N	9 25E
Bonaire, I.	167	12 10N	68 15W
Bonang	141	37 11S	148 41E
Bonanza	166	13 54N	84 35W
Bonaparte Archipelago	136	14 0S	124 30E
Boñar	56	42 52N	5 19W
Bonarbridge	37	57 53N	4 20W
Bonäset	72	63 16N	18 45E
Bonaventure	151	48 5N	65 32W
Bonavista	151	48 40N	53 5W
Bonavista, C.	151	48 42N	53 5W
Bonchester Bri.	35	55 23N	2 36W
Bonchurch	28	50 36N	1 11W
Bondeno	63	44 53N	11 22E
Bondo	124	3 55N	23 53E
Bondoukoro	120	9 51N	4 25W
Bondoukou	120	8 2N	2 47W
Bondowoso	120	7 56S	113 49E
Bondyug	84	60 29N	55 56E
Bone Rate, I.	103	7 25S	121 5E
Bone Rate, Kepulauan	103	6 30S	121 10E
Bone, Teluk	103	4 10S	120 50E
Bonefro	65	41 42N	14 55E
Bo'ness	35	56 0N	3 38W
Bong Son = Hoai Nhon	100	14 26N	109 1E
Bongandanga	124	1 24N	21 3E
Bonge	123	6 5N	37 16E
Bongor	117	10 35N	15 20E
Bongouanou	120	6 42N	4 15W
Bonham	159	33 30N	96 10W
Bonherden	47	51 1N	4 32E
Bonifacio	45	41 24N	9 10E
Bonifacio, Bouches de	64	41 12N	9 15E
Bonin Is.	130	27 0N	142 0E
Bonito de Santa Fé	171	7 19S	38 31W
Bonn	48	50 43N	7 6E
Bonnat	44	46 20N	1 53E
Bonne B.	151	40 31N	58 0W
Bonne Espérance, I.	151	51 24N	57 40W
Bonne Terre	159	37 55N	90 38W
Bonners Ferry	160	48 38N	116 21W
Bonnert	47	49 43N	5 49E
Bonnétable	42	48 11N	0 25E
Bonneuil Matours	42	46 41N	0 34E
Bonneville	45	46 5N	6 24E
Bonney, L.	140	37 50S	140 20E
Bonnie Doon	141	37 2S	145 53E
Bonnie Rock	137	30 29S	118 22E
Bonny, France	43	47 34N	2 50E
Bonny, Nigeria	121	4 25N	7 13E
Bonny, Bight of	121	3 30N	9 20E
Bonny, R.	121	4 20N	7 14E
Bonnyrigg	35	55 52N	3 8W
Bonnyville	153	54 20N	110 45W
Bonoi	103	1 45S	137 41E
Bonorva	64	40 25N	8 47E
Bonsall	163	33 16N	117 14W
Bontang	102	0 10N	117 30E
Bonthain	103	5 34S	119 56E
Bonthe	120	7 30N	12 33W
Bonyeri	120	5 1N	2 46W
Bonyhád	53	46 18N	18 32E
Bonython Ra.	136	23 40S	128 45E
Boogardie	137	28 2S	117 45E
Bookabie P.O.	137	31 50S	132 41E
Booker	159	36 29N	100 30W
Boolaboolka, L.	140	32 38S	143 10E
Boolarra	141	38 20S	146 20E
Boolathanna	137	21 40S	113 41E
Boolcoomata	140	31 57S	140 33E
Booleroo Centre	140	32 53S	138 21E
Booligal	141	33 58S	144 53E
Booloo Downs	137	23 52S	119 33E
Boom	47	51 6N	4 20E
Boonah	139	27 58S	152 41E
Boondall	108	27 20S	153 4E
Boone, Iowa, U.S.A.	158	42 5N	93 53W
Boone, N.C., U.S.A.	157	36 14N	81 43W
Booneville, Ark., U.S.A.	159	35 10N	93 54W
Booneville, Miss., U.S.A.	157	34 39N	88 34W
Boongoondoo	138	22 55S	145 55E
Boonville, Ind., U.S.A.	156	38 3N	87 13W
Boonville, Mo., U.S.A.	158	38 57N	92 45W
Boonville, N.Y., U.S.A.	162	43 31N	75 20W
Booral	141	32 30S	151 56E

Boorindal **Bramminge**

Boorindal	**139**	30 22 S	146 11 E
Booroomugga	**141**	31 17 S	146 27 E
Boorowa	**141**	34 28 S	148 44 E
Boot	**32**	54 24 N	3 18 W
Boothia, Gulf of	**149**	71 0 N	91 0 W
Boothia Pen.	**148**	71 0 N	94 0 W
Bootle, Cumb., U.K.	**32**	54 17 N	3 24 W
Bootle, Merseysude, U.K.	**32**	53 28 N	3 1 W
Booué	**124**	0 5 S	11 55 E
Bopeechee	**139**	29 36 S	137 22 E
Bophuthatswana □	**126**	26 0 S	26 0 E
Bopo	**79**	7 33 N	7 50 E
Boppard	**49**	50 13 N	7 36 E
Boquete	**166**	8 46 N	82 27 W
Boquillas	**164**	29 17 N	102 53 W
Bor	**52**	49 41 N	12 45 E
Bôr	**123**	6 10 N	31 40 E
Bor, Sweden	**73**	57 9 N	14 10 E
Bor, Yugo.	**66**	44 8 N	22 7 E
Borah, Mt.	**160**	44 19 N	113 46 W
Borang	**123**	4 50 N	30 59 E
Borås	**73**	57 43 N	12 56 E
Borås	**73**	57 43 N	12 56 E
Borazjan	**93**	29 22 N	51 10 E
Borba, Brazil	**174**	4 12 S	59 34 W
Borba, Port.	**57**	38 50 N	7 26 W
Borborema, Planalto da	**170**	7 0 S	37 0 W
Borçka	**83**	41 25 N	41 41 E
Borculo	**46**	52 7 N	6 31 E
Borda, C.	**140**	35 45 S	136 34 E
Bordeaux	**44**	44 50 N	0 36 W
Borden, Austral.	**137**	34 3 S	118 12 E
Borden, Can.	**151**	46 18 N	63 47 W
Borden I.	**12**	78 30 N	111 30 W
Borders □	**35**	55 45 N	2 50 W
Bordertown	**140**	36 19 S	140 45 E
Borðeyri	**74**	65 12 N	21 6 W
Bordighera	**62**	43 47 N	7 40 E
Bordj bou Arridj	**119**	36 4 N	4 45 E
Bordj Djeneiene	**119**	31 47 N	10 3 E
Bordj el Hobra	**119**	32 9 N	4 51 E
Bordj Fly Ste. Marie	**118**	27 19 N	2 32 W
Bordj-in-Eker	**119**	24 9 N	5 3 E
Bordj Ménaiel	**119**	36 46 N	3 43 E
Bordj Nili	**118**	33 28 N	3 2 E
Bordj Zelfana	**119**	32 27 N	4 15 E
Bordoba	**85**	39 31 N	73 16 E
Bordon Camp	**29**	51 6 N	0 52 W
Borea Creek	**141**	35 5 S	146 35 E
Borehamwood	**29**	51 40 N	0 15 W
Borek Wlkp.	**54**	51 54 N	17 11 E
Boreland	**35**	55 12 N	3 16 W
Boremore	**141**	33 15 S	149 0 E
Borensberg	**73**	58 34 N	15 17 E
Borgarnes	**74**	64 32 N	21 55 W
Borgefjellet	**74**	65 20 N	13 45 E
Borger, Neth.	**46**	52 54 N	6 33 E
Borger, U.S.A.	**159**	35 40 N	101 20 W
Borgerhout	**47**	51 12 N	4 28 E
Borghamn	**73**	58 23 N	14 41 E
Borgholm	**73**	56 52 N	16 39 E
Bórgia	**65**	38 50 N	16 30 E
Borgie R.	**37**	58 28 N	4 20 W
Borgo San Dalmazzo	**62**	44 19 N	7 29 E
Borgo San Lorenzo	**63**	43 57 N	11 21 E
Borgo Val di Taro	**62**	44 29 N	9 47 E
Borgomanero	**62**	45 41 N	8 28 E
Borgonovo Val Tidone	**62**	45 1 N	9 28 E
Borgorose	**63**	42 12 N	13 14 E
Borgosésia	**62**	45 43 N	8 17 E
Borgvattnet	**72**	63 26 N	15 48 E
Borhaug	**71**	58 6 N	6 33 E
Borikhane	**100**	18 33 N	103 43 E
Borisoglebsk	**81**	51 27 N	42 5 E
Borisoglebskiy	**81**	56 28 N	43 59 E
Borisov	**80**	54 17 N	28 28 E
Borisovka	**85**	43 15 N	68 10 E
Borisovo-Sudskoye	**81**	59 58 N	35 57 E
Borispol	**80**	50 21 N	30 59 E
Borja, Peru	**174**	4 20 S	77 40 W
Borja, Spain	**58**	41 48 N	1 34 W
Borjas Blancas	**58**	41 31 N	0 52 E
Borkou	**117**	18 15 N	18 50 E
Borlänge	**72**	60 29 N	15 26 E
Borley, C.	**13**	66 15 S	52 30 E
Bormida, R.	**62**	44 35 N	8 10 E
Bórmio	**62**	46 28 N	10 22 E
Born	**47**	51 2 N	5 49 E
Borna	**48**	51 8 N	12 31 E
Borndiep, Str.	**46**	53 27 N	5 35 E
Borne	**46**	52 18 N	6 46 E
Bornem	**47**	51 6 N	4 14 E
Borneo, I.	**102**	1 0 N	115 0 E
Bornholm, I.	**73**	55 10 N	15 0 E
Bornholmsgattet	**73**	55 15 N	14 20 E
Borno □	**121**	12 30 N	12 30 E
Bornos	**57**	36 48 N	5 42 W
Bornu Yassa	**121**	12 14 N	12 25 E
Borodino	**80**	55 31 N	35 40 E
Borogontsy	**77**	62 42 N	131 8 E
Boromo	**120**	11 45 N	2 58 W
Boron	**163**	35 0 N	117 39 W
Boronga Is.	**98**	19 58 N	93 6 E
Borongan	**103**	11 37 N	125 26 E
Bororen	**138**	24 13 S	151 33 E
Borotangba Mts.	**123**	6 30 N	25 0 E
Boroughbridge	**33**	54 6 N	1 23 W
Borovan	**67**	43 27 N	23 45 E
Borovichi	**80**	58 25 N	33 55 E
Borovsk, Moscow, U.S.S.R.	**81**	55 12 N	36 24 E
Borovsk, Urals, U.S.S.R.	**84**	59 43 N	56 40 E
Borovskoye	**84**	53 48 N	64 12 E
Borradaile, Mt.	**136**	12 5 S	132 51 E
Borrby	**73**	55 27 N	14 10 E
Borrego Springs	**163**	33 15 N	116 23 W
Borriol	**58**	40 4 N	0 4 W
Borris	**39**	32 36 N	6 57 W
Borris-in-Ossory	**39**	52 57 N	7 40 W
Borrisokane	**39**	53 0 N	8 8 W
Borrisoleigh	**39**	52 48 N	7 58 W
Borroloola	**138**	16 4 S	136 17 E
Borrowdale	**32**	54 31 N	3 10 W
Borsa	**70**	47 41 N	24 50 E
Borsod-Abaúj-Zemplén □	**53**	48 20 N	21 0 E
Borssele	**47**	51 26 N	3 45 E
Bort-les-Orgues	**44**	45 24 N	2 29 E
Borth	**31**	52 29 N	4 3 W
Borujerd	**92**	33 55 N	48 50 E
Borve	**36**	58 25 N	6 28 W
Borzhomi	**83**	41 48 N	43 28 E
Borzna	**80**	51 18 N	32 26 E
Borzya	**77**	50 24 N	116 31 E
Bos. Dubica	**63**	45 10 N	16 50 E
Bos. Gradiška	**66**	45 10 N	17 15 E
Bos. Grahovo	**63**	44 12 N	16 26 E
Bos. Kostajnica	**63**	45 11 N	16 33 E
Bos. Krupa	**63**	44 53 N	16 10 E
Bos. Novi	**63**	45 2 N	16 22 E
Bos. Petrovac	**63**	44 35 N	16 21 E
Bos. Samac	**66**	45 3 N	18 29 E
Bosa	**64**	40 17 N	8 32 E
Bosaga	**85**	37 33 N	65 41 E
Bosanska Brod	**66**	45 10 N	18 0 E
Bosanski Novi	**63**	45 2 N	16 22 E
Bosavi, Mt.	**135**	6 30 S	142 49 E
Bosbury	**28**	52 5 N	2 27 W
Boscastle	**30**	50 42 N	4 42 W
Boscotrecase	**65**	40 46 N	14 28 E
Bosham	**29**	50 50 N	0 51 W
Boshoek	**128**	25 30 S	27 9 E
Boshof	**128**	28 31 S	25 13 E
Boshrūyeh	**93**	33 50 N	57 30 E
Bosilegrad	**66**	42 30 N	22 27 E
Boskoop	**46**	52 4 N	4 40 E
Boskovice	**53**	49 29 N	16 40 E
Bosna i Hercegovina □	**66**	44 0 N	18 0 E
Bosna, R.	**66**	44 50 N	18 10 E
Bosnia = Bosna	**66**	44 0 N	18 0 E
Bosnik	**103**	1 5 S	136 10 E
Bōsō-Hantō	**111**	35 20 N	140 20 E
Bosobolo	**124**	4 15 N	19 50 E
Bosporus = Karadeniz Boğazı	**92**	41 10 N	29 10 E
Bossangoa	**117**	6 35 N	17 30 E
Bossekop	**74**	69 57 N	23 15 E
Bossembélé	**117**	5 25 N	17 40 E
Bossier City	**159**	32 28 N	93 38 W
Bosso	**121**	13 43 N	13 19 E
Bossut C.	**136**	18 42 S	121 35 E
Boston, U.K.	**33**	52 59 N	0 2 W
Boston, U.S.A.	**162**	42 20 N	71 0 W
Boston Bar	**152**	49 52 N	121 22 W
Bosut, R.	**66**	45 5 N	19 2 E
Boswell, Can.	**152**	49 28 N	116 45 W
Boswell, U.S.A.	**159**	34 1 N	95 30 W
Botad	**94**	22 15 N	71 40 E
Botany Bay	**139**	34 0 S	151 14 E
Botene	**100**	17 35 N	101 12 E
Botevgrad	**67**	42 55 N	23 47 E
Bothaville	**128**	27 23 S	26 34 E
Bothel	**32**	54 43 N	3 16 W
Bothnia, G. of	**74**	63 0 N	21 0 E
Bothwell	**138**	42 20 S	147 1 E
Boticas	**56**	41 41 N	7 40 W
Botletle R.	**128**	20 10 S	24 10 E
Botoroaga	**70**	44 8 N	25 32 E
Botoşani	**70**	47 42 N	26 41 E
Botoşani □	**70**	47 50 N	26 50 E
Botro	**120**	7 51 N	5 19 W
Botswana ■	**125**	22 0 S	24 0 E
Bottesford	**33**	52 57 N	0 48 W
Bottineau	**158**	48 49 N	100 25 W
Bottrop	**48**	51 34 N	6 59 E
Botucatu	**173**	22 55 S	48 30 W
Botwood	**151**	49 6 N	55 23 W
Bou Alam	**118**	33 50 N	1 26 E
Bou Ali	**118**	27 11 N	0 4 W
Bou Djébéha	**120**	18 25 N	2 45 W
Bou Garfa	**118**	27 4 N	7 59 W
Bou Guema	**118**	28 49 N	0 19 E
Bou Iblane, Djebel	**118**	33 50 N	4 0 W
Bou Ismail	**118**	36 38 N	2 42 E
Bou Izakarn	**118**	29 12 N	6 46 W
Bou Kahil, Djebel	**118**	34 22 N	9 23 E
Bou Saâda	**119**	35 11 N	4 9 E
Bou Salem	**119**	36 45 N	9 2 E
Bouaké	**120**	7 40 N	5 2 W
Bouar	**124**	6 0 N	15 40 E
Bouârfa	**118**	32 32 N	1 58 E
Bouca	**117**	6 45 N	18 25 E
Boucau	**44**	43 32 N	1 29 W
Boucaut B.	**138**	12 0 S	134 25 E
Bouches-du-Rhône □	**45**	43 37 N	5 2 E
Bouda	**118**	27 50 N	0 27 W
Boudenib	**118**	31 59 N	3 31 W
Boudry	**50**	46 57 N	6 50 E
Boufarik	**118**	36 34 N	2 58 E
Bougainville C.	**136**	13 57 S	126 4 E
Bougainville I.	**135**	6 0 S	155 0 E
Bougainville Reef	**138**	15 30 S	147 5 E
Bougaroun, C.	**119**	37 6 N	6 30 E
Bougie = Béjaïa	**119**	36 42 N	5 2 E
Bougouni	**120**	11 30 N	7 20 W
Bouillon	**47**	49 44 N	5 3 E
Bouïra	**119**	36 20 N	3 59 E
Boujad	**118**	32 46 N	6 24 W
Bouladuff	**39**	52 42 N	7 55 W
Boulder, Austral.	**132**	30 46 S	121 30 E
Boulder, Colo., U.S.A.	**158**	40 3 N	105 10 W
Boulder, Mont., U.S.A.	**160**	46 14 N	112 4 W
Boulder City	**161**	36 0 N	114 50 W
Boulder Creek	**163**	37 7 N	122 7 W
Boulder Dam = Hoover Dam	**161**	36 0 N	114 45 W
Bouleau, Lac au	**150**	47 40 N	77 35 W
Boulhaut	**118**	33 30 N	7 1 W
Boulia	**138**	22 52 S	139 51 E
Bouligny	**43**	49 17 N	5 45 E
Boulogne, R.	**42**	46 50 N	1 25 W
Boulogne-sur-Gesse	**44**	43 18 N	0 38 E
Boulogne-sur-Mer	**43**	50 42 N	1 36 E
Boulsa	**121**	12 39 N	0 34 W
Boultoum	**121**	14 45 N	10 25 E
Boumalne	**118**	31 25 N	6 0 W
Boun Neua	**100**	21 38 N	101 54 E
Boun Tai	**100**	21 23 N	101 58 E
Bouna	**120**	9 10 N	3 0 W
Boundary	**147**	64 11 N	141 2 W
Boundary Pk.	**163**	37 51 N	118 21 W
Boundiali	**120**	9 30 N	6 20 W
Bountiful	**160**	40 57 N	111 58 W
Bounty I.	**130**	46 0 S	180 0 E
Bour Khaya	**77**	71 50 N	133 10 E
Bourbon-l'Archambault	**44**	46 36 N	3 4 E
Bourbon-Lancy	**44**	46 37 N	3 45 E
Bourbonnais	**44**	46 28 N	3 0 E
Bourbonne	**43**	47 59 N	5 45 E
Bourem	**121**	17 0 N	0 24 W
Bourg	**44**	45 3 N	0 34 W
Bourg-Argental	**45**	45 18 N	4 32 E
Bourg-de-Péage	**45**	45 2 N	5 3 E
Bourg-en-Bresse	**45**	46 13 N	5 12 E
Bourg-St.-Andéol	**45**	44 23 N	4 39 E
Bourg-St.-Maurice	**45**	45 35 N	6 46 E
Bourg-St.-Pierre	**50**	45 57 N	7 12 E
Bourganeuf	**44**	45 57 N	1 45 E
Bourges	**43**	47 9 N	2 25 E
Bourget, L. du	**45**	45 44 N	5 52 E
Bourgneuf	**42**	47 2 N	1 58 W
Bourgneuf, B. de	**42**	47 3 N	2 10 W
Bourgneuf, Le	**42**	48 10 N	0 59 W
Bourgogne	**43**	47 0 N	4 30 E
Bourgoin-Jallieu	**45**	45 36 N	5 17 E
Bourke	**139**	30 8 S	145 55 E
Bourlamaque	**150**	48 5 N	77 56 W
Bourne	**29**	52 46 N	0 22 W
Bournemouth	**28**	50 43 N	1 53 W
Bourriot-Bergonce	**44**	44 7 N	0 14 W
Bourton-on-the-Water	**28**	51 53 N	1 45 W
Bouscat, Le	**44**	44 53 N	0 32 W
Boussac	**44**	46 22 N	2 13 E
Boussens	**44**	43 12 N	0 58 E
Bousso	**117**	10 34 N	16 52 E
Boussu	**47**	50 26 N	3 48 E
Bouthillier, Le	**151**	47 47 N	64 55 W
Boutilimit	**120**	17 45 N	14 40 W
Bouvet I.	**15**	55 0 S	3 30 E
Bouznika	**118**	33 46 N	7 6 W
Bouzonville	**43**	49 17 N	6 32 E
Bova Marina	**65**	37 59 N	15 56 E
Bovalino Marina	**65**	38 9 N	16 10 E
Bovec	**63**	46 20 N	13 33 E
Bovenkarspel	**46**	52 41 N	5 14 E
Bòves	**62**	44 19 N	7 29 E
Boves	**62**	44 19 N	7 33 E
Bovey Tracey	**30**	50 36 N	3 40 W
Bovigny	**47**	50 12 N	5 55 E
Bovill	**160**	46 58 N	116 27 W
Bovino	**65**	41 15 N	15 20 E
Bow Island	**152**	49 50 N	111 23 W
Bow, R.	**152**	51 10 N	115 0 W
Bowbells	**158**	48 47 N	102 19 W
Bowdle	**158**	45 30 N	100 2 W
Bowelling	**137**	33 25 S	116 30 E
Bowen	**138**	20 0 S	148 16 E
Bowen Mts.	**141**	37 0 S	148 0 E
Bowen, R.	**138**	20 24 S	147 20 E
Bowes	**32**	54 31 N	1 59 W
Bowie, U.S.A.	**162**	39 0 N	76 47 W
Bowie, Ariz., U.S.A.	**161**	32 15 N	109 30 W
Bowie, Tex., U.S.A.	**159**	33 33 N	97 50 W
Bowland, Forest of	**32**	54 0 N	2 30 W
Bowling Green, Ky., U.S.A.	**156**	37 0 N	86 25 W
Bowling Green, Ohio, U.S.A.	**156**	41 22 N	83 40 W
Bowling Green, Va., U.S.A.	**162**	38 3 N	77 21 W
Bowling Green, C.	**138**	19 19 S	147 25 E
Bowman	**158**	46 12 N	103 21 W
Bowman, I.	**13**	65 0 S	104 0 E
Bowmans	**140**	34 10 S	138 17 E
Bowmanville	**150**	43 55 N	78 41 W
Bowmore	**34**	55 45 N	6 18 W
Bowness, Can.	**152**	50 55 N	114 25 W
Bowness, Solway, U.K.	**32**	54 57 N	3 13 W
Bowness, Windermere, U.K.	**32**	54 22 N	2 56 W
Bowral	**141**	34 26 S	150 27 E
Bowraville	**139**	30 37 S	152 52 E
Bowron, R.	**152**	54 3 N	121 50 W
Bowser L.	**152**	56 30 N	129 30 W
Bowsman	**153**	52 14 N	101 12 W
Bowutu Mts.	**135**	7 45 S	147 10 E
Bowwood	**127**	17 5 S	26 20 E
Box	**28**	51 24 N	2 16 W
Box Hill	**29**	51 16 N	0 16 W
Boxelder Creek	**160**	47 20 N	108 30 W
Boxholm	**73**	58 12 N	15 3 E
Boxley	**29**	51 17 N	0 34 E
Boxmeer	**47**	51 38 N	5 56 E
Boxtel	**47**	51 36 N	5 9 E
Boyabat	**82**	41 28 N	34 42 E
Boyacá □	**174**	5 30 N	72 30 W
Boyanup	**137**	33 30 S	115 40 E
Boyce	**159**	31 25 N	92 39 W
Boyd L.	**150**	61 30 N	103 20 W
Boyer, R.	**152**	58 27 N	115 57 W
Boyle	**38**	53 58 N	8 19 W
Boyne City	**156**	45 13 N	85 1 W
Boyne, R.	**38**	53 40 N	6 34 W
Boynton Beach	**157**	26 31 N	80 3 W
Boyoma, Chutes	**124**	0 12 N	25 25 E
Boyup Brook	**137**	33 50 S	116 23 E
Bozburun	**69**	36 43 N	28 8 E
Bozcaada	**68**	39 49 N	26 3 E
Bozeat	**29**	52 14 N	0 41 W
Bozeman	**160**	45 40 N	111 0 W
Bozepole Wlk.	**54**	54 33 N	17 56 E
Bozevac	**66**	44 32 N	21 24 E
Bozouls	**44**	44 28 N	2 43 E
Bozoum	**117**	6 25 N	16 35 E
Bozovici	**70**	44 56 N	22 1 E
Bra	**62**	44 41 N	7 50 E
Brabant □	**47**	50 46 N	4 30 E
Brabant L.	**153**	54 18 N	108 5 W
Brabrand	**73**	56 9 N	10 7 E
BraC	**63**	43 20 N	16 40 E
Bracadale	**36**	57 22 N	6 24 W
Bracadale, L.	**36**	57 20 N	6 30 W
Bracciano	**63**	42 6 N	12 10 E
Bracciano, L. di	**63**	42 8 N	12 11 E
Bracebridge	**150**	45 2 N	79 19 W
Bracebridge Heath	**33**	53 13 N	0 32 W
Brach	**119**	27 31 N	14 20 E
Bracieux	**43**	47 30 N	1 30 E
Bräcke	**72**	62 45 N	15 26 E
Brackettville	**159**	29 21 N	100 20 W
Brackley	**28**	52 3 N	1 9 W
Bracknell	**29**	51 24 N	0 45 W
Braco	**35**	56 16 N	3 55 W
Brad	**70**	46 10 N	22 50 E
Brădano, R.	**65**	40 41 N	16 20 E
Bradda Hd.	**32**	54 6 N	4 46 W
Bradenton	**157**	27 25 N	82 35 W
Bradford, U.K.	**33**	53 47 N	1 45 W
Bradford, Pa., U.S.A.	**156**	41 58 N	78 41 W
Bradford, Vt., U.S.A.	**162**	43 59 N	72 9 W
Bradford-on-Avon	**28**	51 20 N	2 15 W
Brading	**28**	50 41 N	1 9 W
Bradley, Ark., U.S.A.	**159**	33 7 N	93 39 W
Bradley, Calif., U.S.A.	**163**	35 52 N	120 48 W
Bradley, S.D., U.S.A.	**158**	45 10 N	97 40 W
Bradley Institute	**127**	17 7 S	31 25 E
Bradore Bay	**151**	51 27 N	57 18 W
Bradshaw	**136**	15 21 S	130 16 E
Bradwell-on-Sea	**29**	51 44 N	0 55 E
Bradworthy	**30**	50 54 N	4 22 W
Brady	**159**	31 8 N	99 25 W
Brae	**36**	60 23 N	1 20 W
Brae, oilfield	**19**	58 45 N	1 18 E
Brædstrup	**73**	55 58 N	9 37 E
Braemar, Queens., Austral.	**139**	25 35 S	152 20 E
Braemar, S. Austral., Austral.	**140**	33 12 S	139 35 E
Braemar, U.K.	**37**	57 2 N	3 20 W
Braemar, dist.	**37**	57 2 N	3 20 W
Braemore, Grampian, U.K.	**37**	58 16 N	3 33 W
Braemore, Highland, U.K.	**36**	57 45 N	5 2 W
Braeriach Mt.	**37**	57 4 N	3 44 W
Braga	**56**	41 35 N	8 25 W
Braga □	**56**	41 30 N	8 30 W
Bragado	**172**	35 2 S	60 27 W
Bragança, Brazil	**170**	1 0 S	47 2 W
Bragança, Port.	**56**	41 48 N	6 50 W
Bragança □	**56**	41 30 N	6 45 W
Bragança Paulista	**173**	22 55 S	46 32 W
Brahmanbaria	**98**	23 50 N	91 15 E
Brahmani, R.	**96**	21 0 N	85 15 E
Brahmaputra, R.	**98**	26 30 N	93 30 E
Brahmaur	**93**	32 28 N	76 32 E
Braich-y-Pwll	**31**	52 47 N	4 46 W
Braidwood	**141**	35 27 S	149 49 E
Brailsford	**33**	52 58 N	1 35 W
Braine-l'Alleud	**47**	50 42 N	4 23 E
Braine-le-Comte	**47**	50 37 N	4 8 E
Brainerd	**158**	46 20 N	94 10 W
Braintree, U.K.	**29**	51 53 N	0 34 E
Braintree, U.S.A.	**162**	42 11 N	71 0 W
Braithwaite Pt.	**138**	12 5 S	133 50 E
Brak, R.	**128**	29 50 S	23 10 E
Brake	**48**	53 19 N	8 30 E
Brakel	**46**	51 49 N	5 5 E
Bräkne-Hoby	**73**	56 12 N	15 8 E
Bräkne-Hoby	**73**	56 14 N	15 6 E
Brakpan	**129**	26 13 S	28 20 E
Brakwater	**128**	22 28 S	17 3 E
Brålanda	**73**	58 34 N	12 21 E
Brålanda	**73**	58 34 N	12 21 E
Brăila	**70**	45 19 N	27 59 E
Brăila □	**70**	45 5 N	27 30 E
Bralorne	**152**	50 50 N	123 15 W
Bramford	**29**	52 5 N	1 6 E
Bramminge	**73**	55 28 N	8 42 E

Bramon Brøttum

Bramon 72 62 14N 17 40 E
Brampton, Can. 150 43 45N 79 45W
Brampton, Cambs., U.K. 29 52 19N 0 13W
Brampton, Cumb., U.K. 32 54 56N 2 43W
Bramsche 48 52 25N 7 58 E
Bramshott 29 51 5N 0 47W
Bramwell 138 12 8 S 142 37 E
Brancaster 29 52 58N 0 40 E
Branco, Cabo 170 7 9 S 34 47W
Branco, R. 174 0 0 61 15W
Brande 73 55 57N 9 8 E
Brandenburg 48 52 24N 12 33 E
Brander, Pass of 34 56 25N 5 10W
Branderburgh 37 57 43N 3 17W
Brandfort 128 28 40 S 26 30 E
Brandon, Can. 153 49 50N 99 57W
Brandon, Durham, U.K. 33 54 46N 1 37W
Brandon, Suffolk, U.K. 29 52 27N 0 37 E
Brandon, U.S.A. 156 43 48N 73 4W
Brandon, U.S.A. 162 44 2N 73 5W
Brandon B. 39 52 17N 10 8W
Brandon, Mt. 39 52 15N 10 15W
Brandon Pt. 39 52 18N 10 10W
Brandsen 172 35 10 S 58 15W
Brandval 71 60 19N 12 1 E
Brandvlei 128 30 25 S 20 30 E
Brandýs 52 50 10N 14 40 E
Branford 162 41 15N 72 48W
Braniewo 54 54 25N 19 50 E
Brännarp 73 56 46N 12 38 E
Bransby 139 28 10 S 142 0 E
Bransfield Str. 13 63 0 S 59 0W
Branson, Colo., U.S.A. 159 37 4N 103 53W
Branson, Mo., U.S.A. 159 36 40N 93 18W
Branston 33 53 13N 0 28W
Brantford 150 43 15N 80 15W
Brantôme 44 45 22N 0 39 E
Branxholme 140 37 52 S 141 49 E
Branxton 141 32 38 S 151 21 E
Branzi 62 46 0N 9 46 E
Bras d'or, L. 151 45 50N 60 50W
Brasiléia 174 11 0 S 68 45W
Brasília 171 15 47 S 47 55 E
Braslav 80 55 38N 27 0 E
Braslovče 63 46 21N 15 3 E
Braşov 70 45 38N 25 35 E
Braşov □ 70 45 45N 25 15 E
Brass 121 4 35N 6 14 E
Brass, R. 121 4 15N 6 13 E
Brasschaat 47 51 19N 4 27 E
Brassey, Barisan 102 5 0N 117 15 E
Brassey Ra. 137 25 8 S 122 15 E
Brasstown Bald, Mt. 157 34 54N 83 45W
Brassus, Le 50 46 35N 6 13 E
Brasted 29 51 16N 0 8 E
Bratislava 53 48 10N 17 7 E
Bratsk 77 56 10N 101 30 E
Bratteborg 73 57 37N 14 4 E
Brattleboro 162 42 53N 72 37W
Brattvær 71 63 25N 7 48 E
Braţul Chilia, R. 70 45 25N 29 20 E
Braţul Sfîntu Gheorghe, R. 70 45 0N 29 20 E
Braţul Sulina, R. 70 45 10N 29 20 E
Bratunac 66 44 13N 19 21 E
Braunau 52 48 15N 13 3 E
Braunschweig 48 52 17N 10 28 E
Braunton 30 51 6N 4 9W
Brava 91 1 20N 44 8 E
Bråvikeh 72 58 38N 16 32 E
Bravo del Norte, R. 164 30 30N 105 0W
Brawley 163 32 58N 115 30W
Bray, France 43 49 15N 1 40 E
Bray, Ireland 39 53 12N 6 6W
Bray, U.K. 29 51 30N 0 42W
Bray Hd. 39 51 52N 10 26W
Bray, Mt. 138 14 0N 134 30 E
Bray-sur-Seine 43 48 25N 3 14 E
Brazeau, R. 152 52 55N 115 14W
Brazil 156 39 30N 87 8W
Brazil ■ 174 5 0N 20 0W
Brazilian Highlands 170 18 0 S 46 30W
Brazo Sur, R. 172 25 30 S 58 0W
Brazos, R. 159 30 30N 96 20W
Brazzaville 124 4 9 S 15 12 E
Brčko 66 44 54N 18 46 E
Breadalbane, Austral. 138 23 50 S 139 35 E
Breadalbane, U.K. 34 56 30N 4 15W
Breaden, L. 137 25 51 S 125 28 E
Breage 30 50 6N 5 17W
Breaksea Sd. 143 45 35 S 166 35 E
Bream Bay 142 35 56 S 174 28 E
Bream Head 142 35 51 S 174 36 E
Bream Tail 142 36 3 S 174 36 E
Breamish, R. 35 55 30N 1 55W
Breas 172 25 29 S 70 24W
Brebes 103 6 52 S 109 3 E
Brechin 37 56 44N 2 40W
Brecht 47 51 21N 4 38 E
Breckenridge, Colo., U.S.A. 160 39 30N 106 2W
Breckenridge, Minn., U.S.A. 158 46 20N 96 36W
Breckenridge, Tex., U.S.A. 159 32 48N 98 55W
Breckland 23 52 30N 0 40 E
Brecknock (□) 26 51 58N 3 25W
Břeclav 53 48 46N 16 53 E
Brecon 31 51 57N 3 23W
Brecon Beacons 31 51 53N 3 27W
Breda 47 51 35N 4 45 E
Bredaryd 73 57 10N 13 45 E
Bredasdorp 128 34 33 S 20 2 E
Bredbo 141 35 58 S 149 10 E
Brede 29 50 56N 0 37 E
Bredene 47 51 14N 2 59 E
Bredon Hill 28 52 3N 2 2W
Bredy 84 52 26N 60 21 E
Bree 47 51 8N 5 35 E
Breezand 46 52 53N 4 49 E
Bregalnica, R. 66 41 50N 22 20 E
Bregenz 52 47 30N 9 45 E
Bregning 73 56 8N 8 30 E
Bréhal 42 48 53N 1 30W
Bréhat, I. de 42 48 51N 3 0W
Breiðafjörður 74 65 15N 23 15W
Breil 45 43 56N 7 31 E
Breisach 49 48 2N 7 37 E
Brejinho de Nazaré 170 11 1 S 48 34W
Brejo 170 3 41 S 42 47W
Brekke 71 61 1N 5 26 E
Bremangerlandet 71 61 51N 5 0 E
Bremangerpollen 71 61 51N 5 0 E
Bremen 48 53 4N 8 47 E
Bremen □ 48 53 6N 8 46 E
Bremer I. 138 12 5 S 136 45 E
Bremerhaven 48 53 34N 8 35 E
Bremerton 160 47 30N 122 38W
Bremervörde 48 53 28N 9 10 E
Bremgarten 51 47 21N 8 21 E
Bremnes 71 59 47N 5 8 E
Bremsnes 71 63 6N 7 40 E
Brendon Hills 28 51 6N 3 25W
Brenes 57 37 32N 5 54W
Brenham 159 30 5N 96 27W
Brenner Pass 52 47 0N 11 30 E
Breno 62 45 57N 10 20 E
Brent, Can. 150 46 2N 78 29W
Brent, U.K. 29 51 33N 0 18W
Brent, oil and gasfield 19 61 0N 1 45 E
Brenta, R. 63 45 11N 12 18 E
Brentwood, U.K. 29 51 37N 0 19W
Brentwood, U.S.A. 163 37 55N 121 42W
Bréscia 65 45 33N 10 13 E
Breskens 47 51 23N 3 33 E
Breslau = Wrocław. 54 51 5N 17 5 E
Bresle, R. 43 50 4N 1 21 E
Bresles 43 49 25N 2 13 E
Bressanone 63 46 43N 11 40 E
Bressay 36 60 10N 1 6W
Bressay I. 36 60 10N 1 5W
Bressay Sd. 36 60 8N 1 10W
Bresse, La 43 48 0N 6 53 E
Bresse, Plaine de 43 46 20N 5 10 E
Bressuire 42 46 51N 0 30W
Brest, France 42 48 24N 4 31W
Brest, U.S.S.R. 80 52 10N 23 40 E
Bretagne 42 48 0N 3 0W
Bretçu 70 46 7N 26 18 E
Breteuil 43 49 38N 2 18 E
Breton 152 53 7N 114 28W
Breton Sd. 159 29 40N 89 12W
Brett, C. 142 35 10 S 174 20 E
Bretten 49 49 2N 8 43 E
Bretuil 42 48 50N 0 53 E
Breukelen 46 52 10N 5 0 E
Brevard 157 35 19N 82 42W
Breves 170 1 40 S 50 29W
Brevik 71 59 4N 9 42 E
Brewarrina 139 30 0 S 146 51 E
Brewer 151 44 43N 68 50W
Brewer, Mt. 163 36 44N 118 28W
Brewerton 162 43 14N 76 9W
Brewood 28 52 41N 2 10W
Brewster, N.Y., U.S.A. 162 41 23N 73 37W
Brewster, Wash., U.S.A. 160 48 10N 119 51W
Brewster, Kap 12 70 7N 22 0W
Brewton 157 31 9N 87 2W
Breyten 129 26 16 S 30 0 E
Breytovo 81 58 18N 37 50 E
Brézina 118 33 4N 1 14 E
Březnice 52 49 32N 13 57 E
Breznik 66 42 44N 22 50 E
Brezno 53 48 50N 19 40 E
Bria 117 6 30N 21 58 E
Briançon 45 44 54N 6 39 E
Briare 43 47 38N 2 45 E
Bribbaree 141 34 10 S 147 51 E
Bribie I. 139 27 0 S 152 58 E
Brickaville 129 18 49 S 49 4 E
Bricon 43 48 5N 5 0 E
Bricquebec 42 49 29N 1 39W
Bride 32 54 24N 4 23W
Bridestowe 30 50 41N 4 7W
Bridge 29 51 14N 1 8 E
Bridge of Allan 35 56 9N 3 57W
Bridge of Don 37 57 10N 2 8W
Bridge of Earn 35 56 20N 3 25W
Bridge of Orchy 34 56 29N 4 48W
Bridge of Weir 34 55 51N 4 35W
Bridge, R. 152 50 50N 122 40W
Bridgehampton 162 40 56N 72 18W
Bridgend, Islay, U.K. 34 55 46N 6 15W
Bridgend, Mid Glam., U.K. 31 51 30N 3 35W
Bridgeport, Calif., U.S.A. 163 38 14N 119 15W
Bridgeport, Conn., U.S.A. 162 41 12N 73 12W
Bridgeport, Nebr., U.S.A. 158 41 42N 103 10W
Bridgeport, Tex., U.S.A. 159 33 15N 97 45W
Bridger 160 45 20N 108 58W
Bridgeton 162 39 29N 75 10W
Bridgetown, Austral. 137 33 58 S 116 7 E
Bridgetown, Barbados 167 13 0N 59 30W
Bridgetown, Can. 151 44 55N 65 18W
Bridgetown, Ireland 39 52 13N 6 33W
Bridgeville 162 38 45N 75 36W
Bridgewater, Austral. 140 36 36 S 143 59 E
Bridgewater, Can. 151 44 25N 64 31W
Bridgewater, Mass., U.S.A. 162 41 59N 70 56W
Bridgewater, N.Y., U.S.A. 162 42 58N 75 15W
Bridgewater, S.D., U.S.A. 158 43 34N 97 29W
Bridgewater, C. 140 38 23 S 141 23 E
Bridgnorth 28 52 33N 2 25W
Bridgwater 28 51 7N 3 0W
Bridgwater B. 28 51 15N 3 15W
Bridlington 33 54 6N 0 11W
Bridlington B. 33 54 4N 0 10W
Bridport, Austral. 138 40 59 S 147 23 E
Bridport, U.K. 28 50 43N 2 45W
Brie-Comte-Robert 43 48 40N 2 35 E
Brie, Plaine de 43 48 35N 3 10 E
Briec 42 48 6N 4 0W
Brielle 46 51 54N 4 10 E
Brienne-le-Château 43 48 24N 4 30 E
Brienon 43 48 0N 3 35 E
Brienz 50 46 46N 8 2 E
Brienzersee 50 46 44N 7 53 E
Brierfield 32 53 49N 2 15W
Brierley Hill 28 52 29N 2 7W
Briey 43 49 14N 5 57 E
Brig 50 46 18N 7 59 E
Brigantine 162 39 24N 74 22W
Brigg 33 53 33N 0 30W
Briggsdale 158 40 40N 104 20W
Brigham City 160 41 30N 112 1W
Brighouse 33 53 42N 1 47W
Brighstone 29 50 38N 1 36W
Bright 141 36 42 S 146 56 E
Brightlingsea 29 51 49N 1 1 E
Brighton, Austral. 140 35 5 S 138 30 E
Brighton, Can. 150 44 2N 77 44W
Brighton, U.K. 29 50 50N 0 9W
Brighton, U.S.A. 158 39 59N 104 50W
Brightstone 28 50 38N 1 23W
Brightwater 143 41 22 S 173 9 E
Brignogan-Plage 42 48 40N 4 20W
Brignoles 45 43 25N 6 5 E
Brigstock 29 52 27N 0 38W
Brihuega 58 40 45N 2 52W
Brikama 120 13 15N 16 45W
Brill 28 51 49N 1 3W
Brilliant 152 49 19N 117 38W
Brilon 48 51 23N 8 32 E
Brim 140 36 3 S 142 27 E
Brimfield 28 52 18N 2 42W
Bríndisi 65 40 39N 17 55 E
Brinkley 159 34 55N 91 15W
Brinklow 28 52 25N 1 22W
Brinkworth, Austral. 140 33 42 S 138 26 E
Brinkworth, U.K. 28 51 33N 1 59W
Brinyan 37 59 8N 3 0W
Brion I. 151 47 46N 61 26W
Brionne 42 49 11N 0 43 E
Brionski, I. 63 44 55N 13 45 E
Brioude 44 45 18N 3 23 E
Briouze 42 48 42N 0 23W
Brisbane 139 27 25 S 153 2 E
Brisbane, R. 139 27 24 S 153 9 E
Brisignella 63 44 14N 11 46 E
Bristol, U.K. 28 51 26N 2 35W
Bristol, Conn., U.S.A. 162 41 44N 72 57W
Bristol, Pa., U.S.A. 162 40 6N 74 52W
Bristol, R.I., U.S.A. 162 41 40N 71 15W
Bristol, S.D., U.S.A. 158 45 25N 97 43W
Bristol B. 147 58 0N 160 0W
Bristol Channel 30 51 18N 4 30W
Bristol I. 13 58 45 S 28 0W
Bristol L. 161 34 23N 116 0W
Briston 29 52 52N 1 4 E
Bristow 159 35 5N 96 28W
British Antarctic Territory 13 66 0 S 45 0W
British Columbia □ 152 55 0N 125 15W
British Guiana = Guyana 174 5 0N 59 0W
British Honduras = Belize 165 17 0N 88 30W
British Isles 16 55 0N 4 0W
Briton Ferry 31 51 37N 3 50W
Brits 129 25 37 S 27 48 E
Britstown 128 30 37 S 23 30 E
Britt 150 45 46N 80 34W
Brittany = Bretagne 42 48 0N 3 0W
Brittas 39 53 14N 6 29W
Brittatorp 73 57 3N 14 58 E
Britton 158 45 50N 97 47W
Brive-la-Gaillarde 44 45 10N 1 32 E
Briviesca 58 42 32N 3 19W
Brixham 30 50 24N 3 31W
Brixton 138 23 32 S 144 57 E
Brixworth 29 52 20N 0 54W
Brize Norton 28 51 46N 1 35W
Brlik, U.S.S.R. 76 44 0N 74 5 E
Brlik, Kazakh S.S.R., U.S.S.R. 85 44 5N 73 31 E
Brlik, Kazakh S.S.R., U.S.S.R. 85 43 40N 73 49 E
Brno 53 49 10N 16 35 E
Bro 72 59 13N 13 2 E
Broach = Bharuch 96 21 47N 73 0 E
Broad Arrow 137 30 23 S 121 15 E
Broad B. 36 58 14N 6 16W
Broad Chalke 28 51 2N 1 54W
Broad Clyst 30 50 46N 3 27W
Broad Haven, Ireland 38 54 20N 9 55W
Broad Haven, U.K. 31 51 46N 5 6W
Broad Law, Mt. 35 55 30N 3 22W
Broad, R. 157 34 30N 81 26W
Broad Sd., Austral. 138 22 0 S 149 45 E
Broad Sd., U.K. 30 49 56N 6 19W
Broadalbin 162 43 3N 74 12W
Broadford, Austral. 141 37 14 S 145 4 E
Broadford, Clare, Ireland 39 52 48N 8 38W
Broadford, Limerick, Ireland 39 52 21N 8 59W
Broadford, U.K. 36 57 14N 5 55W
Broadhembury 30 50 49N 3 16W
Broadhurst Ra. 136 22 30 S 122 30 E
Broads, The 29 52 45N 1 30 E
Broadsound Ra. 133 22 50 S 149 30 E
Broadstairs 29 51 21N 1 28 E
Broadus 158 45 28N 105 27W
Broadview 153 50 22N 102 35W
Broadway, Ireland 39 52 13N 6 23W
Broadway, U.K. 28 52 2N 1 51W
Broadwindsor 28 50 49N 2 49W
Broager 73 54 53N 9 40 E
Broaryd 73 57 7N 13 15 E
Brochet, Man., Can. 153 57 53N 101 40W
Brochet, Manitoba, Can. 153 57 55N 101 40W
Brochet, Québec, Can. 150 47 12N 72 42W
Brochet, L. 153 58 36N 101 35W
Brock 153 51 26N 108 43W
Brocken 48 51 48N 10 40 E
Brockenhurst 28 50 49N 1 34W
Brocklehurst 141 32 9 S 148 38 E
Brockman Mt. 137 22 25 S 117 15 E
Brockville 150 44 35N 75 41W
Brockway 158 47 18N 105 46W
Brockworth 28 51 51N 2 9W
Brod 66 41 35N 21 17 E
Brodarevo 66 43 14N 19 44 E
Brodeur Pen. 149 72 30N 88 10W
Brodick 34 55 34N 5 9W
Brodnica 54 53 15N 19 25 E
Brodokalmak 84 55 35N 62 6 E
Brody 80 50 5N 25 10 E
Broechem 47 51 11N 4 38 E
Broek 46 52 26N 5 0 E
Broek op Langedijk 46 52 41N 4 49 E
Brogan 160 44 14N 117 32W
Broglie 42 49 0N 0 30 E
Brok 54 52 43N 21 52 E
Broke Inlet 137 34 55 S 116 25 E
Broken Bank, gasfield 19 53 20N 2 4 E
Broken Bow, Nebr., U.S.A. 158 41 25N 99 35W
Broken Bow, Okla., U.S.A. 159 34 2N 94 43W
Broken Hill 140 31 58 S 141 29 E
Broken Hill = Kabwe 127 14 27 S 28 28 E
Brokind 73 58 13N 15 42 E
Bromborough 32 53 20N 3 0W
Bromham 28 51 23N 2 3W
Bromhead 153 49 18N 103 40W
Bromley 29 51 20N 0 5 E
Bromölla 73 56 5N 14 28 E
Brompton 33 54 22N 1 25W
Bromsgrove 28 52 20N 2 3W
Bromyard 28 52 12N 2 30W
Brønderslev 73 57 16N 9 57 E
Brong Ahafo 120 7 50N 2 0 E
Bronkhorstspruit 129 25 46 S 28 45 E
Bronnitsy 81 55 27N 38 10 E
Bronte, Italy 65 37 48N 14 49 E
Bronte, U.S.A. 159 31 54N 100 18W
Bronte Park 138 42 8 S 146 30 E
Brookeborough 38 54 19N 7 23W
Brookfield 158 39 50N 93 4W
Brookhaven 159 31 40N 90 25W
Brookings, Oreg., U.S.A. 160 42 4N 124 10W
Brookings, S.D., U.S.A. 158 44 20N 96 45W
Brooklands 138 18 5 S 144 0 E
Brookmere 152 49 52N 120 53W
Brooks 152 50 35N 111 55W
Brooks B. 152 50 15N 127 55W
Brooks L. 153 61 55N 106 35W
Brooks Ra. 147 68 40N 147 0W
Brooksville 157 28 32N 82 21W
Brookton 137 32 22 S 116 57 E
Brookville 156 39 25N 85 0W
Brooloo 139 26 30 S 152 43 E
Broom, L. 36 57 55N 5 15W
Broome 136 18 0 S 122 15 E
Broomehill 137 31 51 S 117 39 E
Broomfield 28 51 46N 0 28 E
Broomhill 35 55 19N 1 36W
Broons 42 48 20N 2 16W
Brora 37 58 0N 3 50W
Brora L. 37 58 3N 3 58W
Brora, R. 37 58 4N 3 52W
Brosarp 73 55 44N 14 8 E
Brösarp 73 55 43N 14 6 E
Broseley 28 52 36N 2 30W
Brosna, R. 39 53 8N 8 0W
Broşteni 70 47 14N 25 43 E
Brotas de Macaúbas 171 12 0 S 42 38W
Brothers 160 43 56N 120 39W
Brothertoft 33 53 0N 0 5W
Brotton 33 54 34N 0 55W
Brøttum 71 61 2N 10 34 E

Brough Bura

Brough, Cumbria, U.K. 32 54 32N 2 19W
Brough, Humberside, U.K. 33 53 44N 0 35W
Brough Hd. 37 59 8N 3 20W
Broughams Gate 140 30 51 S 140 59 E
Broughshane 38 54 54N 6 12W
Broughton, Austral. 138 20 10 S 146 20 E
Broughton, Borders, U.K. 35 55 37N 3 25W
Broughton, Humberside, U.K. 33 53 33N 0 36W
Broughton, Northampton, U.K. 29 52 22N 0 45W
Broughton, Yorkshire, U.K. 33 54 26N 1 8W
Broughton-in-Furness 32 54 17N 3 12W
Broughty Ferry 35 56 29N 2 50W
Broumov 53 50 35N 16 20 E
Brouwershaven 46 51 45N 3 55 E
Brouwershavensche Gat 46 51 46N 3 50 E
Brovary 80 50 34N 30 48 E
Brovst 73 57 6N 9 31 E
Browerville 158 46 3N 94 50W
Brown, Mt. 140 32 30 S 138 0 E
Brown, Pt. 139 32 32 S 133 50 E
Brown Willy, Mt. 30 50 35N 4 34W
Brownfield 159 33 10N 102 15W
Browngrove 38 53 33N 8 49W
Brownhills 28 52 38N 1 57W
Browning 160 48 35N 113 10W
Brownlee 153 50 43N 106 1W
Browns Bay 142 36 40 S 174 40 E
Brownstown Hd. 39 52 8N 7 8W
Brownsville, Oreg., U.S.A. 160 44 29N 123 0W
Brownsville, Tenn., U.S.A. 159 35 35N 89 15W
Brownsville, Tex., U.S.A. 159 25 56N 97 25W
Brownwood 159 31 45N 99 0W
Brownwood, L. 159 31 51N 98 35W
Browse I. 136 14 7 S 123 33 E
Broxburn 35 55 56N 3 23W
Broye, R. 50 46 52N 6 58 E
Brozas 57 39 37N 6 47W
Bruas 101 4 31N 100 46 E
Bruay-en-Artois 43 50 29N 2 33 E
Bruce Bay 143 43 35 S 169 42 E
Bruce, gasfield 19 59 45N 1 32 E
Bruce Mines 150 46 20N 83 45W
Bruce, Mt. 136 22 37 S 118 8 E
Bruce Rock 137 31 52 S 118 8 E
Bruchsal 49 49 9N 8 39 E
Bruck a.d. Leitha 53 48 1N 16 47 E
Bruck a.d. Mur 52 47 24N 15 16 E
Brückenau 49 50 17N 9 48 E
Brǔdiceni 70 45 3N 23 4 E
Brue, R. 28 51 10N 2 59W
Bruernish Pt. 36 57 0N 7 22W
Bruff 39 52 29N 8 35W
Brugelette 47 50 35N 3 52 E
Bruges = Brugge 47 51 13N 3 13 E
Brugg 50 47 29N 8 11 E
Brugge 47 51 13N 3 13 E
Brühl 48 50 49N 6 51 E
Bruinisse 47 51 40N 4 5 E
Brûlé 152 53 15N 117 58W
Brûlon 42 47 58N 0 15W
Brûly 47 49 58N 4 32 E
Brumado 171 14 14 S 41 40W
Brumado, R. 171 14 13 S 41 40W
Brumath 43 48 43N 7 40 E
Brummen 46 52 5N 6 10 E
Brumunddal 71 60 53N 10 56 E
Brunchilly 138 18 50 S 134 30 E
Brundidge 157 31 43N 85 45W
Bruneau 160 42 57N 115 55W
Bruneau, R. 160 42 45N 115 50W
Brunei = Bandar Seri Begawan 102 4 52N 115 0 E
Brunei ■ 102 4 50N 115 0 E
Brunette Downs 138 18 40 S 135 55 E
Brunflo 72 63 5N 14 50 E
Brunico 63 46 50N 11 55 E
Brünig, Col de 50 46 46N 8 8 E
Brunkeberg 71 59 26N 8 28 E
Brunna 72 59 52N 17 25 E
Brunnen 51 46 59N 8 37 E
Brunner 143 42 27 S 171 20 E
Brunner, L. 143 42 27 S 171 20 E
Brunnsvik 72 60 12N 15 8 E
Bruno 153 52 20N 105 30W
Brunsberg 72 59 38N 12 52 E
Brunsbüttelkoog 48 53 52N 9 13 E
Brunssum 47 50 57N 5 59 E
Brunswick, Ga., U.S.A. 157 31 10N 81 30W
Brunswick, Md., U.S.A. 156 39 20N 77 38W
Brunswick, Me., U.S.A. 151 43 53N 69 50W
Brunswick, Mo., U.S.A. 158 39 26N 93 10W
Brunswick = Braunschweig 48 52 17N 10 28 E
Brunswick B. 136 15 15 S 124 50 E
Brunswick Junction 137 33 15 S 115 50 E
Brunswick, Pen. de 176 53 30 S 71 30W
Bruntál 53 50 0N 17 27 E
Brunton 35 55 2N 2 6W
Bruny I. 138 43 20 S 147 15 E
Bruree 39 52 25N 8 40W
Brus Laguna 166 15 47N 84 35W
Brusartsi 66 43 40N 23 5 E
Brush 158 40 17N 103 33W
Brusio 51 46 14N 10 8 E
Brusque 173 27 5 S 49 0W
Brussel 47 50 51N 4 21 E
Brussels = Bruxelles 47 50 51N 4 21 E
Brustem 47 50 48N 5 14 E
Bruthen 141 37 42 S 147 50 E
Bruton 28 51 6N 2 28W
Bruvik 71 60 29N 5 40 E
Bruxelles 47 50 51N 4 21 E
Bruyères 43 48 10N 6 40 E
Brwinow 54 52 9N 20 40 E
Bryagovo 67 41 58N 25 8 E
Bryan, Ohio, U.S.A. 156 41 30N 84 30W
Bryan, Texas, U.S.A. 159 30 40N 96 27W
Bryan, Mt. 140 33 30 S 139 0 E
Bryansk 80 53 13N 34 25 E
Bryanskoye 83 44 9N 47 10 E
Bryant 58 44 39N 97 26W
Bryggja 71 61 56N 5 27 E
Bryher I. 30 49 57N 6 21W
Brymbo 31 53 4N 3 5W
Brynamman 31 51 49N 3 52W
Bryncethin 31 51 33N 3 34W
Bryne 71 58 44N 5 38 E
Brynmawr 31 51 48N 3 11W
Bryrup 73 56 2N 9 30 E
Bryson City 157 35 28N 83 25W
Bryte 163 38 35N 121 33W
Brza Palanka 66 44 28N 22 37 E
Brzava, R. 66 45 21N 20 45 E
Brzeg 54 50 52N 17 30 E
Brzeg Dln 54 51 16N 16 41 E
Brzesko 54 49 59N 20 34 E
Brześć Kujawski 54 52 36N 18 55 E
Brzeszcze 54 49 59N 19 10 E
Brzeziny 54 51 49N 19 42 E
Brzozów 54 49 41N 22 3 E
Bu Athiah 119 30 1N 15 30 E
Bu Craa 116 26 45N 17 2 E
Buapinang 103 4 40 S 121 30 E
Buayan 103 5 3N 125 28 E
Buba 120 11 40N 14 59W
Bubanza 126 3 6 S 29 23 E
Bucaramanga 174 7 0N 73 0W
Buccaneer Arch. 136 16 7 S 123 20 E
Bucchiánico 63 42 20N 14 10 E
Bucecea 70 47 47N 26 28 E
Bŭceşti 70 46 50N 27 11 E
Buchach 80 49 5N 25 25 E
Buchan, Austral. 141 37 30 S 148 12 E
Buchan, U.K. 37 57 32N 2 8W
Buchan Ness 37 57 29N 1 48W
Buchan, oilfield 19 57 55N 0 0
Buchanan, Can. 153 51 40N 102 45W
Buchanan, Liberia 120 5 57N 10 2W
Buchanan Cr. 138 17 10 S 138 6 E
Buchanan, L., Queens., Austral. 138 21 35 S 145 52 E
Buchanan, L., W. Australia, Austral. 137 25 33 S 123 2 E
Buchanan, L., U.S.A. 159 30 50N 98 25W
Buchans 151 49 50N 56 52W
Bucharest = Bucureşti 70 44 27N 26 10 E
Buchholz 48 53 19N 9 51 E
Buchloe 49 48 3N 10 45 E
Buchlyvie 34 56 7N 4 20W
Buchon, Pt. 163 35 15N 120 54W
Buchs 51 47 10N 9 28 E
Buck Hill Falls 162 41 11N 75 16W
Buck, The, mt. 37 57 19N 3 0W
Buckden 29 52 17N 0 16W
Bückeburg 48 52 16N 9 2 E
Buckeye 161 33 28N 112 40W
Buckfastleigh 30 50 28N 3 47W
Buckhannon 156 39 2N 80 10W
Buckhaven 35 56 10N 3 2W
Buckie 37 57 40N 2 58W
Buckingham, Can. 150 45 37N 75 24W
Buckingham, U.K. 29 52 0N 0 59W
Buckingham □ 29 51 50N 0 55W
Buckingham B. 138 12 10 S 135 40 E
Buckingham Can. 97 14 0N 80 5 E
Buckinguy 139 31 3 S 147 30 E
Buckland 147 66 0N 161 5W
Buckland Brewer 30 50 56N 4 14W
Buckle Hd. 136 14 26 S 127 52 E
Buckleboo 140 32 54 S 136 12 E
Buckley, U.K. 31 53 10N 3 5W
Buckley, U.S.A. 160 47 10N 122 2W
Bucklin 159 37 37N 99 40W
Bucksburn 37 57 10N 2 10W
Bucquoy 43 50 9N 2 43 E
Buctouche 151 46 30N 64 45W
Bucureşti 70 44 27N 26 10 E
Bucyrus 156 40 48N 83 0W
Budacul, Munte 41 47 5N 25 40 E
Budafok 53 47 26N 19 2 E
Budalin 98 22 20N 95 10 E
Budapest 53 47 29N 19 5 E
Budaun 95 28 5N 79 10 E
Budd Coast 13 67 0 S 112 0 E
Buddabadah 141 31 56 S 147 14 E
Buddon Ness 35 56 29N 2 42W
Buddusò 64 40 35N 9 18 E
Bude 30 50 49N 4 33W
Bude Bay 30 50 50N 4 40W
Budel 47 51 17N 5 34 E
Budeşti 70 44 13N 26 30 E
Budge Budge 95 22 30N 88 25 E
Budgewoi Lake 141 33 13 S 151 34 E
Budia 58 40 38N 2 46W
Búdir 74 64 49N 23 23W
Budjala 124 2 50N 19 40 E
Budle B. 35 55 37N 1 45W
Budleigh Salterton 30 50 37N 3 19W
Búdrio 63 44 31N 11 31 E
Budva 66 42 17N 18 50 E
Budzyn 54 52 54N 16 59 E
Buea 121 4 10N 9 9 E
Buellton 163 34 37N 120 12W
Buena 162 39 31N 74 56W
Buena Vista, Colo., U.S.A. 161 38 56N 106 6W
Buena Vista, Va., U.S.A. 156 37 47N 79 23W
Buena Vista L. 163 35 15N 119 21W
Buenaventura 164 29 50N 107 30W
Buenaventura, B. de 174 3 48N 77 17W
Buendia, Pantano de 58 40 25N 2 43W
Buenópolis 171 17 54 S 44 11W
Buenos Aires, Argent. 172 34 30 S 58 20W
Buenos Aires, Colomb. 174 1 36N 73 18W
Buenos Aires, C. Rica 166 9 10N 83 20W
Buenos Aires □ 172 36 30 S 60 0W
Buenos Aires, Lago 176 46 35 S 72 30W
Buesaco 174 1 23N 77 9W
Buffalo, Can. 153 50 49N 110 42W
Buffalo, Mo., U.S.A. 159 37 40N 93 5W
Buffalo, Okla., U.S.A. 159 36 55N 99 42W
Buffalo, S.D., U.S.A. 159 45 39N 103 31W
Buffalo, Wyo., U.S.A. 160 44 25N 106 50W
Buffalo Center 147 64 2N 145 50W
Buffalo Head Hills 152 57 25N 115 55W
Buffalo L. 152 52 27N 112 54W
Buffalo Narrows 153 55 51N 108 29W
Buffalo, R. 152 57 50N 117 1W
Buffels, R. 129 29 36 S 17 15 E
Buford 157 34 5N 84 0W
Bug, R., Poland 54 51 20N 23 40 E
Bug, R., U.S.S.R. 82 48 0N 31 0 E
Buga 174 4 0N 77 0W
Buganda □ 126 0 0N 31 30 E
Buganga 126 0 25N 32 0 E
Bugeat 44 45 36N 1 55 E
Buggenhout 47 51 1N 4 12 E
Buggs I. L. 157 36 20N 78 30W
Buglawton 32 53 12N 2 11W
Bugle 30 50 23N 4 46W
Bugojno 66 44 2N 17 25 E
Bugsuk, I. 102 8 15N 117 15 E
Bugue, Le 44 44 55N 0 56 E
Bugulma 84 54 33N 52 48 E
Buguma 121 4 42N 6 55 E
Bugun Shara 105 49 0N 104 0 E
Buguruslan 84 53 39N 52 26 E
Buheirat-Murrat-el-Kubra 122 30 15N 32 40 E
Buhl, Idaho, U.S.A. 160 42 35N 114 54W
Buhl, Minn., U.S.A. 158 47 30N 92 46W
Buhŭeşti 70 46 47N 27 32 E
Buhuşi 70 46 41N 26 45 E
Buick 159 37 8N 91 2W
Bŭicoi 70 45 3N 25 52 E
Buie L. 34 56 20N 5 55W
Bŭileşti 70 44 01N 23 20 E
Builth Wells 31 52 10N 3 26W
Buina Qara 93 36 20N 67 0 E
Buinsk 81 55 0N 48 18 E
Buique 170 8 37 S 37 9W
Buis-les-Baronnies 45 44 17N 5 16 E
Buit, L. 151 50 59N 63 13W
Buitenpost 46 53 15N 6 9 E
Buitrago 56 41 0N 3 38W
Bujalance 57 37 54N 4 23W
Buján 56 42 59N 8 36W
Bujaraloz 58 41 29N 0 10W
Buje 63 45 24N 13 39 E
Buji 135 9 8 S 142 11 E
Bujnurd 93 37 35N 57 15 E
Bujumbura (Usumbura) 126 3 16 S 29 18 E
Bük 53 47 22N 16 45 E
Buk 54 52 21N 16 17 E
Buka I. 135 5 10 S 154 35 E
Bukachacha 77 52 55N 116 50 E
Bukama 127 9 10 S 25 50 E
Bukandula 126 0 13N 31 50 E
Bukavu 126 2 20 S 28 52 E
Bukene 126 4 15 S 32 48 E
Bukhara 85 39 48N 64 25 E
Bukima 126 1 50 S 33 25 E
Bukit Mertajam 101 5 22N 100 28 E
Bukittinggi 102 0 20 S 100 20 E
Bukkapatnam 97 14 14N 77 46 E
Buklyan 84 55 42N 52 10 E
Bukoba 126 1 20 S 31 49 E
Bukoba □ 126 1 30 S 32 0 E
Bukowno 54 50 17N 19 35 E
Bukrale 123 4 32N 42 0 E
Bukuru 121 9 42N 8 48 E
Bukuya 126 0 40N 31 52 E
Bula 120 12 7N 15 43W
Bülach 51 47 31N 8 32 E
Bulahdelah 141 32 23 S 152 13 E
Bulan 103 12 40N 123 52 E
Bulanash 84 57 16N 62 0 E
Bulandshahr 94 28 28N 77 58 E
Bulanovo 84 52 27N 55 10 E
Bulantai 99 36 33N 92 18 E
Bûlâq 122 25 10N 30 38 E
Bulawayo 127 20 7 S 28 32 E
Buldana 96 20 30N 76 18 E
Buldir I. 147 52 20N 175 55 E
Bulford 28 51 11N 1 45W
Bulgan 105 48 45N 103 34 E
Bulgaria ■ 67 42 35N 25 30 E
Bulgroo 138 25 47 S 143 58 E
Bulgunnia 139 30 10 S 134 53 E
Bulhar 91 10 25N 44 30 E
Buli, Teluk 103 1 5N 128 25 E
Buliluyan, C. 102 8 20N 117 15 E
Bulki 123 6 11N 36 31 E
Bulkington 163 52 29N 1 25W
Bulkley, R. 152 55 15N 127 40W
Bulkur 77 71 50N 126 30 E
Bull Shoals L. 159 36 40N 93 5W
Bullabulling 137 31 1 S 120 32 E
Bullange 47 50 24N 6 15 E
Bullaque, R. 57 39 20N 4 13W
Bullara 136 22 40 S 114 3 E
Bullaring 137 32 30 S 117 45 E
Bullas 59 38 2N 1 40W
Bulle 50 46 37N 7 3 E
Buller Gorge 143 41 40 S 172 10 E
Buller, Mt. 141 37 10 S 146 28 E
Buller, R. 143 41 44 S 171 36 E
Bullfinch 137 30 58 S 119 3 E
Bulli 141 34 15 S 150 57 E
Bullock Cr. 138 17 51 S 143 45 E
Bulloo Downs, Queens., Austral. 139 28 31 S 142 57 E
Bulloo Downs, W.A., Austral. 137 24 0 S 119 32 E
Bulloo L. 139 28 43 S 142 25 E
Bulloo, R. 139 28 43 S 142 30 E
Bulls 142 40 10 S 175 24 E
Bully-les-Mînes 43 50 27N 2 44 E
Bulnes 172 36 42 S 72 19W
Bulo Burti 91 3 50N 45 33 E
Bulolo 135 7 10 S 146 40 E
Bulpunga 140 33 47 S 141 45 E
Bulqiza 68 40 30N 20 21 E
Bulsar 96 20 40N 72 58 E
Bultfontein 128 28 18 S 26 10 E
Bulu Karakelong 103 4 35N 126 50 E
Buluan 103 9 0N 125 30 E
Bŭlŭciţa 70 44 23N 23 8 E
Bulukumba 103 5 33 S 120 11 E
Bulun 77 70 37N 127 30 E
Bulwell 33 53 1N 1 12W
Bumba 124 2 13N 22 30 E
Bumbiri I. 126 1 40 S 31 55 E
Bumble Bee 161 34 8N 112 18W
Bumbum 121 14 10N 8 10 E
Bumhkang 98 26 51N 97 40 E
Bumhpa Bum 98 26 51N 97 14 E
Bumi, R. 127 17 30 S 28 30 E
Bumtang, R. 98 26 56N 90 53 E
Buna, Kenya 124 2 58N 39 30 E
Buna, P.N.G. 135 8 42 S 148 27 E
Bunaiyin 92 23 10N 51 8 E
Bunaw 39 51 47N 9 50W
Bunazi 126 1 3 S 31 23 E
Bunbeg 38 55 4N 8 18W
Bunbury 132 33 20 S 115 35 E
Bunclody 39 52 40N 6 40W
Buncrana 38 55 8N 7 28W
Bundaberg 139 24 54 S 152 22 E
Bünde 48 52 11N 8 33 E
Bundey, R. 138 21 46 S 135 37 E
Bundi 94 25 30N 75 35 E
Bundooma 138 24 54 S 134 16 E
Bundoran 38 54 24N 8 17W
Bundukia 123 5 14N 30 55 E
Bundure 141 35 10 S 146 1 E
Bŭneasa 70 45 56N 27 55 E
Bunessan 34 56 18N 6 15W
Bung Kan 100 18 23N 103 37 E
Bungay 29 52 27N 1 26 E
Bungendore 141 35 14 S 149 30 E
Bungil Cr. 138 27 5 S 149 5 E
Bungō-Suidō 110 33 0N 132 15 E
Bungoma 126 0 34N 34 34 E
Bungotakada 110 33 35N 131 25 E
Bungu 126 7 35 S 39 0 E
Bunguran N. Is. 102 4 45N 108 0 E
Bunia 126 1 35N 30 20 E
Bunji 95 35 45N 74 40 E
Bunju 102 3 35N 117 50 E
Bunker Hill 163 39 15N 117 8W
Bunkerville 161 36 47N 114 6W
Bunkie 159 31 1N 92 12W
Bunmahon 39 52 8N 7 22W
Bunnanaddan 38 54 3N 8 35W
Bunnell 157 29 28N 81 12W
Bunnik 46 52 4N 5 12 E
Bunnyconnellan 38 54 7N 9 1W
Bunnythorpe 142 40 16 S 175 39 E
Buñol 59 39 25N 0 47W
Bunsbeek 47 50 50N 4 56 E
Bunschoten 46 52 14N 5 22 E
Buntingford 29 51 57N 0 1W
Buntok 102 1 40 S 114 58 E
Bununu 121 9 51N 9 32 E
Bununu Doss 121 10 6N 9 25 E
Bunwell 29 52 30N 1 9 E
Bunyoro □ = Western □ 126 1 45N 31 30 E
Bunza 121 12 8N 4 0 E
Búoareyri 74 65 2N 14 13W
Buol 103 1 15N 121 32 E
Buon Brieng 100 13 9N 108 12 E
Buong Long 100 13 44N 106 59 E
Buorkhaya, Mys 77 71 50N 133 10 E
Buqbuq 122 31 29N 25 29 E
Buqei'a 90 32 58N 35 20 E
Bur Acaba 91 3 12N 44 20 E
Bûr Fuad 122 31 15N 32 20 E
Bûr Safâga 122 26 43N 33 57 E
Bûr Sa'îd 122 31 16N 32 18 E
Bûr Sûdân 122 19 32N 37 9 E
Bûr Taufiq 122 29 54N 32 32 E
Bura 126 1 4 S 39 58 E

Buraidah
Caithness, Ord of, C

Buraidah 92 26 20N 44 8 E
Buraimī, Al Wāhāt al 93 24 15N 55 43 E
Burak Sulayman 90 31 42N 35 7 E
Burama 91 9 55N 43 7 E
Burao 91 9 32N 45 32 E
Buras 159 29 20N 89 33W
Burayevo 84 55 50N 55 24 E
Burbage, Derby, U.K. 32 53 15N 1 55W
Burbage, Leics., U.K. 28 52 31N 1 20W
Burbage, Wilts., U.K. 28 51 21N 1 40W
Burbank 163 34 9N 118 23W
Burcher 141 33 30 S 147 16 E
Burdekin, R. 138 19 38 S 147 25 E
Burdett 152 49 50N 111 32W
Burdur 92 37 45N 30 22 E
Burdwan 95 23 16N 87 54 E
Bure 123 10 40N 37 4 E
Bure, R. 29 52 38N 1 45 E
Bureba, La 58 42 36N 3 24W
Buren 46 51 55N 5 20 E
Burfell 74 64 5N 20 56W
Burford 28 51 48N 1 38W
Burg, Magdeburg, Ger. 48 52 16N 11 50 E
Burg, Schleswig-Holstein, Ger. 48 54 25N 11 10 E
Burg el Arab 122 30 54N 29 32 E
Burg et Tuyur 122 20 55N 27 56 E
Burgan 92 29 0N 47 57 E
Burgas 67 42 33N 27 29 E
Burgaski Zaliv 67 42 30N 27 39 E
Burgdorf, Ger. 48 52 27N 10 0 E
Burgdorf, Switz. 50 47 3N 7 37 E
Burgenland □ 53 47 20N 16 20 E
Burgeo 151 47 37N 57 38W
Burgersdorp 128 31 0 S 26 20 E
Burges, Mt. 137 30 50 S 121 5 E
Burgess 162 37 53N 76 21W
Burgess Hill 29 50 57N 0 7W
Burgh-le-Marsh 33 53 10N 0 15 E
Burghclere 28 51 19N 1 20W
Burghead 37 57 42N 3 30W
Burghead B. 37 57 40N 3 33W
Búrgio 64 37 35N 13 18 E
Bürglen 51 46 53N 8 40 E
Burglengenfeld 49 49 11N 12 2 E
Burgo de Osma 58 41 35N 3 4W
Burgohondo 56 40 26N 4 47W
Burgos 58 42 21N 3 41W
Burgos □ 58 42 21N 3 42W
Burgstädt 48 50 55N 12 49 E
Burgsteinfurt 48 52 9N 7 23 E
Burgsvik 73 57 3N 18 19 E
Burguillos del Cerro 57 38 23N 6 35W
Burgundy = Bourgogne 43 47 0N 4 30 E
Burhanpur 96 21 18N 76 20 E
Burhou Rocks 42 49 45N 2 15W
Buri Pen. 123 15 25N 39 55 E
Burias, I. 103 12 55N 123 5 E
Buribay 84 51 57N 58 10 E
Burica, Punta 166 8 3N 82 51W
Burigi, L. 126 2 2 S 31 22 E
Burin, Can. 151 47 1N 55 14W
Burin, Jordan 90 32 11N 35 15 E
Buriram 100 15 0N 103 0 E
Buriti Alegre 171 18 9 S 49 3W
Buriti Bravo 170 5 50 S 43 50W
Buriti dos Lopes 170 3 10 S 41 52W
Burji 123 5 29N 37 51 E
Burkburnett 159 34 7N 98 35W
Burke 160 47 31N 115 56W
Burke, R. 138 23 12 S 139 33 E
Burketown 138 17 45 S 139 33 E
Burk's Falls 150 45 37N 79 24W
Burley, Hants, U.K. 28 50 49N 1 41W
Burley, N. Yorks., U.K. 33 53 55N 1 46W
Burley, U.S.A. 160 42 37N 113 55W
Burlingame 163 37 35N 122 21W
Burlington, Colo., U.S.A. 158 39 21N 102 18W
Burlington, Iowa, U.S.A. 158 40 50N 91 5W
Burlington, Kans., U.S.A. 158 38 15N 95 47W
Burlington, N.C., U.S.A. 157 36 7N 79 27W
Burlington, N.J., U.S.A. 162 40 5N 74 50W
Burlington, Wash., U.S.A. 160 48 29N 122 19W
Burlington, Wis., U.S.A. 156 42 41N 88 18W
Burlyu-Tyube 76 46 30N 79 10 E
Burma ■ 98 21 0N 96 30 E
Burnabbie 137 32 7 S 126 21 E
Burnaby I. 152 52 25N 131 19W
Burnamwood 141 31 7 S 144 53 E
Burnet 159 30 45N 98 11W
Burnett, R. 133 24 45 S 152 23 E
Burney 160 40 56N 121 41W
Burnfoot 38 55 4N 7 15W
Burngup 137 33 2 S 118 42 E
Burnham, Essex, U.K. 29 51 37N 0 50 E
Burnham, Somerset, U.K. 28 51 14N 3 0W
Burnham Market 29 52 57N 0 43 E
Burnie 138 41 4 S 145 56 E
Burnley 32 53 47N 2 15W
Burnmouth 35 55 50N 2 4W
Burnoye 85 42 36N 70 47 E
Burns, Oreg., U.S.A. 160 43 40N 119 4W
Burns, Wyo., U.S.A. 158 41 13N 104 18W
Burns Lake 152 54 20N 125 45W
Burnside, L. 137 25 25 S 123 0 E
Burnt Paw 147 67 2N 142 43W
Burntisland 35 56 4N 3 14W
Burntwood L. 153 55 22N 100 26W
Burntwood, R. 153 56 8N 96 34W
Burqa 90 32 18N 35 11 E
Burra 140 33 40 S 138 55 E
Burragorang, L. 141 33 52 S 150 37 E
Burramurra 138 20 25N 137 15 E
Burravoe 36 60 30N 1 3W
Burray I. 37 58 50N 2 54W
Burreli 68 41 36N 20 1 E
Burrelton 35 56 30N 3 16W
Burren 39 53 9N 9 5W
Burren Junction 139 30 7 S 148 59 E
Burrendong Dam 139 32 39 S 149 6 E
Burrendong Res. 141 32 45 S 149 10 E
Burriana 58 39 50N 0 4W
Burrinjuck Res. 141 35 0 S 148 36 E
Burro, Serranías del 164 29 0N 102 0W
Burrow Hd. 34 54 40N 4 23W
Burrundie 136 13 32 S 131 42 E
Burruyacú 172 26 30 S 64 40W
Burry Port 31 51 41N 4 17W
Bursa 92 40 15N 29 5 E
Burseryd 73 57 12N 13 17 E
Burstall 153 50 39N 109 54W
Burstwick 33 53 43N 0 6W
Burton 32 54 10N 2 43W
Burton Agnes 33 54 4N 0 18W
Burton Bradstock 28 50 41N 2 43W
Burton Fleming 33 54 8N 0 20W
Burton L. 150 54 45N 78 20W
Burton Latimer 29 52 23N 0 41W
Burton upon Stather 33 53 39N 0 41W
Burton-upon-Trent 28 52 48N 1 39W
Burtonport 38 54 59N 8 26W
Burtundy 140 33 45 S 142 15 E
Burtville 137 28 42 S 122 33 E
Buru, I. 103 3 30 S 126 30 E
Burufu 120 10 25N 2 50W
Burujird 92 33 58N 48 41 E
Burullus, Bahra el 122 31 25N 31 0 E
Burunday 85 43 20N 76 51 E
Burundi ■ 126 3 15 S 30 0 E
Burung 102 0 21N 108 25 E
Bururi 126 3 57 S 29 37 E
Burutu 121 5 20N 5 29 E
Burwash 29 50 59N 0 24 E
Burwash Landing 147 61 21N 139 0W
Burwell, U.K. 29 52 17N 0 20 E
Burwell, U.S.A. 158 41 49N 99 8W
Bury 32 53 36N 2 19W
Bury St. Edmunds 29 52 15N 0 42 E
Buryat A.S.S.R. □ 77 53 0N 110 0 E
Burzenin 54 51 28N 18 47 E
Busalla 62 44 34N 8 58 E
Busango Swamp 127 14 15 S 25 45 E
Busayyah 92 30 0N 46 10 E
Busby 152 53 55N 114 0W
Bushati 68 41 58N 19 34 E
Bushell 153 59 31N 108 45W
Bushenyi 126 0 35 S 30 10 E
Bushey 29 51 38N 0 20W
Bushman Land 128 29 30 S 19 30 E
Bushmills 38 55 14N 6 32W
Bushnell, Ill., U.S.A. 158 40 32N 90 30W
Bushnell, Nebr., U.S.A. 158 41 18N 103 50W
Busia □ 126 0 25N 34 6 E
Busie 120 10 29N 2 22W
Businga 124 3 16N 20 59 E
Buskerud fylke □ 75 60 13N 9 0 E
Busko Zdrój 54 50 28N 20 42 E
Busovača 66 44 6N 17 53 E
Busra 92 32 30N 36 25 E
Bussa 121 10 11N 4 32 E
Bussang 43 47 50N 6 50 E
Busselton 137 33 42 S 115 15 E
Bussigny 50 46 33N 6 33 E
Bussum 46 52 16N 5 10 E
Bustard Hd. 133 24 0 S 151 48 E
Busto Arsizio 62 45 40N 8 50 E
Busto, C. 56 43 34N 6 28W
Busu-Djanoa 124 1 50N 21 5 E
Busuangal, I. 103 12 10N 120 0 E
Büsum 48 54 7N 8 50 E
Buta 126 2 50N 24 53 E
Butare 126 2 31 S 29 52 E
Bute 140 33 51 S 138 2 E
Bute (□) 26 55 40N 5 10W
Bute, I. 34 55 48N 5 2W
Bute Inlet 152 50 40N 124 53W
Bute, Kyles of 34 55 55N 5 10W
Bute, Sd. of 34 55 43N 5 8W
Butemba 126 1 9N 31 37 E
Butembo 126 0 9N 29 18 E
Butera 65 37 10N 14 10 E
Bütgenbach 47 50 26N 6 12 E
Buthidaung 98 20 52N 92 32 E
Butiaba 126 1 50N 31 20 E
Butler 158 38 17N 94 18W
Bütschwil 51 47 23N 9 5 E
Butte, Mont., U.S.A. 160 46 0N 112 31W
Butte, Nebr., U.S.A. 158 42 56N 98 54W
Butterfield, Mt. 137 24 45 S 128 7 E
Buttermere 32 54 32N 3 17W
Butterworth 101 5 24N 100 23 E
Buttevant 39 52 14N 8 40 E
Buttfield, Mt. 137 24 45 S 128 9 E
Button B. 153 58 45N 94 23W
Buttonwillow 163 35 24N 119 28W
Butty Hd. 137 33 54 S 121 39 E
Butuan 103 8 57N 125 33 E
Butuku-Luba 121 3 29N 8 33 E
Butung, I. 103 5 0 S 122 45 E
Buturlinovka 81 50 50N 40 35 E
Butzbach 48 50 24N 8 40 E
Buxar 95 25 34N 83 58 E
Buxton, S. Afr. 128 27 38 S 24 42 E
Buxton, U.K. 32 53 16N 1 54W
Buxy 43 46 44N 4 40 E
Buyaga 77 59 50N 127 0 E
Buynaksk 83 42 36N 47 42 E
Buyr Nuur 105 47 50N 117 42 E
Büyük çekmece 67 41 2N 28 35 E
Büyük Kemikli Burun 68 40 20N 26 15 E
Büyük Menderes, R. 79 37 45N 27 40 E
Buzançais 42 46 54N 1 25 E
Buzau, Pasul 70 45 35N 26 12 E
Buzaymah 117 24 35N 22 0 E
Buzen 110 33 35N 131 5 E
Buzet 63 45 24N 13 58 E
Buzi, R. 127 19 52 S 34 30 E
Buziaş 66 45 38N 21 36 E
Buzuluk 84 52 48N 52 12 E
Buzuluk, R. 81 50 50N 52 12 E
Buzŭu 70 45 10N 26 50 E
Buzŭu □ 70 45 20N 26 30 E
Buzŭu, R. 70 45 10N 27 20 E
Buzzards Bay 162 41 45N 70 38W
Bwagaoia 135 10 40 S 152 52 E
Bwana Mkubwe 127 13 8 S 28 38 E
Byala, Ruse, Bulg. 67 43 28N 25 44 E
Byala, Varna, Bulg. 67 42 53N 27 55 E
Byala Slatina 67 43 26N 23 55 E
Byandovan, Mys 83 39 45N 49 28 E
Bychawa 54 51 1N 22 36 E
Byczyha 54 51 7N 18 12 E
Bydgoszcz 54 53 10N 18 0 E
Bydgoszcz □ 54 53 16N 17 33 E
Byelorussian S.S.R. □ 80 53 30N 27 0 E
Byers 158 39 46N 104 13W
Byfield 28 52 10N 1 15W
Bygland 71 58 50N 7 48 E
Byglandsfjord 71 58 40N 7 50 E
Byglandsfjorden 71 58 44N 7 50 E
Byhalia 159 34 53N 89 41W
Bykhov 80 53 31N 30 14 E
Bykle 71 59 20N 7 22 E
Bykovo 83 49 50N 45 25 E
Bylas 161 33 11N 110 9W
Bylchau 31 53 9N 3 32W
Bylderup 73 54 57N 9 6 E
Bylot I. 149 73 13N 78 34W
Byrd Land = Marie Byrd Land 13 79 30 S 125 0W
Byrd Sub-Glacial Basin 13 82 0 S 120 0W
Byro 137 26 5 S 116 11 E
Byrock 141 30 40 S 146 27 E
Byron B. 151 54 42N 57 40W
Byron, C. 133 28 38 S 153 40W
Byrranga, Gory 77 75 0N 100 0 E
Byrum 73 57 16N 11 0 E
Byske 74 64 57N 21 11 E
Byske, R. 74 65 20N 20 0 E
Bystrovka 85 42 47N 75 42 E
Bystrzyca Kłodzka 54 50 19N 16 39 E
Byten 80 52 50N 25 27 E
Bytom 54 50 25N 19 0 E
Bytom Ordz. 54 51 44N 15 48 E
Bytów 54 54 10N 17 30 E
Byumba 126 1 35 S 30 4 E
Byvalla 72 61 22N 16 27 E
Bzéma 117 24 50N 22 20 E
Bzenec 53 48 58N 17 18 E

C

Ca Mau = Quan Long 101 9 7N 105 8 E
Ca Mau, Mui = Bai Bung 101 8 35N 104 42 E
Ca Na 101 11 20N 108 54 E
Ca, R. 100 18 45N 105 45 E
Caacupé 172 25 23N 57 5W
Caamano Sd. 152 52 55N 129 25W
Caatingas 170 7 0 S 52 30W
Caazapá 172 26 8 S 56 19W
Caazapá □ 173 26 10 S 56 0W
Caballería, Cabo de 58 40 5N 4 5 E
Cabañaquinta 56 43 10N 5 38W
Cabanatuan 103 15 30N 121 5 E
Cabanes 58 40 9N 0 2 E
Cabano 151 47 40N 68 56 E
Cabazon 163 33 55N 116 47W
Cabbage Tree Hd. 108 27 20 S 153 5 E
Cabedelo 170 7 0 S 34 50W
Cabeza del Buey 57 38 44N 5 13W
Cabildo 172 32 30 S 71 5W
Cabimas 174 10 30N 71 25W
Cabinda 124 5 40 S 12 11 E
Cabinda □ 124 5 0 S 12 30 E
Cabinet Mts. 160 48 0N 115 30W
Cables 137 27 55 S 123 25 E
Cableskill 162 42 39N 74 30W
Cabo Blanco 176 47 56 S 65 47W
Cabo Delgado □ 127 10 35 S 40 35 E
Cabo Frio 173 22 51 S 42 3W
Cabo Pantoja 174 1 0 S 75 10W
Cabonga Reservoir 150 47 20N 76 40W
Cabool 159 37 10N 92 8W
Caboolture 139 27 5 S 152 58 E
Cabora Bassa Dam 127 15 20 S 32 50 E
Caborca (Heroica) 164 30 40N 112 10W
Cabot Strait 151 47 15N 59 40W
Cabra 57 37 30N 4 28W
Cabra del Santo Cristo 59 37 42N 3 16W
Cabrach 37 57 20N 3 0W
Cabras 64 39 57N 8 30 E
Cabrera, I. 59 39 6N 2 59 E
Cabrera, Sierra 56 42 12N 6 40W
Cabri 153 50 35N 108 25W
Cabriel, R. 59 39 20N 1 20W
Cabruta 174 7 50N 66 10W
Caburan 103 6 3N 125 45 E
Cabuyaro 174 4 18N 72 49W
Çacabelos 56 42 36N 6 44W
ČaCak 66 43 54N 20 20 E
Cáceres, Brazil 174 16 5 S 57 40W
Cáceres, Colomb. 174 7 35N 75 20W
Cáceres, Spain 57 39 26N 6 23W
Cáceres □ 57 39 45N 6 0W
Cache B. 150 46 26N 80 1W
Cache Bay 150 46 22N 80 0W
Cachepo 57 37 20N 7 49W
Cacheu 120 12 14N 16 8W
Cachi 172 25 5 S 66 10W
Cachimbo, Serra do 175 9 30 S 55 0W
Cáchira 174 7 21N 73 17W
Cachoeira 171 12 30 S 39 0W
Cachoeira Alta 171 18 48 S 50 58W
Cachoeira de Itapemirim 173 20 51 S 41 7W
Cachoeira do Sul 173 30 3 S 52 53W
Cachoeiro do Arari 170 1 1 S 48 58W
Cachopo 57 37 20N 7 49W
Cacolo 124 10 9 S 19 21 E
Caconda 125 13 48 S 15 8 E
Caçu 171 18 37 S 51 4W
Caculé 171 14 30 S 42 13W
Cadamstown 39 53 7N 7 39W
Cadarga 139 26 8 S 150 58 E
Çadaux 137 30 48 S 117 15 E
Čadca 53 49 26N 18 45 E
Caddo 159 34 8N 96 18W
Cadenazzo 51 46 9N 8 57 E
Cader Idris 31 52 43N 3 56W
Cadereyta Jiménez 165 25 40N 100 0W
Cadí, Sierra del 58 42 17N 1 42 E
Cadibarrawirracanna, L. 139 28 52 S 135 27 E
Cadillac, Can. 150 48 14N 78 23W
Cadillac, France 44 44 38N 0 20W
Cadillac, U.S.A. 156 44 16N 85 25W
Cadiz 103 11 30N 123 15 E
Cádiz 57 36 30N 6 20W
Cádiz □ 57 36 36N 5 45W
Cádiz, G. de 57 36 40N 7 0W
Cadomin 152 53 2N 117 20W
Cadotte, R. 152 56 43N 117 10W
Cadours 44 43 44N 1 2 E
Cadoux 137 30 46 S 117 7 E
Caen 42 49 10N 0 22W
Caenby Corner 33 53 23N 0 32W
Caergwrle 29 53 6N 3 3W
Caerhun 31 53 14N 3 50W
Caerleon 31 51 37N 2 57W
Caernarfon 31 53 8N 4 17W
Caernarfon B. 31 53 4N 4 40W
Caernarvon = Caernarfon 31 53 8N 4 17W
Caernarvon (□) 26 53 8N 4 17W
Caerphilly 31 51 34N 3 13W
Caersws 31 52 32N 3 27W
Caerwent 31 51 37N 2 47W
Cæsarea = Qesari 90 32 30N 34 53 E
Caeté 171 20 0 S 43 40W
Caetité 171 13 50 S 42 50W
Cafayate 172 26 2 S 66 0W
Cafu 128 16 30 S 15 8 E
Cagayan de Oro 103 8 30N 124 40 E
Cagayan, R. 103 18 25N 121 42 E
Cagli 63 43 32N 12 38 E
Cágliari 64 39 15N 9 6 E
Cágliari, G. di 64 39 8N 9 10 E
Cagnano Varano 65 41 49N 15 47 E
Cagnes-sur-Mer 45 43 40N 7 9 E
Caguas 147 18 14N 66 4W
Caha Mts. 39 51 45N 9 40W
Caher I. 38 53 44N 10 1W
Caherconlish 39 52 36N 8 30W
Cahermore 39 51 35N 10 2W
Cahir 39 52 23N 7 56W
Cahirciveen 39 51 57N 10 13W
Cahore Pt. 39 52 34N 6 11W
Cahors 44 44 27N 1 27 E
Cahuapanas 174 5 15 S 77 0W
Cai Ban, Dao 100 21 10N 107 27 E
Cai Nuoc 101 8 56N 105 1 E
Caianda 127 11 29 S 23 31 E
Caibarién 166 22 30N 79 30W
Caicara 174 7 38N 66 10W
Caicó 170 6 20 S 37 0W
Caicos Is. 167 21 40N 71 40W
Caicos Passage 167 22 45N 72 45W
Caihaique 176 45 30 S 71 45W
Caird Coast 13 75 0 S 25 0W
Cairn Gorm 37 57 7N 3 40W
Cairn Table 35 55 30N 4 0W
Cairngorm Mts. 37 57 6N 3 42W
Cairnryan 34 54 59N 5 0W
Cairns 138 16 57 S 145 45 E
Cairo, Ga., U.S.A. 157 30 52N 84 12W
Cairo, Illinois, U.S.A. 159 37 0N 89 10W
Cairo, N.Y., U.S.A. 162 42 18N 74 0W
Cairo = El Qahîra 122 30 1N 31 14 E
Cairo Montenotte 62 44 23N 8 16 E
Caister-on-Sea 29 52 38N 1 43 E
Caistor 33 53 29N 0 20W
Caithness (□) 26 58 25N 3 25W
Caithness, Ord of, C. 37 58 35N 3 37W

Caiundo Canton

Caiundo 125 15 50S 17 52E
Caiza 174 20 2S 65 40W
Cajamarca 174 7 5S 78 28W
Cajapió 170 2 58S 44 48W
Cajarc 44 44 29N 1 50E
Cajàzeiros 170 7 0S 38 30W
Čajetina 66 43 47N 19 42E
Čajniče 66 43 34N 19 5E
Çakirgöl 83 40 33N 39 40E
Cala 57 37 59N 6 21W
Cala Cadolar 59 38 38N 1 35E
Cala, R. 57 37 50N 6 8W
Calabar 121 4 57N 8 20E
Calabozo 174 9 0N 67 20W
Calábria □ 65 39 24N 16 30E
Calaburras, Pta. de 57 36 30N 4 38W
Calaceite 58 41 1N 0 11E
Calafat 70 43 58N 22 59E
Calafate 176 50 25S 72 25W
Calahorra 58 42 18N 1 59W
Calais, France 43 50 57N 1 56E
Calais, U.S.A. 151 45 5N 67 20W
Calais, Pas de 160 50 57N 1 20E
Calalaste, Sierra de 172 25 0S 67 0W
Calama, Brazil 174 8 0S 62 50W
Calama, Chile 172 22 30S 68 55W
Calamar, Bolívar, Colomb. 174 10 15N 74 55W
Calamar, Vaupés, Colomb. 174 1 58N 72 32W
Calamian Group 103 11 50N 119 55E
Calamocha 58 40 50N 1 17W
Calanaque 174 0 5S 64 0W
Calañas 57 37 40N 6 53W
Calanda 58 40 56N 0 15W
Calang 102 4 30N 95 43E
Calangiánus 64 40 56N 9 12E
Calapan 103 13 25N 121 7E
Calasparra 59 38 14N 1 41W
Calatafimi 64 37 56N 12 50E
Calatayud 58 41 20N 1 40W
Calauag 103 13 55N 122 15E
Calavà, C. 65 38 11N 14 55E
Calavite, Cape 103 13 26N 120 10E
Calbe 48 51 57N 11 47E
Calca 174 13 10S 72 0W
Calci 62 43 44N 10 31E
Calcidica = Khalkidhikí □ 170 40 25N 23 40E
Calcutta 95 22 36N 88 24E
Caldaro 63 46 23N 11 15E
Caldas □ 174 5 15N 75 30W
Caldas da Rainha 57 39 24N 9 8W
Caldas de Reyes 56 42 36N 8 39W
Caldas Novas 171 17 45S 48 38W
Caldbeck 32 54 45N 3 3W
Calder Bridge 32 54 27N 3 31W
Calder Hall 32 54 26N 3 31W
Calder, R. 33 53 44N 1 21W
Caldera 172 27 5S 70 55W
Caldew R. 32 54 54N 2 59W
Caldiran 92 39 7N 44 0E
Caldwell, Idaho, U.S.A. 160 43 45N 116 42W
Caldwell, Kans., U.S.A. 159 37 5N 97 37W
Caldwell, Texas, U.S.A. 159 30 30N 96 42W
Caldy I. 31 51 38N 4 42W
Caledon, S. Afr. 128 34 14S 19 26E
Caledon, U.K. 38 54 22N 6 50W
Caledon B. 138 12 45S 137 0E
Caledon, R. 128 30 0S 26 46E
Caledonian Can. 37 56 50N 5 6W
Calella 58 41 37N 2 40E
Calemba 128 16 0S 15 38E
Calera, La 172 32 50S 71 10W
Calexico 161 32 40N 115 33W
Calf of Man 32 54 4N 4 48W
Calgary, Can. 152 51 0N 114 10W
Calgary, U.K. 34 56 34N 6 17W
Calhoun 157 34 30N 84 55W
Cali 174 3 25N 76 35W
Caliach Pt. 34 56 37N 6 20W
Calicoan, I. 103 10 59N 125 50E
Calicut 93 11 15N 75 43E
Calicut, (Kozhikode) 97 11 15N 75 43E
Caliente 161 37 43N 114 34W
California 158 38 37N 92 30W
California □ 160 37 25N 120 0W
California, Baja 164 32 10N 115 12W
California, Baja, T.N. □ 164 30 0N 115 0W
California, Baja, T.S. □ 164 25 50N 111 50W
California City 163 35 7N 117 57W
California, Golfo de 164 27 0N 111 0W
California Hot Springs 163 35 51N 118 41W
California, Lr. = California, Baja 164 25 50N 111 50W
Calilegua 172 23 45S 64 42W
Călimăneşti 70 45 14N 24 20E
Calingasta 172 31 15S 69 30W
Calipatria 161 33 8N 115 30W
Calistoga 160 38 36N 122 32W
Calitri 65 40 54N 15 25E
Calkiní 165 20 21N 90 3W
Callabonna, L. 139 29 40S 140 5E
Callac 42 48 25N 3 27W
Callafo 91 6 48N 43 47E
Callan 39 52 33N 7 25W
Callanish 36 58 12N 6 43W
Callantsoog 46 52 50N 4 42E
Callao 174 12 0S 77 0W
Callaway 158 41 20N 99 56W
Calles 165 23 2N 98 42W
Callicoon 162 41 46N 75 3W
Callide 138 24 18S 150 28E
Calling Lake 152 55 15N 113 12W
Callington 30 56 30N 4 19W
Calliope 138 24 0S 151 16E
Callosa de Ensarriá. 59 38 40N 0 8W
Callosa de Segura 59 38 1N 0 53W
Callow 38 53 58N 9 2W
Calne 28 51 26N 2 0W
Calola 128 16 25S 17 48E
Calore, R. 65 41 8N 14 45E
Caloundra 139 26 45S 153 10E
Calpe 59 38 39N 0 3E
Calshot 28 50 49N 1 18W
Calstock, Can. 150 49 47N 84 9W
Calstock, U.K. 30 50 30N 4 13W
Caltabellotta 64 37 36N 13 11E
Caltagirone 65 37 13N 14 30E
Caltanissetta 65 37 30N 14 3E
Caluire-et-Cuire 45 45 49N 4 51E
Calulo 124 10 1S 14 56E
Calumbo 124 9 0S 13 20E
Caluso 62 45 18N 7 52E
Calvados □ 42 49 5N 0 15W
Calvert 159 30 59N 96 50W
Calvert Hills 138 17 15S 137 20E
Calvert I. 152 51 30N 128 0W
Calvert, R. 138 16 17S 137 44E
Calvert Ra. 136 24 0S 122 30E
Calvillo 164 21 51N 102 43W
Calvinia 128 31 28S 19 45E
Calwa 163 36 42N 119 46W
Calzada Almuradiel 59 38 32N 3 28W
Calzada de Calatrava 57 38 42N 3 46W
Cam Lam 101 11 54N 109 10E
Cam Pha 100 21 1N 107 18E
Cam, R. 29 52 21N 0 16E
Cam Ranh 101 11 54N 109 12E
Cam Xuyen 100 18 15N 106 0E
Camabatela 124 8 20S 15 26E
Camacã 171 15 24S 39 30W
Camaçari 171 12 41S 38 18W
Camacho 164 24 25N 102 18W
Camaguán 174 8 6N 67 36W
Camagüey 166 21 20N 78 0W
Camaiore 62 43 57N 10 18E
Camamu 171 13 57S 39 7W
Camaná 174 16 30S 72 50W
Camaquã, R. 173 30 50S 52 50W
Camaret 42 48 16N 4 37W
Camargo 174 20 38S 65 15E
Camargue 45 43 34N 4 34E
Camarillo 163 34 13N 119 2W
Camariñas 56 43 8N 9 12W
Camarón, C. 166 16 0N 85 0W
Camarones, Argent. 176 44 50S 65 40W
Camarones, Chile 174 19 0S 69 58W
Camas 160 45 35N 122 24W
Camas Valley 160 43 0N 123 46W
Cambados 56 42 31N 8 49W
Cambará 173 23 2S 50 5W
Cambay 94 22 23N 72 33E
Cambay, G. of 94 20 45N 72 30E
Camberley 29 51 20N 0 44W
Cambil 59 37 40N 3 33W
Cambo 35 55 9N 1 57W
Cambo-les-Bains 44 43 22N 1 23W
Cambodia ■ 100 12 15N 105 0E
Camborne 30 50 13N 5 18W
Cambrai 43 50 11N 3 14E
Cambria 163 35 44N 121 6W
Cambrian Mts. 31 52 25N 3 52W
Cambridge, Can. 150 43 23N 80 15W
Cambridge, Jamaica 166 18 18N 77 54W
Cambridge, N.Z. 142 37 54S 175 29E
Cambridge, U.K. 29 52 13N 0 8E
Cambridge, Idaho, U.S.A. 160 44 36N 116 52W
Cambridge, Mass., U.S.A. 162 42 20N 71 8W
Cambridge, Md., U.S.A. 162 38 33N 76 2W
Cambridge, Minn., U.S.A. 158 45 34N 93 15W
Cambridge, Nebr., U.S.A. 158 40 20N 100 12W
Cambridge, N.Y., U.S.A. 162 43 2N 73 22W
Cambridge, Ohio, U.S.A. 156 40 1N 81 22W
Cambridge Bay 148 69 10N 105 0W
Cambridge Gulf 136 14 45S 128 0E
Cambridgeshire □ 29 52 12N 0 7E
Cambrils 58 41 8N 1 3E
Cambuci 173 21 35S 41 55W
Camden, Austral. 141 34 1S 150 43E
Camden, U.K. 29 51 33N 0 10W
Camden, Ala., U.S.A. 157 31 59N 87 15W
Camden, Ark., U.S.A. 159 33 30N 92 50W
Camden, Del., U.S.A. 162 39 7N 75 33W
Camden, Me., U.S.A. 151 44 14N 69 6W
Camden, N.J., U.S.A. 162 39 57N 75 1W
Camden, N.Y., U.S.A. 162 43 20N 75 45W
Camden, S.C., U.S.A. 157 34 17N 80 34W
Camden, B. 147 71 0N 145 0W
Camden Sound 136 15 27S 124 25E
Camel R. 30 50 28N 4 49W
Camelford 30 50 37N 4 41W
Camembert 42 48 53N 0 10E
Cámeri 62 45 30N 8 40E
Camerino 63 43 10N 13 4E
Cameron, Ariz., U.S.A. 161 35 55N 111 31W
Cameron, La., U.S.A. 159 29 50N 93 18W
Cameron, Mo., U.S.A. 158 39 42N 94 14W
Cameron, Tex., U.S.A. 159 30 53N 97 0W
Cameron Falls 150 49 8N 88 19W
Cameron Highlands 101 4 27N 101 22E
Cameron Hills 152 59 48N 118 0W
Cameron Mts. 143 46 1S 167 0E
Cameroon ■ 124 3 30N 12 30E
Camerota 65 40 2N 15 21E
Cameroun, Mt. 121 4 45N 8 55E
Cameroun, R. 121 4 0N 9 35E
Camerton 28 51 18N 2 27W
Cametá 170 2 0S 49 30W
Caminha 56 41 50N 8 50W
Camino 163 38 47N 120 40W
Camira Creek 139 29 15S 152 58E
Camiranga 170 1 48S 46 17W
Cammachmore 37 57 2N 2 9W
Camocim 170 2 55S 40 50W
Camogli 62 44 21N 9 9E
Camolin 39 52 37N 6 26W
Camooweal 138 19 56S 138 7E
Camopi, R. 175 3 12N 52 17W
Camp Crook 158 45 36N 103 59W
Camp Hill 162 40 15N 76 56W
Camp Nelson 163 36 8N 118 39W
Camp Wood 159 29 47N 100 0W
Campagna 65 40 40N 15 5E
Campana 172 34 10S 58 55W
Campana, I. 176 48 20S 75 10W
Campanario 57 38 52N 5 36W
Campania □ 65 40 50N 14 45E
Campbell 163 37 17N 121 57W
Campbell, C. 143 41 47S 174 18E
Campbell I. 142 52 30S 169 0E
Campbell L. 153 63 14N 106 55W
Campbell River 152 50 5N 125 20W
Campbell Town 138 41 52S 147 30E
Campbellpur 94 33 46N 72 20E
Campbellsville 156 37 23N 85 12W
Campbellton, Alta., Can. 152 53 32N 113 15W
Campbellton, N.B., Can. 151 47 57N 66 43W
Campbelltown, Austral. 141 34 4S 150 49E
Campbelltown, U.K. 37 57 34N 4 2W
Campbeltown 34 55 25N 5 36W
Campeche 165 19 50N 90 32W
Campeche □ 165 19 50N 90 32W
Campeche, Golfo de 165 19 30N 93 0W
Camperdown 140 38 14S 143 9E
Camperville 153 51 59N 100 9W
Campi Salentina 65 40 22N 18 2E
Campidano 64 39 30N 8 40E
Campillo de Altobuey 58 39 36N 1 49W
Campillo de Llerena 57 38 30N 5 50W
Campillos 57 37 4N 4 51W
Campina Grande 170 7 20S 35 47W
Campiña, La 57 37 45N 4 45W
Campina Verde 171 19 31S 49 28W
Campinas 173 22 50S 47 0W
Campine 47 51 8N 5 20E
Campinho 170 14 30S 39 10W
Campli 63 42 44N 13 40E
Campo 124 2 15N 9 58E
Campo Beló 171 21 0S 45 30W
Campo de Criptana 59 39 25N 3 7W
Campo de Gibraltar 57 36 15N 5 25W
Campo Flórido 171 19 47S 48 35W
Campo Formoso 170 10 30S 40 20W
Campo Grande 175 20 25S 54 40W
Campo Maior, Brazil 170 4 50S 42 12W
Campo Maior, Port. 57 38 59N 7 7W
Campo Mourão 171 24 3S 52 22W
Campo Tencia 51 46 26N 8 43E
Campo Túres 63 46 53N 11 55E
Campoalegre 174 2 41N 75 20W
Campobasso 65 41 34N 14 40E
Campobello di Licata 64 37 16N 13 55E
Campobello di Mazara 64 37 38N 12 45E
Campofelice 64 37 54N 13 53E
Camporeale 64 37 53N 13 3E
Campos 173 21 50S 41 20W
Campos Altos 171 19 41S 46 10W
Campos Belos 171 13 10S 46 45W
Campos del Puerto 59 39 26N 3 1E
Campos Novos 173 27 21S 51 20W
Campos Sales 170 7 4S 40 23W
Camprodón 58 42 19N 2 23E
Campsie Fells 23 56 2N 4 20W
Camptown 162 41 44N 76 14W
Campuya, R. 174 1 10S 74 0W
Camrose, Can. 152 53 0N 112 50W
Camrose, U.K. 31 51 50N 5 2W
Camsall L. 153 72 32N 106 47W
Camsell Portage 153 59 37N 109 15W
Camurra 139 29 21S 149 52E
Can Gio 101 10 25N 106 58E
Can Tho 101 10 2N 105 46E
Canada ■ 148 60 0N 100 0W
Cañada de Gómez 73 32 55S 61 30W
Canadian 159 35 56N 100 25W
Canadian, R. 159 36 0N 98 45W
Canairiktok, R. 151 54 30N 62 30W
Canajoharie 162 42 54N 74 35W
Çanakkale 68 40 8N 26 30E
Çanakkale Boğazi 68 40 0N 26 0E
Canal de l'Est 43 48 45N 5 35E
Canal Flats 152 50 10N 115 48W
Canal latéral à la Garonne 44 44 25N 0 15E
Canalejas 172 35 15S 66 34W
Canals 172 33 35S 62 40W
Canals 59 38 58N 0 35W
Canandaigua 156 42 55N 77 18W
Cananea 164 31 0N 110 20W
Canarias, Islas 116 29 30N 17 0W
Canarreos, Arch. de los 166 21 35N 81 40W
Canary Is. = Canarias, Islas 116 29 30N 17 0W
Canastra, Serra da 171 20 0S 46 20W
Canatlán 164 24 31N 104 47W
Canaveral, C. 157 28 28N 80 31W
Cañaveras 58 40 27N 2 14W
Canavieiras 171 15 39S 39 0W
Canbelego 141 31 32S 146 18E
Canberra 141 35 15S 149 8E
Canby, Calif., U.S.A. 160 41 26N 120 58W
Canby, Minn., U.S.A. 158 44 44N 96 15W
Canby, Oregon, U.S.A. 160 45 24N 122 45W
Cancale 42 48 40N 1 50W
Candala 91 11 30N 49 58E
Candas 56 43 35N 5 45W
Candé 42 47 34N 1 0W
Candea = Iráklion 69 35 20N 25 12E
Candela 65 41 8N 15 31E
Candelaria 173 27 29S 55 44W
Candelaria, Pta. de la 56 43 45N 8 0W
Candeleda 56 40 10N 5 14W
Candelo 141 36 47S 149 43E
Candia = Iráklion 69 35 20N 25 12E
Cândido de Abreu 171 24 35S 51 20W
Cândido Mendes 170 1 27S 45 43W
Candle L. 153 53 50N 105 18W
Cando 158 48 30N 99 14W
Canea = Khaniá 69 35 30N 24 4E
Canela 170 10 15S 48 25W
Canelli 62 44 44N 8 18E
Canelones 172 34 32S 56 10W
Canet-Plage 44 42 41N 3 2E
Cañete, Chile 172 37 50S 73 30W
Cañete, Cuba 167 20 36N 74 43W
Cañete, Peru 174 13 0S 76 30W
Cañete, Spain 58 40 3N 1 54W
Cañete de las Torres 57 37 53N 4 19W
Canfranc 58 42 42N 0 31W
Cangamba 125 13 40S 19 54E
Cangas 56 42 16N 8 47W
Cangas de Narcea 56 43 10N 6 32W
Cangas de Onís 56 43 21N 5 8W
Canguaretama 170 6 20S 35 5W
Canguçu 173 31 22S 52 43W
Canhotinho 171 8 53S 36 12W
Cani, Is. 119 36 21N 10 5E
Canicado 125 24 2S 33 2E
Canicattì 64 37 21N 13 50E
Canicattini 65 37 1N 15 3E
Canim, L. 152 51 45N 120 50W
Canim Lake 152 51 17N 120 54W
Canindé 170 4 22S 39 19W
Canindé, R. 170 6 15S 42 52W
Canipaan 102 8 33N 117 15E
Canisbay 37 58 38N 3 6W
Canisp Mt. 36 58 8N 5 5W
Cañitas 164 23 36N 102 43W
Cañiza, La 56 42 13N 8 16W
Cañizal 56 41 20N 5 22W
Canjáyar 59 37 1N 2 44W
Cankırı 92 40 40N 33 30E
Cankuzo 126 3 10S 30 31E
Canlaon, Mt. 103 9 27N 118 25E
Canmore 152 51 7N 115 18W
Cann River 141 37 35S 149 7E
Canna I. 36 57 3N 6 33W
Canna, Sd. of 36 57 1N 6 30W
Cannanore 97 11 53N 75 27E
Cannes 45 43 32N 7 0E
Cannich 37 57 20N 4 48W
Canning Basin 136 19 50S 124 0E
Canning Town 95 22 23N 88 40E
Cannington 28 51 8N 3 4W
Cannock 28 52 42N 2 2W
Cannock Chase, hills 23 52 43N 2 0W
Cannon Ball, R. 158 46 20N 101 20W
Cannondale, Mt. 138 25 13S 148 57E
Caño Colorado 174 2 18N 68 22W
Canoe L. 153 55 10N 108 15W
Canol 147 65 15N 126 50W
Canon City 158 39 30N 105 20W
Canonbie 35 55 4N 2 58W
Canopus 140 33 29S 140 42E
Canora 153 51 40N 102 30W
Canosa di Púglia 65 41 13N 16 4E
Canourgue, Le 44 44 26N 3 13E
Canowindra 141 33 35S 148 38E
Canso 151 45 20N 61 0W
Cantabria, Sierra de 58 42 40N 2 30W
Cantabrian Mts. = Cantábrica 56 43 0N 5 10W
Cantábrica, Cordillera 56 43 0N 5 10W
Cantal □ 44 45 4N 2 45E
Cantanhede 56 40 20N 8 36W
Cantaura 174 9 19N 64 21W
Cantavieja 58 40 31N 0 25W
Čantavir 66 45 55N 19 46E
Canterbury, Austral. 138 25 23S 141 53E
Canterbury, U.K. 29 51 17N 1 5E
Canterbury □ 143 43 45S 171 19E
Canterbury Bight 143 44 16S 171 55E
Canterbury Plains 143 43 55S 171 22E
Cantil 163 35 18N 117 58W
Cantillana 57 37 36N 5 50W
Canto do Buriti 170 8 7S 42 58W
Canton, Ga., U.S.A. 157 34 13N 84 29W
Canton, Ill., U.S.A. 158 40 32N 90 0W
Canton, Mass., U.S.A. 162 42 9N 71 9W
Canton, Miss., U.S.A. 159 32 40N 90 1W
Canton, Mo., U.S.A. 158 40 10N 91 33W
Canton, Ohio, U.S.A. 156 40 47N 81 22W
Canton, Okla., U.S.A. 159 36 5N 98 36W

Canton **Cascade**

Canton, Pa., U.S.A. 162 41 39N 76 51W
Canton, S.D., U.S.A. 158 43 20N 96 35W
Canton = Kuangchou 109 23 10N 113 10 E
Canton I. 130 2 30 S 172 0W
Canton L. 159 36 12N 98 40W
Cantù 62 45 44N 9 8 E
Canudos 174 7 13 S 58 5W
Canulloit 161 31 58N 106 36W
Canutama 174 6 30 S 64 20W
Canvey 29 51 32N 0 35 E
Canyon, Can. 147 47 25N 84 36W
Canyon, Texas, U.S.A. 159 35 0N 101 57W
Canyon, Wyo., U.S.A. 160 44 43N 110 36W
Canyonlands Nat. Park 161 38 25N 109 30W
Canyonville 160 42 55N 123 14W
Canzo 62 45 54N 9 18 E
Cao Bang 100 22 40N 106 15 E
Cao Lanh 101 10 27N 105 38 E
Caoles 34 56 32N 6 43W
Caolisport, Loch 34 55 54N 5 40W
Cáorle 63 45 36N 12 51 E
Cap-aux-Meules 151 47 23N 61 52W
Cap Chat 151 49 6N 66 40W
Cap-de-la-Madeleine 150 46 22N 72 31W
Cap Haïtien 167 19 40N 72 20W
Cap St.-Jacques = Vung Tau 101 10 21N 107 4 E
Capa Stilo 65 38 25N 16 25 E
Capàccio 65 40 26N 15 4 E
Capaia 124 8 27 S 20 13 E
Capanaparo, R. 174 7 0N 67 30W
Capanema 170 1 12 S 47 11W
Caparo, R. 174 7 30N 70 30W
Capatárida 174 11 11N 70 37W
Capbreton 44 43 39N 1 26W
Capdenac 44 44 34N 2 5 E
Cape Barren I. 138 40 25 S 148 15 E
Cape Breton Highlands Nat. Park 151 46 50N 60 40W
Cape Breton I. 151 46 0N 60 30W
Cape Charles 162 37 15N 75 59W
Cape Coast 121 5 5N 1 15W
Cape Cod B. 162 41 50N 70 18W
Cape Dorset 149 64 14N 76 32W
Cape Dyer 149 66 40N 61 22W
Cape Fear, R. 157 34 30N 78 25W
Cape Girardeau 159 37 20N 89 30W
Cape Jervis 140 35 40 S 138 5 E
Cape May 162 39 1N 74 53W
Cape May C.H. 162 39 5N 74 50W
Cape May Pt. 162 38 56N 74 56W
Cape Montague 151 46 5N 62 25W
Cape Palmas 120 4 25N 7 49W
Cape Preston 136 20 51 S 116 12 E
Cape Province □ 128 32 0 S 23 0 E
Cape, R. 138 20 37 S 147 1 E
Cape Tormentine 151 46 8N 63 47W
Cape Town (Kaapstad) 128 33 55 S 18 22 E
Cape Verde Is. 14 17 10N 25 20W
Cape York Peninsula 138 33 34 S 115 33 E
Capel 29 51 8N 0 18W
Capel Curig 31 53 6N 3 55W
Capela 170 10 30 S 37 0W
Capela de Campo 170 4 40 S 41 55W
Capelinha 171 17 42 S 42 31W
Capella 138 23 2 S 148 1 E
Capella, G. 138 4 45 S 140 50 E
Capella, Mt. 135 5 4 S 141 8 E
Capelle, La 43 49 59N 3 50 E
Capendu 44 43 11N 2 31 E
Capernaum = Kefar Nahum 90 32 54N 35 32 E
Capestang 44 43 20N 3 2 E
Capim 170 1 41 S 47 47W
Capim, R. 170 3 0 S 48 0W
Capinópolis 171 18 41 S 49 35W
Capitan 161 33 40N 105 41W
Capitola 163 36 59N 121 57W
Capivara, Serra da 171 14 35 S 45 0W
Capizzi 65 37 50N 14 26 E
Čapljina 66 43 35N 17 43 E
Capoche, R. 127 15 0 S 32 45 E
Cappamore 39 52 38N 8 20W
Cappoquin 39 52 9N 7 46W
Capraia, I. 62 43 2N 9 50 E
Caprarola 63 42 21N 12 11 E
Capreol 150 46 43N 80 56W
Caprera, I. 64 41 12N 9 28 E
Capri, I. 65 40 34N 14 15 E
Capricorn, C. 133 23 30 S 151 13 E
Capricorn Group 138 23 30 S 151 55 E
Capricorn Ra. 136 23 20 S 117 0 E
Caprino Veronese 62 45 37N 10 47 E
Caprivi Strip 128 18 0 S 23 0 E
Captainganj 95 26 55N 83 45 E
Captain's Flat 141 35 35 S 149 27 E
Captieux 44 44 18N 0 16W
Cápua 65 41 7N 14 15 E
Capulin 159 36 48N 103 59W
Caquetá □ 174 1 0N 74 0W
Caquetá, R. 174 1 0N 76 20W
Cáqueza 174 4 25N 73 57W
Carabobo 174 10 10N 68 5W
Caracal 70 44 8N 24 22 E
Caracaraí 174 1 50N 61 8W
Caracas 174 10 30N 66 55W
Caracol, Piauí, Brazil 170 9 15 S 43 45W
Caracol, Rondonia, Brazil 174 9 15 S 64 20W
Caradoc 140 30 35 S 143 5 E
Caragabal 141 33 49 S 147 45 E
Caragh L. 39 52 3N 9 50W
Caráglio 62 44 25N 7 25 E
Caraí 171 17 12 S 41 42W
Carajás, Serra dos 170 6 0 S 51 30W
Caramanta 174 5 33N 75 38W
Carangola 173 20 50 S 42 5W
Carani 137 30 57 S 116 28 E
Caransebeş 70 45 28N 22 18 E
Carapelle, R. 65 41 20N 15 35 E
Caraş Severin □ 66 45 10N 22 10 E
Caraşova 66 45 11N 21 51 E
Caratasca, Laguna 166 15 30N 83 40W
Caratec 42 48 40N 3 55W
Caratinga 171 19 50 S 42 10W
Caratunk 151 45 13N 69 55W
Caraúbas 170 7 43 S 36 31W
Caravaca 59 38 8N 1 52W
Caravággio 62 45 30N 9 39 E
Caravelas 171 17 45 S 39 15W
Caraveli 174 15 45 S 73 25W
Caràzinho 173 28 0 S 53 0W
Carballino 56 42 26N 8 5W
Carballo 56 43 13N 8 41W
Carberry 153 49 50N 99 25W
Carbia 56 42 48N 8 14W
Carbó 164 29 42N 110 58W
Carbon 152 51 30N 113 9W
Carbonara, C. 64 39 8N 9 30 E
Carbondale, Colo, U.S.A. 160 39 30N 107 10W
Carbondale, Ill., U.S.A. 159 37 45N 89 10W
Carbondale, Pa., U.S.A. 162 41 37N 75 30W
Carbonear 151 47 42N 53 13W
Carboneras 59 37 0N 1 53W
Carboneras de Guadazaón 58 39 54N 1 50W
Carbonia 64 39 10N 8 30 E
Carbost 36 57 19N 6 21W
Carbury 38 53 22N 6 58W
Carcabuey 57 37 27N 4 17W
Carcagente 59 39 8N 0 28W
Carcajou 152 57 47N 117 6W
Carcasse, C. 167 18 30N 74 28W
Carcassonne 44 43 13N 2 20 E
Carche 59 38 26N 1 9W
Carcoar 141 33 36 S 149 8 E
Carcross 147 60 13N 134 45W
Cardabia 136 23 2 S 113 55 E
Cardamom Hills 97 9 30N 77 15 E
Cárdenas, Cuba 166 23 0N 81 30W
Cárdenas, San Luis Potosí, Mexico 166 22 0N 99 41W
Cárdenas, Tabasco, Mexico 165 17 59N 93 21W
Cardenete 58 39 46N 1 41W
Cardiff 31 51 28N 3 11W
Cardiff-by-the-Sea 163 33 1N 117 17W
Cardigan 31 52 6N 4 41W
Cardigan (□) 26 52 6N 4 41W
Cardigan B. 31 52 30N 4 30W
Cardington 29 52 7N 0 23W
Cardón 174 11 37N 70 14W
Cardona, Spain 58 41 56N 1 40 E
Cardona, Uruguay 172 33 53 S 57 18W
Cardoner, R. 58 42 0N 1 33 E
Cardross 153 49 50N 105 40W
Cardston 152 49 15N 113 20W
Cardwell 138 18 14 S 146 2 E
Careen L. 153 57 0N 108 11W
Carei 70 47 40N 22 29 E
Carentan 42 49 19N 1 15W
Carey, Idaho, U.S.A. 160 43 19N 113 58W
Carey, Ohio, U.S.A. 156 40 58N 83 22W
Carey, L. 137 29 0 S 122 15 E
Carey L. 153 62 12N 102 55W
Careysburg 120 6 34N 10 30W
Cargados Garajos, Is. 11 17 0 S 59 0 E
Cargelligo, L. 139 33 17 S 146 24 E
Cargèse 45 42 7N 8 35 E
Carhaix-Plouguer 42 48 18N 3 36W
Carhué 172 37 10 S 62 50W
Cariacica 171 20 16 S 40 25W
Cariaco 174 10 29N 63 33W
Caribaná, Pta. 174 8 37N 76 52W
Caribbean Sea 167 15 0N 75 0W
Cariboo Mts. 152 53 0N 121 0W
Caribou, Can. 153 53 15N 121 55W
Caribou, U.S.A. 151 46 55N 68 0W
Caribou I. 150 47 22N 85 49W
Caribou Is. 152 61 55N 113 15W
Caribou L., Man., Can. 153 59 21N 96 10W
Caribou L., Ont., Can. 150 50 25N 89 5W
Caribou Mts. 152 59 12N 115 40W
Caribou, R., Man., Can. 153 59 20N 94 44W
Caribou, R., N.W.T., Can. 152 61 27N 125 45W
Carichic 164 27 56N 107 3W
Carignan 43 49 38N 5 10 E
Carignano 62 44 55N 7 40 E
Carillo 164 26 50N 103 55W
Carinda 141 30 28 S 147 41 E
Cariñena 58 41 20N 1 13W
Carinhanha 171 14 15 S 44 0W
Carinhanha, R. 171 14 20 S 43 47W
Carini 64 38 9N 13 10 E
Carinish 36 57 31N 7 20W
Carinola 64 41 11N 13 58 E
Carinthia □ = Kärnten 52 46 52N 13 30 E
Caripito 174 10 8N 63 6W
Caririacu 171 7 2 S 39 17W
Carisbrooke 28 50 42N 1 19W
Caritianas 174 9 20 S 63 0W
Cark 32 54 11N 2 59W
Carlentini 65 37 15N 15 2 E
Carleton Place 150 45 8N 76 9W
Carleton Rode 29 52 30N 1 6 E
Carletonville 128 26 23 S 27 22 E
Carlin 160 40 50N 116 5W
Carlingford 38 54 3N 6 10W
Carlingford, L. 38 54 0N 6 5W
Carlinville 158 39 20N 89 55W
Carlisle, U.K. 32 54 54N 2 55W
Carlisle, U.S.A. 162 40 12N 77 10W
Carlitte, Pic 44 42 35N 1 43 E
Carloforte 64 39 10N 8 18 E
Carlops 35 55 47N 3 20W
Carlos Casares 172 35 53 S 61 20W
Carlos Chagas 171 17 43 S 40 45W
Carlos Tejedor 172 35 25 S 62 25W
Carlota, La 172 33 30 S 63 20W
Carlow 39 52 50N 6 58W
Carlow □ 39 52 43N 6 50W
Carloway 36 58 17N 6 48W
Carlsbad, Calif., U.S.A. 163 33 11N 117 25W
Carlsbad, N. Mex., U.S.A. 159 32 20N 104 7W
Carlton 33 52 58N 1 6W
Carlton Colville 29 52 27N 1 41 E
Carlton Miniott 33 54 13N 1 22W
Carluke 35 55 44N 3 50W
Carlyle, Can. 153 49 40N 102 20W
Carlyle, U.S.A. 158 38 38N 89 23W
Carmacks 147 62 5N 136 16W
Carmagnola 62 44 50N 7 42 E
Carman 153 49 30N 98 0W
Carmangay 152 50 10N 113 10W
Carmanville 151 49 23N 54 19W
Carmarthen 31 51 52N 4 20W
Carmarthen (□) 26 53 40N 4 18W
Carmarthen B. 31 51 40N 4 30W
Carmaux 44 44 3N 2 10 E
Carmel, Calif., U.S.A. 163 36 38N 121 55W
Carmel, N.Y., U.S.A. 162 41 25N 73 38W
Carmel Hd. 31 53 24N 4 34W
Carmel Mt. 90 32 45N 35 3 E
Carmel Valley 163 36 29N 121 43W
Carmelo 172 34 0 S 58 10W
Carmen, Colomb. 174 9 43N 75 8W
Carmen, Parag. 173 27 13 S 56 12W
Carmen de Patagones 176 40 50 S 63 0W
Carmen, I. 164 26 0N 111 20W
Carmen, R. 164 30 42N 106 29W
Cármenes 56 42 58N 5 34W
Carmensa 172 35 15 S 67 40W
Carmi 156 38 6N 88 10W
Carmichael 163 38 38N 121 19W
Carmila 138 21 55 S 149 24 E
Carmo do Paranaiba 171 18 59 S 46 21W
Carmona 57 37 28N 5 42W
Carmyllie 37 56 36N 2 41W
Carn Ban 37 57 6N 4 15W
Carn Eige 36 57 17N 5 9W
Carn Glas Chorie 37 57 20N 3 50W
Carn Mor 37 57 14N 3 13W
Carn na Saobhaidh 37 57 12N 4 20W
Carna 39 53 20N 9 50W
Carnarvon, Queens., Austral. 138 24 48 S 147 45 E
Carnarvon, W. Austral., Austral. 137 24 51 S 113 42 E
Carnarvon, S. Afr. 128 30 56 S 22 8 E
Carnarvon Ra., Queensland, Austral. 138 25 15 S 148 30 E
Carnarvon Ra., W.A., Austral. 137 25 0 S 120 45 E
Carnaxide 57 38 43N 9 14W
Carncastle 38 54 55N 5 52W
Carndonagh 38 55 15N 7 16W
Carnduff 153 49 10N 101 50W
Carnedd Llewelyn, Mt. 31 53 9N 3 58W
Carnegie, L. 137 26 5 S 122 30 E
Carnew 39 52 43N 6 30W
Carney 38 54 20N 8 30W
Carnforth 32 54 8N 2 47W
Carnic Alps = Karnische Alpen 63 46 34N 12 50 E
Carnlough 38 55 0N 6 0W
Carno 31 52 34N 3 31W
Carnon 44 43 32N 3 59 E
Carnot 124 4 59N 15 56 E
Carnot B. 136 17 20 S 121 30 E
Carnoustie 35 56 30N 2 41W
Carnsore Pt. 39 52 10N 6 20W
Carnwath 35 55 42N 3 38W
Caro 156 43 29N 83 27W
Carolina, Brazil 170 7 10 S 47 30W
Carolina, S. Afr. 129 26 5 S 30 6 E
Carolina, La 57 38 17N 3 38W
Caroline I. 131 9 15 S 150 3W
Caroline Is. 130 8 0N 150 0 E
Caroline Pk. 143 45 57 S 167 15 E
Carolside 152 51 20N 111 40W
Caron 153 50 30N 105 50W
Caroni, R. 174 6 0N 62 40W
Carora 174 10 11N 70 5W
Carovigno 65 40 42N 17 40 E
Carpathians, Mts. 53 46 20N 26 0 E
Carpaţii Meridionali 70 45 30N 25 0 E
Carpenédolo 62 45 22N 10 25 E
Carpentaria Downs 138 18 44 S 144 20 E
Carpentaria, G. of 133 14 0 S 139 0 E
Carpentras 45 44 3N 5 2 E
Carpi 62 44 47N 10 52 E
Carpina 170 7 51 S 35 15W
Carpino 65 41 50N 15 51 E
Carpinteria 163 34 25N 119 31W
Carpio 56 41 13N 5 7W
Carpolac = Morea 140 36 45 S 141 18 E
Carr Boyd Ra. 136 16 15 S 128 35 E
Carra L. 38 53 41N 9 12W
Carrabelle 157 29 52N 84 40W
Carracastle 38 53 57N 8 42W
Carradale 34 55 35N 5 30W
Carraipia 174 11 16N 72 22W
Carrara 62 44 5N 10 7 E
Carrascosa del Campo 58 40 2N 2 45W
Carrauntohill, Mt. 39 52 0N 9 49W
Carraweena 139 29 10 S 140 0 E
Carrbridge 37 57 17N 3 50W
Carriacou, I. 167 12 30N 61 28W
Carribee 140 35 7 S 136 57 E
Carrick 38 54 40N 8 39W
Carrick, dist. 34 55 12N 4 38W
Carrick-on-Shannon 38 53 57N 8 7W
Carrick-on-Suir 39 52 22N 7 30W
Carrick Ra. 143 45 15 S 169 8 E
Carrickart 38 55 10N 7 47W
Carrickbeg 39 52 20N 7 25W
Carrickboy 38 53 36N 7 40W
Carrickfergus 36 54 43N 5 50W
Carrickfergus □ 38 54 43N 5 49W
Carrickmacross 38 54 0N 6 43W
Carrieton 140 32 25 S 138 31 E
Carrigaholt 39 52 37N 9 42W
Carrigahorig 39 53 4N 8 10W
Carrigaline 39 51 49N 8 22W
Carrigallen 38 53 59N 7 40W
Carrigan Hd. 38 54 38N 8 40W
Carrignavar 39 52 0N 8 29W
Carrigtwohill 39 51 55N 8 15W
Carrington 158 47 30N 99 7W
Carrión de los Condes 56 42 20N 4 37W
Carrión, R. 56 42 42N 4 47W
Carrizal 174 12 1N 72 11W
Carrizal Bajo 172 28 5 S 71 20W
Carrizalillo 172 29 0 S 71 30W
Carrizo Cr. 159 36 30N 103 40W
Carrizo Springs 159 28 28N 99 50W
Carrizozo 161 33 40N 105 57W
Carroll 158 42 2N 94 55W
Carrollton, Ga., U.S.A. 157 33 36N 85 5W
Carrollton, Ill., U.S.A. 158 39 20N 90 25W
Carrollton, Ky., U.S.A. 156 38 40N 85 10W
Carrollton, Mo., U.S.A. 158 39 19N 93 24W
Carron L. 36 57 22N 5 35W
Carron R., U.K. 36 57 30N 5 30W
Carron R., U.K. 37 57 51N 4 21W
Carrot, R. 153 53 50N 101 17W
Carrot River 153 53 17N 103 35W
Carrouges 42 48 34N 0 10W
Carrowkeel 38 55 7N 7 12W
Carrowmore L. 38 54 12N 9 48W
Carruthers 153 52 52N 109 16W
Carryduff 38 54 32N 5 52W
Çarşamba 92 41 15N 36 45 E
Carsoli 63 42 7N 13 3 E
Carson 158 46 27N 101 29W
Carson City 160 39 12N 119 46W
Carson Sink 160 39 50N 118 40W
Carsonville 156 43 25N 82 39W
Carsphairn 34 55 13N 4 15W
Carstairs 35 55 42N 3 41W
Cartagena, Colomb. 174 10 25N 75 33W
Cartagena, Spain 59 37 38N 0 59W
Cartago, Colomb. 174 4 45N 75 55W
Cartago, C. Rica 166 9 50N 84 0W
Cartaret 42 49 23N 1 47W
Cartaxo 57 39 10N 8 47W
Cartaya 57 37 16N 7 9W
Cartersville 157 34 11N 84 48W
Carterton 142 41 2 S 175 31 E
Carthage, Ark., U.S.A. 159 34 4N 92 32W
Carthage, Ill., U.S.A. 158 40 25N 91 10W
Carthage, Mo., U.S.A. 159 37 10N 94 20W
Carthage, N.Y., U.S.A. 156 43 59N 75 37W
Carthage, S.D., U.S.A. 158 44 14N 97 38W
Carthage, Texas, U.S.A. 159 32 8N 94 20W
Cartier I. 136 12 31 S 123 29 E
Cartmel 32 54 13N 2 57W
Cartwright 151 53 41N 56 58W
Caruaru 170 8 15 S 35 55W
Carúpano 174 10 45N 63 15W
Carutapera 170 1 13 S 46 1W
Caruthersville 159 36 10N 89 40W
Carvarzere 63 45 8N 12 7 E
Carvin 43 50 30N 2 57 E
Carvoeiro 174 1 30 S 61 59W
Carvoeiro, Cabo 57 39 21N 9 24W
Casa Agapito 174 2 3N 73 58W
Casa Branca, Brazil 171 21 46 S 47 4W
Casa Branca, Port. 57 38 29N 8 12W
Casa Grande 161 32 53N 111 51W
Casa Nova 170 9 10 S 41 5W
Casablanca, Chile 172 33 20 S 71 25W
Casablanca, Moroc. 118 33 36N 7 36W
Casacalenda 65 41 45N 14 50 E
Casalbordino 63 42 10N 14 34 E
Casale Monferrato 62 45 8N 8 28 E
Casalmaggiore 62 44 59N 10 25 E
Casalpusterlengo 62 45 10N 9 40 E
Casamance, R. 120 12 54N 15 0W
Casamássima 65 40 58N 16 55 E
Casanare, R. 174 6 30N 71 20W
Casarano 65 40 0N 18 10 E
Casares 57 36 27N 5 16W
Casas Grandes 164 30 22N 108 0W
Casas IbáPez 59 39 17N 1 30W
Casasimarro 59 39 22N 2 3W
Casatejada 56 39 54N 5 40W
Casavieja 56 40 17N 4 46W
Cascade, Idaho, U.S.A. 160 44 30N 116 2W

Cascade Cepin

Cascade, Mont., U.S.A. 160 47 16N 111 46W
Cascade Locks 160 45 44N 121 54W
Cascade Pt. 143 44 1S 168 20E
Cascade Ra. 160 45 0N 121 30W
Cascais 57 38 41N 9 25W
Cascina 62 43 40N 10 32E
Caselle Torinese 62 45 12N 7 39E
Caserta 65 41 5N 14 20E
Cashel 39 52 31N 7 53W
Cashla B. 39 53 12N 9 37W
Cashmere 160 47 31N 120 30W
Cashmere Downs 137 28 57S 119 35E
Casigua 174 11 2N 71 1W
Casiguran 103 16 15N 122 15E
Casilda 172 33 10S 61 10W
Casimcea 70 44 45N 28 23E
Casino 139 28 52S 153 3E
Casiquiare, R. 174 2 45N 66 20W
Caslan 152 54 38N 112 31W
Casma 174 9 30S 78 20W
Casmalia 163 34 50N 120 32W
Casola Valsenio 63 44 12N 11 40E
Cásoli 63 42 7N 14 18E
Caspe 58 41 14N 0 1W
Casper 160 42 52N 106 27W
Caspian Sea 79 43 0N 50 0E
Casquets 42 49 46N 2 15W
Cass City 156 43 34N 83 15W
Cass Lake 158 47 23N 94 38W
Cassá de la Selva 58 41 53N 2 52E
Cassano Iónio 65 39 47N 16 20E
Cassel 43 50 48N 2 30E
Casselton 158 47 0N 97 15W
Cássia 171 20 36S 46 56W
Cassiar 152 59 16N 129 40W
Cassiar Mts. 152 59 30N 130 30W
Cassils 152 50 29N 112 15W
Cassinga 125 15 5S 16 23E
Cassino 64 41 30N 13 50E
Cassiporé, C. 170 3 50N 51 5W
Cassis 45 43 14N 5 32E
Cassville 159 36 45N 93 59W
Cástagneto Carducci 62 43 9N 10 36E
Castaic 163 34 30N 118 38W
Castanhal 170 1 18S 47 55W
Castanheiro 174 0 17S 65 38W
Casteau 47 50 32N 4 2E
Castéggio 62 45 1N 9 8E
Castejón de Monegros 58 41 37N 0 15W
Castel di Sangro 65 41 41N 14 5E
Castel San Giovanni 62 45 4N 9 25E
Castel San Pietro 63 44 23N 11 30E
Castelbuono 65 37 56N 14 4E
Casteldelfino 62 44 35N 7 4E
Castelfiorentino 62 43 36N 10 58E
Castelfranco Emília 62 44 37N 11 2E
Castelfranco Veneto 63 45 40N 11 56E
Casteljaloux 44 44 19N 0 6E
Castellabate 65 40 18N 14 55E
Castellammare del Golfo 64 38 2N 12 53E
Castellammare di Stábia 65 40 47N 14 29E
Castellammare, G. di 64 38 5N 12 55E
Castellamonte 62 45 23N 7 42E
Castellana Grotte 65 40 53N 17 10E
Castellane 45 43 50N 6 31E
Castellaneta 65 40 40N 16 57E
Castellar de Santisteban 59 38 16N 3 8W
Castelleone 62 45 19N 9 47E
Castelli 172 36 7S 57 47W
Castelló de Ampurias 58 42 15N 3 4E
Castellón □ 58 40 15N 0 5W
Castellón de la Plana 58 39 58N 0 3W
Castellote 58 40 48N 0 15W
Castelltersol 58 41 45N 2 8E
Castelmáuro 65 41 50N 14 40E
Castelnau-de-Médoc 44 45 2N 0 48W
Castelnaudary 44 43 20N 1 58E
Castelnovo ne' Monti 62 44 27N 10 26E
Castelnuovo di Val di Cécina 62 43 12N 10 54E
Castelo 173 20 53S 41 42E
Castelo Branco 56 39 50N 7 31W
Castelo Branco □ 56 39 52N 7 45W
Castelo de Paiva 56 41 2N 8 16W
Castelo de Vide 57 39 25N 7 27W
Castelo do Piauí 170 5 20S 41 33W
Castelsarrasin 44 44 2N 1 7E
Casteltérmini 64 37 32N 13 38E
Castelvetrano 64 37 40N 12 46E
Casterton 140 37 30S 141 30E
Castets 44 43 52N 1 6W
Castiglione del Lago 63 43 7N 12 3E
Castiglione della Pescáia 62 42 46N 10 53E
Castiglione della Stiviere 62 45 23N 10 30E
Castiglione Fiorentino 63 43 20N 11 55E
Castilblanco 57 39 17N 5 5W
Castilla La Nueva 57 39 45N 3 20W
Castilla La Vieja 56 41 55N 4 0W
Castilla, Playa de 57 37 0N 6 33W
Castille = Castilla 56 40 0N 3 30W
Castilletes 174 11 51N 71 19W
Castillón 164 28 20N 103 38W
Castillon-en-Couserans 44 42 56N 1 1E
Castillon-la-Bataille 44 44 51N 0 2W
Castillonès 44 44 39N 0 37E
Castillos 173 34 12S 53 52W
Castle Acre 29 52 42N 0 42W
Castle Cary 28 51 5N 2 32W
Castle Dale 160 39 11N 111 1W
Castle Donington 28 52 50N 1 20W
Castle Douglas 35 54 57N 3 57W
Castle Eden 54 54 45N 1 20W
Castle Point 142 40 54N 176 15E
Castle Rock, Colo., U.S.A. 158 39 26N 104 50W
Castle Rock, Wash., U.S.A. 160 46 20N 122 58W
Castlebar 38 53 52N 9 17W
Castlebay 36 56 57N 7 30W
Castlebellingham 38 53 53N 6 22W
Castleblakeney 38 53 26N 8 28W
Castleblayney 38 54 7N 6 44W
Castlebridge 39 52 23N 6 28W
Castlecliff 142 39 57S 174 59E
Castlecomer 39 52 49N 7 13W
Castleconnell 39 52 44N 8 30W
Castledawson 38 54 47N 6 35W
Castlederg 38 54 43N 7 35W
Castledermot 39 52 55N 6 50W
Castlefinn 38 54 47N 7 35W
Castleford 33 53 43N 1 21W
Castlegar 152 49 20N 117 40W
Castlegate 160 39 45N 110 57W
Castlegregory 39 52 16N 10 0W
Castlehill 38 51 1N 9 49W
Castleisland 39 52 14N 9 28W
Castlemaine, Austral. 140 37 2S 144 12E
Castlemaine, Ireland 39 52 10N 9 42W
Castlemaine Harb. 39 52 8N 9 50W
Castlemartyr 39 51 54N 8 3W
Castlepollard 38 53 40N 7 20W
Castlereagh 38 53 47N 8 30W
Castlereagh □ 38 54 33N 5 33W
Castlereagh B. 138 12 10S 135 10E
Castlereagh, R. 141 30 12S 147 32E
Castleside 32 54 50N 1 52W
Castleton, Derby., U.K. 33 53 20N 1 47W
Castleton, N. Yorks., U.K. 33 54 27N 0 57W
Castleton, U.S.A. 162 43 37N 73 11W
Castletown, Geoghegan, Ireland 38 53 27N 7 30W
Castletown, Laois, Ireland 38 52 58N 7 31W
Castletown, Meath, Ireland 39 53 47N 6 41W
Castletown, I. of Man 32 54 4N 4 40W
Castletown, U.K. 37 58 35N 3 22W
Castletown Bearhaven 39 51 40N 9 54W
Castletownroche 39 52 10N 8 28W
Castletownshend 39 51 31N 9 11W
Castlevale 138 24 30S 146 48E
Castlewellan 38 54 16N 5 57W
Castor 152 52 15N 111 50W
Castorland 162 43 53N 75 31W
Castres 44 43 37N 2 13E
Castricum 46 52 33N 4 40E
Castries 167 14 0N 60 50W
Castril 59 37 48N 2 46W
Castro, Brazil 173 24 45S 50 0W
Castro, Chile 176 42 30S 73 50W
Castro Alves 171 12 46S 39 26W
Castro del Río 57 37 41N 4 29W
Castro Marim 57 37 13N 7 26W
Castro Urdiales 58 43 23N 3 19W
Castro Verde 57 37 41N 8 4W
Castrojeriz 56 42 17N 4 9W
Castropol 56 43 32N 7 0W
Castroreale 65 38 5N 15 15E
Castrovíllari 65 39 49N 16 11E
Castroville, Calif., U.S.A. 163 36 46N 121 45W
Castroville, Tex, U.S.A. 159 29 20N 98 53W
Castuera 57 38 43N 5 37W
Casummit L. 150 51 29N 92 22W
Cat Ba 100 20 50N 107 0E
Cat I., Bahamas 167 24 30N 75 30W
Cat I., U.S.A. 159 30 15N 89 7W
Cat L. 150 51 40N 91 50W
Čata 53 47 58N 18 38E
Catacamas 166 14 54N 85 56W
Catacaos 174 5 20S 80 45W
Cataguases 173 21 23S 42 39W
Catahoula L. 159 31 30N 92 5W
Catalão 171 18 10S 47 57W
Çatalca 92 41 9N 28 28E
Catalina 151 48 31N 53 4W
Catalonia = Cataluña 58 41 40N 1 15E
Cataluña 58 41 40N 1 15E
Catamarca 172 28 30S 65 50W
Catamarca □ 172 28 30S 65 50W
Catanduanas, Is. 103 13 50N 124 20E
Catanduva 173 21 5S 48 58W
Catánia 65 37 31N 15 4E
Catánia, G. di 65 37 25N 15 8E
Catanzaro 65 38 54N 16 38E
Catarman 103 12 28N 124 1E
Catastrophe C. 136 34 59S 136 0E
Catcleugh 35 55 19N 2 22W
Cateau, Le 43 50 6N 3 30E
Cateel 103 7 47N 126 24E
Catende 170 8 40S 35 43W
Caterham 29 51 16N 0 4W
Cathcart, Austral. 141 36 2S 149 24E
Cathcart, S. Afr. 128 32 18S 27 10E
Catine 41 46 30N 0 15W
Catio 120 11 17N 15 15W
Catismiña 174 4 5N 63 52W
Catita 170 9 31S 43 1W
Catlettsburg 156 38 23N 82 38W
Cato I. 133 23 15S 155 32E
Catoche, C. 165 21 40N 87 0W
Catolé 171 7 19S 36 1W
Catolé do Rocha 170 6 21S 37 45W
Caton 32 54 5N 2 41W
Catonsville 162 39 16N 76 44W
Catral 59 38 10N 0 47W
Catria, Mt. 63 43 28N 12 42E
Catrimani 174 0 27N 61 41W
Catrine 34 55 30N 4 20W
Catsfield 29 50 53N 0 28E
Catskill 162 42 14N 73 52W
Catskill Mts. 162 42 15N 74 15W
Catt, Mt. 138 13 49S 134 23E
Catterick 33 54 23N 1 38W
Cattólica 63 43 58N 12 43E
Cattólica Eraclea 64 37 27N 13 24E
Catton 35 54 56N 2 16W
Catu 171 12 21S 38 23W
Catuala 128 16 25S 19 2E
Catur 127 13 45S 35 30E
Catwick Is. 101 10 0N 109 0E
Cauca □ 174 2 30N 76 50W
Cauca, R. 174 7 25N 75 30W
Caucasia 174 8 0N 75 12W
Caucasus Mts. = Bolshoi Kavkas 83 42 50N 44 0E
Cauccaia 170 3 40S 38 35W
Caudebec-en-Caux 42 49 30N 0 42E
Caudete 59 38 42N 1 2W
Caudry 43 50 7N 3 22E
Caulkerbush 35 54 54N 3 40W
Caulnes 42 48 18N 2 10W
Caulónia 65 38 23N 16 25E
Caungula 124 8 15S 18 50E
Cáuquenes 172 36 0S 72 30W
Caura, R. 174 6 20N 64 30W
Cauresi, R. 127 17 40S 33 10E
Causapscal 151 48 19N 67 12W
Causeway 39 52 25N 9 45W
Caussade 44 44 10N 1 33E
Cauterets 44 42 52N 0 8W
Cauvery, R. 93 12 0N 77 45E
Caux 42 49 38N 0 35E
Cava dei Tirreni 65 40 42N 14 42E
Cávado, R. 56 41 37N 8 15W
Cavaillon 45 43 50N 5 2E
Cavalaire-sur-Mer 45 43 10N 6 33E
Cavalcante 171 13 48S 47 30W
Cavalerie, La 44 44 0N 3 10E
Cavalese 63 46 17N 11 29E
Cavalier 158 48 50N 97 39W
Cavalli Is. 142 35 0S 173 58E
Cavallo, I. 45 41 22N 9 16E
Cavally, R. 120 5 0N 7 40W
Cavan 38 54 0N 7 22W
Cavan □ 38 53 58N 7 10W
Cavanagh Ra. 137 26 10S 122 50E
Cavárzere 63 45 8N 12 6E
Cave City 156 37 13N 85 57W
Cavenagh Range 137 26 12S 127 55E
Cavendish 140 37 31S 142 2E
Cavers 150 48 55N 87 41W
Caviana, Ilha 170 0 15N 50 0W
Cavite 103 14 20N 120 55E
Cavour 62 44 47N 7 22E
Cavtat 66 42 35N 18 13E
Cawdor 37 57 31N 3 56W
Cawkers Well 140 31 41S 142 57E
Cawndilla, L. 140 32 30S 142 15E
Cawnpore = Kanpur 95 26 35N 80 20E
Cawood 33 53 50N 1 7W
Cawston 29 52 47N 1 10E
Caxias 174 5 0S 43 27W
Caxias do Sul 173 29 10S 51 10W
Caxine, C. 118 35 56N 0 27W
Caxito 124 8 30S 13 30E
Cay Sal Bank 166 23 45N 80 0W
Cayambe 174 0 3N 78 22W
Cayce 157 33 59N 81 2W
Cayenne 175 5 0N 52 18W
Cayes, Les 167 18 15N 73 46W
Cayeux-sur-Mer. 43 50 10N 1 30E
Cayey 147 18 7N 66 10W
Caylus 44 44 15N 1 47E
Cayman Brac, I. 166 19 43N 79 49W
Cayman Is. 166 19 40N 79 50W
Cayo 165 17 10N 89 0W
Cayo Romano, I. 167 22 0N 73 30W
Cayuga 162 42 28N 76 30W
Cayuga L. 162 42 45N 76 45W
Cazalla de la Sierra 57 37 56N 5 45W
Cazaux et de Sanguinet, Étang de 44 44 29N 1 10W
Cazenovia 162 42 56N 75 51W
Cazères 44 43 13N 1 5E
Çazin 63 44 57N 15 57E
Čazma 63 45 45N 16 39E
Cazombo 125 12 0S 22 48E
Cazorla, Spain 59 37 55N 3 2W
Cazorla, Venez. 174 8 1N 67 0W
Cazorla, Sierra de 59 38 5N 2 55W
Cea, R. 56 42 40N 5 5W
Ceamurlia de Jos 67 44 43N 28 47E
Ceanannas Mor 38 53 42N 6 53W
Ceará = Fortaleza 170 3 35S 38 35W
Ceará □ 170 5 0S 40 0W
Ceará Mirim 170 5 38S 35 25W
Ceauru, L. 70 44 58N 23 11E
Cebaco, I. 166 7 33N 81 9W
Cebollar 172 29 10S 66 35W
Cebollera, Sierra de 58 42 0N 2 30W
Cebreros 56 40 27N 4 28W
Cebú 103 10 18N 123 54E
Cebú, I. 103 10 15N 123 40E
Ceccano 64 41 34N 13 18E
Cece 53 46 46N 18 39E
Cechi 120 6 15N 4 25W
Cecil Plains 139 27 30S 151 11E
Cecilton 162 39 24N 75 52W
Cécina 62 43 19N 10 33E
Cécina, R. 62 43 19N 10 40E
Ceclavin 56 39 50N 6 45W
Cedar City 161 37 41N 113 3W
Cedar Creek Res. 159 32 15N 96 0W
Cedar Falls 158 42 39N 92 29W
Cedar I. 162 37 35N 75 32W
Cedar Key 157 29 9N 83 5W
Cedar L. 153 53 20N 100 10W
Cedar Pt. 162 38 18N 76 25W
Cedar, R. 158 41 50N 91 20W
Cedar Rapids 158 42 0N 91 38W
Cedarburg 156 43 18N 87 55W
Cedartown 157 34 1N 85 15W
Cedarvale 152 55 1N 128 22W
Cedarville 160 41 37N 120 13W
Cedeira 56 43 39N 8 2W
Cedral 164 23 50N 100 42W
Cedrino, R. 64 40 8N 9 25E
Cedro 170 6 34S 39 3W
Cedros, I. de 164 28 10N 115 20W
Ceduna 139 32 7S 133 46E
Cedynia 54 52 53N 14 12E
Ceepeecee 152 49 52N 126 42W
Cefalù 65 38 3N 14 1E
Cega, R. 56 41 17N 4 10W
Cegléd 53 47 11N 19 47E
Céglie Messápico 65 40 39N 17 31E
Cehegín 59 38 6N 1 48W
Cehu-Silvaniei 70 47 24N 23 9E
Ceiba, La 166 15 40N 86 50W
Ceica 70 46 53N 22 10E
Ceira, R. 56 40 15N 7 55W
Cekhira 119 34 20N 10 5E
Celano 63 42 6N 13 30E
Celanova 56 42 9N 7 58W
Celaya 164 20 31N 100 37W
Celbridge 39 53 20N 6 33W
Celebes I. = Sulawesi 103 2 0S 120 0E
Celebes Sea 103 3 0N 123 0E
Celga 123 12 38N 37 3E
Çelina 156 40 32N 84 31W
Čelió 66 44 43N 18 47E
Celje 63 46 16N 15 18E
Cellar Hd. 36 58 25N 6 10W
Celldömölk 53 47 16N 17 10E
Celle 48 52 37N 10 4E
Celles 47 50 42N 3 28E
Celorica da Beira 56 40 38N 7 24W
Cemaes Bay 31 53 24N 4 27W
Cemaes Hd. 31 52 7N 4 44W
Çement 159 34 56N 98 8W
Čemerno 66 43 26N 20 26E
Cemmaes Road 31 52 39N 3 41W
Cenarth 31 52 3N 4 32W
Cenis, Col du Mt. 45 45 15N 6 55E
Ceno, R. 62 44 40N 9 52E
Cenon 44 44 50N 0 33W
Centallo 62 44 30N 7 35E
Centenário do Sul 171 22 48S 51 57W
Center, N.D., U.S.A. 158 47 9N 101 17W
Center, Texas, U.S.A. 159 31 50N 94 10W
Centerfield 160 39 9N 111 56W
Centerville, Ala., U.S.A. 157 32 55N 87 7W
Centerville, Calif., U.S.A. 163 36 44N 119 30W
Centerville, Iowa, U.S.A. 158 40 45N 92 57W
Centerville, Miss., U.S.A. 159 31 10N 91 3W
Centerville, S.D., U.S.A. 158 43 10N 96 58W
Centerville, Tenn., U.S.A. 157 35 46N 87 29W
Centerville, Tex., U.S.A. 159 31 15N 95 56W
Cento 63 44 43N 11 16E
Central 170 11 8S 42 8W
Central □, Kenya 126 0 30S 33 30E
Central □, Malawi 126 13 30S 33 30E
Central □, U.K. 34 56 10N 4 30W
Central □, Zambia 127 14 25S 28 50E
Central African Republic ■ 124 7 0N 20 0E
Central Auckland □ 142 37 30S 175 30E
Central City, Ky., U.S.A. 156 37 20N 87 7W
Central City, Nebr., U.S.A. 158 41 8N 98 0W
Central, Cordillera, C. Rica 166 10 10N 84 5W
Central, Cordillera, Dom. Rep. 167 19 15N 71 0W
Central I., L. Turkana 126 3 30N 36 0E
Central Islip 162 40 49N 73 13W
Central Makran Range 93 26 30N 64 15E
Central Patricia 150 51 30N 90 9W
Central Ra. 135 5 0S 143 0E
Central Russian Uplands 16 54 0N 36 0E
Central Siberian Plateau 77 65 0N 105 0E
Central Square 162 43 17N 76 9W
Centralia, Ill., U.S.A. 158 38 32N 89 5W
Centralia, Mo., U.S.A. 158 39 12N 92 6W
Centralia, Wash., U.S.A. 160 46 46N 122 59W
Centúripe 65 37 37N 14 41E
Cephalonia = Kefallinía 69 38 28N 20 30E
Cepin 66 45 32N 18 34E

Ceprano Château d'Oex

Ceprano 64 41 33N 13 30E
Ceptura 70 45 1N 26 21E
Ceram I. = Seram I. 103 3 10S 129 0E
Ceram Sea 103 2 30S 128 30E
Cerbère 44 42 26N 3 10E
Cerbicales, Îles 45 41 33N 9 22E
Cerbu 70 44 46N 24 46E
Cercal 57 37 48N 8 40W
Cercemaggiore 65 41 27N 14 43E
Cerdaña 58 42 22N 1 35E
Cerdedo 56 42 33N 8 23W
Cerea 63 45 12N 11 13E
Ceres, Argent. 172 29 55S 61 55W
Ceres, Brazil 171 15 17S 49 35W
Ceres, Italy 62 45 19N 7 22E
Ceres, S. Afr. 128 33 21S 19 18E
Ceres, U.K. 35 56 18N 2 57W
Ceres, U.S.A. 163 37 35N 120 57W
Céret 44 42 30N 2 42E
Cerȩté 174 8 53N 75 48W
Cerfontaine 47 50 11N 4 26E
Cerignola 65 41 17N 15 53E
Cerigo = Kíthira 69 36 9N 23 0E
Cérilly 44 46 37N 2 50E
Cerisiers 43 48 8N 3 30E
Cerizay 42 46 50N 0 40W
Çerkeş 92 40 40N 32 58E
Cerknica 63 45 48N 14 21E
Çermerno 66 43 35N 20 25E
Cerna 70 44 4N 28 17E
Cerna, R. 70 44 45N 24 0E
Cernavodů 70 44 22N 28 3E
Cernay 43 47 44N 7 10E
Cerne Abbas 28 50 49N 2 29W
Cernik 66 45 17N 17 22E
Cerralvo, I. 164 24 20N 109 45E
Cerreto Sannita 65 41 17N 14 34E
Cerrig-y-druidion 31 53 2N 3 34W
Cerritos 164 22 20N 100 20W
Cerro 161 36 47N 105 36W
Cêrro Corá 171 6 3S 36 21W
Cerro de Punta, Mt. 147 18 10N 67 0W
Certaldo 62 43 32N 11 2E
Cervaro, R. 65 41 21N 15 30E
Cervera 58 41 40N 1 16E
Cervera de Pisuerga 56 42 51N 4 30W
Cervera del Río Alhama 58 42 2N 1 58W
Cérvia 63 44 15N 12 20E
Cervignano del Friuli 63 45 49N 13 20E
Cervinara 65 41 2N 14 36E
Cervo 56 43 40N 7 24W
Cervoine 45 42 20N 9 29E
Cesanâtico 63 44 12N 12 22E
César □ 174 9 0N 73 30W
Cesaro 65 37 50N 14 38E
Cesena 63 44 9N 12 14E
Cesenático 63 44 12N 12 22E
Çësis 80 57 17N 25 28E
Česká Třebová 53 49 54N 16 27E
Česke Budějovice 52 48 55N 14 25E
České Velenice 52 48 45N 15 1E
Českézemě 52 50 0N 14 0E
Ceskomoravská Vrchovina 52 49 20N 15 45E
Český Brod 52 50 4N 14 52E
Čéský Krumlov 52 48 43N 14 21E
Český Těšin 53 49 45N 18 39E
Çeşme 69 38 20N 26 23E
Cess, R. 120 5 25N 9 35W
Cessnock 141 32 50S 151 21E
Cestos, R. 120 5 30N 9 30W
Cetate 70 44 7N 23 2E
Cetina, R. 63 43 50N 16 30E
Cetinje 66 42 23N 18 59E
Cetraro 65 39 30N 15 56E
Ceuta 118 35 52N 5 18W
Ceva 62 44 23N 8 0E
Cévennes, mts. 44 44 10N 3 50E
Ceylon = Sri Lanka ■ 97 7 30N 80 50E
Cha-am 100 12 48N 99 58E
Cha Pa 100 22 21N 103 50E
Chaam 47 51 30N 4 52E
Chabeuil 45 44 54N 5 1E
Chabjuwardoo B. 137 23 0S 113 30E
Chablais 45 46 20N 6 36E
Chablis 43 47 47N 3 48E
Chabounia 118 35 30N 2 38E
Chacabuco 172 34 40S 60 27W
Chacewater 30 50 15N 5 8W
Chachapoyas 174 6 15S 77 50W
Chachoengsao 100 13 42N 101 5E
Chachran 93 28 55N 70 30E
Chachro 94 25 5N 70 15E
Chaco □ 172 25 0S 61 0W
Chaco Austral 176 27 30S 61 40W
Chaco Boreal 172 22 30S 60 10W
Chaco Central 176 24 0S 61 0W
Chad ■ 117 12 30N 17 15E
Chadan 77 51 17N 91 35E
Chadileuvú, R. 172 37 0S 65 55W
Chadiza 127 14 10S 33 34E
Chadron 158 42 50N 103 0W
Chadyr-Lunga 82 46 3N 28 51E
Chae Hom 100 18 43N 99 35E
Chaem, R. 100 18 11N 98 38E
Chaeryŏng 107 38 24N 125 36E
Chafurray 174 3 10N 73 14W
Chagai 93 29 30N 63 0E
Chagai Hills 93 29 30N 63 0E
Chagda 77 58 45N 130 30E
Chagford 30 50 40N 3 50W
Chagny 43 46 57N 4 45E
Chagoda 80 59 10N 35 25E
Chagos Arch. 86 6 0S 72 0E
Chãh Bahãr 93 25 20N 60 40E
Ch'ahaerhyuichungch'i 106 41 18N 112 48E
Ch'ahanch'elo 106 41 41N 114 15E
Chahar Buriak 93 30 15N 62 0E
Chãhr-e Babak 93 30 10N 55 20E
Chahsikiang 105 32 32N 79 41E
Chahtung 98 26 41N 98 10E
Chai-nat 100 15 11N 100 8E
Chaibasa 99 22 42N 85 49E
Chaillé-les-Marais 44 46 25N 1 2W
Chaise Dieu, La 44 45 20N 3 40E
Chaiya 101 9 23N 99 14E
Chaiyaphum 100 15 48N 102 2E
Chaize-le-Vicomté, La 42 46 40N 1 18W
Chaj Doab 94 32 0N 73 0E
Chajari 172 30 42N 58 0W
Chakaria 98 21 45N 92 5E
Chake Chake 126 5 15S 39 45E
Chakhansur 93 31 10N 62 0E
Chaklashi 94 22 40N 72 52E
Chakonipau, L. 151 56 18N 68 30W
Chakradharpur 95 22 45N 85 40E
Chakwadam 98 27 29N 98 31E
Chakwal 94 32 50N 72 45E
Chala 174 15 48S 74 20W
Chalais 44 45 16N 0 3E
Chalakudi 97 10 18N 76 20E
Chalcatongo 165 17 4N 97 34W
Chalchihuites 164 23 29N 103 53W
Chalcis = Khalkís 69 38 27N 23 42E
Chale 28 50 35N 1 19W
Chaleur B. 151 47 55N 65 30W
Chalfant 163 37 32N 118 21W
Chalfont St. Peter 29 51 36N 0 33W
Chalhuanca 174 14 15S 73 5W
Ch'aling 109 26 47N 113 45E
Chaling Hu 105 34 55N 98 0E
Chalisgaon 96 20 30N 75 10E
Chalkar 83 50 35N 51 52E
Chalkar Oz. 83 50 33N 51 45E
Chalky Inlet 143 46 3S 166 31E
Challans 42 46 50N 1 52W
Challapata 174 19 0S 66 50W
Challerange 43 49 18N 4 46E
Challis 160 44 32N 114 25W
Chalna 95 22 36N 89 35E
Chalon-sur-Saône 43 46 48N 4 50E
Chalonnes 42 47 20N 0 45W
Châlons-sur-Marne 43 48 58N 4 20E
Châlus 44 45 39N 0 58E
Cham, Ger. 49 49 12N 12 40E
Cham, Switz. 51 47 11N 8 28E
Cham, Cu Lao 100 15 57N 108 30E
Chama, R. 127 36 57N 106 37W
Chaman 93 30 58N 66 25E
Chamarajanagar-Ramasamudram 97 11 52N 76 52E
Chamartín de la Rosa 58 40 28N 3 40W
Chamba, India 94 32 35N 76 10E
Chamba, Tanz. 125 11 37S 37 0E
Chambal, R. 94 26 0N 76 55E
Chamberlain, Austral. 136 15 58S 127 54E
Chamberlain, U.S.A. 158 43 50N 99 21W
Chambers 161 35 13N 109 30W
Chambersburg 156 39 53N 77 41W
Chambéry 45 45 34N 5 55E
Chambeshi 127 12 39S 28 1E
Chambeshi, R. 124 10 20S 31 58E
Chambois 42 48 48N 0 6E
Chambon-Feugerolles, Le 45 45 24N 4 18E
Châmbon, Le 45 45 35N 4 26E
Chambord 151 48 25N 72 6W
Chamboulive 44 45 26N 1 42E
Chambri L. 135 4 15S 143 10E
Chamela 164 19 32N 105 5W
Chamical 172 30 22S 66 27W
Chamkar Luong 101 11 0N 103 45E
Chamonix 45 45 55N 6 51E
Champa 95 22 2N 82 43E
Champagne, Can. 152 60 49N 136 30W
Champagne, France 43 49 0N 4 40E
Champagnole 43 46 45N 5 55E
Champaign 156 40 8N 88 14W
Champassak 100 14 53N 105 52E
Champaubert 43 48 50N 3 45E
Champdeniers 44 46 29N 0 25W
Champeix 44 45 37N 3 8E
Champerico 166 14 18N 91 55W
Champier 50 45 27N 5 17E
Champion B. 137 28 44S 114 36E
Champlain 151 46 27N 72 24W
Champotón 165 19 20N 90 50W
Chamusca 57 39 21N 8 29W
Chana 101 6 55N 100 44E
Chañaral 172 26 15S 70 50W
Chanasma 94 23 44N 72 5E
Chanca, R. 57 37 49N 7 15W
Chanchiang 109 21 15N 110 20E
Chancy 50 46 8N 6 0E
Chanda 96 19 57N 79 25E
Chandalar 147 67 30N 148 35W
Chandausi 95 28 27N 78 49E
Chandeleur Is. 59 29 45N 88 53W
Chandeleur Sd. 159 29 58N 88 40W
Chandernagore 95 22 52N 88 24E
Chandigarh 94 30 30N 76 58E
Chandler, Can. 151 48 18N 64 46W
Chandler, Ariz., U.S.A. 161 33 20N 111 56W
Chandler, Okla., U.S.A. 159 35 43N 97 20W
Chandler's Ford 28 50 59N 1 23W
Chandlers Peak 141 30 24S 152 10E
Chandmani 105 45 20N 97 59E
Chandpur, Bangla. 98 22 8N 90 55E
Chandpur, India 94 29 8N 78 19E
Chang 94 26 59N 68 30E
Ch'ang Chiang, R. 109 31 40N 121 50E
Chang, Ko 101 12 0N 102 23E
Changa 95 33 53N 77 35E
Changanacheri 97 9 25N 76 31E
Changane, R. 125 23 30S 33 50E
Ch'anganpao 108 26 9N 109 42E
Changchiak'ou 106 40 50N 114 53E
Ch'angchiang 100 19 19N 108 43E
Ch'angchih 106 36 11N 113 6E
Ch'angchou 109 31 47N 119 58E
Changchou 109 24 31N 117 40E
Ch'angch'un 107 43 58N 125 19E
Ch'angch'unling 107 45 22N 125 28E
Changdori 107 38 30N 127 40E
Ch'angfeng 109 32 27N 117 9E
Changhsing 109 31 0N 119 56E
Ch'anghua 109 30 10N 119 15E
Changhua 109 24 2N 120 30E
Changhŭng 107 34 41N 126 52E
Changhŭngni 107 40 24N 128 19E
Ch'angi 107 36 51N 119 23E
Changjin 107 40 23N 127 15E
Changjin-chŏsuji 107 40 30N 127 15E
Changkuangts'ai Ling 107 45 50N 128 50E
Changli 107 39 40N 119 19E
Ch'angling 107 44 16N 123 57E
Ch'anglo, Fukien, China 109 25 58N 119 31E
Ch'anglo, Fukien, China 109 26 40N 117 20E
Ch'anglo, Kwangtung, China 109 24 4N 115 37E
Changlun 101 6 25N 100 26E
Changming 108 31 44N 104 44E
Ch'angning, Hunan, China 109 26 25N 112 15E
Ch'angning, Szechwan, China 108 28 38N 104 57E
Ch'angning, Yunnan, China 108 24 50N 99 36E
Ch'angpai 107 41 26N 128 0E
Ch'angpai Shan 107 42 25N 129 0E
Changpei 106 41 7N 114 51E
Ch'angp'ing 106 40 12N 116 12E
Changp'ing 109 25 18N 117 24E
Changpu 109 24 2N 117 31E
Ch'angsha 109 28 15N 113 0E
Ch'angshan 109 28 57N 118 31E
Ch'angshou 108 29 50N 107 2E
Ch'angshu 109 31 33N 120 45E
Ch'angshun 108 25 59N 106 25E
Ch'angt'ai 109 24 34N 117 50E
Ch'angte 109 29 5N 111 42E
Ch'angt'ing 109 25 52N 116 20E
Ch'angt'u 107 42 47N 124 0E
Ch'angtu 108 31 10N 97 14E
Ch'angt'u Shan 109 30 15N 122 20E
Ch'angwu 106 35 9N 107 42E
Changwu 107 42 24N 122 30E
Ch'angyang 109 30 28N 111 9E
Ch'angyatien 106 40 40N 108 46E
Changyeh 105 38 56N 100 37E
Changyŏn 107 38 15N 125 6E
Ch'angyüan 106 35 17N 114 50E
Chanhanga 128 16 0S 14 8E
Chanhua 107 37 42N 118 8E
Chani 108 25 36N 103 49E
Channapatna 97 12 40N 77 15E
Channel Is. 42 49 30N 2 40W
Channel Islands 163 33 30N 119 0W
Channing, Mich., U.S.A. 156 46 9N 88 1W
Channing, Tex., U.S.A. 159 35 45N 102 20W
Chantada 56 42 36N 7 46W
Chanthaburi 100 12 38N 102 12E
Chantilly 43 49 12N 2 29E
Chantonnay 42 46 40N 1 3W
Chantrey Inlet 148 67 48N 96 20W
Chanute 159 37 45N 85 25W
Chanyü 107 44 39N 122 45E
Chanza, R. 57 37 49N 7 15W
Ch'ao Hu 109 31 40N 117 30E
Chao Phraya Lowlands 100 15 30N 100 0E
Chao Phraya, R. 100 13 32N 100 36E
Ch'aoan 109 23 41N 116 33E
Chaoan 109 23 47N 117 5E
Chaoch'eng, Shansi, China 106 36 26N 111 43E
Chaoch'eng, Shantung, China 106 36 3N 115 35E
Chaochiao 108 28 1N 102 49E
Chaoch'ing 109 23 7N 112 24E
Chaohsien 106 37 45N 114 46E
Ch'aohsien 109 31 41N 117 49E
Chaop'ing 109 24 1N 110 59E
Chaot'ung 108 27 19N 103 42E
Ch'aoyang, Kwangtung, China 109 23 10N 116 30E
Ch'aoyang, Liaoning, China 107 41 46N 120 16E
Chaoyüan, Heilungkiang, China 107 45 30N 125 8E
Chaoyüan, Shantung, China 107 37 22N 120 24E
Chap Kuduk 76 48 45N 55 5E
Chapala 127 15 50S 37 35E
Chapala, Lago de 164 20 10N 103 20W
Chaparmukh 98 26 12N 92 31E
Chapayevo 83 50 25N 51 10E
Chapayevsk 81 53 0N 49 40E
Chapecó 173 27 14S 52 41W
Chapel-en-le-Frith 32 53 19N 1 54W
Chapel Hill 157 35 53N 79 3W
Chapelle-d'Angillon, La 43 47 21N 2 25E
Chapelle Glain, La 42 47 38N 1 11W
Chapeyevo 84 50 12N 51 10E
Chapleau 150 47 50N 83 24W
Chaplin 153 50 28N 106 40W
Chaplino 82 48 8N 36 15E
Chaplygin 81 53 15N 39 55E
Chapra 95 25 48N 84 50E
Char 116 21 40N 12 45W
Chara 77 56 54N 118 12E
Charadai 172 27 35S 60 0W
Charagua 174 19 45S 63 10W
Charak 93 26 46N 54 18E
Charalá 174 6 17N 73 10W
Charaña 174 17 30S 69 35W
Charapita 174 0 37S 74 21W
Charata 172 27 13S 61 14W
Charcas 164 23 10N 101 20W
Charcoal L. 153 58 49N 102 22W
Charcot I. 13 70 0S 75 0W
Chard, Can. 153 55 55N 111 10W
Chard, U.K. 28 50 52N 2 59W
Chardara 76 41 16N 67 59E
Chardara, Step 85 42 20N 68 0E
Charduar 98 26 51N 92 46E
Chardzhou 85 39 6N 63 34E
Charente-Maritime □ 44 45 50N 0 35W
Charente □ 44 45 50N 0 16W
Charente, R. 44 45 41N 0 30W
Charentsavan 83 40 35N 44 41E
Chârib, G. 122 28 6N 32 54E
Charikar 93 35 0N 69 10E
Charing 29 51 12N 0 49E
Charité, La 43 47 10N 3 0E
Chariton R. 158 39 19N 92 58W
Charkhari 95 25 24N 79 45E
Charkhi Dadri 94 28 37N 76 17E
Charlbury 28 51 52N 1 29W
Charlemont 38 54 26N 6 40W
Charleroi 47 50 24N 4 27E
Charles, C. 162 37 10N 75 52W
Charles City, Iowa, U.S.A. 158 43 2N 92 41W
Charles City, Va., U.S.A. 162 37 20N 77 4W
Charles L. 153 59 50N 110 33W
Charles, Pk. 137 32 53S 121 8E
Charles Town 156 39 20N 77 50W
Charleston, Miss., U.S.A. 159 34 2N 90 3W
Charleston, Mo., U.S.A. 159 36 52N 89 20W
Charleston, S.C., U.S.A. 157 32 47N 79 56W
Charleston, W. Va., U.S.A. 157 38 24N 81 36W
Charlestown, Ireland 38 53 58N 8 48W
Charlestown, S. Afr. 129 27 26S 29 53E
Charlestown, Ind., U.S.A. 156 38 29N 85 40W
Charlestown, N.H., U.S.A. 162 43 14N 72 24W
Charlestown of Aberlour 37 57 27N 3 13W
Charlesville 124 5 27S 20 59E
Charleville 139 26 24S 146 15E
Charleville-Mézières 43 49 44N 4 40E
Charleville = Rath Luirc 39 52 21N 8 40W
Charlevoix 156 45 19N 85 14W
Charlieu 45 46 10N 4 10E
Charlotte, Mich., U.S.A. 156 42 36N 84 48W
Charlotte, N.C., U.S.A. 157 35 16N 80 46W
Charlotte Amalie 147 18 22N 64 56W
Charlotte Harb. 157 26 45N 82 10W
Charlotte Waters 136 25 56N 134 54E
Charlottenberg 72 59 54N 12 17E
Charlottesville 156 38 1N 78 30W
Charlottetown 151 46 14N 63 8W
Charlton, Austral. 140 36 16S 143 24E
Charlton, U.S.A. 158 40 59N 93 20W
Charlton I. 150 52 0N 79 20W
Charlton Kings 28 51 52N 2 3W
Charlwood 29 51 8N 0 12W
Charmes 43 48 22N 6 17E
Charminster 28 50 43N 2 28W
Charmouth 28 50 45N 2 54W
Charnwood Forest 23 52 43N 1 18W
Charny 151 46 43N 71 15W
Charolles 45 46 27N 4 16E
Charost 43 47 0N 2 7E
Charouïne 118 29 0N 0 15W
Charre 127 17 19S 35 10E
Charroux 44 46 9N 0 25E
Charsadda 94 34 7N 71 45E
Charters Towers 138 20 5S 146 13E
Chartham 29 51 14N 1 1E
Chartre, La 42 47 42N 0 34E
Chartres 42 48 29N 1 30E
Chascomús 172 35 30S 58 0W
Chasefu 127 11 55N 32 58E
Chaslands Mistake 143 46 38S 169 22E
Chasseneuil-sur-Bonnieure 44 45 52N 0 29E
Chata 94 27 42N 77 30E
Châtaigneraie, La 42 46 38N 0 45W
Chatal Balkan = Udvoy Balkan 67 42 50N 26 50E
Château-Chinon 43 47 4N 3 56E
Château d'Oex 50 46 28N 7 8E

Château-du-Loir
Ch'iench'engchen

Château-du-Loir 42 47 40N 0 25 E
Château Gontier 42 47 50N 0 42W
Château-la-Vallière 42 47 30N 0 20 E
Château-Landon 43 48 8N 2 40 E
Château, Le 44 45 52N 1 12W
Château Porcien 43 49 31N 4 13 E
Château Renault 42 47 36N 0 56 E
Château-Salins 43 48 50N 6 30 E
Château-Thierry 43 49 3N 3 20 E
Châteaubourg 43 48 7N 1 25W
Châteaubriant 42 47 43N 1 23W
Châteaudun 42 48 3N 1 20 E
Châteaugiron 42 48 3N 1 30W
Châteaulin 42 48 11N 4 8W
Châteaumeillant 44 46 35N 2 12 E
Châteauneuf 42 48 35N 1 15 E
Châteauneuf-du-Faou 42 48 11N 3 50W
Châteauneuf-sur-Charente 44 45 36N 0 3W
Châteauneuf-sur-Cher 43 46 52N 2 18 E
Châteauneuf-sur-Loire 43 47 52N 2 13 E
Châteaurenard 45 43 53N 4 51 E
Châteauroux 43 46 50N 1 40 E
Châtel-Guyon 44 45 55N 3 4 E
Châtel St. Denis 50 46 32N 6 54 E
Châtelaillon-Plage 44 46 5N 1 5W
Châtelard, Le 50 46 4N 6 57 E
Châtelaudren 42 48 33N 2 59W
Chatelet 47 50 24N 4 32 E
Châtelet, Le, Cher, France 44 46 40N 2 20 E
Châtelet, Le, Seine et Marne, France 43 48 30N 2 47 E
Châtellerault 42 46 50N 0 30 E
Châtelus-Malvaleix 44 46 18N 2 1 E
Chatham, N.B., Can. 151 47 2N 65 28W
Chatham, Ont., Can. 150 42 24N 82 11W
Chatham, U.K. 29 51 22N 0 32 E
Chatham, Alaska, U.S.A. 147 57 30N 135 0W
Chatham, La., U.S.A. 159 32 22N 92 26W
Chatham, N.Y., U.S.A. 162 42 21N 73 32W
Chatham Is. 130 44 0S 176 40W
Chatham Str. 152 57 0N 134 40W
Châtillon, Loiret, France 43 47 36N 2 44 E
Châtillon, Marne, France 43 49 5N 3 43 E
Chatillon 62 45 45N 7 40 E
Châtillon-Coligny 43 47 50N 2 51 E
Châtillon-en-Bazois 43 47 3N 3 39 E
Châtillon-en-Diois 45 44 41N 5 29 E
Châtillon-sur-Seine 43 47 50N 4 33 E
Châtillon-sur-Sèvre 42 46 56N 0 45W
Chatkal, R. 85 41 38N 70 1 E
Chatkalskiy Khrebet 85 41 30N 70 45 E
Chatmohar 95 24 15N 89 26 E
Chatra 95 24 12N 84 56 E
Chatrapur 96 19 22N 85 2 E
Châtre, La 44 46 35N 1 59 E
Chatsworth 127 19 32S 30 46 E
Chatta-Hantō 111 34 45N 136 55 E
Chattahoochee 157 30 43N 84 51W
Chattanooga 157 35 2N 85 17W
Chatteris 29 52 27N 0 3 E
Chatton 35 55 34N 1 55W
Chaturat 100 15 34N 101 51 E
Chatyrkel, Ozero 85 40 40N 75 18 E
Chatyrtash 85 40 55N 76 25 E
Chau Phu 101 10 42N 105 7 E
Chaudes-Aigues 44 44 51N 3 1 E
Chauffailes 44 46 13N 4 20 E
Chauk 98 20 53N 94 49 E
Chaukan La 99 27 0N 97 15 E
Chaukan Pass 98 27 8N 97 10 E
Chaulnes 43 49 48N 2 47 E
Chaumont 43 48 7N 5 8 E
Chaumont-en-Vexin 43 49 16N 1 53 E
Chaumont-sur-Loire 42 47 29N 1 11 E
Chaunay 44 46 13N 0 9 E
Chauny 43 49 37N 3 12 E
Chausey, Îs. 42 48 52N 1 49W
Chaussin 43 46 59N 5 22 E
Chauvin 153 52 45N 110 10W
Chaux de Fonds, La 50 47 7N 6 50 E
Chaves, Brazil 170 0 15S 49 55W
Chaves, Port. 56 41 45N 7 32W
Chavuma 125 13 10S 22 55 E
Chawang 101 8 25N 99 30 E
Ch'aya 108 30 35N 98 3 E
Chayan 85 43 5N 69 25 E
Chayek 85 41 55N 74 30 E
Chaykovskiy 84 56 47N 54 9 E
Chazelles-sur-Lyon 45 45 39N 4 22 E
Cheadle, Gr. Manchester, U.K. 32 53 23N 2 14W
Cheadle, Staffs., U.K. 32 52 59N 1 59W
Cheadle Hulme 32 53 22N 2 12W
Cheb (Eger) 52 50 9N 12 20 E
Chebarkul 84 55 0N 60 25 E
Cheboksary 81 56 8N 47 30 E
Cheboygan 156 45 38N 84 29W
Chebsara 81 59 10N 38 45 E
Chech, Erg 118 25 0N 2 15W
Chechaouen 118 35 9N 5 15W
Chechen 83 43 59N 47 40 E
Chech'eng 106 34 4N 115 13 E
Checheno-Ingush, A.S.S.R. □ 83 43 30N 45 29 E
Chechon 107 37 8N 128 12 E
Checiny 54 50 46N 20 37 E
Checleset B. 152 50 5N 127 35W
Checotah 159 35 31N 95 30W
Chedabucto B. 151 45 25N 61 8W
Cheddar 28 51 16N 2 47W
Cheddleton 32 53 5N 2 2W
Cheduba I. 98 18 45N 93 40 E
Cheepie 139 26 43S 144 59 E
Ch'eerhch'en Ho, R. 105 39 30N 88 15 E
Chef-Boutonne 44 46 7N 0 4W
Chefoo = Yent'ai 107 37 30N 121 12 E
Chefornak 147 60 10N 164 15W
Chegdomyn 77 51 7N 132 52 E
Chegga 118 25 15N 5 40W
Chehalis 160 46 44N 122 59W
Cheju 107 33 28N 126 30 E
Cheju Do 107 33 29N 126 34 E
Chejung 109 27 13N 119 52 E
Chekalin 81 54 10N 36 10 E
Chekao 109 31 46N 117 45 E
Chekiang □ 109 29 30N 120 0 E
Chela, Sa. da 128 16 20S 13 20 E
Chelan, Can. 153 52 38N 103 22 E
Chelan, U.S.A. 160 47 49N 120 0W
Chelan, L. 152 48 5N 120 30W
Cheleken 76 39 26N 53 7 E
Chelforó 176 39 0S 66 40W
Chéliff, O. 118 36 0N 0 8 E
Chelkar 76 47 40N 59 32 E
Chelkar Tengiz, Solonchak 76 48 0N 62 30 E
Chellala Dahrania 118 33 2N 0 1 E
Chelles 43 48 52N 2 33 E
Chełm 54 51 8N 23 30 E
Chełm □ 54 51 15N 23 30 E
Chelmarsh 28 52 29N 2 25W
Chełmek 54 50 6N 19 16 E
Chelmer, R. 29 51 45N 0 42 E
Chełmno 54 53 20N 18 30 E
Chelmsford 29 51 44N 0 29 E
Chełmza 54 53 10N 18 39 E
Chelsea, Austral. 141 38 5S 145 8 E
Chelsea, Okla., U.S.A. 159 36 35N 95 25W
Chelsea, Vermont, U.S.A. 162 43 59N 72 27W
Cheltenham 28 51 55N 2 5W
Chelva 58 39 45N 1 0W
Chelyabinsk 84 55 10N 61 24 E
Chelyuskin, C. 86 77 30N 103 0 E
Chemainus 152 48 55N 123 48W
Chemikovsk 78 56 31N 58 11 E
Chemillé 42 47 14N 0 45W
Chemnitz = Karl-Marx-Stadt 48 50 50N 12 55 E
Chemor 101 4 44N 101 6 E
Chemult 160 43 14N 121 54W
Chen, Gora 77 65 10N 141 20 E
Chenab, R. 94 30 40N 73 30 E
Chenachane, O. 118 25 30N 3 30W
Chenan 106 33 16N 109 1 E
Chenango Forks 162 42 15N 75 51W
Chencha 123 6 15N 37 32 E
Ch'ench'i 109 28 1N 110 13 E
Ch'enchiachiang 107 34 25N 119 50 E
Chenchiang 109 32 12N 119 27 E
Chenchieh 108 23 15N 107 9 E
Chênée 47 50 37N 5 37 E
Cheney 160 47 38N 117 34W
Chenfeng 108 25 25N 105 51 E
Chengan 108 28 30N 107 30 E
Ch'engch'eng 106 35 6N 109 52 E
Ch'engchiang 108 24 40N 102 55 E
Chengchou 106 34 38N 113 43 E
Chengchow = Chengchou 106 34 38N 113 43 E
Chengelee 98 28 47N 96 16 E
Chengho 109 27 25N 118 46 E
Ch'enghsi Hu 109 32 22N 116 12 E
Ch'enghsien, Chekiang, China 109 29 30N 120 48 E
Ch'enghsien, Kansu, China 106 33 42N 105 36 E
Ch'engk'ou 108 31 58N 108 48 E
Ch'engku 106 33 9N 107 22 E
Ch'engkung 108 24 53N 102 45 E
Ch'engmai 100 19 44N 109 59 E
Ch'engpu 109 26 12N 110 5 E
Ch'engte 107 41 0N 117 58 E
Chengting 106 38 8N 114 37 E
Ch'engtu 108 30 45N 104 0 E
Ch'engtung Hu 109 32 17N 116 23 E
Ch'engtzut'uan 107 39 30N 122 30 E
Ch'engwu 106 35 0N 115 56 E
Ch'engyang 107 36 20N 120 16 E
Chengyang 109 32 36N 114 23 E
Chengyangkuan 109 32 29N 116 37 E
Chenhai 109 29 57N 121 42 E
Ch'enhsien 109 25 48N 113 2 E
Chenhsiung 108 27 27N 104 50 E
Chenhsü 109 27 20N 120 16 E
Chenkán 165 19 8N 90 58W
Chenk'ang 108 24 4N 99 18 E
Chenlai 107 45 52N 123 12 E
Chenning 108 25 57N 105 51 E
Chenp'ing 106 33 2N 112 14 E
Ch'enp'ing 108 31 52N 109 31 E
Chenyüan, Kansu, China 106 35 59N 107 2 E
Chenyüan, Kweichow, China 108 27 0N 108 20 E
Cheo Reo = Hau Bon 101 13 25N 108 28 E
Cheom Ksan 100 14 13N 104 56 E
Chepelare 67 41 44N 24 40 E
Chepén 174 7 10S 79 15W
Chepes 172 31 20S 66 35W
Chepo 166 9 10N 79 6W
Chepstow 31 51 38N 2 40W
Cheptsa, R. 81 58 36N 50 4 E
Cheptulil, Mt. 126 1 25N 35 35 E
Chequamegon B. 158 46 40N 90 30W
Chequeche 127 14 13S 38 30 E
Cher □ 43 47 10N 2 30 E
Chér, R. 43 47 10N 2 10 E
Cheran 98 25 45N 90 44 E
Cherasco 62 44 39N 7 50 E
Cheratte 47 50 40N 5 41 E
Cheraw 157 34 42N 79 54W
Cherbourg 42 49 39N 1 40W
Cherchell 118 36 35N 2 12 E
Cherdakly 81 54 25N 48 50 E
Cherdyn 84 60 24N 56 29 E
Cheremkhovo 77 53 32N 102 40 E
Cherepanovo 76 54 15N 83 30 E
Cherepovets 81 59 5N 37 55 E
Chergui, Chott Ech 118 34 10N 0 25 E
Cheri 121 13 26N 11 21 E
Cherikov 80 53 32N 31 20 E
Cheriton 28 51 3N 1 9W
Cheriton Fitzpaine 30 50 51N 3 38W
Cherkessk 83 44 25N 42 10 E
Cherlak 76 54 15N 74 55 E
Chermoz 84 58 46N 56 10 E
Chernak 85 43 24N 68 2 E
Chernaya Kholunitsa 84 58 51N 51 52 E
Cherni, Mt. 67 42 35N 23 18 E
Chernigov 80 51 28N 31 20 E
Chernikovsk 84 54 48N 56 8 E
Chernobyl 80 51 13N 30 15 E
Chernogorsk 77 54 5N 91 10 E
Chernomorskoye 82 45 31N 32 46 E
Chernovskoye 81 58 48N 47 20 E
Chernovtsy 82 48 0N 26 0 E
Chernoye 77 70 30N 89 10 E
Chernushka 84 56 29N 56 3 E
Chernyakhovsk 80 54 29N 21 48 E
Chernyshevskiy 77 62 40N 112 30 E
Chernyshkovskiy 83 48 30N 42 28 E
Cherokee, Iowa, U.S.A. 158 42 40N 95 30W
Cherokee, Okla., U.S.A. 159 36 45N 98 25W
Cherokees, L. of the 159 36 50N 95 12W
Cherquenco 176 38 35S 72 0W
Cherrapunji 99 25 17N 91 47 E
Cherry Creek 160 39 50N 114 58W
Cherry Valley, U.S.A. 162 42 48N 74 45W
Cherry Valley, U.S.A. 163 33 59N 116 57W
Cherryvale 159 37 20N 95 33W
Cherskiy 77 68 45N 161 18 E
Cherskogo Khrebet 77 65 0N 143 0 E
Chertkovo 83 49 25N 40 19 E
Chertsey 29 51 23N 0 30W
Cherven 80 53 45N 28 13 E
Cherven-Bryag 67 43 17N 24 7 E
Cherwell, R. 28 51 46N 1 18W
Chesapeake Bay 162 38 0N 76 12W
Chesapeake Beach 162 38 41N 76 32W
Chesha B. = Cheshskaya G. 78 67 20N 47 0 E
Chesham 29 51 42N 0 36W
Cheshire □ 32 53 14N 2 30W
Cheshunt 29 51 42N 0 1W
Chesil Beach 23 50 37N 2 33W
Cheslatta L. 152 53 49N 125 20W
Chesne, Le 43 49 30N 4 45 E
Cheste 59 39 30N 0 41W
Chester, U.K. 32 53 12N 2 53W
Chester, Calif., U.S.A. 160 40 22N 121 22W
Chester, Ill., U.S.A. 158 37 58N 89 50W
Chester, Mont., U.S.A. 160 48 31N 111 0W
Chester, Pa., U.S.A. 162 39 54N 75 20W
Chester, S.C., U.S.A. 157 34 44N 81 13W
Chester, Va., U.S.A. 162 37 21N 77 27W
Chester, Vt., U.S.A. 162 43 16N 72 36W
Chester-le-Street 33 54 53N 1 34W
Chesterfield, Can. 148 63 0N 91 0W
Chesterfield, U.K. 33 53 14N 1 26W
Chesterfield, U.S.A. 162 37 23N 77 31W
Chesterfield I. 129 16 20S 43 58 E
Chesterfield, Îles 133 19 52S 158 15 E
Chesterfield Inlet 148 63 30N 90 45W
Chesterton Range 138 25 30S 147 27 E
Chestertown 162 39 13N 76 4W
Chesuncook L. 151 46 0N 69 10W
Chetaibi 119 37 1N 7 20 E
Cheticamp 151 46 37N 60 59W
Chetumal 165 18 30N 88 20W
Chetumal, Bahía de 165 18 40N 88 10W
Chetwynd 152 55 45N 121 45W
Chevanceaux 44 45 18N 0 14W
Cheviot Hills 35 55 20N 2 30W
Cheviot Ra. 138 25 20S 143 45 E
Cheviot, The 35 55 29N 2 8W
Chew Bahir 123 4 40N 30 50 E
Chew Magna 28 51 21N 2 37W
Chewelah 160 48 17N 117 43W
Cheyenne, Okla., U.S.A. 159 35 40N 99 40W
Cheyenne, Wyo., U.S.A. 158 41 9N 104 49W
Cheyenne, R. 158 44 50N 101 0W
Cheyenne Wells 158 38 51N 102 23W
Cheylard, Le 45 44 55N 4 25 E
Cheyne B. 137 34 35S 118 50 E
Chhabra 94 24 40N 76 54 E
Chhang 102 12 15N 104 14 E
Chhatak 95 25 5N 91 37 E
Chhatarpur 95 24 55N 79 43 E
Chhep 100 13 45N 105 24 E
Chhindwara 95 22 2N 78 59 E
Chhlong 101 12 15N 105 58 E
Chhuk 101 10 46N 104 8 E
Chi, R. 100 15 11N 104 43 E
Chiaho 109 25 33N 112 15 E
Chiahsiang 106 35 25N 116 21 E
Chiahsien, Hensi, China 106 38 6N 110 28 E
Chiahsien, Honan, China 106 33 58N 113 13 E
Chiahsing 109 30 45N 120 43 E
Chiai 109 23 29N 120 25 E
Chiali 109 23 10N 120 11 E
Chialing Chiang, R. 108 30 2N 106 19 E
Chiamussu 105 46 50N 130 21 E
Chian, Kiangsi, China 109 27 8N 115 0 E
Chian, Kirin, China 107 41 6N 126 10 E
Chiang Dao 100 19 22N 98 58 E
Chiang Kham 100 19 32N 100 18 E
Chiang Khan 100 17 52N 101 36 E
Chiang Khong 100 20 17N 100 24 E
Chiang Mai 100 18 47N 98 59 E
Chiang Saen 100 20 16N 100 5 E
Chiangch'eng 108 22 36N 101 50 E
Chiangchiat'un 107 40 54N 120 34 E
Chiangching 108 29 13N 106 15 E
Chiangchun 109 23 5N 120 5 E
Chianghua 109 25 2N 111 45 E
Chiangk'ou 108 27 42N 108 50 E
Chiangling 109 30 21N 112 5 E
Chiangmen 109 22 37N 113 3 E
Chiangpei 108 29 47N 106 29 E
Chiangp'ing 108 21 36N 108 8 E
Chiangshan 109 28 45N 118 37 E
Chiangta 108 31 28N 99 12 E
Chiangti 108 27 1N 103 37 E
Chiangyin 109 31 50N 120 18 E
Chiangyü 108 31 47N 104 45 E
Chiangyung 109 25 16N 111 20 E
Chianie 125 15 35S 13 40 E
Ch'iaochia 108 26 57N 103 3 E
Chiaochou Wan 107 36 10N 120 15 E
Chiaoho, Hopei, China 106 38 1N 116 17 E
Chiaoho, Kirin, China 107 43 42N 127 19 E
Chiaohsien 107 36 20N 120 0 E
Chiaoling 109 24 40N 117 10 E
Chiaotso 106 35 17N 113 18 E
Chiapa de Corzo 165 16 42N 93 0W
Chiapa, R. 165 16 42N 93 0W
Chiapas □ 165 17 0N 92 45W
Chiaramonte Gulfi 65 37 1N 14 41 E
Chiaravalle 63 38 41N 16 24 E
Chiaravalle Centrale 65 38 41N 16 25 E
Chiari 62 45 31N 9 55 E
Chiashan 109 32 37N 118 8 E
Chiasso 51 45 50N 9 0 E
Chiating 109 31 21N 121 15 E
Chiautla 165 18 18N 98 34W
Chiávari 62 44 20N 9 20 E
Chiavenna 62 46 18N 9 23 E
Chiawang 107 34 30N 117 22 E
Chiayü 109 29 59N 113 54 E
Chiba 111 35 30N 140 7 E
Chiba-ken □ 111 35 30N 140 20 E
Chibabava 129 20 25S 33 35 E
Chibemba 125 15 48S 14 8 E
Chibougamau 150 49 56N 74 24W
Chibougamau L. 150 49 50N 74 20W
Chibougamau, R. 150 49 50N 75 40W
Chibuk 121 10 52N 12 50 E
Chibuto 129 24 40S 33 33 E
Chic-Chocs, Mts. 151 48 55N 66 0W
Chic-Chocs, Parc Prov. des 151 48 55N 66 20W
Chicacole = Srikakulam 97 18 14N 84 4 E
Chicago 156 41 53N 87 40W
Chicago Heights 156 41 29N 87 37W
Chicago North 156 42 20N 87 50W
Chichagof I. 152 58 0N 136 0W
Chichaoua 118 31 32N 8 44W
Chichén Itzá 165 20 40N 88 32W
Chichester 29 50 50N 0 47W
Chichester Ra. 136 21 35S 117 45 E
Chich'i 109 30 4N 118 34 E
Ch'ichiang 108 29 0N 106 40 E
Chichibu 111 36 5N 139 10 E
Ch'ich'ihaerh 105 47 22N 123 57 E
Chichiriviche 174 10 56N 68 16W
Ch'ich'un 109 30 14N 115 25 E
Chickasha 159 35 0N 98 0W
Chicken Hd. 31 58 10N 6 15W
Chiclana de la Frontera 57 36 26N 6 9W
Chiclayo 174 6 42S 79 50W
Chico 160 39 45N 121 54W
Chico, R., Chubut, Argent. 160 44 0S 67 0W
Chico, R., Santa Cruz, Argent. 176 49 30S 69 30W
Chicoa 125 15 35S 32 20 E
Chicomo 129 24 31S 34 6 E
Chicontepec 165 20 58N 98 10W
Chicopee 162 42 6N 72 37W
Chicoutimi 151 48 28N 71 5W
Chidambaram 97 11 20N 79 45 E
Chiddingfold 29 51 6N 0 37W
Chidenguele 129 24 55S 34 2 E
Chidley C. 149 60 23N 64 26W
Chiehhsiu 106 37 0N 111 55 E
Ch'iehmo 105 38 8N 85 32 E
Chiehshou 106 33 20N 115 24 E
Chiehyang 109 23 37N 116 19 E
Chiem Hoa 100 22 12N 105 17 E
Chiemsee 49 47 53N 12 27 E
Chiench'ang 107 41 16N 124 28 E
Chiench'angying 107 40 8N 118 50 E
Ch'iench'engchen 108 27 12N 109 50 E

Ch'ienchiang Chomen Swamp

Ch'ienchiang, Hupeh, China 109 30 25N 112 51 E
Ch'ienchiang, Kwangsi-Chuang, China 108 23 40N 108 58 E
Ch'ienchiang, Szechwan, China 108 29 31N 108 46 E
Chiench'uan 108 26 28N 99 52 E
Chiengi 124 8 45 S 29 10 E
Chienho 108 26 39N 108 35 E
Ch'ienhsi 108 27 3N 106 0 E
Ch'ienhsien 106 34 30N 108 10 E
Chienko 108 32 0N 105 23 E
Chienli 109 29 49N 112 53 E
Chienou 109 27 5N 118 20 E
Ch'ienshan, Anhwei, China 109 30 41N 116 35 E
Ch'ienshan, Kiangsi, China 109 28 18N 117 40 E
Chienshih 108 30 40N 109 43 E
Chienshui 108 23 37N 102 49 E
Chiente 109 29 29N 119 16 E
Chienti, R. 63 43 15N 13 30 E
Chienwei 108 29 13N 103 56 E
Chienyang 109 27 21N 118 5 E
Ch'ienyang, Hunan, China 109 27 18N 110 10 E
Ch'ienyang, Kansu, China 106 34 35N 107 2 E
Chienyang 108 30 24N 104 33 E
Chierhkalang 107 43 6N 122 54 E
Chieri 62 45 0N 7 50 E
Chiese, R. 62 45 45N 10 35 E
Chieti 63 42 22N 14 10 E
Chièvres 47 50 35N 3 48 E
Chigasaki 111 35 19N 139 24 E
Chignecto B. 151 45 48N 64 40W
Chignik 147 56 15N 158 27W
Chigorodó 174 7 41N 76 42W
Chiguana 172 21 0 S 67 50W
Chihari 107 38 40N 126 30 E
Ch'ihch'i 109 21 59N 112 58 E
Chihchiang, Hunan, China 108 27 27N 109 41 E
Chihchiang, Hupei, China 109 30 19N 111 30 E
Chihchin 108 26 42N 105 45 E
Ch'ihfeng 107 42 18N 118 57 E
Chihkou 107 35 55N 119 13 E
Chihli, G. of = Po Hai 107 38 40N 119 0 E
Ch'ihshui 108 29 29N 105 38 E
Ch'ihshui Ho, R. 108 28 53N 105 48 E
Chihsi 107 45 20N 130 55 E
Ch'ihsien 106 34 33N 114 47 E
Chihsien, Honan, China 106 35 25N 114 5 E
Chihsien, Hopei, China 106 37 34N 115 34 E
Chihsien, Shansi, China 106 36 8N 110 39 E
Chihtan 106 36 56N 108 47 E
Chihte 109 30 9N 117 0 E
Chihuahua 164 28 40N 106 3W
Chihuahua □ 164 28 40N 106 3W
Chihuatlán 164 19 14N 104 35W
Chiili 85 44 20N 66 15 E
Chik Ballapur 97 13 25N 77 45 E
Chikawawa 127 16 2 S 34 50 E
Chikhli 96 20 20N 76 18 E
Chikmagalur 97 13 15N 75 45 E
Chikodi 96 16 26N 74 38 E
Chikonde 127 12 16 S 31 38 E
Ch'ik'ou 107 38 37N 117 35 E
Chikugo 110 33 14N 130 28 E
Chikuma-Gawa, R. 111 36 59N 138 35 E
Chilac 165 18 20N 97 24W
Chilako, R. 152 53 53N 122 57W
Chilam Chavki 95 35 5N 75 5 E
Chilanga 127 15 33 S 28 16 E
Chilant'ai 106 39 45N 105 45 E
Chilapa 165 17 40N 99 20W
Chilas 95 35 25N 74 5 E
Chilaw 93 7 30N 79 50 E
Chilcotin, R. 152 51 44N 122 23W
Childers 139 25 15 S 152 17 E
Childress 159 34 30N 100 50W
Chile ■ 176 35 0 S 71 15W
Chilecito 172 29 0 S 67 40W
Chilete 174 7 10 S 78 50W
Chilham 29 51 15N 0 59 E
Chilik, Kazakh S.S.R., U.S.S.R. 84 51 7N 53 55 E
Chilik, Kirgiz S.S.R., U.S.S.R. 85 43 33N 78 17 E
Chililabombwe (Bancroft) 125 12 18 S 27 43 E
Chilin 105 43 53N 126 38 E
Ch'ilin Hu 105 31 50N 89 0 E
Chilka L. 96 19 40N 85 25 E
Chilko, L. 152 52 60N 124 10W
Chilko, R. 152 52 6N 124 9W
Chillagoe 138 17 14 S 144 33 E
Chillán 172 36 40 S 72 10W
Chillicothe, Ill., U.S.A. 158 40 55N 89 32W
Chillicothe, Mo., U.S.A. 158 39 45N 93 30W
Chillicothe, Ohio, U.S.A. 156 39 53N 82 58W
Chilliwack 152 49 10N 122 0W
Chilo 94 27 12N 73 32 E
Chiloane, Î. 129 20 40 S 34 55 E
Chiloé, I. de 176 42 50 S 73 45W
Chilpancingo 165 17 30N 99 40W
Chiltern 141 36 10 S 146 36 E
Chiltern Hills 29 51 44N 0 42W
Chilton 156 44 1N 88 12W
Chiluage 124 9 15 S 21 42 E
Chilubula 127 10 14 S 30 51 E
Chilumba 127 10 28 S 34 12 E
Chilung 109 25 3N 121 45 E
Chilwa, L. (Shirwa) 127 15 15 S 35 40 E
Chimacum 160 48 1N 122 53W
Chimaltitán 164 21 46N 103 50W
Chimán 166 8 45N 78 40W
Chimay 47 50 3N 4 20 E
Chimbay 76 42 57N 59 47 E
Chimborazo 174 1 20 S 78 55W
Chimbote 174 9 0 S 78 35W
Ch'imen 109 29 56N 117 47 E
Chimion 85 40 15N 71 32 E
Chimishliya 70 46 34N 28 44 E
Chimkent 85 42 18N 69 36 E
Chimo 107 36 23N 120 27 E
Chimpembe 127 9 31 S 29 33 E
Chin □ 98 22 0N 93 0 E
Chin Chiang, R. 109 28 23N 115 48 E
Chin Hills 98 22 30N 93 30 E
Chin Ho, R. 106 35 2N 113 25 E
Chin Ling Shan 106 34 0N 107 0 E
Ch'in Shui, R. 109 26 13N 115 15 E
China 164 25 40N 99 20W
China ■ 105 30 0N 110 0 E
China Lake 163 35 44N 117 37W
Chinacates 164 25 0N 105 14W
Chinacota 174 7 37N 72 36W
Ch'inan 106 34 50N 105 35 E
Chinan 106 36 32N 117 0 E
Chinandega 166 12 30N 87 0W
Chinati Pk. 159 30 0N 104 25W
Chincha Alta 174 13 20 S 76 0W
Chinch'eng 106 35 30N 112 50 E
Chinchi 106 37 57N 106 6 E
Chinch'i 109 27 54N 116 44 E
Chinchiang, Fukien, China 109 24 54N 118 35 E
Chinchiang, Kiangsi, China 109 29 44N 115 59 E
Chinchiang, Yunnan, China 108 26 14N 100 34 E
Chinchilla 139 26 45 S 150 38 E
Chinchilla de Monte Aragón 59 38 53N 1 40W
Chinchón 58 40 9N 3 26W
Chinchorro, Banco 165 18 35N 87 20W
Ch'inchou 108 21 58N 108 35 E
Chinchou 107 41 8N 121 6 E
Chinch'uan 108 31 30N 101 55 E
Chincoteague 162 37 58N 75 21W
Chincoteague B. 162 38 5N 75 8W
Chinde 127 18 45 S 36 30 E
Chindo 107 34 28N 126 15 E
Chindwin, R. 98 21 26N 95 15 E
Chineni 95 33 2N 75 15 E
Ch'ing Chiang, R. 109 29 51N 112 22 E
Ch'ing Hai 105 37 0N 100 20 E
Ching Ho, R. 106 34 29N 109 5 E
Ching Shan 109 31 40N 111 30 E
Chinga 127 15 13 S 38 35 E
Chingan 109 28 52N 115 22 E
Ch'ingchen 108 26 32N 106 30 E
Ch'ingch'eng 107 37 11N 117 42 E
Chingchiang 109 32 2N 120 16 E
Ch'ingchiang, Kiangsi, China 109 28 5N 115 30 E
Ch'ingchiang, Kiangsu, China 107 33 33N 119 4 E
Ch'ingchien 106 37 12N 110 6 E
Chingch'uan 106 35 15N 107 22 E
Ch'ingfeng 106 35 54N 115 7 E
Chinghai 106 38 56N 116 55 E
Ch'inghomen 107 41 45N 121 25 E
Chinghsi 108 23 8N 106 25 E
Ch'inghsien 106 38 35N 116 48 E
Chinghsien 109 30 42N 118 23 E
Ch'inghsü 106 37 40N 112 20 E
Chinghung 108 22 0N 100 49 E
Chingi Chiang, R. 108 29 32N 103 44 E
Chingku 108 23 28N 100 42 E
Chingleput 97 12 42N 79 58 E
Ch'ingliu 109 26 12N 116 48 E
Chinglo 106 38 24N 111 54 E
Ch'inglung 108 25 48N 105 14 E
Chingmen 109 30 58N 112 6 E
Chingning, Chekiang, China 109 27 58N 119 38 E
Chingning, Kansu, China 106 35 30N 105 45 E
Chingola 127 12 31 S 27 53 E
Chingole 127 13 4 S 34 17 E
Chingpien 106 37 24N 108 36 E
Chingpo Hu 107 43 50N 128 50 E
Ch'ingp'u 109 31 9N 121 6 E
Chingshan 109 31 2N 113 3 E
Chingshih 109 29 40N 111 50 E
Ch'ingshui 106 34 44N 106 2 E
Chingsing 106 38 5N 114 8 E
Chingt'ai 106 37 10N 104 8 E
Ch'ingtao 107 36 5N 120 25 E
Chingte 109 30 19N 118 31 E
Chingtechen 109 29 19N 117 15 E
Ch'ingt'ien 109 28 9N 120 17 E
Chingtung 108 24 22N 100 50 E
Chingtzukuan 106 33 13N 111 2 E
Chinguar 125 12 18 S 16 45 E
Chinguetti 116 20 25N 12 15W
Chingune 129 20 33 S 35 0 E
Ch'ingyang 105 36 5N 107 40 E
Chingyang 106 34 32N 108 52 E
Ch'ingyang, Anhwei, China 109 30 38N 117 50 E
Ch'ingyang, Ningsia Hui, China 106 36 5N 107 40 E
Chingyü 107 42 22N 126 45 E
Chingyüan 106 36 35N 104 40 E
Ch'ingyüan, Chekiang, China 109 27 37N 119 3 E
Ch'ingyüan, Kwangtung, China 109 23 42N 112 58 E
Ch'ingyüan, Liaoning, China 107 42 6N 124 55 E
Ch'ingyün 107 37 53N 117 23 E
Chinhae 107 35 9N 128 40 E
Chinhanguanine 129 25 21 S 32 30 E
Chinhsi 107 40 49N 120 55 E
Chinhsiang 106 35 5N 116 18 E
Chinhsien, Hopei, China 106 38 2N 115 2 E
Chinhsien, Kiangsi, China 109 28 22N 116 14 E
Chinhsien, Liaoning, China 107 39 6N 121 3 E
Chinhua 109 29 9N 119 41 E
Ch'inhuangtao 107 39 57N 119 40 E
Chining, Inner Mongolia, China 106 41 2N 113 8 E
Chining, Shantung, China 106 35 19N 116 36 E
Chiniot 94 31 45N 73 0 E
Chinipas 164 27 22N 108 32W
Chinju 107 35 12N 128 2 E
Chink'ou 109 30 20N 114 7 E
Chinle 161 36 14N 109 38W
Chinmen 109 24 27N 118 21 E
Chinmen Tao, I. 109 24 25N 118 25 E
Chinnamanur 97 9 50N 77 16 E
Chinnampo 107 38 52N 125 28 E
Chinning 108 24 40N 102 35 E
Chinnur 96 18 57N 79 43 E
Chino, Japan 111 35 59N 138 9 E
Chino, U.S.A. 163 34 1N 117 41W
Chino Valley 161 34 54N 112 28W
Chinon 42 47 10N 0 15 E
Chinook, Can. 153 51 28N 110 59W
Chinook, U.S.A. 160 48 35N 109 19W
Chinp'ing, Kweichow, China 108 26 40N 109 7 E
Chinp'ing, Yunnan, China 108 22 46N 103 15 E
Chinsali 124 10 30 S 32 2 E
Chinsha 108 27 29N 106 15 E
Chinsha Chiang, R. = Yangtze Chiang, R. 108 27 30N 99 30 E
Chinshan 109 30 3N 121 13 E
Ch'inshui 106 35 41N 112 11 E
Chintamani 97 13 26N 78 3 E
Chint'an 109 31 45N 119 35 E
Chint'ang 108 30 51N 104 27 E
Chinwangtao = Ch'inhuangtao 107 39 57N 119 40 E
Ch'inyang 106 35 5N 112 55 E
Ch'inyüan 106 36 31N 112 15 E
Chióggia 63 45 13N 12 15 E
Chíos = Khíos 69 38 27N 26 9 E
Chip Lake 152 53 35N 115 35W
Chipai L. 150 52 56N 87 53W
Chipata (Ft. Jameson) 127 13 38 S 32 28 E
Chipewyan L. 153 58 0N 98 27W
Chipinga 127 20 13 S 32 36 E
Chipiona 57 36 44N 6 26W
Chipley 157 30 45N 85 32W
Chiplun 96 17 31N 73 34 E
Chipman 151 46 6N 65 53W
Chipoka 127 13 57 S 34 28 E
Chiporovtsi 66 43 24N 22 52 E
Chippenham 28 51 27N 2 7W
Chippewa Falls 158 44 55N 91 22W
Chippewa, R. 158 44 45N 91 55W
Chipping Campden 28 52 4N 1 48W
Chipping Norton 28 51 56N 1 32W
Chipping Ongar 29 51 43N 0 15 E
Chipping Sodbury 28 51 31N 2 23W
Chiquian 174 10 10 S 77 0W
Chiquimula 166 14 51N 89 37W
Chiquinquirá 174 5 37N 73 50W
Chir, R. 83 48 45N 42 10 E
Chirala 97 15 50N 80 20 E
Chiramba 127 16 55 S 34 39 E
Chiran 110 31 22N 130 27 E
Chiras 93 35 14N 65 40 E
Chirawa 94 28 14N 75 42 E
Chirayinkil 97 8 41N 76 49 E
Chirbury 28 52 35N 3 6W
Chirchik 85 41 29N 69 35 E
Chirfa 117 20 55N 12 14 E
Chiricahua Pk. 161 31 53N 109 14W
Chirikof I. 147 55 50N 155 40W
Chiriquí, Golfo de 166 8 0N 82 10W
Chiriquí, Lago de 166 9 10N 82 0W
Chiriquí, Vol. 166 8 55N 82 35W
Chirivira Falls 127 21 10 S 32 12 E
Chirk 31 52 57N 3 4W
Chirmiri 99 23 15N 82 20 E
Chirnogi 70 44 7N 26 32 E
Chirnside 35 55 47N 2 11W
Chiromo 125 16 30 S 35 7 E
Chirpan 67 42 10N 25 19 E
Chirripó Grande, cerro 166 9 29N 83 29W
Chisamba 127 14 55 S 28 20 E
Chisapani Garhi 99 27 30N 84 2 E
Ch'ishan 106 34 28N 107 35 E
Chishan 106 35 36N 110 59 E
Ch'ishan 109 22 44N 120 31 E
Chishmy 84 54 35N 55 23 E
Chisholm 152 54 55N 114 10W
Chishou 108 28 12N 109 43 E
Chishui 109 27 14N 115 10 E
Chisimba Falls 127 10 12 S 30 56 E
Chisineu Criş 66 46 32N 21 37 E
Chisledon 28 51 30N 1 44W
Chisone, R. 62 45 0N 7 5 E
Chisos Mts. 159 29 20N 103 15W
Chistian Mandi 94 29 50N 72 55 E
Chistopol 81 55 25N 50 38 E
Chita, Colomb. 174 6 11N 72 28W
Chita, U.S.S.R. 77 52 0N 113 25 E
Chitado 125 17 10 S 14 8 E
Ch'it'ai 105 44 1N 89 28 E
Chitapur 96 17 10N 76 50 E
Chitembo 125 13 30 S 16 50 E
Chitina 147 61 30N 144 30W
Chitinghsilin 105 32 51N 92 28 E
Chitipa 127 9 41 S 33 19 E
Chitokoloki 125 13 43 S 23 4 E
Chitorgarh 94 24 52N 74 43 E
Chitrakot 96 19 20N 81 40 E
Chitral 93 35 50N 71 56 E
Chitravati, R. 97 14 30N 78 0 E
Chitré 167 7 59N 80 27W
Chitse 106 36 54N 114 52 E
Chittagong 98 22 19N 91 55 E
Chittagong □ 98 24 5N 91 25 E
Chittoor 97 13 15N 79 5 E
Chittur 97 10 40N 76 45 E
Chitu 123 8 38N 37 58 E
Ch'itung, Hunan, China 109 26 47N 112 7 E
Ch'itung, Kiangsu, China 109 31 49N 121 40 E
Chiuant'u 107 42 33N 128 19 E
Chiuchaohua 108 32 20N 105 45 E
Chiuch'engch'i 108 27 10N 108 42 E
Chiuchiang, Kiangsi, China 109 29 43N 115 55 E
Chiuchiang, Kwangtung, China 109 22 50N 112 50 E
Chiuch'üan 105 39 46N 98 34 E
Chiuhsiangch'eng 109 33 13N 114 50 E
Chiukuanch'eng 106 35 50N 115 22 E
Chiuling Shan 109 28 50N 114 20 E
Chiuliuch'eng 108 24 32N 109 15 E
Chiulung 108 28 59N 101 32 E
Ch'iungchou Haihsia 100 20 10N 110 15 E
Ch'iunghai 100 19 15N 110 26 E
Chiunglai 108 30 25N 103 30 E
Chiunglai Shan 108 31 20N 102 50 E
Ch'iungshan 100 19 51N 110 26 E
Chiuningkang 109 26 48N 114 6 E
Ch'iupei 108 24 3N 104 12 E
Chiushench'iu 106 33 10N 115 8 E
Chiushengch'i 108 27 31N 109 12 E
Chiusi 63 43 1N 11 58 E
Chiut'ai 107 44 10N 125 49 E
Chiutaosha 106 35 39N 103 45 E
Chiuwuch'ing 106 39 23N 116 53 E
Chiva 59 39 27N 0 41W
Chivasso 62 45 10N 7 52 E
Chivilcoy 172 35 0 S 60 0W
Chiwanda 127 11 23 S 34 55 E
Chiwefwe 127 13 37 S 29 31 E
Chiyang 107 37 0N 117 13 E
Ch'iyang 109 20 35N 111 52 E
Chiyüan 106 35 5N 112 39 E
Chiyün 109 28 35N 120 2 E
Chizera 127 13 10 S 25 0 E
Chkalov = Orenburg 78 52 0N 55 5 E
Chkolovsk 81 56 50N 43 10 E
Chlumec 52 50 9N 15 29 E
Chmielnik 54 50 37N 20 43 E
Cho Bo 100 20 46N 105 10 E
Cho Do 107 38 30N 124 40 E
Cho Phuoc 101 10 26N 107 18 E
Choba 126 2 30N 38 5 E
Chobe National Park 128 21 30 S 25 0 E
Chobe, R. 128 18 10 S 24 10 E
Chobol 121 11 53N 13 1 E
Chochiwŏn 107 36 37N 127 18 E
Chocianów 54 51 35N 15 33 E
Chociwel 54 53 29N 15 21 E
Chocó □ 174 6 0N 77 0W
Chocontá 174 5 9N 73 41W
Chodaków 54 52 16N 20 18 E
Chodavaram 96 17 40N 82 50 E
Chodecz 54 52 24N 19 2 E
Chodziez 54 52 58N 17 0 E
Choele Choel 176 39 11 S 65 40W
Chōfu 111 35 39N 139 33 E
Chohsien 106 39 30N 116 0 E
Choiseul I. 130 7 0 S 156 40 E
Choisy-le-Roi 43 48 45N 2 24 E
Choix 164 26 40N 108 10W
Chojna 54 52 58N 14 25 E
Chojnice 54 53 42N 17 40 E
Chojnów 54 51 25N 15 58 E
Choke Mts. 123 11 18N 37 15 E
Chokurdakh 77 70 38N 147 55 E
Cholame 163 35 44N 120 18W
Cholet 42 47 4N 0 52W
Chollerton 35 55 4N 2 7W
Cholpon-Ata 85 42 40N 77 6 E
Cholsey 28 51 34N 1 10W
Cholu 106 40 19N 115 5 E
Choluteca 166 13 20N 87 14W
Choluteca, R. 166 13 5N 87 20W
Chom Bung 100 13 37N 99 36 E
Chom Thong 100 18 25N 98 41 E
Choma 127 16 48 S 26 59 E
Chomen Swamp 123 9 20N 37 10 E

Chomu Clee Hills

Chomu 94 27 15N 75 40E
Chomutov 52 50 28N 13 23E
Chon Buri 100 13 22N 100 59E
Chon Thanh 101 11 24N 106 36E
Chŏnan 107 36 48N 127 9E
Chonburi 101 13 21N 101 1E
Chone 174 0 40S 80 0W
Chong Kai 100 13 57N 103 35E
Chong Mek 100 15 10N 105 27E
Chŏngdo 107 35 38N 128 42E
Chŏngha 107 36 12N 129 21E
Chŏngjin 107 41 47N 129 50E
Chŏngju 107 39 40N 125 5E
Chŏngułp 107 35 35N 126 50E
Chŏnju 107 35 50N 127 4E
Chonos, Arch. de los 176 45 0S 75 0W
Chopda 96 21 20N 75 15E
Chopim, R. 173 25 35S 53 5W
Choptank, R. 162 38 41N 76 0W
Chorbat La 95 34 42N 76 37E
Chorley 32 53 39N 2 39W
Chormet el Melah 119 30 11N 16 29E
Chorolque, Cerro 172 20 59S 66 5W
Choroszcz 54 53 10N 22 59E
Chortkov 80 49 2N 25 46E
Chorul Tso 95 32 30N 82 30E
Chŏrwŏn 107 38 15N 127 10E
Chorzele 54 53 15N 21 2E
Chorzów 54 50 18N 19 0E
Chos-Malal 172 37 15S 70 5W
Chosan 107 40 50N 125 47E
Choshi 111 35 45N 140 45E
Choszczno 54 53 7N 15 25E
Choteau 160 47 50N 112 10W
Chotila 94 22 30N 71 15E
Chotzu 106 40 52N 112 33E
Chou Shan 109 30 2N 122 6E
Chouchih 106 34 8N 108 14E
Chouch'ü 106 33 46N 104 18E
Chouning 109 27 15N 119 13E
Chouts'un 107 36 48N 117 52E
Ch'ouyang 108 23 14N 104 35E
Chowchilla 163 37 11N 120 12W
Chowkham 98 20 52N 97 28E
Choybalsan 105 48 4N 114 30E
Christchurch, N.Z. 143 43 33S 172 47E
Christchurch, U.K. 28 50 44N 1 47W
Christiana, S. Afr. 128 27 52S 25 8E
Christiana, U.S.A. 162 39 40N 75 40W
Christiansfeld 73 55 21N 9 29E
Christiansö, I. 73 55 19N 15 12E
Christiansted 147 17 45N 64 42W
Christie B. 153 62 32N 111 10W
Christina, R. 153 56 40N 111 3W
Christmas Cr. 136 18 53S 125 55E
Christmas Creek 136 18 29S 125 23E
Christmas I., Ind. Oc. 142 10 0S 105 40E
Christmas I., Pac. Oc. 131 1 58N 157 27W
Christopher L. 137 24 49S 127 42E
Chrudim 52 49 58N 15 43E
Chrzanów 54 50 10N 19 21E
Chtimba 127 10 35S 34 13E
Chu 85 43 36N 73 42E
Ch'u Chiang, R. 108 30 2N 106 19E
Chu Chua 152 51 22N 120 10W
Chu Lai 100 15 28N 108 45E
Chu, R., U.S.S.R. 85 45 0N 67 44E
Chu, R., Viet. 100 19 53N 105 45E
Chuadanga 98 23 38N 88 51E
Ch'üanchou, Fukien, China 109 24 56N 118 35E
Ch'üanchou, Kwangsi-Chuang, China 109 25 59N 111 4E
Chuangho 107 39 42N 123 0E
Chüannan 109 24 50N 114 40E
Chūbu □ 112 36 45N 137 30E
Chubut, R. 176 43 0S 70 0W
Chuch'eng 107 36 0N 119 16E
Chuch'i 108 32 19N 109 52E
Chuchi, Chekiang, China 109 29 43N 120 14E
Chuchi, Honan, China 106 34 27N 115 39E
Chuchi L. 152 55 12N 124 30W
Ch'uching 108 25 34N 103 45E
Chuchou 109 27 50N 113 10E
Chudleigh 30 50 35N 3 36W
Chudovo 80 59 10N 31 30E
Chudskoye, Oz. 80 58 13N 27 30E
Ch'üehshan 109 32 48N 114 1E
Chugach Mts. 147 62 0N 146 0W
Chugiak 147 61 7N 149 10W
Chuginadak I. 147 52 50N 169 45W
Chūgoku □ 110 35 0N 133 0E
Chūgoku-Sanchi 110 35 0N 133 0E
Chuguyev 82 49 55N 36 45E
Chugwater 158 41 48N 104 47W
Chuhai 109 22 17N 113 34E
Chühsien 107 35 35N 118 49E
Ch'uhsien, China 109 28 57N 118 58E
Ch'uhsien, China 109 32 18N 118 18E
Chuhsien 105 28 57N 118 58E
Ch'ühsien 108 30 51N 107 1E
Ch'uhsiung 108 25 2N 101 32E
Chüjung 109 31 56N 119 10E
Chukai 101 4 13N 103 25E
Chukhloma 81 58 45N 42 40E
Chūko 111 36 44N 139 27E
Chukotskiy Khrebet 77 68 0N 175 0E
Chukotskiy, Mys 77 66 10N 169 3E
Chukotskoye More 77 68 0N 175 0W
Chula Vista 163 32 39N 117 8W
Chulak-Kurgan 85 43 46N 69 9E
Chülu 106 37 13N 115 1E
Chulucanas 174 5 0S 80 0W
Chum Phae 100 16 32N 102 6E
Chum Saeng 100 15 55N 100 15E
Chumar 95 32 40N 78 35E
Chumatien 109 33 0N 114 4E
Chumbicha 172 29 0S 66 10W
Chumerna 67 42 45N 25 55E
Chumikan 77 54 40N 135 10E
Chumphon 101 10 35N 99 14E
Chumuare 127 14 31S 31 50E
Chumunjin 107 37 55N 127 44E
Chunchŏn 107 37 58N 127 44E
Chunga 127 15 0S 26 2E
Ch'ungan 109 27 45N 118 0E
Ch'ungch'ing, Szechwan, China 108 29 30N 106 30E
Ch'ungch'ing, Szechwan, China 108 30 27N 103 43E
Chungch'üantzu 106 39 22N 102 42E
Chunggang ŭp 107 41 48N 126 48E
Chunghsiang 109 31 10N 112 35E
Chunghsien 108 30 17N 108 4E
Chunghwa 107 38 52N 125 47E
Ch'ungi 109 25 42N 114 19E
Ch'ungjen 109 27 44N 116 2E
Chungju 107 36 58N 127 58E
Chungkang 107 43 42N 127 37E
Chungking = Ch'ungch'ing 108 29 30N 106 30E
Ch'ungli 106 40 5N 115 12E
Chungli 109 24 57N 121 13E
Ch'ungming 109 31 27N 121 24E
Ch'ungming Tao, I. 109 31 35N 121 40E
Chungmu 107 34 50N 128 20E
Chungning 106 35 22N 105 40E
Chungshan, Kwangsi-Chuang, China 109 24 30N 111 17E
Chungshan, Kwangtung, China 109 22 31N 113 20E
Ch'ungshuiho 106 39 54N 111 34E
Ch'ungte 109 30 32N 120 26E
Chungt'iaoshan 106 35 0N 111 30E
Chungtien 108 27 51N 99 42E
Ch'ungtso 108 22 20N 107 20E
Chungtu 108 24 41N 109 42E
Chungwei 106 37 35N 105 10E
Chungyang 106 37 24N 111 10E
Chungyang Shanmo 109 23 10N 121 0E
Chungyüan 100 19 9N 110 28E
Chünhsien 109 32 40N 111 15E
Chunian 94 31 10N 74 0E
Chunya 127 8 30S 33 27E
Chunya □ 126 7 48S 33 0E
Ch'unyang 107 43 42N 129 26E
Chuquibamba 174 15 47N 72 44W
Chuquicamata 172 22 15S 69 0W
Chuquisaca □ 172 23 30S 63 30W
Chur 51 46 52N 9 32E
Churachandpur 98 24 20N 93 40E
Church Hill 38 55 0N 7 53W
Church House 152 50 20N 125 10W
Church Stretton 28 52 32N 2 49W
Churchdown 28 51 53N 2 9W
Churchill 153 58 47N 94 11W
Churchill, C. 153 58 46N 93 12W
Churchill Falls 151 53 36N 64 19W
Churchill L. 153 55 55N 108 20W
Churchill Pk. 152 58 10N 125 10W
Churchill, R., Man., Can. 153 58 47N 94 12W
Churchill, R., Newf., Can. 151 53 19N 60 10W
Churchill, R., Sask., Can. 153 58 47N 94 12W
Churchtown 39 52 12N 6 20W
Churfisten 51 47 8N 9 17E
Churston Ferrers 30 50 23N 3 32W
Churu 94 28 20N 75 0E
Churuguaro 174 10 49N 69 32W
Churwalden 51 46 47N 9 33E
Chusan 109 32 13N 110 24E
Chushul 95 33 40N 78 40E
Chusovaya, R. 84 58 18N 56 22E
Chusovoy 84 58 15N 57 40E
Chust 85 41 0N 71 13E
Ch'ützu 106 36 24N 107 27E
Chuuronjang 107 41 35N 129 40E
Chuvash A.S.S.R. □ 81 55 30N 48 0E
Chuwassu 108 28 48N 97 27E
Ch'üwu 106 35 35N 111 23E
Ch'üyang 106 38 37N 114 41E
Chüyeh 106 35 23N 116 6E
Ciacova 66 45 35N 21 10E
Cicero 156 41 48N 87 48W
Cicero Dantas 170 10 36S 38 23W
Cidacos, R. 58 42 15N 2 10W
Cide 82 41 40N 32 50E
Ciechanów 54 52 52N 20 38E
Ciechanów □ 54 53 0N 20 30E
Ciechocinek 54 52 53N 18 45E
Ciego de Avila 166 21 50N 78 50W
Ciénaga 174 11 1N 74 15W
Ciénaga de Oro 174 8 53N 75 37W
Cienfuegos 166 22 10N 80 30W
Cieplice Śląskie Zdrój 54 50 50N 15 40E
Cierp 44 42 55N 0 40E
Cies, Islas 56 42 12N 8 55W
Cieszyn 54 49 45N 18 35E
Cieza 59 38 17N 1 23W
Cifuentes 58 40 47N 2 37W
Ciha Pa. 101 22 20N 103 47E
Cijara, Pantano de 57 39 18N 4 52W
Cijulang 103 7 42S 108 27E
Cikampek 103 6 23S 107 28E
Cilacap 103 7 43S 109 0E
Cıldır 83 41 10N 43 20E
Cilgerran 31 52 4N 4 39W
Cilician Gates P. 92 37 20N 34 52E
Cilician Taurus 92 36 40N 34 0E
Cîlnicu 70 44 54N 23 4E
Cimarron, Kans., U.S.A. 159 37 50N 100 20W
Cimarron, N. Mex., U.S.A. 159 36 30N 104 52W
Cimarron, R. 159 37 10N 102 10W
Cîmpia Turzii 70 46 34N 23 53E
Cîmpina 70 45 10N 25 45E
Cîmpulung, Argeş, Rumania 70 45 17N 25 3E
Cîmpulung, Suceava, Rumania 70 47 32N 25 30E
Cîmpuri 67 46 0N 26 50E
Cinca, R. 58 42 20N 0 9E
Cincer 66 43 55N 17 5E
Cinch, R. 157 36 0N 84 15W
Cincinnati 156 39 10N 84 26W
Cincinnatus 162 42 33N 75 54W
Cinderford 28 51 49N 2 30W
Cîndeşti 70 45 15N 26 42E
Ciney 47 50 18N 5 5E
Cinigiano 63 42 53N 11 23E
Cinogli 63 43 23N 13 10E
Cinto, Mt. 45 42 24N 8 54E
Cioranii 70 44 45N 26 25E
Çiotat, La 45 43 12N 5 36E
Čiovo 63 43 30N 16 17E
Cipó 171 11 6S 38 31W
Circle, Alaska, U.S.A. 147 65 50N 144 10W
Circle, Montana, U.S.A. 158 47 26N 105 35W
Circleville, Ohio, U.S.A. 156 39 35N 82 57W
Circleville, Utah, U.S.A. 161 38 12N 112 24W
Cirebon 103 6 45S 108 32E
Cirencester 28 51 43N 1 59W
Cireşu 70 44 47N 22 31E
Cirey-sur-Vezouze 43 48 35N 6 57E
Ciriè 62 45 14N 7 35E
Cirò 65 39 23N 17 3E
Cisco 159 32 25N 99 0W
Cislău 70 45 14N 26 33E
Cisna 54 49 12N 22 20E
Cisneros 174 6 33N 75 4W
Cisnădie 70 45 42N 24 9E
Cisterna di Latina 64 41 35N 12 50E
Cisternino 65 40 45N 17 26E
Cité de Cansado 116 20 51N 17 0W
Citega (Kitega) 126 3 30S 29 58E
Citeli-Ckaro 83 41 33N 46 0E
Citlaltépetl, mt. 165 19 0N 97 20W
Citrusdal 128 32 35S 19 0E
Città della Pieve 63 42 57N 12 0E
Città di Castello 63 43 27N 12 14E
Città Sant' Angelo 63 42 32N 14 5E
Cittadella 63 45 39N 11 48E
Cittaducale 63 42 24N 12 58E
Cittanova 65 38 22N 16 0E
Ciucaş, mt. 70 45 31N 25 56E
Ciudad Acuña 164 29 20N 101 10W
Ciudad Altamirano 164 18 20N 100 40W
Ciudad Bolívar 174 8 5N 63 30W
Ciudad Camargo 164 27 41N 105 10W
Ciudad de Valles 165 22 0N 98 30W
Ciudad del Carmen 165 18 20N 97 50W
Ciudad Delicias = Delicias 164 28 10N 105 30W
Ciudad Guerrero 164 28 33N 107 28W
Ciudad Guzmán 164 19 40N 103 30W
Ciudad Juárez 164 31 40N 106 28W
Ciudad Madero 165 22 19N 97 50W
Ciudad Mante 165 22 50N 99 0W
Ciudad Obregón 164 27 28N 109 59W
Ciudad Piar 174 7 27N 63 19W
Ciudad Real 57 38 59N 3 55W
Ciudad Real □ 57 38 50N 4 0W
Ciudad Rodrigo 56 40 35N 6 32W
Ciudad Trujillo = Sto. Domingo 167 18 30N 70 0W
Ciudad Victoria 165 23 41N 99 9W
Ciudadela 58 40 0N 3 50E
Ciulniţa 70 44 26N 27 22E
Civa, B. 82 41 20N 36 40E
Cividale del Friuli 63 46 6N 13 25E
Civita Castellana 63 42 18N 12 24E
Civitanova Marche 63 43 18N 13 41E
Civitavécchia 63 42 6N 11 46E
Civitella del Tronto 63 42 48N 13 40E
Civray 44 46 10N 0 17E
Çivril 92 38 20N 29 55E
Cixerri, R. 64 39 45N 8 40E
Cizre 92 37 19N 42 10E
Clabach 34 56 38N 6 36W
Clabby 38 54 24N 7 22W
Clach Leathad 34 56 36N 7 52W
Clachan, N. Uist., U.K. 36 57 33N 7 20W
Clachan, Strathclyde, U.K. 34 55 45N 5 35W
Clackline 137 31 40S 116 32E
Clackmannan 35 56 10N 3 50W
Clackmannan (□) 26 56 10N 3 47W
Clacton-on-Sea 29 51 47N 1 10E
Cladich 34 56 21N 5 5W
Claire, L. 152 58 35N 112 5W
Clairemont 159 33 9N 100 44W
Clairvaux-les-Laes 45 46 35N 5 45E
Clamecy 43 47 28N 3 30E
Clane 39 53 18N 6 40W
Clanfield 29 50 56N 1 0W
Clanton 157 32 48N 86 36W
Clanwilliam 128 32 11S 18 52E
Clar, L. nan 37 58 17N 4 8W
Clara 39 53 20N 7 38W
Clara, R. 138 19 8S 142 30E
Claraville 163 35 24N 118 20W
Clare, N.S.W., Austral. 140 33 24S 143 54E
Clare, S. Austral., Austral. 140 33 50S 138 37E
Clare, N. Ireland, U.K. 38 54 25N 6 19W
Clare, Suffolk, U.K. 29 52 5N 0 36E
Clare, U.S.A. 156 43 47N 84 45W
Clare □ 39 52 20N 7 38W
Clare I. 38 53 48N 10 0W
Clare, R. 38 53 20N 9 0W
Clarecastle 39 52 50N 8 58W
Clareen 39 53 4N 7 49W
Claregalaway 39 53 20N 8 57W
Claremont 162 43 23N 72 20W
Claremont Pt. 138 14 1S 143 41E
Claremore 159 36 20N 95 20W
Claremorris 38 53 45N 9 0W
Clarence I. 13 61 30S 53 50W
Clarence, I. 176 54 0S 72 0W
Clarence, R., Austral. 139 29 25S 153 22E
Clarence, R., N.Z. 143 42 10S 173 56E
Clarence Str., Austral. 136 12 0S 131 0E
Clarence Str., U.S.A. 152 55 40N 132 10W
Clarence Town 167 23 6N 74 59W
Clarendon, Ark., U.S.A. 159 34 41N 91 20W
Clarendon, Tex., U.S.A. 159 34 58N 100 54W
Clarenville 151 48 10N 54 1W
Claresholm 152 50 0N 113 45W
Clarie Coast 13 67 0S 135 0E
Clarinbridge 39 53 13N 8 55W
Clarinda 158 40 45N 95 0W
Clarion 158 42 41N 93 46W
Clark 158 44 55N 97 45W
Clark Fork 160 48 9N 116 9W
Clark Fork, R. 160 48 0N 115 40W
Clark Hill Res. 157 33 45N 82 20W
Clarkdale 161 34 53N 112 3W
Clarke City 151 50 12N 66 38W
Clarke, I. 138 40 32S 148 10E
Clarke L. 153 54 24N 106 54W
Clarke Ra. 138 20 45S 148 20E
Clarks Fork, R. 160 45 0N 109 30W
Clark's Harbour 151 43 25N 65 38W
Clarks Station 163 38 8N 116 42W
Clarks Summit 162 41 31N 75 44W
Clarksburg 156 39 18N 80 21W
Clarksdale 159 34 12N 90 33W
Clarkston 160 46 28N 117 2W
Clarksville, Ark., U.S.A. 159 35 29N 93 27W
Clarksville, Tenn., U.S.A. 157 36 32N 87 20W
Clarksville, Tex., U.S.A. 159 33 37N 94 59W
Claro, R. 171 19 8S 50 40W
Clashmore 37 57 53N 4 8W
Clatskanie 160 46 9N 123 12W
Clatteringshaws L. 34 55 3N 4 17W
Claude 159 35 8N 101 22W
Claudio 171 20 26S 44 46W
Claudy 38 54 55N 7 10W
Claunie L. 36 57 8N 5 6W
Claveria 103 18 37N 121 15E
Claverley 28 52 32N 2 19W
Clay 163 38 17N 121 10W
Clay Center 158 39 27N 97 9W
Clay Cross 33 53 11N 1 26W
Clay Hd. 32 54 13N 4 23W
Claydon 29 52 6N 1 7E
Clayette, La 45 46 17N 4 19E
Claymont 162 39 48N 75 28W
Claymore, oilfield 19 58 30N 0 15W
Claypool 161 33 27N 110 55W
Clayton, Idaho, U.S.A. 160 44 12N 114 31W
Clayton, N. Mex., U.S.A. 159 36 30N 103 10W
Cle Elum 160 47 15N 120 57W
Cleady 39 51 53N 9 32W
Clear C. 39 51 26N 9 30W
Clear I. 39 51 26N 9 30W
Clear Lake, Calif., U.S.A. 160 39 5N 122 47W
Clear Lake, S.D., U.S.A. 158 44 48N 96 41W
Clear Lake, Wash., U.S.A. 160 48 27N 122 15W
Clear Lake Res. 160 41 55N 121 10W
Clearfield, Pa., U.S.A. 156 41 0N 78 27W
Clearfield, Utah, U.S.A. 160 41 10N 112 0W
Clearmont 160 44 43N 106 29W
Clearwater, Can. 152 51 38N 120 2W
Clearwater, U.S.A. 157 27 58N 82 45W
Clearwater Cr. 152 61 36N 125 30W
Clearwater L. 150 56 10N 75 0W
Clearwater, Mts. 160 46 20N 115 30W
Clearwater Prov. Park 153 54 0N 101 0W
Clearwater, R., Alta., Can. 152 52 22N 114 57W
Clearwater, R., Alta., Can. 153 56 44N 111 23W
Clearwater, R., B.C., Can. 152 51 38N 120 3W
Cleat 37 58 45N 2 56W
Cleator Moor 32 54 30N 3 32W
Cleburne 159 32 18N 97 25W
Cleddau R. 31 51 46N 4 44W
Clee Hills 23 52 26N 2 35W

Cleethorpes Columbia

Cleethorpes 33 53 33N 0 2W
Cleeve Cloud 28 51 56N 2 0W
Cleggan 38 53 33N 10 7W
Clelles 45 44 50N 5 38E
Clemency 47 49 35N 5 53E
Clent 28 52 25N 2 6W
Cleobury Mortimer 28 52 23N 2 28W
Clerke Reef 136 17 22S 119 20E
Clerks Rocks 13 56 0S 36 30W
Clermont 133 22 49S 147 39E
Clermont-en-Argonne 43 49 5N 5 4E
Clermont-Ferrand 44 45 46N 3 4E
Clermont-l'Hérault 44 43 38N 3 26E
Clerval 43 47 25N 6 30E
Cléry-Saint-André 43 47 50N 1 46E
Cles 62 46 21N 11 4E
Clevedon 28 51 26N 2 52W
Cleveland, Austral. 139 27 30S 153 15E
Cleveland, Miss., U.S.A. 159 33 43N 90 43W
Cleveland, Ohio, U.S.A. 156 41 28N 81 43W
Cleveland, Okla., U.S.A. 159 36 21N 96 33W
Cleveland, Tenn., U.S.A. 157 35 9N 84 52W
Cleveland, Tex., U.S.A. 159 30 18N 95 0W
Cleveland □ 33 54 35N 1 8E
Cleveland, C. 138 19 11S 147 1E
Cleveland Hills 33 54 25N 1 11W
Clevelândia 173 26 24S 52 23W
Clevvaux 47 50 4N 6 2E
Clew Bay 38 53 54N 9 50W
Clewiston 157 26 44N 80 50W
Cley 29 52 57N 1 3E
Clifden, Ireland 38 53 30N 10 2W
Clifden, N.Z. 143 46 1S 167 42E
Clifden B. 38 53 29N 10 5W
Cliff 161 33 0N 108 44W
Cliffe 29 51 27N 0 31E
Cliffony 38 54 25N 8 28W
Clifford 28 52 6N 3 6W
Clift Sound 36 60 4N 1 17W
Clifton, Austral. 139 27 59S 151 53E
Clifton, Ariz., U.S.A. 161 33 8N 109 23W
Clifton, Tex., U.S.A. 159 31 46N 97 35W
Clifton Forge 156 37 49N 79 51W
Climax 153 49 10N 108 20W
Clingmans Dome 157 35 35N 83 30W
Clint 161 31 37N 106 11W
Clinton, B.C., Can. 152 51 6N 121 35W
Clinton, Ont., Can. 150 43 37N 81 32W
Clinton, N.Z. 143 46 12S 169 23E
Clinton, Ark., U.S.A. 159 35 37N 92 30W
Clinton, Conn., U.S.A. 162 41 17N 72 32W
Clinton, Ill., U.S.A. 158 40 8N 89 0W
Clinton, Ind., U.S.A. 156 39 40N 87 22W
Clinton, Iowa, U.S.A. 158 41 50N 90 12W
Clinton, Mass., U.S.A. 162 42 26N 71 40W
Clinton, Mo., U.S.A. 158 38 20N 93 46W
Clinton, N.C., U.S.A. 157 35 5N 78 15W
Clinton, Okla., U.S.A. 159 35 30N 99 0W
Clinton, S.C., U.S.A. 157 34 30N 81 54W
Clinton, Tenn., U.S.A. 157 36 6N 84 10W
Clinton C. 138 22 30S 150 45E
Clinton Colden L. 148 64 58N 107 27W
Clintonville 158 44 35N 88 46W
Clipperton, I. 143 10 18N 109 13W
Clipston 29 52 26N 0 58W
Clisson 42 47 5N 1 16W
Clitheroe 32 53 52N 2 23W
Clive 142 39 36S 176 58E
Clive L. 152 63 13N 118 54W
Cloates, Pt. 136 22 43S 113 40E
Clocolan 129 28 55S 27 34E
Clodomira 172 27 35S 64 14W
Clogh 39 52 51N 7 11W
Cloghan, Donegal, Ireland 38 54 50N 7 56W
Cloghan, Offaly, Ireland 39 53 13N 7 53W
Cloghan, W'meath, Ireland 38 53 33N 7 15W
Clogheen 39 52 17N 8 0W
Clogher 38 54 25N 7 10W
Clogher Hd. 38 53 48N 6 15W
Cloghjordan 39 52 57N 8 2W
Cloghran 38 53 26N 6 14W
Clonakilty 39 51 37N 8 53W
Clonakilty B. 39 51 33N 8 50W
Clonbur 38 53 32N 9 21W
Cloncurry, Austral. 138 20 40S 140 28E
Cloncurry, Ireland 38 53 26N 6 47W
Cloncurry, R. 138 18 37S 140 40E
Clondalkin 39 53 20N 6 25W
Clonee 38 53 25N 6 28W
Cloneen 39 52 28N 7 36W
Clones 38 54 10N 7 13W
Clonkeen 39 51 59N 9 20W
Clonmany 38 55 16N 7 24W
Clonmel 39 52 22N 7 42W
Clonmore 39 52 49N 6 35W
Clonroche 39 52 27N 6 42W
Clontarf 38 53 22N 6 10W
Cloonakool 38 54 6N 8 47W
Cloone 38 53 57N 7 47W
Cloonfad 38 53 41N 8 45W
Cloppenburg 48 52 50N 8 3E
Cloquet 158 46 40N 92 30W
Clorinda 172 25 16S 57 45W
Closeburn 35 55 13N 3 45W
Cloud Peak 160 44 30N 107 10W
Cloudcroft 161 33 0N 105 48W
Cloudy B. 143 41 25S 174 10E
Clough, Ballymena, U.K. 38 54 58N 6 16W
Clough, Down, U.K. 38 54 18N 5 50W
Cloughton 33 54 20N 0 27W
Clova 37 56 50N 3 4W
Clovelly 30 51 0N 4 25W
Cloverdale 160 38 49N 123 0W
Clovis, Calif., U.S.A. 163 36 54N 119 45W
Clovis, N. Mex., U.S.A. 159 34 20N 103 10W
Clowne 33 53 18N 1 16W
Cloyne 39 51 52N 8 7W
Club Terrace 141 37 35S 148 58E
Cluj 70 46 47N 23 38E
Cluj □ 70 46 45N 23 30E
Clun 28 52 26N 3 2W
Clun Forest 28 52 27N 3 7W
Clunbury 28 52 25N 2 55W
Clunes, Austral. 140 37 20S 143 45E
Clunes, U.K. 36 56 57N 4 58W
Cluny 45 46 26N 4 38E
Cluses 45 46 5N 6 35E
Clusone 62 45 54N 9 58E
Clutha, R. 143 46 20S 169 49E
Clwyd □ 31 53 5N 3 20W
Clwyd, R. 31 53 12N 3 30W
Clwydian Ra. 31 53 10N 3 15W
Clydach 31 51 42N 3 54W
Clyde, Austral. 139 28 48S 143 40E
Clyde, Can. 149 70 30N 68 30W
Clyde, N.Z. 143 45 12S 169 20E
Clyde, Firth of 34 55 20N 5 0W
Clyde, R. 34 55 46N 4 58W
Clydebank 34 55 54N 4 25W
Clydesdale 35 55 42N 3 50W
Clynnog-fawr 31 53 2N 4 22W
Côa, R. 56 40 45N 7 0W
Coachella 163 33 44N 116 13W
Coachella Canal 163 32 43N 114 57W
Coachford 39 51 54N 8 48W
Coachman's Cove 151 50 6N 56 20W
Coagh 38 54 39N 6 37W
Coahoma 159 32 17N 101 20W
Coahuayana, R. 164 18 41N 103 45W
Coahuayutla 164 18 19N 101 42W
Coahuila □ 164 27 0N 112 30W
Coal Creek Flat 143 45 27S 169 19E
Coal I. 143 46 8S 166 40E
Coal, R. 152 59 39N 126 57W
Coalane 127 17 48S 37 2E
Coalbrookdale 28 52 38N 2 30W
Coalburn 35 55 35N 3 55W
Coalcomán 164 18 40N 103 10W
Coaldale, Can. 152 49 45N 112 35W
Coaldale, U.S.A. 163 38 2N 117 55W
Coaldale, Pa., U.S.A. 162 40 50N 75 54W
Coalgate 159 34 35N 96 13W
Coalinga 163 36 10N 120 21W
Coalisland 38 54 33N 6 42W
Coalspur 152 53 15N 117 0W
Coalville, U.K. 28 52 43N 1 21W
Coalville, U.S.A. 160 40 58N 111 24W
Coamo 147 18 5N 66 22W
Coaraci 171 14 38S 39 32W
Coari 174 4 8S 63 7W
Coast □ 126 2 40S 39 45E
Coast Mts. 152 52 0N 126 0W
Coast Range 163 40 0N 124 0W
Coastal Plains Basin 137 30 10S 115 30E
Coatbridge 35 55 52N 4 2W
Coatepec 165 19 27N 96 58W
Coatepeque 166 14 46N 91 55W
Coatesville 162 39 59N 75 30W
Coaticook 151 45 10N 71 46W
Coats I. 149 62 30N 83 0W
Coats Land 13 77 0S 25 0W
Coatzacoalcos 165 18 7N 94 35W
Cobadin 70 44 5N 28 13E
Cobalt 150 47 25N 79 42W
Cobán 166 15 30N 90 21W
Cobar 141 31 27S 145 48E
Cobb I. 162 37 17N 75 42W
Cobbannah 141 37 37S 147 12E
Cobberas, Mt. 141 36 53S 148 12E
Cobden 140 38 20S 143 3E
Cóbh 39 51 50N 8 18W
Cobija 174 11 0S 68 50W
Cobourg 150 43 58N 78 10W
Cobourg Pen. 136 11 20S 132 15E
Cobram 141 35 54S 145 40E
Cobre 160 41 6N 114 25W
Cóbué 125 12 0S 34 58E
Coburg 49 50 15N 10 58E
Coca 56 41 13N 4 32W
Coca, R. 174 0 25S 77 5W
Cocal 170 3 28S 41 34W
Cocanada = Kakinada 96 16 55N 82 20E
Cocentaina 59 38 45N 0 27W
Cocha, La 172 27 50S 65 40W
Cochabamba 174 17 15S 66 20W
Coche, I. 174 10 47N 63 56W
Cochem 49 50 8N 7 7E
Cochemane 127 17 0S 32 54E
Cochilha Grande de Albardão 173 28 30S 51 30W
Cochin 97 9 55N 76 22E
Cochin China 101 10 30N 106 0E
Cochin China = Nam-Phan 101 10 30N 106 0E
Cochise 161 32 6N 109 58W
Cochran 157 32 25N 83 23W
Cochrane, Alta., Can. 152 51 11N 114 30W
Cochrane, Ont., Can. 150 49 0N 81 0W
Cochrane, L. 176 47 10S 72 0W
Cochrane, R. 153 57 53N 101 34W
Cockatoo I. 136 16 6S 123 37E
Cockburn 140 32 5S 141 0E
Cockburn, Canal 176 54 30S 72 0W
Cockburn, C. 136 11 20S 132 52E
Cockburn I. 150 45 55N 83 22W
Cockburn Ra. 136 15 46S 128 0E
Cockburnspath 35 55 56N 2 23W
Cockenzie 35 55 58N 2 59W
Cockerham 32 53 58N 2 49W
Cockermouth 32 54 40N 3 22W
Cockeysville 162 39 29N 76 39W
Cockfield 29 52 8N 0 47E
Cocklebiddy 137 32 0S 126 3E
Coco Chan. 101 13 50N 93 25E
Coco Is. 101 14 0N 93 12E
Coco, Pta. 174 2 58N 77 43W
Coco, R. (Wanks) 166 14 10N 85 0W
Cocoa 157 28 22N 80 40W
Cocobeach 124 0 59N 9 34E
Cocoli, R. 120 12 0N 14 0W
Cocora 70 44 45N 27 3E
Côcos 171 14 10S 44 33W
Cocos (Keeling) Is. 11 12 12S 96 54E
Côcos, R. 171 12 44S 44 48W
Cod, C. 162 42 8N 70 10W
Cod, gasfield 19 57 8N 2 35E
Codajás 174 3 40S 62 0W
Coddenham 29 52 8N 1 8E
Codera, C. 174 10 35N 66 4W
Coderre 153 50 11N 106 31W
Codigoro 63 44 50N 12 5E
Codó 170 4 30S 43 55W
Codogno 62 45 10N 9 42E
Codróipo 63 45 57N 13 0E
Codru, Munţii 70 46 30N 22 15E
Cods Hd. 39 51 40N 10 7W
Cody 160 44 35N 109 0W
Coe Hill 150 44 52N 77 50W
Coelemu 172 36 30S 72 48W
Coelho Neto 170 4 15S 43 0W
Coen 138 13 52S 143 12E
Coesfeld 48 51 56N 7 10E
Coeur d'Alene 160 47 45N 116 51W
Coevorden 46 52 40N 6 44E
Coffeyville 159 37 0N 95 40W
Coffin B. Pen. 136 34 20S 135 10E
Coffs Harbour 141 30 16S 153 5E
Cofre de Perote, Cerro 165 19 30N 97 10W
Cofrentes 59 39 13N 1 5W
Cogealac 70 44 36N 28 36E
Coggeshall 29 51 53N 0 41E
Coghinas, R. 64 40 55N 8 48E
Cognac 44 45 41N 0 20W
Cogne 62 45 37N 7 21E
Cogolludo 58 40 59N 3 10W
Cohagen 160 47 2N 106 45W
Cohoes 162 42 47N 73 42W
Cohuna 140 35 45S 144 15E
Coiba I. 166 7 30N 81 40W
Coig, R. 176 51 0S 70 20W
Coigach, dist. 36 58 0N 5 10W
Coillore 36 57 21N 6 23W
Coimbatore 97 11 2N 76 59E
Coimbra 56 40 15N 8 27W
Coimbra □ 56 40 12N 8 25W
Coin 57 36 40N 4 48W
Cojedes □ 174 9 20N 68 20W
Cojimies 174 0 20N 80 0W
Cojocna 70 46 45N 23 50E
Cojutepequé 166 13 41N 88 54W
Čoka 66 45 57N 20 12E
Cokeville 160 42 4N 111 0W
Col di Tenda 62 44 7N 7 36E
Colaba Pt. 96 18 54N 72 47E
Colac 140 38 21S 143 35E
Colachel 97 8 10N 77 15E
Colares 57 38 48N 9 30W
Colatina 171 19 32S 40 37W
Colbinabbin 141 36 38S 144 48E
Colby, U.K. 32 54 6N 4 42W
Colby, U.S.A. 158 39 27N 101 2W
Colchagua □ 172 34 30S 71 0W
Colchester 29 51 54N 0 55E
Cold Fell 32 54 54N 2 40W
Coldingham 35 55 53N 2 10W
Coldstream 35 55 39N 2 14W
Coldwater 159 37 18N 99 24W
Coldwell 150 48 45N 86 30W
Colebrook 138 42 31S 147 12E
Colebrooke 30 50 45N 3 44W
Coleford 28 51 46N 2 38W
Coleman, Can. 152 49 40N 114 30W
Coleman, U.S.A. 159 31 52N 99 30W
Coleman, R. 138 15 6S 141 38E
Colenso 129 28 44S 29 50E
Coleraine, Austral. 140 37 36S 141 40E
Coleraine, U.K. 38 55 8N 6 40E
Coleraine □ 38 55 8N 6 40E
Coleridge, L. 143 43 17S 171 30E
Coleroon, R. 97 11 0N 79 0E
Colesberg 128 30 45S 25 5E
Coleshill 28 52 30N 1 42W
Coleville 163 38 44N 119 30W
Colfax, La., U.S.A. 159 31 35N 92 39W
Colfax, Wash., U.S.A. 160 46 57N 117 28W
Colgrave Sd. 36 60 35N 1 0W
Colhué Huapi, L. 176 45 30S 69 0W
Cólico 62 46 8N 9 22E
Coligny 128 46 24N 5 21E
Colima 164 19 10N 103 40W
Colima □ 164 19 10N 103 40W
Colima, Nevado de 164 19 30N 103 40W
Colina 172 33 13S 70 45W
Colina do Norte 120 12 28N 15 0W
Colinas, Goiás, Brazil 171 14 15S 48 2W
Colinas, Maranhão, Brazil 170 6 0S 44 10W
Colinton, Austral. 141 35 50S 149 10E
Colinton, U.K. 35 55 54N 3 17W
Coll, I. 34 56 40N 6 35W
Collaguasi 172 21 5S 68 45W
Collarada, Peña 58 42 43N 0 29W
Collarenebri 139 29 33S 148 36E
Collbran 161 39 16N 107 58W
Colle Salvetti 62 43 34N 10 27E
Colle Sannita 65 41 22N 14 48E
Colléchio 62 44 23N 10 10E
Colleen Bawn 127 21 0S 29 12E
College Park, Ga., U.S.A. 157 33 42N 84 27W
College Park, Md., U.S.A. 162 39 0N 76 55W
Collette 151 46 40N 65 30W
Collie, N.S.W., Austral. 141 31 41S 148 18E
Collie, W. Austral., Austral. 137 33 22S 116 8E
Collier B. 136 16 10S 124 15E
Collier Law Pk. 32 54 47N 1 59W
Collier Ra. 137 24 45S 119 10E
Collin 35 55 4N 3 30W
Colline Metallifere 62 43 10N 11 0E
Collingbourne 28 51 16N 1 39W
Collingswood 162 39 55N 75 4W
Collingwood, Austral. 138 22 20S 142 31E
Collingwood, Can. 150 44 29N 80 13W
Collingwood, N.Z. 143 40 25S 172 40E
Collingwood B. 138 9 30S 149 30E
Collins 150 50 17N 89 27W
Collinsville 138 20 30S 147 56E
Collipulli 172 37 55S 72 30W
Collison Ra. 136 14 49S 127 25E
Collo 119 36 58N 6 37E
Collon 38 53 46N 6 29W
Collonges 45 46 9N 5 52E
Collooney 38 54 11N 8 28W
Colmar 43 48 5N 7 20E
Colmars 45 44 11N 6 39E
Colmenar 57 36 54N 4 20W
Colmenar de Oreja 58 40 6N 3 25W
Colmenar Viejo 56 40 39N 3 47W
Colmor 159 36 18N 104 36W
Colne 32 53 51N 2 11W
Colne, R., Essex, U.K. 29 51 55N 0 50E
Colne, R., Herts., U.K. 29 51 36N 0 30W
Colnett, Cabo 164 31 0N 116 20W
Colo, R. 141 33 25S 150 52E
Cologna Véneta 63 45 19N 11 21E
Colomb-Béchar = Béchar 118 31 38N 2 18E
Colombey-les-Belles 43 48 32N 5 54E
Colombey-les-deux Églises 43 48 20N 4 50E
Colômbia 171 20 10S 48 40W
Colombia 174 3 24N 79 49W
Colombia ■ 174 3 45N 73 0W
Colombier 50 46 58N 6 53E
Colombo 97 6 56N 79 58E
Colombus, Kans., U.S.A. 159 37 15N 94 30W
Colombus, Nebr., U.S.A. 158 41 30N 97 25W
Colombus, N.Mex., U.S.A. 161 31 54N 107 43W
Colome 158 43 20N 99 44W
Colón, Argent. 172 32 12S 58 30W
Colón, Cuba 166 22 42N 80 54W
Colón, Panama 166 9 20N 80 0W
Colonel Hill 167 22 50N 74 21W
Colonella 63 42 52N 13 50E
Colonia del Sacramento 173 34 25S 57 50W
Colonia Dora 172 28 34S 62 59W
Colonia Las Heras 176 46 30S 69 0W
Colonia Sarmiento 176 45 30S 68 15W
Colonial Hts. 162 37 15N 77 25W
Colonne, C. delle 65 39 2N 17 11E
Colonsay 153 51 59N 105 52W
Colonsay, I. 34 56 4N 6 12W
Colorado □ 154 37 40N 106 0W
Colorado Aqueduct 161 34 17N 114 10W
Colorado City 159 32 25N 100 50W
Colorado Desert 154 34 20N 116 0W
Colorado Plateau 161 36 40N 110 30W
Colorado, R., Argent. 172 37 30S 69 0W
Colorado, R., Ariz., U.S.A. 161 33 30N 114 30W
Colorado, R., Calif., U.S.A. 161 34 0N 114 33W
Colorado, R., Tex., U.S.A. 159 29 40N 96 30W
Colorado Springs 158 38 55N 104 50W
Colorno 62 44 55N 10 21E
Colossal 141 30 52S 147 3E
Colotepec 165 15 47N 97 3W
Colotlán 164 22 6N 103 16W
Colpy 37 57 23N 2 35W
Colsterworth 29 52 48N 0 37W
Coltishall 29 52 44N 1 21E
Colton, Calif., U.S.A. 163 34 4N 117 20W
Colton, Wash., U.S.A. 160 46 41N 117 6W
Columbia, La., U.S.A. 159 32 7N 92 5W
Columbia, Miss., U.S.A. 159 31 16N 89 50W
Columbia, Mo., U.S.A. 158 38 58N 92 20W
Columbia, Pa., U.S.A. 162 40 2N 76 30W
Columbia, S.C., U.S.A. 157 34 0N 81 0W

Columbia Coroaci

Columbia, Tenn., U.S.A. 157 35 40N 87 0W
Columbia, C. 12 83 0N 70 0W
Columbia City 156 41 8N 85 30W
Columbia, District of □ 156 38 55N 77 0W
Columbia Falls 160 48 25N 114 16W
Columbia Heights 158 45 5N 93 10W
Columbia, Mt. 152 52 8N 117 20W
Columbia Plateau 160 47 30N 118 30W
Columbia, R. 160 45 49N 120 0W
Columbretes, Is. 58 39 50N 0 50E
Columbus, Ga., U.S.A. 157 32 30N 84 58W
Columbus, Ind., U.S.A. 156 39 14N 85 55W
Columbus, Miss., U.S.A. 157 33 30N 88 26W
Columbus, Mont., U.S.A. 160 45 45N 109 14W
Columbus, N.D., U.S.A. 158 48 52N 102 48W
Columbus, Ohio, U.S.A. 156 39 57N 83 1W
Columbus, Tex., U.S.A. 159 29 42N 96 33W
Columbus, Wis., U.S.A. 158 43 20N 89 2W
Colunda 125 12 7S 23 36E
Colunga 56 43 29N 5 16W
Colusa 160 39 15N 122 1W
Colville 160 48 33N 117 54W
Colville, C. 142 36 29S 175 21E
Colville, R. 147 69 15N 152 0W
Colwell 35 55 4N 2 4W
Colwich 28 52 48N 1 58W
Colwyn 31 53 17N 3 43W
Colwyn Bay 31 53 17N 3 44W
Colyton 30 50 44N 3 4W
Comácchio 63 44 41N 12 10E
Comalcalco 165 18 16N 93 13W
Comallo 176 41 0S 70 5W
Comana 70 44 10N 26 10E
Comanche, Okla., U.S.A. 159 34 27N 97 58W
Comanche, Tex., U.S.A. 159 31 55N 98 35W
Comăneşti 70 46 25N 26 26E
Comayagua 166 14 25N 87 37W
Combahee, R. 157 32 45N 80 50W
Combara 141 31 10S 148 22E
Combe Martin 30 51 12N 4 2W
Combeaufontaine 43 47 38N 5 54E
Comber 38 54 33N 5 45W
Combermere Bay 98 19 37N 93 34E
Comblain 47 50 29N 5 35E
Combles 43 50 0N 2 50E
Combourg 42 48 25N 1 46W
Comboyne 141 31 34S 152 34E
Combronde 44 45 58N 3 5E
Comeragh Mts. 39 52 17N 7 35W
Comercinho 171 16 19S 41 47W
Comet 138 23 36S 148 38E
Comet Vale 137 29 55S 121 4E
Comilla 98 23 28N 91 10E
Comines 47 50 46N 3 0E
Comino, C. 64 40 28N 9 47E
Cómiso 65 36 57N 14 35E
Comitán 165 16 18N 92 9W
Commentry 44 46 20N 2 46E
Commerce, Ga., U.S.A. 157 34 10N 83 25W
Commerce, Tex., U.S.A. 159 33 15N 95 50W
Commercy 43 48 40N 5 34E
Committee B. 149 68 30N 86 30W
Commonwealth B. 13 67 0S 144 0E
Commoron Cr., R. 139 28 22S 150 8E
Communism Pk. = Kommunizma, Pk. 93 38 40N 72 20E
Como 62 45 48N 9 5E
Como, L. di 62 46 5N 9 17E
Comodoro Rivadavia 176 45 50S 67 40W
Comores, Arch. des 11 10 0S 50 0E
Comores, Is. 11 12 10S 44 15E
Comorin, C. 97 8 3N 77 40E
Comorişte 70 45 10N 21 35E
Comoro Is. 11 12 10S 44 15E
Comox 152 49 42N 124 55W
Compiègne 43 49 24N 2 50E
Compíglia Maríttima 62 43 4N 10 37E
Comporta 57 38 22N 8 46W
Compostela 164 21 15N 104 53W
Comprida, I. 173 24 50S 47 42W
Compton, U.K. 28 51 2N 1 19W
Compton, U.S.A. 163 33 54N 118 13W
Compton Downs 139 30 28S 146 30E
Comrie 35 56 22N 4 0W
Con Cuong 100 19 2N 104 54E
Côn Dao 101 8 45N 106 45E
Con Son, Is. 101 8 41N 106 37E
Conakry 120 9 29N 13 49W
Conara Junction 138 41 50S 147 26E
Conargo 141 35 16S 145 10E
Conatlán 164 24 30N 104 42W
Concarneau 42 47 52N 3 56W
Conceição, Brazil 170 7 33S 38 31W
Conceição, Mozam. 127 18 47S 36 7E
Conceição da Barra 171 18 35S 39 45W
Conceição do Araguaia 170 8 0S 49 2W
Conceição do Canindé 170 7 54S 41 34W
Conceição do Mato Dentro 171 19 1S 43 25W
Concepcián 165 18 15N 90 5W
Concepción, Argent. 172 27 20S 65 35W
Concepción, Boliv. 174 15 50S 61 40W
Concepción, Chile 172 36 50S 73 0W
Concepción, Colomb. 174 0 5N 75 37W
Concepción, Parag. 172 23 30S 57 20W
Concepción, Venez. 174 10 48N 71 46W
Concepción □ 172 37 0S 72 30W
Concepcion, C. 154 34 30N 120 34W
Concepción del Oro 164 24 40N 101 30W
Concepción del Uruguay 172 32 35S 58 20W
Concepción, L. 174 17 20S 61 10W
Concepción, La = Ri-Aba 121 3 28N 84 0E
Concepción, Punta 164 26 55N 111 50W
Concepción, R. 164 30 32N 113 2W
Conception B. 128 23 55S 14 22E
Conception I. 167 23 52N 75 9W
Conception, Pt. 163 34 27N 120 28W
Concession 127 17 27S 30 56E
Conchas Dam 159 35 25N 104 10W
Conche 151 50 48N 55 58W
Conches-en-Ouche 50 48 58N 0 58E
Concho 161 34 32N 109 43W
Concho, R. 159 31 30N 100 8W
Conchos, R., Chihnahua, Mexico 164 29 20N 105 0W
Conchos, R., Tamaulipas, Mexico 165 25 0N 97 32W
Concon 172 32 56S 71 33W
Concord, Calif., U.S.A. 163 37 59N 122 2W
Concord, N.C., U.S.A. 157 35 28N 80 35W
Concord, N.H., U.S.A. 162 43 12N 71 30W
Concórdia, Argent. 172 31 20S 58 2W
Concórdia, Brazil 174 4 36S 66 36W
Concordia, Colomb. 174 2 39N 72 47W
Concordia, Mexico 164 23 18N 106 2W
Concordia, U.S.A. 158 39 35N 97 40W
Concordia, La 165 16 8N 92 38W
Concots 44 44 26N 1 40E
Concrete 160 48 35N 121 49W
Condah 140 37 57S 141 44E
Condamine, R. 133 27 7S 149 48E
Condat 44 45 21N 2 46E
Conde 171 11 49S 37 37W
Condé 43 50 26N 3 34E
Conde 158 45 13N 98 5W
Condé-sur-Noireau 42 48 51N 0 33W
Condeúba 171 15 0S 42 0W
Condobolin 141 33 4S 147 6E
Condom 44 43 57N 0 22E
Condon 160 45 15N 120 8W
Condove 62 45 8N 7 19E
Condover 28 52 39N 2 46W
Conegliano 63 45 53N 12 18E
Conejera, I. 59 39 11N 2 58E
Conejos 164 26 14N 103 53W
Conflans-en-Jarnisy 43 49 10N 5 52E
Confolens 44 46 2N 0 40E
Confuso, R. 172 24 10S 59 0W
Congleton 32 53 10N 2 12W
Congo 170 7 48S 36 40W
Congo ■ 124 1 0S 16 0E
Congo Basin 114 0 10S 24 30E
Congo, Democratic Rep. of = Zaïre ■ 124 3 0S 22 0E
Congo (Kinshasa) ■ = Zaïre ■ 124 1 0S 16 0E
Congo, R. = Zaïre, R. 124 1 30N 28 0E
Congonhas 173 20 30S 43 52W
Congresbury 28 51 20N 2 49W
Congress 161 34 11N 112 56W
Congucu 113 31 25S 52 30W
Conil 57 36 17N 6 10W
Coningsby 33 53 7N 0 9W
Conisbrough 33 53 29N 1 12W
Coniston, Can. 150 46 29N 80 51W
Coniston, U.K. 32 54 22N 3 6W
Coniston Water 32 54 20N 3 5W
Conjeevaram = Kancheepuram 97 12 52N 79 45E
Conjuboy 138 18 35S 144 45E
Conklin 153 55 38N 111 5W
Conlea 139 30 7S 144 35E
Conn, L. 38 54 3N 9 15W
Conna 39 52 5N 8 8W
Connacht 38 53 23N 8 40W
Connah's Quay 31 53 13N 3 6W
Conneaut 156 41 55N 80 32W
Connecticut □ 162 41 40N 72 40W
Connecticut, R. 162 41 17N 72 21W
Connel 34 56 27N 5 24W
Connel Park 34 55 22N 4 15W
Connell 160 46 45N 118 58W
Connemara 38 53 29N 9 45W
Conner, La 160 48 22N 122 27W
Connersville 156 39 40N 85 10W
Connonagh 39 51 35N 9 8W
Connor, Mt. 136 14 34S 126 4E
Connors Ra. 138 21 40S 149 10E
Conoble 141 32 55S 144 42E
Cononaco, R. 174 1 20S 76 30W
Conquest 153 51 32N 107 14W
Conquet, Le 42 48 21N 4 46W
Conrad 160 48 11N 112 0W
Conran, C. 141 37 49S 148 44E
Conroe 159 30 15N 95 28W
Conselheiro Lafaiete 173 20 40S 43 48W
Conselheiro Pena 171 19 10S 41 30W
Consett 32 54 52N 1 50W
Conshohocken 162 40 5N 75 18W
Consort 153 52 1N 110 46W
Constance = Konstanz 49 47 39N 9 10E
Constance, L. = Bodensee 51 47 35N 9 25E
Constanţa 70 44 14N 28 38E
Constanţa □ 70 44 15N 28 15E
Constantia 162 43 15N 76 1W
Constantina 57 37 51N 5 40W
Constantine 119 36 25N 6 42E
Constitución, Chile 172 35 20S 72 30W
Constitución, Uruguay 172 31 0S 58 10W
Consuegra 57 39 28N 3 43W
Consul 153 49 20N 109 30W
Contact 160 41 50N 114 56W
Contai 95 21 54N 87 55E
Contamana 174 7 10S 74 55W
Contarina 63 45 2N 12 13E
Contas, R. 171 13 5S 41 53W
Contes 45 43 49N 7 19E
Conthey 50 46 14N 7 28E
Contin 37 57 34N 4 35W
Contoocook 162 43 13N 71 45W
Contra Costa 129 25 9S 33 30E
Contres 43 47 24N 1 26E
Contrexéville 43 48 6N 5 53E
Convención 174 8 28N 73 21W
Conversano 65 40 57N 17 8E
Convoy 38 54 52N 7 40W
Conway, Ark., U.S.A. 159 35 5N 92 30W
Conway, N.H., U.S.A. 162 43 58N 71 8W
Conway, S.C., U.S.A. 157 33 49N 79 2W
Conway = Conwy 31 53 17N 3 50W
Conway, L. 139 28 17S 135 35E
Conwy 31 53 17N 3 50W
Conwy Bay 31 53 17N 3 57W
Conwy, R. 31 53 18N 3 50W
Coober Pedy 136 29 1S 134 43E
Coobina 137 23 22S 120 10E
Cooch Behar 98 26 22N 89 29E
Cook, Austral. 137 30 37S 130 25E
Cook, U.S.A. 158 47 49N 92 39W
Cook, Bahia 176 55 10S 70 0W
Cook Inlet 147 59 0N 151 0W
Cook Is. 131 20 0S 160 0W
Cook, Mount 143 43 36S 170 9E
Cook Strait 143 41 15S 174 29E
Cooke Plains 140 35 23S 139 34E
Cookeville 157 36 12N 85 30W
Cookham 29 51 33N 0 42W
Cookhouse 128 32 44S 25 47E
Cookstown 38 54 40N 6 43W
Cookstown □ 38 54 40N 6 43W
Cooktown 138 15 30S 145 16E
Coolabah 141 31 1S 146 43E
Cooladdi 139 26 37S 145 23E
Coolah 141 31 48S 149 41E
Coolamon 141 34 46S 147 8E
Coolaney 38 54 10N 8 36W
Coolangatta 139 28 11S 153 29E
Coole 38 53 42N 7 23W
Coolgardie 137 30 55S 121 8E
Coolgreany 39 52 46N 6 14W
Coolibah 136 15 33S 130 56E
Coolidge 161 33 1N 111 35W
Coolidge Dam 161 33 10N 110 30W
Coolmore 38 54 33N 8 12W
Cooma 141 36 12S 149 8E
Coomacarrea Mts. 39 51 59N 10 0W
Coonabarabran 141 31 14S 149 18E
Coonalpyn 140 35 43S 139 52E
Coonamble 141 30 56S 148 27E
Coonana 137 31 0S 123 0E
Coondapoor 97 13 42N 74 40E
Coongie 139 27 9S 140 8E
Coongoola 139 27 43S 145 47E
Cooninie, L. 139 26 4S 139 59E
Coonoor 97 11 10N 76 45E
Cooper 159 33 20N 95 40W
Cooper Cr. 139 28 29S 137 46E
Cooper, R. 157 33 0N 79 55W
Coopersburg 162 40 31N 75 23W
Cooperstown, N.D., U.S.A. 158 47 30N 98 14W
Cooperstown, New York, U.S.A. 162 42 42N 74 57W
Coorabie P.O. 137 31 54S 132 18E
Coorabulka 138 23 41S 140 20E
Coorong, The 133 35 50S 139 20E
Coorow 137 29 53S 116 2E
Cooroy 139 26 22S 152 54E
Coos Bay 160 43 26N 124 7W
Cootamundra 141 34 36S 148 1E
Cootehill 38 54 5N 7 5W
Cooyar 139 26 59S 151 51E
Cooyeana 138 24 29S 138 45E
Copahué, Paso 172 37 49S 71 8W
Copainalá 165 17 8N 93 11W
Copake Falls 162 42 7N 73 31W
Copán 166 14 50N 89 9W
Cope 158 39 44N 102 50W
Cope, Cabo 59 37 26N 1 28W
Cope Cope 140 36 27S 143 5E
Copeland I. 38 54 38N 5 33W
Copenhagen 162 43 54N 75 41W
Copenhagen = København 73 55 41N 12 34E
Copertino 65 40 17N 18 2W
Copeville 140 34 47S 139 51E
Copiapó 172 27 15S 70 20E
Copiapó, R. 172 27 19S 70 56W
Copinsay I. 37 58 54N 2 40W
Coplay 162 40 44N 75 29W
Copley 140 30 24S 138 26E
Copp L. 152 60 14N 114 40W
Copparo 63 44 52N 11 49E
Copper Center 147 62 10N 145 25W
Copper Cliff 150 46 28N 81 4W
Copper Harbor 156 47 31N 87 55W
Copper Mountain 152 49 20N 120 30W
Copper Queen 127 17 29S 29 18E
Copper R. 147 61 30N 144 30W
Copperbelt □ 127 13 15N 27 30E
Copperfield 137 29 1S 120 26E
Coppermine 148 67 50N 115 5W
Coppermine, R. 148 67 49N 115 4W
Copperopolis 163 37 58N 120 38W
Cöppingen 49 48 42N 9 40E
Copythorne 28 50 56N 1 34W
Coquet, I. 35 55 21N 1 30W
Coquet, R. 35 55 18N 1 45W
Coquilhatville = Mbandaka 124 0 1N 18 18E
Coquille 160 43 15N 124 6W
Coquimbo 172 30 0S 71 20W
Coquimbo □ 172 31 0S 71 0W
Cora, oilfield 19 55 45N 4 45E
Corabia 70 43 48N 24 30E
Coração de Jesus 171 11 39S 39 56W
Coracora 174 15 5S 73 45W
Coradi, Is. 65 40 27N 71 10E
Coral Harbour 149 64 8N 83 10W
Coral Rapids 150 50 20N 81 40W
Coral Sea 142 15 0S 150 0E
Coral Sea Islands Terr. 133 20 0S 155 0E
Corato 65 41 12N 16 22E
Corbeil-Essonnes 43 48 36N 2 26E
Corbie 43 49 54N 2 30E
Corbières, mts. 44 42 55N 2 35E
Corbigny 43 47 16N 3 40E
Corbin 156 37 0N 84 3W
Corbion 47 49 48N 5 0E
Corbones, R. 57 37 25N 5 35W
Corbridge 35 54 58N 2 0W
Corby, Lincs., U.K. 29 52 49N 0 31W
Corby, Northants., U.K. 29 52 29N 0 41W
Corcoles, R. 59 39 12N 2 40W
Corcoran 163 36 6N 119 35W
Corcubión 56 42 56N 9 12W
Cord. de Caravaya 174 14 0S 70 30W
Cordele 157 31 55N 83 49W
Cordell 159 35 18N 99 0W
Cordenons 63 45 59N 12 42E
Cordes 44 44 5N 1 57E
Cordillera Oriental 174 5 0N 74 0W
Cordisburgo 171 19 7S 44 21W
Córdoba 172 31 20S 64 10W
Cordoba 164 26 20N 103 20W
Córdoba, Mexico 165 18 50N 97 0W
Córdoba, Spain 57 37 50N 4 50W
Córdoba □, Argent. 172 31 22S 64 15W
Córdoba □, Colomb. 174 8 20N 75 40W
Córdoba □, Spain 57 38 5N 5 0W
Córdoba, Sierra de 172 31 10S 64 25W
Cordon 103 16 42N 121 32E
Cordova, Ala., U.S.A. 157 33 45N 87 12W
Cordova, Alaska, U.S.A. 147 60 36N 145 45W
Corella 58 42 7N 1 48W
Corella, R. 138 19 34S 140 47E
Coremas 170 7 1S 37 58W
Corfe Castle 28 50 58N 2 3W
Corfe Mullen 28 50 45N 2 0W
Corfield 138 21 40S 143 21E
Corfu = Kerkira 68 39 38N 19 50E
Corgo 56 42 56N 7 25W
Cori 64 41 39N 12 53E
Coria 56 40 0N 6 33W
Coricudgy, Mt. 141 32 51S 150 24E
Corigliano Cálabro 65 39 36N 16 31E
Coringa Is. 138 16 58S 149 58E
Corinna 138 41 35S 145 10E
Corinth, Miss., U.S.A. 157 34 54N 88 30W
Corinth, N.Y., U.S.A. 162 43 15N 73 50W
Corinth = Korinthos 69 37 56N 22 55E
Corinth Canal 69 37 48N 23 0E
Corinth, G. of = Korinthiakós 69 38 16N 22 30E
Corinto, Brazil 171 18 20S 44 30W
Corinto, Nic. 166 12 30N 87 10W
Corj □ 70 45 5N 23 25E
Cork 39 51 54N 8 30W
Cork □ 39 51 50N 8 50W
Cork Harbour 39 51 46N 8 16W
Corlay 42 48 20N 3 5W
Corleone 64 37 48N 13 16E
Corleto Perticara 65 40 23N 16 2E
Çorlu 67 41 11N 27 49E
Cormack L. 152 60 56N 121 37W
Cormóns 63 45 58N 13 29E
Cormorant 153 54 14N 100 35W
Cormorant L. 153 54 15N 100 50W
Cormorant, oilfield 19 61 0N 1 10E
Corn Hill, Mt. 38 53 48N 7 43W
Corn Is. 167 12 0N 83 0W
Cornelio 164 29 55N 111 8W
Cornélio Procópio 173 23 7S 50 40W
Cornell 158 45 10N 91 8W
Corner Brook 151 48 57N 57 58W
Corner Inlet 133 38 45S 146 20E
Cornforth 33 54 42N 1 28W
Corniglio 62 44 29N 10 5E
Corning, Ark., U.S.A. 159 36 27N 90 34W
Corning, Calif., U.S.A. 160 39 56N 122 9W
Corning, Iowa, U.S.A. 158 40 57N 94 40W
Corning, N.Y., U.S.A. 162 42 10N 77 3W
Cornwall, Austral. 138 41 33S 148 7E
Cornwall, Can. 150 45 2N 74 44W
Cornwall, U.S.A. 162 40 17N 76 25W
Cornwall □ 30 50 26N 4 40W
Cornwall, C. 30 50 8N 5 42W
Cornwallis I. 12 75 8N 95 0W
Corny Pt. 140 34 55S 137 0E
Coro 174 11 25N 69 41W
Coroaci 171 18 35S 42 17W

Coroatá **Crooksville**

Name	Page	Lat.	Long.
Coroatá	**170**	4 20S	44 0W
Corocoro	**174**	17 15S	69 19W
Corofin	**39**	53 27N	8 50W
Coroico	**174**	16 0S	67 50W
Coromandel, Brazil	**171**	18 28S	47 13W
Coromandel, N.Z.	**142**	36 45S	175 31E
Coromandel Coast	**97**	12 30N	81 0E
Coromandel Pen.	**142**	37 0S	175 45E
Coromandel Ra.	**142**	37 0S	175 40E
Coromorant, L.	**153**	54 20N	100 50W
Corona, Austral.	**139**	31 16S	141 24E
Corona, Calif., U.S.A.	**163**	33 49N	117 36W
Corona, N. Mex., U.S.A.	**161**	34 15N	105 32W
Coronada B.	**166**	9 0N	83 40W
Coronado	**163**	32 45N	117 9W
Coronado, Bahía de	**166**	9 0N	83 40W
Coronation	**152**	52 5N	111 27W
Coronation Gulf	**148**	68 25N	112 0W
Coronation I., Antarct.	**13**	60 45S	46 0W
Coronation I., U.S.A.	**152**	55 52N	134 20W
Coronation Is.	**136**	14 57S	124 55E
Coronda	**172**	31 58S	60 56W
Coronel	**172**	37 0S	73 10W
Coronel Bogado	**172**	27 11S	56 18W
Coronel Dorrego	**172**	38 40S	61 10W
Coronel Fabriciano	**171**	19 31S	42 38W
Coronel Murta	**171**	16 37S	42 11W
Coronel Oviedo	**172**	25 24S	56 30W
Coronel Pringles	**172**	38 0S	61 30W
Coronel Suárez	**172**	37 30S	62 0W
Coronel Vidal	**172**	37 28S	57 45W
Coronie	**170**	5 55N	56 25W
Corovoda	**68**	40 31N	20 14E
Corowa	**141**	35 58S	146 21E
Corozal, Belize	**165**	18 30N	88 30W
Corozal, Colomb.	**174**	9 19N	75 18W
Corpach	**36**	56 50N	5 9W
Corps	**45**	44 50N	5 56E
Corpus	**173**	27 10S	55 30W
Corpus Christi	**159**	27 50N	97 28W
Corpus Christi L.	**159**	28 5N	97 54W
Corque	**174**	18 10S	67 50W
Corral de Almaguer	**58**	39 45N	3 10W
Corran	**36**	56 44N	5 14W
Corrandibby Ra.	**137**	26 0S	115 20E
Corraun Pen.	**38**	53 58N	10 15W
Corrégio	**62**	44 46N	10 47E
Corrente	**170**	10 27S	45 10W
Corrente, R.	**170**	13 8S	43 28W
Correntes, C. das	**129**	24 6S	35 34E
Correntina	**171**	13 20S	44 39W
Corrèze □	**44**	45 20N	1 45E
Corrib, L.	**38**	53 25N	9 10W
Corrie	**34**	55 39N	5 10W
Corrientes	**172**	27 30S	58 45W
Corrientes □	**172**	28 0S	57 0W
Corrientes, C., Colomb.	**174**	5 30N	77 34W
Corrientes, C., Cuba	**166**	21 43N	84 30W
Corrientes, C., Mexico	**164**	20 25N	105 42W
Corrientes, R., Argent.	**172**	30 21S	59 33W
Corrientes, R., Colomb.	**174**	3 15S	75 58W
Corrigan	**159**	31 0N	94 48W
Corrigin	**137**	32 20S	117 53E
Corringham	**33**	53 25N	0 42W
Corris	**31**	52 41N	3 49W
Corrowidgie	**141**	36 56S	148 50E
Corry	**156**	41 55N	79 39W
Corryong	**141**	36 12S	147 53E
Corryvrecken, G. of	**34**	56 10N	5 44W
Corse, C.	**45**	43 1N	9 25E
Corse-du-Sud □	**45**	41 45N	9 0E
Corse, Î	**45**	42 0N	9 0E
Corsewall Pt.	**34**	55 0N	5 10W
Corsham	**28**	51 25N	2 11W
Corsica = Corse	**45**	42 0N	9 0E
Corsicana	**159**	32 5N	96 30W
Corsley	**28**	51 12N	2 14W
Corsock	**35**	55 54N	3 56W
Corté	**45**	42 19N	9 11E
Corte do Pinto	**57**	37 42N	7 29W
Cortegana	**57**	37 52N	6 49W
Cortez	**161**	37 24N	108 35W
Cortina d'Ampezzo	**63**	46 32N	12 9E
Cortland	**162**	42 35N	76 11W
Corton	**29**	52 31N	1 46E
Cortona	**63**	43 16N	12 0E
Coruche	**57**	38 57N	8 30W
Çorum	**92**	40 30N	35 5E
Corumbá, Goias, Brazil	**171**	16 0S	48 50W
Corumbá, Mato Grosso, Brazil	**174**	19 0S	57 30W
Corumbá R.	**171**	17 25S	48 30W
Corumbaíba	**171**	18 9S	48 34W
Coruña □	**56**	43 0N	8 37E
Coruña, La	**56**	43 20N	8 25W
Coruña, La □	**56**	43 10N	8 30W
Corund	**70**	46 30N	25 13E
Corunna = La Coruña	**56**	43 20N	8 25W
Coruripe	**171**	10 5S	36 10W
Corvallis	**160**	44 36N	123 15W
Corve, R.	**28**	52 22N	2 43W
Corvette, L. de la	**150**	53 25N	73 55W
Corwen	**31**	52 59N	3 23W
Corydon	**158**	40 42N	93 22W
Cosalá	**164**	24 28N	106 40W
Cosamaloapán	**165**	18 23N	95 50W
Coseley	**28**	52 33N	2 6W
Cosenza	**65**	39 17N	16 14E
Coşereni	**70**	44 38N	26 35E
Cosham	**28**	50 51N	1 3W
Coshocton	**156**	40 17N	81 51W
Cosne-s.-Loire	**43**	47 24N	2 54E
Coso Junction	**163**	36 3N	117 57W
Coso Pk.	**163**	36 13N	117 44W
Cospeito	**56**	43 12N	7 34W
Cosquín	**172**	31 15S	64 30W
Cossato	**62**	45 34N	8 10E
Cossé-le-Vivien	**42**	47 57N	0 54W
Costa Azul	**50**	43 25N	6 50E
Costa Blanca	**59**	38 25N	0 10W
Costa Brava	**58**	41 30N	3 0E
Costa del Sol	**57**	36 30N	4 30W
Costa Dorada	**58**	40 45N	1 15E
Costa Mesa	**163**	33 39N	117 55W
Costa Rica	**164**	31 20N	112 40W
Costa Rica ■	**166**	10 0N	84 0W
Costa Smeralda	**64**	41 5N	9 35E
Costelloe	**39**	53 20N	9 33W
Costessey	**29**	52 40N	1 11E
Costigliole d'Asti	**62**	44 48N	8 11E
Costilla	**161**	37 0N	105 30W
Coştiui	**70**	47 53N	24 2E
Cosumnes, R.	**163**	38 14N	121 25W
Coswig	**48**	51 52N	12 31E
Cotabato	**103**	7 14N	124 15E
Cotabena	**140**	31 42S	138 11E
Cotagaita	**172**	20 45S	65 30W
Côte d'Azur	**45**	43 25N	6 50E
Côte d'Or	**43**	47 10N	4 50E
Côte d'Or □	**43**	47 30N	4 50E
Côte, La	**50**	46 25N	6 15E
Côte-St. André, La	**45**	45 24N	5 15E
Coteau des Prairies	**158**	44 30N	97 0W
Coteau du Missouri, Plat. du	**154**	47 0N	101 0W
Cotegipe	**171**	12 2S	44 15W
Cotentin	**42**	49 30N	1 30W
Côtes de Meuse	**43**	49 15N	5 22E
Côtes-du-Nord □	**42**	48 25N	2 40W
Cotherstone	**32**	54 34N	1 59W
Cotiella	**58**	42 31N	0 19E
Cotina, R.	**66**	43 36N	19 9E
Cotonou	**121**	6 20N	2 25E
Cotopaxi, Vol.	**174**	0 30S	78 30W
Cotronei	**65**	39 9N	16 27E
Cotswold Hills	**28**	51 42N	2 10W
Cottage Grove	**160**	43 48N	123 2W
Cottbus	**48**	51 44N	14 20E
Cottbus □	**48**	51 43N	13 30E
Cottenham	**29**	52 18N	0 8E
Cottingham	**33**	53 47N	0 23W
Cottonwood, Can.	**152**	53 5N	121 50W
Cottonwood, U.S.A.	**161**	34 48N	112 1W
Coubre, Pte. de la	**44**	45 42N	1 15W
Couches	**43**	46 53N	4 30E
Couço	**57**	38 59N	8 17W
Coudersport	**156**	41 45N	78 1W
Couedic, C. du	**140**	36 5S	136 40E
Couëron	**42**	47 13N	1 44W
Coueson, R.	**42**	48 20N	1 15W
Couhé-Vérac	**44**	46 18N	0 12E
Couillet	**47**	50 23N	4 28E
Coulags	**36**	57 26N	5 24W
Coulanges, Deux Sèvres, France	**44**	46 58N	0 35W
Coulanges, Yonne, France	**43**	47 30N	3 30E
Coulee City	**160**	47 44N	119 12W
Coulman I.	**13**	73 35S	170 0E
Coulommiers	**43**	48 50N	3 3E
Coulonge, R.	**150**	45 52N	76 46W
Coulport	**34**	56 3N	4 53W
Coulterville	**163**	37 42N	120 12W
Council	**147**	64 55N	163 45W
Council Bluffs	**158**	41 20N	95 50W
Council Grove	**158**	38 41N	96 30W
Coupar Angus	**35**	56 33N	3 17W
Courantyne, R.	**174**	5 0N	57 45W
Courçon	**44**	46 15N	0 50W
Cours	**45**	46 7N	4 19E
Courseulles	**42**	49 20N	0 29W
Court-St.-Etienne	**47**	50 38N	4 34E
Courtenay	**152**	49 45N	125 0W
Courtine, La	**44**	45 43N	2 16E
Courtland	**163**	38 20N	121 34W
Courtmacsherry	**39**	51 38N	8 43W
Courtmacsherry B.	**39**	51 37N	8 37W
Courtown	**39**	52 39N	6 14W
Courtrai = Kortrijk	**47**	50 50N	3 17E
Courville	**42**	48 28N	1 15E
Coutances	**42**	49 3N	1 28W
Couterne	**42**	48 30N	0 25W
Coutras	**44**	45 3N	0 8W
Coutts	**152**	49 0N	111 57W
Couvet	**50**	46 57N	6 38E
Couvin	**47**	50 3N	4 29E
Covarrubias	**58**	42 4N	3 31W
Covasna	**70**	45 50N	26 10E
Covasna □	**70**	45 50N	26 0E
Cove Bay	**37**	57 5N	2 5W
Coventry	**28**	52 25N	1 31W
Coventry L.	**153**	61 15N	106 15W
Cover R.	**32**	54 14N	1 45W
Coverack	**30**	50 2N	5 6W
Covilhã	**56**	40 17N	7 31W
Covina	**163**	34 5N	117 52W
Covington, Ga., U.S.A.	**157**	33 36N	83 50W
Covington, Ky., U.S.A.	**156**	39 5N	84 30W
Covington, Okla., U.S.A.	**159**	36 21N	97 36W
Covington, Tenn., U.S.A.	**159**	35 34N	89 39W
Cowal Creek Settlement	**138**	10 54S	142 20E
Cowal, dist.	**34**	56 5N	5 8W
Cowal, L.	**141**	33 40S	147 25E
Cowan	**153**	52 5N	100 45W
Cowan, L.	**137**	31 45S	121 45E
Cowan L.	**153**	54 0N	107 15W
Cowangie	**140**	35 12S	141 26E
Coward Springs	**139**	29 24S	136 48E
Cowarie	**139**	27 45S	138 15E
Cowarna	**137**	30 55S	122 40E
Cowbridge	**31**	51 28N	3 28W
Cowcowing Lakes	**137**	30 55S	117 20E
Cowdenbeath	**35**	56 7N	3 20W
Cowell	**140**	33 39S	136 56E
Cowes	**28**	50 45N	1 18W
Cowfold	**29**	50 58N	0 16W
Cowl Cowl	**141**	33 36S	145 18E
Cowley	**28**	51 43N	1 12W
Cowpen	**35**	55 8N	1 34W
Cowra	**141**	33 49S	148 42E
Coxim	**175**	18 30S	54 55W
Cox's Bazar	**98**	21 26N	91 59E
Cox's Cove	**151**	49 7N	58 5W
Coyame	**164**	29 28N	105 6W
Coylton	**34**	55 26N	4 31W
Coyuca de Benítez	**165**	17 1N	100 8W
Coyuca de Catalán	**164**	18 58N	100 41W
Cozad	**158**	40 55N	99 57W
Cozie, Alpi	**62**	44 50N	6 59E
Cozumel	**165**	20 31N	86 55W
Cozumel, Isla de	**165**	20 30N	86 40W
Craanford	**39**	52 40N	6 23W
Craboon	**141**	32 3S	149 30E
Cracow	**139**	25 17S	150 17E
Cradock	**128**	32 8S	25 36E
Craggie	**37**	57 25N	4 6W
Craig, Alaska, U.S.A.	**147**	55 30N	133 5W
Craig, Colo., U.S.A.	**160**	40 32N	107 44W
Craigavon = Portadown	**38**	54 27N	6 26W
Craigavon = Lurgan	**38**	54 28N	6 20W
Craigellachie	**37**	57 29N	3 9W
Craighouse	**34**	55 50N	5 58W
Craigmore	**127**	20 28S	32 30E
Craignish, L.	**34**	56 11N	5 32W
Craigtown	**37**	58 30N	3 53W
Crail	**35**	56 16N	2 38W
Crailsheim	**49**	49 7N	10 5E
Craiova	**70**	44 21N	23 48E
Cramlington	**35**	55 5N	1 36W
Crampel	**117**	7 8N	19 81E
Cramsie	**138**	23 20S	144 15E
Cranberry Portage	**153**	54 35N	101 23W
Cranborne	**28**	50 55N	1 55W
Cranborne Chase	**29**	50 56N	2 6W
Cranbrook, Tas., Austral.	**138**	42 0S	148 5E
Cranbrook, W. Austral., Austral.	**137**	34 18S	117 33E
Cranbrook, Can.	**152**	49 30N	115 46W
Cranbrook, U.K.	**29**	51 6N	0 33E
Crandon	**158**	45 32N	88 52W
Crane, Oregon, U.S.A.	**160**	43 21N	118 39W
Crane, Texas, U.S.A.	**159**	31 26N	102 27W
Cranfield Pt.	**38**	54 1N	6 3W
Cranleigh	**29**	51 8N	0 29W
Cranshaws	**35**	55 51N	2 30W
Cranston	**162**	41 47N	71 27W
Cranwell	**33**	53 4N	0 29W
Craon	**42**	47 50N	0 58W
Craonne	**43**	49 27N	3 46E
Crasna	**70**	46 32N	27 51E
Crasna, R.	**70**	47 44N	27 35E
Crater Lake	**160**	42 55N	122 3W
Crater Mt.	**135**	6 37S	145 7E
Crater Pt.	**135**	5 25S	152 9E
Crateús	**170**	5 10S	40 50W
Crathie	**37**	57 3N	3 12W
Crati, R.	**65**	39 41N	16 30E
Crato, Brazil	**171**	7 10S	39 25W
Crato, Port.	**57**	39 16N	7 39W
Crau	**45**	43 32N	4 40E
Craughwell	**39**	53 15N	8 44W
Craven Arms	**28**	52 27N	2 49W
Crawford, U.K.	**35**	55 28N	3 40W
Crawford, U.S.A.	**158**	42 40N	103 25W
Crawford, oilfield	**19**	59 7N	1 30E
Crawfordsville	**156**	40 2N	86 51W
Crawley	**29**	51 7N	0 10W
Cray	**31**	51 55N	3 38W
Crazy Mts.	**160**	46 14N	110 30W
Creag Meagaidh, mt.	**37**	56 57N	4 38W
Crean L.	**153**	54 5N	106 9W
Crèche, La	**44**	46 23N	0 19W
Crécy-en-Brie	**43**	48 50N	2 53E
Crécy-en-Ponthieu	**43**	50 15N	1 53E
Crécy-sur-Serre	**43**	49 40N	3 32E
Credenhill	**28**	52 6N	2 49W
Crediton	**30**	50 47N	3 39W
Credo	**137**	30 28S	120 45E
Cree L.	**153**	57 30N	106 30W
Cree, R., Can.	**153**	58 57N	105 47W
Cree, R., U.K.	**34**	54 51N	4 24W
Creede	**161**	37 56N	106 59W
Creegh	**39**	52 45N	9 25W
Creel	**164**	27 45N	107 38W
Creeside	**34**	55 4N	4 41W
Creeslough	**38**	55 8N	7 55W
Creetown	**34**	54 54N	4 23W
Creeves	**39**	52 33N	9 3W
Creggan	**38**	54 39N	7 0W
Cregganbaun	**38**	53 42N	9 48W
Creighton	**158**	42 30N	97 52W
Creil	**43**	49 15N	2 34E
Crema	**62**	45 21N	9 40E
Cremona	**62**	45 8N	10 2E
Crepaja	**66**	45 1N	20 38E
Crépy	**43**	49 37N	3 32E
Crépy-en-Valois	**43**	49 14N	2 54E
Cres	**63**	44 58N	14 25E
Cresbard	**158**	45 13N	98 57W
Crescent, Okla., U.S.A.	**159**	35 38N	97 36W
Crescent, Oreg., U.S.A.	**160**	43 30N	121 37W
Crescent City	**160**	41 45N	124 12W
Crescentino	**62**	45 11N	8 7E
Crespino	**63**	44 59N	11 51E
Crespo	**172**	32 2S	60 19W
Cressman	**150**	47 40N	72 55W
Cressy	**140**	38 2S	143 40E
Crest	**45**	44 44N	5 2E
Crested Butte	**161**	38 57N	107 0W
Crestline	**163**	34 14N	117 18W
Creston, Can.	**152**	49 10N	116 31W
Creston, Calif., U.S.A.	**163**	35 32N	120 33W
Creston, Iowa, U.S.A.	**158**	41 0N	94 20W
Creston, Wash., U.S.A.	**160**	47 47N	118 36W
Creston, Wyo., U.S.A.	**160**	41 46N	107 50W
Crestone	**161**	35 2N	106 0W
Crestview, Calif., U.S.A.	**163**	37 46N	118 58W
Crestview, Fla., U.S.A.	**157**	30 45N	86 35W
Creswick	**140**	37 25S	143 51E
Crete	**158**	40 38N	96 58W
Crete = Kriti	**69**	35 15N	25 0E
Crete, La, Can.	**152**	58 10N	116 29W
Crete, La, Alta., Can.	**152**	58 11N	116 24W
Crete, Sea of	**69**	26 0N	25 0E
Cretin, C.	**135**	6 40S	147 53E
Creus, C.	**58**	42 20N	3 19E
Creuse □	**44**	46 0N	2 0E
Creuse, R.	**44**	47 0N	0 34E
Creusot, Le	**43**	46 50N	4 24E
Creuzburg	**48**	51 3N	10 15E
Crevalcore	**63**	44 41N	11 10E
Crèvecœur-le-Grand	**43**	49 37N	2 5E
Crevillente	**59**	38 12N	0 48W
Crewe	**32**	53 6N	2 28W
Crewkerne	**28**	50 53N	2 48W
Crianlarich	**34**	56 24N	4 37W
Crib Point	**139**	38 22S	145 13E
Criccieth	**31**	52 55N	4 15W
Criciúma	**173**	28 40S	49 23W
Crick	**28**	52 22N	1 9W
Crickhowell	**31**	51 52N	3 8W
Cricklade	**28**	51 38N	1 50W
Crieff	**35**	56 22N	3 50W
Criffell Mt.	**35**	54 56N	3 38W
Crikvenica	**63**	45 11N	14 40E
Crillon, Mt.	**152**	58 39N	137 14W
Crimea = Krymskaya	**82**	45 0N	34 0E
Crimmitschau	**48**	50 48N	12 23E
Crimond	**37**	57 35N	1 53W
Crinan Canal	**34**	56 4N	5 30W
Crinkill	**39**	53 5N	7 55E
Cristalândia	**170**	10 36S	49 11W
Cristeşti	**70**	47 15N	26 33E
Cristino Castro	**170**	8 49S	44 13W
Crişul Alb, R.	**66**	46 25N	21 40E
Crişul Negru, R.	**66**	46 38N	22 26E
Crişul Repede, R.	**70**	47 20N	22 25E
Crivitz	**48**	53 35N	11 39E
Crixás	**171**	14 27S	49 58W
Crna Gora □	**66**	42 40N	19 20E
Crna Trava	**66**	42 49N	22 19E
Crni Drim, R.	**66**	41 17N	20 40E
Crni Timok, R.	**66**	43 53N	22 0E
Crnoljeva Planina	**66**	42 20N	21 0E
Črnomeij	**63**	45 33N	15 10E
Croagh Patrick, mt.	**38**	53 46N	9 40W
Croatia = Hrvatska	**63**	45 20N	16 0E
Crocker, Barisan	**102**	5 0N	116 30E
Crocketford	**35**	55 3N	3 49W
Crockets Town	**38**	54 8N	9 7W
Crockett	**159**	31 20N	95 30W
Crocodile Is.	**138**	11 43S	135 8E
Crocodile, R.	**129**	25 30S	31 15E
Crocq	**44**	45 52N	2 21E
Croghan	**38**	53 55N	8 13W
Croglin	**32**	54 50N	2 37W
Crohy Hd.	**38**	54 55N	8 28W
Croisic, Le	**42**	47 18N	2 30W
Croisic, Pte. du.	**42**	47 19N	2 31W
Croix, La, L.	**150**	48 20N	92 15W
Croker, C.	**136**	10 58S	132 35E
Croker, I.	**136**	11 12N	132 32E
Crolly	**38**	55 2N	8 16W
Cromalt Hills	**36**	58 0N	5 2W
Cromarty, Can.	**153**	58 3N	94 9W
Cromarty, U.K.	**37**	57 40N	4 2W
Cromarty Firth	**37**	57 40N	4 15W
Cromdale, Hills of	**37**	57 20N	3 28W
Cromer	**29**	52 56N	1 18E
Cromore	**36**	58 6N	6 23W
Cromwell, N.Z.	**143**	45 3S	169 14E
Cromwell, U.S.A.	**162**	41 36N	72 39W
Cronat	**43**	46 43N	3 40E
Crondall	**29**	51 13N	0 51W
Cronulla	**141**	34 3S	151 8E
Crook	**33**	54 43N	1 45W
Crooked I.	**167**	22 50N	74 10W
Crooked Island Passage	**167**	23 0N	74 30W
Crooked, R., Can.	**152**	54 10N	122 35W
Crooked, R., U.S.A.	**160**	44 30N	121 0W
Crooklands	**32**	54 16N	2 43W
Crookston, Minn., U.S.A.	**158**	47 50N	96 40W
Crookston, Nebr., U.S.A.	**158**	42 56N	100 45W
Crookstown	**39**	51 50N	8 50W
Crooksville	**156**	39 45N	82 8W

Crookwell **Dalandzadgad**

Crookwell	**141**	34 28 S	149 24 E
Croom	**39**	52 32N	8 43W
Crosby, Cumb., U.K.	**32**	54 45N	3 25W
Crosby, Merseyside, U.K.	**32**	53 30N	3 2W
Crosby, Minn., U.S.A.	**158**	46 28N	93 57W
Crosby, N.D., U.S.A.	**153**	48 55N	103 18W
Crosby Ravensworth	**32**	54 34N	2 35W
Crosbyton	**159**	33 37N	101 12W
Cross City	**157**	29 35N	83 5W
Cross Fell	**32**	54 44N	2 29W
Cross L.	**153**	54 45N	97 30W
Cross Plains	**159**	32 8N	99 7W
Cross, R.	**121**	4 46N	8 20 E
Cross River □	**121**	6 0N	8 0 E
Cross Sound	**147**	58 20N	136 30W
Crossakiel	**38**	53 43N	7 2W
Crossbost	**36**	58 8N	6 27W
Crossdoney	**38**	53 57N	7 27W
Crosse, La, Kans., U.S.A.	**158**	38 33N	99 20W
Crosse, La, Wis., U.S.A.	**158**	43 48N	91 13W
Crossett	**159**	33 10N	91 57W
Crossfarnoge Pt.	**39**	52 10N	6 37W
Crossfield	**152**	51 25N	114 0W
Crossgar	**38**	54 22N	5 46W
Crosshaven	**39**	51 48N	8 19W
Crosshill	**34**	55 19N	4 39W
Crossley, Mt.	**143**	42 50 S	172 5 E
Crossmaglen	**38**	54 5N	6 37W
Crossmolina	**38**	54 6N	9 21W
Croton-on-Hudson	**162**	41 12N	73 55W
Crotone	**65**	39 5N	17 6 E
Crouch, R.	**29**	51 37N	0 53 E
Crow Agency	**160**	45 40N	107 30W
Crow Hd.	**39**	51 34N	10 9W
Crow, R.	**152**	59 41N	124 20W
Crow Sound	**30**	49 56N	6 16W
Crowborough	**29**	51 3N	0 9 E
Crowell	**159**	33 59N	99 45W
Crowl Creek	**141**	32 0 S	145 30 E
Crowland	**29**	52 41N	0 10W
Crowle	**33**	53 36N	0 49W
Crowley	**159**	30 15N	92 20W
Crowley, L.	**163**	37 53N	118 42W
Crowlin Is.	**36**	57 20N	5 50W
Crown Point	**156**	41 24N	87 23W
Crows Landing	**163**	37 23N	121 6W
Crows Nest	**139**	27 16 S	152 4 E
Crowsnest Pass	**152**	49 40N	114 40W
Croyde	**30**	51 7N	4 13W
Croydon, Austral.	**138**	18 13 S	142 14 E
Croydon, U.K.	**29**	51 18N	0 5W
Crozet, Île	**11**	46 27 S	52 0 E
Crozon	**42**	48 15N	4 30W
Cruces, Pta.	**174**	6 39N	77 32W
Cruden Bay	**37**	57 25N	1 50W
Crudgington	**28**	52 46N	2 33W
Crumlin	**38**	54 38N	6 12W
Crummer Peaks	**138**	6 40 S	144 0 E
Crummock Water L.	**32**	54 33N	3 18W
Crusheen	**39**	52 57N	8 52W
Cruz, C.	**166**	19 50N	77 50W
Cruz das Almas	**171**	12 40 S	39 6W
Cruz de Malta	**170**	8 15 S	40 20W
Cruz del Eje	**172**	30 45 S	64 50W
Cruz, La, Colomb.	**174**	1 35N	76 58W
Cruz, La, C. Rica	**166**	11 4N	85 39W
Cruz, La, Mexico	**164**	23 55N	106 54W
Cruzeiro	**173**	22 50 S	45 0W
Cruzeiro do Oeste	**173**	23 46 S	53 4W
Cruzeiro do Sul	**174**	7 35 S	72 35W
Cry L.	**152**	58 45N	128 5W
Cryfow Sl.	**54**	51 2N	15 24 E
Crymmych	**31**	51 59N	4 40W
Crystal Brook	**140**	33 21 S	138 12 E
Crystal City, Mo., U.S.A.	**158**	38 15N	90 23W
Crystal City, Tex., U.S.A.	**159**	28 40N	99 50W
Crystal Falls	**156**	46 9N	88 11W
Crystal River	**157**	28 54N	82 35W
Crystal Springs	**159**	31 59N	90 25W
Čáslav	**52**	49 54N	15 22 E
Csongrád	**53**	46 43N	20 12 E
Csongrád □	**53**	46 32N	20 15 E
Csorna	**53**	47 38N	17 18 E
Csurgo	**53**	46 16N	17 9 E
Ctesiphon	**92**	33 9N	44 35 E
Cu Lao Hon	**101**	10 54N	108 18 E
Cua Rao	**100**	19 16N	104 27 E
Cuácua, R.	**127**	18 0 S	36 0 E
Cuamato	**128**	17 2 S	15 7 E
Cuamba = Nova Preixo	**127**	14 45 S	36 22 E
Cuando	**128**	16 25 S	22 2 E
Cuando Cubango □	**128**	16 25 S	20 0 E
Cuando, R.	**125**	14 0 S	19 30 E
Cuangar	**128**	17 28 S	14 40 E
Cuango	**124**	6 15 S	16 35 E
Cuarto, R.	**172**	33 25 S	63 2W
Cuatrociénegas de Carranza	**164**	26 59N	102 5W
Cuauhtémoc	**164**	28 25N	106 52W
Cuba, Port.	**57**	38 10N	7 54W
Cuba, U.S.A.	**161**	36 0N	107 0W
Cuba ■	**166**	22 0N	79 0W
Cuballing	**137**	32 50 S	117 10 E
Cubango, R.	**128**	16 15 S	17 45 E
Cuchi	**125**	14 37 S	17 10 E
Cuchumatanes, Sierra de los	**166**	15 35N	91 25W
Cuckfield	**29**	51 0N	0 8W
Cucurpe	**164**	30 20N	110 43W

Cucurrupí	**174**	4 23N	76 56W
Cúcuta	**174**	7 54N	72 31W
Cudahy	**156**	42 54N	87 50W
Cudalbi	**70**	45 46N	27 41 E
Cuddalore	**97**	11 46N	79 45 E
Cuddapah	**97**	14 30N	78 47 E
Cuddapan, L.	**138**	25 45 S	141 26 E
Cudgewa	**141**	36 10 S	147 42 E
Cudillero	**56**	43 33N	6 9W
Cudworth	**33**	53 35N	1 25W
Cue	**137**	27 25 S	117 54 E
Cuéllar	**56**	41 23N	4 21W
Cuenca, Ecuador	**174**	2 50 S	79 9W
Cuenca, Spain	**58**	40 5N	2 10W
Cuenca □	**58**	40 0N	2 0W
Cuenca, Serranía de	**58**	39 55N	1 50W
Cuencamé	**164**	24 53N	103 41W
Cuerda del Pozo, Pantano de la	**58**	41 51N	2 44W
Cuernavaca	**165**	18 50N	99 20W
Cuero	**159**	29 5N	97 17W
Cuers	**45**	43 14N	6 5 E
Cuervo	**159**	35 5N	104 25W
Cuesmes	**47**	50 26N	3 56 E
Cuevas de Altamira	**56**	43 20N	4 5W
Cuevas del Almanzora	**59**	37 18N	1 58W
Cuevo	**174**	20 25N	63 30W
Cugir	**70**	43 48N	23 25 E
Cugno	**123**	6 14N	42 31 E
Cuhimbre	**174**	0 10 S	75 23W
Cuiabá	**175**	15 30 S	56 0W
Cuiabá, R.	**175**	16 50 S	56 30W
Cuidad Bolivar	**174**	8 21N	70 34W
Cuilcagh, Mt.	**38**	54 12N	7 50W
Cuilco	**166**	15 24N	91 58W
Cuillin Hills	**36**	57 14N	6 15W
Cuillin Sd.	**36**	57 4N	6 20W
Cuima	**125**	13 0 S	15 45 E
Cuiseaux	**45**	46 30N	5 22 E
Cuité	**170**	6 29 S	36 9W
Cuito, R.	**128**	16 50 S	19 30 E
Cuitzeo, L.	**164**	19 55N	101 5W
Cujmir	**70**	44 13N	22 57 E
Culan	**44**	46 34N	2 20 E
Cŭlaraşi	**43**	44 14N	27 23 E
Culbertson	**158**	48 9N	104 30W
Culburra	**140**	35 50 S	139 58 E
Culcairn	**141**	35 41 S	147 3 E
Culdaff	**38**	55 17N	7 10W
Culebra, I.	**147**	18 19N	65 17W
Culebra, Sierra de la	**56**	41 55N	6 20W
Culemborg	**46**	51 58N	5 14 E
Culgoa	**140**	35 44 S	143 6 E
Culgoa, R.	**139**	29 56 S	146 20 E
Culiacán	**164**	24 50N	107 40W
Culiacán, R.	**164**	24 30N	107 42W
Cŭlimani, Munţii	**70**	47 12N	25 0 E
Cŭlineşti	**70**	45 21N	24 18 E
Culion, I.	**103**	11 54N	120 1 E
Cúllar de Baza	**59**	37 35N	2 34W
Cullarin Range	**141**	34 30 S	149 30 E
Cullaville	**38**	54 4N	6 40W
Cullen, Austral.	**136**	13 58 S	131 54 E
Cullen, U.K.	**37**	57 45N	2 50W
Cullen Pt.	**138**	11 57 S	141 54 E
Cullera	**59**	39 9N	0 17W
Cullin L.	**38**	53 58N	9 12W
Cullivoe	**36**	60 43N	1 0W
Cullman	**157**	34 13N	86 50W
Culloden Moor	**37**	57 29N	4 7W
Cullompton	**30**	50 52N	3 23W
Cullyhanna	**38**	54 8N	6 35W
Culm, R.	**30**	50 46N	3 31W
Culoz	**45**	45 47N	5 46 E
Culpataro	**140**	33 40 S	144 22 E
Culpeper	**156**	38 29N	77 59W
Culrain	**37**	57 55N	4 25W
Culross	**35**	56 4N	3 38W
Cults	**37**	57 8N	2 10W
Culuene, R.	**175**	12 15 S	53 10W
Culvain Mt.	**36**	56 55N	5 19W
Culver, Pt.	**137**	32 54 S	124 43 E
Culverden	**143**	42 47 S	172 49 E
Cumali	**69**	36 42N	27 28 E
Cumaná	**174**	10 30N	64 5W
Cumari	**171**	18 16 S	48 11W
Cumberland, Can.	**152**	49 40N	125 0W
Cumberland, Md., U.S.A.	**156**	39 40N	78 43W
Cumberland, Wis., U.S.A.	**158**	45 32N	92 3W
Cumberland (□)	**26**	54 44N	2 55W
Cumberland I.	**157**	30 52N	81 30W
Cumberland Is.	**138**	20 35 S	149 10 E
Cumberland L.	**153**	54 3N	102 18W
Cumberland Pen.	**149**	67 0N	64 0W
Cumberland Plat.	**157**	36 0N	84 30W
Cumberland, R.	**157**	36 15N	87 0W
Cumberland Sd.	**149**	65 30N	66 0W
Cumborah	**139**	29 40 S	147 45 E
Cumbrae Is.	**34**	55 46N	4 54W
Cumbres Mayores	**57**	38 4N	6 39W
Cumbria □	**32**	54 35N	2 55W
Cumbrian Mts.	**32**	54 30N	3 0W
Cumbum	**97**	15 40N	79 10 E
Cuminestown	**37**	57 32N	2 17W
Cummerower See	**48**	53 47N	12 52 E
Cummertrees	**35**	55 0N	3 20W
Cummings Mtn.	**163**	35 2N	118 34W
Cummins	**139**	34 16 S	135 43 E
Cumnock, Austral.	**141**	32 59 S	148 46 E
Cumnock, U.K.	**34**	55 27N	4 18W
Cumnor	**28**	51 44N	1 20W

Cumpas	**164**	30 0N	109 48W
Cumuruxatiba	**171**	17 6 S	39 13W
Cumwhinton	**32**	54 51N	2 49W
Cuñaré	**174**	0 49N	72 32W
Cuncumén	**172**	31 53 S	70 38W
Cunderdin	**137**	31 37 S	117 12 E
Cundinamarca □	**174**	5 0N	74 0W
Cunene, R.	**128**	17 0 S	15 0 E
Cúneo	**62**	44 23N	7 31 E
Cunillera, I.	**59**	38 59N	1 13 E
Cunlhat	**44**	45 38N	3 32 E
Cunnamulla	**139**	28 2 S	145 38 E
Cunninghame, Reg.	**34**	55 38N	4 35W
Cuorgnè	**62**	45 23N	7 39 E
Cupar, Can.	**153**	50 57N	104 10W
Cupar, U.K.	**35**	56 20N	3 0W
Cupica	**174**	6 50N	77 30W
Cupica, Golfo de	**174**	6 25N	77 30W
Ćuprija	**66**	43 57N	21 26 E
Curaçá	**170**	8 59 S	39 54W
Curaçao, I.	**167**	12 10N	69 0W
Curanilahue	**172**	37 29 S	73 28W
Curaray, R.	**174**	1 30 S	75 30W
Curatabaca	**174**	6 19N	62 51W
Curbarado	**174**	7 3N	76 54W
Curbur	**137**	26 28 S	115 55 E
Cure, La	**50**	46 28N	6 4 E
Curepto	**172**	35 8 S	72 1W
Curiapo	**174**	8 33N	61 5W
Curicó	**172**	34 55 S	71 20W
Curicó □	**172**	34 50 S	71 15W
Curimatá	**170**	10 2 S	44 17W
Curiplaya	**174**	0 16N	74 52W
Curitiba	**173**	25 20 S	49 10W
Curlew Mts.	**38**	54 0N	8 20W
Curoca Norte	**128**	16 15 S	12 58 E
Currabubula	**141**	31 16 S	150 44 E
Curracunya	**139**	28 29 S	144 9 E
Curraglass	**39**	52 5N	8 4W
Currais Novos	**170**	6 13 S	36 30W
Curralinho	**170**	1 35 S	49 30W
Curran, L. = Terewah, L.	**139**	29 50 S	147 24 E
Currane L.	**39**	51 50N	10 8W
Currant	**160**	38 51N	115 32W
Curranyalpa	**141**	30 53 S	144 39 E
Curraweena	**141**	30 47 S	145 54 E
Currawilla	**138**	25 10 S	141 20 E
Current, R.	**159**	37 15N	91 10W
Currie, Austral.	**138**	39 56 S	143 53 E
Currie, U.K.	**35**	55 53N	3 17W
Currie, U.S.A.	**160**	40 16N	114 45W
Currie, Mt.	**129**	30 29 S	29 21 E
Currituck Sd.	**157**	36 20N	75 50W
Curry Rivel	**28**	51 2N	2 52W
Curryglass	**39**	51 40N	9 50W
Curtea-de-Argeş	**70**	45 12N	24 42 E
Curtis, Spain	**56**	43 7N	8 4W
Curtis, U.S.A.	**158**	40 41N	100 32W
Curtis, I.	**138**	23 35 S	151 10 E
Curtis, Pt.	**138**	23 53 S	151 21 E
Curuá, I.	**170**	0 48N	50 10W
Curuapanema, R.	**175**	7 0 S	54 30W
Curuçá	**170**	0 35 S	47 50W
Curuguaty	**173**	24 19 S	55 49W
Curupira, Serra	**174**	1 25N	64 30W
Cururupu	**170**	1 50 S	44 50W
Curuzú Cuatiá	**172**	29 50 S	58 5W
Curvelo	**171**	18 45 S	44 27W
Curyo	**140**	35 50 S	142 47 E
Cushendall	**38**	55 5N	6 3W
Cushendun	**38**	55 8N	6 3W
Cushina	**39**	53 11N	7 10W
Cushing, Mt.	**152**	57 35N	126 57W
Cusihuiriáchic	**164**	28 10N	106 50W
Cussabat	**119**	32 39N	14 1 E
Cusset	**44**	46 8N	3 28 E
Custer	**158**	43 45N	103 38W
Cut Bank	**160**	48 40N	112 15W
Cutchogue	**162**	41 1N	72 30W
Cuthbert	**157**	31 47N	84 47W
Cutler	**163**	36 31N	119 17W
Cutra L.	**39**	53 2N	8 48W
Cutro	**65**	39 1N	16 58 E
Cuttaburra, R.	**139**	29 43 S	144 22 E
Cuttack	**96**	20 25N	85 57 E
Cuvier, C.	**137**	23 14 S	113 22 E
Cuvier I.	**142**	36 27 S	175 50 E
Cuxhaven	**48**	53 51N	8 41 E
Cuyabeno	**174**	0 16 S	75 53W
Cuyahoga Falls	**156**	41 8N	81 30W
Cuyo	**103**	10 50N	121 5 E
Cuyuni, R.	**175**	7 0N	59 30W
Cuzco	**174**	13 32 S	72 0W
Cuzco, Mt.	**174**	20 0 S	66 50W
Čŭzŭneşti	**70**	44 36N	27 3 E
Čvrsnica, Mt.	**66**	43 36N	17 35 E
Cwmbran	**31**	51 39N	3 0W
Cwrt	**31**	52 35N	3 55W
Cyangugu	**126**	2 29 S	28 54 E
Cybinka	**54**	52 12N	14 46 E
Cyclades = Kikladhes	**69**	37 20N	24 30 E
Cygnet	**138**	43 8 S	147 1 E
Cymmer	**31**	51 37N	3 38W
Cynthiana	**156**	38 23N	84 10W
Cynwyl Elfed	**31**	51 55N	4 22W
Cypress Hills	**153**	49 40N	109 30W
Cyprus ■	**92**	35 0N	33 0 E
Cyrenaica □	**117**	27 0N	20 0 E
Cyrene	**117**	32 39N	21 18 E
Czaplinek	**54**	53 34N	16 14 E
Czar	**153**	52 27N	110 50W
Czarne	**54**	53 42N	16 58 E

Czarnków	**54**	52 55N	16 38 E
Czechoslovakia ■	**53**	49 0N	17 0 E
Czechowice-Dziedzice	**54**	49 54N	18 59 E
Czeladz	**54**	50 16N	19 2 E
Czempin	**54**	52 9N	16 33 E
Czersk	**54**	53 46N	17 58 E
Czerwiensk	**54**	52 1N	15 13 E
Czerwionka	**54**	50 7N	18 37 E
Częstochowa	**54**	50 49N	19 7 E
Częstochowa □	**54**	50 45N	19 0 E
Czlopa	**54**	53 6N	16 6 E
Człuchów	**54**	53 41N	17 22 E

D

Da Lat	**101**	11 56N	108 25 E
Da Nang	**100**	16 4N	108 13 E
Da, R.	**100**	21 15N	105 20 E
Daarlerveen	**46**	52 26N	6 34 E
Dab'a, Ras el	**122**	31 3N	28 31 E
Dabai	**121**	11 25N	5 15 E
Dabajuro	**174**	11 2N	70 40W
Dabakala	**120**	8 15N	4 20W
Dabatou	**120**	11 50N	9 20W
Dabburiya	**90**	32 42N	35 22 E
Daberas	**128**	25 27 S	18 30 E
Dabhoi	**94**	22 10N	73 20 E
Dabie	**54**	53 27N	14 45 E
Dabola	**120**	10 50N	11 5W
Dabong	**101**	5 23N	103 1 E
Dabou	**120**	5 20N	4 23W
Daboya	**121**	9 30N	1 20W
Dabra Berhan	**123**	9 42N	39 15 E
Dabra Sina	**123**	9 51N	39 45 E
Dabra Tabor	**123**	11 50N	37 58 E
Dabra Zabit	**123**	11 48N	38 30 E
Dabrowa Górnicza	**54**	50 15N	19 10 E
Dabrowa Tarnówska	**54**	50 10N	20 59 E
Dabrówno	**54**	53 27N	20 2 E
Dabus, R.	**123**	10 12N	35 0 E
Dacca	**98**	23 43N	90 26 E
Dacca □	**98**	24 0N	90 25 E
Dachau	**49**	48 16N	11 27 E
Dadanawa	**174**	3 0N	59 30W
Daday	**82**	41 28N	33 35 E
Daddato	**123**	12 24N	42 45 E
Dade City	**157**	28 20N	82 12W
Dadiya	**121**	9 35N	11 24 E
Dadra and Nagar Haveli □	**96**	20 5N	73 0 E
Dadri = Charkhi Dadri	**94**	28 37N	76 17 E
Dadu	**94**	26 45N	67 45 E
Daer R.	**35**	55 23N	3 39W
Daet	**103**	14 2N	122 55 E
Dagaio	**123**	6 8N	40 40 E
Dagana	**120**	16 30N	15 20W
Dagash	**122**	19 19N	33 25 E
Dagestan, A.S.S.R. □	**83**	42 30N	47 0 E
Daggett	**163**	34 43N	116 52W
Daggs Sd.	**143**	45 23 S	166 45 E
Daghfeli	**122**	19 18N	32 40 E
Daghirie	**123**	11 40N	41 50 E
Dagö = Hiiumaa	**80**	58 50N	22 45 E
Dagoreti	**126**	1 18 S	36 4 E
Dagua	**135**	3 27 S	143 20 E
Dagupan	**103**	16 3N	120 20 E
Dahab	**122**	28 30N	34 31 E
Dahlak Kebir	**123**	15 50N	40 10 E
Dahlenburg	**48**	53 11N	10 43 E
Dahlonega	**157**	34 35N	83 59W
Dahme	**48**	51 51N	13 25 E
Daho	**121**	10 28N	11 18 E
Dahomey ■ = Benin ■	**121**	8 0N	2 0 E
Dahra	**120**	15 22N	15 30W
Dahra, Massif de	**118**	36 7N	1 21 E
Dai Hao	**100**	18 1N	106 25 E
Dai-Sen	**110**	35 22N	133 32 E
Daigo	**111**	36 46N	140 21 E
Dailly	**34**	55 16N	4 44W
Daimanji-San	**110**	36 14N	133 20 E
Daimiel	**59**	39 5N	3 35W
Daintree	**138**	16 20 S	145 20 E
Daiō-Misaki	**111**	34 15N	136 45 E
Dairen = Lüta	**107**	38 55N	121 40 E
Dairût	**122**	27 34N	30 43 E
Dairymple	**34**	55 24N	4 36W
Daisetsu-Zan	**112**	43 30N	142 57 E
Daitari	**96**	21 10N	85 46 E
Daitō	**110**	35 19N	132 58 E
Dajarra	**138**	21 42 S	139 30 E
Dak Dam	**100**	12 20N	107 21 E
Dak Nhe	**100**	15 28N	107 48 E
Dak Pek	**100**	15 4N	107 44 E
Dak Song	**101**	12 19N	107 35 E
Dak Sui	**100**	14 55N	107 43 E
Dakala	**121**	14 27N	2 27 E
Dakar	**120**	14 34N	17 29W
Dakhla	**116**	23 50N	15 53W
Dakhla, El Wâhât el-	**122**	25 30N	28 50 E
Dakhovskaya	**83**	44 13N	40 13 E
Dakingari	**121**	11 37N	4 1 E
Dakor	**94**	22 45N	73 11 E
Dakoro	**121**	14 31N	6 46 E
Dakota City	**158**	42 27N	96 28W
Dakota, North	**158**	47 30N	100 0W
Đakovica	**66**	42 22N	20 26 E
Dakovo	**66**	45 19N	18 24 E
Dakra	**120**	15 22N	15 30W
Dalaba	**120**	10 42N	12 15W
Dalälven, L.	**72**	61 27N	17 15 E
Dalandzadgad	**106**	43 27N	104 30 E

Dalarö
Degeh-Bur

Dalarö **75** 59 8N 18 24 E
Dalat **101** 12 3N 108 32 E
Dalbandin **93** 29 0N 4 23 E
Dalbeattie **35** 54 55N 3 50W
Dalbosjön, L. **73** 58 40N 12 45 E
Dalby, Austral. **139** 27 10 S 151 17 E
Dalby, Sweden **73** 55 42N 13 22 E
Dale, Sogn og Fjordane, Norway **71** 61 27N 7 28 E
Dale, Sogn og Fjordane, Norway **71** 61 22N 5 23 E
Dale, U.K. **31** 51 42N 5 11W
Dalen, Neth. **46** 52 42N 6 46 E
Dalen, Norway **71** 59 26N 8 0 E
Dalet **98** 19 59N 93 51 E
Daletme **98** 21 36N 92 46 E
Dalfsen **46** 52 31N 6 16 E
Dalga **122** 27 39N 30 41 E
Dalgaranger, Mt. **137** 27 50 S 117 5 E
Dalhalvaig **37** 58 28N 3 53W
Dalhart **159** 36 0N 102 30W
Dalhousie, Can. **151** 48 0N 66 26W
Dalhousie, India **94** 32 38N 76 0 E
Daliburgh **36** 57 10N 7 23W
Dalj **174** 45 28N 18 58 E
Dalkeith **35** 55 54N 3 5W
Dalkey **39** 53 16N 6 7W
Dall I. **152** 54 59N 133 25W
Dallarnil **139** 25 19 S 152 2 E
Dallas, U.K. **37** 57 33N 3 32W
Dallas, Oregon, U.S.A. **160** 45 0N 123 15W
Dallas, Texas, U.S.A. **159** 32 50N 96 50W
Dallol **123** 14 14N 40 17 E
Dalmacija **66** 43 20N 17 0 E
Dalmally **34** 56 25N 5 0W
Dalmatia = Dalmacija **66** 43 20N 17 0 E
Dalmatovo **84** 56 16N 62 56 E
Dalmellington **34** 55 20N 4 25W
Dalneretchensk **77** 45 50N 133 40 E
Daloa **120** 7 0N 6 30W
Dalry **34** 55 44N 4 42W
Dalrymple, Mt. **133** 21 1 S 148 39 E
Dalsjöfors **73** 57 46N 18 5 E
Dalskog **73** 58 44N 12 18 E
Dalton, Can. **150** 48 11N 84 1W
Dalton, Cumbria, U.K. **33** 54 9N 3 11W
Dalton, Dumfries, U.K. **35** 55 3N 3 22W
Dalton, N. Yorks., U.K. **33** 54 28N 1 32W
Dalton, Ga., U.S.A. **103** 34 45N 85 0W
Dalton, Mass., U.S.A. **162** 42 28N 73 11W
Dalton, Nebr., U.S.A. **158** 41 27N 103 0W
Dalton Post **152** 66 42N 137 0W
Daltonganj **95** 24 0N 84 4 E
Dalvík **74** 65 58N 18 32W
Dalwhinnie **37** 56 56N 4 14W
Daly City **163** 37 42N 122 28W
Daly L. **153** 56 32N 105 39W
Daly, R. **136** 13 21 S 130 18 E
Daly Waters **138** 16 15 S 133 24 E
Dalystown **38** 53 26N 7 23W
Dam **170** 4 45N 55 0W
Dam Doi **101** 8 59N 105 12 E
Dam Gillan **153** 56 20N 94 40W
Dam Ha **100** 21 21N 107 36 E
Dama, Wadi **122** 27 12N 35 50 E
Daman **96** 20 25N 72 57 E
Daman □ **96** 20 25N 72 58 E
Damanhûr **122** 31 0N 30 30 E
Damar, I. **103** 7 15 S 128 30 E
Damaraland **128** 21 0 S 17 0 E
Damascus = Dimashq **92** 33 30N 36 18 E
Damaturu **121** 11 45N 11 55 E
Damãvand **93** 36 0N 52 0 E
Damãvand, Qolleh-ye **93** 35 45N 52 10 E
Damba, Angola **124** 6 44 S 15 29 E
Damba, Ethiopia **123** 15 10N 38 47 E
Dâmbovnic, R. **70** 44 28N 25 18 E
Dame Marie **167** 18 36N 74 26W
Damerham **28** 50 57N 1 52W
Dames Quarter **162** 38 11N 75 54W
Damghan **93** 36 10N 54 17 E
Damietta = Dumyât **122** 31 24N 31 48 E
Damin **93** 27 30N 60 40 E
Damiya **90** 32 6N 35 34 E
Damman **92** 26 25N 50 2 E
Dammarie **43** 48 20N 1 30 E
Dammartin **43** 49 3N 2 41 E
Dammastock **51** 46 38N 8 24 E
Damme **48** 52 32N 8 12 E
Damodar, R. **95** 23 17N 87 35 E
Damoh **95** 23 50N 79 28 E
Dampier **136** 20 41 S 116 42 E
Dampier Arch. **136** 20 38 S 116 32 E
Dampier Downs **136** 18 24 S 123 5 E
Dampier, Selat **103** 0 40 S 131 0 E
Dampier Str. **135** 5 50 S 148 0 E
Damrei, Chuor Phnum **101** 12 30N 103 0 E
Damville **42** 48 51N 1 5 E
Damvillers **43** 49 20N 5 21 E
Dan Chadi **121** 12 47N 5 17 E
Dan Dume **121** 11 28N 7 8 E
Dan Gora **121** 11 30N 8 7 E
Dan Gulbi **121** 11 40N 6 15 E
Dan, oilfield **19** 55 30N 5 10 E
Dan Sadau **121** 11 25N 6 20 E
Dana **103** 11 0 S 122 52 E
Dana, Lac **150** 50 53N 77 20W
Dana, Mt **163** 37 54N 119 12W
Danakil Depression **123** 12 45N 41 0 E
Danao **103** 10 31N 124 1 E
Danbury **162** 41 23N 73 29W
Danby L. **161** 34 17N 115 0W
Dand **94** 31 28N 65 32 E
Dandaragan **137** 30 40 S 115 40 E
Dandeldhura **95** 29 20N 80 35 E
Dandeli **93** 15 5N 74 30 E
Dandenong **141** 38 0 S 145 15 E
Dandkandi **98** 23 32N 90 43 E
Danforth **151** 45 39N 67 57W
Dang Raek **101** 14 40N 104 0 E
Dangara **85** 38 6N 69 22 E
Danger Is. **131** 10 53 S 165 49W
Danger Pt. **128** 34 40 S 19 17 E
Dangla **123** 11 18N 36 56 E
Dangora **121** 11 30N 8 7 E
Dangrek, Phnom **100** 14 15N 105 0 E
Daniel **160** 42 56N 110 2W
Daniel's Harbour **151** 50 13N 57 35W
Danielskull **128** 28 11 S 23 33 E
Danielson **162** 41 50N 71 52W
Danilov **81** 58 16N 40 13 E
Danilovgrad **66** 42 38N 19 9 E
Danilovka **81** 50 25N 44 12 E
Danissa **126** 3 15N 40 58 E
Danja **121** 11 29N 7 30 E
Dankalwa **121** 11 52N 12 12 E
Dankama **121** 13 20N 7 44 E
Dankhar Gompa **93** 32 10N 78 10 E
Dankov **81** 53 20N 39 5 E
Danlí **166** 14 4N 86 35W
Dannemora **75** 60 12N 17 51 E
Dannenberg **48** 53 7N 11 4 E
Dannevirke **142** 40 12 S 176 8 E
Dannhauser **129** 28 0 S 30 3 E
Dansalan **103** 8 2N 124 30 E
Dansville **156** 42 32N 77 41W
Dantan **95** 21 57N 87 20 E
Danube, R. **53** 45 0N 28 20W
Danubyo **98** 17 15N 95 35 E
Danvers **162** 42 34N 70 55 E
Danville, Ill., U.S.A. **156** 40 10N 87 40W
Danville, Ky., U.S.A. **156** 37 40N 84 45W
Danville, Pa., U.S.A. **162** 40 58N 76 37W
Danville, Va., U.S.A. **157** 36 40N 79 20W
Danzig = Gdansk **54** 54 22N 18 40 E
Dão **103** 10 30N 122 6 E
Dão, R. **56** 40 28N 8 0W
Daosa **94** 26 52N 76 20 E
Daoud = Aïn Beida **119** 35 50N 7 29 E
Daoulas **42** 48 22N 4 17W
Dapango **121** 10 55N 0 16 E
Dar al Hamra, Ad **92** 27 22N 37 43 E
Dar es Salaam **126** 6 50 S 39 12 E
Dar'á **90** 32 36N 36 7 E
Darab **93** 28 50N 54 30 E
Darabani **70** 48 10N 26 39 E
Daraj **119** 30 10N 10 28 E
Daraut Kurgan **85** 39 33N 72 11 E
Daravica **66** 42 32N 20 8 E
Daraw **121** 24 22N 32 51 E
Darazo **121** 11 1N 10 24W
Darband **94** 34 30N 72 50 E
Darbhanga **95** 26 15N 86 8 E
Darby **160** 46 2N 114 7W
D'Arcy **152** 50 35N 122 30W
Darda **66** 45 40N 18 41 E
Dardanelle **163** 38 2N 119 50W
Dardanelles = Canakkale Bogłazi **92** 40 0N 26 20 E
Dardenelle **159** 35 12N 93 9W
Darent, R. **29** 51 22N 0 12 E
Darfield **143** 43 29 S 172 7 E
Darfo **62** 45 43N 10 11 E
Dargai **94** 34 25N 71 45 E
Dargan Ata **76** 40 40N 62 20 E
Dargaville **142** 35 57 S 173 52 E
Darharala **120** 8 23N 4 20W
Dari **123** 5 48N 30 26 E
Darién, G. del **174** 9 0N 77 0W
Darién, Serranía del **174** 8 30N 77 30W
Dariganga **106** 45 5N 113 45 E
Darinskoye **84** 51 20N 51 44 E
Darjeeling **95** 27 3N 88 18 E
Dark Cove **151** 48 47N 54 13W
Darkan **137** 33 20 S 116 43 E
Darke Peak **140** 33 27 S 136 12 E
Darkot Pass **95** 36 45N 73 26 E
Darlaston **28** 52 35N 2 1W
Darling Downs **139** 28 30 S 152 0 E
Darling, R. **140** 34 4 S 141 54 E
Darling Ra. **137** 32 30 S 116 0 E
Darlington, U.K. **33** 54 33N 1 33W
Darlington, S.C., U.S.A. **157** 34 18N 79 50W
Darlington, Wis., U.S.A. **158** 42 43N 90 7W
Darlot, L. **137** 27 48 S 121 35 E
Darłowo **54** 54 25N 16 25 E
Darmstadt **49** 49 51N 8 40 E
Darnall **129** 29 23 S 31 18 E
Darnétal **42** 49 25N 1 10 E
Darney **43** 48 5N 6 0 E
Darnick **140** 32 48 S 143 38 E
Darnley B. **147** 69 30N 123 30W
Darnley, C. **13** 68 0 S 69 0 E
Daroca **58** 41 9N 1 25W
Darr **138** 23 13 S 144 7 E
Darr, R. **138** 23 39 S 143 50 E
Darragh **39** 52 47N 9 7W
Darran Mts. **143** 44 37 S 167 59 E
Darrington **160** 48 14N 121 37W
Darror, R. **91** 10 30N 50 0 E
Darsana **98** 23 35N 88 48 E
Darsi **97** 15 46N 79 44 E
Darsser Ort **48** 44 27N 12 30 E
Dart, R., N.Z. **143** 44 20 S 168 20 E
Dart, R., U.K. **30** 50 24N 3 36W
Dartford **29** 51 26N 0 15 E
Dartington **30** 50 26N 3 42W
Dartmoor, Austral. **140** 37 56N 141 19 E
Dartmoor, U.K. **30** 50 36N 4 0W
Dartmouth, Austral. **138** 23 31 S 144 44 E
Dartmouth, Can. **151** 44 40N 63 30W
Dartmouth, U.K. **30** 50 21N 3 35W
Dartmouth, L. **139** 26 4 S 145 18 E
Darton **33** 53 36N 1 32W
Dartuch, C. **58** 39 55N 3 49 E
Daru, P.N.G. **135** 9 3 S 143 13 E
Daru, S. Leone **120** 8 0N 10 52W
Darvel **34** 55 37N 4 20W
Darvel Bay **103** 4 50N 118 20 E
Darwen **32** 53 42N 2 29W
Darwha **96** 20 15N 77 45 E
Darwin, Austral. **136** 12 25 S 130 51 E
Darwin, U.S.A. **163** 36 15N 117 35W
Darwin, Mt. **127** 16 45 S 31 33 E
Darwin River **136** 12 50 S 130 58 E
Daryacheh-ye-Sistan **93** 31 0N 61 0 E
Daryapur **96** 20 55N 77 20 E
Dase **123** 14 53N 37 15 E
Dashato, R. **123** 7 25N 42 40 E
Dashkesan **83** 40 40N 46 0 E
Dasht-e Kavīr **93** 34 30N 55 0 E
Dasht-e Lut **93** 31 30N 58 0 E
Dasht-i-Khash **93** 32 0N 62 0 E
Dasht-i-Margo **93** 30 40N 62 30 E
Dasht-i-Nawar **94** 33 52N 68 0 E
Dasht, R. **93** 25 40N 62 20 E
Daska **94** 32 20N 74 20 E
Dassa-Zoume **121** 7 46N 2 14 E
Dasseneiland **128** 33 37 S 18 3 E
Datça **69** 36 46N 27 40 E
Datia **95** 25 39N 78 27 E
Dattapur **96** 20 45N 78 15 E
Daugava **80** 57 0N 24 0 E
Daugavpils **80** 55 53N 26 32 E
Daulat Yar **93** 34 30N 65 45 E
Daulatabad **96** 19 57N 75 15 E
Daun **49** 50 5N 6 53 E
Dauphin, Can. **153** 51 9N 100 5W
Dauphin, U.S.A. **162** 40 22N 76 56W
Dauphin I. **157** 30 16N 88 10W
Dauphin L. **153** 51 20N 99 45W
Dauphiné **45** 45 15N 5 25 E
Dauqa **122** 19 30N 41 0 E
Daura, Kano, Nigeria **121** 13 2N 8 21 E
Daura, N.-E., Nigeria **121** 11 31N 11 24 E
Davadi **120** 14 10N 16 3W
Davangere **97** 14 25N 75 50 E
Davao **103** 7 0N 125 40 E
Davao, G. of **103** 6 30N 125 48 E
Davar Panab **93** 27 25N 62 15 E
Dave **74** 52 55N 1 50W
Davenport, Calif., U.S.A. **163** 37 1N 122 12W
Davenport, Iowa, U.S.A. **158** 41 30N 90 40W
Davenport, Wash., U.S.A. **160** 47 40N 118 5W
Davenport Downs **138** 24 8 S 141 7 E
Davenport Ra. **138** 20 28 S 134 0 E
Daventry **28** 52 16N 1 10W
David **166** 8 30N 82 30W
David City **158** 41 18N 97 10W
David Gorodok **80** 52 4N 27 8 E
Davidson **153** 51 16N 105 59W
Davik **71** 61 53N 5 33 E
Davis **163** 38 33N 121 45W
Davis Dam **161** 35 11N 114 35W
Davis Inlet **151** 55 50N 60 45W
Davis Mts. **159** 30 42N 104 15W
Davis Str. **149** 65 0N 58 0W
Davlekanovo **84** 54 13N 55 3 E
Davos **51** 46 48N 9 49 E
Davy L. **153** 58 53N 108 18W
Davyhurst **137** 30 2 S 120 40 E
Dawa, R. **123** 5 0N 39 5 E
Dawaki, Jos, Nigeria **121** 9 25N 9 33 E
Dawaki, Kano, Nigeria **121** 12 5N 8 23 E
Dawayima **90** 31 33N 34 55 E
Dawes Ra. **138** 24 40 S 150 40 E
Dawley **28** 52 40N 2 29W
Dawlish **30** 50 34N 3 28W
Dawna Range **98** 16 30N 98 30 E
Dawnyein **98** 15 54N 95 36 E
Dawros Hd. **38** 54 48N 8 32W
Dawson, Can. **147** 64 10N 139 30W
Dawson, Ga., U.S.A. **157** 31 45N 84 28W
Dawson, N.D., U.S.A. **158** 46 56N 99 45W
Dawson Creek **152** 55 45N 120 15W
Dawson, I. **176** 53 50 S 70 50W
Dawson Inlet **153** 61 50N 93 25W
Dawson, R. **133** 23 25 S 150 10 E
Dawson Range **138** 24 30 S 149 48 E
Dawson's **127** 17 0 S 30 57 E
Daylesford **140** 37 21 S 144 9 E
Dayr al-Ghusūn **90** 32 21N 35 4 E
Dayr az Zawr **92** 35 20N 40 5 E
Daysland **152** 52 50N 112 20W
Dayton, Ohio, U.S.A. **156** 39 45N 84 10W
Dayton, Tenn., U.S.A. **157** 35 30N 85 1W
Dayton, Wash., U.S.A. **160** 46 20N 118 0W
Daytona Beach **157** 29 14N 81 0W
Dayville **160** 44 33N 119 37W
De Aar **128** 30 39 S 24 0 E
De Bilt **46** 52 6N 5 11 E
De Funiak Springs **157** 30 42N 86 10W
De Grey **136** 20 12 S 119 12 E
De Grey, R. **136** 20 0 S 119 13 E
De Kalb **158** 41 55N 88 45W
De Koog **46** 53 6N 4 46 E
De Land **157** 29 1N 81 19W
De Leon **159** 32 9N 98 35W
De Long Mts. **147** 68 10N 163 0W
De Long, Ostrova **77** 76 40N 149 20 E
De Panne **47** 51 6N 2 34 E
De Pere **156** 44 28N 88 1W
De Queen **159** 34 3N 94 24W
De Quincy **159** 30 30N 93 27W
De Ridder **159** 30 48N 93 15W
De Rijp **46** 52 33N 4 51 E
De Smet **158** 44 25N 97 35W
De Tour Village **156** 45 49N 83 56W
De Witt **159** 34 19N 91 20W
Dead Sea = Miyet, Bahr el **92** 31 30N 35 30 E
Deadwood **58** 44 25N 103 43W
Deadwood L. **152** 59 10N 128 30W
Deaf Adder Cr. **136** 13 0 S 132 47 E
Deakin **137** 30 46 S 129 58 E
Deal **29** 51 13N 1 25 E
Dealesville **128** 28 41 S 25 44 E
Dean, Forest of **28** 51 50N 2 35W
Deán Funes **172** 30 20 S 64 20W
Dearborn **150** 42 18N 83 15W
Dearham **32** 54 43N 3 28W
Dease L. **152** 58 40N 130 5W
Dease Lake **152** 58 25N 130 6W
Dease, R. **152** 59 56N 128 32W
Death Valley **163** 36 27N 116 52W
Death Valley Junc. **163** 36 21N 116 30W
Death Valley Nat. Monument **163** 36 30N 117 0W
Deauville **42** 49 23N 0 2 E
Deba Habe **121** 10 14N 11 20 E
Debaltsevo **82** 48 22N 38 26 E
Debar **66** 41 21N 20 37 E
Debba **123** 14 20N 41 18 E
Debden **153** 53 30N 106 50W
Debdou **118** 33 59N 3 0W
Debeeti **128** 23 45 S 26 32 E
Deben, R. **29** 52 4N 1 19 E
Debenham **29** 52 14N 1 10 E
Debessy **84** 57 39N 53 49 E
Dębica **54** 50 2N 21 25 E
Deblin **54** 51 34N 21 50 E
Debo, L. **120** 15 14N 3 57W
Debolt **152** 55 12N 118 1W
Deborah, gasfield **19** 53 4N 1 50 E
Deborah, L. **137** 30 45 S 119 0 E
Debrc **66** 44 38N 19 53 E
Debre Birhan **123** 9 41N 39 31 E
Debre Markos **123** 10 20N 37 40 E
Debre May **123** 11 20N 37 25 E
Debre Sina **123** 9 51N 39 50 E
Debre Tabor **123** 11 50N 38 26 E
Debrecen **53** 47 33N 21 42 E
Dečani **66** 42 30N 20 10 E
Decatur, Ala., U.S.A. **157** 34 35N 87 0W
Decatur, Ga., U.S.A. **157** 33 47N 84 17W
Decatur, Ill., U.S.A. **158** 39 50N 89 0W
Decatur, Ind., U.S.A. **156** 40 52N 85 28W
Decatur, Texas, U.S.A. **159** 33 15N 97 35W
Decazeville **44** 44 34N 2 15 E
Deccan **97** 14 0N 77 0 E
Deception I. **13** 63 0 S 60 15W
Deception L. **153** 56 33N 104 13W
Deception, Mt. **140** 30 42 S 138 16 E
Decize **43** 46 50N 3 28 E
Decollatura **65** 39 2N 16 21 E
Decorah **158** 43 20N 91 50W
Deda **70** 46 56N 24 50 E
Dedaye **98** 16 24N 95 53 E
Deddington **28** 51 58N 1 19W
Dedemsvaavt **46** 52 36N 6 28 E
Dedham **162** 42 14N 71 10W
Dedilovo **81** 53 59N 37 50 E
Dédougou **120** 12 30N 3 35W
Deduru Oya **97** 7 32N 81 45 E
Dedza **127** 14 20 S 34 20 E
Dee, R., Eng.-Wales, U.K. **31** 53 15N 3 7W
Dee, R., Scot., U.K. **37** 57 4N 2 7W
Deel R. **38** 53 35N 7 9W
Deelish **39** 51 41N 9 18W
Deep B. **152** 61 15N 116 35W
Deep Lead **140** 37 0 S 142 43 E
Deep Well **138** 24 20 S 134 0 E
Deepdale **136** 26 22 S 114 20 E
Deeping Fen **29** 52 45N 0 15W
Deeping, St. Nicholas **29** 52 44N 0 11W
Deepwater **139** 29 25 S 151 51 E
Deer I. **147** 54 55N 162 20W
Deer Lake, Newf., Can. **151** 49 11N 57 27W
Deer Lake, Ontario, Can. **153** 52 36N 94 20W
Deer Lodge **160** 46 25N 112 40W
Deer Park **160** 47 55N 117 21W
Deer, R. **153** 58 23N 94 13W
Deer River **158** 47 21N 93 44W
Deer Sound **37** 58 58N 2 50W
Deeral **138** 17 14 S 145 55 E
Deerdepoort **128** 24 37 S 26 27 E
Deering **147** 66 5N 162 50W
Deerlijk **47** 50 51N 3 22 E
Deerness **37** 58 57N 2 44W
Deesa **94** 24 18N 72 10 E
Deferiet **162** 44 2N 75 41W
Defiance **156** 41 20N 84 20W
Deganwy **31** 53 18N 3 49W
Deganya **90** 32 43N 35 34 E
Degebe, R. **57** 38 21N 7 37W
Degeh-Bur **91** 8 11N 43 31 E

FHK

Degema **Dieuze**

Degema 121 4 50N 6 48 E
Degerfors 74 64 16N 19 46 E
Degersfor 73 59 20N 14 28 E
Degersheim 51 47 23N 9 12 E
Degersiö 72 63 13N 18 3 E
Deggendorf 49 48 49N 12 59 E
Degloor 96 18 34N 77 33 E
Deh Bīd 93 30 39N 53 11 E
Deh Kheyr 93 28 45N 54 40 E
Deh Titan 93 33 45N 63 50 E
Dehibat 119 32 0N 10 47 E
Dehiwala 97 6 50N 79 51 E
Dehkhvareqan 92 37 50N 45 55 E
Dehra Dun 94 30 20N 78 4 E
Dehri 95 24 50N 84 15 E
Deinze 47 50 59N 3 32 E
Deir Abu Sa'id 90 32 30N 38 42 E
Deir Dibwan 90 31 55N 35 15 E
Dej 70 47 10N 23 52 E
Deje 72 59 35N 13 29 E
Dekar 128 18 30 S 23 10 E
Dekemhare 123 15 6N 39 0 E
Dekese 124 3 24 S 21 24 E
Dekhkanabad 85 38 21N 66 30 E
Del Mar 163 32 58N 117 16W
Del Norte 161 37 47N 106 27W
Del Rey, Rio 121 4 30N 8 48 E
Del Rio, Mexico 164 29 22N 100 54W
Del Rio, U.S.A. 159 29 15N 100 50W
Delabole 30 50 37N 4 45W
Delagoa B. 129 25 50 S 32 45 E
Delagua 159 32 35N 104 40W
Delai 122 17 21N 36 6 E
Delambre I. 136 20 27 S 117 4 E
Delano 163 35 48N 119 13W
Delareyville 128 26 41 S 25 26 E
Delavan 158 42 40N 88 39W
Delaware 156 40 20N 83 0W
Delaware □ 162 39 0N 75 40W
Delaware B. 162 38 50N 75 0W
Delaware City 162 39 34N 75 36W
Delaware, R. 162 39 20N 75 25W
Delčevo 66 41 58N 22 46 E
Delchirach 37 57 23N 3 20W
Delegate 141 37 4 S 148 56 E
Delémont 50 47 22N 7 20 E
Delft 46 52 1N 4 22 E
Delft I. 97 9 30N 79 40 E
Delfzijl 46 53 20N 6 55 E
Delgado, C. 127 10 45 S 40 40 E
Delgerhet 106 45 50N 110 30 E
Delgo 122 20 6N 30 40 E
Delhi, India 94 28 38N 77 17 E
Delhi, U.S.A. 162 42 17N 74 56W
Deli Jovan 66 44 13N 22 9 E
Delia 152 51 38N 112 23W
Delice, R. 92 39 45N 34 15 E
Delicias 164 28 10N 105 30W
Delicias, Laguna 164 28 7N 105 40W
Delimiro Gouveia 170 9 23 S 37 59W
Delitzsch 48 51 32N 12 22 E
Dell City 161 31 58N 105 19W
Dell Rapids 158 43 53N 96 44W
Delle 43 47 30N 7 2 E
Dellys 119 36 50N 3 57 E
Delmar, Del., U.S.A. 162 38 27N 75 34W
Delmar, N.Y., U.S.A. 162 42 5N 73 50W
Delmenhorst 48 53 3N 8 37 E
Delmiro 170 9 24 S 38 6W
Delnice 63 45 23N 14 50 E
Deloraine, Austral. 138 41 30 S 146 40 E
Deloraine, Can. 153 49 15N 100 29W
Delorme, L. 151 54 31N 69 52W
Delovo 66 44 55N 20 52 E
Delphi 156 40 37N 86 40W
Delphos 156 40 51N 84 17W
Delportshoop 128 28 22 S 24 20 E
Delray Beach 157 26 27N 80 4W
Delsbo 72 61 48N 16 32 E
Delta, Colo., U.S.A. 161 38 44N 108 5W
Delta, Utah, U.S.A. 160 39 21N 112 29W
Delta Amacuro □ 174 8 30N 61 30W
Deltaville 162 37 33N 76 20W
Delungra 139 29 39 S 150 51 E
Delvin 38 53 37N 7 8W
Delvina 68 39 59N 20 4 E
Delvinákion 68 39 57N 20 32 E
Demak 103 6 50 S 110 40 E
Demanda, Sierra de la 58 42 15N 3 0W
Demba 124 5 28 S 22 15 E
Dembecha 123 10 32N 37 30 E
Dembi 123 8 5N 36 25 E
Dembia 126 3 33N 25 48 E
Dembidolo 123 8 34N 34 50 E
Demchok 93 32 40N 79 29 E
Demer, R. 47 51 0N 5 8 E
Demerais, L. 150 47 35N 77 0W
Demerara, R. 174 7 0N 58 0W
Demidov 80 55 10N 31 30 E
Deming 161 32 10N 107 50W
Demini, R. 174 0 46N 62 56W
Demmin 48 53 54N 13 2 E
Demmit 152 55 20N 119 50W
Demnate 118 31 44N 6 59W
Demonte 62 44 18N 7 18 E
Demopolis 157 32 30N 87 48W
Dempo, Mt. 102 4 10 S 103 15 E
Demyansk 80 57 30N 32 27 E
Den Bemmel 46 51 54N 4 26 E
Den Burg 46 53 3N 4 47 E
Den Chai 100 17 59N 100 4 E
Den Dungen 47 51 41N 5 22 E
Den Haag = 's Gravenhage 46 52 7N 4 17 E
Den Ham 46 52 28N 6 30 E
Den Helder 46 52 57N 4 45 E
Den Hulst 46 52 36N 6 16 E
Den Oever 46 52 56N 5 2 E
Denain 43 50 20N 3 22 E
Denair 163 37 32N 120 48W
Denau 85 38 16N 67 54 E
Denbigh 31 53 12N 3 26W
Denbigh (□) 26 53 8N 3 30W
Denby Dale 33 53 35N 1 40W
Denchin 99 31 35N 95 15 E
Dendang 102 3 7 S 107 56 E
Dender, R. 47 51 2N 4 6 E
Denderhoutem 47 50 53N 4 2 E
Denderleeuw 47 50 54N 4 5 E
Dendermonde 47 51 2N 4 5 E
Deneba 123 9 47N 39 10 E
Denekamp 46 52 22N 7 1 E
Denezhkin Kamen, Gora 84 60 25N 59 32 E
Denge 121 12 52N 5 21 E
Dengi 121 9 25N 9 55 E
Denham 137 25 56 S 113 31 E
Denham Ra. 138 21 55 S 147 46 E
Denham Sd. 137 25 45 S 113 15 E
Denholm 153 52 40N 108 0W
Denia 59 38 49N 0 8 E
Denial B. 139 32 14 S 133 32 E
Deniliquin 141 35 30 S 144 58 E
Denison, Iowa, U.S.A. 158 42 0N 95 18W
Denison, Texas, U.S.A. 159 33 50N 96 40W
Denison Plains 136 18 35 S 128 0 E
Denison Range 136 28 30 S 136 5 E
Denisovka 84 52 28N 61 46 E
Denizli 92 37 42N 29 2 E
Denkez Iyesus 123 12 27N 37 43 E
Denman 141 32 24 S 150 42 E
Denmark 137 34 59 S 117 18 E
Denmark ■ 73 55 30N 9 0 E
Denmark Str. 14 66 0N 30 0W
Dennis Hd. 37 59 23N 2 26W
Denniston 143 41 45 S 171 49 E
Denny 35 56 1N 3 55W
Denpasar 102 8 45 S 115 5 E
Dent 32 54 17N 2 28W
Denton, E. Sussex, U.K. 29 50 48N 0 5 E
Denton, Gr. Manchester, U.K. 32 53 26N 2 10W
Denton, Lincs., U.K. 33 52 52N 0 42W
Denton, Md., U.S.A. 162 38 53N 75 50W
Denton, Mont., U.S.A. 160 47 25N 109 56W
Denton, Texas, U.S.A. 159 33 12N 97 10W
D'Entrecasteaux, C. 137 34 50 S 115 59 E
D'Entrecasteaux Is. 135 9 0 S 151 0 E
D'Entrecasteaux Pt. 137 34 50 S 115 57 E
Dents du Midi 50 46 10N 6 56 E
Denu 121 6 4N 1 8 E
Denver, Colo., U.S.A. 158 39 45N 105 0W
Denver, Pa., U.S.A. 162 40 14N 76 8W
Denver City 159 32 58N 102 48W
Deoband 94 29 42N 77 43 E
Deobhog 96 19 53N 82 44 E
Deogarh 96 21 32N 84 45 E
Deoghar 95 24 30N 86 59 E
Deolali 96 19 50N 73 50 E
Deoli 94 25 50N 75 50 E
Deoria 95 26 31N 83 48 E
Deosai, Mts. 95 35 40N 75 0 E
Deposit 162 42 5N 75 23W
Depot Spring 137 27 55 S 120 3 E
Depuch I. 136 20 35 S 117 44 E
Deputatskiy 77 69 18N 139 54 E
Dera Ghazi Khan 94 30 5N 70 43 E
Dera Ismail Khan 94 31 50N 70 50 E
Dera Ismail Khan □ 94 32 30N 70 0 E
Derati Wells 126 3 52N 36 37 E
Derbent 74 42 5N 48 15 E
Derby, Austral. 136 17 18 S 123 38 E
Derby, U.K. 33 52 55N 1 28W
Derby, U.S.A. 162 41 20N 73 5W
Derby □ 33 52 55N 1 28W
Derecske 53 47 20N 21 33 E
Derg, L. 39 53 0N 8 20W
Derg, R. 38 54 42N 7 26W
Dergachi 81 50 3N 36 3 E
Dergaon 99 26 45N 94 0 E
Dermantsi 67 43 8N 24 17 E
Derna 117 32 40N 22 35 E
Dernieres Isles 159 29 0N 90 45W
Derriana, L. 39 51 54N 10 1W
Derrinallum 140 37 57 S 143 15 E
Derry R. 39 52 43N 6 35W
Derrybrien 39 53 4N 8 38W
Derrygonnelly 38 54 25N 7 50W
Derrygrogan 39 53 19N 7 23W
Derrykeighan 38 55 8N 6 30W
Derrylin 38 54 12N 7 34W
Derry = Londonderry 38 55 0N 7 19W
Derrynasaggart Mts. 39 51 58N 9 15W
Derryrush 38 53 23N 9 40W
Derryveagh Mts. 38 55 0N 8 40W
Derudub 122 17 31N 36 7 E
Dervaig 34 56 35N 6 13W
Derval 42 47 40N 1 41W
Dervéni 69 38 8N 22 25 E
Derwent 153 53 41N 110 58W
Derwent, R., Derby, U.K. 33 52 53N 1 17W
Derwent, R., N. Yorks., U.K. 33 53 45N 0 57W
Derwent, R., Tyne & Wear, U.K. 35 54 58N 1 40W
Derwentwater, L. 32 53 34N 3 9W
Des Moines, Iowa, U.S.A. 158 41 35N 93 37W
Des Moines, N. Mex., U.S.A. 159 36 50N 103 51W
Des Moines, R. 158 40 23N 91 25W
Desaguadero, R., Argent. 172 33 28 S 67 15W
Desaguadero, R., Boliv. 174 17 30 S 68 0W
Desborough 29 52 27N 0 50W
Deschaillons 151 46 32N 72 7W
Descharme, R. 153 56 51N 109 13W
Deschutes, R. 160 45 30N 121 0W
Dese 123 11 5N 39 40 E
Deseado, R. 176 40 0 S 69 0W
Desemboque 164 30 30N 112 27W
Deseñzano del Gardo 62 45 28N 10 32 E
Desert Center 161 33 45N 115 27W
Desert Hot Springs 163 33 58N 116 30W
Desertmartin 38 54 47N 6 40W
Desford 28 52 38N 1 19W
Désirade, I. 167 16 18N 61 3W
Deskenatlata L. 152 60 55N 112 3W
Desna, R. 80 52 0N 33 15 E
Desnǔtui, R. 70 44 15N 23 27 E
Desolación, I. 176 53 0 S 74 0W
Despeñaperros, Paso 59 38 24N 3 30W
Despotovac 66 44 6N 21 30 E
Dessa 121 14 44N 1 6 E
Dessau 48 51 49N 12 15 E
Dessel 47 51 15N 5 7 E
Dessye = Dese 123 11 5N 39 40 E
D'Estress B. 140 35 55 S 137 45 E
Desuri 94 25 18N 73 35 E
Desvrès 43 50 40N 1 48 E
Det Udom 100 14 54N 105 5 E
Detinjá, R. 66 43 51N 19 45 E
Detmold 48 51 55N 8 50 E
Detour Pt. 156 45 37N 86 35W
Detroit, Mich., U.S.A. 150 42 13N 83 22W
Detroit, Tex., U.S.A. 159 33 40N 95 10W
Detroit Lakes 158 46 50N 95 50W
Dett 127 18 32 S 26 57 E
Dettifoss 74 65 49N 16 24W
Děčin 52 50 47N 14 12 E
Deurne, Belg. 47 51 12N 4 24 E
Deurne, Neth. 47 51 27N 5 49 E
Deutsche Bucht 48 54 10N 7 51 E
Deutschlandsberg 52 46 49N 15 14 E
Deux-Acren, Les 47 50 44N 3 51 E
Deux-Sèvres □ 42 46 35N 0 20W
Deva 70 45 53N 22 55 E
Devakottai 97 9 55N 78 45 E
Devaprayag 95 30 13N 78 35 E
Dévaványa 53 47 2N 20 59 E
Deveci Daği 82 40 10N 36 0 E
Devecser 53 47 6N 17 26 E
Deventer 46 52 15N 6 10 E
Deveron, R. 37 57 40N 2 31W
Devesel 70 44 28N 22 41 E
Devgad, I. 97 14 48N 74 5 E
Devil R., Pk. 143 40 56 S 172 37 E
Devils Bridge 31 52 23N 3 50W
Devils Den 163 35 46N 119 58W
Devils Lake 158 48 5N 98 50W
Devils Paw, mt. 152 58 47N 134 0W
Devils Pt. 97 9 26N 80 6 E
Devilsbit Mt. 39 52 50N 7 58W
Devin 67 41 44N 24 24 E
Devizes 28 51 21N 2 0W
Devnya 67 43 13N 27 33 E
Devolli, R. 68 40 57N 20 15 E
Devon 152 53 24N 113 44W
Devon I. 12 75 47N 88 0W
Devonport, Austral. 138 41 10 S 146 22 E
Devonport, N.Z. 142 36 49 S 174 49 E
Devonport, U.K. 30 50 23N 4 11W
Devonshire □ 30 50 50N 3 40W
Dewas 94 22 59N 76 3 E
Dewetsdorp 128 29 33 S 26 39 E
Dewgad Baria 94 22 40N 73 55 E
Dewsbury 33 53 42N 1 38W
Dexter, Mo., U.S.A. 159 36 50N 90 0W
Dexter, N. Mex., U.S.A. 159 33 15N 104 25W
Dey-Dey, L. 137 29 12 S 131 4 E
Deyhuk 93 33 15N 104 25W
Deyyer 93 27 55N 51 55 E
Dezadeash L. 152 60 28N 136 58W
Dezfūl 92 32 20N 48 30 E
Dezh Shanpur 92 35 30N 46 25 E
Dezhneva, Mys 77 66 10N 169 3 E
Dhaba 92 27 25N 35 40 E
Dháfni 69 37 48N 22 1 E
Dhahaban 122 21 58N 39 3 E
Dhahiriya = Qz Zahiriya 90 31 25N 34 58 E
Dhahran 92 26 9N 50 10 E
Dhama Dzong 99 28 15N 91 15 E
Dhamási 68 39 43N 22 11 E
Dhampur 95 29 19N 78 33 E
Dhamtari 96 20 42N 81 35 E
Dhanbad 95 23 50N 86 30 E
Dhangarhi 99 28 55N 80 40 E
Dhankuta 95 26 55N 87 20 E
Dhanora 96 20 20N 80 22 E
Dhar 94 22 35N 75 26 E
Dharampur, Mad. P., India 94 22 13N 75 18 E
Dharampur, Maharashtra, India 96 20 32N 73 17 E
Dharapuram 97 10 45N 77 34 E
Dharmapuri 97 12 10N 78 10 E
Dharmavaram 97 14 29N 77 44 E
Dharmsala, (Dharamsala) 94 32 16N 73 23 E
Dhaulagiri Mt. 95 28 45N 83 45 E
Dhebar, L. 94 24 10N 74 0 E
Dhenkanal 96 20 45N 85 35 E
Dhenoúsa 69 37 8N 25 48 E
Dhesfina 69 38 25N 22 31 E
Dheskáti 68 39 55N 21 49 E
Dhespotikó 69 36 57N 24 58 E
Dhidhimótikhon 68 41 22N 26 29 E
Dhikti, Mt. 69 35 8N 25 29 E
Dhilianáta 69 38 15N 20 34 E
Dhílos 69 37 23N 25 15 E
Dhimitsána 69 37 36N 22 3 E
Dhirfis, Mt. 69 38 40N 23 54 E
Dhodhekánisos 69 36 35N 27 0 E
Dhofar 91 17 0N 54 10 E
Dhokós 69 37 20N 23 20 E
Dholiana 68 39 54N 20 32 E
Dholka 94 22 44N 72 29 E
Dholpur 94 26 45N 77 59 E
Dhomokós 69 39 10N 22 18 E
Dhond 96 18 26N 74 40 E
Dhoraji 94 21 45N 70 37 E
Dhoxáthon 68 41 9N 24 16 E
Dhragonisi 69 37 27N 25 29 E
Dhrangadhra 94 22 59N 71 31 E
Dhriopós 69 37 35N 24 35 E
Dhrol 94 22 40N 70 25 E
Dhubaibah 93 23 25N 54 35 E
Dhubri 98 26 2N 90 2 E
Dhulasar 98 21 52N 90 14 E
Dhulia 96 20 58N 74 50 E
Dhupdhara 98 25 58N 91 4 E
Dhurm 122 20 18N 42 53 E
Di Linh 101 11 35N 108 4 E
Di Linh, Cao Nguyen 101 11 30N 108 0 E
Día, I. 69 35 26N 25 13 E
Diable, Mt. 163 37 53N 121 56W
Diablerets, Les 50 46 22N 7 10 E
Diablo Range 163 37 0N 121 5W
Diafarabé 120 14 17N 4 57W
Diala 120 13 59N 10 0W
Dialakoro 120 12 18N 7 54W
Diallassagou 120 13 47N 3 41W
Diamante 172 32 5 S 60 40W
Diamante, R. 172 34 31 S 66 56W
Diamantina 171 18 5 S 43 40W
Diamantina, R. 138 22 25 S 142 20 E
Diamantino 175 14 30 S 56 30W
Diamond Harbour 95 22 11N 88 14 E
Diamond Is. 138 17 25 S 151 5 E
Diamond Mts. 160 40 0N 115 58W
Diamond Springs 163 38 42N 120 49W
Diamondville 160 41 51N 110 30W
Diano Marina 62 43 55N 8 3 E
Dianópolis 171 11 38 S 46 50W
Dianra 120 8 45N 6 14W
Diaole, Î. du. 170 5 15N 52 45W
Diapaga 121 12 5N 1 46 E
Diapangou 121 12 5N 0 10 E
Diapur 140 36 19 S 141 29 E
Diariguila 120 10 35N 10 2W
Dibai (Dubai) 93 25 15N 55 20 E
Dibaya 124 6 20 S 22 0 E
Dibaya Lubue 124 4 12 S 19 54 E
Dibba 93 25 45N 56 16 E
Dibbi 123 4 10N 41 52 E
Dibden 28 50 53N 1 24W
Dibega 92 35 50N 43 46 E
Dibër 68 41 38N 20 15 E
Dibete 128 23 45 S 26 32 E
Dibi 123 4 10N 41 52 E
Dibrugarh 98 27 29N 94 55 E
Dibulla 174 11 17N 73 19W
Dickinson 158 46 50N 102 40W
Dickson 157 36 5N 87 22W
Dickson City 162 41 29N 75 40W
Dicomano 63 43 53 S 11 30 E
Didam 46 51 57N 6 8 E
Didcot 28 51 36N 1 14W
Didesa, W. 123 9 40N 35 50 E
Didiéni 120 14 5N 7 50W
Didsbury 152 51 35N 114 10W
Didwana 94 27 17N 74 25 E
Die 45 44 47N 5 22 E
Diébougou 120 11 0N 3 15W
Diefenbaker L. 153 51 0N 106 55W
Diego Garcia, I. 11 9 50 S 75 0 E
Diégo Suarez 129 12 25 S 49 20 E
Diekirch 47 49 52N 6 10 E
Diélette 42 49 33N 1 52W
Diéma 120 14 32N 9 3W
Diemen 46 52 21N 4 58 E
Diemering 120 12 29N 16 47W
Dien Ban 100 15 53N 108 16 E
Diên Biên Phu 100 21 20N 103 0 E
Dien Khanh 101 12 15N 109 6 E
Diepenheim 46 52 12N 6 33 E
Diepenveen 46 52 18N 6 9 E
Diepholz 48 52 37N 8 22 E
Diepoldsau 51 47 23N 9 40 E
Dieppe 42 49 54N 1 4 E
Dieren 46 52 3N 6 6 E
Dierks 159 34 9N 94 0W
Diessen 47 51 29N 5 10 E
Diessenhofen 51 47 42N 8 46 E
Diest 47 50 58N 5 4 E
Dietikon 51 47 24N 8 24 E
Dieulefit 45 44 32N 5 4 E
Dieuze 43 48 30N 6 40 E

Diever Donskoy

Diever **46** 52 51N 6 19 E
Diffa **121** 13 34N 12 33 E
Differdange **47** 49 81N 5 54 E
Dig **94** 27 28N 77 20 E
Digba **126** 4 25N 25 42 E
Digboi **98** 27 23N 95 38 E
Digby **151** 44 41N 65 50W
Digges **153** 58 40N 94 0W
Digges Is. **149** 62 40N 77 50W
Digges Lamprey **153** 58 33N 94 8W
Dighinala **98** 23 15N 92 5 E
Dighton **158** 38 30N 100 26W
Digne **45** 44 5N 6 12 E
Digoin **44** 46 29N 3 58 E
Digos **103** 6 45N 125 20 E
Digranes **74** 66 4N 14 44 E
Digras **96** 20 6N 77 45 E
Dihang, R. **99** 27 30N 96 30 E
Dijlah **92** 37 0N 42 30 E
Dijle, R. **47** 50 58N 4 41 E
Dijon **43** 47 20N 5 0 E
Dikala **123** 4 45N 31 28 E
Dikhal **123** 11 8N 42 20 E
Dikomu di Kai, Mt. **128** 24 51 S 24 36 E
Diksmuide **47** 51 2N 2 52 E
Dikson **76** 73 40N 80 5 E
Dikumbiya **123** 14 45N 37 30 E
Dikwa **121** 12 4N 13 30 E
Dila **123** 6 14N 38 22 E
Dilam **92** 23 55N 47 10 E
Dilbeek **47** 50 51N 4 17 E
Dili **103** 8 39 S 125 34 E
Dilizhan **83** 41 46N 44 57 E
Dillenburg **48** 50 44N 8 17 E
Dilley **159** 28 40N 99 12W
Dilling **123** 12 3N 29 35 E
Dillingen **49** 49 22N 6 42 E
Dillingham **147** 59 5N 158 30W
Dillon, Can. **153** 55 56N 108 56W
Dillon, Mont., U.S.A. **160** 45 9N 112 36W
Dillon, S.C., U.S.A. **157** 34 26N 79 20W
Dillon, R. **153** 55 56N 108 56W
Dillsburg **162** 40 7N 77 2W
Dilolo **14** 10 28 S 22 18 E
Dilsen **47** 51 2N 5 44 E
Dilston **138** 41 22 S 147 10 E
Dima **123** 6 19N 36 15 E
Dimapur **98** 25 54N 93 45 E
Dimas **164** 23 43N 106 47W
Dimashq **92** 33 30N 36 18 E
Dimbelenge **124** 4 30N 23 0 E
Dimbokro **120** 6 45N 4 30W
Dimboola **140** 36 28 S 142 0 E
Dîmboviţa □ **70** 45 0N 25 30 E
Dîmbovita, R. **70** 44 40N 26 0 E
Dimbulah **138** 17 2 S 145 4 E
Dimitriya Lapteva, Proliv **77** 73 0N 140 0 E
Dimitrovgrad, Bulg. **67** 42 5N 25 35 E
Dimitrovgrad, U.S.S.R. **81** 54 25N 49 33 E
Dimitrovgrad, Yugo. **66** 43 0N 22 48 E
Dimmitt **159** 34 36N 102 16W
Dimo **123** 5 19N 29 10 E
Dimona **90** 31 2N 35 1 E
Dimovo **66** 43 43N 22 50 E
Dinagat I. **103** 10 10N 125 40 E
Dinajpur **98** 25 33N 88 43 E
Dinan **42** 48 28N 2 2W
Dinant **47** 50 16N 4 55 E
Dinapore **95** 25 38N 85 5 E
Dinar **92** 38 5N 30 15 E
Dinard **42** 48 38N 2 6W
Dinaric Alps **16** 44 0N 17 30 E
Dinas Hd. **31** 52 2N 4 56W
Dinas Mawddwy **31** 52 44N 3 41W
Dinas Powis **31** 51 25N 3 14W
Dinder, Nahr ed **123** 12 32N 35 0 E
Dindi, R. **96** 16 24N 78 15 E
Dindigul **97** 10 25N 78 0 E
Dingelstädt **48** 51 19N 10 19 E
Dingila **126** 3 25N 26 25 E
Dingle **39** 52 9N 10 17W
Dingle B. **39** 52 3N 10 20W
Dingle Harbour **39** 52 7N 10 12W
Dingmans Ferry **162** 41 13N 74 55W
Dingo **138** 23 38 S 149 19 E
Dingolfing **49** 48 38N 12 30 E
Dinguiraye **120** 11 30N 10 35W
Dingwall **37** 57 36N 4 26W
Dingyadi **121** 13 0N 0 53 E
Dinh Lap **100** 21 33N 107 6 E
Dinh, Mui **101** 11 22N 109 1 E
Dinhata **98** 26 8N 89 27 E
Dinkel **46** 52 30N 6 58 E
Dinokwe (Palla Road) **128** 23 29 S 26 37 E
Dinosaur National Monument **160** 40 30N 108 45W
Dinslaken **47** 51 34N 6 41 E
Dintel, R. **47** 51 39N 4 22 E
Dinuba **163** 36 37N 119 22W
Dinxperlo **46** 51 52N 6 30 E
Dio **73** 56 37N 14 15 E
Diosgyör **53** 48 7N 20 43 E
Diosig **70** 47 18N 22 2 E
Dioundiou **121** 12 37N 3 33 E
Diourbel **120** 14 39N 16 12W
Diphu Pass **98** 28 9N 97 20 E
Diplo **94** 24 25N 69 35 E
Dipolog **103** 8 36N 123 20 E
Dipşa **70** 46 58N 24 27 E
Dipton **143** 45 54 S 168 22 E
Dir **93** 35 08N 71 59 E
Diré **120** 15 20N 3 25W
Dire Dawa **123** 9 35N 41 45 E
Direction, C. **138** 12 51 S 143 32 E
Diriamba **166** 11 51N 86 19W
Dirico **125** 17 50 S 20 42 E
Dirk Hartog I. **137** 25 50 S 113 5 E
Dirranbandi **139** 28 33 S 148 17 E
Disa **123** 12 5N 34 15 E
Disappointment, C. **160** 46 20N 124 0W
Disappointment L. **136** 23 20 S 122 40 E
Disaster B. **141** 37 15 S 150 0 E
Discovery **148** 63 0N 115 0W
Discovery B. **140** 38 10 S 140 40 E
Disentis **51** 46 42N 8 50 E
Dishna **122** 26 9N 32 32 E
Disina **121** 11 35N 9 50 E
Disko **12** 69 45N 53 30W
Disko Bugt **12** 69 10N 52 0W
Disna **80** 55 32N 28 11 E
Disna, R. **80** 55 20N 27 30 E
Dison **47** 50 37N 5 51 E
Diss **29** 52 23N 1 6 E
Disteghil Sar **95** 36 20N 75 5 E
Distington **32** 54 35N 3 33W
District Heights **162** 38 51N 76 53W
District of Columbia □ **162** 38 55N 77 0W
Distrito Federal □, Brazil **171** 15 45 S 47 45W
Distrito Federal □, Venez. **174** 10 30N 66 55W
Disûq **122** 31 8N 30 35 E
Ditchingham **29** 52 28N 1 26 E
Ditchling & Beacon **29** 50 59N 0 7W
Ditinn **120** 10 53N 12 11W
Dittisham **30** 50 22N 3 36W
Ditton Priors **28** 52 30N 2 33W
Diu, I. **94** 20 45N 70 58 E
Diver **150** 46 44N 79 30W
Dives **42** 49 18N 0 8W
Dives, R. **42** 49 18N 0 7W
Divi Pt. **97** 15 59N 81 9 E
Divichi **83** 41 15N 48 57 E
Divide **160** 45 48N 112 47W
Dividing Ra. **137** 27 45 S 116 0 E
Divinopólis **171** 20 10 S 44 54W
Divisões, Serra dos **171** 17 0 S 51 0W
Divnoye **83** 45 55N 43 27 E
Divo **120** 5 48N 5 15W
Diwal Kol **94** 34 23N 67 52 E
Dixie **160** 45 37N 115 27W
Dixon, Calif., U.S.A. **163** 38 27N 121 49W
Dixon, Ill., U.S.A. **158** 41 50N 89 30W
Dixon, Mont., U.S.A. **160** 47 19N 114 25W
Dixon, N. Mex., U.S.A. **161** 36 15N 105 57W
Dixon Entrance **153** 54 30N 132 0W
Dixonville **152** 56 32N 117 40W
Diyarbakir **92** 37 55N 40 18 E
Dizzard Pt. **30** 50 46N 4 38W
Djabotaoure **121** 8 35N 0 58 E
Djado **119** 21 4N 12 14 E
Djado, Plateau du **119** 21 29N 12 21 E
Djakarta = Jakarta **103** 6 9 S 106 49 E
Djakovo **66** 45 19N 18 24 E
Djamâa **119** 33 32N 5 59 E
Djamba **128** 16 45 S 13 58 E
Djambala **124** 2 20 S 14 30 E
Djanet **119** 24 35N 9 32 E
Djang **121** 5 30N 10 5 E
Djaul I. **135** 2 58 S 150 57 E
Djawa = Jawa **103** 7 0 S 110 0 E
Djebiniana **119** 35 1N 11 0 E
Djelfa **118** 34 40N 3 15 E
Djema **126** 6 9N 25 15 E
Djeneïene **119** 31 45N 10 9 E
Djenné **120** 14 0N 4 30W
Djenoun, Garet el **119** 25 4N 5 31 E
Djerba **119** 33 52N 10 51 E
Djerba, Île de **119** 33 56N 11 0 E
Djerid, Chott **119** 33 42N 8 30 E
Djibo **121** 14 15N 1 35W
Djibouti **123** 11 30N 43 5 E
Djibouti ■ **123** 11 30N 42 15 E
Djidjelli **119** 36 52N 5 50 E
Djirlange **101** 11 44N 108 15 E
Djofra **119** 28 59N 15 47 E
Djolu **124** 0 45N 22 5 E
Djorf el Youdi **118** 32 14N 9 8W
Djougou **121** 9 40N 1 45 E
Djoum **124** 2 41N 12 35 E
Djourab, Erg du **117** 16 40N 18 50 E
Djugu **126** 1 55N 30 35 E
Djúpivogur **74** 64 39N 14 17W
Djursholm **72** 59 25N 18 6 E
Djursland **73** 56 27N 10 45 E
Dmitriev-Lgovskiy **80** 52 10N 35 0 E
Dmitriya Lapteva, Proliv **77** 73 0N 140 0 E
Dmitrov **81** 56 25N 37 32 E
Dmitrovsk Orlovskiy **80** 52 29N 35 10 E
Dneiper, R. = Dnepr **82** 52 29N 35 10 E
Dnepr, R. **82** 50 0N 31 0 E
Dneprodzerzhinsk **82** 48 32N 34 30 E
Dneprodzerzhinskoye Vdkhr. **77** 49 0N 34 0 E
Dnepropetrovsk **82** 48 30N 35 0 E
Dneprorudnoye **82** 47 21N 34 58 E
Dnestr, R. **82** 48 30N 26 30 E
Dnestrovski = Belgorod **82** 50 35N 36 35 E
Dniester = Dnestr **82** 48 30N 26 30 E
Dno **80** 57 50N 29 58 E
Doan Hung **100** 21 38N 105 10 E
Doba **117** 8 40N 16 50 E
Dobané **126** 6 20N 24 39 E
Dobbiaco **63** 46 44N 12 13 E
Dobbyn **138** 19 44 S 139 59 E
Dobczyce **54** 49 52N 20 25 E
Döbeln **48** 51 7N 13 10 E
Doberai, Jazirah **103** 1 25 S 133 0 E
Dobiegniew **54** 52 59N 15 45 E
Doblas **172** 37 5 S 64 0W
Dobo **103** 5 45 S 134 15 E
Doboj **66** 44 46N 18 6 E
Dobra, Poland **54** 53 34N 15 20 E
Dobra, Dîmboviţa, Rumania **67** 44 52N 25 40 E
Dobra, Hunedoara, Rumania **70** 45 54N 22 36 E
Dobre Miasto **54** 53 58N 20 26 E
Dobrinishta **67** 41 49N 23 34 E
Dobriš **52** 49 46N 14 10 E
Dobrodzien **54** 50 45N 18 25 E
Dobrogea **70** 44 30N 28 15 E
Dobruja = Dobrogea **70** 44 30N 28 15 E
Dobrush **80** 52 28N 30 35 E
Dobryanka **84** 58 27N 56 25 E
Dobrzyn n. Wisła **54** 52 39N 19 22 E
Dobtong **123** 6 25N 31 40 E
Doc, Mui **100** 17 58N 106 30 E
Doce, R. **171** 19 37 S 39 49W
Docking **29** 52 55N 0 39 E
Doda **95** 33 10N 75 34 E
Döda Fallet **72** 63 4N 16 35 E
Doddington **29** 52 29N 0 3 E
Dodecanese = Dhodhekánisos **69** 36 35N 27 0 E
Dodewaard **46** 51 55N 5 39 E
Dodge Center **158** 44 1N 92 57W
Dodge City **159** 37 42N 100 0W
Dodge L. **153** 59 50N 105 36W
Dodgeville **158** 42 55N 90 8W
Dodman Pt. **30** 50 13N 4 49W
Dodo **123** 5 10N 29 57 E
Dodola **123** 6 59N 39 11 E
Dodoma **126** 6 8 S 35 45 E
Dodoma □ **126** 6 0 S 36 0 E
Dodsland **153** 51 50N 108 45W
Dodson **160** 48 23N 108 4W
Doesburg **46** 52 1N 6 9 E
Doetinchem **46** 51 59N 6 18 E
Doftana **70** 45 17N 25 45 E
Dog Creek **152** 51 35N 122 14W
Dog L., Man., Can. **152** 51 2N 98 31W
Dog L., Ont., Can. **150** 48 12N 89 16W
Dog, R. **152** 57 50N 94 40W
Doganbey **69** 37 40N 27 10 E
Dogi **93** 32 20N 62 50 E
Dogliani **62** 44 35N 7 55 E
Dōgo **110** 36 15N 133 16 E
Dōgo-San **110** 35 2N 133 13 E
Dògondoutchi **121** 13 38N 4 2 E
Dogoraoua **121** 14 0N 5 31 E
Dogran **94** 31 48N 73 35 E
Dohad **94** 22 50N 74 15 E
Dohazari **99** 22 10N 92 5 E
Doheny **150** 47 4N 72 35W
Doherty **150** 46 58N 79 44W
Doi, I. **103** 2 21N 127 49 E
Doi Luang **101** 18 20N 101 30 E
Doi Saket **100** 18 52N 99 9 E
Doig, R., Alta., Can. **152** 56 57N 120 0W
Doig, R., B.C., Can. **152** 56 25N 120 40W
Dois Irmãos, Serra **171** 8 30 S 41 5W
Dokka **71** 60 49N 10 7 E
Dokka, R. **71** 61 7N 10 0 E
Dokkum **46** 53 20N 5 59 E
Dokkumer Ee, R. **46** 53 18N 5 52 E
Dokri Mohenjodaro **94** 27 25N 68 7 E
Dol **42** 48 34N 1 47W
Dolak, Pulau = Kolepom, P. **103** 8 0 S 138 30 E
Doland **158** 44 55N 98 5W
Dolbeau **151** 48 53N 72 18W
Dôle **43** 47 7N 5 31 E
Doleib, W. **123** 10 30N 33 15 E
Dolgarrog **31** 53 11N 3 50W
Dolgellau **31** 52 44N 3 53W
Dolgelly = Dolgellau **31** 52 44N 3 53W
Dolginovo **80** 54 39N 27 29 E
Dolianovo **64** 39 23N 9 11 E
Dolinskaya **82** 48 16N 32 36 E
Dolisie **124** 4 0 S 13 10 E
Dolj □ **70** 44 10N 23 30 E
Dolla **39** 52 47N 8 12W
Dollar **35** 56 9N 3 41W
Dollart **46** 53 20N 7 10 E
Dolna Banya **67** 42 18N 23 44 E
Dolni Dubnik **67** 43 24N 24 26 E
Dolo **63** 45 25N 12 4 E
Dolo Bay **123** 4 11N 42 3 E
Dolomites = Dolomiti **63** 46 30N 11 40 E
Dolomiti **63** 46 30N 11 40 E
Dolores, Argent. **172** 36 20 S 57 40W
Dolores, Mexico **164** 28 53N 108 27W
Dolores, Uruguay **172** 33 34 S 58 15W
Dolores, Colo., U.S.A. **161** 37 30N 108 30W
Dolores, Tex., U.S.A. **159** 27 40N 99 38W
Dolores, R. **159** 38 30N 108 55W
Đolovo **66** 44 55N 20 52 E
Dolphin and Union Str. **148** 69 5N 114 45W
Dolphin C. **176** 51 10 S 50 0W
Dolphinton **35** 55 42N 3 28W
Dolsk **54** 51 59N 17 3 E
Dolton **30** 50 53N 4 2W
Dolwyddelan **31** 53 3N 3 53W
Dom **50** 46 6N 7 50 E
Dom Joaquim **171** 18 57 S 43 16W
Dom Pedrito **173** 31 0 S 54 40W
Dom Pedro **170** 4 29 S 44 27W
Doma **121** 8 25N 8 18 E
Domasi **127** 15 22 S 35 10 E
Domat Ems **51** 46 50N 9 27 E
Domazlice **52** 49 28N 13 0 E
Dombarovskiy **84** 50 46N 59 32 E
Dombås **71** 62 6N 9 4 E
Dombasle **43** 49 8N 5 10 E
Dombe Grande **125** 12 56 S 13 8 E
Dombes **45** 46 3N 5 0 E
Dombóvár **53** 46 21N 18 9 E
Dombrád **53** 48 13N 21 54 E
Domburg **47** 51 34N 3 30 E
Domel, I = Letsok-aw-kyun **101** 11 30N 98 25 E
Domérat **44** 46 21N 2 32 E
Domett **143** 42 53 S 173 12 E
Domeyko **172** 29 0 S 71 30W
Domeyko, Cordillera **172** 24 30 S 69 0W
Domfront **42** 48 37N 0 40W
Dominador **172** 24 21 S 69 20W
Dominica I. **167** 15 20N 61 20W
Dominica Passage **167** 15 10N 61 20W
Dominican Rep. ■ **167** 19 0N 70 30W
Dömitz **48** 53 9N 11 13 E
Domme **44** 44 48N 1 12 E
Dommel, R. **47** 51 30N 5 20 E
Dommerby **73** 56 33N 9 5 E
Domo **91** 7 50N 47 10 E
Domodossóla **62** 46 6N 8 19 E
Dompaire **43** 48 14N 6 14 E
Dompierre **44** 46 31N 3 41 E
Dompin **120** 5 10N 2 5W
Domrémy **43** 48 26N 5 40 E
Domsjö **72** 63 16N 18 41 E
Domville, Mt. **139** 28 1 S 151 15 E
Domvraina **69** 38 15N 22 59 E
Domzale **63** 46 9N 3 6 E
Don Benito **57** 38 53N 5 51W
Don, C. **136** 11 18 S 131 46 E
Don Duong **101** 11 51N 108 35 E
Don Martín, Presa de **164** 27 30N 100 50W
Don Pedro Res. **163** 37 43N 120 24W
Don, R., India **97** 16 40N 75 55W
Don, R., Eng., U.K. **33** 53 41N 0 51W
Don, R., Scot., U.K. **37** 57 14N 2 5W
Don, R., U.S.S.R. **83** 49 35N 41 40 E
Dona Ana **127** 17 25 S 35 17 E
Donabate **38** 53 30N 6 9W
Donadea **38** 53 20N 6 45W
Donaghadee **38** 54 38N 5 32W
Donaghmore, Ireland **39** 52 54N 7 37W
Donaghmore, U.K. **38** 54 33N 6 50W
Donald **140** 36 23 S 143 0 E
Donalda **152** 52 35N 112 34W
Donaldsonville **159** 30 2N 91 50W
Donalsonville **157** 31 3N 84 52W
Donard **39** 53 1N 6 37W
Donau-Kanal **49** 49 1N 11 27 E
Donau, R. **53** 47 55N 17 20 E
Donaueschingen **49** 47 57N 8 30 E
Donawitz **52** 47 22N 15 4 E
Doncaster **33** 53 31N 1 9W
Dondo, Angola **74** 9 45 S 14 25 E
Dondo, Mozam. **127** 19 33 S 34 46 E
Dondo, Teluk **103** 0 29N 120 45 E
Dondra Head **97** 5 55N 80 40 E
Donegal **38** 54 39N 8 8W
Donegal □ **38** 54 53N 8 0W
Donegal B. **38** 54 30N 8 35W
Donegal Har. **38** 54 35N 8 15W
Donegal Pt. **39** 52 44N 9 38W
Doneraile **39** 52 13N 8 37W
Donets, R. **81** 48 50N 38 45 E
Donetsk **82** 48 0N 37 45 E
Dong **121** 9 20N 12 15 E
Dong Ba Thin **101** 12 8N 109 13 E
Dong Dang **100** 21 4N 106 57 E
Dong Giam **100** 19 15N 105 31 E
Dong Ha **100** 16 49N 107 8 E
Dong Hene **100** 16 16N 105 18 E
Dong Hoi **100** 17 29N 106 36 E
Dong Khe **100** 22 26N 106 27 E
Dong Van **100** 23 16N 105 22 E
Dong Xoai **101** 11 32N 106 55 E
Donga **121** 7 45N 10 2 E
Dongara **137** 29 14 S 114 57 E
Dongargarh **96** 21 10N 80 40 E
Dongen **47** 51 38N 4 56 E
Donges **42** 47 18N 2 4W
Donggala **103** 0 30 S 119 40 E
Dongola **122** 19 9N 30 22 E
Dongou **124** 2 0N 18 5 E
Donhead **28** 51 1N 2 8W
Donington **33** 52 54N 0 12W
Donington, C. **140** 34 45 S 136 0 E
Doniphan **159** 36 40N 90 50W
Donja Stubica **63** 45 59N 16 0 E
Donji Dušnik **66** 43 12N 22 5 E
Donji Miholjac **66** 45 45N 18 10 E
Donji Milanovac **66** 44 28N 22 6 E
Donji Vakuf **66** 44 8N 17 24 E
Donjon, Le **44** 46 22N 3 48 E
Dønna **74** 66 6N 12 30 E
Donna **74** 66 6N 12 30 E
Donna **159** 26 12N 98 2W
Donna Nook, Pt. **33** 53 29N 0 9 E
Donnaconna **151** 46 41N 71 41W
Donnelly's Crossing **142** 35 42 S 173 38 E
Donnybrook **137** 33 34 S 115 48 E
Donor's Hills **138** 18 42 S 140 33 E
Donoughmore **39** 52 0N 8 42W
Donskoy **81** 53 55N 38 15W

Donya Lendava Duncan Town

Donya Lendava 63 46 35N 16 25 E
Donzère 45 44 28N 4 43 E
Donzy 43 47 20N 3 6 E
Dooagh 38 53 59N 10 7W
Doochary 38 54 54N 8 10W
Doodlakine 137 31 34 S 117 51 E
Dooega Hd. 38 53 54N 10 3W
Doon L. 34 55 15N 4 22W
Doon, R. 34 55 26N 4 41W
Doonbeg 39 52 44N 9 31W
Doonbeg R. 39 52 42N 9 20W
Doorn 46 52 2N 5 20 E
Dor (Tantura) 90 32 37N 34 55 E
Dora Báltea, R. 62 45 42N 7 25 E
Dora, L. 136 22 0 S 123 0 E
Dora Riparia, R. 62 45 7N 7 24 E
Dorada, La 174 5 30N 74 40W
Dorading 123 8 30N 33 5 E
Doran L. 153 61 13N 108 6W
Dorat, Le 44 46 14N 1 5 E
Dörby 73 56 20N 16 12 E
Dorchester, Dorset, U.K. 28 50 42N 2 28W
Dorchester, Oxon., U.K. 28 51 38N 1 10W
Dorchester, C. 149 65 27N 77 27W
Dordogne □ 44 45 5N 0 40 E
Dordogne, R. 44 45 2N 0 36W
Dordrecht, Neth. 46 51 48N 4 39 E
Dordrecht, S. Afr. 128 31 20 S 27 3 E
Doré L. 153 54 46N 107 17W
Doré Lake 153 54 38N 107 54W
Dore, Mt. 44 45 32N 2 50 E
Dore, R. 44 45 59N 3 28 E
Dores 37 57 22N 4 20W
Dores do Indaiá 171 19 27 S 45 36W
Dorfen 49 48 16N 12 10 E
Dorgali 64 40 18N 9 35 E
Dori 121 14 3N 0 2W
Doring, R. 128 32 30 S 19 30 E
Dorion 150 45 23N 74 3W
Dorking 29 51 14N 0 20W
Dormaa-Ahenkro 120 7 15N 2 52W
Dormo, Ras 123 13 14N 42 35 E
Dornach 50 47 29N 7 37 E
Dornberg 63 45 45N 13 50 E
Dornbirn 52 47 25N 9 45 E
Dornes 43 46 48N 3 18 E
Dornie 36 57 17N 5 30W
Dornoch 37 57 52N 4 0W
Dornoch, Firth of 37 57 52N 4 0W
Dornogovi □ 106 44 0N 110 0 E
Doro 121 16 9N 0 51W
Dorog 53 47 42N 18 45 E
Dorogobuzh 80 54 50N 33 10 E
Dorohoi 70 47 56N 26 30 E
Döröö Nuur 105 47 40N 93 30 E
Dorre I. 137 25 13 S 113 12 E
Dorrigo 141 30 20 S 152 44 E
Dorris 160 41 59N 121 58W
Dorset □ 28 50 48N 2 25W
Dorsten 48 51 40N 6 55 E
Dorstone 28 52 4N 3 0W
Dortmund 48 51 32N 7 28 E
Dörtyol 92 36 52N 36 12 E
Dorum 48 53 40N 8 33 E
Doruma 126 4 42N 27 33 E
Dorya, W. 123 5 15N 41 30 E
Dos Bahías, C. 176 44 58 S 65 32W
Dos Cabezas 161 32 1N 109 37W
Dos Hermanas 57 37 16N 5 55W
Dos Palos 163 36 59N 120 37W
Dosara 121 12 20N 6 5 E
Doshi 93 35 35N 68 50 E
Dosso 121 13 0N 3 13 E
Döstrup 73 56 41N 9 42 E
Dot 152 50 12N 121 25W
Dothan 157 31 10N 85 25W
Dottignies 47 50 44N 3 19 E
Dotty, gasfield 19 53 3N 1 48 E
Douai 43 50 21N 3 4 E
Douala 121 4 0N 9 45 E
Douarnenez 42 48 6N 4 21W
Double Island Pt. 139 25 56 S 153 11 E
Doubrava, R. 52 49 40N 15 30 E
Doubs □ 43 47 10N 6 20 E
Doubs, R. 43 46 53N 5 1 E
Doubtful B. 137 34 15 S 119 28 E
Doubtful Sd. 143 45 20 S 166 49 E
Doubtless B. 142 34 55 S 173 26 E
Doucet 150 48 15N 76 35W
Doudeville 42 49 43N 0 47 E
Doué 42 47 11N 0 20W
Douentza 120 14 58N 2 48W
Douglas, S. Afr. 128 29 4 S 23 46 E
Douglas, U.K. 32 54 9N 4 29W
Douglas, U.K. 35 55 33N 3 50W
Douglas, Alaska, U.S.A. 147 58 23N 134 32W
Douglas, Ariz., U.S.A. 161 31 21N 109 30W
Douglas, Ga., U.S.A. 157 31 32N 82 52W
Douglas, Wyo., U.S.A. 158 42 45N 105 20W
Douglas Hd. 32 54 9N 4 28W
Douglastown 151 48 46N 64 24W
Douglasville 157 33 46N 84 43W
Douirat 118 33 2N 4 11W
Doukáton, Ákra 69 38 34N 20 30 E
Doulevant 43 48 22N 4 53 E
Doullens 43 50 10N 2 20 E
Doulus Hd. 39 51 57N 10 19W
Doumé 124 4 15N 13 25 E
Douna 120 12 40N 6 0W
Dounby 37 59 4N 3 13W
Doune 35 56 12N 4 3W
Dounreay 37 58 40N 3 28W
Dour 47 50 24N 3 46 E
Dourada, Serra 171 13 10 S 48 45W
Dourados 173 22 9 S 54 50W
Dourados, R. 173 21 58 S 54 18W
Dourdan 43 48 30N 2 0 E
Douro Litoral □ 55 41 10N 8 20W
Douro, R. 56 41 1N 8 16W
Douŭzeci Si Trei August 70 43 50N 28 40 E
Douvaine 45 46 19N 6 16 E
Douz 119 33 25N 9 0 E
Dove 32 52 51N 1 36W
Dove Brook 151 53 40N 57 40W
Dove Creek 161 37 53N 108 59W
Dove Dale 33 53 10N 1 47W
Dove, R. 33 54 20N 0 55W
Dover, Austral. 138 43 18 S 147 2 E
Dover, U.K. 29 51 7N 1 19 E
Dover, Del., U.S.A. 162 39 10N 75 31W
Dover, N.H., U.S.A. 162 43 5N 70 51W
Dover, N.J., U.S.A. 162 40 53N 74 34W
Dover, Ohio, U.S.A. 156 40 32N 81 30W
Dover-Foxcroft 151 45 14N 69 14W
Dover Plains 162 41 43N 73 35W
Dover, Pt. 137 32 32 S 125 32 E
Dover, Str. of 16 51 0N 1 30 E
Doveridge 32 52 54N 1 49 E
Dovey, R. 31 52 32N 4 0W
Dovre 71 62 0N 9 15 E
Dovrefjell 71 62 15N 9 33 E
Dowa 127 13 38 S 33 58 E
Dowagiac 156 42 0N 86 8W
Dowlatabad 93 28 20N 50 40 E
Down □ 38 54 20N 5 50W
Down, Co. 38 54 20N 6 0W
Downey 160 42 29N 112 3W
Downham 29 52 26N 0 15 E
Downham Market 29 52 36N 0 22 E
Downhill 38 55 10N 6 48W
Downieville 160 39 34N 120 50W
Downpatrick 38 54 20N 5 43W
Downpatrick Hd. 38 54 20N 9 21W
Downs Division 139 27 10 S 150 44 E
Downs, The 38 53 30N 7 15W
Downsville 162 42 5N 74 60W
Downton 28 51 0N 1 44W
Dowra 38 54 11N 8 2W
Doylestown 162 40 21N 75 10W
Doyung 99 33 40N 99 25 E
Dra, Cap 118 28 58N 11 0W
Draa, O. 118 30 29N 6 1W
Drachten 46 53 7N 6 5 E
Drăgăneşti 70 44 9N 24 32 E
Drăgăneşti-Viaşca 70 44 5N 25 33 E
Dragaš 66 42 5N 20 35 E
Drăgăsani 70 44 39N 24 17 E
Dragina 66 44 30N 19 25 E
Dragocvet 66 44 0N 21 15 E
Dragonera, I. 58 39 35N 2 19 E
Dragon's Mouth 174 11 0N 61 50W
Dragovistica, (Berivol) 66 42 22N 22 39 E
Draguignan 45 43 30N 6 27 E
Drain 160 43 45N 123 17W
Drake, Austral. 139 28 55 S 152 25 E
Drake, U.S.A. 158 47 56N 100 31W
Drake Passage 13 58 0 S 68 0W
Drakensberg 129 31 0 S 25 0 E
Dráma 68 41 9N 24 10 E
Dráma □ 68 41 10N 24 0 E
Drammen 71 59 42N 10 12 E
Drangajökull 74 66 9N 22 15W
Drangan 39 52 32N 7 36W
Drangedal 71 59 6N 9 3 E
Dranov, Ostrov 70 44 55N 29 30 E
Draperstown 38 54 48N 6 47 E
Dras 95 34 25N 75 48 E
Drau, R. 52 47 46N 13 33 E
Drava, R. 66 45 50N 18 0W
Draveil 43 48 41N 2 25 E
Dravograd 63 46 36N 15 5 E
Drawa, R. 54 53 6N 15 56 E
Drawno 54 53 13N 15 46 E
Drawsko Pom 54 53 35N 15 50 E
Drayton Valley 152 53 25N 114 58W
Dreghorn 34 55 36N 4 30W
Dreibergen 46 52 3N 5 17 E
Drejö 73 54 58N 10 25 E
Dren 66 43 8N 20 44 E
Drenagh 38 55 3N 6 55W
Drenthe □ 54 52 52N 6 40 E
Drentsche Hoofdvaart 46 52 39N 6 4 E
Dresden 48 51 2N 13 45 E
Dresden □ 48 51 12N 14 0 E
Dreumel 47 51 51N 5 26 E
Dreux 42 48 44N 1 23 E
Drezdenko 54 52 50N 15 49 E
Driel 46 51 57N 5 49 E
Driffield 33 54 0N 0 25W
Driftwood 150 49 8N 81 23 E
Drigana 119 20 51N 12 17 E
Driggs 160 43 50N 111 8W
Drimnin 36 56 36N 6 0W
Drimoleague 39 51 40N 9 15W
Drin-i-zi, R. 68 41 37N 20 28 E
Drina, R. 66 44 30N 19 10 E
Drincea, R. 70 44 20N 22 55 E
Drînceni 70 46 49N 28 10 E
Drini, R. 68 42 20N 20 0 E
Drinjača, R. 66 44 20N 19 0 E
Driva 71 62 33N 9 38 E
Driva, R. 71 62 34N 9 33 E
Drivstua 71 62 26N 9 37 E
Drniš 63 43 51N 16 10 E
Drøbak 71 59 39N 10 39 E
Dröbak 75 59 39N 10 48 E
Drobbakk 71 59 39N 10 39 E
Drobin 54 52 42N 19 58 E
Drogheda 38 53 45N 6 20W
Drogichin 80 52 15N 25 8 E
Drogobych 80 49 20N 23 30 E
Droichead Nua 39 53 11N 6 50W
Droitwich 28 52 16N 2 10W
Dromahair 38 54 13N 8 18W
Dromara 38 54 21N 6 1W
Dromard 38 54 14N 8 40W
Drôme □ 45 44 38N 5 15 E
Drôme, R. 45 44 46N 4 46 E
Dromedary, C. 141 36 17 S 150 10 E
Dromiskin 38 53 56N 6 25W
Dromod 38 53 52N 7 55W
Dromore, Down, U.K. 38 54 24N 6 10W
Dromore, Tyrone, U.K. 38 54 31N 7 28W
Dromore West 38 54 15N 8 50W
Dronero 62 44 29N 7 22 E
Dronfield, Austral. 138 21 12 S 140 3 E
Dronfield, U.K. 33 53 18N 1 29W
Dronninglund 73 57 10N 10 19 E
Dronrijp 46 53 11N 5 39 E
Drosendorf 52 48 52N 15 37 E
Drouin 141 38 10 S 145 53 E
Drouzhba 67 43 22N 28 0 E
Drum 38 54 6N 7 9W
Drumbeg, N. Ire., U.K. 38 54 33N 6 0W
Drumbeg, Scot., U.K. 36 58 15N 5 12W
Drumcard 38 54 14N 7 42W
Drumcliffe 38 54 20N 8 30W
Drumcondra 38 53 50N 6 40W
Drumheller 152 51 25N 112 40W
Drumjohn 34 55 14N 4 15W
Drumkeerin 38 54 10N 8 8W
Drumlish 38 53 50N 7 47W
Drummond 160 46 46N 113 4W
Drummond I. 150 46 0N 83 40W
Drummond Pt. 139 34 9 S 135 16 E
Drummond Ra. 138 23 45 S 147 10 E
Drummondville 150 45 55N 72 25W
Drummore 34 54 41N 4 53W
Drumquin 38 54 38N 7 30W
Drumright 159 35 59N 96 38W
Drumshanbo 38 54 2N 8 4W
Drumsna 38 53 57N 8 0W
Drunen 47 51 41N 5 8 E
Druridge B. 35 55 16N 1 32W
Druskinankaj 80 54 3N 23 58 E
Drut, R. 80 52 32N 30 0 E
Druten 46 51 53N 5 36 E
Druya 80 55 45N 27 15 E
Druzhina 77 68 14N 145 18 E
Drvar 63 44 21N 16 2 E
Drvenik 63 43 27N 16 3 E
Dry Tortugas 166 24 38N 82 55W
Dryanovo 67 42 59N 25 28 E
Dryden, Can. 153 49 50N 92 50W
Dryden, N.Y., U.S.A. 162 42 30N 76 18W
Dryden, Tex., U.S.A. 159 30 3N 102 3W
Drygalski I. 13 66 0 S 92 0 E
Drygarn Fawr 31 52 13N 3 39W
Drymen 70 56 4N 4 28W
Drynoch 36 57 17N 6 18W
Drysdale I. 138 11 41 S 136 0 E
Drysdale, R. 136 13 59 S 126 51 E
Dschang 121 5 32N 10 3 E
Du 121 10 26N 1 34W
Du Bois 156 41 8N 78 46W
Du Quoin 158 38 0N 89 10W
Duanesburg 162 42 45N 74 11W
Duaringa 138 23 42 S 149 42 E
Duba 92 27 10N 35 40 E
Dubai = Dubayy 93 24 10N 55 20 E
Dubawnt, L. 153 63 4N 101 42W
Dubawnt, R. 153 64 33N 100 6W
Dubbayy 93 24 10N 55 20 E
Dubbeldam 46 51 47N 4 43 E
Dubbo 141 32 11 S 148 35 E
Dubele 126 2 56N 29 35 E
Dübendorf 51 47 24N 8 37 E
Dubenskiy 84 51 27N 56 38 E
Dubh Artach 34 56 8N 6 40W
Dubica 63 45 17N 16 48 E
Dublin, Ireland 38 53 20N 6 18W
Dublin, Ga., U.S.A. 157 32 30N 83 0W
Dublin, Tex., U.S.A. 159 32 0N 98 20W
Dublin □ 38 53 24N 6 20W
Dublin, B. 39 53 24N 6 20W
Dubna 81 54 8N 36 52 E
Dubno 80 50 25N 25 45 E
Dubois 160 44 7N 112 9W
Dubossary 82 47 15N 29 10 E
Dubossasy Vdkhr. 82 47 30N 29 0 E
Dubovka 83 49 5N 44 50 E
Dubovskoye 83 47 28N 42 40 E
Dubrajpur 95 23 48N 87 25 E
Dubrékah 120 9 46N 13 31W
Dubrovitsa 80 51 31N 26 35 E
Dubrovnik 66 42 39N 18 6 E
Dubrovskoye 77 58 55N 111 0 E
Dubuque 158 42 30N 90 41W
Duchesne 160 40 14N 110 22W
Duchess 138 21 20 S 139 50 E
Ducie I. 131 24 47 S 124 40W
Duck Cr., N.S.W., Austral. 139 31 4 S 147 6 E
Duck Cr., W. Australia, Austral. 136 22 37 S 116 53 E
Duck Lake 153 52 50N 106 16W
Duck, Mt. 153 51 27N 100 35W
Duck Mt. Prov. Parks 153 51 45N 101 0W
Duckwall Mtn. 163 37 58N 120 7W
Duddington 29 52 36N 0 32W
Duddon R. 32 54 12N 3 15W
Düdelange 47 49 29N 6 5 E
Duderstadt 48 51 30N 10 15 E
Dudhi 99 24 15N 83 10 E
Dudhnai 98 25 59N 90 47 E
Düdingen 50 46 52N 7 12 E
Dudinka 77 69 30N 86 0 E
Dudley 28 52 30N 2 5W
Dudna, R. 96 19 36N 76 20 E
Dueñas 56 41 52N 4 33W
Düeni 70 44 51N 28 10 E
Dueodde 73 54 59N 15 4 E
Dueré 171 11 20 S 49 17W
Duero, R. 56 41 37N 4 25W
Duff Is. 142 9 0 S 167 0 E
Duffel 47 51 6N 4 30 E
Duffield 33 52 59N 1 30W
Dufftown 37 57 26N 3 9W
Dufourspitz 50 45 56N 7 52 E
Dugi, I. 63 44 0N 15 0 E
Dugo Selo 63 45 51N 16 18 E
Duhak 93 33 20N 57 30 E
Duifken Pt. 138 12 33 S 141 38 E
Duisburg 48 51 27N 6 42 E
Duitama 174 5 50N 73 2W
Duiveland 47 51 38N 4 0 E
Duiwelskloof 129 23 42 S 30 10 E
Dukana 126 3 59N 37 20 E
Dukati 68 40 16N 19 32 E
Duke I. 152 54 50N 131 20W
Dukhan 93 25 25N 50 50 E
Dukhovshchina 80 55 15N 32 27 E
Duki 93 30 14N 68 25 E
Dukla 54 49 30N 21 35 E
Duku, North-Eastern, Nigeria 121 10 43N 10 43 E
Duku, North-Western, Nigeria 121 11 11N 4 55 E
Dulas B. 31 53 22N 4 16W
Dulawan 103 7 5N 124 20 E
Dulce, Golfo 166 8 40N 83 20W
Dulce, R. 172 29 30 S 63 0W
Duleek 38 53 40N 6 24W
Dŭlgopol 67 43 3N 27 22 E
Dullewala 94 31 50N 71 25 E
Dülmen 48 51 49N 7 18 E
Dulnain Bridge 37 57 19N 3 40W
Dulovo 67 43 48N 27 9 E
Dululu 138 23 48 S 150 15 E
Duluth 158 46 48N 92 10W
Dulverton 28 51 2N 3 33W
Dum Dum 95 22 39N 88 26 E
Dum Duma 99 27 40N 95 40 E
Dumaguete 103 9 17N 123 15 E
Dumai 102 1 35N 101 20 E
Dumaran I. 103 10 33N 119 50 E
Dumaring 103 1 46N 118 10 E
Dumas, Ark., U.S.A. 159 33 52N 91 30W
Dumas, Okla., U.S.A. 159 35 50N 101 58W
Dûmat al Jandal 92 29 55N 39 40 E
Dumba I. 71 61 43N 4 50 E
Dumbarton 34 55 58N 4 35W
Dumbleyung 137 33 17 S 117 42 E
Dumbrăveni 70 46 14N 24 34 E
Dumfries 35 55 4N 3 37W
Dumfries & Galloway □ 35 54 30N 4 0W
Dumfries (□) 26 55 0N 3 30W
Dŭmienesti 70 46 44N 27 1 E
Dumka 95 24 0N 87 22 E
Dumoine L. 150 46 55N 77 55W
Dumoine, R. 150 46 13N 77 51W
Dumraon 95 25 33N 84 8 E
Dumyât 122 31 24N 31 48 E
Dumyât, Masabb 122 31 28N 32 0 E
Dun Laoghaire, (Dunleary) 39 53 17N 6 9W
Dun-le-Palestel 44 46 18N 1 39 E
Dun-sur-Auron 43 46 53N 2 33 E
Duna, R. 53 45 51N 18 48 E
Dunaff Hd. 38 55 18N 7 30W
Dunaföldvár 53 46 50N 18 57 E
Dunai, R. 53 47 50N 18 52 E
Dunaj, R. 67 45 17N 29 32 E
Dunajec, R. 54 50 12N 20 52 E
Dunajska Streda 53 48 0N 17 37 E
Dunamanagh 38 54 53N 7 20W
Dunans 34 56 4N 5 9W
Dunany Pt. 38 53 51N 6 15W
Dunapatai 53 46 39N 19 4 E
Dunaszekcsö 53 46 22N 18 45 E
Dunaújváros 53 47 0N 18 57 E
Dunav, R. 66 45 0N 20 21 E
Dunavtsi 66 43 57N 22 53 E
Dunback 143 45 23 S 170 36 E
Dunbar, Austral. 138 16 0 S 142 22 E
Dunbar, U.K. 35 56 0N 2 32W
Dunbarton (□) 26 56 4N 4 42W
Dunbeath 37 58 15N 3 25W
Dunblane 35 56 10N 3 58W
Dunboyne 38 53 25N 6 30W
Duncan, Can. 152 48 45N 123 40W
Duncan, Ariz., U.S.A. 161 32 46N 109 6W
Duncan, Okla., U.S.A. 159 34 25N 98 0W
Duncan L. 152 62 51N 113 58W
Duncan, L., Brit. Col., Can. 150 50 20N 117 0W
Duncan, L., Qué., Can. 152 53 29N 77 58W
Duncan Pass. 101 11 0N 92 30 E
Duncan Town 166 22 15N 75 45W

Duncansby **Ecoporanga**

Duncansby	**37**	58 37N	3 3W
Duncansby Head	**37**	58 39N	3 0W
Dunchurch	**28**	52 21N	1 19W
Duncormick	**39**	53 14N	6 40W
Dundalk, Ireland	**38**	53 55N	6 45W
Dundalk, U.S.A.	**162**	39 15N	76 31W
Dundalk, B.	**38**	53 55N	6 15W
Dundas	**150**	43 17N	79 59W
Dundas I.	**152**	54 30N	130 50W
Dundas, L.	**137**	32 35S	121 50E
Dundas Str.	**136**	11 15S	131 35E
Dundee, S. Afr.	**129**	28 11S	30 15E
Dundee, U.K.	**35**	56 29N	3 0W
Dundee, U.S.A.	**162**	42 32N	76 59W
Dundgovi □	**106**	45 10N	106 0E
Dundo	**124**	7 23S	20 48E
Dundonald	**38**	54 37N	5 50W
Dundoo	**139**	27 40S	144 37E
Dundrennan	**35**	54 49N	3 56W
Dundrum, Ireland	**39**	53 17N	6 15W
Dundrum, U.K.	**38**	54 17N	5 50W
Dundwara	**95**	27 48N	79 9E
Dunedin, N.Z.	**143**	45 50S	170 33E
Dunedin, U.S.A.	**157**	28 1N	82 45W
Dunedin, R.	**152**	59 30N	124 5W
Dunfanaghy	**38**	55 10N	7 59W
Dunfermline	**35**	56 5N	3 28W
Dungannon	**38**	54 30N	6 47W
Dungannon □	**38**	54 30N	6 55W
Dungarpur	**94**	23 52N	73 45E
Dungarvan	**39**	52 6N	7 40W
Dungarvan Harb.	**39**	52 5N	7 35W
Dungas	**121**	13 4N	9 20E
Dungavel	**35**	55 37N	4 7W
Dungbura La	**99**	34 41N	93 18E
Dungeness	**29**	50 54N	0 59E
Dungiven	**38**	54 55N	6 56W
Dunglow	**38**	54 57N	8 20W
Dungo, L. do	**128**	17 15S	19 0E
Dungog	**141**	32 22S	151 40E
Dungourney	**39**	51 58N	8 5W
Dungu	**124**	2 32N	28 22E
Dungunâb	**122**	21 10N	37 9E
Dungunâb, Khalîg	**122**	21 5N	37 12E
Dunhinda Falls	**97**	7 5N	81 6E
Dunières	**45**	45 13N	4 20E
Dunk I.	**138**	17 59S	146 14E
Dunkeld, Austral.	**140**	37 40S	142 22E
Dunkeld, U.K.	**37**	56 34N	3 36W
Dunkerque	**43**	51 2N	2 20E
Dunkery Beacon	**28**	51 15N	3 37W
Dunkineely	**38**	54 38N	8 22W
Dunkirk	**156**	42 30N	79 18W
Dunkirk = Dunkerque	**43**	51 2N	2 20E
Dunkuj	**123**	11 15N	33 0E
Dunkur	**123**	11 58N	35 58E
Dunkwa, Central, Ghana	**120**	6 0N	1 47W
Dunkwa, Central, Ghana	**121**	5 30N	1 0W
Dunlap	**158**	41 50N	95 30W
Dunlavin	**39**	53 3N	6 40W
Dunleary = Dun Laoghaire	**39**	53 17N	6 8W
Dunleer	**38**	53 50N	6 23W
Dunlin, oilfield	**19**	61 12N	1 40E
Dunloe, Gap of	**39**	52 2N	9 40W
Dunlop	**34**	55 43N	4 32W
Dunloy	**38**	55 1N	6 25W
Dunmanus B.	**39**	51 31N	9 50W
Dunmanway	**39**	51 43N	9 8W
Dunmara	**138**	16 42S	133 25E
Dunmod	**105**	47 45N	106 58E
Dunmore, Ireland	**38**	53 37N	8 44W
Dunmore, U.S.A.	**162**	41 27N	75 38W
Dunmore East	**39**	52 9N	7 0W
Dunmore Town	**166**	25 30N	76 39W
Dunmurry	**38**	54 33N	6 0W
Dunn	**157**	35 18N	78 36W
Dunnellon	**157**	29 4N	82 28W
Dunnet	**37**	58 37N	3 20W
Dunnet B.	**37**	58 37N	3 23W
Dunnet Hd.	**37**	58 38N	3 22W
Dunning, U.K.	**35**	56 18N	3 37W
Dunning, U.S.A.	**158**	41 52N	100 4W
Dunolly	**140**	36 51S	143 44E
Dunoon	**34**	55 57N	4 56W
Dunqul	**122**	23 40N	31 10E
Duns	**35**	55 47N	2 20W
Dunscore	**35**	55 8N	3 48W
Dunseith	**158**	48 49N	100 2W
Dunsford	**30**	50 41N	3 40W
Dunshaughlin	**38**	53 31N	6 32W
Dunsmuir	**160**	41 0N	122 10W
Dunstable	**29**	51 53N	0 31W
Dunstan Mts.	**143**	44 53S	169 35E
Dunster, Can.	**152**	53 8N	119 50W
Dunster, U.K.	**28**	51 11N	3 28W
Dunston	**28**	52 46N	2 7W
Duntelchaig, L.	**37**	57 20N	4 18W
Dunton Green	**29**	51 17N	0 11E
Duntroon	**143**	44 51S	170 40E
Dunŭrea, R.	**70**	45 0N	29 40E
Dunvegan	**36**	57 26N	6 35W
Dunvegan Hd.	**36**	57 30N	6 42W
Dunvegan L.	**153**	60 8N	107 10W
Duong Dong	**101**	10 13N	103 58E
Dupree	**158**	45 4N	101 35W
Dupuyer	**160**	48 11N	112 31W
Duque de Caxias	**173**	22 45S	43 19W
Dura	**90**	31 31N	35 1E
Durack	**136**	15 33S	127 52E
Durack Ra.	**136**	16 50S	127 40E
Durance, R.	**45**	43 55N	4 45E
Durand	**156**	42 54N	83 58W
Durango, Mexico	**164**	24 3N	104 39W
Durango, Spain	**58**	43 13N	2 40W
Durango, U.S.A.	**161**	37 10N	107 50W
Durango □	**164**	25 0N	105 0W
Duranillin	**137**	33 30S	116 45E
Durant	**159**	34 0N	96 25W
Duratón, R.	**56**	41 27N	4 0W
Durazno	**172**	33 25S	56 38W
Durazzo = Durrësi	**68**	41 19N	19 28E
Durban, France	**44**	43 0N	2 49W
Durban, S. Afr.	**129**	29 49S	31 1E
Dúrcal	**57**	37 0N	3 34W
Đurdevac	**66**	46 2N	17 3E
Düren	**48**	50 48N	6 30E
Durg	**96**	21 15N	81 22E
Durgapur	**95**	23 30N	87 9E
Durham, Can.	**150**	44 10N	80 49W
Durham, U.K.	**33**	54 47N	1 34W
Durham, N.C., U.S.A.	**157**	36 0N	78 55W
Durham, N.H., U.S.A.	**162**	43 8N	70 56W
Durham □	**32**	54 42N	1 45W
Durham Downs	**139**	26 6S	149 3E
Durlstone Hd.	**28**	50 35N	1 58W
Durmitor Mt.	**66**	43 18N	19 0E
Dûrmûneşti	**70**	46 21N	26 33E
Durness	**37**	58 34N	4 45W
Durness, Kyle of	**37**	58 35N	4 55W
Durrandella	**138**	24 3S	146 35E
Durrësi	**68**	41 19N	19 28E
Durrie	**138**	25 40S	140 15E
Durrington	**28**	51 12N	1 47W
Durrow	**39**	53 20N	7 31W
Durrus	**39**	51 37N	9 32W
Dursey Hd.	**39**	51 34N	10 41W
Dursey I.	**39**	51 36N	10 12W
Dursley	**28**	51 41N	2 21W
Durtal	**42**	47 40N	0 18W
Duru	**126**	4 20N	28 50E
Durup	**73**	56 45N	8 57E
D'Urville Island	**143**	40 50S	173 55E
Duryea	**162**	41 20N	75 45W
Dusa Mareb	**91**	5 40N	46 33E
Dûsh	**122**	24 35N	30 41E
Dushak	**76**	37 20N	60 10E
Dushanbe	**85**	38 33N	68 48E
Dusheti	**83**	42 0N	44 55E
Dushore	**162**	41 31N	76 24W
Dusky Sd.	**143**	45 47S	166 30E
Dussejour, C.	**136**	14 45S	128 13E
Düsseldorf	**48**	51 15N	6 46E
Dussen	**46**	51 44N	4 59E
Duszniki Zdrój	**54**	51 26N	16 22E
Dutch Harbour	**147**	53 54N	166 35W
Dutlhe	**128**	23 58S	23 46E
Dutsan Wai	**121**	10 50N	8 10E
Dutton, R.	**138**	20 44S	143 10E
Duvan	**84**	55 42N	57 54E
Duved	**72**	63 24N	12 55E
Duvno	**66**	43 42N	17 13E
Duwadami	**92**	24 35N	44 15E
Duzdab = Zāhedān	**93**	29 30N	60 50E
Dve Mogili	**67**	43 47N	25 55E
Dvina, Sev.	**78**	56 30N	24 0E
Dvina, Zap.	**80**	61 40N	45 30E
Dvinsk = Daugavpils	**80**	55 33N	26 32E
Dvinskaya Guba	**78**	65 0N	39 0E
Dvor	**63**	45 4N	16 22E
Dvorce	**53**	49 50N	17 34E
Dvur Králové	**52**	50 27N	15 50E
Dwarka	**94**	22 18N	69 8E
Dwellingup	**137**	32 43S	116 4E
Dwight	**156**	41 5N	88 25W
Dyakovskoya	**81**	60 5N	41 12E
Dyatkovo	**80**	53 48N	34 27E
Dyaul, I.	**138**	3 0S	150 55E
Dyce	**37**	57 12N	2 11W
Dyer	**163**	37 40N	118 5W
Dyer, C.	**149**	67 0N	61 0W
Dyerbeldzhin	**85**	41 13N	74 54E
Dyersburg	**159**	36 2N	89 20W
Dyfed □	**31**	52 0N	4 30W
Dyje, R.	**53**	48 50N	16 45E
Dyke Acland Bay	**138**	8 45S	148 45E
Dykehead	**37**	56 43N	3 0W
Dyle, R.	**47**	50 58N	4 41E
Dymchurch	**29**	51 2N	1 0E
Dymock	**28**	51 58N	2 27W
Dynevor Downs	**139**	28 10S	144 20E
Dynów	**54**	49 50N	22 11E
Dypvag	**71**	79 40N	9 8E
Dyrnes	**71**	63 25N	7 52E
Dysart, Can.	**153**	50 57N	104 2W
Dysart, U.K.	**35**	56 8N	3 8W
Dysjön	**72**	62 38N	15 31E
Dyulgeri	**67**	42 18N	27 23E
Dyurtyuli	**84**	55 9N	54 4E
Dzambeyty	**83**	50 15N	52 30E
Dzaudzhikau = Ordzhonikidze	**83**	43 0N	44 35E
Dzerzhinsk	**80**	53 40N	27 7E
Dzhailma	**76**	51 30N	61 50E
Dzhalal-Abad	**84**	40 56N	73 0E
Dzhalinda	**77**	53 40N	124 0E
Dzhambeyty	**84**	50 16N	52 35E
Dzhambul	**85**	42 54N	71 22E
Dzhambul, Gora	**85**	44 54N	73 0E
Dzhankoi	**82**	45 40N	34 30E
Dzhanybek	**83**	49 25N	46 50E
Dzhardzhan	**77**	68 10N	123 5E
Dzharkurgan	**85**	37 31N	67 25E
Dzhelinde	**77**	70 0N	114 20E
Dzherzhinsk	**80**	53 48N	27 19E
Dzhetygara	**84**	52 11N	61 12E
Dzhetym, Khrebet	**85**	41 30N	77 0E
Dzhezkazgan	**76**	47 10N	67 40E
Dzhizak	**85**	40 6N	67 50E
Dzhugdzur, Khrebet	**77**	57 30N	138 0E
Dzhuma	**85**	39 42N	66 40E
Dzhumgoltau, Khrebet	**85**	42 15N	74 30E
Dzhungarskiye Vorota	**76**	45 0N	82 0E
Dzhvari	**83**	42 42N	42 4E
Działdowo	**54**	53 15N	20 15E
Działoszyce	**54**	50 22N	20 20E
Działoszyn	**54**	51 6N	18 50E
Dzibilchaltún	**165**	21 5N	89 36W
Dzierzgon	**54**	53 58N	19 20E
Dzierzoniow	**54**	50 45N	16 39E
Dzilam de Bravo	**165**	21 24N	88 53W
Dzioua	**119**	33 14N	5 14E
Dziwnów	**54**	54 2N	14 45E
Dzungaria	**105**	44 10N	88 0E
Dzungarian Gates = Dzhungarskiye V.	**105**	45 0N	82 0E
E			
Eabamet, L.	**150**	51 30N	87 46W
Eads	**158**	38 30N	102 46W
Eagle, Alaska, U.S.A.	**147**	64 44N	141 29W
Eagle, Colo., U.S.A.	**160**	39 45N	106 55W
Eagle Butt	**158**	45 1N	101 12W
Eagle Grove	**158**	42 37N	93 53W
Eagle L., Calif., U.S.A.	**160**	40 35N	120 50W
Eagle L., Me., U.S.A.	**151**	46 23N	69 22W
Eagle Lake	**159**	29 35N	96 21W
Eagle Nest	**161**	36 33N	105 13W
Eagle Pass	**159**	28 45N	100 35W
Eagle Pk.	**163**	38 10N	119 25W
Eagle Pt.	**136**	16 11S	124 23E
Eagle, R.	**151**	53 36N	57 26W
Eagle River	**158**	45 55N	89 17W
Eaglehawk	**140**	36 43S	144 16E
Eagles Mere	**162**	41 25N	76 33W
Eaglesfield	**35**	55 3N	3 12W
Eagleshan	**34**	55 44N	4 18W
Eakring	**33**	53 9N	0 59W
Ealing	**29**	51 30N	0 19W
Earaheedy	**137**	25 34S	121 29E
Earby	**32**	53 55N	2 8W
Eardisland	**28**	52 14N	2 50W
Eardisley	**28**	52 8N	3 0W
Earith	**29**	52 21N	0 1E
Earl Grey	**153**	50 57N	104 43W
Earl Shilton	**28**	52 35N	1 20W
Earl Soham	**29**	52 14N	1 15E
Earle	**159**	35 18N	90 26W
Earlimart	**163**	35 53N	119 16W
Earls Barton	**29**	52 16N	0 44W
Earl's Colne	**29**	51 56N	0 43E
Earlsferry	**35**	56 11N	2 50W
Earlston	**35**	55 39N	2 40W
Earn, L.	**34**	56 23N	4 14W
Earn, R.	**35**	56 20N	3 19W
Earnslaw, Mt.	**143**	44 32S	168 27E
Earoo	**137**	29 34S	118 22E
Earsdon	**35**	55 4N	1 30W
Earth	**159**	34 18N	102 30W
Easebourne	**29**	51 0N	0 42W
Easington, Durham, U.K.	**33**	54 50N	1 24W
Easington, Yorks., U.K.	**33**	54 40N	0 7W
Easington Colliery	**33**	54 49N	1 19W
Easingwold	**33**	54 8N	1 11W
Easky	**38**	54 17N	8 58W
Easley	**157**	34 52N	82 35W
East Aberthaw	**31**	51 23N	3 23W
East Anglian Hts.	**29**	52 10N	0 17E
East Angus	**151**	45 30N	71 40W
East, B.	**159**	29 2N	89 16W
East Barming	**29**	51 15N	0 29E
East Bathurst	**151**	47 35N	65 40W
East Bengal	**99**	24 0N	90 0E
East Bergholt	**29**	51 58N	1 2E
East Beskids, mts.	**53**	49 30N	18 45E
East Brent	**28**	51 14N	2 55W
East C., N.Z.	**142**	37 42S	178 35E
East C., P.N.G.	**135**	10 13S	150 53E
East Chicago	**156**	41 40N	87 30W
East China Sea	**105**	30 5N	126 0E
East Coulee	**152**	51 23N	112 27W
East Cowes	**28**	50 45N	1 17W
East Dereham	**29**	52 40N	0 57E
East Falkland	**176**	51 30S	58 30W
East Fen	**33**	53 4N	0 5E
East Florenceville	**151**	46 26N	67 36W
East Grand Forks	**158**	47 55N	97 5W
East Greenwich	**162**	41 40N	71 27W
East Grinstead	**29**	51 8N	0 1W
East Harling	**29**	52 26N	0 55E
East Hartford	**162**	41 46N	72 39W
East Helena	**160**	46 37N	111 58W
East Ilsley	**28**	51 33N	1 15W
East Indies	**102**	0 0	120 0E
East Jordan	**156**	45 10N	85 7W
East Kilbride	**35**	55 46N	4 10W
East Kirkby	**33**	53 5N	1 15W
East Lansing	**156**	42 44N	84 37W
East Linton	**35**	56 0N	2 40W
East Liverpool	**156**	40 39N	80 35W
East London	**129**	33 0S	27 55E
East Looe	**30**	50 22N	4 28W
East Los Angeles	**163**	34 1N	118 9W
East Lynne	**141**	35 35S	150 16E
East Main (Eastmain)	**151**	52 20N	78 30W
East Markham	**33**	53 15N	0 53W
East Midlands, oilfield	**19**	53 20N	0 45W
East Moor	**33**	53 15N	1 30W
East, Mt.	**137**	29 0S	122 30E
East Orange	**162**	40 46N	74 13W
East P.	**151**	46 27N	61 58W
East Pakistan = Bangladesh	**99**	24 0N	90 0E
East Pine	**152**	55 48N	120 5W
East Point	**157**	33 40N	84 28W
East Providence	**162**	41 49N	71 23W
East Retford	**33**	53 19N	0 55W
East St. Louis	**158**	38 36N	90 10W
East Schelde, R.	**47**	51 38N	3 40E
E. Siberian Sea	**77**	73 0N	160 0E
East Stroudsburg	**162**	41 0N	75 11W
East Sussex □	**29**	50 55N	0 20E
East Tawas	**156**	44 17N	83 31W
East Toorale	**139**	30 27S	145 28E
East Walker, R.	**163**	38 52N	119 10W
East Wemyss	**35**	56 8N	3 5W
East Woodhay	**28**	51 21N	1 26W
Eastbourne, N.Z.	**142**	41 19S	174 55E
Eastbourne, U.K.	**29**	50 46N	0 18E
Eastchurch	**29**	51 23N	0 53E
Eastend	**153**	49 32N	108 50W
Easter Islands	**143**	27 0S	109 0W
Easter Ross, dist.	**37**	57 50N	4 35W
Easter Skeld	**36**	60 12N	1 27W
Eastern □	**126**	0 0S	38 30E
Eastern Cr.	**138**	20 40S	141 35E
Eastern Ghats	**97**	15 0N	80 0E
Eastern Group, Is.	**137**	33 30S	124 30E
Eastern Province □	**120**	8 15N	11 0W
Easterville	**153**	53 8N	99 49W
Easthampton	**162**	42 16N	72 40W
Eastland	**159**	32 26N	98 45W
Eastleigh	**28**	50 58N	1 21W
Eastmain (East Main)	**150**	52 20N	78 30W
Eastmain, R.	**150**	52 27N	72 26W
Eastman	**157**	32 13N	83 41W
Eastnor	**28**	52 2N	2 22W
Easton, Dorset, U.K.	**28**	50 32N	2 27W
Easton, Northants., U.K.	**29**	52 37N	0 31W
Easton, Somerset, U.K.	**28**	51 28N	2 42W
Easton, Md., U.S.A.	**162**	38 47N	76 7W
Easton, Pa., U.S.A.	**162**	40 41N	75 15W
Easton, Wash., U.S.A.	**160**	47 14N	121 8W
Eastport, Maine, U.S.A.	**151**	44 57N	67 0W
Eastport, N.Y., U.S.A.	**162**	40 50N	72 44W
Eastry	**29**	51 15N	1 19E
Eastview	**150**	45 27N	75 40W
Eastville	**162**	37 21N	75 57W
Eastwood	**33**	53 2N	1 17W
Eaton, U.K.	**29**	52 52N	0 46W
Eaton, U.S.A.	**158**	40 35N	104 42W
Eaton, L.	**136**	22 55S	130 57E
Eaton Socon	**29**	52 13N	0 18W
Eatonia	**153**	51 13N	109 25W
Eatonton	**157**	33 22N	83 24W
Eatontown	**162**	40 18N	74 7W
Eau Claire, S.C., U.S.A.	**157**	34 5N	81 2W
Eau Claire, Wis., U.S.A.	**158**	44 46N	91 30W
Eauze	**44**	43 53N	0 7E
Eaval, Mt.	**36**	57 33N	7 12W
Ebagoola	**138**	14 15S	143 12E
Eban	**121**	9 40N	4 50E
Ebberston	**33**	54 14N	0 35W
Ebbw Vale	**31**	51 47N	3 12W
Ebeggui	**119**	26 2N	6 0E
Ebeltoft	**75**	56 12N	10 41E
Ebensee	**52**	47 48N	13 46E
Eberbach	**49**	49 27N	8 59E
Eberswalde	**48**	52 49N	13 50E
Ebikon	**51**	47 5N	8 21E
Ebingen	**49**	48 13N	9 1E
Ebino	**110**	32 2N	130 48E
Ebnat-Kappel	**51**	47 16N	9 7E
Eboli	**65**	40 39N	15 2E
Ebolowa	**121**	2 55N	11 10E
Ebony	**128**	22 6S	15 15E
Ébrié, Lagune	**120**	5 12N	4 40W
Ebro, Pantano del	**56**	43 0N	3 58W
Ebro, R.	**58**	41 49N	1 5W
Ebstorf	**48**	53 2N	10 23E
Ecaussines-d' Enghien	**47**	50 35N	4 11E
Ecclefechan	**35**	55 3N	3 18W
Eccleshall	**28**	52 52N	2 14W
Eceabat	**68**	40 11N	26 21E
Éceuillé	**42**	47 10N	1 19E
Ech Chebbi	**118**	26 41N	0 29E
Echallens	**50**	46 38N	6 38E
Echaneni	**77**	27 33S	32 6E
Echelles, Les	**45**	45 27N	5 45E
Echizen-Misaki	**111**	35 59N	135 57E
Echmiadzin	**83**	40 12N	44 19E
Echo Bay, N.W.T., Can.	**148**	66 10N	117 40W
Echo Bay, Ont., Can.	**150**	46 29N	84 4W
Echoing, R.	**153**	55 51N	92 5W
Echt, Neth.	**47**	51 7N	5 52E
Echt, U.K.	**37**	57 8N	2 26W
Echternach	**47**	49 49N	6 3E
Echuca	**141**	36 3S	144 46E
Ecija	**57**	37 30N	5 10W
Eck L.	**34**	56 5N	5 0W
Eckernförde	**48**	54 26N	9 50E
Eckington	**33**	53 19N	1 21W
Eclipse Is.	**136**	13 54S	126 19E
Écommoy	**42**	47 50N	0 17E
Ecoporanga	**171**	18 23S	40 50W

Écos Eldorado

Écos	**43**	49 9N	1 35E
Écouché	**42**	48 42N	0 10W
Ecuador ■	**174**	2 0S	78 0W
Ed	**73**	58 55N	11 55E
Ed Dabbura	**122**	17 40N	34 15E
Ed Damer	**122**	17 27N	34 0E
Ed Debba	**122**	18 0N	30 51E
Ed-Déffa	**122**	30 40N	26 30E
Ed Deim	**123**	10 10N	28 20E
Ed Dueim	**123**	14 0N	32 10E
Ed Dzong	**99**	32 11N	90 12E
Edah	**137**	28 16S	117 10E
Edam, Can.	**153**	53 11N	108 46W
Edam, Neth.	**46**	52 31N	5 3E
Edapally	**97**	11 19N	78 3E
Eday, I.	**37**	59 11N	2 47W
Eday Sd.	**37**	59 12N	2 45W
Edd	**123**	14 0N	41 30E
Edda, oilfield	**19**	56 25N	3 15E
Edderton	**37**	57 50N	4 10W
Eddrachillis B.	**36**	58 16N	5 10W
Eddystone	**30**	50 11N	4 16W
Eddystone Pt.	**138**	40 59S	148 20E
Ede, Neth.	**46**	52 4N	5 40E
Ede, Nigeria	**121**	7 45N	4 29E
Ede, Sweden	**72**	62 10N	16 50E
Édea	**121**	3 51N	10 9E
Edegem	**47**	51 10N	4 27E
Edehon L.	**153**	60 25N	97 15W
Edekel, Adrar	**119**	23 56N	6 47E
Eden, Austral.	**141**	37 3S	149 55E
Eden, U.K.	**38**	54 44N	5 47W
Eden, Tex., U.S.A.	**159**	31 16N	99 50W
Eden, Wyo., U.S.A.	**160**	42 2N	109 27W
Eden L.	**153**	56 38N	100 15W
Eden, R.	**32**	54 57N	3 2W
Edenbridge	**29**	51 12N	0 4E
Edenburg	**128**	29 43S	25 58E
Edendale	**143**	46 19S	168 48E
Edenderry	**39**	53 21N	7 3W
Edenton	**157**	36 5N	76 36W
Edenville	**129**	27 37S	27 34E
Ederny	**38**	54 32N	7 40W
Edgar	**158**	40 25N	98 0W
Edgartown	**162**	41 22N	70 28W
Edge Hill	**28**	52 7N	1 28W
Edge I.	**12**	77 45N	22 30E
Edgecumbe	**142**	37 59S	176 47E
Edgefield	**157**	33 43N	81 59W
Edgeley	**158**	46 27N	98 41W
Edgemont	**158**	43 15N	103 53W
Edgeøya	**12**	77 45N	22 30E
Edgeworthstown = Mostrim	**38**	53 42N	7 36W
Edhessa	**68**	40 48N	22 5E
Edievale	**143**	45 49S	169 22E
Edina, Liberia	**120**	6 0N	10 19W
Edina, U.S.A.	**158**	40 6N	92 10W
Edinburg	**159**	26 22N	98 10W
Edinburgh	**35**	55 57N	3 12W
Edington	**28**	51 17N	2 6W
Edirne	**67**	41 40N	26 45E
Edison	**163**	35 21N	118 52W
Edithburgh	**140**	35 5S	137 43E
Edjeleh	**119**	28 25N	9 40E
Edjudina	**137**	29 48S	122 23E
Edmeston	**162**	42 42N	75 15W
Edmond	**159**	35 37N	97 30W
Edmondbyers	**32**	54 50N	1 59W
Edmonds	**160**	47 47N	122 22W
Edmonton, Austral.	**138**	17 2S	145 46E
Edmonton, Can.	**152**	53 30N	113 30W
Edmund L.	**153**	54 45N	93 17W
Edmundston	**151**	47 23N	68 20W
Edna	**159**	29 0N	96 40W
Edna Bay	**152**	55 55N	133 40W
Edolo	**62**	46 10N	10 21E
Edouard, L.	**126**	0 25S	29 40E
Edremit	**92**	39 40N	27 0E
Edsbyn	**72**	61 23N	15 49E
Edsel Ford Ra.	**13**	77 0S	143 0W
Edsele	**72**	63 25N	16 32E
Edson	**152**	53 40N	116 28W
Eduardo Castex	**172**	35 50S	64 25W
Edward I.	**150**	48 22N	88 37W
Edward, L. = Idi Amin Dada, L.	**126**	0 25S	29 40E
Edward, R.	**140**	35 0S	143 30E
Edward VII Pen.	**13**	80 0S	160 0W
Edwards	**163**	34 55N	117 51W
Edwards Plat.	**159**	30 30N	101 5W
Edwardsville	**162**	41 15N	75 56W
Edzell	**37**	56 49N	2 40W
Edzo	**152**	62 49N	116 4W
Eefde	**46**	52 10N	6 13E
Eek	**147**	60 10N	162 0W
Eekloo	**47**	51 11N	3 33E
Eelde	**46**	53 8N	6 34E
Eem, R.	**46**	52 16N	5 20E
Eems Kanaal	**46**	53 18N	6 46E
Eems, R.	**46**	53 26N	6 57E
Eenrum	**46**	53 22N	6 28E
Eernegem	**47**	51 8N	3 2E
Eerste Valthermond	**46**	52 53N	6 58E
Eersterivier	**128**	34 0S	18 45E
Efate, I. (Vate)	**46**	17 40S	168 25E
Eferding	**52**	48 18N	14 1E
Eferi	**119**	24 30N	9 28E
Effingham	**156**	39 8N	88 30W
Effiums	**121**	6 35N	8 0E
Effretikon	**51**	47 25N	8 42E
Efiduasi	**121**	6 45N	1 25W
Eforie Sud	**70**	44 1N	28 37E
Ega, R.	**58**	42 32N	1 58W
Égadi, Ísole	**64**	37 55N	12 10E
Eganville	**150**	45 32N	77 5W
Egeland	**158**	48 42N	99 6W
Egenolf L.	**153**	59 3N	100 0W
Eger	**53**	47 53N	20 27E
Eger, R.	**53**	47 43N	20 32E
Egersund = Eigersund	**75**	58 26N	6 1E
Egerton, Mt.	**137**	24 42S	117 44E
Egg L.	**153**	55 5N	105 30W
Eggenburg	**52**	48 38N	15 50E
Eggiwil	**50**	46 52N	7 47E
Egham	**29**	51 25N	0 33W
Egilsay I.	**37**	59 10N	2 56W
Eginbah	**136**	20 53S	119 47E
Egletons	**44**	45 24N	2 3E
Eglisau	**51**	47 35N	8 31E
Egmond-aan-Zee	**46**	52 37N	4 38E
Egmont, C.	**142**	39 16S	173 45E
Egmont, Mt.	**142**	39 17S	174 5E
Egogi Bad	**123**	13 10N	41 30E
Egremont	**32**	54 28N	3 33W
Eğridir Gölü	**92**	37 53N	30 50E
Egton	**33**	54 27N	0 45W
Egtved	**73**	55 38N	9 18E
Égua	**174**	5 5N	68 0W
Éguas, R.	**171**	13 26S	44 14W
Égume	**121**	7 30N	7 14E
Éguzon	**44**	46 27N	1 33E
Egvekinot	**77**	66 19N	179 50W
Egyek	**53**	47 39N	20 52E
Egypt ■	**122**	28 0N	31 0E
Eha Amufu	**121**	6 30N	7 40E
Ehime-ken □	**110**	33 30N	132 40E
Ehingen	**49**	48 16N	9 43E
Ehrwald	**52**	47 24N	10 56E
Eibar	**58**	43 11N	2 28W
Eibergen	**46**	52 6N	6 39E
Eichstätt	**49**	48 53N	11 12E
Eidanger	**71**	59 7N	9 43E
Eide	**71**	60 31N	6 44E
Eider, R.	**48**	54 15N	8 50E
Eidsberg	**71**	59 32N	11 16E
Eidsfoss	**71**	59 36N	10 2E
Eidsvold	**139**	25 25S	151 12E
Eidsvoll	**75**	60 19N	11 14E
Eifel	**49**	50 10N	6 45E
Eiffel Flats	**127**	18 20S	30 0E
Eigersund	**71**	58 26N	6 1E
Eigg, I.	**36**	56 54N	6 10W
Eigg, Sd. of	**36**	56 52N	6 15W
Eighty Mile Beach	**136**	19 30S	120 40E
Eil	**91**	8 0N	49 50E
Eil, L.	**36**	56 50N	5 15W
Eilat	**90**	29 30N	34 56E
Eildon	**141**	37 14S	145 55E
Eildon, L.	**139**	37 10S	146 0E
Eileen L.	**153**	62 16N	107 37W
Eilenburg	**48**	51 28N	12 38E
Ein 'Arik	**90**	31 54N	35 8E
Ein el Luweiqa	**123**	14 5N	33 50E
Einasleigh	**138**	18 32S	144 5E
Einasleigh, R.	**138**	17 30S	142 17E
Einbeck	**48**	51 48N	9 50E
Eindhoven	**47**	51 26N	5 30E
Einsiedeln	**51**	47 7N	8 46E
Eiríksjökull	**74**	64 46N	20 24W
Eirlandsche Gat	**46**	53 12N	4 54E
Eirunepé	**174**	6 35S	70 0W
Eisden	**47**	50 59N	5 42E
Eisenach	**48**	50 58N	10 18E
Eisenberg	**48**	50 59N	11 50E
Eisenerz	**52**	47 32N	15 54E
Eisenhüttenstadt	**48**	52 9N	14 41E
Eisenkappel	**52**	46 29N	14 36E
Eisenstadt	**53**	47 51N	16 31E
Eiserfeld	**47**	50 50N	8 0E
Eisfeld	**49**	50 25N	10 54E
Eishort, L.	**36**	57 9N	6 0W
Eisleben	**48**	51 31N	11 31E
Eizariya (Bethany)	**90**	31 47N	35 15E
Ejby	**73**	55 25N	9 56E
Eje, Sierra del	**56**	42 24N	6 54W
Ejea de los Caballeros	**58**	42 7N	1 9W
Ejido	**174**	8 33N	71 14W
Ejura	**121**	7 25N	1 25E
Ejutla	**165**	16 34N	96 44W
Ekalaka	**158**	45 55N	104 30E
Ekawasaki	**110**	33 13N	132 46E
Ekeryd	**73**	57 37N	14 6E
Eket	**121**	4 38N	7 56W
Eketahuna	**142**	40 38S	175 43E
Ekhínos	**68**	41 16N	25 1W
Ekibastuz	**76**	51 40N	75 22E
Ekimchan	**77**	53 0N	133 0W
Ekofisk, oilfield	**19**	56 35N	3 30E
Ekofisk, W., oilfield	**19**	56 35N	3 5E
Ekoli	**126**	0 23S	24 13E
Ekoln, I.	**72**	59 45N	17 40E
Eksjö	**73**	57 40N	14 58W
Ekwan Pt.	**150**	53 16N	82 7W
Ekwan, R.	**150**	53 12N	82 15W
El Abiodh	**118**	32 53N	0 31E
El Aïoun	**118**	34 33N	2 30W
El 'Aiyat	**122**	29 36N	31 15E
El Alamein	**122**	30 48N	28 58E
El Aqaba	**90**	29 31N	35 0E
El Arahal	**57**	37 15N	5 33W
El Araq	**122**	28 40N	26 20E
El Arba	**118**	36 28N	3 12E
El Arba du Rharb	**118**	34 50N	5 59W
El Aricha	**118**	34 13N	1 16W
El Arīhā	**90**	31 52N	35 27E
El Arish	**138**	17 49S	146 1E
El 'Arîsh	**122**	31 8N	33 50E
El Arnaud	**119**	36 7N	5 49E
El Arrouch	**119**	36 37N	6 53E
El Asnam	**118**	36 10N	1 20E
El Astillero	**56**	43 24N	3 49W
El Badâri	**122**	27 4N	31 25E
El Bahrein	**122**	28 30N	26 25E
El Ballâs	**122**	26 2N	32 43E
El Balyana	**122**	26 10N	32 3E
El Baqeir	**122**	18 40N	33 40E
El Barco de Ávila	**56**	40 21N	5 31W
El Barco de Valdeorras	**56**	42 23N	7 0W
El Bauga	**122**	18 18N	33 52E
El Baúl	**174**	8 57N	68 17W
El Bawiti	**122**	28 25N	28 45E
El Bayadh	**118**	33 40N	1 1E
El Bierzo	**56**	42 45N	6 30W
El Biodh	**118**	26 0N	6 32W
El Bluff	**166**	11 59N	83 40W
El Bonillo	**59**	38 57N	2 35W
El Cajon	**163**	32 49N	117 0W
El Callao	**174**	7 25N	61 50W
El Camp	**58**	41 5N	1 10E
El Campo	**159**	29 10N	96 20W
El Carmen	**174**	1 16N	66 52W
El Castillo	**57**	37 41N	6 19W
El Centro	**161**	32 50N	115 40W
El Cerro, Boliv.	**174**	17 30S	61 40W
El Cerro, Spain	**57**	37 45N	6 57W
El Cocuy	**174**	6 25N	72 27W
El Coronil	**57**	37 5N	5 38W
El Cuy	**176**	39 55S	68 25W
El Cuyo	**165**	21 30N	87 40W
El Dab'a	**122**	31 0N	28 27E
El Dátil	**164**	30 7N	112 15W
El Deir	**122**	25 25N	32 20E
El Dere	**91**	3 50N	47 8E
El Díaz	**165**	21 1N	87 17W
El Dificul	**174**	9 51N	74 14W
El Díos	**164**	20 40N	87 20W
El Diviso	**174**	1 22N	78 14W
El Djouf	**120**	20 0N	11 30E
El Dorado, Colomb.	**174**	1 11N	71 52W
El Dorado, Ark., U.S.A.	**159**	33 10N	92 40W
El Dorado, Kans., U.S.A.	**159**	37 55N	96 56W
El Dorado, Venez.	**174**	6 55N	61 30W
El Dorado Springs	**159**	37 54N	93 59W
El Eglab	**118**	26 20N	4 30W
El Escorial	**56**	40 35N	4 7W
El Faiyûm	**122**	29 19N	30 50E
El Fâsher	**123**	13 33N	25 26E
El Fashn	**122**	28 50N	30 54E
El Ferrol	**56**	43 29N	3 14W
El Fifi	**123**	10 4N	25 0E
El Fuerte	**164**	26 30N	108 40W
El Gal	**91**	10 58N	50 20E
El Gebir	**123**	13 40N	29 40E
El Gedida	**122**	25 40N	28 30E
El Geneina	**117**	13 27N	22 45E
El Geteina	**123**	14 50N	32 27E
El Gezira	**123**	14 0N	33 0E
El Gezira □	**123**	15 0N	33 0E
El Gîza	**122**	30 0N	31 10E
El Goléa	**118**	30 30N	2 50E
El Guettar	**119**	34 5N	4 38E
El Hadjire	**119**	32 36N	5 30E
El Hagiz	**123**	15 15N	35 50E
El Hajeb	**118**	33 41N	5 23W
El Hammâm	**122**	30 52N	29 25E
El Hank, Alg.	**118**	25 38N	5 29W
El Hank, Maurit.	**118**	24 37N	7 0W
El Haql	**122**	29 15N	34 59E
El Hawata	**123**	13 25N	34 42E
El Heiz	**122**	27 50N	28 40E
El 'Idisât	**122**	25 30N	32 35E
El Iskandarîya	**122**	31 0N	30 0E
El Istwâ'ya □	**123**	5 0N	30 0E
El Jadida	**118**	33 16N	9 31W
El Jorf Lasfar, C.	**118**	33 5N	8 54W
El Kab	**122**	19 27N	32 46E
El Kala	**119**	36 50N	8 30E
El Kamlin	**123**	15 3N	33 11E
El Kantara, Alg.	**119**	35 14N	5 45E
El Kantara, Tunisia	**119**	33 45N	10 58E
El Karaba	**122**	18 32N	33 41E
El Kef	**119**	36 12N	8 47E
El Keläa des Srarhna	**118**	32 4N	7 27W
El Khandaq	**122**	18 30N	30 30E
El Khârga	**122**	25 30N	30 33E
El Khartûm	**123**	15 31N	32 35E
El Khartûm Bahrî	**123**	15 40N	32 31E
El-Khroubs	**119**	36 10N	6 55E
El Khureiba	**122**	28 3N	35 10E
El Kseur	**119**	36 46N	4 49E
El Ksiba	**118**	32 45N	6 1W
El Kuntilla	**122**	30 1N	34 45E
El Ladhiqiya	**92**	35 20N	35 30E
El Laqeita	**122**	25 50N	33 15E
El Leiya	**123**	16 15N	35 28E
El Mafâza	**123**	13 38N	34 30E
El Mahalla el Kubra	**122**	31 0N	31 0E
El Mahârîq	**122**	25 35N	30 35E
El Maiz	**118**	28 19N	0 9W
El-Maks el-Bahari	**122**	24 30N	30 40E
El Manshâh	**122**	26 26N	31 50E
El Mansour	**118**	27 47N	0 14W
El Mansûra	**122**	31 0N	31 19E
El Mantico	**174**	7 27N	62 32W
El Manzala	**122**	31 10N	31 50E
El Marâgha	**122**	26 35N	31 10E
El Masid	**123**	15 15N	33 0E
El Matariya	**122**	31 15N	32 0E
El Meghaier	**119**	33 55N	5 58E
El Melfa	**119**	31 58N	15 18E
El Meraguen	**118**	28 0N	0 7W
El Metemma	**123**	16 50N	33 10E
El Miamo	**174**	7 39N	61 46W
El Milagro	**172**	30 59S	65 59W
El Milheas	**118**	25 27N	6 57W
El Milia	**119**	36 51N	6 13E
El Minyâ	**122**	28 7N	30 33E
El Molar	**58**	40 42N	3 45W
El Monte	**163**	34 4N	118 2W
El Mreyye	**120**	18 0N	6 0W
El Obeid	**123**	13 8N	30 10E
El Oro = Sta. María del Oro	**164**	25 50N	105 20W
El Oro de Hidalgo	**165**	19 48N	100 8W
El Oued	**119**	33 20N	6 58E
El Ouig	**120**	19 31N	0 27E
El Palmar	**174**	7 58N	61 53W
El Palmito, Presa	**164**	25 40N	105 3W
El Panadés	**58**	41 10N	1 30E
El Pao	**174**	9 38N	68 8W
El Pardo	**56**	40 31N	3 47W
El Paso	**161**	31 50N	106 30W
El Paso Robles	**163**	35 38N	120 41W
El Pedernoso	**59**	39 29N	2 45W
El Pedroso	**57**	37 51N	5 45W
El Pilar	**174**	10 32N	63 9W
El Pobo de Dueñas	**58**	40 46N	1 39W
El Portal	**163**	37 44N	119 49W
El Porvenir, Mexico	**164**	31 15N	105 51W
El Porvenir, Venez.	**174**	4 42N	71 19W
El Prat de Llobregat	**58**	41 18N	2 3E
El Progreso	**166**	15 26N	87 51W
El Provencío	**59**	39 23N	2 35W
El Pueblito	**164**	29 3N	105 4W
El Qahîra	**122**	30 1N	31 14E
El Qantara	**122**	30 51N	32 20E
El Qasr	**122**	25 44N	28 42E
El Qubba	**123**	11 10N	27 5E
El Quseima	**122**	30 40N	34 15E
El Qusîya	**122**	27 29N	30 44E
El Râshda	**122**	25 35N	28 57E
El Reno	**159**	35 30N	98 0W
El Rheauya	**118**	25 52N	6 30W
El Ribero	**56**	42 30N	8 30W
El Rîdisiya	**122**	24 56N	32 51E
El Rio	**163**	34 14N	119 10W
El Ronquillo	**57**	37 44N	6 10W
El Rubio	**57**	37 22N	5 0W
El Saff	**122**	29 34N	31 16E
El Salado	**174**	8 56N	73 55W
El Salto	**164**	23 47N	105 22W
El Salvador ■	**166**	13 50N	89 0W
El Sancejo	**57**	37 4N	5 6W
El Sauce	**166**	13 0N	86 40W
El Shallal	**122**	24 0N	32 53E
El Suweis	**122**	29 58N	32 31E
El Temblador	**174**	8 59N	62 44W
El Thamad	**122**	29 40N	34 28E
El Tigre	**174**	8 55N	64 15W
El Tocuyo	**174**	9 47N	69 48W
El Tofo	**172**	29 22S	71 18W
El Tránsito	**172**	28 52S	70 17W
El Tûr	**122**	28 14N	33 36E
El Turbio	**176**	51 30S	72 40W
El Uqsur	**122**	25 41N	32 38E
El Vado	**58**	41 2N	3 18W
El Vallés	**58**	41 35N	2 20E
El Vigía	**174**	8 38N	71 39W
El Wak	**124**	2 49N	40 56E
El Waqf	**122**	25 45N	32 15E
El Wâsta	**122**	29 19N	31 12E
El Weguet	**123**	5 28N	42 17E
Ela	**123**	12 50N	42 20E
Elafónisos	**69**	36 29N	22 56E
Elaine	**140**	37 44S	144 2E
Elamanchili = Yellamanchilli	**96**	17 26N	82 50E
Elan R.	**31**	52 17N	3 40W
Elan Village	**31**	52 18N	3 34W
Elands	**141**	31 37S	152 20E
Elandsvlei	**128**	32 19S	19 31E
Elassa	**69**	35 18N	26 21E
Elassón	**68**	39 53N	22 12E
Elat	**103**	5 40S	133 5E
Elateia	**69**	38 37N	22 46E
Elâziğ	**92**	38 37N	39 22E
Elba	**157**	31 27N	86 4W
Elba, I.	**62**	42 48N	10 15E
Elbasani	**68**	41 9N	20 9E
Elbasani-Berati	**68**	40 58N	20 0E
Elbe, R.	**48**	53 15N	10 7E
Elbert, Mt.	**161**	39 12N	106 36W
Elberta	**156**	44 35N	86 14W
Elberton	**157**	34 7N	82 51W
Elbeuf	**42**	49 17N	1 2E
Elbląg □	**54**	54 15N	19 30E
Elbląg (Elbing)	**54**	54 10N	19 25E
Elbow	**153**	51 7N	106 35W
Elbrus, Mt.	**83**	43 30N	42 30E
Elburg	**46**	52 26N	5 50E
Elburz Mts. = Alborz	**93**	36 0N	52 0E
Elche	**59**	38 15N	0 42W
Elche de la Sierra	**59**	38 27N	2 3W
Elcho I.	**138**	11 55S	135 45E
Elda	**59**	38 29N	0 47W
Eldfisk, oilfield	**19**	56 25N	3 30E
Eldon, Iowa, U.S.A.	**97**	40 50N	92 12W
Eldon, Mo., U.S.A.	**158**	38 20N	92 38W
Eldora	**158**	42 20N	93 5W
Eldorado, Argent.	**173**	26 28S	54 43W

Eldorado **Ermelo**

Eldorado, Ont., Can. **97** 44 40N 77 32W
Eldorado, Sask., Can. **153** 59 35N 108 30W
Eldorado, Mexico **164** 24 0N 107 30W
Eldorado, Ill., U.S.A. **156** 37 50N 88 25W
Eldorado, Tex., U.S.A. **159** 30 52N 100 35W
Eldoret **126** 0 30N 35 25 E
Electra **159** 34 0N 99 0W
Eleele **147** 21 54N 159 35W
Elefantes, R. **129** 24 0 S 32 30 E
Elektrogorsk **81** 55 56N 38 50 E
Elektrostal **81** 55 41N 38 32 E
Elele **121** 5 5N 6 50 E
Elena **67** 42 55N 25 53 E
Elephant Butte Res. **161** 33 45N 107 30W
Elephant I. **13** 61 0 S 55 0W
Elephant Pass **97** 9 35N 80 25 E
Elesbão Veloso **170** 6 13 S 42 8W
Eleshnitsa **67** 41 52N 23 36 E
Eleuthera I. **166** 25 0N 76 20W
Elevsís **69** 38 4N 23 26 E
Elevtheroúpolis **68** 40 52N 24 20 E
Elfin Cove **147** 58 11N 136 20W
Elgåhogna, Mt. **72** 62 7N 12 7 E
Elgepiggen **71** 62 10N 11 21 E
Elgeyo-Marakwet □ **126** 0 45N 35 30 E
Elgg **51** 47 29N 8 52 E
Elgin, Can. **151** 45 48N 65 10W
Elgin, U.K. **37** 57 39N 3 20W
Elgin, Ill., U.S.A. **156** 42 0N 88 20W
Elgin, N.D., U.S.A. **158** 46 24N 101 46W
Elgin, Nebr., U.S.A. **158** 41 58N 98 3W
Elgin, Nev., U.S.A. **161** 37 27N 114 36W
Elgin, Oreg., U.S.A. **160** 45 37N 118 0W
Elgin, Texas, U.S.A. **159** 30 21N 97 22W
Elgol **36** 57 9N 6 6W
Elgon, Mt. **126** 1 10N 34 30 E
Elham **29** 51 9N 1 7 E
Eliase **103** 8 10 S 130 55 E
Elida **159** 33 56N 103 41W
Elie **153** 49 48N 97 52W
Elie de Beaumont, Mt. **143** 43 30 S 170 20 E
Elikón, Mt. **69** 38 18N 22 45 E
Elim **147** 64 35N 162 20W
Elin Pelin **126** 42 40N 23 38 E
Elisabethville = Lubumbashi **127** 11 32 S 27 38 E
Eliseu Martins **170** 8 13 S 43 42W
Elishaw **35** 55 16N 2 14W
Elista **83** 46 16N 44 14 E
Elit **123** 15 10N 37 0 E
Elizabeth, Austral. **140** 34 42 S 138 41 E
Elizabeth, U.S.A. **162** 40 37N 74 12W
Elizabeth City **157** 36 18N 76 16W
Elizabetha **126** 1 3N 23 37 E
Elizabethton **157** 36 20N 82 13W
Elizabethtown, Ky., U.S.A. **156** 37 40N 85 54W
Elizabethtown, Pa., U.S.A. **162** 40 8N 76 36W
Elizondo **58** 43 12N 1 30W
Elk City **159** 35 25N 99 25W
Elk Grove **163** 38 25N 121 22W
Elk Island Nat. Park **152** 53 47N 112 59W
Elk Lake **150** 47 40N 80 25W
Elk Point **153** 53 54N 110 55W
Elk River, Idaho, U.S.A. **160** 46 50N 116 8W
Elk River, Minn., U.S.A. **158** 45 17N 93 34W
Elkedra **138** 21 9 S 135 26 E
Elkedra, R. **138** 21 8 S 136 22 E
Elkhart, Ind., U.S.A. **156** 41 42N 85 55W
Elkhart, Kans., U.S.A. **159** 37 3N 101 54W
Elkhorn **153** 49 59N 101 14W
Elkhorn, R. **158** 42 0N 98 15W
Elkhotovo **83** 43 19N 44 15 E
Elkhovo **67** 42 10N 26 40 E
Elkin **157** 36 17N 80 50W
Elkins **156** 38 53N 79 53W
Elko, Can. **152** 49 20N 115 10W
Elko, U.S.A. **160** 40 40N 115 50W
Elkton **162** 39 36N 75 50W
Ell, L. **137** 29 13 S 127 46 E
Elland **33** 53 41N 1 49W
Ellecom **46** 52 2N 6 6 E
Ellef Ringnes I. **12** 78 30N 102 2W
Ellen, Mt. **161** 38 4N 110 56W
Ellen R. **32** 54 44N 3 24W
Ellendale, Austral. **136** 17 56 S 124 48 E
Ellendale, U.S.A. **158** 46 3N 98 30W
Ellensburg **160** 47 0N 120 30W
Ellenville **162** 41 42N 74 23W
Eller Beck Bri. **33** 54 23N 0 40W
Ellerston **141** 31 49 S 151 20 E
Ellery, Mt. **141** 37 28 S 148 40 E
Ellesmere **32** 52 55N 2 53W
Ellesmere I. **12** 79 30N 80 0W
Ellesmere, L. **131** 43 46 S 172 27 E
Ellesmere Port **32** 53 17N 2 55W
Ellesworth Land **13** 74 0 S 85 0W
Ellezelles **47** 50 44N 3 42 E
Ellice Is. **130** 8 0 S 176 0 E
Ellicott City **162** 39 16N 76 48W
Ellington **35** 55 14N 1 34W
Ellinwood **158** 38 27N 98 37W
Elliot, Austral. **138** 17 33 S 133 32 E
Elliot, S. Afr. **129** 31 22 S 27 48 E
Elliot Lake **150** 46 35N 82 35W
Ellis **158** 39 0N 99 39W
Ellisville **157** 31 38N 89 12W
Ellon **37** 57 21N 2 5W
Ellore = Eluru **96** 16 48N 81 8 E
Ells, R. **152** 57 18N 111 40W
Ellsworth **158** 38 47N 98 15W
Ellsworth Land **13** 76 0 S 89 0W
Ellwangen **49** 48 57N 10 9 E
Ellwood City **156** 40 52N 80 19W
Elm **51** 46 54N 9 10 E
Elma, Can. **153** 49 52N 95 55W
Elma, U.S.A. **160** 47 0N 123 30 E
Elmer **162** 39 36N 75 10W
Elmhurst **156** 41 52N 87 58W
Elmina **121** 5 5N 1 21W
Elmira, Can. **151** 46 30N 61 59W
Elmira, U.S.A. **162** 42 8N 76 49W
Elmira Heights **162** 42 8N 76 50W
Elmore, Austral. **140** 36 30 S 144 37 E
Elmore, U.S.A. **163** 33 7N 115 49W
Elmshorn **48** 53 44N 9 40 E
Elmswell **29** 52 14N 0 53 E
Elorza **174** 7 3N 69 31W
Eloy **161** 32 46N 111 46W
Éloyes **43** 48 6N 6 36 E
Elphin, Ireland **38** 53 50N 8 11W
Elphin, U.K. **36** 58 4N 5 3W
Elphinstone **138** 21 30 S 148 17 E
Elrose **153** 51 12N 108 0W
Elsas **150** 48 32N 82 55W
Elsinore, Austral. **141** 31 35 S 145 11 E
Elsinore, Cal., U.S.A. **163** 33 40N 117 15W
Elsinore, Utah, U.S.A. **161** 38 40N 112 2W
Elsinore = Helsingor **73** 56 2N 12 35 E
Elspe **48** 51 10N 8 1 E
Elspeet **46** 52 17N 5 48 E
Elst **46** 51 55N 5 51 E
Elsterwerda **48** 51 27N 13 32 E
Elstree **29** 51 38N 0 16W
Elten **46** 51 52N 6 9 E
Eltham, Austral. **141** 37 43 S 145 12 E
Eltham, N.Z. **142** 39 26 S 174 19 E
Elton **83** 49 5N 46 52 E
Eluru **96** 16 48N 81 8 E
Elvas **57** 38 50N 7 17W
Elven **42** 47 44N 2 36W
Elverum **71** 60 53N 11 34 E
Elvire, Mt. **137** 21 52 S 116 50 E
Elvire, R. **136** 17 51 S 128 11 E
Elvo, R. **62** 45 32N 8 14 E
Elvran **71** 63 24N 11 3 E
Elwood, Ind., U.S.A. **156** 40 20N 85 50W
Elwood, Nebr., U.S.A. **158** 40 38N 99 51W
Ely, U.K. **29** 52 24N 0 16 E
Ely, Minn., U.S.A. **158** 47 54N 91 52W
Ely, Nev., U.S.A. **160** 39 10N 114 50W
Elyashiv **90** 32 23N 34 55 E
Elyria **156** 41 22N 82 8W
Emådalen **72** 61 20N 14 44 E
Emaiygi, R. **80** 58 30N 26 30 E
Emba **76** 48 50N 58 8 E
Embarcación **172** 23 10 S 64 0W
Embarras Portage **153** 58 27N 111 28W
Embleton **35** 55 30N 1 38W
Embo **37** 57 55N 4 0W
Embóna **69** 36 13N 27 51 E
Embrach **51** 47 30N 8 36 E
Embrun **45** 44 34N 6 30 E
Embu **126** 0 32 S 37 38 E
Embu □ **126** 0 30 S 37 35 E
Emden **48** 53 22N 7 12 E
Emeq Hula **90** 33 5N 35 8 E
'Emeq Yizre'el **90** 32 35N 35 12 E
Emerald **138** 23 32 S 148 10 E
Emerson **153** 49 0N 97 10W
Emery **161** 38 59N 111 17W
Emery Park **161** 32 10N 110 59W
Emi Koussi, Mt. **117** 20 0N 18 55 E
Emilia-Romagna □ **62** 44 33N 10 40 E
Emilius, Mt. **62** 45 41N 7 23 E
Eminabad **94** 32 2N 74 8 E
Emine **67** 42 40N 27 56 E
Emlichheim **48** 52 37N 6 51 E
Emly **39** 52 28N 8 20W
Emmaboda **73** 56 37N 15 32 E
Emmaus **162** 40 32N 75 30W
Emme, R. **50** 47 0N 7 42 E
Emmeloord **46** 52 44N 5 46 E
Emmen, Neth. **47** 52 48N 6 57 E
Emmen, Switz. **51** 47 4N 8 17 E
Emmendingen **49** 48 7N 7 51 E
Emmental **50** 47 0N 7 35 E
Emmer-Compascum **46** 52 49N 7 2 E
Emmerich **48** 51 50N 6 12 E
Emmet **138** 24 45 S 144 30 E
Emmetsburg **158** 43 3N 94 40W
Emmett **160** 43 51N 116 33W
Emöd **53** 47 57N 20 47 E
Emona **67** 42 43N 27 53 E
Empalme **164** 28 1N 110 49W
Empangeni **129** 28 50 S 31 52 E
Empedrado **172** 28 0 S 58 46W
Empoli **62** 43 43N 10 57 E
Emporia, Kans., U.S.A. **158** 38 25N 96 16W
Emporia, Va., U.S.A. **157** 36 41N 77 32W
Emporium **156** 41 30N 78 17W
Empress **153** 50 57N 110 0W
Emptinne **47** 50 19N 5 8 E
Ems, R. **48** 52 37N 7 16 E
Emsdetten **48** 52 11N 7 31 E
Emsworth **29** 50 51N 0 56 E
Emu **140** 36 44 S 143 26 E
Emu Park **138** 23 13 S 150 50 E
Emu Ra. **136** 23 0 S 122 0 E
Emyvale **38** 54 20N 6 57W
En Gedi **90** 31 28N 35 25 E
En Harod **90** 32 33N 35 22 E
'En Kerem **90** 31 47N 35 6 E
En Nahud **123** 12 45N 28 25 E
en Namous, O. **118** 31 15N 0 10W
Ena **111** 35 25N 137 25 E
Ena-San **111** 35 26N 137 36 E
Enafors **72** 63 17N 12 20 E
Enambú **174** 1 1N 70 17W
Enana **128** 17 30 S 16 23 E
Enånger **72** 61 30N 17 9 E
Enard B. **36** 58 5N 5 20W
Enbetsu **112** 44 44N 141 47 E
Encantadas, Serra **173** 30 40 S 53 0W
Encanto, Cape **103** 20 20N 121 40 E
Encarnación **173** 27 15 S 56 0W
Encarnación de Diaz **164** 21 30N 102 20W
Ench'eng **106** 37 9N 116 16 E
Enchi **120** 5 53N 2 48W
Encinal **159** 28 3N 99 25W
Encinillas **164** 33 3N 117 17W
Encinitas **163** 33 3N 117 17W
Encino **161** 34 46N 106 16W
Encounter B. **140** 35 45 S 138 45 E
Encruzilhada **171** 15 31 S 40 54W
Endau **101** 2 40N 103 38 E
Endau, R. **101** 2 30N 103 30 E
Ende **103** 8 45 S 121 30 E
Endeavour **153** 52 10N 102 39W
Endeavour Str. **138** 10 45 S 142 0 E
Endelave **73** 55 46N 10 18 E
Enderbury I. **131** 3 8 S 171 5W
Enderby, Can. **152** 50 35N 119 10W
Enderby, U.K. **28** 52 35N 1 15W
Enderby I. **136** 20 35 S 116 30 E
Enderby Land **13** 66 0 S 53 0 E
Enderlin **158** 46 45N 97 41W
Endicott, N.Y., U.S.A. **162** 42 6N 76 2W
Endicott, Wash., U.S.A. **160** 47 0N 117 45W
Endicott Mts. **147** 68 0N 152 30W
Endröd **53** 46 55N 20 47 E
Endyalgout I. **136** 11 40 S 132 35 E
Enebakk **71** 59 46N 11 9 E
Enez **68** 40 45N 26 5 E
Enfida **119** 36 6N 10 28 E
Enfield, U.K. **29** 51 39N 0 4W
Enfield, U.S.A. **162** 43 34N 71 57W
Engadin **51** 46 45N 10 10 E
Engadine, Lower = Engiadina Bassa **51** 46 51N 10 18 E
Engadine, Upper = Engiadin 'Ota **51** 46 38N 10 0 E
Engano, C. **167** 18 30N 68 20W
Engaño, C. **103** 18 35N 122 23 E
Engeddi **90** 31 28N 35 25 E
Engelberg **51** 46 48N 8 26 E
Engels **81** 51 28N 46 6 E
Engemann L. **153** 55 55N 106 55W
Enger **71** 60 35N 10 20 E
Enggano, I. **102** 5 20 S 102 40 E
Enghien **47** 50 37N 4 2 E
Engiadin 'Ota **51** 46 38N 10 0 E
Engiadina Bassa **51** 46 51N 10 18 E
Engkilili **102** 1 3N 111 42 E
England **159** 34 30N 91 58W
England □ **27** 53 0N 2 0W
Englee **151** 50 45N 56 5W
Englefield **140** 37 21 S 141 48 E
Englehart **150** 47 49N 79 52W
Engler L. **153** 59 8N 106 52W
Englewood, Colo., U.S.A. **158** 39 40N 105 0W
Englewood, Kans., U.S.A. **159** 37 7N 99 59W
Englewood, N.J., U.S.A. **162** 40 54N 73 59W
English Bazar **95** 24 58N 88 21 E
English Channel **42** 50 0N 2 0W
English Company Is. **133** 12 0 S 137 0 E
English, R. **153** 50 30N 93 50W
English River **150** 49 20N 91 0W
Enid **159** 36 26N 97 52W
Enipévs, R. **68** 39 22N 22 17 E
Eniwetok **131** 11 30N 152 16 E
Enjil **118** 33 12N 4 32W
Enkeldoorn **127** 19 2 S 30 52 E
Enkhuizen **46** 52 42N 5 17 E
Enköping **72** 59 37N 17 4 E
Enlo **108** 24 0N 107 7 E
Enna **65** 37 34N 14 15 E
Ennadai **153** 61 8N 100 53W
Ennadai L. **153** 61 0N 101 0W
Ennedi **117** 17 15N 22 0 E
Ennell L. **38** 53 29N 7 25W
Ennerdale Water **32** 54 32N 3 24W
Enngonia **139** 29 21 S 145 50 E
Enningdal **71** 58 59N 11 33 E
Ennis, Ireland **39** 52 51N 8 59W
Ennis, Mont., U.S.A. **160** 45 27N 111 48W
Ennis, Texas, U.S.A. **159** 32 15N 96 40W
Enniscorthy **39** 52 30N 6 35W
Enniskean **39** 51 44N 8 56W
Enniskerry **39** 53 12N 6 10W
Enniskillen **38** 54 20N 7 40W
Ennistimon **39** 52 56N 9 18W
Enns **52** 48 12N 14 28 E
Enns, R. **52** 48 8N 14 27 E
Enoggera Range **108** 27 26 S 152 56 E
Enoggera Res. **109** 27 27 S 152 55 E
Enontekiö **74** 68 23N 23 37 E
Enp'ing **109** 22 11N 112 18 E
Enriquillo, L. **167** 18 20N 72 5W
Ens **46** 52 38N 5 50 E
Enschede **46** 52 13N 6 53 E
Ensenada, Argent. **172** 34 55 S 57 55W
Ensenada, Mexico **164** 31 50N 116 50W
Enshih **108** 30 18N 109 27 E
Enshū-Nada **111** 34 27N 137 38 E
Ensisheim **43** 47 50N 7 20 E
Enstone **28** 51 55N 1 25W
Entebbe **126** 0 4N 32 28 E
Enter **46** 52 17N 6 35 E
Enterprise, Can. **152** 60 47N 115 45W
Enterprise, Oreg., U.S.A. **160** 45 30N 117 11W
Enterprise, Utah, U.S.A. **161** 37 37N 113 36W
Entlebuch **50** 46 59N 8 4 E
Entrance **152** 53 25N 117 50W
Entre Ríos, Boliv. **172** 21 30 S 64 25W
Entre Ríos, Mozam. **127** 14 57 S 37 20 E
Entre Ríos □ **172** 30 30 S 58 30W
Entre Rios, Bahia **171** 11 56 S 38 5W
Entrecasteaux, Pt. d' **137** 34 50 S 115 56 E
Entrepeñas, Pantano de **58** 40 34N 2 42W
Entwistle **152** 53 30N 115 0W
Enugu **121** 6 30N 7 30 E
Enugu Ezike **121** 7 0N 7 29 E
Enumclaw **160** 47 12N 122 0W
Envermeu **42** 49 53N 1 15 E
Envigado **174** 6 10N 75 35W
Enza, R. **62** 44 33N 10 22 E
Enzan **111** 35 42N 138 44 E
Eólie o Lípari, Is. **65** 38 30N 14 50 E
Epa **138** 8 28 S 146 52 E
Epanomí **68** 40 25N 22 59 E
Epe, Neth. **47** 52 21N 5 59 E
Epe, Nigeria **121** 6 36N 3 59 E
Épernay **43** 49 3N 3 56 E
Épernon **43** 48 35N 1 40 E
Ephesus **92** 38 0N 27 30 E
Ephraim **160** 39 30N 111 37W
Ephrata, Pa., U.S.A. **162** 40 11N 76 11W
Ephrata, Wash., U.S.A. **160** 47 28N 119 32W
Epila **58** 41 36N 1 17W
Épinac-les-Mines **43** 46 59N 4 31 E
Épinal **43** 48 19N 6 27 E
Episcopia Bihorului **70** 47 12N 21 55 E
Epitálion **69** 37 37N 21 30 E
Eport L. **36** 57 33N 7 10W
Epping **29** 51 42N 0 8 E
Epping Forest **29** 51 40N 0 5 E
Epsom **29** 51 19N 0 16W
Epukiro **125** 21 30 S 19 0 E
Epworth **33** 53 30N 0 50W
Equatorial Guinea ■ **124** 2 0 S 78 0W
Équeurdreville-Hainneville **42** 49 40N 1 40W
Er Rahad **123** 12 45N 30 32 E
Er Rif **118** 35 1N 4 1W
Er Roseires **123** 11 55N 34 30 E
Er Rumman **90** 32 9N 35 48 E
Eradu **137** 28 40 S 115 2 E
Erandol **96** 20 56N 75 20 E
Erap **135** 6 37 S 146 51 E
Erāwadī Myit, R. = Irrawaddy, R. **98** 19 30N 95 15 E
Erba, Italy **62** 45 49N 9 12 E
Erba, Sudan **122** 19 5N 36 40 E
Ercha **77** 69 45N 147 20 E
Erciyas Daği **92** 38 30N 35 30 E
Erdene **106** 44 30N 111 10 E
Erding **49** 48 18N 11 55 E
Erebus, Mt. **13** 77 35 S 167 0 E
Erechim **173** 27 35 S 52 15W
Ereğli **92** 41 15N 31 30 E
Erei, Monti **65** 37 20N 14 20 E
Erembodegem **47** 50 56N 4 4 E
Eresma, R. **56** 41 13N 4 30W
Eressós **69** 39 11N 25 57 E
Erewadi Myitwanya **99** 15 30N 95 0 E
Erfenis Dam **128** 28 30 S 26 50 E
Erfjord **71** 59 20N 6 14 E
Erfoud **118** 31 30N 4 15W
Erfurt **48** 50 58N 11 2 E
Erfurt □ **48** 51 10N 10 30 E
Ergani **92** 38 26N 39 49 E
Ergene, R. **67** 41 20N 27 0 E
Ergeni Vozyshennost **83** 47 0N 44 0 E
Erhlien **106** 43 42N 112 2 E
Erhlin **109** 23 54N 120 22 E
Erhtao Chiang, R. **107** 42 35N 128 10 E
Erhyüan **108** 26 7N 99 57 E
Eria, R. **56** 42 10N 6 8W
Eriba **123** 16 40N 36 10 E
Eriboll, L. **37** 58 28N 4 41W
Erica **46** 52 43N 6 56 E
Érice **64** 38 4N 12 34 E
Ericht, L. **37** 56 50N 4 25W
Erie **156** 42 10N 80 7W
Erigavo **91** 10 35N 47 35 E
Erikoúsa **68** 39 55N 19 14 E
Eriksdale **153** 50 52N 98 7W
Erikslund **72** 62 31N 15 54 E
Erimanthos **69** 37 57N 21 50 E
Erimo-misaki **112** 41 50N 143 15 E
Eriskay I. **36** 57 4N 7 18W
Eriskay, Sd. of **36** 57 5N 7 20W
Erisort L. **36** 58 5N 6 30W
Eriswil **50** 47 5N 7 46 E
Erith **152** 53 25N 116 46W
Erithrai **69** 38 13N 23 20 E
Eritrea □ **123** 14 0N 41 0 E
Erjas, R. **56** 39 45N 6 52W
Erker, L. **72** 59 51N 18 29 E
Erlangen **49** 49 35N 11 0 E
Erldunda **138** 25 14 S 133 12 E
Ermelo, Neth. **46** 52 35N 5 35 E
Ermelo, S. Afr. **129** 26 31 S 29 59 E

Ermenak **Fairmount**

Ermenak	**92**	36 44N	33 0E
Ermióni	**69**	37 23N	23 15E
Ermoúpolis = Siros	**69**	37 28N	24 57E
Ernakulam	**97**	9 59N	76 19E
Erne, Lough	**38**	54 26N	7 46W
Erne, R.	**38**	54 30N	8 16W
Ernée	**42**	48 18N	0 56W
Ernest Giles Ra.	**137**	27 0S	123 45E
Erode	**97**	11 24N	77 45E
Eromanga	**139**	26 40S	143 11E
Erongo	**128**	21 39S	15 58E
Erongoberg	**128**	21 45S	15 32E
Erp	**47**	51 36N	5 37E
Erquelinnes	**47**	50 19N	4 8E
Erquy	**42**	48 38N	2 29W
Erquy, Cap d'	**42**	48 39N	2 29W
Err, Piz d'	**51**	46 34N	9 43E
Errabiddy	**137**	25 25S	117 5E
Erramala Hills	**97**	15 30N	78 15E
Errer, R.	**123**	42 35N	8 40E
Errigal, Mt.	**38**	55 2N	8 8W
Errill	**39**	52 52N	7 40W
Erris Hd.	**38**	54 19N	10 0W
Errochty, L.	**37**	56 45N	4 10W
Errogie	**37**	57 16N	4 23W
Errol	**35**	56 24N	3 13W
Erseka	**68**	40 22N	20 40E
Erskine	**158**	47 37N	96 0W
Erstein	**43**	48 25N	7 38E
Erstfeld	**51**	46 50N	8 38E
Ertil	**81**	51 55N	40 50E
Ertvågøy	**71**	63 12N	8 25E
Ertvelde	**47**	51 11N	3 45E
Erundu	**128**	20 39S	16 26E
Eruwa	**121**	7 33N	3 26E
Ervalla	**72**	59 28N	15 16E
Ervy-le-Châtel	**43**	48 2N	3 55E
Erwin	**157**	36 10N	82 28W
Erzgebirge	**48**	50 25N	13 0E
Erzin	**77**	50 15N	95 10E
Erzincan	**92**	39 46N	39 30E
Erzurum	**92**	39 57N	41 15E
Es Sahrâ' Esh Sharqîya	**122**	26 0N	33 30E
Es Sider	**119**	30 50N	18 21E
Es Sînâ'	**122**	29 0N	34 0E
Es Souk	**121**	18 48N	1 2E
Es Sûkî	**123**	13 20N	34 58E
Esa'ala	**135**	9 45S	150 49E
Esambo	**126**	3 48S	23 30E
Esan-misaki	**112**	41 40N	141 10E
Esbjerg	**73**	55 29N	8 29E
Escada	**170**	8 22S	35 14W
Escalante	**161**	37 47N	111 37W
Escalante, R.	**161**	37 45N	111 0W
Escalón	**164**	26 40N	104 20W
Escalona	**56**	40 9N	4 29W
Escambia, R.	**157**	30 45N	87 15W
Escanaba	**156**	45 44N	87 5W
Escant, R.	**47**	51 2N	3 45E
Esch-sur-Alzette	**47**	49 32N	6 0E
Eschallens	**50**	46 39N	6 38E
Eschede	**48**	52 44N	10 13E
Escholzmatt	**50**	46 55N	7 56E
Eschwege	**48**	51 10N	10 3E
Eschweiler	**48**	50 49N	6 14E
Escondida, La	**164**	24 6N	99 55W
Escondido	**163**	33 9N	117 4W
Escrick	**33**	53 53N	1 3W
Escuinapa	**164**	22 50N	105 50W
Escuintla	**166**	14 20N	90 48W
Escuminac	**151**	48 0N	67 0W
Escutillas = Ceba	**174**	6 33N	70 24W
Eséka	**121**	3 41N	10 44E
Esens	**48**	53 40N	7 35E
Esera, R.	**58**	42 24N	0 22E
Esfahan □	**93**	33 0N	53 0E
Esgueva, R.	**56**	41 46N	4 14W
Esh Sham = Dimashq	**92**	33 30N	36 18E
Esh Shamâlîya □	**122**	19 0N	31 0E
Esha Ness	**36**	60 30N	1 36W
Eshowe	**129**	28 50S	31 30E
Eshta' ol	**90**	31 47N	35 0E
Esiama	**120**	4 48N	2 25W
Esino, R.	**63**	43 28N	13 8E
Esk R.	**32**	54 23N	3 21W
Esk, R., Dumfries, U.K.	**35**	54 58N	3 4W
Esk, R., N. Yorks., U.K.	**33**	54 27N	0 36W
Eskdale	**35**	55 12N	3 4W
Eskifjördur	**74**	65 3N	13 55W
Eskilstuna	**72**	59 22N	16 32E
Eskimo Ls.	**147**	69 15N	132 17W
Eskimo Pt.	**153**	61 10N	94 3W
Eskişehir	**92**	39 50N	30 35E
Esla, R.	**56**	41 45N	5 50W
Eslöv	**73**	55 50N	13 20E
Esmeralda, La	**172**	22 16S	62 33W
Esmeraldas	**174**	1 0N	79 40W
Esneux	**47**	50 32N	5 33E
Espa	**71**	60 35N	11 15E
Espada, Pta.	**174**	12 5N	71 7W
Espalion	**44**	44 32N	2 47E
Espalmador, I.	**59**	38 48N	1 26E
Espanola	**150**	46 15N	81 46W
Espardell, I. del	**59**	38 47N	1 25E
Esparraguera	**58**	41 33N	1 52E
Esparta	**166**	9 59N	84 40W
Espejo	**57**	37 40N	4 34W
Espenberg, C.	**147**	66 35N	163 40W
Esperança	**170**	7 1S	35 51W
Esperance	**137**	33 45S	121 55E
Esperance B.	**137**	33 48S	121 55E
Esperantinópolis	**170**	4 53S	44 53W
Esperanza	**172**	31 29S	61 3W
Esperanza, La, Argent.	**172**	24 9S	64 52W
Esperanza, La, Boliv.	**174**	14 20S	62 0W
Esperanza, La, Cuba	**166**	22 46N	83 44W
Esperanza, La, Hond.	**166**	14 15N	88 10W
Espéraza	**44**	42 56N	2 14E
Espevær Lt. Ho.	**71**	59 35N	5 7E
Espichel, C.	**57**	38 22N	9 16W
Espiel	**57**	38 11N	5 1W
Espigão, Serra do	**173**	26 35S	50 30W
Espinal	**174**	4 9N	74 53W
Espinazo, Sierra del = Espinhaço, Serra do	**171**	17 30S	43 30W
Espinhaço, Serra do	**171**	17 30S	43 30W
Espinho	**56**	41 1N	8 38W
Espinilho, Serra do	**173**	28 30S	55 0W
Espino	**174**	8 34N	66 1W
Espinosa de los Monteros	**56**	43 5N	3 34W
Espírito Santo □	**171**	20 0S	40 45W
Espíritu Santo, B. del	**165**	19 15N	79 40W
Espíritu Santo, I.	**164**	24 30N	110 23W
Espita	**165**	21 1N	88 19W
Esplanada	**171**	11 47S	37 57W
Espluga de Francolí	**58**	41 24N	1 7E
Espuña, Sierra de	**59**	37 51N	1 35W
Espungabera	**129**	20 29S	32 45E
Esquel	**176**	42 40S	71 20W
Esquimalt	**148**	48 30N	123 23W
Esquina	**172**	30 0S	59 30W
Essaouira (Mogador)	**118**	31 32N	9 42W
Essarts, Les	**42**	46 47N	1 12W
Essebie	**126**	2 58N	30 40E
Essen, Belg.	**47**	51 28N	4 28E
Essen, Ger.	**48**	51 28N	6 59E
Essendon, Mt.	**137**	25 0S	120 30E
Essequibo, R.	**174**	5 45N	58 50W
Essex	**162**	39 18N	76 29W
Essex □	**29**	51 48N	0 30E
Esslingen	**49**	48 43N	9 19E
Essonne □	**43**	48 30N	2 20E
Essvik	**72**	62 18N	17 24E
Estadilla	**58**	42 4N	0 16E
Estados, I. de los	**176**	54 40S	64 30W
Estagel	**44**	42 47N	2 40E
Estância	**170**	11 16S	37 26W
Estancia	**161**	34 50N	106 1W
Estarreja	**56**	40 45N	8 35W
Estats, P. d'	**44**	42 40N	1 40E
Estavayer le Lac	**50**	46 51N	6 51E
Estcourt	**129**	28 58S	29 53E
Este	**63**	45 12N	11 40E
Esteban	**56**	43 33N	6 5W
Estelí	**166**	13 9N	86 22W
Estella	**58**	42 40N	2 0W
Estelline, S.D., U.S.A.	**158**	44 39N	96 52W
Estelline, Texas, U.S.A.	**159**	34 35N	100 27W
Estena, R.	**57**	39 23N	4 44W
Estepa	**57**	37 17N	4 52W
Estepona	**57**	36 24N	5 7W
Esterhazy	**153**	50 37N	102 5W
Esternay	**43**	48 44N	3 33E
Esterri de Aneu	**58**	42 38N	1 5E
Estevan	**153**	49 10N	102 59W
Estevan Group	**152**	53 3N	129 38W
Estherville	**158**	43 25N	94 50W
Estissac	**43**	48 16N	3 48E
Eston, Can.	**153**	51 8N	108 40W
Eston, U.K.	**33**	54 33N	1 6W
Estonian S.S.R. □	**80**	48 30N	25 30E
Estoril	**57**	38 42N	9 23W
Estrada, La	**56**	42 43N	8 27W
Estrêla, Serra da	**56**	40 10N	7 45W
Estrella	**59**	38 25N	3 35W
Estremadura	**57**	39 0N	9 0W
Estremoz	**57**	38 51N	7 39W
Estrondo, Serra do	**170**	7 20S	48 0W
Esztergom	**53**	47 47N	18 44E
Et Tieta	**118**	29 37N	9 15W
Et Turra	**90**	32 39N	35 39E
Étables-sur-Mer	**42**	48 38N	2 51W
Etah	**95**	27 35N	78 40E
Étain	**43**	49 13N	5 38E
Etalle	**47**	49 40N	5 36E
Etamamu	**151**	50 18N	59 59W
Étampes	**43**	48 26N	2 10E
Étang	**43**	46 52N	4 10E
Etanga	**128**	17 55S	13 00E
Étaples	**43**	50 30N	1 39E
Etawah	**95**	26 48N	79 6E
Etawah, R.	**157**	34 20N	84 15W
Etawney L.	**153**	57 50N	96 50W
Etchingham	**29**	51 0N	0 27E
Eteh	**121**	7 2N	7 28E
Etelia	**121**	19 10N	0 55E
Éthe	**47**	49 35N	5 35E
Ethel Creek	**136**	22 55S	120 11E
Ethel, Oued el	**118**	28 31N	3 37W
Ethelbert	**153**	51 32N	100 25W
Ethiopia ■	**91**	8 0N	40 0E
Ethiopian Highlands	**114**	10 0N	37 0E
Etive, L.	**34**	56 30N	5 12W
Etna, Mt.	**65**	37 45N	15 0E
Etne	**71**	59 40N	5 56E
Etoile	**127**	11 33S	27 30E
Etolin I.	**152**	56 5N	132 20W
Eton	**29**	51 29N	0 37W
Etoshapan	**128**	18 40S	16 30E
Etowah	**157**	35 20N	84 30W
Etrépagny	**42**	49 18N	1 36E
Étretat	**42**	49 42N	0 12E
Etroits, Les	**151**	47 24N	68 54W
Etropole	**68**	43 50N	24 0E
Ettelbrüch	**47**	49 50N	6 5E
Ettelbruck	**47**	49 51N	6 5E
Etten	**47**	51 34N	4 38E
Ettington	**28**	52 8N	1 38W
Ettlingen	**49**	48 58N	8 25E
Ettrick Forest	**35**	55 30N	3 0W
Ettrick Water	**35**	55 31N	2 55W
Etuku	**126**	3 42S	25 45E
Etzatlán	**164**	20 48N	104 5W
Etzna	**165**	19 35N	90 15W
Eu	**42**	50 3N	1 26E
Euboea = Évvoia	**69**	38 40N	23 40E
Euchareena	**141**	32 57S	149 6E
Eucla Basin	**137**	31 19S	126 9E
Euclid	**156**	41 32N	81 31W
Euclides da Cunha	**170**	10 31S	39 1W
Eucumbene, L.	**141**	36 2S	148 40E
Eudora	**159**	33 5N	91 17W
Eudunda	**140**	34 12S	139 7E
Eufaula, Ala., U.S.A.	**157**	31 55N	85 11W
Eufaula, Okla., U.S.A.	**159**	35 20N	95 33W
Eufaula, L.	**159**	35 15N	95 28W
Eugene	**160**	44 0N	123 8W
Eugenia, Punta	**164**	27 50N	115 5W
Eugowra	**141**	33 22S	148 24E
Eulo	**139**	28 10S	145 3E
Eumungerie	**141**	31 56N	148 36E
Eunice, La., U.S.A.	**159**	30 35N	92 28W
Eunice, N. Mex., U.S.A.	**159**	32 30N	103 10W
Eupen	**47**	50 37N	6 3E
Euphrates = Furat, Nahr al	**92**	33 30N	43 0E
Eure □	**42**	49 6N	1 0E
Eure-et-Loir □	**42**	48 22N	1 30E
Eureka, Can.	**12**	80 0N	85 56W
Eureka, Calif., U.S.A.	**160**	40 50N	124 0W
Eureka, Kans., U.S.A.	**159**	37 50N	96 20W
Eureka, Mont., U.S.A.	**160**	48 53N	115 6W
Eureka, Nev., U.S.A.	**160**	39 32N	116 2W
Eureka, S.D., U.S.A.	**158**	45 49N	99 38W
Eureka, Utah, U.S.A.	**160**	40 0N	112 0W
Eureka, Mt.	**137**	26 35S	121 35E
Eurelia	**140**	32 33S	138 35E
Euroa	**141**	36 44S	145 35E
Europa, Île	**125**	22 20S	40 22E
Europa, Picos de	**56**	43 10N	5 0W
Europa Pt.	**55**	36 2N	6 32W
Europa Pt. = Europa, Pta. de	**57**	36 3N	5 21W
Europa, Pta. de	**57**	36 3N	5 21W
Europe	**16**	20 0N	20 0E
Europoort	**46**	51 57N	4 10E
Euskirchen	**48**	50 40N	6 45E
Eustis	**157**	28 54N	81 36W
Eutin	**48**	54 7N	10 38E
Eutsuk L.	**152**	53 20N	126 45W
Euxton	**32**	53 41N	2 42W
Eva Downs	**138**	18 1S	134 52E
Eval, Mt.	**90**	32 15N	35 15E
Evanger	**71**	60 39N	6 7E
Evans	**158**	40 25N	104 43W
Evans Head	**139**	29 7S	153 27E
Evans L.	**150**	50 50N	77 0W
Evans P.	**158**	41 0N	105 35W
Evanston, Ill., U.S.A.	**156**	42 0N	87 40W
Evanston, Wy., U.S.A.	**160**	41 10N	111 0W
Evansville, Ind., U.S.A.	**156**	38 0N	87 35W
Evansville, Wis., U.S.A.	**158**	42 47N	89 18W
Evanton	**37**	57 40N	4 20W
Evato	**129**	20 37S	47 10E
Évaux-les-Bains	**44**	46 12N	2 29E
Eveleth	**158**	47 35N	92 40W
Even Yahuda	**90**	32 16N	34 53E
Evensk	**77**	61 57N	159 14E
Evenstad	**71**	61 25N	11 7E
Everard, C.	**141**	37 49S	149 17E
Everard, L.	**139**	31 30S	135 0E
Everard Ras.	**137**	27 5S	132 28E
Evercreech	**28**	51 8N	2 30W
Everdale	**141**	31 52S	144 46E
Evere	**47**	50 52N	4 25E
Everest, Mt.	**95**	28 5N	86 58E
Everett	**160**	48 0N	122 10W
Evergem	**47**	51 7N	3 43E
Everglades	**157**	26 0N	80 30W
Evergreen	**157**	31 28N	86 55W
Everöd	**73**	55 53N	14 5E
Everson	**160**	48 57N	122 22W
Everton	**141**	36 25S	146 33E
Evesham	**28**	52 6N	1 57W
Evian-les-Bains	**45**	46 24N	6 35E
Evinayong	**124**	1 50N	10 35E
Évinos, R.	**69**	38 27N	21 40E
Evisa	**45**	42 15N	8 48E
Évora	**57**	38 33N	7 57W
Évora □	**57**	38 33N	7 50W
Évreux	**42**	49 0N	1 8E
Évritania □	**69**	39 5N	21 30E
Évron	**42**	48 23N	1 58W
Évros □	**68**	41 10N	26 0E
Evrótas, R.	**69**	36 50N	22 40E
Évvoia	**69**	38 30N	24 0E
Évvoia □	**69**	38 40N	23 40E
Ewe, L.	**36**	57 49N	5 38W
Ewell	**29**	51 20N	0 15W
Ewhurst	**29**	51 9N	0 25W
Ewing	**158**	42 18N	98 22W
Ewo	**124**	0 48S	14 45E
Exaltación	**174**	13 10S	65 20W
Excelsior	**139**	33 6S	149 59W
Excelsior Springs	**158**	39 20N	94 10W
Excideuil	**44**	45 20N	1 4E
Exe, R.	**30**	50 38N	3 27W
Exeter, U.K.	**30**	50 43N	3 31W
Exeter, Calif., U.S.A.	**163**	36 17N	119 9W
Exeter, Nebr., U.S.A.	**158**	40 43N	97 30W
Exeter, N.H., U.S.A.	**162**	43 0N	70 58W
Exford	**28**	51 8N	3 39W
Exloo	**46**	52 53N	6 52E
Exmes	**42**	48 45N	0 10E
Exminster	**30**	50 40N	3 29W
Exmoor	**30**	51 10N	3 59W
Exmore	**162**	37 32N	75 50W
Exmouth, Austral.	**136**	22 6S	114 0E
Exmouth, U.K.	**30**	50 37N	3 26W
Exmouth G.	**136**	22 15S	114 15E
Expedition Range	**138**	24 30S	149 12E
Exton	**29**	52 42N	0 38W
Extremadura	**57**	39 30N	6 5W
Exu	**171**	7 31S	39 43W
Exuma Sound	**166**	24 30N	76 20W
Eyam	**33**	53 17N	1 40W
Eyasi, L.	**126**	3 30S	35 0E
Eyawaddi Myii	**98**	15 50N	95 6E
Eye, Camb., U.K.	**29**	52 36N	0 11W
Eye, Norfolk, U.K.	**29**	52 19N	1 9E
Eye Pen.	**36**	58 13N	6 10W
Eyeberry L.	**153**	63 8N	104 43W
Eyemouth	**35**	55 53N	2 5W
Eygurande	**44**	45 40N	2 26E
Eyhatten	**47**	50 43N	6 1E
Eyisen	**82**	41 0N	36 50E
Eyjafjorður	**74**	66 15N	18 30W
Eymet	**44**	44 40N	0 25E
Eymoutiers	**44**	45 40N	1 45E
Eynhallow Sd.	**37**	59 8N	3 7W
Eynort, L.	**36**	57 13N	7 18W
Eynsham	**28**	51 47N	1 21W
Eyrarbakki	**74**	63 52N	21 9W
Eyre	**137**	32 15S	126 18E
Eyre Cr.	**138**	26 40S	139 0E
Eyre, L.	**133**	29 30S	137 26E
Eyre L., (North)	**139**	28 30S	137 20E
Eyre L., (South)	**139**	29 18S	137 25E
Eyre Mts.	**143**	45 25S	168 25E
Eyre Pen.	**139**	33 30S	137 17E
Eyrecourt	**39**	53 12N	8 8W
Ez Zeidab	**122**	17 25N	33 55E
Ez Zergoun, W.	**118**	32 45N	2 25E
Ezcaray	**58**	42 19N	3 0W
Ezine	**68**	39 48N	26 12E

F

Fabens	**161**	31 30N	106 8W
Fåborg	**73**	55 6N	10 15E
Fabriano	**63**	43 20N	12 52E
Fabrizia	**43**	38 29N	16 19E
Făcăeni	**70**	44 32N	27 53E
Facatativá	**174**	4 49N	74 22W
Facture	**44**	44 39N	0 58W
Fada	**117**	17 13N	21 34E
Fada-n-Gourma	**121**	12 10N	0 30E
Fadd	**53**	46 28N	18 49E
Faddeyevski, Ostrov	**77**	76 0N	150 0E
Fadhili	**92**	26 55N	49 10E
Fadlab	**122**	17 42N	34 2E
Faenza	**63**	44 17N	11 53E
Fafa	**121**	15 22N	0 48E
Fafe	**56**	41 27N	8 11W
Fagam	**121**	11 1N	10 1E
Fågelsjö	**72**	61 50N	14 35E
Fagerhult	**73**	57 8N	15 40E
Fagernes	**75**	60 59N	9 14E
Fagersta	**72**	60 1N	15 46E
Fåglavik	**73**	58 6N	13 6E
Fagnano Castello	**65**	39 31N	16 4E
Fagnano, L.	**176**	54 30S	68 0W
Fagnières	**43**	48 58N	4 20E
Fahral	**93**	29 0N	59 0E
Fahūd	**93**	22 18N	56 28E
Faid	**92**	27 1N	42 52E
Faido	**51**	46 29N	8 48E
Fair, C.	**138**	12 24S	143 16E
Fair Hd.	**38**	55 14N	6 10W
Fair Isle	**23**	59 30N	1 40W
Fair Oaks	**163**	38 39N	121 16W
Fairbank	**161**	31 44N	110 12W
Fairbanks	**147**	64 59N	147 40W
Fairbourne	**31**	52 42N	4 3W
Fairbury	**158**	40 5N	97 5W
Fairfax, Okla., U.S.A.	**159**	36 37N	96 45W
Fairfax, Va., U.S.A.	**162**	38 51N	77 18W
Fairfield, Austral.	**141**	33 53S	150 57E
Fairfield, Ala., U.S.A.	**157**	33 30N	87 0W
Fairfield, Calif., U.S.A.	**163**	38 14N	122 1W
Fairfield, Conn., U.S.A.	**162**	41 8N	73 16W
Fairfield, Idaho, U.S.A.	**160**	43 27N	114 52W
Fairfield, Ill., U.S.A.	**156**	38 20N	88 20W
Fairfield, Iowa, U.S.A.	**158**	41 0N	91 58W
Fairfield, Mont., U.S.A.	**160**	47 40N	112 0W
Fairfield, Texas, U.S.A.	**159**	31 40N	96 0W
Fairford, Can.	**153**	51 37N	98 38W
Fairford, U.K.	**28**	51 42N	1 48W
Fairhope	**157**	30 35N	87 50W
Fairlie, N.Z.	**143**	44 5S	170 49E
Fairlie, U.K.	**34**	55 44N	4 52W
Fairlight	**29**	50 53N	0 40E
Fairmead	**163**	37 5N	120 10W
Fairmont, Minn., U.S.A.	**158**	43 37N	94 30W
Fairmont, W. Va., U.S.A.	**156**	39 29N	80 10W
Fairmont Hot Springs	**152**	50 20N	115 56W
Fairmount	**163**	34 45N	118 26W

Fairplay Field

Fairplay 161 39 9N 107 0W
Fairport 156 43 8N 77 29W
Fairview, Austral. 138 15 31S 144 17E
Fairview, Can. 152 56 5N 118 25W
Fairview, N. Dak., U.S.A. 158 47 49N 104 7W
Fairview, Okla., U.S.A. 159 36 19N 98 30W
Fairview, Utah, U.S.A. 160 39 50N 111 0W
Fairweather, Mt. 147 58 55N 137 45W
Faith 158 45 2N 102 4W
Faither, The, C. 36 60 34N 1 30W
Faizabad, Afghan. 93 37 7N 70 33E
Faizabad, India 95 26 45N 82 10E
Faizpur 96 21 14N 75 49E
Fajardo 147 18 20N 65 39W
Fakenham 29 52 50N 0 51E
Fakfak 103 3 0S 132 15E
Fakiya 170 42 10N 27 4E
Fakobli 120 7 23N 7 23W
Fakse 73 55 15N 12 8E
Fakse B. 73 55 11N 12 15E
Fakse Ladeplads 73 55 16N 12 9E
Fak'u 107 42 31N 123 26E
Falaise 42 48 54N 0 12W
Falaise, Mui 100 19 6N 105 45E
Falakrón Óros 68 41 15N 23 58E
Falam 98 23 0N 93 45E
Falcarragh 38 55 8N 8 8W
Falces 58 42 24N 1 48W
Falcón □ 174 11 0N 69 50W
Falcon, C. 118 35 50N 0 50W
Falcón Dam 159 26 50N 99 20W
Falconara Marittima 63 43 37N 13 23E
Faldingworth 33 53 21N 0 22W
Faléa 120 12 16N 11 17W
Falelatai 84 13 55S 171 59W
Falenki 84 58 22N 51 35E
Faleshty 82 47 32N 27 44E
Falfurrias 159 27 8N 98 8W
Falher 152 55 44N 117 15W
Falkenberg, Ger. 48 51 34N 13 13E
Falkenberg, Sweden 73 56 54N 12 30E
Falkensee 48 52 35N 13 6E
Falkenstein 48 50 27N 12 24E
Falkirk 35 56 0N 3 47W
Falkland 35 56 15N 3 13W
Falkland Is. 176 51 30S 59 0W
Falkland Is. Dep. 13 57 0S 40 0W
Falkland Sd. 176 52 0S 60 0W
Falkonéra 69 36 50N 23 52E
Falköping 73 58 12N 13 33E
Fall Brook 161 33 25N 117 12W
Fall River 162 41 45N 71 5W
Fall River Mills 160 41 1N 121 30W
Fallbrook 163 33 23N 117 15W
Fallmore 38 54 6N 10 5W
Fallon, Mont., U.S.A. 158 46 52N 105 8W
Fallon, Nev., U.S.A. 160 39 31N 118 51W
Falls Church 162 38 53N 77 11W
Falls City, Nebr., U.S.A. 158 40 0N 95 40W
Falls City, Oreg., U.S.A. 160 44 54N 123 29W
Falmey 121 12 36N 2 51E
Falmouth, Jamaica 166 18 30N 77 40W
Falmouth, U.K. 30 50 9N 5 5W
Falmouth, Ky., U.S.A. 156 38 40N 84 20W
Falmouth, Mass., U.S.A. 162 41 34N 70 38W
Falmouth B. 30 50 7N 5 3E
False B. 128 34 15S 18 40E
False Divi Pt. 97 15 35N 80 50E
Falset 58 41 7N 0 50E
Falso, C. 166 15 12N 83 21W
Falster 73 54 45N 11 55E
Falsterbo 73 55 23N 12 50E
Falsterbokanalen 73 55 25N 12 56E
Falstone 35 55 10N 2 26W
Faluja 90 31 48N 31 37E
Falun 72 60 37N 15 37E
Famagusta 92 35 8N 33 55E
Famaka 123 11 24N 34 52E
Famatina, Sierra, de 172 29 5S 68 0W
Family L. 153 51 54N 95 27W
Famoso 163 35 37N 119 12W
Fampotabe 129 15 56S 50 8E
Fan i Madh, R. 68 41 56N 20 16E
Fana, Mali 120 13 0N 6 56W
Fana, Norway 71 60 16N 5 20E
Fanad Hd. 38 55 17N 7 40W
Fanambana 129 13 34S 50 0E
Fanárion 68 39 24N 21 47E
Fanch'ang 109 31 2N 118 13E
Fanchiat'un 107 43 42N 125 5E
Fanchih 106 39 14N 113 19E
Fandriana 129 20 14S 47 21E
Fang 100 19 55N 99 13E
Fangch'eng, Honan, China 106 33 16N 112 59E
Fangch'eng, Kwangsi-Chuang, China 108 21 46N 108 21E
Fanghsien 109 32 0N 111 0E
Fangliao 109 22 22N 130 35E
Fangshan 106 38 0N 111 16E
Fangtzu 107 36 39N 119 15E
Fannich, L. 36 57 40N 5 0W
Fanning I. 131 3 51N 159 22W
Fanny Bay 152 49 27N 124 48W
Fanø 73 55 25N 8 25E
Fano 63 43 50N 13 0E
Fanø, I. 73 55 25N 8 25E
Fanshaw 152 57 11N 133 30W
Fao (Al Fāw) 92 30 0N 48 30E
Faqirwali 94 29 27N 73 0E
Fara in Sabina 63 42 13N 12 44E
Farab 85 39 9N 63 36E
Faraday Seamount Group 14 50 0N 27 0W
Faradje 126 3 50N 29 45E
Farafangana 129 22 49S 47 50E
Farâfra, El Wâhât el- 122 27 15N 28 20E
Farah 93 32 20N 62 7E
Farah □ 93 32 25N 62 10E
Farahalana 129 14 26S 50 10E
Faraid, Gebel 122 23 33N 35 19E
Faraid Hd. 37 58 35N 4 48W
Faramana 120 11 56N 4 45W
Faranah 120 10 3N 10 45W
Farasān, Jazā'ir 91 16 45N 41 55E
Farasan Kebir 91 16 40N 42 0E
Faratsiho 129 19 24S 46 57E
Fardes, R. 59 37 25N 3 10W
Fareham 28 50 52N 1 11W
Farewell 147 62 30N 154 0W
Farewell, C. 143 40 29S 172 43E
Farewell C. = Farvel, K. 12 59 48N 43 55W
Farewell Spit 143 40 35S 173 0E
Farfán 174 0 16N 76 41W
Fargo 158 47 0N 97 0W
Faria, R. 90 32 12N 35 27E
Faribault 158 44 15N 93 19W
Faridkot 94 30 44N 74 45E
Faridpur, Bangla. 98 23 15N 90 0E
Faridpur, India 95 18 14N 79 34E
Farila 72 61 48N 15 50E
Färila 72 61 48N 15 50E
Farim 120 12 27N 15 17W
Farimān 93 35 40N 60 0E
Farina 139 30 3S 138 15E
Faringdon 28 51 39N 1 34W
Faringe 72 59 55N 18 7E
Farinha, R. 170 6 15S 47 30W
Färjestaden 73 56 38N 16 25E
Farmakonisi 69 37 17N 27 8E
Farmerville 159 32 48N 92 23W
Farmingdale 162 40 12N 74 10W
Farmington, Calif., U.S.A. 163 37 56N 121 0W
Farmington, N. Mex., U.S.A. 161 36 45N 108 28W
Farmington, N.H., U.S.A. 162 43 25N 71 3W
Farmington, Utah, U.S.A. 160 41 0N 111 58W
Farmington, R. 162 41 51N 72 38W
Farmville 156 37 19N 78 22W
Farnborough 29 51 17N 0 46W
Farne Is. 35 55 38N 1 37W
Farnham 29 51 13N 0 49W
Farnham, Mt. 152 45 20N 72 55W
Farnworth 32 53 33N 2 24W
Faro, Brazil 175 2 0S 56 45W
Faro, Port. 57 37 2N 7 55W
Fårö 75 58 0N 19 10E
Faro □ 57 37 12N 8 10W
Faroe Is. 16 62 0N 7 0W
Farquhar, C. 137 23 38S 113 36E
Farquhar, Mt. 136 22 18S 116 53E
Farr 37 57 21N 4 13W
Farranfore 39 52 10N 9 32W
Farrars, Cr. 138 25 35S 140 43E
Farrashband 93 28 57N 52 5E
Farrell 156 41 13N 80 29W
Farrell Flat 140 33 48S 138 48E
Farrukhabad 95 27 30N 79 32E
Fars □ 93 29 30N 55 0E
Fársala 68 39 17N 22 23E
Farsø 73 56 46N 9 19E
Farsö 73 56 48N 9 20E
Farstrup 73 56 59N 9 28E
Farsund 71 58 5N 6 55E
Fartura, Serra da 173 26 21S 52 52W
Faru 121 12 48N 6 12E
Farum 73 55 49N 12 21E
Farvel, Kap 12 59 48N 43 55W
Farwell 159 34 25N 103 0W
Faryab 93 28 7N 57 14E
Fasa 93 29 0N 53 32E
Fasag 36 57 33N 5 32W
Fasano 65 40 50N 17 20E
Fashoda 123 9 50N 32 2E
Faskari 79 11 42N 6 58E
Faslane 34 56 3N 4 49W
Fastnet Rock 39 51 22N 9 37W
Fastov 80 50 7N 29 57E
Fatehgarh 95 27 25N 79 35E
Fatehpur, Raj., India 94 28 0N 75 4E
Fatehpur, Ut. P., India 95 27 8N 81 7E
Fatick 120 14 19N 16 27W
Fatima 151 47 24N 61 53W
Fátima 57 39 37N 8 39W
Fatoya 120 11 37N 9 10W
Faucilles, Monts 43 48 5N 5 50E
Fauldhouse 35 55 50N 3 44W
Faulkton 158 45 4N 99 8W
Faulquemont 43 49 3N 6 36E
Fauquemberques 43 50 36N 2 5E
Faure I. 137 25 52S 113 50E
Fauresmith 128 29 44S 25 17E
Fauske 74 67 17N 15 25E
Fauvillers 47 49 51N 5 40E
Faux-Cap 129 25 33S 45 32E
Favara 64 37 19N 13 39E
Faversham 29 51 18N 0 54E
Favignana 64 37 56N 12 18E
Favone 45 41 47N 9 26E
Favourable Lake 150 52 50N 93 39W
Fawley 28 50 49N 1 20W
Fawn, R. 150 52 22N 88 20W
Fawnskin 163 34 16N 116 56W
Faxaflói 74 64 29N 23 0W
Faxäiven 72 63 13N 17 13E
Faya = Largeau 117 17 58N 19 6E
Fayence 45 43 38N 6 42E
Fayette, Ala., U.S.A. 157 33 40N 87 50W
Fayette, La., U.S.A. 156 40 22N 86 52W
Fayette, Mo., U.S.A. 158 39 10N 92 40W
Fayetteville, Ark., U.S.A. 159 36 0N 94 5W
Fayetteville, N.C., U.S.A. 157 35 0N 78 58W
Fayetteville, Tenn., U.S.A. 157 35 0N 86 30W
Fayón 58 41 15N 0 20E
Fazeley 28 52 36N 1 42W
Fazenda Nova 171 16 11S 50 48W
Fazilka 94 30 27N 74 2E
Fazilpur 94 29 18N 70 29E
F'Derik 116 22 40N 12 45W
Fé, La 166 22 2N 84 15W
Feakle 39 52 56N 8 41W
Feale, R. 39 52 26N 9 28W
Fear, C. 157 33 45N 78 0W
Fearn 37 57 47N 4 0W
Fearnan 37 56 34N 4 6W
Feather, R. 160 39 30N 121 20W
Featherston 142 41 6S 175 20E
Featherstone 127 18 42S 30 55E
Fécamp 42 49 45N 0 22E
Fedala = Mohammeda 118 33 44N 7 21W
Fedamore 39 52 33N 8 36W
Federación 172 31 0S 57 55W
Federalsburg 162 38 42N 75 47W
Fedjadj, Chott el 119 33 52N 9 14E
Fedje 71 60 47N 4 43E
Fedorovka 84 53 38N 62 42E
Feeagh L. 38 53 56N 9 35W
Feeny 38 54 54N 7 0W
Fehérgyarmat 53 48 0N 22 30E
Fehmarn 48 54 26N 11 10E
Fehmarn Bælt 73 54 35N 11 20E
Feihsiang 106 36 32N 114 47E
Feihsien 107 35 12N 118 0E
Feilding 142 40 13S 175 35E
Feira 65 15 35S 30 16E
Feira de Santana 171 12 15S 38 57W
Fejér □ 53 47 9N 18 30E
Fejø 73 54 55N 11 30E
Felanitx 59 39 27N 3 7E
Feldbach 52 46 57N 15 52E
Feldberg 48 53 20N 13 26E
Feldberg, mt. 49 47 51N 7 58E
Feldis 51 46 48N 9 26E
Feldkirch 52 47 15N 9 37E
Feldkirchen 52 46 44N 14 6E
Felhit 123 16 40N 38 1E
Felipe Carrillo Puerto 165 19 38N 88 3W
Felixlândia 171 18 47S 44 55W
Felixstowe 29 51 58N 1 22W
Felletin 44 45 53N 2 11E
Felpham 29 50 47N 0 38W
Felton, U.K. 35 55 18N 1 42W
Felton, U.S.A. 163 37 3N 122 4W
Feltre 63 46 1N 11 55E
Feltwell 29 52 29N 0 32E
Femø 73 54 58N 11 53E
Femunden 71 62 10N 11 53E
Fen Ho, R. 106 35 36N 110 42E
Fench'ing 108 24 35N 99 54E
Fénérive 129 17 22S 49 25E
Fenerwa 123 13 5N 39 3E
Fengári 68 40 25N 25 32E
Fengchen 106 40 30N 113 0E
Fengch'eng, Kiangsi, China 109 28 10N 115 43E
Fengch'eng, Liaoning, China 107 40 30N 124 2E
Fengchieh 108 31 3N 109 28E
Fengch'iu 106 35 2N 114 24E
Fenghsiang 106 34 26N 107 18E
Fenghsien, Kiangsu, China 106 34 42N 116 34E
Fenghsien, Shanghai, China 109 30 55N 121 27E
Fenghsien, Shensi, China 106 33 56N 106 41E
Fenghsin 109 28 42N 115 23E
Fenghua 109 29 40N 121 24E
Fenghuang 108 27 58N 109 19E
Fenghuangtsui 106 33 30N 109 27E
Fengi 108 25 35N 100 18E
Fengjun 107 39 51N 118 8E
Fengk'ai 109 23 26N 111 30E
Fengkang 108 27 58N 107 47E
Fengloho 109 31 29N 112 29E
Fengning 106 41 12N 116 32E
Fengshan, Hopei, China 107 41 13N 117 6E
Fengshan, Kwangsi-Chuang, China 108 24 32N 107 3E
Fengt'ai, Anhwei, China 109 32 44N 116 43E
Fengt'ai, Peip'ing, China 106 39 51N 116 17E
Fengteng 106 36 25N 114 14E
Fengtu 108 29 58N 107 59E
Fengyuang 109 32 52N 117 32E
Fenhsi 106 36 38N 111 31E
Feni 109 27 48N 114 41E
Feni Is. 135 4 0S 153 40E
Fenit 39 52 17N 9 51W
Fennagh 39 52 42N 6 50W
Fennimore 158 42 58N 90 41W
Fenny 98 22 55N 91 32E
Fenny Bentley 33 53 4N 1 43W
Fenny Compton 28 52 9N 1 20W
Fenny Stratford 29 51 59N 0 42W
Feno, C. de 45 41 58N 8 33E
Fenoarivo 129 18 26S 46 34E
Fens, The 29 52 45N 0 2E
Fenton, Can. 153 53 0N 105 35W
Fenton, U.S.A. 156 42 47N 83 44W
Fenwick 34 55 38N 4 25W
Fenyang 106 37 19N 111 46E
Feodosiya 82 45 2N 35 28E
Fer, C. de 119 37 3N 7 10E
Ferbane 39 53 17N 7 50W
Ferdows 93 33 58N 58 2E
Fère-Champenoise 43 48 45N 4 0E
Fère-en-Tardenois 43 49 10N 3 30E
Fère, La 43 49 40N 3 20E
Ferentino 64 41 42N 13 14E
Ferfer 91 5 18N 45 20E
Fergana 85 40 23N 71 46E
Ferganskaya Dolina 85 40 50N 71 30E
Ferganskiy Khrebet 85 41 0N 73 50E
Fergus 150 43 43N 80 24W
Fergus Falls 158 46 25N 96 0W
Fergus, R. 39 52 45N 9 0W
Ferguson 150 47 50N 73 30W
Fergusson I. 135 9 30S 150 45E
Fériana 119 34 59N 8 33E
FeriCanci 66 45 32N 18 0E
Ferkane 119 34 37N 7 26E
Ferkéssédougou 120 9 35N 5 6W
Ferlach 52 46 32N 14 18E
Ferland 150 50 19N 88 27W
Ferlo, Vallée du 120 15 15N 14 15W
Fermanagh (□) 38 54 21N 7 40W
Fermo 63 43 10N 13 42E
Fermoselle 56 41 19N 6 27W
Fermoy 39 52 4N 8 18W
Fernagh 38 54 2N 7 51W
Fernan Nuñ,z 57 37 40N 4 44W
Fernández 172 27 55S 63 50W
Fernandina 157 30 40N 81 30W
Fernando de Noronha, I. 170 4 0S 33 10W
Fernando do Noronho □ 170 4 0S 33 10W
Fernando Póo = Macias Nguema Biyoga 113 3 30N 8 40E
Fernandópolis 171 20 16S 50 14W
Ferndale, Calif., U.S.A. 160 40 37N 124 12W
Ferndale, Wash., U.S.A. 160 48 51N 122 41W
Ferness 37 57 28N 3 44W
Fernhurst 29 51 3N 0 43W
Fernie 152 49 30N 115 5W
Fernilea 36 57 18N 6 24W
Fernlees 138 23 51S 148 7E
Fernley 160 39 42N 119 20W
Feroke 97 11 9N 75 46E
Ferozepore 94 30 55N 74 40E
Férrai 68 40 53N 26 10E
Ferrandina 65 40 30N 16 28E
Ferrara 63 44 50N 11 36E
Ferrato, C. 64 39 18N 9 39E
Ferreira do Alentejo 57 38 4N 8 6W
Ferreñafe 174 6 35S 79 50W
Ferret, C. 44 44 38N 1 15W
Ferrette 43 47 30N 7 20E
Ferriday 159 31 35N 91 33W
Ferrières 43 48 5N 2 48E
Ferriete 62 44 40N 9 30E
Ferrol 56 43 29N 8 15W
Ferron 160 39 3N 111 3W
Ferros 171 19 14S 43 2W
Ferryhill 33 54 42N 1 32W
Ferryland 151 47 2N 52 53W
Ferté Bernard, La 42 48 10N 0 40E
Ferté, La 43 48 57N 3 6E
Ferté-Mace, La 42 48 35N 0 21W
Ferté-St. Aubin, La 43 47 42N 1 57E
Ferté-Vidame, La 42 48 37N 0 53E
Fertile 158 47 37N 96 18W
Fertília 64 40 37N 8 13E
Fertöszentmiklós 53 47 35N 16 53E
Fès 118 34 0N 5 0W
Feschaux 47 50 9N 4 54E
Feshi 124 6 0S 18 10E
Fessenden 158 47 42N 99 44W
Fet 71 59 57N 11 12E
Feteşti 70 44 22N 27 51E
Fethaland, Pt. 36 60 39N 1 20W
Fethard 39 52 29N 7 42W
Fethiye 92 36 36N 29 10E
Fetlar, I. 36 60 36N 0 52W
Fettercairn 37 56 50N 2 33W
Feuerthalen 51 47 32N 8 38E
Feurs 45 45 45N 4 13E
Fezzan 117 27 0N 15 0E
Ffestiniog 31 52 58N 3 56W
Fforest Fawr, mt. 31 51 52N 3 35W
Fiambalá 172 27 45S 67 37W
Fianarantsoa 125 21 20S 46 45E
Fianarantsoa □ 129 19 30S 47 0E
Fianga 117 9 55N 15 20E
Fibiş 66 45 57N 21 26E
Fichot, I. 151 51 12N 55 40W
Fichtelgebirge 49 50 10N 12 0E
Ficksburg 129 28 51S 27 53E
Fiddown 39 52 20N 7 20W
Fidenza 62 44 51N 10 3E
Field 150 46 31N 80 1W

Field I Fort Garland

Field I. 136 12 5 S 132 23 E
Field, R. 138 23 48 S 138 0 E
Fields Finds 137 29 0 S 117 10 E
Fierenana 129 18 29 S 48 24 E
Fiéri 68 40 43N 19 33 E
Fiesch 50 46 25N 8 12 E
Fife □ 35 56 13N 3 2W
Fife Ness 35 56 17N 2 35W
Fifth Cataract 123 18 15N 33 50 E
Figeac 44 44 37N 2 2 E
Figline Valdarno 63 43 37N 11 28 E
Figtree 127 20 22 S 28 20 E
Figueira da Foz 56 40 7N 8 54W
Figueiró dos Vinhos 56 39 55N 8 16W
Figueras 58 42 18N 2 58 E
Figuig 118 32 5N 1 11W
Fihaonana 129 18 36 S 47 12 E
Fiherenana, R. 129 22 50 S 44 0 E
Fiji ■ 142 17 20 S 179 0 E
Fiji Is. 130 17 20 S 179 0 E
Fik 90 32 46N 35 41 E
Fika 121 11 15N 11 13 E
Filabres, Sierra de los 59 37 13N 2 20W
Filadélfia, Brazil 170 7 21 S 47 30W
Filadélfia, Italy 65 38 47N 16 17 E
Filadelfia 172 22 25 S 60 0W
Fil'akovo 53 48 17N 19 50 E
Filby 29 52 40N 1 39 E
Filchner Ice Shelf 13 78 0 S 60 0W
Filer 160 42 30N 114 35W
Filey 33 54 13N 0 18W
Filey B. 33 54 12N 0 15W
Filiaşi 70 44 32N 23 31 E
Filiátes 68 39 38N 20 16 E
Filiatrá 69 37 9N 21 35 E
Filicudi, I. 65 38 35N 14 33 E
Filiourí, R. 68 41 15N 25 40 E
Filipstad 72 59 43N 14 9 E
Filisur 51 46 41N 9 40 E
Fillmore, Can. 153 49 50N 103 25W
Fillmore, U.S.A. 163 34 23N 118 58W
Filottrano 63 43 28N 13 20 E
Filton 28 51 29N 2 34 E
Filyos 82 41 34N 32 4 E
Filyos çayi 92 41 35N 32 10 E
Finale Ligure 62 44 10N 8 21 E
Finale nell' Emília 63 44 50N 11 18 E
Fiñana 59 37 10N 2 50W
Fincham 29 52 38N 0 30 E
Findhorn 37 57 39N 3 36W
Findhorn, R. 37 57 38N 3 38W
Findlay 156 41 0N 83 41W
Findon 29 50 53N 0 24W
Finea 38 53 46N 7 23W
Finedon 29 52 20N 0 40W
Finger L. 153 53 9N 93 30W
Fingest 29 51 35N 0 52W
Finglas 38 53 22N 6 18W
Fingõe 127 15 12 S 31 50 E
Finike 92 36 21N 30 10 E
Finistère □ 42 48 20N 4 0W
Finisterre 56 42 54N 9 16W
Finisterre, C. 56 42 50N 9 19W
Finisterre Ra. 135 6 0 S 146 30 E
Finke 138 25 34 S 134 35 E
Finke, R. 138 24 54 S 134 16 E
Finland ■ 78 70 0N 27 0 E
Finland, G. of 78 60 0N 26 0 E
Finlay, R. 152 55 50N 125 10W
Finley, Austral. 141 35 38 S 145 35 E
Finley, U.S.A. 158 47 35N 97 50W
Finn, R. 38 54 50N 7 55W
Finnart 34 56 7N 4 48W
Finnigan, Mt. 138 15 49 S 145 17 E
Finniss 140 35 24 S 138 48 E
Finniss, C. 139 33 38 S 134 51 E
Finnmark fylke □ 74 69 30N 25 0 E
Finschhafen 135 6 33 S 147 50 E
Finse 71 60 36N 7 30 E
Finspång 73 58 45N 15 43 E
Finsta 72 59 45N 18 34 E
Finsteraarhorn 50 46 31N 8 10 E
Finsterwalde 48 51 37N 13 42 E
Finsterwolde 46 53 12N 7 6 E
Finstown 37 59 0N 3 8W
Fintona 38 54 30N 7 20W
Fintown 38 54 52N 8 8W
Finucanel I. 132 20 19 S 118 30 E
Finvoy 38 55 0N 6 29W
Fionn L. 36 57 46N 5 30W
Fionnphort 34 56 19N 6 23W
Fiora, R. 63 42 25N 11 35 E
Fiordland National Park 143 45 0 S 167 50 E
Fiorenzuola d'Arda 62 44 56N 9 54 E
Fiq 90 32 46N 35 41 E
Fire River 150 48 47N 83 36W
Firebag, R. 153 57 45N 111 21W
Firebaugh 163 36 52N 120 27W
Firedrake L. 153 61 25N 104 30W
Firenze 63 43 47N 11 15 E
Firkessédougou 120 9 35N 5 6W
Firmi 44 44 32N 2 19 E
Firminy 45 45 23N 4 18 E
Firoz Kohi 93 34 45N 63 0 E
Firozabad 95 27 10N 78 25 E
First Cataract 122 24 1N 32 51 E
Fīrūzābād 93 28 52N 52 35 E
Firuzkuh 93 35 50N 52 40 E
Firvale 152 52 27N 126 13W
Fish, R. 128 27 40 S 17 30 E
Fisher 137 30 30 S 131 0 E
Fisher B. 153 51 35N 97 13W
Fishguard 31 51 59N 4 59W
Fishguard B. 31 52 2N 4 58W
Fishing L. 153 52 10N 95 24W
Fishkill 162 41 32N 73 53W
Fishtoft 33 52 27N 0 2 E
Fishtown 120 4 24N 7 45 E
Fiskivötn 74 64 50N 20 45W
Fiskum 71 59 42N 9 46 E
Fismes 43 49 20N 3 40 E
Fister 71 59 10N 6 5 E
Fitchburg 162 42 35N 71 47W
Fitero 58 42 4N 1 52W
Fitful Hd. 36 59 54N 1 20W
Fitjar 71 59 55N 5 17 E
Fitri, L. 124 12 50N 17 28 E
Fitz Roy 176 47 10 S 67 0W
Fitzgerald, Can. 152 59 51N 111 36W
Fitzgerald, U.S.A. 157 31 45N 83 10W
Fitzmaurice, R. 136 14 50 S 129 50 E
Fitzpatrick 150 47 29N 72 46W
Fitzroy Crossing 136 18 9 S 125 38 E
Fitzroy, R., Queens., Austral. 138 23 32 S 150 52 E
Fitzroy, R., W. Australia, Austral. 136 17 25 S 124 0 E
Fiume = Rijeka 63 45 20N 14 21 E
Fiumefreddo Brúzio 65 39 14N 16 4 E
Five Alley 39 53 9N 7 51W
Five Points 163 36 26N 120 6W
Fivemiletown 38 54 23N 7 20W
Fizi 126 4 17 S 28 55 E
Fjæra 71 59 52N 6 22 E
Fjaere 71 58 23N 8 36 E
Fjellerup 73 56 29N 10 34 E
Fjerritslev 73 57 5N 9 15 E
Fkih ben Salah 118 32 45N 6 45W
Fla 71 60 25N 9 26 E
Flå 71 63 13N 10 18 E
Flagler 158 39 20N 103 4W
Flagstaff 161 35 10N 111 40W
Flagstone 152 49 4N 115 10W
Flaherty, I. 150 56 15N 79 15W
Flåm 75 60 52N 7 14 E
Flambeau, R. 158 45 40N 90 50W
Flamborough 33 54 7N 0 7W
Flamborough Hd. 33 54 8N 0 4W
Flaming Gorge Dam 160 40 50N 109 25W
Flaming Gorge L. 160 41 15N 109 30W
Flamingo, Teluk 103 5 30 S 138 0 E
Flanders = Flandres 47 51 10N 3 15 E
Flandre Occidental □ 47 51 0N 3 0 E
Flandre Orientale □ 47 51 0N 4 0 E
Flandreau 158 44 5N 96 38W
Flandres, Plaines des 47 51 10N 3 15 E
Flannan Is. 23 58 9N 7 52W
Flaren L. 73 57 2N 14 5 E
Flåsjön 74 64 5N 15 50 E
Flat, R. 152 61 51N 128 0W
Flat River 159 37 50N 90 30W
Flatey, Barðastrandarsýsla, Iceland 74 66 10N 17 52W
Flatey, Suður-þingeyjarsýsla, Iceland 74 65 22N 22 56W
Flathead L. 160 47 50N 114 0W
Flattery, C., Austral. 138 14 58 S 145 21 E
Flattery, C., U.S.A. 160 48 21N 124 43W
Flavy-le-Martel 43 49 43N 3 12 E
Flawil 51 47 26N 9 11 E
Flaxton 158 48 52N 102 24W
Flèche, La 42 47 42N 0 5W
Fleeming, C. 136 11 15 S 131 21 E
Fleet 29 51 16N 0 50W
Fleetwood, U.K. 32 53 55N 3 1W
Fleetwood, U.S.A. 162 40 27N 75 49W
Flekkefjord 71 58 18N 6 39 E
Flémalle 47 50 36N 5 28 E
Flensburg Fjord 73 54 50N 9 40 E
Flensburg 48 54 46N 9 28 E
Flers 42 48 47N 0 33W
Flesberg 71 59 51N 9 22 E
Fletton 29 52 34N 0 13W
Fleurance 44 43 52N 0 40 E
Fleurier 50 46 54N 6 35 E
Fleurus 47 50 29N 4 32 E
Flickerbäcken 72 61 47N 12 34 E
Flims 51 46 50N 9 17 E
Flin Flon 153 54 46N 101 53W
Flinders B. 137 34 19 S 115 9 E
Flinders Group, Is. 138 14 11 S 144 15 E
Flinders I. 138 40 0 S 148 0 E
Flinders, R. 138 17 36 S 140 36 E
Flinders Ranges 140 31 30 S 138 30 E
Flinders Reefs 138 17 37 S 148 31 E
Flint 156 43 5N 83 19W
Flint (□) 26 53 15N 3 12W
Flint, I. 131 11 26 S 151 48W
Flint, R. 157 31 20N 84 10W
Flinton 139 27 55 S 149 32 E
Fliseryd 73 57 6N 16 15 E
Flitwick 29 51 59N 0 30W
Flix 58 41 14N 0 32 E
Flixecourt 43 50 0N 2 5 E
Flobecq 47 50 44N 3 45 E
Floda 72 60 30N 14 53 E
Flodden 35 55 37N 2 8W
Floodwood 158 46 55N 92 55W
Flora, N. Tröndelag, Norway 71 63 27N 11 22 E
Flora, Sogn & Fjordane, Norway 71 61 35N 5 1 E
Flora, U.S.A. 156 38 40N 88 30W
Florac 44 44 20N 3 37 E
Florala 157 31 0N 86 20W
Florânia 170 6 8 S 36 49W
Floreffe 47 50 26N 4 46 E
Florence, Ala., U.S.A. 157 34 50N 87 50W
Florence, Ariz., U.S.A. 161 33 0N 111 25W
Florence, Colo., U.S.A. 158 38 26N 105 0W
Florence, Oreg., U.S.A. 160 44 0N 124 3W
Florence, S.C., U.S.A. 157 34 5N 79 50W
Florence = Firenze 63 43 47N 11 15 E
Florence, L. 139 28 53 S 138 9 E
Florennes 47 50 15N 4 35 E
Florensac 44 43 23N 3 28 E
Florenville 47 49 40N 5 19 E
Flores, Azores 16 39 13N 31 13W
Flores, Brazil 170 7 51 S 37 59W
Flores, Guat. 166 16 50N 89 40W
Flores I. 152 49 20N 126 10W
Flores, I. 103 8 35 S 121 0 E
Flores Sea 102 6 30 S 124 0 E
Floresta 170 9 46 S 37 26W
Floresville 159 29 10N 98 10W
Floriano 170 6 50 S 43 0W
Florianópolis 173 27 30 S 48 30W
Florida, Cuba 166 21 32N 78 14W
Florida, Uruguay 173 34 7 S 56 10W
Florida □ 157 28 30N 82 0W
Florida B. 167 25 0N 81 20W
Florida Keys 167 25 0N 80 40W
Florida, Strait of 167 25 0N 80 0W
Florídia 65 37 6N 15 9 E
Flórina 68 40 48N 21 26 E
Flórina □ 68 40 45N 21 20 E
Florningen 72 61 50N 12 16 E
Florø 71 61 35N 5 1 E
Flosta 71 58 32N 8 56 E
Flower's Cove 151 51 14N 56 46W
Floydada 159 33 58N 101 18W
Flüela Pass 51 46 45N 9 57 E
Fluk 103 1 42 S 127 38 E
Flumen, R. 58 41 50N 0 25W
Flumendosa, R. 64 39 30N 9 25 E
Fluminimaggiore 64 39 25N 8 30 E
Flums 51 47 6N 9 21 E
Flushing = Vlissingen 47 51 26N 3 34 E
Fluviá, R. 58 42 12N 3 7 E
Fly, R. 135 8 25 S 143 0 E
Foam Lake 153 51 40N 103 32W
Foča 66 43 31N 18 47 E
Focşani 70 45 41N 27 15 E
Fofo Fofo 138 8 9 S 147 6 E
Foggaret el Arab 118 27 3N 2 59 E
Foggaret ez Zoua 118 27 20N 3 0 E
Fóggia 65 41 28N 15 31 E
Foggo 121 11 21N 9 57 E
Foglia, R. 63 43 50N 12 32 E
Fogo 151 49 43N 54 17W
Fogo I. 151 49 40N 54 5W
Fohnsdorf 52 47 12N 14 40 E
Föhr 48 54 40N 8 30 E
Foia, Cerro da 57 37 19N 8 10W
Foix 44 42 58N 1 38 E
Fojnica 66 43 59N 17 51 E
Fokang 109 23 52N 113 31 E
Fokino 80 53 30N 34 10 E
Fokís □ 69 38 30N 22 15 E
Fokstua 71 62 8N 9 16 E
Folda, Nord-Trøndelag, Norway 74 64 41N 10 50 E
Folda, Nordland, Norway 74 67 38N 14 50 E
Földeák 53 46 19N 20 30 E
Folette, La 157 36 23N 84 9W
Foley 128 30 25N 87 40W
Foleyet 150 48 15N 82 25W
Folgefonni 71 60 23N 6 34 E
Foligno 63 42 58N 12 40 E
Folkestone 29 51 5N 1 11 E
Folkston 157 30 55N 82 0W
Follett 159 36 30N 100 12W
Follónica 62 42 55N 10 45 E
Folsom 160 38 41N 121 7W
Fond-du-Lac 153 59 19N 107 12W
Fond du Lac 158 43 46N 88 26W
Fond-du-Lac, R. 153 59 17N 106 0W
Fondak 118 35 34N 5 35W
Fondi 64 41 21N 13 25 E
Fonfría 56 41 37N 6 9W
Fongen 71 63 11N 11 38 E
Fonni 64 40 5N 9 16 E
Fonsagrada 56 43 8N 7 4W
Fonseca, G. de 166 13 10N 87 40W
Fontaine-Française 43 47 32N 5 21 E
Fontainebleau 43 48 24N 2 40 E
Fontas, R. 152 58 14N 121 48W
Fonte Boa 174 2 25 S 66 0W
Fontem 121 5 32N 9 52 E
Fontenay-le-Comte 44 46 28N 0 48W
Fontenelle 151 48 54N 64 33W
Fontur 74 66 23N 14 32W
Fonyód 53 46 44N 17 33 E
Foochow = Fuchou 109 26 5N 119 18 E
Foping 106 33 22N 108 19 E
Foppiano 62 46 21N 8 24 E
Föra 73 57 1N 16 51 E
Forbach 43 49 10N 6 52 E
Forbes 141 33 22 S 148 0 E
Forbesganj 95 26 17N 87 18 E
Forcados 121 5 26N 5 26 E
Forcados, R. 121 5 25N 5 20 E
Forcall, R. 58 40 40N 0 12W
Forcalquier 45 43 58N 5 47 E
Forchheim 49 49 42N 11 4 E
Forclaz, Col de la 50 46 3N 7 1 E
Ford City 163 35 9N 119 27W
Førde 71 61 27N 5 53 E
Fordingbridge 28 50 56N 1 48W
Fordongianus 44 40 0N 8 50 E
Fords Bridge 139 29 41 S 145 29 E
Fordyce 159 33 50N 92 20W
Forécariah 120 9 20N 13 10W
Forel 12 66 52N 36 55W
Foremost 152 49 26N 111 25W
Forenza 65 40 50N 15 50 E
Forest, Belg. 47 50 49N 4 20 E
Forest, U.S.A. 159 32 21N 89 27W
Forest City, Ark., U.S.A. 159 35 0N 90 50W
Forest City, Iowa, U.S.A. 158 43 12N 93 39W
Forest City, N.C., U.S.A. 157 35 23N 81 50W
Forest Grove 160 45 31N 123 4W
Forest Lawn 152 51 4N 114 0W
Forest Row 29 51 6N 0 3 E
Forestburg 152 52 35N 112 1W
Forestier Pen. 138 43 0 S 148 0 E
Forestville, Can. 151 48 48N 69 20W
Forestville, U.S.A. 156 44 41N 87 29W
Forez, Mts. du 44 45 40N 3 50 E
Forfar 37 56 40N 2 53W
Forges-les-Eaux 43 49 37N 1 30 E
Forget 150 49 40N 102 50W
Forked River 162 39 50N 74 12W
Forks 160 47 56N 124 23W
Forksville 162 41 29N 76 35W
Forli 63 44 14N 12 2 E
Forman 158 46 9N 97 43W
Formazza 62 46 23N 8 26 E
Formby Pt. 32 53 33N 3 7W
Formentera, I. 59 38 40N 1 30 E
Formentor, C. de 58 39 58N 3 13 E
Fórmia 64 41 15N 13 34 E
Formiga 171 20 27 S 45 25W
Formigine 62 44 37N 10 51 E
Formiguères 44 42 37N 2 5 E
Formosa, Argent. 172 26 15 S 58 10W
Formosa, Brazil 171 15 32 S 47 20W
Formosa = Taiwan ■ 109 24 0N 121 0 E
Formosa □ 172 26 5 S 58 10W
Formosa Bay 126 2 40 S 40 20 E
Formosa Strait 109 24 40N 120 0 E
Formoso, R. 171 10 34 S 49 56W
Fornaes, C. 73 56 27N 10 58 E
Fornells 58 40 4N 4 4 E
Fornos de Algodres 56 40 38N 7 32W
Fornovo di Taro 62 44 42N 10 7 E
Forres 37 57 37N 3 38W
Forrest, Vic., Austral. 140 38 22 S 143 40 E
Forrest, W. Australia, Austral. 137 30 51 S 128 6 E
Forrest Lakes 137 29 12 S 128 46 E
Forrest, Mt. 137 24 48 S 127 45 E
Forrières 47 50 8N 5 17 E
Fors, Jämtland, Sweden 72 63 0N 16 40 E
Fors, Kopparberg, Sweden 72 60 14N 16 20 E
Forsa 72 61 44N 16 55 E
Forsand 71 58 54N 6 5 E
Forsayth 138 18 33 S 143 34 E
Forsbacka 72 60 39N 16 54 E
Forse 72 63 8N 17 1 E
Forserum 73 57 42N 14 30 E
Forshaga 72 59 33N 13 29 E
Forshem 73 58 38N 13 30 E
Forsmo 72 63 16N 17 11 E
Forst 48 51 43N 14 37 E
Forster 141 32 12 S 152 31 E
Forsyth, Ga., U.S.A. 157 33 4N 83 55W
Forsyth, Mont., U.S.A. 160 46 14N 106 37W
Forsyth I. 143 40 58 S 174 5 E
Fort Albany 150 52 15N 81 35W
Fort Ann 162 43 25N 73 30W
Fort Apache 161 33 50N 110 0W
Fort Archambault = Sarh 117 9 5N 18 23 E
Fort Assiniboine 152 54 20N 114 45W
Fort Augustus 37 57 9N 4 40W
Fort Babine 152 55 22N 126 37W
Fort Beaufort 128 32 46 S 26 40 E
Fort Benton 160 47 50N 110 40W
Fort Bragg 160 39 28N 123 50W
Fort Bretonnet = Bousso 117 10 34N 16 52 E
Fort Bridger 160 41 22N 110 20W
Fort Charlet = Djanet 121 24 35N 9 32 E
Fort Chimo 149 58 6N 68 25W
Fort Chipewyan 153 58 42N 111 8W
Fort Collins 158 40 30N 105 4W
Fort Coulonge 150 45 50N 76 45W
Fort Crampel = Crampel 117 7 8N 19 18 E
Fort-Dauphin 129 25 2 S 47 0 E
Fort Davis 159 30 38N 103 53W
Fort-de-France 167 14 36N 61 2W
Fort de Polignac = Illizi 119 26 31N 8 32 E
Fort de Possel = Possel 124 5 5N 19 10 E
Fort Defiance 161 35 47N 109 4W
Fort Dodge 158 42 29N 94 10W
Fort Flatters = Zaouiet El-Khala 119 27 10N 6 40 E
Fort Foureau = Kousseri 117 12 0N 14 55 E
Fort Frances 153 48 35N 93 25W
Fort Franklin 148 65 30N 123 45W
Fort Garland 161 37 28N 105 30W

Fort George

Frýdek-Místek

Fort George 151 53 50N 79 0W
Fort George, R. 150 53 50N 77 0W
Fort Good-Hope 147 66 14N 128 40W
Fort Gouraud = F'Dérik 116 22 40N 12 45W
Fort Grahame 152 56 30N 124 35W
Fort Hancock 161 31 19N 105 56W
Fort Hauchuca 161 31 32N 110 30W
Fort Hertz (Putao) 99 27 28N 97 30 E
Fort Hope 150 51 30N 88 10W
Fort Irwin 163 35 16N 116 34W
Fort Jameson = Chipata 127 13 38 S 32 38 E
Fort Johnston 127 14 25 S 35 16 E
Fort Kent 151 47 12N 68 30W
Fort Klamath 160 42 45N 122 0W
Fort Lallemand 119 31 13N 6 17 E
Fort-Lamy = Ndjamena 117 12 4N 15 8 E
Fort Lapperrine = Tamanrasset 119 22 56N 5 30 E
Fort Laramie 158 42 15N 104 30W
Fort Lauderdale 157 26 10N 80 5W
Fort Liard 152 60 20N 123 30W
Fort Liberté 167 19 42N 71 51W
Fort Lupton 158 40 8N 104 48W
Fort Mackay 152 57 12N 111 41W
Fort McKenzie 151 57 20N 69 0W
Fort Macleod 152 49 45N 113 30W
Fort MacMahon 118 29 51N 1 45 E
Fort McMurray 152 56 44N 111 23W
Fort McPherson 147 67 30N 134 55W
Fort Madison 158 40 39N 91 20W
Fort Meade 157 27 45N 81 45W
Fort Miribel 118 29 31N 2 55 E
Fort Morgan 158 40 10N 103 50W
Fort Myers 157 26 30N 82 0W
Fort Nelson 152 58 50N 122 38W
Fort Nelson, R. 152 59 32N 124 0W
Fort Norman 147 64 57N 125 30W
Fort Pacot (Chirfa) 119 20 55N 12 14 E
Fort Payne 157 34 25N 85 44W
Fort Peck 160 47 1N 105 30W
Fort Peck Dam 160 48 0N 106 20W
Fort Peck Res. 160 47 40N 107 0W
Fort Pierce 158 27 29N 80 19W
Fort Pierre 158 44 25N 100 25W
Fort Pierre Bordes 118 20 0N 2 55 E
Fort Portal 126 0 40N 30 20 E
Fort Providence 152 61 21N 117 40W
Fort Qu'Appelle 153 50 45N 103 50W
Fort Randall 147 55 10N 162 48W
Fort Reliance 153 63 0N 109 20W
Fort Resolution 152 61 10N 113 40W
Fort Rixon 127 20 2 S 29 17 E
Fort Roseberry = Mansa 127 11 10 S 28 50 E
Fort Rupert (Rupert House) 150 51 30N 78 40W
Fort Saint 119 30 13N 9 31 E
Fort St. James 152 54 30N 124 10W
Fort St. John 152 56 15N 120 50W
Fort Sandeman 94 31 20N 69 25 E
Fort Saskatchewan 152 53 40N 113 15W
Fort Scott 159 38 0N 94 40W
Fort Selkirk 147 62 43N 137 22W
Fort Severn 150 56 0N 87 40W
Fort Shevchenko 83 44 30N 50 10W
Fort Sibut = Sibut 117 5 52N 19 10 E
Fort Simpson 152 61 45N 121 23W
Fort Smith, Can. 152 60 0N 111 51W
Fort Smith, U.S.A. 159 35 25N 94 25W
Fort Stanton 161 33 33N 105 36W
Fort Stockton 159 30 48N 103 2W
Fort Sumner 159 34 24N 104 8W
Fort Thomas 161 33 2N 109 59W
Fort Trinquet = Bir Mogrein 116 25 10N 11 25W
Fort Valley 157 32 33N 83 52W
Fort Vermilion 152 58 24N 116 0W
Fort Victoria 127 20 8 S 30 55 E
Ft. Walton Beach 157 30 25N 86 40W
Fort Wayne 156 41 5N 85 10W
Fort William 36 56 48N 5 8W
Fort William = Thunder Bay 150 48 20N 89 10W
Fort Worth 159 32 45N 97 25W
Fort Yates 158 46 8N 100 38W
Fort Yukon 147 66 35N 145 12W
Fortaleza 170 3 35 S 38 35W
Forte Coimbra 174 19 55 S 57 48W
Forte Rocadas 125 16 38 S 15 22 E
Forteau 151 51 28N 57 1W
Fortescue 136 21 4 S 116 4 E
Fortescue, R. 136 21 20 S 116 5 E
Forth, Firth of 35 56 5N 2 55W
Forthassa Rharbia 118 32 52N 1 11W
Forties, oilfield 19 57 40N 1 0 E
Fortin Corrales 174 22 21 S 60 35W
Fortín Guachalla 174 22 22 S 62 23W
Fortín Rojas Silva 172 22 40 S 59 3W
Fortín Siracuas 174 21 3 S 61 46W
Fortín Teniente Montania 172 22 1 S 59 45W
Fortore, R. 63 41 40N 15 0 E
Fortrose 143 46 38 S 168 45 E
Fortuna, Spain 59 38 11N 1 7W
Fortuna, Cal., U.S.A. 160 48 38N 124 8W
Fortuna, N.D., U.S.A. 158 48 55N 103 48W
Fortune Bay 151 47 30N 55 22W
Forty Mile 147 64 20N 140 30W
Forūr 93 26 20N 54 30 E
Fos 62 43 20N 4 57 E
Fos do Jordão 174 9 30 S 72 14W
Fos-sur-Mer 45 43 26N 4 56 E
Foshan 109 23 4N 113 5 E
Fossacesia 63 42 15N 14 30 E
Fossano 62 44 39N 7 40 E
Fosses-la-Ville 47 50 24N 4 41 E
Fossil 160 45 0N 120 9W
Fossilbrook 138 17 47 S 144 29 E
Fossombrone 63 43 41N 12 49 E
Fosston 158 47 33N 95 39W
Foster, R. 153 55 47N 105 49W
Fosters Ra. 138 21 35 S 133 48 E
Fostoria 156 41 8N 83 25W
Fou Chiang, R. 108 30 3N 106 21 E
Fouch'eng 106 37 52N 116 8 E
Fougamou 124 1 38 S 11 39 E
Fougéres 42 48 21N 1 14W
Fouhsinshih 107 42 13N 121 51 E
Foul Pt. 97 8 35N 81 25 E
Foula, I. 23 60 10N 2 5W
Fouling 108 29 40N 107 20 E
Foulpointe 129 17 41 S 49 31 E
Foum el Alba 118 20 45N 3 0W
Foum el Kreneg 118 29 0N 0 58W
Foum Tatahouine 119 32 57N 10 29 E
Foum Zguid 118 30 2N 6 59W
Foumban 121 5 45N 10 50 E
Foundiougne 120 14 5N 16 32W
Founing 107 33 47N 119 48 E
Fountain, Colo., U.S.A. 158 38 42N 104 40W
Fountain, Utah, U.S.A. 160 39 41N 111 50W
Fountain Springs 163 35 54N 118 51W
Foup'ing 106 38 55N 114 13 E
Four Mts., Is. of the 147 52 0N 170 30W
Fourchambault 43 47 0N 3 3 E
Fourchu 151 45 43N 60 17W
Fourcroy, C. 136 11 45 S 130 2 E
Fourmies 43 50 1N 4 2 E
Fournás 69 39 3N 21 52 E
Foúrnoi 69 37 36N 26 32 E
Fours 43 46 50N 3 42 E
Foushan 106 35 58N 111 51 E
Fouta Djalon 120 11 20N 12 10W
Foux, Cap-à- 167 19 43N 73 27W
Fouyang 109 32 55N 115 52 E
Foveaux Str. 143 46 42 S 168 10 E
Fowler, Calif., U.S.A. 163 36 41N 119 41W
Fowler, Colo., U.S.A. 158 38 10N 104 0W
Fowler, Kans., U.S.A. 159 37 28N 100 7W
Fowlers B. 137 31 59 S 132 34 E
Fowlers Bay 137 32 0 S 132 29 E
Fowlerton 159 28 26N 98 50W
Fox Is. 147 52 30N 166 0W
Fox, R. 153 56 3N 93 18W
Fox Valley 153 50 30N 109 25W
Foxboro 162 42 4N 71 16W
Foxe Basin 149 68 30N 77 0W
Foxe Channel 149 66 0N 80 0W
Foxe Pen. 149 65 0N 76 0W
Foxen, L. 72 59 25N 11 55 E
Foxhol 46 53 10N 6 43 E
Foxpark 160 41 4N 106 6W
Foxton 142 40 29 S 175 18 E
Foyle, Lough 38 55 6N 7 8W
Foynes 38 52 30N 9 5W
Foz 56 43 33N 7 20W
Foz do Cunene 128 17 15 S 11 55 E
Foz do Gregório 174 6 47 S 71 0W
Foz do Iguaçu 173 25 30 S 54 30W
Frackville 162 40 46N 76 15W
Fraga 58 41 32N 0 21 E
Fraire 47 50 16N 4 31 E
Frameries 47 50 24N 3 54 E
Framlingham 29 52 14N 1 20 E
Franca 171 20 25 S 47 30W
Francavilla al Mare 63 42 25N 14 16 E
Francavilla Fontana 65 40 32N 17 35 E
France ■ 41 47 0N 3 0 E
Frances 140 36 41 S 140 55 E
Frances Creek 136 13 25 S 132 3 E
Frances L. 152 61 23N 129 30W
Frances, R. 152 60 16N 129 10W
Francés Viejo, C. 167 19 40N 70 0W
Franceville 124 1 40 S 13 32 E
Franche Comté □ 43 46 30N 5 50 E
Franches Montagnes 50 47 10N 7 0 E
Francis-Garnier 118 36 30N 1 30 E
Francis Harbour 151 52 34N 55 44W
Francisco I. Madero, Coahuila, Mexico 164 25 48N 103 18W
Francisco I. Madero, Durango, Mexico 164 24 32N 104 22W
Francisco Sá 171 16 28 S 43 30W
Francistown 125 21 7 S 27 33 E
Francofonte 65 37 13N 14 50 E
François 151 47 35N 56 45W
Francois L. 152 54 0N 125 30W
François, Le 167 14 38N 60 57W
Francorchamps 47 50 27N 5 57 E
Franeker 46 53 12N 5 33 E
Frankado 123 12 30N 43 12 E
Frankenberg 48 51 3N 8 47 E
Frankenthal 49 49 32N 8 21 E
Frankford = Kilcormac 39 53 10N 7 43W
Frankfort, Ind., U.S.A. 156 40 20N 86 33W
Frankfort, Kans., U.S.A. 158 39 42N 96 26W
Frankfort, Ky., U.S.A. 156 38 12N 84 52W
Frankfort, Mich., U.S.A. 156 44 38N 86 14W
Frankfort, N.Y., U.S.A. 162 43 2N 75 4W
Frankfurt □ 48 52 30N 14 0 E
Frankfurt am Main 49 50 7N 8 40 E
Frankfurt an der Oder 48 52 50N 14 31 E
Fränkische Alb 49 49 20N 11 30 E
Fränkische Saale 49 50 7N 9 49 E
Fränkische Saale, R. 49 50 7N 9 49 E
Fränkische Schweiz 49 49 45N 11 10 E
Frankland, R. 137 35 0 S 116 48 E
Franklin, Ky., U.S.A. 157 36 40N 86 30W
Franklin, La., U.S.A. 159 29 45N 91 30W
Franklin, Mass., U.S.A. 162 42 4N 71 23W
Franklin, Nebr., U.S.A. 158 40 9N 98 55W
Franklin, N.H., U.S.A. 162 43 28N 71 39W
Franklin, N.J., U.S.A. 162 41 9N 74 38W
Franklin, Pa., U.S.A. 156 41 22N 79 45W
Franklin, Tenn., U.S.A. 157 35 54N 86 53W
Franklin, Va., U.S.A. 157 36 40N 76 58W
Franklin, W. Va., U.S.A. 156 38 38N 79 21W
Franklin □ 149 71 0N 99 0W
Franklin B. 147 69 45N 126 0W
Franklin D. Roosevelt L. 160 48 30N 118 16W
Franklin I. 13 76 10 S 168 30 E
Franklin, L. 160 40 20N 115 26W
Franklin Mts., Can. 148 66 0N 125 0W
Franklin Mts., N.Z. 143 44 55 S 167 45 E
Franklin Str. 148 72 0N 96 0W
Franklinton 159 30 53N 90 10W
Franklyn Mt. 143 42 4 S 172 42 E
Franks Peak 160 43 50N 109 5W
Frankston 141 38 8 S 145 8 E
Frankton Junc. 142 37 47 S 175 16 E
Fränsta 72 62 30N 16 11 E
Frant 29 51 5N 0 17 E
Frantsa Josifa, Zemlya 76 76 0N 62 0 E
Franz 150 48 25N 84 30W
Franz Josef Fd. 12 73 20N 22 0 E
Franz Josef Land = Frantsa Josifa 76 76 0N 62 0 E
Franzburg 48 54 9N 12 52 E
Frascati 64 41 48N 12 41 E
Fraser I. 139 25 15 S 153 10 E
Fraser L. 152 54 0N 124 50W
Fraser, Mt. 137 25 35 S 118 20 E
Fraser, R., B.C., Can. 152 49 7N 123 11W
Fraser, R., Newf., Can. 151 56 39N 63 10W
Fraserburg 128 31 55 S 21 30 E
Fraserburgh 37 57 41N 2 0W
Fraserdale 150 49 55N 81 37W
Frasertown 142 38 58 S 177 28 E
Frashëri 68 40 23N 20 26 E
Frasne 43 46 50N 6 10 E
Frater 150 47 20N 84 25W
Frauenfeld 51 47 34N 8 54 E
Fray Bentos 172 33 10 S 58 15W
Frazier Downs P.O. 136 18 48 S 121 42 E
Frechilla 56 42 8N 4 50W
Fredericia 73 55 34N 9 45 E
Frederick, Md., U.S.A. 162 39 25N 77 23W
Frederick, Okla., U.S.A. 159 34 22N 99 0W
Frederick, S.D., U.S.A. 158 45 55N 98 29W
Frederick Reef 133 20 58 S 154 23 E
Frederick Sd. 153 57 10N 134 0W
Fredericksburg, Tex., U.S.A. 159 30 17N 98 55W
Fredericksburg, Va., U.S.A. 162 38 16N 77 29W
Frederickstown 159 37 35N 90 15W
Fredericton 151 45 57N 66 40W
Fredericton Junc. 151 45 41N 66 40W
Frederiksberg 72 60 12N 14 25 E
Frederiksborg Amt □ 73 55 50N 12 10 E
Frederikshåb 12 62 0N 49 30W
Frederikshavn 73 57 28N 10 31 E
Frederikssund 73 55 50N 12 3 E
Frederiksted 147 17 43N 64 53W
Fredonia, Ariz., U.S.A. 161 36 59N 112 36W
Fredonia, Kans., U.S.A. 159 37 34N 95 50W
Fredonia, N.Y., U.S.A. 156 42 26N 79 20W
Fredrikstad 71 59 13N 10 57 E
Freehold 162 40 15N 74 18W
Freel Pk. 163 38 52N 119 53W
Freeland 162 41 3N 75 48W
Freeling, Mt. 136 22 35 S 133 06 E
Freels, C. 151 49 15N 53 30W
Freeman, Calif., U.S.A. 163 35 35N 117 53W
Freeman, S.D., U.S.A. 158 43 25N 97 20W
Freeport, Bahamas 167 25 45N 88 30 E
Freeport, Can. 151 44 15N 66 20W
Freeport, Ill., U.S.A. 158 42 18N 89 40W
Freeport, N.Y., U.S.A. 162 40 39N 73 35W
Freeport, Tex., U.S.A. 159 28 55N 95 22W
Freetown 120 8 30N 13 10W
Freevater Forest 37 57 51N 4 45W
Fregenal de la Sierra 57 38 10N 6 39W
Fregene 64 41 50N 12 12 E
Fregeneda, La 56 40 58N 6 54W
Fréhel C. 42 48 40N 2 20W
Freiberg 48 50 55N 13 20 E
Freibourg = Fribourg 50 46 49N 7 9 E
Freiburg, Baden, Ger. 49 48 0N 7 52 E
Freiburg, Sachsen, Ger. 48 53 49N 9 17 E
Freiburger Alpen 50 46 37N 7 10 E
Freire 176 39 0 S 72 50W
Freirina 172 28 30 S 70 27W
Freising 49 48 24N 11 47 E
Freistadt 52 48 30N 14 30 E
Freital 48 51 0N 13 40 E
Fréjus 45 43 25N 6 44 E
Fremantle 137 32 1 S 115 47 E
Fremont, Calif., U.S.A. 163 37 32N 122 57W
Fremont, Mich., U.S.A. 156 43 29N 85 59W
Fremont, Nebr., U.S.A. 158 41 30N 96 30W
Fremont, Ohio, U.S.A. 156 41 20N 83 5W
Fremont, L. 160 43 0N 109 50W
Fremont, R. 161 38 15N 110 20W
French Camp 163 37 53N 121 16W
French Cr. 156 41 30N 80 2W
French Guiana ■ 175 4 0N 53 0W
French I. 141 38 20 S 145 22 E
French Terr. of Afars & Issas □ = Djibouti 123 11 30N 42 15 E
Frenchglen 160 42 56N 119 0W
Frenchman Butte 153 53 36N 109 36W
Frenchman Creek, R. 158 40 34N 101 35W
Frenchman, R. 160 49 25N 108 20W
Frenchpark 38 53 53N 8 25W
Frenda 118 35 2N 1 1 E
Fresco, R. 175 7 15 S 51 30W
Freshfield, C. 13 68 25 S 151 10 E
Freshford 39 52 45N 7 25W
Freshwater 28 50 42N 1 31W
Fresnillo 164 23 10N 103 0W
Fresno 163 36 47N 119 50W
Fresno Alhandiga 56 40 42N 5 37W
Fresno Res. 160 48 47N 110 0W
Freswick 37 58 35N 3 5W
Freuchie 35 56 14N 3 8W
Freudenstadt 49 48 27N 8 25 E
Freux 47 49 59N 5 27 E
Frévent 43 50 15N 2 17 E
Frew, R. 138 20 0 S 135 38 E
Frewena 138 19 50 S 135 50 E
Freycinet, C. 137 34 9 S 115 0 E
Freycinet Pen. 138 42 10 S 148 25 E
Fria 120 10 27N 13 32W
Fría, La 174 8 13N 72 15W
Friant 163 36 59N 119 43W
Frías 172 28 40 S 65 5W
Fribourg 50 46 49N 7 9 E
Fribourg □ 50 45 40N 7 0 E
Frick 50 47 31N 8 1 E
Fridafors 73 56 25N 14 39 E
Fridaythorpe 33 54 2N 0 40W
Friedberg, Bayern, Ger. 49 48 21N 10 59 E
Friedberg, Hessen, Ger. 10 50 19N 8 45 E
Friedland 49 53 40N 13 33 E
Friedrichshafen 49 47 39N 9 29 E
Friedrichskoog 48 54 1N 8 52 E
Friedrichsort 48 54 24N 10 11 E
Friedrichstadt 48 54 23N 9 6 E
Friendly (Tonga) Is. 130 19 50 S 174 30W
Friesach 52 46 57N 14 24 E
Friesack 48 52 43N 12 35 E
Friesche Wad 46 53 22N 5 44 E
Friesland □ 46 53 5N 5 50 E
Friesoythe 48 53 1N 7 51 E
Frigate, L. 150 53 15N 74 45W
Frigg E., gasfield 19 59 50N 2 20 E
Frigg, gasfield 19 59 50N 2 15 E
Frigg N.E., gasfield 19 60 0N 2 17 E
Frillesås 73 57 20N 12 12 E
Frimley 29 51 18N 0 43W
Frinnaryd 73 57 55N 14 50 E
Frinton-on-Sea 29 51 50N 1 16 E
Frio, C. 128 18 0 S 12 0 E
Frio, R. 159 29 40N 99 40W
Friockheim 37 56 39N 2 40W
Friona 159 34 40N 102 42W
Frisa, Loch 34 56 34N 6 5W
Frisian Is. 48 53 30N 6 0 E
Fristad 73 57 50N 13 0 E
Fritch 159 35 40N 101 35W
Fritsla 73 57 33N 12 47 E
Fritzlar 48 51 8N 9 19 E
Friuli-Venezia-Giulia □ 63 46 0N 13 0 E
Frizington 32 54 33N 3 30W
Frobisher B. 149 63 0N 67 0W
Frobisher L. 153 56 20N 108 15W
Frobisher Sd. 149 62 30N 66 0W
Frodsham 32 53 17N 2 45W
Frogmore 141 34 15 S 148 52 E
Frohavet 74 64 5N 9 35 E
Froid 158 48 20N 104 29W
Froid-Chapelle 47 50 9N 4 19 E
Frolovo 83 49 45N 43 30 E
Fromberg 160 45 19N 108 58W
Frombork 54 54 21N 19 41 E
Frome 28 51 16N 2 17W
Frome Downs 140 31 13 S 139 46 E
Frome, L. 140 30 45 S 139 45 E
Frome, R. 28 50 44N 2 5W
Fromentine 42 46 53N 2 9W
Frómista 56 42 16N 4 25W
Front Range 160 40 0N 105 10W
Front Royal 156 38 55N 78 10W
Fronteira 57 39 3N 7 39W
Fronteiras 170 7 5 S 40 37W
Frontera 165 18 30N 92 40W
Frontignan 44 43 27N 3 45 E
Frosinone 64 41 38N 13 20 E
Frosolone 65 41 34N 14 27 E
Frostburg 156 39 43N 78 57W
Frostisen 74 68 14N 17 10 E
Frouard 43 48 47N 6 8 E
Frövi 72 59 28N 15 24 E
Frower Pt. 39 51 40N 8 30W
Froya 71 63 43N 8 40 E
Frøya 71 63 43N 8 40 E
Fröya I. 74 63 45N 8 45 E
Fruges 43 50 30N 2 8 E
Frumoasa 70 46 28N 25 48 E
Frunze 85 42 54N 74 36 E
Fruška Gora 66 45 7N 19 30 E
Frutal 171 20 0 S 49 0W
Frutigen 50 46 35N 7 38 E
Frýdek-Místek 53 49 40N 18 20 E

Frýdlant Garibaldi Prov. Park

Frýdlant, Severočeský, Czech. 52 50 56N 15 9E
Frýdlant, Severomoravský, Czech. 53 49 35N 18 20E
Fryvaldov = Jesenik 53 50 0N 17 8E
Fthiótis □ 69 38 50N 22 25E
Fu 72 60 57N 14 44E
Fuan 109 27 9N 119 38E
Fucécchio 62 43 44N 10 51E
Fuch'ing 109 25 43N 119 22E
Fuchou, Fukien, China 109 26 5N 119 18E
Fuchou, Liaoning, China 107 39 45N 121 45E
Fuchū 110 34 34N 133 14E
Fūchū 111 35 40N 139 29E
Fuch'üan 108 26 42N 107 33E
Fuch'uan 109 24 50N 111 16E
Fucino, L. 44 42 0N 13 30E
Fuencaliente 57 38 25N 4 18W
Fuengirola 57 36 32N 4 41W
Fuente-Alamo 59 38 44N 1 24W
Fuente de Cantos 57 38 15N 6 18W
Fuente de San Esteban, La 56 40 49N 6 15W
Fuente del Maestre 57 38 31N 6 28W
Fuente el Fresno 57 39 14N 3 46W
Fuente Ovejuna 57 38 15N 5 25W
Fuentes de Andalucía 57 37 28N 5 20W
Fuentes de Ebro 58 41 31N 0 38W
Fuentes de León 57 38 5N 6 32W
Fuentes de Oñoro 56 40 33N 6 52W
Fuentesaúco 56 41 15N 5 30W
Fuerte Olimpo 172 21 0S 58 0W
Fuerte, R. 164 26 0N 109 0W
Fuerteventura, I. 116 28 30N 14 0W
Fuertey 38 53 37N 8 16W
Fufeng 106 34 20N 107 51E
Fŭget 70 45 52N 22 10E
Fŭget, Munţii 70 45 50N 22 9E
Fugløysund 74 70 15N 20 20E
Fŭgŭraş 70 45 48N 24 58E
Fŭgŭraş, Munţii 70 45 40N 24 40E
Fuhai 105 47 6N 87 23E
Fuhsien, Liaoning, China 107 39 38N 122 0E
Fuhsien, Shensi, China 106 36 2N 109 20E
Fuhsingchen 108 22 47N 101 5E
Fujaira 93 25 7N 56 18E
Fuji 111 35 9N 138 39E
Fuji-no-miya 111 35 20N 138 40E
Fuji-San 111 35 22N 138 44E
Fuji-yoshida 111 35 50N 138 46E
Fujieda 111 34 52N 138 16E
Fujioka 111 36 15N 139 5E
Fujisawa 111 35 22N 139 29E
Fukien □ 109 26 0N 117 30E
Fukou 106 34 3N 114 27E
Fuku 106 39 2N 111 3E
Fukuchiyama 111 35 25N 135 9E
Fukui 111 36 0N 136 10E
Fukui-ken □ 111 36 0N 136 12E
Fukuma 110 33 46N 130 28E
Fukung 108 26 58N 98 54E
Fukuoka 110 33 30N 130 30E
Fukuoka-ken □ 110 33 30N 131 0E
Fukuroi 111 34 45N 137 55E
Fukushima 112 37 30N 140 15E
Fukushima-ken □ 112 37 30N 140 15E
Fukuyama 110 34 35N 133 20E
Fŭlciu 70 46 17N 28 7E
Fulda 48 50 32N 9 41E
Fullerton, Calif., U.S.A. 163 33 52N 117 58W
Fullerton, Nebr., U.S.A. 158 41 25N 98 0W
Fulmar, oilfield 19 56 30N 2 8E
Fülöpszállás 53 46 49N 19 16E
Fŭlticeni 70 47 21N 26 20W
Fulton, Mo., U.S.A. 158 38 50N 91 55W
Fulton, N.Y., U.S.A. 162 43 20N 76 22W
Fuluälven 72 61 18N 13 4E
Fulufjället 72 61 32N 12 41E
Fulungch'üan 107 44 24N 124 37E
Fülüpszállás 53 46 49N 19 16E
Fumay 43 50 0N 4 40E
Fumbusi 121 10 25N 1 20W
Fumel 44 44 30N 0 58E
Fumin 108 25 14N 102 29E
Funabashi 111 35 45N 140 0E
Funafuti, I. 130 8 30S 179 0E
Funchal 116 32 45N 16 55W
Fundación 174 10 31N 74 11W
Fundão, Brazil 171 19 55S 40 24W
Fundão, Port. 56 40 8N 7 30W
Fundu 127 14 58S 30 14E
Fundy, B. of 151 45 0N 56 0W
Funes 174 1 0N 77 28W
Funing, Hopei, China 107 39 54N 119 12E
Funing, Yunnan, China 108 23 37N 105 36E
Funiu Shan 106 33 40N 112 30E
Funsi 120 10 21N 1 54W
Funtua 121 11 30N 7 18E
Fupien 108 31 18N 102 27E
Fup'ing 106 34 47N 109 7E
Fur 73 56 50N 9 0E
Furat, Nahr al 92 33 30N 43 0E
Furbero 165 20 22N 97 31W
Furka Pass 51 46 34N 8 35E
Furmanov 81 57 25N 41 3E
Furmanovka 85 44 17N 72 57E
Furmanovo 83 49 42N 49 25E
Furnas, Represa de 173 20 50S 45 0W
Furneaux Group 138 40 10S 147 50E
Furness, Pen. 32 54 12N 3 10W
Fürstenau 48 52 32N 7 40E
Fürstenfeld 52 47 3N 16 3E
Fürstenfeldbruck 49 48 10N 11 15E
Fürstenwalde 48 52 20N 14 3E
Fürth 49 49 29N 11 0E
Fürth i. Wald 49 49 19N 12 51E
Furtwangen 49 48 3N 8 14E
Furudal 72 61 10N 15 11E
Furukawa 111 36 14N 137 11E
Furusund 72 59 40N 18 55E
Fury and Hecla Str. 149 69 56N 84 0W
Fusa 71 60 12N 5 37E
Fusagasugá 174 4 21N 74 22W
Fuscaldo 65 39 25N 16 1E
Fushan 107 37 30N 121 5E
Fushë Arrëzi 68 42 4N 20 2E
Fushun, Liaoning, China 107 41 50N 123 55E
Fushun, Szechwan, China 108 29 13N 105 0E
Fush'un Chiang, R. 109 30 5N 120 5E
Fusio 51 46 27N 8 40E
Füssen 49 47 35N 10 43E
Fusui 108 22 35N 107 58E
Fusung 107 42 15N 127 20E
Futago-Yama 110 33 35N 131 36E
Futing 109 27 15N 120 10E
Futuk 121 9 45N 10 56E
Futuna I. 130 14 25S 178 20E
Fŭurei 70 45 6N 27 19E
Fuwa 122 31 12N 30 33E
Fuyang 109 30 5N 119 56E
Fuyang Ho, R. 106 38 14N 116 5E
Fuyü 107 45 10N 124 50E
Fuyüan 105 47 40N 132 30E
Füzesgyarmat 53 47 6N 21 14E
Fwaka 125 12 5S 29 25E
Fylde 32 53 50N 2 58W
Fylingdales Moor 33 54 22N 0 32W
Fyn 73 55 20N 10 30E
Fyne, L. 34 56 0N 5 20W
Fyns Amt □ 73 55 15N 10 30E
Fynshav 73 54 59N 9 59E
Fyresvatn 71 59 6N 8 10E
Fyvie 37 57 26N 2 24W

G

Gaanda 121 10 10N 12 27E
Gaba 123 6 20N 35 7E
Gaba Tula 82 0 20N 38 35E
Gabah, C. 91 8 0N 50 0E
Gabarin 121 11 8N 10 27E
Gabbs 163 38 52N 117 55W
Gabela 124 11 0S 14 37E
Gaberones = Gaborone 128 24 37S 25 57E
Gabès 119 33 53N 10 2E
Gabès, Golfe de 119 34 0N 10 30E
Gabgaba, W. 122 22 10N 33 5E
Gabin 54 52 23N 19 41E
Gabon ■ 124 0 10S 10 0E
Gaborone 128 24 37S 25 57E
Gabrovo 67 42 52N 25 27E
Gacé 42 48 49N 0 20E
Gach Saran 93 30 15N 50 45E
Gacko 66 43 10N 18 33E
Gada 121 13 38N 5 36E
Gadag 97 15 30N 75 45E
Gadamai 123 17 11N 36 10E
Gadap 94 25 5N 67 28E
Gadarwara 95 22 50N 78 50E
Gäddede 74 64 30N 14 15E
Gadebusch 48 53 41N 11 6E
Gadein 123 8 10N 28 45E
Gadhada 94 22 0N 71 35E
Gadmen 51 46 45N 8 16E
Gádor, Sierra de 59 36 57N 2 45W
Gadsden, Ala., U.S.A. 157 34 1N 86 0W
Gadsden, Ariz., U.S.A. 161 32 35N 114 47W
Gadwal 96 16 10N 77 50E
Gaerwen 31 53 13N 4 17W
Gaeta 64 41 12N 13 35E
Gaeta, G. di 64 41 0N 13 25E
Gaffney 157 35 10N 81 31W
Gafsa 119 34 24N 8 51E
Gagarin (Gzhatsk) 80 55 30N 35 0E
Gagetown 151 45 46N 66 29W
Gagino 81 55 15N 45 10E
Gagliano del Capo 65 39 50N 18 23E
Gagnef 72 60 36N 15 5E
Gagnoa 120 6 4N 5 55W
Gagnon 151 51 50N 68 5W
Gagnon, L. 153 62 3N 110 27W
Gagra 83 43 20N 40 10E
Gah 44 43 12N 0 27W
Gahini 126 1 50S 30 30E
Gahmar 95 25 27N 83 55E
Gaibandha 98 25 20N 89 36E
Gaïdhouronísi 69 34 53N 25 41E
Gail 159 32 48N 101 25W
Gail, R. 52 46 37N 13 15E
Gaillac 44 43 54N 1 54E
Gaillon 42 49 10N 1 20E
Gaima 135 8 9S 142 59E
Gainesville, Fla., U.S.A. 157 29 38N 82 20W
Gainesville, Ga., U.S.A. 157 34 17N 83 47W
Gainesville, Mo., U.S.A. 159 36 35N 92 26W
Gainesville, Tex., U.S.A. 159 33 40N 97 10W
Gainford 33 54 34N 1 44W
Gainsborough 33 53 23N 0 46W
Gairdner L. 140 31 30S 136 0E
Gairloch 36 57 42N 5 40W
Gairloch L. 36 57 43N 5 45W
Gairlochy 36 56 55N 5 0W
Gairsay, I. 37 59 4N 2 59W
Gais 51 47 22N 9 27E
Gaithersburg 162 39 9N 77 12W
Gaj 66 45 28N 17 3E
Gajale 121 11 25N 8 10E
Gajiram 121 12 29N 13 9E
Gakuch 95 36 7N 73 45E
Gal Oya Res. 97 8 5N 80 55E
Galachipa 98 22 8N 90 26E
Galadi 121 13 5N 6 20E
Galán, Cerro 172 25 55S 66 52W
Galana, R. 126 3 0S 39 10E
Galangue 125 13 48S 16 3E
Galanta 53 48 11N 17 45E
Galápagos, Is. 131 0 0 89 0W
Galas, R. 101 4 55N 101 57E
Galashiels 35 55 37N 2 50W
Galatás 69 37 30N 23 26E
Galatea 142 38 24S 176 45E
Galaţi 70 45 27N 28 2E
Galaţi □ 70 45 45N 27 30E
Galatina 65 40 10N 18 10E
Galátone 65 40 8N 18 3E
Galax 157 36 42N 80 57W
Galaxídhion 69 38 22N 22 23E
Galbally 39 52 24N 8 17W
Galbraith 138 16 25S 141 30E
Galdhøpiggen 71 61 38N 8 18E
Galeana 164 24 50N 100 4W
Galela 103 1 50N 127 55E
Galena, Austral. 137 27 48S 114 42E
Galena, U.S.A. 147 64 42N 157 0W
Galeota Point 167 10 8N 61 0W
Galera 59 37 45N 2 33W
Galera, Pta. de la 174 10 48N 75 16W
Galesburg 158 40 57N 90 23W
Galey R. 39 52 30N 9 23W
Galgate 32 53 59N 2 47W
Galheirão, R. 171 12 23S 45 5W
Galheiros 171 13 18S 46 25W
Galicea Mare 70 44 4N 23 19E
Galich, R.S.F.S.R., U.S.S.R. 81 58 23N 42 18E
Galich, Uk., U.S.S.R. 80 49 10N 24 40E
Galiche 67 43 34N 23 50E
Galicia 56 42 43N 8 0W
Galijp 46 53 10N 5 58E
Galilee = Hagalil 90 32 53N 35 18E
Galilee, L. 138 22 20S 145 50E
Galite, Is. de la 119 37 30N 8 59E
Galivro Mts. 161 32 40N 110 30W
Gallan Hd. 36 58 14N 7 0W
Gallarate 62 45 40N 8 48E
Gallatin 157 36 24N 86 27W
Galle 97 6 5N 80 10E
Gallego 164 29 49N 106 22W
Gállego, R. 58 42 23N 0 30W
Gallegos, R. 176 51 50S 71 0W
Galley Hd. 39 51 32N 8 56W
Galliate 62 45 27N 8 44E
Gallinas, Pta. 174 12 28N 71 40W
Gallipoli 65 40 8N 18 0E
Gallipoli = Gelibolu 68 40 28N 26 43E
Gallipolis 156 38 50N 82 10W
Gällivare 74 67 9N 20 40E
Gällö 72 62 56N 15 15E
Gallo, C. di 64 38 13N 13 19E
Gallocanta, Laguna de 58 40 58N 1 30W
Galloway 34 55 0N 4 25W
Galloway, Mull of 34 54 38N 4 50W
Gallup 161 35 30N 108 54W
Gallur 58 41 52N 1 19W
Gallyaaral 85 40 2N 67 35E
Galmi 121 13 58N 5 41E
Gal'on 90 31 38N 34 51E
Galong 141 34 37S 148 34E
Galoya 93 8 10N 80 55E
Galston 34 55 36N 4 22W
Galt, Can. 150 43 21N 80 19W
Galt, U.S.A. 163 38 15N 121 18W
Galtström 72 62 10N 17 30E
Galtür 52 46 58N 10 11E
Galty Mts. 39 52 22N 8 10W
Galtymore, Mt. 39 52 22N 8 12W
Galva 158 41 10N 90 0W
Galve de Sorbe 58 41 13N 3 10W
Galveston 159 29 15N 94 48W
Galveston B. 159 29 30N 94 50W
Gálvez, Argent. 172 32 0S 61 20W
Gálvez, Spain 57 39 42N 4 16W
Galway 39 53 16N 9 4W
Galway □ 38 53 16N 9 3W
Galway B. 39 53 10N 9 20W
Gam, R. 100 21 55N 105 12E
Gamagōri 111 34 50N 137 14E
Gamare, L. 123 11 32N 41 40E
Gamarra 174 8 20N 73 45W
Gamawa 121 12 10N 10 31E
Gambaga 121 10 30N 0 28W
Gambat 94 27 17N 68 26E
Gambela 123 8 14N 34 38E
Gambell 147 63 55N 171 50W
Gambia ■ 120 13 25N 16 0W
Gambia, R. 120 13 20N 15 45W
Gambier, C. 136 11 56S 130 57E
Gambier Is. 140 35 3S 136 30E
Gamboli 94 29 53N 68 24E
Gamboma 124 1 55S 15 52E
Gamboola 138 16 29S 143 43E
Gameleira 170 7 50S 50 0W
Gamerco 161 35 33N 108 56W
Gamleby 73 57 54N 16 20W
Gamlingay 29 52 9N 0 11W
Gammelgarn 171 57 24N 18 49E
Gammon, R. 153 51 24N 95 44W
Gamōda-Saki 110 33 50N 134 45E
Gan (Addu Atoll) 87 0 10S 71 10E
Gan Shemu'el 90 32 28N 34 56E
Gan Yavne 90 31 48N 34 42E
Ganado, Ariz., U.S.A. 161 35 46N 109 41W
Ganado, Tex., U.S.A. 159 29 4N 96 31W
Gananoque 150 44 20N 76 10W
Ganaveh 93 29 35N 50 35E
Gand 47 51 2N 3 37E
Gandak, R. 95 27 0N 84 8E
Gandava 94 28 32N 67 32E
Gander 151 48 58N 54 29W
Gander L. 151 48 58N 54 35W
Ganderowe Falls 127 17 20S 29 10E
Gandesa 58 41 3N 0 26E
Gand = Gent 47 51 2N 3 37E
Gandhi Sagar 94 24 40N 75 40E
Gandi 121 12 55N 5 49E
Gandía 59 38 58N 0 9W
Gandino 62 45 50N 9 52E
Gandole 121 8 28N 11 35E
Gandu 171 13 45S 39 30W
Ganedidalem = Gani 103 0 48S 128 14E
Ganetti 122 18 0N 31 10E
Ganga, Mouths of the 95 21 30N 90 0E
Ganga, R. 95 25 0N 88 0E
Ganganagar 94 29 56N 73 56E
Gangapur 94 26 32N 76 37E
Gangara 121 14 35N 8 40E
Gangavati 97 15 30N 76 36E
Gangaw 98 22 5N 94 15E
Ganges 44 43 56N 3 42E
Ganges = Ganga, R. 95 25 0N 88 0E
Gangoh 94 29 46N 77 18E
Gangtok 98 27 20N 88 37E
Ganj 95 27 45N 78 47E
Ganmain 141 34 47S 147 1E
Gannat 44 46 7N 3 11E
Gannett Pk. 160 43 15N 109 47W
Gannvalley 158 44 3N 98 57W
Ganserdorf 53 48 20N 16 43E
Ganta (Gompa) 120 7 15N 8 59W
Gantheaume B. 137 27 40S 114 10E
Gantheaume, C. 140 36 4S 137 25E
Gantsevichi 80 52 42N 26 30E
Ganyushkino 83 46 35N 49 20E
Ganzi 123 4 30N 31 15E
Gao □ 121 18 0N 1 0E
Gao Bang 101 22 37N 106 18E
Gaoua 120 10 20N 3 8W
Gaoual 120 11 45N 13 25W
Gaouz 118 31 52N 4 20W
Gap 45 44 33N 6 5E
Gar Dzong 93 32 20N 79 55E
Gara, L. 38 53 57N 8 26W
Garachiné 166 8 0N 78 12W
Garanhuns 170 8 50S 36 30W
Garawe 120 4 35N 8 0W
Garba Tula 126 0 30N 38 32E
Garber 159 36 30N 97 36W
Garberville 160 40 11N 123 50W
Garboldisham 29 52 24N 0 57E
Garça 171 22 14S 49 37W
Garças, R. 170 8 43S 39 41W
Gard □ 45 44 2N 4 10E
Garda, L. di 62 45 40N 10 40E
Gardanne 45 43 27N 5 27E
Garde L. 153 62 50N 106 13W
Gardelegen 48 52 32N 11 21E
Garden City, Kans., U.S.A. 159 38 0N 100 45W
Garden City, Tex., U.S.A. 159 31 52N 101 28W
Garden Grove 163 33 47N 117 55W
Gardenstown 37 57 40N 2 20W
Gardez 94 33 31N 68 59E
Gardhiki 69 38 50N 21 55E
Gardian 117 15 45N 19 40E
Gardiner, Can. 150 49 19N 81 2W
Gardiner, Mont., U.S.A. 160 45 3N 110 53W
Gardiner, New Mexico, U.S.A. 159 36 55N 104 29W
Gardiners I. 162 41 4N 72 5W
Gardner 162 42 35N 72 0W
Gardner Canal 152 53 27N 128 8W
Gardnerville 160 38 59N 119 47W
Gardo 91 9 18N 49 20E
Gare, L. 34 56 1N 4 50W
Garelochhead 34 56 7N 4 50W
Gareloi I. 147 51 49N 178 50W
Garešnica 66 45 36N 16 56E
Garéssio 62 44 12N 8 1E
Garey 163 34 53N 120 19W
Garfield, Utah, U.S.A. 160 40 45N 112 15W
Garfield, Wash., U.S.A. 160 47 3N 117 8W
Garforth 33 53 48N 1 22W
Gargaliánoi 69 37 4N 21 38E
Gargano, Mte. 65 41 43N 15 43E
Gargans, Mt. 44 45 37N 1 39E
Gargantua, C. 150 47 35N 85 0W
Gargoune 121 15 56N 0 13E
Gargrave 32 53 58N 2 7W
Garhshankar 94 31 13N 76 11E
Gari 84 59 26N 62 21E
Garibaldi 152 49 56N 123 15W
Garibaldi Prov. Park 152 49 50N 122 40W

Garies Ghent

Garies	125	30 32 S	17 59 E
Garigliano, R.	64	41 13N	13 44 E
Garissa	126	0 25 S	39 40 E
Garissa □	126	0 20 S	40 0 E
Garkida	121	10 27N	12 36 E
Garko	121	11 45N	8 53 E
Garland	160	41 47N	112 10W
Garlasco	62	45 11N	8 55 E
Garlieston	34	54 47N	4 22W
Garm	85	39 0N	70 20 E
Garmab	94	32 50N	65 30 E
Garmisch-Partenkirchen	49	47 30N	11 5 E
Garmo	126	61 51N	8 48 E
Garmouth	37	57 40N	3 8W
Garmsar	93	35 20N	52 25 E
Garner	158	43 4N	93 37W
Garnett	158	38 18N	95 12W
Garo Hills	95	25 30N	90 30 E
Garoe	91	8 35N	48 40 E
Garoke	139	36 45 S	141 30 E
Garona, R.	58	42 55N	0 45 E
Garonne, R.	44	45 2N	0 36W
Garoua (Garwa)	121	9 19N	13 21 E
Garraway	120	4 35N	8 0W
Garrel	48	52 58N	7 59 E
Garrigues	44	43 40N	3 30 E
Garrison, Ireland	38	54 25N	8 5W
Garrison, Mont., U.S.A.	160	46 37N	112 56W
Garrison, N.D., U.S.A.	158	31 50N	94 28W
Garrison, Tex., U.S.A.	159	47 39N	101 27W
Garrison Res.	158	47 30N	102 0W
Garron Pt.	38	55 3N	6 0W
Garrovillas	57	39 40N	6 33W
Garrucha	59	37 11N	1 49W
Garry L., Can.	148	65 58N	100 18W
Garry L., U.K.	37	57 5N	4 52W
Garry, R.	37	56 47N	3 47W
Garsdale Head	32	54 19N	2 19W
Garsen	124	2 20 S	40 5 E
Garson L., Alta., Can.	153	56 19N	110 2W
Garson L., Sask., Can.	153	56 20N	110 1W
Garstang	32	53 53N	2 47W
Garston	32	53 21N	2 55W
Gartempe, R.	44	46 47N	0 49 E
Gartok	93	31 59N	80 30 E
Gartz	48	54 17N	13 21 E
Garu, Ghana	121	10 55N	0 20W
Garu, Nigeria	121	13 35N	5 25 E
Garub	128	26 37 S	16 0 E
Garupá	170	1 25 S	51 35W
Garut	103	7 14 S	107 53 E
Garvagh	38	55 0N	6 41W
Garvaghey	38	54 29N	7 8W
Garvald	35	55 55N	2 39W
Garvão	57	37 42N	8 21W
Garvellachs, Is.	34	56 14N	5 48W
Garvie Mts.	143	45 30 S	168 50 E
Garwa	95	24 11N	83 47 E
Garwolin	54	51 55N	21 38 E
Gary	156	41 35N	87 20W
Garzón	174	2 10N	75 40W
Gasan Kuli	76	37 40N	54 20 E
Gascogne	44	43 45N	0 20 E
Gascogne, G. de	58	44 0N	2 0W
Gascony = Gascogne	44	43 45N	0 20 E
Gascoyne Junc. Teleg. Off.	137	25 2 S	115 17 E
Gascoyne, R.	137	24 52 S	113 37 E
Gascueña	58	40 18N	2 31W
Gash, W.	123	15 0N	37 15 E
Gashaka	121	7 20N	11 29 E
Gasherbrum	95	35 40N	76 40 E
Gashua	121	12 54N	11 0 E
Gasmata	138	6 15 S	150 30 E
Gaspé	151	48 52N	64 30W
Gaspé, C.	151	48 48N	64 7W
Gaspé Pass.	151	49 10N	64 0W
Gaspé Pen.	151	48 45N	65 40W
Gaspésie, Parc Prov. de la	151	48 55N	65 50W
Gaspesian Prov. Park	151	49 0N	66 45W
Gassaway	156	38 42N	80 43W
Gasselte	46	52 58N	6 48 E
Gasselternijveen	46	52 59N	6 51 E
Gássino Torinese	62	45 8N	7 50 E
Gassol	121	8 34N	10 25 E
Gastonia	157	35 17N	81 10W
Gastoúni	69	37 51N	21 15 E
Gastoúri	68	39 34N	19 54 E
Gastre	176	42 10 S	69 15W
Gata, C. de	59	36 41N	2 13W
Gata, Sierra de	56	40 20N	6 20W
Gataga, R.	152	58 35N	126 59W
Gatchina	80	59 35N	30 0 E
Gatehouse of Fleet	34	54 53N	4 10W
Gateshead	35	54 57N	1 37W
Gatesville	159	31 29N	97 45W
Gaths	127	26 2 S	30 32 E
Gatico	172	22 40 S	70 20W
Gatinais	43	48 5N	2 40 E
Gâtine, Hauteurs de	44	46 35N	0 45W
Gatineau, Parc de la	150	45 20N	76 0W
Gatineau, R.	150	45 27N	75 42W
Gatley	32	53 25N	2 15W
Gatooma	125	18 20 S	29 52 E
Gattinara	62	45 37N	8 22 E
Gatun, L.	166	9 7N	79 56W
Gaucín	57	36 31N	5 19W
Gaud-i-Zirreh	93	29 45N	62 0 E
Gauer L.	153	57 0N	97 50W
Gauhati	98	26 10N	91 45 E
Gauja, R.	80	57 10N	24 45 E
Gaula, R.	71	62 57N	11 0 E
Gaurain-Ramecroix	47	50 36N	3 30 E
Gaurdak	85	37 50N	66 4 E
Gaussberg, Mt.	13	66 45 S	89 0 E
Gausta	71	59 50N	8 37 E
Gausta, Mt.	75	59 48N	8 40 E
Gavá	58	41 18N	2 0 E
Gavarnie	44	42 44N	0 3W
Gavater	93	25 10N	61 23 E
Gavdhopoúla	69	34 56N	24 0 E
Gávdhos	69	34 50N	24 5 E
Gavere	47	50 55N	3 40 E
Gavião	57	39 28N	7 50W
Gaviota	163	34 29N	120 13W
Gavle	72	60 41N	17 13 E
Gävle	72	60 40N	17 9 E
Gävleborgs Lan □	72	61 20N	16 15 E
Gavorrano	62	42 55N	10 55 E
Gavray	42	49 55N	1 20W
Gavrilov Yam	81	57 10N	39 37 E
Gávrion	69	37 54N	24 44 E
Gawachab	128	27 4 S	17 55 E
Gawai	98	27 56N	97 40 E
Gawilgarh Hills	96	21 15N	76 45 E
Gawler	140	34 30 S	138 42 E
Gawler Ranges	136	32 30 S	135 45 E
Gawthwaite	32	54 16N	3 6W
Gay	84	51 27N	58 27 E
Gaya, India	95	24 47N	85 4 E
Gaya, Niger	121	11 58N	3 28 E
Gaya, Nigeria	121	11 57N	9 0 E
Gaylord	156	45 1N	84 35W
Gayndah	139	25 35 S	151 39 E
Gayny	84	60 18N	54 19 E
Gaysin	82	48 57N	28 25 E
Gayton	29	52 45N	0 35 E
Gayvoron	82	48 22N	29 45 E
Gaywood	29	52 46N	0 26 E
Gaza	90	31 30N	34 28 E
Gaza □	129	23 10 S	32 45 E
Gaza Strip	90	31 29N	34 25 E
Gazaoua	121	13 32N	7 55 E
Gazelle Pen.	135	4 40 S	152 0 E
Gazi	126	1 3N	24 30 E
Gaziantep	92	37 6N	37 23 E
Gbanga	120	7 19N	9 13W
Gbekebo	121	6 26N	4 48 E
Gboko	121	7 17N	9 4 E
Gbongan	121	7 28N	4 20 E
Gcuwa	129	32 20 S	28 11 E
Gdansk	54	54 22N	18 40 E
Gdansk □	54	54 10N	18 30 E
Gdanska, Zatoka	54	54 30N	19 20 E
Gdov	80	58 40N	27 55 E
Gdynia	54	54 35N	18 33 E
Geashill	39	53 14N	7 20W
Gebe, I.	103	0 5N	129 25 E
Gebeit Mine	122	21 3N	36 29 E
Gecoa	123	7 30N	35 18 E
Gedaref	123	14 2N	35 28 E
Gedera	90	31 49N	34 46 E
Gedinne	47	49 59N	4 56 E
Gedney	29	52 47N	0 5W
Gedo	123	9 2N	37 25 E
Gèdre	44	42 47N	0 2 E
Gedser	73	54 35N	11 55 E
Gedser Odde, C.	73	54 30N	12 5 E
Geel	47	51 10N	4 59 E
Geelong	140	38 10 S	144 22 E
Geelvink Chan.	137	28 30 S	114 0 E
Geer, R.	47	50 51N	5 42 E
Geestenseth	48	53 31N	8 51 E
Geesthacht	48	53 25N	10 20 E
Geffen	46	51 44N	5 28 E
Geh	126	26 10N	60 0 E
Geia	90	31 38N	34 37 E
Geidam	121	12 57N	11 57 E
Geikie, R.	153	57 45N	103 52W
Geilenkirchen	48	50 58N	6 8 E
Geili	123	16 1N	32 37 E
Geilo	71	60 32N	8 14 E
Geinica	53	48 51N	20 55 E
Geisingen	49	47 55N	8 37 E
Geita	126	2 48 S	32 12 E
Geita □	126	2 50 S	32 10 E
Gel, R.	123	7 5N	29 10 E
Gel River	123	7 5N	29 10 E
Gela, Golfo di	65	37 0N	14 8 E
Geladi	91	6 59N	46 30 E
Gelderland □	46	52 5N	6 10 E
Geldermalsen	46	51 53N	5 17 E
Geldern	48	51 32N	6 18 E
Geldrop	47	51 25N	5 32 E
Geleen	47	50 57N	5 49 E
Gelehun	120	8 20N	11 40W
Gelendzhik	82	44 33N	38 17 E
Gelibolu	68	40 28N	26 43 E
Gelnhausen	49	50 12N	9 12 E
Gelsenkirchen	48	51 30N	7 5 E
Gelting	48	54 43N	9 53 E
Gemas	101	2 37N	102 36 E
Gembloux	47	50 34N	4 43 E
Gembu	121	8 58N	12 31 E
Gemena	124	3 20N	19 40 E
Gemerek	92	39 15N	36 10 E
Gemert	47	51 33N	5 41 E
Gemiston	128	26 15 S	28 10 E
Gemlik	92	40 28N	29 13 E
Gemmi	50	46 25N	7 37 E
Gemona del Friuli	63	46 16N	13 7 E
Gemsa	122	27 39N	33 35 E
Gemu-Gofa □	123	5 40N	36 40 E
Gemünden	49	50 3N	9 43 E
Genale	123	6 0N	39 30 E
Genappe	47	50 37N	4 27 E
Gençay	44	46 23N	0 23 E
Gendringen	46	51 52N	6 21 E
Gendt	46	51 53N	5 59 E
Geneina, Gebel	122	29 2N	33 55 E
Genemuiden	46	52 38N	6 2 E
General Acha	172	37 20 S	64 38W
General Alvear, B. A., Argent.	172	36 0 S	60 0W
General Alvear, Mend., Argent.	172	35 0 S	67 40W
General Artigas	172	26 52 S	56 16W
General Belgrano	172	36 0 S	58 30W
General Cabrera	172	32 53 S	63 58W
General Cepeda	164	25 23N	101 27W
General Guido	172	36 40 S	57 50W
General Juan Madariaga	172	37 0 S	57 0W
General La Madrid	172	37 30 S	61 10W
General MacArthur	103	11 18N	125 28 E
General Martin Mignuel de Güemes	172	24 50 S	65 0W
General Paz	172	27 45 S	57 36W
General Paz, L.	176	44 0 S	72 0W
General Pico	172	35 45 S	63 50W
General Pinedo	172	27 15 S	61 30W
General Pinto	172	34 45 S	61 50W
General Roca	176	30 0 S	67 40W
General Sampaio	170	4 2 S	39 29W
General Santos	103	6 12N	125 14 E
General Toshevo	67	43 42N	28 6 E
General Treviño	165	26 14N	99 29W
General Trías	164	28 21N	106 22W
General Viamonte	172	35 1 S	61 3W
General Villegas	172	35 0 S	63 0W
Generoso, Mte.	51	45 56N	9 2 E
Genesee	160	46 31N	116 59W
Genesee, R.	156	41 35N	78 0W
Geneseo, Ill., U.S.A.	158	41 25N	90 10W
Geneseo, Kans., U.S.A.	158	38 32N	98 8W
Geneva, Ala., U.S.A.	157	31 2N	85 52W
Geneva, Nebr., U.S.A.	158	40 35N	97 35W
Geneva, N.Y., U.S.A.	162	42 53N	77 0W
Geneva, Ohio, U.S.A.	156	41 49N	80 58W
Geneva = Genève	50	46 12N	6 9 E
Geneva, L.	156	42 38N	88 30W
Geneva, L. = Léman, Lac	50	46 26N	6 30 E
Genève	50	46 12N	6 9 E
Genève □	50	46 10N	6 10 E
Gengenbach	49	48 25N	8 0 E
Genichesk	82	46 12N	34 50 E
Genil, R.	57	37 12N	3 50W
Génissiat, Barrage de	45	46 1N	5 48 E
Genk	47	50 58N	5 32 E
Genkai-Nada	110	34 0N	130 0 E
Genlis	43	47 15N	5 12 E
Gennargentu, Mt. del	64	40 0N	9 10 E
Gennep	47	51 41N	5 59 E
Gennes	42	47 20N	0 17W
Genoa, Austral.	141	37 29 S	149 35 E
Genoa, Nebr., U.S.A.	158	41 31N	97 44W
Genoa, N.Y., U.S.A.	162	42 40N	76 32W
Genoa = Génova	62	44 24N	8 57 E
Génova	62	44 24N	8 56 E
Génova, Golfo di	62	44 0N	9 0 E
Gent	47	51 2N	3 37 E
Gentbrugge	47	51 3N	3 47 E
Genteng	103	7 25 S	106 23 E
Genthin	48	52 24N	12 10 E
Gentio do Ouro	170	11 25 S	42 30W
Geographe B.	137	33 30 S	113 20 E
Geographe Chan.	137	24 30 S	113 0 E
Geokchay	83	40 42N	47 43 E
George, Can.	151	46 12N	62 32W
George, S. Afr.	128	33 58 S	22 29 E
George, L., New South Wales, Austral.	141	35 10 S	149 25 E
George, L., S. Austral., Austral.	140	37 25 S	140 0 E
George, L., W. A., Austral.	137	22 45 S	123 40 E
George, L., Uganda	126	0 5N	30 10 E
George, L., Fla., U.S.A.	157	29 15N	81 35W
George, L., N.Y., U.S.A.	162	43 30N	73 30W
George, Mt.	137	25 17 S	119 0 E
George, R.	151	58 49N	66 10W
George River = Port Nouveau	149	58 30N	65 50W
George Sound	143	44 52 S	167 25 E
George Town, Austral.	138	41 5 S	146 49 E
George Town, Bahamas	166	23 33N	75 47W
George Town, Malay.	101	5 25N	100 19 E
George V Coast	13	67 0 S	148 0 E
George West	159	28 18N	98 5W
Georgetown, Austral.	133	18 17 S	143 33 E
Georgetown, Ont., Can.	150	43 40N	80 0W
Georgetown, P.E.I., Can.	151	46 13N	62 24W
Georgetown, Cay. Is.	166	19 20N	81 24W
Georgetown, Gambia	120	13 30N	14 47W
Georgetown, Guyana	174	6 50N	58 12W
Georgetown, Colo., U.S.A.	160	39 46N	105 49W
Georgetown, Del., U.S.A.	162	38 42N	75 23W
Georgetown, N.Y., U.S.A.	162	42 46N	75 44W
Georgetown, Ohio, U.S.A.	156	38 50N	83 50W
Georgetown, S.C., U.S.A.	157	33 22N	79 15W
Georgetown, Tex., U.S.A.	159	30 45N	98 10W
Georgi Dimitrov	67	42 15N	23 54 E
Georgia □	156	32 0N	82 0W
Georgia, Str. of	152	49 25N	124 0W
Georgian B.	150	45 15N	81 0W
Georgian S.S.R. □	83	41 0N	45 0 E
Georgievsk	83	44 12N	43 28 E
Georgina Downs	138	21 10 S	137 40 E
Georgina, R.	138	23 30 S	139 47 E
Georgiu-Dezh	81	51 3N	39 20 E
Georgiyevka	85	43 3N	74 43 E
Gera	48	50 53N	12 5 E
Gera □	48	50 45N	11 30 E
Geraardsbergen	47	50 45N	3 53 E
Geral de Goias, Serra	171	12 0 S	46 0W
Geral do Paranã Serra	171	15 0 S	47 0W
Geral, Serra, Bahia, Brazil	171	14 0 S	41 0W
Geral, Serra, Goiás, Brazil	170	11 15 S	46 30W
Geral, Serra, Santa Catarina, Brazil	173	26 25 S	50 0W
Geraldine, N.Z.	143	44 5 S	171 15 E
Geraldine, U.S.A.	160	47 45N	110 18W
Geraldton, Austral.	137	28 48 S	114 32 E
Geraldton, Can.	150	49 44N	86 59W
Geranium	140	35 23 S	140 11 E
Gerardmer	43	48 3N	6 50 E
Gerdine, Mt.	147	61 32N	152 30W
Gerede	82	40 45N	32 10 E
Gérgal	59	37 7N	2 31W
Geriban	91	7 10N	48 55 E
Gerik	101	5 25N	100 8 E
Gering	158	41 51N	103 40W
Gerizim	90	32 13N	35 15 E
Gerlach	160	40 43N	119 27W
Gerlachovka, Mt.	53	49 11N	20 7 E
Gerlafingen	50	47 10N	7 34 E
Gerlev	73	56 36N	10 9 E
Gerlogubi	91	6 53N	45 3 E
German Planina	66	42 33N	22 0 E
Germansen Landing	152	55 43N	124 40W
Germany, East ■	48	52 0N	12 0 E
Germany, West ■	48	52 0N	9 0 E
Germersheim	49	49 13N	8 0 E
Germiston	125	26 11 S	28 10 E
Gernsheim	49	49 44N	8 29 E
Gero	111	35 48N	137 14 E
Gerogery	141	35 50 S	147 1 E
Gerolstein	49	50 12N	6 24 E
Gerona	58	41 58N	2 46 E
Gerona □	58	42 11N	2 30 E
Gérouville	47	49 37N	5 26 E
Gerrans B.	30	50 12N	4 57W
Gerrard	152	50 30N	117 17W
Gerrards Cross	29	51 35N	0 32W
Gerrild	73	56 30N	10 50 E
Gerringong	141	34 46 S	150 47 E
Gers □	44	43 35N	0 38 E
Gersau	51	47 0N	8 32 E
Gersoppa Falls	97	14 12N	74 46 E
Gerufa	128	19 8 S	26 0 E
Gerze	92	41 45N	35 10 E
Geseke	48	51 38N	8 29 E
Geser	103	3 50N	130 35 E
Gesso, R.	62	44 21N	7 20 E
Gesves	47	50 24N	5 4 E
Getafe	56	40 18N	3 44W
Gethsémani	151	50 13N	60 40W
Gettysburg, Pa., U.S.A.	156	39 47N	77 18W
Gettysburg, S.D., U.S.A.	158	45 3N	99 56W
Getz Ice Shelf	13	75 0 S	130 0W
Geul, R.	47	50 53N	5 43 E
Geurie	141	32 22 S	148 50 E
Gevaudan	44	44 40N	3 40 E
Gevgelija	66	41 9N	22 30 E
Gévora, R.	57	38 53N	6 57W
Gex	45	46 21N	6 3 E
Geyikli	68	39 50N	26 12 E
Geyser	160	47 17N	110 30W
Geysir	74	64 19N	20 18W
Geyve	82	40 32N	30 18 E
Ghaghara, R.	95	26 0N	84 20 E
Ghail	92	21 40N	46 20 E
Ghalla, Wadi el	123	12 0N	28 58 E
Ghana ■	121	6 0N	1 0W
Ghandhi Dam	93	24 30N	75 35 E
Ghansor	95	22 39N	80 1 E
Ghanzi	128	21 50 S	21 45 E
Ghanzi □	128	21 50 S	21 45 E
Gharbîya, Es Sahrâ el	122	27 40N	26 30 E
Ghard Abû Muharik	122	26 50N	30 0 E
Ghardaïa	118	32 31N	3 37 E
Gharyān	119	32 10N	13 0 E
Ghāt	119	24 59N	10 19 E
Ghat Ghat	92	26 0N	45 5 E
Ghatal	95	22 40N	87 46 E
Ghatampur	95	26 8N	80 13 E
Ghatprabha, R.	96	16 15N	75 20 E
Ghazal, Bahr el	117	15 0N	17 0 E
Ghazaouet	118	35 8N	1 50W
Ghaziabad	94	28 42N	77 35 E
Ghazipur	95	25 38N	83 35 E
Ghazni	94	33 30N	68 17 E
Ghazni □	93	33 0N	68 0 E
Ghedi	62	45 24N	10 16 E
Ghelari	70	45 42N	22 45 E
Ghelinsor	91	6 35N	46 55 E
Ghent = Gand	47	51 4N	3 43 E

Gheorghe Gheorghiu-Dej **Gobo**

Gheorghe Gheorghiu-Dej	**70**	46 17N	26 47 E
Gheorgheni	**70**	46 43N	25 41 E
Ghergani	**70**	44 37N	25 37 E
Gherla	**70**	47 0N	23 57 E
Ghilarza	**64**	40 8N	8 50 E
Ghisonaccia	**45**	42 1N	9 26 E
Ghizao	**94**	33 30N	65 59 E
Ghizar, R.	**95**	36 10N	73 4 E
Ghod, R.	**96**	18 40N	74 15 E
Ghorat □	**93**	34 0N	64 20 E
Ghost River, Can.	**150**	50 10N	91 27W
Ghost River, Ont., Can.	**150**	51 25N	83 20W
Ghot Ogrein	**122**	31 10N	25 20 E
Ghotaru	**94**	27 20N	70 1 E
Ghotki	**94**	28 5N	69 30 E
Ghudâmis	**119**	30 11N	9 29 E
Ghugri	**95**	22 39N	80 41 E
Ghugus	**96**	20 0N	79 0 E
Ghulam Mohammad Barrage	**94**	25 30N	67 0 E
Ghuriân	**93**	34 17N	61 25 E
Gia Dinh	**101**	10 49N	106 42 E
Gia Lai = Pleiku	**101**	14 3N	108 0 E
Gia Nghia	**101**	12 0N	107 42 E
Gia Ngoc	**100**	14 50N	108 58 E
Gia Vuc	**100**	14 42N	108 34 E
Giamda Dzong	**99**	30 3N	93 2 E
Giannutri, I.	**62**	42 16N	11 5 E
Giant Forest	**163**	36 36N	118 43W
Giant Mts. = Krkonose	**52**	50 50N	16 10 E
Giant's Causeway	**38**	55 15N	6 30W
Giarabub = Jaghbub	**117**	29 42N	24 38 E
Giarre	**65**	37 44N	15 10 E
Giaveno	**62**	45 3N	7 20 E
Gibara	**166**	21 0N	76 20W
Gibbon	**158**	40 49N	98 45W
Gibe, R.	**123**	6 25N	36 10 E
Gibellina	**64**	37 48N	13 0 E
Gibeon	**128**	25 7 S	17 45 E
Gibraléon	**57**	37 23N	6 58W
Gibraltar	**57**	36 7N	5 22W
Gibraltar Pt.	**33**	53 6N	0 20 E
Gibraltar, Str. of	**57**	35 55N	5 40W
Gibson Des.	**136**	24 0 S	126 0 E
Gibsons	**152**	49 24N	123 32W
Gida. G.	**12**	72 30N	77 0 E
Giddalur	**97**	15 20N	78 57 E
Gidde	**123**	5 40N	37 25 E
Giddings	**159**	30 11N	96 58W
Gide	**123**	9 52N	35 5 E
Gien	**43**	47 40N	2 36 E
Giessen	**48**	50 34N	8 40 E
Gieten	**46**	53 0N	6 46 E
Gif-sur-Yvette	**46**	48 42N	2 8 E
Gifatin, Geziret	**122**	27 10N	33 50 E
Gifford	**35**	55 54N	2 45W
Gifford Creek	**137**	24 3 S	116 16 E
Gifhorn	**48**	52 29N	10 32 E
Gifu	**111**	35 30N	136 45 E
Gifu-ken □	**111**	36 0N	137 0 E
Gigant	**83**	46 28N	41 30 E
Giganta, Sa. de la	**164**	25 30N	111 30W
Gigen	**67**	43 40N	24 28 E
Giggleswick	**32**	54 5N	2 19W
Gigha, I.	**39**	55 42N	5 45W
Giglio, I.	**62**	42 20N	10 52 E
Gignac	**44**	43 39N	3 32 E
Gigüela, R.	**58**	39 47N	3 0W
Gijón	**56**	43 32N	5 42W
Gil I.	**152**	53 12N	129 15W
Gila Bend	**161**	33 0N	112 46W
Gila Bend Mts.	**161**	33 15N	113 0W
Gila, R.	**161**	33 5N	108 40W
Gilau	**138**	5 38 S	149 3 E
Gilbedi	**121**	13 40N	5 45 E
* Gilbert Is.	**130**	1 0 S	176 0 E
Gilbert Plains	**153**	51 9N	100 28W
Gilbert, R.	**138**	16 35 S	141 15 E
Gilbert River	**138**	18 9 S	142 52 E
Gilberton	**138**	19 16 S	143 35 E
Gilbués	**170**	9 50 S	45 21W
Gilford	**38**	54 23N	6 20W
Gilford I.	**152**	50 40N	126 30W
Gilgai	**137**	31 15 S	119 56 E
Gilgandra	**141**	31 43 S	148 39 E
Gilgil	**126**	0 30 S	36 20 E
Gilgit	**95**	35 50N	74 15 E
Gilgit, R.	**95**	35 50N	74 25 E
Gilgunnia	**141**	32 26 S	146 2 E
Giligulgul	**139**	26 26 S	150 0 E
Gilima	**126**	3 53N	28 15 E
Giljeva Planina	**66**	43 9N	20 0 E
Gill L.	**38**	54 15N	8 25W
Gillam	**153**	56 20N	94 40W
Gilleleje	**73**	56 8N	12 19 E
Gillen, L.	**137**	26 11 S	124 38 E
Gilles, L.	**140**	32 50 S	136 45 E
Gillespie Pt.	**143**	43 24 S	169 49 E
Gillett	**162**	41 57N	76 48W
Gillette	**158**	44 20N	105 38W
Gilliat	**138**	20 40 S	141 28 E
Gillingham, Dorset, U.K.	**28**	51 2N	2 15W
Gillingham, Kent, U.K.	**29**	51 23N	0 48 E
Gilmer	**159**	32 44N	94 55W
Gilmore	**141**	35 14 S	148 12 E
Gilmore, L.	**137**	32 29 S	121 37 E
Gilmour	**150**	44 48N	77 37W
Gilo	**123**	7 35N	34 30 E
Gilo, R.	**161**	33 5N	108 40W
Gilort, R.	**70**	44 38N	23 32 E
Gilroy	**163**	37 1N	121 37W
Gilsland	**32**	55 0N	2 34W
Gilău	**70**	46 45N	23 23W
Giluwe, Mt.	**135**	6 8 S	143 52 E
Gilwern	**31**	51 49N	3 5W
Gilze	**47**	51 32N	4 57 E
Gimåfors	**72**	62 40N	16 25 E
Gimbi	**123**	9 3N	35 42 E
Gimigliano	**65**	38 53N	16 32 E
Gimli	**153**	50 40N	97 10W
Gimmi	**123**	9 0N	37 20 E
Gimo	**72**	60 11N	18 12 E
Gimont	**44**	43 38N	0 52 E
Gimzo	**90**	31 56N	34 56 E
Gin Ganga	**97**	6 5N	80 7 E
Gin Gin	**139**	25 0 S	151 44 E
Ginâh	**122**	25 21N	30 30 E
Gindie	**138**	23 44 S	148 8 E
Gineta, La	**59**	39 8N	2 1W
Gingin	**137**	31 22 S	115 54 E
Gîngiova	**70**	43 54N	23 50 E
Ginir	**123**	7 12N	40 40 E
Ginosa	**65**	40 35N	16 45 E
Ginowan	**112**	26 15N	127 47 E
Ginzo de Limia	**56**	42 3N	7 47W
Giohar	**91**	2 20N	45 15 E
Gióia del Colle	**65**	40 49N	16 55 E
Gióia, G. di	**65**	38 30N	15 50 E
Gióia Táuro	**65**	38 26N	15 53 E
Gioiosa Iónica	**65**	38 20N	16 19 E
Gióna, Óros	**69**	38 38N	22 14 E
Giong, Teluk	**103**	4 50N	118 20 E
Giovi, P. dei	**45**	44 30N	8 55 E
Giovinazzo	**65**	41 10N	16 40 E
Gippsland	**133**	37 45 S	147 15 E
Gir Hills	**94**	21 0N	71 0 E
Girab	**94**	26 2N	70 38 E
Giralla	**136**	22 31 S	114 15 E
Giraltovce	**53**	49 7N	21 32 E
Girard	**159**	37 30N	94 50W
Girardot	**174**	4 18N	74 48W
Girdle Ness	**37**	57 9N	2 2W
Giresun	**92**	40 45N	38 30 E
Girga	**122**	26 17N	31 55 E
Girgir, C.	**135**	3 50 S	144 35 E
Giridih	**95**	24 10N	86 21 E
Girifalco	**65**	38 49N	16 25 E
Girilambone	**141**	31 16 S	146 57 E
Girishk	**93**	31 47N	64 24 E
Giro	**121**	11 7N	4 42 E
Giromagny	**43**	47 44N	6 50 E
Gironde □	**44**	44 45N	0 30W
Gironde, R.	**44**	45 27N	0 53W
Gironella	**58**	42 2N	1 53 E
Giru	**138**	19 30 S	147 5 E
Girvan	**34**	55 15N	4 50W
Girvan R.	**34**	55 18N	4 51W
Gisborne	**142**	38 39 S	178 5 E
Gisburn	**32**	53 56N	2 16W
Gisenyi	**126**	1 41 S	29 30 E
Giske	**71**	62 30N	6 3 E
Gisla	**36**	58 7N	6 53W
Gislaved	**73**	57 19N	13 32 E
Gisors	**43**	49 15N	1 40 E
Gissarskiy, Khrebet	**85**	39 0N	69 0 E
Gistel	**47**	51 9N	2 59 E
Giswil	**50**	46 50N	8 11 E
Gitega (Kitega)	**126**	3 26 S	29 56 E
Gits	**47**	51 0N	3 6 E
Giubiasco	**51**	46 11N	9 1 E
Giugliano in Campania	**65**	40 55N	14 12 E
Giulianova	**63**	42 45N	13 58 E
Giurgeni	**70**	44 45N	27 38 E
Giurgiu	**70**	43 52N	25 57 E
Giv'at Brenner	**90**	31 52N	34 47 E
Give	**73**	55 51N	9 13 E
Givet	**43**	50 8N	4 49 E
Givors	**45**	45 35N	4 45 E
Givry, Belg.	**47**	50 23N	4 2 E
Givry, France	**43**	46 41N	4 46 E
Giza (El Giza)	**122**	30 1N	31 11 E
Gizhduvan	**85**	40 6N	64 41 E
Gizhiga	**77**	62 0N	150 27 E
Gizhiginskaya, Guba	**77**	61 0N	158 0 E
Gizycko	**54**	54 2N	21 48 E
Gizzeria	**65**	38 57N	16 10 E
Gjegjan	**68**	41 58N	20 3 E
Gjerpen	**71**	59 15N	9 33 E
Gjerstad	**71**	58 54N	9 0 E
Gjiri-i-Vlorës	**68**	40 29N	19 27 E
Gjirokastër	**68**	40 7N	20 16 E
Gjoa Haven	**148**	68 20N	96 0W
Gjovdal	**71**	58 52N	8 19 E
Gjøvik	**71**	60 47N	10 43 E
Glace Bay	**151**	46 11N	59 58W
Glacier B.	**152**	58 30N	136 10W
Glacier Nat. Park	**152**	51 15N	117 30W
Glacier National Park	**160**	48 35N	113 40W
Glacier Peak Mt.	**160**	48 7N	121 7W
Gladewater	**159**	32 30N	94 58W
Gladstone, Queens., Austral.	**74**	23 52 S	151 16 E
Gladstone, S.A., Austral.	**140**	33 15 S	138 22 E
Gladstone, W. Australia, Austral.	**137**	25 57 S	114 17 E
Gladstone, Can.	**153**	50 13N	98 57W
Gladstone, U.S.A.	**156**	45 52N	87 1W
Gladwin	**156**	43 59N	84 29W
Gladys L.	**152**	59 50N	133 0W
Glafsfjorden	**72**	59 30N	12 45 E
Głagów Małapolski	**53**	50 10N	21 56 E
Gláma	**74**	65 48N	23 0W
Glåma, R.	**71**	60 30N	12 8 E
Glamis	**37**	56 37N	3 0W
Glamorgan (□)	**26**	51 37N	3 35W
Glamorgan, Vale of	**23**	50 45N	3 15W
Glan, Phil.	**103**	5 45N	125 20 E
Glan, Sweden	**73**	58 37N	16 0 E
Glanaman	**31**	51 48N	3 56W
Glanaruddery Mts.	**39**	52 20N	9 27W
Glandore	**39**	51 33N	9 7W
Glandore Harb.	**39**	51 33N	9 8W
Glanerbrug	**46**	52 13N	6 58 E
Glanton	**35**	55 25N	1 54W
Glanworth	**39**	52 10N	8 25W
Glarner Alpen	**51**	46 50N	9 0 E
Glärnisch	**51**	47 0N	9 0 E
Glarus	**51**	47 3N	9 4 E
Glarus □	**51**	47 0N	9 5 E
Glas Maol	**37**	56 52N	3 20W
Glasco, Kans., U.S.A.	**158**	39 25N	97 50W
Glasco, N.Y., U.S.A.	**162**	42 3N	73 57W
Glasgow, U.K.	**34**	55 52N	4 14W
Glasgow, Ky., U.S.A.	**156**	37 2N	85 55W
Glasgow, Mont., U.S.A.	**160**	48 12N	106 35W
Glasnevin	**38**	53 22N	6 18W
Glassboro	**162**	39 42N	75 7W
Glasslough	**38**	54 20N	6 53W
Glastonbury, U.K.	**28**	51 9N	2 42W
Glastonbury, U.S.A.	**162**	41 42N	72 27W
Glatt, R.	**51**	47 28N	8 32 E
Glattfelden	**51**	47 33N	8 30 E
Glauchau	**48**	50 50N	12 33 E
Glazov	**81**	58 9N	52 40 E
Glbovo	**67**	42 1N	24 43 E
Gleichen	**152**	50 50N	113 0W
Gleisdorf	**52**	47 6N	15 44 E
Glemsford	**29**	52 6N	0 41 E
Glen Affric	**36**	57 15N	5 0W
Glen Afton	**142**	37 46 S	175 4 E
Glen Almond	**35**	56 28N	3 50W
Glen B.	**38**	54 43N	8 45W
Glen Burnie	**162**	39 10N	76 37W
Glen Canyon Dam	**161**	37 0N	111 25W
Glen Canyon Nat. Recreation Area	**161**	37 30N	111 0W
Glen Coe	**23**	56 40N	5 0W
Glen Cove	**162**	40 51N	73 37W
Glen Esk	**37**	56 53N	2 50W
Glen Etive	**34**	56 37N	5 0W
Glen Florrie	**136**	22 55 S	115 59 E
Glen Garry, Inv., U.K.	**36**	57 3N	5 7W
Glen Garry, Per., U.K.	**37**	56 47N	4 5W
Glen Gowrie	**140**	31 4 S	143 10 E
Glen Helen	**32**	54 14N	4 35W
Glen Innes	**139**	29 40 S	151 39 E
Glen Lyon, U.K.	**37**	56 35N	4 20W
Glen Lyon, U.S.A.	**162**	41 10N	76 7W
Glen Massey	**142**	37 38 S	175 2 E
Glen Mor	**37**	57 12N	4 37 E
Glen Moriston	**36**	57 10N	4 58W
Glen Orchy	**34**	56 27N	4 52W
Glen Orrin	**37**	57 30N	4 45W
Glen Oykel	**37**	58 5N	4 50W
Glen, R.	**29**	52 50N	0 7W
Glen Shee	**37**	56 45N	3 25W
Glen Shiel	**36**	57 8N	5 20W
Glen Spean	**37**	56 53N	4 40W
Glen Trool Lodge	**34**	55 5N	4 30W
Glen Ullin	**158**	46 48N	101 46W
Glen Valley	**141**	36 54 S	147 28 E
Glenade	**38**	54 22N	8 17W
Glenamoy	**38**	54 14N	9 40W
Glénans, Is. de	**42**	47 42N	4 0W
Glenariff	**141**	30 50 S	146 33 E
Glenarm	**38**	54 58N	5 58W
Glenart Castle	**39**	52 48N	6 12W
Glenavy, N.Z.	**143**	44 54 S	171 7 E
Glenavy, U.K.	**38**	54 36N	6 12W
Glenbarr	**34**	55 34N	5 40W
Glenbeigh	**39**	52 3N	9 57W
Glenbrittle	**36**	57 13N	6 18W
Glenbrook	**142**	33 46 S	150 37 E
Glenburn	**141**	37 37 S	145 26 E
Glencoe, S. Afr.	**129**	28 11 S	30 11 E
Glencoe, U.S.A.	**158**	44 45N	94 10W
Glencolumbkille	**38**	54 43N	8 41W
Glendale, Can.	**150**	46 45N	84 2W
Glendale, Rhod.	**127**	17 22 S	31 5 E
Glendale, Ariz., U.S.A.	**161**	33 40N	112 8W
Glendale, Calif., U.S.A.	**163**	34 7N	118 18W
Glendale, Oreg., U.S.A.	**160**	42 44N	123 29W
Glendive	**158**	47 7N	104 40W
Glendo	**158**	42 30N	105 0W
Glendora	**163**	34 8N	117 52W
Gleneagles	**35**	56 16N	3 44W
Glenealy	**39**	52 59N	6 10W
Gleneely	**38**	52 14N	7 8W
Glenelg, Austral.	**140**	34 58 S	138 31 E
Glenelg, U.K.	**36**	57 13N	5 37W
Glenelg, R.	**140**	38 4 S	140 59 E
Glenfarne	**38**	54 17N	8 0W
Glenfield	**162**	43 43N	75 24W
Glenfinnan	**36**	56 52N	5 28W
Glengad Hd.	**38**	55 19N	7 11W
Glengariff	**39**	51 45N	9 33W
Glengormley	**38**	54 41N	5 57W
Glengyle	**138**	24 48 S	139 37 E
Glenham	**143**	46 26 S	168 52 E
Glenhope	**143**	41 40 S	172 39 E
Glenisland	**38**	53 54N	9 24W
Glenkens, The	**34**	55 10N	4 15W
Glenluce	**34**	54 53N	4 50W
Glenmary, Mt.	**143**	44 0 S	169 55 E
Glenmaye	**32**	54 11N	4 42W
Glenmora	**159**	31 1N	92 34W
Glenmorgan	**139**	27 14 S	149 42 E
Glenn, oilfield	**19**	57 55N	0 15 E
Glennagevlagh	**38**	53 36N	9 41W
Glennamaddy	**38**	53 37N	8 33W
Glenn's Ferry	**160**	43 0N	115 15W
Glenoe	**38**	54 47N	5 50W
Glenorchy, S. Austral., Austral.	**140**	31 55 S	139 46 E
Glenorchy, Tas., Austral.	**138**	42 49 S	147 18 E
Glenorchy, Vic., Austral.	**140**	36 55 S	142 41 E
Glenore	**138**	17 50 S	141 12 E
Glenormiston	**138**	22 55 S	138 50 E
Glenreagh	**139**	30 2 S	153 1 E
Glenrock	**160**	42 53N	105 55W
Glenrothes	**35**	56 12N	3 11W
Glenrowan	**141**	36 29 S	146 13 E
Glenroy, S. Australia, Austral.	**140**	37 13 S	140 48 E
Glenroy, W. Australia, Austral.	**136**	17 16 S	126 14 E
Glenroy, S. Afr.	**132**	26 23 S	28 17 E
Glens Falls	**162**	43 19N	73 39W
Glentane	**38**	53 25N	8 30W
Glenties	**38**	54 48N	8 18W
Glenville	**156**	38 56N	80 50W
Glenwood, Alta., Can.	**152**	49 21N	113 31W
Glenwood, Newf., Can.	**151**	49 0N	54 47W
Glenwood, Ark., U.S.A.	**159**	34 20N	93 30W
Glenwood, Hawaii, U.S.A.	**147**	19 29N	155 10W
Glenwood, Iowa, U.S.A.	**158**	41 7N	95 41W
Glenwood, Minn., U.S.A.	**158**	45 38N	95 21W
Glenwood Sprs.	**160**	39 39N	107 15W
Gletsch	**51**	46 34N	8 22 E
Glettinganes	**51**	65 30N	13 37W
Glin	**39**	52 34N	9 17W
Glina	**63**	45 20N	16 6 E
Glinojeck	**54**	52 49N	20 21 E
Glinsk	**39**	53 23N	9 49W
Glittertind	**71**	61 40N	8 32 E
Gliwice (Gleiwitz)	**54**	50 22N	18 41 E
Globe	**161**	33 25N	110 53W
Glodeanu-Siliştea	**70**	44 50N	26 48 E
Glödnitz	**52**	46 53N	14 7 E
Glodyany	**70**	47 45N	27 31 E
Gloggnitz	**52**	47 41N	15 56 E
Głogów	**54**	51 37N	16 5 E
Głogowek	**54**	50 21N	17 53 E
Gloria, La	**174**	8 37N	73 48W
Glorieuses, Îs.	**129**	11 30 S	47 20 E
Glossop	**32**	53 27N	1 56W
Gloucester, Austral.	**141**	32 0 S	151 59 E
Gloucester, U.K.	**28**	51 52N	2 15W
Gloucester, U.S.A.	**162**	42 38N	70 39W
Gloucester, Va., U.S.A.	**162**	37 25N	76 32W
Gloucester, C.	**135**	5 26 S	148 21 E
Gloucester City	**162**	39 54N	75 8W
Gloucester, I.	**138**	20 0 S	148 30 E
Gloucestershire □	**28**	51 44N	2 10W
Gloversville	**162**	43 5N	74 18W
Glovertown	**151**	48 40N	54 03W
Głubczyce	**54**	50 13N	17 52 E
Glubokiy	**83**	48 35N	40 25 E
Glubokoye	**80**	55 10N	27 45 E
Głucholazy	**54**	50 19N	17 24 E
Glücksburg	**48**	54 48N	9 34 E
Glückstadt	**48**	53 46N	9 28 E
Gluepot	**140**	33 45 S	140 0 E
Glukhov	**80**	51 40N	33 50 E
Glussk	**80**	52 53N	28 41 E
Gł ó wno	**54**	51 59N	19 42 E
Glyn-ceiriog	**31**	52 56N	3 12W
Glyn Neath	**31**	51 45N	3 37W
Glyncorrwg	**31**	51 40N	3 39W
Glyngøre	**73**	56 46N	8 52 E
Glynn	**39**	52 29N	6 55W
Gmünd, Kärnten, Austria	**52**	46 54N	13 31 E
Gmünd, Niederösterreich, Austria	**52**	48 45N	15 0 E
Gmunden	**52**	47 55N	13 48 E
Gnarp	**72**	62 3N	17 16 E
Gnesta	**72**	59 3N	17 17 E
Gniew	**54**	53 50N	18 50 E
Gniewkowo	**54**	52 54N	18 25 E
Gniezno	**54**	52 30N	17 35 E
Gnoien	**48**	53 58N	12 41 E
Gnopp	**123**	8 47N	29 50 E
Gnosall	**28**	52 48N	2 15W
Gnosjö	**73**	57 22N	13 43 E
Gnowangerup	**137**	33 58 S	117 59 E
Go Cong	**101**	10 22N	106 40 E
Gō-no-ura	**110**	33 44N	129 40 E
Goa	**97**	15 33N	73 59 E
Goa □	**97**	15 33N	73 59 E
Goageb	**128**	26 49 S	17 15 E
Goalen Hd.	**141**	36 33 S	150 4 E
Goalpara	**98**	26 10N	90 40 E
Goalundo	**95**	23 50N	89 47 E
Goaso	**120**	6 48N	2 30W
Goat Fell	**34**	55 37N	5 11W
Goba, Ethiopia	**123**	7 1N	39 59 E
Goba, Mozam.	**125**	26 15 S	32 13 E
Gobabis	**128**	22 16 S	19 0 E
Gobi, desert	**105**	44 0N	111 0 E
Gobichettipalayam	**97**	11 31N	77 21 E
Gobō	**111**	33 53N	135 10 E
Gobo	**123**	5 40N	30 10 E

** Renamed Kiribati*

Goch Grand Bassa

Goch	48	51 40N	6 9 E
Gochas	125	24 59 S	19 25 E
Godalming	29	51 12N	0 37W
Godavari Point	96	17 0N	82 20 E
Godavari, R.	96	19 5N	79 0 E
Godbout	151	49 20N	67 38W
Godda	95	24 50N	87 20 E
Goddua	119	26 26N	14 19 E
Godech	66	43 1N	23 4 E
Godegård	73	58 43N	15 8 E
Goderich	150	43 45N	81 41W
Goderville	42	49 38N	0 22 E
Godhavn	12	69 15N	53 38W
Godhra	94	22 49N	73 40 E
Godmanchester	29	52 19N	0 11W
Gödöllö	53	47 38N	19 25 E
Godoy Cruz	172	32 56 S	68 52W
Godrevy Pt.	30	50 15N	5 24W
Gods L.	153	54 40N	94 15W
Gods, R.	153	56 22N	92 51W
Godshill	28	50 38N	1 13W
Godstone	29	51 15N	0 3W
Godthåb	12	64 10N	51 46W
Godwin Austen (K2)	93	36 0N	77 0 E
Goeie Hoop, Kaap die	128	34 24 S	18 30 E
Goeland, L.	150	49 50N	76 48W
Goeree	46	51 50N	4 0 E
Goes	47	51 30N	3 55 E
Goffstown	162	43 1N	71 36W
Gogama	150	47 35N	81 43W
Gogango	138	23 40 S	150 2 E
Gogebic, L.	158	46 30N	89 34W
Gogha	94	21 32N	72 9 E
Gogolin	54	50 30N	18 0 E
Gogra, R. = Ghaghara	99	26 0N	84 20 E
Gogriâl	123	8 30N	28 0 E
Goiana	170	7 33 S	34 59W
Goiandira	171	11 46 S	46 40W
Goianésia	171	15 18 S	49 7W
Goiânia	171	16 35 S	49 20W
Goiás	171	15 55 S	50 10W
Goiás □	170	12 10 S	48 0W
Goiatuba	171	18 1 S	49 23W
Goil L.	34	56 8N	4 52W
Goirle	47	51 31N	5 4 E
Góis	56	40 10N	8 6W
Goisern	52	47 38N	13 38 E
Gojam □	123	10 55N	36 30 E
Gojeb, W.	123	7 12N	36 40 E
Gojō	111	34 21N	135 42 E
Gojra	94	31 10N	72 40 E
Gokak	97	16 11N	74 52 E
Gokarannath	95	27 57N	80 39 E
Gokarn	97	14 33N	74 17 E
Gökçeada	68	40 10N	26 0 E
Gokteik	99	22 26N	97 0 E
Gokurt	94	29 47N	67 26 E
Gøl	73	57 4N	9 42 E
Gola	95	28 3N	80 32 E
Gola I.	38	55 4N	8 20W
Golaghat	98	26 30N	94 0 E
Golakganj	95	26 8N	89 52 E
Golaya Pristen	82	46 29N	32 23 E
Golchikha	12	71 45N	84 0 E
Golconda	160	40 58N	117 32W
Gold Beach	160	42 25N	124 25W
Gold Coast, Austral.	139	28 0 S	153 25 E
Gold Coast, W. Afr.	121	4 0N	1 40W
Gold Creek	147	62 45N	149 45W
Gold Hill	160	42 28N	123 2W
Gold Point	163	37 21N	117 21W
Gold River	152	49 40N	126 10 E
Goldach	51	47 28N	9 28 E
Goldau	51	47 3N	8 33 E
Goldberg	48	53 34N	12 6 E
Golden, Can.	152	51 20N	117 0W
Golden, Ireland	39	52 30N	8 0W
Golden, U.S.A.	158	39 42N	105 30W
Golden Bay	143	40 40 S	172 50 E
Golden Gate	160	37 54N	122 30W
Golden Hinde, mt.	152	49 40N	125 44W
Golden Prairie	153	50 13N	109 37W
Golden Rock	97	10 45N	78 48 E
Golden Vale	39	52 33N	8 17W
Goldendale	160	45 53N	120 48W
Goldfield	163	37 45N	117 13W
Goldfields	153	59 28N	108 29W
Goldpines	153	50 45N	93 05W
Goldsand L.	153	57 2N	101 8W
Goldsboro	157	35 24N	77 59W
Goldsmith	159	32 0N	102 40W
Goldsworthy	136	20 21 S	119 30 E
Goldsworthy, Mt.	136	20 23 S	119 31 E
Goldthwaite	159	31 25N	98 32W
Goleen	39	51 30N	9 43W
Golegã	57	39 24N	8 29W
Goleniów	54	53 35N	14 50 E
Goleta	163	34 27N	119 50W
Golfito	166	8 41N	83 5W
Golfo degli Aranci	65	41 0N	9 38 E
Goliad	159	28 40N	97 22W
Golija	66	43 22N	20 15 E
Golija, Mts.	66	43 5N	18 45 E
Golina	54	52 15N	18 4 E
Golo, R.	45	42 31N	9 32 E
Golovanesvsk	82	48 25N	30 30 E
Gölpazari	82	40 17N	30 17 E
Golra	94	33 37N	72 56 E
Golspie	37	57 58N	3 58W
Golub Dobrzyn	54	53 7N	19 2 E
Golubac	66	44 38N	21 38 E
Golyama Kamchiya, R.	67	43 2N	27 18 E
Goma, Ethiopia	123	8 29N	36 53 E
Goma, Rwanda	126	2 11 S	29 18 E
Goma, Zaïre	126	1 37 S	29 10 E
Gomare	128	19 25 S	22 8 E
Gomati, R.	95	26 30N	81 50 E
Gombari	126	2 45N	29 3 E
Gombe	121	10 19N	11 2 E
Gombe, R.	126	4 30 S	32 50 E
Gombi	121	10 12N	12 45 E
Gomel	80	52 28N	31 0 E
Gomera, I.	116	28 10N	17 5W
Gometra I.	34	56 30N	6 18W
Gómez Palacio	164	25 40N	104 40W
Gommern	48	52 54N	11 47 E
Gomogomo	103	6 25 S	134 53 E
Gomoh	99	23 52N	86 10 E
Gomotartsi	66	44 6N	22 57 E
Goms	50	46 30N	8 15 E
Gonābād	93	34 15N	58 45 E
Gonaïves	167	19 20N	72 50W
Gonâve, G. de la	167	19 29N	72 42W
Gonâve, I. de la	167	18 45N	73 0W
Gönc	53	48 28N	21 14 E
Gonda	95	27 9N	81 58 E
Gondab-e Kāvūs	93	37 20N	55 25 E
Gondal	94	21 58N	70 52 E
Gonder	123	12 23N	37 30 E
Gondia	96	21 30N	80 10 E
Gondola	127	19 4 S	33 37 E
Gondomar, Port.	56	41 10N	8 35W
Gondomar, Spain	56	42 7N	8 45W
Gondrecourt-le-Château	43	48 26N	5 30 E
Gongola □	121	8 0N	12 0 E
Gongola, R.	121	10 30N	10 22 E
Goniadz	54	53 30N	22 44 E
Goniri	121	11 30N	12 15 E
Gonnesa	64	39 17N	8 27 E
Gonno-Altaysk	76	51 50N	86 5 E
Gonnos	68	39 52N	22 29 E
Gonnosfanadiga	64	39 30N	8 39 E
Gonzales, Calif., U.S.A.	163	36 35N	121 30W
Gonzales, Tex., U.S.A.	159	29 30N	97 30W
González Chaves	172	38 02 S	60 05W
Good Hope, C. of = Goeie Hoop	128	34 24 S	18 30 E
Goode	139	31 58 S	133 45 E
Goodenough I.	135	9 20 S	150 15 E
Gooderham	150	44 54N	78 21W
Goodeve	153	51 4N	103 10W
Gooding	160	43 0N	114 50W
Goodland	158	39 22N	101 44W
Goodnight	159	35 4N	101 13W
Goodooga	139	29 1 S	147 28 E
Goodrich	28	51 52N	2 38W
Goodsoil	153	54 24N	109 13W
Goodsprings	161	35 51N	115 30W
Goodwick	31	52 0N	5 0W
Goodwin, Mt.	136	14 13 S	129 32 E
Goodwood	29	50 53N	0 44W
Goole	33	53 42N	0 52W
Goolgowi	141	33 58 S	145 41 E
Goolwa	140	35 30 S	138 47 E
Goomalling	137	31 15 S	116 42 E
Goombalie	139	29 59 S	145 26 E
Goonalga	140	31 45 S	143 37 E
Goonda	127	19 48 S	33 57 E
Goondiwindi	139	28 30 S	150 21 E
Goongarrie	137	30 2 S	121 8 E
Goonumbla	141	32 59 S	148 11 E
Goonyella	138	21 47 S	147 58 E
Goor	46	52 13N	6 33 E
Gooray	139	28 25 S	150 2 E
Goose Bay	151	53 15N	60 20W
Goose L.	160	42 0N	120 30W
Goose R.	151	53 20N	60 35W
Goothinga	138	17 36 S	140 50 E
Gooty	97	15 7N	77 41 E
Gop	93	22 5N	69 50 E
Gopalganj, Bangla.	98	23 1N	89 50 E
Gopalganj, India	95	26 28N	84 30 E
Goppenstein	50	46 23N	7 46 E
Göppingen	49	48 42N	9 40 E
Gor	59	37 23N	2 58W
Góra	54	51 40N	16 31 E
Gorakhpur	95	26 47N	83 32 E
Gorbatov	81	56 12N	43 2 E
Gorbea, Peña	58	43 1N	2 50W
Gorda	163	35 53N	121 26W
Gorda, Punta	166	14 10N	83 10W
Gordon, Austral.	140	32 7 S	138 20 E
Gordon, U.K.	35	55 41N	2 32W
Gordon, U.S.A.	158	42 49N	102 6W
Gordon B.	136	11 35 S	130 10 E
Gordon Downs	136	18 48 S	128 40 E
Gordon L., Alta., Can.	153	56 30N	110 25W
Gordon L., N.W.T., Can.	152	63 5N	113 11W
Gordon, R.	138	42 27 S	145 30 E
Gordon River	137	34 10 S	117 15 E
Gordonia	128	28 13 S	21 10 E
Gordonvale	138	17 5 S	145 50 E
Gore	139	28 17 S	151 30 E
Goré	117	7 59N	16 49 E
Gore, Ethiopia	123	8 12N	35 32 E
Gore, N.Z.	143	46 5 S	168 58 E
Gore B.	150	45 57N	82 28W
Gorebridge	35	55 51N	3 2W
Goresbridge	39	52 38N	7 0W
Gorey	39	52 41N	6 18W
Gorgan	93	36 55N	54 30 E
Gorge, The	138	18 27 S	145 30 E
Gorgona, I.	174	3 0N	78 10W
Gorgona I.	62	43 27N	9 52 E
Gorgora	123	12 15N	37 17 E
Gori	83	42 0N	44 7 E
Gorinchem	46	51 50N	4 59 E
Goring, Oxon, U.K.	28	51 31N	1 8W
Goring, Sussex, U.K.	29	50 49N	0 26W
Gorinhatã	171	19 15 S	49 45W
Goritsy	81	57 4N	36 43 E
Gorízia	63	45 56N	13 37 E
Gorka	54	51 39N	16 58 E
Gorki = Gorkiy	81	56 20N	44 0 E
Gorkiy	81	57 20N	44 0 E
Gorkovskoye Vdkhr.	81	57 2N	43 4 E
Gorleston	29	52 35N	1 44 E
Gorlev	73	55 30N	11 15 E
Gorlice	54	49 35N	21 11 E
Görlitz	54	51 10N	14 59 E
Gorlovka	81	48 25N	37 58 E
Gorman, Calif., U.S.A.	163	34 47N	118 51W
Gorman, Tex., U.S.A.	159	32 15N	98 43W
Gorna Oryakhovitsa	67	43 7N	25 40 E
Gorna Radgona	63	46 40N	16 2 E
Gornja Tuzla	66	44 35N	18 46 E
Gornji Grad	63	46 20N	14 52 E
Gornji Milanovac	66	44 00N	20 29 E
Gornji Vafuk	66	43 57N	17 34 E
Gorno Ablanovo	67	43 37N	25 43 E
Gorno Filinskoye	76	60 5N	70 0 E
Gornyy	81	51 50N	48 30 E
Gorodenka	82	48 41N	25 29 E
Gorodets	81	56 38N	43 28 E
Gorodische	81	53 13N	45 40 E
Gorodnitsa	80	50 46N	27 26 E
Gorodnya	80	51 55N	31 33 E
Gorodok, Byelorussia, U.S.S.R.	80	55 30N	30 3 E
Gorodok, Ukraine, U.S.S.R.	80	49 46N	23 32 E
Goroka	135	6 7 S	145 25 E
Goroke	140	36 43 S	141 29 E
Gorokhov	80	50 15N	24 45 E
Gorokhovets	81	56 13N	42 39 E
Gorom Gorom	121	14 26N	0 14W
Goromonzi	127	17 52 S	31 22 E
Gorong, Kepulauan	103	4 5 S	131 15 E
Gorongosa, Sa. da	127	18 27 S	32 2 E
Gorongose, R.	129	20 30 S	34 40 E
Gorontalo	103	0 35N	123 13 E
Goronyo	121	13 29N	5 39 E
Gorredijk	46	53 0N	6 3 E
Gorron	42	48 25N	0 50W
Gorseinon	31	51 40N	4 2W
Gorssel	46	52 12N	6 12 E
Gort	39	53 4N	8 50W
Gortin	38	54 43N	7 13W
Gorumahisani	96	22 20N	86 24 E
Gorumna I.	39	53 15N	9 44W
Gorzkowice	54	51 13N	19 36 E
Gorzno	54	53 12N	19 38 E
Gorzów Slaski	54	51 3N	18 22 E
Gorzów Wielkopolski	54	52 43N	15 15 E
Gorzów Wielkopolski □	54	52 45N	15 30 E
Gosainthan, Mt.	99	28 20N	85 45 E
Gosberton	33	52 52N	0 10W
Göschenen	51	46 40N	8 36 E
Göse	111	34 27N	135 44 E
Gosford	141	33 23N	151 18 E
Gosforth	32	54 24N	3 27W
Goshen, S. Afr.	128	25 50 S	25 0 E
Goshen, Calif., U.S.A.	163	36 21N	119 25W
Goshen, Ind., U.S.A.	156	41 36N	85 46W
Goshen, N.Y., U.S.A.	162	41 23N	74 21W
Goslar	48	51 55N	10 23 E
Gospič	63	44 35N	15 23 E
Gosport	28	50 48N	1 8W
Gossa, I.	71	62 52N	6 50 E
Gossau	51	47 25N	9 15 E
Gosse, R.	138	19 32 S	134 37 E
Gostivar	66	41 48N	20 57 E
Gostyn	54	51 50N	17 3 E
Gostynin	54	52 26N	19 29 E
Göta	73	58 6N	12 10 E
Göta älv	73	57 42N	11 54 E
Göta Kanal	73	58 35N	14 15 E
Götaland, reg.	73	58 0N	14 0 E
Göteborg	73	57 43N	11 59 E
Göteborg & Bohus □	75	58 20N	11 50 E
Gotemba	111	35 18N	138 56 E
Götene	73	58 32N	13 30 E
Gotha	48	50 56N	10 42 E
Gothenburg	158	40 58N	100 8W
Gothenburg = Göteborg	73	57 43N	11 59 E
Gotse Delchev (Nevrokop)	67	41 43N	23 46 E
Gotska Sandön	75	58 24N	19 15 E
Gōtsu	110	35 0N	132 14 E
Göttingen	48	51 31N	9 55 E
Gottwaldov (Zlin)	53	49 14N	17 40 E
Gouda	46	52 1N	4 42 E
Goudhurst	29	51 7N	0 28 E
Goudiry	120	14 15N	12 45 E
Gough I.	15	40 10 S	9 45W
Gouin Res.	150	48 35N	74 40W
Gouitafla	120	7 30N	5 53W
Goula Touila	118	21 50N	1 57 E
Goulburn	141	34 44 S	149 44 E
Goulburn Is.	138	11 40 S	133 20 E
Gould, mt.	137	25 46 S	117 18 E
Goulia	120	10 1N	7 11W
Goulimine	118	28 50N	10 0W
Goulmima	118	31 41N	4 57W
Gouménissa	68	40 56N	22 37 E
Goumeur	119	20 40N	18 30 E
Goundam	135	16 25N	3 45W
Gounou-Gaya	124	9 38N	15 31 E
Goúra	69	37 56N	22 20 E
Gourara	118	29 0N	0 30 E
Gouraya	118	36 31N	1 56 E
Gourdon, France	44	44 44N	1 23 E
Gourdon, U.K.	37	56 50N	2 15W
Gouré	121	14 0N	10 10 E
Gourits, R.	128	34 15 S	21 45 E
Gourma Rharous	121	16 55N	2 5W
Gournay-en-Bray	43	49 29N	1 44 E
Gouro	117	19 30N	19 30 E
Gourock	34	55 58N	4 49W
Gourock Ra.	141	36 0 S	149 25 E
Gourselik	121	13 31N	10 52 E
Goursi	120	12 42N	2 37W
Gouvêa	171	18 27 S	43 44W
Gouzon	44	46 12N	2 14 E
Govan	153	51 20N	105 0W
Gove	133	12 25 S	136 55 E
Goverla	82	49 9N	24 30 E
Governador Valadares	171	18 15 S	41 57W
Governor's Harbour	166	25 10N	76 14W
Gowan	138	25 0 S	145 0 E
Gowanda	156	42 29N	78 58W
Gower, The	31	51 35N	4 10W
Gowerton	31	51 38N	4 2W
Gowna, L.	38	53 52N	7 35W
Gowran	39	52 38N	7 5W
Goya	172	29 10 S	59 10W
Goyder's Lagoon	139	27 3 S	139 58 E
Goyllarisquizga	174	10 19 S	76 31W
Goz Beïda	117	12 20N	21 30 E
Goz Regeb	123	16 3N	35 33 E
Gozdnica	54	51 28N	15 4 E
Gozo (Ghaudex)	60	36 0N	14 13 E
Graaff-Reinet	128	32 13 S	24 32 E
Graasten	73	54 57N	9 34 E
Grabow	48	53 17N	11 31 E
Grabów	54	51 31N	18 7 E
Grabs	51	47 11N	9 27 E
Gračac	63	44 18N	15 57 E
Gračanica	66	44 43N	18 18 E
Graçay	43	47 10N	1 50 E
Grace	160	42 38N	111 46W
Grace, L., (North)	137	33 10 S	118 20 E
Grace, L., (South)	137	33 15 S	118 25 E
Graceville	158	45 36N	96 23W
Grachevka	84	52 55N	52 52 E
Gracias a Dios, C.	166	15 0N	83 20W
Gradačac	66	44 52N	18 26 E
Gradaús	170	7 43 S	51 11W
Gradaús, Serra dos	170	8 0 S	50 45W
Gradeska Planina	66	41 30N	22 15 E
Gradets	67	42 46N	26 30 E
Gradignan	44	44 47N	0 36W
Gradnitsa	67	42 57N	24 58 E
Grado, Italy	63	45 40N	13 20 E
Grado, Spain	56	43 23N	6 4W
Gradule	139	28 32 S	149 15 E
Grady	159	34 52N	103 15W
Graeca, Lacul	70	44 5N	26 10 E
Graemsay I.	37	58 56N	3 17W
Graénalon, L.	74	64 10N	17 20W
Grafham Water	29	52 18N	0 17W
Grafton, Austral.	139	29 38 S	152 58 E
Grafton, U.S.A.	158	48 30N	97 25W
Grafton, C.	133	16 51 S	146 0 E
Gragnano	65	40 42N	14 30 E
Graham, Can.	150	49 20N	90 30W
Graham, N.C., U.S.A.	157	36 5N	79 22W
Graham, Tex., U.S.A.	159	33 7N	98 38W
Graham Bell, Os.	76	80 5N	70 0 E
Graham I.	152	53 40N	132 30W
Graham Land	13	65 0 S	64 0W
Graham Mt.	161	32 46N	109 58W
Graham, R.	152	56 31N	122 17W
Grahamdale	153	51 23N	98 30W
Grahamstown	128	33 19 S	26 31 E
Grahamsville	162	41 51N	74 33W
Grahovo	66	42 40N	18 4 E
Graïba	119	34 30N	10 13 E
Graide	47	49 58N	5 4 E
Graigue	39	52 51N	6 56W
Graiguenamanagh	39	52 32N	6 58W
Grain Coast	120	4 20N	10 0W
Grainthorpe	33	53 27N	0 5 E
Graivoron	80	50 29N	35 39 E
Grajaú	170	5 50 S	46 30W
Grajaú, R.	170	3 41 S	44 48W
Grajewo	54	53 39N	22 30 E
Gramada	66	43 49N	22 39 E
Gramat	44	44 48N	1 43 E
Gramisdale	36	57 29N	7 18W
Grammichele	65	37 12N	14 37 E
Grampian □	37	57 0N	3 0W
Grampians, Mts.	140	37 0 S	142 20 E
Gran Canaria	116	27 55N	15 35W
Gran Chaco	156	25 0 S	61 0W
Gran Paradiso	62	49 33N	7 17 E
Gran Sabana, La	174	5 30N	61 30W
Gran Sasso d'Italia, Mt.	44	42 25N	13 30 E
Granada, Nic.	166	11 58N	86 0W
Granada, Spain	59	37 10N	3 35W
Granada, U.S.A.	158	38 5N	102 13W
Granada □	57	37 5N	4 30W
Granard	38	53 47N	7 30W
Granbo	72	61 16N	16 33 E
Granbury	159	32 28N	97 48W
Granby	150	45 25N	72 45W
Grand Bahama I.	166	26 40N	78 30W
Grand Bank	151	47 6N	55 48W
Grand Bassa	120	6 0N	10 2W

Grand Bassam
Grillby

Grand Bassam 120 5 10N 3 49W
Grand Béréby 120 4 38N 6 55W
Grand-Bourg 167 15 53N 61 19W
Grand Canal 39 53 15N 8 10W
Grand Canyon National Park 161 36 15N 112 20W
Grand Cayman 166 19 20N 81 20W
Grand Cess 120 4 40N 8 12W
Grand 'Combe, La 45 44 13N 4 2E
Grand Coulee 160 47 48N 119 1W
Grand Coulee Dam 160 48 0N 118 50W
Grand Erg Occidental 118 30 20N 1 0E
Grand Erg Oriental 119 30 0N 6 30E
Grand Falls 151 47 2N 67 46W
Grand Forks, Can. 152 49 0N 118 30W
Grand Forks, U.S.A. 158 48 0N 97 3W
Grand-Fougeray 42 47 43N 1 44W
Grand Fougeray, Le 42 47 44N 1 43W
Grand Haven 156 43 3N 86 13W
Grand I. 150 46 30N 86 40W
Grand Island 158 40 59N 98 25W
Grand Isle 159 29 15N 89 58W
Grand Junction 161 39 0N 108 30W
Grand L., N.B., Can. 151 45 57N 66 7W
Grand L., Newf., Can. 151 48 45N 57 45W
Grand L., Newf., Can. 151 53 40N 60 30W
Grand L., Newf., Can. 151 49 0N 57 30W
Grand L., U.S.A. 159 29 55N 92 45W
Grand Lac 150 47 35N 77 35W
Grand Lahou 120 5 10N 5 0W
Grand Lake 160 40 20N 105 54W
Grand-Leez 47 50 35N 4 45E
Grand Lieu, Lac de 42 47 6N 1 40W
Grand Manan I. 151 44 45N 66 52W
Grand Marais, Can. 158 47 45N 90 25W
Grand Marais, U.S.A. 156 46 39N 85 59W
Grand Mère 150 46 36N 72 40W
Grand Motte, La 45 48 35N 1 4E
Grand Popo 121 6 15N 1 44E
Grand Portage 150 47 58N 89 41W
Grand Pressigny, Le 42 46 55N 0 48E
Grand, R., Mo., U.S.A. 160 39 23N 93 27W
Grand, R., S.D., U.S.A. 160 45 45N 101 30W
Grand Rapids, Can. 153 53 12N 99 19W
Grand Rapids, Mich., U.S.A. 156 42 57N 85 40W
Grand Rapids, Minn., U.S.A. 158 47 19N 93 29W
Grand St.-Bernard, Col. du 50 45 53N 7 11E
Grand Teton 160 43 45N 110 57W
Grand Valley 160 39 30N 108 2W
Grand View 153 51 11N 100 51W
Grandas de Salime 56 43 13N 6 53W
Grande 170 11 30S 44 30W
Grande, B. 176 50 30S 68 20W
Grande Baie 151 48 19N 70 52W
Grande Cache 152 53 53N 119 8W
Grande, Coxilha 173 28 18S 51 30W
Grande de Santiago, R. 164 21 20N 105 50W
Grande Dixence, Barr. de la 50 46 5N 7 23E
Grande-Entrée 151 47 30N 61 40W
Grande, I. 171 23 9S 44 14W
Grande, La 160 45 15N 118 0W
Grande Prairie 152 55 15N 118 50W
Grande, R., Jujuy, Argent. 172 23 9S 65 52W
Grande, R., Mendoza, Argent. 172 36 52S 69 45W
Grande R. 174 18 35S 63 0W
Grande, R., Brazil 171 20 0S 50 0W
Grande, R., Spain 59 39 6N 0 48W
Grande, R., U.S.A. 159 29 20N 100 40W
Grande Rivière 151 48 26N 64 30W
Grande, Serra, Goiás, Brazil 170 11 15S 46 30W
Grande, Serra, Maranhao, Brazil 170 4 30S 41 20W
Grande, Serra, Piauí, Brazil 170 8 0S 45 0W
Grande Vallée 151 49 14N 65 8W
Grandes Bergeronnes 151 48 16N 69 35W
Grandfalls 159 31 21N 102 51W
Grandglise 47 50 30N 3 42E
Grandoe Mines 152 56 29N 129 54W
Grândola 57 38 12N 8 35W
Grandpré 43 49 20N 4 50E
Grandson 50 46 49N 6 39E
Grandview, Can. 153 51 10N 100 42W
Grandview, U.S.A. 160 46 13N 119 58W
Grandvilliers 43 49 40N 1 57E
Graneros 172 34 5S 70 45W
Graney L. 39 53 0N 8 40W
Grange 38 54 24N 8 32W
Grange, La, Austral. 136 18 45S 121 43E
Grange, La, U.S.A. 163 37 42N 120 27W
Grange, La, Ga., U.S.A. 157 33 4N 85 0W
Grange, La, Ky., U.S.A. 156 38 20N 85 20W
Grange, La, Tex., U.S.A. 159 29 54N 96 52W
Grange-over-Sands 32 54 12N 2 55W
Grangemouth 35 56 1N 3 43W
Granger 160 46 25N 120 5W
Grangesberg 72 60 6N 15 1E
Grängesberg 72 60 6N 15 1E
Grangetown 33 54 36N 1 7W
Grangeville 160 45 57N 116 4W
Granite City 158 38 45N 90 3W
Granite Falls 158 44 45N 95 35W
Granite Mtn. 163 33 5N 116 28W
Granite Peak 137 25 40S 121 20E
Granite Pk., mt. 160 45 8N 109 52W
Granitnyy, Pik 85 39 32N 70 20E
Granity 143 41 39S 171 51E
Granja 170 3 17S 40 50W
Granja de Moreruela 56 41 48N 5 44W
Granja de Torrehermosa 57 38 19N 5 35W
Gränna 73 58 1N 14 28E
Granollers 58 41 39N 2 18E
Gransee 48 53 0N 13 10E
Grant, Can. 150 50 6N 86 18W
Grant, U.S.A. 158 40 53N 101 42W
Grant City 158 40 30N 94 25W
Grant, I. 136 11 10S 132 52E
Grant, Mt. 163 38 34N 118 48W
Grant Range Mts. 161 38 30N 115 30W
Grantham 33 52 55N 0 39W
Grantown-on-Spey 37 57 19N 3 36W
Grants 161 35 14N 107 57W
Grant's Pass 160 42 30N 123 22W
Grantsburg 158 45 46N 92 44W
Grantshouse 35 55 53N 2 17W
Grantsville 160 40 35N 112 32W
Granville, France 42 48 50N 1 35W
Granville, U.K. 38 54 30N 6 47W
Granville, N.D., U.S.A. 158 48 18N 100 48W
Granville, N.Y., U.S.A. 162 43 24N 73 16W
Granville L. 153 56 18N 100 30W
Grao de Gandía 59 39 0N 0 27W
Grapeland 159 31 30N 95 25W
Gras, L. de 148 64 30N 110 30W
Graskop 129 24 56S 30 49E
Gräsmark 72 59 58N 12 44E
Grasmere, Austral. 139 35 1S 117 45E
Grasmere, U.K. 32 54 28N 3 2W
Gräsö 72 60 21N 18 28E
Graso 72 60 28N 18 35E
Grasonville 162 38 57N 76 13W
Grass, R. 153 56 3N 96 33W
Grass Range 160 47 0N 109 0W
Grass River Prov. Park 153 54 40N 100 50W
Grass Valley, Calif., U.S.A. 160 39 18N 121 0W
Grass Valley, Oreg., U.S.A. 160 45 28N 120 48W
Grassano 65 40 38N 16 17E
Grasse 45 43 38N 6 56E
Grassington 32 54 5N 2 0W
Grassmere 140 31 24S 142 38E
Grate's Cove 151 48 8N 53 0W
Graubünden (Grisons) □ 51 46 45N 9 30E
Graulhet 44 43 45N 1 58E
Graus 58 42 11N 0 20E
Gravatá 170 6 59S 35 29W
Grave 46 51 46N 5 44E
Grave, Pte. de 44 45 34N 1 4W
's-Graveland 46 52 15N 5 7E
Gravelbourg 153 49 50N 106 35W
Gravelines 43 51 0N 2 10E
's-Gravendeel 46 51 47N 4 37E
's-Gravenhage 46 52 7N 4 17E
's-Gravenpolder 47 51 28N 3 54E
's-Gravensance 46 52 0N 4 9E
Graversfors 73 58 42N 16 8E
Gravesend, Austral. 139 29 35S 150 20E
Gravesend, U.K. 29 51 25N 0 22E
Gravina di Púglia 65 40 48N 16 25E
Gravir 36 58 2N 6 25W
Gravois, Pointe-à 167 16 15N 73 45W
Gravone, R. 45 42 3N 8 54E
Grävsnäs 73 58 5N 12 29E
Gray 43 47 27N 5 35E
Grayling 156 44 40N 84 42W
Grayling, R. 152 59 21N 125 0W
Grayrigg 32 54 22N 2 40W
Grays Harbor 160 46 55N 124 8W
Grays L. 160 43 8N 111 30W
Grays Thurrock 29 51 28N 0 23E
Grayson 153 50 45N 102 40W
Grayvoron 80 50 29N 35 39E
Graz 52 47 4N 15 27E
Grazalema 57 36 46N 5 23W
Grdelica 66 42 55N 22 3E
Greasy L. 152 62 55N 122 12W
Great Abaco I. 166 26 15N 77 10W
Great Australia Basin 133 26 0S 140 0E
Great Australian Bight 137 33 30S 130 0E
Great Ayton 33 54 29N 1 8W
Great Baddow 29 51 43N 0 31E
Great Bahama Bank 166 23 15N 78 0W
Great Barrier I. 142 36 11S 175 25E
Great Barrier Reef 138 19 0S 149 0E
Great Barrington 162 42 11N 73 22W
Great Basin 154 40 0N 116 30W
Great Bear L. 148 65 0N 120 0W
Great Bear, R. 148 65 0N 124 0W
Great Belt 73 55 20N 11 0E
Great Bena 162 41 57N 75 45W
Great Bend 158 38 25N 98 55W
Great Bentley 29 51 51N 1 5E
Great Bernera, I. 137 58 15N 6 50W
Great Bitter Lake 122 30 15N 32 40E
Great Blasket, I. 39 52 5N 10 30W
Great Britain 16 54 0N 2 15W
Great Bushman Land 128 29 20S 19 20E
Great Central 152 49 20N 125 10W
Great Chesterford 29 52 4N 0 11E
Great Clifton 32 54 39N 3 29W
Great Coco I. 101 14 10N 93 25E
Great Divide 141 23 0S 146 0E
Great Dunmow 29 51 52N 0 22E
Great Exuma I. 166 23 30N 75 50W
Great Falls, Can. 153 50 27N 96 1W
Great Falls, U.S.A. 160 47 27N 111 12W
Great Fish R., S. Afr. 128 33 28S 27 5E
Great Fish R., S. Afr. 128 31 30S 20 16E
Great Gonerby 33 52 56N 0 40W
Great Guana Cay 166 24 0N 76 20W
Great Hanish 123 13 40N 43 0E
Great Harbour Deep 151 50 35N 56 25W
Great Harwood 32 52 41N 2 49W
Great I., Can. 153 58 53N 96 35W
Great I., Ireland 39 51 52N 8 15W
Great Inagua I. 167 21 0N 73 20W
Gt. Indian Desert = Thar Desert 94 28 0N 72 0E
Great Jarvis 151 47 39N 57 12W
Great Karoo = Groot Karoo 128 32 30S 23 0E
Great Lake 138 41 50S 146 30E
Great Lakes 153 44 0N 82 0W
Great Malvern 28 52 7N 2 19W
Great Massingham 29 52 47N 0 41E
Great Missenden 29 51 42N 0 42W
Gt. Namaqualand = Groot Namakwaland 128 26 0S 18 0E
Great Orme's Head 31 53 20N 3 52W
Great Ouse, R. 29 52 20N 0 8E
Great Palm I. 138 18 45S 146 40E
Great Papuan Plateau 135 6 30S 142 25E
Great Plains 50 45 0N 100 0W
Great Ruaha, R. 126 7 30S 35 0E
Great Salt Lake 160 41 0N 112 30W
Great Salt Lake Desert 160 40 20N 113 50W
Great Salt Plains Res. 159 36 40N 98 15W
Great Sandy Desert 136 21 0S 124 0E
Great Sandy I. = Fraser I. 139 25 15S 153 0E
Great Scarcies, R. 120 9 30N 12 40W
Great Shefford 28 51 29N 1 27W
Great Shelford 29 52 9N 0 9E
Great Shunner Fell 32 54 22N 2 16W
Great Sitkin I. 147 52 0N 176 10W
Great Slave L. 152 61 23N 115 38W
Great Stour, R. 29 51 21N 1 15E
Gt. Sugar Loaf, mt. 39 53 10N 6 10W
Great Torrington 30 50 57N 4 9W
Gt. Victoria Des. 137 29 30S 126 30E
Great Wall 106 38 30N 109 30E
Gt. Waltham 29 51 47N 0 29E
Great Whale, R. 150 55 20N 75 30W
Great Whernside, mt. 147 54 9N 1 59W
Great Winterhoek, mt. 128 33 07S 19 10E
Great Wyrley 28 52 40N 2 1W
Great Yarmouth 29 52 40N 1 45E
Great Yeldham 29 52 1N 0 33E
Greater Antilles 167 17 40N 74 0W
Greater Manchester □ 32 53 30N 2 15W
Greatham 33 54 38N 1 14W
Grebbestad 73 58 42N 11 15E
Grebenka 80 50 9N 32 22E
Greco, Mt. 64 41 48N 14 0E
Gredos, Sierra de 56 40 20N 5 0W
Greece ■ 68 40 0N 23 0E
Greeley, Colo., U.S.A. 158 40 30N 104 40W
Greeley, Nebr., U.S.A. 158 41 36N 98 32W
Green B. 156 45 0N 87 30W
Green Bay 156 44 30N 88 0W
Green C. 141 37 13S 150 1E
Green Cove Springs 157 29 59N 81 40W
Green Hammerton 33 54 2N 1 17W
Green Hd. 137 30 5S 114 56E
Green Is. 135 4 35S 154 10E
Green Island 143 45 55S 170 26E
Green Lowther, Mt. 35 55 22N 3 44W
Green R., Ky., U.S.A. 156 37 54N 87 30W
Green R., Utah, U.S.A. 161 39 0N 110 6W
Green R., Wyo., U.S.A. 160 43 2N 110 2W
Green R., Wyo., U.S.A. 160 41 44N 109 28W
Greenbush 158 48 46N 96 10W
Greencastle, U.K. 38 54 2N 6 5W
Greencastle, U.S.A. 156 39 40N 86 48W
Greene 162 42 20N 75 45W
Greenfield, Calif., U.S.A. 163 35 15N 119 0W
Greenfield, Calif., U.S.A. 163 36 19N 121 15W
Greenfield, Ind., U.S.A. 156 39 47N 85 51W
Greenfield, Iowa, U.S.A. 158 41 18N 94 28W
Greenfield, Mass., U.S.A. 162 42 38N 72 38W
Greenfield, Miss., U.S.A. 159 37 28N 93 50W
Greenhead 35 54 58N 2 31W
Greening 150 48 10N 74 55W
Greenisland 38 54 42N 5 50W
Greenland 12 66 0N 45 0W
Greenland Sea 12 73 0N 10 0W
Greenlaw 35 55 42N 2 28W
Greenock 34 55 57N 4 46W
Greenodd 32 54 14N 3 3W
Greenore 38 54 2N 6 8W
Greenore Pt. 39 52 15N 6 20W
Greenough, R. 137 28 54S 115 36E
Greenport 162 41 5N 72 23W
Greensboro, Ga., U.S.A. 157 33 34N 83 12W
Greensboro, Md., U.S.A. 162 38 59N 75 48W
Greensboro, N.C., U.S.A. 157 36 7N 79 46W
Greensburg, Ind., U.S.A. 156 39 20N 85 30W
Greensburg, Kans., U.S.A. 159 37 38N 99 20W
Greensburg, Pa., U.S.A. 156 40 18N 79 31W
Greenstone Pt. 36 57 55N 5 38W
Greenville, Liberia 120 5 7N 9 6W
Greenville, Ala., U.S.A. 157 31 50N 86 37W
Greenville, Calif., U.S.A. 160 40 8N 121 0W
Greenville, Ill., U.S.A. 158 38 53N 89 22W
Greenville, Me., U.S.A. 151 45 30N 69 32W
Greenville, Mich., U.S.A. 156 43 12N 85 14W
Greenville, Miss., U.S.A. 159 33 25N 91 0W
Greenville, N.C., U.S.A. 157 35 37N 77 26W
Greenville, N.H., U.S.A. 162 42 46N 71 49W
Greenville, N.Y., U.S.A. 162 42 25N 74 1W
Greenville, Ohio, U.S.A. 156 40 5N 84 38W
Greenville, Pa., U.S.A. 156 41 23N 80 22W
Greenville, S.C., U.S.A. 157 34 54N 82 24W
Greenville, Tenn., U.S.A. 157 36 13N 82 51W
Greenville, Tex., U.S.A. 159 33 5N 96 5W
Greenwater Lake Prov. Park 153 52 32N 103 30W
Greenway 31 51 56N 4 49W
Greenwich, U.K. 29 51 28N 0 0
Greenwich, Conn., U.S.A. 162 41 1N 73 38W
Greenwich, N.Y., U.S.A. 162 43 2N 73 36W
Greenwood, Can. 152 49 10N 118 40W
Greenwood, Miss., U.S.A. 159 33 30N 90 4W
Greenwood, S.C., U.S.A. 157 34 13N 82 13W
Greenwood, Mt. 136 13 48S 130 4E
Gregory 158 43 14N 99 20W
Gregory Downs 138 18 35S 138 45E
Gregory, L. 139 28 55S 139 0E
Gregory L. 136 20 5S 127 0E
Gregory, L. 137 25 38S 119 58E
Gregory Lake 136 20 10S 127 30E
Gregory, R. 138 17 53S 139 17E
Gregory Ra., Queens., Austral. 138 19 30S 143 40E
Gregory Ra., W. Austral., Austral. 136 21 20S 121 12E
Greian Hd. 36 57 1N 7 30W
Greiffenberg 48 53 6N 13 57E
Greifswald 48 54 6N 13 23E
Greifswalder Bodden 48 54 12N 13 35E
Greifswalder Oie 48 54 15N 13 55E
Grein 52 48 14N 14 51E
Greiner Wald 52 48 30N 15 0E
Greiz 48 50 39N 12 12E
Gremikha 78 67 50N 39 40E
Grenå 73 56 25N 10 53E
Grenada 159 33 45N 89 50W
Grenada I. ■ 167 12 10N 61 40W
Grenade 44 43 47N 1 17E
Grenadines 167 12 40N 61 20W
Grenchen 50 47 12N 7 24E
Grenen 73 57 44N 10 40E
Grenfell, Austral. 141 33 52S 148 8E
Grenfell, Can. 153 50 30N 102 56W
Grenoble 45 45 12N 5 42E
Grenora 158 48 38N 103 54W
Grenville, C. 138 12 0S 143 13E
Grenville Chan. 152 53 40N 129 46W
Gréoux-les-Bains 45 43 55N 5 52E
Gresham 160 45 30N 122 31W
Gresik 103 9 13S 112 38E
Gressoney St. Jean 62 45 49N 7 47E
Greta 32 54 9N 2 36W
Greta R. 32 54 36N 3 5W
Gretna, U.K. 35 54 59N 3 4W
Gretna, U.S.A. 159 30 0N 90 2W
Gretna Green 35 55 0N 3 3W
Gretton 29 52 33N 0 40W
Grevelingen Krammer 46 51 44N 4 0E
Greven 48 52 7N 7 36E
Grevená 68 40 4N 21 25E
Grevená □ 68 40 2N 21 25E
Grevenbroich 48 51 6N 6 32E
Grevenmacher 47 49 41N 6 26E
Grevesmühlen 48 53 51N 11 10E
Grevie 73 56 22N 12 46E
Grevinge 73 55 48N 11 34E
Grey, C. 138 13 0S 136 35E
Grey, R. 143 42 27S 171 12E
Grey Range 133 27 0S 143 30E
Grey Res. 151 48 20N 56 30W
Greyabbey 38 54 32N 5 35W
Greybull 160 44 30N 108 3W
Greystone 32 54 39N 2 52W
Greystones 39 53 9N 6 4W
Greytown, N.Z. 142 41 5S 175 29E
Greytown, S. Afr. 129 29 1S 30 36E
Gribanovskiy 81 51 28N 41 50E
Gribbell I. 152 53 23N 129 0W
Gribbin Head 30 50 18N 4 41W
Gridley 160 39 27N 121 47W
Griekwastad 128 28 49S 23 15E
Griffin 157 33 17N 84 14W
Griffith 141 34 18S 146 2E
Griffith Mine 153 50 47N 93 25W
Grigoryevka 84 50 48N 58 18E
Grijalva, R. 164 16 20N 92 20W
Grijpskerk 46 53 16N 6 18E
Grillby 72 59 38N 17 15E

Grim, C Gus

Grim, C. 133 40 45 S 144 45 E
Grimaïlov 80 49 20N 26 5 E
Grimari 117 5 43N 20 0 E
Grimbergen 47 50 56N 4 22 E
Grimeton 73 57 6N 12 25 E
Griminish Pt. 36 57 40N 7 30W
Grimma 48 51 14N 12 44 E
Grimmen 48 54 6N 13 2 E
Grimsay I. 36 57 29N 7 12W
Grimsby 33 53 35N 0 5W
Grimsel Pass 51 46 34N 8 23 E
Grímsey 74 66 33N 18 0W
Grimshaw 152 56 10N 117 40W
Grimstad 71 58 22N 8 35 E
Grindelwald 50 46 38N 8 2 E
Grindsted 73 55 46N 8 55 E
Grindstone Island 151 47 25N 62 0W
Grindu 70 44 44N 26 50 E
Grinduşul, Mt. 70 46 40N 26 7 E
Griñón 56 40 13N 3 51W
Grinnell 158 41 45N 92 43W
Grip 71 63 16N 7 37 E
Griqualand East 129 30 30 S 29 0 E
Griqualand West 128 28 40 S 23 30 E
Griquet 151 51 30N 55 35W
Grisolles 44 43 49N 1 19 E
Grisons □ 49 46 40N 9 30 E
Grisslehamm 72 60 5N 18 49 E
Grita, La 174 8 8N 71 59W
Gritley 37 58 56N 2 45W
Grivegnée 47 50 37N 5 36 E
Griz Nez 43 50 50N 1 35 E
Grizebeck 32 54 16N 3 10W
Grmeč Planina 63 44 43N 16 16 E
Groais I. 151 50 55N 55 35W
Groblersdal 129 25 15 S 29 25 E
Grobming 52 47 27N 13 54 E
Grocka 66 44 40N 20 42 E
Grodek 80 52 46N 23 38 E
Grodkow 54 50 43N 17 40 E
Grodno 80 53 42N 23 52 E
Grodzisk Mazowiecki 54 52 7N 20 37 E
Grodzisk Wlkp. 54 52 15N 16 22 E
Grodzyanka 80 53 31N 28 42 E
Groenlo 46 52 2N 6 37 E
Groesbeck 159 31 32N 96 34W
Groesbeek 46 51 47N 5 58 E
Groix 42 47 38N 3 29W
Groix, I. de 42 47 38N 3 28W
Grójec 54 51 50N 20 58 E
Grolloo 46 52 56N 6 41 E
Gronau 48 52 13N 7 2 E
Grong 74 64 25N 12 8 E
Groningen 46 53 15N 6 35 E
Groningen □ 46 53 16N 6 40 E
Groninger Wad 46 53 27N 6 30 E
Grönskåra 73 57 5N 15 43 E
Gronsveld 47 50 49N 5 44 E
Groom 159 35 12N 100 59W
Groomsport 38 54 41N 5 37W
Groot Berg, R. 128 32 50 S 18 20 E
Groot-Brakrivier 128 34 2 S 22 18 E
Groot Karoo 128 32 35 S 23 0 E
Groot Namakwaland = Namaland 128 26 0 S 18 0 E
Groot, R. 128 33 10 S 23 35 E
Groote Eylandt 138 14 0 S 136 50 E
Grootebroek 46 52 41N 5 13 E
Grootfontein 128 19 31 S 18 6 E
Grootlaagte, R. 128 21 10 S 21 20 E
Gros C. 152 61 59N 113 32W
Grosa, Punta 59 39 6N 1 36 E
Grósio 62 46 18N 10 17 E
Grosne, R. 45 46 30N 4 40 E
Gross Glockner 52 47 5N 12 40 E
Gross Ottersleben 48 52 5N 11 33 E
Grossa, Pta. 170 1 20N 50 0W
Grossenbrode 48 54 21N 11 4 E
Grossenhain 48 51 17N 13 32 E
Grosseto 62 42 45N 11 7 E
Grossgerungs 52 48 34N 14 57 E
Grosswater B. 151 54 20N 57 40W
Grote Gette, R. 47 50 51N 5 6 E
Grote Nete, R. 47 51 8N 4 34 E
Groton, U.S.A. 162 41 22N 72 12W
Groton, U.S.A. 162 42 36N 76 22W
Grottaglie 65 40 32N 17 25 E
Grottaminarda 65 41 5N 15 4 E
Grouard Mission 152 55 33N 116 9W
Grouin, Pointe du 42 48 43N 1 51W
Groundhog, R. 150 48 45N 82 20W
Grouse Creek 160 41 51N 113 57W
Grouw 46 53 5N 5 51 E
Groveland 163 37 50N 120 14W
Grovelsjön 72 62 6N 12 16 E
Grover City 163 35 7N 120 37W
Groveton 159 31 5N 95 4W
Groznjan 63 45 22N 13 43 E
Groznyy 83 43 20N 45 45 E
Grubbenvorst 47 51 25N 6 9 E
Grubišno Polje 66 45 44N 17 12 E
Grudusk 54 53 3N 20 38 E
Grudziadz 54 53 30N 18 47 E
Gruinard B. 36 57 56N 5 35W
Gruissan 44 43 8N 3 7 E
Grumo Áppula 65 41 2N 16 43 E
Grums 72 59 22N 13 5 E
Grünau 125 27 45 S 18 26 E
Grünberg 48 50 37N 8 55 E
Grundy Center 158 42 22N 92 45W
Grungedal 71 59 44N 7 43 E
Gruting Voe 36 60 12N 1 32W
Gruver 159 36 19N 101 20W
Gruyères 50 46 35N 7 4 E
Gruza 66 43 54N 20 46 E
Gryazi 81 52 30N 39 58 E
Gryazovets 81 58 50N 40 20 E
Grybów 54 49 36N 20 55 E
Grycksbo 72 60 40N 15 29 E
Gryfice 54 53 55N 15 13 E
Gryfino 54 53 16N 14 29 E
Grytgöl 73 58 49N 15 33 E
Grythyttan 72 59 41N 14 32 E
Grytviken 13 53 50 S 37 10W
Gstaad 50 46 28N 7 18 E
Gua 99 22 18N 85 20 E
Gua Musang 101 4 53N 101 58 E
Guacanayabo, Golfo de 166 20 40N 77 20W
Guacara 174 10 14N 67 53W
Guachípas 172 25 40 S 65 30W
Guachiría, R. 174 5 30N 71 30W
Guadajoz, R. 57 37 50N 4 51W
Guadalajara, Mexico 164 20 40N 103 20W
Guadalajara, Spain 58 40 37N 3 12W
Guadalajara □ 58 40 47N 3 0W
Guadalcanal 57 38 5N 5 52W
Guadalcanal, I. 130 9 32 S 160 12 E
Guadalén, R. 59 38 30N 3 7W
Guadales 172 34 30 S 67 55W
Guadalete, R. 57 36 45N 5 47W
Guadalhorce, R. 57 36 50N 4 42W
Guadalimar, R. 59 38 10N 2 53W
Guadalmena, R. 59 38 31N 2 50W
Guadalmez, R. 57 38 33N 4 42W
Guadalope, R. 58 41 0N 0 13W
Guadalquivir, R. 57 38 0N 4 0W
Guadalupe, Brazil 170 6 44 S 43 47W
Guadalupe, Spain 57 39 27N 5 17W
Guadalupe, U.S.A. 163 34 59N 120 33W
Guadalupe Bravos 164 31 20N 106 10W
Guadalupe de los Reyes 164 25 23N 104 15W
Guadalupe I. 143 21 20N 118 50W
Guadalupe Pk. 161 31 50N 105 30W
Guadalupe, R. 159 29 25N 97 30W
Guadalupe, Sierra de 55 39 28N 5 30W
Guadalupe y Calvo 164 26 6N 106 58W
Guadarrama, Sierra de 56 41 0N 4 0W
Guadeloupe, I. 167 16 20N 61 40W
Guadeloupe Passage 167 16 50N 68 15W
Guadiamar, R. 57 37 9N 6 20W
Guadiana Menor, R. 59 37 45N 3 7W
Guadiana, R. 57 37 45N 7 35W
Guadiaro, R. 57 36 39N 5 17W
Guadiato, R. 57 37 55N 4 53W
Guadiela, R. 58 40 30N 2 23W
Guadix 59 37 18N 3 11W
Guafo, Boca del 176 43 35 S 74 0W
Guaina 174 5 9N 63 36W
Guainía □ 174 2 30N 69 00W
Guaíra 173 24 5 S 54 10W
Guaira, La 174 10 36N 66 56W
Guaitecas, Islas 176 44 0 S 74 30W
Guajará-Mirim 174 10 50 S 65 20W
Guajira, La □ 174 11 30N 72 30W
Guajira, Pen. de la 167 12 0N 72 0W
Gualan 166 15 8N 89 22W
Gualdo Tadino 63 43 14N 12 46 E
Gualeguay 172 33 10 S 59 20W
Gualeguaychú 172 33 3 S 58 31W
Guam I. 130 13 27N 144 45 E
Guamá 170 1 37 S 47 29W
Guama 174 10 16N 68 49W
Guamá, R. 170 1 29 S 48 30W
Guamareyes 174 0 30 S 73 0W
Guaminí 172 37 1 S 62 28W
Guampí, Sierra de 174 6 0N 65 35W
Guamuchil 164 25 25N 108 3W
Guanabacoa 166 23 8N 82 18W
Guanabara □ 173 23 0 S 43 25W
Guanacaste 166 10 40N 85 30W
Guanacaste, Cordillera del 166 10 40N 85 4W
Guanacevío 164 25 40N 106 0W
Guanajay 166 22 56N 82 42W
Guanajuato 164 21 0N 101 20W
Guanajuato □ 164 20 40N 101 20W
Guanambi 171 14 13 S 42 47W
Guanare 174 8 42N 69 12W
Guanare, R. 174 8 50N 68 50W
Guandacol 172 29 30 S 68 40W
Guane 166 22 10N 84 0W
Guanhães 171 18 47 S 42 57W
Guanica 147 17 58N 66 55W
Guanipa, R. 174 9 20N 63 30W
Guanta 174 10 14N 64 36W
Guantánamo 167 20 10N 75 20W
Guapí 174 2 36N 77 54W
Guápiles 166 10 10N 83 46W
Guaporé 173 12 0 S 64 0W
Guaporé, R. 174 13 0 S 63 0W
Guaqui 174 16 41 S 68 54W
Guara, Sierra de 58 42 19N 0 15W
Guarabira 170 6 51 S 35 29W
Guarapari 173 20 40 S 40 30W
Guarapuava 171 25 20 S 51 30W
Guaratinguetá 173 22 49 S 45 9W
Guaratuba 173 25 53 S 48 38W
Guard Bridge 35 56 21N 2 52W
Guarda 56 40 32N 7 20W
Guarda □ 56 40 40N 7 20W
Guardafui, C. = Asir, Ras 91 11 55N 51 10 E
Guardamar del Segura 59 38 5N 0 39W
Guardavalle 65 38 31N 16 30 E
Guardia, La 56 41 56N 8 52W
Guardiagrele 63 42 11N 14 11 E
Guardo 56 42 47N 4 50W
Guareña 57 38 51N 6 6W
Guareña, R. 56 41 25N 5 25W
Guaria □ 172 25 45N 56 30W
Guárico □ 174 8 40N 66 35W
Guarujá 173 24 2 S 46 25W
Guarus 173 21 30 S 41 20W
Guasave 164 25 34N 108 27W
Guasdualito 174 7 15N 70 44W
Guasipati 174 7 28N 61 54W
Guasopa 135 9 12 S 152 56 E
Guastalla 62 44 55N 10 40 E
Guatemala 166 14 40N 90 30W
Guatemala ■ 166 15 40N 90 30W
Guatire 174 10 28N 66 32W
Guaviare, R. 174 3 30N 71 0W
Guaxupé 173 21 10 S 47 5W
Guayabal 174 4 43N 71 37W
Guayama 147 17 59N 66 7W
Guayaquil 174 2 15 S 79 52W
Guayaquil, Golfo de 174 3 10 S 81 0W
Guaymallen 172 32 50 S 68 45W
Guaymas 164 27 50N 111 0W
Guba, Ethiopia 123 4 52N 39 18 E
Guba, Zaïre 127 10 38 S 26 27 E
Gubakha 84 58 52N 57 36 E
Gubam 135 8 39 S 141 53 E
Gúbbio 63 43 20N 12 34 E
Gubio 121 12 30N 12 42 E
Gubkin 81 51 17N 37 32 E
Guča 66 43 46N 20 15 E
Guchil 101 5 35N 102 10 E
Gudalur 97 11 30N 76 29 E
Gudata 83 43 7N 40 32 E
Gudbrandsdal 75 61 33N 10 0 E
Guddu Barrage 93 28 30N 69 50 E
Gudenå 73 56 27N 9 40 E
Gudermes 83 43 24N 46 20 E
Gudhjem 73 55 12N 14 58 E
Gudiña, La 56 42 4N 7 8W
Gudivada 96 16 30N 81 15 E
Gudiyatam 97 12 57N 78 55 E
Gudmundra 72 62 56N 17 47 E
Gudrun, gasfield 19 58 50N 1 48 E
Gudur 97 14 12N 79 55 E
Guebwiller 43 47 55N 7 12 E
Guecho 58 43 21N 2 59W
Guéckédou 120 8 40N 10 5W
Guelma 119 36 25N 7 29 E
Guelph 150 43 35N 80 20W
Guelt es Stel 118 35 12N 3 1 E
Guelttara 118 29 23N 2 10W
Guemar 119 33 30N 6 57 E
Guéméné-Penfao 42 47 38N 1 50W
Guéméné-sur-Scorff 42 48 4N 3 13W
Güemes 172 24 50 S 65 0W
Guéné 121 11 44N 3 16 E
Guer 42 47 54N 2 8W
Guérande 42 47 20N 2 26W
Guerche, La 42 47 57N 1 16W
Guerche-sur-l'Aubois, La 43 46 58N 2 56 E
Guercif 118 34 14N 3 21W
Guéréda 124 14 31N 22 5 E
Guéret 44 46 11N 1 51 E
Guérigny 43 47 6N 3 10 E
Guernica 58 43 19N 2 40W
Guernsey 158 42 19N 104 45W
Guernsey I. 42 49 30N 2 35W
Guerrara, Oasis, Alg. 119 32 51N 4 35 E
Guerrara, Saoura, Alg. 118 28 5N 0 8W
Guerrero □ 165 17 30N 100 0W
Guerzim 118 29 45N 1 47W
Güeş ti 70 44 48N 25 19 E
Guestling Green 29 50 53N 0 40 E
Gueugnon 45 45 36N 4 3 E
Gueydan 159 30 3N 92 30W
Guezendi = Ghesendor 119 21 14N 18 14 E
Guglia, P. dal 51 46 28N 9 45 E
Guglionesi 63 51 55N 14 54 E
Guhra 93 27 36N 56 8 E
Guia Lopes da Laguna 173 21 26 S 56 7W
Guiana Highlands 174 5 0N 60 0W
Guibes 128 26 41 S 16 49 E
Guider 121 9 55N 13 59 E
Guidimouni 121 13 42N 9 31 E
Guiglo 120 6 45N 7 30W
Guija 125 34 35 S 33 15 E
Guijo de Coria 56 40 6N 6 28W
Guildford 29 51 14N 0 34W
Guilford, Conn., U.S.A. 162 41 15N 72 40W
Guilford, Me., U.S.A. 151 45 12N 69 25W
Guillaumes 45 44 5N 6 52 E
Guillestre 45 44 39N 6 40 E
Guilsfield 31 52 42N 3 9W
Guilvinec 42 47 48N 4 17W
Guimarães 170 2 9 S 44 35W
Guimarāis 56 41 28N 8 24W
Guimaras I. 103 10 35N 122 37 E
Guinea ■ 120 10 20N 10 0W
Guinea Bissau ■ 120 12 0N 15 0W
Guinea, Gulf of 121 3 0N 2 30 E
Guinea, Port. = Guinea Bissau 120 12 0N 15 0W
Güines 166 22 50N 82 0W
Guingamp 42 48 34N 3 10W
Guipavas 42 48 26N 4 29W
Guipúzcoa □ 58 43 12N 2 15W
Guir, O. 118 39 29N 2 58W
Guirgo 121 11 54N 1 21W
Güiria 174 10 32N 62 18W
Guisborough 33 54 32N 1 2W
Guiscard 43 49 40N 3 0 E
Guise 43 49 52N 3 35 E
Guitiriz 56 43 11N 7 50W
Guivan 103 11 5N 125 55 E
Gujan-Mestras 44 44 38N 1 4W
Gujar Khan 84 33 15N 73 21 E
Gujarat □ 94 23 20N 71 0 E
Gujranwala 94 32 10N 74 12 E
Gujrat 94 32 40N 74 2 E
Gukhothae 101 17 2N 99 50 E
Gukovo 83 48 1N 39 58 E
Gulak 121 10 50N 13 30 E
Gulargambone 141 31 20 S 148 30 E
Gulbahar 93 35 5N 69 10 E
Gulbargâ 96 17 20N 76 50 E
Gulbene 80 57 8N 26 52 E
Gulcha 85 40 19N 73 26 E
Guldborg Sd. 73 54 39N 11 50 E
Guledgud 97 16 3N 75 48 E
Gulf Basin 136 15 20 S 129 0 E
Gulfport 159 30 28N 89 3W
Gulgong 141 32 20 S 149 30 E
Gulistan, Pak. 94 30 36N 66 35 E
Gulistan, U.S.S.R. 85 40 29N 68 46 E
Gulkana 147 62 15N 145 48W
Gull Lake 153 50 10N 108 29W
Gullane 35 56 2N 2 50W
Gullegem 47 50 51N 3 13 E
Gullringen 73 57 48N 15 44 E
Güllük 69 37 12N 27 36 E
Gulma 121 12 40N 4 23 E
Gulmarg 95 34 3N 74 25 E
Gulnam 123 6 55N 29 30 E
Gulnare 140 33 27 S 138 27 E
Gulpaigan 92 33 26N 50 20 E
Gulpen 47 50 49N 5 53 E
Gülpinar 68 39 32N 26 10 E
Gulshad 76 46 45N 74 25 E
Gulsvik 71 60 24N 9 38 E
Gulu 126 2 48N 32 17 E
Gulwe 126 6 30 S 36 25 E
Gulyaypole 82 47 45N 36 21 E
Gum Lake 140 32 42 S 143 9 E
Gumal, R. 94 32 5N 70 5 E
Gumbaz 94 30 2N 69 0 E
Gumel 121 12 39N 9 22 E
Gumiel de Hizán 58 41 46N 3 41W
Gumlu 138 19 53 S 147 41 E
Gumma-ken □ 111 36 30N 138 20 E
Gummersbach 48 51 2N 7 32 E
Gummi 121 12 4N 5 9 E
Gümüsane 92 40 30N 39 30 E
Gümuşhaciköy 82 40 50N 35 18 E
Gumzai 103 5 28 S 134 42 E
Guna 94 24 40N 77 19 E
Guna Mt. 123 11 50N 37 40 E
Gundagai 141 35 3 S 148 6 E
Gundih 103 7 10 S 110 56 E
Gundlakamma, R. 97 15 30N 80 15 E
Gunebang 141 33 5 S 146 38 E
Gungal 141 32 17 S 150 32 E
Gungi 123 10 20N 38 3 E
Gungu 124 5 43 S 19 20 E
Gunisao L. 153 53 33N 96 15W
Gunisao, R. 153 53 56N 97 53W
Gunnedah 141 30 59 S 150 15 E
Gunniguldrie 141 33 12 S 146 8 E
Gunningbar Cr. 141 31 14 S 147 6 E
Gunnison, Colo., U.S.A. 161 38 32N 106 56W
Gunnison, Utah, U.S.A. 160 39 11N 111 48W
Gunnison, R. 161 38 50N 108 30W
Gunnworth 153 51 20N 108 9W
Guntakal 97 15 11N 77 27 E
Guntersville 157 34 18N 86 16W
Guntong 101 4 36N 101 3 E
Guntur 96 16 23N 80 30 E
Gunungapi 103 6 45 S 126 30 E
Gunungsitoli 102 1 15N 97 30 E
Gunungsugih 102 4 58 S 105 7 E
Gunupur 96 19 5N 83 50 E
Gunworth 153 51 20N 108 10W
Gunza 124 10 50 S 13 50 E
Gunzenhausen 49 49 6N 10 45 E
Gupis 95 36 15N 73 20 E
Gura 94 25 12N 71 39 E
Gura Humorului 70 47 35N 25 53 E
Gura Teghii 70 45 30N 26 25 E
Gurage, mt. 123 8 20N 38 20 E
Gurchan 92 34 55N 49 25 E
Gurdaspur 94 32 5N 75 25 E
Gurdon 159 33 55N 93 10W
Gurdzhaani 83 41 43N 45 52 E
Gurgan 93 36 51N 54 25 E
Gurgaon 94 28 33N 77 10 E
Gurghiu, Munţii 70 46 41N 25 15 E
Gurguéia, R. 170 6 50 S 43 24W
Guria 62 44 30N 9 0 E
Gurk, R. 52 46 48N 14 20 E
Gurkha 95 28 5N 84 40 E
Gurla Mandhata 95 30 30N 81 10 E
Gurley 139 29 45 S 149 48 E
Gurnard's Head 30 50 12N 5 37W
Gurnet Pt. 162 42 1N 70 34W
Gurrumbah 138 17 30 S 144 55 E
Gurun 101 5 49N 100 27 E
Gürün 92 38 41N 37 22 E
Gurupá 175 1 20 S 51 45W
Gurupá, I. Grande de 175 1 0 S 51 45W
Gurupi 171 11 43 S 49 4W
Gurupi, R. 170 3 20 S 47 20W
Gurupi, Serra do 170 5 0 S 47 30W
Guryev 83 47 5N 52 0 E
Gus 126 3 2N 36 57 E

Gus-Khrsutalnyy Han Chiang, R

Gus-Khrsutalnyy 81 55 42N 40 35 E
Gusau 121 12 18N 6 31 E
Gusev 80 54 35N 22 20 E
Gushiago 121 9 55N 0 15W
Gusinje 66 42 35N 19 50 E
Gùspini 64 39 32N 8 38 E
Gusselby 72 59 38N 15 14 E
Güssing 53 47 3N 16 20 E
Gustanj 63 46 36N 14 49 E
Gustavus 147 58 25N 135 58W
Gustine 163 37 21N 121 0W
Güstrow 48 53 47N 12 12 E
Gusum 73 58 16N 16 30 E
Gûtaia 70 45 26N 21 30 E
Gütersloh 48 51 54N 8 25 E
Gutha 137 28 58 S 115 55 E
Guthalungra 138 19 52 S 147 50 E
Guthrie 159 35 55N 97 30W
Guttannen 51 46 38N 8 18 E
Guttenberg 158 42 46N 91 10W
Guyana ■ 174 5 0N 59 0W
Guyenne 44 44 30N 0 40 E
Guyman 159 36 45N 101 30W
Guyra 139 30 15 S 151 40 E
Guzar 85 38 36N 66 15 E
Guzmán, Laguna de 164 31 25N 107 25W
Gwa 98 17 30N 94 40 E
Gwaai 127 19 15 S 27 45 E
Gwabegar 141 30 31 S 149 0 E
Gwadabawa 121 13 20N 5 15 E
Gwādar 93 25 10N 62 18 E
Gwagwada 121 10 15N 7 15 E
Gwalchmai 31 53 16N 4 23W
Gwalia 137 28 54 S 121 20 E
Gwalior 94 26 12N 78 10 E
Gwanara 121 18 55N 3 10 E
Gwanda 127 20 55 S 29 0 E
Gwandu 121 12 30N 4 41 E
Gwane 126 4 45N 25 48 E
Gwaram 121 11 15N 9 51 E
Gwarzo 121 12 20N 8 55 E
Gwasero 121 9 30N 8 30 E
Gwaun-Cae-Gurwen 31 51 46N 3 51W
Gweebarra B. 38 54 52N 8 21W
Gweedore 38 55 4N 8 15W
Gweek 30 50 6N 5 12W
Gwelo 125 19 28 S 29 45 E
Gwennap 30 50 12N 5 9W
Gwent □ 31 51 45N 2 55W
Gweta 128 20 12 S 25 17 E
Gwi 121 9 0N 7 10 E
Gwinn 156 46 15N 87 29W
Gwio Kura 121 12 40N 11 2 E
Gwolu 120 10 58N 1 59W
Gwoza 121 11 12N 13 40 E
Gwyddelwern 31 53 2N 3 23W
Gwydir, R. 139 29 27 S 149 48 E
Gwynedd □ 31 53 0N 4 0W
Gya La 95 28 45N 84 45 E
Gyangtse 99 28 50N 89 33 E
Gydanskiy P-ov. 76 70 0N 78 0 E
Gyland 71 58 24N 6 45 E
Gympie 139 26 11 S 152 38 E
Gyobingauk 98 18 13N 95 39 E
Gyoda 111 36 10N 139 30 E
Gyoma 53 46 56N 20 58 E
Gyöngyös 53 47 48N 20 15 E
Györ 53 47 41N 17 40 E
Györ-Sopron □ 53 47 40N 17 20 E
Gypsum Palace 140 32 37 S 144 9 E
Gypsum Pt. 152 61 53N 114 35W
Gypsumville 153 51 45N 98 40W
Gyttorp 72 59 31N 14 58 E
Gyula 53 46 38N 21 17 E
Gzhatsk = Gagarin 80 55 30N 35 0 E

H

Ha Coi 100 21 26N 107 46 E
Ha Dong 100 20 58N 105 46 E
Ha Giang 100 22 50N 104 59 E
Ha Nam = Phu-Ly 100 20 35N 105 50 E
Ha Tien 101 10 23N 104 29 E
Ha Tinh 100 18 20N 105 54 E
Ha Trung 100 20 0N 105 50 E
Haa, The 36 60 20N 1 0 E
Haacht 47 50 59N 4 37 E
Haag 49 48 11N 12 12 E
Haaksbergen 46 52 9N 6 45 E
Haaltert 47 50 55N 4 1 E
Haamstede 47 51 42N 3 45 E
Haapamäki 74 62 18N 24 28 E
Haapsalu 80 58 56N 23 30 E
Haarby 73 55 13N 10 8 E
Haarlem 46 52 23N 4 39 E
Haast 143 43 51 S 169 1 E
Haast P. 143 44 6 S 169 21 E
Haast, R. 143 43 50 S 169 2 E
Haastrecht 46 52 0N 4 47 E
Hab Nadi Chauki 94 25 0N 66 50 E
Hab, R. 93 25 15N 67 8 E
Haba 92 27 10N 47 0 E
Habana, La 166 23 8N 82 22W
Habaswein 126 1 2N 39 30 E
Habay 152 58 50N 118 44W
Habay-la-Neuve 47 49 44N 5 38 E
Habiganj 98 24 24N 91 30 E
Hablingbo 73 57 12N 18 16 E
Habo 73 57 55N 14 6 E
Haccourt 47 50 44N 5 40 E
Hachenburg 48 50 40N 7 49 E
Hachijō-Jima 111 33 5N 139 45 E
Hachinohe 112 40 30N 141 29 E
Hachiōji 111 35 30N 139 30 E
Hachŏn 107 40 29N 129 2 E
Hachy 47 49 42N 5 41 E
Hacketstown 39 52 52N 6 35W
Hackett 152 52 9N 112 28W
Hackettstown 162 40 51N 74 50W
Hackney 29 51 33N 0 2W
Hackthorpe 32 54 37N 2 42W
Hadali 94 32 16N 72 11 E
Hadarba, Ras 122 22 4N 36 51 E
Hadd, Ras al 93 22 35N 59 50 E
Haddenham 29 51 46N 0 56W
Haddington 35 55 57N 2 48W
Haddon Rig 141 31 27 S 147 52 E
Hadeija 121 12 30N 10 5 E
Hadeija, R. 121 12 20N 9 30W
Haden 139 27 13 S 151 54 E
Hadera 90 32 27N 34 55 E
Haderslev 73 55 15N 9 30 E
Hadhra 122 20 10N 41 5 E
Hadhramaut = Hadramawt 91 15 30N 49 30 E
Hadibu 91 12 35N 54 2 E
Hadjeb el Aïoun 119 35 21N 9 32 E
Hadleigh 29 52 3N 0 58 E
Hadley 28 52 42N 2 28W
Hadlow 29 51 12N 0 20 E
Hadong 107 35 5N 127 44 E
Hadramawt 91 15 30N 49 30 E
Hadrians Wall 35 55 0N 2 30W
Hadsten 73 56 19N 10 3 E
Hadsund 73 56 44N 10 8 E
Haeju 107 38 3N 125 45 E
Haenam 107 34 34N 126 15 E
Haerhpin 107 45 45N 126 45 E
Hafar al Batin 92 28 25N 46 50 E
Hafizabad 94 32 5N 73 40 E
Haflong 98 25 10N 93 5 E
Hafnarfjörður 74 64 4N 21 57W
Haft-Gel 92 31 30N 49 32 E
Hafun 91 10 25N 51 16 E
Hafun, Ras 91 10 29N 51 20 E
Hagalil 90 32 53N 35 18 E
Hagar Banga 117 10 40N 22 45 E
Hagari, R. 97 14 0N 76 45 E
Hagemeister I. 147 58 42N 161 0W
Hagen 48 51 21N 7 29 E
Hagenow 48 53 25N 11 10 E
Hagerman 159 33 5N 104 22W
Hagerstown 156 39 39N 77 46W
Hagetmau 44 43 39N 0 37W
Hagfors 72 60 3N 13 45 E
Häggenås 72 63 24N 14 55 E
Hagi, Iceland 74 65 28N 23 25W
Hagi, Japan 110 34 30N 131 30 E
Hagion Evstratios 68 39 30N 25 0 E
Hagion Óros 68 40 37N 24 6 E
Hags Hd. 39 52 57N 9 30W
Hague, C. de la 42 49 44N 1 56W
Hague, The = s'-Gravenhage 47 52 7N 4 17 E
Haguenau 43 48 49N 7 47 E
Hai □ 126 3 10 S 37 10 E
Hai Duong 100 20 56N 106 19 E
Haian, Kiangsu, China 109 32 37N 120 33 E
Haian, Kwangtung, China 109 20 18N 110 11 E
Haich'eng, Fukien, China 109 24 24N 117 51 E
Haich'eng, Liaoning, China 107 40 52N 122 45 E
Haichou 107 34 34N 119 6 E
Haichou Wan 107 35 0N 119 30 E
Haidar Khel 94 33 58N 68 38 E
Haifa 90 32 46N 35 0 E
Haifeng 109 22 59N 115 21 E
Haig 137 30 55 S 126 10 E
Haiger 48 50 44N 8 12 E
Haik'ang 109 20 56N 110 4 E
Haik'ou 100 20 5N 110 20 E
Hā'il 92 27 28N 42 2 E
Hailaerh 105 49 12N 119 42 E
Hailakandi 98 24 42N 92 34 E
Hailey 160 43 30N 114 15W
Haileybury 150 47 30N 79 38W
Hailin 107 44 32N 129 24 E
Hailing Tao 109 21 37N 111 65 E
Hailsham 29 50 52N 0 17 E
Hailun 105 47 27N 126 56 E
Hailung 107 42 30N 125 40 E
Hailuoto 74 65 3N 24 45 E
Haimen, Chekiang, China 109 28 39N 121 25 E
Haimen, Kwangtung, China 109 23 15N 116 35 E
Hainan 100 19 0N 110 0 E
Hainan Str. = Ch'iungcho Haihsia 100 20 10N 110 15 E
Hainaut □ 47 50 30N 4 0 E
Hainburg 53 48 9N 16 56 E
Haines, Alaska, U.S.A. 147 59 20N 135 36W
Haines, Oreg., U.S.A. 160 44 51N 117 59W
Haines City 157 28 6N 81 35W
Haines Junction 147 60 45N 137 30W
Hainfeld 52 48 3N 15 48 E
Haining 109 30 23N 120 30 E
Hainton 33 53 21N 0 13W
Haiphong 100 20 47N 106 35 E
Hait'an Tao 109 25 35N 119 45 E
Haiti ■ 167 19 0N 72 30W
Haiya Junc. 122 18 20N 36 40 E
Haiyang 107 36 45N 121 15 E
Haiyen 109 30 28N 120 57 E
Haiyüan, Kwangsi-Chuang, China 108 22 6N 107 25 E
Haiyüan, Ningsia Hui, China 106 36 32N 105 40 E
Haja 103 3 19 S 129 37 E
Hajdú-Bihar □ 53 47 30N 21 30 E
Hajdúböszörmény 53 47 40N 21 30 E
Hajdúdurog 53 47 48N 21 30 E
Hajdúhadház 53 47 40N 21 40 E
Hajdúnánás 53 47 50N 21 26 E
Hajdúsámson 53 47 37N 21 42 E
Hajdúszobaszló 53 47 27N 21 22 E
Haji Langar 93 35 50N 79 20 E
Hajiganj 98 23 15N 90 50 E
Hajipur 95 25 45N 85 20 E
Hajr 93 24 0N 56 34 E
Haka 98 22 39N 93 37 E
Hakansson, Mts. 127 8 40 S 25 45 E
Hakantorp 73 58 18N 12 55 E
Håkantorp 73 58 18N 12 55 E
Hakataramea 143 44 30 S 170 30 E
Hakataramea, R. 143 44 35 S 170 40 E
Hakken-Zan 111 34 10N 135 54 E
Hakodate 112 41 45N 140 44 E
Hakota 111 36 5N 140 30 E
Haku-San 111 36 9N 136 46 E
Hakun 98 26 46N 95 42 E
Hala 93 25 43N 68 20 E
Hala Hu 105 38 15N 97 40 E
Halab = Aleppo 92 36 10N 37 15 E
Halabjah 92 35 10N 45 58 E
Halaib 122 22 5N 36 30 E
Halanzy 47 49 33N 5 44 E
Halawa 147 21 9N 156 47W
Halbe 122 19 40N 42 15 E
Halberstadt 48 51 53N 11 2 E
Halberton 30 50 55N 3 24W
Halcombe 142 40 8 S 175 30 E
Halcyon, Mt. 103 13 0N 121 30 E
Halden 72 59 7N 11 23 E
Haldensleben 48 52 17N 11 30 E
Haldia 99 22 5N 88 3 E
Haldwani 95 29 25N 79 30 E
Hale 32 53 24N 2 21W
Hale, R. 138 24 56 S 135 53 E
Haleakala Crater 147 20 43N 156 12W
Halen 47 50 57N 5 6 E
Halesowen 28 52 27N 2 2W
Halesworth 29 52 21N 1 30 E
Haleyville 157 34 15N 87 40W
Half Assini 120 5 1N 2 50W
Halfmoon B. 143 46 50 S 168 5 E
Halfway 160 44 56N 117 8W
Halfway, R. 152 56 12N 121 32W
Halhul 90 31 35N 35 7 E
Hali 122 18 40N 41 15 E
Haliburton 150 45 3N 78 30W
Halibut, oilfield 19 61 20N 1 36 E
Halifax, Austral. 138 18 32 S 146 22 E
Halifax, Can. 151 44 38N 63 35W
Halifax, U.K. 32 53 43N 1 51W
Halifax, U.S.A. 162 40 25N 76 55W
Halifax B. 138 18 50 S 147 0 E
Halifax I. 128 26 38 S 15 4 E
Halil, R. 93 27 40N 58 30 E
Halkirk 37 58 30N 3 30W
Hall 52 47 17N 11 30 E
Hall Land 12 81 20N 60 0W
Hall Pt. 136 15 40 S 124 23 E
Hallabro 73 56 22N 15 5 E
Halland 73 56 55N 12 50 E
Hallands län □ 73 56 50N 12 50 E
Hallands Väderö 73 56 27N 12 34 E
Hallandsås 73 56 22N 13 0 E
Halle, Belg. 47 50 44N 4 13W
Halle, Nordrhein-Westfalen, Ger. 48 52 4N 8 20 E
Halle, Sachsen-Anhalt, Ger. 48 51 29N 12 0 E
Halle □ 48 51 28N 11 58 E
Hällefors 72 59 47N 14 31 E
Hallein 52 47 40N 13 5 E
Hällekis 73 58 38N 13 27 E
Hallett 140 33 25 S 138 55 E
Hallettsville 159 29 28N 96 57W
Hallevadsholm 73 58 37N 11 33 E
Hällevadsholm 73 58 35N 11 33 E
Halley Bay 13 75 31 S 26 36W
Hallia, R. 96 16 55N 79 10 E
Halliday 158 47 20N 102 25W
Halliday L. 153 61 21N 108 56W
Hallim 107 33 24N 126 15 E
Hallingdal, R. 75 60 34N 9 12 E
Hallingskeid 71 60 40N 7 17 E
Hällnäs 74 64 19N 19 36 E
Hallock 153 48 47N 97 57W
Hallow 28 52 14N 2 15W
Hall's Creek 136 18 16 S 127 46 E
Hallsberg 72 59 5N 15 7 E
Hallstahammar 72 59 38N 16 15 E
Hallstatt 52 47 33N 13 38 E
Hallstavik 72 60 5N 18 37 E
Hallstead 162 41 56N 75 45W
Hallwiler See 50 47 16N 8 12 E
Hallworthy 30 50 38N 4 34W
Halmahera, I. 103 0 40N 128 0 E
Halmeu 70 47 57N 23 2 E
Halmstad 73 56 41N 12 52 E
Halq el Oued 119 36 53N 10 10 E
Hals 73 56 59N 10 18 E
Halsa 71 63 3N 8 14 E
Halsafjorden 71 63 5N 8 10 E
Hälsingborg = Helsingborg 73 56 3N 12 42 E
Halstad 158 47 21N 96 41W
Halstead 29 51 59N 0 39 E
Haltdalen 71 62 56N 11 8 E
Haltern 48 51 44N 7 10 E
Haltwhistle 35 54 58N 2 27W
Ham 128 49 44N 3 3 E
Ham Tan 101 10 40N 107 45 E
Ham Yen 100 22 4N 105 3 E
Hamā 92 35 5N 36 40 E
Hamab 128 28 7 S 19 16 E
Hamad 123 15 20N 33 32 E
Hamada 110 34 50N 132 10 E
Hamadān 92 34 52N 48 32 E
Hamadān □ 92 35 0N 49 0 E
Hamadh 122 24 55N 39 3 E
Hamadia 118 35 28N 1 57 E
Hamakita 111 34 45N 137 47 E
Hamale 120 10 56N 2 45W
Hamamatsu 111 34 45N 137 45 E
Hamar 71 60 48N 11 7 E
Hamar Koke 123 51 5N 36 45 E
Hamarøy 74 68 5N 15 38 E
Hamâta, Gebel 122 24 17N 35 0 E
Hambantota 93 6 10N 81 10 E
Hamber Prov. Park 152 52 20N 118 0W
Hambledon 28 50 56N 1 6W
Hambleton Hills 33 54 17N 1 12W
Hamburg, Ger. 48 53 32N 9 59 E
Hamburg, Ark., U.S.A. 159 33 15N 91 47W
Hamburg, Iowa, U.S.A. 158 40 37N 95 38W
Hamburg, Pa., U.S.A. 162 40 33N 76 0W
Hamburg □ 48 53 30N 10 0 E
Hamden 162 41 21N 72 56W
Hame 75 61 30N 24 0 E
Hämeen Lääni 75 61 24N 24 10 E
Hämeenlinna 75 61 0N 24 28 E
Hamelin Pool 137 26 22 S 114 20 E
Hamelin Pool Bay 137 26 10 S 114 5 E
Hameln 48 52 7N 9 24 E
Hamersley 136 22 20 S 117 37 E
Hamersley Ra. 136 22 0 S 117 45 E
Hamhung 107 40 0N 127 30 E
Hami 105 42 47N 93 32 E
Hamilton, Austral. 140 37 45 S 142 2 E
Hamilton, Can. 150 43 20N 79 50W
Hamilton, N.Z. 142 37 47 S 175 19 E
Hamilton, U.K. 35 55 47N 4 2W
Hamilton, Alas., U.S.A. 147 62 55N 164 0W
Hamilton, Mont., U.S.A. 160 46 20N 114 6W
Hamilton, N.Y., U.S.A. 162 42 49N 75 31W
Hamilton, Ohio, U.S.A. 156 39 20N 84 35W
Hamilton, Tex., U.S.A. 159 31 40N 98 5W
Hamilton Downs 106 21 25 S 142 23 E
Hamilton, gasfield 19 56 54N 2 13 E
Hamilton Hotel 138 22 45 S 140 40 E
Hamilton Inlet 151 54 0N 57 30W
Hamilton Mt. 162 43 25N 74 22W
Hamilton, R., Queens., Austral. 138 23 30 S 139 47 E
Hamilton, R., S. Austral., Austral. 136 26 40 S 134 20 E
Hamiota 153 50 11N 100 38W
Hamlet 157 34 56N 79 40W
Hamley Bridge 140 34 17 S 138 35 E
Hamlin 159 32 58N 100 8W
Hamm 48 51 40N 7 58 E
Hammam bou Hadjar 118 35 23N 0 58W
Hammamet 119 36 24N 10 38 E
Hammamet, G. de 119 36 10N 10 48 E
Hammarö, I. 72 59 20N 13 30 E
Hammarstrand 72 63 7N 16 20 E
Hamme 47 51 6N 4 8 E
Hamme-Mille 47 50 47N 4 43 E
Hammel 73 56 16N 9 52 E
Hammelburg 49 50 7N 9 54 E
Hammenton 156 39 40N 74 47W
Hammeren 73 55 18N 14 47 E
Hammerfest 74 70 39N 23 41 E
Hammersmith 29 51 30N 0 15W
Hammond, Ind., U.S.A. 156 41 40N 87 30W
Hammond, La., U.S.A. 159 30 32N 90 30W
Hammonton 162 39 38N 74 48W
Hamnavoe 36 60 25N 1 5W
Hamneda 73 56 41N 13 51 E
Hamoir 47 50 25N 5 32 E
Hamont 47 51 15N 5 32 E
Hampden 143 45 18 S 170 50 E
Hampshire □ 28 51 3N 1 20W
Hampshire Downs 28 51 10N 1 10W
Hampton, Ark., U.S.A. 159 33 35N 92 29W
Hampton, Iowa, U.S.A. 158 42 42N 93 12W
Hampton, N.H., U.S.A. 162 42 56N 70 48W
Hampton, S.C., U.S.A. 157 32 52N 81 2W
Hampton, Va., U.S.A. 162 37 4N 76 18W
Hampton Bays 162 40 53N 72 31W
Hampton Harbour 136 20 30 S 116 30 E
Hampton in Arden 28 52 26N 1 42W
Hampton Tableland 137 32 0N 127 0 E
Hamra 92 24 2N 38 55 E
Hamrange 72 60 59N 17 5 E
Hamrat esh Sheykh 123 14 45N 27 55 E
Hamre 71 60 33N 5 20 E
Hamun Helmand 93 31 15N 61 15 E
Hamun-i-Lora, Pak. 93 29 38N 64 58 E
Hamun-i-Lora, Pak. 93 29 38N 64 58 E
Hamun-i-Mashkel 93 28 30N 63 0 E
Hamyang 107 35 32N 127 42 E
Han Chiang, R., Hupeh, China 109 30 35N 114 15 E

Han Chiang, R **Hawzen**

Han Chiang, R., Kwangtung, China 109 23 30N 116 48 E
Hana 147 20 45N 155 59W
Hanak 122 25 32N 37 0 E
Hanamaki 112 39 23N 141 7 E
Hanang □ 126 4 10 S 35 40 E
Hanang, mt. 126 4 30 S 35 25 E
Hanau 49 50 8N 8 56 E
Hanbogd 106 43 11N 107 10 E
Hanch'eng 106 35 30N 110 30 E
Hanchiang 109 25 29N 119 5 E
Hanch'uan 109 30 39N 113 46 E
Hanchuang 107 34 36N 117 22 E
Hanchung 106 33 10N 107 2 E
Hancock, Mich., U.S.A. 158 47 10N 88 35W
Hancock, Minn., U.S.A. 158 45 26N 95 46W
Hancock, Pa., U.S.A. 162 41 57N 75 19W
Handa, Japan 111 34 53N 137 0 E
Handa, Somalia 91 10 37N 51 2 E
Handa I. 36 58 23N 5 10W
Handen 72 59 12N 18 12 E
Handeni 124 5 25 S 38 2 E
Handeni □ 126 5 30 S 38 0 E
Handlová 155 48 45N 18 35 E
Handub 122 19 15N 37 25 E
Handwara 95 34 21N 74 20 E
Handzame 47 51 2N 3 0 E
Hanegev 90 30 50N 35 0 E
Haney 152 49 12N 122 40W
Hanford 163 36 25N 119 39W
Hang Chat 100 18 20N 99 21 E
Hang Dong 100 18 41N 98 55 E
Hangang, R. 107 37 50N 126 30 E
Hangayn Nuruu 105 47 30N 100 0 E
Hangchinch'i 106 39 54N 108 56 E
Hangchinhouch'i 106 41 55N 107 15 E
Hangchou 109 30 15N 120 8 E
Hangchou Wan 109 30 30N 121 30 E
Hanger 73 57 6N 13 58 E
Hangklip, K. 128 34 26 S 18 48 E
Hangö (Hanko) 75 59 59N 22 57 E
Hanhongor 106 43 55N 104 28 E
Hanish J. 91 13 45N 42 46 E
Hanita 90 33 5N 35 10 E
Hankinson 158 46 9N 96 58W
Hanko = Hangö 75 59 59N 22 57 E
Hank'ou 109 30 40N 114 18 E
Hankow = Hank'ou 109 30 40N 114 18 E
Hanksville 161 38 19N 110 45W
Hanku 107 39 16N 117 50 E
Hanle 95 32 42N 79 4 E
Hanmer 143 42 32 S 172 50 E
Hann, Mt. 136 16 0 S 126 0 E
Hann, R. 136 17 26 S 126 17 E
Hanna 152 51 40N 111 54W
Hannaford 158 47 23N 98 18W
Hannah 158 48 58N 98 42W
Hannah B. 150 51 40N 80 0W
Hannahs Bridge 141 31 55 S 149 41 E
Hannibal, Mo., U.S.A. 158 39 42N 91 22W
Hannibal, N.Y., U.S.A. 162 43 19N 76 35W
Hannik 122 18 12N 32 20 E
Hanningfield Water 29 51 40N 0 30 E
Hannover 48 52 23N 9 43 E
Hannut 47 50 40N 5 4 E
Hanö 73 56 0N 14 50 E
Hanö, I. 73 56 2N 14 50 E
Hanöbukten 73 55 35N 14 30 E
Hanoi 100 21 5N 105 55 E
Hanover, S. Afr. 128 31 4 S 24 29 E
Hanover, N.H., U.S.A. 162 43 43N 72 17W
Hanover, Pa., U.S.A. 162 39 46N 76 59W
Hanover, Va., U.S.A. 162 37 46N 77 22W
Hanover = Hannover 48 52 23N 9 43 E
Hanover, I. 176 51 0 S 74 50W
Hanpan, C. 135 5 0 S 154 35 E
Hans Meyer Ra. 135 4 20 S 152 55 E
Hansholm 73 57 8N 8 38 E
Hanshou 109 28 55N 111 58 E
Hansi 94 29 10N 75 57 E
Hansjö 72 61 10N 14 40 E
Hanson, L. 140 31 0 S 136 15 E
Hanson Range 136 27 0 S 136 30 E
Hansted 73 57 8N 8 36 E
Hantan 105 36 42N 114 30 E
Hante 47 50 19N 4 11 E
Hanton 106 36 42N 114 30 E
Hanwood 141 34 26 S 146 3 E
Hanyang 109 30 35N 114 0 E
Hanyin 108 32 53N 108 37 E
Hanyü 111 36 10N 139 32 E
Hanyüan 108 29 21N 102 43 E
Haoch'ing 108 26 34N 100 12 E
Haokang 105 47 25N 132 8 E
Haopi 106 35 57N 114 13 E
Haparanda 74 65 52N 24 8 E
Hapert 47 51 22N 5 15 E
Happy 159 34 47N 101 50W
Happy Camp 160 41 52N 123 30W
Happy Valley 151 53 15N 60 20W
Hapsu 107 41 13N 128 51 E
Hapur 94 28 45N 77 45 E
Haql 92 29 10N 35 0 E
Har 103 5 16 S 133 14 E
Har-Ayrag 106 45 47N 109 16 E
Har Tuv 90 31 46N 35 0 E
Har Us Nuur 105 48 0N 92 10 E
Har Yehuda 90 31 35N 34 57 E
Harad 92 24 15N 49 0 E
Haradera 91 4 33N 47 38 E
Haradh 92 24 15N 49 0 E
Haramsøya 71 62 39N 6 12 E
Haran 92 36 48N 39 0 E
Harat 123 16 5N 39 26 E
Haraze 117 14 20N 19 12 E
Haraze-Mangueigne 117 7 22N 17 3 E
Harbin = Haerhpin 107 45 45N 126 45 E
Harboør 73 56 38N 8 10 E
Harbor Beach 156 43 50N 82 38W
Harbor Springs 156 45 28N 85 0W
Harbour Breton 151 47 29N 55 50W
Harbour Deep 151 50 25N 56 30W
Harbour Grace 151 47 40N 53 22W
Harburg 48 53 27N 9 58 E
Hårby 73 55 13N 10 7 E
Harcourt 138 24 17 S 149 55 E
Harda 94 22 27N 77 5 E
Hardangerfjorden. 71 60 15N 6 0 E
Hardangerjøkulen 71 60 30N 7 0 E
Hardangervidda 71 60 20N 7 20 E
Hardap Dam 128 24 32 S 17 50 E
Hardegarijp 46 53 13N 5 57 E
Harden 141 34 32 S 148 24 E
Hardenberg 46 52 34N 6 37 E
Harderwijk 46 52 21N 5 38 E
Hardey, R. 136 22 45 S 116 8 E
Hardin 160 45 50N 107 35W
Harding 129 30 22 S 29 55 E
Harding Ra. 136 16 17 S 124 55 E
Hardisty 152 52 40N 111 18W
Hardman 160 45 12N 119 49W
Hardoi 95 27 26N 80 15 E
Hardwar 94 29 58N 78 16 E
Hardy 159 36 20N 91 30W
Hardy, Pen. 176 55 30 S 68 20W
Hare B. 151 51 15N 55 45W
Hare Gilboa 90 32 31N 35 25 E
Hare Meron 90 32 59N 35 24 E
Harelbeke 47 50 52N 3 20 E
Haren, Ger. 48 52 47N 7 18 E
Haren, Neth. 46 53 11N 6 36 E
Harer 123 9 20N 42 8 E
Harer □ 123 7 12N 42 0 E
Hareto 123 9 23N 37 6 E
Harfleur 42 49 30N 0 10 E
Hargeisa 91 9 30N 44 2 E
Hargshamn 72 60 12N 18 30 E
Hari, R., Afghan. 93 34 20N 64 30 E
Hari, R., Indon. 102 1 10 S 101 50 E
Haricha, Hamada el 118 22 40N 3 15W
Harihar 97 14 32N 75 44 E
Harim, J. al 60 26 0N 56 10 E
Harima-Nada 110 34 30N 134 35 E
Haringey 29 51 35N 0 7W
Haringhata, R. 98 22 0N 89 58 E
Haringvliet 46 51 48N 4 10 E
Haripad 97 9 14N 76 28 E
Harirúd 93 35 0N 61 0 E
Harkat 122 20 25N 39 40 E
Harlan, Iowa, U.S.A. 158 41 37N 95 20W
Harlan, Tenn., U.S.A. 157 36 58N 83 20W
Harlech 31 52 52N 4 7W
Harlem 160 48 29N 108 39W
Harleston 29 52 25N 1 18 E
Harlingen, Neth. 46 53 11N 5 25 E
Harlingen, U.S.A. 159 26 30N 97 50W
Harlow 29 51 47N 0 9 E
Harlowton 160 46 30N 109 54W
Harmånger 72 61 55N 17 20 E
Harmil 123 16 30N 40 10 E
Harney Basin 160 43 30N 119 0W
Harney L. 160 43 0N 119 0W
Harney Pk. 158 43 52N 103 33W
Härnön 72 62 36N 18 0 E
Härnösand 72 62 38N 18 5 E
Haro 58 42 35N 2 55W
Haro, C. 164 27 50N 110 55W
Haroldswick 36 60 48N 0 50W
Håroy 73 55 13N 10 8 E
Harp L. 151 55 5N 61 50W
Harpe, La 158 40 30N 91 0W
Harpenden 29 51 48N 0 20W
Harpenhalli 97 14 47N 76 2 E
Harper 120 4 25N 7 43 E
Harper Mt. 147 64 15N 143 57W
Harplinge 73 56 45N 12 45 E
Harport L. 36 57 20N 6 20W
Harput 92 38 48N 39 15 E
Harrand 94 29 28N 70 3 E
Harrat al Kishb 92 22 30N 40 15 E
Harrat al Umuirid 92 26 50N 38 0 E
Harrat Khaibar 122 25 45N 40 0 E
Harrat Nawāsīf 122 21 30N 42 0 E
Harray, L. of 37 59 0N 3 15W
Harricana, R. 150 50 30N 79 10W
Harrietsham 29 51 15N 0 41 E
Harriman 157 36 0N 84 35W
Harrington, U.K. 32 54 37N 3 55W
Harrington, U.S.A. 162 38 56N 75 35W
Harrington Harbour 151 50 31N 59 30W
Harris 36 57 50N 6 55W
Harris L. 136 31 10 S 135 10 E
Harris Mts. 143 44 49 S 168 49 E
Harris, Sd. of 36 57 44N 7 6W
Harrisburg, Ill., U.S.A. 159 37 42N 88 30W
Harrisburg, Nebr., U.S.A. 158 41 36N 103 46W
Harrisburg, Oreg., U.S.A. 160 44 25N 123 10W
Harrisburg, Pa., U.S.A. 162 40 18N 76 52W
Harrismith 129 28 15 S 29 8 E
Harrison, Ark., U.S.A. 159 36 10N 93 4W
Harrison, Idaho, U.S.A. 160 47 30N 116 51W
Harrison, Nebr., U.S.A. 158 42 42N 103 52W
Harrison B. 147 70 25N 151 0W
Harrison, C. 151 55 0N 58 0W
Harrison L. 152 49 33N 121 50W
Harrisonburg 156 38 28N 78 52W
Harrisonville 158 38 45N 93 45W
Harriston 150 43 57N 80 53W
Harrisville 150 44 40N 83 19W
Harrogate 33 53 59N 1 32W
Harrow 29 51 35N 0 15W
Harry, L. 139 29 23 S 138 19 E
Harsefeld 48 53 26N 9 31 E
Harskamp 46 52 8N 5 46 E
Harstad 74 68 48N 16 30 E
Hart 156 43 42N 86 21W
Hart, L. 140 31 10 S 136 25 E
Hartbees, R. 128 29 8 S 20 48 E
Hartberg 52 47 17N 15 58 E
Harteigen, Mt. 71 60 11N 7 5 E
Hartest 29 52 7N 0 41 E
Hartford, Conn., U.S.A. 162 41 47N 72 41W
Hartford, Ky., U.S.A. 156 37 26N 86 50W
Hartford, S.D., U.S.A. 158 43 40N 96 58W
Hartford, Wis., U.S.A. 158 43 18N 88 25W
Hartford City 156 40 22N 85 20W
Harthill 35 55 52N 3 45W
Hartland, Can. 151 46 20N 67 32W
Hartland, U.K. 30 50 59N 4 29W
Hartland Pt. 30 51 2N 4 32W
Hartlebury 28 52 20N 2 13W
Hartlepool 33 54 42N 1 11W
Hartley, Rhod. 127 18 10 S 30 7 E
Hartley, U.K. 35 55 5N 1 27W
Hartley Bay 152 53 25N 129 15W
Hartmannberge 128 17 0 S 13 0 E
Hartney 153 49 30N 100 35W
Hartpury 28 51 55N 2 18W
Hartselle 157 34 25N 86 55W
Hartshorne 159 34 51N 95 30W
Hartsville 157 34 23N 80 2W
Hartwell 157 34 21N 82 52W
Harunabad 94 29 35N 73 2 E
Harur 97 12 3N 78 29 E
Harvard, Mt. 161 39 0N 106 5W
Harvey, Austral. 137 33 5 S 115 54 E
Harvey, Ill., U.S.A. 156 41 40N 87 50W
Harvey, N.D., U.S.A. 158 47 50N 99 58W
Harwell 28 51 40N 1 17W
Harwich 29 51 56N 1 18 E
Harwood 33 53 54N 1 30W
Haryana □ 94 29 0N 76 10 E
Harz 48 51 40N 10 40 E
Harzé 47 50 27N 5 40 E
Harzgerode 48 51 38N 11 8 E
Hasa 92 26 0N 49 0 E
Hasaheisa 123 14 25N 33 20 E
Hasani 122 25 0N 37 8 E
Hasanpur 94 28 51N 78 9 E
Haselünne 48 52 40N 7 30 E
Hasharon 90 32 12N 34 49 E
Hashefela 90 31 30N 34 43 E
Hashima 111 35 20N 136 40 E
Hashimoto 111 34 19N 135 37 E
Hasjö 72 63 2N 16 20 E
Håsjö 72 63 1N 16 5 E
Haskell, Kans., U.S.A. 159 35 51N 95 40W
Haskell, Tex., U.S.A. 159 33 10N 99 45W
Haskier Is. 36 57 42N 7 40W
Haslach 49 48 16N 8 7 E
Hasle 73 55 11N 14 44 E
Haslemere 29 51 5N 0 41W
Haslev 73 55 18N 11 57 E
Haslingden 32 53 43N 2 20W
Hasparren 44 43 24N 1 18W
Hassan 92 13 0N 76 5 E
Hasselt, Belg. 47 50 56N 5 21 E
Hasselt, Neth. 46 52 36N 6 6 E
Hassene, Ad. 118 21 0N 4 0 E
Hassfurt 49 50 2N 10 30 E
Hassi Berrekrem 119 33 45N 5 16 E
Hassi Daoula 119 33 4N 5 38 E
Hassi el Biod 119 28 30N 6 0 E
Hassi el Heïda 74 29 34N 0 14W
Hassi Inifel 118 29 50N 3 41 E
Hassi Marroket 119 30 10N 3 0 E
Hassi Messaoud 119 31 43N 6 8 E
Hassi Taguenza 172 29 8N 0 23W
Hassi Zerzour 118 30 51N 3 56W
Hässleby 73 57 37N 15 30 E
Hässleholmen 73 56 9N 13 45 E
Hastière-Lavaux 47 50 13N 4 49 E
Hastigrow 37 58 32N 3 15W
Hastings, Austral. 141 38 18 S 145 12 E
Hastings, N.Z. 142 39 39 S 176 52 E
Hastings, U.K. 29 50 51N 0 36 E
Hastings, Mich., U.S.A. 156 42 40N 82 20W
Hastings, Minn., U.S.A. 158 44 41N 92 51W
Hastings, Nebr., U.S.A. 158 40 34N 98 22W
Hastings Ra. 141 31 15 S 152 14 E
Hästveda 73 56 17N 13 55 E
Hat Nhao 101 14 46N 106 32 E
Hat Yai 101 7 1N 100 27 E
Hatanbulag 106 43 8N 109 14 E
Hatano 111 35 22N 139 14 E
Hatch 161 32 45N 107 8W
Hatches Creek 138 20 56 S 135 12 E
Hatchet L. 153 58 36N 103 40W
Haţeg 70 45 36N 22 55 E
Haţeg, Mţii 70 45 25N 23 0 E
Hatert 46 51 49N 5 50 E
Hatfield 29 51 46N 0 11W
Hatfield Broad Oak 29 51 48N 0 16 E
Hatfield Post Office 140 33 54N 143 49 E
Hatgal 105 50 26N 100 9 E
Hatherleigh 30 50 49N 4 4W
Hathersage 33 53 20N 1 39W
Hathras 94 27 36N 78 6 E
Hatia 99 22 30N 91 5 E
Hato de Corozal 174 6 11N 71 45W
Hato Mayor 167 18 46N 69 15W
Hattah 140 34 48N 142 17 E
Hattem 46 52 28N 6 4 E
Hatteras, C. 157 35 10N 75 30W
Hattiesburg 159 31 20N 89 20W
Hatton, Can. 153 50 2N 109 50W
Hatton, U.K. 37 57 24N 1 57W
Hatvan 53 47 40N 19 45 E
Hau Bon (Cheo Reo) 100 13 25N 108 28 E
Hau Duc 100 15 20N 108 13 E
Hauchinango 164 20 12N 97 45W
Haug 71 60 23N 10 26 E
Haugastøl 71 60 30N 7 50 E
Haugesund 71 59 23N 5 13 E
Haugh of Urr 35 55 0N 3 51W
Haughangaroa Ra. 142 38 42 S 175 40 E
Haughley 29 52 13N 0 59 E
Haukelisæter 71 59 51N 7 9 E
Haulerwijk 46 53 4N 6 20 E
Haultain, R. 153 55 51N 106 46W
Haungpa 98 25 29N 96 7 E
Haura 91 13 50N 47 35 E
Hauraki Gulf 142 36 35 S 175 5 E
Hausruck 52 48 6N 13 30 E
Haut Atlas 118 32 0N 7 0W
Haut-Rhin □ 43 48 0N 7 15 E
Haut Zaïre □ 126 2 20N 26 0 E
Hauta Oasis 92 23 40N 47 0 E
Hautah, Wahāt al 92 23 40N 47 0 E
Haute-Corse □ 45 42 30N 9 30 E
Haute-Garonne □ 44 43 28N 1 30 E
Haute-Loire □ 44 45 5N 3 50 E
Haute-Marne □ 43 48 10N 5 20 E
Haute-Saône □ 43 47 45N 6 10 E
Haute-Savoie □ 45 46 0N 6 20 E
Haute-Vienne □ 44 45 50N 1 10 E
Hauterive 151 49 10N 68 16W
Hautes-Alpes □ 45 44 42N 6 20 E
Hautes Fagnes 47 50 34N 6 6 E
Hautes-Pyrénées □ 44 43 0N 0 10 E
Hauteville-Lompnes 45 45 59N 5 35 E
Hautmont 43 50 15N 3 55 E
Hautrage 47 50 29N 3 46 E
Hauts-de-Seine □ 43 48 52N 2 15 E
Hauts Plateaux 118 34 14N 1 0 E
Hauxley 35 55 21N 1 35W
Havana 158 40 19N 90 3W
Havana = La Habana 166 23 8N 82 22W
Havant 29 50 51N 0 59W
Havasu, L. 161 34 18N 114 8W
Havdhem 73 57 10N 18 20 E
Havelange 47 50 23N 5 15 E
Havelian 94 34 2N 73 10 E
Havelock, N.B., Can. 151 46 2N 65 24W
Havelock, Ont., Can. 150 44 26N 77 53W
Havelock, N.Z. 143 41 17 S 173 48 E
Havelock I. 101 11 55N 93 2 E
Havelte 46 52 46N 6 14 E
Haverfordwest 31 51 48N 4 59W
Haverhill, U.K. 29 52 6N 0 27 E
Haverhill, U.S.A. 162 42 50N 71 2W
Haveri 97 14 53N 75 24 E
Haverigg 32 54 12N 3 16W
Havering 29 51 33N 0 20 E
Haverstraw 162 41 12N 73 58W
Håverud 73 58 50N 12 28 E
Havîrna 70 48 4N 26 43 E
Havlíčkuv Brod 52 49 36N 15 33 E
Havnby 73 55 5N 8 34 E
Havre 160 48 40N 109 34W
Havre-Aubert 151 47 12N 62 0W
Havre de Grace 162 39 33N 76 6W
Havre, Le 42 49 30N 0 5 E
Havre St. Pierre 151 50 18N 63 33W
Havza 92 41 0N 35 35 E
Haw, R. 157 37 43N 80 52W
Hawaii □ 147 20 30N 157 0W
Hawaii I. 147 20 0N 155 0W
Hawaiian Is. 147 20 30N 156 0W
Hawarden, Can. 153 51 25N 106 36W
Hawarden, U.K. 31 53 11N 3 2W
Hawarden, U.S.A. 158 43 2N 96 28W
Hawea Flat 143 44 40 S 169 19 E
Hawea Lake 143 44 28 S 169 19 E
Hawera 142 39 35 S 174 19 E
Hawes 32 54 18N 2 12W
Hawes Water, L. 32 54 32N 2 48W
Hawick 35 55 25N 2 48W
Hawk Junction 150 48 5N 84 38W
Hawkchurch 30 50 47N 2 56W
Hawkdun Ra. 143 44 53 S 170 5 E
Hawke B. 142 39 25 S 177 20 E
Hawker 28 31 59 S 138 22 E
Hawke's Bay □ 142 39 45 S 176 35 E
Hawke's Harbour 151 53 2N 55 50W
Hawkesbury 150 45 35N 74 40W
Hawkesbury I. 152 53 37N 129 3W
Hawkesbury Pt. 138 11 55 S 134 5 E
Hawkesbury River 133 33 50 S 151 44W
Hawkesbury Upton 28 51 34N 2 19W
Hawkhurst 29 51 2N 0 31 E
Hawkinsville 157 32 17N 83 30W
Hawkshead 32 54 23N 3 0W
Hawkwood 139 25 45 S 150 50 E
Hawley, Minn., U.S.A. 158 46 58N 96 20W
Hawley, Pa., U.S.A. 162 41 28N 75 11W
Haworth 32 53 50N 1 57W
Hawsker 33 54 27N 0 34W
Hawthorne 163 38 31N 118 37W
Hawzen 123 13 58N 39 28 E

Haxby Higashiōsaka

Haxby	**33**	54	1N	1	4W
Haxtun	**158**	40	40N	102	39W
Hay, Austral.	**141**	34	30 S	144	51 E
Hay, U.K.	**31**	52	4N	3	9W
Hay, C.	**136**	14	5 S	129	29 E
Hay L.	**152**	58	50N	118	50W
Hay Lakes	**152**	53	12N	113	2W
Hay, R., Austral.	**138**	24	10 S	137	20 E
Hay, R., Can.	**152**	60	0N	116	56W
Hay River	**152**	60	51N	115	44W
Hay Springs	**158**	42	40N	102	38W
Hayange	**43**	49	20N	6	2 E
Hayato	**110**	31	40N	130	43 E
Hayburn Wyke	**33**	54	22N	0	28W
Haycock	**147**	65	10N	161	20W
Hayden, Ariz., U.S.A.	**161**	33	2N	110	54W
Hayden, Wyo., U.S.A.	**160**	40	30N	107	22W
Haydenville	**162**	42	22N	72	42W
Haydon	**138**	18	0 S	141	30 E
Haydon Bridge	**35**	54	58N	2	15W
Haye Descartes, La	**42**	46	58N	0	42 E
Haye-du-Puits, La	**42**	49	17N	1	33W
Hayes	**158**	44	22N	101	1W
Hayes Pen.	**12**	75	30N	65	0W
Hayes, R.	**153**	57	3N	92	12W
Hayle	**30**	50	12N	5	25W
Haymana	**92**	39	30N	32	35 E
Haynesville	**159**	33	0N	93	7W
Hays, Can.	**152**	50	6N	111	48W
Hays, U.S.A.	**158**	38	55N	99	25W
Hayton	**32**	54	55N	2	45W
Hayward, Calif., U.S.A.	**163**	37	40N	122	5W
Hayward, Wis., U.S.A.	**158**	46	2N	91	30W
Hayward's Heath	**29**	51	0N	0	5W
Hazard	**156**	37	18N	83	10W
Hazaribagh	**95**	23	58N	85	26 E
Hazaribagh Road	**95**	24	12N	85	57 E
Hazebrouck	**43**	50	42N	2	31 E
Hazelton, Can.	**152**	55	20N	127	42W
Hazelton, U.S.A.	**158**	46	30N	100	15W
Hazen	**160**	39	37N	119	2W
Hazerswoude	**46**	52	5N	4	36 E
Hazlehurst	**157**	31	50N	82	35W
Hazleton	**156**	40	58N	76	0W
Hazlett, L.	**136**	21	30 S	128	48 E
Hazrat Imam	**93**	37	15N	68	50 E
Heacham	**29**	52	55N	0	30 E
Head of Bight	**137**	31	30 S	131	25 E
Headcorn	**29**	51	10N	0	39 E
Headford	**38**	53	28N	9	6W
Headington	**28**	51	46N	1	13W
Headlands	**127**	18	15 S	32	2 E
Healdsburg	**160**	38	33N	122	51W
Healdton	**159**	34	16N	97	31W
Healesville	**141**	37	35 S	145	30 E
Heanor	**33**	53	1N	1	20W
Heard I.	**11**	53	0 S	74	0 E
Hearne	**159**	30	54N	96	35W
Hearne B.	**153**	60	10N	99	10W
Hearne L.	**152**	62	20N	113	10W
Hearst	**150**	49	40N	83	41W
Heart, R.	**158**	46	40N	101	30W
Heart's Content	**151**	47	54N	53	27W
Heath Mts.	**143**	45	39 S	167	9 E
Heath Pt.	**151**	49	8N	61	40W
Heath Steele	**151**	47	17N	66	5W
Heathcote	**141**	36	56 S	144	45 E
Heather, oilfield	**19**	60	55N	0	50 E
Heathfield	**29**	50	58N	0	18 E
Heathsville	**162**	37	55N	76	28W
Heavener	**159**	34	54N	94	36W
Hebbronville	**159**	27	20N	98	40W
Hebburn	**35**	54	59N	1	30W
Hebden Bridge	**32**	53	45N	2	0W
Hebel	**139**	28	58 S	147	47 E
Heber Springs	**159**	35	29N	91	39W
Hebgen, L.	**160**	44	50N	111	15W
Hebrides, U.K.	**36**	57	30N	7	0W
Hebrides, Inner Is., U.K.	**36**	57	20N	6	40W
Hebrides, Outer Is., U.K.	**36**	57	50N	7	25W
Hebron, Can.	**149**	58	12N	62	38W
Hebron, N.D., U.S.A.	**158**	46	56N	102	2W
Hebron, Nebr., U.S.A.	**158**	40	15N	97	33W
Hebron (Al Khalil)	**90**	31	32N	35	6 E
Heby	**72**	59	56N	16	53 E
Hecate Str.	**152**	53	10N	130	30W
Hechingen	**49**	48	20N	8	58 E
Hechtel	**47**	51	8N	5	22 E
Heckington	**33**	52	59N	0	17W
Hecla	**158**	45	56N	98	8W
Hecla I.	**153**	51	10N	96	43W
Hecla Mt.	**36**	57	18N	7	15W
Heddal	**71**	59	36N	9	20 E
Heddon	**35**	55	0N	1	47W
Hédé	**42**	48	18N	1	49W
Hede	**72**	62	23N	13	30 E
Hedemora	**72**	60	18N	15	58 E
Hedgehope	**143**	46	12 S	168	34 E
Hedley	**159**	34	53N	100	39W
Hedmark □	**75**	61	17N	11	40 E
Hedmark fylke □	**71**	61	17N	11	40 E
Hednesford	**28**	52	43N	2	0W
Hedon	**33**	53	44N	0	11W
Hedrum	**71**	59	7N	10	5 E
Heeg	**46**	52	58N	5	37 E
Heegermeer	**46**	52	56N	5	32 E
Heemskerk	**46**	52	31N	4	40 E
Heemstede	**46**	52	22N	4	37 E
Heer	**47**	50	50N	5	43 E
Heerde	**46**	52	24N	6	2 E
's Heerenburg	**46**	51	53N	6	16 E
's Heerenloo	**46**	52	19N	5	36 E
Heerenveen	**46**	52	57N	5	55 E
Heerhugowaard	**46**	52	40N	4	51 E
Heerlen	**47**	50	55N	6	0 E
Heerlerheide	**47**	50	54N	5	58 E
Heers	**47**	50	45N	5	18 E
Heesch	**46**	51	44N	5	32 E
Heestert	**47**	50	47N	3	25 E
Heeze	**47**	51	23N	5	35 E
Hegyalja, Mts.	**53**	48	25N	21	25 E
Heich'engchen	**106**	36	16N	106	19 E
Heide	**48**	54	10N	9	7 E
Heide, oilfield	**19**	54	5N	9	5 E
Heidelberg, Ger.	**49**	49	23N	8	41 E
Heidelberg, C. Prov., S. Afr.	**128**	34	6 S	20	59 E
Heidelberg, Trans., S. Afr.	**129**	26	30 S	28	23 E
Heidenheim	**49**	48	40N	10	10 E
Heigun-To	**110**	33	47N	132	14 E
Heikant	**47**	51	15N	4	1 E
Heilam	**37**	58	31N	4	40W
Heilbron	**129**	27	16 S	27	59 E
Heilbronn	**49**	49	8N	9	13 E
Heiligenblut	**52**	47	2N	12	51 E
Heiligenhafen	**48**	54	21N	10	58 E
Heiligenstadt	**48**	51	22N	10	9 E
Heilungkiang □	**46**	48	0N	128	0 E
Heim	**71**	63	26N	9	5 E
Heimdal, gasfield	**19**	59	35N	2	15 E
Heino	**46**	52	26N	6	14 E
Heinola	**75**	61	13N	26	24 E
Heinsburg	**153**	53	50N	110	30W
Heinsch	**47**	49	42N	5	44 E
Heinsun	**98**	25	52N	95	35 E
Heinze Is.	**101**	14	25N	97	45 E
Heirnkut	**98**	25	14N	94	44 E
Heishan	**107**	41	40N	122	3 E
Heishui, Liaoning, China	**107**	42	6N	119	22 E
Heishui, Szechwan, China	**108**	32	15N	103	0 E
Heist	**47**	51	20N	3	15 E
Heist-op-den-Berg	**47**	51	5N	4	44 E
Heistad	**71**	59	35N	9	40 E
Hejaz = Hijāz	**92**	26	0N	37	30 E
Hekelegem	**47**	50	55N	4	7 E
Hekimhan	**92**	38	50N	38	0 E
Hekinan	**111**	34	52N	137	0 E
Hekla	**74**	63	56N	19	35W
Hel	**60**	54	38N	18	50 E
Helagsfjället	**72**	62	54N	12	25 E
Helchteren	**47**	51	4N	5	22 E
Helden	**47**	51	19N	6	0 E
Helechosa	**57**	39	22N	4	53W
Helena, Ark., U.S.A.	**159**	34	30N	90	35W
Helena, Mont., U.S.A.	**160**	46	40N	112	0W
Helendale	**163**	34	45N	117	19W
Helensburgh, Austral.	**141**	34	11 S	151	1 E
Helensburgh, U.K.	**34**	56	0N	4	44W
Helensville	**142**	36	41 S	174	29 E
Helets	**90**	31	36N	34	39 E
Helgasjön	**73**	57	0N	14	50 E
Helgeland	**74**	66	20N	13	30 E
Helgeroa	**71**	59	0N	9	45 E
Helgoland, I.	**48**	54	10N	7	51 E
Helgum	**72**	63	25N	16	50 E
Heligoland = Helgoland	**48**	54	10N	7	51 E
Heliopolis	**122**	30	6N	31	17 E
Hell-Ville	**129**	13	25 S	48	16 E
Hellebæk	**73**	56	4N	12	32 E
Helleland	**71**	58	33N	6	7 E
Hellendoorn	**46**	52	24N	6	27 E
Hellertown	**162**	40	35N	75	21W
Hellevoetsluis	**46**	51	50N	4	8 E
Helli Ness	**36**	60	3N	1	10W
Hellick Kenyon Plateau	**13**	82	0 S	110	0W
Hellifield	**32**	54	0N	2	13W
Hellín	**59**	38	31N	1	40W
Hellum	**73**	57	16N	10	10 E
Helmand □	**93**	31	20N	64	0 E
Helmand, R.	**94**	34	0N	67	0 E
Helmond	**47**	51	29N	5	41 E
Helmsdale	**37**	58	7N	3	40W
Helmsley	**33**	54	15N	1	2W
Helmstedt	**48**	52	16N	11	0 E
Helnæs	**73**	55	9N	10	0 E
Helper	**160**	39	44N	110	56W
Helperby	**33**	54	8N	1	20W
Helsby	**32**	53	16N	2	47W
Helsingborg	**73**	56	3N	12	42 E
Helsinge	**73**	56	2N	12	12 E
Helsingfors = Helsinki	**75**	60	15N	25	3 E
Helsingør	**73**	56	2N	12	35 E
Helsinki (Helsingfors)	**75**	60	15N	25	3 E
Helston	**30**	50	7N	5	17W
Helvick Hd.	**39**	52	3N	7	33W
Helvoirt	**47**	51	38N	5	14 E
Helwân	**122**	29	50N	31	20 E
Hem	**71**	59	26N	10	0 E
Hemavati, R.	**97**	12	50N	67	0 E
Hemel Hempstead	**29**	51	45N	0	28W
Hemet	**163**	33	45N	116	59W
Hemingford	**158**	42	21N	103	4W
Hemphill	**159**	31	21N	93	49W
Hempstead	**159**	30	5N	96	5W
Hempton	**29**	52	50N	0	49 E
Hemse	**73**	57	15N	18	22 E
Hemsö, I.	**72**	62	43N	18	5 E
Hemsön	**72**	62	42N	18	5 E
Hemsworth	**33**	53	37N	1	21W
Hemyock	**30**	50	55N	1	13W
Hen & Chicken Is.	**142**	35	58 S	174	45 E
Henares, R.	**58**	40	55N	3	0W
Hendaye	**44**	43	23N	1	47W
Henderson, Argent.	**172**	36	18 S	61	43W
Henderson, U.K.	**36**	57	42N	5	47W
Henderson, Ky., U.S.A.	**156**	37	50N	87	38W
Henderson, Nev., U.S.A.	**161**	36	2N	115	0W
Henderson, Pa., U.S.A.	**157**	35	25N	88	40W
Henderson, Tex., U.S.A.	**159**	32	5N	94	49W
Hendersonville	**157**	35	21N	82	28W
Hendon	**139**	28	5 S	151	50 E
Hendorf	**70**	46	4N	24	5 E
Henfield	**29**	50	56N	0	17W
Hengch'eng	**106**	38	26N	106	26 E
Hengelo, Gelderland, Neth.	**46**	52	3N	6	19 E
Hengelo, Overijssel, Neth.	**46**	52	16N	6	48 E
Hengfeng	**109**	28	25N	117	35 E
Henghsien	**108**	22	36N	109	16 E
Hengoed	**31**	51	39N	3	14W
Hengshan, Hunan, China	**109**	27	15N	112	51 E
Hengshan, Shansi, China	**106**	37	56N	108	53 E
Hengshui	**106**	37	43N	115	42 E
Hengtaohotze	**107**	44	55N	129	3 E
Hengyang	**109**	26	51N	112	30 E
Hengyanghsien	**109**	26	58N	112	21 E
Hénin-Beaumont	**43**	50	25N	2	58 E
Henley	**29**	51	32N	0	53W
Henley-in-Arden	**28**	52	18N	1	47W
Henllan	**31**	53	13N	3	29W
Henlopen, C.	**162**	38	48N	75	5W
Henlow	**29**	51	2N	0	18W
Hennan, L.	**72**	62	3N	15	55 E
Henne	**73**	55	44N	8	11 E
Hennebont	**42**	47	49N	3	19W
Hennenman	**128**	27	59 S	27	1 E
Hennessy	**159**	36	8N	97	53W
Hennigsdorf	**48**	52	38N	13	13 E
Henribourg	**153**	53	25N	105	38W
Henrichemont	**43**	47	20N	2	21 E
Henrietta	**159**	33	50N	98	15W
Henrietta Maria C.	**150**	55	9N	82	20W
Henry	**158**	41	5N	89	20W
Henryetta	**159**	35	2N	96	0W
Henstridge	**28**	50	59N	2	24W
Hentiyn Nuruu	**105**	48	30N	108	30 E
Henty	**141**	35	30N	147	0 E
Henzada	**98**	17	38N	95	35 E
Heppner	**160**	45	27N	119	34W
Herad	**71**	58	8N	6	47 E
Héraðsflói	**74**	65	42N	14	12W
Héradsvötn	**74**	65	25N	19	5W
Herald Cays	**138**	16	58 S	149	9 E
Herāt	**93**	34	20N	62	7 E
Herāt □	**93**	35	0N	62	0 E
Hérault □	**44**	43	34N	3	15 E
Hérault, R.	**44**	43	20N	3	32 E
Herbert	**153**	50	30N	107	10W
Herbert Downs	**138**	23	7 S	139	9 E
Herbert I.	**147**	52	49N	170	10W
Herbert, R.	**138**	18	31 S	146	17 E
Herberton	**138**	17	28 S	145	25 E
Herbertstown	**39**	52	32N	8	29W
Herbiers, Les	**42**	46	52N	1	0W
Herbignac	**42**	47	27N	2	18W
Herborn	**48**	50	40N	8	19 E
Herby	**54**	50	45N	18	50 E
Hercegnovi	**66**	42	30N	18	33 E
Herðubreið	**74**	65	11N	16	21W
Herdla	**71**	60	34N	4	56 E
Hereford, U.K.	**28**	52	4N	2	42W
Hereford, U.S.A.	**159**	34	50N	102	28W
Hereford and Worcester □	**28**	52	10N	2	30W
Herefordshire □	**26**	52	15N	2	50W
Herefoss	**71**	58	32N	8	32 E
Herekino	**142**	35	18 S	173	11 E
Herent	**47**	50	54N	4	40 E
Herentals	**47**	51	12N	4	51 E
Herenthout	**47**	51	8N	4	45 E
Herfølge	**73**	55	26N	12	9 E
Herford	**48**	52	7N	8	40 E
Héricourt	**43**	47	32N	6	55 E
Herington	**158**	38	43N	97	0W
Herisau	**51**	47	22N	9	17 E
Hérisson	**44**	46	32N	2	42 E
Herjehogna	**75**	61	43N	12	7 E
Herk, R.	**47**	50	56N	5	12 E
Herkenbosch	**47**	51	9N	6	4 E
Herkimer	**162**	43	0N	74	59W
Herm I.	**42**	49	30N	2	28W
Herma Ness	**36**	60	50N	0	54W
Hermagor	**52**	46	38N	13	23 E
Herman	**158**	45	51N	96	8W
Hermandez	**163**	36	24N	120	46W
Hermann	**158**	38	40N	91	25W
Hermannsburg	**48**	52	49N	10	6 E
Hermannsburg Mission	**136**	23	57 S	132	45 E
Hermanus	**128**	34	27 S	19	12 E
Herment	**44**	45	45N	2	24 E
Hermidale	**141**	31	30 S	146	42 E
Hermiston	**160**	45	50N	119	16W
Hermitage	**143**	43	44 S	170	5 E
Hermitage B.	**151**	47	33N	56	10W
Hermite, Is.	**176**	55	50 S	68	0W
Hermon, Mt. = Sheikh, J. ash	**92**	33	20N	36	0 E
Hermosillo	**164**	29	10N	111	0W
Hernad, R.	**53**	48	20N	21	15 E
Hernandarias	**173**	25	20 S	54	40W
Hernando, Argent.	**172**	32	28 S	63	40W
Hernando, U.S.A.	**159**	34	50N	89	59W
Herndon	**162**	40	43N	76	51W
Herne, Belg.	**47**	50	44N	4	2 E
Herne, Ger.	**48**	51	33N	7	12 E
Herne Bay	**29**	51	22N	1	8 E
Herne Hill	**137**	31	45 S	116	5 E
Herning	**73**	56	8N	8	58 E
Heroica Nogales	**164**	31	14N	110	56W
Heron Bay	**150**	48	40N	85	25W
Heröy	**71**	62	18N	5	45 E
Herreid	**158**	45	53N	100	5W
's Herrenbroek	**46**	52	32N	6	1 E
Herrera	**57**	39	12N	4	50W
Herrera de Alcántar	**57**	39	39N	7	25W
Herrera de Pisuerga	**56**	42	35N	4	20W
Herrera del Duque	**57**	39	10N	5	3W
Herrero, Punta	**165**	19	17N	87	27W
Herrick	**138**	41	5 S	147	55 E
Herrin	**159**	37	50N	89	0W
Herrljunga	**73**	58	5N	13	1 E
Hersbruck	**49**	49	30N	11	25 E
Herschel I.	**147**	69	35N	139	5W
Herseaux	**47**	50	43N	3	15 E
Herselt	**47**	51	3N	4	53 E
Herserange	**47**	49	30N	5	48 E
Hershey	**162**	40	17N	76	39W
Herstal	**47**	50	40N	5	38 E
Herstmonceux	**29**	50	53N	0	21 E
Hersvik	**71**	61	10N	4	53 E
Hertford	**29**	51	47N	0	4W
Hertford □	**29**	51	51N	0	5W
's Hertogenbosch	**47**	51	42N	5	18 E
Hertzogville	**128**	28	9 S	25	30 E
Hervás	**56**	40	16N	5	52W
Herve	**47**	50	38N	5	48 E
Hervey B.	**133**	25	0 S	152	52 E
Hervey Is.	**131**	19	30 S	159	0W
Hervey Junction	**150**	46	50N	72	29W
Herwijnen	**46**	51	50N	5	7 E
Herzberg, Cottbus, Ger.	**48**	51	40N	13	13 E
Herzberg, Niedersachsen, Ger.	**48**	51	38N	10	20 E
Herzele	**47**	50	53N	3	53 E
Herzliyya	**90**	32	10N	34	50 E
Herzogenbuchsee	**50**	47	11N	7	42 E
Herzogenburg	**52**	48	17N	15	41 E
Hesdin	**43**	50	21N	2	0 E
Hesel	**48**	53	18N	7	36 E
Heskestad	**71**	58	28N	6	22 E
Hesperange	**47**	49	35N	6	10 E
Hesperia	**163**	34	25N	117	18W
Hesse = Hessen	**48**	50	57N	9	20 E
Hessen □	**48**	50	57N	9	20 E
Hessle	**33**	53	44N	0	28 E
Hetch Hetchy Aqueduct	**163**	37	36N	121	25W
Heteren	**46**	51	58N	5	46 E
Hethersett	**29**	52	35N	1	10 E
Hettinger	**158**	46	8N	102	38W
Hetton-le-Hole	**35**	54	49N	1	26W
Hettstedt	**48**	51	39N	11	30 E
Heugem	**47**	50	49N	5	42 E
Heule	**47**	50	51N	3	15 E
Heusden, Belg.	**47**	51	2N	5	17 E
Heusden, Neth.	**46**	51	44N	5	8 E
Hève, C. de la	**42**	49	30N	0	5 E
Heverlee	**47**	50	52N	4	42 E
Heves □	**53**	47	50N	20	0 E
Hevron, N.	**90**	31	28N	34	52 E
Hewett, C.	**149**	70	16N	67	45W
Hewett, gasfield	**19**	53	5N	1	50 E
Hex River	**128**	33	30 S	19	35 E
Hexham	**35**	54	58N	2	7W
Heybridge	**29**	51	44N	0	42 E
Heyfield	**141**	37	59 S	146	47 E
Heysham	**32**	54	5N	2	53W
Heytesbury	**28**	51	11N	2	7W
Heythuysen	**47**	51	15N	5	55 E
Heywood, Austral.	**140**	38	8 S	141	37 E
Heywood, U.K.	**32**	53	36N	2	13W
Hi-no-Misaki	**110**	35	26N	132	38 E
Hi Vista	**163**	34	45N	117	46W
Hiamen	**109**	31	52N	121	15 E
Hiawatha, Kans., U.S.A.	**158**	39	55N	95	33W
Hiawatha, Utah, U.S.A.	**160**	39	37N	111	1W
Hibbing	**158**	47	30N	93	0W
Hibbs B.	**138**	42	35 S	145	15 E
Hibbs, Pt.	**138**	42	38 S	145	15 E
Hibernia Reef	**136**	12	0 S	123	23 E
Hibiki-Nada	**110**	34	0N	130	0 E
Hickman	**159**	36	35N	89	8W
Hickory	**157**	35	46N	81	17W
Hicks Bay	**142**	37	34 S	178	21 E
Hicksville	**162**	40	46N	73	30W
Hida-Gawa	**70**	47	10N	23	9 E
Hida-Gawa, R.	**111**	35	26N	137	3 E
Hida-Sammyaku	**111**	36	30N	137	40 E
Hida-Sanchi	**111**	36	10N	137	0 E
Hidaka	**110**	35	30N	134	44 E
Hidalgo □	**164**	20	30N	99	10W
Hidalgo del Parral	**164**	26	58N	105	40W
Hidalgo, Presa M.	**164**	26	30N	108	35W
Hiddensee	**48**	54	30N	13	6 E
Hidrolândia	**171**	17	0 S	49	15W
Hieflau	**52**	47	36N	14	46 E
Hiendelaencina	**58**	41	5N	3	0W
Hierro I.	**116**	27	57N	17	56 E
Higashi-matsuyama	**111**	36	2N	139	25 E
Higashiōsaka	**111**	34	40N	135	37 E

Higasi-Suidō
Hong Kong ■

Higasi-Suidō 110 34 0N 129 30 E
Higgins 159 36 9N 100 1W
Higginsville 137 31 42S 121 38 E
Higgs I. L. 157 36 20N 78 30W
High Atlas = Haut Atlas 118 32 30N 5 0W
High Bentham 32 54 8N 2 31W
High Borrow Bri. 32 54 26N 2 43W
High Bridge 162 40 40N 74 54W
High Ercall 28 52 46N 2 37W
High Hesket 32 54 47N 2 49W
High I. 151 56 40N 61 10W
High Island 159 29 32N 94 22W
High Level 152 58 31N 117 8W
High Pike, mt. 32 54 43N 3 4W
High Point 157 35 57N 79 58W
High Prairie 152 55 30N 116 30W
High River 152 50 30N 113 50W
High Springs 157 29 50N 82 40W
High Tatra 53 49 30N 20 00 E
High Veld = Hoëveld 129 26 30S 30 0 E
High Willhays, hill 30 50 41N 3 59W
High Wycombe 29 51 37N 0 45W
Higham Ferrers 29 52 18N 0 36W
Highbank 138 47 34S 171 45 E
Highbridge 28 51 13N 2 59W
Highbury 138 16 25S 143 9 E
Highclere 28 51 20N 1 22W
Highland □ 36 57 30N 5 0W
Highland Pk. 156 42 10N 87 50W
Highland Springs 162 37 33N 77 20W
Highley 28 52 25N 2 23W
Highmore 158 44 35N 99 26W
Highrock L. 153 57 5N 105 32W
Hightae 35 55 5N 3 27W
Hightstown 162 40 16N 74 31W
Highworth 28 51 38N 1 42W
Higley 161 33 27N 111 46W
Higüay 167 18 37N 68 42W
Higüero, Pta. 147 18 22N 67 16W
Hiiumaa 80 58 50N 22 45 E
Híjar 58 41 10N 0 27W
Hijāz 91 26 0N 37 30 E
Hiji 110 33 22N 131 32 E
Hijken 46 52 54N 6 30 E
Hikari 110 33 58N 131 58 E
Hiketa 110 34 13N 134 24 E
Hiko 161 37 30N 115 13W
Hikone 111 35 15N 136 10 E
Hikurangi, East Court 142 37 55S 178 4 E
Hikurangi, Mt. 142 37 55S 178 4 E
Hilawng 98 21 23N 93 48 E
Hildburghhausen 49 50 24N 10 43 E
Hildesheim 48 52 9N 9 55 E
Hilgay 29 52 34N 0 23 E
Hill 150 45 40N 74 45W
Hill City, Idaho, U.S.A. 160 43 20N 115 2W
Hill City, Kans., U.S.A. 158 39 25N 99 51W
Hill City, Minn., U.S.A. 158 46 57N 93 35W
Hill City, S.D., U.S.A. 158 43 58N 103 35W
Hill End 141 38 1S 146 9 E
Hill Island L. 153 60 30N 109 50W
Hill, R. 137 30 23S 115 3 E
Hilla, Iraq 92 32 30N 44 27 E
Hilla, Si Arab. 92 23 35N 46 50 E
Hillared 73 57 37N 13 10 E
Hillegom 46 52 18N 4 35 E
Hillerød 73 55 56N 12 19 E
Hillerstorp 73 57 20N 13 52 E
Hilli 98 25 17N 89 1 E
Hillingdon 29 51 33N 0 29W
Hillman 156 45 5N 83 52W
Hillmond 153 53 26N 109 41W
Hillsboro, Kans., U.S.A. 158 38 28N 97 10W
Hillsboro, N. Mex., U.S.A. 161 33 0N 107 35W
Hillsboro, N. Mex., U.S.A. 161 33 0N 107 35W
Hillsboro, N.D., U.S.A. 158 47 23N 97 9W
Hillsboro, N.H., U.S.A. 156 43 8N 71 56W
Hillsboro, Oreg., U.S.A. 160 45 31N 123 0W
Hillsboro, Tex., U.S.A. 159 32 0N 97 10W
Hillsborough, U.K. 38 54 28N 6 6W
Hillsborough, W. Indies 167 12 28N 61 28W
Hillsdale, Mich., U.S.A. 156 41 55N 84 40W
Hillsdale, N.Y., U.S.A. 162 42 11N 73 30W
Hillside 136 21 45S 119 23 E
Hillsport 150 49 27N 85 34W
Hillston 141 33 30S 145 31 E
Hillswick 36 60 29N 1 28W
Hilltown 38 54 12N 6 8W
Hilo 147 19 44N 155 5W
Hilonghilong, mt. 103 9 10N 125 45 E
Hilpsford Pt. 32 54 4N 3 12W
Hilvarenbeek 47 51 29N 5 8 E
Hilversum 46 52 14N 5 10 E
Himachal Pradesh □ 94 31 30N 77 0 E
Himalaya 99 29 0N 84 0 E
Himara 68 40 8N 19 43 E
Himatnagar 93 23 37N 72 57 E
Hime-Jima 110 33 43N 131 40 E
Himeji 110 34 50N 134 40 E
Himi 111 36 50N 137 0 E
Himmerland 73 56 45N 9 30 E
Hims = Homs 92 34 40N 36 45 E
Hinako, Kepulauan 102 0 50N 97 20 E
Hinche 167 19 9N 72 1W
Hinchinbrook I. 138 18 20S 146 15 E
Hinckley, U.K. 28 52 33N 1 21W
Hinckley, U.S.A. 160 39 18N 112 41W
Hindås 73 57 42N 12 27 E
Hindaun 94 26 44N 77 5 E
Hinde Rapids (Hells Gate) 126 5 25S 27 3 E
Hinderwell 33 54 32N 0 45W
Hindhead 29 51 6N 0 42W
Hindley 32 53 32N 2 35W
Hindmarsh L. 140 36 5S 141 55 E
Hindol 95 20 40N 85 10 E
Hinds 143 43 59S 171 36 E
Hindsholm 73 55 30N 10 40 E
Hindu Bagh 94 30 56N 67 57 E
Hindu Kush 93 36 0N 71 0 E
Hindubagh 93 30 56N 67 57 E
Hindupur 97 13 49N 77 32 E
Hines Creek 152 56 20N 118 40W
Hinganghat 96 20 30N 78 59 E
Hingeon 47 50 32N 4 59 E
Hingham, U.K. 29 52 35N 0 59 E
Hingham, U.S.A. 160 48 40N 110 29W
Hingol, R. 93 25 30N 65 30 E
Hingoli 96 19 41N 77 15 E
Hinkley Pt. 28 50 59N 3 32W
Hinlopenstretet 12 79 35N 18 40 E
Hinna 121 10 25N 11 28 E
Hinnøy 74 68 40N 16 28 E
Hino 111 35 0N 136 15 E
Hinojosa 55 38 30N 5 17W
Hinojosa del Duque 57 38 30N 5 17W
Hinokage 110 32 39N 131 24 E
Hinsdale 160 48 26N 107 2W
Hinstock 28 52 50N 2 28W
Hinterrhein, R. 51 46 40N 9 25 E
Hinton, Can. 152 53 26N 117 34W
Hinton, U.S.A. 156 37 40N 80 51W
Hinwil 51 47 18N 8 51 E
Hippolytushoef 46 52 54N 4 58 E
Hirado 110 33 22N 129 33 E
Hirado-Shima 110 33 20N 129 30 E
Hirakarta 111 34 48N 135 40 E
Hirakud 96 21 32N 83 51 E
Hirakud Dam 96 21 32N 83 45 E
Hirara 112 24 48N 125 17 E
Hirata 110 35 24N 132 49 E
Hiratsuka 111 35 19N 139 21 E
Hirhafok 119 23 49N 5 45 E
Hirlŭu 70 47 23N 27 0 E
Hiromi 110 33 13N 132 36 E
Hirosaki 112 40 34N 140 28 E
Hiroshima 110 34 30N 132 30 E
Hiroshima-ken □ 112 34 50N 133 0 E
Hiroshima-Wan 110 34 5N 132 20 E
Hirsoholmene 73 57 30N 10 36 E
Hirson 43 49 55N 4 4 E
Hîrşova 70 44 40N 27 59 E
Hirtshals 73 57 36N 9 57 E
Hirwaun 31 51 43N 3 30W
Hisoy 71 58 26N 8 44 E
Hispaniola, I. 165 19 0N 71 0W
Hissar 94 29 12N 75 45 E
Histon 29 52 15N 0 6 E
Hita 110 33 20N 130 58 E
Hitachi 111 36 36N 140 39 E
Hitachiota 111 36 30N 140 30 E
Hitchin 29 51 57N 0 16W
Hitoyoshi 110 32 13N 130 45 E
Hitra 71 63 30N 8 45 E
Hitzacker 48 53 9N 11 1 E
Hiuchi-Nada 110 34 5N 133 20 E
Hjalmar L. 153 61 33N 109 25W
Hjälmare Kanal 72 59 20N 15 59 E
Hjälmaren 72 59 18N 15 40 E
Hjartdal 71 59 37N 8 41 E
Hjärtsäter 73 58 35N 12 3 E
Hjerkinn 71 62 13N 9 33 E
Hjerpsted 73 55 2N 8 39 E
Hjo 73 58 22N 4 17 E
Hjørring 73 57 29N 9 59 E
Hjorted 73 57 37N 16 19 E
Hjortkvarn 73 58 54N 15 26 E
Hko-ut 98 21 40N 97 46 E
Hkyenhpa 98 27 43N 97 25 E
Hlaingbwe 98 17 8N 97 50 E
Hlinsko 52 49 45N 15 54 E
Hlohovec 53 48 26N 17 49 E
Hlwaze 98 18 54N 96 37 E
Ho 121 6 37N 0 27 E
Ho Chi Minh, Phanh Bho 101 10 58N 106 40 E
Ho Thuong 100 19 32N 105 48 E
Hoa Binh 100 20 50N 105 20 E
Hoa Da (Phan Ri) 101 11 16N 108 40 E
Hoa Hiep 101 11 34N 105 51 E
Hoadley 152 52 45N 114 30W
Hoai Nhon (Bon Son) 100 14 28N 109 1 E
Hoare B. 149 65 17N 62 55W
Hobart, Austral. 138 42 50S 147 21 E
Hobart, U.S.A. 159 35 0N 99 5W
Hobbs 159 32 40N 103 3W
Hobjærg 73 56 19N 9 32 E
Hobo 174 2 35N 75 30W
Hoboken, Belg. 47 51 11N 4 21 E
Hoboken, U.S.A. 162 40 45N 74 4W
Hobro 73 56 39N 9 46 E
Hobscheid 47 49 42N 5 57 E
Hoburg C. 73 56 54N 18 8 E
Hoburgen 73 56 55N 18 7 E
Hochang 108 27 8N 104 45 E
Hochatown 159 34 11N 94 39W
Hochdorf 51 47 10N 8 17 E
Hochiang 108 28 48N 105 48 E
Hochien 106 38 26N 116 5 E
Hoch'ih 108 24 43N 108 2 E
Hoching 106 35 37N 110 43 E
Hoch'iu 109 32 21N 116 13 E
Höchst 49 50 6N 8 33 E
Hoch'ü 106 39 26N 111 8 E
Hoch'uan 108 30 2N 106 18 E
Hockenheim 49 49 18N 8 33 E
Hod, oilfield 19 56 10N 3 25 E
Hodaka-Dake 111 36 17N 137 39 E
Hodde 73 55 42N 8 39 E
Hodder R. 32 53 57N 2 27W
Hoddesdon 29 51 45N 0 1W
Hodeïda 91 14 50N 43 0 E
Hodge, R. 33 54 14N 0 55W
Hodgson 153 51 13N 97 36W
Hódmezóvásárhely 53 46 28N 20 22 E
Hodna, Chott el 119 35 30N 5 0 E
Hodonín 53 48 50N 17 0 E
Hodsager 73 56 19N 8 51 E
Hoeamdong 107 42 30N 130 16 E
Hoëdic, I. 42 47 21N 2 52W
Hoegaarden 47 50 47N 4 53 E
Hoek van Holland 46 52 0N 4 7 E
Hoeksche Waard 46 51 46N 4 25 E
Hoenderloo 46 52 7N 5 52 E
Hoengsŏng 107 37 29N 127 59 E
Hoensbroek 47 50 55N 5 55 E
Hoeryong 107 42 30N 129 58 E
Hoeselt 47 50 51N 5 29 E
Hoëveld 129 26 30S 30 0 E
Hoeven 47 51 35N 4 35 E
Hoeyang 107 38 43N 127 36 E
Hof, Ger. 49 50 18N 11 55 E
Hof, Iceland 74 64 33N 14 40W
Höfðakaupstaður 74 65 50N 20 19W
Hofei 109 31 52N 117 15 E
Hoff 32 54 34N 2 31W
Hofgeismar 48 51 29N 9 23 E
Hofors 72 60 35N 16 15 E
Hofsjökull 74 64 49N 18 48W
Hofsós 74 65 53N 19 26W
Hōfu 110 34 3N 131 34 E
Hofuf 92 25 20N 49 40 E
Hög-Gia, Mt. 71 62 23N 10 7 E
Hog I. 162 37 26N 75 42W
Hogan Group 139 39 13S 147 1 E
Höganäs 73 56 13N 12 34 E
Hogansville 157 33 14N 84 50W
Hogarth, Mt. 138 21 50S 137 0 E
Hogeland 160 48 51N 108 40W
Högen 72 61 47N 14 11 E
Hogenaki Falls 97 12 6N 77 50 E
Högfors, Örebro, Sweden 72 59 58N 15 3 E
Högfors, Västmanlands, Sweden 72 60 2N 16 3 E
Hoggar = Ahaggar 119 23 0N 6 30 E
Hōgo-Kaikyo 110 33 20N 131 58 E
Hog's Back, hill 29 51 13N 0 40W
Hogs Hd. 39 51 46N 10 13W
Högsäter 73 58 38N 12 5 E
Högsby 73 57 10N 16 1 E
Högsjo 72 59 4N 15 44 E
Hogsthorpe 33 53 13N 0 19 E
Hogsty Reef 167 21 41N 73 48W
Hohe Rhön 49 50 24N 9 58 E
Hohe Tauern 52 47 11N 12 40 E
Hohenau 53 48 36N 16 55 E
Hohenems 52 47 22N 9 42 E
Hohenstein Ernstthal 48 50 48N 12 43 E
Hohenwald 157 35 35N 87 30W
Hohenwestedt 48 54 6N 9 40 E
Hohoe 121 7 8N 0 32 E
Hohsi 108 24 9N 102 38 E
Hohsien, Anhwei, China 109 31 43N 118 22 E
Hohsien, Kwangsi-Chuang, China 109 24 25N 111 31 E
Hohsüeh 109 30 2N 112 25 E
Hôi An 100 15 30N 108 19 E
Hoi Xuan 100 20 25N 105 9 E
Hoisington 158 38 33N 98 50W
Højer 73 54 58N 8 42 E
Hōjō 110 33 58N 132 46 E
Hok 73 57 31N 14 16 E
Hökensås 73 58 0N 14 5 E
Hökensås 73 58 0N 14 5 E
Hökerum 73 57 51N 13 16 E
Hokianga Harbour 142 35 31S 173 22 E
Hokitika 143 42 42S 171 0 E
Hokkaidō 112 43 30N 143 0 E
Hokkaidō □ 112 43 30N 143 0 E
Hokksund 71 59 44N 9 59 E
Hok'ou, Kansu, China 106 36 9N 103 29 E
Hok'ou, Kwantang, China 109 23 13N 112 45 E
Hok'ou, Yunnan, China 108 22 39N 103 57 E
Hokow 101 22 39N 103 57 E
Hol-Hol. 123 11 20N 42 50 E
Holan Shan 106 38 50N 105 50 E
Holbæk 73 55 43N 11 43 E
Holbeach 29 52 48N 0 1 E
Holbeach Marsh 29 52 52N 0 5 E
Holborn Hd. 37 58 37N 3 30W
Holbrook, Austral. 141 35 42S 147 18 E
Holbrook, U.S.A. 161 35 0N 110 0W
Holden 152 53 13N 112 11W
Holden Fillmore 160 39 0N 112 26W
Holdenville 159 35 5N 96 25W
Holder 140 34 21S 140 0 E
Holderness 33 53 45N 0 5W
Holdfast 153 50 58N 105 25W
Holdrege 153 40 25N 99 30W
Hole 71 60 6N 10 12 E
Hole-Narsipur 97 12 48N 76 16 E
Holešov 53 49 20N 17 35 E
Holguín 166 20 50N 76 20W
Holinkoerh 106 40 23N 111 53 E
Holič 53 48 49N 17 10 E
Holkham 29 52 57N 0 48 E
Holla, Mt. 123 7 5N 36 35 E
Hollabrunn 52 48 34N 16 5 E
Hollams Bird I. 128 24 40S 14 30 E
Holland 156 42 47N 86 7W
Holland Fen 33 53 0N 0 8W
Holland-on-Sea 29 51 48N 1 12 E
Hollandia = Jajapura 103 2 28S 140 38 E
Hollands Bird I. 128 24 40S 14 30 E
Hollandsch Diep 47 51 41N 4 30 E
Hollandsch IJssel, R. 46 51 55N 4 34 E
Hollandstoun 37 59 22N 2 25W
Höllen 71 58 6N 7 49 E
Holleton 137 31 55S 119 0 E
Hollidaysburg 156 40 26N 78 25W
Hollis 159 34 45N 99 55W
Hollister 161 36 51N 121 24W
Hollum 46 53 26N 5 38 E
Holly 158 38 7N 102 7W
Holly Hill 157 29 15N 81 3W
Holly Springs 159 34 45N 89 25W
Hollymount 38 53 40N 9 7W
Hollywood, Ireland 39 53 6N 6 35W
Hollywood, Calif., U.S.A. 154 34 7N 118 25W
Hollywood, Fla., U.S.A. 157 26 0N 80 9W
Holm 72 62 40N 16 40 E
Holman Island 148 71 0N 118 0W
Hólmavík 74 65 42N 21 40W
Holme, Humberside,, U.K. 33 53 50N 0 48W
Holme, N. Yorks., U.K. 32 53 34N 1 50W
Holmedal 71 59 46N 5 50 E
Holmedal, Fjordane 71 61 22N 5 11 E
Holmegil 72 59 10N 11 44 E
Holmes Chapel 32 53 13N 2 21W
Holmes Reefs 138 16 27S 148 0 E
Holmestrand 71 59 31N 10 14 E
Holmfirth 33 53 34N 1 48W
Holmsbu 71 59 32N 10 27 E
Holmsjön 72 62 26N 15 20 E
Holmsland Klit 73 56 0N 8 5 E
Holmsund 74 63 41N 20 20 E
Holmwood 29 51 12N 0 19W
Hölö 72 59 3N 17 36 E
Holo Ho, R. 107 44 54N 122 22 E
Holod 70 46 49N 22 8 E
Holon 90 32 2N 34 47 E
Holroyd, R. 138 14 10S 141 36 E
Holsen 71 61 25N 6 8 E
Holstebro 73 56 22N 8 37 E
Holsworthy 30 50 48N 4 21W
Holt, Iceland 74 63 33N 19 48W
Holt, Clwyd, U.K. 31 53 4N 2 52W
Holt, Norfolk, U.K. 29 52 55N 1 4 E
Holte 73 55 50N 12 29 E
Holten 46 52 17N 6 26 E
Holton Harbour 151 54 31N 57 12W
Holton le Clay 33 53 29N 0 3W
Holtville 161 32 50N 115 27W
Holum 71 58 6N 7 32 E
Holwerd 46 53 22N 5 54 E
Holy Cross 147 62 10N 159 52W
Holy I., England, U.K. 35 55 42N 1 48W
Holy I., Scotland, U.K. 34 55 31N 5 4W
Holy I., Wales, U.K. 31 53 17N 4 37W
Holyhead 31 53 18N 4 38W
Holyhead B. 31 53 20N 4 35W
Holyoke, Mass., U.S.A. 162 42 14N 72 37W
Holyoke, Nebr., U.S.A. 158 40 39N 102 18W
Holyrood 151 47 27N 53 8W
Holywell 31 53 16N 3 14W
Holywood 38 54 38N 5 50W
Holzminden 48 51 49N 9 31 E
Homa Bay 126 0 36S 34 22 E
Homa Bay □ 126 0 50S 34 30 E
Homalin 98 24 55N 95 0 E
Homberg 48 51 2N 9 20 E
Hombori 121 15 20N 1 38W
Homburg 49 49 19N 7 21 E
Home B. 149 68 40N 67 10W
Home Hill 138 19 43S 147 25 E
Homedale 160 43 42N 116 59W
Homer, Alaska, U.S.A. 147 59 40N 151 35W
Homer, La., U.S.A. 159 32 50N 93 4W
Homestead, Austral. 138 20 20S 145 40 E
Homestead, U.S.A. 157 25 29N 80 27W
Hominy 159 36 26N 96 24W
Homnabad 96 17 45N 77 5 E
Homoine 129 23 55S 35 8 E
Homorod 70 46 5N 25 15 E
Homs = Al Khums 119 32 40N 14 17 E
Homs (Hims) 92 34 40N 36 45 E
Hon Chong 101 10 16N 104 38 E
Hon Me 100 19 23N 105 56 E
Honan □ 106 34 10N 113 10 E
Honbetsu 112 43 7N 143 37 E
Honda 174 5 12N 74 45W
Hondeklipbaai 125 30 19S 17 17 E
Hondo, Japan 110 32 27N 130 12 E
Hondo, U.S.A. 159 29 22N 99 6W
Hondo, R. 165 18 25N 88 21W
Honduras ■ 166 14 40N 86 30W
Honduras, Golfo de 166 16 50N 87 0W
Hönefoss 71 60 10N 10 12 E
Honey L. 160 40 13N 120 14W
Honfleur 42 49 25N 0 13 E
Höng 73 55 30N 11 14 E
Hong Gai 100 20 57N 107 5 E
Hong Kong ■ 109 22 11N 114 14 E

Hong, R Hsiushui

Hong, R. 100 20 17N 106 34 E
Hongchŏn 107 37 44N 127 53 E
Hongha, R. 101 22 0N 104 0 E
Hongor 106 45 56N 112 50 E
Hongsa 100 19 43N 101 20 E
Hongsŏng 107 36 37N 126 38 E
Honguedo, Détroit d' 151 49 15N 64 0W
Hongwon 107 40 0N 127 56 E
Honiara 142 9 30 S 160 0 E
Honington 33 52 58N 0 35W
Honiton 30 50 48N 3 11W
Honjo, Akita, Japan 112 39 23N 140 3 E
Honjo, Gumma, Japan 111 36 14N 139 11 E
Honkawane 111 35 5N 138 5 E
Honkorâb, Ras 122 24 35N 35 10 E
Honolulu 147 21 19N 157 52W
Honshū 112 36 0N 138 0 E
Hontoria del Pinar 58 41 50N 3 10W
Hoo 29 51 25N 0 33 E
Hood Mt. 160 45 15N 122 0W
Hood, Pt. 137 34 23 S 119 34 E
Hood Pt. 135 10 4 S 147 45 E
Hood River 160 45 45N 121 37W
Hoodsport 160 47 24N 123 7W
Hooge 48 54 31N 8 36 E
Hoogerheide 47 51 26N 4 20 E
Hoogeveen 46 52 44N 6 30 E
Hoogeveensche Vaart 46 52 42N 6 12 E
Hoogezand 46 53 11N 6 45 E
Hooghly-Chinsura 95 22 53N 88 27 E
Hooghly, R. 95 21 59N 88 10 E
Hoogkerk 46 53 13N 6 30 E
Hooglede 47 50 59N 3 5 E
Hoogstraten 47 51 24N 4 46 E
Hoogvliet 46 51 52N 4 21 E
Hook 29 51 17N 0 55W
Hook Hd. 39 52 8N 6 57W
Hook I. 138 20 4 S 149 0 E
Hook of Holland = Hoek v. Holland 47 52 0N 4 7 E
Hooker 159 36 55N 101 10W
Hooker Cr. 136 18 23 S 130 50 E
Hoonah 147 58 15N 135 30W
Hooper Bay 147 61 30N 166 10W
Hoopersville 162 38 16N 76 11W
Hoopeston 156 40 30N 87 40W
Hoopstad 128 27 50 S 25 55 E
Höör 73 55 55N 13 33 E
Hoorn 46 52 38N 5 4 E
Hoover Dam 161 36 0N 114 45W
Hop Bottom 162 41 41N 75 47W
Hopà 83 41 28N 41 30 E
Hope, Can. 152 49 25N 121 25 E
Hope, U.K. 31 53 7N 3 2W
Hope, Ark., U.S.A. 159 33 40N 93 30W
Hope, N.D., U.S.A. 158 47 21N 97 42W
Hope Bay 13 65 0 S 55 0W
Hope, L. 139 28 24 S 139 18 E
Hope L. 37 58 24N 4 38W
Hope Pt. 147 68 20N 166 50W
Hope Town 157 26 30N 76 30W
Hopedale, Can. 151 55 28N 60 13W
Hopedale, U.S.A. 162 42 8N 71 33W
Hopefield 128 33 3 S 18 22 E
Hopei □ 107 39 25N 116 45 E
Hopelchén 165 19 46N 89 50W
Hopeman 37 57 42N 3 26W
Hopen 71 63 27N 8 2 E
Hopetoun 137 33 57 S 120 7 E
Hopetown, Austral. 140 35 42 S 142 22 E
Hopetown, S. Afr. 128 29 34 S 24 3 E
Hopewell 162 37 18N 77 17W
Hopien-Ts'un 108 27 40N 101 55 E
Hopin 98 21 14N 96 53 E
Hop'ing 109 24 26N 114 56 E
Hopkins 158 40 31N 94 45W
Hopkins, L. 136 24 15 S 128 35 E
Hopkinsville 157 36 52N 87 26W
Hopland 160 39 0N 123 7W
Hopo 108 31 24N 99 0 E
Hoptrup 73 55 11N 9 28 E
Hop'u 108 21 41N 109 10 E
Hoquiam 160 46 50N 123 55W
Hōrai 111 34 58N 137 32 E
Horazdovice 52 49 19N 13 42 E
Hörby 73 55 50N 13 44 E
Horcajo de Santiago 58 39 50N 3 1W
Hordaland fylke □ 71 60 25N 6 15 E
Horden 33 54 45N 1 17W
Hordern Hills 136 20 40 S 130 20 E
Hordio 91 10 36N 51 8 E
Horezu 70 45 6N 24 0 E
Horgen 51 47 15N 8 35 E
Horgoš 66 46 10N 20 0 E
Horice 52 50 21N 15 39 E
Horley 29 51 10N 0 10W
Horlick Mts. 13 84 0 s 102 0W
Hormoz 93 27 35N 55 0 E
Hormuz, I. 93 27 8N 56 28 E
Hormuz Str. 93 26 30N 56 30 E
Horn, Austria 52 48 39N 15 40 E
Horn, Isafjarðarsýsla, Iceland 74 66 28N 22 28W
Horn, Suður-Múlasýsla, Iceland 74 65 10N 13 31W
Horn, Neth. 47 51 12N 5 57 E
Horn, Cape = Hornos, C. de 176 55 50 S 67 30W
Horn Head 38 55 13N 8 0W
Horn I., Austral. 138 10 37 S 142 17 E
Horn I., P.N.G. 135 10 35 S 142 20 E
Horn, I. 157 30 17N 88 40W
Horn Mts. 152 62 15N 119 15W
Horn, R. 152 61 30N 118 1W
Hornachuelos 57 37 50N 5 14W
Hornavan 74 66 15N 17 30 E
Hornbæk, Frederiksborg, Denmark 73 56 5N 12 26 E
Hornbæk, Viborg, Denmark 73 56 28N 9 58 E
Hornbeck 159 31 22N 93 20W
Hornbrook 160 41 58N 122 37W
Hornburg 48 52 2N 10 36 E
Hornby 143 43 33 S 172 33 E
Horncastle 33 53 13N 0 8W
Horndal 72 60 18N 16 23 E
Horndean 29 50 56N 1 5W
Hornell 156 42 23N 77 41W
Hornell L. 152 62 20N 119 25W
Hornepayne 150 49 14N 84 48W
Hornindal 71 61 58N 6 30 E
Horningsham 28 51 11N 2 16W
Hornitos 163 37 30N 120 14W
Hornnes 71 58 34N 7 45 E
Hornos, Cabo de 176 55 50 S 67 30 E
Hornoy 43 49 50N 1 54 E
Hornsberg, Jamtland, Sweden 72 63 14N 14 40 E
Hornsberg, Kronobergs, Sweden 72 56 37N 13 47 E
Hornsby 141 33 42 S 151 2 E
Hornsea 33 53 55N 0 10W
Hornslandet Pen. 72 61 35N 17 37 E
Hornslet 73 56 18N 10 19 E
Hornu 47 50 26N 3 50 E
Hörnum 73 54 44N 8 18 E
Horovice 52 49 48N 13 53 E
Horqueta 172 23 15 S 56 55W
Horra, La 56 41 44N 3 53W
Horred 73 57 22N 12 28 E
Horse Cr. 158 41 33N 104 45W
Horse Is. 151 50 15N 55 50W
Horsefly L. 152 52 25N 121 0W
Horseheads 162 42 10N 76 49W
Horseleap 38 53 25N 7 34W
Horsens 73 55 52N 9 51 E
Horsens Fjord 73 55 50N 10 0 E
Horseshoe 137 25 27 S 118 31 E
Horseshoe Dam 161 33 45N 111 35W
Horsforth 33 53 50N 1 39W
Horsham, Austral. 140 36 44 S 142 13 E
Horsham, U.K. 29 51 4N 0 20W
Horsham St. Faith 29 52 41N 1 15 E
Horsovsky Tyn 52 49 31N 12 58 E
Horst 47 51 27N 6 3 E
Horsted Keynes 29 51 2N 0 1W
Horten 71 59 25N 10 32 E
Hortobágy, R. 53 47 30N 21 6 E
Horton 158 39 42N 95 30W
Horton-in-Ribblesdale 32 54 9N 2 19W
Horton, R. 147 69 56N 126 52W
Hörvik 73 56 2N 14 45 E
Horw 51 47 1N 8 19 E
Horwich 32 53 37N 2 33W
Horwood, L. 150 48 10N 82 20W
Hosaina 123 7 30N 37 47 E
Hosdurga 97 13 40N 76 17 E
Hose, Pegunungan 102 2 5N 114 6 E
Hoshan 109 31 24N 116 20 E
Hoshangabad 94 22 45N 77 45 E
Hoshiarpur 94 31 30N 75 58 E
Hoshui 106 36 0N 107 59 E
Hoshun 106 37 19N 113 34 E
Hosingen 47 50 1N 6 6 E
Hoskins 135 5 29 S 150 27 E
Hosmer 158 45 36N 99 29W
Hososhima 110 32 26N 131 40 E
Hospental 51 46 37N 8 34 E
Hospet 97 15 15N 76 20 E
Hospital 39 52 30N 8 28W
Hospitalet de Llobregat 58 41 21N 2 6 E
Hospitalet, L' 44 42 36N 1 47 E
Hoste, I. 176 55 0 S 69 0W
Hostens 44 44 30N 0 40W
Hoswick 36 60 0N 1 15W
Hot 100 18 8N 98 29 E
Hot Creek Ra. 160 39 0N 116 0W
Hot Springs, Ark, U.S.A. 159 34 30N 93 0W
Hot Springs, S.D., U.S.A. 158 43 25N 103 30W
Hotagen, L. 74 63 50N 14 30 E
Hotazel 128 27 17 S 23 00 E
Hotchkiss 161 38 55N 107 47W
Hotham, C. 136 12 2 S 131 18 E
Hot'ien 105 37 7N 79 55 E
Hoting 74 64 8N 16 15 E
Hotolishti 68 41 10N 20 25 E
Hotse 106 35 14N 115 27 E
Hotte, Massif de la 167 18 30N 73 45W
Hottentotsbaai 128 26 8 S 14 59 E
Hotton 47 50 16N 5 26 E
Houat, I. 42 47 24N 2 58W
Houck 161 35 15N 109 15W
Houdan 43 48 48N 1 35 E
Houdeng-Goegnies 47 50 29N 4 10 E
Houei Sai 100 20 18N 100 26 E
Houffalize 47 50 8N 5 48 E
Houghton 158 47 9N 88 39W
Houghton L. 156 44 20N 84 40W
Houghton-le-Spring 35 54 51N 1 28W
Houghton Regis 29 51 54N 0 32W
Houhora 142 34 49 S 173 9 E
Houille, R. 47 50 8N 4 50 E
Houlton 151 46 5N 68 0W
Houma 159 29 35N 90 50W
Houmt Souk = Djerba 119 33 53N 10 37 E
Houndé 120 11 34N 3 31W
Hounslow 29 51 29N 0 20W
Hourn L. 36 57 7N 5 35W
Hourtin 44 45 11N 1 4W
Housatonic, R. 162 41 10N 73 7W
Houston, Can. 152 54 25N 126 30W
Houston, Mo., U.S.A. 159 37 20N 92 0W
Houston, Tex., U.S.A. 159 29 50N 95 20W
Houten 46 52 2N 5 10 E
Houthalen 47 51 2N 5 23 E
Houthem 47 50 48N 2 57 E
Houthulst 47 50 59N 2 57 E
Houtman Abrolhos 137 28 43 S 113 48 E
Houyet 47 50 11N 5 1 E
Hova 73 58 53N 14 14 E
Høvag 71 58 10N 8 15 E
Hövåg 71 58 10N 8 16 E
Hovd 105 48 1N 91 39 E
Hovden 71 59 33N 7 22 E
Hove 29 50 50N 0 10W
Hoveton 29 52 45N 1 23 E
Hovingham 33 54 10N 0 59W
Hovmantorp 73 56 47N 15 7 E
Hövsgöl 106 43 37N 109 39 E
Hovsta 72 59 22N 15 15 E
Howakil 123 15 10N 40 16 E
Howar, W., (Shau) 123 17 0N 25 30 E
Howard, Austral. 139 25 16 S 152 32 E
Howard, Kans., U.S.A. 159 37 30N 96 16W
Howard, S.D., U.S.A. 158 44 2N 97 30W
Howard I. 138 12 10 S 135 24 E
Howard L. 153 62 15N 105 57W
Howatharra 137 28 29 S 114 33 E
Howden 33 53 45N 0 52W
Howe 160 43 48N 113 0W
Howe, C. 141 37 30 S 150 0 E
Howell 156 42 38N 84 0W
Howick, N.Z. 142 36 54 S 174 48 E
Howick, S. Afr. 129 29 28 S 30 14 E
Howick Group 138 14 20 S 145 30 E
Howitt, L. 139 27 40 S 138 40 E
Howley 151 49 12N 57 2W
Howmore 36 57 18N 7 23W
Howrah 95 22 37N 88 27 E
Howth 38 53 23N 6 3W
Howth Hd. 38 53 21N 6 0W
Hoxne 29 52 22N 1 11 E
Höxter 48 51 45N 9 26 E
Hoy I. 37 58 50N 3 15W
Hoy Sd. 37 58 57N 3 20W
Hoya 48 52 47N 9 10 E
Høyanger 71 61 25N 6 50 E
Höydalsmo 71 59 30N 8 15 E
Hoyerswerda 48 51 26N 14 14 E
Hoylake 32 53 24N 3 11W
Höyland 71 58 50N 5 43 E
Hoyleton 140 34 2 S 138 34 E
Hoyos 56 40 9N 6 45W
Hoyüan 109 23 50N 114 40 E
Hpawlum 98 27 12N 98 12 E
Hpettintha 98 24 14N 95 23 E
Hpizow 98 26 57N 98 24 E
Hpungan Pass 99 27 30N 96 55 E
Hrádec Králové 52 50 15N 15 50 E
Hrádek 53 48 46N 16 16 E
Hranice 53 49 34N 17 45 E
Hron, R. 53 48 0N 18 4 E
Hrubieszów 54 50 49N 23 51 E
Hrubý Nizký Jeseník 53 50 7N 17 10 E
Hrvatska 63 45 20N 16 0 E
Hsenwi 98 23 22N 97 55 E
Hsi Chiang, R. 109 22 20N 113 20 E
Hsiach'engtzu, Heilungkiang, China 107 44 41N 130 27 E
Hsiach'engtzu, Schechwan, China 108 29 24N 101 46 E
Hsiachiang 109 27 33N 115 10 E
Hsiaching 106 36 57N 115 59 E
Hsiach'uan Shan 109 21 40N 112 37 E
Hsiahsien 106 35 12N 111 11 E
Hsiai 106 34 17N 116 11 E
Hsiakuan 108 25 39N 100 9 E
Hsiamen 109 24 30N 118 7 E
Hsian 106 34 17N 109 0 E
Hsiang Chiang, R. 109 29 30N 113 10 E
Hsiangch'eng, Honan, China 106 33 50N 113 29 E
Hsiangch'eng, Honan, China 106 33 13N 114 50 E
Hsiangch'eng, Szechwan, China 108 29 0N 99 46 E
Hsiangchou 108 23 58N 109 41 E
Hsiangfan 109 32 7N 112 9 E
Hsianghsiang 109 27 46N 112 30 E
Hsiangning 106 36 1N 110 47 E
Hsiangshan 109 29 18N 121 37 E
Hsiangshuik'ou 107 34 12N 119 34 E
Hsiangt'an 109 27 55N 112 52 E
Hsiangtu 108 23 14N 106 57 E
Hsiangyang 109 32 2N 112 6 E
Hsiangyin 109 28 40N 112 53 E
Hsiangyüan 106 36 32N 113 2 E
Hsiangyün 108 25 29N 100 35 E
Hsiaochin 108 31 1N 102 23 E
Hsiaofeng 109 30 36N 119 33 E
Hsiaohsien 106 34 2N 116 56 E
Hsiaohsinganling Shanmo 105 48 45N 127 0 E
Hsiaoi 106 37 7N 111 46 E
Hsiaokan 109 30 57N 113 53 E
Hsiaoshan 109 30 10N 120 15 E
Hsiaot'ai Shan 107 36 18N 116 38 E
Hsiap'u 109 26 58N 119 57 E
Hsiawa 107 42 38N 120 31 E
Hsich'ang 108 27 50N 102 18 E
Hsichieht'o 108 30 24N 108 13 E
Hsich'uan 109 33 0N 111 24 E
Hsich'ung 108 31 0N 105 48 E
Hsiehch'eng 107 34 48N 117 15 E
Hsiehmaho 109 31 38N 111 12 E
Hsienchü 109 28 51N 120 44 E
Hsienfeng 108 29 40N 109 7 E
Hsienhsien 106 38 2N 116 12 E
Hsienning 109 29 51N 114 15 E
Hsienshui Ho, R. 108 30 5N 101 5 E
Hsienyang 106 34 22N 108 48 E
Hsienyu 109 25 24N 118 40 E
Hsifei Ho, R. 109 32 38N 116 39 E
Hsifeng, Kweichow, China 108 27 5N 106 42 E
Hsifeng, Liaoning, China 107 42 44N 124 42 E
Hsifengchen 106 35 40N 107 42 E
Hsifengk'ou 107 40 24N 118 19 E
Hsiho 106 34 2N 105 12 E
Hsihsia, Honan, China 106 33 30N 111 30 E
Hsihsia, Shantung, China 107 37 25N 120 48 E
Hsihsiang 108 33 1N 107 40 E
Hsihsien, Honan, China 109 32 24N 114 52 E
Hsihsien, Shensi, China 106 36 41N 110 56 E
Hsihua 106 33 47N 114 31 E
Hsilamunlun Ho, R. 107 43 24N 123 42 E
Hsiliao Ho, R. 107 43 24N 123 42 E
Hsilin 108 24 30N 105 3 E
Hsin Chiang, R. 109 28 50N 116 40 E
Hsin Ho, R. 107 43 33N 123 31 E
Hsinchan 107 43 52N 127 20 E
Hsinch'ang 109 29 30N 120 54 E
Hsincheng 106 34 25N 113 46 E
Hsinch'eng, Hopei, China 106 39 15N 115 59 E
Hsinch'eng, Kwangsi-Chuang, China 108 24 4N 108 40 E
Hsinchiang 106 35 40N 111 15 E
Hsinchien 108 23 58N 102 47 E
Hsinchin 107 39 25N 121 59 E
Hsinching 108 30 25N 103 49 E
Hsinchi'u 107 41 53N 119 40 E
Hsinchou 109 30 52N 114 48 E
Hsinchu 109 24 48N 120 58 E
Hsinfeng, Kiangsi, China 109 25 27N 114 58 E
Hsinfeng, Kiangsi, China 109 26 7N 116 11 E
Hsinfeng, Kwangtung, China 109 24 4N 114 12 E
Hsingan 109 25 39N 110 39 E
Hsingch'eng 107 40 40N 120 48 E
Hsingho 106 40 52N 113 58 E
Hsinghsien 106 38 31N 111 4 E
Hsinghua 107 32 55N 119 52 E
Hsinghua Wan 109 25 20N 119 20 E
Hsingi 108 25 5N 104 55 E
Hsinging 109 26 25N 110 44 E
Hsingjen 108 25 26N 105 14 E
Hsingjenp'ao 106 37 0N 105 0 E
Hsingkuo 109 26 26N 115 16 E
Hsinglung 107 40 29N 117 32 E
Hsingning 109 24 8N 115 43 E
Hsingp'ing 106 34 18N 108 26 E
Hsingshan 109 31 10N 110 51 E
Hsingt'ai 106 37 5N 114 38 E
Hsingyeh 108 22 45N 109 52 E
Hsinhailien = Lienyünchiangshih 107 34 37N 119 13 E
Hsinhsiang 106 35 15N 113 54 E
Hsinhsien, Shansi, China 106 38 24N 112 47 E
Hsinhsien, Shantung, China 106 36 15N 115 40 E
Hsinhsing 109 22 45N 112 11 E
Hsinhua 109 27 43N 111 18 E
Hsinhui 109 22 32N 113 0 E
Hsini 109 22 12N 110 53 E
Hsining 105 36 37N 101 46 E
Hsink'ai Ho, R. 107 41 10N 122 5 E
Hsinkan 109 27 45N 115 21 E
Hsinkao Shan 109 23 25N 120 52 E
Hsinlit'un 107 42 2N 122 19 E
Hsinlo 106 38 15N 114 40 E
Hsinmin 107 42 0N 122 52 E
Hsinpaoan 106 40 27N 115 23 E
Hsinpin 107 41 43N 125 2 E
Hsinp'ing 108 24 6N 101 58 E
Hsinshao 109 27 20N 111 26 E
Hsint'ai 107 35 54N 117 44 E
Hsint'ien 109 25 56N 112 13 E
Hsints'ai 109 32 44N 114 59 E
Hsinyang 109 32 10N 114 6 E
Hsinyeh 109 37 31N 112 21 E
Hsinyü 109 27 48N 114 56 E
Hsipaw 98 22 37N 97 18 E
Hsip'ing, Honan, China 106 33 34N 110 45 E
Hsip'ing, Honan, China 106 33 23N 114 2 E
Hsishni 109 30 27N 115 13 E
Hsitalahai 106 40 38N 109 38 E
Hsiu Shui, R. 109 29 13N 116 0 E
Hsiujen 109 24 26N 110 14 E
Hsiunghsien 106 38 50N 116 11 E
Hsiungyüeh 107 40 12N 122 12 E
Hsiuning 109 29 51N 118 15 E
Hsiushan 108 28 27N 108 59 E
Hsiushui 109 29 2N 114 34 E

Hsiuwen Ibara

Hsiuwen 108 26 52N 106 35 E
Hsiuyen 107 40 19N 123 15 E
Hsiyang 106 37 27N 113 46 E
Hsüanch'eng 109 30 54N 118 41 E
Hsüanen 108 29 59N 109 24 E
Hsüanhan 108 31 25N 107 38 E
Hsüanhua 106 40 38N 115 5 E
Hsüanwei 108 26 13N 104 5 E
Hsüch'ang 106 34 1N 113 53 E
Hsüchou 107 34 15N 117 10 E
Hsüehfeng Shan 109 27 0N 110 30 E
Hsüehweng Shan 109 24 24N 121 12 E
Hsun Chiang, R. 109 23 30N 111 30 E
Hsünhsien 106 35 40N 114 32 E
Hsüni 106 35 6N 108 20 E
Hsüntien 108 25 33N 103 15 E
Hsünwu 109 24 57N 115 28 E
Hsünyang 108 32 48N 109 27 E
Hsüp'u 109 27 56N 110 36 E
Hsüshui 106 39 1N 115 39 E
Hsüwen 109 20 20N 110 9 E
Hsüyung 108 28 6N 105 21 E
Htawgaw 98 25 57N 98 23 E
Hua Hin 100 12 34N 99 58 E
Huaan 109 25 1N 117 33 E
Huachacalla 164 18 45 S 68 17W
Huachinera 164 30 9N 108 55W
Huachipato 172 36 45 S 73 09W
Huacho 174 11 10 S 77 35W
Huachón 174 10 35 S 76 0W
Huachou 109 21 38N 110 35 E
Huacrachuco 174 8 35 S 76 50W
Huahsien, Honan, China 106 35 33N 114 34 E
Huahsien, Shensi, China 106 34 31N 109 46 E
Huai Yot 101 7 45N 99 37 E
Huaiachen 106 40 33N 114 30 E
Huaian, Hopei, China 106 40 33N 114 30 E
Huaian, Kiangsu, China 107 33 31N 119 8 E
Huaichi 109 24 0N 112 8 E
Huaihua 109 27 34N 109 56 E
Huaijen 106 39 50N 113 7 E
Huaijou 106 40 20N 116 37 E
Huainan 109 32 39N 117 2 E
Huaining 109 30 21N 116 42 E
Huaite 107 43 30N 124 50 E
Huaitechen 107 43 52N 124 45 E
Huaiyang 106 33 50N 115 2 E
Huaiyüan, Anhwei, China 109 32 58N 117 13 E
Huaiyüan, Kwangsi-Chuang, China 108 24 36N 108 27 E
Huajuapan 165 17 50N 98 0W
Huajung 109 29 34N 112 34 E
Hualien 109 24 0N 121 30 E
Huallaga, R. 174 5 30 S 76 10W
Hualpai Pk. 161 35 8N 113 58W
Huan Chiang, R. 106 36 4N 107 40 E
Huancabamba 174 5 10 S 79 15W
Huancané 174 15 10 S 69 50W
Huancapi 174 13 25 S 74 0W
Huancavelica 174 12 50 S 75 5W
Huancayo 174 12 5 S 75 0W
Huanchiang 108 24 50N 108 15 E
Huang Ho, R. 107 36 50N 118 20 E
Huangchiakopa 106 40 20N 109 18 E
Huangch'uan 109 32 8N 115 4 E
Huanghsien, Hunen, China 108 27 22N 109 10 E
Huanghsien, Shantung, China 107 37 38N 120 30 E
Huangkang 109 30 27N 114 50 E
Huanglienp'u 108 25 32N 99 44 E
Huangling 106 35 36N 109 17 E
Huangliu 105 18 20N 108 50 E
Huanglung 106 35 37N 109 58 E
Huanglungt'an 109 32 38N 110 33 E
Huangmei 109 30 4N 115 56 E
Huangshih 109 30 10N 115 2 E
Huangt'uan 107 36 55N 121 41 E
Huangyang 109 26 37N 111 42 E
Huangyen 109 28 37N 121 12 E
Huanhsien 106 36 32N 107 10 E
Huaning 108 24 12N 102 55 E
Huanjen 107 41 16N 125 21 E
Huanp'ing 108 26 54N 107 55 E
Huant'ai 107 36 57N 118 5 E
Huánuco 174 9 55 S 76 15W
Huap'ing 108 26 37N 101 13 E
Huap'itientzu 107 43 30N 130 2 E
Huaraz 174 9 30 S 77 32W
Huarmey 174 10 5 S 78 5W
Huasamota 164 22 30N 104 30W
Huascarán 174 9 0 S 77 30W
Huasco 172 28 24 S 71 15W
Huasco, R. 172 28 27 S 71 13W
Huasna 163 35 6N 120 24W
Huatabampo 164 26 50N 109 50W
Huate 106 41 57N 114 4 E
Huatien 107 42 58N 126 50 E
Huauchinango 165 20 11N 98 3W
Huautla 164 18 20N 96 50W
Huautla de Jiménez 165 18 8N 96 51W
Huay Namota 164 21 56N 104 30W
Huayin 106 34 36N 110 2 E
Huayllay 174 11 03 S 76 21W
Huayüan 108 28 30N 109 25 E
Hubbard 159 31 50N 96 50W
Hubbart Pt. 153 59 21N 94 41W
Hubli-Dharwar 97 15 22N 75 15 E
Huchang 107 41 25N 127 2 E
Huchuetenango 164 15 25N 91 30W
Hückelhoven-Ratheim 48 51 6N 6 3 E
Hucknall 33 53 3N 1 12W
Huddersfield 33 53 38N 1 49W
Hudi 122 17 43N 34 28 E
Hudiksvall 72 61 43N 17 10 E
Hudson, Can. 153 50 6N 92 09W
Hudson, Mich., U.S.A. 156 41 50N 84 20W
Hudson, N.H., U.S.A. 162 42 46N 71 26W
Hudson, N.Y., U.S.A. 162 42 15N 73 46W
Hudson, Wis., U.S.A. 158 44 57N 92 45W
Hudson, Wyo., U.S.A. 160 42 54N 108 37W
Hudson B. 153 59 0N 91 0W
Hudson Bay, Can. 149 60 0N 86 0W
Hudson Bay, Sask., Can. 153 52 51N 102 23W
Hudson Falls 162 43 18N 73 34W
Hudson, R. 162 40 42N 74 2W
Hudson Str. 148 62 0N 70 0W
Hudson's Hope 152 56 0N 121 54W
Hué 100 16 30N 107 35 E
Huebra, R. 56 40 54N 6 28W
Huedin 70 46 52N 23 2 E
Huehuetenango 166 15 20N 91 28W
Huejúcar 164 22 21N 103 13W
Huelgoat 42 48 22N 3 46W
Huelma 59 37 39N 3 28W
Huelva 57 37 18N 6 57W
Huelva □ 57 37 40N 7 0W
Huelva, R. 57 37 46N 6 15W
Huentelauquén 172 31 38 S 71 33W
Huércal Overa 59 37 23N 1 57W
Huerta, Sa. de la 172 31 10 S 67 30W
Huertas, C. de las 59 38 21N 0 24W
Huerva, R. 58 41 13N 1 15W
Huesca 58 42 8N 0 25W
Huesca □ 58 42 20N 0 1 E
Huéscar 59 37 44N 2 35W
Huétamo 164 18 36N 100 54W
Huete 58 40 10N 2 43W
Hugh, R. 138 25 1 S 134 10 E
Hugh Town 30 49 55N 6 19W
Hughenden 138 20 52 S 144 10 E
Hughes, Austral. 137 30 42 S 129 31 E
Hughes, U.S.A. 147 66 0N 154 20W
Hughesville 162 41 14N 76 44W
Hugo, Colo., U.S.A. 158 39 12N 103 27W
Hugo, Okla., U.S.A. 159 34 0N 95 30W
Hugoton 159 37 18N 101 22W
Huhehot = Huhohaot'e 106 40 50N 110 39 E
Huhohaot'e 106 40 50N 110 39 E
Huhsien 106 34 8N 108 34 E
Huian 109 25 4N 118 47 E
Huianp'u 106 37 30N 106 40 E
Huiarau Ra. 142 38 45 S 176 55 E
Huich'ang 109 25 32N 115 45 E
Huichapán 165 20 24N 99 40W
Huichou 109 23 5N 114 24 E
Huifa Ho, R. 107 43 6N 126 53 E
Huihsien, Honan, China 106 35 32N 113 54 E
Huihsien, Kansu, China 106 33 46N 106 6 E
Huila 128 15 30 S 15 0 E
Huila □ 174 2 30N 75 45W
Huila, Nevado del 174 3 0N 76 0W
Huilai 109 23 4N 116 18 E
Huili 108 26 39N 102 11 E
Huimin 107 37 29N 117 29 E
Huinan 107 42 40N 126 5 E
Huinca Renancó 172 34 51 S 64 22W
Huining 106 35 41N 105 8 E
Huinung 106 39 0N 106 45 E
Huiroa 142 39 15 S 174 30 E
Huise 47 50 54N 3 36 E
Huishui 108 26 8N 106 35 E
Huissen 46 51 57N 5 57 E
Huiting 106 34 6N 116 4 E
Huitse 108 26 22N 103 15 E
Huit'ung 108 26 56N 109 36 E
Huixtla 165 15 9N 92 28W
Huiya 92 24 40N 49 15 E
Huizen 46 52 18N 5 14 E
Hukawng Valley 99 26 30N 96 30 E
Hukou 109 29 45N 116 13 E
Hukuma 123 14 55N 36 2 E
Hukuntsi 128 23 58 S 21 45 E
Hula 123 6 33N 38 30 E
Hulaifa 92 25 58N 41 0 E
Hulan 105 46 0N 126 44 E
Huld 106 45 5N 105 30 E
Hülda 90 31 50N 34 51 E
Hull, Can. 150 45 20N 75 40W
Hull, U.K. 33 53 45N 0 20W
Hullavington 28 51 31N 2 9W
Hulme End 32 53 8N 1 51W
Hulst 47 51 17N 4 2 E
Hultsfred 73 57 30N 15 52 E
Hulun Ch'ih 105 49 1N 117 32 E
Humacao 147 18 9N 65 50W
Humahuaca 172 23 10 S 65 25W
Humaitá 174 7 35 S 62 40W
Humaita 172 27 2 S 58 31W
Humansdorp 128 34 2 S 24 46 E
Humber, Mouth of 33 53 32N 0 8 E
Humber, R. 33 53 40N 0 10W
Humberside □ 33 53 50N 0 30W
Humbert River 136 16 30 S 130 45 E
Humble 159 29 59N 95 10W
Humboldt, Can. 153 52 15N 105 9W
Humboldt, Iowa, U.S.A. 158 42 42N 94 15W
Humboldt, Tenn., U.S.A. 157 35 50N 88 55W
Humboldt Gletscher 12 79 30N 62 0W
Humboldt, R. 160 40 55N 116 0W
Humbolt Mts. 143 44 30 S 168 15 E
Hume 163 36 48N 118 54W
Hume, L. 141 36 0 S 147 0 E
Humenné 53 48 55N 21 50 E
Humphreys, Mt. 163 37 17N 118 40W
Humphreys Pk. 161 35 24N 111 38W
Humpolec 52 49 31N 15 20 E
Humshaugh 35 55 3N 2 8W
Humula 141 35 30 S 147 46 E
Hün 119 29 2N 16 0 E
Hun Chiang, R. 107 40 52N 125 42 E
Huna Floi 74 65 50N 20 50W
Hunan □ 109 27 30N 111 30 E
Hunch'un 107 42 52N 130 21 E
Hundested 73 55 58N 11 52 E
Hundred House 31 52 11N 3 17W
Hundred Mile House 152 51 38N 121 18W
Hundshögen, mt. 72 62 57N 13 46 E
Hunedoara 70 45 40N 22 50 E
Hunedoara □ 70 45 45N 22 54 E
Hünfeld 48 50 40N 9 47 E
Hung Chiang, R. 108 27 7N 109 57 E
Hung Ho, R. 109 32 24N 115 32 E
Hung Liu Ho, R. 106 38 3N 109 10 E
Hung Yen 100 20 39N 106 4 E
Hungan 109 31 18N 114 33 E
Hungary ■ 53 47 20N 19 20 E
Hungary, Plain of 16 47 0N 20 0 E
Hungchiang 109 27 6N 110 0 E
Hungerford, Austral. 139 28 58 S 144 24 E
Hungerford, U.K. 28 51 25N 1 30W
Hunghai Wan 109 22 45N 115 15 E
Hunghu 109 29 49N 113 30 E
Hüngnam 107 39 55N 127 45 E
Hungshui Ho, R. 108 23 24N 110 12 E
Hungtech'eng 106 36 48N 107 6 E
Hungt'ou Hsü 109 22 4N 121 25 E
Hungt'se Hu 107 33 15N 118 45 E
Hungtung 106 36 15N 111 37 E
Hungya 108 29 56N 103 25 E
Hungyüan 108 32 46N 102 42 E
Huni Valley 120 5 33N 1 56W
Hunmanby 33 54 12N 0 19W
Hunsberge 128 27 58 S 17 5 E
Hunsrück, mts. 49 50 0N 7 30 E
Hunstanton 29 52 57N 0 30 E
Hunsur 97 12 16N 76 16 E
Hunte, R. 48 52 47N 8 28 E
Hunter, N.Z. 143 44 36 S 171 2 E
Hunter, N.D., U.S.A. 158 47 12N 97 17W
Hunter, N.Y., U.S.A. 162 42 13N 74 13W
Hunter Hills, The 143 44 26 S 170 46 E
Hunter, I. 138 40 30 S 144 54 E
Hunter I. 152 51 55N 128 0W
Hunter Mts. 143 45 43 S 167 25 E
Hunter, R. 143 44 21 S 169 27 E
Hunter Ra. 141 32 45 S 150 15 E
Hunters Road 127 19 9 S 29 49 E
Hunterston 34 55 43N 4 55W
Hunterton 139 26 12 S 148 30 E
Hunterville 142 39 56 S 175 35 E
Huntingburg 156 38 20N 86 58W
Huntingdon, Can. 150 45 10N 74 10W
Huntingdon, U.K. 29 52 20N 0 11W
Huntingdon, N.Y., U.S.A. 162 40 52N 73 25W
Huntingdon, Pa., U.S.A. 156 40 28N 78 1W
Huntingdon & Peterborough (□) 26 52 23N 0 10W
Huntingdon I. 151 53 48N 56 45W
Huntington, U.K. 33 54 0N 1 4W
Huntington, Id., U.S.A. 160 44 22N 117 21W
Huntington, Ind., U.S.A. 156 40 52N 85 30W
Huntington, Ut., U.S.A. 160 39 24N 111 1W
Huntington, W. Va., U.S.A. 156 38 20N 82 30W
Huntington Beach 163 33 40N 118 0W
Huntington Park 161 34 58N 118 15W
Huntly, N.Z. 142 37 34 S 175 11 E
Huntly, U.K. 37 57 27N 2 48W
Huntsville, Can. 150 45 20N 79 14W
Huntsville, Ala., U.S.A. 157 34 45N 86 35W
Huntsville, Tex., U.S.A. 159 30 50N 95 35W
Hunyani Dams. 127 18 0 S 31 10 E
Hunyani, R. 127 18 0 S 31 10 E
Hunyüan 106 39 44N 113 42 E
Hunza, R. 95 36 24N 75 50 E
Huohsien 106 36 38N 111 43 E
Huon, G. 135 7 0 S 147 30 E
Huon Pen. 135 6 20 S 147 30 E
Huong Hoa 100 16 37N 106 45 E
Huong Khe 100 18 13N 105 41 E
Huonville 138 43 0 S 147 5 E
Huoshaop'u 107 43 23N 130 26 E
Hupei □ 109 31 5N 113 5 E
Hurbanovo 53 47 51N 18 11 E
Hurezani 70 44 49N 23 40 E
Hurghada 122 27 15N 33 50 E
Hŭrghita □ 70 46 30N 25 30 E
Hŭrghita Mţii 70 46 25N 25 35 E
Hurley, N. Mex., U.S.A. 161 32 45N 108 7W
Hurley, Wis., U.S.A. 158 46 26N 90 10W
Hurlford 34 55 35N 4 29W
Hurliness 37 58 47N 3 15W
Hurlock 162 38 38N 75 52W
Huron, Calif., U.S.A. 163 36 12N 120 6W
Huron, S.D., U.S.A. 158 44 30N 98 20W
Hurricane 161 37 10N 113 12W
Hursley 28 51 1N 1 23W
Hurso 123 9 35N 41 33 E
Hurstbourne Tarrant 28 51 17N 1 27W
Hurstpierpoint 29 50 56N 0 11W
Hurum, Buskerud, Norway 71 59 36N 10 23 E
Hurum, Oppland, Norway 71 61 9N 8 46 E
Hurunui, R. 143 42 54 S 173 18 E
Hurup 73 56 46N 8 25 E
Husaby 73 58 35N 13 25 E
Húsavík 74 66 3N 17 21W
Husband's Bosworth 28 52 27N 1 3W
Husi 70 46 41N 28 7 E
Husinish Pt. 36 57 59N 7 6W
Huskvarna 73 57 47N 14 15 E
Huslia 147 65 40N 156 30W
Husøy 71 61 3N 4 44 E
Hussar 152 51 3N 112 41W
Hussein (Allenby) Br. 90 31 53N 35 33 E
Hustopéce 53 48 57N 16 43 E
Husum, Ger. 48 54 27N 9 3 E
Husum, Sweden 72 63 21N 19 12 E
Hutchinson, Kans., U.S.A. 159 38 3N 97 59W
Hutchinson, Minn, U.S.A. 158 44 50N 94 22W
Huttenberg 52 46 56N 14 33 E
Hüttental 47 50 53N 8 1 E
Huttig 159 33 5N 92 10W
Hutton, Mt. 139 25 51 S 148 20 E
Hutton, oilfield 19 61 0N 1 30 E
Hutton Ra. 137 24 45 S 124 30 E
Huttwil 50 47 7N 7 50 E
Huwarā 90 32 9N 35 15 E
Huwun 123 4 23N 40 6 E
Huy 47 50 31N 5 15 E
Huyton 32 53 25N 2 52W
Hvaler 71 59 4N 11 1 E
Hvammsfjörður 74 65 4N 22 5W
Hvammur 74 65 13N 21 49W
Hvar 63 43 10N 16 45 E
Hvar, I. 63 43 11N 16 28 E
Hvarski Kanal 63 43 15N 16 35 E
Hvítá, Arnessýsla, Iceland 74 64 0N 20 58W
Hvítá, Mýrasýsla, Iceland 74 64 40N 21 5W
Hvítárvatn 74 63 37N 19 50W
Hvitsten 71 59 35N 10 42 E
Hwachon-chŏsuji 107 38 5N 127 50 E
Hwang Ho = Huang Ho, R. 107 36 50N 118 20 E
Hwekum 98 26 7N 95 22 E
Hyannis, Mass., U.S.A. 162 41 39N 70 17W
Hyannis, Nebr., U.S.A. 158 41 60N 101 45W
Hyargas Nuur 105 49 12N 93 34 E
Hyattsville 162 38 59N 76 55W
Hybo 72 61 49N 16 15 E
Hydaburg 147 55 15N 132 45W
Hyde, N.Z. 143 45 18 S 170 16 E
Hyde, U.K. 32 53 26N 2 6W
Hyde Park 162 41 47N 73 56W
Hyden 137 32 24 S 118 46 E
Hyderabad, India 96 17 10N 78 29 E
Hyderabad, Pak. 94 25 23N 68 36 E
Hyderabad □ 94 25 3N 68 24 E
Hyères 45 43 8N 6 9 E
Hyères, Is. d' 45 43 0N 6 28 E
Hyesan 107 41 20N 128 10 E
Hyland Post 139 57 40N 128 10W
Hyland, R. 152 59 52N 128 12W
Hylestad 71 59 6N 7 29 E
Hyllested 71 56 17N 10 46 E
Hyltebruk 73 56 59N 13 15 E
Hymia 95 33 40N 78 2 E
Hyndman Pk. 160 44 4N 114 0W
Hynish 34 56 27N 6 54W
Hynish B. 34 56 29N 6 40W
Hyōgo-ken □ 110 35 15N 135 0 E
Hyrum 160 41 35N 111 56W
Hysham 160 46 21N 107 11W
Hythe 29 51 4N 1 5 E
Hyūga 110 32 25N 131 35 E
Hyvinkä 75 60 38N 24 50 E

I

I Ho, R. 107 34 10N 118 4 E
I-n-Azaoua 119 20 45N 7 31 E
I-n-Échaïe 118 20 10N 2 5W
I-n-Gall 121 6 51N 7 1 E
I-n-Tabedog 118 19 54N 1 3 E
Iabès, Erg 118 27 30N 2 2W
Iaco, R. 174 10 25 S 70 30W
Iaçu 171 12 45 S 40 13W
Iakora 129 23 6 S 46 40 E
Ialomiţa □ 70 44 30N 27 30 E
Ianca 70 45 6N 27 29 E
Iar Connacht 39 53 20N 9 20W
Iara 70 46 31N 23 35 E
Iaşi □ 70 47 20N 27 0 E
Iaşi (Jassy) 70 47 10N 27 40 E
Iauaretê 174 0 30N 69 5W
Iaucdjovac, (Port Harrison) 149 58 25N 78 15W
Iba 103 15 22N 120 0 E
Ibadan 121 7 22N 3 58 E
Ibagué 174 4 27N 73 14W
Ibaiti 171 23 50 S 50 10W
Iballja 68 42 12N 20 0 E
Ibar, R. 66 43 15N 20 40 E
Ibara 110 34 36N 133 28 E

Ibaraki-ken □ **Inhambane**

Ibaraki-ken □ **111** 36 10N 140 10 E
Ibararaki **111** 34 49N 135 34 E
Ibarra **174** 0 21N 78 7W
Ibba **123** 4 49N 29 2 E
Ibba, Bahr el **123** 5 30N 28 55 E
Ibbenbüren **48** 52 16N 7 41 E
Ibembo **126** 2 35N 23 35 E
Ibera, Laguna **172** 28 30 S 57 9W
Iberian Peninsula **16** 40 0N 5 0W
Iberville **150** 45 19N 73 17W
Iberville, Lac d' **150** 55 55N 73 15W
Ibi **121** 8 15N 9 50 E
Ibiá **171** 19 30 S 46 30W
Ibicaraí **171** 14 51 S 39 36W
Ibicuí **171** 14 51 S 39 59W
Ibicuy **172** 33 55 S 59 10W
Ibioapaba, Serra da **170** 20 14 S 40 25W
Ibipetuba **171** 11 0 S 44 32W
Ibiracu **171** 19 50 S 40 30W
Ibitiara **171** 12 39 S 42 13W
Ibiza **59** 38 54N 1 26 E
Ibiza, I. **59** 39 0N 1 30 E
Íblei, Monti **65** 37 15N 14 45 E
Ibo **127** 12 22 S 40 32 E
Ibonma **103** 3 22 S 133 31 E
Ibotirama **171** 12 13 S 43 12W
Ibriktepe **68** 41 2N 26 33 E
Ibshawâi **122** 29 21N 30 40 E
Ibstock **28** 52 42N 1 23W
Ibu **103** 1 35N 127 25 E
Ibuki-Sanchi **111** 35 25N 136 34 E
Ibŭneşti **70** 46 45N 24 50 E
Iburg **48** 52 10N 8 3 E
Ibusuki **110** 31 12N 130 32 E
Ibwe Munyama **127** 16 5 S 28 31 E
Ica **174** 14 0 S 75 30W
Ica, R. **174** 2 55 S 69 0W
Icabarú **174** 4 20N 61 45W
Içana **174** 1 21N 69 0W
Icatu **170** 2 46 S 44 4W
Iceland, I. ■ **74** 65 0N 19 0W
Icha **77** 55 30N 156 0 E
Ichang **109** 25 25N 112 55 E
Ich'ang **109** 30 40N 111 20 E
Ichchapuram **96** 19 10N 84 40 E
Icheng **109** 32 16N 119 12 E
Ich'eng, Hupeh, China **109** 31 43N 112 12 E
Ich'eng, Shansi, China **106** 35 42N 111 40 E
Ichihara **111** 35 28N 140 5 E
Ichikawa **111** 35 44N 139 55 E
Ichilo, R. **174** 16 30 S 64 45W
Ichinomiya, Gifu, Japan **111** 35 18N 136 48 E
Ichinomiya, Kumamoto, Japan **110** 32 58N 131 5 E
Ichinoseki **112** 38 55N 141 8 E
Ichŏn **107** 37 17N 127 27 E
Icht **118** 29 6N 8 54W
Ichtegem **47** 51 5N 3 1 E
Ich'uan **106** 36 4N 110 6 E
Ich'un **105** 47 42N 128 54 E
Ichün **106** 35 23N 109 7 E
Ich'un, Heilungkiang, China **105** 47 42N 128 54 E
Ich'un, Kiangsi, China **109** 27 47N 114 22 E
Icó **170** 6 24 S 38 51W
Icoraci **170** 1 18 S 48 28W
Icy C. **12** 70 25N 162 0W
Icy Str. **153** 58 20N 135 30W
Ida Grove **158** 42 20N 95 25W
Ida Valley **137** 28 42 S 120 29 E
Idabel **159** 33 53N 94 50W
Idaga Hamus **123** 14 13N 39 35 E
Idah **121** 6 10N 6 40 E
Idaho □ **160** 44 10N 114 0W
Idaho City **160** 43 50N 115 52W
Idaho Falls **160** 43 30N 112 10W
Idaho Springs **160** 39 49N 105 30W
Idanha-a-Nova **56** 39 50N 7 15W
Idanre **121** 7 8N 5 5 E
Idar-Oberstein **49** 49 43N 7 19 E
Idd el Ghanam **117** 11 30N 24 25 E
Iddan **91** 6 10N 49 5 E
Idehan **119** 27 10N 11 30 E
Idehan Marzūq **119** 24 50N 13 51 E
Idelès **119** 23 58N 5 53 E
Idfû **122** 25 0N 32 49 E
Idhi Oros **69** 35 15N 24 45 E
Idhra **69** 37 20N 23 28 E
Idi **102** 4 55N 97 45 E
Idi Amin Dada, L. **93** 0 25 S 29 40 E
Idiofa **124** 4 55 S 19 42 E
Idkerberget **72** 60 22N 15 15 E
Idle **33** 53 50N 1 45W
Idle, R. **33** 53 27N 0 49W
Idmiston **28** 51 8N 1 43W
Idna **90** 31 34N 34 58 E
Idria **163** 36 25N 120 41W
Idrija **63** 46 0N 14 5 E
Idritsa **80** 56 25N 28 57 E
Idstein **49** 50 13N 8 17 E
Idsworth **29** 50 56N 0 56W
Idutywa **125** 32 8 S 28 18 E
Ieper **47** 50 51N 2 53 E
Ierápetra **69** 35 0N 25 44 E
Ierissós **68** 40 22N 23 52 E
Ierissóu Kólpos **68** 40 27N 23 57 E
Ierzu **64** 39 48N 9 32 E
Ieshima-Shotō **110** 34 40N 134 32 E
Iesi **63** 43 32N 13 12 E
Ifach, Punta **59** 38 38N 0 5 E
Ifanadiana **129** 21 29 S 47 39 E
Ife **121** 7 30N 4 31 E
Iférouâne **121** 19 5N 8 35 E
Ifni **118** 29 25N 10 10W
Ifon **121** 6 58N 5 40 E
Iga **111** 34 45N 136 10 E
Iganga **126** 0 30N 33 28 E
Igarapava **171** 20 3 S 47 47W
Igarapé Açu **170** 1 4 S 47 33W
Igarapé-Mirim **170** 1 59 S 48 58W
Igarka **77** 67 30N 87 20 E
Igatimi **173** 24 5 S 55 30W
Igatpuri **96** 19 40N 73 35 E
Igbetti **121** 8 44N 4 8 E
Igbo-Ora **121** 7 10N 3 15 E
Igboho **121** 8 40N 3 50 E
Iggesund **72** 61 39N 17 10 E
Igherm **118** 30 7N 8 18W
Ighil Izane **118** 35 44N 0 31 E
Iglene **118** 22 57N 4 58 E
Iglésias **64** 39 19N 8 27 E
Igli **118** 30 25N 2 12W
Iglino **84** 54 50N 56 26 E
Igloolik Island **149** 69 20N 81 30W
Igma **118** 29 9N 6 11W
Igma, Gebel el **122** 28 55N 34 0 E
Ignace **150** 49 30N 91 40W
Igoshevo **81** 59 25N 42 35 E
Igoumenítsa **68** 39 32N 20 18 E
Igra **84** 57 33N 53 7 E
Iguaçu, Cat. del **173** 25 41N 54 26W
Iguaçu, R. **173** 25 30 S 53 10W
Iguala **165** 18 20N 99 40W
Igualada **58** 41 37N 1 37 E
Iguape **171** 24 43 S 47 33W
Iguape, R. **173** 24 40 S 48 0W
Iguassu = Iguaçu **173** 25 41N 54 26W
Iguatu **170** 6 20 S 39 18W
Iguéla **124** 2 0 S 9 16 E
Igumale **121** 6 47N 7 55 E
Igunga □ **126** 4 20 S 33 45 E
Ihiala **121** 5 40N 6 55 E
Ihosy **129** 22 24 S 46 8 E
Ihotry, L. **129** 21 56 S 43 41 E
Ihsien, Anwhei, China **109** 29 53N 117 57 E
Ihsien, Hopeh, China **106** 39 21N 115 29 E
Ihsien, Liaoning, China **107** 41 34N 121 15 E
Ihsien, Shantung, China **107** 37 11N 119 55 E
Ihuang **109** 27 32N 115 57 E
Ii **74** 65 15N 25 30 E
Iida **111** 35 35N 138 0 E
Iiey **138** 18 53 S 141 12 E
Iijoki **74** 65 20N 26 15 E
Iisalmi **74** 63 32N 27 10 E
Iizuka **110** 33 38N 130 42 E
Ijebu-Igbo **121** 6 56N 4 1 E
Ijebu-Ode **121** 6 47N 3 52 E
IJmuiden **46** 52 28N 4 35 E
IJssel, R. **46** 52 35N 5 50 E
IJsselmeer **46** 52 45N 5 20 E
IJsselmuiden **46** 52 34N 5 57 E
IJsselstein **46** 52 1N 5 2 E
Ijuí, R. **173** 27 58 S 55 20W
Ijūin **110** 31 37N 130 24 E
IJzendijke **47** 51 19N 3 37 E
IJzer, R. **47** 51 9N 2 44 E
Ik, R. **84** 55 55N 52 36 E
Ikamatua **141** 42 15 S 171 41 E
Ikare **121** 7 18N 5 40 E
Ikaria, I. **69** 37 35N 26 10 E
Ikast **73** 56 8N 9 10 E
Ikawa **111** 35 13N 138 15 E
Ikeda **111** 34 1N 133 48 E
Ikeja **121** 6 28N 3 45 E
Ikela **124** 1 0 S 23 35 E
Ikerre **121** 7 25N 5 19 E
Ikhtiman **67** 42 27N 23 48 E
Iki **110** 33 45N 129 42 E
Iki-Kaikyō **110** 33 40N 129 45 E
Ikimba L. **126** 1 30 S 31 20 E
Ikire **121** 7 10N 4 15 E
Ikirun **121** 7 54N 4 40 E
Ikitsuki-Shima **110** 33 23N 129 26 E
Ikole **121** 7 40N 5 37 E
Ikom **121** 6 0N 8 42 E
Ikopa, R. **129** 17 45 S 46 40 E
Ikot Ekpene **121** 5 12N 7 40 E
Ikungu **126** 1 33 S 33 42 E
Ikuno **110** 35 10N 134 48 E
Ila **121** 8 0N 4 51 E
Ilam **95** 26 58N 87 58 E
Ilan, China **105** 46 14N 129 33 E
Ilan, Taiwan **109** 24 45N 121 44 E
Ilanskiy **77** 56 14N 96 3 E
Ilanz **51** 46 46N 9 12 E
Ilaomita, R. **47** 44 47N 27 0 E
Ilaro Agege **121** 6 53N 3 3 E
Ilayangudi **97** 9 34N 78 37 E
Ilbilbie **138** 21 45 S 149 20 E
Ilchester **28** 51 0N 2 41W
Ile-à-la Crosse **153** 55 27N 107 53W
Ile-à-la-Crosse, Lac **153** 55 40N 107 45W
Ile Bouchard, L' **42** 47 7N 0 26 E
Ile de France □ **43** 49 0N 2 20 E
Ilebo **124** 4 17 S 20 47 E
Ileje □ **127** 9 30 S 33 25 E
Ilek **84** 51 32N 53 21 E
Ilek, R. **84** 51 30N 53 22 E
Ilen R. **39** 51 38N 9 19W
Ilero **121** 8 0N 3 20 E
Ilesha, West-Central, Nigeria **121** 7 37N 4 40 E
Ilesha, Western, Nigeria **121** 8 57N 3 28 E
Ilford **153** 56 4N 95 35W
Ilfov □ **70** 44 20N 26 0 E
Ilfracombe, Austral. **138** 23 30 S 144 30 E
Ilfracombe, U.K. **30** 51 13N 4 8W
Ilha Grande, Baia da **171** 23 9 S 44 30W
Ílhavo **56** 40 33N 8 43W
Ilheus **171** 14 49 S 39 2W
Ili **85** 45 53N 77 10 E
Ilia **70** 45 57N 22 40 E
Ilia □ **69** 37 45N 21 35 E
Iliamna L. **147** 59 35N 155 30W
Iliang, Yunnan, China **108** 24 54N 103 9 E
Iliang, Yunnan, China **108** 27 35N 104 1 E
Ilich **85** 40 50N 68 27 E
Ilico **172** 34 50 S 72 20W
Iliff **158** 40 50N 103 3W
Ilíki **69** 38 24N 23 15 E
Ilio Pt. **147** 21 13N 157 16W
Iliodhrómia **68** 39 12N 23 50 E
Ilion **162** 43 0N 75 3W
Ilirska Bistrica **63** 45 34N 14 14 E
Iliysk **76** 44 10N 77 20 E
Ilkal **97** 15 57N 76 8 E
Ilkeston **33** 52 59N 1 19W
Ilkley **21** 53 56N 1 49W
Illana B. **103** 7 35N 123 45 E
Illapel **172** 32 0 S 71 10W
'Illar **90** 32 23N 35 7 E
Ille **44** 42 40N 2 37 E
Ille-et-Vilaine □ **42** 48 10N 1 30W
Iller, R. **49** 47 53N 10 10 E
Illescás **56** 40 8N 3 51W
Illig **91** 7 47N 49 45 E
Illimani, Mte. **174** 16 30 S 67 50W
Illinois □ **155** 40 15N 89 30W
Illinois, R. **155** 40 10N 90 20W
Illizi **119** 26 31N 8 32 E
Illora **57** 37 17N 3 53W
Ilmen, Oz. **80** 58 15N 31 10 E
Ilmenau **48** 50 41N 10 55 E
Ilminster **28** 50 55N 2 56W
Ilo **174** 17 40 S 71 20W
Ilobu **121** 7 45N 4 25 E
Ilohuli Shan **105** 51 20N 124 20 E
Iloilo **103** 10 45N 122 33 E
Ilok **66** 45 15N 19 20 E
Ilora **121** 7 45N 3 50 E
Ilorin **121** 8 30N 4 35 E
Ilovatka **81** 50 30N 46 50 E
Ilovlya **83** 49 15N 44 2 E
Ilovlya, R. **83** 49 38N 44 20 E
Ilowa **54** 51 30N 15 10 E
Ilubabor □ **123** 7 25N 35 0 E
Ilukste **80** 55 55N 26 20 E
Ilung **108** 31 34N 106 24 E
Ilva Micá **70** 47 17N 24 40 E
Ilwaki **103** 7 55 S 126 30 E
Ilyichevsk **82** 46 10N 30 35 E
Imabari **110** 34 4N 133 0 E
Imadahane **118** 32 8N 7 0W
Imaichi **111** 36 6N 139 16 E
Imaloto, R. **129** 23 10 S 45 15 E
Iman = Dalneretchensk **77** 45 50N 133 40 E
Imari **110** 33 15N 129 52 E
Imasa **122** 18 0N 36 12 E
Imathía □ **68** 40 30N 22 15 E
Imbâbah **122** 30 5N 31 12 E
Imbler **160** 45 31N 118 0W
Imbros = Imroz **68** 40 10N 26 0 E
Imen **108** 24 40N 102 9 E
Imeni Panfilova **85** 43 23N 77 7 E
Imeni Poliny Osipenko **77** 55 25N 136 29 E
Imeri, Serra **174** 0 50N 65 25W
Imerimandroso **129** 17 26 S 48 35 E
Imi (Hinna) **123** 6 35N 42 30 E
Imi n'Tanoute **118** 31 13N 8 51 E
Imienp'o **107** 45 0N 128 16 E
Imishly **83** 39 49N 48 4 E
Imiteg **118** 29 43N 8 10W
Imlay **160** 40 45N 118 9W
Immingham **33** 53 37N 0 12W
Immokalee **157** 26 25N 81 20W
Imo □ **121** 5 15N 7 20 E
Imola **63** 44 20N 11 42 E
Imotski **66** 43 27N 17 21 E
Imperatriz **170** 5 30 S 47 29W
Impéria **62** 43 52N 8 0 E
Imperial, Can. **153** 51 21N 105 28W
Imperial, Calif., U.S.A. **161** 32 52N 115 34W
Imperial, Nebr., U.S.A. **158** 40 38N 101 39W
Imperial Beach **163** 32 35N 117 8W
Imperial Dam **161** 32 50N 114 30W
Imperial Valley **163** 32 55N 115 30W
Imperieuse Reef **136** 17 36 S 118 50 E
Impfondo **124** 1 40N 18 0 E
Imphal **98** 24 48N 93 56 E
Imphy **43** 46 56N 3 15 E
Imroz = Gökçeada **68** 40 10N 26 0 E
Imst **52** 47 15N 10 44 E
Imuruan B. **103** 10 40N 119 10 E
In Belbel **118** 27 55N 1 12 E
In Delimane **121** 15 52N 1 31 E
In-Gall **121** 16 51N 7 1 E
In Rhar **118** 27 10N 1 59 E
In Salah **118** 27 10N 1 59 E
In Tallak **121** 16 19N 3 15 E
Ina **111** 35 50N 138 0 E
Ina-Bonchi **111** 35 45N 137 58 E
Inagh **39** 52 53N 9 11W
Inajá **170** 8 54 S 37 49W
Inangahua Junc. **143** 41 52 S 171 59 E
Inanwatan **103** 2 10 S 132 5 E
Iñapari **174** 11 0 S 69 40W
Inari **74** 68 54N 27 5 E
Inari, L. **74** 69 0N 28 0 E
Inazawa **111** 35 15N 136 47 E
Inca **58** 39 43N 2 54 E
Incaguasi **172** 29 12 S 71 5W
Ince **32** 53 32N 2 38W
Ince Burnu **92** 42 2N 35 0 E
Inch **39** 52 42N 8 8W
Inch Br. **39** 52 49N 9 6W
Inchard, Loch **36** 58 28N 5 2W
Inchcape Rock **35** 56 26N 2 24W
Inchigeelagh **39** 51 50N 9 8W
Inchini **123** 8 55N 37 37 E
Inchkeith, I. **35** 56 2N 3 8W
Inchnadamph **36** 58 9N 5 0W
Inch'ŏn **107** 37 27N 126 40 E
Inchture **35** 56 26N 3 8W
Incio **56** 42 39N 7 21W
Incomáti, R. **129** 25 15 S 32 35 E
Incudine, Mte. l' **45** 41 50N 9 12 E
Inda Silase **123** 14 10N 38 15 E
Indaal L. **34** 55 44N 6 20W
Indalsälven **72** 62 36N 17 30 E
Indaw **98** 24 15N 96 5 E
Indbir **123** 8 7N 37 52 E
Indefatigable, gasfield **19** 53 20N 2 40 E
Independence, Calif., U.S.A. **163** 36 51N 118 7W
Independence, Iowa, U.S.A. **158** 42 27N 91 52W
Independence, Kans., U.S.A. **159** 37 10N 95 50W
Independence, Mo., U.S.A. **158** 39 3N 94 25W
Independence, Oreg., U.S.A. **160** 44 53N 123 6W
Independence Fjord **12** 82 10N 29 0W
Independence Mts. **160** 41 30N 116 2W
Independência **170** 5 30 S 40 19W
Independencia, La **165** 16 31N 91 47W
Independenţa **70** 45 25N 27 42 E
Inderborskiy **83** 48 30N 51 42 E
India ■ **87** 20 0N 80 0 E
Indian Cabins **152** 59 52N 117 2W
Indian Harbour **151** 54 27N 57 13W
Indian Head **153** 50 30N 103 35W
Indian House L. **151** 56 30N 64 30W
Indian Lake **162** 43 47N 74 16W
Indian Ocean **11** 5 0 S 75 0 E
Indian River B. **162** 38 36N 75 4W
Indiana **156** 40 38N 79 9W
Indiana □ **156** 40 0N 86 0W
Indianapolis **156** 39 42N 86 10W
Indianola, Iowa, U.S.A. **158** 41 20N 93 38W
Indianola, Miss., U.S.A. **159** 33 27N 90 40W
Indianópolis **171** 19 2 S 47 55 E
Indiapora **171** 19 57 S 50 17W
Indiaroba **171** 11 32 S 37 31W
Indiga **78** 67 50N 48 50 E
Indigirka, R. **77** 69 0N 147 0 E
Indija **66** 45 6N 20 7 E
Indio **163** 33 46N 116 15W
Indonesia ■ **102** 5 0 S 115 0 E
Indore **94** 22 42N 75 53 E
Indramaju **103** 6 21 S 108 20 E
Indramaju, Tg. **103** 6 20 S 108 20 E
Indravati, R. **96** 19 0N 81 15 E
Indre □ **43** 47 12N 1 39 E
Indre-et-Loire □ **42** 47 12N 0 40 E
Indre, R. **42** 47 2N 1 8 E
Indre Söndeled **71** 58 46N 9 5 E
Indus, Mouth of the **94** 24 00N 68 00 E
Indus, R. **94** 28 40N 70 10 E
Inebolu **92** 41 55N 33 40 E
Infante, Kaap **128** 34 27 S 20 51 E
Infantes **59** 38 43N 3 1W
Infiernillo, Presa del **164** 18 9N 102 0W
Infiesto **56** 43 21N 5 21W
Ingá **171** 7 17 S 35 36W
Ingatestone **29** 51 40N 0 23W
Ingelmunster **47** 50 56N 3 16 E
Ingende **124** 0 12 S 18 57 E
Ingenio Santa Ana **172** 27 25 S 65 40W
Ingesvang **73** 56 10N 9 20 E
Ingham **138** 18 43 S 146 10 E
Ingichka **85** 39 47N 65 58 E
Ingleborough, mt. **32** 54 11N 2 23W
Inglefield Land **143** 78 30N 70 0W
Ingleton **32** 54 9N 2 29W
Inglewood, Queensland, Austral. **139** 28 25 S 151 8 E
Inglewood, Vic., Austral. **140** 36 29 S 143 53 E
Inglewood, N.Z. **142** 39 9 S 174 14 E
Inglewood, U.S.A. **163** 33 58N 118 21W
Ingoldmells, Pt. **33** 53 11N 0 21 E
Ingólfshöfði **74** 63 48N 16 39W
Ingolstadt **49** 48 45N 11 26 E
Ingomar **160** 46 43N 107 37W
Ingonish **151** 46 42N 60 18W
Ingore **120** 12 24N 15 48W
Ingul, R. **82** 47 30N 32 15 E
Ingulec **82** 47 42N 33 4 E
Ingulets, R. **82** 47 20N 33 20 E
Inguri, R. **83** 42 58N 42 17 E
Inhaca, I. **129** 26 1 S 32 57 E
Inhafenga **129** 20 36 S 33 47 E
Inhambane **125** 23 54 S 35 30 E

Inhambane □ Itaueira

Inhambane □ 129 22 30 S 34 20 E
Inhambupe 171 11 47 S 38 21W
Inhaminga 127 18 26 S 35 0 E
Inharrime 129 24 30 S 35 0 E
Inharrime, R. 129 24 30 S 35 0 E
Inhassoro 127 21 50 S 35 15 E
Inhuma 170 6 40 S 41 42W
Inhumas 171 16 22 S 49 30W
Iniesta 59 39 27N 1 45W
Ining, Kwangsi-Chuang, China 109 25 8N 109 57 E
Ining, Sinkiang-Uigur, China 105 43 54N 81 21 E
Inírida, R. 174 3 0N 68 40W
Inishark 38 53 36N 10 17W
Inishark I. 38 53 38N 10 17W
Inishbofin I., Donegal, Ireland 38 55 10N 8 10W
Inishbofin I., Galway, Ireland 38 53 35N 10 12W
Inisheer 39 53 3N 9 32W
Inishfree B. 38 55 4N 8 20W
Inishkea Is. 38 54 8N 10 10W
Inishmaan I. 39 53 5N 9 35W
Inishmore, I. 39 53 8N 9 45W
Inishmurray I. 38 54 26N 8 40W
Inishowen Hd. 38 55 14N 6 56W
Inishowen, Pen. 38 55 14N 7 15W
Inishrush 38 54 52N 6 32W
Inishtooskert I. 39 52 10N 10 35W
Inishturk I. 38 53 42N 10 8W
Inishvickillane 39 52 3N 10 37W
Inistioge 39 52 30N 7 5W
Injune 139 25 46 S 148 32 E
Inkberrow 28 52 13N 1 59W
Inklin 152 58 56N 133 5W
Inklin, R. 152 58 50N 133 10W
Inkom 160 42 51N 112 7W
Inkpen Beacon 28 51 22N 1 28W
Inle Aing 98 20 30N 96 58 E
Inn, R. 49 48 35N 13 28 E
Innamincka 139 27 44 S 140 46 E
Innellan 34 55 54N 4 58W
Inner Mongolia □ 106 44 50N 117 40 E
Inner Sound 36 57 30N 5 55W
Innerleithen 35 55 37N 3 4W
Innertkirchen 50 46 43N 8 14 E
Innetalling I. 150 56 0N 79 0W
Innfield 38 53 25N 6 50W
Inniscrone 38 54 13N 69 0W
Innisfail, Austral. 138 17 33 S 146 5 E
Innisfail, Can. 152 52 0N 113 57W
Innishannon 39 51 45N 8 40W
Inniskeen 38 54 0N 6 35W
In'no-shima 110 34 19N 133 10 E
Innsbruck 52 47 16N 11 23 E
Ino 110 33 33N 133 26 E
Inocência 171 19 47 S 51 48W
Inongo 124 1 35 S 18 30 E
Inosu 174 12 22N 71 38W
Inoucdjouac (Port Harrison) 149 58 27N 78 6W
Inowrocław 54 52 50N 18 20 E
Inpundong 107 41 25N 126 34 E
Inquisivi 174 16 50 S 66 45W
Ins 50 47 1N 7 7 E
Insch 37 57 20N 2 39W
Inscription, C. 137 25 29 S 112 59 E
Insein 98 17 15N 96 0 E
Însurăţei 70 44 50N 27 40 E
Intendente Alvear 172 35 12 S 63 32W
Interior 158 43 46N 101 59W
Interlaken, Switz. 50 46 41N 7 50 E
Interlaken, U.S.A. 162 42 37N 76 43W
International Falls 158 48 36N 93 25W
Interview I. 101 12 55N 92 42 E
Inthanon, Mt. 101 18 35N 98 29 E
Intiyaco 172 28 50 S 60 0W
Intragna 51 46 11N 8 42 E
Inubō-Zaki 111 35 42N 140 52 E
Inútil, B. 176 53 30 S 70 15W
Inuvik 147 68 16N 133 40W
Inuyama 111 35 23N 136 56 E
Inver B. 38 54 35N 8 28W
Inverallochy 37 57 40N 1 56W
Inveran, Ireland 39 53 14N 9 28W
Inveran, U.K. 37 57 58N 4 26W
Inveraray 34 56 13N 5 5W
Inverbervie 37 56 50N 2 17W
Invercargill 143 46 24 S 168 24 E
Inverell 139 29 45 S 151 8 E
Invergarry 37 57 5N 4 48W
Invergordon 37 57 41N 4 10W
Invergowrie 35 56 29N 3 5W
Inverie 36 57 2N 5 40W
Inverkeilor 37 56 38N 2 33W
Inverkeithing 35 56 2N 3 24W
Inverleigh 140 38 6 S 144 3 E
Invermere 152 50 30N 116 2W
Invermoriston 37 57 13N 4 38W
Inverness, Can. 151 46 15N 61 19W
Inverness, U.K. 37 57 29N 4 12W
Inverness, U.S.A. 157 28 50N 82 20W
Inverness (□) 26 57 6N 4 40W
Invershiel 36 57 13N 5 25W
Inverurie 37 57 15N 2 21W
Inverway 136 17 50 S 129 38 E
Investigator Group 136 34 45 S 134 20 E
Investigator Str. 140 35 30 S 137 0 E
Inyanga 127 18 12 S 32 40 E
Inyangahi, mt. 127 18 20 S 32 20 E
Inyantue 127 18 30 S 26 40 E
Inyazura 127 18 40 S 31 40 E
Inyo Range 161 37 0N 118 0W
Inyokern 163 35 37N 117 54W
Inywa 98 22 4N 94 44 E
Inza 81 53 55N 46 25 E
Inzell 49 47 48N 12 15 E
Inzer 84 54 14N 57 34 E
Inzhavino 81 52 22N 42 23 E
Ioánnina (Janinà) □ 68 39 39N 20 57 E
Iōhen 110 32 58N 132 32 E
Iola 159 38 0N 95 20W
Ioma 135 8 19 S 147 52 E
Ion Corvin 70 44 7N 27 50 E
Iona I. 34 56 20N 6 25W
Ionava 80 55 8N 24 12 E
Ione, Calif., U.S.A. 163 38 20N 121 0W
Ione, Wash., U.S.A. 160 48 44N 117 29W
Ionia 156 42 59N 85 7W
Ionian Is. = Ionioi Nisoi 69 38 40N 20 0 E
Ionian Sea 61 37 30N 17 30 E
Iónioi Nísoi 69 38 40N 20 8 E
Ioniškis 80 56 13N 23 35 E
Iori, R. 83 41 12N 46 10 E
Íos, I. 69 36 41N 25 20 E
Iowa □ 158 42 18N 93 30W
Iowa City 158 41 40N 91 35W
Iowa Falls 158 42 30N 93 15W
Ipala 126 4 30 S 33 5 E
Ipameri 171 17 44 S 48 9W
Ipanema 75 9 48 S 41 45W
Ipáti 69 38 52N 22 14 E
Ipatovo 83 45 45N 42 50 E
Ipel, R. 53 48 10N 19 35 E
Ipiales 174 0 50N 77 37W
Ipiaú 171 14 8 S 39 44W
Ipin 108 28 48N 104 33 E
Ipinlang 108 25 5N 101 58 E
Ipirá 171 12 10 S 39 44W
Ipiros □ 68 39 30N 20 30 E
Ipixuna 174 7 0 S 71 40W
Ipoh 101 4 35N 101 5 E
Iporá 171 16 28 S 51 7W
Ippy 117 6 5N 21 7 E
Ipsárion Óros 68 40 40N 24 40 E
Ipswich, Austral. 139 27 35 S 152 46 E
Ipswich, U.K. 29 52 4N 1 9 E
Ipswich, N.H., U.S.A. 162 42 40N 70 50W
Ipswich, S.D., U.S.A. 158 45 28N 99 20W
Ipu 170 4 23 S 40 44W
Ipueiras 170 4 33 S 40 43W
Ipupiara 171 11 49 S 42 37W
Iput, R. 80 53 0N 32 10 E
Iquique 174 20 19 S 70 5W
Iquitos 174 3 45 S 73 10W
Iracoubo 175 5 30N 53 10W
Iráklia, I. 69 36 50N 25 28 E
Iráklion 69 35 20N 25 12 E
Iráklion □ 69 35 10N 25 10 E
Irako-Zaki 111 34 35N 137 1 E
Irala 173 25 55 S 54 35W
Iramba □ 126 4 30 S 34 30 E
Iran ■ 93 33 0N 53 0 E
Iran, Pegunungan 102 2 20N 114 50 E
Iran, Plateau of 43 33 00N 55 0 E
Iranamadu Tank 97 9 23N 80 29 E
Iranshahr 93 27 75N 60 40 E
Irapa 174 10 34N 62 35W
Irapuato 164 20 40N 101 40W
Iraq ■ 92 33 0N 44 0 E
Irarrar, W. 118 20 10N 1 30 E
Irati 173 25 25 S 50 38W
Irbid 90 32 35N 35 48 E
Irbit 84 57 41N 63 3 E
Irchester 29 52 17N 0 40W
Irebu 124 0 40 S 17 55 E
Irecê 170 11 18 S 41 52W
Iregua, R. 58 42 22N 2 24 E
Ireland ■ 38 53 0N 8 0W
Ireland's Eye 38 53 25N 6 4W
Irele 121 7 40N 5 40 E
Iremel, Gora 84 54 33N 58 50 E
Iret 77 60 10N 154 5 E
Irgiz, Bol. 81 52 10N 49 10 E
Irharharene 119 27 37N 7 30 E
Irharrhar, O. 119 27 30N 6 0 E
Irhyangdong 107 41 15N 129 30 E
Iri 107 35 59N 127 0 E
Irian Jaya □ 103 4 0 S 137 0 E
Iriba 124 15 7N 22 15 E
Irié 120 8 15N 9 10W
Iriklinskiy 84 51 39N 58 38 E
Iringa 126 7 48 S 35 43 E
Iringa □, Tanz. 126 7 48 S 35 43 E
Iringa □, Tanz. 127 9 0 S 35 0 E
Irinjalakuda 97 10 21N 76 14 E
Iriomote-Jima 112 24 19N 123 48 E
Iriona 166 15 57N 85 11W
Irish Sea 32 54 0N 5 0W
Irish Town 93 40 55 S 145 9 E
Irkeshtam 85 39 41N 73 55 E
Irkutsk 77 52 10N 104 20 E
Irlam 32 53 26N 2 27W
Irma 153 52 55N 111 14W
Irmak 92 39 58N 33 25 E
Irō-Zaki 111 34 36N 138 51 E
Iroise 42 48 15N 4 45W
Iron Baron 140 33 3 S 137 11 E
Iron Gate = Porţile de Fier 70 44 42N 22 30 E
Iron Knob 140 32 46 S 137 8 E
Iron, L. 38 53 37N 7 34W
Iron Mountain 156 45 49N 88 4W
Iron River 158 46 6N 88 40W
Ironbridge 28 52 38N 2 29W
Ironhurst 138 18 5 S 143 28 E
Ironstone Kopje, Mt. 128 25 17 S 24 5 E
Ironton, Mo., U.S.A. 159 37 40N 90 40W
Ironton, Ohio, U.S.A. 156 38 35N 82 40W
Ironwood 158 46 30N 90 10W
Iroquois Falls 150 48 46N 80 41W
Irpen 80 50 30N 30 8 E
Irrara Cr. 139 29 35 S 145 31 E
Irrawaddy 98 17 0N 95 0 E
Irrawaddy □ 98 17 0N 95 0 E
Irrawaddy, R. 98 15 50N 95 6 E
Irsina 65 40 45N 16 15 E
Irt R. 32 54 24N 3 25W
Irthing R. 35 54 25N 2 48W
Irthlingborough 29 52 20N 0 37W
Irtysh, R. 76 53 36N 75 30 E
Irumu 126 1 32N 29 53 E
Irún 58 43 20N 1 52W
Irurzun 58 42 55N 1 50W
Irvine, Can. 153 49 57N 110 16W
Irvine, U.K. 34 55 37N 4 40W
Irvine, U.S.A. 156 37 42N 83 58W
Irvinestown 38 54 28N 7 38W
Irwin, Pt. 137 35 5 S 116 55 E
Irwin, R. 137 29 15 S 114 54 E
Irymple 140 34 14 S 142 8 E
Is-sur-Tille 43 47 30N 5 10 E
Isa 121 13 14N 6 24 E
Isaac, R. 138 22 55 S 149 20 E
Isabel 158 45 27N 101 22W
Isabela, Dom. Rep. 167 19 58N 71 2W
Isabela, Pto Rico 147 18 30N 67 01W
Isabela, Cord. 166 13 30N 85 25W
Isabela, I. 164 21 51N 105 55W
Isabella Ra. 136 21 0 S 121 4 E
Ísafjarðardjúp 74 66 10N 23 0W
Ísafjörður 74 66 5N 23 9W
Isagarh 94 24 48N 77 51 E
Isahaya 110 32 52N 130 2 E
Isaka 126 3 56 S 32 59 E
Isakly 84 54 8N 51 32 E
Isangi 124 0 52N 24 10 E
Isar, R. 49 48 40N 12 30 E
Isarco, R. 63 46 40N 11 35 E
Isari 69 37 22N 22 0 E
Isbergues 43 50 36N 2 24 E
Isbiceni 70 43 45N 24 40 E
Ischia, I. 64 40 45N 13 51 E
Iscuandé 174 2 28N 77 59W
Isdell, R. 136 16 27 S 124 51 E
Ise 111 34 25N 136 45 E
Ise-Heiya 111 34 40N 136 30 E
Ise-Wan 111 34 43N 136 43 E
Isefjord 73 55 53N 11 50 E
Iseltwald 50 46 43N 7 58 E
Isenthal 51 46 55N 8 34 E
Iseo 62 45 40N 10 3 E
Iseo, L. di 62 45 45N 10 3 E
Iseramagazi 126 4 37 S 32 10 E
Isère □ 45 45 15N 5 40 E
Isère, R. 44 45 15N 5 30 E
Iserlohn 48 51 22N 7 40 E
Isérnia 65 41 35N 14 12 E
Isesaki 111 36 19N 139 12 E
Iset, R. 84 56 36N 66 24 E
Iseyin 121 8 0N 3 36 E
Isfara 85 40 7N 70 38 E
Ishan 108 24 30N 108 41 E
Ishara 121 6 40N 3 40 E
Ishigaki 112 24 20N 124 10 E
Ishikari-Wan 112 43 20N 141 20 E
Ishikawa 112 26 25N 127 48 E
Ishikawa-ken □ 111 36 30N 136 30 E
Ishim 76 56 10N 69 18 E
Ishim, R. 76 57 45N 71 10 E
Ishimbay 84 53 28N 56 2 E
Ishinomaki 112 38 32N 141 20 E
Ishioka 111 36 11N 140 16 E
Ishizuchi-Yama 110 33 45N 133 6 E
Ishkashim 85 36 44N 71 37 E
Ishkuman 95 36 30N 73 50 E
Ishmi 68 41 33N 19 34 E
Ishpeming 156 46 30N 87 40W
Ishua 121 7 15N 5 50 E
Ishui 107 35 50N 118 32 E
Ishurdi 98 24 9N 89 3 E
Isigny-sur-Mer 42 49 19N 1 6W
Işik 82 40 40N 32 35 E
Isil Kul 76 54 55N 71 16 E
Isili 44 39 45N 9 6 E
Isiolo 126 0 24N 37 33 E
Isipingo 129 30 00 S 30 57 E
Isipingo Beach 129 30 00 S 30 57 E
Isiro 126 2 53N 27 58 E
Iskander 85 41 36N 69 41 E
Iskenderun 92 36 32N 36 10E
Iskilip 82 40 50N 34 20E
Iskut, R. 152 56 45N 131 49W
Iskyr, R. 67 43 35N 24 20 E
Isla Cristina 57 37 13N 7 17W
Isla, La 174 6 51N 76 56W
Isla, R. 37 56 32N 3 20W
Islamabad 94 33 40N 73 0 E
Islamkot 94 24 42N 70 13 E
Islampur 96 17 2N 72 9 E
Island Falls, Can. 150 49 35N 81 20W
Island Falls, U.S.A. 151 46 0N 68 25W
Island L. 153 53 47N 94 25W
Island Lagoon 140 31 30 S 136 40 E
Island Pt. 137 30 20 S 115 1 E
Island Pond 156 44 50N 71 50W
Island, R. 152 60 25N 121 12W
Islands, B. of, Can. 151 49 11N 58 15W
Islands, B. of, N.Z. 142 35 20 S 174 20 E
Islay, I. 34 55 46N 6 10W
Islay Sound 34 55 45N 6 5W
Isle-Adam, L' 43 49 6N 2 14 E
Isle aux Morts 151 47 35N 59 0W
Isle-Jourdain, L', Gers, France 44 43 36N 1 5 E
Isle-Jourdain, L', Vienne, France 42 46 13N 0 31 E
Isle, L', Tarn, France 44 43 52N 1 49 E
Isle, L', Vaucluse, France 45 43 55N 5 3 E
Isle of Whithorn 34 54 42N 4 22W
Isle of Wight □ 28 50 40N 1 20W
Isle Ornsay 36 57 9N 5 50W
Isle Royale 158 48 0N 88 50W
Isle-sur-la-Sorgue, L' 45 43 55N 5 2 E
Isle-sur-le-Doubs, L' 43 47 26N 6 34 E
Isle Vista 163 34 27N 119 52W
Isleham 29 52 21N 0 24 E
Islet, L' 151 47 4N 70 23W
Isleta 161 34 58N 106 46W
Isleton 163 38 10N 121 37W
Islip 28 51 49N 1 12W
Ismail 82 45 22N 28 46 E
Ismâ'ilîya 122 30 37N 32 18 E
Ismay 158 46 33N 104 44W
Isna 122 25 17N 32 30 E
Isogstalo 95 34 15N 78 46 E
Isola del Liri 64 41 39N 13 32 E
Isola della Scala 62 45 16N 11 0 E
Isola di Capo Rizzuto 65 38 56N 17 5 E
Isparta 92 37 47N 30 30 E
Isperikh 67 43 43N 26 50 E
Ispica 65 36 47N 14 53 E
Israel ■ 90 32 0N 34 50 E
Isseka 137 28 22 S 114 35 E
Issia 120 6 33N 6 33W
Issoire 44 45 32N 3 15 E
Issoudun 43 46 57N 2 0 E
Issyk-Kul, Ozero 85 42 25N 77 15 E
İstanbul 92 41 0N 29 0E
Istmina 174 5 10N 76 39W
Istok 66 42 45N 20 24 E
Istokpoga, L. 157 27 22N 81 14W
Istra, U.S.S.R. 81 55 55N 36 50 E
Istra, Yugo. 63 45 10N 14 0 E
Istranca Dağlari 67 41 48N 27 30 E
Istres 45 43 31N 4 59 E
Istria = Istra 63 45 10N 14 0 E
Itá 172 25 29N 57 21W
Itabaiana, Paraíba, Brazil 170 7 18 S 35 19W
Itabaiana, Sergipe, Brazil 170 10 41 S 37 26W
Itabaianinha 170 11 16 S 37 47W
Itaberaba 171 12 32 S 40 18W
Itaberaí 171 16 2 S 49 48W
Itabira 171 19 37 S 43 13W
Itabirito 173 20 15 S 43 48W
Itabuna 171 14 48 S 39 16W
Itacaiunas, R. 170 5 21 S 49 8W
Itacajá 170 8 19 S 47 46W
Itaete 171 13 0 S 41 5W
Itaguaçu 171 19 48 S 40 51W
Itaguari, R. 171 14 11 S 44 40W
Itaguatins 170 5 47 S 47 29W
Itaim, R. 170 7 2 S 42 2W
Itainópolis 170 7 24 S 41 31W
Itaituba 175 4 10 S 55 50W
Itajaí 173 27 0 S 48 45W
Itajubá 173 22 24 S 45 30W
Itajuípe 171 14 41 S 39 22W
Itaka 127 8 50 S 32 49 E
Itako 111 35 56N 140 33 E
Italy ■ 60 42 0N 13 0 E
Itamataré 170 2 16 S 46 24W
Itambacuri 171 18 1 S 41 42W
Itambé 171 15 15 S 40 37W
Itambe, mt. 170 18 30 S 43 15W
Itampolo 129 24 41 S 43 57 E
Itanhaém 121 24 9 S 46 47W
Itanhém 171 17 9 S 40 20W
Itano 110 34 1N 134 28 E
Itapaci 171 14 57 S 49 34W
Itapagé 170 3 41 S 39 34W
Itaparica, I. de 171 12 54 S 38 42W
Itapebi 171 15 56 S 39 32W
Itapecerica 171 20 28 S 45 7W
Itapecuru-Mirim 170 3 24 S 44 20W
Itapecuru, R. 170 3 20 S 44 15W
Itaperuna 171 21 10 S 42 0W
Itapetinga 171 15 15 S 40 15W
Itapetininga 173 23 36 S 48 7W
Itapeva 173 23 59 S 48 59W
Itapicuru 170 10 50 S 38 40W
Itapicuru, R. 170 5 40 S 44 30W
Itapipoca 170 3 30 S 39 35W
Itapiúna 170 4 33 S 38 57W
Itaporanga 171 7 18 S 38 10W
Itapuá □ 173 26 40 S 55 40W
Itapuranga 171 15 35 S 49 59W
Itaquari 173 20 12 S 40 25W
Itaquatiana 174 2 58 S 58 30W
Itaquí 172 29 0 S 56 30W
Itararé 173 24 6 S 49 23W
Itarsi 94 22 36N 77 51 E
Itarumã 171 18 42 S 51 25W
Itati 172 27 16 S 58 15W
Itatira 170 4 30 S 39 37W
Itatuba 174 5 40 S 63 20W
Itaueira 170 7 36 S 43 2W

Itaueira, R Jedrzejów

Itaueira, R. 170 6 41 S 42 55 W
Itaúna 171 20 4 S 44 34 W
Itchen, R. 28 50 57 N 1 20 W
Itéa 69 38 25 N 22 25 E
Ithaca 162 42 25 N 76 30 W
Ithaca = Itháki 69 38 25 N 20 43 E
Itháki, I. 69 38 25 N 20 40 E
Ithon R. 31 52 16 N 3 23 W
It'iaoshan 106 37 10 N 104 2 E
Itinga 171 16 36 S 41 47 W
Itiruçu 171 13 31 S 40 9 W
Itiúba 171 10 43 S 39 51 W
Ito 111 34 58 N 139 5 E
Itonamas, R. 174 13 0 S 64 25 W
Itsa 122 29 15 N 30 40 E
Itsukaichi 110 34 22 N 132 8 E
Itsuki 110 32 24 N 130 50 E
Itteville 46 48 31 N 2 21 E
Ittiri 64 40 38 N 8 32 E
Itu, Brazil 173 23 10 S 47 15 W
Itu, Hupeh, China 109 30 24 N 111 26 E
Itu, Shantung, China 107 36 41 N 118 28 E
Itu, Nigeria 121 5 10 N 7 58 E
Ituaçu 171 13 50 S 41 18 W
Ituango 174 7 4 N 75 45 W
Ituiutaba 171 19 0 S 49 25 W
Itumbiara 171 18 20 S 49 10 W
Ituna 153 51 10 N 103 30 W
It'ung 107 43 20 N 125 17 E
Itunge Port 127 9 40 S 33 55 E
Itupiranga 170 5 9 S 49 20 W
Iturama 171 19 44 S 50 11 W
Iturbe 172 23 0 S 65 25 W
Ituri, R. 126 1 45 N 26 45 E
Iturup, Ostrov 77 45 0 N 148 0 E
Ituverava 171 20 20 S 47 47 W
Ituyuro, R. 172 22 40 S 63 50 W
Itzehoe 48 53 56 N 9 31 E
Ivalo 74 68 38 N 27 35 E
Ivalojoki 74 68 30 N 27 0 E
Ivanaj 68 42 17 N 19 25 E
Ivanhoe, N.S.W., Austral. 140 32 56 S 144 20 E
Ivanhoe, N.T., Austral. 136 15 41 S 128 41 E
Ivanhoe, U.S.A. 163 36 23 N 119 13 W
Ivanhoe L. 153 60 25 N 106 30 W
Ivanió Grad 63 45 41 N 16 25 E
Ivanjica 66 43 35 N 20 12 E
Ivanjscie 63 46 12 N 16 13 E
Ivankovskoye Vdkhr. 81 56 48 N 36 55 E
Ivano-Frankovsk, (Stanislav) 80 49 0 N 24 40 E
Ivanovka 84 52 34 N 53 23 E
Ivanovo, Byelorussia, U.S.S.R. 80 52 7 N 25 29 E
Ivanovo, R.S.F.S.R., U.S.S.R. 81 57 5 N 41 0 E
Ivato 129 20 37 S 47 10 E
Ivaylovgrad 67 41 32 N 26 8 E
Ivinghoe 29 51 50 N 0 38 W
Ivinheima, R. 173 21 48 S 54 15 W
Iviza = Ibiza 59 39 0 N 1 30 E
Ivohibe 129 22 31 S 46 57 E
Ivolândia 171 16 34 S 50 51 W
Ivory Coast ■ 120 7 30 N 5 0 W
Ivösjön 73 56 8 N 14 25 E
Ivrea 62 45 30 N 7 52 E
Ivugivik, (N.D. d'Ivugivic) 149 62 24 N 77 55 W
Ivybridge 30 50 24 N 3 56 W
Iwahig 102 8 35 N 117 32 E
Iwai-Jima 110 33 47 N 131 58 E
Iwaki 112 37 3 N 140 55 E
Iwakuni 110 34 15 N 132 8 E
Iwami 110 35 32 N 134 15 E
Iwamisawa 112 43 12 N 141 46 E
Iwanai 112 42 58 N 140 30 E
Iwanuma 112 38 7 N 140 58 E
Iwase 110 36 21 N 140 6 E
Iwata 111 34 49 N 137 59 E
Iwate-ken □ 112 39 30 N 141 30 E
Iwate-San 112 39 51 N 141 0 E
Iwo 121 7 39 N 4 9 E
Iwonicz-Zdroj 54 49 37 N 21 47 E
Ixiamas 174 13 50 S 68 5 W
Ixopo 129 30 11 S 30 5 E
Ixtepec 165 16 40 N 95 10 W
Ixtlán de Juárez 165 17 23 N 96 28 W
Ixtlán del Rio 164 21 5 N 104 28 W
Ixworth 29 52 18 N 0 50 E
Iyang, Honan, China 106 34 9 N 112 25 E
Iyang, Hunan, China 109 28 36 N 112 20 E
Iyang, Kiangsi, China 109 28 23 N 117 25 E
Iyo 110 33 45 N 132 45 E
Iyo-mishima 110 33 58 N 133 30 E
Iyo-Nada 110 33 40 N 132 20 E
Izabal, L. 166 15 30 N 89 10 W
Izamal 165 20 56 N 89 1 W
Izberbash 83 42 35 N 47 45 E
Izbica Kujawski 54 52 25 N 18 30 E
Izegem 47 50 55 N 3 12 E
Izgrev 67 43 36 N 26 58 E
Izh, R. 84 55 58 N 52 38 E
Izhevsk 84 56 51 N 53 14 E
Izmail 82 45 22 N 28 46 E
Izmir (Smyrna) 79 38 25 N 27 8 E
Izmit 92 40 45 N 29 50 E
Izola 63 45 32 N 13 39 E
Izu-Hantō 111 34 45 N 139 0 E
Izuhara 110 34 12 N 129 17 E
Izumi 110 32 5 N 130 22 E
Izumiotsu 111 34 30 N 135 24 E
Izumisano 111 34 40 N 135 43 E
Izumo 110 35 20 N 132 55 E
Izyaslav 80 50 5 N 25 50 E
Izyum 82 49 12 N 37 28 E

J

Jaba 123 6 20 N 35 7 E
Jaba' 90 32 20 N 35 13 E
Jabaliya 90 31 32 N 34 27 E
Jabalón, R. 59 38 45 N 3 35 W
Jabalpur 95 23 9 N 79 58 E
Jablah 92 35 20 N 36 0 E
Jablanac 63 44 42 N 14 56 E
Jablonec 52 50 43 N 15 10 E
Jablonica 53 48 37 N 17 26 E
Jabłonowo 54 53 23 N 19 10 E
Jaboatão 170 8 7 S 35 1 W
Jaboticabal 173 21 15 S 48 17 W
Jabukovac 66 44 22 N 22 21 E
Jaburu 174 5 30 S 64 0 W
Jaca 58 42 35 N 0 33 W
Jacala 165 21 1 N 99 11 W
Jacaré, R. 170 10 3 S 42 13 W
Jacareí 173 23 20 S 46 0 W
Jacarèzinho 173 23 5 S 50 0 W
Jáchal 172 30 5 S 69 0 W
Jáchymov 52 50 22 N 12 55 E
Jacinto 171 16 10 S 40 17 W
Jack Lane B. 151 55 45 N 60 35 W
Jackfish 150 48 45 N 87 0 W
Jackman 151 45 35 N 70 17 W
Jacksboro 159 33 14 N 98 15 W
Jackson, Austral. 139 26 39 S 149 39 E
Jackson, Ala., U.S.A. 157 31 32 N 87 53 W
Jackson, Calif., U.S.A. 159 37 25 N 89 42 W
Jackson, Ill., U.S.A. 163 38 25 N 120 47 W
Jackson, Ky., U.S.A. 156 37 35 N 83 22 W
Jackson, Mich., U.S.A. 156 42 18 N 84 25 W
Jackson, Minn., U.S.A. 158 43 35 N 95 30 W
Jackson, Miss., U.S.A. 159 32 20 N 90 10 W
Jackson, Ohio, U.S.A. 156 39 0 N 82 40 W
Jackson, Tenn., U.S.A. 157 35 40 N 88 50 W
Jackson, Wyo., U.S.A. 160 43 30 N 110 49 W
Jackson Bay, Can. 152 50 32 N 125 57 W
Jackson Bay, N.Z. 143 43 58 S 168 42 E
Jackson, C. 143 40 59 S 174 20 E
Jackson, L. 160 43 55 N 110 40 W
Jacksons 143 42 46 S 171 32 E
Jacksonville, Ala., U.S.A. 157 33 49 N 85 45 W
Jacksonville, Calif., U.S.A. 163 37 52 N 120 24 W
Jacksonville, Fla., U.S.A. 157 30 15 N 81 38 W
Jacksonville, Ill., U.S.A. 158 39 42 N 90 15 W
Jacksonville, N.C., U.S.A. 157 34 50 N 77 29 W
Jacksonville, Oreg., U.S.A. 160 42 13 N 122 56 W
Jacksonville, Tex., U.S.A. 159 31 58 N 95 12 W
Jacksonville Beach 157 30 19 N 81 26 W
Jacmel 167 18 20 N 72 40 W
Jacob Lake 161 36 45 N 112 12 W
Jacobabad 94 28 20 N 68 29 E
Jacobeni 70 47 25 N 25 20 E
Jacobina 170 11 11 S 40 30 W
Jacob's Well 90 32 13 N 35 13 E
Jacques Cartier, Mt. 151 48 57 N 66 0 W
Jacques Cartier Pass 151 49 50 N 62 30 W
Jacqueville 120 5 12 N 4 25 W
Jacuí, R. 173 30 2 S 51 15 W
Jacuipe, R. 171 12 30 S 39 5 W
Jacundá, R. 170 1 57 S 50 26 W
Jade 48 53 22 N 8 14 E
Jadebusen, B. 48 53 30 N 8 15 E
Jadoigne 47 50 43 N 4 52 E
Jadotville = Likasi 127 10 55 S 26 48 E
Jadovnik 66 43 20 N 19 45 E
Jadraque 58 40 55 N 2 55 W
Jādū 119 32 0 N 12 0 E
Jaén, Peru 174 5 25 S 78 40 W
Jaén, Spain 57 37 44 N 3 43 W
Jaén □ 57 37 50 N 3 30 W
Jafène 118 20 35 N 5 30 W
Jaffa = Tel Aviv-Yafo 90 32 4 N 34 48 E
Jaffa, C. 140 36 58 S 139 40 E
Jaffna 97 9 45 N 80 2 E
Jaffrey 162 42 50 N 72 4 W
Jagadhri 94 30 10 N 77 20 E
Jagadishpur 95 25 30 N 84 21 E
Jagdalpur 96 19 3 N 82 6 E
Jagersfontein 128 29 44 S 25 27 E
Jaghbub 117 29 42 N 24 38 E
Jagraon 93 30 50 N 75 25 E
Jagst, R. 49 49 13 N 10 0 E
Jagtial 96 18 50 N 79 0 E
Jaguaquara 171 13 32 S 39 58 W
Jaguariaíva 173 24 10 S 49 50 W
Jaguaribe 170 5 53 S 38 37 W
Jaguaribe, R. 170 6 0 S 38 35 W
Jaguaruana 170 4 50 S 37 47 W
Jagüey 166 22 35 N 81 7 W
Jagungal, Mt. 141 36 8 S 148 22 E
Jahangirabad 94 28 19 N 78 4 E
Jahrom 92 28 30 N 53 31 E
Jaicós 170 7 21 S 41 8 W
Jainti 98 26 45 N 89 40 E
Jaintiapur 98 25 8 N 92 7 E
Jaipur 94 27 0 N 76 10 E
Jajarm 93 37 5 N 56 20 E
Jajce 66 44 19 N 17 17 E
Jajere 121 11 58 N 11 25 E
Jajpur 96 20 53 N 86 22 E
Jakarta 103 6 9 S 106 49 E
Jakobstad (Pietarsaari) 74 63 40 N 22 43 E
Jakupica 66 41 45 N 21 22 E
Jal 159 32 8 N 103 8 W
Jala 93 27 30 N 62 40 E
Jalalabad, Afghan. 94 34 30 N 70 29 E
Jalalabad, India 95 26 41 N 79 42 E
Jalalpur Jattan 94 32 38 N 74 19 E
Jalama 163 34 29 N 120 29 W
Jalapa, Guat. 166 14 45 N 89 59 W
Jalapa, Mexico 165 19 30 N 96 50 W
Jalas, Jabal al 92 27 30 N 36 30 E
Jalaun 95 26 8 N 79 25 E
Jales 171 20 16 S 50 33 W
Jaleswar 95 26 38 N 85 48 E
Jalgaon, Maharashtra, India 96 21 2 N 76 31 E
Jalgaon, Maharashtra, India 96 21 0 N 75 42 E
Jalhay 47 50 33 N 5 58 E
Jalingo 121 8 55 N 11 25 E
Jalisco □ 164 20 0 N 104 0 W
Jalkot 95 35 20 N 73 24 E
Jallas, R. 56 42 57 N 9 0 W
Jallumba 140 36 55 N 141 57 E
Jalna 96 19 48 N 75 57 E
Jalón, R. 58 41 20 N 1 40 W
Jalpa 164 21 38 N 102 58 W
Jalpaiguri 98 26 32 N 88 46 E
Jalq 93 27 35 N 62 33 E
Jaluit I. 130 6 0 N 169 30 E
Jamaari 121 11 44 N 9 53 E
Jamaica, I. ■ 166 18 10 N 77 30 W
Jamalpur, Bangla. 98 24 52 N 90 2 E
Jamalpur, India 95 25 18 N 86 28 E
Jamalpurganj 95 23 2 N 88 1 E
Jamanxim, R. 175 6 30 S 55 50 W
Jambe 103 1 15 S 132 10 E
Jambes 47 50 27 N 4 52 E
Jambi 102 1 38 S 103 30 E
Jambusar 94 22 3 N 72 51 E
Jamdena, I. = Yamdena 103 7 45 S 131 20 E
James B. 150 53 30 N 80 0 W
James, R., Dak., U.S.A. 158 44 50 N 98 0 W
James, R., Va., U.S.A. 162 37 0 N 76 27 W
James Ranges 136 24 10 S 132 0 E
James Ross I. 13 63 58 S 50 94 W
Jamestown, Austral. 140 33 10 S 138 32 E
Jamestown, S. Afr. 128 31 6 S 26 45 E
Jamestown, Ky., U.S.A. 156 37 0 N 85 5 W
Jamestown, N.D., U.S.A. 158 47 0 N 98 30 W
Jamestown, N.Y., U.S.A. 156 42 5 N 79 18 W
Jamestown, Tenn., U.S.A. 157 36 25 N 85 0 W
Jamestown, Va., U.S.A. 162 37 12 N 76 46 W
Jamiltepec 165 16 17 N 97 49 W
Jamkhandi 97 16 30 N 75 15 E
Jamma'in 90 32 8 N 35 12 E
Jammalamadugu 97 14 51 N 78 25 E
Jammerbugt 73 57 15 N 9 20 E
Jammu 94 32 43 N 74 54 E
Jammu & Kashmir □ 95 34 25 N 77 0 E
Jamnagar 94 22 30 N 70 0 E
Jamner 96 20 45 N 75 45 E
Jamoigne 47 49 41 N 5 24 E
Jampur 94 29 39 N 70 32 E
Jamrud 94 34 2 N 71 24 E
Jamshedpur 95 22 44 N 86 20 E
Jamtara 95 23 59 N 86 41 E
Jämtlands län □ 72 62 40 N 13 50 E
Jamuna, R. 98 23 51 N 89 45 E
Jamurki 98 24 9 N 90 2 E
Jan Kemp 128 27 55 S 24 51 E
Jan L. 153 54 56 N 102 55 W
Jan Mayen Is. 12 71 0 N 11 0 W
Janaúba 171 15 48 S 43 19 W
Janaucu, I. 170 0 30 N 50 10 W
Jand 94 33 30 N 72 0 E
Janda, Laguna de la 57 36 15 N 5 45 W
Jandaia 171 17 6 S 50 7 W
Jandaq 92 34 3 N 54 22 E
Jandola 94 32 20 N 70 9 E
Jandowae 139 26 45 S 151 7 E
Jandrain-Jandrenouilles 47 50 40 N 4 58 E
Jándula, R. 57 38 25 N 3 55 W
Jane Pk. 142 45 15 S 168 20 E
Janesville 158 42 39 N 89 1 W
Janga 121 10 5 N 1 0 W
Jangaon 96 17 44 N 79 5 E
Janhtang Ga 98 26 32 N 96 38 E
Jani Khel 93 32 45 N 68 25 E
Janja 66 44 40 N 19 17 E
Janjevo 66 42 35 N 21 19 E
Janjina 66 42 58 N 17 25 E
Janos 164 30 45 N 108 10 W
Jánoshalma 53 46 18 N 19 21 E
Jánosháza 53 47 8 N 17 12 E
Jánossomorja 53 47 47 N 17 11 E
Janów 54 50 43 N 22 30 E
Janów Lubelski 54 50 48 N 22 23 E
Janów Podlaski 54 52 11 N 23 11 E
Janowiec Wlkp. 54 52 45 N 17 30 E
Januária 171 15 25 S 44 25 W
Janub Dârfûr □ 123 11 0 N 25 0 E
Janub Kordofân □ 123 12 0 N 30 0 E
Janville 43 48 10 N 1 50 E
Janzé 42 47 55 N 1 28 W
Jaop'ing 109 23 43 N 117 0 E
Jaora 94 23 40 N 75 10 E
Jaoyang 106 38 14 N 115 44 E
Japan ■ 112 36 0 N 136 0 E
Japan, Sea of 112 40 0 N 135 0 E
Japan Trench 142 28 0 N 145 0 E
Japara 103 6 30 S 110 40 E
Japen, I. = Yapen 103 1 50 S 136 0 E
Japero 103 4 59 S 137 11 E
Japurá 174 1 48 S 66 30 W
Japurá, R. 174 3 8 S 64 46 W
Jaque 174 7 27 N 78 15 W
Jaques Cartier, Détroit de 151 50 0 N 63 30 W
Jara, La 161 37 16 N 106 0 W
Jaraguá 171 15 45 S 49 20 W
Jaraicejo 57 39 40 N 5 49 W
Jaraiz 56 40 4 N 5 45 W
Jarales 161 34 44 N 106 51 W
Jarama, R. 58 40 50 N 3 20 W
Jarandilla 56 40 8 N 5 39 W
Jaranwala 94 31 15 N 73 20 E
Jarash 90 32 17 N 35 54 E
Järbo 72 60 42 N 16 38 E
Jarbridge 160 41 56 N 115 27 W
Jardim 172 21 28 S 56 9 W
Jardín, R. 59 38 50 N 2 10 W
Jardines de la Reina, Is. 166 20 50 N 78 50 W
Jargalant = Hovd 105 48 1 N 91 38 E
Jargeau 43 47 50 N 2 7 E
Jarmen 48 53 56 N 13 20 E
Järna, Kopp., Sweden 72 60 33 N 14 26 E
Järna, Stockholm, Sweden 72 59 7 N 17 35 E
Jarnac 44 45 40 N 0 11 W
Jarny 43 49 9 N 5 53 E
Jarocin 54 51 59 N 17 29 E
Jaroměr 52 50 22 N 15 52 E
Jarosław 54 50 2 N 22 42 E
Järpås 73 58 23 N 12 57 E
Järpås 73 58 23 N 12 57 E
Järpen 72 63 21 N 13 26 E
Jarrahdale 137 32 24 S 116 5 E
Jarres, Plaine des 100 19 27 N 103 10 E
Jarrow 35 54 58 N 1 28 W
Jarso 123 5 15 N 37 30 E
Järved 72 63 16 N 18 43 E
Jarvis I. 131 0 15 S 159 55 W
Jarvornik 53 50 23 N 17 2 E
Jarwa 95 27 45 N 82 30 E
Jaša Tomió 66 45 26 N 20 50 E
Jasien 54 51 46 N 15 0 E
Jasin 101 2 20 N 102 26 E
Jäsk 93 25 38 N 57 45 E
Jasło 54 49 45 N 21 30 E
Jasper, Can. 152 52 55 N 118 5 W
Jasper, Ala., U.S.A. 157 33 48 N 87 16 W
Jasper, Ark., U.S.A. 97 36 0 N 93 10 W
Jasper, Fla., U.S.A. 157 30 31 N 82 58 W
Jasper, La., U.S.A. 159 30 59 N 93 58 W
Jasper, S.D., U.S.A. 158 43 52 N 96 22 W
Jasper Nat. Park 152 52 50 N 118 8 W
Jasper Place 152 53 33 N 113 25 W
Jastrebarsko 63 45 41 N 15 39 E
Jastrowie 54 53 26 N 16 49 E
Jastrzebie Zdroj 54 49 57 N 18 35 E
Jászapáti 53 47 32 N 20 10 E
Jászárokszállás 53 47 39 N 20 1 E
Jászberény 53 47 30 N 19 55 E
Jászkiser 53 47 27 N 20 20 E
Jászladány 53 47 23 N 20 18 E
Jatai 171 17 50 S 51 45 W
Jati 94 24 27 N 68 19 E
Jatibarang 103 6 28 S 108 18 E
Jatinegara 103 6 13 S 106 52 E
Játiva 59 39 0 N 0 32 W
Jatobal 170 4 35 S 49 33 W
Jatt 90 32 24 N 35 2 E
Jaú 173 22 10 S 48 30 W
Jau al Milah 91 15 15 N 45 40 E
Jauche 47 50 41 N 4 57 E
Jauja 174 11 45 S 75 30 W
Jaunelgava 80 56 35 N 25 0 E
Jaunpur 95 25 46 N 82 44 E
Java = Jawa 103 7 0 S 110 0 E
Java Sea 102 4 35 S 107 15 E
Javadi Hills 97 12 40 N 78 40 E
Jávea 59 38 48 N 0 10 E
Javhlant = Ulyasutay 105 47 45 N 96 49 E
Javla 96 17 18 N 75 9 E
Javron 42 48 25 N 0 25 W
Jawa 103 7 0 S 110 0 E
Jawor 54 51 4 N 16 11 E
Jaworzno 54 50 13 N 19 22 E
Jay 159 33 17 N 94 46 W
Jayawijaya, Pengunungan 103 7 0 S 139 0 E
Jaydot 153 49 15 N 110 15 W
Jaynagar 99 26 43 N 86 9 E
Jayton 159 33 17 N 100 35 W
Jazminal 164 24 56 N 101 25 W
Jean 161 35 47 N 115 20 W
Jean Marie River 152 61 32 N 120 38 W
Jean Rabel 167 19 50 N 73 30 W
Jeanerette 159 29 52 N 91 38 W
Jebba, Moroc. 118 35 11 N 4 43 W
Jebba, Nigeria 121 9 9 N 4 48 E
Jebel 66 40 35 N 21 15 E
Jebel Aulia 123 15 10 N 32 31 E
Jebel Qerri 123 16 16 N 32 50 E
Jedburgh 35 55 28 N 2 33 W
Jedlicze 54 49 43 N 21 40 E
Jedlnia-Letnisko 54 51 25 N 21 19 E
Jedrzejów 54 50 35 N 20 15 E

Jedway Kaboudia, Rass

Jedway 152 52 17N 131 14W
Jeetze, R. 48 52 58N 11 6E
Jefferson, Iowa, U.S.A. 158 42 3N 94 25W
Jefferson, Tex., U.S.A. 159 32 45N 94 23W
Jefferson, Wis., U.S.A. 158 43 0N 88 49W
Jefferson City 157 36 8N 83 30W
Jefferson, Mt., Calif., U.S.A. 163 38 51N 117 0W
Jefferson, Mt., Oreg., U.S.A. 160 44 45N 121 50W
Jeffersonville 156 38 20N 85 42W
Jega 121 12 15N 4 23E
Jekabpils 80 56 29N 25 57E
Jelenia Góra 54 50 50N 15 45E
Jelenia Góra □ 54 51 0N 15 30E
Jelgava 80 56 41N 22 49E
Jelica 66 43 50N 20 17E
Jelli 123 5 25N 31 45E
Jellicoe 150 49 40N 87 30W
Jelšava 53 48 37N 20 15E
Jemaja 103 3 5N 105 45E
Jemaluang 101 2 16N 103 52E
Jemappes 47 50 27N 3 54E
Jember 103 8 11S 113 41E
Jembongan, I. 102 6 45N 117 20E
Jemmapes = Azzaba 119 36 48N 7 6E
Jemnice 52 49 1N 15 34E
Jena, Ger. 48 50 56N 11 33E
Jena, U.S.A. 159 31 41N 92 7W
Jench'iu 106 38 43N 116 5E
Jendouba 119 36 29N 8 47E
Jenhochieh 108 26 29N 101 45E
Jenhsien 106 37 8N 114 37E
Jenhua 109 25 5N 113 45E
Jenhuai 108 27 53N 106 17E
Jenin 90 32 28N 35 18E
Jenkins 156 37 13N 82 41W
Jennings 159 30 10N 92 45W
Jennings, R. 152 59 38N 132 5W
Jenny 73 57 47N 16 35E
Jeparit 140 36 8S 142 1E
Jequié 171 13 51S 40 5W
Jequitaí, R. 171 17 4S 44 50W
Jequitinhonha 171 16 30S 41 0W
Jequitinhonha, R. 171 15 51S 38 53W
Jerada 118 34 40N 2 10W
Jerantut 101 3 56N 102 22E
Jérémie 167 18 40N 74 10W
Jeremoabo 170 10 4S 38 21W
Jerez de García Salinas 164 22 39N 103 0W
Jerez de la Frontera 57 36 41N 6 7W
Jerez de los Caballeros 57 38 20N 6 45W
Jerez, Punta 165 22 58N 97 40W
Jericho 138 23 38S 146 6E
Jericho = El Arīhā 90 31 52N 35 27E
Jerichow 48 52 30N 12 2E
Jerilderie 141 35 20S 145 41E
Jermyn 162 41 31N 75 31W
Jerome 161 34 50N 112 0W
Jersey City 162 40 41N 74 8W
Jersey, I. 42 49 13N 2 7W
Jersey Shore 156 41 17N 77 18W
Jerseyville 158 39 5N 90 20W
Jerumenha 171 7 5S 43 30W
Jerusalem 90 31 47N 35 10E
Jervaulx 33 54 19N 1 41W
Jervis B. 141 35 8S 150 46E
Jervis, C. 139 35 38S 138 6E
Jesenice 63 46 28N 14 3E
Jesenik 53 50 0N 17 8E
Jeseník (Frývaldov) 53 50 15N 17 11E
Jesenske 53 48 20N 20 10E
Jesselton = Kota Kinabalu 102 6 0N 116 12E
Jessnitz 48 51 42N 12 19E
Jessore 98 23 10N 89 10E
Jesup 157 31 30N 82 0W
Jesús Carranza 165 17 28N 95 1W
Jesús María 172 30 59S 64 5W
Jetmore 159 38 10N 99 57W
Jetpur 94 21 45N 70 10E
Jette 47 50 53N 4 20E
Jevnaker 71 60 15N 10 26E
Jewett 159 31 20N 96 8W
Jewett City 162 41 36N 72 0W
Jeypore 96 18 50N 82 38E
Jeziorany 54 53 58N 20 46E
J.F. Rodrigues 170 2 55S 50 20W
Jhajjar 94 28 37N 76 14E
Jhal Jhao 93 26 20N 65 35E
Jhalakati 99 22 39N 90 12E
Jhalawar 94 24 35N 76 10E
Jhang Maghiana 94 31 15N 72 15E
Jhansi 95 25 30N 78 36E
Jharia 95 23 45N 86 18E
Jharsaguda 99 21 50N 84 5E
Jharsuguda 96 21 50N 84 5E
Jhelum 94 33 0N 73 45E
Jhelum, R. 95 31 50N 72 10E
Jhunjhunu 94 28 10N 75 20E
Jiangshan 95 28 45N 118 37E
Jibão, Serra do 171 14 48S 45 0W
Jibiya 121 13 5N 7 12E
Jibou 70 47 15N 23 17E
Jicín 52 50 25N 15 20E
Jicarón, I. 166 7 10N 81 50W
Jiddah 92 21 29N 39 16E
Jido 99 29 2N 94 58E
Jifna 90 31 58N 35 13E
Jiggalong 136 23 24S 120 47E
Jihk'atse 107 29 15N 88 53E
Jihlava 52 49 28N 15 35E
Jihočeský □ 52 49 8N 14 35E
Jihomoravský □ 53 49 5N 16 30E
Jiht'u 105 33 27N 79 42E
Jijiga 91 9 20N 42 50E
Jijona 59 38 34N 0 30W
Jikamshi 121 12 12N 7 45E
Jiloca, R. 58 41 0N 1 20W
Jílové 52 49 52N 14 29E
Jim Jim Cr. 136 12 50S 132 32E
Jima 123 7 40N 36 55E
Jimbolia 66 45 47N 20 57E
Jimena de la Frontera 57 36 27N 5 24W
Jimenbuen 141 36 42S 148 53E
Jiménez 164 27 10N 105 0W
Jind 94 29 19N 76 16E
Jindabyne 141 36 25S 148 35E
Jindrichuv Hradeç 52 49 10N 15 2E
Jinja 126 0 25N 33 12E
Jinjang 101 3 13N 101 39E
Jinjini 120 7 20N 3 42W
Jinnah Barrage 93 32 58N 71 33E
Jinotega 166 13 6N 85 59W
Jinotepe 166 11 50N 86 10W
Jiparaná (Machado), R. 174 8 45S 62 20W
Jipijapa 174 1 0S 80 40W
Jiquilpán 164 19 57N 102 42W
Jisresh Shughur 92 35 49N 36 18E
Jitarning 137 32 48S 117 57E
Jitra 101 6 16N 100 25E
Jiu, R. 70 44 50N 23 20E
Jiuchin 109 25 53N 116 0E
Jiuli 108 24 6N 97 54E
Jizera, R. 52 50 21N 14 48E
Jizl Wadi 122 26 30N 38 0E
Jizō-zaki 110 35 34N 133 20E
Joaçaba 173 27 5S 51 31W
Joaíma 171 16 39S 41 2W
João 170 2 46S 50 59W
João Amaro 171 12 46S 40 22W
João Câmara 170 5 32S 35 48W
João de Almeida 125 15 10S 13 50E
João Pessoa 170 7 10S 34 52W
João Pinheiro 171 17 45S 46 10W
Joaquim Távora 171 23 30S 49 58W
Joaquín V. González 172 25 10S 64 0W
Jobourg, Nez de 42 49 41N 1 57W
Joch'iang 105 39 2N 88 0E
Jódar 59 37 50N 3 21W
Jodhpur 94 26 23N 73 2E
Joe Batt's Arm 151 49 44N 54 10W
Joensuu 78 62 37N 29 49E
Joeuf 43 49 12N 6 1E
Jofane 125 21 15S 34 18E
Joggins 151 45 42N 64 27W
Jogjakarta = Yogyakarta 103 7 49S 110 22E
Jōhana 111 36 37N 136 57E
Johannesburg, S. Afr. 129 26 10S 28 8E
Johannesburg, U.S.A. 163 35 22N 117 38W
Johannisnäs 72 62 45N 16 15E
Johansfors, Halland, Sweden 73 56 50N 12 58E
Johansfors, Kronoberg, Sweden 73 56 42N 15 32E
John Days, R. 160 45 0N 120 0W
John o' Groats 37 58 39N 3 3W
Johnshaven 37 56 48N 2 20W
Johnson 159 37 35N 101 48W
Johnson City, N.Y., U.S.A. 162 42 7N 75 57W
Johnson City, Tenn., U.S.A. 157 36 18N 82 21W
Johnson City, Tex., U.S.A. 159 30 15N 98 24W
Johnson Cy. 156 42 9N 67 0W
Johnson Ra. 137 29 40S 119 15E
Johnsondale 163 35 58N 118 32W
Johnsons Crossing 152 60 29N 133 18W
Johnsonville 142 41 13S 174 48E
Johnston 31 51 45N 5 5W
Johnston Falls = Mambilima Falls 127 10 31S 28 45E
Johnston I. 131 17 10N 169 8E
Johnston Lakes 137 32 20S 120 45E
Johnston Ra. 137 29 40S 119 20E
Johnstone 34 55 50N 4 31W
Johnstone Str. 152 50 28N 126 0W
Johnstown, Ireland 39 52 46N 7 34W
Johnstown, N.Y., U.S.A. 162 43 1N 74 20W
Johnstown, Pa., U.S.A. 156 40 19N 78 53W
Johnstown Bridge 38 53 23N 6 53W
Johor □ 101 2 5N 103 20E
Johor Baharu 101 1 28N 103 46E
Johor, S. 101 1 45N 103 47E
Joigny 43 48 0N 3 20E
Joinvile 173 26 15S 48 55E
Joinville 43 48 27N 5 10E
Joinville I. 13 63 15N 55 30W
Jojutla 165 18 37N 99 11W
Jokkmokk 74 66 35N 19 50E
Jökulsá á Brú 74 65 40N 14 16W
Jökulsá Fjöllum 74 65 30N 16 15W
Jökulsa R. 74 65 30N 16 15W
Jolan 163 35 58N 121 9W
Joliet 156 41 30N 88 0W
Joliette 150 46 3N 73 24W
Jolo I. 103 6 0N 121 0E
Jome, I. 103 1 16S 127 30E
Jönåker 73 58 44N 16 40E
Jönaker 73 58 48N 16 43E
Jones C. 150 54 33N 79 35W
Jones Sound 12 76 0N 89 0W
Jonesboro, Ark., U.S.A. 159 35 50N 90 45W
Jonesboro, Ill., U.S.A. 159 37 26N 89 18W
Jonesboro, La., U.S.A. 159 32 15N 92 41W
Jonesport 151 44 32N 67 38W
Jönköping 73 57 45N 14 10E
Jönköpings län □ 75 57 30N 14 30E
Jonquière 151 48 27N 71 14W
Jonsberg 73 58 30N 16 48E
Jonsered 73 57 45N 12 10E
Jonzac 44 45 27N 0 28W
Joplin 159 37 0N 94 25W
Jordan, Phil. 103 10 41N 122 38E
Jordan, Mont., U.S.A. 160 47 25N 106 58W
Jordan, N.Y., U.S.A. 162 43 4N 76 29W
Jordan ■ 92 31 0N 36 0E
Jordan, R. 90 32 10N 35 32E
Jordan Valley 160 43 0N 117 2W
Jordânia 171 15 45S 40 11W
Jordanów 54 49 41N 19 49E
Jorhat 98 26 45N 94 20E
Jörn 74 65 4N 20 1E
Jørpeland 71 59 3N 6 1E
Jorquera, R. 172 28 3S 69 58W
Jos 121 9 53N 8 51E
Jošanička Banja 66 43 24N 20 47E
José Batlle y OrdóPez 173 33 20S 55 10W
Josefow 54 52 10N 21 11E
Joseni 70 47 42N 25 29E
Joseph 160 45 27N 117 13W
Joseph Bonaparte G. 136 14 35S 128 50E
Joseph City 161 35 0N 110 16W
Joseph, Lac 151 52 45N 65 18W
Josephine, oilfield 19 58 35N 2 45E
Joshua Tree 163 34 8N 116 19W
Joshua Tree Nat. Mon. 163 33 56N 116 5W
Josselin 42 47 57N 2 33W
Jostedal 71 61 35N 7 15E
Jostedalsbre, Mt. 71 61 45N 7 0E
Jotunheimen 71 61 35N 8 25E
Jounieh 92 33 59N 35 30E
Jourdanton 159 28 54N 98 32W
Journe 46 52 58N 5 48E
Joussard 152 55 22N 115 57W
Joux, Lac de 50 46 39N 6 18E
Jouzjan □ 93 36 10N 66 0E
Jovellanos 166 22 40N 81 10W
Jowai 98 25 26N 92 12E
Joyce's Country, dist. 38 53 32N 9 30W
Joyeuse 45 44 29N 4 16E
Jozini Dam 129 27 27S 32 7E
Ju Shui, R. 109 28 36N 116 4E
Juan Aldama 164 24 20N 103 23W
Juan Bautista 161 36 55N 121 33W
Juan Bautista Alberdi 172 34 26S 61 48W
Juan de Fuca Str. 160 48 15N 124 0W
Juan de Nova, I. 129 17 3S 42 45E
Juan Fernández, Arch. de 131 33 50S 80 0W
Juan José Castelli 172 25 57S 60 37W
Juan L. Lacaze 172 34 26S 57 25W
Juárez, Argent. 172 37 40S 59 43W
Juárez, Mexico 164 27 37N 100 44W
Juárez, Sierra de 164 32 0N 116 0W
Juatinga, Ponta de 171 23 17S 44 30W
Juàzeiro 170 9 30S 40 30W
Juàzeiro do Norte 170 7 10S 39 18W
Jûbâ 123 4 57N 31 35E
Juba, R. 91 1 30N 42 35E
Jubaila 92 24 55N 46 25E
Jûbâl 122 27 30N 34 0E
Jubbulpore = Jabalpur 95 23 9N 79 58E
Jübek 48 54 31N 9 24E
Jubga 83 44 19N 38 48E
Jubilee L. 137 29 0S 126 50E
Juby, C. 116 28 0N 12 59W
Júcar, R. 58 40 8N 2 13W
Júcaro 166 21 37N 78 51W
Juch'eng 109 25 32N 113 39E
Juchitán 165 16 27N 95 5W
Judaea = Yehuda 90 31 35N 34 57E
Judenburg 52 47 12N 14 38E
Judith Gap 160 46 48N 109 46W
Judith Pt. 162 41 20N 71 30W
Judith, R. 160 47 30N 109 30W
Juian 109 27 45N 120 38E
Juich'ang 109 29 40N 115 39E
Juigalpa 166 12 6N 85 26W
Juillac 44 45 20N 1 19E
Juist, I. 48 53 40N 7 0E
Juiz de Fora 171 21 43S 43 19W
Jujuy 172 24 10S 65 25W
Jujuy □ 172 23 20S 65 40W
Jukao 109 32 24N 120 35E
Julesberg 158 41 0N 102 20W
Juli 174 16 10S 69 25W
Julia Cr. 138 20 0S 141 11E
Julia Creek 138 20 39S 141 44E
Juliaca 174 15 25S 70 10W
Julian 163 33 4N 116 38W
Julian Alps = Julijske Alpe 63 46 15N 14 1E
Julianakanaal 47 51 6N 5 52E
Julianehåb 12 60 43N 46 0W
Julianstown 38 53 40N 6 16W
Jülich 48 50 55N 6 20E
Julier P. 51 46 28N 9 32E
Julijske Alpe 63 46 15N 14 1E
Julimes 164 28 25N 105 27W
Jullundur 94 31 20N 75 40E
Jumbo 127 17 30S 30 58E
Jumento, Cayos 167 23 0N 75 40E
Jumet 47 50 27N 4 25E
Jumilla 59 38 28N 1 19W
Jumla 95 29 15N 82 13E
Jumna, R. = Yamuna 94 27 0N 78 30E
Junagadh 94 21 30N 70 30E
Junan 109 32 58N 114 31E
Junction, Tex., U.S.A. 159 30 29N 99 48W
Junction, Utah, U.S.A. 161 38 10N 112 15W
Junction B. 138 11 52S 133 55E
Junction City, Kans., U.S.A. 158 39 4N 96 55W
Junction City, Oreg., U.S.A. 160 44 20N 123 12W
Jundah 138 24 46S 143 2E
Jundiaí 173 23 10S 47 0W
Juneau 147 58 26N 134 30W
Junee 141 34 53S 147 35E
Jung Chiang, R. 108 23 25N 110 0E
Jungan 108 25 14N 109 23E
Jungch'ang 108 29 27N 105 33E
Jungch'eng 107 37 9N 122 23E
Jungchiang 108 25 56N 108 31E
Jungching 108 29 49N 102 55E
Jungfrau 50 46 32N 7 58E
Jungho 106 35 21N 110 32E
Junghsien, Kwangsi-Chuang, China 109 22 52N 110 33E
Junghsien, Szechwan, China 108 29 29N 104 22E
Junglinster 47 49 43N 6 15E
Jungshahi 94 24 52N 67 44E
Jungshui 108 24 14N 109 23E
Juniata, R. 162 40 30N 77 40W
Junín 172 34 33S 60 57W
Junín de los Andes 176 39 45S 71 0W
Junnar 96 19 12N 73 58E
Junquera, La 58 42 25N 2 53E
Junta, La 159 38 0N 103 30W
Juntura 160 43 44N 119 4W
Juparanã, Lagoa 171 19 35S 40 18W
Jupiter, R. 151 49 29N 63 37W
Juquiá 171 24 19S 47 38W
Jur, Nahr el 123 8 45N 29 0E
Jura 43 46 35N 6 5E
Jura □ 43 46 47N 5 45E
Jura, I. 34 56 0N 5 50W
Jura, Paps of, mts. 34 55 55N 6 0W
Jura, Sd. of 34 55 57N 5 45W
Jura Suisse 50 47 10N 7 0E
Jurado 174 7 7N 77 46W
Jurby Hd. 32 54 23N 4 31W
Jurien B. 132 30 17S 115 0E
Jurilovca 70 44 46N 28 52W
Jurm 93 36 50N 70 45E
Juruá, R. 174 2 30S 66 0W
Juruena, R. 174 7 20S 58 3W
Juruti 175 2 9S 56 4W
Jushan 107 36 54N 121 30E
Jussey 43 47 50N 5 55E
Justo Daract 172 33 52S 65 12W
Jüterbog 48 51 59N 13 6E
Juticalpa 166 14 40N 85 50W
Jutland 16 56 0N 8 0E
Jutphaas 46 52 2N 5 6E
Jutung 109 32 19N 121 14E
Juvigny-sous-Andaine 42 48 32N 0 30W
Juvisy 43 48 43N 2 23E
Juwain 93 31 45N 61 30E
Juyüan 109 24 46N 113 16E
Juzennecourt 43 48 10N 5 0E
Jye-kundo 99 33 0N 96 50E
Jylhama 74 64 34N 26 40E
Jylland 73 56 15N 9 20E
Jylland (Jutland) 73 56 25N 9 30E
Jyväskylä 74 62 14N 25 44E

K

K. Sedili Besar 101 1 55N 104 5E
K2, Mt. 95 36 0N 77 0E
Ka Lae (South C.) 147 18 55N 155 41W
Kaaia, Mt. 147 21 31N 158 9W
Kaap die Goeie Hoop 128 34 24S 18 30E
Kaap Plato 128 28 30S 24 0E
Kaapkruis 128 21 43S 14 0E
Kaapstad = Cape Town 125 33 56S 18 27E
Kaatsheuvel 47 51 39N 5 2E
Kabaena, I. 103 5 15S 122 0E
Kabala 120 9 38N 11 37W
Kabale 126 1 15S 30 0E
Kabalo 126 6 0S 27 0E
Kabambare 126 4 41S 27 39E
Kabango 127 8 35S 28 30E
Kabanjahe 102 8 2N 98 27E
Kabara 120 16 40N 2 50W
Kabardinka 82 44 40N 37 57E
Kabardino-Balkar, A.S.S.R. □ 83 43 30N 43 30E
Kabarega Falls 126 2 15N 31 38E
Kabasalan 103 7 47N 122 44E
Kabba 121 7 57N 6 3E
Kabe 110 34 31N 132 31E
Kabi 121 13 30N 12 35E
Kabin Buri 100 13 57N 101 43E
Kabinakagami L. 150 48 54N 84 25W
Kabinda 126 6 23S 24 28E
Kablungu, C. 135 6 20S 150 1E
Kabna 122 19 6N 32 40E
Kabompo 127 13 30S 24 14E
Kabompo, R. 127 13 50S 24 10E
Kabondo 127 8 58S 25 40E
Kabongo 126 7 22S 25 33E
Kabou 121 9 28N 0 55E
Kaboudia, Rass 119 35 13N 11 10E

Kabra Kandalakshkiyzaliv

Kabra 138 23 25S 150 25E
Kabūd Gonbad 93 37 5N 59 45E
Kabuiri 121 11 30N 13 30E
Kabul 94 34 28N 69 18E
Kabul □ 93 34 0N 68 30E
Kabul, R. 94 34 30N 69 13E
Kabunga 126 1 38S 28 3E
Kaburuang 103 3 50N 126 30E
Kabushiya 123 16 54N 33 41E
Kabwe 127 14 30S 28 29E
Kabwum 135 6 11S 147 15E
Kačanik 66 42 13N 21 12E
Kachanovo 80 57 25N 27 38E
Kachebera 127 13 56S 32 50E
Kachin □ 98 26 0N 97 0E
Kachira, Lake 126 0 40S 31 0E
Kachiry 76 53 10N 75 50E
Kachisi 123 9 40N 37 57E
Kachkanar 84 58 42N 59 33E
Kachot 101 11 30N 103 3E
Kaçkar 83 40 45N 41 30E
Kadaingti 98 17 37N 97 32E
Kadan Kyun, I. 101 12 30N 98 20E
Kadanai, R. 94 32 0N 66 10E
Kadarkút 53 46 13N 17 39E
Kadayanallur 97 9 3N 77 22E
Kaddi 121 13 40N 5 40E
Kade 121 6 7N 0 56W
Kadgo, L. 137 25 30S 125 30E
Kadi 94 23 18N 72 23E
Kadina 140 34 0S 137 43E
Kadiri 97 14 12N 78 13E
Kadiyevka 83 48 35N 38 30E
Kadoka 158 43 50N 101 31W
Kadom 81 54 37N 42 24E
Kaduna 121 10 30N 7 21E
Kaduna □ 121 11 0N 7 30E
Kaduna, R. 121 10 5N 8 10E
Kadyoha 120 8 58N 5 53W
Kadzhi-Say 85 42 8N 77 10E
Kaedi 120 16 9N 13 28W
Kaelé 121 10 15N 14 15E
Kaena Pt. 147 21 35N 158 17W
Kaeng Khoï 100 14 35N 101 0E
Kaeo 142 35 6S 173 49E
Kaerh, China 105 31 45N 80 22E
Kaerh, Sudan 123 5 35N 31 20E
Kaesŏng 107 37 58N 126 35E
Kaf 92 31 25N 37 20E
Kafakumba 124 9 38S 23 46E
Kafan 79 39 18N 46 15E
Kafanchan 121 9 40N 8 20E
Kafareti 121 10 25N 11 12E
Kaffrine 120 14 8N 15 36W
Kafia Kingi 117 9 20N 24 25E
Kafinda 127 12 32S 30 20E
Kafirévs, Ákra 69 38 9N 24 8E
Kafiristan 93 35 0N 70 30E
Kafr Ana 70 32 2N 34 48E
Kafr 'Ein 90 32 3N 35 7E
Kafr el Dauwâr 122 31 8N 30 8E
Kafr Kama 90 32 44N 35 26E
Kafr Kannã 90 32 45N 35 20E
Kafr Malik 90 32 0N 35 18E
Kafr Mandã 90 32 49N 35 15E
Kafr Quaddum 90 32 14N 35 7E
Kafr Ra'i 90 32 23N 35 9E
Kafr Sir 90 33 19N 35 23E
Kafr Yasif 90 32 58N 35 10E
Kafue 127 15 46S 28 9E
Kafue Flats 127 15 32S 27 0E
Kafue Gorge 127 16 0S 28 0E
Kafue Hook 127 14 58S 26 0E
Kafue Nat. Park 65 15 30S 25 40E
Kafue, R. 125 15 30S 26 0E
Kafulwe 127 9 0S 29 1E
Kaga, Afghan. 94 34 14N 70 10E
Kaga, Japan 111 36 16N 136 15E
Kagamil I. 147 53 0N 169 40W
Kagan 85 39 43N 64 33E
Kagawa-ken □ 110 34 15N 134 0E
Kagera R. 126 1 15S 31 20E
Kagoshima 110 31 36N 130 40E
Kagoshima-ken □ 110 30 0N 130 0E
Kagoshima-Wan 110 31 0N 130 40E
Kagul 82 45 50N 28 15E
Kahajan, R. 102 2 10S 114 0E
Kahama 126 4 8S 32 30E
Kahama □ 126 3 40S 32 0E
Kahang 101 2 12N 103 32E
Kahe 126 3 30S 37 25E
Kahemba 124 7 18S 18 55E
Kaherekoua Mts. 143 45 45S 167 15E
Kahniah, R. 152 58 15N 120 55W
Kahnuj 93 27 55N 57 40E
Kahoka 158 40 25N 91 42W
Kahoolawe, I. 147 20 33N 156 35W
Kahuku & Pt. 147 21 41N 157 57W
Kahului 147 20 54N 156 28W
Kahurangi, Pt. 143 40 50S 172 10E
Kahuta 94 33 35N 73 24E
Kai Kai 128 19 52S 21 15E
Kai, Kepulauan 103 5 55S 132 45W
Kaiama 121 9 36N 4 1E
Kaiapit 135 6 18S 146 18E
Kaiapoi 143 42 24S 172 40E
Kaibara 111 35 8N 135 5E
K'aichien 109 23 45N 111 47E
K'aifeng 106 34 50N 114 27E
Kaihsien 107 40 25N 122 25E
K'aihsien 108 31 12N 108 25E
K'aihua 109 29 9N 118 24E
Kaiingveld 128 30 0S 22 0E
Kaikohe 142 35 25S 173 49E
Kaikoura 143 42 25S 173 43E
Kaikoura Pen. 143 42 25S 173 43E
Kaikoura Ra. 143 41 59S 173 41E
Kailahun 120 8 18N 10 39W
Kailashahar 98 25 19N 92 0E
Kaili 108 26 32N 107 57E
K'ailu 107 43 35N 121 12E
Kailua 147 19 39N 156 0W
Kaimana 103 3 30S 133 45E
Kaimanawa Mts. 142 39 15S 175 56E
Kaimata 143 42 34S 171 28E
Kaimganj 95 27 33N 79 24E
Kaimon-Dake 110 31 11N 130 32E
Kaimur Hill 95 24 30N 82 0E
Kainan 110 34 9N 135 12E
Kainantu 135 6 18S 145 52E
Kaingaroa Forest 142 38 30S 176 30E
Kainji Res. 121 10 1N 4 40E
Kaipara Harb. 142 36 25S 174 14E
K'aip'ing 109 22 31N 112 32E
Kaipokok B. 151 54 54N 59 47W
Kairana 94 29 33N 77 15E
Kairiru, I. 138 3 20S 143 20E
Kaironi 103 0 47S 133 40E
Kairouan 119 35 45N 10 5E
Kairuku 135 8 51S 146 35E
Kaiserslautern 49 49 30N 7 43E
Kaitaia 142 35 8S 173 17E
Kaitangata 143 46 17S 169 51E
Kaithal 94 29 48N 76 26E
Kaitu, R. 94 33 20N 70 20E
Kaiwi Channel 147 21 13N 157 30W
K'aiyang 108 27 4N 106 55E
K'aiyüan, Liaoning, China 107 42 33N 124 4E
K'aiyüan, Yunnan, China 108 23 47N 103 10E
Kaiyuh Mts. 147 63 40N 159 0W
Kajaani 74 64 17N 27 46E
Kajabbi 138 20 0S 140 1E
Kajan, R. 102 2 40N 116 40E
Kajang 101 2 59N 101 48E
Kajeli 103 3 20S 127 10E
Kajiado 126 1 53S 36 48E
Kajiki 110 31 44N 130 40E
Kajo Kaji 123 3 58N 31 40E
Kajoa, I. 103 0 1N 127 28E
Kajuagung 102 32 8S 104 46E
Kakabeka Falls 150 48 24N 89 37W
Kakamas 125 28 45S 20 33E
Kakamega 126 0 20N 34 46E
Kakamega □ 126 0 20N 34 46E
Kakamigahara 111 35 28N 136 48E
Kakanj 66 44 9N 18 7E
Kakanui Mts. 143 45 10S 170 30E
Kakapotahi 143 43 0S 170 45E
Kake, Japan 110 34 36N 132 19E
Kake, U.S.A. 147 57 0N 134 0W
Kakegawa 111 34 45N 138 1E
Kakhib 83 42 28N 46 34E
Kakhovskoye Vdkhr. 82 47 5N 34 16E
Kakia 125 24 48S 23 22E
Kakinada = Cocanada 99 16 50N 82 11E
Kakinada (Cocanada) 96 16 50N 82 11E
Kakisa L. 152 60 56N 117 43W
Kakisa, R. 152 61 3N 117 10W
Kakogawa 110 34 46N 134 51E
Kaktovik 147 70 8N 143 50W
Kakwa, R. 152 54 37N 118 28W
Kala 121 12 2N 14 40E
Kala Oya. 97 8 15N 80 0E
Kala Shank'ou 95 35 42N 78 20E
Kalaa-Kebira 119 35 59N 10 32E
Kalabagh 94 33 0N 71 28E
Kalabáka 68 39 42N 21 39E
Kalabo 125 14 58S 22 33E
Kalach 81 50 22N 41 0E
Kaladan, R. 99 21 30N 92 45E
Kalahari, Des. 128 24 0S 22 0E
Kalahari Gemsbok Nat. Pk. 128 26 0S 20 30E
Kalahasti 97 13 45N 79 44E
Kalai-Khumb 85 38 28N 70 46E
Kalaja e Turrës 68 41 10N 19 28E
Kalakamati 129 20 40S 27 25E
Kalakan 77 55 15N 116 45E
K'alak'unlun Shank'ou 95 35 33N 77 46E
Kalam 95 35 34N 72 30E
Kalama, U.S.A. 160 46 0N 122 55W
Kalama, Zaïre 126 2 52S 28 35E
Kalamariá 68 40 33N 22 55E
Kalamata 69 37 3N 22 10E
Kalamazoo 156 42 20N 85 35W
Kalamazoo, R. 156 42 40N 86 12W
Kalamb 96 18 3N 74 48E
Kalambo Falls 127 8 37S 31 35E
Kálamos, I. 69 38 37N 20 55E
Kalamoti 69 38 15N 26 4E
Kalamunda 137 32 0S 116 0E
Kalangadoo 140 37 34S 140 41E
Kalannie 137 30 22S 117 5E
Kalao, I. 103 7 21S 121 0E
Kalaotoa, I. 103 7 20S 121 50E
Kälarne 72 62 59N 16 8E
Kalárovo 53 47 54N 18 0E
Kalasin 100 16 26N 103 30E
Kalat 93 29 8N 66 31E
Kalat □ 93 27 0N 64 30E
Kalat-i-Ghilzai 93 32 15N 66 58E
Kálathos (Calato) 69 36 9N 28 8E
Kalaupapa 147 21 12N 156 59W
Kalaus, R. 83 45 40N 43 30E
Kalávrita 69 38 3N 22 8E
Kalaw 98 16 24N 97 30E
Kalba 120 9 30N 2 42W
Kalbarri 137 27 40S 114 10E
Kaldhovd 71 60 5N 8 20E
Kalecik 82 40 4N 33 26E
Kalegauk Kyun 99 15 33N 97 35E
Kalehe 126 2 6S 28 50E
Kalema 126 1 12S 31 55E
Kalemie 124 5 55S 29 9E
Kalemyo 98 23 11N 94 4E
Kalety 54 50 35N 18 52E
Kalewa 98 22 41N 95 32E
Kálfafellsstaður 74 64 11N 15 53W
Kalgan = Changchiak'ou 106 40 50N 114 53E
Kalgoorlie 137 30 40S 121 22E
Kaliakra, Nos 67 43 21N 28 30E
Kalianda 102 5 50S 105 45E
Kalibo 103 11 43N 122 22E
Kaliganj Town 98 23 25N 89 8E
Kalima 126 2 33S 26 32E
Kalimantan Barat □ 102 0 0 110 30E
Kalimantan Selatan □ 102 4 10S 115 30E
Kalimantan Tengah □ 102 2 0S 113 30E
Kalimantan Timor □ 102 1 30N 116 30E
Kálimnos, I. 69 37 0N 27 0E
Kalimpong 95 27 4N 88 35E
Kalinadi, R. 97 14 50N 74 20E
Kalinin 81 56 55N 35 55E
Kaliningrad 80 54 42N 20 32E
Kalinino 83 45 12N 38 59E
Kalininskoye 85 42 50N 73 49E
Kalinkovichi 80 52 12N 29 20E
Kalinovik 66 43 31N 18 29E
Kalipetrovo (Starčevo) 67 44 5N 27 14E
Kaliro 126 0 56N 33 30E
Kalirrákhi 68 40 40N 24 35E
Kalispell 160 48 10N 114 22W
Kalisz 54 51 45N 18 8E
Kalisz □ 54 51 30N 18 0E
Kalisz Pom 54 53 17N 15 55E
Kaliua 126 5 5S 31 48E
Kaliveli Tank 97 12 5N 79 50E
Kalix R. 74 67 0N 22 0E
Kalka 94 30 56N 76 57E
Kalkaroo 140 31 12S 143 54E
Kalkaska 150 44 44N 85 11W
Kalkfeld 128 20 57S 16 14E
Kalkfontein 128 22 4S 20 57E
Kalkfontein Dam 128 29 30S 24 15E
Kalkrand 128 24 1S 17 35E
Kall L. 72 63 35N 13 10E
Kallakurichi 97 11 44N 79 1E
Kållandsö 73 58 40N 13 5E
Källby 73 58 30N 13 8E
Kallia 86 31 46N 35 30E
Kallidaikurichi 97 8 38N 77 31E
Kallinge 73 56 15N 15 18E
Kallithéa 69 37 55N 23 41E
Kallmeti 68 41 51N 19 41E
Kallonís, Kólpos 69 39 10N 26 10E
Kallsjön 74 63 38N 13 0E
Kalltorp 73 58 23N 13 20E
Kalmalo 121 13 40N 5 20E
Kalmar 73 56 40N 16 20E
Kalmar län □ 73 57 25N 16 15E
Kalmar sund 73 56 40N 16 25E
Kalmthout 47 51 23N 4 29E
Kalmyk A.S.S.R. □ 83 46 5N 46 1E
Kalmykovo 83 49 0N 51 35E
Kalna 95 23 13N 88 25E
Kalo 135 10 1S 147 48E
Kalocsa 53 46 32N 19 0E
Kalofer 67 42 37N 24 59E
Kalol, Gujarat, India 94 23 15N 72 33E
Kalol, Gujarat, India 94 22 37N 73 31E
Kalola 127 10 0S 28 0E
Kalolímnos 69 37 4N 27 8E
Kalomo 127 17 0S 26 30E
Kalonerón 69 37 20N 21 38E
Kalpi 95 26 8N 79 47E
Kalrayan Hills 97 11 45N 78 40E
Kalsubai, Mt. 96 17 35N 73 45E
Kaltbrunn 51 47 13N 9 2E
Kaltungo 121 9 48N 11 19E
Kalu 94 25 5N 67 39E
Kaluga 81 54 35N 36 10E
Kalulushi 127 12 50S 28 3E
Kalundborg 73 55 41N 11 5E
Kalush 80 42 9N 24 12E
Kałuszyn 54 52 13N 21 52E
Kalutara 97 6 35N 80 0E
Kalwaria 54 49 53N 19 41E
Kalya 84 60 15N 59 59E
Kalyan, Austral. 140 34 55S 139 49E
Kalyan, India 96 20 30N 74 3E
Kalyani 174 17 53N 76 59E
Kalyazin 81 57 15N 37 45E
Kam Keut 101 18 20N 104 48E
Kama, Burma 98 22 10N 95 10E
Kama, Zaïre 126 3 30S 27 5E
Kama, R. 84 60 0N 53 0E
Kamachumu 126 1 37S 31 37E
Kamae 110 32 48N 131 56E
Kamaguenam 121 13 36N 10 30E
Kamaing 98 24 26N 94 55E
Kamaishi 112 39 20N 142 0E
Kamakura 111 35 19N 139 33E
Kamalia 94 30 44N 72 42E
Kamalino 147 21 50N 160 14W
Kamamaung 98 17 21N 97 40E
Kamango 126 0 40N 29 52E
Kamapanda 127 12 5S 24 0E
Kamaran 91 15 28N 42 35E
Kamashi 85 38 51N 65 23E
Kamativi 127 18 15S 0 27E
Kamba 121 11 50N 3 45E
Kambalda 137 31 10S 121 37E
Kambam 97 9 45N 77 16E
Kambar 94 27 37N 68 1E
Kambarka 84 56 15N 54 11E
Kambia 120 9 3N 12 53W
Kambolé 127 8 47S 30 48E
Kambove 127 10 51S 26 33E
Kamchatka, P-ov. 77 57 0N 160 0E
Kamde 138 8 0S 140 58E
Kamen 76 53 50N 81 30E
Kamen Kashirskiy 80 51 39N 24 56E
Kamenica 66 44 25N 19 40E
Kamenice 52 49 18N 15 2E
Kamenjak, Rt. 63 44 47N 13 55E
Kamenka, R.S.F.S.R., U.S.S.R. 78 65 58N 44 0E
Kamenka, R.S.F.S.R., U.S.S.R. 81 50 47N 39 20E
Kamenka Bugskaya 80 50 8N 24 16E
Kamenka Dneprovskaya 82 47 29N 34 14E
Kamensk 76 56 25N 62 45E
Kamensk Shakhtinskiy 83 48 23N 40 20E
Kamensk-Uralskiy 84 56 25N 62 2E
Kamenskiy 81 50 48N 45 25E
Kamenskoye 77 62 45N 165 30E
Kamenyak 67 43 24N 26 57E
Kamenz 48 51 17N 14 7E
Kameoka 111 35 0N 135 35E
Kames 34 55 53N 5 15W
Kameyama 111 34 51N 126 27E
Kami 68 42 17N 20 18E
Kami-Jima 110 32 27N 130 20E
Kami-koshiki-Jima 110 31 50N 129 52E
Kamiah 160 46 12N 116 2W
Kamien Krajenskie 54 53 32N 17 32E
Kamien Pomorski 54 53 57N 14 43E
Kamiensk 54 51 12N 19 29E
Kamitsu 110 34 6N 134 22E
Kamilonísion 69 35 50N 26 15E
Kamilukuak, L. 153 62 22N 101 40W
Kamina 127 8 45S 25 0E
Kaminak L. 153 62 10N 95 0W
Kamioka 111 36 25N 137 15E
Kamituga Mungombe 126 3 2S 28 10E
Kamiyaku 112 30 25N 130 30E
Kamloops 152 50 40N 120 20W
Kamo 143 35 42S 174 20E
Kamogawa 111 35 5N 140 5E
Kamoke 94 32 4N 74 4E
Kamono 124 3 10S 13 20E
Kamp, R. 52 48 35N 15 26E
Kampala 126 0 20N 32 30E
Kampar 101 4 18N 101 9E
Kampar, R. 102 0 30N 102 0E
Kampen 46 52 33N 5 53E
Kamperland 47 51 34N 3 43E
Kamphaeng Phet 100 16 28N 99 30E
Kampolombo, L. 127 11 30S 29 35E
Kampong Ayer Puteh 101 4 15N 103 10E
Kampong Jerangau 101 4 50N 103 10E
Kampong Raja 101 5 45N 102 35E
Kampong Sedili Besar 101 1 56N 104 8E
Kampong To 101 6 3N 101 13E
Kampot 101 10 36N 104 10E
Kamptee 94 21 9N 79 19E
Kampti 120 10 7N 3 25W
Kampuchea ■ = Cambodia 100 12 15N 105 0E
Kamrau, Teluk 103 3 30S 133 45E
Kamsack 153 51 34N 101 54W
Kamskove Ustye 81 55 10N 49 20E
Kamskoye Vdkhr. 78 58 0N 56 0E
Kamuchawie L. 153 56 18N 101 59W
Kamui-Misaki 112 45 3N 142 30E
Kamyshin 81 50 10N 45 30E
Kamyshlov 84 56 50N 62 43E
Kamyzyak 83 46 4N 48 10E
Kan 98 20 53N 93 49E
Kan Chiang, R. 109 29 45N 116 10E
Kanaaupscow 150 54 2N 76 30W
Kanab 161 37 3N 112 29W
Kanab Creek 161 37 0N 112 40W
Kanaga I. 147 51 45N 177 22W
Kanagawa-ken □ 111 35 20N 139 20E
Kanairiktok, R. 151 55 2N 60 18W
Kanakanak 147 59 0N 158 58W
Kanakapura 97 12 33N 77 28E
Kanália 68 39 30N 22 53E
Kananga 124 5 55S 22 18E
Kanarraville 161 37 34N 113 12W
Kanash 81 55 48N 47 32E
Kanawha, R. 156 39 40N 82 0W
Kanayis, Ras el 122 31 30N 28 5E
Kanazawa 111 36 30N 136 38E
Kanbalu 98 17 55N 85 24E
Kanchanaburi 100 14 8N 99 31E
Kanchenjunga, Mt. 95 27 50N 88 10E
Kanchipuram (Conjeeveram) 97 12 52N 79 45E
Kanchou 109 25 51N 114 59E
Kanch'üan 106 36 19N 109 19E
Kanda Kanda 124 6 52S 23 48E
Kandagach 79 49 20N 57 15E
Kandahar 94 31 32N 65 30E
Kandahar □ 94 31 0N 65 0E
Kandalaksha 78 67 9N 32 30E
Kandalakshkiyzaliv 78 66 0N 35 0E

Kandalu Kástron

Kandalu 93 29 55N 63 20 E
Kandangan 102 2 50S 115 20 E
Kandanos 69 35 19N 23 44 E
Kandé 121 9 57N 1 53 E
Kandep 135 5 54S 143 32 E
Kander, R. 50 46 33N 7 38 E
Kandersteg 50 46 30N 7 40 E
Kandewu 127 14 1S 26 16 E
Kandhíla 69 37 46N 22 22 E
Kandhkot 94 28 16N 69 8 E
Kandhla 94 29 18N 77 19 E
Kandi, Benin 121 11 7N 2 55 E
Kandi, India 95 23 58N 88 5 E
Kandinduna 127 13 58S 24 19 E
Kandira 92 41 5N 30 10 E
Kandla 94 23 0N 70 10 E
Kandos 141 32 45S 149 58 E
Kandrach 93 25 30N 65 30 E
Kandrian 135 6 14S 149 37 E
Kandukur 95 15 12N 79 57 E
Kandy 97 7 18N 80 43 E
Kane 156 41 39N 78 53W
Kane Bassin 12 79 30N 68 0W
Kanel 120 13 18N 14 35W
Kaneohe 147 21 25N 157 48W
Kanevskaya 83 46 3N 39 3 E
Kanfanar 63 45 7N 13 50 E
Kang 93 30 55N 61 55 E
Kangaba 120 11 56N 8 25W
Kangar 101 6 27N 100 12 E
Kangaroo I. 140 35 45S 137 0 E
Kangaroo Mts. 138 23 25S 142 0 E
Kangavar 92 34 40N 48 0 E
Kangean, Kepulauan 102 6 55S 115 23 E
Kangerdlugsuaé 12 68 10N 32 20W
Kanggye 107 41 0N 126 35 E
Kanggyŏng 107 36 10N 126 0 E
Kanghwa 107 37 45N 126 30 E
K'angkang 108 32 46N 101 3 E
Kangnŭng 107 37 45N 128 54 E
Kango 124 0 11N 10 5 E
K'angp'ing 107 43 45N 123 20 E
Kangpokpi 98 25 8N 93 58 E
K'angting 108 30 2N 102 0 E
Kangtissu Shan 95 31 0N 82 0 E
Kangto, Mt. 99 27 50N 92 35 E
Kangyao 107 44 15N 126 40 E
Kangyidaung 98 16 56N 94 54 E
Kanhangad 97 12 21N 74 58 E
Kanheri 96 19 13N 72 50 E
Kani, China 99 29 25N 95 25 E
Kani, Ivory C. 120 8 29N 6 36W
Kaniama 126 7 30S 24 12 E
Kaniapiskau L. 151 54 10N 69 55W
Kaniapiskau, R. 151 57 40N 69 30 E
Kanibadam 85 40 17N 70 25 E
Kanin Nos, Mys 78 68 45N 43 20 E
Kanin, P-ov. 78 68 0N 45 0 E
Kanina 68 40 23N 19 30 E
Kaniva 140 36 22S 141 18 E
Kanjiza 66 46 3N 20 4 E
Kanjut Sar 95 36 15N 75 25 E
Kankakee 156 41 6N 87 50W
Kankakee, R. 156 41 13N 87 0W
Kankan 120 10 30N 9 15W
Kanker 96 20 10N 81 40 E
Kankouchen 107 40 30N 119 27 E
Kanku 106 34 45N 105 12 E
Kankunskiy 77 57 37N 126 8 E
Kanmuri-Yama 110 34 30N 132 4 E
Kannabe 110 34 32N 133 23 E
Kannapolis 157 35 32N 80 37W
Kannauj 95 27 3N 79 26 E
Kannod 93 22 45N 76 40 E
Kano 121 12 2N 8 30 E
Kano □ 121 12 30N 9 0 E
Kan'onji 110 34 7N 133 39 E
Kanoroba 120 9 7N 6 8W
Kanowit 102 2 14N 112 20 E
Kanowna 137 30 32S 121 31 E
Kanoya 110 31 25N 130 50 E
Kanózuga 54 49 58N 22 25 E
Kanpetlet 98 21 10N 93 59 E
Kanpur 95 26 35N 80 20 E
Kansas □ 158 38 40N 98 0W
Kansas City, Kans., U.S.A. 158 39 0N 94 40W
Kansas City, Mo., U.S.A. 158 39 3N 94 30W
Kansas, R. 158 39 15N 96 20W
Kansenia 127 10 20S 26 0 E
Kansk 77 56 20N 95 37 E
Kansŏng 107 38 24N 128 30 E
Kansu □ 105 35 30N 104 30 E
Kant 85 42 53N 74 51 E
Kant'angtzu 106 37 28N 104 33 E
Kantché 121 13 31N 8 30 E
Kantemirovka 83 49 43N 39 55 E
Kantharalak 100 14 39N 104 39 E
Kantishna 147 63 31N 151 5W
Kantō □ 111 36 0N 140 0 E
Kantō-Heiya 111 36 0N 139 30 E
Kantō-Sanchi 111 35 50N 138 50 E
Kantu-long 98 19 57N 97 36 E
Kanturk 39 52 10N 8 55W
Kantzu 108 31 37N 100 0 E
Kanuma 111 36 44N 139 42 E
Kanus 128 27 50S 18 39 E
Kanye 128 25 0S 25 28 E
Kanyu 128 20 7S 24 37 E
Kanyü 107 34 53N 119 9 E
Kanzene 127 10 30S 25 12 E
Kanzi, Ras 126 7 1S 39 33 E
Kaoan 109 28 25N 115 22 E
Kaochou 109 21 55N 110 52 E
Kaohofu 109 30 43N 116 49 E
Kaohsien 108 28 21N 104 31 E
Kaohsiung 109 22 35N 120 16 E
Kaok'eng 109 27 39N 114 4 E
Kaoko Otavi 125 18 12S 13 45 E
Kaokoveld 128 19 0S 13 0 E
Kaolack 120 14 5N 16 8W
Kaolan Shan 109 21 55N 113 15 E
Kaolikung Shan 108 26 0N 98 55 E
Kaomi 107 36 25N 119 45 E
Kaopao Hu 109 32 50N 119 15 E
Kaop'ing 106 35 48N 112 55 E
K'aoshant'un 107 44 25N 124 27 E
Kaot'ang 106 36 51N 116 13 E
Kaoyang 106 38 42N 115 47 E
Kaoyu 109 32 46N 119 32 E
Kaoyüan 107 37 7N 118 0 E
Kapaa 147 22 5N 159 19W
Kapadvanj 94 23 5N 73 0 E
Kapagere 135 9 46S 147 42 E
Kapanga 124 8 30S 22 40 E
Kapanovka 83 47 28N 46 50 E
Kapata 127 14 16S 26 15 E
Kapellen 47 51 19N 4 25 E
Kapello, Ákra 69 36 9N 23 3 E
Kapema 127 10 45S 28 22 E
Kapfenberg 52 47 26N 15 18 E
Kapiri Mposhi 127 13 59S 28 43 E
Kapiskau 150 52 50N 82 1W
Kapiskau, R. 150 52 47N 81 55W
Kapit 102 2 0N 113 5 E
Kapiti I. 142 40 50S 174 56 E
Kaplice 52 48 42N 14 30 E
Kapoe 101 9 34N 98 32 E
Kapoeta 123 4 50N 33 35 E
Kápolnásnyék 53 47 16N 18 41 E
Kaponga 143 39 29S 174 9 E
Kapos, R. 53 46 30N 18 20 E
Kaposvár 53 46 25N 17 47 E
Kappeln 48 54 37N 9 56 E
Kapps 128 22 32S 17 18 E
Kaprije 63 43 42N 15 43 E
Kaprijke 47 51 13N 3 38 E
Kapsan 107 41 4N 128 19 E
Kapsukas 80 54 33N 23 19 E
Kapuas Hulu, Pegunungan 102 1 30N 113 30 E
Kapuas, R. 102 0 20N 111 40 E
Kapuka 127 10 30S 32 55 E
Kapulo 127 8 18S 29 15 E
Kapunda 140 34 20S 138 56 E
Kapurthala 94 31 23N 75 25 E
Kapuskasing 150 49 25N 82 30W
Kapuskasing, R. 150 49 49N 82 0W
Kapustin Yar 83 48 37N 45 40 E
Kaputar, Mt. 139 30 15S 150 10 E
Kaputir 126 2 5N 35 28 E
Kapuvár 53 47 36N 17 1 E
Kara, Turkey 69 38 29N 26 19 E
Kara, U.S.S.R. 76 69 10N 65 25 E
Kara Bogaz Gol, Zaliv 76 41 0N 53 30 E
Kara Burun 69 38 41N 26 28 E
Kara, I. 69 36 58N 27 30 E
Kara Kalpak A.S.S.R. □ 76 43 0N 60 0 E
Kara Kum 76 39 30N 60 0 E
Kara-Saki 110 34 41N 129 30 E
Kara Sea 76 75 0N 70 0 E
Kara Su 85 40 44N 72 53 E
Kara, Wadi 122 20 40N 42 0 E
Karabash 84 55 29N 60 14 E
Karabekaul 85 38 30N 64 8 E
Karabük 82 41 10N 32 30 E
Karabulak 85 44 54N 78 30 E
Karaburuni 68 40 25N 19 20 E
Karabutak 84 49 59N 60 14 E
Karachala 83 39 45N 48 53 E
Karachayevsk 83 43 50N 42 0 E
Karachev 80 53 10N 35 5 E
Karachi 94 24 53N 67 0 E
Karachi □ 94 25 30N 67 0 E
Karad 96 17 15N 74 10 E
Karadeniz Boğazı 92 41 10N 29 5 E
Karadeniz Dağlari 92 41 30N 35 0 E
Karaga 121 9 58N 0 28W
Karagajly 76 49 26N 76 0 E
Karaganda 76 49 50N 73 0 E
Karaginskiy, Ostrov 77 58 45N 164 0 E
Karagwe □ 126 2 0S 31 0 E
Karaikal 97 10 59N 79 50 E
Karaikkudi 97 10 0N 78 45 E
Karaitivu I. 97 9 45N 79 52 E
Karaj 93 35 4N 51 0 E
Karak, Jordan 90 31 14N 35 40 E
Karak, Malay. 101 3 25N 102 2 E
Karakas 76 48 20N 83 30 E
Karakitang 103 3 14N 125 28 E
Karakobis 128 22 3S 20 37 E
Karakoram 95 35 20N 76 0 E
Karakoram P. = K'alak'unlun Shank'ou 95 35 33N 77 46 E
Karakoram Pass 93 35 20N 78 0 E
Karakul, Tadzhik, S.S.R., U.S.S.R. 85 39 2N 73 33 E
Karakul, Uzbek S.S.R., U.S.S.R. 85 39 22N 63 50 E
Karakuldzha 85 40 39N 73 26 E
Karakulino 84 56 1N 53 43 E
Karalon 77 57 5N 115 50 E
Karaman 92 37 14N 33 13 E
Karambu 102 3 53S 116 6 E
Karamea 143 41 14S 172 6 E
Karamea Bight 143 41 22S 171 40 E
Karamea, R. 143 41 13S 172 26 E
Karamet Niyaz 85 37 45N 64 34 E
Karamoja □ 126 3 0N 34 15 E
Karamsad 94 22 35N 72 50 E
Karanganjar 103 7 38S 109 37 E
Karanja 96 20 29N 77 31 E
Karapoit 142 37 53S 175 32 E
Karaşar 82 40 21N 31 55 E
Karasburg 128 28 0S 18 44 E
Karasino 76 66 50N 86 50 E
Karasjok 74 69 27N 25 30 E
Karasuk 76 53 44N 78 2 E
Karasuk □ 126 2 12N 35 15 E
Karasuyama 111 36 39N 140 9 E
Karatau 85 43 10N 70 28 E
Karatau, Khrebet 85 43 30N 69 30 E
Karativu, I. 97 8 22N 79 52 E
Karatiya 90 31 39N 34 43 E
Karatobe 84 49 44N 53 30 E
Karatoya, R. 98 24 7N 89 36 E
Karaturuk 85 43 35N 78 0 E
Karaul-Bazar 85 39 30N 64 48 E
Karauli 94 26 30N 77 4 E
Karavasta 68 40 53N 19 28 E
Karawa 124 3 18N 20 17 E
Karawanken 52 46 30N 14 40 E
Karazhal 76 48 2N 70 49 E
Karbala 92 32 47N 44 3 E
Kårböle 72 61 59N 15 22 E
Karcag 53 47 19N 21 1 E
Karcha, R. 95 34 15N 75 57 E
Kärda 73 57 10N 13 49 E
Kardeljevo 66 43 2N 17 27 E
Kardhámila 69 38 35N 26 5 E
Kardhítsa 68 39 23N 21 54 E
Kardhítsa □ 68 39 15N 21 50 E
Kärdla 80 58 50N 22 40 E
Kareeberge 128 30 50S 22 0 E
Kareima 122 18 30N 31 49 E
Karelian A.S.S.R. □ 78 65 30N 32 30 E
Karema, P.N.G. 135 9 12S 147 18 E
Karema, Tanz. 126 6 49S 30 24 E
Karen 101 12 49N 92 53 E
Karganrud 92 37 55N 49 0 E
Kargapolye 84 55 57N 64 24 E
Kargasok 76 59 3N 80 53 E
Kargat 76 55 10N 80 15 E
Kargı 82 41 11N 34 30 E
Kargil 95 34 32N 76 12 E
Kargowa 54 52 5N 15 51 E
Karguéri 121 13 36N 10 30 E
Kariai 69 40 14N 24 19 E
Kariba 127 16 28S 28 36 E
Kariba Dam 125 16 30S 28 35 E
Kariba Gorge 127 16 30S 28 35 E
Kariba Lake 127 16 40S 28 25 E
Karibib 128 21 0S 15 56 E
Karikal 97 10 59N 79 50 E
Karikkale 92 39 55N 33 30 E
Karimata, Kepulauan 102 1 40S 109 0 E
Karimata, Selat 102 2 0S 108 20 E
Karimnagar 96 18 26N 79 10 E
Karimundjawa, Kepulauan 102 5 50S 110 30 E
Karin 91 10 50N 45 52 E
Káristos 69 38 1N 24 29 E
Karitane 51 45 38S 170 39 E
Kariya 111 34 58N 137 1 E
Karkal 97 13 15N 74 56 E
Karkar I. 135 4 40S 146 0 E
Karkinitskiy Zaliv 82 45 36N 32 35 E
Karkur 90 32 29N 34 57 E
Karkur Tohl 122 22 5N 25 5 E
Karl Libknekht 80 51 40N 35 45 E
Karl-Marx-Stadt 48 50 50N 12 55 E
Karl-Marx-Stadt □ 48 50 45N 13 0 E
Karla, L = Voiviis, Limni 68 39 35N 22 45 E
Karlino 54 54 3N 15 53 E
Karlobag 63 44 32N 15 5 E
Karlovac 63 45 31N 15 36 E
Karlovka 82 49 29N 35 8 E
Karlovy Vary 52 50 13N 12 51 E
Karlsborg 73 58 33N 14 33 E
Karlshamn 73 56 10N 14 51 E
Karlskoga 72 59 22N 14 33 E
Karlskrona 73 56 10N 15 35 E
Karlsruhe 49 49 3N 8 23 E
Karlstad, Sweden 72 59 23N 13 30 E
Karlstad, U.S.A. 158 48 38N 96 30W
Karmøy 71 59 15N 5 15 E
Karnal 94 29 42N 77 2 E
Karnali, R. 95 29 0N 82 0 E
Karnaphuli Res. 98 22 40N 92 20 E
Karnataka □ 97 13 15N 77 0 E
Karnes City 159 28 53N 97 53W
Karni 120 10 45N 2 40W
Karnische Alpen 52 46 36N 13 0 E
Karnobat 67 42 40N 27 0 E
Kärnten □ 52 46 52N 13 30 E
Karo 120 12 16N 2 22W
Karoi 127 16 48S 29 45 E
Karonga 127 9 57S 33 55 E
Karoonda 140 35 1S 139 59 E
Karos, Is. 69 36 54N 25 40 E
Karousâdhes 68 39 47N 19 45 E
Karpalund 73 56 4N 14 5 E
Kárpathos, I. 69 35 37N 27 10 E
Kárpathos, Stenón 69 36 0N 27 30 E
Karpinsk 84 59 45N 60 1 E
Karpogory 78 63 59N 44 27 E
Karrebaek 73 55 12N 11 39 E
Kars 92 40 40N 43 5 E
Karsakpay 76 47 55N 66 40 E
Karsha 83 49 45N 51 35 E
Karshi 85 38 53N 65 48 E
Karsun 81 54 14N 46 57 E
Kartál Óros 68 41 15N 25 13 E
Kartaly 84 53 3N 60 40 E
Kartapur 94 31 27N 75 32 E
Kartuzy 54 54 22N 18 10 E
Karuah 141 32 37S 151 56 E
Karufa 103 3 50S 133 20 E
Karumba 138 17 31S 140 50 E
Karumo 126 2 25S 32 50 E
Karumwa 126 3 12S 32 38 E
Karungu 126 0 50S 34 10 E
Karunjie 136 16 18S 127 12 E
Karup 73 56 19N 9 10 E
Karur 97 10 59N 78 2 E
Karviná 53 49 53N 18 25 E
Karwar 93 14 55N 74 13 E
Karwi 95 25 12N 80 57 E
Kas Kong 101 11 27N 102 12 E
Kasache 127 13 25S 34 20 E
Kasai 110 34 55N 134 52 E
Kasai Occidental □ 127 6 30S 22 30 E
Kasai Oriental □ 126 5 0S 24 30 E
Kasai, R. 124 8 20S 22 0 E
Kasaji 127 10 25S 23 27 E
Kasama, Japan 111 36 23N 140 16 E
Kasama, Zambia 127 10 16S 31 9 E
Kasandong 107 41 18N 126 55 E
Kasane 128 17 34S 24 50 E
Kasanga 127 8 30S 31 10 E
Kasangulu 124 4 15S 15 15 E
Kasaoka 110 34 30N 133 30 E
Kasaragod 97 12 30N 74 58 E
Kasat 98 15 56N 98 13 E
Kasba 98 25 51N 87 37 E
Kasba L. 153 60 20N 102 10W
Kasba Tadla 118 32 36N 6 17W
Kaschmar 93 35 16N 58 26 E
Kaseberga 73 55 24N 14 8 E
Kaseda 110 31 25N 130 19 E
Kasempa 127 13 30S 25 44 E
Kasenga 127 10 20S 28 45 E
Kasese 126 0 13N 30 3 E
Kasewa 127 14 28S 28 53 E
Kasganj 95 27 48N 78 42 E
Kashabowie 150 48 40N 90 26W
Kashan 93 34 5N 51 30 E
Kashgar = K'oshin 105 39 29N 75 58 E
Kashihara 111 34 35N 135 37 E
Kashima, Ibaraki, Japan 111 35 58N 140 38 E
Kashima, Saga, Japan 110 33 7N 130 6 E
Kashima-Nada 111 36 0N 140 45 E
Kashimbo 127 11 12S 26 19 E
Kashin 81 57 20N 37 36 E
Kashipur, Orissa, India 96 19 16N 83 3 E
Kashipur, Ut. P., India 95 29 15N 79 0 E
Kashira 81 54 45N 38 10 E
Kashiwa 111 35 52N 139 59 E
Kashiwazaki 112 37 22N 138 33 E
Kashkasu 85 39 54N 72 44 E
Kashmir □ 95 32 44N 74 54 E
Kashmor 94 28 28N 69 32 E
Kashpirovka 81 53 0N 48 30 E
Kashum Tso 99 34 45N 86 0 E
Kashun Noerh 105 42 25N 101 0 E
Kasimov 81 54 55N 41 20 E
Kasing 126 6 15S 26 58 E
Kaskaskia, R. 158 37 58N 89 57W
Kaskattama, R. 153 57 3N 90 4W
Kaskelan 85 43 20N 76 35 E
Kaskinen (Kaskö) 74 62 22N 21 15 E
Kaskö (Kaskinen) 74 62 22N 21 15 E
Kasli 84 55 53N 60 46 E
Kaslo 152 49 55N 117 0W
Kasmere L. 153 59 34N 101 10W
Kasonawedjo 127 1 50S 137 41 E
Kasongo 126 4 30S 26 33 E
Kasongo Lunda 124 6 35S 17 0 E
Kásos, I. 69 35 20N 26 55 E
Kásos, Stenón 69 35 30N 26 30 E
Kaspi 83 41 54N 44 17 E
Kaspiysk 83 42 45N 47 40 E
Kaspiyskiy 83 45 22N 47 23 E
Kassab ed Doleib 123 13 30N 33 35 E
Kassaba 122 22 40N 29 55 E
Kassala 123 15 23N 36 26 E
Kassala □ 123 15 20N 36 26 E
Kassan 85 39 2N 65 35 E
Kassandra 68 40 0N 23 30 E
Kassansay 85 41 15N 71 31 E
Kassel 48 51 19N 9 32 E
Kassinger 122 18 46N 31 51 E
Kassíopi 80 39 48N 19 55 E
Kassue 103 6 58S 139 21 E
Kastamonu 92 41 25N 33 43 E
Kastav 63 45 22N 14 20 E
Kastélli 69 35 29N 23 38 E
Kastéllion 69 35 12N 25 20 E
Kastellorizon = Megiste 61 36 8N 29 34 E
Kastellou, Ákra 69 35 30N 27 15 E
Kasterlee 47 51 15N 4 59 E
Kastlösa 73 56 26N 16 25 E
Kastó, I. 69 38 35N 20 55 E
Kastóri 69 37 10N 22 17 E
Kastoria 68 40 30N 21 19 E
Kastoria □ 68 40 30N 21 15 E
Kastorías 68 40 30N 21 20 E
Kastornoye 81 51 55N 38 2 E
Kástron 68 39 53N 25 8 E

Kermãn □ **Killavullen**

Kermãn □	**93**	30 0N	57 0 E
Kermanshah	**92**	34 23N	47 0 E
Kermanshah □	**92**	34 0N	46 30 E
Kerme Körfezi	**69**	36 55N	27 50 E
Kermen	**67**	42 30N	26 16 E
Kermit	**159**	31 56N	103 3W
Kern, R.	**163**	35 16N	119 18W
Kerns	**51**	46 54N	8 17 E
Kernville	**163**	35 45N	118 26W
Keroh	**101**	5 43N	101 1 E
Kerr, Pt.	**142**	34 25 S	173 5 E
Kerrera I.	**34**	56 24N	5 32W
Kerrobert	**157**	52 0N	109 11W
Kerrville	**159**	30 1N	99 8W
Kerry	**31**	52 28N	3 16W
Kerry □	**39**	52 7N	9 35W
Kerry Hd.	**39**	52 26N	9 56W
Kerrysdale	**36**	57 41N	5 39W
Kersa	**123**	9 28N	41 48 E
Kerstinbo	**72**	60 16N	16 58 E
Kerteminde	**73**	55 28N	10 39 E
Kertosono	**103**	7 38 S	112 9 E
Keru	**123**	15 40N	37 5 E
Kerulen, R.	**105**	48 48N	117 0 E
Kerzaz	**118**	29 29N	1 25W
Kerzers	**50**	46 59N	7 12 E
Kesagami L.	**150**	50 23N	80 15W
Kesagami, R.	**150**	51 4N	79 45W
Kesan	**68**	41 49N	26 38 E
Kesch, Piz	**51**	46 38N	9 53 E
Kesh	**38**	54 31N	7 43W
Keski Suomen □	**74**	62 45N	25 15 E
Kessel, Belg.	**47**	51 8N	4 38 E
Kessel, Neth.	**47**	51 17N	6 3 E
Kessel-Lo	**47**	50 53N	4 43 E
Kessingland	**29**	52 25N	1 41 E
Kestell	**129**	28 17 S	28 42 E
Kestenga	**78**	66 0N	31 50 E
Kesteren	**46**	51 56N	5 34 E
Keswick	**32**	54 35N	3 9W
Keszthely	**53**	46 50N	17 15 E
Keta	**121**	5 49N	1 0 E
Ketapang	**102**	1 55 S	110 0 E
Ketchikan	**147**	55 25N	131 40W
Ketchum	**160**	43 50N	114 27W
Kete Krachi	**121**	7 55N	0 1W
Ketef, Khalîg Umm el	**122**	23 40N	35 35 E
Ketelmeer	**46**	32 36N	5 46 E
Keti Bandar	**94**	24 8N	67 27 E
Ketri	**94**	28 1N	75 50 E
Ketrzyn	**54**	54 7N	21 22 E
Kettering	**29**	52 24N	0 44W
Kettla, Ness	**36**	60 3N	1 20W
Kettle Falls	**160**	48 41N	118 2W
Kettle Ness	**33**	54 32N	0 41W
Kettle, R.	**153**	56 23N	94 34W
Kettleman City	**163**	36 1N	119 58W
Kettlewell	**32**	54 8N	2 2W
Kety	**54**	49 51N	19 16 E
Kevin	**160**	48 45N	111 58W
Kewanee	**158**	41 18N	90 0W
Kewaunee	**156**	44 27N	87 30W
Keweenaw B.	**156**	46 56N	88 23W
Keweenaw Pen.	**156**	47 30N	88 0W
Keweenaw Pt.	**156**	47 26N	87 40W
Kexby	**33**	53 21N	0 41W
Key Harbour	**150**	45 50N	80 45W
Key, L.	**38**	54 0N	8 15W
Key West	**166**	24 40N	82 0W
Keyingham	**33**	53 42N	0 7W
Keyling Inlet	**136**	14 50 S	129 40 E
Keymer	**29**	50 55N	0 5W
Keynsham	**28**	51 25N	2 30W
Keynshamburg	**127**	19 15 S	29 40 E
Keyport	**162**	40 26N	74 12W
Keyser	**156**	39 26N	79 0W
Keystone, S.D., U.S.A.	**158**	43 54N	103 27W
Keystone, W. Va., U.S.A.	**156**	37 30N	81 30W
Keyworth	**28**	52 52N	1 8W
Kez	**84**	57 55N	53 46 E
Kezhma	**77**	59 15N	100 57 E
Kezmarok	**53**	49 10N	20 28 E
Khabarovo	**76**	69 30N	60 30 E
Khabarovsk	**77**	48 20N	135 0 E
Khachmas	**83**	41 31N	48 42 E
Khachraud	**94**	23 25N	75 20 E
Khadari, W. el	**123**	10 35N	26 16 E
Khadro	**94**	26 11N	68 50 E
Khadyzhensk	**83**	44 26N	39 32 E
Khadzhilyangar	**95**	35 45N	79 20 E
Khagaria	**95**	25 18N	86 32 E
Khaibar	**92**	25 38N	39 28 E
Khaibor	**122**	25 49N	39 16 E
Khaipur, Bahawalpur, Pak.	**94**	29 34N	72 17 E
Khaipur, Hyderabad, Pak.	**94**	27 32N	68 49 E
Khair	**94**	27 57N	77 46 E
Khairabad	**95**	27 33N	80 47 E
Khairagarh	**95**	21 27N	81 2 E
Khairpur	**93**	27 32N	68 49 E
Khairpur □	**94**	23 30N	69 8 E
Khakhea	**125**	24 48 S	23 22 E
Khalach	**85**	38 4N	64 52 E
Khalfallah	**118**	34 33N	0 16 E
Khalij-e-Fars □	**93**	28 20N	51 45 E
Khalilabad	**95**	26 48N	83 5 E
Khálki	**68**	39 36N	22 30 E
Khálki, I.	**69**	36 15N	27 35 E
Khalkidhiki □	**68**	40 25N	23 20 E
Khalkís	**69**	38 27N	23 42 E
Khalmer-Sede = Tazovskiy	**76**	67 30N	78 30 E
Khalmer Yu	**76**	67 58N	65 1 E
Khalturin	**81**	58 40N	48 50 E
Kham Kent	**100**	18 15N	104 43 E
Khamaria	**96**	23 10N	80 52 E
Khama's Country	**128**	21 45 S	26 30 E
Khamba Dzong	**99**	28 25N	88 30W
Khambhalia	**94**	22 14N	69 41 E
Khamgaon	**96**	20 42N	76 37 E
Khammam	**96**	17 11N	80 6 E
Khān Yūnis	**90**	31 21N	34 18 E
Khan Yunus	**90**	31 21N	34 18 E
Khanabad, Afghan.	**93**	36 45N	69 5 E
Khanabad, U.S.S.R.	**85**	40 59N	70 38 E
Khānaqin	**92**	34 23N	45 25 E
Khandrá	**69**	35 3N	26 8 E
Khandwa	**96**	21 49N	76 22 E
Khandyga	**77**	62 30N	134 50 E
Khanewal	**94**	30 20N	71 55 E
Khanga Sidi Nadji	**119**	34 50N	6 50 E
Khanh Duong	**100**	12 44N	108 44 E
Khanh Hung	**101**	9 36N	105 58 E
Khaniá	**69**	35 30N	24 4 E
Khaniá □	**69**	35 0N	24 0 E
Khanion Kólpos	**69**	35 33N	23 55 E
Khanka, Oz.	**76**	45 0N	132 30 E
Khanna	**94**	30 42N	76 16 E
Khanpur	**94**	28 42N	70 35 E
Khantau	**85**	44 13N	73 48 E
Khanty-Mansiysk	**76**	61 0N	69 0 E
Khapalu	**95**	35 10N	76 20 E
Kharagpur	**95**	22 20N	87 25 E
Kharaij	**122**	21 25N	41 0 E
Kharan Kalat	**93**	28 34N	65 21 E
Kharanaq	**93**	32 20N	54 45 E
Kharda	**96**	18 40N	75 40 E
Khardung La	**95**	34 20N	77 43 E
Kharfa	**92**	22 0N	46 35 E
Kharg, Jazireh	**92**	29 15N	50 28 E
Khârga, El Wâhât el	**122**	25 0N	30 0 E
Khargon, India	**93**	21 45N	75 35 E
Khargon, India	**96**	21 45N	75 40 E
Kharit, Wadi el	**122**	24 5N	34 10 E
Kharkov	**82**	49 58N	36 20 E
Kharmanli	**67**	41 55N	25 55 E
Kharovsk	**81**	59 56N	40 13 E
Kharsaniya	**92**	27 10N	49 10 E
Khartoum = El Khartûm	**123**	15 31N	32 35 E
Khartoum □	**123**	16 0N	33 0 E
Khasab	**93**	26 14N	56 15 E
Khasavyurt	**83**	43 30N	46 40 E
Khasebake	**128**	20 42 S	24 29 E
Khash	**93**	28 15N	61 5 E
Khashm el Girba	**123**	14 59N	35 58 E
Khasi Hills	**98**	25 30N	91 30 E
Khaskovo	**67**	41 56N	25 30 E
Khatanga	**77**	72 0N	102 20 E
Khatanga, Zaliv	**12**	66 0N	112 0 E
Khatauli	**94**	29 17N	77 43 E
Khatyrchi	**85**	40 2N	65 58 E
Khatyrka	**77**	62 3N	175 15 E
Khavar □	**92**	37 20N	46 0 E
Khavast	**85**	40 10N	68 49 E
Khawa	**122**	29 45N	40 25 E
Khaydarken	**85**	39 57N	71 20 E
Khazzân Jabal el Awliyâ	**123**	15 24N	32 20 E
Khe Bo	**100**	19 8N	104 41 E
Khe Long	**100**	21 29N	104 46 E
Khed, Maharashtra, India	**96**	18 51N	73 56 E
Khed, Maharashtra, India	**96**	17 43N	73 27 E
Khed Brahma	**93**	24 7N	73 5 E
Khekra	**94**	28 52N	77 20 E
Khemarak Phouminville	**101**	11 37N	102 59 E
Khemis Miliana	**118**	36 11N	2 14 E
Khemisset	**118**	33 50N	6 1W
Khemmarat	**100**	16 10N	105 15 E
Khenchela	**119**	35 28N	7 11 E
Khenifra	**118**	32 58N	5 46W
Khenmarak Phouminville	**102**	11 40N	102 58 E
Kherrata	**119**	36 27N	5 13 E
Kherson	**82**	46 35N	32 35 E
Khersónisos Akrotíri	**69**	35 30N	24 10 E
Khetinsiring	**99**	32 54N	92 50 E
Khiliomódhion	**69**	37 48N	22 51 E
Khilok	**77**	51 30N	110 45 E
Khimki	**81**	55 50N	37 20 E
Khingan, mts.	**86**	47 0N	119 30 E
Khíos	**69**	38 27N	26 9 E
Khisar-Momina Banya	**67**	42 30N	24 44 E
Khiuma = Hiiumaa	**80**	58 50N	22 45 E
Khiva	**76**	41 30N	60 18 E
Khiyav	**92**	38 30N	47 45 E
Khlaouia	**118**	25 50N	6 32W
Khlong Khlung	**100**	16 12N	99 43 E
Khlong, R.	**101**	15 30N	98 50 E
Khmelnitsky	**82**	49 23N	27 0 E
Khmer Republic ■ = Cambodia	**100**	12 15N	105 0 E
Khoai, Hon	**101**	8 26N	104 50 E
Khodzhent	**85**	40 14N	69 37 E
Khoi	**92**	38 40N	45 0 E
Khojak P.	**93**	30 55N	66 30 E
Khok Kloi	**101**	8 17N	98 19 E
Khok Pho	**101**	6 43N	101 6 E
Khokholskiy	**81**	51 35N	38 50 E
Kholm	**80**	57 10N	31 15 E
Kholmsk	**77**	35 5N	139 48 E
Khomas Hochland	**128**	22 40 S	16 0 E
Khomayn	**92**	33 40N	50 7 E
Khomo	**128**	21 7 S	24 35 E
Khon Kaen	**100**	16 30N	102 47 E
Khong, Camb.	**101**	13 55N	105 56 E
Khong, Laos	**100**	14 7N	105 51 E
Khong, R., Laos	**101**	15 0N	106 50 E
Khong, R., Thai.	**101**	17 45N	104 20 E
Khong Sedone	**100**	15 34N	105 49 E
Khonh Hung (Soc Trang)	**101**	9 37N	105 50 E
Khonu	**77**	66 30N	143 25 E
Khoper, R.	**81**	52 0N	43 20 E
Khor el 'Atash	**123**	13 20N	34 15 E
Khóra	**69**	37 3N	21 42 E
Khóra Sfákion	**69**	35 15N	24 9 E
Khorasan □	**93**	34 0N	58 0 E
Khorat = Nakhon Ratchasima	**100**	14 59N	102 12 E
Khorat, Cao Nguyen	**100**	15 30N	102 50 E
Khorat Plat.	**101**	15 30N	102 50 E
Khorb el Ethel	**118**	28 44N	6 11W
Khorog	**85**	37 30N	71 36 E
Khorol	**82**	49 48N	33 15 E
Khorramabad	**92**	33 30N	48 25 E
Khorramshahr	**92**	30 29N	48 15 E
Khota Kota	**127**	12 55 S	34 15 E
Khotan = Hot'ien	**105**	37 7N	79 55 E
Khotin	**82**	48 31N	26 27 E
Khouribga	**118**	32 58N	6 50W
Khowai	**98**	24 5N	91 40 E
Khoyniki	**80**	51 54N	29 55 E
Khrami, R.	**83**	41 30N	44 30 E
Khrenovoye	**81**	51 4N	40 6 E
Khristianá, I.	**69**	36 14N	25 13 E
Khromtau	**84**	50 17N	58 27 E
Khtapodhiá, I.	**69**	37 24N	25 34 E
Khu Khan	**100**	14 42N	104 12 E
Khufaifiya	**92**	24 50N	44 35 E
Khugiani	**94**	31 28N	66 14 E
Khulna	**98**	22 45N	89 34 E
Khulna □	**98**	22 45N	89 35 E
Khulo	**83**	41 33N	42 19 E
Khunzakh	**83**	42 35N	46 42 E
Khur	**93**	32 55N	58 18 E
Khurai	**94**	24 3N	78 23 E
Khurais	**92**	24 55N	48 5 E
Khurja	**94**	28 15N	77 58 E
Khurma	**92**	21 58N	42 3 E
Khūryān Mūryān, Jazā 'ir	**91**	17 30N	55 58 E
Khush	**93**	32 55N	62 10 E
Khushab	**94**	32 20N	72 20 E
Khuzdar	**94**	27 52N	66 30 E
Khuzestan □	**92**	31 0N	50 0 E
Khvalynsk	**81**	52 30N	48 2 E
Khvatovka	**81**	52 24N	46 32 E
Khvor	**93**	33 45N	55 0 E
Khvormuj	**93**	28 40N	51 30 E
Khvoy	**92**	38 35N	45 0 E
Khvoynaya	**80**	58 49N	34 28 E
Khwaja Muhammad	**93**	36 0N	70 0 E
Khyber Pass	**94**	34 10N	71 8 E
Kiabukwa	**127**	8 40 S	24 48 E
Kiadho, R.	**96**	19 50N	76 55 E
Kiama	**141**	34 40 S	150 50 E
Kiamba	**126**	6 0N	124 40 E
Kiambi	**126**	7 15 S	28 0 E
Kiambu	**126**	1 8 S	36 50 E
Kiangsi □	**109**	27 20N	115 40 E
Kiangsu □	**109**	33 0N	119 50 E
Kiania	**129**	20 18 S	47 8 E
Kiaohsien = Chiaohsien	**107**	36 20N	120 0 E
Kibæk	**73**	56 2N	8 51 E
Kibanga Port	**126**	0 10 S	32 58 E
Kibangou	**124**	3 18 S	12 22 E
Kibara	**126**	2 8 S	33 30 E
Kibara, Mts.	**126**	8 25 S	27 10 E
Kibombo	**126**	3 57 S	25 53 E
Kibondo	**126**	3 35 S	30 45 E
Kibondo □	**126**	4 0 S	30 55 E
Kibumbu	**126**	3 32 S	29 45 E
Kibungu	**126**	2 10 S	30 32 E
Kibuye, Burundi	**126**	3 39 S	29 59 E
Kibuye, Rwanda	**126**	2 3 S	29 21 E
Kibwesa	**126**	6 30 S	29 58 E
Kibwezi	**124**	2 27 S	37 57 E
Kibworth Beauchamp	**29**	52 33N	0 59W
Kičevo	**66**	41 34N	20 59 E
Kichiga	**77**	59 50N	163 5 E
Kicking Horse Pass	**152**	51 27N	116 25W
Kidal	**121**	17 50N	1 22 E
Kidderminster	**28**	52 24N	2 13W
Kidete	**126**	6 25 S	37 17 E
Kidira	**120**	14 28N	12 13W
Kidlington	**28**	51 49N	1 18W
Kidnappers, C.	**142**	39 38 S	177 5 E
Kidsgrove	**32**	53 6N	2 15W
Kidston	**138**	18 52 S	144 8 E
Kidstones	**32**	54 15N	2 2W
Kidugalle	**126**	6 49 S	38 15 E
Kidwelly	**31**	51 44N	4 20W
Kiel	**48**	54 16N	10 8 E
Kiel Canal = Nord-Ostee-Kanal	**48**	54 15N	9 40 E
Kielce	**54**	50 58N	20 42 E
Kielce □	**54**	51 0N	20 40 E
Kielder	**35**	55 14N	2 35W
Kieldrecht	**47**	51 17N	4 11 E
Kieler Bucht	**48**	54 30N	10 30 E
Kien Binh	**101**	9 55N	105 19 E
Kien Hung	**101**	9 43N	105 17 E
Kien Tan	**101**	10 7N	105 17 E
Kienchwan	**99**	26 30N	99 45 E
Kienge	**127**	10 30 S	27 30 E
Kiessé	**121**	13 29N	4 1 E
Kieta	**135**	6 12 S	155 36 E
Kiev = Kiyev	**80**	50 30N	30 28 E
Kiffa	**120**	16 50N	11 15W
Kifisiá	**69**	38 4N	23 49 E
Kifissós, R.	**69**	38 30N	23 0 E
Kifri	**92**	34 45N	45 0 E
Kigali	**126**	1 5 S	30 4 E
Kigarama	**126**	1 1 S	31 50 E
Kigoma □	**126**	5 0 S	30 0 E
Kigoma-Ujiji	**126**	5 30 S	30 0 E
Kigomasha, Ras	**126**	4 58 S	38 58 E
Kihee	**139**	27 23 S	142 37 E
Kihikihi	**142**	38 2 S	175 22 E
Kii-Hantō	**111**	34 0N	135 45 E
Kii-Sanchi	**111**	34 20N	136 0 E
Kijik	**147**	60 20N	154 20W
Kikai-Jima	**112**	28 19N	129 58 E
Kikinda	**66**	45 50N	20 30 E
Kikládhes □	**69**	37 0N	25 0 E
Kikládhes, Is.	**69**	37 20N	24 30 E
Kikoira	**141**	33 59 S	146 40 E
Kikori	**135**	7 13 S	144 15 E
Kikori, R.	**135**	7 5 S	144 0 E
Kikuchi	**110**	32 59N	130 47 E
Kikwit	**124**	5 5 S	18 45 E
Kil	**72**	59 30N	13 20 E
Kilafors	**72**	61 14N	16 36 E
Kilakarai	**97**	9 12N	78 47 E
Kilauea	**147**	22 13N	159 25W
Kilauea Crater	**147**	19 24N	155 17W
Kilbaha	**39**	52 35N	9 51W
Kilbeggan	**38**	53 22N	7 30W
Kilbeheny	**39**	52 18N	8 13W
Kilbennan	**38**	53 33N	8 54W
Kilbirnie	**34**	55 46N	4 42W
Kilbrannan Sd.	**34**	55 40N	5 23W
Kilbride	**39**	52 56N	6 5W
Kilbrien	**39**	52 12N	7 40W
Kilbrittain	**39**	51 40N	8 42W
Kilbuck Mts.	**147**	60 30N	160 0W
Kilchberg	**51**	47 18N	8 33 E
Kilchoan	**36**	56 42N	6 8W
Kilcock	**38**	53 24N	6 40W
Kilcoe	**39**	51 33N	9 26W
Kilcogan	**39**	53 13N	8 52W
Kilconnell	**39**	53 20N	8 25W
Kilcoo	**38**	54 14N	6 1W
Kilcormac	**39**	53 11N	7 44W
Kilcoy	**139**	26 59 S	152 30 E
Kilcreggan	**34**	55 59N	4 50W
Kilcrohane	**39**	51 35N	9 44W
Kilcullen	**39**	53 8N	6 45W
Kilcurry	**38**	54 3N	6 26W
Kildare	**39**	53 10N	6 50W
Kildare □	**39**	53 10N	6 50W
Kildavin	**39**	52 41N	6 42W
Kildemo	**39**	52 37N	8 50W
Kildonan	**37**	58 10N	3 50W
Kildorrery	**39**	52 15N	8 25W
Kilembe	**126**	0 15N	30 3 E
Kilfenora	**39**	53 0N	9 13W
Kilfinan	**34**	55 57N	5 19W
Kilfinnane	**39**	52 21N	8 30W
Kilgarvan	**39**	51 54N	9 28W
Kilgore	**159**	32 22N	94 40W
Kilham	**33**	54 4N	0 22W
Kilian Qurghan	**93**	36 52N	78 3 E
Kilifi	**126**	3 40 S	39 48 E
Kilifi □	**126**	3 30 S	39 40 E
Kilimanjaro □	**126**	4 0 S	38 0 E
Kilimanjaro, Mt.	**126**	3 7 S	37 20 E
Kilinailau, Is.	**135**	4 45 S	155 20 E
Kilindini	**126**	4 4 S	39 40 E
Kilis	**92**	36 50N	37 10 E
Kiliya	**82**	45 28N	29 16 E
Kilju	**107**	40 57N	129 25 E
Kilkea	**39**	52 57N	6 55W
Kilkee	**39**	52 41N	9 40W
Kilkeel	**38**	54 4N	6 0W
Kilkelly	**38**	53 53N	8 50W
Kilkenny	**39**	52 40N	7 17W
Kilkenny □	**39**	52 35N	7 15W
Kilkerrin	**38**	52 32N	8 36W
Kilkhampton	**30**	50 53N	4 30W
Kilkieran	**39**	53 20N	9 45W
Kilkieran B.	**38**	53 18N	9 45W
Kilkís	**68**	40 58N	22 57 E
Kilkís □	**68**	41 5N	22 50 E
Kilkishen	**39**	52 49N	8 45W
Kilknock	**38**	53 42N	8 53W
Kill	**39**	52 11N	7 20W
Killadoon	**38**	53 44N	9 53W
Killadysert	**39**	52 40N	9 7W
Killala	**38**	54 13N	9 12W
Killala B.	**38**	54 20N	9 12W
Killaloe	**39**	52 48N	8 28W
Killam	**152**	52 47N	111 51W
Killane	**39**	53 20N	7 6W
Killard, Pt.	**38**	54 18N	5 31W
Killare	**38**	53 28N	7 34W
Killarney, Man., Can.	**150**	49 10N	99 40W
Killarney, Ont., Can.	**153**	45 55N	81 30W
Killarney, Ireland	**39**	52 2N	9 30W
Killarney, L's. of	**39**	52 0N	9 30W
Killary Harb.	**38**	53 38N	9 52W
Killashandra	**38**	54 1N	7 32W
Killashee	**38**	53 40N	7 52W
Killavally	**38**	53 22N	7 23W
Killavullen	**39**	52 8N	8 32W

Killchianaig **Kíthnos**

Killchianaig	34	56 2N	5 48W
Killdeer, Can.	153	49 6N	106 22W
Killdeer, U.S.A.	158	47 26N	102 48W
Killeagh	39	51 56N	8 0W
Killean	34	55 38N	5 40W
Killeen	159	31 7N	97 45W
Killeenleigh	39	51 58N	8 49W
Killeigh	39	53 14N	7 27W
Killenaule	39	52 35N	7 40W
Killianspick	39	52 21N	7 18W
Killiecrankie P.	37	56 44N	3 46W
Killimor	39	53 10N	8 17W
Killin	34	56 28N	4 20W
Killiney	39	53 15N	6 8W
Killingdal	71	62 47N	11 26 E
Killinghall	33	54 1N	1 33W
Killíni	69	37 55N	21 8 E
Killíni, Mts.	69	37 54N	22 25 E
Killinick	39	52 15N	6 29W
Killorglin	39	52 6N	9 48W
Killough	38	54 16N	5 40W
Killtullagh	39	53 17N	8 37W
Killucan	38	53 30N	7 10W
Killurin	39	52 23N	6 35W
Killybegs	38	54 38N	8 26W
Killyleagh	38	54 24N	5 40W
Kilmacolm	34	55 54N	4 39W
Kilmacthomas	39	52 13N	7 27W
Kilmaganny	39	52 26N	7 20W
Kilmaine	38	53 33N	9 10W
Kilmaley	39	52 50N	9 11W
Kilmallock	39	52 22N	8 35W
Kilmaluag	36	57 40N	6 18W
Kilmanagh	39	52 38N	7 28W
Kilmarnock, U.K.	34	55 36N	4 30W
Kilmarnock, U.S.A.	162	37 43N	76 23W
Kilmartin	34	56 8N	5 29W
Kilmaurs	34	55 37N	4 33W
Kilmeaden	39	52 15N	7 15W
Kilmeedy	39	52 25N	8 55W
Kilmelford	34	56 16N	5 30W
Kilmez	84	56 58N	50 55 E
Kilmez, R.	84	56 58N	50 28 E
Kilmichael	39	51 49N	9 4W
Kilmichael Pt.	39	52 44N	6 8W
Kilmihill	39	52 44N	9 18W
Kilmore, Austral.	141	37 25 S	144 53 E
Kilmore, Ireland	39	52 12N	6 35W
Kilmore Quay	39	52 10N	6 36W
Kilmuir	37	57 44N	4 7W
Kilmurry	39	52 47N	9 30W
Kilmurvy	39	53 9N	9 46W
Kilnaleck	38	53 52N	7 21W
Kilninver	34	56 20N	5 30W
Kilombero □	127	8 0 S	37 0 E
Kilondo	127	9 45 S	34 20 E
Kilosa	126	6 48 S	37 0 E
Kilosa □	126	6 48 S	37 0 E
Kilpatrick	39	51 46N	8 42W
Kilrea	38	54 58N	6 34W
Kilrenny	35	56 15N	2 40W
Kilronan	39	53 8N	9 40W
Kilrush	39	52 39N	9 30W
Kilsby	28	52 20N	1 11W
Kilsheelan	39	52 23N	7 37W
Kilsmo	72	59 6N	15 35 E
Kilsyth	35	55 58N	4 3W
Kiltamagh	38	53 52N	9 0W
Kiltealy	39	52 34N	6 45W
Kiltegan	39	52 53N	6 35W
Kiltoom	38	53 30N	8 0W
Kilwa □	127	9 0 S	39 0 E
Kilwa Kisiwani	127	8 58 S	39 32 E
Kilwa Kivinje	127	8 45 S	39 25 E
Kilwa Masoko	127	8 55 S	39 30 E
Kilwinning	34	55 40N	4 41W
Kilworth	39	52 10N	8 15W
Kilworth, mts.	39	52 10N	8 15W
Kim	159	37 18N	103 20W
Kimamba	126	6 45 S	37 10 E
Kimba	140	33 8 S	136 23 E
Kimball, Nebr., U.S.A.	158	41 17N	103 20W
Kimball, S.D., U.S.A.	158	43 47N	98 57W
Kimbe	135	5 33 S	150 11 E
Kimbe B.	135	5 15 S	150 30 E
Kimberley, N.S.W., Austral.	140	32 50 S	141 4 E
Kimberley, W. Australia, Austral.	136	16 20 S	127 0 E
Kimberley, Can.	152	49 40N	115 59W
Kimberley, S. Afr.	128	28 43 S	24 46 E
Kimberley, dist.	132	16 20 S	127 0 E
Kimberley Downs	136	17 24 S	124 22 E
Kimberly	160	42 33N	114 25W
Kimbolton	29	52 17N	0 23W
Kimchŏn	107	36 11N	128 4 E
Kími	69	38 38N	24 6 E
Kimje	107	35 48N	126 45 E
Kimmeridge, oilfield	19	50 36N	2 6W
Kímolos	69	36 48N	24 37 E
Kímolos, I.	69	36 48N	24 35 E
Kimovsk	81	54 0N	38 29 E
Kimparana	120	12 48N	5 0W
Kimry	81	56 55N	37 15 E
Kimsquit	152	52 45N	126 57W
Kimstad	73	58 35N	15 58 E
Kinabalu, mt.	102	6 0N	116 0 E
Kínaros, I.	69	36 59N	26 15 E
Kinaskan L.	152	57 38N	130 8W
Kinawley	38	54 14N	7 40W
Kinbrace	37	58 16N	3 56W
Kincaid	153	49 40N	107 0W
Kincardine, Can.	150	44 10N	81 40W

Kincardine, Fife, U.K.	35	56 4N	3 43W
Kincardine, Highland, U.K.	37	57 52N	4 20W
Kincardine (□)	26	56 56N	2 28W
Kincraig	37	57 8N	3 57W
Kindersley	153	51 30N	109 10W
Kindia	120	10 0N	12 52W
Kindu	126	2 55 S	25 50 E
Kinel	84	53 15N	50 40 E
Kineshma	81	57 30N	42 5 E
Kinesi	126	1 25 S	33 50 E
Kineton	28	52 10N	1 30W
King and Queen	162	37 42N	76 50W
King City	163	36 11N	121 8W
King Cr.	138	24 35 S	139 30 E
King Edward, R.	136	14 14 S	126 35 E
King Frederick VI Land	12	63 0N	43 0W
King Frederick VIII Land	12	77 30N	25 0W
King George	162	38 15N	77 10W
King George B.	176	51 30 S	60 30W
King George I.	13	60 0 S	60 0W
King George Is.	149	53 40N	80 30W
King George Sd.	132	35 5 S	118 0 E
King I., Austral.	138	39 50 S	144 0 E
King I., Can.	152	52 10N	127 40W
King I. = Kadah Kyun	101	12 30N	98 20 E
King, L.	137	33 10 S	119 35 E
King Leopold Ranges	136	17 20 S	124 20 E
King, Mt.	138	25 10 S	147 30 E
King Sd.	136	16 50 S	123 20 E
King William I.	148	69 10N	97 25W
King William, L.	50	42 14 S	146 15 E
King William's Town	128	32 51 S	27 22 E
Kingairloch, dist.	36	56 37N	5 30W
Kingaroy	139	26 32 S	151 51 E
Kingarrow	38	54 55N	8 5W
Kingarth	34	55 45N	5 2W
Kingfisher	159	35 50N	97 55W
Kinghorn	35	56 4N	3 10W
Kingisepp	80	59 25N	28 40 E
Kingisepp (Kuressaare)	80	58 15N	22 15 E
Kingman, Ariz., U.S.A.	161	35 12N	114 2W
Kingman, Kans., U.S.A.	159	37 41N	96 9W
Kings B.	12	78 0N	15 0 E
Kings Canyon National Park	163	37 0N	118 35W
King's Lynn	29	52 45N	0 25 E
Kings Mountain	157	35 13N	81 20W
Kings Park	162	40 53N	73 16W
King's Peak	160	40 46N	110 27W
King's, R.	39	52 32N	7 12W
Kings, R.	163	36 10N	119 50W
King's Sutton	28	52 1N	1 16W
King's Worthy	28	51 6N	1 18W
Kingsbarns	35	56 18N	2 40W
Kingsbridge	30	50 17N	3 46W
Kingsburg	163	36 35N	119 36W
Kingsbury	28	52 33N	1 41W
Kingscote	140	35 33 S	137 31 E
Kingscourt	38	53 55N	6 48W
Kingskerswell	30	50 30N	3 34W
Kingsland	28	52 15N	2 49W
Kingsley	158	42 37N	95 58W
Kingsley Dam	158	41 20N	101 40W
Kingsport	157	36 33N	82 36W
Kingsteignton	30	50 32N	3 35W
Kingston, Can.	150	44 14N	76 30W
Kingston, Jamaica	166	18 0N	76 50W
Kingston, N.Z.	143	45 20 S	168 43 E
Kingston, U.K.	28	51 23N	1 40W
Kingston, N.Y., U.S.A.	162	41 55N	74 0W
Kingston, Pa., U.S.A.	162	41 19N	75 58W
Kingston, R.I., U.S.A.	162	41 29N	71 30W
Kingston South East	140	36 51 S	139 55 E
Kingston-upon-Thames	29	51 23N	0 20W
Kingstown, Austral.	141	30 29 S	151 6 E
Kingstown, St. Vinc.	167	13 10N	61 10W
Kingstree	157	33 40N	79 48W
Kingsville, Can.	150	42 2N	82 45W
Kingsville, U.S.A.	159	27 30N	97 53W
Kingswear	30	50 21N	3 33W
Kingswood	28	51 26N	2 31W
Kington	28	52 12N	3 2W
Kingtung	99	24 30N	100 50 E
Kingussie	37	47 5N	4 2W
Kinistino	153	52 57N	105 2W
Kinkala	124	4 18 S	14 49 E
Kinki □	111	35 0N	135 30 E
Kinleith	142	38 20 S	175 56 E
Kinloch, N.Z.	143	44 51 S	168 20 E
Kinloch, L. More, U.K.	37	58 17N	4 50W
Kinloch, Rhum, U.K.	36	57 0N	6 18W
Kinloch Rannoch	37	56 41N	4 12W
Kinlochbervie	36	58 28N	5 5W
Kinlochewe	36	57 37N	5 20W
Kinlochiel	36	56 52N	5 20W
Kinlochleven	36	56 42N	4 59W
Kinlochmoidart	36	56 47N	5 43W
Kinloss	37	57 38N	3 37W
Kinlough	38	54 27N	8 16W
Kinn	71	61 34N	4 45 E
Kinna	73	57 32N	12 42 E
Kinnaird	152	49 17N	117 39W
Kinnaird's Hd.	37	57 40N	2 0W
Kinnared	73	57 2N	13 7 E
Kinnegad	38	53 28N	7 8W
Kinneret	90	32 44N	35 34 E
Kinneret, Yam	90	32 45N	35 35 E
Kinneviken, B.	73	58 38N	18 20 E
Kinnitty	39	53 6N	7 44W
Kino	164	28 45N	111 59W
Kinoje, R.	150	52 8N	81 25W

Kinomoto	111	35 30N	136 13 E
Kinoni, C. Afr. Emp.	123	5 40N	26 10 E
Kinoni, Uganda	126	0 41 S	30 28 E
Kinping	101	22 56N	103 15 E
Kinrooi	47	51 9N	5 45 E
Kinross	35	56 13N	3 25W
Kinross (□)	26	56 13N	3 25W
Kinsale	39	51 42N	8 31W
Kinsale Harbour	39	51 40N	8 30W
Kinsale Head, gasfield	19	51 20N	8 0W
Kinsale Old Hd.	39	51 37N	8 32W
Kinsarvik	71	60 22N	6 43 E
Kinshasa	124	4 20 S	15 15 E
Kinsley	159	37 57N	99 30W
Kinston	157	35 18N	77 35W
Kintampo	121	8 5N	1 41W
Kintap	102	3 51 S	115 13 E
Kintaravay	36	58 4N	6 42W
Kintore	37	57 14N	2 20W
Kintore Ra.	137	23 15 S	128 47 E
Kintyre, Mull of	34	55 17N	5 4W
Kintyre, pen.	34	55 30N	5 35W
Kinu	98	22 46N	95 37 E
Kinu-Gawa, R.	111	35 36N	139 57 E
Kinushseo, R.	150	55 15N	83 45W
Kinuso	152	55 25N	115 25W
Kinvara	39	53 8N	8 57W
Kinyangiri	126	4 35 S	34 37 E
Kióni	69	38 27N	20 41 E
Kiosk	150	46 6N	78 53W
Kiowa, Kans., U.S.A.	159	37 3N	98 30W
Kiowa, Okla., U.S.A.	159	34 45N	95 50W
Kipahigan L.	153	55 20N	101 55W
Kipanga	126	6 15 S	35 20 E
Kiparissía	69	37 15N	21 40 E
Kiparissiakós Kólpos	69	37 25N	21 25 E
Kipawa Res. Prov. Park	150	47 0N	78 30W
Kipembawe	124	7 38 S	33 27 E
Kipengere Ra.	127	9 12 S	34 15 E
Kipili	126	7 28 S	30 32 E
Kipini	126	2 30 S	40 32 E
Kipling	153	50 6N	102 38W
Kipnuk	147	59 55N	164 7W
Kippen	34	56 8N	4 12W
Kippure, Mt.	39	53 11N	6 23W
Kipushi	127	11 48 S	27 12 E
Kir	124	1 29 S	19 25 E
Kirandul	96	18 33N	81 10 E
Kiratpur	94	29 32N	78 12 E
Kirchberg	50	47 5N	7 35 E
Kirchhain	48	50 49N	8 54 E
Kirchheim	49	48 38N	9 20 E
Kirchheim Bolanden	49	49 40N	8 0 E
Kirchschlag	53	47 30N	16 19 E
Kircubbin	38	54 30N	5 33W
Kirensk	77	57 50N	107 55 E
Kirgiz S.S.R. □	85	42 0N	75 0 E
Kirgiziya Steppe	79	50 0N	55 0 E
Kiri	124	1 29 S	19 25 E
Kiriburu	96	22 0N	85 0 E
Kirikkale	92	39 51N	33 32 E
Kirikopuni	142	35 50 S	174 1 E
Kirillov	81	59 51N	38 14 E
Kirin □	107	43 50N	125 45 E
Kirindi, R.	97	6 15N	81 20 E
Kirishi	80	51 28N	31 59 E
Kirishima-Yama	110	31 58N	130 55 E
Kiriwina Is. = Trobriand Is.	138	8 40 S	151 0 E
Kirk Michael	32	54 17N	4 35W
Kirkbean	35	54 56N	3 35W
Kirkbride	32	54 54N	3 13W
Kirkburton	33	53 36N	1 42W
Kirkby	32	53 29N	2 54W
Kirkby-in-Ashfield	33	53 6N	1 15W
Kirkby Lonsdale	32	54 13N	2 36W
Kirkby Malzeard	33	54 10N	1 38W
Kirkby Moorside	33	54 16N	0 56W
Kirkby Steven	32	54 27N	2 23W
Kirkby Thore	32	54 38N	2 34W
Kirkcaldy	35	56 7N	3 10W
Kirkcolm	34	54 59N	5 4W
Kirkconnel	35	55 23N	4 0W
Kirkcowan	34	54 53N	4 38W
Kirkcudbright	35	54 50N	4 3W
Kirkcudbright (□)	26	55 4N	4 0W
Kirkcudbright B.	35	54 46N	4 0W
Kirkeby	73	55 7N	8 33 E
Kirkee	96	18 34N	73 56 E
Kirkenær	71	60 27N	12 3 E
Kirkenes	74	69 40N	30 5 E
Kirkham	32	53 47N	2 52W
Kirkinner	34	54 59N	4 28W
Kirkintilloch	35	55 57N	4 10W
Kirkjubæjarklaustur	74	63 47N	18 4W
Kirkland, Ariz., U.S.A.	161	34 29N	112 46W
Kirkland, Wash., U.S.A.	160	47 40N	122 10W
Kirkland Lake	150	48 9N	80 2W
Kırklareli	67	41 44N	27 15 E
Kirkliston	35	55 55N	3 27W
Kirkliston Ra.	143	44 25 S	170 34 E
Kirkmichael	37	56 43N	3 31W
Kirkoswald	32	54 46N	2 41W
Kirkoswold	34	55 19N	4 48W
Kirkstone P.	32	54 29N	2 55W
Kirksville	158	40 8N	92 35W
Kirkuk	92	35 30N	44 21 E
Kirkwall	37	58 59N	2 59W
Kirkwhelpington	35	55 9N	2 0W
Kirkwood	128	33 22 S	25 15 E
Kirlampudi	96	17 12N	82 12 E
Kirn	49	49 46N	7 29 E

Kirov, R.S.F.S.R., U.S.S.R.	81	54 3N	34 12 E
Kirov, R.S.F.S.R., U.S.S.R.	84	58 35N	49 40 E
Kirovabad	83	40 45N	46 10 E
Kirovakan	83	41 0N	44 0 E
Kirovo	85	40 26N	70 36 E
Kirovo-Chepetsk	81	58 28N	50 0 E
Kirovograd	82	48 35N	32 20 E
Kirovsk, R.S.F.S.R., U.S.S.R.	78	67 48N	33 50 E
Kirovsk, Ukraine, U.S.S.R.	83	48 35N	38 30 E
Kirovski	83	45 51N	48 11 E
Kirovskiy	85	44 52N	78 12 E
Kirovskoye	85	42 39N	71 35 E
Kirriemuir, Can.	153	51 56N	110 20W
Kirriemuir, U.K.	37	56 41N	3 0W
Kirs	84	59 21N	52 14 E
Kirsanov	81	52 35N	42 40 E
Kirşehir	92	39 14N	34 5 E
Kirstonia	128	25 30 S	23 45 E
Kirtachi	121	12 52N	2 30 E
Kirthar Range	93	27 0N	67 0 E
Kirtling	29	52 11N	0 27 E
Kirtlington	28	51 54N	1 9W
Kirton	39	52 56N	0 3W
Kirton-in-Lindsey	33	53 29N	0 35W
Kiruna	74	67 52N	20 15 E
Kirundu	124	0 50 S	25 35 E
Kirup	137	33 40 S	115 50 E
Kiryū	111	36 24N	139 20 E
Kiryu	81	55 5N	46 45 E
Kirzhach	81	56 12N	38 50 E
Kisa	73	58 0N	15 39 E
Kisaga	126	4 30 S	34 23 E
Kisalaya	166	14 40N	84 3W
Kisámou, Kólpos	69	35 30N	23 38 E
Kisanga	126	2 30N	26 35 E
Kisangani	126	0 35N	25 15 E
Kisar, I.	103	8 5 S	127 10 E
Kisaran	102	2 47N	99 29 E
Kisarawe	126	6 53 S	39 0 E
Kisarawe □	126	7 3 S	39 0 E
Kisarazu	111	35 23N	139 55 E
Kisbér	53	47 30N	18 0 E
Kiselevsk	76	54 5N	86 6 E
Kishanganga, R.	95	34 50N	74 15 E
Kishanganj	95	26 3N	88 14 E
Kishangarh	94	27 50N	70 30 E
Kishi	121	9 1N	3 45 E
Kishinev	82	47 0N	28 50 E
Kishinoi	82	47 1N	28 50 E
Kishiwada	111	34 28N	135 22 E
Kishkeam	39	52 15N	9 12 E
Kishon	90	32 33N	35 12 E
Kishorganj	98	24 26N	90 40 E
Kishorn L.	36	57 22N	5 40W
Kishtwar	95	33 20N	75 48 E
Kisii	126	0 40 S	34 45 E
Kisii □	126	0 40 S	34 45 E
Kisiju	124	7 23 S	39 19 E
Kısır, Dağ	83	41 0N	43 5 E
Kisizi	126	1 0 S	29 58 E
Kiska I.	147	52 0N	177 30 E
Kiskatinaw, R.	152	56 8N	120 10W
Kiskittogisu L.	153	54 13N	98 20W
Kiskomárom = Zalakomár	53	46 33N	17 10 E
Kiskörös	53	46 37N	19 20 E
Kiskundorozsma	53	46 16N	20 5 E
Kiskunfelégyháza	53	46 42N	19 53 E
Kiskunhalas	53	46 28N	19 37 E
Kiskunmajsa	53	46 30N	19 48 E
Kislovodsk	83	43 50N	42 45 E
Kismayu	113	0 20 S	42 30 E
Kiso-Gawa, R.	111	35 2N	136 45 E
Kiso-Sammyaku	111	35 30N	137 45 E
Kisofukushima	111	35 52N	137 43 E
Kisoro	126	1 17 S	29 48 E
Kispest	53	47 27N	19 9 E
Kissidougou	120	9 5N	10 0W
Kissimmee	157	28 18N	81 22W
Kissimmee, R.	157	27 20N	81 0W
Kississing L.	153	55 34N	100 47W
Kistanje	63	43 58N	15 55 E
Kisterenye	53	48 3N	19 50 E
Kisújszállás	53	47 12N	20 50 E
Kisuki	110	35 17N	132 54 E
Kisumu	126	0 3 S	34 45 E
Kisvárda	53	48 14N	22 4 E
Kiswani	126	4 5 S	37 57 E
Kiswere	127	9 27 S	39 30 E
Kit Carson	158	38 48N	102 45W
Kita	120	13 5N	9 25W
Kita-Ura	111	36 0N	140 34 E
Kitab	85	39 7N	66 52 E
Kitakami, R.	112	38 25N	141 19 E
Kitakyūshū	110	33 50N	130 50 E
Kitale	126	1 0N	35 12 E
Kitami	112	43 48N	143 54 E
Kitangiri, L.	126	4 5 S	34 20 E
Kitano-Kaikyō	110	34 17N	134 58 E
Kitaya	127	10 38 S	40 8 E
Kitchener, Austral.	137	30 55 S	124 8 E
Kitchener, Can.	150	43 27N	80 29W
Kitchigami, R.	150	50 35N	78 5W
Kitega = Citega	126	3 30 S	29 58 E
Kiteto □	126	5 0 S	37 0 E
Kitgum Matidi	126	3 17N	32 52 E
Kíthira	69	36 9N	23 0 E
Kíthira, I.	69	36 15N	23 0 E
Kíthnos	69	37 26N	24 27 E

Kíthnos, I **Konstantinovski**

Kíthnos, I. 69 37 25N 24 25 E
Kitimat 152 54 3N 128 38W
Kitinen, R. 74 67 34N 26 40 E
Kitiyab 123 17 13N 33 35 E
Kítros 68 40 22N 22 34 E
Kitsuki 110 33 35N 131 37 E
Kittakittaooloo, L. 139 28 3 S 138 14 E
Kittanning 156 40 49N 79 30W
Kittatinny Mts. 162 41 0N 75 0W
Kittery 162 43 7N 70 42W
Kitui 126 1 17 S 38 0 E
Kitui □ 126 1 30 S 38 25 E
Kitwe 127 12 54 S 28 7 E
Kitzbühel 52 47 27N 12 24 E
Kitzingen 49 49 44N 10 9 E
Kivalina 147 67 45N 164 40W
Kivalo 74 66 18N 26 0 E
Kivarli 94 24 33N 72 46 E
Kivotós 68 40 13N 21 26 E
Kivu □ 126 3 10 S 27 0 E
Kivu, L. 126 1 48 S 29 0 E
Kiwai I. 135 8 35 S 143 30 E
Kiyev 80 50 30N 30 28 E
Kiyevskoye Vdkhr. 80 51 0N 30 0 E
Kizel 84 59 3N 57 40 E
Kiziguru 126 1 46 S 30 23 E
Kizil Jilga 95 35 26N 79 50 E
Kizil Kiya 76 40 20N 72 35 E
Kızılcahaman 82 40 30N 32 30 E
Kızılırmak 83 39 15N 36 0 E
Kizilskoye 84 52 44N 58 54 E
Kizimkazi 126 6 28 S 39 30 E
Kizlyar 83 43 51N 46 40 E
Kizyl-Arvat 76 38 58N 56 15 E
Kjellerup 73 56 17N 9 25 E
Klabat, Teluk 102 1 30 S 105 40 E
Kladanj 66 44 14N 18 42 E
Kladnica 66 43 23N 20 2 E
Kladno 52 50 10N 14 7 E
Kladovo 66 44 36N 22 33 E
Klaeng 100 12 47N 101 39 E
Klagenfurt 52 46 38N 14 20 E
Klagerup 73 55 36N 13 17 E
Klagshamn 73 55 32N 12 53 E
Klagstorp 73 55 22N 13 23 E
Klaipeda 80 55 43N 21 10 E
Klakring 73 55 42N 9 59 E
Klamath Falls 160 42 20N 121 50W
Klamath Mts. 160 41 20N 123 0W
Klamath, R. 160 41 40N 123 30W
Klang = Kelang 101 3 1N 101 33 E
Klangklang 98 22 41N 93 26 E
Klanjec 63 46 3N 15 45 E
Klappan, R. 152 58 0N 129 43W
Klarälven 72 60 32N 13 15 E
Klaten 103 7 43 S 110 36 E
Klatovy 52 49 23N 13 18 E
Klawak 152 55 35N 133 0W
Klawer 128 31 44 S 18 36 E
Klazienaveen 46 52 44N 7 0 E
Kłecko 54 52 38N 17 25 E
Kleczew 54 52 22N 18 9 E
Kleena Kleene 152 52 0N 124 50W
Klein 160 46 26N 108 31W
Klein-Karas 128 27 33 S 18 7 E
Klein Karoo 128 33 45 S 21 30 E
Kleine Gette, R. 47 50 51N 5 6 E
Kleine Nete, R. 47 51 12N 4 46 E
KlekovaCa, mt. 63 44 25N 16 32 E
Klemtu 152 52 35N 128 55W
Klenovec, Czech. 53 48 36N 19 54 E
Klenovec, Yugo. 66 31 32N 20 49 E
Klepp 71 59 48N 5 36 E
Klerksdorp 128 26 51 S 26 38 E
Kletnya 80 53 30N 33 2 E
Kletsk 80 53 5N 26 45 E
Kletskiy 83 49 20N 43 0 E
Kleve 48 51 46N 6 10 E
Klickitat 160 45 50N 12 10W
Klimovichi 80 53 36N 32 0 E
Klin 81 56 28N 36 48 E
Klinaklini, R. 152 51 21N 125 40W
Klinte 73 53 35N 10 12 E
Klintehamn 73 57 22N 18 12 E
Klintsey 80 52 50N 32 10 E
Klipplaat 128 33 0 S 24 22 E
Klisura 67 42 40N 24 28 E
Klitmøller 73 57 3N 8 30 E
Kljajićevo 66 45 45N 19 17 E
Ključ 63 44 32N 16 48 E
Kłobuck 54 50 55N 19 5 E
Kłodzko 54 50 28N 16 38 E
Kloetinge 47 51 30N 3 56 E
Klondike 147 64 0N 139 26W
Kloosterzande 47 51 22N 4 1 E
Klosi 68 41 28N 20 10 E
Klosterneuburg 53 48 18N 16 19 E
Klosters 51 46 52N 9 52 E
Kloten, Sweden 72 59 54N 15 19 E
Kloten, Switz. 51 47 27N 8 35 E
Klötze 48 52 38N 11 9 E
Klouto 121 6 57N 0 44 E
Klovborg 73 55 56N 9 30 E
Klövsjöfj, mt. 72 62 36N 13 57 E
Kluane, L. 147 61 15N 138 40W
Kluang = Keluang 101 1 59N 103 20 E
Kluczbork 54 50 58N 18 12 E
Klundert 47 51 40N 4 32 E
Klyuchevskaya, Guba 83 55 50N 160 30 E
Kmelnitski 80 49 23N 27 0 E
Knapdale, dist. 34 55 55N 5 30W
Knaresborough 33 54 1N 1 29W
Knebworth 29 51 52N 0 11W
Knee L., Man., Can. 153 55 3N 94 45W
Knee L., Sask., Can. 153 55 51N 107 0W
Knesselare 47 51 9N 3 26 E
Knezha 67 43 30N 23 56 E
Knic 66 43 53N 20 45 E
Knight Inlet 152 50 45N 125 40W
Knighton 31 52 21N 3 2W
Knights Ferry 163 37 50N 120 40W
Knight's Landing 160 38 50N 121 43W
Knin 63 44 1N 16 17 E
Knittelfeld 52 47 13N 14 51 E
Knjazevac 66 43 35N 22 18 E
Knob, C. 137 34 32 S 119 16 E
Knock 38 53 48N 8 55W
Knockananna 39 52 52N 6 34W
Knockhoy Mt. 39 51 49N 9 27W
Knocklayd Mt. 38 55 10N 6 15W
Knocklofty 39 52 20N 7 49W
Knockmahon 39 52 8N 7 21W
Knockmealdown Mts. 39 52 16N 8 0W
Knocknaskagh Mt. 39 52 7N 8 25W
Knokke 47 51 20N 3 17 E
Knott End 32 53 55N 3 0W
Knottingley 33 53 42N 1 15W
Knowle 28 52 23N 1 43W
Knox 156 41 18N 86 36W
Knox, C. 152 54 11N 133 5W
Knox City 159 33 26N 99 38W
Knox Coast 13 66 30 S 108 0 E
Knoxville, Iowa, U.S.A. 158 41 20N 93 5W
Knoxville, Pa., U.S.A. 157 41 57N 77 26W
Knoxville, Tenn., U.S.A. 157 35 58N 83 57W
Knoydart, dist. 36 57 3N 5 33W
Knurów 54 50 13N 18 38 E
Knutsford 32 53 18N 2 22W
Knutshø 71 62 18N 9 41 E
Knysna 128 34 2 S 23 2 E
Knyszyn 54 53 20N 22 56 E
Ko Chang 101 12 0N 102 20 E
Ko Ho, R. 109 32 58N 117 13 E
Ko Kha 100 18 11N 99 24 E
Ko Kut 101 11 40N 102 32 E
Ko Phangan 101 9 45N 100 10 E
Ko Phra Thong 101 9 6N 98 15 E
Kō-Saki 110 34 5N 129 13 E
Ko Samui 101 9 30N 100 0 E
Koartac (Notre Dame de Koartac) 149 61 5N 69 36 E
Koba, Aru, Indon. 103 6 37 S 134 37 E
Koba, Bangka, Indon. 102 2 26 S 106 14 E
Kobarid 63 46 15N 13 30 E
Kobayashi 110 31 56N 130 59 E
Kōbe 111 34 45N 135 10 E
Kobelyaki 82 49 11N 34 9 E
København 73 55 41N 12 34 E
Koblenz, Ger. 49 50 21N 7 36 E
Koblenz, Switz. 50 47 37N 8 14 E
Kobo 123 12 2N 39 56 E
Kobrin 80 52 15N 24 22 E
Kobroor, Kepulauan 103 6 10 S 134 30 E
Kobuchizawa 111 35 52N 138 19 E
Kobuk 147 66 55N 157 0W
Kobuk, R. 147 66 55N 157 0W
Kobuleti 83 41 55N 41 45 E
Kobylin 54 51 43N 17 12 E
Kobyłka 54 52 21N 21 10 E
Kobylkino 81 54 8N 43 46 E
Kobylnik 80 54 58N 26 39 E
Kočani 66 41 55N 22 25 E
Koçarli 69 37 45N 27 43 E
Koceljevo 66 44 28N 19 50 E
Kočevje 63 45 39N 14 50 E
Kochang 107 35 41N 127 55 E
Kochas 95 25 15N 83 56 E
Kōchi 110 33 30N 133 35 E
Kōchi-Heiya 110 33 28N 133 30 E
Kōchi-ken □ 110 33 40N 133 30 E
Kochiu 108 23 25N 103 7 E
Kochkor-Ata 85 41 1N 72 29 E
Kochkorka 85 42 13N 75 46 E
Kodaikanai 97 10 13N 77 32 E
Kodaira 111 35 44N 139 29 E
Koddiyar Bay 97 8 33N 81 15 E
Kodiak 147 57 30N 152 45W
Kodiak I. 147 57 30N 152 45W
Kodiang 101 6 21N 100 18 E
Kodinar 94 20 46N 70 46 E
Kodori, R. 83 43 0N 41 40 E
Koekelare 47 51 5N 2 59 E
K'oerch'inyuich-'iench'i 107 46 5N 122 5 E
Koerhmu 105 36 22N 94 55 E
Koersel 47 51 3N 5 17 E
Koes 125 26 0 S 19 15 E
Köflach 13 47 4N 15 4 E
Koforidua 121 6 3N 0 17W
Kōfu 111 35 40N 138 30 E
Koga 111 36 11N 139 43 E
Kogaluk, R. 151 56 12N 61 44W
Kogan 139 27 2 S 150 40 E
Kogin Baba 121 7 55N 11 35 E
Kogizman 92 40 5N 43 10 E
Kogon 121 11 20N 14 32W
Kogota 112 38 33N 141 3 E
Koh-i-Bab, mts. 93 34 30N 67 0 E
Koh-i-Khurd 94 33 30N 65 59 E
Koh-i-Mazar 94 32 30N 66 25 E
Kohat 94 33 40N 71 29 E
Kohima 98 25 35N 94 10 E
Kohler Ra. 13 77 0N 110 0W
Kohtla-Järve 80 59 20N 27 20 E
Kohukohu 142 36 31 S 173 38 E
Koindong 107 40 28N 126 18 E
Kojabuti 103 2 36 S 140 37 E
Kojetin 53 49 21N 17 20 E
Kojima 110 34 20N 133 38 E
Kōjo 110 34 33N 133 55 E
Kojō 107 38 58N 127 58 E
Kojonup 137 33 48 S 117 10 E
Kok Yangak 85 41 2N 73 12 E
Koka 122 20 5N 30 35 E
Kokand 85 40 30N 70 57 E
Kokanee Glacier Prov. Park 152 49 47N 117 10W
Kokas 103 2 42 S 132 26 E
Kokava 53 48 35N 19 50 E
Kokchetav 76 53 20N 69 10 E
Kokemäenjoki 75 61 32N 21 44 E
Kokemäenjoki = Kumo älv 75 61 32N 21 44 E
Kokhma 81 56 55N 41 18 E
Kokkola (Gamlakarleby) 74 63 50N 23 8 E
Koko, Mid-Western, Nigeria 121 6 5N 5 28 E
Koko, North-Western, Nigeria 121 11 28N 4 29 E
Koko Kyunzu 101 14 10N 93 25 E
Koko-Nor = Ch'ing Hai 105 37 0N 100 20 E
Koko Shili 99 35 20N 91 0 E
Kokoda 135 8 54 S 147 47 E
Kokolopozo 120 5 8N 6 5W
Kokomo 156 40 30N 86 6W
Kokopo 135 4 22 S 152 19 E
Kokoro 121 14 12N 0 55 E
Kokoura 77 71 35N 144 50 E
Koksan 107 38 46N 126 40 E
Koksengir, Gora 85 44 21N 65 6 E
Koksoak, R. 149 54 5N 64 10W
Kokstad 125 30 32 S 29 29 E
Kokubu 110 31 44N 130 46 E
Kola 78 68 45N 33 8 E
Kola, I. 103 5 35 S 134 30 E
Kola Pen. = Kolskiy P-ov. 78 67 30N 38 0 E
Kolagede 103 7 54 S 110 26 E
Kolahoi 95 34 12N 75 22 E
Kolahun 120 8 15N 10 4W
Kolaka 103 4 3 S 121 46 E
K'olamai 105 45 30N 84 55 E
K'olan 106 38 43N 111 32 E
Kolar 97 13 12N 78 15 E
Kolar Gold Fields 97 12 58N 78 16 E
Kolari 74 67 20N 23 48 E
Kolarovgrad 67 43 27N 26 42 E
Kolarovo 53 47 56N 18 0 E
Kolašin 66 42 50N 19 31 E
Kolayat 93 27 50N 72 50 E
Kolby 73 55 49N 10 33 E
Kolby Kås 73 55 48N 10 32 E
Kolchugino 81 56 17N 39 22 E
Kolda 120 12 55N 14 50W
Koldewey I. 12 77 0N 18 0W
Kolding 73 55 30N 9 29 E
Kole 124 3 16 S 22 42 E
Koléa 118 36 38N 2 46 E
Kolepom, Pulau 103 8 0 S 138 30 E
Kölfors 72 62 9N 16 30 E
Kolguyev, Ostrov 78 69 20N 48 30 E
Kolham 46 53 11N 6 44 E
Kolhapur 96 16 43N 74 15 E
Kolia 120 9 46N 6 28W
Kolin 52 50 2N 15 9 E
Kolind 73 56 21N 10 34 E
Kölleda 48 51 11N 11 14 E
Kollegal 97 12 9N 77 9 E
Kolleru L. 96 16 40N 81 10 E
Kollum 46 53 17N 6 10 E
Kolmanskop 128 26 45 S 15 14 E
Köln 48 50 56N 9 58 E
Koło 54 52 14N 18 40 E
Kołobrzeg 54 54 10N 15 35 E
Kologriv 81 58 48N 44 25 E
Kolokani 120 13 35N 7 45W
Kolomna 81 55 8N 38 45 E
Kolomyya 82 48 31N 25 2 E
Kolondiéba 120 11 5N 6 54W
Kolonodale 103 2 3 S 121 25 E
Kolosib 98 24 15N 92 45 E
Kolpashevo 76 58 20N 83 5 E
Kolpino 80 59 44N 30 39 E
Kolpny 81 52 12N 37 10 E
Kolskiy Poluostrov 78 67 30N 38 0 E
Kolskiy Zaliv 78 69 23N 34 0 E
Koltubanovskiy 84 52 57N 52 2 E
Kolubara, R. 66 44 35N 20 15 E
Kolumna 54 51 36N 19 14 E
Koluszki 54 51 45N 19 46 E
Kolwezi 124 10 40 S 25 25 E
Kolyberovo 81 55 15N 38 40 E
Kolyma, R. 77 64 40N 153 0 E
Kolymskoye, Okhotsko 77 63 0N 157 0 E
Kôm Ombo 122 24 25N 32 52 E
Komagene 111 35 44N 137 58 E
Komaki 111 35 17N 136 55 E
Komandorskiye Ostrava 77 55 0N 167 0 E
Komárno 53 47 49N 18 5 E
Komárom 53 47 43N 18 7 E
Komárom □ 53 47 35N 18 20 E
Komarovo 80 58 38N 33 40 E
Komatsu 111 36 25 S 136 30 E
Komatsukima 110 34 0N 134 35 E
Kombissiri 121 12 4N 1 20W
Kombori 120 13 26N 3 56W
Kombóti 69 39 6N 21 5 E
Komen 63 45 49N 13 45 E
Komenda 121 5 4N 1 28W
Komi, A.S.S.R. □ 84 64 0N 55 0 E
Komiza 63 43 3N 16 11 E
Komló 53 46 15N 18 16 E
Kommamur Canal 97 16 0N 80 25 E
Kommunarsk 83 48 30N 38 45 E
Kommunizma, Pik 85 39 0N 72 2 E
Komnes 71 59 30N 9 55 E
Komodo 103 8 37 S 119 20 E
Komoé 120 5 12N 3 44W
Komono 124 3 15 S 13 20 E
Komoran, Pulau 103 8 18 S 138 45 E
Komoro 111 36 19N 138 26 E
Komorze 54 62 8N 17 38 E
Komotiri 68 41 9N 25 26 E
Kompong Bang 101 12 24N 104 40 E
Kompong Cham 101 11 54N 105 30 E
Kompong Chhnang 101 12 20N 104 35 E
Kompong Chikreng 100 13 5N 104 18 E
Kompong Kleang 101 13 6N 104 8 E
Kompong Luong 101 11 49N 104 48 E
Kompong Pranak 101 13 35N 104 55 E
Kompong Som 101 10 38N 103 30 E
Kompong Som, Chhung 101 10 50N 103 32 E
Kompong Speu 101 11 26N 104 32 E
Kompong Sralao 100 14 5N 105 46 E
Kompong Thom 100 12 35N 104 51 E
Kompong Trabeck, Camb. 100 13 6N 105 14 E
Kompong Trabeck, Camb. 101 11 9N 105 28 E
Kompong Trach, Camb. 101 11 25N 105 48 E
Kompong Trach, Camb. 118 10 34N 104 28 E
Kompong Tralach 101 11 54N 104 47 E
Komrat 82 46 18N 28 40 E
Komsberge 128 32 40 S 20 45 E
Komsomolabad 85 38 50N 69 55 E
Komsomolets 84 53 45N 62 2 E
Komsomolets, Ostrov 77 80 30N 95 0 E
Komsomolsk, R.S.F.S.R., U.S.S.R. 77 50 30N 137 0 E
Komsomolsk, Turkmen S.S.R., U.S.S.R. 85 39 2N 63 36 E
Komsomolskiy 81 53 30N 49 40 E
Kona, Niger 121 13 33N 8 3 E
Kona, Nigeria 121 8 58N 11 15 E
Konakovo 81 56 52N 36 45 E
Konam Dzong 99 29 5N 93 0 E
Konawa 159 34 59N 96 46W
Kondagaon 96 19 35N 81 35 E
Konde 126 4 57 S 39 45 E
Kondiá 68 39 52N 25 10 E
Kondinin 137 32 34 S 118 8 E
Kondoa 126 4 55 S 35 50 E
Kondoa □ 126 5 0 S 36 0 E
Kondratyevo 77 57 30N 98 30 E
Konduga 121 11 35N 13 26 E
Kong 120 8 54N 4 36W
Kong Christian IX.s Land 12 68 0N 36 0W
Kong Christian X.s Land 12 74 0N 29 0W
Kong Frederik VIII.s Land 12 78 30N 26 0W
Kong Frederik VI.s Kyst 12 63 0N 43 0W
Kong, Koh 101 11 20N 103 0 E
Kong Oscar Fjord 12 72 20N 24 0W
Kong, R. 100 13 32N 105 58 E
Konga 73 56 30N 15 6 E
Kongeå 73 55 24N 8 39 E
Kongju 107 36 30N 127 0 E
Konglu 98 27 13N 97 57 E
Kongolo 126 5 22 S 27 0 E
Kongoussi 121 13 19N 1 32W
Kongsberg 71 59 39N 9 39 E
Kongsvinger 71 60 12N 12 2 E
Kongsvoll 71 62 20N 9 36 E
Kongwa 126 6 11 S 36 26 E
Koni 127 10 40 S 27 11 E
Koni, Mts. 127 10 36 S 27 10 E
Koniecpol 54 50 46N 19 40 E
Königsberg = Kaliningrad 80 54 42N 20 32 E
Königslutter 48 52 14N 10 50 E
Königswusterhausen 48 52 19N 13 38 E
Konin 54 52 12N 18 15 E
Konin □ 54 52 15N 18 30 E
Konispol 68 39 42N 20 10 E
Kónitsa 68 40 5N 20 48 E
Köniz 50 46 56N 7 25 E
Konjic 66 43 42N 17 58 E
Konjice 63 46 20N 15 28 E
Konkouré, R. 120 10 30N 13 40W
Könnern 48 51 40N 11 45 E
Konnur 96 16 14N 74 49 E
Kono 120 8 30N 11 5W
Konoğlu 82 40 35N 31 50 E
Konolfingen 50 46 54N 7 38 E
Konongo 121 6 40N 1 15W
Konos 135 3 10 S 151 44 E
Konosha 78 61 0N 40 5 E
Kōnosu 111 36 3N 139 31 E
Konotop 80 51 12N 33 7 E
Konskaya, R. 82 47 30N 35 0 E
Konskie 54 51 15N 20 23 E
Konsmo 71 58 16N 7 23 E
Konstantinovka 82 48 32N 37 39 E
Konstantinovski, R.S.F.S.R., U.S.S.R. 81 57 45N 39 35 E

Konstantinovski Krokom

Konstantinovski, R.S.F.S.R., U.S.S.R. 83 47 33N 41 10 E
Konstantynów Łódzki 54 51 45N 19 20 E
Konstanz 49 47 39N 9 10 E
Kontagora 121 10 23N 5 27 E
Kontich 47 51 8N 4 26 E
Kontum 100 14 24N 108 0 E
Kontum, Plat. du 100 14 30N 108 0 E
Konya 92 37 52N 32 35 E
Konyin 98 22 58N 94 42 E
Konz Karthaus 49 49 41N 6 36 E
Konza 124 1 45S 37 0 E
Konzhakovskiy Kamen, Gora 84 59 38N 59 8 E
Koog 12 52 27N 4 49 E
Kookynie 137 29 17S 121 22 E
Koolan I. 136 16 0S 123 45 E
Kooline 136 22 57S 116 20 E
Kooloonong 140 34 48S 143 10 E
Koolyanobbing 137 30 48S 119 36 E
Koolymilka P.O. 140 30 58S 136 32 E
Koondrook 140 35 33S 144 8 E
Koorawatha 141 34 2S 148 33 E
Koorda 137 30 48S 117 35 E
Kooskia 160 46 9N 115 59W
Koostatak 153 51 26N 97 26W
Kootenai, R. 160 48 30N 115 30W
Kootenay L. 153 49 45N 117 0W
Kootenay Nat. Park 152 51 0N 116 0W
Kootingal 173 31 1S 151 3 E
Kopa 85 43 31N 75 50 E
Kopaonik Planina 66 43 10N 21 0 E
Kopargaon 96 19 51N 74 28 E
Kópavogur 74 64 6N 21 55W
Koper 63 45 31N 13 44 E
Kopervik 71 59 17N 5 17 E
Kopeysk 84 55 7N 61 37 E
Kopi 139 33 24S 135 40 E
Köping 72 59 31N 16 3 E
Kopiste 63 42 48N 16 42 E
Kopliku 68 42 15N 19 25 E
Köpmanholmen 72 63 10N 18 35 E
Köpmannebro 73 58 45N 12 30 E
Koppal 97 15 23N 76 5 E
Koppang 71 61 34N 11 3 E
Kopparberg 75 59 52N 15 0 E
Kopparbergs län □ 147 61 20N 14 15 E
Koppeh Dāgh 93 38 0N 58 0 E
Kopperå 71 63 24N 11 50 E
Kopperå 71 63 24N 11 52 E
Koppio 140 34 26S 135 51 E
Koppom 72 59 43N 12 10 E
Koprivlen 67 41 36N 23 53 E
Koprivnica 63 46 12N 16 45 E
Koprivshtitsa 67 42 40N 24 19 E
Kopychintsy 80 49 7N 25 58 E
Korab, mt. 66 41 44N 20 40 E
Korakiána 68 39 42N 19 45 E
Koraput 96 18 50N 82 40 E
Korba 95 22 20N 82 45 E
Korbach 48 51 17N 8 50 E
Korbu, G. 101 4 41N 101 18 E
Korça 68 40 37N 20 50 E
Korça □ 68 40 40N 20 50 E
Korčula 63 42 57N 17 8 E
Korčula, I. 63 42 57N 17 0 E
Korčulanski Kanal 63 43 3N 16 40 E
Kordestān □ 92 36 0N 47 0 E
Korea 107 40 0N 127 0 E
Korea Bay 107 39 0N 124 0 E
Korea, South ■ 107 36 0N 128 0 E
Korea Strait 107 34 0N 129 30 E
Koregaon 96 17 40N 74 10 E
Korenevo 80 51 27N 34 55 E
Korenovsk 83 45 12N 39 22 E
Korets 80 50 40N 27 5 E
Korgus 122 19 16N 33 48 E
Korhogo 120 9 29N 5 28W
Koribundu 120 7 41N 11 46W
Koridina 139 29 42S 143 25 E
Korim 103 0 58S 136 10 E
Korinthía □ 69 37 50N 22 35 E
Korinthiakós Kólpos 69 38 16N 22 30 E
Kórinthos 69 37 56N 22 55 E
Korioumé 120 16 35N 3 0W
Kōriyama 112 37 24N 140 23 E
Korkino 84 54 54N 61 23 E
Körmend 53 47 5N 16 35 E
Kornat, I. 63 43 50N 15 20 E
Korneshty 82 47 21N 28 1 E
Korneuburg 53 48 20N 16 20 E
Korning 73 56 30N 9 44 E
Kornsjø 71 58 57N 11 39 E
Kornstad 71 62 59N 7 27 E
Koro, Ivory C. 120 8 32N 7 30W
Koro, Mali 120 14 1N 2 58W
Koroba 135 5 44S 142 47 E
Korocha 81 50 55N 37 30 E
Korogwe 124 5 5S 38 25 E
Korogwe □ 126 5 0S 38 20 E
Koroit 140 38 18S 142 24 E
Korong Vale 140 36 22S 143 45 E
Koróni 69 36 48N 21 57 E
Korónia, Limni 68 40 47N 23 37 E
Koronis 69 37 12N 25 35 E
Koronowo 54 53 19N 17 55 E
Koror 103 7 20N 134 28 E
Körös, R. 53 46 45N 20 20 E
Köröstarcsa 53 46 53N 21 3 E
Korosten 80 50 57N 28 25 E
Korotoyak 81 51 1N 39 2 E
Korraraika, B. de 129 17 45S 43 57 E
Korsakov 77 46 30N 142 42 E
Korshavn 71 58 2N 7 0 E
Korshunovo 77 58 37N 110 10 E
Korsör 73 55 20N 11 9 E
Korsze 54 54 11N 21 9 E
Kortemark 47 51 2N 3 3 E
Kortessem 47 50 52N 5 23 E
Korti 122 18 0N 31 40 E
Kortrijk 47 50 50N 3 17 E
Korumburra 141 38 26S 145 50 E
Korwai 94 24 7N 78 5 E
Koryakskiy Khrebet 77 61 0N 171 0 E
Koryŏng 107 35 44N 128 15 E
Kos 69 36 52N 27 19 E
Kos, I. 69 36 50N 27 15 E
Kosa, Ethiopia 123 7 50N 36 50 E
Kosa, U.S.S.R. 84 59 56N 55 0 E
Kosa, R. 84 60 11N 55 10 E
Kosaya Gora 81 54 10N 37 30 E
Koschagy 79 46 40N 54 0 E
Kosciusko 159 33 3N 89 34W
Kosciusko, I. 152 56 0N 133 40W
Kosciusko, Mt. 141 36 27S 148 16 E
Kösély, R. 53 47 25N 21 30 E
Kosgi 96 16 58N 77 43 E
Kosha 122 20 50N 30 30 E
Koshigaya 111 35 54N 139 48 E
K'oshih 105 39 29N 75 58 E
K'oshihk'ot'engch'i 107 43 17N 117 24 E
Koshiki-Rettō 110 31 45N 129 49 E
Kōshoku 111 36 38N 138 6 E
Koshtëbë 85 41 5N 74 15 E
Kosi 94 27 48N 77 29 E
Kosi-meer 129 27 0S 32 50 E
Košice 53 48 42N 21 15 E
Kosjerič 66 44 0N 19 55 E
Koslan 78 63 28N 48 52 E
Kosŏng 107 38 48N 128 24 E
Kosovska-Mitrovica 66 42 54N 20 52 E
Kościan 54 52 5N 16 40 E
Kościerzyna 54 54 8N 17 59 E
Kosso 120 5 3N 5 47W
Kostajnica 63 45 17N 16 30 E
Kostanjevica 63 45 51N 15 27 E
Kostelec 53 50 14N 16 35 E
Kostenets 67 42 15N 23 52 E
Koster 128 25 52S 26 54 E
Kôstî 123 13 8N 32 43 E
Kostolac 66 44 43N 21 15 E
Kostroma 81 57 50N 41 58 E
Kostromskoye Vdkhr. 81 57 52N 40 49 E
Kostrzyn 54 52 24N 17 14 E
Kostyukovichi 80 53 10N 32 4 E
Koszalin 54 54 12N 16 8 E
Koszalin □ 54 54 10N 16 10 E
Köszeg 53 47 23N 16 33 E
Kot Adu 94 30 30N 71 0 E
Kot Moman 94 32 13N 73 0 E
Kota 94 25 14N 75 49 E
Kota Baharu 101 6 7N 102 14 E
Kota Kinabalu 102 6 0N 116 12 E
Kota-Kota = Khota Kota 127 12 55S 34 15 E
Kota Tinggi 101 1 44N 103 53 E
Kotaagung 102 5 38S 104 29 E
Kotabaru 102 3 20S 116 20 E
Kotabumi 102 4 49S 104 46 E
Kotamobagu 103 0 57N 124 31 E
Kotaneelee, R. 152 60 11N 123 42W
Kotawaringin 102 2 28S 111 27 E
Kotchandpur 98 23 24N 89 1 E
Kotcho L. 152 59 7N 121 12W
Kotel 67 42 52N 26 26 E
Kotelnich 81 58 20N 48 10 E
Kotelnikovo 83 47 45N 43 15 E
Kotelnyy, Ostrov 77 75 10N 139 0 E
Kothagudam 96 17 30N 80 40 E
Kothapet 96 19 21N 79 28 E
Köthen 48 51 44N 11 59 E
Kothi 95 24 45N 80 40 E
Kotiro 94 26 17N 67 13 E
Kotka 75 60 28N 26 58 E
Kotlas 78 61 15N 47 0 E
Kotlenska Planina 67 42 56N 26 30 E
Kotli 94 33 30N 73 55 E
Kotmul 95 35 32N 75 10 E
Kotohira 110 34 11N 133 49 E
Kotonkoro 121 11 3N 5 58 E
Kotor 66 42 25N 18 47 E
Kotor Varoš 66 44 38N 17 22 E
Kotoriba 63 46 23N 16 48 E
Kotovo 81 50 22N 44 45 E
Kotovsk 82 47 55N 29 35 E
Kotputli 94 27 43N 76 12 E
Kotri 94 25 22N 68 22 E
Kotri, R. 96 19 45N 80 35 E
Kótronas 69 36 38N 22 29 E
Kötschach-Mauthern 52 46 41N 13 1 E
Kottayam 97 9 35N 76 33 E
Kottur 97 10 34N 76 56 E
Kotturu 93 14 45N 76 10 E
Kotuy, R. 77 70 30N 103 0 E
Kotzebue 147 66 50N 162 40W
Kotzebue Sd. 147 66 30N 164 0W
Kouango 124 5 0N 20 10 E
Koudekerke 47 51 29N 3 33 E
Koudougou 120 12 10N 2 20W
Koufonísi, I. 69 34 56N 26 8 E
Koufonísia, I. 69 36 57N 25 35 E
Kougaberge 128 33 48S 24 20 E
Kouibli 120 7 15N 7 14W
Kouilou, R. 124 4 10S 12 5 E
Kouki 124 7 22N 17 3 E
Koula Moutou 124 1 15S 12 25 E
Koulen 100 13 50N 104 40 E
Koulikoro 120 12 40N 7 50W
Koumala 138 21 38S 149 15 E
Koumankoun 120 11 58N 6 6W
Koumbia, Guin. 120 11 54N 13 40W
Koumbia, Upp. Vol. 120 11 10N 3 50W
Koumboum 120 10 25N 13 0W
Koumpenntoum 120 13 59N 14 34W
Koumra 117 8 50N 17 35 E
Koumradskiy 76 47 20N 75 0 E
Koundara 120 12 29N 13 18W
Kountze 159 30 20N 94 22W
Koupangtzu 107 41 22N 121 46 E
Koupéla 121 12 11N 0 21 E
Kourizo, Passe de 119 22 28N 15 27 E
Kouroussa 120 10 45N 9 45W
Koussané 120 14 53N 11 14W
Kousseri 117 12 0N 14 55 E
Koutiala 120 12 25N 5 35W
Kouto 120 9 53N 6 25W
Kouvé 121 6 25N 0 59 E
KovaČica 66 45 5N 20 38 E
Kovel 80 51 10N 24 20 E
Kovilpatti 97 9 10N 77 50 E
Kovin 66 44 44N 20 59 E
Kovrov 81 56 25N 41 25 E
Kovur, Andhra Pradesh, India 96 17 3N 81 39 E
Kovur, Andhra Pradesh, India 97 14 30N 80 1 E
Kowal 54 52 32N 19 7 E
Kowalewo Pomorskie 54 53 10N 18 52 E
Kowkash 150 50 20N 87 20W
Kowloon 109 22 20N 114 15 E
Kowŏn 107 39 26N 127 14 E
Kōyama 110 31 20N 130 56 E
Koyan, Pegunungan 102 3 15N 114 30 E
Koyang 106 33 31N 116 11 E
Koytash 85 40 11N 67 19 E
Koyuk 147 64 55N 161 20W
Koyukuk, R. 147 65 45N 156 30W
Koyulhisar 82 40 20N 37 52 E
Koza 112 26 19N 127 46 E
Kozan 92 37 35N 35 50 E
Kozàni 68 40 19N 21 47 E
Kozàni □ 68 40 18N 21 45 E
Kozara, Mts. 63 45 0N 17 0 E
Kozarac 63 44 58N 16 48 E
Kozelsk 80 54 2N 35 38 E
Kozhikode = Calicut 97 11 15N 75 43 E
Kozhva 78 65 10N 57 0 E
Koziegłowy 54 50 37N 19 8 E
Kozje 63 46 5N 15 35 E
Kozle 54 50 20N 18 8 E
Kozlodui 67 43 45N 23 42 E
Kozlovets 67 43 30N 25 20 E
Kozmin 54 51 48N 17 27 E
Kōzu-Shima 111 34 13N 139 10 E
Kozuchów 54 51 45N 15 31 E
Kpabia 121 9 10N 0 20W
Kpandae 121 8 30N 0 2W
Kpandu 121 7 2N 0 18 E
Kpessi 121 8 4N 1 16 E
Kra Buri 101 10 22N 98 46 E
Kra, Isthmus of = Kra, Kho Khot 101 10 15N 99 30 E
Kra, Kho Khot 101 10 15N 99 30 E
Krabbendijke 47 51 26N 4 7 E
Krabi 101 8 4N 98 55 E
Kragan 103 6 43S 111 38 E
Kragerø 71 58 52N 9 25 E
Kragujevac 66 44 2N 20 56 E
Krajenka 54 53 18N 16 59 E
Krakatau = Rakata, Pulau 102 6 10S 105 20 E
Krakor 100 12 32N 104 12 E
Kraków 54 50 4N 19 57 E
Kraków □ 53 50 0N 20 0 E
Kraksaan 103 7 43S 113 23 E
Kraksmala 73 57 2N 15 20 E
Kråkstad 71 59 40N 10 50 E
Kråkstad 71 59 39N 10 55 E
Kralanh 100 13 35N 103 25 E
Králiky 53 50 6N 16 45 E
Kraljevo 66 43 44N 20 41 E
Kralovice 52 49 59N 13 29 E
Královsky Chlmec 53 48 27N 22 0 E
Kralupy 52 50 13N 14 20 E
Kramatorsk 82 48 50N 37 30 E
Kramer 161 35 0N 117 38W
Kramfors 72 62 55N 17 48 E
Kramis, C. 118 36 26N 0 45 E
Krångede 72 63 9N 16 10 E
Krångede 72 63 9N 16 6 E
Kraniá 68 39 53N 21 18 E
Kranidhion 69 37 20N 23 10 E
Kranj 63 46 16N 14 22 E
Kranjska Gora 63 46 29N 13 48 E
Kranzberg 128 21 59S 15 37 E
Krapina 63 46 10N 15 52 E
Krapina, R. 63 46 0N 15 55 E
Krapivna 81 53 58N 37 10 E
Krapkowice 54 50 29N 17 56 E
Kras Polyana 83 43 40N 40 25 E
Krashyy Klyuch 84 55 23N 56 39 E
Kraskino 77 42 44N 130 48 E
Krāslāva 80 55 52N 27 12 E
Kraslice 52 50 19N 12 31 E
Krasnaya Gorbatka 81 55 52N 41 45 E
Krasnik Fabryezny 54 50 58N 22 11 E
Krasnoarmeisk 82 48 18N 37 11 E
Krasnoarmeysk, R.S.F.S.R., U.S.S.R. 81 50 32N 45 50 E
Krasnoarmeysk, R.S.F.S.R., U.S.S.R. 83 48 30N 44 25 E
Krasnodar 83 45 5N 38 50 E
Krasnodonetskaya 83 48 5N 40 50 E
Krasnog Dardeiskoye 82 45 32N 34 16 E
Krasnogorskiy 81 56 10N 48 28 E
Krasnograd 82 49 27N 35 27 E
Krasnogvardeysk 85 39 46N 67 16 E
Krasnogvardeyskoye 83 45 52N 41 33 E
Krasnoïarsk 77 56 8N 93 0 E
Krasnokamsk 84 58 4N 55 48 E
Krasnokutsk 80 50 10N 34 50 E
Krasnoperekopsk 82 46 0N 33 54 E
Krasnoselkupsk 76 65 20N 82 10 E
Krasnoslobodsk 83 48 42N 44 33 E
Krasnoturinsk 84 59 46N 60 12 E
Krasnoufimsk 84 56 57N 57 46 E
Krasnouralsk 84 58 21N 60 3 E
Krasnousolskiy 84 53 54N 56 27 E
Krasnovishersk 84 60 23N 57 3 E
Krasnovodsk 79 40 0N 52 52 E
Krasnoyarsk 77 56 8N 93 0 E
Krasnoyarskiy 84 51 58N 59 55 E
Krasnoye, Kal., U.S.S.R. 83 46 16N 45 0 E
Krasnoye, R.S.F.S.R., U.S.S.R. 81 59 15N 47 40 E
Krasnoye, Ukr., U.S.S.R. 80 49 56N 24 42 E
Krasnozavodsk 81 56 38N 38 16 E
Krasny Liman 82 48 58N 37 50 E
Krasny Sulin 83 47 52N 40 8 E
Krasnystaw 54 50 57N 23 5 E
Krasnyy 80 49 56N 24 42 E
Krasnyy Kholm, R.S.F.S.R., U.S.S.R. 81 58 10N 37 10 E
Krasnyy Kholm, R.S.F.S.R., U.S.S.R. 84 51 35N 54 9 E
Krasnyy Kut 81 50 50N 47 0 E
Krasnyy Luch 83 48 13N 39 0 E
Krasnyy Yar, Kal., U.S.S.R. 83 46 43N 48 23 E
Krasnyy Yar, R.S.F.S.R., U.S.S.R. 81 50 42N 44 45 E
Krasnyy Yar, R.S.F.S.R., U.S.S.R. 81 53 30N 50 22 E
Krasnyyoskolskoye, Vdkhr. 82 49 30N 37 30 E
Kraśnik 54 50 55N 22 5 E
Kraszna, R. 53 48 0N 22 20 E
Kratie 100 12 32N 106 10 E
Kratke Ra. 135 6 45S 146 0 E
Kratovo 66 42 6N 22 10 E
Kravanh, Chuor Phnum 101 12 0N 103 32 E
Krawang 103 6 19N 107 18 E
Krefeld 48 51 20N 6 22 E
Kremaston, Límni 69 38 52N 21 30 E
Kremenchug 82 49 5N 33 25 E
Kremenchugskoye Vdkhr. 82 49 20N 32 30 E
Kremenets 82 50 8N 25 43 E
Kremenica 66 40 55N 21 25 E
Kremennaya 82 49 1N 38 10 E
Kremikovtsi 67 42 46N 23 28 E
Kremmen 48 52 45N 13 1 E
Kremmling 160 40 10N 106 30W
Kremnica 53 48 45N 18 50 E
Krems 52 48 25N 15 36 E
Kremsmünster 52 48 3N 14 8 E
Kretinga 80 55 53N 21 15 E
Krettamia 118 28 47N 3 27W
Krettsy 80 58 15N 32 30 E
Kreuzlingen 51 47 38N 9 10 E
Kribi 121 2 57N 9 56 E
Krichem 67 46 16N 24 28 E
Krichev 80 53 45N 31 50 E
Kriens 51 47 2N 8 17 E
Krim, mt. 63 45 53N 14 30 E
Krimpen 46 51 55N 4 34 E
Krionéri 69 38 20N 21 35 E
Krishna, R. 96 16 30N 77 0 E
Krishnagiri 97 12 32N 78 16 E
Krishnanagar 95 23 24N 88 33 E
Krishnaraja Sagara 97 12 20N 76 30 E
Kristianopel 73 56 12N 16 0 E
Kristiansand 71 58 9N 8 1 E
Kristianstad 73 56 2N 14 9 E
Kristianstad □ 75 56 15N 14 0 E
Kristiansund 71 63 7N 7 45 E
Kristiinankaupunki 74 62 16N 21 21 E
Kristinehamn 72 59 18N 14 13 E
Kristinestad 74 62 16N 21 21 E
Kríti, I. 69 35 15N 25 0 E
Kritsá 69 35 10N 25 41 E
Kriva Palanka 66 42 11N 22 19 E
Kriva, R. 66 42 12N 22 18 E
Krivaja, R. 66 44 15N 18 22 E
Krivelj 66 44 8N 22 5 E
Krivoy Rog 82 47 51N 33 20 E
Krizevci 63 46 3N 16 32 E
Krk 63 45 5N 14 36 E
Krk, I. 63 45 8N 14 40 E
Krka, R. 63 45 50N 15 30 E
Krkonoše 52 50 50N 16 10 E
Krnov 53 50 5N 17 40 E
Krobia 54 51 47N 16 59 E
Kročehlavy 52 50 8N 14 9 E
Kroeng Krai 101 14 55N 98 30 E
Krokawo 54 54 47N 18 9 E
Krokeai 69 36 53N 22 32 E
Kroken, Norway 71 58 57N 9 8 E
Kroken, Sweden 71 59 2N 11 23 E
Krokom 72 63 20N 14 30 E

Krolevets **Kuybyshevskoye Vdkhr**

Krolevets 80 51 35N 33 20 E
Kroměríz 53 49 18N 17 21 E
Krommenie 46 52 30N 4 46 E
Krompachy 53 48 54N 20 52 E
Kromy 80 52 40N 35 48 E
Kronobergs län □ 73 56 45N 14 30 E
Kronprins Harald Kyst 13 70 0S 35 1 E
Kronprins Olav Kyst 13 69 0S 42 0 E
Kronprinsesse Märtha Kyst 13 73 30S 10 0W
Kronshtadt 80 60 5N 29 35 E
Kroonstad 125 27 43S 27 19 E
Kröpelin 48 54 4N 11 48 E
Kropotkin 77 45 25N 40 35 E
Kropp 48 54 24N 9 32 E
Krósniewice 54 52 15N 19 11 E
Krosno 54 49 35N 21 56 E
Kroşno □ 54 49 30N 22 0 E
Krosno Odrz 54 52 3N 15 7 E
Krosścienko 54 49 29N 20 25 E
Krotoszyn 54 51 42N 17 23 E
Krotovka 84 53 18N 51 10 E
Krraba 68 41 13N 20 0 E
Krško 63 45 57N 15 30 E
Krstača, mt. 66 42 57N 20 8 E
Kruger Nat. Pk. 129 24 0S 31 40 E
Krugersdorp 129 26 5S 27 46 E
Kruidfontein 128 32 48S 21 59 E
Kruiningen 47 51 27N 4 2 E
Kruis, Kaap 128 21 55S 13 57 E
Kruishoutem 47 50 54N 3 32 E
Kruisland 47 51 34N 4 25 E
Kruja 68 41 32N 19 46 E
Krulevshchina 80 55 5N 27 45 E
Kruma 68 42 37N 20 28 E
Krumovgrad 67 41 29N 25 38 E
Krung Thep 100 13 45N 100 35 E
Krupanj 66 44 25N 19 22 E
Krupina 53 48 22N 19 5 E
Krupinica, R. 53 48 15N 19 5 E
Kruševac 66 43 35N 21 28 E
Krušovo 66 41 23N 21 19 E
Kruszwica 54 52 40N 18 20 E
Kruzof I. 152 57 10N 135 40W
Krylbo 72 60 7N 16 15 E
Krymsk Abinsk 82 44 50N 38 0 E
Krymskaya 82 45 0N 34 0 E
Krynica 54 49 25N 20 57 E
Krynica Morska 54 54 23N 19 28 E
Krynki 54 53 17N 23 43 E
Kryulyany 70 47 12N 29 9 E
Krzepice 54 50 58N 18 50 E
Krzeszowice 54 50 8N 19 37 E
Krzywin 54 51 58N 16 50 E
Krzyz 54 52 52N 16 0 E
Ksabi, Alg. 118 29 8N 0 58W
Ksabi, Moroc. 118 32 51N 4 13W
Ksar Chellala 118 35 13N 2 19 E
Ksar el Boukhari 118 35 51N 2 52 E
Ksar el Kebir 118 35 0N 6 0W
Ksar es Souk 118 31 58N 4 20W
Ksar Rhilane 119 33 0N 9 39 E
Ksiba 118 32 46N 6 0W
Ksour, Mts. des 118 32 45N 0 30W
Kstovo 81 56 12N 44 13 E
Kuachou 109 32 14N 119 24 E
Kuala 102 2 46N 105 47 E
Kuala Berang 101 5 5N 103 1 E
Kuala Dungun 101 4 45N 103 25 E
Kuala Kangsar 101 4 46N 100 56 E
Kuala Kerai 101 5 30N 102 12 E
Kuala Klawang 101 2 56N 102 5 E
Kuala Kubu Baharu 101 3 34N 101 39 E
Kuala Lipis 101 4 10N 102 3 E
Kuala Lumpur 101 3 9N 101 41 E
Kuala Marang 101 5 12N 103 13 E
Kuala Nerang 101 6 16N 100 37 E
Kuala Pilah 101 2 45N 102 15 E
Kuala Rompin 101 2 49N 103 29 E
Kuala Selangor 101 3 20N 101 15 E
Kuala Terengganu 101 5 20N 103 8 E
Kuala Trengganu 101 5 20N 103 8 E
Kualakahi Chan 147 22 2N 159 53W
Kualakapuas 102 2 55S 114 20 E
Kualakurun 102 1 10S 113 50 E
Kualapembuang, Indon. 102 3 14S 112 38 E
Kualapembuang, Indon. 102 2 52S 111 45 E
Kuanaan 107 34 8N 119 24 E
Kuanch'eng 107 40 39N 118 32 E
Kuandang 103 0 56N 123 1 E
Kuangan 108 30 30N 106 35 E
Kuangch'ang 109 26 50N 116 15 E
Kuangchou 109 23 10N 113 12 E
Kuangfeng 109 28 26N 118 12 E
Kuanghan 108 30 56N 104 15 E
Kuanghua 109 32 22N 111 43 E
Kuangjao 107 37 5N 118 25 E
Kuangling 106 39 47N 114 10 E
Kuangnan 108 24 3N 105 3 E
Kuangning 109 23 40N 112 23 E
Kuangshi 109 29 55N 115 25 E
Kuangshun 108 26 5N 106 16 E
Kuangte 109 30 54N 119 26 E
Kuangtse 109 27 30N 117 24 E
Kuangwuch'eng 106 37 49N 108 51 E
Kuangyüan 108 32 22N 105 50 E
Kuanhsien 108 31 0N 103 40 E
Kuanling 108 25 55N 105 35 E
Kuanp'ing 109 31 39N 110 16 E
Kuantan 101 3 49N 103 20 E
Kuant'ao 106 36 31N 115 16 E
Kuantaok'ou 106 34 18N 111 1 E
K'uantien 107 40 47N 124 43 E
Kuanyang 109 25 29N 111 9 E
Kuanyün 107 34 17N 119 15 E
Kuaram 123 12 25N 39 30 E
Kuba 83 41 21N 48 32 E
Kubak 93 27 10N 63 10 E
Kuban, R. 82 45 5N 38 0 E
Kubenskoye, Oz. 81 59 40N 39 25 E
Kuberle 83 47 0N 42 20 E
Kubokawa 110 33 12N 133 8 E
Kubor 135 6 10S 144 44 E
Kubrat 67 43 49N 26 31 E
Kučevo 66 44 30N 21 40 E
Kucha Gompa 95 34 25N 76 56 E
Kuchaman 94 27 13N 74 47 E
Kuch'ang 108 24 58N 102 45 E
Kuchang 109 28 37N 109 56 E
K'uche K'uerhlo 105 41 43N 82 54 E
Kuchenspitze 49 47 3N 10 14 E
Kuchiang 109 27 11N 114 47 E
Kuching 102 1 33N 110 25 E
Kuchinoerabu-Jima 112 30 28N 130 11 E
Kuchinotsu 110 32 36N 130 11 E
Kuçove = Qytet Stalin 68 40 47N 19 57 E
Kud, R. 94 26 30N 66 12 E
Kuda 93 23 10N 71 15 E
Kudalier, R. 96 18 20N 78 40 E
Kudamatsu 110 34 0N 131 52 E
Kudara 85 38 25N 72 39 E
Kudat 102 6 55N 116 55 E
Kudremukh, Mt. 97 13 15N 75 20 E
Kuduarra Well 136 20 38S 126 20 E
Kudus 103 6 48S 110 51 E
Kudymkar 84 59 1N 54 39 E
Kuei Chiang, R. 109 23 33N 111 18 E
Kueich'i 109 28 17N 117 11 E
Kueich'ih 109 30 42N 117 30 E
Kueichu 108 26 25N 106 40 E
Kueihsien 108 23 6N 109 36 E
Kueilin 109 25 20N 110 18 E
Kueip'ing 108 23 24N 110 5 E
Kueiting 108 26 30N 107 17 E
Kueitung 109 26 12N 114 0 E
Kueiyang, Hunan, China 109 25 44N 112 43 E
Kueiyang, Kweichow, China 108 26 35N 106 43 E
K'uerhlo 105 41 44N 86 9 E
Kufra, El Wâhât el 117 24 17N 23 15 E
Kufrinja 90 32 20N 35 41 E
Kufstein 52 47 35N 12 11 E
Kugmallit B. 147 29 0N 134 0W
Kugong, I. 150 56 18N 79 50W
Kūh-e-Alijuq 93 31 30N 51 41 E
Kūh-e-Dinar 93 30 10N 51 0 E
Kūh-e-Hazaran 93 29 35N 57 20 E
Kūh-e-Jebel Barez 93 29 0N 58 0 E
Kūh-e-Sorkh 93 35 30N 58 45 E
Kūh-e-Taftan 93 28 40N 61 0 E
Kūhak 93 27 12N 63 10 E
Kūhha-ye-Bashakerd 93 26 45N 59 0 E
Kūhha-ye Sabalān 93 38 15N 47 45 E
Kuhnsdorf 52 46 37N 14 38 E
Kuhpayeh 93 32 44N 52 20 E
Kui Buri 101 12 3N 99 52 E
Kuinre 46 52 47N 5 51 E
Kuiseb, R. 125 23 40S 15 30 E
Kuiu I. 147 56 40N 134 15W
Kujangdong 107 39 57N 126 1 E
Kuji 112 40 11N 141 46 E
Kujū-San 110 33 5N 131 15 E
Kujukuri-Heiya 111 35 45N 140 30 E
Kukavica, mt. 66 42 48N 21 57 E
Kukawa 121 12 58N 13 27 E
Kukerin 137 33 13S 118 0 E
Kukësi 68 42 5N 20 20 E
Kukësi □ 68 42 25N 20 15 E
Kukko 123 8 26N 41 35 E
Kukmor 84 56 11N 50 54 E
Kukup 101 1 20N 103 27 E
K'uk'ushihli Shanmo 105 35 20N 91 0 E
Kukvidze 81 50 40N 43 15 E
Kula, Bulg. 66 43 52N 22 36 E
Kula, Yugo. 66 45 37N 19 32 E
Kulai 101 1 44N 103 35 E
Kulal, Mt. 126 2 42N 36 57 E
Kulaly, O. 83 45 0N 50 0 E
Kulanak 85 41 22N 75 30 E
Kulasekharapattanam 97 8 20N 78 0 E
Kuldiga 80 56 58N 21 59 E
Kuldja = Ining 105 43 54N 81 21 E
Kuldu 123 12 50N 28 30 E
Kulebaki 81 55 22N 42 25 E
Kulen Vakuf 63 44 35N 16 2 E
Kulgam 95 33 36N 75 2 E
Kuli 83 42 2N 46 12 E
Kulim 101 5 22N 100 34 E
Kulin 137 32 40S 118 2 E
Kulja 137 30 28S 117 18 E
Küllük 69 37 12N 27 36 E
Kulm 158 46 22N 98 58W
K'uloch'akonnoerh 106 43 25N 114 50 E
Kulsary 76 46 59N 54 1 E
Kultay 83 45 5N 51 40 E
Kulti 95 23 43N 86 50 E
Kulu 93 37 12N 115 2 E
Kulumadau 138 9 15S 152 50 E
K'ulunch'i 107 42 44N 121 44 E
Kulunda 76 52 45N 79 15 E
Kulungar 94 34 0N 69 2 E
Kulwin 140 35 0S 142 42 E
Kulyab 85 37 55N 69 50 E
Kum Tekei 76 43 10N 79 30 E
Kuma 110 33 39N 132 54 E
Kuma, R. 83 44 55N 45 57 E
Kumaganum 121 13 8N 10 38 E
Kumagaya 111 36 9N 139 22 E
Kumak 84 51 10N 60 8 E
Kumamoto 110 32 45N 130 45 E
Kumamoto-ken □ 110 32 30N 130 40 E
Kumano 111 33 54N 136 5 E
Kumano-Nada 111 33 47N 136 20 E
Kumanovo 66 42 9N 21 42 E
Kumara 143 42 37S 171 12 E
Kumarkhali 98 23 51N 89 15 E
Kumarl 137 32 47S 121 33 E
Kumasi 120 6 41N 1 38W
Kumba 121 4 36N 9 24 E
Kumbakonam 97 10 58N 79 25 E
Kumbarilla 139 27 15S 150 55 E
Kumbo 121 6 15N 10 36 E
Kumbukkan Oya 97 6 35N 81 40 E
Kümchŏn 107 38 10N 126 29 E
Kumdok 95 33 32N 78 10 E
Kumeny 81 58 10N 49 47 E
Kümhwa 107 38 17N 127 28 E
Kumi 126 1 30N 33 58 E
Kumkale 68 40 30N 26 13 E
Kumla 72 59 8N 15 10 E
Kumo 121 10 1N 11 12 E
Kumon Bum 98 26 30N 97 15 E
Kumotori-Yama 111 35 51N 138 57 E
Kumta 97 14 29N 74 32 E
Kumtorkala 83 43 2N 46 50 E
Kumukahi, C. 147 19 31N 154 49W
Kumusi, R. 135 8 16S 148 13 E
Kumylzhenskaya 83 49 51N 42 38 E
Kunágota 53 46 26N 21 3 E
Kunama 141 35 35S 148 4 E
Kunar 93 34 30N 71 3 E
Kunashir, Ostrov 77 44 0N 146 0 E
Kunch 95 26 0N 79 10 E
Kunda 80 59 30N 26 34 E
Kundiawa 135 6 2S 145 1 E
Kundip 137 33 42S 120 10 E
Kundla 94 21 21N 71 25 E
Kunduz 93 36 50N 68 50 E
Kunduz □ 93 36 50N 68 50 E
Kunene, R. 128 17 15S 13 40 E
Kungala 139 29 58S 153 7 E
Kungälv 73 57 53N 11 59 E
Kungan 109 30 4N 112 12 E
Kungch'eng 109 24 50N 110 49 E
K'ungch'iao Ho 105 41 48N 86 47 E
Küngdong 107 39 9N 126 5 E
Kungey Alatau, Khrebet 85 42 50N 77 0 E
Kunghit I. 152 52 6N 131 3W
Kungho 105 36 28N 100 45 E
Kungka 108 28 44N 100 22 E
Kungkuan 108 21 51N 109 33 E
Kungrad 76 43 6N 58 54 E
Kungsbacka 73 57 30N 12 5 E
Kungshan 108 27 41N 97 37 E
Kungt'an 108 28 49N 108 38 E
Kungur 84 57 25N 56 57 E
Kungurri 138 21 3S 148 46 E
Kungyangon 98 16 27N 96 1 E
Kungyingtzu 107 43 38N 121 0 E
Kunhar, R. 95 35 0N 73 40 E
Kunhegyes 53 47 22N 20 36 E
Kunimi-Dake 110 32 33N 131 1 E
Kuningan 103 6 59S 108 29 E
Kunisaki 110 33 33N 131 45 E
Kunlara 140 34 54S 139 55 E
Kunlong 98 23 20N 98 50 E
Kunlun Shan 105 36 0N 86 30 E
Kunmadaras 53 47 28N 20 45 E
K'unming 108 25 5N 102 40 E
Kunnamkulam 97 10 38N 76 7 E
Kunrade 47 50 53N 5 57 E
Kunsan 107 35 59N 126 45 E
K'unshan 109 31 22N 121 0 E
Kunszentmárton 53 46 50N 20 20 E
Kununurra 136 15 40S 128 39 E
Kunwarara 138 22 55S 150 9 E
Kuohsien 106 38 57N 112 46 E
Kuopio 74 62 53N 27 35 E
Kuopion Lääni □ 74 63 25N 27 10 E
Kupa, R. 63 45 30N 16 10 E
Kupang 103 10 19S 123 39 E
Kupeik'ou 107 40 42N 117 9 E
Kupiano 135 10 4S 148 14 E
Kupreanof I. 147 56 50N 133 30W
Kupres 66 44 1N 17 15 E
Kupyansk 82 49 45N 37 35 E
Kupyansk-Uzlovoi 82 49 52N 37 34 E
Kur, R. 98 26 50N 91 0 E
Kura, R. 83 40 20N 47 30 E
Kurahashi-Jima 110 34 8N 132 31 E
Kuranda 138 16 48S 145 35 E
Kurandvad 96 16 45N 74 39 E
Kurashiki 110 34 40N 133 50 E
Kurayoshi 110 35 26N 133 50 E
Kurday 85 43 21N 74 59 E
Kurdistan, reg. 92 37 30N 42 0 E
Kurduvadi 96 18 8N 75 29 E
Kure 110 34 14N 132 32 E
Kuressaare = Kingisepp 80 58 15N 22 15 E
Kurgaldzhino 76 50 35N 70 20 E
Kurgan, R.S.F.S.R., U.S.S.R. 77 64 5N 172 50W
Kurgan, R.S.F.S.R., U.S.S.R. 84 55 26N 65 18 E
Kurgan-Tyube 85 37 50N 68 47 E
Kuria Muria I = Khy ryān Muryān J. 91 17 30N 55 58 E
Kurichchi 97 11 36N 77 35 E
Kuridala 138 21 16S 140 29 E
Kurigram 98 25 49N 89 39 E
Kurihashi 111 36 8N 139 42 E
Kuril Trench 142 44 0N 153 0 E
Kurilskiye Ostrova 77 45 0N 150 0 E
Kuring Kuru 128 17 42S 18 32 E
Kuringen 47 50 56N 5 18 E
Kurino 110 31 57N 130 43 E
KüRKkkuyu 68 39 35N 26 27 E
Kurkur 122 23 50N 32 0 E
Kurkûrah 119 31 30N 20 1 E
Kurla 96 19 5N 72 52 E
Kurlovski 81 55 25N 40 40 E
Kurma 123 13 55N 24 40 E
Kurmuk 123 10 33N 34 21 E
Kurnalpi 137 30 29S 122 16 E
Kurnool 97 15 45N 78 0 E
Kurobe-Gawe, R. 111 36 55N 137 25 E
Kurogi 110 33 12N 130 40 E
Kurovskoye 81 55 35N 38 55 E
Kurow 143 44 4S 170 29 E
Kurrajong, N.S.W., Austral. 141 33 33S 150 42 E
Kurrajong, W.A., Austral. 137 28 39S 120 59 E
Kurram, R. 94 33 30N 70 15 E
Kurri Kurri 141 32 50S 151 28 E
Kuršenai 80 56 1N 23 3 E
Kurseong 95 26 56N 88 18 E
Kursk 81 51 42N 36 11 E
Kuršumlija 66 43 9N 21 19 E
Kuršumlijska Banja 66 43 3N 21 11 E
Kurtalon 92 37 55N 41 40 E
Kurtamysh 84 54 55N 64 27 E
Kurty, R. 85 44 16N 76 42 E
Kuru (Chel), Bahr el 123 8 10N 26 50 E
Kuruman 128 27 28S 23 28 E
Kurume 110 33 15N 130 30 E
Kurunegala 97 7 30N 80 18 E
Kurya 77 61 15N 108 10 E
Kusa 84 55 20N 59 29 E
Kuşadası 69 37 52N 27 15 E
Kuşadası Körfezı 69 37 56N 27 0 E
Kusatsu, Gumma, Japan 111 36 37N 138 36 E
Kusatsu, Shiga, Japan 111 34 58N 136 5 E
Kusawa L. 152 60 20N 136 13W
Kusel 49 49 31N 7 25 E
Kushchevskaya 83 46 33N 39 35 E
Kushikino 110 31 44N 130 16 E
Kushima 110 31 29N 131 14 E
Kushimoto 111 33 28N 135 47 E
Kushin 109 32 12N 115 48 E
Kushiro 112 43 0N 144 25 E
Kushiro, R. 112 42 59N 144 23 E
Kushk 93 34 55N 62 30 E
Kushka 76 35 20N 62 18 E
Kushmurun 84 52 27N 64 36 E
Kushmurun, Ozero 84 52 40N 64 48 E
Kushnarenkovo 84 55 6N 55 22 E
Kushol 95 33 40N 76 36 E
Kushrabat 85 40 18N 66 32 E
Kushtia 98 23 55N 89 5 E
Kushum, R. 83 50 40N 50 20 E
Kushva 84 58 18N 59 45 E
Kuskokwim Bay 147 59 50N 162 56W
Kuskokwim Mts. 147 63 0N 156 0W
Kuskokwim, R. 147 61 48N 157 0W
Küsnacht 51 47 19N 8 15 E
Kussa 123 4 9N 38 58 E
Küssnacht 51 47 5N 8 26 E
Kustanay 84 53 10N 63 35 E
Kusu 110 33 16N 131 9 E
Kusung 108 28 25N 105 12 E
Kut, Ko 101 11 40N 102 35 E
Kutá Horq 52 49 57N 15 16 E
Kutahya 92 39 30N 30 2 E
Kutaisi 83 42 19N 42 40 E
Kutaradja = Banda Aceh 102 5 35N 95 20 E
Kutatjane 102 3 45N 97 50 E
Kutch, G. of 94 22 50N 69 15 E
Kutch, Rann of 94 24 0N 70 0 E
Kut'ien 109 26 36N 118 48 E
Kutina 63 45 29N 16 48 E
Kutiyana 94 21 36N 70 2 E
Kutjevo 66 45 23N 17 55 E
Kutkai 98 23 27N 97 56 E
Kutkashen 83 40 58N 47 47 E
Kutná Hora 52 49 57N 15 16 E
Kutno 54 52 15N 19 23 E
Kuttabul 138 21 5S 148 48 E
Kutu 124 2 40S 18 11 E
Kutum 123 14 20N 24 10 E
Kúty 53 48 40N 17 3 E
Kuŭptong 107 40 45N 126 1 E
Kuurne 47 50 51N 3 18 E
Kuvandyk 84 51 28N 57 21 E
Kuvasay 85 40 18N 71 59 E
Kuvshinovo 80 57 2N 34 11 E
Kuwait = Al Kuwayt 92 29 30N 47 30 E
Kuwait ■ 92 29 30N 47 30 E
Kuwana 111 35 0N 136 43 E
Kuyang 106 41 8N 110 1 E
Kuybyshev 81 55 27N 78 19 E
Kuybyshevo, Ukraine S.S.R., U.S.S.R. 82 47 25N 36 40 E
Kuybyshevo, Uzbek S.S.R., U.S.S.R. 85 40 20N 71 15 E
Kuybyshevskiy 85 37 52N 68 44 E
Kuybyshevskoye Vdkhr. 81 55 2N 49 30 E

Kuyeh Ho, R Lambay I

Kuyeh Ho, R. 106 38 30N 110 44 E
Kuylyuk 85 41 14N 69 17 E
Kuyto, Oz. 78 64 40N 31 0 E
Kuyüan, Hopeh, China 106 41 34N 115 38 E
Kuyüan, Ningsia Hui, China 106 36 1N 106 17 E
Kuzhithura 97 8 18N 77 11 E
Kuzino 84 57 1N 59 27 E
Kuzmin 66 45 2N 19 25 E
Kuznetsk 81 53 12N 46 40 E
Kuzomen 78 66 22N 36 50 E
Kvænangen 74 69 55N 21 15 E
Kvam 71 61 40N 9 42 E
Kvamsøy 71 61 7N 6 28 E
Kvarken 74 63 30N 21 0 E
Kvarner 63 44 50N 14 10 E
Kvarnerič 63 44 43N 14 37 E
Kvarnsveden 72 60 32N 15 25 E
Kvarntorp 72 59 8N 15 17 E
Kvås 71 58 16N 7 14 E
Kvernes 71 63 1N 7 44 E
Kvillsfors 73 57 24N 15 29 E
Kvina, R. 71 58 43N 6 52 E
Kvinesdal 71 58 18N 6 59 E
Kviteseid 71 59 24N 8 29 E
Kwabhaca 129 30 51 S 29 0 E
Kwadacha, R. 152 57 28N 125 38W
Kwakhanai 128 21 39 S 21 16 E
Kwakoegron 175 5 25N 55 25W
Kwale, Kenya 126 4 15 S 39 31 E
Kwale, Nigeria 121 6 18N 5 28 E
Kwale □ 126 4 15 S 39 10 E
Kwamouth 124 3 9 S 16 20 E
Kwando, R. 128 16 48 S 22 45 E
Kwangdaeri 107 40 31N 127 32 E
Kwangju 107 35 9N 126 54 E
Kwangsi-Chuang A.R. □ 109 24 0N 109 0 E
Kwangtung □ 109 23 45N 114 0 E
Kwara □ 121 8 0N 5 0 E
Kwaraga 128 20 26 S 24 32 E
Kwataboahegan, R. 150 51 9N 80 50W
Kwatisore 103 3 7 S 139 59 E
Kweichow □ 108 27 20N 107 0 E
Kweiyang = Kueiyang 108 26 35N 106 43 E
Kwethluk 147 60 45N 161 34W
Kwidzyn 54 54 45N 18 58 E
Kwigillingok 147 59 50N 163 10W
Kwiguk 147 63 45N 164 35W
Kwikila 135 9 49 S 147 38 E
Kwimba □ 126 3 0 S 33 0 E
Kwinana 137 32 15 S 115 47 E
Kwitaba 126 3 56 S 29 39 E
Kya-in-Seikkyi 98 16 2N 98 8 E
Kyabe 117 9 30N 19 0 E
Kyabra Cr. 139 25 36 S 142 55 E
Kyabram 139 36 19 S 145 4 E
Kyaiklat 98 16 46N 96 52 E
Kyaikmaraw 98 16 23N 97 44 E
Kyaikthin 98 23 32N 95 40 E
Kyaikto 100 17 20N 97 3 E
Kyakhta 77 50 30N 106 25 E
Kyangin 98 18 20N 95 20 E
Kyaring Tso 99 31 5N 88 25 E
Kyaukhnyat 98 18 15N 97 31 E
Kyaukpadaung 99 20 52N 95 8 E
Kyaukpyu 99 19 28N 93 30 E
Kyaukse 98 21 36N 96 10 E
Kyauktaw 98 21 16N 96 44 E
Kyawkku 98 21 48N 96 56 E
Kyburz 163 38 47N 120 18W
Kybybolite 140 36 53 S 140 55 E
Kyegegwa 126 0 30N 31 0 E
Kyeintali 98 18 0N 94 29 E
Kyela □ 127 9 45 S 34 0 E
Kyenjojo 126 0 40N 30 37 E
Kyidaunggan 98 19 53N 96 12 E
Kyle Dam 127 20 15 S 31 0 E
Kyle, dist. 34 55 32N 4 25W
Kyle of Lochalsh 36 57 17N 5 43W
Kyleakin 36 57 16N 5 44W
Kyneton 140 37 10 S 144 29 E
Kynuna 138 21 37 S 141 55 E
Kyō-ga-Saki 111 35 45N 135 15 E
Kyoga, L. 126 1 35N 33 0 E
Kyogle 139 28 40 S 153 0 E
Kyongju 107 35 51N 129 14 E
Kyongpyaw 99 17 12N 95 10 E
Kyŏngsŏng 107 41 35N 129 36 E
Kyōto 111 35 0N 135 45 E
Kyōto-fu □ 111 35 15N 135 30 E
Kyrínia 92 35 20N 33 20 E
Kyritz 48 52 57N 12 25 E
Kyrkebyn 72 59 18N 13 3 E
Kyrping 71 59 45N 6 5 E
Kyshtym 84 55 42N 60 34 E
Kystatyam 77 67 20N 123 10 E
Kytalktakh 77 65 30N 123 40 E
Kytlym 84 59 30N 59 12 E
Kyu-hkok 98 24 4N 98 4 E
Kyulyunken 77 64 10N 137 5 E
Kyunhla 98 23 25N 95 15 E
Kyuquot 152 50 3N 127 25W
Kyuquot Sd. 83 50 0N 127 25W
Kyurdamir 83 40 25N 48 3 E
Kyūshū 110 33 0N 131 0 E
Kyūshū □ 110 33 0N 131 0 E
Kyūshū-Sanchi 110 32 45N 131 40 E
Kyustendil 66 42 25N 22 41 E
Kyusyur 77 70 39N 127 15 E
Kywong 141 34 58 S 146 44 E
Kyzyl 77 51 50N 94 30 E
Kyzyl-Kiya 85 40 16N 72 8 E
Kyzyl Orda 85 44 56N 65 30 E
Kyzyl Rabat 76 37 45N 74 55 E
Kyzylkum 84 42 30N 65 0 E
Kyzylsu, R. 85 39 11N 72 2 E
Kzyl-orda 85 44 48N 65 28 E

L

Laa 53 48 43N 16 23 E
Laage 48 53 55N 12 21 E
Laasphe 48 50 56N 8 23 E
Laau Pt. 147 21 57N 159 40W
Laba, R. 83 45 0N 40 30 E
Laban, Burma 98 25 52N 96 40 E
Laban, Ireland 39 53 8N 8 50W
Labasheeda 39 52 37N 9 15W
Labastide 44 43 28N 2 39 E
Labastide-Murat 44 44 39N 1 33 E
Labbézenga 121 15 2N 0 48 E
Labdah = Leptis Magna 119 32 40N 14 12 E
Labé 120 11 24N 12 16W
Labe, R. 52 50 3N 15 20 E
Laberec, R. 53 21 57N 49 7 E
Laberge, L. 152 61 11N 135 12W
Labin 63 45 5N 14 8 E
Labinsk 83 44 40N 40 48W
Labis 101 2 22N 103 2 E
Labiszyn 54 52 57N 17 54 E
Laboa 103 8 6 S 122 50 E
Laboe 48 54 25N 10 13 E
Labouheyre 44 44 13N 0 55W
Laboulaye 172 34 10 S 63 30W
Labrador City 151 52 57N 66 55W
Labrador, Coast of ■ 149 53 20N 61 0W
Labranzagrande 174 5 33N 72 34W
Lábrea 174 7 15 S 64 51W
Labrède 44 44 41N 0 32W
Labuan, I. 102 5 15N 115 38W
Labuha 103 0 30 S 127 30 E
Labuhan 103 6 26 S 105 50 E
Labuhanbajo 103 8 28 S 120 1 E
Labuissière 47 50 19N 4 11 E
Labuk, Telok 102 6 10N 117 50 E
Labutta 98 16 9N 94 46 E
Labytnangi 78 66 29N 66 40 E
Lac Allard 151 50 33N 63 24W
Lac Bouchette 151 48 16N 72 11W
Lac du Flambeau 158 46 1N 89 51W
Lac Édouard 151 47 40N 72 16W
Lac la Biche 152 54 45N 111 58W
Lac-Mégantic 151 45 35N 70 53W
Lac Seul 153 50 28N 92 0W
Lac Thien 100 12 25N 108 11 E
Lacanau, Étang de 44 44 58N 1 7W
Lacanau Médoc 44 44 59N 1 5W
Lacantum, R. 165 16 36N 90 40W
Lacara, R. 57 39 7N 6 25W
Lacaune 44 43 43N 2 40 E
Lacaune, Mts. de 44 43 43N 2 50 E
Laccadive Is. = Lakshadweep Is. 86 10 0N 72 30 E
Laceby 33 53 32N 0 10W
Lacepede B. 140 36 40 S 139 40 E
Lacepede Is. 136 16 55 S 122 0 E
Lacerdónia 127 18 3 S 35 35 E
Lachen, Sikkim 98 47 12N 8 51 E
Lachen, Switz. 51 47 12N 8 51 E
Lachi 94 33 25N 71 20 E
Lachine 150 45 30N 73 40W
Lachlan 139 42 50 S 147 3 E
Lachlan, R. 140 34 22 S 143 55 E
Lachmangarh 94 27 50N 75 4 E
Lachute 150 45 39N 74 21 E
Lackagh Hills 38 54 14N 8 0W
Lackawanna 156 42 49N 78 50W
Lackawaxen 162 41 29N 74 59W
Lacock 28 51 24N 2 8W
Lacombe 152 52 30N 113 44W
Lacona 162 43 37N 76 5W
Láconi 64 39 54N 9 4 E
Laconia 162 43 32N 71 30W
Lacq 44 43 25N 0 35W
Lacrosse 160 46 51N 117 58W
Ladainha 171 17 39 S 41 44W
Ladakh Ra. 95 34 0N 78 0 E
Ladder Hills 37 57 14N 3 13W
Ladhar Bheinn 36 57 5N 5 37W
Ladhon, R. 69 37 40N 21 50 E
Lâdik 82 40 57N 35 58 E
Ladismith 128 33 28 S 21 15 E
Lādiz 93 28 55N 61 15 E
Ladnun 94 27 38N 74 25 E
Ladock 30 50 19N 4 58W
Ladoga, L. = Ladozhskoye Oz. 78 61 15N 30 30 E
Ladon 43 48 0N 2 30 E
Ladozhskoye Ozero 76 61 15N 30 30 E
Ladrone Is. = Mariana Is. 130 17 0N 145 0 E
Lady Babbie 127 18 30 S 29 20 E
Lady Beatrix L. 150 5 20N 76 50W
Lady Edith Lagoon 136 20 36 S 126 47 E
Lady Grey 128 30 43 S 27 13 E
Ladybank 35 56 16N 3 8W
Ladybrand 128 29 9 S 27 29 E
Lady's I. Lake 39 52 12N 6 23W
Ladysmith, Can. 152 49 0N 123 49W
Ladysmith, S. Afr. 129 28 32 S 29 46 E
Ladysmith, U.S.A. 158 45 27N 91 4W
Lae 135 6 40 S 147 2 E
Laem Ngop 101 12 10N 102 26 E
Laem Pho 101 6 55N 101 19 E
Læsø 73 57 15N 10 53 E
Læsø Rende 73 57 20N 10 45 E
Lafayette, Colo., U.S.A. 158 40 0N 105 2W
Lafayette, Ga., U.S.A. 157 34 44N 85 15W
Lafayette, La., U.S.A. 159 30 18N 92 0W
Lafayette, Tenn., U.S.A. 157 36 35N 86 0W
Laferté 150 48 37N 78 48W
Laferte, R. 152 61 53N 117 44W
Laffan's Bridge 39 52 36N 7 45W
Lafia 121 8 30N 8 34 E
Lafiagi 121 8 52N 5 20 E
Lafleche 153 49 45N 106 40W
Lafon 123 5 5N 32 29 E
Laforest 150 47 4N 81 12W
Laforsen 72 61 56N 15 3 E
Lagaip, R. 135 5 4 S 141 52 E
Lagan 73 56 32N 12 58 E
Lagan, R. 38 54 35N 5 55W
Lagarfljót 74 65 40N 14 18W
Lagarto 170 10 54 S 37 41W
Lagarto, Serra do 173 23 0 S 57 15W
Lage, Ger. 48 52 0N 8 47 E
Lage, Spain 56 43 13N 9 0W
Lage-Mierde 47 51 25N 5 9 E
Lågen 71 61 29N 10 2 E
Lågen, R. 75 61 30N 10 20 E
Lägerdorf 48 53 53N 9 35 E
Lagg 34 56 57N 5 50W
Laggan, Grampian, U.K. 37 57 24N 3 6W
Laggan, Highland, U.K. 37 57 3N 4 48W
Laggan B. 34 55 40N 6 20W
Laggan L. 37 56 57N 4 30W
Laggers Pt. 139 30 52 S 153 4 E
Laghman □ 93 34 20N 70 0 E
Laghouat 118 33 50N 2 59 E
Laghy 38 54 37N 8 7W
Lagnieu 45 45 55N 5 20 E
Lagny 43 48 52N 2 40 E
Lago 65 39 9N 16 8 E
Lagôa 57 37 8N 8 27W
Lagoaça 56 41 11N 6 44W
Lagodekhi 83 41 50N 46 22 E
Lagónegro 65 40 8N 15 45 E
Lagonoy Gulf 103 13 50N 123 50 E
Lagos, Nigeria 121 6 25N 3 27 E
Lagos, Port. 57 37 5N 8 41W
Lagos de Moreno 164 21 21N 101 55W
Lagrange 136 14 13 S 125 46 E
Lagrange B. 136 18 38 S 121 42 E
Laguardia 58 42 33N 2 35W
Laguépie 44 44 8N 1 57 E
Laguna, Brazil 173 28 30 S 48 50W
Laguna, U.S.A. 161 35 3N 107 28W
Laguna Beach 163 33 31N 117 52W
Laguna Dam 161 32 55N 114 30W
Laguna de la Janda 57 36 15N 5 45W
Laguna Limpia 172 26 32 S 59 45W
Laguna Madre 165 27 0N 97 20W
Laguna Veneta 63 45 23N 12 25 E
Lagunas, Chile 172 21 0 S 69 45W
Lagunas, Peru 174 5 10 S 75 35W
Lagunillas 174 10 8N 71 16W
Lahad Datu 103 5 0N 118 30 E
Lahaina 147 20 52N 156 41W
Lahan Sai 100 14 25N 102 52 E
Lahanam 100 16 16N 105 16 E
Lahardaun 38 54 2N 9 20W
Laharpur 95 27 43N 80 56 E
Lahat 102 3 45 S 103 30 E
Lahe 98 19 18N 93 36 E
Lahewa 102 1 22N 97 12 E
Lahijan 93 37 10N 50 6 E
Lahn, R. 48 50 52N 8 35 E
Laholm 73 56 30N 13 2 E
Laholmsbukten 73 56 30N 12 45 E
Lahontan Res. 160 39 28N 118 58W
Lahore 94 31 32N 74 22 E
Lahore □ 94 31 55N 74 5 E
Lahpongsel 98 27 7N 98 25 E
Lahr 49 48 20N 7 52 E
Lahti 75 60 58N 25 40 E
Lai (Béhagle) 117 9 25N 16 30 E
Lai Chau 100 22 5N 103 3 E
Lai-hka 98 21 16N 97 40 E
Laiagam 135 5 33 S 143 30 E
Laian 109 32 27N 118 25 E
Laichou Wan 107 37 30N 119 30 E
Laidley 139 27 39 S 152 20 E
Laidon L. 37 56 40N 4 40W
Laifeng 108 29 31N 109 18 E
Laigle 42 48 46N 0 38 E
Laignes 43 47 50N 4 20 E
Laihsi 107 36 51N 120 30 E
Laikipia □ 126 0 30N 36 30 E
Laila 92 22 10N 46 40 E
Laillahue, Mt. 174 17 0 S 69 30W
Laingsburg 128 33 9 S 20 52 E
Laipin 108 23 42N 109 16 E
Lairg 37 58 1N 4 24W
Lais 102 3 35 S 102 0 E
Laishui 106 39 23N 115 42 E
Laiwu 107 36 12N 117 38 E
Laiyang 107 36 58N 120 41 E
Laiyüan 106 39 19N 114 41 E
Laja, R. 164 20 55N 100 46W
Lajes, Rio Grande d. N., Brazil 170 5 41 S 36 14W
Lajes, Sta. Catarina, Brazil 173 27 48 S 50 20W
Lajinha 171 20 9 S 41 37W
Lajkovac 66 44 27N 20 14 E
Lajosmizse 53 47 3N 19 32 E
Lak Sao 100 18 11N 104 59 E
Laka Chih 95 30 40N 81 10 E
Lakaband 94 31 2N 69 15 E
Lakar 103 8 15 S 128 17 E
Lake Alpine 163 38 29N 120 0W
Lake Andes 158 43 10N 98 32W
Lake Anse 156 46 42N 88 25W
Lake Arthur 159 30 8N 92 40W
Lake Brown 137 30 56 S 118 20 E
Lake Cargelligo 141 33 15 S 146 22 E
Lake Charles 159 31 10N 93 10W
Lake City, Colo, U.S.A. 161 38 3N 107 27W
Lake City, Fla., U.S.A. 157 30 10N 82 40W
Lake City, Iowa, U.S.A. 158 42 12N 94 42W
Lake City, Mich., U.S.A. 156 44 20N 85 10W
Lake City, Minn., U.S.A. 158 44 28N 92 21W
Lake City, S.C., U.S.A. 157 33 51N 79 44W
Lake Coleridge 143 43 17 S 171 30 E
Lake District 23 54 30N 3 10W
Lake George 162 43 25N 73 43W
Lake Grace 137 33 7 S 118 28 E
Lake Harbour 149 62 30N 69 50W
Lake Havasu City 161 34 25N 114 29W
Lake Hughes 163 34 41N 118 26W
Lake Isabella 163 35 38N 118 28W
Lake King 137 33 5 S 119 45 E
Lake Lenore 153 52 24N 104 59W
Lake Louise 152 51 30N 116 10W
Lake Mason 137 27 30 S 119 30 E
Lake Mead Nat. Rec. Area 161 36 0N 114 30W
Lake Mills 158 43 23N 93 33W
Lake Murray 135 6 48 S 141 29 E
Lake Nash 138 20 57 S 138 0 E
Lake of the Woods 155 49 0N 95 0W
Lake Pleasant 162 43 28N 74 25W
Lake Providence 159 32 49N 91 12W
Lake River 150 54 22N 82 31W
Lake Superior Prov. Park 150 47 45N 84 45W
Lake Tekapo 143 43 55 S 170 30 E
Lake Traverse 150 45 56N 78 4W
Lake Varley 137 32 48 S 119 30 E
Lake Village 159 33 20N 91 19W
Lake Wales 157 27 55N 81 32W
Lake Worth 157 26 36N 80 3W
Lakefield 150 44 25N 78 16W
Lakehurst 162 40 1N 74 19W
Lakeland 157 28 0N 82 0W
Lakenheath 29 52 25N 0 30 E
Lakes Entrance 141 37 50 S 148 0 E
Lakeside, Ariz., U.S.A. 161 34 12N 109 59W
Lakeside, Calif., U.S.A. 163 32 52N 116 55W
Lakeside, Nebr., U.S.A. 158 42 5N 102 24W
Lakeview, N.Y., U.S.A. 156 42 43N 78 57W
Lakeview, Oreg., U.S.A. 160 42 15N 120 22W
Lakewood, Calif., U.S.A. 163 33 51N 118 8W
Lakewood, N.J., U.S.A. 162 40 5N 74 13W
Lakhaniá 69 35 58N 27 54 E
Lákhi 69 35 24N 23 27 E
Lakhimpur 95 27 14N 94 7 E
Lakhipur, Assam, India 98 24 48N 93 0 E
Lakhipur, Assam, India 98 26 2N 90 18 E
Lakhonpheng 100 15 54N 105 34 E
Lakhpat 94 23 48N 68 47 E
Laki 74 64 4N 18 14W
Lakin 159 37 58N 101 18W
Lakitusaki, R. 150 54 21N 82 25W
Lakki 93 32 38N 70 50 E
Lakonia □ 69 36 55N 22 30 E
Lakonikós Kólpos 69 36 40N 22 40 E
Lakor, I. 103 8 15 S 128 17 E
Lakota, Ivory C. 120 5 50N 5 30W
Lakota, U.S.A. 158 48 0N 98 22W
Laksefjorden 74 70 45N 26 50 E
Lakselv 74 70 2N 24 56 E
Lakselvibukt 74 69 26N 19 40 E
Lakshadweep Is. 86 10 0N 72 30 E
Laksham 98 23 14N 91 8 E
Lakshmi Kantapur 95 22 5N 88 20 E
Lakshmipur 98 22 38N 90 16 E
Lakuramau 135 2 54 S 151 15 E
Lala Ghat 99 24 30N 92 40 E
Lala Musa 94 32 40N 73 57 E
Lalago 126 3 28 S 33 58 E
Lalapanzi 127 19 20 S 30 15 E
Lalganj 95 25 52N 85 13 E
Lalibala 123 12 8N 39 10 E
Lalin 107 45 14N 126 52 E
Lalin 56 42 40N 8 5W
Lalin Ho, R. 107 45 28N 125 43 E
Lalinde 44 44 50N 0 44 E
Lalitapur 99 26 36N 85 32 E
Lalitpur 95 24 42N 78 28 E
Lam 100 21 21N 106 31 E
Lam Pao Res. 100 16 50N 103 15 E
Lama Kara 121 9 30N 1 15 E
Lamaing 99 15 25N 97 53 E
Lamaipum 98 25 40N 97 57 E
Lamar, Colo., U.S.A. 158 38 9N 102 35W
Lamar, Mo., U.S.A. 159 37 30N 94 20W
Lamas 174 6 28 S 76 31W
Lamastre 45 44 59N 4 35 E
Lamaya 108 29 50N 99 56 E
Lamb Hd. 37 59 5N 2 32W
Lambach 52 48 6N 13 51 E
Lamballe 42 48 29N 2 31W
Lambaréné 124 0 20 S 10 12 E
Lambay I. 38 53 30N 6 0W

Lambayeque □ Lawrenceville

Lambayeque □ 174 6 45 S 80 0W
Lamberhurst 29 51 5N 0 21 E
Lambert 158 47 44N 104 39W
Lambert, C. 135 4 11 S 151 31 E
Lambert Land 12 79 12N 20 30W
Lambesc 45 43 39N 5 16 E
Lambeth 29 51 27N 0 7W
Lambi Kyun, (Sullivan I.) 101 10 50N 98 20 E
Lámbia 69 37 52N 21 53 E
Lambley 35 54 56N 2 30W
Lambon 135 4 45 S 152 48 E
Lambourn 28 51 31N 1 31W
Lambro, R. 62 45 18N 9 20 E
Lambs Hd. 39 51 44N 10 10W
Lame 121 10 27N 9 12 E
Lame Deer 160 45 45N 106 40W
Lamego 56 41 5N 7 52W
Lameque 151 47 45N 64 38W
Lameroo 140 35 19 S 140 33 E
Lamesa 159 32 45N 101 57W
Lamhult 73 57 12N 14 36 E
Lamía 69 38 55N 22 41 E
Lamitan 103 6 40N 122 10 E
Lammermuir 35 55 50N 2 25W
Lammermuir Hills 35 55 50N 2 40W
Lamoille 160 40 47N 115 31W
Lamon Bay 103 14 30N 122 20 E
Lamont, Can. 152 53 46N 112 50W
Lamont, U.S.A. 163 35 15N 118 55W
Lampa 174 15 10 S 70 30W
Lampang 100 18 18N 99 31 E
Lampasas 159 31 5N 98 10W
Lampaul 42 48 28N 5 7W
Lampazos de Naranjo 164 27 2N 100 32W
Lampedusa, I. 60 35 36N 12 40 E
Lampeter 31 52 6N 4 6W
Lampione, I. 119 35 33N 12 20 E
Lampman 153 49 25N 102 50W
Lamprechtshausen 52 48 0N 12 58 E
Lampung 102 1 48 S 115 0 E
Lamu, Burma 98 19 14N 94 10 E
Lamu, Kenya 126 2 10 S 40 55 E
Lamy 161 35 30N 105 58W
Lan Tsan Kiang (Mekong) 87 18 0N 104 15 E
Lanai City 147 20 50N 156 56W
Lanai I. 147 20 50N 156 55W
Lanak La 95 34 27N 79 32 E
Lanaken 47 50 53N 5 39 E
Lanak'o Shank'ou = Lanak La 95 34 27N 79 32 E
Lanao, L. 103 7 52N 124 15 E
Lanark 35 55 40N 3 48W
Lanark (□) 26 55 37N 3 50W
Lancashire □ 32 53 40N 2 30W
Lancaster, Can. 151 45 17N 66 10W
Lancaster, U.K. 32 54 3N 2 48W
Lancaster, Calif., U.S.A. 163 34 47N 118 8W
Lancaster, Ky., U.S.A. 156 37 40N 84 40W
Lancaster, Pa., U.S.A. 162 40 4N 76 19W
Lancaster, S.C., U.S.A. 157 34 45N 80 47W
Lancaster, Va., U.S.A. 162 37 46N 76 28W
Lancaster, Wis., U.S.A. 158 42 48N 90 43W
Lancaster Sd. 12 74 13N 84 0W
Lancer 153 50 48N 108 53W
Lanchester 33 54 50N 1 44W
Lanch'i 109 29 11N 119 30 E
Lanchou 106 36 5N 103 55 E
Lanciano 63 42 15N 14 22 E
Lancing 29 50 49N 0 19W
Łancut 54 50 10N 22 20 E
Lancy 50 46 12N 6 8 E
Lândana 124 5 11 S 12 5 E
Landau 49 49 12N 8 7 E
Landeck 52 47 9N 10 34 E
Landen 47 50 45N 5 3 E
Lander, Austral. 136 20 25 S 132 0 E
Lander, U.S.A. 160 42 50N 108 49W
Landerneau 42 48 28N 4 17W
Landeryd 73 57 7N 13 15 E
Landes □ 44 43 57N 0 48W
Landes, Les 44 44 20N 1 0W
Landete 58 39 56N 1 25W
Landi Kotal 94 34 7N 71 6 E
Landivisiau 42 48 31N 4 6W
Landkey 30 51 2N 4 0W
Landor 137 25 10 S 117 0 E
Landquart 51 46 58N 9 32 E
Landquart, R. 51 46 50N 9 47 E
Landrecies 43 50 7N 3 40 E
Land's End, Can. 12 76 10N 123 0W
Land's End, U.K. 30 50 4N 5 43W
Landsberg 49 48 3N 10 52 E
Landsborough Cr. 138 22 28 S 144 35 E
Landsbro 73 57 24N 14 56 E
Landschaft 50 47 28N 7 40 E
Landshut 48 48 31N 12 10 E
Landskrona 73 56 53N 12 50 E
Landvetter 73 57 41N 12 17 E
Lane 73 58 25N 12 3 E
Laneffe 47 50 17N 4 35 E
Lanesboro 162 41 57N 75 34W
Lanesborough 38 53 40N 8 0W
Lanett 157 33 0N 85 15W
Lang Bay 152 49 17N 124 21W
Lang Qua 100 22 16N 104 27 E
Lang Shan 106 41 0N 106 20 E
Lang Suan 101 9 57N 99 4 E
Langaa 73 56 23N 9 51 E
Lángadhás 68 40 46N 23 2 E
Langádhia 69 37 43N 22 1 E
Långan 72 63 19N 14 44 E
Langara I. 152 54 14N 133 1W
Langavat L. 36 58 4N 6 48W
Langchen Khambah (Sutlej) 95 31 25N 80 0 E
Langch'i 109 31 10N 119 10 E
Langchung 108 31 31N 105 58 E
Langdon 158 48 47N 98 24W
Langdorp 47 50 59N 4 52 E
Langeac 44 45 7N 3 29 E
Langeb, R. 122 17 28N 36 50 E
Langeberge, C. Prov., S. Afr. 128 28 15 S 22 33 E
Langeberge, C. Prov., S. Afr. 128 33 55 S 21 20 E
Langeland 73 54 56N 10 48 E
Langelands Bælt 73 54 55N 10 56 E
Langemark 47 50 55N 2 55 E
Langen 49 53 36N 8 36 E
Langenburg 153 50 51N 101 43W
Langeness 48 54 34N 8 35 E
Langenlois 52 48 29N 15 40 E
Langensalza 48 51 6N 10 40 E
Langenthal 50 47 13N 7 47 E
Langeoog 48 53 44N 7 33 E
Langeskov 73 55 22N 10 35 E
Langesund 71 59 0N 9 45 E
Langhem 73 57 36N 13 14 E
Länghem 73 57 36N 13 14 E
Langhirano 62 44 39N 10 16 E
Langholm 35 55 9N 2 59W
Langidoon 140 31 36 S 142 2 E
Langjökull 74 64 39N 20 12W
Langkawi I. 101 6 20N 99 45 E
Langkawi, P. 101 6 25N 99 45 E
Langkon 102 6 30N 116 40 E
Langk'ouhsü 109 26 8N 115 10 E
Langlade, Can. 150 48 14N 76 10W
Langlade, St. P. & M. 151 46 50N 56 20W
Langlo 139 26 26 S 146 5 E
Langlois 160 42 54N 124 26W
Langnau 50 46 56N 7 47 E
Langness 32 54 3N 4 37W
Langogne 44 44 43N 3 50 E
Langon 44 44 33N 0 16W
Langøya 74 68 45N 15 10 E
Langport 28 51 2N 2 51W
Langres 43 47 52N 5 20 E
Langres, Plateau de 43 47 45N 5 20 E
Langsa 102 4 30N 97 57 E
Långsele 72 63 12N 17 4 E
Långshyttan 72 60 27N 16 2 E
Langson 100 21 52N 106 42 E
Langstrothdale Chase 32 54 14N 2 13W
Langtai 108 26 6N 105 20 E
Langtao 98 27 15N 97 34 E
Langting 98 25 31N 93 7 E
Langtoft 29 52 42N 0 19W
Langtree 30 55 N 4 11W
Langtry 159 29 50N 101 33W
Langu 101 6 53N 99 47 E
Languedoc □ 44 43 58N 3 22 E
Langwies 51 46 50N 9 44 E
Lanhsien 106 38 17N 111 38 E
Lanigan 153 51 51N 105 2W
Lank'ao 106 34 50N 114 49 E
Lanna 72 59 16N 14 56 E
Lannemezan 44 43 8N 0 23 E
Lannercost 138 18 35 S 146 0 E
Lannilis 42 48 35N 4 32W
Lannion 42 48 46N 3 29W
Lanouaille 44 45 24N 1 9 E
Lanp'ing 108 26 25N 99 24 E
Lansdale 162 40 14N 75 18W
Lansdowne 141 31 48 S 152 30 E
Lansdowne House 150 52 14N 87 53W
Lansford 162 40 48N 75 55W
Lanshan 109 25 18N 112 6 E
Lansing 156 42 47N 84 32W
Lanslebourg-Mont-Cenis 45 45 17N 6 52 E
Lanta Yai, Ko 101 7 35N 99 3 E
Lant'ien 106 34 3N 109 20 E
Lants'ang 108 22 40N 99 58 E
Lants'ang Chiang, R. 108 30 0N 98 0 E
Lantsien 99 32 4N 96 6 E
Lants'un 107 36 24N 120 10 E
Lantuna 103 8 19 S 124 8 E
Lanus 172 34 44 S 58 27W
Lanusei 64 39 53N 9 31 E
Lanzarote, I. 116 29 0N 13 40W
Lanzo Torinese 62 45 16N 7 29 E
Lao Bao 100 16 35N 106 30 E
Lao Cai 100 22 30N 103 57 E
Lao, R. 65 39 45N 15 45 E
Laoag 103 18 7N 120 34 E
Laoang 103 12 32N 125 8 E
Laoha Ho, R. 107 43 24N 120 39 E
Laois □ 39 53 0N 7 20W
Laon 43 49 33N 3 35 E
Laona 156 45 32N 88 41W
Laos ■ 100 17 45N 105 0 E
Lapa 173 25 46 S 49 44W
Lapalisse 44 46 15N 3 44 E
Laparan Cap, I. 103 6 0N 120 0 E
Lapeer 156 43 3N 83 20W
Lapford 30 50 52N 3 49W
Lapi □ 74 67 0N 27 0 E
Lapland = Lappland 74 68 7N 24 0 E
Laporte 162 41 27N 76 30W
Lapovo 66 44 10N 21 2 E
Lappland 74 68 7N 24 0 E
Laprida 172 37 34 S 60 45W
Laptev Sea 77 76 0N 125 0 E
Lapush 160 47 56N 124 33W
Lăpusu, R. 70 47 25N 23 40 E
Lar 93 27 40N 54 14 E
Lara 140 38 2 S 144 26 E
Lara □ 174 10 10N 69 50W
Larabanga 120 9 16N 1 56W
Laracha 56 43 15N 8 35W
Larache 118 35 10N 6 5W
Laragh 39 53 0N 6 20W
Laragne-Montéglin 45 44 18N 5 49 E
Laramie 158 41 15N 105 29W
Laramie Mts. 158 42 0N 105 30W
Laranjeiras 170 10 48 S 37 10W
Laranjeiras do Sul 173 25 23 S 52 23W
Larantuka 103 8 5 S 122 55 E
Larap 103 14 18N 122 39 E
Larat, I. 103 7 0 S 132 0 E
Larbert 35 56 2N 3 50W
Lärbro 73 57 47N 18 50 E
Larch, R. 149 57 30N 71 0W
Lårdal 71 59 20N 8 25 E
Lårdal 71 59 25N 8 10 E
Larde 127 16 28 S 39 43 E
Larder Lake 150 48 5N 79 40W
Lárdhos, Ákra 69 36 4N 28 10 E
Laredo, Spain 58 43 26N 3 28W
Laredo, U.S.A. 159 27 34N 99 29W
Laredo Sd. 152 52 30N 128 53W
Laren 46 52 16N 5 14 E
Largeau (Faya) 117 17 58N 19 6 E
Largentière 45 44 34N 4 18 E
Largs 34 55 48N 4 51W
Lari 62 43 34N 10 35 E
Lariang 103 1 35 S 119 25 E
Larimore 158 47 55N 97 35W
Larino 65 41 48N 14 54 E
Lárisa 68 39 38N 22 28 E
Lárisa □ 68 39 39N 22 24 E
Larkana 94 27 32N 68 2 E
Larkollen 71 59 20N 10 41 E
Larnaca 92 35 0N 33 35 E
Lárnax 92 35 0N 33 35 E
Larne 38 54 52N 5 50W
Larne L. 38 54 52N 5 50W
Larned 158 38 15N 99 10W
Laroch 36 56 40N 5 9W
Larochette 47 49 47N 6 13 E
Laroquebrou 44 44 58N 2 12 E
Larrey, Pt. 136 19 55 S 119 7 E
Larrimah 136 15 35 S 133 12 E
Larsen Ice Shelf 13 67 0 S 62 0W
Larteh 121 5 50N 0 5W
Laru 126 2 54N 24 25 E
Larvik 71 59 4N 10 0 E
Laryak 76 61 15N 80 0 E
Larzac, Causse du 44 44 0N 3 17 E
Las Animas 159 38 8N 103 18W
Las Anod 91 8 26N 47 19 E
Las Blancos 59 37 38N 0 49W
Las Bonitas 174 7 50N 65 40W
Las Brenãs 172 27 5 S 61 7W
Las Cabezas de San Juan 57 37 0N 5 58W
Las Cruces 161 32 25N 106 50W
Las Flores 172 36 0 S 59 0W
Las Heras, Mendoza, Argent. 173 32 51 S 68 49W
Las Heras, Santa Cruz, Argent. 176 46 30 S 69 0W
Las Huertas, Cabo de 59 38 22N 0 24W
Las Khoreh 91 11 4N 48 20 E
Las Lajas 176 38 30 S 70 25W
Las Lajitas 174 6 55N 65 39W
Las Lomitas 172 24 35 S 60 50W
Las Marismas 57 37 5N 6 20W
Las Mercedes 174 9 7N 66 24W
Las Navas de la Concepción 57 37 56N 5 30W
Las Navas de Tolosa 57 38 18N 3 38W
Las Palmas, Argent. 172 27 8 S 58 45W
Las Palmas, Canary Is. 116 28 10N 15 28W
Las Palmas □ 116 28 10N 15 28W
Las Piedras 173 34 35 S 56 20W
Las Plumas 176 43 40 S 67 15W
Las Rosas 172 32 30 S 61 40W
Las Tablas 166 7 49N 80 14W
Las Termas 172 27 29 S 64 52W
Las Tres Marías, Is. 164 20 12N 106 30W
Las Varillas 172 32 0 S 62 50W
Las Vegas, Nev., U.S.A. 161 36 10N 115 5W
Las Vegas, N.M., U.S.A. 161 35 35N 105 10W
Lascano 173 33 35 S 54 18W
Lascaux 44 45 5N 1 10 E
Lashburn 153 53 10N 109 40W
Lashio 98 22 56N 97 45 E
Lashkar 94 26 10N 78 10 E
Łasin 54 53 30N 19 2 E
Lasithi □ 69 35 5N 25 50 E
Lask 54 51 34N 19 8 E
Laskill 33 54 19N 1 6W
Laško 63 46 10N 15 16 E
Lassance 171 17 54 S 44 34W
Lassay 42 48 27N 0 30W
Lassen, Pk. 160 40 20N 121 0W
Lasswade 35 55 53N 3 8W
Last Mountain L. 153 51 5N 105 14W
Lastoursville 124 0 55 S 12 38 E
Lastovo 63 42 46N 16 55 E
Lastovo, I. 63 42 46N 16 55 E
Lastovski Kanal 63 42 50N 17 0 E
Lat Yao 100 15 45N 99 48 E
Latacunga 174 0 50 S 78 35W
Latakia = Al Ladhiqiya 92 35 30N 35 45 E
Latchford 150 47 20N 79 50W
Laterza 65 40 38N 16 47 E
Latham 137 29 44 S 116 20 E
Lathen 48 52 51N 7 21 E
Latheron 37 58 17N 3 20W
Lathrop Wells 163 36 39N 116 24W
Latiano 65 40 33N 17 43 E
Latina 64 41 26N 12 53 E
Latisana 63 45 47N 13 1 E
Latium = Lazio 63 42 0N 12 30 E
Laton 163 36 26N 119 41W
Latorica, R. 53 48 31N 22 0 E
Latouche 147 60 0N 148 0W
Latouche Treville, C. 136 18 27 S 121 49 E
Latrobe 138 38 8 S 146 44 E
Latrobe, Mt. 139 39 0 S 146 23 E
Latrónico 65 40 5N 16 0 E
Latrun 90 31 50N 34 58 E
Latur 96 18 25N 76 40 E
Latvia, S.S.R. □ 80 56 50N 24 0 E
Latzu 105 29 10N 87 45 E
Lauchhammer 48 51 35N 13 40 E
Laudal 71 58 15N 7 30 E
Lauder 35 55 43N 2 45W
Lauderdale 35 55 43N 2 44W
Lauenburg 48 53 23N 10 33 E
Läufelfingen 50 47 24N 7 52 E
Laufen 50 47 25N 7 30 E
Laugarbakki 74 65 20N 20 55W
Laugharne 31 51 45N 4 28W
Laujar 59 37 0N 2 54W
Launceston, Austral. 138 41 24 S 147 8 E
Launceston, U.K. 30 50 38N 4 21W
Laune, R. 39 52 5N 9 40W
Launglon Bok 101 13 50N 97 54 E
Laupheim 49 48 13N 9 53 E
Laura, Queens., Austral. 133 15 32 S 144 32 E
Laura, S.A., Austral. 140 33 10 S 138 18 E
Lauragh 39 51 46N 9 46W
Laureana di Borrello 65 38 28N 16 5 E
Laurel, Del., U.S.A. 162 38 33N 75 34W
Laurel, Md., U.S.A. 162 39 6N 76 51W
Laurel, Miss., U.S.A. 159 31 50N 89 0W
Laurel, Mont., U.S.A. 160 45 46N 108 49W
Laurencekirk 37 56 50N 2 30W
Laurencetown 39 53 14N 8 11W
Laurens 157 34 32N 82 2W
Laurentian Plat. 151 52 0N 70 0W
Laurentides, Parc Prov. des 151 47 45N 71 15W
Lauria 65 40 3N 15 50 E
Laurie I. 13 60 0 S 46 0W
Laurie L. 153 56 35N 101 57W
Laurieston 35 54 57N 4 2W
Laurinburg 157 34 50N 79 25W
Laurium 156 47 14N 88 26W
Lausanne 50 46 32N 6 38 E
Laut Kecil, Kepulauan 102 4 45 S 115 40 E
Laut, Kepulauan 102 4 45N 108 0 E
Lauterbach 48 50 39N 9 23 E
Lauterbrunnen 50 46 36N 7 55 E
Lauterecken 49 49 38N 7 35 E
Lauwe 47 50 47N 3 12 E
Lauwers 46 53 32N 6 23 E
Lauwers Zee 46 53 21N 6 13 E
Lauzon 151 46 48N 71 10W
Lava Hot Springs 160 42 38N 112 1W
Lavadores 56 42 14N 8 41W
Lavagna 62 44 18N 9 22 E
Laval 42 48 4N 0 48W
Lavalle 172 28 15 S 65 15W
Lavandou, Le 45 43 8N 6 22 E
Lâvara 68 41 19N 26 22 E
Lavardac 44 44 12N 0 20 E
Lavaur 44 43 42N 1 49 E
Lavaux 50 46 30N 6 45 E
Lavaveix 44 46 5N 2 8 E
Lavelanet 44 42 57N 1 51 E
Lavello 65 41 4N 15 47 E
Lavendon 29 52 11N 0 39W
Lavenham 29 52 7N 0 48 E
Laverendrye Prov. Park 150 46 15N 17 15W
Laverne 159 36 43N 99 58W
Lavers Hill 140 38 40 S 143 25 E
Laverton 137 28 44 S 122 29 E
Lavi 90 32 47N 35 25 E
Lavik 71 61 6N 5 25 E
Lávkos 69 39 9N 23 14 E
Lavos 56 40 6N 8 49W
Lavras 173 21 20 S 45 0W
Lavre 57 38 46N 8 22W
Lavrentiya 77 65 35N 171 0W
Lávrion 69 37 40N 24 4 E
Lavumisa 129 27 20 S 31 55 E
Lawas 102 4 55N 115 40 E
Lawele 103 5 16 S 123 3 E
Lawers 35 56 31N 4 9W
Lawksawk 98 21 15N 96 52 E
Lawn Hill 138 18 36 S 138 33 E
Lawng Pit 99 26 45N 98 35 E
Lawra 120 10 39N 2 51W
Lawrence, Austral. 173 29 30 S 153 8 E
Lawrence, Kans., U.S.A. 158 39 0N 95 10W
Lawrence, Mass., U.S.A. 162 42 40N 71 9W
Lawrenceburg, Ind., U.S.A. 156 39 5N 84 50W
Lawrenceburg, Tenn., U.S.A. 157 35 12N 87 19W
Lawrenceville, Ga., U.S.A. 157 33 55N 83 59W

Lawrenceville **Lexington**

Lawrenceville, Pa., U.S.A. **162** 42 0N 77 8W
Laws **163** 37 24N 118 20W
Lawton **159** 34 33N 98 25W
Lawu Mt. **103** 7 40S 111 13E
Laxa **72** 59 0N 14 37E
Laxey **32** 54 15N 4 23W
Laxfield **29** 52 18N 1 23E
Laxford, L. **36** 58 25N 5 10W
Laxmeshwar **97** 15 9N 75 28E
Laysan I. **143** 25 30N 167 0W
Laytonville **160** 39 44N 123 29W
Laytown **38** 53 40N 6 15W
Laza **98** 26 30N 97 38E
Lazarevac **66** 44 23N 20 17E
Lazio □ **63** 42 10N 12 30E
Lazonby **32** 54 45N 2 42W
Łazy **54** 50 27N 19 24E
Łbzenica **54** 53 18N 17 15E
Lea **33** 53 22N 0 45W
Lea, R. **29** 51 40N 0 3W
Leach **101** 12 21N 103 46E
Lead **158** 44 20N 103 40W
Leadenham **33** 53 5N 0 33W
Leader **153** 50 50N 109 30W
Leadhills **35** 55 25N 3 47W
Leadville **161** 39 17N 106 23W
Leaf, R., Can. **149** 58 47N 70 4W
Leaf, R., U.S.A. **159** 31 45N 89 20W
Leakey **159** 29 45N 99 45W
Leaksville **157** 36 30N 79 49W
Lealui **125** 15 10S 23 2E
Leamington, Can. **150** 42 3N 82 36W
Leamington, N.Z. **130** 37 55S 175 29E
Leamington, U.K. **28** 52 18N 1 32W
Leamington, U.S.A. **160** 39 37N 112 17W
Leandro Norte Alem **173** 27 34S 55 15W
Leane L. **39** 52 2N 9 32W
Leaoto, Mt. **70** 45 20N 25 20E
Leap **39** 51 34N 9 11W
Learmonth **136** 22 40S 114 10E
Leask **153** 53 5N 106 45W
Leatherhead **29** 51 18N 0 20W
Leavenworth, Mo., U.S.A. **158** 39 25N 95 0W
Leavenworth, Wash., U.S.A. **160** 47 44N 120 37W
Łeba **54** 54 45N 17 32E
Lebak **103** 6 32N 124 5E
Lebane **66** 42 56N 21 44E
Lebanon, Ind., U.S.A. **156** 40 3N 86 55W
Lebanon, Kans., U.S.A. **158** 39 50N 98 35W
Lebanon, Ky., U.S.A. **156** 37 35N 85 15W
Lebanon, Mo., U.S.A. **159** 37 40N 92 40W
Lebanon, Oreg., U.S.A. **160** 44 31N 122 57W
Lebanon, Pa., U.S.A. **162** 40 20N 76 28W
Lebanon, Tenn., U.S.A. **157** 36 15N 86 20W
Lebanon ■ **92** 34 0N 36 0E
Lebbeke **47** 51 0N 4 8E
Lebec **163** 34 36N 118 59W
Lebedin **80** 50 35N 34 30E
Lebedyan **81** 53 0N 39 10E
Lebomboberge **129** 24 30S 32 0E
Łebork **54** 54 33N 17 46E
Lebrija **57** 36 53N 6 5W
Lebu **172** 37 40S 73 47W
Lecce **65** 40 20N 18 10E
Lecco **62** 45 50N 9 27E
Lecco, L. di. **62** 45 51N 9 22E
Lécera **58** 41 13N 0 43W
Lech **52** 47 13N 10 9E
Lech, R. **49** 48 45N 10 45E
Lechlade **28** 51 42N 1 40W
Lechtaler Alpen **52** 47 15N 10 30E
Lectoure **44** 43 56N 0 38E
Łeczyca **54** 52 5N 19 45E
Ledbury **28** 52 3N 2 25W
Lede **47** 50 58N 3 59E
Ledeberg **47** 51 2N 3 45E
Ledec **52** 49 41N 15 18E
Ledesma **56** 41 6N 5 59W
Leduc **152** 53 20N 113 30W
Ledyczek **54** 53 33N 16 59E
Lee, U.K. **28** 50 47N 1 11W
Lee, U.S.A. **160** 40 35N 115 36W
Lee Vining **163** 37 58N 119 7W
Leech L. **158** 47 9N 94 23W
Leedey **159** 35 53N 99 24W
Leeds, U.K. **33** 53 48N 1 34W
Leeds, U.S.A. **157** 33 32N 86 30W
Leek, Neth. **46** 53 10N 6 24E
Leek, U.K. **32** 53 7N 2 2W
Leende **47** 51 21N 5 33E
Leer **48** 53 13N 7 29E
Leerdam **46** 51 54N 5 6E
Leersum **46** 52 0N 5 26E
Leesburg **157** 28 47N 81 52W
Leeston **143** 43 45N 172 19E
Leesville **159** 31 12N 93 15W
Leeton **141** 34 23S 146 23E
Leeuwarden **46** 53 15N 5 48E
Leeuwin, C. **137** 34 20S 115 9E
Leeward Is. **167** 16 30N 63 30W
Lefors **159** 35 30N 100 50W
Lefroy, L. **137** 31 21S 121 40E
Legal **152** 53 55N 113 45W
Legendre I. **136** 20 22S 116 55E
Leghorn = Livorno **62** 43 32N 10 18E
Legion **127** 21 25S 28 30E
Legionowo **54** 52 25N 20 50E
Léglise **47** 49 48N 5 32E
Legnago **63** 45 10N 11 19E
Legnano **62** 45 35N 8 55E
Legnica **54** 51 12N 16 10E
Legnica □ **54** 51 30N 16 0E
Legoniel **38** 54 38N 6 0W
Legrad **63** 46 17N 16 51E
Legume **139** 28 20S 152 12E
Leh **95** 34 15N 77 35E
Lehi **160** 40 20N 112 0W
Lehighton **162** 40 50N 75 44W
Lehinch **39** 52 56N 9 21E
Lehliu **70** 44 29N 26 20E
Lehrte **48** 52 22N 9 58E
Lehua, I. **147** 22 1N 160 6W
Lehututu **128** 23 54S 21 55E
Lei Shui, R. **109** 26 56N 112 39E
Leiah **94** 30 58N 70 58E
Leibnitz **52** 46 47N 15 34E
Leicester **28** 52 39N 1 9W
Leicester □ **28** 52 40N 1 10W
Leichhardt, R. **133** 17 50S 139 49E
Leichhardt Ra. **138** 20 46S 147 40E
Leichou Chiang, R. **109** 20 52N 110 10E
Leichou Pantao **108** 20 40N 110 10E
Leiden **46** 52 9N 4 30E
Leiderdorp **46** 52 9N 4 32E
Leidschendam **46** 52 5N 4 24E
Leie, R. **47** 51 2N 3 45E
Leigh, Gr. Manch., U.K. **32** 53 29N 2 31W
Leigh, Here. & Worcs., U.K. **28** 52 10N 2 21W
Leigh Creek **140** 30 28S 138 24E
Leighlinbridge **39** 52 45N 7 2W
Leighton Buzzard **29** 51 55N 0 39W
Leignon **47** 50 16N 5 7E
Leiktho **98** 19 13N 96 35E
Leinster, Mt. **39** 52 38N 6 47W
Leinster, prov. **39** 53 0N 7 10W
Leintwardine **28** 52 22N 2 51W
Leipo **108** 28 15N 103 34E
Leipzig **48** 51 20N 12 23E
Leipzig □ **48** 51 20N 12 30E
Leiria **57** 39 46N 8 53W
Leiria □ **57** 39 46N 8 53W
Leisler, Mt. **136** 23 23S 129 30E
Leiston **29** 52 13N 1 35E
Leith **35** 55 59N 3 10W
Leith Hill **29** 51 10N 0 23W
Leitha, R. **53** 47 57N 17 5E
Leitholm **35** 55 42N 2 16W
Leitrim **38** 54 0N 8 5W
Leitrim □ **38** 54 8N 8 0W
Leiyang **109** 26 24N 112 51E
Leiza **58** 43 5N 1 55W
Lek, R. **46** 51 54N 4 38E
Lekáni **68** 41 10N 24 35E
Leke **47** 51 6N 2 54E
Lekhainá **69** 37 57N 21 16E
Lekkerkerk **46** 51 54N 4 41E
Leknice **61** 51 34N 14 45E
Leksula **103** 3 46S 126 31E
Leland **159** 33 25N 90 52W
Leland Lakes **153** 60 0N 110 59W
Lelant **30** 50 11N 5 26W
Leleque **176** 42 15S 71 0W
Lelu **98** 19 4N 95 30E
Lelystad **46** 52 30N 5 25E
Lema **121** 12 58N 4 13E
Lemagrut, mt. **123** 3 9S 35 22E
Leman Bank, gasfield **19** 53 5N 2 20E
Léman, Lac **50** 46 26N 6 30E
Lemelerveld **46** 52 26N 6 20E
Lemera **126** 3 0S 28 55E
Lemery **103** 13 58N 120 56E
Lemesós **92** 34 42N 33 1E
Lemgo **48** 52 2N 8 52E
Lemhi Ra. **160** 44 30N 113 30W
Lemmer **46** 52 51N 5 43E
Lemmon **158** 45 59N 102 10W
Lemon Grove **163** 32 45N 117 2W
Lemoore **163** 36 23N 119 46W
Lempdes **44** 45 22N 3 17E
Lemvig **73** 56 33N 8 20E
Lemyethna **98** 21 10N 95 52E
Lena, R. **77** 64 30N 127 0E
Lenadoon Pt. **38** 54 19N 9 3W
Lencloître **42** 46 50N 0 20E
Lençóis **171** 12 35S 41 43W
Lendalfoot **34** 55 12N 4 55W
Lendelede **47** 50 53N 3 16E
Lendinara **63** 45 4N 11 37E
Lene L. **38** 53 40N 7 12W
Lengau de Vaca, Punta **172** 30 14S 71 38W
Lenger **85** 42 12N 69 54E
Lengerich **48** 52 12N 7 50E
Lenggong **101** 5 6N 100 58E
Lengyeltóti **53** 46 40N 17 40E
Lenham **29** 51 14N 0 44E
Lenhovda **73** 57 0N 15 16E
Lenia **123** 4 10N 37 25E
Lenin **83** 48 20N 40 56E
Lenina, Pik **85** 39 20N 72 55E
Leninabad **85** 40 17N 69 37E
Leninakan **83** 41 0N 42 50E
Leningrad **80** 59 55N 30 20E
Leninogorsk, Kazakh S.S.R., U.S.S.R. **76** 50 20N 83 30E
Leninogorsk, R.S.F.S.R., U.S.S.R. **84** 54 36N 52 30E
Leninpol **85** 42 29N 71 55E
Leninsk, R.S.F.S.R., U.S.S.R. **83** 48 40N 45 15E
Leninsk, Uzbek S.S.R., U.S.S.R. **85** 40 38N 72 15E
Leninsk-Kuznetskiy **76** 55 10N 86 10E
Leninskaya **81** 56 7N 44 29E
Leninskoye, R.S.F.S.R., U.S.S.R. **77** 47 56N 132 38E
Leninskoye, R.S.F.S.R., U.S.S.R. **81** 58 23N 47 3E
Leninskoye, Uzbek S.S.R., U.S.S.R. **85** 41 45N 69 23E
Lenk **50** 46 27N 7 28E
Lenkoran **79** 39 45N 48 50E
Lenmalu **103** 1 58S 130 0E
Lennard, R. **136** 17 22S 124 20E
Lennox Hills **34** 56 3N 4 12W
Lennoxtown **34** 55 58N 4 14W
Leno **62** 45 24N 10 14E
Lenoir **157** 35 55N 81 36W
Lenoir City **157** 35 40N 84 20W
Lenora **158** 39 39N 100 1W
Lenore L. **153** 52 30N 104 59W
Lenox **162** 42 20N 73 18W
Lens, Belg. **47** 50 33N 3 54E
Lens, France **43** 50 26N 2 50E
Lens St. Remy **47** 50 39N 5 7E
Lensk (Mukhtuya) **77** 60 48N 114 55E
Lenskoye **82** 45 3N 34 1E
Lent **46** 51 52N 5 52E
Lentini **65** 37 18N 15 0E
Lenwood **163** 34 53N 117 7W
Lenzburg **50** 47 23N 8 11E
Lenzen **48** 53 6N 11 26E
Lenzerheide **51** 46 44N 9 34E
Léo **120** 11 3N 2 2W
Leoben **52** 47 22N 15 5E
Leola **158** 45 47N 98 58W
Leominster, U.K. **28** 52 15N 2 43W
Leominster, U.S.A. **162** 42 32N 71 45W
Léon **44** 43 53N 1 18W
León, Mexico **164** 21 7N 101 30W
León, Nic. **166** 12 20N 86 51W
León, Spain **56** 42 38N 5 34W
Leon **158** 40 40N 93 40W
León □ **56** 42 40N 5 55W
León, Montañas de **56** 42 30N 6 18W
Leonardtown **162** 38 19N 76 39W
Leonel, Mte. **50** 46 15N 8 5E
Leonforte **65** 37 39N 14 22E
Leongatha **141** 38 30S 145 58E
Leonídhion **69** 37 9N 22 52E
Leonora **137** 28 49S 121 19E
Leonora Downs **140** 32 29S 142 5E
Léopold II, Lac = Mai-Ndombe **124** 2 0S 18 0E
Leopoldina **173** 21 28S 42 40W
Leopoldo Bulhões **171** 16 37S 48 46W
Leopoldsburg **47** 51 7N 5 13E
Léopoldville = Kinshasa **124** 4 20S 15 15E
Leoti **158** 38 31N 101 19W
Leoville **153** 53 39N 107 33W
Lépa, L. do **128** 17 0S 19 0E
Lepe **57** 37 15N 7 12W
Lepel **80** 54 50N 28 40E
Lephin **36** 57 26N 6 43W
Lepikha **77** 64 45N 125 55E
Lépo, L. do **128** 17 0S 19 0E
Lepontine Alps **62** 46 22N 8 27E
Lepsény **53** 47 0N 18 15E
Leptis Magna **119** 32 40N 14 12E
Lequeitio **58** 43 20N 2 32W
Lerbäck **72** 58 56N 15 2E
Lercara Friddi **64** 37 42N 13 36E
Lerdo **164** 25 32N 103 32W
Léré **124** 9 39N 14 13E
Lere **121** 9 43N 9 18E
Leribe **129** 28 51S 28 3E
Lérici **62** 44 4N 9 48E
Lérida **58** 41 37N 0 39E
Lérida □ **58** 42 6N 1 0E
Lérins, Is. de **45** 43 31N 7 3E
Lerma **56** 42 0N 3 47W
Léros, I. **69** 37 10N 26 50E
Lérouville **43** 48 50N 5 30E
Lerrig **39** 52 22N 9 47W
Lerwick **36** 60 10N 1 10W
Les **70** 46 58N 21 50E
Lesbos, I. = Lésvos **69** 39 0N 26 20E
Lesbury **35** 55 25N 1 37W
Lésina, L. di **63** 41 53N 15 25E
Lesja **71** 62 7N 8 51E
Lesjaverk **71** 62 12N 8 34E
Lesko **54** 49 30N 22 23E
Leskov, I. **13** 56 0S 28 0W
Leskovac **68** 43 0N 21 58E
Leskovec **68** 40 10N 20 34E
Leslie, U.K. **35** 56 12N 3 12W
Leslie, U.S.A. **159** 35 50N 92 35W
Lesmahagow **35** 55 38N 3 55W
Lesna **54** 51 0N 15 15E
Lesneven **42** 48 35N 4 20W
Lesnič a **66** 44 39N 19 20E
Lesnoy **84** 59 47N 52 9E
Lesnoye **80** 58 15N 35 31E
Lesotho ■ **129** 29 40S 28 0E
Lesozavodsk **77** 45 30N 133 20E
Lesparre-Médoc **44** 45 18N 0 57W
Lessay **42** 49 14N 1 30W
Lesse, R. **47** 50 15N 4 54E
Lesser Antilles **167** 12 30N 61 0W
Lesser Slave L. **152** 55 30N 115 25W
Lessines **47** 50 42N 3 50E
Lestock **153** 51 19N 103 59W
Lesuer I. **136** 13 50S 127 17E
Lesuma **128** 17 58S 25 12E
Lésvos, I. **69** 39 0N 26 20E
Leswalt **34** 54 56N 5 6W
Leszno **54** 51 50N 16 30E
Leszno □ **54** 51 45N 16 30E
Letchworth **29** 51 58N 0 13W
Letea, Ostrov **70** 45 18N 29 20E
Lethbridge **152** 49 45N 112 45W
Lethero **140** 33 33S 142 30E
Lethlhakeng **128** 24 0S 24 59E
Leti **103** 8 10S 127 40E
Leti, Kepulauan **103** 8 10S 128 0E
Letiahau, R. **128** 21 40S 23 30E
Leticia **174** 4 0S 70 0W
Letpadan **98** 17 45N 96 0E
Letpan **98** 19 28N 93 52E
Letsôk-aw-Kyun (Domel I.) **101** 11 30N 98 25E
Letterbreen **38** 54 18N 7 43W
Letterfrack **38** 53 33N 9 58W
Letterkenny **38** 54 57N 7 42W
Lettermacaward **38** 54 51N 8 18W
Lettermore I. **39** 53 18N 9 40W
Lettermullan **39** 53 15N 9 44W
Letterston **31** 51 56N 5 0W
Lettoch **37** 57 22N 3 30W
Leu **70** 44 10N 24 0E
Leucadia **163** 33 4N 117 18W
Leucate **44** 42 56N 3 3E
Leucate, Étang de **44** 42 50N 3 0E
Leuchars **35** 56 23N 2 53W
Leuk **50** 46 19N 7 37E
Leukerbad **50** 46 24N 7 36E
Leupegem **47** 50 50N 3 36E
Leuser, G. **102** 4 0N 96 51E
Leutkirch **49** 47 49N 10 1E
Leuven (Louvain) **47** 50 52N 4 42E
Leuze, Hainaut, Belg. **47** 50 36N 3 37E
Leuze, Namur, Belg. **47** 50 33N 4 54E
Lev Tolstoy **81** 53 13N 39 29E
Levádhia **69** 38 27N 22 54E
Levan **160** 39 37N 111 32W
Levanger **74** 63 45N 11 19E
Levani **68** 40 40N 19 28E
Lévanto **62** 44 10N 9 37E
Levanzo, I. **64** 38 0N 12 19E
Levelland **159** 33 38N 102 17W
Leven, Fife, U.K. **35** 56 12N 3 0W
Leven, Humb., U.K. **33** 53 54N 0 18W
Leven, Banc du **129** 12 30S 47 45E
Leven, L. **35** 56 12N 3 22W
Leven R. **33** 54 27N 1 15W
Levens **45** 43 50N 7 12E
Leveque C. **136** 16 20S 123 0E
Leverano **65** 40 16N 18 0E
Leverburgh **36** 57 46N 7 0W
Leverkusen **48** 51 2N 6 59E
Levet **43** 46 56N 2 22E
Levice **53** 48 13N 18 35E
Levick, Mt. **13** 75 0S 164 0E
Levico **63** 46 0N 11 18E
Levie **45** 41 40N 9 7E
Levier **43** 46 58N 6 8E
Levin **142** 40 37S 175 18E
Levis **151** 46 48N 71 9W
Levis, L. **152** 62 37N 117 58W
Levítha, I. **69** 37 0N 26 28E
Levittown, N.Y., U.S.A. **162** 40 41N 73 31W
Levittown, Pa., U.S.A. **162** 40 10N 74 51W
Levka **67** 41 52N 26 15E
Lévka, Mt. **69** 35 18N 24 3E
Levkás **69** 38 48N 20 43E
Levkás, I. **69** 38 40N 20 43E
Levkimmi **68** 39 25N 20 3E
Levkôsia = Nicosia **92** 35 10N 33 25E
Levoč a **53** 48 59N 20 35E
Levroux **43** 47 0N 1 38E
Levski **67** 43 21N 25 10E
Levskigrad **67** 42 38N 24 47E
Lewe **98** 19 38N 96 7E
Lewellen **158** 41 22N 102 5W
Lewes, U.K. **29** 50 53N 0 2E
Lewes, U.S.A. **156** 38 45N 75 8W
Lewes, L. **148** 60 30N 134 20W
Lewin Brzeski **54** 50 45N 17 37E
Lewis, Butt of **36** 58 30N 6 12W
Lewis, I. **36** 58 10N 6 40W
Lewis, R. **160** 48 0N 113 15W
Lewis Ra. **136** 20 3S 128 50E
Lewisburg, Pa., U.S.A. **162** 40 57N 76 57W
Lewisburg, Tenn., U.S.A. **157** 35 29N 86 46W
Lewisham **29** 51 27N 0 1W
Lewisporte **151** 49 15N 55 3W
Lewiston, U.K. **37** 57 19N 4 30W
Lewiston, Idaho, U.S.A. **160** 45 58N 117 0W
Lewiston, Utah, U.S.A. **160** 42 0N 111 56W
Lewistown, Mont., U.S.A. **160** 47 0N 109 25W
Lewistown, Pa., U.S.A. **156** 40 37N 77 33W
Lexington, Ill., U.S.A. **158** 40 37N 88 47W
Lexington, Ky., U.S.A. **156** 38 6N 84 30W
Lexington, Md., U.S.A. **162** 38 16N 76 27W
Lexington, Miss., U.S.A. **159** 33 8N 90 2W
Lexington, Mo., U.S.A. **158** 39 7N 93 55W
Lexington, N.C., U.S.A. **157** 35 50N 80 13W
Lexington, Nebr., U.S.A. **158** 40 48N 99 45W
Lexington, N.Y., U.S.A. **162** 42 15N 74 22W
Lexington, Oreg., U.S.A. **160** 45 29N 119 46W

Lexington **Litija**

Lexington, Tenn., U.S.A. 157 35 38N 88 25W
Leyburn 33 54 19N 1 50W
Leyland 32 53 41N 2 42W
Leysdown on Sea 29 51 23N 0 57E
Leysin 50 46 21N 7 0E
Leyte, I. 103 11 0N 125 0E
Lezay 44 46 17N 0 0E
Lèze, R. 44 43 28N 1 25E
Lezha 68 41 47N 19 42E
Lézignan-Corbières 44 43 13N 2 43E
Lezoux 44 45 49N 3 21E
Lgov 80 51 42N 35 10E
Lhanbryde 37 57 38N 3 12W
Lhariguo 99 30 29N 93 4E
Lhasa 105 29 39N 91 6E
Lhokseumawe 102 5 20N 97 10E
Lhuntsi Dzong 98 27 39N 91 10E
Li, Finland 74 65 20N 25 20E
Li, Thai. 100 17 48N 98 57E
Li Shui, R. 109 29 24N 112 1E
Liádhoi, I. 69 36 50N 26 11E
Liang Liang 103 5 58N 121 30E
Liang Shan 108 23 42N 99 48E
Lianga 103 8 38N 126 6E
Liangch'eng, Inner Mongolia, China 106 40 26N 112 14E
Liangch'eng, Shantung, China 107 35 35N 119 32E
Lianghok'ou 108 29 10N 108 44E
Lianghsiang 106 39 44N 116 8E
Liangp'ing 108 30 41N 107 49E
Liangpran, Gunong 102 1 0N 114 23E
Liangtang 106 33 56N 106 12E
Liao Ho, R. 107 40 39N 122 12E
Liaoch'eng 106 36 26N 115 58E
Liaochung 107 41 23N 122 42E
Liaoning □ 107 41 15N 122 0E
Liaotung Pantao 107 40 0N 122 22E
Liaotung Wan 107 40 30N 121 30E
Liaoyang 107 41 17N 123 11E
Liaoyüan 107 42 55N 125 10E
Liapádhes 68 39 42N 19 40E
Liard, R. 152 61 51N 121 18W
Liari 94 25 37N 66 30E
Libau = Liepaja 80 56 30N 21 0E
Libby 160 48 20N 115 10W
Libenge 124 3 40N 18 55E
Liberal, Kans., U.S.A. 159 37 4N 101 0W
Liberal, Mo., U.S.A. 159 37 35N 94 30W
Liberec 52 50 47N 15 7E
Liberia 166 10 40N 85 30W
Liberia ■ 120 6 30N 9 30W
Libertad 174 8 20N 69 37W
Libertad, La 166 16 47N 90 7W
Liberty, Mo., U.S.A. 158 39 15N 94 24W
Liberty, N.Y., U.S.A. 162 41 48N 74 45W
Liberty, Pa., U.S.A. 162 41 34N 77 6W
Liberty, Tex., U.S.A. 159 30 5N 94 50W
Libiaz 53 50 7N 19 21E
Libin 47 49 59N 5 15E
Lîbîya, Sahrâ' 114 27 35N 25 0E
Libohava 68 40 3N 20 10E
Libourne 44 44 55N 0 14W
Libramont 47 49 55N 5 23E
Librazhdi 68 41 12N 20 22E
Libreville 124 0 25N 9 26E
Libya ■ 117 28 30N 17 30E
Libyan Plateau = Ed-Déffa 122 30 40N 26 30E
Licantén 172 34 55S 72 0W
Licata 64 37 6N 13 55E
Lich'eng 106 36 59N 113 31E
Lichfield 28 52 40N 1 50W
Lichiang 108 26 54N 100 12E
Lichin 107 37 32N 118 20E
Lichtaart 47 51 13N 4 55E
Lichtenburg 128 26 8S 26 8E
Lichtenfels 49 50 7N 11 4E
Lichtenvoorde 46 51 59N 6 34E
Lichtervelde 47 51 2N 3 9E
Lich'uan, Hupeh, China 109 30 18N 108 51E
Lich'uan, Kiangsi, China 109 27 14N 116 51E
Licosa, Punta 65 40 15N 14 53E
Lida, U.S.A. 163 37 30N 117 30W
Lida, U.S.S.R. 80 53 53N 25 15E
Lidhult 73 56 50N 13 27E
Lidingö 73 59 22N 18 8E
Lidköping 73 58 31N 13 14E
Lido, Italy 63 45 25N 12 23E
Lido, Niger 121 12 54N 3 44E
Lido di Ostia 64 41 44N 12 14E
Lidzbark 54 53 15N 19 49E
Lidzbark Warminski 54 54 7N 20 34E
Liebenwalde 48 52 51N 13 23E
Lieberose 48 51 59N 14 18E
Liebling 66 45 36N 21 20E
Liechtenstein ■ 49 47 8N 9 35E
Liederkerke 47 50 52N 4 5E
Liège 47 50 38N 5 35E
Liège □ 47 50 32N 5 35E
Liegnitz = Legnica 54 51 12N 16 10E
Liempde 47 51 35N 5 23E
Lienart 126 3 3N 25 31E
Lienartville 126 3 3N 25 31E
Liench'eng 109 25 47N 116 48E
Lienchiang, Fukien, China 109 26 11N 119 32E
Lienchiang, Kwangtung, China 109 21 36N 110 16E
Lienhsien 109 24 50N 112 23E
Lienp'ing 109 24 22N 114 30E
Lienshan, Kwangtung, China 109 24 37N 112 2E
Lienshan, Yunnan, China 108 24 48N 97 54E
Lienshankuan 107 40 58N 123 46E
Lienshui 107 33 46N 119 18E
Lienyüan 109 27 41N 111 40E
Lienyünchiang 107 34 47N 119 30E
Lienyünchiangshih 107 34 37N 119 13E
Lienz 52 46 50N 12 46E
Liepāja 80 56 30N 21 0E
Lier 47 51 7N 4 34E
Lierneux 47 50 17N 5 47E
Lieshout 47 51 31N 5 36E
Lieşta 70 45 38N 27 34E
Liestal 50 47 29N 7 44E
Lieşti 70 45 38N 27 34E
Liévin 43 50 24N 2 47E
Lièvre, R. 150 45 31N 75 26W
Liezen 52 47 34N 14 15E
Liffey, R. 39 53 21N 6 20W
Lifford 38 54 50N 7 30W
Liffré 42 48 12N 1 30W
Lifjell 71 59 27N 8 45E
Lightning Ridge 139 29 22S 148 0E
Lignano 63 45 42N 13 8E
Ligny-er-Barrois 43 48 36N 5 20E
Ligny-le-Châtel 43 47 54N 3 45E
Ligoúrion 69 37 37N 23 2E
Ligua, La 172 32 30S 71 16W
Liguria □ 62 44 30N 9 0E
Ligurian Sea 62 43 20N 9 0E
Lihir Group 135 3 0S 152 35E
Lihou Reefs and Cays 138 17 25S 151 40E
Lihsien, Hopeh, China 106 38 29N 115 34E
Lihsien, Hunan, China 109 29 38N 111 45E
Lihsien, Kansu, China 106 34 11N 105 2E
Lihsien, Szechwan, China 108 31 28N 103 17E
Lihue 147 21 59N 159 24W
Lihwa 99 30 4N 100 18E
Likasi 127 10 55S 26 48E
Likati 124 3 20N 24 0E
Likhoslavl 80 57 12N 35 30E
Likhovski 83 48 10N 40 10E
Likoma I. 127 12 3S 34 45E
Likumburu 127 9 43S 35 8E
Liling 109 27 40N 113 30E
Lill 47 51 15N 4 50E
Lille 43 50 38N 3 3E
Lille Bælt 73 55 30N 9 45E
Lillebonne 42 49 30N 0 32E
Lillehammer 71 61 8N 10 30E
Lillers 43 50 35N 2 28E
Lillesand 71 58 15N 8 23E
Lillestrøm 71 59 58N 11 5E
Lillian Point, Mt. 137 27 40S 126 6E
Lillo 58 39 45N 3 20W
Lillooet, R. 152 49 15N 121 57W
Lilongwe 127 14 0S 33 48E
Liloy 103 8 4N 122 39E
Lilun 108 28 3N 100 27E
Lim, R. 66 43 0N 19 40E
Lima, Indon. 103 3 37S 128 4E
Lima, Peru 174 12 0S 77 0W
Lima, Sweden 72 60 55N 13 20E
Lima, Mont., U.S.A. 160 44 41N 112 38W
Lima, Ohio, U.S.A. 156 40 42N 84 5W
Lima, R. 56 41 50N 8 18W
Limanowa 54 49 42N 20 22E
Limassol 92 34 42N 33 1E
Limavady 38 55 3N 6 58W
Limavady □ 38 55 0N 6 55W
Limay Mahuida 172 37 10S 66 45W
Limay, R. 176 39 40S 69 45W
Limbang 102 4 42N 115 6E
Limbara, Monti 64 40 50N 9 10E
Limbdi 94 22 34N 71 51E
Limbourg 47 50 37N 5 56E
Limbourg □ 47 51 2N 5 25E
Limbri 141 31 3S 151 5E
Limbunya 136 17 14S 129 50E
Limburg 49 50 22N 8 4E
Limburg □ 47 51 20N 5 55E
Limedsforsen 72 60 52N 13 25E
Limeira 173 22 35S 47 28W
Limenária 68 40 38N 24 32E
Limerick 39 52 40N 8 38W
Limerick □ 39 52 30N 8 50W
Limerick Junction 39 52 30N 8 12W
Limestone, R. 153 56 31N 94 7W
Limfjorden 73 56 55N 9 0E
Limia, R. 56 41 55N 8 8W
Limmared 73 57 34N 13 20E
Limmat, R. 51 47 26N 8 20E
Limmen 46 52 34N 4 42E
Limmen Bight 138 14 40S 135 35E
Limmen Bight R. 138 15 7S 135 44E
Límni 69 38 43N 23 18E
Límnos, I. 68 39 50N 25 5E
Limoeiro 170 7 52S 25 27W
Limoeiro do Norte 170 5 5S 38 0W
Limoges 44 45 50N 1 15E
Limón 167 10 0N 83 2W
Limon 158 39 18N 103 38W
Limone 62 44 12N 7 32E
Limousin 44 46 0N 1 0E
Limousin, Plateau de 44 46 0N 1 0E
Limoux 44 43 4N 2 12E
Limpopo, R. 129 23 15S 32 5E
Limpsfield 29 51 15N 0 1E
Limu Ling, mts. 100 19 0N 109 20E
Limuru 126 1 2S 36 35E
Lin 68 41 4N 20 38E
Linan 109 30 13N 119 40E
Linares 172 35 50S 71 40W
Linàres 174 1 23N 77 31W
Linares, Mexico 165 24 50N 99 40W
Linares, Spain 59 38 10N 3 40W
Linares □ 172 36 0S 71 0W
Linas Mte. 64 39 25N 8 38E
Linchenchen 106 36 28N 110 0E
Linch'eng 106 37 26N 114 34E
Linch'i 106 35 46N 113 53E
Linchiang 107 41 50N 126 55E
Linchin 106 35 6N 110 33E
Linch'ing 106 36 56N 115 45E
Linch'ü 107 36 30N 118 32E
Linch'uan 109 28 0N 116 20E
Lincluden 35 55 5N 3 40W
Lincoln, Argent. 172 34 55N 61 30W
Lincoln, N.Z. 143 43 38S 172 30E
Lincoln, U.K. 33 53 14N 0 32W
Lincoln, Ill., U.S.A. 158 40 10N 89 20W
Lincoln, Kans., U.S.A. 158 39 6N 98 9W
Lincoln, Maine, U.S.A. 151 45 27N 68 29W
Lincoln, N. Mex., U.S.A. 161 33 30N 105 26W
Lincoln, Nebr., U.S.A. 158 40 50N 96 42W
Lincoln, N.H., U.S.A. 162 44 3N 71 40W
Lincoln □ 33 53 14N 0 32W
Lincoln Sea 12 84 0N 55 0W
Lincoln Wolds 33 53 20N 0 5W
Lincolnton 157 35 30N 81 15W
Lind, Austral. 138 18 58S 144 30E
Lind, U.S.A. 160 47 0N 118 33W
Lindale 32 54 14N 2 54W
Lindås 71 60 44N 5 10E
Lindås, Norway 71 60 44N 5 9E
Lindås, Sweden 73 56 38N 15 35E
Lindau 49 47 33N 9 41E
Linde 46 52 50N 6 57E
Linden, Guyana 174 6 0N 58 10W
Linden, Calif., U.S.A. 163 38 1N 121 5W
Linden, Tex., U.S.A. 159 33 0N 94 20W
Lindenheuvel 47 50 59N 5 48E
Lindenwold 162 39 49N 72 59W
Linderöd 73 55 56N 13 47E
Linderödsåsen 73 55 53N 13 53E
Lindesberg 72 59 36N 15 15E
Lindesnes 71 57 58N 7 3E
Lindfield 29 51 2N 0 5W
Lindi 127 9 58S 39 38E
Lindi □ 127 9 40S 38 30E
Lindi, R. 126 1 25N 25 50E
Lindoso 56 41 52N 8 11W
Lindow 48 52 58N 12 58E
Lindsay, Can. 150 44 22N 78 43W
Lindsay, Calif., U.S.A. 163 36 14N 119 6W
Lindsay, Okla., U.S.A. 159 34 51N 97 37W
Lindsborg 158 38 35N 97 40W
Línea de la Concepción, La 55 36 15N 5 23W
Línea de la Concepción, La 57 36 15N 5 23W
Linfen 106 36 5N 111 32E
Lingakok 99 29 55N 87 38E
Lingayer 103 16 1N 120 14E
Lingayer G. 103 16 10N 120 15E
Lingch'iu 106 39 28N 114 10E
Lingch'uan, Kwangsi Chuang, China 109 25 25N 110 20E
Lingch'uan, Shansi, China 106 35 46N 113 26E
Lingen 48 52 32N 7 21E
Lingfield 29 51 11N 0 1W
Lingga, Kepulauan 102 0 10S 104 30E
Linghed 72 60 48N 15 55E
Linghsien, Hunan, China 109 26 26N 113 45E
Linghsien, Shantung, China 106 37 21N 116 34E
Lingle 158 42 10N 104 18W
Lingling 109 26 13N 111 37E
Lingpi 107 33 33N 117 33E
Lingshan 108 22 26N 109 17E
Lingshih 106 36 51N 111 47E
Lingshou 106 38 18N 114 22E
Lingshui 100 18 27N 110 0E
Lingt'ai 106 35 4N 107 37E
Linguéré 120 15 25N 15 5W
Lingwu 106 38 5N 106 20E
Lingyün 108 24 24N 106 31E
Linh Cam 100 18 31N 105 31E
Linhai 109 28 51N 121 7E
Linhares 171 19 25S 40 4W
Linho 106 40 50N 107 30E
Linhsi 107 43 37N 118 8E
Linhsia 105 35 36N 103 5E
Linhsiang 109 29 29N 113 30E
Linhsien 106 37 57N 110 57E
Lini 107 35 5N 118 20E
Linju 106 34 14N 112 45E
Link 68 41 4N 20 38E
Linkao 100 19 56N 109 42E
Linkinhorne 30 50 31N 4 22W
Linköping 73 58 28N 15 36E
Link'ou 107 45 18N 130 15E
Linli 109 29 27N 111 39E
Linlithgow 35 55 58N 3 38W
Linn, Mt. 160 40 0N 123 0W
Linney Head 31 51 37N 5 4W
Linnhe, L. 34 56 36N 5 25W
Linosa 119 35 51N 12 50E
Lins 173 21 40S 49 44W
Linshui 108 30 18N 106 55E
Linslade 29 51 55N 0 40W
Lint'ao 106 35 20N 104 0E
Linth, R. 49 46 54N 9 0E
Linthal 51 46 54N 9 0E
Lintlaw 153 52 4N 103 14W
Linton, Can. 151 47 15N 72 16W
Linton, U.K. 29 52 6N 0 19E
Linton, Ind., U.S.A. 156 39 0N 87 10W
Linton, N. Dak., U.S.A. 158 46 21N 100 12W
Lints'ang 108 23 54N 100 0E
Lint'ung 106 34 24N 109 13E
Linville 139 26 50S 152 11E
Linwu 109 25 17N 112 33E
Linxe 44 43 56N 1 13W
Linyanti, R. 128 18 10S 24 10E
Linyüan 107 41 18N 119 15E
Linz, Austria 52 48 18N 14 18E
Linz, Ger. 48 50 33N 7 18E
Lion-d'Angers, Le 42 47 37N 0 43W
Lion, G. du 44 43 0N 4 0E
Lioni 65 40 52N 15 10E
Lion's Den 127 17 15S 30 5E
Lion's Head 150 44 58N 81 15W
Liozno 80 55 0N 30 50E
Lipali 127 15 50S 35 50E
Lipari 65 38 26N 14 58E
Lipari, Is. 65 38 40N 15 0E
Lipetsk 81 52 45N 39 35E
Lipiany 54 53 2N 14 58E
Lip'ing 108 26 16N 109 8E
Lipkany 82 48 14N 26 25E
Lipljan 66 42 31N 21 7E
Lipnik 53 49 32N 17 36E
Lipno 54 52 49N 19 15E
Lipo 108 25 25N 107 53E
Lipova 66 46 8N 21 42E
Lipovets 82 49 12N 29 1E
Lippstadt 48 51 40N 8 19E
Lipsco 54 51 10N 21 36E
Lipscomb 159 36 16N 100 28W
Lipsko 54 51 9N 21 40E
Lipsói, I. 69 37 19N 26 50E
Liptovsky Svaty Milkula 53 49 6N 19 35E
Liptrap C. 141 38 50S 145 55E
Lip'u 109 24 30N 110 23E
Lira 126 2 17N 32 57E
Liri, R. 64 41 25N 13 45E
Liria 58 39 37N 0 35W
Lisala 124 2 12N 21 38E
Lisbellaw 38 54 20N 7 32W
Lisboa 57 38 42N 9 10W
Lisboa □ 57 39 0N 9 12W
Lisbon 158 46 30N 97 46W
Lisbon = Lisboa 57 38 42N 9 10W
Lisburn 38 54 30N 6 9W
Lisburne, C. 147 68 50N 166 0W
Liscannor 39 52 57N 9 24W
Liscannor, B. 39 52 57N 9 24W
Liscarroll 39 52 15N 8 44W
Liscia, R. 64 41 5N 9 17E
Liscomb 151 45 2N 62 0W
Lisdoonvarna 39 53 2N 9 18W
Lishe Ho, R. 108 24 18N 101 32E
Lishih 106 37 30N 111 7E
Lishu 107 43 20N 124 37E
Lishuchen 107 45 5N 130 40E
Lishui, Chekiang, China 109 28 27N 119 54E
Lishui, Kiangsu, China 109 31 38N 119 2E
Lisianski I. 130 25 30N 174 0W
Lisieux 42 49 10N 0 12E
Lisischansk 83 48 55N 38 30E
Liskeard 30 50 27N 4 29W
Lismore, N.S.W., Austral. 139 28 44S 153 21E
Lismore, Vic., Austral. 133 37 58S 143 21E
Lismore, Ireland 39 52 8N 7 58W
Lismore I. 34 56 30N 5 30W
Lisnacree 38 54 4N 6 5W
Lisnaskea 38 54 15N 7 27W
Liss 29 51 3N 0 53W
Lissatinning Bri. 39 51 55N 10 1W
Lisse 46 52 16N 4 33E
Lisselton 39 52 30N 9 34W
Lissycasey 39 52 44N 9 12W
List 48 55 1N 8 26E
Lista, Norway 71 58 7N 6 39E
Lista, Sweden 75 59 19N 16 16E
Lister, Mt. 13 78 0S 162 0E
Liston 139 28 39S 152 6E
Listowel, Can. 150 43 44N 80 58W
Listowel, Ireland 39 52 27N 9 30W
Listowel Dns. 139 25 10S 145 12E
Lit-et-Mixe 44 44 2N 1 15W
Lit'ang, Kwangsi-Chuang, China 108 23 11N 109 5E
Lit'ang, Szechwan, China 108 30 4N 100 18E
Litang 103 5 27N 118 31E
Lit'ang Ho, R. 108 28 5N 101 28E
Litcham 29 52 43N 0 49E
Litchfield, Austral. 140 36 18S 142 52E
Litchfield, Conn., U.S.A. 162 41 44N 73 12W
Litchfield, Ill., U.S.A. 158 39 10N 89 40W
Litchfield, Minn., U.S.A. 158 45 5N 95 0W
Liteni 70 47 32N 26 32E
Litherland 32 53 29N 3 0W
Lithgow 141 33 25S 150 8E
Lithinon, Ákra 69 34 55N 24 44E
Lithuania S.S.R. □ 80 55 30N 24 0E
Litija 63 46 3N 14 50E

Lititz	**162**	40 9N	76 18W
Litókhoron	**68**	40 8N	22 34 E
Litoměrice	**52**	50 33N	14 10 E
Litomysi	**53**	49 52N	16 20 E
Litschau	**52**	48 58N	15 4 E
Little Abaco I.	**157**	26 50N	77 30W
Little Aden	**91**	12 41N	45 6 E
Little America	**13**	79 0N	160 0W
Little Andaman I.	**101**	10 40N	92 15 E
Little Barrier I.	**142**	36 12 S	175 8 E
Little Belt	**72**	55 8N	9 55 E
Little Belt Mts.	**160**	46 50N	111 0W
Little Blue, R.	**158**	40 18N	97 45W
Little Bushman Land	**128**	29 10 S	18 10 E
Little Cadotte, R.	**152**	56 41N	117 6W
Little Cayman, I.	**166**	19 41N	80 3W
Little Churchill, R.	**153**	57 30N	95 22W
Little Coco I.	**101**	14 0N	93 15 E
Little Colorado, R.	**161**	36 0N	111 31W
Little Current	**150**	45 55N	82 0W
Little Current, R.	**150**	50 57N	84 36W
Little Egg Inlet	**162**	39 30N	74 20W
Little Falls, Minn., U.S.A.	**158**	45 58N	94 19W
Little Falls, N.Y., U.S.A.	**162**	43 3N	74 50W
Lit. Grand Rapids	**153**	52 0N	95 29W
Lit. Humbaldt, R.	**160**	41 20N	117 27W
Lit. Inagua I.	**167**	21 40N	73 50W
Little Lake	**163**	35 58N	117 58W
Little Longlac	**150**	49 42N	86 58W
Little Marais	**158**	47 24N	91 8W
Little Mecatiná I.	**151**	50 30N	59 25W
Little Minch	**36**	57 35N	6 45W
Lit. Miquelon I.	**151**	46 45N	56 25W
Lit. Missouri R.	**158**	46 40N	103 50W
Little Namaqualand	**128**	29 0 S	17 9 E
Little Ormes Hd.	**31**	53 19N	3 47W
Little Ouse, R.	**29**	52 25N	0 50 E
Little Para, R.	**109**	34 47 S	138 25 E
Little Rann of Kutch	**94**	23 25N	71 25 E
Little Red, R.	**159**	35 40N	92 15W
Little River	**143**	43 45 S	172 49 E
Little Rock	**159**	34 41N	92 10W
Little Ruaha, R.	**126**	7 50 S	35 30 E
Little Sable Pt.	**156**	43 40N	86 32W
Little Scarcies, R.	**125**	9 30N	12 25W
Little Sioux, R.	**147**	42 20N	95 55W
Little Smoky	**152**	54 44N	117 11W
Little Smoky River	**152**	55 40N	117 38W
Little Snake, R.	**160**	40 45N	108 15W
Little Wabash, R.	**156**	38 40N	88 20W
Little Walsingham	**29**	52 53N	0 51 E
Little Whale, R.	**150**	55 50N	75 0W
Littleborough	**32**	53 38N	2 8W
Littlefield	**159**	33 57N	102 17W
Littlefork	**158**	48 24N	93 35W
Littlehampton, Austral.	**109**	35 3 S	138 52 E
Littlehampton, U.K.	**29**	50 48N	0 32W
Littlemill	**37**	57 31N	3 49W
Littleport	**29**	52 27N	0 18 E
Littlestone-on-Sea	**29**	50 59N	0 59 E
Littlestown	**162**	39 45N	77 3W
Littleton Common	**162**	42 32N	71 28W
Litu	**108**	28 24N	101 16 E
Liuan	**109**	31 45N	116 30 E
Liuch'eng	**108**	24 39N	109 14 E
Liuchou	**108**	24 15N	109 22 E
Liuchuang	**107**	33 9N	120 18 E
Liuheng Tao	**109**	29 43N	122 8 E
Liuho, Kiangsu, China	**109**	32 20N	118 51 E
Liuho, Kirin, China	**107**	42 16N	125 42 E
Liukou	**107**	40 57N	118 18 E
Liuli	**127**	11 3 S	34 38 E
Liupa	**106**	33 40N	107 0 E
Liuwa Plain	**125**	14 20 S	22 30 E
Liuyang	**109**	28 9N	113 38 E
Livada	**70**	47 52N	23 5 E
Livadherón	**68**	40 2N	21 57 E
Livanovka	**84**	52 6N	61 59 E
Livarot	**42**	49 0N	0 9 E
Live Oak	**157**	30 17N	83 0W
Liveringa	**136**	18 3 S	124 10 E
Livermore	**163**	37 41N	121 47W
Livermore, Mt.	**159**	30 45N	104 8W
Liverpool, Austral.	**141**	33 54 S	150 58 E
Liverpool, Can.	**151**	44 5N	64 41W
Liverpool, U.K.	**32**	53 25N	3 0W
Liverpool, U.S.A.	**162**	43 6N	76 13W
Liverpool Bay, Can.	**147**	70 0N	128 0W
Liverpool Bay, U.K.	**23**	53 30N	3 20W
Liverpool Plains	**141**	31 15 S	150 15 E
Liverpool Ra.	**141**	31 50 S	150 30 E
Livingston, Guat.	**166**	15 50N	88 50W
Livingston, U.K.	**45**	55 52N	3 33W
Livingston, Calif., U.S.A.	**163**	37 23N	120 43W
Livingston, Mont., U.S.A.	**160**	45 40N	110 40W
Livingstone	**159**	30 44N	94 54W
Livingstone Falls	**126**	5 25 S	13 35 E
Livingstone I.	**13**	63 0 S	60 15W
Livingstone (Maramba)	**127**	17 46 S	25 52 E
Livingstone Memorial	**127**	12 20 S	30 18 E
Livingstone Mts., N.Z.	**143**	45 15 S	168 9 E
Livingstone Mts., Tanz.	**127**	9 40 S	34 20 E
Livingstonia	**127**	10 38 S	34 5 E
Livno	**66**	43 50N	17 0 E
Livny	**81**	52 30N	37 30 E
Livorno	**62**	43 32N	10 18 E
Livramento	**173**	30 55 S	55 30W
Livramento do Brumado	**171**	13 39 S	41 50W

Livron-sur-Drôme	**45**	44 46N	4 51 E
Liwale	**127**	9 48 S	37 58 E
Liwale □	**127**	9 0 S	38 0 E
Liwale Chini	**127**	9 40 S	38 0 E
Lixnaw	**39**	52 24N	9 37W
Lixoúrion	**69**	38 14N	20 24 E
Liyang	**109**	31 22N	119 30 E
Lizard	**30**	49 58N	5 10W
Lizard I.	**138**	14 42 S	145 30 E
Lizard Pt.	**30**	49 57N	5 11W
Lizarda	**170**	9 36 S	46 41W
Lizzano	**65**	40 23N	17 25 E
Ljig	**66**	44 13N	20 18 E
Ljubija	**63**	44 55N	16 35 E
Ljubinje	**66**	42 58N	18 5 E
Ljubljana	**63**	46 4N	14 33 E
Ljubno	**63**	46 25N	14 46 E
Ljubovija	**66**	44 11N	19 22 E
Ljubuški	**66**	43 12N	17 34 E
Ljung	**73**	58 1N	13 3 E
Ljungan	**72**	62 18N	17 23 E
Ljungan, R.	**74**	62 30N	14 30 E
Ljungaverk	**72**	62 30N	16 5 E
Ljungby	**73**	56 49N	13 55 E
Ljusdal	**72**	61 46N	16 3 E
Ljusnan	**72**	61 12N	17 8 E
Ljusnan, R.	**75**	62 0N	15 20 E
Ljusne	**72**	61 13N	17 7 E
Ljutomer	**63**	46 31N	16 11 E
Lki	**67**	41 28N	23 43 E
Llagostera	**58**	41 50N	2 54 E
Llanaber	**31**	52 45N	4 5W
Llanaelhaiarn	**31**	52 59N	4 24W
Llanafan-fawr	**31**	52 12N	3 29W
Llanarmon Dyffryn Ceiriog	**31**	52 53N	3 15W
Llanarth	**31**	52 12N	4 19W
Llanarthney	**31**	51 51N	4 9W
Llanbedr	**31**	52 40N	4 7W
Llanbedrog	**31**	52 52N	4 29W
Llanberis	**31**	53 7N	4 7W
Llanbister	**31**	52 22N	3 19W
Llanbrynmair	**31**	52 36N	3 19W
Llancanelo, Salina	**172**	35 40 S	69 8W
Llandaff	**31**	51 29N	3 13W
Llanddewi-Brefi	**31**	52 11N	3 57W
Llandilo	**31**	51 45N	4 0W
Llandogo	**31**	51 44N	2 40W
Llandovery	**31**	51 59N	3 49W
Llandrillo	**31**	52 56N	3 27W
Llandrindod Wells	**31**	52 15N	3 23W
Llandudno	**31**	53 19N	3 51W
Llandybie	**31**	51 49N	4 0W
Llandyfriog	**31**	52 2N	4 26W
Llandygwydd	**31**	52 3N	4 33W
Llandyrnog	**31**	53 10N	3 19W
Llandyssul	**31**	52 3N	4 20W
Llanelli	**31**	51 41N	4 11W
Llanelltyd	**31**	52 45N	3 54W
Llanenddwyn	**31**	52 48N	4 7W
Llanerchymedd	**31**	53 20N	4 22W
Llanes	**56**	43 25N	4 50W
Llanfaelog	**31**	53 13N	4 29W
Llanfair Caereinion	**31**	52 39N	3 20W
Llanfair Talhaiarn	**31**	53 13N	3 37W
Llanfairfechan	**31**	53 15N	3 58W
Llanfechell	**31**	53 23N	4 25W
Llanfyllin	**31**	52 47N	3 17W
Llangadog	**31**	51 56N	3 53W
Llangefni	**31**	53 15N	4 20W
Llangelynin	**31**	52 39N	4 7W
Llangennech	**31**	51 41N	4 10W
Llangerniew	**31**	53 12N	3 41W
Llangollen	**31**	52 58N	3 10W
Llangranog	**31**	52 11N	4 29W
Llangurig	**31**	52 25N	3 36W
Llangynog	**31**	52 50N	3 24W
Llanharan	**31**	51 32N	3 28W
Llanidloes	**31**	52 28N	3 31W
Llanilar	**31**	52 22N	4 2W
Llanllyfni	**31**	53 2N	4 18W
Llannor	**31**	52 55N	4 25W
Llano Estacado	**154**	34 0N	103 0W
Llano R.	**159**	30 50N	99 0W
Llanon	**31**	52 17N	4 9W
Llanos	**174**	3 25N	71 35W
Llanpumpsaint	**31**	51 56N	4 19W
Llanrhaedr-ym-Mochnant	**31**	52 50N	3 18W
Llanrhidian	**31**	51 36N	4 11W
Llanrhystyd	**31**	52 19N	4 9W
Llanrwst	**31**	53 8N	3 49W
Llansannan	**31**	53 10N	3 35W
Llansawel	**31**	52 0N	4 1W
Llanstephan	**31**	51 46N	4 24W
Llanthony	**31**	51 57N	3 2W
Llantrisant	**31**	51 33N	3 22W
Llanuwchllyn	**31**	52 52N	3 41W
Llanvihangel Crucorney	**31**	51 53N	2 58W
Llanwenog	**31**	52 6N	4 11W
Llanwrda	**31**	51 58N	3 52W
Llanwrtyd Wells	**31**	52 6N	3 39W
Llanybydder	**28**	52 47N	3 8W
Llanybyther	**31**	52 4N	4 10W
Llanymynech	**28**	52 48N	3 6W
Llanystymdwy	**31**	52 56N	4 17W
Llera	**165**	23 19N	99 1W
Llerena	**57**	38 17N	6 0W
Llethr Mt.	**31**	52 47N	3 58W
Lleyn Peninsula	**31**	52 55N	4 35W
Llico	**172**	34 46 S	72 5W
Llobregat, R.	**58**	41 19N	2 9 E
Lloret de Mar	**58**	41 41N	2 53 E

Lloyd B.	**138**	12 45 S	143 27 E
Lloyd Barrage	**95**	27 46N	68 50 E
Lloyd L.	**153**	57 22N	108 57W
Lloydminster	**153**	53 20N	110 0W
Lluchmayor	**59**	39 29N	2 53 E
Llullaillaco, volcán	**172**	24 30 S	68 30W
Llwyngwril	**31**	52 41N	4 6W
Llyswen	**31**	52 2N	3 18W
Lo	**47**	50 59N	2 45 E
Lo Ho, Honan, China	**106**	34 48N	113 4 E
Lo Ho, Shensi, China	**106**	34 41N	110 6 E
Lo, R.	**100**	21 18N	105 25 E
Loa	**161**	38 18N	111 46W
Loa, R.	**172**	21 30 S	70 0W
Loan	**109**	27 24N	115 49 E
Loanhead	**35**	55 53N	3 10W
Loano	**62**	44 8N	8 14 E
Loans	**34**	55 33N	4 39W
Lobatse	**125**	25 12 S	25 40 E
Löbau	**48**	51 5N	14 42 E
Lobaye, R.	**128**	4 30N	17 0 E
Lobbes	**47**	50 21N	4 16 E
Lobenstein	**48**	50 25N	11 39 E
Lobería	**172**	38 10 S	58 40W
Łobez	**54**	53 38N	15 39 E
Lobito	**125**	12 18 S	13 35 E
Lobón, Canal de	**57**	38 50N	6 55W
Lobos	**172**	35 2 S	59 0W
Lobos, I.	**164**	21 27N	97 13W
Lobos, Is.	**168**	6 35 S	80 45W
Lobstick L.	**151**	54 0N	65 12W
Lobva	**84**	59 10N	60 30 E
Lobva, R.	**84**	59 8N	60 48 E
Loc Binh	**100**	21 46N	106 54 E
Loc Ninh	**101**	11 50N	106 34 E
Locarno	**51**	46 10N	8 47 E
Loch Raven Res.	**162**	39 26N	76 33W
Lochaber	**36**	56 55N	5 0W
Lochailort	**36**	56 53N	5 40W
Lochaline	**36**	56 32N	5 47W
Loch'ang	**109**	25 10N	113 20 E
Lochans	**34**	54 52N	5 1W
Lochboisdale	**36**	57 10N	7 20W
Lochbuie	**34**	56 21N	5 52W
Lochcarron	**36**	57 25N	5 30W
Lochdonhead	**34**	56 27N	5 40W
Loche L., La	**153**	56 40N	109 30W
Loche, La	**153**	56 29N	109 26W
Lochearnhead	**34**	56 24N	4 19W
Lochem	**46**	52 9N	6 26 E
Loch'eng	**108**	24 47N	108 54 E
Loches	**42**	47 7N	1 0 E
Lochgelly	**35**	56 7N	3 18W
Lochgilphead	**34**	56 2N	5 37W
Lochgoilhead	**34**	56 10N	4 54W
Lochiang	**108**	31 21N	104 28 E
Lochih	**108**	30 18N	105 0 E
Loch'ing	**109**	28 8N	120 57 E
Loch'ing Wan	**109**	28 4N	121 5 E
Lochinver	**36**	58 9N	5 15W
Lochlaggan Hotel	**37**	56 59N	4 25W
Lochmaben	**35**	55 8N	3 27W
Lochmaddy	**36**	57 36N	7 10W
Lochnagar, Queens., Austral.	**138**	24 34 S	144 52 E
Lochnagar, Queens., Austral.	**138**	23 33 S	145 38 E
Lochnagar, Mt.	**37**	56 57N	3 14W
Łochow	**54**	52 33N	21 42 E
Lochranza	**34**	55 42N	5 18W
Lochs Park, Reg.	**36**	58 7N	6 33W
Loch'uan	**106**	35 48N	109 35 E
Lochwinnoch	**34**	55 47N	4 39W
Lochy, L.	**37**	56 58N	4 55W
Lochy, R.	**36**	56 52N	5 3W
Lock	**139**	33 34 S	135 46 E
Lock Haven	**156**	41 7N	77 31W
Lockeford	**163**	38 10N	121 9W
Lockeport	**151**	43 47N	65 4W
Lockerbie	**35**	55 7N	3 21W
Lockhart, Austral.	**141**	35 14 S	146 40 E
Lockhart, U.S.A.	**159**	29 55N	97 40W
Lockhart, L.	**137**	33 15 S	119 3 E
Lockington	**140**	36 16 S	144 34 E
Lockport	**156**	43 12N	78 42W
Locle, Le	**50**	47 3N	6 44 E
Locminé	**42**	47 54N	2 51W
Locri	**65**	38 14N	16 14 E
Locronan	**42**	48 7N	4 15W
Loctudy	**42**	47 50N	4 12W
Lod	**90**	31 57N	34 54 E
Lodalskåpa	**71**	61 47N	7 13 E
Loddon	**29**	52 32N	1 29 E
Lodève	**44**	43 44N	3 19 E
Lodge Grass	**160**	45 21N	107 27W
Lodgepole	**158**	41 12N	102 40W
Lodgepole Cr.	**158**	41 20N	104 30W
Lodhran	**94**	29 32N	71 30 E
Lodi, Italy	**62**	45 19N	9 30 E
Lodi, U.S.A.	**163**	38 12N	121 16W
Lodja	**124**	3 30 S	23 23 E
Lodji	**103**	1 38 S	127 28 E
Lodosa	**58**	42 25N	2 4W
Lodose	**73**	58 5N	12 10 E
Lödöse	**73**	58 2N	12 9 E
Lodwar	**126**	3 10N	35 40 E
Łodz	**54**	51 45N	19 27E
Łodz □	**54**	51 45N	19 27E
Loengo	**126**	4 48 S	26 30 E
Lofer	**52**	47 35N	12 41 E
Lofoten	**74**	68 10N	13 0 E
Lofoten Is.	**74**	68 30N	15 0 E
Lofsen	**72**	62 7N	13 57 E

Loftahammar	**73**	57 54N	16 41 E
Loftsdalen	**72**	62 10N	13 20 E
Loftus	**33**	54 33N	0 52W
Lofty Ra.	**136**	24 15 S	119 30 E
Loga	**121**	13 37N	3 14 E
Logan, Kans., U.S.A.	**158**	39 23N	99 35W
Logan, Ohio, U.S.A.	**156**	39 25N	82 22 E
Logan, Utah, U.S.A.	**160**	41 45N	111 50W
Logan, Mt.	**147**	60 41N	140 22W
Logan Pass	**152**	48 41N	113 44W
Logansport	**156**	31 58N	93 58W
Loganville	**162**	39 51N	76 42W
Logo	**123**	5 20N	30 18 E
Logo Dergo	**123**	6 10N	29 18 E
Logroño	**58**	42 28N	2 32W
Logroño □	**58**	42 28N	2 27W
Logrosán	**57**	39 20N	5 32W
Løgstør	**73**	56 58N	9 14 E
Lohardaga	**95**	23 27N	84 45 E
Loheia	**91**	15 45N	42 40 E
Lohja	**75**	60 12N	24 5 E
Loho	**106**	33 33N	114 5 E
Lohr	**49**	50 0N	9 35 E
Loikaw	**98**	19 40N	97 17 E
Loimaa	**75**	60 50N	23 5 E
Loir-et-Cher □	**43**	47 40N	1 20 E
Loire □	**45**	45 40N	4 5 E
Loire-Atlantique □	**42**	47 25N	1 40W
Loire, R.	**42**	47 16N	2 10W
Loiret □	**43**	47 58N	2 10 E
Loitz	**48**	53 58N	13 8 E
Loja, Ecuador	**174**	3 59 S	79 16W
Loja, Spain	**57**	37 10N	4 10W
Lojung	**108**	24 27N	109 36 E
Loka	**123**	4 13N	31 0 E
Lokandu	**124**	2 30 S	25 45 E
Løken	**71**	59 48N	11 29 E
Lokerane	**128**	24 54 S	24 42 E
Lokeren	**47**	51 6N	3 59 E
Lokhvitsa	**80**	50 25N	33 18 E
Lokichokio	**126**	4 19N	34 13 E
Lokitaung	**124**	4 12N	35 48 E
Lokka	**74**	67 49N	27 45 E
Løkken, Denmark	**73**	57 22N	9 41 E
Løkken, Norway	**71**	63 8N	9 45 E
Loknya	**80**	56 49N	30 4 E
Lokobo	**123**	4 20N	30 30 E
Lokoja	**121**	7 47N	6 45 E
Lokolama	**124**	2 35 S	19 50 E
Loktung	**100**	18 41N	109 5 E
Lokuti	**123**	4 21N	33 15 E
Lokwei	**100**	19 12N	110 30 E
Lol	**123**	5 28N	29 36 E
Lol, R.	**123**	9 0N	28 10 E
Lola	**120**	7 52N	8 29W
Lolibai, Gebel	**123**	3 50N	33 50 E
Lolimi	**123**	4 35N	34 0 E
Loliondo	**124**	2 2 S	35 39 E
Lolland	**73**	54 45N	11 30 E
Lollar	**48**	50 39N	8 43 E
Lolo	**160**	46 50N	114 8W
Lolodorf	**121**	3 16N	10 49 E
Lolungchung	**126**	30 43N	96 7 E
Lom	**67**	43 48N	23 20 E
Lom Kao	**100**	16 53N	101 14 E
Lom, R.	**66**	43 45N	23 7 E
Lom Sak	**100**	16 47N	101 15 E
Loma	**160**	47 59N	110 29W
Loma Linda	**163**	34 3N	117 16W
Lomami, R.	**126**	1 0 S	24 40 E
Lomas de Zamóra	**172**	34 45 S	58 25W
Lombadria	**136**	16 31 S	122 54 E
Lombard	**160**	46 7N	111 28W
Lombardia □	**62**	45 35N	9 45 E
Lombardy = Lombardia	**62**	45 35N	9 45 E
Lombez	**44**	43 29N	0 55 E
Lomblen, I.	**103**	8 30 S	123 32 E
Lombok, I.	**102**	8 35 S	116 20 E
Lomé	**121**	6 9N	1 20 E
Lomela	**124**	2 5 S	23 52 E
Lomela, R.	**124**	1 30 S	22 50 E
Lomello	**62**	45 11N	8 46 E
Lometa	**159**	31 15N	98 25W
Lomie	**124**	3 13N	13 38 E
Loming	**123**	4 27N	33 40W
Lomma	**73**	55 43N	13 6 E
Lomme, R.	**47**	50 8N	5 10 E
Lommel	**47**	51 14N	5 19 E
Lomond	**152**	50 24N	112 36W
Lomond, gasfield	**19**	57 18N	1 12 E
Lomond, L.	**34**	56 8N	4 38W
Lomond, mt.	**139**	30 0 S	151 45 E
Lomphat	**101**	13 30N	106 59 E
Lompobatang, mt.	**103**	5 24 S	119 56 E
Lompoc	**163**	34 41N	120 32W
Lomsegga	**71**	61 49N	8 21 E
Łomza	**54**	53 10N	22 2 E
Łomza □	**54**	53 0N	22 30 E
Lonan	**106**	34 6N	110 10 E
Lonavla	**96**	18 46N	73 29 E
Loncoche	**176**	39 20 S	72 50W
Londa	**97**	15 30N	74 30 E
Londe, La	**45**	43 8N	6 14 E
Londerzeel	**47**	51 0N	4 19 E
Londiani	**126**	0 10 S	35 33 E
Londinières	**42**	49 50N	1 25 E
London, Can.	**150**	43 0N	81 15W
London, U.K.	**29**	51 30N	0 5W
London, Ky., U.S.A.	**156**	37 11N	84 5W
London, Ohio, U.S.A.	**156**	39 54N	83 28W
London □	**29**	51 30N	0 5W
Londonderry	**38**	55 0N	7 20W

Lugansk McIlwraith Ra

Lugansk = Voroshilovgrad 83 48 35N 39 29 E
Lugard's Falls 126 3 6S 38 41 E
Lugela 127 16 25S 36 43 E
Lugenda, R. 127 12 35S 36 50 E
Lugh Ganana 91 3 48N 42 40 E
Lugnaquilla, Mt. 39 52 48N 6 28W
Lugnvik 72 62 56N 17 55 E
Lugo, Italy 63 44 25N 11 53 E
Lugo, Spain 56 43 2N 7 35W
Lugo □ 56 43 0N 7 30W
Lugoj 66 45 42N 21 57 E
Lugones 56 43 26N 5 50W
Lugovoy 76 43 0N 72 20 E
Lugovoye 85 42 55N 72 43 E
Lugwardine 28 52 4N 2 38W
Luhe, R. 48 53 7N 10 0 E
Luhsi, Yunan, China 108 24 31N 103 46 E
Luhsi, Yunnan, China 108 24 27N 98 36 E
Luhuo 108 31 24N 100 41 E
Lui 106 33 52N 115 28 E
Luiana 125 17 25S 22 30W
Luichart L. 37 57 36N 4 43W
Luichow Pen. = Leichou Pantao 108 20 40N 110 5 E
Luing I. 34 56 15N 5 40W
Luino 62 46 0N 8 42 E
Luís 164 26 36N 109 11W
Luís Correia 170 3 0S 41 35W
Luís Gomes 171 6 25S 38 23W
Luís Gonçalves 170 5 37S 50 25W
Luisa 124 7 40S 22 30 E
Luiza 124 7 40S 22 30 E
Luizi 126 6 0S 27 25 E
Luján 172 34 45S 59 5W
Lukanga Swamp 127 14 30S 27 40 E
Lukenie, R. 124 3 0S 18 50 E
Lukhisaral 95 27 11N 86 5 E
Lukolela 124 1 10S 17 12 E
Lukosi 127 18 30S 26 30 E
Lukovit 67 43 13N 24 11 E
Lukoyanov 81 55 2N 44 20 E
Lukuhu 108 27 46N 100 50 E
Lukulu 125 14 35S 23 25 E
Lula 126 0 30N 25 10 E
Lule, R. 74 65 35N 22 10 E
Luleå 74 65 35N 22 10 E
Lüleburgaz 67 41 23N 27 28 E
Luliang 108 25 3N 103 39 E
Luling 159 29 45N 97 40W
Lulonga, R. 124 1 0N 19 0 E
Lulua, R. 124 6 30S 22 50 E
Luluabourg = Kananga 124 5 55S 22 18 E
Lulung 107 39 55N 118 57 E
Lumai 125 13 20S 21 25 E
Lumajang 103 8 8S 113 16 E
Lumbala, Angola 125 12 36S 22 30 E
Lumbala, Angola 125 14 18S 21 18 E
Lumberton, Miss., U.S.A. 159 31 4N 89 28W
Lumberton, N. Mex., U.S.A. 161 36 58N 106 57W
Lumberton, N.C., U.S.A. 157 34 37N 78 59W
Lumbres 43 50 40N 2 5 E
Lumbwa 126 0 12S 35 28 E
Lumby 152 50 10N 118 50W
Lumding 98 25 46N 93 10 E
Lumege 125 11 45S 20 50 E
Lumeyen 123 4 55N 33 28 E
Lumi 135 3 30S 142 2 E
Lummen 47 50 59N 5 12 E
Lumphanan 37 57 8N 2 41W
Lumsden, N.Z. 143 45 44S 168 27 E
Lumsden, U.K. 37 57 16N 2 51W
Lumut 101 4 13N 100 37 E
Lumut, Tg. 102 3 50S 105 58 E
Lunan 108 24 47N 103 16 E
Lunan B. 37 56 40N 2 25W
Lunavada 94 23 8N 73 37 E
Lunca 70 47 22N 25 1 E
Lund, Norway 74 68 42N 18 9 E
Lund, Sweden 73 55 41N 13 12 E
Lund, U.S.A. 160 38 53N 115 0W
Lunda 124 9 40S 20 12 E
Lundazi 125 12 20S 33 7 E
Lunde 71 59 17N 9 5 E
Lunderskov 73 55 29N 9 19 E
Lundi, R. 127 21 15S 31 25 E
Lundu 102 1 40N 109 50 E
Lundy, I. 30 51 10N 4 41W
Lune, R. 32 54 0N 2 51W
Lüneburg 48 53 15N 10 23 E
Lüneburg Heath = Lüneburger Heide 48 53 0N 10 0 E
Lüneburger Heide 48 53 0N 10 0 E
Lunel 45 43 39N 4 9 E
Lünen 48 51 36N 7 31 E
Lunenburg 151 44 22N 64 18W
Lunéville 43 48 36N 6 30 E
Lung Chiang, R. 108 24 30N 109 15 E
Lunga, R. 127 13 0S 26 33 E
Lungan 108 23 11N 107 41 E
Lungch'ang 108 29 20N 105 19 E
Lungch'ih 108 29 25N 103 24 E
Lungchou 108 22 24N 106 50 E
Lungch'üan 109 28 5N 119 7 E
Lungch'uan, Kwangtung, China 109 24 6N 115 15 E
Lungch'uan, Yunnan, China 108 24 16N 97 58 E
Lungern 50 46 48N 8 10 E
Lungholt 74 63 35N 18 10 E
Lunghsi 106 35 3N 104 38 E
Lunghsien 106 34 47N 107 0 E
Lunghua 107 41 18N 117 42 E
Lunghui 109 27 18N 110 52 E
Lungi Airport 120 8 40N 16 47 E
Lungk'ou 107 37 42N 120 21 E
Lungkuan 106 40 45N 115 43 E
Lungkukang 108 32 18N 99 7 E
Lungleh 98 22 55N 92 45 E
Lungli 108 26 27N 106 58 E
Lunglin 108 24 43N 105 26 E
Lungling 108 24 38N 98 35 E
Lungmen 109 23 44N 114 15 E
Lungming 108 23 4N 107 14 E
Lungnan 109 24 54N 114 47 E
Lungngo 98 21 57N 93 36 E
Lungshan 108 29 27N 109 23 E
Lungsheng 109 25 48N 110 0 E
Lungte 106 35 38N 106 6 E
Lungyen 109 25 9N 117 0 E
Lungyu 109 29 2N 119 10 E
Luni 94 26 0N 73 6 E
Luni, R. 94 25 40N 72 20 E
Luninets 80 52 15N 27 0 E
Luning 163 38 30N 118 10W
Lunino 81 53 35N 45 6 E
Lunna Ness 36 60 27N 1 4W
Lunner 71 60 19N 10 35 E
Lunsemfwa Falls 127 14 30S 29 6 E
Lunsemfwa, R. 127 14 50S 30 10 E
Lunteren 46 52 5N 5 38 E
Luofu 126 0 1S 29 15 E
Luozi 124 4 54S 14 0 E
Lupeni 70 45 21N 23 13 E
Łupków 53 49 15N 22 4 E
Lupundu 127 14 18S 26 45 E
Luque, Parag. 172 25 19S 57 25W
Luque, Spain 57 37 35N 4 16W
Luray 156 38 39N 78 26W
Lure 43 47 40N 6 30 E
Luremo 124 8 30S 17 50 E
Lurgainn L. 36 58 1N 5 15W
Lurgan 38 54 28N 6 20W
Luristan 92 33 20N 47 0 E
Lusaka 127 15 28S 28 16 E
Lusambo 126 4 58S 23 28 E
Luseland 153 52 5N 109 24W
Lushan, Honan, China 106 33 45N 113 10 E
Lushan, Kweichow, China 108 26 33N 107 58 E
Lushan, Szechwan, China 108 30 10N 102 59 E
Lushih 106 34 4N 110 2 E
Lushnja 68 40 55N 19 41 E
Lushoto 126 4 47S 38 20 E
Lushoto □ 126 4 45S 38 20 E
Lushui 108 25 51N 98 55 E
Lüshun 107 38 48N 121 16 E
Lusignan 44 46 26N 0 8 E
Lusigny-sur-Barse 43 48 16N 4 15 E
Lusk, Ireland 38 53 32N 6 10W
Lusk, U.S.A. 158 42 47N 104 27W
Luss 34 56 6N 4 40W
Lussac-les-Châteaux 44 46 24N 0 43 E
Lussanvira 171 20 42S 51 7W
Lüta 107 38 55N 121 40 E
Luti 108 7 14S 157 0 E
Luting 108 29 56N 102 12 E
Luton 29 51 53N 0 24W
Lutong 102 4 30N 114 0 E
Lutry 50 46 31N 6 42 E
Lutsk 80 50 50N 25 15 E
Lutterworth 28 52 28N 1 12W
Luverne 158 43 35N 96 12W
Luvua 127 8 48S 25 17 E
Luwegu, R. 127 9 30S 36 20 E
Luwingu, Mt. 124 10 15S 30 2 E
Luwuk 103 10 0S 122 40 E
Luxembourg 47 49 37N 6 9 E
Luxembourg □ 47 49 58N 5 30 E
Luxembourg ■ 47 50 0N 6 0 E
Luxeuil-les-Bains 43 47 49N 6 24 E
Luxor = El Uqsur 122 25 41N 32 38 E
Luy de Béarn, R. 44 43 39N 0 48W
Luy de France, R. 44 43 39N 0 48W
Luy, R. 44 43 39N 1 9W
Luyksgestel 47 51 17N 5 20 E
Luz, Brazil 171 19 48S 45 40W
Luz, France 44 42 53N 0 1 E
Luzern 51 47 3N 8 18 E
Luzern □ 50 47 2N 7 55 E
Luzerne 162 41 17N 75 54W
Luziânia 171 16 20S 48 0W
Luzilândia 170 3 28S 42 22W
Luzon, I. 103 16 0N 121 0 E
Luzy 43 46 47N 3 58 E
Luzzi 65 39 28N 16 17 E
Lvov 80 49 40N 24 0 E
Lwówek 54 52 28N 16 10 E
Lwówek Śląski 54 51 7N 15 38 E
Lyakhovichi 80 53 2N 26 32 E
Lyakhovskiye, Ostrova 77 73 40N 141 0 E
Lyaki 83 40 34N 47 22 E
Lyall Mt. 142 45 16S 167 32 E
* Lyallpur 94 31 30N 73 5 E
Lyalya, R. 84 59 9N 61 29 E
Lyaskovets 67 43 6N 25 44 E
Lybster 37 58 18N 3 16W
Lychen 48 53 13N 13 20 E
Lyckeby 73 56 12N 15 37 E
Lycksele 74 64 38N 18 40 E
Lydd 29 50 57N 0 56 E
Lydda = Lod 90 31 57N 34 54 E
Lydenburg 129 25 10S 30 29 E
Lydford 30 50 38N 4 7W
Lydham 28 52 31N 2 59W
Lyell 143 41 48S 172 4 E
Lyell I. 152 52 40N 131 35W
Lyell, oilfield 19 60 55N 1 12 E
Lyell Range 143 41 38S 172 20 E
Lygnern 73 57 30N 12 15 E
Lykens 162 40 34N 76 42W
Lykling 71 59 42N 5 12 E
Lyman 160 41 24N 110 15W
Lyme Bay 23 50 36N 2 55W
Lyme Regis 30 50 44N 2 57W
Lyminge 29 51 7N 1 6 E
Lymington 28 50 46N 1 32W
Lymm 32 53 23N 2 30W
Lympne 29 51 4N 1 2 E
Lynchburg 156 37 23N 79 10W
Lynd, R. 138 16 28S 143 18 E
Lynd Ra. 139 25 30S 149 20 E
Lynden 160 48 56N 122 32W
Lyndhurst, N.S.W., Austral. 138 33 41S 149 2 E
Lyndhurst, Queens., Austral. 138 19 12S 144 20 E
Lyndhurst, S. Australia, Austral. 139 30 15S 138 18 E
Lyndhurst, U.K. 28 50 53N 1 33W
Lyndon, R. 137 23 29S 114 6 E
Lyneham 28 51 30N 1 57W
Lyngdal, Agder, Norway 71 58 8N 7 7 E
Lyngdal, Buskerud, Norway 71 59 54N 9 32 E
Lynher Reef 136 15 27S 121 55 E
Lynmouth 30 51 14N 3 50W
Lynn 162 42 28N 70 57W
Lynn Canal 152 58 50N 135 20W
Lynn L. 153 56 30N 101 40W
Lynn Lake 153 56 51N 101 3W
Lynton 30 51 14N 3 50W
Lyntupy 80 55 4N 26 23 E
Lynx L. 153 62 25N 106 15W
Lyø 73 55 3N 10 9 E
Lyon 45 45 46N 4 50 E
Lyonnais 45 45 45N 4 15 E
Lyons, Colo., U.S.A. 158 40 17N 105 15W
Lyons, Ga., U.S.A. 157 32 10N 82 15W
Lyons, Kans., U.S.A. 158 38 24N 98 13W
Lyons, N.Y., U.S.A. 162 43 3N 77 0W
Lyons = Lyon 45 45 46N 4 50 E
Lyons Falls 162 43 37N 75 22W
Lyons, R. 137 25 2S 115 9 E
Lyrestad 73 58 48N 14 4 E
Lysá 52 50 11N 14 51 E
Lysekil 73 58 17N 11 26 E
Lyskovo 81 56 0N 45 3 E
Lyss 50 47 4N 7 19 E
Lysva 84 58 07N 57 49 E
Lysvik 72 60 1N 13 9 E
Lytchett Minster 28 50 44N 2 3W
Lytham St. Anne's 32 53 45N 2 58W
Lythe 33 54 30N 0 40W
Lytle 159 29 14N 98 46W
Lyttelton 143 43 35S 172 44 E
Lytton 152 50 13N 121 31W
Lyuban 80 59 16N 31 18 E
Lyubim 81 58 20N 40 50 E
Lyubimets 67 41 50N 26 5 E
Lyuboml 81 51 10N 24 2 E
Lyubotin 82 50 0N 36 4 E
Lyubytino 80 58 50N 33 16 E
Lyudinovo 80 53 52N 34 28 E

M

Ma, R. 100 19 47N 105 56 E
Ma'ad 90 32 37N 35 36 E
Maam Cross 38 53 28N 9 32W
Maamba 128 17 17S 26 28 E
Ma'an 92 30 12N 35 44 E
Maanshan 109 31 40N 118 30 E
Maarheeze 47 51 19N 5 36 E
Maarianhamina 75 60 5N 19 55 E
Maarn 47 52 3N 5 22 E
Maarssen 46 52 9N 5 2 E
Maartensdijk 46 52 9N 5 10 E
Maas 38 54 49N 8 21W
Maas, R. 47 51 48N 4 55 E
Maasbracht 47 51 9N 5 54 E
Maasbree 47 51 22N 6 3 E
Maasdan 46 51 48N 4 34 E
Maasdijk 46 51 58N 4 13 E
Maaseik 47 51 6N 5 45 E
Maasin 102 10 5N 124 55 E
Maasland 46 51 57N 4 16 E
Maasniel 47 51 12N 6 1 E
Maassluis 47 51 56N 4 16 E
Maastricht 47 50 50N 5 40 E
Maatin-es-Sarra 117 21 45N 22 0 E
Maave 129 21 4S 34 47 E
Mabein 98 23 29N 96 37 E
Mabel L. 152 50 35N 118 43W
Mabel, oilfield 19 58 6N 1 36 E
Mabenge 126 4 15N 24 12 E
Mablethorpe 33 53 21N 0 14 E
Mabrouk 121 19 29N 1 15W
Mabton 127 46 13N 120 1W
Mac Bac 101 9 46N 106 7 E
Mc Grath 147 62 58N 155 40W
Macachin 172 37 10S 63 43W
Macadam Ra. 136 14 40S 129 50 E
Macaé 173 22 20S 41 55W
Macaguane 174 6 35N 71 43W
Macaiba 170 5 15S 35 21W
Macajuba 171 12 9S 40 22W
McAlester 159 34 57N 95 40W
Macamic 150 48 45N 79 0W
Macão 57 39 35N 7 59W
Macao = Macau ■ 109 22 16N 113 35 E
Macapá 175 0 5N 51 10W
Macarani 171 15 33S 40 24W
Macarena, Serranía de la 174 2 45N 73 55W
Macarthur 140 38 5S 142 0 E
McArthur, R. 136 16 45S 136 0 E
McArthur River 138 16 27S 137 7 E
Macau 170 5 0S 36 40W
Macau ■ 109 22 16N 113 35 E
Macaúbas 171 13 2S 42 42W
McBride 152 53 20N 120 10W
McCamey 159 31 8N 102 15W
McCammon 160 42 41N 112 11W
McCarthy 147 61 25N 143 0W
McCauley I. 152 53 40N 130 15W
Macclesfield 32 53 16N 2 9W
McClintock 153 57 50N 94 10W
McClintock Chan. 148 72 0N 102 0W
McClintock Ra., Mts. 136 18 44S 127 38 E
McCloud 160 41 14N 122 5W
McCluer Gulf 103 2 20S 133 0 E
McCluer I. 136 11 5S 133 0 E
McClure, L. 163 37 35N 120 16W
McClusky 158 47 30N 100 31W
McComb 159 31 20N 90 30W
McConnell Creek 152 56 53N 126 30W
McCook 158 40 15N 100 35W
McCulloch 152 49 45N 119 15W
McCusker, R. 153 55 32N 108 39W
McDame 152 59 44N 128 59W
McDermitt 160 42 0N 117 45W
McDonald I. 11 54 0S 73 0 E
Macdonald L. 137 23 30S 129 0 E
Macdonald Ra. 136 15 35S 124 50 E
Macdonnell Ranges 136 23 40S 133 0 E
McDouall Peak 139 29 51S 134 55 E
Macdougall L. 148 66 00N 98 27W
McDougalls Well 140 31 8S 141 15 E
MacDowell L. 150 52 15N 92 45W
Macduff 37 57 40N 2 30W
Mace 150 48 55N 80 0W
Maceda 56 42 16N 7 39W
Macedo da Cavaleiros 124 11 25S 16 45 E
Macedo de Cavaleiros 56 41 31N 6 57W
Macedonia = Makedonija 66 41 53N 21 40 E
Macedonia = Makhedonía 68 40 39N 22 0 E
Maceió 170 9 40S 35 41W
Maceira 57 39 41N 8 55W
Macenta 120 8 35N 9 20W
Macerata 63 43 19N 13 28 E
McFarland 163 35 41N 119 14W
Macfarlane, L. 140 32 0S 136 40 E
McFarlane, R. 153 59 12N 107 58W
McGehee 159 33 40N 91 25W
McGill 160 39 27N 114 50W
Macgillycuddy's Reeks, mts. 39 52 2N 9 45W
McGraw 162 42 35N 76 4W
MacGregor 153 49 57N 98 48W
McGregor, Iowa, U.S.A. 158 42 58N 91 15W
McGregor, Minn., U.S.A. 158 46 37N 93 17W
McGregor, R. 152 55 10N 122 0W
McGregor Ra. 139 27 0S 142 45 E
Mach 93 29 50N 67 20 E
Machacalis 171 17 5S 40 45W
Machachi 174 0 30S 78 15W
Machado, R. = Jiparana 174 8 45S 62 20W
Machagai 172 26 56S 60 2W
Machakos 126 1 30S 37 15 E
Machakos □ 126 1 30S 37 15 E
Machala 174 3 10S 79 50W
Machanga 129 20 59S 35 0 E
Machar Marshes 123 9 28N 33 21 E
Machattie, L. 138 24 50S 139 48 E
Machava 129 25 54S 32 28 E
Machece 127 19 15S 35 32 E
Machecoul 42 47 0N 1 49W
Machelen 47 50 55N 4 26 E
Mach'eng 109 31 11N 115 2 E
Mcherrah 118 27 0N 4 30W
Machevna 77 61 20N 172 20 E
Machezo, mt. 57 39 21N 4 20W
Machiang 108 26 30N 107 35 E
Mach'iaoho 107 44 41N 130 32 E
Machias 151 44 40N 67 34W
Machichaco, Cabo 58 43 28N 2 47W
Machichi, R. 153 57 3N 92 6W
Machida 111 35 28N 139 23 E
Machilipatnam 99 16 12N 81 12 E
Machilipatnam = Masulipatnam 96 16 12N 131 15 E
Machine, La 43 46 54N 3 27 E
Mchinja 127 9 44S 39 45 E
Mchinji 127 13 47S 32 58 E
Machiques 174 10 0N 72 34W
Machrihanish 34 55 25N 5 42W
Machupicchu 174 13 8S 72 30W
Machynlleth 31 52 36N 3 51W
Macias Nguema Biyoga 113 3 30N 8 40 E
McIlwraith Ra. 138 13 50S 143 20 E

* Renamed Shah Faisalabad

Macina Makgobistad

Macina	**120**	14 40N	4 50W
Macina, Canal de	**120**	13 50N	5 40W
McIntosh	**158**	45 57N	101 20W
McIntosh L.	**153**	55 11N	104 41W
MacIntosh Range, Mts.	**137**	24 45S	121 33E
Macintyre, R.	**139**	28 37S	149 40E
Macizo Galaico	**56**	42 30N	7 30W
Mackay, Austral.	**138**	21 8S	149 11E
Mackay, U.S.A.	**160**	43 58N	113 37W
Mackay, L.	**136**	22 30S	129 0E
Mackay, R.	**152**	57 10N	111 38W
McKay Ra.	**137**	23 0S	122 30E
McKeesport	**156**	40 21N	79 50W
Mackenzie	**152**	55 20N	123 05W
McKenzie	**157**	36 10N	88 31W
Mackenzie Bay	**147**	69 0N	137 30W
Mackenzie City = Linden	**174**	6 0N	58 10W
Mackenzie Highway	**152**	58 0N	117 15W
Mackenzie Mts.	**147**	64 0N	128 0W
Mackenzie Plains	**143**	44 10S	170 25W
Mackenzie, R., Austral.	**138**	23 38S	149 46E
Mackenzie, R., Can.	**148**	69 10N	134 20W
McKenzie, R.	**160**	44 2N	122 30W
Mackenzie, Terr.	**149**	61 30N	144 30W
McKerrow L.	**143**	44 25S	168 5E
Mackinaw City	**156**	45 47N	84 44W
McKinlay	**138**	21 16S	141 18E
McKinlay, R.	**138**	20 50S	141 28E
McKinley, Mt.	**147**	63 10N	151 0W
McKinley Sea	**12**	84 0N	10 0W
McKinney	**159**	33 10N	96 40W
Mackinnon Road	**126**	3 40S	39 1E
Mackintosh Ra.	**137**	27 39S	125 32E
McKittrick	**163**	35 18N	119 39W
Mackmyra	**72**	60 40N	17 3E
Macksville	**141**	30 40S	152 56E
McLaren Vale	**140**	35 13S	138 31E
McLaughlin	**158**	45 50N	100 50W
Maclean	**139**	29 26S	153 16E
McLean	**159**	35 15N	100 35W
McLeansboro	**158**	38 5N	88 30W
Maclear	**129**	31 2S	28 23E
Macleay, R.	**141**	30 56S	153 0E
McLennan	**152**	55 42N	116 50W
MacLeod, B.	**152**	62 53N	110 0W
McLeod L.	**137**	24 9S	113 47E
McLeod, L.	**137**	24 50S	114 0E
MacLeod Lake	**152**	54 58N	123 0W
McIlwraith Ra., Mts.	**138**	13 43S	143 23E
McLoughlin, Mt.	**160**	42 30N	122 30W
McLure	**152**	51 2N	120 13W
McMillan L.	**159**	32 40N	104 20W
McMinnville, Oreg., U.S.A.	**160**	45 16N	123 11W
McMinnville, Tenn., U.S.A.	**157**	35 43N	85 45W
McMorran	**153**	51 19N	108 42W
McMurdo Sd.	**13**	77 0S	170 0E
McMurray = Fort McMurray	**152**	56 45N	111 27W
McNary	**161**	34 4N	109 53W
McNaughton L.	**152**	52 0N	118 10W
Macnean L.	**38**	54 19N	7 52W
MacNutt	**153**	51 5N	101 36W
Macodoene	**129**	23 32S	35 5E
Macomb	**158**	40 25N	90 40W
Macomer	**64**	40 16N	8 48E
Mâcon	**45**	46 19N	4 50E
Macon, Ga., U.S.A.	**157**	32 50N	83 37W
Macon, Miss., U.S.A.	**157**	33 7N	88 31W
Macon, Mo., U.S.A.	**158**	39 40N	92 26W
Macondo	**125**	12 37S	23 46E
Macosquink	**38**	55 5N	6 43W
Macossa	**127**	17 55S	33 56E
Macoun L.	**153**	56 32N	103 50W
Macovane	**129**	21 30S	35 0E
McPherson	**158**	38 25N	97 40W
McPherson Pk.	**163**	34 53N	119 53W
Macpherson Ra.	**139**	28 15S	153 15E
Macquarie Harbour	**138**	42 15S	145 15E
Macquarie Is.	**130**	50 0S	160 0E
Macquarie, R.	**139**	30 50S	147 30E
McRae, Mt.	**136**	22 17S	117 35E
MacRobertson Coast	**13**	68 30S	63 0E
Macroom	**39**	51 54N	8 57W
McSwyne's B.	**38**	54 37N	8 25W
Macu	**174**	0 25N	69 15W
Macugnaga	**62**	45 57N	7 58E
Macuirima	**127**	19 14S	35 5E
Macuiza	**127**	8 7S	34 29E
Macujer	**174**	0 24N	73 0W
Macumba, R.	**133**	27 11S	136 0E
Macuse	**127**	17 45S	37 17E
Macuspana	**165**	17 46N	92 36W
Macusse	**128**	17 48S	20 23E
Mácuzari, Presa	**164**	27 10N	109 10W
Macuze	**127**	17 45S	37 17E
Madā 'in Sālih	**122**	26 51N	37 58E
Madagali	**121**	10 56N	13 33E
Madagascar ■	**129**	20 0S	47 0E
Madagascar, I.	**129**	20 0S	47 0E
Madam	**120**	7 58N	3 32W
Madama	**119**	22 0N	14 0E
Madame I.	**151**	45 30N	60 58W
Madanapalle	**97**	13 33N	78 34E
Madang	**135**	5 12S	145 49E
Madaoua	**121**	14 5N	6 27E
Madara	**121**	11 45N	10 35E
Madaripur	**98**	23 2N	90 15E
Madauk	**98**	17 56N	96 52E
Madawaska	**150**	45 30N	77 55W
Madawaska, R.	**150**	45 27N	76 21W
Madaya	**98**	22 20N	96 10E
Madbar	**123**	6 17N	30 45E
Maddalena, I.	**64**	41 15N	9 23E
Maddalena, La	**64**	41 13N	9 25E
Maddaloni	**65**	41 4N	14 23E
Maddy, L.	**36**	57 36N	7 8W
Made	**47**	51 41N	4 49E
Madebele	**123**	12 30N	41 10E
Madeira, Is.	**116**	32 50N	17 0W
Madeira, R.	**174**	5 30S	61 20W
Madeleine, Is. de la	**151**	47 30N	61 40W
Madeley	**28**	52 38N	2 28W
Madely	**32**	52 59N	2 20W
Madenda	**127**	13 42S	35 1W
Madera	**163**	37 0N	120 1W
Madha	**96**	18 0N	75 55E
Madhubani	**95**	26 21N	86 7E
Madhumati, R.	**98**	22 53N	89 52E
Madhupur	**126**	24 18N	86 37E
Madhya Pradesh □	**94**	21 50N	81 0E
Madi Opei	**126**	3 47N	33 5E
Madill	**159**	34 5N	96 49W
Madimba, Mozam.	**127**	4 58S	15 6E
Madimba, Zaïre	**124**	5 0S	15 0E
Madinat al Shaab	**91**	12 50N	45 0E
Madingou	**124**	4 10S	13 33E
Madirovalo	**129**	16 26S	46 32E
Madison, Fla., U.S.A.	**157**	30 29N	83 26W
Madison, Ind., U.S.A.	**156**	38 42N	85 20W
Madison, Nebr., U.S.A.	**158**	41 53N	97 25W
Madison, S.D., U.S.A.	**158**	44 0N	97 8W
Madison, Wis., U.S.A.	**158**	43 5N	89 25W
Madison City	**158**	43 5N	93 10W
Madison Junc.	**160**	44 42N	110 56W
Madison, R.	**160**	45 0N	111 48W
Madisonville	**156**	37 42N	87 30W
Madista	**128**	21 15S	25 6E
Madiun	**103**	7 38S	111 32E
Madol	**123**	9 3N	27 45E
Madona	**80**	56 53N	26 5E
Madonie, Le, Mts.	**64**	37 50N	13 50E
Madoonga	**174**	26 56S	117 35E
Madras, India	**97**	13 8N	80 19E
Madras, U.S.A.	**160**	44 40N	121 10W
Madras = Tamil Nadu □	**97**	11 0N	77 0E
Madre de Dios, I.	**176**	50 20N	75 10W
Madre de Dios, R.	**174**	11 30S	67 30W
Madre del Sur, Sierra	**165**	17 30N	100 0W
Madre, Laguna	**165**	25 0N	97 30W
Madre Occidental, Sierra	**164**	27 0N	107 0W
Madre Oriental, Sierra	**164**	25 0N	100 0W
Madre, Sierra, Mexico	**165**	16 0N	93 0W
Madre, Sierra, Phil.	**103**	17 0N	122 0E
Madri	**94**	24 16N	73 32E
Madrid	**56**	40 25N	3 45W
Madrid □	**56**	40 30N	3 45W
Madridejos	**57**	39 28N	3 33W
Madrigal de las Altas Torres	**56**	41 5N	5 0W
Madrona, Sierra	**57**	38 27N	4 16W
Madroñera	**57**	39 26N	5 42W
Madu	**123**	14 37N	26 4E
Madura Motel	**137**	31 55S	127 0E
Madura, Selat	**103**	7 30S	113 20E
Madurai	**97**	9 55N	78 10E
Madurantakam	**97**	12 30N	79 50E
Madurta	**109**	35 1S	138 44E
Maduru Oya	**97**	7 40N	81 7E
Madzhalis	**83**	42 9N	47 47E
Mae Chan	**100**	20 9N	99 52E
Mae Hong Son	**100**	19 16N	98 8E
Mae Khlong, R.	**100**	13 24N	100 0E
Mae Phrik	**100**	17 27N	99 7E
Mae Ramat	**100**	16 58N	98 31E
Mae Rim	**100**	18 54N	98 57E
Mae Sot	**100**	16 43N	98 34E
Mae Suai	**100**	19 39N	99 33E
Mae Tha	**100**	18 28N	99 8E
Maebaru	**110**	33 33N	130 12E
Maebashi	**111**	36 24N	139 4E
Maella	**58**	41 8N	0 7E
Maentwrog	**31**	52 57N	4 0W
Maerhk'ang	**108**	31 51N	102 28E
Mâeruş	**70**	45 53N	25 31E
Maesteg	**31**	51 36N	3 40W
Maestra, Sierra	**166**	20 15N	77 0W
Maestrazgo, Mts. del	**58**	40 30N	0 25W
Maevatanana	**125**	16 56N	46 49E
Ma'fan	**119**	25 56N	14 56E
Mafeking, Can.	**153**	52 40N	101 10W
Mafeking, S. Afr.	**128**	25 50S	25 38E
Maféré	**120**	5 30N	3 2W
Mafeteng	**128**	29 51S	27 15E
Maffe	**47**	50 21N	5 19E
Maffra	**141**	37 53S	146 58E
Mafia □	**126**	7 50S	39 45E
Mafia I.	**126**	7 45S	39 50E
Mafou	**109**	31 34N	115 15E
Mafra, Brazil	**173**	26 10N	50 0W
Mafra, Port.	**57**	38 55N	9 20W
Mafungabusi Plateau	**127**	18 30S	29 8E
Magadan	**77**	59 30N	151 0E
Magadi	**126**	1 54S	36 19E
Magadi, L.	**126**	1 54S	36 19E
Magaliesburg	**129**	26 1S	27 32E
Magallanes, Estrecho de	**176**	52 30S	75 0W
Magangué	**174**	9 14N	74 45W
Magaria	**121**	13 4N	9 5W
Magburaka	**120**	8 47N	12 0W
Magdal	**90**	32 51N	35 30E
Magdalen Is. = Madeleine, Is. de la	**151**	47 30N	61 40W
Magdalena, Argent.	**172**	35 5S	57 30W
Magdalena, Boliv.	**174**	13 13S	63 57W
Magdalena, Mexico	**164**	30 50N	112 0W
Magdalena, U.S.A.	**161**	34 10N	107 20W
Magdalena □	**174**	10 0N	74 0W
Magdalena, B.	**164**	24 30N	112 10W
Magdalena, I.	**164**	24 40N	112 15W
Magdalena, Llano de la	**164**	25 0N	111 30W
Magdalena, mt.	**102**	4 25N	117 55E
Magdalena, R., Colomb.	**174**	8 30N	74 0W
Magdalena, R., Mexico	**164**	30 50N	112 0W
Magdeburg	**48**	52 8N	11 36E
Magdeburg □	**48**	52 20N	11 40E
Magdelaine Cays	**138**	16 33S	150 18E
Magdiel	**90**	32 10N	34 54E
Magdub	**123**	13 42N	25 5E
Magee	**159**	31 53N	89 45W
Magee, I.	**38**	54 48N	5 44W
Magelang	**103**	7 29S	110 13E
Magellan's Str.	**176**	52 30S	75 0W
Magellan's Str. = Magallanes, Est. de	**176**	52 30S	75 0W
Magenta, Austral.	**140**	33 51S	143 34E
Magenta, Italy	**62**	45 28N	8 53E
Magenta, L.	**137**	33 30S	119 10E
Maggea	**140**	34 28S	140 2E
Maggia	**51**	46 15N	8 42E
Maggia, R.	**51**	46 18N	8 36E
Maggiorasca, Mt.	**62**	44 33N	9 29E
Maggiore, L.	**62**	46 0N	8 35E
Maghama	**120**	15 32N	12 57W
Maghar	**90**	32 54N	35 24E
Maghera	**38**	54 51N	6 40W
Magherafelt	**38**	54 44N	6 37W
Maghnia	**118**	34 50N	1 43W
Maghull	**32**	53 31N	2 56W
Magilligan	**38**	55 10N	6 53W
Magilligan Pt.	**38**	55 10N	6 58W
Magione	**63**	43 10N	12 12E
Maglaj	**66**	44 33N	18 7E
Magliano in Toscana	**63**	42 36N	11 18E
Máglie	**65**	40 8N	18 17E
Magnac-Laval	**44**	46 13N	1 11E
Magnetic Pole, 1976, (South)	**13**	68 48S	139 30E
Magnetic Pole, 1976(North)	**12**	76 12N	100 12W
Magnisia □	**69**	39 24N	22 46E
Magnitogorsk	**84**	53 27N	59 4E
Magnolia, Ark., U.S.A.	**159**	33 18N	93 12W
Magnolia, Miss., U.S.A.	**159**	31 8N	90 28W
Magnor	**71**	59 56N	12 15E
Magnus, oilfield	**19**	61 40N	1 20E
Magny-en-Vexin	**43**	49 9N	1 47E
Mâgoé	**127**	15 45S	31 42E
Magog	**151**	45 18N	72 9W
Magoro	**126**	1 45N	34 12E
Magosta = Famagusta	**92**	35 8N	33 55E
Magoye	**127**	16 1S	27 30E
Magpie L.	**151**	51 0N	64 40W
Magrath	**152**	49 25N	112 50W
Magro, R.	**59**	39 20N	0 45W
Magruder Mt.	**163**	37 25N	117 33W
Magrur, W.	**123**	16 5N	26 30E
Magu □	**126**	2 45S	33 15E
Maguarinho, C.	**170**	0 15S	48 30W
Maguire's Bri.	**38**	54 18N	7 28W
Maguse L.	**153**	61 40N	95 10W
Maguse Pt.	**153**	61 20N	93 50W
Maguse River	**153**	61 20N	94 25W
Magwe	**98**	20 10N	95 0E
Maha Sarakham	**100**	16 12N	103 16E
Mahābād	**92**	36 50N	45 45E
Mahabaleshwar	**96**	17 58N	73 50E
Mahabarat Lekh	**95**	28 30N	82 0E
Mahabo	**129**	20 23S	44 40E
Mahad	**96**	18 6N	73 29E
Mahadeo Hills	**94**	22 20N	78 30E
Mahadeopur	**96**	18 48N	80 0E
Mahagi	**126**	2 20N	31 0E
Mahajamba, B. de la	**129**	15 24S	47 5E
Mahajamba, R.	**129**	17 0S	47 30E
Mahajan	**94**	28 48N	73 56E
Mahajilo, R.	**129**	19 30S	46 0E
Mahakam, R.	**102**	1 0N	114 40E
Mahalapye	**128**	23 1S	26 51E
Mahalla el Kubra	**122**	31 10N	31 0E
Mahallât	**93**	33 55N	50 30E
Mahanadi R.	**96**	20 33N	85 0E
Mahanagh	**38**	53 31N	8 42W
Mahanoro	**129**	19 54S	48 48E
Mahanoy City	**162**	40 48N	76 10W
Maharashtra □	**96**	19 30N	75 30E
Maharès	**119**	34 32N	10 29E
Mahari Mts.	**126**	6 20S	30 0E
Mahasolo	**129**	19 7S	46 22E
Mahaweli Ganga	**97**	8 0N	81 10E
Mahaxay	**100**	17 22N	105 48E
Mahboobabad	**96**	17 42N	80 2E
Mahbubnagar	**96**	16 45N	77 59E
Mahd Dhahab	**92**	25 55N	45 30E
Mahdia	**119**	35 28N	11 0E
Mahé	**97**	11 42N	75 34E
Mahe	**95**	33 10N	78 32E
Mahendra Giri, mt.	**97**	8 20N	77 30E
Mahendraganj	**98**	25 20N	89 45E
Mahenge	**127**	8 45S	36 35E
Maheno	**143**	45 10S	170 50E
Mahia Pen.	**142**	39 9S	177 55E
Mahirija	**118**	34 0N	3 16W
Mahlaing	**98**	21 6N	95 39E
Mahmiya	**123**	17 5N	33 50E
Mahmud Kot	**94**	30 16N	71 0E
Mahmudia	**70**	45 5N	29 5E
Mahnomen	**158**	47 22N	95 57W
Mahoba	**95**	25 15N	79 55E
Mahón	**58**	39 50N	4 18E
Mahone Bay	**151**	44 30N	64 20W
Mahopac	**162**	41 22N	73 45W
Mahsü	**108**	30 31N	100 19E
Mahukona	**147**	20 11N	155 52W
Mahuta	**121**	11 32N	4 58E
Mai-Ndombe, L.	**124**	2 0S	18 0E
Mai-Sai	**100**	20 20N	99 55E
Maibara	**111**	35 19N	136 17E
Maîche	**43**	47 16N	6 48E
Maicuru, R.	**175**	1 0S	54 30W
Máida	**65**	38 51N	16 21E
Maidan Khula	**94**	33 36N	69 50E
Maiden Bradley	**28**	51 9N	2 18W
Maiden Newton	**28**	50 46N	2 35W
Maidenhead	**29**	51 31N	0 42W
Maidi	**123**	16 20N	42 45E
Maidstone, Can.	**153**	53 5N	109 20W
Maidstone, U.K.	**29**	51 16N	0 31E
Maiduguri	**121**	12 0N	13 20E
Maignelay	**43**	49 32N	2 30E
Maigualida, Sierra	**174**	5 30N	65 10W
Maijdi	**98**	22 48N	91 10E
Maikala Ra.	**96**	22 0N	81 0E
Mailly-le-Camp	**43**	48 41N	4 12E
Mailsi	**94**	29 48N	72 15E
Maimana	**93**	35 53N	64 38E
Main Barrier Ra.	**133**	31 10S	141 20E
Main Centre	**153**	50 35N	107 21W
Main Coast Ra.	**138**	16 22S	145 10E
Main, R., Ger.	**49**	50 13N	11 0E
Main, R., U.K.	**38**	54 49N	6 20W
Mainburg	**49**	48 37N	11 49E
Maindargi	**96**	17 33N	74 21E
Maine	**42**	48 0N	0 0E
Maine □	**151**	45 20N	69 0W
Maine-et-Loire □	**42**	47 31N	0 30W
Maine, R.	**39**	52 10N	9 40W
Maïne-Soroa	**121**	13 13N	12 2E
Maingkwan	**98**	26 15N	96 45E
Mainit, L.	**103**	9 31N	125 30E
Mainkaing	**98**	24 48N	95 16E
Mainland, I., Orkneys, U.K.	**37**	59 0N	3 10W
Mainland, I., Shetlands, U.K.	**36**	60 15N	1 22W
Mainpuri	**95**	27 18N	79 4E
Maintenon	**43**	48 35N	1 35E
Maintirano	**129**	18 3S	44 1E
Mainvault	**47**	50 39N	3 43E
Mainz	**49**	50 0N	8 17E
Maipú	**172**	37 0S	58 0W
Maipures	**174**	5 11N	67 49W
Maiquetía	**174**	10 36N	66 57W
Maira, R.	**62**	44 29N	7 15E
Mairabari	**98**	26 30N	92 30E
Mairipotaba	**171**	17 18S	49 28W
Maisi	**167**	20 17N	74 9W
Maisi, C.	**167**	20 10N	74 10W
Maisse	**43**	48 24N	2 21E
Maissin	**47**	49 58N	5 10E
Maitland, N.S.W., Austral.	**141**	32 44S	151 36E
Maitland, S. Australia, Austral.	**140**	34 23S	137 40E
Maitland, L.	**137**	27 11S	121 3E
Maiyema	**121**	12 5N	4 25E
Maiz, Islas del	**166**	12 15N	83 4W
Maizuru	**111**	35 25N	135 22E
Majagual	**174**	8 33N	74 38W
Majalengka	**103**	6 55S	108 14E
Majd el Kurum	**90**	32 56N	35 15E
Majene	**103**	3 27S	118 57E
Majevica Planina	**66**	44 45N	18 50E
Maji	**123**	6 20N	35 30E
Major	**153**	51 52N	109 37W
Majorca, I. = Mallorca, I.	**58**	39 30N	3 0E
Majors Creek	**141**	35 33S	149 45E
Majunga	**125**	15 40S	46 25E
Majunga □	**129**	17 0S	47 0E
Maka	**120**	13 40N	14 10W
Makak	**121**	3 36N	11 0E
Makale	**103**	3 6S	119 51E
Makamba	**126**	4 8S	29 49E
Makamik	**150**	48 45N	79 0W
Makapuu Hd.	**147**	21 19N	157 39W
Makarewa	**143**	46 20S	168 21E
Makari	**124**	12 35N	14 28E
Makarikari = Makgadikgadi	**128**	20 40S	25 45E
Makarovo	**77**	57 40N	107 45E
Makarska	**66**	43 20N	17 2E
Makaryev	**81**	57 52N	43 50E
Makasar = Ujung Pandang	**103**	5 10S	119 20E
Makasar, Selat	**103**	1 0S	118 20E
Makat	**76**	47 39N	53 19E
Makedhonia □	**68**	40 39N	22 0E
Makedonija □	**66**	41 53N	21 40E
Makena	**147**	20 39N	156 27W
Makeni	**120**	8 55N	12 5W
Maker	**30**	50 20N	4 10W
Makeyevka	**82**	48 0N	38 0E
Makgadikgadi	**128**	20 40S	25 45E
Makgadikgadi Salt Pans	**128**	20 40S	25 45E
Makgobistad	**128**	25 45S	25 12E

Makhachkala **Manitou I**

Makhachkala **83** 43 0N 47 15 E
Makharadze **83** 41 55N 42 2 E
Makian, I. **103** 0 12N 127 20 E
Makin, I. **130** 3 30N 174 0 E
Makindu **124** 2 7 S 37 40 E
Makinsk **76** 52 37N 70 26 E
Makkah **122** 21 30N 39 54 E
Makkovik **151** 55 0N 59 10W
Makkum **46** 53 3N 5 25 E
Maklakovo **77** 58 16N 92 29 E
Makó **53** 46 14N 20 33 E
Makokou **124** 0 40N 12 50 E
Makongo **126** 3 15N 26 17 E
Makoro **126** 3 10N 29 59 E
Makoua **124** 0 5 S 15 50 E
Maków Podhal **54** 49 43N 19 45 E
Makrá, I. **69** 36 15N 25 54 E
Makrai **93** 22 2N 77 0 E
Makran **93** 26 13N 61 30 E
Makran Coast Range **93** 25 40N 4 0 E
Makrana **94** 27 2N 74 46 E
Mákri **68** 40 52N 25 40 E
Maksimkin Yar **76** 58 58N 86 50 E
Maktar **119** 35 48N 9 12 E
Mākū **92** 39 15N 44 31 E
Makuan **108** 23 2N 104 24 E
Makum **98** 27 30N 95 23 E
Makumbe **128** 20 15 S 24 26 E
Makumbi **124** 5 50 S 20 43 E
Makunda **128** 22 30 S 20 7 E
Makurazaki **110** 31 15N 130 20 E
Makurdi **120** 7 43N 8 28 E
Makwassie **128** 27 17 S 26 0 E
Mal **98** 26 51N 86 45 E
Mal B. **39** 52 50N 9 30W
Mal-i-Gjalicës së Lumës **68** 42 2N 20 25 E
Mal i Gribës **68** 40 17N 9 45 E
Mal i Nemërçkës **68** 40 15N 20 15 E
Mal i Tomorit **68** 40 42N 20 11 E
Mala Kapela **63** 44 45N 15 30 E
Mala, Pta. **166** 7 28N 80 2W
Malabang **103** 7 36N 124 3 E
Malabar Coast **97** 11 0N 75 0 E
Malacca = Melaka **101** 2 15N 102 15 E
Malacca, Str. of **101** 3 0N 101 0 E
Malacky **53** 48 27N 17 0 E
Malad City **160** 41 10N 112 20 E
Maladetta, Mt. **59** 42 40N 0 30 E
Malafaburi **123** 10 37N 40 30 E
Málaga, Colomb. **174** 6 42N 72 44W
Málaga, Spain **57** 36 43N 4 23W
Malaga **159** 32 12N 104 2W
Málaga □ **57** 36 38N 4 58W
Malagarasi **126** 5 5 S 30 50 E
Malagarasi, R. **126** 3 50 S 30 30 E
Malagasy Rep. ■ = Madagascar ■ **129** 20 0 S 47 0 E
Malagón **57** 39 11N 3 52W
Malagón, R. **57** 37 40N 7 20W
Malahide **38** 53 26N 6 10W
Malaimbandy **129** 20 20 S 45 36 E
Malakâl **123** 9 33N 31 50 E
Malakand **94** 34 40N 71 55 E
Malakoff **159** 32 10N 95 55W
Malakwa **152** 50 55N 118 50W
Malamyzh **77** 50 0N 136 50 E
Malang **103** 7 59 S 112 35 E
Malanje **124** 9 30 S 16 17 E
Mälaren **72** 59 30N 17 10 E
Malargüe **172** 35 40 S 69 30W
Malartic **150** 48 9N 78 9W
Malatya **92** 38 25N 38 20 E
Malawi ■ **127** 13 0 S 34 0 E
Malawi, L. (Lago Niassa) **127** 12 30 S 34 30 E
Malay Pen. **101** 7 25N 100 0 E
• Malaya □ **101** 4 0N 102 0 E
Malaya Belözerka **82** 47 12N 34 56 E
Malaya Vishera **80** 58 55N 32 25 E
Malaybalay **103** 8 5N 125 15 E
Malayer **92** 34 19N 48 51 E
Malaysia ■ **102** 5 0N 110 0 E
• Malaysia, Western □ **101** 5 0N 102 0 E
Malazgirt **92** 39 10N 42 33 E
Malbaie, La **151** 47 40N 70 10W
Malbon **138** 21 5 S 140 17 E
Malbooma **139** 30 41 S 134 11 E
Malbork **54** 54 3N 19 10 E
Malca Dube **123** 6 40N 41 52 E
Malchin **48** 53 43N 12 44 E
Malchow **48** 53 29N 12 25 E
Malcolm **137** 28 51 S 121 25 E
Malcolm, Pt., S. Australia, Austral. **109** 34 52 S 138 29 E
Malcolm, Pt., W. Australia, Austral. **137** 33 48 S 123 45 E
Malczyce **54** 51 14N 16 29 E
Maldegem **47** 51 14N 3 26 E
Malden, Mass., U.S.A. **162** 42 26N 71 5W
Malden, Mo., U.S.A. **159** 36 35N 90 0W
Malden I. **143** 4 3 S 155 1W
Maldive Is. ■ **86** 2 0N 73 0W
Maldon, Austral. **140** 37 0 S 144 6 E
Maldon, U.K. **29** 51 43N 0 41 E
Maldonado **173** 35 0 S 55 0W
Maldonado, Punta **165** 16 19N 98 35W
Malé **62** 46 20N 10 55 E
Malé Karpaty **53** 48 30N 17 20 E
Maléa, Ákra **69** 36 28N 23 7 E
Malegaon **96** 20 30N 74 30 E
Malei **127** 17 12 S 36 58 E
Malela **126** 4 22 S 26 8 E
Malenge **127** 12 40 S 26 42 E

Målerås **73** 56 54N 15 34 E
Malerkotla **94** 30 32N 75 58 E
Máles **69** 36 6N 25 35 E
Malesherbes **43** 48 15N 2 24 E
Maleske Planina **66** 41 38N 23 7 E
Malestroit **42** 47 49N 2 25W
Malfa **65** 38 35N 14 50 E
Malgobek **83** 43 30N 44 52 E
Malgomaj L. **74** 64 40N 16 30 E
Malgrat **58** 41 39N 2 46 E
Malham Tarn **32** 54 6N 2 11W
Malhão, Sa. do **55** 37 25N 8 0W
Malheur L. **160** 43 19N 118 42W
Malheur, R. **160** 43 55N 117 55W
Mali **120** 12 10N 12 20W
Mali ■ **121** 15 0N 10 0W
Mali H Ka R. **98** 25 42N 97 30 E
Mali Kanal **66** 45 36N 19 24 E
Mali Kyun, I. **101** 13 0N 98 20 E
Mali, R. **99** 26 20N 97 40 E
Malibu **163** 34 2N 118 41W
Malih, Nahr al **90** 32 20N 35 29 E
Malik **103** 0 39 S 123 16 E
Malili **103** 2 42 S 121 23 E
Malimba, Mts. **126** 7 30 S 29 30 E
Malin, Ireland **38** 55 18N 7 16W
Malin, U.S.S.R. **80** 50 46N 29 15 E
Malin Hd. **38** 55 18N 7 16W
Malin Pen. **38** 55 20N 7 17W
Malinau **102** 3 35N 116 30 E
Malindi **126** 3 12 S 40 5 E
Maling, Mt. **103** 1 0N 121 0 E
Malingping **103** 6 45 S 106 2 E
Malinyi **127** 8 56 S 36 0 E
Maliqi **68** 40 45N 20 48 E
Malita **103** 6 19N 125 39 E
Malkapur, Maharashtra, India **96** 16 57N 74 0W
Malkapur, Maharashtra, India **96** 20 53N 76 17 E
Małkinia Grn. **54** 52 42N 21 58 E
Malko Turnovo **67** 41 59N 27 31 E
Mallacoota **141** 37 40 S 149 40 E
Mallacoota Inlet **141** 37 40 S 149 40 E
Mallaha **90** 33 6N 35 35 E
Mallaig **36** 57 0N 5 50W
Mallala **140** 34 26 S 138 30 E
Mallawan **95** 27 4N 80 12 E
Mallawi **122** 27 44N 30 44 E
Mallemort **45** 43 44N 5 11 E
Málles Venosta **62** 46 42N 10 32 E
Mállia **69** 35 17N 25 27 E
Mallina P.O. **136** 20 53 S 118 2 E
Mallorca, I. **58** 39 30N 3 0 E
Mallow **39** 52 8N 8 40W
Malltraeth B. **31** 53 7N 4 30W
Mallwyd **31** 52 43N 3 41W
Malmbäck **73** 57 34N 14 28 E
Malmberget **74** 67 11N 20 40 E
Malmèdy **47** 50 25N 6 2 E
Malmesbury, S. Afr. **128** 33 28 S 18 41 E
Malmesbury, U.K. **28** 51 35N 2 5W
Malmö **75** 55 36N 12 59 E
Malmöhus län □ **73** 55 45N 13 30 E
Malmslätt **73** 58 27N 15 33 E
Malmyzh **84** 56 31N 50 41 E
Malmyzh Mozhga **81** 56 35N 50 30 E
Malnaş **70** 46 2N 25 49 E
Malo Konare **67** 42 12N 24 24 E
Maloarkhangelsk **81** 52 28N 36 30 E
Maloja **51** 46 25N 9 35 E
Maloja Pass **51** 46 23N 9 42 E
Malolos **103** 14 50N 121 2 E
Malomalsk **84** 58 45N 59 53 E
Malombe L. **127** 14 40 S 35 15 E
Malomir **67** 42 16N 26 30 E
Malone **156** 44 50N 74 19W
Malorad **67** 43 28N 23 41 E
Malorita **80** 51 41N 24 3 E
Maloyaroslovets **81** 55 2N 36 20 E
Malozemelskaya Tundra **78** 67 0N 50 0 E
Malpartida **57** 39 26N 6 30W
Malpas **32** 53 3N 2 47W
Malpelo I. **174** 4 3N 80 35W
Malpica **56** 43 19N 8 50W
Malprabha, R. **97** 15 40N 74 50 E
Malta, Brazil **170** 6 54 S 37 31W
Malta, Idaho, U.S.A. **160** 42 15N 113 50W
Malta, Mont., U.S.A. **160** 48 20N 107 55W
Malta Channel **64** 36 40N 14 0 E
Maltahöhe **125** 24 55 S 17 0 E
Maltby **33** 53 25N 1 12W
Malters **50** 47 3N 8 11 E
Malton **33** 54 9N 0 48W
Maluku □ **103** 3 0 S 128 0 E
Maluku, Kepulauan **103** 3 0 S 128 0 E
Malumfashi **121** 11 48N 7 39 E
Malung, China **108** 25 18N 103 20 E
Malung, Sweden **72** 60 42N 13 44 E
Malvalli **97** 12 28N 77 8 E
Malvan **97** 16 2N 73 30 E
Malvern, U.K. **28** 52 7N 2 19W
Malvern, U.S.A. **159** 34 22N 92 50W
Malvern Hills **28** 52 0N 2 19W
Malvern Wells **28** 52 4N 2 19W
Malvérnia **129** 22 6 S 31 42 E
Malvik **71** 63 25N 10 40 E
Malvinas Is. = Falkland Is. **174** 51 30 S 59 0W
Malya **126** 3 5 S 33 38 E
Malybay **85** 43 30N 78 25 E
Mama **77** 58 18N 112 54 E

Mamadysh **81** 55 44N 51 23 E
Mamaia **70** 44 18N 28 37 E
Mamaku **142** 38 5 S 176 8 E
Mamanguape **170** 6 50 S 35 4W
Mamasa **103** 2 55 S 119 20 E
Mambasa **126** 1 22N 29 3 E
Mamberamo, R. **103** 2 0 S 137 50 E
Mambilima Falls **127** 10 31 S 28 45 E
Mambirima **127** 11 25 S 27 33 E
Mambo **126** 4 52 S 38 22 E
Mambrui **126** 3 5 S 40 5 E
Mameigwess L. **150** 52 35N 87 50W
Mamer **47** 49 38N 6 2 E
Mamers **42** 48 21N 0 22 E
Mamfe **121** 5 50N 9 15 E
Mammamattawa **150** 50 25N 84 23W
Mámmola **65** 38 23N 16 13 E
Mammoth **161** 32 46N 110 43W
Mamoré, R. **175** 9 55 S 65 20W
Mamou **120** 10 15N 12 0W
Mampatá **120** 11 54N 14 53W
Mampawah **102** 0 30N 109 5 E
Mampong **121** 7 6N 1 26W
Mamuju **103** 2 50 S 118 50 E
Man **120** 7 30N 7 40W
Man, I. of **32** 54 15N 4 30W
Man Na **98** 23 27N 97 19 E
Man O' War Peak **151** 56 58N 61 40W
Man, R. **96** 17 20N 75 0 E
Man Tun **98** 23 2N 98 38 E
Mana, Fr. Gui. **175** 5 45N 53 55W
Mana, U.S.A. **147** 22 3N 159 45W
Mana, R. **123** 6 20N 40 41 E
Måna, R. **71** 59 55N 8 50 E
Manaar, Gulf of **97** 8 30N 79 0 E
Manacacías, R. **174** 4 23N 72 4W
Manacapuru **174** 3 10 S 60 50W
Manacles, The **30** 50 3N 5 5W
Manacor **58** 39 32N 3 12 E
Manage **47** 50 31N 4 15 E
Managua **166** 12 0N 86 20W
Managua, L. **166** 12 20N 86 30W
Manaia **142** 39 33 S 174 8 E
Manakana **129** 13 45 S 50 4 E
Manakara **129** 22 8 S 48 1 E
Manakau Mt. **143** 42 15 S 173 42 E
Manam I. **135** 4 5 S 145 0 E
Manamāh, Al **93** 26 11N 50 35 E
Manambao, R. **129** 17 35 S 44 45 E
Manambato **129** 13 43 S 49 7 E
Manambolo, R. **129** 19 20 S 45 0 E
Manambolosy **129** 16 2 S 49 40 E
Mananara **129** 16 10 S 49 30 E
Mananara, R. **129** 23 25 S 48 10 E
Mananjary **129** 21 13 S 48 20 E
Manantenina **129** 24 17 S 47 19 E
Manaos = Manaus **174** 3 0 S 60 0W
Manapouri **143** 45 34 S 167 39 E
Manapouri, L. **143** 45 32 S 167 32 E
Manar, R. **96** 18 50N 77 20 E
Manas, Gora **85** 42 22N 71 2 E
Manas, R. **99** 26 12N 90 40 E
Manasarowar, L. **105** 30 45N 81 20 E
Manasarowar L. **105** 30 45N 81 20 E
Manasir **93** 24 30N 51 10 E
Manaslu, Mt. **95** 28 33N 84 33 E
Manasquan **162** 40 7N 74 3W
Manassa **161** 37 12N 105 58W
Manassas **162** 38 45N 77 28W
Manassu **105** 44 18N 86 13 E
Manati **147** 18 26N 66 29W
Manaung Kyun **98** 18 45N 93 40 E
Manaus **174** 3 0 S 60 0W
Manawan L. **153** 55 24N 103 14W
Manawatu, R. **142** 40 28 S 175 12 E
Manay **103** 7 17N 126 33 E
Manby **33** 53 22N 0 6 E
Mancelona **156** 44 54N 85 5W
Mancha, La **59** 39 10N 2 54W
Mancha Real **57** 37 48N 3 39W
Manchaster, L. **108** 27 29 S 152 46 E
Manche □ **42** 49 10N 1 20W
Manchester, U.K. **32** 53 30N 2 15W
Manchester, Conn., U.S.A. **162** 41 47N 72 30W
Manchester, Ga., U.S.A. **157** 32 53N 84 32W
Manchester, Iowa, U.S.A. **158** 42 28N 91 27W
Manchester, Ky., U.S.A. **156** 38 40N 83 45W
Manchester, N.H., U.S.A. **162** 42 58N 71 29W
Manchester, Pa., U.S.A. **162** 40 4N 76 43W
Manchester, Vt., U.S.A. **162** 43 10N 73 5W
Manchester L. **153** 61 28N 107 29W
Manchouli **105** 49 46N 117 24 E
Manchuria = Tung Pei **107** 44 0N 126 0 E
Manciano **63** 42 35N 11 30 E
Mancifa **123** 6 53N 41 50 E
Mand, R. **93** 28 20N 52 30 E
Manda, Chunya, Tanz. **127** 6 51 S 32 29 E
Manda, Jombe, Tanz. **127** 10 30 S 34 40 E
Mandabé **125** 21 0 S 44 55 E
Mandaguari **173** 23 32 S 51 42W
Mandah **106** 44 27N 108 20 E
Mandal **71** 58 2N 7 25 E
Mandalay **99** 22 0N 96 10 E
Mandalay = Mandale **98** 22 0N 96 10 E
Mandale **99** 22 0N 96 10 E
Mandalgovi **106** 45 45N 106 20 E
Mandali **92** 33 52N 45 28 E
Mandalya Körfezi **69** 37 15N 27 20 E

Mandan **158** 46 50N 101 0W
Mandapeta **96** 16 47N 81 56 E
Mandar, Teluk **103** 3 35 S 119 4 E
Mandas **64** 39 40N 9 8 E
Mandasaur **93** 24 3N 75 8 E
Mandasor (Mandsaur) **94** 24 3N 75 8 E
Mandawai (Katingan), R. **102** 1 30 S 113 0 E
Mandelieu-la-Napoule **45** 43 34N 6 57 E
Mandera **126** 3 55N 41 42 E
Mandera □ **126** 3 30N 41 0 E
Manderfeld **47** 50 20N 6 20 E
Mandi, India **94** 31 39N 76 58 E
Mandi, Zambia **127** 14 30 S 23 45 E
Mandimba **125** 14 20 S 35 40 E
Mandioli **103** 0 40 S 127 20 E
Mandla **95** 22 39N 80 30 E
Mandø **73** 55 18N 8 33 E
Mandoto **129** 19 34 S 46 17 E
Mandoúdhion **69** 38 48N 23 29 E
Mandra **94** 33 23N 73 12 E
Mandráki **69** 36 36N 27 11 E
Mandrase, R. **129** 25 10 S 46 30 E
Mandritsara **129** 15 50 S 48 49 E
Mandsaur (Mandasor) **94** 24 3N 75 8 E
Mandurah **137** 32 36 S 115 48 E
Mandúria **65** 40 25N 17 38 E
Mandvi **96** 22 51N 69 22 E
Mandya **97** 12 30N 77 0 E
Mandzai **94** 30 55N 67 6 E
Mané **121** 12 59N 1 21W
Manea **29** 52 29N 0 10 E
Maner, R. **97** 18 30N 79 40 E
Maneroo **138** 23 22 S 143 53 E
Maneroo Cr. **138** 23 21 S 143 53 E
Manfalût **122** 27 20N 30 52 E
Manfred **140** 33 19 S 143 45 E
Manfredónia **65** 41 40N 15 55 E
Manfredónia, G. di **65** 41 30N 16 10 E
Manga, Brazil **171** 14 46 S 43 56W
Manga, Upp. Vol. **121** 11 40N 1 4W
Mangabeiras, Chapada das **170** 10 0 S 46 30W
Mangahan **142** 40 26 S 175 48 E
Mangalagiri **96** 16 26N 80 36 E
Mangaldai **98** 26 26N 92 2 E
Mangalia **70** 43 50N 28 35 E
Mangalore, Austral. **141** 36 56 S 145 10 E
Mangalore, India **97** 12 55N 74 47 E
Manganeses **56** 41 45N 5 43W
Mangaon **96** 18 15N 73 20 E
Manger **71** 60 38N 5 3W
Mangerton Mt. **39** 51 59N 9 30W
Manggar **102** 2 50 S 108 10 E
Manggawitu **103** 4 8 S 133 32 E
Mangin Range **98** 24 15N 95 45 E
Mangla Dam **95** 33 32N 73 50 E
Manglaur **94** 29 44N 77 49 E
Mangoche **125** 14 25 S 35 16 E
Mangoky, R. **129** 21 55 S 44 40 E
Mangole I. **103** 1 50 S 125 55 E
Mangombe **126** 1 20 S 26 48 E
Mangonui **142** 35 1 S 173 32 E
Mangotsfield **28** 51 29N 2 29W
Mangualde **56** 40 38N 7 48W
Mangueigne **117** 10 40N 21 5 E
Mangueira, Lagoa da **173** 33 0 S 52 50W
Manguéni, Hamada **119** 22 47N 12 56 E
Mangum **159** 34 50N 99 30W
Mangyai **105** 37 50N 91 38 E
Mangyshlak P-ov. **83** 43 40N 52 30 E
Manhattan, Kans., U.S.A. **158** 39 10N 96 40W
Manhattan, Nev., U.S.A. **163** 38 31N 117 3W
Manhiça **129** 25 23 S 32 49 E
Manhuaçu **171** 20 15 S 42 2W
Manhui **106** 41 1N 107 14 E
Manhumirim **171** 20 22 S 41 57W
Mani **99** 34 52N 87 11 E
Maní **174** 4 49N 72 17W
Mania, R. **129** 19 55 S 46 10 E
Maniago **63** 46 11N 12 40 E
Manica **127** 18 58 S 32 59 E
Manica e Sofala □ **129** 19 10 S 33 45 E
Manicaland □ **127** 19 0 S 32 30 E
Manicoré **174** 6 0 S 61 10W
Manicouagan L. **151** 51 25N 68 15W
Manicouagan, R. **151** 49 30N 68 30W
Manifah **92** 27 30N 49 0 E
Manifold **138** 22 41 S 150 40 E
Manigotagan **153** 51 6N 96 8W
Manigotagan L. **153** 50 52N 95 37W
Manihiki I. **131** 10 24 S 161 1W
Manika, Plat. de **127** 10 0 S 25 5 E
Manikganj **98** 23 52N 90 0 E
Manila, Phil. **103** 14 40N 121 3 E
Manila, U.S.A. **160** 41 0N 109 44W
Manila B. **103** 14 0N 120 0 E
Manilla **141** 30 45 S 150 43 E
Manimpé **120** 14 11N 5 28W
Maningory **129** 17 9 S 49 30 E
Manipur □ **98** 24 30N 94 0 E
Manipur, R. **98** 23 45N 93 40 E
Manisa **92** 38 38N 27 30 E
Manistee **156** 44 15N 86 20W
Manistee, R. **156** 44 15N 86 21W
Manistique **156** 45 59N 86 18W
Manito L. **153** 52 43N 109 43W
Manitoba □ **153** 55 30N 97 0W
Manitoba, L. **153** 51 0N 98 45W
Manitou **153** 49 15N 98 32W
Manitou I. **150** 47 22N 87 30W

• Renamed Peninsular Malaysia

Manitou Is **Marosakoa**

Manitou Is. **156** 45 8N 86 0W
Manitou L., Ont., Can. **153** 49 15N 93 0W
Manitou L., Qué., Can. **151** 50 55N 65 17W
Manitoulin I. **150** 45 40N 82 30W
Manitowaning **150** 45 46N 81 49W
Manitowoc **156** 44 8N 87 40W
Manizales **174** 5 5N 75 32W
Manja **129** 21 26 S 44 20 E
Manjacaze **125** 24 45 S 34 0 E
Manjakandriana **129** 18 55 S 47 47 E
Manjeri **97** 11 7N 76 11 E
Manjhand **94** 25 50N 68 10 E
Manjil **92** 36 46N 49 30 E
Manjimup **137** 34 15 S 116 6 E
Manjra, R. **96** 18 20N 77 20 E
Mankaiana **129** 26 38 S 31 6 E
Mankato, Kans., U.S.A. **158** 39 49N 98 11W
Mankato, Minn., U.S.A. **158** 44 8N 93 59W
Mankono **120** 8 10N 6 10W
Mankota **153** 49 25N 107 5W
Manlay **106** 44 9N 106 50 E
Manlleu **58** 42 2N 2 17 E
Manly, N.S.W., Austral. **141** 33 48 S 151 17 E
Manly, Queens., Austral. **108** 27 27 S 153 11 E
Manmad **96** 20 18N 74 28 E
Mann Ranges, Mts. **137** 26 6 S 130 5 E
Manna **102** 4 25 S 102 55 E
Mannahill **140** 32 25 S 140 0 E
Mannar **97** 9 1N 79 54 E
Mannar, G. of **97** 8 30N 79 0 E
Mannar I. **97** 9 5N 79 45 E
Mannargudi **97** 10 45N 79 32 E
Männedorf **51** 47 15N 8 43 E
Mannheim **49** 49 28N 8 29 E
Manning, Can. **152** 56 53N 117 39W
Manning, U.S.A. **157** 33 40N 80 9W
Manning Prov. Park **152** 49 5N 120 45W
Mannington **156** 39 35N 80 25W
Manningtree **29** 51 56N 1 3 E
Mannu, C. **64** 40 2N 8 24 E
Mannu, R. **64** 39 35N 8 56 E
Mannum **140** 34 57 S 139 12 E
Mano **120** 8 3N 12 12W
Manokwari **103** 0 54 S 134 0 E
Manolás **69** 38 4N 21 21 E
Manombo **129** 22 57 S 43 28 E
Manono **124** 7 15 S 27 25 E
Manorbier **31** 51 38N 4 48W
Manorhamilton **38** 54 19N 8 11W
Manosque **45** 43 49N 5 47 E
Manouane L. **151** 50 45N 70 45W
Manpojin **107** 41 6N 126 24 E
Manresa **58** 41 48N 1 50 E
Mans, Le **42** 48 0N 0 10 E
Mansa, Gujarat, India **94** 23 27N 72 45 E
Mansa, Punjab, India **94** 30 0N 75 27 E
Mansa, Zambia **127** 11 13 S 28 55 E
Mansel I. **149** 62 0N 79 50W
Mansenra **94** 34 20N 73 11 E
Mansfield, Austral. **141** 37 4 S 146 6 E
Mansfield, U.K. **33** 53 8N 1 12W
Mansfield, La., U.S.A. **159** 32 2N 93 40W
Mansfield, Mass., U.S.A. **162** 42 2N 71 12W
Mansfield, Ohio, U.S.A. **156** 40 45N 82 30W
Mansfield, Pa., U.S.A. **162** 41 48N 77 4W
Mansfield, Wash., U.S.A. **160** 47 51N 119 44W
Mansfield Woodhouse **33** 53 11N 1 11W
Mansi **98** 24 40N 95 44 E
Mansidão **170** 10 43 S 44 2W
Mansilla de las Mulas **56** 42 30N 5 25W
Mansle **44** 45 52N 0 9 E
Manso, R. **171** 14 0 S 52 0W
Mansôa **120** 12 0N 15 20W
Manson Cr. **152** 55 37N 124 25W
Mansoura, Djebel **119** 36 1N 4 31 E
Manta **174** 1 0 S 80 40W
Mantalingajan, Mt. **102** 8 55N 117 45 E
Mantare **126** 2 42 S 33 13 E
Manteca **163** 37 50N 121 12W
Mantecal **174** 7 34N 69 17W
Mantekomu Hu **99** 34 40N 89 0 E
Mantena **171** 18 47 S 40 59W
Manteo **157** 35 55N 75 41W
Mantes-la-Jolie **43** 49 0N 1 41 E
Manthani **96** 18 40N 79 35 E
Manthelan **42** 47 9N 0 47 E
Manti **160** 39 23N 111 32W
Mantiqueira, Serra da **173** 22 0 S 44 0W
Manton, U.K. **29** 52 37N 0 41W
Manton, U.S.A. **156** 44 23N 85 25W
Mantorp **73** 58 21N 15 20 E
Mántova **62** 45 10N 10 47 E
Mänttä **74** 62 0N 24 40 E
Mantua = Mántova **62** 45 10N 10 47 E
Mantung **140** 34 35 S 140 3 E
Manturova **81** 58 10N 44 30 E
Manu **174** 12 10 S 71 0W
Manucan **103** 8 14N 123 3 E
Manuel Alves Grande, R. **170** 7 27 S 47 35W
Manuel Alves, R. **171** 11 19 S 48 28W
Manui I. **103** 3 35 S 123 5 E
Manukau **142** 37 1 S 174 55 E
Manukau Harbour **142** 37 3 S 174 45 E
Manunui **142** 38 54 S 175 21 E
Manus I. **135** 2 0 S 147 0 E
Manvi **97** 15 57N 76 59 E
Manville, R.I., U.S.A. **162** 41 58N 71 28W
Manville, Wyo., U.S.A. **158** 42 48N 104 36W
Manwath **96** 19 19N 76 32 E
Many **159** 31 36N 93 28W
Manyane **128** 23 21 S 21 42 E
Manyara L. **126** 3 40 S 35 50 E
Manych-Gudilo, Oz. **83** 46 24N 42 38 E
Manych, R. **83** 47 0N 41 15 E
Manyonga, R. **126** 4 5 S 34 0 E
Manyoni **126** 5 45 S 34 55 E
Manyoni □ **126** 6 30 S 34 30 E
Manzai **94** 32 20N 70 15 E
Manzala, Bahra el **122** 31 10N 31 56 E
Manzanares **59** 39 0N 3 22W
Manzaneda, Cabeza de **56** 42 12N 7 15W
Manzanillo, Cuba **166** 20 20N 77 10W
Manzanillo, Mexico **164** 19 0N 104 20W
Manzanillo, Pta. **166** 9 30N 79 40W
Manzano Mts. **161** 34 30N 106 45W
Manzini **129** 26 30 S 31 25 E
Mao **117** 14 4N 15 19 E
Maohsing **107** 45 31N 124 32 E
Maoke, Pengunungan **102** 3 40 S 137 30 E
Maolin **107** 43 55N 123 25 E
Maoming **109** 21 39N 110 54 E
Maopi T'ou **109** 21 56N 120 43 E
Maoping **109** 30 51N 110 54 E
Maowen **108** 31 41N 103 52 E
Mapastepec **165** 15 26N 92 54W
Mapia, Kepulauan **103** 0 50N 134 20 E
Mapien **108** 28 48N 103 39 E
Mapimí **164** 25 50N 103 31W
Mapimí, Bolsón de **164** 27 30N 103 15W
Map'ing **109** 31 36N 113 33 E
Mapinga **126** 6 40 S 39 12 E
Mapinhane **129** 22 20 S 35 0 E
Maple Creek **153** 49 55N 109 29W
Mapleton **160** 44 4N 123 58W
Maplewood **158** 38 33N 90 18W
Mappinga **109** 34 58 S 138 52 E
Maprik **135** 3 44 S 143 3 E
Mapuca **97** 15 36N 73 46 E
Mapuera, R. **174** 0 30 S 58 25W
Maputo **129** 25 58 S 32 32 E
Maqnā **92** 28 25N 34 50 E
Maquela do Zombo **124** 6 0 S 15 15 E
Maquinchao **176** 41 15 S 68 50W
Maquoketa **158** 42 4N 90 40W
Mar Chiquita, L. **172** 30 40 S 62 50W
Mar del Plata **172** 38 0 S 57 30W
Mar Menor, L. **59** 37 40N 0 45W
Mar, Reg. **37** 57 11N 2 53W
Mar, Serra do **173** 25 30 S 49 0W
Mara, Bangla. **98** 28 11N 94 7 E
Mara, Tanz. **126** 1 30 S 34 32 E
Mara □, Tanz. **126** 1 45 S 34 20 E
Mara □, Tanz. **126** 1 30 S 34 32 E
Maraã **174** 1 43 S 65 25W
Marabá **170** 5 20 S 49 5W
Maracá, I. de **170** 2 10N 50 30W
Maracaibo **174** 10 40N 71 37W
Maracaibo, Lago de **174** 9 40N 71 30W
Maracaju **173** 21 38 S 55 9W
Maracanã **170** 0 46 S 47 27W
Maracás **171** 13 26 S 40 27W
Maracay **174** 10 15N 67 36W
Marādah **119** 29 4N 19 4 E
Maradi **121** 13 35N 8 10 E
Maradun **121** 12 35N 6 18 E
Marāgheh **92** 37 30N 46 12 E
Maragogipe **171** 12 46 S 38 55W
Marajó, B. de **170** 1 0 S 48 30W
Marajó, Ilha de **170** 1 0 S 49 30W
Maralal **124** 1 0N 36 38 E
Maralinga **137** 29 45 S 131 15 E
Marama **140** 35 10 S 140 10 E
Marampa **120** 8 45N 10 28W
Maramureş □ **70** 47 45N 24 0 E
Maran **101** 3 35N 102 45 E
Marana **161** 32 30N 111 9W
Maranboy **136** 14 40 S 132 40 E
Maranchón **58** 41 6N 2 15W
Marand **92** 38 30N 45 45 E
Marandellas **127** 18 5 S 31 42 E
Maranguape **170** 3 55 S 38 50W
Maranhão = São Luis **170** 2 31 S 44 16W
Maranhão □ **170** 5 0 S 46 0W
Marañ ó n, R. **174** 4 50 S 75 35W
Marano, L. di **63** 45 42N 13 13 E
Maranoa R. **139** 27 50 S 148 37 E
Maraş **92** 37 37N 36 53 E
Mărăşeşti **70** 45 52N 27 5 E
Maratea **65** 39 59N 15 43 E
Marateca **57** 38 34N 8 40W
Marathókambos **69** 37 43N 26 42 E
Marathon, Austral. **138** 20 51 S 143 32 E
Marathon, Can. **150** 48 44N 86 23W
Marathón **69** 38 11N 23 58 E
Marathon, N.Y., U.S.A. **162** 42 25N 76 3W
Marathon, Tex., U.S.A. **159** 30 15N 103 15W
Maratua, I. **103** 2 10N 118 35 E
Maraú **171** 14 6 S 39 0W
Marazion **30** 50 8N 5 29W
Marbat **91** 17 0N 54 45 E
Marbella **57** 36 30N 4 57W
Marble Bar **136** 21 9 S 119 44 E
Marble Falls **159** 30 30N 98 15W
Marblehead **162** 42 29N 70 51W
Marburg **48** 50 49N 8 44 E
Marby **72** 63 7N 14 18 E
Marcal, R. **53** 47 21N 17 15 E
Marcali **53** 46 35N 17 25 E
Marcaria **62** 45 7N 10 34 E
March **29** 52 33N 0 5 E
Marchand = Rommani **118** 33 20N 6 40W
Marché **44** 46 0N 1 20 E
Marche □ **63** 43 22N 13 10 E
Marche-en-Famenne **47** 50 14N 5 19 E
Marchena **57** 37 18N 5 23W
Marches = Marche **63** 43 22N 13 10 E
Marciana Marina **62** 42 44N 10 12 E
Marcianise **65** 41 3N 14 16 E
Marcigny **45** 46 17N 4 2 E
Marcillac-Vallon **44** 44 29N 2 27 E
Marcillat **44** 46 12N 2 38 E
Marcinelle **47** 50 24N 4 26 E
Marck **43** 50 57N 1 57 E
Marckolsheim **43** 48 10N 7 30 E
Marcos Juárez **172** 32 42 S 62 5W
Marcus I. **130** 24 0N 153 45 E
Mardan **94** 34 20N 72 0 E
Marden **28** 52 7N 2 42W
Mardie **136** 21 12 S 115 59 E
Mardin **92** 37 20N 40 36 E
Marechal Deodoro **170** 9 43 S 35 54W
Maree L. **36** 57 40N 5 30W
Mareeba **138** 16 59 S 145 28 E
Mareham le Fen **33** 53 7N 0 3W
Marek **103** 4 41 S 120 24 E
Marek = Stanke Dimitrov **66** 42 27N 23 9 E
Maremma **62** 42 45N 11 15 E
Maréna **120** 14 0N 7 30W
Marenberg **63** 46 38N 15 13 E
Marengo **158** 41 42N 92 5W
Marennes **126** 45 49N 1 5W
Marenyi **126** 4 22 S 39 8 E
Marerano **129** 21 23 S 44 52 E
Marèttimo, I. **64** 37 58N 12 5 E
Mareuil-sur-Lay **44** 46 32N 1 14W
Marfa **159** 30 15N 104 0W
Marfleet **33** 53 45N 0 15W
Margable **123** 12 54N 42 38 E
Margam **31** 51 33N 3 45W
Marganets **82** 47 40N 34 40 E
Margao **97** 14 12N 73 58 E
Margaree Harbour **151** 46 26N 61 8W
Margaret Bay **152** 51 20N 127 20W
Margaret L. **152** 58 56N 115 25W
Margaret, R. **136** 12 57 S 131 16 E
Margaret River **137** 33 57 S 115 7 E
Margarita, Isla de **174** 11 0N 64 0W
Margarítion **68** 39 22N 20 26 E
Margate, S. Afr. **129** 30 50 S 30 20 E
Margate, U.K. **29** 51 23N 1 24 E
Margate City **162** 39 20N 74 31W
Margelan **85** 40 27N 71 42 E
Margeride, Mts. de la **44** 44 43N 3 38 E
Margherita **98** 27 16N 95 40 E
Margherita di Savola **65** 41 25N 16 5 E
Marghita **70** 47 22N 22 22 E
Margonin **54** 52 58N 17 5 E
Margreten **47** 50 49N 5 49 E
Marguerite **152** 52 30N 122 25W
Marhoum **118** 34 27N 0 11W
Mari, A.S.S.R. □ **81** 56 30N 48 0 E
María Elena **172** 22 18 S 69 40W
María Grande **172** 31 45 S 59 55W
Maria, I. **138** 14 52 S 135 45 E
Maria I. **138** 42 35 S 148 0 E
Maria van Diemen, C. **142** 34 29 S 172 40 E
Mariager **73** 56 40N 10 0 E
Mariager Fjord **73** 56 42N 10 19 E
Mariakani **126** 3 50 S 39 27 E
Marian L. **152** 63 0N 116 15W
Mariana **171** 20 23 S 43 25W
Mariana Is. **130** 17 0N 145 0 E
Mariana Trench **130** 13 0N 145 0W
Marianao **166** 23 8N 82 24W
Mariani **98** 26 39N 94 19 E
Marianna, Ark., U.S.A. **159** 34 48N 90 48W
Marianna, Fla., U.S.A. **157** 30 45N 85 15W
Mariannelund **73** 57 37N 15 35 E
Mariánské Lázně **52** 49 57N 12 41 E
Marias, R. **160** 48 26N 111 40W
Mariato, Punta **166** 7 12N 80 52W
Mariazell **52** 47 47N 15 19 E
Marib **91** 15 25N 45 20 E
Maribo **73** 54 48N 11 30 E
Maribor **63** 46 36N 15 40 E
Marico, R. **128** 24 25 S 26 30 E
Maricopa, Ariz., U.S.A. **161** 33 5N 112 2W
Maricopa, Calif., U.S.A. **163** 35 7N 119 27W
Marîdî **123** 4 55N 29 25 E
Marîdî, W. **123** 5 25N 29 21 E
Marie Galante, I. **167** 15 56N 61 16W
Mariecourt **149** 61 30N 72 0W
Mariefred **72** 59 15N 17 12 E
Mariehamn (Maarianhamina) **75** 60 5N 19 57 E
Marienberg, Ger. **48** 50 40N 13 10 E
Marienberg, Neth. **47** 52 30N 6 35 E
Marienberg, P.N.G. **138** 3 54 S 144 10 E
Marienbourg **47** 50 6N 4 31 E
Mariental **128** 24 36 S 18 0 E
Mariestad **73** 58 43N 13 50 E
Marietta, Ga., U.S.A. **157** 34 0N 84 30W
Marietta, Ohio, U.S.A. **156** 39 27N 81 27W
Marignane **45** 43 25N 5 13 E
Mariinsk **76** 56 10N 87 20 E
Mariinskiy Posad **81** 56 10N 47 45 E
Marilia **173** 22 0 S 50 0W
Marillana **136** 22 37 S 119 24 E
Marín **56** 42 23N 8 42W
Marina **163** 36 41N 121 48W
Marina di Cirò **65** 39 22N 17 8 E
Mariña, La **56** 43 30N 7 40W
Marina Plains **138** 14 37 S 143 57 E
Marinduque, I. **103** 13 25N 122 0 E
Marine City **156** 42 45N 82 29W
Marinel, Le **127** 10 25 S 25 17 E
Marineo **64** 37 57N 13 23 E
Marinette, Ariz., U.S.A. **161** 33 41N 112 16W
Marinette, Wis., U.S.A. **156** 45 4N 87 40W
Maringá **173** 23 35 S 51 50W
Marinha Grande **57** 39 45N 8 56W
Marino **109** 35 3 S 138 31 E
Marino Rocks **109** 35 3 S 138 31 E
Marion, Austral. **109** 34 59 S 138 33 E
Marion, Ala., U.S.A. **157** 32 33N 87 20W
Marion, Ill., U.S.A. **159** 37 45N 88 55W
Marion, Ind., U.S.A. **156** 40 35N 85 40W
Marion, Iowa, U.S.A. **158** 42 2N 91 36W
Marion, Kans., U.S.A. **158** 38 25N 97 2W
Marion, Mich., U.S.A. **156** 44 7N 85 8W
Marion, N.C., U.S.A. **157** 35 42N 82 0W
Marion, Ohio, U.S.A. **156** 40 38N 83 8W
Marion, S.C., U.S.A. **157** 34 11N 79 22W
Marion, Va., U.S.A. **157** 36 51N 81 29W
Marion Bay **140** 35 12 S 136 59 E
Marion, L. **157** 33 30N 80 15W
Marion Reef **138** 19 10 S 152 17 E
Maripa **174** 7 26N 65 9W
Mariposa **163** 37 31N 119 59W
Mariscal Estigarribia **172** 22 3 S 60 40W
Maritime Alps = Alpes Maritimes **62** 44 10N 7 10 E
Maritsa **67** 42 1N 25 50 E
Maritsá **69** 36 22N 28 10 E
Maritsa, R. **67** 42 15N 24 0 E
Mariyampole = Kapsukas **80** 54 33N 23 19 E
Marjan **93** 32 5N 68 20 E
Mark **34** 55 2N 5 1W
Marka **122** 18 14N 41 19 E
Markapur **97** 15 44N 79 19 E
Markaryd **73** 56 28N 13 35 E
Marke **47** 50 48N 3 14 E
Marked Tree **159** 35 35N 90 24W
Markelo **46** 52 14N 6 30 E
Markelsdorfer Huk **48** 54 33N 11 0 E
Marken **46** 52 26N 5 12 E
Markerwaard **46** 52 33N 5 15 E
Market Bosworth **28** 52 37N 1 24W
Market Deeping **29** 52 40N 0 20W
Market Drayton **32** 52 55N 2 30W
Market Harborough **29** 52 29N 0 55W
Market Lavington **28** 51 17N 1 59W
Market Rasen **33** 53 24N 0 20W
Market Weighton **33** 53 52N 0 40W
Markethill **38** 54 18N 6 31W
Markfield **28** 52 42N 1 18W
Markham I. **12** 84 0N 0 45W
Markham L. **153** 62 30N 102 35W
Markham Mts. **13** 83 0 S 164 0 E
Markham, R. **135** 6 41 S 147 2 E
Marki **54** 52 20N 21 2 E
Markinch **35** 56 12N 3 9W
Markleeville **163** 38 42N 119 47W
Markoupoulon **69** 37 53N 23 57 E
Markovac **66** 44 14N 21 7 E
Markovo **77** 64 40N 169 40 E
Markoye **121** 14 39N 0 2 E
Marks **81** 51 45N 46 50 E
Marks Tey **29** 51 53N 0 48 E
Marksville **159** 31 10N 92 2W
Markt Schwaben **49** 48 14N 11 49 E
Marktredwitz **49** 50 1N 12 2 E
Marlboro, Can. **152** 53 30N 116 50W
Marlboro, U.S.A. **162** 42 19N 71 33W
Marlboro, N.Y., U.S.A. **162** 41 36N 73 58W
Marlborough, Austral. **138** 22 46 S 149 52 E
Marlborough, U.K. **28** 51 26N 1 44W
Marlborough □ **143** 41 45 S 173 33 E
Marlborough Downs **28** 51 25N 1 55W
Marle **43** 49 43N 3 47 E
Marlin **159** 31 25N 96 50W
Marlow, Austral. **141** 35 17 S 149 55 E
Marlow, Ger. **48** 54 8N 12 34 E
Marlow, U.K. **29** 51 34N 0 47W
Marlow, U.S.A. **159** 34 40N 97 58W
Marly-le-Grand **50** 46 47N 7 10 E
Marmagao **97** 15 25N 73 56 E
Marmande **44** 44 30N 0 10 E
Marmara denizi **92** 40 45N 28 15 E
Marmara, I. **82** 40 35N 27 38 E
Marmara, Sea of = Marmara denizi **92** 40 45N 28 15 E
Marmaris **92** 36 50N 28 14 E
Marmarth **158** 46 21N 103 52W
Marmion L. **150** 48 55N 91 30W
Marmion Mt. **137** 29 16 S 119 50 E
Marmolada, Mte. **63** 46 25N 11 55 E
Marmolejo **57** 38 3N 4 13W
Marmora **150** 44 28N 77 41W
Marnay **43** 47 20N 5 48 E
Marne **48** 53 57N 9 1 E
Marne □ **43** 49 0N 4 10 E
Marne, R. **43** 48 53N 4 25 E
Marnhull **28** 50 58N 2 20W
Maro **124** 8 30N 19 0 E
Maroa **174** 2 43N 67 33W
Maroala **129** 15 23 S 47 59 E
Maroantsetra **129** 15 26 S 49 44 E
Marocco ■ **129** 32 0N 5 50W
Maromandia **129** 14 13 S 48 5 E
Maroni, R. **175** 4 0N 52 0W
Marónia **68** 40 53N 25 24 E
Maroochydore **139** 26 29 S 153 5 E
Maroona **140** 37 27 S 142 54 E
Maros, R. **53** 46 25N 20 20 E
Marosakoa **129** 15 26 S 46 38 E

Marostica Maya, R

Marostica	63	45 44N	11 40E
Maroua	121	10 40N	14 20E
Marovoay	129	16 6S	46 39E
Marple	32	53 23N	2 5W
Marquard	128	28 40S	27 28E
Marqueira	57	38 41N	9 9W
Marquesas Is. = Marquises	131	9 30S	140 0W
Marquette	156	46 30N	87 21W
Marquise	43	50 50N	1 40E
Marquises, Is.	131	9 30S	140 0W
Marra	139	31 12S	144 10E
Marra, Gebet	123	7 20N	27 35E
Marradi	63	44 5N	11 37E
Marrakech	118	31 40N	8 0W
Marrat	92	25 0N	45 35E
Marrawah	138	40 55S	144 42E
Marrecas, Serra das	170	9 0S	41 0W
Marree	139	29 39S	138 1E
Marrimane	129	22 58S	33 34E
Marromeu	125	18 40S	36 25E
Marroqui, Punta	56	36 0N	5 37W
Marrowie Creek	141	33 23S	145 40E
Marrubane	127	18 0S	37 0E
Marrum	46	53 19N	5 48E
Marrupa	127	13 8S	37 30E
Mars, Le	158	43 0N	96 0W
Marsa Susa (Apollonia)	117	32 52N	21 59E
Marsabit	126	2 18N	38 0E
Marsabit □	126	2 45N	37 45E
Marsala	64	37 48N	12 25E
Marsciano	63	42 54N	12 20E
Marsden	141	33 47N	147 32E
Marsdiep	46	52 58N	4 46E
Marseillan	44	43 23N	3 31E
Marseille	45	43 18N	5 23E
Marseilles = Marseille	45	43 18N	5 23E
Marsh I.	159	29 35N	91 50W
Marshall, Liberia	120	6 8N	10 22W
Marshall, Ark., U.S.A.	159	35 58N	92 40W
Marshall, Mich., U.S.A.	156	42 17N	84 59W
Marshall, Minn., U.S.A.	158	44 25N	95 45W
Marshall, Mo., U.S.A.	158	39 8N	93 15W
Marshall, Tex., U.S.A.	159	32 29N	94 20W
Marshall Is.	130	9 0N	171 0E
Marshall, R.	138	22 59S	136 59E
Marshalltown	158	42 0N	93 0W
Marshfield, U.K.	28	51 27N	2 18W
Marshfield, Mo., U.S.A.	159	37 20N	92 58W
Marshfield, Wis., U.S.A.	158	44 42N	90 10W
Mársico Nuovo	65	40 26N	15 43E
Marske by the sea	33	54 35N	1 0W
Märsta	72	59 37N	17 52E
Marstal	73	54 51N	10 30E
Marston Moor	33	53 58N	1 17W
Marstrand	73	57 53N	11 35E
Mart	159	31 34N	96 51W
Marta, R.	63	42 18N	11 47E
Martaban	98	16 30N	97 35E
Martaban, G. of	98	15 40N	96 30E
Martano	65	40 14N	18 18E
Martapura	102	3 22S	114 56E
Marte	121	12 23N	13 46E
Martebo	73	57 45N	18 30E
Martelange	47	49 49N	5 43E
Martés, Sierra	59	39 20N	1 0W
Marthaguy Creek	141	30 50S	147 45E
Martham	29	52 42N	1 38E
Martha's Vineyard	162	41 25N	70 35W
Martigné Ferchaud	42	47 50N	1 20W
Martigny	50	46 6N	7 3E
Martigues	45	43 24N	5 4E
Martil	118	35 36N	5 15W
Martin, Czech.	53	49 6N	18 48E
Martin, S.D., U.S.A.	158	43 11N	101 45W
Martin, Tenn., U.S.A.	159	36 23N	88 51W
Martin, L.	157	32 45N	85 50W
Martín, R.	58	41 2N	0 43W
Martina	51	46 53N	10 28E
Martina Franca	65	40 42N	17 20E
Martinborough	142	41 14S	175 29E
Martinez	163	38 1N	122 8W
Martinho Campos	171	19 20S	45 13W
Martinique, I.	167	14 40N	61 0W
Martinique Passage	167	15 15N	61 0W
Martínon	69	38 25N	23 15E
Martinópolis	173	22 11S	51 12W
Martins	171	6 5S	37 55W
Martinsberg	52	48 22N	15 9E
Martinsburg	156	39 30N	77 57W
Martinsville, Ind., U.S.A.	156	39 29N	86 23W
Martinsville, Va., U.S.A.	157	36 41N	79 52W
Martley	28	52 14N	2 22W
Martock	28	50 58N	2 47W
Marton	142	40 4S	175 23E
Martorell	58	41 28N	1 56E
Martos	57	37 44N	3 58W
Martre, La, L.	148	63 8N	117 16W
Martre, La, R.	148	63 0N	118 0W
Martuk	84	50 46N	56 31E
Martuni	83	40 9N	45 10E
Maru	121	12 22N	6 22E
Marudi	102	4 10N	114 25E
Maruf	93	31 30N	67 0E
Marugame	110	34 15N	133 55E
Maruggio	65	40 20N	17 33E
Marui	135	4 4S	143 2E
Maruim	170	10 45S	37 5W
Marulan	141	34 43S	150 3E
Marum	46	53 9N	6 16E
Marunga	128	17 20S	20 2E
Marungu, Mts.	126	7 30S	30 0E
Maruoka	111	36 9N	136 16E
Marvejols	44	44 33N	3 19E
Marvine Mt.	161	38 44N	111 40W
Marwar	94	25 43N	73 45E
Mary	76	37 40N	61 50E
Mary Frances L.	153	63 19N	106 13W
Mary Kathleen	138	20 35S	139 48E
Maryborough, Queens., Austral.	139	25 31S	152 37E
Maryborough, Vic., Austral.	140	37 0S	143 44E
Maryets	81	56 17N	49 47E
Maryfield	153	49 50N	101 35W
Marykirk	37	56 47N	2 30W
Maryland □	156	39 10N	76 40W
Maryland Jc.	127	12 45S	30 31E
Maryport	32	54 43N	3 30W
Mary's Harbour	151	52 18N	55 51W
Marystown	151	47 10N	55 10W
Marysvale	161	38 25N	112 17W
Marysville, Can.	152	49 35N	116 0W
Marysville, Calif., U.S.A.	160	39 14N	121 40W
Marysville, Kans., U.S.A.	158	39 50N	96 38W
Marysville, Ohio, U.S.A.	156	40 15N	83 20W
Marytavy	30	50 34N	4 6W
Maryvale	139	28 4S	152 12E
Maryville	157	35 50N	84 0W
Marywell	37	56 35N	2 31W
Marzo, Punta	174	6 50N	77 42W
Marzuq	119	25 53N	14 10E
Masada = Mesada	90	31 20N	35 19E
Masafa	127	13 50S	27 30E
Masai	101	1 29N	103 55E
Masai Steppe	126	4 30S	36 30E
Masaka	126	0 21S	31 45E
Masakali	121	13 2N	12 32E
Masalima, Kepulauan	102	5 10S	116 50E
Masamba	103	2 30S	120 15E
Masan	107	35 11N	128 32E
Masanasa	59	39 25N	0 25W
Masandam, Ras	93	26 30N	56 30E
Masasi	127	10 45S	38 52E
Masasi □	127	10 45S	38 50E
Masaya	166	12 0N	86 7W
Masba	121	10 35N	13 1E
Mascara	118	35 26N	0 6E
Mascota	164	20 30N	104 50W
Masela	103	8 9S	129 51E
Maseme	147	18 46S	25 3E
Maseru	128	29 18S	27 30E
Mashaba	127	20 2S	30 29E
Mashabih	92	25 35N	36 30E
Masham	33	54 15N	1 40W
Mashan	108	23 44N	108 14E
Masherbrum, mt.	95	35 38N	76 18E
Mashhad	93	36 20N	59 35E
Mashi	121	13 0N	7 54E
Mashiki	110	32 51N	130 53E
Mashki Chah	93	29 5N	62 30E
Mashkode	150	47 2N	84 7W
Mashonaland, North, □	127	16 30S	30 0E
Mashonaland, South, □	127	18 0S	31 30E
Mashtagi	83	40 35N	50 0E
Masi	74	69 26N	23 50E
Masi-Manimba	124	4 40S	18 5E
Masindi	126	1 40N	31 43E
Masindi Port	126	1 43N	32 2E
Masirah	91	20 25N	58 50E
Masisea	174	8 35S	74 15W
Masisi	126	1 23S	28 49E
Masjed Solyman	92	31 55N	49 25E
Mask, L.	38	53 36N	9 24W
Maski	97	15 56N	76 46E
Maslen Nos	67	42 18N	27 48E
Maslinica	63	43 24N	16 13E
Masnou	58	41 28N	2 20E
Masoala, C.	129	15 59S	50 13E
Masoarivo	129	19 3S	44 19E
Masohi	103	3 2S	128 15E
Masomeloka	129	20 17S	48 37E
Mason, Nev., U.S.A.	163	38 56N	119 8W
Mason, S.D., U.S.A.	158	45 12N	103 27W
Mason, Tex., U.S.A.	159	30 45N	99 15W
Mason B.	143	46 55S	167 45E
Mason City	160	48 0N	119 0W
Masqat	93	23 37N	58 36E
Massa	62	44 2N	10 7E
Massa Maríttima	62	43 3N	10 52E
Massa, O.	118	30 0N	9 30W
Massachusetts □	162	42 25N	72 0W
Massachusetts B.	162	42 30N	70 0W
Massada	90	33 12N	35 45E
Massafra	65	40 35N	17 8E
Massaguet	124	12 28N	15 26E
Massakory	117	13 0N	15 49E
Massangena	129	21 34S	33 0E
Massapê	170	3 31S	40 19W
Massarosa	62	43 53N	10 17E
Massat	44	42 53N	1 21E
Massava	84	60 40N	62 6E
Massawa = Mitsiwa	123	15 35N	39 25E
Massena	156	44 52N	74 55W
Massenya	117	11 30N	16 25E
Masset	152	54 0N	132 0W
Massiac	44	45 15N	3 11E
Massif Central	44	45 30N	2 21E
Massillon	156	40 47N	81 30W
Massinga	125	23 15S	35 22E
Massingir	129	23 46S	32 4E
Mässlingen	98	62 42N	12 48E
Massman	138	16 25S	145 25E
Masson I.	13	66 10S	93 20E
Mastaba	122	20 52N	39 30E
Mastanli = Momchilgrad	21	41 33N	25 23E
Masterton	142	40 56S	175 39E
Mástikho, Ákra	68	38 10N	26 2E
Mastuj	95	36 20N	72 36E
Mastung	93	29 50N	66 42E
Mastura	122	23 7N	38 52E
Masuda	110	34 40N	131 51E
Masulipatam	96	16 12N	81 12E
Maswa □	126	1 20S	34 0E
Mat, R.	68	41 40N	20 0E
Mata de São João	171	12 31S	38 17W
Matabeleland North □	127	20 0S	28 0E
Matabeleland South □	127	19 0S	29 0E
Mataboor	103	1 41S	138 3E
Matachel, R.	57	38 32N	6 0W
Matachewan	150	47 56N	80 39W
Matad	105	47 12N	115 29E
Matadi	124	5 52S	13 31E
Matador	153	50 49N	107 56W
Matagalpa	166	13 10N	85 40W
Matagami	150	49 45N	77 34W
Matagami, L.	150	49 50N	77 40W
Matagorda	159	28 43N	96 0W
Matagorda, B.	159	28 30N	96 15W
Matagorda I.	159	28 10N	96 40W
Matak, P.	101	3 18N	106 16E
Matakana	141	32 59S	145 54E
Matale	97	7 30N	80 44E
Matam	120	15 34N	13 17W
Matamata	142	37 48S	175 47E
Matameye	121	13 26N	8 28E
Matamoros, Campeche, Mexico	165	25 53N	97 30W
Matamoros, Coahuila, Mexico	164	25 45N	103 1W
Matamoros, Puebla, Mexico	165	18 2N	98 17W
Matamoros, Tamaulipas, Mexico	165	25 50N	97 30W
Matana, D.	103	2 30S	121 25E
Matandu, R.	127	8 35S	39 40E
Matane	151	48 50N	67 33W
Mat'ang, Szechwan, China	108	31 54N	102 55E
Mat'ang, Yunnan, China	108	23 30N	104 4E
Matankari	121	13 46N	4 1E
Matanuska	148	61 38N	149 0W
Matanzá	174	7 22N	73 2W
Matanzas	166	23 0N	81 40W
Matapá, Ákra	69	36 22N	22 27E
Matapedia	151	48 0N	66 59W
Matara	97	5 58N	80 30E
Mataram	102	8 41S	116 10E
Matarani	174	16 50S	72 10W
Mataranka	136	14 55S	133 4E
Mataró	58	41 32N	2 29E
Matarraña, R.	58	40 55N	0 8E
Mataruška Banja	66	43 40N	20 45E
Matata	142	37 54S	176 48E
Matatiele	129	30 20S	28 49E
Mataura	143	46 11S	168 51E
Mataura, R.	143	45 49S	168 44E
Matehuala	164	23 40N	100 50W
Mateira	171	18 54S	50 30W
Mateke Hills	127	21 48S	31 0E
Matélica	63	43 15N	13 0E
Matera	65	40 40N	16 37E
Mátészalka	53	47 58N	22 20E
Matetsi	127	18 12S	26 0E
Mateur	119	37 0N	9 48E
Mateyev Kurgan	83	47 35N	38 47E
Matfors	72	62 21N	17 2E
Matha	44	45 52N	0 20W
Matheson I.	153	51 45N	96 56W
Mathews	162	37 26N	76 19W
Mathias Pass	143	43 7S	171 6E
Mathis	159	28 4N	97 48W
Mathoura	141	35 50S	144 55E
Mathry	31	51 56N	5 6W
Mathura	94	27 30N	77 48E
Mati	103	6 55N	126 15E
Mati, R.	68	41 40N	20 0E
Matías Romero	165	16 53N	95 2W
Matibane	127	14 49S	40 45E
Matien	109	32 55N	116 26E
Matlock	33	53 8N	1 32W
Matmata	119	33 30N	9 59E
Matna	123	13 49N	35 10E
Mato Grosso □	175	14 0S	55 0W
Mato Grosso, Planalto do	174	15 0S	54 0W
Mato Verde	171	15 23S	42 52W
Matochkin Shar	76	73 10N	56 40E
Matong	135	5 36S	151 50E
Matopo Hills	127	20 36S	28 20E
Matopos	127	20 20S	28 29E
Matour	45	46 19N	4 29E
Matozinhos	56	41 11N	8 42W
Matrah	93	23 37N	58 30E
Matrûh	122	31 19N	27 9E
Matsang Tsangpo (Brahmaputra), R.	99	29 25N	88 0E
Matsena	121	13 5N	10 5E
Matsesta	83	43 34N	39 44E
Matsu Tao	109	26 9N	119 56E
Matsubara	111	34 33N	135 34E
Matsudo	111	35 47N	139 54E
Matsue	110	35 25N	133 10E
Matsumae	112	41 26N	140 7E
Matsumoto	111	36 15N	138 0E
Matsusaka	111	34 34N	136 32E
Matsutō	111	36 31N	136 34E
Matsuura	110	33 20N	129 49E
Matsuyama	110	33 45N	132 45E
Mattagami, R.	150	50 43N	81 29W
Mattancheri	97	9 50N	76 15E
Mattawa	150	46 20N	78 45W
Mattawamkeag	151	45 30N	68 30W
Matterhorn, mt.	50	45 58N	7 39E
Mattersburg	53	47 44N	16 24E
Matthew Town	167	20 57N	73 40W
Matthew's Ridge	174	7 37N	60 10W
Mattice	150	49 40N	83 20W
Mattituck	162	40 58N	72 32W
Mattmar	72	63 18N	13 54E
Mattoon	156	39 30N	88 20W
Matua	102	2 58S	110 52E
Matuba	129	24 28S	32 49E
Matucana	174	11 55S	76 15W
Matun	94	33 22N	69 58E
Maturín	174	9 45N	63 11W
Matutina	171	19 13S	45 58W
Matzuzaki	111	34 43N	138 50E
Mau-é-ele	129	24 18S	34 2E
Mau Escarpment	126	0 40S	36 0E
Mau Ranipur	95	25 16N	79 8E
Mauagami, R.	150	49 30N	82 0W
Maubeuge	43	50 17N	3 57E
Maubourguet	44	43 29N	0 1E
Mauchline	34	55 31N	4 23W
Maud	37	57 30N	2 8W
Maud, Pt.	137	23 6S	113 45E
Maude	140	34 29S	144 18E
Maudheim	13	71 5S	11 0W
Maudin Sun	99	16 0N	94 30E
Mauês	174	3 20S	57 45W
Mauganj	99	24 50N	81 55E
Maughold	32	54 18N	4 17W
Maughold Hd.	32	54 18N	4 17W
Maui I.	147	20 45N	156 20E
Maulamyaing	99	16 30N	97 40E
Maule □	172	36 5S	72 30W
Mauleon	44	43 14N	0 54W
Maulvibazar	98	24 29N	91 42E
Maum	38	53 31N	9 35W
Maumee	156	41 35N	83 40W
Maumee, R.	156	41 42N	83 28W
Maumere	103	8 38S	122 13E
Maumturk Mts.	38	53 32N	9 42W
Maun	128	20 0S	23 26E
Mauna Kea, Mt.	147	19 50N	155 28W
Mauna Loa, Mt.	147	19 50N	155 28W
Maunath Bhanjan	95	25 56N	83 33E
Maungaturoto	142	36 6S	174 23E
Maungdow	98	21 14N	94 5E
Maungmagan Is.	99	14 0S	97 48E
Maungmagan Kyunzu	101	14 0N	97 48E
Maupin	160	45 12N	121 9W
Maure-de-Bretagne	42	47 53N	2 0W
Maureen, oilfield	19	58 5N	1 45E
Maurepas L.	159	30 18N	90 35W
Maures, mts.	45	43 15N	6 15E
Mauriac	44	45 13N	2 19E
Maurice L.	137	29 30S	131 0E
Mauriceville	142	40 45S	175 35E
Maurienne	45	45 15N	6 20E
Mauritania ■	116	20 50N	10 0W
Mauritius ■	11	20 0S	57 0E
Mauron	42	48 9N	2 18W
Maurs	44	44 43N	2 12E
Maurthe, R.	43	48 47N	6 9E
Mauston	158	43 48N	90 5W
Mauterndorf	52	47 9N	13 40E
Mauvezin	44	43 44N	0 53E
Mauzé-sur le Mignon	44	46 12N	0 41W
Mavelikara	97	9 14N	76 32E
Mavinga	125	15 50S	20 10E
Mavli	94	24 45N	73 55E
Mavqi'im	90	31 38N	34 32E
Mavrova	68	40 26N	19 32E
Mavuradonha Mts.	127	16 30S	31 30E
Mawa	126	2 45N	26 33E
Mawana	94	29 6N	77 58E
Mawand	94	29 33N	68 38E
Mawer	153	50 46N	106 22W
Mawgan	30	50 4N	5 10W
Mawkmai	98	20 14N	97 50E
Mawlaik	98	23 40N	94 26E
Mawlawkho	98	17 50N	97 38E
Mawson Base	13	67 30N	65 0E
Max	158	47 50N	101 20W
Maxcanú	165	20 40N	90 10W
Maxhamish L.	152	59 50N	123 17W
Maxixe	129	23 54S	35 17E
Maxwellheugh	35	55 35N	2 23W
Maxwelltown	142	39 51S	174 49E
Maxwelton, Queens., Austral.	138	15 45S	142 30E
Maxwelton, Queens., Austral.	138	20 43S	142 41E
May Downs	138	22 38S	148 55E
May, I. of	35	56 11N	2 32W
May Nefalis	123	15 0N	38 12E
May Pen	166	17 58N	77 15W
May River	135	4 19S	141 58E
Maya	58	43 12N	1 29W
Maya Gudo, Mt.	123	7 30N	37 8E
Maya Mts.	165	16 30N	89 0W
Maya, R.	77	58 20N	135 0E

Mayaguana Island Menglien

Mayaguana Island 167 21 30N 72 44W
Mayagüez 147 18 12N 67 9W
Mayahi 121 13 58N 7 40E
Mayals 58 41 22N 0 30E
Mayang 108 27 53N 109 48E
Mayanup 137 33 58S 116 25E
Mayapán 165 20 38N 89 27W
Mayarf 167 20 40N 75 39W
Mayarí 167 20 40N 75 41W
Mayavaram = Mayuram 97 11 3N 79 42E
Maybell 160 40 30N 108 4W
Maybole 34 55 21N 4 41W
Maychew 123 12 50N 39 42E
Maydena 138 42 45S 146 39E
Maydos 68 40 13N 26 20E
Mayen 49 50 18N 7 10E
Mayenne 42 48 20N 0 38W
Mayenne □ 42 48 10N 0 40W
Mayer 161 34 28N 112 17W
Mayerthorpe 152 53 57N 115 8W
Mayfield, Derby., U.K. 33 53 1N 1 47W
Mayfield, E. Sussex, U.K. 29 51 1N 0 17E
Mayfield, Ky., U.S.A. 157 36 45N 88 40W
Mayfield, N.Y., U.S.A. 162 43 6N 74 16W
Mayhill 161 32 58N 105 30W
Maykop 83 44 35N 40 25E
Mayli-Say 85 41 17N 72 24E
Maymyo 100 22 2N 96 28E
Maynard 162 42 30N 71 33W
Maynard Hills 137 28 35S 119 50E
Mayne, Le, L. 151 57 5N 68 30W
Mayne, R. 138 23 40S 142 10E
Maynooth, Can. 150 45 14N 77 56W
Maynooth, Ireland 38 53 22N 6 38W
Mayo 147 63 38N 135 57W
Mayo □ 139 53 47N 9 7W
Mayo Bridge 38 54 11N 6 13W
Mayo L. 147 63 45N 135 0W
Mayo, R. 164 26 45N 109 47W
Mayon, Mt. 103 13 15N 123 42E
Mayor I. 142 37 16S 176 17E
Mayorga 56 42 10N 5 16W
Mays Landing 162 39 27N 74 44W
Mayskiy 83 43 47N 43 59E
Mayson L. 153 57 55N 107 10W
Maysville 156 38 43N 84 16W
Mayu, I. 103 1 30N 126 30E
Mayuram 97 11 3N 79 42E
Mayville 158 47 30N 97 23W
Mayya 77 61 44N 130 18E
Mazabuka 127 15 52S 27 44E
Mazagán = El Jadida 118 33 11N 8 17W
Mazagão 175 0 20S 51 50W
Mazama 152 49 43N 120 8W
Mazamet 44 43 30N 2 20E
Mazán 174 3 15S 73 0W
Mazapil 164 24 38N 101 34W
Mazar-i-Sharif 93 36 41N 67 0E
Mazar, O. 118 32 0N 1 38E
Mazara del Vallo 64 37 40N 12 34E
Mazarredo 176 47 10S 66 50W
Mazarrón 59 37 38N 1 19W
Mazarrón, Golfo de 59 37 27N 1 19W
Mazaruni, R. 174 6 15N 60 0W
Mazatán 164 29 0N 110 8W
Mazatenango 166 14 35N 91 30W
Mazatlán 164 23 10N 106 30W
Māzhān 93 32 30N 59 0E
Mazheikyai 80 56 20N 22 20E
Mazinān 93 36 25N 56 48E
Mazoe 127 17 28S 30 58E
Mazoe R. 125 16 45S 32 30E
Mazoi 127 16 42S 33 7E
Mazrûb 123 14 0N 29 20E
Mazurian Lakes = Mazurski, Pojezierze 54 53 50N 21 0E
Mazurski, Pojezierze 54 53 50N 21 0E
Mazzarino 65 37 19N 14 12E
Mbaba 120 14 59N 16 44W
Mbabane 129 26 18S 31 6E
Mbagne 120 16 6N 14 47W
M'bahiakro 120 7 33N 4 19W
M'Baiki 124 3 53N 18 1E
Mbala 127 8 46S 31 17E
Mbale 126 1 8N 34 12E
Mbalmayo 121 3 33N 11 33E
Mbamba Bay 127 11 13S 34 49E
Mbandaka 124 0 1S 18 18E
Mbanga 121 4 30N 9 33E
Mbanza Congo 124 6 18S 14 16E
Mbanza Ngungu 124 5 12S 14 53E
Mbarara 126 0 35S 30 25E
Mbatto 120 6 28N 4 22W
Mbenkuru, R. 127 9 25S 39 50E
Mberubu 121 6 10N 7 38E
Mbesuma 127 10 0S 32 2E
Mbeya 127 8 54S 33 29E
Mbeya □ 126 8 15S 33 30E
Mbia 123 6 15N 29 18E
Mbimbi 127 13 25S 23 2E
Mbinga 127 10 50S 35 0E
Mbinga □ 127 10 50S 35 0E
Mbini □ 124 1 30N 10 0E
Mbiti 123 5 42N 28 3E
Mboki 123 5 19N 25 58E
Mboro 120 15 9N 16 54W
Mboune 120 14 42N 13 34W
Mbour 120 14 22N 16 54W
Mbout 120 16 1N 12 38W
Mbozi □ 127 9 0S 32 50E
Mbuji-Mayi 126 6 9S 23 40E
Mbulu 124 3 45S 35 30E
Mbulu □ 126 3 52S 35 33E
Mbumbi 128 18 26S 19 59E
Mburucuyá 172 28 1S 58 14W
M'chounech 119 34 57N 6 1E
M'Clure Str., Can. 10 75 0N 118 0W
M'Clure Str., Can. 12 74 0N 120 0W
Mdennah 118 24 37N 6 0W
Mead L. 161 36 1N 114 44W
Meade, Can. 150 49 26N 83 51W
Meade, U.S.A. 159 37 18N 100 25W
Meadow 137 26 35S 114 40E
Meadow Lake 153 54 10N 108 26W
Meadow Lake Prov. Park 153 54 27N 109 0W
Meadville 156 41 39N 80 9W
Meaford 150 44 36N 80 35W
Mealfuarvonie, Mt. 37 57 15N 4 34W
Mealhada 56 40 22N 8 27W
Mealsgate 32 54 46N 3 14W
Mealy Mts. 151 53 10N 60 0W
Meander, R. = Menderes, Büyük 92 37 45N 27 40E
Meander River 152 59 2N 117 42W
Meare's, C. 160 45 37N 124 0W
Mearim, R. 170 3 4S 44 35W
Mearns, Howe of the 37 56 52N 2 26W
Measham 28 52 43N 1 30W
Meath □ 38 53 32N 6 40W
Meath Park 153 53 27N 105 22W
Meatian 140 35 34S 143 21E
Meaulne 44 46 36N 2 28E
Meaux 43 48 58N 2 50E
Mecanhelas 127 15 12S 35 54E
Mecca 163 33 37N 116 3W
Mecca = Makkah 122 21 30N 39 54E
Mechanicsburg 162 40 12N 77 0W
Mechanicville 162 42 54N 73 41W
Mechara 123 8 36N 40 20E
Mechelen, Anvers, Belg. 47 51 2N 4 29E
Mechelen, Limbourg, Belg. 47 50 58N 5 41E
Méchéria 118 33 35N 0 18W
Mechernich 48 50 35N 6 39E
Mechetinskaya 83 46 45N 40 32E
Mecidiye 68 40 38N 26 32E
Mecitözü 82 40 32N 35 25E
Mecklenburg B. 48 54 20N 11 40E
Meconta 127 14 59S 39 50E
Meda 56 40 57N 7 18W
Meda P.O. 136 17 22S 123 59E
Meda, R. 136 17 20S 124 30E
Medaguine 118 33 41N 3 26E
Medak 96 18 1N 78 15E
Medan 102 3 40N 98 38E
Medanosa, Pta. 176 48 0S 66 0W
Medawachchiya 97 8 30N 80 30E
Meddouza, cap 118 32 33N 9 9W
Médéa 118 36 12N 2 50E
Mededa 66 43 44N 19 15E
Medeiros Neto 171 17 20S 40 14W
Medel, Pic 51 46 37N 8 55E
Medellín 174 6 15N 75 35W
Medemblik 46 52 46N 5 8E
Meder 123 14 42N 40 44E
Mederdra 120 17 0N 15 38W
Medford, Oreg., U.S.A. 160 42 20N 122 52W
Medford, Wis., U.S.A. 158 45 9N 90 21W
Medford Lakes 162 39 52N 74 48W
Medgidia 70 44 15N 28 19E
Medi 123 5 4N 30 42E
Media 162 39 55N 75 23W
Media Agua 172 31 58S 68 25W
Media Luna 172 34 45S 66 44W
Mediaş 70 46 9N 24 22E
Medical Lake 160 47 41N 117 42W
Medicina 63 44 29N 11 38E
Medicine Bow 160 41 56N 106 11W
Medicine Hat 153 50 0N 110 45W
Medicine Lake 158 48 30N 104 30W
Medicine Lodge 159 37 20N 98 37W
Medina, Brazil 171 16 15S 41 29W
Medina, Colomb. 174 4 30N 73 21W
Medina, N.D., U.S.A. 158 46 57N 99 20W
Medina, N.Y., U.S.A. 156 43 15N 78 27W
Medina, Ohio, U.S.A. 156 41 9N 81 50W
Medina = Al Madīnah 92 24 35N 39 52E
Medina de Ríoseco 56 41 53N 5 3W
Medina del Campo 56 41 18N 4 55W
Medina L. 159 29 35N 98 58W
Medina, R. 159 29 10N 98 20W
Medina-Sidonia 57 36 28N 5 57W
Medinaceli 58 41 12N 2 30W
Mediterranean Sea 60 35 0N 15 0E
Medjerda, O. 119 36 35N 8 30E
Medkovets 67 43 37N 23 10E
Medley 153 54 25N 110 16W
Mednogorsk 84 51 24N 57 37E
Médoc 44 45 10N 0 56W
Medstead, Can. 153 53 19N 108 5W
Medstead, U.K. 28 51 7N 1 4W
Medulin 63 44 49N 13 55E
Medveda 66 42 50N 21 32E
Medveditsa, R. 81 50 30N 44 0E
Medvedok 81 57 20N 50 1E
Medvezhi, Ostrava 77 71 0N 161 0E
Medvezhyegorsk 78 63 0N 34 25E
Medway, R. 29 51 12N 0 23E
Medyn 81 54 59N 35 56E
Medzev 53 48 43N 20 55E
Medzilaborce 53 49 17N 21 52E
Meeandh 108 27 26S 153 6E
Meeberrie 137 26 57S 116 0E
Meekatharra 137 26 32S 118 29E
Meeker 160 40 1N 107 58W
Meelpaeg L. 151 48 18N 56 35W
Meeniyan 141 38 35S 146 0E
Meer 47 51 27N 4 45E
Meerane 48 50 51N 12 30E
Meerbeke 47 50 50N 4 3E
Meerle 47 51 29N 4 48E
Meerssen 47 50 53N 5 50E
Meerut 94 29 1N 77 50E
Meeteetsa 160 44 10N 108 56W
Meeuwen 47 51 6N 5 31E
Mega 123 3 57N 38 30E
Megálo Khorío 69 36 27N 27 24E
Megálo Petalí, I. 69 38 0N 24 15E
Megalópolis 69 37 25N 22 7E
Meganísi, I. 69 38 39N 20 48E
Mégantic 151 45 36N 70 56W
Mégara 69 37 58N 23 22E
Megarine 119 33 14N 6 2E
Megdhova, R. 69 39 10N 21 45E
Megen 46 51 49N 5 34E
Mégève 45 45 51N 6 37E
Meghalaya □ 98 25 50N 91 0E
Meghalayap 99 25 40N 89 55E
Meghezez, Mt. 123 9 18N 39 26E
Meghna, R. 98 23 45N 90 40E
Megiddo 90 32 36N 35 11E
Mégiscane, L. 150 48 35N 75 55W
Megiste 61 36 8N 29 34E
Mehadia 70 44 56N 22 23E
Mehaigne, R. 47 50 32N 5 13E
Mehaïguene, O. 118 32 20N 2 45E
Meharry, Mt. 132 22 59S 118 35E
Mehedinti □ 70 44 40N 22 45E
Meheisa 122 19 38N 32 57E
Mehndawal 95 26 58N 83 5E
Mehsana 94 23 39N 72 26E
Mehun-sur-Yèvre 43 47 10N 2 13E
Mei Chiang, R. 109 24 24N 116 35E
Meia Ponte, R. 171 18 32S 49 36W
Meichuan 109 30 9N 115 33E
Meidrim 31 51 51N 4 3W
Meiganga 124 6 20N 14 10E
Meigh 38 54 8N 6 22W
Meihsien, Kwangtung, China 109 24 18N 116 7E
Meihsien, Shensi, China 106 34 16N 107 42E
Meijel 47 51 21N 5 53E
Meiktila 98 21 0N 96 0E
Meilen 51 47 16N 8 39E
Meiningen 48 50 32N 10 25E
Meio, R. 171 13 36S 49 7W
Meira, Sierra de 56 43 15N 7 15W
Meiringen 50 46 43N 8 12E
Meishan 108 30 3N 103 51E
Meissen 48 51 10N 13 29E
Meit'an 108 27 48N 107 28E
Meithalun 90 32 21N 35 16E
Méjean 44 44 15N 3 30E
Mejillones 172 23 10S 70 30W
Meka 137 27 25S 116 48E
Mekambo 124 1 2N 14 5E
Mekdela 123 11 24N 39 10E
Mekhtar 93 30 30N 69 15E
Meklong = Samut Songkhram 101 13 24N 100 1E
Meknès 118 33 57N 5 33W
Meko 121 7 27N 2 52E
Mekong, R. 101 18 0N 104 15E
Mekongga 103 3 50S 121 30E
Mekoryok 147 60 20N 166 20W
Melagiri Hills 97 12 20N 77 30E
Melah, Sebkhet el 118 29 20N 1 30W
Melaka 101 2 15N 102 15E
Melaka □ 101 2 20N 102 15E
Melalap 102 5 10N 116 5E
Mélambes 69 35 8N 24 40E
Melanesia 130 4 0S 155 0E
Melapalaiyam 97 8 39N 77 44E
Melbost 36 58 12N 6 20W
Melbourn 29 52 5N 0 1E
Melbourne, Austral. 141 37 50S 145 0E
Melbourne, U.K. 28 52 50N 1 25W
Melbourne, U.S.A. 157 28 13N 80 14W
Melcésine 62 45 46N 10 48E
Melchor Múzquiz 164 27 50N 101 40W
Melchor Ocampo (San Pedro Ocampo) 164 24 52N 101 40W
Mèldola 63 44 7N 12 3E
Meldorf 48 54 5N 9 5E
Mêle-sur-Sarthe, Le 42 48 31N 0 22E
Melegnano 62 45 21N 9 20E
Melekess = Dimitrovgrad 81 54 25N 49 33E
Melenci 66 45 32N 20 20E
Melenki 81 55 20N 41 37E
Meleuz 84 52 58N 55 55E
Melfi, Chad 117 11 0N 17 59E
Melfi, Italy 65 41 0N 15 40E
Melfort, Can. 153 52 50N 104 37W
Melfort, Rhod. 127 18 0S 31 25E
Melfort, Loch 34 56 13N 5 33W
Melgaço 56 42 7N 8 15W
Melgar de Fernamental 56 42 27N 4 17W
Melhus 71 63 17N 10 18E
Melick 47 51 10N 6 1E
Melide 51 45 57N 8 57E
Meligalá 69 37 15N 21 59E
Melilla 118 35 21N 2 57W
Melilot 42 31 22N 34 37E
Melipilla 172 33 42S 71 15W
Mélissa Óros 69 37 32N 26 4E
Melita 153 49 15N 101 5W
Mélito di Porto Salvo 65 37 55N 15 47E
Melitopol 82 46 50N 35 22E
Melk 52 48 13N 15 20E
Melksham 28 51 22N 2 9W
Mellan-Fryken 72 59 45N 13 10E
Mellansel 74 63 25N 18 17E
Melle, Belg. 47 51 0N 3 49E
Melle, France 44 46 14N 0 10W
Melle, Ger. 48 52 12N 8 20E
Mellègue, O. 119 36 32N 8 51E
Mellen 158 46 19N 90 36W
Mellerud 73 58 41N 12 28E
Mellette 158 45 11N 98 29W
Mellid 56 42 55N 8 1W
Mellish Reef 133 17 25S 155 50E
Mellit 123 14 15N 25 40E
Mellon Charles 36 57 52N 5 37W
Melmerby 32 54 44N 2 35W
Melnik 67 40 58N 23 25E
Mělník 52 50 22N 14 23E
Melo 173 32 20S 54 10W
Melolo 103 9 53S 120 40E
Melones Res. 163 37 57N 120 31W
Melouprey 100 13 48N 105 16E
Melovoye 83 49 25N 40 5E
Melrhir, Chott 119 34 25N 6 24E
Melrose, N.S.W., Austral. 141 32 42S 146 57E
Melrose, W. Australia, Austral. 137 27 50S 121 15E
Melrose, U.K. 35 55 35N 2 44W
Melrose, U.S.A. 159 34 27N 103 33W
Mels 51 47 3N 9 25E
Melsele 47 51 13N 4 17E
Melsonby 33 54 28N 1 41W
Melstone 160 46 45N 108 0W
Melsungen 48 51 8N 9 34E
Melton 29 52 51N 1 1E
Melton Constable 29 52 52N 1 1E
Melton Mowbray 29 52 46N 0 52W
Melun 43 48 32N 2 39E
Melunga 128 17 15S 16 22E
Melur 97 10 2N 78 23E
Melut 123 10 30N 32 20E
Melvaig 36 57 48N 5 49W
Melvich 37 58 33N 3 55W
Melville 153 50 55N 102 50W
Melville B. 138 12 0S 136 45E
Melville, C. 138 14 11S 144 30E
Melville I., Austral. 136 11 30S 131 0E
Melville I., Can. 12 75 30N 111 0W
Melville, L., Newf., Can. 151 53 45N 59 40W
Melville, L., Newf., Can. 151 59 30N 53 40W
Melville Pen. 149 68 0N 84 0W
Melvin L. 38 54 26N 8 10W
Melvin, R. 152 59 11N 117 31W
Mélykút 53 46 11N 19 25E
Memaliaj 68 40 25N 19 58E
Memba 127 14 11S 40 30E
Memboro 103 9 30S 119 30E
Membrilla 59 38 59N 3 21W
Memel 129 27 38S 29 36E
Memel = Klaipeda 80 55 43N 21 10E
Memmingen 49 47 59N 10 12E
Memphis, Tenn., U.S.A. 159 35 7N 90 0W
Memphis, Tex., U.S.A. 159 34 45N 100 30W
Mena 159 34 40N 94 15W
Menai Bridge 31 53 14N 4 11W
Menai Strait 31 53 7N 4 20W
Ménaka 121 15 59N 2 18E
Menaldum 46 53 13N 5 40E
Menamurtee 140 31 25S 143 11E
Menarandra, R. 129 25 0S 44 50E
Menard 159 30 57N 99 58W
Menasha 156 44 13N 88 27W
Menate 102 0 12S 112 47E
Mendawai, R. 102 1 30S 113 0E
Mende 44 44 31N 3 30E
Mendebo Mts. 123 7 0N 39 22E
Mendenhall, C. 147 59 44N 166 10W
Menderes, R. 92 37 25N 28 45E
Mendez 165 25 7N 98 34W
Mendhar 95 33 35N 74 10E
Mendi, Ethiopia 123 9 47N 35 4E
Mendi, P.N.G. 135 6 11S 143 47E
Mendip Hills 28 51 17N 2 40W
Mendlesham 29 52 15N 1 4E
Mendocino 160 39 26N 123 50W
Mendong Gompa 95 31 16N 85 11E
Mendota, Calif., U.S.A. 163 36 46N 120 24W
Mendota, Ill., U.S.A. 158 41 35N 89 5W
Mendoza 172 32 50S 68 52W
Mendoza □ 172 33 0S 69 0W
Mendrisio 51 45 52N 8 59E
Mene Grande 174 9 49N 70 56W
Menemen 92 38 18N 27 10E
Menen 47 50 47N 3 7E
Menfi 64 37 36N 12 57E
Meng-pan 99 23 5N 100 19E
Meng-so 101 22 33N 99 31E
Meng-wang 99 22 17N 100 32E
Meng Wang 101 22 18N 100 31E
Mengch'eng 106 33 17N 116 34E
Mengeš 63 46 24N 14 35E
Menggala 102 4 20S 105 15E
Menghai 108 21 58N 100 28E
Menghsien 106 34 54N 112 47E
Mengíbar 57 37 58N 3 48W
Mengla 108 21 28N 101 35E
Menglien 108 22 21N 99 36E

Mengoub Mikołajki

Mengoub 118 29 49N 5 26W
Mengpolo 108 24 24N 99 14E
Mengshan 109 24 12N 110 31E
Mengting 108 23 33N 98 5E
Mengtz = Mengtzu 108 23 25N 103 20E
Mengtzu 108 23 25N 103 20E
Mengyin 107 35 40N 117 55E
Menihek L. 151 54 0N 67 0W
Menin 47 50 47N 3 7E
Menindee 140 32 20N 142 25E
Menindee, L. 140 32 20N 142 25E
Meningie 140 35 43S 139 20E
Menkúng 99 28 38N 98 24E
Menlo Park 163 37 27N 122 12W
Menominee 156 45 9N 87 39W
Menominee, R. 156 45 30N 87 50W
Menomonie 158 44 50N 91 54W
Menor, Mar 59 37 43N 0 48W
Menorca, I. 58 40 0N 4 0E
Mentawai, Kepulauan 102 2 0S 99 0E
Mentekab 101 3 29N 102 21E
Menton 45 43 50N 7 29E
Menyamya 135 7 10S 145 59E
Menzel-Bourguiba 119 39 9N 9 49E
Menzel Chaker 119 35 0N 10 26E
Menzelinsk 84 55 53N 53 1E
Menzies 137 29 40S 120 58E
Me'ona (Tarshiha) 90 33 1N 35 15E
Meoqui 164 28 17N 105 29W
Mepaco 127 15 57S 30 48E
Meppel 47 52 42N 6 12E
Meppen 48 52 41N 7 20E
Mequinenza 58 41 22N 0 17E
Mer Rouge 159 32 47N 91 48W
Merabéllou, Kólpos 69 35 10N 25 50E
Merai 135 4 52S 152 19E
Merak 103 5 55S 106 1E
Meramangye, L. 137 28 25S 132 13E
Merano (Meran) 63 46 40N 11 10E
Merate 62 45 42N 9 23E
Merauke 103 8 29S 140 24E
Merbabu, Mt. 103 7 30S 110 40E
Merbein 140 34 10S 142 2E
Merca 91 1 48N 44 50E
Mercadal 58 39 59N 4 5E
Mercara 97 12 30N 75 45E
Mercato Saraceno 63 43 57N 12 11E
Merced 163 37 18N 120 30W
Merced Pk. 163 37 36N 119 24W
Merced, R. 163 37 21N 120 58W
Mercedes, Buenos Aires, Argent. 172 34 40S 59 30W
Mercedes, Corrientes, Argent. 172 29 10S 58 5W
Mercedes, San Luis, Argent. 172 33 5S 65 21W
Mercedes, Uruguay 172 33 12S 58 0W
Merceditas 172 28 20S 70 35W
Mercer 142 37 16S 175 5E
Merchtem 47 50 58N 4 14E
Mercy C. 149 65 0N 62 30W
Merdrignac 42 48 11N 2 27W
Mere, Belg. 47 50 55N 3 58E
Mere, U.K. 28 51 5N 2 16W
Meredith C. 176 52 15S 60 40W
Meredith, L. 159 35 30N 101 35W
Merei 70 45 7N 26 43E
Merelbeke 47 51 0N 3 45E
Méréville 43 48 20N 2 5E
Merewa 123 7 40N 36 54E
Mergenevo 84 49 56N 51 18E
Mergenevskiy 83 49 59N 51 15E
Mergui 101 12 30N 98 35E
Mergui Arch. = Myeik Kyunzu 101 11 30N 97 30E
Meribah 140 34 43S 140 51E
Mérida, Mexico 165 20 50N 89 40W
Mérida, Spain 57 38 55N 6 25W
Mérida, Venez. 174 8 36N 71 8W
Mérida □ 174 8 30N 71 10W
Mérida, Cord. de 174 9 0N 71 0W
Meriden, U.K. 28 52 27N 1 36W
Meriden, U.S.A. 162 41 33N 72 47W
Meridian, Idaho, U.S.A. 160 43 41N 116 25W
Meridian, Miss., U.S.A. 157 32 20N 88 42W
Meridian, Tex., U.S.A. 159 31 55N 97 37W
Mering 49 48 15N 11 0E
Merioneth (□) 26 52 49N 3 55W
Merirumã 175 1 15N 54 50W
Merke 85 42 52N 73 11E
Merkel 159 32 30N 100 0W
Merkem 47 50 57N 2 51E
Merksem 47 51 16N 4 25E
Merksplas 47 51 22N 4 52E
Merlebach 43 49 5N 6 52E
Merlerault, Le 42 48 41N 0 16E
Mermaid Mt. 108 27 29S 152 49E
Mermaid Reef 136 17 6S 119 36E
Mern 73 55 3N 12 3E
Merowe 122 18 29N 31 46E
Merredin 137 31 28S 118 18E
Merrick, Mt. 34 55 8N 4 30W
Merrill, Oregon, U.S.A. 160 42 2N 121 37W
Merrill, Wis., U.S.A. 158 45 11N 89 41W
Merrimack, R. 162 42 49N 70 49W
Merritt 152 50 10N 120 45W
Merriwa 141 32 6S 150 22E
Merriwagga 141 33 47S 145 43E
Merroe 137 27 53S 117 50E
Merry I. 150 55 29N 77 31W
Merrygoen 141 31 51S 149 12E
Merryville 159 30 47N 93 31W
Mersa Fatma 123 14 57N 40 17E
Mersch 47 49 44N 6 7E
Merse, dist. 35 55 40N 2 30W
Mersea I. 29 51 48N 0 55E
Merseburg 48 51 20N 12 0E
Mersey, R. 32 53 20N 2 56W
Merseyside □ 32 53 25N 2 55W
Mersin 92 36 51N 34 36E
Mersing 101 2 25N 103 50E
Merta 94 26 39N 74 4E
Mertert 47 49 43N 6 29E
Merthyr Tydfil 31 51 45N 3 23W
Mértola 57 37 40N 7 40E
Merton 29 51 25N 0 13W
Mertzig 47 49 51N 6 1E
Mertzon 159 31 17N 100 48W
Méru 43 49 13N 2 8E
Meru 126 0 3N 37 40E
Meru □ 126 0 3N 37 46E
Meru, mt. 126 3 15S 36 46E
Merville 43 50 38N 2 38E
Méry-sur-Seine 43 48 31N 3 54E
Merzifon 82 40 53N 35 32E
Merzig 49 49 26N 6 37E
Merzouga, Erg Tin 119 24 0N 11 4E
Mesa 161 33 20N 111 56W
Mesa, La, Colomb. 174 4 38N 74 28W
Mesa, La, Calif., U.S.A. 163 32 48N 117 5W
Mesa, La, N. Mex., U.S.A. 161 32 6N 106 48W
Mesach Mellet 119 24 30N 11 30E
Mesada 90 31 20N 35 19E
Mesagne 65 40 34N 17 48E
Mesaras, Kólpos 69 35 6N 24 47E
Meschede 48 51 20N 8 17E
Mesfinto 123 13 30N 37 22E
Mesgouez, L. 150 51 20N 75 0W
Meshchovsk 80 54 22N 35 17E
Meshed = Mashhad 93 36 20N 59 35E
Meshoppen 162 41 36N 76 3W
Mesick 156 44 24N 85 42W
Mesilinka, R. 152 56 6N 124 30W
Mesilla 161 32 20N 107 0W
Meslay-du-Maine 42 47 58N 0 33W
Mesocco 51 46 23N 9 12E
Mesolóngion 69 38 27N 21 28E
Mesopotamia, reg. 92 33 30N 44 0E
Mesoraca 65 39 5N 16 47E
Mésou Volímais 69 37 53N 27 35E
Mess Cr. 152 57 55N 131 14W
Messac 42 47 49N 1 50W
Messad 118 34 8N 3 30E
Méssaména 121 3 48N 12 49E
Messancy 47 49 36N 5 49E
Messeix 44 45 37N 2 33E
Messina, Italy 65 38 10N 15 32E
Messina, S. Afr. 129 22 20S 30 12E
Messina, Str. di 65 38 5N 15 35E
Messíni 69 37 4N 22 1E
Messínia □ 69 37 10N 22 0E
Messiniakós, Kólpos 69 36 45N 22 5E
Mestà, Ákra 69 38 16N 25 53E
Mesta, R. 67 41 30N 24 0E
Mestanza 57 38 35N 4 4W
Město Teplá 52 49 59N 12 52E
Mestre 63 45 30N 12 13E
Mestre, Espigão 171 12 30S 46 10W
Městys Zelezná Ruda 52 49 8N 13 15E
Meta □ 174 3 30N 73 0W
Meta, R. 174 6 20N 68 5W
Metagama 150 47 0N 81 55W
Metaline Falls 160 48 52N 117 22W
Metán 172 25 30S 65 0W
Metauro, R. 63 43 45N 12 59E
Metchosin 152 48 15N 123 37W
Metehara 123 8 58N 39 57E
Metema 123 12 56N 36 13E
Metengobalame 127 14 49S 34 30E
Méthana 69 37 35N 23 23E
Metheringham 33 53 9N 0 22W
Methlick 37 57 26N 2 13W
Methóni 69 36 49N 21 42E
Methuen, Mt. 136 15 54S 124 44E
Methven, N.Z. 143 43 38S 171 40E
Methven, U.K. 35 56 25N 3 35W
Methwin, Mt. 137 25 3S 120 45E
Methwold 29 52 30N 0 33E
Methy L. 153 56 28N 109 30W
Metil 125 16 24S 39 0E
Metkovets 67 43 37N 23 10E
Metkovió 66 43 6N 17 39E
Metlakatla 147 55 10N 131 33W
Metlaoui 119 34 24N 8 24E
Metlika 63 45 40N 15 20E
Metowra 139 25 3S 146 15E
Metropolis 159 37 10N 88 47W
Métsovon 68 39 48N 21 12E
Mettet 47 50 19N 4 41E
Mettuppalaiyam 97 11 18N 76 59E
Mettur 97 11 48N 77 47E
Mettur Dam 95 11 45N 77 45E
Metulla 90 33 17N 35 34E
Metz 43 49 8N 6 10E
Meulaboh 102 4 11N 96 3E
Meulan 43 49 0N 1 52E
Meung-sur-Loire 43 47 50N 1 40E
Meureudu 102 5 19N 96 10E
Meurthe-et-Moselle □ 43 48 52N 6 0E
Meuse □ 43 49 8N 5 25E
Meuse, R. 47 50 45N 5 41E
Meuselwitz 48 51 3N 12 18E
Mevagissey 30 50 16N 4 48W
Mevagissey Bay 30 50 15N 4 40W
Mexborough 33 53 29N 1 18W
Mexia 159 31 38N 96 32W
Mexiana, I. 170 0 0 49 30W
Mexicali 164 32 40N 115 30W
México 165 19 20N 99 10W
Mexico, Me., U.S.A. 156 44 35N 70 30W
Mexico, Mo., U.S.A. 158 39 10N 91 55W
Mexico, N.Y., U.S.A. 162 43 28N 76 18W
Mexico ■ 164 20 0N 100 0W
México □ 164 19 20N 99 10W
Mexico, G. of 165 25 0N 90 0W
Mey 37 58 38N 3 14W
Meyenburg 48 53 19N 12 15E
Meymac 44 45 32N 2 10E
Meyrargues 45 43 38N 5 32E
Meyrueis 44 44 12N 3 27E
Meyssac 44 45 3N 1 40E
Mezdra 67 43 12N 23 35E
Mèze 44 43 27N 3 36E
Mezen 78 65 50N 44 20E
Mezha, R. 80 55 50N 31 45E
Mezhdurechenskiy 84 59 36N 65 56E
Mezidon 42 49 5N 0 1W
Mézières 43 49 45N 4 42E
Mézilhac 45 44 49N 4 21E
Mézin 44 44 4N 0 16E
Mezőberény 53 46 49N 21 3E
Mezőfalva 53 46 55N 18 49E
Mezőhegyes 53 46 19N 20 49E
Mezokövácsháza 53 46 25N 20 57E
Mezőkövesd 53 47 49N 20 35E
Mézos 44 44 5N 1 10W
Mezőtúr 53 47 0N 20 41E
Mezquital 164 23 29N 104 23W
Mezzolombardo 62 46 13N 11 5E
Mgeta 127 8 22S 38 6E
Mglin 80 53 2N 32 50E
Mhlaba Hills 127 18 30S 30 30E
Mhow 94 22 33N 75 50E
Mi-Shima 110 34 46N 131 9E
Miahuatlán 165 16 21N 96 36W
Miajadas 57 39 9N 5 54W
Mialar 94 26 15N 70 20E
Miallo 138 16 28S 145 22E
Miami, Ariz., U.S.A. 161 33 25N 111 0W
Miami, Fla., U.S.A. 157 25 52N 80 15W
Miami, Tex., U.S.A. 159 35 44N 100 38W
Miami Beach 157 25 49N 80 6W
Miami, R. 156 39 20N 84 40W
Miamisburg 156 39 40N 84 11W
Miandowāb 92 37 0N 46 5E
Miandrivazo 125 19 50S 45 56E
Miāneh 92 37 30N 47 40E
Mianwali 94 32 38N 71 28E
Miaoli 109 24 34N 120 48E
Miarinarivo 129 18 57S 46 55E
Miass 84 54 59N 60 6E
Miass, R. 84 56 6N 64 30E
Miasteczko Kraj 54 53 7N 17 1E
Miastko 54 54 0N 16 58E
Mica Dam 152 52 5N 118 32W
Mica Res. 152 51 55N 118 00W
Michael, Mt. 135 6 27S 145 22E
Michalovce 29 48 44N 21 54E
Micheldever 28 51 7N 1 17W
Michelson, Mt. 147 69 20N 144 20W
Michelstadt 49 49 40N 9 0E
Michigan □ 155 44 40N 85 40W
Michigan City 156 41 42N 86 56W
Michigan, L. 156 44 0N 87 0W
Michih 106 37 49N 110 7E
Michikamau L. 151 54 0N 64 0W
Michipicoten 150 47 55N 84 55W
Michipicoten I. 150 47 40N 85 50W
Michoacan □ 164 19 0N 102 0W
Michurin 67 42 9N 27 51E
Michurinsk 81 52 58N 40 27E
Mickle Fell 32 54 38N 2 16W
Mickleover 33 52 55N 1 32W
Mickleton, Oxon., U.K. 28 52 5N 1 45W
Mickleton, Yorks., U.K. 32 54 36N 2 3W
Miclere 138 22 34S 147 32E
Micronesia 130 17 0N 160 0E
Micŭsasa 70 46 7N 24 7E
Mid Calder 35 55 53N 3 23W
Mid Glamorgan □ 31 51 40N 3 25W
Mid Yell 36 60 36N 1 5W
Midai, P. 101 3 0N 107 47E
Midale 153 49 25N 103 20W
Midas 160 41 14N 116 56W
Middagsfjället 72 63 27N 12 19E
Middelbeers 47 51 28N 5 15E
Middelburg, Neth. 47 51 30N 3 36E
Middelburg, C. Prov., S. Afr. 128 31 30S 25 0E
Middelburg, Trans., S. Afr. 129 25 49N 29 28E
Middelfart 73 55 30N 9 43E
Middelharnis 47 51 46N 4 10E
Middelkerke 47 51 11N 2 49E
Middelrode 47 51 41N 5 26E
Middelveld 128 29 45S 22 30E
Middle Alkali L. 160 41 30N 120 3W
Middle Andaman I. 101 12 30N 92 30E
Middle Brook 151 48 40N 54 20W
Middle I. 137 28 55S 113 55E
Middle River 162 39 19N 76 25W
Middle Zoy 28 51 5N 2 54W
Middleboro 162 41 49N 70 55W
Middleburg, N.Y., U.S.A. 162 42 36N 74 19W
Middleburg, Pa., U.S.A. 162 40 47N 77 3W
Middlebury 162 44 0N 73 9W
Middleham 33 54 17N 1 49W
Middlemarch 143 45 30S 170 9E
Middlemarsh 28 50 51N 2 29W
Middleport 156 39 0N 82 5W
Middlesbrough 33 54 35N 1 14W
Middlesex, Belize 165 17 2N 88 31W
Middlesex, U.S.A. 162 40 36N 74 30W
Middleton, Can. 151 44 57N 65 4W
Middleton, Gr. Manchester, U.K. 32 53 33N 2 12W
Middleton, Norfolk, U.K. 29 52 43N 0 29E
Middleton Cheney 28 52 4N 1 17W
Middleton Cr. 138 22 35S 141 51E
Middleton I. 147 59 30N 146 28W
Middleton-in-Teesdale 32 54 38N 2 5W
Middleton in the Wolds 33 53 56N 0 35W
Middleton P.O. 138 22 22S 141 32E
Middletown, U.K. 38 54 18N 6 50W
Middletown, Conn., U.S.A. 162 41 37N 72 40W
Middletown, Del., U.S.A. 162 39 30N 84 21W
Middletown, N.Y., U.S.A. 162 41 28N 74 28W
Middletown, Pa., U.S.A. 162 40 12N 76 44W
Middlewich 32 53 12N 2 28W
Midelt 118 32 46N 4 44W
Midhurst, N.Z. 142 39 17S 174 18E
Midhurst, U.K. 29 50 59N 0 44W
Midi, Canal du 44 43 45N 1 21E
Midi d'Ossau 58 42 50N 0 25W
Midland, Austral. 137 31 54S 115 59E
Midland, Can. 150 44 45N 79 50W
Midland, Mich., U.S.A. 156 43 37N 84 17W
Midland, Tex., U.S.A. 159 32 0N 102 3W
Midland Junc. 137 31 50S 115 58E
Midlands □ 127 19 40S 29 0E
Midleton 39 51 52N 8 12W
Midlothian, Austral. 138 17 10S 141 12E
Midlothian, U.S.A. 159 32 30N 97 0W
Midlothian (□) 26 55 45N 3 15W
Midnapore 95 22 25N 87 21E
Midongy du Sud 129 23 35S 47 1E
Midongy, Massif de 129 23 30S 47 0E
Midskog 73 58 56N 14 5E
Midsomer Norton 28 51 17N 2 29W
Midvale 160 40 39N 111 58W
Midway Is. 130 28 13N 177 22W
Midwest 160 43 27N 106 11W
Midwolda 46 53 12N 6 52E
Midzur 66 43 24N 22 40E
Mie-ken □ 111 34 30N 136 10E
Miechów 54 50 21N 20 5E
Miedzyborz 54 51 39N 17 24E
Miedzychód 54 52 35N 15 53E
Miedzylesie 54 50 41N 16 40E
Miedzyrzec Podlaski 54 51 58N 22 45E
Miedzyrzecz 54 52 26N 15 35E
Miedzyzdroje 54 53 56N 14 26E
Miejska Górka 54 51 39N 16 58E
Miélan 44 43 27N 0 19E
Mielelek 138 6 1S 148 58E
Miench'ih 106 34 48N 111 40E
Mienchu 108 31 22N 104 7E
Mienga 128 17 12S 19 48E
Mienhsien 106 33 11N 106 36E
Mienning 108 28 30N 102 10E
Mienyang, Hupei, China 109 30 10N 113 20E
Mienyang, Szechwan, China 108 31 28N 104 46E
Miercurea Ciuc 70 46 21N 25 48E
Mieres 56 43 18N 5 48W
Mierlo 47 51 27N 5 37E
Mieso 123 9 15N 40 43E
Mieszkowice 54 52 47N 14 30E
Migdal 90 32 51N 35 30E
Migdal Afeq 90 32 5N 34 58E
Migennes 43 47 58N 3 31E
Migliarino 63 44 54N 11 56E
Miguel Alemán, Presa 165 18 15N 96 40W
Miguel Alves 170 4 11S 42 55W
Miguel Calmon 170 11 26S 40 36W
Mihara 110 34 24N 133 5E
Mihara-Yama 111 34 43N 139 23E
Mihsien 106 34 31N 113 22E
Mii 108 26 50N 102 3E
Mijares, R. 58 40 15N 0 50W
Mijas 57 36 36N 4 40W
Mijdrecht 46 52 13N 4 53E
Mijilu 121 10 22N 13 19E
Mikese 126 6 48S 37 55E
Mikha Tskhakaya 83 42 15N 42 7E
Mikhailovgrad 67 43 27N 23 16E
Mikhailovka 82 47 16N 35 27E
Mikhaylov 81 54 20N 39 0E
Mikhaylovka, Azerbaijan, U.S.S.R. 83 41 31N 48 52E
Mikhaylovka, R.S.F.S.R., U.S.S.R. 81 50 3N 43 5E
Mikhaylovski 84 56 27N 59 7E
Mikhnevo 81 55 4N 37 59E
Miki, Hyōgō, Japan 110 34 48N 134 59E
Miki, Kagawa, Japan 110 34 12N 134 7E
Mikinai 69 37 43N 22 46E
Mikindani 127 10 15S 40 2E
Mikkeli 75 61 43N 27 25E
Mikkeli □ 74 62 0N 28 0E
Mikkelin Lääni □ 74 61 56N 28 0E
Mikkwa, R. 152 58 25N 114 46W
Mikniya 123 17 0N 33 45E
Mikołajki 54 53 49N 21 37E

Mjörn Montcornet

Mjörn	73	57 55N	12 25 E
Mjøsa	71	60 40N	11 0 E
Mkata	126	5 45 S	38 20 E
Mkokotoni	126	5 55 S	39 15 E
Mkomazi	126	4 40 S	38 7 E
Mkulwe	127	8 37 S	32 20 E
Mkumbi, Ras	126	7 38 S	39 55 E
Mkushi	127	14 25 S	29 15 E
Mkushi River	127	13 40 S	29 30 E
Mkuze, R.	129	27 45 S	32 30 E
Mkwaya	126	6 17 S	35 40 E
Mladá Boleslav	52	50 27N	14 53 E
Mladenovac	66	44 28N	20 44 E
Mlala Hills	126	6 50 S	31 40 E
Mlange	127	16 2 S	35 33 E
Mlava, R.	66	44 35N	21 18 E
Mława	54	53 9N	20 25 E
Mlinište	63	44 15N	16 50 E
Mljet, I.	66	42 43N	17 30 E
Młynary	54	54 12N	19 46 E
Mme	121	6 18N	10 14 E
Mo, Hordaland, Norway	71	60 49N	5 48 E
Mo, Telemark, Norway	71	59 28N	7 50 E
Mo, Sweden	72	61 19N	16 47 E
Mo i Rana	74	66 15N	14 7 E
Moa, I.	103	8 0 S	128 0 E
Moa, R.	120	7 0N	11 40W
Moab	161	38 40N	109 35W
Moabi	124	2 24 S	10 59 E
Moalie Park	139	29 42 S	143 3 E
Moaña	56	42 18N	8 43W
Moanda	124	1 28 S	13 21 E
Moapo	161	36 45N	114 37W
Moate	39	53 25N	7 43W
Moba	126	7 0 S	29 48 E
Mobara	111	35 25N	140 18 E
Mobaye	124	4 25N	21 5 E
Mobayi	124	4 15N	21 8 E
Moberley	158	39 25N	92 25W
Moberly, R.	152	56 12N	120 55W
Mobert	150	48 41N	85 40W
Mobile	157	30 41N	88 3W
Mobile B.	157	30 30N	88 0W
Mobile, Pt.	157	30 15N	88 0W
Mobjack B.	162	37 16N	76 22W
Möborg	73	56 24N	8 21 E
Mobridge	158	45 40N	100 28W
Mobutu Sese Seko, L.	126	1 30N	31 0 E
Moc Chav	100	20 50N	104 38 E
Moc Hoa	101	10 46N	105 56 E
Mocabe Kasari	127	9 58 S	26 12 E
Mocajuba	170	2 35 S	49 30W
Moçambique	127	15 3 S	40 42 E
Moçambique □	127	14 45 S	38 30 E
Mocanaqua	162	41 9N	76 8W
Mochiang	108	23 25N	101 44 E
Mochiara Grove	128	20 43 S	21 50 E
Mochudi	128	24 27 S	26 7 E
Mocimboa da Praia	127	11 25 S	40 20 E
Mociu	70	46 46N	24 3 E
Möckeln	73	56 40N	14 15 E
Mockhorn I.	162	37 10N	75 52W
Moclips	160	47 14N	124 10W
Moçâmedes □	128	16 35 S	12 30 E
Mocoa	174	1 15N	76 45W
Mococa	173	21 28 S	47 0W
Mocorito	164	25 20N	108 0W
Moctezuma	164	30 12N	106 26W
Moctezuma, R.	165	21 59N	98 34W
Mocuba	125	16 54 S	37 25 E
Moda	98	24 22N	96 29 E
Modane	45	45 12N	6 40 E
Modasa	94	23 30N	73 21 E
Modave	47	50 27N	5 18 E
Modbury, Austral.	109	34 50 S	138 41 E
Modbury, U.K.	30	50 21N	3 53W
Modder, R.	128	28 50 S	24 50 E
Modderrivier	128	29 2 S	24 38 E
Módena	62	44 39N	10 55 E
Modena	161	37 55N	113 56W
Modesto	163	37 43N	121 0W
Módica	65	36 52N	14 45 E
Modigliana	63	44 9N	11 48 E
Modjokerto	103	7 29 S	112 25 E
Modlin	54	52 24N	20 41 E
Mödling	53	48 5N	16 17 E
Modo	123	5 31N	30 33 E
Modra	53	48 19N	17 20 E
Modreeny	39	52 57N	8 6W
Modriča	66	44 57N	18 17 E
Moe	141	38 12 S	146 19 E
Moebase	127	17 3 S	38 41 E
Moei, R.	101	17 25N	98 10 E
Moëlan-s-Mer	42	47 49N	3 38W
Moelfre	31	53 21N	4 15W
Moengo	175	5 45N	54 20W
Moergestel	47	51 33N	5 11 E
Moësa, R.	51	46 12N	9 10 E
Moffat	35	55 20N	3 27W
Moga	94	30 48N	75 8 E
Mogadiscio = Mogadishu	91	2 2N	45 25 E
Mogadishu	91	2 2N	45 25 E
Mogador = Essaouira	118	31 32N	9 42W
Mogadouro	56	41 22N	6 47W
Mogami-gawa, R.	112	38 45N	140 0 E
Mogaung	98	25 20N	97 0 E
Møgeltønder	73	54 57N	8 48 E
Mogente	59	38 52N	0 45W
Moggil	108	27 34 S	152 52 E
Mogho	123	4 54N	40 16 E
Mogi das Cruzes	173	23 45 S	46 20W
Mogi-Guaçu, R.	173	20 53 S	48 10W
Mogi-Mirim	173	22 20 S	47 0W
Mogielnica	54	51 42N	20 41 E
Mogilev	80	53 55N	30 18 E
Mogilev Podolskiy	82	48 20N	27 40 E
Mogilno	54	52 39N	17 55 E
Mogincual	125	15 35 S	40 25 E
Mogliano Veneto	63	45 33N	12 15 E
Mogocha	77	53 40N	119 50 E
Mogoi	103	1 55 S	133 10 E
Mogok	98	23 0N	96 40 E
Mogollon	161	33 25N	108 55W
Mogollon Mesa	161	43 40N	111 0W
Mogriguy	141	32 3 S	148 40 E
Moguer	57	37 15N	6 52W
Mogumber	137	31 2 S	116 3 E
Mohács	53	45 58N	18 41 E
Mohaka, R.	142	39 7 S	177 12 E
Mohall	158	48 46N	101 30W
Mohammadābād	93	37 30N	59 5 E
Mohammedia	118	33 44N	7 21W
Mohave Desert	161	35 0N	117 30W
Mohawk	161	32 45N	113 50W
Mohawk, R.	162	42 47N	73 42W
Moheda	73	57 1N	14 35 E
Mohembo	125	18 15 S	21 43 E
Moher, Cliffs of	39	52 58N	9 30W
Mohican, C.	147	60 10N	167 30W
Mohill	38	53 57N	7 52W
Möhne, R.	48	51 29N	8 10 E
Mohnyin	98	24 47N	96 22 E
Moholm	73	58 37N	14 5 E
Mohon	43	49 45N	4 44 E
Mohoro	126	8 6 S	39 8 E
Moia	123	5 3N	28 2 E
Moidart, L.	36	56 47N	5 40W
Moinabad	96	17 44N	77 16 E
Moineşti	70	46 28N	26 21 E
Mointy	76	47 40N	73 45 E
Moira	38	54 28N	6 16W
Moirais	69	35 4N	24 56 E
Moirans	45	45 20N	5 33 E
Moirans-en-Montagne	45	46 26N	5 43 E
Moisäkula	80	58 3N	24 38 E
Moisie	151	50 7N	66 1W
Moisie, R.	151	50 6N	66 5W
Moissac	44	44 7N	1 5 E
Moita	57	38 38N	8 58W
Mojácar	59	37 6N	1 55W
Mojados	56	41 26N	4 40W
Mojave	163	35 8N	118 8W
Mojave Desert	163	35 0N	116 30W
Mojo, Boliv.	172	21 48 S	65 33W
Mojo, Ethiopia	123	8 35N	39 5 E
Mojo, I.	102	8 10 S	117 40 E
Moju, R.	170	1 40 S	48 25W
Mokai	142	38 32 S	175 56 E
Mokambo	127	12 25 S	28 20 E
Mokameh	95	25 24N	85 55 E
Mokau, R.	142	38 35 S	174 55 E
Mokelumne Hill	163	38 18N	120 43W
Mokelumne, R.	163	38 23N	121 25W
Mokhós	69	35 16N	25 27 E
Mokhotlong	129	29 22 S	29 2 E
Mokihinui	143	41 33 S	171 58 E
Moknine	119	35 35N	10 58 E
Mokokchung	99	26 15N	94 30 E
Mokpalin	98	17 26N	96 53 E
Mokpo	107	34 50N	126 30 E
Mokra Gora	66	42 50N	20 30 E
Mokronog	63	45 57N	15 9 E
Moksha, R.	81	54 45N	43 40 E
Mokshan	81	52 25N	44 35 E
Mokta Spera	120	16 38N	9 6W
Moktama Kwe	99	15 40N	96 30 E
Mol	47	51 11N	5 5 E
Mola, C. de la	58	39 53N	4 20 E
Mola di Bari	65	41 3N	17 5 E
Moland	71	59 11N	8 6 E
Moláoi	69	36 49N	22 56 E
Molat, I.	63	44 15N	14 50 E
Molchanovo	76	57 40N	83 50 E
Mold	31	53 10N	3 10W
Moldava nad Bodvou	53	48 38N	21 0 E
Moldavia = Moldova	70	46 30N	27 0 E
Moldavian S.S.R.□	82	47 0N	28 0 E
Molde	71	62 45N	7 9 E
Moldotau, Khrebet	85	41 35N	75 0 E
Moldova	70	46 30N	27 0 E
Moldova Nouă	70	44 45N	21 41 E
Moldoveanu, mt.	67	45 36N	24 45 E
Mole Creek	138	41 32 S	146 24 E
Mole, R.	29	51 13N	0 15W
Molepolole	125	24 28 S	25 28 E
Moléson	50	46 33N	7 1 E
Molesworth	143	42 5 S	173 16 E
Molfetta	65	41 12N	16 35 E
Molina de Aragón	58	40 46N	1 52W
Moline	158	41 30N	90 30W
Molinella	63	44 38N	11 40 E
Molinos	172	25 28 S	66 15W
Moliro	126	8 12 S	30 30 E
Molise □	63	41 45N	14 30 E
Moliterno	65	40 14N	15 50 E
Mollahat	98	22 56N	89 48 E
Mölle	73	56 17N	12 31 E
Molledo	56	43 8N	4 6W
Mollendo	174	17 0 S	72 0W
Mollerin, L.	137	30 30 S	117 35 E
Mollerusa	58	41 37N	0 54 E
Mollina	57	37 8N	4 38W
Mölln	48	53 37N	10 41 E
Mollösund	73	58 4N	11 30 E
Mölltorp	73	58 30N	14 26 E
Mölndal	73	57 40N	12 3 E
Mölnlycke	73	57 40N	12 8 E
Molo	98	23 22N	96 53 E
Molochansk	82	47 15N	35 23 E
Molochaya, R.	82	47 0N	35 30 E
Molodechno	80	54 20N	26 50 E
Molokai, I.	147	21 8N	157 0W
Moloma, R.	81	59 0N	48 15 E
Molong	141	33 5 S	148 54 E
Molopo, R.	125	25 40 S	24 30 E
Mólos	69	38 47N	22 37 E
Molotov, Mys	77	81 10N	95 0 E
Moloundou	124	2 8N	15 15 E
Molsheim	43	48 33N	7 29 E
Molson L.	153	54 22N	95 32W
Molteno	128	31 22 S	26 22 E
Molu, I.	103	6 45 S	131 40 E
Molucca Sea	103	4 0 S	124 0 E
Moluccas = Maluku, Is.	103	1 0 S	127 0 E
Molusi	128	20 21 S	24 29 E
Moma, Mozam.	127	16 47 S	39 4 E
Moma, Zaïre	126	1 35 S	23 52 E
Momanga	128	18 7 S	21 41 E
Momba	140	30 58 S	143 30 E
Mombaça	170	15 43 S	48 43W
Mombasa	126	4 2 S	39 43 E
Mombetsu, Hokkaido, Japan	112	42 27N	142 4 E
Mombetsu, Hokkaido, Japan	112	44 21N	143 22 E
Mombuey	56	42 3N	6 20W
Momchilgrad	67	41 33N	25 23 E
Momi	126	1 42 S	27 0 E
Momignies	47	50 2N	4 10 E
Mompós	174	9 14N	74 26W
Møn	73	54 57N	12 15 E
Mon, R.	99	20 25N	94 30 E
Mona, Canal de la	167	18 30N	67 45W
Mona, I.	167	18 5N	67 54W
Mona Passage	167	18 0N	67 40W
Mona, Punta, C. Rica	166	9 37N	82 36W
Mona, Punta, Spain	57	36 43N	3 45W
Monach Is.	36	57 32N	7 40W
Monach, Sd. of	36	57 34N	7 26W
Monaco ■	44	43 46N	7 23 E
Monadhliath Mts.	37	57 10N	4 4W
Monadnock Mt.	162	42 52N	72 7W
Monagas □	174	9 20N	63 0W
Monaghan	38	54 15N	6 58W
Monaghan □	38	54 10N	7 0W
Monahans	159	31 35N	102 50W
Monapo	127	14 50 S	40 12 E
Monar For.	36	57 27N	5 10W
Monar L.	36	57 26N	5 8W
Monarch Mt.	152	51 55N	125 57W
Monasterevan	39	53 10N	7 5W
Monastier-sur-Gazeille, Le	44	44 57N	3 59 E
Monastir	119	35 50N	10 49 E
Monastyriska	80	49 8N	25 14 E
Monavullagh Mts.	39	52 14N	7 35W
Moncada	58	39 30N	0 24W
Moncalieri	62	45 0N	7 40 E
Moncalvo	62	45 3N	8 15 E
Moncarapacho	57	37 5N	7 46W
Moncayo, Sierra del	58	41 48N	1 50W
Mönchengladbach	48	51 12N	6 23 E
Monchique	57	37 19N	8 38W
Monchique, Sa. de,	55	37 18N	8 39W
Monclova	164	26 50N	101 30W
Monção	56	42 4N	8 27W
Moncontant	42	46 43N	0 36W
Moncontour	42	48 22N	2 38W
Moncton	151	46 7N	64 51W
Mondego, Cabo	56	40 11N	8 54W
Mondego, R.	56	40 28N	8 0W
Mondeodo	103	3 21 S	122 9 E
Mondolfo	63	43 45N	13 8 E
Mondoñedo	56	43 25N	7 23W
Mondovi	62	44 23N	7 56 E
Mondovi	158	44 37N	91 40W
Mondragon	45	44 13N	4 44 E
Mondragone	64	41 8N	13 52 E
Mondrain I.	137	34 9 S	122 14 E
Monduli □	126	3 0 S	36 0 E
Monemvasia	69	36 41N	23 3 E
Monessen	156	40 9N	79 50W
Monesterio	57	38 6N	6 15W
Monestier-de-Clermont	45	44 55N	5 38 E
Monet	150	48 10N	75 40W
Monêtier-les-Bains, Le	45	44 58N	6 30 E
Monett	159	36 55N	93 56W
Moneygall	39	52 54N	7 59W
Moneymore	38	54 42N	6 40W
Monfalcone	63	45 49N	13 32 E
Monflanquin	44	44 32N	0 47 E
Monforte	57	39 6N	7 25W
Monforte de Lemos	56	42 31N	7 33W
Mong Cai	101	21 27N	107 54 E
Möng Hsu	99	21 54N	98 30 E
Möng Hta	98	19 50N	98 35 E
Mong Ket	98	23 8N	98 22 E
Möng Kung	98	21 35N	97 35 E
Möng Kyawt	98	19 56N	98 45 E
Mong Lang	101	20 29N	97 52 E
Möng Nai	98	20 32N	97 55 E
Möng Pai	98	19 40N	97 15 E
Mong Pawk	99	22 4N	99 16 E
Mong Ping	98	21 22N	99 2 E
Mong Pu	98	20 55N	98 44 E
Mong Ton	98	20 25N	98 45 E
Mong Tung	98	22 2N	97 41 E
Mong Wa	99	21 26N	100 27 E
Mong Yai	98	22 28N	98 3 E
Mongalla	123	5 8N	31 55 E
Monger, L.	137	29 25 S	117 5 E
Monghyr	95	25 23N	86 30 E
Mongla	98	22 8N	89 35 E
Mongngaw	98	22 47N	96 59 E
Mongo	117	12 14N	18 43 E
Mongolia ■	105	47 0N	103 0 E
Mongonu	121	12 40N	13 32 E
Mongororo	124	12 22N	22 26 E
Mongoumba	124	3 33N	18 40 E
Mongpang	101	23 5N	100 25 E
Mongu	125	15 16 S	23 12 E
Mongua	128	16 43 S	15 20 E
Moniaive	35	55 11N	3 55W
Monifieth	35	56 30N	2 48W
Monistral-St.-Loire	45	45 17N	4 11 E
Monitor, Pk.	163	38 52N	116 35W
Monitor, Ra.	163	38 30N	116 45W
Monivea	38	53 22N	8 42W
Monk	153	47 7N	69 59W
Monkey Bay	127	14 7 S	35 1 E
Monkey River	165	16 22N	88 29W
Monki	54	53 23N	22 48 E
Monkira	138	24 46 S	140 30 E
Monkoto	124	1 38 S	20 35 E
Monmouth, U.K.	31	51 48N	2 43W
Monmouth, U.S.A.	158	40 50N	90 40W
Monmouth (□)	26	51 34N	3 5W
Monnow R.	28	51 54N	2 48W
Mono, L.	163	38 0N	119 9W
Mono, Punta del	166	12 0N	83 30W
Monolith	163	35 7N	118 22W
Monópoli	65	40 57N	17 18 E
Monor	53	47 21N	19 27 E
Monóvar	59	38 28N	0 53W
Monowai	143	45 53 S	167 25 E
Monowai, L.	143	45 53 S	167 25 E
Monreal del Campo	58	40 47N	1 20W
Monreale	64	38 6N	13 16 E
Monroe, La., U.S.A.	159	32 32N	92 4W
Monroe, Mich., U.S.A.	156	41 55N	83 26W
Monroe, N.C., U.S.A.	157	35 2N	80 37W
Monroe, Utah, U.S.A.	161	38 45N	111 39W
Monroe, Wis., U.S.A.	158	42 38N	89 40W
Monroe City	158	39 40N	91 40W
Monroeton	162	41 43N	76 29W
Monroeville	157	31 33N	87 15W
Monrovia, Liberia	120	6 18N	10 47W
Monrovia, U.S.A.	161	34 7N	118 1W
Mons	47	50 27N	3 58 E
Møns Klint	73	54 57N	12 33 E
Monsaraz	57	38 28N	7 22W
Monse	103	4 0 S	123 10 E
Monségur	44	44 38N	0 4 E
Monsélice	63	43 13N	11 45 E
Monster	46	52 1N	4 10 E
Mont-aux-Sources	129	28 44 S	28 52 E
Mont-de-Marsin	44	43 54N	0 31W
Mont d'Or, Tunnel	43	46 45N	6 18 E
Mont-Dore, Le	44	45 35N	2 50 E
Mont Joli	151	48 37N	68 10W
Mont Laurier	150	46 35N	75 30W
Mont Luis	151	42 31N	2 6 E
Mont St. Michel	42	48 40N	1 30W
Mont-sur-Marchienne	47	50 23N	4 24 E
Mont Tremblant Prov. Park	150	46 30N	74 30W
Montabaur	48	50 26N	7 49 E
Montacute	109	34 53 S	138 45 E
Montagnac	44	43 29N	3 28 E
Montagnana	63	45 13N	11 29 E
Montagu	128	33 45 S	20 8 E
Montagu, I.	164	58 30 S	26 15W
Montague, Can.	151	46 10N	62 39W
Montague, Calif., U.S.A.	160	41 47N	122 30W
Montague, Mass., U.S.A.	162	42 31N	72 33W
Montague, I.	164	31 40N	144 46W
Montague I.	147	60 0N	147 0W
Montague Ra.	137	29 15 S	119 30 E
Montague Sd.	136	14 28 S	125 20 E
Montaigu	42	46 59N	1 18W
Montalbán	58	40 50N	0 45W
Montalbano di Elicona	65	38 1N	15 0 E
Montalbano Iónico	65	40 17N	16 33 E
Montalbo	58	39 53N	2 42W
Montalcino	63	43 4N	11 30 E
Montalegre	56	41 49N	7 47W
Montalto di Castro	63	42 20N	11 36 E
Montalto Uffugo	65	39 25N	16 9 E
Montalvo	163	34 15N	119 12W
Montamarta	56	41 39N	5 49W
Montaña	174	6 0 S	73 0W
Montana	50	46 19N	7 29 E
Montana □	154	47 0N	110 0W
Montánchez	57	39 15N	6 8W
Montañita	174	1 30N	75 28W
Montargis	43	48 0N	2 43 E
Montauban	44	44 0N	1 21 E
Montauk	162	41 3N	71 57W
Montauk Pt.	162	41 4N	71 52W
Montbard	43	47 38N	4 20 E
Montbéliard	43	47 31N	6 48 E
Montblanch	58	41 23N	1 4 E
Montbrison	45	45 36N	4 3 E
Montcalm, Pic de	44	42 40N	1 25 E
Montceau-les-Mines	43	46 40N	4 23 E
Montchanin	62	46 47N	4 30 E
Montclair	162	40 53N	74 49W
Montcornet	43	49 40N	4 0 E

Montcuq Morvan, Mts. du

Montcuq 44 44 21N 1 13 E
Montdidier 43 49 38N 2 35 E
Monte Albán 165 17 2N 96 45W
Monte Alegre 175 2 0S 54 0W
Monte Alegre de Goiás 171 13 14S 47 10W
Monte Alegre de Minas 171 18 52S 48 52W
Monte Azul 171 15 9S 42 53W
Monte Bello Is. 136 20 30S 115 45 E
Monte Carlo 45 43 46N 7 23 E
Monte Carmelo 171 18 43S 47 29W
Monte Caseros 172 30 10S 57 50W
Monte Comán 172 34 40S 68 0W
Monte Cristi 167 19 52N 71 39W
Monte Libano 16 8 5N 75 29W
Monte Lindo, R. 172 25 30S 58 40W
Monte Quemado 172 25 53S 62 41W
Monte Redondo 56 39 53N 8 50W
Monte San Savino 63 43 20N 11 42 E
Monte Sant' Angelo 65 41 42N 15 59 E
Monte Santo, C. di 64 40 5N 9 42 E
Monte Visto 161 37 40N 106 8W
Monteagudo 173 27 14S 54 8W
Montealegre 59 38 48N 1 17W
Montebello 150 45 40N 74 55W
Montebelluna 63 45 47N 12 3 E
Montebourg 42 49 30N 1 20W
Montecastrilli 63 42 40N 12 30 E
Montecatini Terme 62 43 55N 10 48 E
Montecito 163 34 26N 119 40W
Montecristi 174 1 0S 80 40W
Montecristo, I. 62 42 20N 10 20 E
Montefalco 63 42 53N 12 38 E
Montefiascone 63 42 31N 12 2 E
Montefrío 57 37 20N 3 39W
Montegnée 47 50 38N 5 31 E
Montego B. 166 18 30N 78 0W
Montegranaro 63 43 13N 13 38 E
Monteiro 170 7 22S 37 38W
Monteith 140 35 11S 139 23 E
Montejicar 59 37 33N 3 30W
Montejinnie 136 16 40S 131 45 E
Montekomu Hu 99 34 40N 89 0 E
Montelibano 174 8 5N 75 29W
Montélimar 45 44 33N 4 45 E
Montella 65 40 50N 15 0 E
Montellano 57 36 59N 5 36W
Montello 158 43 49N 89 21W
Montelupo Fiorentino 62 43 44N 11 2 E
Montemór-o-Novo 57 38 40N 8 12W
Montemór-o-Velho 56 40 11N 8 40W
Montemorelos 165 25 11N 99 42W
Montendre 44 45 16N 0 26W
Montenegro 173 29 39S 51 29W
Montenegro □ 66 42 40N 19 20 E
Montenero di Bisaccia 63 42 0N 14 47 E
Montepuez 127 13 8S 38 59 E
Montepuez, R. 127 12 40S 40 15 E
Montepulciano 63 43 5N 11 46 E
Montereale 63 42 31N 13 13 E
Montereau 43 48 22N 2 57 E
Monterey 163 36 35N 121 57W
Monterey, B. 163 36 50N 121 55W
Montería 174 8 46N 75 53W
Monteros 172 27 11S 65 30W
Monterotondo 63 42 3N 12 36 E
Monterrey 164 25 40N 100 30W
Montes Altos 170 5 50S 47 4W
Montes Claros 171 16 30S 43 50W
Montes de Toledo 57 39 35N 4 30W
Montesano 160 47 0N 123 39W
Montesárchio 65 41 5N 14 37 E
Montescaglioso 65 40 34N 16 40 E
Montesilvano 63 42 30N 14 8 E
Montevarchi 63 43 30N 11 32 E
Monteverde 124 8 45S 16 45 E
Montevideo 173 34 50S 56 11W
Montezuma 158 41 32N 92 35W
Montfaucon, Haute-Loire, France 45 45 11N 4 20 E
Montfaucon, Meuse, France 43 49 16N 5 8 E
Montfort 47 51 7N 5 58 E
Montfort-l'Amaury 43 48 47N 1 49 E
Montfort-sur-Meu 42 48 8N 1 58W
Montgenèvre 45 44 56N 6 42 E
Montgomery, U.K. 31 52 34N 3 9W
Montgomery, Ala., U.S.A. 157 32 20N 86 20W
Montgomery, Pa., U.S.A. 162 41 10N 76 53W
Montgomery, W. Va., U.S.A. 156 38 9N 81 21W
Montgomery = Sahiwal 94 30 45N 73 8 E
Montgomery (□) 26 52 34N 3 9W
Montgomery Pass 163 37 58N 118 20W
Montguyon 44 45 12N 0 12W
Monthey 50 46 15N 6 56 E
Monticelli d'Ongina 62 45 3N 9 56 E
Monticello, Ark., U.S.A. 159 33 40N 91 48W
Monticello, Fla., U.S.A. 157 30 35N 83 50W
Monticello, Ind., U.S.A. 156 40 40N 86 45W
Monticello, Iowa, U.S.A. 158 42 18N 91 18W
Monticello, Ky., U.S.A. 157 36 52N 84 50W
Monticello, Minn., U.S.A. 158 45 17N 93 52W
Monticello, Miss., U.S.A. 159 31 35N 90 8W
Monticello, N.Y., U.S.A. 162 41 37N 74 42W
Monticello, Utah, U.S.A. 161 37 55N 109 27W
Montichiari 62 45 28N 10 29 E
Montieri 43 48 30N 4 45 E
Montignac 44 45 4N 1 10 E
Montignies-sur-Sambre 47 50 24N 4 29 E
Montigny-les-Metz 43 49 7N 6 10 E
Montigny-sur-Aube 43 47 57N 4 45 E
Montijo 57 38 52N 6 39W
Montijo, Presa de 57 38 55N 6 26W
Montilla 57 37 36N 4 40W
Montivideo 158 44 55N 95 40W
Montlhéry 43 48 39N 2 15 E
Montluçon 44 46 22N 2 36 E
Montmagny 151 46 58N 70 34W
Montmarault 53 46 11N 2 54 E
Montmartre 153 50 14N 103 27W
Montmédy 43 49 30N 5 20 E
Montmélian 45 45 30N 6 4 E
Montmirail 43 48 51N 3 30 E
Montmoreau-St.-Cybard 44 45 23N 0 8 E
Montmorency 151 46 53N 71 11W
Montmorillon 44 46 26N 0 50 E
Montmort 43 48 55N 3 49 E
Monto 138 24 52S 151 12 E
Montório al Vomano 63 42 35N 13 38 E
Montoro 57 38 1N 4 27W
Montour Falls 162 42 20N 76 51W
Montpelier, Idaho, U.S.A. 160 42 15N 111 29W
Montpelier, Ohio, U.S.A. 156 41 34N 84 40W
Montpelier, Vt., U.S.A. 156 44 15N 72 38W
Montpellier 44 43 37N 3 52 E
Montpezat-de-Quercy 44 44 15N 1 30 E
Montpon-Ménestrol 44 45 2N 0 11 E
Montréal, Can. 150 45 31N 73 34W
Montréal, France 44 43 13N 2 8 E
Montréal L. 153 54 20N 105 45W
Montreal Lake 153 54 3N 105 46W
Montredon-Labessonnié 44 43 45N 2 18 E
Montréjeau 44 43 6N 0 35 E
Montrésor 42 47 10N 1 10 E
Montreuil 43 50 27N 1 45 E
Montreuil-Bellay 42 47 8N 0 9W
Montreux 50 46 26N 6 55 E
Montrevault 42 47 17N 1 2W
Montrevel-en-Bresse 45 46 21N 5 8 E
Montrichard 42 47 20N 1 10 E
Montrose, U.K. 37 56 43N 2 28W
Montrose, Col., U.S.A. 161 38 30N 107 52W
Montrose, Pa., U.S.A. 162 41 50N 75 55W
Montrose, oilfield 19 57 20N 1 35 E
Montross 162 38 6N 76 50W
Monts, Pte des 151 49 27N 67 12W
Montsalvy 44 44 41N 2 30 E
Montsant, Sierra de 58 41 17N 0 1 E
Montsauche 43 47 13N 4 0 E
Montsech, Sierra del 58 42 0N 0 45 E
Montseny 58 42 29N 1 2 E
Montserrat, I. 167 16 40N 62 10W
Montserrat, mt. 58 41 36N 1 49 E
Montuenga 56 41 3N 4 38W
Montuiri 58 39 34N 2 59 E
Monveda 124 2 52N 21 30 E
Monymusk 37 57 13N 2 32W
Monyo 98 17 59N 95 30 E
Mônywa 98 22 7N 95 11 E
Monza 62 45 35N 9 15 E
Monze 127 16 17S 27 29 E
Monze, C. 94 24 47N 66 37 E
Monzón 58 41 52N 0 10 E
Mook 46 51 46N 5 54 E
Mo'oka 111 36 26N 140 1 E
Moolawatana 139 29 55S 139 45 E
Mooleulooloo 140 31 36S 140 32 E
Mooliabeenee 137 31 20S 116 2 E
Mooloogool 137 26 2S 119 5 E
Moomin, Cr. 139 29 44S 149 20 E
Moonah, R. 138 22 3S 138 33 E
Moonbeam 150 49 20N 82 10W
Mooncoin 39 52 18N 7 17W
Moonie 139 27 46S 150 20 E
Moonie, R. 139 27 45S 150 0 E
Moonta 140 34 6S 137 32 E
Moora 137 30 37S 115 58 E
Mooraberree 138 25 13S 140 54 E
Moorarie 137 25 56S 117 35 E
Moorcroft 158 44 17N 104 58W
Moore, L. 137 29 50S 117 35 E
Moore, R. 137 31 22S 115 30 E
Moore Reefs 138 16 0S 149 5 E
Moore River Native Settlement 137 31 1S 115 56 E
Moorebank 47 33 56S 150 56 E
Moorefield 156 39 5N 78 59W
Mooresville 157 35 36N 80 45W
Moorfoot Hills 35 55 44N 3 8W
Moorhead 158 47 0N 97 0W
Moorland 141 31 46S 152 38 E
Mooroopna 141 36 25S 145 22 E
Moorpark 163 34 17N 118 53W
Moorreesburg 128 33 6S 18 38 E
Moorslede 47 50 54N 3 4 E
Moosburg 49 48 28N 11 57 E
Moose Factory 150 51 20N 80 40W
Moose I. 153 51 42N 97 10W
Moose Jaw 153 50 24N 105 30W
Moose Jaw R. 153 50 34N 105 18W
Moose Lake, Can. 153 53 43N 100 20W
Moose Lake, U.S.A. 158 46 27N 92 48W
Moose Mountain Cr. 153 49 13N 102 12W
Moose Mtn. Prov. Park 153 49 48N 102 25W
Moose, R. 150 51 20N 80 25W
Moose River 150 50 48N 81 17W
Moosehead L. 151 45 40N 69 40W
Moosomin 153 50 9N 101 40W
Moosonee 150 51 17N 80 39W
Moosup 162 41 44N 71 52W
Mopeia 125 17 30S 35 40 E
Mopipi 128 21 6S 24 55 E
Mopoi 123 5 6N 26 54 E
Moppin 139 29 12S 146 45 E
Mopti 120 14 30N 4 0W
Moqatta 123 14 38N 35 50 E
Moquegua 174 17 15S 70 46W
Mór 53 47 25N 18 12 E
Móra 57 38 55N 8 10W
Mora, Sweden 72 61 2N 14 38 E
Mora, Minn., U.S.A. 158 45 52N 93 19W
Mora, N. Mex., U.S.A. 161 35 58N 105 21W
Mora de Ebro 58 41 6N 0 38 E
Mora de Rubielos 58 40 15N 0 45W
Mora la Nueva 58 41 7N 0 39 E
Morača, R. 66 42 40N 19 20 E
Morada Nova 170 5 7S 38 23W
Morada Nova de Minas 171 18 37S 45 22W
Moradabad 94 28 50N 78 50 E
Morafenobe 129 17 50S 44 53 E
Morag 54 53 55N 19 56 E
Moral de Calatrava 59 38 51N 3 33W
Moraleja 56 40 6N 6 43W
Morales 174 2 45N 76 38W
Moramanga 125 18 56S 48 12 E
Moran, Kans., U.S.A. 159 37 53N 94 35W
Moran, Wyo., U.S.A. 160 43 53N 110 37W
Morano Cálabro 65 39 51N 16 8 E
Morant Cays 166 17 22N 76 0W
Morant Pt. 166 17 55N 76 12W
Morar 36 56 58N 5 49W
Morar L. 36 56 57N 5 40W
Moratalla 59 38 14N 1 49W
Moratuwa 97 6 45N 79 55 E
Morava, R. 53 49 50N 16 50 E
Moravatío 164 19 51N 100 25W
Moravia, Iowa, U.S.A. 158 40 50N 92 50W
Moravia, N.Y., U.S.A. 162 42 43N 76 25W
Moravian Hts. = Ceskemoravská V. 52 49 30N 15 40 E
Moravica, R. 66 43 40N 20 8 E
Moravice, R. 53 49 50N 17 43 E
Moravita 66 45 17N 21 14 E
Moravska Trebová 53 49 45N 16 40 E
Moravské Budějovice 52 49 4N 15 49 E
Morawa 137 29 13S 116 0 E
Morawhanna 174 8 30N 59 40W
Moray (□) 26 57 32N 3 25W
Moray Firth 37 57 50N 3 30W
Morbach 49 49 48N 7 7 E
Morbegno 62 46 8N 9 34 E
Morbihan □ 42 47 55N 2 50W
Morcenx 44 44 0N 0 55W
Mordelles 42 48 5N 1 52W
Morden 153 49 15N 98 10W
Mordovian S.S.R. □ 81 54 20N 44 30 E
Mordovo 81 52 13N 40 50 E
More L. 37 58 18N 4 52W
Møre og Romsdal □ 71 63 0N 9 0 E
Morea 140 36 45S 141 18 E
Moreau, R. 158 45 15N 102 45W
Morebattle 35 55 30N 2 20W
Morecambe 32 54 5N 2 52W
Morecambe B. 32 54 7N 3 0W
Morecambe, gasfield 19 53 57N 3 40W
Moree 139 29 28S 149 54 E
Morehead, P.N.G. 135 8 41S 141 41 E
Morehead, U.S.A. 156 38 12N 83 22W
Morehead City 157 34 46N 76 44W
Moreira 174 0 34S 63 26W
Morelia 164 19 40N 101 11W
Morella, Austral. 138 23 0S 143 47 E
Morella, Spain 58 40 35N 0 2 E
Morelos 164 26 42N 107 40W
Morelos □ 165 18 40N 99 10W
Morena, Sierra 57 38 20N 4 0W
Morenci 161 33 7N 109 20W
Moreni 70 44 59N 25 36 E
Moreno 171 8 7S 35 6W
Mores, I. 157 26 15N 77 35W
Moresby I. 152 52 30N 131 40W
Morestel 45 45 40N 5 28 E
Moret 43 48 22N 2 48 E
Moreton B. 133 27 10S 153 10 E
Moreton, I. 139 27 10S 153 25 E
Moreton-in-Marsh 28 51 59N 1 42W
Moreton Telegraph Office 138 12 22S 142 30 E
Moretonhampstead 30 50 39N 3 45W
Moreuil 43 49 46N 2 30 E
Morez 45 46 31N 6 2 E
Morgan, Austral. 140 34 0S 139 35 E
Morgan, U.S.A. 160 41 3N 111 44W
Morgan City 159 29 40N 91 15W
Morgan Hill 163 37 8N 121 39W
Morganfield 156 37 40N 87 55W
Morganton 157 35 46N 81 48W
Morgantown 156 39 39N 79 58W
Morganville, Queens., Austral. 139 25 10S 152 0 E
Morganville, S. Australia, Austral. 140 33 10S 140 32 E
Morgat 42 48 15N 4 32 E
Morgenzon 129 26 45S 29 36 E
Morges 50 46 31N 6 29 E
Morhange 43 48 55N 6 38 E
Mori 62 45 51N 10 59 E
Morialmée 47 50 17N 4 30 E
Morialta Falls Reserve 109 34 54S 138 43 E
Moriarty 161 35 3N 106 2W
Morice L. 152 53 50N 127 40W
Morichal 174 2 10N 70 34W
Morichal Largo, R. 174 8 55N 63 0W
Moriguchi 111 34 44N 135 34 E
Moriki 121 12 52N 6 30 E
Morinville 152 53 49N 113 41W
Morioka 112 39 45N 141 8 E
Moris 164 28 8N 108 32W
Morisset 141 33 6S 151 30 E
Morkalla 140 34 23S 141 10 E
Morlaàs 44 43 21N 0 18W
Morlaix 42 48 36N 3 52W
Morlanwelz 47 50 28N 4 15 E
Morley 33 53 45N 1 36W
Mormanno 65 39 53N 15 59 E
Mormant 43 48 37N 2 52 E
Morney 139 25 22S 141 23 E
Morningside 108 27 28S 153 4 E
Mornington, Victoria, Austral. 141 38 15S 145 5 E
Mornington, W. Australia, Austral. 136 17 31S 126 6 E
Mornington, Ireland 38 53 42N 6 17W
Mornington I. 138 16 30S 139 30 E
Mornington, I. 176 49 50S 75 30W
Mórnos, R. 69 38 30N 22 0 E
Moro 123 10 50N 30 9 E
Moro G. 103 6 30N 123 0 E
Morobe 135 7 49S 147 38 E
Morocco ■ 118 32 0N 5 50W
Morococha 174 11 40S 76 5W
Morogoro 126 6 50S 37 40 E
Morogoro □ 126 8 0S 37 0 E
Morokweng 125 26 12S 23 45 E
Moroleón 164 20 8N 101 32W
Morombé 129 21 45S 43 22 E
Moron 172 34 39S 58 37W
Morón 166 22 0N 78 30W
Morón de Almazán 58 41 29N 2 27W
Morón de la Frontera 57 37 6N 5 28W
Morondava 129 20 17S 44 17 E
Morondo 120 8 57N 6 47W
Morongo Valley 163 34 3N 116 37W
Moronou 120 6 16N 4 59W
Morotai, I. 103 2 10N 128 30 E
Moroto 124 2 28N 34 42 E
Moroto Summit, Mt. 126 2 30N 34 43 E
Morozov (Bratan), mt. 67 42 30N 25 10 E
Morozovsk 83 48 25N 41 50 E
Morpeth 35 55 11N 1 41W
Morrelganj 98 22 28N 89 51 E
Morrilton 159 35 10N 92 45W
Morrinhos, Ceara, Brazil 170 3 14S 40 7W
Morrinhos, Minas Gerais, Brazil 171 17 45S 49 10W
Morrinsville 142 37 40S 175 32 E
Morris, Can. 153 49 25N 97 22W
Morris, Ill., U.S.A. 156 41 20N 88 20W
Morris, Minn., U.S.A. 158 45 33N 95 56W
Morris, N.Y., U.S.A. 162 42 33N 75 15W
Morris, Mt. 137 26 9S 131 4 E
Morrisburg 150 44 55N 75 7W
Morrison 158 41 47N 90 0W
Morristown, Ariz., U.S.A. 161 33 54N 112 45W
Morristown, N.J., U.S.A. 162 40 48N 74 30W
Morristown, S.D., U.S.A. 158 45 57N 101 44W
Morristown, Tenn., U.S.A. 157 36 18N 83 20W
Morrisville, N.Y., U.S.A. 162 42 54N 75 39W
Morrisville, Pa., U.S.A. 162 40 13N 74 47W
Morro Agudo 171 20 44S 48 4W
Morro Bay 163 35 27N 120 54W
Morro do Chapéu 171 11 33S 41 9W
Morro, Pta. 172 27 6S 71 0W
Morros 170 2 52S 44 3W
Morrosquillo, Golfo de 167 9 35N 75 40W
Morrum 73 56 12N 14 45 E
Morrumbene 125 23 31S 35 16 E
Mors 73 56 50N 8 45 E
Morshank 81 53 28N 41 50 E
Mörsil 72 63 19N 13 40 E
Mortagne, Charente Maritime, France 44 45 28N 0 49W
Mortagne, Orne, France 42 48 30N 0 32 E
Mortagne, Vendée, France 42 46 59N 0 57W
Mortagne-au-Perche 42 48 31N 0 33 E
Mortagne, R. 43 48 30N 6 30 E
Mortain 42 48 40N 0 57W
Mortara 62 45 15N 8 43 E
Morte Bay 30 51 10N 4 13W
Morte Pt. 30 51 13N 4 14W
Morteau 43 47 3N 6 35 E
Mortehoe 30 51 12N 4 12W
Morteros 172 30 50S 62 0W
Mortes, R. das 171 11 45S 50 44W
Mortimer's Cross 28 52 17N 2 50W
Mortlake 140 38 5S 142 50 E
Morton, Tex., U.S.A. 159 33 39N 102 49W
Morton, Wash., U.S.A. 160 46 33N 122 17W
Morton Fen 29 52 45N 0 23W
Mortsel 47 51 11N 4 27 E
Morundah 141 34 57S 146 19 E
Moruya 141 35 58S 150 3 E
Morvan, Mts. du 43 47 5N 4 0 E

Morven Mukden

Morven, Austral. 139 26 22S 147 5E
Morven, N.Z. 143 44 50S 171 6E
Morven, dist. 34 56 38N 5 44W
Morven, mt., Grampian, U.K. 37 57 8N 3 1W
Morven, mt., Highland, U.K. 37 58 15N 3 40W
Morvern 36 56 38N 5 44W
Morwell 141 38 10S 146 22E
Moryn 54 52 51N 14 22E
Mosalsk 80 54 30N 34 55E
Mosbach 49 49 21N 9 9E
Mosciano Sant' Ángelo 63 42 42N 13 52E
Moscos Is. 101 14 0N 97 30E
Moscow, Idaho, U.S.A. 160 46 45N 116 59W
Moscow, Pa., U.S.A. 162 41 20N 75 31W
Moscow = Moskva 81 55 45N 37 35E
Mosel, R. 49 50 22N 7 36E
Moselle □ 43 48 59N 6 33E
Moselle, R. 47 50 22N 7 36E
Moses Lake 160 47 16N 119 17W
Mosgiel 143 45 53S 170 21E
Moshi 126 3 22S 37 18E
Moshi □ 126 3 22S 37 18E
Moshupa 128 24 46S 25 29E
Mósina 54 52 15N 16 50E
Mosjøen 74 65 51N 13 12E
Moskenesøya 74 67 58N 13 0E
Moskenstraumen 74 67 47N 13 0E
Moskva 81 55 45N 37 35E
Moskva, R. 81 55 5N 38 51E
Moslavačka Gora 63 45 40N 16 37E
Mošóenice 63 45 17N 14 16E
Mosomane (Artesia) 128 24 2S 26 19E
Mosonmagyaróvár 53 47 52N 17 18E
Mo orin 66 45 19N 20 4E
Mospino 82 47 52N 38 0E
Mosquera 174 2 35N 78 30W
Mosquero 159 35 48N 103 57W
Mosqueruela 58 40 21N 0 27W
Mosquitia 166 15 20N 84 10W
Mosquitos, Golfo de los 166 9 15N 81 10W
Moss 71 59 27N 10 40E
Moss Vale 141 34 32S 150 25E
Mossaka 124 1 15S 16 45E
Mossâmedes, Angola 125 15 7S 12 11E
Mossâmedes, Brazil 171 16 7S 50 11W
Mossbank 153 49 56N 105 56W
Mossburn 143 45 41S 168 15E
Mosselbaai 128 34 11S 22 8E
Mossendjo 124 2 55S 12 42E
Mosses, Col des 50 46 25N 7 7E
Mossgiel 140 33 15S 144 30E
Mossley 32 53 31N 2 1W
Mossman 138 16 28S 145 23E
Mossoró 170 5 10S 37 15W
Mossuril 127 14 58S 40 42E
Mossy, R. 153 54 5N 102 58W
Most 52 50 31N 13 38E
Mostar 66 43 22N 17 50E
Mostardas 173 31 2S 50 51W
Mostefa, Rass 119 36 55N 11 3E
Mosterøy 71 59 5N 5 37E
Mostiska 80 49 48N 23 4E
Mostrim 38 53 42N 7 38W
Mosty 80 53 27N 24 38E
Mostyn 31 53 18N 3 14W
Mosul = Al Mawsil 92 36 20N 43 5E
Mosulpo 107 33 20N 126 17E
Mosvatn, L. 71 59 52N 8 5E
Mota del Cuervo 58 39 30N 2 52W
Mota del Marqués 56 41 38N 5 11W
Motagua, R. 166 15 44N 88 14W
Motala 73 58 32N 15 1E
Motcombe 28 51 1N 2 12W
Motegi 111 36 32N 140 11E
Mothe-Achard, La 42 46 37N 1 40W
Motherwell 35 55 48N 4 0W
Motihari 95 26 37N 85 1E
Motilla del Palancar 58 39 34N 1 55W
Motnik 63 46 14N 14 54E
Motocurunya 174 4 24N 64 5W
Motovun 63 45 20N 13 50E
Motozintea de Mendoza 165 15 21N 92 14W
Motril 59 36 44N 3 37W
Motrul, R. 70 44 44N 22 59E
Mott 158 46 25N 102 14W
Motte-Chalançon, La 45 44 30N 5 21E
Motte, La 45 44 20N 6 3E
Mottisfont 28 51 22N 1 32W
Mottola 65 40 38N 17 0E
Motueka 143 41 7S 173 1E
Motul 165 21 0N 89 20W
Motupena Pt. 135 6 30S 155 10E
Mouchalagane, R. 151 50 56N 68 41W
Moúdhros 68 39 50N 25 18E
Moudjeria 120 17 50N 12 15W
Moudon 50 46 40N 6 49E
Mouila 124 1 50S 11 0E
Moulamein 140 35 3S 144 1E
Moule, Le 167 16 20N 61 22W
Moulins 44 46 35N 3 19E
Moulmein 98 16 30N 97 40E
Moulmeingyun 98 16 23N 95 16E
Moulouya, O. 118 35 8N 2 22W
Moulton, U.K. 29 52 17N 0 51W
Moulton, U.S.A. 159 29 35N 97 8W
Moultrie 157 31 11N 83 47W
Moultrie, L. 157 33 25N 80 10W
Mound City, Mo., U.S.A. 158 40 2N 95 25W
Mound City, S.D., U.S.A. 158 45 46N 100 3W
Moúnda, Ákra 69 38 5N 20 45E
Moundou 117 8 40N 16 10E
Moundsville 156 39 53N 80 43W
Moung 100 12 46N 103 27E
Mount Airy 162 36 31N 80 37W
Mount Amherst 136 18 24S 126 58E
Mount Angel 160 45 4N 122 46W
Mount Augustus 137 24 20S 116 56E
Mount Barker, S.A., Austral. 140 35 5S 138 52E
Mount Barker, W.A., Austral. 137 34 38S 117 40E
Mount Barker Junc. 109 35 1S 138 52E
Mount Beauty 141 36 47S 147 10E
Mount Bellew Bridge 38 53 28N 8 30W
Mount Buckley 138 20 6S 148 0E
Mount Carmel, Ill., U.S.A. 156 38 20N 87 48W
Mount Carmel, Pa., U.S.A. 162 40 46N 76 25W
Mount Clemens 150 42 35N 82 50W
Mount Coolon 138 21 25S 147 25E
Mount Cootatha Park 108 27 29S 152 57E
Mount Crosby 108 27 32S 152 48E
Mount Darwin 125 16 47S 31 38E
Mount Desert I. 151 44 25N 68 25W
Mount Dora 157 28 49N 81 32W
Mount Douglas 138 21 35S 146 50E
Mount Edgecumbe 147 57 8N 135 22W
Mount Elizabeth 136 16 0S 125 50E
Mount Enid 136 21 42S 116 26E
Mount Forest 150 43 59N 80 43W
Mount Fox 138 18 45S 145 45E
Mount Gambier 140 37 50S 140 46E
Mount Garnet 138 17 37S 145 6E
Mount Goldsworthy 132 20 25S 119 39E
Mount Gravatt 108 27 32S 153 5E
Mount Hagen 135 5 52S 144 16E
Mount Hope, N.S.W., Austral. 141 32 51S 145 51E
Mount Hope, S.A., Austral. 139 34 7S 135 23E
Mount Hope, U.S.A. 156 37 52N 81 9W
Mount Horeb 158 43 0N 89 42W
Mount Howitt 139 26 31S 142 16E
Mount Isa 138 20 42S 139 26E
Mount Ive 140 32 25S 136 5E
Mount Keith 137 27 15S 120 30E
Mount Kisco 162 41 12N 73 44W
Mount Laguna 163 32 52N 116 25W
Mount Larcom 138 23 48S 150 59E
Mount Lavinia 93 6 50N 79 50E
Mount Lofty Ra. 133 34 35S 139 5E
Mount McKinley Nat. Pk. 147 64 0N 150 0W
Mount Magnet 137 28 2S 117 47E
Mount Manara 140 32 29S 143 58E
Mount Margaret 139 26 54S 143 21E
Mount Maunganui 142 37 40S 176 14E
Mount Monger 137 31 0S 122 0E
Mount Morgan 138 23 40S 150 25E
Mount Morris 156 42 43N 77 50W
Mount Mulligan 138 16 45S 144 47E
Mount Narryer 137 26 30S 115 55E
Mount Newman 136 23 18S 119 45E
Mount Nicholas 137 22 54S 120 27E
Mount Oxide 138 19 30S 139 29E
Mount Pearl 151 47 31N 52 47W
Mount Penn 162 40 20N 75 54W
Mount Perry 139 25 13S 151 42E
Mount Phillips 137 24 25S 116 15E
Mount Pleasant, Iowa, U.S.A. 158 41 0N 91 35W
Mount Pleasant, Mich., U.S.A. 156 43 35N 84 47W
Mount Pleasant, S.C., U.S.A. 157 32 45N 79 48W
Mount Pleasant, Tenn., U.S.A. 157 35 31N 87 11W
Mount Pleasant, Tex., U.S.A. 159 33 5N 95 0W
Mount Pleasant, Ut., U.S.A. 160 39 40N 111 29W
Mount Pocono 162 41 8N 75 21W
Mount Rainier Nat. Park. 160 46 50N 121 43W
Mount Revelstoke Nat. Park 152 51 5N 118 30W
Mount Robson 152 52 56N 119 15W
Mount Robson Prov. Park 152 53 0N 119 0W
Mount Samson 108 27 18S 152 51E
Mount Sandiman 137 24 25S 115 30E
Mount Shasta 160 41 20N 122 18W
Mount Somers 143 43 45S 171 27E
Mount Sterling, Ill., U.S.A. 158 40 0N 90 40W
Mount Sterling, Ky., U.S.A. 158 38 0N 84 0W
Mount Surprise 138 18 10S 144 17E
Mount Talbot 38 53 31N 8 18W
Mount Tom Price 137 22 50S 117 40E
Mount Upton 162 42 26N 75 23W
Mount Vernon, Austral. 137 24 15S 118 15E
Mount Vernon, D.C., U.S.A. 162 38 47N 77 10W
Mount Vernon, Ill., U.S.A. 162 38 17N 88 57W
Mount Vernon, Ind., U.S.A. 158 38 17N 88 57W
Mount Vernon, N.Y., U.S.A. 156 40 57N 73 49W
Mount Vernon, Ohio, U.S.A. 156 40 20N 82 30W
Mount Vernon, Wash., U.S.A. 160 48 27N 122 18W
Mount Victor 140 32 11S 139 44E
Mount Whaleback 132 23 18S 119 44E
Mount Willoughby 139 27 58S 134 8E
Mountain Ash 31 51 42N 3 22W
Mountain Center 163 33 42N 116 44W
Mountain City, Nev., U.S.A. 160 41 54N 116 0W
Mountain City, Tenn., U.S.A. 157 36 30N 81 50W
Mountain Dale 162 41 41N 74 32W
Mountain Grove 159 37 5N 92 20W
Mountain Home, Ark., U.S.A. 159 36 20N 92 25W
Mountain Home, Idaho, U.S.A. 160 43 11N 115 45W
Mountain Iron 158 47 30N 92 87W
Mountain Park. 152 52 50N 117 15W
Mountain View, Ark., U.S.A. 159 35 52N 92 10W
Mountain View, Calif., U.S.A. 161 37 26N 122 5W
Mountain Village 147 62 10N 163 50W
Mountainair 161 34 35N 106 15W
Mountcharles 38 54 37N 8 12W
Mountfield 38 54 34N 7 10W
Mountmellick 39 53 7N 7 20W
Mountnorris 38 54 15N 6 29W
Mountnorris B. 136 11 25S 132 45E
Mountrath 39 53 0N 7 30W
Mounts Bay 30 50 3N 5 27W
Mountsorrel 28 52 43N 1 9W
Mountvernon 152 48 25N 122 20W
Mouping 107 37 24N 121 35E
Moura, Austral. 138 24 35S 149 58E
Moura, Brazil 174 1 25S 61 45W
Moura, Port. 57 38 7N 7 30W
Mourão 57 38 22N 7 22W
Mourdi, Depression du 117 18 10N 23 0E
Mourdiah 120 14 35N 7 25W
Moure, La 158 46 27N 98 17W
Mourenx 44 43 23N 0 36W
Mouri 121 5 6N 1 14W
Mourilyan 138 17 35S 146 3E
Mourmelon-le-Grand 43 49 8N 4 22E
Mourne Mts. 38 54 10N 6 0W
Mourne, R. 38 54 45N 7 39W
Mouroubra 137 29 42S 117 52E
Mourzouq 119 25 53N 14 10W
Mousa I. 36 60 0N 1 10W
Mouscron 47 50 45N 3 12E
Moussoro 117 13 50N 16 35E
Mouthe 43 46 44N 6 12E
Moutier 50 47 16N 7 21E
Moutiers 45 45 29N 6 31E
Mouting 108 25 22N 101 32E
Moutong 103 0 28N 121 13E
Mouy 43 49 18N 2 20E
Mouzáki 68 39 25N 21 37E
Movas 164 28 10N 109 25W
Moville 38 55 11N 7 3W
Moxhe 47 50 38N 5 5E
Moxotó, R. 170 9 19S 38 14W
Moy, Inverness, U.K. 37 57 22N 4 3W
Moy, Ulster, U.K. 38 54 27N 6 40W
Moy, R. 38 54 5N 8 50W
Moyagee 137 27 48S 117 48E
Moyahua 164 21 16N 103 10W
Moyale, Ethiopia 123 3 34N 39 4E
Moyale, Kenya 126 3 30N 39 0E
Moyamba 120 8 15N 12 30W
Moyasta 39 52 40N 9 31W
Moycullen 39 53 20N 9 10W
Moyie 152 49 17N 115 50W
Moyle □ 38 55 10N 6 15W
Moylett 38 53 57N 7 7W
Moynalty 38 53 48N 6 52W
Moyne 39 52 45N 7 43W
Moyobamba 174 6 0S 77 0W
Moyvalley 38 53 26N 6 55W
Moza 90 31 48N 35 8E
Mozambique = Moçambique 125 15 3S 40 42E
Mozambique ■ 129 19 0S 35 0E
Mozambique Chan. 129 20 0S 39 0E
Mozdok 83 43 45N 44 48E
Mozhaisk 81 55 30N 36 2E
Mozhga 84 56 26N 52 15E
Mozirje 63 46 22N 14 58E
Mozua 126 3 57N 24 2E
Mozyr 80 52 0N 29 15E
Mpanda 126 6 23S 31 40E
Mpanda □ 126 6 23S 31 40E
Mpésoba 120 12 31N 5 39W
Mpika 127 11 51S 31 25E
Mpraeso 121 6 50N 0 50W
Mpulungu 127 8 51S 31 5E
Mpwapwa 124 6 30S 36 30E
Mpwapwa □ 126 6 30S 36 20E
Mragowo 54 53 57N 21 18E
Mrakovo 84 52 43N 56 38E
Mramor 66 43 20N 21 45E
Mrhaïer 119 33 55N 5 58E
Mrimina 118 29 50N 7 9W
Mrkonjió Grad 66 44 26N 17 4E
Mrkopalj 63 45 21N 14 52E
Mrocza 54 53 16N 17 35E
Msab, Oued en 119 32 35N 5 20E
Msaken 119 35 49N 10 33E
M'Salu, R. 127 12 25S 39 15E
Msambansovu, mt. 127 15 50S 30 3E
M'sila 119 35 46N 4 30E
Msoro 125 13 35S 31 50E
Msta, R. 80 58 30N 33 30E
Mstislavl 80 54 0N 31 50E
Mszana Dolna 54 49 41N 20 5E
Mszczonów 54 51 58N 20 33E
Mtama 127 10 17S 39 21E
Mtilikwe, R. 127 21 0S 31 12E
Mtsensk 81 53 25N 36 30E
Mtskheta 83 41 52N 44 45E
Mtwara 124 10 20S 40 20E
Mtwara □ 126 1 0S 39 0E
Mtwara-Mikindani 127 10 20S 40 20E
Mu Gia, Deo 100 17 40N 105 47E
Mu Ness 36 60 41N 0 50W
Mu, R. 98 21 56N 95 38E
Muaná 170 1 25S 49 15W
Muanda 124 6 0S 12 20E
Muang Chiang Rai 100 19 52N 99 50E
Muang Kalasin 101 16 26N 103 30E
Muang Lampang 101 18 16N 99 32E
Muang Lamphun 100 18 40N 98 53E
Muang Nan 101 18 52N 100 42E
Muang Phetchabun 101 16 23N 101 12E
Muang Phichit 101 16 29N 100 21E
Muang Ubon 101 15 15N 104 50E
Muang Yasothon 101 15 50N 104 10E
Muar 101 2 3N 102 34E
Muar, R. 101 2 15N 102 48E
Muarabungo 102 1 40S 101 10E
Muaradjuloi 102 0 12S 114 3E
Muaraenim 102 3 40S 103 50E
Muarakaman 102 0 2S 116 45E
Muaratebo 102 1 30S 102 26E
Muaratembesi 102 1 42S 103 2E
Muaratewe 102 0 50S 115 0E
Mubairik 92 23 22N 39 8E
Mubarakpur 95 26 12N 83 24E
Mubende 126 0 33N 31 22E
Mubi 121 10 18N 13 16E
Mubur, P. 101 3 20N 106 12E
Mucajaí, Serra do 174 2 23N 61 10W
Much Dewchurch 28 51 58N 2 45W
Much Marcle 28 51 59N 2 27W
Much Wenlock 28 52 36N 2 34W
Muchalls 37 57 2N 2 10W
Mücheln 48 51 18N 11 49E
Muchinga Mts. 127 11 30S 31 30E
Muchkapskiy 81 51 52N 42 28E
Mŭcin 70 45 16N 28 8E
Muck, I. 36 56 50N 6 15W
Muckadilla 139 26 35S 148 23E
Muckle Roe I. 36 60 22N 1 22W
Muckross Hd. 38 54 37N 8 35W
Mucubela 129 16 53S 37 49E
Mucugê 171 13 5S 37 49E
Mucuri 171 18 0S 40 0W
Mucurici 171 18 6S 40 31W
Mud I. 108 27 20S 153 14E
Mud L. 160 40 15N 120 15W
Mudanya 82 40 25N 28 50E
Muddy, R. 161 38 30N 110 55W
Mudgee 141 32 32S 149 31E
Mudhnib 92 25 50N 44 18E
Mudjatik, R. 153 56 1N 107 36W
Mudon 98 16 15N 97 44E
Muecate 127 14 55S 39 34E
Muêda 127 11 36S 39 28E
Muela, La 58 41 36N 1 7W
Mueller Ra., Mts. 136 18 18S 126 46E
Muerto, Mar 165 16 10N 94 10W
Muff 38 55 4N 7 16W
Mufindi □ 127 8 30S 35 20E
Mufou Shan 109 29 15N 114 20E
Mufulira 127 12 32S 28 15E
Mufumbiro Range 126 1 25S 29 30E
Mugardos 56 43 27N 8 15W
Muge 57 39 3N 8 40W
Muge, R. 57 39 15N 8 18W
Múggia 63 45 36N 13 47E
Mugi 110 33 40N 134 25E
Mugia 56 43 3N 9 17W
Mugila, Mts. 126 7 0S 28 50E
Muğla 92 37 15N 28 28E
Mŭglizh 67 42 37N 25 32E
Mugu 95 29 45N 82 30E
Muhammad Qol 122 20 53N 37 9E
Muhammad Râs 122 27 50N 34 0E
Muhammadabad 95 26 4N 83 25E
Muharraqa = Sa'ad 90 31 28N 34 33E
Muhesi, R. 126 6 40S 35 5E
Muheza □ 126 5 0S 39 0E
Mühldorf 49 48 14N 12 23E
Mühlhausen 48 51 12N 10 29E
Mühlig-Hofmann-fjella 13 72 30S 5 0E
Muhutwe 126 1 35S 31 45E
Mui Bai Bung 101 8 35N 104 42E
Mui Ron 101 18 7N 106 27E
Muiden 46 52 20N 5 4E
Muine Bheag 39 52 42N 6 59W
Muiños 56 41 58N 7 59W
Muir, L. 137 34 30S 116 40E
Muir of Ord 37 57 30N 4 35W
Muirdrum 35 56 31N 2 40W
Muirkirk 35 55 31N 4 6W
Muja 123 12 2N 39 30E
Mukachevo 80 48 27N 22 45E
Mukah 102 2 55N 112 5E
Mukalla 91 14 33N 49 2E
Mukawwa, Geziret 122 23 55N 35 53E
Mukdahan 100 16 32N 104 43E
Mukden = Shenyang 107 41 48N 123 27E

Mukeiras Nabari

Mukeiras **91** 13 59N 45 52 E
Mukhtolovo **81** 55 29N 43 15 E
Mukinbudin **137** 30 55 S 118 5 E
Mukombwe **127** 15 48 S 26 32 E
Mukomuko **102** 2 20 S 101 10 E
Mukomwenze **126** 6 49 S 27 15 E
Mukry **85** 37 54N 65 12 E
Muktsar **94** 30 30N 74 30 E
Muktsar Bhatinda **94** 30 15N 74 57 E
Mukur **94** 32 50N 67 50 E
Mukutawa, R. **153** 53 10N 97 24W
Mukwela **127** 17 0 S 26 40 E
Mula **59** 38 3N 1 33W
Mula, R. **96** 19 16N 74 20 E
Mulanay **103** 13 30N 122 30 E
Mulange **126** 3 40 S 27 10 E
Mulatas, Arch. de las **166** 6 51N 78 31W
Mulchén **172** 37 45 S 72 20W
Mulde, R. **48** 50 55N 12 42 E
Mule Creek **158** 43 19N 104 8W
Muleba **126** 1 50 S 31 37 E
Muleba □ **126** 2 0 S 31 30 E
Mulegé **164** 26 53N 112 1W
Mulegns **51** 46 32N 9 38 E
Mulengchen **107** 44 32N 130 14 E
Muleshoe **159** 34 17N 102 42W
Mulga Valley **140** 31 8 S 141 3 E
Mulgathing **139** 30 15 S 134 0 E
Mulgrave **151** 45 38N 61 31W
Mulgrave I. **135** 10 5 S 142 10 E
Mulhacén **59** 37 4N 3 20W
Mülheim **48** 51 26N 6 53W
Mulhouse **43** 47 40N 7 20 E
Muli, China **99** 28 21N 100 40 E
Muli, China **108** 27 50N 101 15 E
Mull Head **37** 59 23N 2 53W
Mull I. **34** 56 27N 6 0W
Mull, Ross of, dist. **34** 56 20N 6 15W
Mull, Sound of **34** 56 30N 5 50W
Mullagh **39** 53 13N 8 25W
Mullaghareirk Mts. **39** 52 20N 9 10W
Mullaittvu **97** 9 15N 80 55 E
Mullardoch L. **36** 57 30N 5 0W
Mullen **158** 42 5N 101 0W
Mullengudgery **141** 31 43 S 147 29 E
Mullens **156** 37 34N 81 22W
Muller, Pegunungan **102** 0 30N 113 30 E
Muller Ra. **138** 5 30 S 143 0 E
Mullet Pen. **38** 54 10N 10 2W
Mullewa **137** 28 29 S 115 30 E
Mullheim **49** 47 48N 7 37 E
Mulligan, R. **138** 26 40 S 139 0 E
Mullin **159** 31 33N 98 38W
Mullinahone **39** 52 30N 7 31W
Mullinavat **39** 52 23N 7 10W
Mullingar **38** 53 31N 7 20W
Mullins **157** 34 12N 79 15W
Mullion **30** 50 1N 5 15W
Mullsjö **73** 57 56N 13 55 E
Mullumbimby **139** 28 30 S 153 30 E
Mulobezi **127** 16 45 S 25 7 E
Mulrany **38** 53 54N 9 47W
Mulroy B. **38** 55 15N 7 45W
Mulshi L. **96** 18 30N 73 20 E
Multai **96** 21 39N 78 15 E
Multan **94** 30 15N 71 30 E
Multan □ **94** 30 29N 72 29 E
Multrå **72** 63 10N 17 24 E
Mulumbe, Mts. **127** 8 40 S 27 30 E
Mulungushi Dam **127** 14 48 S 28 48 E
Mulvane **159** 37 30N 97 15W
Mulwad **122** 18 45N 30 39 E
Mulwala **141** 35 59 S 146 0 E
Mumbles **31** 51 34N 4 0W
Mumbles Hd. **31** 51 33N 4 0W
Mumbwa **125** 15 0 S 27 0 E
Mumeng **135** 7 1 S 146 37 E
Mumra **83** 45 45N 47 41 E
Mun **101** 15 17N 103 0 E
Mun, R. **100** 15 19N 105 30 E
Muna, I. **103** 5 0 S 122 30 E
Muna Sotuta **165** 20 29N 89 43W
Munawwar **95** 32 47N 74 27 E
Münchberg **49** 50 11N 11 48 E
Müncheberg **48** 52 30N 14 9 E
München **49** 48 8N 11 33 E
Munchen-Gladbach = Mönchengladbach **48** 51 12N 6 23 E
Muncho Lake **152** 59 0N 125 50W
Munchŏn **107** 39 14N 127 19 E
Münchwilen **51** 47 38N 8 59 E
Muncie **156** 40 10N 85 20W
Mundakayam **97** 9 30N 76 32 E
Mundala, Puncak **103** 4 30 S 141 0 E
Mundare **152** 53 35N 112 20W
Munday **159** 33 26N 99 39W
Münden **48** 51 25N 9 42 E
Mundesley **29** 52 53N 1 24 E
Mundiwindi **136** 23 47 S 120 9 E
Mundo Novo **171** 11 50 S 40 29W
Mundo, R. **59** 38 30N 2 15W
Mundra **94** 22 54N 69 26 E
Mundrabilla **137** 31 52 S 127 51 E
Munera **59** 39 2N 2 29W
Muneru, R. **96** 16 45N 80 3 E
Mungallala **139** 26 25 S 147 34 E
Mungallala Cr. **139** 28 53 S 147 5 E
Mungana **138** 17 8 S 144 27 E
Mungaoli **94** 24 24N 78 7 E
Mungari **127** 17 12 S 33 42 E
Mungbere **124** 2 36N 28 28 E
Mungindi **139** 28 58 S 149 1 E
Munhango **125** 12 10 S 18 38 E
Munhango R. **125** 11 30 S 19 30 E
Munich = München **49** 48 8N 11 35 E
Munising **156** 46 25N 86 39W
Munjiye **122** 18 47N 41 20W
Munka-Ljungby **73** 56 16N 12 58 E
Munkedal **73** 58 28N 11 40 E
Munkfors **72** 59 50N 13 30 E
Muñoz Gamero, Pen. **176** 52 30 S 73 5 E
Munro **141** 37 56 S 147 11 E
Munroe L. **153** 59 13N 98 35W
Munsan **107** 37 51N 126 48 E
Munshiganj **98** 23 33N 90 32 E
Münsingen **50** 46 52N 7 32 E
Munster **43** 48 2N 7 8 E
Münster, Niedersachsen, Ger. **48** 52 59N 10 5 E
Münster, Nordrhein-Westfalen, Ger. **48** 51 58N 7 37 E
Münster, Switz. **51** 46 30N 8 17 E
Munster □ **39** 52 20N 8 40W
Muntadgin **137** 31 45 S 118 33 E
Muntele Mare **70** 46 30N 23 12 E
Muntok **102** 2 5 S 105 10 E
Muon Pak Beng **101** 19 51N 101 4 E
Muong Beng **100** 20 23N 101 46 E
Muong Boum **100** 22 24N 102 49 E
Muong Er **100** 20 49N 104 1 E
Muong Hai **100** 21 3N 101 49 E
Muong Hiem **100** 20 5N 103 22 E
Muong Houn **100** 20 8N 101 23 E
Muong Hung **100** 20 56N 103 53 E
Muong Kau **100** 15 6N 105 47 E
Muong Khao **100** 19 47N 103 29 E
Muong Khoua **100** 21 5N 102 31 E
Muong La **101** 20 52N 102 5 E
Muong Liep **100** 18 29N 101 40 E
Muong May **100** 14 49N 106 56 E
Muong Ngeun **100** 20 36N 101 3 E
Muong Ngoi **100** 20 43N 102 41 E
Muong Nhie **100** 22 12N 102 28 E
Muong Nong **100** 16 22N 106 30 E
Muong Ou Tay **100** 22 7N 101 48 E
Muong Oua **100** 18 18N 101 20 E
Muong Pak Bang **100** 19 54N 101 8 E
Muong Penn **100** 20 13N 103 52 E
Muong Phalane **100** 16 39N 105 34 E
Muong Phieng **100** 19 6N 101 32 E
Muong Phine **100** 16 32N 106 2 E
Muong Sai **100** 20 42N 101 59 E
Muong Saiapoun **100** 18 24N 101 31 E
Muong Sen **100** 19 24N 104 8 E
Muong Sing **100** 21 11N 101 9 E
Muong Son **100** 20 27N 103 19 E
Muong Soui **100** 19 33N 102 52 E
Muong Va **100** 21 53N 102 19 E
Muong Xia **100** 20 19N 104 50 E
Muonio **74** 67 57N 23 40 E
Muonio älv **74** 67 48N 23 25 E
Muotathal **51** 46 58N 8 46 E
Muotohora **142** 38 18 S 177 40 E
Mupa **125** 16 5 S 15 50 E
Muqaddam, Wadi **123** 17 0N 32 0 E
Mur-de-Bretagne **42** 48 12N 3 0W
Mur, R. **52** 47 7N 13 55 E
Mura, R. **63** 46 37N 16 9 E
Murallón, Cuerro **176** 49 55 S 73 30W
Muralto **51** 46 11N 8 49 E
Muranda **126** 1 52 S 29 20 E
Murang'a **126** 0 45 S 37 9 E
Murashi **81** 59 30N 49 0 E
Murat **44** 45 7N 2 53 E
Murau **52** 47 6N 14 10 E
Muravera **64** 39 25N 9 35 E
Murça **56** 41 24N 7 28W
Murchison **143** 41 49 S 172 21 E
Murchison Downs **137** 26 45 S 118 55 E
Murchison Falls = Kabarega Falls **126** 2 15N 31 38 E
Murchison House **137** 27 39 S 114 14 E
Murchison Mts. **143** 45 13 S 167 23 E
Murchison, oilfield **19** 61 25N 1 40 E
Murchison, R. **137** 26 45 S 116 15 E
Murchison Ra. **138** 20 0 S 134 10 E
Murchison Rapids **127** 15 55 S 34 35 E
Murcia **59** 38 2N 1 10W
Murcia □ **59** 37 50N 1 30W
Murdo **158** 43 56N 100 43W
Murdoch Pt. **138** 14 37 S 144 55 E
Murdock Hill **109** 34 59 S 138 55 E
Mure, La **45** 44 55N 5 48 E
Mureş □ **70** 46 45N 24 40 E
Mureşul, R. **70** 46 15N 20 13 E
Muret **44** 43 30N 1 20 E
Murfatlar **70** 44 10N 28 26 E
Murfreesboro **157** 35 50N 86 21W
Murg **51** 47 8N 9 13 E
Murgab **85** 38 10N 73 59 E
Murgeni **70** 46 12N 28 1 E
Murgenthal **50** 47 16N 7 50 E
Murgon **139** 26 15 S 151 54 E
Murgoo **137** 27 24 S 116 28 E
Muri **51** 47 17N 8 21 E
Muriaé **173** 21 8 S 42 23W
Murias de Paredes **56** 42 52N 6 19W
Murici **170** 9 19 S 35 56W
Muriel Mine **127** 17 14 S 30 40 E
Muritiba **171** 12 55 S 39 15W
Murits see **48** 53 25N 12 40 E
Murjo Mt. **103** 6 36 S 110 53 E
Murka **126** 3 27 S 38 0 E
Murmansk **78** 68 57N 33 10 E
Murmerwoude **46** 53 18N 6 0 E
Murnau **49** 47 40N 11 11 E
Muro, France **45** 42 34N 8 54 E
Muro, Spain **58** 39 45N 3 3 E
Muro, C. di **45** 41 44N 8 37 E
Muro Lucano **65** 40 45N 15 30 E
Murom **81** 55 35N 42 3 E
Muroran **112** 42 25N 141 0 E
Muros **56** 42 45N 9 5W
Muros y de Noya, Ria de **56** 42 45N 9 0W
Muroto **110** 33 18N 134 9 E
Muroto-Misaki **110** 33 15N 134 10 E
Murowana Gosślina **54** 52 35N 17 0 E
Murphy **160** 43 11N 116 33W
Murphys **163** 38 8N 120 28W
Murphysboro **159** 37 50N 89 20W
Murrat **122** 18 51N 29 33 E
Murray, Ky., U.S.A. **157** 36 40N 88 20W
Murray, Utah, U.S.A. **160** 40 41N 111 58W
Murray Bridge **140** 35 6 S 139 14 E
Murray Downs **138** 21 4 S 134 40 E
Murray Harb. **151** 46 0N 62 28W
Murray, L., P.N.G. **135** 7 0 S 141 35 E
Murray, L., U.S.A. **157** 34 8N 81 30W
Murray, R., S. Australia, Austral. **140** 35 20 S 139 22 E
Murray, R., W. Australia, Austral. **133** 32 33 S 115 45 E
Murray, R., Can. **152** 56 11N 120 45W
Murraysburg **128** 31 58 S 23 47 E
Murree **94** 33 56N 73 28 E
Murrieta **163** 33 33N 117 13W
Murrin Murrin **137** 28 50 S 121 45 E
Murrough **39** 53 7N 9 18W
Murrumbidgee, R. **140** 34 40 S 143 0 E
Murrumburrah **141** 34 32 S 148 22 E
Murrurundi **141** 31 42 S 150 51 E
Murshid **122** 21 40N 31 10 E
Murshidabad **95** 24 11N 88 19 E
Murska Sobota **63** 46 39N 16 12 E
Murtazapur **96** 20 40N 77 25 E
Murten **50** 46 56N 6 7 E
Murten-see **50** 46 56N 7 4 E
Murtle L. **152** 52 8N 119 38W
Murtoa **140** 36 35 S 142 28 E
Murton **33** 54 51N 1 22W
Murtosa **56** 40 44N 8 40W
Muru **123** 6 36N 29 16 E
Murungu **126** 4 12 S 31 10 E
Murupara **142** 38 28 S 176 42 E
Murwara **95** 23 46N 80 28 E
Murwillumbah **139** 28 18 S 153 27 E
Mürz, R. **52** 47 30N 15 25 E
Mürzzuschlag **52** 47 36N 15 41 E
Muş **92** 38 45N 41 30 E
Musa, Gebel (Sinai) **122** 28 32N 33 59 E
Musa Khel **94** 30 29N 69 52 E
Musa Qala (Musa Kala) **93** 32 20N 64 50 E
Musa, R. **135** 9 3 S 148 55 E
Musaffargarh **93** 30 10N 71 10 E
Musairik, Wadi **122** 19 30N 43 10 E
Musala, I. **102** 1 41N 98 28 E
Musalla, mt. **67** 42 13N 23 37 E
Musan **107** 42 12N 129 12 E
Musangu **127** 10 28 S 23 55 E
Musasa **126** 3 25 S 31 30 E
Musashino **111** 35 42N 139 34 E
Muscat = Masqat **93** 23 37N 58 36 E
Muscat & Oman = Oman **91** 23 0N 58 0 E
Muscatine **158** 41 25N 91 5W
Musel **56** 43 34N 5 42W
Musetula **127** 14 28 S 24 1 E
Musgrave Ras. **137** 26 0 S 132 0 E
Mushie **124** 2 56 S 17 4 E
Mushin **121** 6 32N 3 21 E
Musi, R., India **96** 17 10N 79 25 E
Musi, R., Indon. **102** 2 55 S 103 40 E
Muskeg, R. **152** 60 20N 123 20W
Muskegon **156** 43 15N 86 17W
Muskegon Hts. **156** 43 12N 86 17W
Muskegon, R. **156** 43 25N 86 0W
Muskogee **159** 35 50N 95 25W
Muskwa, R. **152** 58 47N 122 48W
Musmar **122** 18 6N 35 40 E
Musofu **127** 13 30 S 29 0 E
Musoma **126** 1 30 S 33 48 E
Musoma □ **126** 1 50 S 34 30 E
Musquaro, L. **151** 50 38N 61 5W
Musquodoboit Harbour **151** 44 50N 63 9W
Mussau I. **135** 1 30 S 149 40 E
Musselburgh **35** 55 57N 3 3W
Musselkanaal **46** 52 57N 7 0 E
Musselshell, R. **160** 46 30N 108 15W
Mussidan **44** 45 2N 0 22 E
Mussomeli **64** 37 35N 13 43 E
Musson **47** 49 33N 5 42 E
Mussooree **94** 30 27N 78 6 E
Mussuco **128** 17 2 S 19 3 E
Mustafa Kemalpaşa **92** 40 3N 28 25 E
Mustajidda **92** 26 30N 41 50 E
Mustang **95** 29 10N 83 55 E
Mustapha, C. **119** 36 55N 11 3 E
Musters, L. **176** 45 20 S 69 25W
Musudan **107** 40 50N 129 43 E
Muswellbrook **141** 32 16 S 150 56 E
Muszyna **53** 49 22N 20 55 E
Mût **122** 25 28N 28 58 E
Mut **92** 36 40N 33 28 E
Mutan Chiang, R. **107** 46 18N 129 31 E
Mutanchiang **107** 44 40N 129 35 E
Mutanda, Mozam. **129** 21 0 S 33 34 E
Mutanda, Zambia **127** 12 15 S 26 13 E
Muthill **35** 56 20N 3 50W
Mutis **174** 1 4N 77 25W
Mutooroo **140** 32 26 S 140 55 E
Mutshatsha **127** 10 35 S 24 20 E
Mutsu-Wan **112** 41 5N 140 55 E
Muttaburra **138** 22 38 S 144 29 E
Muttama **141** 34 46 S 148 8 E
Mutton Bay **151** 50 50N 59 2W
Mutton I. **39** 52 50N 9 31W
Mutuáli **127** 14 55 S 37 0 E
Mutung **108** 29 35N 106 51 E
Mutunópolis **171** 13 40 S 49 15W
Muvatupusha **97** 9 53N 76 35 E
Muxima **124** 9 25 S 13 52 E
Muy, Le **45** 43 28N 6 34 E
Muy Muy **166** 12 39N 85 36W
Muya **77** 56 27N 115 39 E
Muyaga **126** 3 14 S 30 33 E
Muyunkum, Peski **85** 44 12N 71 0 E
Muzaffarabad **95** 34 25N 73 30 E
Muzaffargarh **94** 30 5N 71 14 E
Muzaffarnagar **94** 29 26N 77 40 E
Muzaffarpur **95** 26 7N 85 32 E
Muzhi **76** 65 25N 64 40 E
Muzillac **42** 47 35N 2 30W
Muzkol, Khrebet **85** 38 22N 73 20 E
Muzo **174** 5 32N 74 6W
Muzon C. **152** 54 40N 132 40W
Mvôlô **123** 6 10N 29 53 E
Mwadui **126** 3 35 S 33 40 E
Mwandi Mission **127** 17 30 S 24 51 E
Mwango **126** 6 48 S 24 12 E
Mwanza, Katanga, Congo **126** 7 55 S 26 43 E
Mwanza, Kwango, Congo **127** 5 29 S 17 43 E
Mwanza, Malawi **126** 16 58 S 24 28 E
Mwanza, Tanz. **126** 2 30 S 32 58 E
Mwanza □ **126** 2 0 S 33 0 E
Mwaya **126** 9 32 S 33 55 E
Mweelrea, Mt. **38** 53 37N 9 48W
Mweka **124** 4 50 S 21 40 E
Mwenga **126** 3 1 S 28 21 E
Mwepo **127** 11 50 S 26 10 E
Mweru, L. **127** 9 0 S 29 0 E
Mweza Range **127** 21 0 S 30 0 E
Mwimbi **127** 8 38 S 31 39 E
Mwinilunga **127** 11 43 S 24 25 E
Mwinilunga, Mt. **127** 11 43 S 24 25 E
My Tho **101** 10 29N 106 23 E
Mya, O. **119** 30 46N 4 44 E
Myadh **124** 1 16N 13 10 E
Myanaung **98** 18 25N 95 10 E
Myaungmya **98** 16 30N 95 0 E
Mybster **37** 58 27N 3 24W
Myddfai **31** 51 59N 3 47W
Myddle **28** 52 49N 2 47W
Myerstown **162** 40 22N 76 18W
Myingyan **98** 21 30N 95 30 E
Myitkyina **98** 25 30N 97 26 E
Myittha, R. **98** 16 15N 94 34 E
Myjava **53** 48 41N 17 37 E
Mylor **109** 35 3 S 138 46 E
Mymensingh **98** 24 45N 90 24 E
Myndmere **158** 46 23N 97 7W
Mynydd Bach, Hills **31** 52 16N 4 6W
Mynydd Eppynt, Mts. **31** 52 4N 3 30W
Mynydd Prescelly, mt. **31** 51 57N 4 48W
Mynzhilgi, Gora **85** 43 48N 68 51 E
Myogi **101** 21 24N 96 28 E
Myrdal **71** 60 43N 7 10 E
Mýrdalsjökull **74** 63 40N 19 6W
Myrrhee **136** 36 46 S 146 17 E
Myrtle Beach **157** 33 43N 78 50W
Myrtle Creek **160** 43 0N 123 19W
Myrtle Point **160** 43 0N 124 4W
Myrtleford **141** 36 34 S 146 44 E
Myrtletown **108** 27 23 S 153 8 E
Mysen **71** 59 33N 11 20 E
Myslenice **54** 49 51N 19 57 E
Myslibórz **54** 52 55N 14 50 E
Mysłowice **54** 50 15N 19 12 E
Mysore **97** 12 17N 76 41 E
Mysore □ = Karnataka **142** 13 15N 77 0 E
Mystic **162** 41 21N 71 58W
Mystishchi **81** 55 50N 37 50 E
Myszkow **54** 50 45N 19 22 E
Mythen **51** 47 2N 8 42 E
Myton **160** 40 10N 110 2W
Mývatn **74** 65 36N 17 0W
Mze, R. **52** 49 47N 12 50 E
Mzimba **127** 11 48 S 33 33 E
Mzuzu **127** 11 30 S 33 55 E

N

N' Dioum **120** 16 31N 14 39W
Na-lang **98** 22 42N 97 33 E
Na Noi **100** 18 19N 100 43 E
Na Phao **100** 17 35N 105 44 E
Na Sam **100** 22 3N 106 37 E
Na San **100** 21 12N 104 2 E
Naaldwijk **46** 51 59N 4 13 E
Naalehu **147** 19 4N 155 35W
Na'am **123** 9 42N 28 27 E
Na'an **90** 31 53N 34 52 E
Naantali **75** 60 29N 22 2 E
Naarden **46** 52 18N 5 9 E
Naas **39** 53 12N 6 40W
Nababeep **128** 29 36 S 17 46 E
Nabadwip **95** 23 34N 88 20 E
Nabari **111** 34 37N 136 5 E

Nabas Nashville

Nabas 103 11 47N 122 6E
Nabberu, L. 137 25 30S 120 30E
Naberezhnyye Chelny 84 55 42N 52 19E
Nabesna 147 62 33N 143 10W
Nabeul 119 36 30N 10 51E
Nabha 94 30 26N 76 14E
Nabi Rubin 90 31 56N 34 44E
Nabire 103 3 15S 136 27E
Nabisar 94 25 8N 69 40E
Nabispi, R. 151 50 14N 62 13W
Nabiswera 126 1 27N 32 15E
Nablus = Nābulus 90 32 14N 35 15E
Naboomspruit 129 24 32S 28 40E
Nābulus 90 32 14N 35 15E
Nabúri 127 16 53S 38 59E
Nacala-Velha 127 14 32S 40 34E
Nacaome 166 13 31N 87 30W
Nacaroa 127 14 22S 39 56E
Naches 160 46 48N 120 49W
Nachikatsuura 111 33 33N 135 58E
Nachingwea 127 10 49S 38 49E
Nachingwea □ 127 10 30S 38 30E
Nachna 94 27 34N 71 41E
Náchod 53 50 25N 16 8E
Nacimento Res. 163 35 46N 120 53W
Nacka 72 59 17N 18 12E
Nackara 140 32 48S 139 12E
Naco, Mexico 164 31 20N 109 56W
Naco, U.S.A. 161 31 24N 109 58W
Nacogdoches 159 31 33N 95 30W
Nácori Chico 164 29 39N 109 1W
Nacozari 164 30 30N 109 50W
Nadi 122 18 40N 33 41E
Nadiad 94 22 41N 72 56E
Nador 118 35 14N 2 58W
Nadushan 93 32 2N 53 35E
Nadvornaya 80 48 40N 24 35E
Nadym 76 63 35N 72 42E
Nadym, R. 76 65 30N 73 0E
Nærbø 71 58 40N 5 39E
Næstved 73 55 13N 11 44E
Nafada 121 11 8N 11 20E
Näfels 51 47 6N 9 4E
Nafferton 33 54 1N 0 24W
Naft Shāh 92 34 0N 45 30E
Nafūd ad Dahy 92 22 0N 45 0E
Nafūsah, Jabal 119 32 12N 12 30E
Nag Hammâdi 122 26 2N 32 18E
Naga 103 13 38N 123 15E
Naga Hills 99 26 0N 94 30E
Naga, Kreb en 118 24 12N 6 0W
Naga-Shima, Kagoshima, Japan 110 32 10N 130 9E
Naga-Shima, Yamaguchi, Japan 110 33 55N 132 5E
Nagagami, R. 150 49 40N 84 40W
Nagahama, Ehime, Japan 111 33 36N 132 29E
Nagahama, Shiga, Japan 111 35 23N 136 16E
Nagai Parkar 94 24 28N 70 46E
Nagaland □ 98 26 0N 94 30E
Nagambie 141 36 47S 145 10E
Nagano 111 36 40N 138 10E
Nagano-ken □ 111 36 15N 138 0E
Nagaoka 112 37 27N 138 50E
Nagappattinam 97 10 46N 79 51E
Nagar Parkar 93 24 30N 70 35E
Nagara-Gawa, R. 111 35 1N 136 43E
Nagari Hills 97 15 30N 79 45E
Nagarjuna Sagar 96 16 35N 79 17E
Nagasaki 110 32 47N 129 50E
Nagasaki-ken □ 110 32 50N 129 40E
Nagato 110 34 19N 131 5E
Nagaur 94 27 15N 73 45E
Nagbhir 96 20 34N 79 42E
Nagchu Dzong 99 31 22N 91 54E
Nagercoil 97 8 12N 77 33E
Nagina 95 29 30N 78 30E
Nagineh 93 34 20N 57 15E
Nagold 49 48 38N 8 40E
Nagoorin 138 24 17S 151 15E
Nagorsk 81 59 18N 50 48E
Nagorum 126 4 1N 34 33E
Nagoya 111 35 10N 136 50E
Nagpur 96 21 8N 79 10E
Nagrong 99 32 46N 84 16E
Nagua 167 19 23N 69 50W
Nagyatád 53 46 14N 17 22E
Nagyecsed 53 47 53N 22 24E
Nagykanizsa 53 46 28N 17 0E
Nagykörös 53 46 55N 19 48E
Nagyléta 53 47 23N 21 55E
Naha 112 26 13N 127 42E
Nahalal 90 32 41N 35 12E
Nahanni Butte 152 61 2N 123 20W
Nahanni Nat. Pk. 152 61 15N 125 0W
Naharayim 90 32 28N 35 33E
Nahariyya 90 33 1N 35 5E
Nahāvand 92 34 10N 48 30E
Nahe, R. 49 49 48N 7 33E
Nahf 90 32 56N 35 18E
Nahîya, Wadi 122 27 37N 32 0E
Nahlin 152 58 55N 131 38W
Nahud 122 18 12N 41 40E
Naiapu 70 44 12N 25 47E
Naicá 164 27 53N 105 31W
Naicam 153 52 30N 104 30W
Na'ifah 91 19 59N 50 46E
Naila 49 50 19N 11 43E
Nailsea 28 51 25N 2 44W
Nailsworth 28 51 41N 2 12W
Nain 151 56 34N 61 40W
Na'in 93 32 54N 53 0E
Naini Tal 95 29 23N 79 30E
Nainpur 93 22 30N 80 10E
Naintré 42 46 46N 0 29E
Naira, I. 103 4 28S 130 0E
Nairn 37 57 35N 3 54W
Nairn (□) 26 57 28N 3 52W
Nairn R. 37 57 32N 3 58W
Nairobi 126 1 17S 36 48E
Naivasha 126 0 40S 36 30E
Naivasha □ 126 0 40S 36 30E
Naivasha L. 126 0 48S 36 20E
Najac 44 44 14N 1 58E
Najafābād 93 32 40N 51 15E
Najd 92 26 30N 42 0E
Nájera 58 42 26N 2 48W
Najerilla, R. 58 42 15N 2 45W
Najibabad 94 29 40N 78 20E
Najin 107 42 12N 130 15E
Naju 107 35 3N 126 43E
Naka-Gawa, R. 111 36 20N 140 36E
Naka-no-Shima 112 29 51N 129 46E
Nakalagba 126 2 50N 27 58E
Nakama 110 33 56N 130 43E
Nakaminato 111 36 21N 140 36E
Nakamura 110 33 0N 133 0E
Nakanai Mts. 135 5 40S 151 0E
Nakano 111 36 45N 138 22E
Nakanojō 111 36 35N 138 51E
Nakatane 112 30 31N 130 57E
Nakatsu 110 33 40N 131 15E
Nakatsugawa 111 35 29N 137 30E
Nakelele Pt. 147 21 2N 156 35W
Nakfa 123 16 40N 38 25E
Nakhichevan, A.S.S.R. □ 79 39 14N 45 30E
Nakhl 122 29 55N 33 43E
Nakhl Mubarak 92 24 10N 38 10E
Nakhodka 77 43 10N 132 45E
Nakhon Nayok 100 14 12N 101 13E
Nakhon Pathom 100 13 49N 100 3E
Nakhon Phanom 100 17 23N 104 43E
Nakhon Ratchasima (Khorat) 100 14 59N 102 12E
Nakhon Sawan 100 15 35N 100 10E
Nakhon Si Thammarat 100 8 29N 100 0E
Nakhon Thai 100 17 17N 100 50E
Nakina, B.C., Can. 152 59 12N 132 52W
Nakina, Ont., Can. 150 50 10N 86 40W
Nakło n. Noteoja 54 53 9N 17 38E
Naknek 147 58 45N 157 0W
Nakodar 94 31 8N 75 31E
Nakomis 127 39 19N 89 19W
Nakskov 73 54 50N 11 8E
Näkten 72 62 48N 14 38E
Naktong, R. 107 35 7N 128 57E
Nakur 94 30 2N 77 32E
Nakuru 126 0 15S 35 5E
Nakuru □ 126 0 15S 35 5E
Nakuru, L. 126 0 23S 36 5E
Nakusp 152 50 20N 117 45W
Nal, R. 94 27 0N 65 50E
Nalchik 83 43 30N 43 33E
Nälden 72 63 21N 14 14E
Näldsjön 72 63 25N 14 15E
Nalerigu 121 10 35N 0 25W
Nalgonda 96 17 6N 79 15E
Nalhati 95 24 17N 87 52E
Nalinnes 47 50 19N 4 27E
Nallamalai Hills 97 15 30N 78 50E
Nalón, R. 56 43 35N 6 10W
Nālūt 119 31 54N 11 0E
Nam Can 101 8 46N 104 59E
Nam Dinh 100 20 25N 106 5E
Nam Du, Hon 101 9 41N 104 21E
'Nam', gasfields 19 53 17N 3 36E
Nam Ngum 100 18 35N 102 34E
'Nam', oilfield 19 54 50N 4 40E
Nam-Phan 101 10 30N 106 0E
Nam Phong 100 16 42N 102 52E
Nam Tha 100 20 58N 101 30E
Nam Tok 100 14 14N 99 4E
Nam Tso = Namu Hu 105 30 45N 90 30E
Namacurra 125 17 30S 36 50E
Namakkal 97 11 13N 78 13E
Namaland, Africa 128 26 0S 18 0E
Namaland, S. Afr. 128 30 0S 18 0E
Namangan 85 41 0N 71 40E
Namapa 127 13 43S 39 50E
Namasagali 126 1 2N 33 0E
Namatanai 135 3 40S 152 29E
Nambala 120 14 1N 5 58W
Namber 103 1 2S 134 57E
Nambour 139 26 32S 152 58E
Nambucca Heads 141 30 37S 153 0E
Namcha Barwa 105 29 40N 95 10E
Namche Bazar 95 27 51N 86 47E
Namchonjŏm 107 38 15N 126 26E
Namêche 47 50 28N 5 0E
Namecund 127 14 54S 37 37E
Nameh 102 2 34N 116 21E
Nameponda 127 15 50S 39 50E
Namerikawa 111 36 46N 137 20E
Námestovo 53 49 24N 19 25E
Nametil 127 15 40S 39 15E
Náměšt nad Oslavou 53 49 12N 16 10E
Namew L. 153 54 14N 101 56W
Namhsan 98 22 48N 97 42E
Nami 101 6 2N 100 46E
Namib Desert = Namib Woestyn 128 22 30S 15 0E
Namib-Woestyn 128 22 30S 15 0E
Namibia □ 128 22 0S 18 9E
Namiquipa 164 29 15N 107 25W
Namja Pass 95 30 0N 82 25E
Namkhan 98 23 50N 97 41E
Namlea 103 3 10S 127 5E
Namoi, R. 141 30 12S 149 30E
Namous, O. 118 30 44N 0 18W
Nampa 160 43 40N 116 40W
Nampula 127 15 6S 39 7E
Namrole 103 3 46S 126 46E
Namsen 74 64 27N 11 42E
Namsen, R. 74 64 40N 12 45E
Namsos 74 64 28N 11 0E
Namtu 98 23 5N 97 28E
Namtumbo 127 10 30S 36 4E
Namu 152 51 52N 127 41W
Namu Hu 105 30 45N 90 30E
Namur 47 50 27N 4 52E
Namur □ 47 50 17N 5 0E
Namutoni 128 18 49S 16 55E
Namwala 127 15 44S 26 30E
Namwŏn 107 35 23N 127 23E
Namysłow 54 51 6N 17 42E
Nan 100 18 48N 100 46E
Nan Ling 109 25 0N 112 30E
Nan, R. 100 15 42N 100 9E
Nan Shan 105 38 30N 99 0E
Nana 70 44 17N 26 34E
Nānā, W. 119 30 0N 15 24E
Nanaimo 152 49 10N 124 0W
Nanam 107 41 44N 129 40E
Nan'an 109 24 58N 118 23E
Nanango 139 26 40S 152 0E
Nanao 109 23 26N 117 1E
Nanch'ang 109 28 40N 115 50E
Nanchang, Fukien, China 109 24 26N 117 18E
Nanchang, Hupei, China 109 31 47N 111 42E
Nanch'eng 109 27 33N 116 35E
Nancheng = Hanchung 106 33 10N 107 2E
Nanchiang 108 32 21N 106 50E
Nanchiao 108 22 2N 100 15E
Nanchien 106 25 5N 100 30E
Nanching 109 32 3N 118 47E
Nanchishan Liehtao 108 27 28N 121 4E
Nanch'uan 108 29 7N 107 16E
Nanch'ung 108 30 50N 106 4E
Nancy 43 48 42N 6 12E
Nanda Devi, Mt. 95 30 30N 80 30E
Nandan 110 34 10N 134 42E
Nander 96 19 10N 77 20E
Nandewar Ra. 139 30 15S 150 35E
Nandi □ 126 0 15N 35 0E
Nandikotkur 97 15 52N 78 18E
Nandura 96 20 52N 76 25E
Nandurbar 96 21 20N 74 15E
Nandyal 97 15 30N 78 30E
Nanfeng 109 27 10N 116 24E
Nanga 137 26 7S 113 45E
Nanga Eboko 121 4 41N 12 22E
Nanga Parbat, mt. 95 35 10N 74 35E
Nangade 127 11 5S 39 36E
Nangapinoh 102 0 20S 111 14E
Nangarhar □ 93 34 20N 70 0E
Nangatajap 102 1 32S 110 34E
Nangeya Mts. 126 3 30N 33 30E
Nangis 43 48 33N 3 0E
Nangodi 121 10 58N 0 42W
Nangola 120 12 41N 6 35W
Nangwarry 140 37 33S 140 48E
Nanhsien 109 29 22N 112 25E
Nanhsiung 109 25 10N 114 18E
Nanhua 108 25 10N 101 20E
Nanhui 109 31 3N 121 46E
Nani Hu 109 31 10N 118 55E
Nanjangud 97 12 6N 76 43E
Nanjeko 127 5 31S 23 30E
Nanjirinji 127 9 41S 39 5E
Nankana Sahib 94 31 27N 73 38E
Nank'ang 109 25 38N 114 45E
Nanking = Nanching 109 32 5N 118 45E
Nankoku 110 33 29N 133 38E
Nankung 106 37 22N 115 20E
Nanling 109 30 56N 118 19E
Nannine 137 26 51S 118 18E
Nanning 108 22 48N 108 20E
Nannup 137 33 59S 115 48E
Nanpa 108 32 13N 104 51E
Nanp'an Chiang, R. 108 25 0N 106 11E
Nanpara 95 27 52N 81 33E
Nanp'i 106 38 4N 116 34E
Nanp'ing, Fukien, China 109 26 38N 118 10E
Nanp'ing, Hupeh, China 109 29 55N 112 2E
Nanpu 108 31 19N 106 2E
Nanripe 127 13 52S 38 52E
Nansei-Shotō 112 26 0N 128 0E
Nansen Sd. 12 81 0N 91 0W
Nansio 126 2 3S 33 4E
Nanson 137 28 35S 114 45E
Nant 44 44 1N 3 18E
Nantes 42 47 12N 1 33W
Nanteuil-le-Haudouin 43 49 9N 2 48E
Nantiat 44 46 1N 1 11E
Nanticoke 162 41 12N 76 1W
Nanticoke, R. 162 38 16N 75 56W
Nanton, Can. 152 50 21N 113 46W
Nanton, China 108 24 59N 107 32E
Nantua 45 46 10N 5 35E
Nantucket 162 41 17N 70 6W
Nantucket I. 155 41 16N 70 3W
Nantucket Sd. 162 41 30N 70 15W
Nant'ung 109 32 0N 120 55E
Nantwich 32 53 5N 2 31W
Nanuque 171 17 50S 40 21W
Nanutarra 136 22 32S 115 30E
Nanyang 106 33 0N 112 32E
Nan'yō 110 34 3N 131 49E
Nanyüan 106 39 48N 116 24E
Nanyuki 126 0 2N 37 4E
Nao, C. de la 59 38 44N 0 14E
Nao Chou Tao 109 20 55N 110 35E
Nao, La, Cabo de 59 38 44N 0 14E
Naococane L. 151 52 50N 70 45W
Naogaon 98 24 52N 88 52E
Napa 163 38 18N 122 17W
Napa, R. 163 38 10N 122 19W
Napamute 147 61 30N 158 45W
Napanee 150 44 15N 77 0W
Napanoch 162 41 44N 74 2W
Nape 100 18 18N 105 6E
Nape Pass = Keo Neua, Deo 100 18 23N 105 10E
Napf 50 47 1N 7 56E
Napiéolédougou 120 9 18N 5 35W
Napier 142 39 30S 176 56E
Napier Broome B. 136 14 2S 126 37E
Napier Downs 136 17 11S 124 36E
Napier Pen. 138 12 4S 135 43E
Naples 157 26 10N 81 45W
Naples = Nápoli 65 40 50N 14 5E
Nap'o 108 23 44N 106 49E
Napo □ 174 0 30S 77 0W
Napo, R. 174 3 5S 73 0W
Napoleon, N. Dak., U.S.A. 158 46 32N 99 49W
Napoleon, Ohio, U.S.A. 156 41 24N 84 7W
Nápoli 65 40 50N 14 5E
Nápoli, G. di 65 40 40N 14 10E
Napopo 126 4 15N 28 0E
Napoule, La 45 43 31N 6 56E
Nappa 32 53 58N 2 14W
Nappa Merrie 139 27 36S 141 7E
Naqâda 122 25 53N 32 42E
Nara, Japan 111 34 40N 135 49E
Nara, Mali 120 15 25N 7 20W
Nara, Canal 94 26 0N 69 20E
Nara-ken □ 111 34 30N 136 0E
Nara Visa 159 35 39N 103 10W
Naracoorte 140 36 58S 140 45E
Naradhan 141 33 34S 146 17E
Narasapur 96 16 26N 81 50E
Narasaropet 96 16 14N 80 4E
Narathiwat 101 6 40N 101 55E
Narayanganj 98 23 31N 90 33E
Narayanpet 96 16 45N 77 30E
Narberth 31 51 48N 4 45W
Narbonne 44 43 11N 3 0E
Narborough 28 52 34N 1 12W
Narcea, R. 56 43 15N 6 30W
Nardò 65 40 10N 18 0E
Nare Head 30 50 12N 4 55W
Narembeen 137 32 7S 118 17E
Naretha 137 31 0S 124 45E
Nari, R. 94 29 10N 67 50E
Narin 93 36 5N 69 0E
Narinda, B. de 129 14 55S 47 30E
Narino □ 174 1 30N 78 0W
Narita 111 35 47N 140 19E
Narmada, R. 94 22 40N 77 30E
Narnaul 94 28 5N 76 11E
Narni 63 42 30N 12 30E
Naro, Ghana 120 10 22N 2 27W
Naro, Italy 64 37 18N 13 48E
Naro Fominsk 81 55 23N 36 32E
Narodnaya, G. 78 65 5N 60 0E
Narok 126 1 20S 33 30E
Narok □ 126 1 20S 33 30E
Narón 56 43 32N 8 9W
Narooma 141 36 14S 150 4E
Narowal 94 32 6N 74 52E
Narrabri 139 30 19S 149 46E
Narran, R. 139 28 37S 148 12E
Narrandera 141 34 42S 146 31E
Narraway, R. 152 55 44N 119 55W
Narrogin 137 32 58S 117 14E
Narromine 141 32 12S 148 12E
Narrows, str. 36 57 20N 6 5W
Narsampet 96 17 57N 79 58E
Narsinghpur 95 22 54N 79 14E
Naruto 110 34 11N 134 37E
Narutō 111 35 36N 140 25E
Naruto-Kaikyō 110 34 14N 134 39E
Narva 80 59 10N 28 5E
Narva, R. 80 59 10N 27 50E
Narvik 74 68 28N 17 26E
Narvskoye Vdkhr. 80 59 10N 28 5E
Narwana 94 29 39N 76 6E
Naryan-Mar 78 68 0N 53 0E
Naryilco 139 28 37S 141 53E
Narym 76 59 0N 81 58E
Narymskoye 76 49 10N 84 15E
Naryn 85 41 26N 75 58E
Naryn, R. 85 40 52N 71 36E
Nasa 74 66 29N 15 23E
Nasa, mt. 74 66 32N 15 23E
Nasarawa 121 8 32N 7 41E
Naseby, N.Z. 143 45 1S 170 10E
Naseby, U.K. 29 52 24N 0 59W
Naser, Buheirat en 122 23 0N 32 30E
Nash Pt. 31 51 24N 3 34W
Nashua, Iowa, U.S.A. 158 42 55N 92 34W
Nashua, Mont., U.S.A. 160 48 10N 106 25W
Nashua, N.H., U.S.A. 162 42 50N 71 25W
Nashville, Ark., U.S.A. 159 33 56N 93 50W

Nashville Nevillé-Pont-Pierre

Nashville, Ga., U.S.A.	157	31 13N	83 15W
Nashville, Tenn., U.S.A.	157	36 12N	86 46W
Našice	66	45 32N	18 4E
Nasielsk	54	52 35N	20 50E
Nasik	96	20 2N	73 50E
Nasirabad, Bangla.	95	24 42N	90 30E
Nasirabad, India	94	26 15N	74 45E
Nasirabad, Pak.	96	28 25N	68 25E
Naskaupi, R.	151	53 47N	60 51W
Naso	65	38 8N	14 46E
Nass, R.	152	55 0N	129 40W
Nassau, Bahamas	166	25 0N	77 30W
Nassau, U.S.A.	162	42 30N	73 34W
Nassau, Bahia	176	55 20S	68 0W
Nasser City = Kôm Ombo	122	24 25N	32 52E
Nasser, L. = Naser, Buheiret en	122	23 0N	32 30E
Nassian	120	7 58N	2 57W
Nässjö	73	57 38N	14 45E
Nastopoka Is.	150	57 0N	77 0W
Näsum	73	56 10N	14 29E
Näsviken	72	61 46N	16 52E
Nata, Bots.	128	20 7S	26 4E
Nata, China	100	19 37N	109 17E
Nata, Si Arab.	92	27 15N	48 35E
Nata, Tanz.	125	2 0S	34 25E
Natagaima	174	3 37N	75 6W
Natal, Brazil	170	5 47S	35 13W
Natal, Can.	152	49 43N	114 51W
Natal, Indon.	102	0 35N	99 0E
Natal □	129	28 30S	30 30E
Natalinci	66	44 15N	20 49E
Natanz	93	33 30N	51 55E
Natashquan	151	50 14N	61 46W
Natashquan Pt.	151	50 8N	61 40W
Natashquan, R.	151	50 7N	61 50W
Natchez	159	31 35N	91 25W
Natchitoches	159	31 47N	93 4W
Naters	50	46 19N	8 0E
Nathalia	141	36 1S	145 7E
Nathdwara	94	24 55N	73 50E
Natick	162	42 16N	71 19W
Natih	93	22 25N	56 30E
Natimuk	140	36 42S	142 0E
Nation, R.	152	55 30N	123 32W
National City	163	32 45N	117 7W
National Mills	153	52 52N	101 40W
Natitingou	121	10 20N	1 26E
Natividad, I. de	164	27 50N	115 10W
Natkyizin	101	14 57N	97 59E
Natogyi	98	21 25N	95 39E
Natoma	158	39 14N	99 0W
Natron L.	126	2 20S	36 0E
Natrûn, W. el.	122	30 25N	30 0E
Natuna Besar, Kepulauan	101	4 0N	108 15E
Natuna Selatan, Kepulauan	101	2 45N	109 0E
Naturaliste, C.	132	33 32S	115 0E
Naturaliste C.	138	40 50S	148 15E
Naturaliste Channel	137	25 20S	113 0E
Natya	140	34 57S	143 13E
Nau	85	40 9N	69 22E
Nau-Nau	128	18 57S	21 4E
Nau Qala	94	34 5N	68 5E
Naubinway	150	46 7N	85 27W
Naucelle	44	44 13N	2 20E
Nauders	52	46 54N	10 30E
Nauen	48	52 36N	12 52E
Naujoji Vilnia	80	54 48N	25 27E
Naumburg	48	51 10N	11 48E
Nauru I.	130	0 25N	166 0E
Naurzum	84	51 32N	64 34E
Naushahra	93	34 0N	72 0E
Nauta	174	4 20S	73 35W
Nautanwa	99	27 20N	83 25E
Nautla	165	20 20N	96 50W
Nava	164	28 25N	100 46W
Nava del Rey	56	41 22N	5 6W
Navacerrada, Puerto de	56	40 47N	4 0W
Navahermosa	57	39 41N	4 28W
Navalcarnero	56	40 17N	4 5W
Navalmoral de la Mata	56	39 52N	5 16W
Navalvillar de Pela	57	39 9N	5 24W
Navan = An Uaimh	38	53 39N	6 40W
Navarino, I.	176	55 0S	67 30W
Navarra □	58	42 40N	1 40W
Navarre	44	43 15N	1 20E
Navarreux	44	43 20N	0 47W
Navasota	159	30 20N	96 5W
Navassa I.	167	18 30N	75 0W
Nave	62	45 35N	10 17E
Navenby	33	53 7N	0 32W
Naver L.	37	58 18N	4 20W
Naver, R.	37	58 34N	4 15W
Navia	56	43 24N	6 42W
Navia de Suarna	56	42 58N	6 59W
Navia, R.	56	43 15N	6 50W
Navidad	172	33 57S	71 50W
Navlya	80	52 53N	34 15E
Navoi	85	40 9N	65 22E
Navojoa	164	27 0N	109 30W
Navolato	164	24 47N	107 42W
Navolok	78	62 33N	39 57E
Návpaktos	69	38 23N	21 42E
Návplion	69	37 33N	22 50E
Navrongo	121	10 57N	0 58W
Navsari	96	20 57N	72 59E
Nawa Kot	94	28 21N	71 24E
Nawabganj	98	24 35N	81 14E
Nawabganj, Bara Banki	95	26 56N	81 14E
Nawabganj, Bareilly	95	28 32N	79 40E
Nawabshah	94	26 15N	68 25E
Nawada	95	24 50N	85 25E
Nawakot	95	28 0N	85 10E
Nawalgarh	96	27 50N	75 15E
Nawansnahr	95	32 33N	74 48E
Nawapara	95	20 52N	82 33E
Nawi	122	18 32N	30 50E
Nawng Hpa	98	21 52N	97 52E
Náxos	69	37 8N	25 25E
Náxos, I.	69	37 5N	25 30E
Nay	44	43 10N	0 18W
Nay Band	93	27 20N	52 40E
Naya	174	3 13N	77 22W
Naya, R.	174	3 13N	77 22W
Nayakhan	77	62 10N	159 0E
Nayarit □	164	22 0N	105 0W
Nayé	120	14 28N	12 12W
Nayung	108	26 50N	105 17E
Nazaré, Bahia, Brazil	171	13 0S	39 0W
Nazaré, Goiás, Brazil	170	6 23S	47 40W
Nazaré, Port.	57	39 36N	9 4W
Nazaré Antônio de Jesus	171	13 2S	39 0W
Nazaré da Mata	171	7 44S	35 14W
Nazareth, Israel	90	32 42N	35 17E
Nazareth, U.S.A.	162	40 44N	75 19W
Nazas	164	25 10N	104 0W
Nazas, R.	164	25 20N	104 4W
Naze	112	28 22N	129 27E
Naze, The	29	51 43N	1 19E
Nazeret	123	8 45N	39 15E
Nazir Hat	98	22 35N	91 55E
Nazko	152	53 1N	123 37W
Nazko, R.	152	53 7N	123 34W
Nchacoongo	129	24 20S	35 9E
Nchanga	127	12 30S	27 49E
Ncheu	127	14 50S	34 37E
Ndala	126	4 45S	33 23E
Ndali	121	9 50N	2 46E
Ndareda	126	4 12S	35 30E
Ndélé	117	8 25N	20 36E
Ndendeé	124	2 29S	10 46E
Ndjamena	117	12 4N	15 8E
Ndjolé	124	0 10S	10 45E
Ndola	127	13 0S	28 34E
Ndoto Mts.	126	2 0N	37 0E
Ndrhamcha, Sebkra de	120	18 30N	15 55W
Nduguti	126	4 18S	34 41E
NE Frt. Agency = Arun. Pradesh □	98	28 0N	95 0E
Nea	71	63 15N	11 0E
Néa Epidhavros	69	37 40N	23 7E
Néa Filippiás	68	39 12N	20 53W
Néa Kallikrátiá	68	40 21N	23 1E
Néa Vissi	68	41 34N	26 33E
Neagari	111	36 26N	136 25E
Neagh, Lough	38	54 35N	6 25W
Neah Bay	160	48 25N	124 40W
Neale L.	137	24 15S	130 0E
Neamarrói	127	15 58S	36 50E
Neamţ □	70	47 0N	26 20E
Neápolis, Kozan, Greece	68	40 20N	21 24E
Neápolis, Kriti, Greece	69	35 15N	25 36E
Neápolis, Lakonia, Greece	69	36 27N	23 8E
Near Is.	147	53 0N	172 0W
Neath	31	51 39N	3 49W
Neath, R.	23	51 46N	3 35W
Nebbou	121	11 9N	1 51W
Nebine Cr.	139	29 7S	146 56E
Nebo	138	21 42S	148 42E
Nebolchy	81	59 12N	32 58E
Nebraska □	158	41 30N	100 0W
Nebraska City	158	40 40N	95 52W
Necedah	158	44 2N	90 7W
Nechako, R.	152	53 30N	122 44W
Neches, R.	159	31 80N	94 20W
Neckar, R.	49	48 43N	9 15E
Necochea	172	38 30S	58 50W
Nectar Brook	140	32 43S	137 57E
Nedelišće	63	46 23N	16 22E
Neder Rijn, R.	46	51 57N	6 2E
Nederbrakel	47	50 48N	3 46E
Nederlandsöy I.	71	62 20N	5 35E
Nederweert	47	51 17N	5 45E
Nedha, R.	69	37 25N	21 45E
Nedroma	118	35 1N	1 45W
Nedstrand	71	59 21N	5 49E
Neede	46	52 8N	6 37E
Needham Market	29	52 9N	1 2E
Needilup	137	33 55S	118 45E
Needles	161	34 50N	114 35W
Needles, Pt.	142	36 3S	175 25E
Needles, The	28	50 48N	1 19W
Ñeembucú □	172	27 0S	58 0W
Neemuch (Nimach)	94	24 30N	74 50E
Neenah	156	44 10N	88 30W
Neepawa	153	50 20N	99 30W
Neer	47	51 16N	5 59E
Neerheylissem	47	51 5N	5 42E
Neeroeteren	47	50 44N	4 58E
Neerpelt	47	51 13N	5 26E
Nefta	119	33 53N	7 58E
Neftah Sidi Boubekeur	118	35 1N	0 4E
Neftegorsk	83	44 25N	39 45E
Neftenbach	51	47 32N	8 41E
Neftyannye Kamni	79	40 20N	50 55E
Nefyn	31	52 57N	4 29W
Negapatam = Nagappattinam	97	10 46N	79 38E
Negaunee	156	46 30N	87 36W
Negba	90	31 40N	34 41E
Negele	123	5 20N	39 30E
Negeri Sembilan □	101	2 50N	102 10E
Negev = Hanegev	90	30 50N	35 0E
Negolu	70	45 48N	24 32E
Negombo	97	7 12N	79 50E
Negotin	66	44 16N	22 37E
Negotino	66	41 29N	22 9E
Negra, La	172	23 46S	70 18W
Negra, Peña	56	42 11N	6 30W
Negra Pt.	103	18 40N	120 50E
Negrais C.	98	16 0N	94 30E
Negreira	56	42 54N	8 45W
Negreşti	70	46 50N	27 30E
Négrine	119	34 30N	7 30E
Negro, C.	118	35 40N	5 11W
Negro, R., Argent.	176	40 0S	64 0W
Negro, R., Brazil	174	0 25S	64 0W
Negro, R., Uruguay	173	32 30S	55 30W
Negros, I.	103	10 0N	123 0E
Negru Vodǎ	70	43 47N	28 21E
Nehbandān	93	31 35N	60 5E
Neheim-Hüsten	48	51 27N	7 58E
Nehoiaşu	70	45 24N	26 20E
Neichiang	108	29 35N	105 0E
Neich'iu	106	37 17N	114 31E
Neidpath	153	50 12N	107 20W
Neihart	160	47 0N	110 52W
Neihsiang	106	33 3N	111 53E
Neilrex	141	31 44S	149 20E
Neilston	34	55 47N	4 27W
Neilton	160	47 24N	123 59W
Neira de Jusá	56	42 53N	7 14W
Neisse, R.	48	51 0N	15 0E
Neiva	174	2 56N	75 18W
Nejanilini L.	153	59 33N	97 48W
Nejo	123	9 30N	35 28E
Nekemte	123	9 4N	36 30E
Nêkheb	122	25 10N	33 0E
Neksø	73	55 4N	15 8E
Nelas	56	40 32N	7 52W
Nelaug	71	58 39N	8 40E
Nelgowrie	141	30 54S	148 7E
Nelia	138	20 39S	142 12E
Nelidovo	80	56 13N	32 49E
Neligh	158	42 11N	98 2W
Nelkan	77	57 50N	136 15E
Nellikuppam	97	11 46N	79 43E
Nellore	97	14 27N	79 59E
Nelma	77	47 30N	139 0E
Nelson, Can.	152	49 30N	117 20W
Nelson, N.Z.	143	41 18S	173 16E
Nelson, U.K.	32	53 50N	2 14W
Nelson, Ariz., U.S.A.	161	35 35N	113 24W
Nelson, Nev., U.S.A.	161	35 46N	114 55W
Nelson □	143	42 11S	172 15E
Nelson, C., Austral.	140	38 26S	141 32E
Nelson, C., P.N.G.	135	9 0S	149 20E
Nelson, Estrecho	176	51 30S	75 0W
Nelson Forks	152	59 30N	124 0W
Nelson House	153	55 47N	98 51W
Nelson I.	147	60 40N	164 40W
Nelson L.	153	55 48N	100 7W
Nelson, R.	153	54 33N	98 2W
Nelspruit	126	25 29S	30 59E
Néma	120	16 40N	7 15W
Neman (Nemunas), R.	80	53 30N	25 10E
Neméa	69	37 49N	22 40E
Nemegos	150	47 40N	83 15W
Nemeiben L.	153	55 20N	105 20W
Nemira, Mt.	70	46 17N	26 19E
Nemiscau	150	49 30N	111 15W
Nemours	43	48 16N	2 40E
Nemunas, R.	80	55 25N	21 10E
Nemuro	112	43 20N	145 35E
Nemuro-Kaikyō	112	43 30N	145 30E
Nemuy	77	55 40N	135 55E
Nenagh	39	52 52N	8 11W
Nenana	147	64 30N	149 0W
Nenasi	101	3 9N	103 23E
Nenchiang	105	49 11N	125 13E
Nene, R.	29	52 38N	0 7E
Neno	127	15 25S	34 40E
Nenusa, Kepulauan	103	4 45N	127 1E
Neodesha	159	37 30N	95 37W
Néon Petrítsi	68	41 16N	23 15E
Neópolis	170	10 18S	36 35W
Neosho	159	36 56N	94 28W
Neosho, R.	159	35 59N	95 10W
Nepal ■	95	28 0N	84 30E
Nepalganj	95	28 0N	81 40E
Nephi	160	39 43N	111 52W
Nephin Beg Ra.	38	54 0N	9 40W
Nephin, Mt.	38	54 1N	9 21W
Nepomuk	52	49 29N	13 35E
Neptune City	162	40 13N	74 4W
Néra, R.	66	44 52N	21 45E
Nerac	44	44 19N	0 20E
Nerchinsk	77	52 0N	116 39E
Nerchinskiy Zavod	77	51 10N	119 30E
Nereju	70	45 43N	26 43E
Nerekhta	81	57 26N	40 38E
Neret L.	151	54 45N	70 44W
Neretva, R.	66	43 30N	17 50E
Neretvanski	66	43 7N	17 10E
Neringa	80	55 21N	21 5E
Nerja	57	36 43N	3 55W
Nerl, R.	81	56 30N	40 30E
Nerokoúrou	69	35 29N	24 3E
Nerpio	59	38 11N	2 16W
Nerva	57	37 42N	6 30W
Nes, Iceland	74	65 53N	17 24W
Nes, Neth.	46	53 26N	5 47E
Nes Ziyyona	90	31 56N	34 48W
Nesbyen	71	60 34N	9 6E
Nescopeck	162	41 3N	76 12W
Nesebyr	67	42 41N	27 46E
Nesflaten	71	59 38N	6 48E
Neskaupstaður	74	65 9N	13 42W
Nesland	71	59 31N	7 59E
Neslandsvatn	71	58 57N	9 10E
Nesle	43	49 45N	2 53E
Nesodden	71	59 48N	10 40E
Ness, dist.	36	58 27N	6 20W
Ness, Loch	37	57 15N	4 30W
Nesslau	51	47 14N	9 13E
Neston	32	53 17N	3 3W
Nestórion Óros	68	40 24N	21 16E
Néstos, R.	68	41 20N	24 35E
Nesttun	71	60 19N	5 21E
Nesvizh	80	53 14N	26 38E
Netanya	90	32 20N	34 51E
Nèthe, R.	47	51 5N	4 55E
Netherdale	138	21 10S	148 33E
Netherlands ■	47	52 0N	5 30E
Netherlands Guiana = Surinam	170	4 0N	56 0W
Nethy Bridge	37	57 15N	3 40W
Netley	28	50 53N	1 21W
Netley Gap	28	32 43S	139 59E
Netley Marsh	28	50 55N	1 32W
Neto, R.	65	39 10N	16 58E
Netrakong	98	24 53N	90 47E
Nettancourt	43	48 51N	4 57E
Nettilling L.	149	66 30N	71 0W
Nettlebed	29	51 34N	0 54W
Nettleham	33	53 15N	0 28W
Nettuno	64	41 29N	12 40E
Netzahualcoyotl, Presa	165	17 10N	93 30W
Neu-Isenburg	49	50 3N	8 42E
Neu Ulm	49	48 23N	10 2E
Neubrandenburg	48	53 33N	13 17E
Neubrandenburg □	48	53 30N	13 20E
Neubukow	48	54 1N	11 40E
Neuburg	49	48 43N	11 11E
Neuchâtel	50	47 0N	6 55E
Neuchâtel □	50	47 0N	6 55E
Neuchâtel, Lac de	50	46 53N	6 50E
Neudau	52	47 11N	16 6E
Neuenegg	50	46 54N	7 18E
Neuenhaus	48	52 30N	6 55E
Neuf-Brisach	43	48 0N	7 30E
Neufchâteau, Belg.	47	49 50N	5 25E
Neufchâteau, France	43	48 21N	5 40E
Neufchâtel	43	49 43N	1 30E
Neufchâtel-sur-Aisne	43	49 26N	4 0E
Neuhaus	48	53 16N	10 54E
Neuhausen	51	47 41N	8 37E
Neuilly-St. Front	43	49 10N	3 15E
Neukalen	49	53 49N	12 48E
Neumarkt	49	49 16N	11 28E
Neumünster	48	54 4N	9 58E
Neung-sur-Beuvron	43	47 30N	1 50E
Neunkirchen, Austria	52	47 43N	16 4E
Neunkirchen, Ger.	49	49 23N	7 6E
Neuquén	176	38 0S	68 0E
Neuquén □	172	38 0S	69 50W
Neuruppin	48	52 56N	12 48E
Neuse, R.	157	35 5N	77 40W
Neusiedl	53	47 57N	16 50E
Neusiedler See	53	47 50N	16 47E
Neuss	48	51 12N	6 39E
Neussargues-Moissac	44	45 9N	3 1E
Neustadt, Bay., Ger.	49	49 42N	12 10E
Neustadt, Bay., Ger.	49	48 48N	11 47E
Neustadt, Bay., Ger.	49	49 34N	10 37E
Neustadt, Bay., Ger.	49	50 23N	11 0E
Neustadt, Gera, Ger.	48	50 45N	11 43E
Neustadt, Hessen, Ger.	48	50 51N	9 9E
Neustadt, Niedersachsen, Ger.	48	52 30N	9 30E
Neustadt, Potsdam, Ger.	48	52 50N	12 27E
Neustadt, Rhld-Pfz., Ger.	49	49 21N	8 10E
Neustadt, S.-Holst., Ger.	48	54 6N	10 49E
Neustrelitz	48	53 22N	13 4E
Neuveville, La	50	47 4N	7 6E
Neuvic	44	45 23N	2 16E
Neuville, Belg.	95	50 11N	4 32E
Neuville, France	43	45 52N	4 51E
Neuville-aux-Bois	43	48 4N	2 3E
Neuvy-St.-Sépulchure	44	46 35N	1 48E
Neuvy-sur-Barangeon	43	47 20N	2 15E
Neuwerk, I.	48	53 55N	8 30E
Neuwied	48	50 26N	7 29E
Neva, R.	78	59 50N	30 30E
Nevada	159	37 20N	94 40W
Nevada □	160	39 20N	117 0W
Nevada City	163	39 20N	121 0W
Nevada de Sta. Marta, Sa.	174	10 55N	73 50W
Nevada, Sierra, Spain	59	37 3N	3 15W
Nevada, Sierra, U.S.A.	160	39 0N	120 30W
Nevado, Cerro	172	35 30S	68 20W
Nevado de Colima, Mt.	164	19 35N	103 45W
Nevanka	77	56 45N	98 55E
Nevasa	94	19 34N	75 0E
Nevel	80	56 0N	29 55E
Nevele	47	51 3N	3 28E
Nevern	31	52 2N	4 49W
Nevers	43	47 0N	3 9E
Nevertire	141	31 50S	147 44E
Neville	153	49 58N	107 39W
Nevillé-Pont-Pierre	42	47 33N	0 33E

Nevinnomyssk **Nîl el Abyad, Bahr**

Nevinnomyssk	**83**	44 40N	42 0E
Nevis I.	**167**	17 0N	62 30W
Nevis, L.	**36**	57 0N	5 43W
Nevlunghavn	**71**	58 58N	9 53E
Nevoria	**137**	31 25S	119 25E
Nevrokop = Gotse Delchev	**67**	41 43N	23 46E
Nevşehir	**92**	38 33N	34 40E
Nevyansk	**84**	57 30N	60 13E
New Abbey	**35**	54 59N	3 38W
New Aberdour	**37**	57 39N	2 12W
New Adawso	**121**	6 50N	0 2W
New Albany, Ind., U.S.A.	**156**	38 20N	85 50W
New Albany, Miss., U.S.A.	**159**	34 30N	89 0W
New Albany, Pa., U.S.A.	**162**	41 35N	76 28W
New Alresford	**28**	51 6N	1 10W
New Amsterdam	**174**	6 15N	57 30W
New Angledool	**139**	29 10S	147 55E
New Bedford	**162**	41 40N	70 52W
New Berlin, N.Y., U.S.A.	**162**	42 38N	75 20W
New Berlin, Pa., U.S.A.	**162**	40 50N	76 57W
New Bern	**157**	35 8N	77 3W
New Birmingham	**39**	52 36N	7 38W
New Boston	**159**	33 27N	94 21W
New Braunfels	**159**	29 43N	98 9W
New Brighton, N.Z.	**143**	43 29S	172 43E
New Brighton, U.K.	**32**	53 27N	3 2W
New Britain	**162**	41 41N	72 47W
New Britain, I.	**135**	5 50S	150 20E
New Brunswick	**162**	40 30N	74 28W
New Brunswick □	**151**	46 50N	66 30W
New Buildings	**38**	54 57N	7 21W
New Bussa	**121**	9 53N	4 31E
New Byrd	**13**	80 0S	120 0W
New Caledonia, I.	**130**	21 0S	165 0E
New Castile = Castilla La Neuva	**57**	39 45N	3 20W
New Castle, Del., U.S.A.	**162**	39 40N	75 34W
New Castle, Ind., U.S.A.	**156**	39 55N	85 23W
New Castle, Pa., U.S.A.	**156**	41 0N	80 20W
New Chapel Cross	**39**	51 51N	10 12W
New City	**162**	41 8N	74 0W
New Cumnock	**34**	55 24N	4 13W
New Cuyama	**163**	34 57N	119 38W
New Deer	**37**	57 30N	2 10W
New Delhi	**94**	28 37N	77 13E
New Denver	**152**	50 0N	117 25W
New England	**158**	46 36N	102 47W
New England Ra.	**139**	30 20S	151 45E
New Forest	**28**	50 53N	1 40W
New Freedom	**162**	39 44N	76 42W
New Galloway	**35**	55 4N	4 10W
New Glasgow	**151**	45 35N	62 36W
New Gretna	**162**	39 35N	74 28W
New Guinea, I.	**135**	4 0S	136 0E
New Hampshire □	**156**	43 40N	71 40W
New Hampton	**158**	43 2N	92 20W
New Hanover	**129**	29 22S	30 31E
New Hanover I.	**135**	2 30S	150 10E
New Hartford	**162**	43 4N	75 18W
New Haven	**162**	41 20N	72 54W
New Hazelton	**152**	55 20N	127 30W
• New Hebrides, Is.	**130**	15 0S	168 0E
New Holland, U.K.	**33**	53 42N	0 22W
New Holland, U.S.A.	**162**	40 6N	76 5W
New Iberia	**159**	30 2N	91 54W
New Inn	**39**	53 5N	7 10W
New Ireland, I.	**135**	3 20S	151 50E
New Jersey □	**162**	39 50N	74 10W
New Kensington	**156**	40 36N	79 43W
New Kent	**162**	37 31N	76 59W
New Lexington	**156**	39 40N	82 15W
New Liskeard	**150**	47 31N	79 41W
New London, Conn., U.S.A.	**162**	41 23N	72 8W
New London, Minn., U.S.A.	**158**	45 17N	94 55W
New London, Wis., U.S.A.	**158**	44 23N	88 43W
New Luce	**34**	54 57N	4 50W
New Madrid	**159**	36 40N	89 30W
New Meadows	**160**	45 0N	116 10W
New Mexico □	**154**	34 30N	106 0W
New Milford, Conn., U.S.A.	**162**	41 35N	73 25W
New Milford, Pa., U.S.A.	**162**	41 50N	75 45W
New Mills	**32**	53 22N	2 0W
New Norcia	**137**	30 57S	116 13E
New Norfolk	**138**	42 46S	147 2E
New Orleans	**159**	30 0N	90 5W
New Oxford	**162**	39 52N	77 4W
New Philadelphia	**156**	40 29N	81 25W
New Pitsligo	**37**	57 35N	2 11W
New Plymouth, Bahamas	**166**	26 56N	77 20W
New Plymouth, N.Z.	**142**	39 4S	174 5E
New Point Comfort	**162**	37 18N	76 15W
New Providence I.	**166**	25 0N	77 30W
New Quay	**31**	52 13N	4 21W
New Radnor	**31**	52 15N	3 10W
New Richmond	**158**	45 6N	92 34W
New Roads	**159**	30 43N	91 30W
New Rockford	**158**	47 44N	99 7W
New Romney	**29**	50 59N	0 57E
New Ross	**39**	52 24N	6 58W
New Rossington	**33**	53 30N	1 4W
New Salem	**158**	46 51N	101 25W
New Siberian Is. = Novosibirskiye Os.	**77**	75 0N	140 0E
New Smyrna Beach	**157**	29 0N	80 50W
New South Wales □	**139**	33 0S	146 0E
New Springs	**137**	25 49S	120 1E
New Tamale	**121**	9 10N	1 10W
New Tredegar	**31**	51 43N	3 15W
New Ulm	**158**	44 15N	94 30W
New Waterford	**151**	46 13N	60 4W
New Westminster	**152**	49 10N	122 52W
New York □	**156**	42 40N	76 0W
New York City	**162**	40 45N	74 0W
New Zealand ■	**143**	40 0S	176 0E
Newala	**127**	10 58S	39 10E
Newala □	**127**	10 46S	39 20E
Newark, U.K.	**33**	53 6N	0 48W
Newark, Del., U.S.A.	**162**	39 42N	75 45W
Newark, N.J., U.S.A.	**162**	40 41N	74 12W
Newark, N.Y., U.S.A.	**162**	43 2N	77 10W
Newark, Ohio, U.S.A.	**156**	40 5N	82 30W
Newark Valley	**162**	42 14N	76 11W
Newberg	**160**	45 22N	123 0W
Newberry	**156**	46 20N	85 32W
Newberry Springs	**163**	34 50N	116 41W
Newbiggin-by-the-Sea	**35**	55 12N	1 31W
Newbigging	**35**	55 42N	3 33W
Newbliss	**38**	54 10N	7 8W
Newborough	**31**	53 10N	4 22W
Newbridge, Kildare, Ireland	**39**	53 11N	6 50W
Newbridge, Limerick, Ireland	**38**	52 33N	9 0W
Newbridge-on-Wye	**31**	52 13N	3 27W
Newbrook	**152**	54 24N	112 57W
Newburgh, Fife, U.K.	**35**	56 21N	3 15W
Newburgh, Grampian, U.K.	**37**	57 19N	2 0W
Newburgh, U.S.A.	**162**	41 30N	74 1W
Newburn	**35**	54 57N	1 45W
Newbury	**28**	51 24N	1 19W
Newburyport	**162**	42 48N	70 50W
Newby Bridge	**32**	54 16N	2 59W
Newbyth	**37**	57 35N	2 17W
Newcastle, Austral.	**141**	33 0S	151 40E
Newcastle, Can.	**151**	47 1N	65 38W
Newcastle, Ireland	**39**	53 5N	6 4W
Newcastle, S. Afr.	**125**	27 45S	29 58E
Newcastle, U.K.	**38**	54 13N	5 54W
Newcastle, U.S.A.	**158**	43 50N	104 12W
Newcastle Emlyn	**31**	52 2N	4 29W
Newcastle Ra.	**136**	15 45S	130 15E
Newcastle-under-Lyme	**32**	53 2N	2 15W
Newcastle-upon-Tyne	**35**	54 59N	1 37W
Newcastle Waters	**136**	17 30S	133 28E
Newcastle West	**38**	52 27N	9 3W
Newcastleton	**35**	55 10N	2 50W
Newchurch	**31**	52 9N	3 10W
Newdegate	**137**	33 6S	119 0E
Newe Etan	**90**	32 30N	35 32E
Newe Sha'anan	**90**	32 47N	34 59E
Newe Zohar	**90**	31 9N	35 21E
Newell	**158**	44 48N	103 25W
Newenham, C.	**147**	58 40N	162 15W
Newent	**28**	51 56N	2 24W
Newfield, N.J., U.S.A.	**162**	39 33N	75 1W
Newfield, N.Y., U.S.A.	**162**	42 18N	76 33W
Newfound L.	**162**	43 40N	71 47W
Newfoundland	**151**	48 30N	56 0W
Newfoundland □	**151**	48 28N	56 0W
Newhalem	**152**	48 41N	121 16W
Newhalen	**147**	59 40N	155 0W
Newhall	**163**	34 23N	118 32W
Newham	**29**	51 31N	0 2E
Newhaven	**29**	50 47N	0 4E
Newington, N. Kent, U.K.	**29**	51 21N	0 40E
Newington, S. Kent, U.K.	**29**	51 5N	1 8E
Newinn	**39**	52 28N	7 54W
Newkirk	**159**	36 52N	97 3W
Newlyn	**30**	50 6N	5 33W
Newlyn East	**30**	50 22N	5 3W
Newmachar	**37**	57 16N	2 11W
Newman	**163**	37 19N	121 1W
Newman, Mt.	**137**	23 20S	119 34E
Newmarket, Ireland	**39**	52 13N	9 0W
Newmarket, Lewis, U.K.	**36**	58 14N	6 24W
Newmarket, Norfolk, U.K.	**29**	52 15N	0 23E
Newmarket, U.S.A.	**162**	43 4N	70 57W
Newmarket-on-Fergus	**39**	52 46N	8 54W
Newmill	**37**	57 34N	2 58W
Newmills	**38**	54 56N	7 49W
Newmilns	**34**	55 36N	4 20W
Newnan	**157**	33 22N	84 48W
Newnes	**139**	33 9S	150 16E
Newnham	**28**	51 48N	2 27W
Newport, Essex, U.K.	**29**	51 58N	0 13E
Newport, Gwent, U.K.	**31**	51 35N	3 0W
Newport, I. of W., U.K.	**28**	50 42N	1 18W
Newport, Salop, U.K.	**28**	52 47N	2 22W
Newport, Ark., U.S.A.	**159**	35 38N	91 15W
Newport, Ky., U.S.A.	**156**	39 5N	84 23W
Newport, N.H., U.S.A.	**162**	43 23N	72 8W
Newport, Oreg., U.S.A.	**160**	44 41N	124 2W
Newport, R.I., U.S.A.	**162**	41 30N	71 19W
Newport, Tenn., U.S.A.	**157**	35 39N	83 12W
Newport, Wash., U.S.A.	**160**	48 11N	117 2W
Newport B.	**38**	53 52N	9 38W
Newport Beach	**163**	33 40N	117 58W
Newport News	**162**	37 2N	76 54W
Newport on Tay	**35**	56 27N	2 56W
Newport Pagnell	**29**	52 5N	0 42W
Newquay	**30**	50 24N	5 6W
Newry	**38**	54 10N	6 20W
Newry & Mourne □	**38**	54 10N	6 15W
Newton, Iowa, U.S.A.	**158**	41 40N	93 3W
Newton, Kans., U.S.A.	**159**	38 2N	97 30W
Newton, Mass., U.S.A.	**156**	42 21N	71 10W
Newton, N.C., U.S.A.	**157**	35 42N	81 10W
Newton, N.J., U.S.A.	**162**	41 3N	74 46W
Newton, Texas, U.S.A.	**159**	30 54N	93 42W
Newton Abbot	**30**	50 32N	3 37W
Newton Arlosh	**32**	54 53N	3 15W
Newton-Aycliffe	**33**	54 36N	1 33W
Newton Boyd	**139**	29 45S	152 16E
Newton Ferrers	**30**	50 19N	4 3W
Newton le Willows	**32**	53 28N	3 27W
Newton St. Cyres	**30**	50 46N	3 35W
Newton Stewart	**34**	54 57N	4 30W
Newtonabbey □	**38**	54 45N	6 0W
Newtongrange	**35**	55 52N	3 4W
Newtonhill	**37**	57 1N	20 52E
Newtonmore	**37**	57 4N	4 7W
Newtown, Ireland	**39**	52 20N	8 47W
Newtown, Scot, U.K.	**35**	55 34N	2 38W
Newtown, Wales, U.K.	**31**	52 31N	3 19W
Newtown Crommelin	**38**	54 59N	6 13W
Newtown Cunningham	**38**	55 0N	7 32W
Newtown Forbes	**38**	53 46N	7 50W
Newtown Gore	**38**	54 3N	7 41W
Newtown Hamilton	**38**	54 12N	6 35W
Newtownabbey	**38**	54 40N	5 55W
Newtownards	**38**	54 37N	5 40W
Newtownbutler	**38**	54 12N	7 22W
	39	53 5N	6 7W
Newtownstewart	**38**	54 43N	7 22W
Nexon	**48**	45 41N	1 10E
Neya	**81**	58 21N	43 49E
Neyland	**31**	51 43N	4 58W
Neyrīz	**93**	29 15N	54 55E
Neyshābūr	**93**	36 10N	58 20E
Neyyattinkara	**97**	8 26N	77 5E
Nezhin	**80**	51 5N	31 55E
Nezperce	**160**	46 13N	116 15W
Ngabang	**102**	0 30N	109 55E
Ngaiphaipi	**98**	22 14N	93 15E
Ngambé	**121**	5 48N	11 29E
Ngami Depression	**128**	20 30S	22 46E
Ngamo	**127**	19 3S	27 25E
Ngandjuk	**103**	7 32S	111 55E
Ngao	**100**	18 46N	99 59E
Ngaoundéré	**124**	7 15N	13 35E
Ngapara	**143**	44 57S	170 46E
Ngara	**126**	2 29S	30 40E
Ngara □	**126**	2 29S	30 40E
Ngaruawahia	**142**	37 42S	175 11E
Ngatapa	**142**	38 32S	177 45E
Ngathainggyaung	**98**	17 24N	95 5E
Ngauruhoe, Mt.	**142**	39 13S	175 45E
Ngawi	**103**	7 24S	111 26E
Ngetera	**121**	12 40S	12 46E
Ngha Lo	**101**	21 33N	104 28E
Nghia Lo	**100**	21 33N	104 28E
Ngoma	**127**	13 8S	33 45E
Ngomahura	**127**	20 33S	30 57E
Ngomba	**127**	8 20S	32 53E
Ngonye Falls	**128**	16 35S	23 30E
Ngop	**123**	6 17N	30 9E
Ngorkou	**120**	15 40N	3 41W
Ngorongoro	**126**	3 11S	35 32E
Ngozi	**126**	2 54S	29 50E
Ngudu	**126**	2 58S	33 25E
N'Guigrai	**117**	14 20N	13 20E
Nguna, I.	**100**	17 26S	168 21E
Ngunga	**126**	3 37S	33 37E
Ngungu	**143**	6 15N	28 16E
Ngunguru	**94**	35 37S	174 30E
Nguru	**121**	12 56N	10 29E
Nguru Mts.	**126**	6 0S	37 30E
Nguyen Binh	**100**	22 39N	105 56E
Ngwenya	**129**	26 5S	31 7E
Nha Trang	**101**	12 16N	109 10E
Nhacoongo	**129**	24 18S	35 14E
Nhangutazi, Lago	**129**	24 0S	34 30E
Nhill	**140**	36 18S	141 40E
Nho Quan	**100**	20 18N	105 45E
Nhulunbuy	**138**	12 10S	136 45E
Nia-nia	**126**	1 30N	27 40E
Niafounké	**120**	16 0N	4 5W
Niagara	**156**	45 45N	88 0W
Niagara Falls, Can.	**150**	43 7N	79 5W
Niagara Falls, N. Amer.	**150**	43 5N	79 5W
Niah	**102**	3 58N	113 46E
Niamey	**121**	13 27N	2 6E
Nianforando	**120**	9 37N	10 36W
Nianfors	**72**	61 36N	16 46E
Niangara	**126**	3 50N	27 50E
Niantic	**162**	41 19N	72 12W
Nias, I.	**102**	1 0N	97 40E
Niassa □	**127**	13 30S	36 0E
Niassa, Lago	**127**	12 30S	34 30E
Nibbiano	**62**	44 54N	9 20E
Nibe	**73**	56 59N	9 38E
Nibong Tebal	**101**	5 10N	100 29E
Nicaragua ■	**166**	11 40N	85 30W
Nicaragua, Lago de	**166**	12 50N	85 30W
Nicastro	**65**	39 0N	16 18E
Nice	**45**	43 42N	7 14E
Niceville	**157**	30 30N	86 30W
Nichinan	**110**	31 38N	131 23E
Nicholas, Chan.	**166**	23 30N	80 30W
Nicholasville	**156**	37 54N	84 31W
Nichols	**162**	42 1N	76 22W
Nicholson, Austral.	**136**	18 2S	128 54E
Nicholson, Can.	**150**	47 58N	83 47W
Nicholson, U.S.A.	**162**	41 37N	75 47W
Nicholson, R.	**138**	17 31S	139 36E
Nicholson Ra.	**137**	27 15S	116 30E
Nicobar Is.	**86**	9 0N	93 0E
Nicoclí	**174**	8 26N	76 48W
Nicola	**152**	50 8N	120 40W
Nicolet	**150**	46 17N	72 35W
Nicolls Town	**166**	25 8N	78 0W
Nicosia, Cyprus	**92**	35 10N	33 25E
Nicosia, Italy	**65**	37 45N	14 22E
Nicótera	**65**	38 33N	15 57E
Nicoya	**166**	10 9N	85 27W
Nicoya, Golfo de	**166**	10 0N	85 0W
Nicoya, Pen. de	**166**	9 45N	85 40W
Nidau	**50**	47 7N	7 15E
Nidd, R.	**33**	54 1N	1 32W
Nidda	**48**	50 24N	9 2E
Nidda, R.	**49**	50 25N	9 2E
Nidderdale	**33**	54 5N	1 46W
Nidzica	**54**	53 25N	20 28E
Niebüll	**48**	54 47N	8 49E
Niederaula	**48**	50 48N	9 37E
Niederbipp	**50**	47 16N	7 42E
Niederbronn	**43**	48 57N	7 39E
Niedere Tauern	**93**	47 18N	14 0E
Niedermarsberg	**48**	51 28N	8 52E
Niederösterreich □	**52**	48 25N	15 40E
Niedersachsen □	**48**	54 45N	9 0E
Niel	**47**	51 7N	4 20E
Niellé	**120**	10 5N	5 38W
Niemba	**126**	5 58S	28 24E
Niemcza	**54**	50 42N	16 47E
Niemodlin	**54**	50 38N	17 38E
Niemur	**140**	35 17S	144 9E
Nienburg	**48**	52 38N	9 15E
Nienchʼingtʼangkula Shan	**105**	30 10N	90 0E
Niepołomice	**54**	50 3N	20 13E
Niesen	**50**	46 38N	7 39E
Niesky	**48**	51 18N	14 48E
Nieszawa	**54**	52 52N	18 42E
Nieuw Amsterdam	**46**	52 43N	6 52E
Nieuw Beijerland	**46**	51 49N	4 20E
Nieuw-Buinen	**46**	52 58N	6 56E
Nieuw-Dordrecht	**46**	52 45N	6 59E
Nieuw Hellevoet	**46**	51 51N	4 8E
Nieuw Loosdrecht	**46**	52 12N	5 8E
Nieuw Nickerie	**175**	6 0N	57 10W
Nieuw-Schoonebeek	**46**	52 39N	7 0E
Nieuw-Vassemeer	**47**	51 34N	4 12E
Nieuw-Vennep	**46**	52 16N	4 38E
Nieuw-Weerdinge	**46**	52 51N	6 59E
Nieuwe-Niedorp	**46**	52 44N	4 54E
Nieuwe-Pekela	**46**	53 5N	6 58E
Nieuwe-Schans	**46**	53 11N	7 12E
Nieuwe-Tonge	**47**	51 43N	4 10E
Nieuwendijk	**46**	51 46N	4 55E
Nieuwerkerken	**47**	50 52N	5 12E
Nieuwkoop	**46**	52 9N	4 48E
Nieuwleusen	**46**	52 34N	6 17E
Nieuwnamen	**47**	51 18N	4 9E
Nieuwolda	**46**	53 15N	6 58E
Nieuwpoort	**47**	51 8N	2 45E
Nieuwveen	**46**	52 12N	4 46E
Nieves	**56**	42 7N	8 26W
Nièvre □	**43**	47 10N	5 40E
Nigata	**110**	34 13N	132 39E
Nigde	**92**	38 0N	34 40E
Nigel	**129**	26 27S	28 25E
Niger □	**121**	10 0N	5 0E
Niger ■	**121**	13 30N	10 0E
Niger, R.	**121**	10 0N	4 40E
Nigeria ■	**121**	8 30N	8 0E
Nigg B.	**37**	57 41N	4 5W
Nightcaps	**143**	45 57S	168 14E
Nigrita	**68**	40 56N	23 29E
Nihtaur	**94**	29 27N	78 23E
Nii-Jima	**111**	34 20N	139 15E
Niigata	**112**	37 58N	139 0E
Niigata-ken □	**112**	37 15N	138 45E
Niihama	**110**	33 55N	133 10E
Niihau, I.	**147**	21 55N	160 10W
Niimi	**110**	34 59N	133 28E
Nijar	**59**	36 53N	2 15W
Nijkerk	**47**	52 13N	5 30E
Nijlen	**47**	51 10N	4 40E
Nijmegen	**47**	51 50N	5 52E
Nijverdal	**46**	52 22N	6 28E
Nike	**121**	6 26N	7 29E
Nikel	**74**	69 30N	30 5E
Nikiniki	**103**	9 40S	124 30E
Nikitas	**68**	40 17N	23 34E
Nikki	**121**	9 58N	3 21E
Nikkō	**111**	36 45N	139 35E
Nikolayev	**82**	46 58N	32 7E
Nikolayevsk-na-Amur	**77**	53 40N	140 50E
Nikolayevski	**81**	50 10N	45 35E
Nikolsk	**81**	59 30N	45 28E
Nikolski	**147**	53 0N	168 50W
Nikolskoye, Amur, U.S.S.R.	**77**	47 50N	131 5E
Nikolskoye, Kamandorskiye, U.S.S.R.	**77**	55 12N	166 0E
Nikopol, Bulg.	**67**	43 43N	24 54E
Nikopol, U.S.S.R.	**82**	47 35N	34 25E
Niksar	**82**	40 31N	37 2E
Nīkshah	**93**	26 15N	60 10E
Nik ió	**66**	42 50N	18 57E
Nîl el Abyad, Bahr	**123**	9 30N	31 40E

• *Renamed Vanuatu*

Nîl el Azraq □ N. Taranaki Bt

Nîl el Azraq □	**123**	12 30N	34 30 E
Nîl el Azraq, Bahr	**123**	10 30N	35 0 E
Nîl, Nahr el	**122**	27 30N	30 30 E
Nila	**103**	8 24 S	120 29 E
Niland	**161**	33 16N	115 30W
Nile □	**126**	2 0N	31 30 E
Nile Delta	**122**	31 40N	31 0 E
Nile, R. = Nîl, Nahr el	**122**	27 30N	30 30 E
Niles	**156**	41 8N	80 40W
Nilgiri Hills	**97**	11 30N	76 30 E
Nilo Peçanha	**171**	13 37 S	39 6W
Nilpena	**140**	30 58 S	138 20 E
Nimach = Neemuch	**94**	24 30N	74 50 E
Nimar	**96**	21 49N	76 22 E
Nimba, Mt.	**120**	7 39N	8 30W
Nimbahera	**94**	24 37N	74 45 E
Nîmes	**45**	43 50N	4 23 E
Nimfaíon, Ákra	**68**	40 5N	24 20 E
Nimingarra	**132**	20 31 S	119 55 E
Nimmitabel	**141**	36 29 S	149 15 E
Nimneryskiy	**77**	58 0N	125 10 E
Nimule	**123**	3 32N	32 3 E
Nimy	**47**	50 28N	3 57 E
Nin	**63**	44 16N	15 12 E
Nindigully	**139**	28 21 S	148 50 E
Ninemile	**152**	56 0N	130 7W
Ninemilehouse	**39**	52 28N	7 29W
Ninety Mile Beach	**130**	34 45 S	173 0 E
Ninety Mile Beach, The	**133**	38 15 S	147 24 E
Nineveh	**92**	36 25N	43 10 E
Ninfield	**29**	50 53N	0 26 E
Ningaloo	**136**	22 41 S	113 41 E
Ningan	**107**	44 23N	129 26 E
Ningch'eng	**107**	41 34N	119 20 E
Ningch'iang	**106**	32 49N	106 13 E
Ningchin	**106**	37 37N	114 55 E
Ningching Shan	**108**	31 45N	97 15 E
Ninghai	**109**	29 18N	121 25 E
Ninghsiang	**109**	28 15N	112 30 E
Ninghsien	**106**	35 35N	107 58 E
Ninghua	**109**	26 14N	116 36 E
Ningkang	**109**	26 45N	113 58 E
Ningkuo	**109**	30 38N	118 58 E
Ninglang	**108**	27 19N	100 53 E
Ningling	**106**	34 27N	115 19 E
Ningming	**108**	22 12N	107 5 E
Ningnan	**108**	27 7N	102 42 E
Ningpo	**109**	29 53N	121 33 E
Ningshan	**106**	33 12N	108 29 E
Ningsia Hui A.R. □	**106**	37 45N	106 0 E
Ningte	**109**	26 45N	120 0 E
Ningtsin	**99**	29 44N	98 28 E
Ningtu	**109**	26 22N	115 48 E
Ningwu	**106**	29 2N	112 15 E
Ningyang, Fukien, China	**109**	25 44N	117 8 E
Ningyang, Shantung, China	**106**	35 46N	116 47 E
Ningyüan	**109**	25 36N	111 54 E
Ninh Binh	**100**	20 15N	105 55 E
Ninh Giang	**100**	20 44N	106 24 E
Ninh Hoa	**100**	12 30N	109 7 E
Ninh Ma	**100**	12 48N	109 21 E
Ninian, oilfield	**19**	60 42N	1 30 E
Ninove	**47**	50 51N	4 2 E
Nioaque	**173**	21 5 S	55 50W
Niobrara	**158**	42 48N	97 59W
Niobrara R.	**158**	42 30N	103 0W
Nioki	**124**	2 47 S	17 40 E
Niono	**120**	14 15N	6 0W
Nioro	**120**	15 30N	9 30W
Nioro du Rip	**120**	13 40N	15 50W
Nioro du Sahel	**120**	15 30N	9 30W
Niort	**44**	46 19N	0 29W
Niou	**121**	12 42N	2 1W
Nipa	**135**	6 9 S	143 29 E
Nipan	**138**	24 45 S	150 0 E
Nipani	**96**	16 20N	74 25 E
Nipawin	**153**	53 20N	104 0W
Nipawin Prov. Park	**153**	54 0N	104 37W
Nipigon	**150**	49 0N	88 17W
Nipigon, L.	**150**	49 50N	88 30W
Nipin, R.	**153**	55 46N	109 2W
Nipishish L.	**151**	54 12N	60 45W
Nipissing L.	**150**	46 20N	80 0W
Nipomo	**163**	35 4N	120 29W
Niquelândia	**171**	14 33 S	48 23W
Nira, R.	**96**	18 5N	74 25 E
Nirasaki	**111**	35 42N	138 27 E
Nirmal	**96**	19 3N	78 20 E
Nirmali	**95**	26 20N	86 35 E
Niš	**66**	43 19N	21 58 E
Nisa	**57**	39 30N	7 41W
Nisab	**91**	14 25N	46 29 E
Nišava, R.	**66**	43 20N	22 10 E
Niscemi	**65**	37 8N	14 21 E
Nishi-Sonogi-Hantō	**110**	32 55N	129 45 E
Nishinomiya	**111**	34 45N	135 20 E
Nishinoomote	**112**	30 43N	130 59 E
Nishio	**111**	34 52N	137 3 E
Nishiwaki	**110**	34 59N	134 48 E
Nisiros, I.	**69**	36 35N	27 12 E
Niskibi, R.	**150**	56 29N	88 9W
Nisko	**54**	50 35N	22 7 E
Nispen	**47**	51 29N	4 28 E
Nisporeny	**70**	47 4N	28 10 E
Nissafors	**73**	57 25N	13 37 E
Nissan	**73**	56 40N	12 51 E
Nissan I.	**138**	4 30 S	154 10 E
Nissedal	**71**	59 10N	8 30 E
Nisser	**71**	59 7N	8 28 E
Nissum Fjord	**73**	56 20N	8 11 E
Nistelrode	**47**	51 42N	5 34 E
Nisutlin, R.	**152**	60 14N	132 34W
Nitchequon	**151**	53 10N	70 58W
Niterói	**173**	22 52 S	43 0W
Nith, R.	**35**	55 20N	3 5W
Nithsdale	**35**	55 14N	3 50W
Niton	**28**	50 35N	1 14W
Nitra	**53**	48 19N	18 4 E
Nitra, R.	**53**	48 30N	18 7 E
Nitsa, R.	**84**	57 29N	64 33 E
Nittedal	**71**	60 1N	10 57 E
Niuchieh	**108**	27 47N	104 16 E
Niuchuang	**107**	40 58N	122 38 E
Niue I. (Savage I.)	**130**	19 2 S	169 54W
Niulan Chiang, R.	**108**	27 24N	103 9 E
Niut, Mt.	**102**	0 55N	109 30 E
Nivelles	**47**	50 35N	4 20 E
Nivernais	**43**	47 0N	3 40 E
Nixon, Nev., U.S.A.	**160**	39 54N	119 22W
Nixon, Tex., U.S.A.	**159**	29 17N	97 45W
Nizam Sagar	**96**	18 10N	77 58 E
Nizamabad	**96**	18 45N	78 7 E
Nizamghat	**98**	28 20N	95 45 E
Nizhanaya Tunguska	**77**	64 20N	93 0 E
Nizhiye Sergi	**84**	56 40N	59 18 E
Nizhne Kolymsk	**77**	68 40N	160 55 E
Nizhne-Vartovskoye	**76**	60 56N	76 38 E
Nizhneangarsk	**77**	56 0N	109 30 E
Nizhnegorskiy	**82**	45 27N	34 38 E
Nizhneudinsk	**77**	55 0N	99 20 E
Nizhniy Lomov	**81**	53 34N	43 38 E
Nizhniy Novgorod = Gorkiy	**81**	56 20N	44 0 E
Nizhniy Pyandzh	**85**	37 12N	68 35 E
Nizhniy Tagil	**84**	57 55N	59 57 E
Nizhny Salda	**84**	58 8N	60 42 E
Nizké Tatry	**53**	48 55N	20 0 E
Nizza Monferrato	**62**	44 46N	8 22 E
Njakwa	**127**	11 1 S	33 56 E
Njinjo	**127**	8 34 S	38 44 E
Njombe	**124**	9 20 S	34 50 E
Njombe □	**127**	9 20 S	34 49 E
Njombe, R.	**126**	7 15 S	34 30 E
Nkambe	**121**	6 35N	10 40 E
Nkana	**127**	13 0 S	28 8 E
Nkawkaw	**121**	6 36N	0 49W
Nkhata Bay	**124**	11 33 S	34 16 E
Nkhota Kota	**127**	12 56 S	34 15 E
Nkongsamba	**121**	4 55N	9 55 E
Nkunka	**127**	14 57 S	25 58 E
Nkwanta	**120**	6 10N	2 10W
Nmai Pit, R.	**99**	25 30N	98 0 E
Nmai, R.	**99**	25 30N	98 0 E
Nmaushahra	**95**	33 11N	74 15 E
Nnewi	**121**	6 0N	6 59 E
Noakhali = Maijdi	**98**	22 50N	90 45 E
Noatak	**147**	67 32N	163 10W
Noatak, R.	**147**	68 0N	161 0W
Nobber	**38**	53 49N	6 45W
Nobeoka	**110**	32 36N	131 41 E
Nōbi-Heiya	**111**	35 15N	136 45 E
Noblejas	**58**	39 58N	3 26W
Noblesville	**156**	40 1N	85 59W
Noce, R.	**62**	46 22N	11 0 E
Nocera Inferiore	**65**	40 45N	14 37 E
Nocera Terinese	**65**	39 2N	16 9 E
Nocera Umbra	**63**	43 8N	12 47 E
Nochixtlán	**165**	17 28N	97 14W
Noci	**65**	40 47N	17 7 E
Nockatunga	**139**	27 42 S	142 42 E
Nocona	**159**	33 48N	97 45W
Nocrich	**70**	45 55N	24 26 E
Noda, Japan	**111**	35 56N	139 52 E
Noda, U.S.S.R.	**77**	47 30N	142 5 E
Noel	**159**	36 36N	94 29W
Nogales, Mexico	**164**	31 36N	94 29W
Nogales, U.S.A.	**161**	31 33N	115 50W
Nōgata	**110**	33 48N	130 54 E
Nogent-en-Bassigny	**43**	48 0N	5 20 E
Nogent-le-Rotrou	**42**	48 20N	0 50 E
Nogent-sur-Seine	**43**	48 30N	3 30 E
Noggerup	**137**	33 32 S	116 5 E
Noginsk, Moskva, U.S.S.R.	**81**	55 50N	38 25 E
Noginsk, Sib., U.S.S.R.	**77**	64 30N	90 50 E
Nogoa, R.	**138**	23 33 S	148 32 E
Nogoyá	**172**	32 24 S	59 48W
Nógrád □	**53**	48 0N	19 30 E
Nogueira de Ramuin	**56**	42 21N	7 43W
Noguera Pallaresa, R.	**58**	42 15N	1 0 E
Noguera Ribagorzana, R.	**58**	42 15N	0 45 E
Nohar	**94**	29 11N	74 49 E
Noi, R.	**101**	14 50N	100 15 E
Noire, Mts.	**42**	48 11N	3 40W
Noirétable	**44**	45 48N	3 46 E
Noirmoutier	**42**	47 0N	2 15W
Noirmoutier, Î. de	**42**	46 58N	2 10W
Nojane	**128**	23 15 S	20 14 E
Nojima-Zaki	**111**	34 54N	139 53 E
Nok Kundi	**93**	28 50N	62 45 E
Nokaneng	**128**	19 47 S	22 17 E
Nokhtuysk	**77**	60 0N	117 45 E
Nokomis	**153**	51 35N	105 0W
Nokomis L.	**153**	57 0N	103 0W
Nokou	**124**	14 35N	14 47 E
Nol	**73**	57 56N	12 5 E
Nola, C. Afr. Emp.	**124**	3 35N	16 10 E
Nola, Italy	**65**	40 54N	14 29 E
Nolay	**43**	46 58N	4 35 E
Nolby	**72**	62 17N	17 26 E
Noli, C. di	**62**	44 12N	8 26 E
Nolinsk	**84**	57 28N	49 57 E
Noma Omuramba, R.	**128**	19 6 S	20 30 E
Noma-Saki	**110**	31 25N	130 7 E
Nomad	**135**	6 19 S	142 13 E
Noman L.	**153**	62 15N	108 55W
Nombre de Dios	**166**	9 34N	79 28W
Nome	**147**	64 30N	165 30W
Nomo-Zaki	**110**	32 35N	129 44 E
Nonacho L.	**153**	61 57N	109 28W
Nonancourt	**42**	48 47N	1 11 E
Nonant-le-Pin	**42**	48 42N	0 12 E
Nonda	**138**	20 40 S	142 28 E
Nong Chang	**100**	15 23N	99 51 E
Nong Het	**100**	19 29N	103 59 E
Nong Khae	**101**	14 29N	100 53 E
Nong Khai	**100**	17 50N	102 46 E
Nonoava	**164**	27 22N	106 38W
Nonopapa	**147**	21 50N	160 15W
Nonthaburi	**100**	13 51N	100 34 E
Nontron	**44**	45 31N	0 40 E
Noonamah	**136**	12 40 S	131 4 E
Noonan	**158**	48 51N	102 59W
Noondoo	**139**	28 35 S	148 30 E
Noonkanbah	**102**	18 30 S	124 50 E
Noord-Bergum	**46**	53 14N	6 1 E
Noord Brabant □	**47**	51 40N	5 0 E
Noord Holland □	**46**	52 30N	4 45 E
Noordbeveland	**47**	51 45N	3 50 E
Noordeloos	**46**	51 55N	4 56 E
Noordhollandsch Kanaal	**46**	52 55N	4 48 E
Noordhorn	**46**	53 16N	6 24 E
Noordoostpolder	**46**	52 45N	5 45 E
Noordwijk aan Zee	**46**	52 14N	4 26 E
Noordwijk-Binnen	**46**	52 14N	4 27 E
Noordwijkerhout	**46**	52 16N	4 30 E
'Noordwinning', gasfield	**19**	53 13N	3 10 E
Noordzee Kanaal	**46**	52 28N	4 35 E
Noorvik	**147**	66 50N	161 14W
Noorwolde	**46**	52 54N	6 8 E
Nootka	**152**	49 38N	126 38W
Nootka I.	**152**	49 40N	126 50W
Noqui	**124**	5 55 S	13 30 E
Nora, Ethiopia	**123**	16 6N	40 4 E
Nora, Sweden	**72**	59 32N	15 2 E
Noranda	**150**	48 20N	79 0W
Norberg	**72**	60 4N	15 56 E
Norbottens län □	**74**	66 58N	20 0 E
Nórcia	**63**	42 50N	13 5 E
Norco	**163**	33 56N	117 33W
Nord □	**43**	50 15N	3 30 E
Nord-Ostee Kanal	**48**	54 5N	9 15 E
Nord-Süd Kanal	**48**	53 0N	10 32 E
Nord-Trondelag Fylke □	**74**	64 20N	12 0 E
Nordagutu	**71**	59 25N	9 20 E
Nordaustlandet	**12**	79 55N	23 0 E
Nordborg	**73**	55 5N	9 50 E
Nordby, Fanø, Denmark	**73**	55 27N	8 24 E
Nordby, Samsø, Denmark	**73**	55 58N	10 32 E
Norddal	**71**	62 15N	7 14 E
Norddalsfjord kpl.	**71**	61 39N	5 23 E
Norddeich	**48**	53 37N	7 10 E
Nordegg	**152**	52 29N	116 5W
Nordelph	**29**	52 34N	0 18 E
Norden	**48**	53 35N	7 12 E
Nordenham	**48**	53 29N	8 28 E
Norderhov	**71**	60 7N	10 17 E
Norderney	**48**	53 42N	7 9 E
Norderney, I.	**48**	53 42N	7 15 E
Nordfjord	**71**	61 55N	5 30 E
Nordfriesische Inseln	**48**	54 40N	8 20 E
Nordhausen	**48**	51 29N	10 47 E
Nordhorn	**48**	52 27N	7 4 E
Nordjyllands Amt □	**73**	57 0N	10 0 E
Nordkapp, Norway	**74**	71 10N	25 44 E
Nordkapp, Svalb.	**12**	80 31N	20 0 E
Nordkinn	**16**	71 3N	28 0 E
Nordland Fylke □	**74**	65 40N	13 0 E
Nördlingen	**49**	48 50N	10 30 E
Nordrhein-Westfalen □	**48**	51 45N	7 30 E
Nordstrand, I.	**48**	54 27N	8 50 E
Nordvik	**77**	73 40N	110 57 E
Nore	**71**	60 10N	9 0 E
Nore R.	**39**	52 40N	7 20W
Noreena Cr.	**136**	22 20 S	120 25 E
Norefjell	**71**	60 16N	9 29 E
Norembega	**150**	48 59N	80 43W
Noresund	**71**	60 11N	9 37 E
Norfolk, Nebr., U.S.A.	**158**	42 3N	97 25W
Norfolk, Va., U.S.A.	**156**	36 52N	76 15W
Norfolk □	**29**	52 39N	1 0 E
Norfolk Broads	**29**	52 30N	1 15 E
Norfolk I.	**130**	28 58 S	168 3 E
Norfork Res.	**159**	36 25N	92 0W
Norg	**46**	53 4N	6 28 E
Norham	**35**	55 44N	2 9W
Norilsk	**77**	69 20N	88 0 E
Norley	**139**	27 45 S	143 48 E
Normal	**158**	40 30N	89 0W
Norman	**159**	35 12N	97 30W
Norman, R.	**138**	19 20 S	142 35 E
Norman Wells	**147**	65 17N	126 45W
Normanby	**142**	39 32 S	174 18 E
Normanby I.	**135**	10 55 S	151 5 E
Normanby, R.	**138**	14 23 S	144 10 E
Normandie	**42**	48 45N	0 10 E
Normandie, Collines de	**42**	48 55N	0 45W
Normandin	**150**	48 49N	72 31W
Normandy = Normandie	**42**	48 45N	0 10 E
Normanhurst, Mt.	**137**	25 13 S	122 30 E
Normanton, Austral.	**138**	17 40 S	141 10 E
Normanton, U.K.	**33**	53 41N	1 26W
Normanville	**140**	35 27 S	138 18 E
Norna, Mt.	**138**	20 55 S	140 42 E
Nornalup	**137**	35 0 S	116 48 E
Norquay	**153**	51 53N	102 5W
Ñorquinco	**176**	41 51 S	70 55W
Norrahammar	**73**	57 43N	14 7 E
Norrbottens län □	**74**	66 50N	18 0 E
Norrby	**74**	64 55N	18 15 E
Nørre Åby	**73**	55 27N	9 52 E
Nørre Nebel	**73**	55 47N	8 17 E
Nørresundby	**73**	57 5N	9 52 E
Norris	**160**	45 40N	111 48W
Norristown	**162**	40 9N	75 15W
Norrköping	**73**	58 37N	16 11 E
Norrland □	**74**	66 50N	18 0 E
Norrtälje	**72**	59 46N	18 42 E
Norseman	**137**	32 8 S	121 43 E
Norsholm	**73**	58 31N	15 59 E
Norsk	**77**	52 30N	130 0 E
Norte de Santander □	**174**	8 0N	73 0W
North Adams	**162**	42 42N	73 6W
North America	**50**	40 0N	70 0W
North Andaman I.	**101**	13 15N	92 40 E
North Atlantic Ocean	**14**	30 0N	50 0W
North Ballachulish	**36**	56 42N	5 9W
North Battleford	**153**	52 50N	108 17W
North Bay	**150**	46 20N	79 30W
North Belcher Is.	**150**	56 50N	79 50W
North Bend, Can.	**152**	49 50N	121 35W
North Bend, U.S.A.	**160**	43 28N	124 7W
North Bennington	**162**	42 56N	73 15W
North Berwick, U.K.	**35**	56 4N	2 44W
North Berwick, U.S.A.	**162**	43 18N	70 43W
North Br., Ashburton R.	**143**	43 30 S	171 30 E
North Buganda □	**126**	1 0N	32 0 E
North Canadian, R.	**159**	36 48N	103 0W
North C., Antarct.	**13**	71 0N	166 0 E
North C., Can.	**151**	47 2N	60 20W
North, Cape	**151**	47 2N	60 25W
North C., N.Z.	**142**	34 23 S	173 4 E
North C., P.N.G.	**135**	2 32 S	150 50 E
North C., Spitsbergen	**12**	80 40N	20 0 E
North Caribou L.	**150**	52 50N	90 40W
North Carolina □	**157**	35 30N	80 0W
North Cerney	**28**	51 45N	1 58W
North Channel, Br. Is.	**34**	55 0N	5 30W
North Channel, Can.	**150**	46 0N	83 0W
North Chicago	**156**	42 19N	87 50W
North Collingham	**33**	53 8N	0 46W
North Dakota □	**158**	47 30N	100 0W
North Dandalup	**137**	32 30 S	116 2 E
N. Dorset Downs	**28**	50 50N	2 30W
North Down □	**38**	54 40N	5 45W
North Downs	**29**	51 17N	0 30W
North East	**162**	39 36N	75 56W
North Eastern □	**126**	1 30N	40 0 E
North Esk, R.	**37**	56 44N	2 25W
North European Plain	**16**	55 0N	20 0 E
N. Foreland, Pt.	**29**	51 22N	1 28 E
North Fork	**163**	37 14N	119 29W
N. Frisian Is. = Nordfr'sche Inseln	**48**	54 50N	8 20 E
N. Harris, dist.	**36**	58 0N	6 55W
North Henik L.	**153**	61 45N	97 40W
North Hill	**30**	50 33N	4 26W
North Horr	**126**	3 20N	37 8 E
North Hykeham	**33**	53 10N	0 35W
North I., Kenya	**126**	4 5N	36 5 E
North I., N.Z.	**143**	38 0 S	175 0 E
North Kamloops	**152**	50 40N	120 25W
North Kessock	**37**	57 30N	4 15W
North Knife L., Can.	**153**	58 0N	97 0W
North Knife L., Man., Can.	**153**	58 5N	97 5W
North Knife, R.	**153**	58 53N	94 45W
North Koel, R.	**95**	23 50N	84 5 E
North Korea ■	**105**	40 0N	127 0 E
N. Lakhimpur	**99**	27 15N	94 10 E
N. Las Vegas	**161**	36 15N	115 6W
North Mara □	**126**	1 20 S	34 20 E
North Minch	**36**	58 5N	5 55W
North Molton	**30**	51 3N	3 48W
North Nahanni, R.	**152**	62 15N	123 20W
North Ossetian A.S.S.R. □	**83**	43 30N	44 30 E
North Palisade	**163**	37 6N	118 32W
North Petherton	**28**	51 6N	3 1W
North Platte	**158**	41 10N	100 50W
North Platte, R.	**160**	42 50N	106 50W
North Pt., Austral.	**108**	27 23 S	153 14 E
North Pt., Can.	**151**	47 5N	65 0W
North Pole	**12**	90 0N	0 0 E
North Portal	**153**	49 0N	102 33W
North Powder	**160**	45 2N	117 59W
North Queensferry	**35**	56 1N	3 22W
North Riding (□)	**26**	54 22N	1 30W
North Roe, dist.	**36**	60 40N	1 22W
North Ronaldsay, I.	**37**	59 20N	2 30W
North Sea	**19**	56 0N	4 0 E
North Sentinel, I.	**101**	11 35N	92 15 E
North Somercotes	**33**	53 28N	0 9 E
North Sound	**39**	53 10N	9 48W
North Sound, The	**37**	59 18N	2 45W
North Sporades = Voriai Sporádhes	**69**	39 0N	24 10 E
North Stradbroke I.	**133**	27 35 S	153 28 E
North Sunderland	**33**	55 35N	1 40W
North Sydney	**151**	46 12N	60 21W
North Syracuse	**162**	43 8N	76 7W
N. Taranaki Bt.	**82**	38 45 S	174 20 E

North Tawton Nyirbátor

North Tawton 30 50 48N 3 55W
North Thompson, R. 152 50 40N 120 20W
North Thoresby 33 53 27N 0 3W
North Tidworth 28 51 14N 1 40W
North Tolsta 36 58 21N 6 13W
N. Tonawanda 156 43 5N 78 50W
N. Truchas Pk. 161 36 0N 105 30W
North Twin I. 150 53 20N 80 0W
North Tyne, R. 35 54 59N 2 7W
North Uist I. 36 57 40N 7 15W
North Vancouver 152 49 25N 123 20W
North Vermilion 152 58 25N 116 0W
North Vernon 156 39 0N 85 35W
North Vietnam ■ 100 22 0N 105 0 E
North Wabasca L. 152 56 0N 113 55W
North Walsham 29 52 49N 1 22 E
North West C. 136 21 45 S 114 9 E
North West Highlands 36 57 35N 5 2W
North West River 151 53 30N 60 10W
North Western □ 127 13 30 S 25 30 E
North York Moors 33 54 25N 0 50W
North Yorkshire □ 33 54 15N 1 25W
Northallerton 33 54 20N 1 26W
Northam, Austral. 132 31 35 S 116 42 E
Northam, S. Afr. 137 24 55 S 27 15 E
Northam, U.K. 30 51 2N 4 13W
Northampton, Austral. 137 28 21 S 114 33 E
Northampton, U.K. 29 52 14N 0 54W
Northampton, Mass., U.S.A. 162 42 22N 72 39W
Northampton, Pa., U.S.A. 162 40 38N 75 24W
Northampton □ 29 52 16N 0 55W
Northampton Downs 138 24 35 S 145 48 E
Northbridge 162 42 12N 71 40W
Northcliffe 137 34 39 S 116 7 E
N.E. Land 12 80 0N 24 0 E
N.E. Providence Chan. 166 26 0N 76 0W
Northeast Providence Channel 166 26 0N 76 0W
Northeim 48 51 42N 10 0 E
Northern □, Malawi 127 11 0 S 34 0 E
Northern □, Uganda 126 3 5N 32 30 E
Northern □, Zambia 127 10 30 S 31 0 E
Northern Circars 96 17 30N 82 30 E
Northern Indian L. 153 57 20N 97 20W
Northern Ireland □ 38 54 45N 7 0W
Northern Light, L. 150 48 15N 90 39W
Northern Province □ 120 9 0 S 11 30W
Northern Territory □ 136 16 0 S 133 0 E
Northfield, Minn., U.S.A. 158 44 37N 93 10W
Northfield, N.J., U.S.A. 162 39 22N 74 33W
Northfleet 29 51 26N 0 20 E
Northiam 29 50 59N 0 39 E
Northland □ 143 35 30 S 173 30 E
Northleach 28 51 49N 1 50W
Northome 158 47 53N 94 15W
Northop 31 53 13N 3 8W
Northport, Ala., U.S.A. 157 33 15N 87 35W
Northport, Mich., U.S.A. 156 45 8N 85 39W
Northport, N.Y., U.S.A. 162 40 53N 73 20W
Northport, Wash., U.S.A. 160 48 55N 117 48W
Northrepps 29 52 53N 1 20 E
Northumberland □ 35 55 12N 2 0W
Northumberland, C. 140 38 5 S 140 40 E
Northumberland Is. 138 21 30 S 149 50 E
Northumberland Str. 151 46 20N 64 0W
Northville 162 43 13N 74 11W
Northway Junction 147 63 0N 141 55W
N.W. Providence Chan. 166 26 0N 78 0W
Northwest Terr. 148 65 0N 100 0W
N.W.Basin 137 25 45 S 115 0 E
Northwich 32 53 16N 2 30W
Northwold 29 52 33N 0 37 E
Northwood, Iowa, U.S.A. 158 43 27N 93 12W
Northwood, N.D., U.S.A. 158 47 44N 97 30W
Norton, Rhod. 127 17 52 S 30 40 E
Norton, N. Yorks., U.K. 33 54 9N 0 48W
Norton, Suffolk, U.K. 29 52 15N 0 52 E
Norton, U.S.A. 158 39 50N 100 0W
Norton B. 147 64 40N 162 0W
Norton Fitzwarren 28 51 1N 3 10W
Norton Sd. 147 64 0N 165 0W
Norton Summit 109 34 56 S 138 43 E
Nortorf 48 54 14N 9 47 E
Norwalk, Calif., U.S.A. 163 33 54N 118 5W
Norwalk, Conn., U.S.A. 162 41 9N 73 25W
Norwalk, Ohio, U.S.A. 156 41 13N 82 38W
Norway 156 45 46N 87 57W
Norway ■ 74 67 0N 11 0 E
Norway House 153 53 59N 97 50W
Norwegian Dependency 13 66 0N 15 0 E
Norwegian Sea 14 66 0N 1 0 E
Norwich, U.K. 29 52 38N 1 17 E
Norwich, Conn., U.S.A. 162 41 33N 72 5W
Norwich, N.Y., U.S.A. 162 42 32N 75 30W
Norwood, Austral. 109 34 56 S 138 39 E
Norwood, U.S.A. 162 42 10N 71 10W
Noshiro 112 40 12N 140 0 E
Noshiro, R. 112 40 15N 140 15 E
Nosok 76 70 10N 82 20 E
Nosovka 80 50 50N 31 30 E
Nosratābād 93 29 55N 60 0 E
Noss Hd. 37 58 29N 3 4W
Noss, I. of 36 60 8N 1 1W
Nossa Senhora da Glória 170 10 14 S 37 25W
Nossa Senhora das Dores 170 10 29 S 37 13W
Nossebro 73 58 12N 12 43 E
Nossob 128 22 15 S 17 48 E
Nossob, R. 128 25 15 S 20 30 E
Nosy Bé, I. 125 13 25 S 48 15 E
Nosy Mitsio, I. 125 12 54 S 48 36 E
Nosy Varika 125 20 35 S 48 32 E
Notigi Dam 153 56 40N 99 10W
Notikewin 152 56 55N 117 50W
Notikewin, R. 152 56 59N 117 38W
Notios Evvoïkós Kólpos 69 38 20N 24 0 E
Noto 65 36 52N 15 4 E
Noto, G. di 65 36 50N 15 10 E
Notodden 71 59 35N 9 17 E
Notre Dame 151 46 18N 64 46W
Notre Dame B. 151 49 45N 55 30W
Notre Dame de Koartac 149 60 55N 69 40W
Notre Dame d'Ivugivic 149 62 20N 78 0W
Nottaway, R. 150 51 22N 78 55W
Nøtterøy 71 59 14N 10 24 E
Nottingham 33 52 57N 1 10W
Nottingham □ 33 53 10N 1 0W
Nottoway, R. 156 37 0N 77 45W
Notwani, R. 128 24 14 S 26 20 E
Nouadhibou 116 21 0N 17 0W
Nouakchott 120 18 20N 15 50W
Nouméa 130 22 17 S 166 30 E
Noup Hd. 37 59 20N 3 2W
Noupoort 128 31 10 S 24 57 E
Nouveau Comptoir (Paint Hills) 150 53 0N 78 49W
Nouvelle Calédonie 142 21 0 S 165 0 E
Nouzonville 43 49 48N 4 44 E
Nova-Annenskiy 81 50 32N 42 39 E
Nová Bana 53 48 28N 18 39 E
Nová Bystrice 52 49 2N 15 8 E
Nova Chaves 124 10 50 S 21 15 E
Nova Cruz 170 6 28 S 35 25W
Nova Era 171 19 45 S 43 3W
Nova Esperança 173 23 8 S 52 13W
Nova Friburgo 173 22 10 S 42 30W
Nova Gaia 124 10 10 S 17 35 E
Nova Gradiška 66 45 17N 17 28 E
Nova Granada 171 20 30 S 49 20W
Nova Iguaçu 173 22 45 S 43 28W
Nova Iorque 170 7 0 S 44 5W
Nova Lamego 120 12 19N 14 11W
Nova Lima 173 19 59 S 43 51W
Nova Lisboa = Huambo 125 12 42 S 15 54 E
Nova Lusitânia 127 19 50 S 34 34 E
Nova Mambone 129 21 0 S 35 3 E
Nova Mesto 63 45 47N 15 12 E
Nova Paka 52 50 29N 15 30 E
Nova Ponte 171 19 8 S 47 41W
Nova Preixo 127 14 45 S 36 22 E
Nova Scotia □ 151 45 10N 63 0W
Nova Sofala 129 20 7 S 34 48 E
Nova Varoš 66 43 29N 19 48 E
Nova Venécia 171 18 45 S 40 24W
Nova Zagora 67 42 32N 25 59 E
Novaci, Rumania 70 45 10N 23 42 E
Novaci, Yugo. 66 41 5N 21 29 E
Novaleksandrovskaya 83 45 29N 41 17 E
Novalorque 171 6 48 S 44 0W
Novara 62 45 27N 8 36 E
Novato 163 38 6N 122 35W
Novaya Kakhovka 82 46 42N 33 27 E
Novaya Ladoga 78 60 7N 32 16 E
Novaya Lyalya 84 58 50N 60 35 E
Novaya Sibir, O. 77 75 10N 150 0 E
Novaya Zemlya 76 75 0N 56 0 E
Novelda 59 38 24N 0 45W
Novellara 62 44 50N 10 43 E
Noventa Vicentina 63 45 18N 11 30 E
Novgorod 80 58 30N 31 25 E
Novgorod Severskiy 80 52 2N 33 10 E
Novgorod Volynski 80 50 38N 27 47 E
Novi Bečej. 66 45 36N 20 10 E
Novi Grad 63 45 19N 13 33 E
Novi Knezeva 66 46 4N 20 8 E
Novi Krichim 67 42 22N 24 31 E
Novi Ligure 62 44 45N 8 47 E
Novi-Pazar 67 43 25N 27 15 E
Novi Pazar 66 43 12N 20 28 E
Novi Sad 66 45 18N 19 52 E
Novi Vinodolski 63 45 10N 14 48 E
Novigrad 63 44 10N 15 32 E
Noville 47 50 4N 5 46 E
Novo Acôrdo 170 13 10 S 46 48W
Nôvo Cruzeiro 171 17 29 S 41 53W
Novo Freixo 127 14 49 S 36 30 E
Nôvo Hamburgo 173 29 37 S 51 7W
Novo Horizonte 171 21 25 S 49 10W
Novo Luso 103 4 3 S 126 6 E
Novo Redondo 124 11 10 S 13 48 E
Novo Selo 66 44 11N 22 47 E
Novo-Sergiyevskiy 84 52 5N 53 38 E
Novo-Zavidovskiy 81 56 32N 36 29 E
Novoalekseyevka 84 50 8N 55 39 E
Novoataysk 76 53 30N 84 0 E
Novoazovsk 82 47 15N 38 4 E
Novobelitsa 80 52 27N 31 2 E
Novobogatinskoye 83 47 26N 51 17 E
Novocherkassk 83 47 27N 40 5 E
Novodevichye 81 53 37N 48 58 E
Novograd Volynskiy 80 50 40N 27 35 E
Novogrudok 80 53 40N 25 50 E
Novokayakent 83 42 45N 42 52 E
Novokazalinsk 76 45 40N 61 40 E
Novokhopersk 81 51 5N 41 50 E
Novokuybyshevsk 84 53 7N 49 58 E
Novokuznetsk 76 54 0N 87 10 E
Novomirgorod 82 48 57N 31 33 E
Novomoskovsk, R.S.F.S.R., U.S.S.R. 81 54 5N 38 15 E
Novomoskovsk, Ukrainian S.S.R., U.S.S.R. 81 48 33N 35 17 E
Novoorsk 84 51 21N 59 2 E
Novopolotsk 80 55 38N 28 37 E
Novorossiysk 82 44 43N 37 52 E
Novorzhev 80 57 3N 29 25 E
Novoselitsa 82 48 14N 26 15 E
Novoshakhtinsk 83 47 39N 39 58 E
Novosibirsk 76 55 0N 83 5 E
Novosibirskiye Ostrava 77 75 0N 140 0 E
Novosil 81 52 58N 36 58 E
Novosokolniki 80 56 33N 28 42 E
Novotroitsk 84 51 10N 58 15 E
Novotroitskoye 85 43 42N 73 46 E
Novotulskiy 81 54 10N 37 36 E
Novoukrainka 82 48 25N 31 30 E
Novouzensk 81 50 32N 48 17 E
Novovolynsk 80 50 45N 24 4 E
Novovyatsk 84 58 24N 49 45 E
Novozybkov 80 52 30N 32 0 E
Novska 66 45 19N 17 0 E
Novy Bug 82 47 34N 34 29 E
Nový Bydzov 52 50 14N 15 29 E
Novy Dwór Mazowiecki 54 52 26N 20 44 E
Nový Jičin 53 49 15N 18 0 E
Novyy Oskol 81 50 44N 37 55 E
Novyy Port 76 67 40N 72 30 E
Novyye Aneny 70 46 51N 29 13 E
Now Shahr 93 36 40N 51 40 E
Nowa Deba 54 50 26N 21 41 E
Nowa Nowa 141 37 44 S 148 3 E
Nowa Skalmierzyce 54 51 43N 18 0 E
Nowa Sól 54 51 48N 15 44 E
Nowe 54 53 41N 18 44 E
Nowe Miasteczko 54 51 42N 15 42 E
Nowe Miasto 54 51 38N 20 34 E
Nowe Miasto Lubawskie 54 53 27N 19 33 E
Nowe Warpno 54 53 42N 14 18 E
Nowen Hill 39 51 42N 9 15W
Nowendoc 141 31 32 S 151 44 E
Nowgong 98 26 20N 92 50 E
Nowingi 140 34 33 S 142 15 E
Nowogard 54 53 41N 15 10 E
Nowogród 54 53 14N 21 53 E
Nowra 141 34 53 S 150 35 E
Nowthanna Mt. 137 27 0 S 118 40 E
Nowy Dwór 54 53 40N 23 0 E
Nowy Korczyn 54 50 19N 20 48 E
Nowy Sącz 54 49 40N 20 41 E
Nowy Sącz □ 54 49 30N 20 30 E
Nowy Staw 54 54 13N 19 2 E
Nowy Targ 53 49 30N 20 2 E
Nowy Tomyśl 54 52 19N 16 10 E
Noxen 162 41 25N 76 4W
Noxon 160 48 0N 115 54W
Noya 56 42 48N 8 53W
Noyant 42 47 30N 0 6 E
Noyers 43 47 40N 4 0 E
Noyes, I. 152 55 30N 133 40W
Noyon 43 49 34N 3 0 E
Nriquinha 125 16 0 S 21 25 E
Nsa, O. en 119 32 23N 5 20 E
Nsanje 127 16 55 S 35 12 E
Nsawam 121 5 50N 0 24W
Nsomba 127 10 45 S 29 59 E
Nsopzup 98 25 51N 97 30 E
Nsukka 121 7 0N 7 50 E
Nuanetsi 125 21 15 S 30 48 E
Nuanetsi, R. 127 21 10 S 31 20 E
Nuatja 121 7 0N 1 10 E
Nuba Mts. = Nubāh, Jibālan 123 12 0N 31 0 E
Nubāh, Jibālan 123 12 0N 31 0 E
Nûbîya, Es Sahrâ En 122 21 30N 33 30 E
Ñuble □ 172 37 0 S 72 0W
Nuboai 103 2 10 S 136 30 E
Nubra, R. 95 34 50N 77 25 E
Nudgee 108 27 22 S 153 5 E
Nudgee Beach 108 27 21 S 153 6 E
Nũdlac 66 46 10N 20 50 E
Nudo Ausangate, Mt. 174 13 45 S 71 10W
Nudo de Vilcanota 174 14 30 S 70 0W
Nueces, R. 159 28 18N 98 39W
Nueltin L. 153 60 30N 99 30W
Nuenen 47 51 29N 5 33 E
Nueva Antioquia 174 6 5N 69 26W
Nueva Casas Grandes 164 30 25N 107 55W
Nueva Esparta □ 174 11 0N 64 0W
Nueva Gerona 166 21 53N 82 49W
Nueva Imperial 176 38 45 S 72 58W
Nueva Palmira 172 33 52 S 58 20W
Nueva Rosita 164 28 0N 101 20W
Nueva San Salvador 166 13 40N 89 25W
Nuéve de Julio 172 35 30 S 61 0W
Nuevitas 166 21 30N 77 20W
Nuevo, Golfo 176 43 0 S 64 30W
Nuevo Guerrero 165 26 34N 99 15W
Nuevo Laredo 165 27 30N 99 40W
Nuevo León □ 164 25 0N 100 0W
Nuevo Rocafuerte 174 0 55 S 76 50W
Nugget Pt. 143 46 27 S 169 50 E
Nugrus Gebel 122 24 58N 39 34 E
Nuhaka 142 39 3 S 177 45 E
Nuhurowa, I. 103 5 30 S 132 45 E
Nuits 43 47 10N 4 56 E
Nuits-St.-Georges 43 47 10N 4 56 E
Nukey Bluff, Mt. 132 32 32 S 135 40 E
Nukheila (Merga) 122 19 1N 26 21 E
Nukus 76 42 20N 59 40 E
Nuland 46 51 44N 5 26 E
Nulato 147 64 40N 158 10W
Nules 58 39 51N 0 9W
Nullagine 136 21 53 S 120 6 E
Nullagine, R. 136 21 20 S 120 20 E
Nullarbor 137 31 28 S 130 55 E
Nullarbor Plain 137 30 45 S 129 0 E
Numalla, L. 139 28 43 S 144 20 E
Numan 121 9 29N 12 3 E
Numansdorp 46 51 43N 4 26 E
Numata 111 36 45N 139 4 E
Numatinna, W. 123 6 38N 27 15 E
Numazu 111 35 7N 138 51 E
Numbulwar 138 14 15 S 135 45 E
Numfoor, I. 103 1 0 S 134 50 E
Numurkah 141 36 0 S 145 26 E
Nun, R. 105 47 30N 124 40 E
Nunaksaluk, I. 151 55 49N 60 20W
Nundah 108 27 24 S 152 54 E
Nuneaton 28 52 32N 1 29W
Nungo 127 13 23 S 37 43 E
Nungwe 126 2 48 S 32 2 E
Nunivak I. 147 60 0N 166 0W
Nunkun, Mt. 95 33 57N 76 8 E
Nunney 28 51 13N 2 20W
Nunspeet 46 52 21N 5 45 E
Nuoro 64 40 20N 9 20 E
Nũousa 68 40 42N 22 9 E
Nuqayy, Jabal 119 23 11N 19 30 E
Nuquí 174 5 42N 77 17W
Nurata 85 40 33N 65 41 E
Nuratau, Khrebet 85 40 40N 66 30 E
Nure, R. 62 44 40N 9 32 E
Nuremburg = Nürnberg 49 49 26N 11 5 E
Nuri 164 28 2N 109 22W
Nurina 137 30 44 S 126 23 E
Nuriootpa 140 34 27 S 139 0 E
Nurlat 84 54 29N 50 45 E
Nürnberg 49 49 26N 11 5 E
Nurrari Lakes 137 29 1 S 130 5 E
Nurri 64 39 43N 9 13 E
Nusa Barung 103 8 22 S 113 20 E
Nusa Kambangan 103 7 47 S 109 0 E
Nusa Tenggara □ 102 7 30 S 117 0 E
Nusa Tenggara Barat 102 8 50 S 117 30 E
Nusa Tenggara Timur 103 9 30 S 122 0 E
Nushki 94 29 35N 65 65 E
Nũsũud 70 47 19N 24 29 E
Nutak 149 57 28N 61 52W
Nuth 47 50 55N 5 53 E
Nutwood Downs 138 15 49 S 134 10 E
Nuwaiba 122 28 58N 34 40 E
Nuwakot 95 28 10N 83 55 E
Nuwara Eliya 97 6 58N 80 55 E
Nuwefontein 128 28 1 S 19 6 E
Nuweveldberge 128 32 10 S 21 45 E
Nuyts Arch. 139 32 12 S 133 20 E
Nuyts, C. 137 32 2 S 132 21 E
Nuyts, Pt. 132 35 4 S 116 38 E
Nuzvid 96 16 47N 80 53 E
NW Tor, oilfield 19 56 42N 3 13 E
Nyaake (Webo) 120 4 52N 7 37W
Nyabing 137 33 30 S 118 7 E
Nyack 162 41 5N 73 57W
Nyadal 72 62 48N 17 59 E
Nyagyn 76 62 8N 63 36 E
Nyah West 140 35 11 S 143 21 E
Nyahanga 126 2 20 S 33 37 E
Nyahua 126 5 25 S 33 23 E
Nyahururu 126 0 2N 36 27 E
Nyahururu Falls 126 0 2N 36 27 E
Nyakanazi 126 3 2 S 31 10 E
Nyakasu 126 3 58 S 30 6 E
Nyakrom 121 5 40N 0 50W
Nyâlâ 123 12 2N 24 58 E
Nyamandhlovu 127 19 55 S 28 16 E
Nyambiti 126 2 48 S 33 27 E
Nyamwaga 126 1 27 S 34 33 E
Nyandekwa 126 3 57 S 32 32 E
Nyanga, L. 137 29 57 S 126 10 E
Nyangana 128 18 0 S 20 40 E
Nyanguge 126 2 30 S 33 12 E
Nyangwena 127 15 18 S 28 45 E
Nyanji 127 14 25 S 31 46 E
Nyankpala 121 9 21N 0 58W
Nyanza, Burundi 126 4 21 S 29 36 E
Nyanza, Rwanda 126 2 20 S 29 42 E
Nyanza □ 126 0 10 S 34 15 E
Nyarling, R. 152 60 41N 113 23W
Nyasa, L. = Malawi, L. 127 12 0 S 34 30 E
Nyaunglebin 98 17 52N 96 42 E
Nyazepetrovsk 84 56 3N 59 36 E
Nyazwidzi, R. 127 19 35 S 32 0 E
Nyborg 73 55 18N 10 47 E
Nybro 73 56 44N 15 55 E
Nybster 37 58 34N 3 6W
Nyda 76 66 40N 73 10 E
Nyenchen Tanglha Shan 99 30 30N 95 0 E
Nyeri 126 0 23 S 36 56 E
Nyeri □ 126 0 25 S 56 55 E
Nyerol 123 8 41N 32 1 E
Nyhem 72 62 54N 15 37 E
Nyiel 123 6 9N 31 4 E
Nyika Plat. 127 10 30 S 36 0 E
Nyilumba 127 10 30 S 40 22 E
Nyinahin 120 6 43N 2 3W
Nyirbátor 53 47 49N 22 9 E

Nyíregyháza Oldmeldrum

Nyíregyháza	53	48 0N	21 47 E
Nykarleby (Uusikaarlepyy)	74	63 32N	22 31 E
Nykobing	73	54 56N	11 52 E
Nykøbing, Falster, Denmark	73	54 56N	11 52 E
Nykøbing, Mors, Denmark	73	56 48N	8 51 E
Nykøbing, Sjælland, Denmark	73	55 55N	11 40 E
Nyköbing	73	56 49N	8 50 E
Nyköping	73	58 45N	17 0 E
Nykroppa	72	59 37N	14 18 E
Nykvarn	72	59 11N	17 25 E
Nyland	72	63 1N	17 45 E
Nylstroom	129	24 42 S	28 22 E
Nymagee	141	32 7 S	146 20 E
Nymburk	52	50 10N	15 1 E
Nymindegab	73	55 50N	8 12 E
Nynäshamn	72	58 54N	17 57 E
Nyngan	141	31 30 S	147 8 E
Nyon	50	46 23N	6 14 E
Nyons	45	44 22N	5 10 E
Nyora	141	38 20 S	145 41 E
Nyord	73	55 4N	12 13 E
Nysa	54	50 40N	17 22 E
Nysa, R.	54	52 4N	14 46 E
Nyssa	160	43 56N	117 2W
Nysted	73	54 40N	11 44 E
Nytva	84	57 56N	55 20 E
Nyūgawa	110	33 56N	133 5 E
Nyunzu	126	5 57 S	27 58 E
Nyurba	77	63 17N	118 20 E
Nzega	126	4 10 S	33 12 E
Nzega □	126	4 10 S	33 10 E
N'Zérékoré	120	7 49N	8 48W
Nzilo, Chutes de	127	10 18 S	25 27 E
Nzubuka	126	4 45 S	32 50 E

O

O-Shima, Fukuoka, Japan	110	33 54N	130 25 E
O-Shima, Nagasaki, Japan	110	33 29N	129 33 E
O-Shima, Shizuoka, Japan	111	34 44N	139 24 E
Oa, Mull of	34	55 35N	6 20W
Oa, The, Pen.	34	55 36N	6 17W
Oacoma	158	43 50N	99 26W
Oadby	28	52 37N	1 7W
Oahe	158	44 33N	100 29W
Oahe Dam	158	44 28N	100 25W
Oahe Res	158	45 30N	100 15W
Oahu I.	147	21 30N	158 0W
Oak Creek	160	40 15N	106 59W
Oak Harb.	160	48 20N	122 38W
Oak Lake	153	49 45N	100 45W
Oak Park	156	41 55N	87 45W
Oak Ridge	157	36 1N	84 5W
Oak View	163	34 24N	119 18W
Oakbank, S. Australia, Austral.	109	34 59 S	138 51 E
Oakbank, S. Australia, Austral.	140	33 4 S	140 33 E
Oakdale, Calif., U.S.A.	163	37 49N	120 56W
Oakdale, La., U.S.A.	159	30 50N	92 38W
Oakengates	28	52 42N	2 29W
Oakes	158	46 14N	98 4W
Oakesdale	160	47 11N	117 9W
Oakey	139	27 25 S	151 43 E
Oakham	29	52 40N	0 43W
Oakhill	156	38 0N	81 7W
Oakhurst	163	37 19N	119 40W
Oakland	163	37 50N	122 18W
Oakland City	156	38 20N	87 20W
Oaklands, N.S.W., Austral.	141	35 34 S	146 10 E
Oaklands, S. Australia, Austral.	109	35 1 S	138 32 E
Oakley	160	42 14N	113 55W
Oakley Creek	141	31 37 S	149 46 E
Oakover, R.	136	20 43 S	120 33 E
Oakridge	160	43 47N	122 31W
Oakwood	159	31 35N	95 47W
Oamaru	143	45 5 S	170 59 E
Oamishirasato	111	35 23N	140 18 E
Oarai	111	36 21N	140 40 E
Oasis, Calif., U.S.A.	163	33 28N	116 6W
Oasis, Nev., U.S.A.	163	37 29N	117 55W
Oates Coast	13	69 0 S	160 0 E
Oatman	161	35 1N	114 19W
Oaxaca	165	17 2N	96 40W
Oaxaca □	165	17 0N	97 0W
Ob, R.	76	62 40N	66 0 E
Oba	150	49 4N	84 7W
Obala	121	4 9N	11 32 E
Obama, Eukui, Japan	111	35 30N	135 45 E
Obama, Nagasaki, Japan	110	32 43N	130 13 E
Oban, N.Z.	143	46 55 S	168 10 E
Oban, U.K.	34	56 25N	5 30W
Obatogamau L.	150	49 34N	74 26W
Obbia	91	5 25N	48 30 E
Obdam	46	52 41N	4 55 E
Obed	152	53 30N	117 10W
Obeh	93	34 28N	63 10 E
Ober-Aagau	50	47 10N	7 45 E
Obera	173	27 21 S	55 2W
Oberalppass	51	46 39N	8 35 E
Oberalpstock	51	46 45N	8 47 E
Oberammergau	49	47 35N	11 3 E
Oberdrauburg	52	46 44N	12 58 E
Oberengadin	51	46 35N	9 55 E
Oberentfelden	50	47 21N	8 2 E
Oberhausen	48	51 28N	6 50 E
Oberkirch	49	48 31N	8 5 E
Oberland	50	46 30N	7 30 E
Oberlin, Kans., U.S.A.	158	39 52N	100 31W
Oberlin, La., U.S.A.	159	30 42N	92 42W
Obernai	43	48 28N	7 30 E
Oberndorf	49	48 17N	8 35 E
Oberon	141	33 45 S	149 52 E
Oberösterreich □	52	48 10N	14 0 E
Oberpfalzer Wald	49	49 30N	12 25 E
Oberseebach	51	48 53N	7 58 E
Obersiggenthal	51	47 29N	8 18 E
Oberstdorf	49	47 25N	10 16 E
Oberwil	50	47 32N	7 33 E
Obi, Kepulauan	103	1 30 S	127 30 E
Obiaruku	121	5 51N	6 9 E
Óbidos, Brazil	175	1 50 S	55 30W
Óbidos, Port.	57	39 19N	9 10W
Obihiro	112	42 25N	143 12 E
Obilnoye	83	47 32N	44 30 E
Obisfelde	48	52 27N	10 57 E
Objat	44	45 16N	1 24 E
Obluchye	77	49 10N	130 50 E
Obninsk	81	55 8N	36 13 E
Obo, C. Afr. Emp.	123	5 20N	26 32 E
Obo, Ethiopia	123	3 34N	38 52 E
Oboa, Mt.	126	1 45N	34 45 E
Obock	123	12 0N	43 20 E
Oborniki	54	52 39N	16 59 E
Oborniki Śl.	54	51 17N	16 53 E
Obot	123	4 32N	37 13 E
Obout	121	3 28N	11 47 E
Oboyan	81	51 20N	36 28 E
Obrenovac	66	44 40N	20 11 E
O'Briensbridge	39	52 46N	8 30W
Obrovac	63	44 11N	15 41 E
Observatory Inlet	152	55 25N	129 45W
Obshchi Syrt	16	52 0N	53 0 E
Obskaya Guba	76	70 0N	73 0 E
Obuasi	121	6 17N	1 40W
Obubra	121	6 8N	8 20 E
Obyachevo	84	60 20N	49 37 E
Obzor	67	42 50N	27 52 E
Ocala	157	29 11N	82 5W
Ocampo	164	28 9N	108 8W
Ocaña	58	39 55N	3 30W
Ocanomowoc	158	43 7N	88 30W
Ocate	159	36 12N	104 59W
Occidental, Cordillera	174	5 0N	76 0W
Ocean City, Md., U.S.A.	162	38 20N	75 5W
Ocean City, N.J., U.S.A.	162	39 18N	74 34W
Ocean Falls	152	52 25N	127 40W
Ocean I.	130	0 45 S	169 50 E
Ocean Park	160	46 30N	124 2W
Oceanlake	160	45 0N	124 0W
Oceano	163	35 6N	120 37W
Oceanside	163	33 13N	117 26W
Ochagavia	58	42 55N	1 5W
Ochakov	82	46 35N	31 30 E
Ochamchire	83	42 46N	41 32 E
Ochamps	47	49 56N	5 16 E
Och'eng	109	30 20N	114 51 E
Ocher	84	57 53N	54 42 E
Ochiai	110	35 1N	133 45 E
Ochil Hills	35	56 14N	3 40W
Ochiltree	34	55 26N	4 23W
Ochre River	153	51 4N	99 47W
Ochsenfurt	49	49 38N	10 3 E
Ocilla	157	31 35N	83 12W
Ockelbo	72	60 54N	16 45 E
Ocmulgee, R.	157	32 0N	83 19W
Ocna Mureş	70	46 23N	23 49 E
Ocna-Sibiului	70	45 52N	24 2 E
Ocnele Mari	70	45 8N	24 18 E
Oconee, R.	157	32 30N	82 55W
Oconto	156	44 52N	87 53W
Oconto Falls	156	44 52N	88 10W
Ocós	166	14 31N	92 11W
Ocosingo	165	18 4N	92 15W
Ocotal	166	13 41N	86 41W
Ocotlán	164	20 21N	102 42W
Ocquier	47	50 24N	5 24 E
Ocreza, R.	56	39 50N	7 35W
Ócsa	53	47 17N	19 15 E
Octave	161	34 10N	112 43W
Octeville	42	49 38N	1 40W
Octyabrskoy Revolyutsii, Os.	77	79 30N	97 0 E
Ocumare del Tuy	174	10 7N	66 46W
Ocussi	103	9 20 S	124 30 E
Oda, Ghana	121	5 50N	1 5W
Oda, Ehime, Japan	110	33 36N	132 53 E
Oda, Shimane, Japan	110	35 11N	132 30 E
Ödåkra	73	56 9N	12 45 E
Ödåkra	73	56 7N	12 45 E
Odanakumadona	128	20 55 S	24 46 E
Ódáoahraun	74	65 5N	17 0W
Odate	112	40 16N	140 34 E
Odawara	111	35 20N	139 6 E
Odda	71	60 3N	6 35 E
Odder	73	55 58N	10 10 E
Oddobo	123	12 21N	42 6 E
Oddur	91	4 0N	43 35 E
Ödeborg	73	58 32N	11 58 E
Odei, R.	153	56 6N	96 54W
Odemira	57	37 35N	8 40W
Ödemiş	92	38 15N	28 0 E
Odense	73	55 22N	10 23 E
Odenton	162	39 5N	76 42W
Odenwald	48	49 18N	9 0 E
Oder, R.	48	53 0N	14 12 E
Oderzo	63	45 47N	12 29 E
Odessa, Del., U.S.A.	162	39 27N	75 40W
Odessa, Tex., U.S.A.	159	31 51N	102 23W
Odessa, Wash., U.S.A.	160	47 25N	118 35W
Odessa, U.S.S.R.	82	46 30N	30 45 E
Odiel, R.	57	37 30N	6 55W
Odienné	120	9 30N	7 34W
Odiham	29	51 16N	0 56W
Odin, gasfield	19	60 5N	2 10 E
Odoben	121	5 38N	0 56W
Odobeşti	70	45 43N	27 4 E
Odolanów	54	51 34N	17 40 E
O'Donnell	159	33 0N	101 48W
Odoorn	46	52 51N	6 51 E
Odorheiul Secuiesc	70	46 21N	25 21 E
Odoyevo	81	53 56N	36 42 E
Odra, R., Czech.	53	49 43N	17 47 E
Odra, R., Poland	54	52 40N	14 28 E
Odra, R., Spain	56	42 30N	4 15W
Odzaci	66	45 30N	19 17 E
Odzak	66	45 3N	18 18 E
Odzi	125	19 0 S	32 20 E
Oedelem	47	51 10N	3 21 E
Oegstgeest	46	52 11N	4 29 E
Oeiras, Brazil	170	7 0 S	42 8W
Oeiras, Port.	57	38 41N	9 18W
Oelrichs	158	43 11N	103 14W
Oelsnitz	48	50 24N	12 11 E
Oenpelli	136	12 20 S	133 4 E
Oensingen	50	47 17N	7 43 E
Oerhtossu, reg.	106	39 20N	108 30 E
Ofanto, R.	65	41 8N	15 50 E
Ofen Pass	51	46 37N	10 17 E
Offa	121	8 13N	4 42 E
Offaly □	39	53 15N	7 30W
Offenbach	49	50 6N	8 46 E
Offenbeek	47	51 17N	6 5 E
Offenburg	126	48 27N	7 56 E
Offerdal	72	63 28N	14 0 E
Offida	63	42 56N	13 40 E
Offranville	42	49 52N	1 0 E
Ofidhousa, I.	69	36 33N	26 8 E
Ofotfjorden	74	68 27N	16 40 E
Oga-Hantō	111	39 58N	139 59 E
Ogahalla	150	50 6N	85 51W
Ōgaki	111	35 21N	136 37 E
Ogallala	158	41 12N	101 40W
Ogbomosho	121	8 1N	3 29 E
Ogden, Iowa, U.S.A.	158	42 3N	94 0W
Ogden, Utah, U.S.A.	160	41 13N	112 1W
Ogdensburg	156	44 40N	75 27W
Ogeechee, R.	157	32 30N	81 32W
Oglio, R.	62	45 15N	10 15 E
Ogmore	138	22 37 S	149 35 E
Ogmore, R.	31	51 29N	3 37W
Ogmore Vale	30	51 35N	3 32W
Ogna	71	58 31N	5 48 E
Ognon, R.	43	47 43N	6 32 E
Ogoja	121	6 38N	8 39 E
Ogoki	150	51 35N	86 0W
Ogoki L.	150	50 50N	87 10W
Ogoki, R.	150	51 38N	85 57W
Ogoki Res.	150	50 45N	88 15W
Ogooué, R.	124	1 0 S	10 0 E
Ogori	110	34 6N	131 24 E
Ogosta, R.	67	43 35N	23 35 E
Ogowe, R. = Ogooué, R.	124	1 0 S	10 0 E
Ograzden	66	41 30N	22 50 E
Ogrein	122	17 55N	34 50 E
Ogulin	63	45 16N	15 16 E
Ogun □	121	7 0N	3 0 E
Oguni	110	33 4N	131 2 E
Oguta	121	5 44N	6 44 E
Ogwashi-Uku	121	6 15N	6 30 E
Ogwe	121	5 0N	7 14 E
Ohai	143	44 55 S	168 0 E
Ohakune	142	39 24 S	175 24 E
Ohara	111	35 15N	140 23 E
Ohau, L.	143	44 15 S	169 53 E
Ohaupo	142	37 56 S	175 20 E
Ohey	47	50 26N	5 8 E
O'Higgins □	172	34 15 S	71 1W
Ohio □	156	40 20N	83 0W
Ohio, R.	156	38 0N	86 0W
Ohiwa Harbour	142	37 59 S	177 10 E
Ohre, R.	52	50 10N	12 30 E
Ohrid	66	41 8N	20 52 E
Ohridsko, Jezero	66	41 8N	20 52 E
Ohrigstad	129	24 41 S	30 36 E
Öhringen	49	49 11N	9 31 E
Oi Ho	108	28 37N	98 16 E
Oignies	47	50 28N	3 0 E
Oil City	156	41 26N	79 40W
Oildale	163	35 25N	119 1W
Oilgate	39	52 25N	6 30W
Oinousa, I.	69	38 33N	26 14 E
Oirschot	47	51 30N	5 18 E
Oise □	43	49 28N	2 30 E
Oise, R.	43	49 53N	3 50 E
Oisterwijk	47	51 35N	5 12 E
Oita	110	33 14N	131 36 E
Oita-ken □	110	33 15N	131 30 E
Oiticica	170	5 3 S	41 5W
Ojai	163	34 28N	119 16W
Ojinaga	164	29 34N	104 25W
Ojocaliente	164	30 25N	106 30W
Ojos del Salado	172	27 0 S	68 40W
Oka, R.	81	56 20N	43 59 E
Okahandja	128	22 0 S	16 59 E
Okahukura	142	38 48N	175 14 E
Okaihau	142	35 19 S	173 36 E
Okakune	142	39 26 S	175 24 E
Okanagan L.	152	50 0N	119 30W
Okanogan	160	48 22N	119 35W
Okanogan, R.	160	48 40N	119 24W
Okány	53	46 52N	21 21 E
Okapa	135	6 38 S	145 39 E
Okaputa	128	20 5 S	17 0 E
Okara	94	30 50N	73 25 E
Okarito	143	43 15 S	170 9 E
Okato	142	39 12 S	173 53 E
Okaukuejo	125	19 10 S	16 0 E
Okavango, R. = Cubango, R.	125	16 15 S	18 0 E
Okavango Swamp	128	19 30 S	23 0 E
Okawa	110	33 9N	130 21 E
Okaya	111	36 0N	138 10 E
Okayama	110	34 40N	133 54 E
Okayama-ken □	110	35 0N	133 50 E
Okazaki	111	34 57N	137 10 E
Oke-Iho	121	8 1N	3 18 E
Okeechobee	157	27 16N	80 46W
Okeechobee L.	157	27 0N	80 50W
Okefenokee Swamp	157	30 50N	82 15W
Okehampton	30	50 44N	4 1W
Okene	121	7 32N	6 11 E
Oker, R.	48	52 7N	10 34 E
Okha	77	53 40N	143 0 E
Ókhi Óros	69	38 5N	24 25 E
Okhotsk	77	59 20N	143 10 E
Okhotsk, Sea of	77	55 0N	145 0 E
Okhotskiy Perevoz	77	61 52N	135 35 E
Okhotsko Kolymskoy	77	63 0N	157 0 E
Oki-no-Shima	110	32 44N	132 33 E
Oki-Shotō	110	36 15N	133 15 E
Okiep	128	29 39 S	17 53 E
Okigwi	121	5 52N	7 20 E
Okija	121	5 54N	6 55 E
Okinawa-Jima	112	26 32N	128 0 E
Okinawa-Shotō	112	27 0N	128 0 E
Okinoerabu-Jima	112	27 21N	128 33 E
Okitipupa	121	6 31N	4 50 E
Oklahoma □	159	35 20N	97 30W
Oklahoma City	159	35 25N	97 30W
Okmulgee	159	35 38N	96 0W
Oknitsa	82	48 25N	27 20 E
Okolo	126	2 37N	31 8 E
Okondeka	128	21 38 S	15 37 E
Okondja	124	0 35 S	13 45 E
Okonek	54	53 32N	16 51 E
Okrika	121	4 47N	7 4 E
Oksby	73	55 33N	8 8 E
Oktyabr	85	43 41N	77 12 E
Oktyabrskiy	84	54 28N	53 28 E
Okuchi	110	32 4N	130 37 E
Okulovka	80	58 19N	33 28 E
Okuru	143	43 55 S	168 55 E
Okushiri-Tō	112	42 15N	139 30 E
Okuta	121	9 14N	3 12 E
Okwa, R.	128	22 25 S	22 30 E
Okwoga	121	7 3N	7 42 E
Ola	159	35 2N	93 10W
Ólafsfjörður	74	66 4N	18 39W
Ólafsvík	74	64 53N	23 43W
Olancha	163	36 15N	118 1W
Olancha Pk.	163	36 15N	118 7W
Olanchito	167	15 30N	86 30W
Öland	73	56 45N	16 50 E
Olargues	44	43 34N	2 53 E
Olary	140	32 18 S	140 19 E
Olascoaga	172	35 15 S	60 39W
Olathe	158	38 50N	94 50W
Olavarría	172	36 55 S	60 20W
Oława	54	50 57N	17 20 E
Olbia	64	40 55N	9 30 E
Olbia, G. di	64	40 55N	9 35 E
Old Bahama Chan.	166	22 10N	77 30W
Old Baldy Pk = San Antonio, Mt.	163	34 17N	117 38W
Old Castile = Castilla la Vieja	56	41 55N	4 0W
Old Castle	38	53 46N	7 10W
Old Cork	138	22 57 S	142 0 E
Old Dale	163	34 8N	115 47W
Old Deer	37	57 30N	2 3W
Old Dongola	122	18 11N	30 44 E
Old Factory	150	52 36N	78 43W
Old Forge, N.J., U.S.A.	162	43 43N	74 58W
Old Forge, N.Y., U.S.A.	162	43 43N	74 58W
Old Forge, Pa., U.S.A.	162	41 20N	75 46W
Old Fort, R.	153	58 36N	110 24W
Old Harbor	147	57 12N	153 22W
Old Kilpatrick	34	55 56N	4 34W
Old Leake	33	53 2N	0 6 E
Old Leighlin	39	52 46N	7 2W
Old Man of Hoy	37	58 53N	3 25W
Old Point Comfort	162	37 0N	76 20W
Old Radnor	31	52 14N	3 7W
Old Serenje	127	13 7 S	30 45 E
Old Shinyanga	126	3 33 S	33 27 E
Old Town	151	45 0N	68 50W
Old Wives L.	153	50 5N	106 0W
Oldbury	28	52 30N	2 0W
Oldeani	126	3 22 S	35 35 E
Oldenburg, Niedersachsen, Ger.	48	53 10N	8 10 E
Oldenburg, S.-Holst, Ger.	48	54 16N	10 53 E
Oldenzaal	46	52 19N	6 53 E
Oldham	32	53 33N	2 8W
Oldman, R.	152	49 57N	111 42W
Oldmeldrum	37	57 20N	2 19W

Örkény Owen

Örkény 53 47 9N 19 26 E
Orkla 71 63 18N 9 51 E
Orkla, R. 74 63 18N 9 51 E
Orkney 128 26 42 S 26 40 E
Orkney □ 37 59 0N 3 0W
Orkney Is. 37 59 0N 3 0W
Orland 160 39 46N 122 12W
Orlando 157 28 30N 81 25W
Orlando, C.d' 65 38 10N 14 43 E
Orléanais 43 48 0N 2 0 E
Orléans 43 47 54N 1 52 E
Orleans, I. d' 156 46 54N 70 58W
Orlice, R. 52 50 5N 16 10 E
Orlické Hory 53 50 15N 16 30 E
Orlov 53 49 17N 20 51 E
Orlov Gay 81 51 4N 48 19 E
Orlovat 66 45 14N 20 33 E
Ormara 93 25 16N 64 33 E
Ormea 62 44 9N 7 54 E
Ormesby St. Margaret 29 52 39N 1 42 E
Ormília 68 40 16N 23 33 E
Ormoc 103 11 0N 124 37 E
Ormond, N.Z. 142 38 33 S 177 56 E
Ormond, U.S.A. 157 29 13N 81 5W
Ormondville 142 40 5 S 176 19 E
Ormoz 63 46 25N 16 10 E
Ormskirk 32 53 35N 2 53W
Ornans 43 47 7N 6 10 E
Orne □ 42 48 40N 0 0 E
Orneta 54 54 8N 20 9 E
Ørnhøj 73 56 13N 8 34 E
Ornö 72 59 4N 18 24 E
Örnsköldsvik 72 63 17N 18 40 E
Oro Grande 163 34 36N 117 20W
Oro, R. 164 26 8N 105 58W
Orocué 174 4 48N 71 20W
Orodo 121 5 34N 7 4 E
Orogrande 161 32 20N 106 4W
Orol 56 43 34N 7 39W
Oromocto 151 45 54N 66 29W
Oron, Israel 90 30 55N 35 1 E
Oron, Nigeria 121 4 48N 8 14 E
Oron, Switz. 50 46 34N 6 50 E
Oron, R. 77 69 21N 95 43 E
Oronsay I. 34 56 0N 6 14W
Oronsay, Pass of 34 56 0N 6 10W
Oropesa 56 39 57N 5 10W
Oroquieta 103 8 32N 123 44 E
Orori 107 40 1N 127 27 E
Orós 170 6 15 S 38 55W
Orosei, G. di 64 40 15N 9 40 E
Orosháza 53 46 32N 20 42 E
Orotukan 77 62 16N 151 42 E
Oroville, Calif., U.S.A. 160 39 31N 121 30W
Oroville, Wash., U.S.A. 158 48 58N 119 30W
Orowia 143 46 1 S 167 50 E
Orphir 37 58 56N 3 8W
Orrefors 73 56 50N 15 45 E
Orroroo 140 32 43 S 138 38 E
Orsa 72 61 7N 14 37 E
Orsara di Puglia 65 41 17N 15 16 E
Orsasjön 72 61 7N 14 37 E
Orsha 80 54 30N 30 25 E
Orsières 50 46 2N 7 9 E
Orsk 84 51 12N 58 34 E
Ørslev 73 55 23N 11 56 E
Orsogna 63 42 13N 14 17 E
Orşova 70 44 41N 22 25 E
Ørsted 73 56 30N 10 20 E
Orta, L. d' 62 45 48N 8 21 E
Orta Nova 65 41 20N 15 40 E
Orte 63 42 28N 12 23 E
Ortegal, C. 56 43 43N 7 52W
Orthez 44 43 29N 0 48W
Ortho 47 50 8N 5 37 E
Ortigueira 56 43 40N 7 50W
Ortles, mt. 62 46 31N 10 33 E
Orto, Tokay 82 42 20N 76 1 E
Ortón, R. 174 10 50 S 67 0W
Orton Tebay 32 54 28N 2 35W
Ortona 63 42 21N 14 24 E
Orune 64 40 25N 9 20 E
Oruro 174 18 0 S 67 19W
Orust 73 58 10N 11 40 E
Orüştie 70 45 50N 23 10 E
Oruzgan 94 32 30N 66 35 E
Orvault 42 47 17N 1 38 E
Orvieto 63 42 43N 12 8 E
Orwell 162 43 35N 75 60W
Orwell, R. 29 52 2N 1 12 E
Orwigsburg 162 40 38N 76 6W
Oryakhovo 66 43 40N 23 57 E
Orzinuovi 62 45 24N 9 55 E
Orzysz 54 53 50N 21 58 E
Os 71 60 9N 5 30 E
Osa 84 57 17N 55 26 E
Osa, Pen. de 166 8 0N 84 0W
Osage, Iowa, U.S.A. 158 43 15N 92 50W
Osage, Wyo., U.S.A. 158 43 59N 104 25W
Osage City 158 38 43N 95 51W
Osage, R. 158 38 15N 92 30W
Ōsaka 111 34 30N 135 30 E
Osaka-fu □ 111 34 40N 135 30 E
Osaka-Wan 111 34 30N 135 18 E
Osan 107 37 11N 127 4 E
Osawatomie 158 38 30N 94 55W
Osborne 158 39 30N 98 45W
Osby 73 56 23N 13 59 E
Osceola, Ark., U.S.A. 159 35 40N 90 0W
Osceola, Iowa, U.S.A. 158 41 0N 93 20W
Oschatz 48 51 17N 13 8 E
Oschersleben 48 52 2N 11 13 E
Öschiri 64 40 43N 9 7 E
Osečina 66 44 23N 19 34 E
Ösel = Saaremaa 80 58 30N 22 30W
Osenovka 66 70 40N 120 50 E
Osëry 81 54 52N 38 28 E
Osh 85 40 37N 72 49 E
Oshan 108 24 11N 102 24 E
Oshawa 150 43 50N 78 45W
Oshikango 128 17 9 S 16 10 E
Oshima 110 33 11N 132 24 E
Oshkosh, Nebr., U.S.A. 156 41 27N 102 20W
Oshkosh, Wis., U.S.A. 156 44 3N 88 35W
Oshmyany 80 54 26N 25 58 E
Oshogbo 121 7 48N 4 37 E
Oshwe 124 3 25 S 19 28 E
Osica de Jos 70 44 14N 24 20 E
Osieczna 54 51 55N 16 40 E
Osijek 66 45 34N 18 41 E
Osilo 64 40 45N 8 41 E
Osimo 63 43 40N 13 30 E
Osintorf 80 54 34N 30 31 E
Osipovichi 80 53 25N 28 33 E
Oskaloosa 158 41 18N 92 40W
Oskarshamn 73 57 15N 16 27 E
Oskelaneo 150 48 5N 75 15W
Oskol, R. 81 50 20N 38 0 E
Oslo 71 59 55N 10 45 E
Oslob 103 9 31N 123 26 E
Oslofjorden 71 59 20N 10 35 E
Osmanabad 96 18 5N 76 10 E
Osmancık 82 40 45N 34 47 E
Osmand Ra. 136 17 10 S 128 45 E
Osmaniye 92 37 5N 36 10 E
Osmo 72 58 58N 17 55 E
Osmotherley 33 54 22N 1 18W
Osnabrück 48 52 16N 8 2 E
Osobláha 53 50 17N 17 44 E
Osolo 71 59 53N 10 52 E
Osona 128 22 3 S 16 59 E
Osorio 173 29 53 S 50 17W
Osorno, Chile 176 40 25 S 73 0W
Osorno, Spain 56 42 24N 4 22W
Osorno, Vol. 176 41 0N 72 30W
Osoyoos 152 49 0N 119 30W
Ospika, R. 152 56 20N 124 0W
Osprey Reef 138 13 52 S 146 36 E
Oss 46 51 46N 5 32 E
Ossa de Montiel 59 38 58N 2 45W
Ossa, Mt. 138 41 52 S 146 3 E
Ossa, Oros 68 39 47N 22 42 E
Ossabaw I. 157 31 45N 81 8W
Ossendrecht 47 51 24N 4 20 E
Ossett 33 53 40N 1 35W
Ossining 162 41 9N 73 50W
Ossipee 162 43 41N 71 9W
Osśno Lubuskie 54 52 28N 14 51 E
Ossokmanuan L. 151 53 25N 65 0W
Ossora 77 59 20N 163 13 E
Osświecim 54 50 2N 19 11 E
Ostashkov 80 57 4N 33 2 E
Oste, R. 48 53 30N 9 12 E
Ostend = Oostende 47 51 15N 2 50 E
Oster 80 50 57N 30 46 E
Osterburg 48 52 47N 11 44 E
Österby 72 60 13N 17 55 E
Österbymo 73 57 49N 15 15 E
Österdalälven 72 61 30N 13 45 E
Östergötlands Län □ 73 58 35N 15 45 E
Osterholz-Scharmbeck 48 53 14N 8 48 E
Østerild 73 57 3N 8 50 E
Østerild 73 57 2N 8 51 E
Österkorsberga 73 57 18N 15 6 E
Ostermundigen 50 46 58N 7 30 E
Osterøya 71 60 32N 5 30 E
Östersund 72 63 10N 14 38 E
Østfold fylke □ 71 59 25N 11 25 E
Ostfriesische Inseln 48 53 45N 7 15 E
Ostia Lido (Lido di Roma) 64 41 43N 12 17 E
Ostiglia 63 45 4N 11 9 E
Ostrava 53 49 51N 18 18 E
Ostrgrog 54 52 37N 16 33 E
Ostróda 54 53 42N 19 58 E
Ostrog 80 50 20N 26 30 E
Ostrogozhsk 81 50 55N 39 7 E
Ostrołeka 54 53 4N 21 38 E
Ostrołeka □ 54 53 0N 21 30 E
Ostrov, Bulg. 67 43 40N 24 9 E
Ostrov, Rumania 70 44 6N 27 24 E
Ostrov, U.S.S.R. 80 57 25N 28 20 E
Ostrów Mazowiecka 54 52 50N 21 51 E
Ostrów Wielkopolski 54 51 36N 17 44 E
Ostrowiec-Swietokrzyski 54 50 55N 21 22 E
Ostrozac 66 43 43N 17 49 E
Ostrzeszów 54 51 25N 17 52 E
Ostseebad-Kühlungsborn 48 54 10N 11 40 E
Östsinni 71 60 53N 10 3 E
Ostuni 65 40 44N 17 34 E
Osum, R. 67 43 35N 25 0 E
Osumi-Hanto 110 31 20N 130 55 E
Osumi-Kaikyō 112 30 55N 130 50 E
Osumi, R. 68 40 40N 20 10 E
Osumi-Shoto 112 30 30N 130 40 E
Osuna 57 37 14N 5 8W
Oswaldtwistle 32 53 44N 2 27W
Oswego 162 43 29N 76 30W
Oswestry 28 52 52N 3 3W
Ota, Japan 111 35 11N 136 38 E
Ota, Japan 111 36 18N 139 22 E
Ota-Gawa 110 34 21N 132 18 E
Otago □ 143 45 20 S 169 20 E
Otago Harb. 143 45 47 S 170 42 E
Otago Pen. 143 45 48 S 170 45 E
Otahuhu 142 36 56 S 174 51 E
Otake 110 34 12N 132 13 E
Otaki, Japan 111 35 17N 140 15 E
Otaki, N.Z. 142 40 45 S 175 10 E
Otane 142 39 54 S 176 39 E
Otar 85 43 32N 75 12 E
Otaru 112 43 10N 141 0 E
Otaru-Wan 112 43 25N 141 1 E
Otautau 143 46 9 S 168 1 E
Otava, R. 52 49 16N 13 32 E
Otavalo 174 0 20N 78 20W
Otavi 128 19 40 S 17 24 E
Otchinjau 128 16 30 S 13 56 E
Otelec 66 45 36N 20 50 E
Otero de Rey 56 43 6N 7 36W
Othello 160 46 53N 119 8W
Othonoi, I. 68 39 52N 19 22 E
Othris, Mt. 69 39 4N 22 42 E
Otira 143 42 49 S 171 35 E
Otira Gorge 143 42 53 S 171 33 E
Otis 158 40 12N 102 58W
Otjiwarongo 128 20 30 S 16 33 E
Otley 33 53 54N 1 41W
Otmuchow 54 50 28N 17 10 E
Otočac 63 44 53N 15 12 E
Otoineppu 112 44 44N 142 16 E
Otorohanga 142 38 12 S 175 14 E
Otoskwin, R. 150 52 13N 88 6W
Otosquen 153 53 17N 102 1W
Otoyo 110 33 43N 133 45 E
Otra 71 58 8N 8 1 E
Otranto 65 40 9N 18 28 E
Otranto, C.d' 65 40 7N 18 30 E
Otranto, Str. of 65 40 15N 18 40 E
Otrøy 71 62 43N 6 50 E
Otsuki 111 35 36N 138 57 E
Otta 71 61 46N 9 32 E
Ottapalam 97 10 46N 76 23 E
Ottawa, Can. 150 45 27N 75 42W
Ottawa, Ill., U.S.A. 156 41 20N 88 55W
Ottawa, Kans., U.S.A. 158 38 40N 95 10W
Ottawa Is. 149 59 35N 80 16W
Ottawa, R. 150 47 45N 78 35W
Ottélé 121 3 38N 11 19 E
Ottenby 73 56 15N 16 24 E
Otter L. 153 55 35N 104 39W
Otter R. 30 50 47N 3 12W
Otter Rapids, Ont., Can. 150 50 11N 81 39W
Otter Rapids, Sask., Can. 153 55 38N 104 44W
Otterburn 35 55 14N 2 12W
Otterndorf 48 53 47N 8 52 E
Otteröy, I. 71 62 45N 6 50 E
Ottersheim 52 48 21N 14 12 E
Otterup 73 55 30N 10 22 E
Ottery St. Mary 30 50 45N 3 16W
Ottignies 47 50 40N 4 33 E
Otto Beit Bridge 127 15 59 S 28 56 E
Ottosdal 128 26 46 S 25 59 E
Ottoshoop 128 25 45 S 26 58 E
Ottsjö 72 63 13N 13 2 E
Ottter Ferry 34 56 1N 5 20W
Ottumwa 158 41 0N 92 25W
Otu 121 8 14N 3 22 E
Otukpa (Al Owuho) 121 7 9N 7 41 E
Oturkpo 121 7 10N 8 15 E
Otway, Bahia 176 53 30 S 74 0W
Otway, C. 140 38 52 S 143 30 E
Otwock 54 52 5N 21 20 E
Ötz 52 47 13N 10 53 E
Ötz, Fl. 52 47 13N 10 53 E
Ötz, R. 52 47 14N 10 50 E
Ötztaler Alpen 52 46 58N 11 0 E
Ou, Neua 100 22 18N 101 48 E
Ou, R. 100 20 4N 102 13 E
Ouachita Mts. 159 34 50N 94 30W
Ouachita, R. 159 33 0N 92 15W
Ouadane 116 20 50N 11 40W
Ouadda 117 8 15N 22 20 E
Ouagadougou 121 12 25N 1 30W
Ouahigouya 120 13 40N 2 25W
Ouahila 118 27 50N 5 0W
Ouahran = Oran 118 35 37N 0 39W
Oualâta 121 17 20N 6 55W
Ouallene 118 24 41N 1 11 E
Ouanda Djallé 117 8 55N 22 53 E
Ouango 124 4 19N 22 30 E
Ouargla 119 31 59N 5 25 E
Ouarkziz, Djebel 118 28 50N 8 0W
Ouarzazate 118 30 55N 6 55W
Ouatagouna 121 15 11N 0 43 E
Oubangi, R. 124 1 0N 17 50 E
Oubarakai, O. 119 27 20N 9 0 E
Ouche, R. 43 47 11N 5 10 E
Oud-Gastel 47 51 35N 4 28 E
Oud Turnhout 47 51 19N 5 0 E
Ouddorp 46 51 50N 3 57 E
Oude-Pekela 46 53 6N 7 0 E
Oude Rijn, R. 46 52 12N 4 24 E
Oudega 46 53 8N 6 0 E
Oudenaarde 47 50 50N 3 37 E
Oudenbosch 47 51 35N 4 32 E
Oudenburg 47 51 11N 3 1 E
Ouderkerk, Holl. Mérid., Neth. 46 51 56N 4 38 E
Ouderkerk, Utrecht, Neth. 46 52 18N 4 55 E
Oudeschild 46 53 2N 4 50 E
Oudewater 46 52 2N 4 52 E
Oudkarspel 46 52 43N 4 49 E
Oudon 42 47 22N 1 19W
Oudon, R. 42 47 47N 1 2W
Oudtshoorn 128 33 35 S 22 14 E
Oued Sbita 118 25 50N 5 2W
Ouellé 120 7 26N 4 1W
Ouessa 120 11 4N 2 47W
Ouessant, Île d' 42 48 28N 5 6W
Ouesso 124 1 37N 16 5 E
Ouezzane 118 34 51N 5 42W
Ouffet 47 50 26N 5 28 E
Oughter L. 38 54 2N 7 30W
Oughterard 38 53 26N 9 20W
Ougrée 47 50 36N 5 32 E
Ouidah 121 6 25N 2 0 E
Ouimet 150 48 43N 88 35W
Ouistreham 42 49 17N 0 18W
Ouj, R. 118 51 15N 29 45 E
Oujda □ 118 33 18N 1 25W
Oujeft 116 20 2N 13 0W
Oulad Naïl, Mts. des 118 34 30N 3 30 E
Ouled Djellal 119 34 28N 5 2 E
Oulmès 118 33 17N 6 0W
Oulton 29 52 29N 1 40 E
Oulton Broad 29 52 28N 1 43 E
Oulu 74 65 1N 25 29 E
Oulu □ 74 65 10N 27 20 E
Oulujärvi 74 64 25N 27 0 E
Oulujoki 74 64 45N 26 30 E
Oulun Lääni □ 74 64 36N 27 20 E
Oulx 62 45 2N 6 49 E
Oum el Bouaghi 119 35 55N 7 6 E
Oum el Ksi 118 29 4N 6 59W
Oum-er-Rbia 118 32 30N 6 30W
Oum-er-Rbia, O. 118 32 30N 6 30W
Oumè 120 5 21N 5 27W
Ounane, Dj. 119 25 4N 7 10 E
Ounasjoki 74 66 31N 25 44 E
Oundle 29 52 28N 0 28W
Ounguati 128 21 54 S 15 46 E
Ounianga Kébir 117 19 4N 20 29 E
Ounlivou 121 7 20N 1 34 E
Our, R. 47 49 55N 6 5 E
Ouray 161 38 3N 107 48W
Oureg, Oued el 118 32 34N 2 10 E
Ourém 170 1 33 S 47 6W
Ouricuri 170 7 53 S 40 5W
Ourinhos 173 23 0 S 49 54W
Ourini 117 16 7N 22 25 E
Ourique 57 37 38N 8 16W
Ouro Fino 173 22 16 S 46 25W
Ouro Prêto 173 20 20 S 43 30W
Ouro Sogui 120 15 36N 13 19W
Oursi 121 14 41N 0 27W
Ourthe, R. 47 50 29N 5 35 E
Ouse 138 42 25 S 146 42 E
Ouse, R., Sussex, U.K. 29 50 58N 0 3 E
Ouse, R., Yorks., U.K. 33 54 3N 0 7 E
Oust 44 42 52N 1 13 E
Oust, R. 42 48 8N 2 49W
Out Skerries, Is. 36 60 25N 0 50W
Outardes, R. 151 50 0N 69 4W
Outer Hebrides, Is. 36 57 30N 7 40W
Outer I. 151 51 10N 58 35W
Outes 56 42 52N 8 55W
Outjo 128 20 5 S 16 7 E
Outlook, Can. 153 51 30N 107 0W
Outlook, U.S.A. 158 48 53N 104 46W
Outreau 43 50 40N 1 36 E
Outwell 29 52 36N 0 14 E
Ouyen 140 35 1 S 142 22 E
Ouzouer-le-Marché 42 47 54N 1 32 E
Ovada 62 44 39N 8 40 E
Ovalle 172 30 33 S 71 18W
Ovamboland = Owambo 128 17 20 S 16 30 E
Ovar 56 40 51N 8 40W
Ovejas 174 9 32N 75 14W
Ovens 141 36 35 S 146 46 E
Over Flakkee, I. 47 51 45N 4 5 E
Over Wallop 28 51 9N 1 35W
Overbister 37 59 16N 2 33W
Overdinkel 46 52 14N 7 2 E
Overflakkee 46 51 44N 4 10 E
Overijse 47 50 47N 4 32 E
Overijssel 46 50 46N 4 32 E
Overijssel □ 46 52 25N 6 35 E
Overijsselsch Kanaal 46 52 31N 6 6 E
Överkalix 74 66 19N 22 50 E
Overpelt 47 51 12N 5 20 E
Overstand 29 52 55N 1 20W
Overton, Clwyd, U.K. 31 52 58N 2 56W
Overton, Hants, U.K. 28 51 14N 1 16W
Overton, U.S.A. 161 36 32N 114 31W
Övertorneå 74 66 23N 23 40 E
Overum 73 58 0N 16 20 E
Ovid, Colo., U.S.A. 158 41 0N 102 17W
Ovid, N.Y., U.S.A. 162 42 41N 76 49W
Ovidiopol 82 46 15N 30 30 E
Oviedo 56 43 25N 5 50W
Oviedo □ 56 43 20N 6 0W
Oviken 72 63 0N 14 23 E
Oviksfjällen 72 63 0N 13 49 E
Övör Hangay □ 106 45 0N 102 30 E
Ovoro 121 5 26N 7 16 E
Övre Sirdal 71 58 48N 6 43 E
Øvre Sirdal 71 58 48N 6 47 E
Ovruch 80 51 25N 28 45 E
Owaka 143 46 27 S 169 40 E
Owambo 128 17 20 S 16 30 E
Owasco L. 162 42 50N 76 31W
Owase 111 34 7N 136 5 E
Owatonna 158 44 3N 93 17W
Owego 162 42 6N 76 17W
Owel, L. 38 53 34N 7 24W
Owen 140 34 15 S 138 32 E

Owen Falls **Pang-Yang**

Owen Falls	**126**	0 30N	33 5E
Owen Mt.	**143**	41 35S	152 33E
Owen Sound	**150**	44 35N	80 55W
Owen Stanley Range	**135**	8 30S	147 0E
Owendo	**124**	0 17N	9 30E
Oweniny R.	**38**	54 13N	9 32W
Owenkillew R.	**38**	54 44N	7 15W
Owens L.	**163**	36 20N	118 0W
Owens, R.	**163**	36 32N	117 59W
Owensboro	**156**	37 40N	87 5W
Owensville	**158**	38 20N	91 30W
Owerri	**121**	5 29N	7 0E
Owhango	**142**	39 51S	175 20E
Owl, R.	**153**	57 51N	92 44W
Owo	**121**	7 18N	5 30E
Owosso	**156**	43 0N	84 10W
Owston Ferry	**33**	53 28N	0 47W
Owyhee	**160**	42 0N	116 3W
Owyhee, R.	**160**	43 10N	117 37W
Owyhee Res.	**160**	43 30N	117 30W
Ox Mts.	**38**	54 6N	9 0W
Oxberg	**72**	61 7N	14 11E
Oxelösund	**73**	58 43N	17 15E
Oxford, N.Z.	**143**	43 18S	172 11E
Oxford, U.K.	**28**	51 45N	1 15W
Oxford, Mass., U.S.A.	**162**	42 7N	71 52W
Oxford, Miss., U.S.A.	**159**	34 22N	89 30W
Oxford, N.C., U.S.A.	**157**	36 19N	78 36W
Oxford, N.Y., U.S.A.	**162**	42 27N	75 36W
Oxford, Ohio, U.S.A.	**156**	39 30N	84 40W
Oxford, Pa., U.S.A.	**162**	39 47N	75 59W
Oxford □	**28**	51 45N	1 15W
Oxford L.	**153**	54 51N	95 37W
Oxilithos	**69**	38 35N	24 7E
Oxley	**140**	34 11S	144 6E
Oxley Cr.	**108**	27 35S	153 0E
Oxnard	**163**	34 10N	119 14W
Oya	**102**	2 55N	111 55E
Oyabe	**111**	36 47N	136 56E
Oyama	**111**	36 18N	139 48E
Oyana	**110**	32 32N	130 18E
Oyem	**124**	1 42N	11 43E
Oyen	**153**	51 22N	110 28W
Øyeren	**71**	59 48N	11 14E
Oyeren	**71**	59 50N	11 15E
Oykel Bridge	**37**	57 58N	4 45W
Oykell, R.	**37**	57 55N	4 26W
Oymyakon	**77**	63 25N	143 10E
Oyo	**121**	7 46N	3 56E
Oyo □	**121**	8 0N	3 30E
Oyonnax	**45**	46 16N	5 40E
Oyster B.	**138**	42 15S	148 5E
Öystese	**71**	60 22N	6 9E
Øystese	**71**	60 24N	6 12E
Oytal	**85**	42 54N	73 17E
Ozamis (Mizamis)	**103**	8 15N	123 50E
Ozark, Ala., U.S.A.	**157**	31 29N	85 39W
Ozark, Ark., U.S.A.	**159**	35 30N	93 50W
Ozark, Mo., U.S.A.	**159**	37 0N	93 15W
Ozark Plateau	**159**	37 20N	91 40W
Ozarks, L. of	**158**	38 10N	93 0W
Ózd	**53**	48 14N	20 15E
Ozerhinsk	**80**	53 40N	27 7E
Ozërnyy	**84**	51 8N	60 50E
Ozieri	**64**	40 35N	9 0E
Ozimek	**54**	50 41N	18 11E
Ozona	**159**	30 43N	101 11W
Ozorków	**54**	51 57N	19 16E
Ozren, Mt.	**66**	43 55N	18 29E
Ozu	**110**	33 30N	132 33E
Ozu Kumamoto	**110**	32 52N	130 52E
Ozuluama	**165**	21 40N	97 50W
Ozun	**70**	45 47N	25 50E
P			
Pa	**120**	11 33N	3 19W
Pa-an	**98**	16 45N	97 40E
Pa Mong Dam	**100**	18 0N	102 22E
Pa Sak, R.	**101**	15 30N	101 0E
Paal	**47**	51 2N	5 10E
Paar, R.	**49**	48 42N	11 27E
Paarl	**128**	33 45S	18 56E
Paatsi, R.	**74**	68 55N	29 0E
Paauilo	**147**	20 3N	155 22W
Pab Hills	**94**	26 30N	66 45E
Pabbay I.	**36**	57 46N	7 12W
Pabbay, Sd. of	**36**	57 45N	7 4W
Pabianice	**54**	51 40N	19 20E
Pabna	**98**	24 1N	89 18E
Pabo	**126**	2 56N	32 3E
Pacajá, R.	**170**	1 56S	50 50W
Pacajus	**170**	4 10S	38 38W
Pacasmayo	**174**	7 20S	79 35W
Pacaudière, La	**43**	46 11N	3 52E
Paceco	**64**	37 59N	12 32E
Pachhar	**94**	24 40N	77 42E
Pachino	**65**	36 43N	15 4E
Pacho	**174**	5 8N	74 10W
Pachora	**96**	20 38N	75 29E
Pachpadra	**93**	25 58N	72 10E
Pachuca	**165**	20 10N	98 40W
Pachung	**108**	31 58N	106 40E
Pacific	**152**	54 48N	128 28W
Pacific Grove	**163**	36 38N	121 58W
Pacific Ocean	**143**	10 0N	140 0W
Pacifica	**163**	37 36N	122 30W
Packsaddle	**140**	30 36S	141 58E
Pacoh	**152**	53 0N	132 30W
Pacov	**52**	49 27N	15 0E
Pacsa	**53**	46 44N	17 2E
Pacuí, R.	**171**	16 46S	45 1W
Pacy-sur-Eure	**171**	49 1N	1 23E
Paczkow	**54**	50 28N	17 0E
Padaido, Kepulauan	**103**	1 5S	138 0E
Padalarang	**103**	7 50S	107 30E
Padang	**102**	1 0S	100 20E
Padang, I.	**102**	1 0S	100 10E
Padangpanjang	**102**	0 30S	100 20E
Padangsidimpuan	**102**	1 30N	99 15E
Padatchuang	**98**	19 41N	96 35E
Padborg	**73**	54 49N	9 21E
Paddock Wood	**29**	51 13N	0 24E
Paddockwood	**153**	53 30N	105 30W
Paderborn	**48**	51 42N	8 44E
Padesul	**70**	45 40N	22 22E
Padiham	**32**	53 48N	2 20W
Padina	**70**	44 50N	27 8E
Padlei	**153**	62 10N	97 5W
Padloping Island	**149**	67 0N	63 0W
Padma, R.	**98**	23 22N	90 32E
Padmanabhapuram	**97**	8 16N	77 17E
Pádova	**63**	45 24N	11 52E
Padra	**94**	22 15N	73 7E
Padrauna	**95**	26 54N	83 59E
Padre I.	**159**	27 0N	97 20W
Padrón	**56**	42 41N	8 39W
Padstow	**32**	50 33N	4 57W
Padstow Bay	**30**	50 35N	4 58W
Padua = Pádova	**63**	45 24N	11 52E
Paducah, Ky., U.S.A.	**156**	37 0N	88 40W
Paducah, Tex., U.S.A.	**159**	34 3N	100 16W
Padul	**57**	37 1N	3 38W
Padula	**65**	40 20N	15 40E
Padwa	**96**	18 27N	82 37E
Paekakariki	**142**	40 59S	174 58E
Paektu-san	**107**	42 0N	128 3E
Paengaroa	**142**	37 49S	176 29E
Paengnyŏng Do	**107**	37 57N	124 40E
Paeroa	**142**	37 23S	175 41E
Paesana	**62**	44 40N	7 18E
Pag	**63**	44 27N	15 5E
Pag, I.	**63**	44 50N	15 0E
Paga	**121**	11 1N	1 8W
Pagadian	**103**	7 55N	123 30E
Pagai Selatan, I.	**102**	3 0S	100 15W
Pagai Utara, I.	**102**	2 35S	100 0E
Pagalu, I.	**114**	1 35S	3 35E
Pagaralam	**102**	4 0S	103 17E
Pagastikós Kólpos	**68**	39 15N	23 12E
Pagatan	**102**	3 33S	115 59E
Page	**158**	47 11N	97 37W
Paglieta	**63**	42 10N	14 30E
Pagnau	**123**	8 15N	34 7E
Pagny-sur-Moselle	**43**	48 59N	6 2E
Pagosa Springs	**161**	37 16N	107 4W
Pagwa River	**150**	50 2N	85 14W
Pahala	**147**	20 25N	156 0W
Pahang □	**101**	3 40N	102 20E
Pahang, R.	**101**	3 30N	103 9E
Pahang, st.	**101**	3 30N	103 9E
Pahiatua	**142**	40 27S	175 50E
Pahoa	**147**	19 30N	154 57W
Pahokee	**157**	26 50N	80 30W
Pahrump	**161**	36 15N	116 0W
Pahsien	**106**	39 10N	116 20E
Pahsientung	**107**	43 11N	120 57E
Pai	**100**	19 19N	98 27E
Paia	**147**	20 54N	156 22W
Paible	**36**	57 35N	7 30W
Paich'eng	**105**	45 40N	122 52E
Paich'i	**109**	28 2N	111 18E
P'aichou	**109**	30 12N	113 56E
Paicines	**163**	36 44N	121 17W
Paide	**80**	58 57N	25 31E
Paignton	**30**	50 26N	3 33W
Paiho, China	**109**	32 49N	110 3E
Paiho, Taiwan	**109**	23 21N	120 25E
Paihok'ou	**109**	31 46N	110 13E
Päijänne	**75**	61 30N	25 30E
Pailin	**101**	12 46N	102 36E
Pailolo Chan.	**147**	21 5N	156 42W
Paimbœuf	**42**	47 17N	2 0W
Paimboeuf	**44**	47 17N	2 2W
Paimpol	**42**	48 48N	3 4W
Painan	**102**	1 15S	100 40E
Painesville	**156**	41 42N	81 18W
Painiu	**109**	32 51N	112 10E
Painscastle	**31**	52 7N	3 13W
Painswick	**28**	51 47N	2 11W
Paint l.	**153**	55 28N	97 57W
Painted Desert	**161**	36 40N	112 0W
Paintsville	**156**	37 50N	82 50W
Paipa	**174**	5 47N	73 7W
Paise	**108**	23 55N	106 28E
Paisha	**106**	34 23N	112 32E
Paisley, U.K.	**34**	55 51N	4 27W
Paisley, U.S.A.	**160**	42 43N	120 40W
Paita	**174**	5 5S	81 0W
Paiva, R.	**56**	40 50N	7 55W
Paiyin	**105**	36 45N	104 4E
Paiyü	**99**	31 12N	98 45E
Paiyunopo	**106**	41 46N	109 58E
Pajares	**56**	39 57N	1 48W
Pak Lay	**100**	18 15N	101 27E
Pak Phanang	**101**	8 21N	100 12E
Pak Sane	**100**	18 22N	103 39E
Pak Song	**100**	15 11N	106 14E
Pak Suong	**100**	19 58N	102 15E
Pakala	**97**	13 29N	79 8E
Pakanbaru	**102**	0 30N	101 15E
Pakaraima, Sierra	**174**	6 0N	60 0W
Pakemba	**127**	13 3S	29 58E
Pakenham	**141**	38 6S	145 30E
Pakhoi = Peihai	**108**	21 30N	109 5E
Pakhtakor	**85**	40 2N	65 46E
Pakistan ■	**93**	30 0N	70 0E
Pakistan, East = Bangladesh ■	**99**	24 0N	90 0E
Pakkading	**100**	18 19N	103 59E
Paknam = Samut Prakan	**100**	13 36N	100 36E
P'ako	**105**	30 52N	81 19E
Pakokku	**98**	21 30N	95 0E
Pakpattan	**94**	30 25N	73 16E
Pakrac	**66**	45 27N	17 12E
Paks	**53**	46 38N	18 55E
Pakse	**100**	15 5N	105 52E
Paksikori	**107**	42 27N	130 31E
Paktya □	**93**	33 0N	69 15E
Pakwach	**126**	2 28N	31 27E
Pal	**93**	33 45N	79 33E
Pala, Chad	**117**	9 25N	15 5E
Pala, U.S.A.	**163**	33 22N	117 5W
Pala, Zaïre	**126**	6 45S	29 30E
Palabek	**126**	3 22N	32 33E
Palacious	**159**	28 44N	96 12W
Palafrugell	**58**	41 55N	3 10E
Palagiano	**65**	40 35N	17 0E
Palagonia	**65**	37 20N	14 43E
Palagruza	**63**	42 24N	16 15E
Palaiókastron	**69**	35 12N	26 18E
Palaiokhora	**69**	35 16N	23 39E
Pálairos	**69**	38 45N	20 51E
Palais, Le	**42**	47 20N	3 10W
Palakol	**96**	16 31N	81 46E
Palam	**96**	19 0N	77 0E
Palamás	**68**	39 26N	22 4E
Palamós	**58**	41 50N	3 10E
Palampur	**94**	32 10N	76 30E
Palana, Austral.	**138**	39 45S	147 55E
Palana, U.S.S.R.	**77**	59 10N	160 10E
Palanan	**103**	17 8N	122 29E
Palandri	**95**	33 42N	73 40E
Palanpur	**94**	24 10N	72 25E
Palapye	**128**	22 30S	27 7E
Palar, R.	**97**	12 27N	80 13E
Palas	**95**	35 4N	73 4E
Palatka	**157**	29 40N	81 40W
Palau Is.	**130**	7 30N	134 30E
Palauig	**103**	15 26N	119 54E
Palauk	**101**	13 10N	98 40E
Palavas	**44**	43 32N	3 56E
Palawan, I.	**102**	10 0N	119 0E
Palayancottai	**97**	8 45N	77 45E
Palazzo San Gervásio	**65**	40 53N	15 58E
Palazzolo Acreide	**65**	37 4N	14 43E
Paldiski	**80**	59 23N	24 9E
Pale	**66**	43 50N	18 38E
Palel	**98**	24 27N	94 2E
Paleleh	**103**	1 10N	121 50E
Palembang	**102**	3 0S	104 50E
Palencia	**56**	42 1N	4 34W
Palencia □	**56**	42 31N	4 33W
Palermo, Colomb.	**174**	2 54N	75 26W
Palermo, Italy	**64**	38 8N	13 20E
Palermo, U.S.A.	**160**	39 30N	121 37W
Palestine, Asia	**90**	32 0N	35 0E
Palestine, U.S.A.	**159**	31 42N	95 35W
Palestrina	**64**	41 50N	12 52E
Paletwa	**98**	21 30N	92 50E
Palghat	**97**	10 46N	76 42E
Palgrave	**29**	52 22N	1 7E
Palgrave, Mt.	**136**	23 22S	115 58E
P'ali	**105**	27 45N	89 10E
Pali	**94**	25 50N	73 20E
Palik'un	**105**	43 35N	92 51E
Palimé	**121**	6 57N	0 37E
Palintaoch'i	**107**	43 59N	119 20E
Palinuro, C.	**65**	40 1N	15 14E
Palinyuch'i (Tapanshang)	**107**	43 40N	118 20E
Palisade	**158**	40 35N	101 10W
Paliseul	**47**	49 54N	5 8E
Palitana	**94**	21 32N	71 49E
Palizada	**165**	18 18N	92 8W
Palizzi	**65**	37 58N	15 59E
Palk Bay	**97**	9 30N	79 30E
Palk Strait	**97**	10 0N	80 0E
Palkonda	**96**	18 36N	83 48E
Palkonda Ra.	**97**	13 50N	79 20E
Pallasgreen	**39**	52 35N	8 22W
Pallaskenry	**39**	52 39N	8 53W
Pallasovka	**81**	50 4N	47 0E
Palleru, R.	**96**	17 30N	79 40E
Pallinup	**137**	34 0S	117 55E
Pallisa	**126**	1 12N	33 43E
Palliser Bay	**142**	41 26S	175 5E
Palliser, C.	**142**	41 37S	175 14E
Pallu	**94**	28 59N	74 14E
Palm Beach	**157**	26 46N	80 0W
Palm Desert	**163**	33 43N	116 22W
Palm Is.	**138**	18 40S	146 35E
Palm Springs	**163**	33 51N	116 35W
Palma, Canary Is.	**16**	28 40N	17 50W
Palma, Mozam.	**127**	10 46S	40 29E
Palma, Spain	**58**	39 33N	2 39E
Palma, Bahía de	**59**	39 30N	2 39E
Palma del Rio	**57**	37 43N	5 17W
Palma di Montechiaro	**64**	37 12N	13 46E
Palma, I.	**116**	28 45N	17 50W
Palma, La, Panama	**166**	8 15N	78 0W
Palma, La, Spain	**57**	37 21N	6 38W
Palma, R.	**171**	10 10N	71 50W
Palma Soriano	**166**	20 15N	76 0W
Palmanova	**63**	45 54N	13 18E
Palmares	**170**	8 41S	35 36W
Palmarito	**174**	7 37N	70 10W
Palmarola, I.	**64**	40 57N	12 50E
Palmas	**173**	26 29S	52 0W
Palmas, C.	**120**	4 27N	7 46W
Palmas de Monte Alto	**171**	14 16S	43 10W
Pálmas, G. di	**64**	39 0N	8 30E
Palmdale	**163**	34 36N	118 7W
Palmeira	**171**	25 25S	50 0W
Palmeira dos Índios	**170**	9 25S	36 37W
Palmeirais	**170**	12 31S	41 34W
Palmeiras, R.	**171**	12 22S	47 8W
Palmeirinhas, Pta. das	**124**	9 2S	12 57E
Palmela	**57**	38 32N	8 57W
Palmelo	**171**	17 20S	48 27W
Palmer, Alaska, U.S.A.	**147**	61 35N	149 10W
Palmer, Mass., U.S.A.	**162**	42 9N	72 21W
Palmer Arch	**13**	64 15S	65 0W
Palmer Lake	**158**	39 10N	104 52W
Palmer Pen.	**13**	73 0S	60 0W
Palmer, R., N. Terr., Austral.	**138**	24 30S	133 0E
Palmer, R., Queens., Austral.	**138**	16 5S	142 43E
Palmerston	**142**	45 29S	170 43E
Palmerston, C.	**133**	21 32S	149 29E
Palmerston North	**143**	40 21S	175 39E
Palmerton	**162**	40 47N	75 36W
Palmetto	**157**	27 33N	82 33W
Palmi	**65**	38 21N	15 51E
Palmira, Argent.	**172**	32 59S	68 25W
Palmira, Colomb.	**174**	3 32N	76 16W
Palmyra, Mo., U.S.A.	**158**	39 45N	91 30W
Palmyra, N.J., U.S.A.	**162**	40 0N	75 1W
Palmyra, Pa., U.S.A.	**162**	40 18N	76 36W
Palmyra = Tadmor	**92**	34 30N	37 55E
Palni	**97**	10 30N	77 30E
Palni Hills	**97**	10 14N	77 33E
Palo Alto	**163**	37 25N	122 8W
Palo del Colle	**65**	41 4N	16 43E
Paloe	**103**	8 20S	121 43E
Paloma, La	**172**	30 35S	71 0W
Palombara Sabina	**63**	42 4N	12 45E
Palopo	**103**	3 0S	120 16E
Palos, Cabo de	**59**	37 38N	0 40W
Palos Verdes	**163**	33 48N	118 23W
Palos Verdes, Pt.	**163**	33 43N	118 26W
Palouse	**160**	46 59N	117 5W
Palparara	**138**	24 47S	141 22E
Pålsboda	**73**	59 3N	15 22E
Palu, Indon.	**103**	1 0S	119 59E
Palu, Turkey	**92**	38 45N	40 0E
Paluan	**103**	13 35N	120 29E
Palwal	**94**	28 8N	77 19E
Pama, China	**108**	24 9N	107 15E
Pama, Upp. Vol.	**121**	11 19N	0 44E
Pamanukan	**103**	6 16S	107 49E
Pamban I.	**97**	9 24N	79 15E
Pamekasan	**103**	7 10S	113 29E
Pameungpeuk	**103**	7 38S	107 44E
Pamiench'eng	**107**	43 13N	124 2E
Pamiers	**44**	43 7N	1 39E
Pamir, R.	**85**	37 1N	72 41E
Pamirs, Ra.	**85**	37 40N	73 0E
Pamlico, R.	**157**	35 25N	76 40W
Pamlico Sd.	**157**	35 20N	76 0W
Pampa	**159**	35 35N	100 58W
Pampa de las Salinas	**172**	32 1S	66 58W
Pampa, La □	**172**	36 50S	66 0W
Pampanua	**103**	4 22S	120 14E
Pamparato	**62**	44 16N	7 54E
Pampas, Argent.	**172**	34 0S	64 0W
Pampas, Peru	**174**	12 20S	74 50W
Pamplona, Colomb.	**174**	7 23N	72 39W
Pamplona, Spain	**58**	42 48N	1 38W
Pampoenpoort	**128**	31 3S	22 40E
Pamunkey, R.	**162**	37 32N	76 50W
Pana	**158**	39 25N	89 0W
Panaca	**161**	37 51N	114 50W
Panagyurishte	**67**	42 49N	24 15E
Panaitan, I.	**103**	6 35S	105 10E
Panaji (Panjim)	**97**	15 25N	73 50E
Panamá	**166**	9 0N	79 25W
Panama ■	**166**	8 48N	79 55W
Panama Canal	**166**	9 10N	79 56W
Panama Canal Zone	**166**	9 10N	79 56W
Panama City	**157**	30 10N	85 41W
Panamá, Golfo de	**166**	8 4N	79 20W
Panamint Mts.	**161**	36 15N	117 20W
Panamint Springs	**163**	36 20N	117 28W
Panão	**174**	9 55S	75 55W
Panare	**101**	6 51N	101 30E
Panarea, I.	**65**	38 38N	15 3E
Panaro, R.	**62**	44 48N	11 5E
Panarukan	**103**	7 40S	113 52E
Panay, G.	**103**	11 0N	122 30E
Panay I.	**103**	11 10N	122 30E
Pancake Ra.	**161**	38 30N	116 0W
Pančevo	**66**	44 52N	20 41E
Panciu	**70**	45 54N	27 8E
Pancorbo, Paso	**58**	42 32N	3 5W
Pandan	**103**	11 45N	122 10E
Pandangpanjang	**102**	0 40S	100 20E
Pandeglang	**103**	6 25S	106 0E
Pandharpur	**96**	17 41N	75 20E
Pandhurna	**96**	21 36N	78 35E
Pandilla	**58**	41 32N	3 43W
Pando	**173**	34 30S	56 0W
Pando, L. = Hope L.	**139**	28 24S	139 18E
Panevėzys	**80**	55 42N	24 25E
Panfilov	**76**	44 30N	80 0E
Panfilovo	**81**	50 25N	42 46E
Pang-Long	**99**	23 11N	98 45E
Pang-Yang	**99**	22 7N	98 48E

Panga Paulista

Panga 126 1 52N 26 18 E
Pangaion Óros 68 40 50N 24 0 E
Pangalanes, Canal des 129 22 48 S 47 50 E
Pangani 126 5 25 S 38 58 E
Pangani □ 126 5 25 S 39 0 E
Pangani, R. 126 4 40 S 37 50 E
Pangbourne 28 51 28N 1 5W
P'angchiang 106 42 50N 113 1 E
Pangfou 109 32 55N 117 25 E
Pangi 126 3 10 S 26 35 E
Pangkai 98 22 40N 97 31 E
Pangkalanberandan 102 4 1N 98 20 E
Pangkalansusu 102 4 2N 98 42 E
Pangkoh 102 3 5 S 114 8 E
Pangnirtung 149 66 0N 66 0W
Pangong Tso, L. 95 34 0N 78 20 E
Pangrango 103 6 46 S 107 1 E
Pangsau Pass 98 27 15N 96 10 E
Pangta 105 30 14N 97 24 E
Pangtara 98 20 57N 96 40 E
Panguitch 161 37 52N 112 30W
Pangutaran Group 103 6 18N 120 34 E
Panhandle 159 35 23N 101 23W
P'anhsien 108 25 46N 104 39 E
Pani Mines 94 22 29N 73 50 E
Panipat 94 29 25N 77 2 E
Panjal Range 94 32 30N 76 50 E
Panjgur 93 27 0N 64 5 E
Panjim = Panaji 93 15 25N 73 50 E
Panjinad Barrage 93 29 22N 71 15 E
Panjwai 94 31 26N 65 27 E
Pankadjene 103 4 46 S 119 34 E
Pankal Pinang 102 2 0 S 106 0 E
Pankshin 121 9 25N 9 25 E
P'anlung Chiang, R. 108 21 18N 105 25 E
Panmunjŏm 107 37 59N 126 38 E
Panna 95 24 40N 80 15 E
Panna Hills 95 24 40N 81 15 E
Pannuru 97 16 5N 80 34 E
Panorama 173 21 21 S 51 51W
Panruti 97 11 46N 79 35 E
P'anshan 107 41 12N 122 4 E
P'anshih 107 42 55N 126 3 E
Pant'anching 106 39 7N 103 52 E
Pantano 161 32 0N 110 32W
Pantar, I. 103 8 28 S 124 10 E
Pantelleria 64 36 52N 12 0 E
Pantelleria, I. 64 36 52N 12 0 E
Pantha 98 24 7N 94 17 E
Pantin Sakan 98 18 38N 97 33 E
Pantjo 103 8 42 S 118 40 E
Pantón 56 42 31N 7 37W
Pantukan 103 7 17N 125 58 E
Panuco 165 22 0N 98 25W
Panyam 121 9 27N 9 8 E
P'anyü 109 23 2N 113 20 E
Pão de AçIcar 171 9 45 S 37 26W
Paoan 109 22 32N 114 8 E
Paoch'eng 106 33 14N 106 56 E
Paochi 106 34 25N 107 11 E
Paochiatun 107 33 56N 120 12 E
Paoching 108 28 41N 109 35 E
Paok'ang 109 31 57N 111 20 E
Paokuot'u 107 42 20N 120 42 E
Páola 65 39 21N 16 2 E
Paola 158 38 36N 94 50W
Paonia 161 38 56N 107 37W
Paoshan, Shanghai, China 109 31 25N 121 29 E
Paoshan, Yunnan, China 105 25 7N 99 9 E
Paote 106 39 7N 111 13 E
Paoti 107 39 44N 117 18 E
Paoting 106 38 50N 115 30 E
Paot'ou 106 40 35N 110 3 E
Paoua 117 7 25N 16 30 E
Paoying 107 33 15N 119 20 E
Papá 53 47 22N 17 30 E
Papa Sd. 37 59 20N 2 56W
Papa, Sd. of 36 60 19N 1 40W
Papa Stour I. 36 60 20N 1 40W
Papa Stronsay I. 37 59 10N 2 37W
Papa Westray I. 37 59 20N 2 55W
Papagayo, Golfo de 166 10 4N 85 50W
Papagayo, R., Brazil 164 12 30 S 58 10W
Papagayo, R., Mexico 165 16 36N 99 43W
Papagni R. 97 14 10N 78 30 E
Papaikou 147 19 47N 155 6W
Papakura 142 37 4 S 174 59 E
Papaloapan, R. 164 18 2N 96 51W
Papantla 165 20 45N 97 21W
Papar 102 5 45N 116 0 E
Paparoa 142 36 6 S 174 16 E
Paparoa Range 143 42 5 S 171 35 E
Pápas, Ákra 69 38 13N 21 6 E
Papatoetoe 142 36 59 S 174 51 E
Papenburg 48 53 7N 7 25 E
Papien Chiang, R. (Da) 108 22 56N 101 47 E
Papigochic, R. 164 29 9N 109 40W
Paposo 172 25 0 S 70 30W
Paps, The, mts. 39 52 0N 9 15W
Papua, Gulf of 135 9 0 S 144 50 E
Papua New Guinea ■ 135 8 0 S 145 0 E
PapuCa 63 44 22N 15 30 E
Papudo 172 32 29 S 71 27W
Papuk, mts. 66 45 30N 17 30 E
Papun 98 18 0N 97 30 E
Pará = Belém 170 1 20 S 48 30W
Pará □ 175 3 20 S 52 0W
Parábita 65 40 3N 18 8 E
Paracatú 171 17 10 S 46 50W
Paracatu, R. 171 16 30 S 45 4W
Paracel Is. 102 16 49N 111 2 E
Parachilna 140 31 10 S 138 21 E
Parachinar 94 34 0N 70 5 E
Paracombe 109 34 51 S 138 47 E
Paracuru 170 3 24 S 39 4W
Paradas 57 37 18N 5 29W
Paradela 56 42 44N 7 37W
Paradip 95 20 15N 86 35 E
Paradise 160 47 27N 114 54W
Paradise, R. 151 53 27N 57 19W
Paradise Valley 160 41 30N 117 28W
Parado 103 8 42 S 118 30 E
Paradyz 54 51 19N 20 2 E
Parafield 109 34 47 S 138 38 E
Parafield Airport 109 34 48 S 138 38 E
Paragould 159 36 5N 90 30W
Paragua, La 174 6 50N 63 20W
Paragua, R. 174 6 30N 63 30W
Paraguaçu Paulista 173 22 22 S 50 35W
Paraguaçu, R. 171 12 45 S 38 54W
Paraguai, R. 174 16 0 S 57 52W
Paraguaipoa 174 11 21N 71 57W
Paraguana, Pen. de 174 12 0N 70 0W
Paraguarí 172 25 36 S 57 0W
Paraguarí □ 172 26 0 S 57 10W
Paraguay ■ 172 23 0 S 57 0W
Paraguay, R. 172 27 18 S 58 38W
Paraíba = Joéo Pessoa 164 7 10 S 35 0W
Paraiba □ 170 7 0 S 36 0W
Paraíba do Sul, R. 173 21 37 S 41 3W
Paraibano 171 6 30 S 44 1W
Parainen 75 60 18N 22 18 E
Paraíso 165 19 3 S 52 59W
Paraiso 165 18 24N 93 14W
Parakhino Paddubye 80 58 46N 33 10 E
Parakou 121 9 25N 2 40 E
Parakylia 140 30 24 S 136 25 E
Paralion-Astrous 69 37 25N 22 45 E
Paramagudi 97 9 31N 78 39 E
Paramaribo 175 5 50N 55 10W
Parambu 170 6 13 S 40 43W
Paramillo, Nudo del 174 7 4N 75 55W
Paramirim 171 13 26 S 42 15W
Paramirim, R. 171 11 34 S 43 18W
Paramithiá 68 39 30N 20 35 E
Paramushir, Ostrov 77 40 24N 156 0 E
Paran, N. 90 30 14N 34 48 E
Paraná 172 32 0 S 60 30W
Paranã 171 12 30 S 47 40W
Paraná □ 173 24 30 S 51 0W
Paraná, R. 172 33 43 S 59 15W
Paranã, R. 171 22 25 S 53 1W
Paranaguá 173 25 30 S 48 30W
Paranaíba, R. 171 18 0 S 49 12W
Paranapanema, R. 173 22 40 S 53 9W
Paranapiacaba, Serra do 173 24 31 S 48 35W
Paranavaí 173 23 4 S 52 28W
Parang, Jolo, Phil. 103 5 55N 120 54 E
Parang, Mindanao, Phil. 103 7 23N 124 16 E
Parangaba 170 3 45 S 38 33W
Paraóin 66 43 54N 21 27 E
Paraparanma 143 40 57 S 175 3 E
Parapóla, I. 69 36 55N 23 27 E
Paraspóri, Ákra 69 35 55N 27 15 E
Paratinga 171 12 40 S 43 10W
Paratoo 140 32 42 S 139 22 E
Parattah 138 42 22 S 147 23 E
Paraúna 171 17 2 S 50 26W
Paray-le-Monial 45 46 27N 4 7 E
Parbati, R. 94 25 51N 76 34 E
Parbatipur 98 25 39N 88 55 E
Parbhani 96 19 8N 76 52 E
Parchim 48 53 25N 11 50 E
Parczew 54 51 9N 22 52 E
Pardee Res. 163 38 16N 120 51W
Pardes Hanna 90 32 28N 34 57 E
Pardilla 56 41 33N 3 43W
Pardo, R., Bahia, Brazil 171 15 40 S 39 0W
Pardo, R., Mato Grosso, Brazil 171 21 0 S 53 25W
Pardo, R., Minas Gerais, Brazil 171 15 48 S 44 48W
Pardo, R., São Paulo, Brazil 171 20 45 S 48 0W
Pardubice 52 50 3N 15 45 E
Pare 103 7 43 S 112 12 E
Pare □ 126 4 10 S 38 0 E
Pare Mts. 126 4 0 S 37 45 E
Pare Pare 103 4 0 S 119 45 E
Parecis, Serra dos 174 13 0 S 60 0W
Paredes de Nava 56 42 9N 4 42W
Parelhas 170 6 41 S 36 39W
Paren 77 62 45N 163 0 E
Parengarenga Harbour 142 34 31 S 173 0 E
Parent 150 47 55N 74 35W
Parent, Lac. 150 48 31N 77 1W
Parentis-en-Born 44 44 21N 1 4W
Parepare 103 4 0 S 119 40 E
Parfino 80 57 59N 31 34 E
Parfuri 129 22 28 S 31 17 E
Paria, Golfo de 174 10 20N 62 0W
Paria, Pen. de 174 10 50N 62 30W
Pariaguán 174 8 51N 64 43W
Pariaman 102 0 47 S 100 11 E
Paricutín, Cerro 164 19 28N 102 15W
Parigi 103 0 50 S 120 5 E
Parika 174 6 50N 58 20W
Parima, Serra 174 2 30N 64 0W
Parinari 174 4 35 S 74 25W
Parincea 70 46 27N 27 9 E
Parîng, mt. 70 45 20N 23 37 E
Parintins 175 2 40 S 56 50W
Paripart Kyun 99 14 55 S 93 45 E
Paris, Can. 150 43 12N 80 25W
Paris, France 43 48 50N 2 20 E
Paris, Idaho, U.S.A. 160 42 13N 111 30W
Paris, Ky., U.S.A. 156 38 12N 84 12W
Paris, Tenn., U.S.A. 157 36 20N 88 20W
Paris, Tex., U.S.A. 159 33 40N 95 30W
Parish 162 43 24N 76 9W
Pariti 103 9 55 S 123 30 E
Park City 160 40 42N 111 35W
Park Falls 158 45 58N 90 27 E
Park Range 160 40 0N 106 30W
Park Rapids 158 46 56N 95 0W
Park River 158 48 25N 97 17W
Park Rynie 129 30 25 S 30 35 E
Park View 161 36 45N 106 37W
Parkent 85 41 18N 69 40 E
Parker, Ariz., U.S.A. 161 34 8N 114 16W
Parker, S.D., U.S.A. 158 43 25N 97 7W
Parker Dam 161 34 13N 114 5W
Parkersburg 156 39 18N 81 31W
Parkerview 153 51 21N 103 18W
Parkes, A.C.T., Austral. 133 35 18 S 149 8 E
Parkes, N.S.W., Austral. 141 33 9 S 148 11 E
Parkfield 163 35 54N 120 26W
Parkhar 85 37 30N 69 34 E
Parknasilla 39 51 49N 9 50W
Parkside 153 53 10N 106 33W
Parkston 158 43 25N 98 0W
Parksville 152 49 20N 124 21W
Parkville 162 39 23N 76 33W
Parlakimedi 96 18 45N 84 5 E
Parma, Italy 62 44 50N 10 20 E
Parma, U.S.A. 160 43 49N 116 59W
Parna, R. 62 44 27N 10 3 E
Parnaguá 170 10 10 S 44 10W
Parnaiba, Piauí, Brazil 170 3 0 S 41 40W
Parnaíba, São Paulo, Brazil 170 19 34 S 51 14W
Parnaíba, R. 170 3 35 S 43 0W
Parnamirim 170 8 5 S 39 34W
Parnarama 170 5 41 S 43 6W
Parnassós, mt. 69 38 17N 21 30 E
Parnassus 143 42 42 S 173 23 E
Párnis, mt. 69 38 14N 23 45 E
Párnon Óros 69 37 15N 22 45 E
Pärnu 80 58 12N 24 33 E
Parola 96 20 47N 75 7 E
Paroo Chan. 133 30 50 S 143 35 E
Paroo, R. 139 30 0 S 144 5 E
Paropamisus Range = Fīroz Kohi 93 34 45N 63 0 E
Páros 69 37 5N 25 9 E
Páros, I. 69 37 5N 25 12 E
Parowan 161 37 54N 112 56W
Parpaillon, mts. 45 44 30N 6 40 E
Parracombe 30 51 11N 3 55W
Parral 172 36 10 S 72 0W
Parramatta 141 33 48 S 151 1 E
Parramore I. 162 37 32N 75 39W
Parras 164 25 30N 102 20W
Parrett, R. 28 51 7N 2 58W
Parris I. 157 32 20N 80 30W
Parrsboro 151 45 30N 64 10W
Parry 153 49 47N 104 41W
Parry, C. 147 70 20N 123 38W
Parry Is. 12 77 0N 110 0W
Parry Sound 150 45 20N 80 0W
Parshall 158 47 56N 102 11W
Parsnip, R. 152 55 10N 123 2W
Parsons 159 37 20N 95 10W
Parsons Ra., Mts. 138 13 30 S 135 15 E
Partabpur 96 20 0N 80 42 E
Partanna 64 37 43N 12 51 E
Partapgarh 94 24 2N 74 40 E
Parthenay 42 46 38N 0 16W
Partille 73 57 48N 12 18 E
Partinico 64 38 3N 13 6 E
Partney 33 53 12N 0 7 E
Parton 32 54 34N 3 35W
Partry Mts. 38 53 40N 9 28W
Partur 96 19 40N 76 14 E
Paru, R. 175 0 20 S 53 30W
Parur 97 10 13N 76 14 E
Paruro 174 13 45 S 71 50W
Parvatipuram 96 18 50N 83 25 E
Parwan □ 93 35 0N 69 0 E
Påryd 73 56 34N 15 55 E
Parys 128 26 52 S 27 29 E
Parys, Mt. 31 53 23N 4 18W
Pas-de-Calais □ 43 50 30N 2 30 E
Pasadena, Calif., U.S.A. 163 34 5N 118 9W
Pasadena, Tex., U.S.A. 159 29 45N 95 14W
Pasaje 174 3 10 S 79 40W
Pasaje, R. 172 25 35 S 64 57W
Pascagoula 159 30 30N 88 30W
Pascagoula, R. 159 30 40N 88 35W
Paşcani 70 47 14N 26 45 E
Pasco 160 46 10N 119 0W
Pasco, Cerro de 174 10 45 S 76 10W
Pascoag 162 41 57N 71 42W
Pascoe, Mt. 137 27 25 S 120 40 E
Pasewalk 48 53 30N 14 0 E
Pasfield L. 153 58 24N 105 20W
Pasha, R. 80 60 20N 33 0 E
Pashiwari 95 34 40N 75 10 E
Pashiya 84 58 33N 58 26 E
Pashmakli = Smolyan 67 41 36N 24 38 E
Pasighat 98 28 4N 95 21 E
Pasir Mas 101 6 2N 102 8 E
Pasir Puteh 101 5 50N 102 24 E
Pasirian 103 8 13 S 113 8 E
Pasley, C. 137 33 52 S 123 35 E
Pasman I. 63 43 58N 15 20 E
Pasmore, R. 140 31 5 S 139 49 E
Pasni 93 25 15N 63 27 E
Paso de Indios 176 43 55 S 69 0W
Paso de los Libres 172 29 44 S 57 10W
Paso de los Toros 172 32 36 S 56 37W
Paso Robles 161 35 40N 120 45W
Paspebiac 151 48 3N 65 17W
Pasrur 94 32 16N 74 43 E
Passage East 39 52 15N 7 0W
Passage West 39 51 52N 8 20W
Passaic 162 40 50N 74 8W
Passau 49 48 34N 13 27 E
Passendale 47 50 54N 3 2 E
Passero, C. 65 36 42N 15 8 E
Passo Fundo 173 28 10 S 52 30W
Passos 171 20 45 S 46 37W
Passow 48 53 13N 14 3 E
Passwang 50 47 22N 7 41 E
Passy 43 45 55N 6 41 E
Pastaza, R. 174 2 45 S 76 50W
Pastek 54 54 3N 19 41 E
Pasto 174 1 13N 77 17W
Pasto Zootécnico do Cunene 128 16 20 S 15 20 E
Pastos Bons 170 6 36 S 44 5W
Pastrana 58 40 27N 2 53W
Pasuruan 103 7 40 S 112 53 E
Pasym 54 53 48N 20 49 E
Pásztó 53 47 52N 19 43 E
Patagonia, Argent. 176 45 0 S 69 0W
Patagonia, U.S.A. 161 31 35N 110 45W
Patan, India 93 23 54N 72 14 E
Patan, Gujarat, India 96 17 22N 73 48 E
Patan, Maharashtra, India 94 23 54N 72 14 E
Patan (Lalitapur) 99 27 40N 85 20 E
Pat'ang Szechwan 105 30 2N 98 58 E
Patani 103 0 20N 128 50 E
Pataohotzu 107 43 5N 127 33 E
Patapsco Res. 162 39 27N 76 55W
Pataudi 94 28 18N 76 48 E
Patay 43 48 2N 1 40 E
Patcham 29 50 52N 0 9W
Patchewollock 140 35 22 S 142 12 E
Patchogue 162 40 46N 73 1W
Patea 142 39 45 S 174 30 E
Pategi 121 8 50N 5 45 E
Pateley Bridge 33 54 5N 1 45W
Patensie 128 33 46 S 24 49 E
Paternò 65 37 34N 14 53 E
Paternoster, Kepulauan 102 7 5 S 118 15 E
Pateros 160 48 4N 119 58W
Paterson, Austral. 141 32 37 S 151 39 E
Paterson, U.S.A. 162 40 55N 74 10W
Paterson Inlet 143 46 56 S 168 12 E
Paterson Ra. 136 21 45 S 122 10 E
Paterswolde 46 53 9N 6 34 E
Pathankot 94 32 18N 75 45 E
Patharghata 98 22 2N 89 58 E
Pathfinder Res. 160 42 0N 107 0W
Pathiu 101 10 42N 99 19 E
Pathum Thani 100 14 1N 100 32 E
Páti 103 6 45 S 111 3 E
Patiala 94 30 23N 76 26 E
Patine Kouta 120 12 45N 13 45W
Patjitan 103 8 12 S 111 8 E
Patkai Bum 98 27 0N 95 30 E
Pátmos 69 37 21N 26 36 E
Pátmos, I. 69 37 21N 26 36 E
Patna, India 95 25 35N 85 18 E
Patna, U.K. 34 55 21N 4 30W
Patonga 126 2 45N 33 15 E
Patos 170 7 1 S 37 16W
Patos de Minas 171 18 35 S 46 32W
Patos, Lag. dos 173 31 20 S 51 0 E
Patosi 68 40 42N 19 38 E
Patquía 172 30 0 S 66 55W
Pátrai 69 38 14N 21 47 E
Pátraikos, Kólpos 69 38 17N 21 30 E
Patrick 32 54 13N 4 41W
Patrocinio 171 18 57 S 47 0W
Patta 126 2 10 S 41 0 E
Patta, I. 126 2 10 S 41 0 E
Pattada 64 40 35N 9 7 E
Pattanapuram 97 9 6N 76 33 E
Pattani 101 6 48N 101 15 E
Patten 151 45 59N 68 28W
Patterdale 32 54 33N 2 55W
Patterson, Calif., U.S.A. 163 37 30N 121 9W
Patterson, La., U.S.A. 159 29 44N 91 20W
Patterson, Mt. 163 38 29N 119 20W
Patti 94 31 17N 74 54 E
Patti Castroreale 65 38 8N 14 57 E
Pattoki 94 31 5N 73 52 E
Pattukkottai 97 10 25N 79 20 E
Patu 170 6 6 S 37 38W
Patuakhali 98 22 20N 90 25 E
Patuca, Punta 166 15 49N 84 14W
Patuca, R. 166 15 20N 84 40W
Patung 109 31 0N 110 30 E
Pâturages 47 50 25N 3 52 E
Patutahi 142 38 38 S 177 55 E
Pátzcuaro 164 19 30N 101 40W
Pau 44 43 19N 0 25W
Pau d' Arco 170 7 30 S 49 22W
Pau dos Ferros 170 6 7 S 38 10W
Pauillac 44 45 11N 0 46W
Pauini, R. 174 1 42 S 62 50W
Pauk 98 21 55N 94 30 E
Paul I. 151 56 30N 61 20W
Paulatuk 147 69 25N 124 0W
Paulhan 44 43 33N 3 28 E
Paulis = Isiro 126 2 53N 27 58 E
Paulista 170 7 57 S 34 53W

Paulistana **Perryton**

Paulistana 170 8 9S 41 9W
Paull 33 53 42N 0 12W
Paullina 158 42 55N 95 40W
Paulo Afonso 170 9 21S 38 15W
Paulo de Faria 171 20 2S 49 24W
Paulpietersburg 129 27 23S 30 50E
Paul's Valley 159 34 40N 97 17W
Pauma Valley 163 33 16N 116 58W
Paungde 98 18 29N 95 30E
Pauni 96 20 48N 79 40E
Pavelets 81 53 49N 39 14E
Pavia 62 45 10N 9 10E
Pavlikeni 67 43 14N 25 20E
Pavlodar 76 52 33N 77 0E
Pavlof Is. 147 55 30N 161 30W
Pavlograd 82 48 30N 35 52E
Pavlovo, Gorkiy, U.S.S.R. 81 55 58N 43 5E
Pavlovo, Yakut A.S.S.R., U.S.S.R. 77 63 5N 115 25E
Pavlovsk 81 50 26N 40 5E
Pavlovskaya 83 46 17N 39 47E
Pavlovskiy Posad 81 55 37N 38 42E
Pavullo nel Frignano 62 44 20N 10 50E
Pawahku 98 26 11N 98 40E
Pawhuska 159 36 40N 96 25W
Pawling 162 41 35N 73 37W
Pawnee 159 36 24N 96 50W
Pawnee City 158 40 8N 96 10W
Pawtucket 162 41 51N 71 22W
Paximádhia 69 35 0N 24 35E
Paxoi, I. 68 39 14N 20 12E
Paxton, Ill., U.S.A. 156 40 25N 88 0W
Paxton, Nebr., U.S.A. 158 41 12N 101 27W
Paya Bakri 101 2 3N 102 44E
Payakumbah 102 0 20S 100 35E
Payenhaot'e (Alashantsoch'i) 106 38 50N 105 32E
Payenk'ala Shan 105 34 20N 97 0E
Payerne 50 46 49N 6 56E
Payette 160 44 0N 117 0W
Paymogo 57 37 44N 7 21W
Payne L. 149 59 30N 74 30W
Payne, R. 149 60 0N 70 0W
Payneham 109 34 54S 138 39E
Paynes Find 137 29 15S 117 42E
Paynesville, Liberia 120 6 20N 10 45W
Paynesville, U.S.A. 158 45 21N 94 44W
Paysandú 172 32 19S 58 8W
Payson, Ariz., U.S.A. 161 34 17N 111 15W
Payson, Utah, U.S.A. 160 40 8N 111 41W
Paz, Bahía de la 164 24 15N 110 25W
Paz Centro, La 166 12 20N 86 41W
Paz, La, Entre Ríos, Argent. 172 30 50S 59 45W
Paz, La, San Luis, Argent. 172 33 30S 67 20W
Paz, La, Boliv. 174 16 20S 68 10W
Paz, La, Hond. 166 14 20N 87 47W
Paz, La, Mexico 164 24 10N 110 20W
Paz, La, Bahía de 164 24 20N 110 40W
Paz, R. 166 13 44N 90 10W
Pazar 92 41 10N 40 50E
Pazardzhik 67 42 12N 24 20E
Pazin 63 45 14N 13 56E
Pčinja, R. 66 42 0N 21 45E
Pe Ell 160 46 30N 123 18W
Peabody 162 42 31N 70 56W
Peace Point 152 59 7N 112 27W
Peace, R. 152 59 0N 111 25W
Peace River 152 56 15N 117 18W
Peace River Res. 152 55 40N 123 40W
Peacehaven 29 50 47N 0 1E
Peach Springs 161 35 36N 113 30W
Peak Downs 138 22 55S 148 0E
Peak Downs Mine 138 22 17S 148 11E
Peak Hill, N.S.W., Austral. 141 32 39S 148 11E
Peak Hill, W. A., Austral. 137 25 35S 118 43E
Peak Range 138 22 50S 148 20E
Peak, The 32 53 24N 1 53W
Peake 140 35 25S 140 0E
Peake Cr. 139 28 2S 136 7E
Peale Mt. 161 38 25N 109 12W
Pearblossom 163 34 30N 117 55W
Pearce 161 31 57N 109 56W
Pearl Banks 97 8 45N 79 45E
Pearl City 147 2 21N 158 0W
Pearl Harbor 147 21 20N 158 0W
Pearl, R. 159 31 50N 90 0W
Pearsall 159 28 55N 99 8W
Pearse I. 152 54 52N 130 14W
Peary Land 12 82 40N 33 0W
Pease, R. 159 34 18N 100 15W
Peasenhall 29 52 17N 1 24E
Pebane 127 17 10S 38 8E
Pebas 174 3 10S 71 55W
Pebble Beach 163 36 34N 121 57W
Peçanha 171 18 33S 42 34W
Péccioli 62 43 32N 10 43E
Pechea 70 45 36N 27 49E
Pechenezhin 82 48 30N 24 48E
Pechenga 78 69 30N 31 25E
Pechnezhskoye Vdkhr. 81 50 0N 36 50E
Pechora, R. 78 62 30N 56 30E
Pechorskaya Guba 78 68 40N 54 0E
Pechory 80 57 48N 27 40E
Pecica 66 46 10N 21 3E
Pečka 66 44 18N 19 33E
Pécora, C. 64 39 28N 8 23E
Pecos 159 31 25N 103 35W
Pecos, R. 159 31 22N 102 30W
Pecqueuse 47 48 39N 2 3E
Pécs 53 46 5N 18 15E
Pedasí 166 7 32N 80 3W
Peddapalli 96 18 40N 79 24E
Peddapuram 96 17 6N 82 5E
Peddavagu, R. 96 16 33N 79 8E
Pedder, L. 138 42 55S 146 10E
Pedernales 167 18 2N 71 44W
Pedirka 139 26 40S 135 14E
Pedjantan, I. 102 0 5S 106 15E
Pedra Azul 171 16 2S 41 17W
Pedra Grande, Recifes do 171 17 45S 38 58W
Pedras, Pta. de 171 7 38S 34 47W
Pedreiras 170 4 32S 44 40W
Pedrera, La 174 1 18S 69 43W
Pedro Afonso 170 9 0S 48 10W
Pedro Antonio Santos 165 18 54N 88 15W
Pedro Cays 166 17 5N 77 48W
Pedro Chico 174 1 4N 70 25W
Pedro de Valdivia 172 22 33S 69 38W
Pedro Juan Caballero 173 22 30S 55 40W
Pedro Muñoz 59 39 25N 2 56W
Pedrógão Grande 56 39 55N 8 0W
Peebinga 140 34 52S 140 57E
Peebles 35 55 40N 3 12W
Peebles (□) 26 55 37N 3 4W
Peekshill 162 41 18N 73 57W
Peel, Austral. 139 33 20S 149 38E
Peel, I. of Man 32 54 14N 4 40W
Peel Fell, mt. 35 55 17N 2 35W
Peel, R., Austral. 141 30 50S 150 29E
Peel, R., Can. 147 67 0N 135 0W
Peelwood 141 34 7S 149 27E
Peene, R. 48 53 53N 13 53E
Peera Peera Poolanna L. 139 26 30S 138 0E
Peers 152 53 40N 116 0W
Pegasus Bay 143 43 20S 173 10E
Peggau 52 47 12N 15 21E
Pego 59 38 51N 0 8W
Pegswood 35 55 12N 1 38W
Pegu 99 17 20N 96 29E
Pegu Yoma, mts. 98 19 0N 96 0E
Pegwell Bay 29 51 18N 1 22E
Pehčevo 66 41 41N 22 55E
Pehuajó 172 36 0S 62 0W
Pei Chiang, R. 109 23 12N 112 45E
Pei Wan 107 36 25N 120 45E
Peian 105 48 16N 126 36E
Peichen 107 41 38N 121 50E
Peichengchen 107 44 30N 123 27E
Peichiang 109 23 0N 120 0E
Peihai 108 21 30N 109 5E
P'eihsien, Kiangsu, China 106 34 44N 116 55E
P'eihsien, Kiangsu, China 107 34 20N 117 57E
Peiliu 109 22 45N 110 20E
Peine, Chile 172 23 45S 68 8W
Peine, Ger. 48 52 19N 10 12E
Peip'an Chiang, R. 108 25 0N 106 11E
Peip'ei 105 29 49N 106 27E
Peip'iao 107 41 48N 120 44E
Peip'ing 106 39 45N 116 25E
Peissenberg 49 47 48N 11 4E
Peitz 48 51 50N 14 23E
Peixe 171 12 0S 48 40W
Peixe, R. 171 21 31S 51 58W
Peize 46 53 9N 6 30E
Pek, R. 66 44 58N 21 55E
Pekalongan 103 6 53S 109 40E
Pekan 101 3 30N 103 25E
Pekin 158 40 35N 89 40W
Peking = Peip'ing 106 39 45N 116 25E
Pelabuhan Ratu, Teluk 103 7 5S 106 30E
Pelabuhanratu 103 7 0S 106 32E
Pélagos, I. 68 39 17N 24 4E
Pelagruza, Is. 63 42 24N 16 15E
Pelaihari 102 3 55S 114 45E
Pełczyce 54 53 3N 15 16E
Peleaga, mt. 70 45 22N 22 55E
Pelee I. 150 41 47N 82 40W
Pelée, Mt. 167 14 40N 61 0W
Pelee, Pt. 150 41 54N 82 31W
Pelekech, mt. 126 3 52N 35 8E
Peleng, I. 103 1 20S 123 30E
Pelham 157 31 5N 84 6W
Pelhrimov 52 49 24N 15 12E
Pelican 147 58 12N 136 28W
Pelican L. 153 52 28N 100 20W
Pelican Narrows 153 55 10N 102 56W
Pelican Portage 152 55 51N 113 0W
Pelican Rapids 153 52 45N 100 42W
Peligre, L. de 167 19 1N 71 58W
Pelkosenniemi 74 67 6N 27 28E
Pella 158 41 20N 93 0W
Pélla □ 68 40 52N 22 0E
Péllaro 65 38 1N 15 40E
Pellworm, I. 48 54 30N 8 40E
Pelly Bay 149 68 0N 89 50W
Pelly L. 148 66 0N 102 0W
Pelly, R. 147 62 15N 133 30W
Peloponnese = Pelóponnisos 69 37 10N 22 0E
Pelopónnisos Kai Dhitikí Iprotikí Ellas □ 69 37 10N 22 0E
Peloritani, Monti 65 38 2N 15 15E
Peloro, C. 65 38 15N 15 40E
Pelorus Sound 143 40 59S 173 59E
Pelotas 173 31 42S 52 23W
Pelòvo 67 43 26N 24 17E
Pelvoux, Massif de 45 44 52N 6 20E
Pelym R. 84 59 39N 63 6E
Pemalang 103 6 53S 109 23E
Pematang Siantar 102 2 57N 99 5E
Pemba, Mozam. 127 12 58S 40 30E
Pemba, Zambia 127 16 30S 27 28E
Pemba Channel 126 5 0S 39 37E
Pemba, I. 126 5 0S 39 45E
Pemberton, Austral. 137 34 30S 116 0E
Pemberton, Can. 152 50 25N 122 50W
Pembina 153 48 58N 97 15W
Pembina, R. 153 49 0N 98 12W
Pembine 156 45 38N 87 59W
Pembrey 31 51 42N 4 17W
Pembroke, Can. 150 45 50N 77 7W
Pembroke, N.Z. 143 44 33S 169 9E
Pembroke, U.K. 31 51 41N 4 57W
Pembroke, U.S.A. 157 32 5N 81 32W
Pembroke (□) 26 51 40N 5 0W
Pembroke Dock 31 51 41N 4 57W
Pembury 29 51 8N 0 20E
Pen-y-Ghent 32 54 10N 2 15W
Pen-y-groes, Dyfed, U.K. 31 51 48N 4 3W
Pen-y-groes, Gwynedd, U.K. 31 53 3N 4 18W
Peñíscola 58 40 22N 0 24E
Peña de Francia, Sierra de 56 40 32N 6 10W
Peña Roya, mt. 58 40 24N 0 40W
Peña, Sierra de la 58 42 32N 0 45W
Penafiel 56 41 12N 8 17W
Peñafiel 56 41 35N 4 7W
Peñaflor 57 37 43N 5 21W
Peñalara, Pico 56 40 51N 3 57W
Penally 31 51 39N 4 44W
Penalva 170 3 18S 45 10W
Penamacôr 56 40 10N 7 10W
Penang = Pinang 101 5 25N 100 15E
Penápolis 173 21 30S 50 0W
Peñaranda de Bracamonte 56 40 53N 5 13W
Peñarroya-Pueblonuevo 57 38 19N 5 16W
Penarth 31 51 26N 3 11W
Peñas, C. de 56 43 42N 5 52W
Peñas de San Pedro 59 38 44N 2 0W
Peñas, G. de 176 47 0S 75 0W
Peñas, Pta. 174 11 17N 70 28W
Pench'i 107 41 20N 123 48E
Pencoed 31 51 31N 3 30W
Pend Oreille, L. 160 48 0N 116 30W
Pend Oreille, R. 160 49 4N 117 37W
Pendálofon 68 40 14N 21 12E
Pendeen 30 50 11N 5 39W
Pendelikón 69 38 5N 23 53E
Pendembu 120 9 7N 12 14W
Pendências 170 5 15S 36 43W
Pender B. 136 16 45S 122 42E
Pendine 31 51 44N 4 33W
Pendle Hill 32 53 53N 2 18W
Pendleton, Calif., U.S.A. 163 33 16N 117 23W
Pendleton, Oreg., U.S.A. 160 45 35N 118 50W
Pendzhikent 85 39 29N 67 37E
Penedo 170 10 15S 36 36W
Penetanguishene 150 44 50N 79 55W
Penfield 109 34 44S 138 38E
Pengalengan 103 7 9S 107 30E
P'engch'i 108 30 50N 105 42E
Penge, Kasai, Congo 126 5 30S 24 33E
Penge, Kivu, Congo 126 4 27S 28 25E
P'enghsien 108 30 59N 103 56E
P'enghu Liehtao 109 22 30N 119 30E
P'englai 107 37 49N 120 47E
P'engshui 108 29 19N 108 12E
P'engtse 109 29 53N 116 32E
Penguin 138 41 8S 146 6E
Penhalonga 127 18 52S 32 40E
Peniche 57 39 19N 9 22W
Penicuik 35 55 50N 3 14W
Penida, I. 102 8 45S 115 30E
Penistone 33 53 31N 1 38W
Penitentes, Serra dos 170 8 45S 46 20W
Penkridge 28 52 44N 2 8W
Penmachno 31 53 2N 3 47W
Penmaenmawr 31 53 16N 3 55W
Penmarch 42 47 49N 4 21W
Penmarch, Pte. de 42 47 48N 4 22W
Penn Yan 162 42 39N 77 7W
Pennabilli 63 43 50N 12 17E
Pennant 153 50 32N 108 14W
Penne 63 42 28N 13 56E
Penner, R. 97 14 50N 78 20E
Penneshaw 140 35 44S 137 56E
Pennines 32 54 50N 2 20W
Pennino, Mte. 63 43 6N 12 54E
Pennsburg 162 40 23N 75 30W
Pennsville 162 39 39N 75 31W
Pennsylvania □ 156 40 50N 78 0W
Penny 152 53 51N 121 48W
Peno 80 57 2N 32 33E
Penola 140 37 25S 140 47E
Penong 139 31 59S 133 5E
Penonomé 166 8 31N 80 21W
Penpont 35 55 14N 3 49W
Penrhyn Is. 131 9 0S 150 30W
Penrith, Austral. 141 33 43S 150 38E
Penrith, U.K. 32 54 40N 2 45W
Penryn 30 50 10N 5 7W
Pensacola 157 30 30N 87 10W
Pensacola Mts. 13 84 0S 40 0W
Pense 153 50 25N 104 59W
Penshurst, Austral. 140 37 49S 142 20W
Penshurst, U.K. 29 51 10N 0 12E
Pentecoste 170 3 48S 37 17W
Penticton 152 49 30N 119 30W
Pentire Pt. 30 50 35N 4 57W
Pentland 138 20 32S 145 25E
Pentland Firth 37 58 43N 3 10W
Pentland Hills 35 55 48N 3 25W
Pentland Skerries 37 58 41N 2 53W
Pentraeth 31 53 17N 4 13W
Pentre Foelas 31 53 2N 3 41W
Penukonda 97 14 5N 77 38E
Penwortham 32 53 45N 2 44W
Penybont 31 52 17N 3 18W
Penylan L. 153 61 50N 106 20W
Penza 81 53 15N 45 5E
Penzance 30 50 7N 5 32W
Penzberg 49 47 46N 11 23E
Penzhinskaya Guba 77 61 30N 163 0E
Penzlin 48 53 32N 13 6E
Peó 66 42 40N 20 17E
Peoria, Ariz., U.S.A. 161 33 40N 112 15W
Peoria, Ill., U.S.A. 158 40 40N 89 40W
Pepacton Res. 162 42 5N 74 58W
Pepingen 47 50 46N 4 10E
Pepinster 47 50 34N 5 47E
Pepmbridge 28 52 13N 2 54W
Pepperwood 160 40 23N 124 0W
Peqini 68 41 4N 19 44E
Pera Hd. 138 12 55S 141 37E
Perabumilih 102 3 27S 104 15E
Perakhóra 69 38 2N 22 56E
Peraki, R. 101 5 10N 101 4E
Perales de Alfambra 58 40 38N 1 0W
Perales del Puerto 56 40 10N 6 40W
Peralta 58 42 21N 1 49W
Pérama 69 35 20N 24 22E
Perast 66 42 31N 18 47E
Percé 151 48 31N 64 13W
Perche 42 48 31N 1 1E
Perche, Collines de la 42 42 30N 2 5E
Percival Lakes 136 21 25S 125 0E
Percy 42 48 55N 1 11W
Percy Is. 138 21 39S 150 16E
Percyville 138 19 2S 143 45E
Perdido, Mte. 58 42 40N 0 50E
Pereira 174 4 49N 75 43W
Pereira Barreto 171 20 38S 51 7W
Pereira de Eóa 128 16 48S 15 50E
Perekerten 140 34 55S 143 40E
Perenjori 137 29 26S 116 16E
Pereslavi-Zelesskiy 80 56 45N 38 58E
Pereyaslav-Khmelnitskiy 80 50 3N 31 28E
Perez, I. 165 22 24N 89 42W
Perg 52 48 15N 14 38E
Pergamino 172 33 52S 60 30W
Pergine Valsugano 63 46 4N 11 15E
Pérgola 63 43 35N 12 50E
Perham 158 46 36N 95 36W
Perham Down Camp 28 51 14N 1 38W
Perhentian, Kepulauan 101 5 54N 102 42E
Peri, L. 140 30 45S 143 35E
Periam 66 46 2N 20 59E
Peribonca, L. 151 50 1N 71 10W
Péribonca, R. 151 48 45N 72 5W
Perico 172 24 20S 65 5W
Pericos 164 25 3N 107 42W
Périers 42 49 11N 1 25W
Périgord 44 45 0N 0 40E
Périgueux 44 45 10N 0 42E
Perija, Sierra de 174 9 30N 73 3W
Perim, I. 91 12 39N 43 25E
Peristera, I. 69 39 15N 23 58E
Peritoró 170 4 20S 44 18W
Periyakulam 97 10 5N 77 30E
Periyar, L. 97 9 25N 77 10E
Periyar, R. 97 10 15N 78 10E
Perkam, Tg. 103 1 35S 137 50E
Perkasie 162 40 22N 75 18W
Perkovió 63 43 41N 16 10E
Perlas, Arch. de las 166 8 41N 79 7W
Perlas, Punta de 166 11 30N 83 30W
Perleberg 48 53 5N 11 50E
Perlevka 81 51 56N 38 57E
Perlez 66 45 11N 20 22E
Perlis □ 101 5 30N 100 15E
Perm (Molotov) 84 58 0N 57 10E
Përmeti 68 40 15N 20 21E
Pernambuco = Recife 170 8 0S 35 0W
Pernambuco □ 170 8 0S 37 0W
Pernatty Lagoon 140 31 30S 137 12E
Peron, C. 137 25 30S 113 30E
Peron Is. 136 13 9S 130 4E
Peron Pen. 137 26 0S 113 10E
Péronne 43 49 55N 2 57E
Péronnes 47 50 27N 4 9E
Perosa Argentina 62 44 57N 7 11E
Perouse Str., La 86 45 40N 142 0E
Perow 152 54 35N 126 10W
Perpendicular Pt. 139 31 37S 152 52E
Perpignan 44 42 42N 2 53E
Perranporth 30 50 21N 5 9W
Perranzabuloe 30 50 18N 5 7W
Perris 163 33 47N 117 14W
Perros-Guirec 42 48 49N 3 28W
Perry, Fla., U.S.A. 157 30 9N 83 10W
Perry, Ga., U.S.A. 157 32 25N 83 41W
Perry, Iowa, U.S.A. 158 41 48N 94 5W
Perry, Maine, U.S.A. 157 44 59N 67 20W
Perry, Okla., U.S.A. 159 36 20N 97 20W
Perry, Mt. 139 25 12S 151 41E
Perryton 159 36 28N 100 48W

Pingaring **Polcura**

Pingaring **137** 32 40 S 118 32 E
P'ingch'ang **108** 31 33 N 107 6 E
P'ingchiang **109** 28 42 N 113 35 E
P'ingch'uan **107** 41 0 N 118 36 E
Pingelly **137** 32 29 S 116 59 E
P'ingho **109** 24 18 N 117 2 E
P'inghsiang, Kiangsi, China **109** 27 39 N 113 50 E
P'inghsiang, Kwangsi Chuang, China **108** 22 6 N 106 44 E
P'inghu **109** 30 38 N 121 0 E
P'ingi, Shantung, China **107** 35 30 N 117 36 E
P'ingi, Yünnan, China **108** 25 40 N 104 14 E
P'ingkuo **108** 23 20 N 107 34 E
P'ingli **108** 32 26 N 109 22 E
P'ingliang **105** 35 32 N 106 50 E
Pinglo, Kwangsi-Chuang, China **109** 24 30 N 110 45 E
Pinglo, Ningsia Hui, China **106** 38 58 N 106 30 E
P'inglu **106** 37 32 N 112 14 E
P'ingluch'eng **106** 39 46 N 112 6 E
P'ingnan, Fukien, China **109** 26 56 N 119 3 E
P'ingnan, Kwangsi-Chiang, China **109** 23 33 N 110 23 E
P'ingpa **108** 26 25 N 106 15 E
P'ingpien **108** 22 54 N 103 40 E
Pingrup **137** 33 32 S 118 29 E
P'ingt'an **109** 25 31 N 119 47 E
P'ingt'ang **108** 25 50 N 107 19 E
P'ingting **106** 37 48 N 113 37 E
P'ingt'ingshan **106** 33 43 N 113 28 E
P'ingtu **107** 36 47 N 119 56 E
P'ingtung **105** 22 38 N 120 30 E
Pingwu **105** 32 27 N 104 25 E
P'ingwu **108** 32 25 N 104 36 E
P'ingyang **109** 27 40 N 120 33 E
P'ingyangchen **107** 45 11 N 131 15 E
P'ingyao **106** 37 12 N 112 10 E
P'ingyin **106** 36 18 N 116 26 E
P'ingyüan, Kwangtung, China **109** 24 34 N 115 54 E
P'ingyüan, Ningsia Hui, China **106** 37 9 N 116 25 E
Pinhai **107** 34 0 N 119 50 E
Pinhal **173** 22 10 S 46 46 W
Pinheiro **170** 2 31 S 45 5 W
Pinhel **56** 40 18 N 7 0 W
Pinhoe **30** 50 44 N 3 29 W
Pinhsien, Heilung Kiang, China **107** 45 44 N 127 27 E
Pinhsien, Shensi, China **106** 35 10 N 108 10 E
Pini, I. **102** 0 10 N 98 40 E
Piniós, R., Ilia, Greece **69** 37 38 N 21 20 E
Piniós, R., Trikkala, Greece **68** 39 55 N 22 10 E
Pinjarra **137** 32 37 S 115 52 E
Pink, R. **153** 56 50 N 103 50 W
Pinkafeld **53** 47 22 N 16 9 E
Pinlebu **98** 24 5 N 95 22 E
Pinnacles, Austral. **137** 28 12 S 120 26 E
Pinnacles, U.S.A. **163** 36 33 N 121 8 W
Pinnaroo **140** 35 13 S 140 56 E
Pinon Hills **163** 34 26 N 117 39 W
Pinos **164** 22 20 N 101 40 W
Pinos, I. de **166** 21 40 N 82 40 W
Pinos, Mt **163** 34 49 N 119 8 W
Pinos Pt. **161** 36 50 N 121 57 W
Pinos Puente **57** 37 15 N 3 45 W
Pinotepa Nacional **165** 16 25 N 97 55 W
Pinrang **103** 3 46 S 119 34 E
Pinsk **80** 52 10 N 26 8 E
Pintados **174** 20 35 S 69 40 W
Pinto Butte Mt. **153** 49 22 N 107 27 W
Pintumba **137** 31 50 S 132 18 E
Pinwherry **34** 55 9 N 4 50 W
Pinyang **108** 23 17 N 108 47 E
Pinyug **78** 60 5 N 48 0 E
Pinzolo **62** 46 9 N 10 45 E
Pio XII **170** 3 53 S 45 17 W
Pioche **161** 38 0 N 114 35 W
Piombino **62** 42 54 N 10 30 E
Pioner, I. **77** 79 50 N 92 0 E
Pionki **54** 51 29 N 21 28 E
Piorini, L. **174** 3 15 S 62 35 W
Piotrków Trybunalski **54** 51 23 N 19 43 E
Piotrków Trybunalski □ **54** 51 30 N 19 45 E
Piove di Sacco **63** 45 18 N 12 1 E
Pip **93** 26 45 N 60 10 E
Pipar **94** 26 25 N 73 31 E
Pipariya **96** 22 45 N 78 23 E
Piper, oilfield **19** 58 30 N 0 15 E
Pipéri, I. **68** 39 20 N 24 19 E
Pipestone **158** 44 0 N 96 20 W
Pipestone Cr. **153** 53 37 N 109 46 W
Pipestone, R. **150** 52 53 N 89 23 W
Pipinas **172** 35 30 S 57 19 W
Pipiriki **142** 38 28 S 175 5 E
Pipmuacan Res. **151** 49 40 N 70 25 W
Pippingarra **136** 20 27 S 118 42 E
Pipriac **42** 47 49 N 1 58 W
Piqua **156** 40 10 N 84 10 W
Piquet Carneiro **171** 5 48 S 39 25 W
Piquiri, R. **173** 24 3 S 54 14 W
Piracanjuba **171** 17 18 S 49 1 W
Piracicaba **173** 22 45 S 47 30 W
Piracuruca **170** 3 50 S 41 50 W
Piræus = Piraiévs **69** 37 57 N 23 42 E
Piraiévs **69** 37 57 N 23 42 E
Piraiévs □ **69** 37 0 N 23 30 E
Piráino **65** 38 10 N 14 52 E
Pirajuí **173** 21 59 S 49 29 W
Piran (Pirano) **63** 45 31 N 13 33 E
Pirane **172** 25 25 S 59 30 W
Piranhas **170** 9 27 S 37 46 W
Pirapemas **170** 3 43 S 44 14 W
Pirapora **171** 17 20 S 44 56 W
Piratyin **80** 50 15 N 32 25 E
Pirbright **29** 51 17 N 0 40 W
Pirdop **67** 42 40 N 24 10 E
Pires do Rio **171** 17 18 S 48 17 W
Pirganj **98** 25 51 S 88 24 E
Pirgos, Ilia, Greece **69** 37 40 N 21 27 E
Pirgos, Messinia, Greece **69** 36 50 N 22 16 E
Pirgovo **67** 43 44 N 25 43 E
Piriac-sur-Mer **42** 47 22 N 2 33 W
Piribebuy **172** 25 26 S 57 2 W
Pirin Planina **67** 41 40 N 23 30 E
Pirineos, mts. **58** 42 40 N 1 0 E
Piripiri **170** 4 15 S 41 46 W
Piritu **174** 9 23 N 69 12 W
Pirmasens **49** 49 12 N 7 30 E
Pirna **48** 50 57 N 13 57 E
Pirojpur **98** 22 35 N 90 1 E
Pirot **66** 43 9 N 22 39 E
Pirsagat, R. **83** 40 15 N 48 45 E
Pirtleville **161** 31 25 N 109 35 W
Piru **163** 34 25 N 118 48 W
Piryí **69** 38 13 N 25 59 E
Pisa **62** 43 43 N 10 23 E
Pisa Ra. **143** 44 52 S 169 12 E
Pisagua **174** 19 40 S 70 15 W
Pisarovina **63** 45 35 N 15 50 E
Pisciotta **65** 40 7 N 15 12 E
Pisco **174** 13 50 S 76 5 W
Piscu **70** 45 30 N 27 43 E
Písek **52** 49 19 N 14 10 E
Pisham **108** 29 37 N 106 13 E
P'ishan **105** 37 38 N 78 19 E
Pishin Lora, R. **94** 30 15 N 66 5 E
Pising **103** 5 8 S 121 53 E
Pismo Beach **163** 35 9 N 120 38 W
Pissos **44** 44 19 N 0 49 W
Pisticci **65** 40 24 N 16 33 E
Pistoia **62** 43 57 N 10 53 E
Pistol B. **153** 62 25 N 92 37 W
Pisuerga, R. **56** 42 10 N 4 15 W
Pisz **54** 53 38 N 21 49 E
Pitalito **174** 1 51 N 76 2 W
Pitanga **171** 24 46 S 51 44 W
Pitangui **171** 19 40 S 44 54 E
Pitarpunga, L. **140** 34 24 S 143 30 E
Pitcairn I. **131** 25 5 S 130 5 W
Pite älv **74** 65 44 N 20 50 W
Piteå **74** 65 20 N 21 25 E
Piteşti **70** 44 52 N 24 54 E
Pithapuram **96** 17 10 N 82 15 E
Pithara **137** 30 20 S 116 35 E
Pithion **68** 41 24 N 26 40 W
Pithiviers **43** 48 10 N 2 13 E
Pitigliano **63** 42 38 N 11 40 E
Pitiquito **164** 30 42 N 112 2 W
Pitlochry **37** 56 43 N 3 43 W
Pitt I. **152** 53 30 N 129 50 W
Pittem **47** 51 1 N 3 13 E
Pittenweem **35** 56 13 N 2 43 W
Pittsburg, Calif., U.S.A. **163** 38 1 N 121 50 W
Pittsburg, Kans., U.S.A. **159** 37 21 N 94 43 W
Pittsburg, Tex., U.S.A. **159** 32 59 N 94 58 W
Pittsburgh **156** 40 25 N 79 55 W
Pittsfield, Ill., U.S.A. **158** 39 35 N 90 46 W
Pittsfield, N.H., U.S.A. **162** 43 17 N 71 18 W
Pittston **162** 41 19 N 75 50 W
Pittsworth **139** 27 41 S 151 37 E
Pituri, R. **138** 22 35 S 138 30 E
Pitzewo **107** 39 28 N 122 30 E
Piuí **171** 20 28 S 45 58 W
Pium **170** 10 27 S 49 11 W
Piura **174** 5 5 S 80 45 W
Piva, R. **66** 43 15 N 18 50 E
Pivijay **174** 10 28 N 74 37 W
Piwniczna **54** 49 27 N 20 42 E
Pixariá Óros **69** 38 42 N 23 39 E
Pixley **163** 35 58 N 119 18 W
Piyai **68** 39 17 N 21 25 E
Piyang **109** 32 50 N 113 30 E
Piz Bernina **49** 46 23 N 9 45 E
Pizarro **174** 4 58 N 77 22 W
Pizol **51** 46 57 N 9 23 E
Pizzo **65** 38 44 N 16 10 E
Placentia **151** 47 20 N 54 0 W
Placentia B. **151** 47 0 N 54 40 W
Placerville **160** 38 47 N 120 51 W
Placetas **166** 22 15 N 79 44 W
'Placid', gasfield **19** 53 25 N 4 20 E
Plačkovica, mts. **66** 41 45 N 22 30 E
Pladda, I. **34** 55 25 N 5 7 W
Plaffein **50** 46 45 N 7 17 E
Plain Dealing **159** 32 56 N 93 41 W
Plainfield **162** 40 37 N 74 28 W
Plains, Kans., U.S.A. **159** 37 20 N 100 35 W
Plains, Mont., U.S.A. **160** 47 27 N 114 57 W
Plains, Tex., U.S.A. **159** 33 11 N 102 50 W
Plainview, Nebr., U.S.A. **158** 42 25 N 97 48 W
Plainview, Tex., U.S.A. **159** 34 10 N 101 40 W
Plainville **158** 39 18 N 99 19 W
Plainwell **156** 42 28 N 85 40 W
Plaisance **44** 43 36 N 0 3 E
Pláka **68** 36 45 N 24 26 E
Plakhino **76** 67 45 N 86 5 E
Planá **52** 49 50 N 12 44 E
Plana Cays **167** 22 38 N 73 30 W
Planada **163** 37 18 N 120 19 W
Planaltina **171** 15 30 S 47 45 W
Plancoët **42** 48 32 N 2 13 W
Plandisšte **66** 45 16 N 21 10 E
Planeta Rica **174** 8 25 N 75 36 W
Planina, Slovenija, Yugo. **63** 45 47 N 14 19 E
Planina, Slovenija, Yugo. **63** 46 10 N 15 12 E
Plankinton **158** 43 45 N 98 27 W
Plano **159** 33 0 N 96 45 W
Plant City **157** 28 0 N 82 15 W
Plant, La **158** 45 11 N 100 40 W
Plaquemine **159** 30 20 N 91 15 W
Plasencia **56** 40 3 N 6 8 W
Plaški **63** 45 4 N 15 22 E
Plassen **72** 61 9 N 12 30 E
Plast **84** 54 22 N 60 50 E
Plaster Rock **151** 46 53 N 67 22 W
Plata, La, Argent. **172** 35 0 S 57 55 W
Plata, La, U.S.A. **162** 38 32 N 76 59 W
Plata, La, Rio de **172** 35 0 S 56 40 W
Platani, R. **64** 37 28 N 13 23 E
Plateau **13** 70 55 S 40 0 E
Plateau □ **121** 9 0 N 9 0 E
Plateau du Coteau du Missouri **158** 47 9 N 101 5 W
Platí, Ákra **68** 40 27 N 24 0 E
Platinum **147** 59 2 N 161 50 W
Plato **174** 9 47 N 74 47 W
Platte **158** 43 28 N 98 50 W
Platte, Piz **51** 46 30 N 9 35 E
Platte, R. **158** 41 0 N 98 0 W
Platteville **158** 40 18 N 104 47 W
Plattling **49** 48 46 N 12 53 E
Plattsburgh **156** 44 41 N 73 30 W
Plattsmouth **158** 41 0 N 96 0 W
Plau **48** 53 27 N 12 16 E
Plauen **48** 50 29 N 12 9 E
Plav **66** 42 38 N 19 57 E
Plavnica **66** 42 10 N 19 20 E
Plavsk **81** 53 40 N 37 18 E
Playa Azul **164** 17 59 N 102 24 W
Playa de Castilla **57** 41 25 N 0 12 W
Playgreen L. **153** 54 0 N 98 15 W
Pleasant Bay **151** 46 51 N 60 48 W
Pleasant Hill **158** 38 48 N 94 14 W
Pleasant Hills **141** 35 28 S 146 50 E
Pleasant Mount **162** 41 44 N 75 26 W
Pleasant Pt. **143** 44 16 S 171 9 E
Pleasanton **159** 29 0 N 98 30 W
Pleasantville **162** 39 25 N 74 30 W
Pléaux **44** 45 8 N 2 13 E
Pleiku (Gia Lai) **101** 14 3 N 108 0 E
Plélan-le-Grand **42** 48 0 N 2 7 W
Plémet **42** 48 11 N 2 36 W
Pléneuf-Val-André **42** 48 35 N 2 32 W
Pleniţa **70** 44 14 N 23 10 E
Plenty, Bay of **142** 37 45 S 177 0 E
Plenty, R. **138** 23 25 S 136 31 E
Plentywood **158** 48 45 N 104 35 W
Plesetsk **78** 62 40 N 40 10 E
Plessisville **151** 46 14 N 71 47 W
Plestin-les-Grèves **42** 48 40 N 3 39 W
Pleszew **54** 51 53 N 17 47 E
Pleternica **66** 45 17 N 17 48 E
Pletipi L. **151** 51 44 N 70 6 W
Pleven **67** 43 26 N 24 37 E
Plevlja **66** 43 21 N 19 21 E
Płock **54** 52 32 N 19 40 E
Płock □ **54** 52 30 N 19 45 E
Plöcken Passo **63** 46 37 N 12 57 E
Plockton **36** 57 20 N 5 40 W
Ploegsteert **47** 50 44 N 2 53 E
Ploëmeur **42** 47 44 N 3 26 W
Ploërmel **42** 47 55 N 2 26 W
Ploieşti **70** 44 57 N 26 5 E
Plomárion **69** 38 58 N 26 24 E
Plomb du Cantal **44** 45 2 N 2 48 E
Plombières **43** 47 59 N 6 27 E
Plomin **63** 45 8 N 14 10 E
Plön **48** 54 8 N 10 22 E
Plöner See **48** 53 9 N 15 5 E
Plonge, Lac La **153** 55 8 N 107 20 W
Płonsk **54** 52 37 N 20 21 E
Płoty **54** 53 48 N 15 18 E
Plouay **42** 47 55 N 3 21 W
Ploudalmézeau **42** 48 34 N 4 41 W
Plougasnou **42** 48 42 N 3 49 W
Plouha **42** 48 41 N 2 57 W
Plouhinec **42** 48 0 N 4 29 W
Plovdiv **67** 42 8 N 24 44 E
Plum I. **162** 41 10 N 72 12 W
Plumbridge **38** 54 46 N 7 15 W
Plummer **160** 47 21 N 116 59 W
Plumtree **127** 20 27 S 27 55 E
Plunge **80** 55 53 N 21 51 E
Pluvigner **42** 47 46 N 3 1 W
Plymouth, U.K. **30** 50 23 N 4 9 W
Plymouth, Calif., U.S.A. **163** 38 29 N 120 51 W
Plymouth, Ind., U.S.A. **156** 41 20 N 86 19 W
Plymouth, Mass., U.S.A. **162** 41 58 N 70 40 W
Plymouth, N.C., U.S.A. **157** 35 54 N 76 55 W
Plymouth, N.H., U.S.A. **162** 43 44 N 71 41 W
Plymouth, Pa., U.S.A. **162** 41 17 N 76 0 W
Plymouth, Wis., U.S.A. **156** 43 42 N 87 58 W
Plymouth Sd. **30** 50 20 N 4 10 W
Plympton **30** 50 24 N 4 2 W
Plymstock **30** 50 22 N 4 6 W
Plynlimon = Pumlumon Fawr **31** 52 29 N 3 47 W
Plyussa **80** 47 40 N 29 0 E
Plyussa, R. **80** 58 40 N 28 30 E
Plzen **52** 49 45 N 13 22 E
Pniewy **54** 52 31 N 16 16 E
Pô **121** 11 14 N 1 5 W
Po Hai **107** 38 30 N 119 0 E
Po, R. **62** 45 0 N 10 45 E
Poai **106** 35 10 N 113 4 E
Pobé **121** 7 0 N 2 38 E
Pobedino **76** 49 51 N 142 49 E
Pobedy Pik **76** 40 45 N 79 58 E
Pobiedziska **54** 52 29 N 17 19 E
Pobla de Lillet, La **58** 42 16 N 1 59 E
Pobla de Segur **58** 42 15 N 0 58 E
Pobladura de Valle **56** 42 6 N 5 44 W
Pocahontas, Arkansas, U.S.A. **159** 37 18 N 81 20 W
Pocahontas, Iowa, U.S.A. **158** 42 41 N 94 42 W
Pocatello **160** 42 50 N 112 25 W
Pochep **80** 52 58 N 33 15 E
Pochinki **81** 54 41 N 44 59 E
Pochinok **80** 54 28 N 32 29 E
Pöchlarn **52** 48 12 N 15 12 E
Pochontas **152** 53 0 N 117 51 W
Pochutla **165** 15 50 N 96 31 W
Pocinhos **170** 7 4 S 36 3 W
Pocita Casas **164** 28 32 N 111 6 W
Pocklington **33** 53 56 N 0 48 W
Poções **171** 14 31 S 40 21 W
Pocomoke City **162** 38 4 N 75 32 W
Pocomoke, R. **162** 38 5 N 75 34 W
Poços de Caldas **173** 21 50 S 46 45 W
Pocrane **171** 19 37 S 41 37 W
PoC!tky **52** 49 15 N 15 14 E
Poddebice **54** 51 54 N 18 58 E
Poděbrady **52** 50 9 N 15 8 E
Podensac **44** 44 40 N 0 22 W
Podgorica = Titograd **66** 42 30 N 19 19 E
Podkamennaya Tunguska **77** 61 50 N 90 26 E
Podlapac **63** 44 45 N 15 47 E
Podmokly **52** 50 48 N 14 10 E
Podoleni **70** 46 46 N 26 39 E
Podolínec **53** 49 16 N 20 31 E
Podolsk **81** 55 25 N 37 30 E
Podor **120** 16 40 N 14 50 W
Podporozhy **78** 60 55 N 34 2 E
Podravska Slatina **66** 45 42 N 17 45 E
Podsreda **63** 45 42 N 15 45 E
Podu Turcului **70** 46 11 N 27 25 E
Podujevo **66** 42 54 N 21 10 E
Poel, I. **48** 54 0 N 11 25 E
Pofadder **128** 29 10 S 19 22 E
Pogamasing **150** 46 55 N 81 50 W
Poggiardo **65** 40 3 N 18 21 E
Poggibonsi **63** 43 27 N 11 8 E
Pogoanele **70** 44 55 N 27 0 E
Pogorzela **54** 51 50 N 17 12 E
Pogradeci **68** 40 57 N 20 48 E
Poh **103** 0 46 S 122 51 E
Pohang **107** 36 1 N 129 23 E
Pohorelá **53** 48 50 N 20 2 E
Pohorelice **53** 48 59 N 16 31 E
Pohorje, mts. **63** 46 30 N 15 7 E
Poiana Mare **70** 43 57 N 23 5 E
Poiana Ruscŭi, Munţii **70** 45 45 N 22 25 E
Pt. Augusta **140** 32 30 S 137 50 E
Point Baker **147** 56 20 N 133 35 W
Point Cloates **137** 22 40 S 113 45 E
Point Edward **150** 43 10 N 82 30 W
Point Fortin **167** 10 9 N 61 46 W
Point Hope **147** 68 20 N 166 50 W
Point Lay **147** 69 45 N 163 10 W
Point Pass **140** 34 5 S 139 5 E
Point Pedro **97** 9 50 N 80 15 E
Point Pleasant, N.J., U.S.A. **162** 40 5 N 74 4 W
Point Pleasant, W. Va., U.S.A. **156** 38 50 N 82 7 W
Point Reyes Nat. Seashore **163** 38 0 N 122 58 W
Point Rock **159** 31 30 N 99 56 W
Pointe-à-la Hache **159** 29 35 N 89 55 W
Pointe-à-Pitre **167** 16 10 N 61 30 W
Pointe-Noire **124** 4 48 S 12 0 E
Poirino **62** 44 55 N 7 50 E
Poisonbush Ra. **136** 22 30 S 121 30 E
Poissy **43** 48 55 N 2 0 E
Poitiers **42** 46 35 N 0 20 W
Poitou, Plaines du **44** 46 30 N 0 1 W
Poix **43** 49 47 N 2 0 E
Poix-Terron **43** 49 38 N 4 38 E
Pojoaque **161** 35 55 N 106 0 W
Pojuca **171** 12 21 S 38 20 W
Pokaran **93** 27 0 N 71 50 E
Pokataroo **139** 29 30 S 148 34 E
Poko, Sudan **123** 5 41 N 31 55 E
Poko, Zaïre **126** 3 7 N 26 52 E
Pok'ot'u **105** 48 46 N 121 54 E
Pokrovka **85** 42 20 N 78 0 E
Pokrovsk **77** 61 29 N 129 6 E
Pokrovsk-Uralskiy **84** 60 10 N 59 49 E
Pol **56** 43 9 N 7 20 W
Pola **80** 57 30 N 32 0 E
Pola de Allande **56** 43 16 N 6 37 W
Pola de Gordón, La **56** 42 51 N 5 41 W
Pola de Lena **56** 43 10 N 5 49 W
Pola de Siero **56** 43 24 N 5 39 W
Pola de Somiedo **56** 43 5 N 6 15 W
Polacca **161** 35 52 N 110 25 W
Polan **93** 25 30 N 61 10 E
Poland ■ **54** 52 0 N 20 0 E
Polanów **54** 54 7 N 16 41 E
Polar Bear Prov. Park **150** 54 30 N 83 20 W
Polcura **172** 37 10 S 71 50 W

Połcyn Zdrój Portel

Połcyn Zdrój 54 53 47N 16 5 E
Polden Hills 28 51 7N 2 50W
Polegate 29 50 49N 0 15 E
Polessk 80 54 50N 21 8 E
Polesworth 28 52 37N 1 37W
Polevskoy 84 56 26N 60 11 E
Polewali, Sulawesi, Indon. 103 4 8 S 119 43 E
Polewali, Sulawesi, Indon. 103 3 21 S 119 31 E
Polgar 53 47 54N 21 6 E
Pŏlgyo-ri 107 34 51N 127 21 E
Poli 124 8 34N 12 54 E
Políaigos, I. 69 36 45N 24 38 E
Policastro, Golfo di 65 39 55N 15 35 E
Police 54 53 33N 14 33 E
Polička 53 49 43N 16 15 E
Polignano a Mare 65 41 0N 17 12 E
Poligny 43 46 50N 5 42 E
Polikhnitas 69 39 4N 26 10 E
Polillo I. 103 14 56N 122 0 E
Polis 92 35 3N 32 30 E
Polístena 65 38 25N 16 4 E
Políyiros 68 40 23N 23 25 E
Polkowice 54 51 29N 16 3 E
Polla 65 40 31N 15 27 E
Pollachi 97 10 35N 77 0 E
Pollensa 58 39 54N 3 2 E
Pollensa, B. de 58 39 55N 3 5 E
Póllica 65 40 13N 15 3 E
Pollino, Mte. 65 39 54N 16 13 E
Pollock 158 45 58N 100 18W
Pollremon 38 53 40N 8 38W
Polna 80 58 31N 28 0 E
Polnovat 76 63 50N 66 5 E
Polo, Kwangtung, China 109 23 9N 114 17 E
Polo, S.-U., China 105 44 59N 81 57 E
Polo, U.S.A. 158 42 0N 89 38W
Pologi 82 47 29N 36 15 E
Polonnoye 80 50 6N 27 30 E
Polossu 108 31 12N 98 36 E
Polotsk 80 55 30N 28 50 E
Polperro 30 50 19N 4 31W
Polruan 30 50 17N 4 36W
Polski Trmbesh 67 43 20N 25 38 E
Polsko Kosovo 67 43 23N 25 38 E
Polson 160 47 45N 114 12W
Poltava 82 49 35N 34 35 E
Polur 97 12 32N 79 11 E
Polyarny 78 69 8N 33 20 E
Pomarance 62 43 18N 10 51 E
Pomarico 65 40 31N 16 33 E
Pomaro 164 18 20N 103 18W
Pombal, Brazil 170 6 55 S 37 50W
Pombal, Port. 56 39 55N 8 40W
Pómbia 69 35 0N 24 51 E
Pomeroy, U.K. 38 54 36N 6 56W
Pomeroy, Ohio, U.S.A. 156 39 0N 82 0W
Pomeroy, Wash., U.S.A. 160 46 30N 117 33W
Pomio 135 5 32 S 151 33 E
Pomona 163 34 2N 117 49W
Pomorie 67 42 26N 27 41 E
Pompano 157 26 12N 80 6W
Pompei 65 40 45N 14 30 E
Pompey 43 48 50N 6 2 E
Pompeys Pillar 160 46 0N 108 0W
Ponape I. 130 6 55N 158 10 E
Ponask, L. 150 54 0N 92 41W
Ponass L. 153 52 16N 103 58W
Ponca 158 42 38N 96 41W
Ponca City 159 36 40N 97 5W
Ponce 147 18 1N 66 37W
Ponchatoula 159 30 27N 90 25W
Poncheville, L. 150 50 10N 76 55W
Poncin 45 46 6N 5 25 E
Pond 163 35 43N 119 20W
Pond Inlet 149 72 30N 75 0W
Pondicherry 97 11 59N 79 50 E
Pondoland 129 31 10 S 29 30W
Pondooma 140 33 29 S 136 59 E
Pondrôme 47 50 6N 5 0 E
Ponds, I. of 151 53 27N 55 52W
Ponferrada 56 42 32N 6 35W
Pongaroa 142 40 33 S 176 15 E
Pôngo , Ponte de 127 19 0 S 34 0 E
Pongo, W. 123 8 0N 27 20 E
Poniatowa 54 51 11N 22 3 E
Poniec 54 51 48N 16 50 E
Ponnaiyar, R. 97 11 50N 79 45 E
Ponnani 97 10 45N 75 59 E
Ponnani, R. 97 10 45N 75 59 E
Ponneri 97 13 20N 80 15 E
Ponnyadaung 99 22 0N 94 10 E
Ponoi 78 67 0N 41 0 E
Ponoi, R. 78 67 10N 39 0 E
Ponoka 152 52 42N 113 40W
Ponomarevka 84 53 19N 54 8 E
Ponorogo 103 7 52 S 111 29 E
Pons, France 44 45 35N 0 34W
Pons, Spain 58 41 55N 1 12 E
Ponsul, R. 57 39 54N 8 45 E
Pont-à-Celles 47 50 30N 4 22 E
Pont-à-Mousson 43 45 54N 6 1 E
Pont Audemer 42 49 21N 0 30 E
Pont Aven 42 47 51N 3 47W
Pont Canavese 62 45 24N 7 33 E
Pont Château 42 47 26N 2 8W
Pont-de-Roide 43 47 23N 6 45 E
Pont-de-Salars 44 44 18N 2 44 E
Pont-de-Vaux 43 46 26N 4 56 E
Pont-de-Veyle 45 46 17N 4 53 E
Pont-l'Abbé 42 47 52N 4 15W
Pont Lafrance 151 47 40N 64 58W
Pont, Le 50 46 41N 6 20 E
Pont-l'Eveque 42 49 18N 0 11 E
Pont-St.-Esprit 45 44 16N 4 40 E
Pont-sur-Yonne 43 48 18N 3 10 E
Ponta de Pedras 170 1 23 S 48 52W
Ponta Grossa 173 25 0 S 50 10W
Ponta Pora 173 22 20 S 55 35W
Ponta São Sebastião 129 22 2 S 35 25 E
Pontacq 44 43 11N 0 8W
Pontailler 43 47 18N 5 24 E
Pontal, R. 170 9 8 S 40 12W
Pontalina 171 17 31 S 49 27W
Pontardawe 31 51 43N 3 51W
Pontardulais 31 51 42N 4 3W
Pontarlier 43 46 54N 6 20 E
Pontassieve 63 43 47N 11 25 E
Pontaubault 42 48 40N 1 20W
Pontaumur 44 45 52N 2 40 E
Pontcharra 45 45 26N 6 1 E
Pontchartrain, L. 159 30 12N 90 0W
Pontchâteau 42 47 25N 2 5W
Ponte Alta do Norte 170 10 45 S 47 34W
Ponte Alta, Serra do 171 19 42 S 47 40W
Ponte da Barca 56 41 48N 8 25W
Ponte de Sor 57 39 17N 7 57W
Ponte dell 'Olio 62 44 52N 9 39 E
Ponte di Legno 62 46 15N 10 30 E
Ponte do Lima 56 41 46N 8 35W
Ponte do Pungué 127 19 30 S 34 33 E
Ponte Leccia 45 42 28N 9 13 E
Ponte nell' Alpi 63 46 10N 12 18 E
Ponte Nova 173 20 25 S 42 54W
Ponte San Martino 62 45 36N 7 47 E
Ponte San Pietro 62 45 42N 9 35 E
Pontebba 63 46 30N 13 17 E
Pontecorvo 64 41 28N 13 40 E
Pontedera 62 43 40N 10 37 E
Pontefract 33 53 42N 1 19W
Ponteix 153 49 46N 107 29W
Ponteland 35 53 3N 1 45W
Pontelandolfo 65 41 17N 14 41 E
Pontemacassar Naikliu 103 9 30 S 123 58 E
Pontevedra 56 42 26N 8 40W
Pontevedra □ 56 42 25N 8 39W
Pontevedra, R. de 56 42 22N 8 45W
Pontevico 62 45 16N 10 6 E
Ponthierville = Ubundi 126 0 22 S 25 30 E
Pontiac, Ill., U.S.A. 158 40 50N 88 40W
Pontiac, Mich., U.S.A. 156 42 40N 83 20W
Pontian Kechil 101 1 29N 103 23 E
Pontianak 102 0 3 S 109 15 E
Pontine Is. = Ponziane, Isole 64 40 55N 13 0 E
Pontine Mts. = Karadeniz D. 92 41 30N 35 0 E
Pontínia 64 41 25N 13 2 E
Pontivy 42 48 5N 3 0W
Pontoise 43 49 3N 2 5 E
Ponton, R. 152 58 27N 116 11W
Pontorson 42 48 34N 1 30W
Pontrémoli 62 44 22N 9 52 E
Pontresina 51 46 29N 9 48 E
Pontrhydfendigaid 31 52 17N 3 50W
Pontrieux 28 48 42N 3 10W
Pontrilas 28 51 56N 2 53W
Ponts-de Cé, Les 42 47 25N 0 30W
Pontypool 31 51 42N 3 1W
Pontypridd 31 51 36N 3 21W
Ponza, I. 64 40 55N 12 57 E
Ponziane, Isole 64 40 55N 13 0 E
Poochera 139 32 43 S 134 51 E
Poole 28 50 42N 2 2W
Poole Harb. 28 50 41N 2 0W
Poolewe 36 57 45N 5 38W
Pooley Bridge 32 54 37N 2 49W
Pooley I. 152 52 45N 128 15W
Poonamallee 97 13 3N 80 10 E
Poona = Pune 96 18 29N 73 57 E
Pooncarie 140 33 22 S 142 31 E
Poonindie 140 34 34 S 135 54 E
Poopelloe, L. 140 31 40 S 144 0 E
Poopó, Lago de 174 18 30 S 67 35W
Poor Knights Is. 142 35 29 S 174 43 E
Pooraka 109 34 50 S 138 38 E
Poorman 147 64 5N 155 48W
Popai 108 22 13N 109 55 E
Popak 101 22 15N 109 56 E
Popakai, Austral. 170 32 12 S 141 46 E
Popakai, Surinam 170 3 20N 55 30W
Popanyinning 137 32 40 S 117 2 E
Popayán 174 2 27N 76 36W
Poperinge 47 50 51N 2 42 E
Popigay 77 71 55N 110 47 E
Popilta, L. 140 33 10 S 141 42 E
Popio, L. 140 33 10 S 141 52 E
Poplar 158 48 3N 105 9W
Poplar Bluff 159 36 45N 90 22W
Poplar, R., Man., Can. 153 53 0N 97 19W
Poplar, R., N.W.T., Can. 152 61 22N 121 52W
Poplarville 159 30 55N 89 30W
Popocatepetl, vol. 165 19 10N 98 40W
Popokabaka 124 5 49 S 16 40 E
Pópoli 63 42 12N 13 50 E
Popondetta 135 8 48 S 148 17 E
Popovača 63 45 30N 16 41 E
Popovo 67 43 21N 26 18 E
Poppel 47 51 27N 5 2 E
Poprád 53 49 3N 20 18 E
Poprád, R. 53 49 15N 20 30 E
Poquoson 162 37 7N 76 21W
Poradaha 98 23 51N 89 1 E
Porali, R. 94 27 15N 66 24 E
Porangahau 142 40 17 S 176 37 E
Porangatu 171 13 26 S 49 10W
Porbandar 94 21 44N 69 43 E
Porcher I. 152 53 50N 130 30W
Porcos, R. 171 12 42 S 45 7W
Porcuna 57 37 52N 4 11W
Porcupine, R., Can. 153 59 11N 104 46W
Porcupine, R., U.S.A. 147 67 0N 143 0W
Pordenone 63 45 58N 12 40 E
Pordim 67 43 23N 24 51 E
Pore 174 5 43N 72 0W
Poreč 63 45 14N 13 36 E
Porecatu 171 22 43 S 51 24W
Poretskoye 81 55 9N 46 21 E
Pori 75 61 29N 21 48 E
Porirua 142 41 8 S 174 52 E
Porjus 74 66 57N 19 50 E
Porkhov 80 57 45N 29 38 E
Porkkala 75 59 59N 24 26 E
Porlamar 174 10 57N 63 51W
Porlezza 62 46 2N 9 8 E
Porlock 28 51 13N 3 36W
Porlock B. 28 51 14N 3 37W
Porlock Hill 28 51 12N 3 40W
Porma, R. 56 42 45N 5 21W
Pornic 42 47 7N 2 5W
Poronaysk 77 49 20N 143 0 E
Póros 69 37 30N 23 30 E
Póros, I. 69 37 30N 23 30 E
Poroshiri-Dake 112 42 41N 142 52 E
Poroszló 53 47 39N 20 40 E
Poroto Mts. 127 9 0 S 33 30 E
Porraburdoo 137 23 15 S 117 28 E
Porrentruy 50 47 25N 7 6 E
Porreras 58 39 29N 3 2 E
Porsangen 74 70 40N 25 40 E
Porsgrunn 71 59 10N 9 40 E
Port 43 47 43N 6 4 E
Port Adelaide 140 34 46 S 138 30 E
Port Alberni 152 49 15N 124 50W
Port Albert 141 38 42 S 146 42 E
Port Albert Victor 94 21 0N 71 30 E
Port Alexander 147 56 13N 134 40W
Port Alfred, Can. 151 48 18N 70 53W
Port Alfred, S. Afr. 125 33 36 S 26 55 E
Port Alice 152 50 25N 127 25W
Port Allegany 156 41 49N 78 17W
Port Allen 159 30 30N 91 15W
Port Alma 138 23 38 S 150 53 E
Port Angeles 160 48 7N 123 30W
Port Antonio 166 18 10N 76 30W
Port Aransas 159 27 49N 97 4W
Port Arthur, Austral. 138 43 7 S 147 50 E
Port Arthur, U.S.A. 159 30 0N 94 0W
Port Arthur = Lüshun 107 38 51N 121 20 E
Port Arthur = Thunder Bay 150 48 25N 89 10W
Port Askaig 34 55 51N 6 8W
Port au Port B. 151 48 40N 58 50W
Port-au-Prince 167 18 40N 72 20W
Port Augusta West 140 32 29 S 137 47 E
Port Austin 150 44 3N 82 59W
Port aux Basques 151 47 32N 59 8W
Port Awanui 142 37 50 S 178 29 E
Port Bannatyne 34 55 51N 5 4W
Port Bell 126 0 18N 32 35 E
Port Bergé Vaovao 129 15 33 S 47 40 E
Port Blair 101 11 40N 92 30 E
Port Blandford 151 48 30N 53 50W
Port Bolivar 159 29 20N 94 40W
Port Bou 58 42 25N 3 9 E
Port Bouet 120 5 16N 4 57W
Port Bradshaw 138 12 30 S 137 0 E
Port Broughton 140 33 37 S 137 56 E
Port Burwell 150 42 40N 80 48W
Port Campbell 140 35 37 S 143 1 E
Port Canning 95 22 17N 88 48 E
Port Carlisle 32 54 56N 3 12W
Port-Cartier 151 50 10N 66 50W
Port Chalmers 143 45 49 S 170 30 E
Port Charlotte 34 55 44N 6 22W
Port Chester 162 41 0N 73 41W
Port Clements 152 53 40N 132 10W
Port Clinton 156 41 30N 83 0W
Port Colborne 150 42 50N 79 10W
Port Coquitlam 152 49 20N 122 45W
Port Curtis 138 24 0 S 151 34 E
Port Darwin, Austral. 136 12 24 S 130 45 E
Port Darwin, Falk. Is. 176 51 50 S 59 0W
Port Davey 138 43 16 S 145 55 E
Port-de-Bouc 45 43 24N 4 59 E
Port de Paix 167 19 50N 72 50W
Port Deposit 162 39 37N 76 5W
Port Dickson 101 2 30N 101 49 E
Port Dinorwic 31 53 11N 4 12W
Port Douglas 138 16 30 S 145 30 E
Port Edward 152 54 12N 130 10W
Port Elgin 150 44 25N 81 25W
Port Elizabeth 128 33 58 S 25 40 E
Port Ellen 34 55 38N 6 10W
Port Erin 32 54 5N 4 45W
Port Erroll 37 57 25N 1 50W
Port Essington 136 11 15 S 132 10 E
Port Étienne = Nouadhibou 116 21 0N 17 0W
Port Ewen 162 41 54N 73 59W
Port Fairy 140 38 22 S 142 12 E
Port Fitzroy 142 36 8 S 175 20 E
Port Fouâd = Bûr Fuad 122 31 15N 32 20 E
Port Francqui 124 4 17 S 20 47 E
Port-Gentil 124 0 47 S 8 40 E
Port Gibson 159 31 57N 91 0W
Port Glasgow 34 55 57N 4 40W
Port Gregory 137 27 40 S 114 0 E
Port Harcourt 121 4 40N 7 10 E
Port Hardy 152 50 41N 127 30W
Port Harrison 149 58 25N 78 15W
Port Hawkesbury 151 45 36N 61 22W
Port Hedland 136 20 25 S 118 35 E
Port Heiden 147 57 0N 158 40W
Port Hood 151 46 0N 61 32W
Port Hope 150 44 0N 78 20W
Port Hueneme 163 34 7N 119 12W
Port Huron 156 43 0N 82 28W
Port Isaac 30 50 35N 4 50W
Port Isaac B. 30 50 36N 4 50W
Port Isabel 159 26 12N 97 9W
Port Jackson 133 33 50 S 151 18 E
Port Jefferson 162 40 58N 73 5W
Port Jervis 162 41 22N 74 42W
Port Joinville 42 46 45N 2 23W
Port Kaituma 174 8 3N 59 58W
Port Katon 83 46 27N 38 56 E
Port Kelang 101 3 0N 101 23 E
Port Kembla 141 34 29 S 150 56 E
Port La Nouvelle 44 43 1N 3 3 E
Port Laoise 39 53 2N 7 20W
Port Lavaca 159 28 38N 96 38W
Port Leyden 162 43 35N 75 21W
Port Lincoln 140 34 42 S 135 52 E
Port Logan 34 54 42N 4 57W
Port Loko 120 8 48N 12 46W
Port Louis 42 47 42N 3 22W
Port Lyautey = Kenitra 118 34 15N 6 40W
Port Lyttelton 143 43 37N 172 50 E
Port Macdonnell 140 38 0 S 140 39 E
Port Macquarie 141 31 25 S 152 54 E
Port Maitland 151 44 0N 66 2W
Port Maria 166 18 25N 76 55W
Port Mellon 152 49 32N 123 31W
Port Menier 151 49 51N 64 15W
Port Morant 166 17 54N 76 19W
Port Moresby 135 9 24 S 147 8 E
Port Mouton 151 43 58N 64 50W
Port Musgrave 138 11 55 S 141 50 E
Port Navalo 42 47 34N 2 54W
Port Nelson 153 57 3N 92 36W
Port Nicholson 142 41 20 S 174 52 E
Port Nolloth 128 29 17 S 16 52 E
Port Norris 162 39 15N 75 2W
Port Nouveau-Quebec (George R.) 149 58 30N 65 50W
Port O'Connor 159 28 26N 96 24W
Port of Ness 36 58 29N 6 13W
Port of Spain 167 10 40N 61 20W
Port Orchard 160 47 31N 122 38W
Port Oxford 160 42 45N 124 28W
Port Pegasus 143 47 12 S 167 41 E
Port Perry 150 44 6N 78 56W
Port Phillip B. 139 38 10 S 144 50 E
Port Pirie 140 33 10 S 137 58 E
Port Pólnocny □ 54 54 25N 18 42 E
Port Radium = Echo Bay 148 66 10N 117 40W
Port Renfrew 152 48 30N 124 20W
Port Roper 138 14 45 S 134 47 E
Port Rowan 150 42 40N 80 30W
Port Royal 162 38 10N 77 12W
Port Safaga = Bûr Safâga 122 26 43N 33 57 E
Port Said = Bûr Sa'îd 122 31 16N 32 18 E
Port St. Joe 157 29 49N 85 20W
Port St. Johns = Umzimvubu 129 31 38 S 29 33 E
Port-St. Louis 45 43 23N 4 50 E
Port St. Louis 129 13 7 S 48 48 E
Port-St.-Louis-du-Rhône 45 43 23N 4 49 E
Port St. Mary 32 54 5N 4 45W
Port St. Servain 151 51 21N 58 0W
Port Sanilac 150 43 26N 82 33W
Port Saunders 151 50 40N 57 18W
Port Shepstone 129 30 44 S 30 28 E
Port Simpson 152 54 30N 130 20W
Port Stanley 150 42 40N 81 10W
Port Sudan = Bôr Sôdân 122 19 32N 37 9 E
Port Sunlight 32 53 22N 3 0W
Port Talbot 31 51 35N 3 48W
Port Taufiq = Bûr Taufiq 122 29 54N 32 32 E
Port Townsend 160 48 7N 122 50W
Port-Vendres 44 42 32N 3 8 E
Port Victoria 140 34 30 S 137 29 E
Port Wakefield 140 34 12 S 138 10 E
Port Washington 156 43 25N 87 52W
Port Weld 101 4 50N 100 38 E
Port William 34 54 46N 4 35W
Portachuelo 174 17 10 S 63 20W
Portacloy 38 54 20N 9 48W
Portadown (Craigavon) 38 54 27N 6 26W
Portaferry 38 54 23N 5 32W
Portage, Can. 151 46 40N 64 5W
Portage, U.S.A. 158 43 31N 89 25W
Portage la Prairie 153 49 58N 98 18W
Portage Mt. Dam 152 56 0N 122 0W
Portageville 159 36 25N 89 40W
Portaguiran 36 58 15N 6 10W
Portalegre 57 39 19N 7 25W
Portalegre □ 57 39 20N 7 40W
Portales 159 34 12N 103 25W
Portarlington 39 53 10N 7 10W
Porte, La 156 41 40N 86 40W
Porteirinha 171 15 44 S 43 2W
Portel, Brazil 170 1 57 S 50 49W

Portel Prochowice

Portel, Port. 57 38 19N 7 41W
Porter L., N.W.T., Can. 153 61 41N 108 5W
Porter L., Sask., Can. 153 56 20N 107 20W
Porterville, S. Afr. 128 33 0S 18 57E
Porterville, U.S.A. 163 36 5N 119 0W
Portet 44 43 34N 0 11W
Porteynon 31 51 33N 4 13W
Portglenone 38 54 53N 6 30W
Portgordon 37 57 40N 3 1W
Porth Neigwl 31 52 48N 4 35W
Porth Neigwl, B. 31 52 48N 4 33W
Porthcawl 31 51 28N 3 42W
Porthill 160 49 0N 116 30W
Porthleven 30 50 5N 5 19W
Porthmadog 31 52 55N 4 13W
Portile de Fier 70 44 42N 22 30E
Portimão 57 37 8N 8 32W
Portishead 28 51 29N 2 46W
Portknockle 37 57 40N 2 52W
Portland, N.S.W., Austral. 141 33 20S 150 0E
Portland, Victoria, Austral. 140 38 20S 141 35E
Portland, Conn., U.S.A. 162 41 34N 72 39W
Portland, Me., U.S.A. 151 43 40N 70 15W
Portland, Mich., U.S.A. 156 42 52N 84 58W
Portland, Oreg., U.S.A. 160 45 35N 122 40W
Portland B. 140 38 15S 141 45E
Portland Bill 28 50 31N 2 27W
Portland, C. 133 40 46S 148 0E
Portland I. 142 39 20S 177 51E
Portland, I. of 28 50 32N 2 25W
Portland, Pa. 162 40 55N 75 6W
Portland Prom. 149 58 40N 78 33W
Portlaw 39 52 18N 7 20W
Portmagee 39 51 53N 10 22W
Portmahomack 37 57 50N 3 50W
Portmarnock 38 53 25N 6 10W
Portnacroish 34 56 34N 5 24W
Portnahaven 34 55 40N 6 30W
Portneuf 151 46 43N 71 55W
Pôrto, Brazil 170 3 54S 42 42W
Pôrto, Port. 56 41 8N 8 40W
Pôrto □ 56 41 8N 8 20W
Pôrto Alegre, Mato Grosso, Brazil 170 21 40S 53 30W
Pôrto Alegre, Rio Grande do Sul, Brazil 173 30 5S 51 3W
Porto Alexandre 128 15 55S 11 55E
Porto Amboim = Gunza 124 10 50S 13 50E
Porto Amelia = Pemba 127 12 58S 40 30E
Porto Argentera 62 44 15N 7 27E
Porto Azzurro 62 42 46N 10 24E
Porto Botte 64 39 3N 8 33E
Pôrto Calvo 171 9 4S 35 24W
Porto Civitanova 63 43 19N 13 44E
Pôrto da Fôlha 170 9 55S 37 17W
Pôrto de Moz 170 1 41S 52 22W
Pôrto de Pedras 170 9 10S 35 17W
Porto Empédocle 64 37 18N 13 30E
Pôrto Esperança 174 19 37S 57 29W
Pôrto Franco 170 6 20S 47 24W
Porto Garibaldi 63 44 41N 12 14E
Porto, G. de 45 42 17N 8 34E
Pôrto Lago 68 41 1N 25 6E
Porto Mendes 173 24 30S 54 15W
Porto Murtinho 174 21 45S 57 55W
Pôrto Nacional 170 10 40S 48 30W
Porto Novo, Benin 121 6 23N 2 42E
Porto Novo, India 97 11 30N 79 38E
Porto Recanati 63 43 26N 13 40E
Porto San Giorgio 63 43 11N 13 49E
Porto San Stéfano 68 42 26N 11 6E
Porto Santo, I. 116 33 45S 16 25W
Pôrto São José 173 22 43S 53 10W
Pôrto Seguro 171 16 26S 39 5W
Porto Tolle 63 44 57N 12 20E
Porto Tórres 64 40 50N 8 23E
Pôrto União 173 26 10S 51 10W
Pôrto Válter 174 8 5S 72 40W
Porto-Vecchio 45 41 35N 9 16E
Pôrto Velho 174 8 46S 63 54W
Portobelo 166 9 35N 79 42W
Portoferráio 62 42 50N 10 20E
Portogruaro 63 45 47N 12 50E
Portola 160 39 49N 120 28W
Portomaggiore 63 44 41N 11 47E
Porton Camp 28 51 8N 1 42W
Portoscuso 64 39 12N 8 22E
Portovénere 62 44 2N 9 50E
Portoviejo 174 1 0S 80 20W
Portpatrick 34 54 50N 5 7W
Portree 36 57 25N 6 11W
Portroe 39 52 53N 8 20W
Portrush 38 55 13N 6 40W
Portsall 42 48 37N 4 45W
Portsalon 38 55 12N 7 37W
Portskerra 37 58 35N 3 55W
Portslade 29 50 50N 0 11W
Portsmouth, Domin. 167 15 34N 61 27W
Portsmouth, U.K. 28 50 48N 1 6W
Portsmouth, N.H., U.S.A. 162 43 5N 70 45W
Portsmouth, Ohio, U.S.A. 156 38 45N 83 0W
Portsmouth, R.I., U.S.A. 162 41 35N 71 44W
Portsmouth, Va., U.S.A. 156 36 50N 76 20W
Portsoy 37 57 41N 2 41W
Portstewart 38 55 12N 6 43W
Porttipahta 74 68 5N 26 30E
Portugal ■ 56 40 0N 7 0W
Portugalete 58 43 19N 3 4W
Portuguesa □ 174 9 10N 69 15W
Portuguese Guinea = Guinea Bissau 120 12 0N 15 0W
Portuguese Timor ■ = Timor 103 8 0S 126 30E
Portumna 39 53 5N 8 12W
Porvenir 176 53 10S 70 30W
Porvoo 75 60 24N 25 40E
Porzuna 57 39 9N 4 9W
Posada, R. 64 40 40N 9 35E
Posadas, Argent. 173 27 30S 56 0W
Posadas, Spain 57 37 47N 5 11W
Poschiavo 51 46 19N 10 4E
Posets, mt. 58 42 39N 0 25E
Poshan 107 36 30N 117 50E
Posidhio, Ákra 68 39 57N 23 30E
Poso 103 1 20S 120 55E
Poso Colorado 172 23 30S 58 45W
Poso, D. 103 1 20S 120 55E
Posong 107 34 46N 129 5E
Posse 171 14 4S 46 18W
Possel 124 5 5N 19 10E
Possession I. 13 72 4S 172 0E
Pössneck 48 50 42N 11 34E
Possut'eng Hu 105 42 0N 87 0E
Post 159 33 13N 101 21W
Post Falls 160 47 50N 116 59W
Postavy 80 55 4N 26 58E
Postbridge 30 50 36N 3 54W
Poste-de-la-Baleine 30 50 36N 3 54W
Poste Maurice Cortier (Bidon 5) 118 22 14N 1 2E
Postiljon, Kepulauan 103 6 30S 118 50E
Postmasburg 128 28 18S 23 5E
Postojna 63 45 46N 14 12E
Potamós 69 39 38N 19 53E
Potchefstroom 125 26 41S 27 7E
Potcoava 70 44 30N 24 39E
Poté 171 17 49S 41 49W
Poteau 159 35 5N 94 37W
Poteet 159 29 4N 98 35W
Potelu, Lacul 70 43 44N 24 20E
Potenza 65 40 40N 15 50E
Potenza Picena 63 43 22N 13 37E
Poteriteri, L. 143 46 5S 167 10E
Potes 56 43 15N 4 42W
Potgietersrus 129 24 10S 29 3E
Poti 83 42 10N 41 38E
Potiraguá 171 15 36S 39 53W
Potiskum 121 11 39N 11 2E
Potlogi 70 44 34N 25 34E
Potomac, R. 162 38 0N 76 23W
Potosí 174 19 38S 65 50W
Potosí □ 174 20 31S 67 0W
Pot'ou 106 37 57N 116 39E
Potrerillos 172 26 20S 69 30W
Potros, Cerro del 172 28 32S 69 0W
Potsdam, Ger. 48 52 23N 13 4E
Potsdam, U.S.A. 156 44 40N 74 59W
Potsdam □ 48 52 40N 12 50E
Potter 158 41 15N 103 20W
Potter Heigham 29 52 44N 1 33E
Potterne 28 51 19N 2 0W
Potters Bar 29 51 42N 0 11W
Potterspury 29 52 5N 0 52W
Pottery Hill = Abu Ballas 122 24 26N 27 36E
Pottstown 162 40 17N 75 40W
Pottsville 162 40 39N 76 12W
Pottuvil 93 6 55N 81 50E
P'otzu 109 23 30N 120 25E
Pouancé 42 47 44N 1 10W
Pouce Coupé 152 55 40N 120 10W
Poughkeepsie 162 41 40N 73 57W
Pouilly 43 47 18N 2 57E
Poulaphouca Res. 39 53 8N 6 30W
Pouldu, Le 42 47 41N 3 36W
Poulsbo 160 47 45N 122 39W
Poultney 162 43 31N 73 14W
Poulton le Fylde 32 53 51N 2 59W
Poundstock 30 50 44N 4 34W
Pouso Alegre, Mato Grosso, Brazil 175 11 55S 57 0W
Pouso Alegre, Minas Gerais, Brazil 173 22 14S 45 57W
Pouzages 44 46 40N 0 50W
Povenets 78 62 50N 34 50E
Poverty Bay 142 38 43S 178 2E
Póvoa de Lanhosa 56 41 33N 8 15W
Póvoa de Varzim 56 41 25N 8 46W
Povorino 81 51 12N 42 28E
Powassan 150 46 5N 79 25W
Poway 163 32 58N 117 2W
Powder, R. 158 46 47N 105 12W
Powell 160 44 45N 108 45W
Powell Creek 136 18 6S 133 46E
Powell River 152 49 22N 125 31W
Powers, Mich., U.S.A. 156 45 40N 87 32W
Powers, Oreg., U.S.A. 160 42 53N 124 2W
Powers Lake 158 48 37N 102 38W
Powick 28 52 9N 2 15W
Powis, Vale of 23 52 40N 3 10W
Powys □ 31 52 20N 3 20W
P'oyang 109 29 1N 116 38E
Poyang Hu 109 29 10N 116 10E
Poyarkovo 77 49 36N 128 41E
Poyntzpass 38 54 17N 6 22W
Poysdorf 53 48 40N 16 37E
Poza de la Sal 58 42 35N 3 31W
Poza Rica 165 20 33N 97 27W
Pozarevac 66 44 35N 21 18E
Pozega 66 45 21N 17 41E
Pozhva 84 59 5N 56 5E
Poznan 54 52 25N 17 0E
Pozo 163 35 20N 120 24W
Pozo Alcón 59 37 42N 2 56W
Pozo Almonte 174 20 10S 69 50W
Pozoblanco 57 38 23N 4 51W
Pozzallo 65 36 44N 15 40E
Pra, R. 121 5 30N 1 38W
Prabuty 54 53 47N 19 15E
Prača 66 43 47N 18 43E
Prachatice 52 49 1N 14 0E
Prachin Buri 100 14 0N 101 25E
Prachuap Khiri Khan 101 11 49N 99 48E
Pradelles 44 44 46N 3 52E
Pradera 174 3 25N 76 15W
Prades 44 42 38N 2 23E
Prado 171 17 20S 39 13W
Prado del Rey 57 36 48N 5 33W
Præstø 73 55 8N 12 2E
Pragersko 63 46 27N 15 42E
Prague = Praha 52 50 5N 14 22E
Praha 52 50 5N 14 22E
Prahecq 44 46 19N 0 26W
Prahita, R. 97 19 0N 79 55E
Prahova □ 70 44 50N 25 50E
Prahova, R. 70 44 50N 25 50E
Prahova, Reg. 70 44 50N 25 50E
Prahovo 66 44 18N 22 39E
Praid 70 46 32N 25 10E
Prainha, Amazonas, Brazil 174 7 10S 60 30W
Prainha, Pará, Brazil 175 1 45S 53 30W
Prairie, Queens., Austral. 138 20 50S 144 35E
Prairie, S. Australia, Austral. 109 34 51S 138 49E
Prairie City 160 45 27N 118 44W
Prairie du Chien 158 43 1N 91 9W
Prairie, R. 159 34 45N 101 15W
Praja 102 8 39S 116 27E
Prajeczno 54 51 10N 19 0E
Pramánda 68 39 32N 21 8E
Pran Buri 100 12 23N 99 55E
Prang 121 8 1N 0 56W
Prapat 102 2 41N 98 58E
Praszka 54 51 32N 18 31E
Prata, Minas Gerais, Brazil 171 19 25S 49 0W
Prata, Pará, Brazil 170 1 10S 47 35W
Prática di Mare 64 41 40N 12 26E
Prato 62 43 53N 11 5E
Prátola Peligna 63 42 7N 13 51E
Pratovécchio 63 43 44N 11 43E
Prats-de-Molló 44 42 25N 2 27E
Pratt 159 37 40N 98 45W
Pratteln 50 47 31N 7 41E
Prättigau 51 46 56N 9 44E
Prattville 157 32 30N 86 28W
Pravara, R. 96 19 30N 74 28E
Pravdinsk 81 56 29N 43 28E
Pravia 56 43 30N 6 12W
Prawle Pt. 30 50 13N 3 41W
Pré-en-Pail 42 48 28N 0 12W
Pré St. Didier 62 45 45N 7 0E
Precordillera 172 30 0S 69 1W
Predáppio 63 44 7N 11 58E
Predazzo 63 46 19N 11 37E
Predejane 66 42 51N 22 9E
Preeceville 153 51 57N 102 40W
Prees 32 52 54N 2 40W
Preesall 32 53 55N 2 58W
Préfailles 42 47 9N 2 11W
Pregonero 174 8 1N 71 46W
Pregrada 63 46 11N 15 45E
Preko 63 44 7N 15 14E
Prelate 153 50 51N 109 24W
Prelog 63 46 18N 16 32E
Premier 152 56 4N 129 56W
Premier Downs 137 30 30S 126 30E
Premont 159 27 19N 91 8W
Premuda, I. 63 44 20N 14 36E
Prenj, mt. 66 43 33N 17 53E
Prenjasi 68 41 6N 20 32E
Prentice 158 45 31N 90 19W
Prenzlau 48 53 19N 13 51E
Prepansko Jezero 68 40 45N 21 0E
Preparis I. 99 14 55N 93 45E
Preparis North Channel 101 15 12N 93 40E
Preparis South Channel 101 14 36N 93 40E
Prerov 53 49 28N 17 27E
Prescot 32 53 27N 2 49W
Prescott, Can. 150 44 45N 75 30W
Prescott, Ariz., U.S.A. 161 34 35N 112 30W
Prescott, Ark., U.S.A. 159 33 49N 93 22W
Preservation Inlet 143 46 8S 166 35E
Preševo 66 42 19N 21 39E
Presho 158 43 56N 100 4W
Preshute 28 51 24N 1 45W
Presicce 65 39 53N 18 13E
Presidencia de la Plaza 172 27 0S 60 0W
Presidencia Roque Sáenz Peña 172 26 45S 60 30W
Presidente Dutra 164 5 15S 44 30W
Presidente Epitácio 171 21 46S 52 6W
Presidente Hayes □ 172 24 0S 59 0W
Presidente Hermes 174 11 0S 61 55W
Presidente Prudente 173 22 5S 51 25W
Presidente Rogue Saena Peña 172 34 33S 58 30W
Presidio, Mexico 164 29 29N 104 23W
Presidio, U.S.A. 159 29 30N 104 20W
Preslav 67 43 10N 26 52E
Prespa, L. = Prepansko Jezero 68 40 45N 21 0E
Prespa, mt. 67 41 44N 25 0E
Presque Isle 151 46 40N 68 0W
Prestatyn 31 53 20N 3 24W
Prestea 120 5 22N 2 7W
Presteigne 31 52 17N 3 0W
Preštice 52 49 34N 13 20E
Preston, Borders, U.K. 35 55 48N 2 18W
Preston, Dorset, U.K. 28 50 38N 2 26W
Preston, Lancs., U.K. 32 53 46N 2 42W
Preston, Idaho, U.S.A. 160 42 0N 112 0W
Preston, Minn., U.S.A. 158 43 39N 92 3W
Preston, Nev., U.S.A. 160 38 59N 115 2W
Preston, C. 136 20 51S 116 12E
Prestonpans 35 55 58N 3 0W
Prestwich 32 53 32N 2 18W
Prestwick 34 55 30N 4 38W
Prêto, R., Bahia 170 11 21S 43 52W
Pretoria 129 25 44S 28 12E
Prettyboy Res. 162 39 37N 76 43W
Preuilly-sur-Claise 42 46 51N 0 56E
Préveza 69 38 57N 20 47E
Préveza □ 68 39 20N 20 40E
Prey-Veng 101 11 35N 105 29E
Priazovskoye 82 46 22N 35 28E
Pribilov Is. 12 56 0N 170 0W
Priboj 66 43 35N 19 32E
Pribram 52 49 41N 14 2E
Price 160 39 40N 110 48W
Price I. 152 52 23N 128 41W
Prichalnaya 83 48 57N 44 33E
Priego 58 40 38N 2 21W
Priego de Córdoba 57 37 27N 4 12W
Priekule 80 57 27N 21 45E
Prieska 128 29 40S 22 42E
Priest Gully Cr. 108 27 29S 153 11E
Priest L. 160 48 30N 116 55W
Priest River 160 48 11N 117 0W
Priest Valley 163 36 10N 120 39W
Priestly 152 54 8N 125 20W
Prievidza 53 48 46N 18 36E
Prijedor 63 44 58N 16 41E
Prijepolje 66 43 27N 19 40E
Prilep 66 41 21N 21 37E
Priluki 80 50 30N 32 15E
Prime Seal I. 138 40 3S 147 43E
Primeira Cruz 170 2 30S 43 26W
Primorsko 67 42 15N 27 44E
Primorsko-Akhtarsk 82 46 2N 38 10E
Primrose L. 153 54 55N 109 45W
Prince Albert 153 53 15N 105 50W
Prince Albert Nat. Park 153 54 0N 106 25W
Prince Albert Pen. 148 72 30N 116 0W
Prince Alfred C. 12 74 20N 124 40W
Prince Charles I. 149 67 47N 76 12W
Prince Edward I. □. 151 44 2N 77 20W
Prince Edward Is. 11 45 15S 39 0E
Prince Frederick 162 38 33N 76 35W
Prince George 152 53 50N 122 50W
Prince of Wales, C. 147 65 50N 168 0W
Prince of Wales I. 147 73 0N 99 0W
Prince of Wales, I. 147 53 30N 131 30W
Prince of Wales Is. 135 10 40S 142 10E
Prince Patrick I. 12 77 0N 120 0W
Prince Regent Inlet 12 73 0N 90 0W
Prince Rupert 152 54 20N 130 20W
Prince William Sd. 147 60 20N 146 30W
Princenhage 47 51 9N 4 45E
Princes Risborough 29 51 43N 0 50W
Princesa Isabel 170 7 44S 38 0W
Princess Anne 162 38 12N 75 41W
Princess Charlotte B. 138 14 25S 144 0E
Princess Mary Ranges 136 15 30S 125 30E
Princess Royal I. 152 53 0N 128 40W
Princeton, Can. 152 49 27N 120 30W
Princeton, Ill., U.S.A. 158 41 25N 89 25W
Princeton, Ind., U.S.A. 156 38 20N 87 35W
Princeton, Ky., U.S.A. 156 37 6N 87 55W
Princeton, Mo., U.S.A. 158 40 23N 93 35W
Princeton, N.J., U.S.A. 162 40 18N 74 40W
Princeton, W. Va., U.S.A. 156 37 21N 81 8W
Princetown 30 50 33N 4 0W
Principe Chan. 152 53 28N 130 0W
Principe da Beira 174 12 20S 64 30W
Principe, I. de 114 1 37N 7 27E
Prineville 160 44 17N 120 57W
Prins Albert 128 33 12S 22 2E
Prins Harald Kyst 13 70 0S 35 1E
Prinzapolca 166 13 20N 83 35W
Prior, C. 56 43 34N 8 17W
Pripet Marshes = Polesye 80 52 0N 28 10E
Pripet, R. = Pripyat, R. 80 51 30N 30 0E
Pripyat, R. 80 51 30N 30 0E
Prislop, Pasul 70 47 37N 25 15E
Pristen 81 51 15N 12 40E
Priština 66 42 40N 21 13E
Pritchard 157 30 47N 88 5W
Pritzwalk 48 53 10N 12 11E
Privas 45 44 45N 4 37E
Priverno 64 41 29N 13 10E
Privolzhsk 81 57 9N 14 9E
Privolzhskaya Vozvyshennest 81 51 0N 46 0E
Privolzhskiy 81 51 25N 46 3E
Privolzhye 81 52 52N 48 33E
Privutnoye 83 47 12N 43 30E
Prizren 66 42 13N 20 45E
Prizzi 64 37 44N 13 24E
Prnjavor 66 44 52N 17 43E
Probolinggo 103 7 46S 113 13E
Probus 30 50 17N 4 55W
Prochowice 54 51 17N 16 20E

Procida, I Qattâra, Munkhafed el

Procida, I. 64 40 46N 14 0 E
Proctor 162 43 40N 73 2W
Proddatur 97 14 45N 78 30 E
Proença-a-Nova 57 39 45N 7 54W
Profondeville 47 50 23N 4 52 E
Progreso 165 21 20N 89 40W
Prokhladnyy 83 43 50N 44 2 E
Prokletije 68 42 30N 19 45 E
Prokopyevsk 76 54 0N 87 3 E
Prokuplje 66 43 16N 21 36 E
Proletarskaya 83 46 42N 41 50 E
Prome = Pyè 99 18 45N 95 30 E
Prophet, R. 152 58 48N 122 40W
Propriá 170 10 13 S 36 51W
Propriano 45 41 41N 8 52 E
Proserpine 138 20 21 S 148 36 E
Prospect, Austral. 109 34 53 S 138 36 E
Prospect, U.S.A. 162 43 18N 75 9W
Prosser 160 46 11N 119 52W
Prostějov 53 49 30N 17 9 E
Proston 139 26 14 S 151 32 E
Proszowice 54 50 13N 20 16 E
Protection 159 37 16N 99 30W
Próti, I. 69 37 5N 21 32 E
Provadija 67 43 12N 27 30 E
Proven 47 50 54N 2 40 E
Provence 45 43 40N 5 46 E
Providence, Ky., U.S.A. 156 37 25N 87 46W
Providence, R.I., U.S.A. 162 41 41N 71 15W
Providence Bay 150 45 41N 82 15W
Providence C. 143 45 59 S 166 29 E
Providence Mts. 161 35 0N 115 30W
Providencia 174 0 28 S 76 28W
Providencia, I. de 166 13 25N 81 26W
Provideniya 77 64 23N 173 18 E
Province Wellesley 101 5 15N 100 20 E
Provincetown 162 42 5N 70 11W
Provins 43 48 33N 3 15 E
Provo 160 40 16N 111 37W
Provost 153 52 25N 110 20W
Prozor 66 43 50N 17 34 E
Prudentópolis 171 25 12 S 50 57W
Prudhoe 35 54 57N 1 52W
Prudhoe Bay, Austral. 138 21 30 S 149 30W
Prudhoe Bay, U.S.A. 147 70 20N 148 20W
Prudhoe I. 138 21 23 S 149 45 E
Prudhoe Land 12 78 1N 65 0W
Prud'homme 153 52 20N 105 54W
Prudnik 54 50 20N 17 38 E
Prüm 49 50 14N 6 22 E
Pruszcz 54 54 17N 19 40 E
Pruszków 54 52 9N 20 49 E
Prut, R. 70 46 3N 28 10 E
Prvič, I. 63 44 55N 14 47 E
Prvomay 67 42 8N 25 17 E
Prydz B. 13 69 0 S 74 0 E
Pryor 159 36 17N 95 20W
Przasnysz 54 53 2N 20 45 E
Przedbórz 54 51 6N 19 53 E
Przedecz 54 52 20N 18 53 E
Przemyśl 54 49 50N 22 45 E
Przemyśl □ 54 80 0N 23 0 E
Przeworsk 54 50 6N 22 32 E
Przewóz 54 51 28N 14 57 E
Przhevalsk 85 42 30N 78 20 E
Przysucha 54 51 22N 20 38 E
Psakhná 69 38 34N 23 35 E
Psarà, I. 69 38 37N 25 38 E
Psathoúra, I. 68 39 30N 24 12 E
Psel, R. 82 49 25N 33 50 E
Pserimos, I. 69 36 56N 27 12 E
Pskem, R. 85 41 38N 70 1 E
Pskemskiy Khrebet 85 42 0N 70 45 E
Pskent 85 40 54N 69 20 E
Pskov 80 57 50N 28 25 E
Psunj, mt. 66 45 25N 17 19 E
Pszczyna 54 49 59N 18 58 E
Pteleón 69 39 3N 22 57 E
Ptich, R. 80 52 30N 28 45 E
Ptolemais 68 40 30N 21 43 E
Ptuj 63 46 28N 15 50 E
Ptujska Gora 63 46 23N 15 47 E
Pua 100 19 11N 100 55 E
Puán 172 37 30 S 63 0W
P'uan 108 25 47N 104 57 E
Puan 107 35 44N 126 7 E
Pubnico 151 43 47N 65 50W
Pucallpa 174 8 25 S 74 30W
P'uchen 107 37 21N 118 1 E
P'uch'eng 109 27 45N 118 47 E
Pucheni 70 45 12N 25 17 E
P'uch'i 109 29 43N 113 53 E
Pucisce 63 43 22N 16 43 E
Puck 54 54 45N 18 23 E
Puddletown 28 50 45N 2 21W
Pudsey 33 53 47N 1 40W
Pudukkottai 97 10 28N 78 47 E
Puebla 165 19 0N 98 10W
Puebla □ 165 18 30N 98 0W
Puebla de Alcocer 57 38 59N 5 14W
Puebla de Don Fadrique 59 37 58N 2 25W
Puebla de Don Rodrigo 57 39 5N 4 37W
Puebla de Guzmán 57 37 37N 7 15W
Puebla de los Infantes, La 57 37 47N 5 24W
Puebla de Montalbán, La 56 39 52N 4 22W
Puebla de Sanabria 56 42 4N 6 38W
Puebla de Trives 56 42 20N 7 10W
Puebla del Caramiñal 56 42 37N 8 56W
Puebla, La 58 39 50N 3 0 E
Pueblo 158 38 20N 104 40W
Pueblo Bonito 161 36 4N 107 57W
Pueblo Hundido 172 26 20 S 69 30W
Pueblo Nuevo 174 8 26N 71 26W
Pueblonuevo 55 38 16N 5 16W
Puelches 172 38 5 S 66 0W
Puelén 172 37 32 S 67 38W
Puente Alto 172 33 32 S 70 35W
Puente del Arzobispo 56 39 48N 5 10W
Puente Genil 57 37 22N 4 47W
Puente la Reina 58 42 40N 1 49W
Puentearas 56 42 10N 8 28W
Puentedeume 56 43 24N 8 10W
Puentes de García Rodríguez 56 43 27N 7 51W
Puerco, R. 161 35 10N 109 45W
Puerh 105 23 11N 100 56 E
P'uerh 108 23 5N 101 5 E
Puerhching 105 47 43N 86 53 E
Puerta, La 59 38 22N 2 45W
Puerto Aisén 176 45 10 S 73 0W
Puerto Angel 165 15 40N 96 29W
Puerto Arista 165 15 56N 93 48W
Puerto Armuelles 166 8 20N 83 10W
Puerto Ayacucho 174 5 40N 67 35W
Puerto Barrios 166 15 40N 88 40W
Puerto Bermejo 172 26 55 S 58 34W
Puerto Bermúdez 174 10 20 S 75 0W
Puerto Bolívar 174 3 10 S 79 55W
Puerto Cabello 174 10 28N 68 1W
Puerto Cabezas 166 14 0N 83 30W
Puerto Cabo Gracias a Dios 166 15 0N 83 10W
Puerto Capaz = Jebba 118 35 11N 4 43W
Puerto Carreño 174 6 12N 67 22W
Puerto Casado 172 22 19 S 57 56W
Puerto Castilla 166 16 0N 86 0W
Puerto Chicama 174 7 45 S 79 20W
Puerto Coig 176 50 54 S 69 15W
Puerto Columbia 174 10 59N 74 58W
Puerto Cortés, C. Rica 166 8 20N 82 20W
Puerto Cortés, Hond. 166 15 51N 88 0W
Puerto Cuemani 174 0 5N 73 21W
Puerto Cumarebo 174 11 29N 69 21W
Puerto de Cabras 116 28 40N 13 30W
Puerto de Morelos 165 20 49N 86 52W
Puerto de Santa María 57 36 36N 6 13W
Puerto Deseado 176 47 45 S 66 0W
Puerto Heath 174 12 25 S 68 45W
Puerto Huitoto 174 0 18N 74 3W
Puerto Juárez 165 21 11N 86 49W
Puerto La Cruz 174 10 13N 64 38W
Puerto Leguízamo 174 0 12 S 74 46W
Puerto Libertad 164 29 55N 112 41W
Puerto Limón, Meta, Colomb. 174 3 23N 73 30W
Puerto Limón, Putumayo, Colomb. 174 1 3N 76 30W
Puerto Lobos 176 42 0 S 65 3W
Puerto López 174 4 5N 72 58W
Puerto Lumbreras 59 37 34N 1 48W
Puerto Madryn 176 42 48 S 65 4W
Puerto Maldonado 174 12 30 S 69 10W
Puerto Manotí 166 21 22N 76 50W
Puerto Mazarrón 59 37 34N 1 15W
Puerto Mercedes 174 1 11N 72 53W
Puerto Montt 176 41 28 S 72 40W
Puerto Natales 176 51 45 S 72 25W
Puerto Nuevo 174 5 53N 69 56W
Puerto Ordaz 174 8 16N 62 44W
Puerto Padre 166 21 13N 76 35W
Puerto Páez 174 6 13N 67 28W
Puerto Peñasco 164 31 20N 113 33W
Puerto Pinasco 172 22 43 S 57 50W
Puerto Pirámides 176 42 35 S 64 20W
Puerto Plata 167 19 40N 70 45W
Puerto Princesa 94 9 44N 118 44 E
Puerto Quellón 176 43 7 S 73 37W
Puerto Quepos 166 9 29N 84 6W
Puerto Real 57 36 33N 6 12W
Puerto Rico 174 1 54N 75 10W
Puerto Rico ■ 147 18 15N 66 45W
Puerto Rico Trough 14 20 0N 63 0W
Puerto Sastre 172 22 25 S 57 55W
Puerto Suárez 174 18 58 S 57 52W
Puerto Tejada 174 3 14N 76 24W
Puerto Umbria 174 0 52N 76 33W
Puerto Vallarta 164 20 26N 105 15W
Puerto Villamizar 174 8 25N 72 30W
Puerto Wilches 174 7 21N 73 54W
Puertollano 57 38 43N 4 7W
Puertomarín 56 42 48N 7 37W
Pueyrredón, L. 176 47 20 S 72 0W
Puffin I., Ireland 39 51 50N 10 25W
Puffin I., U.K. 31 53 19N 4 1W
Pugachev 81 52 0N 48 55 E
Puge 126 4 45 S 33 11 E
Puget Sd. 160 47 15N 123 30W
Puget-Théniers 45 43 58N 6 53 E
Púglia 65 41 0N 16 30 E
Pugŏdong 107 42 5N 130 0 E
Pugu 126 6 55 S 39 4 E
Puha 142 38 30 S 177 50 E
P'uhsien 106 36 25N 110 4 E
Puhute Mesa 163 37 25N 116 50W
Pui 70 45 30N 23 4 E
Puieşti 70 46 25N 27 33 E
Puig Mayor, Mte. 58 39 49N 2 47 E
Puigcerdá 58 42 24N 1 50 E
Puigmal, Mt. 58 42 23N 2 7 E
Puisaye, Collines de 43 47 34N 3 28 E
Puiseaux 43 48 11N 2 30 E
Pujon-chosuji 107 40 35N 127 35 E
Puka 68 42 2N 19 53 E
Pukaki L. 143 44 4 S 170 1 E
Pukatawagan 153 55 45N 101 20W
Pukchin 107 40 12N 125 45 E
Pukchŏng 107 40 14N 128 18 E
Pukearuhe 142 38 55 S 174 31 E
Pukekohe 142 37 12 S 174 55 E
Puketeraki Ra. 143 42 58 S 172 13 E
Pukeuri 143 45 4 S 171 2 E
P'uko 108 27 27N 102 34 E
Pukoo 147 21 4N 156 48W
P'uk'ou 109 32 7N 118 43 E
Pula 64 39 0N 9 0 E
Pula (Pola) 63 44 54N 13 57 E
Pulaski, N.Y., U.S.A. 162 43 32N 76 9W
Pulaski, Tenn., U.S.A. 157 35 10N 87 0W
Pulaski, Va., U.S.A. 156 37 4N 80 49W
Puławy 54 51 23N 21 59 E
Pulborough 29 50 58N 0 30W
Pulgaon 96 20 44N 78 21 E
Pulham Market 29 52 25N 1 15 E
Pulham St. Mary 29 52 25N 1 14 E
Pulicat, L. 97 13 40N 80 15 E
Puliyangudi 97 9 11N 77 24 E
Pullabooka 141 33 44 S 147 46 E
Pullen Cr. 108 27 33 S 152 54 E
Pullman 160 46 49N 117 10W
Pulmakong 121 11 2N 0 2 E
Pulog, Mt. 103 16 40N 120 50 E
Puloraja 102 4 55N 95 24 E
Pułtusk 54 52 43N 21 6 E
Pumlumon Fawr 31 52 29N 3 47W
Pumpsaint 31 52 3N 3 58W
Puna 174 19 45 S 65 28W
Puna de Atacama 172 25 0 S 67 0W
Puná, I. 174 2 55 S 80 5W
Punakha 98 27 42N 89 52 E
Punalur 97 9 0N 76 56 E
Punasar 94 27 6N 73 6 E
Punata 174 17 25 S 65 50W
Punch 95 33 48N 74 4 E
Pune 96 18 29N 73 57 E
Pungsan 107 40 50N 128 9 E
P'uning 109 23 19N 116 9 E
Punjab □ 94 31 0N 76 0 E
Punkatawagon 153 55 44N 101 20W
Puno 174 15 55 S 70 3W
Punt, La 51 46 35N 9 56 E
Punta Alta 176 38 53 S 62 4W
Punta Arenas 176 53 0 S 71 0W
Punta de Díaz 172 28 0 S 70 45W
Punta de Piedras 174 10 54N 64 6W
Punta del Lago Viedma 176 49 45 S 72 0W
Punta Gorda, Belize 165 16 10N 88 45W
Punta Gorda, U.S.A. 157 26 55N 82 0W
Punta Prieta 164 28 58N 114 17W
Puntabie 139 32 12 S 134 5 E
Puntarenas 166 10 0N 84 50W
Puntes de García Rodríguez 56 43 27N 7 50W
Punto Fijo 174 11 42N 70 13W
Punxsutawney 156 40 56N 79 0W
P'upei 108 22 16N 109 33 E
Puquio 174 14 45 S 74 10W
Pur, R. 76 65 30N 77 40 E
Purace, vol. 174 2 21N 76 23W
Puračió 66 44 33N 18 28 E
Purari, R. 135 7 49 S 145 0 E
Purbeck, Isle of 28 50 40N 2 5W
Purcell 159 35 0N 97 25W
Purchena Tetica 59 37 21N 2 21W
Purdy Is. 138 3 0 S 146 0 E
Purfleet 29 51 29N 0 15 E
Puri 96 19 50N 85 58 E
Purificación 174 3 51N 74 55W
Purísima, La 164 26 10N 112 4W
Purley 28 51 29N 1 4W
Purli 96 18 50N 76 35 E
Purmerend 47 52 30N 4 58 E
Purna, R. 96 19 55N 76 20 E
Purnea 95 25 45N 87 31 E
Pursat 101 12 34N 103 50 E
Puruey 174 7 35N 64 48W
Purukcahu 102 0 35 S 114 35 E
Purulia 95 23 17N 86 33 E
Purus, R. 174 5 25 S 64 0W
Purwakarta 103 6 35 S 107 29 E
Purwodadi, Jawa, Indon. 103 7 7 S 110 55 E
Purwodadi, Jawa, Indon. 103 7 51 S 110 0 E
Purworejo 103 7 43 S 110 2 E
Puryŏng 107 42 0N 129 43 E
Pus, R. 96 19 50N 77 45 E
Pusad 96 19 56N 77 36 E
Pusan 107 35 5N 129 0 E
Pushchino 77 54 20N 158 10 E
Pushkin 80 59 45N 30 25 E
Pushkino 81 51 16N 47 9 E
Puskitamika L. 150 49 20N 76 30W
Püspökladány 53 47 19N 21 6 E
Pussa 129 24 30 S 33 55 E
Pustoshka 80 56 11N 29 30 E
Puszczykowo 54 52 18N 16 49 E
Putahow L. 153 59 54N 100 40W
Putao 98 27 28N 97 30 E
Putaruru 142 38 2 S 175 50 E
Putbus 48 54 19N 13 29 E
Put'ehach'i 105 48 0N 122 43 E
Puţeni 70 45 49N 27 42 E
Puthein Myit, R. 99 15 56N 94 18 E
P'ut'ien 109 25 27N 118 59 E
Putignano 65 40 50N 17 5 E
P'uting 108 26 19N 105 45 E
Putlitz 48 53 15N 12 3 E
Putna 70 47 50N 25 33 E
Putna, R. 70 45 42N 27 26 E
Putnam 162 41 55N 71 55W
Putnok 53 48 18N 20 26 E
P'ut'o 109 29 58N 122 15 E
Putorana, Gory 77 69 0N 95 0 E
Putorino 142 39 4 S 177 9 E
Putta 47 51 4N 4 38 E
Puttalam 93 8 1N 79 55 E
Puttalam Lagoon 97 8 15N 79 45 E
Putte 47 51 22N 4 24 E
Putten 46 52 16N 5 36 E
Puttgarden 48 54 28N 11 15 E
Puttur 97 12 46N 75 12 E
Putty 141 32 57 S 150 42 E
Putumayo □ 174 1 30 S 70 0W
Putumayo, R. 174 1 30 S 70 0W
Putussibau, G. 102 0 45N 113 50 E
Pututahi 142 38 39 S 177 53 E
Puurs 47 51 5N 4 17 E
Puy-de-Dôme 44 45 46N 2 57 E
Puy-de-Dôme □ 44 45 47N 3 0 E
Puy-de-Sancy 44 45 32N 2 41 E
Puy Guillaume 44 45 57N 3 28 E
Puy, Le 44 45 3N 3 52 E
Puy l'Evêque 44 44 31N 1 9 E
Puyallup 160 47 10N 122 22W
P'uyang 106 35 41N 115 0 E
Puylaurens 44 43 35N 2 0 E
Puyôo 44 43 33N 0 56W
Pwalagu 121 10 38N 0 50W
Pwani □, Tanz. 126 7 0 S 39 0 E
Pwani □, Tanz. 126 7 0 S 39 30 E
Pweto 127 8 25 S 28 51 E
Pwinbyu 98 20 23N 94 40 E
Pwllheli 31 52 54N 4 26W
Pya Ozero 78 66 8N 31 22 E
Pyana, R. 81 55 30N 45 0 E
Pyandzh 85 37 14N 69 6 E
Pyandzh, R. 85 37 6N 68 20 E
Pyapon 98 16 5N 95 50 E
Pyasina, R. 77 72 30N 90 30 E
Pyatigorsk 83 44 2N 43 0 E
Pyatikhatki 82 48 28N 33 38 E
Pyaye 98 19 12N 95 10 E
Pyè 98 18 49N 95 13 E
Pyinbauk 98 19 10N 95 12 E
Pyinmana 98 19 45N 96 20 E
Pyŏktong 107 40 37N 125 26 E
Pyŏnggang 107 38 24N 127 17 E
Pyŏngtaek 107 37 1N 127 4 E
P'yŏngyang 107 39 0N 125 45 E
Pyote 159 31 34N 103 5W
Pyramid L. 160 40 0N 119 30W
Pyramid Pk. 163 36 25N 116 37W
Pyramids 122 29 58N 31 9 E
Pyrenees 44 42 45N 0 18 E
Pyrénées-Atlantiques □ 44 43 15N 1 0W
Pyrénées-Orientales □ 44 42 35N 2 26 E
Pyrzyce 54 53 10N 14 55 E
Pyshchug 81 58 57N 45 27 E
Pyshma, R. 84 57 8N 66 18 E
Pytalovo 80 57 5N 27 55 E
Python 127 17 56 S 29 10 E
Pyttegga 71 62 13N 7 42 E
Pyu 98 18 30N 96 35 E
Pyzdry 54 52 11N 17 42 E

Q

Qaar Zeitun 122 29 10N 25 48 E
Qabalon 90 32 8N 35 17 E
Qabatiya 90 32 25N 35 16 E
Qadam 93 32 55N 66 45 E
Qadhimah 92 22 20N 39 13 E
Qadian 94 31 51N 74 19 E
Qal at Shajwa 122 25 2N 38 57 E
Qala-i-Jadid (Spin Baldak) 94 31 1N 66 25 E
Qala-i-Kirta 93 32 15N 63 0 E
Qala Nau 93 35 0N 63 5 E
Qala Punja 93 37 0N 72 40 E
Qala Yangi 94 34 20N 66 30 E
Qal'at al Akhdhar 92 28 0N 37 10 E
Qal'at Saura 122 26 10N 38 40 E
Qal'eh Shaharak 93 34 10N 64 20 E
Qalqīlya 90 32 12N 34 58 E
Qalyûb 122 30 12N 31 11 E
Qam 90 32 36N 35 43 E
Qamar, Ghubbat al 91 16 20N 52 30 E
Qamruddin Karez 94 31 45N 68 20 E
Qana 90 33 12N 35 17 E
Qâra 122 29 38N 26 30 E
Qara Qash, R. 95 35 45N 78 45 E
Qara Tagh La = Kala Shank'ou 95 35 42N 78 20 E
Qarachuk 92 37 0N 42 2 E
Qarah 92 29 55N 40 3 E
Qardud 123 10 20N 29 56 E
Qarrasa 123 14 38N 32 5 E
Qarsa 123 9 28N 41 48 E
Qaşr Bū Hadi 119 31 1N 16 45 E
Qasr-e-Qand 93 26 15N 60 45 E
Qasr Farâfra 122 27 0N 28 1 E
Qastina 90 31 44N 34 45 E
Qatar ■ 93 25 30N 51 15 E
Qattâra 122 30 12N 27 3 E
Qattara Depression = Q. Munkhafed el 122 29 30N 27 30 E
Qattâra, Munkhafed el 122 29 30N 27 30 E

Qayen Rancharia

Qayen 93 33 40N 59 10 E
Qazvin 92 36 15N 50 0 E
Qena 122 26 10N 32 43 E
Qena, Wadi 122 26 57N 32 50 E
Qendrevca 68 40 20N 19 48 E
Qesari 90 32 30N 34 53 E
Qeshm 93 26 55N 56 10 E
Qeshm, I. 93 26 50N 56 0 E
Qila Safed 93 29 0N 61 30 E
Qila Saifulla 94 30 45N 68 17 E
Qiryat 'Anivim 90 31 49N 35 7 E
Qiryat Bialik 90 32 50N 35 5 E
Qiryat 'Eqron 90 31 52N 34 49 E
Qiryat Hayyim 90 32 49N 35 4 E
Qiryat Shemona 90 33 13N 35 35 E
Qiryat Yam 90 32 51N 35 4 E
Qishon, R. 90 32 42N 35 7 E
Qishran 122 20 14N 40 2 E
Qizan 123 16 57N 42 34 E
Qom 93 34 40N 51 0 E
Quabbin Res. 162 42 17N 72 21W
Quabbo 123 12 2N 39 56 E
Quackenbrück 48 52 40N 7 59 E
Quadring 33 52 53N 0 9W
Quainton 29 51 51N 0 53W
Quairading 137 32 0S 117 21 E
Quakerstown 162 40 27N 75 20W
Qualeup 137 33 48S 116 48 E
Quambatook 138 35 49S 143 34 E
Quambone 141 30 57S 147 53 E
Quan Long 101 9 7N 105 8 E
Quanan 159 34 20N 99 45W
Quandialla 141 34 1S 147 47 E
Quang Nam 101 15 55N 108 15 E
Quang Ngai 101 15 13N 108 58 E
Quang Yen 100 21 3N 106 52 E
Quantock Hills, The 28 51 8N 3 10W
Quaraî 172 30 15S 56 20W
Quarré les Tombes 43 47 21N 4 0 E
Quarryville 162 39 54N 76 10W
Quartu Sant' Elena 64 39 15N 9 10 E
Quartzsite 161 33 44N 114 16W
Quatsino 152 50 30N 127 40W
Quatsino Sd. 152 50 42N 127 58W
Qubab = Mishmar Aiyalon 90 31 52N 34 57 E
Qûchãn 93 37 10N 58 27 E
Que Que 127 18 58S 29 48 E
Queanbeyan 141 35 17S 149 14 E
Québec 151 46 52N 71 13W
Québec □ 151 50 0N 70 0W
Quedlinburg 48 51 47N 11 9 E
Queen Alexandra Ra. 13 85 0S 170 0 E
Queen Anne 162 38 55N 75 57W
Queen Bess Mt. 152 51 13N 124 35W
Queen Charlotte 152 53 15N 132 2W
Queen Charlotte Is. 152 53 20N 132 10W
Queen Charlotte Sd. 143 41 10S 174 15 E
Queen Charlotte Str. 152 51 0N 128 0W
Queen Elizabeth Is. 10 78 0N 95 0W
Queen Elizabeth Nat. Pk. 126 0 0S 30 0 E
Queen Mary Coast 13 70 0S 95 0 E
Queen Maud G. 148 68 15N 102 30W
Queenborough 29 51 24N 0 46 E
Queen's Chan. 136 15 0S 129 30 E
Queensbury 32 53 46N 1 50W
Queenscliff 138 38 16S 144 39 E
Queensferry 35 56 0N 3 25W
Queensland □ 138 15 0S 142 0 E
Queenstown, Austral. 138 42 4S 145 35 E
Queenstown, N.Z. 143 45 1S 168 40 E
Queenstown, S. Afr. 125 31 52S 26 52 E
Queguay Grande, R. 172 32 9S 58 9W
Queimadas 170 11 0S 39 38W
Quela 124 9 10S 16 56 E
Quelimane 127 17 53S 36 58 E
Quemado, N. Mex., U.S.A. 161 34 17N 108 28W
Quemado, Tex., U.S.A. 159 28 58N 100 35W
Quemoy, I. = Chinmen Tao, I. 109 24 25N 118 25 E
Quemú-Quemú 172 36 3S 63 36W
Quendale, B. of 36 59 53N 1 20W
Quequén 172 38 30S 58 30W
Querein 123 13 30N 34 50 E
Querétaro 164 20 40N 100 23W
Querétaro □ 164 20 30N 100 30W
Querfurt 48 51 22N 11 33 E
Quesada 59 37 51N 3 4W
Quesnel 152 53 5N 122 30W
Quesnel L. 152 52 30N 121 20W
Quesnel, R. 152 52 58N 122 29W
Quest, Pte. 151 49 52N 64 40W
Questa 161 36 45N 105 35W
Questembert 42 47 40N 2 28W
Quetico 150 48 45N 90 55W
Quetico Prov. Park 150 48 30N 91 45W
Quetta 93 30 15N 66 55 E
Quetta □ 93 30 15N 66 55 E
Quezaltenango 166 14 40N 91 30W
Quezon City 103 14 38N 121 0 E
Qui Nhon 101 13 40N 109 13 E
Quiaca, La 172 22 5S 65 35W
Quibaxi 124 8 24S 14 27 E
Quibdó 174 5 42N 76 40W
Quiberon 42 47 29N 3 9W
Quíbor 174 9 56N 69 37W
Quick 152 54 36N 126 54W
Quickborn 48 53 42N 9 52 E
Quiet L. 152 61 5N 133 5W
Quiévrain 47 50 24N 3 41 E
Quiindy 172 25 58S 57 14W
Quila 164 24 23N 107 13W
Quilán, C. 176 43 15S 74 30W
Quilengues 125 14 12S 14 12 E
Quilimarí 172 32 5S 70 30W
Quilino 172 30 14S 64 29W
Quillabamba 174 12 50S 72 50W
Quillagua 172 21 40S 69 40W
Quillaicillo 172 31 17S 71 40W
Quillan 44 42 53N 2 10 E
Quillebeuf 42 49 28N 0 30 E
Quillota 172 32 54S 71 16W
Quilmes 172 34 43S 58 15W
Quilon 97 8 50N 76 38 E
Quilpie 139 26 35S 144 11 E
Quilpué 172 33 5S 71 33W
Quilty 39 52 50N 9 27W
Quilua 127 16 17S 39 54 E
Quimilí 172 27 40S 62 30W
Quimper 42 48 0N 4 9W
Quimperlé 42 47 53N 3 33W
Quin 39 52 50N 8 52W
Quinag 36 58 13N 5 5W
Quincy, Calif., U.S.A. 160 39 56N 121 0W
Quincy, Fla., U.S.A. 157 30 34N 84 34W
Quincy, Ill., U.S.A. 158 39 55N 91 20W
Quincy, Mass., U.S.A. 162 42 14N 71 0W
Quincy, Wash., U.S.A. 160 47 22N 119 56W
Quines 172 32 13S 65 48W
Quinga 127 15 49S 40 15 E
Quingey 43 47 7N 5 52 E
Quinhagak 147 59 45N 162 0W
Quintana de la Serena 57 38 45N 5 40W
Quintana Roo □ 165 19 0N 88 0W
Quintanar de la Orden 58 39 36N 3 5W
Quintanar de la Sierra 58 41 57N 2 55W
Quintanar del Rey 59 39 21N 1 56W
Quintero 172 32 45S 71 30W
Quintin 42 48 26N 2 56W
Quinto 58 41 25N 0 32W
Quinyambie 139 30 15S 141 0 E
Quípar, R. 59 37 58N 2 3W
Quirihue 172 36 15S 72 35W
Quirindi 141 31 28S 150 40 E
Quiriquire 174 9 59N 63 13W
Quiroga 56 42 28N 7 18W
Quirpon I. 151 51 32N 55 28W
Quisiro 174 10 53N 71 17W
Quissac 45 43 55N 4 0 E
Quissanga 127 12 24S 40 28 E
Quitilipi 172 26 50S 60 13W
Quitman, Ga., U.S.A. 157 30 49N 83 35W
Quitman, Miss., U.S.A. 157 32 2N 88 42W
Quitman, Tex., U.S.A. 159 32 48N 95 25W
Quito 174 0 15S 78 35W
Quixadá 170 4 55S 39 0W
Quixaxe 127 15 17S 40 4 E
Quixeramobim 170 5 12S 39 17W
Qul'ân, Jazâ'ir 122 24 22N 35 31 E
Qumran 90 31 43N 35 27 E
Quneitra 90 33 7N 35 48 E
Quoich L. 36 57 4N 5 20W
Quoile, R. 38 54 21N 5 40W
Quoin I. 136 14 54S 129 32 E
Quoin Pt., N.Z. 143 46 19S 170 11 E
Quoin Pt., S. Afr. 128 34 46S 19 37 E
Quondong 140 33 6S 140 18 E
Quorn, Austral. 140 32 25S 138 0 E
Quorn, Can. 150 49 25N 90 55W
Quorndon 28 52 45N 1 10W
Qûs 122 25 55N 32 50 E
Quseir 122 26 7N 34 16 E
Qusra 90 32 5N 35 20 E
Quthing 129 30 25S 27 36 E
Quynh Nhai 100 21 49N 103 33 E
Qytet Stalin (Kuçove) 68 40 47N 19 57 E

R

Ra, Ko 101 9 13N 98 16 E
Raa. 73 56 0N 12 45 E
Råa 73 56 0N 12 45 E
Raahana 90 32 12N 34 52 E
Raahe 74 64 40N 24 28 E
Raalte 46 52 23N 6 16 E
Raamsdonksveer 47 51 43N 4 52 E
Raasay I. 36 57 25N 6 4W
Raasay, Sd. of 36 57 30N 6 8W
Rab 63 44 45N 14 45 E
Rab, I. 63 44 45N 14 45 E
Raba 103 8 36S 118 55 E
Rába, R. 54 47 38N 17 38 E
Rabaçal, R. 56 41 41N 7 15W
Rabah 121 13 5N 5 30 E
Rabai 126 3 50S 39 31 E
Rabaraba 135 9 58S 149 49 E
Rabastens 44 43 50N 1 43 E
Rabastens, Hautes Pyrénées 44 43 25N 0 10 E
Rabat 118 34 2N 6 48W
Rabaul 135 4 24S 152 18 E
Rabbalshede 73 58 40N 11 27 E
Rabbit L. 153 47 0N 79 38W
Rabbit Lake 153 53 8N 107 46W
Rabbit, R. 152 59 41N 127 12W
Rabbitskin, R. 152 61 47N 120 42W
Rabigh 92 22 50N 39 5 E
Rabka 54 49 37N 19 59 E
Rača 66 44 14N 21 0 E
Rácale 65 39 57N 18 6 E
Racalmuto 64 37 25N 13 41 E
Racconigi 62 44 47N 7 41 E
Race, C. 151 46 40N 53 5W
Raceview 108 27 38S 152 47 E
Rach Gia 101 10 5N 105 5 E
Raciaz 54 52 46N 20 10 E
Racibórz (Ratibor) 54 50 7N 18 18 E
Racine 156 42 41N 87 51W
Rackheath 29 52 41N 1 22 E
Rackwick 37 58 52N 3 23W
Radama, Îs. 129 14 0S 47 47 E
Radama, Presqu'île d' 129 14 16S 47 53 E
Radan, mt. 66 42 59N 21 29 E
Radbuza, R. 52 49 35N 13 5 E
Radcliffe, Gr. Manch., U.K. 32 53 35N 2 19W
Radcliffe, Notts., U.K. 33 52 57N 1 3W
Rade 71 59 21N 10 53 E
Radeburg 48 51 6N 13 45 E
Radeče 63 46 5N 15 14 E
Radekhov 80 50 25N 24 32 E
Radford 156 37 8N 80 32W
Radhanpur 94 23 50N 71 38 E
Radika, R. 66 41 38N 20 37 E
Radisson 153 52 30N 107 20W
Radium Hill 133 32 30S 140 42 E
Radium Hot Springs 152 50 48N 116 12W
Radkow 54 50 30N 16 24 E
Radley 28 51 42N 1 14W
Radlin 54 50 3N 18 29 E
Radna 66 46 7N 21 41 E
Radnevo 67 42 17N 25 58 E
Radnice 52 49 51N 13 35 E
Radnor (□) 26 52 20N 3 20W
Radnor Forest 31 52 17N 3 10W
Radom 54 51 23N 21 12 E
Radom □ 54 51 30N 21 0 E
Radomir 66 42 37N 23 4 E
Radomsko 54 51 5N 19 28 E
Radomyshl 80 50 30N 29 12 E
Radomysl Wielki 54 50 14N 21 15 E
Radoszyce 54 51 4N 20 15 E
Radoviš 66 41 38N 22 28 E
Radovljica 63 46 22N 14 12 E
Radöy I. 71 60 40N 4 55 E
Radstadt 52 47 24N 13 28 E
Radstock 28 51 17N 2 25W
Radstock, C. 139 33 12S 134 20 E
Raduša 66 42 7N 21 15 E
Radviliškis 80 55 49N 23 33 E
Radville 153 49 30N 104 15W
Radymno 54 49 59N 22 52 E
Radyr 31 51 32N 3 16W
Radzanów 54 52 56N 20 8 E
Radziejów 54 52 40N 18 30 E
Radzyn Chełminski 54 53 23N 18 55 E
Rae 152 62 50N 116 3W
Rae Bareli 95 26 18N 81 20 E
Rae Isthmus 149 66 40N 87 30W
Raeside, L. 137 29 20S 122 0 E
Raetihi 142 39 25S 175 17 E
Rafaela 172 31 10S 61 30W
Rafah 122 31 18N 34 14 E
Rafai 126 4 59N 23 58 E
Raffadali 64 37 23N 13 29 E
Rafhã 92 29 35N 43 35 E
Rafid 90 32 57N 35 52 E
Rafsanjãn 93 30 30N 56 5 E
Raft Pt. 136 16 4S 124 26 E
Ragag 123 10 59N 24 40 E
Ragama 93 7 0N 79 50 E
Ragged Mt. 137 33 27S 123 25 E
Raglan, Austral. 138 23 42S 150 49 E
Raglan, N.Z. 142 37 55S 174 55 E
Raglan, U.K. 31 51 46N 2 51W
Ragueneau 151 49 11N 68 18W
Ragunda 72 63 6N 16 23 E
Ragusa 65 36 56N 14 42 E
Raha 103 8 20S 118 40 E
Rahad el Berdi 117 11 20N 23 40 E
Rahad, Nahr er 123 12 40N 35 30 E
Rahden 48 52 26N 8 36 E
Raheita 123 12 46N 43 4 E
Raheng = Tak 100 17 5N 99 10 E
Rahimyar Khan 94 28 30N 70 25 E
Rahotu 142 39 20S 173 49 E
Raichur 96 16 10N 77 20 E
Raiganj 95 25 37N 88 10 E
Raigarh, Madhya Pradesh, India 96 21 56N 83 25 E
Raigarh, Orissa, India 96 19 51N 82 6 E
Raiis 92 23 33N 38 43 E
Raijua 103 10 37S 121 36 E
Railton 138 41 25S 146 28 E
Rainbow 140 35 55S 142 0 E
Rainbow Lake 152 58 30N 119 23W
Rainham 29 51 22N 0 36 E
Rainier 160 46 4N 123 0W
Rainier, Mt. 160 46 50N 121 50W
Rainworth 33 53 8N 1 6W
Rainy L. 153 48 30N 92 30W
Rainy River 153 48 50N 94 30W
Raipur 96 21 17N 81 45 E
Raith 150 48 50N 90 0W
Raj Nandgaon 99 21 0N 81 0 E
Raja Empat, Kepulauan 103 0 30S 129 40 E
Raja-Jooseppi 74 68 28N 28 29 E
Raja, Ujung 102 3 40N 96 25 E
Rajahmundry 96 17 1N 81 48 E
Rajang, R. 102 2 30N 113 30 E
Rajapalaiyarm 97 9 25N 77 35 E
Rajasthan □ 94 26 45N 73 30 E
Rajasthan Canal 94 30 31N 71 0 E
Rajauri 95 33 25N 74 21 E
Rajbari 98 23 47N 89 41 E
Rajgarh, Mad. P., India 94 24 2N 76 45 E
Rajgarh, Raj., India 94 28 40N 75 25 E
Rajgród 54 53 42N 22 42 E
Rajhenburg 63 46 1N 15 29 E
Rajkot 94 22 15N 70 56 E
Rajmahal Hills 95 24 30N 87 30 E
Rajnandgaon 96 21 5N 81 5 E
Rajojooseppi 74 68 25N 28 30 E
Rajpipla 96 21 50N 73 30 E
Rajpura 94 30 32N 76 32 E
Rajshahi 98 24 22N 88 39 E
Rajshahi □ 95 25 0N 89 0 E
Rakaia 143 43 45S 172 1 E
Rakaia, R. 143 43 26S 171 47 E
Rakan, Ras 93 26 10N 51 20 E
Rakaposhi 95 36 10N 74 0 E
Rakaposhi, mt. 93 36 20N 74 30 E
Rakha 122 18 25N 41 30 E
Rakhni 94 30 4N 69 56 E
Rakitovo 67 41 59N 24 5 E
Rakkestad 71 59 25N 11 21 E
Rakoniewice 54 52 10N 16 16 E
Rakops 128 21 1S 24 28 E
Rákospalota 53 47 30N 19 5 E
Rakovica 63 44 59N 15 38 E
Rakovník 52 50 6N 13 42 E
Rakovski 67 42 21N 24 57 E
Raleigh, Can. 150 49 30N 92 5W
Raleigh, U.S.A. 150 35 46N 78 38W
Raleigh B. 157 34 50N 76 15W
Ralja 66 44 33N 20 34 E
Ralls 159 33 40N 101 20W
Ralston 162 41 30N 76 57W
Rãm Allãh 90 31 55N 35 10 E
Ram Hd. 141 37 47S 149 30 E
Ram, R. 152 62 1N 123 41W
Rama, Israel 90 32 56N 35 21 E
Rama, Nic. 166 12 9N 84 15W
Ramacca 65 37 24N 14 40 E
Ramachandrapuram 96 16 50N 82 4 E
Ramadi 92 33 28N 43 15 E
Ramales de la Victoria 58 43 15N 3 28W
Ramalho, Serra do 171 13 45S 44 0W
Raman 101 6 29N 101 18 E
Ramanathapuram 97 9 25N 78 55 E
Ramanetaka, B. de 129 14 13S 47 52 E
Ramas C. 97 15 5N 73 55 E
Ramat Gan 90 32 4N 34 48 E
Ramatlhabama 128 25 37S 25 33 E
Ramban 95 33 14N 75 12 E
Rambervillers 43 48 20N 6 38 E
Rambipudji 103 8 12S 113 37 E
Rambla, La 57 37 37N 4 45W
Rambouillet 43 48 40N 1 48 E
Rambre Kyun 98 19 0N 94 0 E
Ramdurg 97 15 58N 75 22 E
Rame Head 30 50 19N 4 14W
Ramechhap 95 27 25N 86 10 E
Ramelau, Mte. 103 8 55S 126 22 E
Ramenskoye 81 55 32N 38 15 E
Ramgarh, Bihar, India 95 23 40N 85 35 E
Ramgarh, Rajasthan, India 94 27 16N 75 14 E
Ramgarh, Rajasthan, India 94 27 30N 70 36 E
Ramhormoz 92 31 15N 49 35 E
Ramla 90 31 55N 34 52 E
Ramlat Zalṭan 119 28 30N 19 30 E
Ramlu Mt. 123 13 32N 41 40 E
Ramme 73 56 30N 8 11 E
Rammun 90 31 55N 35 17 E
Ramna Stacks, Is. 36 60 40N 1 20W
Ramnad = Ramanathapuram 97 9 25N 78 55 E
Ramnagar 95 32 47N 75 18 E
Ramnäs 72 59 46N 16 12 E
Ramon 81 52 8N 39 21 E
Ramona 163 33 1N 116 56W
Ramor L. 38 53 50N 7 5W
Ramore 150 48 30N 80 25W
Ramos Arizpe 164 23 35N 100 59W
Ramos, R. 164 25 35N 105 3W
Ramoutsa 128 24 50S 25 52 E
Rampart 147 65 0N 150 15W
Rampside 32 54 6N 3 10W
Rampur, H.P., India 94 31 26N 77 43 E
Rampur, M.P., India 94 23 25N 73 53 E
Rampur, Orissa, India 96 21 48N 83 58 E
Rampur, U.P., India 94 28 50N 79 5 E
Rampura 94 24 30N 75 27 E
Rampurhat 95 24 10N 87 50 E
Ramsbottom 32 53 36N 2 20W
Ramsbury 28 51 26N 1 37W
Ramsel 47 51 2N 4 50 E
Ramsele 74 63 31N 16 27 E
Ramsey, Can. 150 47 25N 82 20W
Ramsey, Cambs., U.K. 29 52 27N 0 6W
Ramsey, Essex, U.K. 29 51 55N 1 12 E
Ramsey, I. of M., U.K. 32 54 20N 4 21W
Ramsgate 29 51 20N 1 25 E
Ramshai 98 26 44N 88 51 E
Rämshyttan 72 60 17N 15 15 E
Ramsjö 72 62 11N 15 37 E
Ramtek 96 21 20N 79 15 E
Ramu, R. 135 4 0S 144 41 E
Ramvik 72 62 49N 17 51 E
Ranaghat 95 23 15N 88 35 E
Ranahu 94 25 55N 69 45 E
Ranau 102 6 2N 116 40 E
Rancagua 172 34 10S 70 50W
Rance 47 50 9N 4 16 E
Rance, R. 42 48 34N 1 59W
Rancharia 171 22 15S 50 55W

Rancheria, R Rennell Sd

Rancheria, R. 152 60 13N 129 7W
Ranchester 160 44 57N 107 12W
Ranchi 95 23 19N 85 27 E
Rancu 70 44 32N 24 15 E
Rand 141 35 33 S 146 32 E
Randallstown 162 39 22N 76 48W
Randalstown 38 54 45N 6 20W
Randan 44 46 2N 3 21 E
Randazzo 65 37 53N 14 56 E
Randböl 73 55 43N 9 17 E
Randers 73 56 29N 10 1 E
Randers Fjord 73 56 37N 10 20 E
Randfontein 129 26 8 S 27 45 E
Randolph, Mass., U.S.A. 162 42 10N 71 3W
Randolph, Utah, U.S.A. 160 41 43N 111 10W
Randolph, Vt., U.S.A. 162 43 55N 72 39W
Randsburg 163 35 26N 117 44W
Randsfjord 71 60 15N 10 25 E
Råne älv 74 66 26N 21 10 E
Råneå 74 65 53N 22 18 E
Ranfurly 143 45 7 S 170 6 E
Rangae 101 6 19N 101 44 E
Rangamati 98 22 38 S 92 12 E
Rangataua 142 39 26 S 175 28 E
Rangaunu B. 142 34 51 S 173 15 E
Rångedala 73 57 47N 13 9 E
Rangeley 156 44 58N 70 33W
Rangely 160 40 3N 108 53W
Ranger 159 32 30N 98 42W
Rangia 98 26 15N 91 20 E
Rangiora 143 43 19 S 172 36 E
Rangitaiki 130 38 52 S 176 23 E
Rangitaiki, R. 142 37 54 S 176 49 E
Rangitata, R. 143 43 45 S 171 15 E
Rangitikei, R. 142 40 17 S 175 15 E
Rangitoto Range 142 38 25 S 175 35 E
Rangkasbitung 103 6 22 S 106 16 E
Rangon 99 16 45N 96 20 E
Rangon, R. 99 16 28N 96 40 E
Rangoon 98 16 45N 96 20 E
Rangpur 98 25 42N 89 22 E
Rangsit 100 13 59N 100 37 E
Ranibennur 97 14 35N 75 30 E
Raniganj 95 23 40N 87 15 E
Ranipet 97 12 56N 79 23 E
Raniwara 93 24 50N 72 10 E
Ranken, R. 138 20 31 S 137 36 E
Rankin 159 31 16N 101 56W
Rankin Inlet 148 62 30N 93 0W
Rankin's Springs 141 33 49 S 146 14 E
Rannes 138 24 6 S 150 11 E
Rannoch L. 37 56 41N 4 20W
Rannoch Moor 34 56 38N 4 48W
Rannoch Sta. 37 56 40N 4 32W
Ranobe, B. de 129 23 3 S 43 33 E
Ranohira 129 22 29 S 45 24 E
Ranomafana, Tamatave, Madag. 129 18 57 S 48 50 E
Ranomafana, Tuléar, Madag. 129 24 34 S 47 0 E
Ranong 101 9 56N 98 40 E
Rantau 102 4 15N 98 5 E
Rantauprapat 102 2 15N 99 50 E
Rantemario 103 3 15 S 119 57 E
Rantis 90 32 4N 35 3 E
Rantoul 156 40 18N 88 10W
Ranum 73 56 54N 9 14 E
Ranwanlenau 128 19 37 S 22 49 E
Raon-l' Étape 43 48 24N 6 50 E
Raoui, Erg er 118 29 0N 2 0W
Rapa Iti, I. 131 27 35 S 144 20W
Rapallo 62 44 21N 9 12 E
Rapang 103 3 45 S 119 55 E
Râpch 93 25 40N 59 15 E
Raphoe 38 54 52N 7 36W
Rapid City 158 44 0N 103 0W
Rapid, R. 152 59 15N 129 5W
Rapid River 156 45 55N 87 0W
Rapides des Joachims 150 46 13N 77 43W
Rapla 80 58 88N 24 52 E
Rapness 37 59 15N 2 51W
Raposos 171 19 57 S 43 48W
Rappahannock, R. 162 37 35N 76 17W
Rapperswil 51 47 14N 8 45 E
Raqqa 92 36 0N 38 55 E
Raquete 127 14 8 S 38 13 E
Raquette Lake 162 43 49N 74 40W
Rareagh 38 53 37N 8 37W
Rarotonga, I. 131 21 30 S 160 0W
Ras al Khaima 93 25 50N 56 5 E
Ra's Al-Unūf 119 30 25N 18 15 E
Ra's at Tannurah 92 26 40N 50 10 E
Ras Dashan, mt. 123 13 8N 37 45 E
Ras el Ma 118 34 26N 0 50W
Ras Gharib 122 28 6N 33 18 E
Ras Mallap 122 29 18N 32 50 E
Rasa, Punta 176 40 50 S 62 15W
Rasboda 72 60 8N 16 58 E
Raseiniai 80 55 25N 23 5 E
Rashad 123 11 55N 31 0 E
Rashîd 122 31 21N 30 22 E
Rashîd, Masabb 122 31 22N 30 17 E
Rasht 92 37 20N 49 40 E
Rasi Salai 100 15 20N 104 9 E
Rasipuram 97 11 30N 78 25 E
Raška 66 43 19N 20 39 E
Raso, C. 170 1 50N 50 0W
Rason, L. 137 28 45 S 124 25 E
Raşova 70 44 15N 27 55 E
Rasovo 67 43 42N 23 17 E
Rasra 95 25 50N 83 50 E
Rass el Oued 119 35 57N 5 2 E
Rasskazovo 81 52 35N 41 50 E
Rastatt 49 48 50N 8 12 E
Rastu 70 43 53N 23 16 E
Raszków 54 51 43N 17 40 E
Rat Buri 100 13 30N 99 54 E
Rat, Is. 147 51 50N 178 15 E
Rat, R. 152 56 0N 99 30W
Rat River 152 61 7N 112 36W
Rätan 72 62 27N 14 33 E
Ratangarh 94 28 5N 74 35 E
Rath 95 25 36N 79 37 E
Rath Luirc (Charleville) 39 52 21N 8 40W
Rathangan 39 53 13N 7 0W
Rathconrah 38 53 30N 7 32W
Rathcoole 39 53 17N 6 29W
Rathcormack 39 52 5N 8 19W
Rathdowney 39 52 52N 7 36W
Rathdrum, Ireland 39 52 57N 6 13W
Rathdrum, U.S.A. 160 47 50N 116 58W
Ratheclaung 98 20 29N 92 45 E
Rathen 37 57 38N 1 58W
Rathenow 48 52 38N 12 23 E
Rathfriland 38 54 12N 6 12W
Rathkeale 39 52 32N 8 57W
Rathkenny 38 53 45N 6 39W
Rathlin I. 38 55 18N 6 14W
Rathlin O'Birne I. 38 54 40N 8 50W
Rathmelton 38 55 3N 7 35W
Rathmolyon 38 53 30N 6 49W
Rathmore, Cork, Ireland 39 51 30N 9 21W
Rathmore, Kerry, Ireland 39 52 5N 9 12W
Rathmore, Kildare, Ireland 39 53 13N 6 35W
Rathmullen 38 55 6N 7 32W
Rathnure 39 52 30N 6 47W
Rathvilly 72 52 54N 6 42W
Ratlam 94 23 20N 75 0 E
Ratnagiri 96 16 57N 73 18 E
Ratnapura 97 6 40N 80 20 E
Ratoath 38 53 30N 6 27W
Raton 159 37 0N 104 30W
Rattaphum 101 7 8N 100 16 E
Ratten 52 47 28N 15 44 E
Rattray 37 56 36N 3 20W
Rattray Hd. 37 57 38N 1 50W
Rättvik 72 60 52N 15 7 E
Ratz, Mt. 152 57 23N 132 12W
Ratzeburg 48 53 41N 10 46 E
Raub 101 3 47N 101 52 E
Rauch 172 36 45 S 59 5W
Raufarhöfn 74 66 27N 15 57W
Raufoss 71 60 44N 10 37 E
Raukumara Ra. 142 38 5 S 177 55 E
Raul Soares 171 20 5 S 42 22W
Rauland 71 59 43N 8 0 E
Rauma 75 61 10N 21 30 E
Rauma, R. 71 62 34N 7 43 E
Raundal 71 60 40N 6 37 E
Raunds 29 52 20N 0 32W
Raung, Mt. 103 8 8 S 114 4 E
Raurkela 96 22 14N 84 50 E
Rava Russkaya 80 50 15N 23 42 E
Ravanusa 64 37 16N 13 58 E
Ravar 93 31 20N 56 51 E
Ravels 47 51 22N 5 0 E
Ravena 162 42 28N 73 49W
Ravenglass 32 54 21N 3 25W
Ravenna, Italy 63 44 28N 12 15 E
Ravenna, U.S.A. 158 41 3N 98 58W
Ravensburg 49 47 48N 9 38 E
Ravenshoe 138 17 37 S 145 29 E
Ravenstein 46 51 47N 5 39 E
Ravensthorpe 137 33 35 S 120 2 E
Ravenstonedale 32 54 26N 2 26W
Ravenswood, Austral. 138 20 6 S 146 54 E
Ravenswood, U.S.A. 156 38 58N 81 47W
Ravensworth 141 32 26 S 151 4 E
Raventasón 174 6 10 S 81 0W
Ravi, R. 94 31 0N 73 0 E
Ravna Gora 63 45 24N 14 50 E
Ravna Reka 66 43 59N 21 35 E
Ravnstrup 73 56 27N 9 17 E
Rawa Mazowiecka 54 51 46N 20 12 E
Rawalpindi 94 33 38N 73 8 E
Rawalpindi □ 93 33 10N 72 50 E
Rawāndūz 92 36 40N 44 30 E
Rawang 101 3 20N 101 35 E
Rawdon 150 46 3N 73 40W
Rawene 142 35 25 S 173 32 E
Rawicz 54 51 36N 16 52 E
Rawlinna 137 30 58 S 125 28 E
Rawlins 160 41 50N 107 20W
Rawlinson Range 137 24 40 S 128 30 E
Rawmarsh 33 53 27N 1 20W
Rawson 176 43 15 S 65 0W
Rawtenstall 32 53 42N 2 18W
Rawuya 121 12 10N 6 50 E
Ray, N. Mex., U.S.A. 159 35 57N 104 8W
Ray, N.D., U.S.A. 158 48 21N 103 6W
Ray, C. 151 47 33N 59 15W
Ray Mts. 147 66 0N 152 10W
Rayachoti 97 14 4N 78 50 E
Rayadrug 97 14 40N 76 50 E
Rayagada 96 19 15N 83 20 E
Raychikhinsk 77 49 46N 129 25 E
Rayevskiy 84 54 4N 54 56 E
Rayin 93 29 40N 57 22 E
Rayleigh 29 51 36N 0 38 E
Raymond, Can. 152 49 30N 112 35W
Raymond, Calif., U.S.A. 163 37 13N 119 54W
Raymond, Wash., U.S.A. 160 46 45N 123 48W
Raymond Terrace 141 32 45 S 151 44 E
Raymondville 159 26 30N 97 50W
Raymore 153 51 25N 104 31W
Rayne 159 30 16N 92 16W
Rayón 164 29 43N 110 35W
Rayong 100 12 40N 101 20 E
Rayville 159 32 30N 91 45W
Raz, Pte. du 42 48 2N 4 47W
Razana 66 44 6N 19 55 E
Razanj 66 43 40N 21 31 E
Razdelna 67 43 13N 27 41 E
Razelm, Lacul 70 44 50N 29 0 E
Razgrad 67 43 33N 26 34 E
Razlog 67 41 53N 23 28 E
Razmak 94 32 45N 69 50 E
Razole 96 16 56N 81 48 E
Razor Back Mt. 152 51 32N 125 0W
Ré, Île de 44 46 12N 1 30W
Rea, L. 39 53 10N 8 32W
Reading, U.K. 29 51 27N 0 57W
Reading, U.S.A. 162 40 20N 75 53W
Realicó 172 35 0 S 64 15W
Réalmont 44 43 48N 2 10 E
Ream 101 10 34N 103 39 E
Reata 164 26 8N 101 5W
Reay 37 58 33N 3 48W
Rebais 43 48 50N 3 10 E
Rebecca L. 137 30 0 S 122 30 E
Rebi 103 5 30 S 134 7 E
Rebiana 117 24 12N 22 10 E
Rebun-Tō 112 45 23N 141 2 E
Recanati 63 43 24N 13 32 E
Recaş 66 45 46N 21 30 E
Recess 38 53 29N 9 4W
Recherche, Arch. of the 137 34 15 S 122 50 E
Rechitsa 80 52 13N 30 15 E
Recht 47 50 20N 6 3 E
Recife 170 8 0 S 35 0W
Recklinghausen 48 51 36N 7 10 E
Reconquista 172 29 10 S 59 45W
Recreo 172 29 25 S 65 10W
Reculver 29 51 22N 1 12 E
Recz 54 53 16N 15 31 E
Red B. 38 55 4N 6 2W
Red Bank 162 40 21N 74 4W
Red Bay 151 51 44N 56 25W
Red Bluff 160 40 11N 122 11W
Red Bluff L. 159 31 59N 103 58W
Red Cliffs 140 34 19 S 142 11 E
Red Cloud 158 40 8N 98 33W
Red Creek 162 43 14N 76 45W
Red Deer 152 52 20N 113 50W
Red Deer L. 153 52 55N 101 20W
Red Deer, R. 152 50 58N 110 0W
Red Deer R. 153 52 53N 101 1W
Red Dial 32 54 48N 3 9W
Red Hook 162 41 55N 73 53W
Red Indian L. 151 48 35N 57 0W
Red L. 158 48 0N 95 0W
Red Lake 153 51 1N 94 1W
Red Lake Falls 158 47 54N 96 30W
Red Lion 162 39 54N 76 36W
Red Lodge 160 45 10N 109 10W
Red Mountain 163 35 37N 117 38W
Red Oak 158 41 0N 95 10W
Red Point Rock 137 32 13 S 127 32 E
Red, R., Can. 153 50 24N 96 48W
Red, R., Minn., U.S.A. 158 48 10N 97 0W
Red, R., Tex., U.S.A. 159 33 57N 95 30W
Red, R. = Hong, R. 100 20 17N 106 34 E
Red Rock 150 48 55N 88 15W
Red Rock, L. 158 41 30N 93 15W
Red Sea 91 25 0N 36 0 E
Red Slate Mtn. 163 37 31N 118 52W
Red Sucker L 153 54 9N 93 40W
Red Tower Pass = Turnu Rosu P. 70 45 33N 24 17 E
Red Wharf Bay 31 53 18N 4 10W
Red Wing 158 44 32N 92 35W
Reda 54 54 40N 18 19 E
Rédange 47 49 46N 5 52 E
Redbank 108 27 25N 152 52 E
Redbridge 29 51 35N 0 7 E
Redcar 33 54 37N 1 4W
Redcliff 153 50 10N 110 50W
Redcliffe 139 27 12 S 153 0 E
Redcliffe, Mt. 137 28 30 S 121 30 E
Redcliffs 139 34 16 S 142 10 E
Reddersburg 128 29 41 S 26 10 E
Redding 160 40 30N 122 25W
Redditch 28 52 18N 1 57W
Rede, R. 35 55 8N 2 12W
Redenção 170 4 13 S 38 43W
Redesmouth 35 55 7N 2 12W
Redfield 158 45 0N 98 30W
Redhill 29 51 14N 0 10W
Redknife, R. 152 61 14N 119 22W
Redland 37 59 6N 3 4W
Redlands 163 34 0N 117 11W
Redlynch 28 50 59N 1 42W
Redmile 33 52 54N 0 48W
Redmire 32 54 19N 1 55W
Redmond, Austral. 137 34 55 S 117 40 E
Redmond, U.S.A. 160 44 19N 121 11W
Redon 42 47 40N 2 6W
Redonda, I. 167 16 58N 62 19W
Redondela 56 42 15N 8 38W
Redondo 57 38 39N 7 37W
Redondo Beach 163 33 52N 118 26W
Redrock Pt. 152 62 11N 115 2W
Redruth 30 50 14N 5 14W
Redvers 153 49 35N 101 40W
Redwater 152 53 55N 113 6W
Redwood City 163 37 30N 122 15W
Redwood Falls 158 44 30N 95 2W
Ree, L. 38 53 35N 8 0W
Reed City 156 43 52N 85 30W
Reed L. 153 54 38N 100 30W
Reed, Mt. 151 52 5N 68 5W
Reeder 158 47 7N 102 52W
Reedham 29 52 34N 1 33 E
Reedley 163 36 36N 119 27W
Reedsburg 158 43 34N 90 5W
Reedsport 160 43 45N 124 4W
Reedy Creek 140 36 58 S 140 2 E
Reef Pt. 142 35 10 S 173 5 E
Reefton, N.S.W., Austral. 141 34 15 S 147 27 E
Reefton, S. Australia, Austral. 109 34 57 S 138 55 E
Reefton, N.Z. 143 42 6 S 171 51 E
Reepham 29 52 46N 1 6 E
Reeth 32 54 23N 1 56W
Refsnes 71 61 9N 7 14 E
Reftele 73 57 11N 13 35 E
Refugio 159 28 18N 97 17W
Rega, R. 54 53 52N 15 16 E
Regalbuto 65 37 40N 14 38 E
Regar 85 38 30N 68 14 E
Regavim 90 32 32N 35 2 E
Regen 49 48 58N 13 9 E
Regeneração 170 6 15 S 42 41W
Regensburg 49 49 1N 12 7 E
Regensdorf 51 47 26N 8 28 E
Réggio di Calábria 65 38 7N 15 38 E
Réggio nell' Emilia 62 44 42N 10 38 E
Regina 153 50 30N 104 35W
Registan □ 93 30 15N 65 0 E
Registro 173 24 29 S 47 49W
Reguengos de Monsaraz 57 38 25N 7 32W
Rehar 95 23 36N 82 52 E
Rehoboth, Damaraland, Namibia 128 23 15 S 17 4 E
Rehoboth, Ovamboland, Namibia 128 17 55 S 15 5 E
Rehoboth Beach 162 38 43N 75 5W
Rehovot 90 31 54N 34 48 E
Reichenbach, Ger. 48 50 36N 12 19 E
Reichenbach, Switz. 50 46 38N 7 42 E
Reid 137 30 49 S 128 26 E
Reid River 138 19 40 S 146 48 E
Reiden 50 47 14N 7 59 E
Reidsville 157 36 21N 79 40W
Reigate 29 51 14N 0 11W
Reillo 58 39 54N 1 53W
Reims 43 49 15N 4 0 E
Reina 90 32 43N 35 18 E
Reina Adelaida, Arch. 176 52 20 S 74 0W
Reinach, Aargau, Switz. 50 47 14N 8 11 E
Reinach, Basel, Switz. 50 47 29N 7 35 E
Reinbeck 158 42 18N 92 40W
Reindeer I. 153 52 30N 98 0W
Reindeer L. 153 57 15N 102 15W
Reindeer, R. 153 55 36N 103 11W
Reine, La 150 48 50N 79 30W
Reinga, C. 142 34 25 S 172 43 E
Reinosa 56 43 2N 4 15W
Reinosa, Paso 56 42 56N 4 10W
Reira 123 15 25N 34 50 E
Reiss 37 58 29N 3 7W
Reisterstown 162 39 28N 76 50W
Reitdiep 46 53 20N 6 20 E
Reitz 129 27 48 S 28 29 E
Reivilo 128 27 36 S 24 8 E
Rejmyra 73 58 50N 15 55 E
Reka, R. 63 45 40N 14 0 E
Rekovac 66 43 51N 21 3 E
Remad, Ouedber 118 33 28N 1 20W
Remanso 170 9 41 S 42 4W
Remarkable, Mt. 140 32 48 S 138 10 E
Rembang 103 6 42 S 111 21 E
Remchi 118 35 2N 1 26W
Remedios, Colomb. 174 7 2N 74 41W
Remedios, Panama 166 8 15N 81 50W
Remeshk 93 26 55N 58 50 E
Remetea 70 46 45N 29 29 E
Remich 47 49 32N 6 22 E
Remiremont 43 48 0N 6 36 E
Remo 123 6 48N 41 20 E
Remontnoye 83 47 44N 43 37 E
Remoulins 45 43 55N 4 35 E
Remscheid 48 51 11N 7 12 E
Remsen 162 43 19N 75 11W
Rena 71 61 8N 11 20 E
Renda 123 14 30N 40 0 E
Rende 65 39 19N 16 11 E
Rendeux 47 50 14N 5 30 E
Rendina 69 39 4N 21 58 E
Rendsburg 48 54 18N 9 41 E
Rene 77 66 2N 179 25W
Renee, oilfield 19 58 4N 0 16 E
Renens 50 46 31N 6 34 E
Renfrew, Can. 150 45 30N 76 40W
Renfrew, U.K. 34 55 52N 4 24W
Renfrew (□) 26 55 50N 4 30W
Rengat 102 0 30 S 102 45 E
Rengo 172 34 24 S 70 50W
Reni 82 45 28N 28 15 E
Renigunta 97 13 38N 79 30 E
Renish Pt. 36 57 44N 6 59W
Renkum 46 51 58N 5 43 E
Renmark 140 34 11 S 140 43 E
Rennell Sd. 152 53 23N 132 35W

Renner Springs Teleg. Off **Riverton**

Renner Springs Teleg. Off. **138** 18 20 S 133 47 E
Rennes **42** 48 7N 1 41W
Rennesøy **71** 59 6N 5 43 E
Reno **160** 39 30N 119 50W
Reno, R. **63** 44 45N 11 40 E
Renovo **156** 41 20N 77 47W
Rens **55** 54 54N 9 5 E
Rensselaer, Ind., U.S.A. **156** 41 0N 87 10W
Rensselaer, N.Y., U.S.A. **162** 42 38N 73 41W
Rentería **58** 43 19N 1 54W
Renton **160** 47 30N 122 9W
Renwicktown **143** 41 30 S 173 51 E
Réo **120** 12 28N 2 35 E
Réole, La **44** 44 35N 0 1W
Reotipur **95** 25 33N 83 45 E
Repalle **97** 16 2N 80 45 E
Répcelak **53** 47 24N 17 1 E
Repton **28** 52 50N 1 32W
Republic, Mich., U.S.A. **156** 46 25N 87 59W
Republic, Wash., U.S.A. **160** 48 38N 118 42W
Republican City **158** 40 9N 99 20W
Republican, R. **158** 40 0N 98 30W
Repulse B., Antarct. **13** 64 30 S 99 30 E
Repulse B., Austral. **133** 20 31 S 148 45 E
Repulse Bay **149** 66 30N 86 30W
Requena, Peru **174** 5 5 S 73 52W
Requena, Spain **59** 39 30N 1 4W
Resele **72** 63 20N 17 5 E
Resen **66** 41 5N 21 0 E
Reserve, Can. **153** 52 28N 102 39W
Reserve, U.S.A. **161** 33 50N 108 54W
Resht = Rasht **92** 37 20N 49 40 E
Resistencia **172** 27 30 S 59 0W
Reşiţa **66** 45 18N 21 53 E
Resko **54** 53 47N 15 25 E
Resolution I., Can. **149** 61 30N 65 0W
Resolution I., N.Z. **143** 45 40 S 166 40 E
Resolven **31** 51 43N 3 42W
Resplandes **170** 6 17 S 45 13W
Resplendor **171** 19 20 S 41 15W
Ressano Garcia **129** 25 25 S 32 0 E
Rest Downs **141** 31 48 S 146 21 E
Reston, Can. **153** 49 33N 101 6W
Reston, U.K. **35** 55 51N 2 11W
Restrepo **174** 4 15N 73 33W
Reszel **54** 54 4N 21 10 E
Retalhuleu **166** 14 33N 91 46W
Reteag **70** 47 10N 24 0 E
Retem, O. el **119** 33 40N 0 40 E
Retenue, Lac de **127** 11 0 S 27 0 E
Rethel **43** 49 30N 4 20 E
Rethem **48** 52 47N 9 25 E
Réthímnon **69** 35 15N 24 40 E
Réthímnon □ **69** 35 23N 24 28 E
Retie **47** 51 16N 5 5 E
Rétiers **42** 47 55N 1 25W
Retiro **172** 35 59 S 71 47W
Retortillo **56** 40 48N 6 21W
Rétság **53** 47 58N 19 10 E
Reuland **47** 50 12N 6 8 E
Réunion, Î. **11** 22 0 S 56 0 E
Reus **58** 41 10N 1 5 E
Reusel **47** 51 21N 5 9 E
Reuss, R. **51** 47 16N 8 24 E
Reuterstadt-Stavenhagen **48** 53 41N 12 54 E
Reutlingen **49** 48 28N 9 13 E
Reutte **52** 47 29N 10 42 E
Reuver **47** 51 17N 6 5 E
Revda **84** 56 48N 59 57 E
Revel **44** 43 28N 2 0 E
Revelganj **95** 25 50N 84 40 E
Revelstoke **152** 51 0N 118 0W
Revigny **43** 48 50N 5 0 E
Revilla Gigedo, Is. de **131** 18 40N 112 0W
Revillagigedo I. **152** 55 50N 131 20W
Revin **43** 49 55N 4 39 E
Revolyutsii, Pix **85** 38 31N 72 21 E
Revuè, R. **127** 19 30 S 33 35 E
Rewa **95** 24 33N 81 25 E
Rewari **94** 28 15N 76 40 E
Rex **147** 64 10N 149 20W
Rexburg **160** 43 45N 111 50W
Rey Bouba **117** 8 40N 14 15 E
Rey Malabo **121** 3 45N 8 50 E
Reyes, Pt. **163** 37 59N 123 2W
Reykjahlið **74** 65 40N 16 55W
Reykjanes **74** 63 48N 22 40W
Reykjavík **74** 64 10N 21 57 E
Reynolds **153** 49 40N 95 55W
Reynolds Ra. **136** 22 30 S 133 0 E
Reynosa **165** 26 5N 98 18W
Reza'iyeh **92** 37 40N 45 0 E
Rezã'iyeh, Daryãchech-ye **92** 37 30N 45 30 E
Rèzekne **80** 56 30N 27 17 E
Rezh **84** 57 23N 61 24 E
Rezina **70** 47 45N 29 0 E
Rezovo **67** 42 0N 28 0 E
Rgotina **67** 44 1N 22 18 E
Rhaeadr Ogwen **31** 53 8N 4 0W
Rharis, O. **119** 26 30N 5 4 E
Rhayader **31** 52 19N 3 30W
Rheden **46** 52 0N 6 3 E
Rheidol, R. **31** 52 25N 3 57W
Rhein **153** 51 25N 102 15W
Rhein, R. **48** 51 42N 6 20 E
Rheinbach **48** 50 38N 6 54 E
Rheine **48** 52 17N 7 25 E
Rheineck **51** 47 28N 9 31 E
Rheinfelden **50** 47 32N 7 47 E
Rheinland-Pfalz □ **49** 50 50N 7 0 E
Rheinsberg **48** 53 6N 12 52 E
Rheinwaldhorn **51** 46 30N 9 3 E
Rhenen **46** 51 58N 5 33 E
Rheydt **48** 51 10N 6 24 E
Rhin, R. **48** 51 42N 6 20 E
Rhinau **43** 48 19N 7 43 E
Rhine, R. = Rhein **47** 51 42N 6 20 E
Rhinebeck **162** 41 56N 73 55W
Rhinelander **158** 45 38N 89 29W
Rhino Camp **126** 3 0N 31 22 E
Rhisnes **47** 50 31N 4 48 E
Rhiw **31** 52 49N 4 37W
Rho **62** 45 31N 9 2 E
Rhode Island □ **162** 41 38N 71 37W
Rhodes = Ródhos **69** 36 15N 28 10 E
Rhodes' Tomb **127** 20 30 S 28 30 E
Rhodesia ■ **127** 20 0 S 30 0 E
Rhodope Mts. = Rhodopi Planina **67** 41 40N 24 20 E
Rhodopi Planina **67** 41 40N 24 20 E
Rhondda **31** 51 39N 3 30W
Rhône □ **45** 45 54N 4 35 E
Rhône, R. **45** 43 28N 4 42 E
Rhos-on-Sea **31** 53 18N 3 46W
Rhosllanerchrugog **31** 53 3N 3 4W
Rhossilli **31** 51 34N 4 18W
Rhu Coigach, C. **36** 58 6N 5 27W
Rhuddlan **31** 53 17N 3 28W
Rhum, I. **36** 57 0N 6 20W
Rhyl **31** 53 19N 3 29W
Rhymney **31** 51 45N 3 17W
Rhynie **37** 57 20N 2 50W
Ri-Aba **121** 3 28N 8 40 E
Riachão **170** 7 20 S 46 37W
Riachão do Jacuípe **171** 11 48 S 39 21W
Riacho de Santana **171** 13 37 S 42 57W
Rialma **171** 15 18 S 49 34W
Rialto **163** 34 6N 117 22W
Riang **98** 27 31N 92 56 E
Riaño **56** 42 59N 5 0W
Rians **45** 43 37N 5 44 E
Riansares, R. **58** 40 0N 3 0W
Riasi **95** 33 10N 74 50 E
Riau □ **102** 0 0 102 35 E
Riau, Kepulauan **102** 0 30N 104 20 E
Riaza **58** 41 18N 3 30W
Riaza, R. **58** 41 16N 3 29W
Riba de Saelices **58** 40 55N 2 18 E
Ribadavia **56** 42 17N 8 8W
Ribadeo **56** 43 35N 7 5W
Ribadesella **56** 43 30N 5 7W
Ribamar **170** 2 33 S 44 3W
Ribas **58** 42 19N 2 15 E
Ribat **125** 29 50N 60 55 E
Ribatejo □ **55** 39 15N 8 30W
Ribble, R. **32** 54 13N 2 20W
Ribe **73** 55 19N 8 44 E
Ribe Amt □ **73** 55 34N 8 30 E
Ribeauvillé **43** 48 10N 7 20 E
Ribécourt **43** 49 30N 2 55 E
Ribeira **56** 42 36N 8 58W
Ribeira do Pombal **170** 10 50 S 38 32W
Ribeirão Prêto **173** 21 10 S 47 50W
Ribeiro Gonçalves **170** 7 32 S 45 14W
Ribémont **43** 49 47N 3 27 E
Ribera **64** 37 30N 13 13 E
Ribérac **44** 45 15N 0 20 E
Riberalta **174** 11 0 S 66 0W
Ribnica **63** 45 45N 14 45 E
Ribnitz-Dangarten **48** 54 14N 12 24 E
Ričany **52** 50 0N 14 40 E
Riccall **33** 53 50N 1 4W
Riccarton **143** 43 32 S 172 37 E
Riccia **65** 41 30N 14 50 E
Riccione **63** 44 0N 12 39 E
Rice Lake **158** 45 30N 91 42W
Rich **118** 32 16N 4 30W
Rich Hill **159** 38 5N 94 22W
Richards B. **129** 28 48 S 32 6 E
Richards Deep **15** 25 0 S 73 0W
Richards L. **153** 59 10N 107 10W
Richardson Mts. **143** 44 49 S 168 34 E
Richardson, R. **153** 58 25N 111 14W
Richardton **158** 46 56N 102 22W
Riche, C. **137** 34 36 S 118 47 E
Richelieu **42** 47 0N 0 20 E
Richey **158** 47 42N 105 5W
Richfield, Idaho, U.S.A. **160** 43 2N 114 5W
Richfield, Utah, U.S.A. **161** 38 50N 112 0W
Richfield Springs **162** 42 51N 74 59W
Richibucto **151** 46 42N 64 54W
Richland, Ga., U.S.A. **157** 32 7N 84 40W
Richland, Oreg., U.S.A. **160** 44 49N 117 9W
Richland, Wash., U.S.A. **160** 46 15N 119 15W
Richland Center **158** 43 21N 90 22W
Richlands **156** 37 7N 81 49W
Richmond, N.S.W., Austral. **141** 33 35 S 150 42 E
Richmond, Queens., Austral. **138** 20 43 S 143 8 E
Richmond, N.Z. **143** 41 4 S 173 12 E
Richmond, S. Afr. **125** 29 51 S 30 18 E
Richmond, N. Yorks., U.K. **33** 54 24N 1 43W
Richmond, Surrey, U.K. **29** 51 28N 0 18W
Richmond, Calif., U.S.A. **163** 38 0N 122 21W
Richmond, Ind., U.S.A. **156** 39 50N 84 50W
Richmond, Ky., U.S.A. **156** 37 40N 84 20W
Richmond, Mo., U.S.A. **158** 39 15N 93 58W
Richmond, Tex., U.S.A. **159** 29 32N 95 42W
Richmond, Va., U.S.A. **162** 37 33N 77 27W
Richmond Gulf **150** 56 20N 75 50W
Richmond, Mt. **143** 41 32 S 173 22 E
Richmond, Ra. **139** 29 0 S 152 45 E
Richmond Ra. **143** 41 32 S 173 22 E
Richterswil **51** 47 13N 8 43 E
Richton **157** 31 23N 88 58W
Richwood **156** 38 17N 80 32W
Rickmansworth **29** 51 38N 0 28W
Ricla **58** 41 31N 1 24W
Riddarhyttan **72** 59 49N 15 33 E
Ridderkerk **46** 51 52N 4 35 E
Riddes **50** 46 11N 7 14 E
Ridgecrest **163** 35 38N 117 40W
Ridgedale **153** 53 0N 104 10W
Ridgefield **162** 41 17N 73 30W
Ridgeland **157** 32 30N 80 58W
Ridgelands **138** 23 16 S 150 17 E
Ridgetown **150** 42 26N 81 52W
Ridgewood **162** 40 59N 74 7W
Ridgway **156** 41 25N 78 43W
Riding Mt. Nat. Park **153** 50 50N 100 0W
Ridley Mt. **137** 33 12 S 122 7 E
Ridsdale **35** 55 9N 2 8W
Ried **52** 48 14N 13 30 E
Riehen **50** 47 35N 7 39 E
Riel **47** 51 31N 5 1 E
Rienne **47** 50 0N 4 53 E
Rienza, R. **63** 46 49N 11 47 E
Riesa **48** 51 19N 13 19 E
Riesi **65** 37 16N 14 4 E
Rietfontein **128** 26 44 S 20 1 E
Rieti **63** 42 23N 12 50 E
Rieupeyroux **44** 44 19N 2 12 E
Rievaulx **33** 54 16N 1 7W
Riez **45** 43 49N 6 6 E
Rifle **160** 39 40N 107 50W
Rifstangi **74** 66 32N 16 12W
Rift Valley **126** 0 20N 36 0 E
Rig Rig **117** 14 13N 14 25 E
Riga **80** 56 53N 24 8 E
Riga, G. of = Rīgas Jūras Līcis **80** 57 40N 23 45 E
Rīgas Jūras Līcis **80** 57 40N 23 45 E
Rigby **160** 43 41N 111 58W
Riggins **160** 45 29N 116 26W
Rignac **44** 44 25N 2 16 E
Rigo **138** 9 41 S 147 31 E
Rigolet **151** 54 10N 58 23W
Riihimäki **75** 60 45N 24 48 E
Riiser-Larsen halvøya **13** 68 0 S 35 0 E
Riishiri-Tō **112** 45 11N 141 15 E
Rijau **121** 11 8N 5 17 E
Rijeka Crnojevica **66** 42 24N 19 1 E
Rijeka (Fiume) **63** 45 20N 14 21 E
Rijen **47** 51 35N 4 55 E
Rijkevorsel **47** 51 21N 4 46 E
Rijn, R. **47** 52 5N 4 50 E
Rijnsberg **46** 52 11N 4 27 E
Rijsbergen **47** 51 31N 4 41 E
Rijssen **46** 52 19N 6 30 E
Rijswijk **46** 52 4N 4 22 E
Rike **123** 10 50N 39 53 E
Rikita **123** 5 5N 28 29 E
Rila **67** 42 7N 23 7 E
Rila Planina **66** 42 10N 23 30 E
Rillington **33** 54 10N 0 41W
Rilly **43** 49 11N 4 3 E
Rima **99** 28 35N 97 5 E
Rima, R. **121** 13 15N 5 15 E
Rimavská Sobota **53** 48 22N 20 2 E
Rimbey **152** 52 35N 114 15W
Rimbo **72** 59 44N 18 21 E
Rimforsa **73** 58 8N 15 42 E
Rimi **121** 12 58N 7 43 E
Rímini **63** 44 3N 12 33 E
Rîmna, R. **70** 45 36N 27 3 E
Rîmnicu Sůrat **70** 45 26N 27 3 E
Rîmnicu Vîlcece **70** 45 9N 24 21 E
Rimouski **151** 48 27N 68 30W
Rinca **103** 8 45 S 119 35 E
Rincón de Romos **164** 22 14N 102 18W
Rinconada **172** 22 26 S 66 10W
Ringarum **73** 58 21N 16 26 E
Ringe **73** 55 13N 10 28 E
Ringel Spitz **51** 46 53N 9 19 E
Ringford **35** 54 55N 4 3W
Ringim **121** 12 13N 9 10 E
Ringkøbing **73** 56 5N 8 15 E
Ringkøbing Amt □ **73** 56 15N 8 30 E
Ringling **160** 46 16N 110 56W
Ringmer **29** 50 53N 0 5 E
Ringmoen **71** 60 21N 10 6 E
Ringsaker **71** 60 54N 10 45 E
Ringsend **38** 55 2N 6 45W
Ringsjön L. **73** 55 55N 13 30 E
Ringsted **73** 55 25N 11 46 E
Ringvassøy **74** 69 36N 19 15 E
Ringville **39** 52 3N 7 37W
Ringwood **28** 5C 50N 1 48W
Rinía, I. **69** 37 23N 25 13 E
Rinjani **65** 8 20 S 116 30 E
Rinns, The, Reg. **34** 54 52N 5 3W
Rintein **48** 52 11N 9 3 E
Rio Arica **174** 1 35 S 75 30W
Rio Branco **174** 9 58 S 67 49W
Río Branco **173** 32 40 S 53 40W
Rio Brilhante **173** 21 48 S 54 33W
Río Chico **174** 10 19N 65 59W
Rio Claro, Brazil **173** 22 19 S 47 35W
Rio Claro, Trin **167** 10 20N 61 25W
Río Colorado **176** 39 0 S 64 0W
Río Cuarto **172** 33 10 S 64 25W
Rio das Pedras **129** 23 8 S 35 28 E
Rio de Contas **171** 13 36 S 41 48W
Rio de Janeiro **173** 23 0 S 43 12W
Rio de Janeiro □ **173** 22 50 S 43 0W
Rio del Rey **121** 4 42N 8 37 E
Rio do Prado **171** 16 35 S 40 34W
Rio do Sul **173** 27 95 S 49 37W
Río Gallegos **176** 51 35 S 69 15W
Río Grande **176** 53 50 S 67 45W
Rio Grande **173** 32 0 S 52 20W
Río Grande, Mexico **164** 23 50N 103 2W
Río Grande, Nic. **166** 12 54N 83 33W
Rio Grande City **159** 26 30N 91 55W
Río Grande del Norte, R. **154** 26 0N 97 0W
Río Grande do Norte □ **170** 5 40 S 36 0W
Rio Grande do Sul □ **173** 30 0 S 53 0W
Rio Grande, R. **161** 37 47N 106 15W
Río Hato **166** 8 22N 80 10W
Rio Lagartos **165** 21 36N 88 10W
Rio Largo **171** 9 28 S 35 50W
Rio Maior **57** 39 19N 8 57W
Rio Marina **62** 42 48N 10 25 E
Río Mulatos **174** 19 40 S 66 50W
Rio Muni □ = Mbini □ **124** 1 30N 10 0 E
Rio Negro **173** 26 0 S 50 0W
Río Oriente **166** 22 17N 81 13W
Rio Pardo, Minas Gerais, Brazil **171** 15 55 S 42 30W
Rio Pardo, Rio Grande do Sul, Brazil **173** 30 0 S 52 30W
Rio Prêto, Serra do **171** 13 29 S 39 55W
Rio, Punta del **59** 36 49N 2 24W
Rio Real **171** 11 28 S 37 56W
Río Segundo **172** 31 40 S 63 59W
Río Tercero **172** 32 15 S 64 8W
Rio Tinto, Brazil **170** 6 48 S 35 5W
Rio Tinto, Port. **56** 41 11N 8 34W
Rio Verde **170** 17 50 S 51 0W
Río Verde **165** 21 56N 99 59W
Rio Vista **163** 38 11N 121 44W
Ríobamba **174** 1 50 S 78 45W
Riohacha **174** 11 33N 72 55W
Rioja, La, Argent. **172** 29 20 S 67 0W
Rioja, La, Spain **58** 42 20N 2 20W
Rioja, La □ **172** 29 30 S 67 0W
Riom **44** 45 54N 3 7 E
Riom-és-Montagnes **44** 45 17N 2 39 E
Rion-des-Landes **44** 43 55N 0 56W
Rionegro **174** 6 9N 75 22W
Rionero in Vúlture **65** 40 55N 15 40 E
Ríos **56** 41 58N 7 16W
Riosucio, Caldas, Colomb. **174** 5 30N 75 40W
Riosucio, Choco, Colomb. **174** 7 27N 77 7W
Riou L. **153** 59 7N 106 25W
Riparia, Dora, R. **62** 45 7N 7 24 E
Ripatransone **63** 43 0N 13 45 E
Ripley, Derby, U.K. **33** 53 3N 1 24W
Ripley, N. Yorks, U.K. **33** 54 3N 1 34W
Ripley, U.S.A. **159** 35 43N 89 34W
Ripoll **58** 42 15N 2 13 E
Ripon, Calif., U.S.A. **163** 37 44N 121 7W
Ripon, Wis., U.S.A. **156** 43 51N 88 50W
Riposto **65** 37 44N 15 12 E
Risalpur **94** 34 3N 71 59 E
Risan **66** 42 32N 18 42 E
Risca **31** 51 36N 3 6W
Riscle **44** 43 39N 0 5W
Rishon Le Zion **90** 31 58N 34 48 E
Rishpon **90** 32 12N 34 49 E
Rishton **32** 53 46N 2 26W
Riska **71** 58 56N 5 52 E
Risle, R. **42** 48 55N 0 41 E
Rîsnov **70** 45 35N 25 27 E
Rison **159** 33 57N 92 11W
Risør **71** 58 43N 9 13 E
Ritchie's Archipelago **101** 12 5N 94 0 E
Riti **121** 7 57N 9 41 E
Ritzville **160** 47 10N 118 21W
Riu **98** 28 19N 95 3 E
Riva Bella Ouistreham **42** 49 17N 0 18W
Riva del Garda **62** 45 53N 10 50 E
Rivadavia, Buenos Aires, Argent. **172** 35 29 S 62 59W
Rivadavia, Mendoza, Argent. **172** 33 13 S 68 30W
Rivadavia, Salta, Argent. **172** 24 5 S 63 0W
Rivadavia, Chile **172** 29 50 S 70 35W
Rivarolo Canavese **62** 45 20N 7 42 E
Rivas **166** 11 30N 85 50W
Rive-de-Gier **45** 45 32N 4 37 E
River Cess **120** 5 30N 9 25W
Rivera **173** 31 0 S 55 50W
Riverchapel **39** 52 38N 6 14W
Riverdale **163** 36 26N 119 52W
Riverhead **162** 40 53N 72 40W
Riverhurst **153** 50 55N 106 50W
Riverina **136** 29 45 S 120 40 E
Riverina, dist. **133** 35 30 S 145 20 E
Rivers **153** 50 2N 100 14W
Rivers □ **121** 5 0N 6 30 E
Rivers Inlet **152** 51 40N 127 20W
Rivers, L. of the **153** 49 49N 105 44W
Riversdal **128** 34 7 S 21 15 E
Riverside, Calif., U.S.A. **163** 34 0N 117 22W
Riverside, Wyo., U.S.A. **160** 41 12N 106 57W
Riversleigh **138** 19 5 S 138 48 E
Riverton, Austral. **140** 34 10 S 138 46 E

* *Renamed Zimbabwe*

Riverton **Ross and Cromarty (□)**

Riverton, Can.	**153**	51 5N	97 0W
Riverton, N.Z.	**143**	46 21S	168 0E
Riverton, U.S.A.	**160**	43 1N	108 27W
Riverview	**108**	27 36S	152 51E
Rives	**45**	45 21N	5 31E
Rivesaltes	**44**	42 47N	2 50E
Riviera	**62**	44 0N	8 30E
Rivière à Pierre	**151**	46 57N	72 12W
Rivière-au-Renard	**151**	48 59N	64 23W
Rivière Bleue	**151**	47 26N	69 2W
Rivière-du-Loup	**151**	47 50N	69 30W
Rivière Pontecôte	**151**	49 57N	67 1W
Rivoli	**62**	45 3N	7 31E
Rivoli B.	**140**	37 32S	140 3E
Rivungo	**128**	16 9S	21 51E
Riwaka	**143**	41 5S	172 59E
Rixensart	**47**	50 43N	4 32E
Riyadh = Ar Riyad	**92**	24 41N	46 42E
Rize	**92**	41 0N	40 30E
Rizzuto, C.	**65**	38 54N	17 5E
Rjukan	**71**	59 54N	8 33E
Roa, Norway	**71**	60 17N	10 37E
Roa, Spain	**56**	41 41N	3 56W
Road Town	**167**	18 27N	64 37W
Road Weedon	**28**	52 14N	1 6W
Roade	**29**	52 10N	0 53W
Roadhead	**32**	55 4N	2 44W
Roag, L.	**36**	58 10N	6 55W
Roan Antelope	**127**	13 2S	28 19E
Roanne	**45**	46 3N	4 4E
Roanoke, Ala., U.S.A.	**157**	33 9N	85 23W
Roanoke, Va., U.S.A.	**156**	37 19N	79 55W
Roanoke I.	**157**	35 55N	75 40W
Roanoke, R.	**157**	36 15N	77 20W
Roanoke Rapids	**157**	36 36N	77 42W
Roaringwater B.	**39**	51 30N	9 30W
Roatán	**166**	16 18N	86 35W
Robbins I.	**138**	40 42S	145 0E
Robe, R., Austral.	**136**	21 42S	116 15E
Robe, R., Ireland	**38**	53 38N	9 10W
Röbel	**48**	53 24N	12 37E
Robert Lee	**159**	31 55N	100 26W
Robert Pt.	**137**	32 34S	115 40E
Roberton	**35**	55 24N	2 53W
Roberts	**160**	43 44N	112 8W
Robertsganj	**95**	24 44N	83 12E
Robertson, Austral.	**132**	34 37S	150 36E
Robertson, S. Afr.	**128**	33 46S	19 50E
Robertson I.	**13**	68 0S	75 0W
Robertson Ra.	**136**	23 15S	121 0E
Robertsport	**120**	6 45N	11 26W
Robertstown, Austral.	**140**	33 58S	139 5E
Robertstown, Ireland	**39**	53 16N	6 50W
Roberval	**150**	48 32N	72 15W
Robeson Kanal	**12**	82 0N	61 30W
Robesonia	**162**	40 21N	76 8W
Robin Hood's B.	**33**	54 26N	0 31W
Robinson Crusoe I.	**143**	33 50S	78 30W
Robinson, R.	**138**	16 3S	137 16E
Robinson Ranges	**137**	25 40S	118 0E
Robinson River	**138**	16 45S	136 58E
Robinvale	**140**	34 40S	142 45E
Robla, La	**56**	42 50N	5 41W
Roblin	**153**	51 14N	101 21W
Roboré	**174**	18 10S	59 45W
Robson, Mt.	**152**	53 10N	119 10W
Robstown	**159**	27 47N	97 40W
Roca, C. da	**57**	38 40N	9 31W
Roca Partida, I.	**164**	19 1N	112 2W
Roçadas	**128**	16 45S	15 0E
Rocas, I.	**170**	4 0S	34 1W
Rocca d'Aspidé	**65**	40 27N	15 10E
Rocca San Casciano	**63**	44 3N	11 30E
Roccalbegna	**63**	42 47N	11 30E
Roccastrada	**63**	43 0N	11 10E
Rocella Iónica	**65**	38 20N	16 24E
Rocester	**32**	52 56N	1 50W
Rocha	**173**	34 30S	54 25W
Rochdale	**32**	53 36N	2 10W
Roche	**30**	50 24N	4 50W
Roche-Bernard, La	**42**	47 31N	2 19W
Roche-Canillac, La	**44**	45 12N	1 57E
Roche-en-Ardenne, La	**47**	50 11N	5 35E
Roche, La, France	**45**	46 4N	6 19E
Roche, La, Switz.	**50**	46 42N	7 7E
Roche-sur-Yon, La	**42**	46 40N	1 25W
Rochechouart	**44**	45 50N	0 49E
Rochefort, Belg.	**47**	50 9N	5 12E
Rochefort, France	**44**	45 56N	0 57W
Rochefort-en-Terre	**42**	47 42N	2 22W
Rochefoucauld, La	**44**	45 44N	0 24E
Rochelle	**158**	41 55N	89 5W
Rochelle, La	**44**	46 10N	1 9W
Rocher River	**152**	61 23N	112 44W
Rocherath	**47**	50 26N	6 18E
Rocheservière	**42**	46 57N	1 30W
Rochester, Austral.	**140**	36 22S	144 41E
Rochester, Can.	**152**	54 22N	113 27W
Rochester, Kent, U.K.	**29**	51 22N	0 30E
Rochester, Northum., U.K.	**35**	55 16N	2 16W
Rochester, Ind., U.S.A.	**156**	41 5N	86 15W
Rochester, Minn., U.S.A.	**158**	44 1N	92 28W
Rochester, N.H., U.S.A.	**162**	43 19N	70 57W
Rochester, N.Y., U.S.A.	**156**	43 10N	77 40W
Rochford	**29**	51 36N	0 42E
Rochfortbridge	**38**	53 25N	7 19W
Rociana	**57**	37 19N	6 35W
Rociu	**70**	44 43N	25 2E
Rock Flat	**141**	36 21S	149 13E
Rock Hall	**162**	39 8N	76 14W
Rock Hill	**157**	34 55N	81 2W
Rock Island	**158**	41 30N	90 35W
Rock Lake	**158**	48 50N	99 13W
Rock, R.	**152**	60 7N	127 7W
Rock Rapids	**158**	43 25N	96 10W
Rock River	**160**	41 49N	106 0W
Rock Sound	**166**	24 54N	76 12W
Rock Sprs., Ariz., U.S.A.	**161**	34 2N	112 11W
Rock Sprs., Mont., U.S.A.	**160**	46 55N	106 11W
Rock Sprs., Tex., U.S.A.	**159**	30 2N	100 11W
Rock Sprs., Wyo., U.S.A.	**160**	41 40N	109 10W
Rock Valley	**158**	43 10N	96 17W
Rockall I.	**16**	57 37N	13 42W
Rockanje	**46**	51 52N	4 4E
Rockcliffe	**32**	54 58N	3 0W
Rockcorry	**38**	54 7N	7 0W
Rockdale	**159**	30 40N	97 0W
Rockefeller Plat.	**13**	84 0S	130 0W
Rockford	**158**	42 20N	89 0W
Rockglen	**153**	49 11N	105 57W
Rockhampton	**138**	23 22S	150 32E
Rockhampton Downs	**138**	18 57S	135 10E
Rockhill	**39**	52 25N	8 44W
Rockingham, Austral.	**137**	32 15S	115 38E
Rockingham, U.K.	**29**	52 32N	0 43W
Rockingham B.	**138**	18 5S	146 10E
Rockingham For.	**29**	52 28N	0 42W
Rockland, Idaho, U.S.A.	**160**	42 37N	112 57W
Rockland, Me., U.S.A.	**151**	44 0N	69 0W
Rockland, Mich., U.S.A.	**158**	46 40N	89 10W
Rockmart	**157**	34 1N	85 2W
Rockmills	**39**	52 13N	8 25W
Rockport, Mass., U.S.A.	**162**	42 39N	70 36W
Rockport, Mo., U.S.A.	**158**	40 26N	95 30W
Rockport, Tex., U.S.A.	**159**	28 2N	97 3W
Rockville, Conn., U.S.A.	**162**	41 51N	72 27W
Rockville, Md., U.S.A.	**162**	39 7N	77 10W
Rockwall	**159**	32 55N	96 30W
Rockwell City	**158**	42 20N	94 35W
Rockwood	**157**	35 52N	84 40W
Rocky Ford	**158**	38 7N	103 45W
Rocky Gully	**137**	34 30S	117 0E
Rocky Lane	**152**	58 31N	116 22W
Rocky Mount	**157**	35 55N	77 48W
Rocky Mountain House	**152**	52 22N	114 55W
Rocky Mts.	**152**	55 0N	121 0W
Rocky Pt.	**137**	33 30S	123 57E
Rockyford	**152**	51 14N	113 10W
Rocroi	**43**	49 55N	4 30E
Rod	**93**	28 10N	63 5E
Roda, La, Albacete, Spain	**59**	39 13N	2 15W
Roda, La, Sevilla, Spain	**57**	37 12N	4 46W
Rødberg	**71**	60 17N	8 56E
Rødby	**73**	54 41N	11 23E
Rødby Havn	**73**	54 39N	11 22E
Roddickton	**151**	50 51N	56 8W
Rødding	**73**	55 23N	9 3E
Rødekro	**73**	55 4N	9 20E
Rodel	**36**	57 45N	6 57W
Roden	**46**	53 8N	6 26E
Rødenes	**71**	59 35N	11 34E
Rodenkirchen	**48**	53 24N	8 26E
Roderick I.	**152**	52 38N	128 22W
Rodez	**44**	44 21N	2 33E
Rodholívas	**68**	40 55N	24 0E
Rodhópi □	**68**	41 10N	25 30E
Ródhos	**69**	36 15N	28 10E
Ródhos, I.	**69**	36 15N	28 10E
Roding R.	**29**	51 31N	0 7E
Rödjenäs	**73**	57 33N	14 50E
Rodna	**70**	47 25N	24 50E
Rodney, C.	**142**	36 17S	174 50E
Rodniki	**81**	57 7N	41 37E
Rodriguez, I.	**11**	20 0S	65 0E
Roe, R.	**38**	55 0N	6 56W
Roebling	**162**	40 7N	74 45W
Roebourne	**136**	20 44S	117 9E
Roebuck B.	**136**	18 5S	122 20E
Roebuck Plains P.O.	**136**	17 56S	122 28E
Roelofarendsveen	**46**	52 12N	4 38E
Roer, R.	**47**	51 12N	5 59E
Roermond	**47**	51 12N	6 0E
Roes Welcome Sd.	**149**	65 0N	87 0W
Roeselare	**47**	50 57N	3 7E
Rœulx	**47**	50 31N	4 7E
Rogachev	**80**	53 8N	30 5E
Rogagua, L.	**174**	14 0S	66 50W
Rogaland fylke □	**75**	59 12N	6 20E
Rogans Seat, Mt.	**32**	54 25N	2 10W
Rogaóica	**66**	44 4N	19 40E
Rogaška Slatina	**63**	46 15N	15 42E
Rogate	**29**	51 0N	0 51W
Rogatec	**63**	46 15N	21 46E
Rogatin	**80**	29 24N	24 36E
Rogers	**159**	36 20N	94 0W
Rogers City	**156**	45 25N	83 49W
Rogerson	**160**	42 10N	114 40W
Rogersville	**157**	36 27N	83 1W
Roggan River	**151**	54 25N	79 32W
Roggel	**47**	51 16N	5 56E
Roggeveldberge	**128**	32 10S	20 10E
Roggiano Gravina	**65**	39 37N	16 9E
Rogliano, France	**45**	42 57N	9 30E
Rogliano, Italy	**65**	39 11N	16 20E
Rogoaguado, L.	**174**	13 0S	65 30W
Rogowo	**54**	52 43N	17 38E
Rogozno	**54**	52 45N	16 59E
Rogue, R.	**160**	42 30N	124 0W
Rohan	**42**	48 4N	2 45W
Rohnert Park	**163**	38 16N	122 40W
Rohrbach	**43**	49 3N	7 15E
Rohri	**94**	27 45N	68 51E
Rohri Canal	**94**	26 15N	68 27E
Rohtak	**94**	28 55N	76 43E
Roi Et	**100**	15 56N	103 40E
Roisel	**43**	49 58N	3 6E
Rojas	**172**	34 10S	60 45W
Rojo, C., Mexico	**165**	21 33N	97 20W
Rojo, C., W. Indies	**147**	17 56N	67 11W
Rokan, R.	**102**	1 30N	100 50E
Rokeby	**138**	13 39S	142 40E
Rokiskis	**80**	55 55N	25 35E
Rokitnoye	**81**	50 57N	35 56E
Rokycany	**52**	49 43N	13 35E
Rolândia	**173**	23 5S	52 0W
Røldal	**71**	59 47N	6 50E
Rolde	**46**	52 59N	6 39E
Rolette	**158**	48 42N	99 50W
Rolfstorp	**73**	57 11N	12 27E
Rolla, Kansas, U.S.A.	**159**	37 10N	101 40W
Rolla, Missouri, U.S.A.	**159**	38 0N	91 42W
Rolla, N. Dak., U.S.A.	**158**	48 50N	99 36W
Rollag	**71**	60 2N	9 18E
Rollands Plains	**141**	31 17S	152 42E
Rolle	**50**	46 28N	6 20E
Rolleston, Austral.	**138**	24 28S	148 35E
Rolleston, N.Z.	**143**	43 35S	172 24E
Rollingstone	**138**	19 2S	146 24E
Rom	**123**	9 54N	32 16E
Roma, Austral.	**139**	26 32S	148 49E
Roma, Italy	**64**	41 54N	12 30E
Roma, Sweden	**73**	57 32N	18 26E
Roman, Bulg.	**67**	43 8N	23 54E
Roman, Rumania	**70**	46 57N	26 55E
Romana, La	**167**	18 27N	68 57W
Romang, I.	**103**	7 30S	127 20E
Rômani	**122**	30 59N	32 38E
Romanija planina	**66**	43 50N	18 45E
Romano, Cayo	**166**	22 0N	77 30W
Romano di Lombardía	**62**	45 32N	9 45E
Romanovka = Bessarabka	**82**	46 21N	28 51E
Romans	**62**	45 3N	5 3E
Romanshorn	**51**	47 33N	9 22E
Romanzof, C.	**147**	62 0N	165 50W
Rombo □	**126**	3 10S	37 30E
Rome, U.S.A.	**162**	41 51N	76 21W
Rome, Ga., U.S.A.	**157**	34 20N	85 0W
Rome, N.Y., U.S.A.	**162**	43 14N	75 29W
Rome = Roma	**64**	41 54N	12 30E
Romeleåsen	**73**	55 34N	13 33E
Romenây	**45**	46 30N	5 1E
Romeo	**151**	47 28N	57 4W
Romerike	**71**	60 7N	11 10E
Romilly	**43**	48 31N	3 44E
Romîni	**70**	44 59N	24 11E
Rommani	**118**	33 31N	6 40W
Romney	**156**	39 21N	78 45W
Romney Marsh	**29**	51 0N	1 0E
Romny	**80**	50 48N	33 28E
Rømø	**73**	55 10N	8 30E
Romodan	**80**	50 0N	33 15E
Romodanovo	**81**	54 26N	45 23E
Romont	**50**	46 42N	6 54E
Romorantin-Lanthenay	**43**	47 21N	1 45E
Romsdal, R.	**71**	62 25N	8 0E
Romsdalen	**74**	62 25N	7 50E
Romsey	**28**	51 0N	1 29W
Ron	**100**	17 53N	106 27E
Rona I.	**36**	57 33N	6 0W
Ronan	**160**	47 30N	114 11W
Ronas Hill	**36**	60 33N	1 25W
Ronay I.	**36**	57 30N	7 10W
Roncador Cay	**166**	13 40N	80 4W
Roncador, Serra do	**171**	12 30S	52 30W
Roncesvalles, Paso	**58**	43 1N	1 19W
Ronceverte	**156**	37 45N	80 28W
Ronciglione	**63**	42 18N	12 12E
Ronco, R.	**63**	44 26N	12 15E
Ronda	**57**	36 46N	5 12W
Ronda, Serrania de	**57**	36 44N	5 3W
Rondane	**71**	61 57N	9 50E
Rondón	**174**	6 17N	71 6W
Rondônia □	**174**	11 0S	63 0W
Rong, Koh	**101**	10 45N	103 15E
Ronge, La, Can.	**153**	55 5N	105 20W
Ronge, La, Sask., Can.	**153**	55 6N	105 17W
Ronge, Lac La	**153**	55 10N	105 0W
Rongotea	**142**	40 19S	175 25E
Rønne	**73**	55 6N	14 44E
Ronne Land	**13**	83 0S	70 0W
Ronneby	**73**	56 12N	15 17E
Ronsard, C.	**137**	24 46S	113 10E
Ronse	**47**	50 45N	3 35E
Roodepoort-Maraisburg	**125**	26 8S	27 52E
Roodeschool	**46**	53 25N	6 46E
Roof Butte	**161**	36 29N	109 5W
Roompot	**47**	51 37N	3 44E
Roorkee	**94**	29 52N	77 59E
Roosendaal	**47**	51 32N	4 29E
Roosevelt, Minn., U.S.A.	**158**	48 51N	95 2W
Roosevelt, Utah, U.S.A.	**160**	40 19N	110 1W
Roosevelt I.	**13**	79 0S	161 0W
Roosevelt, Mt.	**152**	58 20N	125 20W
Roosevelt Res.	**161**	33 46N	111 0W
Roosky	**38**	53 50N	7 55W
Ropczyce	**54**	50 4N	21 38E
Roper, R.	**138**	14 43S	135 27E
Ropesville	**159**	33 25N	102 10W
Ropsley	**33**	52 53N	0 31W
Roque Pérez	**172**	35 25S	59 24W
Roquefort	**44**	44 2N	0 20W
Roquefort-sur-Souizon	**44**	43 58N	2 59E
Roquemaure	**45**	44 3N	4 48E
Roquetas	**58**	40 50N	0 30E
Roquevaire	**45**	43 20N	5 36E
Roraima □	**174**	2 0N	61 30W
Roraima, Mt.	**174**	5 10N	60 40W
Rorketon	**153**	51 24N	99 35W
Røros	**71**	62 35N	11 23E
Rorschach	**51**	47 28N	9 30E
Rørvik	**74**	64 54N	11 15E
Rosa, U.S.A.	**160**	38 15N	122 16W
Rosa, Zambia	**127**	9 33S	31 15E
Rosa Brook	**137**	33 57S	115 10E
Rosa, C.	**119**	37 0N	8 16E
Rosa, Monte	**50**	45 57N	7 53E
Rosal	**56**	41 57N	8 51W
Rosal de la Frontera	**57**	37 59N	7 13W
Rosalia	**160**	47 26N	117 25W
Rosamund	**163**	34 52N	118 10W
Rosans	**45**	44 24N	5 29E
Rosario	**172**	33 0S	60 50W
Rosário, Maran., Brazil	**170**	3 0S	44 15W
Rosário, Rio Grande do Sul, Brazil	**176**	30 15S	55 0W
Rosario, Baja California, Mexico	**164**	30 0N	116 0W
Rosario, Durango, Mexico	**164**	26 30N	105 35W
Rosario, Sinaloa, Mexico	**164**	23 0N	106 0W
Rosario, Venez.	**174**	10 19N	72 19W
Rosario de la Frontera	**172**	25 50S	65 0W
Rosario de Lerma	**172**	24 59S	65 35W
Rosario del Tala	**172**	32 20S	59 10W
Rosário do Sul	**173**	30 15S	54 55W
Rosarito	**164**	28 38N	114 4W
Rosarno	**65**	38 29N	15 59E
Rosas	**58**	42 19N	3 10E
Rosas, G. de,	**55**	42 10N	3 15E
Rosburgh	**143**	45 33S	169 19E
Roscoe	**162**	41 56N	74 55W
Roscoff	**42**	48 44N	4 0W
Roscommon, Ireland	**38**	53 38N	8 11W
Roscommon, U.S.A.	**156**	44 27N	84 35W
Roscommon □	**38**	53 40N	8 15W
Roscrea	**39**	52 58N	7 50W
Rose Blanche	**151**	47 38N	58 45W
Rose Harbour	**152**	52 15N	131 10W
Rose Ness	**37**	58 52N	2 50W
Rose Pt.	**152**	54 11N	131 39W
Rose, R.	**138**	14 16S	135 45E
Rose Valley	**153**	52 19N	103 49W
Roseau, Domin.	**167**	15 20N	61 30W
Roseau, U.S.A.	**158**	48 51N	95 46W
Rosebery	**138**	41 46S	145 33E
Rosebud, Austral.	**141**	38 21S	144 54E
Rosebud, U.S.A.	**159**	31 5N	97 0W
Roseburg	**160**	43 10N	123 10W
Rosedale, Austral.	**138**	24 38S	151 53E
Rosedale, U.S.A.	**159**	33 51N	91 0W
Rosedale Abbey	**33**	54 22N	0 51W
Rosée	**47**	50 14N	4 41E
Rosegreen	**39**	52 28N	7 51W
Rosehall	**37**	57 59N	4 36W
Rosehearty	**37**	57 42N	2 8W
Rosemarkie	**37**	57 35N	4 8W
Rosemary	**152**	50 46N	112 5W
Rosenallis	**39**	53 10N	7 25W
Rosenberg	**159**	29 30N	95 48W
Rosendaël	**43**	51 3N	2 24E
Rosenheim	**49**	47 51N	12 9E
Roseto degli Abruzzi	**63**	42 40N	14 2E
Rosetown	**153**	51 35N	108 3W
Rosetta = Rashîd	**122**	31 21N	30 22E
Roseville	**160**	38 46N	121 17W
Rosewood, N.S.W., Austral.	**141**	35 38S	147 52E
Rosewood, N.T., Austral.	**136**	16 28S	128 58E
Rosewood, Queens., Austral.	**139**	27 38S	152 36E
Rosh Haniqra, Kefar	**90**	33 5N	35 5E
Rosh Pinna	**90**	32 58N	35 32E
Rosh Ze'ira	**90**	31 14N	35 15E
Roshage C.	**73**	57 7N	8 35E
Rosières	**43**	48 36N	6 20E
Rosignano Marittimo	**62**	43 23N	10 28E
Rosignol	**174**	6 15N	57 30W
Roşiori-de-Vede	**70**	44 9N	25 0E
Rositsa	**67**	43 57N	27 57E
Rositsa, R.	**67**	43 10N	25 30E
Roskeeragh Pt.	**38**	54 22N	8 40W
Roskhill	**36**	57 24N	6 31W
Roskilde	**73**	55 38N	12 3E
Roskilde Amt □	**73**	55 35N	12 5E
Roskilde Fjord	**73**	55 50N	12 2E
Roskill, Mt.	**142**	36 55S	174 45E
Roslavl	**80**	53 57N	32 55E
Roslyn	**141**	34 29S	149 37E
Rosmaninhal	**57**	39 44N	7 5W
Røsnæs	**73**	55 44N	10 55E
Rosneath	**34**	56 1N	4 49W
Rosolini	**65**	36 49N	14 58E
Rosporden	**42**	47 57N	3 50W
Ross, Austral.	**138**	42 2S	147 30E
Ross, N.Z.	**143**	42 53S	170 49E
Ross, U.K.	**28**	51 55N	2 34W
Ross and Cromarty (□)	**26**	57 43N	4 50W

Ross Dependency Sabang, O

Ross Dependency 13 70 0S 170 5W
Ross I. 13 77 30S 168 0E
Ross Ice Shelf 13 80 0S 180 0W
Ross L. 160 48 50N 121 0W
Ross on Wye 28 51 55N 2 34W
Ross River, Austral. 138 19 15S 146 51E
Ross River, Can. 147 62 30N 131 30W
Ross Sea 13 74 0S 178 0E
Rossa 51 46 23N 9 8E
Rossall Pt. 32 53 55N 3 2W
Rossan Pt. 38 54 42N 8 47W
Rossano Cálabro 65 39 36N 16 39E
Rossburn 153 50 40N 100 49W
Rosscahill 38 53 23N 9 15W
Rosscarbery 39 51 39N 9 1W
Rosscarbery B. 39 51 32N 9 0W
Rossel I. 138 11 30S 154 30E
Rosses B. 38 55 2N 8 30W
Rosses Point 38 54 17N 8 34W
Rosses, The 38 55 2N 8 20W
Rossignol, L., N.S., Can. 151 44 12N 65 0W
Rossignol, L., Qué., Can. 150 52 43N 73 40W
Rossing 128 22 30S 14 50E
Rossland 152 49 6N 117 50W
Rosslare 39 52 17N 6 23W
Rosslau 48 51 52N 12 15E
Rosslea 38 54 15N 7 11W
Rosso 120 16 40N 15 45W
Rossosh 83 50 15N 39 20E
Rossport 150 48 50N 87 30W
Rossum 46 51 48N 5 20E
Røssvatnet 74 65 45N 14 5E
Rossville 138 15 48S 145 15E
Rosthern 153 52 40N 106 20W
Rostock 48 54 4N 12 9E
Rostock □ 48 54 10N 12 30E
Rostov, Don, U.S.S.R. 83 47 15N 39 45E
Rostov, Moskva, U.S.S.R. 81 57 14N 39 25E
Rostrenen 42 48 14N 3 21W
Rostrevor 38 54 7N 6 12W
Roswell 159 33 26N 104 32W
Rosyth 35 56 2N 3 26W
Rota 57 36 37N 6 20W
Rotälven 72 61 30N 14 10E
Rotan 159 32 52N 100 30W
Rotem 47 51 3N 5 45E
Rotenburg 48 53 6N 9 24E
Rothbury 35 55 19N 1 55W
Rothbury Forest 35 55 19N 1 50W
Rothenburg 51 47 6N 8 16E
Rothenburg ob der Tauber 49 49 21N 10 11E
Rother, R. 29 50 59N 0 40W
Rotherham 33 53 26N 1 21W
Rothes 37 57 31N 3 12W
Rothesay, Can. 151 45 23N 66 0W
Rothesay, U.K. 34 55 50N 5 3W
Rothhaar G., mts. 50 51 6N 8 10E
Rothienorman 37 57 24N 2 28W
Rothrist 50 47 18N 8 54E
Rothwell, Northants, U.K. 29 52 25N 0 48W
Rothwell, W. Yorks., U.K. 33 53 46N 1 29W
Roti, I. 103 10 50S 123 0E
Rotkop 128 26 44S 15 27E
Roto 141 33 0S 145 30E
Roto Aira L. 142 39 3S 175 55E
Rotoehu L. 142 38 1S 176 32E
Rotoiti L. 142 41 51S 172 49E
Rotoma L. 142 38 2S 176 35E
Rotondella 65 40 10N 16 30E
Rotoroa Lake 143 41 55S 172 39E
Rotorua 142 38 9S 176 16E
Rotorua, L. 142 38 5S 176 18E
Rotselaar 47 50 57N 4 42E
Rottal 37 56 48N 3 1W
Rotten, R. 50 46 18N 7 36E
Rottenburg 49 48 28N 8 56E
Rottenmann 52 47 31N 14 22E
Rotterdam 46 51 55N 4 30E
Rottingdean 29 50 48N 0 3W
Rottnest I. 137 32 0S 115 27E
Rottumeroog 46 53 33N 6 34E
Rottweil 49 48 9N 8 38E
Rotuma, I. 130 12 25S 177 5E
Roubaix 43 50 40N 3 10E
Roudnice 52 50 25N 14 15E
Rouen 42 49 27N 1 4E
Rouergue 44 44 20N 2 20E
Rough, gasfield 19 53 50N 0 27E
Rough Pt. 39 52 19N 10 0W
Rough Ridge 143 45 10S 169 55E
Rouillac 44 45 47N 0 4W
Rouleau 153 50 10N 104 56W
Round Mt. 139 30 26S 152 16E
Round Mountain 163 38 46N 117 3W
Roundstone 38 53 24N 9 55W
Roundup 160 46 25N 108 35W
Roundwood 39 53 4N 6 14W
Rourkela 95 22 14N 84 50E
Rousay, I. 37 59 10N 3 2W
Rousky 38 54 44N 7 10E
Rousse, L'Île 45 43 27N 8 57E
Roussillon 45 45 24N 4 49E
Rouveen 46 52 37N 6 11E
Rouxville 128 30 11S 26 50E
Rouyn 150 48 20N 79 0W
Rovaniemi 74 66 29N 25 41E
Rovato 62 45 34N 10 0E
Rovenki 83 48 5N 39 27E
Rovereto 62 45 53N 11 3E
Rovigo 63 45 4N 11 48E
Rovinari 70 46 56N 23 10E
Rovinj 63 45 18N 13 40E
Rovira 174 4 15N 75 20W
Rovno 80 50 40N 26 10E
Rovnoye 81 50 52N 46 3E
Rovuma, R. 127 11 30S 36 10E
Rowanburn 35 55 5N 2 54W
Rowena 139 29 48S 148 55E
Rowes 141 37 0S 149 6E
Rowley Shoals 136 17 40S 119 20E
Rowood 161 32 18N 112 54W
Rowrah 32 54 34N 3 26W
Roxa 120 11 15N 15 45W
Roxas 103 11 36N 122 49E
Roxboro 157 36 24N 78 59W
Roxborough Downs 138 22 20S 138 45E
Roxburgh, N.Z. 143 45 33S 169 19E
Roxburgh, U.K. 35 55 34N 2 30W
Roxburgh (□) 26 55 30N 2 30W
Roxby 33 53 38N 0 37W
Roxen 73 58 30N 15 40E
Roy 160 47 17N 109 0W
Roy Hill 136 22 37S 119 58E
Roy, Le 159 38 8N 95 35W
Roya, Peña 58 40 25N 0 40W
Royal Canal 38 53 29N 7 0W
Royal Oak 156 42 30N 83 5W
Royalla 141 35 30S 149 9E
Royan 44 45 37N 1 2W
Roybridge 37 56 53N 4 50W
Roye 43 47 40N 6 31E
Røyken 71 59 45N 10 23E
Royston 29 52 3N 0 1W
Royton 32 53 34N 2 7W
Rozaj 66 42 50N 20 15E
Rozan 54 52 52N 21 25E
Rozdol 80 49 30N 24 1E
Rozier, Le 44 44 13N 3 12E
Roznava 53 48 37N 20 35E
Rozoy 43 48 40N 2 56E
Rozoy-sur-Serre 43 49 40N 4 8E
Rozwadów 54 50 37N 22 2E
Rrësheni 68 41 47N 19 49E
Rtanj, mt. 66 43 45N 21 50W
Rtem, Oued el 119 33 40N 5 34E
Rtishchevo 81 52 35N 43 50E
Rúa 56 42 24N 7 6W
Ruacaná 128 17 20S 14 12E
Ruahine Ra. 142 39 55S 176 2E
Ruamahanga, R. 142 41 24S 175 8E
Ruapehu 142 39 17S 175 35E
Ruapuke I. 143 46 46S 168 31E
Ruatoria 142 37 55S 178 20E
Ruãus, W. 119 30 14N 15 0E
Ruawai 142 36 15S 173 59E
Rub 'al Khali 91 21 0N 51 0E
Rubeho, mts. 126 6 50S 36 25E
Rubery 28 52 24N 1 59W
Rubezhnoye 82 49 6N 38 25E
Rubha Ardvule C. 36 57 17N 7 32W
Rubha Hunish, C. 36 57 42N 6 20W
Rubh'an Dunain, C. 36 57 10N 6 20W
Rubiataba 171 15 8S 49 48W
Rubicone, R. 63 44 0N 12 20E
Rubim 171 16 23S 40 32W
Rubinéia 171 20 13S 51 2W
Rubino 120 6 4N 4 18W
Rubio 174 7 43N 72 22W
Rubona 126 0 29N 30 9E
Rubtsovsk 76 51 30N 80 50E
Ruby 147 64 40N 155 35W
Ruby L. 160 40 10N 115 28W
Ruby Mts. 160 40 30N 115 30W
Rubyvale 138 23 25S 147 45E
Rucava 80 56 9N 20 32E
Ruciane-Nida 54 53 40N 21 32E
RûcûSdia 66 44 59N 21 36E
Rud 71 60 1N 10 1E
Ruda 73 57 6N 16 7E
Ruda Slaska 53 50 16N 18 50E
Rudall 140 33 43S 136 17E
Rudbar 93 30 0N 62 30E
Ruden, I. 48 54 13N 13 47E
Rüdersdorf 48 52 28N 13 48E
Rudewa 127 10 7S 34 47E
Rudgwick 29 51 7N 0 54W
Rudkøbing 73 54 56N 10 41E
Rudna 54 51 30N 16 17E
Rudnichnyy 84 59 38N 52 26E
Rudnik, Bulg. 67 42 36N 27 30E
Rudnik, Yugo. 67 44 7N 20 35E
Rudnik, mt. 67 44 7N 20 35E
Rudnogorsk 77 57 15N 103 42E
Rudnya 80 54 55N 31 13E
Rudnyy 84 52 57N 63 7E
Rudo 66 43 41N 19 23E
Rudolstadt 48 50 44N 11 20E
Rudozem 67 41 29N 24 51E
Rudston 33 54 6N 0 19W
Rûducaneni 70 46 58N 27 54E
Rûdûuţi 70 47 50N 25 59E
Rudyard 156 46 14N 84 35E
Rue 43 50 15N 1 40E
Ruelle 44 45 41N 0 14E
Rufa'a 123 14 44N 33 32E
Ruffec Charente 44 46 2N 0 12E
Rufi 123 5 58N 30 18E
Rufiji □ 126 8 0S 38 30E
Rufiji, R. 124 7 50S 38 15E
Rufino 172 34 20S 62 50W
Rufisque 120 14 40N 17 15W
Rufunsa 127 15 4S 29 34E
Rugby, U.K. 28 52 23N 1 16W
Rugby, U.S.A. 158 48 21N 100 0W
Rugeley 28 52 47N 1 56W
Rügen, I. 48 54 22N 13 25E
Rugezi 126 2 6S 33 18E
Rugles 42 48 50N 0 40E
Ruhāma 90 31 31N 34 43E
Ruhea 98 26 10N 88 25E
Ruhengeri 126 1 30S 29 36E
Ruhla 48 50 53N 10 21E
Ruhland 48 51 27N 13 52E
Ruhr, R. 48 51 25N 7 15E
Ruhuhu, R. 127 10 15S 34 55E
Rui Barbosa 171 12 18S 40 27W
Ruidosa 159 29 59N 104 39W
Ruidoso 161 33 19N 105 39W
Ruinen 46 52 46N 6 21E
Ruinen A Kanaal 46 52 54N 7 8E
Ruinerwold 46 52 44N 6 15E
Ruj, mt. 66 42 52N 22 42E
Rujen, mt. 66 42 9N 22 30E
Ruk 94 27 50N 68 42E
Rukwa □, Tanz. 126 7 0S 31 30E
Rukwa □, Tanz. 126 7 0S 31 30E
Rukwa L. 126 7 50S 32 10E
Rulhieres, C. 136 13 56S 127 22E
Rulles 47 49 43N 5 32E
Rully 167 46 52N 4 44E
Rum Jungle 136 13 0S 130 59E
Ruma 66 45 8N 19 50E
Rumah 92 25 35N 47 10E
Rumania ■ 61 46 0N 25 0E
Rumbalara 138 25 20S 134 29E
Rumbek 123 6 54N 29 37E
Rumbeke 47 50 56N 3 10E
Rumburk 52 50 57N 14 32E
Rumelange 47 49 27N 6 2E
Rumford 156 44 30N 70 30W
Rumia 54 54 37N 18 25E
Rumilly 45 45 53N 5 56E
Rumney 31 51 32N 3 7W
Rumoi 112 43 56N 141 39W
Rumonge 126 3 59S 29 26E
Rumsey 152 51 51N 112 48W
Rumson 162 40 23N 74 0W
Rumula 138 16 35S 145 20E
Rumuruti 126 0 17N 36 32E
Runabay Hd. 38 55 10N 6 2W
Runanga 143 42 25S 171 15E
Runaway, C. 142 37 32S 178 2E
Runcorn, Austral. 108 27 36S 153 4E
Runcorn, U.K. 32 53 20N 2 44W
Rungwa 126 6 55S 33 32E
Rungwa, R. 126 7 15S 33 10E
Rungwe 127 9 11S 33 32E
Rungwe □ 127 9 25S 33 32E
Runka 121 12 28N 7 20E
Runn 72 60 30N 15 40E
Rupa 98 27 15N 92 30E
Rupar 94 31 2N 76 38E
Rupat, I. 102 1 45N 101 40E
Rupea 61 46 2N 25 13E
Rupert House = Fort Rupert 150 51 30N 78 40W
Rupert, R. 150 51 29N 78 45W
Rupsa 98 21 44N 87 20E
Rupununi, R. 175 3 30N 59 30W
Ruquka Gie La 99 31 35N 97 55E
Rurrenabaque 174 14 30S 67 32W
Rus, R. 58 39 30N 2 30W
Rusambo 127 16 30S 32 4E
Rusape 125 18 35S 32 8E
Ruschuk = Ruse 67 43 48N 25 59E
Ruse 67 43 48N 25 59E
Rusetu 70 44 57N 27 14E
Rush 38 53 31N 6 7W
Rushden 29 52 17N 0 37W
Rushford 158 43 48N 91 46W
Rushville, Ill., U.S.A. 158 40 6N 90 35W
Rushville, Ind., U.S.A. 156 39 38N 85 22W
Rushville, Nebr., U.S.A. 158 42 43N 102 35W
Rushworth 141 36 32S 145 1E
Rusken 73 57 15N 14 20E
Ruskington 33 53 5N 0 23W
Russas 171 4 56S 38 2W
Russell, Can. 153 50 50N 101 20W
Russell, N.Z. 142 35 16S 174 10E
Russell, U.S.A. 158 38 56N 98 55W
Russell L., Man., Can. 153 56 15N 101 30W
Russell L., N.W.T., Can. 152 63 5N 115 44W
Russellkonda 96 19 57N 84 42E
Russellville, Ala., U.S.A. 157 34 30N 87 44W
Russellville, Ark., U.S.A. 159 35 15N 93 0W
Russellville, Ky., U.S.A. 157 36 50N 86 50W
Russi 63 44 21N 12 1E
Russian Mission 147 61 45N 161 25W
Russian S.F.S.R. □ 77 62 0N 105 0E
Russkoye Ustie 12 71 0N 149 0E
Rust 53 47 49N 16 42E
Rustam 94 34 25N 72 13E
Rustam Shahr 94 26 58N 66 6E
Rustavi 83 40 45N 44 30E
Rustenburg 128 25 41S 27 14E
Ruston 159 32 30N 92 40W
Ruswil 50 47 5N 8 8E
Rutana 126 3 55S 30 0E
Rutba 92 33 4N 40 15E
Rute 57 37 19N 4 29W
Ruteng 103 8 26S 120 30E
Ruth 160 39 15N 115 1W
Ruth, oilfield 19 55 33N 4 55E
Rutherglen, Austral. 141 36 5S 146 29E
Rutherglen, U.K. 34 55 50N 4 11W
Ruthin 31 53 7N 3 20W
Ruthven 37 57 4N 4 2W
Ruthwell 35 55 0N 3 24W
Rüti 51 47 16N 8 51E
Rutigliano 65 41 1N 17 0E
Rutland 162 43 38N 73 0W
Rutland (□) 26 52 38N 0 40W
Rutland I. 101 11 25N 92 40E
Rutland Plains 138 15 38S 141 49E
Rutledge L. 153 61 33N 110 47W
Rutledge, R. 153 61 4N 112 0W
Rutshuru 126 1 13S 29 25E
Ruurlo 46 52 5N 6 24E
Ruvo di Púglia 65 41 7N 16 27E
Ruvu 126 6 49S 38 43E
Ruvu, R. 126 7 25S 38 15E
Ruvuma □ 127 10 20S 36 0E
Ruvuma, R. 127 11 30S 36 10E
Ruwaidha 92 23 40N 44 40E
Ruwandiz 92 36 40N 44 32E
Ruwenzori Mts. 126 0 30N 29 55E
Ruwenzori, mt. 126 0 30N 29 55E
Ruyigi 126 3 29S 30 15E
Ruzayevka 81 54 10N 45 0E
Ruzhevo Konare 67 42 23N 24 46E
Ruzomberok 53 49 3N 19 17E
Rwanda ■ 126 2 0S 30 0E
Ryaberg 73 56 47N 13 15E
Ryakhovo 67 44 0N 26 18E
Ryan, L. 34 55 0N 5 2W
Ryazan 81 54 50N 39 40E
Ryazhsk 81 53 45N 40 3E
Rybache 76 46 40N 81 20E
Rybachi Poluostrov 78 69 43N 32 0E
Rybachye 85 42 26N 76 12E
Rybinsk (Shcherbakov) 81 58 5N 38 50E
Rybinsk Vdkhr. 81 58 30N 38 0E
Rybnik 54 50 6N 18 32E
Rybnitsa 82 47 45N 29 0E
Rychwał 54 52 4N 18 10E
Ryd 73 56 27N 14 42E
Rydal 32 54 28N 2 59W
Ryde 28 50 44N 1 9W
Rydö 73 56 58N 13 10E
Rydsnäs 73 57 47N 15 9E
Rydułtowy 54 50 4N 18 23E
Rydzyna 54 51 47N 16 39E
Rye, Denmark 73 56 5N 9 45E
Rye, U.K. 29 50 57N 0 46E
Rye Patch Res. 160 40 45N 118 20W
Rye, R. 33 54 12N 0 53W
Ryegate 160 46 21N 109 27W
Ryhope 35 54 52N 1 22W
Rylsk 80 51 30N 34 51E
Rylstone 141 32 46S 149 58E
Rymanów 54 49 35N 21 51E
Ryn 54 53 57N 21 34E
Ryningsnäs 73 57 17N 15 58E
Ryōhaku-Sanchi 111 36 0N 136 49E
Rypin 54 53 3N 19 32E
Ryton, Tyne & Wear, U.K. 35 54 58N 1 44W
Ryton, Warwick, U.K. 28 52 23N 1 25W
Ryūgasaki 111 35 54N 140 11E
Ryūkyū Is. = Nansei-Shotō 112 26 0N 128 0E
Rzepin 54 52 20N 14 49E
Rzeszów 54 50 5N 21 58E
Rzeszów □ 54 50 0N 22 0E
Rzhev 80 56 20N 34 20E

S

s'-Hertogenbosch 47 51 42N 5 17E
Sa 100 18 34N 100 45E
Sa. da Canastra 125 19 30S 46 5W
Sa Dec 101 10 20N 105 46E
Sa-Koi 98 19 54N 97 3E
Sa'ad (Muharraga) 90 31 28N 34 33E
Sa'ādatabād 93 30 10N 53 5E
Saale, R. 48 51 25N 11 56E
Saaler Bodden 48 54 20N 12 25E
Saalfelden 70 47 26N 12 51E
Saalfield 48 50 39N 11 21E
Saane, R. 50 46 23N 7 18E
Saanen 50 46 29N 7 15E
Saar (Sarre), □ 43 49 20N 6 45E
Saarbrücken 49 49 15N 6 58E
Saarburg 49 49 36N 6 32E
Saaremaa 80 58 30N 22 30E
Saariselkä 74 68 16N 28 15E
Saarland □ 131 49 20N 6 45E
Saarlouis 49 49 19N 6 45E
Saas Fee 50 46 7N 7 56E
Saas-Grund 50 46 7N 7 57E
Saba I. 167 17 30N 63 10W
Sabac 66 44 48N 19 42E
Sabadell 58 41 28N 2 7E
Sabae 111 35 57N 136 11E
Sabagalel 102 1 36S 98 40E
Sabah □ 102 6 0N 117 0E
Sabak 100 3 46N 100 58E
Sábana de la Mar 167 19 7N 69 40W
Sábanalarga 174 10 38N 74 55W
Sabang, O. 102 5 50N 95 15E

Sabará **St. Lawrence**

Sabará 171 19 55 S 43 55W
Sabarania 103 2 5 S 138 18 E
Sabari, R. 96 18 0N 81 25 E
Sabastiya 90 32 17N 35 12 E
Sabaudia 64 41 17N 13 2 E
Sabderat 123 15 26N 36 42 E
Sabhah 119 27 9N 14 29 E
Sabie 129 25 4 S 30 48 E
Sabinal, Mexico 164 30 50N 107 25W
Sabinal, U.S.A. 159 29 20N 99 27W
Sabinal, Punta del 59 36 43N 2 44W
Sabinas 164 27 50N 101 10W
Sabinas Hidalgo 164 26 40N 100 10W
Sabinas, R. 164 27 37N 100 42W
Sabine 159 29 42N 93 54W
Sabine, R. 159 31 30N 93 35W
Sabinópolis 171 18 40 S 43 6W
Sabinov 53 49 6N 21 5 E
Sabirabad 83 40 0N 48 30 E
Sabkhat Tawurgha 119 31 48N 15 30 E
Sablayan 103 12 5N 120 50 E
Sable 42 47 50N 0 21W
Sable, C., Can. 151 43 29N 65 38W
Sable, C., U.S.A. 166 25 5N 81 0W
Sable I. 151 44 0N 60 0W
Sablé-sur-Sarthe 42 47 50N 0 20W
Sables-D'Olonne, Les 44 46 30N 1 45W
Saboeiro 170 6 32 S 39 54W
Sabor, R. 56 41 16N 7 10W
Sabou 120 12 1N 2 28W
Sabrâtah 119 32 47N 12 29 E
Sabrina Coast 13 67 0 S 120 0 E
Sabugal 56 40 20N 7 5W
Sabzevar 93 36 15N 57 40 E
Sabzvaran 93 28 45N 57 50 E
Sac City 158 42 26N 95 0W
Sacandaga Res. 162 43 6N 74 16W
Sacedón 58 40 29N 2 41W
Sachigo, L. 150 53 50N 92 12W
Sachigo, R. 150 55 6N 88 58W
Sachinbulako 106 43 5N 111 47 E
Sachkhere 83 42 25N 43 28 E
Sachseln 51 46 52N 8 15 E
Sacile 63 45 58N 16 7 E
Säckingen 49 47 34N 7 56 E
Saco, Me., U.S.A. 162 43 30N 70 27W
Saco, Mont., U.S.A. 160 48 28N 107 19W
Sacquoy Hd. 37 59 12N 3 5W
Sacramento, Brazil 171 19 53 S 47 27W
Sacramento, U.S.A. 163 38 39N 121 30 E
Sacramento Mts. 161 32 30N 105 30W
Sacramento, R. 163 38 3N 121 56W
Sacratif, Cabo 59 36 42N 3 28W
Sacriston 33 54 49N 1 38W
Sada 56 43 22N 8 15W
Sada-Misaki-Hantō 110 33 22N 132 1 E
Sadaba 58 2 19N 1 12W
Sa'dani 124 5 58 S 38 35 E
Sadao 101 6 38N 100 26 E
Sadasivpet 96 17 38N 77 50 E
Sadberge 33 54 32N 1 30W
Sadd el Aali 122 24 5N 32 54 E
Saddell 34 55 31N 5 30W
Saddle, Hd. 38 54 0N 10 10W
Saddle, The 36 57 10N 5 27W
Sade 121 11 22N 10 45 E
Sadiba 128 18 53 S 23 1 E
Sadimi 127 9 25 S 23 32 E
Sado 112 38 0N 138 25 E
Sado, R. 57 38 10N 8 22W
Sadon, Burma 99 25 28N 98 0 E
Sadon, U.S.S.R. 83 42 52N 43 58 E
Sadri 94 24 28N 74 30 E
Saduya 98 27 50N 95 40 E
Sæby 73 57 21N 10 30 E
Saelices 58 39 55N 2 49W
Safâga 122 26 42N 34 0 E
Safaha 122 26 25N 39 0 E
Safaniya 92 28 5N 48 42 E
Safárikovo 53 48 25N 20 20 E
Safed Koh, Mts. 94 34 15N 64 0 E
Safford 61 32 54N 109 52W
Saffron Walden 29 52 2N 0 15 E
Safi, Jordan 90 31 2N 35 28 E
Safi, Moroc. 118 32 18N 9 14W
Safiah 42 31 27N 34 46 E
Safonovo 80 65 40N 47 50 E
Safranbolu 82 41 15N 32 34 E
Sag Harbor 162 40 59N 72 17W
Sag Sag 135 5 32 S 148 23 E
Saga, Indon. 103 2 40 S 132 55 E
Saga, Kōchi, Japan 110 33 5N 133 6 E
Saga, Saga, Japan 110 33 15N 130 16 E
Saga-ken □ 110 33 15N 130 20 E
Sagåg 71 59 46N 5 25 E
Sagaing 98 23 30N 95 30 E
Sagaing □ 98 22 0N 95 30 E
Sagala 120 14 9N 6 38W
Sagami-Nada 111 34 58N 139 23 E
Sagami-Wan 111 35 15N 139 25 E
Sagamihara 111 35 33N 139 25 E
Saganoseki 110 33 15N 131 53 E
Sagar 93 23 50N 78 50 E
Sagara, India 97 14 14N 75 6 E
Sagara, Japan 111 34 41N 138 12 E
Sagara, L. 126 5 20 S 31 0 E
Sagawa 110 33 28N 133 11 E
Sågen 72 60 17N 14 10 E
Sagil 105 50 20N 91 40 E
Saginaw 156 43 26N 83 55W
Saginaw B. 150 43 50N 83 40W
Sagleipie 45 45 25N 7 0 E
Saglouc (Sugluk) 149 62 30N 74 15W
Sagone 45 42 7N 8 42 E
Sagone, G. de 45 42 4N 8 40 E
Sagori 107 35 25N 126 49 E
Sagra, La, Mt. 59 38 0N 2 35W
Sagres 57 37 0N 8 58W
Sagu 98 20 13N 94 46 E
Sagua la Grande 166 22 50N 80 10W
Saguache 161 38 10N 106 4W
Saguenay, R. 151 48 22N 71 0W
Sagunto 58 39 42N 0 18W
Sahaba 122 18 57N 30 25 E
Sahagún, Colomb. 174 8 57N 75 27W
Sahagún, Spain 56 42 18N 5 2W
Saham 90 32 42N 35 46 E
Sahara 118 23 0N 5 0W
Saharanpur 94 29 58N 77 33 E
Saharien Atlas 118 34 9N 3 29 E
Sahasinaka 129 21 49 S 47 49 E
Sahaswan 95 28 5N 78 45 E
Sahel, Canal du 120 14 20N 6 0W
Sahibganj 95 25 12N 87 55 E
Sahiwal 94 30 45N 73 8 E
Sahl Arraba 90 37 26N 35 12 E
Sahtaneh, R. 152 59 2N 122 28W
Sahuaripa 164 29 30N 109 0W
Sahuarita 161 31 58N 110 59W
Sahuayo 164 20 4N 102 43W
Sahy 53 48 4N 18 55 E
Sai Buri 101 6 43N 101 39 E
Saibai I. 135 9 25 S 142 40 E
Sa'id Bundas 117 8 24N 24 48 E
Saïda 118 34 50N 0 11 E
Sa'idabad 93 29 30N 55 45 E
Saidapet 97 13 0N 80 15 E
Saidor 135 5 40 S 146 29 E
Saidu 95 34 50N 72 15 E
Säle 72 59 8N 12 55 E
Saighan 93 35 10N 67 55 E
Saignelégier 50 47 15N 7 0 E
Saignes 44 45 20N 2 31 E
Saigō 110 36 12N 133 20 E
Saigon = Phanh Bho Ho Chi Minh 101 10 58N 106 40 E
Saih-al-Malih 93 23 37N 58 31 E
Saihut 91 15 12N 51 10 E
Saijō, Ehima, Japan 110 33 55N 133 11 E
Saijō, Hiroshima, Japan 110 34 25N 132 45 E
Saikhoa Ghat 99 27 50N 95 40 E
Saiki 110 32 58N 131 57 E
Saillans 45 44 42N 5 12 E
Sailolof 103 1 7 S 130 46 E
Saima 107 40 59N 124 15 E
Saimaa, L. 78 61 15N 28 15 E
St. Abbs 35 55 54N 2 7W
St. Abb's Head 35 55 55N 2 10W
St. Aegyd 52 47 52N 15 33 E
St. Affrique 44 43 57N 2 53 E
St. Agnes 30 50 18N 5 13W
St. Agnes Hd. 30 50 19N 5 14W
St. Agnes I. 30 49 53N 6 20W
St.-Agrève 45 45 0N 4 23 E
St.-Aignan 42 47 16N 1 22 E
St. Albans, Austral. 138 24 43 S 139 56 E
St. Albans, Can. 151 47 51N 55 50W
St. Albans, U.K. 29 51 44N 0 19W
St. Albans, Vt., U.S.A. 156 44 49N 73 7W
St. Albans, W. Va., U.S.A. 156 38 21N 81 50W
St. Alban's Head 28 50 34N 2 3W
St. Albert 152 53 37N 113 40W
St. Amand 43 50 25N 3 6 E
St.-Amand-en-Puisaye 43 47 32N 3 5 E
St.-Amand-Mont-Rond 44 46 43N 2 30 E
St.-Amarin 43 47 54N 7 0 E
St.-Amour 45 46 26N 5 21 E
St. Andrä 52 46 46N 14 50 E
St. André, C. 129 16 11 S 44 27 E
St.-André-de-Cubzac 44 44 59N 0 26W
St. André de l'Eure 42 48 54N 1 16 E
St.-André-les-Alpes 45 43 58N 6 30 E
St. Andrews, Can. 151 47 45N 59 15W
St. Andrews, N.Z. 143 44 33 S 171 10 E
St. Andrews, U.K. 35 56 20N 2 48W
St. Ann B. 151 46 22N 60 25W
St. Anne 42 49 43N 2 11W
St. Anne's 32 53 45N 3 2W
St. Ann's 35 55 14N 3 28W
St. Ann's Bay 166 18 26N 77 15W
St. Ann's Hd. 31 51 41N 5 11W
St. Anthony, Can. 151 51 22N 55 35W
St. Anthony, U.S.A. 160 44 0N 111 49W
St.-Antonin-Noble-Val 44 44 10N 1 45 E
St. Arnaud 140 36 32 S 143 16 E
St. Arnaud Ra. 143 42 1 S 172 53 E
St. Arthur 151 47 47N 67 46W
St. Asaph 31 53 15N 3 27W
St. Astier 44 45 8N 0 31 E
St.-Aubin 50 46 54N 6 47 E
St.-Aubin-du-Cormier 42 48 15N 1 26W
St. Augustin 129 23 33 S 43 46 E
St-Augustin-Saguenay 151 51 13N 58 38W
St. Augustine 157 29 52N 81 20W
St. Austell 30 50 20N 4 48W
St.-Avold 43 49 6N 6 43 E
St. Barthélemy, I. 167 17 50N 62 50W
St. Bathans 143 44 53 S 170 0 E
St. Bathan's Mt. 143 44 45 S 169 45 E
St. Bees 32 54 29N 3 36W
St. Bee's Hd. 32 54 30N 3 38 E
St.-Benoît-du-Sault 44 46 26N 1 24 E
St. Bernard, Col du Grand 50 45 53N 7 11 E
St.-Blaise 50 47 1N 6 59 E
St. Blazey 32 50 22N 4 48W
St. Boniface 153 49 50N 97 10W
St. Bonnet 45 44 40N 6 5 E
St. Boswells 35 55 34N 2 39W
St.-Brévin-les-Pins 42 47 14N 2 10W
St. Briavels 28 51 44N 2 39W
St.-Brice-en-Coglès 42 48 25N 1 22W
St. Bride's 151 46 56N 54 10W
St. Bride's B. 31 51 48N 5 15W
St.-Brieuc 42 48 30N 2 46W
St. Budeaux 30 50 23N 4 10W
St. Buryan 30 50 4N 5 34W
St.-Calais 42 47 55N 0 45 E
St.-Cast 42 48 37N 2 18W
St. Catharines 150 43 10N 79 15W
St. Catherine's I. 157 31 35N 81 10W
St. Catherine's Pt. 28 50 34N 1 18W
St.-Céré 44 44 51N 1 54 E
St. Cergue 50 46 27N 6 10 E
St. Cernin 44 45 5N 2 25 E
St.-Chamond 45 45 28N 4 31 E
St. Charles, Ill., U.S.A. 156 41 55N 88 21W
St. Charles, Mo., U.S.A. 158 38 46N 90 30W
St.-Chély-d'Apcher 44 44 48N 3 17 E
St.-Chinian 44 43 25N 2 56 E
St. Christopher (St. Kitts) 167 17 20N 62 40W
St.-Ciers-sur-Gironde 44 45 17N 0 37W
St. Clair 162 40 42N 76 12W
St. Clair, L. 150 42 30N 82 45W
St.-Claud 44 45 54N 0 28 E
St. Claude 153 49 40N 98 20W
St.-Claude 45 46 22N 5 52 E
St. Clears 31 51 48N 4 30W
St.-Cloud 42 48 51N 2 12 E
St. Cloud, Fla., U.S.A. 157 28 15N 81 15W
St. Cloud, Minn., U.S.A. 158 45 30N 94 11W
St. Coeur de Marie 151 48 39N 71 43W
St. Columb Major 30 50 26N 4 56W
St. Combs 37 57 40N 1 55W
St. Cricq, C. 137 25 17 S 113 6 E
St. Croix Falls 158 45 18N 92 22W
St. Croix, I. 147 17 45N 64 45W
St. Croix, R. 158 45 20N 92 50W
St. Cyprien 44 42 37N 3 0 E
St.-Cyr 45 43 11N 5 43 E
St. Cyrus 36 56 47N 2 25W
St. David's, Can. 151 48 12N 58 52W
St. David's, U.K. 31 51 54N 5 16W
St. David's Head 31 51 54N 5 16W
St.-Denis 43 48 56N 2 22 E
St.-Denis-d'Orques 42 48 2N 0 17W
St. Dennis 30 50 23N 4 53W
St.-Dié 43 48 17N 6 56 E
St. Dizier 43 48 40N 5 0 E
St. Dogmaels 31 52 6N 4 42W
St. Dominick 30 50 28N 4 15W
St. Donats 31 51 23N 3 32W
St.-Egrève 45 45 14N 5 41 E
St. Elias, Mt. 147 60 20N 141 59W
St. Elias Mts. 147 59 30N 137 30W
St. Eloy 44 46 10N 2 51 E
St. Emilon 44 44 53N 0 9W
St. Endellion 30 50 33N 4 49W
St. Enoder 30 50 22N 4 57W
St. Erth 30 50 10N 5 26W
St. Étienne 45 45 27N 4 22 E
St.-Étienne-de-Tinée 45 44 16N 6 56 E
St. Eustatius I. 167 17 20N 63 0W
St. Félicien 150 48 40N 72 25W
St. Fergus 37 57 33N 1 50W
St. Fillans 35 56 25N 4 7W
St. Finian's B. 39 51 50N 10 22W
St. Fintan's 151 48 10N 58 50W
St.-Florent 45 42 41N 9 18 E
St.-Florent-sur-Cher 43 46 59N 2 15 E
St.-Florentin 43 48 0N 3 45 E
St.-Flour 44 45 2N 3 6 E
St.-Fons 45 45 42N 4 52 E
St. Francis 158 39 48N 101 47W
St. Francis C. 128 34 14 S 24 49 E
St. Francis, R. 159 32 25N 90 36W
St.-Fulgent 42 46 50N 1 10W
St. Gabriel de Brandon 150 46 17N 73 24W
St.-Gengoux-le-National 45 46 37N 4 40 E
St.-Geniez-d'Olt 44 44 27N 2 58 E
St. George, Austral. 139 28 1 S 148 41 E
St. George, Can. 151 45 11N 66 50W
St. George, P.N.G. 135 4 10 S 152 20 E
St. George, S.C., U.S.A. 157 33 13N 80 37W
St. George, Utah, U.S.A. 161 37 10N 113 35W
St. George, C., Can. 151 48 30N 59 16W
St. George, C., P.N.G. 135 4 49 S 152 53 E
St. George, C., U.S.A. 157 29 36N 85 2W
St. George Hd. 139 35 11 S 150 45 E
St. George Ra., Mts. 136 18 40 S 125 0 E
St. George West 153 50 33N 96 7W
St.-Georges 47 50 37N 4 20 E
St. George's 151 48 26N 58 31W
St. Georges, Qué., Can. 151 46 8N 70 40W
St. Georges, Quebec, Can. 150 46 42N 72 35W
St. Georges, Fr. Gui. 175 4 0N 52 0W
St. George's 167 12 5N 61 43W
St. George's B. 151 48 24N 58 53W
St. George's Channel 147 52 0N 6 0W
St. Georges-de-Didonne 44 45 36N 1 0W
St. Georges Head 141 35 12 S 150 42 E
St.-Gérard 47 50 21N 4 44 E
St. Germain 43 48 53N 2 5 E
St.-Germain-Lembron 44 45 27N 3 14 E
St.-Germain-de-Calberte 44 44 13N 3 48 E
St.-Germain-des-Fossés 44 46 12N 3 26 E
St.-Germain-du-Plain 43 46 42N 4 58 E
St.-Germain-Laval 45 45 50N 4 1 E
St. Germans 30 50 24N 4 19W
St. Gervais, Haute Savoie, France 45 45 53N 6 42 E
St. Gervais, Puy de Dôme, France 44 46 4N 2 50 E
St.-Gervais-les-Bains 43 45 53N 6 41 E
St.-Gildas, Pte. de 42 47 8N 2 14W
St.-Gilles 45 43 40N 4 26 E
St. Gilles Croix-de-Vie 42 46 41N 1 55W
St.-Gingolph 50 46 24N 6 48 E
St.-Girons 44 42 59N 1 8 E
St. Gla, L. 72 59 35N 12 30 E
St. Goar 49 50 31N 7 43 E
St. Gotthard P. = San Gottardo 51 46 33N 8 33 E
St. Govan's Hd. 31 51 35N 4 56W
St.-Guadens 44 43 6N 0 44 E
St.-Gualtier 42 46 39N 1 26 E
St.-Guénolé 42 47 49N 4 23W
St. Harmon 31 52 21N 3 29W
St. Heddinge 73 55 9N 12 26 E
St. Helena 160 38 29N 122 30W
St. Helena, I. 15 15 55 S 5 44W
St. Helenabaai 128 32 40 S 18 10 E
St. Helens, Austral. 138 41 20 S 148 15 E
St. Helens, I.o.W., U.K. 28 50 42N 1 6W
St. Helens, Merseyside, U.K. 32 53 28N 2 44W
St. Helens, U.S.A. 160 45 55N 122 50W
St. Helier 42 49 11N 2 6W
St. Hilaire 42 48 35N 1 7W
St. Hippolyte 43 47 20N 6 50 E
St. Hippolyte-du-Fort 44 43 58N 3 52 E
St.-Honoré 43 46 54N 3 50 E
St.-Hubert 47 50 2N 5 23 E
St. Hyacinthe 150 45 40N 72 58W
St. Ignace 156 45 53N 84 43W
St. Ignace I. 150 48 45N 88 0W
St. Ignatius 160 47 25N 114 2W
St.-Imier 50 47 9N 6 58 E
St. Issey 30 50 30N 4 55W
St. Ives, Cambs., U.K. 29 52 20N 0 5W
St. Ives, Cornwall, U.K. 30 50 13N 5 29W
St. Ives Bay 30 50 15N 5 27W
St.-James 42 48 31N 1 20W
St. James 158 43 57N 94 40W
St. James C. 152 51 55N 131 0W
St. Jean 150 45 20N 73 50W
St.-Jean 45 48 57N 3 1 E
St. Jean Baptiste 153 49 15N 97 20W
St. Jean, C. 124 1 5N 9 20 E
St.-Jean-de-Maurienne 45 45 16N 6 28 E
St.-Jean-de-Luz 44 43 23N 1 39W
St.-Jean-de-Monts 42 46 47N 2 4W
St.-Jean-du-Gard 44 47 7N 3 52 E
St.-Jean-en-Royans 45 45 1N 5 18 E
St.-Jean, L. 151 48 40N 72 0W
St. Jean-Port-Joli 151 47 15N 70 13W
St.-Jean, R. 151 50 17N 64 20W
St. Jérôme, Qué., Can. 150 45 47N 74 0W
St. Jérôme, Qué., Can. 151 48 26N 71 53W
St. John, Can. 151 45 20N 66 8W
St. John, Kans., U.S.A. 159 37 59N 98 45W
St. John, N.D., U.S.A. 158 48 58N 99 40W
St. John, C. 151 50 0N 55 32W
St. John, I. 147 18 20N 64 45W
St. John, R. 151 45 15N 66 4W
St. Johns 167 17 6N 61 51W
St. John's, Can. 151 47 35N 52 40W
St. John's, U.K. 32 54 13N 4 38W
St. Johns, Ariz., U.S.A. 161 34 31N 109 26W
St. Johns, Mich., U.S.A. 156 43 0N 84 38W
St. Johns Chapel 32 54 43N 2 10W
St. John's Pt., Ireland 38 54 35N 8 26W
St. John's Pt., U.K. 38 54 14N 5 40W
St. Johns, R. 157 30 20N 81 30W
St. Johnsbury 156 44 25N 72 1W
St. Johnston 38 54 56N 7 29W
St. Johnsville 162 43 0N 74 43W
St. Joseph, La., U.S.A. 159 31 55N 91 15W
St. Joseph, Mo., U.S.A. 158 39 40N 94 50W
St. Joseph, I. 150 46 12N 83 58W
St. Joseph, L. 150 51 10N 90 35W
St. Joseph, R. 156 42 7N 86 30W
St. Joseph's 156 42 5N 86 30W
St. Jovite 150 46 8N 74 38W
St. Juéry 44 43 55N 2 42 E
St. Julien 45 46 8N 6 5 E
St.-Julien-Chapteuil 45 45 2N 4 4 E
St. Julien du Sault 43 48 1N 3 17 E
St.-Junien 44 45 53N 0 55 E
St. Just 30 50 7N 5 41W
St.-Just-en-Chaussée 43 49 30N 2 25 E
St.-Just-en-Chevalet 44 45 55N 3 50 E
St.-Justin 44 43 59N 0 14W
St. Karlsö, I. 73 57 17N 17 58 E
St. Keverne 30 50 3N 5 5W
St. Kew 30 50 34N 4 48W
St. Kilda 143 45 53 S 170 31 E
St. Kilda, I. 23 57 40N 8 50W
St. Kitts, I. 167 17 20N 62 40W
St. Laurent 153 50 25N 97 58W
St.-Laurent-du-Pont 45 45 23N 5 45 E
St.-Laurent-en-Grandvaux 45 46 35N 5 45 E
St. Lawrence, Austral. 138 22 16 S 149 31 E
St. Lawrence, Can. 151 46 54N 55 23W

St. Lawrence, Gulf of Sam Ngao

St. Lawrence, Gulf of **151** 48 25N 62 0W
St. Lawrence, I. **147** 63 0N 170 0W
St. Lawrence, R. **151** 49 30N 66 0W
St.-Léger **47** 49 37N 5 39E
St. Leonard **151** 47 12N 67 58W
St.-Léonard-de-Noblat **44** 45 49N 1 29E
St. Leonards **29** 50 51N 0 34E
St. Levan **30** 50 3N 5 36W
St Lewis, R. **151** 52 26N 56 11W
St. Lin **150** 45 44N 73 46W
St.-Lô **42** 49 7N 1 5W
St. Louis, Senegal **120** 16 8N 16 27W
St. Louis, Mich., U.S.A. **156** 43 27N 84 38W
St. Louis, Mo., U.S.A. **158** 38 40N 90 12W
St. Louis R. **158** 47 15N 92 45W
St.-Loup-sur-Semouse **43** 47 53N 6 16E
St. Lucia, C. **129** 28 32S 32 29E
St. Lucia Channel **167** 14 15N 61 0W
St. Lucia I. **167** 14 0N 60 50W
St. Lucia, Lake **129** 28 5S 32 30E
St. Lunaire-Griquet **151** 51 31N 55 28W
St. Maarten, I. **167** 18 0N 63 5W
St. Mabyn **30** 50 30N 4 45W
St. Magnus B. **36** 60 25N 1 35W
St.-Maixent-l'École **44** 46 24N 0 12W
St.-Malo **42** 48 39N 2 1W
St. Malo, G. de **42** 48 50N 2 30W
St. Mandrier **45** 43 4N 5 56E
St. Marc **167** 19 10N 72 50W
St.-Marcellin **45** 45 9N 5 20E
St. Marcouf, Is. **42** 49 30N 1 10W
St.-Mard **47** 49 2N 2 42E
St. Margaret's-at-Cliffe **29** 51 10N 1 23E
St. Margaret's Hope **37** 58 49N 2 58W
St. Maries **160** 47 17N 116 34W
St. Martin **43** 50 42N 1 38E
St.-Martin, I. **167** 18 0N 63 0W
St. Martin L. **153** 51 40N 98 30W
St. Martin-Tende-Vésubie **45** 44 4N 7 15E
St. Martins **151** 45 22N 65 25W
St. Martin's I. **30** 49 58N 6 16W
St. Martinsville **159** 30 10N 91 50W
St.-Martory **44** 43 9N 0 56E
St. Mary B. **151** 46 50N 53 50W
St. Mary Bourne **28** 51 16N 1 24W
St. Mary C. **120** 13 24N 13 10E
St. Mary Is. **97** 13 20N 74 35E
St. Mary, Mt. **135** 8 8S 146 54E
St. Mary Pk. **140** 31 32S 138 34E
St. Marys, N.S.W., Austral. **133** 33 44S 150 49E
St. Marys, Tas., Austral. **138** 41 32S 148 11E
St. Mary's, Can. **151** 46 56N 53 34W
St. Mary's, U.K. **37** 58 53N 2 55W
St. Mary's, Ohio, U.S.A. **156** 40 33N 84 20W
St. Mary's, Pa., U.S.A. **156** 41 30N 78 33W
St Marys Bay **151** 44 25N 66 10W
St. Mary's, C. **151** 46 50N 54 12W
St. Mary's I. **30** 49 55N 6 17W
St. Mary's Pk. **133** 31 30S 138 33E
St. Mary's Sd. **30** 49 53N 6 19W
St. Mathews I. = Zadetkyi Kyun **101** 10 0N 48 25E
St.-Mathieu, Pte. de **42** 48 20N 4 45W
St. Matthias Grp. **135** 1 30S 150 0E
St.-Maur-des-Fosses **43** 48 48N 2 30E
St. Maurice **50** 46 13N 7 0E
St. Maurice R. **150** 47 20N 72 50W
St. Mawes **30** 50 10N 5 1W
St.-Médard-de-Guizières **44** 45 1N 0 4W
St.-Méen-le-Grand **42** 48 11N 2 12W
St. Merryn **30** 50 31N 4 58W
St. Michael **147** 63 30N 162 30W
St. Michaels, Arizona, U.S.A. **161** 35 45N 109 5W
St. Michaels, Maryland, U.S.A. **162** 38 47N 76 14W
St. Michael's Mt. **30** 50 7N 5 30W
St. Michel **45** 45 15N 6 29E
St. Mihiel **43** 48 54N 5 30E
St. Minver **30** 50 34N 4 52W
St. Monans **35** 56 13N 2 46W
St.-Nazaire **42** 47 17N 2 12W
St. Neots **29** 52 14N 0 16W
St.-Nicholas-de-Port **43** 48 38N 6 18E
St. Niklaus **50** 46 10N 7 49E
St. Ninian's, I. **36** 59 59N 1 20W
St. Olaf **73** 55 40N 14 12E
St.-Omer **43** 50 45N 2 15E
St. Osyth **29** 51 47N 1 4E
St. Ouen **43** 48 50N 2 20E
St. Pacome **151** 47 24N 69 58W
St. Palais **44** 45 40N 1 8W
St. Pamphile **151** 46 58N 69 48W
St.-Pardoux-la-Rivière **44** 45 29N 0 45E
St. Pascal **151** 47 32N 69 48W
St. Patrickswell **39** 52 36N 8 43W
St. Paul, Can. **152** 54 59N 111 17W
St. Paul, France **44** 43 44N 1 3W
St. Paul, Minn., U.S.A. **158** 44 54N 93 5W
St. Paul, Nebr., U.S.A. **158** 41 15N 98 30W
St. Paul-de-Fenouillet **44** 42 50N 2 28E
St. Paul, I., Atl. Oc. **14** 0 50N 31 40W
St. Paul, I., Can. **151** 47 12N 60 9W
St. Paul, I., Ind. Oc. **11** 30 40S 77 34E
St. Paul's B. **151** 49 48N 57 58W
St.-Peray **45** 44 57N 4 50E
St.-Père-en-Retz **42** 47 11N 2 2W
St. Peter **158** 44 15N 93 57W
St. Peter Port **42** 49 27N 2 31W
St. Peters, N.S., Can. **151** 45 40N 60 53W
St. Peters, P.E.I., Can. **151** 46 25N 62 35W
St. Petersburg **157** 27 45N 82 40W
St.-Philbert-de-Grand-Lieu **42** 47 2N 1 39W
St Pierre **151** 46 40N 56 0W
St.-Pierre-d'Oleron **44** 45 57N 1 19W
St.-Pierre-Église **42** 49 40N 1 24W
St.-Pierre-en-Port **42** 49 48N 0 30E
Saint-Pierre et Miquelon □ **151** 46 55N 56 10W
St-Pierre, L. **150** 46 12N 72 52W
St.-Pierre-le-Moûtier **43** 46 47N 3 7E
St. Pierre-sur-Dives **42** 49 2N 0 1W
St.-Pieters Leew **47** 50 47N 4 16E
St. Pol **43** 50 21N 2 20E
St.-Pol-de-Léon **42** 48 41N 4 0W
St.-Pol-sur-Mer **43** 51 1N 2 20E
St. Pons **44** 43 30N 2 45E
St.-Pourçain-sur-Sioule **43** 46 18N 3 18E
St.-Quay-Portrieux **42** 48 39N 2 51W
St.-Quentin **43** 49 50N 3 16E
St. Rambert-d'Albon **45** 45 17N 1 35E
St.-Raphaël **45** 43 25N 6 46E
St. Regis **160** 47 20N 115 3W
St.-Rémy-de-Provence **45** 43 48N 4 50E
St.-Renan **42** 48 26N 4 37W
St.-Saëns **42** 49 41N 1 16E
St.-Sauveur-en-Puisaye **43** 47 37N 3 12E
St.-Sauveur-le-Vicomte **42** 49 23N 1 32W
St. Savin **44** 46 34N 0 50E
St.-Savinien **44** 45 53N 0 42W
St. Sebastien, C. **129** 12 26S 48 44E
St.-Seine-l'Abbaye **43** 47 26N 4 47E
St. Sernin **44** 43 54N 2 35E
St.-Servan-sur-Mer **42** 48 38N 2 0E
St.-Sever-Calvados **42** 48 50N 1 3W
St. Simeon **151** 47 51N 69 54W
St. Stephen, Can. **151** 45 16N 67 17W
St. Stephen, U.K. **30** 50 20N 4 52W
St.-Sulpice **44** 43 46N 1 41E
St.-Sulpice-Laurière **44** 46 3N 1 29E
St. Teath **30** 50 34N 4 45W
St.-Thegonnec **42** 48 31N 3 57W
St. Thomas **150** 42 45N 81 10W
St. Thomas, I. **147** 18 21N 64 55W
St. Tite **150** 46 45N 72 40W
St. Tropez **45** 43 17N 6 38E
St. Troud **47** 50 48N 5 10E
St. Tudwal's Is. **31** 52 48N 4 28W
St. Tudy **30** 50 33N 4 45W
St.-Vaast-la-Hougue **42** 49 35N 1 17W
St. Valéry **43** 50 10N 1 38E
St.-Valéry-en-Caux **42** 49 52N 0 43E
St.-Vallier **45** 45 11N 4 50E
St.-Vallier-de-Thiey **45** 43 42N 6 51E
St.-Varent **42** 46 53N 0 13W
St. Vincent **14** 18 0N 26 1W
St. Vincent C. **125** 21 58S 43 20E
St. Vincent, C. = São Vincente **57** 37 0N 9 0W
St. Vincent-de-Tyrosse **44** 43 39N 1 18W
St. Vincent, G. **140** 35 0S 138 0E
St. Vincent, I. **167** 13 10N 61 10W
St. Vincent Passage **167** 13 30N 61 0W
St.-Vith **47** 50 17N 6 9E
St.-Yrieux-la-Perche **44** 45 31N 1 12E
Ste.-Adresse **42** 49 31N 0 5E
Ste.-Agathe-des-Monts **150** 46 3N 74 17W
Ste. Anne **167** 14 26N 60 53W
Ste. Anne de Beaupré **151** 47 2N 70 58W
Ste. Anne de Portneuf **151** 48 38N 69 8W
Ste.-Anne-des-Monts **151** 49 8N 66 30W
Ste. Benoîte **43** 49 47N 3 30E
Ste. Cecile **151** 47 56N 64 34W
Ste.-Croix **43** 46 49N 6 34W
Ste.-Enimie **44** 44 22N 3 26E
Ste.-Foy-la-Grande **44** 44 50N 0 13E
Ste. Genevieve **158** 37 59N 90 2W
Ste. Germaine **151** 46 24N 70 24W
Ste.-Hermine **44** 46 32N 1 4W
Ste.-Livrade-sur-Lot **44** 44 24N 0 36E
Ste. Marguerite, R. **151** 50 9N 66 36W
Ste. Marie **167** 14 48N 61 1W
Ste.-Marie-aux-Mines **43** 48 10N 7 12E
Ste. Marie, C. **129** 25 36S 45 8E
Ste. Marie de la Madeleine **151** 46 26N 71 0W
Ste. Marie, I. **129** 16 50S 49 55E
Ste.-Maure-de-Touraine **42** 47 7N 0 37E
Ste.-Maxime **45** 43 19N 6 39E
Ste.-Menehould **43** 49 5N 4 54E
Ste.-Mère-Église **42** 49 24N 1 19W
Ste. Rose **167** 16 20N 61 45W
Ste. Rose du lac **153** 51 41N 99 30W
Ste. Teresa **172** 33 33S 60 54W
Saintes **44** 45 45N 0 37W
Saintes, I. des **167** 15 50N 61 35W
Saintes-Maries-de-la-Mer **45** 43 26N 4 26E
Saintes Maries, Les **45** 43 27N 4 25E
Saintfield **38** 54 28N 5 50W
Saintonge **44** 45 40N 0 50W
Sairang **99** 23 50N 92 45E
Sairecábur, Cerro **172** 22 43S 67 54W
Saitama-ken □ **111** 36 25N 137 0E
Saito **110** 32 3N 131 18E
Sajama, Nevada **174** 18 0S 68 55W
Sajan **66** 45 50N 20 58E
Sajószentpéter **53** 48 12N 20 44E
Sajum, mt. **95** 33 20N 79 0E
Saka Ilkalat **93** 27 20N 64 7E
Sakai **111** 34 30N 135 30E
Sakaide **110** 34 15N 133 56E
Sakaiminato **110** 35 38N 133 11E
Sakaka **92** 30 0N 40 8E
Sakami, L. **150** 53 15N 76 45W
Sâkâne, 'Erg i-n **118** 20 30N 1 30W
Sakania **127** 12 43S 28 30E
Sakar, I. **138** 5 30S 148 0E
Sakarya, R. **82** 40 5N 31 0E
Sakata **112** 36 38N 138 19E
Sakchu **107** 40 23N 125 2E
Sakeny, R. **129** 20 0S 45 25E
Sakété **121** 6 40N 2 32E
Sakhalin, Ostrov **77** 51 0N 143 0E
Sakhi Gopal **96** 19 58N 85 50E
Sakhnin **90** 32 52N 35 12E
Saki **82** 45 16N 33 34E
Sakiai **80** 54 59N 23 0E
Sakmara **84** 52 0N 55 20E
Sakmara, R. **84** 51 46N 55 1E
Sakołow Małopolski **54** 50 10N 22 9E
Sakon Nakhon **100** 17 10N 104 9E
Sakrand **94** 26 10N 68 15E
Sakri **96** 21 2N 74 40E
Sakskøbing **73** 54 49N 11 39E
Saku **111** 36 11N 138 31E
Sakuma **111** 35 3N 137 56E
Sakurai **111** 34 30N 135 51E
Sakuru **111** 35 43N 140 14E
Säkylä **75** 61 4N 22 20E
Sal, R. **83** 47 25N 42 20E
Sal'a **53** 48 10N 17 50E
Sala **72** 59 58N 16 35E
Sala Consilina **65** 40 23N 15 35E
Sala-y-Gomez, I. **131** 26 28S 105 28W
Salaberry-de-Valleyfield **150** 45 15N 74 8W
Salada, La **164** 24 30N 111 30W
Saladas **172** 28 15S 58 40W
Saladillo **172** 35 40S 59 55W
Salado, R., Buenos Aires, Argent. **172** 35 40S 58 10W
Salado, R., Santa Fe, Argent. **172** 27 0S 63 40W
Salado, R., Mexico **164** 26 52N 99 19W
Salaga **121** 8 31N 0 31W
Salala, Liberia **120** 6 42N 10 7W
Salala, Sudan **122** 21 17N 36 16E
Salalah **91** 16 56N 53 59E
Salama **90** 32 3N 34 48E
Salamanca, Chile **172** 32 0S 71 25W
Salamanca, Spain **56** 40 58N 5 39W
Salamanca, U.S.A. **156** 42 10N 78 42W
Salamanca □ **56** 40 57N 5 40W
Salamaua **138** 7 10S 147 0E
Salamina **174** 5 25N 75 29W
Salamis **69** 37 56N 23 30E
Salar de Atacama **176** 23 30S 68 25W
Salar de Uyuni **174** 20 30S 67 45W
Salard **70** 47 12N 22 3E
Salas **56** 43 25N 6 15W
Salas de los Infantes **58** 42 2N 3 17W
Salavat **84** 53 21N 55 55E
Salaverry **174** 8 15S 79 0W
Salawe **126** 3 17S 32 56E
Salayar, I. **103** 6 15S 120 30E
Salazar, R. **58** 42 45N 1 8W
Salbohed **72** 59 55N 16 22E
Salbris **43** 47 25N 2 3E
Salcia **70** 43 56N 24 55E
Salcombe **30** 50 14N 3 47W
Salcombe Regis **30** 50 41N 3 11W
Saldaña **56** 42 32N 4 48W
Saldanha **128** 33 0S 17 58E
Saldanhabaai **128** 33 6S 18 0E
Saldus **80** 56 45N 22 37E
Sale **141** 38 6S 147 6E
Salé **118** 34 3N 6 48W
Sale **32** 53 26N 2 19W
Saléa-koïra **121** 16 54N 0 46W
Salebabu **103** 3 45N 125 55E
Salehabad **93** 35 40N 61 2E
Salekhard **76** 66 30N 66 25E
Salem, India **97** 11 40N 78 11E
Salem, Ind., U.S.A. **156** 38 38N 86 16W
Salem, Mass., U.S.A. **162** 42 29N 70 53W
Salem, Mo., U.S.A. **159** 37 40N 91 30W
Salem, N.H., U.S.A. **162** 42 47N 71 12W
Salem, N.J., U.S.A. **162** 39 34N 75 29W
Salem, N.Y., U.S.A. **162** 43 10N 73 20W
Salem, Ohio, U.S.A. **156** 40 52N 80 50W
Salem, Oreg., U.S.A. **160** 45 0N 123 0W
Salem, Va., U.S.A. **156** 37 19N 80 8W
Salembu, Kepulauan **102** 5 35S 114 30E
Salemi **64** 37 49N 12 47E
Salen, Norway **75** 64 41N 11 27E
Salen, Highland, U.K. **36** 56 42N 5 48W
Salen, Strathclyde, U.K. **34** 56 31N 5 57W
Salernes **45** 43 34N 6 15E
Salerno **65** 40 40N 14 44E
Salerno, G. di **65** 40 35N 14 45E
Salfit **90** 32 5N 35 11E
Salford **32** 53 30N 2 17W
Salford Priors **28** 52 10N 1 52W
Salgir, R. **82** 45 30N 34 30E
Salgótarján **53** 48 5N 19 47E
Salgueiro **170** 8 4S 39 6W
Salies-de-Béarn **44** 43 28N 0 56W
Salima **125** 13 47S 34 28E
Salin **98** 20 35N 94 40E
Salina **158** 38 50N 97 40W
Salina Cruz **165** 16 10N 95 10W
Salina, I. **65** 38 35N 14 50E
Salina, La **174** 10 22N 71 27W
Salinas, Brazil **171** 16 20S 42 10W
Salinas, Chile **172** 23 31S 69 29W
Salinas, Ecuador **174** 2 10S 80 50W
Salinas, Mexico **164** 23 37N 106 8W
Salinas, U.S.A. **163** 36 40N 121 31W
Salinas Ambargasta **172** 29 0S 65 30W
Salinas, B. de **166** 11 4N 85 45W
Salinas, Cabo de **59** 39 16N 3 4E
Salinas (de Hidalgo) **164** 22 30N 101 40W
Salinas Grandes **172** 30 0S 65 0W
Salinas, Pampa de las **172** 31 58S 66 42W
Salinas, R., Mexico **165** 16 28N 90 31W
Salinas, R., U.S.A. **163** 36 45N 121 48W
Saline, R. **158** 39 10N 99 5W
Salines-les-Bains **43** 46 58N 5 52E
Salinópolis **170** 0 40S 47 20W
Salir **57** 37 14N 8 2W
Salisbury, Austral. **140** 34 46S 138 40E
Salisbury, Rhod. **127** 17 50S 31 2E
Salisbury, U.K. **28** 51 4N 1 48W
Salisbury, Md., U.S.A. **162** 38 20N 75 38W
Salisbury, N.C., U.S.A. **157** 35 42N 80 29W
Salisbury Plain **28** 51 13N 1 50W
Salitre, R. **170** 9 29S 40 39W
Salka **121** 10 20N 4 58E
Salle, La **158** 41 20N 89 5W
Sallent **58** 41 49N 1 54E
Salles-Curan **44** 44 11N 2 48E
Salling **73** 56 40N 8 55E
Sallisaw **159** 35 26N 94 45W
Sallom Junc. **122** 19 23N 37 6E
Sally Gap, Mt. **39** 53 7N 6 18W
Salmerón **58** 40 33N 2 29W
Salmo **152** 49 10N 117 20W
Salmon **160** 45 12N 113 56W
Salmon Arm **152** 50 40N 119 15W
Salmon Falls **160** 42 55N 114 59W
Salmon Gums **137** 32 59S 121 38E
Salmon, R., Can. **152** 54 3N 122 40W
Salmon, R., U.S.A. **160** 46 0N 116 30W
Salmon Res. **151** 48 05N 56 00W
Salmon River Mts. **160** 45 0N 114 30W
Salo **75** 60 22N 23 3E
Salò **62** 45 37N 10 32E
Salobreña **57** 36 44N 3 35W
Salome **161** 33 51N 113 37W
Salon-de-Provence **45** 43 39N 5 6E
Salonica = Thessaloniki **68** 40 38N 22 58E
Salonta **70** 46 49N 21 42E
Salop □ **28** 52 36N 2 45W
Salor, R. **57** 39 39N 7 3W
Salou, Cabo **58** 41 3N 1 10E
Salsacate **172** 31 20S 65 5W
Salsaker **72** 62 59N 18 20E
Salses **44** 42 50N 2 55E
Salsette I. **96** 19 5N 72 50E
Salsk **83** 46 28N 41 30E
Salso, R. **65** 37 6N 13 55E
Salsomaggiore **62** 44 48N 9 59E
Salt **90** 32 2N 35 43E
Salt Creek **140** 36 8S 139 38E
Salt Creek Telegraph Office **139** 36 0S 139 35E
Salt Fork R. **159** 37 25N 98 40W
Salt Lake City **160** 40 45N 111 58W
Salt, R., Can. **152** 60 0N 112 25W
Salt, R., U.S.A. **161** 33 50N 110 25W
Salt Range **94** 32 30N 72 25E
Salta **172** 24 47S 65 25W
Salta □ **172** 24 48S 65 30W
Saltash **30** 50 25N 4 13W
Saltburn by Sea **33** 54 35N 0 58W
Saltcoats **34** 55 38N 4 47W
Saltee Is. **39** 52 7N 6 37W
Saltergate **33** 54 20N 0 40W
Saltfjorden **74** 67 15N 14 20E
Saltfleet **33** 53 25N 0 11E
Saltfleetby **33** 53 23N 0 10E
Salthill **39** 53 15N 9 6W
Saltholm **73** 55 38N 12 43E
Salthólmavík **74** 65 24N 21 57W
Saltillo **164** 25 30N 100 57W
Salto, Argent. **172** 34 20S 60 15W
Salto, Uruguay **172** 31 20S 57 59W
Salto □ **172** 31 20S 57 59W
Salto Augusto, falls **172** 8 30S 58 0W
Salto da Divisa **171** 16 0S 39 57W
Salton City **163** 33 21N 115 59W
Salton Sea **163** 33 20N 115 50W
Saltpond **121** 5 15N 1 3W
Saltsjöbaden **73** 59 15N 18 20E
Saltspring **152** 48 54N 123 37W
Saltwood **29** 51 4N 1 5E
Saluda **162** 37 36N 76 36W
Salula, R. **157** 34 12N 81 45W
Salûm **122** 31 31N 25 7E
Salûm, Khâlig el **122** 31 30N 25 9E
Salur **96** 18 27N 83 18E
Saluzzo **62** 44 39N 7 29E
Salvador, Brazil **171** 13 0S 38 30W
Salvador, Can. **153** 52 10N 109 25W
Salvador ■ **164** 13 50N 89 0W
Salvador, L. **159** 29 46N 90 16W
Salvaterra **170** 0 46S 48 31W
Salvaterra de Magos **57** 39 1N 8 47W
Sálvora, Isla **56** 42 30N 8 58W
Salwa **93** 24 45N 50 55E
Salween, R. **98** 16 31N 97 37E
Salza, R. **52** 47 43N 15 0E
Salzach, R. **52** 47 15N 12 25E
Salzburg **52** 47 48N 13 2E
Salzgitter **48** 52 2N 10 22E
Salzwedel **48** 52 50N 11 11E
Sam Neua **100** 20 29N 104 0E
Sam Ngao **100** 17 18N 99 0E

Sam Rayburn Res San Quintín

Sam Rayburn Res. **159** 31 15N 94 20W
Sam Son **100** 19 44N 105 54E
Sam Ten **100** 19 59N 104 38E
Sama **84** 60 12N 60 22E
Sama de Langreo **56** 43 18N 5 40W
Samales Group **103** 6 0N 122 0E
Samalkot **96** 17 3N 82 13E
Samâlût **122** 28 20N 30 42E
Samana **94** 30 10N 76 13E
Samana Cay **167** 23 3N 73 45W
Samanco **174** 9 10S 78 30W
Samanga **127** 8 20S 39 13E
Samangan **93** 36 15N 67 40E
Samangwa **126** 4 23S 24 10E
Samani **112** 42 7N 142 56E
Samar, I. **103** 12 0N 125 0E
Samara, R. **84** 53 10N 50 4E
Samaria **135** 10 39S 150 41E
Samaria = Shomron **90** 32 15N 35 13E
Samarkand **85** 39 40N 67 0E
Samarra **92** 34 16N 43 55E
Samastipur **95** 25 50N 85 50E
Samatan **44** 43 29N 0 55E
Samba, Kashmir **95** 32 32N 75 10E
Samba, Zaïre **126** 4 38S 26 22E
Sambaíba **170** 7 8S 45 21W
Sambaina **129** 19 37S 47 8E
Sambaise **65** 38 58N 16 16E
Sambalpur **96** 21 28N 83 58E
Sambas, S. **102** 1 20N 109 20E
Sambava **129** 14 16S 50 10E
Sambawizi **127** 18 24S 26 13E
Sambhal **95** 28 35N 78 37E
Sambhar **94** 26 52N 75 10E
Sambonifacio **62** 45 24N 11 16E
Sambor, Camb. **100** 12 46N 106 0E
Sambor, U.S.S.R. **80** 49 30N 23 10E
Sambre, R. **47** 50 27N 4 52E
Sambuca **64** 37 39N 13 6E
Samburu □ **126** 1 10N 37 0E
Sambusu **128** 17 55S 19 21E
Samchök **107** 37 30N 129 10E
Samchonpo **107** 34 54N 128 6E
Same **126** 4 2S 37 38E
Samedan **51** 46 32N 9 52E
Samer **43** 50 38N 1 44E
Samfya **127** 11 16S 29 31E
Sámi **69** 38 15N 20 39E
Samna **122** 25 12N 37 17E
Samnager **71** 60 23N 5 39E
Samnaun **51** 46 57N 10 22E
Samnu **119** 27 15N 14 55E
Samo Alto **172** 30 22S 71 0W
Samoan Is. **10** 14 0S 171 0W
Samobor **63** 45 47N 15 44E
Samoëns **45** 46 5N 6 45E
Samoorombón, Bahía **172** 36 5S 57 20W
Samorogouan **120** 11 21N 4 57W
Samos **56** 42 44N 7 20W
Samoš **66** 45 13N 20 49E
Sámos, I. **69** 37 45N 26 50E
Samosir, P. **102** 2 35N 98 50E
Samothráki **68** 40 28N 25 38E
Samothráki, I. **68** 40 25N 25 40E
Sampa **120** 8 0N 2 36W
Sampacho **172** 33 20S 64 50W
Sampang **103** 7 11S 113 13E
Samper de Calanda **58** 41 11N 0 2W
Sampford Courtenay **30** 50 47N 3 58W
Sampit **102** 2 20S 113 0E
Samra **92** 25 35N 41 0E
Samreboi **120** 5 34N 7 28E
Samrée **47** 50 13N 5 39E
Samrong, Camb. **100** 14 15N 103 30E
Samrong, Thai. **100** 15 10N 100 40E
Samsø **73** 55 50N 10 35E
Samsø Bælt **73** 55 45N 10 45E
Samsonovo **85** 37 53N 65 15E
Samsun **92** 41 15N 36 15E
Samsun Daği **69** 37 45N 27 10E
Samtredia **83** 42 7N 42 24E
Samui, Ko **101** 9 30N 100 0E
Samur, R. **83** 41 30N 48 0E
Samusole **127** 10 2S 24 0E
Samut Prakan **100** 13 32N 100 40E
Samut Sakhon **100** 13 31N 100 20E
Samut Songkhram (Mekong) **100** 13 24N 100 1E
Samwari **94** 28 5N 66 46E
Samyo La **99** 29 55N 84 46E
San **120** 13 15N 4 45W
San Adrián, C. de **56** 43 21N 8 50W
San Adrián, G. de **56** 43 21N 8 50W
San Agustín **174** 1 53N 76 16W
San Agustin, C. **103** 6 20N 126 13E
San Agustín de Valle Fértil **172** 30 35S 67 30W
San Ambrosio, I. **131** 26 35S 79 30W
San Andreas **163** 38 17N 120 39W
San Andrés, I. de **166** 12 42N 81 46W
San Andres Mts. **161** 33 0N 106 45W
San Andrés Tuxtla **165** 18 30N 95 20W
San Angelo **159** 31 30N 100 30W
San Anselmo **163** 37 49N 122 34W
San Antonio, Belize **165** 16 15N 89 2W
San Antonio, Chile **172** 33 40S 71 40W
San Antonio, N. Mex., U.S.A. **161** 33 58N 106 57W
San Antonio, Tex., U.S.A. **159** 29 30N 98 30W
San Antonio, Venez. **174** 3 30N 66 44W
San Antonio Abad **59** 38 59N 1 19E
San Antonio, C., Argent. **172** 36 15S 56 40W
San Antonio, C., Cuba **166** 21 50N 84 57W
San Antonio, C. de **59** 38 48N 0 12E
San Antonio de Caparo **174** 7 35N 71 27W
San Antonio de los Baños **166** 22 54N 82 31W
San Antonio de los Cobres **172** 24 16S 66 2W
San Antonio do Zaire **124** 6 8S 12 11E
San Antonio, Mt. (Old Baldy Pk.) **163** 34 17N 117 38W
San Antonio Oeste **176** 40 40S 65 0W
San Antonio, R. **159** 28 30N 97 14W
San Ardo **163** 36 1N 120 54W
San Bartolomeo in Galdo **65** 41 23N 15 2E
San Benedetto **62** 45 2N 10 57E
San Benedetto del Tronto **63** 42 57N 13 52E
San Benedicto, I. **164** 19 18N 110 49W
San Benito **159** 26 5N 97 32W
San Benito Mtn. **163** 36 22N 120 37W
San Benito, R. **163** 36 53N 121 50W
San Bernardino **163** 34 7N 117 18W
San Bernardino, Paso del **51** 46 28N 9 11E
San Bernardo **172** 33 40S 70 50W
San Bernardo, I. de **174** 9 45N 75 50W
San Blas **164** 26 10N 108 40W
San Blas, C. **157** 29 40N 85 25W
San Blas, Cord. de **166** 9 15N 78 30W
San Borja **174** 15 0S 67 12W
San Buenaventura **164** 27 5N 101 32W
San Buenaventura = Ventura **163** 34 17N 119 18W
San Carlos, Argent. **172** 33 50S 69 0W
San Carlos, Mexico **164** 29 0N 101 10W
San Carlos, Nic. **166** 11 12N 84 50W
San Carlos, Phil. **103** 10 29N 123 25E
San Carlos, Uruguay **173** 34 46S 54 58W
San Carlos, U.S.A. **161** 33 24N 110 27W
San Carlos, Amazonas, Venez. **174** 1 55N 67 4W
San Carlos, Cojedes, Venez. **174** 9 40N 68 36W
San Carlos de Bariloche **176** 41 10S 71 25W
San Carlos de la Rápita **58** 40 37N 0 35E
San Carlos del Zulia **174** 9 1N 71 55W
San Carlos L. **161** 33 20N 110 10W
San Carlos = Butuku-Luba **121** 3 29N 8 33E
San Cataldo **64** 37 30N 13 58E
San Celoni **58** 41 42N 2 30E
San Clemente, Chile **172** 35 30S 71 39W
San Clemente, Spain **59** 39 24N 2 25W
San Clemente, U.S.A. **163** 33 29N 117 45W
San Clemente I. **163** 32 53N 118 30W
San Constanzo **63** 43 46N 13 5E
San Cristóbal, Argent. **172** 30 20S 61 10W
San Cristóbal, Dom. Rep. **167** 18 25N 70 6W
San Cristóbal, Venez. **174** 7 46N 72 14W
San Cristóbal de las Casas **165** 16 50N 92 33W
San Damiano d'Asti **62** 44 51N 8 4E
San Daniel del Friuli **63** 46 10N 13 0E
San Demétrio Corone **65** 39 34N 16 22E
San Diego, Calif., U.S.A. **163** 32 43N 117 10W
San Diego, Tex., U.S.A. **159** 27 47N 98 15W
San Diego, C. **176** 54 40S 65 10W
San Diego de la Unión **164** 21 28N 100 52W
San Donà di Piave **63** 45 38N 12 34E
San Elpídio a Mare **63** 43 16N 13 41E
San Estanislao **172** 24 39S 56 26W
San Esteban de Gormaz **58** 41 34N 3 13W
San Felice sul Panaro **62** 44 51N 11 9E
San Felipe, Chile **172** 32 43S 70 50W
San Felipe, Mexico **164** 31 0N 114 52W
San Felipe, Venez. **174** 10 20N 68 44W
San Felipe, R. **163** 33 12N 115 49W
San Feliu de Guixols **58** 41 45N 3 1E
San Feliu de Llobregat **58** 41 23N 2 2E
San Félix **174** 8 20N 62 35W
San Felix, I. **131** 26 30S 80 0W
San Fernando, Chile **172** 34 30S 71 0W
San Fernando, Mexico **164** 30 0N 115 10W
San Fernando, Luzon, Phil. **103** 15 5N 120 37E
San Fernando, Luzon, Phil. **103** 16 40N 120 23E
San Fernando, Spain **57** 36 22N 6 17W
San Fernando, Trin **167** 10 20N 61 30W
San Fernando, U.S.A. **163** 34 15N 118 29W
San Fernando de Apure **174** 7 54N 67 28W
San Fernando de Atabapo **174** 4 3N 67 42W
San Fernando di Puglia **65** 41 18N 16 5E
San Fernando, R. **164** 25 0N 99 0W
San Francisco, Córdoba, Argent. **172** 31 30S 62 5W
San Francisco, San Luis, Argent. **172** 32 45S 66 10W
San Francisco, U.S.A. **163** 37 47N 122 30W
San Francisco de Macorís **167** 19 19N 70 15W
San Francisco del Monte de Oro **172** 32 36S 66 8W
San Francisco del Oro **164** 26 52N 105 50W
San Francisco Javier **59** 38 40N 1 25E
San Francisco, Paso de **172** 35 40S 70 24W
San Francisco, R. **161** 33 30N 109 0W
San Francisco Solano, Pta. **174** 6 18N 77 29W
San Francisville **159** 30 48N 91 22W
San Fratello **65** 38 1N 14 33E
San Gabriel **174** 0 36N 77 49W
San Gavino Monreale **64** 39 33N 8 47E
San German **147** 18 5N 67 3W
San Gil **174** 6 33N 73 8W
San Gimignano **62** 43 28N 11 3E
San Giórgio di Nogaro **63** 45 50N 13 13E
San Giórgio Iónico **65** 40 27N 17 23E
San Giovanni Bianco **62** 45 52N 9 40E
San Giovanni in Fiore **65** 39 16N 16 42E
San Giovanni in Persiceto **63** 44 39N 11 12E
San Giovanni Rotondo **65** 41 41N 15 42E
San Giovanni Valdarno **63** 43 32N 11 30E
San Giuliano Terme **62** 43 45N 10 26E
San Gorgonio Mtn. **163** 34 7N 116 51W
San Gottardo, Paso del **51** 46 33N 8 33E
San Gregorio, Uruguay **173** 32 37S 55 40W
San Gregorio, U.S.A. **163** 37 20N 122 23W
San Guiseppe Iato **64** 37 37N 13 11E
San Ignacio, Boliv. **174** 16 20S 60 55W
San Ignacio, Mexico **164** 27 27N 112 51W
San Ignacio, Parag. **172** 26 52S 57 3W
San Ignacio, Laguna **164** 26 50N 113 11W
San Ildefonso, C. **103** 16 0N 122 10E
San Isidro **172** 34 29S 58 31W
San Jacinto, Colomb. **174** 9 50N 75 8W
San Jacinto, U.S.A. **163** 33 47N 116 57W
San Javier, Misiones, Argent. **173** 27 55S 55 5W
San Javier, Santa Fe, Argent. **172** 30 40S 59 55W
San Javier, Boliv. **174** 16 18S 62 30W
San Javier, Chile **172** 35 40S 71 45W
San Javier, Spain **59** 37 49N 0 50W
San Jerónimo, Sa. de **174** 8 0N 75 50W
San Joaquin **163** 36 36N 120 11W
San Joaquín **174** 10 16N 67 47W
San Joaquin R. **163** 38 4N 121 51W
San Joaquin Valley **163** 37 0N 120 30W
San Jorge **172** 31 54S 61 50W
San Jorge, Bahía de **164** 31 20N 113 20W
San Jorge, Golfo de **176** 46 0S 66 0W
San Jorge, G. de **58** 40 50N 0 55W
San José, Boliv. **174** 17 45S 60 50W
San José, C. Rica **166** 10 0N 84 2W
San José, Guat. **164** 14 0N 90 50W
San José, Luzon, Phil. **103** 15 45N 120 55E
San José, Mindoro, Phil. **103** 10 50N 122 5E
San José, Spain **59** 38 55N 1 18E
San Jose, Calif., U.S.A. **163** 37 20N 121 53W
San Jose, N. Mex., U.S.A. **159** 35 26N 105 30W
San José Carpizo **165** 19 26N 90 32W
San José de Feliciano **172** 30 26S 58 46W
San José de Jáchal **172** 30 5S 69 0W
San José de Mayo **172** 34 27S 56 27W
San José de Ocuné **174** 4 15N 70 20W
San José del Cabo **164** 23 0N 109 50W
San José del Guaviare **174** 2 35N 72 38W
San José, I. **164** 25 0N 110 50W
San Juan, Argent. **172** 31 30S 68 30W
San Juan, Antioquía, Colomb. **174** 8 46N 76 32W
San Juan, Meta, Colomb. **174** 3 26N 73 50W
San Juan, Dom. Rep. **147** 18 49N 71 12W
San Juan, Coahuila, Mexico **164** 29 34N 101 53W
San Juan, Jalisco, Mexico **164** 21 20N 102 50W
San Juan, Querétaro, Mexico **164** 20 25N 100 0W
San Juan, Phil. **103** 8 35N 126 20E
San Juan, Pto Rico **147** 18 28N 66 37W
San Juan □ **172** 31 9S 69 0W
San Juan Bautista, Parag. **172** 26 37S 57 6W
San Juan Bautista, Spain **59** 39 5N 1 31E
San Juan Bautista, U.S.A. **163** 36 51N 121 32W
San Juan, C. **147** 18 23N 65 37W
San Juan Capistrano **163** 33 29N 117 40W
San Juan de Guadalupe **164** 24 38N 102 44W
San Juan de los Cayos **174** 11 10N 68 25W
San Juan de los Morros **174** 9 55N 67 21W
San Juan de Norte, B. de **166** 11 30N 83 40W
San Juan del Norte **166** 10 58N 83 40W
San Juan del Puerto **57** 37 20N 6 50W
San Juan del Río **165** 24 47N 104 27W
San Juan del Sur **166** 11 20N 86 0W
San Juan Mts. **161** 38 30N 108 30W
San Juan, Presa de **164** 17 45N 95 15W
San Juan, R., Argent. **172** 32 20S 67 25W
San Juan, R., Colomb. **174** 4 0N 77 20W
San Juan, R., Nic. **166** 11 0N 84 30W
San Juan, R., Calif., U.S.A. **163** 36 14N 121 9W
San Juan, R., Utah, U.S.A. **161** 37 20N 110 20W
San Julián **176** 49 15S 68 0W
San Just, Sierra de **58** 40 45N 0 41W
San Justo **172** 30 55S 60 30W
San Kamphaeng **100** 18 45N 99 8E
San Lázaro, C. **164** 24 50N 112 18W
San Lázaro, Sa. de **164** 23 25N 110 0W
San Leandro **163** 37 40N 122 6W
San Leonardo **58** 41 51N 3 5W
San Lorenzo, Argent. **172** 32 45S 60 45W
San Lorenzo, Ecuador **174** 1 15N 78 50W
San Lorenzo, Parag. **172** 25 20S 57 32W
San Lorenzo, Venez. **174** 9 47N 71 4W
San Lorenzo de la Parilla **58** 39 51N 2 22W
San Lorenzo de Morunys **58** 42 8N 1 35E
San Lorenzo, I., Mexico **164** 28 35N 112 50W
San Lorenzo, I., Peru **174** 12 20S 77 35W
San Lorenzo, Mt. **176** 47 40S 72 20W
San Lorenzo, R. **164** 24 15N 107 24W
San Lucas, Boliv. **174** 20 5S 65 0W
San Lucas, Baja California S., Mexico **164** 27 10N 112 14W
San Lucas, Baja California S., Mexico **164** 22 53N 109 54W
San Lucas, U.S.A. **163** 36 8N 121 1W
San Lucas, C. de **164** 22 50N 110 0W
San Lucido **65** 39 18N 16 3E
San Luis, Argent. **172** 33 20S 66 20W
San Luis, Cuba **166** 22 17N 83 46W
San Luis, Guat. **166** 16 14N 89 27W
San Luis, U.S.A. **161** 37 14N 105 26W
San Luis, Venez. **174** 11 7N 69 42W
San Luis □ **172** 34 0S 66 0W
San Luís de la Loma **164** 17 18N 100 55W
San Luís de la Paz **164** 21 19N 100 32W
San Luís de Potosí **164** 22 9N 100 59W
San Luís de Potosí □ **164** 22 10N 101 0W
San Luis, I. **164** 29 58N 114 26W
San Luis Obispo **161** 35 21N 120 38W
San Luis Res. **163** 37 4N 121 5W
San Luis Río Colorado **164** 32 29N 114 48W
San Luis, Sierra de **172** 37 25N 66 10W
San Marco Argentano **65** 39 34N 16 8E
San Marco dei Cavoti **65** 41 20N 14 50E
San Marco in Lámis **65** 41 43N 15 38E
San Marcos, Guat. **166** 14 59N 91 52W
San Marcos, U.S.A. **159** 29 53N 98 0W
San Marcos, I. **164** 27 13N 112 6W
San Marino **63** 43 56N 12 25E
San Marino ■ **63** 43 56N 12 25E
San Martín, Argent. **172** 33 5S 68 28W
San Martín, Colomb. **174** 3 42N 73 42W
San Martín de Valdeiglesias **56** 40 21N 4 24W
San Martín, L. **176** 48 50S 72 50W
San Martino de Calvi **62** 45 57N 9 41E
San Mateo, Spain **58** 40 28N 0 10E
San Mateo, U.S.A. **163** 37 32N 122 19W
San Matías **174** 16 25S 58 20W
San Matías, Golfo de **176** 41 30S 64 0W
San Miguel, El Sal. **166** 13 30N 88 12W
San Miguel, Panama **166** 8 27N 78 55W
San Miguel, Spain **59** 39 3N 1 26E
San Miguel, U.S.A. **163** 35 45N 120 42W
San Miguel, Venez. **174** 9 40N 65 11W
San Miguel de Salinas **59** 37 59N 0 47W
San Miguel de Tucumán **172** 26 50S 65 20W
San Miguel del Monte **172** 35 23S 58 50W
San Miguel I. **163** 34 2N 120 23W
San Miguel, R., Boliv. **174** 16 0S 62 45W
San Miguel, R., Ecuador/Ecuador **174** 0 25N 76 30W
San Miniato **62** 43 40N 10 50E
San Narcisco **103** 15 2N 120 3E
San Nicolás de los Arroyas **172** 33 17S 60 10W
San Nicolas I. **154** 33 16N 119 30W
San Onafre **163** 33 22N 117 34W
San Onofre **174** 9 44N 75 32W
San Pablo, Boliv. **172** 21 43S 66 38W
San Pablo, Colomb. **174** 5 27N 70 56W
San Paolo di Civitate **65** 41 44N 15 16E
San Pedro, Buenos Aires, Argent. **173** 33 43S 59 45W
San Pedro, Jujuy, Argent. **172** 24 12S 64 55W
San Pedro, Chile **172** 21 58S 68 30W
San Pedro, Colomb. **174** 4 56N 71 53W
San Pedro, Dom. Rep. **167** 18 30N 69 18W
San Pedro, Ivory C. **120** 4 50N 6 33W
San Pedro, Mexico **164** 23 55N 110 17W
San Pedro □ **172** 24 0S 57 0W
San Pedro Channel **163** 33 35N 118 25W
San Pedro de Arimena **174** 4 37N 71 42W
San Pedro de Atacama **172** 22 55S 68 15W
San Pedro de Jujuy **172** 24 12S 64 55W
San Pedro de las Colonias **164** 25 50N 102 59W
San Pedro de Lloc **174** 7 15S 79 28W
San Pedro del Norte **166** 13 4N 84 33W
San Pedro del Paraná **172** 26 43S 56 13W
San Pedro del Pinatar **59** 37 50N 0 50W
San Pedro Mártir, Sierra **164** 31 0N 115 30W
San Pedro Mixtepec **165** 16 2N 97 0W
San Pedro Ocampo = Melchor Ocampo **164** 24 52N 101 40W
San Pedro, Pta. **172** 25 30S 70 38W
San Pedro, R., Chihuahua, Mexico **164** 28 20N 106 10W
San Pedro, R., Michoacan, Mexico **164** 19 23N 103 51W
San Pedro, R., Nayarit, Mexico **164** 21 45N 105 30W
San Pedro, R., U.S.A. **161** 32 45N 110 35W
San Pedro, Sierra de **57** 39 18N 6 40W
San Pedro Sula **166** 15 30N 88 0W
San Pedro Tututepec **165** 16 9N 97 38W
San Pedro,Pta. **172** 25 30S 70 38W
San Pietro, I. **64** 39 9N 8 17E
San Pietro Vernotico **65** 40 28N 18 0E
San Quintín, Mexico **164** 30 29N 115 57W

San Quintín Santiago

San Quintín, Phil. 103 16 1N 120 56 E
San, R. 54 50 25N 22 20 E
San Rafael, Argent. 172 34 40 S 68 30W
San Rafael, Colomb. 174 6 2N 69 45W
San Rafael, Calif., U.S.A. 163 38 0N 122 32W
San Rafael, N. Mex., U.S.A. 161 35 6N 107 58W
San Rafael, Venez. 174 10 42N 71 46W
San Rafael Mtn. 163 34 41N 119 52W
San Ramón de la Nueva Orán 172 23 10 S 64 20W
San Remo 62 43 48N 7 47 E
San Román, C. 174 12 12N 70 0W
San Roque, Argent. 172 28 15 S 58 45W
San Roque, Spain 57 36 17N 5 21W
San Rosendo 172 37 10 S 72 50W
San Saba 159 31 12N 98 45W
San Salvador 166 13 40N 89 20W
San Salvador de Jujuy 172 23 30 S 65 40W
San Salvador (Watlings) I. 167 24 0N 74 40W
San Sebastián, Argent. 176 53 10 S 68 30W
San Sebastián, Spain 58 43 17N 1 58W
San Sebastián, Venez. 174 9 57N 67 11W
San Serverino 63 43 13N 13 10 E
San Severo 63 41 41N 15 23 E
San Simeon 163 35 39N 121 11W
San Simon 161 32 14N 109 16W
San Stéfano di Cadore 63 46 34N 12 33 E
San Telmo 164 30 58N 116 6W
San Tiburcio 164 24 8N 101 32W
San Valentin, Mte. 176 46 30 S 73 30W
San Vicente de Alcántara 57 39 22N 7 8W
San Vicente de la Barquera 56 43 30N 4 29W
San Vicente del Caguán 174 2 7N 74 46W
San Vicenzo 93 43 9N 10 32 E
San Vito al Tagliamento 63 45 55N 12 50 E
San Vito, C. 64 38 11N 12 41 E
San Vito Chietino 63 42 19N 14 27 E
San Vito dei Normanni 65 40 40N 17 40 E
San Yanaro 174 2 47N 69 42W
San Ygnacio 159 27 6N 92 24W
San Ysidro 161 32 33N 117 5W
San'a 91 15 27N 44 12 E
Sana, R. 63 44 40N 16 43 E
Sanaba 120 12 25N 3 47W
Sanabria, La 56 42 0N 6 30W
Sanâfir 122 27 49N 34 37 E
Sanaga, R. 121 3 35N 9 38 E
Sanak I 147 53 30N 162 30W
Sanaloa, Presa 164 24 50N 107 20W
Sanana 103 2 5 S 125 50 E
Sanand 94 22 59N 72 25 E
Sanandaj 92 35 25N 47 7 E
Sanandita 172 21 40 S 63 35W
Sanary 45 43 7N 5 48 E
Sanawad 94 22 11N 76 5 E
Sanbe-San 110 35 6N 132 38 E
Sancergues 43 47 10N 2 54 E
Sancerre 43 47 20N 2 50 E
Sanch'a Ho 108 26 55N 106 6 E
Sanch'aho 107 44 59N 126 1 E
Sánchez 167 19 15N 69 36W
Sanchiang 108 25 22N 109 26 E
Sanchor 94 24 52N 71 49 E
Sanco, Pt. 103 8 15N 126 24 E
Sancoins 43 46 47N 2 55 E
Sancti-Spíritus 166 21 52N 79 33W
Sand Lake 150 47 46N 84 31W
Sand Point 147 55 20N 160 32W
Sand, R. 129 22 25 S 30 5 E
Sand Springs 159 36 12N 96 5W
Sanda 111 34 53N 135 14 E
Sanda I. 34 55 17N 5 35W
Sandah 122 20 35N 39 32 E
Sandakan 102 5 53N 118 10 E
Sandalwood 140 34 55 S 140 9 E
Sandan 101 12 46N 106 0 E
Sandanski 67 41 35N 23 16 E
Sandaré 120 14 40N 10 15W
Sanday I. 36 57 2N 6 30W
Sanday, I. 37 59 15N 2 30W
Sanday Sd. 37 59 11N 2 31W
Sandbach 32 53 9N 2 23W
Sandbank 34 55 58N 4 57W
Sande, Möre og Romsdal, Norway 71 62 15N 5 27 E
Sande, Sogn og Fjordane, Norway 71 61 20N 5 47 E
Sandefjord 71 59 10N 10 15 E
Sandeid 71 59 33N 5 52 E
Sanders 161 35 12N 109 25W
Sanderson 159 30 5N 102 30W
Sanderston 140 34 46 S 139 15 E
Sandfell 74 63 57N 16 48W
Sandfly L. 153 55 43N 106 6W
Sandgate, Austral. 139 27 18 S 153 3 E
Sandgate, U.K. 29 51 5N 1 9 E
Sandhammaren, C. 73 55 23N 14 14 E
Sandhead 34 54 48N 4 58W
Sandhurst 29 51 21N 0 48W
Sandia 174 14 10 S 69 30W
Sandikli 92 38 30N 30 20 E
Sandiman, Mt. 137 24 21 S 115 20 E
Sandnes 71 58 50N 5 45 E
Sandness 37 60 18N 1 38W
Sandoa 124 9 48 S 23 0 E
Sandomierz 54 50 40N 21 43 E
Sandona 174 1 17N 77 28W
Sandover, R. 138 21 43 S 136 32 E
Sandoway 99 18 20N 94 30 E
Sandown 28 50 39N 1 9W
Sandpoint 160 48 20N 116 40W
Sandray, I. 36 56 53N 7 30W
Sandringham 29 52 50N 0 30 E
Sandslån 72 63 2N 17 49 E
Sandspit 152 53 14N 131 49W
Sandston 162 37 31N 77 19W
Sandstone 137 27 59 S 119 16 E
Sandusky, Mich., U.S.A. 150 43 26N 82 50W
Sandusky, Ohio, U.S.A. 156 41 25N 82 40W
Sandveld 128 32 0 S 18 15 E
Sandvig, Denmark 73 55 18N 14 48 E
Sandvig, Sweden 72 55 32N 14 47 E
Sandvika 71 59 54N 10 29 E
Sandviken 72 60 38N 16 46 E
Sandwich 29 51 16N 1 21 E
Sandwich B., Can. 151 53 40N 57 15W
Sandwich B., S. Afr. 128 23 25 S 14 20 E
Sandwich, C. 138 18 14 S 146 18 E
Sandwich Group 13 57 0 S 27 0W
Sandwip Chan. 99 22 35N 91 35 E
Sandy 29 53 8N 0 18W
Sandy Bight 137 33 50 S 123 20 E
Sandy C., Queens., Austral. 139 24 42 S 153 15 E
Sandy C., Tas., Austral. 138 41 25 S 144 45 E
Sandy Cay 167 23 13N 75 18W
Sandy Cr. 160 42 20N 109 30W
Sandy L. 150 53 2N 93 0W
Sandy Lake 150 53 0N 93 15W
Sandy Narrows 153 55 5N 103 4W
Sanford, Fla., U.S.A. 157 28 45N 81 20W
Sanford, Me., U.S.A. 162 43 28N 70 47W
Sanford, N.C., U.S.A. 157 35 30N 79 10W
Sanford, Mt. 136 16 58 S 130 32 E
Sanford Mt. 148 62 30N 143 0W
Sanford, R. 137 27 22 S 115 53 E
Sang-i-Masha 94 33 16N 67 5 E
Sanga 127 12 22 S 35 21 E
Sanga, R. 124 1 0N 16 30 E
Sanga Tolon 77 61 50N 149 40 E
Sangamner 96 19 30N 74 15 E
Sangar, Afghan. 94 32 56N 65 30 E
Sangar, U.S.S.R. 77 63 55N 127 31 E
Sangar Sarcai 94 34 27N 70 35 E
Sangasanga 102 0 29 S 117 13 E
Sangchen La 99 31 30N 84 40 E
Sangchih 109 29 25N 109 30 E
Sange 126 6 58 S 84 40 E
Sangeang, I. 103 8 12 S 119 6 E
Sanger 163 36 47N 119 35W
Sangerhausen 48 51 28N 11 18 E
Sanggau 102 0 5N 110 30 E
Sangihe, Kep. 103 3 0N 126 0 E
Sangihe, P. 103 3 45N 125 30 E
Sangju 107 36 25N 128 10 E
Sangkan Ho 106 40 24N 115 19 E
Sangkapura 102 5 52 S 112 40 E
Sangkhla 100 15 7N 98 28 E
Sangli 96 16 55N 74 33 E
Sangmélina 121 2 57N 12 1 E
Sangonera, R. 59 37 39N 2 0W
Sangpang Bum 98 26 30N 95 50 E
Sangre de Cristo Mts. 159 37 0N 105 0W
Sangro, R. 63 42 10N 14 30 E
Sangudo 152 53 50N 114 54W
Sangüesa 58 42 37N 1 17W
Sanguinaires, I. 45 41 51N 8 36 E
Sanhala 120 10 3N 6 51W
Sanho 107 39 59N 117 4 E
Sani R. 100 13 32N 105 57 E
Sanish 158 48 0N 102 30W
Sanje 126 0 49 S 31 30 E
Sankaranayinarkovil 97 9 10N 77 35 E
Sankeshwar 96 16 23N 74 23 E
Sankosh, R. 98 26 24N 89 47 E
Sankt Andra 52 46 46N 14 50 E
Sankt Antönien 51 46 58N 9 48 E
Sankt Blasien 49 47 47N 8 7 E
Sankt Gallen 51 47 26N 9 22 E
Sankt Gallen □ 51 47 25N 9 22 E
Sankt Ingbert 49 49 16N 7 6 E
Sankt Johann 52 47 22N 13 12 E
Sankt Margrethen 51 47 28N 9 37 E
Sankt Moritz 51 46 30N 9 50 E
Sankt Olof 73 55 37N 14 8 E
Sankt Pölten 52 48 12N 15 38 E
Sankt Valentin 52 48 11N 14 33 E
Sankt Veit 52 46 54N 14 22 E
Sankt Wendel 49 49 27N 7 9 E
Sankt Wolfgang 52 47 43N 13 27 E
Sankuru, R. 124 4 17 S 20 25 E
Sanlúcar de Barrameda 57 37 26N 6 18W
Sanlucár la Mayor 57 37 26N 6 18W
Sanluri 64 39 35N 8 55 E
Sanmártin 70 46 19N 25 58 E
Sanmen 109 29 5N 121 35 E
Sanmenhsia 106 34 46N 111 30 E
Sanming 109 26 13N 117 35 E
Sannan 111 35 2N 135 1 E
Sannaspos 128 29 6 S 26 34 E
Sannicandro Gargánico 65 41 50N 15 34 E
Sânnicolaul-Maré 66 46 5N 20 39 E
Sannidal 71 58 55N 9 15 E
Sannieshof 128 26 30 S 25 47 E
Sano 111 36 19N 139 35 E
Sanok 54 49 35N 22 10 E
Sanokwelle 120 7 19N 8 38W
Sanpa 108 29 42N 99 33 E
Sanpah 139 30 32 S 141 12 E
Sanquhar 35 55 21N 3 56W
Sansanding Dam 120 13 37N 6 0W
Sansanné-Mango 121 10 20N 0 30 E
Sansepolcro 63 43 34N 12 8 E
Sanshui 109 23 11N 112 53 E
Sanski Most 63 44 46N 16 40 E
Sansui 108 26 57N 108 37 E
Sant' Ágata de Gati 65 41 6N 14 30 E
Sant' Ágata di Militello 65 38 2N 14 40 E
Santa Ana, Ecuador 174 1 10 S 80 20W
Santa Ana, El Sal. 166 14 0N 89 40W
Santa Ana, Mexico 164 30 31N 111 8W
Santa Ana, U.S.A. 163 33 48N 117 55W
Santa Ána, El Beni 174 13 50 S 65 40W
Sant' Ángelo Lodigiano 62 45 14N 9 25 E
Sant' Antíoco 64 39 2N 8 30 E
Sant' Antíoco, I. 64 39 2N 8 30 E
Sant' Arcángelo di Romagna 63 44 4N 12 26 E
Santa Bárbara, Brazil 171 16 0 S 59 0W
Santa Bárbara, Colomb. 174 5 53N 75 35W
Santa Barbara 166 14 53N 88 14W
Santa Bárbara, Mexico 164 26 48N 105 50W
Santa Bárbara, Spain 58 40 42N 0 29 E
Santa Barbara 163 34 25N 119 40W
Santa Bárbara 174 7 47N 71 10W
Santa Barbara Channel 163 34 20N 120 0W
Santa Barbara I. 163 33 29N 119 2W
Santa Barbara Is. 161 33 31N 119 0W
Santa Bárbara, Mt. 59 37 23N 2 50W
Santa Catalina 174 10 36N 75 17W
Santa Catalina, G. of 163 33 0N 118 0W
Santa Catalina, I., Mexico 164 25 40N 110 50W
Santa Catalina, I., U.S.A. 163 33 20N 118 30W
Santa Catarina □ 173 27 25 S 48 30W
Santa Catarina, I. de 173 27 30 S 48 40W
Santa Caterina 65 37 37N 14 1 E
Santa Cecília 173 26 56 S 50 27W
Santa Clara, Cuba 166 22 20N 80 0W
Santa Clara, Calif., U.S.A. 163 37 21N 122 0W
Santa Clara, Utah, U.S.A. 161 37 10N 113 38W
Santa Clara de Olimar 173 32 50 S 54 54W
Santa Clotilde 174 2 25 S 73 45W
Santa Coloma de Farnés 58 41 50N 2 39 E
Santa Coloma de Gramanet 58 41 27N 2 13 E
Santa Comba 56 43 2N 8 49W
Santa Croce Camerina 65 36 50N 14 30 E
Santa Cruz, Argent. 176 50 0 S 68 50W
Santa Cruz, Boliv. 174 17 43 S 63 10W
Santa Cruz, Brazil 170 7 57 S 36 12W
Santa Cruz, Canary Is. 116 28 29N 16 26W
Santa Cruz, Chile 172 34 38 S 71 27W
Santa Cruz, C. Rica 166 10 15N 85 41W
Santa Cruz, Phil. 103 14 20N 121 30 E
Santa Cruz, Calif., U.S.A. 163 36 55N 122 1W
Santa Cruz, N. Mexico, U.S.A. 161 35 59N 106 1W
Santa Cruz □ 174 17 43 S 63 10W
Santa Cruz Cabrália 171 16 17 S 39 2W
Santa Cruz de Barahona 167 18 12N 71 6W
Santa Cruz de Mudela 59 38 39N 3 28W
Santa Cruz de Tenerife □ 72 28 10N 17 20W
Santa Cruz del Norte 166 23 9N 81 55W
Santa Cruz del Retamar 56 40 8N 4 14W
Santa Cruz del Sur 166 20 50N 78 0W
Santa Cruz do Rio Pardo 173 22 54 S 49 37W
Santa Cruz do Sul 173 29 42 S 52 25W
Santa Cruz I. 154 34 0N 119 45W
Santa Cruz, Is. 130 10 30 S 166 0 E
Santa Cruz, R. 176 50 10 S 70 0W
Santa Elena, Argent. 172 30 58 S 59 47W
Santa Elena, Ecuador 174 2 16 S 80 52W
Santa Elena C. 167 10 54N 85 56W
Santa Enimie 44 44 24N 3 26 E
Sant' Eufémia, Golfo di 65 38 50N 16 10 E
Santa Eulalia 59 40 34N 1 20W
Santa Fe, Argent. 172 31 35 S 60 41W
Santa Fe, Spain 57 37 11N 3 43W
Santa Fe, U.S.A. 161 35 40N 106 0W
Santa Fé □ 172 31 50 S 60 55W
Santa Filomena 170 9 0 S 45 50W
Santa Genoveva, Mt. 164 23 18N 109 52W
Santa Groce di Magliano 65 41 43N 14 59 E
Santa Helena 170 2 14 S 45 18W
Santa Helena de Goiás 171 17 43 S 50 35W
Santa Inês 171 13 17 S 39 48W
Santa Inés, I. 176 54 0 S 73 0W
Santa Inés, Mt. 57 38 32N 5 37W
Santa Isabel, Argent. 172 36 10 S 67 0W
Santa Isabel, Brazil 171 13 45 S 56 30W
Santa Isabel = Rey Malabo 121 3 45N 8 50 E
Santa Isabel do Araguaia 170 6 7 S 48 19W
Santa Isabel, Pico 121 4 43N 8 49 E
Santa Juliana 171 19 19 S 47 32W
Santa Lucía, Corrientes, Argent. 172 28 58 S 59 5W
Santa Lucía, San Juan, Argent. 172 31 30 S 68 45W
Santa Lucía, Spain 59 37 35N 0 58W
Santa Lucia 172 34 27 S 56 24W
Santa Lucia Range 163 36 0N 121 20W
Santa Luzia 170 6 53 S 36 56W
Santa Magdalena, I. 164 24 50N 112 15W
Santa Margarita, Argent. 172 38 18 S 61 35W
Santa Margarita, U.S.A. 163 35 23N 120 37W
Santa Margarita, I. 164 24 30N 112 0W
Santa Margarita, R. 163 33 13N 117 23W
Santa Margherita 62 44 20N 9 11 E
Santa María, Argent. 172 26 40 S 66 0W
Santa Maria, Brazil 173 29 40 S 53 40W
Santa Maria 65 41 3N 14 29 E
Santa Maria 164 27 40N 114 40W
Santa María, Spain 58 39 39N 2 45 E
Santa Maria, Switz. 51 46 36N 10 25 E
Santa Maria, U.S.A. 163 34 58N 120 29W
Santa Maria, Zambia 127 11 5 S 29 58 E
Santa María, Bahía de 164 25 10N 108 40W
Santa Maria, Cabo de 57 36 39N 7 53W
Santa Maria da Vitória 171 13 24 S 44 12W
Santa María del Oro 164 25 30N 105 20W
Santa Maria di Leuca, C. 65 39 48N 18 20 E
Santa Maria do Suaçuí 171 18 12 S 42 25W
Santa María la Real de Nieva 56 41 4N 4 24W
Santa María, R. 164 31 0N 107 14W
Santa Marta, Colomb. 174 11 15N 74 13W
Santa Marta, Spain 57 38 37N 6 39W
Santa Marta Grande, C. 173 28 43 S 48 50W
Santa Marta, Ría de 56 43 44N 7 45W
Santa Marta, Sierra Nevada de 147 10 55N 73 50W
Santa Monica 163 34 0N 118 30W
Santa Napa 160 38 28N 122 45W
Santa Olalla, Huelva, Spain 57 37 54N 6 14W
Santa Olalla, Toledo, Spain 56 40 2N 4 25W
Sant' Onofrio 65 38 42N 16 10 E
Santa Paula 163 34 20N 119 2W
Santa Pola 59 38 13N 0 35W
Santa Quitéria 170 4 20 S 40 10W
Santa Rita, U.S.A. 161 32 50N 108 0W
Santa Rita, Guarico, Venez. 174 8 8N 66 16W
Santa Rita, Zulia, Venez. 174 10 32N 71 32W
Santa Rosa, La Pampa, Argent. 172 36 40 S 64 30W
Santa Rosa, San Luis, Argent. 172 32 30 S 65 10W
Santa Rosa, Boliv. 174 10 25 S 67 20W
Santa Rosa, Brazil 173 27 52 S 54 29W
Santa Rosa, Colomb. 174 3 32N 69 48W
Santa Rosa, Hond. 164 14 40N 89 0W
Santa Rosa, Calif., U.S.A. 163 38 26N 122 43W
Santa Rosa, N. Mexico, U.S.A. 159 34 58N 104 40W
Santa Rosa, Amazonas, Venez. 174 1 29N 66 55W
Santa Rosa, Apure, Venez. 174 6 37N 67 57W
Santa Rosa de Cabal 174 4 52N 75 38W
Santa Rosa de Copán 166 14 47N 88 46W
Santa Rosa de Osos 174 6 39N 75 28W
Santa Rosa de Río Primero 172 31 8 S 63 20W
Santa Rosa de Viterbo 174 5 53N 72 59W
Santa Rosa I., Calif., U.S.A. 163 34 0N 120 6W
Santa Rosa I., Fla., U.S.A. 157 30 23N 87 0W
Santa Rosa Mts. 160 41 45N 117 30W
Santa Rosalia 164 27 20N 112 30W
Santa Sofia 63 43 57N 11 55 E
Santa Sylvina 172 27 50 S 61 10W
Santa Tecla = Nueva San Salvador 164 13 40N 89 25W
Santa Teresa, Argent. 172 33 25 S 60 47W
Santa Teresa, Brazil 171 19 55 S 40 36W
Santa Teresa, Mexico 165 25 17N 97 51W
Santa Teresa, Venez. 174 4 43N 61 4W
Santa Teresa di Riva 63 37 58N 15 21 E
Santa Teresa Gallura 64 41 14N 9 12 E
Santa Teresinha 170 12 45 S 50 40W
Santa Vitória 171 18 50 S 50 8W
Santa Vitória do Palmar 173 33 32 S 53 25W
Santa Ynez 163 34 37N 120 5W
Santa Ynez, R. 163 34 37N 120 41W
Santa Ysabel 163 33 7N 116 40W
Sant'ai 108 31 5N 105 2 E
Santadi 64 39 5N 8 42 E
Santahar 98 24 48N 88 59 E
Santaluz 171 11 15 S 39 22W
Santana 171 13 2 S 44 5W
Santana, Coxilha de 173 30 50 S 55 35W
Santana do Ipanema 170 9 22 S 37 14W
Santana do Livramento 173 30 55 S 55 30W
Santander, Colomb. 174 3 1N 76 28W
Santander, Spain 56 43 27N 3 51W
Santander □ 56 43 25N 4 0W
Santander Jiménez 165 24 11N 98 29W
Santañy 59 39 20N 3 5 E
Santaquin 160 40 0N 111 51W
Santarém, Brazil 175 2 25 S 54 42W
Santarém, Port. 57 39 12N 8 42W
Santarém □ 57 39 10N 8 40W
Santaren Channel 166 24 0N 79 30W
Santèramo in Colle 65 40 48N 16 45 E
Santerno, R. 63 44 10N 11 38 E
Santhia 62 45 20N 8 10 E
Santiago, Brazil 173 29 11 S 54 52W
Santiago, Chile 172 33 24 S 70 50W
Santiago, Dom. Rep. 167 19 30N 70 40W

Santiago Sayville

Santiago, Panama 166 8 0N 81 0W
Santiago □ 172 33 30S 70 50W
Santiago de Compostela 56 42 52N 8 37W
Santiago de Cuba 166 20 0N 75 49W
Santiago del Estero 172 27 50S 64 15W
Santiago del Estero □ 172 27 50S 64 20W
Santiago do Cacém 57 38 1N 8 42W
Santiago Ixcuintla 164 21 50N 105 11W
Santiago Papasquiaro 164 25 0N 105 20W
Santiago, Punta de 121 3 12N 8 40E
Santiaguillo, L. de 164 24 50N 104 50W
Santillana del Mar 56 43 24N 4 6W
Santipur 95 23 17N 88 25E
Säntis 51 47 15N 9 22E
Santisteban del Puerto 59 38 17N 3 15W
Santo Amaro 171 12 30S 38 50W
Santo Anastácio 173 21 58S 51 39W
Santo André 173 23 39S 46 29W
Santo Ângelo 173 28 15S 54 15W
Santo Antonio 170 15 50S 56 0W
Santo Antônio de Jesus 171 12 58S 39 16W
Santo Antonio do Zaire 124 6 7S 12 20E
Santo Corazón 174 18 0S 58 45W
Santo Domingo, Dom. Rep. 167 18 30N 70 0W
Santo Domingo, Baja Calif. N., Mexico 164 30 43N 115 56W
Santo Domingo, Baja Calif. S., Mexico 164 25 32N 112 2W
Santo Domingo, Nic. 166 12 14N 84 59W
Santo Domingo de la Calzada 58 42 26N 2 27W
Santo Isabel do Morro 171 11 34S 50 40W
Santo Stéfano di Camastro 65 38 1N 14 22E
Santo Stino di Livenza 63 45 45N 12 40E
Santo Tirso 56 41 29N 8 18W
Santo Tomas 164 31 33N 116 24W
Santo Tomás 174 14 34S 72 30W
Santo Tomé 173 28 40S 56 5W
Santoña 56 43 29N 3 20W
Santos 173 24 0S 46 20W
Santos Dumont 173 22 55S 43 10W
Santos, Sierra de los 57 38 7N 5 12W
Santport 46 52 26N 4 39E
Santu 108 25 59N 107 52E
Sanur 90 32 22N 35 15E
Sanvignes-les-Mines 43 46 40N 4 18E
San'yō 110 34 2N 131 5E
Sanyuki-Sammyaku 110 34 5N 133 0E
Sanza Pombo 124 7 18S 15 56E
São Anastacio 173 22 0S 51 40W
São Bartolomeu de Messines 57 37 15N 8 17W
São Benedito 170 4 3S 40 53W
São Bento 170 2 42S 44 50W
São Bento do Norte 170 5 4S 36 2W
São Borja 173 28 45S 56 0W
São Bras d'Alportel 57 37 8N 7 58W
São Caitano 170 8 21S 36 6W
São Carlos 173 22 0S 47 50W
São Cristóvão 170 11 15S 37 15W
São Domingos, Brazil 171 13 25S 46 10W
São Domingos, Guin.-Biss. 170 12 22N 16 8W
São Domingos do Maranhão 170 5 42S 44 22W
São Félix, Bahia, Brazil 171 12 38S 38 58W
São Félix, Mato Grosso, Brazil 171 11 36S 50 39W
Sao Francisco 171 16 0S 44 50W
Sao Francisco do Maranhão 170 6 15S 42 52W
São Francisco do Sul 173 26 15S 48 36W
São Francisco, R. 170 10 30S 36 24W
São Gabriel 173 30 10S 54 30W
São Gabriel da Palha 171 18 47S 40 59W
São Gonçalo 173 22 48S 43 5W
São Gotardo 171 19 19S 46 3W
Sao Hill 127 8 20S 35 18E
São João da Boa Vista 173 22 0S 46 52W
São João da Pesqueira 56 41 8N 7 24W
São João da Ponte 171 15 56S 44 1W
São João del Rei 173 21 8S 44 15W
São João do Araguaia 170 5 23S 48 46W
São João do Paraíso 171 15 19S 42 1W
São João do Piauí 170 8 10S 42 15W
São João dos Patos 170 6 30S 43 42W
São João Evangelista 171 18 32S 42 45W
São Joaquim da Barra 171 20 35S 47 53W
São José, B. de 170 2 38S 44 4W
São José da Laje 170 9 1S 36 3W
São José de Mipibu 170 6 5S 35 15W
São José do Peixe 170 7 24S 42 34W
São José do Rio Prêto 173 20 50S 49 20W
São José dos Campos 173 23 7S 45 52W
São Leopoldo 173 29 50S 51 10W
São Lourenço, Mato Grosso, Brazil 173 16 30S 55 5W
São Lourenço, Minas Gerais, Brazil 171 22 7S 45 3W
São Lourenço, R. 175 16 40S 56 0W
São Luís do Curu 170 3 40S 39 14W
São Luis Gonzaga 173 28 25S 55 0W
São Luís (Maranhão) 170 2 39S 44 15W
Sao Marcelino 174 1 0N 67 12W
São Marcelino 174 1 0N 67 12W
São Marcos, B. de 170 2 0S 44 0W
São Marcos, R. 171 18 15S 47 37W
São Martinho 56 39 30N 9 8W
São Mateus 171 18 44S 39 50W
São Mateus, R. 171 18 35S 39 44W
São Miguel 16 37 33N 25 27W
São Miguel do Araguaia 171 13 19S 50 13W
São Miguel dos Campos 170 9 47S 36 5W
São Nicolau, R. 170 5 45S 42 2W
São Paulo 173 23 40S 46 50W
São Paulo □ 173 22 0S 49 0W
São Pedro do Piaui 171 5 56S 42 43W
São Pedro do Sul 56 40 46N 8 4W
São Rafael 170 5 47S 36 55W
São Raimundo das Mangabeiras 170 7 1S 45 29W
São Raimundo Nonato 170 9 1S 42 42W
São Romão, Amazonas, Brazil 174 5 53S 67 50W
São Romão, Minas Gerais, Brazil 171 16 22S 45 4W
São Roque, C. de 170 5 30S 35 10W
São Sebastião do Paraíso 173 20 54S 46 59W
São Sebastião, I. 173 23 50S 45 18W
São Simão 171 18 56S 50 30W
São Teotónio 57 37 30N 8 42W
São Tomé 170 5 58S 36 4W
São Tomé, C. de 173 22 0S 41 10W
São Tomé, I. 114 0 10N 7 0E
São Vicente 173 23 57S 46 23W
São Vicente, Cabo de 57 37 0N 9 0W
Saona, I. 167 18 10N 68 40W
Saône-et-Loire □ 43 46 25N 4 50E
Saône, R. 43 46 25N 4 50E
Saonek 103 0 28S 130 47E
Saoura, O. 118 29 55N 1 50W
Sapai 68 41 2N 25 43E
Sapão, R. 170 11 1S 45 32W
Saparua, I. 103 3 33S 128 40E
Sapé 170 7 6S 35 13W
Sapele 121 5 50N 5 40E
Sapelo I. 157 31 28N 81 15W
Sapiéntza I. 69 36 33N 21 43E
Sapodnyy Sayan 77 52 30N 94 0E
Sapone 121 12 3N 1 35W
Saposoa 174 6 55S 76 30W
Sapozhok 81 53 59N 40 51E
Sappemeer 46 53 10N 6 48E
Sapporo 112 43 0N 141 15E
Sapri 65 40 5N 15 37E
Sapudi, I. 103 7 2S 114 17E
Sapulpa 159 36 0N 96 40W
Sapur 95 34 18N 74 27E
Saqota 123 12 40N 39 1E
Saqqez 92 36 15N 46 20E
Sar-i-Pul 93 36 10N 66 0E
Sar Planina 66 42 10N 21 0E
Sara 120 11 40N 3 53W
Sara Buri 100 14 30N 100 55E
Sarab 92 38 0N 47 30E
Sarada, R. 99 28 15N 80 30E
Saragossa = Zaragoza 58 41 39N 0 53W
Saraguro 174 3 35S 79 16W
Sarai 70 44 43N 28 10E
Saraipalli 96 21 20N 82 59E
Sarajevo 66 43 52N 18 26E
Saraktash 84 51 47N 56 22E
Saramati 98 25 44N 95 2E
Saran 122 19 35N 40 30E
Saran, G. 102 0 30S 111 25E
Saranac Lake 156 44 20N 74 10W
Saranda, Alb. 68 39 59N 19 55E
Saranda, Tanz. 126 5 45S 34 59E
Sarandí del Yi 173 33 18S 55 38W
Sarandí Grande 172 33 20S 55 50W
Sarangani B. 103 6 0N 125 13E
Sarangani Is. 103 5 25N 125 25E
Sarangarh 96 21 30N 82 57E
Saransk 81 54 10N 45 10E
Sarapul 84 56 28N 53 48E
Sarasota 157 27 10N 82 30W
Saratoga, Calif., U.S.A. 163 37 16N 122 2W
Saratoga, Wyo., U.S.A. 160 41 30N 106 56W
Saratoga Springs 162 43 5N 73 47W
Saratok 102 3 5S 110 50E
Saratov 81 51 30N 46 2E
Saravane 100 15 43N 106 25E
Sarawak □ 102 2 0N 113 0E
Saraya 120 12 50N 11 45W
Sarbaz 93 26 38N 61 19E
Sarbisheh 93 32 30N 59 40E
Sârbogârd 53 46 55N 18 40E
Sarca, R. 62 46 5N 10 45E
Sardalas 119 25 50N 10 54E
Sardarshahr 94 28 30N 74 29E
Sardegna, I. 64 39 57N 9 0E
Sardhana 94 29 9N 77 39E
Sardinata 174 8 5N 72 48W
Sardinia = Sardegna 64 39 57N 9 0E
Sardo 123 11 56N 41 14E
Sarektjåkkå 74 67 27N 17 43E
Sarengrad 66 45 14N 19 16E
Saréyamou 120 16 25N 3 10W
Sargasso Sea 14 27 0N 72 0W
Sargent 158 41 42N 99 24W
Sargodha 94 32 10N 72 40E
Sargodha □ 94 31 50N 72 0E
Sarh 117 9 5N 18 23E
Sarhro, Jebel 118 31 6N 5 0W
Sári 93 36 30N 53 11E
Sária, I. 69 35 54N 27 17E
Sarichef C. 147 54 38N 164 59W
Sarida, R. 90 32 4N 35 3E
Sarikamiş 92 40 22N 42 35E
Sarikei 102 2 8N 111 30E
Sarina 138 21 22S 149 13E
Sarine, R. 50 46 32N 7 4E
Sariñena 58 41 47N 0 10W
Sarír Tibasti 119 22 50N 18 30E
Sarita 159 27 14N 90 49W
Sariwołn 107 38 31N 125 46E
Sariyer 67 41 10N 29 3E
Sark, I. 42 49 25N 2 20W
Sarkad 53 46 47N 21 17E
Sarlat-la-Canéda 44 44 54N 1 13E
Sarles 158 48 58N 98 57W
Sarmi 103 1 49S 138 38E
Särna 72 61 41N 12 58E
Sarnano 63 43 2N 13 17E
Sarnen 50 46 53N 8 13E
Sarnia 150 42 58N 82 23W
Sarno 65 40 48N 14 35E
Sarnowa 54 51 39N 16 53E
Sarny 80 51 17N 26 40E
Särö 73 57 31N 11 57E
Sarolangun 102 2 30S 102 30E
Saronikós Kólpos 69 37 45N 23 45E
Saros Körfezi 68 40 30N 26 15E
Sárospatak 53 48 18N 21 33E
Sarosul Romanesc 66 45 34N 21 43E
Sarpsborg 71 59 16N 11 12E
Sarracín 58 42 15N 3 45W
Sarralbe 43 48 55N 7 1E
Sarraz, La 50 46 38N 6 30E
Sarre, La 150 48 45N 79 15W
Sarre, R. 43 48 49N 7 0E
Sarre-Union 43 48 55N 7 4E
Sarrebourg 43 48 43N 7 3E
Sarreguemines 43 49 1N 7 4E
Sarriá 56 42 41N 7 29W
Sarrión 58 40 9N 0 49W
Sarro 120 13 40N 5 5W
Sarstedt 48 52 13N 9 50E
Sartène 45 41 38N 9 0E
Sarthe □ 42 47 58N 0 10E
Sarthe, R. 42 47 33N 0 31W
Sartilly 42 48 45N 1 28W
Sartynya 76 63 30N 62 50E
Sarum 122 21 11N 39 10E
Sarúr 93 23 17N 58 4E
Sárvár 53 47 15N 16 56E
Sarveston 93 29 20N 53 10E
Särvfjället 72 62 42N 13 30E
Sárviz, R. 53 46 40N 18 40E
Sary Ozek 85 44 22N 77 59E
Sary-Tash 85 39 44N 73 15E
Saryagach 85 41 27N 69 9E
Sarych, Mys. 82 44 25N 33 25E
Sarykolskiy Khrebet 85 38 30N 74 30E
Sarykopa, Ozero 84 50 22N 64 6E
Sarymoin, Ozero 84 51 36N 64 30E
Saryshagan 76 46 12N 73 48E
Sarzana 70 44 7N 9 57E
Sarzeau 42 47 31N 2 48W
Sas van Gent 47 51 14N 3 48E
Sasa 90 33 2N 35 23E
Sasabeneh 91 7 59N 44 43E
Sasaram 95 24 57N 84 5E
Sasayama 111 35 4N 135 13E
Sasca Montanŭ 66 44 41N 21 45E
Sasebo 110 33 10N 129 43E
Saser Mt. 95 34 50N 77 50E
Saskatchewan □ 153 54 40N 106 0W
Saskatchewan, R. 153 53 12N 99 16W
Saskatoon 153 52 10N 106 38W
Sasolburg 129 26 46S 27 49E
Sasovo 81 54 25N 41 55E
Sassandra 120 5 0N 6 8W
Sassandra, R. 120 5 0N 6 8W
Sássari 64 40 44N 8 33E
Sassenheim 46 52 14N 4 31E
Sassnitz 48 54 29N 13 39E
Sasso Marconi 63 44 22N 11 12E
Sassocorvaro 63 43 47N 12 30E
Sassoferrato 63 43 26N 12 51E
Sassuolo 62 44 31N 10 47E
Sástago 58 41 19N 0 21W
Sastown 120 4 45N 8 27W
Sasumua Dam 126 0 54S 36 46E
Sasyk, Ozero 70 45 45N 30 0E
Sasykkul 85 37 41N 73 11E
Sata-Misaki 110 30 59N 130 40E
Satadougou 120 12 40N 11 25W
Satanta 159 37 30N 101 0W
Satara 96 17 44N 73 58E
Satilla, R. 157 31 15N 81 50W
Satka 84 55 3N 59 1E
Satkania 98 22 4N 92 3E
Satkhira 98 22 43N 89 8E
Satmala Hills 96 20 15N 74 40E
Satna 95 24 35N 80 50E
Sator, mt. 63 44 11N 16 43E
Sátoraljaújhely 53 48 25N 21 41E
Satpura Ra. 94 21 40N 75 0E
Satrup 48 54 39N 9 38E
Satsuma-Hantō 110 31 25N 130 25E
Satsuna-Shotō 112 30 0N 130 0E
Sattahip 100 12 41N 100 54E
Sattenpalle 96 16 25N 80 6E
Satu Mare 70 47 46N 22 55E
Satui 102 3 50S 115 20E
Satumare □ 70 47 45N 23 0E
Satun 101 6 43N 100 2E
Saturnina, R. 174 12 15S 58 10W
Sauce 172 30 5S 58 46W
Sauceda 164 25 46N 101 19W
Saucillo 164 28 1N 105 17W
Sauda 71 59 38N 6 21E
Saúde 170 10 56S 40 24W
Sauðarkrókur 74 65 45N 19 40W
Saudi Arabia ■ 92 26 0N 44 0E
Sauerland 48 51 0N 8 0E
Saugerties 162 42 4N 73 58W
Saugues 44 44 58N 3 32E
Sauherad 71 59 25N 9 15E
Sauid el Amia 118 25 57N 6 8W
Saujon 44 45 41N 0 55W
Sauk Center 158 45 42N 94 56W
Sauk Rapids 158 45 35N 94 10W
Saulgau 49 48 4N 9 32E
Saulieu 43 47 17N 4 14E
Sault 45 44 6N 5 24E
Sault Ste. Marie, Can. 150 46 30N 84 20W
Sault Ste. Marie, U.S.A. 156 46 27N 84 22W
Saumlaki 103 7 55S 131 20E
Saumur 42 47 15N 0 5W
Saunders 152 52 58N 115 40W
Saunders C. 143 45 53S 170 45E
Saunders I. 13 57 30S 27 30W
Saunders Point, Mt. 137 27 52S 125 38E
Saundersfoot 31 51 43N 4 42W
Saurbær, Borgarfjarðarsýsla, Iceland 74 64 24N 21 35W
Saurbær, Eyjafjarðarsýsla, Iceland 74 65 27N 18 13W
Sauri 121 11 50N 6 44E
Sausalito 163 37 51N 122 29W
Sautatá 174 7 50N 77 4W
Sauveterre, B. 44 43 25N 0 57W
Sauzé-Vaussais 44 46 8N 0 8E
Savá 166 15 32N 86 15W
Sava 65 40 28N 17 32E
Sava, R. 63 44 40N 19 50E
Savage 158 47 43N 104 20W
Savalou 121 7 57N 2 4E
Savanah Downs 138 19 30S 141 30E
Savane 127 19 37S 35 8E
Savanna 158 42 5N 90 10W
Savanna la Mar 166 18 10N 78 10W
Savannah, Ga., U.S.A. 157 32 4N 81 4W
Savannah, Mo., U.S.A. 158 39 55N 94 46W
Savannah, Tenn., U.S.A. 157 35 12N 88 18W
Savannah Downs 138 19 28S 141 47E
Savannah, R. 157 33 0N 81 30W
Savannakhet 100 16 30N 104 49E
Savant L. 150 50 14N 90 6W
Savant Lake 150 50 30N 90 25W
Savantvadi 97 15 55N 73 54E
Savanur 97 14 59N 75 28E
Savda 96 21 9N 75 56E
Savé 121 8 2N 2 17E
Save R. 125 21 16S 34 0E
Saveh 92 35 2N 50 20E
Savelovo 81 56 51N 37 20E
Savelugu 121 9 38N 0 54W
Savenay 42 47 20N 1 55W
Saverdun 44 43 14N 1 34E
Saverne 43 48 39N 7 20E
Savièse 50 46 17N 7 22E
Savigliano 62 44 39N 7 40E
Savigny-sur-Braye 44 47 53N 0 49E
Saviñao 56 42 35N 7 38W
Savio, R. 63 43 58N 12 10E
Savnik 66 42 59N 19 10E
Savognin 51 46 36N 9 37E
Savoie □ 45 45 26N 6 35E
Savona 62 44 19N 8 29E
Savonlinna 78 61 55N 28 55E
Sävsjö 73 57 20N 14 40E
Sävsjøström 73 57 1N 15 25E
Sawahlunto 102 0 52S 100 52E
Sawai 103 3 0S 129 5E
Sawai Madhopur 94 26 0N 76 25E
Sawang Daen Din 100 17 28N 103 28E
Sawankhalok 100 17 19N 99 50E
Sawara 111 35 55N 140 30E
Sawatch Mts. 161 38 30N 106 30W
Sawbridgeworth 29 51 49N 0 10E
Sawdā, Jabal as 119 28 51N 15 12E
Sawel, Mt. 38 54 48N 7 5W
Sawfajjin, W. 119 31 46N 14 30E
Sawi 101 10 14N 99 5E
Sawmills 127 19 30S 28 2E
Sawston 29 52 7N 0 11E
Sawtry 29 52 26N 0 17W
Sawu, I. 103 10 35S 121 50E
Sawu Sea 103 9 30S 121 50E
Saxby, R. 138 18 25S 140 53E
Saxilby 33 53 16N 0 40W
Saxlingham Nethergate 29 52 33N 1 16E
Saxmundham 29 52 13N 1 29E
Saxon 50 46 9N 7 11E
Saxony, Lower = Niedersachsen 48 52 45N 9 0E
Say 121 13 8N 2 22E
Saya 121 9 30N 3 18E
Sayabec 151 48 35N 67 41W
Sayaboury 100 19 15N 101 45E
Sayán 174 11 0S 77 25W
Sayan, Vostochnyy 77 54 0N 96 0E
Sayan, Zapadnyy 77 52 30N 94 0E
Sayasan 83 42 56N 46 15E
Sayda 92 33 35N 35 25E
Sayhan Ovoo 106 45 27N 103 54E
Sayhandulaan 106 44 40N 109 1E
Saynshand 106 44 55N 110 11E
Sayō 110 34 59N 134 22E
Sayre, Okla., U.S.A. 159 35 20N 99 40W
Sayre, Pa., U.S.A. 162 42 0N 76 30W
Sayula 164 19 50N 103 40W
Sayville 162 40 45N 73 7W

Sazan	68	40 30N	19 20 E
Sazin	95	35 35N	73 30 E
Sazlika, R.	67	42 15N	25 50 E
Sbeïtla	119	35 12N	9 7 E
Scaër	42	48 2N	3 42W
Scalasaig	34	56 4N	6 10W
Scalby	33	54 18N	0 26W
Scalby Ness	33	54 18N	0 25W
Scalea	65	39 49N	15 47 E
Scalloway	36	60 9N	1 16W
Scalpay, I., Inner Hebrides, U.K.	36	57 18N	6 0W
Scalpay, I., Outer Hebrides, U.K.	36	57 51N	6 40W
Scamblesby	33	53 17N	0 5W
Scammon Bay	147	62 0N	165 49W
Scandia	152	50 20N	112 0W
Scandiano	62	44 36N	10 40 E
Scandinavia	16	64 0N	12 0 E
Scansano	63	42 40N	11 20 E
Scapa Flow	37	58 52N	3 6W
Scarastovore	36	57 50N	7 2W
Scarba, I.	34	56 10N	5 42W
Scarborough, Trin	167	11 11N	60 42W
Scarborough, U.K.	33	54 17N	0 24W
Scargill	143	42 56S	172 58 E
Scariff	39	52 55N	8 32W
Scariff I.	39	51 43N	10 15W
Scarinish	34	56 30N	6 48W
Scarning	29	52 40N	0 53W
Scarp, I.	36	58 1N	7 8W
Scarpe, R.	43	50 31N	3 27 E
Scarsdale	140	37 41S	143 39 E
Scattery I.	39	52 37N	9 30W
Scavaig, L.	36	57 8N	6 10W
Scebeli, Uebi	91	2 0N	44 0 E
Scédro, I.	63	43 6N	16 43 E
Scenic	158	43 49N	102 32W
Schaal See	48	53 40N	10 57 E
Schaan	51	47 10N	9 31 E
Schaesberg	47	50 54N	6 0 E
Schaffen	47	51 0N	5 5 E
Schaffhausen	51	47 42N	8 39 E
Schaffhausen □	51	47 42N	8 36 E
Schagen	47	52 49N	4 48 E
Schaghticoke	162	42 54N	73 35W
Schalkhaar	46	52 17N	6 12 E
Schalkwijk	46	52 0N	5 11 E
Schangnau	50	46 50N	7 47 E
Schänis	51	47 10N	9 3 E
Schärding	52	48 27N	13 27 E
Scharhörn, I.	48	53 58N	8 24 E
Scharnitz	52	47 23N	11 15 E
Scheessel	48	53 10N	9 33 E
Schefferville	151	54 48N	66 50W
Scheibbs	52	48 1N	15 9 E
Schelde, R.	47	51 10N	4 20 E
Scheldewindeke	47	50 56N	3 46 E
Schenectady	162	42 50N	73 58W
Schenevus	162	42 33N	74 50W
Scherfede	48	51 32N	9 2 E
Scherpenheuvel	47	50 58N	4 58 E
Scherpenisse	47	51 33N	4 6 E
Scherpenzeel	46	52 5N	5 30 E
Schesaplana	51	47 5N	9 43 E
Scheveningen	46	52 6N	4 16 E
Schichallion, Mt.	37	56 40N	4 6W
Schiedam	46	51 55N	4 25 E
Schiermonnikoog	46	53 29N	6 10 E
Schiermonnikoog, I.	46	53 30N	6 15 E
Schiers	51	47 58N	9 41 E
Schifferstadt	49	49 22N	8 23 E
Schifflange	47	49 30N	6 1 E
Schijndel	47	51 37N	5 27 E
Schiltigheim	43	48 35N	7 45 E
Schio	63	45 42N	11 21 E
Schipbeek	46	52 14N	6 10 E
Schipluiden	46	51 59N	4 19 E
Schirmeck	43	48 29N	7 12 E
Schladming	52	47 23N	13 41 E
Schlei, R.	48	54 45N	9 52 E
Schleiden	48	50 32N	6 26 E
Schleswig	48	54 32N	9 34 E
Schleswig-Holstein □	48	54 10N	9 40 E
Schlieren	51	47 28N	8 27 E
Schlüchtern	49	50 20N	9 32 E
Schmalkalden	48	50 43N	10 28 E
Schmölln	48	50 54N	12 22 E
Schneeberg, Austria	52	47 53N	15 55 E
Schneeberg, Ger.	48	50 35N	12 39 E
Schoenberg	47	50 17N	6 16 E
Schofield	158	44 54N	89 39W
Schoharie	162	42 40N	74 19W
Schoharie, R.	162	42 56N	74 18W
Schönberg, Rostock, Ger.	48	53 50N	10 55 E
Schönberg, Schleswig-Holstein, Ger.	48	54 23N	10 20 E
Schönebeck	48	52 2N	11 42 E
Schönenwerd	50	47 23N	8 0 E
Schöningen	48	52 8N	10 57 E
Schoondijke	47	51 21N	3 33 E
Schoonebeek	46	52 39N	6 52 E
Schoonebeek, oilfield	19	52 45N	6 50 E
Schoonhoven	46	51 57N	4 51 E
Schoonoord	46	52 51N	6 46 E
Schoorl	46	52 42N	4 42 E
Schors	80	51 48N	31 56 E
Schortens	48	53 37N	7 51 E
Schoten	47	51 16N	4 30 E
Schouten, Kepulauan	103	1 0S	136 0 E
Schouter I.	138	42 20S	148 20 E
Schouwen, I.	47	51 43N	3 45 E
Schramberg	49	48 12N	8 24 E
Schrankogl	52	47 3N	11 7 E
Schreckhorn	50	46 36N	8 7 E
Schreiber	150	48 45N	87 20W
Schroon Lake	162	43 47N	73 46W
Schruns	52	47 5N	9 56 E
Schuler	153	50 20N	110 6W
Schuls	51	46 48N	10 18 E
Schumacher	150	48 30N	81 16W
Schüpfen	50	47 2N	7 24 E
Schüpfheim	50	46 57N	8 2 E
Schurz	163	38 57N	118 48W
Schuyler	158	41 30N	97 3W
Schuylerville	162	43 6N	73 35W
Schuylkill Haven	162	40 37N	76 11W
Schuylkill, R.	162	39 53N	75 12W
Schwabach	49	49 19N	11 3 E
Schwäbisch Gmünd	49	48 49N	9 48 E
Schwäbisch Hall	49	49 7N	9 45 E
Schwäbischer Alb	49	48 30N	9 30 E
Schwanden	51	47 1N	9 5 E
Schwarzach, R.	52	50 30N	11 30 E
Schwarzenberg	48	50 31N	12 49 E
Schwarzenburg	50	46 49N	7 20 E
Schwarzwald	49	48 0N	8 0 E
Schwaz	52	47 20N	11 44 E
Schwedt	48	53 4N	14 18 E
Schweinfurt	49	50 3N	10 12 E
Schweizer Mittelland	50	47 0N	7 15 E
Schweizer Reneke	128	27 11S	25 18 E
Schwerin	48	53 37N	11 22 E
Schwerin □	48	53 35N	11 20 E
Schweriner See	48	53 45N	11 26 E
Schwetzingen	49	49 22N	8 35 E
Schwyz	51	47 2N	8 39 E
Schwyz □	51	47 2N	8 39 E
Sciacca	64	37 30N	13 3 E
Scicli	65	36 48N	14 41 E
Scie, La	151	49 57N	55 36W
Scillave	91	6 22N	44 32 E
Scilly, Isles of	30	49 55N	6 15W
Scinawa	54	51 25N	16 26 E
Scioto, R.	156	39 0N	83 0W
Scituate	162	42 12N	70 44W
Sclayn	47	50 29N	5 2 E
Scobey	158	48 47N	105 30W
Scole	29	52 22N	1 10 E
Scone	141	32 0S	150 52 E
Scopwick	33	53 6N	0 24W
Scórdia	65	37 19N	14 50 E
Score Hd.	36	60 12N	1 5W
Scoresby Sund	12	70 20N	23 0W
Scorno, Punta dello	64	41 7N	8 23 E
Scotia, Calif., U.S.A.	160	40 36N	124 4W
Scotia, N.Y., U.S.A.	162	42 50N	73 58W
Scotia Sea	13	56 5S	56 0W
Scotland	158	43 10N	97 45W
Scotland □	51	57 0N	4 0W
Scotland Neck	157	36 6N	77 24W
Scott	13	77 0S	165 0 E
Scott, C., Antarct.	13	71 30S	168 0 E
Scott, C., Austral.	136	13 30S	129 49 E
Scott City	158	38 30N	100 52W
Scott, I.	13	67 0S	179 0 E
Scott Inlet	149	71 0N	71 0W
Scott Is.	152	50 48N	128 40W
Scott L.	153	59 55N	106 18W
Scott Reef	136	14 0S	121 50 E
Scottburgh	129	30 15S	30 47 E
Scottsbluff	158	41 55N	103 35W
Scottsboro	157	34 40N	86 0W
Scottsburg	156	38 40N	85 46W
Scottsdale	138	41 9S	147 31 E
Scottsville	157	36 48N	86 10W
Scottville, Austral.	138	20 33S	147 49 E
Scottville, U.S.A.	156	43 57N	86 18W
Scourie	36	58 20N	5 10W
Scousburgh	36	59 58N	1 20W
Scrabby	38	53 53N	7 32W
Scrabster	37	58 36N	3 31W
Scram, gasfield	19	52 55N	2 42 E
Scramoge	38	53 46N	8 4W
Scranton	162	41 22N	75 41W
Screebe Lodge	38	53 23N	9 33W
Screggan	42	53 15N	7 32W
Scremerston	35	55 44N	1 59W
Scridain, L.	34	56 23N	6 7W
Scunthorpe	33	53 35N	0 38W
Scuol	51	46 48N	10 17 E
Scusciuban	91	10 28N	50 5 E
SE Tor, oilfield	19	56 38N	3 27 E
Sea Isle City	162	39 9N	74 42W
Seabra	171	12 25S	41 46W
Seabrook, L.	137	30 55S	119 40 E
Seaford, Austral.	141	38 10S	145 11 E
Seaford, U.K.	29	50 46N	0 8 E
Seaford, U.S.A.	162	38 37N	75 36W
Seaforth	150	43 35N	81 25W
Seaforth, L.	36	57 52N	6 36W
Seagraves	159	32 56N	102 30W
Seaham	35	54 51N	1 20W
Seahouses	35	55 35N	1 39W
Seal Cove	151	49 57N	56 22W
Seal L.	151	54 20N	61 30W
Seal, R.	153	58 50N	97 30W
Sealga, L. na	36	57 50N	5 18W
Sealy	159	29 46N	96 9W
Seamer	33	54 14N	0 27W
Sean, gasfield	19	53 13N	2 50 E
Searchlight	161	35 31N	114 55W
Searcy	159	35 15N	91 45W
Searles, L.	163	35 47N	117 17W
Seascale	32	54 24N	3 29W
Seaside, Calif., U.S.A.	163	36 37N	121 50W
Seaside, Oreg., U.S.A.	160	46 12N	121 55W
Seaside Park	162	39 55N	74 5W
Seaspray	141	38 25S	147 15 E
Seaton, U.K.	30	50 42N	3 3W
Seaton, U.K.	32	54 40N	3 31W
Seaton Delaval	35	55 5N	1 33W
Seattle	160	47 41N	122 15W
Seaview Ra.	138	18 40S	145 45 E
Seaward Kaikouras, Mts.	143	42 10S	173 44 E
Sebago Lake	162	43 50N	70 35W
Sebastián Vizcaíno, Bahía	164	28 0N	114 30W
Sebastopol	160	38 24N	122 49W
Sebastopol = Sevastopol	82	44 35N	33 30 E
Sebderat	123	15 26N	36 42 E
Sebdou	118	34 38N	1 19W
Sebeşului, Mţii.	70	45 56N	23 40 E
Sebewaing	156	43 45N	83 27W
Sebezh	80	56 14N	28 22 E
Sebi	120	15 50N	4 12W
Sebinkarahisar	82	40 22N	38 28 E
Sebiş	70	46 23N	22 13 E
Sebkra Azzel Mati	118	26 10N	0 43 E
Sebkra Mekerghene	118	26 21N	1 30 E
Sebou, Oued	118	34 16N	6 40W
Sebring	157	27 36N	81 47W
Sebta = Ceuta	118	35 52N	5 26W
Sebuku, I.	102	3 30S	116 25 E
Sebuku, Teluk	102	4 0N	118 10 E
Sečanj	66	45 25N	20 47 E
Secchia, R.	62	44 30N	10 40 E
Sechelt	152	49 25N	123 42W
Sechura, Desierto de	174	6 0S	80 30W
Seclin	43	50 33N	3 2 E
Secondigny	42	46 37N	0 26W
Sečovce	53	48 42N	21 40 E
Secretary I.	143	45 15S	166 56 E
Secunderabad	96	17 28N	78 30 E
Seda, R.	57	39 6N	7 53W
Sedalia	158	38 40N	93 18W
Sedan, Austral.	140	34 34S	139 19 E
Sedan, France	43	49 43N	4 57 E
Sedan, U.S.A.	159	37 10N	96 11W
Sedano	58	42 43N	3 49W
Sedbergh	32	54 20N	2 31W
Seddon	143	41 40S	174 7 E
Seddonville	143	41 33S	172 1 E
Sede Ya'aqov	90	32 43N	35 7 E
Sederberg, Mt.	128	32 22S	19 7 E
Sedgefield	33	54 40N	1 27W
Sedgewick	152	52 48N	111 41W
Sedhiou	120	12 50N	15 30W
Sedičany	52	49 40N	14 25 E
Sedico	63	46 8N	12 6 E
Sedinenie	67	42 16N	24 33 E
Sedley	153	50 10N	104 0W
Sedom	90	31 5N	35 20 E
Sedova, Pik	76	73 20N	55 10 E
Sédrata	119	36 7N	7 31 E
Sedro Woolley	160	48 30N	122 15W
Sedrun	51	46 36N	8 47 E
Seduva	80	55 45N	23 45 E
Sędziszów Małapolski	54	50 5N	21 45 E
Seebad Ahlbeck	48	53 56N	14 10 E
Seefeld	52	51 53N	13 17 E
Seehausen	48	52 52N	11 43 E
Seeheim	128	26 32S	17 52 E
Seekoe, R.	128	30 34S	24 45 E
Seeland	50	47 0N	7 6 E
Seelaw	48	52 32N	14 22 E
Seend	28	51 20N	2 2W
Sées	42	48 38N	0 10 E
Seesen	48	51 53N	10 10 E
Sefadu	120	8 35N	10 58W
Séfeto	120	14 8N	9 49W
Sefrou	118	33 52N	4 52W
Sefton	143	43 15S	172 41 E
Sefton Mt.	143	43 40S	170 5 E
Sefuri-San	110	33 28N	130 18 E
Sefwi Bekwai	120	6 10N	2 25W
Seg-ozero	76	63 0N	33 10 E
Segamat	101	2 30N	102 50 E
Segarcea	70	44 6N	23 43 E
Segbwema	120	8 0N	11 0W
Segeston	31	51 41N	4 48W
Seget	103	1 24S	130 58 E
Seggueur, O.	118	32 4N	2 4 E
Segid	123	16 55N	42 0 E
Segonzac	44	45 36N	0 14W
Segorbe	58	39 50N	0 30W
Ségou	120	13 30N	6 10W
Segovia	56	40 57N	4 10W
Segovia □	56	40 55N	4 10W
Segré	42	47 40N	0 52W
Segre, R.	58	41 40N	0 43 E
Seguam	147	52 0N	172 30W
Seguam Pass.	147	53 0N	175 30W
Séguéla	120	7 55N	6 40W
Segula I.	147	52 0N	178 5W
Segundo	159	37 12N	104 50W
Segundo, R.	172	30 53S	62 44W
Segura, R.	59	38 9N	0 40W
Segura, Sierra de	59	38 5N	2 45W
Sehithwa	125	20 30S	22 30 E
Sehore	94	23 10N	77 5 E
Sehwan	94	26 28N	67 53 E
Seica Mare	70	46 1N	24 7 E
Seikpyu	98	20 54N	94 48 E
Seil, I.	34	56 17N	5 37W
Seilandsjøkelen	74	70 25N	23 16 E
Seiling	159	36 10N	99 5W
Seille, R.	45	46 31N	4 57 E
Seilles	47	50 30N	5 6 E
Sein, I. de	42	48 2N	4 52W
Seinäjoki	74	62 48N	22 43 E
Seine-Maritime □	42	49 40N	1 0 E
Seine □	43	49 0N	3 0 E
Seine-et-Marne □	43	48 45N	3 0 E
Seine, R.	42	49 28N	0 15 E
Seine-Saint-Denis □	43	48 58N	2 24 E
Seini	70	47 44N	23 21 E
Seistan	93	30 50N	61 0 E
Seiyala	122	22 57N	32 41 E
Sejal	174	2 45N	68 0W
Sejerby	73	55 54N	11 10 E
Sejerø	73	55 54N	11 15 E
Sejerø Bugt	73	55 53N	11 9 E
Seka	123	8 10N	36 52 E
Sekaju	102	2 58S	103 58 E
Seke	126	3 20S	33 31 E
Sekenke	126	4 18S	34 11 E
Seki	111	35 29N	136 55 E
Sekigahara	111	35 22N	136 28 E
Sekiu	160	48 30N	124 29W
Sekkane, Erg in	118	20 30N	1 30W
Sekondi	120	5 2N	1 48W
Sekondi-Takoradi	120	5 0N	1 48W
Sekuma	128	24 36S	23 57 E
Sela Dingay	123	9 58N	39 32 E
Selah	160	46 44N	120 30W
Selama	101	5 12N	100 42 E
Selangor □	101	3 20N	101 30 E
Selargius	64	39 14N	9 14 E
Selaru, I.	103	8 18S	131 0 E
Selat Bangka	102	2 30S	105 30 E
Selawik	147	66 55N	160 10W
Selb	49	50 9N	12 9 E
Selborne	29	51 5N	0 55W
Selby, U.K.	33	53 47N	1 5W
Selby, U.S.A.	158	45 34N	99 55W
Selbyville	162	38 28N	75 13W
Selce	63	43 20N	16 50 E
Selden	158	39 24N	100 39W
Seldovia	147	59 30N	151 45W
Sele, R.	65	40 27N	15 0 E
Selenica	68	40 33N	19 39 E
Selenter See	48	54 19N	10 26 E
Selestat	43	48 10N	7 26 E
Selet	72	63 15N	15 45 E
Seletan, Tg.	102	4 10S	114 40 E
Seletin	70	47 50N	25 12 E
Selevac	66	44 44N	20 52 E
Selfridge	158	46 3N	100 57W
Sélibaby	120	15 20N	12 15W
Seliger, Oz.	80	57 15N	33 0 E
Seligman	161	35 17N	112 56W
Selim, C. Afr. Emp.	126	5 31N	23 48 E
Selim, Turkey	83	40 15N	42 48 E
Selîma, El Wâhât el	122	21 28N	29 31 E
Selinda Spillway	128	18 35S	23 10 E
Selinoús	69	37 35N	21 37 E
Selinsgrove	162	40 48N	76 52W
Selipuk Gompa	95	31 23N	82 49 E
Selizharovo	80	57 1N	33 17 E
Selje	71	62 3N	5 22 E
Seljord	71	59 30N	8 40 E
Selkirk, Can.	153	50 10N	97 20W
Selkirk, U.K.	35	55 33N	2 50W
Selkirk (□)	26	55 30N	3 0W
Selkirk I.	153	53 20N	99 6W
Selkirk Mts.	152	51 15N	117 40W
Selles-sur-Cher	43	47 16N	1 33 E
Sellières	43	46 50N	5 32 E
Sells	161	31 57N	111 57W
Sellye	53	45 52N	17 51 E
Selma, Ala., U.S.A.	157	32 30N	87 0W
Selma, Calif., U.S.A.	163	36 39N	119 39W
Selma, N.C., U.S.A.	157	35 32N	78 15W
Selmer	157	35 9N	88 36W
Sélo, Óros	68	41 10N	126 0 E
Selongey	43	47 36N	5 10 E
Selowandoma Falls	127	21 15S	31 50 E
Selpele	103	0 1S	130 5 E
Selsey	29	50 44N	0 47W
Selsey Bill	29	50 44N	0 47W
Seltz	43	48 48N	8 4 E
Selu, I.	103	7 26S	130 55 E
Selukwe	127	19 40S	30 0 E
Sélune, R.	42	48 38N	1 22W
Selva, Argent.	172	29 50S	62 0W
Selva, Spain	58	41 13N	1 8 E
Selva Beach, La	163	36 56N	121 51W
Selva, La	58	42 0N	2 45 E
Selvas	174	6 30S	67 0W
Selwyn	133	21 30S	140 29 E
Selwyn L.	153	60 0N	104 30W
Selwyn Mts.	147	63 0N	130 0W
Selwyn P.O.	138	21 32S	140 30 E
Selwyn Ra.	138	21 10S	140 0 E
Semani, R.	68	40 45N	19 50 E
Semarang	103	7 0S	110 26 E
Sembabule	126	0 4S	31 25 E
Semeih	123	12 43N	30 53 E
Semenov	81	56 43N	44 30 E
Semenovka	82	49 37N	33 2 E
Semeru, Mt.	103	8 4S	113 3 E
Sémi	120	15 4N	13 41W
Semiluki	81	51 41N	39 10 E
Seminoe Res.	160	42 0N	107 0W
Seminole, Okla., U.S.A.	159	35 15N	96 45W
Seminole, Tex., U.S.A.	159	32 41N	102 38W
Semiozernoye	84	52 22N	64 8 E
Semipalatinsk	76	50 30N	80 10 E
Semirara Is.	103	12 0N	121 20 E

Semisopochnoi I Shawbost

Semisopochnoi I. 147 52 0N 179 40W
Semitau 102 0 29N 111 57 E
Semiyarskoye 76 50 55N 78 30 E
Semmering Pass. 52 47 41N 15 45 E
Semnan 93 35 55N 53 25 E
Semnan □ 93 36 0N 54 0 E
Semois, R. 47 49 53N 4 44 E
Semporna 103 4 30N 118 33 E
Semuda 102 2 51S 112 58 E
Semur-en-Auxois 43 47 30N 4 20 E
Sen. R. 101 13 45N 105 12 E
Sena Madureira 174 9 5S 68 45W
Senador Pompeu 170 5 40S 39 20W
Senai 101 1 38N 103 38 E
Senaja 102 6 49S 117 2 E
Senanga 128 16 2S 23 14 E
Senatobia 159 34 38N 89 57W
Sendafa 123 9 11N 39 3 E
Sendai, Kagoshima, Japan 110 31 50N 130 20 E
Sendai, Miyagi, Japan 112 38 15N 141 0 E
Sendamangalam 97 11 17N 78 17 E
Sendeling's Drift 128 28 12S 16 52 E
Sendenhorst 48 51 50N 7 49 E
Sendurjana 96 21 32N 78 24 E
Senec 53 48 12N 17 23 E
Seneca, Oreg., U.S.A. 160 44 10N 119 2W
Seneca, S.C., U.S.A. 157 34 43N 82 59W
Seneca Falls 162 42 55N 76 50W
Seneca L. 162 42 40N 76 58W
Seneffe 47 50 32N 4 16 E
Senegal ■ 120 14 30N 14 30W
Senegal, R. 120 16 30N 15 30W
Senekal 129 28 18S 27 36 E
Senftenberg 48 51 30N 13 51 E
Senga Hill 127 9 19S 31 11 E
Senge Khambab (Indus), R. 94 28 40N 70 10 E
Sengerema □ 126 2 10S 32 20 E
Sengiley 81 53 58N 48 54 E
Sengwa, R. 127 17 10S 28 15 E
Senhor-do-Bonfim 170 10 30S 40 10W
Senica 53 48 41N 17 25 E
Senigállia 63 43 42N 13 12 E
Seniku 98 25 32N 97 48 E
Senio, R. 63 44 18N 11 47 E
Senj 63 45 0N 14 58 E
Senja 74 69 25N 17 20 E
Senlis 43 49 13N 2 35 E
Senmonorom 100 12 27N 107 12 E
Sennâr 123 13 30N 33 35 E
Senne, R. 47 50 42N 4 13 E
Sennen 30 50 4N 5 42W
Senneterre 150 48 25N 77 15W
Senno 80 54 45N 29 58 E
Sennori 64 40 49N 8 36 E
Senny Bridge 31 51 57N 3 35W
Seno 100 16 41N 105 1 E
Senonches 42 48 34N 1 2 E
Senorbi 64 39 33N 9 8 E
Senozeče 63 45 43N 14 3 E
Sens 43 48 11N 3 15 E
Senta 66 45 55N 20 3 E
Sentein 44 42 53N 0 58 E
Senteny 126 5 17S 25 42 E
Sentier, Le 51 46 37N 6 15 E
Sentinel 161 32 56N 113 13W
Sento Sé 170 9 40S 41 18W
Sentolo 103 7 55S 110 13 E
Senya Beraku 121 5 28N 0 31W
Seo de Urgel 58 42 22N 1 23 E
Seohara 95 29 15N 78 33 E
Seoni 95 22 5N 79 30 E
Seorinayan 96 21 45N 82 34 E
Separation Point 151 53 37N 57 25W
Seph, R. 33 54 17N 1 9W
Sepik, R. 135 3 49S 144 30 E
Sepólno Krajenskie 54 53 26N 17 30 E
Sepone 100 16 45N 106 13 E
Sepopa 128 18 49S 22 12 E
Sepopol 54 54 16N 21 2 E
Sepori 107 38 57N 127 25 E
Sept Îles 151 50 13N 66 22W
Septemvri 67 42 13N 24 6 E
Septimus 138 21 13S 148 47 E
Sepúlveda 56 41 18N 3 45W
Sequeros 56 40 31N 6 2W
Sequim 160 48 3N 123 9W
Sequoia Nat. Park 163 36 30N 118 30W
Serafimovich 83 49 30N 42 50 E
Seraing 47 50 35N 5 32 E
Seraja 101 2 41N 108 35 E
Seram, I. 103 3 10S 129 0 E
Serampore 95 22 44N 88 30 E
Serang 103 6 8S 106 10 E
Serasan 101 2 31N 109 2 E
Serasan, I. 102 2 29N 109 4 E
Seravezza 62 43 59N 10 13 E
Serbia = Srbija 66 43 30N 21 0 E
Sercaia 70 45 49N 25 9 E
Serdo 123 11 56N 41 14 E
Serdobsk 81 52 28N 44 10 E
Seredka 80 58 12N 28 3 E
Seregno 62 45 40N 9 12 E
Seremban 101 2 43N 101 53 E
Serena, La, Chile 172 29 55S 71 10W
Serena, La, Spain 57 38 45N 5 40W
Serengeti □ 126 2 0S 34 30 E
Serengeti Plain 126 2 40S 35 0 E
Serenje 125 13 14S 30 15 E
Sergach 81 55 30N 45 30 E
Serge, R. 58 42 5N 1 21 E
Sergievsk 81 54 0N 51 10 E
Sergipe □ 170 10 30S 37 30W
Seria 102 4 37N 114 30 E
Serian 102 1 10N 110 40 E
Seriate 62 45 42N 9 43 E
Sérifontaine 43 49 20N 1 45 E
Sérifos, I. 69 37 9N 24 30 E
Sérignan 44 43 17N 3 17 E
Serik 92 36 55N 31 10 E
Seringapatam Reef 136 13 38S 122 5 E
Sermaize-les-Bains 43 48 47N 4 54 E
Sermata, I. 103 8 15S 128 50 E
Sérmide 63 45 0N 11 17 E
Sernovdsk 76 61 20N 73 28 E
Sernovodsk 84 53 54N 51 16 E
Sero 120 14 42N 10 59W
Serón 59 37 20N 2 29W
Serós 58 41 27N 0 24 E
Serov 84 59 36N 60 35 E
Serowe 128 22 25S 26 43 E
Serpa 57 37 57N 7 38 E
Serpeddi, Punta 64 39 19N 9 28 E
Serpentara 64 39 8N 9 38 E
Serpentine 137 32 23S 115 58 E
Serpentine L. 137 28 30S 129 10 E
Serpent's Mouth 174 10 0N 61 30W
Serpis, R. 59 38 45N 0 21W
Serpukhov 81 54 55N 37 28 E
Serra 171 20 7S 40 18W
Serra Capriola 65 41 47N 15 12 E
Serra do Salitre 74 19 6S 46 41W
Serra Talhada 170 7 59S 38 18W
Serradilla 56 39 50N 6 9W
Sérrai □ 68 41 5N 23 37 E
Serramanna 64 39 26N 8 56 E
Serranía de Cuenca 58 40 10N 1 50W
Serrat, C. 119 37 14N 9 10 E
Serres 45 44 26N 5 43 E
Serrezuela 172 30 40S 65 20W
Serrinha 171 11 39S 39 0W
Serrita 170 7 56S 39 19W
Serro 171 18 37S 43 23W
Sersale 65 39 1N 16 44 E
Sertã 56 39 48N 8 6W
Sertânia 170 8 5S 37 20W
Sertanópolis 173 23 4S 51 2W
Sertão 170 10 0S 40 20W
Sertig 51 46 44N 9 52 E
Serua, P. 103 6 18S 130 1 E
Serui 103 1 45S 136 10 E
Serule 128 21 57S 27 11 E
Sérvia 68 40 9N 21 58 E
Sesajap Lama 102 3 32N 117 11 E
Sese Is. 126 0 30S 32 30 E
Sesepe 103 1 30S 127 59 E
Sesfontein 128 19 7S 13 39 E
Sesheke 128 17 29S 24 13 E
Sesia, R. 62 45 35N 8 23 E
Sesimbra 57 38 28N 9 20W
Seskanore 38 54 31N 7 15W
Sessa Aurunca 64 41 14N 13 55 E
Sestao 58 43 18N 3 0W
Sesto S. Giovanni 62 45 32N 9 14 E
Sestri Levante 62 44 17N 9 22 E
Sestrières 62 44 58N 6 56 E
Sestrunj, I. 63 44 10N 15 0 E
Sestu 64 39 18N 9 6 E
Sesvenna 62 46 42N 10 25 E
Seta 108 32 20N 100 41 E
Setaka 110 33 9N 130 28 E
Setana 112 42 26N 139 51 E
Sète 44 43 25N 3 42 E
Sete Lagoas 171 19 27S 44 16W
Sétif 119 36 9N 5 26 E
Seto 111 35 14N 137 6 E
Seto Naikai 110 34 20N 133 30 E
Setouchi 112 28 8N 129 19 E
Setsan 98 16 3N 95 23 E
Settat 118 33 0N 7 40W
Setté Cama 124 2 32S 9 57 E
Séttimo Tor 62 45 9N 7 46 E
Setting L. 153 55 0N 98 38W
Settle 32 54 5N 2 18W
Settlement Pt. 157 26 40N 79 0W
Setto Calende 62 45 44N 8 37 E
Setúbal 57 38 30N 8 58W
Setúbal □ 57 38 25N 8 35W
Setúbal, B. de 57 38 40N 8 56W
Seul L. 150 50 25N 92 30W
Seul Reservoir, Lac 150 50 25N 92 30W
Seulimeum 102 5 27N 95 15 E
Seuzach 51 47 32N 8 49 E
Sevastopol 82 44 35N 33 30 E
Sevelen 51 47 7N 9 30 E
Seven Emu 138 16 20S 137 8 E
Seven Heads 39 51 35N 8 43W
Seven Hogs, Is. 39 52 20N 10 0W
Seven, R. 33 54 11N 0 51W
Seven Sisters 31 51 46N 3 43W
Seven Sisters, mt 152 54 56N 128 10W
Sevenoaks 29 51 16N 0 11 E
Sevenum 47 51 25N 6 2 E
Sever, R. 57 39 40N 7 32W
Sévérac-le-Chateau 44 44 20N 3 5 E
Severn Beach 28 51 34N 2 39W
Severn L. 150 53 54N 90 48W
Severn, R., Can. 150 56 2N 87 36W
Severn, R., U.K. 28 51 35N 2 38W
Severn Stoke 28 52 5N 2 13W
Severnaya Zemlya 77 79 0N 100 0 E
Severnyye Uvaly 78 58 0N 48 0 E
Severo-Kurilsk 77 50 40N 156 8 E
Severodonetsk 83 48 50N 38 30 E
Severodvinsk 78 64 27N 39 58 E
Severomoravsky □ 53 49 38N 17 40 E
Severouralsk 84 60 9N 59 57 E
Sevier 161 38 39N 112 11W
Sevier L. 160 39 0N 113 20W
Sevier, R. 161 39 10N 112 50W
Sevilla, Colomb. 174 4 16N 75 57W
Sevilla, Spain 57 37 23N 6 0W
Sevilla □ 57 37 0N 6 0W
Seville = Sevilla 57 37 23N 6 0W
Sevnica 63 46 2N 15 19 E
Sevsk 80 52 10N 34 30 E
Seward 147 60 0N 149 40W
Seward Pen. 147 65 0N 164 0W
Sewell 172 34 10S 70 45W
Sewer 103 5 46S 134 40 E
Sexbierum 46 53 13N 5 29 E
Sexsmith 152 55 21N 118 47W
Seychelles, Is. 11 5 0S 56 0 E
Seyðisfjörður 74 65 16N 14 0W
Seym, R. 80 51 45N 35 0 E
Seymchan 77 62 40N 152 30 E
Seymour, Austral. 141 37 0S 145 10 E
Seymour, Conn., U.S.A. 162 41 23N 73 5W
Seymour, Ind., U.S.A. 156 39 0N 85 50W
Seymour, Tex., U.S.A. 159 33 35N 99 18W
Seymour, Wis., U.S.A. 156 44 30N 88 20W
Seyne 45 44 21N 6 22 E
Seyne-sur-Mer, La 45 43 7N 5 52 E
Sezana 63 45 43N 13 41 E
Sézanne 43 48 40N 3 40 E
Sezze 64 41 30N 13 3 E
Sfântu Gheorghe 70 45 52N 25 48 E
Sfax 119 34 49N 10 48 E
Sgurr Mor 36 57 42N 5 0W
Sgurr na Ciche 36 57 0N 5 29W
Sgurr na Lapaich 36 57 23N 5 5W
Sha Ch'i, R. 109 26 35N 118 8 E
Shaartuz 85 37 16N 68 8 E
Shaba 126 8 0S 25 0 E
Shaba Gamba 99 32 8N 88 55 E
Shaballe, R. 123 5 0N 44 0 E
Shabani 127 20 17S 30 2 E
Shabbear 30 50 52N 4 12W
Shabla 67 43 31N 28 32 E
Shabogamo L. 151 48 40N 77 0W
Shabunda 126 2 40S 27 16 E
Shackleton 13 78 30S 36 1W
Shackleton Inlet 13 83 0S 160 0 E
Shaddad 122 21 25N 40 2 E
Shadi 95 33 24N 77 14 E
Shadrinsk 84 56 5N 63 58 E
Shadwân 122 27 30N 34 0 E
Shaffa 121 10 30N 12 6 E
Shafter 163 35 32N 119 14W
Shaftesbury 28 51 0N 2 12W
Shag Pt. 143 45 29S 170 52 E
Shagamu 121 6 51N 3 39 E
Shagram 95 36 24N 72 20 E
Shah Bunder 94 24 13N 67 50 E
Shahabad, And. P., India 96 17 10N 78 11 E
Shahabad, Punjab, India 94 30 10N 76 55 E
Shahabad, Raj., India 94 25 15N 77 11 E
Shahabad, Uttar Pradesh, India 95 27 36N 79 56 E
Shāhābād 93 37 40N 56 50 E
Shahada 96 21 33N 74 30 E
Shahapur 96 15 50N 74 34 E
Shāhbād 92 34 10N 46 30 E
Shahdād 93 30 30N 57 40 E
Shahdadkot 94 27 50N 67 55 E
Shahddpur 94 25 55N 68 35 E
Shahganj 95 26 3N 82 44 E
Shahgarh 93 27 15N 69 50 E
Shahhat (Cyrene) 117 32 40N 21 35 E
Shāhī 93 36 30N 52 55 E
Shahjahanpur 95 27 54N 79 57 E
Shaho 106 36 31N 114 35 E
Shahpur, Mad. P., India 94 22 12N 77 58 E
Shahpur, Mysore, India 97 16 40N 76 48 E
Shahpur, Iran 92 38 12N 44 45 E
Shahpur, Pak. 94 28 46N 68 27 E
Shahpura 95 23 10N 80 45 E
Shahr-e Babak 93 30 10N 55 20 E
Shahr Kord 93 32 15N 50 55 E
Shahraban 92 34 0N 45 0 E
Shahreza 93 32 0N 51 55 E
Shahrig 94 30 15N 67 40 E
Shahriza 93 32 0N 51 50 E
Shahrud 93 36 30N 55 0 E
Shahrukh 93 33 50N 60 10 E
Shahsavar 93 36 45N 51 12 E
Shahsien 109 26 25N 117 50 E
Shahuk'ou 106 40 20N 112 18 E
Shaibâra 123 25 26N 36 47 E
Shaikhabad 94 34 0N 68 45 E
Shaim 84 60 21N 64 10 E
Shajapur 94 23 20N 76 15 E
Shakargarh 94 32 17N 75 43 E
Shakawe 128 18 28S 21 49 E
Shakhristan 85 39 47N 68 49 E
Shakhrisyabz 85 39 3N 66 50 E
Shakhty 83 47 40N 40 10 E
Shakhunya 81 57 40N 47 0 E
Shaki 121 8 41N 3 21 E
Shakopee 158 44 45N 93 30W
Shaktolik 147 64 30N 161 15W
Shala Lake 123 7 30N 38 30 E
Shaldon 30 50 32N 3 31W
Shalkar Karashatau, Ozero 84 50 26N 61 12 E
Shalkar Yega Kara, Ozero 84 50 45N 60 54 E
Sham, J. ash 93 23 10N 57 5 E
Shama 121 5 1N 1 42W
Shamâl Dâfû □ 123 15 0N 25 0 E
Shamâl Kordofân □ 123 15 0N 30 0 E
Shamar, Jabal 92 27 40N 41 0 E
Shamattawa 153 55 51N 92 5W
Shamattawa, R. 150 55 1N 85 23W
Shambe 123 7 2N 30 46 E
Shambu 123 9 32N 37 3 E
Shamgong Dzong 98 27 19N 90 35 E
Shamil, India 94 29 32N 77 18 E
Shamil, Iran 93 27 30N 56 55 E
Shamkhor 83 40 56N 46 0 E
Shamo, L. 123 5 45N 37 30 E
Shamokin 162 40 47N 76 33W
Shamrock 159 35 15N 100 15W
Shamva 125 17 20S 31 32 E
Shan □ 98 21 30N 98 30 E
Shanagolden 39 52 35N 9 6W
Shanan, R. 123 8 0N 40 20 E
Shanch'eng 109 31 45N 115 30 E
Shandon 163 35 39N 120 23W
Shandon Downs 138 17 45S 134 50 E
Shanga 121 9 1N 5 2 E
Shangalowe 127 10 50S 26 30 E
Shangani 127 19 1S 28 51 E
Shangani, R. 127 18 35S 27 45 E
Shangchih, (Chuho) 107 45 10N 127 59 E
Shangching 106 33 9N 110 2 E
Shangch'iu 105 34 26N 115 40 E
Shangch'uan Shan, I. 109 21 45N 112 45 E
Shanghai 109 31 10N 121 25 E
Shanghang 109 25 5N 116 30 E
Shangho 107 37 19N 117 9 E
Shanghsien 106 33 30N 109 58 E
Shangjao 109 28 25N 117 57 E
Shangkao 109 28 16N 114 50 E
Shanglin 108 23 26N 108 36 E
Shangnan 106 33 35N 110 49 E
Shangpanch'eng 107 40 50N 118 0 E
Shangshui 106 33 35N 114 34 E
Shangssu 108 22 10N 108 0 E
Shangtsei 106 33 15N 114 20 E
Shangtu 106 41 31N 113 35 E
Shangyu 109 25 59N 114 29 E
Shanhaikuan 107 40 0N 119 48 E
Shanhot'un 107 44 42N 127 12 E
Shanhsien 106 34 51N 116 9 E
Shani 121 10 14N 12 2 E
Shaniko 160 45 0N 120 15W
Shanklin 28 50 39N 1 9W
Shannon, Greenl. 12 75 10N 18 30W
Shannon, N.Z. 142 40 33S 175 25 E
Shannon Airport 39 52 42N 8 57W
Shannon Bridge 39 53 17N 8 2W
Shannon I. 12 75 0N 18 0W
Shannon, Mouth of the 39 52 30N 9 55W
Shannon, R. 39 53 10N 8 10W
Shansi □ 106 37 30N 112 15 E
Shantar, Ostrov Bolshoi 77 55 9N 137 40 E
Shant'ou 109 23 28N 116 40 E
Shantung □ 105 36 0N 117 30 E
Shantung Pantao 107 37 5N 121 0 E
Shanyang 106 33 39N 110 2 E
Shanyin 106 39 34N 112 50 E
Shaohing 109 30 0N 120 32 E
Shaokuan 109 24 50N 113 35 E
Shaowu 109 27 25N 117 30 E
Shaoyang 109 27 10N 111 30 E
Shap 32 54 32N 2 40W
Shap'ing 109 22 46N 112 57 E
Shapinsay, I. 37 59 2N 2 50W
Shapinsay Sd. 37 59 0N 2 51W
Shaqra 92 25 15N 45 16 E
Sharafa (Ogr) 123 11 59N 27 7 E
Sharavati, R. 97 14 32N 74 0 E
Sharhjui 93 32 30N 67 22 E
Shari 92 27 20N 43 45 E
Sharjah 93 25 23N 55 26 E
Shark B., N. Territory, Austral. 132 11 20S 130 35 E
Shark B., W. Australia, Austral. 137 25 55S 113 32 E
Sharm el Sheikh 122 27 53N 34 15 E
Sharon, Mass., U.S.A. 162 42 5N 71 11W
Sharon, Pa., U.S.A. 156 41 18N 80 30W
Sharon, Plain of = Hasharon 90 32 12N 34 49 E
Sharon Springs 162 42 48N 74 37W
Sharp Pt. 138 10 58S 142 43 E
Sharpe, L. 150 54 10N 93 21W
Sharpe L. 153 50 23N 95 30W
Sharpness 28 51 43N 2 28W
Sharya 81 58 12N 45 40 E
Shasha 123 6 29N 35 59 E
Shashemene 123 7 13N 38 33 E
Shashi 125 21 15S 27 27 E
Shashi, R. 127 21 40S 28 40 E
Shashih 109 30 19N 112 14 E
Shasta, Mt. 160 41 45N 122 0W
Shasta Res. 160 40 50N 122 15W
Shati 109 26 6N 114 51 E
Shatsk 81 54 0N 41 45 E
Shattuck 159 36 17N 99 55W
Shaumyani 83 41 13N 44 45 E
Shaunavon 153 49 35N 108 25W
Shaver Lake 163 37 9N 119 18W
Shaw I. 138 20 30S 149 2 E
Shaw, R. 136 20 21S 119 17 E
Shawan 105 44 21N 85 37 E
Shawangunk Mts. 162 41 40N 74 25W
Shawano 156 44 45N 88 38W
Shawbost 36 58 20N 6 40W

FHK

Siddipet **Skaneateles**

Siddipet 96 18 0N 79 0E
Sidensjo 72 63 20N 18 20E
Sidéradougou 120 10 42N 4 12W
Siderno Marina 65 38 16N 16 17E
Sidheros, Ákra 69 35 19N 26 19E
Sidhirókastron 68 37 20N 21 46E
Sidhpur 94 23 56N 71 25E
Sîdi Abd el Rahman 122 30 55N 28 41E
Sîdi Barrâni 122 31 32N 25 58E
Sidi-Bel-Abbès 118 35 13N 0 10W
Sidi Bennour 118 32 40N 9 26W
Sidi Haneish 122 31 10N 27 35E
Sidi Ifni 118 29 29N 10 3W
Sidi Kacem 118 34 11N 5 40W
Sīdī Miftāh 119 31 8N 16 58E
Sidi Moussa, O. 118 33 0N 8 50W
Sidi Omar 122 31 24N 24 57E
Sīdī Yahya 119 30 55N 16 30E
Sidlaw Hills 35 56 32N 3 10W
Sidlesham 29 50 46N 0 46W
Sidmouth 30 50 40N 3 13W
Sidmouth, C. 138 13 25S 143 36E
Sidney, Can. 152 48 39N 123 24W
Sidney, Mont., U.S.A. 158 47 51N 104 7W
Sidney, N.Y., U.S.A. 162 42 18N 75 20W
Sidney, Ohio, U.S.A. 156 40 18N 84 6W
Sidoardjo 103 7 30S 112 46E
Sidoktaya 98 20 27N 94 15E
Sidon, (Saida) 92 33 38N 35 28E
Sidra, G. of = Khalīj Surt 61 31 40N 18 30E
Siedlce 54 52 10N 22 20E
Siedlce □ 54 52 0N 22 0E
Siegburg 48 50 48N 7 12E
Siegen 48 50 52N 8 2E
Siem Pang 100 14 7N 106 23E
Siem Reap 100 13 20N 103 52E
Siena 63 43 20N 11 20E
Sieniawa 54 50 11N 22 38E
Sieradź 54 51 37N 18 41E
Sieradź □ 54 51 30N 19 0E
Sieraków 54 52 39N 16 2E
Sierck-les-Bains 43 49 26N 6 20E
Sierpc 54 52 55N 19 43E
Sierpe, Bocas de la 174 10 0N 61 30W
Sierra Alta 58 40 31N 1 30W
Sierra Blanca 161 31 11N 105 17W
Sierra Blanca, mt. 161 33 20N 105 54W
Sierra City 160 39 34N 120 42W
Sierra Colorado 176 40 35S 67 50W
Sierra de Gädor 59 36 57N 2 45W
Sierra de Yeguas 57 37 7N 4 52W
Sierra Gorda 172 23 0S 69 15W
Sierra Leone ■ 120 9 0N 12 0W
Sierra Majada 164 27 19N 103 42W
Sierre 50 46 17N 7 31E
Sífnos 69 37 0N 24 45E
Sifton 153 51 21N 100 8W
Sifton Pass 152 57 52N 126 15W
Sig 118 35 32N 0 12W
Sigaboy 103 6 39N 126 10E
Sigdal 71 60 4N 9 38E
Sigean 44 43 2N 2 58E
Sighetul Marmatiei 70 47 57N 23 52E
Sighişoara 70 46 12N 24 50E
Sighty Crag 35 55 8N 2 37W
Sigli 102 5 25N 96 0E
Siglufjörður 74 66 12N 18 55W
Sigma 103 11 29N 122 40E
Sigmaringen 49 48 5N 9 13E
Signakhi 83 40 52N 45 57E
Signau 50 46 56N 7 45E
Signy I. 13 60 45S 46 30W
Signy-l'Abbaye 43 49 40N 4 25E
Sigsig 174 3 0S 78 50W
Sigtuna 72 59 36N 17 44E
Sigüenza 58 41 3N 2 40W
Siguiri 120 11 31N 9 10W
Sigulda 80 57 10N 24 55E
Sigurd 161 38 57N 112 0W
Sihanoukville = Kompong Som 101 10 40N 103 30E
Si'ir 90 31 35N 35 9E
Siirt 92 37 57N 41 55E
Sijarira, Ra. 127 17 36S 27 45E
Sijsele 13 51 12N 3 20E
Sikandarabad 94 28 30N 77 39E
Sikandra Rao 93 27 43N 78 24E
Sikar 94 27 39N 75 10E
Sikasso 120 11 7N 5 35W
Sikerete 128 19 0S 20 48E
Sikeston 159 36 52N 89 35W
Sikhote Alin, Khrebet 77 46 0N 136 0E
Sikiá. 68 40 2N 23 56E
Síkinos, I. 69 36 40N 25 8E
Sikionia 69 38 0N 22 44E
Sikkani Chief, R. 152 57 47N 122 15W
Sikkim ■ 98 27 50N 88 50E
Siklós 53 45 50N 18 19E
Sikoro 120 12 19N 7 8W
Sikqo 101 7 34N 99 21E
Sil, R. 56 42 23N 7 30W
Sila, La, Mts. 65 39 15N 16 35E
Silacayoapán 165 17 30N 98 9W
Silandro 62 46 38N 10 48E
Sīlat adh Dhahr 90 32 19N 35 11E
Silba 63 44 24N 14 41E
Silba, I. 63 44 24N 14 41E
Silchar 98 24 49N 92 48E
Silcox 153 57 12N 94 10W
Silenrieux 47 50 14N 4 27E
Siler City 157 35 44N 79 30W
Sileru, R. 96 18 0N 82 0E
Silesia = Slask 54 51 0N 16 30E
Silet 118 22 44N 4 37E
Silgarhi Doti 95 29 15N 82 0E
Silghat 98 26 35N 93 0E
Silifke 92 36 22N 33 58E
Siliguri 98 26 45N 88 25E
Siliqua 64 39 20N 8 49E
Silistra 67 44 6N 27 19E
Siljan, L. 72 60 55N 14 45E
Silkeborg 73 56 10N 9 32E
Sillajhuay, Cordillera 174 19 40S 68 40W
Sillé-le Guillaume 42 48 10N 0 8W
Silloth 32 54 53N 3 25W
Siloam Springs 159 36 15N 94 31W
Silogui 102 1 10S 98 46E
Silsbee 159 30 20N 94 8W
Silsden 32 53 55N 1 55W
Silute 80 55 21N 21 33E
Silva Porto = Bié 125 12 22S 16 55E
Silvaplana 51 46 28N 9 48E
Silver City, Calif., U.S.A. 160 36 19N 119 44W
Silver City, N. Mex., U.S.A. 161 32 50N 108 18W
Silver Cr., R. 160 43 30N 119 30W
Silver Creek 156 42 33N 79 9W
Silver L. 163 38 39N 120 6W
Silver Lake, Calif., U.S.A. 163 35 21N 116 7W
Silver Lake, Oreg., U.S.A. 160 43 9N 121 4W
Silver Springs 162 39 2N 77 3W
Silverhojden 72 60 2N 15 0E
Silvermine, Mts. 39 52 47N 8 15W
Silvermines 39 52 48N 8 15W
Silverpeak, Ra. 163 37 35N 117 45W
Silverstone 28 52 5N 1 3W
Silverton, Austral. 140 31 52S 141 10E
Silverton, U.K. 30 50 49N 3 29W
Silverton, Colo., U.S.A. 161 37 51N 107 45W
Silverton, Tex., U.S.A. 159 34 30N 101 16W
Silves 57 37 11N 8 26W
Silvia 174 2 37N 76 21W
Silvies, R. 160 43 57N 119 5W
Silvolde 46 51 55N 6 23E
Silvretta Gruppe 51 46 50N 10 6E
Silwa Bahari 122 24 45N 32 55E
Silwan 90 31 59N 35 15E
Silwani 93 23 18N 78 27E
Silz 52 47 16N 10 56E
Sim, C. 118 31 26N 9 51W
Simanggang 102 1 15N 111 25E
Simão Dias 170 10 44S 37 49W
Simard, L. 150 47 40N 78 40W
Simarun 93 31 16N 51 40E
Simba 126 1 41S 34 12E
Simbach 49 48 16N 13 3E
Simbo 126 4 51S 29 41E
Simcoe 150 42 50N 80 20W
Simcoe, L. 150 44 25N 79 20W
Simenga 77 62 50N 107 55E
Simeon 47 50 45N 5 36E
Simeulue, I. 102 2 45N 95 45E
Simferopol 82 44 55N 34 3E
Sími 69 36 35N 27 50E
Sími, I. 69 36 35N 27 50E
Simi Valley 163 34 16N 118 47W
Simikot 95 30 0N 81 50E
Simití 174 7 58N 73 57W
Simitli 66 41 52N 23 7E
Simla 94 31 2N 77 15E
Simleu-Silvaniei 70 47 17N 22 50E
Simme, R. 50 46 38N 7 25E
Simmern 48 49 59N 7 32E
Simmie 153 49 56N 108 6W
Simmler 163 35 21N 119 59W
Simões 170 7 30S 40 49W
Simojärvi 74 66 5N 27 10E
Simojoki 74 65 46N 25 15E
Simojovel 165 17 12N 92 38W
Simonette, R. 152 55 9N 118 15W
Simonsbath 28 51 8N 3 45W
Simonside, Mt. 35 55 17N 2 0W
Simonstown 128 34 14S 18 26E
Simontornya 53 46 45N 18 33E
Simpang 101 4 50N 100 40E
Simpleveld 47 50 50N 5 58E
Simplício Mendes 170 7 51S 41 54W
Simplon 50 46 12N 8 4E
Simplon Pass 50 46 15N 8 0E
Simplon Tunnel 50 46 15N 8 7E
Simpson Des. 138 25 0S 137 0E
Simpungdong 107 41 56N 129 29E
Simrishamn 73 55 33N 14 22E
Simsbury 162 41 52N 72 48W
Simunjan 102 1 25N 110 45E
Sîmŭrtin 70 46 19N 25 58E
Simushir, Ostrov 77 46 50N 152 30E
Sina, R. 97 18 25N 75 28E
Sinaai 47 51 9N 4 2E
Sinabang 102 2 30N 46 30E
Sinai = Es Sînâ' 122 29 0N 34 0E
Sinai, Mt. = Musa, G. 122 28 32N 33 59E
Sinaia 70 45 21N 25 38E
Sinaloa 164 25 50N 108 20W
Sinaloa □ 164 25 0N 107 30W
Sinalunga 63 43 12N 11 43E
Sinamaica 174 11 5N 71 51W
Sînandrei 70 45 52N 21 13E
Sīnāwan 119 31 0N 10 30E
Sinbaung we 98 19 43N 95 10E
Sinbo 98 24 46N 97 3E
Sincé 174 9 15N 75 9W
Sincelejo 174 9 18N 75 24W
Sinchangni, Kor., N. 107 40 7N 128 28E
Sinchangni, Kor., N. 107 39 24N 126 8E
Sinclair 160 41 47N 107 35W
Sinclair Mills 152 54 5N 121 40W
Sinclair's B. 37 58 30N 3 0W
Sincorá, Serra do 171 13 30S 41 0W
Sind, R. 95 34 18N 75 0E
Sind Sagar Doab 94 32 0N 71 30E
Sinda 127 17 28S 25 51E
Sindal 73 57 28N 10 10E
Sindangan 103 8 10N 123 5E
Sindangbarang 103 7 27S 107 9E
Sindjai 103 5 0S 120 20E
Sinelnikovo 82 48 25N 35 30E
Sines 57 37 56N 8 51W
Sines, Cabo de 57 37 58N 8 53W
Sineu 58 39 39N 3 0E
Sinewit, Mt. 135 4 44S 152 2E
Sinfra 120 6 35N 5 56W
Sing Buri 100 14 53N 100 25E
Singa 123 13 10N 33 57E
Singanallurt 97 11 2N 77 1E
Singaparna 103 7 23S 108 4E
Singapore ■ 101 1 17N 103 51E
Singapore, Straits of 101 1 15N 104 0E
Singaraja 102 8 15S 115 10E
Singen 49 47 45N 8 50E
Singida 126 4 49S 34 48E
Singida □ 126 6 0S 34 30E
Singitikós, Kólpos 68 40 6N 24 0E
Singkaling Hkamti 98 26 0N 95 45E
Singkang 103 4 8S 120 1E
Singkawang 102 1 0N 109 5E
Singkep, I. 102 0 30S 104 20E
Singleton, Austral. 141 32 33S 151 10E
Singleton, U.K. 29 50 55N 0 45W
Singleton, Mt. 137 29 27S 117 15E
Singö 72 60 12N 18 45E
Singoli 94 25 0N 75 16E
Singora = Songkhla 101 7 12N 100 36E
Singosan 107 38 52N 127 25E
Sinhailian (Lienyünchiangshih) 107 34 31N 118 15E
Sinhung 107 40 11N 127 34E
Siniatsikon, Óros 68 40 25N 21 35E
Siniscóla 64 40 35N 9 40E
Sinj 63 43 42N 16 39E
Sinjajevina, Planina 66 42 57N 19 22E
Sinjil 90 32 3N 35 15E
Sinkat 122 18 55N 36 49E
Sinkiang-Uighur □ 105 42 0N 86 0E
Sinmark 107 38 25N 126 14E
Sinnai Sardinia 64 39 18N 9 13E
Sinnar 96 19 48N 74 0E
Sinni, R. 65 40 6N 16 15E
Sînnicolau-Maré 70 46 5N 20 39E
Sinnûris 122 29 26N 30 31E
Sinoe, L. 70 44 35N 28 50E
Sinoia 127 17 20S 30 8E
Sinop 92 42 1N 35 11E
Sinop, R. 82 42 1N 35 2E
Sinpo 107 40 0N 128 13E
Sins 51 47 12N 8 24E
Sinskoye 77 61 8N 126 48E
Sint Annaland 47 51 36N 4 6E
Sint Annaparochie 46 53 16N 5 40E
Sint-Denijs 47 50 45N 3 23E
Sint Eustatius, I. 167 17 30N 62 59W
Sint-Genesius-Rode 47 50 45N 4 22E
Sint-Gillis-Waas 47 51 13N 4 6E
Sint-Huibrechts-Lille 47 51 13N 5 29E
Sint-Katelinje-Waver 47 51 5N 4 32E
Sint-Kruis 47 51 13N 3 15E
Sint-Laureins 47 51 14N 3 32E
Sint Maarten, I. 167 18 4N 63 4W
Sint-Michiels 47 51 11N 3 15E
Sint Nicolaasga 46 52 55N 5 45E
Sint Niklaas 47 51 10N 4 9E
Sint Oedenrode 47 51 35N 5 29E
Sint Pancras 46 52 40N 4 48E
Sint-Pauwels 47 51 11N 3 57E
Sint Philipsland 47 51 37N 4 10E
Sint Truiden 47 50 48N 5 12E
Sint Willebroad 47 51 33N 4 33E
Sîntana Ano 70 46 20N 21 30E
Sintang 102 0 5N 111 35E
Sintjohannesga 46 52 55N 5 52E
Sinton 159 28 1N 97 30W
Sintra 57 38 47N 9 25W
Sinŭiju 107 40 5N 124 24E
Sinuk 147 64 42N 166 22W
Sinyang = Hsinyang 109 32 10N 114 6E
Sinyukha, R. 82 48 31N 30 31E
Siófok 53 46 54N 18 4E
Sióma 128 16 25S 23 28E
Sion 50 46 14N 7 20E
Sion Mills 38 54 47N 7 29W
Sioua, El Wâhât es 122 29 10N 25 30E
Sioux City 158 42 32N 96 25W
Sioux Falls 158 43 35N 96 40W
Sioux Lookout 150 50 10N 91 50W
Sip Song Chaw Thai, reg. 100 21 30N 103 30E
Sipan 66 42 45N 17 52E
Sipera, I. 102 2 18S 99 40E
Sipiwesk L. 153 55 5N 97 35W
Sipul 138 5 50S 148 28E
Siquia, R. 166 12 30N 84 30W
Siquijor, I. 103 9 12N 123 45E
Siquirres 166 10 6N 83 30W
Siquisique 174 10 34N 69 42W
Sir Edward Pellew Group 138 15 40S 137 10E
Sir Graham Moore Is. 136 13 53S 126 34E
Sir Samuel Mt. 137 27 45S 120 40E
Sir Thomas, Mt. 137 27 10S 129 45E
Sira 97 13 41N 76 49E
Sira, R. 71 58 43N 6 40E
Siracusa 65 37 4N 15 17E
Sirajganj 95 24 25N 89 47E
Sirake 138 9 1S 141 2E
Sirakoro 120 12 41N 9 14W
Sirasso 120 9 16N 6 6W
Siret 70 47 55N 26 5E
Siret, R. 70 47 58N 26 5E
Siria 66 46 16N 21 38E
Sirinhaém 171 8 35S 35 7W
Sirkall (Shivali) 97 11 15N 79 41E
Sírna, I. 69 36 22N 26 42E
Sirnach 51 47 28N 8 59E
Sirohi 94 24 52N 72 53E
Siroki Brijeg 66 43 21N 17 36E
Sironj 94 24 5N 77 45E
Síros 69 37 28N 24 57E
Síros, I. 69 37 28N 24 57E
Sirretta Pk. 163 35 56N 118 19W
Sirsa 94 29 33N 75 4E
Sirsi 97 14 40N 74 49E
Siruela 57 38 58N 5 3W
Sisak 63 45 30N 16 21E
Sisaket 100 15 8N 104 23E
Sisante 59 39 25N 2 12W
Sisargas, Islas 56 43 21N 8 50W
Sishen 128 27 55S 22 59E
Sisipuk I. 153 55 40N 102 0W
Sisipuk L. 153 55 45N 101 50W
Sisophon 100 13 31N 102 59E
Sissach 50 47 27N 7 48E
Sisseton 158 45 43N 97 3W
Sissonne 43 49 34N 3 51E
Sistan-Baluchistan □ 93 27 0N 62 0E
Sistema Central 56 40 40N 5 55W
Sistema Ibérico 58 41 0N 2 10W
Sisteron 45 44 12N 5 57E
Sisters 160 44 21N 121 32W
Sitamarhi 95 26 37N 85 30E
Sitapur 95 27 38N 80 45E
Siteki 129 26 32S 31 58E
Sitges 58 41 17N 1 47E
Sithoniá 68 40 0N 23 45E
Sitia 69 35 13N 26 6E
Sítio da Abadia 171 14 48S 46 16W
Sitka 147 57 9N 134 58W
Sitona 123 14 25N 37 23E
Sitoti 128 23 15S 23 40E
Sitra 122 28 40N 26 53E
Sittang Myit, R. 99 18 20N 96 45E
Sittang, R. 98 17 10N 96 58E
Sittard 47 51 0N 5 52E
Sittaung 98 24 10N 94 35E
Sittensen 48 53 17N 9 32E
Sittingbourne 29 51 20N 0 43E
Sittwe 99 20 15N 92 45E
Situbondo 103 7 45S 114 0E
Siuch'uan 109 26 20N 114 30E
Siuna 166 13 37N 84 45W
Sivaganga 97 9 50N 78 28E
Sivagiri 97 9 16N 77 26E
Sivakasi 97 9 24N 77 47E
Sivand 93 30 5N 52 55E
Sivas 92 39 43N 36 58E
Siverek 92 37 50N 39 25E
Sivrihisar 92 39 30N 31 35E
Sivry 47 50 10N 4 12E
Sîwa 122 29 11N 25 31E
Siwalik Range 95 28 0N 83 0E
Siwan 95 26 13N 84 27E
Sixmile Cross 38 54 34N 7 7W
Sixmilebridge 39 52 45N 8 46W
Siyâl, Jazâ'ir 122 22 49N 36 6E
Siyana 94 28 37N 78 6E
Sizewell 29 52 13N 1 38E
Sjaelland 73 55 30N 11 30E
Sjaellands Odde 73 56 0N 11 15E
Själevad 72 63 18N 18 36E
Sjarinska Banja 66 42 45N 21 38E
Sjenica 66 43 16N 20 0E
Sjernarőy 71 59 15N 5 50E
Sjoa 71 61 41N 9 40E
Sjöbo 73 55 37N 13 45E
Sjöholt 71 62 27N 6 52E
Sjönsta 74 67 10N 16 3E
Sjösa 73 58 47N 17 4E
Skadovsk 82 46 17N 32 52E
Skælskör 73 55 16N 11 18E
Skagafjörður 74 65 54N 19 35W
Skagastölstindane, mt. 75 61 25N 8 10E
Skagen 75 68 37N 14 27E
Skagen, pt. 73 57 43N 10 35E
Skagern 72 59 0N 14 20E
Skagerrak 73 57 30N 9 0E
Skagway 147 59 30N 135 20W
Skaidi 74 70 26N 24 30E
Skala Podolskaya 82 48 50N 26 15E
Skalat 80 49 23N 25 55E
Skalbmierz 54 56 22N 12 30E
Skalderviken 73 56 22N 12 30E
Skalicd 53 48 50N 17 15E
Skallingen, Odde 73 55 32N 8 13E
Skalni Dol = Kamenyak 67 43 24N 26 57E
Skals 73 56 34N 9 24E
Skanderborg 73 56 2N 9 55E
Skaneateles 162 42 57N 76 26W

Soller Speer

Soller 58 39 43N 2 45 E
Sollerön 72 60 54N 14 38 E
Solna 72 59 22N 18 1 E
Solnechnogorsk 81 56 10N 36 57 E
Sölnkletten, Mt. 71 61 55N 10 18 E
Sologne 59 47 40N 2 0 E
Solojärg 73 56 50N 10 8 E
Solok 102 0 55 S 100 40 E
Sololá 166 14 49N 91 10 E
Solomon Is. ■ 135 6 0 S 155 0 E
Solomon, N. Fork, R. 158 39 45N 99 0W
Solomon Sea 135 7 0 S 150 0 E
Solomon, S. Fork, R. 158 39 25N 99 12W
Solomon's Pools = Burak Sulayman 90 31 42N 35 7 E
Solon Springs 158 46 19N 91 47W
Solonópole 170 5 44 S 39 1W
Solor, I. 103 8 27 S 123 0 E
Solotcha 81 54 48N 39 53 E
Solothurn 50 47 13N 7 32 E
Solothurn □ 50 47 18N 7 40 E
Solotobe 85 44 37N 66 3 E
Solsona 58 42 0N 1 31 E
Solt 53 46 45N 19 1 E
Solta, I. 63 43 24N 16 15 E
Soltanabad 93 36 29N 58 5 E
Soltaniyeh 92 36 20N 48 55 E
Soltau 48 52 59N 9 50 E
Soltsy 80 58 10N 30 10 E
Solun 105 46 40N 120 40 E
Solund 71 61 5N 4 50 E
Solund I. 71 61 7N 4 50 E
Solunska Glava 66 41 44N 21 31 E
Solva 31 51 52N 5 12W
Solvang 163 34 36N 120 8W
Solvay 162 43 5N 76 17W
Solvesborg 73 56 5N 14 35 E
Sölvesborg 73 56 5N 14 35 E
Solway Firth 32 54 45N 3 38W
Solwezi 127 12 20 S 26 21 E
Somali Rep. ■ 91 7 0N 47 0 E
Somaliland 123 12 0N 43 0 E
Sombe Dzong 98 27 13N 89 8 E
Sombernon 43 47 20N 4 40 E
Sombor 66 45 46N 19 17 E
Sombrerete 164 23 40N 103 40W
Sombrero I. 167 18 30N 63 30W
Somerby 29 52 42N 0 49W
Someren 47 51 23N 5 42 E
Somers 160 48 4N 114 18W
Somerset, Austral. 138 10 45 S 142 25 E
Somerset, Can. 153 49 25N 98 39W
Somerset, Colo., U.S.A. 161 38 55N 107 30W
Somerset, Ky., U.S.A. 156 37 5N 84 40W
Somerset, Mass., U.S.A. 162 41 45N 71 10W
Somerset □ 28 51 9N 3 0W
Somerset East 128 32 42 S 25 35 E
Somerset, I. 148 73 30N 93 0W
Somerset West 128 34 8 S 18 50 E
Somersham 29 52 24N 0 0W
Somersworth 162 43 15N 70 51W
Somerton, U.K. 28 51 3N 2 45W
Somerton, U.S.A. 161 32 41N 114 47W
Somerville 162 40 34N 74 36W
Someş, R. 70 47 15N 23 45 E
Someşul Mare, R. 70 47 18N 24 30 E
Somma Lombardo 62 45 41N 8 42 E
Somma Vesuviana 65 40 52N 14 23 E
Sommariva 139 26 24 S 146 36 E
Sommatino 65 37 20N 14 0 E
Somme □ 43 50 0N 2 20 E
Somme, B. de la 42 5 22N 1 30 E
Sommelsdijk 46 51 46N 4 9 E
Sommen 73 58 12N 15 0 E
Sommen, L. 73 58 0N 15 15 E
Sommepy-Tahure 43 49 15N 4 31 E
Sömmerda 48 51 10N 11 8 E
Sommersted 73 55 19N 9 18 E
Sommesous 43 48 44N 4 12 E
Sommières 45 43 47N 4 6 E
Somogy □ 53 46 19N 17 30 E
Somogyszob 53 46 18N 17 20 E
Somoto 166 13 28N 86 37W
Sompolno 54 52 26N 18 45 E
Somport, Paso 58 42 48N 0 31W
Somport, Puerto de 58 42 48N 0 31W
Sompting 29 50 51N 0 20W
Son, Neth. 47 51 31N 5 30 E
Son, Norway 71 59 32N 10 42 E
Son, Spain 56 42 43N 8 58W
Son Hoa 100 13 2N 108 58 E
Son La 100 21 20N 103 50 E
Son Ma 100 15 3N 108 34 E
Son Tay 100 21 8N 105 30 E
Soná 166 8 0N 81 10W
Sonamarg 95 34 18N 75 21 E
Sonamukhi 95 23 18N 87 27 E
Sonamura 98 23 29N 91 15 E
Sönchön 107 39 48N 124 55 E
Soncino 62 45 24N 9 52 E
Sondags, R. 128 32 10N 24 40 E
Søndala 62 46 20N 10 20 E
Sondar 95 33 28N 75 56 E
Sönder Hornum 73 56 32N 9 38 E
Sønder Omme 73 55 50N 8 54 E
Sønderborg 73 54 55N 9 49 E
Sonderhausen 48 51 22N 10 50 E
Sønderjyllands Amt □ 73 55 10N 9 10 E
Sondre Höland 71 59 44N 11 30 E
Sondre Land 71 60 44N 10 21 E
Söndre Stromfjord 12 66 30N 50 52W
Söndrio 62 46 10N 9 53 E
Sone 127 17 23 S 34 55 E
Sonepat 94 29 0N 77 5 E
Sonepur 96 20 55N 83 50 E
Song 100 18 28N 100 11 E
Song Cau 100 13 20N 109 18 E
Songa, R. 71 59 57N 7 30 E
Söngchön 107 39 12N 126 15 E
Songea 127 10 40 S 35 40 E
Songea □ 127 10 30 S 36 0 E
Songeons 43 49 32N 1 50 E
Songjin 107 40 40N 129 10 E
Songjŏngni 107 35 8N 126 47 E
Songkhla 101 7 13N 100 37 E
Songnim 107 38 45N 125 39 E
Songwe, Malawi 127 9 44 S 33 58 E
Songwe, Zaïre 127 3 20 S 26 16 E
Sonkel, Ozero 85 41 50N 75 12 E
Sonkovo 81 57 50N 37 5 E
Sonmiani 94 25 25N 66 40 E
Sonning 29 51 28N 0 53W
Sonnino 64 41 25N 13 13 E
Sono, R., Goias, Brazil 170 8 58 S 48 11W
Sono, R., Minas Gerais, Brazil 171 17 2 S 45 32W
Sonobe 111 35 6N 135 28 E
Sonogno 51 46 22N 8 47 E
Sonoma 163 38 17N 122 27W
Sonora, Calif., U.S.A. 163 37 59N 120 27W
Sonora, Texas, U.S.A. 159 30 33N 100 37W
Sonora □ 164 28 0N 111 0W
Sonora P. 160 38 17N 119 35W
Sonora, R. 164 28 30N 111 33W
Sonoyta 164 31 51N 112 50W
Sönsan 107 36 14N 128 17 E
Sonskyn 128 30 47 S 26 28 E
Sonsonate 166 13 43N 89 44W
Sonthofen 49 47 31N 10 16 E
Soo Junction 156 46 20N 85 14W
Soochow = Suchou 109 31 15N 120 40 E
Sööner Nissum 73 56 19N 8 11 E
Sop Hao 100 20 33N 104 27 E
Sop Prap 100 17 53N 99 20 E
Sopi 103 2 40N 128 28 E
Sopo, Nahr 123 8 40N 26 30 E
Sopot, Poland 54 54 27N 18 31 E
Sopot, Yugo. 66 44 29N 20 30 E
Sopotnica 66 41 23N 21 13 E
Sopron 49 47 41N 16 37 E
Sop's Arm 151 49 46N 56 56W
Sör-Fron 71 61 35N 9 59 E
Sor, R. 57 39 7N 9 52 E
Sør-Rondane 13 72 0 S 25 0 E
Sør Trøndelag fylke □ 71 63 0N 11 0 E
Sora 64 41 45N 13 36 E
Sorada 96 19 32N 84 45 E
Sorah 94 27 13N 68 56 E
Söråker 72 62 30N 17 32 E
Sorano 63 42 40N 11 42 E
Sorata 174 15 50 S 68 50W
Sorbas 59 37 6N 2 7W
Sorbie 34 54 46N 4 26W
Sordale 37 58 33N 3 26W
Sordeval 42 48 44N 0 55W
Sorel 150 46 0N 73 10W
Sörenberg 50 46 50N 8 2 E
Soresina 62 45 17N 9 51 E
Sörfold 74 67 5N 14 20 E
Sorgues 45 44 1N 4 53 E
Soria 58 41 43N 2 32W
Soria □ 58 41 46N 2 28W
Soriano 172 33 24 S 58 19W
Soriano □ 176 33 30 S 58 0W
Sorisdale 34 56 40N 6 28W
Sorn 34 55 31N 4 18W
Sorø 73 55 26N 11 32 E
Soro 120 10 9N 9 48W
Sorocaba 173 23 31 S 47 35W
Sorochinsk 84 52 26N 53 10 E
Soroki 82 48 8N 28 12 E
Soroksár 53 47 24N 19 9 E
Soron 94 27 55N 78 45 E
Sorong 103 0 55 S 131 15 E
Sororoca 174 0 43N 61 31W
Soroti 126 1 43N 33 35 E
Soröy Sundet 74 70 25N 23 0 E
Soröya 74 70 35N 22 45 E
Soroyane 71 62 25N 5 32 E
Sorraia, R. 57 38 55N 8 35W
Sorrento, Austral. 139 38 22 S 144 47 E
Sorrento, Italy 65 40 38N 14 23 E
Sorris Sorris 128 21 0 S 14 46 E
Sorsele 74 65 31N 17 30 E
Sorso 64 40 50N 8 34 E
Sorsogon 103 13 0N 124 0 E
Sortat 37 58 32N 3 12W
Sortino 65 37 9N 15 1 E
Sos 58 42 30N 1 13W
Sŏsan 107 36 47N 126 27 E
Soscumica, L. 150 50 15N 77 27W
Sosdala 73 56 2N 13 41 E
Sosna, R. 81 52 30N 38 0 E
Sosnowiec 54 50 20N 19 10 E
Sospel 45 43 52N 7 27 E
Soštanj 63 46 23N 15 4 E
Sösura 107 42 16N 130 36 E
Sosva 84 59 10N 61 50 E
Sosva, R. 84 59 32N 62 20 E
Soto la Marina, R. 165 23 40N 97 40W
Soto y Amío 56 42 46N 5 53W
Sotra I. 71 60 15N 5 0 E
Sotteville 42 49 24N 1 5 E
Souanké 124 2 10N 14 10 E
Souderton 162 40 19N 75 19W
Soufi 120 15 13N 12 17W
Souflíon 68 41 12N 26 18 E
Soufrière 167 13 51N 61 4W
Soufrière, vol. 167 13 10N 61 10W
Sougne-Remouchamps 47 50 29N 5 42 E
Souillac 44 44 53N 1 29 E
Souk-Ahras 119 36 17N 7 57 E
Souk el Arba du Rharb 118 34 50N 5 59W
Souk el Khemis 119 36 36N 8 58 E
Soukhouma 100 14 38N 105 48 E
Sŏul 105 37 31N 127 6 E
Soulac-sur-Mer 44 45 30N 1 7W
Soultz 43 48 57N 7 52 E
Soumagne 47 50 37N 5 44 E
Sound, The 75 56 7N 12 30 E
Soúnion, Ákra 69 37 37N 24 1 E
Sour el Ghozlane 119 36 10N 3 45 E
Sources, Mt. aux 129 28 45 S 28 50 E
Sourdeval 42 48 43N 0 55W
Soure, Brazil 170 0 35 S 48 30W
Soure, Port. 56 40 4N 8 38W
Souris, Man., Can. 153 49 40N 100 20W
Souris, P.E.I., Can. 151 46 21N 62 15W
Souris, R. 153 49 40N 99 34W
Soúrpi 69 39 6N 22 54 E
Sous, R. 118 30 31N 9 27W
Sousa 170 6 45 S 38 10W
Sousel, Brazil 170 2 38 S 52 29W
Sousel, Port. 57 38 57N 7 40W
Souss, O. 118 30 23N 8 24W
Sousse 119 35 50N 10 38 E
Soustons 44 43 45N 1 19W
Souterraine, La 44 46 15N 1 30 E
South Africa, Rep. of, ■ 125 30 0 S 25 0 E
South Amboy 162 40 29N 74 17W
South America 168 10 0 S 60 0W
South Auckland & Bay of Plenty □ 142 38 30 S 177 0 E
South Aulatsivik I. 151 56 45N 61 30W
South Australia □ 136 32 0 S 139 0 E
South Baldy, Mt. 161 34 6N 107 27W
South Bend, Indiana, U.S.A. 156 41 38N 86 20W
South Bend, Wash., U.S.A. 160 46 44N 123 52W
South Benfleet 29 51 33N 0 34 E
South Blackwater 138 24 00 S 148 35 E
South Boston 157 36 42N 78 58W
South Br. Ashburton, R. 143 43 30 S 171 15 E
South Branch, Can. 151 47 55N 59 2W
South Branch, U.S.A. 151 44 30N 83 55W
South Brent 30 50 26N 3 50W
South Brook 151 49 26N 56 5W
South Buganda □ 126 0 15 S 31 30 E
South Cape 147 18 58N 155 24 E
South Carolina □ 157 33 45N 81 0W
South Cave 33 53 46N 0 37W
South Charleston 156 38 20N 81 40W
South China Sea 101 7 0N 107 0 E
South Dakota □ 158 45 0N 100 0W
South Dell 36 58 28N 6 20W
South Dorset Downs 28 50 40N 2 26W
South Downs 29 50 53N 0 10W
South East C. 138 43 40 S 146 50 E
South East Is. 137 34 17 S 123 30 E
South Elkington 33 53 22N 0 5W
South Esk, R. 37 56 44N 3 3W
South Foreland 29 51 7N 1 23 E
S. Fork, American, R. 163 38 45N 121 5W
South Fork, R. 160 47 54N 113 15W
South Gamboa 164 9 4N 79 40W
South Gate 163 33 57N 118 12W
South Georgia 13 54 30 S 37 0W
South Glamorgan □ 31 51 30N 3 20W
South Grafton 139 29 41 S 152 47 E
South Harris, district 36 56 51N 3 10W
South Haven 156 42 22N 86 20W
South Hayling 29 50 47N 0 56W
South Henik, L. 153 61 30N 97 30W
South Horr 126 2 12N 36 56 E
South I., Kenya 126 2 35N 36 35 E
South I., N.Z. 143 43 0 S 170 0 E
South Invercargill 143 46 26N 168 23 E
South Kirby 33 53 35N 1 25W
South Knife, R. 153 58 55N 94 37W
S. Kolok 101 6 2N 101 58 E
South Korea ■ 107 36 0N 128 0 E
S. Lembing 101 3 55N 103 3 E
South Magnetic Pole 13 66 30 S 139 30 E
South Marsh Is. 162 38 6N 76 1W
South Milwaukee 156 42 50N 87 52W
South Molton 30 51 1N 3 50W
South Nahanni, R. 152 61 3N 123 21W
South Nesting B. 36 60 18N 1 5W
South Orkney Is. 13 63 0 S 45 0W
South Pass 160 42 20N 108 58W
South Passage 137 26 07 S 113 09 E
S. Petani 101 5 37N 100 30 E
South Petherton 28 50 57N 2 49W
South Petherwin 30 50 35N 4 22W
South Pines 157 35 10N 79 25W
South Platte, R. 158 40 50N 102 45W
South Pt. 151 49 6N 62 11W
South Pole 13 90 0 S 0 0 E
South Porcupine 150 48 30N 81 12W
South Portland 162 43 38N 70 15W
South River, Can. 150 45 52N 79 29W
South River, U.S.A. 162 40 27N 74 23W
South Ronaldsay, I. 37 58 46N 2 58W
S. Sandwich Is. 15 57 0 S 27 0W
South Saskatchewan, R. 153 53 15N 105 5W
South Sd. 39 53 4N 9 28W
South Seal, R. 153 58 48N 98 8W
South Sentinel, I. 101 11 1N 92 16 E
South Shetland Is. 13 62 0 S 59 0W
South Shields 35 54 59N 1 26W
South Sioux City 158 42 30N 96 30W
South Taranaki Bight 142 39 40 S 174 5 E
South Tawton 30 50 44N 3 55W
South Thompson, R. 152 50 40N 120 20W
South Twin I. 150 53 7N 79 52W
South Tyne, R. 35 54 46N 2 25W
South Uist, I. 37 57 4N 7 21W
South Ulvön, I. 72 63 0N 18 45 E
South Walls, I. 37 58 45N 3 7W
South West Africa ■ = Namibia 128 22 0 S 18 9 E
South West C. 138 43 34 S 146 3 E
South West Cape 143 47 16 S 167 31 E
South Williamsport 162 41 14N 77 0W
South Yarmouth 162 41 35N 70 10W
South Yemen ■ 91 15 0N 48 0 E
South Yorkshire □ 33 53 30N 1 20W
Southam 28 52 16N 1 24W
Southampton, Can. 150 44 30N 81 25W
Southampton, U.K. 28 50 54N 1 23W
Southampton, U.S.A. 162 40 54N 72 22W
Southampton I. 149 64 30N 84 0W
Southampton Water 28 50 52N 1 21W
Southborough 29 51 10N 0 15 E
Southbridge, N.Z. 143 43 48 S 172 16 E
Southbridge, U.S.A. 162 42 4N 72 2W
Southeast C. 147 62 55N 169 40W
Southend, Can. 153 56 19N 103 14W
Southend, U.K. 34 55 18N 5 38W
Southend-on-Sea 29 51 32N 0 42 E
Southern □, Malawi 127 15 0 S 35 0 E
Southern □, S. Leone 120 0 8N 12 30 E
Southern □, Uganda 122 0 30 S 30 30 E
Southern □, Zambia 127 16 20 S 26 20 E
Southern Alps 143 43 41 S 170 11 E
Southern Cross 137 31 12 S 119 15 E
Southern Hills 137 32 15 S 122 40 E
Southern Indian L. 153 57 10N 98 30W
Southern Indian Lake 153 57 0N 99 0W
Southern Ocean 13 62 0 S 160 0W
Southern Uplands 35 55 30N 3 3W
Southery 29 52 32N 0 23 E
Southington 162 41 37N 72 53W
Southland □ 143 45 51 S 168 13 E
Southminster 29 51 40N 0 51 E
Southold 162 41 4N 72 26W
Southport, Austral. 139 27 58 S 153 25 E
Southport, U.K. 32 53 38N 3 1W
Southport, U.S.A. 157 33 55N 78 0W
Southwark 29 51 29N 0 5W
Southwell 33 53 4N 0 57W
Southwick 29 50 50N 0 14W
Southwold 29 52 19N 1 41 E
Soutpansberge 129 23 0 S 29 30 E
Souvigny 44 46 33N 3 10 E
Sovata 70 46 35N 25 3 E
Sovetsk, Lithuania, U.S.S.R. 80 55 6N 21 50 E
Sovetsk, R.S.F.S.R., U.S.S.R. 81 57 38N 48 53 E
Sovetskaya Gavan 77 48 50N 140 0 E
Sovicille 63 43 16N 11 12 E
Sovra 66 42 44N 17 34 E
Sowerby 33 54 13N 1 19W
Söya-Misaki 112 45 30N 142 0 E
Soyopa 164 28 41N 109 37W
Sozh, R. 80 53 50N 31 50 E
Sozopol 67 42 23N 27 42 E
Spa 47 50 29N 5 53 E
Spain ■ 55 40 0N 5 0W
Spakenburg 46 52 15N 5 22 E
Spalding, Austral. 140 33 30 S 138 37 E
Spalding, U.K. 29 52 47N 0 9W
Spalding, U.S.A. 158 41 45N 98 27W
Spandet 73 55 15N 8 54 E
Spånga 72 59 23N 17 55 E
Spångenäs 73 57 36N 16 7 E
Spangereid 71 58 3N 7 9 E
Spaniard's Bay 151 47 38N 53 20W
Spanish 150 46 12N 82 20W
Spanish Fork 160 40 10N 111 37W
Spanish Pt. 39 52 51N 9 27W
Spanish Sahara □ = Western Sahara 116 25 0N 13 0W
Spanish Town 166 18 0N 77 20W
Sparkford 28 51 2N 2 33W
Sparrows Point 162 39 13N 76 29W
Sparta, Ga., U.S.A. 157 33 18N 82 59W
Sparta, N.J., U.S.A. 162 41 2N 74 38W
Sparta, Wis., U.S.A. 158 43 55N 91 10W
Sparta = Spárti 69 37 5N 22 25 E
Spartanburg 157 35 0N 82 0W
Spartel, C. 118 35 47N 5 56W
Spárti 69 37 5N 22 25 E
Spartivento, C., Calabria, Italy 65 37 56N 16 4 E
Spartivento, C., Sard., Italy 65 38 52N 8 50 E
Spas-Demensk 80 54 20N 34 0 E
Spas-Klepiki 81 54 34N 40 2 E
Spassk-Dalniy 77 44 40N 132 40 E
Spassk-Ryazanskiy 81 54 30N 40 25 E
Spatha Ákra. 69 35 42N 23 43 E
Spatsizi, R. 152 57 42N 128 7W
Spean Bridge 36 56 53N 4 55W
Spearfish 158 44 32N 103 52W
Spearman 159 36 15N 101 10W
Speculator 162 43 30N 74 25W
Speed 140 35 21 S 142 27 E
Speer 51 47 12N 9 8 E

Speers Stíra

Speers 153 52 43N 107 34W
Speightstown 167 13 15N 59 39W
Speke 32 53 21N 2 51W
Speke Gulf, L. Victoria 126 2 20S 32 50E
Spekholzerheide 47 50 51N 6 2E
Spelve, L. 34 56 22N 5 45W
Spenard 147 61 5N 149 50W
Spencer, Idaho, U.S.A. 160 44 18N 112 8W
Spencer, Iowa, U.S.A. 158 43 5N 95 3W
Spencer, Nebr., U.S.A. 158 42 52N 98 43W
Spencer, N.Y., U.S.A. 162 42 14N 76 30W
Spencer, W. Va., U.S.A. 156 38 47N 81 24W
Spencer B. 128 25 30S 14 47E
Spencer Bay 148 69 32N 93 32W
Spencer, C. 140 35 20S 136 45E
Spencer G. 140 34 0S 137 20E
Spences Bridge 152 50 25N 121 20W
Spennymoor 33 54 43N 1 35W
Spenser Mts. 143 42 15S 172 45E
Sperkhiós, R. 69 38 57N 22 3E
Sperrin Mts. 38 54 50N 7 0W
Spessart 49 50 0N 9 20E
Spetsai 69 37 16N 23 9E
Spétsai, I. 69 37 15N 23 10E
Spey B. 37 57 41N 3 0W
Spey Bay 37 57 39N 3 4W
Spey, R. 37 57 26N 3 25W
Speyer 49 49 19N 8 26E
Speyer, R. 41 49 18N 7 52E
Spezia = La Spézia 62 44 7N 9 49E
Spézia, La 62 44 8N 9 50E
Spezzano Albanese 65 39 41N 16 19E
Spiddal 39 53 14N 9 19W
Spiekeroog, I. 48 53 45N 7 42E
Spielfeld 63 46 43N 15 38E
Spiez 50 46 40N 7 40E
Spijk 46 53 24N 6 50E
Spijkenisse 46 51 51N 4 20E
Spili 69 35 13N 24 31E
Spilimbergo 63 46 7N 12 53E
Spillimacheen 152 51 6N 117 0W
Spilsby 33 53 10N 0 6E
Spin Baldak 93 31 3N 66 16E
Spinazzola 65 40 58N 16 5E
Spincourt 43 49 20N 5 39E
Spind 71 58 6N 6 53E
Spineni 70 44 43N 24 37E
Spirit Lake 160 47 56N 116 56W
Spirit River 152 55 45N 118 50W
Spiritwood 153 53 24N 107 33W
Spišská Nová Ves 53 48 58N 20 34E
Spišské Podhradie 53 49 0N 20 48E
Spit Pt. 136 20 4S 118 59E
Spithead 29 50 43N 0 56W
Spittal 52 46 48N 13 31E
Spitzbergen (Svalbard) 12 78 0N 17 0E
Split 63 43 31N 16 26E
Split L. 153 56 8N 96 15W
Splitski Kan 63 43 31N 16 20E
Splügen 51 46 34N 9 21E
Splügenpass 51 46 30N 9 20E
Spoffard 159 29 10N 100 27W
Spofforth 33 53 57N 1 28W
Spokane 160 47 45N 117 25W
Sponvika 71 59 7N 11 15E
Spooner 158 45 49N 91 51W
Sporádhes 69 37 0N 27 0E
Sporyy Navolok, M. 76 75 50N 68 40E
Spotswood 162 40 23N 74 23W
Spragge 150 46 15N 82 40W
Sprague 160 47 25N 117 59W
Sprague River 160 42 49N 121 31W
Spratly, I. 102 8 20N 112 0E
Spray 160 44 56N 119 46W
Spree, R. 48 52 23N 13 52E
Sprimont 47 50 30N 5 40E
Spring City, Pa., U.S.A. 162 40 11N 75 33W
Spring City, Utah, U.S.A. 160 39 31N 111 28W
Spring Grove 162 39 55N 76 56W
Spring Hill 141 33 23S 149 9E
Spring Mts. 161 36 20N 115 43W
Spring Valley, Minn., U.S.A. 158 43 40N 92 30W
Spring Valley, N.Y., U.S.A. 162 41 7N 74 4W
Springbok 128 29 42S 17 54E
Springburn 143 43 40S 171 32E
Springdale, Can. 151 49 30N 56 6W
Springdale, Ark., U.S.A. 159 36 10N 94 5W
Springdale, Wash., U.S.A. 160 48 1N 117 50W
Springe 48 52 12N 9 35E
Springerville 161 34 10N 109 16W
Springfield, N.Z. 143 43 19S 171 56E
Springfield, Colo., U.S.A. 159 37 26N 102 40W
Springfield, Ill., U.S.A. 158 39 48N 89 40W
Springfield, Mass., U.S.A. 162 42 8N 72 37W
Springfield, Mo., U.S.A. 159 37 15N 93 20W
Springfield, Ohio, U.S.A. 156 39 50N 83 48W
Springfield, Oreg., U.S.A. 160 44 2N 123 0W
Springfield, Tenn., U.S.A. 157 36 35N 86 55W
Springfield, Va., U.S.A. 162 38 45N 77 13W
Springfield, Vt., U.S.A. 162 43 20N 72 30W
Springfontein 128 30 15S 25 40E
Springhill 151 45 40N 64 4W
Springhouse 152 51 56N 122 7W
Springhurst 141 36 10S 146 31E
Springs 129 26 13S 28 25E
Springsure 138 24 8S 148 6E
Springvale, Queens., Austral. 138 23 33S 140 42E
Springvale, W. Australia, Austral. 136 17 48S 127 41E
Springvale, U.S.A. 162 43 28N 70 48W
Springville, Calif., U.S.A. 163 36 8N 118 49W
Springville, N.Y., U.S.A. 156 42 31N 78 41W
Springville, Utah, U.S.A. 160 40 14N 111 35W
Springwater 153 51 58N 108 23W
Sproatley 33 53 46N 0 9W
Spur 159 33 28N 100 50W
Spurn Hd. 33 53 34N 0 8E
Spuz 66 42 32N 19 10E
Spuzzum 152 49 37N 121 23W
Spydeberg 71 59 37N 11 4E
Squam L. 162 43 45N 71 32W
Squamish 152 49 45N 123 10W
Square Islands 151 52 47N 55 47W
Squillace, Golfo di 65 38 43N 16 35E
Squinzano 65 40 27N 18 1E
Squires, Mt. 137 26 14S 127 46E
Sragen 103 7 28S 110 59E
Srbac 66 45 7N 17 30E
Srbija □ 66 43 30N 21 0E
Srbobran 66 45 32N 19 48E
Sre Khtum 101 12 10N 106 52E
Sre Umbell 101 11 8N 103 46E
Srebrnica 66 44 10N 19 18E
Sredinyy Khrebet 77 57 0N 160 0E
Središce 63 46 24N 16 17E
Sredna Gora 67 42 40N 25 0E
Sredne Tambovskoye 77 50 55N 137 45E
Srednekolymsk 77 67 20N 154 40E
Srednevilyuysk 77 63 50N 123 5E
Sredni Rodopi 67 41 40N 24 45E
Sredniy Ural, mts. 166 59 0N 59 0E
Srem 54 52 6N 17 2E
Srepok, R. 100 13 33N 106 16E
Sretensk 77 52 10N 117 40E
Sri Lanka ■ 97 7 30N 80 50E
Sriharikota, I. 97 13 40N 81 30E
Srikakulam 96 18 14N 84 4E
Srinagar 95 34 12N 74 50E
Sripur 98 24 14N 90 30E
Srirangam 97 10 54N 78 42E
Srirangapatnam 97 12 26N 76 43E
Śrivilliputtur 97 9 31N 77 40E
Środa Wlkp. 54 52 15N 17 19E
Srpska Crnja 66 45 38N 20 44E
Srpska Itabej 66 45 35N 20 44E
Ssu Chiao 109 30 43N 122 28E
Ssuhsien 107 33 25N 117 54E
Ssuhui 109 23 20N 112 41E
Ssunan 108 27 56N 108 14E
Ssup'ing 105 43 10N 124 25E
Ssushui, Honan, China 106 34 51N 113 12E
Ssushui, Shantung, China 107 35 39N 117 15E
Ssutzuwangch'i 106 41 30N 111 37E
Staaten, R. 138 16 24S 141 17E
Stabroek 47 51 20N 4 22E
Stack's Mts. 39 52 20N 9 34W
Stad Delden 46 52 16N 6 43E
Stade 48 53 35N 9 31E
Staden 47 50 59N 3 1E
Staðarhólskirkja 74 65 23N 21 58W
Stadil 73 56 12N 8 12E
Städjan 72 61 56N 12 30E
Stadlandet 71 62 10N 5 10E
Stadsforsen 72 63 0N 16 45E
Stadskanaal 46 53 4N 6 48E
Stadthagen 48 52 20N 9 14E
Stadtlohn 48 51 59N 6 52E
Stadtroda 48 50 51N 11 44E
Stäfa 51 47 14N 8 45E
Stafafell 74 64 25N 14 52W
Staffa, I. 34 56 26N 6 21W
Stafford, U.K. 28 52 49N 2 9W
Stafford, Kansas, U.S.A. 159 38 0N 98 35W
Stafford, Va., U.S.A. 162 38 2S 77 30W
Stafford □ 28 52 53N 2 10W
Stafford Springs 162 41 58N 72 20W
Stagnone, I. 64 37 50N 12 28E
Staindrop 33 54 35N 1 49W
Staines 29 51 26N 0 30W
Stainforth 33 53 37N 0 59W
Stainmore For. 32 54 29N 2 5W
Stainton 33 53 17N 0 23W
Stainz 52 46 53N 15 17E
Staithes 33 54 33N 0 47W
Stakkroge 73 55 53N 8 51E
Stalač 66 43 43N 21 28E
Stalbridge 28 50 57N 2 22W
Stalden 50 46 14N 7 52E
Stalham 29 52 46N 1 31E
Stalingrad = Volgograd 83 48 40N 44 25E
Staliniri = Tskhinvali 83 42 14N 44 1E
Stalino = Donetsky 82 48 0N 37 45E
Stalinogorsk = Novomoskovsk 81 54 5N 38 15E
Stallingborough 33 53 36N 0 11W
Stalowa Wola 54 50 34N 22 3E
Stalybridge 32 53 29N 1 56W
Stamford, Austral. 138 21 15S 143 46E
Stamford, U.K. 29 52 39N 0 29W
Stamford, Conn., U.S.A. 162 41 5N 73 30W
Stamford, N.Y., U.S.A. 162 42 25N 74 37W
Stamford, Tex., U.S.A. 159 32 58N 99 50W
Stamford Bridge 33 53 59N 0 53W
Stamfordham 35 55 3N 1 53W
Stampersgat 47 51 37N 4 26E
Stamps 159 33 22N 93 30W
Stanberry 158 40 12N 94 32W
Standerton 129 26 55S 29 13E
Standish, U.K. 32 53 35N 2 39W
Standish, U.S.A. 156 43 58N 83 57W
Standon 29 51 53N 0 2E
Stanford 160 47 11N 110 10W
Stanford on Teme 28 52 17N 2 26W
Stange Hedmark 71 60 43N 11 11E
Stanger 129 29 18S 31 21E
Stanhope, Austral. 141 36 27S 144 59E
Stanhope, U.K. 32 54 45N 2 0W
Stanišic 53 45 53N 19 12E
Stanislaus, R. 163 37 40N 121 15W
Stanislav = Ivano-Frankovsk 80 49 0N 24 40E
Stanke Dimitrov 66 42 27N 23 9E
Stanley, Austral. 138 40 46S 145 19E
Stanley, N.B., Can. 151 46 20N 66 50W
Stanley, Sask., Can. 153 55 24N 104 22W
Stanley, Falk. Is. 176 51 40S 58 0W
Stanley, Durham, U.K. 33 54 53N 1 42W
Stanley, Tayside, U.K. 35 56 29N 3 28W
Stanley, Idaho, U.S.A. 160 44 10N 114 59W
Stanley, N.D., U.S.A. 158 48 20N 102 23W
Stanley, Wis., U.S.A. 158 44 57N 91 0W
Stanley Res. 97 11 50N 77 40E
Stanleyville = Kisangani 126 0 35N 25 15E
Stanlow 32 53 17N 2 52W
Stann Creek 165 17 0N 88 20W
Stannington 35 55 7N 1 41W
Stanovoy Khrebet 77 55 0N 130 0E
Stans 51 46 58N 8 21E
Stansmore Ra. 136 21 23S 128 33E
Stansted Mountfitchet 29 51 54N 0 13E
Stanthorpe 139 28 36S 151 59E
Stanton, Can. 147 69 45N 128 52W
Stanton, U.S.A. 159 32 8N 101 45W
Stantsiya Karshi 85 38 49N 65 47E
Stanwix 32 54 54N 2 56W
Staphorst 46 52 39N 6 12E
Stapleford 33 52 56N 1 16W
Staplehurst 29 51 9N 0 35E
Stapleton 158 41 30N 100 31W
Staporkow 54 51 9N 20 31E
Star City 153 52 55N 104 20W
Stara-minskaya 83 46 33N 39 0E
Stara Moravica 66 45 50N 19 30E
Stara Pazova 66 45 0N 20 10E
Stara Planina 67 43 15N 23 0E
Stara Zagora 67 42 26N 25 39E
Starachowice-Wierzbnik 54 51 3N 21 2E
Staraya Russa 80 57 58N 31 10E
Starbuck I. 131 5 37S 155 55W
Stargard 48 53 29N 13 19E
Stargard Szczecinski 54 53 20N 15 0E
Stari Bar 66 42 7N 19 13E
Stari Trg. 63 45 29N 15 7E
Staritsa 80 56 33N 35 0E
Starke 157 30 0N 82 10W
Starkville, Colo., U.S.A. 159 37 10N 104 31W
Starkville, Miss., U.S.A. 157 33 26N 88 48W
Starnberg 49 48 0N 11 20E
Starnberger See 49 48 0N 11 0E
Starobelsk 83 49 27N 39 0E
Starodub 80 52 30N 32 50E
Starogard 54 53 55N 18 30E
Start Bay 30 50 15N 3 35W
Start Pt., Devon, U.K. 30 50 13N 3 38W
Start Pt., Orkney, U.K. 37 59 17N 2 25W
Stary Sacz 54 49 33N 20 26E
Staryy Biryuzyak 83 44 46N 46 50E
Staryy Kheydzhan 77 60 0N 144 50E
Staryy Krym 82 44 48N 35 8E
Staryy Oskol 81 51 12N 37 55E
Stassfurt 48 51 51N 11 34E
State College 156 40 47N 77 49W
State Is. 150 48 40N 87 0W
Staten I. 162 40 35N 74 10W
Staten, I. = Los Estados, I. de 176 54 40S 64 0W
Statesboro 157 32 26N 81 46W
Statesville 157 35 48N 80 51W
Statfjord, oilfield 19 61 15N 1 50E
Stathelle 71 59 3N 9 41E
Stauffer 163 34 45N 119 3W
Staunton, U.K. 28 51 58N 2 19W
Staunton, Ill., U.S.A. 158 39 0N 89 49W
Staunton, Va., U.S.A. 156 38 7N 79 4W
Stavanger 159 58 57N 5 40E
Staveley, Cumbria, U.K. 32 54 24N 2 49W
Staveley, Derby, U.K. 33 53 16N 1 20W
Stavelot 47 50 23N 5 55E
Stavenisse 47 51 35N 4 1E
Staveren 46 52 53N 5 22E
Stavern 71 59 0N 10 1E
Stavfjord 71 61 30N 5 0E
Stavre 72 62 51N 15 19E
Stavropol 83 45 5N 42 0E
Stavroúpolis 68 41 12N 24 45E
Stavsjö 73 48 42N 16 30E
Stawell 140 37 5S 142 47E
Stawell, R. 138 20 38S 142 55E
Stawiszyn 54 51 56N 18 4E
Staxigoe 37 58 28N 3 2W
Steamboat Springs 160 40 30N 106 58W
Stebark 54 53 30N 20 10E
Stebleva 68 41 18N 20 33E
Steckborn 51 47 44N 8 59E
Steele 158 46 56N 99 52W
Steelton 162 40 17N 76 50W
Steelville 159 37 57N 91 21W
Steen, R. 152 59 35N 117 10W
Steen River 152 59 40N 117 12W
Steenbergen 47 51 35N 4 19E
Steenvoorde 43 50 48N 2 33E
Steenwijk 46 52 47N 6 7E
Steep Pt. 137 26 08S 113 8E
Steep Rock 153 51 30N 98 48W
Steep Rock Lake 150 48 50N 91 38W
Stefănesti 70 47 44N 27 15E
Stefanie L. = Chew Bahir 123 4 40N 30 50E
Steffisburg 50 46 47N 7 38E
Stefŭnesti 70 47 44N 27 15E
Stege 73 55 0N 12 18E
Steierdorf Anina 66 45 6N 21 51E
Steiermark □ 52 47 26N 15 0E
Steigerwald 49 49 45N 10 30E
Stein, Neth. 47 50 58N 5 45E
Stein, Switz. 51 47 40N 8 50E
Stein, U.K. 36 57 30N 6 35W
Steinbach 153 49 32N 96 40W
Steinfort 47 49 39N 5 55E
Steinheim 48 51 50N 9 6E
Steinkjer 74 63 59N 11 31E
Steinkopf 125 29 15S 17 48E
Stekene 47 51 12N 4 2E
Stella Land 128 26 45S 24 50E
Stellarton 151 45 32N 62 45W
Stellenbosch 128 33 58S 18 50E
Stellendam 46 51 49N 4 1E
Stelvio, Paso dello 51 46 32N 10 27E
Stemshaug 71 63 19N 8 44E
Stendal 48 52 36N 11 50E
Stene 47 51 12N 2 56E
Stenhousemuir 35 56 2N 3 46W
Stenmagle 73 55 49N 11 39E
Stenness, L., of 37 59 0N 3 15W
Stensele 74 65 3N 17 8E
Stenstorp 73 58 17N 13 45E
Stenungsund 73 58 6N 11 50E
Stepanakert 79 40 0N 46 25E
Stephan 158 48 30N 96 53W
Stephens Cr. 140 32 15S 141 55E
Stephens I., Can. 152 54 10N 130 45W
Stephens I., N.Z. 143 40 40S 174 1E
Stephenville, Can. 151 48 31N 58 30W
Stephenville, U.S.A. 159 32 12N 98 12W
Stepnica 54 53 38N 14 36E
Stepnoi = Elista 83 46 25N 44 17E
Stepnoye 84 54 4N 60 26E
Sterkstroom 128 31 32S 26 32E
Sterlego, Mys 12 80 30N 90 0E
Sterling, Colo., U.S.A. 158 40 40N 103 15W
Sterling, Ill., U.S.A. 158 41 45N 89 45W
Sterling, Kans., U.S.A. 158 38 17N 98 13W
Sterling City 159 31 50N 100 59W
Sterlitamak 84 53 40N 56 0E
Sternberg 48 53 42N 11 48E
Sternberk 53 49 45N 17 15E
Stettin = Szczecin 54 53 27N 14 27E
Stettiner Haff 48 53 50N 14 25E
Stettler 152 52 19N 112 40W
Steubenville 156 40 21N 80 39W
Stevenage 29 51 54N 0 11W
Stevens Port 158 44 32N 89 34W
Stevens Village 147 66 0N 149 10W
Stevenson L. 153 53 55N 95 9W
Stevenson, R. 136 46 15S 134 10E
Stevenston 34 55 38N 4 46W
Stevns Klint 73 55 17N 12 28E
Stewart 152 55 56N 129 57W
Stewart, C. 138 11 57S 134 45E
Stewart, I. 176 54 50S 71 30W
Stewart I. 143 46 58S 167 54E
Stewart River 147 63 19N 139 26W
Stewarton 34 55 40N 4 30W
Stewartstown 38 54 35N 6 40W
Stewiacke 151 45 9N 63 22W
Steyning 29 50 54N 0 19W
Steynsburg 128 31 15S 25 49E
Steyr 52 48 3N 14 25E
Steyr, R. 52 48 57N 14 15E
Steytlerville 128 33 17S 24 19E
Stia 63 43 48N 11 41E
Stiens 46 53 16N 5 46E
Stigler 159 35 19N 95 6W
Stigliano 65 40 24N 16 13E
Stigsnæs 73 55 13N 11 18E
Stigtomta 73 58 47N 16 48E
Stikine Mts. 148 59 30N 129 30W
Stikine, R. 147 58 0N 131 12W
Stilfontein 128 26 50S 26 50E
Stilís 69 38 55N 22 37E
Stillington 33 54 7N 1 5W
Stillwater, Minn., U.S.A. 158 45 3N 92 47W
Stillwater, N.Y., U.S.A. 162 42 55N 73 41W
Stillwater, Okla., U.S.A. 159 36 5N 97 3W
Stillwater Mts. 160 39 45N 118 6W
Stilwell 159 35 52N 94 36W
Stimfalias, L. 69 37 51N 22 27E
Stimson 150 48 58N 80 30W
Stinchar, R. 34 55 10N 4 50W
Stingray Pt. 162 37 35N 76 15W
Stip 66 41 42N 22 10E
Stiperstones Mt. 28 52 36N 2 57W
Stíra 69 38 9N 24 14E

Stiring Wendel **Sukkur**

Stiring Wendel	**43**	49 12N	6 57 E
Stirling, Austral.	**138**	17 12 S	141 35 E
Stirling, Can.	**152**	49 30N	112 30W
Stirling, N.Z.	**143**	46 14 S	169 49 E
Stirling, U.K.	**35**	56 17N	3 57W
Stirling (□)	**26**	56 3N	4 10W
Stirling Ra.	**137**	34 0 S	118 0 E
Stjárneborg	**73**	57 53N	14 45 E
Stjarnsfors	**72**	60 2N	13 45 E
Stjördalshalsen	**71**	63 29N	10 51 E
Stobo	**35**	55 38N	3 18W
Stoborough, oilfield	**19**	50 38N	2 8W
Stockaryd	**73**	57 19N	14 36 E
Stockbridge	**28**	51 7N	1 30W
Stockerau	**53**	48 24N	16 12 E
Stockett	**160**	47 23N	111 7W
Stockholm	**72**	59 20N	18 3 E
Stockholms län □	**72**	59 30N	18 20 E
Stockhorn	**50**	46 42N	7 33 E
Stockport	**32**	53 25N	2 11W
Stocksbridge	**33**	53 30N	1 36W
Stockton, Austral.	**141**	32 56 S	151 47 E
Stockton, Calif., U.S.A.	**163**	38 0N	121 20W
Stockton, Kans., U.S.A.	**158**	39 30N	99 20W
Stockton, Mo., U.S.A.	**159**	37 40N	93 48W
Stockton-on-Tees	**33**	54 34N	1 20W
Stockvik	**72**	62 17N	17 23 E
Stoczek Łukowski	**54**	51 58N	22 22 E
Stode	**72**	62 28N	16 35 E
Stoer	**36**	58 12N	5 20W
Stogovo, mts.	**66**	41 31N	20 38 E
Stoke, N.Z.	**143**	41 19N	173 14 E
Stoke, U.K.	**29**	51 26N	0 41 E
Stoke Ferry	**29**	52 34N	0 31 E
Stoke Fleming	**30**	50 19N	3 36W
Stoke Mandeville	**29**	51 46N	0 47W
Stoke Prior	**28**	52 18N	2 5W
Stokenham	**30**	50 15N	3 40W
Stokes Bay	**150**	45 0N	81 22W
Stokes Pt.	**138**	40 10 S	143 56 E
Stokes Ra.	**136**	15 50 S	130 50 E
Stokesley	**33**	54 27N	1 12W
Stokke	**71**	59 13N	10 17 E
Stokkem	**47**	51 1N	5 45 E
Stokken	**71**	58 31N	8 53 E
Stokkseyri	**74**	63 50N	20 58W
Stokkes	**74**	64 14N	14 58W
Stolac	**66**	43 8N	17 59 E
Stolberg, Germ., E.	**48**	51 33N	11 0 E
Stolberg, Germ., W.	**48**	50 48N	6 13 E
Stolbovaya, R.S.F.S.R., U.S.S.R.	**77**	64 50N	153 50 E
Stolbovaya, R.S.F.S.R., U.S.S.R.	**81**	55 10N	37 32 E
Stolbtsy	**80**	53 22N	26 43 E
Stolin	**80**	51 53N	26 50 E
Stolnici	**70**	44 31N	24 48 E
Stolwijk	**46**	51 59N	4 47 E
Ston	**66**	42 51N	17 43 E
Stone, Bucks., U.K.	**29**	51 48N	0 52W
Stone, Stafford, U.K.	**32**	52 55N	2 10W
Stone Harbor	**162**	39 3N	74 45W
Stonecliffe	**150**	46 13N	77 56W
Stonehaven	**37**	56 58N	2 11W
Stonehenge, Austral.	**138**	24 22 S	143 17 E
Stonehenge, U.K.	**28**	51 9N	1 45W
Stonehouse, Glous., U.K.	**28**	51 45N	2 18W
Stonehouse, Strathclyde, U.K.	**35**	55 42N	4 0W
Stonewall	**153**	50 10N	97 19W
Stongfjord	**71**	61 28N	14 0 E
Stonham Aspall	**29**	52 11N	1 7 E
Stony L.	**153**	58 51N	98 40W
Stony Point	**162**	41 14N	73 59W
Stony Rapids	**153**	59 16N	105 50W
Stony River	**147**	61 48N	156 48W
Stony Stratford	**29**	52 4N	0 51W
Stony Tunguska = Tunguska, Nizhmaya	**77**	64 0N	95 0 E
Stopnica	**54**	50 27N	20 57 E
Stor Elvdal	**71**	61 30N	11 1 E
Stora Borge Fjell, Mt.	**48**	65 12N	14 0 E
Stora Gla	**72**	59 30N	12 30 E
Stora Karlsö	**73**	57 17N	17 59 E
Stora Lulevatten	**74**	67 10N	19 30 E
Stora Sjøfallet	**74**	67 29N	18 40 E
Storavan	**74**	65 45N	18 10 E
Stord Leirvik, I.	**71**	59 48N	5 27 E
Store Bælt	**73**	55 20N	11 0 E
Store Creek	**141**	32 54 S	149 6 E
Store Heddinge	**73**	55 18N	12 23 E
Storen	**71**	63 3N	10 18 E
Storfjorden	**71**	62 25N	6 30 E
Storm B.	**138**	43 10 S	147 30 E
Storm Lake	**158**	42 35N	95 5W
Stormberg	**125**	31 16 S	26 17 E
Stormsrivier	**128**	33 59 S	23 52 E
Stornoway	**36**	58 12N	6 23W
Storozhinets	**82**	48 14 S	25 45 E
Storr, The, mt.	**36**	57 30N	6 12W
Storrs	**162**	41 48N	72 15W
Storsjö	**72**	62 49N	13 5 E
Storsjöen, Hedmark, Norway	**71**	60 20N	11 40 E
Storsjöen, Hedmark, Norway	**71**	61 30N	11 14 E
Storsjön, Gavleborg, Sweden	**72**	60 35N	16 45 E
Storsjön, Jämtland, Sweden	**72**	62 50N	13 8 E
Storstroms Amt □	**73**	49 50N	11 45 E
Stort, R.	**29**	51 50N	0 7 E
Storuman	**74**	65 5N	17 10 E
Storuman, L.	**74**	65 5N	17 10 E
Storvätteshagna, Mt.	**72**	62 6N	12 30 E
Storvik	**72**	60 35N	16 33 E
Stotfold	**29**	52 2N	0 13W
Stoughton	**153**	49 40N	103 0W
Stour, R., Dorset, U.K.	**28**	50 48N	2 7W
Stour, R., Heref. & Worcs., U.K.	**28**	52 25N	2 13W
Stour, R., Kent, U.K.	**29**	51 15N	0 57 E
Stour, R., Suffolk, U.K.	**29**	51 55N	1 5 E
Stourbridge	**28**	52 28N	2 8W
Stourport	**28**	52 21N	2 18W
Stout, L.	**153**	52 0N	94 40W
Stove Pipe Wells Village	**163**	36 35N	117 11W
Stow	**35**	55 41N	2 50W
Stow Bardolph	**29**	52 38N	0 24 E
Stow-on-the-Wold	**28**	51 55N	1 42W
Stowmarket	**29**	52 11N	1 0 E
Stowupland	**29**	52 12N	1 3 E
Strabane	**38**	54 50N	7 28W
Strabane □	**38**	54 45N	7 25W
Strachan	**37**	57 1N	2 31W
Strachur	**34**	56 10N	5 5W
Stracin	**66**	42 13N	22 2 E
Stradbally, Kerry, Ireland	**39**	52 15N	10 4W
Stradbally, Laoighis, Ireland	**39**	53 2N	7 10W
Stradbally, Waterford, Ireland	**39**	52 7N	7 28W
Stradbroke	**29**	52 19N	1 16 E
Strade	**38**	53 56N	9 8W
Stradella	**62**	45 4N	9 20 E
Stradone	**38**	54 0N	7 12W
Strahan	**138**	42 9 S	145 20 E
Straldzha	**67**	42 35N	26 40 E
Stralkonice	**52**	49 15N	13 53 E
Stralsund	**48**	54 17N	13 5 E
Strand, Hedmark, Norway	**71**	61 18N	11 15 E
Strand, Rogaland, Norway	**71**	59 3N	5 56 E
Strand, S. Afr.	**128**	34 9 S	18 48 E
Stranda	**71**	62 19N	6 58 E
Strandby	**73**	56 47N	9 13 E
Strandebarm	**71**	60 17N	6 0 E
Strandhill	**38**	54 16N	8 34W
Strandvik	**71**	60 9N	5 41 E
Strangford	**38**	54 23N	5 34W
Strängnäs	**72**	59 23N	17 8 E
Stranorlar	**38**	54 58N	7 47W
Stranraer	**34**	54 54N	5 0W
Strasbourg, Can.	**153**	51 4N	104 55W
Strasbourg, France	**43**	48 35N	7 42 E
Strasburg, Ger.	**48**	53 30N	13 44 E
Strasburg, U.S.A.	**158**	46 12N	101 9W
Strassen	**47**	49 37N	6 4 E
Stratford, N.S.W., Austral.	**141**	32 7 S	151 55 E
Stratford, Vic., Austral.	**141**	37 59 S	147 7 E
Stratford, Can.	**150**	43 23N	81 0W
Stratford, N.Z.	**142**	39 20 S	174 19 E
Stratford, Calif., U.S.A.	**163**	36 10N	119 49W
Stratford, Conn., U.S.A.	**162**	41 13N	73 8W
Stratford, Tex., U.S.A.	**159**	36 20N	102 3W
Stratford-on-Avon	**28**	52 12N	1 42W
Stratford St. Mary	**29**	51 58N	0 59 E
Strath Avon	**37**	57 19N	3 23W
Strath Dearn	**37**	57 20N	4 0W
Strath Earn	**35**	56 20N	3 50W
Strath Glass	**37**	57 20N	4 40W
Strath Naver	**37**	58 24N	4 12W
Strath Spey	**37**	57 15N	3 40W
Strathalbyn	**140**	35 13 S	138 53 E
Strathaven	**35**	55 40N	4 4W
Strathbogie, Dist.	**37**	57 25N	2 45W
Strathclyde □	**34**	56 0N	4 50W
Strathcona Prov. Park	**152**	49 38N	125 40W
Strathdon	**37**	57 12N	3 4W
Strathkanaird	**36**	57 58N	5 5W
Strathmore, Austral.	**138**	17 50 S	142 35 E
Strathmore, Can.	**152**	51 5N	113 25W
Strathmore, Highland, U.K.	**37**	58 20N	4 40W
Strathmore, Tayside, U.K.	**37**	56 40N	3 4W
Strathmore, U.S.A.	**163**	36 9N	119 4W
Strathnaver	**152**	53 20N	122 33W
Strathpeffer	**37**	57 35N	4 32W
Strathroy	**150**	42 58N	81 38W
Strathy	**37**	58 30N	4 0W
Strathy Pt.	**37**	58 35N	4 0W
Strathyre	**34**	56 14N	4 20W
Stratmiglo Scot.	**35**	56 16N	3 15W
Stratton, U.K.	**30**	50 49N	4 31W
Stratton, U.S.A.	**158**	39 20N	102 36W
Stratton St. Margaret	**28**	51 35N	1 45W
Straubing	**49**	48 53N	12 35 E
Straumnes	**74**	66 26N	23 8W
Straumsnes Åsskard	**71**	63 4N	8 2 E
Strausberg	**48**	52 40N	13 52 E
Strawberry Res.	**160**	40 0N	111 0W
Strawn	**159**	32 36N	98 30W
Strážnice	**53**	48 54N	17 19 E
Streaky B.	**139**	32 51 S	134 18 E
Streaky Bay	**139**	32 48 S	134 13 E
Streatley	**28**	51 31N	1 9W
Streator	**158**	41 9N	88 52W
Středočeský □	**52**	49 55N	14 30 E
Stredoslovenský □	**53**	48 30N	19 15 E
Streé	**47**	50 17N	4 18 E
Street	**28**	51 7N	2 43W
Strehaia	**70**	44 37N	23 10 E
Strelcha	**67**	42 30N	24 19 E
Strelka	**77**	58 5N	93 10 E
Streng, R.	**100**	13 12N	103 37 E
Strengelvåg	**74**	68 58N	15 11 E
Strensall	**33**	54 3N	1 2W
Stretford	**32**	53 27N	2 19W
Stretton	**32**	53 21N	2 34W
Strezhevoy	**76**	60 42N	77 34 E
Strezhnoye	**76**	57 45N	84 2 E
Stribro	**52**	49 44N	13 0 E
Strichen	**37**	57 35N	2 5W
Strickland, R.	**135**	7 35 S	141 36 E
Strijen	**46**	51 45N	4 33 E
Strimón, R.	**68**	41 0N	23 30 E
Strimonikós Kólpos	**68**	40 33N	24 0 E
Striven, L.	**34**	55 58N	5 9W
Strofadhes, I.	**69**	37 15N	21 0 E
Strokestown	**38**	53 47N	8 6W
Strom	**71**	60 17N	11 44 E
Ström	**72**	61 52N	17 20 E
Stroma, I. of	**37**	58 40N	3 8W
Strombacka	**72**	61 58N	16 44 E
Strómboli, I.	**65**	38 48N	15 12 E
Stromeferry	**36**	57 20N	5 33W
Stromemore	**36**	57 22N	5 33W
Stromness	**37**	58 58N	3 18W
Ströms Vattudal L.	**74**	64 0N	15 30 E
Stromsberg	**72**	60 28N	17 44 E
Strömsnäsbruk	**73**	56 35N	13 45 E
Strömstad	**72**	58 55N	11 15 E
Stromsund	**74**	63 51N	15 35 E
Stronachlachar	**34**	56 15N	4 35W
Strone	**34**	55 59N	4 54W
Stróngoli	**65**	39 16N	17 2 E
Stronsay Firth	**37**	59 4N	2 50W
Stronsay, I.	**37**	59 8N	2 38W
Strontian	**36**	56 42N	5 32W
Strood	**29**	51 23N	0 30 E
Stroove	**38**	55 13N	6 57W
Stropkov	**53**	49 13N	21 39 E
Stroud	**28**	51 44N	2 12W
Stroud Road	**141**	32 18 S	151 57 E
Stroudsberg	**162**	40 59N	75 15W
Struer	**73**	56 30N	8 35 E
Struga	**66**	41 13N	20 44 E
Strugi Krasnye	**80**	58 21N	28 51 E
Struma, R.	**67**	41 50N	23 18 E
Strumble Hd.	**31**	52 3N	5 6W
Strumica	**66**	41 28N	22 41 E
Strumica, R.	**66**	41 26N	27 46 E
Strusshamn	**71**	60 24N	5 10 E
Struthers	**150**	48 41N	85 51W
Struy	**37**	57 25N	4 40W
Stryama	**67**	42 16N	24 54 E
Stryi	**80**	49 16N	23 48 E
Stryker	**152**	48 40N	114 44W
Stryków	**54**	51 55N	19 33 E
Strzegom	**54**	50 58N	16 20 E
Strzelce Krajenskie	**54**	52 52N	15 33 E
Strzelecki Creek	**139**	29 37 S	139 59 E
Strzelin	**54**	50 46N	17 2 E
Strzelno	**54**	52 35N	18 9 E
Strzyzów	**54**	49 52N	21 47 E
Stuart, Fla., U.S.A.	**157**	27 11N	80 12W
Stuart, Nebr., U.S.A.	**158**	42 39N	99 8W
Stuart I.	**147**	63 55N	164 50W
Stuart L.	**152**	54 30N	124 30W
Stuart Mts.	**143**	45 2 S	167 39 E
Stuart, R.	**152**	54 0N	123 35W
Stuart Range	**139**	29 10 S	134 56 E
Stuart's Ra.	**136**	29 10 S	135 0 E
Stubbekøbing	**73**	54 53N	12 9 E
Stuben	**52**	46 58N	10 31 E
Stuberhuk	**48**	54 23N	11 18 E
Studholme Junc.	**143**	44 42 S	171 9 E
Studland	**28**	50 39N	1 58W
Studley	**28**	52 16N	1 54W
Stugsund	**72**	61 16N	17 18 E
Stugun	**72**	63 10N	15 40 E
Stull, L.	**153**	54 24N	92 34W
Stung-Treng	**100**	13 31N	105 58 E
Stupart, R.	**153**	56 0N	93 25W
Stupino	**81**	54 57N	38 2 E
Sturgeon B.	**153**	52 0N	97 50W
Sturgeon Bay	**156**	44 52N	87 20W
Sturgeon Falls	**150**	46 25N	79 57W
Sturgeon L., Alta., Can.	**152**	55 6N	117 32W
Sturgeon L., Ont., Can.	**150**	50 0N	90 45W
Sturgis, Mich., U.S.A.	**156**	41 50N	85 25W
Sturgis, S.D., U.S.A.	**158**	44 25N	103 30W
Sturko, I.	**73**	56 5N	15 42 E
Sturminster Marshall	**28**	50 48N	2 4W
Sturminster Newton	**28**	50 56N	2 18W
Stúrovo	**53**	47 48N	18 41 E
Sturt Cr.	**136**	19 0 S	128 15 E
Sturt Creek	**136**	19 0 S	128 15 E
Sturt, R.	**136**	34 58 S	138 31 E
Sturton	**33**	53 22N	0 39W
Sturts Meadows	**140**	31 18 S	141 42 E
Stutterheim	**128**	32 33 S	27 28 E
Stuttgart, Ger.	**49**	48 46N	9 10 E
Stuttgart, U.S.A.	**159**	34 30N	91 33W
Stuyvesant	**162**	42 23N	73 45W
Stykkishólmur	**74**	65 2N	22 40W
Styr, R.	**80**	51 4N	25 20 E
Styria = Steiermark	**52**	47 26N	15 0 E
Su-no-Saki	**111**	34 58N	139 45 E
Suakin	**122**	19 0N	37 20 E
Suan	**107**	38 42N	126 22 E
Suaqui	**164**	29 12N	109 41W
Suay Rieng	**101**	11 9N	105 45 E
Subang	**103**	7 30 S	107 45 E
Subansiri, R.	**98**	26 48N	93 50 E
Subi	**101**	2 55N	108 50 E
Subi, I.	**102**	2 58N	108 50 E
Subiaco	**63**	41 56N	13 5 E
Subotica	**66**	46 6N	19 29 E
Success	**153**	50 28N	108 6W
Suceava	**70**	47 38N	26 16 E
Suceava □	**70**	47 37N	26 18 E
Suceava, R.	**70**	47 38N	26 16 E
Sucha-Beskidzka	**54**	49 44N	19 35 E
Suchan	**54**	53 18N	15 18 E
Suchedniów	**54**	51 3N	20 49 E
Such'i	**109**	21 23N	110 16 E
Suchien	**107**	33 58N	118 17 E
Suchil	**164**	23 38N	103 55W
Suchitoto	**166**	13 56N	89 0W
Suchou	**109**	31 15N	120 40 E
Süchow = Hsüchou	**107**	34 15N	117 10 E
Suchowola	**54**	53 33N	23 3 E
Sucio, R.	**174**	6 40N	77 0W
Suck, R.	**39**	53 17N	8 10W
Suckling, Mt.	**135**	9 43 S	148 59 E
Sucre, Boliv.	**174**	19 0 S	65 15W
Sucre, Venez.	**174**	10 25N	64 5W
Sucre □, Colomb.	**174**	8 50N	75 40W
Sucre □, Venez.	**174**	10 25N	63 30W
Sŭcueni	**70**	47 20N	22 5 E
Sucunduri, R.	**174**	6 20N	58 35W
SuCuraj	**63**	43 10N	17 8 E
Sucuriju	**170**	1 39N	49 57W
Sud-Ouest, Pte. du	**151**	49 23N	63 36W
Sud, Pte.	**151**	49 3N	62 14W
Suda, R.	**81**	59 40N	36 30 E
Sudak	**82**	44 51N	34 57 E
Sudan ■	**117**	15 0N	30 0 E
Sudan, The	**114**	11 0N	9 0 E
Suday	**81**	59 0N	43 15 E
Sudbury, Can.	**150**	46 30N	81 0W
Sudbury, Derby, U.K.	**33**	52 53N	1 43W
Sudbury, Suffolk, U.K.	**29**	52 2N	0 44 E
Sûdd	**123**	8 20N	29 30 E
Süderbrarup	**48**	54 38N	9 47 E
Süderlügum	**48**	54 50N	8 46 E
Sudetan Mts. = Sudety	**53**	50 20N	16 45 E
Sudety	**53**	50 20N	16 45 E
Sudi	**127**	10 11 S	39 57 E
Sudirman, Pengunungan	**103**	4 30N	137 0 E
Suditi	**70**	44 35N	27 38 E
Sudogda	**81**	55 55N	40 50 E
Sudr	**122**	29 40N	32 42 E
Sudzha	**80**	51 14N	34 25 E
Sueca	**59**	39 12N	0 21W
Sueur, Le	**158**	44 25N	93 52W
Suez = Suweis	**122**	28 40N	33 0 E
Suf	**90**	32 19N	35 49 E
Sufaina	**92**	23 6N	40 44 E
Suffield	**153**	50 12N	111 10W
Suffolk	**156**	36 47N	76 33W
Suffolk □	**29**	52 16N	1 0 E
Suffolk, East, □	**29**	52 16N	1 10 E
Suffolk, West, □	**29**	52 16N	0 45 E
Sufi-Kurgan	**85**	40 2N	73 30 E
Sufuk	**93**	23 50N	51 50 E
Suga no-Sen	**110**	35 25N	134 25 E
Sugag	**70**	45 47N	23 37 E
Sugar City	**158**	38 18N	103 38W
Sugarloaf Pt.	**126**	32 22 S	152 30 E
Sugluk = Sagloue	**149**	62 10N	75 40W
Sugny	**47**	49 49N	4 54 E
Suhaia, L.	**70**	43 45N	25 15 E
Suhār	**93**	24 20N	56 40 E
Suhbaatar	**105**	46 54N	113 25 E
Suhl	**48**	50 35N	10 40 E
Suhl □	**48**	50 37N	10 43 E
Suhr	**50**	47 22N	8 5 E
Suhsien	**106**	33 40N	117 0 E
Suhum	**121**	6 5N	0 27W
Suian	**109**	29 28N	118 44 E
Suica	**66**	43 52N	17 11 E
Suich'ang	**109**	28 36N	119 16 E
Suichiang	**108**	28 40N	103 58 E
Suifenho	**107**	44 30N	131 2 E
Suihsien	**109**	31 41N	113 20 E
Suihua	**98**	46 37N	127 0 E
Suilu	**108**	22 20N	107 48 E
Suining, Hunan, China	**108**	26 21N	110 0 E
Suining, Kiangsu, China	**107**	33 54N	117 56 E
Suining, Szechwan, China	**108**	30 31N	105 34 E
Suippes	**43**	49 8N	4 30 E
Suir, R.	**39**	52 31N	7 59W
Suita	**111**	34 45N	135 32 E
Suiteh	**106**	37 35N	110 5 E
Suiyang, Heilungkiang, China	**107**	44 26N	130 51 E
Suiyang, Kweichow, China	**108**	27 57N	107 11 E
Sujangarh	**94**	27 42N	47 31 E
Sukabumi	**103**	6 56 S	106 57 E
Sukadana	**102**	1 10 S	110 0 E
Sukandja	**102**	2 28 S	110 25 E
Sukarnapura = Jajapura	**103**	2 28N	140 38 E
Sukarno, G. = Jaja, Puncak	**103**	3 57 S	137 17 E
Sukchŏn	**107**	39 22N	125 35 E
Sukhinichi	**80**	54 8N	35 10 E
Sukhona, R.	**78**	60 30N	45 0 E
Sukhothai	**100**	17 1N	99 49 E
Sukhoy Log	**84**	56 55N	62 1 E
Sukhumi	**83**	43 0N	41 0 E
Sukkur	**94**	27 50N	68 46 E

Syke Tambelan, Kepulauan

Syke **48** 52 55N 8 50 E
Syktyvkar **78** 61 45N 50 40 E
Sylacauga **157** 33 10N 86 15W
Sylarna, Mt. **72** 63 2N 12 11 E
Sylhet **98** 24 54N 91 52 E
Sylt, I. **48** 54 50N 8 20 E
Sylva, R. **84** 58 0N 56 54 E
Sylvan Beach **162** 43 12N 75 44W
Sylvan Lake **152** 52 20N 114 10W
Sylvania **157** 32 45N 81 37W
Sylvester **157** 31 31N 83 50W
Sym **76** 60 20N 87 50 E
Symington **35** 55 35N 3 36W
Symón **164** 24 42N 102 35W
Symonds Yat **28** 51 50N 2 38W
Synnott Ra. **136** 16 30 S 125 20 E
Syr Darya **76** 45 0N 65 0 E
Syracuse, Kans., U.S.A. **159** 38 0N 101 40W
Syracuse, N.Y., U.S.A. **162** 43 4N 76 11W
Syrdarya **85** 40 50N 68 40 E
Syria ■ **92** 35 0N 38 0 E
Syriam **98** 16 44N 96 19 E
Syrian Des. **92** 31 30N 40 0 E
Sysert **84** 56 29N 60 49 E
Syston **28** 52 42N 1 5W
Syuldzhyukyor **77** 63 25N 113 40 E
Syutkya, mt. **67** 41 50N 24 16 E
Syzran **81** 53 12N 48 30 E
Szabolcs-Szatmár □ **53** 48 2N 21 45 E
Szamocin **54** 53 2N 17 7 E
Szamotuły **54** 52 35N 16 34 E
Szaraz, R. **53** 46 28N 20 44 E
Szazhalombatta **53** 47 20N 18 58 E
Szczara, R. **53** 53 15N 25 10 E
Szczebrzeszyn **54** 50 42N 22 59 E
Szczecin **54** 53 27N 14 27 E
Szczecin □ **54** 53 25N 14 32 E
Szczecinek **54** 53 43N 16 41 E
Szczekocimy **54** 50 38N 19 48 E
Szczrk **53** 49 42N 19 1 E
Szczuczyn **54** 53 36N 22 19 E
Szczytno **54** 53 33N 21 0 E
Szechwan □ **109** 30 15N 103 15 E
Szécsény **53** 48 7N 19 30 E
Szeged **53** 46 16N 20 10 E
Szeghalom **53** 47 1N 21 10 E
Székesfehérvár **53** 47 15N 18 25 E
Szekszárd **53** 46 22N 18 42 E
Szendrö **53** 48 24N 20 41 E
Szentendre **53** 47 39N 19 4 E
Szentes **53** 46 39N 20 21 E
Szentgotthárd **53** 46 58N 16 19 E
Szentlörinc **53** 46 3N 18 1 E
Szerencs **53** 48 10N 21 12 E
Szeshui **33** 34 50N 113 20 E
Szigetvár **53** 46 3N 17 46 E
Szlichtyogowa **54** 51 42N 16 15 E
Szob **53** 47 48N 18 53 E
Szolnok **53** 47 10N 20 15 E
Szolnok □ **53** 47 15N 20 30 E
Szombathely **53** 47 14N 16 38 E
Szprotawa **54** 51 33N 15 35 E
Sztum **54** 53 55N 19 1 E
Sztuto **54** 54 20N 19 15 E
Sztutowo **54** 54 20N 19 15 E
Szürvas **53** 46 50N 20 38 E
Szydłowiec **54** 51 15N 20 51 E
Szypliszki **54** 54 17N 23 2 E

T

't Harde **46** 52 24N 5 54 E
't Zandt **46** 53 22N 6 46 E
Ta-erh Po, L. **106** 43 15N 116 35 E
Ta Khli Khok **100** 15 18N 100 20 E
Ta Lai **101** 11 24N 107 23 E
Taalintehdas **74** 60 2N 22 30 E
Taan **107** 45 30N 124 18 E
Taavetti **75** 60 56N 27 32 E
Taba **92** 26 55N 42 30 E
Tabacal **172** 23 15 S 64 15W
Tabaco **103** 13 22N 123 44 E
Tabagné **120** 7 59N 3 4W
Tabar Is. **135** 2 50 S 152 0 E
Tabarca, Isla de **59** 38 17N 0 30W
Tabarka **119** 36 56N 8 46 E
Tabarra **59** 38 37N 1 44 E
Tabas, Khorasan, Iran **93** 33 35N 56 55 E
Tabas, Khorasan, Iran **93** 32 48N 60 12 E
Tabasará, Serrania de **166** 8 35N 81 40W
Tabasco □ **165** 17 45N 93 30W
Tabatinga **174** 4 11 S 69 58W
Tabatinga, Serra da **170** 10 30 S 44 0W
Tabayin **98** 22 42N 95 20 E
Tabelbala, Kahal de **118** 28 47N 2 0W
Taber **152** 49 47N 112 8W
Taberg **162** 43 18N 75 37W
Tabernas **59** 37 4N 2 26W
Tabernas de Valldigna **59** 39 5N 0 13W
Tabigha **90** 32 53N 35 33 E
Tabira **170** 7 35 S 37 33W
Tablas, I. **103** 12 25N 122 2 E
Table B. **151** 53 40N 56 25W
Table Mt. **128** 34 0 S 18 22 E
Table Top, Mt. **138** 23 24 S 147 11 E
Tableland **136** 17 16 S 126 51 E
Tabletop, mt. **137** 22 32 S 123 50 E
Tábor **52** 49 25N 14 39 E
Tabor **90** 32 42N 35 24 E
Tabora **126** 5 2 S 32 57 E
Tabora □ **126** 5 0 S 33 0 E
Tabory **84** 58 31N 64 33 E
Tabou **120** 4 30N 7 20W
Tabouda **118** 34 44N 5 14W
Tabrīz **92** 38 7N 46 20 E
Tabūk **92** 28 30N 36 25 E
Täby **72** 59 29N 18 4 E
Tacámbaro **164** 19 14N 101 28W
Tacarigua, L. de **174** 11 3N 68 25W
Tach'aitan **105** 37 50N 95 18 E
T'ach'eng **105** 46 45N 82 57 E
Tach'eng **106** 38 35N 116 39 E
Tach'engtzu **107** 41 44N 118 52 E
Tach'i **109** 24 51N 121 14 E
Tachia **109** 24 25N 120 28 E
Tachiai **108** 23 44N 103 57 E
Tachibana-Wan **110** 32 45N 130 7 E
Tachikawa **111** 35 42N 139 25 E
Tach'in Ch'uan, R. **108** 31 57N 102 11 E
Tach'ing Shan, mts. **106** 40 50N 111 0 E
Tachira **174** 8 7N 72 21W
Tachira □ **174** 8 7N 72 15W
Tachov **52** 49 47N 12 39 E
Tachu **108** 30 45N 107 13 E
Tacina, R. **65** 39 5N 16 51 E
Tacloban **103** 11 15N 124 58 E
Tacna **174** 18 0 S 70 20W
Tacoma **160** 47 15N 122 30W
Tacuarembó **173** 31 45 S 56 0W
Tacumshin L. **39** 52 12N 6 28W
Tadcaster **33** 53 53N 1 16W
Tademaït, Plateau du **118** 28 30N 2 30 E
Tadent, O. **119** 22 30N 7 0 E
Tadjerdjert, O. **119** 26 0N 8 0W
Tadjerouna **118** 33 31N 2 3 E
Tadjettaret, O. **119** 22 0N 7 30W
Tadjmout, O. **118** 25 37N 3 48 E
Tadjoura **123** 11 50N 42 55 E
Tadjoura, Golfe de **123** 11 50N 43 0 E
Tadley **28** 51 21N 1 8W
Tadmor, N.Z. **143** 41 27 S 172 45 E
Tadmor, Syria **92** 34 30N 37 55 E
Tado **174** 5 16N 76 32W
Tadotsu **110** 34 16N 133 45 E
Tadoule L **153** 58 36N 98 20W
Tadoussac **151** 48 11N 69 42W
Tadzhik S.S.R. □ **85** 35 30N 70 0 E
Taechŏnni **107** 36 21N 126 36 E
Taegu **107** 35 50N 128 37 E
Taegwandong **107** 40 13N 125 12 E
Taejŏn **107** 36 20N 127 28 E
Taerhhanmaoming-anlienhoch'i **106** 41 50N 110 27 E
Taerhting **105** 37 15N 92 36 E
Taf, R. **31** 51 55N 4 36W
Tafalla **58** 42 30N 1 41W
Tafang **108** 27 10N 105 39 E
Tafar **123** 6 52N 28 15 E
Tafas **90** 32 44N 36 5 E
Tafassasset, O. **119** 23 0N 9 11 E
Tafelbaai **128** 33 35 S 18 25 E
Tafelney, C. **118** 31 3N 9 51W
Tafermaar **103** 6 47 S 134 10 E
Tafi Viejo **172** 26 43 S 65 17W
Tafiré **120** 9 4N 5 10W
Tafnidilt **118** 28 47N 10 58W
Tafraout **118** 29 50N 8 58W
Taft, Phil. **103** 11 57N 125 30 E
Taft, Ala., U.S.A. **163** 35 10N 119 28W
Taft, Tex., U.S.A. **159** 27 58N 97 23W
Taga Dzong **98** 27 5N 90 0 E
Taganrog **83** 47 12N 38 50 E
Taganrogskiy Zaliv **82** 47 0N 38 30 E
Tagant **120** 18 20N 11 0W
Tagap Ga **98** 26 56N 96 13 E
Tagbilaran **103** 9 39N 123 51 E
Tage **135** 6 19 S 143 20 E
Tággia **62** 43 52N 7 50 E
Taghmon **39** 52 19N 6 40W
Taghrīfat **119** 29 5N 17 26 E
Taghzout **118** 33 30N 4 49W
Tagish **152** 60 19N 134 16W
Tagish L. **147** 60 10N 134 20W
Tagliacozzo **63** 42 4N 13 13 E
Tagliamento, R. **63** 45 38N 13 5 E
Táglio di Po **63** 45 0N 12 12 E
Tagomago, Isla de **59** 39 2N 1 39 E
Tagua, La **174** 0 3N 74 40W
Taguatinga **171** 12 26 S 46 26W
Tagula **135** 11 22 S 153 15 E
Tagula I. **135** 11 30 S 153 30 E
Tagum (Hijo) **103** 7 33N 125 53 E
Tagus = Tajo, R. **55** 39 44N 5 50W
Tahahbala, I. **102** 0 30 S 98 30 E
Tahakopa **143** 46 30 S 169 23 E
Tahala **118** 34 0N 4 28W
Tahan, Gunong **101** 4 45N 102 25 E
Tahara **111** 34 40N 137 16 E
Tahat Mt. **119** 23 18N 5 21 E
Tāherī **93** 27 43N 52 20 E
Tahiti, I. **131** 17 37 S 149 27W
Tahoe **160** 39 12N 120 9W
Tahoe, L. **160** 39 0N 120 9W
Tahora **142** 39 2 S 174 49 E
Tahoua **121** 14 57N 5 16 E
Tahsien **108** 31 17N 107 30 E
Tahsin **108** 22 48N 107 23 E
Tahsinganling Shanmo **105** 49 0N 122 0 E
Tahsingkou **107** 43 23N 129 39 E
Tahsintien **107** 37 37N 120 50 E
Tahsüeh Shan, mts. **108** 31 15N 101 20 E
Tahta **122** 26 44N 31 32 E
Tahulandang, I. **103** 2 27N 125 23 E
Tahuna **103** 3 45N 125 30 E
Tahung Shan, mts. **109** 31 30N 112 50 E
Tai **108** 30 41N 103 29 E
Taï **120** 5 55N 7 30W
T'ai Hu **105** 31 10N 120 0 E
Tai Shan **109** 30 17N 122 10 E
T'aian **107** 36 12N 117 7 E
T'aichiang **108** 26 40N 108 19 E
T'aichou **109** 32 22N 119 45 E
T'aichou Liehtao **109** 28 30N 121 53 E
T'aichung **105** 24 9N 120 37 E
T'aichunghsien **109** 24 15N 120 35 E
Taieri, R. **143** 46 3 S 170 12 E
Taiga Madema **119** 23 46N 15 25 E
T'aihang Shan, mts. **106** 35 40N 113 20 E
Taihape **142** 39 41 S 175 48 E
T'aiho, Anhwei, China **109** 33 10N 115 36 E
T'aiho, Kiangsi, China **109** 26 50N 114 53 E
T'aihsien **109** 32 17N 120 10 E
T'aihsing **109** 32 10N 120 4 E
Taihu **109** 30 30N 116 25 E
T'aik'ang **106** 34 4N 114 52 E
Taikkyi **98** 17 20N 96 0 E
T'aiku **106** 37 23N 112 34 E
Tailem Bend **140** 35 12 S 139 29 E
Tailfingen **49** 48 15N 9 1 E
Taïma **92** 27 35N 38 45 E
Taimyr = Taymyr **77** 75 0N 100 0 E
Taimyr, Oz. **77** 74 20N 102 0 E
Tain **37** 57 49N 4 4W
T'ainan **109** 23 0N 120 10 E
T'ainanhsien **109** 23 21N 120 17 E
Tainaron, Akra **69** 36 22N 22 27 E
Tainggya **98** 17 49N 94 29 E
T'aining **109** 26 55N 117 12 E
Taintignies **47** 50 33N 3 22 E
Taiobeiras **171** 15 49 S 42 14W
T'aipei **109** 25 2N 121 30 E
T'aip'ing **109** 30 18N 118 6 E
Taiping **101** 4 51N 100 44 E
Taipu **170** 5 37 S 35 36W
T'aip'ussuchi **106** 41 55N 115 23 E
Taisha **110** 35 24N 132 40 E
T'aishan **109** 22 17N 112 43 E
Taishun **109** 27 33N 119 43 E
Taita □ **126** 4 0 S 38 30 E
Taita Hills **126** 3 25 S 38 15 E
Taitao, Pen. de **176** 46 30 S 75 0W
T'aitung **105** 22 43N 121 4 E
Taivalkoski **74** 65 33N 28 12 E
Taiwan (Formosa) ■ **109** 23 30N 121 0 E
Taiwara **93** 33 30N 64 24 E
Taïyetos Óros **69** 37 0N 22 23 E
Taiyiba, Israel **90** 32 36N 35 27 E
Taiyiba, Jordan **90** 31 55N 35 17 E
T'aiyüan **106** 37 55N 112 40 E
Ta'izz **91** 13 43N 44 7 E
Tajapuru, Furo do **170** 1 50 S 50 25W
Tajarhī **119** 24 15N 14 46 E
Tajicaringa **164** 23 15N 104 44W
Tajima **112** 35 19N 135 8 E
Tajimi **111** 35 19N 137 8 E
Tajimi Gifu **55** 35 25N 137 5 E
Tajitos **164** 30 58N 112 18W
Tajo, R. **57** 40 35N 1 52W
Tajumulco, Volcán de **165** 15 20N 91 50W
Tājūrā **119** 32 51N 13 27 E
Tak **100** 16 52N 99 8 E
Takachiho **110** 32 42N 131 18 E
Takahashi **110** 34 51N 133 39 E
Takaka **143** 40 51N 172 50 E
Takamatsu **110** 34 20N 134 5 E
Takanabe **110** 32 8N 131 30 E
Takaoka **111** 36 40N 137 0 E
Takapau **142** 40 2 S 176 21 E
Takapuna **142** 36 47 S 174 47 E
Takasago **110** 34 45N 134 48 E
Takasaki **111** 36 20N 139 0 E
Takase **110** 34 7N 133 48 E
Takatsuki **111** 34 51N 135 37 E
Takaungu **126** 3 38 S 39 52 E
Takawa **110** 33 47N 130 51 E
Takayama **111** 36 18N 137 11 E
Takayama-Bonchi **111** 36 0N 137 18 E
Takefu **111** 35 50N 136 10 E
Takehara **110** 34 21N 132 55 E
Takeley **29** 51 52N 0 16 E
Takeo, Camb. **101** 10 59N 104 47 E
Takeo, Japan **110** 33 12N 130 1 E
Tåkern **73** 58 22N 14 45 E
Takestan **92** 36 0N 49 50 E
Taketa **110** 32 58N 131 24 E
Takh **95** 33 6N 77 32 E
Takhman **101** 11 29N 104 57 E
Taki **135** 6 29 S 155 52 E
Takingeun **102** 4 45N 96 50 E
Takla L. **152** 55 15N 125 45W
Takla Landing **152** 55 30N 125 50W
Takla Makan **105** 39 0N 83 0 E
Takoradi **120** 4 58N 1 55W
Taku, China **107** 38 59N 117 41 E
Taku, Japan **110** 33 18N 130 3 E
Taku, R. **152** 58 30N 133 50W
Takuan **108** 27 44N 103 53 E
Takum **121** 7 18N 9 36 E
Takuma **110** 34 13N 133 40 E
Takushan **107** 39 55N 123 30 E
Tal-y-llyn **31** 52 40N 3 44W
Tal-y-sarn **31** 53 3N 4 12W
Tala, Uruguay **173** 34 21 S 55 46W
Tala, U.S.S.R. **77** 72 40N 113 30 E
Talach'in **106** 36 42N 104 54 E
Talagante **172** 33 40 S 70 50W
Talaint **118** 29 37N 9 45W
Talak **121** 18 0N 5 0 E
Talamanca, Cordillera de **166** 9 20N 83 20W
Talara **174** 4 30 S 81 10 E
Talas **85** 42 45N 72 0 E
Talas, R. **85** 44 0N 70 20 E
Talasea **135** 5 20 S 150 2 E
Talasskiy, Khrebet **85** 42 15N 72 0 E
Talata Mafara **121** 12 38N 6 4 E
Talaud, Kepulauan **103** 4 30N 127 10 E
Talavera de la Reina **56** 39 55N 4 46W
Talawana **136** 22 51 S 121 9 E
Talawgyi **98** 25 4N 97 19 E
Talayan **103** 6 52N 124 24 E
Talbot, C. **136** 13 48 S 126 43 E
Talbragar, R. **141** 32 5 S 149 15 E
Talca **172** 35 20 S 71 46W
Talca □ **172** 35 20 S 71 46W
Talcahuano **172** 36 40 S 73 10W
Talcher **96** 20 55N 85 3 E
Talcho **121** 14 35N 3 22 E
Taldom **81** 56 45N 37 29 E
Taldy Kurgan **76** 45 10N 78 45 E
Taleqan □ **93** 36 40N 69 30 E
Talesh, Kūlhā-Ye **92** 39 0N 48 30 E
Talfit **90** 32 5N 35 17 E
Talga, R. **136** 21 2 S 119 51 E
Talgar **85** 43 19N 77 15 E
Talgar, Pic **85** 43 5N 77 20 E
Talgarth **31** 51 59N 3 15W
Talguharai **122** 18 19N 35 56 E
Talguppa **93** 14 10N 74 45 E
Tali, Shensi, China **106** 34 48N 109 48 E
Tali, Yunnan, China **108** 25 45N 100 5 E
Tali Post **123** 5 55N 30 44 E
Taliabu, I. **103** 1 45 S 125 0 E
Taliang Shan **108** 28 0N 103 0 E
Talibong, Ko **101** 7 15N 99 23 E
Talihina **159** 34 45N 95 1W
Talikoti **96** 16 29N 76 17 E
Talimardzhan **85** 38 23N 65 37 E
Taling Ho, R. **107** 40 54N 121 38 E
Taling Sung **101** 15 5N 99 11 E
Talitsa **84** 57 0N 63 43 E
Taliwang **102** 8 50 S 116 55 E
Talkeetna **147** 62 20N 150 0W
Talkeetna Mts. **147** 62 20N 149 0W
Tall 'Asūr **90** 31 59N 35 17 E
Talla **122** 28 5N 30 43 E
Talladale **36** 57 41N 5 20W
Talladega **157** 33 28N 86 2W
Tallahassee **157** 30 25N 84 15W
Tallangatta **141** 36 15 S 147 10 E
Tallarook **141** 37 5 S 145 6 E
Tallåsen **72** 61 52N 16 2 E
Tallawang **141** 32 12 S 149 28 E
Tällberg **72** 60 51N 15 2 E
Tallebung **141** 32 42 S 146 34 E
Tallering Pk **137** 28 6 S 115 37 E
Tallinn (Reval) **80** 59 29N 24 58 E
Tallow **39** 52 6N 8 0W
Tallowbridge **39** 52 6N 8 1W
Tallulah **159** 32 25N 91 12W
Talluza **90** 32 17N 35 18 E
Talmage **153** 49 46N 103 40W
Talmest **118** 31 48N 9 21W
Talmont **44** 46 27N 1 37W
Talnoye **82** 48 57N 30 35 E
Taloda **96** 21 34N 74 19 E
Talodi **123** 10 35N 30 22 E
Talou Shan, mts. **108** 28 20N 107 10 E
Talovaya **81** 51 13N 40 38 E
Talpa de Allende **164** 20 23N 104 51W
Talsarnau **31** 52 54N 4 4W
Talsinnt **118** 32 33N 3 27W
Taltal **172** 25 23 S 70 40W
Taltson L. **153** 61 30N 110 15W
Taltson R. **152** 61 24N 112 46W
Talwood **139** 28 29 S 149 29 E
Talyawalka Cr. **140** 32 28 S 142 22 E
Talybont **31** 52 29N 3 59W
Tam Chau **101** 10 48N 105 12 E
Tam Ky **100** 15 34N 108 29 E
Tam Quan **100** 14 35N 109 3 E
Tama **158** 41 56N 92 37W
Tama Abu, Pegunungan **102** 3 10N 115 0 E
Tamala **137** 26 35 S 113 40 E
Tamalameque **174** 8 52N 73 49W
Tamale **121** 9 22N 0 50W
Taman **82** 45 14N 36 41 E
Tamana **110** 32 58N 130 32 E
Tamanar **118** 31 1N 9 46W
Tamano **110** 34 35N 133 59 E
Tamanrasset **119** 22 56N 5 30 E
Tamanrasset, O. **118** 22 0N 2 0 E
Tamanthi **98** 25 19N 95 17 E
Tamaqua **162** 40 46N 75 58W
Tamar, R. **30** 50 33N 4 15W
Támara **174** 5 50N 72 10W
Tamarang **141** 31 27 S 150 5 E
Tamarite de Litera **58** 41 52N 0 25 E
Tamashima **110** 34 32N 133 40 E
Tamási **53** 46 40N 18 18 E
Tamaské **121** 14 55N 5 55 E
Tamatave **129** 18 10 S 49 25 E
Tamatave □ **129** 18 0 S 49 0 E
Tamaulipas □ **165** 24 0N 99 0W
Tamaulipas, Sierra de **165** 23 30N 98 20W
Tamazula **164** 24 55N 106 58W
Tamazunchale **165** 21 16N 98 47W
Tambacounda **120** 13 55N 13 45W
Tambai **123** 16 32N 37 13 E
Tambelan, Kepulauan **102** 1 0N 107 30 E

Tambellup Taunton

Tambellup	137	34 4 S	117 37 E
Tambo	138	24 54 S	146 14 E
Tambo de Mora	174	13 30 S	76 20W
Tambohorano	129	17 30 S	43 58 E
Tambora, G.	102	8 12 S	118 5 E
Tamboritha, Mt.	141	37 31 S	146 51 E
Tambov	81	52 45N	41 20 E
Tambre, R.	56	42 55N	8 30W
Tambuku, G.	103	7 8 S	113 40 E
Tamburâ	123	5 40N	27 25 E
Tamchaket	120	17 25N	10 40W
Tamchok Khambab (Brahmaputra)	99	29 25N	88 0 E
Tamdybulak	85	41 46N	64 36 E
Tame	174	6 28N	71 44W
Tame, R.	28	52 43N	1 45W
Tamega, R.	56	41 12N	8 5W
Tamelelt	119	26 30N	6 14 E
Tamenglong	98	25 0N	93 35 E
Tamerfors	75	61 30N	23 50 E
Tamerlanovka	85	42 36N	69 17 E
Tamerton Foliot	30	50 25N	4 10W
Tamerza	119	34 23N	7 58 E
Tamgak, Mts.	121	19 12N	8 35 E
Tamiahua, Laguna de	165	21 30N	97 30W
Tamil Nadu □	97	11 0N	77 0 E
Tamines	47	50 26N	4 36 E
Taming	106	36 20N	115 10 E
Tamins	51	46 50N	9 24 E
Tamluk	95	22 18N	87 58 E
Tammisaari (Ekenäs)	75	60 0N	23 26 E
Tammun'	90	32 18N	35 23 E
Tamnaren	72	60 10N	17 25 E
Tamou	121	12 45N	2 11 E
Tampa	157	27 57N	82 30W
Tampa B.	157	27 40N	82 40W
Tampere	75	61 30N	23 50 E
Tampico	165	22 20N	97 50W
Tampin	101	2 28N	102 13 E
Tamri	118	30 49N	9 50W
Tamrida = Hadibu	91	12 35N	54 2 E
Tamsagbulag	105	47 14N	117 21 E
Tamsagout	118	24 5N	6 35W
Tamsalu	80	59 11N	26 8 E
Tamsweg	52	47 7N	13 49 E
Tamu	99	24 13N	94 12 E
Tamuja, R.	57	39 33N	6 8W
Tamworth, Austral.	141	31 0 S	150 58 E
Tamworth, U.K.	28	52 38N	1 41W
Tamyang	107	35 19N	126 59 E
Tan An	101	10 32N	106 25 E
Tana	74	70 7N	28 5 E
Tana Fd.	74	70 35N	28 30 E
Tana, L.	123	13 5N	37 30 E
Tana, R., Kenya	126	0 50 S	39 45 E
Tana, R., Norway	48	69 50N	26 0 E
Tanabe	111	33 44N	135 22 E
Tanabi	171	20 37 S	49 37W
Tanacross	147	63 40N	143 30W
Tanafjorden	74	70 45N	28 25 E
Tanagro, R.	65	40 35N	15 25 E
Tanahdjampea, I.	103	7 10 S	120 35 E
Tanahgrogot	102	1 55 S	116 15 E
Tanahmasa, I.	102	0 5 S	98 29 E
Tanahmerah	103	6 0 S	140 7 E
Tanami	136	19 59 S	129 43 E
Tanami Des.	136	18 50 S	132 0 E
Tanana	147	65 10N	152 15W
Tanana, R.	147	64 25N	145 30W
Tananarive	129	18 55 S	47 31 E
Tananarive □	129	19 0 S	47 0 E
Tananarive = Antananarivo	125	18 55 S	47 31 E
Tananger	71	58 57N	5 37 E
Tanant	118	31 54N	6 56W
Tánaro, R.	62	44 9N	7 50 E
Tanaunelia	64	40 42N	9 45 E
Tanba-Sanchi	111	35 7N	135 48 E
Tanbar	97	25 55 S	142 0 E
Tancarville	42	49 29N	0 28 E
Tanchai	108	25 58N	107 49 E
T'anch'eng	107	34 38N	118 21 E
Tanda, U.P., India	95	26 33N	82 35 E
Tanda, U.P., India	95	28 57N	78 56 E
Tanda, Ivory C.	120	7 48N	3 10W
Tandag	103	9 4N	126 9 E
Tandala	127	9 25 S	34 15 E
Tândârei	70	44 39N	27 40 E
Tandil	172	37 15 S	59 6W
Tandjungpandan	102	2 43 S	107 38 E
Tandlianwald	94	31 3N	73 9 E
Tando Adam	94	25 45N	68 40 E
Tandou L.	140	32 40 S	142 5 E
Tandragee	38	54 22N	6 23W
Tandsbyn	72	63 0N	14 45W
Tandur	96	19 11N	79 30 E
Tane-ga-Shima	112	30 35N	130 59 E
Taneatua	142	38 4 S	177 1 E
Tanen Range	101	19 40N	99 0 E
Tanen Tong Dan, Burma	99	16 30N	98 30 E
Tanen Tong Dan, Thai.	100	19 43N	98 30 E
Taneytown	162	39 40N	77 10W
Tanezrouft	118	23 9N	0 11 E
Tanfeng	106	33 45N	110 18 E
Tang	38	53 31N	7 49W
Tang, Koh	101	10 16N	103 7 E
Tang Krasang	101	12 34N	105 3 E
Tang La	99	32 59N	92 17 E
Tang Pass	99	32 59N	92 17 E
Tanga	99	5 5 S	39 2 E
Tanga □	126	5 20 S	38 0 E
Tanga Is.	135	3 20 S	153 15 E
Tangail	98	24 15N	89 55 E
Tanganyika, L.	126	6 40 S	30 0 E
T'angch'i	109	29 3N	119 24 E
Tanger	118	35 50N	5 49W
Tangerang	103	6 12 S	106 39 E
Tangerhütte	48	52 26N	11 50 E
Tangermünde	48	52 32N	11 57 E
T'angho	109	32 10N	112 20 E
Tangier	162	37 49N	75 59W
Tangier = Tanger	118	35 50N	5 49W
Tangier I.	162	37 50N	76 0W
Tangier Sd.	162	38 3N	75 5W
Tangkak	101	2 18N	102 34 E
T'angku	107	39 4N	117 45 E
T'angkula Shanmo	98	33 0N	92 0 E
Tanglha Shan	99	33 0N	90 0 E
Tangorin P.O.	138	21 47 S	144 12 E
Tangra Tso	99	31 25N	85 30 E
Tangshan	106	34 25N	116 24 E
T'angshan	107	39 40N	118 10 E
T'angt'ang	108	26 29N	104 12 E
T'angt'ou	107	35 21N	118 32 E
Tangt'u	109	31 34N	118 29 E
Tanguiéta	121	10 40N	1 21 E
Tangyang, Chekiang, China	109	29 17N	120 14 E
Tangyang, Hupeh, China	109	30 50N	111 45 E
Tangyen Ho, R.	108	28 55N	108 36 E
Tanimbar, Kepulauan	103	7 30 S	131 30 E
Taning	106	36 32N	110 47 E
Taniyama	110	31 31N	130 31 E
Tanjay	103	9 30N	123 5 E
Tanjore = Thanjavur	97	10 48N	79 12 E
Tanjung	102	2 10 S	115 25 E
Tanjung Malim	101	3 42N	101 31 E
Tanjungbalai	101	2 55N	99 44 E
Tanjungbatu	102	2 23N	118 3 E
Tanjungkarang	102	5 20 S	105 10 E
Tanjungpinang	102	1 5N	104 30 E
Tanjungpriok	103	6 8 S	106 55 E
Tanjungredeb	102	2 9N	117 29 E
Tanjungselor	102	2 55N	117 25 E
Tank	94	32 14N	70 25 E
Tankan Shan	109	22 3N	114 16 E
Tanleng	108	30 2N	103 33 E
Tanndalen	72	62 33N	12 18 E
Tannin	150	49 40N	91 0W
Tannis B.	73	57 40N	10 15 E
Tano, R.	120	6 0N	2 30W
Tanoumrout	119	23 2N	5 31 E
Tanout	121	14 50N	8 55 E
Tanquinho	171	12 42 S	39 43W
Tanshui	109	25 10N	121 28 E
Tanta	122	30 45N	30 57 E
Tantan	118	28 29N	11 1W
Tantoyuca	165	21 21N	98 10W
Tantung	107	40 10N	124 23 E
Tantura = Dor	90	32 37N	34 55 E
Tanuku	96	16 45N	81 44 E
Tanum	73	58 42N	11 20 E
Tanunda	140	34 30 S	139 0 E
Tanur	97	11 1N	75 46 E
Tanus	44	44 8N	2 19 E
Tanworth	28	52 20N	1 50W
Tanzania ■	126	6 40 S	34 0 E
Tanzawa-Sanchi	111	35 27N	139 0 E
Tanzilla, R.	152	58 8N	130 43W
T'aoan	107	45 20N	122 50 E
Taoch'eng	108	29 3N	100 10 E
Taoerh Ho	107	45 42N	124 5 E
Taofu	108	31 0N	101 9 E
Taohsien	109	25 37N	111 24 E
T'aohua Tao	109	29 48N	122 17 E
T'aolo	106	38 45N	106 40 E
Taormina	65	37 52N	15 16 E
Taos	161	36 28N	105 35W
Taoudenni	118	22 40N	3 55W
Taoudrart, Adrar	118	24 25N	2 24 E
Taounate	118	34 32N	4 41W
Taourirt, Alg.	118	26 37N	0 8 E
Taourirt, Moroc.	118	34 20N	2 47W
Taouz	118	31 2N	4 0W
T'aoyüan, China	109	28 54N	111 29 E
T'aoyüan, Taiwan	109	25 0N	121 4 E
Tapa	80	59 15N	26 0 E
Tapa Shan	108	31 45N	109 30 E
Tapachula	165	14 54N	92 17W
Tapah	101	4 12N	101 15 E
Tapajós, R.	175	4 30 S	56 10W
Tapaktuan	102	3 30N	97 10 E
Tapanui	143	45 56 S	169 18 E
Tapauá	174	5 40 S	64 20W
Tapauá, R.	174	6 0 S	65 40W
Tapeta	120	6 36N	8 52W
Taphan Hin	100	16 13N	100 16 E
Tapia	56	43 34N	6 56W
Tapieh Shan, mts.	109	31 20N	115 30 E
T'ap'ingchen	106	33 42N	111 44 E
Tapini	135	8 19 S	147 0 E
Tápiószele	53	47 45N	19 55 E
Tapiraí	171	19 52 S	46 1W
Tapirapé, R.	170	10 41 S	50 38W
Tapirapecó, Serra	174	1 10N	65 0W
Taplan	140	34 33 S	140 52 E
Tapolca	53	46 53N	17 29 E
Tappahannock	162	37 56N	76 50W
Tapsing	99	30 22N	96 25 E
Tapti, R.	96	21 25N	75 0 E
Tapu	109	24 31N	116 41 E
Tapuaenuku, Mt.	143	41 55 S	173 50 E
Tapul Group, Is.	103	5 35N	120 50 E
Tapun	98	18 22N	95 27 E
Taquara	173	29 36N	50 46W
Taquari, R.	173	18 10 S	56 0W
Taquaritinga	171	21 24 S	48 30W
Tara, Austral.	139	27 17 S	150 31 E
Tara, Japan	110	33 2N	130 11 E
Tara, U.S.S.R.	76	56 55N	74 30 E
Tara, Zambia	127	16 58 S	26 45 E
Tara-Dake	110	32 58N	130 6 E
Tara, R.	66	43 10N	19 20 E
Tarabagatay, Khrebet	77	48 0N	83 0 E
Tarābulus, Leb.	92	34 31N	33 52 E
Tarābulus, Libya	119	32 49N	13 7 E
Taradale	142	39 33 S	176 53 E
Tarahouahout	119	22 47N	5 59 E
Tarakan	102	3 20N	117 35 E
Tarakit, Mt.	126	2 2N	35 10 E
Taralga	141	34 26 S	149 52 E
Taramakau, R.	143	42 34 S	171 8 E
Tarana	141	33 31 S	149 52 E
Taranagar	94	28 43N	75 9 E
Taranaki □	142	39 5 S	174 51 E
Tarancón	58	40 1N	3 1W
Taranga	94	23 56N	72 43 E
Taranga Hill	94	24 0N	72 40 E
Taransay, I.	36	57 54N	7 0W
Taransay, Sd. of	36	57 52N	7 0W
Táranto	65	40 30N	17 11 E
Táranto, G. di	65	40 0N	17 15 E
Tarapacá	174	2 56 S	69 46W
Tarapacá □	172	20 45 S	69 30W
Tarare	45	45 54N	4 26 E
Tararua Range	142	40 45 S	175 25 E
Tarascon, Ariège, France	44	42 50N	1 37 E
Tarascon, Bouches-du-Rhône, France	45	43 48N	4 39 E
Tarashcha	82	49 30N	30 31 E
Tarat, Bj.	119	26 4N	9 7 E
Tarauacá	174	8 6 S	70 48W
Tarauacá, R.	174	7 30 S	70 30W
Taravo, R.	45	41 48N	8 52 E
Tarawera	142	39 2 S	176 36 E
Tarawera L.	142	38 13 S	176 27 E
Tarawera Mt.	142	38 14 S	176 32 E
Tarazat, Massif de	119	20 2N	8 30 E
Tarazona	58	41 55N	1 43W
Tarazona de la Mancha	59	39 16N	1 55W
Tarbat Ness	37	57 52N	3 48W
Tarbela Dam	94	34 0N	72 52 E
Tarbert, Ireland	39	52 34N	9 22W
Tarbert, Strathclyde, U.K.	34	55 55N	5 25W
Tarbert, W. Isles, U.K.	36	57 54N	6 49W
Tarbert, L. E.	36	57 50N	6 45W
Tarbert, L. W., Strathclyde, U.K.	34	55 58N	5 30W
Tarbert, L. W., W. Isles, U.K.	36	57 55N	6 56W
Tarbes	44	43 15N	0 3 E
Tarbet, Highland, U.K.	36	56 58N	5 38W
Tarbet, Strathclyde, U.K.	34	56 13N	4 44W
Tarbolton	34	55 30N	4 30W
Tarboro	157	35 55N	77 3W
Tarbrax	138	21 7 S	142 26 E
Tarbū	119	26 0N	15 5 E
Tarcento	63	46 12N	13 12 E
Tarcoola	139	30 44 S	134 36 E
Tarcoon	139	30 15 S	146 35 E
Tarcău, Munţii	70	46 39N	26 7 E
Tardets-Sorholus	44	43 17N	0 52W
Taree	141	31 50 S	152 30 E
Tarentaise	45	45 30N	6 35 E
Tarf Shaqq al Abd	122	26 50N	36 6 E
Tarfa, Wadi el	122	28 16N	31 15 E
Tarfaya	116	27 55N	12 55W
Targon	44	44 44N	0 16W
Targuist	118	34 59N	4 14W
Tarhbalt	118	30 48N	5 10W
Tarhit	118	30 58N	2 0W
Tarhūnah	119	32 15N	13 28 E
Tari	135	5 54 S	142 59 E
Tarib, Wadi	122	18 30N	43 23 E
Táriba	174	7 49N	72 13W
Tarifa	57	36 1N	5 36W
Tarija	172	21 30 S	64 40W
Tarija □	172	21 30 S	63 30W
Tarim, R.	105	41 5N	86 40 E
Tarime □	126	1 15 S	34 0 E
Taringo Downs	141	32 13 S	145 33 E
Taritoe, R.	103	3 0 S	138 5 E
Tarka, R.	128	32 10 S	26 0 E
Tarkastad	128	32 0 S	26 16 E
Tarkhankut, Mys	82	45 25N	32 30 E
Tarko Sale	76	64 55N	77 50 E
Tarkwa	120	5 20N	2 0W
Tarlac	103	15 29N	120 35 E
Tarland	37	57 8N	2 51W
Tarleton	32	53 41N	2 50W
Tarlsland	152	57 03N	111 40W
Tarlton Downs	138	22 40 S	136 45 E
Tarm	73	55 56N	8 31 E
Tarma	174	11 25 S	75 45W
Tarn □	44	43 49N	2 8 E
Tarn-et-Garonne □	44	44 8N	1 20 E
Tarn, R.	44	44 5N	1 2 E
Tärna	74	65 45N	15 10 E
Tarna, R.	53	48 0N	20 5 E
Tårnby	73	55 37N	12 36 E
Tarnobrzeg □	54	50 40N	22 0 E
Tarnów	54	50 3N	21 0 E
Tarnów □	54	50 0N	21 0 E
Tarnowskie Góry	54	50 27N	18 54 E
Táro, R.	62	44 37N	9 58 E
Tarong	139	26 47 S	151 51 E
Taroom	139	25 36 S	149 48 E
Taroudannt	118	30 30N	8 52W
Tarp	48	54 40N	9 25 E
Tarpon Springs	157	28 8N	82 42W
Tarporley	32	53 10N	2 42W
Tarquínia	63	42 15N	11 45 E
Tarqumiyah	90	31 35N	35 1 E
Tarragona	58	41 5N	1 17 E
Tarragona □	58	41 0N	1 0 E
Tarrasa	58	41 26N	2 1 E
Tárrega	58	41 39N	1 9 E
Tarrytown	162	41 5N	73 52W
Tarshiha = Me'ona	90	33 1N	35 15 E
Tarso Emissi	119	21 27N	18 36 E
Tarso Ovrari	119	21 27N	17 27 E
Tarsus	92	36 58N	34 55 E
Tartagal	172	22 30 S	63 50W
Tartan, oilfield	19	58 22N	0 5 E
Tartas	44	43 50N	0 49W
Tartna Point	140	32 54 S	142 24 E
Tartu	80	58 25N	26 58 E
Tartus	92	34 55N	35 55 E
Tarumirim	171	19 16 S	41 59W
Tarumizu	110	31 29N	130 42 E
Tarussa	81	54 44N	37 10 E
Tarutao, Ko	101	6 33N	99 40 E
Tarutung	102	2 0N	99 0 E
Tarves	37	57 22N	2 13W
Tarvisio	63	46 31N	13 35 E
Tarz Ulli	119	25 46N	9 44 E
Tas-Buget	85	44 46N	65 33 E
Tasahku	98	27 33N	97 52 E
Tasāwah	119	26 0N	13 37 E
Taschereau	150	48 40N	78 40W
Taseko, R.	152	52 4N	123 9W
Tasgaon	96	17 2N	74 39 E
Ta'shan	123	16 31N	42 33 E
Tashauz	76	42 0N	59 20 E
Tashet'ai	106	41 0N	109 21 E
Tashi Chho Dzong	98	27 31N	89 45 E
Tashihch'iao (Yingk'ou)	107	40 38N	122 30 E
T'ashihk'uerhkan	85	37 47N	75 14 E
Tashkent	85	41 20N	69 10 E
Tashkumyr	85	41 40N	72 10 E
Tashkurghan	93	36 45N	67 40 E
Tashtagol	76	52 47N	87 53 E
Tasikmalaya	103	7 18 S	108 12 E
Tasjön	74	64 15N	15 45 E
Taşköpru	82	41 30N	34 15 E
Tasman Bay	143	40 59 S	173 25 E
Tasman Glacier	143	43 45 S	170 20 E
Tasman, Mt.	143	43 34 S	170 12 E
Tasman Mts.	143	41 3 S	172 25 E
Tasman Pen.	138	43 10 S	148 0 E
Tasman, R.	143	43 48 S	170 8 E
Tasman Sea	142	36 0 S	160 0 E
Tasmania, I., □	138	49 0 S	146 30 E
Tassil Tin-Rerhoh	118	20 5N	3 55 E
Tassili n-Ajjer	119	25 47N	8 1 E
Tassili-Oua-Ahaggar	119	20 41N	5 30 E
Tasty	85	44 47N	69 7 E
Tasu Sd.	152	52 47N	132 2W
Tata, Hung.	53	47 37N	18 19 E
Tata, Moroc.	118	29 46N	7 50W
Tatabánya	53	47 32N	18 25 E
Tatar A.S.S.R. □	84	55 30N	51 30 E
Tatarsk	76	55 20N	75 50 E
Tatarskiy Proliv	77	54 0N	141 0 E
Tatebayashi	111	36 15N	139 32 E
Tateshina-Yama	111	36 8N	138 11 E
Tateyama	111	35 0N	139 50 E
Tathlina L.	152	60 33N	117 39W
Tathra	141	36 44 S	149 59 E
Tat'ien, Fukien, China	109	25 42N	117 50 E
Tat'ien, Szechwan, China	108	26 18N	101 45 E
Tatinnai L.	153	60 55N	97 40W
Tatlayoka Lake	152	51 35N	124 24W
Tatnam, C.	153	57 16N	91 0W
Tato Ho, R.	108	31 25N	100 42 E
Tatra = Tatry	54	49 20N	20 0 E
Tatry	54	49 20N	20 0 E
Tatsu	108	29 40N	105 45 E
Tatsuno	110	34 52N	134 33 E
Tatta	94	24 42N	67 55 E
Tattenhall	32	53 7N	2 47W
Tatu Ho, R.	108	29 35N	103 47 E
Tatuí	173	23 25 S	48 0W
Tatum	159	33 16N	103 16W
Tat'ung, Anhwei, China	109	30 48N	117 44 E
Tat'ung, Shansi, China	106	40 9N	113 19 E
Tatura	141	36 29 S	145 16 E
Tatvan	92	37 28N	42 27 E
Tauá	170	6 1 S	40 26W
Taubaté	173	23 5 S	45 30W
Tauberbischofsheim	49	49 37N	9 40 E
Taucha	48	51 22N	12 31 E
Tauern, mts.	52	47 15N	12 40 E
Tauern-tunnel	52	47 0N	13 12 E
Taufikia	123	9 24N	31 37 E
Taumarunui	142	38 53 S	175 15 E
Taumaturgo	174	9 0 S	73 50W
Taung	128	27 33 S	24 47 E
Taungdwingyi	98	20 1N	95 40 E
Taunggyi	98	20 50N	97 0 E
Taungtha	98	20 45N	94 50 E
Taungup	98	18 51N	94 14 E
Taungup Pass	98	18 40N	94 45 E
Taungup Taunggya	99	18 20N	93 40 E
Taunsa Barrage	95	31 0N	71 0 E
Taunton, U.K.	28	51 1N	3 7W

Taunton Tetbury

Taunton, U.S.A. 162 41 54N 71 6W
Taunus 49 50 15N 8 20 E
Taupo 142 38 41 S 176 7 E
Taupo, L. 142 38 46 S 175 55 E
Tauq 92 35 12N 44 29 E
Taurage 80 55 14N 22 28 E
Tauramena 174 5 1N 72 45W
Tauranga 142 37 35 S 176 11 E
Tauranga Harb. 142 37 30 S 176 5 E
Taureau, Lac 150 46 50N 73 40W
Tauri, R. 135 8 8 S 146 8 E
Taurianova 65 38 22N 16 1 E
Taurus Mts. = Toros Dağlari 92 37 0N 35 0 E
Táuste 58 41 58N 1 18W
Tauz 83 41 0N 45 40 E
Tavani 153 62 10N 93 30W
Tavannes 50 47 13N 7 12 E
Tavas 92 37 35N 29 8 E
Tavda 84 58 7N 65 8 E
Tavda, R. 84 59 30N 63 0 E
Taverny 43 49 2N 2 13 E
Taveta 124 3 31N 37 37 E
Taviche 165 16 38N 96 32W
Tavignano, R. 45 42 7N 9 33 E
Tavira 57 37 8N 7 40W
Tavistock 30 50 33N 4 9W
Tavolara, I. 64 40 55N 9 40 E
Távora, R. 56 41 0N 7 30W
Tavoy 101 14 7N 98 18 E
Tavoy, I. = Mali Kyun 99 13 0N 98 20 E
Taw, R. 30 50 58N 3 58W
Tawang 99 27 37N 91 50 E
Tawas City 156 44 16N 83 31W
Tawau 102 4 20N 117 55 E
Tawngche 98 26 34N 95 38 E
Tawnyinah 38 53 55N 8 45W
Tāworgha' 119 32 1N 15 2 E
Taxila 94 33 42N 72 52 E
Tay Bridge 35 56 28N 3 0W
Tay, Firth of 35 56 25N 3 8W
Tay, L., Austral. 137 32 55 S 120 48 E
Tay, L., U.K. 35 56 30N 4 10W
Tay Ninh 101 11 20N 106 5 E
Tay, R. 35 56 37N 3 38W
Tay Strath 37 56 38N 3 40W
Tayabamba 174 8 15 S 77 10W
Tayao 108 25 41N 101 18 E
Tayaparva La 95 31 35N 83 20 E
Tayeh 109 30 5N 114 57 E
Taylor, Can. 152 56 13N 120 40W
Taylor, Alaska, U.S.A. 147 65 40N 164 50W
Taylor, Pa., U.S.A. 162 41 23N 75 43W
Taylor, Tex., U.S.A. 159 30 30N 97 30W
Taylor, Mt. 143 43 30 S 171 20 E
Taylor Mt. 161 35 16N 107 50W
Taylorville 158 39 32N 89 20W
Taymyr, Oz. 77 74 50N 102 0 E
Taymyr, P-ov. 77 75 0N 100 0 E
Taynuilt 34 56 25N 5 15W
Tayport 34 56 27N 2 52W
Tayr Zebna 90 33 14N 35 23 E
Tayshet 77 55 58N 97 25 E
Tayside □ 35 56 25N 3 30W
Taytay 103 10 45N 119 30 E
Tayu 109 25 38N 114 9 E
Tayülo 105 29 13N 98 13 E
Tayung 109 29 8N 110 30 E
Taz, R. 76 65 40N 82 0 E
Taza 118 34 10N 4 0W
Taze 98 22 57N 95 24 E
Tazenakht 118 30 46N 7 3W
Tazin L. 153 59 44N 108 42W
Tazin, R. 153 60 26N 110 45W
Tazoult 119 35 29N 6 11 E
Tazovskiy 76 67 30N 78 30 E
Tbilisi (Tiflis) 83 41 50N 44 50 E
Tchad (Chad) ■ 117 12 30N 17 15 E
Tchad, Lac 117 13 30N 14 30 E
Tchaourou 121 8 58N 2 40 E
Tchentlo L. 152 55 15N 125 0W
Tchibanga 124 2 45 S 11 12 E
Tchin Tabaraden 121 15 58N 5 50 E
Tczew 54 54 8N 18 50 E
Te Anau L. 143 45 15 S 167 45 E
Te Araroa 142 37 39 S 178 25 E
Te Aroha 142 37 32 S 175 44 E
Te Awamutu 142 38 1 S 175 20 E
Te Horo 142 40 48 S 175 6 E
Te Kaha 142 37 44 S 177 44 E
Te Karaka 142 38 26 S 177 53 E
Te Kauwhata 142 37 25 S 175 9 E
Te Kinga 143 42 35 S 171 31 E
Te Kopuru 142 36 2 S 173 56 E
Te Kuiti 142 38 20 S 175 11 E
Te Puke 142 37 46 S 176 22 E
Te Waewae B. 143 46 13 S 167 33 E
Tea Tree 136 22 11 S 133 17 E
Teaca 70 46 55N 24 30 E
Teague 159 31 40N 96 20W
Tean 109 29 21N 115 42 E
Teangue 36 57 7N 5 52W
Teano 65 41 15N 14 1 E
Teapa 165 17 35N 92 56W
Teba 57 36 59N 4 55W
Tebay 32 54 25N 2 35W
Teberda 83 43 30N 43 54 E
Tébessa 119 35 22N 8 8 E
Tebicuary, R. 172 26 36 S 58 16W
Tebing Tinggi 102 3 38 S 102 1 E
Tébourba 119 36 49N 9 51 E
Téboursouk 119 36 29N 9 10 E
Tebulos 83 42 36N 45 25 E
Tecapa 163 35 51N 116 14W
Tecate 164 32 34N 116 38W
Techa, R. 84 56 13N 62 58 E
Tech'ang 108 27 22N 102 10 E
Techiang 108 28 19N 108 5 E
Techiman 120 7 35N 1 58W
Tech'in 108 28 30N 98 52 E
Tech'ing 109 23 8N 111 46 E
Techirghiol 70 44 4N 28 32 E
Techou 106 37 19N 116 19 E
Tecomán 164 18 55N 103 53W
Tecoripa 164 28 37N 109 57W
Tecuci 70 45 51N 27 27 E
Tecumseh 156 42 1N 83 59W
Tedavnet 38 54 19N 7 2W
Tedesa 123 5 10N 37 40 E
Tedzhen 76 37 23N 60 31 E
Tees B. 72 54 37N 1 10W
Tees, R. 33 54 36N 1 25W
Teesdale 32 54 37N 2 10W
Teesside 33 54 37N 1 13W
Tefé 174 3 25 S 64 50W
Tegal 103 6 52 S 109 8 E
Tegelen 47 51 20N 6 9 E
Teggiano 65 40 24N 15 32 E
Teghra 95 25 30N 85 34 E
Tegid, L. 31 52 53N 3 38W
Tegina 121 10 5N 6 11 E
Tegucigalpa 166 14 10N 87 0W
Tehachapi 163 35 11N 118 29W
Tehachapi Mts. 163 35 0N 118 40W
Tehamiyam 122 18 26N 36 45 E
Tehilla 122 17 42N 36 6 E
Téhini 120 9 39N 3 32W
Tehrān 93 35 44N 51 30 E
Tehrān □ 93 35 0N 49 30 E
Tehsing 109 28 54N 117 34 E
Tehua 109 25 30N 118 14 E
Tehuacán 165 18 20N 97 30W
Tehuantepec 165 16 10N 95 19W
Tehuantepec, Golfo de 165 15 50N 95 0W
Tehuantepec, Istmo de 165 17 0N 94 30W
Tehui 107 44 32N 125 42 E
Teich, Le 44 44 38N 0 59W
Teifi, R. 31 52 4N 4 14W
Teign, R. 30 50 41N 3 42W
Teignmouth 30 50 33N 3 30W
Teikovo 81 56 55N 40 30 E
Teil, Le 45 44 33N 4 40 E
Teilleul, Le 42 48 32N 0 53W
Teishyai 80 55 59N 22 14 E
Teiuş 70 46 12N 23 40 E
Teixeira 170 7 13 S 37 15W
Teixeira de Sousa = Luau 124 10 40 S 22 10 E
Teixeira Pinto 120 12 10N 13 55 E
Tejo, R. 57 39 15N 8 35W
Tejon Pass 163 34 49N 118 53W
Tejung 108 28 46N 99 19 E
Tekamah 158 41 48N 96 14W
Tekapo, L. 143 43 53 S 170 33 E
Tekax 165 20 20N 89 30W
Tekeli 85 44 50N 79 0 E
Tekeze, W. 123 13 50N 37 50 E
Tekija 66 44 42N 22 26 E
Tekirdağ 92 40 58N 27 30 E
Tekkali 96 18 43N 84 24 E
Teko 108 31 49N 98 40 E
Tekoa 160 47 19N 117 4W
Tekoulât, O. 118 22 30N 2 20 E
Tel Adashim 90 32 39N 35 17 E
Tel Aviv-Yafo 90 32 4N 34 48 E
Tel Hanan 90 32 47N 35 3 E
Tel Hazor 90 33 2N 35 2 E
Tel Lakhish 90 31 34N 34 51 E
Tel Malhata 90 31 13N 35 2 E
Tel Megiddo 90 32 35N 38 11 E
Tel Mond 90 32 15N 34 56 E
Tela 166 15 40N 87 28W
Télagh 118 34 51N 0 32W
Telanaipura = Jambi 102 1 38 S 103 30 E
Telavi 83 42 0N 45 30 E
Telciu 70 47 25N 24 24 E
Telefomin 135 5 10 S 141 40 E
Telega = Doftana 70 45 17N 25 45 E
Telegraph Cr. 152 58 0N 131 10W
Telekhany 80 52 30N 25 46 E
Telemark fylke □ 71 59 25N 8 30 E
Telén 172 36 15 S 65 31W
Teleneshty 70 47 35N 28 24 E
Teleño 56 42 23N 6 22W
Teleorman □ 70 44 0N 25 0 E
Teleorman, R. 70 44 15N 25 20 E
Teles Pires (São Manuel), R. 174 8 40 S 57 0W
Telescope Peak, Mt. 163 36 6N 117 7W
Teletaye 121 16 31N 1 30 E
Telford 28 52 42N 2 31W
Telfs 52 47 19N 11 4 E
Telgte 48 51 59N 7 46 E
Telichie 139 31 45 S 139 59 E
Télimélé 120 10 54N 13 2W
Telkwa 152 54 41N 126 56W
Tell 90 32 12N 35 12 E
Tell City 156 38 0N 86 44W
Teller 147 65 12N 166 24W
Tellicherry 97 11 45N 75 30 E
Tellin 47 50 5N 5 13 E
Telluride 161 37 58N 107 54W
Telok Anson 101 4 3N 101 0 E
Teloloapán 165 18 21N 99 51W
Telom, R. 101 4 20N 101 46 E
Telpos Iz. 78 63 35N 57 30 E
Telsen 176 42 30 S 66 50W
Teltow 48 52 24N 13 15 E
Telukbetung 102 5 29 S 105 17 E
Telukbutun 101 4 5N 108 7 E
Telukdalem 102 0 45N 97 50 E
Tema 121 5 41N 0 0 E
Temagami L. 150 47 0N 80 10W
Temanggung 103 7 18 S 110 10 E
Temapache 165 21 4N 97 38W
Temax 165 21 10N 88 50W
Tembe 126 0 30 S 28 25 E
Tembeling, R. 101 4 20N 102 23 E
Tembleque 58 39 41N 3 30W
Temblor Ra, mts. 163 35 30N 120 0W
Tembuland □ 129 31 35 S 28 0 E
Teme, R. 28 52 23N 2 15W
Temecula 163 33 26N 117 6W
Temelelt 118 31 50N 7 32W
Temerloh 101 3 27N 102 25 E
Temir Tau 76 53 10N 87 20 E
Temirtau 76 50 5N 72 56 E
Témiscaming 150 46 44N 79 5W
Temma 138 41 12 S 144 42 E
Temnikov 81 54 40N 43 11 E
Temo, R. 64 40 20N 8 30 E
Temora 141 34 30 S 147 30 E
Temosachic 164 28 58N 107 50W
Tempe, S. Afr. 161 29 1 S 26 13 E
Tempe, U.S.A. 161 33 26N 111 59W
Tempe Downs 136 24 22 S 132 24 E
Temperanceville 162 37 54N 75 33W
Tempestad 174 1 20 S 74 56W
Tempino 102 1 55 S 103 23 E
Témpio Pausania 64 40 53N 9 6 E
Temple 159 31 5N 97 28W
Temple B. 138 12 15 S 143 3 E
Temple Combe 28 51 0N 2 25W
Temple Ewell 29 51 9N 1 16W
Temple Sowerby 30 54 38N 2 33W
Templemore 39 52 48N 7 50W
Templenoe 39 51 52N 9 40W
Templeton, Austral. 138 18 30 S 142 30 E
Templeton, U.K. 31 51 46N 4 45W
Templeton, U.S.A. 163 35 33N 120 42W
Templeton, R. 138 21 0 S 138 40 E
Templeuve 47 50 39N 3 17 E
Templin 48 53 8N 13 31 E
Tempo 38 54 23N 7 28W
Tempoal 165 21 31N 98 23W
Temryuk 82 45 15N 37 11 E
Temse 47 51 7N 4 13 E
Temska, R. 66 43 17N 22 33 E
Temuco 176 38 50 S 72 50W
Temuka 143 44 14 S 171 17 E
Ten Boer 46 53 16N 6 42 E
Tena 174 0 59 S 77 49W
Tenabo 165 20 2N 90 12W
Tenaha 159 31 57N 94 15W
Tenali 96 16 15N 80 35 E
Tenancingo 165 19 0N 99 33W
Tenango 165 19 0N 99 40W
Tenasserim 100 12 6N 99 3 E
Tenasserim □ 100 14 0N 98 30 E
Tenay 45 45 55N 5 30 E
Tenbury 28 52 18N 2 35W
Tenby 31 51 40N 4 42W
Tenda 45 44 5N 7 34 E
Tenda, Col de 45 44 9N 7 32 E
Tendaho 123 11 39N 40 54 E
Tende 45 44 5N 7 35 E
Tendelti 123 13 1N 31 55 E
Tendjedi, Adrar 119 23 41N 7 32 E
Tendrara 118 33 3N 1 58W
Tendre, Mt. 50 46 35N 6 18 E
Teneida 122 25 30N 29 19 E
Ténéré 119 23 2N 16 0 E
Tenerife, I. 116 28 20N 16 40W
Ténès 118 36 31N 1 14 E
T'eng Ch'ung 99 25 9N 98 22 E
Teng, R. 101 20 30N 98 10 E
Tengah □ 103 2 0 S 122 0 E
Tengah Kepulauan 102 7 5 S 118 15 E
Tengchow = P'englai 107 37 49N 120 47 E
Tengch'uan 108 26 0N 100 4 E
Tengch'ung 108 25 2N 98 28 E
Tengfeng 106 34 27N 113 2 E
Tenggara □ 103 3 0 S 122 0 E
Tenggol, P. 101 4 48N 103 41 E
T'enghsien, Honan, China 109 32 41N 112 5 E
T'enghsien, Kwangsi Chuang, China 109 23 23N 110 54 E
T'enghsien, Shantung, China 105 35 8N 117 9 E
Tengiz, Ozero 76 50 30N 69 0 E
Tengko 99 32 30N 98 0 E
Tengk'o 108 32 32N 97 35 E
Tengk'ou 106 40 18N 106 59 E
Tenigerbad 51 46 42N 8 57 E
Tenille 157 32 58N 82 50W
Tenindewa 137 28 30 S 115 20 E
Tenkasi 97 8 55N 77 20 E
Tenke, Congo 127 11 22 S 26 40 E
Tenke, Zaîre 127 10 32 S 26 7 E
Tenkodogo 121 12 0N 0 10W
Tenna, R. 63 43 12N 13 43 E
Tennant Creek 136 19 30 S 134 0 E
'Tenneco', oilfield 19 54 6N 4 42 E
Tennessee □ 155 36 0N 86 30W
Tenneville 47 50 6N 5 32 E
Tennsift, Oued 118 32 3N 9 28W
Tenom 102 5 4N 115 38 E
Tenosique 165 17 30N 91 24W
Tenri 111 34 46N 135 55 E
Tenryū 111 34 52N 137 55 E
Tent L. 153 62 25N 107 54W
Tenterden 29 51 4N 0 42 E
Tenterfield 139 29 0 S 152 0 E
Teófilo Otôni 171 17 50 S 41 30W
Tepa 120 6 57N 2 30W
Tepalcatepec, R. 164 18 35N 101 59W
Tepao 108 23 21N 106 33 E
Tepehuanes 164 25 21N 105 44W
Tepetongo 164 22 28N 103 9W
Tepic 164 21 30N 104 54W
Tepi'ng 107 37 28N 116 67 E
Teploklyuchenka 85 42 30N 78 30 E
Tepoca, C. 164 29 20N 112 25W
Tequila 164 20 54N 103 47W
Ter Apel 46 52 53N 7 5 E
Ter, R. 58 42 0N 2 30 E
Téra 121 14 0N 0 57 E
Tera, R. 56 41 54N 5 44W
Téramo 63 42 40N 13 40 E
Terang 140 38 15 S 142 55 E
Terawhiti, C. 142 41 16 S 174 38 E
Terborg 46 51 56N 6 22 E
Tercan 92 39 50N 40 30 E
Terceira 16 38 43N 27 13W
Tercero, R. 172 32 58 S 61 47W
Terdal 96 16 33N 75 9 E
Terebovlya 80 49 18N 25 44 E
Teregova 70 45 10N 22 16 E
Terek-Say 85 41 30N 71 11 E
Terembone Cr. 139 30 25 S 148 50 E
Terengganu □ 101 4 55N 103 0 E
Tereshka, R. 81 52 0N 46 36 E
Teresina 170 5 2 S 42 45W
Terewah L. 139 29 52 S 147 35 E
Terezinha 174 0 44N 69 27W
Terges, R. 57 37 49N 7 41W
Tergnier 43 49 40N 3 17 E
Terhazza 118 23 45N 4 59W
Terheijden 47 51 38N 4 45 E
Teriang 101 3 15N 102 26 E
Terkezi 117 18 27N 21 40 E
Terlizzi 65 41 8N 16 32 E
Termas de Chillan 172 36 50 S 71 31W
Terme 82 41 11N 37 0 E
Termez 85 37 0N 67 15 E
Términi Imerese 43 37 59N 13 51 E
Términos, Laguna de 165 18 35N 91 30W
Termoli 63 42 0N 15 0 E
Termon 38 55 3N 7 50W
Termonfeckin 38 53 47N 6 15W
Tern, oilfield 19 61 17N 0 55 E
Ternate 103 0 45N 127 25 E
Terneuzen 47 51 20N 3 50 E
Terney 77 45 3N 136 37 E
Terni 63 42 34N 12 38 E
Ternitz 52 47 43N 16 2 E
Ternopol 80 49 30N 25 40 E
Terowie, N.S.W., Austral. 139 32 27 S 147 52 E
Terowie, Vic., Austral. 140 33 10 S 138 50 E
Terra Bella 163 35 58N 119 3W
Terra Nova B. 13 74 50 S 164 40 E
Terrace 152 54 30N 128 35W
Terrace Bay 150 48 47N 87 10W
Terracina 64 41 17N 13 12 E
Terralba 64 39 42N 8 38 E
Terranuova 63 43 38N 11 35 E
Terrasini Favarotta 64 38 10N 13 4 E
Terrasson 44 45 7N 1 19 E
Terrebonne B. 159 29 15N 90 28W
Terrecht 118 20 10N 0 10W
Terrell 159 32 44N 96 19W
Terrenceville 151 47 40N 54 44W
Terrick Terrick 138 24 44 S 145 5 E
Terry 158 46 47N 105 20W
Terryglass 39 53 3N 8 14W
Terryville 162 41 41N 73 1W
Terschelling, I. 46 53 25N 5 20 E
Terskey Alatau, Khrebet 85 41 50N 77 0 E
Terter, R. 83 40 5N 46 15 E
Teruel 58 40 22N 1 8W
Teruel □ 58 40 48N 1 0W
Tervel 67 43 45N 27 28 E
Tervola 74 66 6N 24 49 E
Teryaweyna L. 140 32 18 S 143 22 E
Tešanj 66 44 38N 17 59 E
Teseney 123 15 5N 36 42 E
Tesha, R. 81 55 32N 43 0 E
Teshio 112 44 53N 141 44 E
Teshio-Gawa, R. 112 44 53N 141 45 E
Tešica 66 43 27N 21 45 E
Tesiyn Gol, R. 105 50 28N 93 4 E
Teslin 147 60 10N 132 43W
Teslin L. 152 60 15N 132 57W
Teslin, R. 152 61 34N 134 35W
Teslió 66 44 37N 17 54 E
Teso □ = Eastern □ 126 1 50N 33 45 E
Tessalit 121 20 12N 1 0 E
Tessaoua 121 13 47N 7 56 E
Tessenderlo 47 51 4N 5 5 E
Tessier 153 51 48N 107 26W
Tessin 48 54 2N 12 28 E
Tessit 121 15 13N 0 18 E
Test, R. 28 51 7N 1 30W
Testa del Gargano 65 41 50N 16 10 E
Teste, La 44 44 37N 1 8W
Tét 53 47 30N 17 33 E
Tetachuck L. 152 53 18N 125 55W
Tetas, Pta. 172 23 31 S 70 38W
Tetbury 28 51 37N 2 9W

Tete **Tijibadok**

Tete	127	16 13 S	33 33 E
Tete □	127	15 15 S	32 40 E
Teterev, R.	80	50 30N	29 30 E
Teteringen	47	51 37N	4 49 E
Teterow	48	53 45N	12 34 E
Teteven	67	42 58N	24 17 E
Tethull, R.	152	60 35N	112 12W
Tetiyev	82	49 22N	29 38 E
Tetlin	147	63 14N	142 50W
Tetlin Junction	147	63 29N	142 55W
Tetney	33	53 30N	0 1W
Teton, R.	160	47 58N	111 0W
Tétouan	118	35 35N	5 21W
Tetovo	66	42 1N	21 2 E
Tettenhall	28	52 35N	2 7W
Tetuán = Tétouan	118	35 30N	5 25W
Tetyukhe	77	44 45N	135 40 E
Teuco, R.	172	25 30 S	60 25W
Teufen	51	47 24N	9 23 E
Teulada	64	38 59N	8 47 E
Teulon	153	50 23N	97 16W
Tevere, R.	63	42 30N	12 20 E
Teviot, R.	35	55 21N	2 51W
Teviotdale	35	55 25N	2 50W
Teviothead	35	55 19N	2 55W
Tewantin	139	26 27 S	153 3 E
Tewkesbury	28	51 59N	2 8W
Texada I.	152	49 40N	124 25W
Texarkana, Ark., U.S.A.	159	33 25N	94 0W
Texarkana, Tex., U.S.A.	159	33 25N	94 3W
Texas	139	28 49 S	151 15 E
Texas □	159	31 40N	98 30W
Texas City	159	27 20N	95 20W
Texel, I.	46	53 5N	4 50 E
Texhoma	159	36 32N	101 47W
Texline	159	36 26N	103 0W
Texoma L.	159	34 0N	96 38W
Teyang	108	31 8N	104 24 E
Teykovo	81	56 55N	40 30 E
Teynham	29	51 19N	0 50 E
Teyr Zebna	90	33 14N	35 23 E
Teza, R.	81	56 41N	41 45 E
Tezin	94	34 24N	69 30 E
Teziutlán	165	19 50N	97 30W
Tezpur	98	26 40N	92 45 E
Tezzeron L.	152	54 43N	124 30W
Tha-anne, R.	153	60 31N	94 37W
Tha Deua, Laos	100	17 57N	102 38 E
Tha Deua, Laos	100	19 26N	101 50 E
Tha Nun	101	8 12N	98 17 E
Tha Pia	100	17 48N	100 32 E
Tha Rua	100	14 34N	100 44 E
Tha Sala	101	8 40N	99 56 E
Tha Song Yang	101	17 34N	97 55 E
Thaba Putsoa, mt.	129	29 45 S	28 0 E
Thabana Ntlenyana, Mt.	129	29 30 S	29 9 E
Thabazimbi	129	24 40 S	26 4 E
Thabeikkyin	98	22 53N	95 59 E
Thai Binh	100	20 27N	106 20 E
Thai Muang	101	8 24N	98 16 E
Thai Nguyen	100	21 35N	105 46 E
Thailand (Siam) ■	100	16 0N	102 0 E
Thakhek	100	17 25N	104 45 E
Thakurgaon	98	26 2N	88 28 E
Thal	94	33 28N	70 33 E
Thal Desert	93	31 0N	71 30 E
Thala	119	35 35N	8 40 E
Thala La	99	28 25N	97 23 E
Thalabarivat	100	13 33N	105 57 E
Thalkirch	51	46 39N	9 17 E
Thallon	139	28 30 S	148 57 E
Thalwil	51	47 17N	8 35 E
Thame	29	51 44N	0 58W
Thame, R.	29	51 52N	0 47W
Thames	142	37 7 S	175 34 E
Thames, Firth of	142	37 0 S	175 25 E
Thames, R., Can.	150	42 20N	82 25W
Thames, R., N.Z.	142	37 32 S	175 45 E
Thames, R., U.K.	28	51 30N	0 35 E
Thames, R., U.S.A.	162	41 18N	72 9W
Thāmit, W.	119	30 51N	16 14 E
Than Uyen	100	22 0N	103 54 E
Thana	96	19 12N	72 59 E
Thanbyuzayat	98	15 58N	97 44 E
Thanesar	94	30 1N	76 52 E
Thanet, I. of	29	51 21N	1 20 E
Thang Binh	101	15 50N	108 20 E
Thangoo P.O.	136	18 10 S	122 22 E
Thangool	138	24 29 S	150 35 E
Thanh Hoa	100	19 48N	105 46 E
Thanh Hung	101	9 55N	105 43 E
Thanh Thuy	100	22 55N	104 51 E
Thanjavur (Tanjore)	97	10 48N	79 12 E
Thanlwin myit, R.	99	20 0N	98 0 E
Thann	43	47 48N	7 5 E
Thaon	43	48 15N	6 25 E
Thap Sakae	101	11 30N	99 37 E
Thap Than	100	15 27N	99 54 E
Thar (Great Indian) Desert	94	28 25N	72 0 E
Tharad	94	24 30N	71 30 E
Thargomindah	139	27 58 S	143 46 E
Tharrawaddy	98	17 38N	95 48 E
Tharrawaw	98	17 41N	95 28 E
Tharthār, Bahr ath	92	34 0N	43 0 E
Thasopoúla, I.	68	40 49N	24 45 E
Thásos	68	40 50N	24 50 E
Thásos, I.	68	40 40N	24 40 E
That Khe	100	22 16N	106 28 E
Thatcham	28	51 24N	1 17W
Thatcher, Ariz., U.S.A.	161	32 54N	109 46W
Thatcher, Colo., U.S.A.	161	37 38N	104 6W
Thaton	98	16 55N	97 22 E
Thau, Étang de	44	43 23N	3 36 E
Thaungdut	98	24 30N	94 40 E
Thaxted	29	51 57N	0 20 E
Thayer	159	36 34N	91 34W
Thayetmyo	98	19 20N	95 18 E
Thayngen	51	47 49N	8 43 E
Thazi	99	21 0N	96 5 E
The Alberga, R.	139	27 6 S	135 33 E
The Bight	167	24 19N	75 24W
The Corrong	139	36 0 S	139 30 E
The Dalles	160	45 40N	121 11W
The Diamantina	139	26 45 S	139 30 E
The English Company's Is.	138	11 50 S	136 32 E
The Entrance	141	33 21 S	151 30 E
The Four Archers	138	15 31 S	135 22 E
The Frome, R.	139	29 8 S	137 54 E
The Granites	136	20 35 S	130 21 E
The Great Divide	141	35 0 S	149 17 E
The Grenadines, Is.	167	12 30N	61 30W
The Hague (s'Gravenhage)	47	52 7N	7 14 E
The Hamilton, R.	139	26 40 S	135 19 E
The Johnston Lakes	137	32 25 S	120 30 E
The Lake	167	21 5N	73 34W
The Loup	38	54 42N	6 32W
The Macumba, R.	139	27 52 S	137 12 E
The Neales, R.	139	28 8 S	136 47 E
The Oaks	141	34 3 S	150 34 E
The Officer, R.	137	27 46 S	129 46 E
The Pas	153	53 45N	101 15W
The Range	127	19 2 S	31 2 E
The Rock	141	35 15 S	147 2 E
The Salt Lake	139	30 6 S	142 8 E
The Stevenson, R.	139	27 6 S	135 33 E
The Thumbs, Mts.	143	43 35 S	170 40 E
The Warburton, R.	139	28 4 S	137 28 E
Theale	28	51 26N	1 5W
Thebes	122	25 40N	32 35 E
Thedford	158	41 59N	100 31W
Theebine	139	25 57 S	152 34 E
Thekulthili L.	153	61 3N	110 0W
Thelma, oilfield	19	58 25N	1 18 E
Thelon, R.	153	62 35N	104 3W
Thénezay	42	46 44N	0 2W
Thenon	44	45 9N	1 4 E
Theodore	138	24 55 S	150 3 E
Thepha	101	6 52N	100 58 E
Thérain, R.	43	49 15N	2 27 E
Thermaïkos Kólpos	68	40 15N	22 45 E
Thermopilai P.	69	38 48N	22 45 E
Thermopolis	160	43 14N	108 10W
Thesprotía □	68	39 27N	20 22 E
Thessalía □	68	39 30N	22 0 E
Thessalon	150	46 20N	83 30W
Thessaloníki	68	40 38N	23 0 E
Thessaloníki □	68	40 45N	23 0 E
Thessaly = Thessalía	68	39 30N	22 0 E
Thetford	29	52 25N	0 44 E
Thetford Mines	151	46 8N	71 18W
Theun, R.	100	18 19N	104 0 E
Theunissen	128	28 26 S	26 43 E
Theux	47	50 32N	5 49 E
Thevenard	139	32 9 S	133 38 E
Thiámis, R.	68	39 34N	20 18 E
Thiberville	42	49 8N	0 27 E
Thicket Portage	153	55 19N	97 42W
Thief River Falls	159	48 15N	96 10W
Thiel	120	14 55N	15 5W
Thiene	63	45 42N	11 29 E
Thierache	43	49 51N	3 45 E
Thiers	44	45 52N	3 33 E
Thies	120	14 50N	16 51W
Thiet	123	7 37N	28 49 E
Thika	126	1 1 S	37 5 E
Thika □	126	1 1 S	37 5 E
Thille-Boubacar	120	16 31N	15 5W
Thillot, Le	43	47 53N	6 46 E
Thimphu (Tashi Chho Dzong)	98	27 31N	89 45 E
Þingvallavatn	74	64 11N	21 9W
Thionville	43	49 20N	6 10 E
Thirá	69	36 23N	25 27 E
Thirasiá, I.	69	36 26N	25 21 E
Thirlmere, L.	32	54 32N	3 4W
Thirsk	33	54 15N	1 20W
Thisted	75	56 58N	8 40 E
Thistle I.	140	35 0 S	136 8 E
Thistle, oilfield	19	61 20N	1 35 E
Thitgy	98	18 15N	96 13 E
Thitpokpin	98	19 24N	96 1 E
Thiu Khao Phetchabun	101	16 20N	100 55 E
Thívai	69	38 19N	23 19 E
Thiviers	44	45 25N	0 54 E
Thizy	45	46 2N	4 18 E
Þjorsa	74	63 47N	20 48W
Thlewiaza, R., Man., Can.	153	59 43N	100 5W
Thlewiaza, R., N.W.T., Can.	153	60 29N	94 40W
Thmar Puok	100	13 57N	103 4 E
Tho Vinh	100	19 16N	105 42 E
Thoa, R.	153	60 31N	109 47W
Thoen	100	17 36N	99 12 E
Thoeng	100	19 41N	100 12 E
Thoissey	45	46 12N	4 48 E
Tholdi	95	35 5N	76 6 E
Tholen	47	51 32N	4 13 E
Thomas, Okla., U.S.A.	159	35 48N	98 48W
Thomas, W. Va., U.S.A.	156	39 10N	79 30W
Thomas, L.	139	26 4 S	137 58 E
Thomas Street	38	53 27N	8 15W
Thomastown	39	52 32N	7 10W
Thomasville, Ala., U.S.A.	157	31 55N	87 42W
Thomasville, Fla., U.S.A.	157	30 50N	84 0W
Thomasville, N.C., U.S.A.	157	35 5N	80 4W
Thommen	47	50 14N	6 5 E
Thompson, Can.	153	55 45N	97 52W
Thompson, U.S.A.	162	41 52N	75 31W
Thompson Falls	160	47 37N	115 26W
Thompson Landing	153	62 56N	110 40W
Thompson, R., Can.	152	50 15N	121 24W
Thompson, R., U.S.A.	158	39 46N	93 37W
Thompsons	161	39 0N	109 50W
Thompsonville	162	42 0N	72 37W
Thomson, R.	138	25 11 S	142 53 E
Thomson's Falls = Nyahururu Falls	126	0 2N	36 27 E
Thon Buri	100	13 43N	100 29 E
Thonburi	101	13 50N	100 36 E
Thônes	45	45 54N	6 18 E
Thongwa	98	16 45N	96 33 E
Thonon-les-Bains	45	46 22N	6 29 E
Thonze	98	17 38N	95 47 E
Thorez	83	48 4N	38 34 E
Þorlákshöfn	74	63 51N	21 22W
Thornaby on Tees	33	54 36N	1 19W
Thornborough	138	16 54 S	145 2 E
Thornbury, N.Z.	143	46 17 S	168 9 E
Thornbury, U.K.	28	51 36N	2 31W
Thorndon	29	52 16N	1 8 E
Thorne, U.K.	33	53 36N	0 56W
Thorne, U.S.A.	163	38 36N	118 34W
Thorne Glacier	13	87 30N	150 0 E
Thorney	29	52 37N	0 8W
Thornham	29	52 59N	0 35 E
Thornhill	35	55 15N	3 46W
Thornthwaite	32	54 36N	3 13W
Thornton-Beresfield	141	32 50 S	151 40 E
Thornton Celveleys	32	53 52N	3 1W
Thornton Dale	33	54 14N	0 41W
Thorpe	29	52 38N	1 20 E
Thorpe le Soken	29	51 50N	1 11 E
Thouarcé	43	47 17N	0 30W
Thouin, C.	136	20 20 S	118 10 E
Thousand Oakes	163	34 10N	118 50W
Thrace = Thráki	68	41 10N	25 30 E
Thráki	68	41 9N	25 30 E
Thrakikón Pélagos	68	40 30N	25 0 E
Thrapston	29	52 24N	0 32W
Three Bridges	29	51 7N	0 9W
Three Forks	160	45 5N	111 40W
Three Hills	152	51 43N	113 15W
Three Hummock I.	138	40 25 S	144 55 E
Three Kings Is.	142	34 10 S	172 10 E
Three Lakes	158	45 41N	89 10W
Three Pagodas P.	100	15 16N	98 23 E
Three Points, C.	120	4 42N	2 6W
Three Rivers, Austral.	137	25 10 S	119 5 E
Three Rivers, Calif., U.S.A.	163	36 26N	118 54W
Three Rivers, Tex., U.S.A.	159	28 30N	98 10W
Three Sisters, Mt.	160	44 10N	121 52W
Threlkeld	32	54 37N	3 2W
Threshfield	32	54 5N	2 2W
Þórisvatn	74	64 50N	19 26W
Throssell, L.	137	27 27 S	124 16 E
Throssell Ra.	136	17 24 S	126 4 E
Þórshöfn	74	66 12N	15 20W
Thrumster	37	58 24N	3 8W
Thuan Moa	101	8 58N	105 30 E
Thubun Lakes	153	61 30N	112 0W
Thueyts	45	44 41N	4 9 E
Thuillies	47	50 18N	4 20 E
Thuin	47	50 20N	4 17 E
Thuir	44	42 38N	2 45 E
Thule	12	77 30N	69 0W
Thun	50	46 45N	7 38 E
Thundelarra	137	28 53 S	117 7 E
Thunder B.	156	45 0N	83 20W
Thunder Bay	150	48 20N	89 0W
Thunder River	152	52 13N	119 20W
Thundulda	137	32 15 S	126 3 E
Thunersee	50	46 43N	7 39 E
Thung Song	101	8 10N	99 40 E
Thunkar	98	27 55N	91 0 E
Thuong Tra	100	16 2N	107 42 E
Thur, R.	51	47 32N	9 10 E
Thurgau □	51	47 34N	9 10 E
Thüringer Wald	48	50 35N	11 0 E
Thurlby	29	52 45N	0 21W
Thurles	39	52 40N	7 53W
Thurloo Downs	139	29 15 S	143 30 E
Thurmaston	28	52 40N	1 8W
Thurmont	162	39 37N	77 25W
Thurn P.	49	47 20N	12 15 E
Thursby	32	54 40N	3 3W
Thursday I.	138	10 30 S	142 3 E
Thurso, Can.	150	45 36N	75 15W
Thurso, U.K.	37	58 34N	3 31W
Thurso, R.	37	58 36N	3 30W
Thurston I.	13	72 0 S	100 0W
Thury-Harcourt	42	49 0N	0 30W
Thusis	51	46 42N	9 26 E
Thutade L.	152	57 0N	126 55W
Thuy, Le	100	17 14N	106 49 E
Thylungra	139	26 4 S	143 28 E
Thyolo	127	16 7 S	35 5 E
Thysville = Mbanza Ngungu	124	5 12 S	14 53 E
Ti-n-Amzi, O.	121	17 35N	4 20 E
Ti-n-Barraouene, O.	121	18 40N	4 5 E
Ti-n-Emensan	118	22 59N	4 45 E
Ti-n-Geloulet	118	25 58N	4 2 E
Ti-n-Medjerdam, O.	118	25 45N	1 30W
Ti-n-Tarabine, O.	119	21 37N	7 11 E
Ti-n-Zaouatène	118	48 55 S	77 9W
Tia	141	31 10 S	151 50 E
Tiahualilo	164	26 20N	103 30W
Tianguá	170	3 44 S	40 59W
Tiankoura	120	10 47N	3 17W
Tiaret (Tagdent)	118	35 28N	1 21 E
Tiarra	141	32 46 S	145 1 E
Tiassalé	120	5 58N	4 57W
Tibagi	173	24 30 S	50 24W
Tibagi, R.	173	22 47 S	51 1W
Tibari	123	5 2N	31 48 E
Tibati	121	6 22N	12 30 E
Tiber = Tevere, R.	63	42 30N	12 20 E
Tiber Res.	160	48 20N	111 15W
Tiberias	90	32 47N	35 32 E
Tiberias, L. = Kinneret, Yam	90	32 49N	35 36 E
Tibesti	119	21 0N	17 30 E
Tibet	99	32 30N	86 0 E
Tibet □	105	32 30N	86 0 E
Tibiri	121	13 34N	7 4 E
Tibleş, mt.	70	47 32N	24 15 E
Tibleş, Mţii	70	47 41N	24 6 E
Tibnīn	90	33 12N	35 24 E
Tibooburra	139	29 26 S	142 1 E
Tibro	73	58 28N	14 10 E
Tibugá, Golfo de	174	5 45N	77 20W
Tiburón, I.	164	29 0N	112 30W
Ticehurst	29	51 2N	0 23 E
Tichit	120	18 35N	9 20W
Ticino □	51	46 20N	8 45 E
Ticino, R.	62	45 23N	8 47 E
Tickhill	33	53 25N	1 8W
Ticonderoga	162	43 50N	73 28W
Ticul	165	20 20N	89 50W
Tidaholm	73	58 12N	13 55 E
Tiddim	98	23 20N	93 45 E
Tideridjaouine, Adrar	118	23 0N	2 15 E
Tideswell	33	53 17N	1 46W
Tidikelt	118	26 58N	1 30 E
Tidjikdja	120	18 4N	11 35W
Tidore	103	0 40N	127 25 E
Tidra, I.	120	19 45N	16 20W
Tiébélé	121	11 6N	0 59W
Tiébissou	120	7 9N	5 18W
Tiéboro	119	21 20N	17 7 E
Tiefencastel	51	46 40N	9 33 E
Tiego	120	12 6N	2 38 E
T'iehling	107	42 17N	123 50 E
Tiel	46	51 53N	5 26 E
Tielt	47	51 0N	3 20 E
Tien Shan	85	42 0N	80 0 E
Tien Yen	100	21 20N	107 24 E
T'ienchang	107	32 41N	118 59 E
T'ienchen	106	40 30N	114 6 E
Tiench'eng	109	21 31N	111 18 E
T'ienching	107	39 10N	117 15 E
T'ienchu	108	26 55N	109 12 E
T'ienchüan	108	30 4N	102 50 E
T'ienchuangt'ai	107	40 49N	122 6 E
Tienen	47	50 48N	4 57 E
T'ienho	108	24 47N	108 42 E
T'ienhsi	108	24 26N	106 5 E
Tiénigbé	120	8 11N	5 43W
Tienkianghsien	69	30 25N	107 30 E
T'ienlin	108	24 19N	106 15 E
T'ienmen	109	30 37N	113 10 E
T'ieno	108	25 9N	106 57 E
Tienpai	109	21 30N	111 1 E
T'ienshui	105	34 35N	105 15 E
T'ient'ai	109	29 9N	121 2 E
Tientsin = T'ienching	105	39 10N	117 15 E
T'ientung	108	23 39N	107 8 E
T'ienyang	108	23 43N	106 44 E
Tierp	72	60 20N	17 30 E
Tierra Alta	174	8 11N	76 4W
Tierra Amarilla	172	27 28 S	70 18W
Tierra Colorada	165	17 10N	99 35W
Tierra de Barros	57	38 40N	6 30W
Tierra de Campos	56	42 10N	4 50W
Tierra del Fuego, I. Gr. de	176	54 0 S	69 0W
Tiétar, R.	56	39 55N	5 50W
Tieté, R.	171	20 40 S	51 35W
Tieyon	139	26 12 S	133 52 E
Tiffin	156	41 8N	83 10W
Tifi	123	6 12N	36 55 E
Tiflèt	118	33 54N	6 20W
Tiflis = Tbilisi	83	41 50N	44 50 E
Tifrah	90	31 19N	34 42 E
Tifton	157	31 28N	83 32W
Tifu	103	3 39 S	126 18 E
Tigalda I.	147	54 9N	165 0W
Tighnabruaich	34	55 55N	5 13W
Tigil	77	58 0N	158 10 E
Tignish	151	46 58N	64 2W
Tigre □	123	13 35N	39 15 E
Tigre, R.	174	3 30 S	74 58W
Tigu	99	29 48N	91 38 E
Tiguentourine	119	28 8N	8 58 E
Tiguila	121	14 44N	1 50W
Tigveni	70	45 10N	24 31 E
Tigyaing	98	23 45N	96 10 E
Tîh, Gebel el	122	29 32N	33 26 E
Tihodaine, Dunes de	119	25 15N	7 15 E
Tijī	119	32 0N	11 18 E
Tijiamis	103	7 16 S	108 29 E
Tijibadok	103	6 53 S	106 47 E

Tijirit, O Tolox

Tijirit, O. 120 19 30N 6 15W
Tijuana 164 32 30N 117 3W
Tikal 166 17 2N 89 35W
Tikamgarh 95 24 44N 78 57E
Tikan 138 5 58S 149 2E
Tikhoretsk 83 45 56N 40 5E
Tikhvin 80 59 35N 33 30E
Tikkadouine, Adrar 118 24 28N 1 30E
Tiko 121 4 4N 9 20E
Tikrit 92 34 35N 43 37E
Tiksi 77 71 50N 129 0E
Tilamuta 103 0 40N 122 15E
Tilburg 47 51 31N 5 6E
Tilbury, Can. 150 42 17N 84 23W
Tilbury, U.K. 29 51 27N 0 24E
Tilcara 172 23 30S 65 23W
Tilden 158 42 3N 97 45W
Tilemsès 121 15 37N 4 44E
Tilemsi, Vallée du 121 17 42N 0 15E
Tilghman 162 38 42N 76 20W
Tilhar 95 28 0N 79 45E
Tilia, O. 118 27 32N 0 55E
Tilichiki 77 61 0N 166 5E
Tiligul, R. 82 47 35N 30 30E
Tililane 118 27 49N 0 6W
Tilin 98 21 41N 94 6E
Tílissos 69 38 15N 25 0E
Till, R. 35 55 35N 2 3W
Tillabéri 121 14 7N 1 28E
Tillamook 160 45 29N 123 55W
Tillberga 72 59 42N 16 39E
Tilley 152 50 28N 111 38W
Tillia 121 16 8N 4 47E
Tillicoultry 35 56 9N 3 44W
Tillsonburg 150 42 53N 80 44W
Tilmanstone 29 51 13N 1 18E
Tílos, I. 69 36 27N 27 27E
Tilpa 139 30 57S 144 24E
Tilrhemt 118 33 9N 3 22E
Tilsit = Sovetsk 80 55 6N 21 50E
Tilt, R. 37 56 50N 3 50W
Tilton 162 43 25N 71 36W
Timahoe 39 52 59N 7 12W
Timanskiy Kryazh 78 65 58N 50 5E
Timaru 143 44 23S 171 14E
Timashevo 84 53 22N 51 9E
Timashevsk 83 45 35N 39 0E
Timau 126 0 4N 37 15E
Timbákion 69 35 4N 24 45E
Timbaúba 170 7 31S 35 19W
Timbédra 120 16 17N 8 16W
Timber L. 158 45 29N 101 0W
Timber Mtn. 163 37 6N 116 28W
Timbío 174 2 20N 76 40W
Timbiqui 174 2 46N 77 42W
Timboon 140 38 30S 142 58E
Timbuktu = Tombouctou 120 16 50N 3 0W
Timdjaouine 118 21 47N 4 30E
Timétrine Montagnes 121 19 25N 1 0W
Timfi Óros 68 39 59N 20 45E
Timfristós, Óros 69 38 57N 21 50E
Timhadite 118 33 15N 5 4W
Timimoun 118 29 14N 0 16E
Timimoun, Sebkha de 118 28 50N 0 46E
Timiris, C. 120 19 15N 16 30W
Timiş □ 66 45 40N 21 30E
Timiş, R. 70 45 30N 21 0E
Timişoara 66 45 43N 21 15E
Timmins 150 48 28N 81 25W
Timmoudi 118 29 20N 1 8W
Timok, R. 66 44 10N 22 40E
Timoleague 39 51 40N 8 51W
Timolin 39 52 59N 6 49W
Timon 170 5 8S 42 52W
Timor □ 103 8 0S 126 30E
Timor, I. 103 9 0S 125 0E
Timor Sea 136 10 0S 127 0E
Timur □ 103 9 0S 125 0E
Tin Alkoum 119 24 30N 10 17E
Tin Gornai 121 16 38N 0 38W
Tin Mtn. 163 36 54N 117 28W
Tîna, Khalîg el 122 31 20N 32 42E
Tinaca Pt. 103 5 30N 125 25E
Tinaco 174 9 42N 68 26W
Tinafak, O. 119 27 10N 7 0W
Tinahely 39 52 48N 6 28W
Tinambacan 103 12 5N 124 32E
Tinapagee 139 29 25S 144 15E
Tinaquillo 174 9 55N 68 18W
Tinaroo Falls 138 17 5S 145 4E
Tinca 70 46 46N 21 58E
Tinchebray 42 48 47N 0 45W
Tindivanam 97 12 15N 79 35E
Tindouf 118 27 50N 8 4W
Tindzhe Dzong 95 28 20N 88 8E
Tineo 56 43 21N 6 27W
Tinerhir 118 31 29N 5 31W
Tinfouchi 118 28 58N 5 54W
T'ing Chiang, R. 109 24 24N 116 35E
Tingan 100 19 42N 110 18E
Tingch'u, R. 108 28 20N 99 12E
Tingewick 28 51 59N 1 4W
Tinggi, Pulau, Is. 101 2 18N 104 7E
Tinghai 109 30 0N 122 10E
Tinghsi 106 35 33N 104 32E
Tinghsiang 106 38 32N 112 59E
Tinghsien 106 38 30N 115 0E
Tingkawk Sakun 98 26 4N 96 44E
Tingk'ouchen 106 39 48N 106 36E
Tinglev 73 54 57N 9 13E
Tingnan 109 24 47N 115 2E
Tingo María 174 9 10S 76 0W
Tingpien 106 37 36N 107 38E
Tingshan 109 31 16N 119 51E
Tingsryd 73 56 31N 15 0E
Tingt'ao 106 35 4N 115 34E
Tingvalla 73 58 47N 12 2E
Tingyüan 109 32 32N 117 41E
Tinh Bien 101 10 36N 104 57E
Tinharé, I. de 171 13 30S 38 58W
Tinié 121 14 17N 1 30W
Tinioulig, Sebkra 118 22 30N 6 45W
Tinjoub 118 29 45N 5 40W
Tinkurrin 137 32 59S 117 46E
Tinnia 172 27 0S 62 45W
Tinnoset 71 59 45N 9 3E
Tinnsjø 71 59 55N 8 54E
Tinogasta 172 28 0S 67 40W
Tínos 69 37 33N 25 8E
Tiñoso, C. 59 37 32N 1 6W
Tinsukia 98 27 29N 95 26E
Tintagel 30 50 40N 4 45W
Tintagel Hd. 30 50 40N 4 46W
Tintern 31 51 42N 2 41W
Tintern Abbey 39 52 14N 6 50W
Tintigny 47 49 41N 5 31E
Tintina 172 27 2S 62 45W
Tintinara 140 35 48S 140 2E
Tinto, R. 57 37 30N 5 33W
Tinui 142 40 52S 176 5E
Tinwald 143 43 55S 171 43E
Tioga 162 41 54N 77 9W
Tioman, I. 101 2 50N 104 10E
Tioman, Pulau, Is. 101 2 50N 104 10E
Tionaga 150 48 0N 82 0W
Tione di Trento 62 46 3N 10 44E
Tior 123 6 26N 31 11E
Tioulilin 118 27 1N 0 2W
Tipongpani 99 27 20N 95 55E
Tipperary 39 52 28N 8 10W
Tipperary □ 39 52 37N 7 55W
Tipton, U.K. 28 52 32N 2 4W
Tipton, Calif., U.S.A. 163 36 3N 119 19W
Tipton, Ind., U.S.A. 156 40 17N 86 30W
Tipton, Iowa, U.S.A. 158 41 45N 91 12W
Tiptonville 159 36 22N 89 30W
Tiptree 29 51 48N 0 46E
Tiptur 97 13 15N 76 26E
Tira 90 32 14N 34 56E
Tiracambu, Serra do 170 3 15S 46 30W
Tirahart, O. 118 23 55N 2 0W
Tiran 93 32 45N 51 0E
Tirân 122 27 56N 34 35E
Tirana 68 41 18N 19 49E
Tirana-Durrësi □ 68 41 35N 20 0E
Tirano 62 46 13N 10 11E
Tirarer, Mont 121 19 35N 1 10W
Tiraspol 82 46 55N 29 35E
Tirat Carmel 90 32 46N 34 58E
Tirat Tsevi 90 32 26N 35 31E
Tirat Yehuda 90 32 1N 34 56E
Tiratimine 118 25 56N 3 37E
Tirdout 121 16 7N 1 5W
Tire 92 38 5N 27 50E
Tirebolu 92 40 58N 38 45E
Tiree, I. 34 56 31N 6 55W
Tiree, Passage of 34 56 30N 6 30W
Tîrgoviste 70 44 55N 25 27E
Tîrgu Frumos 70 47 12N 27 2E
Tîrgu-Jiu 70 45 5N 23 19E
Tîrgu Mureş 70 46 31N 24 38E
Tîrgu Neamţ 70 47 12N 26 25E
Tîrgu Ocna 70 46 16N 26 39E
Tîrgu Secuiesc 70 46 0N 26 10E
Tirich Mir Mt. 93 36 15N 71 35E
Tiriola 65 38 57N 16 32E
Tiririca, Serra da 171 17 6S 47 6W
Tirlyanskiy 84 54 14N 58 35E
Tirna, R. 96 18 5N 76 30E
Tîrnava = Botoroaga 70 44 8N 25 32E
Tîrnava Mare, R. 70 46 15N 24 30E
Tîrnava Mica, R. 70 46 17N 24 30E
Tírnavos 68 39 45N 22 18E
Tîrnova 70 45 23N 22 1E
Tîrnŭveni 70 46 19N 24 13E
Tirodi 96 21 35N 79 35E
Tirol □ 52 47 3N 10 43E
Tiros 171 19 0S 45 58W
Tirschenreuth 49 49 51N 12 20E
Tirso, L. 64 40 8N 8 56E
Tirso, R. 64 40 33N 9 12E
Tirstrup 73 56 18N 10 42E
Tirua 142 38 25S 174 40E
Tiruchchirappalli 97 10 45N 78 45E
Tiruchendur 97 8 30N 78 11E
Tiruchengodu 97 11 23N 77 56E
Tirumangalam 97 9 49N 77 58E
Tirunelveli (Tinnevelly) 97 8 45N 77 45E
Tirupati 97 13 45N 79 30E
Tiruppattur 97 12 30N 78 30E
Tiruppur 97 11 12N 77 22E
Tiruturaipundi 97 10 32N 79 41E
Tiruvadaimarudur 97 11 2N 79 27E
Tiruvallar 97 13 9N 79 57E
Tiruvannamalai 97 12 10N 79 12E
Tiruvarur (Negapatam) 97 10 46N 79 38E
Tiruvatipuram 97 12 39N 79 33E
Tiruvottiyur 97 13 10N 80 22E
Tisa, R. 66 45 30N 20 20E
Tisdale 153 52 50N 104 0W
Tiseirhatène, Mares de 118 22 51N 9 30W
Tishomingo 159 34 14N 96 38W
Tisjön 72 60 56N 13 0E
Tisnaren 72 58 58N 15 56E
Tisno 63 44 45N 15 41E
Tišnov 53 49 21N 16 25E
Tisovec 53 48 41N 19 56E
Tissemsilt 118 35 35N 1 50E
Tissit, O. 119 27 28N 9 58W
Tissø 73 55 35N 11 18E
Tista, R. 98 25 23N 89 43E
Tisted 73 56 58N 8 40E
Tisza, R. 53 47 38N 20 44E
Tiszaföldvár 53 47 0N 20 14E
Tiszafüred 53 47 38N 20 50E
Tiszalök 53 48 0N 21 10E
Tiszavasvári 53 47 58N 21 18E
Tit, Alg. 118 27 0N 1 37E
Tit, Alg. 119 23 0N 5 10E
Tit-Ary 77 71 50N 126 30E
Titaguas 58 39 53N 1 6W
Titahi Bay 142 41 6S 174 50E
Titai Damer 123 16 43N 37 25E
Titchfield 28 50 51N 1 13W
Titel 66 45 29N 20 18E
Tithwal 95 34 21N 73 50E
Titicaca, L. 174 15 30S 69 30W
Titilagarh 96 20 15N 83 5E
Tititira Head 98 43 38S 169 26E
Titiwa 121 12 14N 12 53E
Titlis 51 46 46N 8 27E
Titograd 66 42 30N 19 19E
Titov Veles 66 41 46N 21 47E
Titova Korenica 63 44 45N 15 41E
Titovo Uzice 66 43 55N 19 50E
Titule 126 3 15N 25 31E
Titumate 174 8 19N 77 5W
Titusville 156 41 35N 79 39W
Tiumpan Hd. 36 58 15N 6 10W
Tivaouane 120 14 56N 16 45W
Tivat 66 42 28N 18 43E
Tiveden 73 58 50N 14 30E
Tiverton 30 50 54N 3 30W
Tívoli 63 41 58N 12 45E
Tiwi 93 22 45N 59 12E
Tiyo 123 14 41N 40 57E
Tizga 118 32 1N 5 9W
Tizi n'Isly 118 32 28N 5 47W
Tizi Ouzou 119 36 42N 4 3E
Tizmín 165 21 0N 88 1W
Tiznados, R. 174 8 50N 67 50W
Tiznit 118 29 48N 9 45W
Tjalang 103 4 30N 95 43E
Tjangkuang, Tg. 102 7 0S 105 0E
Tjareme, G. 103 6 55S 108 27E
Tjeggelvas 74 66 37N 17 45E
Tjepu 103 7 12S 111 31E
Tjeukemeer 46 52 53N 5 48E
Tjiandjur 103 6 51S 107 7E
Tjibatu 103 7 8S 107 59E
Tjikadjang 103 7 25S 107 48E
Tjimahi 103 6 53S 107 33E
Tjirebon = Cirebon 103 6 45S 108 32E
Tjöllong 71 59 6N 10 3E
Tjöme 71 59 8N 10 26E
Tjonger Kanaal 46 52 52N 6 52E
Tjörn 73 58 0N 11 35E
Tjörnes 74 66 12N 17 9W
Tjuls 73 57 30N 18 15E
Tjurup 102 4 26S 102 13E
Tkibuli 83 42 26N 43 0E
Tkvarcheli 83 42 47N 41 52E
Tlacolula 165 16 57N 96 29W
Tlacotalpán 165 18 37N 95 40W
Tlaquepaque 164 20 39N 103 19W
Tlaxcala 165 19 20N 98 14W
Tlaxcala □ 165 19 30N 98 20W
Tlaxiaco 165 17 10N 97 40W
Tlell 152 53 34N 131 56W
Tlemcen 118 34 52N 1 15W
Tleta di Sidi Bouguedra 118 32 16N 8 58W
Tleta Sidi Bouguedra 118 32 16N 9 59W
Tlumach 80 48 46N 25 0E
Tłuszcz 54 52 25N 21 25E
Tlyarata 83 42 9N 46 26E
Tmassah 119 26 19N 15 51E
Tmisan 119 27 23N 13 30E
To Bong 100 12 45N 109 16E
T'o Chiang, R. 108 28 56N 105 33E
To-Shima 111 34 31N 139 17E
Toad, R. 152 59 25N 124 57W
Toay 172 36 50S 64 30W
Toba 111 34 30N 136 45E
Toba Kakar 94 31 30N 69 0E
Toba, L. 102 2 40N 98 50E
Toba Tek Singh 94 30 55N 72 25E
Tobago, I. 167 11 10N 60 30W
Tobarra 59 38 35N 1 41W
Tobelo 103 1 25N 127 56E
Tobercurry 38 54 3N 8 43W
Tobermore 38 54 49N 6 43W
Tobermorey 138 22 12S 138 0E
Tobermory, Can. 150 45 12N 81 40W
Tobermory, U.K. 34 56 37N 6 4W
Tobin, L. 136 21 45S 125 49E
Tobin L. 153 53 35N 103 30W
Toboali 102 3 0S 106 25E
Tobol 84 52 40N 62 39E
Tobol, R. 84 58 10N 68 12E
Toboli 103 0 38S 120 12E
Tobolsk 84 58 0N 68 10E
Tobruk = Tubruq 117 32 7N 23 55E
Tobyhanna 162 41 10N 75 15W
Tocantínia 170 9 33S 48 22W
Tocantinópolis 170 6 20S 47 25W
Tocantins, R. 170 14 30S 49 0W
Tocca 157 34 6N 83 17W
Toce, R. 62 46 5N 8 29E
Tochigi 111 36 25N 139 45E
Tochigi-ken □ 111 36 45N 139 45E
Tocina 57 37 37N 5 44W
Toconao 172 34 35N 83 19W
Toconhão, Serra do 171 14 30S 47 46W
Tocópero 174 11 30N 69 16W
Tocopilla 172 22 5S 70 10W
Tocumwal 141 35 45S 145 31E
Tocuyo, R. 174 10 50N 69 0W
Todd, R. 138 24 52S 135 48E
Toddington 29 51 57N 0 31W
Todeli 103 1 38S 124 34E
Todenyang 126 4 35N 35 56E
Todi 63 42 47N 12 24E
Tödi 51 46 48N 8 55E
Todjo 103 1 20S 121 15E
Todmorden 32 53 43N 2 7W
Todos os Santos, Baía de 171 12 48S 38 38W
Todos Santos 164 23 27N 110 13W
Todos Santos, Bahia de 164 31 48N 116 42W
Todtnau 49 47 50N 7 56E
Toe Hd., Ireland 39 51 29N 9 13W
Toe Hd., U.K. 36 57 50N 7 10W
Toecé 121 11 50N 1 16W
Toetoes B. 143 46 42S 168 41E
Tofield 152 53 25N 112 40W
Tofino 152 49 11N 125 55W
Töfsingdalems National Park 72 62 15N 12 44E
Tofta 73 57 11N 12 20E
Toftlund 73 55 11N 9 2E
Tōgane 111 35 33N 140 22E
Togba 120 17 26N 10 25W
Toggenburg 51 47 16N 9 9E
Togian, Kepulauan 103 0 20S 121 50E
Togliatti 81 53 37N 49 18E
Togo ■ 121 6 15N 1 35E
Toguzak, R. 84 54 3N 62 44E
Tōhoku □ 112 39 50N 141 45E
Toi 111 34 54N 134 47E
Toinya 123 6 17N 29 46E
Toiyabe Dome 163 38 51N 117 22W
Toiyabe, Ra. 163 39 10N 117 10W
Tōjō 110 34 53N 133 16E
Tok, R. 84 52 46N 52 22E
Tokaanu 142 38 58S 175 46E
Tokachi, R. 112 42 44N 143 42E
Tokaj 53 48 8N 21 27E
Tokala, G. 103 1 30S 121 40E
Tokanui 143 46 34S 168 56E
Tokarahi 143 44 56S 170 39E
Tokat 92 40 22N 36 35E
Tŏkchŏn 107 39 45N 126 18E
Tokelau Is. 130 9 0S 172 0W
Toki 111 35 18N 137 8E
Tokmak, Kirgizia, U.S.S.R. 84 42 55N 75 45E
Tokmak, Ukraine, U.S.S.R. 82 47 16N 35 42E
Toko Ra. 138 23 5S 138 20E
Tokomaru Bay 142 38 8S 178 22E
Tokombere 121 11 18N 3 30E
Tókomlós 53 46 24N 20 45E
Tokoname 111 34 53N 136 51E
Tokong 101 5 27N 100 23E
Tokoroa 142 38 20S 175 50E
Tokorozawa 111 35 47N 139 28E
T'ok'ot'o 106 40 15N 111 12E
Toktogul 85 41 50N 72 50E
Tokuii 110 34 11N 131 42E
Tokule 123 14 54N 38 26E
Tokunoshima 112 27 56N 128 55E
Tokushima 110 34 4N 134 34E
Tokushima-ken □ 110 35 50N 134 30E
Tokuyama 110 34 0N 131 50E
Tōkyō 111 35 45N 139 45E
Tōkyō-to □ 111 35 40N 139 30E
Tōkyō-Wan 111 35 25N 139 47E
Tolaerh 105 35 8N 81 33E
Tolaga Bay 142 38 21S 178 20E
Tolageak 147 70 2N 162 50W
Tolbukhin 67 43 37N 27 49E
Toledo, Spain 56 39 50N 4 2W
Toledo, Ohio, U.S.A. 156 41 37N 83 33W
Toledo, Oreg., U.S.A. 160 44 40N 123 59W
Toledo, Wash., U.S.A. 160 42 29N 122 58W
Toledo, Montes de 57 39 33N 4 20W
Tolentino 63 43 12N 13 17E
Tolfino 152 49 6N 125 54W
Tolga, Alg. 119 34 46N 5 22E
Tolga, Norway 71 62 26N 11 1E
Tolima □ 174 3 45N 75 15W
Tolima, Vol. 174 4 40N 75 19W
Tolitoli 103 1 5N 120 50E
Tolkamer 46 51 52N 6 6E
Tolkmicko 54 54 19N 19 31E
Tollarp 73 55 55N 13 58E
Tollesbury 29 51 46N 0 51E
Tolleson 161 33 29N 112 10W
Tollhouse 163 37 1N 119 24W
Tolmachevo 80 58 56N 29 57E
Tolmezzo 63 46 23N 13 0E
Tolmino 63 46 11N 13 45E
Tolna 53 46 25N 18 48E
Tolna □ 53 46 30N 18 30E
Tolne 73 57 28N 10 20E
Tolo 124 2 50S 18 40E
Tolo, Teluk 103 2 20S 122 10E
Tolokiwa I. 138 5 30S 147 30E
Tolon 121 9 26N 1 3W
Tolosa 58 43 8N 2 5W
Tolox 57 36 41N 4 54W

Tolsta Hd **Tregnago**

Tolsta Hd. **36** 58 20N 6 10W
Toluca **165** 19 20N 99 50W
Tolun **106** 42 22N 116 30 E
Tom Burke **129** 23 5 S 28 4 E
Tomahawk **158** 45 28N 89 40W
Tomakomai **112** 42 38N 141 36 E
Tomales **163** 38 15N 122 53W
Tomales B. **163** 38 15N 123 58W
Tomar **57** 39 36N 8 25W
Tómaros Óros **68** 39 29N 20 48 E
Tomaszów Lubelski **54** 50 29N 23 23 E
Tomaszów Mazowiecki **54** 51 30N 19 57 E
Tomatin **37** 57 20N 4 0W
Tomatlán **164** 19 56N 105 15W
Tombé **123** 5 53N 31 40 E
Tombigbee, R. **157** 32 0N 88 6W
Tombodor, Serra do **171** 12 0 S 41 30W
Tombouctou **120** 16 50N 3 0W
Tombstone **161** 31 40N 110 4W
Tomdoun **36** 57 4N 5 2W
Tomé **172** 36 36 S 73 6W
Tomé-Açu **170** 2 25 S 48 9W
Tomelilla **73** 55 33N 13 58 E
Tomelloso **59** 39 10N 3 2W
Tomingley **141** 32 31 S 148 16 E
Tomini **103** 0 30N 120 30 E
Tomini, Teluk **103** 0 10 S 122 0 E
Tominian **120** 13 17N 4 35W
Tomiño **56** 41 59N 8 46W
Tomintoul **37** 57 15N 3 22W
Tomioka **111** 36 15N 138 54 E
Tomkinson Ranges **137** 26 11 S 129 5 E
Tommot **77** 58 50N 126 20 E
Tomnavoulin **37** 57 19N 3 18W
Tomnop Ta Suos **101** 11 20N 104 15 E
Tomo, Colomb. **174** 2 38N 67 32W
Tomo, Japan **110** 34 23N 133 23 E
Tomobe **111** 36 40N 140 41 E
Toms Place **163** 37 34N 118 41W
Toms River **162** 39 59N 74 12W
Tomsk **76** 56 30N 85 12 E
Tomtabacken **73** 57 30N 14 30 E
Tonalá **165** 16 8N 93 41W
Tonale, Passo del **62** 46 15N 10 34 E
Tonalea **161** 36 17N 110 58W
Tonami **111** 36 56N 136 58 E
Tonantins **174** 2 45 S 67 45W
Tonasket **160** 48 45N 119 30W
Tonawanda **156** 43 0N 78 54W
Tonbridge **29** 51 12N 0 18 E
Tondano **103** 1 35N 124 54 E
Tondela **56** 40 31N 8 5W
Tønder **73** 54 58N 8 50 E
Tondi **97** 9 45N 79 4 E
Tondi Kiwindi **121** 14 28N 2 02 E
Tondibi **121** 16 39N 0 14W
Tone-Gawa, R. **111** 35 44N 140 51 E
Tone, R. **137** 34 23 S 116 25 E
Tone R. **30** 50 59N 3 15W
Tong **28** 52 39N 2 18W
Tonga Is. ■ **130** 20 0 S 173 0W
Tonga Trench **143** 18 0 S 175 0W
Tongaat **129** 29 33 S 31 9 E
Tongala **141** 36 14 S 144 56 E
Tongaland **129** 27 0 S 32 0 E
Tongareva I **143** 9 0 S 158 0W
Tongariro, mt. **142** 39 7 S 175 50 E
Tongchŏnni **107** 39 50N 127 25 E
Tongeren **47** 50 47N 5 28 E
Tongio **141** 37 14 S 147 44 E
Tongjosŏn Man **107** 39 30N 128 0 E
Tongking = Bac-Phan **101** 21 30N 105 0 E
Tongking, G. of **101** 20 0N 108 0 E
Tongnae **107** 35 12N 129 5 E
Tongobory **129** 23 32 S 44 20 E
Tongoy **172** 30 25 S 71 40W
Tongres = Tongeren **47** 50 47N 5 28 E
Tongsa Dzong **98** 27 31N 90 31 E
Tongue **37** 58 29N 4 25W
Tongue, Kyle of **37** 58 30N 4 30W
Tongue, R. **160** 48 30N 106 30W
Tongyang **107** 39 9N 126 53 E
Tonj **123** 7 20N 28 44 E
Tonk **94** 26 6N 75 54 E
Tonkawa **159** 36 44N 67 22W
Tonkin = Bac-Phan **100** 22 0N 105 0 E
Tonkin, G. of **100** 20 0N 108 0 E
Tonlé Sap **100** 13 0N 104 0 E
Tonnay-Charente **44** 45 56N 0 55W
Tonneins **44** 44 24N 0 20 E
Tonnerre **43** 47 51N 3 59 E
Tönning **48** 54 18N 8 57 E
Tonopah **163** 38 4N 117 12W
Tonoshō **110** 34 29N 134 11 E
Tonosí **166** 7 20N 80 20W
Tonsberg **71** 59 19N 10 25 E
Tonstad **71** 58 40N 6 45 E
Tonto Basin **61** 33 58N 111 15W
Tonyrefail **31** 51 35N 3 26W
Tonzang **98** 23 36N 93 42 E
Tonzi **98** 24 39N 94 57 E
Tooele **160** 40 30N 112 20W
Toolonda **140** 36 58 S 141 5 E
Toombeolo **38** 53 26N 9 52W
Toomevara **39** 52 50N 8 2W
Toompine **139** 27 15 S 144 19 E
Toongi **141** 32 28 S 148 30 E
Toonpan **138** 19 28 S 146 48 E
Toora **141** 38 39 S 146 23 E
Toora-Khem **77** 52 28N 96 9 E
Toormore **39** 51 31N 9 41W
Toowoomba **139** 27 32 S 151 56 E
Top **93** 34 15N 68 35 E
Top Ozero **78** 65 35N 32 0 E
Topalu **70** 44 31N 28 3 E
Topaz **163** 38 41N 119 30W
Topeka **158** 39 3N 95 40W
Topki **76** 55 25N 85 20 E
Topla, R. **53** 49 0N 21 36 E
Topley **152** 54 32N 126 5W
Toplica, R. **66** 43 15N 21 30 E
Toplița **70** 46 55N 25 27 E
Topocalma, Pta. **172** 34 10 S 72 2W
Topock **161** 34 46N 114 29W
Topola **66** 44 17N 20 32 E
Topol'čany **53** 48 35N 18 12 E
Topoli **83** 47 59N 51 45 E
Topolnitsa, R. **67** 42 21N 24 0 E
Topolobampo **164** 25 40N 109 10W
Topolovgrad **67** 42 5N 26 20 E
TopolvŭT Mare **66** 45 46N 21 41 E
Toppenish **160** 46 27N 120 16W
Topsham **30** 50 40N 3 27W
Topusko **63** 45 18N 15 59 E
Toquima, Ra. **163** 39 0N 117 0W
Tor Bay, Austral. **137** 35 5 S 117 50 E
Tor Bay, U.K. **23** 50 26N 3 31W
Tor Ness **37** 58 47N 3 18W
Tor, oilfield **19** 56 40N 3 35 E
Torå **58** 41 49N 1 25 E
Tora Kit **123** 11 2N 32 30 E
Torata **174** 17 3 S 70 1W
Torbat-e Heydarīyeh **93** 35 15N 59 12 E
Torbat-e Jām **93** 35 8N 60 35 E
Torbay, Can. **151** 47 40N 52 42W
Torbay, U.K. **30** 50 26N 3 31W
Torchin **80** 50 45N 25 0 E
Tordal **71** 59 10N 8 45 E
Tordesillas **56** 41 30N 5 0W
Tordoya **56** 43 6N 8 36W
Töre **74** 65 55N 22 40 E
Töreboda **73** 58 41N 14 7 E
Torfajökull **74** 63 54N 19 0W
Torgau **48** 51 32N 13 0 E
Torgelow **48** 53 40N 13 59 E
Torhout **47** 51 5N 3 7 E
Tori **123** 7 53N 33 35 E
Torigni-sur-Vire **42** 49 3N 0 58W
Torija **58** 40 44N 3 2W
Torin **164** 27 33N 110 5W
Toriñana, C. **56** 43 3N 9 17W
Torino **62** 45 4N 7 40 E
Torit **123** 4 20N 32 55 E
Torkovichi **80** 58 51N 30 30 E
Tormac **66** 45 30N 21 30 E
Tormentine **151** 46 6N 63 46W
Tormes, R. **56** 41 7N 6 0W
Tornado Mt. **152** 49 55N 114 40W
Tornby **73** 57 32N 9 56 E
Torne älv **74** 65 50N 24 12 E
Torneå = Tornio **74** 65 50N 24 12 E
Torness **37** 57 18N 4 22W
Torneträsk **74** 68 24N 19 15 E
Tornio **74** 65 50N 24 12 E
Tornionjoki **74** 65 50N 24 12 E
Tornquist **172** 38 0 S 62 15W
Toro **56** 41 35N 5 24W
Torö **73** 58 48N 17 50 E
Toro, Cerro del **172** 29 0 S 69 50W
Toro Pk. **163** 33 34N 116 24W
Törökszentmjklés **53** 47 11N 20 27 E
Toronátos Kólpos **68** 40 5N 23 30 E
Toronto, Austral. **141** 33 0 S 151 30 E
Toronto, Can. **150** 43 39N 79 20W
Toronto, U.S.A. **156** 40 27N 80 36W
Toronto, L. **164** 27 40N 105 30W
Toropets **80** 56 30N 31 40 E
Tororo **126** 0 45N 34 12 E
Toros Dağlari **92** 37 0N 35 0 E
Torphins **37** 57 7N 2 37W
Torpoint **30** 50 23N 4 12W
Torpshammar **72** 62 29N 16 20 E
Torquay, Austral. **140** 38 20 S 144 19 E
Torquay, Can. **153** 49 9N 103 30W
Torquay, U.K. **30** 50 27N 3 31W
Torquemada **56** 42 2N 4 19W
Torralba de Calatrava **57** 39 1N 3 44W
Torran Rocks **34** 56 14N 6 24W
Torrance **163** 33 50N 118 19W
Torrão **57** 38 16N 8 11W
Torre Annunziata **64** 40 45N 14 26 E
Tôrre de Moncorvo **56** 41 12N 7 8W
Torre del Greco **65** 40 47N 14 22 E
Torre del Mar **57** 36 44N 4 6W
Torre-Pacheco **29** 37 44N 0 57W
Torre Pellice **62** 44 49N 7 13 E
Torreblanca **58** 40 14N 0 12 E
Torrecampo **57** 38 29N 4 41W
Torrecilla en Cameros **58** 42 15N 2 38W
Torredembarra **58** 41 9N 1 24W
Torredonjimeno **57** 37 46N 3 57W
Torrejoncillo **56** 39 54N 6 28W
Torrelaguna **58** 40 50N 3 38W
Torrelavega **56** 43 20N 4 5W
Torremaggiore **65** 41 42N 15 17 E
Torremolinos **57** 36 38N 4 30W
Torrens Cr. **138** 22 23 S 145 9 E
Torrens Creek **138** 20 48 S 145 3 E
Torrens, L. **140** 31 0 S 137 50 E
Torrente **59** 39 27N 0 28W
Torrenueva **59** 38 38N 3 22W
Torreón **164** 25 33N 103 25W
Torreperogil **59** 38 2N 3 17W
Torres, Mexico **164** 28 46N 110 47W
Torres, Spain **57** 41 6N 5 0W
Tôrres Novas **57** 39 27N 8 33W
Torres Strait **135** 9 50 S 142 20 E
Torres Vedras **57** 39 5N 9 15W
Torrevieja **59** 37 59N 0 42W
Torrey **161** 38 12N 111 30W
Torridge, R. **30** 50 51N 4 10W
Torridon **36** 57 33N 5 34W
Torridon, L. **36** 57 35N 5 50W
Torrijos **56** 39 59N 4 18W
Törring **73** 55 52N 9 29 E
Torrington, Conn., U.S.A. **162** 41 50N 73 9W
Torrington, Wyo., U.S.A. **158** 42 5N 104 8W
Torroboll **37** 58 0N 4 23W
Torroella de Montgri **58** 42 2N 3 8 E
Torrox **57** 36 46N 3 57W
Torsås **73** 56 24N 16 0 E
Torsby **72** 60 7N 13 0 E
Torsjok **72** 57 5N 34 55 E
Torsö **73** 58 48N 13 45 E
Torthorwald **35** 55 7N 3 30W
Tortola, I. **147** 18 19N 65 0W
Tórtoles de Esgueva **56** 41 49N 4 2W
Tortona **62** 44 53N 8 54 E
Tortoreto **63** 42 50N 13 55 E
Tortorici **65** 38 2N 14 48 E
Tortosa **58** 40 49N 0 31 E
Tortosa C. **58** 40 41N 0 52 E
Tortosendo **56** 40 15N 7 31W
Tortue, I. de la **167** 20 5N 72 57W
Tortuga, Isla la **167** 11 8N 67 2W
Torud **93** 35 25N 55 5 E
Torugart, Pereval **85** 40 32N 75 24 E
Torun **54** 53 0N 18 39 E
Torup **73** 56 57N 13 5 E
Torvastad **71** 59 23N 5 15 E
Torver **32** 54 20N 3 7W
Tory I. **38** 55 17N 8 12W
Torysa, R. **53** 48 50N 21 15 E
Torzhok **80** 57 5N 34 55 E
Tosa **110** 33 24N 133 23 E
Tosa-shimizu **110** 32 52N 132 58 E
Tosa-Wan **110** 33 15N 133 30 E
Tosa-yamada **110** 33 36N 133 38 E
Toscaig **36** 57 23N 5 49W
Toscana **62** 43 30N 11 5 E
Tosno **80** 59 30N 30 58 E
Töss, R. **51** 47 32N 8 39 E
Tossa **58** 41 43N 2 56 E
Tostado **172** 29 15 S 61 50W
Tostedt **48** 53 17N 9 42 E
Tosu **110** 33 22N 130 31 E
Toszek **54** 50 27N 18 32 E
Totak **71** 59 40N 7 45 E
Totana **59** 37 45N 1 30W
Toten **71** 60 37N 10 53 E
Toteng **128** 20 22 S 22 58 E
Tôtes **42** 49 41N 1 3 E
Totland **28** 50 41N 1 32W
Totley **33** 53 18N 1 32W
Totma **81** 60 0N 42 40 E
Totnes **30** 50 26N 3 41W
Totonicapán **166** 14 50N 91 20W
Totskoye **84** 52 32N 52 45 E
Tottenham **141** 32 14 S 147 21 E
Totton **28** 50 55N 1 29W
Tottori **110** 35 30N 134 15 E
Tottori-ken □ **110** 35 30N 134 12 E
Touamotou, Archipel des **131** 17 0 S 144 0W
Touat **118** 27 30N 0 30 E
Touba **120** 8 15N 7 40W
Toubkal, Djebel **118** 31 0N 8 0W
Toubouai, Îles **131** 25 0 S 150 0W
Toucy **43** 47 44N 3 15 E
Tougan **120** 13 11N 2 58W
Touggourt **119** 33 10N 6 0 E
Tougué **120** 11 25N 11 50W
Toukmatine **119** 24 49N 7 11 E
Toul **43** 48 40N 5 53 E
Toulepleu **120** 6 32N 8 24W
Toulon **45** 43 10N 5 55 E
Toulouse **44** 43 37N 1 27 E
Toummo **119** 22 45N 14 8 E
Toummo Dhoba **119** 22 30N 14 31 E
Toumodi **120** 6 32N 5 4W
Tounan **109** 23 41N 120 28 E
Tounassine, Hamada **118** 28 48N 5 0W
Toungoo **98** 19 0N 96 30 E
Touques, R. **42** 49 22N 0 8 E
Touquet, Le **43** 50 30N 1 36 E
Tour-du-Pin, La **45** 45 33N 5 27 E
Touraine **42** 47 20N 0 30 E
Tourane = Da Nang **100** 16 4N 108 13 E
Tourcoing **43** 50 42N 3 10 E
Tourcoingbam **121** 13 23N 1 33W
Tournai **47** 50 35N 3 25 E
Tournan-en-Brie **43** 48 44N 2 46 E
Tournay **44** 43 13N 0 13 E
Tournon **45** 45 4N 4 50 E
Tournon-St.-Martin **42** 46 45N 0 58 E
Tournus **45** 46 35N 4 54 E
Touros **170** 5 12 S 35 28W
Tours **42** 47 22N 0 40 E
Touside, Pic **119** 21 1N 16 18 E
T'outaokou **107** 42 44N 129 12 E
Touwsrivier **128** 33 20 S 20 0 E
Tovar **174** 8 20N 71 46W
Tovarkovskiy **81** 53 40N 38 5 E
Tovdal **71** 58 47N 8 10 E
Tovdalselva **71** 58 20N 8 16 E
Towamba **141** 37 6 S 149 43 E
Towanda **162** 41 46N 76 30W
Towcester **29** 52 7N 0 56W
Tower **158** 47 49N 92 17W
Towerhill Cr. **138** 22 28 S 144 35 E
Town Yetholm **35** 55 33N 2 19W
Towner **158** 48 25N 100 26W
Townsend **160** 46 25N 111 32W
Townshend, C. **133** 22 18 S 150 30 E
Townshend, I. **138** 22 16 S 150 31 E
Townsville **138** 19 15 S 146 45 E
Towson **162** 39 26N 76 34W
Toyah **159** 31 20N 103 48W
Toyahvale **159** 30 58N 103 45W
Toyama **111** 36 40N 137 15 E
Toyama-ken □ **111** 36 45N 137 30 E
Tōyō **110** 33 26N 134 16 E
Toyohashi **111** 34 45N 137 25 E
Toyokawa **111** 34 48N 137 27 E
Toyonaka **111** 34 50N 135 28 E
Toyooka **110** 35 35N 134 55 E
Toyota **111** 35 3N 137 7 E
Toyoura **110** 34 6N 130 57 E
Toytepa **85** 41 3N 69 20 E
Tozeur **119** 33 56N 8 8 E
Tra On **101** 9 58N 105 55 E
Trabancos, R. **56** 41 0N 5 3 E
Trabzon **92** 41 0N 39 45 E
Tracadie **151** 47 30N 64 55W
Tracy, Calif., U.S.A. **163** 37 46N 121 27W
Tracy, Minn., U.S.A. **158** 44 12N 95 3W
Tradate **62** 45 43N 8 54 E
Trafalgar **141** 38 14 S 146 12 E
Trafalgar, C. **57** 36 10N 6 2W
Traghan **119** 26 0N 14 30 E
Traian **70** 45 2N 28 15 E
Trail **152** 49 5N 117 40W
Trainor L. **152** 60 24N 120 17W
Traipu **171** 9 58 S 37 1W
Tralee **39** 52 16N 9 42W
Tralee B. **39** 52 17N 9 55W
Tramelan **50** 47 13N 7 7 E
Tramore **39** 52 10N 7 10W
Tramore B. **39** 52 9N 7 10W
Tran Ninh, Cao Nguyen **100** 19 30N 103 10 E
Tranas **73** 58 3N 14 59 E
Tranås **73** 55 37N 13 59 E
Trancas **172** 26 20 S 65 20W
Tranche-sur-Mer, La **42** 46 20N 1 27W
Trancoso **56** 40 49N 7 21W
Tranebjerg **73** 55 51N 10 36 E
Tranemo **73** 57 30N 13 20 E
Tranent **35** 55 57N 2 58W
Trang **101** 7 33N 99 38 E
Trangahy **129** 19 7 S 44 43 E
Trangan, I. **103** 6 40 S 134 20 E
Trangie **141** 32 4 S 148 0 E
Trångsviken **72** 63 19N 14 0 E
Trani **65** 41 17N 16 24 E
Tranoroa **129** 24 42 S 45 4 E
Tranquebar **97** 11 1N 79 54 E
Tranqueras **173** 31 8 S 56 0W
Trans Nzoia □ **126** 1 0N 35 0 E
Transcona **153** 49 50N 97 0W
Transilvania **70** 46 19N 25 0 E
Transkei □ **129** 32 15 S 28 15 E
Transtrand **72** 61 6N 13 20 E
Transvaal □ **128** 25 0 S 29 0 E
Transylvania = Transilvania **70** 46 19N 25 0 E
Transylvanian Alps **70** 45 30N 25 0 E
Trápani **64** 38 1N 12 30 E
Trappe Peak, Mt. **160** 45 56N 114 29W
Traqowel **140** 35 50 S 144 0 E
Traralgon **141** 38 12 S 146 34 E
Traryd **73** 56 35N 13 45 E
Trarza □ **120** 17 30N 15 0W
Tras os Montes e Alto-Douro □ **55** 41 25N 7 20W
Trasacco **63** 41 58N 13 30 E
Trasimeno, L. **63** 43 10N 12 5 E
Träslöv **73** 57 8N 12 21 E
Trat **101** 12 14N 102 33 E
Traun **52** 48 14N 14 15 E
Traun-see **49** 47 48N 13 45 E
Traunstein **49** 47 52N 12 40 E
Trävad **73** 58 15N 13 5 E
Traveller's L. **140** 33 20 S 142 0 E
Travemünde **48** 53 58N 10 52 E
Travers, Mt. **143** 42 1 S 172 45 E
Traverse City **156** 44 45N 85 39W
Traverse I. **13** 48 0 S 28 0 E
Travnik **66** 44 17N 17 39 E
Trawbreaga B. **38** 55 20N 7 25W
Trawsfynydd **31** 52 54N 3 55W
Trayning **137** 31 7 S 117 46 E
Traynor **153** 52 20N 108 32W
Trazo **56** 43 0N 8 30W
Trbovlje **63** 46 12N 15 5 E
Trebbia, R. **62** 44 52N 9 30 E
Trebel, R. **48** 54 0N 12 50 E
Trebinje **66** 42 44N 18 22 E
Trebisacce **65** 39 52N 16 32 E
Trebišnica, R. **66** 42 47N 18 8 E
Trebišov **53** 48 38N 21 41 E
Trebizat **66** 43 15N 17 30 E
Třebon **52** 48 59N 14 48 E
Trebujena **57** 36 52N 6 11W
Trecate **62** 45 29N 8 42 E
Tredegar **31** 51 47N 3 16W
Trefeglwys **31** 52 31N 3 31W
Trefriw **31** 53 9N 3 50W
Tregaron **31** 52 14N 3 56W
Trégastel-Plage **42** 48 49N 3 31W
Tregnago **63** 45 31N 11 10 E

Tregrasse Is
Tullow

Tregrasse Is. 138 17 41S 150 43E
Tréguier 42 48 47N 3 16W
Trégunc 42 47 51N 3 51W
Tregynon 31 52 32N 3 19W
Treharris 31 51 40N 3 17W
Treherne 153 49 38N 98 42W
Tréia 63 43 30N 13 20E
Treig, L. 37 56 48N 4 42W
Treignac 44 45 32N 1 48E
Treinta y Tres 173 33 10S 54 50W
Treis 49 50 9N 7 19E
Trekveid 128 30 35S 19 45E
Trelde Næs 73 55 38N 9 53E
Trelech 31 51 56N 4 28W
Trelew 176 43 10S 65 20W
Trélissac 44 45 11N 0 47E
Trelleborg 73 55 20N 13 10E
Trélon 43 50 5N 4 6E
Tremadoc 31 52 57N 4 9W
Tremadoc, Bay 31 52 51N 4 18W
Tremblade, La 44 45 46N 1 8W
Tremelo 47 51 0N 4 42E
Trementina 159 35 27N 105 30W
Tremiti, I. 63 42 8N 15 30E
Tremonton 160 41 45N 112 10W
Tremp 58 42 10N 0 52E
Trenary 156 46 12N 86 59W
Trenčin 53 48 52N 18 4E
Trenche, R. 150 47 46N 72 53W
Trenggalek 103 8 5S 111 44E
Trenque Lauquen 172 36 0S 62 45W
Trent, R. 33 53 33N 0 44W
Trentham 32 52 59N 2 12W
Trentino-Alto Adige □ 62 46 5N 11 0E
Trento 62 46 5N 11 8E
Trenton, Can. 150 44 10N 77 40W
Trenton, Mo., U.S.A. 158 40 5N 93 37W
Trenton, Nebr., U.S.A. 158 40 14N 101 4W
Trenton, N.J., U.S.A. 162 40 15N 74 41W
Trenton, Tenn., U.S.A. 159 35 58N 88 57W
Trepassey 151 46 43N 53 25W
Tréport, Le 42 50 3N 1 20E
Treptow 48 53 42N 13 15E
Trepuzzi 65 40 26N 18 4E
Tres Arroyos 172 38 20S 60 20W
Três Corações 173 21 30S 45 30W
Três Lagoas 171 20 50S 51 50W
Tres Marías, Is. 164 21 25N 106 28W
Três Marias, Represa 171 18 12S 45 15W
Tres Montes, C. 176 47 0S 75 35W
Tres Pinos 163 36 48N 121 19W
Três Pontas 173 21 23S 45 29W
Tres Puentes 172 27 50S 70 15W
Três Puntas, C. 176 47 0S 66 0W
Tres Rios 173 22 20S 43 30W
Tres Valles 165 18 15N 96 8W
Tresco I. 30 49 57N 6 20W
Treshnish Is. 34 56 30N 6 25W
Treska, R. 66 41 45N 21 11E
Treskavika Planina 66 43 40N 18 20E
Trespaderne 58 42 47N 3 24W
Tretower 31 51 53N 3 11W
Trets 45 43 27N 5 41E
Treuchtlingen 49 48 58N 10 55E
Treuddyn 31 53 7N 3 8W
Treuenbrietzen 48 52 6N 12 51E
Treungen 75 59 1N 8 31E
Trevíglio 62 45 31N 9 35E
Trevinca, Peña 56 42 15N 6 46W
Treviso 63 45 40N 12 15E
Trevose Hd. 30 50 33N 5 3W
Trévoux 45 45 57N 4 47E
Trgovište 66 42 20N 22 10E
Triabunna 138 42 30S 147 55E
Triánda 69 36 25N 28 10E
Triang 101 3 13N 102 27E
Triangle 162 38 33N 77 20W
Triaucourt-en-Argonne 43 48 59N 5 2E
Tribsees 48 54 4N 12 46E
Tribulation, C. 138 16 5S 145 29E
Tribune 158 38 30N 101 45W
Tricárico 65 40 37N 16 9E
Tricase 65 39 56N 18 20E
Trichinopoly = Tiruchchirappalli 97 10 45N 78 45E
Trichur 97 10 30N 76 18E
Trida 141 33 1S 145 1E
Trier 49 49 45N 6 37E
Trieste 63 45 39N 13 45E
Trieste, G. di 63 45 37N 13 40E
Triggiano 65 41 4N 16 58E
Triglav 63 46 30N 13 45E
Trigno, R. 63 41 55N 14 37E
Trigueros 57 37 24N 6 50W
Tríkeri 69 39 6N 23 5E
Tríkhonis, Límni 69 38 34N 21 30E
Tríkkala 68 39 34N 21 47E
Tríkkala □ 68 39 41N 21 30E
Trikora, G. 103 4 11S 138 0E
Trilj 63 43 38N 16 42E
Trillick 38 54 27N 7 30W
Trillo 58 40 42N 2 35W
Trim 38 53 34N 6 48W
Trimdon 33 54 43N 1 23W
Trimley 29 51 59N 1 19E
Trincomalee 97 8 38N 81 15E
Trindade 171 16 40S 49 30W
Trindade, I. 15 20 20S 29 50W
Trinidad, Boliv. 174 14 54S 64 50W
Trinidad, Colomb. 174 5 25N 71 40W
Trinidad, Cuba 166 21 40N 80 0W
Trinidad, Uruguay 172 33 30S 56 50W
Trinidad, U.S.A. 159 37 15N 104 30W
Trinidad & Tobago ■ 167 10 30N 61 20W
Trinidad, I., Argent. 176 39 10S 62 0W
Trinidad, I., S. Amer. 167 10 30N 61 15W
Trinidad, R. 165 17 49N 95 9W
Trinitápoli 65 41 22N 16 5E
Trinity, Can. 151 48 22N 53 29W
Trinity, U.S.A. 159 30 50N 95 20W
Trinity B., Austral. 133 16 30S 146 0E
Trinity B., Can. 151 48 20N 53 10W
Trinity Mts. 159 40 20N 118 50W
Trinity R. 159 30 30N 95 0W
Trino 62 45 10N 8 18E
Trion 157 34 35N 85 18W
Trionto C. 65 34 38N 16 47E
Triora 62 44 0N 7 46E
Tripoli = Tarabulus 92 34 31N 33 52E
Tripoli = Tarābulus 119 32 49N 13 7E
Trípolis 69 37 31N 22 25E
Tripp 158 43 16N 97 58W
Tripura □ 98 24 0N 92 0E
Trischen, I. 48 54 3N 8 32E
Tristan da Cunha, I. 15 37 6S 12 20W
Trivandrum 97 8 31N 77 0E
Trivento 65 41 48N 14 31E
Trnava 53 48 23N 17 35E
Trobriand Is. 135 8 30S 151 0E
Trochu 152 51 50N 113 13W
Trodely I. 150 52 15N 79 26W
Trogir 63 43 32N 16 15E
Troglav, mt. 63 43 56N 16 36E
Trögstad 71 59 37N 11 16E
Tróia 65 41 22N 15 19E
Troilus, L. 150 50 50N 74 35W
Troina 65 37 47N 14 34E
Trois Fourches, Cap des 118 35 26N 2 58W
Trois Pistoles 151 48 5N 69 10W
Trois-Riviéres 150 46 25N 72 40W
Troisvierges 47 50 8N 6 0E
Troitsk 84 54 10N 61 35E
Troitskiy 84 55 29N 37 18E
Troitsko-Pechorsk 78 62 40N 56 10E
Trölladyngja 74 64 54N 17 15W
Trolladyngja 74 64 49N 17 29W
Trollhättan 73 58 17N 12 20E
Trollheimen 71 62 46N 9 1E
Tromöy 71 58 28N 8 53E
Troms fylke □ 74 68 56N 19 0E
Tromsø 74 69 40N 18 56E
Trøna 163 35 46N 117 23W
Tronador, Mt. 176 41 53S 71 0W
Tröndelag, N. □ 74 65 0N 12 0E
Tröndelag, S. □ 71 62 0N 10 0E
Trondheim 71 63 25N 10 25E
Trondheimsfjorden 74 63 35N 10 30E
Trönninge 73 56 38N 12 59E
Trönö 72 61 22N 16 54E
Tronto, R. 63 42 50N 13 46E
Troodos, mt. 128 34 58N 32 55E
Troon 34 55 33N 4 40W
Tropea 65 38 40N 15 53E
Tropic 161 37 44N 112 4W
Tropoja 68 42 23N 20 10E
Trossachs, The 34 56 14N 4 24W
Trostan Mt. 38 55 4N 6 10W
Trostberg 49 48 2N 12 33E
Trotternish, dist. 36 57 32N 6 15W
Troup 159 32 10N 95 3W
Troup Hd. 37 57 41N 2 18W
Trout L., N.W. Terr., Can. 152 60 40N 121 40W
Trout L., Ont., Can. 153 51 20N 93 15W
Trout Lake 150 46 10N 85 2W
Trout, R. 152 61 19N 119 51W
Trout River 151 49 29N 58 8W
Trout Run 162 41 23N 77 3W
Trouville 42 49 21N 0 5E
Trowbridge 28 51 18N 2 12W
Troy, Turkey 92 39 55N 26 20E
Troy, Alabama, U.S.A. 157 31 50N 85 58W
Troy, Kans., U.S.A. 158 39 47N 95 2W
Troy, Mo., U.S.A. 158 38 56N 90 59W
Troy, Montana, U.S.A. 160 48 30N 115 58W
Troy, N.Y., U.S.A. 162 42 45N 73 39W
Troy, Ohio, U.S.A. 156 40 0N 84 10W
Troy, Pa., U.S.A. 162 41 47N 76 47W
Troyan 67 42 57N 24 43E
Troyes 43 48 19N 4 3E
Trpanj 66 43 1N 17 15E
Trstena 53 49 21N 19 37E
Trstenik 66 43 36N 21 0E
Trubchevsk 80 52 33N 33 47E
Truc Giang 101 10 14N 106 22E
Trucial States = Utd. Arab Emirates 93 24 0N 54 30E
Truckee 160 39 20N 120 11W
Trujillo, Colomb. 174 4 10N 76 19W
Trujillo, Hond. 166 16 0N 86 0W
Trujillo, Peru 174 8 0S 79 0W
Trujillo, Spain 57 39 28N 5 55W
Trujillo, U.S.A. 159 35 34N 104 44W
Trujillo, Venez. 174 9 22N 70 26W
Truk Is. 131 7 25N 151 46E
Trull 28 50 58N 3 8W
Trumann 159 35 42N 90 32W
Trumansburg 162 42 33N 76 40W
Trumbull, Mt. 161 36 25N 113 32W
Trumpington 29 52 11N 0 6E
Trún 66 42 51N 22 38E
Trun, France 42 48 50N 0 2E
Trun, Switz. 51 46 45N 8 59E
Trundle 141 32 53S 147 42E
Trung-Phan, reg. 100 16 0N 108 0E
Truro, Austral. 140 34 24S 139 9E
Truro, Can. 151 45 21N 63 14E
Truro, U.K. 30 50 17N 5 2W
Trûscûu, Muntii 70 46 14N 23 14E
Truskmore, mt. 38 54 23N 8 20W
Truslove 137 33 20S 121 45E
Trustrup 73 56 20N 10 46E
Truth or Consequences 161 33 9N 107 16W
Trutnov 52 50 37N 15 54E
Truxton 162 42 45N 76 2W
Truyère, R. 44 44 38N 2 34E
Trwyn Cilan 31 52 47N 4 31W
Tryavna 67 42 54N 25 25E
Tryon 157 35 15N 82 16W
Trzciarka 54 53 3N 16 25E
Trzciel 54 52 23N 15 50E
Trzcinsko-Zdroj 54 52 58N 14 35E
Trzebiez 54 53 38N 14 31E
Trzebinia 54 50 11N 19 30E
Trzeblatów 54 54 3N 15 18E
Trzebnica 54 51 20N 17 1E
Trzemeszno 54 52 33N 17 48E
Tržič 63 46 22N 14 18E
Tsafriya 90 31 59N 34 51E
Tsaidam 105 37 0N 95 0E
Tsak'o 108 31 56N 99 35E
Tsamandás 68 39 46N 20 21E
Tsamkong = Chanchiang 109 21 15N 110 20E
Tsana Dzong 99 28 0N 91 55E
Tsanga 99 30 43N 100 32E
Ts'angchi 108 31 48N 105 57E
Ts'angchou 106 38 10N 116 50E
Tsangpo 99 29 40N 89 0E
Ts'angyüan 108 23 9N 99 15E
Ts'ao Ho, R. 107 40 32N 124 11E
Tsaochuang 107 34 30N 117 49E
Tsaochwang 174 35 11N 115 28E
Ts'aohsien 106 34 50N 115 31E
Tsaoyang 109 32 8N 112 42E
Tsaratanana 129 16 47S 47 39E
Tsaratanana, Mt. de 129 14 0S 49 0E
Tsarevo = Michurin 67 42 9N 27 51E
Tsaring Nor 99 34 40N 97 20E
Tsaritsáni 68 39 53N 15 14E
Tsau 128 20 8S 22 29E
Tsaukaib 128 26 37S 15 39E
Tsebrikovo 82 47 9N 30 10E
Ts'ehung 108 25 2N 105 47E
Tselinograd 76 51 10N 71 30E
Tsengch'eng 109 23 17N 113 49E
Ts'enkung 108 27 13N 108 45E
Tsetserleg 105 47 36N 101 32E
Tshabong 128 26 2S 22 29E
Tshane 125 24 5S 21 54E
Tshela 124 5 4S 13 0E
Tshesebe 129 20 43S 27 32E
Tshhinvali 83 42 14N 44 1E
Tshibeke 126 2 40S 28 35E
Tshibinda 126 2 23S 28 30E
Tshikapa 124 6 17S 21 0E
Tshilenge 126 6 12S 23 40E
Tshinsenda 127 12 15N 28 0E
Tshofa 124 5 8S 25 8E
Tshombe 129 25 18S 45 29E
Tshwane 128 22 24S 22 1E
Tsigara 128 20 22S 25 54E
Tsihombe 125 25 10S 45 41E
Tsilmamo 123 6 1N 35 10E
Tsimlyansk 83 47 45N 42 0E
Tsimlyanskoye Vdkhr. 83 48 0N 43 0E
Tsinan = Chinan 106 36 32N 117 0E
Tsineng 128 27 05S 23 05E
Tsínga, mt. 68 41 23N 24 44E
Tsinghai □ 105 36 0N 96 0E
Tsingtao = Ch'ingtao 107 36 5N 120 25E
Tsinjomitondraka 129 15 40S 47 8E
Tsiroanomandidy 129 18 46S 46 2E
Tsivilsk 81 55 50N 47 25E
Tsivory 129 24 4S 46 5E
Tskhinali 79 42 22N 43 52E
Tso Chiang, R. 108 22 52N 108 5E
Tso Morari, L. 95 32 50N 78 20E
Tsochou 108 22 36N 107 36E
Tsoch'üan 106 37 3N 113 27E
Tsodilo Hill 128 18 49S 21 43E
Tsogttsetsiy 106 43 43N 105 35E
Tsokung 108 29 55N 97 44E
Tsona Dzong 99 28 0N 91 55E
Tsoshui 106 33 40N 109 9E
Tsouhsien 106 35 24N 116 58E
Tsu 111 34 45N 136 25E
Tsu L. 152 60 40N 111 52W
Tsuchiura 111 36 12N 140 15E
Tsugaru-Kaikyō 112 41 35N 141 0E
Tsukumi 110 33 4N 131 52E
Tsukushi-Sanchi 110 33 25N 130 30E
Tsumeb 128 19 9S 17 44E
Tsumis 128 23 39S 17 29E
Tsuna 110 34 28N 134 56E
Ts'ungchiang 108 25 45N 108 54E
Tsunhua 107 40 12N 117 56E
Tsuni 108 27 43N 106 52E
Tsuno-Shima 110 34 21N 130 52E
Tsuru 111 35 31N 138 57E
Tsuruga 111 35 45N 136 2E
Tsuruga-Wan 111 35 50N 136 3E
Tsurugi 111 36 37N 136 37E
Tsurugi-San 110 33 51N 134 6E
Tsurumi-Saki 110 32 56N 132 5E
Tsuruoka 112 38 44N 139 50E
Tsurusaki 110 33 14N 131 41E
Tsushima 111 35 10N 136 43E
Tsushima, I. 110 34 20N 129 20E
Tsvetkovo 82 49 15N 31 33E
Tu, R. 98 22 50N 97 15E
Tua, R. 57 41 19N 7 15W
Tuai 143 38 47S 177 15E
Tuakau 142 37 16S 174 59E
Tual 103 5 30S 132 50E
Tuam 38 53 30N 8 50W
Tuamarina 143 41 25S 173 59E
Tuamgraney 39 52 54N 8 32W
Tuamotu Arch = Touamotou 131 17 0S 144 0W
Tuan 108 23 59N 108 3E
T'uanch'i 108 27 28N 107 7E
T'uanfeng 109 30 38N 114 52E
Tuao 103 17 47S 121 30E
Tuapse 83 44 5N 39 10E
Tuatapere 143 46 8S 167 41E
Tuath, Loch 34 56 30N 6 15W
Tuba City 161 36 8N 111 12W
Tubac 161 31 45N 111 2W
Tubai Is. = Toubouai, Îles 131 25 0S 150 0W
Tuban 102 6 57S 112 4E
Tubarão 173 28 30S 49 0W
Tubas 90 32 20N 35 22E
Tubau 102 3 10N 113 40E
Tubayq, Jabal at 122 29 30N 27 30E
Tubbergen 46 52 24N 6 48E
Tübingen 48 48 31N 9 4E
Tubize 47 50 42N 4 13E
Tubja, W. 122 25 27N 38 55E
Tubruq, (Tobruk) 117 32 7N 23 55E
Tubuai, Îles 131 25 0S 150 0W
Tuc Trung 101 11 1N 107 12E
Tucacas 174 10 48N 68 19W
Tucano 170 10 58S 38 48W
Tuch'ang 109 29 15N 116 13E
T'uch'ang 109 24 42N 121 25E
Tuchodi, R. 152 58 17N 123 42W
Tuchola 54 53 33N 17 52E
Tuchów 54 49 54N 21 1E
T'uch'üan 107 45 22N 121 41E
Tuckanarra 137 27 8S 118 1E
Tuckernuck I. 162 41 15N 70 17W
Tucson 161 32 14N 110 59W
Tucumán 172 26 50S 65 20W
Tucumán □ 172 26 48S 66 2W
Tucumcari 159 35 12N 103 45W
Tucupido 174 9 17N 65 47W
Tucupita 174 9 14N 62 3W
Tucuracas 174 11 45N 72 22W
Tucuruí 170 3 42S 49 27W
Tuczno 54 53 13N 16 10E
Tudela 58 42 4N 1 39W
Tudela de Duero 56 41 37N 4 39W
Tudor, Lac 151 55 50N 65 25W
Tudora 70 47 31N 26 45E
Tudweiliog 31 52 54N 4 37W
Tuella, R. 56 41 50N 7 10W
Tuen 139 28 33S 145 37E
Tueré, R. 170 2 48S 50 59W
Tufi 135 9 8S 149 19E
Tugidak I. 147 56 30N 154 40W
Tuguegarao 103 17 35N 121 42E
Tugur 77 53 50N 136 45E
Tugwa 128 17 27S 18 33E
Tukangbesi, Kepulauan 103 6 0S 124 0E
Tukarak I. 150 56 15N 78 45W
Tukobo 120 5 1N 2 47W
Tūkrah 119 32 30N 20 37E
Tuku, mt. 123 9 10N 36 43E
Tukums 80 57 2N 23 3E
Tukuyu 127 9 17S 33 35E
Tukzar 93 35 55N 66 25E
Tula, Hidalgo, Mexico 165 20 0N 99 20W
Tula, Tamaulipas, Mexico 165 23 0N 99 40W
Tula, Nigeria 121 9 51N 11 27E
Tula, U.S.S.R. 81 54 13N 37 32E
Tulak 93 33 55N 63 40E
Tulancingo 165 20 5N 98 22W
Tulanssu 105 36 52N 98 24E
Tulare 163 36 15N 119 26W
Tulare Basin 163 36 0N 119 48W
Tulare Lake 161 36 0N 119 53W
Tularosa 161 33 4N 106 1W
Tulbagh 128 33 16S 19 6E
Tulcán 174 0 48N 77 43W
Tulcea 70 45 13N 28 46E
Tulcea □ 70 45 0N 29 0E
Tulchin 82 48 41N 28 55E
Tuléar 129 23 21S 43 40E
Tuléar □ 129 21 0S 45 0E
Tulemalu L. 153 62 58N 99 25W
Tulgheş 70 4 58N 25 45E
Tuli, Indon. 103 1 24S 122 26E
Tuli, Rhod. 127 21 58S 29 13E
Tuliuchen 106 39 1N 116 54E
Tulkarm 90 32 19N 35 10E
Tulla, Ireland 39 52 53N 8 45W
Tulla, U.S.A. 159 34 35N 101 44W
Tulla, L. 34 56 33N 4 47W
Tullaghoge 38 54 36N 6 43W
Tullaghought 39 52 25N 7 22W
Tullahoma 157 35 23N 86 12W
Tullamore, Austral. 141 32 39S 147 36E
Tullamore, Ireland 39 53 17N 7 30W
Tullaroan 39 52 40N 7 27W
Tulle 44 45 16N 0 47E
Tullibigeal 141 33 25S 146 44E
Tullins 45 45 18N 5 29E
Tulln 52 48 20N 16 4E
Tullow 39 52 48N 6 45W

Tullus Uddingston

Tullus	123	11 7N	24 40 E
Tully, Austral.	138	17 56 S	145 55 E
Tully, Ireland	38	53 44N	8 9W
Tully, U.S.A.	162	42 48N	76 7W
Tully Cross	38	53 35N	9 59W
Tŭlmaciu	70	45 38N	24 19 E
Tulmaythah	117	32 40N	20 55 E
Tulmur	138	22 40 S	142 20 E
Tulnici	70	45 51N	26 38 E
Tulovo	67	42 33N	25 32 E
Tulsa	159	36 10N	96 0W
Tulsequah	152	58 39N	133 35W
Tulsk	38	53 47N	8 15W
Tulu Milki	123	9 55N	38 14 E
Tulu Welel, Mt.	123	8 56N	35 30 E
Tulua	174	4 6N	76 11W
T'ulufan	105	42 56N	89 10 E
Tulun	77	54 40N	100 10 E
Tulungagung	103	8 5 S	111 54 E
Tum	103	3 28 S	130 21 E
Tuma	81	55 10N	40 30 E
Tuma, R.	166	13 18N	84 50W
Tumaco	174	1 50N	78 45W
Tumatumari	174	5 20N	58 55W
Tumba	72	59 12N	17 48 E
Tumba, L.	124	0 50 S	18 0 E
Tumbarumba	141	35 44 S	148 0 E
Tumbaya	172	23 50 S	65 20W
Tumbes	174	3 30 S	80 20W
Tumbwa	127	11 25 S	27 15 E
Tumby B.	140	34 21 S	136 8 E
T'umen	107	42 55N	129 50 E
T'umen Kiang, R.	107	42 18N	130 41 E
Tumeremo	174	7 18N	61 30W
Tumiritinga	171	18 58 S	41 38W
Tumkur	97	13 18N	77 12 E
Tumleberg	73	58 16N	12 52 E
Tummel, L.	37	56 43N	3 55W
Tummel, R.	37	56 42N	4 5W
T'umot'eyuch'i	106	40 42N	111 8 E
Tump	93	26 7N	62 16 E
Tumpat	101	6 11N	102 10 E
Tumsar	96	21 26N	79 45 E
Tumu	120	10 56N	1 56W
Tumucumaque, Serra de	175	2 0N	55 0W
Tumut	141	35 16 S	148 13 E
Tumutuk	84	55 1N	53 19 E
Tumwater	160	47 0N	122 58W
Tuna, Pta.	147	17 59N	65 53W
Tunas de Zaza	166	21 39N	79 34W
Tunbridge Wells	29	51 7N	0 16 E
T'unch'i	105	29 50N	118 26 E
Tuncurry	141	32 9 S	152 29 E
Tunduru	127	11 0 S	37 25 E
Tunduru □	127	11 5 S	37 22 E
Tundzha, R.	67	42 0N	26 35 E
Tune	71	59 16N	11 2 E
Tung Chiang, R.	109	22 55N	113 35 E
Tung-Pei	77	44 0N	126 0 E
Tunga La	99	29 0N	94 14 E
Tunga Pass	98	29 0N	94 14 E
Tunga, R.	97	13 42N	75 20 E
Tungabhadra Dam	97	15 21N	76 23 E
Tungabhadra, R.	97	15 30N	77 0 E
Tungachen	106	36 15N	165 12 E
Tungan	109	26 24N	111 17 E
T'ungan	109	24 44N	118 9 E
T'ungcheng, Anhwei, China	109	31 3N	116 58 E
T'ungcheng, Hupeh, China	109	29 15N	113 49 E
Tungch'i	108	28 43N	106 42 E
T'ungchiang, Heilungkiang, China	105	47 40N	132 30 E
T'ungchiang, Szechwan, China	108	31 56N	107 15 E
Tungchingch'eng	107	44 9N	129 7 E
Tungchuan	105	35 4N	109 2 E
T'ungch'uan	106	35 95N	109 5 E
Tungch'uan	108	26 9N	103 7 E
Tungfanghsien, (Paso)	100	18 50N	108 33 E
Tungfeng	107	42 40N	125 34 E
T'unghai	108	24 8N	102 43 E
Tunghai Tao	109	21 2N	110 25 E
Tunghsiang	109	28 14N	116 35 E
T'unghsien	105	39 45N	116 43 E
T'unghsin	106	37 9N	106 28 E
T'unghua	107	41 45N	126 0 E
Tungi	98	23 53N	90 24 E
T'ungjen	105	27 43N	109 10 E
Tungkan	108	23 22N	105 9 E
Tungkou	107	39 52N	124 8 E
Tungku	108	31 52N	100 14 E
T'ungku	109	28 32N	114 23 E
Tungkuan	109	23 0N	113 39 E
T'ungkuan	105	34 37N	110 27 E
Tungkuang	106	37 53N	116 32 E
Tungla	166	13 24N	84 15W
Tunglan	108	24 30N	107 23 E
T'ungliang	108	29 52N	106 2 E
T'ungliao	107	43 37N	122 16 E
Tungling	109	31 0N	117 54 E
Tungliu	109	30 13N	116 55 E
T'unglu	109	29 49N	119 40 E
Tungnafellsjökull	74	64 45N	17 55W
T'ungnan	108	30 14N	105 48 E
Tungning	107	44 3N	131 7 E
T'ungpai	109	32 22N	113 24 E
Tungp'ing	106	35 55N	116 18 E
Tungpu	99	31 42N	98 19 E
Tungshan	109	23 40N	117 31 E
Tungshih	109	24 12N	120 43 E
Tungsten, Can.	152	61 57N	128 16W
Tungsten, U.S.A.	160	40 50N	118 10W
Tungt'ai	109	32 50N	120 46 E
T'ungtao	108	26 21N	109 36 E
T'ungtien	108	26 40N	99 32 E
Tungt'ing Hu	109	29 18N	112 45 E
Tungtzu	108	28 8N	106 49 E
Tunguchumuch'inch'i	106	45 33N	116 50 E
Tunguska, Nizhmaya, R.	77	64 0N	95 0 E
Tunguska, Podkammenaya, R.	77	61 0N	98 0 E
T'ungwei	106	35 18N	105 10 E
T'ungyü	107	44 48N	123 6 E
Tunhua	107	43 20N	128 10 E
Tunhuang	105	40 10N	94 50 E
Tuni	96	17 22N	82 43 E
Tunia	174	2 41N	76 31W
Tunica	159	34 43N	90 23W
Tunis	119	36 50N	10 11 E
Tunis, Golfe de	119	37 0N	10 30 E
Tunisia ■	119	33 30N	9 10 E
Tunja	174	5 40N	73 25W
Tunkhannock	162	41 32N	75 56W
T'unliu	106	36 19N	112 54 E
Tunnsjøen	74	64 45N	13 25 E
Tuno I.	73	55 58N	10 27 E
T'unpuli Shan	105	35 0N	89 30 E
Tunstall	29	52 7N	1 28 E
Tuntatuliag	147	60 20N	162 45W
Tunungayualuk I.	151	56 0N	61 0W
Tunuyán	172	33 55 S	69 0W
Tunuyán, R.	172	33 33 S	67 30W
Tuolumne	163	37 59N	120 16W
Tuolumne, R.	163	37 36N	121 13W
Tuoy-Khaya	77	62 32N	111 18 E
Tupã	173	21 57 S	50 28W
Tupaciguara	171	18 35 S	48 42W
Tuparro, R.	174	5 0N	68 40W
Tupelo	157	34 15N	88 42W
Tupik	77	54 26N	119 57 E
Tupinambaranas, I.	174	3 0 S	58 0W
Tupirama	170	8 58 S	48 12W
Tupiratins	170	8 23 S	48 8W
Tupiza	172	21 30 S	65 40W
Tupman	163	35 18N	119 21W
Tupper	152	55 32N	120 1W
Tupper L.	156	44 18N	74 30W
Tupungato, Cerro	172	33 15 S	69 50W
Tuque, La	150	47 30N	72 50W
Túquerres	174	1 5N	77 37W
Tur	90	31 47N	35 14 E
Tura, India	98	25 30N	90 16 E
Tura, U.S.S.R.	77	64 20N	99 30 E
Tura, R.	84	57 12N	66 56 E
Turaba, W.	122	21 15N	41 32 E
Turagua, Serrania	174	7 20N	64 35W
Turaiyur	97	11 9N	78 38 E
Turakina	142	40 3 S	175 16 E
Turakirae Hd.	142	41 26 S	174 56 E
Tūrān	93	35 45N	56 50 E
Turan	77	51 38N	101 40 E
Turbenthal	51	47 27N	8 51 E
Tureburg	72	59 30N	17 58 E
Turégano	56	41 9N	4 1W
Turek	54	52 3N	18 30 E
Turen	174	9 17N	69 6W
Turfan Depression	105	42 45N	89 0 E
Turgay	84	49 38N	63 30 E
Turgay, R.	84	48 1N	62 45 E
Tŭrgovishte	67	43 17N	26 38 E
Turgutlu	92	38 30N	27 48 E
Turhal	82	40 24N	36 19 E
Turia, R.	58	39 43N	1 0W
TuriaçI	170	1 40 S	45 28W
TuriaçI, R.	170	3 0 S	46 0W
Turigshih	100	18 42N	109 27 E
Turin = Torino	62	45 3N	7 40 E
Turin Taber	152	49 47N	112 24W
Turinsk	84	58 3N	63 42 E
Turkana □	126	3 0N	35 30 E
Turkana, L.	80	4 10N	32 10 E
Turkestan	76	43 10N	68 10 E
Turkestanskiy, Khrebet	85	39 35N	69 0 E
Túrkeve	53	47 6N	20 44 E
Turkey ■	92	39 0N	36 0 E
Turkey Creek P.O.	136	17 2 S	128 12 E
Turki	81	52 0N	43 15 E
Turkmen S.S.R. □	85	39 0N	59 0 E
Turks Is.	167	21 20N	71 20W
Turks Island Passage	167	21 30N	71 20W
Turku (Åbo)	75	60 30N	22 19 E
Turku-Pori □	75	60 27N	22 15 E
Turkwell, R.	126	2 30N	35 20 E
Turlock	163	37 30N	120 55W
Turnagain, C.	142	40 28 S	176 38 E
Turnagain, R.	152	59 12N	127 35W
Turnberry, Can.	153	53 25N	101 45W
Turnberry, U.K.	34	55 19N	4 50W
Turneffe Is.	165	17 20N	87 50W
Turner	160	48 52N	108 25W
Turner Pt.	138	11 47 S	133 32 E
Turner River	136	17 52 S	128 16 E
Turner Valley	152	50 40N	114 17W
Turners Falls	162	42 36N	72 34W
Turnhout	47	51 19N	4 57 E
Türnitz	52	47 55N	15 29 E
Turnor L.	153	56 35N	108 35W
Turnov	52	50 34N	15 10 E
Turnovo	67	43 5N	25 41 E
Turnovo □	67	43 4N	25 39 E
Turnu Mŭgurele	70	43 46N	24 56 E
Turnu Roşu Pasul	70	45 33N	24 17 E
Turnu-Severin	70	44 39N	22 41 E
Turö	73	55 2N	10 40 E
Turon	159	37 48N	98 27W
Tuross Head	141	36 3 S	150 8 E
Turriff	37	57 32N	2 28W
Tursha	81	56 50N	47 45 E
Tursi	65	40 15N	16 27 E
Turtle Hd. I.	138	10 50 S	142 37 E
Turtle L., Can.	153	53 36N	108 38W
Turtle L., N.D., U.S.A.	158	47 30N	100 55W
Turtle L., Wis., U.S.A.	158	45 22N	92 10W
Turtleford	153	53 23N	108 57W
Turua	142	37 14 S	175 35 E
Turubah	92	28 20N	43 15 E
Turukhansk	77	65 50N	87 50 E
Turun ja Porin lääni □	75	60 27N	22 15 E
Turzovka	53	49 25N	18 41 E
Tuscaloosa	157	33 13N	87 31W
Tuscánia	63	42 25N	11 53 E
Tuscany = Toscana	62	43 28N	11 15 E
Tuscola, Ill., U.S.A.	156	39 48N	88 15W
Tuscola, Tex., U.S.A.	159	32 15N	99 48W
Tuscumbia	157	34 42N	87 42W
Tushan	106	25 50N	107 33 E
Tushino	81	55 44N	37 29 E
Tuskar Rock	39	52 12N	6 10W
Tuskegee	157	32 24N	85 39W
Tŭšnad	70	47 30N	22 33 E
Tustna	71	63 10N	8 5 E
Tuszyn	54	51 36N	19 33 E
Tutaryd	73	56 54N	13 59 E
Tutbury	28	52 52N	1 41W
Tutikorin	97	8 50N	78 12 E
Tutin	66	43 0N	20 20 E
Tutóia	170	2 45 S	42 20W
Tutoko Mt.	143	44 35 S	168 1 E
Tutong	102	4 47N	114 34 E
Tutova, R.	70	46 20N	27 30 E
Tutrakan	67	44 2N	26 40 E
Tutshi L.	152	59 56N	134 30W
Tuttlingen	49	47 59N	8 50 E
Tutuaia	103	8 25 S	127 15 E
Tutye	140	35 12 S	141 29 E
Tuva, A.S.S.R. □	77	51 30N	95 0 E
Tuxford	33	53 14N	0 52W
Tuxpan	165	20 50N	97 30W
Tuxtla Gutiérrez	165	16 50N	93 10W
Tuy	56	42 3N	8 39W
Tuy An	100	13 17N	109 16 E
Tuy Doc	101	12 15N	107 27 E
Tuy Hoa	100	13 5N	109 17 E
Tuy Phong	101	11 14N	108 43 E
Tuya L.	152	59 7N	130 35W
Tuyen Hoa	100	17 50N	106 10 E
Tuyen Quang	100	21 50N	105 10 E
Tuymazy	84	54 36N	53 42 E
Tuyun	108	26 15N	107 32 E
Tuz Gölü	92	38 45N	33 30 E
Tuz Khurmatli	92	34 52N	44 41 E
Tuz Khurmatu	92	34 50N	44 45 E
Tuzkan, Ozero	85	40 35N	67 28 E
Tuzla	66	44 34N	18 41 E
Tuzlov, R.	83	47 28N	39 45 E
Tvåaker	73	57 4N	12 25 E
Tværsted	73	57 36N	10 12 E
Tvarskog	73	56 34N	16 0 E
Tved	73	56 12N	10 25 E
Tvedestrand	71	58 38N	8 58 E
Tveitsund	71	59 2N	8 31 E
Tvelt	71	60 30N	7 11 E
Tvyrditsa	67	42 42N	25 53 E
Twain Harte	163	38 2N	120 14W
Twardogóra	54	51 23N	17 28 E
Twatt	37	59 6N	3 15W
Tweed, R.	35	55 42N	2 10W
Tweede Exploërmond	46	52 55N	6 56 E
Tweedmouth	35	55 46N	2 1W
Tweedshaws	35	55 26N	3 29W
Tweedsmuir Prov. Park	152	52 55N	126 20W
Twello	46	52 14N	6 6 E
Twelve Pins	38	53 32N	9 50W
Twentynine Palms	163	34 10N	116 4W
Twillingate	151	49 42N	54 45W
Twin Bridges	160	45 33N	112 23W
Twin Falls	160	42 30N	114 30W
Twin Valley	158	47 18N	96 15W
Twinnge	98	21 58N	96 23 E
Twisp	160	48 21N	120 5W
Twistringen	48	52 48N	8 38 E
Two Harbors	158	47 1N	91 40W
Two Hills	152	53 43N	111 45W
Two Mile Borris	39	52 41N	7 43W
Two Rivers	156	44 10N	87 31W
Two Thumbs Ra.	143	43 45 S	170 44 E
Two Tree	138	18 25 S	140 3 E
Twofold B.	141	37 8 S	149 59 E
Twong	123	5 18N	28 29 E
Twyford, Berks., U.K.	29	51 29N	0 51W
Twyford, Hants., U.K.	28	51 1N	1 19W
Ty	73	56 27N	8 32 E
Tyborön	73	56 42N	8 12 E
Tychy	54	50 9N	18 59 E
Tyczyn	54	49 58N	22 2 E
Tydd St. Mary	29	52 45N	0 9 E
Tykocin	54	53 13N	22 46 E
Tyldal	71	62 8N	10 48 E
Tyldesley	32	53 31N	2 29W
Tyler, Minn., U.S.A.	158	44 18N	96 15W
Tyler, Tex., U.S.A.	159	44 18N	96 15W
Tylldal	71	62 7N	10 45 E
Tylösand	73	56 33N	12 40 E
Týn nad Vltavou	52	49 13N	14 26 E
Tynagh	39	53 10N	8 22W
Tyndall, Mt.	143	43 15 S	170 55 E
Tyndinskiy	77	55 10N	124 43 E
Tyndrum	34	56 26N	4 41W
Tyne & Wear □	35	54 55N	1 35W
Tyne, R., Eng., U.K.	35	54 58N	1 28W
Tyne, R., Scot., U.K.	35	55 58N	2 45W
Tynemouth	35	55 1N	1 27W
Tynset	71	62 17N	10 47 E
Tyre = Sūr	90	33 19N	35 16 E
Tyrifjorden	71	60 2N	10 8 E
Tyringe	73	56 9N	13 35 E
Tyristrand	71	60 5N	10 5 E
Tyrnyauz	83	43 21N	42 45 E
Tyrol = Tirol	52	46 50N	11 20 E
Tyrone □	38	54 40N	7 15W
Tyrone, Co.	38	54 40N	7 15W
Tyrrell Arm	153	62 27N	97 30W
Tyrrell, L.	140	35 20 S	142 50 E
Tyrrell L.	153	63 7N	105 27W
Tyrrell, R.	140	35 26 S	142 51 E
Tyrrhenian Sea	60	40 0N	12 30 E
Tysfjörden	74	68 10N	16 10 E
Tysmenitsa	80	48 58N	24 50 E
Tysnes	71	60 1N	5 30 E
Tyssedal	71	60 7N	6 35 E
Tystberga	73	58 51N	17 15 E
Tyulgan	84	52 22N	56 12 E
Tyumen	84	57 0N	65 18 E
Tyumen-Aryk	85	44 2N	67 1 E
Tyup	85	42 45N	78 20 E
Tyvoll	71	62 43N	11 21 E
Tywardreath	30	50 21N	4 40W
Tywi, R.	31	51 48N	4 20W
Tywyn	31	52 36N	4 5W
Tzaneen	129	23 47 S	30 9 E
Tzefa	90	31 7N	35 12 E
Tzermiadhes Neapolis	69	35 11N	25 29 E
Tzoumérka, Óros	68	39 30N	21 26 E
Tzu Shui, R.	109	29 2N	112 55 E
Tzuch'ang	106	37 12N	109 44 E
Tzuch'eng	107	36 39N	117 56 E
Tzuch'i	109	27 42N	116 58 E
Tz'uch'i	109	29 59N	121 14 E
Tzuchien	99	27 43N	98 34 E
Tzuchin	109	23 38N	115 10 E
Tzuchung	108	29 49N	104 55 E
Tz'uhsien	106	36 22N	114 23 E
Tzuhsing	109	25 58N	113 24 E
Tzukuei	105	31 0N	110 38 E
Tzukung	108	29 20N	104 50 E
Tz'uli	109	29 25N	111 6 E
Tzummarum	46	53 14N	5 32 E
Tzupo	105	36 49N	118 5 E
T'zuyang	108	32 31N	108 32 E
Tzuyang	108	30 7N	104 39 E
Tzuyün	108	25 45N	106 5 E

U

U Taphao	100	12 35N	101 0 E
Uad Erni, O.	118	26 30N	9 30W
Uainambi	174	1 43N	69 51W
Uanda	138	21 37 S	144 55 E
Uarsciek	91	2 28N	45 55 E
Uasadi-jidi, Sierra	174	4 54N	65 18W
Uasin □	126	0 30N	35 20 E
Uassem	90	32 59N	36 2 E
Uato-Udo	103	4 3 S	126 6 E
Uatumã, R.	174	1 30 S	59 25W
Uauá	170	9 50 S	39 28W
Uaupés	174	0 8 S	67 5W
Uaxactún	166	17 25N	89 29W
Ub	66	44 28N	20 6 E
Ubá	173	21 0 S	43 0W
Ubaitaba	171	14 18 S	39 20W
Ubangi, R. = Oubangi	124	1 0N	17 50 E
Ubaté	174	5 19N	73 49W
Ubauro	94	28 15N	69 45 E
Ube	110	33 56N	131 15 E
Ubeda	59	38 3N	3 23W
Uberaba	171	19 50 S	47 55W
Uberlândia	171	19 0 S	48 20W
Ubiaja	121	6 41N	6 22 E
Ubolratna Phong, L.	100	16 45N	102 30 E
Ubombo	129	27 31 S	32 4 E
Ubon Ratchathani	100	15 15N	104 50 E
Ubondo	126	0 55 S	25 42 E
Ubort, R.	80	51 45N	28 30 E
Ubrique	57	36 41N	5 27W
Ubundi	126	0 22 S	25 30 E
Ucayali, R.	174	6 0 S	75 0W
Uccle	47	50 48N	4 22 E
Uchaly	84	54 19N	59 27 E
Uchi Lake	153	51 10N	92 40W
Uchiko	110	33 33N	132 39 E
Uchiura-Wan	112	42 25N	140 40 E
Uchte	48	52 29N	8 52 E
Uchterek	85	41 45N	73 12 E
Uckerath	48	50 44N	7 22 E
Uckfield	29	50 58N	0 6 E
Ucluelet	152	48 57N	125 32W
Ucolta	107	32 56 S	138 59 E
Ucuriş	70	46 41N	21 58 E
Uda, R.	77	54 42N	135 14 E
Udaipur	94	24 36N	73 44 E
Udaipur Garhi	95	27 0N	86 35 E
Udamalpet	97	10 35N	77 15 E
Udbina	63	44 31N	15 47 E
Uddeholm	72	60 1N	13 38 E
Uddel	46	52 15N	5 48 E
Uddevalla	73	58 21N	11 55 E
Uddingston	35	55 50N	4 3W

Uddjaur **Ust Kuyga**

Uddjaur 74 65 55N 17 50 E
Uden 47 51 40N 5 37 E
Udgir 96 18 25N 77 5 E
Udhampur 95 33 0N 75 5 E
Udi 121 6 23N 7 21 E
Udine 63 46 5N 13 10 E
Udine □ 63 46 3N 13 13 E
Udipi 97 13 25N 74 42 E
Udmurt, A.S.S.R. □ 84 57 30N 52 30 E
Udon Thani 100 17 29N 102 46 E
Udubo 121 11 52N 10 35 E
Udvoj Balken 67 42 50N 26 50 E
Udzungwa Range 127 11 15 S 35 10 E
Ueckermünde 48 53 45N 14 1 E
Ueda 111 36 24N 138 16 E
Uedineniya, Os. 12 78 0N 85 0 E
Uele, R. 124 3 50N 22 40 E
Uelen 77 66 10N 170 0W
Uelzen 48 53 0N 10 33 E
Ueno 111 34 53N 136 14 E
Uere, R. 124 3 45N 24 45 E
Uetendorf 50 46 47N 7 34 E
Ufa 84 54 45N 55 55 E
Ufa, R. 84 56 30N 58 10 E
Uffculme 30 50 45N 3 19W
Ufford 29 52 6N 1 22 E
Ugad R. 125 20 55 S 14 30 E
Ugalla, R. 126 6 0 S 32 0 E
Ugamas 128 28 0 S 19 41 E
Uganda ■ 126 2 0N 32 0 E
Ugborough 30 50 22N 3 53W
Ugchelen 46 52 11N 5 56 E
Ugento 65 39 55N 18 10 E
Ugep 121 5 53N 8 2 E
Ugie 129 31 10 S 28 13 E
Ugijar 59 36 58N 3 7W
Ugine 45 45 45N 6 25 E
Ugla 122 25 40N 37 42 E
Uglich 81 57 33N 38 13 E
Ugljane 63 43 35N 16 46 E
Ugra, R. 80 54 45N 35 30 E
Ugurchin 67 43 6N 24 26 E
Uh, R. 53 48 40N 22 0 E
Uherske Hradiště 53 49 4N 17 30 E
Uhersky Brod 53 49 1N 17 40 E
Uhrichsville 156 40 23N 81 22W
Uig, Lewis, U.K. 36 58 13N 7 1W
Uig, Skye, U.K. 36 57 35N 6 20W
Uinta Mts. 160 40 45N 110 30W
Uitenhage 128 33 40 S 25 28 E
Uitgeest 46 52 32N 4 43 E
Uithoorn 46 52 14N 4 50 E
Uithuizen 46 53 24N 6 41 E
Uitkerke 47 51 18N 3 9 E
Ujda = Oujda 118 34 45N 2 0W
Ujfehértó 53 47 49N 21 41 E
Ujh, R. 95 32 40N 75 30 E
Ujhani 95 28 0N 79 6 E
Uji 111 34 53N 135 48 E
Ujjain 94 23 9N 75 43 E
Ujpest 53 47 22N 19 6 E
Ujszász 53 47 19N 20 7 E
Ujung Pandang 103 5 10 S 119 20 E
Uka 77 57 50N 162 0 E
Ukara I. 126 1 44 S 33 0 E
Ukehe 121 6 40N 7 24 E
Ukerewe □ 126 2 0 S 32 30 E
Ukerewe Is. 126 2 0 S 33 0 E
Ukholovo 81 54 47N 40 30 E
Ukhrul 98 25 10N 94 25 E
Ukhta 78 63 55N 54 0 E
Ukiah 160 39 10N 123 9W
Ukki Fort 95 33 28N 76 54 E
Ukmerge 80 55 15N 24 45 E
Ukraine S.S.R. □ 82 48 0N 35 0 E
Uksyanskoye 84 55 57N 63 1 E
Ukwi 128 23 29 S 20 30 E
Ulaanbaatar 105 47 55N 106 53 E
Ulaangom 105 49 58N 92 2 E
Ulak I. 147 51 24N 178 58W
Ulamambri 141 31 19 S 149 23 E
Ulamba 127 9 3 S 23 38 E
Ulan Bator = Ulaanbaatar 105 47 55N 106 53 E
Ulan Ude 77 52 0N 107 30 E
Ulanbel 85 44 50N 71 7 E
Ulanga □ 127 8 40 S 36 50 E
Ulanów 54 50 30N 22 16 E
Ulaya, Morogoro, Tanz. 126 7 3 S 36 55 E
Ulaya, Shinyanga, Tanz. 126 4 25 S 33 30 E
Ulbster 37 58 21N 3 9W
Ulceby Cross 33 53 14N 0 6 E
Ulcinj 66 41 58N 19 10 E
Ulco 128 28 21 S 24 15 E
Ulefoss 71 59 17N 9 16 E
Ulëza 68 41 46N 19 57 E
Ulfborg 73 56 16N 8 20 E
Ulft 46 51 53N 6 23 E
Ulhasnagar 96 19 15N 73 10 E
Ulinda 141 31 35 S 149 30 E
Uljma 66 45 2N 21 10 E
Ulla, R. 56 42 45N 8 30W
Ulladulla 141 35 21 S 150 29 E
Ullånger 72 62 58N 18 16 E
Ullapool 36 57 54N 5 10W
Ullared 73 57 8N 12 42 E
Ulldecona 58 40 36N 0 20 E
Ullswater, L. 32 54 35N 2 52W
Ullvättern, L. 72 59 30N 14 21 E
Ulm 49 48 23N 10 0 E
Ulmarra 139 29 37 S 153 4 E
Ulmeni 70 45 4N 46 40 E
Ulricehamn 73 57 46N 13 26 E
Ulrum 46 53 22N 6 20 E
Ulsberg 71 62 45N 9 59 E
Ulsfeinvik 71 62 21N 5 53 E
Ulster □ 38 54 45N 6 30W
Ulster Canal 38 54 15N 7 0W
Ulstrem 67 42 1N 26 27 E
Ultima 140 35 22 S 143 18 E
Ulubaria 95 22 31N 88 4 E
Ulugh Muztagh 99 36 40N 87 30 E
Uluguru Mts. 126 7 15 S 37 30 E
Ulva, I. 34 56 30N 6 12W
Ulvenhout 47 51 33N 4 48 E
Ulverston 32 54 13N 3 7W
Ulverstone 138 41 11 S 146 11 E
Ulvik 71 60 35N 6 54 E
Ulvo 73 56 40N 14 37 E
Ulya 77 59 10N 142 0 E
Ulyanovsk 81 54 25N 48 25 E
Ulyasutay 105 47 45N 96 49 E
Ulysses 159 37 39N 101 25W
Ulzio 62 45 2N 6 49 E
Um Qeis 90 32 40N 35 41 E
Umag 63 45 26N 13 31 E
Umala 174 17 25 S 68 5W
Uman 82 48 40N 30 12 E
Umánaé 12 70 40N 52 10W
Umánaé Fjord 10 70 40N 52 0W
Umaria 99 23 35N 80 50 E
Umarkhed 96 19 37N 77 38 E
Umarkot 93 25 15N 69 40 E
Umatilla 160 45 58N 119 17W
Umba 78 66 50N 34 20 E
Umbertide 63 43 18N 12 20 E
Umboi I. 135 5 40 S 148 0 E
Umbrella Mts. 143 45 35 S 169 5 E
Umbria □ 63 42 53N 12 30 E
Ume, R. 74 64 45N 18 30 E
Umeå 74 63 45N 20 20 E
Umera 103 0 12 S 129 30 E
Umfuli, R. 127 17 50 S 29 40 E
Umgusa 127 19 29 S 27 52 E
Umi 110 33 34N 130 30 E
Umiat 147 69 25N 152 20W
Umka 66 44 40N 20 19 E
Umkomaas 129 30 13 S 30 48 E
Umm al Aranib 119 26 10N 14 54 E
Umm al Qaiwain 93 25 30N 55 35 E
Umm Arda 123 15 17N 32 31 E
Umm az Zamul 93 22 35N 55 18 E
Umm Bel 123 13 35N 28 0 E
Umm Digulgulaya 123 10 28N 24 58 E
Umm Dubban 123 15 23N 32 52 E
Umm el Fahm 90 32 31N 35 9 E
Umm Hagar 123 14 20N 36 41 E
Umm Koweika 123 13 10N 32 16 E
Umm Lajj 92 25 0N 37 23 E
Umm Merwa 122 18 4N 32 30 E
Umm Qurein 123 16 3N 28 49 E
Umm Rumah 122 25 50N 36 30 E
Umm Ruwaba 123 12 50N 31 10 E
Umm Said 93 25 0N 51 40 E
Umm Sidr 123 14 29N 25 10 E
Ummanz I. 48 54 29N 13 9 E
Umnak. 147 53 20N 168 20W
Umnak I. 147 53 0N 168 0W
Umniati, R. 127 18 0 S 29 0 E
Umpang 101 16 3N 98 54 E
Umpqua, R. 160 43 30N 123 30W
Umrer 96 20 51N 79 18 E
Umreth 94 22 41N 73 4 E
Umshandige Dam 127 20 10 S 30 40 E
Umtali 127 18 58 S 32 38 E
Umtata 129 31 36 S 28 49 E
Umuahia-Ibeku 121 5 33N 7 29 E
Umvukwe Ra.. 127 16 45 S 30 45 E
Umvuma 127 19 16 S 30 30 E
Umzimvubu, R. 129 31 38 S 29 33 E
Umzingwane, R. 127 21 30 S 29 30 E
Umzinto 129 30 15 S 30 45 E
Una 94 20 46N 71 8 E
Una, Mt. 143 42 13 S 172 36 E
Una, R. 63 44 50N 16 15 E
Unac, R. 63 44 42N 16 15 E
Unadilla 162 42 20N 75 17W
Unalanaska I. 147 54 0N 164 30W
Uncastillo 58 42 21N 1 8W
Uncia 174 18 25 S 66 40W
Uncompahgce Pk., Mt. 161 38 5N 107 32W
Unden 73 58 45N 14 25 E
Underbool 140 35 10 S 141 51 E
Undersaker 72 63 19N 13 21 E
Undersvik 72 61 36N 16 20 E
Undredal 71 60 57N 7 6 E
Unecha 80 52 50N 32 37 E
Ungarie 141 33 38 S 146 56 E
Ungarra 140 34 12 S 136 2 E
Ungava B. 149 59 30N 67 30W
Ungava Pen. 50 60 0N 75 0W
Ungeny 82 47 11N 27 51 E
Unggi 105 42 16N 130 28 E
Ungwatiri 123 16 52N 36 10 E
Uni 84 56 44N 51 47 E
União 170 4 50 S 37 50W
União da Vitória 173 26 5 S 51 0W
União dos Palamares 170 9 10 S 36 2W
Uniejów 54 51 59N 18 46 E
Unije, I. 63 44 40N 14 15 E
Unimak I. 147 54 30N 164 30W
Unimak Pass. 148 53 30N 165 15W
Union, Mo., U.S.A. 158 38 25N 91 0W
Union, S.C., U.S.A. 157 34 49N 81 39W
Union City, N.J., U.S.A. 162 40 47N 74 5W
Union City, Ohio, U.S.A. 156 40 11N 84 49W
Union City, Pa., U.S.A. 156 41 53N 79 50W
Union Gap 157 46 38N 120 29W
Unión, La, Chile 176 40 10 S 73 0W
Unión, La, Colomb. 174 1 35N 77 5W
Unión, La, El Sal. 165 13 20N 87 50W
Unión, La 164 17 58N 101 49W
Unión, La, Spain 59 37 38N 0 53W
Unión, La, Venez. 174 7 28N 67 53W
Union, Mt. 161 34 34N 112 21W
Union of Soviet Soc. Rep. ■ 77 47 0N 100 0 E
Union Springs 157 32 9N 85 44W
Uniondale Road 128 33 39 S 23 7 E
Uniontown 156 39 54N 79 45W
Unirea 70 44 15N 27 35 E
United Arab Emirates ■ 93 23 50N 54 0 E
United Arab Republic ■ 113 27 5N 30 0 E
United Kingdom ■ 27 55 0N 3 0W
United States of America ■ 155 37 0N 96 0W
Unity 153 52 30N 109 5W
Unjha 94 23 46N 72 24 E
Unnao 95 26 35N 80 30 E
Uno, Ilha 120 11 15N 16 13W
Unshin, R. 38 54 8N 8 26W
Unst, I. 36 60 50N 0 55W
Unstrut, R. 48 51 16N 11 29 E
Unter-Engadin 51 46 48N 10 20 E
Unterägeri 51 47 8N 8 36 E
Unterkulm 50 47 18N 8 7 E
Unterseen 50 46 41N 7 50 E
Unterwalden nid dem Wald □ 51 46 50N 8 25 E
Unterwalden ob dem Wald □ 51 46 55N 8 15 E
Unterwaldner Alpen 51 46 55N 8 15 E
Unterwasser 51 46 32N 8 21 E
Unturán, Sierra de 174 1 35N 64 40W
Unuk, R. 152 56 5N 131 3W
Ünye 82 41 5N 37 15 E
Unzen-Dake 111 32 45N 130 17 E
Unzha 81 57 40N 44 8 E
Unzha, R. 81 58 0N 43 40 E
Uors 51 46 42N 9 12 E
Uozu 111 36 48N 137 24 E
Upa, R. 53 50 45N 16 15 E
Upal 123 6 56N 34 12 E
Upata 174 8 1N 62 24W
Upavon 28 51 17N 1 49W
Upemba, L. 127 8 30 S 26 20 E
Upernavik 12 72 49N 56 20W
Upington 128 28 25 S 21 15 E
Upleta 94 21 46N 70 16 E
Upolu Pt. 147 20 16N 155 52W
Upper Alkali Lake 160 41 47N 120 0W
Upper Arrow L. 152 50 30N 117 50W
Upper Austria = Oberösterreich 52 48 15N 14 10 E
Upper Chapel 31 52 3N 3 26W
Upper Foster L. 153 56 47N 105 20W
Upper Heyford 28 51 54N 1 16W
Upper Hutt 142 41 8 S 175 5 E
Upper Klamath L. 160 42 16N 121 55W
Upper L. Erne 38 54 14N 7 22W
Upper Lake 160 39 10N 122 55W
Upper Manilla 141 30 38 S 150 40 E
Upper Marlboro 162 38 49N 76 45W
Upper Musquodoboit 151 45 10N 62 58W
Upper Sandusky 156 40 50N 83 17W
Upper Volta ■ 120 12 0N 0 30W
Upperchurch 39 52 43N 8 2W
Upphärad 73 58 9N 12 19 E
Uppingham 29 52 36N 0 43W
Uppsala 72 59 53N 17 38 E
Uppsala län □ 72 60 0N 17 30 E
Upshi 95 33 48N 77 52 E
Upstart, C. 138 19 41 S 147 45 E
Upton, U.K. 32 53 14N 2 52W
Upton, U.S.A. 158 44 8N 104 35W
Upton-upon-Severn 28 52 4N 2 12W
Upwey 28 50 40N 2 29W
Ur 92 30 55N 46 25 E
Ura-Tyube 85 39 55N 69 1 E
Urabá, Golfo de 174 8 25N 76 53W
Uracará 174 2 20 S 57 50W
Urach 49 48 29N 9 25 E
Uraga-Suidō 111 35 13N 139 45 E
Urakawa 112 42 9N 142 47 E
Ural, Mt. 141 33 21 S 146 12 E
Ural Mts. = Uralskie Gory 78 60 0N 59 0 E
Ural, R. 84 49 0N 52 0W
Uralla 141 30 37 S 151 29 E
Uralsk 84 51 20N 51 20 E
Uralskie Gory 78 60 0N 59 0 E
Urambo 126 5 4 S 32 47 E
Urambo □ 126 5 0 S 32 0 E
Urana 141 35 15 S 146 21 E
Urandangi 138 21 32 S 138 14 E
Uranium City 153 59 34N 108 37W
Uraricaá, R. 174 3 20N 61 56W
Uravakonda 97 14 57N 77 12 E
Urawa 111 35 50N 139 40 E
Uray 76 60 5N 65 15 E
Urbana, Ill., U.S.A. 156 40 7N 88 12W
Urbana, Ohio, U.S.A. 156 40 9N 83 44W
Urbana, La 174 7 8N 66 56W
Urbánia 63 43 40N 12 31 E
Urbano Santos 170 3 12 S 43 23W
Urbel, R. 58 42 30N 3 49W
Urbino 63 43 43N 12 38 E
Urbión, Picos de 58 42 1N 2 52W
Urcos 174 13 30 S 71 30W
Urda, Spain 57 39 25N 3 43W
Urda, U.S.S.R. 83 48 52N 47 23 E
Urdinarrain 172 32 37 S 58 52W
Urdos 44 42 51N 0 35W
Urdzhar 76 47 5N 81 38 E
Ure, R. 33 54 20N 1 25W
Uren 81 57 35N 45 55 E
Ures 164 29 30N 110 30W
Ureshino 110 33 6N 129 59 E
Urfa 92 37 12N 38 50 E
Urfahr 52 48 19N 14 17 E
Urgench 76 41 40N 60 30 E
Urgun 93 32 55N 69 12 E
Urgut 85 39 23N 67 15 E
Uri 95 34 8N 74 2 E
Uri □ 51 46 43N 8 35 E
Uribante, R. 174 7 25N 71 50W
Uribe 174 3 13N 74 24W
Uribia 174 11 43N 72 16W
Urim 90 31 18N 34 32 E
Uriondo 172 21 41 S 64 41W
Urique 164 27 13N 107 55W
Urique, R. 164 26 29N 107 58W
Urirotstock 51 46 52N 8 32 E
Urk 46 52 39N 5 36 E
Urla 92 38 20N 26 55 E
Urlati 70 44 59N 26 15 E
Urlingford 39 52 43N 7 35W
Urmia, L. 92 37 30N 45 30 E
Urmia (Rezā'iyeh) 92 37 40N 45 0 E
Urmston 32 53 28N 2 22W
Urner Alpen 51 46 45N 8 45 E
Uroševac 66 42 23N 21 10 E
Urrao 174 6 20N 76 11W
Urshult 73 56 31N 14 50 E
Urso 123 9 35N 41 33 E
Ursus 54 52 21N 20 53 E
Uruaca 171 15 30 S 49 41W
Uruaçu 171 14 30 S 49 10W
Uruapán 164 19 30N 102 0W
Urubamba 174 13 5 S 72 10W
Urubamba, R. 174 11 0 S 73 0W
Uruçuca 171 14 35 S 39 16W
Uruçuí 170 7 20 S 44 28W
Uruçuí Prêto, R. 170 7 20 S 44 38W
Uruçuí, Serra do 170 9 0 S 44 45W
Urucuia, R. 171 16 8 S 45 5W
Uruguai, R. 173 24 0 S 53 30W
Uruguaiana 172 29 50 S 57 0W
Uruguay ■ 172 32 30 S 55 30W
Uruguay, R. 172 28 0 S 56 0W
Urumchi = Wulumuchi 105 43 40N 87 50 E
Urup, I. 77 43 0N 151 0 E
Urup, R. 83 44 19N 41 30 E
Urutaí 171 17 28 S 48 12W
Uruyén 174 5 41N 62 25W
Uruzgan □ 93 33 30N 66 0 E
Uryupinsk 81 50 45N 42 3 E
Urzhum 81 57 10N 49 56 E
Urziceni 70 44 46N 26 42 E
Usa 110 33 31N 131 21 E
Usa, R. 78 66 20N 56 0 E
Uşak 92 38 43N 29 28 E
Usakos 128 22 0 S 15 31 E
Usambara Mts. 126 4 50 S 38 20 E
Usedom 48 53 50N 13 55 E
Useko 124 5 8 S 32 24 E
Usfan 122 21 58N 39 27 E
Ush-Tobe 76 45 16N 78 0 E
Ushakova, O. 12 82 0N 80 0 E
Ushant = Ouessant, Île d' 42 48 25N 5 5W
Ushashi 126 1 59 S 33 57 E
Ushat 123 7 59N 29 28 E
Ushibuka 110 32 11N 130 1 E
Ushuaia 176 54 50 S 68 23W
Ushumun 77 52 47N 126 32 E
Usk 31 51 42N 2 53W
Usk, R. 31 51 37N 2 56W
Uskedal 71 59 56N 5 53 E
Üsküdar 92 41 0N 29 5 E
Uslar 48 51 39N 9 39 E
Usman 81 52 5N 39 48 E
Usoga □ 126 0 5N 33 30 E
Usoke 126 5 7 S 32 19 E
Usolye Sibirskoye 77 52 40N 103 40 E
Usoro 121 5 33N 6 11 E
Uspallata, P. de 172 32 30 S 69 28W
Uspenskiy 76 48 50N 72 55 E
Usquert 46 53 24N 6 36 E
Ussel 44 45 32N 2 18 E
Ussuriysk 77 43 40N 131 50 E
Ust 52 50 41N 14 2 E
Ust Aldan = Batamay 77 63 30N 129 15 E
Ust Amginskoye = Khandyga 77 62 30N 134 50 E
Ust-Bolsheretsk 77 52 40N 156 30 E
Ust Buzulukskaya 81 50 8N 42 11 E
Ust Doneckij 83 47 35N 40 55 E
Ust Donetskiy 83 47 35N 40 55 E
Ust Ilga 77 55 5N 104 55 E
Ust Ilimpeya = Yukti 77 63 20N 105 0 E
Ust-Ilimsk 77 58 3N 102 39 E
Ust Ishim 76 57 45N 71 10 E
Ust Kamchatsk 77 56 10N 162 0 E
Ust Kamenogorsk 76 50 0N 82 20 E
Ust Karenga 77 54 40N 116 45 E
Ust Khayryuzova 77 57 15N 156 55 E
Ust Kut 77 56 50N 105 10 E
Ust Kuyga 77 70 1N 135 36 E

Ust Labinsk **Vatoloha, Mt**

Ust Labinsk	**83**	45 15N	39 50 E
Ust Luga	**80**	59 35N	28 26 E
Ust Maya	**77**	60 30N	134 20 E
Ust Mil	**77**	59 50N	133 0 E
Ust Nera	**77**	64 35N	143 15 E
Ust Olenek	**77**	73 0N	120 10 E
Ust-Omchug	**77**	61 9N	149 38 E
Ust Port	**76**	70 0N	84 10 E
Ust Tsilma	**78**	65 25N	52 0 E
Ust-Tungir	**77**	55 25N	120 15 E
Ust Urt = Ustyurt	**76**	44 0N	55 0 E
Ust Usa	**78**	66 0N	56 30 E
Ust-Uyskoye	**84**	54 16N	63 54 E
Ust Vorkuta	**76**	67 7N	63 35 E
Ustaoset	**71**	60 30N	8 2 E
Ustaritz	**44**	43 24N	1 27W
Uste	**81**	59 35N	39 40 E
Uster	**51**	47 22N	8 43 E
Ustí na Orlici	**53**	49 58N	16 38 E
Ustí nad Labem	**52**	50 41N	14 3 E
Ustica, I.	**64**	38 42N	13 10 E
Ustka	**54**	54 35N	16 55 E
Ustron	**54**	49 45N	18 48 E
Ustrzyki Dolne	**54**	49 27N	22 40 E
Ustye	**77**	55 30N	97 30 E
Ustyurt, Plato	**76**	44 0N	55 0 E
Ustyuzhna	**81**	58 50N	36 32 E
Ušće	**66**	43 43N	20 39 E
Usuki	**110**	33 8N	131 49 E
Usulután	**166**	13 25N	88 28W
Usumacinta, R.	**165**	17 0N	91 0W
Usva	**84**	58 41N	57 37 E
Uta	**66**	45 24N	21 13 E
Utah □	**160**	39 30N	111 30W
Utah, L.	**160**	40 10N	111 58W
Ute Cr.	**159**	36 5N	103 45W
Utena	**80**	55 27N	25 40 E
Utersen	**48**	53 40N	9 40 E
Utete	**124**	8 0S	38 45 E
Uthai Thani	**100**	15 22N	100 3 E
Uthal	**94**	25 44N	66 40 E
Uthmaniyah	**92**	25 5N	49 6 E
Utiariti	**174**	13 0S	58 10W
Utica	**162**	43 5N	75 18W
Utiel	**58**	39 37N	1 11W
Utik L.	**153**	55 15N	96 0W
Utikuma L.	**152**	55 50N	115 30W
Utinga	**171**	12 6S	41 5W
Uto	**110**	32 41N	130 40 E
Utrecht, Neth.	**46**	52 3N	5 8 E
Utrecht, S. Afr.	**129**	27 38S	30 20 E
Utrecht □	**46**	52 6N	5 7 E
Utrera	**57**	37 12N	5 48W
Utsjoki	**74**	69 51N	26 59 E
Utsunomiya	**111**	36 30N	139 50 E
Uttar Pradesh □	**95**	27 0N	80 0 E
Uttaradit	**100**	17 36N	100 5 E
Uttersberg	**72**	59 45N	15 39 E
Uttersley	**73**	54 56N	11 11 E
Uttoxeter	**32**	52 53N	1 50W
Utva, R.	**84**	51 28N	52 40 E
Ütze	**48**	52 28N	10 11 E
Uudenmaan lääni □	**75**	60 25N	25 0 E
Uusikaarlepyy	**74**	63 32N	22 31 E
Uusikaupunki	**75**	60 47N	21 25 E
Uva	**84**	56 59N	52 13 E
Uvac, R.	**66**	43 35N	19 40 E
Uvalde	**159**	29 15N	99 48W
Uvarovo	**81**	51 59N	42 14 E
Uvat	**76**	59 5N	68 50 E
Uvelskiy	**84**	54 26N	61 22 E
Uvinza	**126**	5 5S	30 24 E
Uvira	**126**	3 22S	29 3 E
Uvlova, R.	**52**	49 34N	13 20 E
Uvs Nuur, L.	**105**	50 20N	92 45 E
Uwa	**110**	33 22N	132 31 E
Uwainhid	**92**	24 50N	46 0 E
Uwajima	**110**	33 10N	132 35 E
Uxmal	**165**	20 22N	89 46W
Uyeasound	**36**	60 42N	0 55W
Uyo	**121**	5 1N	7 53 E
Uyu, R.	**98**	24 51N	94 57 E
Uyuk	**85**	43 36N	71 16 E
Uyuni	**172**	20 35S	66 55W
Uyuni, Salar de	**172**	20 10S	68 0W
Uzbekistan S.S.R. □	**85**	40 5N	65 0 E
Uzen, Bol.	**81**	50 0N	49 30 E
Uzen, Mal.	**81**	50 0N	48 30 E
Uzerche	**44**	45 25N	1 35 E
Uzès	**45**	44 1N	4 26 E
Uzgen	**85**	40 46N	73 18 E
Uzh, R.	**80**	51 15N	29 45 E
Uzhgorod	**80**	48 36N	22 18 E
Uzlovaya	**81**	54 0N	38 5 E
Uzun-Agach	**85**	43 35N	76 20 E
Uzunköprü	**67**	41 16N	26 43 E
Uzure	**126**	4 40S	34 22 E
Uzwil	**51**	47 26N	9 9 E

V

Vaal, R.	**128**	27 40S	25 30 E
Vaaldam	**129**	27 0S	28 14 E
Vaals	**47**	50 46N	6 1 E
Vaalwater	**129**	24 15S	28 8 E
Vaasa	**74**	63 16N	21 35 E
Vaasan lääni □	**74**	63 2N	22 50 E
Vaassen	**46**	52 17N	5 58 E
Vabre	**44**	43 42N	2 24 E
Vác	**53**	47 49N	19 10 E
Vacaria	**173**	28 31S	50 52W
Vacaville	**163**	38 21N	122 0W
Vach, R.	**76**	60 56N	76 38 E
Vache, I.-à	**167**	18 2N	73 35W
Väddö	**72**	59 55N	18 50 E
Väderum	**73**	57 32N	16 11 E
Vadnagar	**94**	23 47N	72 40 E
Vado Ligure	**62**	44 16N	8 26 E
Vadodara	**94**	22 20N	73 10 E
Vadsø	**74**	70 3N	29 50 E
Vadstena	**73**	58 28N	14 54 E
Vaduz	**51**	47 8N	9 31 E
Vaerøy, Nordland Fylke, Norway	**74**	67 40N	12 40 E
Vaerøy, Sogn og Fjordane, Norway	**71**	61 17N	4 45 E
Vagney	**43**	48 1N	6 43 E
Vagnhärad	**72**	58 57N	17 33 E
Vagos	**56**	40 33N	8 42W
Vagsöy, I.	**71**	62 0N	5 0 E
Váh, R.	**53**	49 10N	18 20 E
Vaigach	**76**	70 10N	59 0 E
Vaigai, R.	**97**	9 47N	78 23 E
Vaiges	**42**	48 2N	0 30W
Vaihingen	**49**	48 44N	8 58 E
Vaihsel B.	**13**	75 0S	35 0W
Vaijapur	**96**	19 58N	74 45 E
Vaikam	**97**	9 45N	76 25 E
Vaila I.	**36**	60 12N	1 34W
Vailly Aisne	**43**	49 25N	3 30 E
Vaippar, R.	**97**	9 0N	78 25 E
Vaison	**45**	44 14N	5 4 E
Vajpur	**96**	21 24N	73 45 E
Vakarel	**67**	42 35N	23 40 E
Vakhsh, R.	**85**	37 6N	68 18 E
Vaksdal	**71**	60 29N	5 45 E
Vál	**53**	47 22N	18 40 E
Val d' Ajol, Le	**43**	47 55N	6 30 E
Val-de-Marne □	**43**	48 45N	2 28 E
Val-d'Oise □	**43**	49 5N	2 0 E
Val d'Or	**150**	48 7N	77 47W
Val Marie	**153**	49 15N	107 45W
Val-St.-Germain	**47**	48 34N	2 4 E
Valadares	**56**	41 5N	8 38W
Valahia	**70**	44 35N	25 0 E
Valais □	**50**	46 12N	7 45 E
Valais, Alpes du	**50**	46 47N	7 30 E
Valandovo	**66**	41 19N	22 34 E
Valasské MeziríU5	**53**	49 29N	17 59 E
Valaxa, I.	**69**	38 50N	24 29 E
Valcheta	**176**	40 40S	66 20W
Valdagno	**63**	45 38N	11 18 E
Valdahon, Le	**43**	47 8N	6 20 E
Valday	**80**	57 58N	31 9 E
Valdayskaya Vozvyshennost	**80**	57 0N	33 40 E
Valdeazogues, R.	**57**	38 45N	4 55W
Valdemarsvik	**73**	58 14N	16 40 E
Valdepeñas, Ciudad Real, Spain	**57**	38 43N	3 25W
Valdepeñas, Jaén, Spain	**57**	37 33N	3 47W
Valderaduey, R.	**56**	42 30N	5 0W
Valderrobres	**58**	40 53N	0 9 E
Valdes Pen.	**176**	42 30S	63 45W
Valdez	**147**	61 14N	146 10W
Valdivia	**176**	39 50S	73 14W
Valdivia □	**176**	40 0S	73 0W
Valdivia, La	**172**	34 43S	72 5W
Valdobbiádene	**63**	45 53N	12 0 E
Valdosta	**157**	30 50N	83 48W
Valdoviño	**56**	43 36N	8 8W
Valdres	**71**	60 55N	9 28 E
Vale, U.S.A.	**160**	44 0N	117 15W
Vale, U.S.S.R.	**83**	41 30N	42 58 E
Valea lui Mihai	**70**	47 32N	22 11 E
Valença, Brazil	**171**	13 20S	39 5W
Valença, Port.	**56**	42 1N	8 34W
Valença do Piauí	**170**	6 20S	41 45W
Valence	**45**	44 57N	4 54 E
Valence-d'Agen	**44**	44 8N	0 54 E
Valencia, Spain	**59**	39 27N	0 23W
Valencia, Venez.	**174**	10 11N	68 0W
Valencia □	**59**	39 20N	0 40W
Valencia, Albufera de	**59**	39 20N	0 27W
Valencia de Alcántara	**57**	39 25N	7 14W
Valencia de Don Juan	**56**	42 17N	5 31W
Valencia des Ventoso	**57**	38 15N	6 29W
Valencia, G. de	**59**	39 30N	0 20 E
Valencia, L. de	**167**	10 13N	67 40W
Valenciennes	**43**	50 20N	3 34 E
Valensole	**45**	43 50N	5 59 E
Valentia Hr.	**39**	51 56N	10 17W
Valentia I.	**39**	51 54N	10 22W
Valentine, Nebr., U.S.A.	**158**	42 50N	100 35W
Valentine, Tex., U.S.A.	**159**	30 36N	104 28W
Valenton	**160**	48 45N	2 28 E
Valenza	**62**	45 2N	8 39 E
Våler	**71**	60 41N	11 50 E
Valera	**174**	9 19N	70 37W
Valguarnera Caropepe	**65**	37 30N	14 22 E
Valhall, oilfield	**19**	56 17N	3 25 E
Valier	**160**	48 15N	112 9W
Valinco, G. de	**45**	41 40N	8 52 E
Valjevo	**66**	44 18N	19 53 E
Valkeakoski	**75**	61 16N	24 2 E
Valkenburg	**47**	50 52N	5 50 E
Valkenswaard	**47**	51 21N	5 29 E
Vall de Uxó	**58**	40 49N	0 15W
Valla	**72**	59 2N	16 20 E
Valladolid, Mexico	**165**	20 30N	88 20W
Valladolid, Spain	**56**	41 38N	4 43W
Valladolid □	**56**	41 38N	4 43W
Vallata	**65**	41 3N	15 16 E
Valldalssæter	**71**	59 56N	6 57 E
Valle	**71**	59 13N	7 33 E
Valle d'Aosta □	**62**	45 45N	7 22 E
Valle de Arán	**58**	42 50N	0 55 E
Valle de Cabuérniga	**56**	43 14N	4 18W
Valle de la Pascua	**174**	9 13N	66 0W
Valle de Santiago	**164**	20 25N	101 15W
Valle de Zaragoza	**164**	27 28N	105 49W
Valle del Cauca □	**174**	3 45N	76 30W
Valle Fértil, Sierra del	**172**	30 20S	68 0W
Valle Hermosa	**165**	25 35N	102 25 E
Valle Nacional	**165**	17 47N	96 19W
Vallecas	**56**	40 23N	3 41W
Valledupar	**174**	10 29N	73 15W
Vallejo	**163**	38 12N	122 15W
Vallenar	**172**	28 30S	70 50W
Valleraugue	**44**	44 6N	3 39 E
Vallet	**42**	47 10N	1 15W
Valletta	**60**	35 54N	14 30 E
Valley	**31**	53 17N	4 31W
Valley Center	**163**	33 13N	117 2W
Valley City	**158**	46 57N	98 0W
Valley Falls	**160**	42 33N	120 8W
Valley Okolona	**159**	34 0N	88 45W
Valley Springs	**163**	38 11N	120 50W
Valley View	**162**	40 39N	76 33W
Valleyfield	**150**	45 15N	74 8W
Valleyview	**152**	55 5N	117 17W
Valli di Comácchio	**63**	44 40N	12 15 E
Vallimanca, Arroyo	**172**	35 40S	59 10W
Vallo della Lucánia	**65**	40 14N	15 16 E
Vallon	**45**	44 25N	4 23 E
Vallorbe	**50**	46 42N	6 20 E
Valls	**58**	41 18N	1 15 E
Vallsta	**72**	61 31N	16 22 E
Valmaseda	**58**	43 11N	3 12W
Valmiera	**80**	57 37N	25 38 E
Valmont	**42**	49 45N	0 30 E
Valmontone	**64**	41 48N	12 55 E
Valmy	**43**	49 5N	4 45 E
Valnera, Mte.	**58**	43 9N	3 40W
Valognes	**42**	49 30N	1 28W
Valona (Vlora)	**68**	40 32N	19 28 E
Valongo	**56**	40 37N	8 27W
Valpaços	**56**	41 36N	7 17W
Valparaíso, Chile	**172**	33 2S	71 40W
Valparaíso, Mexico	**164**	22 50N	103 32W
Valparaiso	**156**	41 27N	87 2W
Valparaíso □	**172**	33 2S	71 40W
Valpovo	**66**	45 39N	18 25 E
Valréas	**45**	44 24N	5 0 E
Vals	**51**	46 39N	10 11 E
Vals-les-Bains	**45**	44 42N	4 24 E
Vals, R.	**128**	27 28S	26 52 E
Vals, Tanjung	**103**	8 32S	137 32 E
Valsbaai	**128**	34 15S	18 40 E
Valskog	**72**	59 27N	15 57 E
Válta	**68**	40 3N	23 25 E
Valtellina	**62**	46 9N	10 2 E
Valverde del Camino	**57**	37 35N	6 47W
Valverde del Fresno	**56**	40 15N	6 51W
Valyiki	**81**	50 10N	38 5 E
Vama	**70**	47 34N	25 42 E
Vambarra Ra.	**136**	15 13S	130 24 E
Vamdrup	**50**	55 26N	9 10 E
Vammala	**75**	61 20N	22 55 E
Vámos	**69**	35 24N	24 13 E
Vamsadhara, R.	**96**	18 22N	84 15 E
Van	**92**	38 30N	43 20 E
Van Alstyne	**159**	33 25N	96 36W
Van Bruyssel	**151**	47 56N	72 9W
Van Buren, Can.	**151**	47 10N	67 55W
Van Buren, Ark., U.S.A.	**159**	35 28N	94 18W
Van Buren, Me., U.S.A.	**157**	47 10N	68 1W
Van Buren, Mo., U.S.A.	**159**	37 0N	91 0W
Van Canh	**100**	13 37N	109 0 E
Van der Kloof Dam	**128**	30 04S	24 40 E
Van Diemen, C., N.T., Austral.	**136**	11 9S	130 24 E
Van Diemen, C., Queens., Austral.	**138**	16 30S	139 46 E
Van Diemen G.	**136**	11 45S	131 50 E
Van Gölü	**92**	38 30N	43 0 E
Van Horn	**161**	31 3N	104 55W
Van Ninn	**100**	12 42N	109 14 E
Van Reenen P.	**129**	28 22S	29 27 E
Van Tassell	**158**	42 40N	104 3W
Van Tivu, I.	**97**	8 51N	78 15 E
Van Wert	**156**	40 52N	84 31W
Van Yen	**100**	21 4N	104 42 E
Vanavara	**77**	60 22N	102 16 E
Vancouver, Can.	**152**	49 20N	123 10W
Vancouver, U.S.A.	**160**	45 44N	122 41W
Vancouver, C.	**137**	35 2S	118 11 E
Vancouver I.	**152**	49 50N	126 0W
Vandalia, Ill., U.S.A.	**158**	38 57N	89 4W
Vandalia, Mo., U.S.A.	**158**	39 18N	91 30W
Vandeloos Bay	**97**	8 0N	81 45 E
Vandenburg	**163**	34 35N	120 44W
Vanderbijlpark	**86**	26 42S	27 54 E
Vanderhoof	**152**	54 0N	124 0W
Vanderlin I.	**138**	15 44S	137 2 E
Vandyke	**138**	24 10S	147 51 E
Vänern	**73**	58 47N	13 30 E
Vänersborg	**73**	58 26N	12 27 E
Vang Vieng	**100**	18 58N	102 32 E
Vanga	**126**	4 35S	39 12 E
Vangaindrano	**129**	23 21S	47 36 E
Vanguard	**153**	49 55N	107 20W
Vanier	**150**	45 27N	75 40W
Vanimo	**135**	2 42S	141 21 E
Vanivilasa Sagara	**97**	13 45N	76 30 E
Vaniyambadi	**97**	12 46N	78 44 E
Vankleek Hill	**150**	45 32N	75 40W
Vanna	**74**	70 6N	19 50 E
Vannas	**74**	63 58N	19 48 E
Vannes	**42**	47 40N	2 47W
Vanoise, Massif de la	**45**	45 25N	6 40 E
Vanrhynsdorp	**128**	31 36S	18 44 E
Vanrook	**138**	16 57S	141 57 E
Vans, Les	**45**	44 25N	4 7 E
Vansbro	**72**	60 32N	14 15 E
Vanse	**71**	58 6N	6 41 E
Vansittart B.	**136**	14 3S	126 17 E
Vanthli	**94**	21 28N	70 25 E
Vanua Levu, I.	**130**	16 33S	178 8 E
Vanwyksvlei	**128**	30 18S	21 49 E
Vanylven	**71**	62 5N	5 33 E
Vapnyarka	**82**	48 32N	28 45 E
Var □	**45**	43 27N	6 18 E
Vara	**73**	58 16N	12 55 E
Varada, R.	**97**	14 46N	75 15 E
Varades	**42**	47 25N	1 1W
Varaita, R.	**62**	44 35N	7 15 E
Varaldsöy	**71**	60 6N	5 59 E
Varallo	**62**	45 50N	8 13 E
Varanasi (Benares)	**95**	25 22N	83 8 E
Varangerfjorden	**74**	70 3N	29 25 E
Varazdin	**63**	46 20N	16 20 E
Varazze	**62**	44 21N	8 36 E
Varberg	**73**	57 17N	12 20 E
Vardar, R.	**66**	41 25N	22 20 E
Varde	**73**	55 38N	8 29 E
Varde Å	**73**	55 35N	8 19 E
Vardø	**74**	70 23N	31 5 E
Varel	**48**	53 23N	8 9 E
Varella, Mui	**100**	12 54N	109 26 E
Varena	**80**	54 12N	24 30 E
Vårendseke	**73**	57 4N	15 0 E
Varennes-sur-Allier	**44**	49 12N	5 0 E
Vareš	**66**	44 12N	18 23 E
Varese	**62**	45 49N	8 50 E
Varese Ligure	**62**	44 22N	9 33 E
Vårgårda	**73**	58 2N	12 49 E
Vargem Bonita	**171**	20 20S	46 22W
Vargem Grande	**170**	3 33S	43 56W
Varginha	**173**	21 33S	45 25W
Vargön	**73**	58 22N	12 20 E
Varhaug	**71**	58 37N	5 41 E
Varillas	**172**	24 0S	70 10W
Varing	**73**	58 30N	14 0 E
Värmdö, I.	**72**	59 18N	18 45 E
Värmeln	**72**	59 35N	13 0 E
Värmlands län □	**72**	59 45N	13 20 E
Varmlandssaby	**72**	59 7N	14 15 E
Varna, Bulg.	**67**	43 13N	27 56 E
Varna, U.S.S.R.	**84**	53 24N	60 58 E
Varna, R.	**96**	17 13N	73 50 E
Varnamo	**73**	57 10N	14 3 E
Varnsdorf	**52**	49 56N	14 38 E
Värö	**73**	51 16N	12 15 E
Varpelev	**73**	55 22N	12 17 E
Värsjö	**73**	56 23N	13 27 E
Varsseveld	**46**	51 56N	6 29 E
Varteig	**71**	59 23N	11 12 E
Varto	**92**	39 10N	41 28 E
Vartofta	**73**	58 6N	13 40 E
Vartry Res.	**39**	53 3N	6 12W
Varvarin	**66**	43 43N	21 20 E
Varzaneh	**93**	32 25N	52 40 E
Várzea Alegre	**170**	6 47S	39 17W
Várzea da Palma	**171**	17 36S	44 44W
Varzi	**62**	44 50N	9 12 E
Varzo	**62**	46 12N	8 15 E
Varzy	**43**	47 22N	3 20 E
Vas □	**53**	47 10N	16 55 E
Vasa	**74**	63 6N	21 38 E
Vasa Barris, R.	**170**	11 10S	37 10W
Vásárosnamény	**53**	48 9N	22 19 E
Väsby	**73**	56 13N	12 37 E
Vascão, R.	**57**	37 44N	8 15W
Vascongadas	**58**	42 50N	2 45W
Vaşcǎu	**70**	46 28N	22 30 E
Väse	**72**	59 23N	13 52 E
Vasht = Khāsh	**93**	28 20N	61 6 E
Vasii Levski	**67**	43 23N	25 26 E
Vasilevichi	**80**	52 15N	29 50 E
Vasilikón	**69**	38 25N	23 40 E
Vasilkov	**80**	50 7N	30 28 E
Vaslui	**70**	46 38N	27 42 E
Vaslui □	**71**	46 30N	27 30 E
Väsman	**72**	60 9N	15 5 E
Vassa	**74**	63 6N	21 38 E
Vassar, Can.	**153**	49 10N	95 55W
Vassar, U.S.A.	**156**	43 23N	83 33W
Vast Silen, L.	**72**	59 15N	12 15 E
Västerås	**73**	59 37N	16 38 E
Västerbottens län □	**74**	64 58N	18 0 E
Västerdalälven	**72**	60 30N	13 25 E
Västernorrlands län □	**72**	63 30N	17 40 E
Västervik	**73**	57 43N	16 43 E
Västmanland □	**72**	59 55N	16 30 E
Vasto	**63**	42 8N	14 40 E
Vasvár	**53**	47 3N	16 47 E
Vatan	**43**	47 4N	1 50 E
Vaternish Pt.	**36**	57 36N	6 40W
Vatersay, I.	**36**	56 55N	7 32W
Vathí	**69**	37 46N	27 1 E
Váthia	**69**	36 29N	22 29 E
Vatican City ■	**63**	41 54N	12 27 E
Vatin	**66**	45 12N	21 20 E
Vatnajökull	**74**	64 30N	16 48W
Vatnås	**71**	59 58N	9 37 E
Vatne	**71**	62 33N	6 38 E
Vatneyri	**74**	65 35N	24 0W
Vatoloha, Mt.	**129**	17 52S	47 48 E

Vatomandry Vijayadurg

Vatomandry 129 19 20S 48 59E
Vatra-Dornei 70 47 22N 25 22E
Vats 71 59 29N 5 45E
Vättern, L. 73 58 25N 14 30E
Vättis 51 46 55N 9 27E
Vaucluse □ 45 44 3N 5 10E
Vaucouleurs 43 48 37N 5 40E
Vaud □ 50 46 35N 6 30E
Vaughan 161 34 37N 105 12W
Vaughn 160 47 37N 111 36W
Vaulruz 50 46 38N 7 0E
Vaupés □ 174 1 0N 71 0W
Vaupés, R. 174 1 0N 71 0W
Vauvert 45 43 42N 4 17E
Vauxhall 152 50 5N 112 9W
Vavincourt 43 48 49N 5 12E
Vavoua 120 7 23N 6 29W
Vaxholm 72 59 25N 18 20E
Växjö 73 56 52N 14 50E
Vaygach, Ostrov 76 70 0N 60 0E
Vaza Barris, R. 171 10 0S 37 30W
Veadeiros 171 14 7S 47 31W
Veagh L. 38 55 3N 7 57W
Vechta 48 52 47N 8 18E
Vechte, R. 46 52 34N 6 6E
Vecilla, La 56 42 51N 5 27W
Vecsés 53 47 26N 19 19E
Vedaraniam 97 10 25N 79 50E
Vedbæk 73 55 50N 12 33E
Veddige 73 57 17N 12 20E
Vedea, R. 70 44 0N 25 20E
Vedelgem 47 51 7N 3 10E
Vedia 172 34 30S 61 31W
Vedra, Isla del 59 38 52N 1 12E
Vedrin 47 50 30N 4 52E
Veendam 46 53 5N 6 52E
Veenendaal 46 52 2N 5 34E
Veenwouden 46 53 14N 6 0E
Veerle 47 51 4N 4 59E
Vefsna 74 65 48N 13 10E
Vega, Norway 74 65 40N 11 55E
Vega, U.S.A. 159 35 18N 102 26W
Vega Baja 147 18 27N 66 23W
Vega Fd. 74 65 37N 12 0E
Vega, I. 74 65 42N 11 50E
Vega, La 167 19 20N 70 30W
Vegadeo 56 43 27N 7 4W
Vegesack 48 53 10N 8 38E
Vegfjorden 74 65 37N 12 0E
Veggerby 73 56 54N 9 39E
Veggli 71 60 3N 9 9E
Veghel 47 51 37N 5 32E
Vegorritis, Limni 68 40 45N 21 45E
Vegreville 152 53 30N 112 5W
Vegusdal 71 58 32N 8 10E
Veii 63 42 0N 12 24E
Veinticino de Mayo 172 38 0S 67 40W
Veitch 140 34 39S 140 31E
Vejen 73 55 30N 9 9E
Vejer de la Frontera 57 36 15N 5 59W
Vejle 73 55 43N 9 30E
Vejle Amt □ 73 55 2N 11 22E
Vejle Fjord 73 55 40N 9 50E
Vejlo 73 55 10N 11 45E
Vela Luka 63 42 59N 16 44E
Velanai I. 97 9 45N 79 45E
Velarde 161 36 11N 106 1W
Velas, C. 166 10 21N 85 52W
Velasco 159 29 0N 95 20W
Velasco, Sierra de. 172 29 20S 67 10W
Velay, Mts. du 44 45 0N 3 40E
Velb 46 52 0N 5 59E
Velddrif 128 32 42S 18 11E
Velden 47 51 25N 6 10E
Veldhoven 47 51 24N 5 25E
Veldwezelt 47 50 52N 5 38E
Velebit Planina 63 44 50N 15 20E
Velebitski Kanal 63 44 45N 14 55E
Veleka, R. 67 42 4N 27 30E
Velenje 63 46 23N 15 8E
Velestinon 68 39 23N 22 43E
Vélez 174 6 1N 73 41W
Velez 66 43 19N 18 2E
Vélez Blanco 57 37 41N 2 5W
Vélez Málaga 57 36 48N 4 5W
Vélez Rubio 59 37 41N 2 5W
Velhas, R. 171 17 13S 44 49W
Velika 66 45 27N 17 40E
Velika Goricá 63 45 44N 16 5E
Velika Kapela 63 45 10N 15 5E
Velika Kladuša 63 45 11N 15 48E
Velika Morava, R. 66 44 30N 21 9E
Velika Plana 66 44 20N 21 1E
Velikaya, R. 80 56 40N 28 40E
Veliké Kapušany 53 48 34N 22 5E
Velike Lašče 63 45 49N 14 45E
Veliki Backa Kanal 68 45 45N 19 15E
Veliki Jastrebac 66 43 25N 21 30E
Veliki Ustyug 78 60 47N 46 20E
Velikiye Luki 80 56 25N 30 32E
Velíko Turnovo 67 43 5N 25 41E
Velikonda Range 97 14 45N 79 10E
Velikoye, Oz. 81 55 15N 40 0E
Velingrad 67 42 4N 23 58E
Velino, Mt. 63 42 10N 13 20E
Velizh 80 55 30N 31 11E
Velké Karlovice 53 49 20N 18 17E
Velke Mezirici 52 49 21N 16 1E
Velký ostrov Zitný 53 48 5N 17 20E
Vellar, R. 97 11 30N 79 36E
Velletri 64 41 43N 12 43E
Velling 73 56 2N 8 20E
Vellinge 73 55 29N 13 0E
Vellir 74 65 55N 18 28W
Vellore 97 12 57N 79 10E
Velsen-Noord 46 52 27N 4 40E
Velsk 78 61 10N 42 5E
Velten 48 52 40N 13 11E
Veluwe Meer 46 52 24N 5 44E
Velva 158 48 6N 100 56W
Velvendós 68 40 15N 22 6E
Vem 73 56 21N 8 21E
Vembanad Lake 97 9 36N 76 15E
Veme 71 60 14N 10 7E
Ven 73 55 55N 12 45E
Vena 73 57 31N 16 0E
Venado 164 22 50N 101 10W
Venado Tuerto 172 33 50S 62 0W
Venafro 65 41 28N 14 3E
Venarey-les-Laumes 43 47 32N 4 26E
Venaria 62 45 12N 7 39E
Ven čane 66 44 24N 20 28E
Vence 45 43 43N 7 6E
Vendas Novas 57 38 39N 8 27W
Vendée 42 46 50N 1 35W
Vendée □ 44 46 40N 1 20W
Vendée, Collines de 42 46 35N 0 45W
Vendée, R. 42 46 30N 0 45W
Vendeuvre-sur-Barse 43 48 14N 4 28E
Vendôme 42 47 47N 1 3E
Vendrell 58 41 10N 1 30E
Vendsyssel 73 57 22N 10 0E
Veneta, Laguna 63 45 19N 12 13E
Venetie 147 67 0N 146 30W
Véneto □ 63 45 30N 12 0E
Venev 81 54 22N 38 17E
Venézia 63 45 27N 12 20E
Venézia, Golfo di 63 45 20N 13 0E
Venezuela ■ 174 8 0N 65 0W
Venezuela, Golfo de 174 11 30N 71 0W
Vengurla 97 15 53N 73 45E
Vengurla Rocks 97 15 50N 73 22E
Venice = Venézia 63 45 27N 12 20E
Vénissieux 45 45 43N 4 53E
Venjansjön 72 60 58N 14 2E
Venkatagiri 97 14 0N 79 35E
Venkatapuram 96 18 20N 80 30E
Venlo 47 51 22N 6 11E
Vennesla 71 58 15N 8 0E
Venø, Is. 73 56 33N 8 38E
Venraij 47 51 31N 6 0E
Venta de Cardeña 57 38 16N 4 20W
Venta de San Rafael 56 40 42N 4 12W
Venta, La 165 18 8N 94 3W
Ventana, Punta de la 164 24 4N 109 48W
Ventersburg 128 28 7S 27 9E
Ventimíglia 62 43 50N 7 39E
Ventnor 28 50 35N 1 12W
Ventotene, I. 64 40 48N 13 25E
Ventry 39 52 8N 10 21W
Ventspils 80 57 25N 21 32E
Ventuari, R. 174 5 20N 66 0W
Ventucopa 163 34 50N 119 29W
Ventura 163 34 16N 119 18W
Ventura, La 164 24 38N 100 54W
Venturosa, La 174 6 8N 68 48W
Venus B. 141 38 40S 145 42E
Veoy 71 62 45N 7 30E
Veoy Is. 71 62 45N 7 30E
Vera, Argent. 172 29 30S 60 20W
Vera, Spain 59 37 15N 1 15W
Veracruz 165 19 10N 96 10W
Veracruz □ 165 19 0N 96 15W
Veraval 94 20 53N 70 27E
Verbánia 62 45 50N 8 55E
Verbicaro 65 39 46N 15 54E
Verbier 50 46 6N 7 13E
Vercelli 62 45 19N 8 25E
Verdalsøra 74 63 48N 11 30E
Verde Grande, R. 171 16 13S 43 49W
Verde Pequeno, R. 171 14 48S 43 31W
Verde, R., Argent. 176 41 55S 66 0W
Verde, R., Goiás, Brazil 171 18 1S 50 14W
Verde, R., Goiás, Brazil 171 19 11S 50 44W
Verde, R., Chihuahua, Mexico 164 26 59N 107 58W
Verde, R., Oaxaca, Mexico 164 15 59N 97 50W
Verde, R., Veracruz, Mexico 165 21 10N 102 50W
Verde, R., Parag. 172 23 9S 57 37W
Verden 48 52 58N 9 18E
Verdhikoúsa 68 39 47N 21 59E
Verdigre 158 42 38N 98 0W
Verdon-sur-Mer, Le 44 45 33N 1 4W
Verdun 43 49 12N 5 24E
Verdun-sur-le Doubs 43 46 54N 5 0E
Vereeniging 129 26 38S 27 57E
Vérendrye, Parc Prov. de 150 47 20N 76 40W
Vereshchagino 84 58 5N 54 40E
Verga, C. 120 10 30N 14 10W
Vergara 58 43 9N 2 28W
Vergato 62 44 18N 11 8E
Vergemont 138 23 33S 143 1E
Vergemont Cr. 138 24 16S 143 16E
Vergt 44 45 2N 0 43E
Verín 56 41 57N 7 27W
Veriña 56 43 32N 5 43W
Verkhnedvinsk 80 55 45N 27 58E
Verkhneuralsk 84 53 53N 59 13E
Verkhniy-Avzyan 84 53 32N 57 33E
Verkhniy Baskunchak 83 48 5N 46 50E
Verkhniy Tagil 84 57 22N 59 56E
Verkhniy Ufaley 84 56 4N 60 14E
Verkhniye Kigi 84 55 25N 58 37E
Verkhnyaya Salda 84 58 2N 60 33E
Verkhoturye 84 58 52N 60 48E
Verkhovye 81 52 55N 37 15E
Verkhoyansk 77 67 50N 133 50E
Verkhoyanskiy Khrebet 77 66 0N 129 0E
Verlo 153 50 19N 108 35W
Verma 71 62 21N 8 3E
Vermenton 43 47 40N 3 42E
Vermilion 153 53 20N 110 50W
Vermilion, B. 159 29 45N 91 55W
Vermilion Bay 153 49 50N 93 20W
Vermilion Chutes 152 58 22N 114 51W
Vermilion, R., Alta., Can. 153 53 22N 110 51W
Vermilion, R., Qué., Can. 150 47 38N 72 56W
Vermillion 158 42 50N 96 56W
Vermont □ 156 43 40N 72 50W
Vern, oilfield 19 55 35N 4 45E
Vernal 160 40 28N 109 35W
Vernalis 163 37 36N 121 17W
Vernayez 50 46 8N 7 3E
Verner 150 46 25N 80 8W
Verneuil, Bois de 50 48 59N 1 59E
Verneuil-sur-Avre 42 48 45N 0 55E
Vernier 50 46 13N 6 5E
Vernon, Can. 152 50 20N 119 15W
Vernon, France 42 49 5N 1 30E
Vernon, U.S.A. 159 34 0N 99 15W
Vero Beach 157 27 39N 80 23W
Véroia 68 40 34N 22 18E
Verolanuova 62 45 20N 10 5E
Véroli 64 41 43N 13 24E
Verona 62 45 27N 11 0E
Veropol 77 66 0N 168 0E
Verrieres, Les 50 46 55N 6 28E
Versailles 43 48 48N 2 8E
Versoix 50 46 17N 6 10E
Vert, C. 120 14 45N 17 30W
Vertou 42 47 10N 1 28W
Vertus 43 48 54N 4 0E
Verulam 129 29 38S 31 2E
Verviers 47 50 37N 5 52E
Vervins 43 49 50N 3 53E
Verwood, Can. 153 49 30N 105 40W
Verwood, U.K. 28 50 53N 1 53W
Veryan 30 50 13N 4 56W
Veryan Bay 30 50 12N 4 51W
Verzej 63 46 34N 16 13E
Vesdre, R. 47 50 36N 6 0E
Veseli nad Luznicí 52 49 12N 14 15E
Veselie 67 42 18N 27 38E
Veselovskoye Vdkhr. 83 47 0N 41 0E
Veselyy Res. 83 47 0N 41 0E
Veshenskaya 83 49 35N 41 44E
Vesle, R. 43 49 17N 3 50E
Veslyana, R. 84 60 20N 54 0E
Vesoul 43 60 40N 6 11E
Vessigebro 73 56 58N 12 40E
Vest-Agder fylke □ 71 58 30N 7 15E
Vest Fjorden 71 68 0N 15 0E
Vesta 166 9 43N 83 3W
Vestby 71 59 37N 10 45E
Vester Hassing 73 57 4N 10 8E
Vesterålen 74 68 45N 14 30E
Vestersche Veld 46 52 52N 6 9E
Vestfjorden 74 67 55N 14 0E
Vestfold fylke □ 71 59 15N 10 0E
Vestmannaeyjar 74 63 27N 20 15W
Vestmarka 71 59 56N 11 59E
Vestnes 71 62 39N 7 5E
Vestone 62 45 43N 10 25E
Vestsjaellands Amt □ 73 55 30N 11 20E
Vestspitsbergen 12 78 40N 17 0E
Vestvågøy 74 68 18N 13 50E
Vesuvio 65 40 50N 14 22E
Vesuvius, Mt. = Vesuvio 65 40 50N 14 22E
Veszprém 53 47 8N 17 57E
Veszprém □ 53 47 5N 17 55E
Vésztö 53 46 55N 21 16E
Vetapalam 97 15 47N 80 18E
Vetlanda 73 57 24N 15 3E
Vetluga 81 57 53N 45 45E
Vetluzhskiy 81 57 17N 45 12E
Vetovo 67 43 42N 26 16E
Vetralia 63 42 20N 12 2E
Vetren 67 42 15N 24 3E
Vettore, Mte. 63 44 38N 7 5E
Veurne 47 51 5N 2 40E
Vevey 50 46 28N 6 51E
Vévi 68 40 47N 21 38E
Veys 92 31 30N 49 0E
Vézelise 43 48 30N 6 5E
Vezhen, mt. 67 42 50N 24 20E
Vi Thanh 101 9 42N 105 26E
Viacha 174 16 30S 68 5W
Viadana 62 44 55N 10 30E
Viana, Brazil 170 3 0S 44 40W
Viana, Port. 55 38 20N 8 0W
Viana, Spain 58 42 31N 2 22W
Viana do Castelo 56 41 42N 8 50W
Vianden 47 49 56N 6 12E
Vianen 46 51 59N 5 5E
Vianna do Castelo □ 56 41 50N 8 30W
Vianópolis 171 16 40S 48 35W
Viar, R. 56 37 45N 5 54W
Viaréggio 62 43 52N 10 13E
Vibank 153 50 20N 103 56W
Vibey, R. 56 42 21N 7 15E
Vibo Valéntia 65 38 40N 16 5E
Viborg 73 56 27N 9 23E
Viborg Amt □ 73 56 30N 9 20E
Vic-en-Bigorre 44 43 24N 0 3E
Vic-Fezensac 44 43 45N 0 18E
Vic Fézensac 44 43 47N 0 19E
Vic-sur-Cère 44 44 59N 2 38E
Vic-sur-Seille 43 48 45N 6 33E
Vicarstown 39 53 5N 7 7W
Vicenza 63 45 32N 11 31E
Vich 58 41 58N 2 19E
Vichada □ 174 5 0N 69 30W
Vichuga 81 57 25N 41 55E
Vichy 44 46 9N 3 26E
Vickerstown 32 54 8N 3 17W
Vicksburg, Mich., U.S.A. 156 42 10N 85 30W
Vicksburg, Miss., U.S.A. 159 32 22N 90 56W
Vico, L. di 63 42 20N 12 10E
Viçosa, Min. Ger., Brazil 170 20 45S 42 53W
Viçosa, Pernambuco, Brazil 170 9 28S 36 14W
Viçosa do Ceará 170 3 34S 41 5W
Vicosoprano 51 46 22N 9 38E
Victor 158 38 43N 105 7W
Victor Emanuel Ra. 135 5 20S 142 15E
Victor Harbour 139 35 30S 138 37E
Victoria, Argent. 172 32 40S 60 10W
Victoria, Austral. 138 21 16S 149 3E
Victoria, Camer. 121 4 1N 9 10E
Victoria, Can. 152 48 30N 123 25W
Victoria, Chile 176 38 13S 72 20W
Victoria, Guin. 120 10 50N 14 32W
Victoria, H. K. 109 22 25N 114 15E
Victoria, Malay. 102 5 20N 115 20E
Victoria, Tex., U.S.A. 159 28 50N 97 0W
Victoria, Va., U.S.A. 158 38 52N 99 8W
Victoria □, Austral. 131 37 0S 144 0E
Victoria □, Rhod. 127 21 0S 31 30E
Victoria Beach 153 50 40N 96 35W
Victoria de las Tunas 166 20 58N 76 59W
Victoria Falls 127 17 58S 25 45E
Victoria, Grand L. 150 47 31N 77 30W
Victoria Harbour 150 44 45N 79 45W
Victoria I. 148 71 0N 111 0W
Victoria, L., N.S.W., Austral. 140 33 57S 141 15E
Victoria, L., Vic., Austral. 139 38 2S 147 34E
Victoria, L., E. Afr. 126 1 0S 33 0E
Victoria, La 174 10 14N 67 20W
Victoria Ld. 13 75 0S 160 0E
Victoria, Mt., Burma 98 21 15N 93 55E
Victoria, Mt., P.N.G. 135 8 55S 147 32E
Victoria Nile R. 126 2 25N 31 50E
Victoria, R. 136 15 10S 129 40E
Victoria R. Downs 136 16 25S 131 0E
Victoria Ra. 143 42 12S 172 7E
Victoria Res. 151 48 20N 57 27W
Victoria Taungdeik 99 21 15N 93 55E
Victoria West 128 31 25S 23 4E
Victoriaville 151 46 4N 71 56W
Victorica 172 36 20S 65 30W
Victorino 174 2 48N 67 50W
Victorville 163 34 32N 117 18W
Vicuña 172 30 0S 70 50W
Vicuña Mackenna 172 33 53S 64 25W
Vidalia 157 32 13N 82 25W
Vidauban 45 43 25N 6 27E
Videlv, R. 71 58 50N 8 32E
Vidigueira 57 38 12N 7 48W
Vidin 66 43 59N 22 52E
Vidio, Cabo 56 43 35N 6 14W
Vidisha (Bhilsa) 94 23 28N 77 53E
Vidöstern 73 57 5N 14 0E
Vidra 70 45 56N 26 55E
Viduša, mts. 66 42 55N 18 21E
Vidzy 80 54 40N 26 37E
Viedma 176 40 50S 63 0W
Viedma, L. 176 49 30S 72 30W
Vieira 56 41 38N 8 8W
Viejo Canal de Bahama 166 22 10N 77 30W
Viella 58 42 43N 0 44E
Vielsalm 47 50 17N 5 54E
Vien Pou Kha 101 20 45N 101 5E
Vienenburg 48 51 57N 10 35E
Vieng Pou Kha 100 20 41N 101 4E
Vienna, Illinois, U.S.A. 159 37 29N 88 54W
Vienna, Va., U.S.A. 162 38 54N 77 16W
Vienna = Wien 53 48 12N 16 22E
Vienne 45 45 31N 4 53E
Vienne □ 44 45 53N 0 42E
Vienne, R. 42 47 5N 0 30E
Vientiane 100 17 58N 102 36E
Vieques, I. 147 18 8N 65 25W
Vierlingsbeek 47 51 36N 6 1E
Viersen 48 51 15N 6 23E
Vierwaldstättersee 51 47 0N 8 30E
Vierzon 43 47 13N 2 5E
Vieux-Boucau-les-Bains 44 43 48N 1 23W
Vif 45 45 5N 5 41E
Vigan 103 17 35N 120 28E
Vigan, Le 44 44 0N 3 36E
Vigevano 62 45 18N 8 50E
Vigia 170 0 50S 48 5W
Vigia Chico 165 19 46N 87 35W
Vignacourt 43 50 1N 2 15E
Vignemale, Pic du 44 42 47N 0 10W
Vigneulles 43 48 59N 5 40E
Vignola 62 44 29N 11 0E
Vigo 56 42 12N 8 41W
Vigo, Ría de 56 42 15N 8 45W
Vihiers 42 47 10N 0 30W
Vijayadurg 96 16 30N 73 25E

Vijayawada (Bezwada) Voitsberg

Vijayawada (Bezwada) 96 16 31N 80 39 E
Vijfhuizen 46 52 22N 4 41 E
Vikedal 71 59 30N 5 55 E
Viken, L. 73 58 40N 10 2 E
Vikersund 71 59 58N 10 2 E
Viking 152 53 7N 111 50W
Viking, gasfield 19 53 30N 2 20 E
Vikna 74 64 52N 10 57 E
Vikramasingapuram 97 8 40N 76 47 E
Viksjö 72 62 45N 17 26 E
Vikulovo 76 56 50N 70 40 E
Vila Alferes Chamusca 129 24 27 S 33 0 E
Vila Arriaga 125 14 35 S 13 30 E
Vila Bittencourt 174 1 20 S 69 20W
Vila Cabral = Lichinga 127 13 13 S 35 11 E
Vila Caldas Xavier 127 14 28 S 33 0 E
Vila Coutinho 127 14 37 S 34 19 E
Vila da Maganja 127 17 18 S 37 30 E
Vila da Ponte 125 14 35 S 16 40 E
Vila de Aljustrel 125 13 30 S 19 45 E
Vila de João Belo = Xai-Xai 129 25 6 S 33 31 E
Vila de Liquica 103 8 40 S 125 20 E
Vila de Manica 125 18 58 S 32 59 E
Vila de Rei 57 39 41N 8 9W
Vila de Sena = Sena 127 17 25 S 35 0 E
Vila do Bispo 57 37 5N 8 53W
Vila do Conde 56 41 21N 8 45W
Vila Fontes 125 17 51 S 35 24 E
Vila Fontes Velha 127 17 51 S 35 24 E
Vila Franca de Xira 57 38 57N 8 59W
Vila Gamito 127 14 12 S 33 0 E
Vila General Machado 125 11 58 S 17 22 E
Vila Gomes da Costa 129 24 20 S 33 37 E
Vila Henrique de Carvalho = Lunda 124 9 40 S 20 12 E
Vila Junqueiro 127 15 25 S 36 58 E
Vila Luiza 129 25 45 S 32 35 E
Vila Luso = Moxico 125 11 53 S 19 55 E
Vila Machado 127 19 15 S 34 14 E
Vila Marechal Carmona = Uige 124 7 30 S 14 40 E
Vila Mariano Machado 125 13 3 S 14 35 E
Vila Moatize 127 16 11 S 33 40 E
Vila Mouzinho 127 14 48 S 34 25 E
Vila Murtinho 174 10 20 S 65 20W
Vila Nova de Fozcôa 56 41 5N 7 9W
Vila Nova de Ourém 57 39 40N 8 35W
Vila Nova do Seles 125 11 35 S 14 22 E
Vila Novo de Gaia 56 41 4N 8 40W
Vila Paiva Couceiro 125 14 37 S 14 40 E
Vila Paiva de Andrada 127 18 37 S 34 2 E
Vila Pery = Chimoio 127 19 4 S 33 30 E
Vila Pouca de Aguiar 56 41 30N 7 38W
Vila Real 56 41 17N 7 48W
Vila Real de Santo Antonio 57 37 10N 7 28W
Vila Robert Williams 125 12 46 S 15 30 E
Vila Salazar, Angola 124 9 12 S 14 48 E
Vila Salazar, Indon. 103 5 25 S 123 50 E
Vila Teixeira da Silva 125 12 10 S 15 0 E
Vila Vasco da Gama 127 14 54 S 32 14 E
Vila Velha 173 20 20 S 40 17W
Vila Verissimo Sarmento 124 8 15 S 20 50 E
Vila Viçosa 57 38 45N 7 27W
Vilaboa 56 42 21N 8 39W
Vilaine, R. 42 47 35N 2 10W
Vilanculos 129 22 1 S 35 17 E
Vilar Formosa 56 40 38N 6 45W
Vilareal □ 56 41 36N 7 35W
Vileyka 80 54 30N 27 0 E
Vilhelmina 74 64 35N 16 39 E
Vilhena 174 12 30 S 60 0W
Viliga 77 60 2N 156 56 E
Viliya, R. 80 54 57N 24 35 E
Viljandi 80 58 28N 25 30 E
Villa Abecia 172 21 0 S 68 18W
Villa Ahumada 164 30 30N 106 40W
Villa Ana 172 28 28 S 59 40W
Villa Angela 172 27 34 S 60 45W
Villa Bella 174 10 25 S 65 30W
Villa Bens (Tarfaya) 116 27 55N 12 55W
Villa Cañas 172 34 0 S 61 35W
Villa Cisneros = Dakhla 116 23 50N 15 53W
Villa Colón 172 31 38 S 68 20W
Villa Constitución 172 33 15 S 60 20W
Villa de Cura 174 10 2N 67 29W
Villa de María 172 30 0 S 63 43W
Villa de Rosario 172 24 30 S 57 35W
Villa Dolores 172 31 58 S 65 15W
Villa Franca 172 26 14 S 58 20W
Villa Frontera 164 26 56N 101 27W
Villa Guillermina 172 28 15 S 59 29W
Villa Hayes 172 25 0 S 57 20W
Villa Iris 172 38 12 S 63 12W
Villa Julia Molina 167 19 5N 69 45W
Villa Madero 164 24 28N 104 10W
Villa María 172 32 20 S 63 10W
Villa Mazán 172 28 40 S 66 30W
Villa Mentes 172 21 10 S 63 30W
Villa Minozzo 62 44 21N 10 30 E
Villa Montes 172 21 10 S 63 30W
Villa Ocampo, Argent. 172 28 30 S 59 20W
Villa Ocampo, Mexico 164 26 29N 105 30W
Villa Ojo de Agua 172 29 30 S 63 44W
Villa San Agustín 172 30 35 S 67 30W
Villa San Giovanni 65 38 13N 15 38 E
Villa San José 172 32 12 S 58 15W
Villa San Martín 172 28 9 S 64 9W
Villa Santina 63 46 25N 12 55 E
Villa Unión 164 23 12N 106 14W
Villablino 56 42 57N 6 19W
Villabruzzi 91 3 3N 45 18 E
Villacampo, Pantano de 56 41 31N 6 0W
Villacañas 58 39 38N 3 20W
Villacarlos 58 39 53N 4 17 E
Villacarriedo 58 43 14N 3 48W
Villacarrillo 59 38 7N 3 3W
Villacastín 56 40 46N 4 25W
Villach 52 46 37N 13 51 E
Villaciaro 64 39 27N 8 45 E
Villada 56 42 15N 4 59W
Villadiego 56 42 31N 4 1W
Villadossóla 62 46 4N 8 16 E
Villafeliche 58 41 10N 1 30W
Villafranca 58 42 17N 1 46W
Villafranca de los Barros 57 38 35N 6 18W
Villafranca de los Caballeros 59 39 26N 3 21W
Villafranca del Bierzo 56 42 38N 6 50W
Villafranca del Cid 58 40 26N 0 16W
Villafranca del Panadés 58 41 21N 1 40 E
Villafranca di Verona 62 45 20N 10 51 E
Villagarcía de Arosa 56 42 34N 8 46W
Villagrán 165 24 29N 99 29W
Villaguay 172 32 0 S 58 45W
Villaharta 57 38 9N 4 54W
Villahermosa, Mexico 165 17 45N 92 50W
Villahermosa, Spain 59 38 46N 2 52W
Villaines-la-Juhel 42 48 21N 0 20W
Villajoyosa 59 38 30N 0 12W
Villalba 56 40 36N 3 59W
Villalba de Guardo 56 42 42N 4 49W
Villalón de Campos 56 42 5N 5 4W
Villalpando 56 41 51N 5 25W
Villaluenga 56 40 2N 3 54W
Villamañán 56 42 19N 5 35W
Villamartín 56 36 52N 5 38W
Villamayor 58 41 42N 0 43W
Villamblard 44 45 2N 0 32 E
Villanova Monteleone 64 40 30N 8 28 E
Villanueva, Colomb. 174 10 37N 72 59W
Villanueva, U.S.A. 161 35 16N 105 31W
Villanueva de Castellón 59 39 5N 0 31W
Villanueva de Córdoba 57 38 20N 4 38W
Villanueva de la Fuente 59 38 42N 2 42W
Villanueva de la Serena 57 38 59N 5 50W
Villanueva de la Sierra 56 40 12N 6 24W
Villanueva de los Castillejos 57 37 30N 7 15W
Villanueva del Arzobispo 59 38 10N 3 0W
Villanueva del Duque 57 38 20N 4 38W
Villanueva del Fresno 57 38 23N 7 10W
Villanueva y Geltrú 58 41 13N 1 40 E
Villaodrid 56 43 20N 7 11W
Villaputzu 64 39 28N 9 33 E
Villar del Arzobispo 58 39 44N 0 50W
Villar del Rey 57 39 7N 6 50W
Villarcayo 58 42 56N 3 34W
Villard 45 45 4N 5 33 E
Villard-Bonnot 45 45 14N 5 53 E
Villard-de-Lans 45 45 3N 5 33 E
Villarino de los Aires 56 41 18N 6 23W
Villarosa 65 37 36N 14 9 E
Villarramiel 56 42 2N 4 55W
Villarreal 58 39 55N 0 3W
Villarrica, Chile 176 39 15 S 72 30W
Villarrica, Parag. 172 25 40 S 56 30W
Villarrobledo 59 39 18N 2 36W
Villarroya de la Sierra 58 41 27N 1 46W
Villarrubia de los Ojos 59 39 14N 3 36W
Villars 45 46 0N 5 2 E
Villarta de San Juan 59 39 15N 3 25W
Villasayas 58 41 24N 2 39W
Villaseca de los Gamitos 56 41 2N 6 7W
Villastar 58 40 17N 1 9W
Villatobas 58 39 54N 3 20W
Villavicencio, Argent. 172 32 28 S 69 0W
Villavicencio, Colomb. 174 4 9N 73 37W
Villaviciosa 56 43 32N 5 27W
Villazón 172 22 0 S 65 35W
Ville de Paris □ 43 48 50N 2 20 E
Ville Marie 150 47 20N 79 30W
Ville Platte 159 30 45N 92 17W
Villedieu 42 48 50N 1 12W
Villefort 44 44 28N 3 56 E
Villefranche 43 47 19N 146 0 E
Villefranche-de-Lauragais 44 43 25N 1 44 E
Villefranche-de-Rouergue 44 44 21N 2 2 E
Villefranche-du-Périgord 44 44 38N 1 5 E
Villefranche-sur-Saône 45 45 59N 4 43 E
Villel 58 40 14N 1 12W
Villemaur 43 48 14N 3 40 E
Villemur-sur-Tarn 44 43 51N 1 31 E
Villena 59 38 40N 0 52W
Villenauxe 43 48 36N 3 30 E
Villenave 44 44 46N 0 33W
Villeneuve, France 43 48 42N 2 25 E
Villeneuve, Italy 62 45 40N 7 10 E
Villeneuve, Switz. 50 46 24N 6 56 E
Villeneuve-l'Archevèque 43 48 14N 3 32 E
Villeneuve-lès-Avignon 45 43 57N 4 49 E
Villeneuve-sur-Allier 44 46 40N 3 13 E
Villeneuve-sur-Lot 44 44 24N 0 42 E
Villeréal 44 44 38N 0 45 E
Villers Bocage 42 49 3N 0 40W
Villers Bretonneux 43 49 50N 2 30 E
Villers-Cotterets 43 49 15N 3 4 E
Villers-Farlay 47 47 0N 5 45 E
Villers-le-Bouillet 47 50 34N 5 15 E
Villers-le-Gambon 47 50 11N 4 37 E
Villers-sur-Mer 42 49 21N 0 2W
Villersexel 43 47 33N 6 26 E
Villerslev 73 56 49N 8 29 E
Villerupt 43 49 28N 5 55 E
Villerville 42 49 26N 0 5 E
Villiers 129 27 2 S 28 36 E
Villingen = Schwenningen 49 48 3N 8 29 E
Villisca 158 40 55N 94 59W
Villupuram 97 11 59N 79 31 E
Vilna 152 54 7N 111 55W
Vilnius 80 54 38N 25 25 E
Vils 52 47 33N 10 37 E
Vilsbiburg 49 48 27N 12 23 E
Vilslev 73 55 24N 8 42 E
Vilusi 66 42 44N 18 34 E
Vilvoorde 47 50 56N 4 26 E
Vilyuy, R. 77 63 58N 125 0 E
Vilyuysk 77 63 40N 121 20 E
Vimercate 62 45 38N 9 25 E
Vimiosa 56 41 35N 6 13W
Vimmerby 73 57 40N 15 55 E
Vimo 72 60 50N 14 20 E
Vimoutiers 42 48 57N 0 10 E
Vimperk 52 49 3N 13 46 E
Viña del Mar 172 33 0 S 71 30W
Vinaroz 58 40 30N 0 27 E
Vincennes 156 38 42N 87 29W
Vincent 163 34 33N 118 11W
Vinchina 172 28 45 S 68 15W
Vindel älv 74 64 20N 19 20 E
Vindeln 74 64 12N 19 43 E
Vinderup 73 56 29N 8 45 E
Vindhya Ra. 94 22 50N 77 0 E
Vinegar Hill 39 52 30N 6 28W
Vineland 162 39 30N 75 0W
Vinga 66 46 0N 21 14 E
Vingnes 71 61 7N 10 26 E
Vinh 100 18 45N 105 38 E
Vinh Linh 100 17 4N 107 2 E
Vinh Loi 101 9 20N 104 45 E
Vinh Long 101 10 16N 105 57 E
Vinh Yen 100 21 21N 105 35 E
Vinhais 56 41 50N 7 0W
Vinica 63 45 28N 15 16 E
Vinita 159 36 40N 95 12W
Vinkeveen 46 52 13N 4 56 E
Vinkovci 66 45 19N 18 48 E
Vinnitsa 82 49 15N 28 30 E
Vinstra 71 61 37N 9 44 E
Vinton, Iowa, U.S.A. 158 42 8N 92 1W
Vinton, La., U.S.A. 159 30 13N 93 35W
Vintu de Jos 70 46 0N 23 30 E
Viöl 48 54 32N 9 12 E
Violet Town 141 36 38 S 145 42 E
Vipava 63 45 51N 13 38 E
Vipiteno 63 46 55N 11 25 E
Viqueque 103 8 42 S 126 30 E
Vir 85 37 45N 72 5 E
Vir, I. 63 44 17N 15 3 E
Virac 103 13 30N 124 20 E
Virachei 100 13 59N 106 49 E
Virago Sd. 152 54 0N 132 42W
Virajpet 97 12 15N 75 50 E
Viramgam 94 23 5N 72 0 E
Virarajendrapet (Virajpet) 97 12 10N 75 50 E
Viravanallur 97 8 40N 79 30 E
Virden 153 49 50N 100 56W
Vire 42 48 50N 0 53W
Virgem da Lapa 171 16 49 S 42 21W
Virgenes, C. 176 52 19 S 68 21W
Virgin Gorda, I. 147 18 45N 64 26W
Virgin Is. 147 18 40N 64 30W
Virgin, R., Can. 153 57 2N 108 17W
Virgin, R., U.S.A. 161 36 50N 114 10W
Virginia, Ireland 38 53 50N 7 5W
Virginia, S. Afr. 128 28 8 S 26 55 E
Virginia, U.S.A. 158 47 30N 92 32W
Virginia □ 156 37 45N 78 0W
Virginia Beach 156 36 54N 75 58W
Virginia City, Mont., U.S.A. 160 45 25N 111 58W
Virginia City, Nev., U.S.A. 160 39 19N 119 39W
Virginia Falls 152 61 38N 125 42W
Virginiatown 150 48 9N 79 36W
Virgins, C. 176 52 10 S 68 30W
Virieu-le-Grand 45 45 51N 5 39 E
Virje 66 46 4N 16 59 E
Viroqua 158 43 33N 90 57W
Virovitica 66 45 51N 17 21 E
Virpaza, R. 66 42 14N 19 6 E
Virserum 73 57 20N 15 35 E
Virton 47 49 35N 5 32 E
Virtsu 80 58 32N 23 33 E
Virudhunagar 97 9 30N 78 0 E
Vis 63 43 0N 16 10 E
Vis, I. 63 43 0N 16 10 E
Vis Kanal 63 43 4N 16 5 E
Visalia 163 36 25N 119 18W
Visayan Sea 103 11 30N 123 30 E
Visby 73 57 37N 18 18 E
Viscount Melville Sd. 12 74 10N 108 0W
Visé 47 50 44N 5 41 E
Višegrad 66 43 47N 19 17 E
Viseu, Brazil 170 1 10 S 46 20W
Viseu, Port. 56 40 40N 7 55W
Vişeu 70 47 45N 24 25 E
Viseu □ 56 40 40N 7 55W
Vishakhapatnam 96 17 45N 83 20 E
Vishera, R. 84 59 55N 56 25 E
Vishnupur 95 23 8N 87 20 E
Visikoi I. 13 56 30 S 26 40 E
Visingsö 73 58 2N 14 20 E
Viskafors 73 57 37N 12 50 E
Vislanda 73 56 46N 14 30 E
Vislinskil Zaliv (Zalew Wislany) 54 54 20N 19 50 E
Visnagar 94 23 45N 72 32 E
Višnja Gora 63 45 58N 14 45 E
Viso del Marqués 59 38 32N 3 34W
Viso, Mte. 62 44 38N 7 5 E
Visoko 66 43 58N 18 10 E
Visp 50 46 17N 7 52 E
Vispa, R. 50 46 9N 7 48 E
Visselhovde 48 52 59N 9 36 E
Vissoie 50 46 13N 7 36 E
Vista 163 33 12N 117 14W
Vistonis, Limni 68 41 0N 25 7 E
Vistula, R. = Wisła, R. 54 53 38N 18 47 E
Vit, R. 67 43 30N 24 30 E
Vitanje 63 46 40N 15 18 E
Vitebsk 80 55 10N 30 15 E
Viterbo 63 42 25N 12 8 E
Viti Levu, I. 143 17 30 S 177 30 E
Vitiaz Str. 135 5 40 S 147 10 E
Vitigudino 56 41 1N 6 35W
Vitim 77 59 45N 112 25 E
Vitim, R. 77 58 40N 112 50 E
Vitína 69 37 40N 22 10 E
Vitina 66 43 17N 17 29 E
Vitória 171 20 20 S 40 22W
Vitoria 58 42 50N 2 41W
Vitória da Conquista 171 14 51 S 40 51W
Vitória de São Antão 170 8 10 S 37 20W
Vitorino Friere 170 4 4 S 45 10W
Vitré 42 48 8N 1 12W
Vitry-le-François 43 48 43N 4 33 E
Vitsi, Mt. 68 40 40N 21 25 E
Vittangi 74 67 41N 21 40 E
Vitteaux 43 47 24N 4 30 E
Vittel 43 48 12N 5 57 E
Vittória 65 36 58N 14 30 E
Vittório Véneto 63 45 59N 12 18 E
Vitu Is. 135 4 50 S 149 25 E
Vivegnis 47 50 42N 5 39 E
Viver 58 39 55N 0 36W
Vivero 56 43 39N 7 38W
Viviers 45 44 30N 4 40 E
Vivonne, Austral. 140 35 59 S 137 9 E
Vivonne, France 44 46 36N 0 15 E
Vivonne B. 140 35 59 S 137 9 E
Vivsta 72 62 30N 17 18 E
Vizcaíno, Desierto de 164 27 40N 113 50W
Vizcaíno, Sierra 164 27 30N 114 0W
Vizcaya □ 58 43 15N 2 45W
Vizianagaram 96 18 6N 83 10 E
Vizille 45 45 5N 5 46 E
Vizinada 63 45 20N 13 46 E
Viziru 70 45 0N 27 43 E
Vizovice 53 49 12N 17 56 E
Vizzini 65 37 9N 14 43 E
Vlaardingen 46 51 55N 4 21 E
Vladicin Han 66 42 42N 22 1 E
Vladimir 81 56 0N 40 30 E
Vladimir Volynskiy 80 50 50N 24 18 E
Vladimirci 66 44 36N 19 45 E
Vladimirovac 66 45 1N 20 53 E
Vladimirovka, U.S.S.R. 83 44 37N 44 41 E
Vladimirovka, U.S.S.R. 83 48 27N 46 5 E
Vladimirovo 67 43 32N 23 22 E
Vladislavovka 82 45 15N 35 15 E
Vladivostok 82 43 10N 131 53 E
Vlamertinge 47 50 51N 2 49 E
Vlaming Head 137 21 48 S 114 5 E
Vlasenica 66 44 11N 18 59 E
Vlasim 52 49 40N 14 53 E
Vlasinsko Jezero 66 42 44N 22 37 E
Vlašió, mt. 66 44 19N 17 37 E
Vlasotinci 66 42 59N 22 7 E
Vleuten 46 52 6N 5 1 E
Vlieland, I. 46 53 30N 4 55 E
Vliestroom 46 53 19N 5 8 E
Vlijmen 47 51 42N 5 14 E
Vlissingen 47 51 26N 3 34 E
Vlora 68 40 32N 19 28 E
Vlora □ 68 40 12N 20 0 E
Vltava, R. 52 49 35N 14 10 E
Vlădeasa, mt. 70 46 47N 22 50 E
Vo Dat 101 11 9N 107 31 E
Vobarno 62 45 38N 10 30 E
Vočin 66 45 37N 17 33 E
Vodice 63 43 47N 15 47 E
Vodnany 52 49 9N 14 11 E
Vodnjan 63 44 59N 13 52 E
Voe 36 60 21N 1 15W
Voga 121 6 23N 1 30 E
Vogelkop = Doberai, Jazirah 103 1 25 S 133 0 E
Vogelsberg 48 50 37N 9 30 E
Voghera 62 44 59N 9 1 E
Vohémar 129 13 25 S 50 0 E
Vohipeno 129 22 22 S 47 51 E
Voi 126 3 25 S 38 32 E
Void 43 48 40N 5 36 E
Voil, L. 34 56 20N 4 25W
Voineşti, Iaşi, Rumania 70 47 5N 27 27 E
Voineşti, Ploeşti, Rumania 70 45 5N 25 14 E
Voiotía □ 69 38 20N 23 0 E
Voiron 45 45 22N 5 35 E
Voiseys B. 151 56 15N 61 50W
Voitsberg 52 47 3N 15 9 E

Voiviis Limni, L
Walla Walla

Voiviis Limni, L. 68 39 30N 22 45 E
Vojens 73 55 16N 9 18 E
Vojmsjön 74 64 55N 16 40 E
Vojnió 63 45 19N 15 43 E
Vojvodina, Auton. Pokragina 66 45 20N 20 0 E
Vokhma 81 59 0N 46 45 E
Vokhma, R. 81 59 0N 46 44 E
Vokhtoga 81 58 46N 41 8 E
Volary 52 48 54N 13 52 E
Volborg 158 45 50N 105 44W
Volchansk 81 50 17N 36 58 E
Volchya, R. 82 48 0N 37 0 E
Volda 71 62 9N 6 5 E
Volendam 46 52 30N 5 4 E
Volga 81 57 58N 38 16 E
Volga Hts. = Privolzhskaya V.S. 79 51 0N 46 0 E
Volga, R. 83 52 20N 48 0 E
Volgodonsk 83 47 33N 42 5 E
Volgograd 83 48 40N 44 25 E
Volgogradskoye Vdkhr. 81 50 0N 45 20 E
Volgorechensk 81 57 28N 41 14 E
Volissós 69 38 29N 25 54 E
Volkerak 47 51 39N 4 18 E
Völkermarkt 52 46 39N 14 39 E
Volkhov 80 59 55N 32 15 E
Volkhov, R. 80 59 30N 32 0 E
Völklingen 49 49 15N 6 50 E
Volkovysk 80 53 9N 24 30 E
Volksrust 129 27 24 S 29 53 E
Vollenhove 46 52 40N 5 58 E
Volnovakha 82 47 35N 37 30 E
Volo 140 31 37 S 143 0 E
Volochayevka 77 48 40N 134 30 E
Volodary 81 56 12N 43 15 E
Vologda 81 59 25N 40 0 E
Volokolamsk 81 56 5N 36 0 E
Volokonovka 81 50 33N 37 58 E
Volontirovka 82 46 28N 29 28 E
Vólos 68 39 24N 22 59 E
Volosovo 80 59 27N 29 32 E
Volozhin 80 54 3N 26 30 E
Volsk 81 52 5N 47 28 E
Volstrup 73 57 19N 10 27 E
Volta, L. 121 7 30N 0 15 E
Volta, R. 121 8 0N 0 10W
Volta Redonda 173 22 31 S 44 5W
Voltaire, C. 136 14 16 S 125 35 E
Volterra 62 43 24N 10 50 E
Voltri 62 44 25N 8 43 E
Volturara Áppula 65 41 30N 15 2 E
Volturno, R. 65 41 18N 14 20 E
Volubilis 118 34 2N 5 33W
Vólvi, L. 68 40 40N 23 34 E
Volzhsk 81 55 57N 48 23 E
Volzhskiy 83 48 56N 44 46 E
Vondrozo 129 22 49 S 47 20 E
Vónitsa 69 38 53N 20 58 E
Voorburg 46 52 5N 4 24 E
Voorne Putten 46 51 52N 4 10 E
Voorst 46 52 10N 6 8 E
Voorthuizen 46 52 11N 5 36 E
Vopnafjörður 74 65 45N 14 40W
Vorarlberg □ 52 47 20N 10 0 E
Vóras Óros 68 40 57N 21 45 E
Vorbasse 73 55 39N 9 6 E
Vorden 46 52 6N 6 19 E
Vorderrheim, R. 51 46 49N 9 25 E
Vordingborg 73 55 0N 11 54 E
Voreppe 45 45 18N 5 39 E
Voríai Sporádhes 69 39 15N 23 30 E
Vórios Evvoïkós Kólpos 69 38 45N 23 15 E
Vorkuta 78 67 48N 64 20 E
Vorma 71 60 9N 11 27 E
Vorona, R. 81 52 0N 42 20 E
Voronezh, R.S.S.R., U.S.S.R. 81 51 40N 39 10 E
Voronezh, Ukraine, U.S.S.R. 80 51 47N 33 28 E
Voronezh, R. 81 52 30N 39 30 E
Vorontsovo-Aleksandrovskoïe = Zelenokumsk. 83 44 30N 44 1 E
Voroshilovgrad 83 48 38N 39 15 E
Voroshilovsk = Kommunarsk 83 48 3N 38 40 E
Vorovskoye 77 54 30N 155 50 E
Vorselaar 47 51 12N 4 46 E
Vorskla, R. 82 49 30N 34 31 E
Vorukh 85 39 52N 70 35 E
Vorupør 73 56 58N 8 22 E
Vosges 43 48 20N 7 10 E
Vosges □ 43 48 12N 6 20 E
Voskopoja 68 40 40N 20 33 E
Voskresensk 81 55 27N 38 31 E
Voskresenskoye 81 56 51N 45 30 E
Voss 71 60 38N 6 26 E
Vosselaar 47 51 19N 4 52 E
Vostok I. 131 10 5 S 152 23W
Vostotnyy Sayan 77 54 0N 96 0 E
Votice 52 49 38N 14 39 E
Votkinsk 84 57 0N 53 55 E
Votkinskoye Vdkhr. 78 57 30N 55 0 E
Vouga, R. 56 40 46N 8 10W
Voulte-sur-Rhône, La 45 44 48N 4 46 E
Vouvry 50 46 21N 6 21 E
Voúxa, Ákra 69 35 37N 20 32 E
Vouzela 56 40 43N 8 7W
Vouziers 43 49 22N 4 40 E
Voves 43 48 15N 1 38 E
Voxna 72 61 20N 15 30 E
Voy 37 59 1N 3 16W
Vozhe Oz. 78 60 45N 39 0 E
Vozhgaly 81 58 24N 50 1 E
Voznesensk 82 47 35N 31 15 E
Voznesenye 78 61 0N 35 45 E
Vráble 53 48 15N 18 16 E
Vrácevšnica 66 44 2N 20 34 E
Vrådal 71 59 20N 8 25 E
Vradiyevka 82 49 56N 30 38 E
Vraka 68 42 8N 19 28 E
Vrakhnéika 69 38 10N 21 40 E
Vrancea □ 70 45 50N 26 45 E
Vrancei, Munţi 70 46 0N 26 30 E
Vrangelja, Ostrov 77 71 0N 180 0 E
Vrangtjarn 72 62 14N 16 37 E
Vranica, mt. 66 43 59N 18 0 E
Vranje 66 42 34N 21 54 E
Vranjska Banja 66 42 34N 22 1 E
Vranov 53 48 53N 21 40 E
Vransko 63 46 17N 14 58 E
Vratsa 67 43 13N 23 30 E
Vratsa □ 67 43 30N 23 30 E
Vrbas 66 45 0N 17 27 E
Vrbas, R. 66 44 30N 17 10 E
Vrbnik 63 45 4N 14 32 E
Vrboviec 63 45 53N 16 28 E
Vrbovsko 63 45 24N 15 5 E
Vrchlabí 52 49 38N 15 37 E
Vrede 129 27 24 S 29 6 E
Vredefort 128 27 0 S 26 58 E
Vredenburg 128 32 51 S 18 0 E
Vredendal 128 31 41 S 18 35 E
Vreeswijk 46 52 1N 5 6 E
Vrena 73 58 54N 16 41 E
Vrgorac 66 43 12N 17 20 E
Vrhnika 63 45 58N 14 15 E
Vriddhachalam 97 11 30N 79 10 E
Vridi 120 5 15N 4 3W
Vridi Canal 120 5 15N 4 3W
Vries 46 53 5N 6 35 E
Vriezenveen 46 52 25N 6 38 E
Vrindaban 94 27 37N 77 40 E
Vrnograč 63 43 12N 17 20 E
Vrondádhes 69 38 25N 26 7 E
Vroomshoop 46 52 27N 6 34 E
Vrpolje 66 43 42N 16 1 E
Vršac 66 45 8N 21 18 E
Vršački Kanal 66 45 15N 21 0 E
Vrsheto 67 43 15N 23 23 E
Vryburg 128 26 55 S 24 45 E
Vryheid 129 27 54 S 30 47 E
Vsetín 53 49 20N 18 0 E
Vu Liet 100 18 43N 105 23 E
Vŭcha, R. 67 41 53N 24 26 E
Vučitrn 66 42 49N 20 59 E
Vught 47 51 38N 5 20 E
Vuka, R. 66 45 28N 18 30 E
Vukovar 66 45 21N 18 59 E
Vulcan, Can. 152 50 25N 113 15W
Vulcan, Rumania 70 45 23N 23 17 E
Vulcan, U.S.A. 156 45 46N 87 51W
Vŭlcani 66 46 0N 20 26 E
Vulcano, I. 65 38 25N 14 58 E
Vulchedrŭma 67 43 42N 23 16 E
Vulci 63 42 23N 11 37 E
Vŭleni 70 44 15N 24 45 E
Vulkaneshty 82 45 35N 28 30 E
Vunduzi, R. 127 18 0 S 33 45 E
Vung Tau 101 10 21N 107 4 E
Vûrbitsa 67 42 59N 26 40 E
Vutcani 70 46 26N 27 59 E
Vuyyuru 96 16 28N 80 50 E
Vvedenka 84 54 0N 63 53 E
Vyara 96 21 8N 73 28 E
Vyasniki 81 56 10N 42 10 E
Vyatka, R. 84 56 30N 51 0 E
Vyatskiye Polyany 84 56 5N 51 0 E
Vyazemskiy 77 47 32N 134 45 E
Vyazma 80 55 10N 34 15 E
Vyborg 78 60 43N 28 47 E
Vychegda R. 78 61 50N 52 30 E
Vychodné Beskydy 53 49 30N 22 0 E
Východočeský □ 52 50 20N 15 45 E
Východoslovenský □ 53 48 50N 21 0 E
Vyg-ozero 78 63 30N 34 0 E
Vyja, R. 81 41 53N 24 26 E
Vypin, I. 97 10 10N 76 15 E
Vyrnwy, L. 31 52 48N 3 30W
Vyrnwy, R. 31 52 43N 3 15W
Vyshniy Volochek 80 57 30N 34 30 E
Vyškov 53 49 17N 17 0 E
Vysoké Mýto 53 49 58N 16 23 E
Vysoké Tatry 53 49 30N 20 0 E
Vysokovsk 81 56 22N 36 30 E
Vysotsk 80 51 43N 36 32 E
Vyssi Brod 92 48 36N 14 20 E
Vytegra 52 61 15N 36 40 E

W

Wa 121 10 7N 2 25W
Waal, R. 46 51 59N 4 8 E
Waalwijk 47 51 42N 5 4 E
Waarschoot 47 51 10N 3 36 E
Waasmunster 47 51 6N 4 5 E
Wabag 135 5 32 S 143 53 E
Wabakimi L. 150 50 38N 89 45W
Wabana 151 47 40N 53 0W
Wabasca 152 55 57N 113 45W
Wabash 156 40 48N 85 46W
Wabash, R. 156 39 10N 87 30W
Wabawng 98 25 18N 97 46 E
Wabeno 156 45 25N 88 40W
Wabi Gestro, R. 123 6 0N 41 35 E
Wabi, R. 123 7 35N 40 5 E
Wabi Shaballe, R. 123 8 0N 40 45 E
Wabigoon, L. 153 49 44N 92 34W
Wabowden 153 54 55N 98 38W
Wabrzezno 54 53 16N 18 57 E
Wabuk Pt. 150 55 20N 85 5W
Wabush City 151 52 55N 66 52W
Wabuska 160 39 16N 119 13W
W.A.C. Bennett Dam 152 56 2N 122 6W
Wachapreague 162 37 36N 75 41W
Wachtebeke 47 51 11N 3 52 E
Waco 159 31 33N 97 5W
Waconichi, L. 150 50 8N 74 0W
Wad ar Rimsa 92 26 5N 41 30 E
Wad Ban Naqa 123 16 32N 33 9 E
Wad Banda 123 13 10N 27 50 E
Wad el Haddad 123 13 50N 33 30 E
Wad en Nau 123 14 10N 33 34 E
Wad Hamid 123 16 20N 32 45 E
Wâd Medanî 123 14 28N 33 30 E
Wad Thana 94 27 22N 66 23 E
Wadayama 110 35 19N 134 52 E
Waddān 119 29 9N 16 45 E
Waddān, Jabal 119 29 0N 16 15 E
Waddeneilanden 46 53 25N 5 10 E
Waddenzee 46 53 6N 5 10 E
Wadderin Hill 137 32 0 S 118 25 E
Waddesdon 29 51 50N 0 54W
Waddingham 33 53 28N 0 31W
Waddington 33 53 10N 0 31W
Waddington, Mt. 152 51 23N 125 15W
Waddinxveen 46 52 2N 4 40 E
Waddy Pt. 139 24 58 S 153 21 E
Wadebridge 30 50 31N 4 51W
Wadena, Can. 153 51 57N 103 38W
Wadena, U.S.A. 158 46 25N 95 2W
Wädenswil 51 47 14N 8 30 E
Wadesboro 157 35 2N 80 2W
Wadhams 152 51 30N 127 30W
Wadhurst 29 51 3N 0 21 E
Wadi 121 13 5N 11 40 E
Wādī ash Shāfi' 119 27 30N 15 0 E
Wādī Banī Walīd 119 31 49N 14 0 E
Wadi Gemâl 122 24 35N 35 10 E
Wadi Halfa 122 21 53N 31 19 E
Wadi Masila 91 16 30N 49 0 E
Wadi Sabha 92 23 50N 48 30 E
Wadlew 54 51 31N 19 23 E
Wadowice 54 49 52N 19 30 E
Wadsworth 160 39 44N 119 22W
Waegwan 107 35 59N 128 23 E
Waenfawr 31 53 7N 4 10W
Wafou Hu 109 32 19N 116 56 E
Wafra 92 28 33N 48 3 E
Wagenberg 47 51 40N 4 46 E
Wageningen 46 51 58N 5 40 E
Wager B. 149 65 26N 88 40W
Wager Bay 149 65 56N 90 49W
Wagga Wagga 141 35 7 S 147 24 E
Waghete 103 4 10 S 135 50 E
Wagin, Austral. 137 33 17 S 117 25 E
Wagin, Nigeria 137 12 42N 7 10 E
Wagon Mound 159 36 10N 105 0W
Wagoner 159 36 0N 95 20W
Wagrowiec 54 52 48N 17 19 E
Wah 94 33 45N 72 40 E
Wahai 103 2 48 S 129 35 E
Wahiawa 147 21 30N 158 2W
Wahnai 94 32 40N 65 50 E
Wahoo 158 41 15N 96 35W
Wahpeton 158 46 20N 96 35W
Wahratta 140 31 58 S 141 50 E
Wai 96 17 56N 73 57 E
Wai, Koh 101 9 55N 102 55 E
Waiai, R. 143 45 36 S 167 45 E
Waianae 147 21 25N 158 8W
Waiau 143 42 39 S 173 5 E
Waiau, R. 143 42 47 S 173 22 E
Waiawe Ganga 97 6 15N 81 0 E
Waibeem 103 0 30 S 132 50 E
Waiblingen 49 48 49N 9 20 E
Waidhofen, Niederösterreich, Austria 52 48 49N 15 17 E
Waidhofen, Niederösterreich, Austria 52 47 57N 14 46 E
Waigeo, I. 103 0 20 S 130 40 E
Waihao Downs 143 44 48 S 170 55 E
Waihao, R. 143 44 52 S 171 11 E
Waiheke Islands 142 36 48 S 175 6 E
Waihi 142 37 23 S 175 52 E
Waihola 143 46 1 S 170 8 E
Waihola L. 143 45 59 S 170 8 E
Waihou, R. 143 37 15 S 175 40 E
Waika 126 2 22 S 25 42 E
Waikabubak 103 9 45 S 119 25 E
Waikaka 143 45 55 S 169 1 E
Waikaoti 131 45 36 S 170 41 E
Waikare, L. 142 37 26 S 175 13 E
Waikaremoana 142 38 42 S 177 12 E
Waikaremoana L. 142 38 49 S 177 9 E
Waikari 143 42 58 S 172 41 E
Waikato, R. 142 37 23 S 174 43 E
Waikawa Harbour 143 46 39 S 169 9 E
Waikerie 140 34 9 S 140 0 E
Waikiekie 142 35 57 S 174 16 E
Waikokopu 142 39 3 S 177 52 E
Waikokopu Harb. 142 39 4 S 177 53 E
Waikouaiti 143 45 36 S 170 41 E
Wailuku 147 20 53N 156 26W
Waimakariri, R. 143 42 23 S 172 42 E
Waimangaroa 143 41 43 S 171 46 E
Waimanola 147 21 19N 157 43W
Waimarie 143 41 35 S 171 58 E
Waimarino 143 40 40 S 175 20 E
Waimate 143 44 53 S 171 3 E
Waimea 147 21 57N 159 39W
Waimea Plain 143 45 55 S 168 35 E
Waimes 47 50 25N 6 7 E
Wainfleet All Saints 33 53 7N 0 16 E
Wainganga, R. 96 21 0N 79 45 E
Waingapu 103 9 35 S 120 11 E
Waingmaw 98 25 21N 97 26 E
Wainiha 147 22 9N 159 34W
Wainuiomata 142 41 17 S 174 56 E
Wainwright, Can. 153 52 50N 110 50W
Wainwright, U.S.A. 147 70 39N 160 10W
Waiotapu 142 38 21 S 176 25 E
Waiouru 142 39 28 S 175 41 E
Waipahi 143 46 6 S 169 15 E
Waipahu 147 21 23N 158 1W
Waipapa Pt. 143 46 40 S 168 51 E
Waipara 143 43 3 S 172 46 E
Waipawa 142 39 56 S 176 38 E
Waipiro 142 38 2 S 176 22 E
Waipori 131 45 50 S 169 52 E
Waipu 142 35 59 S 174 29 E
Waipukurau 142 40 1 S 176 33 E
Wairakei 142 38 37 S 176 6 E
Wairarapa I. 142 41 14 S 175 15 E
Wairau, R. 143 41 32 S 174 7 E
Wairio 143 45 59 S 168 3 E
Wairoa 142 39 3 S 177 25 E
Wairoa, R. 142 36 5 S 173 59 E
Waitaki Plains 143 44 22 S 170 0 E
Waitaki, R. 143 44 23 S 169 55 E
Waitara 142 38 59 S 174 15 E
Waitchie 140 35 22 S 143 8 E
Waitoa 142 37 37 S 175 35 E
Waitotara 142 39 49 S 174 44 E
Waitsburg 160 46 15N 118 10W
Waiuku 142 37 15 S 174 45 E
Wajir 126 1 42N 40 20 E
Wajir □ 126 1 42N 40 20 E
Wakaia 143 45 44 S 168 51 E
Wakasa 110 35 20N 134 24 E
Wakasa-Wan 111 34 45N 135 30 E
Wakatipu, L. 143 45 5 S 168 33 E
Wakaw 153 52 39N 105 44W
Wakayama 111 34 15N 135 15 E
Wakayama-ken □ 111 33 50N 135 30 E
Wake 110 34 48N 134 8 E
Wake Forest 157 35 58N 78 30W
Wake I. 130 19 18N 166 36 E
Wakefield, N.Z. 143 41 24 S 173 5 E
Wakefield, U.K. 33 53 41N 1 31W
Wakefield, Mass., U.S.A. 162 42 30N 71 3W
Wakefield, Mich., U.S.A. 158 46 28N 89 53W
Wakema 98 16 40N 95 18 E
Wakhan □ 93 37 0N 73 0 E
Wakkanai 112 45 28N 141 35 E
Wakkerstroom 129 27 24 S 30 10 E
Wako 150 49 50N 91 22W
Wakool 140 35 28 S 144 23 E
Wakool, R. 140 35 5 S 143 33 E
Wakre 103 0 30 S 131 5 E
Waku 135 6 5 S 149 9 E
Wakuach L. 151 55 34N 67 32W
Walachia □ 70 44 40N 25 0 E
Walamba 127 13 30 S 28 42 E
Walberswick 29 52 18N 1 39 E
Wałbrzych 54 50 45N 16 18 E
Walbury Hill 28 51 22N 1 28W
Walcha 141 30 55 S 151 31 E
Walcha Road 141 30 55 S 151 24 E
Walcheren, I. 46 51 30N 3 35 E
Walcott 160 41 50N 106 55W
Walcz 54 53 17N 16 27 E
Wald 51 47 17N 8 56 E
Waldbröl 48 50 52N 7 36 E
Waldeck 48 51 12N 9 4 E
Walden, Colo., U.S.A. 160 40 47N 106 20W
Walden, N.Y., U.S.A. 162 41 32N 74 13W
Waldenburg 50 47 23N 7 45 E
Waldorf 162 38 37N 76 54W
Waldport 160 44 30N 124 2W
Waldron, Can. 153 50 53N 102 35W
Waldron, U.K. 29 50 56N 0 13 E
Waldron, U.S.A. 159 34 52N 94 4W
Waldshut 49 47 37N 8 12 E
Waldya 123 11 50N 39 34 E
Walebing 137 30 40 S 116 15 E
Walembele 120 10 30N 1 14W
Walensee 51 47 7N 9 13 E
Walenstadt 51 47 8N 9 19 E
Wales 147 65 38N 168 10W
Walewale 121 10 21N 0 50W
Walgett 133 30 0 S 148 5 E
Walhalla, Austral. 141 37 56 S 146 29 E
Walhalla, U.S.A. 153 48 55N 97 55W
Waliso 123 8 33N 38 1 E
Walkaway 137 28 59 S 114 48 E
Walker 158 47 4N 94 35W
Walker L., Man., Can. 153 54 42N 96 57W
Walker L., Qué., Can. 151 50 20N 67 11W
Walker L., U.S.A. 163 38 56N 118 46W
Walkerston 138 21 11 S 149 8 E
Wall 158 44 0N 102 14W
Walla Walla, Austral. 141 35 45 S 146 54 E
Walla Walla, U.S.A. 160 46 3N 118 25W

Wallabadah Weaverham

Wallabadah 138 17 57 S 142 15 E
Wallace, Idaho, U.S.A. 160 47 30N 116 0W
Wallace, N.C., U.S.A. 157 34 50N 77 59W
Wallace, Nebr., U.S.A. 158 40 51N 101 12W
Wallaceburg 150 42 40N 82 23W
Wallacetown 143 46 21 S 168 19 E
Wallachia = Valahia 70 44 35N 25 0 E
Wallal 139 26 32 S 146 7 E
Wallal Downs 136 19 47 S 120 40 E
Wallambin, L. 137 30 57 S 117 35 E
Wallaroo 140 33 56 S 137 39 E
Wallasey 32 53 26N 3 2W
Walldurn 49 49 34N 9 23 E
Wallerawang 141 33 25 S 150 4 E
Wallhallow 138 17 50 S 135 50 E
Wallingford 162 43 27N 72 50W
Wallis Arch. 142 13 20 S 176 20 E
Wallisellen 51 47 25N 8 36 E
Wallowa 160 45 40N 117 35W
Wallowa, Mts. 160 45 20N 117 30W
Walls 36 60 14N 1 32W
Wallsend, Austral. 141 32 55 S 151 40 E
Wallsend, U.K. 35 54 59N 1 30W
Wallula 160 46 3N 118 59W
Wallumbilla 139 26 33 S 149 9 E
Walmer, S. Afr. 128 33 57 S 25 35 E
Walmer, U.K. 29 51 12N 1 23 E
Walmsley, L. 153 63 25N 108 36W
Walney, Isle of 32 54 5N 3 15W
Walnut Ridge 159 36 7N 90 58W
Walpeup 140 35 10 S 142 2 E
Walpole 29 52 44N 0 13 E
Walsall 28 52 36N 1 59W
Walsenburg 159 37 42N 104 45W
Walsh, Austral. 138 16 40 S 144 0 E
Walsh, U.S.A. 159 37 28N 102 15W
Walsh, R. 138 16 31 S 143 42 E
Walshoutem 47 50 43N 5 4 E
Walsoken 29 52 41N 0 12 E
Walsrode 48 52 51N 9 37 E
Waltair 96 17 44N 83 23 E
Walterboro 157 32 53N 80 40W
Walters 159 34 25N 98 20W
Waltershausen 48 50 53N 10 33 E
Waltham, Can. 150 45 57N 76 57W
Waltham, U.K. 29 53 32N 0 6W
Waltham, U.S.A. 34 42 22N 71 12W
Waltham Abbey 29 51 40N 0 1 E
Waltham Forest 29 51 37N 0 2 E
Waltham on the Wolds 29 52 49N 0 48W
Waltman 160 43 8N 107 15W
Walton 162 42 12N 75 9W
Walton-le-Dale 32 53 45N 2 41W
Walton-on-the-Naze 29 51 52N 1 17 E
Walu 98 23 54N 96 57 E
Walvis Ridge 15 30 0 S 3 0 E
Walvisbaai 128 23 0 S 14 28 E
Walwa 141 35 59 S 147 44 E
Wamaza 126 4 12 S 27 2 E
Wamba, Kenya 126 0 58N 37 19 E
Wamba, Nigeria 126 8 58N 8 34 E
Wamba, Zaïre 121 2 10N 27 57 E
Wamego 158 39 14N 96 22W
Wamena 103 3 58 S 138 50 E
Wampo 99 31 30N 86 38 E
Wamsasi 103 3 27 S 126 7 E
Wan Hat 98 20 14N 97 53 E
Wan Kinghao 98 21 34N 98 17 E
Wan Lai-Kam 98 21 21N 98 22 E
Wan Tup 98 21 13N 98 42 E
Wana 94 32 20N 69 32 E
Wanaaring 139 29 38 S 144 0 E
Wanaka L. 143 44 33 S 169 7 E
Wanan 109 26 25N 114 50 E
Wanapiri 103 4 30 S 135 50 E
Wanapitei 150 46 30N 80 45W
Wanapitei L. 150 46 45N 80 40W
Wanaque 162 41 3N 74 17W
Wanbi 140 34 46 S 140 17 E
Wanborough 28 51 33N 1 40W
Wanch'eng 108 22 51N 107 25 E
Wanch'üan 106 35 26N 110 50 E
Wanch'uan 106 40 50N 114 56 E
Wandanian 141 35 6 S 150 30 E
Wanderer 127 19 36 S 30 1 E
Wandiwash 97 12 30N 79 30 E
Wandoan 139 26 5 S 149 55 E
Wandre 47 50 40N 5 39 E
Wandsworth 29 51 28N 0 15W
Wanfercée-Baulet 47 50 28N 4 35 E
Wanfuchuang 107 40 10N 122 34 E
Wang Kai (Ghâbat el Arab) 123 9 3N 29 23 E
Wang Noi 100 14 13N 100 44 E
Wang, R. 100 17 8N 99 2 E
Wang Saphung 100 17 18N 101 46 E
Wang Thong 100 16 50N 100 26 E
Wanga 126 2 58N 29 12 E
Wangal 103 6 8 S 134 9 E
Wanganella 141 35 6 S 144 49 E
Wanganui 142 39 35 S 175 3 E
Wanganui, R., N.I., N.Z. 142 39 25 S 175 4 E
Wanganui, R., S.I., N.Z. 143 43 3 S 170 26 E
Wangaratta 141 36 21 S 146 19 E
Wangchiang 109 30 7N 116 41 E
Wangch'ing 107 43 14N 129 38 E
Wangdu Phodrang 98 27 28N 89 54 E
Wangerooge I. 48 53 47N 7 52 E
Wangi 126 1 58 S 40 58 E
Wangiwangi, I. 103 5 22 S 123 37 E
Wangmo 108 25 14N 105 59 E
Wangts'ang 108 32 12N 106 21 E
Wangtu 106 38 42N 115 4 E
Wanhsien, Hopeh, China 106 38 49N 115 7 E
Wanhsien, Kansu, China 105 36 45N 107 24 E
Wankaner 94 22 42N 71 0 E
Wanki Nat. Park 128 19 0 S 26 30 E
Wankie 127 18 18 S 26 30 E
Wankie □ 127 18 18 S 26 30 E
Wanless 153 54 11N 101 21W
Wanna Lakes 137 28 30 S 128 27 E
Wannien 109 28 40N 116 55 E
Wanon Niwar 100 17 38N 103 46 E
Wanshengch'ang 108 28 58N 106 55 E
Wanssum 47 51 32N 6 5 E
Wanstead 143 40 8 S 176 30 E
Wantage 28 51 35N 1 25W
Wantsai 109 28 5N 114 22 E
Wanyin 98 20 23N 97 15 E
Wanyüan 108 32 4N 108 5 E
Wanzarïk 119 27 3N 13 30 E
Wanze 47 50 32N 5 13 E
Wapakoneta 156 40 35N 84 10W
Wapato 160 46 30N 120 25W
Wapawekka L. 153 54 55N 104 40W
Wapikopa L. 150 42 50N 88 10W
Wapiti, R. 150 55 5N 118 18W
Wappingers Fs. 162 41 35N 73 56W
Wapsipinican, R. 158 41 44N 90 19W
Warabi 111 35 49N 139 41 E
Warandab 91 7 20N 44 2 E
Warangal 96 17 58N 79 45 E
Waratah 138 41 30 S 145 30 E
Waratah B. 139 38 54 S 146 5 E
Warboys 29 52 25N 0 5W
Warburg 48 51 29N 9 10 E
Warburton 141 37 47 S 145 42 E
Warburton, R. 143 27 30 S 138 30 E
Warburton Ra. 137 25 55 S 126 28 E
Ward, Ireland 38 53 25N 6 19W
Ward, N.Z. 143 41 49 S 174 11 E
Ward Cove 152 55 25N 132 10W
Ward Hunt, C. 135 8 2 S 148 10 E
Ward Hunt Str. 135 9 30 S 150 0 E
Ward Mtn. 163 37 12N 118 54W
Ward, R. 139 26 32 S 146 6 E
Warden 129 27 50 S 29 0 E
Wardha 96 20 45N 78 39 E
Wardha, R. 93 19 57N 79 11 E
Wardington 28 52 8N 1 17W
Wardle 32 53 7N 2 35W
Wardlow 152 50 56N 111 31W
Wardoan 133 25 59 S 149 59 E
Wards River 141 32 11 S 151 56 E
Ward's Stone, mt. 32 54 2N 2 39W
Ware, Can. 152 57 26N 125 41W
Ware, U.K. 29 51 48N 0 2W
Ware, U.S.A. 162 42 16N 72 15W
Waregem 47 50 53N 3 27 E
Wareham, U.K. 28 50 41N 2 8W
Wareham, U.S.A. 162 41 45N 70 44W
Wareham, oilfield 19 50 40N 2 8W
Waremme 47 50 43N 5 15 E
Waren 48 53 30N 12 41 E
Warendorf 48 51 57N 8 0 E
Warialda 139 29 29 S 150 33 E
Wariap 103 1 30 S 134 5 E
Warin Chamrap 100 15 12N 104 53 E
Wark 35 55 5N 2 14W
Warkopi 103 1 12 S 134 9 E
Warkworth, N.Z. 142 36 24 S 174 41 E
Warkworth, U.K. 35 55 22N 1 38W
Warley 28 52 30N 2 0W
Warm Springs, Mont., U.S.A. 160 46 11N 112 56W
Warm Springs, Nev., U.S.A. 161 38 16N 116 32W
Warman 153 52 19N 106 30W
Warmbad, Namibia 128 19 14 S 13 51 E
Warmbad, Namibia 128 28 25 S 18 42 E
Warmbad, S. Afr. 129 24 51 S 28 19 E
Warmenhuizen 46 52 43N 4 44 E
Warmeriville 43 49 20N 4 13 E
Warminster 28 51 12N 2 11W
Warmond 46 52 12N 4 30 E
Warnambool Downs 138 22 48 S 142 52 E
Warnemünde 48 54 9N 12 5 E
Warner 152 49 17N 112 12W
Warner Range, Mts. 160 41 30 S 120 20W
Warner Robins 157 32 41N 83 36W
Warneton 47 50 45N 2 57 E
Warnow, R. 48 54 0N 12 9 E
Warnsveld 46 52 8N 6 14 E
Waroona 137 32 50 S 115 58 E
Warora 96 20 14N 79 1 E
Warracknabeal 140 36 9 S 142 26 E
Warragul 141 38 10 S 145 58 E
Warrawaqine 136 20 51 S 120 42 E
Warrayelu 123 10 40N 39 28 E
Warrego, R. 139 30 24 S 145 21 E
Warrego Ra. 138 25 15 S 146 0 E
Warren, Austral. 141 31 42 S 147 51 E
Warren, Ark., U.S.A. 159 33 35N 92 3W
Warren, Pa., U.S.A. 156 41 52N 79 10W
Warren, R.I., U.S.A. 156 41 43N 71 19W
Warrenpoint 38 54 7N 6 15W
Warrens Landing 153 53 40N 98 0W
Warrensburg 158 38 45N 93 45W
Warrenton, S. Afr. 128 28 9 S 24 47 E
Warrenton, U.S.A. 160 46 11N 123 59W
Warrenville 139 25 48 S 147 22 E
Warri 121 5 30N 5 41 E
Warrie 136 22 12 S 119 40 E
Warrina 136 28 12 S 135 50 E
Warrington, N.Z. 143 45 43 S 170 35 E
Warrington, U.K. 32 53 25N 2 38W
Warrington, U.S.A. 157 30 22N 87 16W
Warrnambool 140 38 25 S 142 30 E
Warroad 158 49 0N 95 20W
Warsaw 156 41 14N 85 50W
Warsaw = Warszawa 54 52 13N 21 0 E
Warsop 33 53 13N 1 9W
Warstein 48 51 26N 8 20 E
Warszawa 54 52 13N 21 0 E
Warszawa □ 54 52 30N 17 0 E
Warta 54 51 43N 18 38 E
Warta, R. 54 52 40N 16 10 E
Waru 103 3 30 S 130 36 E
Warud 96 21 30N 78 16 E
Warwick, Austral. 139 28 10 S 152 1 E
Warwick, U.K. 28 52 17N 1 36W
Warwick, N.Y., U.S.A. 162 41 16N 74 22W
Warwick, R.I., U.S.A. 162 41 43N 71 25W
Warwick □ 28 52 20N 1 30W
Wasa 152 49 45N 115 50W
Wasatch, Mt., Ra. 160 40 30N 111 15W
Wasbank 129 28 15 S 30 9 E
Wasbister 37 59 11N 3 2W
Wasco, Calif., U.S.A. 163 35 37N 119 16W
Wasco, Oreg., U.S.A. 160 45 45N 120 46W
Waseca 158 44 3N 93 31W
Wasekamio L. 153 56 45N 108 45W
Wash, The 33 52 58N 0 20W
Washburn, N.D., U.S.A. 158 47 23N 101 0W
Washburn, Wis., U.S.A. 158 46 38N 90 55W
Washford 28 51 9N 3 22W
Washington, U.K. 35 54 55N 1 30W
Washington, D.C., U.S.A. 162 38 52N 77 0W
Washington, Ga., U.S.A. 157 33 45N 82 45W
Washington, Ind., U.S.A. 156 38 40N 87 8W
Washington, Iowa, U.S.A. 158 41 20N 91 45W
Washington, Miss., U.S.A. 158 38 35N 91 20W
Washington, N.C., U.S.A. 157 35 35N 77 1W
Washington, N.J., U.S.A. 162 40 45N 74 59W
Washington, Ohio, U.S.A. 156 39 34N 83 26W
Washington, Pa., U.S.A. 156 40 10N 80 20W
Washington, Utah, U.S.A. 161 37 10N 113 30W
Washington □ 160 47 45N 120 30W
Washington Court House 156 39 34N 83 26W
Washington I., Pac. Oc. 131 4 43N 160 25W
Washington I., U.S.A. 156 45 24N 86 54W
Washington Mt. 156 44 15N 71 18W
Washir 93 32 15N 63 50 E
Wasian 103 1 47 S 133 19 E
Wasilków 54 53 12N 23 13 E
Wasior 103 2 43 S 134 30 E
Waskaiowaka, L. 153 56 33N 96 23W
Waskesiu Lake 153 53 55N 106 5W
Wasm 122 18 2N 41 32 E
Waspik 47 51 41N 4 57 E
Wassen 51 46 42N 8 36 E
Wassenaar 46 52 8N 4 24 E
Wasserburg 49 48 4N 12 15 E
Wassy 43 48 30N 4 58 E
Wast Water, L. 32 54 26N 3 18W
Waswanipi 150 49 40N 75 59W
Waswanipi, L. 150 49 35N 76 40W
Watangpone 103 4 29 S 120 25 E
Wataroa 143 43 18 S 170 24 E
Wataroa, R. 143 43 7 S 170 16 E
Watawaha, P. 103 6 30 S 122 20 E
Watchet 28 51 10N 3 20W
Water Park Pt. 138 22 56 S 150 47 E
Water Valley 159 34 9N 89 38W
Waterberg, Namibia 128 20 30 S 17 18 E
Waterberg, S. Afr. 129 24 14 S 28 0 E
Waterberg, mt. 128 20 26 S 17 13 E
Waterbury 162 41 32N 73 0W
Waterbury L. 153 58 10N 104 22W
Waterford, Ireland 39 52 16N 7 8W
Waterford, S. Afr. 128 33 6 S 25 0 E
Waterford, U.S.A. 163 37 38N 120 46W
Waterford □ 39 51 10N 7 40W
Waterford Harb. 39 52 10N 6 58W
Watergate Bay 30 50 26N 5 4W
Watergrasshill 39 52 1N 8 20W
Waterhen L., Man., Can. 153 52 10N 99 40W
Waterhen L., Sask., Can. 153 54 28N 108 25W
Wateringen 46 52 2N 4 16 E
Waterloo, Belg. 47 50 43N 4 25 E
Waterloo, Can. 150 43 30N 80 32W
Waterloo, S. Leone 120 8 26N 13 8W
Waterloo, U.K. 32 53 29N 3 2W
Waterloo, Ill., U.S.A. 158 38 22N 90 6W
Waterloo, Iowa, U.S.A. 158 42 27N 92 20W
Waterloo, N.Y., U.S.A. 162 42 54N 76 53W
Watermeal-Boitsford 47 50 48N 4 25 E
Watermeet 158 46 15N 89 12W
Waternish 36 57 32N 6 35W
Waterton Lakes Nat. Park 152 49 5N 114 15W
Watertown, Conn., U.S.A. 162 41 36N 73 7W
Watertown, N.Y., U.S.A. 162 43 58N 75 57W
Watertown, S.D., U.S.A. 158 44 57N 97 5W
Watertown, Wis., U.S.A. 158 43 15N 88 45W
Waterval-Boven 129 25 40 S 30 18 E
Waterville, Ireland 39 51 49N 10 10W
Waterville, Me., U.S.A. 151 44 35N 69 40W
Waterville, N.Y., U.S.A. 162 42 56N 75 23W
Waterville, Wash., U.S.A. 160 47 45N 120 1W
Watervliet, Belg. 47 51 17N 3 38 E
Watervliet, U.S.A. 162 42 46N 73 43W
Wates 103 7 53 S 110 6 E
Watford 29 51 38N 0 23W
Watford City 158 47 50N 103 23W
Wath 33 53 29N 1 20W
Wathaman, R. 153 57 16N 102 59W
Watheroo 137 30 15 S 116 0W
Watien 109 32 45N 112 30 E
Wat'ing 106 35 25N 106 46 E
Watkins Glen 162 42 25N 76 55W
Watlings I. 167 24 0N 74 35W
Watlington, Norfolk, U.K. 29 52 40N 0 24 E
Watlington, Oxford, U.K. 29 51 38N 1 0W
Watonga 159 35 51N 98 24W
Watou 47 50 51N 2 38 E
Watraba 139 31 58 S 133 13 E
Watrous, Can. 153 51 40N 105 25W
Watrous, U.S.A. 159 35 50N 104 55W
Watsa 126 3 4N 29 30 E
Watseka 156 40 45N 87 45W
Watson, Austral. 137 30 29 S 131 31 E
Watson, Can. 153 52 10N 104 30W
Watson Lake 147 60 6N 128 49W
Watsontown 162 41 5N 76 52W
Watsonville 163 36 55N 121 49W
Watten 37 21 1 S 144 3 E
Wattenwil 50 46 46N 7 30 E
Wattiwarriganna Cr. 139 28 57 S 136 10 E
Watton 29 52 35N 0 50 E
Wattwil 51 47 18N 9 6 E
Watubela, Kepulauan 103 4 28 S 131 54 E
Wau 135 7 21 S 146 47 E
Waubach 47 50 55N 6 3 E
Waubay 158 45 42N 97 17W
Waubra 140 37 21 S 143 39 E
Wauchope 141 31 28 S 152 45 E
Wauchula 157 27 35N 81 50W
Waugh 153 49 40N 95 20W
Waukegan 156 42 22N 87 54W
Waukesha 156 43 0N 88 15W
Waukon 158 43 14N 91 33W
Wauneta 158 40 27N 101 25W
Waupaca 158 44 22N 89 8W
Waupun 158 43 38N 88 44W
Waurika 159 34 12N 98 0W
Wausau 158 44 57N 89 40W
Wautoma 158 44 3N 89 20W
Wauwatosa 156 43 6N 87 59W
Wave Hill 136 17 32N 131 0 E
Waveney, R. 29 52 24N 1 20 E
Waver R. 32 54 50N 3 15W
Waverley 142 39 46 S 174 37 E
Waverly, Iowa, U.S.A. 158 42 40N 92 30W
Waverly, N.Y., U.S.A. 162 42 0N 76 33W
Wavre 47 50 43N 4 38 E
Wavreille 47 50 7N 5 15 E
Wâw 123 7 45N 28 1 E
Waw an Namus 119 24 24N 18 11 E
Wawa, Can. 150 47 59N 84 47W
Wawa, Nigeria 121 9 54N 4 27 E
Wawa, Sudan 122 20 30N 30 22 E
Wawanesa 153 49 36N 99 40W
Wawoi, R. 135 7 48 S 143 16 E
Wawona 163 37 32N 119 39W
Waxahachie 159 32 22N 96 53W
Waxweiler 49 50 6N 6 22 E
Way, L. 137 26 45 S 120 16 E
Wayabula Rau 103 2 29N 128 17 E
Wayatinah 138 42 19 S 146 27 E
Waycross 157 31 12N 82 25W
Wayi 123 5 8N 30 10 E
Wayne, Nebr., U.S.A. 158 42 16N 97 0W
Wayne, W. Va., U.S.A. 156 38 15N 82 27W
Waynesboro, Miss., U.S.A. 157 31 40N 88 39W
Waynesboro, Pa., U.S.A. 156 39 46N 77 32W
Waynesboro, Va., U.S.A. 156 38 4N 78 57W
Waynesburg 156 39 54N 80 12W
Waynesville 157 35 31N 83 0W
Waynoka 159 36 38N 98 53W
Waza 94 33 22N 69 22 E
Wâzin 119 31 58N 10 51 E
Wazirabad, Afghan. 93 36 44N 66 47 E
Wazirabad, Pak. 94 32 30N 74 8 E
We 102 6 3N 95 56 E
Weald, The 29 51 7N 0 9 E
Wear, R. 35 54 55N 1 22W
Weardale 32 54 44N 2 5W
Wearhead 32 54 45N 2 14W
Weatherford, Okla., U.S.A. 159 35 30N 98 45W
Weatherford, Tex., U.S.A. 159 32 45N 97 48W
Weaver, R. 32 53 17N 2 35W
Weaverham 32 53 15N 2 30W

Webb City Whitby

Webb City 159 37 9N 94 30W
Weber 142 40 24S 176 20E
Webera, Bale, Ethiopia 123 6 29N 40 33E
Webera, Shewa, Ethiopia 123 9 40N 39 0E
Webster, Mass., U.S.A. 162 42 4N 71 54W
Webster, S.D., U.S.A. 158 45 24N 97 33W
Webster, Wis., U.S.A. 158 45 53N 92 25W
Webster City 158 42 30N 93 50W
Webster Green 158 38 38N 90 20W
Webster Springs 156 38 30N 80 25W
Wecliniec 54 51 18N 15 10E
Weda 103 0 30N 127 50E
Weda, Teluk 103 0 30N 127 50E
Weddell I. 176 51 50S 61 0W
Weddell Sea 13 72 30S 40 0W
Wedderburn 140 36 20S 143 33E
Wedge I. 132 30 50S 115 11E
Wedgeport 151 43 44N 65 59W
Wedmore 28 51 14N 2 50W
Wednesbury 28 52 33N 2 1W
Wednesfield 28 52 36N 2 3W
Wedza 127 18 40S 31 33E
Wee Elwah 141 32 2S 145 14E
Wee Waa 139 30 11S 149 26E
Weed 160 41 29N 122 22W
Weedsport 162 43 3N 76 35W
Weemelah 139 29 2S 149 7E
Weenen 129 28 48S 30 7E
Weener 48 53 10N 7 23E
Weert 47 51 15N 5 43E
Weesen 51 47 7N 9 4E
Weesp 46 52 18N 5 2E
Weggis 51 47 2N 8 26E
Wegierska-Gorka 54 49 36N 19 7E
Wegorzewo 54 54 13N 21 43E
Wegroów 54 52 24N 22 0E
Wehl 46 51 58N 6 13E
Wei Ho, R., Honan, China 106 34 58N 113 32E
Wei Ho, R., Shensi, China 106 34 38N 110 20E
Wei-si 99 27 18N 99 18E
Weich'ang 107 41 56N 117 34E
Weichou Tao 108 21 3N 109 2E
Weich'uan 106 34 19N 114 0E
Weida 48 50 47N 12 3E
Weiden 49 49 40N 12 10E
Weifang 107 36 47N 119 10E
Weihai 107 37 30N 122 10E
Weihsi 108 27 18N 99 18E
Weihsin 108 27 48N 105 5E
Weilburg 48 50 28N 8 17E
Weilheim 49 47 50N 11 9E
Weimar 48 51 0N 11 20E
Weinan 106 34 30N 109 35E
Weinfelden 51 47 34N 9 6E
Weingarten 49 47 49N 9 39E
Weinheim 49 49 33N 8 40E
Weining 108 26 50N 104 19E
Weipa 138 12 24S 141 50E
Weir, R., Austral. 139 28 20S 149 50E
Weir, R., Can. 153 56 54N 93 21W
Weir River 153 56 49N 94 6W
Weisen 51 46 42N 9 43E
Weiser 160 44 10N 117 0W
Weishan, Shantung, China 107 34 49N 47 6E
Weishan, Yunnan, China 108 25 16N 100 21E
Weissenburg 49 49 2N 10 58E
Weissenfels 48 51 11N 11 58E
Weisshorn 50 46 7N 7 43E
Weissmies 50 46 8N 8 1E
Weisstannen 51 46 59N 9 22E
Weisswasser 48 51 30N 14 36E
Weiswampach 47 50 8N 6 5E
Wëitra 52 48 41N 14 54E
Weiyüan 106 35 6N 104 14E
Weiyuan 106 35 10N 104 20E
Weiz 52 47 13N 15 39E
Wejherowo 54 54 35N 18 12E
Wekusko 153 54 45N 99 45W
Wekusko L. 153 54 40N 99 50W
Welbourn Hill 139 27 21S 134 6E
Welby 153 50 33N 101 29W
Welch 156 37 29N 81 36W
Welcome 138 15 20S 144 40E
Weldon 35 55 16N 1 46W
Welega □ 123 9 25N 34 20E
Welford, Berks., U.K. 28 51 28N 1 24W
Welford, Northampton, U.K. 28 52 26N 1 5W
Welkenraedt 47 50 39N 5 58E
Welkite 123 8 15N 37 42E
Welkom 128 28 0S 26 50E
Welland 150 43 0N 79 10W
Welland, R. 29 52 43N 0 10W
Wellen 47 50 50N 5 21E
Wellesley Is. 138 17 20S 139 30E
Wellin 47 50 5N 5 6E
Wellingborough 29 52 18N 0 41W
Wellington, Austral. 141 32 35S 148 59E
Wellington, Can. 150 43 57N 77 20W
Wellington, N.Z. 142 41 19S 174 46E
Wellington, S. Afr. 128 33 38S 18 57E
Wellington, U.K. 28 50 58N 3 13W
Wellington, Col., U.S.A. 158 40 43N 105 0W
Wellington, Kans., U.S.A. 159 37 15N 97 25W
Wellington, Nev., U.S.A. 163 38 47N 119 28W
Wellington, Okla., U.S.A. 159 34 55N 100 13W
Wellington □ 143 40 8S 175 36E
Wellington Bridge 39 52 15N 6 45W
Wellington, I. 176 49 30S 75 0W
Wellington, L. 141 38 6S 147 20E
Wellington, Mt. 142 36 55S 174 52E
Wellington (Telford) 28 52 42N 2 31W
Wello, L. 137 26 43S 123 10E
Wellow 28 51 20N 2 22W
Wells, Norfolk, U.K. 29 52 57N 0 51E
Wells, Somerset, U.K. 28 51 12N 2 39W
Wells, Me., U.S.A. 162 43 18N 70 35W
Wells, Minn., U.S.A. 158 43 44N 93 45W
Wells, Nev., U.S.A. 160 41 8N 115 0W
Wells, N.Y., U.S.A. 162 43 24N 74 17W
Wells Gray Prov. Park 152 52 30N 120 15W
Wells L. 137 26 44S 123 15E
Wellsboro 156 41 46N 77 20W
Wellsford 142 36 16S 174 32E
Wellsville, Mo., U.S.A. 158 39 4N 91 30W
Wellsville, N.Y., U.S.A. 156 42 9N 77 53W
Wellsville, Ohio, U.S.A. 156 40 36N 80 40W
Wellsville, Utah, U.S.A. 160 41 35N 111 59W
Wellton 161 32 46N 114 6W
Welmel, W. 123 6 0N 40 20E
Welney 29 52 31N 0 15E
Welo □ 123 11 50N 39 48E
Wels 52 48 9N 14 1E
Welshpool 31 52 40N 3 9W
Welton 33 53 19N 0 29W
Welwel 91 7 5N 45 25E
Welwitschia 128 20 16S 14 59E
Welwyn 153 50 20N 101 30W
Welwyn Garden City 29 51 49N 0 11W
Wem 28 52 52N 2 45W
Wembere, R. 126 4 45S 34 0E
Wembury 30 50 19N 4 6W
Wemmel 47 50 55N 4 18E
Wemyss Bay 34 55 52N 4 54W
Wenatchee 160 47 30N 120 17W
Wench'ang 100 19 38N 110 42E
Wencheng 109 27 48N 120 5E
Wenchi 120 7 46N 2 8W
Wenchiang 108 30 43N 103 56E
Wenchou 109 28 1N 120 39E
Wench'uan 108 31 28N 103 35E
Wendell 160 42 50N 114 51W
Wendesi 103 2 30S 134 10E
Wendo 123 6 40N 38 27E
Wendover, U.K. 29 51 46N 0 45W
Wendover, U.S.A. 160 40 49N 114 1W
Wenduine 47 51 18N 3 5E
Wengan 108 27 0N 107 32E
Wengch'eng 109 24 22N 113 50E
Wenge 126 0 3N 24 0E
Wengen 50 46 37N 7 55E
Wengniut'ech'i 107 42 59N 118 48E
Wengpu 108 32 55N 98 30E
Wengyüan 109 24 21N 114 7E
Wenhsi 106 35 23N 111 8E
Wenhsiang 106 34 36N 110 34E
Wenhsien, Honan, China 106 34 56N 113 4E
Wenhsien, Kansu, China 106 58 0N 104 39E
Wenling 109 28 22N 121 18E
Wenlock 138 13 6S 142 58E
Wenlock Edge 23 52 30N 2 43W
Wenlock, R. 133 12 2S 141 55E
Wenshan 108 23 22N 104 13E
Wenshang 106 35 37N 116 33E
Wenshui, Kweichow, China 108 28 27N 106 31E
Wenshui, Shansi, China 106 37 25N 112 1E
Wensleydale 32 54 18N 2 0W
Wensu 105 41 15N 80 14E
Wenteng 107 37 10N 122 0E
Wentworth 140 34 2S 141 54E
Wentworth, Mt. 138 24 12S 147 1E
Wenut 103 3 11S 133 19E
Weobley 28 52 9N 2 52W
Weott 160 40 19N 123 56W
Wepener 128 29 42S 27 3E
Werbomont 47 50 23N 5 41E
Werda 128 25 24S 23 15E
Werdau 48 50 45N 12 20E
Werder, Ethiopia 91 6 58N 45 1E
Werder, Ger. 48 52 23N 12 56E
Werdohl 48 51 15N 7 47E
Weri 103 3 10S 132 30E
Werkendam 46 51 50N 4 53E
Werne 48 51 38N 7 38E
Wernigerode 48 51 49N 0 45E
Werribee 140 37 54S 144 40E
Werrimull 140 34 25S 141 38E
Werrington 30 50 31N 4 22W
Werris Creek 141 31 18S 150 38E
Wersar 103 1 30S 131 55E
Wertheim 49 49 44N 9 32E
Wervershoof 46 52 44N 5 10E
Wervik 47 50 47N 3 3E
Wesel 48 51 39N 6 34E
Weser, R. 48 53 33N 8 30E
Wesiri 103 7 30S 126 30E
Wesleyville 151 49 8N 53 36W
Wessel, C. 138 10 59S 136 46E
Wessel Is. 138 11 10S 136 45E
Wesselburen 48 54 11N 8 53E
Wessem 47 51 11N 5 49E
Wessington 158 44 30N 98 40W
Wessington Springs 158 44 10N 98 35W
West 159 31 50N 97 5W
West Auckland 33 54 38N 1 42W
West B. 151 45 53N 82 8W
West, B. 159 29 5N 89 27W
West Baines, R. 136 15 36S 129 58E
West Bend 156 43 25N 88 10W
West Bengal □ 95 25 0N 90 0E
West Branch 156 44 16N 84 13W
West Bridgford 33 52 56N 1 8W
West Bromwich 28 52 32N 2 1W
West Burra, I. 36 60 5N 1 21W
West Calder 35 55 51N 3 34W
West Canada Cr. 162 43 1N 74 58W
West Cape Howe 137 35 8S 117 36E
West Chester 162 39 58N 75 36W
West Coker 28 50 55N 2 40W
West Columbia 159 29 10N 95 38W
West Covina 163 34 4N 117 54W
West Derry 162 42 55N 71 19W
West Des Moines 158 41 30N 93 45W
West End 166 26 41N 78 58W
West Falkland Island 176 51 30S 60 0W
West Fen 33 53 5N 0 5W
West Frankfort 158 37 56N 89 0W
West Glamorgan □ 31 51 40N 3 55W
West Grinstead 29 50 58N 0 19W
West Haddon 28 52 21N 1 5W
West Harbour 131 45 51S 170 33E
West Hartford 162 41 45N 72 45W
West Haven 162 41 18N 72 57W
West Hazleton 162 40 58N 76 0W
West Helena 159 34 30N 90 40W
West Hurley 162 41 59N 74 7W
West Indies 158 15 0N 70 0W
West Kilbride 34 55 41N 4 50W
West Kirby 32 53 22N 3 11W
West Lavington 28 51 16N 1 59W
West Linton 35 55 45N 3 24W
West Looe 30 50 21N 4 29W
West Lulworth 28 50 37N 2 14W
West Lunga, R. 127 12 35S 24 45E
West Magpie R. 151 51 2N 64 42W
West Malling 29 51 16N 0 25E
West Memphis 159 35 5N 90 3W
West Meon 28 51 2N 1 3W
West Mersea 29 51 46N 0 55E
West Midlands □ 28 52 30N 1 55W
West Milton 162 41 1N 76 50W
West Monroe 159 32 32N 92 7W
West Nicholson 127 21 2S 29 20E
West Pakistan = Pakistan 93 27 0N 67 0W
West Palm Beach 157 26 44N 80 3W
West Paris 101 44 18N 70 30W
West Parley 28 50 46N 1 52W
West Plains 159 36 45N 91 50W
West Pt. 140 35 1S 135 56E
West Point, Can. 151 49 55N 64 30W
West Point, Jamaica 166 18 14N 78 30W
West Point, Ga., U.S.A. 157 32 54N 85 10W
West Point, Miss., U.S.A. 157 33 36N 88 38W
West Point, Nebr., U.S.A. 158 41 50N 96 43W
West Point, Va., U.S.A. 162 37 35N 76 47W
West Pokot □ 126 1 30N 35 40E
West, R. 162 42 52N 72 33W
West Rasen 33 53 23N 0 23W
West Reading 162 40 20N 75 57W
West Riding (□) 26 53 50N 1 30W
West Road R. 152 53 18N 122 53W
West Rutland 162 43 36N 73 3W
West Schelde = Westerschelde 47 51 23N 3 50E
West Sole, gasfield 19 53 40N 1 15E
West Spitsbergen 12 78 40N 17 0E
West Sussex □ 29 50 55N 0 30W
West-Terschelling 46 53 22N 5 13E
West Virginia □ 156 39 0N 18 0W
West-Vlaanderen □ 47 51 0N 3 0E
West Walker, R. 163 38 54N 119 9W
West Wittering 29 50 44N 0 53W
West Wyalong 141 33 56S 147 10E
West Yellowstone 160 44 47N 111 4W
West York 162 39 57N 76 46W
West Yorkshire □ 33 53 45N 1 40W
Westall 139 32 55S 134 4E
Westbank 152 49 50N 119 25W
Westbourne 29 50 53N 0 55W
Westbrook, Maine, U.S.A. 162 43 40N 70 22W
Westbrook, Tex., U.S.A. 159 32 25N 101 0W
Westbury, Austral. 138 41 30S 146 51E
Westbury, Salop, U.K. 28 52 40N 2 57W
Westbury, Wilts., U.K. 28 51 16N 2 11W
Westbury-on-Severn 28 51 49N 2 24W
Westby 158 48 52N 104 3W
Westend 163 35 42N 117 24W
Wester Ross, dist. 36 57 37N 5 0W
Westerbork 46 52 51N 6 37E
Westerham 29 51 16N 0 5E
Westerland 48 54 51N 8 20E
Western □, Kenya 126 0 30N 34 30E
Western □, Uganda 126 1 45N 31 30E
Western □, Zambia 127 13 15N 27 30E
Western Australia □ 137 25 0S 118 0E
Western Bay 151 46 50N 52 30W
Western Germany ■ 48 50 0N 8 0E
Western Ghats 97 15 30N 74 30E
Western Is. □ 36 57 40N 7 0W
Western River 140 35 42S 136 56E
Western Samoa ■ 130 14 0S 172 0W
Westernport 156 30 30N 79 5W
Westerschelde, R. 47 51 25N 4 0E
Westerstede 48 51 15N 7 55E
Westervoort 46 51 58N 5 59E
Westerwald, mts. 48 50 39N 8 0E
Westfield, U.K. 29 50 53N 0 30E
Westfield, U.S.A. 162 42 9N 72 49W
Westgat 47 51 39N 3 44E
Westhope 158 48 55N 101 0W
Westhoughton 32 53 34N 2 30W
Westkapelle, Belg. 47 51 19N 3 19E
Westkapelle, Neth. 47 51 31N 3 28E
Westland □ 143 43 33S 169 59E
Westland Bight 143 42 55S 170 5E
Westlock 152 54 9N 113 55W
Westmalle 47 51 18N 4 42E
Westmeath □ 38 53 30N 7 30W
Westmine 137 29 2S 116 8E
Westminster 162 39 34S 77 1W
Westmorland 161 33 2N 115 42W
Westmorland (□) 26 54 28N 2 40W
Weston, Malay. 102 5 10N 115 35E
Weston, U.K. 28 52 51N 2 2W
Weston, Oreg., U.S.A. 160 45 50N 118 30W
Weston, W. Va., U.S.A. 156 39 3N 80 29W
Weston I. 150 52 33N 79 36W
Weston-super-Mare 28 51 20N 2 59W
Westport, Ireland 38 53 44N 9 31W
Westport, N.Z. 143 41 46S 171 37E
Westport, U.S.A. 160 46 48N 124 4W
Westport B. 38 53 48N 9 38W
Westray 153 53 36N 101 24W
Westray Firth 37 59 15N 3 0W
Westray, I. 37 59 18N 3 0W
Westree 150 47 26N 81 34W
Westruther 35 55 45N 2 34W
Westview 152 49 50N 124 31W
Westville, Ill., U.S.A. 156 40 3N 87 36W
Westville, Okla., U.S.A. 159 36 0N 94 33W
Westward Ho 30 51 2N 4 16W
Westwood 160 40 26N 121 0W
Wetar, I. 103 7 30S 126 30E
Wetaskiwin 152 52 55N 113 24W
Wetherby 33 53 56N 1 23W
Wethersfield 162 41 43N 72 40W
Wetlet 98 21 13N 95 53E
Wettingen 51 47 28N 8 20E
Wetwang 33 54 2N 0 35W
Wetzikon 51 47 19N 8 48E
Wetzlar 48 50 33N 8 30E
Wevelgem 47 50 49N 3 12E
Wewak 135 3 38S 143 41E
Wewaka 159 35 10N 96 35W
Wexford 39 52 20N 6 28W
Wexford □ 39 52 20N 6 25W
Wexford Harb. 39 52 20N 6 25W
Wey, R. 29 51 19N 0 29W
Weybourne 29 52 57N 1 9E
Weybridge 29 51 23N 0 28W
Weyburn 153 49 40N 103 50W
Weyburn L. 152 63 0N 117 59W
Weyer 52 47 51N 14 40E
Weymouth, Can. 151 44 30N 66 1W
Weymouth, U.K. 28 50 36N 2 28W
Weymouth, U.S.A. 162 42 13N 70 53W
Weymouth, C. 133 12 37S 143 27E
Wezep 46 52 28N 6 0E
Whakamaru 142 38 23S 175 63E
Whakatane 142 37 57S 177 1E
Whale Cove 148 62 11N 92 36W
Whale Firth 36 60 40N 1 10W
Whale, R. 151 58 15N 67 40W
Whales 13 78 0S 165 0W
Whaley Bridge 32 53 20N 2 0W
Whalley 32 53 49N 2 25W
Whalsay, I. 36 60 22N 1 0W
Whalton 35 55 7N 1 46W
Whangamomona 142 39 8S 174 44E
Whangarei 142 35 43S 174 21E
Whangarei Harbour 142 35 45S 174 28E
Whangaroa 142 35 4S 173 46E
Whangumata 142 37 12S 175 53E
Whaplode 29 52 42N 0 3W
Wharanui 143 41 55S 174 6E
Wharfe, R. 33 53 55N 1 30W
Wharfedale 31 54 7N 2 4W
Wharton, N.J., U.S.A. 162 40 53N 74 36W
Wharton, Tex., U.S.A. 159 29 20N 96 6W
Whauphill 34 54 48N 4 31W
Whayjonta 139 29 40S 142 35E
Wheatland 158 42 4N 105 58W
Wheatley Hill 33 54 45N 1 23W
Wheaton, Md., U.S.A. 162 39 3N 77 3W
Wheaton, Minn., U.S.A. 158 45 50N 96 29W
Wheeler, Oreg., U.S.A. 160 45 45N 123 57W
Wheeler, Tex., U.S.A. 159 35 29N 100 15W
Wheeler Peak, Mt. 160 38 57N 114 15W
Wheeler, R. 153 57 34N 104 15W
Wheeler Ridge 163 35 0N 118 57W
Wheeling 156 40 2N 80 41W
Whichham 32 54 14N 3 22W
Whidbey I. 152 48 15N 122 40W
Whidbey Is. 136 34 30S 135 3E
Whiddy, I. 39 51 41N 9 30W
Whimple 30 50 46N 3 21W
Whipsnade 29 51 51N 0 32W
Whiskey Gap 152 49 0N 113 3W
Whiskey Jack L. 153 58 23N 101 55W
Whissendine 29 52 43N 0 46W
Whistleduck Cr. 138 20 15S 135 18E
Whistler 157 30 50N 88 10W
Whiston 32 53 25N 2 45W
Whitburn 35 55 52N 3 41W
Whitby 33 54 29N 0 37W

Winterborne Abbas Yaapeet

Winterborne Abbas 28 50 43N 2 30W
Winters 159 31 58N 99 58W
Winterset 158 41 18N 94 0W
Winterswijk 46 51 58N 6 43E
Winterthur 51 47 30N 8 44E
Winterton, Humberside, U.K. 33 53 39N 0 37W
Winterton, Norfolk, U.K. 29 52 43N 1 43E
Winthrop, Minn., U.S.A. 158 44 31N 94 25W
Winthrop, Wash., U.S.A. 160 48 27N 120 6W
Winton, Austral. 138 22 24S 143 3E
Winton, N.Z. 143 46 8S 168 20E
Winton, U.S.A. 157 36 25N 76 58W
Wirksworth 33 53 5N 1 34W
Wirral 23 53 25N 3 0W
Wirraminna 140 31 12S 136 13E
Wirrulla 139 32 24S 134 31E
Wisbech 29 52 39N 0 10E
Wisborough Green 29 51 2N 0 30W
Wisconsin □ 158 44 30N 90 0W
Wisconsin Dells 158 43 38N 89 45W
Wisconsin, R. 158 45 25N 89 45W
Wisconsin Rapids 158 44 25N 89 50W
Wisdom 147 45 36N 113 1W
Wiserman 147 67 25N 150 15W
Wishaw 35 55 46N 3 55W
Wishek 158 46 20N 99 35W
Wiske, R. 33 54 26N 1 27W
Wisła 53 49 38N 18 53E
Wisła, R. 54 53 38N 18 47E
Wisłok, R. 53 50 7N 22 25E
Wisłoka, R. 53 49 50N 21 28E
Wismar 48 53 53N 11 23E
Wismar B. 48 54 0N 11 15E
Wisner 158 42 0N 96 46W
Wissant 43 50 52N 1 40E
Wissembourg 43 48 57N 7 57E
Wissenkerke 47 51 35N 3 45E
Wistoka, R. 54 49 50N 21 28E
Witbank 129 25 51S 29 14E
Witchita 159 37 40N 97 22W
Witchyburn 37 57 37N 2 37W
Witdraai 128 26 58S 20 48E
Witham 29 51 48N 0 39E
Witham, R. 33 53 3N 0 8W
Withern 33 53 19N 0 9E
Withernsea 33 53 43N 0 2W
Witkowo 54 52 26N 17 45E
Witley 29 51 9N 0 39W
Witmarsum 46 53 6N 5 28E
Witney 28 51 47N 1 29W
Witnossob, R. 128 23 0S 18 40E
Wittdün 48 54 38N 8 23E
Witten 48 51 26N 7 19E
Wittenberg 48 51 51N 12 39E
Wittenberge 48 53 0N 11 44E
Wittenburg 48 53 30N 11 4E
Wittenoom, W. Australia, Austral. 132 22 15S 118 20E
Wittenoom, W. Australia, Austral. 136 18 34S 128 51E
Wittersham 29 51 1N 0 42E
Wittingen 48 52 43N 10 43E
Wittlich 49 50 0N 6 54E
Wittmund 48 53 39N 7 35E
Wittow 48 54 37N 13 21E
Wittstock 48 53 10N 12 30E
Witzenhausen 48 51 20N 9 50E
Wiveliscombe 28 51 2N 3 20W
Wivenhoe 29 51 51N 0 59E
Wiyeb, W. 123 7 15N 40 15E
Wladyslawowo 54 52 6N 18 28E
Wlen 160 51 0N 15 39E
Wlingi 103 8 5S 112 25E
Włocławek 54 52 40N 19 3E
Włodawa 54 51 33N 23 31E
Włoszczowa 54 50 50N 19 55E
Woburn, U.K. 29 51 59N 0 37W
Woburn, U.S.A. 162 42 31N 71 7W
Woburn Sands 29 51 1N 0 38W
Wodonga 141 36 5S 146 50E
Wodzisław Sl. 54 50 1N 18 26E
Woerden 46 52 5N 4 54E
Woerht'ukou 106 42 35N 112 19E
Woerth 43 48 57N 7 45E
Woevre 43 49 15N 5 45E
Wognum 46 52 40N 5 1E
Wohlen 51 47 21N 8 17E
Wokam, I. 103 5 45S 134 28E
Wokha 98 26 6N 94 16E
Woking, Can. 152 55 35N 118 50W
Woking, U.K. 29 51 18N 0 33W
Wokingham 29 51 25N 0 50W
Wolbrom 54 50 24N 19 45E
Woldegk 48 53 27N 13 35E
Wolf Creek 160 47 1N 112 2W
Wolf L. 152 60 24N 133 42W
Wolf Point 158 48 6N 105 40W
Wolf, R. 152 60 17N 132 33W
Wolf Rock 30 49 56N 5 50W
Wolfe I. 150 44 7N 76 20W
Wolfeboro 162 43 35N 71 12W
Wolfenbüttel 48 52 10N 10 33E
Wolfenden 152 52 0N 119 25W
Wolfheze 46 52 0N 5 48E
Wolfram 138 17 6S 145 0E
Wolf's Castle 31 51 53N 4 57W
Wolfsberg 52 46 50N 14 52E
Wolfsburg 48 52 27N 10 49E
Wolgast 48 54 3N 13 46E
Wolhusen 50 47 4N 8 4E
Wolin 54 53 40N 14 37E
Wollaston, Islas 176 55 40S 67 30W
Wollaston L. 153 58 7N 103 10W
Wollaston Pen. 148 69 30N 115 0W
Wollogorang 138 17 13S 137 57E
Wollongong 141 34 25S 150 54E
Wolmaransstad 128 27 12S 26 13E
Wolmirstedt 48 52 15N 11 35E
Wołomin 54 52 19N 21 15E
Wołow 54 51 20N 16 38E
Wolseley, Austral. 140 36 23S 140 54E
Wolseley, Can. 153 50 25N 103 15W
Wolseley, S. Afr. 128 33 26S 19 7E
Wolsingham 32 54 44N 1 52W
Wolstenholme Sound 12 74 30N 75 0W
Wolsztyn 54 52 8N 16 5E
Wolvega 46 52 52N 6 0E
Wolverhampton 28 52 35N 2 6W
Wolverton 29 52 3N 0 48W
Wolviston 33 54 39N 1 25W
Wombera 123 10 45N 35 49E
Wombwell 33 53 31N 1 23W
Wommels 46 53 6N 5 36E
Wonarah P.O. 138 19 55S 136 20E
Wonboyn 141 37 15S 149 55E
Wonck 47 50 46N 5 38E
Wondai 139 26 20S 151 49E
Wondelgem 47 51 5N 3 44E
Wonder Gorge 127 14 40S 29 0E
Wongalarroo L. 140 31 32S 144 0E
Wongan 137 30 51S 116 37E
Wongan Hills 137 30 53S 116 42E
Wongawal 137 25 5S 121 55E
Wonosari 103 7 38S 110 36E
Wŏnsan 107 39 11N 127 27E
Wonston 28 51 9N 1 18W
Wonthaggi 141 38 37S 145 37E
Wonyulgunna Hill, Mt. 137 24 52S 119 44E
Woocalla 140 31 42S 137 12E
Wood Buffalo Nat. Park 152 56 28N 113 41W
Wood Green 138 22 26S 134 12E
Wood Is. 136 16 24S 123 19E
Wood L. 153 55 17N 103 17W
Wood Lake 158 42 38N 100 14W
Wood Mt. 153 49 14N 106 30W
Woodah I. 138 13 27S 136 10E
Woodanilling 137 33 31S 117 24E
Woodbine 162 39 14N 74 49W
Woodbourne 162 41 46N 74 35W
Woodbridge 29 52 6N 1 19E
Woodburn 139 29 6S 153 23E
Woodbury, U.K. 30 50 40N 3 24W
Woodbury, U.S.A. 162 39 50N 75 9W
Woodchopper 147 65 25N 143 30W
Wooden Bridge 39 52 50N 6 13W
Woodend 140 37 20N 144 33E
Woodford 39 53 3N 8 23W
Woodfords 163 38 47N 119 50W
Woodhall Spa. 33 53 10N 0 12W
Woodham Ferrers 29 51 40N 0 37E
Woodlake 163 36 25N 119 6W
Woodland 160 38 40N 121 50W
Woodlands 137 24 46S 118 8E
Woodlark I. 135 9 10S 152 50E
Woodley 29 51 26N 0 54W
Woodpecker 152 53 30N 122 40W
Woodplumpton 32 53 47N 2 46W
Woodridge 153 49 20N 96 9W
Woodroffe, Mt. 137 26 20S 131 45E
Woodruff, Ariz., U.S.A. 161 34 51N 110 1W
Woodruff, Utah, U.S.A. 160 41 30N 111 4W
Woods, L., Austral. 138 17 50S 133 30E
Woods, L., Can. 151 54 30N 65 13W
Woods, Lake of the 153 49 30N 94 30W
Woodside, S. Australia, Austral. 140 34 58S 138 52E
Woodside, Victoria, Austral. 141 38 31S 146 52E
Woodstock, N.S.W., Austral. 141 33 45S 148 53E
Woodstock, Queens., Austral. 138 19 35S 146 50E
Woodstock, W.A., Austral. 136 21 41S 118 57E
Woodstock, N.B., Can. 151 46 11N 67 37W
Woodstock, Ont., Can. 150 43 10N 80 45W
Woodstock, U.K. 28 51 51N 1 20W
Woodstock, Ill., U.S.A. 158 42 17N 88 30W
Woodstock, Vt., U.S.A. 162 43 37N 72 31W
Woodstown 162 39 39N 75 20W
Woodville, N.Z. 142 40 20S 175 53E
Woodville, U.S.A. 159 30 45N 94 25W
Woodward 159 36 24N 99 28W
Woodward, Mt. 137 26 0S 131 0E
Woody 163 35 42N 118 50W
Wookey 28 51 13N 2 41W
Wookey Hole 28 51 13N 2 41W
Wool 28 50 41N 2 13W
Woolacombe 30 51 10N 4 12W
Woolamai, C. 141 38 30S 145 23E
Wooler 35 55 33N 2 0W
Woolgangie 137 31 12S 120 35E
Woolyeenyer, Mt. 137 32 16S 121 47E
Woombye 139 26 40S 152 55E
Woomera 140 31 11S 136 47E
Woonona 141 34 21S 150 54E
Woonsocket 162 42 0N 71 30W
Woonsockett 158 44 5N 98 15W
Wooramel 137 25 45S 114 40E
Wooramel, R. 137 25 30S 114 30E
Wooroloo 137 31 48S 116 18E
Wooroorooka 139 29 0S 145 41E
Wooster 156 40 38N 81 55W
Wootton Bassett 28 51 32N 1 55W
Wootton Wawen 28 52 16N 1 47W
Worb 50 46 56N 7 33E
Worcester, S. Afr. 125 33 39S 19 27E
Worcester, U.K. 28 52 12N 2 12W
Worcester, Mass., U.S.A. 162 42 14N 71 49W
Worcester, N.Y., U.S.A. 162 42 35N 74 45W
Worcestershire (□) 26 52 13N 2 10W
Worfield 28 52 34N 2 22W
Wörgl 52 47 29N 12 3E
Worikambo 121 10 43N 0 11W
Workington 32 54 39N 3 34W
Worksop 33 53 19N 1 9W
Workum 46 52 59N 5 26E
Worland 160 44 0N 107 59W
Wormerveer 46 52 30N 4 46E
Wormhoudt 43 50 52N 2 28E
Wormit 35 56 26N 2 59W
Worms 49 49 37N 8 21E
Worms Head 29 51 33N 4 19W
Worplesdon 29 51 16N 0 36W
Worsley 137 33 15S 116 2E
Wortham, U.K. 29 52 22N 1 3E
Wortham, U.S.A. 159 31 48N 96 27W
Wörther See 52 46 37N 14 19E
Worthing 29 50 49N 0 21W
Worthington 158 43 35N 95 30W
Wosi 103 0 15S 128 0E
Wota (Shoa Ghimirra) 123 7 4N 35 51E
Wotton-under-Edge 28 51 37N 2 20W
Woubrugge 46 52 10N 4 39E
Woudenberg 46 52 5N 5 25E
Woudsend 46 52 56N 5 38E
Wour 119 21 14N 16 0E
Wouw 47 51 31N 4 23E
Wowoni, I. 103 4 5S 123 5E
Woy Woy 141 33 30S 151 19E
Wragby 33 53 17N 0 18W
Wrangell 147 56 30N 132 25W
Wrangell, I. 152 56 20N 132 10W
Wrangell Mts. 147 61 40N 143 30W
Wrangle 33 53 3N 0 9E
Wrath, C. 36 58 38N 5 0W
Wray 158 40 8N 102 18W
Wreck I. 162 37 12N 75 48W
Wrekin, The, Mt. 28 52 41N 2 35W
Wrens 157 33 13N 82 23W
Wrentham 29 52 24N 1 39E
Wrexham 31 53 5N 3 0W
Wriezen 48 52 43N 14 9E
Wright, Can. 152 51 52N 121 40W
Wright, Phil. 103 11 42N 125 2E
Wright, Mt. 151 52 40N 67 25W
Wrightlington 28 51 18N 2 16W
Wrightson, Mt. 161 31 49N 110 56W
Wrightsville 162 40 2N 76 32W
Wrightwood 163 34 21N 117 38W
Wrigley 148 63 16N 123 27W
Writtle 29 51 44N 0 27E
Wrocław 54 51 5N 17 5E
Wrocław □ 54 51 0N 17 0E
Wronki 54 52 41N 16 21E
Wrotham 29 51 18N 0 20E
Wroughton 28 51 31N 1 47W
Wroxham 29 52 42N 1 23E
Września 54 52 21N 17 36E
Wschowa 54 51 48N 16 20E
Wu Chiang, R. 108 29 42N 107 20E
Wu Shui, R. 109 27 7N 109 57E
Wuan 106 36 45N 114 2E
Wubin 137 30 6S 116 37E
Wuch'ang, Heilungkiang, China 107 44 55N 127 10E
Wuch'ang, Hupeh, China 109 30 30N 114 15E
Wuch'eng 108 30 48N 98 46E
Wuch'i 108 31 28N 109 36E
Wuchiang 109 31 10N 120 37E
Wuchih Shan, mts. 100 18 45N 109 45E
Wuch'ing 107 39 25N 117 7E
Wuchou 105 23 33N 111 18E
Wuch'uan, Inner Mong., China 106 41 8N 111 24E
Wuch'uan, Kwangsi-Chuang, China 109 21 29N 110 49E
Wuch'uan, Kweichow, China 108 28 30N 107 58E
Wuchung 106 38 4N 106 12E
Wufeng 109 30 12N 110 36E
Wuhan 109 30 35N 114 15E
Wuho 107 33 9N 117 53E
Wuhsi 105 31 30N 120 20E
Wuhsiang 106 36 50N 112 52E
Wuhsing 109 30 49N 120 5E
Wuhsüan 108 23 36N 109 39E
Wuhu 105 31 18N 118 20E
Wuhu (Wou-tou) 109 31 21N 118 30E
Wui, Anhwei, China 109 28 53N 119 48E
Wui, Hopeh, China 106 37 49N 115 54E
Wui Shan, mts. 105 27 30N 117 30E
Wukang 109 26 50N 110 15E
Wukari 121 7 57N 9 42E
Wulachieh 107 44 5N 126 27E
Wulanhaot'e 105 46 5N 122 5E
Wulanpulang 106 41 8N 110 56E
Wulehe 121 3 42N 0 0E
Wuliang Shan, mts. 108 24 0N 100 55E
Wuliaru, I. 103 7 10S 131 0E
Wulien 107 35 45N 119 12E
Wuluk'omushih Ling 105 36 25N 87 25E
Wulumuchi 105 43 40N 87 50E
Wulunku Ho, R. 105 46 58N 87 28E
Wum 121 6 40N 10 2E
Wuming 108 23 11N 108 12E
Wuneba 123 4 49N 30 22E
Wuning 109 29 16N 115 0E
Wunnummin L. 150 52 55N 89 10W
Wunsiedel 49 50 2N 12 0E
Wunstorf 48 52 26N 9 29E
Wuntho, Burma 98 21 44N 96 2E
Wuntho, Burma 99 23 55N 95 45E
Wupao 106 37 35N 110 45E
Wup'ing 109 25 9N 116 5E
Wuppertal, Ger. 48 51 15N 7 8E
Wuppertal, S. Afr. 128 32 13S 19 12E
Wurarga 137 28 25S 116 15E
Würenlingen 51 47 32N 8 16E
Wurung 138 19 13S 140 38E
Würzburg 49 49 46N 9 55E
Wurzen 48 51 21N 12 45E
Wushan, Kansu, China 106 34 42N 104 58E
Wushan, Szechwan, China 108 31 3N 109 57E
Wushench'i 106 38 57N 109 15E
Wustrow 48 54 4N 11 33E
Wusu 105 44 27N 84 37E
Wutai 106 38 44N 113 18E
Wuti 107 37 46N 117 39E
Wuting 108 25 33N 102 26E
Wuting = Huimin 107 37 32N 117 33E
Wuting Ho, R. 106 37 8N 110 25E
Wut'ungch'iao 108 29 24N 104 0E
Wutunghaolan 107 42 49N 120 11E
Wuustwezel 47 51 23N 4 36E
Wuwei, Anhwei, China 109 31 22N 117 55E
Wuwei, Kansu, China 105 37 55N 102 48E
Wuyang 106 33 25N 113 36E
Wuyo 121 10 23N 11 50E
Wuyüan, Inner Mong., China 106 41 6N 108 16E
Wuyüan, Kiangsi, China 109 29 17N 117 54E
Wuyün 105 49 17N 129 40E
Wyaaba Cr. 138 16 27S 141 35E
Wyalkatchem 137 31 8S 117 22E
Wyalong 139 33 54S 147 16E
Wyalusing 162 41 40N 76 16W
Wyandotte 156 42 14N 83 13W
Wyandra 139 27 12S 145 56E
Wyangala Res. 141 33 54S 149 0E
Wyara, L. 139 28 42S 144 14E
Wych Farm, oilfield 19 50 38N 2 2W
Wycheproof 140 36 0N 143 17E
Wye 29 51 11N 0 56E
Wye, R. 28 52 0N 2 36W
Wyemandoo, Mt. 137 28 28S 118 29E
Wyk 48 54 41N 8 33E
Wylfa Hd. 31 53 25N 4 28W
Wylye, R. 28 51 8N 1 53W
Wymondham, Leicester, U.K. 29 52 45N 0 42W
Wymondham, Norfolk, U.K. 29 52 34N 1 7E
Wymore 158 40 10N 97 8W
Wynberg 128 34 2S 18 28E
Wynbring 139 30 33S 133 32E
Wyndham, Austral. 136 15 33S 128 3E
Wyndham, N.Z. 143 46 20S 168 51E
Wynne 159 35 15N 90 50W
Wynnstay 31 52 36N 3 33W
Wynnum 139 27 27S 153 9E
Wynyard 153 51 45N 104 10W
Wyola, L. 137 29 8S 130 17E
Wyoming □ 154 42 48N 109 0W
Wyong 141 33 14S 151 24E
Wyre Forest 28 52 24N 2 24W
Wyre, I. 37 59 7N 2 58W
Wyre, R. 37 53 52N 2 57W
Wyrzysk 54 53 10N 17 17E
Wysoka 54 53 13N 17 2E
Wyszków 54 52 36N 21 25E
Wyszogród 54 52 23N 20 9E
Wytheville 156 37 0N 81 3W

X

Xai-Xai 129 25 6S 33 31E
Xambioá 170 6 25S 48 40W
Xanten 48 51 40N 6 27E
Xanthí 68 41 10N 24 58E
Xanthí □ 68 41 10N 24 58E
Xapuri 174 10 35S 68 35W
Xau 128 21 15S 24 44E
Xavantina 173 21 15S 52 48W
Xenia 156 39 42N 83 57W
Xieng Khouang 100 19 17N 103 25E
Xilókastron 69 38 4N 22 43E
Xinavane 129 25 2S 32 47E
Xingu, R. 175 2 25S 52 35W
Xiniás, L. 69 39 2N 22 12E
Xique-Xique 170 10 50S 42 40W
Xuan Loc 101 10 56N 107 14E
Xuyen Moc 101 10 34N 107 25E

Y

Ya 'Bud 90 32 27N 35 10E
Yaamba 138 23 8S 150 22E
Yaan 108 30 0N 102 59E
Yaapeet 140 35 45S 142 3E

Yabassi Yorktown

Yabassi	**121**	4 30N	9 57 E
Yabba North	**141**	36 13 S	145 42 E
Yabelo	**123**	4 57N	38 8 E
Yablanitsa	**67**	43 2N	24 5 E
Yablonovyy Khrebet	**77**	53 0N	114 0 E
Yabrīn	**92**	23 7N	48 52 E
Yach'i	**108**	27 35N	106 40 E
Yachiang	**108**	30 4N	101 7 E
Yacuiba	**172**	22 0 S	63 25W
Yadgir	**96**	16 45N	77 5 E
Yadkin, R.	**157**	36 15N	81 0W
Yadrin	**81**	55 57N	46 6 E
Yaeyama-Shotō	**112**	24 25N	124 0 E
Yagaba	**121**	10 14N	1 20W
Yagoua	**124**	10 20N	14 58 E
Yagur	**90**	32 45N	35 4 E
Yaha	**101**	6 29N	101 8 E
Yahk	**152**	49 6N	116 10W
Yahuma	**124**	1 0N	22 5 E
Yaihsien	**100**	18 14N	109 29 E
Yaizu	**111**	34 52N	138 20 E
Yajua	**121**	11 27N	12 49 E
Yakage	**110**	34 37N	133 35 E
Yakataga	**147**	60 5N	142 32W
Yakiang	**99**	30 4N	101 15 E
Yakima	**160**	46 42N	120 30W
Yakima, R.	**160**	47 0N	120 30W
Yako	**120**	12 59N	2 15W
Yakoruda	**67**	42 1N	23 29 E
Yakshur Bodya	**84**	57 11N	53 7 E
Yaku-Jima	**112**	30 20N	130 30 E
Yakut A.S.S.R. □	**77**	62 0N	130 0 E
Yakutat	**147**	59 50N	139 44W
Yakutsk	**77**	62 5N	129 40 E
Yala	**101**	6 33N	101 18 E
Yalabusha, R.	**159**	33 53N	89 50W
Yalbalgo	**137**	25 10 S	114 45 E
Yalboroo	**138**	20 50 S	148 40 E
Yalgoo	**137**	28 16 S	116 39 E
Yalikavak	**69**	37 6N	27 18 E
Yalinga	**117**	6 20N	23 10 E
Yalkubul, Punta	**165**	21 32N	88 37W
Y'allaq, G.	**122**	30 21N	33 31 E
Yalleroi	**138**	24 3 S	145 42 E
Yallourn	**141**	38 10 S	146 18 E
Yalpukh, Oz.	**70**	45 30N	28 41 E
Yalta	**82**	44 30N	34 10 E
Yalu Chiang, R.	**107**	39 45N	124 20 E
Yalung Chiang, R.	**105**	26 35N	101 45 E
Yalutorovsk	**76**	56 30N	65 40 E
Yam Kinneret	**90**	32 49N	35 36 E
Yamada	**110**	33 43N	130 49 E
Yamaga	**110**	33 1N	130 41 E
Yamagata	**112**	38 15N	140 15 E
Yamagata-ken □	**112**	38 30N	140 0 E
Yamagawa	**110**	31 12N	130 39 E
Yamaguchi	**110**	34 10N	131 32 E
Yamaguchi-ken □	**110**	34 20N	131 40 E
Yamal, Poluostrov	**76**	71 0N	70 0 E
Yamana	**92**	24 5N	47 30 E
Yamanaka	**111**	36 15N	136 22 E
Yamanashi-ken □	**111**	35 40N	138 40 E
Yamankhalinka	**83**	47 43N	49 21 E
Yamantau	**78**	54 20N	57 40 E
Yamantau, Gora	**84**	54 15N	58 6 E
Yamato	**111**	35 27N	139 25 E
Yamatotakada	**111**	34 31N	135 45 E
Yamazaki	**110**	35 0N	134 32 E
Yamba, N.S.W., Austral.	**139**	29 26 S	153 23 E
Yamba, S. Australia, Austral.	**140**	34 10 S	140 52 E
Yambah	**138**	23 10 S	133 50 E
Yâmbiô	**123**	4 35N	28 16 E
Yambol	**67**	42 30N	26 36 E
Yamdena	**103**	7 45 S	131 20 E
Yame	**110**	33 13N	130 35 E
Yamethin	**98**	20 29N	96 18 E
Yamil	**121**	12 53N	8 4 E
Yamma-Yamma L.	**139**	26 16 S	141 20 E
Yampa, R.	**160**	40 37N	108 0W
Yampi Sd.	**136**	16 8 S	123 38 E
Yampol	**82**	48 15N	28 15 E
Yamrat	**121**	10 11N	9 55 E
Yamrukohal, Mt.	**67**	42 44N	24 52 E
Yamun	**90**	32 29N	35 14 E
Yamuna (Jumna), R.	**94**	27 0N	78 30 E
Yan	**121**	10 5N	12 11 E
Yan Oya	**97**	9 0N	81 10 E
Yana, R.	**77**	69 0N	134 0 E
Yanac	**140**	36 8 S	141 25 E
Yanagawa	**110**	33 10N	130 24 E
Yanahara	**110**	34 58N	134 2 E
Yanam	**96**	16 47N	82 15 E
Yanaul	**84**	56 25N	55 0 E
Yanbu 'al Bahr	**92**	24 0N	38 5 E
Yancannia	**139**	30 12 S	142 35 E
Yanchep	**137**	31 30 S	115 45 E
Yanco	**141**	34 38 S	146 27 E
Yanco Cr.	**141**	35 14 S	145 35 E
Yandabome	**138**	7 1 S	145 46 E
Yandal	**137**	27 35 S	121 10 E
Yandanooka	**137**	29 18 S	115 29 E
Yandaran	**138**	24 43 S	152 6 E
Yandil	**137**	26 20 S	119 50 E
Yandoon	**98**	17 0N	95 40 E
Yanfolila	**120**	11 11N	8 9W
Yangambi	**126**	0 47N	24 20 E
Yangch'angtzukou	**106**	41 31N	109 1 E
Yangch'eng	**106**	35 32N	112 26 E
Yangchiang	**109**	21 55N	111 55 E
Yangchiaoch'iao	**109**	29 45N	112 45 E
Yangchiapa	**106**	42 6N	113 46 E
Yangchou	**109**	32 24N	119 26 E
Yangchoyung Hu	**105**	29 0N	90 40 E
Yangch'ü = T'aiyüan	**106**	37 55N	112 40 E
Yangch'üan	**106**	37 54N	113 36 E
Yangch'un	**109**	22 10N	111 47 E
Yanghsien	**106**	33 20N	107 30 E
Yanghsin	**109**	29 53N	115 10 E
Yangi-Yer	**76**	40 17N	68 48 E
Yangibazar	**85**	41 40N	70 53 E
Yangikishlak	**85**	40 25N	67 10 E
Yangiyul	**85**	41 0N	69 3 E
Yangku	**106**	36 8N	115 48 E
Yangliuch'ing	**107**	39 11N	117 9 E
Yangp'i	**108**	25 40N	100 0 E
Yangp'ing	**109**	31 13N	111 33 E
Yangp'ingkuan	**106**	33 2N	105 56 E
Yangshan	**109**	24 28N	112 38 E
Yangshuo	**109**	24 45N	110 24 E
Yangtze (Ch'ang Chiang)	**109**	1 48N	121 53 E
Yangyang	**107**	38 4N	128 38 E
Yangyüan	**106**	40 5N	114 12 E
Yanhee Res.	**101**	17 30N	98 45 E
Yanko Cr.	**139**	35 17 S	145 15 E
Yankton	**158**	42 55N	97 25W
Yanna	**139**	26 58 S	146 0 E
Yanonge	**126**	0 35N	24 38 E
Yantabulla	**139**	29 21 S	145 0 E
Yantra, R.	**67**	43 35N	25 37 E
Yany Kurgan	**85**	43 55N	67 15 E
Yao, Chad	**117**	12 56N	17 33 E
Yao, Japan	**111**	34 32N	135 36 E
Yao Yai, Ko	**101**	8 0N	98 35 E
Yaoan	**108**	25 32N	101 12 E
Yaoundé	**121**	3 50N	11 35 E
Yaowan	**107**	34 10N	118 3 E
Yap Is.	**103**	9 30N	138 10 E
Yapen	**103**	1 50 S	136 0 E
Yapen, Selat	**103**	1 20 S	136 10 E
Yapo, R.	**174**	0 30 S	77 0W
Yappar, R.	**138**	18 22 S	141 16 E
Yaqui, R.	**164**	28 28N	109 30W
Yar	**84**	58 14N	52 5 E
Yar-Sale	**76**	66 50N	70 50 E
Yaracuy □	**174**	10 20N	68 45W
Yaraka	**138**	24 53 S	144 3 E
Yaransk	**81**	57 13N	47 56 E
Yaratishky	**80**	54 3N	25 52 E
Yarcombe	**30**	50 51N	3 6W
Yarda	**117**	18 35N	19 0 E
Yardea P.O.	**139**	32 23 S	135 32 E
Yare, R.	**29**	52 36N	1 28 E
Yarensk	**78**	61 10N	49 8 E
Yarfa	**122**	24 40N	38 35 E
Yari, R.	**174**	1 0N	73 40W
Yaringa North	**137**	25 53 S	114 30 E
Yaringa South	**137**	26 3 S	114 28 E
Yarkand = Soch'e	**105**	38 24N	77 20 E
Yarkhun, R.	**95**	36 30N	72 45 E
Yarm	**33**	54 31N	1 21W
Yarmouth, Can.	**151**	43 53N	65 45W
Yarmouth, U.K.	**28**	50 42N	1 29W
Yaroslavl	**81**	57 35N	39 55 E
Yarra Yarra Lakes	**137**	29 40 S	115 45 E
Yarraden	**138**	14 28 S	143 15 E
Yarraloola	**136**	21 33 S	115 52 E
Yarram	**141**	38 29 S	146 40 E
Yarraman	**139**	26 50 S	152 0 E
Yarraman Cr.	**139**	26 46 S	152 1 E
Yarranvale	**139**	26 50 S	145 20 E
Yarras	**141**	31 25 S	152 20 E
Yarrawonga	**141**	36 0 S	146 0 E
Yarrow	**35**	55 32N	3 0W
Yarrowee, R.	**140**	38 18 S	144 30 E
Yarto	**140**	35 28 S	142 16 E
Yartsevo	**77**	60 20N	90 0 E
Yarumal	**174**	6 58N	75 24W
Yaselda, R.	**80**	52 26N	25 30 E
Yashi	**121**	12 23N	7 54 E
Yashiro-Jima	**110**	33 55N	132 15 E
Yasin	**95**	36 24N	73 15 E
Yasinovataya	**82**	48 7N	37 57 E
Yasinski, L.	**150**	53 16N	77 35W
Yasnogorsk	**81**	54 32N	37 38 E
Yasothon	**100**	15 50N	104 10 E
Yass	**141**	34 49 S	148 54 E
Yasugi	**110**	35 26N	133 15 E
Yas'ur	**90**	32 54N	35 10 E
Yatagan	**69**	37 20N	28 10 E
Yate	**28**	51 32N	2 26W
Yates Center	**159**	37 53N	95 45W
Yates Pt.	**143**	44 29 S	167 49 E
Yathkyed L.	**153**	62 40N	98 0W
Yathong	**141**	32 37 S	145 33 E
Yatsuo	**111**	36 34N	137 8 E
Yatsushiro	**110**	32 30N	130 40 E
Yatsushiro-Kai	**110**	32 30N	130 25 E
Yatta	**90**	31 27N	35 6 E
Yatta Plat.	**126**	2 0 S	38 0 E
Yattah	**90**	31 27N	35 6 E
Yatton	**28**	51 23N	2 50W
Yauyos	**174**	12 10 S	75 50W
Yaval	**96**	21 10N	75 42 E
Yavan	**85**	38 19N	69 2 E
Yavari R.	**174**	4 50 S	72 0W
Yavorov	**80**	49 55N	23 20 E
Yawatahama	**110**	33 27N	132 24 E
Yawri B.	**120**	8 22N	13 0W
Yaxley	**29**	52 31N	0 14W
Yazagyo	**98**	23 30N	94 6 E
Yazd (Yezd)	**93**	31 55N	54 27 E
Yazdan	**93**	33 30N	60 50 E
Yazoo City	**159**	32 48N	90 28W
Yazoo, R.	**159**	32 35N	90 50W
Ybbs	**52**	48 12N	15 4 E
Yding Skovhøj	**75**	55 59N	9 46 E
Yea	**141**	37 14 S	145 26 E
Yealering	**137**	32 36 S	117 36 E
Yealmpton	**30**	50 21N	4 0W
Yearinan	**141**	31 10 S	149 11 E
Yebbi-Souma	**119**	21 7N	17 54 E
Yebbigué	**119**	22 30N	17 30 E
Yebel Jarris Tighzert, O.	**118**	28 10N	9 37W
Yebyu	**99**	14 15N	98 13 E
Yechŏn	**107**	36 39N	128 27 E
Yecla	**59**	38 35N	1 5W
Yécora	**164**	28 20N	108 58W
Yedashe	**98**	17 24N	95 50 E
Yeddou	**118**	28 5N	9 2W
Yeeda River	**136**	17 31 S	123 38 E
Yeelanna	**139**	34 9 S	135 45 E
Yefremov	**81**	53 15N	38 3 E
Yegorlyk, R.	**83**	46 15N	41 30 E
Yegorlykskaya	**83**	46 5N	40 35 E
Yegoryevsk	**81**	55 27N	38 55 E
Yegros	**172**	26 20 S	56 25W
Yehchih	**108**	27 39N	99 0 E
Yehsien	**106**	33 37N	113 20 E
Yehud	**90**	32 3N	34 53 E
Yehuda, Midbar	**90**	31 35N	34 57 E
Yei	**123**	4 3N	30 40 E
Yei, Nahr	**123**	5 50N	30 20 E
Yelan	**81**	50 55N	43 43 E
Yelan Kolenovski	**81**	51 16N	40 45 E
Yelandur	**97**	12 6N	77 0 E
Yelanskoye	**77**	61 25N	128 0 E
Yelarbon	**139**	28 33 S	150 49 E
Yelatma	**81**	55 0N	41 52 E
Yelets	**81**	52 40N	38 30 E
Yelimané	**120**	15 9N	22 49 E
Yell, I.	**36**	60 35N	1 5W
Yell Sd.	**36**	60 33N	1 15W
Yellamanchilli (Elamanchili)	**96**	17 26N	82 50 E
Yellow Sea	**105**	35 0N	123 0 E
Yellowdine	**137**	31 17 S	119 40 E
Yellowhead P.	**152**	52 53N	118 25W
Yellowknife	**152**	62 27N	114 21W
Yellowknife, R.	**152**	62 31N	114 19W
Yellowstone L.	**160**	44 30N	110 20W
Yellowstone National Park	**160**	44 35N	110 0W
Yellowstone, R.	**158**	46 35N	105 45W
Yelnya	**80**	54 35N	33 15 E
Yelsk	**80**	51 50N	29 3 E
Yelvertoft	**138**	20 13 S	138 53 E
Yelwa	**122**	10 49N	8 41 E
Yemanzhelinsk	**84**	54 58N	61 18 E
Yemen ■	**91**	15 0N	44 0 E
Yemen, South ■	**74**	15 0N	48 0 E
Yen Bai	**100**	21 42N	104 52 E
Yenakiyevo	**82**	48 15N	38 5 E
Yenan	**106**	36 42N	109 25 E
Yenangyaung	**98**	20 30N	95 0 E
Yenanma	**98**	19 46N	96 48 E
Yenchang	**106**	36 44N	110 2 E
Yench'eng, Honan, China	**106**	33 37N	114 0 E
Yench'eng, Kiangsu, China	**107**	33 24N	120 10 E
Yench'i	**105**	42 6N	86 34 E
Yenchi	**107**	42 53N	129 31 E
Yench'ih	**106**	37 47N	107 24 E
Yenchihsien	**107**	42 46N	129 24 E
Yenchin	**108**	28 4N	104 14 E
Yench'ing	**106**	40 28N	115 58 E
Yenching	**108**	29 7N	98 33 E
Yenchou	**105**	35 40N	116 50 E
Yench'uan	**106**	36 52N	110 11 E
Yenda	**141**	34 13 S	146 14 E
Yendéré	**120**	10 12N	4 59W
Yendi	**121**	9 29N	0 1W
Yenfeng	**108**	25 52N	101 5 E
Yenho	**108**	28 35N	108 28 E
Yenhsing	**108**	25 22N	101 44 E
Yenisaia	**68**	41 1N	24 57 E
Yenisey, R.	**76**	68 0N	86 30 E
Yeniseysk	**77**	58 39N	92 4 E
Yeniseyskiy Zaliv	**76**	72 20N	81 0 E
Yenne	**45**	45 43N	5 44 E
Yenotyevka	**83**	47 15N	47 0 E
Yenpien	**108**	26 54N	101 34 E
Yenshan, Hopeh, China	**107**	38 3N	117 12 E
Yenshan, Yunnan, China	**108**	23 40N	104 22 E
Yenshou	**107**	45 27N	128 19 E
Yent'ai	**107**	37 35N	121 25 E
Yent'ing	**108**	31 19N	105 20 E
Yenyüan	**108**	27 25N	101 33 E
Yenyuka	**77**	58 20N	121 30 E
Yeo, L.	**137**	28 0 S	124 30 E
Yeo, R.	**28**	51 1N	2 46W
Yeola	**96**	20 0N	74 30 E
Yeotmal	**96**	20 20N	78 15 E
Yeoval	**141**	32 41 S	148 39 E
Yeovil	**28**	50 57N	2 38W
Yepes	**56**	39 55N	3 39W
Yeppoon	**138**	23 5 S	150 47 E
Yeráki	**69**	37 0N	22 42 E
Yerbogachen	**77**	61 16N	108 0 E
Yerevan	**83**	40 10N	44 20 E
Yerilla	**137**	29 24 S	121 47 E
Yerington	**163**	38 59N	119 10W
Yerla, R.	**96**	17 35N	74 30 E
Yermakovo	**77**	52 35N	126 20 E
Yermo	**163**	34 58N	116 50W
Yermolayevo	**78**	52 58N	56 12 E
Yerofey Pavlovich	**77**	54 0N	122 0 E
Yerseke	**47**	51 29N	4 3 E
Yershov	**81**	51 15N	48 27 E
Yerūshalayim	**90**	31 47N	35 10 E
Yerville	**42**	49 40N	0 53 E
Yes Tor, Mt.	**30**	50 41N	3 59W
Yesagyo	**98**	21 38N	95 14 E
Yesan	**107**	36 41N	126 51 E
Yeşilirmak	**82**	41 0N	36 40 E
Yeso	**159**	34 29N	104 87W
Yessentuki	**83**	44 0N	42 45 E
Yeste	**59**	38 22N	2 19W
Yeu, I. d'	**42**	46 42N	2 20W
Yevlakh	**83**	40 39N	47 7 E
Yevpatoriya	**82**	45 15N	33 20 E
Yevstratovskiy	**81**	50 11N	39 2 E
Yeya, R.	**83**	46 40N	39 0 E
Yeysk Staro	**82**	46 40N	38 12 E
Yhati	**172**	25 45 S	56 35W
Yhú	**173**	25 0 S	56 0W
Yi, R.	**172**	33 7 S	57 8W
Yiali, I.	**69**	36 41N	27 11 E
Yiáltra	**69**	38 51N	22 59 E
Yianisádhes, I.	**69**	35 20N	26 10 E
Yiannitsa	**68**	40 46N	22 24 E
Yibal	**91**	22 10N	56 8 E
Yidhá	**68**	40 35N	22 53 E
Yinchiang	**108**	27 58N	108 20 E
Yinch'uan	**105**	38 30N	106 20 E
Yindarlgooda, L.	**137**	30 40 S	121 52 E
Ying Ho, R.	**109**	32 30N	116 32 E
Yingch'eng	**109**	30 55N	113 35 E
Yingchiang	**108**	24 48N	98 5 E
Yinghsien	**106**	39 36N	113 12 E
Yingk'ou	**107**	40 38N	122 30 E
Yingp'an, Chiang, G.	**108**	21 20N	109 30 E
Yingp'anshan	**108**	27 56N	105 34 E
Yingshan, Hupeh, China	**109**	31 37N	113 46 E
Yingshan, Hupeh, China	**109**	30 50N	115 45 E
Yingshan, Szechwan, China	**108**	31 6N	106 35 E
Yingshang	**109**	32 36N	116 16 E
Yingtan	**105**	28 12N	117 0 E
Yingte	**109**	24 10N	113 24 E
Yinkanie	**140**	34 22 S	140 17 E
Yinmabin	**99**	22 10N	94 55 E
Yinnietharra	**137**	24 39 S	116 12 E
Yioúra, I.	**68**	39 23N	24 10 E
Yipang	**101**	22 15N	101 26 E
Yirga Alem	**124**	6 34N	38 29 E
Yithion	**69**	36 46N	22 34 E
Yizre'el	**90**	32 34N	35 19 E
Ylitornio	**74**	66 19N	23 39 E
Ylivieska	**74**	64 4N	24 28 E
Yngaren	**73**	58 50N	16 35 E
Ynykchanskiy	**77**	60 15N	137 43 E
Yoakum	**159**	29 20N	97 10W
Yobuko	**110**	33 32N	129 54 E
Yog Pt.	**103**	13 55N	124 20 E
Yogyakarta	**103**	7 49 S	110 22 E
Yoho Nat. Park	**152**	51 25N	116 30W
Yojoa, L. de	**166**	14 53N	88 0W
Yŏju	**107**	37 20N	127 35 E
Yokadouma	**124**	3 35N	14 50 E
Yŏkaichi	**111**	35 6N	136 12 E
Yŏkaichiba	**111**	35 42N	140 33 E
Yokkaichi	**111**	35 0N	136 30 E
Yoko	**121**	5 50N	12 20 E
Yokohama	**111**	35 27N	139 39 E
Yokosuka	**111**	35 20N	139 40 E
Yokote	**112**	39 20N	140 30 E
Yola	**121**	9 10N	12 29 E
Yolaina, Cordillera de	**166**	11 30N	84 0W
Yom Mae Nam	**101**	15 15N	100 20 E
Yonago	**110**	35 25N	133 19 E
Yŏnan	**107**	37 55N	126 11 E
Yonezawa	**112**	37 57N	140 4 E
Yong Peng	**101**	2 0N	103 3 E
Yong Sata	**101**	7 8N	99 41 E
Yongampo	**107**	39 56N	124 23 E
Yŏngchon	**107**	35 58N	128 56 E
Yŏngdŏk	**107**	36 24N	129 22 E
Yŏngdŭngpo	**107**	37 31N	126 54 E
Yŏnghŭng	**107**	39 31N	127 18 E
Yŏngju	**107**	36 50N	128 40 E
Yŏngwŏl	**107**	37 11N	128 28 E
Yonibana	**120**	8 30N	12 19W
Yonker	**153**	52 40N	109 40W
Yonkers	**162**	40 57N	73 51W
Yonne □	**43**	47 50N	3 40 E
Yonne, R.	**43**	48 23N	2 58 E
Yonov	**121**	7 33N	8 42 E
Yoqueam	**90**	32 40N	35 6 E
York, Austral.	**137**	31 52 S	116 47 E
York, U.K.	**33**	53 58N	1 7W
York, Ala., U.S.A.	**157**	32 30N	88 18W
York, Nebr., U.S.A.	**158**	40 55N	97 35W
York, Pa., U.S.A.	**162**	39 57N	76 43W
York, C.	**138**	10 42 S	142 31 E
York Factory	**153**	57 0N	92 18W
York Haven	**162**	40 7N	76 46W
York, Kap	**12**	75 55N	66 25W
York, R.	**162**	37 15N	76 23W
York Sd.	**136**	14 50 S	125 5 E
York, Vale of	**23**	54 15N	1 25W
Yorke Pen.	**140**	34 50 S	137 40 E
Yorkshire Wolds	**33**	54 0N	0 30W
Yorkton	**153**	51 11N	102 28W
Yorktown, Tex., U.S.A.	**159**	29 0N	97 29W

Yorktown Zell

Yorktown, Va., U.S.A. 162 37 14N 76 30W
Yornup 137 34 2S 116 10E
Yoro 166 15 9N 87 7W
Yosemite National Park 163 38 0N 119 30W
Yosemite Village 163 37 45N 119 35W
Yoshii 110 33 16N 129 46E
Yoshimatsu 110 32 0N 130 47E
Yoshkar Ola 81 56 49N 47 10E
Yŏsu 107 34 47N 127 45E
Youanmi 137 28 37S 118 49E
Youbou 152 48 53N 124 13W
Youghal 39 51 58N 7 51W
Youghal B. 39 51 55N 7 50W
Youkounkoun 120 12 35N 13 11W
Young, Austral. 141 34 19S 148 18E
Young, Can. 153 51 47N 105 45W
Young, Uruguay 172 32 44S 57 36W
Young, U.S.A. 161 34 9N 110 56W
Young Ra. 143 44 10S 169 30E
Younghusband, L. 140 30 50S 136 5E
Younghusband Pen. 140 36 0S 139 25E
Youngstown, Can. 153 51 35N 111 10W
Youngstown, U.S.A. 156 41 7N 80 41W
Youssoufia 118 32 16N 8 31W
Yoweragabbie 137 28 14S 117 39E
Yowrie 141 36 17S 149 46E
Yoxall 28 52 45N 1 49W
Yoxford 29 52 16N 1 30E
Yozgat 92 39 51N 34 47E
Ypané, R. 172 23 29S 57 19W
Yport 42 49 45N 0 15E
Ypres 47 50 50N 2 52E
Ypsilanti 156 42 18N 83 40W
Yreka 160 41 44N 122 40W
Ysabel Chan. 135 2 0S 150 0E
Ysbyty Ystwyth 31 52 20N 3 50W
Ysleta 161 31 45N 106 24W
Yssingeaux 45 45 9N 4 8E
Ystad 73 55 26N 13 50E
Ystalyfera 31 51 46N 3 48W
Ystradgynlais 31 51 47N 3 45W
Ystwyth, R. 31 52 24N 4 2W
Ythan, R. 37 57 26N 2 12W
Ytre Adal 71 60 15N 10 14E
Ytterhogdal 72 62 12N 14 56E
Ytyk-Kel 77 62 20N 133 28E
Yü Chiang, R., China 105 22 50N 108 6E
Yü Chiang, R., China 108 22 50N 108 6E
Yu Shui, R. 108 28 37N 110 23E
Yüan Chiang, R. 109 29 0N 111 50E
Yüan Chiang, R (Hong.) 108 29 12N 111 43E
Yüanan 109 31 3N 111 34E
Yüanchiang, Hünan, China 109 28 50N 112 23E
Yüanchiang, Yunnan, China 108 23 40N 102 0E
Yüanch'ü 106 35 18N 111 41E
Yüanli 109 24 27N 120 39E
Yüanlin 109 23 45N 120 30E
Yuanling 109 28 30N 110 5E
Yüanmou 108 25 42N 101 32E
Yuanyang 108 23 10N 102 58E
Yüanyang 108 35 3N 113 57E
Yuat, R. 135 4 10S 143 52E
Yuba City 160 39 12N 121 37W
Yūbari 112 43 4N 141 59E
Yūbetsu 112 43 13N 144 5E
Yucatán □ 165 21 30N 86 30W
Yucatán Basin 14 20 0N 84 0W
Yucatán Channel 166 22 0N 86 30W
Yucca 161 34 56N 114 6W
Yucca Valley 163 34 8N 116 30W
Yücha 108 26 55N 101 24E
Yucheng 106 36 55N 116 40E
Yüch'i 108 24 25N 102 35E
Yuch'i 109 26 10N 118 11E
Yüchiang 109 28 24N 116 53E
Yüch'ien 109 30 12N 119 24E
Yüch'ing 108 27 13N 107 54E
Yudino 76 55 10N 67 55E
Yüehhsi, Anhwei, China 109 30 54N 116 22E
Yüehhsi, Szechwan, China 108 28 36N 102 35E
Yüehyang 109 29 20N 113 7E
Yuendumu 136 22 16S 131 49E
Yufu-Dake 110 33 17N 131 33E
Yugoslavia ■ 66 44 0N 20 0E
Yühsien 106 34 10N 113 30E
Yuhsien, Hunan, China 109 27 2N 113 20E
Yuhsien, Shansi, China 106 38 5N 113 24E
Yühuan Tao, I. 109 28 5N 121 15E
Yukan 109 28 43N 116 35E
Yukhnov 80 54 44N 35 15E
Yūki 111 36 18N 139 53E
Yukon □ 147 63 0N 135 0W
Yukon, R. 147 65 30N 150 0W
Yukti 77 63 20N 105 0E
Yukuhashi 110 33 44N 130 59E
Yule, R. 136 20 24S 118 12E
Yuli 122 9 44N 10 12E
Yülin 100 18 10N 109 31E
Yulin, Guangdong, China 109 22 36N 110 7E
Yulin, Shensi, China 105 38 15N 109 30E
Yuma, Ariz., U.S.A. 161 32 45N 114 37W
Yuma, Colo., U.S.A. 158 40 10N 102 43W
Yuma, B. de 167 18 20N 68 35W
Yumali 140 35 32S 139 45E
Yumbe 126 3 28N 31 15E
Yumbi 126 1 12S 26 15E
Yumbo 174 3 35N 76 28W
Yümenhsien 105 40 17N 97 12E
Yün Ho 107 33 16N 118 45E
Yun Ho 109 35 0N 117 0E
Yuna 137 28 20S 115 0E
Yünan 109 23 14N 111 31E
Yunaska I. 147 52 40N 170 40W
Yünch'eng, Shansi, China 106 35 1N 110 59E
Yünch'eng, Shantung, China 106 35 35N 115 56E
Yunfou 109 22 56N 112 2E
Yungan 109 25 50N 117 25E
Yungas 174 17 0S 66 0W
Yungay 172 37 10S 72 5W
Yungch'eng 106 33 56N 116 22E
Yungchi 106 34 52N 110 26E
Yungch'ing 106 39 19N 116 29E
Yungch'uan 108 20 22N 105 52E
Yungch'un 109 25 19N 118 17E
Yungfeng 109 27 20N 115 27E
Yungfu 109 24 59N 109 59E
Yungho 106 36 44N 110 39E
Yunghsin 109 16 55N 114 18E
Yunghsing 109 26 8N 113 6E
Yunghsiu 109 29 8N 115 42E
Yungjen 108 26 4N 101 42E
Yungk'ang, Chekiang, China 109 28 53N 120 2E
Yungk'ang, Kwangsi Chuang Aut. Region, China 108 22 48N 107 51E
Yungnien 106 36 49N 114 33E
Yungning, Kwangsi Chuang A. R., China 108 22 45N 108 29E
Yungning, Ningsia Hui A. R., China 106 38 18N 106 18E
Yungning, Yunnan, China 108 27 50N 100 40E
Yungningchai 106 36 35N 108 51E
Yungp'ing 108 25 25N 99 36E
Yungshan 108 28 11N 103 35E
Yungsheng 108 26 42N 100 45E
Yungshun, Hunan, China 108 29 3N 109 50E
Yungshun, Kwangsi Chuang, China 108 22 48N 108 55E
Yungt'ai 109 25 52N 118 55E
Yungteng 106 36 44N 103 24E
Yungting 109 24 49N 116 46E
Yunho = Lishui 109 28 6N 119 34E
Yünhsi 109 33 0N 110 22E
Yünhsiao 109 24 1N 117 15E
Yünhsien, Hupeh, China 105 32 50N 110 53E
Yünhsien, Yunnan, China 108 24 25N 100 6E
Yünlin 109 23 42N 120 31E
Yunling Shan, mts. 108 28 30N 98 50E
Yunlung 99 25 50N 99 25E
Yünmeng 109 31 1N 113 39E
Yunnan □ 108 25 0N 102 30E
Yunndaga 137 29 45S 121 0E
Yunomae 110 32 12N 130 59E
Yunotso 110 35 5N 132 21E
Yunquera de Henares 58 40 47N 3 11W
Yunta 140 32 34S 139 36E
Yünyang 108 30 55N 108 56E
Yüp'ing 108 27 14N 108 54E
Yupyongdong 107 41 49N 128 53E
Yur 77 59 52N 137 49E
Yurga 76 55 42N 84 51E
Yuria 84 59 22N 54 10E
Yuribei 76 71 20N 76 30E
Yurimaguas 174 5 55S 76 0W
Yurya 81 59 1N 49 13E
Yuryev Polskiy 81 56 30N 39 47E
Yuryevets 81 57 25N 43 2E
Yuryuzan 84 54 27N 58 28E
Yuscarán 166 13 58N 86 51W
Yusha, Jebel 90 32 4N 35 41E
Yüshan 109 28 40N 118 15E
Yüshanchen 108 29 31N 108 25E
Yushe 106 37 4N 112 58E
Yüshu 105 33 1N 96 44E
Yushu 107 44 46N 126 34E
Yüt'ai 106 35 2N 116 40E
Yüt'ien 107 39 53N 117 45E
Yütu 109 26 0N 115 24E
Yütz'u 106 37 42N 112 44E
Yüwang 106 37 9N 106 28E
Yuyang 108 28 44N 108 46E
Yüyang 109 30 12N 119 56E
Yüyao 109 30 3N 121 9E
Yuyao 109 30 0N 121 20E
Yuyu 105 40 20N 112 30E
Yuyü 106 40 10N 112 25E
Yüyuan 109 28 9N 121 11E
Yuzha 81 56 40N 42 10E
Yuzhno-Sakhalinsk 77 47 5N 142 5E
Yuzhno-Surkhanskoye Vodokhranilishehe 85 37 53N 67 42E
Yuzhno-Uralsk 84 54 26N 61 15E
Yuzhnyy Ural, mts. 84 53 0N 58 0E
Yvelines □ 43 48 40N 1 45E
Yverdon 50 46 47N 6 39E
Yvetot 42 49 37N 0 44E
Yvonand 50 46 48N 6 44E

Z

Za, O. 118 34 5N 2 30W
Zaalayskiy Khrebet 85 39 20N 73 0E
Zaamslag 47 51 19N 3 55E
Zaan, R. 46 52 25N 4 52E
Zaandam 47 52 26N 4 49E
Zab, Monts du 119 34 55N 5 0E
Zabalj, Yugo. 66 45 21N 20 5E
Zabalj, Yugo. 66 45 23N 20 5E
Zabari 66 44 22N 21 15E
Zabarjad 122 23 40N 36 12E
Zabaykalskiy 77 49 40N 117 10E
Zabkowice Slaskie 54 50 22N 19 17E
Zabljak 66 42 19N 19 10E
Zabludow 54 53 0N 23 19E
Zabno 54 50 9N 20 53E
Zābol 93 31 0N 61 25E
Zābolī 93 27 10N 61 35E
Zabré 121 11 12N 0 36W
Zabrze 54 50 24N 18 50E
Zacapa 166 14 59N 89 31W
Zacapu 164 19 50N 101 43W
Zacatecas 164 22 49N 102 34W
Zacatecas □ 164 23 30N 103 0W
Zacatecolua 166 13 29N 88 51W
Zacaultipán 165 20 39N 98 36W
Zacoalco 164 20 10N 103 40W
Zadar 63 44 8N 15 8E
Zadawa 121 11 33N 10 19E
Zadetkyi Kyun 101 10 0N 98 25E
Zadonsk 81 52 25N 38 56E
Zafed 90 32 58N 35 29E
Zafora, I. 69 36 5N 26 24E
Zafra 57 38 26N 6 30W
Zagan 54 51 39N 15 22E
Zagazig 122 30 40N 31 12E
Zaghouan 119 36 23N 10 10E
Zaglivérion 68 40 36N 23 15E
Zaglou 118 27 17N 0 3W
Zagnanado 121 7 18N 2 28E
Zagorá 68 39 27N 23 6E
Zagora 118 30 14N 5 51W
Zagórów 54 52 10N 17 54E
Zagorsk 81 56 20N 38 10E
Zagórz 54 49 30N 22 14E
Zagreb 63 45 50N 16 0E
Zāgros, Kudha-ye 93 33 45N 47 0E
Zagubica 66 44 15N 21 47E
Zaguinaso 120 10 1N 6 14W
Zāhedān 93 29 30N 60 50E
Zahirabad 96 17 43N 77 37E
Zahlah 92 33 52N 35 50E
Zahna 48 51 54N 12 47E
Zahrez Chergui 118 35 0N 3 30E
Zahrez Rharbi 118 34 50N 2 55E
Zailiyskiy Alatau, Khrebet 85 43 5N 77 0E
Zainsk 84 55 18N 52 4E
Zaïr 118 29 47N 5 51W
Zaïre, R. 124 1 30N 28 0E
Zaïre, Rep. of ■ 124 3 0S 23 0E
Zaječar 66 43 53N 22 18E
Zakamensk 77 50 23N 103 17E
Zakariya 90 31 43N 34 57E
Zakataly 83 41 38N 46 35E
Zakavkazye 83 42 0N 44 0E
Zakhu 92 37 10N 42 50E
Zákinthos 69 37 47N 20 54E
Zākinthos, I. 69 37 45N 27 45E
Zakopane 54 49 18N 19 57E
Zala □ 53 46 42N 16 50E
Zala, R. 53 46 53N 17 6E
Zalaegerszeg 53 46 53N 16 47E
Zalakomár 53 46 33N 17 10E
Zalalövö 53 46 51N 16 35E
Zalamea de la Serena 57 38 40N 5 38W
Zalamea la Real 57 37 41N 6 38W
Zalau 121 10 30N 8 58E
Zalazna 84 58 39N 52 31E
Zalec 63 46 16N 15 10E
Zaleshchiki 82 48 45N 25 45E
Zalewo 54 53 55N 19 41E
Zalingei 117 13 5N 23 10E
Zalṭan, Jabal 119 28 46N 19 45E
Zaltbommel 46 51 48N 5 15E
Zalŭ 121 47 12N 23 5E
Zambeke 126 2 8N 25 17E
Zambèze, R. 127 18 46S 36 16E
Zambezi, R. 127 18 46S 36 16E
Zambezia □ 127 16 15S 37 30E
Zambia ■ 125 15 0S 28 0E
Zamboanga 103 6 59N 122 3E
Zambrano 174 9 45N 74 49W
Zametchino 81 53 30N 42 30E
Zamora, Mexico 164 20 0N 102 21W
Zamora, Spain 56 41 30N 5 45W
Zamora □ 56 41 30N 5 46W
Zamość 54 50 50N 23 22E
Zamuro, Sierra del 174 4 0N 62 30W
Zamzam, W. 119 31 0N 14 30E
Zan 121 9 26N 0 17W
Zanaga 124 2 48S 13 48E
Záncara, R. 58 39 20N 3 0W
Zandvoort 46 52 22N 4 32E
Zanesville 156 39 56N 82 2W
Zangue, R. 127 18 5S 35 10E
Zanjan 92 36 40N 48 35E
Zannone, I. 64 40 38N 13 2E
Zante = Zákinthos 69 37 47N 20 54E
Zanthus 137 31 2S 123 34E
Zanzibar 126 6 12S 39 12E
Zanzibar I. 126 6 12S 39 12E
Zanzūr 119 32 55N 13 1E
Zaouatalaz 119 24 57N 8 16E
Zaouiet El Kahla 119 27 10N 6 40E
Zaouiet Reggane 118 26 32N 0 3E
Zapadna Morava, R. 66 43 50N 20 15E
Zapadnaya Dvina 80 56 15N 32 3E
Západné Beskydy 54 49 30N 19 0E
Západočesky □ 52 49 35N 13 0E
Západoslovenský □ 53 48 30N 17 30E
Zapala 176 39 0S 70 5W
Zapaleri, Cerro 172 22 49S 67 11W
Zapata 159 26 56N 92 17W
Zapatón, R. 57 39 0N 6 49W
Zaporozhye 82 47 50N 35 10E
Zapponeta 65 41 27N 15 57E
Zara 92 39 58N 37 43E
Zaragoza, Colomb. 174 7 30N 74 52W
Zaragoza, Coahuila, Mexico 164 28 30N 101 0W
Zaragoza, Nuevo León, Mexico 165 24 0N 99 36W
Zaragoza, Spain 58 41 39N 0 53W
Zaragoza □ 58 41 35N 1 0W
Zarand 93 30 46N 56 34E
Zarasai 80 55 40N 26 12E
Zarate 172 34 7S 59 0W
Zaraysk 81 54 48N 38 53E
Zaraza 174 9 21N 65 19W
Zarembo I. 152 56 20N 132 50W
Zari 73 13 8N 12 37E
Zaria 121 11 0N 7 40E
Zarisberge 128 24 30S 16 15E
Zarki 54 50 38N 19 21E
Zarnów 54 51 16N 20 9E
Zarnuqa 90 31 53N 34 47E
Zarów 54 50 56N 16 29E
Zarqa, R. 90 32 10N 35 37E
Zaruma 174 3 40S 79 30W
Zary 54 51 37N 15 10E
Zarza de Alange 57 38 49N 6 13W
Zarza de Granadilla 56 40 14N 6 3W
Zarza, La 57 37 42N 6 51W
Zarzaïtine 119 28 32N 9 5E
Zarzal 174 4 24N 76 4W
Zarzis 119 33 31N 11 2E
Zas 56 43 4N 8 53W
Zashiversk 77 67 25N 142 40E
Zaskar Mountains 95 33 15N 77 30E
Zaskar, R. 95 33 55N 77 2E
Zastron 128 30 18S 27 7E
Zatec 52 50 20N 13 32E
Zator 54 49 59N 19 28E
Zavala 66 42 50N 17 59E
Zavareh 93 33 35N 52 28E
Zaventem 47 50 53N 4 28E
Zavetnoye 83 47 13N 43 50E
Zavidovici 66 44 27N 18 13E
Zavitinsk 77 50 10N 129 20E
Zavodoski, I. 13 56 0S 27 45W
Zavolzhye 81 56 37N 43 18E
Zawadzkie 54 50 37N 18 28E
Zawidów 54 51 1N 15 1E
Zawiercie 54 50 30N 19 13E
Zâwyet Shammâs 122 31 30N 26 37E
Zâwyet Um el Rakham 122 31 18N 27 1E
Zâwyet Ungeila 122 31 23N 26 42E
Zayandeh, R. 93 32 35N 32 0E
Zayarsk 77 56 20N 102 55E
Zaysan 76 47 28N 84 52E
Zaysan, Oz. 76 48 0N 83 0E
Zāzamt, W. 119 30 29N 14 30E
Zazir, O. 119 22 0N 5 40E
Zázrivá 53 49 16N 19 7E
Zbarazh 80 49 43N 25 44E
Zbaszyn 54 52 14N 15 56E
Zbaszynek 54 52 16N 15 51E
Zblewo 54 53 56N 18 19E
Zdandijk 46 52 82N 4 49E
Zdolbunov 80 50 30N 26 15E
Zdrelo 66 44 16N 21 28E
Zdunska Wola 54 51 37N 18 59E
Zduny 54 51 39N 17 21E
Zeballos 152 49 59N 126 50W
Zebediela 129 24 20S 29 17E
Zedelgem 47 51 8N 3 8E
Zeebrugge 47 51 19N 3 12E
Zeehan 138 41 52S 145 25E
Zeeland 47 51 41N 5 40E
Zeeland □ 47 51 30N 3 50E
Ze'elim 90 31 13N 34 32E
Zeelst 47 51 25N 5 25E
Zeerust 128 25 31S 26 4E
Zefat 90 32 58N 35 29E
Zegdou 118 29 51N 4 53W
Zege 123 11 43N 37 18E
Zegelsem 47 50 49N 3 43E
Zegoua 120 10 32N 5 35W
Zehdenick 48 52 59N 13 20E
Zeil, Mt. 136 23 24S 132 23E
Zeila 91 11 15N 43 30E
Zeist 46 52 5N 5 15E
Zeita 90 32 23N 35 2E
Zeitz 48 51 3N 12 9E
Zele 47 51 4N 4 2E
Zelendolsk 81 55 55N 48 30E
Zelengora, mts. 66 43 22N 18 30E
Zelenika 66 42 27N 18 37E
Zelenogradsk 80 54 53N 20 29E
Zelenokumsk 83 44 30N 44 1E
Zelenovski 83 48 6N 50 45E
Zelhem 47 52 0N 6 21E
Zell 49 47 42N 7 50E

Alternative Spellings

NOTE: The following list gives the principal places where new names or spellings (given first) have been adopted. Earlier forms still in use are cross referenced to the new form. Place names of which the national spelling varies considerably from the English form, e.g. Livorno – Leghorn, are also included.

Aachen, Aix la Chapelle
Aalst: Alost
Abercorn, see Mbala
Åbo, see Turku
Acre, see 'Akko
Adrianople, see Edirne
Affreville, see Khemis Miliana
Agram, see Zagreb
Agrigento: Girgenti
Ahvenanmaa: Åland Is.
Aix la Chapelle, see Aachen
Ain Mokra, see Berrahal
Ain Salah, see In Salah
Ain Touta: MacMahon
'Akko: Acre
Akmolinsk, see Tselinograd
Al Hoceima: Alhucemas,
    Villa Sanjurjo
Al Khalih: Hebron
Al Khums, see Homs
Al Lādhiqiyah: Latakia
Al Marj: Barce
Al Mawsil: Mosul
Al Mukha: Mocha
Al Qasabat: Cussabat
Al Quds: Jerusalem
Åland Is., see Ahvenanmaa
Alashantsoch'i: Payenhaot'e
Alba Iulia: Karlsburg
Albert, L., see Mobutu Sese
    Seko, L.
Albertville, see Kalemie
Alcazarquivir, see Ksar el Kebir
Aleppo, see Halab
Alexandretta, see İskenderun
Alexandria, see Al Iskandarîya
Alhucemas, see Al Hoceima
Allenstein, see Olsztyn
Amraoti: Amravati
An Geata Mór: Binghamstown
An Nhon: Binh Dinh
An Uaimh: Navan
Andulo, see Macedo da Cavaleiros
Ankara: Angora
Annaba: Bône
Annobón, see Pagalu
Antakya: Antioch
Anvers: Antwerp, Antwerpen
Apollonia, see Marsa Susa
Ar Riyâd: Riyadah
Arabian Gulf, see Persian G.
Arkhangelsk: Archangel
Arlon: Aarlen
Artemovsk: Bakhmut
Athinai: Athens
Augusto Cardoso: Metangula
Aumale, see Sour el Ghozlane
Auschwitz, see Oswiecim

Bac Lieu, see Vinh Loi
Bagenalstown, see Muine
    Bheag
Bahia, see Salvador
Baile Átha Cliath: Dublin
Baile Deasmhumhna:
    Ballydesmond
Bakhmut, see Artemovsk
Bakwanga, see Mbuji-Mayi
Ballydesmond, see Baile
    Deasmhumhna
Baltiysk: Pillau
Banaras, see Varanasi
Banda Aceh; Kutaradja
Bandar Maharani, see Muar
Bandar Penggarem, see
    Batu Pahat
Bandundu: Banningville
Banghāzî: Benghazi
Bangladesh: East Pakistan
Banjul: Bathurst
Barce, see Al Marj
Baroda, see Vadodara
Basel: Basle
Basutoland, see Lesotho
Batavia, see Jakarta
Batu Pahat: Bandar Penggarem
Bayan Tumen, see Choybalsan
Béchar: Colomb-Béchar
Bechuanaland Prot. see
    Botswana
Bedeau, see Ras el Ma
Bejaïa: Bougie
Belém: Pará
Belgard, see Białogard
Belize: British Honduras
Belogorsk: Kuibyshevka
    Vostochnaya
Benares, see Varanasi
Benghazi: Banghāzî
Benin: Dahomey
Beograd: Belgrade
Berdyansk: Osipenko
Bern: Berne
Berrahal: Ain Mokra
Bezwada, see Vijayawada
Bharat: India

Bharuch: Broach
Bhavnagar: Bhaunagar
Bhilsa, see Vidisha
Białogard: Belgrad
Binghamstown, see
    An Geata Mór
Binh Dinh, see An Nhon
Bir Mogrein: Fort Trinquet
Bitola: Monastir
Björneborg, see Pori
Bolzano: Bozen
Bône, see Annaba
Borgå, see Porvoo
Botswana: Bechuanaland Prot.
Bougie, see Bejaïa
Brahestad, see Raahe
Braniewo: Braunsberg
Bratislava: Pressburg
Braunsberg, see Braniewo
Breslau, see Wrocław
Bressanone: Brixen
Brest: Brest Litovsk
British Guiana, see Guyana
British Honduras, see Belize
Brixen, see Bressanone
Brno: Brünn
Broach, see Bharuch
Broken Hill, see Kabwe
Brugge: Bruges
Brunico: Bruneck
Brünn, see Brno
Brusa, see Bursa
Bruxelles: Brussel, Brussels
Bucureşti: Bucharest
Budweis, see České
    Budějovice
Bujumbura: Usumbura
Bukavu; Costermansville
Bunclody: Newtownbarry
Bursa: Brusa

Ca Mau, see Quang Long
Caesarea, see Qesari
Cairo, see El Qâhira
Calicut: Kozhikode
Cambridge: Galt
Candia, see Iráklion
Canton, see Kuangchou
Caporetto, see Kobarid
Caribrod, see Dimitrovgrad
Carlsbad, see Karlovy Vary
Carmona: Uige
Cattaro, see Kotor
Cawnpore, see Kanpur
Ceanannus Mór: Kells
Ceará, see Fortaleza
Celebes, see Sulawesi
Cerigo, see Kithira
Cernauti, see Chernovtsy
České Budějovice: Budweis
Ceylon, see Sri Lanka
Chad: Tchad
Changan, see Hsian
Changchiak'ou: Kalgan
Charleville, see Rath Luirc
Chefoo, see Yent'ai
Cheju-do: Quelpart
Chemnitz, see Karl Marx Stadt
Chemulpho, see Inch'ŏn
Cheribon, see Cirebon
Chernovtsy: Cernauti,
    Czernowitz
Chernyakhovsk: Insterberg
Ch'ich'ihaerh: Lungkiang
Chihli: Po Hai
Chilin: Yungki
Chilumba: Deep Bay
Chilung: Keelung
Chios, see Khios
Chipata: Fort Jameson
Chisinau, see Kishinev
Chistyakovo, see Thorez
Chitipa: Fort Hill
Chkalov, see Orenburg
Choybalsan: Bayan Tumen
Chongjin: Seishin
Chtimba: Florence Bay
Churchill, R.: Hamilton R.
Cieszyn: Teschen
Cirebon: Cheribon
Cluj: Klausenburg
Coatzacoalcos: Pto. Mexico
Cocanada, see Kakinada
Colomb-Béchar, see Béchar
Cologne: Köln
Congo (Kinshasa), see
    Zaïre
Conjeeveram, see Kanchipuram
Constance, see Konstanz
Constanţa: Küstenje
Constantinople, see İstanbul
Copenhagen, see København
Coquilhatville, see Mbandaka
Corfu, see Kérkira
Corunna, see La Coruña
Costermansville, see Bukavu

Courtrai, see Kortrijk
Craigavon: Lurgan and
    Portadown
Crete, see Kriti
Cuamba, see Novo Freixo
Cussabat, see Al Qasabat
Cyclades, see Kikládhes
Cyrene, see Shahhat
Czernowitz, see Chernovtsy

Dahomey, see Benin
Dairen, see Lüta
Damascus, see Dimashq
Damietta: Dumyât
Danzig, see Gdańsk
Daugavpils: Dvinsk
Deep Bay, see Chilumba
Deutsch Krone, see Wałcz
Dimashq: Damascus
Dimitrovgrad: Caribrod
Dimitrovo, see Pernik
Djerba: Houmt Souk
Djibouti: Fr. Terr. of the Afars
    & the Issas
Dnepropetrovsk:
    Yekaterinoslav
Dobrich, see Tolbukhin
Donetsk: Stalino
Dor: Tantura
Dorpat, see Tartu
Drissa, see Verchnedvinsk
Droichead Nua: Newbridge
Dublin, see Baile Átha Cliath
Dubrovnik: Ragusa
Dumyât: Damietta
Dunaújváros: Sztalinvaros
Dundo: Portugalia
Dunkerque: Dunquerque,
    Dunkirk
Durrësi: Durazzo
Dushanbe: Stalinbad
Dvinsk, see Daugavpils
Dzaudzhikau, see
    Ordzhonikidze

East Pakistan, see
    Bangladesh
Edirne: Adrianople
Edward, L., see Idi Amin Dada, L.
Eisenhüttenstadt:
    Stalinstadt, Furstenberg
El Asnam: Orléansville
El Bayadh: Géryville
El Eulma: St. Arnaud
El Harrach: Maison Carrée
El Iskandarîya: Alexandria
El Jadida: Mazagan
El Kala: La Calle
El Qâhira: Cairo
El Suweis: Suez
Elbląg: Elbing
Elizabethville, see Lubumbashi
Ellore: Eluru, Elluru
Escaut, see Schelde
Esfahān: Isfahan
Essaouira: Mogador
Evvoia: Euboea

Faizabad: Fyzabad
F'Dérik: Fort Gouraud
Fengtien, see Shenyang
Fernando Póo, see Macias
    Nguema Biyoga
Firenze: Florence
Fiume, see Rijeka
Flanders, see Vlaanderen
Florence Bay, see Chtimba
Florence, see Firenze
Flushing, see Vissingen
Formosa, see Taiwan
Fort de Polignac, see Illizi
Fort Flatters, see
    Zaouiet El-Kahla
Fort Gouraud, see F'Dérik
Fort Hall, see Muranga
Fort Jameson, see Chipata
Fort Lamy, see Ndjamena
Fort Rosebery, see Mansa
Fort Rousset, see Owando
Fort Rupert: Rupert House
Fort Hill, see Chitipa
Fort Manning, see Mchinji
Fort Trinquet, see Bir Mogrein
Forialeza: Ceará
Fredrikshald, see Halden
French Terr. of the Afars & the
    Issas:, see Djibouti
Fribourg: Freibourg
Frunze: Pishpek
Fuchou: Minhow
Fünfkirchen, see Pécs
Fyzabad, see Faizabad

Gagarin: Gzhatsk
Gago Coutinho, see Lumbala
Gallipoli, see Gelibolu

Galt, see Cambridge
Gamlakarleby, see Kokkola
Gand, see Gent
Gävle: Gefle
Gdańsk: Danzig
Gelibolu: Gallipoli
Geneva (Lake), see Léman
Genève: Geneva (Town)
Genoa: Génova
Gent: Gand, Ghent
George River,
    see Port Nouveau-Québec
Géryville, see El Bayadh
Ghazaouet: Nemours
Ghent, see Gent
Girgenti, see Agrigento
Glatz, see Kłodzko
Gliwice: Gleiwitz
Glorenza: Glurns
Glubczyce: Leobschütz
Goleniów: Gollnow
Gorkiy: Nijni Novgorod
Gorodok, see Zakamensk
Göteborg: Gothenburg
Gottwaldov: Zlin
Great Whale River,
    see Poste de la Baleine
Grosswardein, see Oradea
Guardafui, C., see Ras Asir
Guinea-Bissau: Portuguese
    Guinea
Gunza: Porto Amboim
Guyana: British Guiana
Gzhatsk, see Gagarin

Haeju: Haiju
Haerhpin: Pinkiang
Hailaer: Hulun
Halab: Haleb, Aleppo
Halden: Fredrikshald
Haleb, see Halab
Halq el Qued: La Goulette
Hamadia: Victor Hugo
Hamilton R., see Churchill R.
Hämeenlinna: Tavastehus
Hannover: Hanover
Hebron, see Al Khalih
Heijo, see P'yŏngyang
Helsinki: Helsingfors
Hermannstadt, see Sibiu
Hirschberg, see Jelenia Góra
Hollandia, see Jayapura
Homs: Al Khums,
    Leptis Magna
Hot Springs, see Truth or
    Consequences
Hot'ien: Khotan
Houmt Souk, see Djerba
Hovd: Jargalant, Kobdo
Hsian: Changan
Hulun, see Hailaer

Iaşi: Jassy
Ibiza: Iviza
Idi Amin Dada, L.: Edward, L.
Ieper: Ypres
Ighil Izane: Relizane
Ilebo: Port Francqui
Illizi: Fort de Polignac
In Salah: Ain Salah
Inch'ŏn: Chemulpho
India: Bharat
Inoucdjouac: Port Harrison
Insterberg, see Chernyakhovsk
Iráklion: Candia
Iran: Persia
Isfahan, see Esfahān
İskenderun: Alexandretta
Isiro: Paulis
İstanbul: Constantinople
Ivano-Frankovsk: Stanislav
Iviza, see Ibiza
Izmir: Smyrna

Jabalpur: Jubbulpore
Jadotville, see Likasi
Jaffa, see Tel Aviv-Yafo
Jakarta: Batavia
Jambi: Telanaipura
Jamnagar: Navanagar
Jargalant, see Hovd
Jassy, see Iaşi
Javhlant, see Ulyasutay
Jayapura: Sukarnapura, Hollandia
Jelenia Góra: Hirschberg
Jelgava: Mitau
Jerusalem: Al Quds
Jesselton, see Kota Kinabalu
João Pessoa: Paraiba
Jubbulpore, see Jabalpur

Kabwe: Broken Hill
Kakinada: Cocanada
Kalamata: Kalámai
Kalemie: Albertville

Kalgan, see Changchiak'ou
Kalinin: Tver
Kaliningrad: Königsberg
Kananga: Luluabourg
Kanchipuram: Conjeeveram
Kanchow: Kanhsien
Kanpur: Cawnpore
Kaolan, see Lanchou
Karl Marx Stadt: Chemnitz
Karlovac: Karlstadt
Karlsburg, see Alba Iulia
Karlstadt, see Karlovac
Karlovy Vary: Carlsbad
Kaschau, see Košice
Kaskinen: Kaskö
Katowice: Stalinogrod
Kaunas: Kovno
Keelung, see Chilung
Keijo, see Sŏul
Kells, see Ceanannus Mór
Kendrapara: Kendlapara
Kenitra: Port Lyautey
Kérkira: Corfu
Khanh Hung: Soc Trang
Khemelnitski: Proskurov
Khemis Miliana: Affreville
Khios: Chios
Khodzhent, see Leninabad
Khotan, see Hot'ien
Kikládhes: Cyclades
Kinshasa: Leopoldville
Kirov: Viatka, Vyatka
Kirovgrad: Kirovo
    Yelisavetgrad, Zinovyevsk
Kisangani: Stanleyville
Kishinev: Chisinau
Kitakyūshū: Kokura,
    Moji, Tobata,
    Wakamatsu & Yawata
Kithira: Cerigo
Klaipeda: Memel
Klausenburg, see Cluj
Kłodzko: Glatz
Kobarid: Caporetto
Kobdo, see Hovd
København: Copenhagen
Kokkola: Gamlakarleby
Kokura, see Kitakyūshū
Kolarovgrad, see Šumen
Kolchugino, see Leninsk
    Kuznetski
Köln, see Cologne
Kolobrzeg: Kolberg
Kommunarsk: Voroshilovsk,
    Stavropol
Königsberg, see Kaliningrad
Konstanz: Constance
Kortrijk: Courtrai
Košice: Kaschau
Koszalin: Köslin
Kota Kinabalu: Jesselton
Kotor: Cattaro
Kovna, see Kaunas
Kozhikode, see Calicut
Kraljevo: Rankovicevo
Krasnodar: Yekaterinodar
Kristiinankaupunki:
    Kristinestad
Kriti: Krete, Crete
Kropotkin: Romanovsk
Ksar Chellala: Reibell
Ksar el Kebir: Alcazarquivir
Kuangchou: Canton, Panyu
Kuçovë, see Qytet Stalin
Kuybyshev: Samara
Kuibyshevka Vostochnaya,
    see Belogorsk
K'unming: Yunnan
Küstenje, see Constanţa
Kutaraja, see Banda Aceh

La Calle, see El Kala
La Coruña: Corunna
La Goulette, see Halq el Qued
Laibach, see Ljubljana
Lanchou: Kaolan
Lappeenranta: Villmanstrand
Latakia, see Al Lādhiqiyah
Lauenburg, see Lebork
Lebork: Lauenburg
Leeu-Gamka: Fraserburg Road
Leghorn, see Livorno
Legnica: Liegnitz
Léman, Lake: Geneva, Lake
Lemberg, see Lvov
Leninabad: Khodzhent
Leninsk Kuznetski:
    Lenino, Kolchugino
Lensk: Mukhtuya
Leobschütz, see Glubczyce
Leopold II, L., see Mai-Ndombe, L.
Léopoldville, see Kinshasa
Leptis Magna, see Homs
Lesotho: Basutoland
Leuven: Louvain

Liberec: Reichenberg
Liegnitz, see Legnica
Liepaja: Libau
Likasi: Jadotville
Lisboa: Lisbon
Livorno: Leghorn
Llanelli: Llanelly
Ljubljana: Laibach
Lod: Lydda
Lourenço Marques, see Maputo
Louvain, see Leuven
Luau: Lunda
Lubumbashi: Elizabethville
Lucerne, see Luzern
Luena: Moxico
Lugansk, see Voroshilovgrad
Luluabourg, see Kananga
Lumbala: Gago Coutinho
Luofu: Lubero
Lurgan, see Craigavon
Lunda, see Luau
Lungkiang, see Ch'ich'ihaerh
Lüta: Port Arthur and Dairen
Luxembourg: Luxemburg
Luzern: Lucerne
Lvov: Lwow, Lemberg
Lydda, see Lod
Lyon: Lyons

Maas, see Meuse
Macedo da Cavaleiros: Andulo
Machilipatnam: Masulipatnam
Macias Nguema Biyoga:
 Fernando Póo
MacMahon, see Ain Touta
Madura: Madurai
Magallanes, see Punta Arenas
Maghnia: Marnia
Mai-Ndombe, L.: Leopold II, L.
Maison Carrée, see El Harrach
Majorca, see Mallorca
Malawi: Nyasaland
Malawi, L.: L. Nyasa
Malbork: Marienburg
Malines: Mechelen
Mallorca: Majorca
Mandsaur: Mandasor
Mansa: Fort Rosebery
Mantes-la-Jolie: Mantes
 Gassicourt
Mantova: Mantua
Maputo: Lourenço Marques
Maranhão, see São Luís
Marburg, see Maribor
Marchand, see Rommani
Marek, see Stanke Dimitrov
Maria Theresiopel, see Subotica
Mariánské Lázně: Marienbad
Maribor: Marburg
Maricourt: Wakeham Bay
Marienburg, see Malbork
Mariupol, see Zhdanov
Marnia, see Maghnia
Marsa Susa: Apollonia
Marseille: Marseilles
Masulipatnam, see Machilipatnam
Mathura: Muttra
Mayuram: Mayavaram
Mazagan, see El Jadida
Mbala: Abercorn
Mbandaka: Coquilhatville
Mbanza Congo: S. Salvador
 do Congo
Mbini, see Rio Muni
Mbuji-Mayi: Bakwanga
Mchinji: Fort Manning
Meathas Truim:
 Edgeworthstown
Mechelen: Malines
Memel, see Klaipeda
Menorca: Minorca
Menongue: Serpa Pinto
Me'ona: Tarshiha
Merano: Meran
Metangula, see
 Augusto Cardosa
Meuse: Maas
Mikkeli: Sankt Michel
Milano: Milan
Minhow, see Fuchou
Minorca, see Menorca
Misratah: Misurata
Mitau, see Jelgava
Mobutu Sese Seko, L.: Albert, L.
Mocha, see Al Mukha
Mogador, see Essaouira
Mohammedia: Perrégaux
Moji, see Kitakyūshū
Molotov, see Perm
Molotovsk, see Severodvinsk
Monastir, see Bitola
Montagnac, see Remchi
Montgomery, see Sahiwal
Moskva: Moscow
Mosul, see Al Mawsil
Moxico, see Luena
Muar: Bandar Maharani
Mukden, see Shenyang
Muine Bheag: Bagenalstown
Mukhtuya, see Lensk
München: Munich
Muranga: Fort Hall

Muscat & Oman, see Oman
Muttra, see Mathura

Najin: Rashin
Namibia: South West Africa
Namur: Namen
Nanning: Yungning
Nápolí: Naples
Navan, see An Uaimh
Navanagar, see Jamnagar
Ndalatando: Salazar
Ndjamena: Fort Lamy
Neemuch: Nimach
Neisse, see Nysa
Nemours, see Ghazaouet
Netherlands Guiana, see
 Surinam(e)
Neusatz, see Novi Sad
Neustettin, see Szczecinek
Newbridge (Ire.), see
 Droichead Nua
Newtonbarry, see Bunclody
Nictheroy, see Niteroi
Nieuwport: Nieuport
Nijni Novgorod, see Gorkiy
Nikolaistad, see Vaasa
Nimach, see Neemuch
Nisa, see Nysa
Niteroi: Nichteroy
Northern Rhodesia, see Zambia
Nouadhibou: Port Etienne
Nouveau Comptoir: Paint Hills
Nova Freixo: Cuamba
Novi Becej: Volosinovo
Novi Sad: Neusatz
Novokuznetsk: Stalinsk
Novomoskovsk: Stalinogorsk
Novosibirsk: Novo Nikolaevsk
Nsanje: Port Herald
Nürnberg: Nuremberg
Nyahururu: Thompson's Falls
Nyasa, L., see Malawi, L.
Nyasaland: Malawi
Nyasaland, see Malawi
Nykarleby, see Uusikaarlepyy
Nysa: Nisa, Neisse
Nyslott, see Savonlinna
Nystad, see Uusikaupunki

Odenburg, see Sopron
Olomouc: Olmutz
Olsztyn: Allenstein
Oman: Muscat & Oman
Ongiva: Va. Pereira d'Eça
Opole: Oppeln
Oporto, see Pòrto
Oradea: Grosswardein
Oran: Ouahran
Ordzhonikidze: Dzaudzihikau
Orléansville, see El Asnam
Orenburg: Chkalov
Osipenko, see Berdyansk
Ostende: Oostende, Ostend
Oswiecim: Auschwitz
Ouagadougou: Wagadugu
Ouargla: Wargla
Oulu: Uleâborg
Owando: Ft. Rousset

Pagalu: Annobón
Paint Hills, see
 Nouveau Comptoir
Pahangkaraya: Pahandut
Panyu, see Kuangchou
Paoshan: Yungchang
Paoting: Tsingyuan
Papua New Guinea: Papua, N. E.
 New Guinea
Pará, see Belém
Paraiba, see João Pessoa
Pátrai: Patras
Paulis, see Isiro
Payenhaot'e, see Alashantsoch'i
Pécs: Fünfkirchen
Peip'ing: Peking
Perm: Molotov
Pernambuco, see Recife
Pernik: Dimitrovo
Perrégaux, see Mohammedia
Persia, see Iran
Persian Gulf: Arabian G.
Phanh Bho Ho Chi Minh: Saigon
Philippeville, see Skikda
Philippopolis, see Plovdiv
Pillau, see Baltiysk
Pilsen: Plzeň
Pinkiang, see Haerhpin
Piraevs: Piraeus, Peiraieus,
 Pireets
Pishpek, see Frunze
Plovdiv: Philippopolis
Plzeň: Pilsen
Po Hai, see Chihli
Pola, see Pula
Podgorica, see Titograd
Ponthierville, see Ubundı
Poona, see Pune
Pori: Björneborg
Port Arthur, see Lüta
Port Etienne, see Nouadhibou
Port Francqui, see Ilebo
Port Harrison, see Inoucdjouac
Port Herald, see Nsanje

Port Lyautey, see Kenitra
Port Nouveau-Québec:
 George River
Portadown, see Craigavon
Pòrto: Oporto
Porto Amboim, see Gunza
Portugalia, see Dundo
Portuguese Guinea, see Guinea-
 Bissau
Porvoo: Borgå
Poste de la Baleine:
 Great Whale River
Poznan: Posen
Praha: Prague
Pressburg, see Bratislava
Proskurov, see Khmelnitski
Puerto Mexico, see
 Coatzacoalcos
Pula: Pola
Pune: Poona
Punta Arenas: Magallanes
P'yŏngyang: Heijo

Qesari: Caesarea
Quang Long: Ca Mau
Quelpart, see Cheju-do
Qytet Stalin: Kuçovë

Raahe: Brahestad
Raciborz: Ratibor
Ragusa, see Dubrovnik
Rahaeng, see Tak
Rankovicevo, see Kraljevo
Ras Asir: Cape Guardafui
Ras el Ma: Bedeau
Rashīd: Rosetta
Rashin, see Najin
Rass el Oued: Tocqueville
Rath Luirc: Charleville
Ratibor, see Raciborz
Ratisbon, see Regensburg
Recife: Pernambuco
Regensburg: Ratisbon
Reibell, see Ksar Chellala
Reichenberg, see Liberec
Relizanne, see Ighil Izane
Remchi: Montagnac
Revel, see Tallinn
Rezā'iyeh, L.: Urmia, L.
Rhodes, see Rodhós
Rhodesia: Southern Rhodesia,
 Zimbabwe
Rijeka: Fiume
Rio Muni, see Mbini
Riyadah, see Ar Riyād
Rodhós: Rhodes
Roeselare: Roulers
Roma: Rome
Romanovsk, see Kropotkin
Rommani: Marchand
Roraima: Rio Branco
Rosetta: Rashīd
Roulers, see Roeselare
Rovinj: Rovigno
Rudolf, L., see Turkana,L.
Rupert House, see Fort Rupert
Ruse: Ruschuk
Rybinsk: Shcherbakov

Saglouc: Sugluk
Sahiwal: Montgomery
Saïda: Sidon
Saigon, see Phanh Bho Ho Chi Minh
Saint Arnaud, see El Eulma
Saint Denis, see Sig
Saint Gall: Sankt Gallen
Saint Nicolas, see Sint Niklaas
Salazar, see Ndalatando
Salonika, see Thessaloníki
Salvador: Bahia
Samara, see Kuybyshev
Sambor: Sandan
Sankt Gallen, see Saint Gall
Sankt Michel, see Mikkeli
Santo Domingo: Ciudad
 Trujillo
São Luís: Maranhão
S. Salvador do Congo, see
 Mbanza Congo
Saragossa, see Zaragoza
Savonlinna: Nyslott
Schässburg, see Sighişoara
Schelde: Escaut, Scheldt
Schweidnitz, see Świdnica
Scutari (Albania), see Shkodra
Scutari (Turkey), see Usküdar
Sedom: Sodom
Seishin, see Chongjin
Sept Iles: Seven Islands
Serpa Pinto, see Menongue
Severodvinsk: Molotovsk
Sevilla: Seville
's Gravenhage: The Hague
Shahhat: Cyrene
Shcherbakov, see Rybinsk
Sheki: Nukha
Shenyang: Mukden, Fengtien
Shetland: Zetland
Shkodra: Scutari
Siam, see Thailand
Sibiu: Hermannstadt
Sidon, see Saïda

Sig: St. Denis
Sighişoara: Schässburg
Simbirsk, see Ulyanovsk
Singora, see Songkhla
Sint Niklaas: Saint Nicolas
Siracusa: Syracuse
Skikda: Philippeville
Skopje: Skoptje, Usküb
Sliten, see Zlitan
Słupsk: Stolp
Smyrna, see Izmir
Soc Trang, see Khanh Hung
Soch'e: Yarkand
Sodom, see Sedom
Sofiya: Sofia
Sombor: Zombor
Songkhla: Singora
Sopron: Odenburg
Sôul: Keijo
Sour el Ghozlane: Aumale
Sousse: Susa
South West Africa, see Namibia
Southern Rhodesia, see
 Rhodesia
Sovetsk: Tilsit
Split: Spalato
Sri Lanka: Ceylon
Stalin, see Varna
Stalinabad, see Dushanbe
Stalingrad, see Volgograd
Staliniri, see Tskhinvali
Stalino, see Donetsk
Stalinogorsk, see
 Novomoskovsk
Stalinogrod, see Katowice
Stalinsk, see Novokuznetsk
Stalinstad, see Eisenhüttenstadt
Stanislav, see Ivano-Frankovsk
Stanke Dimitrov: Marek
Stanleyville, see Kisangani
Stettin, see Szczecin
Sterzing: Vipiteno
Stolp, see Słupsk
Stolpmünde, see Ustka
Stuhlweissenburg, see
 Székesfehérvár
Subotica: Maria Theresiopel
Suchou: Wuhsien
Suez, see El Suweis
Sugluk, see Saglouc
Sukarnapura, see Jayapura
Sulawesi: Celebes
Šumen: Kolarovgrad
Sūr: Tyre
Surinam(e): Netherlands Guiana
Susa, see Sousse
Sverdlovsk: Yekaterinburg
Świdnica: Schweidnitz
Syracuse, see Siracusa
Szczecin: Stettin
Szczecinek: Neustettin
Székesfehérvár:
 Stuhlweissenburg
Sztalinvaros, see Dunaújváros

Tagdempt, see Tiaret
T'aipei: Taihoku
Taiwan: Formosa
T'aiyüan: Yangku
Tak: Rehaeng
Tallinn: Revel, Reval
Tampere: Tammefors
Tanganyika, see Tanzania
Tantura, see Dor
Tanzania: Tanganyika
 and Zanzibar
Tarābulus, see Tripoli
Tarshiha, see Me'ona
Tartu: Dorpat
Tavastehus, see Hämeenlinna
Tbilisi: Tiflis
Tchad, see Chad
Tel Aviv-Yafo: Jaffa, Tel Aviv
Telanaipura: Jambi
Tende: Tenda
Teschen, see Cieszyn
Thailand: Siam
Thebes, see Thívai
The Hague, see 's-Gravenhage
Thessaloníki: Salonika
Tiaret: Tagdempt
Thívai: Thebes
Thompson's Falls, see Nyahururu
Thorez: Christyakovo
Tiflis, see Tbilisi
Tihwa, see Wulumuchi
Tilsit, see Sovetsk
Timbuktu, see Tombouctou
Tiruchchirappalli: Trichinopoly
Tissemsilt: Vialar
Titograd: Podgorica
Tobata, see Kitakyūshū
Tocqueville, see Rass el Oued
Tolbukhin: Dobrich
Tombouctou: Timbuktu
Torino: Turin
Tornio: Tornea
Tournai: Doornik
Trèves: Trier
Trichinopoly, see
 Tiruchchirappalli
Tripoli: Tarābulus

Trucial States, see United Arab
 Emirates
Truth or Consequences:
 Hot Springs
Tselinograd: Akmolinsk
Tsingyuan, see Paoting
Tskhinvali: Staliniri
Turkana, L.: Rudolf, L.
Turku: Åbo
Turnovo: Veliko Tarnovo
Tver, see Kalinin
Tyre, see Sūr

Ubundi: Ponthierville
Uige, see Carmona
Ulan Ude: Verkhneudinsk
Uleâborg, see Oulu
Ulyanovsk: Simbitsk
Ulyasutay: Javhlant
United Arab Emirates: Trucial
 States
Urmia, L., see Rezā'iyeh, L.
Usküb, see Skopje
Usküdar: Scutari
Ussurysk: Voroshilov
Usumbura, see Bujumbura
Uusikaarlepyy: Nykarleby
Uusikaupunki: Nystad

Vaasa: Nikolaistad
Vadodara: Baroda
Varanasi: Banaras, Benares
Varna: Stalin
Veliko Tarnovo, see Turnovo
Venézia: Venice
Ventspils: Windau, Vindava
Verchnedvinsk: Drissa
Verkhneudinsk, see Ulan Ude
Vialar, see Tissemsilt
Victor Hugo, see Hamadia
Viborg: Viipuri, Vyborg
Vidisha: Bhilsa
Vienna, see Wien
Vijayawada: Bezwada
Vila Pereira d'Eça, see Ongiva
Villa Sanjurjo, see Al Hoceima
Villmanstrand, see
 Lappeenranta
Vilnius: Vilna, Vilno
 Vilnyus, Wilno
Vinh Loi: Bac Lieu
Vindava, see Ventspils
Vipiteno: Sterzing
Vishakhapatnam:
 Vizagapatnam,
 Visakakhapatnam
Vlaanderen: Flanders
Vlissingen: Flushing
Volgograd: Stalingrad
Volosinovo, see Novi Becej
Voroshilov: Ussurysk
Voroshilovgrad: Lugansk
Voroshilovsk, see Kommunarsk
Vyatka, see Kirov

Wagadugu, see Oaugadougou
Wakamatsu, see Kitakyūshū
Wakeham Bay, see Maricourt
Walbrzych: Waldenburg
Walcz: Deutsch Krone
Wanchüan, see Kalgan
Warszawa: Warsaw
Wenchow: Yungkia
Wien: Vienna
Wilno, see Vilnius
Windau, see Ventspils
Wrocław: Breslau
Wuhsien, see Suchou
Wulumuchi: Tihwa

Yanam: Yanaon
Yangku, see T'aiyüan
Yarkand, see Soch'e
Yawata, see Kitakyūshū
Yekaterinburg, see Sverdlovsk
Yekaterinodar, see Krasnodar
Yekaterinoslav, see
 Dnepropetrovsk
Yelisavetgrad, see Kirovgrad
Yent'ai: Chéfoo
Ypres, see leper
Yungchang, see Paoshan
Yungki, see Chilin
Yunkia, see Wenchow
Yungning, see Nanning
Yunnan, see K'unming

Zadar: Zara
Zaire: Congo (Kinshasa)
Zagreb: Agram
Zakamensk: Gorodok
Zambia: Northern Rhodesia
Zaouiet El-Kahla: Fort Flatters
Zaragoza: Saragossa
Zetland: Shetland
Zhdanov: Mariupol
Zimbabwe, see Rhodesia
Zinovyevsk, see Kirovgrad
Zlin, see Gottwaldov
Zlitan: Sliten
Zombor, see Sombor

Geographical Terms

This is a list of some of the geographical words from foreign languages which are found in the place names on the maps and in the index. Each is followed by the language and the English meaning.

Afr. afrikaans
Alb. albanian
Amh. amharic
Ar. arabic
Ber. berber
Bulg. bulgarian
Bur. burmese

Chin. chinese
Cz. czechoslovakian
Dan. danish
Dut. dutch
Fin. finnish
Flem. flemish
Fr. french

Gae. gaelic
Ger. german
Gr. greek
Heb. hebrew
Hin. hindi
I.-C. indo-chinese
Ice. icelandic

It. italian
Jap. japanese
Kor. korean
Lapp. lappish
Lith. lithuanian
Mal. malay
Mong. mongolian

Nor. norwegian
Pash. pashto
Pers. persian
Pol. polish
Port. portuguese
Rum. rumanian
Russ. russian

Ser.-Cr. serbo-croat
Siam. siamese
Sin. sinhalese
Som. somali
Span. spanish
Swed. swedish
Tib. tibetan
Turk. turkish

A. (Ain) *Ar.* spring
–á *Ice.* river
a *Dan., Nor., Swed.* stream
–abad *Pers., Russ.* town
Abyad *Ar.* white
Ad. (Adrar) *Ar., Ber.* mountain
Ada, Adasi *Tur.* island
Addis *Amh.* new
Adrar *Ar., Ber.* mountain
Aïn *Ar.* spring
Ákra *Gr.* cape
Akrotíri *Gr.* cape
Alb *Ger.* mountains
Albufera *Span.* lagoon
–ålen *Nor.* island
Alpen *Ger.* mountain pastures
Alpes *Fr.* mountains
Alpi *It.* mountains
Alto *Port.* high
–älv, –älven *Swed.* stream, river
Amt *Dan.* first-order administrative division
Appennino *It.* mountain range
Arch. (Archipiélago) *Span.* archipelago
Arcipélago *It.* archipelago
Arq. (Arquipélago) *Port.* archipelago
Arr. (Arroyo) *Span.* stream
–Ås, –åsen *Nor., Swed.* hill
Autonomna Oblast *Ser.-Cr.* autonomous region
Ayios *Gr.* island
Ayn *Ar.* well, waterhole

B(a). (Baía) *Port.* bay
B. (Baie) *Fr.* bay
B. (Bahía) *Span.* bay
B. (Ben) *Gae.* mountain
B. (Bir) *Ar.* well
B. (Bucht) *Ger.* bay
B. (Bugt.) *Dan.* bay
Baai, –baai *Afr.* bay
Bâb *Ar.* gate
Bäck, –bäcken *Swed.* stream
Back, backen, *Swed.* hill
Bad, –bad *Ger.* spa
Bâdiya, -t *Ar.* desert
Baek *Dan.* stream
Baelt *Dan.* strait
Bahía *Span.* bay
Bahr *Ar.* sea, river
Bahra *Ar.* lake
Baía *Port.* bay
Baie *Fr.* bay
Bajo, –a, *Span.* lower
Bakke *Nor.* hill
Bala *Pers.* upper
Baltǎ *Rum.* marsh, lake
Banc *Fr.* bank
Bander *Ar., Mal.* port
Bandar *Pers.* bay
Banja *Ser. Cr.* spa. resort
Barat *Mal.* western
Barr. (Barrage) *Fr.* dam
Barracão *Port.* dam, waterfall
Bassin *Fr.* bay
Bayt *Heb.* house, village
Bazar *Hin.* market, bazaar
Be'er *Heb.* well
Beit *Heb.* village
Belo-, Belyy, Belaya,

Beloye, *Russ.* white
Ben *Gae.* mountain
Bender *Somal.* harbour
Berg,(e) (–berg(e) *Afr.* mountain(s)
Berg, –berg *Ger.* mountain
–berg, –et *Nor., Swed.* hill, mountain, rock
Bet *Heb.* house, village
Bir, Bîr *Ar.* well
Birket *Ar.* lake, bay, marsh
Bj. (Bordj) *Ar.* port
–bjerg *Dan.* hill, point
Boca *Span.* river mouth
Bodden *Ger.* bay, inlet
Bogaz, Boğaz, –ı *Tur.* strait
Boka *Ser.-Cr.* gulf, inlet
Bol. (Bolshoi) *Russ.* great, large
Bordj *Ar.* fort
–borg *Dan., Nor., Swed.* castle, fort
–botn *Nor.* valley floor
bouche(s) *Fr.* mouth
Br. (Burnu) *Tur.* cape
Braţul *Rum.* distributary stream
–breen *Nor.* glacier
–bruck *Ger.* bridge
–brunn *Swed.* well, spring
Bucht *Ger.* bay
Bugt, –bugt *Dan.* bay
Buheirat *Ar.* lake
Bukit *Mal.* hill
Bukten *Swed.* bay
–bulag *Mong.* spring
Bûr *Ar.* port
Burg. *Ar.* fort
Burg, –burg *Ger.* castle
Burnu *Tur.* cape
Burun *Tur.* cape
Butt *Gae.* promontory
–by *Dan., Nor., Swed.* town
–byen *Nor., Swed.* town

C. (Cabo) *Port., Span.* headland, cape
C. (Cap) *Fr.* cape
C. (Capo) *It.* cape
Cabeza *Span.* peak, hill
Camp *Port., Span.* land, field
Campo *Span.* plain
Campos *Span.* upland
Can. (Canal) *Fr., Span.* canal
Canale *It.* canal
Canalul *Ser.-Cr.* canal
Cao Nguyên *Thai.* plateau, tableland
Cap *Fr.* cape
Capo *It.* cape
Cataracta *Sp.* cataract
Cauce *Span.* intermittent stream
Causse *Fr.* upland (limestone)
Cayi *Tur.* river
Cayo(s) *Span.* rock(s), islet(s)
Cerro *Span.* hill, peak
Ch. (Chaîne(s)) *Fr.* mountain range(s)
Ch. (Chott) *Ar.* salt lake
Chaco *Span.* jungle
Chaîne(s) *Fr.* mountain range(s)
Chap. (Chapada) *Port.* hills, upland

Chapa *Span.* hills, upland
Chapada *Port.* hills, upland
Chaung *Bur.* stream, river
Chen *Chin.* market town
Ch'eng *Chin.* town
Chiang *Chin.* river
Ch'ih *Chin.* pool
Ch'ŏn *Kor.* river
–chŏsuji *Kor.* reservoir
Chott *Ar.* salt lake, swamp
Chou *Chin.* district
Chu *Tib.* river
Chung *Chin.* middle
Chute *Fr.* waterfall
Co. (Cerro) *Span.* hill, peak
Coch. (Cochilla) *Port.* hills
Col *Fr., It.* Pass
Colline(s) *Fr.* hill(s)
Conca *It.* plain, basin
Cord. (Cordillera) *Span.* mountain chain
Costa *It., Span.* coast
Côte *Fr.* coast, slope, hill
Cuchillas *Spain* hills
Cu-Lao *I.-C.* island

D. (Dolok) *Mal.* mountain
Dâgh *Pers.* mountain
Dağ(ı) *Tur.* mountain(s)
Dağları *Tur.* mountain range
Dake *Jap.* mountain
–dal *Nor.* valley
–dal, –e *Dan., Nor.* valley
–dal, –en *Swed.* valley, stream
Dalay *Mong.* sea, large lake
–dalir *Ice.* valley
–dalur *Ice.* valley
–damm, –en *Swed.* lake
Danau *Mal.* lake
Dao *I.-O.* island
Dar *Ar.* region
Darya *Russ.* river
Daryácheh *Pers.* marshy lake, lake
Dasht *Pers.* desert, steppe
Daung *Bur.* mountain, hill
Dayr *Ar.* depression, hill
Debre *Amh.* hill
Deli *Ser.-Cr.* mountain(s)
Denizi *Tur.* sea
Dépt. (Département) *Fr.* first-order administrative division
Desierto *Span.* desert
Dhar *Ar.* region, mountain chain
Dj. (Djebel) *Ar.* mountain
Dō *Jap., Kor.* island
Dong *Kor.* village, town
Dong *Thai.* jungle region
–dorf *Ger.* village
–dorp *Afr.* village
–drif *Afr.* ford
–dybet *Dan.* marine channel
Dzong *Tib.* town, settlement

Eil.-eiland(en) *Afr., Dut.* island(s)
–elv *Nor.* river
–'emeq *Heb.* plain, valley
'erg *Ar.* desert with dunes
Estrecho *Span.* strait
Estuario *Span.* estuary

Étang *Fr.* lagoon
–ey(jar) *Ice.* island(s)

F. (Fiume) *It.* river
F. Folyó *Hung.* river
Fd. (Fjord) *Nor.* Inlet of sea
–feld *Ger.* field
–fell *Ice.* mountain, hill
–feng *Chin.* mountain
Fiume *It.* river
Fj. (–fjell) *Nor.* mountain
–fjall *Ice.* mountain(s), hill(s)
–fjäll(et) *Swed.* hill(s), mountain(s), ridge
–fjällen *Swed.* mountains
–fjard(en) *Swed.* fjord, bay, lake
Fjeld *Dan.* mountain
–fjell *Nor.* mountain, rock
–fjord(en) *Nor.* inlet of sea
–fjorden *Dan.* bay, marine channel
–fjörður *Ice.* fjord
Fl. (Fleuve) *Fr.* river
Fl. (Fluss) *Ger.* river
–flói *Ice.* bay, marshy country
Fluss *Ger.* river
foce, –i *It.* mouth(s)
Folyó *Hung.* river
–fontein *Afr.* fountain, spring
–fors, –en, *Swed.* rapids, waterfall
Foss *Ice., Nor.* waterfall
–furt *Ger.* ford
Fylke *Nor.* first-order administrative division

G. (Gebel) *Ar.* mountain
G. (Gebirge) *Ger.* hills, mountains
G. (Golfe) *Fr.* gulf
G. (Golfo) *It.* gulf
G. (Gora) *Bulg., Russ., Ser.-Cr.* mountain
G. (Gunong) *Mal.* mountain
–gang *Kor.* river
Ganga *Hin., Sin.* river
–gat *Dan.* sound
–gau *Ger.* district
Gave *Fr.* stream
–gawa *Jap.* river
Geb. (Gebirge) *Ger.* hills, mountains
Gebel *Ar.* mountain
Geziret *Ar.* island
Ghat *Hin.* range of hills
Ghiol *Rum.* lake
Ghubbat *Ar.* bay, inlet
Gji *Alb.* bay
Gjol *Alb.* lagoon, lake
Gl. (Glava) *Ser.-Cr.* mountain, peak
Glen. *Gae.* valley
Gletscher *Ger.* glacier
Gobi *Mong.* desert
Gol *Mong.* river
Golfe *Fr.* gulf
Golfo *It., Span.* gulf
Gomba *Tib.* settlement
Gora *Bulg., Russ., Ser.-Cr.* mountain(s)
Góry *Pol., Russ.* mountain
Gölü *Tur.* lake
–gorod *Russ.* small town
Grad *Bulg., Russ., Ser-Cr.* town, city

Grada *Russ.* mountain range
Guba *Russ.* bay
–Guntô *Jap.* island group
Gunong *Mal.* mountain
Gurǎ *Rum.* passage

H. Hadabat *Ar.* plateau
–hafen *Ger.* harbour, port
Haff *Ger.* bay
Hai *Chin.* sea
Haihsia *Chin.* strait
–hale *Dan.* spit, peninsula
Hals *Dan., Nor.* peninsula, isthmus
Halvø *Dan.* peninsula
Halvøya *Nor.* peninsula
Hāmad, Hamada, Hammādah *Ar.* stony desert, plain
–hamn *Swed., Nor.* harbour, anchorage
Hāmūn *Ar.* plain
Hāmūn *Pers.* low-lying marshy area
–Hantô *Jap.* peninsula
Harju *Fin.* hill
Hassi *Ar.* well
–haug *Nor.* hill
Hav *Swed.* gulf
Havet *Nor.* sea
–havn *Dan., Nor.* harbour
Hegyseg *Hung.* forest
Heide *Ger.* heath
Hi. (hassi) *Ar.* well
Ho *Chin.* river
–hø *Nor.* peak
Hochland *Afr.* highland
Hoek, –hoek *Afr., Dut.* cape
Höfn *Ice.* harbour, port
–hög, –en, –högar, –högarna *Swed.* hill(s), peak, mountain
Höhe *Ger.* hills
Holm *Dan.* island
–holm, –holme, –holzen, *Swed.* island
Hon *I.-C.* island
Hora *Cz.* mountain
–horn *Nor.* peak
Hory *Cz.* mountain range, forest
–hoved *Dan.* point, headland, peninsula
Hráun *Ice.* lava
–hsi *Chin.* mountain, stream
–hsiang *Chin.* village
–hsien *Chin.* district
Hu *Chin.* lake
Huk *Dan., Ger.* point
Huken *Nor.* head

I. (Île) *Fr.* island
I. (Ilha) *Port.* island
I. (Insel) *Ger.* island
I. (Isla) *Span.* island
I. (Isola) *It.* island
Idehan *Ar., Ber.* sandy plain
Île(s) *Fr.* island(s)
Ilha *Port.* island
Insel(n) *Ger.* island(s)
Irmak *Tur.* river
Is. (Inseln) *Ger.* islands
Is. (Islas) *Span.* islands
Is. (Isola) *It.* island
Isola, –e *It.* island(s)
Istmo *Span.* isthmus

J. (Jabal) *Ar.* mountain
J. (Jazira) *Ar.* island
J. (Jebel) *Ar.* mountain
J. (Jezioro) *Pol.* lake
Jabal *Ar.* mountain, range
–jaur *Swed.* lake
–järvi *Fin.* lake, bay, pond
Jasovir *Bulg.* reservoir
Jazā'ir *Ar.* islands
Jazîra *Ar.* island
Jazireh *Pers.* island
Jebel *Ar.* mountain
Jezero *Ser.-Cr.* lake
Jezioro *Pol.* lake
–Jima *Jap.* island
Jøkelen *Nor.* glacier
–joki *Fin.* stream
–jökull *Ice.* glacier
Jūras Līcis *Lat.* bay, gulf

K. (Kap) *Dan.* cape
K (Khalig) *Ar.* gulf
K. (Kiang) *Chin.* river
K. (Kuala) *Mal.* confluence, estuary
Kaap *Afr.* cape
Kai *Jap.* sea
Kaikyō *Jap.* strait
Kamennyy *Russ.* stony
Kampong *Mal.* village
Kan. (Kanal) *Ser.-Cr.* channel, canal
Kanaal *Dut., Flem.* canal
Kanal *Dan.* channel, gulf
Kanal *Ger., Swed.* canal, stream
kanal *Ser.-Cr.* channel, canal
Kang *Kor.* river, bay
Kangri *Tib.* mountain glacier
Kap *Dan., Ger.* cape
Kapp *Nor.* cape
Kas *I.-C.* island
–kaupstaður *Ice.* market town
–kaupunki *Fin.* town
Kavîr *Pers.* salt desert
Kébir *Ar.* great
Kéfar *Heb.* village, hamlet
–ken *Jap.* first-order administrative division
Kep *Alb.* cape
Kepulauan *Mal.* archipelago
Ketjil *Mal.* lesser, little
Khalig, Khalij *Ar.* gulf
khamba, –Idg *Tib.* source, spring
Khawr *Ar.* wadi
Khirbat *Ar.* ruins
Kho Khot *Thai.* isthmus
Khôr *Pers.* creek, estuary
Khrebet *Russ.* mountain range
Kiang *Chin.* river
–klint *Dan.* cliff
–Klintar *Swed.* hills
Kloof *Afr.* gorge
Knude *Dan.* point
Ko *Jap.* lake
Ko *Thai.* island
Kohi *Pash.* mountains
Kol *Russ.* lake
Kolymskoye *Russ.* mountain range
Kólpos *Gr., Tur.* gulf, bay
Kompong *Mal.* landing place
–kop *Afr.* hill

–köping *Swed.* market town
Körfezi *Tur.* gulf
Kosa *Russ.* spit
–koski *Fin.* cataract, rapids
–kraal *Afr.* native village
Krasnyy *Russ.* red
Kryash *Russ.* ridge, hills
Kuala *Mal.* confluence, estuary
kuan *Chin.* pass
Kuh –hha *Pers.* mountains
Kul *Russ.* lake
Kulle *Swed.* hill, shoal
Kum *Russ.* sandy desert
Kumpu *Fin.* hill
Kurgan *Russ.* mound
Kwe *Bur.* bay, gulf
Kyst *Dan.* coast
Kyun, –zu, –umya *Bur.* island(s)

L. (Lac) *Fr.* lake
L. (Lacul) *Rum.* lake
L. (Lago) *It., Span.* lake, lagoon
L. (Lagoa) *Port.* lagoon
L. (Límni) *Gr.* lake
L. (Loch) *Gae.* (lake, inlet)
L. (Lough) *Gae.* (lake, inlet)
La *Tib.* pass
La (Lagoa) *Port.* lagoon
–laagte *Afr.* watercourse
Läani *Fin.* first-order administrative division
Län *Swed.* first-order administrative division
Lac *Fr.* lake
Lacul *Rum.* lake, lagoon
Lago *It., Span.* lake, lagoon
Lagoa *Port.* lagoon
Laguna *It., Span.* lagoon, intermittent lake
Lagune *Fr.* lake
Lahti *Fin.* bay, gulf, cove
Lakhti *Russ.* bay, gulf
Lampi *Fin.* lake
Land *Ger.* first-order administrative division
–land *Dan.* region
–land *Afr., Nor.* land, province
Lido *It.* beach, shore
Liehtao *Chin.* islands
Lilla *Swed.* small
Límni *Gr.* lake
Ling *Chin.* mountain range, ice
Linna *Fin.* historical fort
Llano *Span.* prairie, plain
Loch *Gae.* (lake)
Lough *Gae.* (lake)
Lum *Alb.* river
Lund *Dan.* forest
–lund, –en *Swed.* wood(s)

M. (Maj, Mai) *Alb.* mountain, peak
M. (Mont) *Fr.* mountain peak
M. (Mys) *Russ.* cape
Madīna(h) *Ar.* town, city
Madiq *Ar.* strait
Maj *Alb.* peak
Mäki *Fin.* hill, hillside
Mal *Alb.* mountain
Mal *Russ.* little, small
Mal/a, –i, –o *Ser.-Cr.* small, little
Man *Kor.* bay
Mar *Span.* lagoon, sea
Mare *Rum.* great
Marisma *Span.* marsh
–mark *Dan., Nor.* land
Marsâ *Ar.* anchorage, bay, inlet
Masabb *Ar.* river mouth
Massif *Fr.* upland, plateau
Mato *Port.* forest
Mazar *Pers.* shrine, tomb
Meer *Afr., Dut., Ger.* lake sea

Mi., Mti. (Monti) *It.* mountains
Miao *Chin.* temple, shrine
Midbar *Heb.* wilderness
Mif. (Massif) *Fr.* upland, plateau
Misaki *Jap.* cape, point
–mo *Nor., Swed.* heath, island
–mon *Swed.* heath
Mong *Bur.* town
Mont *Fr.* hill, mountain
Montagna *It.* mountain
Montagne *Fr.* hill, mountain
Montaña *Span.* mountain
Monte *It., Port., Span.* mountain
Monti *It.* mountains
More *Russ.* sea
Mörön *Hung.* river
Mt. (Mont) *Fr.* mountain
Mt. (Monti) *It.* mountain
Mt. (Montaña) *Span.* mountain range
Mte. (Monte) *It., Port., Span.* mountain
Mţi. (Munţi) *Rum.* mountain
Mts. (Monts) *Fr.* mountains
Muang *Mal.* town
Mui *Ar., I.-C.* cape
Mull *Gae.* (promontory)
Mund, –mund *Afr.* mouth
Munkhafed *Ar.* depression
Munte *Rum.* mount
Munţi(i) *Rum.* mountain(s)
Muong *Mal.* village
Myit *Bur.* river
Myitwanya *Bur.* mouths of river
–mýri *Ice.* bog
Mys *Russ.* cape

N. (Nahal) *Heb.* river
Naes *Dan.* point, cape
Nafūd *Ar.* sandy desert
Nahal *Heb.* river
Nahr *Ar.* river, stream
Najd *Ar.* plateau, pass
Nakhon *Thai.* town
Nam *I.-C.* river
–nam *Kor.* south
–näs *Swed.* cape
–nes *Ice., Nor.* cape
Ness, –ness *Gae.* promontory, cape
Nez *Fr.* cape
–niemi *Fin.* cape, point, peninsula, island
Nizhne, –iy *Russ.* lower
Nizmennost *Russ.* plain, lowland
Nísos, Nísoi *Gr.* island(s)
Nor *Chin.* lake
Nor *Tib.* peak
Nos *Bulg., Russ.* cape, point
Nudo *Span.* mountain
Nuruu *Mong.* mountain range
Nuur *Mong.* lake

O. (Ostrov) *Russ.* island
O (Ouâdî, Oued) *Ar.* wadi
–ö *Swed.* island, peninsula, point
–öar, (–na) *Swed.* islands
Oblast *Russ.* administrative division
Öbor *Mong.* inner
Occidental *Fr., Span.* western
Odde *Dan., Nor.* point, peninsula, cape
Oji *Alb.* bay
Ojo *Span.* spring
Oki *Jap.* bay
–ön *Swed.* island peninsula
Ondör *Mong.* high, tall

–ör *Swed.* island, peninsula, point
Oraşul *Rum.* city
Ord *Gae.* point
Óri *Gr.* mountains
Oriental *Span.* eastern
Ôrmos *Gr.* bay
Óros *Gr.* mountain
Ort *Ger.* point, cape
Ostrov(a) *Russ.* island(s)
Otok(–i) *Ser.-Cr.* island(s)
Ouadi, –edi *Ar.* dry watercourse, wadi
Ouzan *Pers.* river
Ova –si) *Tur.* plains, lowlands
–øy, (–a) *Nor.* island(s)
Oya *Hin.* point
Oya *Sin.* river
Oz. (Ozero, a) *Russ.* lake(s)

P. (Passo) *It.* pass
P. (Pasul) *Rum.* pass
P. (Pico) *Span.* peak
P. (Prokhod) *Bulg.* pass
–pää *Fin.* hill(s), mountain
Pahta *Lapp.* hill
Pampa, –s *Span.* plain(s) salt flat(s)
Pan. (Pantano) *Span.* Reservoir
Pantao *Chin.* peninsula
Parbat *Urdu* mountain
Pas *Fr.* gap
Paso *Span.* pass, marine channel
Pass *Ger.* pass
Passo *It.* pass
Pasul *Rum.* pass
Patam *Hin.* small village
Patna, –patnam *Hin.* small village
Pegunungan *Mal.* mountain, range
Pei, –pei *Chin.* north
Pélagos *Gr.* sea
Pen. (Península) *Span.* peninsula
Peña *Span.* rock, peak
Península *Span.* peninsula
Per. (Pereval) *Russ.* pass
Pertuis *Fr.* channel
Peski *Russ.* desert, sands
Phanom *I.-C., Thai.* mountain
Phnom *I.-C.* mountain
Phu *I.-C.* mountain
Pic *Fr.* peak
Pico(s) *Span.* peak(s)
Pik *Russ.* peak
Piz., pizzo *It.* peak
Pl. (Planina) *Ser.-Cr.* mountain, range
Plage *Fr.* beach
Plaine *Fr.* plain
Planalto *Span.* plateau
Planina *Bulg., Ser.-Cr.* mountain, range
Plat. (Plateau) *Fr.* level upland
Plato *Russ.* plateau
Playa *Span.* beach
P-ov. (Poluostrov) *Russ.* peninsula
Pointe *Fr.* point, cape
Pojezierze *Pol.* lakes plateau
Polder *Dut.* reclaimed farmland
–pólis *Gr.* city, town
Poluostrov *Russ.* peninsula
Połwysep *Pol.* peninsula
Pont *Fr.* bridge
Ponta *Port.* point, cape
Ponte *It.* bridge
Poort *Afr.* passage, gate
–poort *Dut.* port
Porta *Port.* pass
Portil, –e *Rum.* gate
Portillo *Span.* pass
Porto *It.* port
Porto *Port., Span.* port

Pot. (Potámi, Potamós) *Gr.* river
Poulo *I.-C.* island
Pr. (Průsmyk) *Cz.* pass
Pradesh *Hin.* state
Presa *Span.* reservoir
Presqu'île *Fr.* peninsula
Prokhod *Bulg.* pass
Proliv *Russ.* strait
Prusmyk *Cz.* pass
Pso. (Passo) *It.* pass
Pta. (Ponta) *Port.* point, cape
Pta. (Punta) *It., Span.* point, cape, peak
Pte. (Pointe) *Fr.* point cape
Puerto *Span.* port, pass
Puig *Cat.* peak
Pulau *Mal.* island
Puna *Span.* desert plateau
Punta *It., Span.* point, peak
Puy *Fr.* hill

Qal'at *Ar.* fort
Qanal *Ar.* canal
Qasr *Ar.* fort
Qiryat *Heb.* town
Qolleh *Pers.* mountain

Ramla *Ar.* sand
Rann *Hin.* swampy region
Rao *I.-C.* river
Ras *Amh.* cape, headland
Räs *Ar.* cape, headland
Recife(s) *Port.* reef(s)
Reka *Bulg., Cz., Russ.* river
Repede *Rum.* rapids
Represa *Port.* dam
Reshteh *Pers.* mountain range
–Rettō *Jap.* group of islands
Ria *Span.* estuary, bay
Ribeirão *Port.* river
Rijeka *Ser.-Cr.* river
Rio *Port.* river
Río *Span.* river
Riv. (Riviera) *It.* coastal plain, coast, river
Rivier *Afr.* river
Riviera *It.* coast
Rivière *Fr.* river
Roche *Fr.* rock
Rog *Russ.* horn
–rück *Ger.* ridge
Rüd *Pers.* stream, river
Rudohorie *Cz.* ore mountains
Rzeka *Pol.* river

S. (Sungei) *Mal.* river
Sa. (Serra) *It., Port.* range of hills
Sa. (Sierra) *Span.* range of hills
–saari *Fin.* island
Sadd *Ar.* dam
Sagar, –ara *Hin., Urdu* lake
Saharā *Ar.* desert
Sahrâ *Ar.* desert
Sa'id *Ar.* highland
Sakar *Fin.* mountain
–Saki *Jap.* point
Sal. (Salar) *Span.* salt pan
Salina(s) *Span.* salt flat(s)
–salmi *Fin.* strait, sound, lake, channel
Saltsjöbad *Swed.* resort
Sammyaku *Jap.* mountain, range
Samut *Thai.* gulf
–San *Jap.* hill, mountain
Sap. (Sapadno) *Russ.* west
Sasso *It.* mountain
Se, Sé *I.-C.* river
Sebkha, –kra *Ar.* salt flats
See *Ger.* lake
–see *Ger.* sea
–şehir *Turk.* town
Selat *Mal.* strait
–selkä *Fin.* bay, lake, sound, ridge, hills

Selva *Span.* forest, wood
Seno *Span.* bay, sound
Serír *Ar.* desert of small stones
Serra *It., Port.* range of hills
Serrania *Span.* mountains
Sev. (Severo) *Russ.* north
–shahr *Pers.* city, town
Shan *Chin.* hills, mountains, pass
Shan-mo *Chin.* mountain range
Shatt *Ar.* river
–Shima *Jap.* island
Shimāli *Ar.* northern
–Shotō *Jap.* group of islands
Shuik'u *Chin.* reservoir
Sierra *Span.* hill, range
Sjö, sjön *Swed.* lake, bay, sea
Sjøen *Dan.* sea
Skär *Swed.* island, rock, cape
Skog *Nor.* forest
–skog, –skogen *Swed.* wood(s)
–skov *Dan.* forest
Slieve *Gae.* range of hills
–sø *Dan., Nor.* lake
Sør *Nor.* south, southern
Solonchak *Russ.* salt lake, marsh
Souk *Ar.* market
Spitze *Ger.* peak, mountain
–spruit *Afr.* stream
–stad *Afr., Nor., Swed.* town
–stadt *Ger.* town
Staður *Ice.* town
Stausee *Ger.* reservoir
Stenón *Gr.* strait, pass
Step *Russ.* plain
Str. (Stretto) *It.* strait
–strand *Dan., Nor.* beach
–strede *Nor.* straits
Strelka *Russ.* spit
–strete *Nor.* straits
Stretto *It.* strait
Stroedet *Dan.* strait
–ström, –strömmen *Swed.* stream(s)
–stroom *Afr.* large river
Suidō *Jap.* strait, channel
Sûn *Bur.* cape
Sund *Dan.* sound
–sund, –sundet *Swed.* sound, estuary, inlet
–sund(et) *Nor.* sound
Sungai, –ei *Mal.* river
Sungei *Mal.* river
Sur *Span.* south, southern
Sveti *Bulg.* pass
Syd *Dan., Swed.* south

Tai –tai *Chin.* tower
Tal *Mong.* plain, steppe
–tal *Ger.* valley
Tall *Ar.* hills, hummocks
Tandjung *Mal.* cape, headland
Tao *Chin.* island
Tassili *Ar.* rocky plateau
Tau *Russ.* mountain, range
Taung *Bur.* mountain, south
Taunggya *Bur.* pass
Télok *I.-C., Mal.* bay bight
Teluk *Mal.* bay, gulf
Tg. (Tandjung) *Mal.* cape, headland
–thal *Ger.* valley
Thok *Tib.* town
Tierra *Span.* land, country
–tind *Nor.* peak
Tjärn, –en, –et *Swed.* lake
Tong *Nor.* village, town
Tong *Bur., Thai.* mountain range
Tonle *I.-C.* large river, lake
–träsk *Swed.* bog, swamp
Tsangpo *Tib.* large river
Tso *Tib.* lake

Tsu *Jap.* entrance, bay
Tulur *Ar.* hill
T'un *Chin.* village
Tung *Chin.* east
Tunnel *Fr.* tunnel
Tunturi *Fin.* hill(s), mountain(s), ridge

Uad *Ar.* dry watercourse, wadi
Udjung *Mal.* cape
Udd, udde, udden *Swed.* point, peninsula
Uebi *Somal.* river
Us *Mong.* water
Ust *Russ.* river mouth
Uul *Mong., Russ.* mountain, range

V. (Volcán) *Span.* volcano
–vaara *Fin.* hill, mountain, ridge, peak
–våg *Nor.* bay
Val *Fr., It.* valley
Valea *Rum.* valley
–vall, –vallen *Swed.* mountain
Valle *Span.* valley
Vallée *Fr.* valley
Valli *It.* lake, lagoon
Väst *Swed.* west
–vatn *Ice., Nor.* lake
Vatten *Swed.* lake
Vdkhr. (Vodokhranilishche) *Russ.* reservoir
–ved, –veden *Swed.* range, hills
Veld, –veld *Afr.* field
Velik/a, –e, –i, –o *Ser.Cr.* large
–vesi *Fin.* water, lake, bay sound, strait
Vest *Dan., Nor.* west
Vf. (vîrful) *Rum.* peak, mountain
–vidda *Nor.* plateau
Vig *Dan.* bay, inlet, cove, lagoon, lake, bight
–vik, –vika, –viken *Nor., Swed.* bay, cove, gulf, inlet, lake
Vila *Port.* small town
Villa *Span.* town
Ville *Fr.* town
Vinh *I.-C.* bay
Vîrful *Rum.* peak, mountain
–vlei *Afr.* pond, pool
Vodokhranilishche *Russ.* reservoir
Vol. (Volcán) *Span.* volcano, mountain
Vorota *Russ.* gate
Vostochnyy *Russ.* eastern
Vozyshennost *Russ.* heights, uplands
Vrata *Bulg.* gate, pass
Vrchovina *Cz.* mountainous country
Vrchy *Cz.* mountain range
Vung *I.-C.* gulf
–vuori *Fin.* mountain, hill

W. (Wādī) *Ar.* dry watercourse
Wâhât *Ar.* oasis
Wald *Ger.* wood, forest
Wan *Chin., Jap.* bay
Webi *Amh.* river
Woestyn *Afr.* desert

Yam *Heb.* sea
Yang *Chin.* ocean
Yazovir *Bulg.* reservoir
Yoma *Bur.* mountain range
–yüan *Chin.* spring

–**Z**aki *Jap.* peninsula
Zalew *Pol.* lagoon, swamp
Zaliv *Russ.* bay
Zan *Jap.* mountain
Zatoka *Pol.* bay
Zee *Dut.* sea
Zemlya *Russ.* land, island(s)